# ENGLISH DRAMA
## 1580-1642

*SELECTED AND EDITED BY*

## C. F. TUCKER BROOKE

STERLING PROFESSOR OF ENGLISH

AND

## NATHANIEL BURTON PARADISE

ASSISTANT PROFESSOR OF ENGLISH
YALE UNIVERSITY

## D. C. HEATH AND COMPANY
Lexington, Massachusetts

Printed in the United States of America.

International Standard Book Number: 0-669-06144-1

# PREFACE

WE HAVE attempted in this volume to illustrate by means of adequate texts, adequately annotated, the main course of English dramatic literature during the sixty years of heyday sometimes termed "Elizabethan." A collection such as this, which offers only some five per cent of the available material, must have deplorable omissions. We regret our inability to find any place for such charming work as is the best of Brome, Field, Day, and Porter, and still more our need of limiting to a single play apiece several dramatists of major rank and maximum productivity. We have, however, made our choice with the interests of the normal reader of a book like this in view, avoiding singularity and keeping in mind the proper representation of types and topics as well as authors. When so judged, we believe that the plays included may fairly challenge preference over any that we have omitted.

The texts rest upon a careful new collation of the original editions, and will be found, we believe, to possess a high degree of accuracy. Variant readings are recorded more fully than may be thought advisable in a book of this nature. Our principle has been to note all readings which can be regarded as possible ones, and all that explain the nature of corruptions in the old copies. In the glossing of archaic or misleading words, we have also intended to err on the side of copiousness; and we hope that the mechanical arrangement of our apparatus will make it easy for the reader to ignore whatever portion of it does not at the moment interest him. We have abstained from note-references in the text, and have distinguished textual from glossarial or exegetical notes by printing the former in parentheses. We have retained spellings and grammatical forms which throw light upon the Elizabethan language, and have not normalized spellings (e.g., 'murther' beside 'murder,' 'farder' beside 'farther,' 'venter' beside 'venture') which indicate the quality of the author's pronunciation. Diacritical marks have been introduced where necessary to guide the reader in accenting words like 'cónfessor,' 'canónize,' 'massácres,' 'revénue.' The syllable –ed in past tenses has been kept only where the reader should give it syllabic value; otherwise we print 'd.

The actual stage directions and scene divisions of the original texts are given, we believe, with the strict fidelity requisite for any intelligent study of early stage practice. Necessary additional matter of this kind, emanating from later editors, is enclosed in square brackets. Occasional directions in parentheses indicate that the matter is to be found, at least essentially, in the originals. In typographical appearance (e.g., the type and language employed for act and scene headings, the appearance of stage directions on the page, etc.) we have sought to give the reader as faithful an impression of the actual look of the old texts as can be done in a two-column book.

In the one-page introductions to the various plays we have attempted to summarize the concrete facts and to give the most useful references, without trespassing upon the field of æsthetic interpretation which should be left free for readers and teachers.

We desire to acknowledge our particular obligations to the authorities of the Huntington Library, to Dr. George Watson Cole, personally, and to the librarians of the Yale University Library and the Elizabethan Club.

C. F. T. B.
N. B. P.

# CONTENTS

v

# ILLUSTRATIONS

*The Araygnement of Paris*
# A PASTORALL.

Prefented before the Queenes
Maieftie, by the Children
of her Chappell.

Imprinted at London by
Henrie Marſh.
*ANNO.* 1584.

BIBLIOGRAPHICAL RECORD. The only early edition of *The Arraignment of Paris* is the quarto issued by Henry Marsh in 1584. The author's name does not appear on the title-page of this volume, nor was the play entered on the Registers of the Stationers' Co.

AUTHORSHIP. Peele's title to the authorship of the play is definitely established by Thomas Nashe in his epistle prefixed to Greene's *Menaphon* (1589). After discussing several English poets, Nashe says of Peele:

> ". . . for the last, thogh not the least of them all, I dare commend him to all that know him, as the chiefe supporter of pleasance nowe liuing, the Atlas of Poetrie, and *primus verborum Artifex:* whose first encrease, the Arraignement of Paris, might plead to your opinions his pregnant dexteritie of wit, and manifold varietie of inuention; wherein (*me iudice*) hee goeth a step beyond all that write."

This attribution is confirmed by the appearance in *England's Helicon* (1600) of passages from the play over the signature "Geo. Peele."

DATE AND STAGE PERFORMANCE. The title-page of the quarto states that the play had been "presented before the Queenes Maiestie, by the Children of her Chappell." This company is known to have acted at court on Jan. 6 (Twelfth Night), and Feb. 2 (Candlemas) in 1584. It seems probable that this play, obviously designed for performance before Queen Elizabeth, was presented on one of these occasions.

STRUCTURE. This pastoral is constructed on classical principles, with five acts and (with a few exceptions) new scenes whenever new characters enter the stage. Modern editors usually amalgamate the shorter scenes, but we have kept the division of the original quarto, which was evidently that of Peele himself. A special feature of the structure of this play which will repay study is the purposeful experimentation with many types of metre. Most of the play is in lyric, riming measures, varying from two-stress to eight-stress verses. Blank verse is employed in only about 190 lines, which have a recitative or oratorical character; and the best of these mark the highest point reached by English blank verse before the advent of Marlowe.

SOURCES. The theme of Paris's judgment among the three goddesses was, of course, a commonplace of classical scholarship; and it has been shown to have been employed frequently before Peele's time to flatter a living queen (see T. S. Graves, "*The Arraignment of Paris* and 16th Century Flattery," *Modern Language Notes*, Feb., 1913). Probably while still at Oxford, about 1580, Peele had written a narrative *Tale of Troy* in decasyllabic couplets, which covers the theme of his play and contains striking anticipations of its phraseology (see T. Larsen, "The Early Years of George Peele, Dramatist," *Transactions of the Royal Society of Canada*, 1928, 294 ff.). Peele's original genius appears chiefly in the play (apart from the remarkable poetry that it contains) in two points: (1) his manipulation of the story into a pastoral drama such as had not previously been attempted in England; and (2) the happy invention by which he develops out of the old myth of Paris's judgment among the goddesses a new myth dealing with Paris's arraignment for that judgment. There seems to be no good reason for believing that Peele was acquainted with an Italian play of similar title, *Il Giuditio di Paride*, by Anello Paulilli, printed at Naples, 1566. (See Miss V. M. Jeffery, *Modern Language Review*, April, 1924; A. H. Gilbert, *Modern Language Notes*, Jan., 1926; and T. Larsen, *loc. cit.*)

The English shepherds, Colin, Hobbinol, Diggon, and Thenot, who appear so surprisingly in Act III, are drawn from Spenser's *Shepherds' Calendar* (1579); and this fixes a *terminus a quo* for the date of the play. Peele's playful handling of the Colin Clout story drew from Spenser a mock-rueful acknowledgment in *Colin Clout's Come Home Again* (1591, lines 392 f.):

> "There eke is *Palin* worthie of great praise,
> Albe he envie at my rustick quill."

# GEORGE PEELE (*c.* 1557–1596)

## THE ARRAIGNMENT OF PARIS

[DRAMATIS PERSONAE

| | | | |
|---|---|---|---|
| SATURN | VULCAN | THENOT | ATE |
| JUPITER | PAN | JUNO | CLOTHO |
| NEPTUNE | FAUNUS | PALLAS | LACHESIS |
| PLUTO | SILVANUS | VENUS | ATROPOS |
| APOLLO | PARIS | DIANA | ŒNONE |
| MARS | COLIN | POMONA | HELEN |
| BACCHUS | HOBBINOL | FLORA | THESTYLIS |
| MERCURY | DIGGON | RHANIS | |

Cupids, Cyclops, Shepherds, Knights, the Muses, a Nymph of Diana, etc.

SCENE: A vale on Mt. Ida: Mt. Olympus.]

### *Ate Prologus*

CONDEMNED soul, Ate, from lowest hell,
And deadly rivers of th' infernal Jove,
Where bloodless ghosts in pains of endless date
Fill ruthless ears with never-ceasing cries,
Behold, I come in place, and bring beside    5
The bane of Troy! behold, the fatal fruit,
Raught from the golden tree of Proserpine!
Proud Troy must fall, so bid the gods above,
And stately Ilium's lofty towers be razed
By conquering hands of the victorious foe;   10
King Priam's palace waste with flaming fire,
Whose thick and foggy smoke, piercing the sky,
Must serve for messenger of sacrifice,
T' appease the anger of the angry heavens;
And Priam's younger son, the shepherd swain,
Paris, th' unhappy organ of the Greeks.   16
So, loath and weary of her heavy load,
The Earth complains unto the hellish prince,
Surcharged with the burden that she nill sustain.
Th' unpartial daughters of Necessity    20
Been aiders in her suit: and so the twine
That holds old Priam's house, the thread of Troy,
Dame Atropos with knife in sunder cuts.
Done be the pleasure of the powers above,
Whose hests men must obey: and I my part   25
Perform in Ida vales. Lordings, adieu!
Imposing silence for your task, I end,
Till just assembly of the goddesses
Make me begin the tragedy of Troy.
*Exit Ate cum aureo pomo.*

### ACT. I. SCENA I

*Pan, Faunus, and Silvanus, with their attendants,
enter to give welcome to the goddesses: Pan's
Shepherd hath a lamb, Faunus' Hunter hath
a fawn, Silvanus' Woodman with an oaken-
bough laden with acorns.*

#### *Pan incipit*

*Pan.* Silvanus, either Flora doth us wrong,
Or Faunus made us tarry all too long,
For by this morning mirth it should appear,
The Muses or the goddesses be near.
*Faun.* My fawn was nimble, Pan, and
    whipp'd apace, —    5
'T was happy that we caught him up at last, —
The fattest, fairest fawn in all the chace;
I wonder how the knave could skip so fast.
*Pan.* And I have brought a twagger for the
    nones,
A bunting lamb; nay, pray you feel; no bones:
Believe me now, my cunning much I miss,   11
If ever Pan felt fatter lamb than this.
*Sil.* Sirs, you may boast your flocks and
    herds that bin both fresh and fair,
Yet hath Silvanus walks, i-wis, that stand in
    wholesome air;
And, lo, the honour of the woods, the gallant
    oakenbough,    15
Do I bestow, laden with acorns and with mast
    enow!
*Pan.* Peace, man, for shame! shalt have
    both lambs and dams and flocks and herds
    and all,

---

**Ate Prologus:** Enter Ate, as speaker of the Prologue    **3 of . . . date:** everlasting    **5 in:** *i.e.,* to
this    **7 Raught:** snatched    **19 nill:** will not    **20 unpartial:** impartial    **21 aiders:** ('aydes' Q)
**29 S. D. cum . . . pomo:** with the golden apple    **S. D. incipit:** begins    **7 chace:** hunting field
**9 twagger:** fat lamb    **nones:** occasion    **10 bunting:** fat

3

And all my pipes to make thee glee; we meet
  not now to brawl.
    *Faun.*   There's no such matter, Pan; we are
  all friends assembled hither,
To bid Queen Juno and her pheeres most hum-
  bly welcome hither:                                        20
Diana, mistress of our woods, her presence will
  not want;
Her courtesy to all her friends, we wot, is nothing scant.

### ACT. I.  SCENA II

*Pomona entereth with her fruit, manentibus Pan
cum reliquis*

    *Pom.*   Yea, Pan, no farther yet, and had the
  start of me?
Why, then Pomona with her fruit comes time
  enough, I see.
Come on a while; with country store, like
  friends, we venter forth:
Think'st, Faunus, that these goddesses will take
  our gifts in worth?
    *Faun.*   Yea, doubtless, for shall tell thee,
  dame, 't were better give a thing,          5
A sign of love, unto a mighty person or a king,
Than to a rude and barbarous swain, but bad
  and basely born,
For gently takes the gentleman that oft the
  clown will scorn.
    *Pan.*   Say'st truly, Faunus; I myself have
  given good tidy lambs
To Mercury, may say to thee, to Phœbus, and
  to Jove;                                             10
When to a country mops, forsooth, chave of-
  fer'd all their dams,
And pip'd and pray'd for little worth, and
  rang'd about the grove.
    *Pom.*   God Pan, that makes your flock so
  thin, and makes you look so lean,
To kiss in corners.
    *Pan.*   Well said, wench! some other thing
  you mean.                                            15
    *Pom.*   Yea, jest it out till it go alone: but
  marvel where we miss
Fair Flora all this merry morn.
    *Faun.*   Some news; see where she is.

### ACT. I.  SCENA III

*Flora entereth to the country gods*

    *Pan.*   Flora, well met, and for thy taken
  pain,
Poor country gods, thy debtors we remain.

    *Flo.*   Believe me, Pan, not all thy lambs and
  yoes,
Nor, Faunus, all thy lusty bucks and does
(But that I am instructed well to know         5
What service to the hills and dales I owe),
Could have enforc'd me to so strange a toil,
Thus to enrich this gaudy, gallant soil.
    *Faun.*   But tell me, wench, hast done 't so
  trick indeed,
That heaven itself may wonder at the deed? 10
    *Flo.*   Not Iris, in her pride and bravery,
Adorns her arch with such variety;
Nor doth the milk-white way, in frosty night,
Appear so fair and beautiful in sight,
As done these fields, and groves, and sweetest
  bowers,                                              15
Bestrew'd and deck'd with parti-colour'd flow-
  ers.
Along the bubbling brooks and silver glide,
That at the bottom doth in silence slide;
The watery flowers and lilies on the banks,
Like blazing comets, burgeon all in ranks;     20
Under the hawthorn and the poplar-tree,
Where sacred Phœbe may delight to be,
The primerose, and the purple hyacinth,
The dainty violet, and the wholesome minth,
The double daisy, and the cowslip, queen       25
Of summer flowers, do overpeer the green;
And round about the valley as ye pass,
Ye may ne see for peeping flowers the grass:
That well the mighty Juno, and the rest,
May boldly think to be a welcome guest         30
On Ida hills, when to approve the thing,
The Queen of Flowers prepares a second spring.
    *Sil.*   Thou gentle nymph, what thanks shall
  we repay
To thee that mak'st our fields and woods so
  gay?
    *Flo.*   Silvanus, when it is thy hap to see 35
My workmanship in portraying all the three:
First stately Juno with her port and grace,
Her robes, her lawns, her crownet, and her
  mace,
Would make thee muse this picture to behold,
Of yellow oxlips bright as burnish'd gold.     40
    *Pom.*   A rare device; and Flora well, perdy,
Did paint her yellow for her jealousy.
    *Flo.*   Pallas in flowers of hue and colours
  red;
Her plumes, her helm, her lance, her Gorgon's
  head,
Her trailing tresses that hang flaring round, 45
Of July-flowers so graffed in the ground,
That, trust me, sirs, who did the cunning see,
Would at a blush suppose it to be she.

²⁰ **pheeres:** companions     S. D. **manentibus . . . reliquis:** Pan remaining with the rest     ³ **venter·
venture     ⁴ in worth:** in good part     ⁸ **that:** that which     ¹¹ **mops:** girl     **chave:** I have
5. D. **country:** pastoral     ³ **yoes:** ewes     ⁹ **trick:** neatly     ¹¹ **bravery:** finery     ³⁷ **port:** stately car·
riage     ³⁸ **lawns:** garments of fine linen     **crownet:** coronet     ⁴¹ **perdy:** indeed (par Dieu)

*Pan.* Good Flora, by my flock, 't was very
good
To dight her all in red, resembling blood.   50
*Flo.*  Fair Venus of sweet violets in blue,
With other flowers infix'd for change of hue;
Her plumes, her pendants, bracelets, and her
rings,
Her dainty fan, and twenty other things,
Her lusty mantle waving in the wind,        55
And every part in colour and in kind;
And for her wreath of roses, she nill dare
With Flora's cunning counterfeit compare.
So that what living wight shall chance to see
These goddesses, each plac'd in her degree,  60
Portray'd by Flora's workmanship alone,
Must say that art and nature met in one.
*Sil.*  A dainty draught to lay her down in
blue,
The colour commonly betokening true.
*Flo.*  This piece of work, compact with many
a flower,                                    65
And well laid in at entrance of the bower,
Where Phœbe means to make this meeting
royal,
Have I prepar'd to welcome them withal.
*Pom.*  And are they yet dismounted, Flora,
say,
That we may wend to meet them on the way? 70
*Flo.*  That shall not need: they are at hand
by this,
And the conductor of the train hight Rhanis.
Juno hath left her chariot long ago,
And hath return'd her peacocks by her rainbow;
And bravely, as becomes the wife of Jove,   75
Doth honour by her presence to our grove.
Fair Venus she hath let her sparrows fly,
To tend on her and make her melody;
Her turtles and her swans unyoked be,
And flicker near her side for company.       80
Pallas hath set her tigers loose to feed,
Commanding them to wait when she hath
need.
And hitherward with proud and stately pace,
To do us honour in the sylvan chace,
They march, like to the pomp of heaven above,
Juno the wife and sister of King Jove,       86
The warlike Pallas, and the Queen of Love.
*Pan.*  Pipe, Pan, for joy, and let thy shep-
herds sing;
Shall never age forget this memorable thing.
*Flo.*  Clio, the sagest of the Sisters Nine, 90
To do observance to this dame divine,
Lady of learning and of chivalry,
Is here arrived in fair assembly;
And wandering up and down th' unbeaten ways,
Rings through the wood sweet songs of Pallas'
praise.                                      95

*Pom.*  Hark, Flora, Faunus! here is melody,
A charm of birds, and more than ordinary.

*An artificial charm of birds being heard within,
Pan speaks*

*Pan.*  The silly birds make mirth; then
should we do them wrong,
Pomona, if we nill bestow an echo to their song.

*An echo to their song*

*The Song. A quire within and without*

*Gods.*  O Ida, O Ida, O Ida, happy hill! 100
This honour done to Ida may it continue still!
*Muses [within.]*  Ye country gods that in this
Ida won,
Bring down your gifts of welcome
For honour done to Ida.
*Gods.*  Behold, in sign of joy we sing,    105
And signs of joyful welcome bring,
For honour done to Ida.
*Muses [within.]*  The Muses give you melody
to gratulate this chance,
And Phœbe, chief of sylvan chace, commands
you all to dance.
*Gods.*  Then round in a circle our sportance
must be;                                     110
Hold hands in a hornpipe, all gallant in glee.
*Dance.*
*Muses [within.]*  Reverence, reverence, most
humble reverence!
*Gods.*  Most humble reverence!


## ACT. I.  SCENA IV

*Pallas, Juno, and Venus enter, Rhanis leading
the way.  Pan alone sings*

THE SONG

The God of Shepherds, and his mates,
With country cheer salutes your states,
Fair, wise, and worthy as you be,
And thank the gracious ladies three
For honour done to Ida.                       5

*The birds sing*

*The song being done, Juno speaks*

*Juno.*  Venus, what shall I say? for, though
I be a dame divine,
This welcome and this melody exceeds these
wits of mine.
*Ven.*  Believe me, Juno, as I hight the Sover-
eign of Love,
These rare delights in pleasures pass the ban-
quets of King Jove.
*Pal.*  Then, Venus, I conclude it easily may
be seen,                                      10

---

⁵⁰ **dight:** dress   ⁷² **hight:** called   ⁹⁵ **Rings:** ('Ringe' Q)   ⁹⁷ **charm:** singing, chorus   ⁹⁸ **silly:**
simple, innocent   ¹⁰² **won:** dwell   ⁵ S. D. **birds:** mechanical birds behind the scenes

That in her chaste and pleasant walks fair
    Phœbe is a queen.
    *Rha.*   Divinest Pallas, and you sacred dames,
Juno and Venus, honour'd by your names,
Juno, the wife and sister of King Jove,
Fair Venus, lady-president of love,      15
If any entertainment in this place,
That can afford but homely, rude, and base,
It please your godheads to accept in gree,
That gracious thought our happiness shall be.
My mistress Dian, this right well I know,    20
For love that to this presence she doth owe,
Accounts more honour done to her this day,
Than ever whilom in these woods of Ida;
And for our country gods, I dare be bold,
They make such cheer, your presence to be-
    hold,      25
Such jouisance, such mirth, and merriment,
As nothing else their mind might more con-
    tent:
And that you do believe it to be so,
Fair goddesses, your lovely looks do show.
It rests in fine, for to confirm my talk,    30
Ye deign to pass along to Dian's walk;
Where she among her troop of maids attends
The fair arrival of her welcome friends.
    *Flo.*   And we will wait with all observance
    due,
And do just honour to this heavenly crew.    35
    *Pan.*   The God of Shepherds, Juno, ere
    thou go,
Intends a lamb on thee for to bestow.
    *Faun.*   Faunus, high ranger in Diana's chace,
Presents a fawn to Lady Venus' grace.
    *Sil.*   Silvanus gives to Pallas' deity    40
This gallant bough raught from the oaken-
    tree.
    *Pom.*   To them that doth this honour to our
    fields
Her mellow apples poor Pomona yields.
    *Juno.*   And, gentle gods, these signs of your
    goodwill
We take in worth, and shall accept them still. 45
    *Ven.*   And, Flora, this to thee among the
    rest, —
Thy workmanship comparing with the best,
Let it suffice thy cunning to have [power]
To call King Jove from forth his heavenly
    bower.
Hadst thou a lover, Flora, credit me,    50
I think thou wouldst bedeck him gallantly.
But wend we on; and, Rhanis, lead the way,
That kens the painted paths of pleasant Ida.
                      *Exeunt omnes.*

## ACT. I. SCENA V. *et ultima*

### *Paris and Œnone*

    *Par.*   Œnone, while we been disposed to
    walk,
Tell me what shall be subject of our talk?
Thou hast a sort of pretty tales in store,
Dare say no nymph in Ida woods hath more:
Again, beside thy sweet alluring face,    5
In telling them thou hast a special grace.
Then, prithee, sweet, afford some pretty thing,
Some toy that from thy pleasant wit doth
    spring.
    *Œn.*   Paris, my heart's contentment and my
    choice,
Use thou thy pipe, and I will use my voice; 10
So shall thy just request not be denied,
And time well spent, and both be satisfied.
    *Par.*   Well, gentle nymph, although thou do
    me wrong,
That can ne tune my pipe unto a song,
Me list this once, Œnone, for thy sake,    15
This idle task on me to undertake.

         *They sit under a tree together.*

    *Œn.*   And whereon, then, shall be my roun-
    delay?
For thou hast heard my store long since, dare
    say;
How Saturn did divide his kingdom tho
To Jove, to Neptune, and to Dis below;    20
How mighty men made foul successless war
Against the gods and state of Jupiter;
How Phorcys' imp, that was so trick and fair,
That tangled Neptune in her golden hair,
Became a Gorgon for her lewd misdeed, — 25
A pretty fable, Paris, for to read,
A piece of cunning, trust me, for the nones,
That wealth and beauty alter men to stones;
How Salmacis, resembling idleness,
Turns men to women all through wantonness;
How Pluto raught Queen Ceres' daughter
    thence,    31
And what did follow of that love-offence;
Of Daphne turn'd into the laurel-tree,
That shows a mirror of virginity;
How fair Narcissus tooting on his shade,    35
Reproves disdain, and tells how form doth vade;
How cunning Philomela's needle tells
What force in love, what wit in sorrow dwells;
What pains unhappy souls abide in hell,
They say because on earth they lived not
    well, —    40
Ixion's wheel, proud Tantal's pining woe.

---

Prometheus' torment, and a many mo;
How Danaus' daughters ply their endless
　　task,
What toil the toil of Sisyphus doth ask:
All these are old and known, I know, yet, if
　　thou wilt have any,　　　　　　　　　45
Choose some of these for, trust me, else Œnone
　　hath not many.
　　*Par.* Nay, what thou wilt: but sith my cun-
　　ning not compares with thine,
Begin some toy that I can play upon this pipe of
　　mine.
　　*Œn.* There is a pretty sonnet, then, we call
　　it Cupid's Curse,
"They that do change old love for new, pray
　　gods they change for worse!"　　　　50
The note is fine and quick withal, the ditty will
　　agree,
Paris, with that same vow of thine upon our
　　poplar-tree.
　　*Par.* No better thing; begin it, then:
　　Œnone, thou shalt see
Our music figure of the love that grows 'twixt
　　thee and me.

*They sing; and while Œnone singeth, he pipeth.*

*Incipit Œnone.*

　　*Œn.* Fair and fair, and twice so fair,　　55
　　　　As fair as any may be;
　　　The fairest shepherd on our green,
　　　　A love for any lady.
　　*Par.* Fair and fair, and twice so fair,
　　　　As fair as any may be;　　　　　60
　　　Thy love is fair for thee alone,
　　　　And for no other lady.
　　*Œn.* My love is fair, my love is gay,
　　　　As fresh as been the flowers in May,
　　　And of my love my roundelay,　　　65
　　　　My merry merry merry roundelay,
　　　　Concludes with Cupid's curse, —
　　　They that do change old love for new,
　　　　Pray gods they change for worse!
*Ambo simul.*
　　　They that do change, &c.　　　　70
　　*Œn.* Fair and fair, &c.
　　*Par.* Fair and fair, &c.
　　　Thy love is fair, &c.
　　*Œn.* My love can pipe, my love can sing,
　　　　My love can many a pretty thing,　75
　　　And of his lovely praises ring
　　　　My merry merry roundelays.
　　　　Amen to Cupid's curse, —
　　　They that do change, &c.
　　*Par.* They that do change, &c.　　　80
*Ambo.* Fair and fair, &c.

*Finis Camœnæ.*

*The song being ended, they rise, and Œnone
　　speaks.*

　　*Œn.* Sweet shepherd, for Œnone's sake be
　　cunning in this song,
And keep thy love, and love thy choice, or else
　　thou dost her wrong.
　　*Par.* My vow is made and witnessed, the
　　poplar will not start,
Nor shall the nymph Œnone's love from forth
　　my breathing heart.　　　　　　　85
I will go bring thee on thy way, my flock are
　　here behind,
And I will have a lover's fee; they say, unkiss'd
　　unkind.

　　　　　　　　　　　*Exeunt ambo.*


## ACT. II.　SCENA I

*Venus, Juno, Pallas*

　　*Ven.* (*ex abrupto.*) But pray you, tell me
　　Juno, was it so,
As Pallas told me here the tale of Echo?
　　*Juno.* She was a nymph indeed, as Pallas
　　tells,
A walker, such as in these thickets dwells;
And as she told what subtle juggling pranks　5
She play'd with Juno, so she told her thanks:
A tattling trull to come at every call,
And now, forsooth, nor tongue nor life at all.
And though perhaps she was a help to Jove,
And held me chat while he might court his love,
Believe me, dames, I am of this opinion,　　11
He took but little pleasure in the minion;
And whatsoe'er his scapes have been beside,
Dare say for him, 'a never stray'd so wide:
A lovely nut-brown lass or lusty trull　　15
Have power perhaps to make a god a bull.
　　*Ven.* Gramercy, gentle Juno, for that jest;
I' faith, that item was worth all the rest.
　　*Pal.* No matter, Venus, howsoe'er you
　　scorn,
My father Jove at that time ware the horn.　20
　　*Juno.* Had every wanton god above, Venus,
　　not better luck,
Then heaven would be a pleasant park, and
　　Mars a lusty buck.
　　*Ven.* Tut, Mars hath horns to butt withal,
　　although no bull 'a shows,
'A never needs to mask in nets, 'a fears no
　　jealous froes.
　　*Juno.* Forsooth, the better is his turn, for,
　　if 'a speak too loud,　　　　　　25
Must find some shift to shadow him, a net or
　　else a cloud.

---

⁴² mo: more　　⁶⁹ S. D. Ambo simul: both together　　⁵¹ S. D. Camœnæ: song　　⁴¹ cunning:
letter-perfect　¹ ex abrupto: suddenly　⁶ her thanks: Juno's punishment of Echo　⁷ trull: wench
¹³ scapes: escapades　²⁴ froes: women　²⁶ shift: device　shadow: conceal

*Pal.* No more of this, fair goddesses; unrip
    not so your shames,
To stand all naked to the world, that been such
    heavenly dames.
    *Juno.* Nay, Pallas, that 's a common trick
    with Venus well we know,
And all the gods in heaven have seen her naked
    long ago.                                        30
    *Ven.* And then she was so fair and bright,
    and lovely and so trim,
As Mars is but for Venus' tooth, and she will
    sport with him:
And, but me list not here to make comparison
    with Jove,
Mars is no ranger, Juno, he, in every open
    grove.
    *Pal.* Too much of this: we wander far, the
    skies begin to scowl;                            35
Retire we to Diana's bower, the weather will be
    foul.

*The storm being past of thunder and lightning,
and Ate having trundled the ball into place,
crying, "Fatum Trojæ," Juno taketh the ball
up and speaketh.*

    *Juno.* Pallas, the storm is past and gone,
    and Phœbus clears the skies,
And, lo, behold a ball of gold, a fair and worthy
    prize!
    *Ven.* This posy wills the apple to the fairest
    given be;
Then is it mine, for Venus hight the fairest of
    the three.                                       40
    *Pal.* The fairest here, as fair is meant, am I,
    ye do me wrong;
And if the fairest have it must, to me it doth
    belong.
    *Juno.* Then Juno may it not enjoy, so every
    one says no,
But I will prove myself the fairest, ere I lose
    it so.

*They read the posy.*

The brief is this, *Detur Pulcherrimæ*,           45
Let this unto the fairest given be,
The fairest of the three, — and I am she.

*Pallas reads.*

*Pal.* *Detur pulcherrimæ,*
Let this unto the fairest given be,
The fairest of the three, — and I am she.         50

*Venus reads.*

*Ven.* *Detur pulcherrimæ,*
Let this unto the fairest given be,
The fairest of the three, — and I am she.

    *Juno.* My face is fair; but yet the majesty,
That all the gods in heaven have seen in me, 55
Have made them choose me, of the planets
    seven,
To be the wife of Jove and queen of heaven.
If, then, this prize be but bequeath'd to beauty,
The only she that wins this prize am I.
    *Ven.* That Venus is the fairest, this doth
    prove,                                           60
That Venus is the lovely Queen of Love:
The name of Venus is indeed but beauty,
And men me fairest call per excellency.
If, then, this prize be but bequeath'd to beauty,
The only she that wins this prize am I.            65
    *Pal.* To stand on terms of beauty as you
    take it,
Believe me, ladies, is but to mistake it.
The beauty that this subtle prize must win,
No outward beauty hight, but dwells within;
And sift it as you please, and you shall find, 70
This beauty is the beauty of the mind:
This fairness virtue hight in general,
That many branches hath in special;
This beauty wisdom hight, whereof am I,
By heaven appointed, goddess worthily.            75
And look how much the mind, the better
    part,
Doth overpass the body in desert,
So much the mistress of those gifts divine
Excels thy beauty, and that state of thine.
Then, if this prize be thus bequeath'd to beauty,
The only she that wins this prize am I.            81
    *Ven.* Nay, Pallas, by your leave, you wan-
    der clean:
We must not conster hereof as you mean,
But take the sense as it is plainly meant;
And let the fairest ha't, I am content.            85
    *Pal.* Our reasons will be infinite, I trow,
Unless unto some other point we grow:
But first here 's none, methinks, dispos'd to
    yield,
And none but will with words maintain the
    field.
    *Juno.* Then, if you will, t' avoid a tedious
    grudge,                                          90
Refer it to the sentence of a judge;
Whoe'er he be that cometh next in place,
Let him bestow the ball and end the case.
    *Ven.* So can it not go wrong with me at
    all.
    *Pal.* I am agreed, however it befall:          95
And yet by common doom, so may it be,
I may be said the fairest of the three.
    *Juno.* Then yonder, lo, that shepherd swain
    is he,
That must be umpire in this controversy!

---

**²⁸ but me list:** though I desire    **⁴⁴ S. D. posy:** inscription    **⁴⁵ brief:** writing    **⁸³ conster:** construe
**⁸⁶ reasons:** arguments    **⁹⁰ grudge:** quarrel    **⁹⁴ at all:** ('not at al' Q)    **⁹⁶ doom:** judgment

## ACT. II. SCENA II

*Paris alone. Manentibus Pal., Junone, Venere*

*Ven.* Juno, in happy time! I do accept the
man;
It seemeth by his looks some skill of love he can.
   *Par.* The nymph is gone, and I, all solitary,
Must wend to tend my charge, oppress'd with
   melancholy.
This day (or else me fails my shepherd's skill)
Will tide me passing good or passing ill.       6
   *Juno.* Shepherd, abash not, though at sud-
   den thus
Thou be arriv'd by ignorance among us,
Not earthly but divine, and goddesses all three;
Juno, Pallas, Venus, these our titles be.       10
Nor fear to speak for reverence of the place,
Chosen to end a hard and doubtful case.
This apple, lo (nor ask thou whence it came),
Is to be given unto the fairest dame!
And fairest is, nor she, nor she, but she,       15
Whom, shepherd, thou shalt fairest name to be.
This is thy charge; fulfil without offence,
And she that wins shall give thee recompense.
   *Pal.* Dread not to speak, for we have chosen
   thee,
Sith in this case we can no judges be.       20
   *Ven.* And, shepherd, say that I the fairest
   am,
And thou shalt win good guerdon for the same.
   *Juno.* Nay, shepherd, look upon my stately
   grace,
Because the pomp that 'longs to Juno's mace
Thou mayst not see; and think Queen Juno's
   name,       25
To whom old shepherds title works of fame,
Is mighty, and may easily suffice,
At Phœbus' hand, to gain a golden prize.
And for thy meed, sith I am queen of riches,
Shepherd, I will reward thee with great mon-
   archies,       30
Empires, and kingdoms, heaps of massy gold,
Sceptres and diadems curious to behold,
Rich robes, of sumptuous workmanship and
   cost,
And thousand things whereof I make no boast:
The mould whereon thou treadest shall be of
   Tagus' sands,       35
And Xanthus shall run liquid gold for thee to
   wash thy hands;
And if thou like to tend thy flock, and not from
   them to fly,
Their fleeces shall be curled gold to please their
   master's eye;

And last, to set thy heart on fire, give this one
   fruit to me,
And, shepherd, lo, this tree of gold will I bestow
   on thee!       40

### Juno's Show

*Hereupon did rise a Tree of Gold laden with
diadems and crowns of gold.*

The ground whereon it grows, the grass, the
   root of gold,
The body and the bark of gold, all glistering to
   behold,
The leaves of burnish'd gold, the fruits that
   thereon grow
Are diadems set with pearl in gold, in gorgeous
   glistering show;
And if this tree of gold in lieu may not suffice, 45
Require a grove of golden trees, so Juno bear
   the prize.

### The Tree sinketh.

*Pal.* Me list not tempt thee with decaying
   wealth,
Which is embas'd by want of lusty health;
But if thou have a mind to fly above,
Y-crown'd with fame, near to the seat of Jove,
If thou aspire to wisdom's worthiness,       51
Whereof thou mayst not see the brightness,
If thou desire honour of chivalry,
To be renown'd for happy victory,
To fight it out, and in the champaign field   55
To shroud thee under Pallas' warlike shield,
To prance on barbed steeds: this honour, lo,
Myself for guerdon shall on thee bestow!
And for encouragement, that thou mayst see
What famous knights Dame Pallas' warriors be,
Behold in Pallas' honour here they come,       61
Marching along with sound of thundering drum.

### Pallas' Show

*Hereupon did enter Nine Knights in armour,
treading a warlike almain, by drum and fife;
and then [they] having marched forth again,
Venus speaketh.*

*Ven.* Come, shepherd, come, sweet shep-
   herd, look on me,
These been too hot alarums these for thee:
But if thou wilt give me the golden ball,       65
Cupid my boy shall ha't to play withal,
That, whensoe'er this apple he shall see,
The God of Love himself shall think on thee,
And bid thee look and choose, and he will
   wound
Whereso thy fancy's object shall be found;   70
And lightly, when he shoots, he doth not miss:

---

² **can:** knows   ⁶ **tide:** betide   ⁷ **abash:** be abashed   ²⁵ **Thou:** ('They' Q)   ²⁶ **shepherds:** *i.e.*,
poets   ²⁹ **meed:** reward   ³¹ **massy:** heavy   ³⁵ **mould:** ground   ⁴⁸ **embas'd:** rendered valueless
⁵⁵ **champaign:** level, open   ⁵⁷ **barbed:** caparisoned in armor   ⁶² S. D. **almain:** dance   ⁷¹ **lightly:**
usually

And I will give thee many a lovely kiss,
And come and play with thee on Ida here;
And if thou wilt a face that hath no peer,
A gallant girl, a lusty minion trull,                75
That can give sport to thee thy bellyfull,
To ravish all thy beating veins with joy,
Here is a lass of Venus' court, my boy!
Here, gentle shepherd, here 's for thee a piece,
The fairest face, the flower of gallant Greece.  80

*Venus' Show*

*Here Helen entereth in her bravery, with four
Cupids attending on her, each having his fan
in his hand to fan fresh air in her face: she
singeth as followeth.*

Se Diana nel cielo è una stella
Chiara e lucente, piena de splendore,
Che porge luc' all' affanato cuore;
Se Diana nel ferno è una dea,
Che da conforto all' anime dannate,          85
Che per amor son morte desperate;
Se Diana, ch' in terra è delle nimphe
Reina imperativa di dolci fiori,
Tra bosch' e selve da morte a pastori;
Io son un Diana dolce e rara,                 90
Che con li guardi io posso far guerra
A Dian' infern', in cielo, e in terra.

*The song being ended, Helen departeth, and Paris
speaketh.*

*Par.*  Most heavenly dames, was never man
    as I,
Poor shepherd swain, so happy and unhappy;
The least of these delights that you devise,  95
Able to rape and dazzle human eyes.
But since my silence may not pardon'd be,
And I appoint which is the fairest she,
Pardon, most sacred dames, sith one, not all,
By Paris' doom must have this golden ball. 100
Thy beauty, stately Juno, dame divine,
That like to Phœbus' golden beams doth shine,
Approves itself to be most excellent;
But that fair face that doth me most content,
Sith fair, fair dames, is neither she nor she, 105
But she whom I shall fairest deem to be,
That face is hers that hight the Queen of
    Love,
Whose sweetness doth both gods and creatures
    move.
            *He giveth the golden ball to Venus.*
And if the fairest face deserve the ball,
Fair Venus, ladies, bears it from ye all.    110

*Ven.*  And in this ball doth Venus more de-
    light
Than in her lovely boy fair Cupid's sight.
Come, shepherd, come; sweet Venus is thy
    friend;
No matter how thou other gods offend.

*Venus taketh Paris with her.  Exeunt.*

*Juno.*  But he shall rue and ban the dismal
    day                                       115
Wherein his Venus bare the ball away;
And heaven and earth just witnesses shall be,
I will revenge it on his progeny.
*Pal.*  Well, Juno, whether we be lief or loath,
Venus hath got the apple from us both.      120
                            *Exeunt ambo.*

## ACT. III.  SCENA I

*Colin, th' enamoured shepherd, singeth his pas-
sion of love.*

### THE SONG

O gentle Love, ungentle for thy deed,
    Thou mak'st my heart
    A bloody mark
With piercing shot to bleed!
Shoot soft, sweet Love, for fear thou shoot
    amiss,                                      5
    For fear too keen
    Thy arrows been,
And hit the heart where my beloved is.
Too fair that fortune were, nor never I
    Shall be so blest,                         10
    Among the rest,
That Love shall seize on her by sympathy.
Then since with Love my prayers bear no boot,
    This doth remain
    To cease my pain,                          15
I take the wound, and die at Venus' foot.
                            *Exit Colin.*

## ACT. III.  SCENA II

*Hobbinol, Diggon, Thenot*

*Hob.*  Poor Colin, woeful man, thy life for-
    spoke by love,
What uncouth fit, what malady, is this that
    thou dost prove?
*Dig.*  Or Love is void of physic clean, or
    Love's our common wrack,

---

⁷² **lovely:** loving        ⁷⁵ **minion:** darling        ⁸¹⁻⁹² If Diana in heaven is a star, bright and
shining, full of splendor, which gives light to troubled hearts; if Diana in hell is a goddess who gives
comfort to damned souls who have died desperate through love; if Diana, who on earth is queen of the
nymphs and ruler of the sweet flowers, among the groves and wooded places gives death to the shepherds; I am a Diana sweet and rare who, with my glances, can make war on Diana in hell, in heaven,
and on earth.        ⁹⁶ **rape:** ravish, delight        ¹³ **boot:** influence        ² **uncouth:** unaccustomed        ³ **wrack:**
destruction, woe

That gives us bane to bring us low, and lets us
    medicine lack.
    *Hob.*   That ever Love had reverence 'mong
    silly shepherd swains!                   5
Belike that humour hurts them most that most
    might be their pains.
    *The.*   Hobbin, it is some other god that cher-
    isheth their sheep,
For sure this Love doth nothing else but make
    our herdmen weep.
    *Dig.*   And what a hap is this, I pray, when
    all our woods rejoice,
For Colin thus to be denied his young and
    lovely choice?                   10
    *The.*   She hight indeed so fresh and fair that
    well it is for thee,
Colin, and kind hath been thy friend, that
    Cupid could not see.
    *Hob.*   And whither wends yon thriveless
    swain, like to the stricken deer?
Seeks he dictamnum for his wound within our
    forest here?
    *Dig.*   He wends to greet the Queen of Love,
    that in these woods doth won,       15
With mirthless lays to make complaint to Venus
    of her son.
    *The.*   Ah, Colin, thou art all deceiv'd! she
    dallies with the boy,
And winks at all his wanton pranks, and thinks
    thy love a toy.
    *Hob.*   Then leave him to his luckless love, let
    him abide his fate;
The sore is rankled all too far, our comfort
    comes too late.                 20
    *Dig.*   Though Thestylis the scorpion be that
    breaks his sweet assault,
Yet will Rhamnusia vengeance take on her dis-
    dainful fault.
    *The.*   Lo, yonder comes the lovely nymph,
    that in these Ida vales
Plays with Amyntas' lusty boy, and coys him
    in the dales!
    *Hob.*   Thenot, methinks her cheer is chang'd,
    her mirthful looks are laid,        25
She frolics not; pray god, the lad have not be-
    guil'd the maid!

## ACT. III. SCENA III

*Œnone entereth with a wreath of poplar on her head.*

### Manent Pastores.

    *Œn.*   Beguil'd, disdain'd, and out of love!
    Live long, thou poplar-tree,
And let thy letters grow in length, to witness
    this with me.

Ah, Venus, but for reverence unto thy sacred
    name,
To steal a silly maiden's love, I might account
    it blame;
And if the tales be true I hear, and blush for to
    recite,                   5
Thou dost me wrong to leave the plains and
    dally out of sight.
False Paris, this was not thy vow, when thou
    and I were one,
To range and change old love for new; but now
    those days be gone.
But I will find the goddess out, that she thy vow
    may read,
And fill these woods with my laments for thy
    unhappy deed.              10
    *Hob.*   So fair a face, so foul a thought to
    harbour in his breast!
Thy hope consum'd, poor nymph, thy hap is
    worse than all the rest.
    *Œn.*   Ah, shepherds, you been full of wiles,
    and whet your wits on books,
And rape poor maids with pipes and songs, and
    sweet alluring looks!
    *Dig.*   Mis-speak not all for his amiss; there
    been that keepen flocks,       15
That never chose but once, nor yet beguiled
    love with mocks.
    *Œn.*   False Paris, he is none of those; his
    trothless double deed
Will hurt a many shepherds else that might go
    nigh to speed.
    *The.*   Poor Colin, that is ill for thee, that art
    as true in trust
To thy sweet smart as to his nymph Paris hath
    been unjust.              20
    *Œn.*   Ah, well is she hath Colin won, that
    nill no other love!
And woe is me, my luck is loss, my pains no
    pity move!
    *Hob.*   Farewell, fair nymph, sith he must
    heal alone that gave the wound;
There grows no herb of such effect upon Dame
    Nature's ground.

*Exeunt Pastores.*

## [SCENA IV.]

*Manet Œnone. Mercury entereth with Vulcan's
Cyclops.*

    *Mer.*   Here is a nymph that sadly sits, and
    she beleek
Can tell some news, Pyracmon, of the jolly
    swain we seek:
Dare wage my wings, the lass doth love, she
    looks so bleak and thin;

---

⁷ **their:** ('her' Q)    ¹² **kind:** nature    ¹⁴ **dictamnum:** an herb which deer were said to eat to
heal their wounds    ²² **Rhamnusia:** Nemesis    ²⁴ **coys:** caresses    ²⁵ **cheer:** expression    ¹⁶ **amiss:**
fault    ¹⁸ **speed:** prosper    ¹ **beleek:** ('belike' Q)    ³ **bleak:** wan

And 't is for anger or for grief: but I will talk
  begin.
*Œn.* Break out, poor heart, and make complaint, the mountain flocks to move,     5
What proud repulse and thankless scorn thou
  hast receiv'd of love.
*Mer.* She singeth; sirs, be hush'd a while.

*Œnone singeth as she sits.*

*Œnone's Complaint.*

Melpomene, the Muse of tragic songs,
With mournful tunes, in stole of dismal hue,
Assist a silly nymph to wail her woe,     10
And leave thy lusty company behind.

Thou luckless wreath! becomes not me to wear
The poplar-tree for triumph of my love:
Then, as my joy, my pride of love, is left,
Be thou unclothed of thy lovely green;     15

And in thy leaves my fortune written be,
And them some gentle wind let blow abroad,
That all the world may see how false of love
False Paris hath to his Œnone been.

*The song ended, Œnone sitting still, Mercury*
*speaketh.*

*Mer.* Good day, fair maid; weary belike
  with following of your game,     20
I wish thee cunning at thy will, to spare or
  strike the same.
*Œn.* I thank you, sir; my game is quick,
  and rids a length of ground,
And yet I am deceiv'd, or else 'a had a deadly
  wound.
*Mer.* Your hand perhaps did swerve awry.
*Œn.* Or else it was my heart.     24
*Mer.* Then sure 'a plied his footmanship.
*Œn.* 'A play'd a ranging part.
*Mer.* You should have given a deeper
  wound.
*Œn.* I could not that for pity.
*Mer.* You should have eyed him better,
  then.
*Œn.* Blind love was not so witty.     27
*Mer.* Why, tell me, sweet, are you in love?
*Œn.* Or would I were not so.
*Mer.* Ye mean because a' does ye wrong.
*Œn.* Perdy, the more my woe.     29
*Mer.* Why, mean ye Love, or him ye lov'd?
*Œn.* Well may I mean them both.
*Mer.* Is love to blame?
*Œn.* The Queen of Love hath made him
  false his troth.     31
*Mer.* Mean ye, indeed, the Queen of Love?
*Œn.* Even wanton Cupid's dame.     32

*Mer.* Why, was thy love so lovely, then?
*Œn.* His beauty hight his shame;
The fairest shepherd on our green.
*Mer.* Is he a shepherd, than?     34
*Œn.* And sometime kept a bleating flock.
*Mer.* Enough, this is the man.
Where wons he, than?
*Œn.* About these woods, far from the
  poplar-tree.
*Mer.* What poplar mean ye?
*Œn.* Witness of the vows 'twixt him and me.
And come and wend a little way, and you shall
  see his skill.     38
*Mer.* Sirs, tarry you.
*Œn.* Nay, let them go.
*Mer.* Nay, not unless you will.
Stay, nymph, and hark to what I say of him
  thou blamest so,
And, credit me, I have a sad discourse to tell
  thee ere I go.     41
Know then, my pretty mops, that I hight Mer-
  cury,
The messenger of heaven, and hither fly,
To seize upon the man whom thou dost love,
To summon him before my father Jove,
To answer matter of great consequence:     46
And Jove himself will not be long from hence.
*Œn.* Sweet Mercury, and have poor Œnon's
  cries
For Paris' fault y-pierc'd th' unpartial skies?
*Mer.* The same is he, that jolly shepherd's
  swain.     50
*Œn.* His flock do graze upon Aurora's plain,
The colour of his coat is lusty green;
That would these eyes of mine had never seen
His 'ticing curled hair, his front of ivory!
Then had not I, poor I, been unhappy.     55
*Mer.* No marvel, wench, although we can-
  not find him,
When all too late the Queen of Heaven doth
  mind him.
But if thou wilt have physic for thy sore,
Mind him who list, remember thou him no
  more,
And find some other game, and get thee gone;
For here will lusty suitors come anon,     61
Too hot and lusty for thy dying vein,
Such as ne'er wont to make their suits in
  vain.

*Exit Mercury cum Cyclop.*

*Œn.* I will go sit and pine under the poplar-
  tree,
And write my answer to his vow, that every eye
  may see.     65

                                    *Exit.*

---

⁹ **stole:** Roman matron's robe     ²² **rids:** moves over     ²⁴ **awry:** ('awarie' Q)     ²⁷ **witty:** wise
³¹ **false:** violate     ³⁴ **than:** then     ⁴¹ **to:** (not in Q)     ⁵³ **That would:** Would that!     ⁵⁴ **front:** brow
⁵⁹ **list:** wishes to     ⁶³ **ne'er wont:** ('were monte' Q)

### ACT. III. SCENA V

*Venus, Paris, and a company of Shepherds*

*Ven.*   Shepherds, I am content, for this sweet
shepherd's sake,
A strange revenge upon the maid and her disdain to take.
Let Colin's corpse be brought in place, and
buried in the plain,
And let this be the verse, *The love whom Thestylis hath slain.*
And, trust me, I will chide my son for partiality,             5
That gave the swain so deep a wound, and let
her scape him by.
  *First Shep.*   Alas that ever Love was blind, to
shoot so far amiss!
  *Ven.*   Cupid my son was more to blame, the
fault not mine, but his.

*Pastores exeunt.   Manent Ven. cum Par.*

  *Par.*   O madam, if yourself would deign the
handling of the bow,
Albeit it be a task, yourself more skill, more
justice know.            10
  *Ven.*   Sweet shepherd, didst thou ever love?
  *Par.*   Lady, a little once.
  *Ven.*   And art thou chang'd?
  *Par.*   Fair Queen of Love, I lov'd not all
attonce.
  *Ven.*   Well, wanton, wert thou wounded so
deep as some have been,       15
It were a cunning cure to heal, and rueful to be
seen.
  *Par.*   But tell me, gracious goddess, for a
start and false offence
Hath Venus or her son the power at pleasure to
dispense?
  *Ven.*   My boy, I will instruct thee in a piece
of poetry,
That haply erst thou hast not heard: in hell
there is a tree,       20
Where once a-day do sleep the souls of false
forsworen lovers,
With open hearts; and there about in swarms
the number hovers
Of poor forsaken ghosts, whose wings from off
this tree do beat
Round drops of fiery Phlegethon to scorch false
hearts with heat.
This pain did Venus and her son entreat the
prince of hell       25
T' impose to such as faithless were to such as
lov'd them well:
And, therefore, this, my lovely boy, fair Venus
doth advise thee,

Be true and steadfast in thy love, beware thou
do disguise thee;
For he that makes but love a jest, when pleaseth
him to start,
Shall feel those fiery water-drops consume his
faithless heart.       30
  *Par.*   Is Venus and her son so full of justice
and severity?
  *Ven.*   Pity it were that love should not be
linked with indifferency.
However lovers can exclaim for hard success in
love,
Trust me, some more than common cause that
painful hap doth move:
And Cupid's bow is not alone his triumph, but
his rod;       35
Nor is he only but a boy, he hight a mighty
god;
And they that do him reverence have reason for
the same,
His shafts keep heaven and earth in awe, and
shape rewards for shame.
  *Par.*   And hath he reason to maintain why
Colin died for love?
  *Ven.*   Yea, reason good, I warrant thee, in
right it might behove.       40
  *Par.*   Then be the name of Love ador'd; his
bow is full of might,
His wounds are all but for desert, his laws are
all but right.
  [*Ven.*]   Well, for this once me list apply my
speeches to thy sense,
And Thestylis shall feel the pain for Love's sup-
pos'd offence.

*The Shepherds bring in Colin's hearse, singing,*

Welladay, welladay, poor Colin, thou art going
to the ground,       45
  The love whom Thestylis hath slain,
  Hard heart, fair face, fraught with disdain,
Disdain in love a deadly wound.
  Wound her, sweet Love, so deep again,
  That she may feel the dying pain      50
  Of this unhappy shepherd's swain,
And die for love as Colin died, as Colin died.
               *Finis camœnæ.*

  *Ven.*   Shepherds, abide; let Colin's corpse
be witness of the pain
That Thestylis endures in love, a plague for her
disdain.
Behold the organ of our wrath, this rusty churl
is he;       55
She dotes on his ill-favour'd face, so much accurs'd is she.

*A foul, crooked Churl enters, and Thestylis, a fair
Lass, wooeth him. She singeth an old song
called,* The Wooing of Colman. *He crab-*

*bedly refuseth her, and goeth out of place: she
tarrieth behind.*

*Par.*   Ah, poor unhappy Thestylis, unpitied
is thy pain!
*Ven.*   Her fortune not unlike to hers whom
cruel thou hast slain.

*Thestylis singeth, and the Shepherds reply.*

THE SONG

*Thest.*   The strange affects of my tormented
heart,
Whom cruel love hath woeful prisoner caught,
Whom cruel hate hath into bondage brought, 61
Whom wit no way of safe escape hath taught,
Enforce me say, in witness of my smart,
There is no pain to foul disdain in hardy suits of
love.
*Shepherds.*   There is no pain, &c.   65
*Thest.*   Cruel, farewell.
*Shepherds.*   Cruel, farewell.
*Thest.*   Most cruel thou, of all that nature
fram'd.
*Shepherds.*   Most cruel, &c.
*Thest.*   To kill thy love with thy disdain. 70
*Shepherds.*   To kill thy love with thy dis-
dain.
*Thest.*   Cruel Disdain, so live thou nam'd.
*Shepherds.*   Cruel Disdain, &c.
*Thest.*   And let me die of Iphis' pain.
*Shepherds.*   A life too good for thy disdain.
*Thest.*   Sith this my stars to me allot,   76
And thou thy love hast all forgot.
*Shepherds.*   And thou, &c.

*Exit Thestylis.*

*The grace of this song is in the Shepherds' echo to
her verse.*

*Ven.*   Now, shepherds, bury Colin's corpse,
perfume his hearse with flowers,
And write what justice Venus did amid these
woods of yours.   80

*The Shepherds carry out Colin.*

How now, how cheers my lovely boy, after this
dump of love?
*Par.*   Such dumps, sweet lady, as been these,
are deadly dumps to prove.
*Ven.*   Cease, shepherd, there are other news,
after this melancholy:
My mind presumes some tempest toward upon
the speech of Mercury.

ACT. III.   SCENA VI

*Mercury with Vulcan's Cyclops enter.*
*Manentibus Ven. cum Par.*

*Mer.*   Fair Lady Venus, let me pardon'd
be,
That have of long been well-belov'd of thee,
If, as my office bids, myself first brings
To my sweet madam these unwelcome tidings.
*Ven.*   What news, what tidings, gentle Mer-
cury,   5
In midst of my delights, to trouble me?
*Mer.*   At Juno's suit, Pallas assisting her,
Sith both did join in suit to Jupiter,
Action is enter'd in the court of heaven;
And me, the swiftest of the planets seven,   10
With warrant they have thence despatch'd
away,
To apprehend and find the man, they say,
That gave from them that self-same ball of
gold,
Which, I presume, I do in place behold;
Which man, unless my marks be taken wide,   15
Is he that sits so near thy gracious side.
This being so, it rests he go from hence,
Before the gods to answer his offence.
*Ven.*   What tale is this?   Doth Juno and her
mate
Pursue this shepherd with such deadly hate,   20
As what was then our general agreement
To stand unto they nill be now content?
Let Juno jet, and Pallas play her part,
What here I have, I won it by desert;
And heaven and earth shall both confounded
be,   25
Ere wrong in this be done to him or me.
*Mer.*   This little fruit, if Mercury can spell,
Will send, I fear, a world of souls to hell.
*Ven.*   What mean these Cyclops, Mercury?
Is Vulcan wax'd so fine,
To send his chimney-sweepers forth to fetter
any friend of mine? —   30
Abash not, shepherd, at the thing; myself thy
bail will be. —
He shall be present at the court of Jove, I war-
rant thee.
*Mer.*   Venus, give me your pledge.
*Ven.*   My ceston, or my fan, or both?
*Mer.*   *(taketh her fan.)*   Nay, this shall
serve: your word to me as sure as is your
oath.   35
At Diana's bower; and, lady, if my wit or policy
May profit him, for Venus' sake let him make
bold with Mercury.

*Exit [with the Cyclops].*

*Ven.*   Sweet Paris, whereon dost thou muse?

---

**58 hers:** ('his' Q)   **59 affects:** passions ('effects' Q)   **81 dump:** melancholy song   **82 prove:**
experience   **84 toward:** at hand   **15 my . . . wide:** I am mistaken   **23 jet:** strut   **34 ceston:** girdle

*Par.*  The angry heavens, for this fatal jar,
Name me the instrument of dire and deadly
   war.                                        40

*Explicit Actus Tertius. Exeunt Venus and Paris.*

## ACT. IIII. SCENA I

*Vulcan, following one of Diana's Nymphs*

*Vul.*  Why, nymph, what need ye run so
   fast?  What though but black I be?
I have more pretty knacks to please than every
   eye doth see;
And though I go not so upright, and though I
   am a smith,
To make me gracious you may have some other
   thing therewith.

## ACT. IIII. SCENA II

*Bacchus, Vulcan, Nymph*

*Bac.*  Yea, Vulcan, will ye so indeed? —
   Nay, turn, and tell him, trull,
He hath a mistress of his own to take his belly-
   full.
*Vul.*  Why sir, if Phœbe's dainty nymphs
   please lusty Vulcan's tooth,
Why may not Vulcan tread awry as well as
   Venus doth?
*Nym.*  Ye shall not taint your troth for me:
   you wot it very well,                          5
All that be Dian's maids are vow'd to halter
   apes in hell.
*Bac.*  I' faith, i' faith, my gentle mops, but I
   do know a cast,
Lead apes who list, that we would help t'un-
   halter them as fast.
*Nym.*  Fie, fie, your skill is wondrous great!
   had thought the God of Wine
Had tended but his tubs and grapes, and not
   been half so fine.                             10
*Vul.*  Gramercy for that quirk, my girl.
*Bac.*  That 's one of dainty's frumps.
*Nym.*  I pray, sir, take 't with all amiss; our
   cunning comes by lumps.
*Vul.*  Sh'ath capp'd his answer in the cue.
*Nym.*  How says 'a, has she so?               13
As well as she that capp'd your head to keep
   you warm below.
*Vul.*  Yea, then you will be curst I see.
*Bac.*  Best let her even alone.
*Nym.*  Yea, gentle gods, and find some other
   string to harp upon.

*Bac.*  Some other string! agreed, i' faith, some
   other pretty thing;                            17
'T were shame fair maids should idle be: how
   say you, will ye sing?
*Nym.*  Some rounds or merry roundelays, we
   sing no other songs;
Your melancholic notes not to our country
   mirth belongs.                                 20
*Vul.*  Here comes a crew will help us trim.

## ACTVS IIII. SCENA III

*Mercury with the Cyclops*

*Mer.*  Yea, now our task is done.
*Bac.*  Then merry, Mercury; more than
   time this round were well begun.

*They sing "Hey down, down, down," &c.*

*The song done, she windeth a horn in Vulcan's
ear, and runneth out.  Manent Vulcan, Bacchus, Mercury, Cyclops.*

*Vul.*  A harlotry, I warrant her.
*Bac.*  A peevish elvish shroe.
*Mer.*  Have seen as far to come as near, for
   all her ranging so.                            5
But, Bacchus, time well-spent I wot, our sacred
   father Jove,
With Phœbus and the God of War are met in
   Dian's grove.
*Vul.*  Then we are here before them yet: but
   stay, the earth doth swell;
God Neptune, too (this hap is good), doth meet
   the Prince of Hell.

*Pluto ascendeth from below in his chair; Neptune
entereth at another way.*

*Plu.*  What jars are these, that call the gods
   of heaven and hell below?                      10
*Nep.*  It is a work of wit and toil to rule a
   lusty shroe.

## ACT. IIII. SCENA IIII

*Enter Jupiter, Saturn, Apollo, Mars, Juno,
Pallas, and Diana.*

*Jupiter speaketh.*

*Jup.*  Bring forth the man of Troy, that he
   may hear
Whereof he is to be arraigned here.
*Nep.*  Lo, where 'a comes, prepar'd to plead
   his case,
Under conduct of lovely Venus' grace!

*[Enter Venus with Paris.]*

---

³⁹ **jar:** quarrel     ² **knacks:** tricks     ⁶ **halter . . . hell:** (Spinsters were proverbially doomed to
lead apes in hell. For 'apes' Q reads 'apples.')     ⁷ **cast:** device     ¹¹ **quirk:** quip     **frumps:**
mocking speeches     ¹⁵ **curst:** ill-tempered     ²¹ **trim:** finely     s. d. **windeth:** bloweth     ³ **harlotry:**
silly girl     ⁴ **shroe:** shrew     IV. iv. s. d. (Q adds names of those already present: Pluto, Neptune,
Bacchus, Vulcan, Mercury, Cyclops.)

*Mer.*  I have not seen a more alluring boy. 5
*Apol.*  So beauty hight the wrack of Priam's
Troy.

*The gods being set in Diana's bower, Juno, Pallas,
Venus, and Paris stand on sides before them.*

*Ven.*  Lo, sacred Jove, at Juno's proud com-
plaint,
As erst I gave my pledge to Mercury,
I bring the man whom he did late attaint,
To answer his indictment orderly; 10
And crave this grace of this immortal senate,
That ye allow the man his advocate.
*Pal.*  That may not be; the laws of heaven
deny
A man to plead or answer by attorney.
*Ven.*  Pallas, thy doom is all too peremptory.
*Apol.*  Venus, that favour is denied him
flatly: 16
He is a man, and therefore by our laws,
Himself, without his aid, must plead his cause.
*Ven.*  Then 'bash not, shepherd, in so good a
case;
And friends thou hast, as well as foes, in place.
*Juno.*  Why, Mercury, why do ye not indict
him? 21
*Ven.*  Soft, gentle Juno, I pray you, do not
bite him.
*Juno.*  Nay, gods, I trow, you are like to
have great silence,
Unless this parrot be commanded hence.
*Jup.*  Venus, forbear, be still. — Speak,
Mercury. 25
*Ven.*  If Juno jangle, Venus will reply.
*Mer.*  Paris, king Priam's son, thou art ar-
raign'd of partiality,
Of sentence partial and unjust; for that with-
out indifferency,
Beyond desert or merit far, as thine accusers
say,
From them, to Lady Venus here, thou gavest
the prize away: 30
What is thine answer?

*Paris' oration to the Council of the Gods.*

Sacred and just, thou great and dreadful Jove,
And you thrice-reverend powers, whom love
nor hate
May wrest awry: if this, to me a man,
This fortune fatal be, that I must plead 35
For safe excusal of my guiltless thought,
The honour more makes my mishap the less,
That I a man must plead before the gods,
Gracious forbearers of the world's amiss,
For her, whose beauty how it hath entic'd, 40
This heavenly senate may with me aver.
But sith nor that nor this may do me boot,

And for myself myself must speaker be,
A mortal man amidst this heavenly presence;
Let me not shape a long defence to them 45
That been beholders of my guiltless thoughts.
Then for the deed, — that I may not deny,
Wherein consists the full of mine offence, —
I did upon command; if then I err'd,
I did no more than to a man belong'd. 50
And if, in verdit of their forms divine,
My dazzled eye did swarve or surfeit more
On Venus' face than any face of theirs,
It was no partial fault, but fault of his,
Belike, whose eyesight not so perfect was 55
As might discern the brightness of the rest.
And if it were permitted unto men,
Ye gods, to parley with your secret thoughts,
There been that sit upon that sacred seat,
That would with Paris err in Venus' praise. 60
But let me cease to speak of error here;
Sith what my hand, the organ of my heart,
Did give with good agreement of mine eye,
My tongue is vow'd with process to maintain.
*Plu.*  A jolly shepherd, wise and eloquent. 65
*Par.*  First, then, arraign'd of partiality,
Paris replies, "Unguilty of the fact;"
His reason is, because he knew no more
Fair Venus' ceston than Dame Juno's mace,
Nor never saw wise Pallas' crystal shield. 70
Then as I look'd, I lov'd and lik'd attonce,
And as it was referr'd from them to me,
To give the prize to her whose beauty best
My fancy did commend, so did I praise
And judge as might my dazzled eye discern. 75
*Nep.*  A piece of art, that cunningly, perdy,
Refers the blame to weakness of his eye.
*Par.*  Now, for I must add reason for my
deed,
Why Venus rather pleas'd me of the three;
First, in the intrails of my mortal ears, 80
The question standing upon beauty's blaze,
The name of her that hight the Queen of Love,
Methought, in beauty should not be excell'd.
Had it been destined to majesty
(Yet will I not rob Venus of her grace), 85
Then stately Juno might have borne the ball.
Had it to wisdom been intituled,
My human wit had given it Pallas then.
But sith unto the fairest of the three
That power, that threw it for my farther ill, 90
Did dedicate this ball; and safest durst
My shepherd's skill adventure, as I thought,
To judge of form and beauty rather than
Of Juno's state or Pallas' worthiness, —
That learn'd to ken the fairest of the flock, 95
And praised beauty but by nature's aim; —
Behold, to Venus Paris gave this fruit,

---

⁴ **s. d. Pallas:** ('Pallas, Diana' Q)  ¹⁸ **aid:** advocate  ³⁹ **forbearers:** interceptors  ⁵¹ **verdit:**
**judgment**  ⁵² **swarve:** swerve  ⁶⁴ **process:** systematic argument  ⁸⁰ **intrails:** sound-passages
⁸¹ **blaze:** proclamation  ⁸⁷ **intituled:** inscribed  ⁹² **adventure:** venture

A daysman chosen there by full consent,
And heavenly powers should not repent their
   deeds.
Where it is said, beyond desert of hers    100
I honour'd Venus with this golden prize,
Ye gods, alas, what can a mortal man
Discern betwixt the sacred gifts of heaven?
Or, if I may with reverence reason thus:
Suppose I gave — and judg'd corruptly then,
For hope of that that best did please my
   thought —    106
This apple, not for beauty's praise alone;
I might offend, sith I was guerdoned,
And tempted more than ever creature was
With wealth, with beauty, and with chivalry,
And so preferr'd beauty before them all,    111
The thing that hath enchanted heaven itself.
And for the one, contentment is my wealth;
A shell of salt will serve a shepherd swain,
A slender banquet in a homely scrip,    115
And water running from the silver spring.
For arms, they dread no foes that sit so low;
A thorn can keep the wind from off my back,
A sheep-cote thatch'd a shepherd's palace hight.
Of tragic Muses shepherds con no skill;    120
Enough is them, if Cupid been displeas'd,
To sing his praise on slender oaten pipe.
And thus, thrice-reverend, have I told my tale,
And crave the torment of my guiltless soul
To be measured by my faultless thought.    125
If warlike Pallas or the Queen of Heaven
Sue to reverse my sentence by appeal,
Be it as please your majesties divine;
The wrong, the hurt, not mine, if any be,
But hers whose beauty claim'd the prize of me.

*Paris having ended, Jupiter speaketh.*

*Jup.* Venus, withdraw your shepherd for a
   space,    131
Till he again be call'd for into place.
                   *Exeunt Venus and Paris.*
Juno, what will ye after this reply,
But doom with sentence of indifferency?
And if you will but justice in the cause,    135
The man must quited be by heaven's laws.
*Juno.* Yea, gentle Jove, when Juno's suits
   are mov'd,
Then heaven may see how well she is belov'd.
*Apol.* But, madam, fits it majesty divine
In any sort from justice to decline?    140
*Pal.* Whether the man be guilty, yea or no,
That doth not hinder our appeal, I trow.
*Juno.* Phœbus, I wot, amid this heavenly
   crew,
There be that have to say as well as you.
*Apol.* And, Juno, I with them, and they
   with me,    145

In law and right must needfully agree.
*Pal.* I grant ye may agree, but be content
To doubt upon regard of your agreement.
*Plu.* And if ye mark'd, the man in his de-
fence
Said thereof as 'a might with reverence.    150
*Vul.* And did ye very well, I promise ye.
*Juno.* No doubt, sir, you could note it cun-
ningly.
*Sat.* Well, Juno, if ye will appeal, ye may,
But first despatch the shepherd hence away.
*Mars.* Then Vulcan's dame is like to have
   the wrong.    155
*Juno.* And that in passion doth to Mars
   belong.
*Jup.* Call Venus and the shepherd in again.

                *[Exit Mercury.]*

*Bac.* And rid the man that he may know his
   pain.
*Apol.* His pain, his pain, his never-dying
   pain,
A cause to make a many mo complain.    160

   *Mercury bringeth in Venus and Paris.*

*Jup.* Shepherd, thou hast been heard with
   equity and law,
And for thy stars do thee to other calling
   draw,
We here dismiss thee hence, by order of our
   senate:
Go take thy way to Troy, and there abide thy
   fate.
*Ven.* Sweet shepherd, with such luck in
   love, while thou dost live,    165
As may the Queen of Love to any lover give.
*Par.* My luck is loss, howe'er my love do
   speed:
I fear me Paris shall but rue his deed.
                      *Paris exit.*
*Apol.* From Ida woods now wends the
   shepherd's boy,
That in his bosom carries fire to Troy.    170
*Jup.* Venus, these ladies do appeal, you
   see,
And that they may appeal the gods agree:
It resteth, then, that you be well content
To stand in this unto our final judgment;
And if King Priam's son did well in this,    175
The law of heaven will not lead amiss.
*Ven.* But, sacred Jupiter, might thy daugh-
   ter choose,
She might with reason this appeal refuse:
Yet if they be unmoved in their shames,
Be it a stain and blemish to their names;    180
A deed, too, far unworthy of the place,
Unworthy Pallas' lance or Juno's mace;

---

**98 daysman:** umpire    **108 guerdoned:** ('pardoned' Q)    **120 con:** know, have    **136 quited:**
acquitted    **148 upon regard:** considering the circumstances    **158 rid:** dismiss

And if to beauty it bequeathed be,
I doubt not but it will return to me.

*She layeth down the ball.*

*Pal.* Venus, there is no more ado than so, 185
It resteth where the gods do it bestow.

*Nep.* But, ladies, under favour of your rage,
Howe'er it be, you play upon the vantage.

*Jup.* Then, dames, that we more freely may
debate,
And hear th' indifferent sentence of this sen-
ate,                                            190
Withdraw you from this presence for a space,
Till we have throughly question'd of the case:
Dian shall be your guide; nor shall you need
Yourselves t' inquire how things do here suc-
ceed;
We will, as we resolve, give you to know, 195
By general doom how everything doth go.

*Dia.* Thy will, my wish. — Fair ladies, will
ye wend?

*Juno.* Beshrew her whom this sentence doth
offend.

*Ven.* Now, Jove, be just; and, gods, you
that be Venus' friends,
If you have ever done her wrong, then may you
make amends.                                   200

*Manent Dii. Exeunt Diana, Pallas, Juno,
Venus.*

*Jup.* Venus is fair, Pallas and Juno too.

*Vul.* But tell me now without some more
ado,
Who is the fairest she, and do not flatter.

*Plu.* Vulcan, upon comparison hangs all the
matter:
That done, the quarrel and the strife were
ended.                                         205

*Mars.* Because 't is known, the quarrel is
pretended.

*Vul.* Mars, you have reason for your speech,
perdy;
My dame, I trow, is fairest in your eye.

*Mars.* Or, Vulcan, I should do her double
wrong.

*Sat.* About a toy we tarry here so long. 210
Give it by voices, voices give the odds;
A trifle so to trouble all the gods!

*Nep.* Believe me, Saturn, be it so for me.

*Bac.* For me.

*Plu.* For me.

*Mars.* For me, if Jove agree.

*Mer.* And, gentle gods, I am indifferent; 215
But then I know who 's likely to be shent.

*Apol.* Thrice-reverend gods, and thou, immortal Jove,

If Phœbus may, as him doth much behove,
Be licensed, according to our laws,
To speak uprightly in this doubted cause   220
(Sith women's wits work men's unceasing
woes),
To make them friends, that now been friendless
foes,
And peace to keep with them, with us, and all,
That make their title to this golden ball
(Nor think, ye gods, my speech doth derogate
From sacred power of this immortal senate); 226
Refer this sentence where it doth belong.
In this, say I, fair Phœbe hath the wrong;
Not that I mean her beauty bears the prize,
But that the holy law of heaven denies    230
One god to meddle in another's power;
And this befell so near Diana's bower,
As for th' appeasing this unpleasant grudge,
In my conceit, she hight the fittest judge.
If Jove control not Pluto's hell with charms, 235
If Mars have sovereign power to manage
arms,
If Bacchus bear no rule in Neptune's sea,
Nor Vulcan's fire doth Saturn's scythe obey,
Suppress not, then, 'gainst law and equity,
Diana's power in her own territory,        240
Whose regiment, amid her sacred bowers,
As proper hight as any rule of yours.
Well may we so wipe all the speech away,
That Pallas, Juno, Venus, hath to say,
And answer that, by justice of our laws,   245
We were not suffer'd to conclude the cause.
And this to me most egal doom appears,
A woman to be judge among her pheeres.

*Mer.* Apollo hath found out the only mean
To rid the blame from us and trouble clean. 250

*Vul.* We are beholding to his sacred wit.

*Jup.* I can commend and well allow of it;
And so derive the matter from us all,
That Dian have the giving of the ball.

*Vul.* So Jove may clearly excuse him in the
case,                                          255
Where Juno else would chide and brawl apace.

*All they rise and go forth.*

*Mer.* And now it were some cunning to divine
To whom Diana will this prize resign.

*Vul.* Sufficeth me, it shall be none of mine.

*Bac.* Vulcan, though thou be black, th' art
nothing fine.                                  260

*Vul.* Go bathe thee, Bacchus, in a tub of
wine;
The ball 's as likely to be mine as thine.

*Exeunt omnes. Explicit Act IV.*

---

**188 vantage:** your special privileges or capacities to influence the judges    **192 throughly:**
thoroughly    **194 succeed:** follow, happen    **196 doom:** announced judgment    **201 s. d. Dii:** the gods
**211 voices:** votes    **216 shent:** blamed    **220 doubted:** doubtful    **234 conceit:** opinion    **237 Neptune's:**
('Neptune' Q)    **241 regiment:** rule    **247 egal:** just    **251 beholding:** indebted    **253 derive:** divert

ACT. V. *et ultimi*, SCENA I

*Diana, Pallas, Juno, Venus*

*Dia.* Lo, ladies, far beyond my hope and
    will, you see,
This thankless office is impos'd to me;
Wherein if you will rest as well content,
As Dian will be judge indifferent,
My egal doom shall none of you offend,     5
And of this quarrel make a final end:
And therefore, whether you be lief or loath,
Confirm your promise with some sacred oath.
   *Pal.* Phœbe, chief mistress of this sylvan
    chace,
Whom gods have chosen to conclude the case 10
That yet in balance undecided lies,
Touching bestowing of this golden prize,
I give my promise and mine oath withal,
By Styx, by heaven's power imperial,
By all that 'longs to Pallas' deity,      15
Her shield, her lance, ensigns of chivalry,
Her sacred wreath of olive and of bay,
Her crested helm, and else what Pallas may,
That wheresoe'er this ball of purest gold,
That chaste Diana here in hand doth hold, 20
Unpartially her wisdom shall bestow,
Without mislike or quarrel any mo,
Pallas shall rest content and satisfied,
And say the best desert doth there abide.
   *Juno.* And here I promise and protest
    withal,      25
By Styx, by heaven's power imperial,
By all that 'longs to Juno's deity,
Her crown, her mace, ensigns of majesty,
Her spotless marriage-rites, her league divine,
And by that holy name of Proserpine,    30
That wheresoe'er this ball of purest gold,
That chaste Diana here in hand doth hold,
Unpartially her wisdom shall bestow,
Without mislike or quarrel any mo,
Juno shall rest content and satisfied,    35
And say the best desert doth there abide.
   *Ven.* And, lovely Phœbe, for I know thy
    doom
Will be no other than shall thee become,
Behold, I take thy dainty hand to kiss,
And with my solemn oath confirm my promise,
By Styx, by Jove's immortal empery,    41
By Cupid's bow, by Venus' myrtle-tree,
By Vulcan's gift, my ceston and my fan,
By this red rose, whose colour first began
When erst my wanton boy (the more his blame)
Did draw his bow awry and hurt his dame, 46
By all the honour and the sacrifice
That from Cithæron and from Paphos rise,

That wheresoe'er this ball of purest gold,
That chaste Diana here in hand doth hold, 50
Unpartially her wisdom shall bestow,
Without mislike or quarrel any mo,
Venus shall rest content and satisfied,
And say the best desert doth there abide.

*Diana, having taken their oaths, speaketh.*

*Diana describeth the Nymph Eliza, a figure of the
              Queen.*

   *Dia.* It is enough, and, goddesses, attend.
There wons within these pleasant shady
    woods,      56
Where neither storm nor sun's distemperature
Have power to hurt by cruel heat or cold,
Under the climate of the milder heaven;
Where seldom lights Jove's angry thunder-
    bolt,      60
For favour of that sovereign earthly peer;
Where whistling winds make music 'mong the
    trees, —
Far from disturbance of our country gods,
Amids the cypress-springs, a gracious nymph,
That honours Dian for her chastity,    65
And likes the labours well of Phœbe's groves;
The place Elyzium hight, and of the place
Her name that governs there Eliza is:
A kingdom that may well compare with mine,
An auncient seat of kings, a second Troy,   70
Y-compass'd round with a commodious sea.
Her people are y-cleped *Angeli*,
Or, if I miss, a letter is the most:
She giveth laws of justice and of peace;
And on her head, as fits her fortune best,    75
She wears a wreath of laurel, gold, and palm;
Her robes of purple and of scarlet dye;
Her veil of white, as best befits a maid:
Her auncestors live in the House of Fame:
She giveth arms of happy victory,    80
And flowers to deck her lions crown'd with
    gold.
This peerless nymph, whom heaven and earth
    beloves,
This paragon, this only, this is she,
In whom do meet so many gifts in one,
On whom our country gods so often gaze,    85
In honour of whose name the Muses sing;
In state Queen Juno's peer, for power in arms
And virtues of the mind Minerva's mate,
As fair and lovely as the Queen of Love,
As chaste as Dian in her chaste desires:    90
The same is she, if Phœbe do no wrong,
To whom this ball in merit doth belong.
   *Pal.* If this be she whom some Zabeta
    call,
To whom thy wisdom well bequeaths the ball.

---

⁷ **or:** ('of' Q)    ⁶⁴ **springs:** groves    ⁶⁵ **honours:** ('honour' Q)    ⁷³ **a . . . most:** *i.e.,* 'Angli'
(English)    ⁹¹ **do . . . wrong:** be not mistaken    ⁹³ **Zabeta:** Elizabeth, so called in Gascoigne's
masque at Kenilworth (1575)

I can remember, at her day of birth,            95
How Flora with her flowers strew'd the earth,
How every power with heavenly majesty
In person honour'd that solemnity.
*Juno.* The lovely Graces were not far away,
They threw their balm for triumph of the day.
*Ven.* The Fates against their kind began a
   cheerful song,                               101
And vow'd her life with favour to prolong.
Then first gan Cupid's eyesight wexen dim;
Belike Eliza's beauty blinded him.
To this fair nymph, not earthly, but divine, 105
Contents it me my honour to resign.
   *Pal.* To this fair queen, so beautiful and
   wise,
Pallas bequeaths her title in the prize.
   *Juno.* To her whom Juno's looks so well be-
   come,
The Queen of Heaven yields at Phœbe's doom;
And glad I am Diana found the art,           111
Without offence so well to please desart.
   *Dia.* Then mark my tale. The usual time is
   nigh,
When wont the Dames of Life and Destiny,
In robes of cheerful colours, to repair      115
To this renowned queen so wise and fair,
With pleasaunt songs this peerless nymph to
   greet;
Clotho lays down her distaff at her feet,
And Lachesis doth pull the thread at length,
The third with favour gives it stuff and
   strength;                                     120
And for contrary kind affords her leave,
As her best likes, her web of life to weave.
This time we will attend, and in the mean-
   while
With some sweet song the tediousness beguile.

*The Music sound, and the Nymphs within sing*
*or solfa with voices and instruments awhile.*
*Then enter Clotho, Lachesis, and Atropos,*
*singing as followeth: the state being in place.*

### THE SONG

*Clo. Humanæ vitæ filum sic volvere Parcæ.*
*Lach. Humanæ vitæ filum sic tendere Par-*
   *cæ.*                                          126
*Atro. Humanæ vitæ filum sic scindere Par-*
   *cæ.*
*Clo. Clotho colum bajulat.*

*Lach. Lachesis trahit.*
*Atro. Atropos occat.*                           130
*Tres Simul. Vive diu felix votis hominumque*
   *deûmque,*
*Corpore, mente, libro, doctissima, candida, casta.*

*They lay down their properties at the Queen's feet.*

   *Clo. Clotho colum pedibus.*
   *Lach. Lachesis tibi pendula fila.*
   *Atro. Et fatale tuis manibus ferrum Atropos*
   *offert.*                                       135
*[Tres Simul]. Vive diu felix, &c.*

*The song being ended, Clotho speaks to the Queen.*

   *Clo.* Gracious and wise, fair Queen of rare
   renown,
Whom heaven and earth beloves, amid thy
   train,
Noble and lovely peers: to honour thee,
And do thee favour more than may belong      140
By nature's law to any earthly wight,
Behold continuance of our yearly due;
Th' unpartial Dames of Destiny we meet,
As have the gods and we agreed in one,
In reverence of Eliza's noble name;          145
And humbly, lo, her distaff Clotho yields!
   *Lach.* Her spindle Lachesis, and her fatal
   reel,
Lays down in reverence at Eliza's feet.
*Te tamen in terris unam tria numina Divam*
*Invita statuunt naturæ lege sorores,*         150
*Et tibi, non aliis, didicerunt parcere Parcæ.*
   *Atro.* Dame Atropos, according as her
   pheeres,
To thee, fair Queen, resigns her fatal knife:
Live long the noble phœnix of our age,
Our fair Eliza, our Zabeta fair!             155
   *Dia.* And, lo, beside this rare solemnity,
And sacrifice these dames are wont to do, —
A favour, far indeed contrary kind, —
Bequeathed is unto thy worthiness
This prize from heaven and heavenly goddesses!

*She delivereth the ball of gold to the Queen's own*
*hands.*

Accept it, then, thy due by Dian's doom,     161
Praise of the wisdom, beauty, and the state,
That best becomes thy peerless excellency.
   *Ven.* So, fair Eliza, Venus doth resign
The honour of this honour to be thine.       165

---

**101** against . . . kind: contrary to their nature   **103** **wexen:** to grow   **121** **And for:** because
**124** S. D. **solfa:** sing the notes of the scale   **state:** royal chair with a canopy   **125** So the Fates spin
the thread of human life.   **126** **tendere:** draw out   **127** **scindere:** cut   **128** Clotho bears the distaff.
**129** **trahit:** draws (the thread)   **130** **occat:** cuts (it)   **131-132** Live long, happy in the prayers of
men and gods, in body, mind, and book (*i.e.,* wisdom or learning), most learned, fair, and chaste.
**133** Clotho (lays) the distaff at your feet.   **134** Lachesis (offers) to you the pendant threads.
**135** And Atropos offers to your hands the fatal knife.   **149-151** But you on earth one goddess the three
sister divinities decree against nature's law, and you, not others, the Fates have learned to spare.
**158** **contrary kind:** contrary to their nature

*Juno.* So is the Queen of Heaven content
   likewise
To yield to thee her title in the prize.
  *Pal.* So Pallas yields the praise hereof to
   thee,
For wisdom, princely state, and peerless beauty.

## EPILOGUS

*Omnes Simul.  Vive diu felix votis hominum-*
   *que deûmque,*            170
*Corpore, mente, libro, doctissima, candida, casta.*
                 *Exeunt omnes.*

FINIS

# THE
# Old Wiues Tale.

A pleafant conceited Comedie, played by the Queenes Ma-
iefties players.

Written by *G. P.*

Printed at London by *Iohn Danter*, and are to
be fold by *Raph Hancocke*, and *Iohn
Hardie.* 1 5 9 5.

BIBLIOGRAPHICAL RECORD. On April 16, 1595, Ralph Hancock *Entred for his Copie vnder thandes* (*i.e.*, the signatures) *of bothe the wardens a booke or interlude intituled a pleasant Conceipte called the owlde wifes tale*. In the same year the only source of our text, a Quarto, appeared, printed by the disorderly John Danter (the printer also of the first edition of *Titus Andronicus*, 1594, and the bad first Quarto of *Romeo and Juliet*, 1597), for sale by Hancock and John Hardy. The last page bears the colophon: *Printed at London by Iohn Danter, for Raph Hancocke, and Iohn Hardie, and are to be solde at the shop ouer against Saint Giles his Church without Criplegate. 1595.*

There were no other early editions, and the play was not reprinted till 1828.

DATE AND STAGE PERFORMANCE. The Queen's players, by whom the comedy was produced (see facsimile title-page) had been organized in 1583 by Sir Francis Walsingham, who selected from among the actors of the day twelve of the best for the Queen's special service, the famous clown, Richard Tarleton, being one. After Tarleton's death in 1588, however, this group was not long able to compete successfully with the other London companies, and in the spring of 1594 they abandoned the effort and retired to the provinces for good. This was doubtless the occasion which made Peele's play, and several by Greene as well, available for printing.

We cannot date the first production of *The Old Wives Tale*, but it occurred in the years when the fortunes of the Queen's Company were declining, and the very brief text that has come down may be a specially shortened version for performance in the country. The play cannot well be earlier than Greene's *Orlando Furioso*, which the Queen's Men bought in 1591, from which are taken the conjurer's name, Sacrapant, and two almost-verbatim quotations (see notes on lines 758 and 990–993). It had no further stage history until very modern times.

AUTHORSHIP. Peele's authorship is attested externally only by the initials, G. P., on the title-page; but this has not been questioned, and the internal evidence of his peculiar genius is abundantly conspicuous.

STRUCTURE. No act or scene division is indicated in the Quarto, and as the text stands none can profitably be attempted. The piece was probably intended from the first as a "pleasant Conceipte" rather than a full-dress comedy, and designed for the simplest stages.

SOURCES. The general idea may well have been suggested by Greene's narrative *Perimedes the Blacksmith* (1588), which deals with the blacksmith and his wife (Delia) and the motive of story-telling. The brilliant interweaving of varied folklore elements is Peele's most genial and characteristic contribution. This has been well studied by Miss S. L. C. Clapp ("Peele's Use of Folk-Lore in *The Old Wives Tale*," Univ. of Texas Studies in English, 1926). It can hardly be doubted that the braggart Huanebango satirizes Gabriel Harvey, whom Nashe, Lyly, and Greene were all ridiculing in the years about 1590, and it is probable that contemporaries saw other topical references in Peele's play. See, however, Gwenan Jones, "The Intention of Peele's *Old Wives Tale*," Aberystwyth Studies, 1925, 79–93. (The influence of the story of Sacrapant, Delia, and the two brothers upon Milton's *Comus* has been often noted.)

# GEORGE PEELE

## THE OLD WIVES TALE

[DRAMATIS PERSONAE

ANTIC,   ⎫<br>
FROLIC,   ⎬ Pages<br>
FANTASTIC, ⎭<br>
CLUNCH, a Smith<br>
MADGE, his Old Wife

CALYPHA, ⎫ Brothers, seeking<br>
THELEA,  ⎭ Delia, their sister<br>
ERESTUS, the Old Man at the Cross<br>
LAMPRISCUS, a Countryman<br>
HUANEBANGO, a Braggart

COREBUS, or BOOBY, the Clown<br>
SACRAPANT, a Magician<br>
EUMENIDES, a Wandering Knight, in love with Delia<br>
WIGGEN, a Parish Unthrift<br>
STEVEN LOACH, a Churchwarden

DELIA, Daughter of the King of Thessaly<br>
VENELIA, Betrothed to Erestus<br>
ZANTIPPA, ⎫ Daughters of<br>
CELANTA,  ⎭ Lampriscus

A Friar; a Sexton; Voice from Well of Life; Ghost of Jack; Hostess; Harvesters; two Furies; Fiddlers.

SCENE: An English wood and Clunch's house on the edge of it.]

*Enter Antic, Frolic, and Fantastic*

*Ant.* How now, fellow Frolic! What, all amort? Doth this sadness become thy madness? What though we have lost our way in the woods, yet never hang the head as though thou hadst no hope to live till to-morrow; for [5 Fantastic and I will warrant thy life to-night for twenty in the hundred.

*Fro.* Antic and Fantastic, as I am frolic franion, never in all my life was I so dead slain. What, to lose our way in the wood, [10 without either fire or candle, so uncomfortable! *O cælum! O terra! O Maria!* O Neptune!

*Fan.* Why makes thou it so strange, seeing Cupid hath led our young master to the fair lady, and she is the only saint that he hath [15 sworn to serve?

*Fro.* What resteth, then, but we commit him to his wench, and each of us take his stand up in a tree, and sing out our ill fortune to the tune of *"O man in desperation"?*    20

*Ant.* Desperately spoken, fellow Frolic, in the dark; but seeing it falls out thus, let us rehearse the old proverb:

"Three merry men, and three merry men,<br>
  And three merry men be we;     25<br>
I in the wood, and thou on the ground,<br>
  And Jack sleeps in the tree."

*Fan.* Hush! a dog in the wood, or a wooden dog! O comfortable hearing! I had even as lief the chamberlain of the White Horse had [30 called me up to bed.

*Fro.* Either hath this trotting cur gone out of his circuit, or else are we near some village, which should not be far off, for I perceive the glimmering of a glow-worm, a candle, or a [35 cat's eye, my life for a halfpenny!

*Enter [Clunch] a smith, with a lantern and candle*

In the name of my own father, be thou ox or ass that appearest, tell us what thou art.

*Smith.* What am I? Why, I am Clunch the smith. What are you? What make you in [40 my territories at this time of the night?

*Ant.* What do we make, dost thou ask? Why, we make faces for fear; such as if thy mortal eyes could behold, would make thee water the long seams of thy side slops, [45 smith.

*Fro.* And, in faith, sir, unless your hospitality do relieve us, we are like to wander, with a sorrowful heigh-ho, among the owlets and hobgoblins of the forest. Good Vulcan, for [50 Cupid's sake that hath cozened us all, befriend us as thou mayst; and command us howsoever, wheresoever, whensoever, in whatsoever, for ever and ever.

---

¹ **Frolic:** ('Franticke' Q)   ² **amort:** dispirited   ²⁻³ **madness: levity**   ⁶⁻⁷ **warrant . . . hundred:** give you one chance in five of surviving   ⁹ **franion:** scamp   ¹² **O . . . Maria:** O heaven! earth! seas! ¹⁴ **O . . . desperation:** a doleful ballad air   ²⁴⁻²⁷ (From a popular song)   ²⁸ **wooden:** (with pun on "wood," mad)   ⁴⁵ **slops:** loose breeches   ⁵⁰ **Vulcan:** the god of smiths   ⁵¹ **cozened:** deceived

*Smith.* Well, masters, it seems to me you [55 have lost your way in the wood; in consideration whereof, if you will go with Clunch to his cottage, you shall have house-room and a good fire to sit by, although we have no bedding to put you in. 60

*All.* O blessed smith, O bountiful Clunch!

*Smith.* For your further entertainment, it shall be as it may be, so and so.
*Here a dog bark.*
Hark! this is Ball my dog, that bids you all welcome in his own language. Come, [65 take heed for stumbling on the threshold. — Open door, Madge; take in guests.

*Enter old woman [Madge]*

*Madge.* Welcome, Clunch, and good fellows all, that come with my good man. For my good man's sake, come on, sit down; here is [70 a piece of cheese, and a pudding of my own making.

*Ant.* Thanks, gammer; a good example for the wives of our town.

*Fro.* Gammer, thou and thy good man [75 sit lovingly together; we come to chat, and not to eat.

*Smith.* Well, masters, if you will eat nothing, take away. Come, what do we to pass away the time? Lay a crab in the fire to [80 roast for lamb's-wool. What, shall we have a game at trump or ruff to drive away the time? How say you?

*Fan.* This smith leads a life as merry as a king with Madge his wife. Sirrah Frolic, I [85 am sure thou art not without some round or other; no doubt but Clunch can bear his part.

*Fro.* Else think you me ill brought up; so set to it when you will. *They sing.*

SONG

Whenas the rye reach to the chin, 90
And chopcherry, chopcherry ripe within,
Strawberries swimming in the cream,
And school-boys playing in the stream;
Then, O, then, O, then, O, my true-love said,
Till that time come again 95
She could not live a maid.

*Ant.* This sport does well; but methinks, gammer, a merry winter's tale would drive away the time trimly. Come, I am sure you are not without a score. 100

*Fan.* I' faith, gammer, a tale of an hour long were as good as an hour's sleep.

*Fro.* Look you, gammer, of the giant and the king's daughter, and I know not what. I have seen the day, when I was a little one, [105

you might have drawn me a mile after you with such a discourse.

*Madge.* Well, since you be so importunate, my good man shall fill the pot and get him to bed; they that ply their work must keep [110 good hours. One of you go lie with him; he is a clean-skinned man, I tell you, without either spavin or wind-gall: so I am content to drive away the time with an old wives' winter's tale.

*Fan.* No better hay in Devonshire; o' [115 my word, gammer, I 'll be one of your audience.

*Fro.* And I another, that 's flat.

*Ant.* Then must I to bed with the good man. — *Bona nox*, gammer. — Good night, Frolic.

*Smith.* Come on, my lad, thou shalt take [120 thy unnatural rest with me.
*Exeunt Antic and the Smith.*

*Fro.* Yet this vantage shall we have of them in the morning, to be ready at the sight thereof extempore.

*Madge.* Now this bargain, my masters, [125 must I make with you, that you will say hum and ha to my tale; so shall I know you are awake.

*Both.* Content, gammer, that will we do.

*Madge.* Once upon a time, there was a [130 king, or a lord, or a duke, that had a fair daughter, the fairest that ever was, as white as snow and as red as blood; and once upon a time his daughter was stolen away; and he sent all his men to seek out his daughter; [135 and he sent so long, that he sent all his men out of his land.

*Fro.* Who dressed his dinner, then?

*Madge.* Nay, either hear my tale, or kiss my tail. [140

*Fan.* Well said! On with your tale, gammer.

*Madge.* O Lord, I quite forgot! There was a conjurer, and this conjurer could do any thing, and he turned himself into a great dragon, and carried the king's daughter away in his [145 mouth to a castle that he made of stone; and there he kept her I know not how long, till at last all the king's men went out so long that her two brothers went to seek her. O, I forget! she (he, I would say,) turned a proper young [150 man to a bear in the night, and a man in the day, and keeps by a cross that parts three several ways; and he made his lady run mad — Gods me bones, who comes here?

*Enter the Two Brothers*

*Fro.* Soft, gammer, here some come to [155 tell your tale for you.

*Fan.* Let them alone; let us hear what they will say.

---

[73] **gammer:** dame   [81] **lamb's-wool:** roasted apple mixed with ale   [82] **trump, ruff:** ancient varieties of whist   [86] **round:** choral song   [123] **ready:** dressed   [150] **proper:** handsome   [152] **keeps:** dwells (*i.e.*, the bear-man, Erestus)   [152-153] **parts . . . ways:** separates three different roads

*1 Bro.* Upon these chalky cliffs of Albion
We are arrived now with tedious toil;        160
And compassing the wide world round about,
To seek our sister, to seek fair Delia forth,
Yet cannot we so much as hear of her.
  *2 Bro.* O fortune cruel, cruel and unkind!
Unkind in that we cannot find our sister,    165
Our sister, hapless in her cruel chance!
Soft! who have we here?

*Enter Senex [Erestus] at the cross, stooping*
*to gather*

  *1 Bro.* Now, father, God be your speed!
What do you gather there?
  *Erest.* Hips and haws, and sticks and [170
straws, and things that I gather on the ground,
my son.
  *1 Bro.* Hips and haws, and sticks and straws!
Why, is that all your food, father?
  *Erest.* Yea, son.                         175
  *2 Bro.* Father, here is an alms-penny for
me; and if I speed in that I go for, I will give
thee as good a gown of grey as ever thou diddest
wear.
  *1 Bro.* And, father, here is another alms- [180
penny for me; and if I speed in my journey, I
will give thee a palmer's staff of ivory, and a
scallop-shell of beaten gold.
  *Erest.* Was she fair?
  *2 Bro.* Ay, the fairest for white, and the [185
purest for red, as the blood of the deer, or the
driven snow.
  *Erest.* Then hark well, and mark well, my
old spell:
Be not afraid of every stranger;
Start not aside at every danger;             190
Things that seem are not the same;
Blow a blast at every flame;
For when one flame of fire goes out,
Then comes your wishes well about:
If any ask who told you this good,           195
Say, the white bear of England's wood.
  *1 Bro.* Brother, heard you not what the old
man said?
"Be not afraid of every stranger;
Start not aside for every danger;
Things that seem are not the same;           200
Blow a blast at every flame;
If any ask who told you this good,
Say, the white bear of England's wood."
  *2 Bro.* Well, if this do us any good,
Well fare the white bear of England's wood!  205
                 *Exeunt [the Two Brothers].*
  *Erest.* Now sit thee here, and tell a heavy
tale,
Sad in thy mood, and sober in thy cheer;

Here sit thee now, and to thyself relate
The hard mishap of thy most wretched state.
In Thessaly I liv'd in sweet content,        210
Until that fortune wrought my overthrow;
For there I wedded was unto a dame,
That liv'd in honour, virtue, love, and fame.
But Sacrapant, that cursed sorcerer,
Being besotted with my beauteous love,       215
My dearest love, my true betrothed wife,
Did seek the means to rid me of my life.
But worse than this, he with his chanting spells
Did turn me straight unto an ugly bear;
And when the sun doth settle in the west,    220
Then I begin to don my ugly hide.
And all the day I sit, as now you see,
And speak in riddles, all inspir'd with rage,
Seeming an old and miserable man,
And yet I am in April of my age.             225

*Enter Venelia his lady, mad; and goes in again.*

See where Venelia, my betrothed love,
Runs madding, all enrag'd, about the woods,
All by his cursed and enchanting spells. —

*Enter Lampriscus with a pot of honey*

But here comes Lampriscus, my discontented
neighbour. How now, neighbour! You [230
look toward the ground as well as I; you
muse on something.
  *Lamp.* Neighbour, on nothing but on the
matter I so often moved to you. If you do
anything for charity, help me; if for neigh- [235
bourhood or brotherhood, help me: never was
one so cumbered as is poor Lampriscus; and
to begin, I pray receive this pot of honey, to
mend your fare.
  *Erest.* Thanks, neighbour, set it down; [240
honey is always welcome to the bear. And
now, neighbour, let me hear the cause of your
coming.
  *Lamp.* I am, as you know, neighbour, a
man unmarried; and lived so unquietly [245
with my two wives, that I keep every year holy
the day wherein I buried them both: the first
was on Saint Andrew's day, the other on
Saint Luke's.
  *Erest.* And now, neighbour, you of this [250
country say, your custom is out. But on with
your tale, neighbour.
  *Lamp.* By my first wife, whose tongue
wearied me alive, and sounded in my ears
like the clapper of a great bell, whose talk [255
was a continual torment to all that dwelt by
her or lived nigh her, you have heard me say
I had a handsome daughter.
  *Erest.* True, neighbour.

---

¹⁸³ **scallop-shell:** badge of a pilgrim    ²¹⁰ **Thessaly:** reputed land of witches    ²¹⁵ **besotted:**
infatuated    ²¹⁸ **chanting:** bewitching    ²³⁴ **moved:** mentioned    ²⁴⁸ **Saint Andrew's day:** Nov. 30
²⁴⁹ **Saint Luke's:** Oct. 18    ²⁵¹ **custom:** customary service or duty    **out:** expired

*Lamp.*  She it is that afflicts me with her [260 continual clamours, and hangs on me like a bur. Poor she is, and proud she is; as poor as a sheep new-shorn, and as proud of her hopes as a peacock of her tail well-grown.

*Erest.*  Well said, Lampriscus!  You [265 speak it like an Englishman.

*Lamp.*  As curst as a wasp, and as froward as a child new-taken from the mother's teat; she is to my age as smoke to the eyes or as vinegar to the teeth.                                      270

*Erest.*  Holily praised, neighbour.  As much for the next.

*Lamp.*  By my other wife I had a daughter so hard-favoured, so foul and ill-faced, that I think a grove full of golden trees, and the [275 leaves of rubies and diamonds, would not be a dowry answerable to her deformity.

*Erest.*  Well, neighbour, now you have spoke, hear me speak.  Send them to the well for the water of life; there shall they find [280 their fortunes unlooked for.  Neighbour, farewell.                                                       *Exit.*

*Lamp.*  Farewell, and a thousand!  And now goeth poor Lampriscus to put in execution this excellent counsel.              *Exit.* [285

*Fro.*  Why, this goes round without a fiddling-stick: but, do you hear, gammer, was this the man that was a bear in the night and a man in the day?

*Madge.*  Ay, this is he; and this man [290 that came to him was a beggar, and dwelt upon a green.  But soft! who comes here?  O, these are the harvest-men.  Ten to one they sing a song of mowing.

*Enter the Harvest-men a-singing, with this song double repeated*

All ye that lovely lovers be,               295
Pray you for me.
Lo, here we come a-sowing, a-sowing,
And sow sweet fruits of love;
In your sweet hearts well may it prove!

*Exeunt.*

*Enter Huanebango with his two-hand sword, and Booby, the clown*

*Fan.*  Gammer, what is he?          300

*Madge.*  O, this is one that is going to the conjurer.  Let him alone; hear what he says.

*Huan.*  Now, by Mars and Mercury, Jupiter and Janus, Sol and Saturnus, Venus and Vesta, Pallas and Proserpina, and by the honour [305

of my house, Polimackeroeplacidus, it is a wonder to see what this love will make silly fellows adventure, even in the wane of their wits and infancy of their discretion.  Alas, my friend! what fortune calls thee forth to seek [310 thy fortune among brazen gates, enchanted towers, fire and brimstone, thunder and lightning?  Beauty, I tell thee, is peerless, and she precious whom thou affectest.  Do off these desires, good countryman; good friend, run [315 away from thyself; and, so soon as thou canst, forget her, whom none must inherit but he that can monsters tame, labours achieve, riddles absolve, loose enchantments, murther magic, and kill conjuring, — and that is the great and [320 mighty Huanebango.

*Booby.*  Hark you, sir, hark you.  First know I have here the flurting feather, and have given the parish the start for the long stock: now, sir, if it be no more but running [325 through a little lightning, and thunder, and "riddle me, riddle me what's this?"  I'll have the wench from the conjurer, if he were ten conjurers.

*Huan.*  I have abandoned the court and [330 honourable company, to do my devoir against this sore sorcerer and mighty magician: if this lady be so fair as she is said to be, she is mine, she is mine; *meus, mea, meum, in contemptum omnium grammaticorum.*     335

*Booby.*  *O falsum Latinum!*
The fair maid is *minum,*
*Cum apurtinantibus gibletis* and all.

*Huan.*  If she be mine, as I assure myself the heavens will do somewhat to reward [340 my worthiness, she shall be allied to none of the meanest gods, but be invested in the most famous stock of Huanebango, — Polimackeroeplacidus my grandfather, my father Pergopolineo, my mother Dionora de Sardinia, [345 famously descended.

*Booby.*  Do you hear, sir?  Had not you a cousin that was called Gusteceridis?

*Huan.*  Indeed, I had a cousin that sometime followed the court infortunately, and [350 his name Bustegusteceridis.

*Booby.*  O Lord, I know him well!  He is the knight of the neat's-feet.

*Huan.*  O, he loved no capon better!  He hath oftentimes deceived his boy of his dinner; [355 that was his fault, good Bustegusteceridis.

*Booby.*  Come, shall we go along?

---

²⁶⁷ **curst:** cross     ²⁷⁵⁻²⁷⁶ **grove . . . diamonds:** (Cf. *Arraignment of Paris,* II. ii. 40–46) ²⁸⁶⁻²⁸⁷ **goes . . . stick:** moves without urging     ²⁹⁷⁻²⁹⁸ **Lo . . . love:** (Gummere suggests that these lines should begin the song, and compares the reaping song, lines 623 ff.)     ²⁹⁹ **S. D. Booby:** later called Corebus     ³⁰⁶ **Polimackeroeplacidus:** Polymachaeroplagides, name of a soldier in the *Pseudolus* of Plautus     ³¹⁴ **Do off:** doff     ³¹⁸⁻³¹⁹ **absolve:** solve     ³¹⁹ **loose:** annul     ³²³ **flurting:** waving     ³²⁴ **given . . . stock:** started the fashion of long hose (?)     ³⁴⁴⁻³⁴⁵ **Pergopolineo:** Pyrgopolinices, the braggart in *Miles Gloriosus* by Plautus

*[Enter Erestus at the cross]*

Soft! here is an old man at the cross; let us
ask him the way thither. — Ho, you gaffer! [360
I pray you tell where the wise man the conjurer dwells.

*Huan.* Where that earthly goddess keepeth
her abode, the commander of my thoughts,
and fair mistress of my heart. 365

*Erest.* Fair enough, and far enough from
thy fingering, son.

*Huan.* I will follow my fortune after mine
own fancy, and do according to mine own
discretion. 370

*Erest.* Yet give something to an old man
before you go.

*Huan.* Father, methinks a piece of this cake
might serve your turn.

*Erest.* Yea, son. 375

*Huan.* Huanebango giveth no cakes for alms;
ask of them that give gifts for poor beggars. —
Fair lady, if thou wert once shrined in this
bosom, I would buckler thee haratantara.
*Exit.*

*Booby.* Father, do you see this man? [380
You little think he 'll run a mile or two for such
a cake, or pass for a pudding. I tell you, father,
he has kept such a begging of me for a piece of
this cake! Whoo! he comes upon me with "a
superfantial substance, and the foison of [385
the earth," that I know not what he means.
If he came to me thus, and said, "My friend
Booby," or so, why, I could spare him a piece
with all my heart; but when he tells me how
God hath enriched me above other fellows [390
with a cake, why, he makes me blind and deaf
at once. Yet, father, here is a piece of cake for
you, as hard as the world goes. *[Gives cake.]*

*Erest.* Thanks, son, but list to me;
He shall be deaf when thou shalt not see. 395
Farewell, my son: things may so hit,
Thou mayst have wealth to mend thy wit.

*Booby.* Farewell, father, farewell; for I must
make haste after my two-hand sword that is
gone before. *Exeunt omnes.* [400

*Enter Sacrapant in his study*

*Sac.* The day is clear, the welkin bright and
grey,
The lark is merry and records her notes;
Each thing rejoiceth underneath the sky,
But only I, whom heaven hath in hate,
Wretched and miserable Sacrapant. 405
In Thessaly was I born and brought up;
My mother Meroe hight, a famous witch,
And by her cunning I of her did learn

To change and alter shapes of mortal men.
There did I turn myself into a dragon, 410
And stole away the daughter to the king,
Fair Delia, the mistress of my heart;
And brought her hither to revive the man
That seemeth young and pleasant to behold,
And yet is aged, crooked, weak, and numb. 415
Thus by enchanting spells I do deceive
Those that behold and look upon my face;
But well may I bid youthful years adieu.

*Enter Delia with a pot in her hand*

See where she comes from whence my sorrows
grow!
How now, fair Delia! where have you been? [420

*Del.* At the foot of the rock for running
water, and gathering roots for your dinner, sir.

*Sac.* Ah, Delia, fairer art thou than the
running water, yet harder far than steel or
adamant! 425

*Del.* Will it please you to sit down, sir?

*Sac.* Ay, Delia, sit and ask me what thou
wilt,
Thou shalt have it brought into thy lap.

*Del.* Then, I pray you, sir, let me have the
best meat from the King of England's table, [430
and the best wine in all France, brought in by
the veriest knave in all Spain.

*Sac.* Delia, I am glad to see you so pleasant.
Well, sit thee down. —
Spread, table, spread, 435
Meat, drink, and bread,
Ever may I have
What I ever crave,
When I am spread,
For meat for my black cock, 440
And meat for my red.

*Enter a Friar with a chine of beef and a pot of
wine*

Here, Delia, will ye fall to?

*Del.* Is this the best meat in England?

*Sac.* Yea.

*Del.* What is it? 445

*Sac.* A chine of English beef, meat for a
king and a king's followers.

*Del.* Is this the best wine in France?

*Sac.* Yea.

*Del.* What wine is it? 450

*Sac.* A cup of neat wine of Orleans, that
never came near the brewers in England.

*Del.* Is this the veriest knave in all Spain?

*Sac.* Yea.

*Del.* What is he, a friar? 455

*Sac.* Yea, a friar indefinite, and a knave
infinite.

---

³⁶⁰ **gaffer:** old man  ³⁷⁹ **haratantara:** (usually "taratantara") the sound of a trumpet  ³⁸² **pass:**
care  ³⁸⁵ **superfantial:** inexpressible  **foison:** plenty  ³⁹³ **as . . . goes:** despite hard times  ⁴⁰¹ **grey:**
blue  ⁴⁰² **records:** warbles  ⁴⁵¹ **neat:** pure

*Del.*  Then, I pray ye, Sir Friar, tell me
before you go, which is the most greediest
Englishman?                                        460
*Fri.*  The miserable and most covetous usurer.
*Sac.*  Hold thee there, friar.      *Exit Friar.*
But, soft!
Who have we here?  Delia, away, begone!

*Enter the Two Brothers*

Delia, away! for beset are we. —
But heaven nor hell shall rescue her for me. 465
          [*Exeunt Delia and Sacrapant.*]
  1 *Bro.*  Brother, was not that Delia did
    appear,
Or was it but her shadow that was here?
  2 *Bro.*  Sister, where art thou? Delia, come
    again!
He calls, that of thy absence doth complain. —
Call out, Calypha, that she may hear,       470
And cry aloud, for Delia is near.
  *Echo.*  Near.
  1 *Bro.*  Near! O, where? Hast thou any
    tidings?
  *Echo.*  Tidings.
  2 *Bro.*  Which way is Delia, then; or that,
    or this?                                        475
  *Echo.*  This.
  1 *Bro.*  And may we safely come where
    Delia is?
  *Echo.*  Yes.
  2 *Bro.*  Brother, remember you the white
bear of England's wood?                          480
"Start not aside for every danger,
Be not afeard of every stranger;
Things that seem are not the same."
  1 *Bro.*  Brother, why do we not, then, courageously enter?                                   485
  2 *Bro.*  Then, brother, draw thy sword and
    follow me.

*Enter [Sacrapant] the Conjurer: it lightens
and thunders; the 2. Brother falls down.*

  1 *Bro.*  What, brother, dost thou fall?
  *Sac.*  Ay, and thou too, Calypha.

*Fall 1. Brother.  Enter Two Furies*

*Adeste, dæmones!*  Away with them:
Go carry them straight to Sacrapanto's cell, 490
There in despair and torture for to dwell.
          [*Exeunt Furies with the Two Brothers.*]
These are Thenores' sons of Thessaly,
That come to seek Delia their sister forth;
But, with a potion I to her have given,
My arts have made her to forget herself.    495
  *He removes a turf, and shows a light in a glass.*
See here the thing which doth prolong my life.
With this enchantment I do any thing;

And till this fade, my skill shall still endure,
And never none shall break this little glass,
But she that's neither wife, widow, nor
  maid.                                            500
Then cheer thyself; this is thy destiny,
Never to die but by a dead man's hand.  *Exit.*

*Enter Eumenides, the wandering knight, and
  [Erestus] the old man at the cross*

  *Eum.*  Tell me, Time,
Tell me, just Time, when shall I Delia see?
When shall I see the loadstar of my life?  505
When shall my wand'ring course end with her
  sight,
Or I but view my hope, my heart's delight?
          [*Seeing Erestus*]
Father, God speed! If you tell fortunes, I
pray, good father, tell me mine.
  *Erest.*  Son, I do see in thy face         510
Thy blessed fortune work apace.
I do perceive that thou hast wit;
Beg of thy fate to govern it,
For wisdom govern'd by advice,
Makes many fortunate and wise.                515
Bestow thy alms, give more than all,
Till dead men's bones come at thy call.
Farewell, my son! Dream of no rest,
Till thou repent that thou didst best.
                          *Exit Old Man.*
  *Eum.*  This man hath left me in a laby-
    rinth:                                         520
He biddeth me give more than all,
"Till dead men's bones come at thy call";
He biddeth me dream of no rest,
Till I repent that I do best.
                  [*Lies down and sleeps.*]

*Enter Wiggen, Corebus, Churchwarden, and
  Sexton*

  *Wig.*  You may be ashamed, you whore- [525
son scald Sexton and Churchwarden, if you had
any shame in those shameless faces of yours, to
let a poor man lie so long above ground unburied.  A rot on you all, that have no more
compassion of a good fellow when he is gone! [530
  *Church.*  What, would you have us to bury
him, and to answer it ourselves to the parish?
  *Sex.*  Parish me no parishes; pay me my fees,
and let the rest run on in the quarter's accounts, and put it down for one of your good [535
deeds, o' God's name! for I am not one that
curiously stands upon merits.
  *Cor.*  You whoreson, sodden-headed sheep's-
face, shall a good fellow do less service and
more honesty to the parish, and will you not, [540
when he is dead, let him have Christmas burial?

⁴⁶⁵ nor: ('or' Q)    ⁴⁸⁹ Adeste: assist ('Adestes' Q)    ⁵²⁴ S. D. Corebus: i.e., "Booby"    ⁵²⁶ scald:
scurvy    ⁵³¹ Church: ('Simon' Q)

*Wig.* Peace, Corebus! As sure as Jack was Jack, the frolic'st franion amongst you, and I, Wiggen, his sweet sworn brother, Jack shall have his funerals, or some of them shall lie [545 on God's dear earth for it, that 's once.

*Church.* Wiggen, I hope thou wilt do no more than thou dar'st answer.

*Wig.* Sir, sir, dare or dare not, more or less, answer or not answer, do this, or have this. [550

*Sex.* Help, help, help!

*Wiggen sets upon the parish with a pike-staff.*

*Eumenides awakes and comes to them*

*Eum.* Hold thy hands, good fellow.

*Cor.* Can you blame him, sir, if he take Jack's part against this shake-rotten parish that will not bury Jack? 555

*Eum.* Why, what was that Jack?

*Cor.* Who, Jack, sir? Who, our Jack, sir? As good a fellow as ever trod upon neat's-leather.

*Wig.* Look you, sir; he gave fourscore [560 and nineteen mourning gowns to the parish when he died, and because he would not make them up a full hundred, they would not bury him: was not this good dealing?

*Church.* O Lord, sir, how he lies! He [565 was not worth a halfpenny, and drunk out every penny; and now his fellows, his drunken companions would have us to bury him at the charge of the parish. An we make many such matches, we may pull down the steeple, sell [570 the bells, and thatch the chancel. He shall lie above ground till he dance a galliard about the church-yard, for Steven Loach.

*Wig.* Sic argumentaris, Domine Loach: — "an we make many such matches, we may [575 pull down the steeple, sell the bells, and thatch the chancel!" — in good time, sir, and hang yourselves in the bell-ropes, when you have done. *Domine opponens, præpono tibi hanc quæstionem,* whether will you have the [580 ground broken or your pates broken first? For one of them shall be done presently, and to begin mine, I 'll seal it upon your coxcomb.

*Eum.* Hold thy hands, I pray thee, good fellow; be not too hasty. 585

*Cor.* You capon's face, we shall have you turned out of the parish one of these days, with never a tatter to your arse; then you are in worse taking than Jack.

*Eum.* Faith, and he is bad enough. This [590 fellow does but the part of a friend, to seek to bury his friend. How much will bury him?

*Wig.* Faith, about some fifteen or sixteen shillings will bestow him honestly.

*Sex.* Ay, even thereabouts, sir. 595

*Eum.* Here, hold it, then: — [*aside*] and I have left me but one poor three half-pence. Now do I remember the words the old man spake at the cross, "Bestow all thou hast," and this is all, "till dead men's bones comes [600 at thy call." — Here, hold it [*gives money*]; and so farewell.

*Wig.* God, and all good, be with you, sir! [*Exit Eumenides.*] Nay, you cormorants, I 'll bestow one peal of Jack at mine own proper [605 costs and charges.

*Cor.* You may thank God the long staff and the bilbo-blade crossed not your coxcomb. — Well, we 'll to the church-stile and have a pot, and so trill-lill. 610

*Church.* } Come, let 's go. *Exeunt.*
*Sex.* }

*Fan.* But, hark you, gammer, methinks this Jack bore a great sway in the parish.

*Madge.* O, this Jack was a marvellous [615 fellow! he was but a poor man, but very well beloved. You shall see anon what this Jack will come to.

*Enter the Harvest-men singing, with women in their hands*

*Fro.* Soft! who have we here? Our amorous harvesters. 620

*Fan.* Ay, ay, let us sit still, and let them alone.

*Here they begin to sing, the song doubled*

Lo, here we come a-reaping, a-reaping,
To reap our harvest-fruit!
And thus we pass the year so long, 625
And never be we mute.

*Exeunt the Harvest-men.*

*Enter Huanebango and [a little later] Corebus, the clown*

*Fro.* Soft! who have we here?

*Madge.* O, this is a choleric gentleman! All you that love your lives, keep out of the smell of his two-hand sword. Now goes he to the [630 conjurer.

---

**546 once:** positive    **550 have this:** receive this (beating)    **551 S. D. parish:** the parochial officers (This S. D. is printed in Q as part of Sexton's speech.)    **554 shake-rotten:** ready to fall to pieces    **570 matches:** bargains    **571 thatch:** replace the costly leaden roof with thatch    **572 galliard:** lively dance    **573 Steven Loach:** the Churchwarden's name (but see note on 531)    **574 Sic argumentaris:** thus you reason    **577 in . . . time:** very well    **579–580 Domine . . . quæstionem:** "Master adversary, I put this question to you." (From the language of academic debate)    **583 begin mine:** open my argument    **588 are:** will be    **589 taking:** predicament    **605 of:** in honor of    **609 church-stile:** edge of church property    **610 trill-lill:** the noise of liquor going down the throat    **620 harvesters:** ('haurest starres' Q)

*Fan.* Methinks the conjurer should put the fool into a juggling-box.

*Huan.* Fee, fa, fum,
    Here is the Englishman, —   635
    Conquer him that can, —
    Came for his lady bright,
    To prove himself a knight,
    And win her love in fight.

*Cor.* Who-haw, Master Bango, are you [640 here? Hear you, you had best sit down here, and beg an alms with me.

*Huan.* Hence, base cullion! Here is he that commandeth ingress and egress with his weapon, and will enter at his voluntary, whosoever [645 saith no.

*A voice and flame of fire; Huanebango falleth down*

*Voice.* No.

*Madge.* So with that they kissed, and spoiled the edge of as good a two-hand sword as ever God put life in. Now goes Corebus in, spite [650 of the conjurer.

*Enter [Sacrapant] the Conjurer and [Two Furies and] strike Corebus blind*

*Sac.* Away with him into the open fields,
To be a ravening prey to crows and kites:
    [*Huan. is carried out by the Two Furies.*]
And for this villain, let him wander up and down,
In naught but darkness and eternal night.  655
*Cor.* Here hast thou slain Huan, a slashing knight,
And robbed poor Corebus of his sight.   *Exit.*
*Sac.* Hence, villain, hence! — Now I have unto Delia
Given a potion of forgetfulness,
That, when she comes, she shall not know her brothers.  660
Lo, where they labour, like to country slaves,
With spade and mattock on this enchanted ground!
Now will I call her by another name;
For never shall she know herself again,
Until that Sacrapant hath breath'd his last.  665
See where she comes.

*Enter Delia*

Come hither, Delia, take this goad; here hard
At hand two slaves do work and dig for gold:
Gore them with this, and thou shalt have enough.    *He gives her a goad.*
*Del.* Good sir, I know not what you mean.  670
*Sac.* [*aside.*] She hath forgotten to be Delia,
But not forgot the same she should forget;

But I will change her name. —
Fair Berecynthia, so this country calls you,
Go ply these strangers, wench; they dig for gold.    *Exit Sacrapant.* [675
*Del.* O heavens, how
Am I beholding to this fair young man!
But I must ply these strangers to their work:
See where they come.

*Enter the Two Brothers in their shirts, with spades, digging*

*1 Bro.* O brother, see where Delia is!  680
*2 Bro.* O Delia,
Happy are we to see thee here!
*Del.* What tell you me of Delia, prating swains?
I know no Delia, nor know I what you mean.
Ply you your work, or else you are like to smart.  685
*1 Bro.* Why, Delia, know'st thou not thy brothers here?
We come from Thessaly to seek thee forth;
And thou deceiv'st thyself, for thou art Delia.
*Del.* Yet more of Delia? Then take this, and smart.    [*Pricks them with the goad.*]
What feign you shifts for to defer your labour?  690
Work, villains, work; it is for gold you dig.
*2 Bro.* Peace, brother, peace: this vild enchanter
Hath ravish'd Delia of her senses clean,
And she forgets that she is Delia.
*1 Bro.* Leave, cruel thou, to hurt the miserable. —  695
Dig, brother, dig, for she is hard as steel.

*Here they dig, and descry the light under a little hill.*

*2 Bro.* Stay, brother; what hast thou descried?
*Del.* Away, and touch it not; it is something that my lord hath hidden there.
                    *She covers it again.*

*Enter Sacrapant*

*Sac.* Well said! thou plyest these pioners [700 well. — Go get you in, you labouring slaves.
             [*Exeunt the Two Brothers.*]
Come, Berecynthia, let us in likewise,
And hear the nightingale record her notes.
                 *Exeunt omnes.*

*Enter Zantippa, the curst daughter, to the Well with a pot in her hand*

*Zan.* Now for a husband, house, and home:
God send a good one or none, I pray God!  705
My father hath sent me to the well for the

---

**643** cullion: rogue  **645 voluntary:** will  **690 What:** why  shifts: tricks  **692 vild:** vile  **700 Well said:** well done  pioners: miners

water of life, and tells me, if I give fair words,
I shall have a husband.

⌈*Celanta,*⌉ *the foul wench, to the Well*
*for water with a pot in her hand*

But here comes Celanta, my sweet sister. I'll
stand by and hear what she says.          710
*Cel.* My father hath sent me to the well for
water, and he tells me, if I speak fair, I shall
have a husband, and none of the worst. Well,
though I am black, I am sure all the world
will not forsake me; and, as the old proverb [715
is, though I am black, I am not the devil.
*Zan.* Marry-gup with a murrain, I know
wherefore thou speakest that: but go thy ways
home as wise as thou cam'st, or I'll set thee
home with a wanion.                       720

*Here she strikes her pitcher against her*
*sister's, and breaks them both, and goes her way.*

*Cel.* I think this be the curstest quean in the
world. You see what she is, a little fair, but as
proud as the devil, and the veriest vixen that
lives upon God's earth. Well, I'll let her alone,
and go home and get another pitcher, and, [725
for all this, get me to the well for water. *Exit.*

*Enter two Furies out of the Conjurer's cell and*
*lays Huanebango by the Well of Life* ⌈*and*
*then exeunt*⌉*. Enter Zantippa with a pitcher*
*to the well.*

*Zan.* Once again for a husband; and, in
faith, Celanta, I have got the start of you; belike husbands grow by the well-side. Now my
father says I must rule my tongue. Why, [730
alas, what am I, then? A woman without a
tongue is as a soldier without his weapon.
But I'll have my water, and be gone.

*Here she offers to dip her pitcher in, and a Head*
*speaks in the well*

*Head.* Gently dip, but not too deep,
For fear you make the golden beard to weep. 735
Fair maiden, white and red,
Stroke me smooth, and comb my head,
And thou shalt have some cockell-bread.
*Zan.* What is this?
"Fair maiden, white and red,        740
Comb me smooth, and stroke my head,
And thou shalt have some cockell-bread"?
"Cockell" callest thou it, boy? Faith, I'll
give you cockell-bread.

*She breaks her pitcher upon his Head: then it*
*thunders and lightens; and Huanebango*
*rises up. Huanebango is deaf and cannot*
*hear.*

*Huan.* Philida, phileridos, pamphilida, flo-
rida, flortos:                            745
Dub dub-a-dub, bounce, quoth the guns, with
a sulphurous huff-snuff:
Wak'd with a wench, pretty peat, pretty love,
and my sweet pretty pigsnie,
Just by thy side shall sit surnamed great
Huanebango:
Safe in my arms will I keep thee, threat Mars
or thunder Olympus.
*Zan.* [*aside.*] Foh, what greasy groom [750
have we here? He looks as though he crept out
of the backside of the well, and speaks like a
drum perish'd at the west end.
*Huan.* O, that I might, — but I may not,
woe to my destiny therefore! —
Kiss that I clasp! but I cannot. Tell me, my
destiny, wherefore?                       755
*Zan.* [*aside.*] Whoop! now I have my dream.
Did you never hear so great a wonder as this?
Three blue beans in a blue bladder, rattle,
bladder, rattle.
*Huan.* [*aside.*] I'll now set my counte- [760
nance, and to her in prose, it may be, this rim-
ram-ruff is too rude an encounter. — Let me,
fair lady, if you be at leisure, revel with your
sweetness, and rail upon that cowardly conjurer, that hath cast me, or congealed me [765
rather, into an unkind sleep, and polluted my
carcass.
*Zan.* [*aside.*] Laugh, laugh, Zantippa; thou
hast thy fortune, a fool and a husband under one.
*Huan.* Truly, sweetheart, as I seem, [770
about some twenty years, the very April of
mine age.
*Zan.* [*aside.*] Why, what a prating ass is this!
*Huan.* Her coral lips, her crimson chin,
Her silver teeth so white within,          775
Her golden locks, her rolling eye,
Her pretty parts, let them go by,
Heigh-ho, hath wounded me,
That I must die this day to see!
*Zan.* By Gogs-bones, thou art a flouting [780
knave. "Her coral lips, her crimson chin"!
ka, wilshaw!
*Huan.* True, my own, and my own because

---

714 **black:** not fair   717 **Marry-gup:** common exclamation of disgust   **murrain:** plague   720 **wanion:**
vengeance   735 **beard:** ('birde' Q)   738 **cockell-bread:** bread moulded with special rites as a love
charm   745 A hexameter in mock-Latin   746 **bounce:** boom!   **huff-snuff:** bluster (parody of
Stanyhurst's translation of Vergil, 1582)   747 **pigsnie:** sweetheart   748 **surnamed . . . Huanebango:**
Huanebango the Great   753 **perish'd:** worn out   754 One of Gabriel Harvey's English hexameters
758-759 **Three . . . rattle:** (This nonsense is found also in the Alleyn MS. of Greene's *Orlando Furioso*,
lines 136-137)   761-762 **rim-ram-ruff:** ("rum, ram, ruf" is Chaucer's term for alliterative verse, Parson's
Prol., 43)   769 **under one:** combined   782 **ka:** quoth he

mine, and mine because mine, ha, ha! Above a thousand pounds in possibility, and things [785 fitting thy desire in possession.

*Zan.* [*aside.*] The sot thinks I ask of his lands. Lob be your comfort, and cuckold be your destiny! — Hear you, sir; an if you will have us, you had best say so betime.     790

*Huan.* True, sweetheart, and will royalize thy progeny with my pedigree.  *Exeunt omnes.*

*Enter Eumenides, the wandering knight*

*Eum.* Wretched Eumenides, still unfortunate,
Envied by fortune and forlorn by fate,
Here pine and die, wretched Eumenides,     795
Die in the spring, the April of my age!
Here sit thee down, repent what thou hast done:
I would to God that it were ne'er begun!

*Enter [the Ghost of] Jack*

*Jack.* You are well overtaken, sir.
*Eum.* Who 's that?     800
*Jack.* You are heartily well met, sir.
*Eum.* Forbear, I say; who is that which pincheth me?
*Jack.* Trusting in God, good Master Eumenides, that you are in so good health as [805 all your friends were at the making hereof, God give you good morrow, sir! Lack you not a neat, handsome, and cleanly young lad, about the age of fifteen or sixteen years, that can run by your horse, and, for a need, make [810 your mastership's shoes as black as ink? How say you, sir?
*Eum.* Alas, pretty lad, I know not how to keep myself, and much less a servant, my pretty boy; my state is so bad.     815
*Jack.* Content yourself, you shall not be so ill a master but I 'll be as bad a servant. Tut, sir, I know you, though you know not me. Are not you the man, sir, — deny it if you can, sir, — that came from a strange [820 place in the land of Catita, where Jack-an-apes flies with his tail in his mouth, to seek out a lady as white as snow and as red as blood? Ha, ha! have I touched you now?
*Eum.* [*aside.*] I think this boy be a spirit. [825 — How know'st thou all this?
*Jack.* Tut, are not you the man, sir, — deny it if you can, sir, — that gave all the money you had to the burying of a poor man, and but one three-half-pence left in your [830 purse? Content you, sir, I 'll serve you, that is flat.
*Eum.* Well, my lad, since thou art so importunate, I am content to entertain thee, not

as a servant, but a copartner in my journey. [835 But whither shall we go? for I have not any money more than one bare three-half-pence.
*Jack.* Well, master, content yourself, for if my divination be not out, that shall be spent at the next inn or alehouse we come [840 to: for, master, I know you are passing hungry; therefore I 'll go before and provide dinner until that you come; no doubt but you 'll come fair and softly after.
*Eum.* Ay, go before; I 'll follow thee.     845
*Jack.* But do you hear, master? Do you know my name?
*Eum.* No, I promise thee, not yet.
*Jack.* Why, I am Jack.
     *Exit [Ghost of] Jack.*
*Eum.* Jack! Why, be it so, then.     850

*Enter the Hostess and Jack, setting meat on the table; and Fiddlers come to play. Eumenides walketh up and down, and will eat no meat.*

*Host.* How say you, sir? Do you please to sit down?
*Eum.* Hostess, I thank you, I have no great stomach.
*Host.* Pray, sir, what is the reason your [855 master is so strange? Doth not this meat please him?
*Jack.* Yes, hostess, but it is my master's fashion to pay before he eats; therefore, a reckoning, good hostess.     860
*Host.* Marry, shall you, sir, presently. *Exit.*
*Eum.* Why, Jack, what dost thou mean? Thou knowest I have not any money; therefore, sweet Jack, tell me, what shall I do?
*Jack.* Well, master, look in your purse. [865
*Eum.* Why, faith, it is a folly, for I have no money.
*Jack.* Why, look you, master; do so much for me.
*Eum.* [*looking into his purse.*] Alas, Jack, [870 my purse is full of money!
*Jack.* "Alas," master! does that word belong to this accident? Why, methinks I should have seen you cast away your cloak, and in a bravado danced a galliard round about [875 the chamber. Why, master, your man can teach you more wit than this.

*[Re-enter Hostess]*

Come, hostess, cheer up my master.
*Host.* You are heartily welcome; and if it please you to eat of a fat capon, a fairer [880 bird, a finer bird, a sweeter bird, a crisper bird, a neater bird, your worship never eat of.

---

⁷⁸⁸ **Lob:** country bumpkin ("Lob's pound" = jail)     ⁷⁸⁹ **an:** ('and' Q)     ⁸³³⁻⁸³⁴ **importunate:** ('imporuate' Q)     ⁸³⁴ **entertain:** employ     ⁸⁵⁰ **S. D. come:** ('came' Q)     ⁸⁶¹ **presently:** at once

*Eum.* Thanks, my fine, eloquent hostess.

*Jack.* But hear you, master, one word by the way. Are you content I shall be halves [885 in all you get in your journey?

*Eum.* I am, Jack, here is my hand.

*Jack.* Enough, master, I ask no more.

*Eum.* Come, hostess, receive your money; and I thank you for my good entertain- [890 ment.                          [*Gives money.*]

*Host.* You are heartily welcome, sir.

*Eum.* Come, Jack, whither go we now?

*Jack.* Marry, master, to the conjurer's presently.                                  895

*Eum.* Content, Jack. — Hostess, farewell.
                                *Exeunt omnes.*

*Enter Corebus [blind], and Celanta, the foul wench, to the Well for water*

*Cor.* Come, my duck, come: I have now got a wife. Thou art fair, art thou not?

*Cel.* My Corebus, the fairest alive; make no doubt of that.                       900

*Cor.* Come, wench, are we almost at the well?

*Cel.* Ay, Corebus, we are almost at the well now. I 'll go fetch some water; sit down while I dip my pitcher in.

*Voice.* Gently dip, but not too deep,     905
For fear you make the golden beard to weep.

*A Head comes up with ears of corn, and she combs them in her lap*

Fair maiden, white and red,
Comb me smooth, and stroke my head,
And thou shalt have some cockell-bread.

   [*Voice.*] Gently dip, but not too deep,   910
For fear thou make the golden beard to weep.

*A [Second] Head comes up full of gold; she combs it into her lap*

Fair maid, white and red,
Comb me smooth, and stroke my head,
And every hair a sheaf shall be,
And every sheaf a golden tree.        915

*Cel.* O, see, Corebus, I have comb'd a great deal of gold into my lap, and a great deal of corn!

*Cor.* Well said, wench! now we shall have just enough. God send us coiners to coin our [920 gold. But come, shall we go home, sweetheart?

*Cel.* Nay, come, Corebus, I will lead you.

*Cor.* So, Corebus, things have well hit;
Thou hast gotten wealth to mend thy wit.
                                        *Exeunt.*

*Enter [the Ghost of] Jack and [Eumenides] the wandering knight*

*Jack.* Come away, master, come.      925
*Eum.* Go along, Jack, I'll follow thee. Jack,

they say it is good to go cross-legged, and say his prayers backward; how sayest thou?

*Jack.* Tut, never fear, master; let me alone. Here sit you still; speak not a word; and [930 because you shall not be enticed with his enchanting speeches, with this same wool I 'll stop your ears: and so, master, sit still, for I must to the conjurer.     *Exit [Ghost of] Jack.*

*Enter [Sacrapant] the Conjurer to the wandering knight*

*Sac.* How now! What man art thou that sits so sad?                                935
Why dost thou gaze upon these stately trees
Without the leave and will of Sacrapant?
What, not a word but mum? Then, Sacrapant,
Thou art betray'd.

*Enter [the Ghost of] Jack invisible, and taketh off Sacrapant's wreath from his head, and his sword out of his hand*

What hand invades the head of Sacrapant? 940
What hateful Fury doth envy my happy state?
Then, Sacrapant, these are thy latest days.
Alas, my veins are numb'd, my sinews shrink,
My blood is pierc'd, my breath fleeting away,
And now my timeless date is come to end! 945
He in whose life his actions hath been so foul,
Now in his death to hell descends his soul.
                                *He dieth.*

*Jack.* O, sir, are you gone? Now I hope we shall have some other coil. — Now, master, how like you this? The conjurer he is [950 dead, and vows never to trouble us more. Now get you to your fair lady, and see what you can do with her. — Alas, he heareth me not all this while; but I will help that.
                *He pulls the wool out of his ears.*

*Eum.* How now, Jack! What news?    955

*Jack.* Here, master, take this sword, and dig with it at the foot of this hill.
         *He digs, and spies a light [in a glass].*

*Eum.* How now, Jack! What is this?

*Jack.* Master, without this the conjurer could do nothing; and so long as this light [960 lasts, so long doth his art endure, and this being out, then doth his art decay.

*Eum.* Why, then, Jack, I will soon put out this light.

*Jack.* Ay, master, how?                965

*Eum.* Why, with a stone I 'll break the glass. and then blow it out.

*Jack.* No, master, you may as soon break the smith's anvil as this little vial; nor the biggest blast that ever Boreas blew cannot [970 blow out this little light; but she that is neither

maid, wife, nor widow.  Master, wind this horn,
and see what will happen.

*He winds the horn.  Here enters Venelia, and
breaks the glass, and blows out the light,
and goeth in again*

So, master, how like you this?  This is she that
ran madding in the woods, his betrothed [975
love that keeps the cross; and now, this light
being out, all are restored to their former
liberty.  And now, master, to the lady that
you have so long looked for.

*He draweth a curtain, and there
Delia sitteth asleep*

*Eum.*  God speed, fair maid, sitting [980
alone, — there is once.  God speed, fair maid,
— there is twice.  God speed, fair maid, — that
is thrice.

*Del.*  Not so, good sir, for you are by.

*Jack.*  Enough, master, she hath spoke; [985
now I will leave her with you.          *[Exit.]*

*Eum.*  Thou fairest flower of these western
parts,
Whose beauty so reflecteth in my sight
As doth a crystal mirror in the sun;
For thy sweet sake I have cross'd the frozen
      Rhine;                                            990
Leaving fair Po, I sail'd up Danuby
As far as Saba, whose enhancing streams
Cuts twixt the Tartars and the Russians;
These have I cross'd for thee, fair Delia:
Then grant me that which I have su'd for
      long.                                              995

*Del.*  Thou gentle knight, whose fortune is
      so good
To find me out and set my brothers free,
My faith, my heart, my hand I give to thee.

*Eum.*  Thanks, gentle madam; but here
comes Jack; thank him, for he is the best [1000
friend that we have.

*Enter [the Ghost of] Jack, with a head in
his hand*

How now, Jack!  What hast thou there?

*Jack.*  Marry, master, the head of the conjurer.

*Eum.*  Why, Jack, that is impossible; [1005
he was a young man.

*Jack.*  Ah, master, so he deceived them that
beheld him!  But he was a miserable, old, and
crooked man, though to each man's eye he
seemed young and fresh; for, master, [1010
this conjurer took the shape of the old man
that kept the cross, and that old man was in
the likeness of the conjurer.  But now, master,
wind your horn.

*He winds his horn.  Enter Venelia, the Two
Brothers, and [Erestus] he that was at the
cross*

*Eum.*  Welcome, Erestus! welcome, fair Ve-
nelia!                                                 1015
Welcome, Thelea and Calypha both!
Now have I her that I so long have sought;
So saith fair Delia, if we have your consent.

*1 Bro.*  Valiant Eumenides, thou well de-
servest
To have our favours; so let us rejoice      1020
That by thy means we are at liberty.
Here may we joy each in other's sight,
And this fair lady have her wandering knight.

*Jack.*  So, master, now ye think you have
done; but I must have a saying to you. [1025
You know you and I were partners, I to have
half in all you got.

*Eum.*  Why, so thou shalt, Jack.

*Jack.*  Why, then, master, draw your sword,
part your lady, let me have half of her [1030
presently.

*Eum.*  Why, I hope, Jack, thou dost but jest.
I promised thee half I got, but not half my
lady.

*Jack.*  But what else, master?  Have [1035
you not gotten her?  Therefore divide her
straight, for I will have half; there is no
remedy.

*Eum.*  Well, ere I will falsify my word unto
my friend, take her all.  Here, Jack, I 'll [1040
give her thee.

*Jack.*  Nay, neither more nor less, master,
but even just half.

*Eum.*  Before I will falsify my faith unto my
friend, I will divide her.  Jack, thou shalt [1045
have half.

*1 Bro.*  Be not so cruel unto our sister, gentle
knight.

*2 Bro.*  O, spare fair Delia!  She deserves no
death.                                                  1050

*Eum.*  Content yourselves; my word is passed
to him. — Therefore prepare thyself, Delia, for
thou must die.

*Del.*  Then farewell, world!  Adieu, Eumenides!

*He offers to strike, and [the Ghost of]
Jack stays him*

*Jack.*  Stay, master; it is sufficient [1055
I have tried your constancy.  Do you now
remember since you paid for the burying of a
poor fellow?

*Eum.*  Ay, very well, Jack.

*Jack.*  Then, master, thank that good [1060

---

<sup>990—993</sup> (A close parody of four lines in scene 1 of Greene's *Orlando Furioso*.)   <sup>1025</sup> **a . . . to:** a
**settlement with**   <sup>1057</sup> **since: when**

deed for this good turn; and so God be with you all!

[*The Ghost of*] *Jack leaps down in the ground.*

*Eum.*  Jack, what, art thou gone?  Then
     farewell, Jack! —
Come, brothers, and my beauteous Delia,
Erestus, and thy dear Venelia,          1065
We will to Thessaly with joyful hearts.

*All.*  Agreed: we follow thee and Delia.

*Exeunt omnes* [*except Frolic, Fantastic, and
     Madge*]

*Fan.*  What, gammer, asleep?

*Madge.*  By the mass, son, 't is almost day;
and my windows shuts at the cock's-crow. [1070

*Fro.*  Do you hear, gammer?  Methinks this
Jack bore a great sway amongst them.

*Madge.*  O, man, this was the ghost of the
poor man that they kept such a coil to bury;
and that makes him to help the wander- [1075
ing knight so much.  But come, let us in: we
will have a cup of ale and a toast this morning,
and so depart.

*Fan.*  Then you have made an end of your
tale, gammer?                                1080

*Madge.*  Yes, faith: when this was done, I
took a piece of bread and cheese, and came my
way; and so shall you have, too, before you go,
to your breakfast.                    [*Exeunt.*]

FINIS

1071–1072 (Cf. lines 613, 614.)    1078 **depart:** part company

# ENDIMION,

# The Man in the
## *Moone*.

Playd before the Queenes Ma-
ieſtie at Greenewich on Candlemas day
at night, by the Chyldren of
Paules.

AT LONDON,
Printed by I. Charlewood, for
the widdowe Broome.
**1591.**

BIBLIOGRAPHICAL RECORD. The only early Quarto is that of 1591, which does not name the author (see facsimile of title-page). There is another text (essentially the same, except that it adds the dumb-show at the end of Act II and the three songs omitted in 1591) in the collective edition of six plays by Lyly, issued in 12mo. by Edward Blount in 1632 with the title: — *Six Court Comedies. Often Presented and Acted before Queene Elizabeth, by the Children of her Maiesties Chappell, and the Children of Paules. Written By the onely Rare Poet of that Time, the Witie, Comicall, Facetiously-Quicke, and vnparalell'd: Iohn Lilly, Master of Arts.* The first play in this volume is *Endymion*.

*Endymion* was entered on the Register of the Stationers' Co., Oct. 4, 1591: — *mystres Broome Wydowe Late Wyfe of William Broome Entred for her copies vnder the hand of the Bishop of London: Three Comedies plaied before her maiestie by the Children of Paules th'one Called Endimion, th'other, Gallathea and th'other, Midas . . . xviij d.*

The printer appended to the Quarto of 1591 the following note to the reader: *Since the Plaies in Paules were dissolued, there are certaine Commedies come to my handes by chaunce, which were presented before her Maiestie at seuerall times by the children of Paules. This is the first, and if in any place it shall dysplease, I will take more paines to perfect the next. I referre it to thy indifferent iudgement to peruse, whome I woulde willinglie please. And if this may passe with thy good lyking, I will then goe forwarde to publish the rest. In the meane time, let this haue thy good worde for my better encouragement. Farewell.*

DATE AND STAGE PERFORMANCE. The company of boy players attached to St. Paul's Cathedral had been favorite entertainers of Queen Elizabeth's court during the early part of her reign. After a period of quiescence they again rose to prominence in the decade 1580–1590, with Lyly as their dramatist and the Earl of Oxford as their patron. The statement on the Quarto title-page concerning the royal performance agrees with the record of payment to Thomas Giles, Master of the Children of Paul's, for a play presented before the Queen at Greenwich Palace, Feb. 2 (Candlemas Day), 1588, and this doubtless dates *Endymion*.

STRUCTURE. The division into acts and scenes is moulded on Latin precedent, and the stage directions are of the classical pattern employed also by Ben Jonson and by Marlowe in *Tamburlaine:* at the head of each scene are listed the characters who take part in it in the order in which they speak or appear. The stage setting, however, is highly romantic. Places separated by vast distances (the lunary bank, castle in the desert, and fountain) were apparently represented by sections of the same simple platform stage — such as could be conveniently set up in Greenwich Palace — and a journey may be visualized by stepping across it (see IV. iii. 67–94). The treatment of time is that of a fairy tale.

PLOT AND ALLEGORY. The fundamental story of Cynthia, the moon-goddess, and Endymion may have been borrowed from one of Lucian's *Dialogues of the Gods* (no. 11). Sir Tophas derives his name and mock-epic exploits from Chaucer's *Tale of Sir Thopas:* in his constant hunger and his boastfulness he is a blend of the Latin parasite and braggart soldier. The main contemporary interest in *Endymion*, as in other plays by Lyly (e.g., *Sapho and Phao* and *Midas*) lay in its reference to persons and incidents of Elizabeth's court. Cynthia is the Queen, and Tellus — in her jealousy, her captivity in a desert castle (Tutbury), and her wiles — must have recalled Mary, Queen of Scots, who was beheaded in 1586. Endymion would naturally suggest the Earl of Leicester, and Eumenides, the good counsellor, Lyly's patron Burghley. Some favorable picture of the Earl of Oxford would be expected, and a case has been made out for him as Endymion; but consistent reproduction of actuality would have been impolitic, and the critics who have sought to find it have unduly disregarded the caveat in Lyly's Prologue to the play.

# JOHN LYLY (1554-1606)

## ENDYMION

### THE MAN IN THE MOON

[DRAMATIS PERSONAE

| | |
|---|---|
| ENDYMION, in love with Cynthia | EPITON, Page to Sir Tophas |
| EUMENIDES, his friend, in love with Semele | |
| CORSITES, a Captain, in love with Tellus | CYNTHIA, the Queen |
| PANELION, } Lords of Cynthia's Court | TELLUS, in love with Endymion |
| ZONTES, } | FLOSCULA, her attendant |
| PYTHAGORAS, the Greek Philosopher | SEMELE, loved by Eumenides |
| GYPTES, an Egyptian Soothsayer | SCINTILLA, } Waiting-maids |
| GERON, an old man, husband to Dipsas | FAVILLA, } |
| SIR TOPHAS, a Braggart | DIPSAS, an old Enchantress |
| DARES, Page to Endymion | BAGOA, her servant |
| SAMIAS, Page to Eumenides | |

A Constable; Watchmen; Fairies; Three Ladies and an Old Man in the Dumb Show.

SCENE: The gardens of Cynthia's palace, a grove with a bank of lunary, a castle in a desert place.]

## THE PROLOGUE

Most high and happy Princess, we must tell you a tale of the Man in the Moon, which, if it seem ridiculous for the method, or superfluous for the matter, or for the means incredible, for three faults we can make but one excuse: it is a tale of the Man in the Moon.

It was forbidden in old time to dispute of Chimæra because it was a fiction: we hope in our times none will apply pastimes, because they are fancies; for there liveth none under the sun [5 that knows what to make of the Man in the Moon. We present neither comedy, nor tragedy, nor story, nor anything but that whosoever heareth may say this: Why, here is a tale of the Man in the Moon.

### Actus primus. Scæna prima.

#### Endymion, Eumenides

*Endymion.* I find, Eumenides, in all things both variety to content, and satiety to glut, saving only in my affections, which are so staid, and withal so stately, that I can neither satisfy my heart with love, nor mine eyes with wonder. [5 My thoughts, Eumenides, are stitched to the stars, which being as high as I can see, thou mayest imagine how much higher they are than I can reach.

*Eum.* If you be enamoured of anything [10 above the moon, your thoughts are ridiculous, for that things immortal are not subject to affections; if allured or enchanted with these transitory things under the moon, you show yourself senseless to attribute such lofty [15 titles to such low trifles.

*End.* My love is placed neither under the moon nor above.

*Eum.* I hope you be not sotted upon the Man in the Moon. 20

*End.* No; but settled either to die or possess the moon herself.

*Eum.* Is Endymion mad, or do I mistake? Do you love the moon, Endymion?

*End.* Eumenides, the moon. 25

*Eum.* There was never any so peevish to imagine the moon either capable of affection or shape of a mistress; for as impossible it is to make love fit to her humour, which no man knoweth, as a coat to her form, which con- [30 tinueth not in one bigness whilst she is measuring. Cease off, Endymion, to feed so much upon

---

Prol. [1] tale . . . Moon: a fable    [5] apply pastimes: interpret the play as referring to actual events or persons    [16] low: ('loue' Q)    [19] sotted: infatuated    [26] peevish: foolish

41

fancies. That melancholy blood must be purged which draweth you to a dotage no less miserable than monstrous.                                    35

*End.* My thoughts have no veins, and yet unless they be let blood, I shall perish.

*Eum.* But they have vanities, which being reformed, you may be restored.

*End.* O, fair Cynthia, why do others term [40 thee unconstant whom I have ever found unmovable? Injurious time, corrupt manners, unkind men, who, finding a constancy not to be matched in my sweet mistress, have christened her with the name of wavering, waxing, and [45 waning! Is she inconstant that keepeth a settled course; which, since her first creation, altereth not one minute in her moving? There is nothing thought more admirable or commendable in the sea than the ebbing and flowing; [50 and shall the moon, from whom the sea taketh this virtue, be accounted fickle for increasing and decreasing? Flowers in their buds are nothing worth till they be blown, nor blossoms accounted till they be ripe fruit; and shall we [55 then say they be changeable for that they grow from seeds to leaves, from leaves to buds, from buds to their perfection? Then, why be not twigs that become trees, children that become men, and mornings that grow to evenings, [60 termed wavering, for that they continue not at one stay? Ay, but Cynthia, being in her fulness, decayeth, as not delighting in her greatest beauty, or withering when she should be most honoured. When malice cannot object [65 anything, folly will, making that a vice which is the greatest virtue. What thing (my mistress excepted), being in the pride of her beauty and latter minute of her age, that waxeth young again? Tell me, Eumenides, what is he that [70 having a mistress of ripe years and infinite virtues, great honours and unspeakable beauty, but would wish that she might grow tender again, getting youth by years, and never-decaying beauty by time; whose fair face neither [75 the summer's blaze can scorch, nor winter's blast chap, nor the numbering of years breed altering of colours? Such is my sweet Cynthia, whom time cannot touch because she is divine, nor will offend because she is delicate. O Cyn- [80 thia, if thou shouldst always continue at thy fulness, both gods and men would conspire to ravish thee. But thou, to abate the pride of our affections, dost detract from thy perfections, thinking it sufficient if once in a month [85 we enjoy a glimpse of thy majesty; and then, to increase our griefs, thou dost decrease thy gleams, coming out of thy royal robes, wherewith thou dazzlest our eyes, down into thy swathe clouts, beguiling our eyes; and then —        90

*Eum.* Stay there, Endymion; thou that committest idolatry, wilt straight blaspheme, if thou be suffered. Sleep would do thee more good than speech: the moon heareth thee not, or if she do, regardeth thee not.        95

*End.* Vain Eumenides, whose thoughts never grow higher than the crown of thy head! Why troublest thou me, having neither head to conceive the cause of my love or a heart to receive the impressions? Follow thou thine own for- [100 tunes, which creep on the earth, and suffer me to fly to mine, whose fall, though it be desperate, yet shall it come by daring. Farewell. [*Exit.*]

*Eum.* Without doubt Endymion is bewitched; otherwise in a man of such rare [105 virtues there could not harbour a mind of such extreme madness. I will follow him, lest in this fancy of the moon he deprive himself of the sight of the sun.                          *Exit.*

### *Actus primus. Scæna secunda.*

#### *Tellus, Floscula*

*Tellus.* Treacherous and most perjured Endymion! Is Cynthia the sweetness of thy life and the bitterness of my death? What revenge may be devised so full of shame as my thoughts are replenished with malice? Tell me, Floscula, [5 if falseness in love can possibly be punished with extremity of hate? As long as sword, fire, or poison may be hired, no traitor to my love shall live unrevenged. Were thy oaths without number, thy kisses without measure, thy sighs [10 without end, forged to deceive a poor credulous virgin, whose simplicity had been worth thy favour and better fortune? If the gods sit unequal beholders of injuries, or laughers at lovers' deceits, then let mischief be as well for- [15 given in women as perjury winked at in men.

*Flosc.* Madam, if you would compare the state of Cynthia with your own, and the height of Endymion his thoughts with the meanness of your fortune, you would rather yield than [20 contend, being between you and her no comparison; and rather wonder than rage at the greatness of his mind, being affected with a thing more than mortal.

*Tellus.* No comparison, Floscula? And [25 why so? Is not my beauty divine, whose body is decked with fair flowers, and veins are vines, yielding sweet liquor to the dullest spirits; whose ears are corn, to bring strength; and whose hairs are grass, to bring abundance? [30 Doth not frankincense and myrrh breathe out of my nostrils, and all the sacrifice of the gods breed in my bowels? Infinite are my creatures, without which neither thou, nor Endymion, nor any, could love or live.        35

---

89-90 **swathe clouts:** swaddling-clothes        13-14 **unequal:** prejudiced

*Flosc.* But know you not, fair lady, that Cynthia governeth all things? Your grapes would be but dry husks, your corn but chaff, and all your virtues vain, were it not Cynthia that preserveth the one in the bud and nourisheth the [40 other in the blade, and by her influence both comforteth all things, and by her authority commandeth all creatures. Suffer, then, Endymion to follow his affections, though to obtain her be impossible, and let him flatter himself in his [45 own imaginations, because they are immortal.

*Tellus.* Loath I am, Endymion, thou shouldest die, because I love thee well; and that thou shouldest live, it grieveth me, because thou lovest Cynthia too well. In these extremities, [50 what shall I do? Floscula, no more words; I am resolved. He shall neither live nor die.

*Flosc.* A strange practice, if it be possible.

*Tellus.* Yes, I will entangle him in such a sweet net that he shall neither find the means [55 to come out, nor desire it. All allurements of pleasure will I cast before his eyes, insomuch that he shall slake that love which he now voweth to Cynthia, and burn in mine, of which he seemeth careless. In this languishing, be- [60 tween my amorous devices and his own loose desires, there shall such dissolute thoughts take root in his head, and over his heart grow so thick a skin, that neither hope of preferment, nor fear of punishment, nor counsel of the wisest, nor [65 company of the worthiest, shall alter his humour, nor make him once to think of his honour.

*Flosc.* A revenge incredible, and, if it may be, unnatural.

*Tellus.* He shall know the malice of a wo- [70 man to have neither mean nor end; and of a woman deluded in love to have neither rule nor reason. I can do it! I must! I will! All his virtues will I shadow with vices; his person (ah, sweet person!) shall he deck with such rich [75 robes as he shall forget it is his own person; his sharp wit (ah, wit too sharp that hath cut off all my joys!) shall he use in flattering of my face and devising sonnets in my favour. The prime of his youth and pride of his time shall be spent [80 in melancholy passions, careless behaviour, untamed thoughts, and unbridled affections.

*Flosc.* When this is done, what then? Shall it continue till his death, or shall he dote forever in this delight? 85

*Tellus.* Ah, Floscula, thou rendest my heart in sunder in putting me in remembrance of the end.

*Flosc.* Why, if this be not the end, all the rest is to no end. 90

*Tellus.* Yet suffer me to imitate Juno, who would turn Jupiter's lovers to beasts on the earth, though she knew afterwards they should be stars in heaven.

*Flosc.* Affection that is bred by enchant- [95 ment is like a flower that is wrought in silk, — in colour and form most like, but nothing at all in substance or savour.

*Tellus.* It shall suffice me if the world talk that I am favoured of Endymion. 100

*Flosc.* Well, use your own will; but you shall find that love gotten with witchcraft is as unpleasant as fish taken with medicines unwholesome.

*Tellus.* Floscula, they that be so poor that [105 they have neither net nor hook will rather poison dough than pine with hunger; and she that is so oppress'd with love that she is neither able with beauty nor wit to obtain her friend, will rather use unlawful means than try un- [110 tolerable pains. I will do it. *Exit.*

*Flosc.* Then about it. Poor Endymion, what traps are laid for thee because thou honourest one that all the world wondereth at! And what plots are cast to make thee unfortunate that [115 studiest of all men to be the faithfulest! *Exit.*

### Actus primus. Scæna tertia.

*Dares, Samias, Sir Tophas, Epiton*

*Dares.* Now our masters are in love up to the ears, what have we to do but to be in knavery up to the crowns?

*Samias.* Oh, that we had Sir Tophas, that brave squire, in the midst of our mirth, — *et* [5 *ecce autem,* "Will you see the Devil," —

#### Enter Sir Tophas [and Epiton]

*Top.* Epi!

*Epi.* Here, sir.

*Top.* I brook not this idle humour of love; it tickleth not my liver, from whence the love- [10 mongers in former age seemed to infer they should proceed.

*Epi.* Love, sir, may lie in your lungs, — [*Aside.*] and I think it doth, and that is the cause you blow and are so pursy. 15

*Top.* Tush, boy, I think it but some device of the poet to get money.

*Epi.* A poet? What 's that?

*Top.* Dost thou not know what a poet is?

*Epi.* No. 20

*Top.* Why, fool, a poet is as much as one should say — a poet. [*He observes Dares and Samias.*] But soft, yonder be two wrens; shall I shoot at them?

*Epi.* They are two lads. 25

*Top.* Larks or wrens, I will kill them.

---

⁵³ **practice:** plot   ¹⁰³ **medicines:** poisoned dough-balls; cf. line 107.   **Sc. III. s. d. Sir Tophas** and Epiton enter by another door, a little after the others.

*Epi.* Larks! Are you blind? They are two little boys.

*Top.* Birds or boys, they are both but a pittance for my breakfast; therefore have at [30 them, for their brains must, as it were, embroider my bolts.

*Sam.* Stay your courage, valiant knight, for your wisdom is so weary that it stayeth itself.

*Dar.* Why, Sir Tophas, have you for- [35 gotten your old friends?

*Top.* Friends? *Nego argumentum.*

*Sam.* And why not friends?

*Top.* Because *amicitia* (as in old annals we find) is *inter pares.* Now, my pretty com- [40 panions, you shall see how unequal you be to me; but I will not cut you quite off; you shall be my half-friends for reaching to my middle; so far as from the ground to the waist I will be your friend.          45

*Dar.* Learnedly. But what shall become of the rest of your body, from the waist to the crown?

*Top.* My children, *quod supra vos nihil ad vos;* you must think the rest immortal, be- [50 cause you cannot reach it.

*Epi.* Nay, I tell ye my master is more than a man.

*Dar.* And thou less than a mouse.

*Top.* But what be you two?        55

*Sam.* I am Samias, page to Eumenides.

*Dar.* And I Dares, page to Endymion.

*Top.* Of what occupation are your masters?

*Dar.* Occupation, you clown! Why, they are honourable and warriors.        60

*Top.* Then are they my prentices.

*Dar.* Thine! And why so?

*Top.* I was the first that ever devised war, and therefore by Mars himself given me for my arms a whole armory; and thus I go, as you [65 see, clothed with artillery. It is not silks, milksops, nor tissues, nor the fine wool of Ceres, but iron, steel, swords, flame, shot, terror, clamour, blood, and ruins, that rocks asleep my thoughts, which never had any other cradle [70 but cruelty. Let me see, do you not bleed?

*Dar.* Why so?

*Top.* Commonly my words wound.

*Sam.* What then do your blows?

*Top.* Not only wound, but also confound. [75

*Sam.* How darst thou come so near thy master, Epi? Sir Tophas, spare us.

*Top.* You shall live: — you, Samias, because you are little; you, Dares, because you are no bigger; and both of you, because you are but [80

two; for commonly I kill by the dozen, and have for every particular adversary a peculiar weapon.

*Sam.* May we know the use, for our better skill in war?

*Top.* You shall. Here is a burbolt for the [85 ugly beast the blackbird.

*Dar.* A cruel sight.

*Top.* Here is the musket for the untamed or, as the vulgar sort term it, the wild mallard.

*Sam.* O desperate attempt!        90

*Epi.* Nay, my master will match them.

*Dar.* Ay, if he catch them.

*Top.* Here is a spear and shield, and both necessary, the one to conquer, the other to subdue or overcome the terrible trout, which al- [95 though he be under the water, yet tying a string to the top of my spear and an engine of iron to the end of my line, I overthrow him, and then herein I put him.

*Sam.* O wonderful war! [*Aside.*] Dares, [100 didst thou ever hear such a dolt?

*Dar.* [*Aside.*] All the better; we shall have good sport hereafter, if we can get leisure.

*Sam.* [*Aside.*] Leisure! I will rather lose my master's service than his company! Look [105 how he struts. [*To Sir Tophas.*] But what is this? Call you it your sword?

*Top.* No, it is my simitar; which I, by construction often studying to be compendious, call my smiter.        110

*Dar.* What, are you also learned, sir?

*Top.* Learned? I am all Mars and Ars.

*Sam.* Nay, you are all mass and ass.

*Top.* Mock you me? You shall both suffer, yet with such weapons as you shall make [115 choice of the weapon wherewith you shall perish. Am I all a mass or lump? is there no proportion in me? Am I all ass? is there no wit in me? Epi, prepare them to the slaughter.

*Sam.* I pray, sir, hear us speak! We call [120 you mass, which your learning doth well understand is all man, for *mas, maris* is a man. Then *as,* as you know, is a weight, and we for your virtues account you a weight.

*Top.* The Latin hath saved your lives, the [125 which a world of silver could not have ransom'd. I understand you, and pardon you.

*Dar.* Well, Sir Tophas, we bid you farewell, and at our next meeting we will be ready to do you service.        130

*Top.* Samias, I thank you: Dares, I thank you: but especially I thank you both.

*Sam.* [*Aside.*] Wisely. Come, next time we'll have some pretty gentlewomen with us to

---

³² **bolts:** blunt arrows    ³⁷ **Nego argumentum:** I deny your argument.    ³⁹⁻⁴⁰ **amicitia . . . pares:** friendship is between equals    ⁴⁹⁻⁵⁰ **quod . . . vos:** what is above you does not concern you (cf. *Friar Bacon and Friar Bungay,* Sc. ii. 22–25)    ⁶⁷ **Ceres:** 'Seres' (Bond), as Ceres was not goddess of flocks. "Wool of Seres" would be "Chinese silk."    ⁵⁶, ⁵⁷ **Eumenides, Endymion:** (transposed in Q, Blount) ⁷⁵ **wound:** ('confound' Q, Blount)    ⁸⁵ **burbolt:** bird-bolt (cf. note on line 32)

walk, for without doubt with them he will [135
be very dainty.

*Dar.* Come, let us see what our masters
do; it is high time.

*Exeunt [Samias and Dares].*

*Top.* Now will I march into the field,
where, if I cannot encounter with my foul [140
enemies, I will withdraw myself to the river,
and there fortify for fish, for there resteth no
minute free from fight.          *Exit [with Epi.].*

## Actus primus. Scæna quarta.

*Tellus, Floscula, [meeting] Dipsas*

*Tellus.* Behold, Floscula, we have met with
the woman by chance that we sought for by
travail. I will break my mind to her without
ceremony or circumstance, lest we lose that
time in advice that should be spent in execu- [5
tion.

*Flosc.* Use your discretion; I will in this case
neither give counsel nor consent, for there cannot be a thing more monstrous than to force
affection by sorcery, neither do I imagine [10
anything more impossible.

*Tellus.* Tush, Floscula, in obtaining of love,
what impossibilities will I not try? And for the
winning of Endymion, what impieties will I not
practise? [*To Dipsas.*] Dipsas, whom as [15
many honour for age as wonder at for cunning,
listen in few words to my tale, and answer in
one word to the purpose, for that neither my
burning desire can afford long speech, nor the
short time I have to stay many delays. Is it [20
possible by herbs, stones, spells, incantation, enchantment, exorcisms, fire, metals, planets, or
any practice, to plant affection where it is not,
and to supplant it where it is?

*Dipsas.* Fair lady, you may imagine that [25
these hoary hairs are not void of experience,
nor the great name that goeth of my cunning
to be without cause. I can darken the sun by
my skill and remove the moon out of her course;
I can restore youth to the aged and make [30
hills without bottoms; there is nothing that I
cannot do but that only which you would have
me do: and therein I differ from the gods, that
I am not able to rule hearts; for were it in my
power to place affection by appointment, I [35
would make such evil appetites, such inordinate
lusts, such cursed desires, as all the world
should be filled both with superstitious heats
and extreme love.

*Tellus.* Unhappy Tellus, whose desires are [40
so desperate that they are neither to be conceived of any creature, nor to be cured by any
art!

*Dipsas.* This I can: breed slackness in love,
though never root it out. What is he whom [45
you love, and what she that he honoureth?

*Tellus.* Endymion, sweet Endymion is he
that hath my heart; and Cynthia, too, too fair
Cynthia, the miracle of nature, of time, of fortune, is the lady that he delights in, and [50
dotes on every day, and dies for ten thousand
times a day.

*Dipsas.* Would you have his love either by
absence or sickness aslaked? Would you that
Cynthia should mistrust him, or be jealous [55
of him without colour?

*Tellus.* It is the only thing I crave, that, seeing my love to Endymion, unspotted, cannot be
accepted, his truth to Cynthia, though it be unspeakable, may be suspected.          60

*Dipsas.* I will undertake it, and overtake
him, that all his love shall be doubted of, and
therefore become desperate: but this will wear
out with time that treadeth all things down but
truth.          65

*Tellus.* Let us go.

*Dipsas.* I follow.          *Exeunt.*

## Actus secundus. Scæna prima.

*Endymion, [later] Tellus*

*Endymion.* O fair Cynthia! O unfortunate
Endymion! Why was not thy birth as high as
thy thoughts, or her beauty less than heavenly;
or why are not thine honours as rare as her
beauty, or thy fortunes as great as thy de- [5
serts? Sweet Cynthia, how wouldst thou be
pleased, how possessed? Will labours, patient
of all extremities, obtain thy love? There is no
mountain so steep that I will not climb, no monster so cruel that I will not tame, no action [10
so desperate that I will not attempt. Desirest
thou the passions of love, the sad and melancholy moods of perplexed minds, the not-to-be-
expressed torments of racked thoughts? Behold
my sad tears, my deep sighs, my hollow [15
eyes, my broken sleeps, my heavy countenance.
Wouldst thou have me vowed only to thy
beauty and consume every minute of time in
thy service? Remember my solitary life almost
these seven years. Whom have I entertained [20
but mine own thoughts and thy virtues? What
company have I used but contemplation? Whom
have I wondered at but thee? Nay, whom have
I not contemned for thee? Have I not crept
to those on whom I might have trodden, [25
only because thou didst shine upon them? Have
not injuries been sweet to me, if thou vouch-
safedst I should bear them? Have I not spent
my golden years in hopes, waxing old with

---

⁵⁴ **aslaked:** abated      ⁵⁶ **colour:** reason, pretext      ⁶¹ **overtake:** overcome

wishing, yet wishing nothing but thy love? [30
With Tellus, fair Tellus, have I dissembled,
using her but as a cloak for mine affections,
that others, seeing my mangled and disordered
mind, might think it were for one that loveth
me, not for Cynthia, whose perfection allow- [35
eth no companion nor comparison. In the midst
of these distempered thoughts of mine thou art
not only jealous of my truth, but careless, suspicious, and secure; which strange humour maketh my mind as desperate as thy conceits are [40
doubtful. I am none of those wolves that bark
most when thou shinest brightest, but that fish
(thy fish, Cynthia, in the flood Araris) which
at thy waxing is as white as the driven snow,
and at thy waning as black as deepest dark- [45
ness. I am that Endymion, sweet Cynthia, that
have carried my thoughts in equal balance with
my actions, being always as free from imagining ill as enterprising; that Endymion whose
eyes never esteemed anything fair but thy [50
face, whose tongue termed nothing rare but thy
virtues, and whose heart imagined nothing miraculous but thy government; yea, that Endymion, who, divorcing himself from the amiableness
of all ladies, the bravery of all courts, the [55
company of all men, hath chosen in a solitary
cell to live, only by feeding on thy favour, ac-
counting in the world — but thyself — nothing
excellent, nothing immortal: thus mayst thou
see every vein, sinew, muscle, and artery of [60
my love, in which there is no flattery, nor
deceit, error, nor art. But soft, here cometh
Tellus. I must turn my other face to her, like
Janus, lest she be as suspicious as Juno.

*Enter Tellus [followed by Floscula
and Dipsas]*

*Tellus.* Yonder I espy Endymion. I will [65
seem to suspect nothing, but soothe him, that
seeing I cannot obtain the depth of his love, I
may learn the height of his dissembling. Floscula and Dipsas, withdraw yourselves out of
our sight, yet be within the hearing of our [70
saluting. [*Floscula and Dipsas withdraw.*]
How now, Endymion, always solitary? No
company but your own thoughts, no friend but
melancholy fancies?

*End.* You know, fair Tellus, that the [75
sweet remembrance of your love is the only
companion of my life, and thy presence, my
paradise; so that I am not alone when nobody
is with me, and in heaven itself when thou art
with me.                                         80

*Tellus.* Then you love me, Endymion?

*End.* Or else I live not, Tellus.

*Tellus.* Is it not possible for you, Endymion,
to dissemble?

*End.* Not, Tellus, unless I could make me [85
a woman.

*Tellus.* Why, is dissembling joined to their
sex inseparable, as heat to fire, heaviness to
earth, moisture to water, thinness to air?

*End.* No, but found in their sex as com- [90
mon as spots upon doves, moles upon faces,
caterpillars upon sweet apples, cobwebs upon
fair windows.

*Tellus.* Do they all dissemble?

*End.* All but one.                              95

*Tellus.* Who is that?

*End.* I dare not tell; for if I should say you,
then would you imagine my flattery to be extreme; if another, then would you think my
love to be but indifferent.                     100

*Tellus.* You will be sure I shall take no vantage of your words. But, in sooth, Endymion,
without more ceremonies, is it not Cynthia?

*End.* You know, Tellus, that of the gods we
are forbidden to dispute, because their dei- [105
ties come not within the compass of our reasons;
and of Cynthia we are allowed not to talk but
to wonder, because her virtues are not within
the reach of our capacities.

*Tellus.* Why, she is but a woman.              110

*End.* No more was Venus.

*Tellus.* She is but a virgin.

*End.* No more was Vesta.

*Tellus.* She shall have an end.

*End.* So shall the world.                      115

*Tellus.* Is not her beauty subject to time?

*End.* No more than time is to standing still.

*Tellus.* Wilt thou make her immortal?

*End.* No, but incomparable.

*Tellus.* Take heed, Endymion, lest like [120
the wrestler in Olympia, that striving to lift an
impossible weight catch'd an incurable strain,
thou, by fixing thy thoughts above thy reach,
fall into a disease without all recure. But I see
thou art now in love with Cynthia.             125

*End.* No, Tellus, thou knowest that the
stately cedar, whose top reacheth unto the
clouds, never boweth his head to the shrubs
that grow in the valley; nor ivy, that climbeth
up by the elm, can ever get hold of the [130
beams of the sun. Cynthia I honour in all humi-
ity, whom none ought or dare adventure to love,
whose affections are immortal, and virtues infinite. Suffer me, therefore, to gaze on the
moon, at whom, were it not for thyself, I [135
would die with wondering.            *Exeunt.*

---

⁴² **fish:** " The fish Scolopidus in the flood Araris at the waxing of the moon is as white as the driven
snow and at the waning as black as the burnt coal." Lyly's *Euphues* (ed. Croll and Clemons, p. 74.)
The Arar is the Saône, and the story comes from a classical treatise on rivers falsely ascribed to Plutarch.
⁶⁶ **soothe:** beguile

## Actus secundus. Scæna secunda.

### Dares, Samias, Scintilla, Favilla

*Dar.* Come, Samias, didst thou ever hear such a sighing, the one for Cynthia, the other for Semele, and both for moonshine in the water?

*Sam.* Let them sigh, and let us sing. How [5 say you, gentlewomen, are not our masters too far in love?

*Scint.* Their tongues, haply, are dipp'd to the root in amorous words and sweet discourses, but I think their hearts are scarce tipp'd on [10 the side with constant desires.

*Dar.* How say you, Favilla, is not love a lurcher, that taketh men's stomachs away that they cannot eat, their spleen that they cannot laugh, their hearts that they cannot fight, [15 their eyes that they cannot sleep, and leaveth nothing but livers to make nothing but lovers!

*Favil.* Away, peevish boy; a rod were better under thy girdle than love in thy mouth! It will be a forward cock that croweth in the [20 shell.

*Dar.* Alas, good old gentlewoman, how it becometh you to be grave!

*Scint.* Favilla, though she be but a spark, yet is she fire.                                        25

*Favil.* And you, Scintilla, be not much more than a spark, though you would be esteemed a flame.

*Sam.* [*Aside to Dares.*] It were good sport to see the fight between two sparks.            30

*Dar.* [*Aside to Samias.*] Let them to it, and we will warm us by their words.

*Scint.* You are not angry, Favilla?

*Favil.* That is, Scintilla, as you list to take it.                                             35

*Sam.* That, that!

*Scint.* This it is to be matched with girls, who coming but yesterday from making of babies, would before to-morrow be accounted matrons.

*Favil.* I cry your matronship mercy. Be- [40 cause your pantables be higher with cork, therefore your feet must needs be higher in the insteps. You will be mine elder because you stand upon a stool and I on the floor.

*Sam.* Good, good!                                    45

*Dar.* [*To Samias.*] Let them alone, and see with what countenance they will become friends.

*Scint.* Nay, you think to be the wiser, because you mean to have the last word.      50

*Sam.* [*To Dares.*] Step between them lest they scratch. — In faith, gentlewomen, seeing we came out to be merry, let not your jarring mar our jests; be friends. How say you?

*Scint.* I am not angry, but it spited me to [55 see how short she was.

*Favil.* I meant nothing till she would needs cross me.

*Dar.* Then, so let it rest.

*Scint.* I am agreed.                                 60

*Favil.* And I. Yet I never took anything so unkindly in my life.                    [*Weeps.*]

*Scint.* 'Tis I have the cause, that never offered the occasion.                     [*Weeps.*]

*Dar.* Excellent, and right like a woman. 65

*Sam.* A strange sight to see water come out of fire.

*Dar.* It is their property to carry in their eyes fire and water, tears and torches, and in their mouths honey and gall.                70

*Scint.* You will be a good one if you live. But what is yonder formal fellow?

### Enter Sir Tophas [and Epiton]

*Dar.* Sir Tophas, Sir Tophas, of whom we told you. If you be good wenches, make as though you love him, and wonder at him.  75

*Favil.* We will do our parts.

*Dar.* But first let us stand aside, and let him use his garb, for all consisteth in his gracing.
                                   [*The four retire.*]

*Top.* Epi!

*Epi.* At hand, sir.                                  80

*Top.* How likest thou this martial life, where nothing but blood besprinkleth our bosoms? Let me see, be our enemies fat?

*Epi.* Passing fat: and I would not change this life to be a lord; and yourself passeth all [85 comparison, for other captains kill and beat, and there is nothing you kill, but you also eat.

*Top.* I will draw out their guts out of their bellies, and tear the flesh with my teeth, so mortal is my hate, and so eager my un- [90 staunched stomach.

*Epi.* [*Aside.*] My master thinks himself the valiantest man in the world if he kill a wren; so warlike a thing he accounteth to take away life, though it be from a lark.               95

*Top.* Epi, I find my thoughts to swell and my spirit to take wings, insomuch that I cannot continue within the compass of so slender combats.

*Favil.* This passeth!                            } 100
*Scint.* Why, is he not mad?        } [*Aside.*]
*Sam.* No, but a little vainglorious. }

*Top.* Epi!

*Epi.* Sir.

*Top.* I will encounter that black and cruel [105

---

¹³ **lurcher:** thief   **stomachs:** appetites   ²⁴ **spark:** Latin **favilla** = glowing ash   ³⁸ **babies:** dolls
⁴¹ **pantables:** shoes   ⁴²⁻⁴³ **higher . . . insteps:** more arrogant   ⁵⁶ **short:** ill-tempered   ⁷⁸ **use his garb:**
**show his style**   ⁸³ **enemies:** the trout, or larks, which Epiton is carrying   ¹⁰⁰ **passeth:** exceeds belief

enemy that beareth rough and untewed locks
upon his body, whose sire throweth down the
strongest walls, whose legs are as many as both
ours, on whose head are placed most horrible
horns by nature as a defence from all harms. [110

*Epi.* What mean you, master, to be so desperate?

*Top.* Honour inciteth me, and very hunger
compelleth me.

*Epi.* What is that monster?             115

*Top.* The monster *Ovis.* I have said, — let
thy wits work.

*Epi.* I cannot imagine it. Yet let me see, —
a black enemy with rough locks. It may be
a sheep, and *Ovis* is a sheep. His sire so [120
strong: a ram is a sheep's sire, that being also
an engine of war. Horns he hath, and four
legs, — so hath a sheep. Without doubt, this
monster is a black sheep. Is it not a sheep that
you mean?                                 125

*Top.* Thou hast hit it: that monster will I
kill and sup with.

*Sam.* [*Aside.*] Come, let us take him off.
[*Samias, Dares, Favilla, and Scintilla come
forward.*] Sir Tophas, all hail!         130

*Top.* Welcome, children; I seldom cast mine
eyes so low as to the crowns of your heads, and
therefore pardon me that I spake not all this
while.

*Dar.* No harm done. Here be fair ladies [135
come to wonder at your person, your valour,
your wit, the report whereof hath made them
careless of their own honours, to glut their eyes
and hearts upon yours.

*Top.* Report cannot but injure me, for [140
that not knowing fully what I am, I fear she
hath been a niggard in her praises.

*Scint.* No, gentle knight, report hath been
prodigal, for she hath left you no equal, nor
herself credit, so much hath she told; yet no [145
more than we now see.

*Dar.* [*Aside.*] A good wench!

*Favil.* If there remain as much pity toward
women as there is in you courage against your
enemies, then shall we be happy, who, hear- [150
ing of your person, came to see it, and seeing it,
are now in love with it.

*Top.* Love me, ladies? I easily believe it,
but my tough heart receiveth no impression
with sweet words. Mars may pierce it, [155
Venus shall not paint on it.

*Favil.* A cruel saying.

*Sam.* [*Aside.*] There 's a girl!

*Dar.* Will you cast these ladies away, and all
for a little love? Do but speak kindly.    160

*Top.* There cometh no soft syllable within

my lips; custom hath made my words bloody
and my heart barbarous. That pelting word
love, how waterish it is in my mouth; it carrieth no sound. Hate, horror, death, are [165
speeches that nourish my spirits. I like honey,
but I care not for the bees; I delight in music,
but I love not to play on the bagpipes; I can
vouchsafe to hear the voice of women, but to
touch their bodies, I disdain it as a thing [170
childish and fit for such men as can disgest
nothing but milk.

*Scint.* A hard heart! Shall we die for your
love and find no remedy?

*Top.* I have already taken a surfeit.    175

*Epi.* Good master, pity them.

*Top.* Pity them, Epi? No, I do not think
that this breast shall be pestered with such a
foolish passion. What is that the gentlewoman
carrieth in a chain?                      180

*Epi.* Why, it is a squirrel.

*Top.* A squirrel? O gods, what things are
made for money!

*Dar.* Is not this gentleman over-wise?

*Favil.* I could stay all day with him, if [185
I feared not to be shent.

*Scint.* Is it not possible to meet again?

*Dar.* Yes, at any time.

*Favil.* Then let us hasten home.

*Scint.* Sir Tophas, the god of war deal [190
better with you than you do with the god of
love.

*Favil.* Our love we may dissemble, disgest
we cannot; but I doubt not but time will hamper you and help us.                      195

*Top.* I defy time, who hath no interest in my
heart. Come, Epi, let me to the battle with
that hideous beast. Love is pap, and hath no
relish in my taste because it is not terrible.

[*Exeunt Sir Tophas and Epiton.*]

*Dar.* Indeed a black sheep is a perilous [200
beast; but let us in till another time.

*Favil.* I shall long for that time.    *Exeunt.*

## Actus secundus. Scæna tertia.

*Endymion, [secretly observed by] Dipsas,
Bagoa*

*End.* No rest, Endymion! Still uncertain
how to settle thy steps by day or thy thoughts
by night! Thy truth is measured by thy fortune, and thou art judged unfaithful because
thou art unhappy. I will see if I can beguile [5
myself with sleep, and if no slumber will take
hold in my eyes, yet will I embrace the golden
thoughts in my head, and wish to melt by musing; that as ebony, which no fire can scorch, is yet

---

¹⁰⁶ **untewed:** uncombed     ¹⁶³ **pelting:** paltry     ¹⁷¹· ¹⁹³ **disgest:** digest     ¹⁸⁶ **shent:** reproved
⁹⁻¹⁰ **ebony . . . savours:** Lyly misunderstands Pliny, who states, in his *Natural History,* that ebony
will burn with a pleasant odor.

consumed with sweet savours, so my heart, [10 which cannot be bent by the hardness of fortune, may be bruised by amorous desires. On yonder bank never grew anything but lunary, and hereafter I will never have any bed but that bank. O Endymion, Tellus was fair. But [15 what availeth beauty without wisdom? Nay, Endymion, she was wise. But what availeth wisdom without honour? She was honourable, Endymion; belie her not. Ay, but how obscure is honour without fortune. Was she not for- [20 tunate whom so many followed? Yes, yes, but base is fortune without majesty. Thy majesty, Cynthia, all the world knoweth and wondereth at, but not one in the world that can imitate it or comprehend it. No more, Endymion. Sleep [25 or die. Nay, die, for to sleep, it is impossible; — and yet I know not how it cometh to pass, I feel such a heaviness both in mine eyes and heart that I am suddenly benumbed, yea, in every joint. It may be weariness, for when [30 did I rest? It may be deep melancholy, for when did I not sigh? Cynthia! Ay, so; — I say, Cynthia! *He falls asleep.*

*[Enter Dipsas and Bagoa]*

*Dipsas.* Little dost thou know, Endymion, when thou shalt wake, for hadst thou placed [35 thy heart as low in love as thy head lieth now in sleep, thou mightest have commanded Tellus, whom now, instead of a mistress, thou shalt find a tomb. These eyes must I seal up by art, not nature, which are to be opened neither by [40 art nor nature. Thou that layest down with golden locks shalt not awake until they be turned to silver hairs; and that chin on which scarcely appeareth soft down shall be filled with bristles as hard as broom. Thou shalt sleep [45 out thy youth and flowering time, and become dry hay before thou knowest thyself green grass; and ready by age to step into the grave when thou wakest, that was youthful in the court when thou laidst thee down to sleep. [50 The malice of Tellus hath brought this to pass, which if she could not have intreated of me by fair means, she would have commanded by menacing, for from her gather we all our simples to maintain our sorceries. *[To Bagoa.]* [55 Fan with this hemlock over his face, and sing the enchantment for sleep, whilst I go in and finish those ceremonies that are required in our art. Take heed ye touch not his face, for the fan is so seasoned that whoso it toucheth with [60

a leaf shall presently die, and over whom the wind of it breatheth, he shall sleep forever. *Exit.*

*Bagoa.* Let me alone; I will be careful. What hap hadst thou, Endymion, to come under the hands of Dipsas? O fair En- [65 dymion, how it grieveth me that that fair face must be turned to a withered skin and taste the pains of death before it feel the reward of love! I fear Tellus will repent that which the heavens themselves seemed to rue. But I hear Dipsas [70 coming! I dare not repine, lest she make me pine, and rock me into such a deep sleep that I shall not awake to my marriage.

*Enter Dipsas*

*Dipsas.* How now, have you finished?
*Bagoa.* Yea. 75
*Dipsas.* Well then, let us in; and see that you do not so much as whisper that I did this, for if you do, I will turn thy hairs to adders and all thy teeth in thy head to tongues. Come away, come away. *Exeunt.* [80

A DUMB SHOW

*Music sounds. Three ladies enter: one with a knife and a looking-glass, who, by the procurement of one of the other two, offers to stab Endymion as he sleeps; but the third wrings her hands, lamenteth, offering still to prevent it, but dares [85 not. At last, the first lady looking in the glass, casts down the knife.* **Exeunt.**
*Enters an ancient man with books with three leaves; offers the same twice. Endymion refuseth. He rendeth two, and offers the third, [90 where he stands awhile; and then Endymion offers to take it.* **Exit [the Old Man].**

## *Actus tertius. Scæna prima.*

*Cynthia, three Lords [i.e., Eumenides, Corsites, Zontes], Tellus [with Semele and Panelion]*

*Cynthia.* Is the report true, that Endymion is stricken into such a dead sleep that nothing can either wake him or move him?
*Eum.* Too true, madam, and as much to be pitied as wondered at. 5
*Tellus.* As good sleep and do no harm as wake and do no good.
*Cynth.* What maketh you, Tellus, to be so short? The time was Endymion only was.
*Eum.* It is an old saying, madam, that a [10

---

[13] **lunary:** moon-wort, a fern. "I have heard of an herb called Lunary, that being bound to the pulses of the sick, causeth nothing but dreams of weddings and dances." Lyly's *Sapho and Phao* (III. iii. 43–45). [49] **was:** *i.e.,* wast [56–57] **sing . . . sleep:** evidently a song sung by Bagoa before the return of Dipsas (line 74). It has not been preserved. [61] **presently:** immediately [80] S. D. **Dumb Show:** (visualizes the dreams which Endymion later reports to Cynthia, V. i. 100 ff. Not in Q.) [90] **rendeth:** ('readeth' Blount. Cf. V. i. 138 ff.) [9] **only was:** was your one thought

waking dog doth afar off bark at a sleeping
lion.

*Sem.* It were good, Eumenides, that you
took a nap with your friend, for your speech
beginneth to be heavy.                          15

*Eum.* Contrary to your nature, Semele,
which hath been always accounted light.

*Cynth.* What, have we here before my face
these unseemly and malapert overthwarts! I
will tame your tongues and your thoughts, [20
and make your speeches answerable to your
duties, and your conceits fit for my dignity, else
will I banish you both my person and the world.

*Eum.* Pardon I humbly ask; but such is my
unspotted faith to Endymion that whatsoever [25
seemeth a needle to prick his finger is a dagger
to wound my heart.

*Cynth.* If you be so dear to him, how hap-
peneth it you neither go to see him, nor search
for remedy for him?                             30

*Eum.* I have seen him to my grief, and sought
recure with despair, for that I cannot imagine
who should restore him that is the wonder to
all men. Your Highness, on whose hands the
compass of the earth is at command, though [35
not in possession, may show yourself both
worthy your sex, your nature, and your favour,
if you redeem that honourable Endymion,
whose ripe years foretell rare virtues, and whose
unmellowed conceits promise ripe counsel. [40

*Cynth.* I have had trial of Endymion, and
conceive greater assurance of his age than I
could hope of his youth.

*Tellus.* But timely, madam, crooks that tree
that will be a cammock, and young it pricks [45
that will be a thorn; and therefore he that
began without care to settle his life, it is a sign
without amendment he will end it.

*Cynth.* Presumptuous girl, I will make thy
tongue an example of unrecoverable dis- [50
pleasure. Corsites, carry her to the castle in
the desert, there to remain and weave.

*Cors.* Shall she work stories or poetries?

*Cynth.* It skilleth not which. Go to, in both;
for she shall find examples infinite in either [55
what punishment long tongues have. Eumenides, if either the soothsayers in Egypt, or the
enchanters in Thessaly, or the philosophers in
Greece, or all the sages of the world can find
remedy, I will procure it; therefore, dispatch [60
with all speed: you, Eumenides, into Thessaly; you, Zontes, into Greece, because you are
acquainted in Athens; you, Panelion, to Egypt;
saying that Cynthia sendeth, and if you will,
commandeth.                                     65

*Eum.* On bowed knee I give thanks, and
with wings on my legs, I fly for remedy.

*Zon.* We are ready at your highness' command, and hope to return to your full content.

*Cynth.* It shall never be said that Cynthia, [70
whose mercy and goodness filleth the heavens
with joys and the world with marvels, will
suffer either Endymion or any to perish, if he
may be protected.

*Eum.* Your Majesty's words have been al- [75
ways deeds, and your deeds virtues. *Exeunt.*

## Actus tertius.  Scæna secunda.

### Corsites, Tellus

*Cors.* Here is the castle, fair Tellus, in which
you must weave, till either time end your days,
or Cynthia her displeasure. I am sorry so fair a
face should be subject to so hard a fortune, and
that the flower of beauty, which is honoured [5
in courts, should here wither in prison.

*Tellus.* Corsites, Cynthia may restrain the
liberty of my body, of my thoughts she cannot;
and therefore do I esteem myself most free,
though I am in greatest bondage.                10

*Cors.* Can you then feed on fancy, and subdue the malice of envy by the sweetness of
imagination?

*Tellus.* Corsites, there is no sweeter music to
the miserable than despair; and therefore [15
the more bitterness I feel, the more sweetness
I find· for so vain were liberty, and so unwelcome the following of higher fortune, that I
choose rather to pine in this castle than to be a
prince in any other court.                      20

*Cors.* A humour contrary to your years and
nothing agreeable to your sex; the one commonly allured with delights, the other always
with sovereignty.

*Tellus.* I marvel, Corsites, that you being [25
a captain, who should sound nothing but terror
and suck nothing but blood, can find in your
heart to talk such smooth words, for that it
agreeth not with your calling to use words so
soft as that of love.                           30

*Cors.* Lady, it were unfit of wars to discourse
with women, into whose minds nothing can sink
but smoothness; besides, you must not think
that soldiers be so rough-hewn, or of such
knotty mettle, that beauty cannot allure, [35
and you, being beyond perfection, enchant.

*Tellus.* Good Corsites, talk not of love, but
let me to my labour. The little beauty I have
shall be bestowed on my loom, which I now
mean to make my lover.                          40

*Cors.* Let us in, and what favour Corsites
can show, Tellus shall command.

*Tellus.* The only favour I desire is now and
then to walk.                           *Exeunt.*

---

¹⁹ **malapert overthwarts:** impertinent wranglings    ⁴⁵ **cammock:** crooked stick    ⁵⁴ **skilleth:** mat·
ters    ⁵⁸ **Thessaly:** fabled abode of witches    ²² **nothing agreeable:** in no way suitable

*Actus tertius.   Scæna tertia.*

*Sir Tophas and Epiton*

*Tophas.*   Epi!
*Epi.*   Here, sir.
*Tophas.*   Unrig me.   Heigho!
*Epi.*   What 's that?
*Tophas.*   An interjection, whereof some are [5
of mourning: as *eho, vah.*
*Epi.*   I understand you not.
*Tophas.*   Thou seest me.
*Epi.*   Ay.
*Tophas.*   Thou hear'st me.                       10
*Epi.*   Ay.
*Tophas.*   Thou feelest me.
*Epi.*   Ay.
*Tophas.*   And not understand'st me?
*Epi.*   No.                                       15
*Tophas.*   Then am I but three-quarters of a
noun substantive.   But alas, Epi, to tell thee
the troth, I am a noun adjective.
*Epi.*   Why?
*Tophas.*   Because I cannot stand without [20
another.
*Epi.*   Who is that?
*Tophas.*   Dipsas.
*Epi.*   Are you in love?
*Tophas.*   No; but love hath, as it were, [25
milk'd my thoughts and drained from my heart
the very substance of my accustomed courage;
it worketh in my head like new wine, so as I
must hoop my sconce with iron, lest my head
break, and so I bewray my brains.   But, I [30
pray thee, first discover me in all parts, that I
may be like a lover, and then will I sigh and
die.   Take my gun and give me a gown: *Cedant
arma togæ.*
*Epi.*   Here.                                     35
*Tophas.*   Take my sword and shield and give
me beard-brush and scissors: *Bella gerant alii,
tu, Pari, semper ama.*
*Epi.*   Will you be trimm'd, sir?
*Tophas.*   Not yet; for I feel a contention [40
within me whether I shall frame the bodkin
beard or the bush.   But take my pike and give
me pen: *Dicere quæ puduit, scribere jussit amor.*
*Epi.*   I will furnish you, sir.
*Tophas.*   Now, for my bow and bolts give [45
me ink and paper, for my smiter a pen-knife;
for

*Scalpellum, calami, atramentum, charta, libelli.
Sint semper studiis arma parata meis.*

*Epi.*   Sir, will you give over wars and play [50
with that bauble called love?
*Tophas.*   Give over wars?   No, Epi, *Militat
omnis amans, et habet sua castra Cupido.*
*Epi.*   Love hath made you very eloquent,
but your face is nothing fair.                     55
*Tophas.*   *Non formosus erat, sed erat facundus
Ulysses.*
*Epi.*   Nay, I must seek a new master if you
can speak nothing but verses.
*Tophas.*   *Quicquid conabar dicere, versus* [60
*erat.*   Epi, I feel all Ovid *De Arte Amandi* lie
as heavy at my heart as a load of logs.   Oh,
what a fine, thin hair hath Dipsas!   What a
pretty low forehead!   What a tall and stately
nose!   What little hollow eyes!   What great [65
and goodly lips!   How harmless she is, being
toothless, — her fingers fat and short, adorned
with long nails like a bitter!   In how sweet a
proportion her cheeks hang down to her breasts
like dugs and her paps to her waist like bags! [70
What a low stature she is, and yet what a great
foot she carrieth!   How thrifty must she be in
whom there is no waist!   How virtuous is she
like to be, over whom no man can be jealous!
*Epi.*   Stay, master, you forget yourself.   75
*Tophas.*   O Epi, even as a dish melteth by the
fire, so doth my wit increase by love.
*Epi.*   Pithily, and to the purpose!   But what,
begin you to nod?
*Tophas.*   Good Epi, let me take a nap; for [80
as some man may better steal a horse than another look over the hedge, so divers shall be
sleepy when they would fainest take rest.
                                      *He sleeps.*
*Epi.*   Who ever saw such a woodcock!   Love
Dipsas!   Without doubt all the world will [85
now account him valiant, that ventureth on her
whom none durst undertake.   But here cometh
two wags.

*Enter Dares and Samias*

*Sam.*   Thy master hath slept his share.
*Dar.*   I think he doth it because he would [90
not pay me my board-wages.

---

⁶ **eho, vah:** Sir Tophas' knowledge of grammar is derived from the famous Latin grammar published
by Lyly's grandfather, William Lilly, in 1549.   ³⁰ **bewray:** expose   ³³⁻³⁴ **Cedant . . . togæ:** Let arms
yield to the toga (*i.e.*, to civil life).   ³⁷⁻³⁸ **Bella . . . ama:** Let others wage wars: do you, Paris, ever
devote yourself to love.   ⁴¹⁻⁴² **bodkin . . . bush:** pointed beard or bushy one   ⁴³ **Dicere . . . amor:**
Love has bidden me write what I was ashamed to say.   ⁴⁸⁻⁴⁹ Let pen-knife, pens, ink, paper, and books
be always ready, the implements for my studies.   ⁵²⁻⁵³ **Militat . . . Cupido:** Every lover is a soldier,
and Cupid has his own camp.   ⁵⁶⁻⁵⁷ **Non . . . Ulysses:** Ulysses was not handsome, but he was eloquent.   ⁶⁰⁻⁶¹ **Quicquid . . . erat:** Whatever I tried to say was verse.   ⁶⁸ **bitter:** old form of "bit-
tern"; cf. l. 121   ⁸⁴ **woodcock:** simpleton

*Sam.* It is a thing most strange: and I think mine will never return, so that we must both seek new masters, for we shall never live by our manners.                                                95

*Epi.* If you want masters, join with me and serve Sir Tophas, who must needs keep more men, because he is toward marriage.

*Sam.* What, Epi, where 's thy master?

*Epi.* Yonder, sleeping in love.            100

*Dar.* Is it possible?

*Epi.* He hath taken his thoughts a hole lower, and saith, seeing it is the fashion of the world, he will vail bonnet to beauty.

*Sam.* How is he attired?                  105

*Epi.* Lovely.

*Dar.* Whom loveth this amorous knight?

*Epi.* Dipsas.

*Sam.* That ugly creature? Why, she is a fool, a scold, fat, without fashion, and quite [110 without favour.

*Epi.* Tush, you be simple; my master hath a good marriage.

*Dar.* Good! As how?

*Epi.* Why, in marrying Dipsas he shall [115 have every day twelve dishes of meat to his dinner, though there be none but Dipsas with him: four of flesh, four of fish, four of fruit.

*Sam.* As how, Epi?

*Epi.* For flesh these: woodcock, goose, [120 bitter, and rail.

*Dar.* Indeed, he shall not miss, if Dipsas be there.

*Epi.* For fish these: crab, carp, lump, and pouting.                                      125

*Sam.* Excellent, for of my word she is both crabbish, lumpish, and carping.

*Epi.* For fruit these: fretters, medlars, hartichokes, and lady-longings. Thus you see he shall fare like a king, though he be but a [130 beggar.

*Dar.* Well, Epi, dine thou with him, for I had rather fast than see her face. But see, thy master is asleep; let us have a song to wake this amorous knight.                           135

*Epi.* Agreed.

*Sam.* Content.

THE FIRST SONG

*Epi.*  Here snores Tophas,
That amorous ass,
Who loves Dipsas,                          140
With face so sweet,
Nose and chin meet.

*All three.* { At sight of her each Fury skips
            { And flings into her lap their whips.

*Dar.* Holla, holla in his ear.             145

*Sam.* The witch, sure, thrust her fingers there.

*Epi.* Cramp him, or wring the fool by th' nose.

*Dar.* Or clap some burning flax to his toes.

*Sam.* What music 's best to wake him?

*Epi.* Bow-wow, let bandogs shake him!      150

*Dar.* Let adders hiss in 's ear;

*Sam.* Else earwigs wriggle there.

*Epi.* No, let him batten; when his tongue Once goes, a cat is not worse strung.       154

*All three.* { But if he ope nor mouth nor eyes,
            { He may in time sleep himself wise.

*Top.* Sleep is a binding of the senses, love a loosing.

*Epi.* [*Aside.*] Let us hear him awhile.

*Top.* There appeared in my sleep a goodly [160 owl, who, sitting upon my shoulder, cried "Twit, twit"; and before mine eyes presented herself the express image of Dipsas. I marvelled what the owl said, till at the last I perceived "Twit, twit," "To it, to it," only [165 by contraction admonished by this vision to make account of my sweet Venus.

*Sam.* Sir Tophas, you have overslept yourself.

*Top.* No, youth, I have but slept over [170 my love.

*Dar.* Love? Why, it is impossible that into so noble and unconquered a courage love should creep, having first a head as hard to pierce as steel, then to pass to a heart [175 arm'd with a shirt of mail.

*Epi.* Ay, but my master yawning one day in the sun, Love crept into his mouth before he could close it, and there kept such a tumbling in his body that he was glad to untruss [180 the points of his heart and entertain Love as a stranger.

*Top.* If there remain any pity in you, plead for me to Dipsas.

*Dar.* Plead! Nay, we will press her to it. [185 [*Aside to Samias.*] Let us go with him to Dipsas, and there shall we have good sport. — But, Sir Tophas, when shall we go? For I find my tongue voluble, and my heart venturous, and all myself like myself.                     190

*Sam.* [*Aside to Dares.*] Come, Dares, let us not lose him till we find our masters, for as long as he liveth, we shall lack neither mirth nor meat.

*Epi.* We will travice. Will you go, sir? [195

*Top.* I præ, sequar.                *Exeunt.*

---

<sup>102–103</sup> **taken . . . lower:** come off his high horse    <sup>104</sup> **vail bonnet:** take off his hat    <sup>106</sup> **lovely:** like a lover    <sup>111</sup> **favour:** good looks    <sup>128</sup> **fretters:** a kind of apple (?)    <sup>129</sup> **lady-longings:** a kind of apple <sup>138</sup> **Song:** (This and the later songs appear first in Blount.)    <sup>150</sup> **bandogs:** fierce dogs    <sup>180–181</sup> **untruss the points:** untie the laces    <sup>195</sup> **travice:** traverse, move away    <sup>196</sup> **I præ, sequar:** You go first: I will follow.

## Actus tertius. Scæna quarta.

### Eumenides, Geron

*Eum.* Father, your sad music being tuned on the same key that my hard fortune is, hath so melted my mind that I wish to hang at your mouth's end till my life end.

*Ger.* These tunes, gentleman, have I been [5 accustomed with these fifty winters, having no other house to shroud myself but the broad heavens; and so familiar with me hath use made misery that I esteem sorrow my chiefest solace, and welcomest is that guest to me [10 that can rehearse the saddest tale or the bloodiest tragedy.

*Eum.* A strange humour. Might I inquire the cause?

*Ger.* You must pardon me if I deny to tell [15 it, for knowing that the revealing of griefs is, as it were, a renewing of sorrow, I have vowed therefore to conceal them, that I might not only feel the depth of everlasting discontentment, but despair of remedy. But whence are you? [20 What fortune hath thrust you to this distress?

*Eum.* I am going to Thessaly, to seek remedy for Endymion, my dearest friend, who hath been cast into a dead sleep almost these twenty years, waxing old and ready for the grave, [25 being almost but newly come forth of the cradle.

*Ger.* You need not for recure travel far, for whoso can clearly see the bottom of this fountain shall have remedy for anything.

*Eum.* That methinketh is unpossible. [30 Why, what virtue can there be in water?

*Ger.* Yes, whosoever can shed the tears of a faithful lover shall obtain anything he would. Read these words engraven about the brim.

*Eum.* Have you known this by experience, [35 or is it placed here of purpose to delude men?

*Ger.* I only would have experience of it, and then should there be an end of my misery; and then would I tell the strangest discourse that ever yet was heard. 40

*Eum.* Ah, Eumenides!

*Ger.* What lack you, gentleman; are you not well?

*Eum.* Yes, father, but a qualm that often cometh over my heart doth now take hold of [45 me. But did never any lovers come hither?

*Ger.* Lusters, but not lovers; for often have I seen them weep, but never could I hear they saw the bottom.

*Eum.* Came there women also? 50

*Ger.* Some.

*Eum.* What did they see?

*Ger.* They all wept, that the fountain overflowed with tears, but so thick became the water with their tears that I could scarce [55 discern the brim, much less behold the bottom.

*Eum.* Be faithful lovers so scant?

*Ger.* It seemeth so, for yet heard I never of any.

*Eum.* Ah, Eumenides, how art thou per- [60 plexed! Call to mind the beauty of thy sweet mistress and the depth of thy never-dying affections. How oft hast thou honoured her, not only without spot, but suspicion of falsehood! And how hardly hath she rewarded thee without [65 cause or colour of despite. How secret hast thou been these seven years, that hast not, nor once darest not to name her, for discontenting her. How faithful, that hast offered to die for her, to please her! Unhappy Eumenides! [70

*Ger.* Why, gentleman, did you once love?

*Eum.* Once? Ay, father, and ever shall.

*Ger.* Was she unkind and you faithful?

*Eum.* She of all women the most froward, and I of all creatures the most fond. 75

*Ger.* You doted then, not loved, for affection is grounded on virtue, and virtue is never peevish; or on beauty, and beauty loveth to be praised.

*Eum.* Ay, but if all virtuous ladies should [80 yield to all that be loving, or all amiable gentlewomen entertain all that be amorous, their virtues would be accounted vices, and their beauties deformities; for that love can be but between two, and that not proceeding of him [85 that is most faithful but most fortunate.

*Ger.* I would you were so faithful that your tears might make you fortunate.

*Eum.* Yea, father, if that my tears clear not this fountain, then may you swear it is but a [90 mere mockery.

*Ger.* So saith every one yet that wept.

*Eum.* Ah, I faint, I die! Ah, sweet Semele, let me alone, and dissolve, by weeping, into water. [*He gazes into the fountain.*] [95

*Ger.* This affection seemeth strange: if he see nothing, without doubt this dissembling passeth, for nothing shall draw me from the belief.

*Eum.* Father, I plainly see the bottom, [100 and there in white marble engraven these words: *Ask one for all, and but one thing at all.*

*Ger.* O fortunate Eumenides, (for so have I heard thee call thyself,) let me see. I cannot discern any such thing. I think thou dreamest. [105

*Eum.* Ah, father, thou art not a faithful lover, and therefore canst not behold it.

*Ger.* Then ask, that I may be satisfied by the event, and thyself blessed.

*Eum.* Ask? So I will. And what shall I [110 do but ask, and whom should I ask but Semele, the possessing of whose person is a pleasure that

94 **dissolve:** *i.e.*, let me dissolve 99 **belief:** *i.e.*, in the magical property of the fountain

cannot come within the compass of comparison; whose golden locks seem most curious when they seem most careless; whose sweet looks [115 seem most alluring when they are most chaste; and whose words the more virtuous they are, the more amorous they be accounted? I pray thee, Fortune, when I shall first meet with fair Semele, dash my delight with some light dis- [120 grace, lest embracing sweetness beyond measure, I take a surfeit without recure. Let her practise her accustomed coyness that I may diet myself upon my desires; otherwise the fulness of my joys will diminish the sweetness, and [125 I shall perish by them before I possess them.

Why do I trifle the time in words? The least minute being spent in the getting of Semele is more worth than the whole world; therefore let me ask. What now, Eumenides! Whither [130 art thou drawn? Hast thou forgotten both friendship and duty: care of Endymion, and the commandment of Cynthia? Shall he die in a leaden sleep because thou sleepest in a golden dream? Ay, let him sleep ever, so I slumber [135 but one minute with Semele. Love knoweth neither friendship nor kindred. Shall I not hazard the loss of a friend for the obtaining of her for whom I would often lose myself? Fond Eumenides, shall the enticing beauty of a [140 most disdainful lady be of more force than the rare fidelity of a tried friend? The love of men to women is a thing common and of course; the friendship of man to man infinite and immortal. Tush! Semele doth possess my love. Ay, [145 but Endymion hath deserved it. I will help Endymion. I found Endymion unspotted in his truth. Ay, but I shall find Semele constant in her love. I will have Semele. What shall I do? Father, thy gray hairs are embassadors of [150 experience. Which shall I ask?

*Ger.* Eumenides, release Endymion, for all things, friendship excepted, are subject to fortune: love is but an eye-worm, which only tickleth the head with hopes and wishes; [155 friendship the image of eternity, in which there is nothing movable, nothing mischievous. As much difference as there is between beauty and virtue, bodies and shadows, colours and life, so great odds is there between love and friend- [160 ship.

Love is a chameleon, which draweth nothing into the mouth but air, and nourisheth nothing in the body but lungs. Believe me, Eumenides, desire dies in the same moment that beauty [165 sickens, and beauty fadeth in the same instant that it flourisheth. When adversities flow, then love ebbs; but friendship standeth stiffly in

storms. Time draweth wrinkles in a fair face, but addeth fresh colours to a fast friend, [170 which neither heat, nor cold, nor misery, nor place, nor destiny, can alter or diminish. O friendship, of all things the most rare, and therefore most rare because most excellent, whose comforts in misery is always sweet, [175 and whose counsels in prosperity are ever fortunate! Vain love, that, only coming near to friendship in name, would seem to be the same or better in nature!

*Eum.* Father, I allow your reasons, and [180 will therefore conquer mine own. Virtue shall subdue affections, wisdom lust, friendship beauty. Mistresses are in every place, and as common as hares in Athos, bees in Hybla, fowls in the air; but friends to be found [185 are like the phœnix in Arabia, but one; or the philadelphi in Arays, never above two. I will have Endymion. Sacred fountain, in whose bowels are hidden divine secrets, I have increased your waters with the tears of un- [190 spotted thoughts, and therefore let me receive the reward you promise. Endymion, the truest friend to me, and faithfulest lover to Cynthia, is in such a dead sleep that nothing can wake or move him.                                                195

*Ger.* Dost thou see anything?

*Eum.* I see in the same pillar these words: *When she whose figure of all is the perfectest, and never to be measured — always one, yet never the same; still inconstant, yet never wavering —* [200 *shall come and kiss Endymion in his sleep, he shall then rise, else never.* This is strange.

*Ger.* What see you else?

*Eum.* There cometh over mine eyes either a dark mist, or upon the fountain a deep [205 thickness, for I can perceive nothing. But how am I deluded, or what difficult, nay impossible, thing is this?

*Ger.* Methinketh it easy.

*Eum.* Good father, and how?                        210

*Ger.* Is not a circle of all figures the perfectest?

*Eum.* Yes.

*Ger.* And is not Cynthia of all circles the most absolute?                                              215

*Eum.* Yes.

*Ger.* Is it not impossible to measure her, who still worketh by her influence, never standing at one stay?

*Eum.* Yes.                                                      220

*Ger.* Is she not always Cynthia, yet seldom in the same bigness; always wavering in her waxing or waning, that our bodies might the better be governed, our seasons the dailier give their

---

[139] **Fond:** foolish    [184] **Athos:** ('Atho' Q, Blount. Lyly is probably referring to the classical Mt. Athos.)    [187] **philadelphi:** the mock-orange (*Philadelphus hirsutus*), the blossoms of which grow in pairs (?).    **Arays:** Aranjuez, where famous gardens had been laid out by Philip II (?).

increase; yet never to be removed from her [225 course, as long as the heavens continue theirs?

*Eum.* Yes.

*Ger.* Then who can it be but Cynthia, whose virtues being all divine must needs bring things to pass that be miraculous? Go, humble thy- [230 self to Cynthia; tell her the success, of which myself shall be a witness. And this assure thyself, that she that sent to find means for his safety will now work her cunning.

*Eum.* How fortunate am I, if Cynthia be [235 she that may do it!

*Ger.* How fond art thou, if thou do not believe it!

*Eum.* I will hasten thither that I may entreat on my knees for succour, and embrace in [240 mine arms my friend.

*Ger.* I will go with thee, for unto Cynthia must I discover all my sorrows, who also must work in me a contentment.

*Eum.* May I now know the cause?    245

*Ger.* That shall be as we walk, and I doubt not but the strangeness of my tale will take away the tediousness of our journey.

*Eum.* Let us go.

*Ger.* I follow.           *Exeunt.* [250

## Actus quartus. Scæna prima.

### Tellus, [and later] Corsites

*Tellus.* I marvel Corsites giveth me so much liberty, — all the world knowing his charge to be so high and his nature to be most strange, — who hath so ill entreated ladies of great honour that he hath not suffered them to look out [5 of windows, much less to walk abroad. It may be he is in love with me, for (Endymion, hardhearted Endymion, excepted) what is he that is not enamour'd of my beauty? But what respectest thou the love of all the world? En- [10 dymion hates thee. Alas, poor Endymion, my malice hath exceeded my love, and thy faith to Cynthia quenched my affections. Quenched, Tellus? Nay, kindled them afresh; insomuch that I find scorching flames for dead embers, [15 and cruel encounters of war in my thoughts instead of sweet parleys. Ah, that I might once again see Endymion! Accursed girl, what hope hast thou to see Endymion, on whose head already are grown gray hairs, and whose life [20 must yield to nature, before Cynthia end her displeasure. Wicked Dipsas, and most devilish Tellus, the one for cunning too exquisite, the other for hate too intolerable! Thou wast commanded to weave the stories and poetries [25 wherein were showed both examples and punishments of tattling tongues, and thou hast only embroidered the sweet face of Endymion, de-

vices of love, melancholy imaginations, and what not, out of thy work, that thou shouldst [30 study to pick out of thy mind. But here cometh Corsites. I must seem yielding and stout; full of mildness, yet tempered with a majesty; for if I be too flexible, I shall give him more hope than I mean; if too froward, enjoy less liberty [35 than I would. Love him I cannot, and therefore will practise that which is most contrary to our sex, to dissemble.

### Enter Corsites

*Cor.* Fair Tellus, I perceive you rise with the lark, and to yourself sing with the nightin- [40 gale.

*Tellus.* My lord, I have no playfellow but fancy; being barred of all company, I must question with myself, and make my thoughts my friends.          45

*Cor.* I would you would account my thoughts also your friends, for they be such as are only busied in wondering at your beauty and wisdom; and some such as have esteemed your fortune too hard; and divers of that kind [50 that offer to set you free, if you will set them free.

*Tellus.* There are no colours so contrary as white and black, nor elements so disagreeing as fire and water, nor anything so opposite as [55 men's thoughts and their words.

*Cor.* He that gave Cassandra the gift of prophesying, with the curse that, spake she never so true, she should never be believed, hath I think poisoned the fortune of men, [60 that uttering the extremities of their inward passions are always suspected of outward perjuries.

*Tellus.* Well, Corsites, I will flatter myself and believe you. What would you do to en- [65 joy my love?

*Cor.* Set all the ladies of the castle free, and make you the pleasure of my life: more I cannot do, less I will not.

*Tellus.* These be great words, and fit your [70 calling; for captains must promise things impossible. But will you do one thing for all?

*Cor.* Anything, sweet Tellus, that am ready for all.

*Tellus.* You know that on the lunary bank [75 sleepeth Endymion.

*Cor.* I know it.

*Tellus.* If you will remove him from that place by force, and convey him into some obscure cave by policy, I give you here the [80 faith of an unspotted virgin that you only shall possess me as a lover, and in spite of malice have me for a wife.

*Cor.* Remove him, Tellus! Yes, Tellus, h<sup>...</sup>

shall be removed, and that so soon as thou [85 shalt as much commend my diligence as my force. I go.

*Tellus.*   Stay, will yourself attempt it?

*Cor.*   Ay, Tellus; as I would have none partaker of my sweet love, so shall none be [90 partners of my labours.   But I pray thee go at your best leisure, for Cynthia beginneth to rise, and if she discover our love, we both perish, for nothing pleaseth her but the fairness of virginity.   All things must be not only without [95 lust but without suspicion of lightness.

*Tellus.*   I will depart, and go you to Endymion.

*Cor.*   I fly, Tellus, being of all men the most fortunate.                                   *Exit.* [100

*Tellus.*   Simple Corsites, I have set thee about a task, being but a man, that the gods themselves cannot perform: for little dost thou know how heavy his head lies, how hard his fortune; but such shifts must women have to deceive [105 men, and under colour of things easy, entreat that which is impossible; otherwise we should be cumbered with importunities, oaths, sighs, letters, and all implements of love, which to one resolved to the contrary are most loath- [110 some.   I will in, and laugh with the other ladies at Corsites' sweating.                          *Exit.*

## Actus quartus.   Scæna secunda.

### Samias, Dares, and [later] Epiton

*Sam.*   Will thy master never awake?

*Dar.*   No; I think he sleeps for a wager.   But how shall we spend the time?   Sir Tophas is so far in love that he pineth in his bed and cometh not abroad.                                              5

*Sam.*   But here cometh Epi in a pelting chafe.

### [Enter Epiton]

*Epi.*   A pox of all false proverbs, and were a proverb a page, I would have him by the ears!

*Sam.*   Why art thou angry?

*Epi.*   Why?   You know it is said, "The [10 tide tarrieth no man."

*Sam.*   True.

*Epi.*   A monstrous lie; for I was tied two hours, and tarried for one to unloose me.

*Dar.*   Alas, poor Epi!                                15

*Epi.*   Poor! No, no, you base-conceited slaves, I am a most complete gentleman, although I be in disgrace with Sir Tophas.

*Dar.*   Art thou out with him?

*Epi.*   Ay, because I cannot get him a lodg- [20 ing with Endymion.   He would fain take a nap for forty or fifty years.

*Dar.*   A short sleep, considering our long life.

*Sam.*   Is he still in love?

*Epi.*   In love?   Why he doth nothing but [25 make sonnets.

*Sam.*   Canst thou remember any one of his poems?

*Epi.*   Ay, this is one:—

> The beggar, Love, that knows not where to lodge,
>    At last within my heart, when I slept,      31
>                                        He crept.
>    I wak'd, and so my fancies began to fodge.

*Sam.*   That 's a very long verse.

*Epi.*   Why, the other was short.   The first [35 is called from the thumb to the little finger; the second from the little finger to the elbow; and some he hath made to reach to the crown of his head, and down again to the sole of his foot.   It is set to the tune of the black [40 Saunce; *ratio est*, because Dipsas is a black saint.

*Dar.*   Very wisely.   But pray thee, Epi, how art thou complete; and being from thy master, what occupation wilt thou take?                45

*Epi.*   Know, my hearts, I am an absolute *Microcosmus*, a petty world of myself: my library is my head, for I have no other books but my brains; my wardrobe on my back, for I have no more apparel than is on my body; [50 my armory at my fingers' ends, for I use no other artillery than my nails; my treasure in my purse.   *Sic omnia mea mecum porto.*

*Dar.*   Good!

*Epi.*   Know, sirs, my palace is pav'd with [55 grass, and tiled with stars, for *Cælo tegitur qui non habet urnam*, — he that hath no house must lie in the yard.

*Sam.*   A brave resolution!   But how wilt thou spend thy time?                                      60

*Epi.*   Not in any melancholy sort; for mine exercise I will walk horses.

*Dar.*   Too bad!

*Epi.*   Why, is it not said, "It is good walking when one hath his horse in his hand"? [65

*Sam.*   Worse and worse!   But how wilt thou live?

*Epi.*   By angling.   Oh, 't is a stately occupation to stand four hours in a cold morning, and to have his nose bitten with frost before his [70 bait be mumbled with a fish.

*Dar.*   A rare attempt!   But wilt thou never travel?

*Epi.*   Yes, in a western barge, when with a

---

**85 as:** that    **6 pelting chafe:** bad humor    **33 fodge:** move    **40–41 black Saunce:** Black Sanctus, a hymn to St. Satan    **46 Know:** ('No' Q, Blount)    **53 Sic . . . porto:** I carry thus all my things with me.    **55 Know:** ('Now' Q, Blount)    **56–57 Cœlo . . . urnam:** He is covered with the sky who does not have a burial urn.

good wind and lusty pugs, one may go ten [75
miles in two days.

*Sam.* Thou art excellent at thy choice. But
what pastime wilt thou use? None?

*Epi.* Yes, the quickest of all.

*Sam.* What, dice?             80

*Epi.* No, when *I* am in haste, one-and-
twenty games at chess, to pass a few minutes.

*Dar.* A life for a little lord, and full of
quickness.

*Epi.* Tush, let me alone! But I must [85
needs see if I can find where Endymion lieth,
and then go to a certain fountain hard by,
where they say faithful lovers shall have all
things they will ask. If I can find out any of
these, *Ego et magister meus erimus in tuto,* I [90
and my master shall be friends. He is resolved
to weep some three or four pailfuls to avoid the
rheum of love that wambleth in his stomach.

*Enter the Watch [i.e., Constable and
two Watchmen]*

*Sam.* Shall we never see thy master, Dares?

*Dar.* Yes; let us go now, for to-morrow [95
Cynthia will be there.

*Epi.* I will go with you; — but how shall we
see for the Watch?

*Sam.* Tush, let me alone! I 'll begin to them.
Masters, God speed you.             100

*1 Watch.* Sir boy, we are all sped already.

*Epi.* [*Aside.*] So methinks, for they smell
all of drink, like a beggar's beard.

*Dar.* But I pray, sirs, may we see Endymion?             105

*2 Watch.* No, we are commanded in Cynthia's name, that no man shall see him.

*Sam.* No man! Why, we are but boys.

*1 Watch.* Mass, neighbours, he says true, for
if I swear I will never drink my liquor by [110
the quart, and yet call for two pints, I think
with a safe conscience I may carouse both.

*Dar.* Pithily, and to the purpose.

*2 Watch.* Tush, tush, neighbours, take me
with you.             115

*Sam.* [*Aside.*] This will grow hot.

*Dar.* [*Aside.*] Let them alone.

*2 Watch.* If I say to my wife, "Wife, I
will have no raisins in my pudding," she puts in
currants; small raisins are raisins, and boys [120
are men: even as my wife should have put no
raisins in my pudding, so shall there no boys
see Endymion.

*Dar.* Learnedly.

*Epi.* Let Master Constable speak; I think [125
he is the wisest among you.

*Master Constable.* You know, neighbours, 't

is an old said saw, "Children and fools speak
true."

*All say.* True!             130

*Mast. Const.* Well, there you see the men be
the fools, because it is provided from the children.

*Dar.* Good.

*Mast. Const.* Then, say I, neighbours, [135
that children must not see Endymion, because
children and fools speak true.

*Epi.* O wicked application!

*Sam.* Scurvily brought about!

*1 Watch.* Nay, he says true, and there- [140
fore till Cynthia have been here, he shall not be
uncovered. Therefore, away!

*Dar.* [*Aside to Sam. and Epi.*] A watch, quoth
you! A man may watch seven years for a
wise word, and yet go without it. Their wits [145
are all as rusty as their bills. — But come on,
Master Constable, shall we have a song before
we go?

*Mast. Const.* With all my heart.

THE SECOND SONG

*Watch.* Stand! Who goes there?      150
We charge you appear
'Fore our constable here,
In the name of the Man in the Moon.
To us billmen relate
Why you stagger so late,        155
And how you come drunk so soon.
*Pages.* What are ye, scabs?
*Watch.*             The Watch;
This the Constable.
*Pages.*             A patch.
*Const.* Knock 'em down unless they all stand:
If any run away.           160
'T is the old watchman's play,
To reach him a bill of his hand.
*Pages.* O gentlemen, hold,
Your gowns freeze with cold,
And your rotten teeth dance in your head; 165
*Epi.* Wine nothing shall cost ye;
*Sam.* Nor huge fires to roast ye;
*Dar.* Then soberly let us be led.
*Const.* Come, my brown bills, we 'll roar,
Bounce loud at tavern door,       170
*Omnes.* And i' th' morning steal all to bed.
                          *Exeunt.*

## Actus quartus. Scæna tertia.

*Corsites solus.* [*Endymion lies asleep on the
lunary bank.*]

*Corsites.* I am come in sight of the lunary
bank. Without doubt Tellus doteth upon me,
and cunningly, that I might not perceive her
love, she hath set me to a task that is done be-

⁷⁵ **pugs:** fellows    ⁹⁰ **Ego . . . tuto:** I and my master shall be in safety.    ⁹³ **wambleth:** rumbleth
⁹⁸ **see for:** take measures about    ¹¹⁴⁻¹¹⁵ **take me with you:** let me understand you    ¹³² **provided:**
*i.e.,* **divided** (?)    ¹⁴⁶ **bills:** halberts    ¹⁵⁷ **scabs:** rogues    ¹⁵⁸ **patch:** fool    ¹⁶⁹ **roar:** swagger

fore it is begun. Endymion, you must change [5
your pillow, and if you be not weary of sleep, I
will carry you where at ease you shall sleep your
fill. It were good that without more ceremonies
I took him, lest being espied, I be entrapp'd, and
so incur the displeasure of Cynthia, who [10
commonly setteth watch that Endymion have
no wrong.                                 *He lifts.*
What now, is your mastership so heavy, or are
you nail'd to the ground? Not stir one whit! Then
use all thy force, though he feel it and wake. [15
What, stone-still? Turn'd, I think, to earth
with lying so long on the earth. Didst not thou,
Corsites, before Cynthia, pull up a tree that
forty years was fastened with roots and
wreathed in knots to the ground? Didst not [20
thou, with main force, pull open the iron gates
which no ram or engine could move? Have my
weak thoughts made brawn-fallen my strong
arms, or is it the nature of love, or the quintessence of the mind, to breed numbness or [25
litherness, or I know not what languishing
in my joints and sinews, being but the base
strings of my body? Or doth the remembrance
of Tellus so refine my spirits into a matter so
subtle and divine that the other fleshy parts [30
cannot work whilst they muse? Rest thyself,
rest thyself; nay, rent thyself in pieces, Corsites, and strive, in spite of love, fortune, and
nature, to lift up this dulled body, heavier than
dead and more senseless than death.        35

### Enter Fairies

But what are these so fair fiends that cause
my hairs to stand upright and spirits to fall
down? Hags, — out alas, nymphs, I crave pardon. Ay me, out! what do I hear!

> *The Fairies dance, and with a song pinch
> him, and he falleth asleep. They
> kiss Endymion and depart.*

#### THE THIRD SONG BY FAIRIES

*Omnes.* Pinch him, pinch him, black and blue,
Saucy mortals must not view          41
What the Queen of Stars is doing,
Nor pry into our fairy wooing.
  1 *Fairy.* Pinch him blue,
  2 *Fairy.* And pinch him black;          45
  3 *Fairy.* Let him not lack
Sharp nails to pinch him blue and red,
Till sleep has rock'd his addle head.
  4 *Fairy.* For the trespass he hath done,
Spots o'er all his flesh shall run.          50
• Kiss Endymion, kiss his eyes,
Then to our midnight heidegyes.
                        *Exeunt [Fairies].*

*[Enter, at the side of the stage opposite Corsites,]
Cynthia, Floscula, Semele, Panelion, Zontes,
Pythagoras, Gyptes. [Corsites sleeps still.]*

*Cynth.* You see, Pythagoras, what ridiculous
opinions you hold, and I doubt not but you are
now of another mind.                        55
*Pythag.* Madam, I plainly perceive that the
perfection of your brightness hath pierced
through the thickness that covered my mind;
insomuch that I am no less glad to be reformed than ashamed to remember my [60
grossness.
*Gyptes.* They are thrice fortunate that live in
your palace where truth is not in colours but
life, virtues not in imagination but execution.
*Cynth.* I have always studied to have rather [65
living virtues than painted gods, the body of
truth than the tomb. But let us walk to Endymion; it may be it lieth in your arts to
deliver him; as for Eumenides, I fear he is
dead.                                        70
*Pythag.* I have alleged all the natural reasons
I can for such a long sleep.
*Gyptes.* I can do nothing till I see him.
*Cynth.* Come, Floscula; I am sure you are
glad that you shall behold Endymion.        75
*Flosc.* I were blessed, if I might have him
recovered.
*Cynth.* Are you in love with his person?
*Flosc.* No, but with his virtue.
*Cynth.* What say you, Semele?             80
*Sem.* Madam, I dare say nothing for fear I
offend.
*Cynth.* Belike you cannot speak except you
be spiteful; but as good be silent as saucy.
Panelion, what punishment were fit for [85
Semele, in whose speech and thoughts is only
contempt and sourness?
*Panel.* I love not, madam, to give any judgment; yet, sith Your Highness commandeth,
I think, to commit her tongue close prisoner [90
to her mouth.
*Cynth.* Agreed. Semele, if thou speak this
twelvemonth, thou shalt forfeit thy tongue.
Behold Endymion! Alas, poor gentleman,
hast thou spent thy youth in sleep, that once [95
vowed all to my service! Hollow eyes, gray
hairs, wrinkled cheeks, and decayed limbs! Is
it destiny or deceit that hath brought this
to pass? If the first, who could prevent thy
wretched stars? If the latter, I would I [100
might know thy cruel enemy. I favoured thee,
Endymion, for thy honour, thy virtues, thy
affections; but to bring thy thoughts within
the compass of thy fortunes, I have seemed
strange, that I might have thee staid; and [105

---

²³ **brawn-fallen:** weak    ²⁶ **litherness:** languor    ³² **rent:** rend; cf. V. iii. 55    ⁵² **heidegyes:** dances
⁶¹ **grossness:** stupidity    ⁶⁷⁻⁶⁸ **walk to Endymion:** The walk is indicated by crossing the stage; cf. line 94.

now are thy days ended before my favour begin.
But whom have we here?  Is it not Corsites?
    *Zon.*  It is, but more like a leopard than a man.
    *Cynth.*  Awake him. [*Zontes wakens Corsites.*]
How now, Corsites, what make you here? [110
How came you deformed?  Look on thy hands,
and then thou seest the picture of thy face.
    *Cors.*  Miserable wretch, and accursed!  How
am I deluded!  Madam, I ask pardon for my offence, and you see my fortune deserveth pity. [115
    *Cynth.*  Speak on; thy offence cannot deserve
greater punishment: but see thou rehearse
the truth, else shalt thou not find me as thou
wishest me.
    *Cors.*  Madam, as it is no offence to be in [120
love, being a man mortal, so I hope can it be no
shame to tell with whom, my lady being heavenly.  Your Majesty committed to my charge fair
Tellus, whose beauty in the same moment took
my heart captive that I undertook to carry [125
her body prisoner.  Since that time have I found
such combats in my thoughts between love
and duty, reverence and affection, that I could
neither endure the conflict, nor hope for the
conquest.                                          130
    *Cynth.*  In love?  A thing far unfitting the
name of a captain, and (as I thought) the
tough and unsmoothed nature of Corsites.  But
forth!
    *Cors.*  Feeling this continual war, I thought [135
rather by parley to yield than by certain danger
to perish.  I unfolded to Tellus the depth of
my affections, and framed my tongue to utter a
sweet tale of love, that was wont to sound nothing but threats of war.  She, too fair to be [140
true and too false for one so fair, after a nice
denial, practised a notable deceit, commanding
me to remove Endymion from this cabin, and
carry him to some dark cave; which I seeking
to accomplish, found impossible; and so by [145
fairies or fiends have been thus handled.
    *Cynth.*  How say you, my lords, is not Tellus
always practising of some deceits?  In sooth,
Corsites, thy face is now too foul for a lover,
and thine heart too fond for a soldier.  You [150
may see when warriors become wantons how
their manners alter with their faces.  Is it not a
shame, Corsites, that having lived so long in
Mars his camp, thou shouldst now be rocked in
Venus' cradle?  Dost thou wear Cupid's [155
quiver at thy girdle and make lances of looks?
Well, Corsites, rouse thyself and be as thou
hast been; and let Tellus, who is made all of
love, melt herself in her own looseness.
    *Cors.*  Madam, I doubt not but to recover [160
my former state, for Tellus' beauty never
wrought such love in my mind as now her deceit

hath despite; and yet to be revenged of a woman
were a thing than love itself more womanish.
    *Gyptes.*  These spots, gentleman, are to be [165
worn out, if you rub them over with this lunary; so that in place where you received this
maim you shall find a medicine.
    *Cors.*  I thank you for that.  The gods bless
me from love and these pretty ladies that [170
haunt this green.
    *Flosc.*  Corsites, I would Tellus saw your ami-
able face.                          [*Semele laughs.*]
    *Zont.*  How spitefully Semele laugheth, that
dare not speak.                                    175
    *Cynth.*  Could you not stir Endymion with
that doubled strength of yours?
    *Cors.*  Not so much as his finger with all my
force.
    *Cynth.*  Pythagoras and Gyptes, what [180
think you of Endymion?  What reason is to be
given, what remedy?
    *Pyth.*  Madam, it is impossible to yield reason
for things that happen not in compass of nature.
It is most certain that some strange en- [185
chantment hath bound all his senses.
    *Cynth.*  What say you, Gyptes?
    *Gyptes.*  With Pythagoras, that it is enchant-
ment, and that so strange that no art can undo
it, for that heaviness argueth a malice unre- [190
movable in the enchantress, and that no power
can end it, till she die that did it, or the heavens
show some means more than miraculous.
    *Flosc.*  O Endymion, could spite itself devise a
mischief so monstrous as to make thee dead [195
with life, and living, being altogether dead?
Where others number their years, their hours,
their minutes, and step to age by stairs, thou only
hast thy years and times in a cluster, being old
before thou rememb'rest thou wast young. [200
    *Cynth.*  No more, Floscula; pity doth him no
good.  I would anything else might; and I vow
by the unspotted honour of a lady he should not
miss it.  But is this all, Gyptes, that is to be
done?                                              205
    *Gyptes.*  All as yet.  It may be that either the
enchantress shall die or else be discovered: if
either happen, I will then practise the utmost
of my art.  In the mean season, about this grove
would I have a watch, and the first living [210
thing that toucheth Endymion to be taken.
    *Cynth.*  Corsites, what say you, will you
undertake this?
    *Cors.*  Good madam, pardon me!  I was over-
taken too late.  I should rather break into [215
the midst of a main battle than again fall into
the hands of those fair babies.
    *Cynth.*  Well, I will provide others.  Pythag-
oras and Gyptes, you shall yet remain in my

court, till I hear what may be done in this [220
matter.
*Pyth.*  We attend.
*Cynth.*  Let us go in.                         *Exeunt.*

### Actus quintus.  Scæna prima.

#### Samias, Dares

*Sam.*  Eumenides hath told such strange
tales as I may well wonder at them, but never
believe them.
*Dar.*  The other old man, what a sad speech
used he, that caused us almost all to weep. [5
Cynthia is so desirous to know the experiment
of her own virtue, and so willing to ease Endymion's hard fortune, that she no sooner heard
the discourse but she made herself in a readiness to try the event.                          10
*Sam.*  We will also see the event. But whist!
here cometh Cynthia with all her train. Let us
sneak in amongst them.

*Enter Cynthia, Floscula, Semele, [Eumenides,]
Panelion, etc.*

*Cynth.*  Eumenides, it cannot sink into my
head that I should be signified by that sa- [15
cred fountain, for many things are there in the
world to which those words may be applied.
*Eum.*  Good madam, vouchsafe but to try;
else shall I think myself most unhappy that I
asked not my sweet mistress.                    20
*Cynth.*  Will you not yet tell me her name?
*Eum.*  Pardon me, good madam, for if Endymion awake, he shall; myself have sworn
never to reveal it.
*Cynth.*  Well, let us to Endymion. I will [25
not be so stately, good Endymion, not to stoop
to do thee good; and if thy liberty consist in a
kiss from me, thou shalt have it; and although
my mouth hath been heretofore as untouched
as my thoughts, yet now to recover thy life, [30
though to restore thy youth it be impossible, I
will do that to Endymion which yet never
mortal man could boast of heretofore, nor shall
ever hope for hereafter.          *She kisseth him.*
*Eum.*  Madam, he beginneth to stir.          35
*Cynth.*  Soft, Eumenides; stand still.
*Eum.*  Ah, I see his eyes almost open.
*Cynth.*  I command thee once again, stir not.
I will stand behind him.
*Pan.*  What do I see? Endymion almost [40
awake?
*Eum.*  Endymion, Endymion, art thou deaf
or dumb, or hath this long sleep taken away thy
memory? Ah, my sweet Endymion, seest thou
not Eumenides, thy faithful friend, thy faith- [45
ful Eumenides, who for thy safety hath been

careless of his own content? Speak, Endymion!
Endymion! Endymion!
*End.*  Endymion? I call to mind such a
name.                                           50
*Eum.*  Hast thou forgotten thyself, Endym-
ion? Then do I not marvel thou rememb'rest
not thy friend. I tell thee thou art Endymion,
and I Eumenides. Behold also Cynthia, by
whose favour thou art awaked, and by whose [55
virtue thou shalt continue thy natural course.
*Cynth.*  Endymion, speak, sweet Endymion!
Knowest thou not Cynthia?
*End.*  O heavens, whom do I behold? Fair
Cynthia, divine Cynthia?                         60
*Cynth.*  I am Cynthia, and thou Endymion.
*End.*  "Endymion!" What do I hear? What,
a gray beard, hollow eyes, withered body, decayed limbs, — and all in one night?
*Eum.*  One night! Thou hast here slept [65
forty years, — by what enchantress as yet it is
not known, — and behold, the twig to which
thou laid'st thy head is now become a tree.
Callest thou not Eumenides to remembrance?
*End.*  Thy name I do remember by the [70
sound, but thy favour I do not yet call to mind;
only divine Cynthia, to whom time, fortune,
destiny, and death are subject, I see and remember, and in all humility I regard and reverence.                                         75
*Cynth.*  You have good cause to remember
Eumenides, who hath for thy safety forsaken
his own solace.
*End.*  Am I that Endymion who was wont in
court to lead my life, and in justs, tourneys, [80
and arms, to exercise my youth? Am I that
Endymion?
*Eum.*  Thou art that Endymion, and I Eumenides: wilt thou not yet call me to remembrance?                                         85
*End.*  Ah, sweet Eumenides, I now perceive
thou art he, and that myself have the name of
Endymion; but that this should be my body I
doubt, for how could my curled locks be turned
to gray hairs and my strong body to a dying [90
weakness, having waxed old, and not knowing
it.
*Cynth.*  Well, Endymion, arise. [*Endymion,
trying to rise, sinks back.*] A while sit down, for
that thy limbs are stiff and not able to stay [95
thee, and tell what hast thou seen in thy sleep
all this while, — what dreams, visions, thoughts,
and fortunes; for it is impossible but in so long
time thou shouldest see things strange.
*End.*  Fair Cynthia, I will rehearse what [100
I have seen, humbly desiring that when I exceed in length, you give me warning, that I
may end; for to utter all I have to speak would

---

²⁰ **asked not:** *i.e.,* asked not for    ⁷¹ **favour:** features    ⁹⁵ **stay:** support

be troublesome, although haply the strangeness may somewhat abate the tediousness.    105

*Cynth.* Well, Endymion, begin.

*End.* Methought I saw a lady passing fair, but very mischievous, who in the one hand carried a knife with which she offered to cut my throat, and in the other a looking-glass, [110 wherein seeing how ill anger became ladies, she refrained from intended violence. She was accompanied with other damsels, one of which, with a stern countenance, and as it were with a settled malice engraven in her eyes, [115 provoked her to execute mischief; another, with visage sad, and constant only in sorrow, with her arms crossed, and watery eyes, seemed to lament my fortune, but durst not offer to prevent the force. I started in my sleep, [120 feeling my very veins to swell and my sinews to stretch with fear, and such a cold sweat bedewed all my body that death itself could not be so terrible as the vision.

*Cynth.* A strange sight! Gyptes, at our [125 better leisure, shall expound it.

*End.* After long debating with herself, mercy overcame anger, and there appeared in her heavenly face such a divine majesty mingled with a sweet mildness that I was ravished [130 with the sight above measure, and wished that I might have enjoyed the sight without end; and so she departed with the other ladies, of which the one retained still an unmovable cruelty, the other a constant pity.    135

*Cynth.* Poor Endymion, how wast thou affrighted! What else?

*End.* After her, immediately appeared an aged man with a beard as white as snow, carrying in his hand a book with three leaves, [140 and speaking, as I remember, these words: "Endymion, receive this book with three leaves, in which are contained counsels, policies, and pictures," and with that he offered me the book, which I rejected; [145 wherewith, moved with a disdainful pity, he rent the first leaf in a thousand shivers. The second time he offered it, which I refused also; at which, bending his brows, and pitching his eyes fast to the ground, as though they were fixed [150 to the earth and not again to be removed, then suddenly casting them up to the heavens, he tore in a rage the second leaf, and offered the book only with one leaf. I know not whether fear to offend or desire to know some [155 strange thing moved me: I took the book, and so the old man vanished.

*Cynth.* What diddest thou imagine was in the last leaf?

*End.* There portray'd to life, with a cold [160 quaking in every joint, I beheld many wolves barking at thee, Cynthia, who having ground their teeth to bite, did with striving bleed themselves to death. There might I see Ingratitude with an hundred eyes gazing for bene- [165 fits, and with a thousand teeth gnawing on the bowels wherein she was bred. Treachery stood all clothed in white, with a smiling countenance, but both her hands bathed in blood. Envy with a pale and meagre face (whose body [170 was so lean that one might tell all her bones, and whose garment was so totter'd that it was easy to number every thread) stood shooting at stars, whose darts fell down again on her own face. There might I behold drones or [175 beetles — I know not how to term them — creeping under the wings of a princely eagle, who, being carried into her nest, sought there to suck that vein that would have killed the eagle. I mused that things so base should [180 attempt a fact so barbarous, or durst imagine a thing so bloody. And many other things, madam, the repetition whereof may at your better leisure seem more pleasing, for bees surfeit sometimes with honey, and the gods are [185 glutted with harmony, and your highness may be dulled with delight.

*Cynth.* I am content to be dieted; therefore, let us in. Eumenides, see that Endymion be well tended, lest either eating immoderately or [190 sleeping again too long, he fall into a deadly surfeit or into his former sleep. See this also be proclaimed: that whosoever will discover this practice shall have of Cynthia infinite thanks and no small rewards. *Exit* [*accompanied*]. 195

*Flosc.* Ah, Endymion, none so joyful as Floscula of thy restoring.

*Eum.* Yes, Floscula, let Eumenides be somewhat gladder, and do not that wrong to the settled friendship of a man as to compare it [200 with the light affection of a woman. Ah, my dear friend Endymion, suffer me to die with gazing at thee.

*End.* Eumenides, thy friendship is immortal and not to be conceived; and thy good [205 will, Floscula, better than I have deserved. But let us all wait on Cynthia. I marvel Semele speaketh not a word.

*Eum.* Because if she do, she loseth her tongue.    210

*End.* But how prospereth your love?

*Eum.* I never yet spake word since your sleep.

*End.* I doubt not but your affection is old and your appetite cold.    215

---

¹⁴⁷ **shivers:** pieces, fragments    ¹⁶⁰⁻¹⁸² Alluding to the plots against the Queen's life in the years before the Armada.    ¹⁷¹ **tell:** count    ¹⁷² **totter'd:** tattered, threadbare    ¹⁸¹ **fact: deed**    ¹⁸⁸ **dieted:** put on a ration    ¹⁹³⁻¹⁹⁴ **discover this practice:** expose this plot

*Eum.* No, Endymion, thine hath made it stronger, and now are my sparks grown to flames and my fancies almost to frenzies: but let us follow, and within we will debate all this matter at large.                                    *Exeunt.* [220

## *Actus quintus.  Scæna secunda.*

### *Sir Tophas, Epiton*

*Top.* Epi, love hath justled my liberty from the wall, and taken the upper hand of my reason.

*Epi.* Let me then trip up the heels of your affection and thrust your good will into the [5 gutter.

*Top.* No, Epi, Love is a lord of misrule and keepeth Christmas in my corpse.

*Epi.* No doubt there is good cheer: what dishes of delight doth his lordship feast you [10 withal?

*Top.* First, with a great platter of plum porridge of pleasure, wherein is stewed the mutton of mistrust.

*Epi.* Excellent love-pap.                              15

*Top.* Then cometh a pie of patience, a hen of honey, a goose of gall, a capon of care, and many other viands, some sweet and some sour, which proveth love to be, as it was said of in old years, *Dulce venenum.*                        20

*Epi.* A brave banquet!

*Top.* But, Epi, I pray thee feel on my chin; something pricketh me. What dost thou feel or see?

*Epi.* There are three or four little hairs.   25

*Top.* I pray thee call it my beard. How shall I be troubled when this young spring shall grow to a great wood!

*Epi.* Oh, sir, your chin is but a quiller yet; you will be most majestical when it is full- [30 fledge. But I marvel that you love Dipsas, that old crone.

*Top.* *Agnosco veteris vestigia flammæ;* I love the smoke of an old fire.

*Epi.* Why she is so cold that no fire can [35 thaw her thoughts.

*Top.* It is an old goose, Epi, that will eat no oats; old kine will kick, old rats gnaw cheese, and old sacks will have much patching. I prefer an old coney before a rabbit-sucker, [40 and an ancient hen before a young chicken-peeper.

*Epi.* [*Aside.*] *Argumentum ab antiquitate;* my master loveth antique work.

*Top.* Give me a pippin that is withered [45 like an old wife!

*Epi.* Good, sir.

*Top.* Then, — *a contrario sequitur argumentum,* — give me a wife that looks like an old pippin.                                             50

*Epi.* [*Aside.*] Nothing hath made my master a fool but flat scholarship.

*Top.* Knowest thou not that old wine is best?

*Epi.* Yes.

*Top.* And thou knowest that like will to [55 like?

*Epi.* Ay.

*Top.* And thou knowest that Venus loved the best wine?

*Epi.* So.                                            60

*Top.* Then I conclude that Venus was an old woman in an old cup of wine, for *est Venus in vinis, ignis in igne fuit.*

*Epi.* *O lepidum caput.* O madcap master! You were worthy to win Dipsas, were she as [65 old again, for in your love you have worn the nap of your wit quite off and made it threadbare. But soft, who comes here?

[*Enter Samias and Dares*]

*Top.* My solicitors.

*Sam.* All hail, Sir Tophas; how feel you [70 yourself?

*Top.* Stately in every joint, which the common people term stiffness. Doth Dipsas stoop? Will she yield? Will she bend?

*Dar.* Oh, sir, as much as you would wish, [75 for her chin almost toucheth her knees.

*Epi.* Master, she is bent, I warrant you.

*Top.* What conditions doth she ask?

*Sam.* She hath vowed she will never love any that hath not a tooth in his head less [80 than she.

*Top.* How many hath she?

*Dar.* One.

*Epi.* That goeth hard, master, for then you must have none.                                    85

*Top.* A small request, and agreeable to the gravity of her years. What should a wise man do with his mouth full of bones like a charnel-house? The turtle true hath ne'er a tooth.

*Sam.* [*To Epi.*] Thy master is in a notable [90 vein, that will lose his teeth to be like a turtle.

*Epi.* [*Aside.*] Let him lose his tongue, too; I care not.

*Dar.* Nay, you must also have no nails, for she long since hath cast hers.                     95

*Top.* That I yield too. What a quiet life

---

**1-2 justled . . . wall:** got the better of    **7 lord of misrule:** a person, often of inferior rank, who presided over the Christmas festivities at such places as the universities or the Inns of Court    **15 love-pap:** ('love lappe' Q, Blount)    **20 Dulce venenum:** sweet poison    **22-31** (Jesting at the boy-actor of Sir Tophas)    **27 spring:** grove    **29 quiller:** unfledged bird    **33 Agnosco . . . flammæ:** I recognize the traces of an old flame.    **40 coney:** rabbit    **rabbit-sucker:** sucking rabbit    **62-63 est . . . fuit:** In wines there is Venus; there was fire in fire.    **64 O . . . caput:** O charming person    **89 turtle:** turtle-dove

shall Dipsas and I lead when we can neither bite nor scratch! You may see, youths, how age provides for peace.

*Sam.* [*Aside.*] How shall we do to make [100 him leave his love, for we never spake to her?

*Dar.* [*Aside.*] Let me alone. [*To Sir Tophas.*] She is a notable witch, and hath turned her maid Bagoa to an aspen tree, for bewraying her secrets.                                            105

*Top.* I honour her for her cunning, for now when I am weary of walking on two legs, what a pleasure may she do me to turn me to some goodly ass, and help me to four.

*Dar.* Nay, then I must tell you the [110 troth. Her husband, Geron, is come home, who this fifty years hath had her to wife.

*Top.* What do I hear? Hath she an husband? Go to the sexton and tell him Desire is dead, and will him to dig his grave. O [115 heavens, an husband! What death is agreeable to my fortune?

*Sam.* Be not desperate, and we will help you to find a young lady.

*Top.* I love no grissels; they are so brit- [120 tle they will crack like glass, or so dainty that if they be touched they are straight of the fashion of wax; *animus majoribus instat*, I desire old matrons. What a sight would it be to embrace one whose hair were as orient as [125 the pearl, whose teeth shall be so pure a watchet that they shall stain the truest turquoise, whose nose shall throw more beams from it than the fiery carbuncle, whose eyes shall be environ'd about with redness ex- [130 ceeding the deepest coral, and whose lips might compare with silver for the paleness! Such a one if you can help me to, I will by piecemeal curtail my affections towards Dipsas, and walk my swelling thoughts till they be cold.   135

*Epi.* Wisely provided. How say you, my friends, will you angle for my master's cause?

*Sam.* Most willingly.

*Dar.* If we speed him not shortly, I will burn my cap. We will serve him of the spades, [140 and dig an old wife out of the grave that shall be answerable to his gravity.

*Top.* Youths, adieu; he that bringeth me first news, shall possess mine inheritance.
                                 [*Exit Sir Tophas.*]

*Dar.* What, is thy master landed?      145

*Epi.* Know you not that my master is *liber tenens?*

*Sam.* What 's that?

*Epi.* A freeholder. But I will after him.

*Sam.* And we to hear what news of En- [150 dymion for the conclusion.                *Exeunt.*

## Actus quintus. Scæna tertia.

### Panelion, Zontes

*Pan.* Who would have thought that Tellus, being so fair by nature, so honourable by birth, so wise by education, would have entered into a mischief to the gods so odious, to men so detestable, and to her friend so malicious?       5

*Zon.* If Bagoa had not bewrayed it, how then should it have come to light? But we see that gold and fair words are of force to corrupt the strongest men, and therefore able to work silly women like wax.                            10

*Pan.* I marvel what Cynthia will determine in this cause.

*Zon.* I fear, as in all causes — hear of it in justice, and then judge of it in mercy; for how can it be that she that is unwilling to punish [15 her deadliest foes with disgrace, will revenge injuries of her train with death?

*Pan.* That old witch, Dipsas, in a rage, having understood her practice to be discovered, turned poor Bagoa to an aspen tree. But let [20 us make haste and bring Tellus before Cynthia, for she was coming out after us.

*Zon.* Let us go.                        *Exeunt.*

*Cynthia, Semele, Floscula, Dipsas, Endymion, Eumenides, [Geron, Pythagoras, Gyptes, and Sir Tophas]*

*Cynth.* Dipsas, thy years are not so many as thy vices, yet more in number than commonly [25 nature doth afford or justice should permit. Hast thou almost these fifty years practised that detested wickedness of witchcraft? Wast thou, so simple as for to know the nature of simples, of all creatures to be most sinful? Thou hast [30 threat'ned to turn my course awry and alter by thy damnable art the government that I now possess by the eternal gods; but know thou, Dipsas, and let all the enchanters know, that Cynthia, being placed for light on earth, is also [35 protected by the powers of heaven. Breathe out thou mayest words; gather thou mayest herbs; find out thou mayest stones agreeable to thine art; yet of no force to appal my heart in which courage is so rooted, and constant [40 persuasion of the mercy of the gods so grounded, that all thy witchcraft I esteem as weak as the world doth thy case wretched. This noble gentleman, Geron, once thy husband but now thy mortal hate, didst thou procure to live in [45 a desert, almost desperate; Endymion, the flower of my court and the hope of succeeding

---

120 **grissels:** young girls   123 **animus . . . instat:** My desire pursues older women.   125 **orient:** whit-ish   127 **watchet:** light blue   139 **speed him:** aid him   145 **landed:** possessed of land   146–147 **liber tenens:** a free man who holds property; pun on "libertine"

time, hast thou bewitched by art, before thou
wouldest suffer him to flourish by nature.

*Dipsas.* Madam, things past may be re- [50
pented, not recalled: there is nothing so wicked
that I have not done, nor anything so wished
for as death. Yet among all the things that I
committed, there is nothing so much tormenteth
my rented and ransack'd thoughts as that in [55
the prime of my husband's youth I divorced him
by my devilish art; for which if to die might
be amends, I would not live till tomorrow. If
to live and still be more miserable would better
content him, I would wish of all creatures to [60
be oldest and ugliest.

*Geron.* Dipsas, thou hast made this difference
between me and Endymion, that being both
young, thou hast caused me to wake in melancholy, losing the joys of my youth, and him [65
to sleep, not remembering youth.

*Cynth.* Stay, here cometh Tellus; we shall
now know all.

*Enter Corsites, Tellus, Panelion, etc.*

*Cors.* I would to Cynthia thou couldest make
as good an excuse in truth as to me thou hast [70
done by wit.

*Tellus.* Truth shall be mine answer, and
therefore I will not study for an excuse.

*Cynth.* Is it possible, Tellus, that so few years
should harbour so many mischiefs? Thy [75
swelling pride have I borne, because it is a thing
that beauty maketh blameless, which the more
it exceedeth fairness in measure, the more it
stretcheth itself in disdain. Thy devices against
Corsites I smile at, for that wits, the sharper [80
they are, the shrewder they are; but this unacquainted and most unnatural practice with a
vile enchantress against so noble a gentleman as
Endymion I abhor as a thing most malicious,
and will revenge as a deed most monstrous. [85
And as for you, Dipsas, I will send you into
the desert amongst wild beasts, and try whether
you can cast lions, tigers, boars, and bears into as
dead a sleep as you did Endymion, or turn them
to trees, as you have done Bagoa. But tell me, [90
Tellus, what was the cause of this cruel part,
far unfitting thy sex, in which nothing should
be but simpleness, and much disagreeing from
thy face, in which nothing seemed to be but
softness.                      95

*Tellus.* Divine Cynthia, by whom I receive
my life and am content to end it, I can neither
excuse my fault without lying, nor confess it
without shame. Yet were it possible that in so
heavenly thoughts as yours there could fall [100
such earthly motions as mine, I would then hope,
if not to be pardoned without extreme punishment, yet to be heard without great marvel.

*Cynth.* Say on, Tellus, I cannot imagine
any thing that can colour such a cruelty.    105

*Tellus.* Endymion, that Endymion, in the
prime of his youth, so ravish'd my heart with
love, that to obtain my desires I could not
find means, nor to resist them reason. What was
she that favoured not Endymion, being [110
young, wise, honourable, and virtuous; besides,
what metal was she made of (be she mortal) that
is not affected with the spice, nay, infected
with the poison of that not-to-be-expressed yet
always-to-be-felt love, which breaketh the [115
brains and never bruiseth the brow, consumeth the heart and never toucheth the skin,
and maketh a deep scar to be seen before any
wound at all be felt. My heart, too tender
to withstand such a divine fury, yielded to [120
love. Madam, I — not without blushing confess — yielded to love.

*Cynth.* A strange effect of love, to work
such an extreme hate. How say you, Endymion? All this was for love?        125

*End.* I say, madam, then the gods send me
a woman's hate.

*Cynth.* That were as bad, for then by contrary you should never sleep. But on, Tellus;
let us hear the end.                130

*Tellus.* Feeling a continual burning in all
my bowels, and a bursting almost in every vein,
I could not smother the inward fire, but it
must needs be perceived by the outward smoke;
and by the flying abroad of divers sparks, [135
divers judged of my scalding flames. Endymion,
as full of art as wit, marking mine eyes, (in
which he might see almost his own), my sighs,
(by which he might ever hear his name
sounded), aimed at my heart, in which he [140
was assured his person was imprinted, and by
questions wrung out that which was ready to
burst out. When he saw the depth of my affections, he sware that mine in respect of his were
as fumes to Ætna, valleys to Alps, ants [145
to eagles, and nothing could be compared to
my beauty but his love and eternity. Thus
drawing a smooth shoe upon a crooked foot, he
made me believe that (which all of our sex willingly acknowledge) I was beautiful, and [150
to wonder (which indeed is a thing miraculous)
that any of his sex should be faithful.

*Cynth.* Endymion, how will you clear yourself?

*End.* Madam, by mine own accuser.    155

*Cynth.* Well, Tellus, proceed; but briefly,
lest taking delight in uttering thy love, thou
offend us with the length of it.

*Tellus.* I will, madam, quickly make an end
of my love and my tale. Finding continual [160

---

⁵⁴ **rented:** torn     ⁸¹ **shrewder:** more malicious
rôle    ¹⁰¹ **motions:** impulses    ¹⁰⁵ **colour:** gloss over

⁸¹⁻⁸² **unacquainted:** unheard of    ⁹¹ **part:** act,
¹⁰⁹ **resist:** ('resite' Q; 'recite' Blount)

increase of my tormenting thoughts, and that the enjoying of my love made deeper wounds than the entering into it, I could find no means to ease my grief but to follow Endymion, and continually to have him in the object of [165 mine eyes who had me slave and subject to his love. But in the moment that I feared his falsehood and tried myself most in mine affections, I found — ah, grief, even then I lost myself! — I found him in most melancholy and desperate [170 terms, cursing his stars, his state, the earth, the heavens, the world, and all for the love of —

*Cynth.* Of whom? Tellus, speak boldly.

*Tellus.* Madam, I dare not utter, for fear to offend.                               175

*Cynth.* Speak, I say; who dare take offence, if thou be commanded by Cynthia?

*Tellus.* For the love of Cynthia.

*Cynth.* For my love, Tellus? That were strange. Endymion, is it true?         180

*End.* In all things, madam, Tellus doth not speak false.

*Cynth.* What will this breed to in the end? Well, Endymion, we shall hear all.

*Tellus.* I, seeing my hopes turned to mis- [185 haps, and a settled dissembling towards me, and an unmovable desire to Cynthia, forgetting both myself and my sex, fell unto this unnatural hate; for knowing your virtues, Cynthia, to be immortal, I could not have an imagination to with- [190 draw him; and finding mine own affections unquenchable, I could not carry the mind that any else should possess what I had pursued. For though in majesty, beauty, virtue, and dignity, I always humbled and yielded myself [195 to Cynthia, yet in affections I esteemed myself equal with the goddesses, and all other creatures, according to their states, with myself; for stars to their bigness have their lights, and the sun hath no more, and little pitchers, when [200 they can hold no more, are as full as great vessels that run over. Thus, madam, in all truth have I uttered the unhappiness of my love and the cause of my hate, yielding wholly to that divine judgment which never erred for want of [205 wisdom or envied for too much partiality.

*Cynth.* How say you, my lords, to this matter? But what say you, Endymion; hath Tellus told troth?

*End.* Madam, in all things but in that [210 she said I loved her and swore to honour her.

*Cynth.* Was there such a time whenas for my love thou didst vow thyself to death, and in respect of it loathed thy life? Speak, Endymion; I will not revenge it with hate.        215

*End.* The time was, madam, and is, and ever shall be, that I honoured your highness

above all the world, but to stretch it so far as to call it love I never durst. There hath none pleased mine eye but Cynthia, none delighted [220 mine ears but Cynthia, none possessed my heart but Cynthia. I have forsaken all other fortunes to follow Cynthia, and here I stand ready to die, if it please Cynthia. Such a difference hath the gods set between our states that all must be [225 duty, loyalty, and reverence; nothing (without it vouchsafe your highness) be termed love. My unspotted thoughts, my languishing body, my discontented life, let them obtain by princely favour that which to challenge they [230 must not presume, only wishing of impossibilities; with imagination of which I will spend my spirits, and to myself, that no creature may hear, softly call it love; and if any urge to utter what I whisper, then will I name it honour. [235 From this sweet contemplation if I be not driven, I shall live of all men the most content, taking more pleasure in mine aged thoughts than ever I did in my youthful actions.

*Cynth.* Endymion, this honourable respect [240 of thine shall be christened love in thee, and my reward for it, favour. Persever, Endymion, in loving me, and I account more strength in a true heart than in a walled city. I have laboured to win all, and study to keep such as I [245 have won; but those that neither my favour can move to continue constant, nor my offered benefits get to be faithful, the gods shall either reduce to truth, or revenge their treacheries with justice. Endymion, continue as thou hast [250 begun, and thou shalt find that Cynthia shineth not on thee in vain.

            [*Endymion throws off the marks
                           of old age.*]

*End.* Your highness hath blessed me, and your words have again restored my youth; methinks I feel my joints strong and these [255 mouldy hairs to moult, and all by your virtue, Cynthia, into whose hands the balance that weigheth time and fortune are committed.

*Cynth.* What, young again! Then it is pity to punish Tellus.                      260

*Tellus.* Ah, Endymion, now I know thee and ask pardon of thee; suffer me still to wish thee well.

*End.* Tellus, Cynthia must command what she will.                          265

*Flosc.* Endymion, I rejoice to see thee in thy former estate.

*End.* Good Floscula, to thee also am I in my former affections.

*Eum.* Endymion, the comfort of my life, [270 how am I ravished with a joy matchless, saving only the enjoying of my mistress.

---

190-191 **could . . . him:** could not imagine that I could withdraw him    192 **carry the mind:** bear to think   199 **to:** according to   242 **Persever:** persevere

*Cynth.* Endymion, you must now tell who Eumenides shrineth for his saint.

*End.* Semele, madam.                             275

*Cynth.* Semele, Eumenides? Is it Semele, the very wasp of all women, whose tongue stingeth as much as an adder's tooth?

*Eum.* It is Semele, Cynthia, the possessing of whose love must only prolong my life.   280

*Cynth.* Nay, sith Endymion is restored, we will have all parties pleased. Semele, are you content after so long trial of his faith, such rare secrecy, such unspotted love, to take Eumenides? Why speak you not? Not a word? [285

*End.* Silence, madam, consents; that is most true.

*Cynth.* It is true, Endymion. Eumenides, take Semele; take her, I say.

*Eum.* Humble thanks, madam; now [290 only do I begin to live.

*Sem.* A hard choice, madam, either to be married if I say nothing, or to lose my tongue if I speak a word. Yet do I rather choose to have my tongue cut out than my heart distem- [295 pered: I will not have him.

*Cynth.* Speaks the parrot! She shall nod hereafter with signs. Cut off her tongue, nay her head, that having a servant of honourable birth, honest manners, and true love, will [300 not be persuaded.

*Sem.* He is no faithful lover, madam, for then would he have asked his mistress.

*Ger.* Had he not been faithful, he had never seen into the fountain, and so lost his friend [305 and mistress.

*Eum.* Thine own thoughts, sweet Semele, witness against thy words, for what hast thou found in my life but love? And as yet what have I found in my love but bitterness? [310 Madam, pardon Semele, and let my tongue ransom hers.

*Cynth.* Thy tongue, Eumenides! What, shouldst thou live wanting a tongue to blaze the beauty of Semele! Well, Semele, I will [315 not command love, for it cannot be enforced; let me entreat it.

*Sem.* I am content your highness shall command, for now only do I think Eumenides faithful, that is willing to lose his tongue for my [320 sake; yet loath, because it should do me better service. Madam, I accept of Eumenides.

*Cynth.* I thank you, Semele.

*Eum.* Ah, happy Eumenides, that hast a friend so faithful and a mistress so fair! [325 With what sudden mischief will the gods daunt this excess of joy? Sweet Semele, I live or die as thou wilt.

*Cynth.* What shall become of Tellus? Tellus,

you know Endymion is vowed to a service [330 from which death cannot remove him. Corsites casteth still a lovely look towards you. How say you, will you have your Corsites, and so receive pardon for all that is past?

*Tellus.* Madam, most willingly.           335

*Cynth.* But I cannot tell whether Corsites be agreed.

*Cors.* Ay, madam, more happy to enjoy Tellus than the monarchy of the world.

*Eum.* Why, she caused you to be pinched [340 with fairies.

*Cors.* Ay, but her fairness hath pinched my heart more deeply.

*Cynth.* Well, enjoy thy love. But what have you wrought in the castle, Tellus?        345

*Tellus.* Only the picture of Endymion.

*Cynth.* Then so much of Endymion as his picture cometh to, possess and play withal.

*Cors.* Ah, my sweet Tellus, my love shall be as thy beauty is, matchless.           350

*Cynth.* Now it resteth, Dipsas, that if thou wilt forswear that vile art of enchanting, Geron hath promised again to receive thee; otherwise, if thou be wedded to that wickedness, I must and will see it punished to the uttermost.  355

*Dipsas.* Madam, I renounce both substance and shadow of that most horrible and hateful trade, vowing to the gods continual penance, and to your highness obedience.

*Cynth.* How say you, Geron; will you [360 admit her to your wife?

*Ger.* Ay, with more joy than I did the first day, for nothing could happen to make me happy but only her forsaking that lewd and detestable course. Dipsas, I embrace thee.   365

*Dipsas.* And I thee, Geron, to whom I will hereafter recite the cause of these my first follies.

*Cynth.* Well, Endymion, nothing resteth now but that we depart. Thou hast my favour; [370 Tellus her friend; Eumenides in paradise with his Semele; Geron contented with Dipsas.

*Top.* Nay, soft; I cannot handsomely go to bed without Bagoa.

*Cynth.* Well, Sir Tophas, it may be there [375 are more virtues in me than myself knoweth of, for Endymion I awaked, and at my words he waxed young. I will try whether I can turn this tree again to thy true love.

*Top.* Turn her to a true love or false, so [380 she be a wench I care not.

*Cynth.* Bagoa, Cynthia putteth an end to thy hard fortunes; for, being turned to a tree for revealing a truth, I will recover thee again, if in my power be the effect of truth.        385

[*Bagoa recovers human shape.*]

---

*Top.* Bagoa, a bots upon thee!

*Cynth.* Come, my lords, let us in. You, Gyptes and Pythagoras, if you can content yourselves in our court, to fall from vain follies of philosophers to such virtues as are here practised, [390 you shall be entertained according to your deserts, for Cynthia is no stepmother to strangers.

*Pythag.* I had rather in Cynthia's court spend ten years than in Greece one hour.

*Gyptes.* And I choose rather to live by [395 the sight of Cynthia than by the possessing of all Egypt.

*Cynth.* Then follow.

*Eum.* We all attend.                    *Exeunt.*

## THE EPILOGUE

A MAN walking abroad, the Wind and Sun strove for sovereignty, the one with his blast, the other with his beams. The Wind blew hard; the man wrapped his garment about him harder: it blustered more strongly; he then girt it fast to him. "I cannot prevail," said the Wind. The Sun, casting her crystal beams, began to warm the man; he unloosed his gown. Yet it shined brighter; he then put it off. "I yield," said the Wind, "for if thou continue shining, he will also put off [5 his coat."

Dread Sovereign, the malicious that seek to overthrow us with threats, do but stiffen our thoughts, and make them sturdier in storms; but if Your Highness vouchsafe with your favourable beams to glance upon us, we shall not only stoop, but with all humility lay both our hands and hearts at Your Majesty's feet.                    10

386 **bots:** plague (*lit.*, worms)

# THE
# HONORABLE HISTORIE
of frier Bacon, and frier Bongay.

As it was plaid by her Maiesties seruants.

Made by *Robert Greene* Maister of Arts.

## LONDON,

Printed for Edward White, and are to be sold at his shop, at
the little North dore of Poules, at the signe of
the Gun. 1594.

BIBLIOGRAPHICAL RECORD. The earliest Quarto of *Friar Bacon and Friar Bungay* appeared in 1594 with the statement that the play had been "made by Robert Greene, Master of Arts." Other editions followed in 1630 and 1655. The play had been entered on the Register of the Stationers' Co., May 14, 1594: — *Edward White. Entred for his Copie vnder th[e h]ands of bothe the wardens a booke entituled the Historye of ffryer Bacon and ffryer Boungaye . . . vjd.*

DATE AND STAGE PERFORMANCE. This play bears a relationship both in plot and in specific passages to Marlowe's *Doctor Faustus*, and has formerly been conjectured to have been written about 1589 in order to compete with the latter by showing an English sorcerer who defeats his German rival. But we have no positive evidence for so early a date, nor is the priority of *Doctor Faustus* to *Friar Bacon* assured (cf. Introduction to *Doctor Faustus*). The emphasis on the establishment of peace in Queen Elizabeth's reign in Bacon's last speech must have been written after the defeat of the Spanish Armada in 1588, but this may be an addition written for a special performance before the Queen. The title-page of the first edition states that the play had been "plaid by her Maiesties seruants." Henslowe records a revival of the play by Lord Strange's Men at the Rose on Feb. 19, 1592, and thereafter, and another revival in April, 1594, by the combined companies of the Queen's Men and Sussex's Men. The Admiral's Men revived the play once more for the Christmas festivities at Court in 1602. Thomas Middleton received five shillings for a prologue and an epilogue to be used at this performance. The title-page of the 1630 Quarto states that the play had been "lately plaid by the Prince Palatine his Seruants." As these players were the direct successors of the Admiral's Men, it is probable that the play had an occasional performance until the closing of the theatres.

STRUCTURE. The play belongs to the "chronicle history" type, presenting a series of interesting events without definite limitation of time, place, or action. Neither acts nor scenes are marked in the early texts, and the nature of the entertainment provided is (as commonly in Greene's plays) generously varied.

SOURCE. Greene's immediate source was a prose narrative called *The Famous History of Friar Bacon*. Although the earliest surviving edition of this tract is dated 1627, the composition of the book clearly belongs to a much earlier period. The Stationers' Register bears witness to the interest in magic and witchcraft, particularly as they were practised by Bacon and Doctor Faustus, which prevailed during the last decade of Greene's life. Mr. P. Z. Round has pointed out (*Modern Language Review*, 1926, pp. 19–23) the use made by Greene of Holinshed's Chronicle.

HISTORICAL BACKGROUND. Although professing to use the material of history, this play is actually almost pure fiction. Neither the Emperor of Germany (Frederick II) nor the King of Castile (Ferdinand III) ever made a visit to England, so far as is known. Prince Edward married Elinor of Castile some sixteen years before the Crusade referred to in the play, and he was represented by proxy at the wedding. He did not ever fight before the walls of Damascus, nor did he have any historical connection with Friar Bacon. The name of Vandermast is unknown in the annals of science and magic. Warren was normally known as Earl of Surrey, not of Sussex, and there is no record of any actual person to correspond to Margaret of Fressingfield.

# ROBERT GREENE (1558–1592)

## THE HONOURABLE HISTORY OF FRIAR BACON AND FRIAR BUNGAY

[DRAMATIS PERSONAE

KING HENRY III of England (1216–1272)
EDWARD, Prince of Wales, his son
FREDERICK, Emperor of Germany
KING OF CASTILE
EDWARD LACY, Earl of Lincoln
EDWARD [or JOHN] WARREN, Earl of Sussex
WILLIAM ERMSBY, a gentleman of the Court
RALPH SIMNELL, the Court Fool

ROGER BACON, a Franciscan Friar (1215?–1292?)
BURDEN, MASON, and CLEMENT: Doctors of Oxford
FRIAR BUNGAY, a Suffolk Conjurer

JAQUES VANDERMAST, a German Conjurer
MILES, Friar Bacon's poor scholar

LAMBERT ⎫ Gentlemen of Suffolk
SERLSBY ⎭
LAMBERT, Jr. ⎫ Oxford Scholars,
SERLSBY, Jr. ⎭ sons of the above
THOMAS and RICHARD: Suffolk rustics

PRINCESS ELINOR of Castile
MARGARET, daughter of the Keeper of Fressing-field Park
JOAN, a Suffolk country wench

The Keeper of the Royal Park of Fressingfield, Suffolk; an Oxford Constable; the Hostess of the Bell Inn, Henley; a Post; Lords, Countrymen, etc.; a Devil; Spirit in shape of Hercules; a Dragon

SCENE: The English Court; Fressingfield and Harleston in Suffolk; Oxford]

[SCENE I. *Fressingfield*]

*Enter Prince Edward malcontented, with Lacy, Earl of Lincoln, John Warren, Earl of Sussex, and Ermsby, gentleman: Ralph Simnell, the King's Fool*

*Lacy.* Why looks my lord like to a troubled sky
When heaven's bright shine is shadow'd with a fog?
Alate we ran the deer, and through the launds
Stripp'd with our nags the lofty frolic bucks
That scudded 'fore the teasers like the wind. 5
Ne'er was the deer of merry Fressingfield
So lustily pull'd down by jolly mates,
Nor shar'd the farmers such fat venison,
So frankly dealt, this hundred years before;
Nor have I seen my lord more frolic in the chase, 10
And now — chang'd to a melancholy dump.
*War.* After the prince got to the Keeper's lodge,
And had been jocund in the house awhile,
Tossing off ale and milk in country cans,
Whether it was the country's sweet content, 15
Or else the bonny damsel fill'd us drink,

That seem'd so stately in her stammel red,
Or that a qualm did cross his stomach then, —
But straight he fell into his passions.
*Erms.* Sirrah Ralph, what say you to your master? 20
Shall he thus all amort live malcontent?
*Ralph.* Hearest thou, Ned? — Nay, look if he will speak to me!
*P. Edw.* What say'st thou to me, fool?
*Ralph.* I prithee, tell me, Ned, art thou in [25 love with the Keeper's daughter?
*P. Edw.* How if I be, what then?
*Ralph.* Why, then, sirrah, I'll teach thee how to deceive Love.
*P. Edw.* How, Ralph? 30
*Ralph.* Marry, Sirrah Ned, thou shalt put on my cap and my coat and my dagger, and I will put on thy clothes and thy sword; and so thou shalt be my fool.
*P. Edw.* And what of this? 35
*Ralph.* Why, so thou shalt beguile Love; for Love is such a proud scab, that he will never meddle with fools nor children. Is not Ralph's counsel good, Ned?
*P. Edw.* Tell me, Ned Lacy, didst thou mark the maid, 40
How lively in her country-weeds she look'd?

S. D. **Prince Edward**: ('Edward the First' Q 1)    ³ **Alate**: of late    **launds**: glades
⁴ **Stripp'd**: outstripped    ⁵ **teasers**: dogs used to rouse the game    ⁹ **frankly dealt**: generously distributed    ¹⁷ **stammel**: coarse woolen cloth    ²⁰ **Ralph**: (spelled 'Raphe' regularly in Q 1)
²¹ **amort**: dejected    ³⁷ **scab**: rogue

71

A bonnier wench all Suffolk cannot yield: —
All Suffolk! nay, all England holds none such.
   *Ralph.* Sirrah Will Ermsby, Ned is deceived.
   *Erms.* Why, Ralph?             45
   *Ralph.* He says all England hath no such,
and I say, and I 'll stand to it, there is one better
in Warwickshire.
   *War.* How provest thou that, Ralph?
   *Ralph.* Why, is not the abbot a learned [50
man, and hath read many books, and thinkest
thou he hath not more learning than thou to
choose a bonny wench? Yes, I warrant thee,
by his whole grammar.
   *Erms.* A good reason, Ralph.      55
   *P. Edw.* I tell thee, Lacy, that her sparkling
     eyes
Do lighten forth sweet love's alluring fire;
And in her tresses she doth fold the looks
Of such as gaze upon her golden hair;
Her bashful white, mix'd with the morning's
   red                      60
Luna doth boast upon her lovely cheeks;
Her front is beauty's table, where she paints
The glories of her gorgeous excellence;
Her teeth are shelves of precious marguerites,
Richly enclos'd with ruddy coral cleeves.  65
Tush, Lacy, she is Beauty's over-match,
If thou survey'st her curious imagery.
   *Lacy.* I grant, my lord, the damsel is as fair
As simple Suffolk's homely towns can yield;
But in the court be quainter dames than she, 70
Whose faces are enrich'd with honour's taint,
Whose beauties stand upon the stage of Fame,
And vaunt their trophies in the Courts of Love.
   *P. Edw.* Ah, Ned, but hadst thou watch'd
     her as myself,
And seen the secret beauties of the maid,  75
Their courtly coyness were but foolery.
   *Erms.* Why, how watch'd you her, my lord?
   *P. Edw.* Whenas she swept like Venus
     through the house,
And in her shape fast folded up my thoughts,
Into the milk-house went I with the maid,  80
And there amongst the cream-bowls she did
   shine
As Pallas 'mongst her princely huswifery.
She turn'd her smock over her lily arms,
And div'd them into milk to run her cheese;
But, whiter than the milk, her crystal skin, 85
Checked with lines of azure, made her blush
That art or nature durst bring for compare.
Ermsby, if thou hadst seen, as I did note it
   well,
How Beauty play'd the huswife, how this girl,
Like Lucrece, laid her fingers to the work,  90

Thou wouldst, with Tarquin, hazard Rome
   and all
To win the lovely maid of Fressingfield.
   *Ralph.* Sirrah Ned, wouldst fain have her?
   *P. Edw.* Ay, Ralph.
   *Ralph.* Why, Ned, I have laid the plot in [95
my head; thou shalt have her already.
   *P. Edw.* I 'll give thee a new coat, an thou
learn me that.
   *Ralph.* Why, Sirrah Ned, we 'll ride to Oxford to Friar Bacon. O, he is a brave scholar, [100
sirrah; they say he is a brave necromancer, that
he can make women of devils, and he can juggle
cats into costermongers.
   *P. Edw.* And how then, Ralph?
   *Ralph.* Marry, sirrah, thou shalt go to [105
him: and because thy father Harry shall not
miss thee, he shall turn me into thee; and I 'll
to the court, and I 'll prince it out; and he shall
make thee either a silken purse full of gold, or
else a fine wrought smock.          110
   *P. Edw.* But how shall I have the maid?
   *Ralph.* Marry, sirrah, if thou be'st a silken
purse full of gold, then on Sundays she 'll hang
thee by her side, and you must not say a word.
Now, sir, when she comes into a great [115
press of people, for fear of the cutpurse, on a
sudden she 'll swap thee into her plackerd;
then, sirrah, being there, you may plead for
yourself.
   *Erms.* Excellent policy!         120
   *P. Edw.* But how if I be a wrought smock?
   *Ralph.* Then she 'll put thee into her chest
and lay thee into lavender, and upon some good
day she 'll put thee on; and at night when you
go to bed, then being turned from a smock [125
to a man, you may make up the match.
   *Lacy.* Wonderfully wisely counselled, Ralph.
   *P. Edw.* Ralph shall have a new coat.
   *Ralph.* God thank you when I have it on my
back, Ned.                130
   *P. Edw.* Lacy, the fool hath laid a perfect
   plot;
For-why our country Margaret is so coy,
And stands so much upon her honest points,
That marriage or no market with the maid.
Ermsby, it must be necromantic spells  135
And charms of art that must enchain her love,
Or else shall Edward never win the girl.
Therefore, my wags, we 'll horse us in the
   morn,
And post to Oxford to this jolly friar:
Bacon shall by his magic do this deed.  140
   *War.* Content, my lord; and that 's a speedy
   way

---

<sup>62</sup> **front:** brow   **table:** tablet   <sup>64</sup> **marguerites:** pearls   <sup>65</sup> **cleeves:** cliffs   <sup>67</sup> **curious imagery:**
rare appearance   <sup>70</sup> **quainter:** more exquisite   <sup>71</sup> **honour's taint:** marks of high breeding   <sup>86</sup> **made:**
*i.e.,* would have made   <sup>97</sup> **an thou:** ('and' Q 1)   <sup>106</sup> **because:** so that   <sup>117</sup> **swap:** sweep   **plackerd:**
**placket**   <sup>132</sup> **For-why:** because   <sup>133</sup> **honest points:** points of honour

To wean these headstrong puppies from the
teat.
 *P. Edw.* I am unknown, not taken for the
prince;
They only deem us frolic courtiers,
That revel thus among our liege's game; 145
Therefore I have devis'd a policy.
Lacy, thou know'st next Friday is Saint
James',
And then the country flocks to Harleston
fair;
Then will the Keeper's daughter frolic there,
And over-shine the troop of all the maids 150
That come to see and to be seen that day.
Haunt thee disguis'd among the country-swains,
Feign th' art a farmer's son, not far from
thence,
Espy her loves, and who she liketh best;
Cote him, and court her, to control the
clown; 155
Say that the courtier tired all in green,
That help'd her handsomely to run her cheese,
And fill'd her father's lodge with venison,
Commends him, and sends fairings to herself.
Buy something worthy of her parentage, 160
Not worth her beauty; for, Lacy, then the
fair
Affords no jewel fitting for the maid.
And when thou talk'st of me, note if she
blush;
O, then she loves: but if her cheeks wax pale,
Disdain it is. Lacy, send how she fares, 165
And spare no time nor cost to win her loves.
 *Lacy.* I will, my lord, so execute this charge
As if that Lacy were in love with her.
 *P. Edw.* Send letters speedily to Oxford of
the news.
 *Ralph.* And, Sirrah Lacy, buy me a thou- [170
sand thousand million of fine bells.
 *Lacy.* What wilt thou do with them, Ralph?
 *Ralph.* Marry, every time that Ned sighs for
the Keeper's daughter, I 'll tie a bell about him;
and so within three or four days I will send [175
word to his father Harry that his son and my
master Ned is become Love's morris-dance.
 *P. Edw.* Well, Lacy, look with care unto
thy charge,
And I will haste to Oxford to the friar,
That he by art and thou by secret gifts 180
Mayst make me lord of merry Fressingfield.
 *Lacy.* God send your honour your heart's
desire.        *Exeunt.*

[SCENE II. *Friar Bacon's Cell at Brasenose
College*]

*Enter Friar Bacon, with Miles his poor Scholar,
with books under his arm; with them
Burden, Mason, Clement, three Doctors*

 *Bacon.* Miles, where are you?
 *Miles.* Hic sum, doctissime et reverendissime
doctor.
 *Bacon.* Attulisti nos libros meos de necroman-
tia? 5
 *Miles.* Ecce quam bonum et quam jucundum
habitare libros in unum!
 *Bacon.* Now, masters of our academic state,
That rule in Oxford, viceroys in your place,
Whose heads contain maps of the liberal arts, 10
Spending your time in depth of learned skill,
Why flock you thus to Bacon's secret cell,
A friar newly stall'd in Brasenose?
Say what 's your mind, that I may make reply.
 *Burd.* Bacon, we hear that long we have
suspect, 15
That thou art read in magic's mystery;
In pyromancy, to divine by flames;
To tell, by hydromantic, ebbs and tides;
By aeromancy to discover doubts,
To plain out questions, as Apollo did. 20
 *Bacon.* Well, Master Burden, what of all this?
 *Miles.* Marry, sir, he doth but fulfil, by re-
hearsing of these names, the fable of the Fox
and the Grapes; that which is above us per-
tains nothing to us. 25
 *Burd.* I tell thee, Bacon, Oxford makes re-
port,
Nay, England, and the court of Henry says,
Th' art making of a brazen head by art,
Which shall unfold strange doubts and apho-
risms,
And read a lecture in philosophy; 30
And, by the help of devils and ghastly fiends,
Thou mean'st, ere many years or days be past,
To compass England with a wall of brass.
 *Bacon.* And what of this?
 *Miles.* What of this, master! Why, he [35
doth speak mystically; for he knows, if your
skill fail to make a brazen head, yet Mother
Waters' strong ale will fit his turn to make him
have a copper nose.
 *Clem.* Bacon, we come not grieving at thy
skill, 40
But joying that our académy yields

---

 ¹⁴⁷ **Saint James':** St. James' Day (July 25)  ¹⁵⁵ **cote:** outstrip, surpass  **control:** overcome
¹⁵⁶ **tired:** attired ¹⁵⁹ **fairings:** gifts ²⁻³ Here I am, most learned and reverend doctor. ⁴⁻⁵ Have
you brought us my books of necromancy? ⁶⁻⁷ See how good and pleasant it is for books to dwell
together in one place (or in unity). (Cf. Psalm cxxxiii. 1) ⁹ **viceroys . . . place:** with viceregal
authority ¹³ **stall'd:** enstalled ¹⁵ **that . . . suspect:** what . . . suspected ¹⁸ **hydromantic:** divination by water ('Hadromaticke' Q 1) ¹⁹ **aeromancy:** divination from the air **discover doubts:**
solve difficulties ²⁰ **plain out:** explain ²⁹ **aphorisms:** statements of scientific principles

A man suppos'd the wonder of the world;
For if thy cunning work these miracles,
England and Europe shall admire thy fame,
And Oxford shall in characters of brass,        45
And statues, such as were built up in Rome,
Etérnize Friar Bacon for his art.
   *Mason.* Then, gentle friar, tell us thy intent.
   *Bacon.* Seeing you come as friends unto the
    friar,
Resolve you, doctors, Bacon can by books     50
Make storming Boreas thunder from his cave,
And dim fair Luna to a dark eclipse.
The great arch-ruler, potentate of hell,
Trembles when Bacon bids him or his fiends
Bow to the force of his pentagonon.             55
What art can work, the frolic friar knows;
And therefore will I turn my magic books,
And strain out necromancy to the deep.
I have contriv'd and fram'd a head of brass
(I made Belcephon hammer out the stuff),        60
And that by art shall read philosophy;
And I will strengthen England by my skill,
That if ten Cæsars liv'd and reign'd in Rome,
With all the legions Europe doth contain,
They should not touch a grass of English
   ground.                                      65
The work that Ninus rear'd at Babylon,
The brazen walls fram'd by Semiramis,
Carv'd out like to the portal of the sun,
Shall not be such as rings the English strand
From Dover to the market-place of Rye.          70
   *Burd.* Is this possible?
   *Miles.* I'll bring ye two or three witnesses.
   *Burd.* What be those?
   *Miles.* Marry, sir, three or four as honest
devils and good companions as any be in hell. [75
   *Mason.* No doubt but magic may do much
   in this;
For he that reads but mathematic rules
Shall find conclusions that avail to work
Wonders that pass the common sense of men.
   *Burd.* But Bacon roves a bow beyond his
   reach,                                        80
And tells of more than magic can perform,
Thinking to get a fame by fooleries.
Have I not pass'd as far in state of schools,
And read of many secrets? Yet to think
That heads of brass can utter any voice,        85
Or more, to tell of deep philosophy, —
This is a fable Æsop had forgot.
   *Bacon.* Burden, thou wrong'st me in detract-
   ing thus;
Bacon loves not to stuff himself with lies.
But tell me 'fore these doctors, if thou dare, 90
Of certain questions I shall move to thee.

   *Burd.* I will: ask what thou can.
   *Miles.* Marry, sir, he'll straight be on your
pick-pack, to know whether the feminine or
the masculine gender be most worthy.
   *Bacon.* Were you not yesterday, Master
Burden, at Henley upon the Thames?
   *Burd.* I was; what then?
   *Bacon.* What book studied you there on all
night?                                          100
   *Burd.* I! none at all; I read not there a line.
   *Bacon.* Then, doctors, Friar Bacon's art
   knows naught.
   *Clem.* What say you to this, Master Burden?
Doth he not touch you?
   *Burd.* I pass not of his frivolous speeches. 105
   *Miles.* Nay, Master Burden, my master, ere
he hath done with you, will turn you from a
doctor to a dunce, and shake you so small, that
he will leave no more learning in you than is in
Balaam's ass.                                   110
   *Bacon.* Masters, for that learned Burden's
   skill is deep,
And sore he doubts of Bacon's cabalism,
I'll show you why he haunts to Henley oft:
Not, doctors, for to taste the fragrant air,
But there to spend the night in alchemy,        115
To multiply with secret spells of art;
Thus private steals he learning from us all.
To prove my sayings true, I'll show you straight
The book he keeps at Henley for himself.
   *Miles.* Nay, now my master goes to conjura-
tion, take heed.                                121
   *Bacon.* Masters, stand still, fear not, I'll
   show you but his book. *Here he conjures.*
*Per omnes deos infernales, Belcephon!*

*Enter a Woman with a shoulder of mutton on a*
*spit, and a Devil*

   *Miles.* O master, cease your conjuration, or
you spoil all; for here's a she-devil come [125
with a shoulder of mutton on a spit. You have
marr'd the devil's supper; but no doubt he
thinks our college fare is slender, and so hath
sent you his cook with a shoulder of mutton, to
make it exceed.                                 130
   *Hostess.* O, where am I, or what's become
   of me?
   *Bacon.* What art thou?
   *Hostess.* Hostess at Henley, mistress of the
   Bell.
   *Bacon.* How camest thou here?
   *Hostess.* As I was in the kitchen 'mongst the
   maids,                                     135
Spitting the meat 'gainst supper for my guests,
A motion mov'd me to look forth of door:

---

    ⁵⁰ **Resolve you:** be assured    ⁵⁵ pentagonon: the five-starred ray used in magic ('pentageron'
Q 1)    ⁸⁰ **roves . . . reach:** shoots with a bow beyond his control    ⁸² **fame:** reputation    ⁹⁴ **pick-**
**pack:** pick-a-back, shoulders    ¹⁰⁵ **pass not of:** care not for    ¹¹² **cabalism:** mystic art    ¹²³ **Per . . .**
**infernales:** by all the infernal gods    ¹³⁶ **guests:** ('guesse' Qq.)    ¹³⁷ **motion:** impulse

No sooner had I pried into the yard,
But straight a whirlwind hoisted me from
    thence,
And mounted me aloft unto the clouds.　140
As in a trance, I thought nor feared naught,
Nor know I where or whither I was ta'en,
Nor where I am nor what these persons be.
    *Bacon.* No? Know you not Master Burden?
    *Hostess.* O, yes, good sir, he is my daily
    guest. —　145
What, Master Burden! 't was but yesternight
That you and I at Henley play'd at cards.
    *Burd.* I know not what we did. — A pox of
all conjuring friars!
    *Clem.* Now, jolly friar, tell us, is this the book
That Burden is so careful to look on?　151
    *Bacon.* It is. — But, Burden, tell me now,
Think'st thou that Bacon's necromantic skill
Cannot perform his head and wall of brass,
When he can fetch thine hostess in such
    post?　155
    *Miles.* I 'll warrant you, master, if Master
Burden could conjure as well as you, he would
have his book every night from Henley to study
on at Oxford.
    *Mason.* Burden,　160
What, are you mated by this frolic friar? —
Look how he droops; his guilty conscience
Drives him to bash, and makes his hostess
    blush.
    *Bacon.* Well, mistress, for I will not have
you miss'd,
You shall to Henley to cheer up your guests　165
'Fore supper gin. — Burden, bid her adieu;
Say farewell to your hostess 'fore she goes. —
Sirrah, away, and set her safe at home.
    *Hostess.* Master Burden, when shall we see
you at Henley?　170
            *Exeunt Hostess and the Devil.*
    *Burd.* The devil take thee and Henley too.
    *Miles.* Master, shall I make a good motion?
    *Bacon.* What 's that?
    *Miles.* Marry, sir, now that my hostess is
gone to provide supper, conjure up another [175
spirit, and send Doctor Burden flying after.
    *Bacon.* Thus, rulers of our academic state,
You have seen the friar frame his art by proof;
And as the college called Brazen-nose
Is under him, and he the master there,　180
So surely shall this head of brass be fram'd,
And yield forth strange and uncouth apho-
    risms,
And hell and Hecate shall fail the friar,
But I will circle England round with brass.
    *Miles.* So be it *et nunc et semper*, amen.　185
            *Exeunt omnes.*

[SCENE III. *Harleston Fair*]

*Enter Margaret, the fair maid of Fressingfiela,
    with Thomas and Joan, and other clowns:
    Lacy disguised in country apparel*

    *Thom.* By my troth, Margaret, here 's a
weather is able to make a man call his father
"whoreson": if this weather hold, we shall
have hay good cheap, and butter and cheese at
Harleston will bear no price.　5
    *Mar.* Thomas, maids when they come to see
    the fair
Count not to make a cope for dearth of hay;
When we have turn'd our butter to the salt,
And set our cheese safely upon the racks,
Then let our fathers price it as they please.　10
We country sluts of merry Fressingfield
Come to buy needless naughts to make us fine,
And look that young men should be frank this
    day,
And court us with such fairings as they can.
Phœbus is blithe, and frolic looks from heaven,
As when he courted lovely Semele,　16
Swearing the pedlars shall have empty packs,
If that fair weather may make chapmen buy.
    *Lacy.* But, lovely Peggy, Semele is dead,
And therefore Phœbus from his palace pries,　20
And, seeing such a sweet and seemly saint,
Shows all his glories for to court yourself.
    *Mar.* This is a fairing, gentle sir, indeed,
To soothe me up with such smooth flattery;
But learn of me, your scoff 's too broad be-
    fore. —　25
Well, Joan, our beauties must abide their jests;
We serve the turn in jolly Fressingfield.
    *Joan.* Margaret, a farmer's daughter for a
    farmer's son:
I warrant you, the meanest of us both
Shall have a mate to lead us from the church.
But, Thomas, what 's the news? What, in a
    dump?　31
Give me your hand, we are near a pedlar's
    shop;
Out with your purse, we must have fairings now.
    *Thom.* Faith, Joan, and shall. I 'll bestow a
fairing on you, and then we will to the tavern, [35
and snap off a pint of wine or two.
            *All this while Lacy whispers
            Margaret in the ear.*
    *Mar.* Whence are you, sir? Of Suffolk? For
    your terms
Are finer than the common sort of men.
    *Lacy.* Faith, lovely girl, I am of Beccles by,
Your neighbour, not above six miles from
    hence,　40

---

<sup>155</sup> **post:** haste　　<sup>161</sup> **mated:** confounded　　<sup>163</sup> **bash:** be abashed　　<sup>4</sup> **good cheap:** at a low price
<sup>7</sup> **cope:** bargain　　<sup>11</sup> **sluts:** girls　　<sup>13</sup> **frank:** generous　　<sup>18</sup> **chapmen:** shoppers　　<sup>25</sup> **scoff:** jest
**broad before:** barefaced

A farmer's son, that never was so quaint
But that he could do courtesy to such dames.
But trust me, Margaret, I am sent in charge
From him that revell'd in your father's house,
And fill'd his lodge with cheer and venison, 45
Tired in green.  He sent you this rich purse,
His token that he help'd you run your cheese,
And in the milkhouse chatted with yourself.
    *Mar.*  To me?
    *Lacy.*        You forget yourself.
    Women are often weak in memory.    50
    *Mar.*  O, pardon, sir, I call to mind the man.
'T were little manners to refuse his gift,
And yet I hope he sends it not for love;
For we have little leisure to debate of that.
    *Joan.*  What, Margaret! blush not; maids
      must have their loves.    55
    *Thom.*  Nay, by the mass, she looks pale as if
she were angry.
    *Rich.*  Sirrah, are you of Beccles?  I pray,
how doth Goodman Cob?  My father bought a
horse of him. —I 'll tell you, Margaret, 'a [60
were good to be a gentleman's jade, for of all
things the foul hilding could not abide a dung-
cart.
    *Mar.* [*Aside.*]  How different is this farmer
      from the rest
That erst as yet hath pleas'd my wand'ring
      sight!    65
His words are witty, quickened with a smile,
His courtesy gentle, smelling of the court;
Facile and debonair in all his deeds,
Proportion'd as was Paris, when, in grey,
He courted Œnon in the vale by Troy.    70
Great lords have come and pleaded for my love;
Who but the Keeper's lass of Fressingfield?
And yet methinks this farmer's jolly son
Passeth the proudest that hath pleas'd mine
    eye.
But, Peg, disclose not that thou art in love, 75
And show as yet no sign of love to him,
Although thou well wouldst wish him for thy
    love;
Keep that to thee till time doth serve thy turn,
To show the grief wherein thy heart doth
    burn. —
Come, Joan and Thomas, shall we to the
    fair? —    80
You, Beccles man, will not forsake us now?
    *Lacy.*  Not whilst I may have such quaint
    girls as you.
    *Mar.*  Well, if you chance to come by Fres-
    singfield,
Make but a step into the Keeper's lodge,
And such poor fare as woodmen can afford, 85

Butter and cheese, cream and fat venison,
You shall have store, and welcome therewithal.
    *Lacy.*  Gramercies, Peggy;  look for me ere
    long.    *Exeunt omnes.*

[SCENE IV.  *King Henry's Court*]

*Enter Henry the third, the Emperor, the King of
    Castile, Elinor, his daughter, Jaques Van-
    dermast, a German*

    *K. Hen.*  Great men of Europe, monarchs of
    the west,
Ring'd with the walls of old Oceanus,
Whose lofty surge is like the battlements
That compass'd high-built Babel in with
    towers,
Welcome, my lords, welcome, brave western
    kings,    5
To England's shore, whose promontory cleeves
Shows Albion is another little world;
Welcome says English Henry to you all;
Chiefly unto the lovely Elinor,
Who dar'd for Edward's sake cut through the
    seas,    10
And venture as Agenor's damsel through the
    deep,
To get the love of Henry's wanton son.
    *K. of Cast.*  England's rich monarch, brave
    Plantagenet,
The Pyren Mounts swelling above the clouds,
That ward the wealthy Castile in with walls, 15
Could not detain the beauteous Elinor;
But, hearing of the fame of Edward's youth,
She dar'd to brook Neptunus' haughty pride,
And bide the brunt of froward Æolus.    19
Then may fair England welcome her the more.
    *Elin.*  After that English Henry by his lords
Had sent Prince Edward's lovely counterfeit,
A present to the Castile Elinor,
The comely portrait of so brave a man,
The virtuous fame discoursed of his deeds, 25
Edward's courageous resolution,
Done at the Holy Land 'fore Damas' walls,
Led both mine eye and thoughts in equal links
To like so of the English monarch's son,
That I attempted perils for his sake.    30
    *Emp.*  Where is the prince, my lord?
    *K. Hen.*  He posted down, not long since,
    from the court,
To Suffolk side, to merry Framlingham,
To sport himself amongst my fallow deer;
From thence, by packets sent to Hampton-
    house,    35
We hear the prince is ridden with his lords
To Oxford, in the académy there

---

<sup>41</sup> **quaint:** fastidious    <sup>49</sup> **You . . . yourself:** (given to Margaret in Qq.)    <sup>62</sup> **hilding:** worthless creature    <sup>69</sup> **grey:** the color of a shepherd's garb    <sup>88</sup> **Gramercies:** thanks    <sup>3</sup> **surge is:** ('surges' Qq.)    <sup>11</sup> **Agenor's damsel:** Europa    <sup>27</sup> **Damas':** Damascus    <sup>33</sup> **Framlingham:** ('Fremingham' Qq.)    <sup>35</sup> **Hampton-house:** Hampton Court (built by Cardinal Wolsey in Henry VIII's reign)

To hear dispute amongst the learned men.
But we will send forth letters for my son,
To will him come from Oxford to the court. 40
  *Emp.* Nay, rather, Henry, let us, as we be,
Ride for to visit Oxford with our train.
Fain would I see your universities,
And what learn'd men your académy yields.
From Hapsburg have I brought a learned clerk
To hold dispute with English orators.    46
This doctor, surnam'd Jaques Vandermast,
A German born, pass'd into Padua,
To Florence and to fair Bolonia,
To Paris, Rheims, and stately Orleans,    50
And, talking there with men of art, put down
The chiefest of them all in aphorisms,
In magic, and the mathematic rules:
Now let us, Henry, try him in your schools.
  *K. Hen.* He shall, my lord; this motion likes
    me well.    55
We 'll progress straight to Oxford with our
    trains,
And see what men our académy brings. —
And, wonder Vandermast, welcome to me.
In Oxford shalt thou find a jolly friar
Call'd Friar Bacon, England's only flower:  60
Set him but nonplus in his magic spells,
And make him yield in mathematic rules,
And for thy glory I will bind thy brows,
Not with a poet's garland made of bays,
But with a coronet of choicest gold.    65
Whilst, then, we set to Oxford with our
    troops,
Let 's in and banquet in our English court.
                        *Exeunt.*

### [SCENE V. *A Street in Oxford*]

*Enter Ralph Simnell in [Prince] Edward's
    apparel; [Prince] Edward, Warren,
    Ermsby, disguised*

  *Ralph.* Where be these vagabond knaves,
that they attend no better on their master?
  *P. Edw.* If it please your honour, we are all
ready at an inch.
  *Ralph.* Sirrah Ned, I 'll have no more post-  [5
horse to ride on: I 'll have another fetch.
  *Erms.* I pray you, how is that, my lord?
  *Ralph.* Marry, sir, I 'll send to the Isle of Ely
for four or five dozen of geese, and I 'll have them
tied six and six together with whip-cord.  [10
Now upon their backs will I have a fair field-
bed with a canopy; and so, when it is my pleasure, I 'll flee into what place I please. This will
be easy.

  *War.* Your honour hath said well; but  [15
shall we to Brasenose College before we pull
off our boots?
  *Erms.* Warren, well motion'd; we will to the
    friar
Before we revel it within the town. —
Ralph, see you keep your countenance like a
    prince.    20
  *Ralph.* Wherefore have I such a company of
cutting knaves to wait upon me, but to keep
and defend my countenance against all mine
enemies? Have you not good swords and buck-
lers?    25

### *Enter Bacon and Miles*

  *Erms.* Stay, who comes here?
  *War.* Some scholar; and we 'll ask him where
Friar Bacon is.
  *Bacon.* Why, thou arrant dunce, shall I never
make thee good scholar? Doth not all the  [30
town cry out and say, Friar Bacon's subsizar is
the greatest blockhead in all Oxford? Why,
thou canst not speak one word of true Latin.
  *Miles.* No, sir? yes. What is this else? *Ego
sum tuus homo,* "I am your man": I warrant  [35
you, sir, as good Tully's phrase as any is in
Oxford.
  *Bacon.* Come on, sirrah; what part of speech
is *Ego?*
  *Miles.* Ego, that is "I"; marry, *nomen*  [40
*substantivo.*
  *Bacon.* How prove you that?
  *Miles.* Why, sir, let him prove himself an 'a
will; I can be heard, felt, and understood.
  *Bacon.* O gross dunce! *Here beat him.*  [45
  *P. Edw.* Come, let us break off this dispute
between these two. — Sirrah, where is Brase-
nose College?
  *Miles.* Not far from Coppersmith's Hall.
  *P. Edw.* What, dost thou mock me?    50
  *Miles.* Not I, sir: but what would you at
Brasenose?
  *Erms.* Marry, we would speak with Friar
Bacon.
  *Miles.* Whose men be you?    55
  *Erms.* Marry, scholar, here 's our master.
  *Ralph.* Sirrah, I am the master of these good
fellows; mayst thou not know me to be a lord
by my reparrel?    59
  *Miles.* Then here 's good game for the hawk;
for here 's the master-fool and a covey of cox-
combs. One wise man, I think, would spring
you all.
  *P. Edw.* Gog's wounds! Warren, kill him.

---

⁴⁵ **Hapsburg:** ('Hasburg' Qq.)    ⁵⁸ **wonder:** wondrous    ⁶⁶ **Whilst:** until    **set:** set out ('fit'
Q 1; 'sit' Q 2)    ⁴ **at an inch:** at any moment    ⁶ **fetch:** trick    ²² **cutting:** swaggering    ³¹ **subsizar:** a student who received free board and tuition in return for menial services (A term used at
Cambridge, not at Oxford)    ⁴⁰⁻⁴⁴ (Cf. Lyly, *Endymion,* III. iii. 8–17.)    ⁵⁹ **reparrel:** error for
"apparel"    ⁶⁴ **Gog's:** (by) God's

*War.* Why, Ned, I think the devil be in |65
my sheath; I cannot get out my dagger.

*Erms.* Nor I mine. 'Swounds, Ned, I think
I am bewitch'd.

*Miles.* A company of scabs! The proudest of
you all draw your weapon, if he can. —   70
                                        [*Aside.*]
See how boldly I speak, now my master is by.

*P. Edw.* I strive in vain; but if my sword be
shut

And conjur'd fast by magic in my sheath,
Villain, here is my fist.
                        *Strike him a box on the ear.*

*Miles.* O, I beseech you conjure his hands |75
too, that he may not lift his arms to his head, for
he is light-fingered!

*Ralph.* Ned, strike him; I 'll warrant thee by
mine honour.

*Bacon.* What means the English prince to
wrong my man?                          80

*P. Edw.* To whom speak'st thou?

*Bacon.* To thee.

*P. Edw.* Who art thou?

*Bacon.* Could you not judge when all your
swords grew fast,
That Friar Bacon was not far from hence?  85
Edward, King Henry's son and Prince of Wales,
Thy fool disguis'd cannot conceal thyself.
I know both Ermsby and the Sussex Earl.
Else Friar Bacon had but little skill.
Thou com'st in post from merry Fressing-
field,                                  90
Fast-fancied to the Keeper's bonny lass,
To crave some succour of the jolly friar;
And Lacy, Earl of Lincoln, hast thou left
To treat fair Margaret to allow thy loves.  94
But friends are men, and love can baffle lords;
The earl both woos and courts her for him-
self.

*War.* Ned, this is strange; the friar knoweth
all.

*Erms.* Apollo could not utter more than this.

*P. Edw.* I stand amaz'd to hear this jolly
friar
Tell even the very secrets of my thoughts. —
But, learned Bacon, since thou know'st the
cause                                   101
Why I did post so fast from Fressingfield,
Help, friar, at a pinch, that I may have
The love of lovely Margaret to myself,  104
And, as I am true Prince of Wales, I 'll give
Living and lands to strength thy college state.

*War.* Good friar, help the prince in this.

*Ralph.* Why, servant Ned, will not the friar
do it? Were not my sword glued to my scab-

bard by conjuration, I would cut off his |110
head, and make him do it by force.

*Miles.* In faith, my lord, your manhood and
your sword is all alike; they are so fast conjured
that we shall never see them.

*Erms.* What, doctor, in a dump? Tush, help
the prince,                            115
And thou shalt see how liberal he will prove.

*Bacon.* Crave not such actions greater dumps
than these?
I will, my lord, strain out my magic spells;
For this day comes the earl to Fressingfield,  119
And 'fore that night shuts in the day with dark,
They 'll be betrothed each to other fast.
But come with me; we 'll to my study straight,
And in a glass prospective I will show
What 's done this day in merry Fressingfield.

*P. Edw.* Gramercies, Bacon; I will quite thy
pain.                                  125

*Bacon.* But send your train, my lord, into
the town;
My scholar shall go bring them to their inn.
Meanwhile we 'll see the knavery of the earl.

*P. Edw.* Warren, leave me: — and, Ermsby,
take the fool;
Let him be master, and go revel it,    130
Till I and Friar Bacon talk awhile.

*War.* We will, my lord.

*Ralph.* Faith, Ned, and I 'll lord it out till
thou comest. I 'll be Prince of Wales over all
the black-pots in Oxford.          *Exeunt.* 135

[SCENE VI.  *Friar Bacon's Cell*]

[*Friar*] *Bacon and* [*Prince*] *Edward goes into
the study.*

*Bacon.* Now, frolic Edward, welcome to my
cell;
Here tempers Friar Bacon many toys,
And holds this place his consistory-court,
Wherein the devils pleads homage to his words.
Within this glass prospective thou shalt see   5
This day what 's done in merry Fressingfield
'Twixt lovely Peggy and the Lincoln Earl.

*P. Edw.* Friar, thou glad'st me. Now shall
Edward try
How Lacy meaneth to his sovereign lord.

*Bacon.* Stand there and look directly in the
glass.                                 10

*Enter Margaret and Friar Bungay*

What sees my lord?

*P. Edw.* I see the Keeper's lovely lass
appear,
As brightsome as the paramour of Mars,

---

⁹¹ **Fast-fancied:** tied by love    ⁹⁴ **treat:** entreat    ¹²³ **glass prospective:** a magical glass which
reflected distant or future events    ¹²⁵ **quite:** requite    ¹³⁵ **black-pots:** leathern ale-jugs    Scene
VI s. d. (The shift of scene is effected by the stepping of Bacon and Edward from the outer to the
rear stage.)    ¹³ **brightsome:** ('bright-sunne' Qq.)

Only attended by a jolly friar.
*Bacon.* Sit still, and keep the crystal in your
    eye.    15
*Mar.* But tell me, Friar Bungay, is it true
That this fair courteous country swain,
Who says his father is a farmer nigh,
Can be Lord Lacy, Earl of Lincolnshire?
*Bun.* Peggy, 't is true, 't is Lacy for my
    life,    20
Or else mine art and cunning both doth fail,
Left by Prince Edward to procure his loves;
For he in green, that holp you run your cheese,
Is son to Henry and the Prince of Wales.
*Mar.* Be what he will, his lure is but for
    lust.    25
But did Lord Lacy like poor Margaret,
Or would he deign to wed a country lass,
Friar, I would his humble handmaid be,
And for great wealth quite him with cour-
    tesy.    29
*Bun.* Why, Margaret, dost thou love him?
*Mar.* His personage, like the pride of vaunt-
    ing Troy,
Might well avouch to shadow Helen's rape:
His wit is quick and ready in conceit,
As Greece afforded in her chiefest prime:
Courteous, ah friar, full of pleasing smiles!    35
Trust me, I love too much to tell thee more;
Suffice to me he 's England's paramour.
*Bun.* Hath not each eye that view'd thy
    pleasing face
Surnamed thee Fair Maid of Fressingfield?
*Mar.* Yes, Bungay; and would God the
    lovely earl    40
Had that in *esse* that so many sought.
*Bun.* Fear not, the friar will not be behind
To show his cunning to entangle love.
*P. Edw.* I think the friar courts the bonny
    wench;
Bacon, methinks he is a lusty churl.    45
*Bacon.* Now look, my lord.

*Enter Lacy [disguised as before]*

*P. Edw.* Gog's wounds, Bacon, here comes
    Lacy!
*Bacon.* Sit still, my lord, and mark the
    comedy.
*Bun.* Here 's Lacy, Margaret; step aside
    awhile.    [*They withdraw.*]
*Lacy.* Daphne, the damsel that caught
    Phœbus fast,    51
And lock'd him in the brightness of her looks,
Was not so beauteous in Apollo's eyes
As is fair Margaret to the Lincoln Earl.
Recant thee, Lacy, thou art put in trust:    55
Edward, thy sovereign's son, hath chosen thee,
A secret friend, to court her for himself,

And dar'st thou wrong thy prince with treach-
    ery?
Lacy, love makes no exception of a friend,
Nor deems it of a prince but as a man.    60
Honour bids thee control him in his lust;
His wooing is not for to wed the girl,
But to entrap her and beguile the lass.
Lacy, thou lov'st, then brook not such abuse,
But wed her, and abide thy prince's frown;    65
For better die than see her live disgrac'd.
*Mar.* Come, friar, I will shake him from his
    dumps. —    [*Comes forward.*]
How cheer you, sir? A penny for your thought!
You 're early up, pray God it be the near.
What, come from Beccles in a morn so soon?    70
*Lacy.* Thus watchful are such men as live in
    love,
Whose eyes brook broken slumbers for their
    sleep.
I tell thee, Peggy, since last Harleston fair
My mind hath felt a heap of passions.
*Mar.* A trusty man, that court it for your
    friend.    75
Woo you still for the courtier all in green?
I marvel that he sues not for himself.
*Lacy.* Peggy,
I pleaded first to get your grace for him;
But when mine eyes survey'd your beauteous
    looks,    80
Love, like a wag, straight div'd into my heart,
And there did shrine the idea of yourself.
Pity me, though I be a farmer's son,
And measure not my riches, but my love.    84
*Mar.* You are very hasty; for to garden well,
Seeds must have time to sprout before they
    spring:
Love ought to creep as doth the dial's shade,
For timely ripe is rotten too-too soon.
*Bun.* [*Coming forward.*] *Deus hic;* room for a
    merry friar!
What, youth of Beccles, with the Keeper's
    lass?    90
'T is well; but tell me, hear you any news?
*Mar.* No, friar. What news?
*Bun.* Hear you not how the pursuivants do
    post
With proclamations through each country-
    town?    94
*Lacy.* For what, gentle friar? Tell the news.
*Bun.* Dwell'st thou in Beccles, and hear'st
    not of these news?
Lacy, the Earl of Lincoln, is late fled
From Windsor court, disguised like a swain,
And lurks about the country here unknown.
Henry suspects him of some treachery,    100
And therefore doth proclaim in every way,
That who can take the Lincoln Earl shall have,

---

²⁹ **for:** in place of    ³² **shadow:** excuse    **rape:** ('cape' Qq.)    ⁶⁹ **near:** nearer (to your purpose)
³¹ **wag:** mischievous child    ⁸⁸ **timely:** prematurely    ⁸⁹ **Deus hic:** may God be here

Paid in the Exchequer, twenty thousand crowns.

*Lacy.*   The Earl of Lincoln! Friar, thou art
  mad.

It was some other; thou mistak'st the man. 105
The Earl of Lincoln! Why, it cannot be.

*Mar.*   Yes, very well, my lord, for you are he:
The Keeper's daughter took you prisoner.
Lord Lacy, yield, I 'll be your gaoler once.

*P. Edw.*   How familiar they be, Bacon! 110

*Bacon.*   Sit still, and mark the sequel of their
  loves.

*Lacy.*   Then am I double prisoner to thyself.
Peggy, I yield. But are these news in jest?

*Mar.*   In jest with you, but earnest unto me;
For-why these wrongs do wring me at the
  heart.                                       115
Ah, how these earls and noblemen of birth
Flatter and feign to forge poor women's ill!

*Lacy.*   Believe me, lass, I am the Lincoln
  Earl;
I not deny but, tired thus in rags,
I liv'd disguis'd to win fair Peggy's love.   120

*Mar.*   What love is there where wedding ends
  not love?

*Lacy.*   I meant. fair girl, to make thee Lacy's
  wife.

*Mar.*   I little think that earls will stoop so low.

*Lacy.*   Say, shall I make thee countess ere I
  sleep?

*Mar.*   Handmaid unto the earl, so please himself;                                        125
A wife in name, but servant in obedience.

*Lacy.*   The Lincoln Countess, for it shall be so:
I 'll plight the bands, and seal it with a kiss.

*P. Edw.*   Gog's wounds, Bacon, they kiss!
I 'll stab them.                              130

*Bacon.*   O, hold your hands, my lord, it is the
  glass!

*P. Edw.*   Choler to see the traitors gree so
  well
Made me think the shadows substances.

*Bacon.*   'T were a long poniard, my lord, to
  reach between
Oxford and Fressingfield; but sit still and see
  more.                                        135

*Bun.*   Well, Lord of Lincoln, if your loves be
  knit.
And that your tongues and thoughts do both
  agree,
To avoid ensuing jars, I 'll hamper up the
  match.
I 'll take my portace forth and wed you
  here:
Then go to bed and seal up your desires.      140

*Lacy.*   Friar, content. — Peggy, how like
  you this?

*Mar.*   What likes my lord is pleasing unto me.

*Bun.*   Then hand-fast hand, and I will to my
  book.

*Bacon.*   What sees my lord now?

*P. Edw.*   Bacon, I see the lovers hand in
  hand,                                        145
The friar ready with his portace there
To wed them both: then am I quite undone.
Bacon, help now, if e'er thy magic serv'd;
Help, Bacon! Stop the marriage now,
If devils or necromancy may suffice,          150
And I will give thee forty thousand crowns.

*Bacon.*   Fear not, my lord, I 'll stop the jolly
  friar
For mumbling up his orisons this day.

*Lacy.*   Why speak'st not, Bungay? Friar, to
  thy book.

     *Bungay is mute, crying,* "Hud, hud."

*Mar.*   How look'st thou, friar, as a man dis-
  traught?                                     155
Reft of thy senses, Bungay? Show by signs,
If thou be dumb, what passions holdeth thee.

*Lacy.*   He 's dumb indeed. Bacon hath with
  his devils
Enchanted him, or else some strange disease
Or apoplexy hath possess'd his lungs.         160
But, Peggy, what he cannot with his book,
We 'll 'twixt us both unite it up in heart.

*Mar.*   Else let me die, my lord, a miscreant.

*P. Edw.*   Why stands Friar Bungay so
  amaz'd?

*Bacon.*   I have struck him dumb, my lord;
  and, if your honour please,                  165
I 'll fetch this Bungay straightway from Fressingfield,
And he shall dine with us in Oxford here.

*P. Edw.*   Bacon, do that, and thou contentest
  me.

*Lacy.*   Of courtesy, Margaret, let us lead the
  friar
Unto thy father's lodge, to comfort him       170
With broths, to bring him from this hapless
  trance.

*Mar.*   Or else, my lord, we were passing unkind
To leave the friar so in his distress.

*Enter a Devil, and carry Bungay on his back.*

O, help, my lord! a devil, a devil, my lord!
Look how he carries Bungay on his back!       175
Let 's hence, for Bacon's spirits be abroad.
                                  *Exeunt.*

*P. Edw.*   Bacon, I laugh to see the jolly friar
Mounted upon the devil, and how the earl
Flees with his bonny lass for fear.
As soon as Bungay is at Brasenose,            180
And I have chatted with the merry friar,
I will in post hie me to Fressingfield,

---

¹¹⁹ **tired:** attired   ¹³⁸ **jars:** discord, quarrels   **hamper:** fasten   ¹³⁹ **portace:** breviary   ¹⁴³ **hand-fast:** clasp   ¹⁵³ **For:** from   ¹⁶⁴ **Bungay:** ('Bacon' Qq.)

And quite these wrongs on Lacy ere 't be long.
*Bacon.* So be it, my lord; but let us to our
dinner;
For ere we have taken our repast awhile,    185
We shall have Bungay brought to Brasenose.
                                        *Exeunt.*

[SCENE VII.    *The Regent-house at Oxford*]

*Enter three doctors, Burden, Mason, Clement*

*Mason.*  Now that we are gather'd in the
Regent-house,
It fits us talk about the king's repair,
For he, trooped with all the western kings,
That lie alongst the Dantzic seas by east,
North by the clime of frosty Germany,    5
The Almain monarch, and the Saxon duke,
Castile and lovely Elinor with him,
Have in their gests resolv'd for Oxford town.
*Burd.*  We must lay plots of stately tragedies.
Strange comic shows, such as proud Roscius    10
Vaunted before the Roman emperors,
To welcome all the western potentates.
*Clem.*  But more; the king by letters hath
foretold
That Frederick, the Almain emperor,
Hath brought with him a German of esteem,    15
Whose surname is Don Jaques Vandermast,
Skilful in magic and those secret arts.
*Mason.*  Then must we all make suit unto
the friar,
To Friar Bacon, that he vouch this task,
And undertake to countervail in skill    20
The German; else there 's none in Oxford can
Match and dispute with learned Vandermast.
*Burd.*  Bacon, if he will hold the German
play,
Will teach him what an English friar can do.
The devil, I think, dare not dispute with him.    25
*Clem.*  Indeed, Mas doctor, he displeasur'd
you,
In that he brought your hostess with her spit
From Henley, posting unto Brasenose.
*Burd.*  A vengeance on the friar for his pains!
But leaving that, let 's hie to Bacon straight,    30
To see if he will take this task in hand.
*Clem.*  Stay, what rumour is this?  The town
is up in a mutiny.  What hurly-burly is this?

*Enter a Constable, with Ralph, Warren, Ermsby
[all three disguised as before], and Miles*

*Cons.*  Nay, masters, if you were ne'er so
good, you shall before the doctors to answer [35
your misdemeanour.

*Burd.*  What's the matter, fellow?
*Cons.*  Marry, sir, here's a company of
rufflers, that, drinking in the tavern, have made
a great brawl, and almost killed the vintner.  40
*Miles.*  *Salve*, Doctor Burden!
This lubberly lurden,
Ill-shap'd and ill-faced,
Disdain'd and disgraced,
What he tells unto *vobis*    45
*Mentitur de nobis.*
*Burd.*  Who is the master and chief of this
crew?
*Miles.*  *Ecce asinum mundi*
*Figura rotundi*,    50
Neat, sheat, and fine,
As brisk as a cup of wine.
*Burd.*  What are you?
*Ralph.*  I am, father doctor, as a man would
say, the bell-wether of this company; these [55
are my lords, and I the Prince of Wales.
*Clem.*  Are you Edward, the king's son?
*Ralph.*  Sirrah Miles, bring hither the tapster
that drew the wine, and, I warrant, when they
see how soundly I have broke his head, [60
they'll say 't was done by no less man than a
prince.
*Mason.*  I cannot believe that this is the
Prince of Wales.
*War.*  And why so, sir?    65
*Mason.*  For they say the prince is a brave
and a wise gentleman.
*War.*  Why, and think'st thou, doctor, that
he is not so?
Dar'st thou detract and derogate from him,
Being so lovely and so brave a youth?    70
*Erms.*  Whose face, shining with many a
sug'red smile,
Bewrays that he is bred of princely race.
*Miles.*  And yet, master doctor,
To speak like a proctor,
And tell unto you    75
What is veriment and true;
To cease of this quarrel,
Look but on his apparel;
Then mark but my talis,
He is great Prince of Walis,    80
The chief of our *gregis*,
And *filius regis*:
Then 'ware what is done,
For he is Henry's white son.
*Ralph.*  Doctors, whose doting night-caps [85
are not capable of my ingenious dignity, know
that I am Edward Plantagenet, whom if you

---

¹ **Regent-house:** meeting place of the governing board of the university    ² **repair:** visit    ⁶ **Saxon:**
('Scocon' Q 1)    ⁸ **gests:** itinerary of a royal progress    ¹² **To . . . potentates:** (Qq. give to Clement)    ¹⁹ **vouch:** deign to do    ²⁴ **Will:** ('Weele' Qq.)    ²⁶ **displeasur'd:** ('pleasured' Qq.)
³² **rumour:** noise    ³⁹ **rufflers:** bullies    ⁴¹ **Salve:** hail    ⁴² **lubberly lurden:** lazy, worthless fellow
⁴⁶ **Mentitur de nobis:** he lies about us    ⁴⁹⁻⁵⁰ **Ecce . . . rotundi:** Lo, the ass of the world, round in shape.
('Fugura' Q 1)    ⁵¹ **sheat:** trim    ⁸¹ **gregis:** band    ⁸² **filius regis:** king's son    ⁸⁴ **white:** darling

displease will make a ship that shall hold all your
colleges, and so carry away the Niniversity with
a fair wind to the Bankside in Southwark. [90
— How say'st thou, Ned Warren, shall I not
do it?

*War.* Yes, my good lord; and, if it please
your lordship, I will gather up all your old
pantofles, and with the cork make you a [95
pinnace of five-hundred ton, that shall serve
the turn marvellous well, my lord.

*Erms.* And I, my lord, will have pioners to
undermine the town, that the very gardens and
orchards be carried away for your summer- [100
walks.

*Miles.* And I, with *scientia*
And great *diligentia*,
Will conjure and charm,
To keep you from harm;                          105
That *utrum horum mavis*,
Your very great *navis*,
Like Barclay's ship,
From Oxford do skip
With colleges and schools,                       110
Full-loaden with fools.
*Quid dicis ad hoc,*
Worshipful *Domine* Dawcock?

*Clem.* Why, hare-brain'd courtiers, are you
    drunk or mad,
To taunt us up with such scurrility?             115
Deem you us men of base and light esteem,
To bring us such a fop for Henry's son? —
Call out the beadles and convey them hence
Straight to Bocardo: let the roisters lie
Close clapp'd in bolts, until their wits be tame.

*Erms.* Why, shall we to prison, my lord? 121

*Ralph.* What say'st, Miles, shall I honour
the prison with my presence?

*Miles.* No, no: out with your blades,
And hamper these jades;                          125
Have a flurt and a crash,
Now play revel-dash,
And teach these sacerdos
That the Bocardos,
Like peasants and elves,                         130
Are meet for themselves.

*Mason.* To the prison with them, constable.

*War.* Well, doctors, seeing I have sported
    me
With laughing at these mad and merry wags,
Know that Prince Edward is at Brasenose, 135
And this, attired like the Prince of Wales,
Is Ralph, King Henry's only loved fool;
I, Earl of Sussex, and this Ermsby,
One of the privy-chamber to the king;

Who, while the prince with Friar Bacon stays,
Have revell'd it in Oxford as you see.       141

*Mason.* My lord, pardon us, we knew not
    what you were:
But courtiers may make greater scapes than
    these.
Wilt please your honour dine with me to-day?

*War.* I will, Master doctor, and satisfy   [145
the vintner for his hurt; only I must desire you
to imagine him all this forenoon the Prince of
Wales.

*Mason.* I will, sir.

*Ralph.* And upon that I will lead the way; [150
only I will have Miles go before me, because I
have heard Henry say that wisdom must go before majesty.                        *Exeunt omnes.*

[SCENE VIII.  *Fressingfield*]

*Enter Prince Edward with his poniard in his
hand, Lacy, and Margaret*

*P. Edw.* Lacy, thou canst not shroud thy
    traitorous thoughts,
Nor cover, as did Cassius, all his wiles;
For Edward hath an eye that looks as far
As Lynceus from the shores of Græcia.
Did not I sit in Oxford by the friar,             5
And see thee court the maid of Fressingfield,
Sealing thy flattering fancies with a kiss?
Did not proud Bungay draw his portace forth,
And, joining hand in hand, had married you,
If Friar Bacon had not struck him dumb,    10
And mounted him upon a spirit's back,
That we might chat at Oxford with the friar?
Traitor, what answer'st? Is not all this true?

*Lacy.* Truth all, my lord; and thus I make
    reply:
At Harleston fair, there courting for your grace,
Whenas mine eye survey'd her curious shape, 16
And drew the beauteous glory of her looks
To dive into the centre of my heart,
Love taught me that your honour did but jest,
That princes were in fancy but as men;      20
How that the lovely maid of Fressingfield
Was fitter to be Lacy's wedded wife
Than concubine unto the Prince of Wales.

*P. Edw.* Injurious Lacy, did I love thee
    more
Than Alexander his Hephæstion?              25
Did I unfold the passions of my love,
And lock them in the closet of thy thoughts?
Wert thou to Edward second to himself,
Sole friend, and partner of his secret loves?
And could a glance of fading beauty break    30

---

⁹⁵ **pantofles:** slippers (with cork soles)    ⁹⁸ **pioners:** diggers    ¹⁰⁸ **Barclay's ship:** The Ship of
Fools    (Qq., 'Bartlets,' perhaps intentionally)    ¹¹² **Quid . . . hoc:** What do you say to this?
¹¹⁹ **Bocardo:** the prison in the old north gate of Oxford    ¹²⁶ **flurt:** flourish    ¹²⁸ **sacerdos:** priests
(apparently for the rhyme)    ¹³⁸ **Sussex:** ('Essex' Qq.)    ¹⁴³ **scapes:** escapades    ¹⁶ **curious:** rare
²⁰ **fancy:** love    ²⁶ **passions:** ('passion' Q 1)

Th' enchained fetters of such private friends?
Base coward, false, and too effeminate
To be corrival with a prince in thoughts!
From Oxford have I posted since I din'd,
To quite a traitor 'fore that Edward sleep.    35
    *Mar.* 'T was I, my lord, not Lacy stept awry:
For oft he su'd and courted for yourself,
And still woo'd for the courtier all in green;
But I, whom fancy made but over-fond,
Pleaded myself with looks as if I lov'd;    40
I fed mine eye with gazing on his face,
And still bewitch'd lov'd Lacy with my looks;
My heart with sighs, mine eyes pleaded with
    tears,
My face held pity and content at once,
And more I could not cipher out by signs,    45
But that I lov'd Lord Lacy with my heart.
Then, worthy Edward, measure with thy mind
If women's favours will not force men fall,
If beauty, and if darts of piercing love,
Is not of force to bury thoughts of friends.    50
    *P. Edw.* I tell thee, Peggy, I will have thy
    loves:
Edward or none shall conquer Margaret.
In frigates bottom'd with rich Sethin planks,
Topp'd with the lofty firs of Lebanon,
Stemm'd and incas'd with burnish'd ivory,    55
And over-laid with plates of Persian wealth,
Like Thetis shalt thou wanton on the waves,
And draw the dolphins to thy lovely eyes,
To dance lavoltas in the purple streams;
Sirens, with harps and silver psalteries,    60
Shall wait with music at thy frigate's stem,
And entertain fair Margaret with their lays.
England and England's wealth shall wait on
    thee;
Britain shall bend unto her prince's love,
And do due homage to thine excellence,    65
If thou wilt be but Edward's Margaret.
    *Mar.* Pardon, my lord: if Jove's great royalty
Sent me such presents as to Danaë;
If Phœbus, tired in Latona's webs,
Come courting from the beauty of his lodge; 70
The dulcet tunes of frolic Mercury, —
Not all the wealth heaven's treasury affords
Should make me leave Lord Lacy or his love.
    *P. Edw.* I have learn'd at Oxford, then, this
    point of schools, —
*Ablata causa, tollitur effectus:*    75
Lacy, the cause that Margaret cannot love
Nor fix her liking on the English prince,
Take him away, and then the effects will fail.
Villain, prepare thyself; for I will bathe
My poniard in the bosom of an earl.    80
    *Lacy.* Rather than live, and miss fair Mar-
    garet's love,

Prince Edward, stop not at the fatal doom,
But stab it home: end both my loves and life.
    *Mar.* Brave Prince of Wales, honour'd for
    royal deeds,
'T were sin to stain fair Venus' courts with
    blood;    85
Love's conquests ends, my lord, in courtesy.
Spare Lacy, gentle Edward; let me die,
For so both you and he do cease your loves.
    *P. Edw.* Lacy shall die as traitor to his lord.
    *Lacy.* I have deserv'd it, Edward; act it
    well.    90
    *Mar.* What hopes the prince to gain by
    Lacy's death?
    *P. Edw.* To end the loves 'twixt him and
    Margaret.
    *Mar.* Why, thinks King Henry's son that
    Margaret's love
Hangs in the uncertain balance of proud time?
That death shall make a discord of our
    thoughts?    95
No, stab the earl, and, 'fore the morning sun
Shall vaunt him thrice over the lofty east,
Margaret will meet her Lacy in the heavens.
    *Lacy.* If aught betides to lovely Margaret
That wrongs or wrings her honour from con-
    tent,    100
Europe's rich wealth nor England's monarchy
Shall not allure Lacy to over-live.
Then, Edward, short my life, and end her loves.
    *Mar.* Rid me, and keep a friend worth
    many loves.
    *Lacy.* Nay, Edward, keep a love worth
    many friends.    105
    *Mar.* An if thy mind be such as fame hath
    blaz'd,
Then, princely Edward, let us both abide
The fatal resolution of thy rage.
Banish thou fancy and embrace revenge,
And in one tomb knit both our carcases,    110
Whose hearts were linked in one perfect love.
    *P. Edw.* [*Aside.*] Edward, art thou that
    famous Prince of Wales,
Who at Damasco beat the Saracens,
And brought'st home triumph on thy lance's
    point?
And shall thy plumes by pull'd by Venus
    down?    115
Is 't princely to dissever lovers' leagues,
To part such friends as glory in their loves?
Leave, Ned, and make a virtue of this fault,
And further Peg and Lacy in their loves:
So in subduing fancy's passion,    120
Conquering thyself, thou gett'st the richest
    spoil. —
Lacy, rise up. Fair Peggy, here 's my hand.

---

³³ **corrival:** equal    ⁵³ **Sethin:** Shittim, acacia    ⁵⁹ **lavoltas:** lively dances    ⁶² **their:** ('her' Qq.)
⁶⁹ **tired:** attired ('tied' Qq.)    **webs:** fabrics    ⁷⁰ **lodge:** *i.e.,* palace of the sun    ⁷⁵ "The cause
having been removed, the effect is removed."    ¹⁰² **over-live:** live after (her)    ¹⁰⁴ **Rid:** get rid of

The Prince of Wales hath conquer'd all his
    thoughts,
And all his loves he yields unto the earl.
Lacy, enjoy the maid of Fressingfield;    125
Make her thy Lincoln Countess at the church,
And Ned, as he is true Plantagenet,
Will give her to thee frankly for thy wife.
    *Lacy.* Humbly I take her of my sover-
    eign,
As if that Edward gave me England's right, 130
And rich'd me with the Albion diadem.
    *Mar.* And doth the English prince mean
    true?
Will he vouchsafe to cease his former loves,
And yield the title of a country maid
Unto Lord Lacy?    135
    *P. Edw.* I will, fair Peggy, as I am true
    lord.
    *Mar.* Then, lordly sir, whose conquest is as
    great,
In conquering love, as Cæsar's victories,
Margaret, as mild and humble in her thoughts
As was Aspasia unto Cyrus' self,    140
Yields thanks, and, next Lord Lacy, doth en-
    shrine
Edward the second secret in her heart.
    *P. Edw.* Gramercy, Peggy. Now that vows
    are past,
And that your loves are not to be revolt,
Once, Lacy, friends again. Come, we will
    post
To Oxford; for this day the king is there,    146
And brings for Edward Castile Elinor.
Peggy, I must go see and view my wife:
I pray God I like her as I lov'd thee.
Beside, Lord Lincoln, we shall hear dispute 150
'Twixt Friar Bacon and learned Vander-
    mast.
Peggy, we 'll leave you for a week or two.
    *Mar.* As it please Lord Lacy; but love's
    foolish looks
Think footsteps miles and minutes to be hours.
    *Lacy.* I 'll hasten, Peggy, to make short
    return. —    155
But please your honour go unto the lodge,
We shall have butter, cheese, and venison;
And yesterday I brought for Margaret
A lusty bottle of neat claret-wine;
Thus can we feast and entertain your grace. 160
    *P. Edw.* 'T is cheer, Lord Lacy, for an em-
    peror,
If he respect the person and the place.
Come, let us in; for I will all this night
Ride post until I come to Bacon's cell.
                            *Exeunt.*

[SCENE IX. *Oxford*]

*Enter* [*King*] *Henry, Emperor, Castile, Elinor,*
    *Vandermast, Bungay*

    *Emp.* Trust me, Plantagenet, these Oxford
    schools
Are richly seated near the river-side:
The mountains full of fat and fallow deer,
The battling pastures laid with kine and
    flocks,
The town gorgeous with high-built colleges,    5
And scholars seemly in their grave attire,
Learned in searching principles of art. —
What is thy judgment, Jacques Vandermast?
    *Van.* That lordly are the buildings of the
    town,    9
Spacious the rooms, and full of pleasant walks;
But for the doctors, how that they be learned,
It may be meanly, for aught I can hear.
    *Bun.* I tell thee, German, Hapsburg holds
    none such,
None read so deep as Oxenford contains.
There are within our academic state    15
Men that may lecture it in Germany
To all the doctors of your Belgic schools.
    *K. Hen.* Stand to him, Bungay, charm this
    Vandermast,
And I will use thee as a royal king.
    *Van.* Wherein darest thou dispute with
    me?    20
    *Bun.* In what a doctor and a friar can.
    *Van.* Before rich Europe's worthies put thou
    forth
The doubtful question unto Vandermast.
    *Bun.* Let it be this, — Whether the spirits
of pyromancy or geomancy be most predomi- [25
nant in magic?
    *Van.* I say, of pyromancy.
    *Bun.* And I, of geomancy.
    *Van.* The cabalists that write of magic
    spells,
As Hermes, Melchie, and Pythagoras,    30
Affirm that, 'mongst the quadruplicity
Of elemental essence, *terra* is but thought
To be a *punctum* squared to the rest;
And that the compass of ascending elements
Exceed in bigness as they do in height;    35
Judging the concave circle of the sun
To hold the rest in his circumference.
If, then, as Hermes says, the fire be great'st,
Purest, and only giveth shapes to spirits,
Then must these dæmones that haunt that place
Be every way superior to the rest.    41
    *Bun.* I reason not of elemental shapes,

---

¹⁴⁰ **Aspasia, Cyrus:** (from Plutarch's Life of Artaxerxes)    ¹⁴² **secret:** sanctuary    ¹⁴⁴ **to be:**
('be' Q 1)    **revolt:** overturned    ¹⁶² **respect:** consider    ⁴ **battling:** fattening    **laid:** covered
³⁰ **Hermes:** Hermes Trismegistus    **Melchie:** Porphyry, a neo-Platonist, author of a life of Pythagoras and works on magic    ³³ **punctum:** atom    **squared to:** compared to

Nor tell I of the concave latitudes,
Noting their essence nor their quality,
But of the spirits that pyromancy calls,    45
And of the vigour of the geomantic fiends.
I tell thee, German, magic haunts the ground,
And those strange necromantic spells,
That work such shows and wondering in the
    world,
Are acted by those geomantic spirits    50
That Hermes calleth *terræ filii*.
The fiery spirits are but transparent shades,
That lightly pass as heralds to bear news;
But earthly fiends, clos'd in the lowest deep,
Dissever mountains, if they be but charg'd,    55
Being more gross and massy in their power.
    *Van.* Rather these earthly geomantic spirits
Are dull and like the place where they re-
    main;
For when proud Lucifer fell from the heavens,
The spirits and angels that did sin with him,    60
Retain'd their local essence as their faults,
All subject under Luna's continent.
They which offended less hang in the fire,
And second faults did rest within the air;
But Lucifer and his proud-hearted fiends    65
Were th.own into the centre of the earth,
Having less understanding than the rest,
As having greater sin and lesser grace.
Therefore such gross and earthly spirits do serve
For jugglers, witches, and vild sorcerers;    70
Whereas the pyromantic genii
Are mighty, swift, and of far-reaching power.
But grant that geomancy hath most force;
Bungay, to please these mighty potentates,
Prove by some instance what thy art can do.    75
    *Bun.* I will.
    *Emp.* Now, English Harry, here begins the
    game;
We shall see sport between these learned men.
    *Van.* What wilt thou do?
    *Bun.* Show thee the tree, leav'd with refined
    gold,    80
Whereon the fearful dragon held his seat,
That watch'd the garden call'd Hesperides,
Subdu'd and won by conquering Hercules.
    *Van.* Well done!

*Here Bungay conjures, and the tree appears
    with the dragon shooting fire.*

    *K. Hen.* What say you, royal lordings, to my
    friar?    85
Hath he not done a point of cunning skill?
    *Van.* Each scholar in the necromantic spells
Can do as much as Bungay hath perform'd.
But as Alcmena's bastard raz'd this tree,
So will I raise him up as when he liv'd,    90
And cause him pull the dragon from his seat,

And tear the branches piecemeal from the root.
Hercules! *Prodi, prodi*, Hercules!

*Hercules appears in his lion's skin.*

    *Her.* *Quis me vult?*
    *Van.* Jove's bastard son, thou Libyan Her-
    cules,    95
Pull off the sprigs from off the Hesperian tree,
As once thou didst to win the golden fruit.
    *Her.* *Fiat.*
        [*Here he begins to break the branches.*
    *Van.* Now, Bungay, if thou canst by magic
    charm
The fiend, appearing like great Hercules,    100
From pulling down the branches of the tree,
Then art thou worthy to be counted learned.
    *Bun.* I cannot.
    *Van.* Cease, Hercules, until I give thee
    charge. —
Mighty commander of this English isle,    105
Henry, come from the stout Plantagenets,
Bungay is learn'd enough to be a friar;
But to compare with Jaques Vandermast,
Oxford and Cambridge must go seek their cells
To find a man to match him in his art.    110
I have given non-plus to the Paduans,
To them of Sien, Florence, and Bologna,
Rheims, Louvain, and fair Rotterdam,
Frankfort, Lutetia, and Orleans:
And now must Henry, if he do me right,    115
Crown me with laurel, as they all have done.

*Enter Bacon*

    *Bacon.* All hail to this royal company,
That sit to hear and see this strange dispute! —
Bungay, how stand'st thou as a man amaz'd?
What, hath the German acted more than
    thou?    120
    *Van.* What art thou that questions thus?
    *Bacon.* Men call me Bacon.
    *Van.* Lordly thou look'st, as if that thou
    wert learn'd;
Thy countenance as if science held her seat
Between the circled arches of thy brows.    125
    *K. Hen.* Now, monarchs, hath the German
    found his match.
    *Emp.* Bestir thee, Jaques, take not now the
    foil,
Lest thou dost lose what foretime thou didst
    gain.
    *Van.* Bacon, wilt thou dispute?
    *Bacon.* No,    130
Unless he were more learn'd than Vandermast:
For yet, tell me, what hast thou done?
    *Van.* Rais'd Hercules to ruinate that tree
That Bungay mounted by his magic spells.
    *Bacon.* Set Hercules to work.    135

*Van.* Now, Hercules, I charge thee to thy task;
Pull off the golden branches from the root.
*Her.* I dare not. See'st thou not great Bacon here,
Whose frown doth act more than thy magic can?
*Van.* By all the thrones, and dominations, 140
Virtues, powers, and mighty hierarchies,
I charge thee to obey to Vandermast.
*Her.* Bacon, that bridles headstrong Belcephon,
And rules Asmenoth, guider of the north,
Binds me from yielding unto Vandermast. 145
*K. Hen.* How now, Vandermast! Have you met with your match?
*Van.* Never before was 't known to Vandermast
That men held devils in such obedient awe.
Bacon doth more than art, or else I fail. 150
*Emp.* Why, Vandermast, art thou overcome? —
Bacon, dispute with him, and try his skill.
*Bacon.* I come not, monarchs, for to hold dispute
With such a novice as is Vandermast;
I come to have your royalties to dine 155
With Friar Bacon here in Brasenose;
And, for this German troubles but the place,
And holds this audience with a long suspense,
I 'll send him to his académy hence. — 159
Thou Hercules, whom Vandermast did raise,
Transport the German unto Hapsburg straight,
That he may learn by travail, 'gainst the spring,
More secret dooms and aphorisms of art.
Vanish the tree, and thou away with him!
*Exit the spirit with Vandermast and the tree.*
*Emp.* Why, Bacon, whither dost thou send him? 165
*Bacon.* To Hapsburg; there your highness at return
Shall find the German in his study safe.
*K. Hen.* Bacon, thou hast honour'd England with thy skill,
And made fair Oxford famous by thine art;
I will be English Henry to thyself. 170
But tell me, shall we dine with thee to-day?
*Bacon.* With me, my lord; and while I fit my cheer,
See where Prince Edward comes to welcome you,
Gracious as the morning-star of heaven. *Exit.*

*Enter [Prince] Edward, Lacy, Warren, Ermsby*

*Emp.* Is this Prince Edward, Henry's royal son? 175

How martial is the figure of his face!
Yet lovely and beset with amorets.
*K. Hen.* Ned, where hast thou been?
*P. Edw.* At Framlingham, my lord, to try your bucks
If they could scape the teasers or the toil. 180
But hearing of these lordly potentates
Landed, and progress'd up to Oxford town,
I posted to give entertain to them:
Chief, to the Almain monarch; next to him,
And joint with him, Castile and Saxony 185
Are welcome as they may be to the English court.
Thus for the men: but see, Venus appears,
Or one that overmatcheth Venus in her shape!
Sweet Elinor, beauty's high-swelling pride,
Rich nature's glory and her wealth at once, 190
Fair of all fairs, welcome to Albion;
Welcome to me, and welcome to thine own,
If that thou deign'st the welcome from myself.
*Elin.* Martial Plantagenet, Henry's high-minded son,
The mark that Elinor did count her aim, 195
I lik'd thee 'fore I saw thee: now I love,
And so as in so short a time I may;
Yet so as time shall never break that "so,"
And therefore so accept of Elinor.
*K. of Cast.* Fear not, my lord, this couple will agree, 200
If love may creep into their wanton eyes: —
And therefore, Edward, I accept thee here,
Without suspense, as my adopted son.
*K. Hen.* Let me that joy in these consorting greets,
And glory in these honours done to Ned, 205
Yield thanks for all these favours to my son,
And rest a true Plantagenet to all.

*Enter Miles with a cloth and trenchers and salt*

*Miles.* Salvete, omnes reges,
That govern your *greges*
In Saxony and Spain, 210
In England and in Almain!
For all this frolic rabble
Must I cover the table
With trenchers, salt, and cloth;
And then look for your broth. 215
*Emp.* What pleasant fellow is this?
*K. Hen.* 'Tis, my lord, Doctor Bacon's poor scholar.
*Miles [Aside.]* My master hath made me sewer of these great lords; and, God knows, [220
I am as serviceable at a table as a sow is under an apple-tree. 'T is no matter; their cheer shall not be great, and therefore what skills where the salt stand, before or behind? *[Exit.]*

---

150 **fail**: am mistaken    162 **spring**: ('springs' Qq.)    177 **amorets**: love-kindling looks    180 **toil**: trap    208 "Hail, all ye kings."    209 **greges**: people    220 **sewer**: servant who sets the table    223 **skills**: matters

*K. of Cast.* These scholars knows more skill
  in axioms,                                         225
How to use quips and sleights of sophistry,
Than for to cover courtly for a king.

*Enter Miles with a mess of pottage and broth;*
  *and, after him, Bacon*

*Miles.* Spill, sir? why, do you think I never
carried twopenny chop before in my life? —
By your leave, *nobile decus,*                       230
For here comes Doctor Bacon's *pecus,*
Being in his full age
To carry a mess of pottage.
  *Bacon.* Lordings, admire not if your cheer
  be this,
For we must keep our academic fare;                  235
No riot where philosophy doth reign:
And therefore, Henry, place these potentates,
And bid them fall unto their frugal cates.
  *Emp.* Presumptuous friar! What, scoff'st
  thou at a king?
What, dost thou taunt us with thy peasants'
  fare,                                              240
And give us cates fit for country swains? —
Henry, proceeds this jest of thy consent,
To twit us with a pittance of such price?
Tell me, and Frederick will not grieve thee long.
  *K. Hen.* By Henry's honour, and the royal
  faith                                              245
The English monarch beareth to his friend,
I knew not of the friar's feeble fare,
Nor am I pleas'd he entertains you thus.
  *Bacon.* Content thee, Frederick, for I
  show'd the cates,
To let thee see how scholars use to feed;           250
How little meat refines our English wits. —
Miles, take away, and let it be thy dinner.
  *Miles.* Marry, sir, I will.
This day shall be a festival-day with me;
For I shall exceed in the highest degree.
                                   *Exit Miles.*
  *Bacon.* I tell thee, monarch, all the German
  peers                                             256
Could not afford thy entertainment such,
So royal and so full of majesty,
As Bacon will present to Frederick.
The basest waiter that attends thy cups             260
Shall be in honours greater than thyself;
And for thy cates, rich Alexandria drugs,
Fetch'd by carvels from Egypt's richest straits,
Found in the wealthy strand of Africa,
Shall royalize the table of my king;                265
Wines richer than th' Egyptian courtesan

Quaff'd to Augustus' kingly countermatch,
Shall be carous'd in English Henry's feasts;
Candy shall yield the richest of her canes;
Persia, down her Volga by canoes,                   270
Send down the secrets of her spicery;
The Afric dates, myrobalans of Spain,
Conserves and suckets from Tiberias,
Cates from Judæa, choicer than the lamp
That fired Rome with sparks of gluttony,            275
Shall beautify the board for Frederick:
And therefore grudge not at a friar's feast.
                                   *[Exeunt.]*

### [SCENE X. *Fressingfield*]

*Enter two gentlemen, Lambert and Serlsby,*
  *with the Keeper*

  *Lam.* Come, frolic Keeper of our liege's game,
Whose table spread hath ever venison
And jacks of wines to welcome passengers,
Know I 'm in love with jolly Margaret,
That overshines our damsels as the moon       5
Dark'neth the brightest sparkles of the night.
In Laxfield here my land and living lies:
I 'll make thy daughter jointer of it all,
So thou consent to give her to my wife;
And I can spend five hundred marks a-year. 10
  *Ser.* I am the lands-lord, Keeper, of thy holds,
By copy all thy living lies in me;
Laxfield did never see me raise my due:
I will enfeoff fair Margaret in all,
So she will take her to a lusty squire.             15
  *Keep.* Now, courteous gentles, if the Keep-
  er's girl
Hath pleas'd the liking fancy of you both,
And with her beauty hath subdu'd your
  thoughts,
'T is doubtful to decide the question.
It joys me that such men of great esteem        20
Should lay their liking on this base estate,
And that her state should grow so fortunate
To be a wife to meaner men than you.
But sith such squires will stoop to keeper's fee,
I will, to avoid displeasure of you both,          25
Call Margaret forth, and she shall make her
  choice.                               *Exit.*
  *Lam.* Content, Keeper; send her unto us.
Why, Serlsby, is thy wife so lately dead,
Are all thy loves so lightly passed over,
As thou canst wed before the year be out?      30
  *Ser.* I live not, Lambert, to content the dead,
Nor was I wedded but for life to her:
The grave ends and begins a married state.

---

²²⁷ **cover:** set the table   ²²⁹ **twopenny chop:** chopped meat in broth (?)   ²³⁰ **nobile decus:** your
noble grace   ²³¹ **pecus:** beast   ²³⁴ **admire:** wonder   ²⁴³ **with:** ('with such' Qq.)   ²⁶² **drugs:**
spices   ²⁶³ **carvels:** small, fast ships   ²⁶⁷ **countermatch:** rival (*i.e.,* Antony)   ²⁶⁹ **Candy:** Crete
²⁷² **myrobalans:** a kind of plums ('mirabiles' Qq.)   ²⁷³ **suckets:** sweetmeats   ²⁷⁴ **lamp:** lamprey
(with pun)   ³ **jacks:** pitchers   **passengers:** wayfarers   ⁸ **jointer:** jointure or jointress   ¹³ **due:**
rents   ²⁴ **fee:** estate   ³³ **grave:** ('graves' Q 1)

*Enter Margaret*

*Lam.*  Peggy, the lovely flower of all towns,
Suffolk's fair Helen, and rich England's star,   35
Whose beauty, tempered with her huswifery,
Makes England talk of merry Fressingfield!
  *Ser.*  I cannot trick it up with poesies,
Nor paint my passions with comparisons,
Nor tell a tale of Phœbus and his loves:   40
But this believe me, — Laxfield here is mine,
Of ancient rent seven hundred pounds a-year,
And if thou canst but love a country squire,
I will enfeoff thee, Margaret, in all.
I cannot flatter; try me, if thou please.   45
  *Mar.*  Brave neighbouring squires, the stay
    of Suffolk's clime,
A keeper's daughter is too base in gree
To match with men accounted of such worth:
But might I not displease, I would reply.
  *Lam.*  Say, Peggy; naught shall make us
    discontent.   50
  *Mar.*  Then, gentles, note that love hath
    little stay,
Nor can the flames that Venus sets on fire
Be kindled but by fancy's motion:
Then pardon, gentles, if a maid's reply
Be doubtful, while I have debated with my-
    self,   55
Who, or of whom, love shall constrain me
    like.
  *Ser.*  Let it be me; and trust me, Margaret,
The meads environ'd with the silver streams,
Whose battling pastures fatt'neth all my flocks,
Yielding forth fleeces stapled with such wool   60
As Lempster cannot yield more finer stuff,
And forty kine with fair and burnish'd heads,
With strouting dugs that paggle to the ground,
Shall serve thy dairy, if thou wed with me.
  *Lam.*  Let pass the country wealth, as flocks
    and kine,   65
And lands that wave with Ceres' golden sheaves,
Filling my barns with plenty of the fields;
But, Peggy, if thou wed thyself to me,
Thou shalt have garments of embroid'red silk,
Lawns, and rich net-works for thy head-at-
    tire:   70
Costly shall be thy fair habiliments,
If thou wilt be but Lambert's loving wife.
  *Mar.*  Content you, gentles, you have prof-
    fer'd fair,
And more than fits a country maid's degree;
But give me leave to counsel me a time,   75
For fancy blooms not at the first assault;
Give me but ten days' respite, and I will
    reply,
Which or to whom myself affectionates.

  *Ser.*  Lambert, I tell thee, thou'rt importu-
    nate;
Such beauty fits not such a base esquire:   80
It is for Serlsby to have Margaret.
  *Lam.*  Think'st thou with wealth to over-
    reach me?
Serlsby, I scorn to brook thy country braves.
I dare thee, coward, to maintain this wrong,
At dint of rapier, single in the field.   85
  *Ser.*  I'll answer, Lambert, what I have
    avouch'd. —
Margaret, farewell; another time shall serve.
                           *Exit Serlsby.*
  *Lam.*  I'll follow. — Peggy, farewell to thy-
    self;
Listen how well I'll answer for thy love.
                           *Exit Lambert.*
  *Mar.*  How Fortune tempers lucky haps with
    frowns,   90
And wrongs me with the sweets of my delight!
Love is my bliss, and love is now my bale.
Shall I be Helen in my froward fates,
As I am Helen in my matchless hue,
And set rich Suffolk with my face afire?   95
If lovely Lacy were but with his Peggy,
The cloudy darkness of his bitter frown
Would check the pride of these aspiring squires.
Before the term of ten days be expir'd,
Whenas they look for answer of their loves,   100
My lord will come to merry Fressingfield,
And end their fancies and their follies both:
Till when, Peggy, be blithe and of good cheer.

*Enter a Post with a letter and a bag of gold.*

  *Post.*  Fair lovely damsel, which way leads
    this path?
How might I post me unto Fressingfield?   105
Which footpath leadeth to the Keeper's lodge?
  *Mar.*  Your way is ready, and this path is
    right;
Myself do dwell hereby in Fressingfield,
And if the Keeper be the man you seek,
I am his daughter: may I know the cause?   110
  *Post.*  Lovely, and once beloved of my lord, —
No marvel if his eye was lodg'd so low,
When brighter beauty is not in the heavens, —
The Lincoln Earl hath sent you letters here,
And, with them, just an hundred pounds in
    gold.   115
Sweet, bonny wench, read them, and make
    reply.
  *Mar.*  The scrolls that Jove sent Danaë,
Wrapp'd in rich closures of fine burnish'd gold,
Were not more welcome than these lines to me.
Tell me, whilst that I do unrip the seals,   120
Lives Lacy well? How fares my lovely lord?

---

⁴⁷ **daughter:** ('daughters' Q 1)   **gree:** degree   ⁵⁵ **while:** until   ⁶⁰ **stapled . . . wool:** of
such quality   ⁶¹ **Lempster:** Leominster (in Herefordshire)   ⁶³ **strouting:** swelling   **paggle:** hang
loosely   ⁸³ **braves:** boasts   ⁹³ **froward:** untoward; ('forward' Qq.)

*Post.* Well, if that wealth may make men to
live well.
                    [*The letter, and Margaret reads it.*]

Mar. *The blooms of the almond-tree grow
in a night, and vanish in a morn; the flies
hæmeræ, fair Peggy, take life with the sun,* [125
*and die with the dew; fancy that slippeth in with
a gaze, goeth out with a wink; and too timely
loves have ever the shortest length. I write this as
thy grief, and my folly, who at Fressingfield lov'd
that which time hath taught me to be but mean* [130
*dainties. Eyes are dissemblers, and fancy is but
queasy; therefore know, Margaret, I have chosen
a Spanish lady to be my wife, chief waiting-woman
to the Princess Elinor; a lady fair, and no less
fair than thyself, honourable and wealthy. In* [135
*that I forsake thee, I leave thee to thine own lik-
ing; and for thy dowry I have sent thee an hundred pounds; and ever assure thee of my favour,
which shall avail thee and thine much.*

        *Farewell.       Not thine, nor his own,* 140
                        *Edward Lacy.*

Fond Ate, doomer of bad-boding fates,
That wraps proud Fortune in thy snaky locks,
Didst thou enchant my birth-day with such stars
As light'ned mischief from their infancy?    145
If heavens had vow'd, if stars had made decree,
To show on me their froward influence, —
If Lacy had but lov'd, heavens, hell, and all
Could not have wrong'd the patience of my mind.

    *Post.* It grieves me, damsel; but the earl is
        forc'd                                    150
To love the lady by the king's command.

    *Mar.* The wealth combin'd within the Eng-
lish shelves,
Europe's commander, nor the English king,
Should not have mov'd the love of Peggy from
        her lord.

    *Post.* What answer shall I return to my
        lord?                                     155

    *Mar.* First, for thou cam'st from Lacy whom
I lov'd, —
Ah, give me leave to sigh at every thought! —
Take thou, my friend, the hundred pound he
        sent,
For Margaret's resolution craves no dower.
The world shall be to her as vanity;             160
Wealth, trash; love, hate; pleasure, despair:
For I will straight to stately Framlingham,
And in the abbey there be shorn a nun,
And yield my loves and liberty to God.
Fellow, I give thee this, not for the news,      165
For those be hateful unto Margaret,
But for th' art Lacy's man, once Margaret's
        love.

*Post.* What I have heard, what passions I
        have seen,
I 'll make report of them unto the earl.
                                *Exit Post.*

*Mar.* Say that she joys his fancies be at
        rest,                                     170
And prays that his misfortune may be hers.
                                        *Exit.*

[SCENE XI.  *Friar Bacon's Cell*]

*Enter Friar Bacon drawing the curtains with a
    white stick, a book in his hand, and a lamp
    lighted by him; and the Brazen Head, and
    Miles with weapons by him*

Bacon. Miles, where are you?
*Miles.* Here, sir.
Bacon. How chance you tarry so long?
*Miles.* Think you that the watching of the
Brazen Head craves no furniture? I warrant [5
you, sir, I have so armed myself that if all your
devils come, I will not fear them an inch.

    *Bacon.* Miles,
Thou know'st that I have dived into hell,
And sought the darkest palaces of fiends;         10
That with my magic spells great Belcephon
Hath left his lodge and kneeled at my cell;
The rafters of the earth rent from the poles,
And three-form'd Luna hid her silver looks,
Trembling upon her concave continent,             15
When Bacon read upon his magic book.
With seven years' tossing necromantic charms,
Poring upon dark Hecat's principles,
I have fram'd out a monstrous head of brass,
That, by the enchanting forces of the devil,      20
Shall tell out strange and uncouth aphorisms,
And girt fair England with a wall of brass.
Bungay and I have watch'd these threescore
        days,
And now our vital spirits crave some rest.
If Argus liv'd, and had his hundred eyes,         25
They could not over-watch Phobetor's night.
Now, Miles, in thee rests Friar Bacon's weal:
The honour and renown of all his life
Hangs in the watching of this Brazen Head;
Therefore I charge thee by the immortal God, 30
That holds the souls of men within his fist,
This night thou watch; for ere the morning-star
Sends out his glorious glister on the north,
The head will speak: then, Miles, upon thy life,
Wake me; for then by magic art I 'll work    35
To end my seven years' task with excellence.
If that a wink but shut thy watchful eye,
Then farewell Bacon's glory and his fame!
Draw close the curtains, Miles: now, for thy life,
Be watchful, and — *Here he falleth asleep.* 40

---

¹²⁵ **hæmeræ:** ephemeræ    ¹²⁷ **timely:** precocious    ¹³² **queasy:** fastidious    ¹⁵² **shelves:** coasts
¹⁶³ **shorn:** The cutting of a nun's hair was a symbol of renouncing the world.    ⁵ **furniture:** equipment    ²¹ **uncouth:** unknown

*Miles.* So; I thought you would talk yourself
asleep anon; and 't is no marvel, for Bungay on
the days, and he on the nights, have watched
just these ten and fifty days: now this is the
night, and 't is my task, and no more. Now, [45
Jesus bless me, what a goodly head it is! and
a nose! you talk of *nos autem glorificare;* but
here 's a nose that I warrant may be called *nos
autem populare* for the people of the parish.
Well, I am furnished with weapons: now, [50
sir, I will set me down by a post, and make it
as good as a watchman to wake me, if I chance
to slumber. I thought, Goodman Head, I would
call you out of your *memento.* (*Sit down and
knock your head.*) Passion o' God, I have al- [55
most broke my pate! Up, Miles, to your task;
take your brown-bill in your hand; here 's some
of your master's hobgoblins abroad.
  *With this a great noise. The Head speaks.*
  *The Brazen Head.* Time is!
*Miles.* Time is! Why, Master Brazen- [60
head, have you such a capital nose, and answer
you with syllables, "Time is"? Is this all my
master's cunning, to spend seven years' study
about "Time is"? Well, sir, it may be we shall
have some better orations of it anon. Well, [65
I 'll watch you as narrowly as ever you were
watch'd, and I 'll play with you as the nightingale with the slow-worm; I 'll set a prick
against my breast. Now rest there, Miles. Lord
have mercy upon me, I have almost killed [70
myself! [*A noise.*] Up, Miles; list how they
rumble.
  *The Brazen Head.* Time was!
*Miles.* Well, Friar Bacon, you spent your
seven-years' study well, that can make [75
your head speak but two words at once, "Time
was." Yea, marry, time was when my master
was a wise man, but that was before he began
to make the Brazen Head. You shall lie while
your arse ache, an your head speak no better. [80
Well, I will watch, and walk up and down, and
be a peripatetian and a philosopher of Aristotle's stamp. [*A noise.*] What, a fresh noise?
Take thy pistols in hand, Miles.

*Here the Head speaks, and a lightning flasheth
    forth, and a hand appears that breaketh down
    the Head with a hammer.*

  *The Brazen Head.* Time is past!      85
*Miles.* Master, master, up! Hell 's broken
loose! Your head speaks; and there 's such a
thunder and lightning, that I warrant all Oxford is up in arms. Out of your bed, and take
a brown-bill in your hand; the latter day is [90
come.

*Bacon.* Miles, I come. O, passing warily
    watch'd!
Bacon will make thee next himself in love.
When spake the head?
*Miles.* When spake the head! Did not [95
you say that he should tell strange principles of
philosophy? Why, sir, it speaks but two words
at a time.
*Bacon.* Why, villain, hath it spoken oft?
*Miles.* Oft! ay, marry, hath it, thrice; [100
but in all those three times it hath uttered but
seven words.
*Bacon.* As how?
*Miles.* Marry, sir, the first time he said,
"Time is," as if Fabius Cumentator should [105
have pronounced a sentence; the second time
he said, "Time was"; and the third time,
with thunder and lightning, as in great choler,
he said, "Time is past."
*Bacon.* 'T is past indeed. Ah, villain! time
    is past:                                110
My life, my fame, my glory, all are past. —
Bacon, the turrets of thy hope are ruin'd down,
Thy seven years' study lieth in the dust:
Thy Brazen Head lies broken through a slave
That watch'd, and would not when the head
    did will. —                           115
What said the head first?
*Miles.* Even, sir, "Time is."
*Bacon.* Villain, if thou hadst call'd to Bacon
    then,
If thou hadst watch'd, and wak'd the sleepy
    friar,
The Brazen Head had uttered aphorisms,   120
And England had been circled round with
    brass:
But proud Asmenoth, ruler of the north,
And Demogorgon, master of the fates,
Grudge that a mortal man should work so much.
Hell trembled at my deep-commanding
    spells,                               125
Fiends frown'd to see a man their over-match;
Bacon might boast more than a man might
    boast.
But now the braves of Bacon hath an end,
Europe's conceit of Bacon hath an end,
His seven years' practice sorteth to ill end:  130
And, villain, sith my glory hath an end,
I will appoint thee to some fatal end.
Villain, avoid! get thee from Bacon's sight!
Vagrant, go roam and range about the world,
And perish as a vagabond on earth!       135
*Miles.* Why, then, sir, you forbid me your
    service?
*Bacon.* My service, villain! with a fatal curse,
That direful plagues and mischief fall on thee.

⁵⁴⁻⁵⁵ S. D. **sit . . . head:** (marginal note in Q 1, from prompt-copy)   ⁵⁷ **brown-bill:** halberd
¹⁰⁵ **Cumentator:** Cunctator, *i.e.,* Fabius Maximus   ¹⁰⁶ **the . . . time:** (not in Qq.)   ¹²⁴ **work:**
accomplish   ¹³² **to . . . fatal:** ('fatal to some' Qq.)

*Miles.* 'T is no matter, I am against you with the old proverb, — The more the fox is [140 cursed, the better he fares. God be with you, sir. I 'll take but a book in my hand, a wide-sleeved gown on my back, and a crowned cap on my head, and see if I can want promotion.

*Bacon.* Some fiend or ghost haunt on thy weary steps,                                              145
Until they do transport thee quick to hell;
For Bacon shall have never merry day,
To lose the fame and honour of his Head.

*Exeunt.*

[SCENE XII.  *At Court*]

*Enter Emperor, Castile, [King] Henry, Elinor, Edward, Lacy, Ralph*

*Emp.*  Now, lovely prince, the prime of Albion's wealth,
How fares the Lady Elinor and you?
What, have you courted and found Castile fit
To answer England in equivalence?
Will 't be a match 'twixt bonny Nell and thee?

*P. Edw.*  Should Paris enter in the courts of Greece,                                              6
And not lie fetter'd in fair Helen's looks?
Or Phœbus scape those piercing amorets
That Daphne glanced at his deity?
Can Edward, then, sit by a flame and freeze, 10
Whose heat puts Helen and fair Daphne down?
Now, monarchs, ask the lady if we gree.

*K. Hen.*  What, madam, hath my son found grace or no?

*Elin.*  Seeing, my lord, his lovely counterfeit,
And hearing how his mind and shape agreed, 15
I come not, troop'd with all this warlike train,
Doubting of love, but so affectionate
As Edward hath in England what he won in Spain.

*K. of Cast.*  A match, my lord; these wantons needs must love:
Men must have wives, and women will be wed.                                                        20
Let 's haste the day to honour up the rites.

*Ralph.*  Sirrah Harry, shall Ned marry Nell?

*K. Hen.*  Ay, Ralph: how then?

*Ralph.*  Marry, Harry, follow my counsel: send for Friar Bacon to marry them, for he 'll [25 so conjure him and her with his necromancy, that they shall love together like pig and lamb whilst they live.

*K. of Cast.*  But hearest thou, Ralph, art thou content to have Elinor to thy lady?          30

*Ralph.*  Ay, so she will promise me two things.

*K. of Cast.*  What 's that, Ralph?

*Ralph.*  That she will never scold with Ned, nor fight with me. — Sirrah Harry, I have put her down with a thing unpossible.          35

*K. Hen.*  What 's that, Ralph?

*Ralph.*  Why, Harry, didst thou ever see that a woman could both hold her tongue and her hands?  No: but when egg-pies grows on apple-trees, then will thy grey mare prove a bag- [40 piper.

*Emp.*  What says the Lord of Castile and the Earl of Lincoln, that they are in such earnest and secret talk?

*K. of Cast.*  I stand, my lord, amazed at his talk,                                              45
How he discourseth of the constancy
Of one surnam'd, for beauty's excellence,
The Fair Maid of merry Fressingfield.

*K. Hen.*  'T is true, my lord, 't is wondrous for to hear;
Her beauty passing Mars's paramour,          50
Her virgin's right as rich as Vesta's was.
Lacy and Ned hath told me miracles.

*K. of Cast.*  What says Lord Lacy?  Shall she be his wife?

*Lacy.*  Or else Lord Lacy is unfit to live. —
May it please your highness give me leave to post                                                  55
To Fressingfield, I 'll fetch the bonny girl,
And prove, in true appearance at the court,
What I have vouched often with my tongue.

*K. Hen.*  Lacy, go to the 'querry of my stable,
And take such coursers as shall fit thy turn; 60
Hie thee to Fressingfield, and bring home the lass;
And, for her fame flies through the English coast,
If it may please the Lady Elinor,
One day shall match your excellence and her.

*Elin.*  We Castile ladies are not very coy; 65
Your highness may command a greater boon:
And glad were I to grace the Lincoln Earl
With being partner of his marriage-day.

*P. Edw.*  Gramercy, Nell, for I do love the lord,
As he that 's second to thyself in love.          70

*Ralph.*  You love her? — Madam Nell, never believe him you, though he swears he loves you.

*Elin.*  Why, Ralph?

*Ralph.*  Why, his love is like unto a tapster's glass that is broken with every touch; for [75 he loved the fair maid of Fressingfield once out of all ho. — Nay, Ned, never wink upon me; I care not, I.

*K. Hen.*  Ralph tells all; you shall have a good secretary of him. —                              80
But, Lacy, haste thee post to Fressingfield;

¹⁴¹ **cursed:** with a pun on *coursed*    ¹⁴⁶ **quick:** alive    ¹ **prime:** ('prince' Qq.)    ¹² **gree:** agree    ¹⁸ **As:** that    ⁶² **for:** because    ⁷⁰ **thyself:** ('myselfe' Qq.)    ⁷⁶⁻⁷⁷ **out . . . ho:** excessively    ⁸⁰ **secretary:** confidant

For ere thou hast fitted all things for her
   state,
The solemn marriage-day will be at hand.
  *Lacy.* I go, my lord.          *Exit Lacy.*
  *Emp.* How shall we pass this day, my lord?85
  *K. Hen.* To horse, my lord; the day is pass-
    ing fair,
We 'll fly the partridge, or go rouse the deer.
Follow, my lords; you shall not want for sport.
                      *Exeunt.*

[SCENE XIII.  *Friar Bacon's Cell*]

*Enter Friar Bacon with Friar Bungay to his
    cell*

  *Bun.* What means the friar that frolick'd it
    of late,
To sit as melancholy in his cell
As if he had neither lost nor won to-day?
  *Bacon.* Ah, Bungay, my Brazen Head is
    spoil'd,
My glory gone, my seven years' study lost!  5
The fame of Bacon, bruited through the world,
Shall end and perish with this deep disgrace.
  *Bun.* Bacon hath built foundation of his fame
So surely on the wings of true report,
With acting strange and uncouth miracles,  10
As this cannot infringe what he deserves.
  *Bacon.* Bungay, sit down, for by prospective
    skill
I find this day shall fall out ominous:
Some deadly act shall 'tide me ere I sleep;
But what and wherein little can I guess.   15
My mind is heavy, whatsoe'er shall hap.

*Enter two Scholars, sons to Lambert and Serlsby
    Knock*

  *Bacon.* Who 's that knocks?
  *Bun.* Two scholars that desires to speak
    with you.
  *Bacon.* Bid them come in. —
Now, my youths, what would you have?   20
  *First Schol.* Sir, we are Suffolk-men and
    neighbouring friends;
Our fathers in their countries lusty squires;
Their lands adjoin: in Cratfield mine doth dwell,
And his in Laxfield. We are college-mates,
Sworn brothers, as our fathers lives as friends.
  *Bacon.* To what end is all this?      26
  *Second Schol.* Hearing your worship kept
    within your cell
A glass prospective, wherein men might see
Whatso their thoughts or hearts' desire could
    wish,
We come to know how that our fathers fare. 30

  *Bacon.* My glass is free for every honest
    man.
Sit down, and you shall see ere long, how
Or in what state your friendly fathers live.
Meanwhile, tell me your names.
  *First Schol.* Mine Lambert.        35
  *Second Schol.* And mine Serlsby.
  *Bacon.* Bungay, I smell there will be a trag-
    edy.

*Enter Lambert and Serlsby with rapiers and
    daggers*

  *Lam.* Serlsby, thou hast kept thine hour like
    a man:
Th' art worthy of the title of a squire,
That durst, for proof of thy affection   40
And for thy mistress' favour, prize thy blood.
Thou know'st what words did pass at Fressing-
    field,
Such shameless braves as manhood cannot brook:
Ay, for I scorn to bear such piercing taunts,
Prepare thee, Serlsby; one of us will die.   45
  *Ser.* Thou see'st I single meet thee in the
    field,
And what I spake, I 'll maintain with my sword.
Stand on thy guard, I cannot scold it out.
An if thou kill me, think I have a son,
That lives in Oxford in the Broadgates-hall,  50
Who will revenge his father's blood with blood.
  *Lam.* And, Serlsby, I have there a lusty
    boy,
That dares at weapon buckle with thy son,
And lives in Broadgates too, as well as thine.
But draw thy rapier, for we 'll have a bout.  55
  *Bacon.* Now, lusty younkers, look within the
    glass,
And tell me if you can discern your sires.
  *First Schol.* Serlsby, 't is hard; thy father
    offers wrong,
To combat with my father in the field.
  *Second Schol.* Lambert, thou liest, my
    father's is th' abuse,   60
And thou shalt find it, if my father harm.
  *Bun.* How goes it, sirs?
  *First Schol.* Our fathers are in combat hard
    by Fressingfield.
  *Bacon.* Sit still, my friends, and see the event.
  *Lam.* Why stand'st thou, Serlsby? Doubt'st
    thou of thy life?   65
A veney, man! fair Margaret craves so much.
  *Ser.* Then this for her.
  *First Schol.* Ah, well thrust!
  *Second Schol.* But mark the ward.

      *They fight and kill each other*

---

  **8 of:** ('on' Qq.)    **16 My . . . hap:** (Qq. give to Bungay)    **23 Cratfield:** ('Crackfield' Q 1)
**33 fathers live:** ('father liues' Q 1)    **41 prize:** risk    **46 meet, in:** (not in Qq.)    **56 younkers:**
young gentlemen    **61 harm:** come to harm    **64 event:** outcome    **66 veney:** bout    **69 ward:**
parry

*Lam*   O, I am slain!                                          70
*Ser.*   And I, — Lord have mercy on me!
*First Schol.*   My father slain! — Serlsby,
ward that.
*Second Schol.*   And so is mine! — Lambert,
I 'll quite thee well.
*The two Scholars stab one another [and die].*
*Bun.*   O strange stratagem!
*Bacon.*   See, friar, where the fathers both lie
dead! —                                                        75
Bacon, thy magic doth effect this massacre:
This glass prospective worketh many woes;
And therefore seeing these brave lusty Brutes,
These friendly youths, did perish by thine
art,
End all thy magic and thine art at once.        80
The poniard that did end the fatal lives,
Shall break the cause efficient of their woes.
So fade the glass, and end with it the shows
That necromancy did infuse the crystal with.
*He breaks the glass.*
*Bun.*   What means learn'd Bacon thus to
break his glass?                                               85
*Bacon.*   I tell thee, Bungay, it repents me sore
That ever Bacon meddled in this art.
The hours I have spent in pyromantic spells,
The fearful tossing in the latest night
Of papers full of necromantic charms,          90
Conjuring and adjuring devils and fiends,
With stole and alb and strange pentagonon;
The wresting of the holy name of God,
As Soter, Eloim, and Adonai,
Alpha, Manoth, and Tetragrammaton,        95
With praying to the five-fold powers of heaven,
Are instances that Bacon must be damn'd
For using devils to countervail his God. —
Yet, Bacon, cheer thee, drown not in despair:
Sins have their salves, repentance can do
much:                                                          100
Think Mercy sits where Justice holds her seat,
And from those wounds those bloody Jews did
pierce,
Which by thy magic oft did bleed afresh,
From thence for thee the dew of mercy drops,
To wash the wrath of high Jehovah's ire,     105
And make thee as a new-born babe from sin. —
Bungay, I 'll spend the remnant of my life
In pure devotion, praying to my God
That he would save what Bacon vainly lost.
*Exeunt.*

[SCENE XIV.  *Fressingfield*]

*Enter Margaret in nun's apparel; Keeper, her
father; and their Friend*

*Keeper.*   Margaret, be not so headstrong in
these vows:
O, bury not such beauty in a cell,

That England hath held famous for the hue!
Thy father's hair, like to the silver blooms
That beautify the shrubs of Africa,            5
Shall fall before the dated time of death,
Thus to forgo his lovely Margaret.
*Mar.*   Ah, father, when the harmony of
heaven
Soundeth the measures of a lively faith,
The vain illusions of this flattering world     10
Seems odious to the thoughts of Margaret.
I loved once, — Lord Lacy was my love;
And now I hate myself for that I lov'd,
And doted more on him than on my God;
For this I scourge myself with sharp repents. 15
But now the touch of such aspiring sins
Tells me all love is lust but love of heavens;
That beauty us'd for love is vanity:
The world contains naught but alluring baits,
Pride, flattery, and inconstant thoughts.     20
To shun the pricks of death, I leave the world,
And vow to meditate on heavenly bliss,
To live in Framlingham a holy nun,
Holy and pure in conscience and in deed;
And for to wish all maids to learn of me     25
To seek heaven's joy before earth's vanity.
*Friend.*   And will you, then, Margaret, be
shorn a nun, and so leave us all?
*Mar.*   Now farewell world, the engine of all
woe!
Farewell to friends and father!   Welcome
Christ!                                                         30
Adieu to dainty robes!   This base attire
Better befits an humble mind to God
Than all the show of rich habiliments.
Love — O love! and, with fond love, farewell
Sweet Lacy, whom I loved once so dear!     35
Ever be well, but never in my thoughts,
Lest I offend to think on Lacy's love:
But even to that, as to the rest, farewell!

*Enter Lacy, Warren, Ermsby, booted and
spurred*

*Lacy.*   Come on, my wags, we 're near the
Keeper's lodge.
Here have I oft walk'd in the watery meads, 40
And chatted with my lovely Margaret.
*War.*   Sirrah Ned, is not this the Keeper?
*Lacy.*   'T is the same.
*Erm.*   The old lecher hath gotten holy mut-
ton to him: a nun, my lord.                      45
*Lacy.*   Keeper, how far'st thou?   Holla, man,
what cheer?
How doth Peggy, thy daughter and my love?
*Keeper.*   Ah, good my lord!   O, woe is me
for Peg!
See where she stands clad in her nun's attire,
Ready for to be shorn in Framlingham;     50
She leaves the world because she left your love.

O, good my lord, persuade her if you can!
   *Lacy.* Why, how now, Margaret! What, a
malcontent?
A nun? What holy father taught you this,
To task yourself to such a tedious life     55
As die a maid? 'T were injury to me,
To smother up such beauty in a cell.
   *Mar.* Lord Lacy, thinking of thy former miss,
How fond the prime of wanton years were
   spent
In love (O, fie upon that fond conceit,   60
Whose hap and essence hangeth in the eye!),
I leave both love and love's content at once,
Betaking me to Him that is true love,
And leaving all the world for love of Him.
   *Lacy.* Whence, Peggy, comes this metamor-
   phosis?   65
What, shorn a nun, and I have from the court
Posted with coursers to convey thee hence
To Windsor, where our marriage shall be kept!
Thy wedding-robes are in the tailor's hands.
Come, Peggy, leave these peremptory vows.   70
   *Mar.* Did not my lord resign his interest,
And make divorce 'twixt Margaret and him?
   *Lacy.* 'T was but to try sweet Peggy's con-
   stancy.
But will fair Margaret leave her love and lord?
   *Mar.* Is not heaven's joy before earth's fad-
   ing bliss,   75
And life above sweeter than life in love?
   *Lacy.* Why, then, Margaret will be shorn a
   nun?
   *Mar.* Margaret hath made a vow which may
not be revok'd.
   *War.* We cannot stay, my lord; and if she be
   so strict,
Our leisure grants us not to woo afresh.   80
   *Erms.* Choose you, fair damsel; yet the
   choice is yours, —
Either a solemn nunnery or the court,
God or Lord Lacy. Which contents you best,
To be a nun or else Lord Lacy's wife?
   *Lacy.* A good motion. — Peggy, your an-
   swer must be short.   85
   *Mar.* The flesh is frail: my lord doth know
   it well,
That when he comes with his enchanting face,
Whatsoe'er betide, I cannot say him nay.
Off goes the habit of a maiden's heart,
And, seeing fortune will, fair Framlingham,   90
And all the show of holy nuns, farewell!
Lacy for me, if he will be my lord.
   *Lacy.* Peggy, thy lord, thy love, thy husband.
Trust me, by truth of knighthood, that the king
Stays for to marry matchless Elinor,   95
Until I bring thee richly to the court,

That one day may both marry her and thee. —
How say'st thou, Keeper? Art thou glad of this?
   *Keep.* As if the English king had given
The park and deer of Fressingfield to me.   100
   *Erm.* I pray thee, my Lord of Sussex, why
art thou in a brown study?
   *War.* To see the nature of women; that
be they never so near God, yet they love to die
in a man's arms.   105
   *Lacy.* What have you fit for breakfast? We
   have hied
And posted all this night to Fressingfield.
   *Mar.* Butter and cheese, and umbles of a deer,
Such as poor keepers have within their lodge.
   *Lacy.* And not a bottle of wine?   110
   *Mar.* We 'll find one for my lord.
   *Lacy.* Come, Sussex, let us in: we shall have
   more,
For she speaks least, to hold her promise sure.
                           *Exeunt.*

## [SCENE XV.]

### *Enter a Devil to seek Miles*

   *Dev.* How restless are the ghosts of hellish
   spirits,
When every charmer with his magic spells
Calls us from nine-fold-trenched Phlegethon,
To scud and over-scour the earth in post
Upon the speedy wings of swiftest winds!   5
Now Bacon hath rais'd me from the darkest
   deep,
To search about the world for Miles his man,
For Miles, and to torment his lazy bones
For careless watching of his Brazen Head.
See where he comes. O, he is mine!   10

### *Enter Miles with a gown and a corner-cap*

   *Miles.* A scholar, quoth you! marry, sir, I
would I had been made a bottle-maker when I
was made a scholar; for I can get neither to
be a deacon, reader, nor schoolmaster, no, not
the clerk of a parish. Some call me dunce; [15
another saith, my head is as full of Latin as an
egg 's full of oatmeal. Thus I am tormented,
that the devil and Friar Bacon haunts me.
— Good Lord, here 's one of my master's devils!
I 'll go speak to him. — What, Master Plu- [20
tus, how cheer you?
   *Dev.* Dost thou know me?
   *Miles.* Know you, sir! Why, are not you
one of my master's devils, that were wont
to come to my master, Doctor Bacon, at [25
Brasenose?
   *Dev.* Yes, marry, am I.
   *Miles.* Good Lord, Master Plutus, I have

⁵⁸ **thy . . . miss:** my former loss of you   ⁶⁰ **fond:** foolish   ¹⁰⁸ **umbles:** liver, kidneys, etc.
¹¹² **let us:** ('lets' Q 1)   **Sc. XV** (This scene cannot be definitely located.)   ¹⁹ S. D. **corner-cap:** academic cap

seen you a thousand times at my master's, and yet I had never the manners to make you [30 drink. But, sir, I am glad to see how conformable you are to the statute. — I warrant you, he's as yeomanly a man as you shall see: mark you, masters, here's a plain honest man, without welt or guard. But I pray you, sir, [35 do you come lately from hell?

*Dev.* Ay, marry: how then?

*Miles.* Faith, 't is a place I have desired long to see. Have you not good tippling-houses there? May not a man have a lusty fire there, a [40 pot of good ale, a pair of cards, a swinging piece of chalk, and a brown toast that will clap a white waistcoat on a cup of good drink?

*Dev.* All this you may have there.

*Miles.* You are for me, friend, and I am for [45 you. But I pray you, may I not have an office there?

*Dev.* Yes, a thousand. What wouldst thou be?

*Miles.* By my troth, sir, in a place where I may profit myself. I know hell is a hot place, [50 and men are marvellous dry, and much drink is spent there; I would be a tapster.

*Dev.* Thou shalt.

*Miles.* There's nothing lets me from going with you, but that 't is a long journey, and [55 I have never a horse.

*Dev.* Thou shalt ride on my back.

*Miles.* Now surely here's a courteous devil, that, for to pleasure his friend, will not stick to make a jade of himself. — But I pray [60 you, goodman friend, let me move a question to you.

*Dev.* What's that?

*Miles.* I pray you, whether is your pace a trot or an amble?                                    65

*Dev.* An amble.

*Miles.* 'T is well; but take heed it be not a trot: but 't is no matter, I 'll prevent it.

*Dev.* What dost?

*Miles.* Marry, friend, I put on my spurs; [70 for if I find your pace either a trot or else uneasy, I 'll put you to a false gallop; I 'll make you feel the benefit of my spurs.

*Dev.* Get up upon my back.

[*Miles mounts on the Devil's back.*]

*Miles.* O Lord, here's even a goodly mar- [75 vel, when a man rides to hell on the devil's back!

*Exeunt, roaring.*

[SCENE XVI. *At Court*]

*Enter the Emperor with a pointless sword: next the King of Castile carrying a sword with a point; Lacy carrying the globe; Edward*

*Warren carrying a rod of gold with a dove on it; Ermsby with a crown and sceptre; the Queen with the Fair Maid of Fressingfield on her left hand; [King] Henry; [Prince Edward]; Bacon; with other Lords attending.*

*P. Edw.* Great potentates, earth's miracles for state,
Think that Prince Edward humbles at your feet,
And, for these favours, on his martial sword
He vows perpetual homage to yourselves,
Yielding these honours unto Elinor.          5

*K. Hen.* Gramercies, lordings; old Plantagenet,
That rules and sways the Albion diadem,
With tears discovers these conceived joys,
And vows requital, if his men-at-arms,
The wealth of England, or due honours done 10
To Elinor, may quite his favourites.
But all this while what say you to the dames
That shine like to the crystal lamps of heaven?

*Emp.* If but a third were added to these two,
They did surpass those gorgeous images     15
That gloried Ida with rich beauty's wealth.

*Mar.* 'T is I, my lords, who humbly on my knee
Must yield her orisons to mighty Jove
For lifting up his handmaid to this state,
Brought from her homely cottage to the court, 20
And grac'd with kings, princes, and emperors;
To whom (next to the noble Lincoln Earl)
I vow obedience, and such humble love
As may a handmaid to such mighty men.

*P. Elin.* Thou martial man that wears the Almain crown,          25
And you the western potentates of might,
The Albion princess, English Edward's wife,
Proud that the lovely star of Fressingfield,
Fair Margaret, Countess to the Lincoln Earl, 29
Attends on Elinor, — gramercies, lord, for her, —
'T is I give thanks for Margaret to you all,
And rest for her due bounden to yourselves.

*K. Hen.* Seeing the marriage is solémnized,
Let 's march in triumph to the royal feast. —
But why stands Friar Bacon here so mute? 35

*Bacon.* Repentant for the follies of my youth,
That magic's secret mysteries misled,
And joyful that this royal marriage
Portends such bliss unto this matchless realm.

*K. Hen.* Why, Bacon,          40
What strange event shall happen to this land?
Or what shall grow from Edward and his queen?

*Bacon.* I find by deep prescience of mine art,
Which once I temp'red in my secret cell,

---

31-32 conformable . . . statute: *i.e.*, in dress     35 welt: trimmings     guard: facings     41 pair: pack     swinging: huge     43 white waistcoat: collar of froth     15 those . . . images: the three goddesses of the choice of Paris. Cf. *Arraignment of Paris*, Act II, Sc. i

That here where Brute did build his Troyno-
 vant,            45
From forth the royal garden of a king
Shall flourish out so rich and fair a bud
Whose brightness shall deface proud Phœbus'
 flower,
And over-shadow Albion with her leaves.
Till then Mars shall be master of the field, 50
But then the stormy threats of wars shall cease:
The horse shall stamp as careless of the pike,
Drums shall be turn'd to timbrels of delight;
With wealthy favours plenty shall enrich
The strand that gladded wand'ring Brute to
 see,              55
And peace from heaven shall harbour in these
 leaves
That gorgeous beautifies this matchless flower:
Apollo's heliotropion then shall stoop,
And Venus' hyacinth shall vail her top;
Juno shall shut her gilliflowers up,   60

And Pallas' bay shall 'bash her brightest green;
Ceres' carnation, in consórt with those,
Shall stoop and wonder at Diana's rose.
 *K. Hen.*  This prophecy is mystical. —
But, glorious commanders of Europa's love, 65
That makes fair England like that wealthy
 isle
Circled with Gihon and swift Euphrates,
In royalizing Henry's Albion
With presence of your princely mightiness, —
Let 's march: the tables all are spread,  70
And viands, such as England's wealth affords,
Are ready set to furnish out the boards.
You shall have welcome, mighty potentates:
It rests, to furnish up this royal feast,
Only your hearts be frolic; for the time  75
Craves that we taste of naught but jouissance.
Thus glories England over all the west.
            *Exeunt omnes.*
 *Omne tulit punctum qui miscuit utile dulci.*

  ⁴⁵ **Brute:** Brutus, the grandson of Æneas **Troynovant:** London ⁴⁷ ff. The usual flattery
of Queen Elizabeth ⁵³ **timbrels:** tambourines ⁵⁹ **vail:** lower ⁶¹ **'bash:** abate ⁶⁷ **swift:** ('first'
Qq.) ⁷⁴ **rests:** remains **furnish up:** make complete ⁷⁵ **Only:** only that ⁷⁸ "He has won every
vote who has mingled profit with pleasure" (Greene's favorite motto).

[The letter is in Kyd's autograph, but unsigned. Omitted letters given in italic.]

Pleaseth it *your* honou*r*able L*ord*shi*p* toching Marlowes monstruous opinions as I
cannot but with an agreved conscience think on him or them so can I but *pa*rticularize
fewe in the respect of them that kept him greater company.  Howbeit in
discharg of dutie both towards God *your* Lord*s*hi*p*s & the world thus much haue I thought
good breiflie to discover in all humblenes
Ffirst it was his custom when I knewe him first & as I heare saie he
contynewd it, in table talk or otherwise to iest at the devine scriptures
gybe at praiers, & stryve in argum*ent* to frustrate & confute what hath byn
spoke or wrytt by prophets & such holie men.

1    He wold report St John to be *our* savio*ur* Christes Alexis I cover it w*i*th reverence
     and trembling that is that Christ did loue him w*i*th an extraordinary loue.

2    That for me to wryte a poem of St paules conversion as I was determined
     he said wold be as if I shold go wryte a book of fast & loose, esteming
     paul a Jugler.

3    That the prodigall Childs portion was but fower nobles he held his
     purse so neere the bottom in all pictures, and that it either was a iest
     or els fowr nobles then was thought a great patrimony not thinking it a
     *pa*rable

4    That things esteemed to be donn by devine power might haue aswell been don
     by observation of men all w*hi*ch he wold so sodenlie take slight occasion to
     slyp out as I & many others in regard of his other rashnes in attempting
     soden pryvie iniuries to men did ouerslypp though often reprehend him for it
     & for which god is my witnes aswell by my lords comaundm*ent* as in hatred
     of his Life & thoughts I left & did refraine his companie.
     He wold *per*swade w*i*th men of quallitie to goe vnto the k of scotts whether
     I heare Royden is gon and where if he had liud he told me when I
     sawe him last he meant to be.

1

2

3

4

BIBLIOGRAPHICAL RECORD. *The Spanish Tragedy* was no less monumentally popular with the reading public than it was on the stage. On Oct. 6, 1592, the following entry was made on the Register of the Stationers' Co.: *Abell Ieffes Entred for his copie vnder thandes of master Hartwell and master Stirrop, a booke whiche is called the Spanishe tragedie of Don Horatio and Bellmipeia* [*sic*] &*c.*

On Dec. 18 of the same year another record (cf. Greg and Boswell, *Records of the Court of the Stationers' Company*, 1930, p. 44) declares that Abell Jeffes, mentioned above, and Edward White, had each offended against the laws of the company: Jeffes by publishing *Arden of Feversham*, the copyright of which belonged to White, and White by publishing *The Spanish Tragedy*, which belonged to Jeffes. The books so printed were confiscated by the company, and the printers fined.

The earliest extant quarto (technically an octavo) of *The Spanish Tragedy*, printed by Edward Allde for Edward White, bears no date, but asserts that it is "Newly corrected and amended of such grosse faults as passed in the first impression." This edition, of which only one copy is known to survive, is doubtless the one which was suppressed. Of the still earlier, and allegedly faultier, one issued by Jeffes we have no trace. In 1594 another edition was printed by Jeffes, "to be sold by Edward White"; and on Aug. 13, 1599, Jeffes transferred his copyright to William White, who, after issuing an edition in that year, surrendered the copyright to Thomas Pavier, Aug. 14, 1600. In 1602 appeared, under the auspices of Pavier, but from the press of William White, a quarto which first contained the famous "additions" (see below). Another quarto has survived with the date 1602 on the title-page, but with a colophon dated 1603; and there were further editions in 1610 (colophon, 1611), 1615 (two issues), 1618, 1623 (two issues), and finally in 1633.

THE ADDITIONS. On Sept. 25, 1601, and June 22, 1602, Philip Henslowe, in behalf of the Admiral's Men, made large payments to Ben Jonson for two sets of "adicyons" to a play referred to under the title of *Jeronimo*. Critics do not see Jonson's hand, however, in the remarkable additions which appear first in the 1602 Quarto, and which we here distinguish by the use of italic type. They are of surprising literary quality, surpassing the original play in this respect, but are not recognizably Jonsonian and probably date from 1597, when Henslowe produced a revival of the play, which he marked as "new." (See W. W. Greg, introduction to Malone Society reprint, 1925, and the Oxford Jonson, II. 238 ff.)

DATE AND STAGE PERFORMANCE. A somewhat blind reference in the Induction to Jonson's *Bartholomew Fair* (1614) refers to *Jeronimo* along with *Titus Andronicus* as a play already twenty-five or thirty years old. This would give 1584–1589 as the period during which the tragedy first appeared, and the lack of any reference to the Armada among the allusions to Anglo-Spanish history in Hieronimo's masque (I. v) suggests a date earlier than 1588. Probably 1586 is not far from correct. Professor T. W. Baldwin (*Modern Language Notes*, June, 1925; *Philological Quarterly*, July, 1927) argues that it cannot be later than the summer of 1585. The play was revived at the Rose Theatre by Strange's Men in 1592, and by the Admiral's at the same house in 1597, Ben Jonson acting the part of Hieronimo. Henslowe records in all twenty-nine performances. Another elaborate revival was doubtless undertaken in 1601–1602, in connection with the additions for which Jonson was paid, but detailed information for this period is lacking.

AUTHORSHIP. The early editions of *The Spanish Tragedy* are all anonymous, and none of the theatrical notices of the play mentions Kyd. We owe our knowledge of his authorship to Thomas Heywood, who quotes three lines (IV. i. 86–88) in his *Apology for Actors*, 1612, with the words: "Therefore, M[aster] Kid, in his *Spanish Tragedy*, upon occasion presenting itself, thus writes."

STRUCTURE. The early quartos divide the play into four acts, but not into scenes. The third act alone is, however, as long as the other three combined, and it may be that the usual five-act division was Kyd's original intention. Many of the devices which he invented or derived from his predecessors in Senecan tragedy passed into the common stock of the Elizabethan theatre. Among them are the idyllic garden scene; the play within the play; the dumb-show, made by Kyd an integral part of the drama; and the careful articulation of the subplot.

SOURCES. Kyd's plot does not correspond with any sequence of events in the history of Spain and Portugal. The time of action is thought of as the very recent past, the conflict in which Andrea lost his life being identifiable with the Battle of Alcantara in 1580. The form of the play is derived from the tragedies of Seneca (two of which are divided like this into four acts). Kyd retained the Senecan chorus, ghost, and spectacular peculiarities of plot, but gave them new vitality. The character of Lorenzo reflects the contemporary conception of Machiavelli's teachings. (The facsimile reproduces Kyd's letter about Marlowe, discovered by F. K. Brown in 1921.)

# THOMAS KYD (1558–1594)

## THE SPANISH TRAGEDY

## ACTUS PRIMUS

### [SCENE I. INDUCTION]

*Enter the Ghost of Andrea, and with him
Revenge*

*Ghost.* When this eternal substance of my
    soul
Did live imprison'd in my wanton flesh,
Each in their function serving other's need,
I was a courtier in the Spanish court.
My name was Don Andrea; my descent,   5
Though not ignoble, yet inferior far
To gracious fortunes of my tender youth:
For there in prime and pride of all my years,
By duteous service and deserving love,
In secret I possess'd a worthy dame,   10
Which hight sweet Bel-imperia by name.
But in the harvest of my summer joys
Death's winter nipp'd the blossoms of my bliss,
Forcing divorce betwixt my love and me.
For in the late conflict with Portingale   15
My valour drew me into danger's mouth,
Till life to death made passage through my
    wounds.
When I was slain, my soul descended straight
To pass the flowing stream of Acheron;
But churlish Charon, only boatman there,   20
Said that, my rites of burial not perform'd,
I might not sit amongst his passengers.
Ere Sol had slept three nights in Thetis' lap,
And slak'd his smoking chariot in her flood,
By Don Horatio, our knight marshal's son,   25
My funerals and obsequies were done.
Then was the ferryman of hell content
To pass me over to the slimy strand,
That leads to fell Avernus' ugly waves.
There, pleasing Cerberus with honey'd speech,   30
I pass'd the perils of the foremost porch.
Not far from hence, amidst ten thousand souls,
Sat Minos, Æacus, and Rhadamanth;
To whom no sooner 'gan I make approach,
To crave a passport for my wand'ring ghost,   35
But Minos, in graven leaves of lottery,
Drew forth the manner of my life and death.
"This knight," quoth he, "both liv'd and died
    in love;
And for his love tried fortune of the wars;
And by war's fortune lost both love and life."   40
"Why then," said Æacus, "convey him hence,
To walk with lovers in our fields of love,
And spend the course of everlasting time
Under green myrtle-trees and cypress shades."

---

¹¹ **hight:** was called   ¹⁵ **Portingale:** Portugal   ¹⁸⁻⁸⁵ (Cf. Æneid, Bk. VI)   ²⁹ **Avernus:** a noisome lake in southern Italy, identified with the entrance to Hell and hence Hell itself   ³⁶ **leaves of lottery:** books of fate

"No, no," said Rhadamanth, "it were not well,          45
With loving souls to place a martialist.
He died in war, and must to martial fields,
Where wounded Hector lives in lasting pain,
And Achilles' Myrmidons do scour the plain."
Then Minos, mildest censor of the three,          50
Made this device to end the difference:
"Send him," quoth he, "to our infernal king,
To doom him as best seems his majesty."
To this effect my passport straight was drawn.
In keeping on my way to Pluto's court,          55
Through dreadful shades of ever-glooming night,
I saw more sights than thousand tongues can tell,
Or pens can write, or mortal hearts can think.
Three ways there were: that on the right-hand side
Was ready way unto the 'foresaid fields,          60
Where lovers live and bloody martialists;
But either sort contain'd within his bounds.
The left-hand path, declining fearfully,
Was ready downfall to the deepest hell,
Where bloody Furies shakes their whips of steel,          65
And poor Ixion turns an endless wheel;
Where usurers are chok'd with melting gold,
And wantons are embrac'd with ugly snakes,
And murderers groan with never-killing wounds,
And perjur'd wights scalded in boiling lead,          70
And all foul sins with torments overwhelm'd.
'Twixt these two ways I trod the middle path,
Which brought me to the fair Elysian green,
In midst whereof there stands a stately tower,
The walls of brass, the gates of adamant.          75
Here finding Pluto with his Proserpine,
I show'd my passport, humbled on my knee;
Whereat fair Proserpine began to smile,
And begg'd that only she might give my doom.
Pluto was pleas'd, and seal'd it with a kiss.          80
Forthwith, Revenge, she rounded thee in th' ear,
And bade thee lead me through the gates of horn,
Where dreams have passage in the silent night.
No sooner had she spoke, but we were here —
I wot not how — in twinkling of an eye.          85
  *Revenge.*  Then know, Andrea, that thou art arriv'd
Where thou shalt see the author of thy death,
Don Balthazar, the prince of Portingale,

Depriv'd of life by Bel-imperia.
Here sit we down to see the mystery,          90
And serve for Chorus in this tragedy.

[SCENE II. *The Court of Spain*]

*Enter Spanish King, General, Castile, Hieronimo*

  *King.*  Now say, lord General, how fares our camp?
  *Gen.*  All well, my sovereign liege, except some few
That are deceas'd by fortune of the war.
  *King.*  But what portends thy cheerful countenance,
And posting to our presence thus in haste?          5
Speak, man, hath fortune given us victory?
  *Gen.*  Victory, my liege, and that with little loss.
  *King.*  Our Portingals will pay us tribute then?
  *Gen.*  Tribute and wonted homage therewithal.
  *King.*  Then bless'd be heaven and guider of the heavens,          10
From whose fair influence such justice flows.
  *Cast.*  *O multum dilecte Deo, tibi militat æther,*
*Et conjuratæ curvato poplite gentes*
*Succumbunt: recti soror est victoria juris.*
  *King.*  Thanks to my loving brother of Castile.          15
But, General, unfold in brief discourse
Your form of battle and your war's success,
That, adding all the pleasure of thy news
Unto the height of former happiness,
With deeper wage and greater dignity          20
We may reward thy blissful chivalry.
  *Gen.*  Where Spain and Portingale do jointly knit
Their frontiers, leaning on each other's bound,
There met our armies in their proud array;
Both furnish'd well, both full of hope and fear,          25
Both menacing alike with daring shows,
Both vaunting sundry colours of device,
Both cheerly sounding trumpets, drums, and fifes,
Both raising dreadful clamours to the sky,
That valleys, hills, and rivers made rebound,          30
And heaven itself was frighted with the sound.
Our battles both were pitch'd in squadron form,

---

**46 martialist:** warlike man     **50 censor:** judge     **53 doom:** judge, sentence     **62 either:** each **his:** its     **81 rounded:** whispered     **82 gates of horn:** gates of Sleep ('Hor' Q 1, 2; 'Horror' Q 3, etc.)     **91 Chorus:** interpreter (as in Greek tragedy)     **12–14 O . . . juris:** O much beloved of God, the heavens fight for thee, and the conspiring nations fall on bended knee; victory is the sister of just law. (Adapted from Claudian. The Latin passages in the play were printed very incorrectly in the quartos. They are given as corrected by modern editors.)     **27 colours of device:** insignia on standards     **30 rebound:** re-echo     **32 battles:** battle-lines     **pitch'd:** drawn up

Each corner strongly fenc'd with wings of shot;
But ere we join'd and came to push of pike,
I brought a squadron of our readiest shot  35
From out our rearward to begin the fight.
They brought another wing t' encounter us.
Meanwhile, our ordnance play'd on either side,
And captains strove to have their valours
    tried.
Don Pedro, their chief horsemen's colonel,  40
Did with his cornet bravely make attempt
To break the order of our battle ranks.
But Don Rogero, worthy man of war,
March'd forth against him with our musketeers,
And stopp'd the malice of his fell approach.  45
While they maintain hot skirmish to and fro,
Both battles join, and fall to handy-blows,
Their violent shot resembling th' ocean's rage,
When, roaring loud, and with a swelling tide,
It beats upon the rampiers of huge rocks,  50
And gapes to swallow neighbour-bounding
    lands.
Now, while Bellona rageth here and there,
Thick storms of bullets ran like winter's hail,
And shiver'd lances dark'd the troubled air.
        *Pede pes et cuspide cuspis;*  55
*Arma sonant armis, vir petiturque viro.*
On every side drop captains to the ground,
And soldiers, some ill-maim'd, some slain out-
    right:
Here falls a body sund'red from his head,
There legs and arms lie bleeding on the grass,  60
Mingled with weapons and unbowell'd steeds,
That scattering overspread the purple plain.
In all this turmoil, three long hours and more,
The victory to neither part inclin'd;
Till Don Andrea, with his brave lanciers,  65
In their main battle made so great a breach,
That, half dismay'd, the multitude retir'd.
But Balthazar, the Portingales' young prince,
Brought rescue, and encourag'd them to stay.
Here-hence the fight was eagerly renew'd,  70
And in that conflict was Andrea slain,
Brave man at arms, but weak to Balthazar.
Yet while the prince, insulting over him,
Breath'd out proud vaunts, sounding to our
    reproach,
Friendship and hardy valour join'd in one  75
Prick'd forth Horatio, our knight marshal's son,
To challenge forth that prince in single fight.
Not long between these twain the fight endur'd,
But straight the prince was beaten from his
    horse,
And forc'd to yield him prisoner to his foe.  80
When he was taken, all the rest they fled,

And our carbines pursu'd them to the death,
Till, Phœbus waving to the western deep,
Our trumpeters were charg'd to sound retreat.
    *King.* Thanks, good lord General, for these
    good news;  85
And for some argument of more to come,
Take this, and wear it for thy sovereign's sake.
                  *Gives him his chain.*
But tell me now, hast thou confirm'd a peace?
    *Gen.* No peace, my liege, but peace con-
    ditional,
That if with homage tribute be well paid,  90
The fury of your forces will be stay'd:
And to this peace their viceroy hath subscrib'd,
                *Gives the King a paper.*
And made a solemn vow that, during life,
His tribute shall be truly paid to Spain.
    *King.* These words, these deeds, become thy
    person well.  95
But now, knight marshal, frolic with thy king,
For 't is thy son that wins this battle's prize.
    *Hier.* Long may he live to serve my sover-
    eign liege,
And soon decay, unless he serve my liege.
    *King.* Nor thou, nor he, shall die without
    reward.             *A tucket afar off.* 100
What means this warning of this trumpet's
    sound?
    *Gen.* This tells me that your grace's men of
    war,
Such as war's fortune hath reserv'd from death,
Come marching on towards your royal seat,
To show themselves before your majesty;  105
For so I gave in charge at my depart.
Whereby by demonstration shall appear
That all, except three hundred or few more,
Are safe return'd, and by their foes enrich'd.

    *The Army enters; Balthazar, between Lo-
    renzo and Horatio, captive*

    *King.* A gladsome sight! I long to see them
    here.          *They enter and pass by.* 110
Was that the warlike prince of Portingale,
That by our nephew was in triumph led?
    *Gen.* It was, my liege, the prince of Portin-
    gale.
    *King.* But what was he that on the other
    side
Held him by th' arm, as partner of the prize? 115
    *Hier.* That was my son, my gracious sover-
    eign;
Of whom though from his tender infancy
My loving thoughts did never hope but well,
He never pleas'd his father's eyes till now,

---

<sup>33</sup> **shot:** musketeers    <sup>34</sup> **push of pike:** fighting at close quarters    <sup>41</sup> **cornet:** wing of an army
<sup>47</sup> **handy-blows:** hand-to-hand fighting    <sup>50</sup> **rampiers:** ramparts    <sup>55-56</sup> **Pede . . . viro:** Foot to
foot and lance to lance, arms clash on arms, and man is assailed by man.    <sup>70</sup> **Here-hence:** Henceforth
<sup>72</sup> **to:** *i.e.,* compared to    <sup>73</sup> **insulting:** exulting contemptuously    <sup>76</sup> **Prick'd:** spurred    <sup>83</sup> **waving:**
declining    <sup>100</sup> S. D. **tucket:** flourish of trumpets

Nor fill'd my heart with over-cloying joys. 120
*King.*  Go, let them march once more about
   these walls,
That, staying them, we may confer and talk
With our brave prisoner and his double guard.
                                    [*Exit a messenger.*]
Hieronimo, it greatly pleaseth us
That in our victory thou have a share, 125
By virtue of thy worthy son's exploit.

*Enter again*

Bring hither the young prince of Portingale:
The rest march on; but, ere they be dismiss'd,
We will bestow on every soldier
Two ducats, and on every leader ten, 130
That they may know our largess welcomes
   them.    *Exeunt all but* [*the King*], *Baltha-*
          *zar, Lorenzo* [*and*] *Horatio.*
Welcome, Don Balthazar! welcome, nephew!
And thou, Horatio, thou art welcome too.
Young prince, although thy father's hard mis-
   deeds,
In keeping back the tribute that he owes, 135
Deserve but evil measure at our hands,
Yet shalt thou know that Spain is honourable.
*Bal.*  The trespass that my father made in
   peace
Is now controll'd by fortune of the wars;
And cards once dealt, it boots not ask why
   so. 140
His men are slain, a weakening to his realm;
His colours seiz'd, a blot unto his name;
His son distress'd, a cor'sive to his heart:
These punishments may clear his late offence.
*King.*  Ay, Balthazar; if he observe this
   truce, 145
Our peace will grow the stronger for these wars.
Meanwhile live thou, though not in liberty,
Yet free from bearing any servile yoke;
For in our hearing thy deserts were great,
And in our sight thyself art gracious. 150
*Bal.*  And I shall study to deserve this grace.
*King.*  But tell me — for their holding makes
   me doubt —
To which of these twain art thou prisoner?
*Lor.*  To me, my liege.
*Hor.*                    To me, my sovereign.
*Lor.*  This hand first took his courser by the
   reins. 155
*Hor.*  But first my lance did put him from
   his horse.
*Lor.*  I seiz'd his weapon, and enjoy'd it first.
*Hor.*  But first I forc'd him lay his weapons
   down.
*King.*  Let go his arm, upon our privilege.
                                    *Let him go.*

Say, worthy prince, to whether did'st thou
   yield? 160
*Bal.*  To him in courtesy, to this perforce.
He spake me fair, this other gave me strokes;
He promis'd life, this other threat'ned death;
He won my love, this other conquer'd me,
And, truth to say, I yield myself to both. 165
*Hier.*  But that I know your grace for just
   and wise,
And might seem partial in this difference,
Enforc'd by nature and by law of arms
My tongue should plead for young Horatio's
   right.
He hunted well that was a lion's death, 170
Not he that in a garment wore his skin;
So hares may pull dead lions by the beard.
*King.*  Content thee, marshal, thou shalt
   have no wrong;
And, for thy sake, thy son shall want no right.
Will both abide the censure of my doom? 175
*Lor.*  I crave no better than your grace
   awards.
*Hor.*  Nor I, although I sit beside my right.
*King.*  Then by my judgment, thus your
   strife shall end:
You both deserve, and both shall have reward.
Nephew, thou took'st his weapon and his
   horse: 180
His weapons and his horse are thy reward.
Horatio, thou didst force him first to yield:
His ransom therefore is thy valour's fee;
Appoint the sum, as you shall both agree.
But, nephew, thou shalt have the prince in
   guard, 185
For thine estate best fitteth such a guest:
Horatio's house were small for all his train.
Yet, in regard thy substance passeth his,
And that just guerdon may befall desert,
To him we yield the armour of the prince. 190
How likes Don Balthazar of this device?
*Bal.*  Right well, my liege, if this proviso
   were,
That Don Horatio bear us company,
Whom I admire and love for chivalry.
*King.*  Horatio, leave him not that loves
   thee so. — 195
Now let us hence to see our soldiers paid,
And feast our prisoner as our friendly guest.
                                    *Exeunt.*

[SCENE III.  *The Court of Portugal*]

*Enter Viceroy, Alexandro, Villuppo*

*Vic.*  Is our ambassador despatch'd for Spain?
*Alex.*  Two days, my liege, are past since his
   depart.

---

¹³⁹ controll'd: overmastered, held in check    ¹⁴³ cor'sive: corrosive    ¹⁶⁰ whether: which of the
two    ¹⁶¹ him: *i.e.,* Lorenzo    ¹⁷⁵ censure: decision    doom: judgment    ¹⁷⁷ sit beside: fail of
¹⁸⁸ in regard: inasmuch as

*Vic.* And tribute-payment gone along with him?
*Alex.* Ay, my good lord.
*Vic.* Then rest we here awhile in our unrest,　5
And feed our sorrows with some inward sighs,
For deepest cares break never into tears.
But wherefore sit I in a regal throne?
This better fits a wretch's endless moan.
　　　　　　　　　*Falls to the ground.*
Yet this is higher than my fortunes reach,　10
And therefore better than my state deserves.
Ay, ay, this earth, image of melancholy,
Seeks him whom fates adjudge to misery.
Here let me lie; now am I at the lowest.
　*Qui jacet in terra, non habet unde cadat.*　15
*In me consumpsit vires fortuna nocendo;*
*Nil superest ut jam possit obesse magis.*
Yes, Fortune may bereave me of my crown.
Here, take it now: let Fortune do her worst,
She will not rob me of this sable weed.　20
O no, she envies none but pleasant things.
Such is the folly of despiteful chance!
Fortune is blind, and sees not my deserts;
So is she deaf, and hears not my laments;
And could she hear, yet is she wilful-mad,　25
And therefore will not pity my distress.
Suppose that she could pity me, what then?
What help can be expected at her hands
Whose foot is standing on a rolling stone,
And mind more mutable than fickle winds?　30
Why wail I, then, where 's hope of no redress?
O yes, complaining makes my grief seem less.
My late ambition hath distain'd my faith;
My breach of faith occasion'd bloody wars;
Those bloody wars have spent my treasure;　35
And with my treasure my people's blood;
And with their blood, my joy and best belov'd,
My best belov'd, my sweet and only son.
O, wherefore went I not to war myself?
The cause was mine; I might have died for both.　40
My years were mellow, his but young and green,
My death were natural, but his was forc'd.
*Alex.* No doubt, my liege, but still the prince survives.
*Vic.* Survives! Ay, where?
*Alex.* In Spain, a prisoner by mischance of war.　45
*Vic.* Then they have slain him for his father's fault.
*Alex.* That were a breach to common law of arms.
*Vic.* They reck no laws that meditate revenge.

*Alex.* His ransom's worth will stay from foul revenge.
*Vic.* No; if he liv'd, the news would soon be here.　50
*Alex.* Nay, evil news fly faster still than good.
*Vic.* Tell me no more of news, for he is dead.
*Vil.* My sovereign, pardon the author of ill news,
And I 'll bewray the fortune of thy son.
*Vic.* Speak on, I 'll guerdon thee, whate'er it be.　55
Mine ear is ready to receive ill news;
My heart grown hard 'gainst mischief's battery.
Stand up, I say, and tell thy tale at large.
*Vil.* Then hear that truth which these mine eyes have seen.
When both the armies were in battle join'd,　60
Don Balthazar, amidst the thickest troops,
To win renown did wondrous feats of arms.
Amongst the rest, I saw him, hand to hand,
In single fight with their lord-general;
Till Alexandro, that here counterfeits　65
Under the colour of a duteous friend,
Discharg'd his pistol at the prince's back
As though he would have slain their general:
But therewithal Don Balthazar fell down;
And when he fell, then we began to fly:　70
But, had he liv'd, the day had sure been ours.
*Alex.* O wicked forgery! O traitorous miscreant!
*Vic.* Hold thou thy peace! But now, Villuppo, say,
Where then became the carcase of my son?
*Vil.* I saw them drag it to the Spanish tents.
*Vic.* Ay, ay, my nightly dreams have told me this. —　76
Thou false, unkind, unthankful, traitorous beast,
Wherein had Balthazar offended thee,
That thou shouldst thus betray him to our foes?
Was 't Spanish gold that bleared so thine eyes　80
That thou couldst see no part of our deserts?
Perchance, because thou art Terceira's lord,
Thou hadst some hope to wear this diadem,
If first my son and then myself were slain.
But thy ambitious thought shall break thy neck.　85
Ay, this was it that made thee spill his blood;
　　　*Take the crown and put it on again.*
But I 'll now wear it till thy blood be spilt.
*Alex.* Vouchsafe, dread sovereign, to hear me speak.

¹⁵⁻¹⁷ **Qui . . . magis:** He who lies on the ground has not whence he may fall.  Against me fortune has consumed her power of doing harm.  Nothing remains that now can hurt me more!　²⁰ **weed:** garment　²⁹ **is:** (not in Qq.)　³³ **distain'd:** sullied　⁵⁴ **bewray:** reveal　⁷⁴ **Where then became:** What then became of　⁸² **Terceira:** an important island in the Azores

*Vic.* Away with him! His sight is second
hell.
Keep him till we determine of his death:     90
                     [*They take him out.*]
If Balthazar be dead, he shall not live.
Villuppo, follow us for thy reward.
                              *Exit Viceroy.*
*Vil.* Thus have I with an envious, forged tale
Deceiv'd the king, betray'd mine enemy,
And hope for guerdon of my villainy. *Exit.* 95

[SCENE IV.   *The Court of Spain*]

*Enter Horatio and Bel-imperia*

*Bel.* Signior Horatio, this is the place and
hour,
Wherein I must entreat thee to relate
The circumstance of Don Andrea's death,
Who, living, was my garland's sweetest flower,
And in his death hath buried my delights.     5
*Hor.* For love of him and service to yourself,
I nill refuse this heavy doleful charge;
Yet tears and sighs, I fear, will hinder me.
When both our armies were enjoin'd in fight,
Your worthy chevalier amidst the thick'st,    10
For glorious cause still aiming at the fairest,
Was at the last by young Don Balthazar
Encount'red hand to hand.  Their fight was
long,
Their hearts were great, their clamours menac-
ing,
Their strength alike, their strokes both dan-
gerous.                                       15
But wrathful Nemesis, that wicked power,
Envying at Andrea's praise and worth,
Cut short his life, to end his praise and worth.
She, she herself, disguis'd in armour's mask —
As Pallas was before proud Pergamus —        20
Brought in a fresh supply of halberdiers,
Which paunch'd his horse, and ding'd him to
the ground.
Then young Don Balthazar with ruthless rage,
Taking advantage of his foe's distress,
Did finish what his halberdiers begun,        25
And left not, till Andrea's life was done.
Then, though too late, incens'd with just re-
morse,
I with my band set forth against the prince,
And brought him prisoner from his halberdiers.
*Bel.* Would thou hadst slain him that so
slew my love!                                 30
But then was Don Andrea's carcase lost?
*Hor.* No, that was it for which I chiefly
strove,
Nor stepp'd I back till I recover'd him.
I took him up, and wound him in mine arms;

And welding him unto my private tent,        35
There laid him down, and dew'd him with my
tears,
And sigh'd and sorrow'd as became a friend.
But neither friendly sorrow, sighs, nor tears
Could win pale Death from his usurped right.
Yet this I did, and less I could not do:      40
I saw him honoured with due funeral.
This scarf I pluck'd from off his lifeless arm,
And wear it in remembrance of my friend.
*Bel.*   I know the scarf: would he had kept it
still!
For had he liv'd, he would have kept it still, 45
And worn it for his Bel-imperia's sake;
For 't was my favour at his last depart.
But now wear thou it both for him and me;
For after him thou hast deserv'd it best.
But for thy kindness in his life and death,   50
Be sure, while Bel-imperia's life endures,
She will be Don Horatio's thankful friend.
*Hor.*   And, madam, Don Horatio will not
slack
Humbly to serve fair Bel-imperia.
But now, if your good liking stand thereto,   55
I 'll crave your pardon to go seek the prince;
For so the duke, your father, gave me charge.
                                        *Exit.*
*Bel.*   Ay, go, Horatio, leave me here alone;
For solitude best fits my cheerless mood.
Yet what avails to wail Andrea's death,       60
From whence Horatio proves my second love?
Had he not lov'd Andrea as he did,
He could not sit in Bel-imperia's thoughts.
But how can love find harbour in my breast
Till I revenge the death of my belov'd?        65
Yes, second love shall further my revenge!
I 'll love Horatio, my Andrea's friend,
The more to spite the prince that wrought his
end;
And where Don Balthazar, that slew my love,
Himself now pleads for favour at my hands,    70
He shall, in rigour of my just disdain,
Reap long repentance for his murderous deed.
For what was 't else but murderous cowardice,
So many to oppress one valiant knight,
Without respect of honour in the fight?        75
And here he comes that murd'red my delight.

*Enter Lorenzo and Balthazar*

*Lor.*   Sister, what means this melancholy
walk?
*Bel.*   That for a while I wish no company.
*Lor.*   But here the prince is come to visit you.
*Bel.*   That argues that he lives in liberty.    80
*Bal.*   No, madam, but in pleasing servitude.
*Bel.*   Your prison then, belike, is your conceit.

---

³ **circumstance:** particulars     ⁷ **nill:** will not     ²² **paunch'd:** stabbed in the belly     **ding'd:**
knocked down     ²⁷ **incens'd:** inflamed     **remorse:** regret, pity     ³⁵ **welding:** carrying (archaic
form of "wielding")     ⁷⁴ **oppress:** overpower     ⁸² **conceit:** fancy

*Bal.* Ay, by conceit my freedom is enthrall'd.
*Bel.* Then with conceit enlarge yourself
again.
*Bal.* What, if conceit have laid my heart to
gage? 85
*Bel.* Pay that you borrow'd, and recover it.
*Bal.* I die, if it return from whence it lies.
*Bel.* A heartless man, and live? A miracle!
*Bal.* Ay, lady, love can work such miracles.
*Lor.* Tush, tush, my lord! let go these am-
bages, 90
And in plain terms acquaint her with your love.
*Bel.* What boots complaint, when there 's no
remedy?
*Bal.* Yes, to your gracious self must I com-
plain,
In whose fair answer lies my remedy,
On whose perfection all my thoughts attend, 95
On whose aspect mine eyes find beauty's bower,
In whose translucent breast my heart is lodg'd.
*Bel.* Alas, my lord, these are but words of
course,
And but devis'd to drive me from this place.
*She, in going in, lets fall her glove, which*
*Horatio, coming out, takes up.*
*Hor.* Madam, your glove. 100
*Bel.* Thanks, good Horatio; take it for thy
pains.
*Bal.* Signior Horatio stoop'd in happy time!
*Hor.* I reap'd more grace than I deserv'd or
hop'd.
*Lor.* My lord, be not dismay'd for what is
past.
You know that women oft are humorous. 105
These clouds will overblow with little wind;
Let me alone, I 'll scatter them myself.
Meanwhile, let us devise to spend the time
In some delightful sports and revelling.
*Hor.* The king, my lords, is coming hither
straight, 110
To feast the Portingal ambassador;
Things were in readiness before I came.
*Bal.* Then here it fits us to attend the king,
To welcome hither our ambassador, 114
And learn my father and my country's health.

[SCENE V. *The Same*]

*Enter the Banquet, Trumpets, the King, and*
*Ambassador*

*King.* See, lord Ambassador, how Spain entreats

Their prisoner Balthazar, thy viceroy's son.
We pleasure more in kindness than in wars.
*Amb.* Sad is our king, and Portingale la-
ments,
Supposing that Don Balthazar is slain; 5
*Bal.* So am I slain, by beauty's tyranny.
You see, my lord, how Balthazar is slain:
I frolic with the Duke of Castile's son,
Wrapp'd every hour in pleasures of the court,
And grac'd with favours of his majesty. 10
*King.* Put off your greetings, till our feast
be done;
Now come and sit with us, and taste our cheer.
*Sit to the banquet.*
Sit down, young prince, you are our second
guest;
Brother, sit down; and, nephew, take your
place.
Signior Horatio, wait thou upon our cup; 15
For well thou hast deserv'd to be honour'd.
Now, lordings, fall to. Spain is Portugal,
And Portugal is Spain; we both are friends;
Tribute is paid, and we enjoy our right.
But where is old Hieronimo, our marshal? 20
He promis'd us, in honour of our guest,
To grace our banquet with some pompous jest.

*Enter Hieronimo, with a drum, three knights,*
*each his scutcheon; then he fetches three*
*kings; they take their crowns and them*
*captive.*

Hieronimo, this masque contents mine eye,
Although I sound not well the mystery.
*Hier.* The first arm'd knight, that hung his
scutcheon up, 25
*He takes the scutcheon and gives it*
*to the King.*
Was English Robert, Earl of Gloucester,
Who, when King Stephen bore sway in Albion,
Arriv'd with five and twenty thousand men
In Portingale, and by success of war
Enforc'd the king, then but a Saracen, 30
To bear the yoke of the English monarchy.
*King.* My lord of Portingale, by this you see
That which may comfort both your king and
you,
And make your late discomfort seem the less.
But say, Hieronimo, what was the next? 35
*Hier.* The second knight, that hung his
scutcheon up, *He doth as he did before.*
Was Edmund, Earl of Kent in Albion,
When English Richard wore the diadem.

84 **enlarge:** set free   85 **to gage:** as a pledge   90 **ambages:** circumlocutions   98 **words of course:** ceremonial phrases   99 **devis'd:** ( 'deuise' Q 1–2)   105 **humorous:** capricious   1 **entreats:** treats   22 **pompous:** stately   26 **English Robert:** Robert of Gloucester seems never to have been in Portugal. Some Englishmen, however, did take part in the capture of Lisbon in 1147.   37 **Edmund:** Edmund Langley, Earl of Kent, went to Portugal during the reign of Richard II, not to attack the king but to aid him against the Spaniards. He was created Duke of York four years later (1385) for his services against the Scots.

He came likewise, and razed Lisbon walls,
And took the King of Portingale in fight;    40
For which and other such-like service done
He after was created Duke of York.
   *King.* This is another special argument,
That Portingale may deign to bear our yoke,
When it by little England hath been yok'd.    45
But now, Hieronimo, what were the last?
   *Hier.* The third and last, not least, in our
     account,                    *Doing as before.*
Was, as the rest, a valiant Englishman,
Brave John of Gaunt, the Duke of Lancaster,
As by his scutcheon plainly may appear.    50
He with a puissant army came to Spain,
And took our King of Castile prisoner.
   *Amb.* This is an argument for our viceroy
That Spain may not insult for her success,
Since English warriors likewise conquer'd
   Spain,                                  55
And made them bow their knees to Albion.
   *King.* Hieronimo, I drink to thee for this
   device,
Which hath pleas'd both the ambassador and
   me:
Pledge me, Hieronimo, if thou love the king.
          *Takes the cup of Horatio.*
My lord, I fear we sit but over-long,    60
Unless our dainties were more delicate;
But welcome are you to the best we have.
Now let us in, that you may be despatch'd:
I think our council is already set.
                 *Exeunt omnes.*

           [*Chorus*]

   *Andrea.* Come we for this from depth of un-
    derground,                              65
To see him feast that gave me my death's
   wound?
These pleasant sights are sorrow to my soul:
Nothing but league, and love, and banqueting?
   *Revenge.* Be still, Andrea; ere we go from
   hence,
I 'll turn their friendship into fell despite,    70
Their love to mortal hate, their day to night,
Their hope into despair, their peace to war,
Their joys to pain, their bliss to misery.


         ACTUS SECUNDUS

   [SCENE I. *The Palace of Don Cyprian*]

     *Enter Lorenzo and Balthazar*

   *Lor.* My lord, though Bel-imperia seem thus
   coy,
Let reason hold you in your wonted joy.

In time the savage bull sustains the yoke,
In time all haggard hawks will stoop to lure,
In time small wedges cleave the hardest oak,    5
In time the flint is pierc'd with softest shower,
And she in time will fall from her disdain,
And rue the sufferance of your friendly pain.
   *Bal.* No, she is wilder, and more hard withal,
Than beast, or bird, or tree, or stony wall.    10
But wherefore blot I Bel-imperia's name?
It is my fault, not she, that merits blame.
My feature is not to content her sight,
My words are rude and work her no delight.
The lines I send her are but harsh and ill,    15
Such as do drop from Pan and Marsyas' quill.
My presents are not of sufficient cost,
And being worthless, all my labour 's lost.
Yet might she love me for my valiancy:
Ay, but that 's sland'red by captivity.    20
Yet might she love me to content her sire:
Ay, but her reason masters his desire.
Yet might she love me as her brother's friend:
Ay, but her hopes aim at some other end.
Yet might she love me to uprear her state:    25
Ay, but perhaps she hopes some nobler mate.
Yet might she love me as her beauty's thrall:
Ay, but I fear she cannot love at all.
   *Lor.* My lord, for my sake leave these ecsta-
   sies,
And doubt not but we 'll find some remedy.    30
Some cause there is that lets you not be lov'd;
First that must needs be known, and then re-
   mov'd.
What, if my sister love some other knight?
   *Bal.* My summer's day will turn to winter's
   night.
   *Lor.* I have already found a stratagem    35
To sound the bottom of this doubtful theme.
My lord, for once you shall be rul'd by me;
Hinder me not, whate'er you hear or see.
By force or fair means will I cast about
To find the truth of all this question out.    40
Ho, Pedringano!
   *Ped.*          *Signior!*
   *Lor.*                    *Vien qui presto.*

      *Enter Pedringano*

   *Ped.* Hath your lordship any service to
   command me?
   *Lor.* Ay, Pedringano, service of import;
And — not to spend the time in trifling words —
Thus stands the case: it is not long, thou
   know'st,                                45
Since I did shield thee from my father's wrath,
For thy conveyance in Andrea's love,

---

  ⁴⁹ **John of Gaunt:** John of Gaunt led an army to Spain in 1386–1387. He claimed the throne of Castile, but failed to capture the king and was finally forced to withdraw. He later married his daughter to the heir to the Castilian throne.   ³⁻⁶ (From Son. 47 of Watson's *Hecatompathia* [1582]. Cf. *Much Ado*, I. i. 271.)   ⁴ **haggard:** untamed   ²⁷ **beauty's:** ('beauteous' Qq.)   ⁴¹ **Vien qui presto:** Come here quickly (Italian).   ⁴⁷ **conveyance:** secret agency

For which thou wert adjudg'd to punishment.
I stood betwixt thee and thy punishment,
And since, thou know'st how I have favour'd
    thee.                                          50
Now to these favours will I add reward,
Not with fair words, but store of golden coin,
And lands and living join'd with dignities,
If thou but satisfy my just demand.
Tell truth, and have me for thy lasting friend. 55
    *Ped.*  Whate'er it be your lordship shall de-
    mand,
My bounden duty bids me tell the truth,
If case it lie in me to tell the truth.
    *Lor.*  Then, Pedringano, this is my demand:
Whom loves my sister Bel-imperia?                  60
For she reposeth all her trust in thee.
Speak, man, and gain both friendship and re-
    ward:
I mean, whom loves she in Andrea's place?
    *Ped.*  Alas, my lord, since Don Andrea's
    death
I have no credit with her as before,              65
And therefore know not, if she love or no.
    *Lor.*  Nay, if thou dally, then I am thy foe,
                              *Draws his sword.*
And fear shall force what friendship cannot
    win.
Thy death shall bury what thy life conceals;
Thou diest for more esteeming her than me. 70
    *Ped.*  O, stay, my lord!
    *Lor.*  Yet speak the truth, and I will guerdon
    thee,
And shield thee from whatever can ensue,
And will conceal whate'er proceeds from thee.
But if thou dally once again, thou diest.         75
    *Ped.*  If madam Bel-imperia be in love —
    *Lor.*  What, villain! Ifs and ands?
                              *Offer to kill him.*
    *Ped.*  O, stay, my lord! She loves Horatio.
                              *Balthazar starts back.*
    *Lor.*  What, Don Horatio, our knight mar-
    shal's son?
    *Ped.*  Even him, my lord.                     80
    *Lor.*  Now say but how know'st thou he is
    her love,
And thou shalt find me kind and liberal.
Stand up, I say, and fearless tell the truth.
    *Ped.*  She sent him letters, which myself
    perus'd,
Full-fraught with lines and arguments of love, 85
Preferring him before Prince Balthazar.
    *Lor.*  Swear on this cross that what thou
    say'st is true,
And that thou wilt conceal what thou hast
    told.
    *Ped.*  I swear to both, by him that made us
    all.

    *Lor.*  In hope thine oath is true, here 's thy
    reward;                                        90
But if I prove thee perjur'd and unjust,
This very sword whereon thou took'st thine
    oath
Shall be the worker of thy tragedy.
    *Ped.*  What I have said is true, and shall —
    for me —
Be still conceal'd from Bel-imperia.              95
Besides, your honour's liberality
Deserves my duteous service, even till death.
    *Lor.*  Let this be all that thou shalt do for
    me:
Be watchful when and where these lovers
    meet,
And give me notice in some secret sort.          100
    *Ped.*  I will, my lord.
    *Lor.*  Then shalt thou find that I am liberal.
Thou know'st that I can more advance thy
    state
Than she; be therefore wise, and fail me not.
Go and attend her, as thy custom is,             105
Lest absence make her think thou dost amiss.
                              *Exit Pedringano.*
Why so: *tam armis quam ingenio:*
Where words prevail not, violence prevails;
But gold doth more than either of them both.
How likes Prince Balthazar this stratagem? 110
    *Bal.*  Both well and ill; it makes me glad and
    sad:
Glad, that I know the hinderer of my love;
Sad, that I fear she hates me whom I love:
Glad, that I know on whom to be reveng'd;
Sad, that she 'll fly me, if I take revenge.      115
Yet must I take revenge, or die myself,
For love resisted grows impatient.
I think Horatio be my destin'd plague:
First, in his hand he brandished a sword,
And with that sword he fiercely waged war, 120
And in that war he gave me dangerous wounds,
And by those wounds he forced me to yield,
And by my yielding I became his slave.
Now in his mouth he carries pleasing words,
Which pleasing words do harbour sweet con-
    ceits,                                         125
Which sweet conceits are lim'd with sly deceits,
Which sly deceits smooth Bel-imperia's ears,
And through her ears dive down into her heart,
And in her heart set him, where I should stand.
Thus hath he ta'en my body by his force, 130
And now by sleight would captivate my soul;
But in his fall I 'll tempt the destinies,
And either lose my life, or win my love.
    *Lor.*  Let 's go, my lord; your staying stays
    revenge.
Do you but follow me, and gain your love: 135
Her favour must be won by his remove. *Exeunt.*

⁶⁶ **If:** in     ⁶⁷ s. d.,     ⁷⁷ s. d.: (added in 1602 and later Qq.)     ⁸⁷ **cross:** sword-hilt     ¹⁰⁷ **tam**
  **. . ingenio:** as much by arms as by cunning

[SCENE II. *The Same*]

*Enter Horatio and Bel-imperia*

*Hor.* Now, madam, since by favour of your
  love
Our hidden smoke is turn'd to open flame,
And that with looks and words we feed our
  thoughts
(Two chief contents, where more cannot be had);
Thus, in the midst of love's fair blandishments, 5
Why show you sign of inward languishments?
                    *Pedringano showeth all to the
                    Prince    and    Lorenzo,
                    placing them in secret.*
*Bel.* My heart, sweet friend, is like a ship at
  sea;
She wisheth port, where, riding all at ease,
She may repair what stormy times have worn,
And leaning on the shore, may sing with joy 10
That pleasure follows pain, and bliss annoy.
Possession of thy love is th' only port,
Wherein my heart, with fears and hopes long
  toss'd,
Each hour doth wish and long to make resort,
There to repair the joys that it hath lost,    15
And, sitting safe, to sing in Cupid's choir
That sweetest bliss is crown of love's desire.
                    *Balthazar [and Lorenzo] above.*
*Bal.* O sleep, mine eyes, see not my love
  profan'd;
Be deaf, my ears, hear not my discontent;
Die, heart; another joys what thou deserv'st. 20
*Lor.* Watch still, mine eyes, to see this love
  disjoin'd;
Hear still, mine ears, to hear them both lament;
Live, heart, to joy at fond Horatio's fall.
*Bel.* Why stands Horatio speechless all this
  while?
*Hor.* The less I speak, the more I medi-
  tate.                                          25
*Bel.* But whereon dost thou chiefly medi-
  tate?
*Hor.* On dangers past, and pleasures to
  ensue.
*Bal.* On pleasures past, and dangers to en-
  sue.
*Bel.* What dangers and what pleasures dost
  thou mean?
*Hor.* Dangers of war, and pleasures of our
  love.                                          30
*Lor.* Dangers of death, but pleasures none
  at all.
*Bel.* Let dangers go, thy war shall be with
  me,
But such a warring as breaks no bond of peace.

Speak thou fair words, I 'll cross them with fair
  words;
Send thou sweet looks, I 'll meet them with
  sweet looks;                                   35
Write loving lines, I 'll answer loving lines;
Give me a kiss, I 'll countercheck thy kiss:
Be this our warring peace, or peaceful war.
*Hor.* But, gracious madam, then appoint
  the field,
Where trial of this war shall first be made.   40
*Bal.* Ambitious villain, how his boldness
  grows!
*Bel.* Then be thy father's pleasant bower
  the field,
Where first we vow'd a mutual amity.
The court were dangerous, that place is safe.
Our hour shall be, when Vesper 'gins to rise, 45
That summons home distressful travellers.
There none shall hear us but the harmless birds;
Happily the gentle nightingale
Shall carol us asleep, ere we be ware,
And, singing with the prickle at her breast,   50
Tell our delight and mirthful dalliance.
Till then each hour will seem a year and more.
*Hor.* But, honey-sweet and honourable love,
Return we now into your father's sight;
Dangerous suspicion waits on our delight.      55
*Lor.* Ay, danger mix'd with jealous despite
Shall send thy soul into eternal night. *Exeunt.*

[SCENE III. *The Court of Spain*]

*Enter King of Spain, Portingale Ambassador,
Don Cyprian, etc.*

*King.* Brother of Castile, to the prince's love
What says your daughter Bel-imperia?
*Cyp.* Although she coy it, as becomes her
  kind,
And yet dissemble that she loves the prince,
I doubt not, I, but she will stoop in time.     5
And were she froward, which she will not be,
Yet herein shall she follow my advice,
Which is to love him, or forgo my love.
*King.* Then, lord Ambassador of Portingale,
Advise thy king to make this marriage up,      10
For strengthening of our late-confirmed league;
I know no better means to make us friends.
Her dowry shall be large and liberal:
Besides that she is daughter and half-heir
Unto our brother here, Don Cyprian,            15
And shall enjoy the moiety of his land,
I 'll grace her marriage with an uncle's gift,
And this it is: in case the match go forward,
The tribute which you pay, shall be releas'd;
And if by Balthazar she have a son,            20
He shall enjoy the kingdom after us.

---

<sup>17</sup> S. D. **above:** on the upper stage    <sup>20</sup> **joys:** enjoys    <sup>23</sup> **fond:** infatuated, foolish    <sup>45</sup> **Vesper:**
the evening star    <sup>46</sup> **travellers:** (meaning both "wanderers" and "laborers")    <sup>3</sup> **coy it:** affect
shyness

*Amb.* I 'll make the motion to my sovereign liege,
And work it, if my counsel may prevail.
*King.* Do so, my lord, and if he give consent,
I hope his presence here will honour us,    25
In celebration of the nuptial day;
And let himself determine of the time.
*Amb.* Will 't please your grace command me aught beside?
*King.* Commend me to the king, and so farewell.
But where 's Prince Balthazar to take his leave?    30
*Amb.* That is perform'd already, my good lord.
*King.* Amongst the rest of what you have in charge,
The prince's ransom must not be forgot.
That 's none of mine, but his that took him prisoner;
And well his forwardness deserves reward.    35
It was Horatio, our knight marshal's son.
*Amb.* Between us there 's a price already pitch'd,
And shall be sent with all convenient speed.
*King.* Then once again farewell, my lord.
*Amb.* Farewell, my lord of Castile, and the rest.                            *Exit.* 40
*King.* Now, brother, you must take some little pains
To win fair Bel-imperia from her will.
Young virgins must be ruled by their friends.
The prince is amiable, and loves her well;
If she neglect him and forgo his love,    45
She both will wrong her own estate and ours.
Therefore, whiles I do entertain the prince
With greatest pleasure that our court affords,
Endeavour you to win your daughter's thought:
If she give back, all this will come to naught. 50
                                    *Exeunt.*

[SCENE IV. *Hieronimo's Garden*]

*Enter Horatio, Bel-imperia, and Pedringano*

*Hor.* Now that the night begins with sable wings
To overcloud the brightness of the sun,
And that in darkness pleasures may be done,
Come, Bel-imperia, let us to the bower,
And there in safety pass a pleasant hour.    5
*Bel.* I follow thee, my love, and will not back,
Although my fainting heart controls my soul.
*Hor.* Why, make you doubt of Pedringano's faith?
*Bel.* No, he is as trusty as my second self. —
Go, Pedringano, watch without the gate,    10
And let us know if any make approach.

*Ped.* [*Aside.*] Instead of watching, I 'll deserve more gold
By fetching Don Lorenzo to this match.
                            *Exit Pedringano.*
*Hor.* What means my love?
*Bel.*            I know not what myself;
And yet my heart foretells me some mischance. 15
*Hor.* Sweet, say not so; fair fortune is our friend,
And heavens have shut up day to pleasure us.
The stars, thou see'st, hold back their twinkling shine,
And Luna hides herself to pleasure us.
*Bel.* Thou hast prevail'd; I 'll conquer my misdoubt,    20
And in thy love and counsel drown my fear.
I fear no more; love now is all my thoughts.
Why sit we not? for pleasure asketh ease.
*Hor.* The more thou sitt'st within these leafy bowers,
The more will Flora deck it with her flowers. 25
*Bel.* Ay, but if Flora spy Horatio here,
Her jealous eye will think I sit too near.
*Hor.* Hark, madam, how the birds record by night,
For joy that Bel-imperia sits in sight.
*Bel.* No, Cupid counterfeits the nightingale,    30
To frame sweet music to Horatio's tale.
*Hor.* If Cupid sing, then Venus is not far:
Ay, thou art Venus, or some fairer star.
*Bel.* If I be Venus, thou must needs be Mars;
And where Mars reigneth, there must needs be wars.    35
*Hor.* Then thus begin our wars: put forth thy hand,
That it may combat with my ruder hand.
*Bel.* Set forth thy foot to try the push of mine.
*Hor.* But first my looks shall combat against thine.
*Bel.* Then ward thyself: I dart this kiss at thee.    40
*Hor.* Thus I retort the dart thou threw'st at me.
*Bel.* Nay then, to gain the glory of the field,
My twining arms shall yoke and make thee yield.
*Hor.* Nay then, my arms are large and strong withal:
Thus elms by vines are compass'd, till they fall.    45
*Bel.* O, let me go; for in my troubled eyes
Now may'st thou read that life in passion dies.
*Hor.* O, stay a while, and I will die with thee;

---

²³ **work:** accomplish    ⁴⁹ **thought:** ( 'thoughts' early Qq.)    ⁵⁰ **give back: refuse**    ⁷ **con-trols: is in conflict with**    ²⁸ **record:** sing    ³⁵ **wars:** ( 'warre' Qq.)

So shalt thou yield, and yet have conquer'd
  me.
*Bel.*   Who's there, Pedringano?  We are be-
tray'd!                                                          50

*Enter Lorenzo, Balthazar, Serberine,
      Pedringano, disguised*

*Lor.*   My lord, away with her, take her
aside.—
O, sir, forbear: your valour is already tried.
Quickly despatch, my masters.
                          *They hang him in the arbour.*
*Hor.*              What, will you murder me?
*Lor.*   Ay, thus, and thus: these are the fruits
ot love.                            *They stab him.*
*Bel.*   O, save his life, and let me die for him! 55
O, save him, brother; save him, Balthazar:
I lov'd Horatio; but he lov'd not me.
*Bal.*   But Balthazar loves Bel-imperia.
*Lor.*   Although his life were still ambitious,
  proud,
Yet is he at the highest now he is dead.     60
*Bel.*   Murder! murder!  Help, Hieronimo,
  help!
*Lor.*   Come, stop her mouth; away with her.
                                          *Exeunt.*

[SCENE V.   *The Same*]

*Enter Hieronimo in his shirt, &c.*

*Hier.*   What outcries pluck me from my
  naked bed,
And chill my throbbing heart with trembling
  fear,
Which never danger yet could daunt before?
Who calls Hieronimo?  Speak, here I am.
I did not slumber; therefore 't was no dream. 5
No, no, it was some woman cried for help,
And here within this garden did she cry,
And in this garden must I rescue her. —
But stay, what murd'rous spectacle is this?
A man hang'd up and all the murderers gone! 10
And in my bower, to lay the guilt on me!
This place was made for pleasure, not for death.
                          *He cuts him down.*
Those garments that he wears I oft have seen —
Alas, it is Horatio, my sweet son!
O no, but he that whilom was my son!     15
O, was it thou that call'dst me from my bed?
O speak, if any spark of life remain:
I am thy father.  Who hath slain my son?
What savage monster, not of human kind,
Hath here been glutted with thy harmless
  blood,                                                         20
And left thy bloody corpse dishonoured here,
For me, amidst these dark and deathful shades,
To drown thee with an ocean of my tears?

O heavens, why made you night to cover sin?
By day this deed of darkness had not been.  25
O earth, why didst thou not in time devour
The vild profaner of this sacred bower?
O poor Horatio, what hadst thou misdone,
To leese thy life, ere life was new begun?
O wicked butcher, whatsoe'er thou wert,     30
How could thou strangle virtue and desert?
Ay me most wretched, that have lost my joy.
In leesing my Horatio, my sweet boy!

*Enter Isabella*

*Isab.*   My husband's absence makes my
  heart to throb: —
Hieronimo!                                                     35
*Hier.*   Here, Isabella, help me to lament;
For sighs are stopp'd, and all my tears are spent.
*Isab.*   What world of grief! my son Horatio!
O, where's the author of this endless woe?
*Hier.*   To know the author were some ease of
  grief.                                                           40
For in revenge my heart would find relief.
*Isab.*   Then is he gone? and is my son gone
  too?
O, gush out, tears, fountains and floods of tears;
Blow, sighs, and raise an everlasting storm;
For outrage fits our cursed wretchedness.     45
[*Ay me, Hieronimo, sweet husband, speak!*
Hier.   *He supp'd with us to-night, frolic and
    merry,*
*And said he would go visit Balthazar*
*At the duke's palace: there the prince doth lodge.*
*He had no custom to stay out so late:*     50
*He may be in his chamber; some go see.*
*Roderigo, ho!*

Enter Pedro and Jaques

Isab.   *Ay me, he raves! — Sweet Hieronimo!*
Hier.   *True, all Spain takes note of it.*
*Besides, he is so generally belov'd;*     55
*His majesty the other day did grace him*
*With waiting on his cup: these be favours,*
*Which do assure me he cannot be short-liv'd.*
Isab.   *Sweet Hieronimo!*
Hier.   *I wonder how this fellow got his clothes! —*
*Sirrah, sirrah, I'll know the truth of all.*     61
*Jaques, run to the Duke of Castile's presently,*
*And bid my son Horatio to come home:*
*I and his mother have had strange dreams to-night.*
*Do ye hear me, sir?*
Jaques.              *Ay, sir.*
Hier.                      *Well, sir, be gone.* 65
*Pedro, come hither; know'st thou who this is?*
Ped.   *Too well, sir.*
Hier.   *Too well! Who, who is it?  Peace, Isa-
  bella!*
*Nay, blush not, man.*

---

²² **these:** ('this' Qq.)   ²⁷ **vild:** vile   ²⁹ **leese:** lose   ⁴⁵ **outrage:** outcry   ⁴⁶⁻⁹⁹ (**First passage
of additions**)

Ped.                    *It is my lord Horatio.*
Hier.    *Ha, ha, St. James! but this doth make*
    *me laugh,*                                                    70
*That there are more deluded than myself.*
Ped.    *Deluded?*
Hier.                    *Ay:*
*I would have sworn myself, within this hour,*
*That this had been my son Horatio:*
*His garments are so like.*                                        75
*Ha! are they not great persuasions?*
Isab.    *O, would to God it were not so!*
Hier.    *Were not, Isabella? Dost thou dream*
    *it is?*
*Can thy soft bosom entertain a thought*
*That such a black deed of mischief should be*
    *done*                                                          80
*On one so pure and spotless as our son?*
*Away, I am ashamed.*
Isab.                    *Dear Hieronimo,*
*Cast a more serious eye upon thy grief;*
*Weak apprehension gives but weak belief.*
Hier.    *It was a man, sure, that was hang'd up*
    *here;*                                                         85
*A youth, as I remember: I cut him down.*
*If it should prove my son now after all —*
*Say you? say you? — Light! lend me a taper;*
*Let me look again. — O God!*
*Confusion, mischief, torment, death and hell,*     90
*Drop all your stings at once in my cold bosom,*
*That now is stiff with horror: kill me quickly!*
*Be gracious to me, thou infective night,*
*And drop this deed of murder down on me;*
*Gird in my waste of grief with thy large dark-*
    *ness,*                                                         95
*And let me not survive to see the light*
*May put me in the mind I had a son.*
Isab.    *O sweet Horatio! O my dearest son!*
Hier.    *How strangely had I lost my way to*
    *grief!]*
Sweet, lovely rose, ill-pluckt before thy time,     100
Fair, worthy son, not conquer'd, but betray'd,
I 'll kiss thee now, for words with tears are
    stay'd.
*Isab.* And I 'll close up the glasses of his sight,
For once these eyes were only my delight.
*Hier.* See'st thou this handkercher be-
    smear'd with blood?                                          105
It shall not from me, till I take revenge.
See'st thou those wounds that yet are bleeding
    fresh?

I 'll not entomb them, till I have reveng'd.
Then will I joy amidst my discontent;
Till then my sorrow never shall be spent.           110
    *Isab.* The heavens are just; murder cannot
    be hid.
Time is the author both of truth and right,
And time will bring this treachery to light.
    *Hier.* Meanwhile, good Isabella, cease thy
    plaints,
Or, at the least, dissemble them awhile:            115
So shall we sooner find the practice out,
And learn by whom all this was brought about.
Come, Isabel, now let us take him up,
                *They take him up.*
And bear him in from out this cursed place.
I 'll say his dirge; singing fits not this case.    120

*O aliquis mihi quas pulchrum ver educat herbas,*
    Hieronimo sets his breast unto his sword.
*Misceat, et nostro detur medicina dolori;*
*Aut, si qui faciunt annorum oblivia, succos*
*Præbeat; ipse metam magnum quæcunque per*
    *orbem*
*Gramina Sol pulchras effert in luminis oras;*      125
*Ipse bibam quicquid meditatur saga veneni,*
*Quicquid et herbarum vi cæca nenia nectit:*
*Omnia perpetiar, lethum quoque, dum semel omnis*
*Noster in extincto moriatur pectore sensus. —*
*Ergo tuos oculos nunquam, mea vita, videbo,*       130
*Et tua perpetuus sepelivit lumina somnus?*
*Emoriar tecum: sic, sic juvat ire sub umbras. —*
*At tamen absistam properato cedere letho,*
*Ne mortem vindicta tuam tam nulla sequatur.*
        Here he throws it from him and
        bears the body away.

*[Chorus]*

    *Andrea.* Brought'st thou me hither to in-
    crease my pain?                                              135
I look'd that Balthazar should have been slain;
But 't is my friend Horatio that is slain,
And they abuse fair Bel-imperia,
On whom I doted more than all the world,
Because she lov'd me more than all the world.
    *Revenge.* Thou talk'st of harvest, when    141
    the corn is green:
The end is crown of every work well done;
The sickle comes not, till the corn be ripe.
Be still; and ere I lead thee from this place,
I 'll show thee Balthazar in heavy case.            145

---

**93** infective: infectious    **102** stay'd: ( 'stain'd' early Qq.)    **104** only my: *i.e.*, my only    121–134 O,
let someone mix for me the herbs which lovely spring brings forth, and let medicine be given to our
pain; or let him provide potions, if any cause forgetfulness of years. May I myself reap throughout
the great earth whatever plants Sol brings forth in the fair realms of light. May I drink whatever
poison the diviner contrives and whatever of herbs of dark power her incantation unites. Let me
endure all things, even death, provided that all our feeling may die at once in a heart that is dead.
Shall I then never again see your eyes, my life? And has eternal sleep buried your light? Let me die
with you! so, so would I go to the shades below! And yet I shall refrain from yielding to a hasty
death lest then no revenge should follow your death.

## ACTUS TERTIUS

[SCENE I. *The Court of Portugal*]

*Enter Viceroy of Portingale, Nobles, Villuppo*

*Vic.* Infortunate condition of kings,
Seated amidst so many helpless doubts!
First we are plac'd upon extremest height,
And oft supplanted with exceeding hate,
But ever subject to the wheel of chance; 5
And at our highest never joy we so
As we both doubt and dread our overthrow.
So striveth not the waves with sundry winds
As Fortune toileth in the affairs of kings,
That would be fear'd, yet fear to be belov'd, 10
Sith fear or love to kings is flattery.
For instance, lordings, look upon your king,
By hate deprived of his dearest son,
The only hope of our successive line.
*Nob.* I had not thought that Alexandro's
heart 15
Had been envenom'd with such extreme hate;
But now I see that words have several works,
And there 's no credit in the countenance.
*Vil.* No; for, my lord, had you beheld the
train
That feigned love had colour'd in his looks, 20
When he in camp consorted Balthazar,
Far more inconstant had you thought the sun,
That hourly coasts the centre of the earth,
Than Alexandro's purpose to the prince.
*Vic.* No more, Villuppo, thou hast said
enough, 25
And with thy words thou slay'st our wounded
thoughts.
Nor shall I longer dally with the world,
Procrastinating Alexandro's death.
Go, some of you, and fetch the traitor forth,
That, as he is condemned, he may die. 30

*Enter Alexandro with a Nobleman and halberts*

*Nob.* In such extremes will nought but pa-
tience serve.
*Alex.* But in extremes what patience shall I
use?
Nor discontents it me to leave the world,
With whom there nothing can prevail but
wrong.
*Nob.* Yet hope the best.
*Alex.* 'T is heaven is my hope. 35
As for the earth, it is too much infect
To yield me hope of any of her mould.
*Vic.* Why linger ye? Bring forth that daring
fiend,
And let him die for his accursed deed.

*Alex.* Not that I fear the extremity of
death 40
(For nobles cannot stoop to servile fear)
Do I, O king, thus discontented live.
But this, O this, torments my labouring soul,
That thus I die suspected of a sin
Whereof, as heavens have known my secret
thoughts, 45
So am I free from this suggestion.
*Vic.* No more, I say! to the tortures!
When?
Bind him, and burn his body in those flames,
*They bind him to the stake.*
That shall prefigure those unquenched fires
Of Phlegethon, prepared for his soul. 50
*Alex.* My guiltless death will be aveng'd on
thee,
On thee, Villuppo, that hath malic'd thus,
Or for thy meed hast falsely me accus'd.
*Vil.* Nay, Alexandro, if thou menace me,
I 'll lend a hand to send thee to the lake 55
Where those thy words shall perish with thy
works,
Injurious traitor! monstrous homicide!

*Enter Ambassador*

*Amb.* Stay, hold a while;
And here — with pardon of his majesty —
Lay hands upon Villuppo.
*Vic.* Ambassador, 60
What news hath urg'd this sudden entrance?
*Amb.* Know, sovereign lord, that Balthazar
doth live.
*Vic.* What say'st thou? Liveth Balthazar,
our son?
*Amb.* Your highness' son, Lord Balthazar,
doth live;
And, well entreated in the court of Spain, 65
Humbly commends him to your majesty.
These eyes beheld; and these my followers,
With these, the letters of the king's commends,
*Gives him letters.*
Are happy witnesses of his highness' health.
*The King looks on the letters, and proceeds.*
*Vic.* "Thy son doth live, your tribute is re-
ceiv'd; 70
Thy peace is made, and we are satisfied.
The rest resolve upon as things propos'd
For both our honours and thy benefit."
*Amb.* These are his highness' farther articles.
*He gives him more letters.*
*Vic.* Accursed wretch, to intimate these
ills 75
Against the life and reputation
Of noble Alexandro! Come, my lord, unbind
him. —

⁴ **hate:** ('heat' Q 1, 2)  ⁷ **doubt:** fear, suspect
²³ **coasts:** circles  ³⁶ **infect:** infected  ⁴⁷ **When:** an expression of impatience  ⁵² **malic'd:** maliciously plotted  ⁶⁸ **commends:** commendations

Let him unbind thee, that is bound to death,
To make a quital for thy discontent.
                 *They unbind him.*
   *Alex.*  Dread lord, in kindness you could do
    no less                    80
Upon report of such a damned fact;
But thus we see our innocence hath sav'd
The hopeless life which thou, Villuppo, sought
By thy suggestions to have massacred.
   *Vic.*  Say, false Villuppo, wherefore didst
    thou thus                  85
Falsely betray Lord Alexandro's life?
Him whom thou know'st that no unkindness
    else
But even the slaughter of our dearest son
Could once have mov'd us to have miscon-
    ceiv'd.
   *Alex.*  Say, treacherous Villuppo, tell the
    king:                    90
Wherein hath Alexandro us'd thee ill?
   *Vil.*  Rent with remembrance of so foul a
    deed,
My guilty soul submits me to thy doom;
For not for Alexandro's injuries,
But for reward and hope to be preferr'd,  95
Thus have I shamelessly hazarded his life.
   *Vic.*  Which, villain, shall be ransom'd with
    thy death;
And not so mean a torment as we here
Devis'd for him who, thou said'st, slew our son,
But with the bitterest torments and extremes
That may be yet invented for thine end.   101
           *Alexandro seems to entreat.*
Entreat me not; go, take the traitor hence:
                  *Exit Villuppo.*
And, Alexandro, let us honour thee
With public notice of thy loyalty. —
To end those things articulated here     105
By our great lord, the mighty King of Spain,
We with our council will deliberate.
Come, Alexandro, keep us company.  *Exeunt.*

    [SCENE II.  *The Court of Spain*]

        *Enter Hieronimo*

   *Hier.*  O eyes! no eyes, but fountains fraught
    with tears;
O life! no life, but lively form of death;
O world! no world, but mass of public wrongs,
Confus'd and fill'd with murder and misdeeds!
O sacred heavens! if this unhallow'd deed,  5
If this inhuman and barbarous attempt,
If this incomparable murder thus
Of mine, but now no more my son,
Shall unreveal'd and unrevenged pass,
How should we term your dealings to be just, 10

If you unjustly deal with those that in your
    justice trust?
The night, sad secretary to my moans,
With direful visions wake my vexed soul,
And with the wounds of my distressful son
Solicit me for notice of his death.          15
The ugly fiends do sally forth of hell,
And frame my steps to unfrequented paths,
And fear my heart with fierce inflamed thoughts.
The cloudy day my discontents records,
Early begins to register my dreams,     20
And drive me forth to seek the murderer.
Eyes, life, world, heavens, hell, night, and day,
See, search, shew, send some man, some mean,
    that may —         *A letter falleth.*
What 's here? a letter? Tush! it is not so! —
A letter written to Hieronimo!   *Red ink.* 25
"For want of ink, receive this bloody writ.
Me hath my hapless brother hid from thee;
Revenge thyself on Balthazar and him:
For these were they that murdered thy son.
Hieronimo, revenge Horatio's death,    30
And better fare than Bel-imperia doth."
What means this unexpected miracle?
My son slain by Lorenzo and the prince!
What cause had they Horatio to malign?
Or what might move thee, Bel-imperia,   35
To accuse thy brother, had he been the mean?
Hieronimo, beware! — thou art betray'd,
And to entrap thy life this train is laid.
Advise thee therefore, be not credulous:
This is devised to endanger thee,     40
That thou, by this, Lorenzo shouldst accuse;
And he, for thy dishonour done, should draw
Thy life in question and thy name in hate.
Dear was the life of my beloved son,
And of his death behoves me be reveng'd;  45
Then hazard not thine own, Hieronimo,
But live t' effect thy resolution.
I therefore will by circumstances try,
What I can gather to confirm this writ;
And, heark'ning near the Duke of Castile's
    house,                   50
Close, if I can, with Bel-imperia,
To listen more, but nothing to bewray.

        *Enter Pedringano*

Now, Pedringano!
   *Ped.*          Now, Hieronimo!
   *Hier.*  Where 's thy lady?
   *Ped.*         I know not; here 's my lord.

        *Enter Lorenzo*

   *Lor.*  How now, who 's this? Hieronimo?
   *Hier.*               My lord. 55
   *Ped.*  He asketh for my lady Bel-imperia.

---

    79 **quital:** requital   80 **kindness:** nature   81 **fact:** deed   91 **wherein:** ('Or wherein' Qq.)   95 **pre-**
**ferr'd:** advanced   98 **mean:** moderate   105 **articulated:** set forth in articles   12 **secretary:** confidant   13 **fear:** affright   38 **train:** snare, trap   48 **circumstances:** indirect methods   51 **Close:** meet

*Lor.* What to do, Hieronimo? The duke,
my father, hath
Upon some disgrace awhile remov'd her hence;
But, if it be aught I may inform her of,
Tell me, Hieronimo, and I 'll let her know it. 60
*Hier.* Nay, nay, my lord, I thank you; it
shall not need.
I had a suit unto her, but too late,
And her disgrace makes me unfortunate.
*Lor.* Why so, Hieronimo? Use me.
*Hier.* O no, my lord, I dare not; it must
not be.                                                    65
I humbly thank your lordship.
[Hier.                        *Who? You, my lord?*
*I reserve your favour for a greater honour;*
*This is a very toy, my lord, a toy.*
    Lor. *All 's one, Hieronimo, acquaint me with*
*it.*
    Hier. *I' faith, my lord, it is an idle thing;* 70
*I must confess I ha' been too slack, too tardy,*
*Too remiss unto your honour.*
    Lor.                        *How now, Hieronimo?*
    Hier. *In troth, my lord, it is a thing of noth-*
*ing:*
*The murder of a son, or so ——*
*A thing of nothing, my lord!*]
    *Lor.*                        Why then, farewell. 75
    *Hier.* My grief no heart, my thoughts no
tongue can tell.                                *Exit.*
    *Lor.* Come hither, Pedringano, see'st thou
this?
    *Ped.* My lord, I see it, and suspect it too.
    *Lor.* This is that damned villain Serberine
That hath, I fear, reveal'd Horatio's death. 80
    *Ped.* My lord, he could not, 't was so lately
done;
And since he hath not left my company.
    *Lor.* Admit he have not, his condition 's
such,
As fear or flattering words may make him false.
I know his humour, and therewith repent 85
That e'er I us'd him in this enterprise.
But, Pedringano, to prevent the worst,
And 'cause I know thee secret as my soul,
Here, for thy further satisfaction, take thou
this,                            *Gives him more gold.*
And hearken to me — thus it is devis'd: 90
This night thou must (and, prithee, so re-
solve)
Meet Serberine at Saint Luigi's Park —
Thou know'st 't is here hard by behind the
house;
There take thy stand, and see thou strike him
sure,
For die he must, if we do mean to live. 95

*Ped.* But how shall Serberine be there, my
lord?
    *Lor.* Let me alone; I 'll send to him to meet
The prince and me, where thou must do this
deed.
    *Ped.* It shall be done, my lord, it shall be
done;
And I 'll go arm myself to meet him there. 100
    *Lor.* When things shall alter, as I hope they
will,
Then shalt thou mount for this; thou know'st
my mind.                                *Exit Pedringano.*
*Che le Ieron!*

*Enter Page*

*Page.*        My lord?
    *Lor.*                        Go, sirrah,
To Serberine, and bid him forthwith meet
The prince and me at Saint Luigi's Park, 105
Behind the house; this evening, boy!
    *Page.*                        I go, my lord.
    *Lor.* But, sirrah, let the hour be eight
o'clock:
Bid him not fail.
    *Page.*                I fly, my lord.        *Exit.*
    *Lor.* Now to confirm the complot thou hast
cast
Of all these practices, I 'll spread the watch, 110
Upon precise commandment from the king,
Strongly to guard the place where Pedringano
This night shall murder hapless Serberine.
Thus must we work that will avoid distrust;
Thus must we practise to prevent mishap, 115
And thus one ill another must expulse.
This sly enquiry of Hieronimo
For Bel-imperia breeds suspicion,
And this suspicion bodes a further ill.
As for myself, I know my secret fault, 120
And so do they; but I have dealt for them.
They that for coin their souls endangered,
To save my life, for coin shall venture theirs;
And better it 's that base companions die
Than by their life to hazard our good haps. 125
Nor shall they live, for me to fear their faith:
I 'll trust myself, myself shall be my friend;
For die they shall, —
Slaves are ordained to no other end.        *Exit.*

[SCENE III.    *Saint Luigi's Park*]

*Enter Pedringano, with a pistol*

    *Ped.* Now, Pedringano, bid thy pistol hold,
And hold on, Fortune! once more favour me;
Give but success to mine attempting spirit,
And let me shift for taking of mine aim.

---

⁶⁶⁻⁷⁵ **Who . . . lord:** (Second passage of additions, replacing lines 65, 66)    ⁸⁵ **humour:** disposition
⁹² **Saint Luigi's:** ('S. Luigis' early Qq.)    ¹⁰³ **Che le Ieron:** (?) 'Chi (qui), il ladrone,' Here, thief!
¹⁰⁹ **cast:** devised    ¹¹⁰ **practices:** tricks    ¹¹⁴ **that:** that which    ¹²⁴ **companions:** fellows    ¹²⁵ **haps:**
fortunes

Here is the gold: this is the gold propos'd;    5
It is no dream that I adventure for,
But Pedringano is possess'd thereof.
And he that would not strain his conscience
For him that thus his liberal purse hath
  stretch'd,
Unworthy such a favour, may he fail,          10
And, wishing, want, when such as I prevail.
As for the fear of apprehension,
I know, if need should be, my noble lord
Will stand between me and ensuing harms;
Besides, this place is free from all suspect:  15
Here therefore will I stay and take my stand.

*Enter the Watch*

1 *Watch.*  I wonder much to what intent it is
That we are thus expressly charg'd to watch.
   2 *Watch.*  'T is by commandment in the
   king's own name.
   3 *Watch.*  But we were never wont to watch
   and ward                                    20
So near the duke his brother's house before.
   2 *Watch.*  Content yourself, stand close,
   there 's somewhat in 't.

*Enter Serberine*

*Ser.*  Here, Serberine, attend and stay thy
  pace;
For here did Don Lorenzo's page appoint
That thou by his command shouldst meet with
  him.                                         25
How fit a place — if one were so dispos'd —
Methinks this corner is to close with one.
   *Ped.*  Here comes the bird that I must seize
   upon.
Now, Pedringano, or never, play the man!
   *Ser.*  I wonder that his lordship stays so
   long,                                       30
Or wherefore should he send for me so late?
   *Ped.*  For this, Serberine! — and thou shalt
   ha 't.                      *Shoots the dag.*
So, there he lies; my promise is perform'd.

*The Watch*

1 *Watch.*  Hark, gentlemen, this is a pistol
  shot.
   2 *Watch.*  And here 's one slain; — stay the
   murderer.                                   35
   *Ped.*  Now by the sorrows of the souls in
   hell,          *He strives with the Watch.*
Who first lays hand on me, I 'll be his priest.
   3 *Watch.*  Sirrah, confess, and therein play
   the priest,
Why hast thou thus unkindly kill'd the man?
   *Ped.*  Why?  Because he walk'd abroad so
   late.                                       40

   3 *Watch.*  Come, sir, you had been better
   kept your bed,
Than have committed this misdeed so late.
   2 *Watch.*  Come, to the marshal's with the
   murderer!
   1 *Watch.*  On to Hieronimo's! help me here
To bring the murd'red body with us too.       45
   *Ped.*  Hieronimo?  Carry me before whom
   you will.
Whate'er he be, I 'll answer him and you;
And do your worst, for I defy you all.  *Exeunt.*

[SCENE IV.   *The Palace of Don Cyprian*]

*Enter Lorenzo and Balthazar*

*Bal.*  How now, my lord, what makes you
  rise so soon?
   *Lor.*  Fear of preventing our mishaps too
   late.
   *Bal.*  What mischief is it that we not mis-
   trust?
   *Lor.*  Our greatest ills we least mistrust, my
   lord,
And inexpected harms do hurt us most.          5
   *Bal.*  Why, tell me, Don Lorenzo, tell me,
   man,
If aught concerns our honour and your own.
   *Lor.*  Nor you, nor me, my lord, but both in
   one;
For I suspect — and the presumption 's great —
That by those base confederates in our fault 10
Touching the death of Don Horatio,
We are betray'd to old Hieronimo.
   *Bal.*  Betray'd, Lorenzo?  Tush! it cannot
   be.
   *Lor.*  A guilty conscience, urged with the
   thought
Of former evils, easily cannot err.           15
I am persuaded — and dissuade me not —
That all 's revealed to Hieronimo.
And therefore know that I have cast it thus: —

*Enter Page*

But here 's the page.  How now? what news
  with thee?
   *Page.*  My lord, Serberine is slain.
   *Bal.*            Who?  Serberine, my man?
   *Page.*  Your highness' man, my lord.
   *Lor.*      Speak, page, who murdered him?  21
   *Page.*  He that is apprehended for the fact.
   *Lor.*  Who?
   *Page.*          Pedringano.
   *Bal.*  Is Serberine slain, that lov'd his lord
   so well?
Injurious villain, murderer of his friend!     25
   *Lor.*  Hath Pedringano murdered Serberine?

---

¹⁵ **suspect:** suspicion    ³² S. D. **dag:** pistol    ³⁷ **be his priest:** be present at his death, murder him
³⁹ **unkindly:** with unnatural cruelty    ³ **mistrust:** suspect

My lord, let me entreat you to take the pains
To exasperate and hasten his revenge
With your complaints unto my lord the king.
This their dissension breeds a greater doubt. 30
   *Bal.*  Assure thee, Don Lorenzo, he shall die,
Or else his highness hardly shall deny.
Meanwhile I 'll haste the marshal-sessions,
For die he shall for this his damned deed.
                  *Exit Balthazar.*
   *Lor.*  Why so, this fits our former policy, 35
And thus experience bids the wise to deal.
I lay the plot; he prosecutes the point:
I set the trap; he breaks the worthless twigs,
And sees not that wherewith the bird was
    lim'd.
Thus hopeful men, that mean to hold their
    own,                     40
Must look like fowlers to their dearest friends.
He runs to kill whom I have holp to catch,
And no man knows it was my reaching fatch.
'T is hard to trust unto a multitude,
Or any one, in mine opinion,      45
When men themselves their secrets will reveal.

       *Enter a Messenger with a letter*

Boy!
   *Page.*  My lord.
   *Lor.*  What 's he?
   *Mes.*        I have a letter to your lordship.
   *Lor.*  From whence?
   *Mes.*     From Pedringano that 's imprisoned.
   *Lor.*  So he is in prison then?
   *Mes.*             Ay, my good lord. 50
   *Lor.*  What would he with us? — He writes
us here,
To stand good lord, and help him in distress. —
Tell him I have his letters, know his mind;
And what we may, let him assure him of.
Fellow, begone; my boy shall follow thee.  55
                  *Exit Messenger.*
This works like wax; yet once more try thy
    wits. —
Boy, go, convey this purse to Pedringano;
Thou know'st the prison, closely give it him.
And be advis'd that none be there about.
Bid him be merry still, but secret;     60
And though the marshal-sessions be to-day,
Bid him not doubt of his delivery.
Tell him his pardon is already sign'd,
And thereon bid him boldly be resolv'd:
For, were he ready to be turned off —    65
As 't is my will the uttermost be tried —
Thou with his pardon shalt attend him still.
Show him this box, tell him his pardon 's in 't;

But open 't not, an if thou lov'st thy life,
But let him wisely keep his hopes unknown. 70
He shall not want while Don Lorenzo lives.
Away!
   *Page.*  I go, my lord, I run.
   *Lor.*  But, sirrah, see that this be cleanly
    done.                 *Exit Page.*
Now stands our fortune on a tickle point,
And now or never ends Lorenzo's doubts.   75
One only thing is uneffected yet,
And that 's to see the executioner.
But to what end? I list not trust the air
With utterance of our pretence therein,
For fear the privy whisp'ring of the wind   80
Convey our words amongst unfriendly ears,
That lie too open to advantages.
*E quel che voglio io, nessun lo sa;*
*Intendo io: quel mi basterà.*      *Exit.*

      [SCENE V.  *A Street*]
      *Enter Boy with the box*

   *Boy.*  My master hath forbidden me to look
in this box; and, by my troth, 't is likely, if he
had not warned me, I should not have had so
much idle time; for we men's-kind in our minority are like women in their uncertainty: [5
that they are most forbidden, they will soonest
attempt: so I now. —— By my bare honesty,
here 's nothing but the bare empty box! Were it
not sin against secrecy, I would say it were a
piece of gentlemanlike knavery. I must go [10
to Pedringano, and tell him his pardon is in
this box; nay, I would have sworn it, had I not
seen the contrary. I cannot choose but smile
to think how the villain will flout the gallows,
scorn the audience, and descant on the [15
hangman, and all presuming of his pardon from
hence. Will 't not be an odd jest for me to stand
and grace every jest he makes, pointing my
finger at this box, as who would say, "Mock on,
here 's thy warrant." Is 't not a scurvy jest [20
that a man should jest himself to death? Alas!
poor Pedringano, I am in a sort sorry for thee;
but if I should be hanged with thee, I cannot
weep.                      *Exit.*

    [SCENE VI.  *A Court of Justice*]
    *Enter Hieronimo and the Deputy*

   *Hier.*  Thus must we toil in other men's ex-
    tremes,
That know not how to remedy our own;
And do them justice, when unjustly we,
For all our wrongs, can compass no redress.

---

   **28 exasperate:** make more severe   **his:** *i.e.*, upon him   **32 hardly . . . deny:** shall resist with difficulty   **37 prosecutes the point:** directs the blow   **39 lim'd:** caught   **43 reaching fatch:** deep-
laid stratagem   **58 closely:** secretly   **65 turned off:** hanged   **73 cleanly:** cleverly   **74 tickle:** critical, precarious   **79 pretence:** intention   **83–84 E . . . basterà:** And what I want, nobody knows.
I understand: that will suffice me. (Ital.)   **15 descant:** comment

But shall I never live to see the day,     5
That I may come, by justice of the heavens,
To know the cause that may my cares allay?
This toils my body, this consumeth age,
That only I to all men just must be,
And neither gods nor men be just to me.    10
   *Dep.* Worthy Hieronimo, your office asks
A care to punish such as do transgress.
   *Hier.* So is 't my duty to regard his death
Who, when he liv'd, deserv'd my dearest blood.
But come, for that we came for: let 's begin, 15
For here lies that which bids me to be gone.

*Enter Officers, Boy, and Pedringano, with a*
     *letter in his hand, bound*

   *Dep.* Bring forth the prisoner, for the court
is set.
   *Ped.* Gramercy, boy, but it was time to
come;
For I had written to my lord anew
A nearer matter that concerneth him,    20
For fear his lordship had forgotten me.
But sith he hath rememb'red me so well —
Come, come, come on, when shall we to this
   gear?
   *Hier.* Stand forth, thou monster, murderer
of men,
And here, for satisfaction of the world,    25
Confess thy folly, and repent thy fault;
For there 's thy place of execution.
   *Ped.* This is short work. Well, to your
marshalship
First I confess — nor fear I death therefore —
I am the man, 't was I slew Serberine.    30
But, sir, then you think this shall be the place,
Where we shall satisfy you for this gear?
   *Dep.* Ay, Pedringano.
   *Ped.*            Now I think not so.
   *Hier.* Peace, impudent; for thou shalt find
it so;
For blood with blood shall, while I sit as
   judge,    35
Be satisfied, and the law discharg'd.
And though myself cannot receive the like,
Yet will I see that others have their right.
Despatch: the fault 's approved and confess'd,
And by our law he is condemn'd to die.    40
   *Hangm.* Come on, sir, are you ready?
   *Ped.* To do what, my fine, officious knave?
   *Hangm.* To go to this gear.
   *Ped.* O sir, you are too forward: thou
wouldst fain furnish me with a halter, to [45
disfurnish me of my habit. So I should go out
of this gear, my raiment, into that gear, the
rope. But, hangman, now I spy your knavery,
I 'll not change without boot, that 's flat.
   *Hangm.* Come, sir.    50

   *Ped.* So, then, I must up?
   *Hangm.* No remedy.
   *Ped.* Yes, but there shall be for my coming
down.
   *Hangm.* Indeed, here 's a remedy for that. 55
   *Ped.* How? Be turn'd off?
   *Hangm.* Ay, truly. Come, are you ready?
I pray, sir, despatch; the day goes away.
   *Ped.* What, do you hang by the hour? If
you do, I may chance to break your old [60
custom.
   *Hangm.* Faith, you have reason; for I am
like to break your young neck.
   *Ped.* Dost thou mock me, hangman? Pray
God, I be not preserved to break your knave's
pate for this.    66
   *Hangm.* Alas, sir! you are a foot too low to
reach it, and I hope you will never grow so high
while I am in the office.
   *Ped.* Sirrah, dost see yonder boy with [70
the box in his hand?
   *Hangm.* What, he that points to it with his
finger?
   *Ped.* Ay, that companion.
   *Hangm.* I know him not; but what of [75
him?
   *Ped.* Dost thou think to live till his old
doublet will make thee a new truss?
   *Hangm.* Ay, and many a fair year after, to
truss up many an honester man than either [80
thou or he.
   *Ped.* What hath he in his box, as thou
think'st?
   *Hangm.* Faith, I cannot tell, nor I care not
greatly; methinks you should rather hearken [85
to your soul's health.
   *Ped.* Why, sirrah, hangman, I take it that
that is good for the body is likewise good for
the soul: and it may be, in that box is balm for
both.    90
   *Hangm.* Well, thou art even the merriest
piece of man's flesh that e'er groan'd at my
office door!
   *Ped.* Is your roguery become an office with
a knave's name?    95
   *Hangm.* Ay, and that shall all they witness
that see you seal it with a thief's name.
   *Ped.* I prithee, request this good company to
pray with me.
   *Hangm.* Ay, marry, sir, this is a good
motion. My masters, you see here 's a good
fellow.    102
   *Ped.* Nay, nay, now I remember me, let
them alone till some other time; for now I have
no great need.    105
   *Hier.* I have not seen a wretch so impu-
pudent.

  **23 gear:** business   **39 approved:** proved   **45 habit:** (The clothes of the criminal were a perqui-
site of the hangman.)

O monstrous times, where murder 's set so
    light,
And where the soul, that should be shrin'd in
    heaven,
Solely delights in interdicted things,
Still wand'ring in the thorny passages,    110
That intercepts itself of happiness.
Murder! O bloody monster! God forbid
A fault so foul should 'scape unpunished.
Despatch, and see this execution done! —
This makes me to remember thee, my son.
                      *Exit Hieronimo.*

*Ped.* Nay, soft, no haste.     116
*Dep.* Why, wherefore stay you? Have you
    hope of life?
*Ped.* Why, ay!
*Hangm.*     As how?
*Ped.* Why, rascal, by my pardon from the
    king.
*Hangm.* Stand you on that? Then you shall
    off with this.     *He turns him off.*
*Dep.* So, executioner; — convey him hence;
But let his body be unburied:     122
Let not the earth be choked or infect
With that which heaven contemns, and men
    neglect.     *Exeunt.*

[SCENE VII. *Hieronimo's House*]

*Enter Hieronimo*

*Hier.* Where shall I run to breathe abroad
    my woes,
My woes, whose weight hath wearied the earth?
Or mine exclaims, that have surcharg'd the air
With ceaseless plaints for my deceased son?
The blust'ring winds, conspiring with my
    words,     5
At my lament have mov'd the leafless trees,
Disrob'd the meadows of their flow'red green,
Made mountains marsh with spring-tides of my
    tears,
And broken through the brazen gates of hell.
Yet still tormented is my tortur'd soul     10
With broken sighs and restless passions,
That, winged, mount; and, hovering in the air,
Beat at the windows of the brightest heavens,
Soliciting for justice and revenge:
But they are plac'd in those imperial heights, 15
Where, countermur'd with walls of diamond,
I find the place impregnable; and they
Resist my woes, and give my words no way.

*Enter Hangman with a letter*

*Hangm.* O lord, sir! God bless you, sir! the
man, sir, Petergade, sir, he that was so full [20
of merry conceits —

*Hier.* Well, what of him?
*Hangm.* O lord, sir, he went the wrong way;
the fellow had a fair commission to the contrary.
Sir, here is his passport; I pray you, sir, we [25
have done him wrong.
*Hier.* I warrant thee, give it me.
*Hangm.* You will stand between the gallows
    and me?
*Hier.* Ay, ay.
*Hangm.* I thank your lordship's worship. 30
                      *Exit Hangman.*
*Hier.* And yet, though somewhat nearer me
    concerns,
I will, to ease the grief that I sustain,
Take truce with sorrow while I read on this.
"My lord, I write, as mine extremes requir'd,
That you would labour my delivery.     35
If you neglect, my life is desperate,
And in my death I shall reveal the truth.
You know, my lord, I slew him for your sake,
And was confederate with the prince and you;
Won by rewards and hopeful promises,     40
I holp to murder Don Horatio." —
Holp he to murder mine Horatio?
And actors in th' accursed tragedy
Wast thou, Lorenzo? Balthazar, and thou?
Of whom my son, my son, deserv'd so well? 45
What have I heard, what have mine eyes be-
    held?
O sacred heavens, may it come to pass
That such a monstrous and detested deed,
So closely smother'd, and so long conceal'd,
Shall thus by this be venged or reveal'd?     50
Now see I what I durst not then suspect,
That Bel-imperia's letter was not feign'd.
Nor feigned she, though falsely they have
    wrong'd
Both her, myself, Horatio, and themselves.
Now may I make compare 'twixt hers and this,
Of every accident I ne'er could find     56
Till now, and now I feelingly perceive
They did what heaven unpunish'd would not
    leave.
O false Lorenzo! are these thy flattering looks?
Is this the honour that thou didst my son?   60
And Balthazar — bane to thy soul and me! —
Was this the ransom he reserv'd thee for?
Woe to the cause of these constrained wars!
Woe to thy baseness and captivity,
Woe to thy birth, thy body, and thy soul,   65
Thy cursed father, and thy conquer'd self!
And bann'd with bitter execrations be
The day and place where he did pity thee!
But wherefore waste I mine unfruitful words,
When naught but blood will satisfy my woes? 70
I will go plain me to my lord the king,

---

111 **intercepts . . . of:** cuts itself off from   124 **heaven:** ('heauens' Q 1)   15 **imperial:** (The
meaning "empyreal" is included.)   16 **countermur'd:** doubly walled   30 **lordship's:** ('L.' Qq.)
34 **write:** Manly emends to *writ.*

And cry aloud for justice through the court,
Wearing the flints with these my wither'd feet;
And either purchase justice by entreats,
Or tire them all with my revenging threats. 75

*Exit.*

[SCENE VIII.  *The Same*]

*Enter Isabella and her Maid*

*Isab.*  So that you say this herb will purge
the eye,
And this, the head? —
Ah! — but none of them will purge the heart!
No, there 's no medicine left for my disease,
Nor any physic to recure the dead.        5

*She runs lunatic.*

Horatio!  O, where 's Horatio?
*Maid.*  Good madam, affright not thus your-
self
With outrage for your son Horatio:
He sleeps in quiet in the Elysian fields.
*Isab.*  Why, did I not give you gowns and
goodly things,                         10
Bought you a whistle and a whipstalk too,
To be revenged on their villainies?
*Maid.*  Madam, these humours do torment
my soul.
*Isab.*  My soul — poor soul, thou talk'st of
things
Thou know'st not what — my soul hath silver
wings,                                 15
That mounts me up unto the highest heavens;
To heaven?  Ay, there sits my Horatio,
Back'd with a troop of fiery Cherubins,
Dancing about his newly healed wounds,
Singing sweet hymns and chanting heavenly
notes,                                 20
Rare harmony to greet his innocence,
That died, ay died, a mirror in our days.
But say, where shall I find the men, the mur-
derers,
That slew Horatio?  Whither shall I run
To find them out that murdered my son?  25

*Exeunt.*

[SCENE IX.  *The Palace of Don Cyprian*]

*Bel-imperia at a window*

*Bel.*  What means this outrage that is off'red
me?
Why am I thus sequest'red from the court?
No notice!  Shall I not know the cause
Of these my secret and suspicious ills?
Accursed brother, unkind murderer,      5
Why bend'st thou thus thy mind to martyr me?
Hieronimo, why writ I of thy wrongs,

Or why art thou so slack in thy revenge?
Andrea, O Andrea! that thou sawest
Me for thy friend Horatio handled thus,  10
And him for me thus causeless murdered! —
Well, force perforce, I must constrain myself
To patience, and apply me to the time,
Till heaven, as I have hop'd, shall set me free.

*Enter Christophil*

*Chris.*  Come, madam Bel-imperia, this may
not be.                          *Exeunt.* 15

[SCENE X.  *The Same*]

*Enter Lorenzo, Balthazar, and the Page*

*Lor.*  Boy, talk no further; thus far
things go well.
Thou art assur'd that thou sawest him dead?
*Page.*  Or else, my lord, I live not.
*Lor.*                          That 's enough.
As for his resolution in his end,
Leave that to him with whom he sojourns
now.                                   5
Here, take my ring and give it Christophil,
And bid him let my sister be enlarg'd,
And bring her hither straight. —   *Exit Page.*
This that I did was for a policy,
To smooth and keep the murder secret,   10
Which, as a nine-days' wonder, being o'erblown,
My gentle sister will I now enlarge.
*Bal.*  And time, Lorenzo; for my lord the
duke,
You heard, enquired for her yester-night.
*Lor.*  Why, and my lord, I hope you heard
me say                                 15
Sufficient reason why she kept away;
But that 's all one.  My lord, you love her?
*Bal.*                                   Ay.
*Lor.*  Then in your love beware; deal cun-
ningly:
Salve all suspicions, only soothe me up;
And if she hap to stand on terms with us — 20
As for her sweetheart and concealment so —
Jest with her gently; under feigned jest
Are things conceal'd that else would breed un-
rest.
But here she comes.

*Enter Bel-imperia*

Now, sister, —
*Bel.*                          Sister?  No!
Thou art no brother, but an enemy;      25
Else wouldst thou not have us'd thy sister so:
First, to affright me with thy weapons drawn,
And with extremes abuse my company;
And then to hurry me, like whirlwind's rage,

11 whipstalk: handle of a whip    14 talk'st: (Q 1623, 'talks,' early Qq.)    4 these: (Q 1633, 'this,' early Qq.)    6 bend'st: (Q 1623, 'bends,' early Qq.)    13 apply me: adapt myself    9 policy: stratagem    10 smooth: beguile    19 soothe me up: confirm what I say    20 stand on terms: haggle over conditions    28 extremes: extremities    company: companion (?), presence (?)

Amidst a crew of thy confederates,                30
And clap me up where none might come at me,
Nor I at any to reveal my wrongs.
What madding fury did possess thy wits?
Or wherein is 't that I offended thee?
 *Lor.* Advise you better, Bel-imperia, 35
For I have done you no disparagement;
Unless, by more discretion than deserv'd,
I sought to save your honour and mine own.
 *Bel.* Mine honour? Why, Lorenzo, wherein
is 't
That I neglect my reputation so 40
As you, or any, need to rescue it?
 *Lor.* His highness and my father were re-
solv'd
To come confer with old Hieronimo
Concerning certain matters of estate
That by the viceroy was determined. 45
 *Bel.* And wherein was mine honour touch'd
in that?
 *Bal.* Have patience, Bel-imperia; hear the
rest.
 *Lor.* Me, next in sight, as messenger they
sent
To give him notice that they were so nigh:
Now when I came, consorted with the prince, 50
And unexpected in an arbour there
Found Bel-imperia with Horatio —
 *Bel.* How then?
 *Lor.* Why, then, remembering that old dis-
grace,
Which you for Don Andrea had endur'd, 55
And now were likely longer to sustain,
By being found so meanly accompanied,
Thought rather — for I knew no readier mean —
To thrust Horatio forth my father's way.
 *Bal.* And carry you obscurely somewhere
else, 60
Lest that his highness should have found you
there.
 *Bel.* Even so, my lord? And you are witness
That this is true which he entreateth of?
You, gentle brother, forg'd this for my sake,
And you, my lord, were made his instrument? 65
A work of worth, worthy the noting too!
But what 's the cause that you conceal'd me
since?
 *Lor.* Your melancholy, sister, since the news
Of your first favourite Don Andrea's death,
My father's old wrath hath exasperate. 70
 *Bal.* And better was 't for you, being in dis-
grace,
To absent yourself, and give his fury place.
 *Bel.* But why had I no notice of his ire?
 *Lor.* That were to add more fuel to your fire,
Who burnt like Ætna for Andrea's loss. 75

 *Bel.* Hath not my father, then, inquir'd for
me?
 *Lor.* Sister, he hath, and thus excus'd I thee.
        *He whispereth in her ear.*
But Bel-imperia, see the gentle prince;
Look on thy love, behold young Balthazar,
Whose passions by thy presence are increas'd; 80
And in whose melancholy thou may'st see
Thy hate, his love; thy flight, his following thee.
 *Bel.* Brother, you are become an orator —
I know not, I, by what experience —
Too politic for me, past all compare, 85
Since last I saw you; but content yourself:
The prince is meditating higher things.
 *Bal.* 'T is of thy beauty, then, that conquers
kings;
Of those thy tresses, Ariadne's twines,
Wherewith my liberty thou hast surpris'd; 90
Of that thine ivory front, my sorrow's map,
Wherein I see no haven to rest my hope.
 *Bel.* To love and fear, and both at once, my
lord,
In my conceit, are things of more import
Than women's wits are to be busied with. 95
 *Bal.* 'T is I that love.
 *Bel.*     Whom?
 *Bal*        Bel-imperia.
 *Bel.* But I that fear.
 *Bal.*      Whom?
 *Bel.*        Bel-imperia.
 *Lor.* Fear yourself?
 *Bel.*     Ay, brother.
 *Lor.*        How?
 *Bel.*       As those
That what they love are loath and fear to lose.
 *Bal.* Then, fair, let Balthazar your keeper
be. 100
 *Bel.* No, Balthazar doth fear as well as we:
*Et tremulo metui pavidum junxere timorem —*
*Est vanum stolidæ proditionis opus.*
 *Lor.* Nay, and you argue things so cun-
ningly,
We 'll go continue this discourse at court. 105
 *Bal.* Led by the loadstar of her heavenly
looks,
Wends poor oppressed Balthazar,
As o'er the mountains walks the wanderer,
Incertain to effect his pilgrimage. *Exeunt.*

#### [SCENE XI. *A Street*]

*Enter two Portingales, and Hieronimo meets*
*them.*

*1 Port.* By your leave, sir.
[Hier. *'T is neither as you think, nor as you*
*think,*

---

 **⁶⁴ forg'd:** devised **⁹¹ front:** forehead **⁹⁴ conceit:** opinion **¹⁰², ¹⁰³ Et . . . opus:** And I feared to add trembling fear to a quaking man; vain is the work of stupid treachery. **²⁻⁴⁸** (Third passage of additions)

*Nor as you think; you 're wide all.*
*These slippers are not mine, they were my son Ho-*
*ratio's.*
*My son? and what 's a son?  A thing begot*      5
*Within a pair of minutes — thereabout;*
*A lump bred up in darkness, and doth serve*
*To ballace these light creatures we call women;*
*And, at nine months' end, creeps forth to light.*
*What is there yet in a son,*      10
*To make a father dote, rave, or run mad?*
*Being born, it pouts, cries, and breeds teeth.*
*What is there yet in a son?  He must be fed,*
*Be taught to go, and speak.  Ay, or yet*
*Why might not a man love a calf as well?*      15
*Or melt in passion o'er a frisking kid,*
*As for a son?  Methinks, a young bacon,*
*Or a fine little smooth horse-colt,*
*Should move a man as much as doth a son:*
*For one of these, in very little time,*      20
*Will grow to some good use; whereas a son,*
*The more he grows in stature and in years,*
*The more unsquar'd, unbevell'd, he appears,*
*Reckons his parents among the rank of fools,*
*Strikes care upon their heads with his mad riots,* 25
*Makes them look old before they meet with*
*   age.*
*This is a son! — And what a loss were this,*
*Consider'd truly? —— O, but my Horatio*
*Grew out of reach of these insatiate humours:*      30
*He lov'd his loving parents;*
*He was my comfort, and his mother's joy,*
*The very arm that did hold up our house:*
*Our hopes were stored up in him,*
*None but a damned murderer could hate him.*
*He had not seen the back of nineteen year,*      35
*When his strong arm unhors'd*
*The proud Prince Balthazar, and his great mind,*
*Too full of honour, took him us to mercy,*
*That valiant, but ignoble Portingale!*
*Well, heaven is heaven still!*      40
*And there is Nemesis, and Furies,*
*And things call'd whips,*
*And they sometimes do meet with murderers:*
*They do not always scape, that 's some comfort.*
*Ay, ay, ay; and then time steals on,*      45
*And steals, and steals, till violence leaps forth*
*Like thunder wrapp'd in a ball of fire,*
*And so doth bring confusion to them all.]*
Good leave have you: nay, I pray you go,
For I 'll leave you, if you can leave me so.      50
   2 *Port.*  Pray you, which is the next way to
      my lord the duke's?
   *Hier.*  The next way from me.
   1 *Port.*                To his house, we mean.
   *Hier.*  O, hard by: 't is yon house that you
      see.

2 *Port.*  You could not tell us if his son were
   there?
*Hier.*  Who, my Lord Lorenzo?
1 *Port.*                          Ay, sir.
      *He goeth in at one door and comes*
         *out at another.*
*Hier.*                          O, forbear! 55
For other talk for us far fitter were.
But if you be importunate to know
The way to him, and where to find him out,
Then list to me, and I 'll resolve your doubt.
There is a path upon your left-hand side      60
That leadeth from a guilty conscience
Unto a forest of distrust and fear —
A darksome place, and dangerous to pass.
There shall you meet with melancholy thoughts,
Whose baleful humours if you but uphold,      65
It will conduct you to despair and death —
Whose rocky cliffs when you have once beheld,
Within a hugy dale of lasting night,
That, kindled with the world's iniquities,
Doth cast up filthy and detested fumes: —      70
Not far from thence, where murderers have built
A habitation for their cursed souls,
There, in a brazen cauldron, fix'd by Jove,
In his fell wrath, upon a sulphur flame,
Yourselves shall find Lorenzo bathing him      75
In boiling lead and blood of innocents.
   1 *Port.*  Ha, ha, ha!
   *Hier.*  Ha, ha, ha! Why, ha, ha, ha! Fare-
      well, good ha, ha, ha!          *Exit.*
   2 *Port.*  Doubtless this man is passing lunatic,
Or imperfection of his age doth make him dote.
Come, let 's away to seek my lord the duke. 81
                                    *Exeunt.*

[SCENE XII.  *The Court of Spain*]

*Enter Hieronimo, with a poniard in one hand*
   *and a rope in the other*

   *Hier.*  Now, sir, perhaps I come and see the
      king;
The king sees me, and fain would hear my
   suit:
Why, is not this a strange and seld-seen thing,
That standers-by with toys should strike me
   mute?
Go to, I see their shifts, and say no more.      5
Hieronimo, 't is time for thee to trudge.
Down by the dale that flows with purple gore
Standeth a fiery tower; there sits a judge
Upon a seat of steel and molten brass,
And 'twixt his teeth he holds a fire-brand,      10
That leads unto the lake where hell doth stand
Away, Hieronimo! to him be gone;
He 'll do thee justice for Horatio's death.

Turn down this path: thou shalt be with him
   straight;
Or this, and then thou need'st not take thy
   breath:                                              15
This way or that way? —— Soft and fair, not
   so:
For if I hang or kill myself, let 's know
Who will revenge Horatio's murder then?
No, no! fie, no! pardon me, I 'll none of that.
      *He flings away the dagger and halter.*
This way I 'll take, and this way comes the
   king:       *He takes them up again.* 20
And here I 'll have a fling at him, that 's flat;
And, Balthazar, I 'll be with thee to bring,
And thee, Lorenzo! Here 's the king — nay,
   stay;
And here, ay here — there goes the hare away.

*Enter King, Ambassador, Castile, and Lorenzo*

   *King.*  Now show, ambassador, what our
     viceroy saith:                                   25
Hath he receiv'd the articles we sent?
   *Hier.*  Justice, O justice to Hieronimo.
   *Lor.*  Back! see'st thou not the king is busy?
   *Hier.*                  O, is he so?
   *King.*  Who is he that interrupts our busi-
     ness?
   *Hier.*  Not I. [*Aside.*] Hieronimo, beware!
   go by, go by!                                        30
   *Amb.*  Renowmed King, he hath receiv'd and
   read
Thy kingly proffers, and thy promis'd league;
And, as a man extremely over-joy'd
To hear his son so princely entertain'd,
Whose death he had so solemnly bewail'd,   35
This for thy further satisfaction
And kingly love he kindly lets thee know:
First, for the marriage of his princely son
With Bel-imperia, thy beloved niece,
The news are more delightful to his soul,   40
Than myrrh or incense to the offended heavens.
In person, therefore, will he come himself,
To see the marriage rites solemnized,
And, in the presence of the court of Spain,
To knit a sure inexplicable band            45
Of kingly love and everlasting league
Betwixt the crowns of Spain and Portingale.
There will he give his crown to Balthazar,
And make a queen of Bel-imperia.
   *King.*  Brother, how like you this our vice-
     roy's love?                                     50
   *Cast.*  No doubt, my lord, it is an argument
Of honourable care to keep his friend,
And wondrous zeal to Balthazar his son;
Nor am I least indebted to his grace,

That bends his liking to my daughter thus. 55
   *Amb.*  Now last, dread lord, here hath his
     highness sent
(Although he send not that his son return)
His ransom due to Don Horatio.
   *Hier.*  Horatio! who calls Horatio?
   *King.*  And well rememb'red: thank his maj-
     esty.                                            60
Here, see it given to Horatio.
   *Hier.*  Justice, O, justice, justice, gentle king!
   *King.*  Who is that? Hieronimo?
   *Hier.*  Justice, O, justice! O my son, my son!
My son, whom naught can ransom or redeem! 65
   *Lor.*  Hieronimo, you are not well-advis'd.
   *Hier.*  Away, Lorenzo, hinder me no more;
For thou hast made me bankrupt of my bliss.
Give me my son! you shall not ransom him.
Away! I 'll rip the bowels of the earth,      70
       *He diggeth with his dagger.*
And ferry over to th' Elysian plains,
And bring my son to show his deadly wounds.
Stand from about me!
I 'll make a pickaxe of my poniard,
And here surrender up my marshalship;        75
For I 'll go marshal up the fiends in hell,
To be avenged on you all for this.
   *King.*  What means this outrage?
Will none of you restrain his fury?
   *Hier.*  Nay, soft and fair! you shall not need
   to strive.                                          80
Needs must he go that the devils drive. *Exit.*
   *King.*  What accident hath happ'd Hier-
     onimo?
I have not seen him to demean him so.
   *Lor.*  My gracious lord, he is with extreme
   pride,
Conceiv'd of young Horatio his son,          85
And covetous of having to himself
The ransom of the young prince Balthazar,
Distract, and in a manner lunatic.
   *King.*  Believe me, nephew, we are sorry for 't:
This is the love that fathers bear their sons. 90
But, gentle brother, go give to him this gold,
The prince's ransom; let him have his due.
For what he hath, Horatio shall not want;
Haply Hieronimo hath need thereof.
   *Lor.*  But if he be thus helplessly distract,  95
'T is requisite his office be resign'd,
And given to one of more discretion.
   *King.*  We shall increase his melancholy so.
'T is best that we see further in it first,
Till when, ourself will execute the place.   100
And, brother, now bring in the ambassador,
That he may be a witness of the match
'Twixt Balthazar and Bel-imperia,

And that we may prefix a certain time.
Wherein the marriage shall be solemnized, 105
That we may have thy lord, the viceroy, here.
   *Amb.* Therein your highness highly shall
    content
His majesty, that longs to hear from hence.
   *King.* On, then, and hear you, lord ambassa-
    dor ——                *Exeunt.*

   [SCENE XIIA.  *Hieronimo's Garden*]

    [*Enter Jaques and Pedro*

   *Jaq.*  I wonder, Pedro, why our master thus
*At midnight sends us with our torches' light,*
*When man and bird and beast are all at rest,*
*Save those that watch for rape and bloody murder.*
   *Ped.*  O Jaques, know thou that our master's
    mind                            5
*Is much distraught, since his Horatio died,*
*And — now his aged years should sleep in rest,*
*His heart in quiet — like a desperate man,*
*Grows lunatic and childish for his son.*
*Sometimes, as he doth at his table sit,*     10
*He speaks as if Horatio stood by him;*
*Then starting in a rage, falls on the earth,*
*Cries out, "Horatio! Where is my Horatio?"*
*So that with extreme grief and cutting sorrow*
*There is not left in him one inch of man.*    15
*See, where he comes.*

      Enter Hieronimo

   *Hier.*  I pry through every crevice of each wall,
*Look on each tree, and search through every brake,*
*Beat at the bushes, stamp our grandam earth,*
*Dive in the water, and stare up to heaven,*   20
*Yet cannot I behold my son Horatio. —*
*How now, who's there? — Sprites! Sprites!*
   *Ped.*  We are your servants that attend you, sir.
   *Hier.*  What make you with your torches in the
    dark?
   *Ped.*  You bid us light them, and attend you
    here.                          25
   *Hier.*  No, no, you are deceiv'd! not I; — you
    are deceiv'd!
*Was I so mad to bid you light your torches now?*
*Light me your torches at the mid of noon,*
*Whenas the sun-god rides in all his glory;*
*Light me your torches then.*
   *Ped.*         Then we burn daylight. 30
   *Hier.*  Let it be burnt; Night is a murderous
    slut,
*That would not have her treasons to be seen;*
*And yonder pale-fac'd Hecate there, the moon,*
*Doth give consent to that is done in darkness;*
*And all those stars that gaze upon her face,*   35
*Are aglets on her sleeve, pins on her train;*
*And those that should be powerful and divine,*
*Do sleep in darkness when they most should shine.*

   *Ped.*  Provoke them not, fair sir, with tempting
    words:
*The heavens are gracious, and your miseries*   40
*And sorrow makes you speak you know not what.*
   *Hier.*  Villain, thou liest! and thou doest naught
*But tell me I am mad. Thou liest, I am not mad!*
*I know thee to be Pedro, and he Jaques.*
*I'll prove it to thee; and were I mad, how could*
    I?                             45
*Where was she that same night when my Horatio*
*Was murd'red? She should have shone: search*
    thou the book.
*Had the moon shone, in my boy's face there was a*
    kind of grace,
*That I know — nay, I do know — had the mur-*
    derer seen him,
*His weapon would have fall'n and cut the earth,* 50
*Had he been fram'd of naught but blood and death.*
*Alack! when mischief doth it knows not what,*
*What shall we say to mischief?*

      Enter Isabella

   *Isab.*  Dear Hieronimo, come in a-doors;
*O, seek not means so to increase thy sorrow.*   55
   *Hier.*  Indeed, Isabella, we do nothing here.
*I do not cry: ask Pedro, and ask Jaques;*
*Not I indeed; we are very merry, very merry.*
   *Isab.*  How? be merry here, be merry here?
*Is not this the place, and this the very tree,*   60
*Where my Horatio died, where he was murdered?*
   *Hier.*  Was — do not say what: let her weep
    it out.
*This was the tree; I set it of a kernel:*
*And when our hot Spain could not let it grow,*
*But that the infant and the human sap*   65
*Began to wither, duly twice a morning*
*Would I be sprinkling it with fountain-water.*
*At last it grew and grew, and bore and bore,*
*Till at the length*
*It grew a gallows, and did bear our son;*   70
*It bore thy fruit and mine — O wicked, wicked*
    plant!
         One knocks within at the door.
*See, who knocks there.*
   *Ped.*         It is a painter, sir.
   *Hier.*  Bid him come in, and paint some com-
    fort,
*For surely there's none lives but painted com-*
    fort.
*Let him come in! — One knows not what may*
    chance.                     75
*God's will, that I should set this tree! — but even so*
*Masters ungrateful servants rear from naught,*
*And then they hate them that did bring them up.*

      Enter the Painter

   *Paint.*  God bless you, sir.

Sc. XIIA (The entire scene is the fourth passage of additions.)   **24 make:** do   **30 burn daylight:**
waste time   **33 Hecate:** ('Hee-cat' Qq.)   **36 aglets:** metal ornaments

Hier. *Wherefore? Why, thou scornful villain?*                                                     80
*How, where, or by what means should I be*
  *bless'd?*
Isab. *What wouldst thou have, good fellow?*
Paint.                              *Justice, madam.*
Hier. *O ambitious beggar!*
*Wouldst thou have that that lives not in the world?*
*Why, all the undelved mines cannot buy*              85
*An ounce of justice!*
*'T is a jewel so inestimable. I tell thee,*
*God hath engross'd all justice in his hands,*
*And there is none but what comes from him.*
Paint.                          *O, then I see*
*That God must right me for my murd'red son.* 90
Hier. *How, was thy son murdered?*
Paint. *Ay, sir; no man did hold a son so*
  *dear.*
Hier. *What, not as thine? That's a lie,*
*As massy as the earth. I had a son*
*Whose least unvalued hair did weigh*               95
*A thousand of thy sons: and he was murdered.*
Paint. *Alas, sir, I had no more but he.*
Hier. *Nor I, nor I: but this same one of*
  *mine*
*Was worth a legion. But all is one.*
*Pedro, Jaques, go in a-doors; Isabella, go,*        100
*And this good fellow here and I*
*Will range this hideous orchard up and down,*
*Like to two lions reaved of their young.*
*Go in a-doors, I say.*

                              Exeunt [Isab., etc.].

              The painter and he sits down.

                      *Come, let's talk wisely now.*
*Was thy son murdered?*
Paint.                              *Ay, sir.*
Hier.                          *So was mine.* 105
*How dost take it? Art thou not sometimes mad?*
*Is there no tricks that comes before thine eyes?*
Paint. *O Lord, yes, sir.*
Hier. *Art a painter? Canst paint me a tear,*
*or a wound, a groan, or a sigh? Canst paint* [110
*me such a tree as this?*
Paint. *Sir, I am sure you have heard of my*
*painting: my name's Bazardo.*
Hier. *Bazardo! Afore God, an excellent fellow. Look you, sir, do you see? I'd have you* [115
*paint me for my gallery, in your oil-colours*
*matted, and draw me five years younger than I am*
*— do ye see, sir, let five years go; let them go like*
*the marshal of Spain — my wife Isabella standing*
*by me, with a speaking look to my son Horatio,* [120
*which should entend to this or some such-like purpose: "God bless thee, my sweet son," and my*

*hand leaning upon his head, thus, sir; do you see?*
*May it be done?*
Paint. *Very well, sir.*                          125
Hier. *Nay, I pray, mark me, sir. Then, sir,*
*would I have you paint me this tree, this very tree.*
*Canst paint a doleful cry?*
Paint. *Seemingly, sir.*
Hier. *Nay, it should cry; but all is one.* [130
*Well, sir, paint me a youth run through and*
*through with villains' swords, hanging upon this*
*tree. Canst thou draw a murderer?*
Paint. *I'll warrant you, sir; I have the pattern*
*of the most notorious villains that ever lived in* [135
*all Spain.*
Hier. *O, let them be worse, worse: stretch thine*
*art, and let their beards be of Judas his own colour;*
*and let their eye-brows jutty over: in any case observe that. Then, sir, after some violent noise,* [140
*bring me forth in my shirt, and my gown under*
*mine arm, with my torch in my hand, and my*
*sword reared up, thus: — and with these words:*
*"What noise is this? Who calls Hieronimo?"*
*May it be done?*                                  145
Paint. *Yea, sir.*
Hier. *Well, sir; then bring me forth, bring me*
*through alley and alley, still with a distracted countenance going along, and let my hair heave up my*
*night-cap. Let the clouds scowl, make the* [150
*moon dark, the stars extinct, the winds blowing, the*
*bells tolling, the owl shrieking, the toads croaking,*
*the minutes jarring, and the clock striking twelve.*
*And then at last, sir, starting, behold a man hanging, and tottering and tottering, as you know the* [155
*wind will wave a man, and I with a trice to cut*
*him down. And looking upon him by the advantage of my torch, find it to be my son Horatio.*
*There you may show a passion, there you may*
*show a passion! Draw me like old Priam of* [160
*Troy, crying, "The house is a-fire, the house is*
*a-fire, as the torch over my head!" Make me curse,*
*make me rave, make me cry, make me mad, make*
*me well again, make me curse hell, invocate heaven,*
*and in the end leave me in a trance — and so forth.*
Paint. *And is this the end?*                      166
Hier. *O no, there is no end; the end is death*
*and madness! As I am never better than when I*
*am mad; then methinks I am a brave fellow, then*
*I do wonders; but reason abuseth me, and* [170
*there's the torment, there's the hell. At the last, sir,*
*bring me to one of the murderers; were he as strong*
*as Hector, thus would I tear and drag him up and*
*down.*

                  He beats the painter in, then comes
                      out again, with a book in his
                      hand.]

---

⁹⁴ **massy**: heavy     ¹⁰³ **reaved**: robbed     ¹⁰⁷ **tricks**: illusory appearances     ¹¹¹ **tree**: ('tear'
Q 1602–1603)     ¹¹⁶ **for**: (not in Qq.)     ¹¹⁷ **matted**: dulled     ¹²¹ **entend**: portend     ¹²⁹ **seemingly**:
in semblance     ¹³⁹ **jutty over**: project     ¹⁴⁸ **alley**: garden-walk     ¹⁵³ **jarring**: ticking     ¹⁵⁰ **show**:
(not in Qq.)

[SCENE XIII. *Hieronimo's House*]

*Enter Hieronimo, with a book in his hand*

Hier.  *Vindicta mihi!*

Ay, heaven will be reveng'd of every ill;
Nor will they suffer murder unrepaid.
Then stay, Hieronimo, attend their will:
For mortal men may not appoint their time! 5
"*Per scelus semper tutum est sceleribus iter.*"
Strike, and strike home, where wrong is off'red
     thee;
For evils unto ills conductors be,
And death's the worst of resolution.
For he that thinks with patience to contend 10
To quiet life, his life shall easily end. —
"*Fata si miseros juvant, habes salutem;
Fata si vitam negant, habes sepulcrum*":
If destiny thy miseries do ease,
Then hast thou health, and happy shalt thou be;
If destiny deny thee life, Hieronimo, 16
Yet shalt thou be assured of a tomb;
If neither, yet let this thy comfort be:
Heaven covereth him that hath no burial.
And to conclude, I will revenge his death! 20
But how?  Not as the vulgar wits of men,
With open, but inevitable ills,
As by a secret, yet a certain mean,
Which under kindship will be cloaked best.
Wise men will take their opportunity, 25
Closely and safely fitting things to time.
But in extremes advantage hath no time;
And therefore all times fit not for revenge.
Thus therefore will I rest me in unrest,
Dissembling quiet in unquietness, 30
Not seeming that I know their villainies,
That my simplicity may make them think
That ignorantly I will let all slip;
For ignorance, I wot, and well they know,
*Remedium malorum iners est.* 35
Nor aught avails it me to menace them,
Who, as a wintry storm upon a plain,
Will bear me down with their nobility.
No, no, Hieronimo, thou must enjoin
Thine eyes to observation, and thy tongue 40
To milder speeches than thy spirit affords,
Thy heart to patience, and thy hands to rest,
Thy cap to courtesy, and thy knee to bow,
Till to revenge thou know when, where, and
     how.                    *A noise within.*
How now, what noise?  What coil is that you
     keep?                                    45

*Enter a Servant*

Serv.  Here are a sort of poor petitioners
That are importunate, and it shall please you,
     sir,
That you should plead their cases to the king.
Hier.  That I should plead their several ac-
     tions?
Why, let them enter, and let me see them.  50

*Enter three Citizens and an Old Man*

1 Cit.  So, I tell you this: for learning and
     for law,
There is not any advocate in Spain
That can prevail, or will take half the pain
That he will, in pursuit of equity.
Hier.  Come near, you men, that thus im-
     portune me. —                           55
[*Aside.*] Now must I bear a face of gravity;
For thus I us'd, before my marshalship,
To plead in causes as corregidor. —
Come on, sirs, what's the matter?
2 Cit.                        Sir, an action.
Hier.  Of battery?
1 Cit.                Mine of debt.
Hier.                            Give place. 60
2 Cit.  No, sir, mine is an action of the case.
3 Cit.  Mine an *ejectione firmæ* by a lease.
Hier.  Content you, sirs; are you deter-
     mined
That I should plead your several actions?
1 Cit.  Ay, sir, and here's my declaration. 65
2 Cit.  And here is my band.
3 Cit.                  And here is my lease.
          *They give him papers.*
Hier.  But wherefore stands yon silly man so
     mute,
With mournful eyes and hands to heaven up-
     rear'd?
Come hither, father, let me know thy cause.
Senex.  O worthy sir, my cause, but slightly
     known,                                   70
May move the hearts of warlike Myrmidons,
And melt the Corsic rocks with ruthful tears.
Hier.  Say, father, tell me, what's thy suit?
Senex.                    No, sir, could my woes
Give way unto my most distressful words,
Then should I not in paper, as you see, 75
With ink bewray what blood began in me.
Hier.  What's here?  "The humble supplica-
     tion
Of Don Bazulto for his murd'red son."

---

¹ **Vindicta mihi:** Vengeance is mine!    ⁶ **Per . . . iter:** The safe way to further crimes is always
through crime.    ⁹ Resolute action can at worst end in death.    ¹²⁻¹³ (Translated in the next four
lines)    ²² Not with open, but inevitable (because secret) injuries (?)    ²⁴ **kindship:** kindness    ³⁰ **Dissembling:** pretending    ³⁵ **Remedium . . . est:** is a futile remedy for ills    ³⁸ **nobility:** high rank
⁴⁵ **coil:** disturbance    ⁴⁶ **sort:** group    ⁴⁷ **and:** if, an    ⁵⁸ **corregidor:** advocate (strictly, magistrate)
⁶¹ **action of the case:** an action for redress of wrongs not specially provided against by law    ⁶² **ejectione firmæ:** a writ to eject a tenant ('firma' Qq.)    ⁶⁶ **band:** bond    ⁶⁷ **silly:** simple, unlearned
⁷² **Corsic:** of Corsica

*Senex.* Ay, sir.

*Hier.*   No, sir, it was my murd'red son:
O my son, my son, O my son Horatio!                    80
But mine, or thine, Bazulto, be content.
Here, take my handkercher and wipe thine eyes,
Whiles wretched I in thy mishaps may see
The lively portrait of my dying self.

                    *He draweth out a bloody napkin.*
O no, not this; Horatio, this was thine;                    85
And when I dy'd it in thy dearest blood,
This was a token 'twixt thy soul and me,
That of thy death revenged I should be.
But here, take this, and this — what, my
    purse? —
Ay, this, and that, and all of them are thine; 90
For all as one are our extremities.

1 *Cit.*   O, see the kindness of Hieronimo!

2 *Cit.*   This gentleness shows him a gentleman.

*Hier.*   See, see, O see thy shame, Hieronimo!
See here a loving father to his son!                    95
Behold the sorrows and the sad laments,
That he delivereth for his son's decease!
If love's effects so strives in lesser things,
If love enforce such moods in meaner wits,
If love express such power in poor estates, 100
Hieronimo, whenas a raging sea,
Toss'd with the wind and tide, o'erturneth then
The upper billows, course of waves to keep,
Whilst lesser waters labour in the deep,
Then sham'st thou not, Hieronimo, to neglect
The sweet revenge of thy Horatio?                    106
Though on this earth justice will not be found,
I'll down to hell, and in this passion
Knock at the dismal gates of Pluto's court,
Getting by force, as once Alcides did,                    110
A troop of Furies and tormenting hags
To torture Don Lorenzo and the rest.
Yet lest the triple-headed porter should
Deny my passage to the slimy strand,
The Thracian poet thou shalt counterfeit.   115
Come on, old father, be my Orpheus,
And if thou canst no notes upon the harp,
Then sound the burden of thy sore heart's grief,
Till we do gain that Proserpine may grant
Revenge on them that murdered my son.   120
Then will I rent and tear them, thus and thus,
Shivering their limbs in pieces with my teeth.

                    *Tear the papers.*

1 *Cit.*   O sir, my declaration!

                    *Exit Hieronimo, and they after.*

2 *Cit.*                    Save my bond!

                    *Enter Hieronimo*

2 *Cit.*   Save my bond!

3 *Cit.*   Alas, my lease! it cost me ten pound,
And you, my lord, have torn the same.   126

*Hier.*   That cannot be, I gave it never a
    wound.
Show me one drop of blood fall from the same!
How is it possible I should slay it then?
Tush, no;  run after, catch me if you can.   130

                    *Exeunt all but the Old Man. Ba-*
                    *zulto remains till Hieronimo*
                    *enters again, who, staring him*
                    *in the face, speaks.*

*Hier.*   And art thou come, Horatio, from the
    depth,
To ask for justice in this upper earth,
To tell thy father thou art unreveng'd,
To wring more tears from Isabella's eyes,
Whose lights are dimm'd with over-long la-
    ments?                    135
Go back, my son, complain to Æacus,
For here's no justice; gentle boy, begone,
For justice is exiled from the earth:
Hieronimo will bear thee company.
Thy mother cries on righteous Rhadamanth 140
For just revenge against the murderers.

*Senex.*   Alas, my lord, whence springs this
    troubled speech?

*Hier.*   But let me look on my Horatio.
Sweet boy, how art thou chang'd in death's
    black shade!
Had Proserpine no pity on thy youth,                    145
But suffer'd thy fair crimson-colour'd spring
With wither'd winter to be blasted thus?
Horatio, thou art older than thy father.
Ah, ruthless fate, that favour thus transforms!

*Baz.*   Ah, my good lord, I am not your young
    son.                    150

*Hier.*   What, not my son?  Thou then a Fury
art,
Sent from the empty kingdom of black night
To summon me to make appearance
Before grim Minos and just Rhadamanth,
To plague Hieronimo that is remiss,                    155
And seeks not vengeance for Horatio's death.

*Baz.*   I am a grieved man, and not a ghost,
That came for justice for my murder'd son.

*Hier.*   Ay, now I know thee, now thou nam'st
    thy son.
Thou art the lively image of my grief;                    160
Within thy face my sorrows I may see.
Thy eyes are gumm'd with tears, thy cheeks
    are wan,
Thy forehead troubled, and thy mutt'ring lips
Murmur sad words abruptly broken off
By force of windy sighs thy spirit breathes; 165
And all this sorrow riseth for thy son:
And selfsame sorrow feel I for my son.
Come in, old man, thou shalt to Isabel.

---

¹⁰¹⁻¹⁰⁴ (A difficult passage, probably corrupt.   None of the emendations suggested is satisfactory.
¹⁰² o'erturneth: ('oreturnest' early Qq.)   ¹¹⁷ canst: knowest   ¹²¹ rent: rend   ¹⁴⁹ fate: ('Father
Qq.)   favour: appearance   ¹⁵⁹ thy: (so Qq. 1623–1633; Q 1, etc., 'my')

Lean on my arm: I thee, thou me, shalt stay,
And thou, and I, and she will sing a song,  170
Three parts in one, but all of discords fram'd —:
Talk not of chords, but let us now be gone,
For with a cord Horatio was slain.        *Exeunt.*

[SCENE XIV.  *The Court of Spain*]

*Enter King of Spain, the Duke, Viceroy, and
    Lorenzo, Balthazar, Don Pedro, and Bel-
    imperia*

*King.*  Go, brother, it is the Duke of Castile's
    cause;
Salute the Viceroy in our name.
    *Cast.*                              I go.
    *Vic.*  Go forth, Don Pedro, for thy nephew's
    sake,
And greet the Duke of Castile.
    *Ped.*                  It shall be so.
    *King.*  And now to meet these Portuguese: 5
For as we now are, so sometimes were these,
Kings and commanders of the western Indies.
Welcome, brave Viceroy, to the court of Spain,
And welcome all his honourable train!
'T is not unknown to us for why you come, 10
Or have so kingly cross'd the seas:
Sufficeth it, in this we note the troth
And more than common love you lend to us.
So is it that mine honourable niece
(For it beseems us now that it be known) 15
Already is betroth'd to Balthazar:
And by appointment and our condescent
To-morrow are they to be married.
To this intent we entertain thyself,
Thy followers, their pleasure, and our peace. 20
Speak, men of Portingale, shall it be so?
If ay, say so; if not, say flatly no.
    *Vic.*  Renowmed King, I come not, as thou
    think'st,
With doubtful followers, unresolved men,
But such as have upon thine articles    25
Confirm'd thy motion, and contented me.
Know, sovereign, I come to solemnize
The marriage of thy beloved niece,
Fair Bel-imperia, with my Balthazar, —
With thee, my son; whom sith I live to see, 30
Here take my crown, I give it her and thee;
And let me live a solitary life,
In ceaseless prayers,
To think how strangely heaven hath thee pre-
    serv'd.
    *King.*  See, brother, see, how nature strives
    in him!                              35
Come, worthy Viceroy, and accompany
Thy friend with thine extremities;
A place more private fits this princely mood.
    *Vic.*  Or here, or where your highness thinks
    it good.  *Exeunt all but Castile and Lorenzo.*

    *Cast.*  Nay, stay, Lorenzo, let me talk with
    you.                                 40
See'st thou this entertainment of these kings?
    *Lor.*  I do, my lord, and joy to see the same.
    *Cast.*  And knowest thou why this meeting is?
    *Lor.*  For her, my lord, whom Balthazar doth
    love,
And to confirm their promis'd marriage.  45
    *Cast.*  She is thy sister?
    *Lor.*                  Who, Bel-imperia?  Ay,
My gracious lord, and this is the day,
That I have long'd so happily to see.
    *Cast.*  Thou wouldst be loath that any fault
    of thine
Should intercept her in her happiness?   50
    *Lor.*  Heavens will not let Lorenzo err so
    much.
    *Cast.*  Why then, Lorenzo, listen to my
    words:
It is suspected, and reported too,
That thou, Lorenzo, wrong'st Hieronimo,
And in his suits towards his majesty      55
Still keep'st him back, and seeks to cross his
    suit.
    *Lor.*  That I, my lord ——?
    *Cast.*  I tell thee, son, myself have heard it
    said,
When, to my sorrow, I have been ashamed
To answer for thee, though thou art my son. 60
Lorenzo, know'st thou not the common love
And kindness that Hieronimo hath won
By his deserts within the court of Spain?
Or see'st thou not the king my brother's care
In his behalf, and to procure his health?  65
Lorenzo, shouldst thou thwart his passions,
And he exclaim against thee to the king,
What honour were 't in this assembly,
Or what a scandal were 't among the kings
To hear Hieronimo exclaim on thee?        70
Tell me — and look thou tell me truly too —
Whence grows the ground of this report in
    court?
    *Lor.*  My lord, it lies not in Lorenzo's power
To stop the vulgar, liberal of their tongues.
A small advantage makes a water-breach,   75
And no man lives that long contenteth all.
    *Cast.*  Myself have seen thee busy to keep
    back
Him and his supplications from the king.
    *Lor.*  Yourself, my lord, hath seen his pas-
    sions,
That ill beseem'd the presence of a king:  80
And, for I pitied him in his distress,
I held him thence with kind and courteous
    words
As free from malice to Hieronimo
As to my soul, my lord.

---

¹⁷ **condescent:** consent   ²³ **Renowmed:** famed   ³⁷ **extremities:** unrestrained emotion   ⁷⁵ **advantage:** occasion   **water-breach:** burst of water through a dike

*Cast.* Hieronimo, my son, mistakes thee
then.                                                                      85
*Lor.* My gracious father, believe me, so he
doth.
But what's a silly man, distract in mind
To think upon the murder of his son?
Alas! how easy is it for him to err!
But for his satisfaction and the world's,          90
'T were good, my lord, that Hieronimo and I
Were reconcil'd, if he misconster me.
*Cast.* Lorenzo, thou hast said; it shall be so.
Go one of you, and call Hieronimo.
*Enter Balthazar and Bel-imperia*
*Bal.* Come, Bel-imperia, Balthazar's con-
tent,                                                                      95
My sorrow's ease and sovereign of my bliss,
Sith heaven hath ordain'd thee to be mine:
Disperse those clouds and melancholy looks,
And clear them up with those thy sun-bright
eyes,
Wherein my hope and heaven's fair beauty
lies.                                                                     100
*Bel.* My looks, my lord, are fitting for my
love,
Which, new-begun, can show no brighter yet.
*Bal.* New-kindled flames should burn as
morning sun.
*Bel.* But not too fast, lest heat and all be
done.
I see my lord my father.
*Bal.*                            Truce, my love;   105
I will go salute him.
*Cast.*                       Welcome, Balthazar,
Welcome, brave prince, the pledge of Castile's
peace!
And welcome, Bel-imperia! — How now, girl?
Why com'st thou sadly to salute us thus?
Content thyself, for I am satisfied:               110
It is not now as when Andrea liv'd;
We have forgotten and forgiven that,
And thou art graced with a happier love. —
But, Balthazar, here comes Hieronimo;
I'll have a word with him.                           115
*Enter Hieronimo and a Servant*
*Hier.* And where's the duke?
*Serv.*                            Yonder.
*Hier.*                            Even so. —
What new device have they devised, trow?
*Pocas palabras!* mild as the lamb!
Is't I will be reveng'd? No, I am not the man.
*Cast.* Welcome, Hieronimo.                  120
*Lor.* Welcome, Hieronimo.
*Bal.* Welcome, Hieronimo.
*Hier.* My lords, I thank you for Horatio.
*Cast.* Hieronimo, the reason that I sent
To speak with you, is this.

*Hier.*                            What, so short? 125
Then I'll be gone, I thank you for 't.
*Cast.* Nay, stay, Hieronimo! — go call him,
son.
*Lor.* Hieronimo, my father craves a word
with you.
*Hier.* With me, sir? Why, my lord, I
thought you had done.
*Lor.* No; [*Aside.*] would he had!
*Cast.*                            Hieronimo, I hear 130
You find yourself aggrieved at my son,
Because you have not access unto the king;
And say 't is he that intercepts your suits.
*Hier.* Why, is not this a miserable thing, my
lord?
*Cast.* Hieronimo, I hope you have no cause,
And would be loath that one of your deserts 136
Should once have reason to suspect my son,
Considering how I think of you myself.
*Hier.* Your son Lorenzo! Whom, my noble
lord?
The hope of Spain, mine honourable friend? 140
Grant me the combat of them, if they dare:
*Draws out his sword.*
I'll meet him face to face, to tell me so!
These be the scandalous reports of such
As loves not me, and hate my lord too much.
Should I suspect Lorenzo would prevent   145
Or cross my suit, that lov'd my son so well?
My lord, I am asham'd it should be said.
*Lor.* Hieronimo, I never gave you cause.
*Hier.* My good lord, I know you did not.
*Cast.*                            There then pause;   150
And for the satisfaction of the world,
Hieronimo, frequent my homely house,
The Duke of Castile, Cyprian's ancient seat;
And when thou wilt, use me, my son, and it:
But here, before Prince Balthazar and me,
Embrace each other, and be perfect friends. 155
*Hier.* Ay, marry, my lord, and shall.
Friends, quoth he? See, I'll be friends with
you all:
Specially with you, my lovely lord;
For divers causes it is fit for us
That we be friends: the world is suspicious, 160
And men may think what we imagine not.
*Bal.* Why, this is friendly done, Hieronimo.
*Lor.* And that I hope old grudges are forgot.
*Hier.* What else? It were a shame it
should not be so.
*Cast.* Come on, Hieronimo, at my request; 165
Let us entreat your company to-day.   *Exeunt.*
*Hier.* Your lordship's to command. — Pah!
keep your way:
*Chi mi fa più carezze che non suole,*
*Tradito mi ha, o tradir mi vuole.*          *Exit.*

⁹² **misconster:** misunderstand    ¹⁰² **no:** (not in Q 1)    ¹¹⁷ **trow:** do you suppose?    ¹¹⁸ **Pocas palabras:** few words (Spanish; a stock phrase) ¹⁶⁸, ¹⁶⁹ **Chi . . . vuole:** He who caresses me more than usual has betrayed me or hopes to betray me. (Ital.)

*[Chorus]*

*Enter Ghost and Revenge*

*Ghost.* Awake, Erichtho! Cerberus, awake!
Solicit Pluto, gentle Proserpine!     171
To combat, Acheron and Erebus!
For ne'er, by Styx and Phlegethon in hell,
O'er-ferried Charon to the fiery lakes
Such fearful sights, as poor Andrea sees.     175
Revenge, awake!
    *Revenge.* Awake? For why?
    *Ghost.* Awake, Revenge; for thou art ill-
advis'd
To sleep away what thou art warn'd to watch!
    *Revenge.* Content thyself, and do not trouble
me.
    *Ghost.* Awake, Revenge, if love — as love
hath had —     180
Have yet the power or prevalence in hell!
Hieronimo with Lorenzo is join'd in league,
And intercepts our passage to revenge.
Awake, Revenge, or we are woe-begone!
    *Revenge.* Thus worldlings ground what they
have dream'd upon.     185
Content thyself, Andrea: though I sleep,
Yet is my mood soliciting their souls.
Sufficeth thee that poor Hieronimo
Cannot forget his son Horatio.
Nor dies Revenge, although he sleep awhile; 190
For in unquiet, quietness is feign'd,
And slumb'ring is a common worldly wile.
Behold, Andrea, for an instance, how
Revenge hath slept, and then imagine thou,
What 't is to be subject to destiny.     195

*Enter a Dumb Show*

    *Ghost.* Awake, Revenge; reveal this mystery.
    *Revenge.* The two first the nuptial torches
bore
As brightly burning as the mid-day's sun;
But after them doth Hymen hie as fast,
Clothed in sable and a saffron robe,     200
And blows them out, and quencheth them with
blood,
As discontent that things continue so.
    *Ghost.* Sufficeth me; thy meaning's under-
stood,
And thanks to thee and those infernal powers
That will not tolerate a lover's woe.     205
Rest thee, for I will sit to see the rest.
    *Revenge.* Then argue, not, for thou last thy
request.     *Exeunt.*

ACTUS QUARTUS

[SCENE I.   *The Palace of Don Cyprian*]

*Enter Bel-imperia and Hieronimo*

    *Bel.* Is this the love thou bear'st Horatio?
Is this the kindness that thou counterfeits?
Are these the fruits of thine incessant tears?
Hieronimo, are these thy passions,
Thy protestations and thy deep laments,     5
That thou wert wont to weary men withal?
O unkind father! O deceitful world!
With what excuses canst thou show thyself
From this dishonour and the hate of men,
Thus to neglect the loss and life of him     10
Whom both my letters and thine own belief
Assures thee to be causeless slaughtered?
Hieronimo, for shame, Hieronimo,
Be not a history to after-times
Of such ingratitude unto thy son.     15
Unhappy mothers of such children then!
But monstrous fathers to forget so soon
The death of those whom they with care and
cost
Have tend'red so, thus careless should be lost.
Myself, a stranger in respect of thee,     20
So lov'd his life, as still I wish their deaths.
Nor shall his death be unreveng'd by me,
Although I bear it out for fashion's sake;
For here I swear, in sight of heaven and earth,
Shouldst thou neglect the love thou shouldst
retain,     25
And give it over and devise no more,
Myself should send their hateful souls to hell
That wrought his downfall with extremest
death.
    *Hier.* But may it be that Bel-imperia
Vows such revenge as she hath deign'd to say? 30
Why, then I see that heaven applies our drift,
And all the saints do sit soliciting
For vengeance on those cursed murderers.
Madam, 't is true, and now I find it so,
I found a letter, written in your name,     35
And in that letter, how Horatio died.
Pardon, O pardon, Bel-imperia,
My fear and care in not believing it;
Nor think I thoughtless think upon a mean
To let his death be unreveng'd at full.     40
And here I vow — so you but give consent,
And will conceal my resolution —
I will ere long determine of their deaths
That causeless thus have murdered my son.
    *Bel.* Hieronimo, I will consent, conceal,     45

---

<sup>171–175</sup> This passage is corrupt in the early quartos and Schick's emendations, given here, are not
wholly satisfactory.    <sup>174</sup> **O'er-ferried:** ('Nor ferried' Q 1)    <sup>175</sup> **sees:** ('see' Q 1)    <sup>178</sup> **what:**
*i.e.,* the time during which    <sup>185</sup> **ground:** build (upon)    <sup>187</sup> **mood:** anger    <sup>9</sup> (Preceded in Qq.
by 'With what dishonour and the hate of men,' duplicating parts of 8 and 9. A line has probably
been lost.)    <sup>23</sup> **bear it out:** pretend    <sup>31</sup> **applies our drift:** furthers our intention    <sup>38</sup> **care:** undue
caution

And aught that may effect for thine avail,
Join with thee to revenge Horatio's death.
    *Hier.*   On, then; whatsoever I devise,
Let me entreat you, grace my practices,
For-why the plot's already in mine head.    50
Here they are.
            *Enter Balthazar and Lorenzo*
    *Bal.*            How now, Hieronimo?
What, courting Bel-imperia?
    *Hier.*                    Ay, my lord;
Such courting as, I promise you,
She hath my heart, but you, my lord, have hers.
    *Lor.*   But now, Hieronimo, or never,    55
We are to entreat your help.
    *Hier.*                    My help?
Why, my good lords, assure yourselves of me;
For you have given me cause, — ay, by my
        faith have you!
    *Bal.*   It pleas'd you, at the entertainment of
        the ambassador,
To grace the king so much as with a show.    60
Now, were your study so well furnished,
As, for the passing of the first night's sport,
To entertain my father with the like,
Or any such-like pleasing motion,
Assure yourself, it would content them well.    65
    *Hier.*   Is this all?
    *Bal.*            Ay, this is all.
    *Hier.*   Why then, I'll fit you; say no more.
When I was young, I gave my mind
And plied myself to fruitless poetry;
Which though it profit the professor naught,    70
Yet is it passing pleasing to the world.
    *Lor.*   And how for that?
    *Hier.*   Marry, my good lord, thus: —
And yet methinks, you are too quick with us —
When in Toledo there I studied,
It was my chance to write a tragedy, —    75
See here, my lords —    *He shows them a book.*
Which, long forgot, I found this other day.
Now would your lordships favour me so much
As but to grace me with your acting it —
I mean each one of you to play a part —    80
Assure you, it will prove most passing strange,
And wondrous plausible to that assembly.
    *Bal.*   What, would you have us play a trag-
        edy?
    *Hier.*   Why, Nero thought it no disparage-
        ment,
And kings and emperors have ta'en delight    85
To make experience of their wits in plays.
    *Lor.*   Nay, be not angry, good Hieronimo;
The prince but ask'd a question.
    *Bal.*   In faith, Hieronimo, and you be in
        earnest,
I'll make one.

    *Lor.*            And I another.    90
    *Hier.*   Now, my good lord, could you entreat
Your sister Bel-imperia to make one?
For what's a play without a woman in it?
    *Bel.*   Little entreaty shall serve me, Hieron-
imo;
For I must needs be employ'd in your play.    95
    *Hier.*   Why, this is well.   I tell you, lordings,
It was determined to have been acted
By gentlemen and scholars too,
Such as could tell what to speak.
    *Bal.*                        And now
It shall be play'd by princes and courtiers,    100
Such as can tell how to speak:
If, as it is our country manner,
You will but let us know the argument.
    *Hier.*   That shall I roundly.   The chronicles
        of Spain
Record this written of a knight of Rhodes:    105
He was betroth'd, and wedded at the length,
To one Perseda, an Italian dame,
Whose beauty ravish'd all that her beheld,
Especially the soul of Soliman,
Who at the marriage was the chiefest guest.    110
By sundry means sought Soliman to win
Perseda's love, and could not gain the same.
Then 'gan he break his passions to a friend,
One of his bashaws, whom he held full dear.
Her had this bashaw long solicited,    115
And saw she was not otherwise to be won,
But by her husband's death, this knight of
        Rhodes,
Whom presently by treachery he slew.
She, stirr'd with an exceeding hate therefore,
As cause of this slew Soliman,    120
And, to escape the bashaw's tyranny,
Did stab herself: and this the tragedy.
    *Lor.*   O excellent!
    *Bel.*                But say, Hieronimo,
What then became of him that was the bashaw?
    *Hier.*   Marry, thus: mov'd with remorse of
        his misdeeds,    125
Ran to a mountain-top, and hung himself.
    *Bal.*   But which of us is to perform that part?
    *Hier.*   O, that will I, my lords; make no
        doubt of it.
I'll play the murderer, I warrant you,
For I already have conceited that.    130
    *Bal.*   And what shall I?
    *Hier.*   Great Soliman, the Turkish emperor.
    *Lor.*   And I?
    *Hier.*            Erastus, the knight of Rhodes.
    *Bal.*   And I?
    *Hier.*            Perseda, chaste and resolute.
And here, my lords, are several abstracts
        drawn,    135

**50 For-why:** because    **64 motion:** puppet show    **70 professor:** practitioner    **82 plausible:**
worthy of applause    **89 and:** if    **104 roundly:** thoroughly    **113 break:** make known    **114 bashaws:**
pashas    **122 this:** this is    **130 conceited:** imagined, thought out    **135 abstracts:** individual parts

For each of you to note your parts,
And act it, as occasion 's off'red you.
You must provide a Turkish cap,
A black mustachio and a falchion;
    *Gives a paper to Balthazar.*
You with a cross, like to a knight of Rhodes; 140
    *Gives another to Lorenzo.*
And, madam, you must attire yourself
    *He giveth Bel-imperia another.*
Like Phœbe, Flora, or the huntress,
Which to your discretion shall seem best.
And as for me, my lords, I 'll look to one,
And, with the ransom that the Viceroy sent, 145
So furnish and perform this tragedy,
As all the world shall say, Hieronimo
Was liberal in gracing of it so.
 *Bal.* Hieronimo, methinks a comedy were
  better.
 *Hier.* A comedy?      150
Fie! comedies are fit for common wits;
But to present a kingly troop withal,
Give me a stately-written tragedy;
*Tragœdia cothurnata*, fitting kings,
Containing matter, and not common things. 155
My lords, all this must be performed,
As fitting for the first night's revelling.
The Italian tragedians were so sharp of wit,
That in one hour's meditation
They would perform anything in action. 160
 *Lor.* And well it may; for I have seen the
  like
In Paris 'mongst the French tragedians.
 *Hier.* In Paris? mass! and well remembered!
There 's one thing more that rests for us to do.
 *Bal.* What 's that, Hieronimo? Forget not
  anything.      165
 *Hier.* Each one of us
Must act his part in unknown languages,
That it may breed the more variety:
As you, my lord, in Latin, I in Greek,
You in Italian; and for because I know 170
That Bel-imperia hath practis'd the French,
In courtly French shall all her phrases be.
 *Bel.* You mean to try my cunning then,
  Hieronimo?
 *Bal.* But this will be a mere confusion
And hardly shall we all be understood. 175
 *Hier.* It must be so; for the conclusion
Shall prove the invention and all was good:
And I myself in an oration,
And with a strange and wondrous show besides,
That I will have there behind a curtain, 180
Assure yourself, shall make the matter known;
And all shall be concluded in one scene,
For there 's no pleasure ta'en in tediousness.
 *Bal.* [*Aside to Lorenzo.*] How like you this?

 *Lor.*      Why, thus my lord:
We must resolve to soothe his humours up. 185
 *Bal.* On then, Hieronimo; farewell till soon.
 *Hier.* You 'll ply this gear?
 *Lor.*      I warrant you.
    *Exeunt all but Hieronimo.*
 *Hier.*      Why so:
Now shall I see the fall of Babylon,
Wrought by the heavens in this confusion.
And if the world like not this tragedy, 190
Hard is the hap of old Hieronimo.  *Exit.*

[SCENE II. *Hieronimo's Garden*]

*Enter Isabella with a weapon*

 *Isab.* Tell me no more! — O monstrous
  homicides!
Since neither piety nor pity moves
The king to justice or compassion,
I will revenge myself upon this place,
Where thus they murdered my beloved son. 5
    *She cuts down the arbour.*
Down with these branches and these loathsome
  boughs
Of this unfortunate and fatal pine!
Down with them, Isabella; rent them up,
And burn the roots from whence the rest is
  sprung!
I will not leave a root, a stalk, a tree, 10
A bough, a branch, a blossom, nor a leaf,
No, not an herb within this garden-plot, —
Accursed complot of my misery!
Fruitless for ever may this garden be,
Barren the earth, and blissless whosoever 15
Imagines not to keep it unmanur'd!
An eastern wind, commix'd with noisome airs,
Shall blast the plants and the young saplings;
The earth with serpents shall be pestered,
And passengers, for fear to be infect, 20
Shall stand aloof, and, looking at it, tell:
"There, murd'red, died the son of Isabel."
Ay, here he died, and here I him embrace:
See, where his ghost solicits with his wounds
Revenge on her that should revenge his death. 25
Hieronimo, make haste to see thy son;
For sorrow and despair hath cited me
To hear Horatio plead with Rhadamanth.
Make haste, Hieronimo, to hold excus'd
Thy negligence in pursuit of their deaths 30
Whose hateful wrath bereav'd him of his breath.
Ah, nay, thou dost delay their deaths,
Forgives the murderers of thy noble son,
And none but I bestir me — to no end!
And as I curse this tree from further fruit, 35
So shall my womb be cursed for his sake;
And with this weapon will I wound the breast,

¹⁴² **huntress:** Diana ¹⁵⁴ **Tragœdia cothurnata:** stately tragedy ¹⁶¹ **may:** may be true ¹⁸⁵ **soothe**
**. . up:** humour him ¹³ **complot:** accomplice (usually conspiracy) ¹⁶ **unmanur'd:** uncultivated
²⁰ **passengers:** travellers ²⁹ **hold excus'd:** make excuses for

The hapless breast, that gave Horatio suck.
*She stabs herself.*

[SCENE III.   *The Palace of Don Cyprian*]

*Enter Hieronimo; he knocks up the curtain.*

*Enter the Duke of Castile*

*Cast.*   How now, Hieronimo, where's your
fellows,
That you take all this pain?
*Hier.*   O sir, it is for the author's credit,
To look that all things may go well.
But, good my lord, let me entreat your grace, 5
To give the king the copy of the play:
This is the argument of what we show.
*Cast.*   I will, Hieronimo.
*Hier.*   One thing more, my good lord.
*Cast.*   What's that?
*Hier.*          Let me entreat your grace 10
That, when the train are pass'd into the gallery,
You would vouchsafe to throw me down the
key.
*Cast.*   I will, Hieronimo.          *Exit Castile.*
*Hier.*   What, are you ready, Balthazar?
Bring a chair and a cushion for the king.     15

*Enter Balthazar, with a chair*

Well done, Balthazar! hang up the title:
Our scene is Rhodes.   What, is your beard on?
*Bal.*   Half on; the other is in my hand.
*Hier.*   Despatch for shame; are you so long?
*Exit Balthazar.*
Bethink thyself, Hieronimo,                      20
Recall thy wits, recount thy former wrongs
Thou hast receiv'd by murder of thy son,
And lastly, not least! how Isabel,
Once his mother and thy dearest wife,
All woe-begone for him, hath slain herself.    25
Behoves thee then, Hieronimo, to be reveng'd!
The plot is laid of dire revenge:
On, then, Hieronimo, pursue revenge;
For nothing wants but acting of revenge!
*Exit Hieronimo.*

[SCENE IV.   *The Same*]

*Enter Spanish King, Viceroy, the Duke of
Castile, and their train*

*King.*   Now, Viceroy, shall we see the tragedy
Of Soliman, the Turkish emperor,
Perform'd of pleasure by your son the prince,
My nephew Don Lorenzo, and my niece.
*Vic.*   Who? Bel-imperia?
*King.*          Ay, and Hieronimo, our marshal, 5
At whose request they deign to do't themselves.
These be our pastimes in the court of Spain.
Here, brother, you shall be the bookkeeper:
This is the argument of that they show.

*He giveth him a book.*
Gentlemen, this play of Hieronimo, in [10
sundry languages, was thought good to be set down
in English, more largely, for the easier understanding to every public reader.

Enter Balthazar, Bel-imperia, and Hieronimo

*Bal.*   *Bashaw, that Rhodes is ours, yield heav-
ens the honour,*
*And holy Mahomet, our sacred prophet!*     15
*And be thou grac'd with every excellence*
*That Soliman can give, or thou desire.*
*But thy desert in conquering Rhodes is less*
*Than in reserving this fair Christian nymph,*
*Perseda, blissful lamp of excellence,*          20
*Whose eyes compel, like powerful adamant,*
*The warlike heart of Soliman to wait.*
*King.*   See, Viceroy, that is Balthazar, your
son,
That represents the emperor Soliman:
How well he acts his amorous passion!          25
*Vic.*   Ay, Bel-imperia hath taught him that.
*Cast.*   That's because his mind runs all on
Bel-imperia.
*Hier.*   *Whatever joy earth yields, betide your
majesty.*
*Bal.*   *Earth yields no joy without Perseda's
love.*
*Hier.*   *Let then Perseda on your grace attend.* 30
*Bal.*   *She shall not wait on me, but I on her:*
*Drawn by the influence of her lights, I yield.*
*But let my friend, the Rhodian knight, come forth.*
*Erasto, dearer than my life to me,*
*That he may see Perseda, my beloved.*          35

*Enter Erasto*

*King.*   Here comes Lorenzo: look upon the
plot,
And tell me, brother, what part plays he?
*Bel.*   *Ah, my Erasto, welcome to Perseda.*
*Lor.*   *Thrice happy is Erasto that thou livest;*
*Rhodes' loss is nothing to Erasto's joy;*        40
*Sith his Perseda lives, his life survives.*
*Bal.*   *Ah, bashaw, here is love betwixt Erasto*
*And fair Perseda, sovereign of my soul.*
*Hier.*   *Remove Erasto, mighty Soliman,*
*And then Perseda will be quickly won.*          45
*Bal.*   *Erasto is my friend; and while he lives,*
*Perseda never will remove her love.*
*Hier.*   *Let not Erasto live to grieve great Soli-
man.*
*Bal.*   *Dear is Erasto in our princely eye.*
*Hier.*   *But if he be your rival, let him die.*  50
*Bal.*   *Why, let him die! — so love commandeth
me.*
*Yet grieve I that Erasto should so die.*
*Hier.*   *Erasto, Soliman saluteth thee,*

<sup>16</sup> **title:** title-board, indicating title or scene of play     <sup>8</sup> **bookkeeper:** prompter     <sup>36</sup> **plot:** man-
uscript schedule

*And lets thee wit by me his highness' will,*
*Which is, thou shouldst be thus employ'd.*
                                                    Stab him.
Bel.                                            *Ay me!* 55
*Erasto! See, Soliman, Erasto's slain!*
Bal.   *Yet liveth Soliman to comfort thee.*
*Fair queen of beauty, let not favour die,*
*But with a gracious eye behold his grief*
*That with Perseda's beauty is increas'd,*      60
*If by Perseda his grief be not releas'd.*
Bel.   *Tyrant, desist soliciting vain suits;*
*Relentless are mine ears to thy laments,*
*As thy butcher is pitiless and base,*
*Which seiz'd on my Erasto, harmless knight.* 65
*Yet by thy power thou thinkest to command,*
*And to thy power Perseda doth obey;*
*But, were she able, thus she would revenge*
*Thy treacheries on thee, ignoble prince:*
                                                 Stab him.
*And on herself she would be thus reveng'd.*    70
                                              Stab herself.
*King.*   Well said! — Old marshal, this was
   bravely done!
*Hier.*   But Bel-imperia plays Perseda well!
*Vic.*   Were this in earnest, Bel-imperia,
You would be better to my son than so.
*King.*   But now what follows for Hiero-
   nimo?                                            75
*Hier.*   Marry, this follows for Hieronimo:
Here break we off our sundry languages,
And thus conclude I in our vulgar tongue.
Haply you think — but bootless are your
   thoughts —
That this is fabulously counterfeit,              80
And that we do as all tragedians do, —
To die to-day, for fashioning our scene,
The death of Ajax or some Roman peer,
And in a minute starting up again,
Revive to please tomorrow's audience.            85
No, princes; know I am Hieronimo,
The hopeless father of a hapless son,
Whose tongue is tun'd to tell his latest tale,
Not to excuse gross errors in the play.
I see, your looks urge instance of these words; 90
Behold the reason urging me to this!
                                       *Shows his dead son.*
See here my show, look on this spectacle!
Here lay my hope, and here my hope hath end;
Here lay my heart, and here my heart was slain;
Here lay my treasure, here my treasure lost; 95
Here lay my bliss, and here my bliss bereft:
But hope, heart, treasure, joy, and bliss,
All fled, fail'd, died, yea, all decay'd with this.
From forth these wounds came breath that gave
   me life;
They murd'red me that made these fatal
   marks.                                         100

The cause was love, whence grew this mortal
   hate;
The hate, Lorenzo and young Balthazar;
The love, my son to Bel-imperia.
But night, the coverer of accursed crimes,
With pitchy silence hush'd these traitors'
   harms,                                        105
And lent them leave, for they had sorted leisure
To take advantage in my garden-plot
Upon my son, my dear Horatio.
There merciless they butcher'd up my boy,
In black, dark night, to pale, dim, cruel
   death.                                        110
He shrieks: I heard — and yet, methinks, I
   hear —
His dismal outcry echo in the air.
With soonest speed I hasted to the noise,
Where hanging on a tree I found my son,
Through-girt with wounds, and slaught'red as
   you see.                                      115
And griev'd I, think you, at this spectacle?
Speak, Portuguese, whose loss resembles mine:
If thou canst weep upon thy Balthazar,
'T is like I wail'd for my Horatio.
And you, my lord, whose reconciled son      120
March'd in a net, and thought himself unseen,
And rated me for brainsick lunacy,
With "God amend that mad Hieronimo!" —
How can you brook our play's catastrophe?
And here behold this bloody handkercher,    125
Which at Horatio's death I weeping dipp'd
Within the river of his bleeding wounds:
It as propitious, see, I have reserv'd,
And never hath it left my bloody heart,
Soliciting remembrance of my vow          130
With these, O, these accursed murderers:
Which now perform'd, my heart is satisfied.
And to this end the bashaw I became
That might revenge me on Lorenzo's life,
Who therefore was appointed to the part,  135
And was to represent the knight of Rhodes,
That I might kill him more conveniently.
So, Viceroy, was this Balthazar, thy son,
That Soliman which Bel-imperia,
In person of Perseda, murdered;           140
Solely appointed to that tragic part
That she might slay him that offended her.
Poor Bel-imperia miss'd her part in this:
For though the story saith she should have
   died,
Yet I of kindness, and of care to her,    145
Did otherwise determine of her end;
But love of him whom they did hate too much
Did urge her resolution to be such.
And, princes, now behold Hieronimo,
Author and actor in this tragedy,         150
Bearing his latest fortune in his fist;

---

[61] **Perseda his:** ('Persedaes' Qq.)   [90] **urge instance:** demand proof   [106] **sorted:** chosen
[115] **Through-girt:** pierced through   [121] **net:** *i.e.,* transparent disguise

And will as resolute conclude his part,
As any of the actors gone before.
And, gentles, thus I end my play;
Urge no more words: I have no more to say. 155
*He runs to hang himself.*
*King.* O hearken, Viceroy! Hold, Hiero-
nimo!
Brother, my nephew and thy son are slain!
*Vic.* We are betray'd; my Balthazar is
slain!
Break ope the doors; run, save Hieronimo.
*They break in and hold Hieronimo.*
Hieronimo, do but inform the king of these
events; 160
Upon mine honour, thou shalt have no harm.
*Hier.* Viceroy, I will not trust thee with my
life,
Which I this day have offer'd to my son.
Accursed wretch!
Why stay'st thou him that was resolv'd to
die? 165
*King.* Speak, traitor! damned, bloody mur-
derer, speak!
For now I have thee, I will make thee speak.
Why hast thou done this undeserving deed?
*Vic.* Why hast thou murdered my Baltha-
zar?
*Cast.* Why hast thou butcher'd both my
children thus? 170
*Hier.* O, good words!
As dear to me was my Horatio
As yours, or yours, or yours, my lord, to you.
My guiltless son was by Lorenzo slain,
And by Lorenzo and that Balthazar 175
Am I at last revenged thoroughly,
Upon whose souls may heavens be yet aveng'd
With greater far than these afflictions.
*Cast.* But who were thy confederates in this?
*Vic.* That was thy daughter Bel-imperia; 180
For by her hand my Balthazar was slain:
I saw her stab him.
*King.* Why speak'st thou not?
*Hier.* What lesser liberty can kings afford
Than harmless silence? Then afford it me.
Sufficeth, I may not, nor I will not tell thee. 185
*King.* Fetch forth the tortures: traitor as
thou art,
I'll make thee tell.
*Hier.* Indeed,
Thou may'st torment me as his wretched son
Hath done in murd'ring my Horatio;
But never shalt thou force me to reveal 190
The thing which I have vow'd inviolate.
And therefore, in despite of all thy threats,
Pleas'd with their deaths, and eas'd with their
revenge,

First take my tongue, and afterwards my heart.
*He bites out his tongue.*
[*Hier.* *But are you sure they are dead?*
*Cast.* *Ay, slave, too sure.* 195
*Hier.* *What, and yours too?*
*Vic.* *Ay, all are dead; not one of them survive.*
*Hier.* *Nay, then I care not; come, and we shall
be friends;*
*Let us lay our heads together:*
*See, here's a goodly noose will hold them all.* 200
*Vic.* *O damned devil, how secure he is!*
*Hier.* *Secure? Why, dost thou wonder at it?*
*I tell thee, Viceroy, this day I have seen revenge,*
*And in that sight am grown a prouder monarch,*
*Than ever sat under the crown of Spain.* 205
*Had I as many lives as there be stars,*
*As many heavens to go to, as those lives,*
*I'd give them all, ay, and my soul to boot,*
*But I would see thee ride in this red pool.*
*Cast.* *Speak, who were thy confederates in this?*
*Vic.* *That was thy daughter Bel-imperia;* 211
*For by her hand my Balthazar was slain:*
*I saw her stab him.*
*Hier.* *O, good words!*
*As dear to me was my Horatio,* 215
*As yours, or yours, or yours, my lord, to you.*
*My guiltless son was by Lorenzo slain,*
*And by Lorenzo and that Balthazar*
*Am I at last revenged thoroughly,*
*Upon whose souls may heavens be yet reveng'd* 220
*With greater far than these afflictions.*
*Methinks, since I grew inward with revenge,*
*I cannot look with scorn enough on death.*
*King.* *What, dost thou mock us, slave? —
Bring tortures forth.*
*Hier.* *Do, do, do: and meantime I'll torture
you.* 225
*You had a son, as I take it; and your son*
*Should ha' been married to your daughter: ha,
was't not so? —*
*You had a son too, he was my liege's nephew;*
*He was proud and politic; had he liv'd,*
*He might ha' come to wear the crown of Spain,* 230
*I think 't was so: — 't was I that kill'd him;*
*Look you, this same hand, 't was it that stabb'd*
*His heart — do you see this hand? —*
*For one Horatio, if you ever knew him:*
*A youth, one that they hang'd up in his father's
garden;* 235
*One that did force your valiant son to yield,*
*While your more valiant son did take him prisoner.*
*Vic.* *Be deaf, my senses; I can hear no more.*
*King.* *Fall, heaven, and cover us with thy sad
ruins.*
*Cast.* *Roll all the world within thy pitchy
cloud.* 240

159 doors: *i.e.*, of the gallery   168 **undeserving:** undeserved   195–244 (Fifth passage of additions, replacing ll. 171–194)   201 **secure:** unconcerned   222 **inward:** intimate   226 **You:** (To the
Viceroy)   227 **your:** (To Castile)   236 **your:** (To the Viceroy)   237 **your:** (To Castile)

*Hier.* *Now do I applaud what I have acted.*
*Nunc iners cadat manus!*
*Now to express the rupture of my part, —*
*First take my tongue, and afterward my heart.*
                              He bites out his tongue.]
*King.* O monstrous resolution of a wretch! 245
See, Viceroy, he hath bitten forth his tongue,
Rather than to reveal what we requir'd.
*Cast.* Yet can he write.
*King.* And if in this he satisfy us not,
We will devise th' extremest kind of death 250
That ever was invented for a wretch.
                    *Then he makes signs for a knife to*
                    *mend his pen.*
*Cast.* O, he would have a knife to mend his
    pen.
*Vic.* Here, and advise thee that thou write
    the truth.
*King.* Look to my brother! save Hieronimo!
        *He with a knife stabs the Duke and*
        *himself.*
What age hath ever heard such monstrous
    deeds?                                      255
My brother, and the whole succeeding hope
That Spain expected after my decease!
Go, bear his body hence, that we may mourn
The loss of our beloved brother's death,
That he may be entomb'd whate'er befall. 260
I am the next, the nearest, last of all.
*Vic.* And thou, Don Pedro, do the like for
    us:
Take up our hapless son, untimely slain;
Set me with him, and he with woeful me,
Upon the main-mast of a ship unmann'd, 265
And let the wind and tide haul me along
To Scylla's barking and untamed gulf,
Or to the loathsome pool of Acheron,
To weep my want for my sweet Balthazar:
Spain hath no refuge for a Portingale. 270
        *The trumpets sound a dead march; the*
        *King of Spain mourning after his*
        *brother's body, and the King of Por-*
        *tingale bearing the body of his son.*

                    [*Chorus*]

            *Enter Ghost and Revenge*

*Ghost.* Ay, now my hopes have end in their
    effects,
When blood and sorrow finish my desires:
Horatio murder'd in his father's bower;
Vild Serberine by Pedringano slain;

False Pedringano hang'd by quaint device; 5
Fair Isabella by herself misdone;
Prince Balthazar by Bel-imperia stabb'd:
The Duke of Castile and his wicked son
Both done to death by old Hieronimo;
My Bel-imperia fall'n as Dido fell, 10
And good Hieronimo slain by himself:
Ay, these were spectacles to please my soul!
Now will I beg at lovely Proserpine
That, by the virtue of her princely doom,
I may consort my friends in pleasing sort, 15
And on my foes work just and sharp revenge.
I'll lead my friend Horatio through those fields,
Where never-dying wars are still inur'd;
I'll lead fair Isabella to that train,
Where pity weeps, but never feeleth pain; 20
I'll lead my Bel-imperia to those joys,
That vestal virgins and fair queens possess;
I'll lead Hieronimo where Orpheus plays,
Adding sweet pleasure to eternal days.
But say, Revenge, for thou must help, or
    none, 25
Against the rest how shall my hate be shown?
*Rev.* This hand shall hale them down to
    deepest hell,
Where none but Furies, bugs, and tortures
    dwell.
*Ghost.* Then, sweet Revenge, do this at my
    request:
Let me be judge, and doom them to unrest. 30
Let loose poor Tityus from the vulture's gripe,
And let Don Cyprian supply his room;
Place Don Lorenzo on Ixion's wheel,
And let the lover's endless pains surcease
(Juno forgets old wrath, and grants him ease);
Hang Balthazar about Chimæra's neck, 36
And let him there bewail his bloody love,
Repining at our joys that are above;
Let Serberine go roll the fatal stone,
And take from Sisyphus his endless moan; 40
False Pedringano, for his treachery,
Let him be dragg'd through boiling Acheron,
And there live, dying still in endless flames,
Blaspheming gods and all their holy names.
*Rev.* Then haste we down to meet thy friends
    and foes: 45
To place thy friends in ease, the rest in woes;
For here though death hath end their misery,
I'll there begin their endless tragedy.
                                        *Exeunt.*

                    FINIS

²⁴² **Nunc . . . manus:** Now let my hand fall idle.    **iners cadat:** ('mors caede' or 'mers cadae'
Qq.)    ²⁵⁴ **King:** (before l. 255 in Qq.)    ²⁶⁷ **gulf:** (Qq. 1623–1633; 'greefe' other Qq.)    ¹ **effects:**
consummation    ⁴ **Vild:** vile    ¹³ **at:** at the hands of    ¹⁵ **consort:** associate with    ¹⁸ **inur'd:** carried on    ²⁸ **bugs:** bugbears    ³² **supply . . . room:** take his place    ³⁵ **him:** *i.e.,* Ixion    ⁴⁷ **hath**
**end:** hath ended ('doth end' Q 1623)

# Tamburlaine

## the Great.

### Who, from a Scythian Shephearde,
by his rare and woonderfull Conquests,
became a most puissant and migh-
tye Monarque.

And (for his tyranny, and terrour in
Warre) was tearmed,

### The Scourge of God.

### Deuided into two Tragicall Dif-
courfes, as they were fundrie times
fhewed vpon Stages in the Citie
of London.

.

By the right honorable the Lord
Admyrall, his feruantes.

Now firft, and newlie publifhed.

LONDON.

Printed by Richard Ihones: at the figne
of the Rofe and Crowne neere Hol-
borne Bridge. 1590.

BIBLIOGRAPHICAL RECORD. Both parts of *Tamburlaine* (of which only the first is here reprinted) were entered on the Stationers' Register, Aug. 14, 1590: — *"xiij die Augusti / Richard Jones / Entred vnto him for his Copye / The twooe commicall discourses of Tomberlein the Cithian shepparde / vnder the handes of Master Abraham Hartewell, and the Wardens vjd."* Four early editions appeared, dated 1590, 1593 or 1592 (the last figure is defaced in the only known copy), 1597, and 1605–1606. These are all strictly octavos rather than quartos, but in the footnotes of the present edition have been referred to by the usual symbol "Q." The play was not again printed for over two hundred years.

AUTHORSHIP. The authorship of *Tamburlaine* is not indicated in any of the early editions, and Marlowe's responsibility for it is not more than strongly implied in any of the contemporary references that have been discovered. But the internal evidence is so strongly in his favor that the skepticism which was current in the early nineteenth century has no support today.

DATE AND STAGE HISTORY. A reference to "daring God out of heauen with that Atheist *Tamburlan"* in Robert Greene's *Perimedes* (which was licensed March 29, 1588) seems to be pointed especially at a passage in the second part of *Tamburlaine;* and since the prologue to the second part says definitely that that play was composed in consequence of the success of Part I, the evidence that Part II was on the stage by March, 1588, indicates 1587 as the latest date for the production of Part I. Sir Edmund Chambers has recently (London *Times Lit. Sup.*, Aug. 28, 1930) discovered another allusion which would indicate that Part II was being acted as early as Nov., 1587. This was the year in which Marlowe left Cambridge and in which he was also engaged in some unexplained services to the state. It is quite possible that the first part was written at Cambridge or during the poet's travels abroad. As the title-page informs us, it was produced by the Lord Admiral's Servants, the company of Edward Alleyn, "upon stages in the City of London," — probably in the innyards for which the extreme simplicity of its staging made it well suited.

Henslowe's Diary records a revival by the Admiral's men at the Rose, Aug. 28, 1594, which brought him the large sum of £3 11s. Between then and Nov. 12, 1595, Part I was given fifteen times, and during the last eleven months of the period most often in conjunction with the second part, on consecutive days. The fustian of the noisier passages was much ridiculed by critical writers, but the large number of parodies and allusions, down to the closing of the theatres in 1642, attest the play's popular vogue. If we can believe Charles Saunders, who produced a play on the same theme in 1681, Marlowe's *Tamburlaine* had been acted at the Cockpit or Phoenix private theatre (which opened in 1617), where the *Jew of Malta* was also produced; but by Saunders' time *Tamburlaine* had been so forgotten that "not a book-seller in London, or scarce the players themselves who acted it formerly, could call [it] to remembrance."

STRUCTURE. *Tamburlaine*, especially the first part, looks like the work of an author to whom the Latin drama is more familiar and attractive than the Elizabethan. It is meticulously divided into acts and scenes and shows Senecan influence also in the emphasis on declamation, the stressing of gory or lurid details, and the scorn of comic intermixture. The stage contemplated is a simple platform such as would serve a college performance, no particular use being made in Part I of the balcony and rear-stage which Marlowe employed so cleverly in later dramas.

SOURCES. Accounts of the meteoric career of the Mongolian emperor Timur (1336–1405) could have been found by Marlowe in a great variety of places. The learning on this subject has been admirably summarized by Miss Ellis-Fermor in her edition of the play (1930). A chapter in Fortescue's *Forest*, translated from the Spanish of Pedro Mexia and twice printed (1571, 1576), probably first attracted the poet to the subject. This he seems to have supplemented from the Latin accounts of Perondinus (*Magni Tamerlanis Scytharum Imperatoris Vita*, 1553) and others. The romantic and amatory elements are mainly Marlowe's independent contribution, and in his treatment of the Persians he writes much more as a student of Herodotus than as a reader of mediæval chronicles. Conspicuous in the list of his sources stands the newly published atlas of Ortelius (*Theatrum Orbis Terrarum*, 1584), whose maps of Asia and Africa were diligently scrutinized by the poet for sonorous place-names and geographical inspiration. Finally Marlowe tapped freely all the store of classic myth, astronomy, and "physic" which he had laid up in his student days.

# CHRISTOPHER MARLOWE (1564–1593)

## TAMBURLAINE THE GREAT

[THE FIRST PART

#### DRAMATIS PERSONAE

MYCETES, King of Persia
COSROE, his Brother
ORTYGIUS,
CENEUS,
MEANDER, } Persian Lords and Captains
MENAPHON,
THERIDAMAS,
TAMBURLAINE, a Scythian Shepherd
TECHELLES,
USUMCASANE, } his Followers
BAJAZETH, Emperor of the Turks
KING OF ARABIA
KING OF FEZ

KING OF MOROCCO
KING OF ARGIER (Algiers)
SOLDAN OF EGYPT
GOVERNOR OF DAMASCUS
AGYDAS,
MAGNETES, } Median Lords
CAPOLIN, an Egyptian Captain
PHILEMUS, a Messenger

ZENOCRATE, Daughter of the Soldan of Egypt
ANIPPE, her Maid
ZABINA, Wife of Bajazeth
EBEA, her Maid

Virgins of Damascus; Bassoes, Lords, Citizens, Moors, Soldiers, and Attendants]

## THE PROLOGUE

FROM jigging veins of rhyming mother wits,
And such conceits as clownage keeps in pay,
We'll lead you to the stately tent of war,
Where you shall hear the Scythian Tamburlaine
Threat'ning the world with high astounding terms,
And scourging kingdoms with his conquering sword.
View but his picture in this tragic glass,
And then applaud his fortunes as you please.

### Actus 1. Scæna 1.

*Mycetes, Cosroe, Meander, Theridamas,*
*Ortygius, Ceneus, [Menaphon,] with others*

*Myc.* Brother Cosroe, I find myself aggriev'd,
Yet insufficient to express the same,
For it requires a great and thund'ring speech.
Good brother, tell the cause unto my lords;
I know you have a better wit than I.      5
    *Cos.* Unhappy Persia! — that in former age
Hast been the seat of mighty conquerors,
That, in their prowess and their policies,
Have triumph'd over Afric and the bounds
Of Europe, where the sun dares scarce appear 10
For freezing meteors and congealed cold, —
Now to be rul'd and governed by a man
At whose birthday Cynthia with Saturn join'd,
And Jove, the Sun, and Mercury denied

To shed their influence in his fickle brain!  15
Now Turks and Tartars shake their swords at thee,
Meaning to mangle all thy provinces.
    *Myc.* Brother, I see your meaning well enough,
And through your planets I perceive you think
I am not wise enough to be a king;      20
But I refer me to my noblemen
That know my wit, and can be witnesses.
I might command you to be slain for this:
Meander, might I not?
    *Meand.* Not for so small a fault, my sovereign lord.      25
    *Myc.* I mean it not, but yet I know I might.
Yet live; yea, live, Mycetes wills it so.
Meander, thou, my faithful counsellor,
Declare the cause of my conceived grief,
Which is, God knows, about that Tamburlaine,

---

Prol. ¹ **jigging**: proper to the "jig," ballad-drama      ² **insufficient**: unable      ⁸ **policies**: diplomacy
¹³ **Cynthia . . . Saturn**: the moon and the planet Saturn, which exerted malign influences on the horoscope      ¹⁵ **their**: ('his' Qq.)      ¹⁶ **thee**: Persia

139

That, like a fox in midst of harvest time,    31
Doth prey upon my flocks of passengers;
And, as I hear, doth mean to pull my plumes:
Therefore 't is good and meet for to be wise.
   *Meand.*  Oft have I heard your majesty
   complain    35
Of Tamburlaine, that sturdy Scythian thief,
That robs your merchants of Persepolis
Treading by land unto the Western Isles,
And in your confines with his lawless train
Daily commits incivil outrages,    40
Hoping (misled by dreaming prophecies)
To reign in Asia, and with barbarous arms
To make himself the monarch of the East;
But ere he march in Asia, or display
His vagrant ensign in the Persian fields,    45
Your grace hath taken order by Theridamas,
Charg'd with a thousand horse, to apprehend
And bring him captive to your highness' throne.
   *Myc.*  Full true thou speak'st, and like thy-
   self, my lord,
Whom I may term a Damon for thy love:    50
Therefore 't is best, if so it like you all,
To send my thousand horse incontinent
To apprehend that paltry Scythian.
How like you this, my honourable lords?
Is it not a kingly resolution?    55
   *Cos.*  It cannot choose, because it comes from
   you.
   *Myc.*  Then hear thy charge, valiant Theri-
   damas,
The chiefest captain of Mycetes' host,
The hope of Persia, and the very legs
Whereon our state doth lean as on a staff,    60
That holds us up, and foils our neighbour foes.
Thou shalt be leader of this thousand horse,
Whose foaming gall with rage and high disdain
Have sworn the death of wicked Tamburlaine.
Go frowning forth; but come thou smiling
   home,    65
As did Sir Paris with the Grecian dame.
Return with speed — time passeth swift away;
Our life is frail, and we may die to-day.
   *Ther.*  Before the moon renew her borrow'd
   light,
Doubt not, my lord and gracious sovereign,    70
But Tamburlaine and that Tartarian rout
Shall either perish by our warlike hands,
Or plead for mercy at your highness' feet.
   *Myc.*  Go, stout Theridamas! thy words are
   swords,    74
And with thy looks thou conquerest all thy foes.

I long to see thee back return from thence,
That I may view these milk-white steeds of mine
All loaden with the heads of killed men,
And from their knees even to their hoofs below
Besmear'd with blood, that makes a dainty
   show.    80
   *Ther.*  Then now, my lord, I humbly take my
   leave.
   *Myc.*  Theridamas, farewell! ten thousand
   times.                               *Exit [Theridamas].*
Ah, Menaphon, why stay'st thou thus behind,
When other men press forward for renown?
Go, Menaphon, go into Scythia;    85
And foot by foot follow Theridamas.
   *Cos.*  Nay, pray you let him stay; a greater
   [trust]
Fits Menaphon than warring with a thief.
Create him Prorex of all Africa,
That he may win the Babylonians' hearts    90
Which will revolt from Persian government,
Unless they have a wiser king than you.
   *Myc.*  "Unless they have a wiser king than
   you!"
These are his words; Meander, set them down.
   *Cos.*  And add this to them — that all Asia    95
Lament to see the folly of their king.
   *Myc.*  Well, here I swear by this my royal
   seat, —
   *Cos.*  You may do well to kiss it then. [*Aside.*]
   *Myc.*  Emboss'd with silk as best beseems
   my state,
To be reveng'd for these contemptuous words.
Oh, where is duty and allegiance now?    101
Fled to the Caspian or the Ocean main?
What shall I call thee? Brother? — No, a foe;
Monster of nature! Shame unto thy stock!
That dar'st presume thy sovereign for to mock!
Meander, come: I am abus'd, Meander.    106
      *Exit [with Meander, &c.]. Manent Cosroe*
      *and Menaphon.*
   *Men.*  How now, my lord? What, mated and
   amaz'd
To hear the king thus threaten like himself!
   *Cos.*  Ah, Menaphon, I pass not for his
   threats;
The plot is laid by Persian noblemen    110
And captains of the Median garrisons
To crown me Emperor of Asia.
But this it is that doth excruciate
The very substance of my vexed soul —
To see our neighbours, that were wont to
   quake    115

---

³²⁻³³ **flocks . . . plumes:** (The suggestion in Mycetes' foolish figure is that the "passengers"
and he himself are geese.)    ³⁷ **Persepolis:** capital of *ancient* Persia (superseded by Shiraz and Ispahan
in Middle Ages)    ³⁸ **Treading:** ('Trading' Q 2)    **Western Isles:** British Isles    ⁴⁰ **incivil:** riotous
⁴¹ **dreaming:** productive of vain dreams    ⁴⁷ **Charg'd with:** put in command of    ⁵² **incontinent:** at
once    ⁵⁶ **choose:** be otherwise    ⁷¹ **rout:** rabble    ⁸⁷ **trust:** (word omitted Qq.)    ⁸⁹ **Prorex:** viceroy
all: (not in Q 1–3)    ⁹⁰ **Babylonians':** (Cairo and Babylon were sometimes confused.)    ¹⁰⁶ **S. D.
Manent:** remain on the stage    ¹⁰⁷ **mated:** cast down    ¹⁰⁹ **pass:** care    ¹¹⁵ **see:** see how

And tremble at the Persian monarch's name,
Now sits and laughs our regiment to scorn;
And that which might resolve me into tears,
Men from the farthest equinoctial line     119
Have swarm'd in troops into the Eastern India,
Lading their ships with gold and precious stones,
And made their spoils from all our provinces.
    *Men.* This should entreat your highness to
      rejoice,
Since Fortune gives you opportunity
To gain the title of a conqueror        125
By curing of this maimed empery.
Afric and Europe bordering on your land,
And continent to your dominions,
How easily may you, with a mighty host,
Pass into Græcia, as did Cyrus once,     130
And cause them to withdraw their forces home,
Lest you subdue the pride of Christendom.
                   [*Trumpet within.*]
    *Cos.* But, Menaphon, what means this trum-
      pet's sound?
    *Men.* Behold, my lord! Ortygius and the
      rest,
Bringing the crown to make you Emperor. 135

*Enter Ortygius and Ceneus, bearing a crown,*
*with others*

    *Orty.* Magnificent and mighty Prince Cosroe,
We, in the name of other Persian states
And commons of this mighty monarchy,
Present thee with th' imperial diadem.
    *Cen.* The warlike soldiers and the gentlemen,
That heretofore have fill'd Persepolis     141
With Afric captains taken in the field,
Whose ransom made them march in coats of
    gold,
With costly jewels hanging at their ears,
And shining stones upon their lofty crests, 145
Now living idle in the walled towns,
Wanting both pay and martial discipline,
Begin in troops to threaten civil war,
And openly exclaim against the king.
Therefore, to stay all sudden mutinies,     150
We will invest your highness Emperor,
Whereat the soldiers will conceive more joy
Than did the Macedonians at the spoil
Of great Darius and his wealthy host.
    *Cos.* Well, since I see the state of Persia
      droop                             155
And languish in my brother's government,
I willingly receive th' imperial crown,
And vow to wear it for my country's good,
In spite of them shall malice my estate.

    *Orty.* And in assurance of desir'd success, 160
We here do crown thee monarch of the East,
Emperor of Asia and of Persia;
Great Lord of Media and Armenia;
Duke of Africa and Albania,
Mesopotamia and of Parthia,            165
East India and the late-discovered isles;
Chief Lord of all the wide, vast Euxine sea,
And of the ever-raging Caspian lake.
Long live Cosroe, mighty Emperor!
    *Cos.* And Jove may never let me longer live
Than I may seek to gratify your love,     171
And cause the soldiers that thus honour me
To triumph over many provinces!
By whose desires and discipline in arms
I doubt not shortly but to reign sole king, 175
And with the army of Theridamas,
(Whither we presently will fly, my lords)
To rest secure against my brother's force.
    *Orty.* We knew, my lord, before we brought
      the crown,
Intending your investion so near        180
The residence of your despised brother,
The lords would not be too exasperate
To injure or suppress your worthy title;
Or, if they would, there are in readiness
Ten thousand horse to carry you from hence,
In spite of all suspected enemies.        186
    *Cos.* I know it well, my lord, and thank you
      all.
    *Orty.* Sound up the trumpets, then. God
      save the King! [*Trumpets sound.*] *Exeunt.*

## Actus 1. Scæna 2.

*Tamburlaine leading Zenocrate: Techelles, Usum-*
*casane, [Agydas, Magnetes and] other Lords,*
*and Soldiers, loaden with treasure*

    *Tamb.* Come, lady, let not this appal your
      thoughts;
The jewels and the treasure we have ta'en
Shall be reserv'd, and you in better state,
Than if you were arriv'd in Syria,
Even in the circle of your father's arms,     5
The mighty Soldan of Egyptia.
    *Zeno.* Ah, shepherd! pity my distressed
      plight,
(If, as thou seemst, thou art so mean a man,)
And seek not to enrich thy followers
By lawless rapine from a silly maid,       10
Who travelling with these Median lords
To Memphis, from my uncle's country of
    Media,

---

¹¹⁷ **sits, laughs:** (plurals)    **regiment:** rule    ¹¹⁸ **resolve:** dissolve    ¹¹⁹ **equinoctial:** equatorial
(men from the distant equator)    ¹²⁸ **continent:** contiguous    ¹³⁰ **Græcia:** possessions of the Greek
Emperor at Constantinople    ¹³² **pride of Christendom:** Constantinople    ¹³⁷ **states:** dignitaries
¹⁶⁹ **them:** those who    ¹⁷⁰ **Jove may:** may Jove    ¹⁷⁴ **and:** ('of' Qq.)    ¹⁸⁰ **investion:** investiture
³ **reserv'd:** safeguarded    **in better state:** better honored    ¹² **of Media:** (Perhaps this should end
previous line and "Median" be omitted )

Where all my youth I have been governed,
Have pass'd the army of the mighty Turk,
Bearing his privy signet and his hand          15
To safe conduct us thorough Africa.
  *Mag.*   And since we have arriv'd in Scythia,
Besides rich presents from the puissant Cham,
We have his highness' letters to command
Aid and assistance, if we stand in need.      20
  *Tamb.*   But now you see these letters and
    commands
Are countermanded by a greater man;
And through my provinces you must expect
Letters of conduct from my mightiness,
If you intend to keep your treasure safe.      25
But, since I love to live at liberty,
As easily may you get the Soldan's crown
As any prizes out of my precinct;
For they are friends that help to wean my state
Till men and kingdoms help to strengthen it, 30
And must maintain my life exempt from servi-
    tude. —
But, tell me, madam, is your grace betroth'd?
  *Zeno.*   I am, my lord — for so you do im-
    port.
  *Tamb.*   I am a lord, for so my deeds shall
    prove:
And yet a shepherd by my parentage.           35
But, lady, this fair face and heavenly hue
Must grace his bed that conquers Asia,
And means to be a terror to the world,
Measuring the limits of his empery
By east and west, as Phœbus doth his course. 40
Lie here, ye weeds that I disdain to wear!
This complete armour and this curtle-axe
Are adjuncts more beseeming Tamburlaine.
And, madam, whatsoever you esteem
Of this success and loss unvalued,            45
Both may invest you Empress of the East;
And these that seem but silly country swains
May have the leading of so great an host,
As with their weight shall make the mountains
    quake,
Even as when windy exhalations,               50
Fighting for passage, tilt within the earth.
  *Tech.*   As princely lions, when they rouse
    themselves,
Stretching their paws, and threat'ning herds of
    beasts,
So in his armour looketh Tamburlaine.
Methinks I see kings kneeling at his feet,     55
And he with frowning brows and fiery looks,
Spurning their crowns from off their captive
    heads.

  *Usum.*   And making thee and me, Techelles,
    kings,
That even to death will follow Tamburlaine.
  *Tamb.*   Nobly resolv'd, sweet friends and fol-
    lowers!                                     60
These lords, perhaps, do scorn our estimates,
And think we prattle with distemper'd spirits;
But since they measure our deserts so mean, —
That in conceit bear empires on our spears,
Affecting thoughts coequal with the clouds, — 65
They shall be kept our forced followers,
Till with their eyes they view us emperors.
  *Zeno.*   The gods, defenders of the innocent,
Will never prosper your intended drifts,
That thus oppress poor friendless passengers. 70
Therefore at least admit us liberty,
Even as thou hop'st to be eternized
By living Asia's mighty Emperor.
  *Agyd.*   I hope our lady's treasure and our own
May serve for ransom to our liberties.         75
Return our mules and empty camels back,
That we may travel into Syria,
Where her betrothed lord Alcidamus,
Expects th' arrival of her highness' person.
  *Mag.*   And wheresoever we repose ourselves,
We will report but well of Tamburlaine.        81
  *Tamb.*   Disdains Zenocrate to live with me?
Or you, my lords, to be my followers?
Think you I weigh this treasure more than you?
Not all the gold in India's wealthy arms       85
Shall buy the meanest soldier in my train.
Zenocrate, lovelier than the love of Jove,
Brighter than is the silver Rhodope,
Fairer than whitest snow on Scythian hills, —
Thy person is more worth to Tamburlaine,       90
Than the possession of the Persian crown,
Which gracious stars have promis'd at my birth.
A hundreth Tartars shall attend on thee,
Mounted on steeds swifter than Pegasus;
Thy garments shall be made of Median silk,     95
Enchas'd with precious jewels of mine own,
More rich and valurous than Zenocrate's.
With milk-white harts upon an ivory sled,
Thou shalt be drawn amidst the frozen pools,
And scale the icy mountains' lofty tops,       100
Which with thy beauty will be soon resolv'd.
My martial prizes, with five hundred men
Won on the fifty-headed Volga's waves,
Shall all we offer to Zenocrate, —
And then myself to fair Zenocrate.             105
  *Tech.*   What now! — in love?
  *Tamb.*   Techelles, women must be flattered:
But this is she with whom I am in love.

---

¹⁵ **hand**: signed passport    ¹⁸ **Cham**: emperor of Tartary    ²⁶ **at liberty**: bounteously    ³³ **so
. . . import**: such you must be    ⁴¹ **weeds**: his shepherd dress    ⁴² **curtle-axe**: cutlass    ⁴³ **adjuncts**: trappings    ⁴⁵ **success**: incident    **unvalued**: of petty value    ⁴⁶ **invest**: cause to be
⁵⁰ **exhalations**: subterranean blasts    ⁶¹ **estimates**: valuations    ⁶⁵ **Affecting**: indulging    ⁶⁹ **drifts**:
designs    ⁷⁰ **passengers**: travelers    ⁷² **eternized**: immortalized    ⁷³ **living**: living to be    ⁷⁶ **empty**:
discharged of the treasure they bore    ⁹⁷ **valurous**: costly

*Enter a Soldier*

*Sold.*  News! news!

*Tamb.*  How now, what's the matter?     110

*Sold.*  A thousand Persian horsemen are at hand,
Sent from the king to overcome us all.

*Tamb.*  How now, my lords of Egypt, and Zenocrate!
Now must your jewels be restor'd again,
And I that triumph'd so be overcome?     115
How say you, lordings, — is not this your hope?

*Agyd.*  We hope yourself will willingly restore them.

*Tamb.*  Such hope, such fortune, have the thousand horse.
Soft ye, my lords, and sweet Zenocrate!
You must be forced from me ere you go.     120
A thousand horsemen! — We five hundred foot! —
An odds too great for us to stand against.
But are they rich?  And is their armour good?

*Sold.*  Their plumed helms are wrought with beaten gold,     124
Their swords enamell'd, and about their necks
Hangs massy chains of gold, down to the waist,
In every part exceeding brave and rich.

*Tamb.*  Then shall we fight courageously with them?
Or look you I should play the orator?

*Tech.*  No; cowards and faint-hearted runaways     130
Look for orations when the foe is near.
Our swords shall play the orators for us.

*Usum.*  Come! let us meet them at the mountain foot,
And with a sudden and an hot alarm,
Drive all their horses headlong down the hill.  135

*Tech.*  Come, let us march!

*Tamb.*  Stay, Techelles! ask a parley first.

*The Soldiers enter*

Open the mails, yet guard the treasure sure;
Lay out our golden wedges to the view,     139
That their reflections may amaze the Persians;
And look we friendly on them when they come.
But if they offer word or violence,
We'll fight five hundred men-at-arms to one,
Before we part with our possession.     144
And 'gainst the general we will lift our swords,
And either lanch his greedy thirsting throat,
Or take him prisoner, and his chain shall serve
For manacles, till he be ransom'd home.

*Tech.*  I hear them come; shall we encounter them?

*Tamb.*  Keep all your standings and not stir a foot,     150

Myself will bide the danger of the brunt.

*Enter Theridamas with others*

*Ther.*  Where is this Scythian Tamburlaine?

*Tamb.*  Whom seek'st thou, Persian? — I am Tamburlaine.

*Ther.*  Tamburlaine! —
A Scythian shepherd so embellished     155
With nature's pride and richest furniture!
His looks do menace Heaven and dare the gods:
His fiery eyes are fix'd upon the earth,
As if he now devis'd some stratagem,     159
Or meant to pierce Avernus' darksome vaults
To pull the triple-headed dog from hell.

*Tamb.*  Noble and mild this Persian seems to be,
If outward habit judge the inward man.

*Tech.*  His deep affections make him passionate.

*Tamb.*  With what a majesty he rears his looks!     165
In thee, thou valiant man of Persia,
I see the folly of thy emperor.
Art thou but captain of a thousand horse,
That by characters graven in thy brows,
And by thy martial face and stout aspect,     170
Deserv'st to have the leading of an host!
Forsake thy king, and do but join with me,
And we will triumph over all the world.
I hold the Fates bound fast in iron chains,
And with my hand turn Fortune's wheel about:
And sooner shall the sun fall from his sphere  176
Than Tamburlaine be slain or overcome.
Draw forth thy sword, thou mighty man-at-arms,
Intending but to raze my charmed skin,
And Jove himself will stretch his hand from Heaven     180
To ward the blow and shield me safe from harm.
See how he rains down heaps of gold in showers,
As if he meant to give my soldiers pay!
And as a sure and grounded argument,
That I shall be the monarch of the East,     185
He sends this Soldan's daughter, rich and brave,
To be my Queen and portly Empress.
If thou wilt stay with me, renowmed man,
And lead thy thousand horse with my conduct,
Besides thy share of this Egyptian prize,     190
Those thousand horse shall sweat with martial spoil
Of conquer'd kingdoms and of cities sack'd.
Both we will walk upon the lofty clifts,
And Christian merchants that with Russian stems
Plough up huge furrows in the Caspian sea,  195
Shall vail to us, as lords of all the lake.

127 **brave:** gay     138 **mails:** coffers     146 **lanch:** pierce     156 **furniture:** equipment     164 **affections:** emotions     187 **portly:** of noble port     189 **conduct:** direction     193 **clifts:** cliffs     194 **stems:** ships
196 **vail:** salute

Both we will reign as consuls of the earth,
And mighty kings shall be our senators.
Jove sometime masked in a shepherd's weed,
And by those steps that he hath scal'd the
    Heavens                                            200
May we become immortal like the gods.
Join with me now in this my mean estate,
(I call it mean because, being yet obscure,
The nations far remov'd admire me not,)        204
And when my name and honour shall be spread
As far as Boreas claps his brazen wings,
Or fair Boötes sends his cheerful light,
Then shalt thou be competitor with me,
And sit with Tamburlaine in all his majesty.
    *Ther.*  Not Hermes, prolocutor to the gods, 210
Could use persuasions more pathetical.
    *Tamb.*  Nor are Apollo's oracles more true
Than thou shalt find my vaunts substantial.
    *Tech.*  We are his friends, and if the Persian
    king
Should offer present dukedoms to our state, 215
We think it loss to make exchange for that
We are assur'd of by our friend's success.
    *Usum.*  And kingdoms at the least we all
    expect,
Besides the honour in assured conquests,
Where kings shall crouch unto our conquering
    swords,                                            220
And hosts of soldiers stand amaz'd at us;
When with their fearful tongues they shall con-
    fess:
These are the men that all the world admires.
    *Ther.*  What strong enchantments 'tice my
    yielding soul
As these resolved noble Scythians?             225
But shall I prove a traitor to my king?
    *Tamb.*  No, but the trusty friend of Tambur-
    laine.
    *Ther.*  Won with thy words, and conquer'd
    with thy looks,
I yield myself, my men, and horse to thee,
To be partaker of thy good or ill,             230
As long as life maintains Theridamas.
    *Tamb.*  Theridamas, my friend, take here my
    hand,
Which is as much as if I swore by Heaven,
And call'd the gods to witness of my vow:
Thus shall my heart be still combin'd with
    thine
Until our bodies turn to elements,             236
And both our souls aspire celestial thrones.
Techelles and Casane, welcome him!
    *Tech.*  Welcome, renowmed Persian, to us all!
    *Usum.*  Long may Theridamas remain with
    us!                                                240

    *Tamb.*  These are my friends, in whom I more
    rejoice
Than doth the King of Persia in his crown,
And by the love of Pylades and Orestes,
Whose statues we adore in Scythia,
Thyself and them shall never part from me 245
Before I crown you kings in Asia.
Make much of them, gentle Theridamas,
And they will never leave thee till the death.
    *Ther.*  Nor thee nor them, thrice noble Tam-
    burlaine,
Shall want my heart to be with gladness pierc'd
To do you honour and security.                 251
    *Tamb.*  A thousand thanks, worthy Therida-
    mas.
And now, fair madam, and my noble lords,
If you will willingly remain with me,
You shall have honours as your merits be; 255
Or else you shall be forc'd with slavery.
    *Agyd.*  We yield unto thee, happy Tambur-
    laine.
    *Tamb.*  For you then, madam, I am out of
    doubt.
    *Zeno.*  I must be pleas'd perforce.  Wretched
    Zenocrate!                               *Exeunt.*

## *Actus 2.  Scæna 1.*

*Cosroe, Menaphon, Ortygius, Ceneus,
with other Soldiers*

    *Cos.*  Thus far are we towards Theridamas,
And valiant Tamburlaine, the man of fame,
The man that in the forehead of his fortune
Bears figures of renown and miracle.
But tell me, that hast seen him, Menaphon, 5
What stature wields he, and what personage?
    *Men.*  Of stature tall, and straightly fash-
    ioned,
Like his desire, lift upwards and divine;
So large of limbs, his joints so strongly knit,
Such breadth of shoulders as might mainly bear
Old Atlas' burthen; 'twixt his manly pitch, 11
A pearl, more worth than all the world, is
    plac'd,
Wherein by curious sovereignty of art
Are fix'd his piercing instruments of sight,
Whose fiery circles bear encompassed        15
A heaven of heavenly bodies in their spheres,
That guides his steps and actions to the throne,
Where honour sits invested royally:
Pale of complexion (wrought in him with pas-
    sion)
Thirsting with sovereignty, with love of arms. 20
His lofty brows in folds do figure death,
And in their smoothness amity and life;

---

²⁰⁶ To the farthest north    ²⁰⁷ **Boötes:** the northern constellation containing Arcturus    ²⁰⁸ **competitor:** partner   ²¹⁰ **prolocutor:** spokesman   ²¹¹ **pathetical:** moving   ²²⁵ **As:** ('Are' Qq.)   ²³⁶ **elements:** earth, air, fire, water   ²⁴⁹ **Nor . . . them:** neither to thee nor to them   ²⁵⁰ **want:** be
wanting   ¹⁰ **mainly:** strongly   ¹¹ **'twixt:** midway of   **pitch:** width of shoulder

About them hangs a knot of amber hair,
Wrapped in curls, as fierce Achilles' was,
On which the breath of Heaven delights to
    play, 25
Making it dance with wanton majesty.
His arms and fingers, long, and sinewy,
Betokening valour and excess of strength —
In every part proportioned like the man
Should make the world subdu'd to Tambur-
    laine. 30
    *Cos.* Well hast thou portray'd in thy terms
    of life
The face and personage of a wondrous man;
Nature doth strive with Fortune and his stars
To make him famous in accomplish'd worth;
And well his merits show him to be made 35
His fortune's master and the king of men,
That could persuade at such a sudden pinch,
With reasons of his valour and his life,
A thousand sworn and overmatching foes.
Then, when our powers in points of swords are
    join'd 40
And clos'd in compass of the killing bullet,
Though strait the passage and the port be
    made
That leads to palace of my brother's life,
Proud is his fortune if we pierce it not.
And when the princely Persian diadem 45
Shall overweigh his weary witless head,
And fall like mellow'd fruit with shakes of
    death,
In fair Persia, noble Tamburlaine
Shall be my regent and remain as king.
    *Orty.* In happy hour we have set the crown 50
Upon your kingly head, that seeks our honour
In joining with the man ordain'd by Heaven
To further every action to the best.
    *Cen.* He that with shepherds and a little
    spoil
Durst, in disdain of wrong and tyranny, 55
Defend his freedom 'gainst a monarchy,
What will he do supported by a king,
Leading a troop of gentlemen and lords,
And stuff'd with treasure for his highest
    thoughts!
    *Cos.* And such shall wait on worthy Tambur-
    laine. 60
Our army will be forty thousand strong,
When Tamburlaine and brave Theridamas
Have met us by the river Araris;
And all conjoin'd to meet the witless king,
That now is marching near to Parthia, 65
And with unwilling soldiers faintly arm'd,
To seek revenge on me and Tamburlaine,
To whom, sweet Menaphon, direct me straight.
    *Men.* I will, my lord.     *Exeunt.*

### Actus 2. Scæna 2.

*Mycetes, Meander, with other Lords
and Soldiers*

    *Myc.* Come, my Meander, let us to this gear.
I tell you true, my heart is swoln with wrath
On this same thievish villain, Tamburlaine,
And of that false Cosroe, my traitorous brother.
Would it not grieve a king to be so abus'd 5
And have a thousand horsemen ta'en away?
And, which is worst, to have his diadem
Sought for by such scald knaves as love him
    not?
I think it would; well then, by Heavens I
    swear,
Aurora shall not peep out of her doors, 10
But I will have Cosroe by the head,
And kill proud Tamburlaine with point of
    sword.
Tell you the rest, Meander; I have said.
    *Meand.* Then having past Armenian deserts
    now, 14
And pitch'd our tents under the Georgian hills,
Whose tops are cover'd with Tartarian thieves,
That lie in ambush, waiting for a prey,
What should we do but bid them battle straight,
And rid the world of those detested troops?
Lest, if we let them linger here awhile, 20
They gather strength by power of fresh supplies.
This country swarms with vile outrageous men
That live by rapine and by lawless spoil,
Fit soldiers for the wicked Tamburlaine;
And he that could with gifts and promises 25
Inveigle him that led a thousand horse,
And make him false his faith unto his king,
Will quickly win such as are like himself.
Therefore cheer up your minds; prepare to
    fight;
He that can take or slaughter Tamburlaine 30
Shall rule the province of Albania:
Who brings that traitor's head, Theridamas,
Shall have a government in Media,
Beside the spoil of him and all his train:
But if Cosroe, (as our spials say, 35
And as we know) remains with Tamburlaine,
His highness' pleasure is that he should live,
And be reclaim'd with princely lenity.

    *[Enter a Spy]*

    *A Spy.* An hundred horsemen of my com-
    pany,
Scouting abroad upon these champion plains, 40
Have view'd the army of the Scythians,
Which make reports it far exceeds the king's.
    *Meand.* Suppose they be in number infinite,

---

²⁷ **sinewy**: ('snowy' Qq.)   ³⁰ **Should**: who should   ³¹ **of life**: vivid   ⁴² **port**: gateway   ¹ **gear**:
business   ⁴ **of**: on   ⁸ **scald**: scurvy   ²⁷ **false**: betray   ³⁵ **spials**: spies   ⁴⁰ **champion**: level.
champain

Yet being void of martial discipline
All running headlong after greedy spoils,     45
And more regarding gain than victory,
Like to the cruel brothers of the earth,
Sprung of the teeth of dragons venomous,
Their careless swords shall lanch their fellows'
     throats,
And make us triumph in their overthrow.     50
    *Myc.* Was there such brethren, sweet Mean-
     der, say,
That sprung of teeth of dragons venomous?
    *Meand.* So poets say, my lord.
    *Myc.* And 't is a pretty toy to be a poet.
Well, well, Meander, thou art deeply read,     55
And having thee, I have a jewel sure.
Go on, my lord, and give your charge, I say;
Thy wit will make us conquerors to-day.
    *Meand.* Then, noble soldiers, to entrap these
     thieves,
That live confounded in disorder'd troops,     60
If wealth or riches may prevail with them,
We have our camels laden all with gold,
Which you that be but common soldiers
Shall fling in every corner of the field;
And while the base-born Tartars take it up,  65
You, fighting more for honour than for gold,
Shall massacre those greedy-minded slaves;
And when their scatter'd army is subdu'd,
And you march on their slaughter'd carcases,
Share equally the gold that bought their lives, 70
And live like gentlemen in Persia.
Strike up the drum and march courageously!
Fortune herself doth sit upon our crests.
    *Myc.* He tells you true, my masters: so he
     does.
Drums, why sound ye not, when Meander
     speaks?     *Exeunt [drums sounding].* 75

### Actus 2.  Scæna 3.

*Cosroe, Tamburlaine, Theridamas, Techelles,
    Usumcasane, Ortygius, with others*

    *Cos.* Now, worthy Tamburlaine, have I re-
     pos'd
In thy approved fortunes all my hope.
What think'st thou, man, shall come of our at-
     tempts?
For even as from assured oracle,
I take thy doom for satisfaction.     5
    *Tamb.* And so mistake you not a whit, my
     lord;
For fates and oracles of Heaven have sworn
To royalize the deeds of Tamburlaine,
And make them blest that share in his at-
     tempts.

And doubt you not but, if you favour me,     10
And let my fortunes and my valour sway
To some direction in your martial deeds,
The world will strive with hosts of men-at-arms,
To swarm unto the ensign I support:
The host of Xerxes, which by fame is said     15
To drink the mighty Parthian Araris,
Was but a handful to that we will have.
Our quivering lances, shaking in the air,
And bullets, like Jove's dreadful thunderbolts,
Enroll'd in flames and fiery smouldering mists, 20
Shall threat the gods more than Cyclopian wars:
And with our sun-bright armour as we march,
We 'll chase the stars from Heaven and dim
     their eyes
That stand and muse at our admired arms.
    *Ther.* You see, my lord, what working words
     he hath;     25
But when you see his actions top his speech,
Your speech will stay or so extol his worth
As I shall be commended and excus'd
For turning my poor charge to his direction.
And these his two renowmed friends, my lord, 30
Would make one thrust and strive to be retain'd
In such a great degree of amity.
    *Tech.* With duty and with amity we yield
Our utmost service to the fair Cosroe.
    *Cos.* Which I esteem as portion of my crown.
Usumcasane and Techelles both,     36
When she that rules in Rhamnus' golden gates,
And makes a passage for all prosperous arms,
Shall make me solely Emperor of Asia,
Then shall your meeds and valours be advanc'd
To rooms of honour and nobility.     41
    *Tamb.* Then haste, Cosroe, to be king alone,
That I with these, my friends, and all my men
May triumph in our long-expected fate.
The king, your brother, is now hard at hand: 45
Meet with the fool, and rid your royal shoulders
Of such a burthen as outweighs the sands
And all the craggy rocks of Caspia.

*[Enter a Messenger]*

    *Mess.* My lord, we have discover'd the enemy
Ready to charge you with a mighty army.     50
    *Cos.* Come, Tamburlaine! now whet thy
     winged sword,
And lift thy lofty arm into the clouds,
That it may reach the King of Persia's crown,
And set it safe on my victorious head.     54
    *Tamb.* See where it is, the keenest curtle-axe
That e'er made passage thorough Persian arms.
These are the wings shall make it fly as swift
As doth the lightning or the breath of Heaven,
And kill as sure as it swiftly flies.     59

---

⁴⁷ **cruel brothers:** (Jason sowed dragon's teeth in the earth, and there sprang up a body of armed
men.)  ⁵ **doom:** judgment  **satisfaction:** complete certainty  ⁷ **of:** (not in Qq.)  ¹⁶ **Araris:** (the
Scamander in Herodotus)  ²⁶ **top:** exceed ('stop' Qq.)  ³¹ **thrust:** push  ³⁷ **she:** Nemesis, goddess of justice  (She had a temple at Rhamnus in Attica.)  ⁴¹ **rooms:** places

*Cos.* Thy words assure me of kind success;
Go, valiant soldier, go before and charge
The fainting army of that foolish king.
   *Tamb.* Usumcasane and Techelles, come!
We are enough to scare the enemy,
And more than needs to make an emperor. 65
                   [*Exeunt*] *to the battle,*

### [SCENE IV]

*and Mycetes comes out alone with his crown in his*
*hand, offering to hide it*

   *Myc.* Accurs'd be he that first invented war!
They knew not, ah, they knew not, simple men,
How those were hit by pelting cannon shot
Stand staggering like a quivering aspen leaf,
Fearing the force of Boreas' boisterous blasts. 5
In what a lamentable case were I,
If Nature had not given me wisdom's lore!
For kings are clouts that every man shoots at,
Our crown the pin that thousands seek to
   cleave;
Therefore in policy I think it good         10
To hide it close; a goodly stratagem,
And far from any man that is a fool:
So shall not I be known; or if I be,
They cannot take away my crown from me.
Here will I hide it in this simple hole.     15

         *Enter Tamburlaine*

   *Tamb.* What, fearful coward, straggling from
   the camp,
When kings themselves are present in the field?
   *Myc.* Thou liest.
   *Tamb.* Base villain! dar'st thou give the lie?
   *Myc.* Away; I am the king; go; touch me
   not.                            20
Thou break'st the law of arms, unless thou
   kneel
And cry me "mercy, noble king."
   *Tamb.* Are you the witty King of Persia?
   *Myc.* Ay, marry am I: have you any suit to
   me?
   *Tamb.* I would entreat you to speak but
   three wise words.                    25
   *Myc.* So I can when I see my time.
   *Tamb.* Is this your crown?
   *Myc.* Ay, didst thou ever see a fairer?
   *Tamb.* You will not sell it, will ye?
   *Myc.* Such another word and I will have [30
thee executed. Come, give it me!
   *Tamb.* No; I took it prisoner.
   *Myc.* You lie; I gave it you.
   *Tamb.* Then 't is mine.
   *Myc.* No; I mean I let you keep it.     35
   *Tamb.* Well; I mean you shall have it again.
Here; take it for a while: I lend it thee,

'Till I may see thee hemm'd with armed men;
Then shalt thou see me pull it from thy head.
Thou art no match for mighty Tamburlaine. 40
                        [*Exit.*]
   *Myc.* O gods! Is this Tamburlaine the thief?
I marvel much he stole it not away.
   *Sound trumpets to the battle, and he runs in.*

### [SCENE V]

*Cosroe, Tamburlaine, Theridamas, Menaphon,*
*Meander, Ortygius, Techelles, Usumcasane,*
*with others*

   *Tamb.* Hold thee, Cosroe! wear two imperial
   crowns.
Think thee invested now as royally,
Even by the mighty hand of Tamburlaine,
As if as many kings as could encompass thee, 4
With greatest pomp, had crown'd thee emperor.
   *Cos.* So do I, thrice renowmed man-at-arms,
And none shall keep the crown but Tambur-
   laine.
Thee do I make my regent of Persia,
And general lieftenant of my armies.
Meander, you, that were our brother's guide, 10
And chiefest counsellor in all his acts,
Since he is yielded to the stroke of war,
On your submission we with thanks excuse,
And give you equal place in our affairs.
   *Meand.* Most happy Emperor, in humblest
   terms,                         15
I vow my service to your majesty,
With utmost virtue of my faith and duty.
   *Cos.* Thanks, good Meander: then, Cosroe,
   reign,
And govern Persia in her former pomp!
Now send ambassage to thy neighbour kings, 20
And let them know the Persian king is chang'd,
From one that knew not what a king should do,
To one that can command what 'longs thereto.
And now we will to fair Persepolis,
With twenty thousand expert soldiers.     25
The lords and captains of my brother's camp
With little slaughter take Meander's course,
And gladly yield them to my gracious rule.
Ortygius and Menaphon, my trusty friends,
Now will I gratify your former good,     30
And grace your calling with a greater sway.
   *Orty.* And as we ever aim'd at your behoof,
And sought your state all honour it deserv'd,
So will we with our powers and our lives
Endeavour to preserve and prosper it.     35
   *Cos.* I will not thank thee, sweet Ortygius,
Better replies shall prove my purposes.
And now, Lord Tamburlaine, my brother's
   camp
I leave to thee and to Theridamas.

---

³ **were:** who were    ⁸ **clouts:** white "bull's-eyes" on archery targets    ⁹ **pin:** the peg in the
middle of the "clout"    ⁷ **keep:** guard    ⁹ **lieftenant:** lieutenant    ³² **behoof:** profit

To follow me to fair Persepolis.          40
Then will we march to all those Indian mines
My witless brother to the Christians lost,
And ransom them with fame and usury.
And till thou overtake me, Tamburlaine,
(Staying to order all the scatter'd troops,)   45
Farewell, lord regent and his happy friends!
I long to sit upon my brother's throne.
   *Meand.*   Your majesty shall shortly have
    your wish,
And ride in triumph through Persepolis.
   *Exeunt. Manent Tamb., Tech., Ther., Usum.*
   *Tamb.* "And ride in triumph through Persep-
    olis!"          50
Is it not brave to be a king, Techelles?
Usumcasane and Theridamas,
Is it not passing brave to be a king,
And ride in triumph through Persepolis?
   *Tech.*   O, my lord, 't is sweet and full of
    pomp.          55
   *Usum.*   To be a king is half to be a god.
   *Ther.*   A god is not so glorious as a king.
I think the pleasure they enjoy in Heaven,
Cannot compare with kingly joys in earth.
To wear a crown enchas'd with pearl and gold,
Whose virtues carry with it life and death;   61
To ask and have, command and be obeyed;
When looks breed love, with looks to gain the
    prize, —
Such power attractive shines in princes' eyes!
   *Tamb.*   Why say, Theridamas, wilt thou be a
    king?          65
   *Ther.*   Nay, though I praise it, I can live
    without it.
   *Tamb.*   What says my other friends?   Will
    you be kings?
   *Tech.*   Ay, if I could, with all my heart, my
    lord.
   *Tamb.*   Why, that's well said, Techelles; so
    would I,
And so would you, my masters, would you not?
   *Usum.*   What then, my lord?          71
   *Tamb.*   Why then, Casane, shall we wish for
    aught
The world affords in greatest novelty,
And rest attemptless, faint, and destitute?
Methinks we should not: I am strongly mov'd,
That if I should desire the Persian crown,   76
I could attain it with a wondrous ease.
And would not all our soldiers soon consent,
If we should aim at such a dignity?
   *Ther.*   I know they would with our persua-
    sions.          80
   *Tamb.* Why then, Theridamas, I 'll first assay
To get the Persian kingdom to myself;

Then thou for Parthia; they for Scythia and
   Media.
And, if I prosper, all shall be as sure
As if the Turk, the Pope, Afric, and Greece, 85
Came creeping to us with their crowns apiece.
   *Tech.*   Then shall we send to this triumphing
    king,
And bid him battle for his novel crown?
   *Usum.*   Nay, quickly then, before his room
    be hot.
   *Tamb.*   'T will prove a pretty jest, in faith,
    my friends.          90
   *Ther.*   A jest to charge on twenty thousand
    men!
I judge the purchase more important far.
   *Tamb.*   Judge by thyself, Theridamas, not
    me;
For presently Techelles here shall haste
To bid him battle ere he pass too far,          95
And lose more labour than the gain will quite.
Then shalt thou see the Scythian Tamburlaine
Make but a jest to win the Persian crown.
Techelles, take a thousand horse with thee,
And bid him turn him back to war with us, 100
That only made him king to make us sport.
We will not steal upon him cowardly,
But give him warning and more warriors.
Haste thee, Techelles; we will follow thee.
            *[Exit Techelles.]*
What saith Theridamas?
   *Ther.*          Go on for me.   *Exeunt.* 105

### Actus 2.   Scæna 6.
*Costoe, Meander, Ortygius, Menaphon,
   with other Soldiers*

   *Cos.*   What means this devilish shepherd to
    aspire
With such a giantly presumption
To cast up hills against the face of Heaven,
And dare the force of angry Jupiter?
But as he thrust them underneath the hills,   5
And press'd out fire from their burning jaws,
So will I send this monstrous slave to hell,
Where flames shall ever feed upon his soul.
   *Meand.*   Some powers divine, or else infernal,
    mix'd
Their angry seeds at his conception;          10
For he was never sprung of human race,
Since with the spirit of his fearful pride
He dare so doubtlessly resolve of rule,
And by profession be ambitious.
   *Orty.*   What god, or fiend, or spirit of the
    earth,          15
Or monster turned to a manly shape,

---

73 **in . . . novelty:** however rare   75 **mov'd:** inwardly assured   85 **Turk . . . Afric . . . Greece:** Bajazeth, the Soldan of Egypt, and the Greek Emperor   86 **apiece:** ('apace' Qq. 1–2)   92 **purchase:** tangible booty   96 **quite:** justify   100 **him back:** ('his back' Qq.)   5 **he:** Jupiter   **them:** the Titans   13 **doubtlessly:** unhesitatingly   15, 16 (Complete the sense by supplying "was his progenitor.")

Or of what mould or mettle he be made,
What star or state soever govern him,
Let us put on our meet encount'ring minds
And in detesting such a devilish thief,    20
In love of honour and defence of right,
Be arm'd against the hate of such a foe,
Whether from earth, or hell, or Heaven he grow.
   *Cos.* Nobly resolv'd, my good Ortygius;
And since we all have suck'd one wholesome air,
And with the same proportion of elements   26
Resolve, I hope we are resembled,
Vowing our loves to equal death and life.
Let's cheer our soldiers to encounter him,
That grievous image of ingratitude,    30
That fiery thirster after sovereignty,
And burn him in the fury of that flame,
That none can quench but blood and empery.
Resolve, my lords and loving soldiers, now
To save your king and country from decay.   35
Then strike up, drum; and all the stars that make
The loathsome circle of my dated life,
Direct my weapon to his barbarous heart,
That thus opposeth him against the gods,
And scorns the powers that govern Persia!   40
                     *[Exeunt.]*

### [SCENE VII]

*Enter to the battle, and after the battle enter Cos-*
*roe, wounded, Theridamas, Tamburlaine,*
*Techelles, Usumcasane, with others*

   *Cos.* Barbarous and bloody Tamburlaine,
Thus to deprive me of my crown and life!
Treacherous and false Theridamas,
Even at the morning of my happy state,
Scarce being seated in my royal throne,    5
To work my downfall and untimely end!
An uncouth pain torments my grieved soul,
And death arrests the organ of my voice,
Who, ent'ring at the breach thy sword hath
   made,
Sacks every vein and artier of my heart. —  10
Bloody and insatiate Tamburlaine!
   *Tamb.* The thirst of reign and sweetness of
   a crown,
That caus'd the eldest son of heavenly Ops
To thrust his doting father from his chair,
And place himself in the empyreal Heaven,  15
Mov'd me to manage arms against their state.
What better precedent than mighty Jove?
Nature that fram'd us of four elements,
Warring within our breasts for regiment,
Doth teach us all to have aspiring minds:   20
Our souls, whose faculties can comprehend
The wondrous architecture of the world,
And measure every wand'ring planet's course,
Still climbing after knowledge infinite,

And always moving as the restless spheres,  25
Wills us to wear ourselves, and never rest,
Until we reach the ripest fruit of all,
That perfect bliss and sole felicity,
The sweet fruition of an earthly crown.
   *Ther.* And that made me to join with Tam-
   burlaine:    30
For he is gross and like the massy earth,
That moves not upwards, nor by princely deeds
Doth mean to soar above the highest sort.
   *Tech.* And that made us the friends of Tam-
   burlaine,
To lift our swords against the Persian king.  35
   *Usum.* For as, when Jove did thrust old Sat-
   urn down,
Neptune and Dis gain'd each of them a crown,
So do we hope to reign in Asia,
If Tamburlaine be plac'd in Persia.
   *Cos.* The strangest men that ever nature
   made!    40
I know not how to take their tyrannies.
My bloodless body waxeth chill and cold,
And with my blood my life slides through my
   wound;
My soul begins to take her flight to hell,
And summons all my senses to depart. —   45
The heat and moisture, which did feed each
   other,
For want of nourishment to feed them both,
Is dry and cold; and now doth ghastly death,
With greedy talons gripe my bleeding heart,
And like a harpy tires on my life.    50
Theridamas and Tamburlaine, I die:
And fearful vengeance light upon you both!
       *[Cosroe dies. Tamburlaine] takes*
          *the crown and puts it on.*
   *Tamb.* Not all the curses which the Furies
   breathe
Shall make me leave so rich a prize as this.
Theridamas, Techelles, and the rest,    55
Who think you now is King of Persia?
   *All.* Tamburlaine! Tamburlaine!
   *Tamb.* Though Mars himself, the angry god
   of arms,
And all the earthly potentates conspire
To dispossess me of this diadem,    60
Yet will I wear it in despite of them,
As great commander of this eastern world,
If you but say that Tamburlaine shall reign.
   *All.* Long live Tamburlaine and reign in
   Asia!
   *Tamb.* So now it is more surer on my head,  65
Than if the gods had held a parliament,
And all pronounc'd me King of Persia.
                     *[Exeunt.*

*Finis Actus 2*

---

   **27 Resolve:** decompose   **resembled:** alike (in spirit)   **37 loathsome circle:** awful aspect (the planetary influence limiting life)   **10 artier:** artery   **13 Ops:** wife of Saturn, mother of Jupiter   **40 tires:** preys

## Actus 3.  Scæna 1.

*Bajazeth, the Kings of Fez, Morocco, and*
*Argier, with others in great pomp*

*Baj.*   Great Kings of Barbary and my portly
   bassoes,
We hear the Tartars and the eastern thieves,
Under the conduct of one Tamburlaine,
Presume a bickering with your emperor,     4
And thinks to rouse us from our dreadful siege
Of the famous Grecian Constantinople.
You know our army is invincible:
As many circumcised Turks we have,
And warlike bands of Christians renied,
As hath the ocean or the Terrene sea       10
Small drops of water when the moon begins
To join in one her semicircled horns.
Yet would we not be brav'd with foreign power,
Nor raise our siege before the Grecians yield,
Or breathless lie before the city walls.    15
   *Fez.*   Renowmed Emperor, and mighty
      general,
What, if you sent the bassoes of your guard
To charge him to remain in Asia,
Or else to threaten death and deadly arms
As from the mouth of mighty Bajazeth?       20
   *Baj.*   Hie thee, my basso, fast to Persia.
Tell him thy Lord, the Turkish Emperor,
Dread Lord of Afric, Europe, and Asia,
Great King and conqueror of Græcia,
The ocean, Terrene, and the Coal-black sea, 25
The high and highest monarch of the world,
Wills and commands (for say not I entreat),
Not once to set his foot in Africa,
Or spread his colours in Græcia,
Lest he incur the fury of my wrath.        30
Tell him I am content to take a truce,
Because I hear he bears a valiant mind:
But if, presuming on his silly power,
He be so mad to manage arms with me,
Then stay thou with him; say, I bid thee so: 35
And if, before the sun have measur'd Heaven
With triple circuit, thou regreet us not,
We mean to take his morning's next arise
For messenger he will not be reclaim'd,
And mean to fetch thee in despite of him.   40
   *Bas.*   Most great and puissant monarch of
      the earth,
Your basso will accomplish your behest,
And show your pleasure to the Persian,
As fits the legate of the stately Turk.
                                    *Exit Bass.*
   *Arg.*   They say he is the king of Persia; 45
But if he dare attempt to stir your siege,
'T were requisite he should be ten times more,

For all flesh quakes at your magnificence.
   *Baj.*   True, Argier; and tremble at my looks.
   *Mor.*   The spring is hind'red by your smoth-
      ering host,                           50
For neither rain can fall upon the earth,
Nor sun reflex his virtuous beams thereon, —
The ground is mantled with such multitudes.
   *Baj.*   All this is true as holy Mahomet;
And all the trees are blasted with our breaths.
   *Fez.*   What thinks your greatness best to
      be achiev'd                           56
In pursuit of the city's overthrow?
   *Baj.*   I will the captive pioners of Argier
Cut off the water that by leaden pipes
Runs to the city from the mountain Carnon. 60
Two thousand horse shall forage up and down,
That no relief or succour come by land:
And all the sea my galleys countermand.
Then shall our footmen lie within the trench,
And with their cannons, mouth'd like Orcus'
   gulf,                                    65
Batter the walls, and we will enter in;
And thus the Grecians shall be conquered.
                                    *Exeunt.*

## Actus 3.  Scæna 2.

*Agydas, Zenocrate, Anippe, with others*

[*Agyd.*]   Madam Zenocrate, may I presume
To know the cause of these unquiet fits,
That work such trouble to your wonted rest?
'T is more than pity such a heavenly face
Should by heart's sorrow wax so wan and pale,  5
When your offensive rape by Tamburlaine
(Which of your whole displeasures should be
   most)
Hath seem'd to be digested long ago.
   *Zeno.*   Although it be digested long ago,
As his exceeding favours have deserv'd,      10
And might content the Queen of Heaven as well
As it hath chang'd my first conceiv'd disdain,
Yet since a farther passion feeds my thoughts
With ceaseless and disconsolate conceits,
Which dyes my looks so lifeless as they are,  15
And might, if my extremes had full events,
Make me the ghastly counterfeit of death.
   *Agyd.*   Eternal heaven sooner be dissolv'd,
And all that pierceth Phœbe's silver eye,
Before such hap fall to Zenocrate!           20
   *Zeno.*   Ah, life and soul, still hover in his
      breast
And leave my body senseless as the earth;
Or else unite you to his life and soul,
That I may live and die with Tamburlaine!

*Enter [behind] Tamburlaine, with Techelles*
*and others*

---

¹ **bassoes:** pashas   ⁹ **renied:** renegade   ¹⁰ **Terrene:** Mediterranean   ¹² To approach the full
of the moon (the period of full tides)   ⁶³ **countermand:** command   ⁶ **rape:** seizure   ¹³ **since:** since
then   ¹⁶ **extremes:** violent passions   **events:** outward manifestation   ¹⁹ **Phœbe's:** the moon's

*Agyd.* With Tamburlaine! Ah, fair Zeno-
crate,    25
Let not a man so vile and barbarous,
That holds you from your father in despite,
And keeps you from the honours of a queen,
(Being suppos'd his worthless concubine,)
Be honour'd with your love but for necessity. 30
So, now the mighty Soldan hears of you,
Your highness needs not doubt but in short
   time
He will with Tamburlaine's destruction
Redeem you from this deadly servitude.
   *Zeno.* Agydas, leave to wound me with these
   words,    35
And speak of Tamburlaine as he deserves.
The entertainment we have had of him
Is far from villainy or servitude,
And might in noble minds be counted princely.
   *Agyd.* How can you fancy one that looks so
   fierce,    40
Only dispos'd to martial stratagems?
Who, when he shall embrace you in his arms,
Will tell how many thousand men he slew;
And when you look for amorous discourse,
Will rattle forth his facts of war and blood, 45
Too harsh a subject for your dainty ears.
   *Zeno.* As looks the Sun through Nilus' flow-
   ing stream,
Or when the Morning holds him in her arms,
So looks my lordly love, fair Tamburlaine;
His talk much sweeter than the Muses' song 50
They sung for honour 'gainst Pierides;
Or when Minerva did with Neptune strive:
And higher would I rear my estimate
Than Juno, sister to the highest god,
If I were match'd with mighty Tamburlaine. 55
   *Agyd.* Yet be not so inconstant in your
   love;
But let the young Arabian live in hope
After your rescue to enjoy his choice.
You see, — though first the King of Persia,
Being a shepherd, seem'd to love you much, —
Now on his majesty he leaves those looks,    61
Those words of favour, and those comfortings,
And gives no more than common courtesies.
   *Zeno.* Thence rise the tears that so distain
   my cheeks,
Fearing his love through my unworthiness. — 65
     *Tamburlaine goes to her and takes*
     *her away lovingly by the hand,*
     *looking wrathfully on Agydas,*
     *and says nothing.* [*Exeunt*
     *all but Agydas.*]
   *Agyd.* Betray'd by fortune and suspicious
   love,
Threat'ned with frowning wrath and jealousy,
Surpris'd with fear of hideous revenge,

I stand aghast; but most astonied
To see his choler shut in secret thoughts,    70
And wrapp'd in silence of his angry soul.
Upon his brows was portray'd ugly death;
And in his eyes the fury of his heart,
That shine as comets, menacing revenge,
And casts a pale complexion on his cheeks. 75
As when the seaman sees the Hyades
Gather an army of Cimmerian clouds,
(Auster and Aquilon with winged steeds,
All sweating, tilt about the watery Heavens,
With shivering spears enforcing thunder claps,
And from their shields strike flames of light-
   ning,)    81
All fearful folds his sails and sounds the
   main,
Lifting his prayers to the Heavens for aid
Against the terror of the winds and waves:
So fares Agydas for the late-felt frowns    85
That sent a tempest to my daunted thoughts,
And makes my soul divine her overthrow.

     *Enter Techelles with a naked dagger*

   *Tech.* See you, Agydas, how the king salutes
   you?
He bids you prophesy what it imports.    *Exit.*
   *Agyd.* I prophesied before, and now I prove 91
The killing frowns of jealousy and love.
He needed not with words confirm my fear,
For words are vain where working tools pre-
   sent
The naked action of my threat'ned end.
It says: "Agydas, thou shalt surely die,    95
And of extremities elect the least;
More honour and less pain it may procure
To die by this resolved hand of thine,
Than stay the torments he and Heaven have
   sworn."    99
Then haste, Agydas, and prevent the plagues
Which thy prolonged fates may draw on thee.
Go, wander, free from fear of tyrant's rage,
Removed from the torments and the hell
Wherewith he may excruciate thy soul,
And let Agydas by Agydas die,    105
And with this stab slumber eternally.
     *Stabs himself.*

     [*Re-enter Techelles with Usumcasane*]

   *Tech.* Usumcasane, see, how right the man
Hath hit the meaning of my lord, the king.
   *Usum.* Faith, and Techelles, it was manly
   done;
And since he was so wise and honourable, 110
Let us afford him now the bearing hence,
And crave his triple-worthy burial.
   *Tech.* Agreed, Casane; we will honour him.
     [*Exeunt bearing out the body.*]

---

³⁵ **Agydas:** (not in Qq.)    ⁴⁵ **facts:** feats    ⁶⁹ **astonied:** astonished    ⁷⁷ **Cimmerian:** black
⁷⁸ **Auster and Aquilon:** winds from the south and north    ⁸² **main:** sea

### Actus 3. Scæna 3.

*Tamburlaine, Techelles, Usumcasane, Therida-
mas, Basso, Zenocrate, [Anippe,] with
others*

*Tamb.*  Basso, by this thy lord and master
knows
I mean to meet him in Bithynia:
See how he comes!  Tush, Turks are full of
brags,
And menace more than they can well perform.
He meet me in the field, and fetch thee hence!
Alas! poor Turk! his fortune is too weak    6
T' encounter with the strength of Tamburlaine.
View well my camp, and speak indifferently:
Do not my captains and my soldiers look
As if they meant to conquer Africa?    10
*Bas.*  Your men are valiant, but their num-
ber few,
And cannot terrify his mighty host.
My lord, the great commander of the world,
Besides fifteen contributory kings,
Hath now in arms ten thousand Janissaries,  15
Mounted on lusty Mauritanian steeds,
Brought to the war by men of Tripoli;
Two hundred thousand footmen that have
serv'd
In two set battles fought in Græcia:
And for the expedition of this war,    20
If he think good, can from his garrisons
Withdraw as many more to follow him.
*Tech.*  The more he brings the greater is the
spoil,
For when they perish by our warlike hands,
We mean to seat our footmen on their steeds,  25
And rifle all those stately Janissars.
*Tamb.*  But will those kings accompany your
lord?
*Bas.*  Such as his highness please; but some
must stay
To rule the provinces he late subdu'd.
*Tamb.* [*To his Officers.*]  Then fight coura-
geously: their crowns are yours;    30
This hand shall set them on your conquering
heads,
That made me Emperor of Asia.
*Usum.*  Let him bring millions infinite of men,
Unpeopling Western Africa and Greece,
Yet we assure us of the victory.    35
*Ther.*  Even he that in a trice vanquish'd two
kings,
More mighty than the Turkish emperor,
Shall rouse him out of Europe, and pursue
His scatter'd army till they yield or die.
*Tamb.*  Well said, Theridamas; speak in that
mood;    40

For *will* and *shall* best fitteth Tamburlaine,
Whose smiling stars gives him assured hope
Of martial triumph ere he meet his foes.
I that am term'd the scourge and wrath of
God,
The only fear and terror of the world,    45
Will first subdue the Turk, and then enlarge
Those Christian captives, which you keep as
slaves,
Burdening their bodies with your heavy chains,
And feeding them with thin and slender fare;
That naked row about the Terrene sea,    50
And when they chance to breathe and rest a
space,
Are punish'd with bastones so grievously,
That they lie panting on the galley's side,
And strive for life at every stroke they give.
These are the cruel pirates of Argier,    55
That damned train, the scum of Africa,
Inhabited with straggling runagates,
That make quick havoc of the Christian blood;
But, as I live, that town shall curse the time
That Tamburlaine set foot in Africa.    60

*Enter Bajazeth with his Bassoes, and contribu-
tory Kings [of Fez, Morocco, and Argier;
Zabina and Ebea]*

*Baj.*  Bassoes and Janissaries of my guard,
Attend upon the person of your lord,
The greatest potentate of Africa.
*Tamb.*  Techelles and the rest, prepare your
swords;
I mean t' encounter with that Bajazeth.    65
*Baj.*  Kings of Fez, Moroccus, and Argier,
He calls me Bajazeth, whom you call Lord!
Note the presumption of this Scythian slave!
I tell thee, villain, those that lead my horse
Have to their names titles of dignity,    70
And dar'st thou bluntly call me Bajazeth?
*Tamb.*  And know thou, Turk, that those
which lead my horse,
Shall lead thee captive thorough Africa;
And dar'st thou bluntly call me Tamburlaine?
*Baj.*  By Mahomet my kinsman's sepulchre,
And by the holy Alcoran I swear,    76
He shall be made a chaste and lustless eunuch,
And in my sarell tend my concubines;
And all his captains that thus stoutly stand,
Shall draw the chariot of my emperess,    80
Whom I have brought to see their overthrow.
*Tamb.*  By this my sword, that conquer'd
Persia,
Thy fall shall make me famous through the
world.
I will not tell thee how I 'll handle thee,
But every common soldier of my camp    85
Shall smile to see thy miserable state.

---

⁸ **indifferently**: without bias    ⁴⁶ **enlarge**: free    ⁵² **bastones**: cudgels    ⁵⁵ **Argier**: Algeria
⁷⁶ **Alcoran**: the Koran    ⁷⁸ **sarell**: harem

*Fez.* What means the mighty Turkish em-
peror,
To talk with one so base as Tamburlaine?
*Mor.* Ye Moors and valiant men of Bar-
bary,
How can ye suffer these indignities?    90
*Arg.* Leave words, and let them feel your
lances' points
Which glided through the bowels of the Greeks.
*Baj.* Well said, my stout contributory kings:
Your threefold army and my hugy host
Shall swallow up these base-born Persians.   95
*Tech.* Puissant, renowm'd, and mighty Tam-
burlaine,
Why stay we thus prolonging all their lives?
*Ther.* I long to see those crowns won by our
swords,
That we may reign as kings of Africa.
*Usum.* What coward would not fight for
such a prize?     100
*Tamb.* Fight all courageously, and be you
kings;
I speak it, and my words are oracles.
*Baj.* Zabina, mother of three braver boys
Than Hercules, that in his infancy
Did pash the jaws of serpents venomous;   105
Whose hands are made to gripe a warlike lance,
Their shoulders broad for complete armour
fit,
Their limbs more large, and of a bigger size,
Than all the brats ysprung from Typhon's
loins;
Who, when they come unto their father's age,
Will batter turrets with their manly fists: — 111
Sit here upon this royal chair of state,
And on thy head wear my imperial crown,
Until I bring this sturdy Tamburlaine
And all his captains bound in captive chains. 115
*Zab.* Such good success happen to Bajazeth!
*Tamb.* Zenocrate, the loveliest maid alive,
Fairer than rocks of pearl and precious stone,
The only paragon of Tamburlaine,
Whose eyes are brighter than the lamps of
Heaven      120
And speech more pleasant than sweet har-
mony!
That with thy looks canst clear the darken'd
sky,
And calm the rage of thund'ring Jupiter: —
Sit down by her, adorned with my crown,
As if thou wert the Empress of the world. 125
Stir not, Zenocrate, until thou see
Me march victoriously with all my men,
Triumphing over him and these his kings,
Which I will bring as vassals to thy feet.
Till then take thou my crown, vaunt of my
worth,      130

And manage words with her, as we will arms.
*Zeno.* And may my love, the King of Persia,
Return with victory and free from wound!
*Baj.* Now shalt thou feel the force of Turk-
ish arms,
Which lately made all Europe quake for fear. 135
I have of Turks, Arabians, Moors, and Jews,
Enough to cover all Bithynia.
Let thousands die; their slaughter'd carcases
Shall serve for walls and bulwarks to the
rest,
And as the heads of Hydra, so my power,   140
Subdued, shall stand as mighty as before.
If they should yield their necks unto the sword,
Thy soldier's arms could not endure to strike
So many blows as I have heads for thee.
Thou know'st not, foolish-hardy Tamburlaine,
What 't is to meet me in the open field,    146
That leave no ground for thee to march upon.
*Tamb.* Our conquering swords shall marshal
us the way.
We use to march upon the slaughter'd foe,
Trampling their bowels with our horses'
hoofs, —      150
Brave horses bred on the white Tartarian hills.
My camp is like to Julius Cæsar's host,
That never fought but had the victory;
Nor in Pharsalia was there such hot war
As these, my followers, willingly would have. 155
Legions of spirits fleeting in the air
Direct our bullets and our weapons' points,
And make our strokes to wound the senseless
air.
And when she sees our bloody colours spread,
Then Victory begins to take her flight,    160
Resting herself upon my milk-white tent. —
But come, my lords, to weapons let us fall;
The field is ours, the Turk, his wife, and all.
                 *Exit with his followers.*
*Baj.* Come, kings and bassoes, let us glut
our swords,      164
That thirst to drink the feeble Persians' blood.
                 *Exit with his followers.*
*Zab.* Base concubine, must thou be plac'd
by me,
That am the empress of the mighty Turk?
*Zeno.* Disdainful Turkess and unreverend
boss!
Call'st thou me concubine, that am betroth'd
Unto the great and mighty Tamburlaine? 170
*Zab.* To Tamburlaine, the great Tartarian
thief!
*Zeno.* Thou wilt repent these lavish words
of thine,
When thy great basso-master and thyself
Must plead for mercy at his kingly feet,
And sue to me to be your advocates.    175

---

⁹⁴ **hugy:** huge    ¹⁰⁵ **pash:** crush    ¹⁵⁶ **fleeting:** hovering    ¹⁵⁸ **air:** ('lure' Qq.)    ¹⁶⁸ **boss:** fat, lazy
woman    ¹⁷⁵ **advocates:** advocate for the two of you

*Zab.* And sue to thee! I tell thee, shameless girl,
Thou shalt be laundress to my waiting maid! —
How lik'st thou her, Ebea? Will she serve?
  *Ebea.* Madam, she thinks, perhaps, she is too fine,
But I shall turn her into other weeds,          180
And make her dainty fingers fall to work.
  *Zeno.* Hear'st thou, Anippe, how thy drudge doth talk?
And how my slave, her mistress, menaceth?
Both for their sauciness shall be employ'd    184
To dress the common soldiers' meat and drink,
For we will scorn they should come near ourselves.
  *Anip.* Yet sometimes let your highness send for them
To do the work my chambermaid disdains.
        *They sound the battle within, and stay.*
  *Zeno.* Ye gods and powers that govern Persia,
And made my lordly love her worthy king, 190
Now strengthen him against the Turkish Bajazeth,
And let his foes, like flocks of fearful roes
Pursu'd by hunters, fly his angry looks,
That I may see him issue conqueror!
  *Zab.* Now, Mahomet, solicit God himself, 195
And make him rain down murthering shot from Heaven
To dash the Scythians' brains, and strike them dead,
That dare to manage arms with him
That offer'd jewels to thy sacred shrine,
When first he warr'd against the Christians! 200
                *To the battle again.*
  *Zeno.* By this the Turks lie welt'ring in their blood,
And Tamburlaine is Lord of Africa.
  *Zab.* Thou art deceiv'd. — I heard the trumpets sound
As when my emperor overthrew the Greeks,
And led them captive into Africa.              205
Straight will I use thee as thy pride deserves:
Prepare thyself to live and die my slave.
  *Zeno.* If Mahomet should come from Heaven and swear
My royal lord is slain or conquered,
Yet should he not persuade me otherwise   210
But that he lives and will be conqueror.

*Bajazeth flies and he pursues him. The battle
short, and they enter. Bajazeth is overcome*

  *Tamb.* Now, king of bassoes, who is conqueror?
  *Baj.* Thou, by the fortune of this damned foil.

  *Tamb.* Where are your stout contributory kings?

*Enter Techelles, Theridamas, Usumcasane*

  *Tech.* We have their crowns, their bodies strow the field.                              215
  *Tamb.* Each man a crown! Why, kingly fought, i' faith.
Deliver them into my treasury.
  *Zeno.* Now let me offer to my gracious lord
His royal crown again so highly won.
  *Tamb.* Nay, take the Turkish crown from her, Zenocrate,                            220
And crown me Emperor of Africa.
  *Zab.* No, Tamburlaine: though now thou gat the best,
Thou shalt not yet be lord of Africa.
  *Ther.* Give her the crown, Turkess: you were best.
        *He takes it from her, and gives it
                Zenocrate.*
  *Zab.* Injurious villains! thieves! runagates!
How dare you thus abuse my majesty?     226
  *Ther.* Here, madam, you are Empress; she is none.
  *Tamb.* Not now, Theridamas; her time is past.
The pillars that have bolster'd up those terms,
Are fallen in clusters at my conquering feet. 230
  *Zab.* Though he be prisoner, he may be ransom'd.
  *Tamb.* Not all the world shall ransom Bajazeth.
  *Baj.* Ah, fair Zabina! we have lost the field;
And never had the Turkish emperor
So great a foil by any foreign foe.            235
Now will the Christians miscreants be glad,
Ringing with joy their superstitious bells,
And making bonfires for my overthrow.
But, ere I die, those foul idolaters
Shall make me bonfires with their filthy bones.
For though the glory of this day be lost,   241
Afric and Greece have garrisons enough
To make me sovereign of the earth again.
  *Tamb.* Those walled garrisons will I subdue,
And write myself great lord of Africa.     245
So from the East unto the furthest West
Shall Tamburlaine extend his puissant arm.
The galleys and those pilling brigandines,
That yearly sail to the Venetian gulf,
And hover in the Straits for Christians' wrack,
Shall lie at anchor in the isle Asant,        251
Until the Persian fleet and men of war,
Sailing along the oriental sea,
Have fetch'd about the Indian continent,
Even from Persepolis to Mexico,            255

---

[180] **weeds:** attire    [188] S. D. **and stay:** The noise of battle behind stage ceases.    [211] S. D. **he:** Tamburlaine    [213] **foil:** defeat ('soil' Qq.)    [248] **pilling:** pillaging    [251] **Asant:** Zante    [255] **to Mexico:** *i.e.,* across the Pacific

And thence unto the straits of Jubalter;
Where they shall meet and join their force in
    one,
Keeping in awe the bay of Portingale,
And all the ocean by the British shore;
And by this means I 'll win the world at last. 260
    *Baj.*   Yet set a ransom on me, Tamburlaine.
    *Tamb.*   What, think'st thou Tamburlaine es-
    teems thy gold?
I 'll make the kings of India, ere I die,
Offer their mines to sue for peace to me,
And dig for treasure to appease my wrath. 265
Come, bind them both, and one lead in the
    Turk;
The Turkess let my love's maid lead away.
                       *They bind them.*
    *Baj.*   Ah, villains! — dare ye touch my sacred
    arms?
O Mahomet! — O sleepy Mahomet!
    *Zab.*   O cursed Mahomet, that makest us
    thus                             270
The slaves to Scythians rude and barbarous!
    *Tamb.*   Come, bring them in; and for this
    happy conquest,
Triumph and solemnise a martial feast. *Exeunt.*

          *Finis Actus Tertii*

### Actus 4. Scæna 1.

*Soldan of Egypt, with three or four Lords,*
*Capolin [and a Messenger]*

    *Sold.*   Awake, ye men of Memphis! Hear
    the clang
Of Scythian trumpets! Hear the basilisks
That, roaring, shake Damascus' turrets down!
The rogue of Volga holds Zenocrate,
The Soldan's daughter, for his concubine,   5
And with a troop of thieves and vagabonds,
Hath spread his colours to our high disgrace,
While you, faint-hearted, base Egyptians,
Lie slumbering on the flowery banks of Nile,
As crocodiles that unaffrighted rest     10
While thund'ring cannons rattle on their skins.
    *Mess.*   Nay, mighty Soldan, did your great-
    ness see
The frowning looks of fiery Tamburlaine,
That with his terror and imperious eyes
Commands the hearts of his associates,   15
It might amaze your royal majesty.
    *Sold.*   Villain, I tell thee, were that Tambur-
    laine
As monstrous as Gorgon, prince of hell,
The Soldan would not start a foot from him.
But speak, what power hath he?
    *Mess.*                  Mighty lord,   20
Three hundred thousand men in armour clad,

Upon their prancing steeds disdainfully
With wanton paces trampling on the ground:
Five hundred thousand footmen threat'ning
    shot,
Shaking their swords, their spears, and iron
    bills,
Environing their standard round, that stood 26
As bristle-pointed as a thorny wood:
Their warlike engines and munition
Exceed the forces of their martial men.
    *Sold.*   Nay, could their numbers countervail
    the stars,                         30
Or ever-drizzling drops of April showers,
Or wither'd leaves that Autumn shaketh down
Yet would the Soldan by his conquering power,
So scatter and consume them in his rage,
That not a man should live to rue their fall. 35
    *Capo.*   So might your highness, had you time
    to sort
Your fighting men, and raise your royal host.
But Tamburlaine, by expedition,
Advantage takes of your unreadiness.
    *Sold.*   Let him take all th' advantages he
    can.                              40
Were all the world conspir'd to fight for him,
Nay, were he devil, as he is no man,
Yet in revenge of fair Zenocrate,
Whom he detaineth in despite of us,
This arm should send him down to Erebus,   45
To shroud his shame in darkness of the night.
    *Mess.*   Pleaseth your mightiness to under-
    stand,
His resolution far exceedeth all.
The first day when he pitcheth down his tents,
White is their hue, and on his silver crest,   50
A snowy feather spangled white he bears,
To signify the mildness of his mind,
That, satiate with spoil, refuseth blood.
But when Aurora mounts the second time
As red as scarlet is his furniture;       55
Then must his kindled wrath be quench'd with
    blood,
Not sparing any that can manage arms.
But if these threats move not submission,
Black are his colours, black pavilion;
His spear, his shield, his horse, his armour,
    plumes,                        60
And jetty feathers menace death and hell!
Without respect of sex, degree, or age,
He razeth all his foes with fire and sword.
    *Sold.*   Merciless villain! Peasant, ignorant
Of lawful arms or martial discipline!     65
Pillage and murder are his usual trades;
The slave usurps the glorious name of war.
See, Capolin, the fair Arabian king,
That hath been disappointed by this slave
Of my fair daughter and his princely love,   70

---

  256 **Jubalter:** Gibraltar     258 **Portingale:** Biscay     2 **basilisks:** large cannon     18 **Gorgon:**
Demogorgon    30 **countervail:** equal

May have fresh warning to go war with us,
And be reveng'd for her disparagement.

*[Exeunt.]*

## Actus 4. Scæna 2.

*Tamburlaine, Techelles, Theridamas, Usumca-
sane, Zenocrate, Anippe, two Moors drawing
Bajazeth in his cage, and his wife [Zabina]
following him*

*Tamb.* Bring out my footstool.

*They take him out of the cage.*

*Baj.* Ye holy priests of heavenly Mahomet,
That, sacrificing, slice and cut your flesh,
Staining his altars with your purple blood!
Make Heaven to frown and every fixed star 5
To suck up poison from the moorish fens,
And pour it in this glorious tyrant's throat.

*Tamb.* The chiefest God, first mover of that
sphere,
Enchas'd with thousands ever-shining lamps,
Will sooner burn the glorious frame of
Heaven, 10
Than it should so conspire my overthrow.
But, villain! thou that wishest this to me,
Fall prostrate on the low disdainful earth,
And be the footstool of great Tamburlaine,
That I may rise into my royal throne. 15

*Baj.* First shalt thou rip my bowels with thy
sword,
And sacrifice my heart to death and hell,
Before I yield to such a slavery.

*Tamb.* Base villain, vassal, slave to Tambur-
laine!
Unworthy to embrace or touch the ground, 20
That bears the honour of my royal weight;
Stoop, villain, stoop! — Stoop! for so he bids
That may command thee piecemeal to be torn,
Or scatter'd like the lofty cedar trees
Struck with the voice of thund'ring Jupiter. 25

*Baj.* Then, as I look down to the damned
fiends,
Fiends, look on me! and thou, dread god of hell,
With ebon sceptre strike this hateful earth,
And make it swallow both of us at once!

*He gets up upon him to his chair.*

*Tamb.* Now clear the triple region of the
air, 30
And let the majesty of Heaven behold
Their scourge and terror tread on emperors.
Smile stars, that reign'd at my nativity,
And dim the brightness of their neighbour
lamps!
Disdain to borrow light of Cynthia! 35
For I, the chiefest lamp of all the earth,
First rising in the East with mild aspect,
But fixed now in the meridian line,

Will send up fire to your turning spheres,
And cause the sun to borrow light of you. 40
My sword struck fire from his coat of steel,
Even in Bithynia, when I took this Turk;
As when a fiery exhalation,
Wrapp'd in the bowels of a freezing cloud,
Fighting for passage, makes the welkin crack,
And casts a flash of lightning to the earth. 46
But ere I march to wealthy Persia,
Or leave Damascus and th' Egyptian fields,
As was the fame of Clymen's brain-sick son,
That almost brent the axle-tree of Heaven, 50
So shall our swords, our lances, and our shot
Fill all the air with fiery meteors:
Then, when the sky shall wax as red as blood,
It shall be said I made it red myself,
To make me think of naught but blood and
war.

*Zab.* Unworthy king, that by thy cruelty 56
Unlawfully usurp'st the Persian seat,
Dar'st thou, that never saw an emperor
Before thou met my husband in the field,
Being thy captive, thus abuse his state? 60
Keeping his kingly body in a cage,
That roofs of gold and sun-bright palaces
Should have prepar'd to entertain his grace?
And treading him beneath thy loathsome feet,
Whose feet the kings of Africa have kiss'd? 65

*Tech.* You must devise some torment worse,
my lord,
To make these captives rein their lavish tongues.

*Tamb.* Zenocrate, look better to your slave.

*Zeno.* She is my handmaid's slave, and she
shall look
That these abuses flow not from her tongue: 70
Chide her, Anippe.

*Anip.* Let these be warnings for you then,
my slave,
How you abuse the person of the king;
Or else I swear to have you whipp'd, stark-
nak'd.

*Baj.* Great Tamburlaine, great in my over-
throw, 75
Ambitious pride shall make thee fall as low,
For treading on the back of Bajazeth,
That should be horsed on four mighty kings.

*Tamb.* Thy names and titles and thy digni-
ties
Are fled from Bajazeth and remain with me, 80
That will maintain 't against a world of kings.
Put him in again.

*[They put him into the cage.]*

*Baj.* Is this a place for mighty Bajazeth?
Confusion light on him that helps thee thus!

*Tamb.* There, whiles he lives, shall Bajazeth
be kept; 85
And, where I go, be thus in triumph drawn.

---

⁷ **glorious:** vaunting ⁴⁵ **welkin:** sky ⁴⁹ **Clymen's:** Clymene, mother of Phaethon ⁵⁰ **brent:**
burned **axle-tree:** mechanism on which the heavens turned

And thou, his wife, shalt feed him with the scraps
My servitors shall bring thee from my board;
For he that gives him other food than this
Shall sit by him and starve to death himself. 90
This is my mind and I will have it so.
Not all the kings and emperors of the earth,
If they would lay their crowns before my feet,
Shall ransom him or take him from his cage.
The ages that shall talk of Tamburlaine, 95
Even from this day to Plato's wondrous year,
Shall talk how I have handled Bajazeth.
These Moors, that drew him from Bithynia
To fair Damascus, where we now remain,
Shall lead him with us wheresoe'er we go. 100
Techelles, and my loving followers,
Now may we see Damascus' lofty towers,
Like to the shadows of Pyramides,
That with their beauties grac'd the Memphian fields.
The golden stature of their feather'd bird 105
That spreads her wings upon the city walls
Shall not defend it from our battering shot.
The townsmen mask in silk and cloth of gold,
And every house is as a treasury:
The men, the treasure, and the town is ours.
    *Ther.*  Your tents of white now pitch'd before the gates, 111
And gentle flags of amity display'd,
I doubt not but the governor will yield,
Offering Damascus to your majesty.
    *Tamb.*  So shall he have his life and all the rest. 115
But if he stay until the bloody flag
Be once advanc'd on my vermilion tent.
He dies, and those that kept us out so long.
And when they see me march in black array,
With mournful streamers hanging down their heads, 120
Were in that city all the world contain'd,
Not one should scape, but perish by our swords.
    *Zeno.*  Yet would you have some pity for my sake,
Because it is my country's, and my father's.
    *Tamb.*  Not for the world, Zenocrate, if I have sworn. 125
Come; bring in the Turk.      *Exeunt.*

### Actus 4. Scæna 3.

*Soldan, [the King of] Arabia, Capolin,*
*with streaming colours, and Soldiers*

    *Sold.*  Methinks we march as Meleager did,
Environed with brave Argolian knights,
To chase the savage Calydonian boar,
Or Cephalus with lusty Theban youths

Against the wolf that angry Themis sent 5
To waste and spoil the sweet Aonian fields.
A monster of five hundred thousand heads,
Compact of rapine, piracy, and spoil,
The scum of men, the hate and scourge of God,
Raves in Egyptia and annoyeth us. 10
My lord, it is the bloody Tamburlaine,
A sturdy felon and a base-bred thief,
By murder raised to the Persian crown,
That dares control us in our territories.
To tame the pride of this presumptuous beast, 15
Join your Arabians with the Soldan's power:
Let us unite our royal bands in one,
And hasten to remove Damascus' siege.
It is a blemish to the majesty
And high estate of mighty emperors, 20
That such a base usurping vagabond
Should brave a king, or wear a princely crown.
    *Arab.*  Renowmed Soldan, have ye lately heard
The overthrow of mighty Bajazeth
About the confines of Bithynia? 25
The slavery wherewith he persecutes
The noble Turk and his great emperess?
    *Sold.*  I have, and sorrow for his bad success;
But, noble lord of great Arabia,
Be so persuaded that the Soldan is 30
No more dismay'd with tidings of his fall
Than in the haven when the pilot stands
And views a stranger's ship rent in the winds,
And shivered against a craggy rock.
Yet in compassion of his wretched state, 35
A sacred vow to Heaven and him I make,
Confirming it with Ibis' holy name,
That Tamburlaine shall rue the day, the hour,
Wherein he wrought such ignominious wrong
Unto the hallow'd person of a prince, 40
Or kept the fair Zenocrate so long
As concubine, I fear, to feed his lust.
    *Arab.*  Let grief and fury hasten on revenge;
Let Tamburlaine for his offences feel
Such plagues as Heaven and we can pour on him. 45
I long to break my spear upon his crest,
And prove the weight of his victorious arm;
For Fame, I fear, hath been too prodigal
In sounding through the world his partial praise.
    *Sold.*  Capolin, hast thou survey'd our powers? 50
    *Capol.*  Great Emperors of Egypt and Arabia,
The number of your hosts united is
A hundred and fifty thousand horse;
Two hundred thousand foot, brave men-at-arms,
Courageous, and full of hardiness. 55
As frolic as the hunters in the chase

---

⁹⁶ **wondrous year:** when the irregularities due to planetary motion are equalized    ¹⁰⁵ **stature:** statue    **bird:** the divine Ibis    ²⁵ **confines:** borders    ²⁸ **his:** Bajazeth's    **success:** outcome, fate    ³⁷ **Ibis':** bird worshiped in Egypt    ⁴⁷ **prove:** test

Of savage beasts amid the desert woods.

*Àrab.* My mind presageth fortunate success;
And, Tamburlaine, my spirit doth foresee
The utter ruin of thy men and thee.        60

*Sold.* Then rear your standards; let your
sounding drums
Direct our soldiers to Damascus' walls.
Now, Tamburlaine, the mighty Soldan comes,
And leads with him the great Arabian king,
To dim thy baseness and obscurity,        65
Famous for nothing but for theft and spoil;
To raze and scatter thy inglorious crew
Of Scythians and slavish Persians.    *Exeunt.*

## Actus 4.  Scæna 4.

*The Banquet; and to it cometh Tamburlaine, all
in scarlet, [Zenocrate,] Theridamas, Techelles, Usumcasane, the Turk [Bajazeth
in his cage, Zabina,] with others*

*Tamb.* Now hang our bloody colours by Da-
mascus,
Reflexing hues of blood upon their heads,
While they walk quivering on their city walls,
Half dead for fear before they feel my wrath:
Then let us freely banquet and carouse        5
Full bowls of wine unto the god of war,
That means to fill your helmets full of gold,
And make Damascus spoils as rich to you
As was to Jason Colchos' golden fleece. —
And now, Bajazeth, hast thou any stomach?  10

*Baj.* Ay, such a stomach, cruel Tamburlaine,
as I could willingly feed upon thy blood-raw
heart.

*Tamb.* Nay, thine own is easier to come by;
pluck out that, and 't will serve thee and thy [15
wife. Well, Zenocrate, Techelles, and the rest,
fall to your victuals.

*Baj.* Fall to, and never may your meat
digest!
Ye Furies, that can mask invisible,
Dive to the bottom of Avernus' pool,        20
And in your hands bring hellish poison up
And squeeze it in the cup of Tamburlaine!
Or, winged snakes of Lerna, cast your stings,
And leave your venoms in this tyrant's dish!

*Zab.* And may this banquet prove as omi-
nous        25
As Progne's to th' adulterous Thracian king,
That fed upon the substance of his child.

*Zeno.* My lord, how can you suffer these
Outrageous curses by these slaves of yours?

*Tamb.* To let them see, divine Zenocrate,  30
I glory in the curses of my foes,
Having the power from the imperial Heaven
To turn them all upon their proper heads.

*Tech.* I pray you give them leave, madam;
this speech is a goodly refreshing to them.  35

*Ther.* But if his highness would let them be
fed, it would do them more good.

*Tamb.* Sirrah, why fall you not to?  Are you
so daintily brought up, you cannot eat your own
flesh?        40

*Baj.* First, legions of devils shall tear thee in
pieces.

*Usum.* Villain, knowest thou to whom thou
speakest?

*Tamb.* O, let him alone. Here; eat, sir; [45
take it from my sword's point, or I 'll thrust it to
thy heart.        *He takes it and stamps upon it.*

*Ther.* He stamps it under his feet, my lord.

*Tamb.* Take it up, villain, and eat it; or I
will make thee slice the brawns of thy arms [50
into carbonadoes and eat them.

*Usum.* Nay, 't were better he kill'd his
wife, and then she shall be sure not to be
starv'd, and he be provided for a month's
victual beforehand.        55

*Tamb.* Here is my dagger: despatch her
while she is fat; for if she live but a while
longer, she will fall into a consumption with fretting, and then she will not be worth the eating.

*Ther.* Dost thou think that Mahomet will [60
suffer this?

*Tech.* 'T is like he will when he cannot let
it.

*Tamb.* Go to; fall to your meat. — What,
not a bit! Belike he hath not been watered [65
today; give him some drink.
*They give him water to drink, and
he flings it on the ground.*

*Tamb.* Fast, and welcome, sir, while hunger make you eat. How now, Zenocrate, doth
not the Turk and his wife make a goodly show
at a banquet?        70

*Zeno.* Yes, my lord.

*Ther.* Methinks, 't is a great deal better
than a consort of music.

*Tamb.* Yet music would do well to cheer up
Zenocrate. Pray thee, tell, why art thou so [75
sad? If thou wilt have a song, the Turk shall
strain his voice. But why is it?

*Zeno.* My lord, to see my father's town be-
sieg'd,
The country wasted where myself was born,
How can it but afflict my very soul?        80
If any love remain in you, my lord,
Or if my love unto your majesty
May merit favour at your highness' hands,
Then raise your siege from fair Damascus' walls,
And with my father take a friendly truce.  85

*Tamb.* Zenocrate, were Egypt Jove's own
land,
Yet would I with my sword make Jove to
stoop.
I will confute those blind geographers

---

⁵¹ **carbonadoes:** steaks    ⁶² **let:** prevent    ⁶⁷ **while:** till    ⁷³ **consort:** band

That make a triple region in the world,
Excluding regions which I mean to trace, 90
And with this pen reduce them to a map,
Calling the provinces, cities, and towns,
After my name and thine, Zenocrate.
Here at Damascus will I make the point
That shall begin the perpendicular; 95
And would'st thou have me buy thy father's
love
With such a loss? — Tell me, Zenocrate.

*Zeno.* Honour still wait on happy Tamburlaine!
Yet give me leave to plead for him, my lord.

*Tamb.* Content thyself: his person shall be
safe, 100
And all the friends of fair Zenocrate,
If with their lives they will be pleas'd to yield,
Or may be forc'd to make me Emperor;
For Egypt and Arabia must be mine. —
Feed, you slave! Thou may'st think thy- [105
self happy to be fed from my trencher.

*Baj.* My empty stomach, full of idle heat,
Draws bloody humours from my feeble parts,
Preserving life by hasting cruel death.
My veins are pale, my sinews hard and dry, 110
My joints benumb'd: unless I eat, I die.

*Zab.* Eat, Bajazeth. Let us live in spite of
them, looking some happy power will pity and
enlarge us.

*Tamb.* Here, Turk; wilt thou have a [115
clean trencher?

*Baj.* Ay, tyrant, and more meat.

*Tamb.* Soft, sir; you must be dieted; too
much eating will make you surfeit.

*Ther.* So it would, my lord, specially [120
having so small a walk and so little exercise.

*Enter a second course, of crowns*

*Tamb.* Theridamas, Techelles, and Casane,
here are the cates you desire to finger, are they
not?

*Ther.* Ay, my lord; but none save kings
must feed with these. 126

*Tech.* 'T is enough for us to see them, and
for Tamburlaine only to enjoy them.

*Tamb.* Well; here is now to the Soldan of
Egypt, the King of Arabia, and the Governor [130
of Damascus. Now take these three crowns, and
pledge me, my contributory kings. I crown you
here, Theridamas, King of Argier; Techelles,
King of Fez; and Usumcasane, King of Moroccus. How say you to this, Turk? These are [135
not your contributory kings.

*Baj.* Nor shall they long be thine, I warrant
them.

*Tamb.* Kings of Argier, Moroccus, and of
Fez,
You that have march'd with happy Tambur-
laine
As far as from the frozen plage of Heaven 140
Unto the watery morning's ruddy bower,
And thence by land unto the torrid zone:
Deserve these titles I endow you with
By valour and by magnanimity.
Your births shall be no blemish to your fame, 145
For virtue is the fount whence honour springs,
And they are worthy she investeth kings.

*Ther.* And since your highness hath so well
vouchsaf'd,
If we deserve them not with higher meeds
Than erst our states and actions have retain'd,
Take them away again and make us slaves. 151

*Tamb.* Well said, Theridamas; when holy
fates
Shall 'stablish me in strong Egyptia,
We mean to travel to th' antartic pole,
Conquering the people underneath our feet, 155
And be renowm'd as never emperors were.
Zenocrate, I will not crown thee yet,
Until with greater honours I be grac'd.
[*Exeunt.*]

*Finis Actus quarti*

## Actus 5. Scæna 1.

*The Governor of Damascus, with three or four
Citizens, and four Virgins, with branches of
laurel in their hands*

*Gov.* Still doth this man, or rather god, of
war
Batter our walls and beat our turrets down;
And to resist with longer stubbornness
Or hope of rescue from the Soldan's power,
Were but to bring our wilful overthrow, 5
And make us desperate of our threat'ned lives.
We see his tents have now been altered
With terrors to the last and cruel'st hue.
His coal-black colours everywhere advanc'd
Threaten our city with a general spoil; 10
And if we should with common rites of arms
Offer our safeties to his clemency,
I fear the custom, proper to his sword, —
Which he observes as parcel of his fame,
Intending so to terrify the world, — 15
By any innovation or remorse
Will never be dispens'd with till our deaths.
Therefore, for these our harmless virgins' sakes,
Whose honours and whose lives rely on him,
Let us have hope that their unspotted prayers,

---

89 **triple:** consisting of Asia, Europe, Africa 91 **pen:** his sword 94–95 **point . . . perpen-**
**dicular:** probably the zero meridian, from which longitude is reckoned 113 **looking:** anticipating
123 **cates:** delicacies 140 **plage:** region ('place' Qq.) 141 *I.e.,* to the farthest east 144 **valour:**
('value' Qq.) 147 **they:** those who 14 **parcel:** part 16 **innovation:** alteration

Their blubber'd cheeks, and hearty, humble
  moans,     21
Will melt his fury into some remorse,
And use us like a loving conqueror.
  *Virg.* If humble suits or imprecations,
(Utter'd with tears of wretchedness and blood 25
Shed from the heads and hearts of all our sex,
Some made your wives and some your children)
Might have entreated your obdurate breasts
To entertain some care of our securities
Whiles only danger beat upon our walls,   30
These more than dangerous warrants of our
  death
Had never been erected as they be,
Nor you depend on such weak helps as we.
  *Gov.* Well, lovely virgins, think our country's
  care,
Our love of honour, loath to be inthrall'd   35
To foreign powers and rough imperious yokes,
Would not with too much cowardice or fear,
(Before all hope of rescue were denied)
Submit yourselves and us to servitude.
Therefore in that your safeties and our own,   40
Your honours, liberties, and lives were weigh'd
In equal care and balance with our own,
Endure as we the malice of our stars,
The wrath of Tamburlaine, and power of wars;
Or be the means the overweighing heavens   45
Have kept to qualify these hot extremes,
And bring us pardon in your cheerful looks.
  *2 Virg.* Then here before the majesty of
  Heaven
And holy patrons of Egyptia,
With knees and hearts submissive we entreat   50
Grace to our words and pity to our looks,
That this device may prove propitious,
And through the eyes and ears of Tamburlaine
Convey events of mercy to his heart.
Grant that these signs of victory we yield   55
May bind the temples of his conquering head,
To hide the folded furrows of his brows,
And shadow his displeased countenance
With happy looks of ruth and lenity.
Leave us, my lord, and loving countrymen;   60
What simple virgins may persuade, we will.
  *Gov.* Farewell, sweet virgins, on whose safe
  return
Depends our city, liberty, and lives.
               *Exeunt [all but the Virgins].*

### Actus 5. Scæna 2.

*Tamburlaine, Techelles, Theridamas, Usumca-*
*  sane, with others. Tamburlaine all in black*
*  and very melancholy*

  *Tamb.* What, are the turtles fray'd out of
  their nests?

Alas, poor fools! must you be first shall feel
The sworn destruction of Damascus?
They know my custom; could they not as well
Have sent ye out when first my milk-white flags,
Through which sweet Mercy threw her gentle
  beams,     6
Reflexing them on your disdainful eyes,
As now, when fury and incensed hate
Flings slaughtering terror from my coal-black
  tents,     9
And tells for truth submissions comes too late?
  *1 Virg.* Most happy King and Emperor of
  the earth,
Image of honour and nobility,
For whom the powers divine have made the
  world,
And on whose throne the holy Graces sit;
In whose sweet person is compris'd the sum   15
Of Nature's skill and heavenly majesty;
Pity our plights! O pity poor Damascus!
Pity old age, within whose silver hairs
Honour and reverence evermore have reign'd!
Pity the marriage bed, where many a lord,   20
In prime and glory of his loving joy,
Embraceth now with tears of ruth and blood
The jealous body of his fearful wife,
Whose cheeks and hearts, so punish'd with con-
  ceit
To think thy puissant, never-stayed arm   25
Will part their bodies, and prevent their souls
From heavens of comfort yet their age might
  bear,
Now wax all pale and withered to the death,
As well for grief our ruthless governor
Have thus refus'd the mercy of thy hand,   30
(Whose sceptre angels kiss and furies dread,)
As for their liberties, their loves, or lives.
O then for these, and such as we ourselves,
For us, for infants, and for all our bloods,
That never nourish'd thought against thy rule,
Pity, O pity, sacred Emperor,   36
The prostrate service of this wretched town,
And take in sign thereof this gilded wreath;
Whereto each man of rule hath given his hand,
And wish'd, as worthy subjects, happy means
To be investers of thy royal brows   41
Even with the true Egyptian diadem!
  *Tamb.* Virgins, in vain ye labour to prevent
That which mine honour swears shall be per-
  form'd.
Behold my sword! what see you at the point?
  *Virg.* Nothing but fear and fatal steel,
  my lord.     46
  *Tamb.* Your fearful minds are thick and
  misty then;
For there sits Death, there sits imperious
  Death,

---

²⁴ **imprecations:** entreaties    ⁵⁴ **events:** results      ¹ **turtles fray'd:** doves scared    ⁵ **flags:**
(Supply "appeared.")    ²⁴ **conceit:** foreboding

Keeping his circuit by the slicing edge.
But I am pleas'd you shall not see him there;
He now is seated on my horsemen's spears, 51
And on their points his fleshless body feeds.
Techelles, straight go charge a few of them
To charge these dames, and show my servant,
    Death,
Sitting in scarlet on their armed spears.    55
    *Omnes.*  O pity us!
    *Tamb.*  Away with them, I say, and show
        them Death.        *They take them away.*
I will not spare these proud Egyptians,
Nor change my martial observations
For all the wealth of Gihon's golden waves, 60
Or for the love of Venus, would she leave
The angry god of arms and lie with me.
They have refus'd the offer of their lives,
And know my customs are as peremptory
As wrathful planets, death, or destiny.    65

                *Enter Techelles*

What, have your horsemen shown the virgins
    Death?
    *Tech.*  They have, my lord, and on Damas-
        cus' walls
Have hoisted up their slaughter'd carcases.
    *Tamb.*  A sight as baneful to their souls, I
        think,
As are Thessalian drugs or mithridate:    70
But go, my lords, put the rest to the sword.
        *Exeunt [all except Tamburlaine].*
Ah, fair Zenocrate! divine Zenocrate!
Fair is too foul an epithet for thee,
That in thy passion for thy country's love,
And fear to see thy kingly father's harm,    75
With hair dishevell'd wip'st thy watery cheeks;
And, like to Flora in her morning's pride
Shaking her silver tresses in the air,
Rain'st on the earth resolved pearl in showers,
And sprinklest sapphires on thy shining face, 80
Where Beauty, mother to the Muses, sits
And comments volumes with her ivory pen,
Taking instructions from thy flowing eyes;
Eyes when that Ebena steps to Heaven,
In silence of thy solemn evening's walk,    85
Making the mantle of the richest night,
The moon, the planets, and the meteors, light.
There angels in their crystal armours fight
A doubtful battle with my tempted thoughts
For Egypt's freedom, and the Soldan's life; 90
His life that so consumes Zenocrate,
Whose sorrows lay more siege unto my soul,
Than all my army to Damascus' walls:
And neither Persia's sovereign, nor the Turk

Troubled my senses with conceit of foil    95
So much by much as doth Zenocrate.
What is beauty, saith my sufferings, then?
If all the pens that ever poets held
Had fed the feeling of their masters' thoughts,
And every sweetness that inspir'd their hearts,
Their minds, and muses on admired themes; 101
If all the heavenly quintessence they still
From their immortal flowers of poesy,
Wherein, as in a mirror, we perceive
The highest reaches of a human wit:    105
If these had made one poem's period,
And all combin'd in beauty's worthiness,
Yet should there hover in their restless heads
One thought, one grace, one wonder, at the
    least,
Which into words no virtue can digest.    110
But how unseemly is it for my sex,
My discipline of arms and chivalry,
My nature, and the terror of my name,
To harbour thoughts effeminate and faint!
Save only that in beauty's just applause,    115
With whose instinct the soul of man is
    touch'd; —
And every warrior that is rapt with love
Of fame, of valour, and of victory,
Must needs have beauty beat on his conceits:
I thus conceiving and subduing both    120
That which hath stoop'd the tempest of the
    gods,
Even from the fiery-spangled veil of Heaven,
To feel the lovely warmth of shepherds' flames,
And mask in cottages of strowed weeds,
Shall give the world to note, for all my birth,
That virtue solely is the sum of glory,    126
And fashions men with true nobility. —
Who 's within there?

            *Enter two or three [Attendants]*

Hath Bajazeth been fed to-day?
    *Atten.*  Ay, my lord.    130
    *Tamb.*  Bring him forth; and let us know if
the town be ransack'd.    *[Exeunt Attendants.]*

        *Enter Techelles, Theridamas, Usumcasane,
                and others*

    *Tech.*  The town is ours, my lord, and fresh
        supply
Of conquest and of spoil is offer'd us.
    *Tamb.*  That 's well, Techelles; what 's the
        news?    135
    *Tech.*  The Soldan and the Arabian king to-
        gether,
March on us with such eager violence

---

⁴⁹ **circuit:** sphere of action    ⁵⁶ **Omnes:** all the virgins    ⁵⁹ **observations:** observances    ⁶⁰ **Gihon:**
one of the four rivers of Paradise (*Genesis* ii. 13)    ⁷⁰ **mithridate:** compound of poisons    ⁷⁹ **resolved
pearl:** *i.e.,* tears    ⁸⁴ **Ebena:** W. Warner (*Pan his Syrinx*, 1584, F 3ᵛ) speaks of sleepers as sacrificing
to "the god of Ebona," a "drowsy deity."    ⁹⁴ **Persia's:** ('Perseans' Qq.)    ¹⁰² **still:** distill    ¹¹⁰ **virtue:**
mental energy    ¹²¹ **tempest . . . gods:** Apollo?    ¹²⁴ **mask:** live disguised ('martch' Qq.)

As if there were no way but one with us.
*Tamb.* No more there is not, I warrant thee,
    Techelles.
            *They bring in the Turk [and Zabina].*
*Ther.* We know the victory is ours, my lord;
But let us save the reverend Soldan's life,   141
For fair Zenocrate that so laments his state.
*Tamb.* That will we chiefly see unto, Theri-
    damas,
For sweet Zenocrate, whose worthiness
Deserves a conquest over every heart.   145
And now, my footstool, if I lose the field,
You hope of liberty and restitution?
Here let him stay, my masters, from the tents,
Till we have made us ready for the field.
Pray for us, Bajazeth; we are going.   150
        *Exeunt [all except Bajazeth and Zabina].*
*Baj.* Go, never to return with victory!
Millions of men encompass thee about,
And gore thy body with as many wounds!
Sharp, forked arrows light upon thy horse!
Furies from the black Cocytus lake   155
Break up the earth, and with their firebrands
Enforce thee run upon the baneful pikes!
Volleys of shot pierce through thy charmed
    skin,
And every bullet dipp'd in poison'd drugs!
Or roaring cannons sever all thy joints,   160
Making thee mount as high as eagles soar!
*Zab.* Let all the swords and lances in the
    field
Stick in his breast as in their proper rooms!
At every pore let blood come dropping forth,
That ling'ring pains may massacre his heart, 165
And madness send his damned soul to hell!
*Baj.* Ah, fair Zabina! we may curse his
    power,
The heavens may frown, the earth for anger
    quake,
But such a star hath influence in his sword, 169
As rules the skies and countermands the gods
More than Cimmerian Styx or Destiny;
And then shall we in this detested guise, —
With shame, with hunger, and with horror
    aye
Griping our bowels with retorqued thoughts, —
And have no hope to end our ecstasies.   175
*Zab.* Then is there left no Mahomet, no God,
No Fiend, no Fortune, nor no hope of end
To our infamous, monstrous slaveries?
Gape, earth, and let the fiends infernal view
A hell as hopeless and as full of fear   180
As are the blasted banks of Erebus,
Where shaking ghosts with ever-howling groans
Hover about the ugly ferryman,
To get a passage to Elysium!

Why should we live? O, wretches, beggars,
    slaves!   185
Why live we, Bajazeth, and build up nests
So high within the region of the air
By living long in this oppression,
That all the world will see and laugh to scorn
The former triumphs of our mightiness   190
In this obscure infernal servitude?
*Baj.* O life, more loathsome to my vexed
    thoughts
Than noisome parbreak of the Stygian snakes,
Which fills the nooks of hell with standing air,
Infecting all the ghosts with cureless griefs! 195
O dreary engines of my loathed sight,
That sees my crown, my honour, and my name
Thrust under yoke and thraldom of a thief,
Why feed ye still on day's accursed beams
And sink not quite into my tortur'd soul?   200
You see my wife, my queen and emperess,
Brought up and propped by the hand of fame,
Queen of fifteen contributory queens,
Now thrown to rooms of black abjection,
Smear'd with blots of basest drudgery,   205
And villeiness to shame, disdain, and misery.
Accursed Bajazeth, whose words of ruth
(That would with pity cheer Zabina's heart,
And make our souls resolve in ceaseless tears)
Sharp hunger bites upon, and gripes the root 210
From whence the issues of my thoughts do
    break.
O poor Zabina! O my queen! my queen!
Fetch me some water for my burning breast,
To cool and comfort me with longer date,
That in the short'ned sequel of my life   215
I may pour forth my soul into thine arms
With words of love, whose moaning intercourse
Hath hitherto been stay'd with wrath and hate
Of our expressless bann'd inflictions.
*Zab.* Sweet Bajazeth, I will prolong thy life,
As long as any blood or spark of breath   221
Can quench or cool the torments of my grief.
                            *She goes out.*
*Baj.* Now, Bajazeth, abridge thy baneful
    days,
And beat thy brains out of thy conquer'd head,
Since other means are all forbidden me   225
That may be ministers of my decay.
O, highest lamp of ever-living Jove,
Accursed day! infected with my griefs,
Hide now thy stained face in endless night,
And shut the windows of the lightsome
    heavens!   230
Let ugly Darkness with her rusty coach,
Engirt with tempests, wrapp'd in pitchy clouds,
Smother the earth with never-fading mists,
And let her horses from their nostrils breathe

---

¹⁵⁵ **Cocytus:** river in hell   ¹⁷² **shall we:** shall we live   ¹⁷⁴ **retorqued:** foiled   ¹⁸⁶⁻¹⁸⁷ **build . . .
air:** make ourselves so conspicuous   ¹⁹³ **parbreak:** vomit   ¹⁹⁴ **standing:** stagnant   ²⁰⁶ **villeiness:** slave   ²⁰⁹ **resolve:** melt   ²¹⁹ **bann'd:** cursed

Rebellious winds and dreadful thunder-claps,
That in this terror Tamburlaine may live, 236
And my pin'd soul, resolv'd in liquid air,
May still excruciate his tormented thoughts!
Then let the stony dart of senseless cold
Pierce through the centre of my wither'd heart,
And make a passage for my loathed life! 241

*He brains himself against the cage.*

*Enter Zabina*

*Zab.* What do mine eyes behold? My husband dead!
His skull all riven in twain! His brains dash'd
out!
The brains of Bajazeth, my lord and sovereign!
O Bajazeth, my husband and my lord! 245
O Bajazeth! O Turk! O Emperor!
Give him his liquor? Not I. Bring milk and
fire, and my blood I bring him again. — Tear me
in pieces! Give me the sword with a ball of wild-
fire upon it. — Down with him! Down with [250
him! — Go to my child! Away! Away! Away!
Ah, save that infant! save him, save him! —
I, even I, speak to her. — The sun was down;
streamers white, red, black, here, here, here!
— Fling the meat in his face — Tamburlaine,
Tamburlaine! — Let the soldiers be buried. [256
— Hell! Death! Tamburlaine! Hell! — Make
ready my coach, my chair, my jewels. I come!
I come! I come!

*She runs against the cage and brains herself.*

*[Enter] Zenocrate with Anippe*

*Zeno.* Wretched Zenocrate! that liv'st to see
Damascus' walls dy'd with Egyptian blood, 261
Thy father's subjects and thy countrymen;
Thy streets strow'd with dissevered joints of
men
And wounded bodies gasping yet for life:
But most accurst, to see the sun-bright troop 265
Of heavenly virgins and unspotted maids
(Whose looks might make the angry god of
arms
To break his sword and mildly treat of love)
On horsemen's lances to be hoisted up
And guiltlessly endure a cruel death: 270
For every fell and stout Tartarian steed,
That stamp'd on others with their thundering
hoofs,
When all their riders charg'd their quivering
spears,
Began to check the ground and rein themselves,
Gazing upon the beauty of their looks. 275
Ah Tamburlaine! wert thou the cause of this,
That term'st Zenocrate thy dearest love?
Whose lives were dearer to Zenocrate
Than her own life, or aught save thine own love.
But see another bloody spectacle! 280
Ah, wretched eyes, the enemies of my heart,

How are ye glutted with these grievous objects,
And tell my soul more tales of bleeding ruth!
See, see, Anippe, if they breathe or no.
*Anippe.* No breath, nor sense, nor motion
in them both. 285
Ah, madam! this their slavery hath enforc'd,
And ruthless cruelty of Tamburlaine.
*Zeno.* Earth, cast up fountains from thy en-
trails,
And wet thy cheeks for their untimely deaths!
Shake with their weight in sign of fear and
grief! 290
Blush, Heaven, that gave them honour at their
birth
And let them die a death so barbarous!
Those that are proud of fickle empery
And place their chiefest good in earthly pomp,
Behold the Turk and his great Emperess! 295
Ah, Tamburlaine! my love! sweet Tambur-
laine!
That fight'st for sceptres and for slippery
crowns,
Behold the Turk and his great Emperess!
Thou, that in conduct of thy happy stars
Sleep'st every night with conquest on thy
brows, 300
And yet would'st shun the wavering turns of
war,
In fear and feeling of the like distress
Behold the Turk and his great Emperess!
Ah, mighty Jove and holy Mahomet,
Pardon my love! — O, pardon his contempt 305
Of earthly fortune and respect of pity,
And let not conquest, ruthlessly pursu'd,
Be equally against his life incens'd
In this great Turk and hapless Emperess!
And pardon me that was not mov'd with ruth
To see them live so long in misery! 311
Ah, what may chance to thee, Zenocrate?
*Anippe.* Madam, content yourself, and be
resolv'd.
Your love hath Fortune so at his command,
That she shall stay and turn her wheel no more,
As long as life maintains his mighty arm 316
That fights for honour to adorn your head.

*Enter [Philemus,] a Messenger*

*Zeno.* What other heavy news now brings
Philemus?
*Phil.* Madam, your father, and th' Arabian
king,
The first affecter of your excellence, 320
Comes now, as Turnus 'gainst Æneas did,
Armed with lance into the Egyptian fields,
Ready for battle 'gainst my lord, the king.
*Zeno.* Now shame and duty, love and fear,
presents
A thousand sorrows to my martyr'd soul. 325

283 **And**: and yet

Whom should I wish the fatal victory,
When my poor pleasures are divided thus
And rack'd by duty from my cursed heart?
My father and my first-betrothed love
Must fight against my life and present love;  330
Wherein the change I use condemns my faith,
And makes my deeds infamous through the
world.
But as the gods, to end the Troyans' toil,
Prevented Turnus of Lavinia
And fatally enrich'd Æneas' love,  335
So, for a final issue to my griefs,
To pacify my country and my love
Must Tamburlaine by their resistless powers,
With virtue of a gentle victory,
Conclude a league of honour to my hope;  340
Then, as the Powers divine have pre-ordain'd,
With happy safety of my father's life
Send like defence of fair Arabia.
    *They sound to the battle [within]: and Tam-
    burlaine enjoys the victory. After, [the
    King of] Arabia enters wounded.*
    *Arab.*  What cursed power guides the mur-
        thering hands
Of this infamous tyrant's soldiers,  345
That no escape may save their enemies,
Nor fortune keep themselves from victory?
Lie down, Arabia, wounded to the death,
And let Zenocrate's fair eyes behold
That, as for her thou bear'st these wretched
    arms,  350
Even so for her thou diest in these arms,
Leaving thy blood for witness of thy love.
    *Zeno.*  Too dear a witness for such love, my
        lord.
Behold Zenocrate! the cursed object,
Whose fortunes never mastered her griefs;  355
Behold her wounded, in conceit, for thee,
As much as thy fair body is for me.
    *Arab.*  Then shall I die with full contented
        heart,
Having beheld divine Zenocrate,
Whose sight with joy would take away my
    life —  360
As now it bringeth sweetness to my wound —
If I had not been wounded as I am.
Ah! that the deadly pangs I suffer now
Would lend an hour's license to my tongue,
To make discourse of some sweet accidents  365
Have chanc'd thy merits in this worthless bond-
    age;
And that I might be privy to the state
Of thy deserv'd contentment, and thy love.
But, making now a virtue of thy sight
To drive all sorrow from my fainting soul,  370
Since death denies me further cause of joy,
Depriv'd of care, my heart with comfort dies,
Since thy desired hand shall close mine eyes.
                              [*He dies.*]

*Enter Tamburlaine, leading the Soidan, Tech-
elles, Theridamas, Usumcasane, with others*

    *Tamb.*  Come, happy father of Zenocrate,
A title higher than thy Soldan's name;  375
Though my right hand have thus enthralled
    thee,
Thy princely daughter here shall set thee free;
She that hath calm'd the fury of my sword,
Which had ere this been bath'd in streams of
    blood
As vast and deep as Euphrates or Nile.  380
    *Zeno.*  O sight thrice welcome to my joyful
        soul,
To see the king, my father, issue safe
From dangerous battle of my conquering love!
    *Sold.*  Well met, my only dear Zenocrate,  384
Though with the loss of Egypt and my crown.
    *Tamb.*  'T was I, my lord, that gat the vic-
        tory,
And therefore grieve not at your overthrow,
Since I shall render all into your hands,
And add more strength to your dominions
Than ever yet confirm'd th' Egyptian crown.
The god of war resigns his room to me,  391
Meaning to make me general of the world.
Jove, viewing me in arms, looks pale and wan,
Fearing my power should pull him from his
    throne.
Where'er I come the Fatal Sisters sweat,  395
And grisly Death, by running to and fro,
To do their ceaseless homage to my sword.
And here in Afric, where it seldom rains,
Since I arriv'd with my triumphant host,
Have swelling clouds, drawn from wide-gasp-
    ing wounds,  400
Been oft resolv'd in bloody purple showers,
A meteor that might terrify the earth,
And make it quake at every drop it drinks.
Millions of souls sit on the banks of Styx,
Waiting the back return of Charon's boat;  405
Hell and Elysium swarm with ghosts of men
That I have sent from sundry foughten fields,
To spread my fame through hell and up to
    Heaven.
And see, my lord, a sight of strange import,  409
Emperors and kings lie breathless at my feet.
The Turk and his great Empress, as it seems,
Left to themselves while we were at the fight,
Have desperately despatch'd their slavish lives;
With them Arabia, too, hath left his life:
All sights of power to grace my victory.  415
And such are objects fit for Tamburlaine;
Wherein, as in a mirror, may be seen
His honour that consists in shedding blood,
When men presume to manage arms with him.
    *Sold.*  Mighty hath God and Mahomet made
        thy hand,  420
Renowmed Tamburlaine! to whom all kings

Of force must yield their crowns and emperies;
And I am pleas'd with this my overthrow,
If, as beseems a person of thy state,
Thou hast with honour us'd Zenocrate.          425
   *Tamb.*   Her state and person wants no pomp,
    you see;
And for all blot of foul inchastity
I record Heaven her heavenly self is clear.
Then let me find no further time to grace     429
Her princely temples with the Persian crown.
But here these kings that on my fortunes
    wait,
And have been crown'd for proved worthiness
Even by this hand that shall establish them,
Shall now, adjoining all their hands with mine,
Invest her here my Queen of Persia.           435
What saith the noble Soldan and Zenocrate!
   *Sold.*   I yield with thanks and protestations
Of endless honour to thee for her love.
   *Tamb.*   Then doubt I not but fair Zenocrate
Will soon consent to satisfy us both.          440
   *Zeno.*   Else should I much forget myself, my
    lord.
   *Ther.*   Then let us set the crown upon her
    head,
That long hath ling'red for so high a seat.
   *Tech.*   My hand is ready to perform the deed;
For now her marriage-time shall work us rest.
   *Usum.*   And here's the crown, my lord; help
    set it on.          446
   *Tamb.*   Then sit thou down, divine Zenocrate;

And here we crown thee Queen of Persia,
And all the kingdoms and dominions
That late the power of Tamburlaine subdu'd.
As Juno, when the giants were suppress'd,     451
That darted mountains at her brother Jove,
So looks my love, shadowing in her brows
Triumphs and trophies for my victories;
Or as Latona's daughter, bent to arms,         455
Adding more courage to my conquering mind.
To gratify the sweet Zenocrate,
Egyptians, Moors, and men of Asia,
From Barbary unto the western Indie,
Shall pay a yearly tribute to thy sire;        460
And from the bounds of Afric to the banks
Of Ganges shall his mighty arm extend.
And now, my lords and loving followers,
That purchas'd kingdoms by your martial
    deeds,
Cast off your armour, put on scarlet robes,   465
Mount up your royal places of estate,
Environed with troops of noblemen,
And there make laws to rule your provinces.
Hang up your weapons on Alcides' post,
For Tamburlaine takes truce with all the world.
Thy first-betrothed love, Arabia,             471
Shall we with honour, as beseems, entomb,
With this great Turk and his fair Emperess.
Then, after all these solemn exequies,
We will our rites of marriage solemnise.       475
                         [*Exeunt.*]
*Finis Actus quinti et ultimi huius primæ partis.*

---

⁴²⁸ **record:** call to witness    ⁴³³ **establish:** make secure    ⁴⁶⁹ **Alcides' post:** door-post of temple
of Hercules

# The Tragicall History
## of the Life and Death
### of Doctor FAVSTVS.

---

With new additions

---

Written by *Ch. Marlot,*

Printed at London for *Iohn Wright*, and are to be sold at his shop without Newgate. 1628.

BIBLIOGRAPHICAL RECORD. On January 7, 1601 (modern reckoning), Thomas Bushell entered for publication "a booke called the plaie of Doctor Faustus." Few items of Elizabethan drama have been more diligently sought than the first edition of this play, which the entry quoted presumably anticipated, but no copy has yet been discovered. The failure does not, however, warrant the inference that *Faustus* was not printed in 1601, for all the many editions were avidly read and thus "thumbed out of existence." Of the Quarto texts which have escaped no less than five appear to survive in single copies. In 1604 Bushell issued the earliest known Quarto, and on September 13, 1610, he transferred his copyright to John Wright, who had for some reason already produced an edition in 1609 (two copies known), and who appears as publisher of all the rest down to and including that of 1631. They are: — 1611 (Huntington Library), 1616 (British Museum), 1619 (Robt. Garrett, Baltimore), 1620 (two copies known), 1624 (British Museum), 1628 (Lincoln Coll., Oxford and Royal Library, Stockholm; see facsimile of title-page), 1631 (five copies known). The latest Quarto of all was published after the Restoration, in 1663, "with new additions as it is now acted." It gives a badly depraved text, and has no real authority.

The early Quartos hand the play down in two radically different versions. The first three (1604, 1609, 1611) give what we refer to in the footnotes as the "A" version. This is undeniably a bad text. It makes the play very short and has probably lost a good deal of the original contents. In a few cases the dropping of necessary lines is definitely provable. Many lines have lost their rhythm, and bits of actors' "gag" are discernible. Moreover, the "A" text, for all its brevity, has sections of farcical matter that offer little suggestion of Marlowe's workmanship: they are probably patches inserted to cover the deletion of original matter.

Quartos 1616–1631 give the "B" text, which, being nearly 600 lines longer, expands the play to normal size. In his recent edition Professor F. S. Boas has argued ably in behalf of this version. It has independent manuscript authority, and certainly improves or usefully supplements the "A" text at various points. We have adopted and noted its readings wherever they seemed definitely better, or of special interest, but have otherwise adhered to the "A" version, since the major part of "B's" additions seems to represent the post-Marlowe expansion mentioned in the next section. (See *Philological Quarterly*, January, 1933, pp. 17–23.)

STAGE HISTORY. The first recorded performance was by the Admiral's company at the Rose Theatre, September 30, 1594, considerably more than a year after Marlowe's death. This can hardly have been the première production, and the play is not marked by Henslowe as new, but it must have been a relative novelty, for it brought in large profits and was repeated 24 times before the end of October, 1597, by which time its drawing power had sunk to little or nothing. The next revival may have been in 1602 and was the occasion of a thorough refurbishing of the old play, for Henslowe notes a payment, November 22, 1602, to William Birde and Samuel Rowley of £4 (half the price of a complete play) "for ther adicyones in doctor fostes." These extensive additions, made subsequently to Bushell's entry of the "A" text in 1601, are in our opinion the main source of the new matter in "B."

After 1600 the regular playing-place of the Admiral's Men (who by their patron's advancement in the peerage were known also as the Earl of Nottingham's) was the Fortune Theatre. A writer of 1620 suggests that *Dr. Faustus* was long popular there: — ". . . men goe to the Fortune in Golding-Lane to see the Tragedie of Doctor Faustus. There indeede a man may behold shaggehayr'd Devills runne roaring over the stage with squibs in their mouthes, while Drummers make Thunder in the Tyring-house, and the twelve-penny Hirelings make artificiall Lightning in their Heavens" (Melton's *Astrologaster*). Other writers mention "Devills in Dr. Faustus when the old Theater crakt and frighted the audience" (T. M., *Black Book*, 1604) and "the visible apparition of the Devill on the stage at the Belsavage playhouse, in Queen Elizabethes dayes . . . while they were there prophanely playing the History of Faustus" (Prynne, *Histriomastix*, 1633). These last two, if they can be relied upon, would apparently carry us back to the period before Henslowe's Rose Theatre was opened. The Belsavage was an innyard, and the "old Theatre" the first of the Elizabethan public playhouses.

The great Faustus was Edward Alleyn, who, according to Rowlands (*Knave of Clubs*, 1609), played the part "in a surplis, with a crosse upon his breast." An anecdote relates that Alleyn's retirement from the trade of acting and devotion of himself to good works came as a result of the horror he felt when once a real devil appeared in answer to his conjuration in *Doctor Faustus*. As has been noted, the play was revived after the Restoration, and in the form of cheap "harlequinades" it remained popular in the eighteenth century. In the Elizabethan age English actors carried it to Germany, where it left its progeny in the numerous German puppet plays of Faust, which retain features of Marlowe's tragedy and drew Goethe's attention to the theme. (See Otto Heller, "*Faust* and *Faustus*: A Study of Goethe's Relation to Marlowe," 1931.)

SOURCE AND DATE. These points must be considered together. There is no question about the first. Marlowe followed, not the German text of the Faustbook (1587), but the free English adaptation of it by "P. F." which was printed in 1592. As we have now no ground for believing that P. F.'s version was in print before 1592 (see Professor Boas's edition, p. 7), we must infer either that Marlowe used the "P. F." text in manuscript or that the play was not written before 1592. The former hypothesis seems the less unlikely of the two, for the other gives a date strangely similar to that of the very different *Edward II;* but in any case *Faustus,* obviously written for Alleyn, must have preceded *Edward II,* which was composed after Marlowe had separated from Alleyn and his company.

STRUCTURE. No formal division into either acts or scenes is found in any text before the peculiarly bad one of 1663. This orders the material (imperfectly) in five acts, and better evidence of some such original intention appears in the choral recitative passages introduced in the earlier texts at points that may have been the openings of Acts I, III, IV, and V. But if the five-act structure was ever clear-cut, it has long since been obscured by revision, and the play now falls most naturally into three parts, dealing with (1) the making of the bond, (2) Faustus's enjoyment of supernatural power, and (3) the fulfilment of the bond. The middle portion, based on episodic material from the Faustbook, has most attracted the corrupter, but behind the corruption can still be traced a rather grandiose design: to secure, as in *Edward II,* a satisfactory illusion of the passage of much time by means of short scenes which, while mutually incongruous, unite in preparing for the tremendous close of the play. The amount of stage spectacle employed was very great: the firing of squibs, the appearances, disappearances, and transformations of infernal visitors, the masque of deadly sins, etc. Henslowe's inventory shows that a dragon was among the properties used, and perhaps also a painted scene of the city of Rome. The revisers added still more of these embellishments, and in the last scene presented the audience with the view of a mechanical heaven and hell.

# CHRISTOPHER MARLOWE

## THE TRAGICAL HISTORY OF DR. FAUSTUS

[DRAMATIS PERSONAE

CHORUS
DOCTOR FAUSTUS
WAGNER, his Famulus or Poor Scholar
(German) VALDES, } Friends of Faustus
CORNELIUS, 

LUCIFER
BELZEBUB
MEPHISTOPHILIS
GOOD ANGEL, } Monitors attendant on Faustus
EVIL ANGEL, 

THE SEVEN DEADLY SINS

THE POPE
CHARLES V of Germany
CARDINAL OF LORRAINE
DUKE OF VANHOLT (Anhalt)
DUCHESS OF VANHOLT

ROBIN, } Clowns
RAFE (Ralph), 

An Old Man; a Knight; a Horse-Courser; a Vintner; a Clown; Scholars, Friars, and Attendants;
Spirits in the form of Alexander the Great, his Paramour, and Helen of Troy; Devils

SCENE: Wittenberg, Rome, Court of Charles V, Anhalt]

*Enter Chorus*

Not marching now in fields of Thrasimene,
Where Mars did mate the Carthaginians;
Nor sporting in the dalliance of love,
In courts of kings where state is overturn'd;
Nor in the pomp of proud audacious deeds, 5
Intends our Muse to daunt his heavenly verse.
Only this, gentlemen, we must perform:
The form of Faustus' fortunes, good or bad.
And now to patient judgments we appeal,
And speak for Faustus in his infancy. 10
Now is he born, his parents base of stock,
In Germany, within a town call'd Rhodes;
Of riper years to Wittenberg he went,
Whereas his kinsmen chiefly brought him up.
So soon he profits in divinity, 15
The fruitful plot of scholarism graz'd,
That shortly he was grac'd with doctor's name,
Excelling all whose sweet delight disputes
In heavenly matters of theology;
Till swollen with cunning, of a self-conceit, 20
His waxen wings did mount above his reach,
And melting heavens conspir'd his overthrow;
For, falling to a devilish exercise,
And glutted now with learning's golden gifts,

He surfeits upon cursed necromancy. 25
Nothing so sweet as magic is to him,
Which he prefers before his chiefest bliss.
And this the man that in his study sits! *Exit.*

[SCENE I]

*Enter Faustus in his Study*

*Faust.* Settle my studies, Faustus, and begin
To sound the depth of that thou wilt profess;
Having commenc'd, be a divine in show,
Yet level at the end of every art,
And live and die in Aristotle's works. 5
Sweet Analytics, 't is thou hast ravish'd me,
*Bene disserere est finis logices.*
Is "to dispute well logic's chiefest end"?
Affords this art no greater miracle?
Then read no more, thou hast attain'd the end;
A greater subject fitteth Faustus' wit. 11
Bid ὂν καὶ μὴ ὂν farewell; Galen come,
Seeing *Ubi desinit philosophus, ibi incipit medi-*
    *cus;*
Be a physician, Faustus, heap up gold,
And be eterniz'd for some wondrous cure. 15
*Summum bonum medicinæ sanitas,*
"The end of physic is our body's health."

S. D. **Chorus:** a single actor ¹ **Thrasimene:** Lake Trasimenus, where Hannibal defeated the Romans ² **mate:** ally himself with ⁶ **daunt:** tame, exhaust ('vaunt' B) ⁹ **And . . . appeal** B: ('To patient judgments we appeal our plaud.' A) ¹² **Rhodes:** *i.e.,* Roda, near Weimar ¹³ **Witten-berg:** ('Wertenberg' two earliest Qq., and so later) ¹⁶ Having nibbled the fruits of learning ¹⁸ **whose . . . disputes:** who find delight in disputation ²¹ **waxen wings:** (alluding to myth of Icarus) ²⁸ **this the man:** (Chorus draws curtain before rear-stage.) ¹ **Settle:** make firm ³ **commenc'd:** graduated ⁴ **level:** aim ⁶ **Analytics:** (Aristotle's logic consisted of "prior" and "posterior" analytics.) ¹² ὂν . . . ὂν: "being and not being," *i.e.,* philosophy **Galen:** the standard classical work on medicine ¹³ "Where the philosopher stops, the doctor begins."

Why, Faustus, hast thou not attain'd that end?
Is not thy common talk sound aphorisms?
Are not thy bills hung up as monuments,          20
Whereby whole cities have escap'd the plague,
And thousand desperate maladies been eas'd?
Yet art thou still but Faustus and a man.
Couldst thou make men to live eternally,
Or, being dead, raise them to life again,          25
Then this profession were to be esteem'd.
Physic, farewell. — Where is Justinian?
                                                  [*Reads.*]
*Si una eademque res legatur duobus, alter rem,*
    *alter valorem rei, &c.*
A pretty case of paltry legacies!          [*Reads.*]
*Exhæreditare filium non potest pater nisi —*          30
Such is the subject of the Institute
And universal body of the law.
His study fits a mercenary drudge,
Who aims at nothing but external trash;
Too servile and illiberal for me.          35
When all is done, divinity is best;
Jerome's Bible, Faustus, view it well.
                                                  [*Reads.*]
*Stipendium peccati mors est.* Ha! *Stipendium,*
    *&c.*
"The reward of sin is death." That's hard.
                                                  [*Reads.*]
*Si peccasse negamus, fallimur, et nulla est in*
    *nobis veritas.*          40
"If we say that we have no sin we deceive our-
selves, and there's no truth in us."
                                    Why, then, belike,
We must sin and so consequently die.
Ay, we must die an everlasting death.
What doctrine call you this! *Che sera sera.*          45
"What will be shall be." Divinity, adieu!
These metaphysics of magicians
And necromantic books are heavenly;
Lines, circles, scenes, letters, and characters,          49
Ay, these are those that Faustus most desires.
O what a world of profit and delight,
Of power, of honour, of omnipotence
Is promis'd to the studious artizan!
All things that move between the quiet poles
Shall be at my command. Emperors and kings

Are but obey'd in their several provinces,          56
Nor can they raise the wind or rend the clouds;
But his dominion that exceeds in this
Stretcheth as far as doth the mind of man.
A sound magician is a mighty god:          60
Here, Faustus, try thy brains to gain a deity.
Wagner!

                    *Enter Wagner*

           Commend me to my dearest friends,
The German Valdes and Cornelius;
Request them earnestly to visit me.
    *Wag.* I will, sir.                    *Exit.* 65
    *Faust.* Their conference will be a greater
help to me
Than all my labours, plod I ne'er so fast.

        *Enter the Good Angel and the Evil Angel*

    *G. Ang.* O Faustus! lay that damned book
aside,
And gaze not on it lest it tempt thy soul,
And heap God's heavy wrath upon thy head.          70
Read, read the Scriptures: that is blasphemy.
    *E. Ang.* Go forward, Faustus, in that famous
art,
Wherein all Nature's treasury is contain'd:
Be thou on earth as Jove is in the sky,
Lord and commander of these elements.          75
                            *Exeunt* [*Angels*].
    *Faust.* How am I glutted with conceit of this!
Shall I make spirits fetch me what I please,
Resolve me of all ambiguities,
Perform what desperate enterprise I will?
I'll have them fly to India for gold,          80
Ransack the ocean for orient pearl,
And search all corners of the new-found world
For pleasant fruits and princely delicates;
I'll have them read me strange philosophy
And tell the secrets of all foreign kings;          85
I'll have them wall all Germany with brass,
And make swift Rhine circle fair Wittenberg;
I'll have them fill the public schools with silk,
Wherewith the students shall be bravely clad;
I'll levy soldiers with the coin they bring,          90
And chase the Prince of Parma from our land,

[19] **sound aphorisms:** valid precepts (The medical precepts of Hippocrates were called aphorisms.)
[20] **bills:** prescriptions    **hung . . . monuments:** posted in public places    [24] **Couldst . . . men** B:
('Wouldst . . . man' A)    [28] "If the same thing is bequeathed to two persons, let one have the thing,
the other its equivalent in other property" (a rule cited in Justinian's *Digest*).    [31] **Institute:** Justinian's *Institutes*, textbook of Roman law    [32] **law** B: ('Church' A)    [33] **His:** Its    [35] **Too servile** B:
('The deuill' A)    [37] **Jerome's Bible:** the Vulgate text, in Latin    [38] (Romans vi. 23)    [40] (I Epist.
of St. John i. 8)    [47] **metaphysics:** supernatural arts    [49] **scenes:** perhaps "schemes," astrologers'
calculations (B omits the word)    [53] **artizan:** virtuoso    [63] **German Valdes** (suggested by the name
of the Spanish humanist, Juan de Valdes?)    **Cornelius:** Cornelius Agrippa, 1486–1535, an alchemist
[75] **elements:** the four elements that made the world    [76] **conceit:** apprehension    [78] **Resolve:** inform
**ambiguities:** disputed questions    [83] **delicates:** delicacies    [84] **strange:** that in unknown tongues
[86] **wall . . . brass:** suggested by the legend of Friar Bacon, who meant to wall England with brass
(See Greene's play, *Friar Bacon and Friar Bungay*.)    [88] **public schools:** university classrooms    **silk:**
(misprinted "skill" in all early editions)    [91] **Prince of Parma:** Philip II's representative in the Nether
ands, 1579–1592

And reign sole king of all our provinces;
Yea, stranger engines for the brunt of war
Than was the fiery keel at Antwerp's bridge,
I 'll make my servile spirits to invent.  95
Come, German Valdes and Cornelius,
And make me blest with your sage conference.

*Enter Valdes and Cornelius*

Valdes, sweet Valdes, and Cornelius,
Know that your words have won me at the last
To practise magic and concealed arts:  100
Yet not your words only, but mine own fantasy,
That will receive no object, for my head
But ruminates on necromantic skill.
Philosophy is odious and obscure,
Both law and physic are for petty wits;  105
Divinity is basest of the three,
Unpleasant, harsh, contemptible, and vild:
'T is magic, magic, that hath ravish'd me.
Then, gentle friends, aid me in this attempt;
And I that have with concise syllogisms  110
Gravell'd the pastors of the German church,
And made the flow'ring pride of Wittenberg
Swarm to my problems, as the infernal spirits
On sweet Musæus, when he came to hell,
Will be as cunning as Agrippa was,  115
Whose shadows made all Europe honour him.
 *Vald.* Faustus, these books, thy wit, and our
  experience
Shall make all nations to canónise us.
As Indian Moors obey their Spanish lords,
So shall the subjects of every element  120
Be always serviceable to us three;
Like lions shall they guard us when we please;
Like Almain rutters with their horsemen's
  staves,
Or Lapland giants, trotting by our sides;
Sometimes like women or unwedded maids, 125
Shadowing more beauty in their airy brows
Than have the white breasts of the queen of love:
From Venice shall they drag huge argosies,
And from America the golden fleece
That yearly stuffs old Philip's treasury;  130
If learned Faustus will be resolute.
 *Faust.* Valdes, as resolute am I in this
As thou to live; therefore object it not.
 *Corn.* The miracles that magic will perform
Will make thee vow to study nothing else.  135
He that is grounded in astrology,

Enrich'd with tongues, well seen in minerals,
Hath all the principles magic doth require.
Then doubt not, Faustus, but to be renowm'd,
And more frequented for this mystery  140
Than heretofore the Delphian Oracle.
The spirits tell me they can dry the sea,
And fetch the treasure of all foreign wracks,
Ay, all the wealth that our forefathers hid
Within the massy entrails of the earth;  145
Then tell me, Faustus, what shall we three
  want?
 *Faust.* Nothing, Cornelius! O this cheers my
  soul!
Come! Show me some demonstrations magical,
That I may conjure in some lusty grove,
And have these joys in full possession.  150
 *Vald.* Then haste thee to some solitary grove,
And bear wise Bacon's and Albanus' works,
The Hebrew Psalter and New Testament;
And whatsoever else is requisite  154
We will inform thee ere our conference cease.
 *Corn.* Valdes, first let him know the words of
  art;
And then, all other ceremonies learn'd,
Faustus may try his cunning by himself.
 *Vald.* First I 'll instruct thee in the rudi-
  ments,
And then wilt thou be perfecter than I.  160
 *Faust.* Then come and dine with me, and
  after meat,
We 'll canvass every quiddity thereof;
For ere I sleep I 'll try what I can do:
This night I 'll conjure though I die therefore.
   *Exeunt.*

[SCENE II. *Near Faustus' house.*]

*Enter two Scholars*

 1 *Scholar.* I wonder what 's become of Faustus that was wont to make our schools ring
with *sic probo?*
 2 *Schol.* That shall we know, for see, here
comes his boy.  5

*Enter Wagner*

 1 *Schol.* How now, sirrah! Where 's thy
master?
 *Wag.* God in heaven knows!
 2 *Schol.* Why, dost not thou know?
 *Wag.* Yes, I know. But that follows not. 10

---

 ⁹² **provinces:** (of the Netherlands)  ⁹⁴ **fiery keel:** the fire-ship employed by the defenders of Antwerp in 1585 to blow up Parma's bridge over the Scheldt river  ¹⁰² **receive no object:** fix upon no
objective  ¹⁰⁶ **basest . . . three:** baser than the other three  ¹⁰⁷ **vild:** vile  ¹¹³ **problems:** demonstrations  ¹¹⁴ **Musæus:** (Cf. *Æneid* vi. 667.)  ¹¹⁶ **shadows:** spirits (Cf. Lyly's *Campaspe,* Prol.:
"Agrippa his shadows, who in the moment they were seen were of any shape one would conceive.")
¹²⁰ **subjects:** disembodied forces  ¹²¹ **serviceable:** obedient  ¹²³ **Almain rutters:** German troopers
¹²⁹ **golden fleece:** alluding to the "plate fleet"  ¹³³ **object:** stress, mention  ¹³⁷ **well seen in minerals:** competent in the use of crystals  ¹³⁹ **renowm'd:** renowned, renommé  ¹⁴⁰ **frequented:** sought
after  ¹⁵² **Albanus':** Petrus de Albano, a 13th century alchemist  ¹⁶² **quiddity:** essential  ³ **sic
probo:** "Thus I prove it"; the phrase with which the philosopher introduced his solution of the problem stated.  ⁵ **boy:** pupil-servant

1 *Schol.* Go to, sirrah! Leave your jesting, and tell us where he is.

*Wag.* That follows not necessary by force of argument, that you, being licentiate, should stand upon 't: therefore, acknowledge your [15 error and be attentive.

2 *Schol.* Why, didst thou not say thou knew'st?

*Wag.* Have you any witness on 't?

1 *Schol.* Yes, sirrah, I heard you.          20

*Wag.* Ask my fellow if I be a thief.

2 *Schol.* Well, you will not tell us?

*Wag.* Yes, sir, I will tell you; yet if you were not dunces, you would never ask me such a question; for is not he *corpus naturale?* and is not that *mobile?* Then wherefore should [26 you ask me such a question? But that I am by nature phlegmatic, slow to wrath, and prone to lechery (to love, I would say), it were not for you to come within forty foot of the place [30 of execution, although I do not doubt to see you both hang'd the next sessions. Thus having triumph'd over you, I will set my countenance like a precisian, and begin to speak thus: — Truly, my dear brethren, my master is within at dinner, with Valdes and Cornelius, as this [36 wine, if it could speak, would inform your worships; and so the Lord bless you, preserve you, and keep you, my dear brethren, my dear brethren.          *Exit.*  40

1 *Schol.* Nay, then, I fear he is fallen into that damned art, for which they two are infamous through the world.

2 *Schol.* Were he a stranger, and not allied to me, yet should I grieve for him. But come, let us go and inform the Rector, and see if he [46 by his grave counsel can reclaim him.

1 *Schol.* O, I fear me nothing can reclaim him.

2 *Schol.* Yet let us try what we can do.  50

          *Exeunt.*

[Scene III. *A grove.*]

*Enter Faustus to conjure*

*Faust.* Now that the gloomy shadow of the earth,
Longing to view Orion's drizzling look,
Leaps from th' antarctic world unto the sky,
And dims the welkin with her pitchy breath,

Faustus, begin thine incantations,          5
And try if devils will obey thy hest,
Seeing thou hast pray'd and sacrific'd to them.
Within this circle is Jehovah's name,
Forward and backward anagrammatiz'd,
The breviated names of holy saints,          10
Figures of every adjunct to the heavens,
And characters of signs and erring stars,
By which the spirits are enforc'd to rise:
Then fear not, Faustus, but be resolute,
And try the uttermost magic can perform.  15

*Sint mihi Dei Acherontis propitii! Valeat numen triplex Jehovæ! Ignei, ærii, aquæ, terræ spiritus, salvete! Orientis princeps, Belzebub, inferni ardentis monarcha, et Demogorgon, propitiamus vos, ut appareat et surgat Mephisto-* [20 *philis. Quid tu moraris? Per Jehovam, Gehennam, et consecratam aquam quam nunc spargo, signumque crucis quod nunc facio, et per vota nostra, ipse nunc surgat nobis dicatus Mephistophilis!*          25

*Enter [Mephistophilis] a Devil*

I charge thee to return and change thy shape;
Thou art too ugly to attend on me.
Go, and return an old Franciscan friar;
That holy shape becomes a devil best.
          *Exit Devil.*
I see there's virtue in my heavenly words;  30
Who would not be proficient in this art?
How pliant is this Mephistophilis,
Full of obedience and humility!
Such is the force of magic and my spells.
No, Faustus, thou art conjuror laureate,  35
That canst command great Mephistophilis:
*Quin redis Mephistophilis fratris imagine.*

*Enter Mephistophilis [like a Franciscan Friar]*

*Meph.* Now, Faustus, what would'st thou have me do?

*Faust.* I charge thee wait upon me whilst I live,
To do whatever Faustus shall command,  40
Be it to make the moon drop from her sphere,
Or the ocean to overwhelm the world.

*Meph.* I am a servant to great Lucifer,
And may not follow thee without his leave;
No more than he commands must we perform.

*Faust.* Did not he charge thee to appear to me?          46

---

[13] **necessary:** as a proper logical deduction   [14] **licentiate:** qualified for an M.A. or higher degree   [17-21] (Omitted in B)   [30-31] **within . . . execution:** within reach of my wrath   [34] **precisian:** puritan   [42] **art:** the black art   [44-50] (Recast as verse in B)   [46] **Rector:** university head   [1] **earth** A: ('night' B)   [2] **drizzling:** betokening rain (Orion is a winter constellation.)   [3] **antarctic world:** southern hemisphere (In winter the earth's shadow is projected from the south.)   [10] **The breviated** A: ('Th' abbreviated' B)   [11] **adjunct:** *i.e.*, fixed star   [12] **signs:** signs of the Zodiac   **erring stars:** planets   [16] **Valeat:** farewell to   [17] **aquæ, terræ:** ('Aquatani' Qq.)   [21] **Quid tu moraris:** Why do you delay? ('quod tumeraris' Qq.)   [35] **No:** (in sense of "why, assuredly")   [37] "Why do you not return in the image of a friar?" ('regis' Qq.)

*Meph.* No, I came now hither of mine own accord.

*Faust.* Did not my conjuring speeches raise thee? Speak.

*Meph.* That was the cause, but yet *per accidens;*

For when we hear one rack the name of God,    50
Abjure the Scriptures and his Saviour Christ,
We fly in hope to get his glorious soul;
Nor will we come, unless he use such means
Whereby he is in danger to be damn'd:
Therefore the shortest cut for conjuring    55
Is stoutly to abjure the Trinity,
And pray devoutly to the Prince of Hell.

*Faust.* So Faustus hath
Already done; and holds this principle,
There is no chief but only Belzebub,    60
To whom Faustus doth dedicate himself.
This word "damnation" terrifies not him,
For he confounds hell in Elysium;
His ghost be with the old philosophers!
But, leaving these vain trifles of men's souls, 65
Tell me what is that Lucifer thy lord?

*Meph.* Arch-regent and commander of all spirits.

*Faust.* Was not that Lucifer an angel once?

*Meph.* Yes, Faustus, and most dearly lov'd of God.

*Faust.* How comes it then that he is prince of devils?    70

*Meph.* O, by aspiring pride and insolence;
For which God threw him from the face of Heaven.

*Faust.* And what are you that live with Lucifer?

*Meph.* Unhappy spirits that fell with Lucifer,
Conspir'd against our God with Lucifer,    75
And are for ever damn'd with Lucifer.

*Faust.* Where are you damn'd?

*Meph.* In hell.

*Faust.* How comes it then that thou art out of hell?

*Meph.* Why this is hell, nor am I out of it. 80
Think'st thou that I who saw the face of God,
And tasted the eternal joys of Heaven,
Am not tormented with ten thousand hells,
In being depriv'd of everlasting bliss?
O Faustus! leave these frivolous demands,    85
Which strike a terror to my fainting soul.

*Faust.* What, is great Mephistophilis so passionate
For being deprived of the joys of Heaven?
Learn thou of Faustus manly fortitude,

And scorn those joys thou never shalt possess.

Go bear these tidings to great Lucifer:    91
Seeing Faustus hath incurr'd eternal death
By desperate thoughts against Jove's deity,
Say he surrenders up to him his soul,
So he will spare him four-and-twenty years, 95
Letting him live in all voluptuousness;
Having thee ever to attend on me;
To give me whatsoever I shall ask,
To tell me whatsoever I demand,
To slay mine enemies, and aid my friends, 100
And always be obedient to my will.
Go and return to mighty Lucifer,
And meet me in my study at midnight,
And then resolve me of thy master's mind.

*Meph.* I will, Faustus.      *Exit.* 105

*Faust.* Had I as many souls as there be stars,
I'd give them all for Mephistophilis.
By him I'll be great Emperor of the world,
And make a bridge through the moving air,
To pass the ocean with a band of men;    110
I'll join the hills that bind the Afric shore,
And make that country continent to Spain,
And both contributory to my crown.
The Emperor shall not live but by my leave,
Nor any potentate of Germany.    115
Now that I have obtain'd what I desire,
I'll live in speculation of this art
Till Mephistophilis return again.      *Exit.*

[SCENE IV]

*Enter Wagner and the Clown*

*Wag.* Sirrah, boy, come hither.

*Clown.* How, boy! Swowns, boy! I hope you have seen many boys with such pickadevaunts as I have. Boy, quotha!

*Wag.* Tell me, sirrah, hast thou any comings in?    6

*Clown.* Ay, and goings out too. You may see else.

*Wag.* Alas, poor slave! See how poverty jesteth in his nakedness! The villain is bare and [10 out of service, and so hungry that I know he would give his soul to the devil for a shoulder of mutton, though it were blood-raw.

*Clown.* How? My soul to the Devil for a shoulder of mutton, though 't were blood-raw! [15 Not so, good friend. By 'r Lady, I had need have it well roasted and good sauce to it, if I pay so dear.

*Wag.* Well, wilt thou serve me, and I'll make thee go like *Qui mihi discipulus?*    20

*Clown.* How, in verse?

*Wag.* No, sirrah; in beaten silk and staves-acre.

*Clown.* How, now, knave's acre! Ay, I thought that was all the land his father left [25 him. Do ye hear? I would be sorry to rob you of your living.

*Wag.* Sirrah, I say in stavesacre.

*Clown.* Oho! Oho! Stavesacre! Why, then, belike if I were your man I should be full of vermin. 31

*Wag.* So thou shalt, whether thou beest with me or no. But, sirrah, leave your jesting, and bind yourself presently unto me for seven years, or I 'll turn all the lice about thee into familiars, and they shall tear thee in pieces. 36

*Clown.* Do you hear, sir? You may save that labour; they are too familiar with me already. Swowns! they are as bold with my flesh as if they had paid for my meat and [40 drink.

*Wag.* Well, do you hear, sirrah? Hold, take these guilders. [*Gives money.*]

*Clown.* Gridirons! what be they?

*Wag.* Why, French crowns. 45

*Clown.* Mass, but for the name of French crowns, a man were as good have as many English counters. And what should I do with these?

*Wag.* Why, now, sirrah, thou art at an [50 hour's warning, whensoever or wheresoever the devil shall fetch thee.

*Clown.* No, no. Here, take your gridirons again.

*Wag.* Truly, I 'll none of them. 55

*Clown.* Truly, but you shall.

*Wag.* Bear witness I gave them him.

*Clown.* Bear witness I give them you again.

*Wag.* Well, I will cause two devils presently to fetch thee away. — Baliol and Belcher! 60

*Clown.* Let your Balio and your Belcher come here, and I 'll knock them, they were never so knock'd since they were devils. Say I should kill one of them, what would folks say? "Do ye see yonder tall fellow in the round [65 slop? — he has kill'd the devil." So I should be call'd Kill-devil all the parish over.

*Enter two Devils, and the Clown runs up and down crying*

*Wag.* Baliol and Belcher! Spirits, away!
*Exeunt [Devils].*

*Clown.* What, are they gone? A vengeance on them, they have vild long nails! There [70 was a he-devil, and a she-devil! I 'll tell you how

you shall know them: all he-devils has horns, and all she-devils has clifts and cloven feet.

*Wag.* Well, sirrah, follow me.

*Clown.* But, do you hear — if I should serve you, would you teach me to raise up Banios [76 and Belcheos?

*Wag.* I will teach thee to turn thyself to anything; to a dog, or a cat, or a mouse, or a rat, or anything. 80

*Clown.* How! a Christian fellow to a dog o˄ a cat, a mouse or a rat! No, no, sir. If you turn me into anything, let it be in the likeness of a little pretty frisking flea, that I may be here and there and everywhere. Oh, I 'll tickle [85 the pretty wenches' plackets; I 'll be amongst them, i' faith.

*Wag.* Well, sirrah, come.

*Clown.* But, do you hear, Wagner?

*Wag.* How! — Baliol and Belcher! 90

*Clown.* O Lord! I pray, sir, let Banio and Belcher go sleep.

*Wag.* Villain, call me Master Wagner, and let thy left eye be diametarily fix'd upon my right heel, with *quasi vestigias nostras insistere.*
*Exit.*

*Clown.* God forgive me, he speaks Dutch [96 fustian. Well, I 'll follow him, I 'll serve him, that 's flat. *Exit.*

[SCENE V]

*Enter Faustus in his study*

*Faust.* Now, Faustus, must
Thou needs be damn'd, and canst thou not be sav'd:
What boots it then to think of God or Heaven?
Away with such vain fancies, and despair:
Despair in God, and trust in Belzebub. 5
Now go not backward: no, Faustus, be resolute.
Why waverest thou? O, something soundeth in mine ears
"Abjure this magic, turn to God again!"
Ay, and Faustus will turn to God again.
To God? — He loves thee not — 10
The God thou serv'st is thine own appetite,
Wherein is fix'd the love of Belzebub;
To him I 'll build an altar and a church,
And offer lukewarm blood of new-born babes.

*Enter Good Angel and Evil*

*G. Ang.* Sweet Faustus, leave that execrable art. 15

*Faust.* Contrition, prayer, repentance! What of them?

*G. Ang.* O, they are means to bring thee unto Heaven.

---

²²⁻²³ **stavesacre:** a plant used for ridding clothes of lice ³⁶ **familiars:** attendant spirits ⁴³ **guilders:** Dutch coins ⁵⁰ **at:** subject to ⁶⁵ **tall:** robust ⁶⁵⁻⁶⁶ **round slop:** wide breeches ⁹⁴ **diametarily:** directly (diametrically) ⁹⁵ **quasi . . . insistere:** as if to tread in our tracks (bad Latin) ⁹⁷ **fustian:** pompous nonsense ⁶ **no:** (Not in B) **Faustus:** (an actor's insertion?)

*E. Ang.* Rather illusions, fruits of lunacy,
That makes men foolish that do trust them
  most.
  *G. Ang.* Sweet Faustus, think of Heaven,
    and heavenly things.               20
  *E. Ang.* No, Faustus, think of honour and
    of wealth.            *Exeunt [Angels].*
  *Faust.* Of wealth!
Why, the signiory of Emden shall be mine.
When Mephistophilis shall stand by me,
What God can hurt thee, Faustus? Thou art
  safe;                      25
Cast no more doubts. Come, Mephistophilis,
And bring glad tidings from great Lucifer; —
Is 't not midnight? Come, Mephistophilis;
*Veni, veni, Mephistophile!*

    *Enter Mephistophilis*

Now tell me, what says Lucifer thy lord?    30
  *Meph.* That I shall wait on Faustus whilst
    he lives,
So he will buy my service with his soul.
  *Faust.* Already Faustus hath hazarded that
    for thee.
  *Meph.* But now thou must bequeath it
    solemnly,
And write a deed of gift with thine own blood,
For that security craves great Lucifer.      36
If thou deny it, I will back to hell.
  *Faust.* Stay, Mephistophilis! tell me what
    good
Will my soul do thy lord.
  *Meph.*            Enlarge his kingdom.
  *Faust.* Is that the reason why he tempts us
    thus?                      40
  *Meph. Solamen miseris socios habuisse dolo-
    ris.*
  *Faust.* Why, have you any pain that tortures
    others?
  *Meph.* As great as have the human souls of
    men.
But tell me, Faustus, shall I have thy soul?
And I will be thy slave, and wait on thee,    45
And give thee more than thou hast wit to ask.
  *Faust.* Ay, Mephistophilis, I give it thee.
  *Meph.* Then stab thine arm courageously,
And bind thy soul that at some certain day
Great Lucifer may claim it as his own;    50
And then be thou as great as Lucifer.
  *Faust. [Stabbing his arm.]* Lo, Mephistoph-
    illis, for love of thee,
I cut mine arm, and with my proper blood
Assure my soul to be great Lucifer's,
Chief lord and regent of perpetual night!    55

View here the blood that trickles from mine
  arm,
And let it be propitious for my wish.
  *Meph.* But, Faustus, thou must
Write it in manner of a deed of gift.
  *Faust.* Ay, so I will. *[Writes.]* But, Mephis-
    tophilis,                   60
My blood congeals, and I can write no more.
  *Meph.* I 'll fetch thee fire to dissolve it
    straight.                  *Exit.*
  *Faust.* What might the staying of my blood
    portend?
Is it unwilling I should write this bill?
Why streams it not that I may write afresh? 65
*Faustus gives to thee his soul.* Ah, there it stay'd.
Why should'st thou not? Is not thy soul thine
  own?
Then write again: — *Faustus gives to thee his
  soul.*

    *Enter Mephistophilis with a chafer of coals*

  *Meph.* Here 's fire. Come, Faustus, set it on.
  *Faust.* So now the blood begins to clear
    again;                    70
Now will I make an end immediately. *[Writes.]*
  *Meph.* O what will not I do to obtain his
    soul!                  *[Aside.]*
  *Faust. Consummatum est:* this bill is ended,
And Faustus hath bequeath'd his soul to Luci-
  fer. —
But what is this inscription on mine arm?    75
*Homo, fuge!* Whither should I fly?
If unto God, he 'll throw me down to hell. —
My senses are deceiv'd; here 's nothing writ: —
I see it plain; here in this place is writ
*Homo, fuge!* Yet shall not Faustus fly.      80
  *Meph.* I 'll fetch him somewhat to delight
    his mind.                *Exit.*

  *Enter [Mephistophilis] with Devils, giving
    crowns and rich apparel to Faustus, and
    dance, and then depart*

  *Faust.* Speak, Mephistophilis, what means
    this show?
  *Meph.* Nothing, Faustus, but to delight thy
    mind withal,
And to show thee what magic can perform.
  *Faust.* But may I raise up spirits when I
    please?                  85
  *Meph.* Ay, Faustus, and do greater things
    than these.
  *Faust.* Then there 's enough for a thousand
    souls.
Here, Mephistophilis, receive this scroll,

---

²³ **Emden:** capital of East Friesland (on particularly friendly terms with England in the Armada
period)    ²⁵ **thee:** ('me' B)    ³⁴ **now** B: ('Faustus' A)    ³⁸ **tell:** ('and tell' Qq.)    ⁴⁰, ⁴² **why:**
(Not in A)    ⁴¹ (A line frequently quoted, but of unknown origin: "Misery loves company.")
⁴² **that tortures:** you who torture    ⁵³ **proper:** own    ⁷³ **Consummatum est:** (Faustus blasphemously
parodies Christ [St. John xix. 30]).    ⁸³ **withal:** (Not in B)    ⁸⁷ (Not in B)

A deed of gift of body and of soul:
But yet conditionally that thou perform          90
All articles prescrib'd between us both.
*Meph.* Faustus, I swear by hell and Lucifer
To effect all promises between us made.
*Faust.* Then hear me read them: *On these*
*conditions following. First, that Faustus may* [95
*be a spirit in form and substance. Secondly, that*
*Mephistophilis shall be his servant, and at his*
*command. Thirdly, that Mephistophilis shall do*
*for him and bring him whatsoever. Fourthly,*
*that he shall be in his chamber or house* [100
*invisible. Lastly, that he shall appear to the*
*said John Faustus, at all times, in what form*
*or shape soever he please: — I, John Faustus, of*
*Wittenberg, Doctor, by these presents do give both*
*body and soul to Lucifer, Prince of the East,* [105
*and his minister, Mephistophilis; and furthermore*
*grant unto them, that four-and-twenty years being*
*expired, the articles above written inviolate, full*
*power to fetch or carry the said John Faustus,*
*body and soul, flesh, blood, or goods, into their* [110
*habitation wheresoever. By me, John Faustus.*
*Meph.* Speak, Faustus, do you deliver this
     as your deed?
*Faust.* Ay, take it, and the devil give thee
     good on 't.
*Meph.* Now, Faustus, ask what thou wilt. 114
*Faust.* First will I question with thee about
     hell.
Tell me, where is the place that men call hell?
*Meph.* Under the heavens.
*Faust.* Ay, but whereabout?
*Meph.* Within the bowels of these elements,
Where we are tortur'd and remain for ever.   120
Hell hath no limits, nor is circumscrib'd
In one self place; for where we are is hell,
And where hell is there must we ever be:
And, to conclude, when all the world dissolves,
And every creature shall be purified,          125
All places shall be hell that is not Heaven.
*Faust.* Come, I think hell 's a fable.
*Meph.* Ay, think so still, till experience
     change thy mind.
*Faust.* Why, think'st thou then that Faustus
     shall be damn'd?                          129
*Meph.* Ay, of necessity, for here 's the scroll
Wherein thou hast given thy soul to Lucifer.
*Faust.* Ay, and body too; but what of that?
Think'st thou that Faustus is so fond to ima-
     gine
That, after this life, there is any pain?      134
Tush; these are trifles, and mere old wives' tales.
*Meph.* But I am an instance to prove the
     contrary,
For I am damned, and am now in hell.

*Faust.* How! now in hell!
Nay, and this be hell, I 'll willingly be damn'd
     here.
What? sleeping, eating, walking, and disputing?
But, leaving off this, let me have a wife,      141
The fairest maid in Germany, for I
Am wanton and lascivious, and can
Not live without a wife.
*Meph.* How — a wife?                          145
I prithee, Faustus, talk not of a wife.
*Faust.* Nay, sweet Mephistophilis, fetch me
     one, for I will have one.
*Meph.* Well — thou wilt have one. Sit
     there till I come:
I 'll fetch thee a wife in the Devil's name.
                                    [*Exit.*]

*Enter* [*Mephistophilis*] *with a Devil dressed like*
     *a woman, with fireworks*

*Meph.* Tell me, Faustus, how dost thou like
     thy wife?                                 150
*Faust.* A plague on her for a hot whore!
*Meph.* Tut, Faustus,
Marriage is but a ceremonial toy;
If thou lovest me, think no more of it.
I 'll cull thee out the fairest courtesans,     155
And bring them every morning to thy bed;
She whom thine eye shall like, thy heart shall
     have,
Be she as chaste as was Penelope,
As wise as Saba, or as beautiful
As was bright Lucifer before his fall.          160
Here, take this book, peruse it thoroughly:
                              [*Gives a book.*]
The iterating of these lines brings gold;
The framing of this circle on the ground
Brings whirlwinds, tempests, thunder and
     lightning;
Pronounce this thrice devoutly to thyself,      165
And men in armour shall appear to thee,
Ready to execute what thou desir'st.
*Faust.* Thanks, Mephistophilis; yet fain
would I have a book wherein I might behold
all spells and incantations, that I might raise [170
up spirits when I please.
*Meph.* Here they are, in this book.
                         *There turn to them.*
*Faust.* Now would I have a book where I
might see all characters and planets of the
heavens, that I might know their motions and
dispositions.                                   176
*Meph.* Here they are too.   *Turn to them.*
*Faust.* Nay, let me have one book more, —
and then I have done, — wherein I might see
all plants, herbs, and trees that grow upon [180
the earth.

---

⁹⁹ **whatsoever:** anything   ¹²³ **there:** (Not in A)   ¹²⁵ **purified:** released from Purgatory   ¹³³ **fond:**
foolish   ¹³⁶ **But:** ('But Faustus' A)   ¹³⁹⁻¹⁴⁶ (Printed as prose in A)   ¹⁴⁰ ('What walking, disputing, &c' A)   ¹⁵⁹ **Saba:** Queen of Sheba   ¹⁶⁸⁻¹⁸⁴ (Probably an actors' addition: not in B)

*Meph.* Here they be.
*Faust.* O, thou art deceived.
*Meph.* Tut, I warrant thee. *Turn to them.*
[*Exeunt.*]

[SCENE VI]

*Enter Faustus in his study, and Mephistophilis*

*Faust.* When I behold the heavens, then I
repent,
And curse thee, wicked Mephistophilis,
Because thou hast depriv'd me of those joys.
*Meph.* Why, Faustus,
Think'st thou Heaven is such a glorious thing?
I tell thee 't is not half so fair as thou,        6
Or any man that breathes on earth.
*Faust.* How provest thou that?
*Meph.* 'T was made for man, therefore is
man more excellent.
*Faust.* If heaven was made for man, 't was
made for me;        10
I will renounce this magic and repent.

*Enter Good Angel and Evil Angel*

*G. Ang.* Faustus, repent; yet God will pity
thee.
*E. Ang.* Thou art a spirit; God cannot pity
thee.
*Faust.* Who buzzeth in mine ears I am a
spirit?
Be I a devil, yet God may pity me;        15
Ay, God will pity me if I repent.
*E. Ang.* Ay, but Faustus never shall repent.
*Exeunt* [*Angels*].
*Faust.* My heart 's so hard'ned I cannot re-
pent.
Scarce can I name salvation, faith, or heaven,
But fearful echoes thunder in mine ears        20
"Faustus, thou art damn'd!" Then swords
and knives,
Poison, guns, halters, and envenom'd steel
Are laid before me to despatch myself,
And long ere this I should have done the deed,
Had not sweet pleasure conquer'd deep despair.
Have not I made blind Homer sing to me        26
Of Alexander's love and Œnon's death?
And hath not he that built the walls of Thebes
With ravishing sound of his melodious harp,
Made music with my Mephistophilis?        30
Why should I die then, or basely despair?
I am resolv'd: Faustus shall ne'er repent.
Come, Mephistophilis, let us dispute again,

And argue of divine astrology.
Speak, are there many spheres above the
moon?        35
Are all celestial bodies but one globe,
As is the substance of this centric earth?
*Meph.* As are the elements, such are the
heavens
Even from the moon unto the empyreal orb,
Mutually folded in each others' spheres,        40
And jointly move upon one axletree
Whose terminine is term'd the world's wide pole;
Nor are the names of Saturn, Mars, or Jupiter
Feign'd, but are erring stars.
*Faust.* But, have they all        45
One motion, both *situ et tempore?*
*Meph.* All jointly move from east to west in
four-and-twenty hours upon the poles of the
world; but differ in their motion upon the poles
of the zodiac.        50
*Faust.* Tush!
These slender trifles Wagner can decide;
Hath Mephistophilis no greater skill?
Who knows not the double motion of the
planets?
The first is finish'd in a natural day;        55
The second thus: as Saturn in thirty years;
Jupiter in twelve; Mars in four; the Sun, Venus,
and Mercury in a year; the moon in twenty-
eight days. Tush, these are freshmen's supposi-
tions. But tell me, hath every sphere a do- [60
minion or *intelligentia?*
*Meph.* Ay.
*Faust.* How many heavens, or spheres, are
there?
*Meph.* Nine: the seven planets, the firma-
ment, and the empyreal heaven.        66
*Faust.* But is there not *cœlum igneum et
cristalinum?*
*Meph.* No, Faustus, they be but fables.
*Faust.* Well, resolve me in this question:
Why have we not conjunctions, oppositions, [70
aspects, eclipses, all at one time, but in some
years we have more, in some less?
*Meph.* *Per inæqualem motum respectu totius.*
*Faust.* Well, I am answered. Tell me who
made the world.
*Meph.* I will not.        75
*Faust.* Sweet Mephistophilis, tell me.
*Meph.* Move me not, for I will not tell thee.
*Faust.* Villain, have I not bound thee to tell
me anything?

---

4 (' 'T was thine own seeking, Faustus, thank thyself.' B)        10 **heaven was** B: ('it were' A)        13 **spirit:**
*i.e.,* you have signed away your human soul        24 **done the deed** B: ('slain myself' A)        27 **Alexander:**
Paris, in love with Œnone and Helen        28 **he:** Amphion        35 **Speak ... spheres** B: ('Tell me ...
heavens' A)        37 **centric:** occupying the centre of the universe        38 **heavens** B: ('spheres' A)        39 (Not
in A)        40 **spheres** B: ('orb' A)        41 **And** B: ('And, Faustus, all' A)        42 **terminine** A: ('termine' B)
46 **situ et tempore:** in direction and period of revolution        49-50 **poles ... zodiac:** ecliptic        59-60 **sup-
positions** A: ('questions' B)        60-61 **dominion or intelligentia:** ruling spirit        67-68 (Not in A)
57 **cœlum igneum et cristalinum:** the fiery (empyrean) and crystalline sphere        73 "By reason of
differences of velocity "

*Meph.* Ay, that is not against our kingdom; but this is.
Think thou on hell, Faustus, for thou art damn'd. 80
*Faust.* Think, Faustus, upon God that made the world.
*Meph.* Remember this!
*Faust.* Ay, go, accursed spirit, to ugly hell.
'T is thou hast damn'd distressed Faustus' soul.
Is 't not too late? 85

*Enter Good Angel and Evil*

*E. Ang.* Too late.
*G. Ang.* Never too late, if Faustus can repent.
*E. Ang.* If thou repent, devils shall tear thee in pieces.
*G. Ang.* Repent, and they shall never raze thy skin.

*Exeunt [Angels].*

*Faust.* Ah, Christ, my Saviour, 90
Seek to save distressed Faustus' soul.

*Enter Lucifer, Belzebub, and Mephistophilis*

*Luc.* Christ cannot save thy soul, for he is just;
There 's none but I have interest in the same.
*Faust.* O, who art thou that look'st so terrible?
*Luc.* I am Lucifer, 95
And this is my companion-prince in hell.
*Faust.* O Faustus! they are come to fetch thy soul!
*Belz.* We come to tell thee thou dost injure us.
*Luc.* Thou call'st on Christ contrary to thy promise.
*Belz.* Thou should'st not think on God. 100
*Luc.* Think on the Devil.
*Belz.* And his dam, too.
*Faust.* Nor will I henceforth: pardon me in this,
And Faustus vows never to look to Heaven,
Never to name God, or to pray to him, 105
To burn his Scriptures, slay his ministers,
And make my spirits pull his churches down.
*Luc.* So shalt thou show thyself an obedient servant,
And we will highly gratify thee for it.
*Belz.* Faustus, we are come from hell in [110
person to show thee some pastime. Sit down, and thou shalt behold the Seven Deadly Sins appear to thee in their proper shapes and likeness.
*Faust.* That sight will be as pleasing unto me,

As Paradise was to Adam the first day 116
Of his creation.
*Luc.* Talk not of Paradise or creation, but mark the show. Go, Mephistophilis, fetch them in. 120

*Enter the Seven Deadly Sins*

Now, Faustus, examine them of their several names and dispositions.
*Faust.* That shall I soon! What art thou, the first?
*Pride.* I am Pride. I disdain to have any [125 parents. I am like to Ovid's flea: I can creep into every corner of a wench; sometimes, like a periwig, I sit upon her brow; or like a fan of feathers, I kiss her lips; indeed I do — what do I not? But, fie, what a scent is here! [130 I 'll not speak another word, except the ground were perfum'd, and covered with cloth of arras.
*Faust.* What art thou, the second?
*Covet.* I am Covetousness, begotten of an [135 old churl in an old leathern bag; and might I have my wish I would desire that this house and all the people in it were turn'd to gold, that I might lock you up in my good chest. O, my sweet gold! 140
*Faust.* What art thou, the third?
*Wrath.* I am Wrath. I had neither father nor mother: I leapt out of a lion's mouth when I was scarce half an hour old; and ever since I have run up and down the world with [145 this case of rapiers wounding myself when I had nobody to fight withal. I was born in hell; and look to it, for some of you shall be my father.
*Faust.* What art thou, the fourth? 150
*Envy.* I am Envy, begotten of a chimney sweeper and an oyster-wife. I cannot read, and therefore wish all books were burnt. I am lean with seeing others eat. O that there would come a famine through all the world, that [155 all might die, and I live alone! then thou should'st see how fat I would be. But must thou sit and I stand! Come down with a vengeance!
*Faust.* Away, envious rascal! What art thou, the fift? 160
*Glut.* Who, I, sir? I am Gluttony. My parents are all dead, and the devil a penny they have left me, but a bare pension, and that is thirty meals a day and ten bevers — a small trifle to suffice nature. O, I come of a royal [165 parentage! My grandfather was a gammon of bacon, my grandmother a hogshead of

⁹⁷ fetch B: ('fetch away' A) ⁹⁸⁻¹⁰² (As in B: one speech in A, assigned to Lucifer) ¹⁰²⁻¹⁰⁴ (Not in B) ¹⁰⁸⁻¹¹⁴ (One speech in A, abbreviated and assigned to Lucifer) ¹¹³⁻¹²⁰ (As in B) ¹²⁶ Ovid's flea: the late Latin poem, *de Pulice*, falsely ascribed to Ovid ¹⁴² Wrath: (B transposes speeches of Wrath and Envy.) ¹⁴⁶ case: pair ¹⁶⁰ fift: fifth ¹⁶⁴ bevers: snacks between meals ¹⁶⁶⁻¹⁶⁷ grandfather . . . grandmother A: ('father . . . mother' B)

claret-wine, my godfathers were these, Peter
Pickleherring, and Martin Martlemas-beef. O,
but my godmother, she was a jolly gentle- [170
woman, and well beloved in every good town
and city: her name was Mistress Margery
Marchbeer. Now, Faustus, thou hast heard all
my progeny, wilt thou bid me to supper?

*Faust.* No, I 'll see thee hanged! thou [175
wilt eat up all my victuals.

*Glut.* Then the Devil choke thee!

*Faust.* Choke thyself, glutton! What art
thou, the sixt?

*Sloth.* Heigh ho! I am Sloth. I was be- [180
gotten on a sunny bank, where I have lain ever
since; and you have done me great injury to
bring me from thence: let me be carried thither
again by Gluttony and Lechery. Heigh ho!
I 'll not speak another word for a king's ransom.

*Faust.* And what are you, Mistress Minx,
the seventh and last?     187

*Lech.* Who, I, sir? I am one that loves an
inch of raw mutton better than an ell of fried
stockfish; and the first letter of my name begins
with Lechery.     191

*Luc.* Away to hell, to hell! *Exeunt the Sins.*
— Now, Faustus, how dost thou like this?

*Faust.* O, this feeds my soul!

*Luc.* Tut, Faustus, in hell is all manner of
delight.     196

*Faust.* O might I see hell, and return again,
How happy were I then!

*Luc.* Thou shalt; I will send for thee at midnight.

In meantime take this book; peruse it throughly
and thou shalt turn thyself into what shape [201
thou wilt.

*Faust.* Great thanks, mighty Lucifer!
This will I keep as chary as my life.

*Luc.* Farewell, Faustus, and think on the
Devil.     205

*Faust.* Farewell, great Lucifer! Come, Mephistophilis.

     *Exeunt omnes.*

*Enter the Chorus*

Learned Faustus,
To find the secrets of astronomy,
Graven in the book of Jove's high firmament,
Did mount him up to scale Olympus' top;
Where, sitting in a chariot burning bright  5

Drawn by the strength of yoked dragons' necks,
He views the clouds, the planets, and the stars,
The tropic zones and quarters of the sky
From the bright circle of the horned moon
Even to the height of *Primum Mobile.*  10
And whirling round with this circumference,
Within the concave compass of the pole,
From east to west his dragons quickly glide,
And in eight days did bring him home again.
Not long he stayed within his quiet house  15
To rest his bones after his weary toil,
But new exploits do hale him out again,
And mounted then upon a dragon's back,
That with his wings did part the subtle air,
He now is gone to prove cosmography,  20
That measures coasts and kingdoms of the earth;
And, as I guess, will first arrive at Rome,
To see the Pope and manner of his court
And take some part of holy Peter's feast,
The which this day is highly solemniz'd.  25

[SCENE VII.  *The Pope's Privy-chamber.*]

*Enter Faustus and Mephistophilis*

*Faust.* Having now, my good Mephistophilis,
Pass'd with delight the stately town of Trier,
Environ'd round with airy mountain-tops,
With walls of flint, and deep entrenched lakes,
Not to be won by any conquering prince;  5
From Paris next, coasting the realm of France,
We saw the river Maine fall into Rhine,
Whose banks are set with groves of fruitful vines;
Then up to Naples, rich Campania,
Whose buildings fair and gorgeous to the eye,  10
The streets straight forth, and pav'd with
    finest brick,
Quarters the town in four equivalents.
There saw we learned Maro's golden tomb,
The way he cut, an English mile in length,
Thorough a rock of stone in one night's space;  15
From thence to Venice, Padua, and the rest,
In one of which a sumptuous temple stands,
That threats the stars with her aspiring top,
Whose frame is pav'd with sundry-colour'd
    stones,
And roof'd aloft with curious work in gold.  20
Thus hitherto hath Faustus spent his time:
But tell me, now, what resting-place is this?
Hast thou, as erst I did command,
Conducted me within the walls of Rome?

169 **Martlemas-beef:** salted beef, prepared about Martinmas (Nov. 11)  179 **sixt:** sixth  180, 184 **Heigh
ho:** (Not in A)  186 **And what** B: ('What' A)  190 **stockfish:** haddock (Lenten fare)  Chorus
1–25 (From B. In A it is reduced to eleven lines and assigned to Wagner, whose rôle was performed
by the same actor.)  10 **Primum Mobile:** the highest celestial sphere  11 Following the motion of
the *Primum Mobile*  12 **compass . . . pole:** arc described by poles of the universe  20 **prove:** test
2 **Trier:** Treves  9 **Campania:** (Misled by a passage in the Faustbook — "Campania in the Kingdom
of Neapolis," p. 54 — Marlowe takes Campania to be a name for the city of Naples.)  12 **equivalents:**
equal sections  13 **Maro's:** Vergil's  14 **way:** the tunnel at Posilippo near Vergil's tomb (cf. Faustbook, p. 54)  17 (Two descriptions in Faustbook, p. 55, are merged.  Lines 17–18 refer to St. Anthony's, Padua; 19–20 to St. Mark's, Venice.)  19, 20 (Not in A)

*Meph.* Faustus, I have; and because we [25
will not be unprovided, I have taken up his
Holiness' privy-chamber for our use.
*Faust.* I hope his Holiness will bid us welcome.
*Meph.* Tut, 't is no matter, man, we 'll be
bold with his good cheer.             30
And now, my Faustus, that thou may'st per-
ceive
What Rome containeth to delight thee with,
Know that this city stands upon seven hills
That underprop the groundwork of the same.
Just through the midst runs flowing Tiber's
     stream,             35
With winding banks that cut it in two parts:
Over the which four stately bridges lean,
That make safe passage to each part of Rome:
Upon the bridge call'd Ponte Angelo
Erected is a castle passing strong,        40
Within whose walls such store of ordnance
     are,
And double cannons, fram'd of carved brass,
As match the days within one complete year;
Beside the gates an high pyramides,
Which Julius Cæsar brought from Africa.    45
*Faust.* Now by the kingdoms of infernal rule,
Of Styx, Acheron, and the fiery lake
Of ever-burning Phlegethon, I swear
That I do long to see the monuments
And situation of bright-splendent Rome.    50
Come, therefore, let 's away.
     *Meph.*    Nay, Faustus, stay; I know you 'd
         see the Pope,    •
And take some part of holy Peter's feast,
Where thou shalt see a troop of bald-pate friars,
Whose *summum bonum* is in belly-cheer.    55
     *Faust.* Well, I 'm content to compass then
some sport,
And by their folly make us merriment.
Then charm me, that I
May be invisible, to do what I please
Unseen of any whilst I stay in Rome.      60
            [*Mephistophilis charms him.*]
     *Meph.* So, Faustus now
Do what thou wilt, thou shalt not be discern'd.

*Sound a sennet. Enter the Pope and the Car-*
     *dinal of Lorraine to the banquet, with Friars*
     *attending.*

     *Pope.* My Lord of Lorraine, will 't please you
draw near?
     *Faust.* Fall to, and the devil choke you and
you spare!
     *Pope.* How now! Who 's that which spake?
— Friars, look about.            65

     *Friar.* Here 's nobody, if it like your Holi-
ness.
     *Pope.* My lord, here is a dainty dish was sent
me from the Bishop of Milan.
     *Faust.* I thank you, sir.          *Snatch it.*
     *Pope.* How now! Who 's that which snatch'd
the meat from me? Will no man look? My [71
lord, this dish was sent me from the Cardinal
of Florence.
     *Faust.* You say true; I 'll ha 't. [*Snatches it.*]
     *Pope.* What again! My lord, I 'll drink to [75
your Grace.
     *Faust.*    I 'll pledge your Grace.
            [*Snatches the cup.*]
     *Lor.* My lord, it may be some ghost newly
crept out of purgatory, come to beg a pardon
of your Holiness.             80
     *Pope.* It may be so. Friars, prepare a dirge
to lay the fury of this ghost. Once again, my
lord, fall to.          *The Pope crosseth himself.*
     *Faust.* What, are you crossing of yourself?
Well, use that trick no more, I would advise
you.             85
            *Cross again.*
Well, there 's the second time. Aware the
     third,
I give you fair warning.
     *Cross again, and Faustus hits him a*
         *box of the ear; and they all run*
         *away.*
Come on, Mephistophilis, what shall we do?
     *Meph.* Nay, I know not. We shall be
curs'd with bell, book, and candle.      90
     *Faust.* How! bell, book, and candle, — can-
dle, book, and bell,
Forward and backward to curse Faustus to
hell!
Anon you shall hear a hog grunt, a calf bleat,
and an ass bray,
Because it is Saint Peter's holiday.

     *Enter all the Friars to sing the Dirge*

     *Friar.* Come, brethren, let 's about our [95
business with good devotion.

     *Sing this:*

Cursed be he that stole away his Holiness' meat
     from the table! *Maledicat Dominus!*
Cursed be he that struck his Holiness a blow
     on the face! *Maledicat Dominus!*
Cursed be he that took Friar Sandelo a blow on
     the pate! *Maledicat Dominus!*
Cursed be he that disturbeth our holy dirge!
     *Maledicat Dominus!*            100

---

<sup></sup> ²⁵⁻³⁰ (Corrupted text; B substitutes a poorly versified equivalent.)    ³⁵,³⁶ (Not in A)    ⁴⁴ **Beside:**
('Besides' A)    **an:** ('and' Qq.)    pyramides: obelisk (In 1586 an obelisk, brought to Rome by Cali-
gula, was set up near St. Peter's. Faustbook, p. 56: "He saw the pyramide that Julius Cæsar brought
out of Africa.")    ⁵⁴ ff. (B substitutes a much longer, heavily rimed amplification of the remainder of
this scene.)    ⁸⁶ **Aware:** beware

Cursed be he that took away his Holiness' wine!
*Maledicat Dominus! Et omnes sancti!
Amen!*
[*Mephistophilis and Faustus*] *beat
the Friars, and fling fireworks
among them: and so exeunt.*

[SCENE VIII. — *An Inn-yard.*]

*Enter Robin the Ostler with a book in his hand.*

*Robin.* O, this is admirable! here I ha' stolen
one of Dr. Faustus' conjuring books, and i'
faith I mean to search some circles for my
own use. Now will I make all the maidens in
our parish dance at my pleasure, stark naked [5
before me; and so by that means I shall see
more than e'er I felt or saw yet.

*Enter Rafe calling Robin*

*Rafe.* Robin, prithee come away; there 's a
gentleman tarries to have his horse, and he
would have his things rubb'd and made clean. [10
He keeps such a chafing with my mistress about
it; and she has sent me to look thee out. Prithee
come away.
*Robin.* Keep out, keep out, or else you are
blown up; you are dismemb'red, Rafe: keep [15
out, for I am about a roaring piece of work.
*Rafe.* Come, what dost thou with that same
book? Thou canst not read.
*Robin.* Yes, my master and mistress shall
find that I can read, he for his forehead, she [20
for her private study; she 's born to bear with
me, or else my art fails.
*Rafe.* Why, Robin, what book is that?
*Robin.* What book! Why, the most intolerable book for conjuring that e'er was invented
by any brimstone devil.                        26
*Rafe.* Canst thou conjure with it?
*Robin.* I can do all these things easily with it:
first, I can make thee drunk with ippocras at
any tabern in Europe for nothing; that 's one
of my conjuring works.                         31
*Rafe.* Our Master Parson says that 's nothing.
*Robin.* True, Rafe; and more, Rafe, if thou
hast any mind to Nan Spit, our kitchenmaid,
then turn her and wind her to thy own use [35
as often as thou wilt, and at midnight.
*Rafe.* O brave Robin, shall I have Nan
Spit, and to mine own use? On that condition
I 'll feed thy devil with horsebread as long as
he lives, of free cost.                         40
*Robin.* No more, sweet Rafe: let 's go and
make clean our boots, which lie foul upon our
hands, and then to our conjuring in the Devil's
name.                                 *Exeunt.*

[SCENE IX]

*Enter Robin and Rafe with a silver goblet.*

*Robin.* Come, Rafe, did not I tell thee we
were for ever made by this Doctor Faustus'
book? *Ecce signum,* here 's a simple purchase
for horsekeepers; our horses shall eat no hay
as long as this lasts.                         5

*Enter the Vintner*

*Rafe.* But, Robin, here comes the vintner.
*Robin.* Hush! I 'll gull him supernaturally.
Drawer, I hope all is paid: God be with you.
Come, Rafe.
*Vint.* Soft, sir; a word with you. I must [10
yet have a goblet paid from you, ere you go.
*Robin.* I, a goblet, Rafe; I, a goblet! I
scorn you, and you are but a &c. I, a goblet!
search me.
*Vint.* I mean so, sir, with your favour.    15
[*Searches him.*]
*Robin.* How say you now?
*Vint.* I must say somewhat to your fellow.
You, sir!
*Rafe.* Me, sir! me, sir! search your fill.
[*Vintner searches him.*] Now, sir, you may be
ashamed to burden honest men with a matter [21
of truth.
*Vint.* Well, t' one of you hath this goblet
about you.
*Robin.* [*Aside.*] You lie, drawer, 't is afore [25
me. — Sirrah you, I 'll teach ye to impeach
honest men; stand by; — I 'll scour you for a
goblet! — Stand aside, you had best. I charge
you in the name of Belzebub. — Look to the
goblet, Rafe.            [*Aside to Rafe.*]  30
*Vint.* What mean you, sirrah?
*Robin.* I 'll tell you what I mean. *He reads.*
*Sanctobulorum, Periphrasticon* — Nay, I 'll
tickle you, vintner. — Look to the goblet,
Rafe.                                    35
*Polypragmos Belseborams framanto pacostiphos
tostu, Mephistophilis, &c.*

*Enter Mephistophilis, sets squibs at their backs
[and then exit]. They run about.*

*Vint.* O *nomine Domine!* what meanst thou,
Robin? Thou hast no goblet.
*Rafe. Peccatum peccatorum!* Here 's [40
thy goblet, good vintner.
[*Gives the goblet to Vintner, who exit.*]
*Robin. Misericordia pro nobis!* What shall
I do? Good Devil, forgive me now, and I 'll
never rob thy library more.

Sc. VIII (Clearly spurious, like Sc. IX which follows. B gives a different version of each scene
and separates them, putting one before and one after the scene at Rome.)    ¹⁶ **roaring:** furious
²⁹ **ippocras:** a compound of wine, spice, and sugar    ³⁰ **tabern:** tavern    ⁴ **purchase:** booty
⁸ **Drawer:** waiter    ¹³ **&c.:** (gag to be added *ad lib.*)    ²² **of truth:** concerning their honesty

*Enter to them Mephistophilis*

*Meph.* Vanish, villains, th' one like an [45 ape, another like a bear, the third an ass for doing this enterprise!
Monarch of hell, under whose black survey
Great potentates do kneel with awful fear,
Upon whose altars thousand souls do lie!    50
How am I vexed with these villains? charms?
From Constantinople am I hither come
Only for pleasure of these damned slaves.
*Robin.* How from Constantinople? You have had a great journey. Will you take sixpence [55 in your purse to pay for your supper, and begone?
*Meph.* Well, villains, for your presumption,
I transform thee into an ape, and thee into a dog; and so begone.                    *Exit.* 60
*Robin.* How, into an ape? That 's brave! I 'll have fine sport with the boys. I 'll get nuts and apples enow.
*Rafe.* And I must be a dog.
*Robin.* I' faith thy head will never be out [65 of the pottage pot.                    *Exeunt.*

*Enter Chorus*

When Faustus had with pleasure ta'en the view
Of rarest things, and royal courts of kings,
He stay'd his course and so returned home;
Where such as bear his absence but with grief,—
I mean his friends and nearest companions, —
Did gratulate his safety with kind words.    6
And in their conference of what befell,
Touching his journey through the world and air,
They put forth questions of astrology,
Which Faustus answer'd with such learned skill
As they admir'd and wonder'd at his wit.    11
Now is his fame spread forth in every land:
Amongst the rest the Emperor is one,
Carolus the Fift, at whose palace now
Faustus is feasted 'mongst his noblemen.    15
What there he did in trial of his art,
I leave untold, — your eyes shall see perform'd.

[SCENE X.    *Court of Charles V.*]

*Enter Emperor, Faustus, [Mephistophilis,] and a Knight, with attendants*

*Emp.* Master Doctor Faustus, I have heard strange report of thy knowledge in the black art, how that none in my empire nor in the whole world can compare with thee for the rare effects of magic. They say thou hast a familiar [5 spirit, by whom thou canst accomplish what thou list. This, therefore, is my request, that thou let me see some proof of thy skill, that mine eyes may be witnesses to confirm what mine ears have heard reported; and here I [10 swear to thee by the honour of mine imperial crown, that, whatever thou doest, thou shalt be no ways prejudiced or endamaged.
*Knight.* I' faith he looks much like a conjuror.                    *Aside.* 15
*Faust.* My gracious sovereign, though I must confess myself far inferior to the report men have published, and nothing answerable to the honour of your imperial majesty, yet for that love and duty binds me thereunto, I am con- [20 tent to do whatsoever your majesty shall command me.
*Emp.* Then, Doctor Faustus, mark what I shall say.
As I was sometime solitary set
Within my closet, sundry thoughts arose    25
About the honour of mine ancestors:
How they had won by prowess such exploits,
Got such riches, subdued so many kingdoms,
As we that do succeed, or they that shall
Hereafter possess our throne, shall    30
(I fear me) never attain to that degree
Of high renown and great authority.
Amongst which kings is Alexander the Great,
Chief spectacle of the world's pre-eminence,
The bright shining of whose glorious acts    35
Lightens the world with his reflecting beams;
As, when I hear but motion made of him,
It grieves my soul I never saw the man.
If, therefore, thou by cunning of thine art    39
Canst raise this man from hollow vaults below,
Where lies entomb'd this famous conqueror,
And bring with him his beauteous paramour,
Both in their right shapes, gesture, and attire
They us'd to wear during their time of life,
Thou shalt both satisfy my just desire,    45
And give me cause to praise thee whilst I live.
*Faust.* My gracious lord, I am ready to accomplish your request so far forth as by art, and power of my Spirit, I am able to perform.    50
*Knight.* I' faith that 's just nothing at all.                    *Aside.*
*Faust.* But, if it like your Grace, it is not in my ability to present before your eyes the true substantial bodies of those two deceased princes, which long since are consumed to dust.    55
*Knight.* Ay, marry, Master Doctor, now there 's a sign of grace in you, when you will confess the truth.                    *Aside.*
*Faust.* But such spirits as can lively resemble Alexander and his paramour shall appear before

---

[45-47] (These lines, not in B, once concluded the scene. Another ending has been tacked on.)
Chorus [1-17] (Not in B. In A this passage is separated by the two Robin-Rafe scenes from the scene at Charles V's court, with which it evidently belongs.)    Sc. X (Expanded into four scenes in B)
[18] **answerable:** fitting    [24] **set:** seated    [36] **his:** its    [37] **As:** so that    **motion:** mention

your Grace in that manner that they both [61
liv'd in, in their most flourishing estate; which
I doubt not shall sufficiently content your imperial majesty.

*Emp.* Go to, Master Doctor, let me see them
presently.                                      66

*Knight.* Do you hear, Master Doctor? You
bring Alexander and his paramour before the
Emperor!

*Faust.* How then, sir?                        70

*Knight.* I' faith that's as true as Diana
turn'd me to a stag!

*Faust.* No, sir, but when Actæon died, he
left the horns for you. Mephistophilis, begone.                    *Exit Mephistophilis.* 75

*Knight.* Nay, and you go to conjuring, I'll
be gone.                          *Exit Kn.*

*Faust.* I'll meet with you anon for inter-
rupting me so. Here they are, my gracious
lord.                                          80

*Enter Mephistophilis with [Spirits in the shape
of] Alexander and his Paramour*

*Emp.* Master Doctor, I heard this lady while
she liv'd had a wart or mole in her neck. How
shall I know whether it be so or no?

*Faust.* Your Highness may boldly go and see.
                    *Exeunt Alex. [and other Spirit].*

*Emp.* Sure these are no spirits, but the [85
true substantial bodies of those two deceased
princes.

*Faust.* Will't please your Highness now to
send for the knight that was so pleasant with
me here of late?                               90

*Emp.* One of you call him forth.
                              *[Exit Attendant.]*


*Enter the Knight with a pair of horns on his head*

How now, sir knight! why I had thought
thou had'st been a bachelor, but now I see thou
hast a wife, that not only gives thee horns, but
makes thee wear them. Feel on thy head.        95

*Knight.* Thou damned wretch and execrable
                              dog,
Bred in the concave of some monstrous rock,
How darst thou thus abuse a gentleman?
Villain, I say, undo what thou hast done!

*Faust.* O, not so fast, sir; there's no haste: [100
but, good, are you rememb'red how you crossed
me in my conference with the Emperor? I
think I have met with you for it.

*Emp.* Good Master Doctor, at my entreaty release him; he hath done penance sufficient. [105

*Faust.* My gracious lord, not so much for

the injury he off'red me here in your presence,
as to delight you with some mirth, hath Faustus
worthily requited this injurious knight; [109
which being all I desire, I am content to release him of his horns: and, sir knight, hereafter speak well of scholars. Mephistophilis,
transform him straight. [*Mephistophilis removes the horns.*] Now, my good lord, having
done my duty I humbly take my leave.      115

*Emp.* Farewell, Master Doctor; yet, ere you
                              go,
Expect from me a bounteous reward.
                    *Exit Emperor [and others]*


[SCENE XI. — *Location Indefinite.*]

[*Enter Faustus and Mephistophilis*]

*Faust.* Now, Mephistophilis, the restless
                              course
That Time doth run with calm and silent foot,
Short'ning my days and thread of vital life,
Calls for the payment of my latest years;
Therefore, sweet Mephistophilis, let us        5
Make haste to Wittenberg.

*Meph.* What, will you go on horseback or on
                              foot?

*Faust.* Nay, till I am past this fair and pleas-
                              ant green,
I'll walk on foot.


*Enter a Horse-Courser*

*Horse-C.* I have been all this day seeking [10
one Master Fustian: mass, see where he is! God
save you, Master Doctor!

*Faust.* What, horse-courser! You are well
met.

*Horse-C.* Do you hear, sir? I have [15
brought you forty dollars for your horse.

*Faust.* I cannot sell him so: if thou lik'st him
for fifty, take him.

*Horse-C.* Alas, sir, I have no more. — I pray
you speak for me.             [*To Meph.*] 20

*Meph.* I pray you let him have him: he is an
honest fellow, and he has a great charge —
neither wife nor child.

*Faust.* Well, come, give me your money.
My boy will deliver him to you. But I must [25
tell you one thing before you have him: ride
him not into the water at any hand.

*Horse-C.* Why, sir, will he not drink of all
waters?

*Faust.* O yes, he will drink of all waters, [30
but ride him not into the water: ride him over
hedge or ditch, or where thou wilt, but not into
the water.

⁶¹ **both:** ('best' A. Cf. Faustbook: "in manner and forme as they both liued in their most
florishing time")   ⁶⁶ **presently:** at once   ⁷⁶ **and:** if, an   ¹⁰¹ **good:** my good sir   ¹⁰³ **met with:**
recompensed   ¹⁰⁹ **injurious:** abusive   Sc. XI (Reduced by nearly half in B)   ⁹ S. D. **Horse-Courser:**
dealer in horses   ²² **charge:** financial burden   ²⁷ **at . . . hand:** in any case

*Horse-C.* Well, sir. — Now am I made man forever. I 'll not leave my horse for forty. If [35 he had but the quality of hey-ding-ding, hey-ding-ding, I 'd make a brave living on him: he has a buttock as slick as an eel. [*Aside.*] Well, God b' wi' ye, sir, your boy will deliver him me: but hark ye, sir; if my horse be sick or ill at [40 ease, if I bring his water to you, you 'll tell me what it is?

*Faust.* Away, you villain; what, dost think I am a horse-doctor? *Exit Horse-Courser.*
What art thou, Faustus, but a man con-
demn'd to die? 45
Thy fatal time doth draw to final end;
Despair doth drive distrust unto my thoughts.
Confound these passions with a quiet sleep:
Tush, Christ did call the thief upon the cross;
Then rest thee, Faustus, quiet in conceit. 50
*Sleep in his chair [on rear-stage].*

*Enter Horse-Courser, all wet, crying*

*Horse-C.* Alas, alas! Doctor Fustian, quotha? Mass, Doctor Lopus was never such a doctor. H'as given me a purgation has purg'd me of forty dollars; I shall never see them more. But yet, like an ass as I was, I would not be ruled [55 by him, for he bade me I should ride him into no water. Now I, thinking my horse had had some rare quality that he would not have had me known of, I, like a venturous youth, rid him into the deep pond at the town's end. I was [60 no sooner in the middle of the pond, but my horse vanish'd away, and I sat upon a bottle of hay, never so near drowning in my life. But I 'll seek out my Doctor, and have my forty dollars again, or I 'll make it the dearest horse! — [65 O, yonder is his snipper-snapper. — Do you hear? You hey-pass, where 's your master?

*Meph.* Why, sir, what would you? You can-not speak with him.

*Horse-C.* But I will speak with him. 70

*Meph.* Why, he 's fast asleep. Come some other time.

*Horse-C.* I 'll speak with him now, or I 'll break his glass windows about his ears.

*Meph.* I tell thee he has not slept this [75 eight nights.

*Horse-C.* And he have not slept this eight weeks, I 'll speak with him.

*Meph.* See where he is, fast asleep.

*Horse-C.* Ay, this is he. God save ye, Mas-[80 ter Doctor! Master Doctor, Master Doctor Fus-tian! — Forty dollars, forty dollars for a bottle of hay!

*Meph.* Why, thou seest he hears thee not.

*Horse-C.* So ho, ho! — so ho, ho! (*Halloo in* [85 *his ear.*) No, will you not wake? I 'll make you wake ere I go. (*Pull him by the leg, and pull it away.*) Alas, I am undone! What shall I do?

*Faust.* O my leg, my leg! Help, Mephistoph-ilis! call the officers. My leg, my leg! 90

*Meph.* Come, villain, to the constable.

*Horse-C.* O lord, sir, let me go, and I 'll give you forty dollars more.

*Meph.* Where be they?

*Horse-C.* I have none about me. Come to my ostry and I 'll give them you. 96

*Meph.* Begone quickly.
*Horse-Courser runs away.*

*Faust.* What, is he gone? Farewell he! Faustus has his leg again, and the horse-courser, I take it, a bottle of hay for his labour. Well, this trick shall cost him forty dollars more. 101

*Enter Wagner*

How now, Wagner, what 's the news with thee?

*Wag.* Sir, the Duke of Vanholt doth ear-nestly entreat your company. 105

*Faust.* The Duke of Vanholt! an honourable gentleman, to whom I must be no niggard of my cunning. Come, Mephistophilis, let 's away to him. *Exeunt.* 109

[SCENE XII. — *Duke of Anhalt's Castle.*]
*Enter to them the Duke and the Duchess. The Duke speaks.*

*Duke.* Believe me, Master Doctor, this mer-riment hath much pleased me.

*Faust.* My gracious lord, I am glad it contents you so well. — But it may be, madam, you take no delight in this. I have heard that great- [5 bellied women do long for some dainties or other. What is it, madam? Tell me, and you shall have it.

*Duchess.* Thanks, good Master Doctor; and for I see your courteous intent to pleasure [10 me, I will not hide from you the thing my heart desires; and were it now summer, as it is Jan-uary and the dead time of the winter, I would desire no better meat than a dish of ripe grapes. 15

*Faust.* Alas, madam, that 's nothing! Meph-istophilis, begone. *Exit Meph.*
Were it a greater thing than this, so it would content you, you should have it.

*Enter Mephistophilis with the grapes*

Here they be, madam; will 't please you taste on them? 21

**34 made:** fortunate   **36 quality, etc.:** ability to dance   **46 fatal:** allotted   **48 Confound:** undo
**50 conceit:** mind   **52 Doctor Lopus:** Dr. Lopez, executed 1594 (a post-Marlovian allusion)   **53 has:** that has   **59 known:** aware   **62 bottle:** bunch   **67 hey-pass:** trickster   **96 ostry:** hostelry
**104 Vanholt:** Anhalt   Sc. XII (Padded with farcical matter in B)

*Duke.* Believe me, Master Doctor, this makes me wonder above the rest, that being in the dead time of winter, and in the month of January, how you should come by these grapes. 25

*Faust.* If it like your Grace, the year is divided into two circles over the whole world, that, when it is here winter with us, in the contrary circle it is summer with them, as in India, Saba, and farther countries in the East; and by means of a swift spirit that I have, [31 I had them brought hither, as ye see. — How do you like them, madam? be they good?

*Duchess.* Believe me, Master Doctor, they be the best grapes that e'er I tasted in my life before.                                                             36

*Faust.* I am glad they content you so, madam.

*Duke.* Come, madam, let us in, where you must well reward this learned man for the great kindness he hath show'd to you.                   40

*Duchess.* And so I will, my lord; and whilst I live, rest beholding for this courtesy.

*Faust.* I humbly thank your Grace.

*Duke.* Come, Master Doctor, follow us and receive your reward.                 *Exeunt.* 45

[SCENE XIII. — *The House of Faustus.*]

*Enter Wagner, solus*

*Wag.* I think my master means to die shortly. He has made his will and given me his wealth: His house, his goods, and store of golden plate, Besides two thousand ducats ready coin'd. And yet, methinks, if that death were near, 5 He would not banquet and carouse and swill Amongst the students, as even now he doth, Who are at supper with such belly-cheer As Wagner ne'er beheld in all his life.           9 See where they come! Belike the feast is ended.

*Enter Faustus, with two or three Scholars [and Mephistophilis]*

1 *Schol.* Master Doctor Faustus, since our conference about fair ladies, which was the beautiful'st in all the world, we have determined with ourselves that Helen of Greece was the admirablest lady that ever lived. Therefore, Master Doctor, if you will do us that favour, [16 as to let us see that peerless dame of Greece, whom all the world admires for majesty, we should think ourselves much beholding unto you.                                                               20

*Faust.* Gentlemen, For that I know your friendship is unfeigned, And Faustus' custom is not to deny The just requests of those that wish him well,

You shall behold that peerless dame of Greece, No otherways for pomp and majesty       25 Than when Sir Paris cross'd the seas with her, And brought the spoils to rich Dardania. Be silent, then, for danger is in words.

*Music sounds, and Helen passeth over the stage.*

2 *Schol.* Too simple is my wit to tell her praise, Whom all the world admires for majesty.   30

3 *Schol.* No marvel though the angry Greeks pursu'd With ten years' war the rape of such a queen, Whose heavenly beauty passeth all compare.

1 *Schol.* Since we have seen the pride of Nature's works, And only paragon of excellence,         35

*Enter an Old Man*

Let us depart; and for this glorious deed Happy and blest be Faustus evermore.

*Faustus.* Gentlemen, farewell — the same I wish to you.

*Exeunt Scholars [and Wagner].*

*Old Man.* Ah, Doctor Faustus, that I might prevail To guide thy steps unto the way of life,   40 By which sweet path thou may'st attain the goal That shall conduct thee to celestial rest! [*O gentle Faustus, leave this damned art, This magic, that will charm thy soul to hell, And quite bereave thee of salvation!*         45 *Though thou hast now offended like a man, Do not persever in it like a devil: Yet, yet, thou hast an amiable soul, If sin by custom grow not into nature. Then, Faustus, will repentance come too late,* 50 *Then thou art banish'd from the sight of heaven. No mortal can express the pains of hell! It may be, this my exhortation Seems harsh and all unpleasant: let it not! For, gentle son, I speak it not in wrath,*   55 *Or envy of thee, but in tender love, And pity of thy future misery. And so have hope that this my kind rebuke, Checking thy body, may amend thy soul.*] Break heart, drop blood, and mingle it with tears,                                                           60 Tears falling from repentant heaviness Of thy most vild and loathsome filthiness, The stench whereof corrupts the inward soul With such flagitious crimes of heinous sins As no commiseration may expel,               65 But mercy, Faustus, of thy Saviour sweet, Whose blood alone must wash away thy guilt.

*Faust.* Where art thou, Faustus? Wretch,
what hast thou done?
Damn'd art thou, Faustus, damn'd; despair
and die!
Hell claims his right, and with a roaring voice 70
Says "Faustus! come! thine hour is almost
come!"
And Faustus now will come to do thee right.
*Mephistophilis gives him a dagger.*
*Old Man.* Ah stay, good Faustus, stay thy
desperate steps!
I see an angel hovers o'er thy head,
And, with a vial full of precious grace, 75
Offers to pour the same into thy soul:
Then call for mercy, and avoid despair.
*Faust.* Ah, my sweet friend, I feel
Thy words to comfort my distressed soul.
Leave me a while to ponder on my sins. 80
*Old Man.* I go, sweet Faustus, but with
heavy cheer,
Fearing the ruin of thy hopeless soul. [*Exit.*]
*Faust.* Accursed Faustus, where is mercy now?
I do repent; and yet I do despair:
Hell strives with grace for conquest in my
breast: 85
What shall I do to shun the snares of death?
*Meph.* Thou traitor, Faustus, I arrest thy soul
For disobedience to my sovereign lord;
Revolt, or I 'll in piecemeal tear thy flesh.
*Faust.* I do repent I e'er offended him. 90
Sweet Mephistophilis, entreat thy lord
To pardon my unjust presumption,
And with my blood again I will confirm
My former vow I made to Lucifer.
*Meph.* Do it then quickly, with unfeigned
heart, 95
Lest greater danger do attend thy drift.
*Faust.* Torment, sweet friend, that base
and crooked age,
That durst dissuade me from thy Lucifer,
With greatest torments that our hell affords.
*Meph.* His faith is great, I cannot touch his
soul; 100
But what I may afflict his body with
I will attempt, which is but little worth.
*Faust.* One thing, good servant, let me crave
of thee,
To glut the longing of my heart's desire, —
That I might have unto my paramour 105
That heavenly Helen, which I saw of late,
Whose sweet embracings may extinguish clean
These thoughts that do dissuade me from my
vow,
And keep mine oath I made to Lucifer.

*Meph.* Faustus, this or what else thou shalt
desire 110
Shall be perform'd in twinkling of an eye.

*Enter Helen [again, passing over between two
Cupids]*

*Faust.* Was this the face that launch'd a
thousand ships,
And burnt the topless towers of Ilium?
Sweet Helen, make me immortal with a kiss.
[*Kisses her.*]
Her lips sucks forth my soul; see where it
flies! — 115
Come, Helen, come, give me my soul again.
[*Kisses her.*]
Here will I dwell, for Heaven be in these lips,
And all is dross that is not Helena.

*Enter Old Man*

I will be Paris, and for love of thee,
Instead of Troy, shall Wittenberg be sack'd; 120
And I will combat with weak Menelaus,
And wear thy colours on my plumed crest;
Yea, I will wound Achilles in the heel,
And then return to Helen for a kiss.
Oh, thou art fairer than the evening air 125
Clad in the beauty of a thousand stars;
Brighter art thou than flaming Jupiter
When he appear'd to hapless Semele;
More lovely than the monarch of the sky
In wanton Arethusa's azur'd arms: 130
And none but thou shalt be my paramour.
*Exeunt [Faustus and Helen].*
*Old Man.* Accursed Faustus, miserable man,
That from thy soul exclud'st the grace of
Heaven,
And fly'st the throne of his tribunal seat!

*Enter the Devils*

Satan begins to sift me with his pride. 135
As in this furnace God shall try my faith,
My faith, vile hell, shall triumph over thee.
Ambitious fiends! see how the heavens smiles
At your repulse, and laughs your state to
scorn!
Hence, hell! for hence I fly unto my God. 140
*Exeunt.*

[SCENE XIV. — *Faustus' Chamber.*]

*Enter Faustus with the Scholars*

*Faust.* Ah, gentlemen!
*1 Schol.* What ails Faustus?
*Faust.* Ah, my sweet chamber-fellow, had I

---

⁷⁰ claims his B: ('calls for' A)  ⁷¹, ⁷² almost, now: (These two words not in A)  ⁷⁴ hovers: which
hovers  ⁸⁹ Revolt: turn back  ⁹⁰ (Not in A)  ⁹⁷ age: old man  ¹¹¹ S. D. again . . . Cupids:
(Added by B)  ¹¹³ topless: immensely high  ¹²⁹ monarch of the sky: Apollo  ¹³⁰ Arethusa's: (The
myth of Apollo and Leucothoe is perhaps referred to; cf. Ovid, *Met.* iv. 230 ff.)  ¹³²⁻¹⁴⁰ (Not in B)
Sc XIV  ¹ (This is preceded by 27 spurious lines in B.)

lived with thee, then had I lived still! but now I die eternally. Look, comes he not, comes he [5 not?

*2 Schol.* What means Faustus?

*3 Schol.* Belike he is grown into some sickness by being over solitary.

*1 Schol.* If it be so, we 'll have physicians to [10 cure him. 'T is but a surfeit. Never fear, man.

*Faust.* A surfeit of deadly sin that hath damn'd both body and soul.

*2 Schol.* Yet, Faustus, look up to Heaven; remember, God's mercies are infinite.    16

*Faust.* But Faustus' offence can ne'er be pardoned. The serpent that tempted Eve may be sav'd, but not Faustus. Ah, gentlemen, hear me with patience, and tremble not at my [20 speeches! Though my heart pants and quivers to remember that I have been a student here these thirty years, oh, would I had never seen Wittenberg, never read book! And what wonders I have done, all Germany can witness, yea, [26 all the world; for which Faustus hath lost both Germany and the world, — yea Heaven itself, Heaven, the seat of God, the throne of the blessed, the kingdom of joy; and must remain in hell for ever: hell, ah, hell, for ever! Sweet friends! what shall become of Faustus being in hell for ever?    32

*3 Schol.* Yet, Faustus, call on God.

*Faust.* On God, whom Faustus hath abjur'd! on God, whom Faustus hath blasphemed! Ah, my God, I would weep, but the Devil draws [36 in my tears. Gush forth, blood, instead of tears! Yea, life and soul! Oh, he stays my tongue! I would lift up my hands, but see, they hold them, they hold them!    40

*All.* Who, Faustus?

*Faust.* Lucifer and Mephistophilis. Ah, gentlemen, I gave them my soul for my cunning! 

*All.* God forbid!    45

*Faust.* God forbade it indeed; but Faustus hath done it. For vain pleasure of four-and-twenty years hath Faustus lost eternal joy and felicity. I writ them a bill with mine own blood: the date is expired; the time will come, and [50 he will fetch me.

*1 Schol.* Why did not Faustus tell us of this before, that divines might have prayed for thee?

*Faust.* Oft have I thought to have done [55 so; but the Devil threat'ned to tear me in pieces if I nam'd God; to fetch both body and soul if I once gave ear to divinity: and now 't is too late. Gentlemen, away! lest you perish with me.

*2 Schol.* Oh, what shall we do to save Faustus?

*Faust.* Talk not of me, but save yourselves, and depart.    62

*3 Schol.* God will strengthen me. I will stay with Faustus.    64

*1 Schol.* Tempt not God, sweet friend; but let us into the next room, and there pray for him.

*Faust.* Ay, pray for me, pray for me! and what noise soever ye hear, come not unto me, for nothing can rescue me.    70

*2 Schol.* Pray thou, and we will pray that God may have mercy upon thee.

*Faust.* Gentlemen, farewell! If I live till morning I 'll visit you: if not, Faustus is gone to hell.    75

*All.* Faustus, farewell!

                       *Exeunt Scholars.*

[Meph. *Ay, Faustus, now thou hast no hope of heaven;*
*Therefore, despair; think only upon hell,*
*For that must be thy mansion, there to dwell.*

Faust. *O thou bewitching fiend! 't was thy temptation*    80
*Hath robb'd me of eternal happiness.*

Meph. *I do confess it, Faustus, and rejoice.*
*'T was I that, when thou wert i' the way to heaven,*
*Damm'd up thy passage; when thou took'st the book*    84
*To view the Scriptures, then I turn'd the leaves*
*And led thine eye.*
*What, weep'st thou? 'T is too late: despair. Farewell.*
*Fools that will laugh on earth must weep in hell.*
                       *Exit.*

Enter the Good Angel and the Bad Angel at several doors

Good. *O Faustus, if thou hadst given ear to me,*
*Innumerable joys had followed thee;*    90
*But thou didst love the world.*

Bad. *Gave ear to me,*
*And now must taste hell's pains perpetually.*

Good. *O what will all thy riches, pleasures, pomps*
*Avail thee now?*

Bad.          *Nothing, but vex thee more,*
*To want in hell, that had on earth such store.*   96

Music while the Throne descends

Good. *O thou hast lost celestial happiness,*
*Pleasures unspeakable, bliss without end!*
*Hadst thou affected sweet divinity,*
*Hell, or the devil, had had no power on thee.*   100
*Hadst thou kept on that way, Faustus, behold*
*In what resplendent glory thou hadst set*
*In yonder throne, like those bright-shining saints,*

---

<sup>77–123</sup> (These obviously spurious lines, added by B, are included for the interest of their melodramatic staging.)

*And triumph'd over hell.  That hast thou lost;* 104
*And now, poor soul, must thy good angel leave*
    *thee.*                    [The Throne ascends.]
*The jaws of hell are open to receive thee.    Exit.*

Hell is discovered

Bad.  *Now, Faustus, let thine eyes with horror*
*stare*
*Into that vast perpetual torture-house.*
*There are the Furies tossing damned souls*
*On burning forks; their bodies broil in lead.* 110
*There are live quarters broiling on the coals,*
*That ne'er can die.  This ever-burning chair*
*Is for o'er-turtur'd souls to rest them in.*
*These, that are fed with sops of flaming fire,*
*Were gluttons. and lov'd only delicates,*        115
*And laugh'd to see the poor starve at their gates.*
*And yet all these are nothing: thou shalt see*
*Ten thousand tortures that more horrid be.*
    Faust.  *O, I have seen enough to torture me.*
    Bad.  *Nay, thou must feel them, taste the smart*
    *of all:*                                      120
*He that loves pleasure must for pleasure fall.*
*And so I leave thee, Faustus, till anon;*
*Then wilt thou tumble in confusion.*       Exit.]

The Clock strikes eleven

*Faust.*    Ah, Faustus,
Now hast thou but one bare hour to live,     125
And then thou must be damn'd perpetually!
Stand still, you ever-moving spheres of Heaven,
That time may cease, and midnight never come!
Fair Nature's eye, rise, rise again and make
Perpetual day;  or let this hour be but     130
A year, a month, a week, a natural day,
That Faustus may repent and save his soul!
*O lente, lente, currite, noctis equi!*
The stars move still, time runs, the clock will
    strike,
The Devil will come, and Faustus must be
    damn'd.                                   135
O, I 'll leap up to my God! Who pulls me down?
See, see where Christ's blood streams in the
    firmament!
One drop would save my soul — half a drop:
    ah, my Christ!
Ah, rend not my heart for naming of my
    Christ!                                   139
Yet will I call on him: O spare me, Lucifer! —
Where is it now? 'T is gone; and see where God
Stretcheth out his arm, and bends his ireful
    brows!
Mountains and hills, come, come and fall on me,

And hide me from the heavy wrath of God!
That when you vomit forth into the air,      145
My limbs may issue from your smoky mouths.
No! no!
Then will I headlong run into the earth;
Earth gape! O no, it will not harbour me!
You stars that reign'd at my nativity,       150
Whose influence hath allotted death and hell,
Now draw up Faustus like a foggy mist
Into the entrails of yon labouring cloud,
So that my soul may but ascend to Heaven. 154
            *The watch strikes [the half hour].*
Ah, half the hour is past! 'T will all be past
    anon!
O God!
If thou wilt not have mercy on my soul,
Yet for Christ's sake whose blood hath ran-
    som'd me,
Impose some end to my incessant pain:        159
Let Faustus live in hell a thousand years —
A hundred thousand, and at last be sav'd!
No end is limited to damned souls!
Why wert thou not a creature wanting soul?
Or why is this immortal that thou hast?
Ah, Pythagóras' metempsýchosis!              165
Were that true,
This soul should fly from me, and I be chang'd
Unto some brutish beast! All beasts are happy,
For, when they die,
Their souls are soon dissolv'd in elements;  170
But mine must live, still to be plagu'd in hell.
Curst be the parents that engend'red me!
No, Faustus: curse thyself: curse Lucifer,
That hath depriv'd thee of the joys of Heaven.
            *The clock striketh twelve.*
O, it strikes, it strikes! Now, body, turn to air,
Or Lucifer will bear thee quick to hell.     176
            *Thunder and lightning.*
O soul, be chang'd into little water-drops,
And fall into the ocean — ne'er be found.
My God! my God! look not so fierce on me!

            *Enter Devils*

Adders and serpents, let me breathe awhile!
Ugly hell, gape not! come not, Lucifer!      18;
I 'll burn my books! — Ah Mephistophilis!
            *Exeunt [Devils with him].*

[SCENE XV

Enter the Scholars

    1.  *Come, gentlemen, let us go visit Faustus,*
*For such a dreadful night was never seen*
*Since first the world's creation did begin.*

---

[129] **eye:** *i.e.,* the sun    [131] **natural:** from sunrise to sunset    [133] (Slightly altered from Ovid, *Amores*
i. 13. 40: "Run slowly, slowly, Horses of the Night!")    [136] **O:** (This unmetrical word looks like
actor's rant; so "half a drop" in 138 and "Ah" in 139)    [145, 146] (We have transposed these lines
from their unmeaning position in earlier editions, after line 153.)    [162] **limited:** measured out    [165] (The
pronunciation indicated was common at the time.)    [170] **elements:** earth, air, fire, water    [176] **quick:**
alive    Sc. XV (Added by B: spurious)

*Such fearful shrieks and cries were never heard.*
*Pray heaven the Doctor have escap'd the danger!* 5
   2.   *O help us heaven! See, here are Faustus'*
      *limbs,*
*All torn asunder by the hand of death.*
   3.   *The devils whom Faustus serv'd have torn*
      *him thus;*
*For 'twixt the hours of twelve and one, methought,*
*I heard him shriek and call aloud for help,*   10
*At which self time the house seem'd all on fire*
*With dreadful horror of these damned fiends.*
   2.   *Well, gentlemen, though Faustus' end be*
      *such*
*As every Christian heart laments to think on;*
*Yet for he was a scholar, once admir'd*   15
*For wondrous knowledge in our German schools,*

*We'll give his mangled limbs due burial;*
*And all the students, cloth'd in mourning black,*
*Shall wait upon his heavy funeral.*     Exeunt.]

*Enter Chorus*

Cut is the branch that might have grown full
    straight,
And burned is Apollo's laurel bough,
That sometime grew within this learned man.
Faustus is gone! Regard his hellish fall,
Whose fiendful fortune may exhort the wise   5
Only to wonder at unlawful things,
Whose deepness doth entice such forward wits
To practice more than heavenly power permits.

*Terminat hora diem, terminat author opus.*

Chorus [1, 2] (Cf. Psalm lxxx. 15, 16; also Churchyard, *Shore's Wife*, st. 24)   [7] **deepness:** obscurity

*The Famous*

# TRAGEDY

OF

# THE RICH IEVV

OF *MALTA.*

AS IT VVAS PLAYD
BEFORE THE KING AND
QVEENE, IN HIS MAJESTIES
Theatre at *White-Hall,* by her Majesties
Servants at the *Cock-pit.*

*Written by* CHRISTOPHER MARLO.

LONDON;
Printed by *I. B.* for *Nicholas Vavasour,* and are to be sold
at his Shop in the Inner-Temple, neere the
Church. 1633.

BIBLIOGRAPHICAL RECORD. The only extant text of the *Jew of Malta* is that of the late and corrupt Quarto of 1633. It had been entered for publication on the Stationers' Register, May 17, 1594, under the title of *the famouse tragedie of the Riche Iewe of Malta*, but was re-entered, November 20, 1632, by Nicholas Vavasour, who published the Quarto from which alone we know the play.

DATE AND STAGE HISTORY. The reference in the third line of the Prologue, "Now the Guise is dead," points to a date subsequent to Guise's assassination (December 23, 1588). Early in 1592 the tragedy was being acted at the Rose Theatre with great success, by Lord Strange's company. The earliest record of performance occurs in an entry near the opening of Henslowe's Diary: — *Received at the Iewe of malltuse the 26 of febrearye 1591 (i.e.,* 1592) *ls (i.e.,* £2 10s). Between this date and June 21, 1596, Henslowe itemizes thirty-six performances, an extraordinary number for the period. The play was apparently Henslowe's private property, or that of his son-in-law, Edward Alleyn, who acted the part of Barabas, and for whom it was probably specifically written by Marlowe. An inventory of the properties of the Admiral's company, March 10, 1598, mentions *1 cauderm* (caldron) *for the Iewe*, evidently employed in the remarkable concluding scene.

A revival took place in 1601, for Henslowe notes purchases as follows: — *Lent vnto Robart shawe & Mr. Jube the 19 of maye 1601 to bye diuers thinges for the Jewe of malta the some of v 11. lent mor to the littell tayller the same daye for more thinges for the Jewe of malta some of x s.* But we have no details about the run at this period. Revived a generation later by the company of Queen Henrietta Maria, it was performed before the King (Charles I) and Queen at Whitehall Palace as well as at the company's private theatre, the Cockpit or Phœnix in Drury Lane. Thomas Heywood supplied a prologue and epilogue on each occasion, sponsoring the tragedy, "writ many years agone, And in that age thought second unto none," and adding a dedication to the printed edition, which, since he alludes to it as a "new year's gift," must have appeared about the beginning of 1633.

On April 24, 1818, Edmund Kean, who had risen to fame four years before by his performance of Shylock, revived *The Jew of Malta* at the Drury Lane Theatre. This production, the first of a play by Marlowe in modern times, led to violent controversies in the press and stimulated the rising interest in the poet. The acting text, prepared by Samson Penley, shows much sophistication of the plot, and is marked by numerous silent insertions of lines from *Edward II*.

STRUCTURE. The Quarto text is divided into acts but not scenes. It observes unity of place and covers a lapse of time of little over a month. The utilization of the threefold Elizabethan stage is very clever in Acts I, II, and V: few plays of the period indeed offer better opportunity for studying theatrical technique. But the tragedy certainly suffered during the forty years of manipulation which it underwent after Marlowe's death. Acts III and IV in particular are stultified by a general crudity that can hardly be ascribed to the author who designed the original plot. It is fair to assume that several successive hands worked at bedizening a tragedy which held the stage through such a long period, but the last revision, upon which our Quarto rests, was doubtless the most destructive. Mr. A. M. Clark has admirably studied the traces of Heywood's hand in *The Jew of Malta* (*Thomas Heywood*, 1931, 287–298), reaching the conclusion that "the chief blame for the corruption of the play must attach to its editor" (*i.e.,* Heywood).

SOURCE. The plot is freely invented, the incidents being unhistorical and dependent in only very slight degree upon earlier narrative. In imagining them Marlowe was influenced by three topics of great contemporary interest: — (1) The "super-man" doctrine of Machiavelli's *Prince;* (2) The traditional Jewish-Christian hostility, which came to a head a little later in the trial and execution of Dr. Lopez (1594); (3) The enterprises of the Turks and Spaniards in the Mediterranean. Malta was never captured by the Turks, but it had sustained a great siege in 1565, and another plot to seize the island was being hatched in Constantinople in 1590–1591, with the secret connivance of the English government, who saw in it a means of weakening Spanish power. A Portuguese Jew, Juan Miques, also known as Joseph Nassi, exerted immense influence at the Turkish court in the third quarter of the sixteenth century and was famous as an arch-contriver of plots against the Christians. Still closer to Barabas in time and incident is the career of another Jew, David Passi, the Sultan's confidential adviser, who was chiefly instrumental in the plot to capture Malta mentioned above and was closely involved with Queen Elizabeth's representatives at Constantinople. He was a notorious diplomatic figure from 1585 and suffered an ignominious fall in 1591 (See *Times Literary Supplement*, June 8, 1922). The story of the two friars, which appears also in two of Heywood's works, was probably added by him. It derives ultimately from a novella of Masuccio.

# CHRISTOPHER MARLOWE

## THE JEW OF MALTA

[DRAMATIS PERSONAE

MACHIAVEL, Speaker of the Prologue
BARABAS, a wealthy Jew
FERNEZE, Governor of Malta
DON LODOWICK, his Son
SELIM CALYMATH, Son of the Sultan
MARTIN DEL BOSCO, Vice-Admiral of Spain
DON MATHIAS, a Gentleman
ITHIMORE, slave of Barabas

JACOMO,
BERNARDINE, } Friars
PILIA-BORZA, a Bully

ABIGAIL, Daughter of Barabas
KATHERINE, mother of Mathias
BELLAMIRA, a Courtesan

An Abbess and Two Nuns; Two Merchants; Three Jews; Knights, Bassoes, Officers, Guard; a
Reader; Messengers, Slaves, and Carpenters

SCENE: Malta]

## [THE PROLOGUE]

MACHIAVEL

ALBEIT the world think Machiavel is dead,
Yet was his soul but flown beyond the Alps,
And, now the Guise is dead, is come from France
To view this land and frolic with his friends.
To some perhaps my name is odious,                                5
But such as love me guard me from their tongues;
And let them know that I am Machiavel,
And weigh not men, and therefore not men's words.
Admir'd I am of those that hate me most.
Though some speak openly against my books,                       10
Yet will they read me, and thereby attain
To Peter's chair; and when they cast me off,
Are poison'd by my climbing followers.
I count religion but a childish toy,
And hold there is no sin but ignorance.                          15
"Birds of the air will tell of murders past!"
I am asham'd to hear such fooleries.
Many will talk of title to a crown:
What right had Cæsar to the empery?
Might first made kings, and laws were then most sure             20
When, like the Draco's, they were writ in blood.
Hence comes it that a strong-built citadel
Commands much more than letters can import;
Which maxim had but Phalaris observ'd,
He had never bellow'd, in a brazen bull,                         25
Of great ones' envy. O' the poor petty wights
Let me be envi'd and not pitied!

¹ **Machiavel:** Niccolo Machiavelli: (d. 1527), regarded as the typical scheming politician    ² **flown
. . . Alps:** *i.e.*, reincarnated in the Duc de Guise (assassinated, Dec., 1588)    ⁴ **his friends:** *i.e.*, the
English devotees of Machiavellian policy    ⁸ **weigh not:** care nothing for    ¹² **Peter's chair:** the
papacy    ¹⁹ **empery:** supreme power ('Empire' Q)    ²¹ **Draco's:** author of the inhumane law code of
early Athens ('Drancus' Q)    ²⁴ **but:** (Not in Q)    **Phalaris:** Sicilian tyrant, burned to death in a
brazen bull

But whither am I bound? I come not, I,
To read a lecture here in Britain,
But to present the tragedy of a Jew,                                    30
Who smiles to see how full his bags are cramm'd,
Which money was not got without my means.
I crave but this: — grace him as he deserves,
And let him not be entertain'd the worse
Because he favours me.                    [*Draws curtain and exit.*] 35

### [ACT I

#### SCENE I]

*Enter Barabas in his counting-house, with
heaps of gold before him*

*Bar.*   So that of thus much that return was
    made:
And of the third part of the Persian ships,
There was the venture summ'd and satisfied.
As for those Samiotes, and the men of Uz,
That bought my Spanish oils and wines of
    Greece,                                        5
Here have I purs'd their paltry silverlings.
Fie, what a trouble 't is to count this trash!
Well fare the Arabians, who so richly pay
The things they traffic for with wedge of gold,
Whereof a man may easily in a day              10
Tell that which may maintain him all his life.
The needy groom that never fing'red groat,
Would make a miracle of thus much coin;
But he whose steel-barr'd coffers are cramm'd
    full,
And all his lifetime hath been tired,          15
Wearying his fingers' ends with telling it,
Would in his age be loath to labour so,
And for a pound to sweat himself to death.
Give me the merchants of the Indian mines,
That trade in metal of the purest mould;      20
The wealthy Moor, that in the eastern rocks
Without control can pick his riches up,
And in his house heap pearl like pebble-stones,
Receive them free, and sell them by the weight;
Bags of fiery opals, sapphires, amethysts,    25
Jacinths, hard topaz, grass-green emeralds,
Beauteous rubies, sparkling diamonds,
And seld-seen costly stones of so great price
As one of them indifferently rated,
And of a carat of this quantity,              30
May serve in peril of calamity
To ransom great kings from captivity.
This is the ware wherein consists my wealth;
And thus methinks should men of judgment
    frame

Their means of traffic from the vulgar trade, 35
And as their wealth increaseth, so enclose
Infinite riches in a little room.
But now how stands the wind?
Into what corner peers my halcyon s bill?
Ha! to the east? Yes. See, how stands the
    vanes?                                         40
East and by south: why, then, I hope my ships
I sent for Egypt and the bordering isles
Are gotten up by Nilus' winding banks;
Mine argosy from Alexandria,
Loaden with spice and silks, now under sail,  45
Are smoothly gliding down by Candy shore
To Malta, through our Mediterranean sea.
But who comes here? How now?

*Enter a Merchant*

*Merch.*   Barabas, thy ships are safe,
Riding in Malta-road: and all the merchants 50
With other merchandise are safe arriv'd,
And have sent me to know whether yourself
Will come and custom them.
    *Bar.*   The ships are safe, thou say'st, and
        richly fraught?
    *Merch.*   They are.
    *Bar.*   Why then go bid them come ashore,
And bring with them their bills of entry.      56
I hope our credit in the custom-house
Will serve as well as I were present there.
Go send 'em threescore camels, thirty mules,
And twenty waggons to bring up the ware.      60
But art thou master in a ship of mine,
And is thy credit not enough for that?
    *Merch.*   The very custom barely comes to
        more
Than many merchants of the town are worth,
And therefore far exceeds my credit, sir.      65
    *Bar.*   Go tell 'em the Jew of Malta sent thee,
    man:
Tush! who amongst 'em knows not Barabas?
    *Merch.*   I go.
    *Bar.*            So then, there 's somewhat come.
Sirrah, which of my ships art thou master of?
    *Merch.*   Of the *Speranza*, sir.

---

S. D. Enter: *i.e.*, is revealed on inner stage    ¹ that return: the aforesaid profit    ⁴ Samiotes: inhabitants of Samos ('Samintes' in Q)    ¹¹ Tell: count    ²⁸ seld-seen: rare    ³⁴ frame: guide, divert    ³⁵ from: away from    ³⁸ (Here Barabas comes forward from the inner stage.)    ³⁹ halcyon's: kingfisher's (Sir Thos. Browne, *Pseudodoxia Ep.*, bk. iii. ch. x, discusses the vulgar error "that a king-fisher hanged by the bill sheweth in what quarter the wind is.")    ⁵³ custom: see through the custom-house

*Bar.*                         And saw'st thou not
Mine argosy at Alexandria?                         71
Thou could'st not come from Egypt, or by Caire,
But at the entry there into the sea,
Where Nilus pays his tribute to the main,
Thou needs must sail by Alexandria.               75
  *Merch.*  I neither saw them, nor inquir'd of
    them:
But this we heard some of our seamen say,
They wond'red how you durst with so much
    wealth
Trust such a crazed vessel, and so far.
  *Bar.*  Tush, they are wise! I know her and
    her strength.                                 80
But go, go thou thy ways, discharge thy ship,
And bid my factor bring his loading in.
                              [*Exit Merch.*]
And yet I wonder at this argosy.

*Enter a second Merchant*

  *2 Merch.*  Thine argosy from Alexandria,
Know, Barabas, doth ride in Malta-road,           85
Laden with riches, and exceeding store
Of Persian silks, of gold, and orient pearl.
  *Bar.*  How chance you came not with those
    other ships
That sail'd by Egypt?
  *2 Merch.*                Sir, we saw 'em not.
  *Bar.*  Belike they coasted round by Candy
    shore                                         90
About their oils, or other businesses.
But 't was ill done of you to come so far
Without the aid or conduct of their ships.
  *2 Merch.*  Sir, we were wafted by a Spanish
    fleet,
That never left us till within a league,          95
That had the galleys of the Turk in chase.
  *Bar.*  O! they were going up to Sicily. —
Well, go,
And bid the merchants and my men despatch
And come ashore, and see the fraught dis-
    charg'd.                                      100
  *2 Merch.*  I go.                         *Exit.*
  *Bar.*  Thus trowls our fortune in by land and
    sea,
And thus are we on every side enrich'd.
These are the blessings promis'd to the Jews,
And herein was old Abram's happiness.            105
What more may Heaven do for earthly man
Than thus to pour out plenty in their laps,
Ripping the bowels of the earth for them,
Making the sea their servant, and the winds
To drive their substance with successful blasts?
Who hateth me but for my happiness?              111

Or who is honour'd now but for his wealth?
Rather had I, a Jew, be hated thus,
Than pitied in a Christian poverty;
For I can see no fruits in all their faith,       115
But malice, falsehood, and excessive pride,
Which methinks fits not their profession.
Haply some hapless man hath conscience,
And for his conscience lives in beggary.
They say we are a scatter'd nation:               120
I cannot tell, but we have scambled up
More wealth by far than those that brag of
    faith.
There 's Kirriah Jairim, the great Jew of Greece,
Obed in Bairseth, Nones in Portugal,
Myself in Malta, some in Italy,                   125
Many in France, and wealthy every one;
Ay, wealthier far than any Christian.
I must confess we come not to be kings:
That 's not our fault: alas, our number 's few,
And crowns come either by succession,            130
Or urg'd by force; and nothing violent,
Oft have I heard tell, can be permanent.
Give us a peaceful rule, make Christians kings,
That thirst so much for principality.
I have no charge, nor many children,             135
But one sole daughter, whom I hold as dear
As Agamemnon did his Iphigen;
And all I have is hers. But who comes here?

*Enter three Jews*

  *1 Jew.*  Tush, tell not me; 't was done of
    policy.
  *2 Jew.*  Come, therefore, let us go to Bara-
    bas,                                          140
For he can counsel best in these affairs;
And here he comes.
  *Bar.*                Why, how now, countrymen!
Why flock you thus to me in multitudes?
What accident 's betided to the Jews?
  *1 Jew.*  A fleet of warlike galleys, Barabas,   145
Are come from Turkey, and lie in our road;
And they this day sit in the council-house
To entertain them and their embassy.
  *Bar.*  Why, let 'em come, so they come not
    to war;
Or let 'em war, so we be conquerors: —            150
Nay, let 'em combat, conquer, and kill all,
So they spare me, my daughter, and my wealth.
                                      *Aside.*
  *1 Jew.*  Were it for confirmation of a league,
They would not come in warlike manner thus.
  *2 Jew.*  I fear their coming will afflict us all.
  *Bar.*  Fond men! what dream you of their
    multitudes?                                   156

---

⁷² **Egypt:** upper Egypt  **Caire:** Cairo    ⁸² **factor:** commercial agent  **loading:** inventory of cargo
⁹⁴ **wafted:** convoyed    ¹⁰⁰ **fraught.** freight    ¹⁰² **trowls:** rolls    ¹⁰⁹ **servant:** ('seruants' Q)
¹²¹ **scambled up:** amassed    ¹³¹ **urg'd by force:** forcibly gained    ¹³⁵ **charge:** burden    ¹⁴² **here he
comes:** Barabas, who has retired into his counting-house (inner stage) at line 138, comes forward again.
¹⁴⁷ **they:** the Christian Knights of Malta    ¹⁵⁶ **Fond:** foolish

What need they treat of peace that are in
    league?
The Turks and those of Malta are in league.
Tut, tut, there is some other matter in 't.
    1 *Jew.*   Why, Barabas, they come for peace
    or war.                                              160
    *Bar.*   Haply for neither, but to pass along
Towards Venice by the Adriatic Sea;
With whom they have attempted many times,
But never could effect their stratagem.
    3 *Jew.*   And very wisely said.  It may be so.
    2 *Jew.*   But there 's a meeting in the senate-
    house,                                               166
And all the Jews in Malta must be there.
    *Bar.*   Hum; all the Jews in Malta must be
    there?
Ay, like enough.  Why, then, let every man
Provide him, and be there for fashion-sake.  170
If anything shall there concern our state,
Assure yourselves I 'll look — unto myself.
                                              *Aside.*
    1 *Jew.*   I know you will.  Well, brethren, let
    us go.
    2 *Jew.*   Let 's take our leaves.  Farewell,
    good Barabas.
    *Bar.*   Do so.  Farewell, Zaareth; farewell,
    Temainte.            [*Exeunt Jews.*]   175
And, Barabas, now search this secret out;
Summon thy senses, call thy wits together:
These silly men mistake the matter clean.
Long to the Turk did Malta contribute;
Which tribute, all in policy, I fear,              180
The Turks have let increase to such a sum
As all the wealth of Malta cannot pay;
And now by that advantage thinks, belike,
To seize upon the town: ay, that he seeks.
Howe'er the world go, I 'll make sure for one,
And seek in time to intercept the worst,          186
Warily guarding that which I ha' got.
*Ego mihimet sum semper proximus.*
Why, let 'em enter, let 'em take the town.
                                              [*Exit*]

[SCENE II. — *Within the Senate-house.*]

*Enter* [*Ferneze,*] *Governor of Malta, Knights,*
    [*and Officers;*] *met by Bassoes of the Turk;*
    *Calymath*

    *Gov.*   Now, Bassoes, what demand you at
    our hands?
    1 *Bas.*   Know, Knights of Malta, that we
    came from Rhodes,
From Cyprus, Candy, and those other Isles
That lie betwixt the Mediterranean seas.
    *Gov.*   What 's Cyprus, Candy, and those
    other Isles                                       5

To us or Malta?  What at our hands demand
    ye?
    *Cal.*   The ten years' tribute that remains
    unpaid.
    *Gov.*   Alas! my lord, the sum is over-great,
I hope your highness will consider us.
    *Cal.*   I wish, grave governor, 't were in my
    power                                             10
To favour you, but 't is my father's cause,
Wherein I may not, nay, I dare not, dally.
    *Gov.*   Then give us leave, great Selim Caly-
    math.   [*Consults apart with the Knights.*]
    *Cal.*   Stand all aside, and let the knights
    determine,
And send to keep our galleys under sail,          15
For happily we shall not tarry here. —
Now, governor, how are you resolv'd?
    *Gov.*   Thus: since your hard conditions are
    such
That you will needs have ten years' tribute past,
We may have time to make collection              20
Amongst the inhabitants of Malta for 't.
    1 *Bas.*   That 's more than is in our com-
    mission.
    *Cal.*   What, Callapine! a little courtesy.
Let 's know their time, perhaps it is not long;
And 't is more kingly to obtain by peace          25
Than to enforce conditions by constraint.
What respite ask you, governor?
    *Gov.*                          But a month.
    *Cal.*   We grant a month, but see you keep
    your promise.
Now launch our galleys back again to sea,
Where we 'll attend the respite you have ta'en,
And for the money send our messenger.            31
Farewell, great governor and brave Knights of
    Malta.
    *Gov.*   And all good fortune wait on Caly-
    math!   *Exeunt* [*Calymath and Bassoes*].
Go one and call those Jews of Malta hither:
Were they not summon'd to appear to-day?  35
    *Off.*   They were, my lord, and here they come.

        *Enter Barabas and three Jews*

    1 *Knight.*   Have you determin'd what to say
    to them?
    *Gov.*   Yes, give me leave: — and, Hebrews,
    now come near.
From the Emperor of Turkey is arriv'd
Great Selim Calymath, his highness' son,          40
To levy of us ten years' tribute past.
Now then, here know that it concerneth us —
    *Bar.*   Then, good my lord, to keep your quiet
    still,
Your lordship shall do well to let them have it.

---

    [163] **With:** against      **attempted:** made raids
but even the great powers made contributions for the purpose of buying peace from the Turks.
    [188] Altered from Terence (*Andria* iv. i. 12): Proximus sum egomet mihi.      [1] **Bassoes:** pashas
    [5] **Candy:** Crete      [16] **happily:** perchance

    [179] Unhistorical in the sense of formal tribute,

*Gov.* Soft, Barabas, there 's more longs to 't
than so.                                              45
To what this ten years' tribute will amount,
That we have cast, but cannot compass it
By reason of the wars that robb'd our store;
And therefore are we to request your aid.
*Bar.* Alas, my lord, we are no soldiers;   50
And what 's our aid against so great a prince?
1 *Knight.* Tut, Jew, we know thou art no
soldier;
Thou art a merchant and a monied man,
And 't is thy money, Barabas, we seek.    54
*Bar.* How, my lord! my money?
*Gov.*                    Thine and the rest.
For, to be short, amongst you 't must be had.
1 *Jew.* Alas, my lord, the most of us are
poor.
*Gov.* Then let the rich increase your por-
tions.
*Bar.* Are strangers with your tribute to be
tax'd?
2 *Knight.* Have strangers leave with us to
get their wealth?                         60
Then let them with us contribute.
*Bar.* How! Equally?
*Gov.*                   No, Jew, like infidels.
For through our sufferance of your hateful
lives,
Who stand accursed in the sight of Heaven,
These taxes and afflictions are befall'n,    65
And therefore thus we are determined.
Read there the articles of our decrees.
*Reader.* "First, the tribute-money of the
Turks shall all be levied amongst the Jews, and
each of them to pay one half of his estate." [70
*Bar.* How, half his estate? — I hope you
mean not mine.              [*Aside.*]
*Gov.* Read on.
*Reader.* "Secondly, he that denies to pay
shall straight become a Christian."
*Bar.* How, a Christian? Hum, what 's here
to do?                      [*Aside.*] 75
*Reader.* "Lastly, he that denies this shall
absolutely lose all he has."
*All three Jews.* O my lord, we will give half.
*Bar.* O earth-mettl'd villains, and no He-
brews born!
And will you basely thus submit yourselves 80
To leave your goods to their arbitrament?
*Gov.* Why, Barabas, wilt thou be christened?
*Bar.* No, governor, I will be no convertite.
*Gov.* Then pay thy half.
*Bar.* Why, know you what you did by this
device?                                       85
Half of my substance is a city's wealth.
Governor, it was not got so easily;
Nor will I part so slightly therewithal.

*Gov.* Sir, half is the penalty of our decree.
Either pay that, or we will seize on all.    90
            [*Exeunt Officers, on a sign from
                    Governor.*]
*Bar.* *Corpo di Dio!* stay! you shall have half;
Let me be us'd but as my brethren are.
*Gov.* No, Jew, thou hast denied the articles,
And now it cannot be recall'd.
*Bar.* Will you then steal my goods?    95
Is theft the ground of your religion?
*Gov.* No, Jew, we take particularly thine
To save the ruin of a multitude;
And better one want for a common good
Than many perish for a private man.    100
Yet, Barabas, we will not banish thee,
But here in Malta, where thou gott'st thy
wealth,
Live still; and, if thou canst, get more.
*Bar.* Christians, what or how can I multiply?
Of naught is nothing made.    105
1 *Knight.* From naught at first thou cam'st
to little wealth,
From little unto more, from more to most.
If your first curse fall heavy on thy head,
And make thee poor and scorn'd of all the world,
'T is not our fault, but thy inherent sin.    110
*Bar.* What, bring you Scripture to confirm
your wrongs?
Preach me not out of my possessions.
Some Jews are wicked, as all Christians are;
But say the tribe that I descended of
Were all in general cast away for sin,    115
Shall I be tried by their transgression?
The man that dealeth righteously shall live;
And which of you can charge me otherwise?
*Gov.* Out, wretched Barabas!
Sham'st thou not thus to justify thyself,    120
As if we knew not thy profession?
If thou rely upon thy righteousness,
Be patient and thy riches will increase.
Excess of wealth is cause of covetousness:
And covetousness, O, 't is a monstrous sin. 125
*Bar.* Ay, but theft is worse. Tush! take not
from me then,
For that is theft; and if you rob me thus,
I must be forc'd to steal and compass more.
1 *Knight.* Grave governor, list not to his ex-
claims.
Convert his mansion to a nunnery;    130

*Enter Officers*

His house will harbour many holy nuns.
*Gov.* It shall be so. Now, officers, have you
done?
*Off.* Ay, my lord, we have seiz'd upon the
goods
And wares of Barabas, which being valued,

---

⁴⁵ **longs:** belongs   ⁴⁷ **cast:** reckoned   **compass:** obtain   ⁷⁹ **earth-mettl'd:** earthy   ¹⁰⁸ **your:**
that of you Jews in general

Amount to more than all the wealth in Malta. 135
And of the other we have seized half.
 [*Gov.*] Then we 'll take order for the residue.
 *Bar.* Well then, my lord, say, are you satis-
fied?
You have my goods, my money, and my wealth,
My ships, my store, and all that I enjoy'd; 140
And, having all, you can request no more;
Unless your unrelenting flinty hearts
Suppress all pity in your stony breasts,
And now shall move you to bereave my life.
 *Gov.* No, Barabas, to stain our hands with
blood                                                      145
Is far from us and our profession.
 *Bar.* Why, I esteem the injury far less
To take the lives of miserable men
Than be the causers of their misery.
You have my wealth, the labour of my life, 150
The comfort of mine age, my children's hope,
And therefore ne'er distinguish of the wrong.
 *Gov.* Content thee, Barabas, thou hast
naught but right.
 *Bar.* Your extreme right does me exceeding
wrong:
But take it to you, i' the devil's name.   155
 *Gov.* Come, let us in, and gather of these
goods
The money for this tribute of the Turk.
 1 *Knight.* 'T is necessary that be look'd
unto;
For if we break our day, we break the league,
And that will prove but simple policy.   160
    *Exeunt [all except Barabas and*
     *the Jews].*
 *Bar.* Ay, policy! that 's their profession,
And not simplicity, as they suggest.
The plagues of Egypt, and the curse of Heaven,
Earth's barrenness, and all men's hatred
Inflict upon them, thou great *Primus Motor!* 165
And here upon my knees, striking the earth,
I ban their souls to everlasting pains
And extreme tortures of the fiery deep,
That thus have dealt with me in my distress.
 1 *Jew.* O yet be patient, gentle Barabas. 170
 *Bar.* O silly brethren, born to see this day,
Why stand you thus unmov'd with my laments?
Why weep you not to think upon my wrongs?
Why pine not I, and die in this distress?
 1 *Jew.* Why, Barabas, as hardly can we
brook                                                     175
The cruel handling of ourselves in this.
Thou seest they have taken half our goods.
 *Bar.* Why did you yield to their extortion?
You were a multitude, and I but one;
And of me only have they taken all.   180

 1 *Jew.* Yet, Brother Barabas, remember
Job.
 *Bar.* What tell you me of Job? I wot his
wealth
Was written thus: he had seven thousand
sheep,
Three thousand camels, and two hundred yoke
Of labouring oxen, and five hundred   185
She-asses: but for every one of those,
Had they been valued at indifferent rate,
I had at home, and in mine argosy,
And other ships that came from Egypt last,
As much as would have bought his beasts and
him,   190
And yet have kept enough to live upon:
So that not he, but I may curse the day,
Thy fatal birth-day, forlorn Barabas;
And henceforth wish for an eternal night, 194
That clouds of darkness may enclose my flesh,
And hide these extreme sorrows from mine eyes:
For only I have toil'd to inherit here
The months of vanity and loss of time,
And painful nights have been appointed me.
 2 *Jew.* Good Barabas, be patient.   200
 *Bar.* Ay, ay;
Pray, leave me in my patience. You that
Were ne'er possess'd of wealth, are pleas'd with
want;
But give him liberty at least to mourn,
That in a field amidst his enemies   205
Doth see his soldiers slain, himself disarm'd,
And knows no means of his recovery.
Ay, let me sorrow for this sudden chance;
'T is in the trouble of my spirit I speak;
Great injuries are not so soon forgot.   210
 1 *Jew.* Come, let us leave him; in his ireful
mood
Our words will but increase his ecstasy.
 2 *Jew.* On, then; but trust me 't is a misery
To see a man in such affliction. —
Farewell, Barabas!   *Exeunt [the three Jews].*
 *Bar.*     Ay, fare you well.   215
See the simplicity of these base slaves,
Who, for the villains have no wit themselves,
Think me to be a senseless lump of clay
That will with every water wash to dirt.
No, Barabas is born to better chance,   220
And fram'd of finer mould than common men,
That measure naught but by the present time.
A reaching thought will search his deepest wits,
And cast with cunning for the time to come:
For evils are apt to happen every day. — 225

   *Enter Abigail, the Jew's daughter*

But whither wends my beauteous Abigail?

<hr>

 ¹³⁶ **other:** other Jews   ¹⁵² **distinguish:** quibble   ¹⁶⁰ **simple:** foolish   ¹⁸³ **written thus:** cf. Job i. 3
¹⁹⁷⁻¹⁹⁹ Cf. Job vii. 3: "So am I made to possess months of vanity, and wearisome nights are appointed
to me."   ²¹² **ecstasy:** mad emotion   ²¹⁷ **for:** because   ²²³ **reaching thought:** ambitious thinker
²²⁴ **cast:** plot

O! what has made my lovely daughter sad?
What, woman! moan not for a little loss:
Thy father has enough in store for thee.
   *Abig.*    Not for myself, but aged Barabas; 230
Father, for thee lamenteth Abigail.
But I will learn to leave these fruitless tears,
And, urg'd thereto with my afflictions,
With fierce exclaims run to the senate-house,
And in the senate reprehend them all,    235
And rent their hearts with tearing of my hair,
Till they reduce the wrongs done to my father.
   *Bar.*    No, Abigail, things past recovery
Are hardly cur'd with exclamations.
Be silent, daughter, sufferance breeds ease, 240
And time may yield us an occasion
Which on the sudden cannot serve the turn.
Besides, my girl, think me not all so fond
As negligently to forgo so much
Without provision for thyself and me:    245
Ten thousand portagues, besides great pearls,
Rich costly jewels, and stones infinite,
Fearing the worst of this before it fell,
I closely hid.
   *Abig.*     Where, father?
   *Bar.*           In my house, my girl.
   *Abig.*    Then shall they ne'er be seen of Bara-
bas:    250
For they have seiz'd upon thy house and wares.
   *Bar.*    But they will give me leave once more,
   I trow,
To go into my house.
   *Abig.*           That may they not:
For there I left the governor placing nuns,
Displacing me; and of thy house they mean 255
To make a nunnery, where none but their own
   sect
Must enter in; men generally barr'd.
   *Bar.*    My gold! my gold! and all my wealth
   is gone!
You partial heavens, have I deserv'd this
   plague?
What, will you thus oppose me, luckless stars,
To make me desperate in my poverty?    261
And knowing me impatient in distress,
Think me so mad as I will hang myself,
That I may vanish o'er the earth in air,
And leave no memory that e'er I was?    265
No, I will live; nor loathe I this my life:
And, since you leave me in the ocean thus
To sink or swim, and put me to my shifts,
I 'll rouse my senses and awake myself.    269
Daughter, I have it! Thou perceiv'st the plight
Wherein these Christians have oppressed me.
Be rul'd by me, for in extremity
We ought to make bar of no policy.
   *Abig.*    Father, whate'er it be to injure them

That have so manifestly wronged us,    275
What will not Abigail attempt?
   *Bar.*           Why, so.
Then thus: thou told'st me they have turn'd
   my house
Into a nunnery, and some nuns are there?
   *Abig.*    I did.
   *Bar.*       Then, Abigail, there must my girl
Entreat the abbess to be entertain'd.    280
   *Abig.*    How, as a nun?
   *Bar.*         Ay, daughter, for religion
Hides many mischiefs from suspicion.
   *Abig.*    Ay, but, father, they will suspect me
   there.
   *Bar.*    Let 'em suspect; but be thou so precise
As they may think it done of holiness.    285
Entreat 'em fair, and give them friendly speech,
And seem to them as if thy sins were great,
Till thou hast gotten to be entertain'd.
   *Abig.*    Thus, father, shall I much dissemble.
   *Bar.*                    Tush!
As good dissemble that thou never mean'st, 290
As first mean truth and then dissemble it.
A counterfeit profession is better
Than unseen hypocrisy.
   *Abig.*    Well, father, say I be entertain'd,
What then shall follow?
   *Bar.*        This shall follow then:
There have I hid, close underneath the plank 296
That runs along the upper-chamber floor,
The gold and jewels which I kept for thee.
But here they come; be cunning, Abigail.
   *Abig.*    Then, father, go with me.
   *Bar.*        No, Abigail, in this
It is not necessary I be seen;    301
For I will seem offended with thee for 't.
Be close, my girl, for this must fetch my gold.
                     [*They retire.*]

*Enter Three Friars and Two Nuns*

   1 *Friar.*    Sisters,    304
We now are almost at the new-made nunnery.
   *Abb.*    The better; for we love not to be seen.
'T is thirty winters long since some of us
Did stray so far amongst the multitude.
   1 *Friar.*    But, madam, this house
And waters of this new-made nunnery    310
Will much delight you.
   *Abb.*    It may be so; but who comes here?
                 [*Abigail comes forward.*]
   *Abig.*    Grave abbess, and you, happy virgins'
   guide,
Pity the state of a distressed maid.
   *Abb.*    What art thou, daughter?    315
   *Abig.*    The hopeless daughter of a hapless
   Jew,

---

²³⁶ **rent:** rend    ²⁴⁶ **portagues:** large Portuguese gold coins (worth about £4)    ²⁸⁰ **entertain'd:** accepted as an inmate    ³⁰³ **close:** secretive    S. D. **Two Nuns:** The first Nun is the Abbess.    ³¹⁰ **waters:** fountains

The Jew of Malta, wretched Barabas;
Sometimes the owner of a goodly house,
Which they have now turn'd to a nunnery.
   *Abb.* Well, daughter, say, what is thy suit
with us?                                                     320
   *Abig.* Fearing the afflictions which my father
feels
Proceed from sin, or want of faith, in us,
I 'd pass away my life in penitence,
And be a novice in your nunnery,
To make atonement for my labouring soul. 325
   1 *Friar.* No doubt, brother, but this pro-
ceedeth of the spirit.
   2 *Friar.* Ay, and of a moving spirit too,
brother; but come,
Let us entreat she may be entertain'd.
   *Abb.* Well, daughter, we admit you for a
nun.                                                        329
   *Abig.* First let me as a novice learn to frame
My solitary life to your strait laws,
And let me lodge where I was wont to lie.
I do not doubt, by your divine precepts
And mine own industry, but to profit much.
   *Bar.* As much, I hope, as all I hid is worth.
                               *Aside.*
   *Abb.* Come, daughter, follow us.           336
   *Bar.* [*Coming forward.*] Why, how now, Abi-
gail!
What mak'st thou amongst these hateful Chris-
tians?
   1 *Friar.* Hinder her not, thou man of little
faith,                                                      339
For she has mortified herself.
   *Bar.*                            How! mortified?
   1 *Friar.* And is admitted to the sister-
hood.
   *Bar.* Child of perdition, and thy father's
shame!
What wilt thou do among these hateful fiends?
I charge thee on my blessing that thou leave
These devils, and their damned heresy.       345
   *Abig.* Father, give me — [*She goes to him.*]
   *Bar.*                         Nay, back, Abigail, —
                          *Whispers to her.*
And think upon the jewels and the gold;
The board is marked thus that covers it. —
Away, accursed, from thy father's sight.
   1 *Friar.* Barabas, although thou art in mis-
belief,                                                     350
And wilt not see thine own afflictions,
Yet let thy daughter be no longer blind.
   *Bar.* Blind, friar; I reck not thy persua-
sions, —
The board is marked thus + that covers it. —
         [*Aside to Abigail in a whisper.*]
For I had rather die than see her thus.       355
Wilt thou forsake me too in my distress,

Seduced daughter? — Go, forget not —
                          *Aside to her.*
Becomes it Jews to be so credulous? —
To-morrow early I 'll be at the door.
                          *Aside to her.*
No, come not at me; if thou wilt be damn'd,
Forget me, see me not, and so be gone. —      361
Farewell, remember to-morrow morning. —
                             *Aside.*
Out, out, thou wretch!
   [*Exeunt severally; as they are going out,*]

               *Enter Mathias*

   *Math.* Who 's this? Fair Abigail, the rich
Jew's daughter,
Become a nun! Her father's sudden fall     365
Has humbled her and brought her down to
this.
Tut, she were fitter for a tale of love,
Than to be tired out with orisons;
And better would she far become a bed,
Embraced in a friendly lover's arms,          370
Than rise at midnight to a solemn mass.

               *Enter Lodowick*

   *Lod.* Why, how now, Don Mathias! in a
dump?
   *Math.* Believe me, noble Lodowick, I have
seen
The strangest sight, in my opinion,
That ever I beheld.
   *Lod.*                    What was 't, I prithee?  375
   *Math.* A fair young maid, scarce fourteen
years of age,
The sweetest flower in Cytherea's field,
Cropt from the pleasures of the fruitful earth,
And strangely metamorphos'd [to a] nun.
   *Lod.* But say, what was she?
   *Math.*                    Why, the rich Jew's daughter.
   *Lod.* What, Barabas, whose goods were
lately seiz'd?                                              381
Is she so fair?
   *Math.*              And matchless beautiful,
As, had you seen her, 't would have mov'd your
heart,
Though countermur'd with walls of brass, to
love,
Or at the least to pity.                                    385
   *Lod.* And if she be so fair as you report,
'T were time well spent to go and visit her.
How say you, shall we?
   *Math.* I must and will, sir; there 's no
remedy.
   *Lod.* And so will I too, or it shall go hard.
Farewell, Mathias.
   *Math.*              Farewell, Lodowick.       391
                     *Exeunt [severally].*

[318] **Sometimes:** formerly    [340] **mortified herself:** died to the world    [353] **reck:** value    [372] **dump:** brown study    [384] **countermur'd:** reinforced (Q 'countermin'd')

## Actus Secundus

[SCENE I. — *Before the New Nunnery.*]

*Enter Barabas with a light*

*Bar.* Thus, like the sad presaging raven,
    that tolls
The sick man's passport in her hollow beak,
And in the shadow of the silent night
Doth shake contagion from her sable wings,
Vex'd and tormented runs poor Barabas    5
With fatal curses towards these Christians.
The incertain pleasures of swift-footed Time
Have ta'en their flight, and left me in despair;
And of my former riches rests no more
But bare remembrance, like a soldier's scar,   10
That has no further comfort for his maim.
O Thou, that with a fiery pillar led'st
The sons of Israel through the dismal shades,
Light Abraham's offspring, and direct the hand
Of Abigail this night; or let the day    15
Turn to eternal darkness after this!
No sleep can fasten on my watchful eyes,
Nor quiet enter my distemper'd thoughts,
Till I have answer of my Abigail.

*Enter Abigail above*

*Abig.* Now have I happily espi'd a time   20
To search the plank my father did appoint;
And here behold, unseen, where I have found
The gold, the pearls, and jewels, which he hid.
    *Bar.* Now I remember those old women's
        words,        24
Who in my wealth would tell me winter's tales,
And speak of spirits and ghosts that glide by
    night
About the place where treasure hath been hid:
And now methinks that I am one of those;
For whilst I live, here lives my soul's sole hope,
And, when I die, here shall my spirit walk.   30
    *Abig.* Now that my father's fortune were so
        good
As but to be about this happy place!
'T is not so happy: yet when we parted last,
He said he would attend me in the morn.
Then, gentle sleep, where'er his body rests,   35
Give charge to Morpheus that he may dream
A golden dream, and of the sudden walk,
Come and receive the treasure I have found.
    *Bar.* *Bueno para todos mi ganado no es.*
As good go on as sit so sadly thus.      40
But stay, what star shines yonder in the east?
The loadstar of my life, if Abigail.
Who 's there?

*Abig.*        Who 's that?
*Bar.*             Peace, Abigail, 't is I.
*Abig.* Then, father, here receive thy happi-
    ness.
*Bar.* Hast thou 't?
*Abig.*      Here!      *Throws down bags.*
              Hast thou 't?     45
There 's more, and more, and more.
    *Bar.*            O my girl!
My gold, my fortune, my felicity!
Strength to my soul, death to mine enemy!
Welcome, the first beginner of my bliss!
O Abigail, Abigail, that I had thee here too!   50
Then my desires were fully satisfied:
But I will practise thy enlargement thence.
O girl! O gold! O beauty! O my bliss!
                 *Hugs his bags.*
    *Abig.* Father, it draweth towards midnight
        now,
And 'bout this time the nuns begin to wake; 55
To shun suspicion, therefore, let us part.
    *Bar.* Farewell, my joy, and by my fingers
        take
A kiss from him that sends it from his soul.
              [*Exit Abigail above.*]
Now Phœbus ope the eyelids of the day,
And for the raven wake the morning lark,   60
That I may hover with her in the air;
Singing o'er these, as she does o'er her young.
*Hermoso placer de los dineros!*      *Exit.*

[SCENE II]

*Enter Governor [Ferneze], Martin del Bosco,
    the Knights*

*Gov.* Now, captain, tell us whither thou art
    bound?
Whence is thy ship that anchors in our road?
And why thou cam'st ashore without our leave?
    *Bosc.* Governor of Malta, hither am I bound;
My ship, *The Flying Dragon*, is of Spain,    5
And so am I: del Bosco is my name;
Vice-admiral unto the Catholic King.
    1 *Knight.* 'T is true, my lord, therefore en-
        treat him well.
    *Bosc.* Our fraught is Grecians, Turks, and
        Afric Moors.
For late upon the coast of Corsica,      10
Because we vail'd not to the Turkish fleet,
Their creeping galleys had us in the chase:
But suddenly the wind began to rise,
And then we luff'd and tack'd and fought at
    ease:
Some have we fir'd, and many have we sunk; 15

---

² **passport:** omen of death    12,13 Cf. Exodus xiii. 21    19 S. D. **above:** on the balcony    37 **walk:**
*i.e.*, as a somnambulist    39 "My earnings are not everybody's property." (Q 'Birn para todos, my
ganada no er.')    52 **enlargement:** liberation    63 "What lovely pleasure money gives!" (Q 'Hermoso
Piarer, de les Denirch.')    7 **Catholic King:** special title of the King of Spain    11 **vail'd:** lowered
**sail in homage**    **Turkish:** ('Spanish' Q)    14 **luff'd and tack'd:** ('left, and tooke' Q)

But one amongst the rest became our prize.
The captain 's slain, the rest remain our slaves,
Of whom we would make sale in Malta here.
   *Gov.* Martin del Bosco, I have heard of thee:
Welcome to Malta, and to all of us;   20
But to admit a sale of these thy Turks
We may not, nay, we dare not, give consent
By reason of a tributary league.
   1 *Knight.* Del Bosco, as thou lov'st and
honour'st us,
Persuade our governor against the Turk;   25
This truce we have is but in hope of gold,
And with that sum he craves might we wage
war.
   *Bosc.* Will Knights of Malta be in league
with Turks,
And buy it basely too for sums of gold?
My lord, remember that, to Europe's shame,   30
The Christian Isle of Rhodes, from whence you
came,
Was lately lost, and you were stated here
To be at deadly enmity with Turks.
   *Gov.* Captain, we know it, but our force is
small.
   *Bosc.* What is the sum that Calymath re-
quires?   35
   *Gov.* A hundred thousand crowns.
   *Bosc.* My lord and king hath title to this isle,
And he means quickly to expel you hence;
Therefore be rul'd by me, and keep the gold.
I 'll write unto his majesty for aid,   40
And not depart until I see you free.
   *Gov.* On this condition shall thy Turks be
sold.
Go, officers, and set them straight in show.
                 *[Exeunt Officers.]*
Bosco, thou shalt be Malta's general;
We and our warlike Knights will follow thee  45
Against these barbarous misbelieving Turks.
   *Bosc.* So shall you imitate those you suc-
ceed:
For when their hideous force environ'd Rhodes,
Small though the number was that kept the
town,
They fought it out, and not a man surviv'd  50
To bring the hapless news to Christendom.
   *Gov.* So will we fight it out. Come, let 's
away!
Proud daring Calymath, instead of gold,
We 'll send thee bullets wrapp'd in smoke and
fire.
Claim tribute where thou wilt, we are resolv'd,
Honour is bought with blood and not with
  gold.               *Exeunt.*  56

[SCENE III. — *The Market-Place.*]

*Enter Officers with [Ithimore and other] Slaves*

   1 *Off.* This is the market-place, here let 'em
stand:
Fear not their sale, for they 'll be quickly
bought.
   2 *Off.* Every one's price is written on his
back,
And so much must they yield or not be sold.
   1 *Off.* Here comes the Jew; had not his
goods been seiz'd,   5
He 'd give us present money for them all.

*Enter Barabas*

   *Bar.* [*Aside.*] In spite of these swine-eating
Christians, —
Unchosen nation, never circumcis'd,
Such as (poor villains!) were ne'er thought
upon
Till Titus and Vespasian conquer'd us, —   10
Am I become as wealthy as I was.
They hop'd my daughter would ha' been a nun;
But she 's at home, and I have bought a house
As great and fair as is the governor's;
And there in spite of Malta will I dwell,   15
Having Ferneze's hand, whose heart I 'll have;
Ay, and his son's too, or it shall go hard.
I am not of the tribe of Levi, I,
That can so soon forget an injury.   19
We Jews can fawn like spaniels when we please,
And when we grin we bite; yet are our looks
As innocent and harmless as a lamb's.
I learn'd in Florence how to kiss my hand,
Heave up my shoulders when they call me
dog,
And duck as low as any barefoot friar;   25
Hoping to see them starve upon a stall,
Or else be gather'd for in our synagogue,
That, when the offering-basin comes to me,
Even for charity I may spit into 't.
Here comes Don Lodowick, the governor's son,
One that I love for his good father's sake.   31

*Enter Lodowick*

   *Lod.* I hear the wealthy Jew walked this
way.
I 'll seek him out, and so insinuate,
That I may have a sight of Abigail;
For Don Mathias tells me she is fair.   35
   *Bar.* [*Aside.*] Now will I show myself
To have more of the serpent than the dove;
That is — more knave than fool.

---

  **30–33** Historically correct. Sultan Solyman II conquered Rhodes in 1522 from the Knights of St.
John, to whom the Emperor Charles V then gave the island of Malta.    **32 stated:** established
**50 not a man surviv'd:** Incorrect. The Knights evacuated Rhodes with their arms and property.
**6 present:** ready   **16 hand:** written guarantee   **18 tribe of Levi:** the priestly, consecrated tribe
of Israel   **23 Florence:** Machiavelli's city   **26 stall:** bench for petty merchandise

*Lod.* Yond walks the Jew; now for fair
   Abigail.
*Bar.* [*Aside.*] Ay, ay, no doubt but she 's at
   your command.                                    40
*Lod.* Barabas, thou know'st I am the gover-
   nor's son.
*Bar.* I would you were his father, too, sir;
That 's all the harm I wish you. [*Aside.*] The
   slave looks
Like a hog's-cheek new singed.
*Lod.* Whither walk'st thou, Barabas?      45
*Bar.* No further: 't is a custom held with
   us,
That when we speak with Gentiles like to you,
We turn into the air to purge ourselves:
For unto us the promise doth belong.
*Lod.* Well, Barabas, canst help me to a dia-
   mond?                                            50
*Bar.* O, sir, your father had my diamonds.
Yet I have one left that will serve your turn: —
I mean my daughter: but ere he shall have her
I 'll sacrifice her on a pile of wood.
I ha' the poison of the city for him,              55
And the white leprosy.               *Aside.*
*Lod.* What sparkle does it give without a
   foil?
*Bar.* The diamond that I talk of ne'er was
   foil'd: —
[*Aside.*] But when he touches it, it will be
   foil'd: —
Lord Lodowick, it sparkles bright and fair.   60
*Lod.* Is it square or pointed, pray let me
   know.
*Bar.* Pointed it is, good sir — but not for
   you.                             *Aside.*
*Lod.* I like it much the better.
*Bar.*                     So do I too.
*Lod.* How shows it by night?
*Bar.*             Outshines Cynthia's rays:
— You 'll like it better far o' nights than days.
                                   *Aside.*
*Lod.* And what 's the price?               66
*Bar.* [*Aside.*] Your life and if you have it. —
O my lord,
We will not jar about the price; come to my
   house
And I will give 't your honour — with a ven-
   geance.                          *Aside.*
*Lod.* No, Barabas, I will deserve it first.  70
*Bar.* Good sir,
Your father has deserv'd it at my hands,
Who, of mere charity and Christian ruth,
To bring me to religious purity,
And as it were in catechising sort,           75
To make me mindful of my mortal sins,
Against my will, and whether I would or no,
Seiz'd all I had, and thrust me out o' doors,

And made my house a place for nuns most
   chaste.
*Lod.* No doubt your soul shall reap the fruit
   of it.                                          80
*Bar.* Ay, but, my lord, the harvest is far
   off.
And yet I know the prayers of those nuns
And holy friars, having money for their pains,
Are wondrous; — and indeed do no man good —
                                   *Aside.*
And seeing they are not idle, but still doing,  85
'T is likely they in time may reap some fruit,
I mean in fulness of perfection.
*Lod.* Good Barabas, glance not at our holy
   nuns.
*Bar.* No, but I do it through a burning
   zeal, —
Hoping ere long to set the house afire;        90
For though they do a while increase and
   multiply,
I 'll have a saying to that nunnery. —   *Aside.*
As for the diamond, sir, I told you of,
Come home and there 's no price shall make
   us part,
Even for your honourable father's sake. —  95
It shall go hard but I will see your death. —
                                   *Aside.*
But now I must be gone to buy a slave.
*Lod.* And, Barabas, I 'll bear thee company.
*Bar.* Come then. Here 's the market-place.
What 's the price of this slave? Two hundred
   crowns!                                        100
Do the Turks weigh so much?
*1 Off.*                Sir, that 's his price.
*Bar.* What, can he steal that you demand
   so much?
Belike he has some new trick for a purse;
And if he has, he is worth three hundred plates,
So that, being bought, the town-seal might be
   got                                            105
To keep him for his lifetime from the gallows.
The sessions day is critical to thieves,
And few or none 'scape but by being purg'd.
*Lod.* Rat'st thou this Moor but at two hun-
   dred plates?
*1 Off.* No more, my lord.                  110
*Bar.* Why should this Turk be dearer than
   that Moor?
*1 Off.* Because he is young and has more
   qualities.
*Bar.* What, hast the philosopher's stone?
And thou hast, break my head with it, I 'll for-
   give thee.                                      115
*Slave.* No, sir; I can cut and shave.
*Bar.* Let me see, sirrah, are you not an old
   shaver?
*Slave.* Alas, sir! I am a very youth.

---

³⁹ **Yond:** yonder   ⁵⁷ **foil:** metal setting   ⁵⁹ **foil'd:** defiled   ⁹² **have a saying to:** settle accounts
with   ¹⁰⁴ **plates:** silver coins   ¹¹⁴ **And:** An, if

*Bar.*  A youth?  I 'll buy you, and marry [120
you to Lady Vanity, if you do well.
*Slave.*  I will serve you, sir.
*Bar.*  Some wicked trick or other.  It may be,
under colour of shaving, thou 'lt cut my throat
for my goods.  Tell me, hast thou thy health
well?                                                    126
*Slave.*  Ay, passing well.
*Bar.*  So much the worse; I must have one
that 's sickly, an 't be but for sparing victuals:
't is not a stone of beef a day will maintain [130
you in these chops; let me see one that 's somewhat leaner.
  1 *Off.*  Here 's a leaner.  How like you him?
*Bar.*  Where wast thou born?
*Ith.*  In Thrace; brought up in Arabia. 135
*Bar.*  So much the better, thou art for my
turn.
An hundred crowns?  I 'll have him; there 's
the coin.                              [*Gives money.*]
  1 *Off.*  Then mark him, sir, and take him
hence.
*Bar.*  Ay, mark him, you were best, for this
is he
That by my help shall do much villainy.    140
                                          [*Aside.*]
My lord, farewell.  Come, sirrah, you are mine.
As for the diamond, it shall be yours;
I pray, sir, be no stranger at my house,
All that I have shall be at your command.

*Enter Mathias and his Mother* [*Katherine*]

*Math.*  What makes the Jew and Lodowick
so private?                                              145
I fear me 't is about fair Abigail.       [*Aside.*]
*Bar.*  Yonder comes Don Mathias, let us
stay;
He loves my daughter, and she holds him dear:
But I have sworn to frustrate both their hopes,
And be reveng'd upon the — governor.       150
                                  [*Exit Lodowick.*]
*Kath.*  This Moor is comeliest, is he not?
Speak, son.
*Math.*  No, this is the better, mother; view
this well.
          [*Kath. scrutinizes one of the slaves.*]
*Bar.*  Seem not to know me here before your
mother,
Lest she mistrust the match that is in hand.
When you have brought her home, come to my
house;                                                   155
Think of me as thy father; son, farewell.
*Math.*  But wherefore talk'd Don Lodowick
with you?

*Bar.*  Tush! man, we talk'd of diamonds, not
of Abigail.
*Kath.*  Tell me, Mathias, is not that the
Jew?
*Bar.*  As for the comment on the Maccabees,
I have it, sir, and 't is at your command.   161
*Math.*  Yes, madam, and my talk with him
was
About the borrowing of a book or two.
*Kath.*  Converse not with him, he is cast off
from heaven.
Thou hast thy crowns, fellow.  Come, let 's
away.                                                    165
*Math.*  Sirrah, Jew, remember the book.
*Bar.*  Marry will I, sir.
            *Exeunt* [*Mathias and his Mother*].
*Off.*                        Come, I have made
A reasonable market; let 's away.
                  [*Exeunt Officers with Slaves.*]
*Bar.*  Now let me know thy name, and there-
withal
Thy birth, condition, and profession.       170
*Ith.*  Faith, sir, my birth is but mean; my
name 's
Ithimore; my profession what you please.
*Bar.*  Hast thou no trade?  Then listen to
my words,
And I will teach that that shall stick by thee:
First be thou void of these affections,      175
Compassion, love, vain hope, and heartless fear;
Be mov'd at nothing, see thou pity none,
But to thyself smile when the Christians moan.
*Ith.*  O brave Master!  I worship your nose
for this.
*Bar.*  As for myself, I walk abroad o' nights
And kill sick people groaning under walls: 181
Sometimes I go about and poison wells;
And now and then, to cherish Christian thieves,
I am content to lose some of my crowns,
That I may, walking in my gallery,         185
See 'em go pinion'd along by my door.
Being young, I studied physic, and began
To practise first upon the Italian;
There I enrich'd the priests with burials,
And always kept the sextons' arms in ure   190
With digging graves and ringing dead men's
knells.
And after that was I an engineer,
And in the wars 'twixt France and Germany,
Under pretence of helping Charles the Fifth,
Slew friend and enemy with my stratagems. 195
Then after that was I an usurer,
And with extorting, cozening, forfeiting,
And tricks belonging unto brokery,

120–121 **youth . . . Lady Vanity:** (alluding to the interlude of *Lusty Juventus*)   129 **an 't:** (‘and ’ Q)
130 **a stone:** 14 pounds   136 **turn:** purpose   144 S. D. (‘Enter Mathias, Mater’ Q)   147 **stay:** break off
165 **fellow:** (addressed to Officer)   169 (The scene now changes to the street in front of Barabas' house.)
174 **that that:** (‘that’ Q)   179 **nose:** (Barabas wore a large artificial nose, the stage mark of the usurer)
190 **ure:** exercise

I fill'd the jails with bankrouts in a year,
And with young orphans planted hospitals, 200
And every moon made some or other mad,
And now and then one hang himself for grief,
Pinning upon his breast a long great scroll
How I with interest tormented him.
But mark how I am blest for plaguing them;
I have as much coin as will buy the town. 206
But tell me now, how hast thou spent thy
    time?
    *Ith.* 'Faith, master,
In setting Christian villages on fire,
Chaining of eunuchs, binding galley-slaves. 210
One time I was an hostler in an inn,
And in the night-time secretly would I steal
To travellers' chambers, and there cut their
    throats.
Once at Jerusalem, where the pilgrims kneel'd,
I strowed powder on the marble stones, 215
And therewithal their knees would rankle so,
That I have laugh'd a-good to see the cripples
Go limping home to Christendom on stilts.
    *Bar.* Why this is something. Make account
    of me
As of thy fellow: we are villains both, 220
Both circumcised, we hate Christians both.
Be true and secret, thou shalt want no gold.
But stand aside, here comes Don Lodowick.

        *Enter Lodowick*

    *Lod.* O Barabas, well met;
Where is the diamond you told me of? 225
    *Bar.* I have it for you, sir; please you walk
    in with me.
What ho, Abigail! open the door, I say.

      *Enter Abigail [with letters]*

    *Abig.* In good time, father; here are letters
    come
From Ormus, and the post stays here within.
    *Bar.* Give me the letters. — Daughter, do
    you hear? 230
Entertain Lodowick, the governor's son,
With all the courtesy you can afford,
Provided that you keep your maidenhead.
Use him as if he were a Philistine,
Dissemble, swear, protest, vow to love him, 235
He is not of the seed of Abraham. — *Aside.*
I am a little busy, sir; pray pardon me.
Abigail, bid him welcome for my sake.
    *Abig.* For your sake and his own he 's wel-
    come hither.
    *Bar.* Daughter, a word more. Kiss him;
    speak him fair, 240
And like a cunning Jew so cast about,
That ye be both made sure ere you come out.
                       *[Aside.]*

    *Abig.* O father! Don Mathias is my love.
    *Bar.* I know it: yet I say, make love to him;
Do, it is requisite it should be so —   *[Aside.]*
Nay, on my life, it is my factor's hand — 246
But go you in, I 'll think upon the account.

  *[Exeunt Abigail and Lodowick into the house]*

The account is made, for Lodowick — dies.
My factor sends me word a merchant 's fled
That owes me for a hundred tun of wine. 250
I weigh it thus much [*snapping his fingers*]; I
    have wealth enough,
For now by this has he kiss'd Abigail;
And she vows love to him, and he to her.
As sure as Heaven rain'd manna for the Jews,
So sure shall he and Don Mathias die: 255
His father was my chiefest enemy.

        *Enter Mathias*

Whither goes Don Mathias? Stay awhile.
    *Math.* Whither, but to my fair love Abigail?
    *Bar.* Thou know'st, and Heaven can witness
    it is true,
That I intend my daughter shall be thine. 260
    *Math.* Ay, Barabas, or else thou wrong'st
    me much.
    *Bar.* O, Heaven forbid I should have such a
    thought.
Pardon me though I weep: the governor's son
Will, whether I will or no, have Abigail:
He sends her letters, bracelets, jewels, rings.
    *Math.* Does she receive them? 266
    *Bar.* She? No, Mathias, no, but sends them
    back,
And when he comes, she locks herself up fast;
Yet through the keyhole will he talk to her,
While she runs to the window looking out, 270
When you should come and hale him from the
    door.
    *Math.* O treacherous Lodowick!
    *Bar.* Even now as I came home, he slipp'd
    me in,
And I am sure he is with Abigail.
    *Math.* I 'll rouse him thence. 275
    *Bar.* Not for all Malta, therefore sheathe
    your sword.
If you love me, no quarrels in my house;
But steal you in, and seem to see him not;
I 'll give him such a warning ere he goes
As he shall have small hopes of Abigail. 280
Away, for here they come.

      *Enter Lodowick, Abigail*

    *Math.* What, hand in hand! I cannot suffer
    this.
    *Bar.* Mathias, as thou lov'st me, not a word.

---

  ¹⁹⁹ **bankrouts:** bankrupts   ²⁰⁰ **planted hospitals:** filled the poorhouses   ²¹⁶ **rankle:** fester
²¹⁷ **a-good:** heartily   ²¹⁸ **stilts:** crutches   ²²⁹ **Ormus:** city on Persian Gulf, famed for exotic wealth
(cf. *Paradise Lost* ii. 3)   ²⁴² **made sure:** betrothed

*Math.* Well, let it pass, another time shall
serve.                    *Exit* [*into the house*].
*Lod.* Barabas, is not that the widow's son?
*Bar.* Ay, and take heed, for he hath sworn
your death.                                        286
*Lod.* My death? What, is the base-born
peasant mad?
*Bar.* No, no, but happily he stands in fear
Of that which you, I think, ne'er dream upon,
My daughter here, a paltry silly girl.        290
*Lod.* Why, loves she Don Mathias?
*Bar.* Doth she not with her smiling answer
you?
*Abig.* [*Aside.*] He has my heart; I smile
against my will.
*Lod.* Barabas, thou know'st I have lov'd
thy daughter long.
*Bar.* And so has she done you, even from
a child.                                          295
*Lod.* And now I can no longer hold my mind.
*Bar.* Nor I the affection that I bear to you.
*Lod.* This is thy diamond. Tell me, shall I
have it?
*Bar.* Win it, and wear it, it is yet unsoil'd.
O! but I know your lordship would disdain 300
To marry with the daughter of a Jew;
And yet I 'll give her many a golden cross
With Christian posies round about the ring.
*Lod.* 'T is not thy wealth, but her that I es-
teem;
Yet crave I thy consent.                         305
*Bar.* And mine you have, yet let me talk to
her. —
This offspring of Cain, this Jebusite,    *Aside.*
That never tasted of the Passover,
Nor e'er shall see the land of Canaan,
Nor our Messias that is yet to come; —       310
This gentle maggot, Lodowick, I mean, —
                                        [*Aloud.*]
Must be deluded. Let him have thy hand,
But keep thy heart till Don Mathias comes.
                                        [*Aside.*]
*Abig.* What, shall I be betroth'd to Lodo-
wick?
*Bar.* It 's no sin to deceive a Christian; 315
For they themselves hold it a principle,
Faith is not to be held with heretics;
But all are heretics that are not Jews.
This follows well, and therefore, daughter, fear
not. —                                  [*Aside.*]
I have entreated her, and she will grant.    320
*Lod.* Then, gentle Abigail, plight thy faith
to me.
*Abig.* I cannot choose, seeing my father bids.
Nothing but death shall part my love and
me.

*Lod.* Now have I that for which my soul
hath long'd.                                     324
*Bar.* So have not I, but yet I hope I shall.
                                        *Aside.*
*Abig.* [*Aside.*] O wretched Abigail, what hast
thou done?
*Lod.* Why on the sudden is your colour
chang'd?
*Abig.* I know not, but farewell, I must be
gone.
*Bar.* Stay her, but let her not speak one word
more.
*Lod.* Mute o' the sudden! Here 's a sudden
change.                                          330
*Bar.* O, muse not at it, 't is the Hebrews'
guise,
That maidens new betroth'd should weep
awhile.
Trouble her not; sweet Lodowick, depart:
She is thy wife, and thou shalt be mine heir.
*Lod.* O, is 't the custom? Then I am re-
solv'd:                                          335
But rather let the brightsome heavens be dim,
And nature's beauty choke with stifling clouds,
Than my fair Abigail should frown on me. —
There comes the villain, now I 'll be reveng'd.

*Enter Mathias*

*Bar.* Be quiet, Lodowick, it is enough   340
That I have made thee sure to Abigail.
*Lod.* Well, let him go.                *Exit.*
*Bar.* Well, but for me, as you went in at
doors
You had been stabb'd, but not a word on 't
now;
Here must no speeches pass, nor swords be
drawn.                                           345
*Math.* Suffer me, Barabas, but to follow him.
*Bar.* No; so shall I, if any hurt be done,
Be made an accessory of your deeds.
Revenge it on him when you meet him next.
*Math.* For this I 'll have his heart.     350
*Bar.* Do so; lo, here I give thee Abigail.
*Math.* What greater gift can poor Mathias
have?
Shall Lodowick rob me of so fair a love?
My life is not so dear as Abigail.
*Bar.* My heart misgives me, that, to cross
your love,                                       355
He 's with your mother; therefore after him.
*Math.* What, is he gone unto my mother?
*Bar.* Nay, if you will, stay till she comes
herself.
*Math.* I cannot stay; for if my mother come,
She 'll die with grief.                          360
                                        *Exit.*

294–295 (Contrast I. ii. 382 ff.)   302 **cross:** crusado (Portuguese coin)   303 **posies:** mottoes
307 **Jebusite:** alien, non-Jew (cf. Judges xix. 12)   319 **follows well:** is logical   326 **thou:** ('thee' Q)
331 **guise:** custom   335 **resolv'd:** satisfied

*Abig.*  I cannot take my leave of him for
tears.
Father, why have you thus incens'd them both?
   *Bar.*  What 's that to thee?
   *Abig.*                I 'll make 'em friends again.
   *Bar.*  You 'll make 'em friends!  Are there
    not Jews enow                                364
In Malta, but thou must dote upon a Christian?
   *Abig.*  I will have Don Mathias; he is my
    love.
   *Bar.*  Yes, you shall have him. — Go, put
    her in.
   *Ith.*  Ay, I 'll put her in.  [*Puts Abigail in.*]
   *Bar.*  Now tell me, Ithimore, how lik'st thou
    this?
   *Ith.*  Faith, master, I think by this     370
You purchase both their lives; is it not so?
   *Bar.*  True; and it shall be cunningly per-
    form'd.
   *Ith.*  O master, that I might have a hand in
    this!
   *Bar.*  Ay, so thou shalt, 't is thou must do
    the deed.
Take this, and bear it to Mathias straight,  375
               [*Gives a letter.*]
And tell him that it comes from Lodowick.
   *Ith.*  'T is poison'd, is it not?
   *Bar.*  No, no, and yet it might be done that
    way.
It is a challenge feign'd from Lodowick.     379
   *Ith.*  Fear not; I 'll so set his heart afire,
That he shall verily think it comes from him.
   *Bar.*  I cannot choose but like thy readiness:
Yet be not rash, but do it cunningly.
   *Ith.*  As I behave myself in this, employ me
    hereafter.
   *Bar.*  Away then.        *Exit* [*Ithimore*].
So, now will I go in to Lodowick,            386
And, like a cunning spirit, feign some lie,
Till I have set 'em both at enmity.    *Exit.*

### Actus Tertius

[SCENE I. — *A Street.*]

*Enter* [*Bellamira,*] *a Courtesan*

   *Bell.*  Since this town was besieg'd, my gain
    grows cold.
The time has been that, but for one bare night,
A hundred ducats have been freely given:
But now against my will I must be chaste;
And yet I know my beauty doth not fail.    5
From Venice merchants, and from Padua
Were wont to come rare-witted gentlemen,
Scholars I mean, learned and liberal;
And now, save Pilia-Borza, comes there none,
And he is very seldom from my house;       10
And here he comes.

*Enter Pilia-Borza*

   *Pilia.*  Hold thee, wench, there 's something
for thee to spend.    [*Shows a bag of silver.*]
   *Bell.*  'T is silver.  I disdain it.
   *Pilia.*  Ay, but the Jew has gold,         15
And I will have it, or it shall go hard.
   *Bell.*  Tell me, how cam'st thou by this?
   *Pilia.*  Faith, walking the back-lanes, through
the gardens, I chanc'd to cast mine eye up to
the Jew's counting-house, where I saw some [20
bags of money, and in the night I clamber'd up
with my hooks, and, as I was taking my choice,
I heard a rumbling in the house; so I took only
this, and run my way.  But here 's the Jew's
man.                                        25

*Enter Ithimore*

   *Bell.*  Hide the bag.
   *Pilia.*  Look not towards him, let 's away.
Zoons, what a looking thou keep'st; thou 'lt
   betray 's anon.
      [*Exeunt Bellamira and Pilia-Borza.*]
   *Ith.*  O the sweetest face that ever I beheld!
I know she is a courtesan by her attire.  Now [30
would I give a hundred of the Jew's crowns
that I had such a concubine.
Well, I have deliver'd the challenge in such sort,
As meet they will, and fighting die; brave
   sport!                                 *Exit.*

[SCENE II. — *Street, beside Barabas' house.*]

*Enter Mathias*

   *Math.*  This is the place; now Abigail shall
    see
Whether Mathias holds her dear or no.

*Enter Lodowick*

   *Math.*  What, dares the villain write in such
    base terms?
   *Lod.*  I did it; and revenge it if thou dar'st.

*Fight: enter Barabas, above*

   *Bar.*  O bravely fought! and yet they thrust
    not home.                              5
Now, Lodowick! now, Mathias!  So ——
                 [*Both fall.*]
So now they have show'd themselves to be tall
   fellows.
   [*Cries*] *within.*  Part 'em, part 'em.
   *Bar.*  Ay, part 'em now they are dead.  Fare-
    well, farewell.                       *Exit.*

*Enter Governor, Mater* [*i.e., Katherine*]

   *Gov.*  What sight is this! — my Lodowick
    slain!                                 10

---

¹ **Since . . . besieg'd:** The siege does not begin till later (cf. Sc. v. below); this scene is probably
misplaced and spurious. Sc. ii.    ² S. D. ('Enter Lodow. reading' Q)    ⁷ **tall:** valiant

These arms of mine shall be thy sepulchre.
*Mater.* Who is this? My son Mathias slain!
*Gov.* O Lodowick! had'st thou perish'd by
the Turk,
Wretched Ferneze might have veng'd thy death.
*Mater.* Thy son slew mine, and I 'll revenge
his death.                                                    15
*Gov.* Look, Katherine, look! — thy son gave
mine these wounds.
*Mater.* O leave to grieve me, I am griev'd
enough.
*Gov.* O that my sighs could turn to lively
breath;
And these my tears to blood, that he might live!
*Mater.* Who made them enemies?           20
*Gov.* I know not, and that grieves me most
of all.
*Mater.* My son lov'd thine.
*Gov.*                     And so did Lodowick him.
*Mater.* Lend me that weapon that did kill
my son,
And it shall murder me.
*Gov.* Nay, madam, stay; that weapon was
my son's,                                                     25
And on that rather should Ferneze die.
*Mater.* Hold, let 's inquire the causers of
their deaths,
That we may venge their blood upon their
heads.
*Gov.* Then take them up, and let them be
interr'd
Within one sacred monument of stone;      30
Upon which altar I will offer up
My daily sacrifice of sighs and tears,
And with my prayers pierce impartial heavens,
Till they reveal the causers of our smarts,
Which forc'd their hands divide united hearts.
Come, Katherina, our losses equal are;     36
Then of true grief let us take equal share.
                              *Exeunt [with the bodies].*

[SCENE III. — *House of Barabas.*]

*Enter Ithimore*

*Ith.* Why, was there ever seen such villainy,
So neatly plotted, and so well perform'd?
Both held in hand, and flatly both beguil'd?

*Enter Abigail*

*Abig.* Why, how now, Ithimore, why
laugh'st thou so?
*Ith.* O mistress, ha! ha! ha!                   5
*Abig.* Why, what ail'st thou?
*Ith.* O my master!
*Abig.* Ha!

*Ith.* O mistress! I have the bravest, grav-
est, secret, subtle, bottle-nos'd knave to my
master, that ever gentleman had.            11
*Abig.* Say, knave, why rail'st upon my father
thus?
*Ith.* O, my master has the bravest policy.
*Abig.* Wherein?
*Ith.* Why, know you not?                      15
*Abig.* Why, no.
*Ith.* Know you not of Mathias' and Don
Lodowick's disaster?
*Abig.* No, what was it?
*Ith.* Why, the devil invented a challenge, [20
my master writ it, and I carried it, first to
Lodowick, and *imprimis* to Mathias.
And then they met, and, as the story says,
In doleful wise they ended both their days.
*Abig.* And was my father furtherer of their
deaths?                                                       25
*Ith.* Am I Ithimore?
*Abig.* Yes.
*Ith.* So sure did your father write, and I
carry the challenge.
*Abig.* Well, Ithimore, let me request thee
this:                                                          30
Go to the new-made nunnery, and inquire
For any of the friars of Saint Jaques,
And say, I pray them come and speak with
me.
*Ith.* I pray, mistress, will you answer me
to one question?                                          35
*Abig.* Well, sirrah, what is 't?
*Ith.* A very feeling one: have not the nuns
fine sport with the friars now and then?
*Abig.* Go to, sirrah sauce, is this your ques-
tion? Get ye gone.                                      40
*Ith.* I will, forsooth, mistress.            *Exit.*
*Abig.* Hard-hearted father, unkind Barabas!
Was this the pursuit of thy policy!
To make me show them favour severally,    44
That by my favour they should both be slain?
Admit thou lov'dst not Lodowick for his sire,
Yet Don Mathias ne'er offended thee:
But thou wert set upon extreme revenge,
Because the sire dispossess'd thee once,
And could'st not venge it, but upon his son,   50
Nor on his son, but by Mathias' means;
Nor on Mathias, but by murdering me.
But I perceive there is no love on earth,
Pity in Jews, nor piety in Turks,              54
But here comes cursed Ithimore, with the friar.

*Enter Ithimore, Friar [Jacomo]*

*F. Jac.* *Virgo, salve.*
*Ith.* When! duck you!

³³ **impartial:** unfriendly   ³⁴ **reveal:** (Not in Q)   ³ **held in hand:** kept in suspense   ²² **im-**
**primis:** first (Ithimore does not know the word's meaning.)   ²³ **and:** (Not in Q)   ³² **friars of Saint**
**Jaques:** Jacobins, French Dominicans ('St. Iaynes' Q)   ⁴³ **pursuit:** aim   ⁴⁶ **sire:** ('sinne Q)
⁴⁹ **sire:** ('Pryor' Q)   ⁵⁷ **When:** exclamation of impatience   **duck:** make obeisance

*Abig.* Welcome, grave friar; Ithimore, be-
gone. *Exit [Ithimore].*
Know, holy sir, I am bold to solicit thee.
*F. Jac.* Wherein? 60
*Abig.* To get me be admitted for a nun.
*F. Jac.* Why, Abigail, it is not yet long since
That I did labour thy admission,
And then thou did'st not like that holy life.
*Abig.* Then were my thoughts so frail and
unconfirm'd, 65
And I was chain'd to follies of the world:
But now experience, purchased with grief,
Has made me see the difference of things.
My sinful soul, alas, hath pac'd too long
The fatal labyrinth of misbelief, 70
Far from the Sun that gives eternal life.
*F. Jac.* Who taught thee this?
*Abig.* The abbess of the house,
Whose zealous admonition I embrace:
O, therefore, Jacomo, let me be one,
Although unworthy, of that sisterhood. 75
*F. Jac.* Abigail, I will, but see thou change
no more,
For that will be most heavy to thy soul.
*Abig.* That was my father's fault.
*F. Jac.* Thy father's! how?
*Abig.* Nay, you shall pardon me. *[Aside.]*
O Barabas,
Though thou deservest hardly at my hands, 80
Yet never shall these lips bewray thy life.
*F. Jac.* Come, shall we go?
*Abig.* My duty waits on you.
*Exeunt.*

[SCENE IV. — *The Same.*]

*Enter Barabas, reading a letter*

*Bar.* What, Abigail become a nun again!
False and unkind; what, hast thou lost thy
father?
And all unknown, and unconstrain'd of me,
Art thou again got to the nunnery?
Now here she writes, and wills me to repent. 5
Repentance! *Spurca!* what pretendeth this?
I fear she knows — 't is so — of my device
In Don Mathias' and Lodovico's deaths.
If so, 't is time that it be seen into;
For she that varies from me in belief 10
Gives great presumption that she loves me not;
Or loving, doth dislike of something done.
But who comes here?

[*Enter Ithimore*]

O Ithimore, come near;
Come near, my love; come near, thy master's
life.
My trusty servant, nay, my second self: 15

For I have now no hope but even in thee,
And on that hope my happiness is built.
When saw'st thou Abigail?
*Ith.* To-day.
*Bar.* With whom?
*Ith.* A friar.
*Bar.* A friar! false villain, he hath done the
deed. 20
*Ith.* How, sir?
*Bar.* Why, made mine Abigail a nun.
*Ith.* That 's no lie, for she sent me for him.
*Bar.* O unhappy day!
False, credulous, inconstant Abigail!
But let 'em go: and, Ithimore, from hence 25
Ne'er shall she grieve me more with her dis-
grace;
Ne'er shall she live to inherit aught of mine,
Be blest of me, nor come within my gates,
But perish underneath my bitter curse,
Like Cain by Adam for his brother's death. 30
*Ith.* O master!
*Bar.* Ithimore, entreat not for her, I am
mov'd,
And she is hateful to my soul and me:
And 'less thou yield to this that I entreat,
I cannot think but that thou hat'st my life. 35
*Ith.* Who, I, master? Why, I 'll run to some
rock,
And throw myself headlong into the sea;
Why, I 'll do anything for your sweet sake.
*Bar.* O trusty Ithimore, no servant, but my
friend,
I here adopt thee for mine only heir, 40
All that I have is thine when I am dead,
And whilst I live use half; spend as myself.
Here take my keys, — I 'll give 'em thee anon.
Go buy thee garments; — but thou shalt not
want.
Only know this, that thus thou art to do: 45
But first go fetch me in the pot of rice
That for our supper stands upon the fire.
*Ith.* [*Aside.*] I hold my head my master 's
hungry. — I go, sir. *Exit.*
*Bar.* Thus every villain ambles after wealth,
Although he ne'er be richer than in hope. 50
But, hush 't!

*Enter Ithimore with the pot*

*Ith.* Here 't is, master.
*Bar.* Well said, Ithimore.
What, hast thou brought the ladle with thee
too?
*Ith.* Yes, sir, the proverb says, he that eats
with the devil had need of a long spoon. I have
brought you a ladle. 55
*Bar.* Very well, Ithimore, then now be secret;

---

81 **bewray:** expose  2 **unkind:** unnatural  6 **Spurca:** fie!  **pretendeth:** portendeth  15 **self:**
('life' Q)  32 **mov'd:** enraged  34 **'less:** unless ('least' Q)  48 **hold:** wager

And for thy sake, whom I so dearly love,
Now shalt thou see the death of Abigail,
That thou may'st freely live to be my heir.
*Ith.* Why, master, will you poison her [60
with a mess of rice porridge? That will preserve
life, make her round and plump, and batten
more than you are aware.
*Bar.* Ay, but, Ithimore, seest thou this?
It is a precious powder that I bought          65
Of an Italian in Ancona once,
Whose operation is to bind, infect,
And poison deeply, yet not appear
In forty hours after it is ta'en.
*Ith.* How, master?                            70
*Bar.* Thus, Ithimore.
This even they use in Malta here, — 't is called
Saint Jaques' Even, — and then I say they use
To send their alms unto the nunneries.
Among the rest bear this, and set it there;    75
There 's a dark entry where they take it in,
Where they must neither see the messenger,
Nor make inquiry who hath sent it them.
*Ith.* How so?
*Bar.* Belike there is some ceremony in 't.    80
There, Ithimore, must thou go place this pot.
Stay, let me spice it first!
*Ith.* Pray do, and let me help you, master.
Pray let me taste first.
*Bar.* Prithee do. [*Ithimore tastes.*] What
   say'st thou now?                            85
*Ith.* Troth, master, I 'm loath such a pot of
pottage should be spoil'd.
*Bar.* Peace, Ithimore, 't is better so than
spar'd.
Assure thyself thou shalt have broth by the eye.
My purse, my coffer, and myself is thine.      90
*Ith.* Well, master, I go.
*Bar.* Stay, first let me stir it, Ithimore.
As fatal be it to her as the draught
Of which great Alexander drunk and died:
And with her let it work like Borgia's wine,   95
Whereof his sire, the Pope, was poisoned.
In few, the blood of Hydra, Lerna's bane,
The juice of hebon, and Cocytus' breath,
And all the poisons of the Stygian pool
Break from the fiery kingdom; and in this      100
Vomit your venom and invenom her
That like a fiend hath left her father thus.
*Ith.* [*Aside.*] What a blessing has he given 't!
Was ever pot of rice porridge so sauc'd! — What
shall I do with it?                            105
*Bar.* O, my sweet Ithimore, go set it down,
And come again so soon as thou hast done,
For I have other business for thee.

*Ith.* Here 's a drench to poison a whole
stable of Flanders mares. I 'll carry 't to [110
the nuns with a powder.
*Bar.* And the horse pestilence to boot;
away!
*Ith.* I am gone.
Pay me my wages, for my work is done. *Exit.*
*Bar.* I 'll pay thee with a vengeance, Ithimore.                                  *Exit.* 115

[SCENE V]

*Enter Governor, [del] Bosco, Knights, Bashaw*

*Gov.* Welcome, great bashaw; how fares
   Calymath?
What wind drives you thus into Malta-road?
*Bas.* The wind that bloweth all the world
   besides, —
Desire of gold.
*Gov.*          Desire of gold, great sir?
That 's to be gotten in the Western Ind:       5
In Malta are no golden minerals.
*Bas.* To you of Malta thus saith Calymath:
The time you took for respite is at hand.
For the performance of your promise pass'd,
And for the tribute-money I am sent.           10
*Gov.* Bashaw, in brief, shalt have no tribute
   here,
Nor shall the heathens live upon our spoil.
First will we raze the city walls ourselves,
Lay waste the island, hew the temples down,
And, shipping of our goods to Sicily,          15
Open an entrance for the wasteful sea,
Whose billows beating the resistless banks,
Shall overflow it with their refluence.
*Bas.* Well, Governor, since thou hast broke
   the league
By flat denial of the promis'd tribute,        20
Talk not of razing down your city walls.
You shall not need trouble yourselves so far,
For Selim Calymath shall come himself,
And with brass bullets batter down your towers,
And turn proud Malta to a wilderness          25
For these intolerable wrongs of yours;
And so farewell.
*Gov.* Farewell.                [*Exit Bashaw.*]
And now, you men of Malta, look about,
And let 's provide to welcome Calymath.        30
Close your portcullis, charge your basilisks,
And as you profitably take up arms,
So now courageously encounter them;
For by this answer broken is the league,
And naught is to be look'd for now but wars,   35
And naught to us more welcome is than wars.
                                    *Exeunt.*

⁶² **batten:** thrive   ⁶⁶ **Ancona:** a refuge for "Marranos," Christianized Jews from Portugal   ⁸⁹ **by the eye:** to your heart's desire   ⁹⁵ **Borgia:** Cæsar Borgia   ⁹⁷ **In few:** in brief   ⁹⁸ **hebon:** the yew tree, *ebenus*, thought poisonous   **Cocytus:** a river in Hades   ¹¹¹ **with a powder:** with violent speed   ¹ **bashaw:** same as "basso"; cf. I. ii ('Bashaws' Q)   ¹⁷ **resistless:** unresisting   ¹⁸ **refluence:** flood-tide   ³¹ **basilisks:** large cannon   ³² **profitably:** in your own interests

[SCENE VI. — *Before the Nunnery.*]

*Enter Two Friars [Jacomo and Bernardine]*

1 *Fri.*   O, brother, brother, all the nuns are
sick,
And physic will not help them; they must die.
2 *Fri.*   The abbess sent for me to be confess'd:
O, what a sad confession will there be!
1 *Fri.*   And so did fair Maria send for me.  5
I 'll to her lodging; hereabouts she lies.   *Exit.*

*Enter Abigail*

2 *Fri.*   What, all dead, save only Abigail?
*Abig.*   And I shall die too, for I feel death
coming.
Where is the friar that convers'd with me?   9
2 *Fri.*   O, he is gone to see the other nuns.
*Abig.*   I sent for him, but seeing you are
come,
Be you my ghostly father: and first know,
That in this house I liv'd religiously,
Chaste, and devout, much sorrowing for my
sins;
But ere I came ——                          15
2 *Fri.*   What then?
*Abig.*   I did offend high Heaven so grievously
As I am almost desperate for my sins;
And one offence torments me more than all.
You knew Mathias and Don Lodowick?    20
2 *Fri.*   Yes, what of them?
*Abig.*   My father did contract me to 'em
both:
First to Don Lodowick; him I never lov'd;
Mathias was the man that I held dear,
And for his sake did I become a nun.      25
2 *Fri.*   So, say how was their end?
*Abig.*   Both jealous of my love, envied each
other,
And by my father's practice, which is there
Set down at large. the gallants were both slain.
[*Gives a paper.*]
2 *Fri.*   O monstrous villainy!           30
*Abig.*   To work my peace, this I confess to
thee;
Reveal it not, for then my father dies.
2 *Fri.*   Know that confession must not be
reveal'd.
The canon law forbids it, and the priest
That makes it known, being degraded first,  35
Shall be condemn'd, and then sent to the fire.
*Abig.*   So I have heard; pray, therefore keep
it close.
Death seizeth on my heart: ah, gentle friar,
Convert my father that he may be sav'd,
And witness that I die a Christian. [*Dies.*]  40

2 *Fri.*   Ay, and a virgin too; that grieves
me most.
But I must to the Jew and exclaim on him,
And make him stand in fear of me.

*Enter 1 Friar [Jacomo]*

1 *Fri.*   O brother, all the nuns are dead, let 's
bury them.
2 *Fri.*   First help to bury this, then go with
me                                          45
And help me to exclaim against the Jew.
1 *Fri.*   Why, what has he done?
2 *Fri.*   A thing that makes me tremble to
unfold.
1 *Fri.*   What, has he crucified a child?
2 *Fri.*   No, but a worse thing: 't was told
me in shrift.                               50
Thou know'st 't is death and if it be reveal'd.
Come, let 's away.                    *Exeunt.*

## Actus Quartus

[SCENE I. — *A Street.*]

*Enter Barabas, Ithimore. Bells within*

*Bar.*   There is no music to a Christian's
knell:
How sweet the bells ring now the nuns are dead,
That sound at other times like tinker's pans!
I was afraid the poison had not wrought;
Or, though it wrought, it would have done no
good,                                        5
For every year they swell, and yet they live;
Now all are dead, not one remains alive.
*Ith.*   That 's brave, master, but think you it
will not be known?
*Bar.*   How can it, if we two be secret?   10
*Ith.*   For my part fear you not.
*Bar.*   I 'd cut thy throat if I did.
*Ith.*   And reason too.
But here 's a royal monastery hard by;
Good master, let me poison all the monks.   15
*Bar.*   Thou shalt not need, for now the nuns
are dead,
They 'll die with grief.
*Ith.*   Do you not sorrow for your daughter's
death?
*Bar.*   No, but I grieve because she liv'd so
long.
An Hebrew born, and would become a Chris-
tian!                                        20
*Cazzo, diabolo.*

*Enter the Two Friars*

*Ith.*   Look, look, master, here come two religious caterpillars.
*Bar.*   I smelt 'em ere they came.         24
*Ith.*   God-a-mercy, nose! Come, let 's begone.

---

²⁸ **practice:** plot   ⁴² **exclaim on:** denounce
term of defiance   ⁵¹ **and if:** if   ¹ **to:** equal to   ²¹ **Cazzo:** Italian

*2 Fri.* Stay, wicked Jew, repent, I say, and stay.

*1 Fri.* Thou hast offended, therefore must be damn'd.

*Bar.* I fear they know we sent the poison'd broth.

*Ith.* And so do I, master; therefore speak 'em fair.

*2 Fri.* Barabas, thou hast —— 30

*1 Fri.* Ay, that thou hast ——

*Bar.* True, I have money. What though I have?

*2 Fri.* Thou art a ——

*1 Fri.* Ay, that thou art, a ——

*Bar.* What needs all this? I know I am a Jew. 35

*2 Fri.* Thy daughter ——

*1 Fri.* Ay, thy daughter ——

*Bar.* O speak not of her! then I die with grief.

*2 Fri.* Remember that ——

*1 Fri.* Ay, remember that —— 40

*Bar.* I must needs say that I have been a great usurer.

*2 Fri.* Thou hast committed ——

*Bar.* Fornification — but that was in another country; and besides, the wench is dead.

*2 Fri.* Ay, but, Barabas, 45 Remember Mathias and Don Lodowick.

*Bar.* Why, what of them?

*2 Fri.* I will not say that by a forg'd challenge they met.

*Bar.* [*Aside.*] She has confess'd, and we are both undone, ——
My bosom inmates! —— but I must dissemble. —— *Aside.*
O holy friars, the burthen of my sins 51
Lie heavy on my soul; then pray you tell me,
Is 't not too late now to turn Christian?
I have been zealous in the Jewish faith,
Hard-hearted to the poor, a covetous wretch, 55
That would for lucre's sake have sold my soul.
A hundred for a hundred I have ta'en;
And now for store of wealth may I compare
With all the Jews in Malta; but what is wealth?
I am a Jew, and therefore am I lost. 60
Would penance serve for this my sin,
I could afford to whip myself to death.

*Ith.* And so could I; but penance will not serve.

*Bar.* To fast, to pray, and wear a shirt of hair,
And on my knees creep to Jerusalem. 65
Cellars of wine, and sollars full of wheat,
Warehouses stuff'd with spices and with drugs,
Whole chests of gold, in bullion, and in coin,

Besides I know not how much weight in pearl,
Orient and round, have I within my house; 70
At Alexandria, merchandise unsold.
But yesterday two ships went from this town:
Their voyage will be worth ten thousand crowns.
In Florence, Venice, Antwerp, London, Seville,
Frankfort, Lubeck, Moscow, and where not, 75
Have I debts owing; and in most of these
Great sums of money lying in the banco.
All this I 'll give to some religious house,
So I may be baptiz'd, and live therein.

*1 Fri.* O good Barabas, come to our house.

*2 Fri.* O no, good Barabas, come to our house; 81
And, Barabas, you know ——

*Bar.* I know that I have highly sinn'd.
You shall convert me, you shall have all my wealth.

*1 Fri.* O Barabas, their laws are strict. 85

*Bar.* I know they are, and I will be with you.

*2 Fri.* They wear no shirts, and they go barefoot too.

*Bar.* Then 't is not for me; and I am resolv'd
You shall confess me, and have all my goods.

*1 Fri.* Good Barabas, come to me. 90

*Bar.* You see I answer him, and yet he stays;
Rid him away, and go you home with me.

*1 Fri.* I 'll be with you to-night.

*Bar.* Come to my house at one o'clock this night.

*1 Fri.* You hear your answer, and you may be gone. 95

*2 Fri.* Why, go, get you away.

*1 Fri.* I will not go for thee.

*2 Fri.* Not! then I 'll make thee, rogue.

*1 Fri.* How, dost call me rogue? *Fight.*

*Ith.* Part 'em, master, part 'em. 100

*Bar.* This is mere frailty, brethren; be content.
Friar Bernardine, go you with Ithimore;
You know my mind, let me alone with him.
[*Aside to F. Bernardine.*]
[*Fri. Jac.*] Why does he go to thy house?
Let him be gone.

*Bar.* I 'll give him something and so stop his mouth. 105
*Exit* [*Ithimore with Friar Bernardine*].
I never heard of any man but he
Malign'd the order of the Jacobins:
But do you think that I believe his words?
Why, brother, you converted Abigail;
And I am bound in charity to requite it, 110
And so I will. O Jacomo, fail not, but come.

*Fri.* [*Jac.*] But, Barabas, who shall be your godfathers?

---

57 A . . . hundred: usury at one hundred per cent    66 sollars: lofts    70 Orient: of rare quality    77 banco: bank (Italian)    87 2 Fri. (assigned to '1' Q)    93 1 Fri. (assigned to '2' Q)    98 rogue: ('goe' Q)

For presently you shall be shriv'd.
  *Bar.* Marry, the Turk shall be one of my
    godfathers,
But not a word to any of your covent.    115
  *Fri.* [*Jac.*] I warrant thee, Barabas.  *Exit.*
  *Bar.* So, now the fear is past, and I am safe,
For he that shriv'd her is within my house;
What if I murder'd him ere Jacomo comes?
Now I have such a plot for both their lives 120
As never Jew nor Christian knew the like:
One turn'd my daughter, therefore he shall die;
The other knows enough to have my life,
Therefore 't is not requisite he should live.
But are not both these wise men to suppose 125
That I will leave my house, my goods, and
  all,
To fast and be well whipp'd? I 'll none of that.
Now, Friar Bernardine, I come to you,
I 'll feast you, lodge you, give you fair words,
And after that, I and my trusty Turk —    130
No more, but so: it must and shall be done.

          *Enter Ithimore*

Ithimore, tell me, is the friar asleep?
  *Ith.* Yes; and I know not what the reason
    is:
Do what I can he will not strip himself,
Nor go to bed, but sleeps in his own clothes. 135
I fear me he mistrusts what we intend.
  *Bar.* No, 't is an order which the friars use.
Yet, if he knew our meanings, could he scape?
  *Ith.* No, none can hear him, cry he ne'er so
    loud.
  *Bar.* Why, true, therefore did I place him
    there.    140
The other chambers open towards the street.
  *Ith.* You loiter, master; wherefore stay we
    thus?
O how I long to see him shake his heels.
  *Bar.* Come on, sirrah.    144
Off with your girdle, make a handsome noose.
    [*Ithimore takes off his girdle and
        ties a noose in it.*]
Friar, awake!
    [*Draws curtain before rear stage,
      revealing Bernardine asleep.*]
  *Fri.* [*Bern.*] What, do you mean to strangle
    me?
  *Ith.* Yes, 'cause you use to confess.
  *Bar.* Blame not us but the proverb, "Con-
fess and be hanged." Pull hard!    150
  *Fri.* [*Bern.*] What, will you have my life?
  *Bar.* Pull hard, I say. — You would have
    had my goods.
  *Ith.* Ay, and our lives too, therefore pull
    amain.    [*They strangle him.*]
'T is neatly done, sir, here 's no print at all.

  *Bar.* Then is it as it should be; take him
    up.    155
  *Ith.* Nay, master, be rul'd by me a little.
[*Stands the body upright against pillar of outer
stage.*] So, let him lean upon his staff. Excel-
lent! he stands as if he were begging of bacon.
  *Bar.* Who would not think but that this
    friar liv'd?    159
What time o' night is 't now, sweet Ithimore?
  *Ith.* Towards one.
  *Bar.* Then will not Jacomo be long from
    hence.    [*They retire.*]

          *Enter Jacomo*

  [*Fri.*] *Jac.* This is the hour wherein I shall
    proceed;
O happy hour wherein I shall convert
An infidel, and bring his gold into    165
Our treasury!
But soft, is not this Bernardine? It is;
And, understanding I should come this way,
Stands here o' purpose, meaning me some
    wrong,
And intercept my going to the Jew. —    170
Bernardine!
Wilt thou not speak? Thou think'st I see thee
    not;
Away, I 'd wish thee, and let me go by.
No, wilt thou not? Nay, then, I 'll force my
    way:    174
And see, a staff stands ready for the purpose:
As thou lik'st that, stop me another time.
          *Strike him.  He falls.*

    *Enter Barabas* [*and Ithimore*]

  *Bar.* Why, how now, Jacomo, what hast
    thou done?
  [*Fri.*] *Jac.* Why, stricken him that would
    have struck at me.
  *Bar.* Who is it? Bernardine! Now out,
    alas, he 's slain!
  *Ith.* Ay, master, he 's slain; look how his
brains drop out on 's nose.    181
  [*Fri.*] *Jac.* Good sirs, I have done 't, but
nobody knows it but you two; I may escape.
  *Bar.* So might my man and I hang with
you for company.    185
  *Ith.* No, let us bear him to the magistrates.
  [*Fri.*] *Jac.* Good Barabas, let me go.
  *Bar.* No, pardon me; the law must have
    his course.
I must be forc'd to give in evidence,
That being importun'd by this Bernardine 190
To be a Christian, I shut him out,
And there he sat. Now I, to keep my word,
And give my goods and substance to your
    house,
Was up thus early with intent to go

---

<sup>113</sup> **presently:** at once   <sup>115</sup> **covent:** religious house   <sup>137</sup> **order:** rule   <sup>142</sup> **stay:** delay   <sup>151</sup> **have:**
('saue' Q)   <sup>163</sup> **proceed:** take a great step forward   <sup>188</sup> **his:** its

Unto your friary, because you stay'd.        195
*Ith.* Fie upon 'em, master; will you turn
Christian when holy friars turn devils and
murder one another?
*Bar.* No, for this example I 'll remain a
Jew:                                         199
Heaven bless me! What, a friar a murderer!
When shall you see a Jew commit the like?
*Ith.* Why, a Turk could ha' done no more.
*Bar.* To-morrow is the sessions; you shall
to it.
Come, Ithimore, let 's help to take him hence.
[*Fri.*] *Jac.* Villains, I am a sacred person;
touch me not.                                205
*Bar.* The law shall touch you, we 'll but
lead you, we.
'Las, I could weep at your calamity!
Take in the staff too, for that must be shown:
Law wills that each particular be known.
                                 *Exeunt.*

[SCENE II. — *Bellamira's House.*]

*Enter Courtesan* [*Bellamira*] *and Pilia-Borza*

*Bell.* Pilia-Borza, did'st thou meet with
Ithimore?
*Pilia.* I did.
*Bell.* And did'st thou deliver my letter?
*Pilia.* I did.
*Bell.* And what think'st thou? Will he
come?                                          5
*Pilia.* I think so, and yet I cannot tell; for
at the reading of the letter he look'd like a man
of another world.
*Bell.* Why so?
*Pilia.* That such a base slave as he should [10
be saluted by such a tall man as I am, from
such a beautiful dame as you.
*Bell.* And what said he?
*Pilia.* Not a wise word, only gave me a nod,
as who should say, "Is it even so?" and so I [15
left him, being driven to a non-plus at the critical aspect of my terrible countenance.
*Bell.* And where didst meet him?
*Pilia.* Upon mine own freehold, within forty
foot of the gallows, conning his neck-verse, [20
I take it, looking of a friar's execution: whom
I saluted with an old hempen proverb, *Hodie
tibi, cras mihi,* and so I left him to the mercy
of the hangman: but the exercise being done,
see where he comes.                            25

*Enter Ithimore*

*Ith.* I never knew a man take his death so
patiently as this friar. He was ready to leap off

ere the halter was about his neck; and when
the hangman had put on his hempen tippet, he
made such haste to his prayers as if he had [30
had another cure to serve. Well, go whither he
will, I 'll be none of his followers in haste: and,
now I think on 't, going to the execution, a fellow met me with a muschatoes like a raven's
wing, and a dagger with a hilt like a warm- [35
ing-pan, and he gave me a letter from one
Madam Bellamira, saluting me in such sort as
if he had meant to make clean my boots with
his lips: the effect was, that I should come to
her house. I wonder what the reason is; it [40
may be she sees more in me than I can find in
myself: for she writes further, that she loves
me ever since she saw me, and who would not
requite such love? Here 's her house, and here
she comes, and now would I were gone; I [45
am not worthy to look upon her.
*Pilia.* This is the gentleman you writ to.
*Ith.* [*Aside.*] Gentleman! he flouts me; what
gentry can be in a poor Turk of tenpence? I 'll
be gone.                                       50
*Bell.* Is 't not a sweet-fac'd youth, Pilia?
*Ith.* [*Aside.*] Again, "sweet youth!" — Did
not you, sir, bring the sweet youth a letter?
*Pilia.* I did, sir, and from this gentlewoman,
who, as myself, and the rest of the family, [55
stand or fall at your service.
*Bell.* Though woman's modesty should hale
me back,
I can withhold no longer. Welcome, sweet love!
*Ith.* [*Aside.*] Now am I clean, or rather
foully, out of the way.                        60
*Bell.* Whither so soon?
*Ith.* [*Aside.*] I 'll go steal some money from
my master to make me handsome. — Pray pardon me, I must go see a ship discharg'd.
*Bell.* Canst thou be so unkind to leave me
thus?                                          65
*Pilia.* And ye did but know how she loves
you, sir.
*Ith.* Nay, I care not how much she loves me —
Sweet Allamira, would I had my master's
wealth for thy sake!
*Pilia.* And you can have it, sir, and if you
please.                                        70
*Ith.* If 't were above ground, I could and
would have it; but he hides and buries it up, as
partridges do their eggs, under the earth.
*Pilia.* And is 't not possible to find it out?
*Ith.* By no means possible.                   75
*Bell.* [*Aside to Pilia-Borza.*] What shall we
do with this base villain then?

____
[20] **neck-verse:** the Latin verse (usually opening of Psalm 51) by which criminals claiming benefit
of clergy were tested   [21] **of:** upon   [22] **hempen:** reeking of the halter   [22-23] **Hodie . . . mihi:** Your
fate to-day, mine to-morrow.   [31] **cure:** parochial appointment   [34] **muschatoes:** moustache
[39] **effect:** purport (of the letter)   [49] **of tenpence:** *i.e.,* a cheap slave (proverbial)   [60] **out of the way:**
lost, bewildered

*Pilia.* [*Aside to her.*] Let me alone; do but
you speak him fair.
But you know some secrets of the Jew,
Which, if they were reveal'd, would do him
    harm.                                               79
*Ith.* Ay, and such as — Go to, no more! I 'll
make him send me half he has, and glad he
scapes so too. Pen and ink! I 'll write unto
him; we 'll have money straight.
*Pilia.* Send for a hundred crowns at least.
*Ith.* Ten hundred thousand crowns. "Mas-
    ter Barabas."                    *He writes.* 85
*Pilia.* Write not so submissively, but threat-
    'ning him.
*Ith.* [*Writing.*] "Sirrah Barabas, send me a
    hundred crowns."
*Pilia.* Put in two hundred at least.
*Ith.* [*Writing.*] " I charge thee send me three
hundred by this bearer, and this shall be [90
your warrant: if you do not — no more, but so."
*Pilia.* Tell him you will confess.
*Ith.* [*Writing.*] "Otherwise I 'll confess all."
— Vanish, and return in a twinkle.
*Pilia.* Let me alone; I 'll use him in his
    kind.                                              95
                [*Exit Pilia-Borza with the letter.*]
*Ith.* Hang him, Jew!
*Bell.* Now, gentle Ithimore, lie in my lap. —
Where are my maids? Provide a running ban-
    quet;
Send to the merchant, bid him bring me silks.
Shall Ithimore, my love, go in such rags?    100
*Ith.* And bid the jeweller come hither too.
*Bell.* I have no husband, sweet; I 'll marry
    thee.
*Ith.* Content: but we will leave this paltry
    land,
And sail from hence to Greece, to lovely Greece.
I 'll be thy Jason, thou my golden fleece;    105
Where painted carpets o'er the meads are
    hurl'd,
And Bacchus' vineyards o'erspread the world;
Where woods and forests go in goodly green;
I 'll be Adonis, thou shalt be Love's Queen.
The meads, the orchards, and the primrose-
    lanes,                                             110
Instead of sedge and reed, bear sugar-canes;
Thou in those groves, by Dis above,
Shalt live with me and be my love.
*Bell.* Whither will I not go with gentle Ithi-
    more?

### Enter Pilia-Borza

*Ith.* How now! hast thou the gold?    115
*Pilia.* Yes.

*Ith.* But came it freely? Did the cow give
down her milk freely?
*Pilia.* At reading of the letter, he star'd and
stamp'd and turn'd aside. I took him by [120
the beard, and look'd upon him thus; told him
he were best to send it. Then he hugg'd and
embrac'd me.
*Ith.* Rather for fear than love.
*Pilia.* Then, like a Jew, he laugh'd and [125
jeer'd, and told me he lov'd me for your sake,
and said what a faithful servant you had been.
*Ith.* The more villain he to keep me thus.
Here 's goodly 'parel, is there not?    129
*Pilia.* To conclude, he gave me ten crowns.
*Ith.* But ten? I 'll not leave him worth a
grey groat. Give me a ream of paper; we 'll
have a kingdom of gold for 't.
*Pilia.* Write for five hundred crowns.    134
*Ith.* [*Writing.*] "Sirrah, Jew, as you love your
life send me five hundred crowns, and give the
bearer one hundred." Tell him I must have 't.
*Pilia.* I warrant your worship shall have 't.
*Ith.* And if he ask why I demand so much,
tell him I scorn to write a line under a hundred
crowns.                                                141
*Pilia.* You 'd make a rich poet, sir. I am
    gone.                                           *Exit.*
*Ith.* Take thou the money; spend it for my
    sake.
*Bell.* 'T is not thy money, but thyself I
    weigh;
Thus Bellamira esteems of gold.    145
                          [*Throws it aside.*]
But thus of thee.                    *Kiss him.*
*Ith.* That kiss again! she runs division of
    my lips.
What an eye she casts on me! It twinkles like
    a star.
*Bell.* Come, my dear love, let 's in and sleep
    together.                                          149
*Ith.* O, that ten thousand nights were put
in one, that we might sleep seven years together
afore we wake!
*Bell.* Come, amorous wag, first banquet, and
then sleep.                    *Exeunt.*

### [SCENE III. — *The Jew's House.*]

#### *Enter Barabas, reading a letter*

*Bar.* "Barabas, send me three hundred
    crowns. —"
Plain Barabas! O, that wicked courtesan!
He was not wont to call me Barabas.
"Or else I will confess:" ay, there it goes:
But, if I get him, *coupe de gorge* for that.    5

---

⁹⁵ **in his kind:** according to his nature    ⁹⁸ **running banquet:** hasty repast    ¹¹² **Dis above:** an
absurdity. (Dis was god of the underworld.)    ¹³² **grey groat:** silver fourpence    **ream:** pun on
"realm," which was often so spelled and pronounced    ¹⁴⁷ **runs division of:** plays on (musical phrase)
⁶ **coupe de gorge:** throat-cutting

He sent a shaggy totter'd staring slave,
That when he speaks draws out his grisly
  beard,
And winds it twice or thrice about his ear;
Whose face has been a grindstone for men's
  swords;
His hands are hack'd, some fingers cut quite
  off;                                            10
Who, when he speaks, grunts like a hog, and
  looks
Like one that is employ'd in catzery
And crossbiting, — such a rogue
As is the husband to a hundred whores:
And I by him must send three hundred crowns!
Well, my hope is, he will not stay there still; 16
And when he comes, — O, that he were but
  here!

*Enter Pilia-Borza*

*Pilia.* Jew, I must ha' more gold.
*Bar.* Why, want'st thou any of thy tale?
*Pilia.* No; but three hundred will not serve
his turn.                                        21
*Bar.* Not serve his turn, sir?
*Pilia.* No, sir; and, therefore, I must have
five hundred more.
*Bar.* I 'll rather ——                           25
*Pilia.* O good words, sir, and send it you
were best! See, there 's his letter. [*Gives letter.*]
*Bar.* Might he not as well come as send?
Pray bid him come and fetch it; what he writes
for you, ye shall have straight.                 30
*Pilia.* Ay, and the rest too, or else ——
*Bar.* [*Aside.*] I must make this villain
away. — Please you dine with me, sir; and you
shall be most heartily — poison'd.      *Aside.*
*Pilia.* No, God-a-mercy. Shall I have these
  crowns?                                         35
*Bar.* I cannot do it, I have lost my keys.
*Pilia.* O, if that be all, I can pick ope your
  locks.
*Bar.* Or climb up to my counting-house win-
dow: you know my meaning.
*Pilia.* I know enough, and therefore talk not
to me of your counting-house. The gold! or [41
know, Jew, it is in my power to hang thee.
*Bar.* [*Aside.*] I am betray'd. —
'T is not five hundred crowns that I esteem,
I am not mov'd at that: this angers me,     45
That he, who knows I love him as myself,
Should write in this imperious vein. Why, sir,
You know I have no child, and unto whom
Should I leave all but unto Ithimore?
*Pilia.* Here 's many words, but no crowns.
  The crowns!                                     50
*Bar.* Commend me to him, sir, most humbly,
And unto your good mistress, as unknown.

*Pilia.* Speak, shall I have 'em, sir?
*Bar.*               Sir, here they are. —
                                  [*Gives money.*]
O, that I should part with so much gold! —
Here, take 'em, fellow, with as good a will ——
As I would see thee hang'd. [*Aside.*] — O, love
  stops my breath:                               56
Never lov'd man servant as I do Ithimore!
*Pilia.* I know it, sir.
*Bar.* Pray, when, sir, shall I see you at my
  house?
*Pilia.* Soon enough, to your cost, sir. Fare
  you well.                               *Exit.* 60
*Bar.* Nay, to thine own cost, villain, if thou
  com'st!
Was ever Jew tormented as I am?
To have a shag-rag knave to come, —
Three hundred crowns, — and then five hun-
  dred crowns!
Well, I must seek a means to rid 'em all,    65
And presently; for in his villainy
He will tell all he knows, and I shall die for 't.
I have it:
I will in some disguise go see the slave,     69
And how the villain revels with my gold. *Exit.*

[SCENE IV. — *Bellamira's House.*]

*Enter Courtesan [Bellamira,] Ithimore,
        Pilia-Borza*

*Bell.* I 'll pledge thee, love, and therefore
  drink it off.
*Ith.* Say'st thou me so? Have at it; and,
  do you hear?                        [*Whispers.*]
*Bell.* Go to, it shall be so.
*Ith.* Of that condition I will drink it up.
Here 's to thee!
*Bell.*            Nay, I 'll have all or none.   5
*Ith.* There, if thou lov'st me, do not leave a
  drop.
*Bell.* Love thee! fill me three glasses.
*Ith.* Three and fifty dozen, I 'll pledge thee.
*Pilia.* Knavely spoke, and like a knight-at-
  arms.
*Ith.* Hey, *Rivo Castiliano!* a man 's a man!
*Bell.* Now to the Jew.                          11
*Ith.* Ha! to the Jew, and send me money he
  were best.
*Pilia.* What would'st thou do if he should
  send thee none?
*Ith.* Do nothing; but I know what I know:
he 's a murderer.                                15
*Bell.* I had not thought he had been so brave
  a man.
*Ith.* You knew Mathias and the governor's
son; he and I killed 'em both, and yet never
touch'd 'em.

---

⁶ **totter'd:** tattered   ¹² **catzery:** roguery   ¹³ **crossbiting:** swindling   ¹⁶ **still:** always   ¹⁹ **tale:**
sum   ⁵² **as:** although   ⁶³ **shag-rag:** ruffianly   ¹² **he:** ('you' Q)

*Pilia.* O, bravely done.                          20
*Ith.* I carried the broth that poison'd the
nuns; and he and I, snickle hand too fast,
strangled a friar.
*Bell.* You two alone?
*Ith.* We two; and 't was never known, nor
never shall be for me.                             26
*Pilia.* [*Aside to Bellamira.*] This shall with
   me unto the governor.
*Bell.* [*Aside to Pilia-Borza.*] And fit it
   should: but first let 's ha' more gold. —
Come, gentle Ithimore, lie in my lap.
*Ith.* Love me little, love me long. Let music
   rumble,                                         30
Whilst I in thy incony lap do tumble.

*Enter Barabas, with a lute, disguis'd*

*Bell.* A French musician! Come, let 's hear
   your skill.
*Bar.* Must tuna my lute for sound, twang,
twang, first.
*Ith.* Wilt drink, Frenchman? Here 's to [35
thee with a —— Pox on this drunken hiccup!
*Bar.* Gramercy, monsieur.
*Bell.* Prithee, Pilia-Borza, bid the fiddler
give me the posy in his hat there.
*Pilia.* Sirrah, you must give my mistress
your posy.                                         41
*Bar.* À votre commandement, madame.
*Bell.* How sweet, my Ithimore, the flowers
   smell!
*Ith.* Like thy breath, sweetheart; no violet
like 'em.                                          45
*Pilia.* Foh! methinks they stink like a holly-
hock.
*Bar.* [*Aside.*] So, now I am reveng'd upon
   'em all.
The scent thereof was death; I poison'd
   it.
*Ith.* Play, fiddler, or I 'll cut your cat's guts
into chitterlings.                                 51
*Bar.* Pardonnez moi, be no in tune yet; so
now, now all be in.
*Ith.* Give him a crown, and fill me out more
   wine.
*Pilia.* There 's two crowns for thee; play. 55
*Bar. Aside.* How liberally the villain gives
me mine own gold!                        [*Plays.*]
*Pilia.* Methinks he fingers very well.
*Bar. Aside.* So did you when you stole my
gold.                                              60
*Pilia.* How swift he runs!
*Bar. Aside.* You run swifter when you
threw my gold out of my window.
*Bell.* Musician, hast been in Malta long?
*Bar.* Two, three, four month, madame.  65
*Ith.* Dost not know a Jew, one Barabas?

*Bar.* Very mush, monsieur; you no be his
man?
*Pilia.* His man?
*Ith.* I scorn the peasant; tell him so.    70
*Bar.* [*Aside.*]  He knows it already.
*Ith.* 'T is a strange thing of that Jew, he
lives upon pickled grasshoppers and sauc'd
mushrooms.
*Bar. Aside.* What a slave 's this?  The gov-
ernor feeds not as I do.                           76
*Ith.* He never put on clean shirt since he was
circumcis'd.
*Bar. Aside.* O rascal!  I change myself
twice a day.                                       80
*Ith.* The hat he wears, Judas left under the
elder when he hang'd himself.
*Bar. Aside.* 'T was sent me for a present
from the great Cham.
*Pilia.* A musty slave he is; — Whither now,
fiddler?                                           86
*Bar.* Pardonnez moi, monsieur, me be no well.
                                             *Exit.*
*Pilia.* Farewell, fiddler! One letter more to
the Jew.
*Bell.* Prithee, sweet love, one more, and
   write it sharp.                                 90
*Ith.* No, I 'll send by word of mouth now.
— Bid him deliver thee a thousand crowns, by
the same token, that the nuns lov'd rice,
that Friar Bernardine slept in his own clothes.
Any of 'em will do it.                             95
*Pilia.* Let me alone to urge it, now I know
the meaning.
*Ith.* The meaning has a meaning. Come,
   let 's in.
To undo a Jew is charity, and not sin. *Exeunt.*

## Actus Quintus

[SCENE I]

*Enter Governor [Ferneze], Knights, Martin
del Bosco, [and Officers]*

*Gov.* Now, gentlemen, betake you to your
   arms,
And see that Malta be well fortifi'd;
And it behoves you to be resolute;
For Calymath, having hover'd here so long,
Will win the town, or die before the walls.   5
*Knight.* And die he shall, for we will never
   yield.

*Enter Courtesan [Bellamira], Pilia-Borza*

*Bell.* O, bring us to the governor.
*Gov.* Away with her! she is a courtesan.
*Bell.* Whate'er I am, yet, governor, hear me
   speak;                                           9

---

²² **snickle:** noose ("too free with our noose-hand" ?)    ³¹ **incony:** delicate    ⁵¹ **chitterlings:**
small intestines of pig, fried or boiled    ⁸⁴ **Cham:** emperor of Tartary

I bring thee news by whom thy son was slain:
Mathias did it not; it was the Jew.
   *Pilia.* Who, besides the slaughter of these
    gentlemen,
Poison'd his own daughter and the nuns,
Strangled a friar and I know not what   14
Mischief beside.
   *Gov.*         Had we but proof of this ——
   *Bell.* Strong proof, my lord; his man 's now
    at my lodging,
That was his agent; he 'll confess it all.
   *Gov.* Go fetch him straight [*Exeunt Officers*].
I always fear'd that Jew.

    *Enter [Officers with] Jew, Ithimore*

   *Bar.* I 'll go alone; dogs! do not hale me
    thus.   19
   *Ith.* Nor me neither. I cannot outrun you,
constable: — O my belly!
   *Bar.* [*Aside.*] One dram of powder more had
    made all sure.
What a damn'd slave was I!
   *Gov.* Make fires, heat irons, let the rack be
    fetch'd.
   *Knight.* Nay, stay, my lord; 't may be he
    will confess.   25
   *Bar.* Confess! what mean you, lords? Who
    should confess?
   *Gov.* Thou and thy Turk; 't was you that
    slew my son.
   *Ith.* Guilty, my lord, I confess. Your son
and Mathias were both contracted unto Abi-
gail; he forg'd a counterfeit challenge.   30
   *Bar.* Who carried that challenge?
   *Ith.* I carried it, I confess; but who writ it?
Marry, even he that strangled Bernardine,
poison'd the nuns and his own daughter.
   *Gov.* Away with him! his sight is death to
    me.   35
   *Bar.* For what, you men of Malta? Hear
    me speak:
She is a courtesan, and he a thief,
And he my bondman. Let me have law,
For none of this can prejudice my life.
   *Gov.* Once more, away with him; you shall
    have law.   40
   *Bar.* [*Aside.*] Devils, do your worst! I
    live in spite of you. —
As these have spoke, so be it to their souls! —
[*Aside.*] I hope the poison'd flowers will work
    anon.    *Exeunt [Officers with Barabas
        and Ithimore, Bellamira and
        Pilia-Borza*].

    *Enter Mater [Katherine]*

   *Mater.* Was my Mathias murder'd by the
    Jew?
Ferneze, 't was thy son that murder'd him.  45

   *Gov.* Be patient, gentle madam, it was he;
He forg'd the daring challenge made them fight.
   *Mater.* Where is the Jew? Where is that
    murderer?
   *Gov.* In prison till the law has pass'd on him.

    *Enter Officer*

   *Off.* My lord, the courtesan and her man
    are dead:   50
So is the Turk and Barabas the Jew.
   *Gov.* Dead!
   *Off.* Dead, my lord, and here they bring
    his body.
   *Bosco.* This sudden death of his is very
    strange.
   *Gov.* Wonder not at it, sir, the Heavens are
    just;   55
Their deaths were like their lives, then think
    not of 'em.
Since they are dead, let them be buried.
For the Jew's body, throw that o'er the
    walls,
To be a prey for vultures and wild beasts. —
So now away, and fortify the town. *Exeunt.* 60

   [SCENE II. — *Outside the City-Wall.*]

    [*Barabas discovered rising*]

   *Bar.* What, all alone? Well fare, sleepy
    drink.
I 'll be reveng'd on this accursed town;
For by my means Calymath shall enter in.
I 'll help to slay their children and their wives,
To fire the churches, pull their houses down. 5
Take my goods too, and seize upon my lands!
I hope to see the governor a slave,
And, rowing in a galley, whipp'd to death.

    *Enter Calymath, Bashaws, Turks*

   *Caly.* Whom have we there, a spy?
   *Bar.* Yes, my good lord, one that can spy a
    place   10
Where you may enter, and surprise the town.
My name is Barabas: I am a Jew.
   *Caly.* Art thou that Jew whose goods we
    heard were sold
For tribute-money?
   *Bar.*       The very same, my lord:
And since that time they have hir'd a slave, my
    man,   15
To accuse me of a thousand villainies:
I was imprisoned, but 'scap'd their hands.
   *Caly.* Did'st break prison?
   *Bar.* No, no;
I drank of poppy and cold mandrake juice; 20
And being asleep, belike they thought me dead,
And threw me o'er the walls: so, or how else,
The Jew is here, and rests at your command.

                   ³⁰ he: (Not in Q)

*Caly.* 'T was bravely done: but tell me, Barabas,                                                24
Canst thou, as thou report'st, make Malta ours?
  *Bar.* Fear not, my lord, for here against the sluice
The rock is hollow, and of purpose digg'd
To make a passage for the running streams
And common channels of the city.
Now, whilst you give assault unto the walls,   30
I 'll lead five hundred soldiers through the vault,
And rise with them i' th' middle of the town,
Open the gates for you to enter in;
And by this means the city is your own.         34
  *Caly.* If this be true, I 'll make thee governor.
  *Bar.* And if it be not true, then let me die.
  *Caly.* Thou 'st doom'd thyself. Assault it presently.                                    *Exeunt.*

### [SCENE III. — *Within the Town.*]

*Alarums. Enter [Calymath,] Turks, Barabas, [with] Governor and Knights prisoners*

  *Caly.* Now vail your pride, you captive Christians,
And kneel for mercy to your conquering foe.
Now where 's the hope you had of haughty Spain?
Ferneze, speak, had it not been much better   4
To 've kept thy promise than be thus surpris'd?
  *Gov.* What should I say? We are captives and must yield.
  *Caly.* Ay, villains, you must yield, and under Turkish yokes
Shall groaning bear the burthen of our ire;
And, Barabas, as erst we promis'd thee,
For thy desert we make thee governor.           10
Use them at thy discretion.
  *Bar.*                              Thanks, my lord.
  *Gov.* O fatal day, to fall into the hands
Of such a traitor and unhallow'd Jew!
What greater misery could Heaven inflict?
  *Caly.* 'T is our command: and, Barabas, we give,                                         15
To guard thy person, these our Janizaries:
Entreat them well, as we have used thee.
And now, brave bashaws, come, we 'll walk about
The ruin'd town, and see the wrack we made.—
Farewell, brave Jew; farewell, great Barabas!                                                  20
    *Exeunt [Calymath and bashaws].*
  *Bar.* May all good fortune follow Calymath!
And now, as entrance to our safety,
To prison with the governor and these
Captains, his consorts and confederates.

  *Gov.* O villain! Heaven will be reveng'd on thee.                                         25
  *Bar.* Away! no more; let him not trouble me.
    *Exeunt [Turks, with Ferneze and Knights].*
Thus hast thou gotten, by thy policy,
No simple place, no small authority.
I now am governor of Malta; true, —
But Malta hates me, and, in hating me,          30
My life 's in danger, and what boots it thee,
Poor Barabas, to be the governor,
Whenas thy life shall be at their command?
No, Barabas, this must be look'd into;
And since by wrong thou gott'st authority,      33
Maintain it bravely by firm policy.
At least unprofitably lose it not:
For he that liveth in authority,
And neither gets him friends, nor fills his bags,
Lives like the ass, that Æsop speaketh of,      40
That labours with a load of bread and wine,
And leaves it off to snap on thistle-tops:
But Barabas will be more circumspect.
Begin betimes; occasion 's bald behind;
Slip not thine opportunity, for fear too late   45
Thou seek'st for much, but canst not compass it. —
Within here!

### *Enter Governor, with a Guard*

  *Gov.* My lord?
  *Bar.*         Ay, "lord;" thus slaves will learn.
Now, governor; — stand by there, wait within.
    *[Exeunt Guard.]*
This is the reason that I sent for thee:
Thou seest thy life and Malta's happiness      50
Are at my arbitrement; and Barabas
At his discretion may dispose of both.
Now tell me, governor, and plainly too,
What think'st thou shall become of it and thee?
  *Gov.* This, Barabas; since things are in thy power,                                        55
I see no reason but of Malta's wrack,
Nor hope of thee but extreme cruelty.
Nor fear I death, nor will I flatter thee.
  *Bar.* Governor, good words; be not so furious.
'T is not thy life which can avail me aught;     60
Yet you do live, and live for me you shall:
And, as for Malta's ruin, think you not
'T were slender policy for Barabas
To dispossess himself of such a place?
For sith, as once you said, within this isle,   65
In Malta here, that I have got my goods,
And in this city still have had success,
And now at length am grown your governor,

---

²⁶ **sluice:** ('Truce' Q)   ²⁹ **channels:** gutters   ⁵ **To 've:** ('To' Q)   ¹⁷ **Entreat:** treat   ²² **entrance:** first step   ⁴⁴ **occasion 's bald behind:** *i.e.,* neglected opportunity is lost   ⁵⁶ **reason:** probability   ⁵⁸ **Nor:** neither   ⁶¹ **for me:** so far as I am concerned   ⁶⁶ **that:** construe with "sith" (l. 65)

Yourselves shall see it shall not be forgot:
For, as a friend not known but in distress, 70
I 'll rear up Malta, now remediless.
    *Gov.* Will Barabas recover Malta's loss?
Will Barabas be good to Christians?
    *Bar.* What wilt thou give me, governor, to procure
A dissolution of the slavish bands 75
Wherein the Turk hath yok'd your land and you?
What will you give me if I render you
The life of Calymath, surprise his men,
And in an outhouse of the city shut
His soldiers, till I have consum'd 'em all with fire? 80
What will you give him that procureth this?
    *Gov.* Do but bring this to pass which thou pretendest,
Deal truly with us as thou intimatest,
And I will send amongst the citizens,
And by my letters privately procure 85
Great sums of money for thy recompense:
Nay more, do this, and live thou governor still.
    *Bar.* Nay, do thou this, Ferneze, and be free.
Governor, I enlarge thee; live with me,
Go walk about the city, see thy friends: 90
Tush, send not letters to 'em, go thyself,
And let me see what money thou canst make.
Here is my hand that I 'll set Malta free:
And thus we cast it. To a solemn feast
I will invite young Selim Calymath, 95
Where be thou present only to perform
One stratagem that I 'll impart to thee,
Wherein no danger shall betide thy life,
And I will warrant Malta free for ever. 99
    *Gov.* Here is my hand; believe me, Barabas,
I will be there, and do as thou desirest.
When is the time?
    *Bar.*         Governor, presently:
For Calymath, when he hath view'd the town,
Will take his leave and sail toward Ottoman.
    *Gov.* Then will I, Barabas, about his coin, 105
And bring it with me to thee in the evening.
    *Bar.* Do so, but fail not; now farewell, Ferneze! —        *[Exit Ferneze.]*
And thus far roundly goes the business:
Thus loving neither, will I live with both,
Making a profit of my policy; 110
And he from whom my most advantage comes
Shall be my friend.
This is the life we Jews are us'd to lead;
And reason too, for Christians do the like.
Well, now about effecting this device; 115
First to surprise great Selim's soldiers,
And then to make provision for the feast,
That at one instant all things may be done.

My policy detests prevention:
To what event my secret purpose drives, 120
I know; and they shall witness with their lives.
                       *Exit.*

### [SCENE IV. — *The Walls.*]

*Enter Calymath, Bashaws*

    *Caly.* Thus have we view'd the city, seen the sack,
And caus'd the ruins to be new-repair'd,
Which with our bombards' shot and basilisk
We rent in sunder at our entry:
And now I see the situation, 5
And how secure this conquer'd island stands,
Environ'd with the Mediterranean Sea,
Strong-countermur'd with other petty isles;
And, toward Calabria, back'd by Sicily,
Where Syracusian Dionysius reign'd, 10
Two lofty turrets that command the town:
I wonder how it could be conquer'd thus.

*Enter a Messenger*

    *Mess.* From Barabas, Malta's governor, I bring
A message unto mighty Calymath:
Hearing his sovereign was bound for sea, 15
To sail to Turkey, to great Ottoman,
He humbly would entreat your majesty
To come and see his homely citadel,
And banquet with him ere thou leav'st the isle.
    *Caly.* To banquet with him in his citadel? 20
I fear me, messenger, to feast my train
Within a town of war so lately pillag'd
Will be too costly and too troublesome:
Yet would I gladly visit Barabas,
For well has Barabas deserv'd of us. 25
    *Mess.* Selim, for that, thus saith the governor,
That he hath in store a pearl so big,
So precious, and withal so orient,
As, be it valued but indifferently,
The price thereof will serve to entertain 30
Selim and all his soldiers for a month.
Therefore he humbly would entreat your highness
Not to depart till he has feasted you.
    *Caly.* I cannot feast my men in Malta-walls,
Except he place his tables in the streets. 35
    *Mess.* Know, Selim, that there is a monastery
Which standeth as an outhouse to the town:
There will he banquet them; but thee at home,
With all thy bashaws and brave followers.
    *Caly.* Well, tell the governor we grant his suit. 40
We 'll in this summer evening feast with him.

---

    ⁷¹ **remediless:** without a doubt    ⁸⁹ **enlarge:** liberate    ⁹⁴ **cast:** plan    ¹⁰⁴ **Ottoman:** the Ottoman capital, Constantinople    ¹¹⁹ **prevention:** forestalling    ³ **bombards':** ancient cannon    ⁸ **countermur'd:** ('countermin'd' Q)    ¹⁰, ¹¹ (Printed in reverse order Q)

*Mess.* I shall, my lord.                    *Exit.*

*Caly.* And now, bold bashaws, let us to our tents,
And meditate how we may grace us best
To solemnize our governor's great feast.    45
                                        *Exeunt.*

[SCENE V. — *A Street.*]

*Enter Governor, Knights, del Bosco*

*Gov.* In this, my countrymen, be rul'd by me.
Have special care that no man sally forth
Till you shall hear a culverin discharg'd
By him that bears the linstock, kindled thus;
Then issue out and come to rescue me,       5
For happily I shall be in distress,
Or you released of this servitude.
  *1 Knight.* Rather than thus to live as Turkish thralls,
What will we not adventure?
  *Gov.* On then, begone.
  *Knights.*        Farewell, grave governor! 10
                                        *Exeunt.*

[SCENE VI. — *Gallery in the Citadel.*]

*Enter [Barabas,] with a hammer, above, very busy; [and Carpenters]*

*Bar.* How stand the cords? How hang these hinges? Fast?
Are all the cranes and pulleys sure?
  *1 Carp.*                    All fast.
  *Bar.* Leave nothing loose, all levell'd to my mind.
Why now I see that you have art indeed.
There, carpenters, divide that gold amongst
  you:                    [*Gives money.*] 5
Go swill in bowls of sack and muscadine!
Down to the cellar, taste of all my wines.
  *1 Carp.* We shall, my lord, and thank you.
                        *Exeunt [Carpenters].*
  *Bar.* And, if you like them, drink your fill and die:
For so I live, perish may all the world!      10
Now, Selim Calymath, return me word
That thou wilt come, and I am satisfied.

*Enter Messenger*

Now, sirrah, what, will he come?
  *Mess.* He will; and has commanded all his men
To come ashore, and march through Malta streets,    15
That thou may'st feast them in thy citadel.
  *Bar.* Then now are all things as my wish would have 'em.

There wanteth nothing but the governor's pelf,
And see, he brings it.

*Enter Governor*

                    Now, governor, the sum?
  *Gov.* With free consent, a hundred thousand pounds.    20
  *Bar.* Pounds, say'st thou, governor? Well, since it is no more,
I'll satisfy myself with that; nay, keep it still,
For if I keep not promise, trust not me.
And, governor, now partake my policy:
First, for his army; they are sent before,    25
Enter'd the monastery, and underneath
In several places are field-pieces pitch'd,
Bombards, whole barrels full of gunpowder,
That on the sudden shall dissever it,
And batter all the stones about their ears,    30
Whence none can possibly escape alive.
Now as for Calymath and his consorts,
Here have I made a dainty gallery,
The floor whereof, this cable being cut,
Doth fall asunder; so that it doth sink      35
Into a deep pit past recovery.
Here, hold that knife [*throws down a knife*], and when thou seest he comes,
And with his bashaws shall be blithely set,
A warning-piece shall be shot off from the tower,
To give thee knowledge when to cut the cord 40
And fire the house. Say, will not this be brave?
  *Gov.* O excellent! here, hold thee, Barabas.
I trust thy word, take what I promis'd thee.
  *Bar.* No, governor, I'll satisfy thee first,
Thou shalt not live in doubt of anything.      45
Stand close, for here they come [*Ferneze retires*]. Why, is not this
A kingly kind of trade to purchase towns
By treachery and sell 'em by deceit?
Now tell me, worldlings, underneath the sun
If greater falsehood ever has been done?       50

*Enter Calymath and Bashaws*

  *Caly.* Come, my companion bashaws; see, I pray,
How busy Barabas is there above
To entertain us in his gallery;
Let us salute him. Save thee, Barabas!
  *Bar.* Welcome, great Calymath!
  *Gov.* [*Aside.*] How the slave jeers at him. 55
  *Bar.* Will 't please thee, mighty Selim Calymath,
To ascend our homely stairs?
  *Caly.*                    Ay, Barabas. —
Come, bashaws, attend.
  *Gov.* [*Coming forward.*] Stay, Calymath!
For I will show thee greater courtesy

---

³ **culverin:** small cannon    ⁴ **linstock:** stick by which the gunner's match was applied    ³ **lev-**
**ell'd . . . mind:** agreeing with my design    ³² **consorts:** companions

Than Barabas would have afforded thee.          60
*Knight.* [*Within.*] Sound a charge there!
*A charge, the cable cut, a caldron discovered.*

[*Enter del Bosco and Knights*]

*Caly.*                    How now! what means this?
*Bar.*   Help, help me! Christians, help!
*Gov.*   See, Calymath, this was devis'd for
  thee!
*Caly.*   Treason! treason! bashaws, fly!
*Gov.*                    No, Selim, do not fly;
See his end first, and fly then if thou canst.  65
*Bar.*   O help me, Selim! help me, Christians!
Governor, why stand you all so pitiless?
*Gov.*   Should I in pity of thy plaints or thee,
Accursed Barabas, base Jew, relent?
No, thus I 'll see thy treachery repaid,          70
But wish thou hadst behav'd thee otherwise.
*Bar.*   You will not help me, then?
*Gov.*                    No, villain, no.
*Bar.*   And, villains, know you cannot help
  me now. —
Then, Barabas, breathe forth thy latest fate,
And in the fury of thy torments strive          75
To end thy life with resolution.
Know, governor, 't was I that slew thy son;
I fram'd the challenge that did make them meet.
Know, Calymath, I aim'd thy overthrow,
And had I but escap'd this stratagem,            80
I would have brought confusion on you all,
Damn'd Christians, dogs, and Turkish infidels!
But now begins the extremity of heat
To pinch me with intolerable pangs.
Die, life! fly, soul! tongue, curse thy fill, and
  die!                    [*Dies.*]  85
*Caly.*   Tell me, you Christians, what doth
  this portend?
*Gov.*   This train he laid to have entrapp'd
  thy life.
Now, Selim, note the unhallow'd deeds of Jews:
Thus he determin'd to have handled thee,
But I have rather chose to save thy life.         90

*Caly.*   Was this the banquet he prepar'd for
  us?
Let 's hence, lest further mischief be pretended.
*Gov.*   Nay, Selim, stay; for since we have
  thee here,
We will not let thee part so suddenly.
Besides, if we should let thee go, all 's one,    95
For with thy galleys could'st thou not get
  hence,
Without fresh men to rig and furnish them.
*Caly.*   Tush, governor, take thou no care for
  that,
My men are all aboard,
And do attend my coming there by this.          100
*Gov.*   Why, heard'st thou not the trumpet
  sound a charge?
*Caly.*   Yes, what of that?
*Gov.*                    Why then the house was fir'd,
Blown up, and all thy soldiers massacred.
*Caly.*   O monstrous treason!
*Gov.*                    A Jew's courtesy:
For he that did by treason work our fall,        105
By treason hath deliver'd thee to us.
Know, therefore, till thy father hath made
  good
The ruins done to Malta and to us,
Thou canst not part; for Malta shall be freed,
Or Selim ne'er return to Ottoman.                110
*Caly.*   Nay, rather, Christians, let me go to
  Turkey,
In person there to mediate your peace;
To keep me here will naught advantage you.
*Gov.*   Content thee, Calymath, here thou
  must stay,
And live in Malta prisoner; for come all the
  world                                          115
To rescue thee, so will we guard us now,
As sooner shall they drink the ocean dry
Than conquer Malta, or endanger us.
So march away, and let due praise be given
Neither to Fate nor Fortune, but to Heaven. 120
                                        *Exeunt.*

[61] S. D. a caldron discovered: (Curtain before inner stage opens and discloses Barabas in the caldron.)   [92] pretended: intended   [112] mediate: ('meditate' Q)   [115] all: ('call' Q)

# The troublesome

raigne and lamentable death of
Edward *the second, King of*
England: with the tragicall
*fall of proud* Mortimer:

As it was sundrie times publiquely acted
*in the honourable citie of London, by the*
right honourable the Earle of Pem-
*brooke his seruants.*

*Written by* Chri. Marlow *Gent.*

Imprinted at London for *William Iones,*
dwelling neere Holbourne conduit at the
*signe of the Gunne,* 1594

BIBLIOGRAPHICAL RECORD. William Jones entered the play for publication on July 6, 1593, five weeks after the author's burial: — "A booke Intituled The troublesom Reign and Lamentable Death of Edward the Second, king of England, with the tragicall fall of proud Mortymer." Good evidence exists that an edition appeared in this year, but the earliest of which a copy is known to survive is that of 1594 (see title-page). Others followed in 1598, 1612, and 1622. *Edward II* was the only play by Marlowe included in the first edition of Dodsley's *Old Plays* (1744). It was reprinted in the second Dodsley (1780) and the third (1825) and in four other editions between 1810 and 1826; and throughout this period was better known than any other of Marlowe's works.

DATE AND STAGE HISTORY. *Edward II* is the latest of Marlowe's dramas, produced by the Earl of Pembroke's Company after the poet had severed his connection with the Admiral-Strange combination that acted all his other plays except the early *Dido*. The earlier half of 1592 is the most likely date of first production, for the theatres were closed in June of that year and remained so (by reason of plague) till after Marlowe's death.

STRUCTURE. The early editions are entirely without indication of act or scene division; and though the material can be easily arranged in five acts (with a light division between II and III), it is evident that the dramatist is seeking a more fluid medium in this treatment of the march of history than was offered by the scheme of a rigid five-act tragedy. It is no less evident that he has turned his back upon the one-man type of play, and is dividing the histrionic opportunity much more equally among his actors; while in Isabella he develops the female interest much further than in any of the plays of the Alleyn-Admiral group. Most interesting of all is the striking emphasis upon stage action everywhere, which shows the practicing playwright superseding the poet. Only in the grand emotional climaxes, the scenes of Edward's deposition and death, is the poet allowed a free rein.

PLOT. The play presents the history of twenty-three years (1307–1330), from the accession of Edward II to the death of Mortimer. Holinshed's *Chronicle* is the main source, with occasional dependence upon Fabyan and Stowe. Holinshed has been very carefully studied and, where it suited the author's purpose, closely followed. But in its general sweep the tragedy is grandiosely unhistoric. Chronology and precise fact are evaded with obvious and intelligent intention, and much foreshortening is employed, in order to focus all attention upon the central theme of the good and ill in Edward and the crushing problem involved in loyalty or disloyalty to such a king. In the characters of Isabella and Young Mortimer Marlowe has carried character "development" to lengths previously unattempted. There are doubtless faulty strokes, but these characters, like the static one of Gaveston, are deeply etched.

# CHRISTOPHER MARLOWE

## THE TRAGEDY OF EDWARD THE SECOND

[DRAMATIS PERSONAE

KING EDWARD THE SECOND
PRINCE EDWARD, his Son, afterwards King Edward the Third
EARL OF KENT, Half-Brother to King Edward the Second
GAVESTON, the King's Favourite
ARCHBISHOP OF CANTERBURY
BISHOPS OF COVENTRY AND WINCHESTER
EARLS OF WARWICK, LANCASTER, PEMBROKE, ARUNDEL, AND LEICESTER
LORD BERKELEY
ROGER MORTIMER, the elder (of Chirk)
ROGER MORTIMER, the younger, his Nephew (of Wigmore)
SIR JOHN OF HAINAULT
SPENCER, the elder

SPENCER, the younger, his Son
BALDOCK, an Oxford Scholar
BEAUMONT,
TRUSSEL, } Court Attendants
LEVUNE,
JAMES, a Soldier of Lord Pembroke's
GURNEY
MATREVIS
LIGHTBORN, a Murderer
RICE AP HOWELL

QUEEN ISABELLA, Wife to King Edward the Second
MARGARET DE CLARE, Niece to King Edward the Second, daughter to the Duke of Gloucester

The King's Champion; an Abbot and Monks; Herald; Three Poor Men; a Mower; Lords, Ladies, Messengers, Soldiers, and Attendants

SCENE: London, various parts of England, Wales, and France]

[ACT I

SCENE I. — *A Street in London.*]

*Enter Gaveston, reading on a letter that was brought him from the King*

Gaveston. "My father is deceas'd! Come, Gaveston,
And share the kingdom with thy dearest friend."
Ah! words that make me surfeit with delight!
What greater bliss can hap to Gaveston
Than live and be the favourite of a king!     5
Sweet prince, I come; these, these thy amorous lines
Might have enforc'd me to have swum from France,
And, like Leander, gasp'd upon the sand,
So thou would'st smile, and take me in thy arms.
The sight of London to my exil'd eyes     10
Is as Elysium to a new-come soul;
Not that I love the city, or the men,
But that it harbours him I hold so dear —
The king, upon whose bosom let me lie,
And with the world be still at enmity.     15
What need the arctic people love starlight,
To whom the sun shines both by day and night?
Farewell base stooping to the lordly peers!
My knee shall bow to none but to the king.
As for the multitude, that are but sparks     20
Rak'd up in embers of their poverty, —
*Tanti!* I 'll fawn first on the wind
That glanceth at my lips, and flyeth away.

*Enter three Poor Men*

But how now, what are these?
*Poor Men.* Such as desire your worship's service.     25
*Gav.* What canst thou do?
1 *P. Man.* I can ride.
*Gav.* But I have no horses. — What art thou?
2 *P. Man.* A traveller.
*Gav.* Let me see: thou would'st do well     30
To wait at my trencher and tell me lies at dinner time;
And as I like your discoursing, I 'll have you. — And what art thou?
3 *P. Man.* A soldier that hath serv'd against the Scot.
*Gav.* Why, there are hospitals for such as     35
you.
I have no war, and therefore, sir, begone.

---

¹⁴ **lie:** ('die' Qq.)   ²¹ **Rak'd up:** as fire was preserved by covering it with ashes   ²² **Tanti:** So much for them! (with a contemptuous gesture)   ³¹ **trencher:** wooden plate   ³⁵ **hospitals:** charitable institutions, almshouses

3 *P. Man.* Farewell, and perish by a sol-
dier's hand,
That would'st reward them with an hospital.
  *Gav.* Ay, ay, these words of his move me as
  much
As if a goose should play the porpentine,   40
And dart her plumes, thinking to pierce my
breast.
But yet it is no pain to speak men fair;
I 'll flatter these, and make them live in
hope. —                          [*Aside.*]
You know that I came lately out of France,
And yet I have not view'd my lord the king; 45
If I speed well, I 'll entertain you all.
  *Omnes.* We thank your worship.
  *Gav.* I have some business: leave me to my-
self.
  *Omnes.* We will wait here about the court.
                                   *Exeunt.*
  *Gav.* Do. — These are not men for me:   50
I must have wanton poets, pleasant wits,
Musicians, that with touching of a string
May draw the pliant king which way I please.
Music and poetry is his delight;
Therefore I 'll have Italian masks by night,   55
Sweet speeches, comedies, and pleasing shows;
And in the day, when he shall walk abroad,
Like sylvan nymphs my pages shall be clad;
My men, like satyrs grazing on the lawns,
Shall with their goat-feet dance an antic hay.
Sometime a lovely boy in Dian's shape,   61
With hair that gilds the water as it glides,
Crownets of pearl about his naked arms,
And in his sportful hands an olive tree,
To hide those parts which men delight to see, 65
Shall bathe him in a spring; and there hard by,
One like Actæon peeping through the grove
Shall by the angry goddess be transform'd,
And running in the likeness of an hart
By yelping hounds pull'd down, and seem to
die; —                               70
Such things as these best please his majesty,
My lord. — Here comes the king, and the
nobles
From the parliament. I 'll stand aside.
                                  [*Retires.*]

*Enter the King, Lancaster, Mortimer Senior,
Mortimer Junior, Edmund Earl of Kent,
Guy Earl of Warwick, &c.*

  *K. Edw.* Lancaster!
  *Lan.* My lord.                        75
  *Gav.* That Earl of Lancaster do I abhor.
                                  [*Aside.*]

  *K. Edw.* Will you not grant me this? — In
spite of them
I 'll have my will; and these two Mortimers,
That cross me thus, shall know I am displeas'd.
                                  [*Aside.*]
  *Mor. Sen.* If you love us, my lord, hate
  Gaveston.                             80
  *Gav.* That villain Mortimer! I 'll be his
  death.                          [*Aside.*]
  *Mor. Jun.* Mine uncle here, this earl, and I
  myself
Were sworn to your father at his death,
That he should ne'er return into the realm;
And know, my lord, ere I will break my oath,
This sword of mine, that should offend your
foes,                                 86
Shall sleep within the scabbard at thy need,
And underneath thy banners march who will,
For Mortimer will hang his armour up.
  *Gav. Mort Dieu!*              [*Aside.*]
  *K. Edw.* Well, Mortimer, I 'll make thee
  rue these words.                      91
Beseems it thee to contradict thy king?
Frown'st thou thereat, aspiring Lancaster?
The sword shall plane the furrows of thy
brows,
And hew these knees that now are grown so
stiff.                                 95
I will have Gaveston; and you shall know
What danger 't is to stand against your king.
  *Gav.* Well done, Ned!          [*Aside.*]
  *Lan.* My lord, why do you thus incense your
  peers,
That naturally would love and honour you 100
But for that base and obscure Gaveston?
Four earldoms have I, besides Lancaster —
Derby, Salisbury, Lincoln, Leicester.
These will I sell, to give my soldiers pay,
Ere Gaveston shall stay within the realm;  105
Therefore, if he be come, expel him straight.
  *Kent.* Barons and earls, your pride hath
  made me mute;
But now I 'll speak, and to the proof, I hope.
I do remember, in my father's days,
Lord Percy of the north, being highly mov'd,
Braved Mowbery in presence of the king;  111
For which, had not his highness lov'd him well,
He should have lost his head; but with his look
The undaunted spirit of Percy was appeas'd,
And Mowbery and he were reconcil'd.  115
Yet dare you brave the king unto his face. —
Brother, revenge it, and let these their heads
Preach upon poles, for trespass of their tongues.
  *War.* O, our heads!

---

⁴⁰ **porpentine:** porcupine   ⁴⁵ **yet:** as yet   ⁴⁶ **entertain:** take into service   ⁵⁹ **grazing:** tending
cattle   ⁶⁰ **hay:** a lively dance   ⁷⁰ **pull'd:** be pulled (This passage describes well the "entertainments" presented to Queen Elizabeth on her "progresses.")   ⁸³ **Were sworn:** swore an oath
⁹⁴ **furrows:** angry folds   ¹¹³ **his look:** that of the King (Edward I)   ¹¹⁸ **Preach upon poles:** be
set up on poles as a lesson to traitors

*K. Edw.* Ay, yours; and therefore I would
wish you grant.                               120
*War.* Bridle thy anger, gentle Mortimer.
*Mor. Jun.* I cannot, nor I will not; I must
speak. —
Cousin, our hands, I hope, shall fence our heads,
And strike off his that makes you threaten
us.                                           124
Come, uncle, let us leave the brain-sick king,
And henceforth parle with our naked swords.
*Mor. Sen.* Wiltshire hath men enough to save
our heads.
*War.* All Warwickshire will love him for my
sake.
*Lan.* And northward Gaveston hath many
friends. —
Adieu, my lord; and either change your
mind,                                         130
Or look to see the throne, where you should sit,
To float in blood; and at thy wanton head,
The glozing head of thy base minion thrown.
*Exeunt Nobiles [leaving King Edward, Kent,
and Gaveston].*
*K. Edw.* I cannot brook these haughty men-
aces.
Am I a king, and must be overrul'd? —        135
Brother, display my ensigns in the field;
I 'll bandy with the barons and the earls,
And either die or live with Gaveston.
*Gav.* I can no longer keep me from my
lord.                        *[Comes forward.]*
*K. Edw.* What, Gaveston! welcome! — Kiss
not my hand.                                  140
Embrace me, Gaveston, as I do thee.
Why should'st thou kneel? Know'st thou not
who I am?
Thy friend, thyself, another Gaveston!
Not Hylas was more mourn'd of Hercules,
Than thou hast been of me since thy exile.   145
*Gav.* And since I went from hence, no soul
in hell
Hath felt more torment than poor Gaveston.
*K. Edw.* I know it. — Brother, welcome
home my friend.
Now let the treacherous Mortimers conspire,
And that high-minded Earl of Lancaster:      150
I have my wish, in that I joy thy sight;
And sooner shall the sea o'erwhelm my land
Than bear the ship that shall transport thee
hence.
I here create thee Lord High Chamberlain,
Chief Secretary to the state and me,         155
Earl of Cornwall, King and Lord of Man.
*Gav.* My lord, these titles far exceed my
worth.

*Kent.* Brother, the least of these may well
suffice
For one of greater birth than Gaveston.
*K. Edw.* Cease, brother, for I cannot brook
these words.                                  160
Thy worth, sweet friend, is far above my gifts.
Therefore, to equal it, receive my heart.
If for these dignities thou be envied,
I 'll give thee more; for, but to honour thee,
Is Edward pleas'd with kingly regiment.      165
Fear'st thou thy person? Thou shalt have a
guard.
Wantest thou gold? Go to my treasury.
Wouldst thou be lov'd and fear'd? Receive my
seal;
Save or condemn, and in our name command
Whatso thy mind affects, or fancy likes.     170
*Gav.* It shall suffice me to enjoy your love,
Which whiles I have, I think myself as great
As Cæsar riding in the Roman street,
With captive kings at his triumphant car.

*Enter the Bishop of Coventry*

*K. Edw.* Whither goes my lord of Coventry
so fast?                                      175
*Bish.* To celebrate your father's exequies. —
But is that wicked Gaveston return'd?
*K. Edw.* Ay, priest, and lives to be reveng'd
on thee,
That wert the only cause of his exile.
*Gav.* 'T is true; and but for reverence of
these robes,                                  180
Thou should'st not plod one foot beyond this
place.
*Bish.* I did no more than I was bound to
do;
And, Gaveston, unless thou be reclaim'd,
As then I did incense the parliament,
So will I now, and thou shalt back to France.
*Gav.* Saving your reverence, you must par-
don me.                                       186
*K. Edw.* Throw off his golden mitre, rend
his stole,
And in the channel christen him anew.
*Kent.* Ah, brother, lay not violent hands on
him!
For he 'll complain unto the see of Rome.    190
*Gav.* Let him complain unto the see of hell;
I 'll be reveng'd on him for my exile.
*K. Edw.* No, spare his life, but seize upon
his goods.
Be thou lord bishop and receive his rents,
And make him serve thee as thy chaplain.     195
I give him thee — here, use him as thou wilt.
*Gav.* He shall to prison, and there die in bolts.

---

[120] **grant:** yield     [123] **fence:** protect     [126] **parle:** parley     [128–129] **love . . . friends:** ironical
[133] **glozing:** flattering     **minion:** favorite     [137] **bandy:** try conclusions     [150] **high-minded:** insolent
[165] **regiment:** rule     [167] **Wantest:** ('Wants' Qq.)     [170] **affects:** inclines to     [183] **reclaim'd:** reformed
[187] **stole:** vestment     [188] **channel:** gutter     [197] **bolts:** fetters

*K. Edw.* Ay, to the Tower, the Fleet, or
where thou wilt.
*Bish.* For this offence, be thou accurst of
God!
*K. Edw.* Who 's there? Convey this priest
to the Tower.                                200
*Bish.* True! true!
*K. Edw.* But in the meantime, Gaveston,
away,
And take possession of his house and goods.
Come, follow me, and thou shalt have my guard
To see it done, and bring thee safe again.   205
   *Gav.* What should a priest do with so fair a
house?
A prison may beseem his holiness.
                                        [*Exeunt.*]

[SCENE II. — *Westminster.*]

*Enter* [*on one side*] *both the Mortimers;* [*on the
other,*] *Warwick and Lancaster*

*War.* 'T is true, the bishop is in the Tower,
And goods and body given to Gaveston.
   *Lan.* What! will they tyrannize upon the
church?
Ah, wicked king! accursed Gaveston!
This ground, which is corrupted with their
steps,                                        5
Shall be their timeless sepulchre or mine.
   *Mor. Jun.* Well, let that peevish Frenchman
guard him sure;
Unless his breast be sword-proof, he shall die.
   *Mor. Sen.* How now! why droops the Earl of
Lancaster?
   *Mor. Jun.* Wherefore is Guy of Warwick dis-
content?                                       10
   *Lan.* That villain Gaveston is made an earl.
   *Mor. Sen.* An earl!
   *War.* Ay, and besides Lord Chamberlain of
the realm,
And Secretary too, and Lord of Man.
   *Mor. Sen.* We may not, nor we will not
suffer this.                                   15
   *Mor. Jun.* Why post we not from hence to
levy men?
   *Lan.* "My Lord of Cornwall" now at every
word!
And happy is the man whom he vouchsafes,
For vailing of his bonnet, one good look.
Thus, arm in arm, the king and he doth march:
Nay more, the guard upon his lordship waits,   21
And all the court begins to flatter him.
   *War.* Thus, leaning on the shoulder of the
king,
He nods and scorns and smiles at those that pass.

   *Mor. Sen.* Doth no man take exceptions at
the slave?                                     25
   *Lan.* All stomach him, but none dare speak
a word.
   *Mor. Jun.* Ah, that bewrays their baseness,
Lancaster!
Were all the earls and barons of my mind,
We 'ld hale him from the bosom of the king,
And at the court-gate hang the peasant up,   30
Who, swoln with venom of ambitious pride,
Will be the ruin of the realm and us.

*Enter the* [*Arch*]*bishop of Canterbury* [*and an
Attendant*]

   *War.* Here comes my lord of Canterbury's
grace.
   *Lan.* His countenance bewrays he is dis-
pleas'd.
   *Arch.* First were his sacred garments rent
and torn,                                      35
Then laid they violent hands upon him; next
Himself imprison'd, and his goods asseiz'd:
This certify the Pope; — away, take horse.
                                        [*Exit Attend.*]
   *Lan.* My lord, will you take arms against the
king?
   *Arch.* What need I? God himself is up in
arms,                                          40
When violence is offer'd to the church.
   *Mor. Jun.* Then will you join with us, that
be his peers,
To banish or behead that Gaveston?
   *Arch.* What else, my lords? for it concerns
me near;
The bishopric of Coventry is his.             45

*Enter the Queen*

   *Mor. Jun.* Madam, whither walks your
majesty so fast?
   *Que.* Unto the forest, gentle Mortimer,
To live in grief and baleful discontent;
For now my lord the king regards me not,
But dotes upon the love of Gaveston.          50
He claps his cheeks, and hangs about his neck,
Smiles in his face, and whispers in his ears;
And when I come he frowns, as who should say,
"Go whither thou wilt, seeing I have Gaveston."
   *Mor. Sen.* Is it not strange that he is thus
bewitch'd?                                     55
   *Mor. Jun.* Madam, return unto the court
again.
That sly inveigling Frenchman we 'll exile,
Or lose our lives; and yet, ere that day come,
The king shall lose his crown; for we have power
And courage too, to be reveng'd at full.      60

---

¹⁹⁸ **Fleet:** Fleet prison   ²⁰¹ **True:** a gibe at the King's "Convey," one meaning of which was to
remove dishonestly   ⁶ **timeless:** untimely   ⁹ **How now:** (At this point the two pairs of nobles
recognize each other.)   ¹⁹ **vailing:** doffing   ²⁶ **stomach:** resent   ²⁹ **We 'ld:** ('Weele' Qq.)   ⁴⁵ **his:**
Gaveston's   ⁴⁷ **Unto the forest:** *i.e.*, out into the wilds

*Que.* But yet lift not your swords against
the king.

*Lan.* No; but we will lift Gaveston from
hence.

*War.* And war must be the means, or he 'll
stay still.

*Que.* Then let him stay; for rather than
my lord

Shall be oppress'd by civil mutinies,          65
I will endure a melancholy life,
And let him frolic with his minion.

*Arch.* My lords, to ease all this, but hear
me speak: —

We and the rest, that are his counsellors,
Will meet, and with a general consent          70
Confirm his banishment with our hands and
seals.

*Lan.* What we confirm the king will frustrate.

*Mor. Jun.* Then may we lawfully revolt
from him.

*War.* But say, my lord, where shall this
meeting be?

*Arch.* At the New Temple.

*Mor. Jun.*                    Content.          75

*Arch.* And, in the meantime, I 'll entreat you all

ſo cross to Lambeth, and there stay with me.

*Lan.* Come then, let 's away.

*Mor. Jun.*                    Madam, farewell!

*Que.* Farewell, sweet Mortimer, and, for
my sake,

Forbear to levy arms against the king.          80

*Mor. Jun.* Ay, if words will serve; if not, I
must.                    [*Exeunt.*]

### [SCENE III]

*Enter Gaveston and the Earl of Kent*

*Gav.* Edmund, the mighty Prince of Lancaster,

That hath more earldoms than an ass can bear,
And both the Mortimers, two goodly men,
With Guy of Warwick, that redoubted knight,
Are gone towards Lambeth — there let them
remain!                    *Exeunt.* 5

### [SCENE IV. — *London: the Temple.*]

*Enter Nobiles [Lancaster, Warwick, Pembroke,
the Elder Mortimer, Young Mortimer, the
Archbishop of Canterbury and Attendants]*

*Lan.* Here is the form of Gaveston's exile:
May it please your lordship to subscribe your
name.

*Arch.* Give me the paper.
          [*He signs, as do the others after him.*]

*Lan.* Quick, quick, my lord; I long to write
my name.

*War.* But I long more to see him banish'd
hence.          5

*Mor. Jun.* The name of Mortimer shall
fright the king,

Unless he be declin'd from that base peasant.

*Enter the King [Kent,] and Gaveston [Gaveston
seats himself beside the King.]*

*K. Edw.* What, are you mov'd that Gaveston
sits here?

It is our pleasure; we will have it so.

*Lan.* Your grace doth well to place him by
your side,          10

For nowhere else the new earl is so safe.

*Mor. Sen.* What man of noble birth can
brook this sight?

*Quam male conveniunt!*

See what a scornful look the peasant casts!

*Pem.* Can kingly lions fawn on creeping
ants?          15

*War.* Ignoble vassal, that like Phaeton
Aspir'st unto the guidance of the sun!

*Mor. Jun.* Their downfall is at hand, their
forces down;

We will not thus be fac'd and over-peer'd.

*K. Edw.* Lay hands on that traitor Mortimer!

*Mor. Sen.* Lay hands on that traitor Gaveston!                    [*They seize Gaveston.*] 21

*Kent.* Is this the duty that you owe your
king?

*War.* We know our duties — let him know
his peers.

*K. Edw.* Whither will you bear him? Stay,
or ye shall die.

*Mor. Sen.* We are no traitors; therefore
threaten not.          25

*Gav.* No, threaten not, my lord, but pay
them home!

Were I a king —

*Mor. Jun.*          Thou villain, wherefore talk'st
thou of a king,

That hardly art a gentleman by birth?

*K. Edw.* Were he a peasant, being my
minion,          30

I 'll make the proudest of you stoop to him.

*Lan.* My lord, you may not thus disparage
us. —

Away, I say, with hateful Gaveston!

---

**61 Que.:** (Qq. assign this speech to the Archbishop.)          **75 New Temple:** the present Temple on the Strand; home of the Knights Templars (who removed thither in 1184 from Holborn)          **76 Arch.:** (Not in Qq.)          **77 Lambeth:** city residence of the Archbishop of Canterbury, south of the Thames     Sc. III. A front-stage scene, marking passage of time and change of place          **1 form:** draft          **7 declin'd:** alienated          **13 Quam male conveniunt:** How ill they agree! Suggested by Ovid, *Met.* II. 846 f.: "Non bene conveniunt, nec in una sede morantur, Majestas et amor." (Majesty and love do not well agree nor can they dwell in one seat.)          **19 over-peer'd:** bullied

*Mo. Sen.* And with the Earl of Kent that
favours him.
        [*Attendants remove Kent and Gaveston.*]
*K. Edw.* Nay, then, lay violent hands upon
your king.                                          35
Here, Mortimer, sit thou in Edward's throne;
Warwick and Lancaster, wear you my crown.
Was ever king thus over-rul'd as I?
    *Lan.* Learn then to rule us better, and the
realm.
    *Mor. Jun.* What we have done, our heart-
blood shall maintain.                               40
    *War.* Think you that we can brook this up-
start pride?
    *K. Edw.* Anger and wrathful fury stops my
speech.
    *Arch.* Why are you mov'd? Be patient,
my lord,
And see what we your counsellors have done.
    *Mor. Jun.* My lords, now let us all be reso-
lute,                                               45
And either have our wills, or lose our lives.
    *K. Edw.* Meet you for this, proud overdaring
peers?
Ere my sweet Gaveston shall part from me,
This isle shall fleet upon the ocean,
And wander to the unfrequented Inde.                50
    *Arch.* You know that I am legate to the
Pope.
On your allegiance to the see of Rome,
Subscribe, as we have done, to his exile.
    *Mor. Jun.* Curse him, if he refuse; and then
may we
Depose him and elect another king.                 55
    *K. Edw.* Ay, there it goes! but yet I will
not yield.
Curse me, depose me, do the worst you can.
    *Lan.* Then linger not, my lord, but do it
straight.
    *Arch.* Remember how the bishop was
abus'd!                                             59
Either banish him that was the cause thereof,
Or I will presently discharge these lords
Of duty and allegiance due to thee.
    *K. Edw.* [*Aside.*] It boots me not to threat;
I must speak fair.
The legate of the Pope will be obey'd. —
My lord, you shall be Chancellor of the realm;
Thou, Lancaster, High Admiral of our fleet; 66
Young Mortimer and his uncle shall be earls;
And you, Lord Warwick, President of the
North;
And thou, of Wales. If this content you not,
Make several kingdoms of this monarchy,            70
And share it equally amongst you all,
So I may have some nook or corner left,
To frolic with my dearest Gaveston.

    *Arch.* Nothing shall alter us, we are re-
solv'd.
    *Lan.* Come, come, subscribe.                   75
    *Mor. Jun.* Why should you love him whom
the world hates so?
    *K. Edw.* Because he loves me more than all
the world.
Ah, none but rude and savage-minded men
Would seek the ruin of my Gaveston;
You that be noble-born should pity him.             80
    *War.* You that are princely-born should
shake him off.
For shame subscribe, and let the lown depart.
    *Mor. Sen.* Urge him, my lord.
    *Arch.* Are you content to banish him the
realm?
    *K. Edw.* I see I must, and therefore am
content.                                            85
Instead of ink, I 'll write it with my tears.
                            [*Subscribes.*]
    *Mor. Jun.* The king is love-sick for his
minion.
    *K. Edw.* 'T is done; and now, accursed
hand, fall off!
    *Lan.* Give it me; I 'll have it publish'd in
the streets.
    *Mor. Jun.* I 'll see him presently despatch'd
away.                                               90
    *Arch.* Now is my heart at ease.
    *War.*                        And so is mine.
    *Pem.* This will be good news to the common
sort.
    *Mor. Sen.* Be it or no, he shall not linger here.
        *Exeunt Nobiles* [*leaving the King*].
    *K. Edw.* How fast they run to banish him I
love!
They would not stir, were it to do me good.   95
Why should a king be subject to a priest?
Proud Rome! that hatchest such imperial
grooms,
For these thy superstitious taper-lights,
Wherewith thy antichristian churches blaze,
I 'll fire thy crazed buildings, and enforce · 100
The papal towers to kiss the lowly ground!
With slaughter'd priests make Tiber's channel
swell,
And banks rais'd higher with their sepulchres!
As for the peers, that back the clergy thus,
If I be king, not one of them shall live.          105

                *Enter Gaveston*

    *Gav.* My lord, I hear it whisper'd everywhere,
That I am banish'd, and must fly the land.
    *K. Edw.* 'T is true, sweet Gaveston — O!
were it false!
The legate of the Pope will have it so,
And thou must hence, or I shall be depos'd. 110

---

⁴⁹ **fleet:** float    ⁶¹ **presently:** immediately
people    ⁹⁷ **imperial:** imperious

⁶⁹ **thou:** Pembroke    ⁸² **lown:** clown    ⁹² **sort.**

But I will reign to be reveng'd of them;
And therefore, sweet friend, take it patiently.
Live where thou wilt, I 'll send thee gold
   enough;
And long thou shalt not stay, or if thou dost, 114
I 'll come to thee; my love shall ne'er de-
   cline.
   *Gav.* Is all my hope turn'd to this hell of
   grief?
   *K. Edw.* Rend not my heart with thy too
   piercing words:
Thou from this land, I from myself am ban-
   ish'd.
   *Gav.* To go from hence grieves not poor
   Gaveston;
But to forsake you, in whose gracious looks 120
The blessedness of Gaveston remains,
For nowhere else seeks he felicity.
   *K. Edw.* And only this torments my
   wretched soul
That, whether I will or no, thou must de-
   part.
Be governor of Ireland in my stead,     125
And there abide till fortune call thee home.
Here take my picture, and let me wear thine.
   [*They exchange pictures.*]
O, might I keep thee here as I do this,
Happy were I! but now most miserable!     129
   *Gav.* 'T is something to be pitied of a king.
   *K. Edw.* Thou shalt not hence — I 'll hide
   thee, Gaveston.
   *Gav.* I shall be found, and then 't will grieve
   me more.
   *K. Edw.* Kind words and mutual talk makes
   our grief greater;
Therefore, with dumb embracement, let us
   part. —
Stay, Gaveston, I cannot leave thee thus.     135
   *Gav.* For every look, my lord, drops down a
   tear.
Seeing I must go, do not renew my sorrow.
   *K. Edw.* The time is little that thou hast to
   stay,
And, therefore, give me leave to look my fill.
But come, sweet friend, I 'll bear thee on thy
   way.     140
   *Gav.* The peers will frown.
   *K. Edw.* I pass not for their anger. — Come,
   let 's go;
·) that we might as well return as go.

   *Enter Edmund [Kent] and Queen Isabel*

   *Que.* Whither goes my lord?
   *K. Edw.* Fawn not on me, French strumpet!
   Get thee gone!     145
   *Que.* On whom but on my husband should
   I fawn?

   *Gav.* On Mortimer! with whom, ungentle
   queen —
I say no more. Judge you the rest, my lord.
   *Que.* In saying this, thou wrong'st me.
   Gaveston.     14
Is 't not enough that thou corrupt'st my lord
And art a bawd to his affections,
But thou must call mine honour thus in ques-
   tion?
   *Gav.* I mean not so; your grace must pardon
   me.
   *K. Edw.* Thou art too familiar with that
   Mortimer,
And by thy means is Gaveston exil'd;     155
But I would wish thee reconcile the lords,
Or thou shalt ne'er be reconcil'd to me.
   *Que.* Your highness knows it lies not in my
   power.
   *K. Edw.* Away then! touch me not. — Come,
   Gaveston.
   *Que.* Villain! 't is thou that robb'st me of
   my lord.     160
   *Gav.* Madam, 't is you that rob me of my
   lord.
   *K. Edw.* Speak not unto her; let her droop
   and pine.
   *Que.* Wherein, my lord, have I deserv'd these
   words?
Witness the tears that Isabella sheds,
Witness this heart, that, sighing for thee,
   breaks,     165
How dear my lord is to poor Isabel.
   *K. Edw.* And witness Heaven how dear thou
   art to me!     [*Spurning her.*]
There weep; for till my Gaveston be repeal'd,
Assure thyself thou com'st not in my sight.
   *Exeunt Edward and Gaveston.*
   *Que.* O miserable and distressed queen!
Would, when I left sweet France and was em-
   bark'd,     171
That charming Circes, walking on the waves,
Had chang'd my shape, or at the marriage-
   day
The cup of Hymen had been full of poison,
Or with those arms that twin'd about my
   neck
I had been stifled, and not liv'd to see     176
The king my lord thus to abandon me!
Like frantic Juno will I fill the earth
With ghastly murmur of my sighs and cries;
For never doted Jove on Ganymede     180
So much as he on cursed Gaveston.
But that will more exasperate his wrath,
I must entreat him, I must speak him fair,
And be a means to call home Gaveston.
And yet he 'll ever dote on Gaveston;     185
And so am I for ever miserable.

---

¹⁴² **pass:** care    ¹⁵⁰ **corrupt'st:** ('corrupts' Qq.)    ¹⁶⁸ **repeal'd:** recalled    ¹⁷² **charming Circes:** the
enchantress Circe    ¹⁷⁸ **frantic:** (because of Jove's infidelities)

*Enter the Nobles [Lancaster, Warwick, Pembroke, the Mortimers] to the Queen*

*Lan.* Look where the sister of the King of France
Sits wringing of her hands, and beats her breast!
*War.* The king, I fear, hath ill-entreated her.
*Pem.* Hard is the heart that injures such a saint. 190
*Mor. Jun.* I know 't is 'long of Gaveston she weeps.
*Mor. Sen.* Why? He is gone.
*Mor. Jun.* Madam, how fares your grace?
*Que.* Ah, Mortimer! now breaks the king's hate forth,
And he confesseth that he loves me not.
*Mor. Jun.* Cry quittance, madam, then; and love not him. 195
*Que.* No, rather will I die a thousand deaths!
And yet I love in vain; — he 'll ne'er love me.
*Lan.* Fear ye not, madam; now his minion 's gone,
His wanton humour will be quickly left. 199
*Que.* O never, Lancaster! I am enjoin'd
To sue unto you all for his repeal;
This wills my lord, and this must I perform,
Or else be banish'd from his highness' presence.
*Lan.* For his repeal? Madam, he comes not back,
Unless the sea cast up his shipwrack'd body. 205
*War.* And to behold so sweet a sight as that,
There 's none here but would run his horse to death.
*Mor. Jun.* But, madam, would you have us call him home?
*Que.* Ay, Mortimer, for till he be restor'd,
The angry king hath banish'd me the court; 210
And, therefore, as thou lov'st and tend'rest me,
Be thou my advocate unto these peers.
*Mor. Jun.* What! would ye have me plead for Gaveston?
*Mor. Sen.* Plead for him he that will, I am resolv'd.
*Lan.* And so am I, my lord. Dissuade the queen. 215
*Que.* O Lancaster! let him dissuade the king,
For 't is against my will he should return.
*War.* Then speak not for him! let the peasant go.
*Que.* 'T is for myself I speak, and not for him.
*Pem.* No speaking will prevail, and therefore cease. 220
*Mor. Jun.* Fair queen, forbear to angle for the fish

Which, being caught, strikes him that takes it dead;
I mean that vile torpedo, Gaveston,
That now, I hope, floats on the Irish seas.
*Que.* Sweet Mortimer, sit down by me awhile, 225
And I will tell thee reasons of such weight
As thou wilt soon subscribe to his repeal.
*Mor. Jun.* It is impossible; but speak your mind.
*Que.* Then thus, — but none shall hear it but ourselves.
[*Talks to Young Mortimer apart.*]
*Lan.* My lords, albeit the queen win Mortimer, 230
Will you be resolute, and hold with me?
*Mor. Sen.* Not I, against my nephew.
*Pem.* Fear not, the queen's words cannot alter him.
*War.* No? Do but mark how earnestly she pleads!
*Lan.* And see how coldly his looks make denial! 235
*War.* She smiles; now for my life his mind is chang'd!
*Lan.* I 'll rather lose his friendship, I, than grant.
*Mor. Jun.* Well, of necessity it must be so.—
My lords, that I abhor base Gaveston,
I hope your honours make no question, 240
And therefore, though I plead for his repeal,
'T is not for his sake, but for our avail;
Nay for the realm's behoof, and for the king's.
*Lan.* Fie, Mortimer, dishonour not thyself!
Can this be true, 't was good to banish him? 245
And is this true, to call him home again?
Such reasons make white black, and dark night day.
*Mor. Jun.* My lord of Lancaster, mark the respect.
*Lan.* In no respect can contraries be true.
*Que.* Yet, good my lord, hear what he can allege. 250
*War.* All that he speaks is nothing; we are resolv'd.
*Mor. Jun.* Do you not wish that Gaveston were dead?
*Pem.* I would he were!
*Mor. Jun.* Why, then, my lord, give me but leave to speak.
*Mor. Sen.* But, nephew, do not play the sophister. 255
*Mor. Jun.* This which I urge is of a burning zeal
To mend the king, and do our country good.
Know you not Gaveston hath store of gold,
Which may in Ireland purchase him such friends

---

[191] **'long:** because   [205] **shipwrack'd:** ('shipwrack' Q 1)   [223] **torpedo:** ray-fish   [248] **respect: relation of events**   [255] **sophister:** sophist

As he will front the mightiest of us all?     260
And whereas he shall live and be belov'd,
'T is hard for us to work his overthrow.
   *War.* Mark you but that, my lord of Lan-
caster.
   *Mor. Jun.* But were he here, detested as he is,
How easily might some base slave be suborn'd
To greet his lordship with a poniard,     266
And none so much as blame the murtherer,
But rather praise him for that brave attempt,
And in the chronicle enrol his name
For purging of the realm of such a plague!     270
   *Pem.* He saith true.
   *Lan.* Ay, but how chance this was not done
before?
   *Mor. Jun.* Because, my lords, it was not
thought upon.
Nay, more, when he shall know it lies in us
To banish him, and then to call him home,     275
'T will make him vail the top-flag of his pride,
And fear to offend the meanest nobleman.
   *Mor. Sen.* But how if he do not, nephew?
   *Mor. Jun.* Then may we with some colour
rise in arms;
For howsoever we have borne it out,     280
'T is treason to be up against the king.
So shall we have the people of our side,
Which for his father's sake lean to the king,
But cannot brook a night-grown mushroom,
Such a one as my lord of Cornwall is,     285
Should bear us down of the nobility.
And when the commons and the nobles join,
'T is not the king can buckler Gaveston;
We 'll pull him from the strongest hold he hath.
My lords, if to perform this I be slack,     290
Think me as base a groom as Gaveston.
   *Lan.* On that condition, Lancaster will grant.
   *War.* And so will Pembroke and I.
   *Mor. Sen.* And I.     294
   *Mor. Jun.* In this I count me highly grati-
fied,
And Mortimer will rest at your command.
   *Que.* And when this favour Isabel forgets,
Then let her live abandon'd and forlorn. —
But see, in happy time, my lord the king,
Having brought the Earl of Cornwall on his
way,     300
Is new return'd. This news will glad him much,
Yet not so much as me. I love him more
Than he can Gaveston; would he lov'd me
But half so much, then were I treble-blest.

     *Enter King Edward, mourning*

   *K. Edw.* He 's gone, and for his absence thus
I mourn.     305
Did never sorrow go so near my heart

As doth the want of my sweet Gaveston;
And could my crown's revénue bring him back,
I would freely give it to his enemies,
And think I gain'd, having bought so dear a
friend.     310
   *Que.* Hark! how he harps upon his minion.
   *K. Edw.* My heart is as an anvil unto sorrow,
Which beats upon it like the Cyclops' hammers,
And with the noise turns up my giddy brain,
And makes me frantic for my Gaveston.     315
Ah! had some bloodless Fury rose from hell,
And with my kingly sceptre struck me dead,
When I was forc'd to leave my Gaveston!
   *Lan.* *Diablo!* What passions call you these?
   *Que.* My gracious lord, I come to bring
you news.     320
   *K. Edw.* That you have parled with your
Mortimer!
   *Que.* That Gaveston, my lord, shall be re-
peal'd.
   *K. Edw.* Repeal'd! The news is too sweet to
be true.
   *Que.* But will you love me, if you find it so?
   *K. Edw.* If it be so, what will not Edward
do?     325
   *Que.* For Gaveston, but not for Isabel.
   *K. Edw.* For thee, fair queen, if thou lov'st
Gaveston.
I 'll hang a golden tongue about thy neck,
Seeing thou hast pleaded with so good success.
   *Que.* No other jewels hang about my neck 330
Than these, my lord; nor let me have more
wealth
Than I may fetch from this rich treasury.
O how a kiss revives poor Isabel!
   *K. Edw.* Once more receive my hand; and
let this be
A second marriage 'twixt thyself and me.     335
   *Que.* And may it prove more happy than
the first!
My gentle lord, bespeak these nobles fair,
That wait attendance for a gracious look,
And on their knees salute your majesty.
   *K. Edw.* Courageous Lancaster, embrace
thy king!     340
And, as gross vapours perish by the sun,
Even so let hatred with thy sovereign's smile.
Live thou with me as my companion.
   *Lan.* This salutation overjoys my heart.
   *K. Edw.* Warwick shall be my chiefest
counsellor:     345
These silver hairs will more adorn my court
Than guady silks, or rich imbrothery.
Chide me, sweet Warwick, if I go astray.
   *War.* Slay me, my lord, when I offend your
grace.

---

   **260 front:** face on equal terms     **268 attempt:** enterprise     **279 colour:** justification     **284 brook:**
endure that     **295 highly gratified:** much obliged     **331 these:** the king's arms     **332 treasury:** his
mouth     **342 sovereign's:** ('soueraigne' Q 1-2)     **347 imbrothery:** embroidery

*K. Edw.* In solemn triumphs, and in public
shows,                                              350
Pembroke shall bear the sword before the king.
*Pem.* And with this sword Pembroke will
fight for you.
*K. Edw.* But wherefore walks young Morti-
mer aside?
Be thou commander of our royal fleet;
Or, if that lofty office like thee not,             355
I make thee here Lord Marshal of the realm.
*Mor. Jun.* My lord, I 'll marshal so your
enemies,
As England shall be quiet, and you safe.
*K. Edw.* And as for you, Lord Mortimer of
Chirke,                                             359
Whose great achievements in our foreign war
Deserves no common place nor mean reward,
Be you the general of the levied troops,
That now are ready to assail the Scots.
*Mor. Sen.* In this your grace hath highly
honour'd me,
For with my nature war doth best agree.     365
*Que.* Now is the King of England rich and
strong,
Having the love of his renowned peers.
*K. Edw.* Ay, Isabel, ne'er was my heart so
light.
Clerk of the crown, direct our warrant forth
For Gaveston to Ireland:

*[Enter Beaumont with warrant]*

                          Beaumont, fly      370
As fast as Iris or Jove's Mercury.
*Beau.* It shall be done, my gracious lord.
                                        *[Exit.]*
*K. Edw.* Lord Mortimer, we leave you to
your charge.
Now let us in, and feast it royally.          374
Against our friend the Earl of Cornwall comes,
We 'll have a general tilt and tournament;
And then his marriage shall be solemniz'd.
For wot you not that I have made him sure
Unto our cousin, the Earl of Gloucester's heir?
*Lan.* Such news we hear, my lord.        380
*K. Edw.* That day, if not for him, yet for my
sake,
Who in the triumph will be challenger,
Spare for no cost; we will requite your love.
*War.* In this, or aught, your highness shall
command us.
*K. Edw.* Thanks, gentle Warwick: come,
let 's in and revel.                          385
    *Exeunt [King and others]. Manent Mor-
    timers*
*Mor. Sen.* Nephew, I must to Scotland; thou
stayest here.

Leave now to oppose thyself against the king.
Thou seest by nature he is mild and calm,
And seeing his mind so dotes on Gaveston,
Let him without controlment have his will.  390
The mightiest kings have had their minions:
Great Alexander loved Hephestion;
The conquering Hercules for Hylas wept;
And for Patroclus stern Achilles droop'd.
And not kings only, but the wisest men:     395
The Roman Tully lov'd Octavius;
Grave Socrates, wild Alcibiades.
Then let his grace, whose youth is flexible,
And promiseth as much as we can wish,
Freely enjoy that vain, light-headed earl;   400
For riper years will wean him from such toys.
*Mor. Jun.* Uncle, his wanton humour grieves
not me;
But this I scorn, that one so basely born
Should by his sovereign's favour grow so pert,
And riot it with the treasure of the realm.   405
While soldiers mutiny for want of pay,
He wears a lord's revénue on his back,
And Midas-like, he jets it in the court,
With base outlandish cullions at his heels,   409
Whose proud fantastic liveries make such show
As if that Proteus, god of shapes, appear'd.
I have not seen a dapper Jack so brisk;
He wears a short Italian hooded cloak
Larded with pearl, and, in his Tuscan cap,
A jewel of more value than the crown.        415
Whiles other walk below, the king and he
From out a window laugh at such as we,
And flout our train, and jest at our attire.
Uncle, 't is this that makes me impatient.
*Mor. Sen.* But, nephew, now you see the
king is chang'd.                              420
*Mor. Jun.* Then so am I, and live to do him
service:
But whiles I have a sword, a hand, a heart,
I will not yield to any such upstart.
You know my mind; come, uncle, let's away.
                                        *Exeunt.*

### [ACT II]

[SCENE I. — *Castle of Gilbert de Clare, Earl of
Gloucester.*]

*Enter [Young] Spencer and Baldock*

*Bald.* Spencer,
Seeing that our lord th' Earl of Gloucester 's
dead,
Which of the nobles dost thou mean to serve?
*Spen.* Not Mortimer, nor any of his side,
Because the king and he are enemies.
Baldock, learn this of me: a factious lord     5
Shall hardly do himself good, much less us.

But he that hath the favour of a king
May with one word advance us while we live.
The liberal Earl of Cornwall is the man    9
On whose good fortune Spencer's hope depends.
    *Bald.* What, mean you then to be his fol-
    lower?
    *Spen.* No, his companion; for he loves me
    well,
And would have once preferr'd me to the king.
    *Bald.* But he is banish'd; there 's small hope
    of him.
    *Spen.* Ay, for a while; but, Baldock,
    mark the end.    15
A friend of mine told me in secrecy
That he 's repeal'd, and sent for back again;
And even now a post came from the court
With letters to our lady from the king;
And as she read she smil'd, which makes me
    think    20
It is about her lover Gaveston.
    *Bald.* 'T is like enough; for since he was
    exil'd
She neither walks abroad, nor comes in sight.
But I had thought the match had been broke
    off,    24
And that his banishment had chang'd her mind.
    *Spen.* Our lady's first love is not wavering;
My life for thine, she will have Gaveston.
    *Bald.* Then hope I by her means to be pre-
    ferr'd,
Having read unto her since she was a child.
    *Spen.* Then, Baldock, you must cast the
    scholar off,    30
And learn to court it like a gentleman.
'T is not a black coat and a little band,
A velvet-cap'd coat, fac'd before with serge,
And smelling to a nosegay all the day,
Or holding of a napkin in your hand,    35
Or saying a long grace at a table's end,
Or making low legs to a nobleman,
Or looking downward with your eyelids close,
And saying, "Truly, an 't may please your
    honour,"
Can get you any favour with great men;    40
You must be proud, bold, pleasant, resolute,
And now and then stab, as occasion serves.
    *Bald.* Spencer, thou know'st I hate such for-
    mal toys,
And use them but of mere hypocrisy.
Mine old lord whiles he liv'd was so precise,    45
That he would take exceptions at my buttons,
And being like pin's heads, blame me for the
    bigness;
Which made me curate-like in mine attire,
Though inwardly licentious enough

And apt for any kind of villainy.    50
I am none of these common pedants, I,
That cannot speak without *propterea quod.*
    *Spen.* But one of those that saith *quando-
    quidem,*
And hath a special gift to form a verb.
    *Bald.* Leave off this jesting, here my lady
    comes.    55

*Enter the Lady [Margaret de Clare]*

    *Lady.* The grief for his exile was not so much
As is the joy of his returning home.
This letter came from my sweet Gaveston.
What need'st thou, love, thus to excuse thyself?
I know thou couldst not come and visit me.    60
[*Reads.*] "I will not long be from thee, though
    I die."
This argues the entire love of my lord;
[*Reads.*] "When I forsake thee, death seize on
    my heart:"
But rest thee here where Gaveston shall sleep.
         [*Puts the letter into her bosom.*]
Now to the letter of my lord the king. —    65
He wills me to repair unto the court,
And meet my Gaveston. Why do I stay,
Seeing that he talks thus of my marriage-day?
Who 's there? Baldock!
See that my coach be ready, I must hence.    70
    *Bald.* It shall be done, madam.
    *Lady.* And meet me at the park-pale pres-
    ently.        *Exit Baldock.*
Spencer, stay you and bear me company,
For I have joyful news to tell thee of.
My lord of Cornwall is a-coming over,    75
And will be at the court as soon as we.
    *Spen.* I knew the king would have him home
    again.
    *Lady.* If all things sort out as I hope they will,
Thy service, Spencer, shall be thought upon.
    *Spen.* I humbly thank your ladyship.    80
    *Lady.* Come, lead the way; I long till I am
    there.        [*Exeunt.*]

[SCENE II. — *Tynemouth Castle, Northumber-
    land.*]

*Enter Edward, the Queen, Lancaster, [Young]
    Mortimer, Warwick, Pembroke, Kent, At-
    tendants*

    *K. Edw.* The wind is good, I wonder why
    he stays;
I fear me he is wrack'd upon the sea.
    *Que.* Look, Lancaster, how passionate he is,
And still his mind runs on his minion!
    *Lan.* My lord, —    5

---

    [13] **preferr'd:** recommended    [32] **band:** clerical collar    [37] **legs:** bows    [45] **precise:** Puritanical
[46] **buttons:** an object of scandal to precisians    [52] **propterea quod:** because (pedantic, prosaic form)
[53] **quandoquidem:** since (poetical and affected)    [54] **form a verb:** say things neatly    [78] **sort out:**
result

*K. Edw.* How now! what news? Is Gaveston
arriv'd?

*Mor. Jun.* Nothing but Gaveston! — What
means your grace?
You have matters of more weight to think upon;
The King of France sets foot in Normandy.

   *K. Edw.* A trifle! we 'll expel him when we
please.                                 10
But tell me, Mortimer, what 's thy device
Against the stately triumph we decreed?

   *Mor. Jun.* A homely one, my lord, not worth
the telling.

   *K. Edw.* Prithee let me know it.

   *Mor. Jun.* But, seeing you are so desirous,
thus it is:                                   15
A lofty cedar-tree, fair flourishing,
On whose top-branches kingly eagles perch,
And by the bark a canker creeps me up,
And gets unto the highest bough of all:
The motto, *Æque tandem.*           20

   *K. Edw.* And what is yours, my lord of Lancaster?

   *Lan.* My lord, mine 's more obscure than
Mortimer's.
Pliny reports there is a flying fish
Which all the other fishes deadly hate,
And therefore, being pursued, it takes the air:
No sooner is it up, but there 's a fowl   26
That seizeth it; this fish, my lord, I bear:
The motto this: *Undique mors est.*

   *K. Edw.* Proud Mortimer! ungentle Lancas-
ter!
Is this the love you bear your sovereign?   30
Is this the fruit your reconcilement bears?
Can you in words make show of amity,
And in your shields display your rancorous
minds!
What call you this but private libelling
Against the Earl of Cornwall and my brother?

   *Que.* Sweet husband, be content, they all
love you.                                  36

   *K. Edw.* They love me not that hate my
Gaveston.
I am that cedar, shake me not too much;
And you the eagles; soar ye ne'er so high,
I have the jesses that will pull you down;   40
And *Æque tandem* shall that canker cry
Unto the proudest peer of Britainy.
Though thou compar'st him to a flying fish,
And threatenest death whether he rise or fall,
'T is not the hugest monster of the sea,   45
Nor foulest harpy that shall swallow him.

   *Mor. Jun.* If in his absence thus he favours
him,

What will he do whenas he shall be present?

   *Lan.* That shall we see; look where his lordship comes.

*Enter Gaveston*

   *K. Edw.* My Gaveston!              50
Welcome to Tynemouth! Welcome to thy
friend!
Thy absence made me droop and pine away;
For, as the lovers of fair Danaë,
When she was lock'd up in a brazen tower,
Desir'd her more, and wax'd outrageous,   55
So did it sure with me; and now thy sight
Is sweeter far than was thy parting hence
Bitter and irksome to my sobbing heart.

   *Gav.* Sweet lord and king, your speech pre-
venteth mine,
Yet have I words left to express my joy:   60
The shepherd nipp'd with biting winter's
rage
Frolics not more to see the painted spring,
Than I do to behold your majesty.

   *K. Edw.* Will none of you salute my Gaveston?

   *Lan.* Salute him? yes. Welcome, Lord
Chamberlain!                          65

   *Mor. Jun.* Welcome is the good Earl of
Cornwall!

   *War.* Welcome, Lord Governor of the Isle
of Man!

   *Pem.* Welcome, Master Secretary!

   *Kent.* Brother, do you hear them?

   *K. Edw.* Still will these earls and barons use
me thus?                               70

   *Gav.* My lord, I cannot brook these injuries.

   *Que.* [*Aside.*] Aye me, poor soul, when these
begin to jar.

   *K. Edw.* Return it to their throats, I 'll be
thy warrant.

   *Gav.* Base, leaden earls, that glory in your
birth,
Go sit at home and eat your tenants' beef;   75
And come not here to scoff at Gaveston,
Whose mounting thoughts did never creep so
low
As to bestow a look on such as you.

   *Lan.* Yet I disdain not to do this for you.
      [*Draws his sword and offers to stab
      Gaveston.*]

   *K. Edw.* Treason! treason! where 's the
traitor?                                80

   *Pem.* Here! here!

   *K. Edw.* Convey hence Gaveston; they 'll
murder him.

---

**11 device:** heraldic emblem   **12 Against:** for use at
"equally at length." (The canker will be as high as the eagle.)   **18 canker:** canker-worm   **20 Æque tandem:**
**27 bear:** *i.e.*, on my shield   **28 Undique,**
**etc.:** Death is everywhere.   **35 brother:** (Gaveston and the king had been brought up as foster-
brothers.)   **40 jesses:** straps by which falcons were controlled ('gresses' Qq.)   **42 Britainy:**
Britain   **56 sure:** surely ('fare' Q 1622)   **59 preventeth:** anticipates   **72 Aye me:** Woe is me.

*Gav.* The life of thee shall salve this foul
  disgrace.
*Mor. Jun.* Villain! thy life, unless I miss
  mine aim.                    [*Wounds Gaveston.*]
*Que.* Ah! furious Mortimer, what hast thou
  done?                                            85
*Mor.* No more than I would answer, were
  he slain.
          [*Exit Gaveston with Attendants.*]
*K. Edw.* Yes, more than thou canst answer,
  though he live.
Dear shall you both abye this riotous deed.
Out of my presence! Come not near the court.
*Mor. Jun.* I 'll not be barr'd the court for
  Gaveston.                                        90
*Lan.* We 'll hale him by the ears unto the
  block.
*K. Edw.* Look to your own heads; his is
  sure enough.
*War.* Look to your own crown, if you back
  him thus.
*Kent.* Warwick, these words do ill beseem
  thy years.
*K. Edw.* Nay, all of them conspire to cross
  me thus;                                          95
But if I live, I 'll tread upon their heads
That think with high looks thus to tread me
  down.
Come. Edmund, let 's away and levy men,
'T is war that must abate these barons' pride.
          *Exit the King* [*with Queen and Kent*].
*War.* Let 's to our castles, for the king is
  mov'd.                                           100
*Mor. Jun.* Mov'd may he be, and perish in
  his wrath!
*Lan.* Cousin, it is no dealing with him now,
He means to make us stoop by force of arms;
And therefore let us jointly here protest,
To prosecute that Gaveston to the death.    105
*Mor. Jun.* By heaven, the abject villain
  shall not live!
*War.* I 'll have his blood, or die in seeking it.
*Pem.* The like oath Pembroke takes.
*Lan.* And so doth Lancaster.
Now send our heralds to defy the king;     110
And make the people swear to put him down.

*Enter a Post*

*Mor. Jun.* Letters! From whence?
*Mess.* From Scotland, my lord.
          [*Giving letters to Mortimer.*]
*Lan.* Why, how now, cousin, how fares all
  our friends?
*Mor. Jun.* My uncle 's taken prisoner by the
  Scots.                                           115

*Lan.* We 'll have him ransom'd, man; be of
  good cheer.
*Mor. Jun.* They rate his ransom at five
  thousand pound.
Who should defray the money but the king,
Seeing he is taken prisoner in his wars?
I 'll to the king.                               120
*Lan.* Do, cousin, and I 'll bear thee company.
*War.* Meantime, my lord of Pembroke and
  myself
Will to Newcastle here, and gather head.
*Mor. Jun.* About it then, and we will follow
  you.
*Lan.* Be resolute and full of secrecy.    125
*War.* I warrant you. [*Exit with Pembroke.*]
*Mor. Jun.* Cousin, and if he will not ransom
  him,
I 'll thunder such a peal into his ears,
As never subject did unto his king.
*Lan.* Content, I 'll bear my part — Holla!
  who 's there?                                   130

*[Enter Guard]*

*Mor. Jun.* Ay, marry, such a guard as this
  doth well.
*Lan.* Lead on the way.
*Guard.*          Whither will your lordships?
*Mor. Jun.* Whither else but to the king? 134
*Guard.* His highness is dispos'd to be alone.
*Lan.* Why, so he may, but we will speak to
  him.
*Guard.* You may not in, my lord.
*Mor.*                May we not?

*[Enter King Edward and Kent on the balcony]*

*K. Edw.*                     How now!
What noise is this? Who have we there?
                    Is 't you? [*Going.*] 140
*Mor.* Nay, stay, my lord, I come to bring
  you news;
Mine uncle 's taken prisoner by the Scots.
*K. Edw.* Then ransom him.
*Lan.* 'T was in your wars; you should ran-
  som him.
*Mor.* And you shall ransom him, or
  else ——                                        145
*Kent.* What! Mortimer, you will not threaten
  him?
*K. Edw.* Quiet yourself: you shall have the
  broad seal,
To gather for him thoroughly the realm.
*Lan.* Your minion Gaveston hath taught
  you this.
*Mor.* My lord, the family of the Morti-
  mers                                            150

---

88 **abye:** pay for   111 S. D. **Post:** messenger   115 This episode is not historical. (The elder Mortimer here passes out of the play.)   123 **Newcastle here:** (nine miles from Tynemouth)   **head:**
armed force   127 **and if:** if   130 S. D. The guard bars the entrance to the rear stage.   147 **broad
seal:** royal endorsement (on a beggar's license)

Are not so poor, but, would they sell their land,
'T would levy men enough to anger you.
We never beg, but use such prayers as these.
   *K. Edw.* Shall I still be haunted thus?
   *Mor.* Nay, now you 're here alone, I 'll speak
my mind. 155
   *Lan.* And so will I, and then, my lord, fare-
well.
   *Mor.* The idle triumphs, masques, lascivious
shows,
And prodigal gifts bestow'd on Gaveston,
Have drawn thy treasure dry, and made thee
weak; 159
The murmuring commons overstretched hath.
   *Lan.* Look for rebellion, look to be depos'd.
Thy garrisons are beaten out of France,
And, lame and poor, lie groaning at the gates.
The wild O' Neill, with swarms of Irish kerns,
Lives uncontroll'd within the English pale. 165
Unto the walls of York the Scots made road,
And unresisted drave away rich spoils.
   *Mor.* The haughty Dane commands the nar-
row seas,
While in the harbour ride thy ships unrigg'd.
   *Lan.* What foreign prince sends thee ambas-
sadors? 170
   *Mor.* Who loves thee, but a sort of flatterers?
   *Lan.* Thy gentle queen, sole sister to Valois,
Complains that thou hast left her all forlorn.
   *Mor.* Thy court is naked, being bereft of
those 174
That makes a king seem glorious to the world;
I mean the peers, whom thou should'st dearly
love.
Libels are cast again thee in the street;
Ballads and rhymes made of thy overthrow.
   *Lan.* The Northern borderers seeing their
houses burnt,
Their wives and children slain, run up and
down, 180
Cursing the name of thee and Gaveston.
   *Mor.* When wert thou in the field with ban-
ner spread,
But once? and then thy soldiers march'd like
players,
With garish robes, not armour; and thyself,
Bedaub'd with gold, rode laughing at the rest,
Nodding and shaking of thy spangled crest, 186
Where women's favours hung like labels down.
   *Lan.* And thereof came it, that the fleering
Scots,
To England's high disgrace, have made this jig:

*Maids of England, sore may you mourn* 190
*For your lemans you have lost at Bannocks-*
   *bourn, —*
   *With a heave and a ho!*
*What, weeneth the King of England*
*So soon to have won Scotland? —*
   *With a rombelow!* 195

   *Mor.* Wigmore shall fly, to set my uncle free.
   *Lan.* And when 't is gone, our swords shall
purchase more.
If ye be mov'd, revenge it as you can;
Look next to see us with our ensigns spread.
                  *Exeunt Nobiles.*
   *K. Edw.* My swelling heart for very anger
breaks! 200
How oft have I been baited by these peers,
And dare not be reveng'd, for their power is
great!
Yet, shall the crowing of these cockerels
Affright a lion? Edward, unfold thy paws,
And let their lives' blood slake thy fury's hun-
ger. 205
If I be cruel and grow tyrannous,
Now let them thank themselves, and rue too
late.
   *Kent.* My lord, I see your love to Gaveston
Will be the ruin of the realm and you,
For now the wrathful nobles threaten wars, 210
And therefore, brother, banish him for ever.
   *K. Edw.* Art thou an enemy to my Gaveston?
   *Kent.* Ay, and it grieves me that I favour'd
him.
   *K. Edw.* Traitor, begone! whine thou with
Mortimer. 214
   *Kent.* So will I, rather than with Gaveston.
   *K. Edw.* Out of my sight, and trouble me no
more!
   *Kent.* No marvel though thou scorn thy
noble peers,
When I thy brother am rejected thus. *Exit.*
   *K. Edw.* Away!
Poor Gaveston, that hast no friend but me! 220
Do what they can, we 'll live in Tynemouth here;
And, so I walk with him about the walls,
What care I though the earls begirt us round?—
Here comes she that 's cause of all these jars.

*Enter the Queen, Ladies Three, [Gaveston,]*
    *Baldock, and Spencer*

   *Que.* My lord, 't is thought the earls are
up in arms. 225

---

152 **'T would:** ('Would' Q 1–2)   153 **these:** (making minatory gestures)   160 **overstretched:** passed
the limits of their patience   164 **kerns:** foot soldiers, "the very dross and scum of the country"   165 **pale:**
the settled district about Dublin   168 **narrow seas:** English Channel   171 **sort:** mob   177 **Libels:**
abusive papers   **again:** agin', against   188 **fleering:** gibing   189 **this jig:** (Copied out of Fabyan's
*Chronicle.* The disastrous Bannockburn campaign occurred several years after the historic date of this
scene.)   191 **lemans:** sweethearts   196 **Wigmore:** Mortimer's estate in Herefordshire   **fly:** be sold
224a S. D. **Ladies Three:** *i.e.,* the king's niece and two attendants

*K. Edw.* Ay, and 't is likewise thought you
favour 'em.

*Que.* Thus do you still suspect me without cause.

*Lady.* Sweet uncle! speak more kindly to
the queen.

*Gav.* My lord, dissemble with her, speak her
fair.

*K. Edw.* Pardon me, sweet, I forgot my-
self.                                                          230

*Que.* Your pardon is quickly got of Isabel.

*K. Edw.* The younger Mortimer is grown so
brave,
That to my face he threatens civil wars.

*Gav.* Why do you not commit him to the
Tower?

*K. Edw.* I dare not, for the people love him
well.                                                          235

*Gav.* Why, then we 'll have him privily made
away.

*K. Edw.* Would Lancaster and he had both
carous'd
A bowl of poison to each other's health!
But let them go, and tell me what are these?

*Lady.* Two of my father's servants whilst he
liv'd,—                                                        240
May 't please your grace to entertain them
now.

*K. Edw.* Tell me, where wast thou born?
What is thine arms?

*Bald.* My name is Baldock, and my gentry
I fetch'd from Oxford, not from heraldry.

*K. Edw.* The fitter art thou, Baldock, for
my turn.                                                       245
Wait on me, and I 'll see thou shalt not
want.

*Bald.* I humbly thank your majesty.

*K. Edw.* Knowest thou him, Gaveston?

*Gav.*                           Ay, my lord;
His name is Spencer, he is well allied.
For my sake, let him wait upon your grace;     250
Scarce shall you find a man of more desert.

*K. Edw.* Then, Spencer, wait upon me; for
his sake
I 'll grace thee with a higher style ere long.

*Spen.* No greater titles happen unto me,
Than to be favour'd of your majesty!           255

*K. Edw.* Cousin, this day shall be your mar-
riage-feast.
And, Gaveston, think that I love thee well,
To wed thee to our niece, the only heir
Unto the Earl of Gloucester late deceas'd.

*Gav.* I know, my lord, many will stomach
me,                                                            260
But I respect neither their love nor hate.

*K. Edw.* The headstrong barons shall not
limit me;

He that I list to favour shall be great.
Come, let 's away; and when the marriage ends,
Have at the rebels, and their 'complices!       265
                                        *Exeunt omnes.*

[SCENE III. — *Near Tynemouth Castle.*]

*Enter Lancaster, Mortimer, Warwick, Pembroke,*
          [*and, at another door,*] *Kent*

*Kent.* My lords, of love to this our native
land
I come to join with you and leave the king;
And in your quarrel and the realm's behoof
Will be the first that shall adventure life.

*Lan.* I fear me, you are sent of policy,         5
To undermine us with a show of love.

*War.* He is your brother, therefore have we
cause
To cast the worst, and doubt of your revolt.

*Kent.* Mine honour shall be hostage of my
truth;
If that will not suffice, farewell, my lords.     10

*Mor.* Stay, Edmund; never was Plantagenet
False of his word, and therefore trust we thee.

*Pem.* But what 's the reason you should
leave him now?

*Kent.* I have inform'd the Earl of Lancaster.

*Lan.* And it sufficeth. Now, my lords, know
this,                                                          15
That Gaveston is secretly arriv'd,
And here in Tynemouth frolics with the king.
Let us with these our followers scale the walls,
And suddenly surprise them unawares.            19

*Mor.* I 'll give the onset.

*War.*                        And I 'll follow thee.

*Mor.* This totter'd ensign of my ancestors,
Which swept the desert shore of that dead
sea
Whereof we got the name of Mortimer,
Will I advance upon these castle-walls.
Drums, strike alarum, raise them from their
sport,                                                         25
And ring aloud the knell of Gaveston!

*Lan.* None be so hardy as to touch the king;
But neither spare you Gaveston nor his friends.
                                              *Exeunt.*

[SCENE IV. — *Outside the Castle.*]

*Enter the King and Spencer. To them* [*later*]
          *Gaveston, &c.*

*K. Edw.* O tell me, Spencer, where is Gaveston?

*Spen.* I fear me he is slain, my gracious lord.

*K. Edw.* No, here he comes; now let them
spoil and kill.

---

²²⁷ **still:** always    ²⁴² **arms:** heraldic badge    ²⁴⁸ **him:** *i.e.,* the other stranger    ²⁵³ **style:** title of
nobility    ⁸ **cast:** reckon    ²¹ **totter'd:** tattered, time-honored

*[Enter Queen Isabella, King Edward's Niece, Gaveston, and Nobles]*

Fly, fly, my lords, the earls have got the hold;
Take shipping and away to Scarborough;       5
Spencer and I will post away by land.
    *Gav.* O stay, my lord, they will not injure you.
    *K. Edw.* I will not trust them; Gaveston, away!
    *Gav.* Farewell, my lord.
    *K. Edw.* Lady, farewell.       10
    *Lady.* Farewell, sweet uncle, till we meet again.
    *K. Edw.* Farewell, sweet Gaveston; and farewell, niece.
    *Que.* No farewell to poor Isabel thy queen?
    *K. Edw.* Yes, yes, for Mortimer, your lover's sake. *Exeunt omnes, manet Isabella.*
    *Que.* Heavens can witness I love none but you!       15
From my embracements thus he breaks away.
O that mine arms could close this isle about,
That I might pull him to me where I would!
Or that these tears that drizzle from mine eyes
Had power to mollify his stony heart,       20
That when I had him we might never part.

*Enter the Barons [Lancaster, Warwick, Mortimer, and others]. Alarums*

    *Lan.* I wonder how he scap'd!
    *Mor.*             Who 's this? The queen!
    *Que.* Ay, Mortimer, the miserable queen,
Whose pining heart her inward sighs have blasted,
And body with continual mourning wasted.       25
These hands are tir'd with haling of my lord
From Gaveston, from wicked Gaveston,
And all in vain; for, when I speak him fair,
He turns away, and smiles upon his minion.
    *Mor.* Cease to lament, and tell us where 's the king?       30
    *Que.* What would you with the king? Is 't him you seek?
    *Lan.* No, madam, but that cursed Gaveston.
Far be it from the thought of Lancaster
To offer violence to his sovereign.
We would but rid the realm of Gaveston:       35
Tell us where he remains, and he shall die.
    *Que.* He 's gone by water unto Scarborough;
Pursue him quickly, and he cannot scape;
The king hath left him, and his train is small.
    *War.* Forslow no time, sweet Lancaster; let 's march.       40
    *Mor.* How comes it that the king and he is parted?

    *Que.* That this your army, going several ways,
Might be of lesser force; and with the power
That he intendeth presently to raise,
Be easily suppress'd; therefore be gone.       45
    *Mor.* Here in the river rides a Flemish hoy;
Let 's all aboard, and follow him amain.
    *Lan.* The wind that bears him hence will fill our sails.
Come, come aboard, 't is but an hour's sailing.
    *Mor.* Madam, stay you within this castle here.       50
    *Que.* No, Mortimer, I 'll to my lord the king.
    *Mor.* Nay, rather sail with us to Scarborough.
    *Que.* You know the king is so suspicious,
As if he hear I have but talk'd with you,
Mine honour will be call'd in question;       55
And therefore, gentle Mortimer, be gone.
    *Mor.* Madam, I cannot stay to answer you,
But think of Mortimer as he deserves.
    *[Exeunt all except Queen Isabella.]*
    *Que.* So well hast thou deserv'd, sweet Mortimer,
As Isabel could live with thee for ever!       60
In vain I look for love at Edward's hand,
Whose eyes are fix'd on none but Gaveston;
Yet once more I 'll importune him with prayers.
If he be strange and not regard my words,
My son and I will over into France,       65
And to the king my brother there complain,
How Gaveston hath robb'd me of his love:
But yet I hope my sorrows will have end,
And Gaveston this blessed day be slain. *Exit.*

### [SCENE V]

*Enter Gaveston, pursued*

    *Gav.* Yet, lusty lords, I have escap'd your hands,
Your threats, your 'larums, and your hot pursuits;
And though divorced from King Edward's eyes,
Yet liveth Pierce of Gaveston unsurpris'd,
Breathing, in hope (*malgrado* all your beards,  5
That muster rebels thus against your king),
To see his royal sovereign once again.

*Enter the Nobles [Warwick, Lancaster, Pembroke, Mortimer, Soldiers]*

    *War.* Upon him, soldiers, take away his weapons.
    *Mor.* Thou proud disturber of thy country's peace,
Corrupter of thy king, cause of these broils, 10
Base flatterer, yield! and were it not for shame,
Shame and dishonour to a soldier's name,

---

    ⁴ **hold:** stronghold    ⁴⁰ **Forslow:** waste
**pris'd:** uncaptured    ⁵ **malgrado:** despite    ⁴⁶ **hoy:** small vessel    ⁶⁴ **strange:** cold    ⁴ **unsur-**

Upon my weapon's point here shouldst thou
fall,
And welter in thy gore.
　*Lan.*　　　　　　Monster of men!
That, like the Greekish strumpet, train'd to
arms　　　　　　　　　　　　　15
And bloody wars so many valiant knights:
Look for no other fortune, wretch, than death!
King Edward is not here to buckler thee.
　*War.*　Lancaster, why talk'st thou to the
slave?　　　　　　　　　　　　19
Go, soldiers, take him hence, for, by my sword,
His head shall off. Gaveston, short warning
Shall serve thy turn; it is our country's cause
That here severely we will execute
Upon thy person. Hang him at a bough.　24
　*Gav.*　My lord! —
　*War.*　　　　　Soldiers, have him away; —
But for thou wert the favourite of a king,
Thou shalt have so much honour at our hands—
　*Gav.*　I thank you all, my lords: then I per-
ceive
That heading is one, and hanging is the other,
And death is all.　　　　　　　30

*Enter Earl of Arundel*

　*Lan.*　How now, my lord of Arundel?
　*Arun.*　My lords, King Edward greets you all
by me.
　*War.*　Arundel, say your message.
　*Arun.*　　　　　　　　His majesty,
Hearing that you had taken Gaveston,
Entreateth you by me, yet but he may　35
See him before he dies; for why, he says,
And sends you word, he knows that die he shall;
And if you gratify his grace so far,
He will be mindful of the courtesy.　　39
　*War.*　How now?
　*Gav.*　　　Renowmed Edward, how thy name
Revives poor Gaveston!
　*War.*　　　　　No, it needeth not;
Arundel, we will gratify the king
In other matters; he must pardon us in this.
Soldiers, away with him!
　*Gav.*　　　　Why, my lord of Warwick,
Will not these delays beget my hopes?　45
I know it, lords, it is this life you aim at,
Yet grant King Edward this.
　*Mor.*　　　　　Shalt thou appoint
What we shall grant? Soldiers, away with him!
Thus we 'll gratify the king:
We 'll send his head by thee; let him bestow　50
His tears on that, for that is all he gets
Of Gaveston, or else his senseless trunk.
　*Lan.*　Not so, my lords, lest he bestow more
cost

In burying him than he hath ever earn'd.
　*Arun.*　My lords, it is his majesty's request,　55
And in the honour of a king he swears,
He will but talk with him, and send him back.
　*War.*　When? can you tell? Arundel, no;
we wot
He that the care of his realm remits,
And drives his nobles to these exigents　60
For Gaveston, will, if he sees him once,
Violate any promise to possess him.
　*Arun.*　Then if you will not trust his grace in
keep,
My lords, I will be pledge for his return.　64
　*Mor.*　It is honourable in thee to offer this;
But for we know thou art a noble gentleman,
We will not wrong thee so, to make away
A true man for a thief.
　*Gav.*　How mean'st thou, Mortimer? That
is over-base.
　*Mor.*　Away, base groom, robber of king's
renown!　　　　　　　　　　70
Question with thy companions and thy mates.
　*Pem.*　My Lord Mortimer, and you, my lords,
each one:
To gratify the king's request therein,
Touching the sending of this Gaveston,
Because his majesty so earnestly　　　75
Desires to see the man before his death,
I will upon mine honour undertake
To carry him, and bring him back again;
Provided this, that you, my lord of Arundel,　79
Will join with me.
　*War.*　　　Pembroke, what wilt thou do?
Cause yet more bloodshed? Is it not enough
That we have taken him, but must we now
Leave him on "had I wist," and let him go?
　*Pem.*　My lords, I will not over-woo your
honours,
But if you dare trust Pembroke with the pris-
oner,　　　　　　　　　　　85
Upon mine oath, I will return him back.
　*Arun.*　My lord of Lancaster, what say you
in this?
　*Lan.*　Why, I say, let him go on Pembroke's
word.
　*Pem.*　And you, Lord Mortimer?　　89
　*Mor.*　How say you, my lord of Warwick?
　*War.*　Nay, do your pleasures, I know how
't will prove.
　*Pem.*　Then give him me.
　*Gav.*　　　　Sweet sovereign, yet I come
To see thee ere I die.
　*War.*　　　　Yet not perhaps,
If Warwick's wit and policy prevail. [*Aside.*]
　*Mor.*　My lord of Pembroke, we deliver
him you;　　　　　　　　　95

¹⁵ Greekish strumpet: Helen　train'd: enticed　³⁶ for why: because　⁵⁹ his: (Not in Qq.)
⁶⁰ exigents: violent courses　⁶¹ sees: ('zease' Q 1)　⁶³ in keep: as keeper　⁸³ "had I wist":
conditions we shall later rue

Return him on your honour.  Sound, away!
　　　　*Exeunt [Mortimer, Warwick, and*
　　　　*Lancaster].  Manent Pembroke,*
　　　　*Arundel, Gaveston & Pembroke's*
　　　　*men, four soldiers.*
*Pem.*  My lord Arundel, you shall go with
　me.
My house is not far hence; out of the way
A little, but our men shall go along.
We that have pretty wenches to our wives, 100
Sir, must not come so near and balk their lips.
　*Arun.*  'T is very kindly spoke, my lord of
　　Pembroke;
Your honour hath an adamant of power
To draw a prince.
　*Pem.*　　So, my lord.  Come hither, James:
　　　　*[Addressing one of the soldiers.]*
I do commit this Gaveston to thee.　　105
Be thou this night his keeper; in the morning
We will discharge thee of thy charge.  Be gone.
　*Gav.*  Unhappy Gaveston, whither goest thou
　now?
　　　　*Exit [Gaveston] cum servis Pen.*
*Horse-boy.*  My lord, we 'll quickly be at
Cobham.　　　　　　　*Exeunt ambo.*

## [ACT III

### SCENE I]

*Enter Gaveston mourning, and the Earl of*
*Pembroke's men [James &c.]*

　*Gav.*  O treacherous Warwick! thus to wrong
　thy friend.
　*James.*  I see it is your life these arms pursue.
　*Gav.*  Weaponless must I fall, and die in
　bands?
O! must this day be period of my life?
Centre of all my bliss!  And ye be men,　　5
Speed to the king.

*Enter Warwick and his company*

　*War.*　　　　My lord of Pembroke's men,
Strive you no longer.  I will have that Gaveston.
　*James.*  Your lordship doth dishonour to
　yourself,
And wrong our lord, your honourable friend.
　*War.*  No, James, it is my country's cause I
　follow.　　10
Go, take the villain, soldiers: come away.
We 'll make quick work.  Commend me to
　your master,
My friend, and tell him that I watch'd it well.

Come, let thy shadow parley with King Ed-
　ward.
　*Gav.*  Treacherous earl, shall I not see the
　king?　　　　　　　　　　　　　　15
　*War.*  The King of Heaven, perhaps; no
　other king.
Away!  *Exeunt Warwick and his men with*
　　　　*Gaveston.  Manet James cum ceteris.*
　*James.*  Come, fellows, it booted not for us to
　strive.
We will in haste go certify our lord.　　*Exeunt.*

[SCENE II. — *Near Boroughbridge, Yorkshire.*]

*Enter King Edward and Spencer, [Baldock*
*and Soldiers] with drums and fifes*

　*K. Edw.*  I long to hear an answer from the
　barons
Touching my friend, my dearest Gaveston.
Ah, Spencer, not the riches of my realm
Can ransom him!  Ah, he is mark'd to die!
I know the malice of the younger Mortimer; 5
Warwick, I know, is rough, and Lancaster
Inexorable, and I shall never see
My lovely Pierce, my Gaveston, again!
The barons overbear me with their pride.
　*Spen.*  Were I King Edward, England's
　sovereign,　　　　　　　　　　　10
Son to the lovely Eleanor of Spain,
Great Edward Longshanks' issue, would I bear
These braves, this rage, and suffer uncontroll'd
These barons thus to beard me in my land,
In mine own realm?  My lord, pardon my
　speech:　　　　　　　　　　　　15
Did you retain your father's magnanimity,
Did you regard the honour of your name,
You would not suffer thus your majesty
Be counterbuff'd of your nobility.
Strike off their heads, and let them preach on
　poles!　　　　　　　　　　　　20
No doubt, such lessons they will teach the rest,
As by their preachments they will profit much,
And learn obedience to their lawful king.
　*K. Edw.*  Yea, gentle Spencer, we have been
　too mild,
Too kind to them; but now have drawn our
　sword,　　　　　　　　　　　　25
And if they send me not my Gaveston,
We 'll steel it on their crest, and poll their
　tops.
　*Bald.*  This haught resolve becomes your
　majesty,
Not to be tied to their affection,

---

**97 Arundel:** (Not in Qq.)　　**101 balk:** leave unsaluted　　**103 adamant:** magnet　　**108** S. D. **cum**
**servis Pen.:** *i.e.*, with James and Pembroke's other soldiers　　**109** S. D. **ambo:** both (*i.e.*, Pembroke, and
Arundel with horse-boy)　　**3 bands:** fetters　　**4 period:** end　　**5 And:** if, an　　**14 shadow:** ghost
**17** S. D. **cum ceteris:** with Pembroke's other men　　**18 booted:** availed　　**15 certify:** inform　　**13 braves:**
defiances　　**19 counterbuff'd of:** buffeted by　　**21 they:** the severed heads　　**27 steel it:** prove its
temper　　**poll:** prune　　**28 haught:** proud

As though your highness were a schoolboy still,
And must be aw'd and govern'd like a child. 31

*Enter Hugh Spencer, an old man,*
*father to the Young Spencer, with*
*his truncheon and Soldiers*

*Spen. pater.* Long live my sovereign, the
  noble Edward,
In peace triumphant, fortunate in wars!
  *K. Edw.* Welcome, old man, com'st thou in
    Edward's aid?
Then tell thy prince, of whence and what thou
  art.                                          35
  *Spen. pa.* Lo, with a band of bowmen and of
pikes,
Brown bills and targeteers, four hundred
strong,
Sworn to defend King Edward's royal right,
I come in person to your majesty,
Spencer, the father of Hugh Spencer there,  40
Bound to your highness everlastingly
For favours done, in him, unto us all.
  *K. Edw.* Thy father, Spencer?
  *Spen. filius.* True, and it like your grace,
That pours, in lieu of all your goodness shown,
His life, my lord, before your princely feet. 45
  *K. Edw.* Welcome ten thousand times, old
    man, again.
Spencer, this love, this kindness to thy king,
Argues thy noble mind and disposition.
Spencer, I here create thee Earl of Wiltshire,
And daily will enrich thee with our favour,  50
That, as the sunshine, shall reflect o'er thee.
Beside, the more to manifest our love,
Because we hear Lord Bruse doth sell his land,
And that the Mortimers are in hand withal,
Thou shalt have crowns of us t' outbid the
  barons:                                      55
And, Spencer, spare them not, but lay it on.
Soldiers, a largess, and thrice welcome all!
  [*Y.*] *Spen.* My lord, here comes the queen.
*Enter the Queen and her son [Prince Edward,]*
*and Levune, a Frenchman*

  *K. Edw.* Madam, what news?
  *Que.* News of dishonour, lord, and discon-
    tent.                                       60
Our friend Levune, faithful and full of trust,
Informeth us, by letters and by words,
That Lord Valois our brother, King of France,
Because your highness hath been slack in hom-
age,
Hath seized Normandy into his hands.         65
These be the letters, this the messenger.
  *K. Edw.* Welcome, Levune. Tush, Sib, if
    this be all,

Valois and I will soon be friends again. —
But to my Gaveston; shall I never see,
Never behold thee now? — Madam, in this mat-
  ter,                                          70
We will employ you and your little son;
You shall go parley with the king of France.—
Boy, see you bear you bravely to the king,
And do your message with a majesty.
  *Prince.* Commit not to my youth things of
    more weight                                 75
Than fits a prince so young as I to bear,
And fear not, lord and father: Heaven's great
  beams
On Atlas' shoulder shall not lie more safe,
Than shall your charge committed to my trust.
  *Que.* Ah, boy! this towardness makes thy
    mother fear                                 80
Thou art not mark'd to many days on earth.
  *K. Edw.* Madam, we will that you with speed
    be shipp'd,
And this our son; Levune shall follow you
With all the haste we can despatch him hence.
Choose of our lords to bear you company,   85
And go in peace; leave us in wars at home.
  *Que.* Unnatural wars, where subjects brave
    their king;
God end them once! My lord, I take my leave,
To make my preparation for France.
                    [*Exit with Prince Edward.*]

*Enter Lord Arundel*

  *K. Edw.* What, Lord Arundel, dost thou
    come alone?                                 90
  *Arun.* Yea, my good lord, for Gaveston is
    dead.
  *K. Edw.* Ah, traitors! have they put my
    friend to death?
Tell me, Arundel, died he ere thou cam'st,
Or didst thou see my friend to take his death?
  *Arun.* Neither, my lord; for as he was sur-
    pris'd,                                     95
Begirt with weapons and with enemies round,
I did your highness' message to them all;
Demanding him of them, entreating rather,
And said, upon the honour of my name,
That I would undertake to carry him          100
Unto your highness, and to bring him back.
  *K. Edw.* And tell me, would the rebels deny
    me that?
  [*Y.*] *Spen.* Proud recreants!
  *K. Edw.*          Yea, Spencer, traitors all.
  *Arun.* I found them at the first inexorable.
The Earl of Warwick would not bide the hear-
  ing,                                         105
Mortimer hardly; Pembroke and Lancaster

---

³¹ S. D. **truncheon**: mace   ⁴⁴ **lieu**: recompense   ⁵⁴ **in hand**: bargaining   ⁶³ **brother**: (really,
uncle)   ⁶⁵ **Normandy**: (really, Aquitaine. Normandy was not an English possession at this time.)
⁶⁷ **Sib**: diminutive of Isabel   ⁷⁷ **beams**: supports   ⁸⁰ **towardness**: precocity   ⁸⁹ S. D. **Arundel**:
('Matre[vis]' Q and so throughout the scene. The rôles of Arundel and Matrevis were doubtless doubled.)

Spake least: and when they flatly had denied,
Refusing to receive me pledge for him,
The Earl of Pembroke mildly thus bespake:
"My lords, because our sovereign sends for him,
And promiseth he shall be safe return'd,      111
I will this undertake, to have him hence,
And see him re-deliver'd to your hands."
  *K. Edw.* Well, and how fortunes it that he
   came not?
  [*Y.*] *Spen.* Some treason, or some villainy,
   was cause.                           115
  *Arun.* The Earl of Warwick seiz'd him on his
   way;
For being deliver'd unto Pembroke's men,
Their lord rode home thinking his prisoner safe;
But ere he came, Warwick in ambush lay,
And bare him to his death; and in a trench 120
Strake off his head, and march'd unto the camp.
  [*Y.*] *Spen.* A bloody part, flatly against
   law of arms!
  *K. Edw.* O shall I speak, or shall I sigh and
   die!
  [*Y.*] *Spen.* My lord, refer your vengeance
   to the sword.
Upon these barons! hearten up your men! 125
Let them not unreveng'd murther your friends!
Advance your standard, Edward, in the field,
And march to fire them from their starting holes.

   *Edward kneels, and saith.*

  [*K. Edw.*]. By earth, the common mother of
   us all,
By Heaven, and all the moving orbs thereof, 130
By this right hand, and by my father's sword,
And all the honours 'longing to my crown,
I will have heads and lives for him, as many
As I have manors, castles, towns, and towers! —
           [*Rises.*]
Treacherous Warwick! traitorous Mortimer! 135
If I be England's king, in lakes of gore
Your headless trunks, your bodies will I trail,
That you may drink your fill, and quaff in blood,
And stain my royal standard with the same,
That so my bloody colours may suggest      140
Remembrance of revenge immortally
On your accursed traitorous progeny,
You villains, that have slain my Gaveston!
And in this place of honour and of trust,
Spencer, sweet Spencer, I adopt thee here: 145
And merely of our love we do create thee
Earl of Gloucester, and Lord Chamberlain,
Despite of times, despite of enemies.
  [*Y.*] *Spen.* My lord, here 's a messenger
   from the barons,
Desires access unto your majesty.          150
  *K. Edw.* Admit him near.

   *Enter the Herald from the Barons with his coat
        of arms*

  *Her.* Long live King Edward, England's
   lawful lord!
  *K. Edw.* So wish not they, I wis, that sent
   thee hither.
Thou com'st from Mortimer and his 'complices:
A ranker rout of rebels never was.          155
Well, say thy message.
  *Her.* The barons, up in arms, by me salute
Your highness with long life and happiness;
And bid me say, as plainer to your grace,
That if without effusion of blood            160
You will this grief have ease and remedy,
That from your princely person you remove
This Spencer, as a putrefying branch,
That deads the royal vine, whose golden leaves
Empale your princely head, your diadem,    165
Whose brightness such pernicious upstarts dim,
Say they;  and lovingly advise your grace,
To cherish virtue and nobility,
And have old servitors in high esteem,
And shake off smooth dissembling flatterers. 170
This granted, they, their honours, and their
  lives,
Are to your highness vow'd and consecrate.
  [*Y.*] *Spen.* Ah, traitors! will they still dis-
   play their pride?
  *K. Edw.* Away, tarry no answer, but be
   gone!
Rebels, will they appoint their sovereign    175
His sports, his pleasures, and his company?
Yet, ere thou go, see how I do divorce
         *Embrace Spencer.*
Spencer from me. — Now get thee to thy lords,
And tell them I will come to chastise them
For murthering Gaveston.  Hie thee, get thee
  gone!                                 180
Edward with fire and sword follows at thy heels.
         [*Exit Herald.*]
My lords, perceive you how these rebels swell?
Soldiers, good hearts, defend your sovereign's
  right,
For now, even now, we march to make them
  stoop.
Away!                              *Exeunt.* 185

  [SCENE III. — *Boroughbridge battlefield,
    Yorkshire.*]

*Alarums, excursions, a great fight, and a retreat.
  Enter the King, Spencer the father, Spencer
  the son, and the Noblemen of the king's side*

  *K. Edw.* Why do we sound retreat?  Upon
   them, lords!

---

<sup>114</sup> **it:** (Not in Qq.)    <sup>128</sup> **starting holes:** fox-holes    <sup>153</sup> **wis:** incorrect form of "wot"    <sup>159</sup> **plainer:** complainant    <sup>161</sup> **will:** wish that    <sup>182</sup> **lords:** ('lord' Qq.)    Scene III (No change of scene on Eliza-bethan stage)

This day i shall pour vengeance with my sword
On those proud rebels that are up in arms
And do confront and countermand their
   king.
*Spen. son.* I doubt it not, my lord, right will
   prevail.     5
*Spen. fa.* 'T is not amiss, my liege, for either
   part
To breathe awhile; our men, with sweat and
   dust
All chok'd, well near begin to faint for heat;
And this retire refresheth horse and man.
*Spen. son.* Here come the rebels.     10

*Enter the Barons, Mortimer, Lancaster, War-
   wick, Pembroke, cum ceteris*

*Mor.* Look, Lancaster, yonder is Edward
Among his flatters.
*Lan.*           And there let him be
Till he pay dearly for their company.
*War.* And shall, or Warwick's sword shall
   smite in vain.
*K. Edw.* What, rebels, do you shrink and
   sound retreat?     15
*Mor.* No, Edward. no; thy flatterers faint
   and fly.
*Lan.* Thou 'd best betimes forsake them,
   and their trains,
For they 'll betray thee, traitors as they are.
*Spen. son.* Traitor on thy face, rebellious
   Lancaster!
*Pem.* Away, base upstart, brav'st thou
   nobles thus?     20
*Spen. fa.* A noble attempt and honourable
   deed,
Is it not, trow ye, to assemble aid,
And levy arms against your lawful king!
*K. Edw.* For which ere long their heads shall
   satisfy,
T' appease the wrath of their offended king. 25
*Mor.* Then, Edward, thou wilt fight it to
   the last,
And rather bathe thy sword in subjects' blood,
Than banish that pernicious company?
*K. Edw.* Ay, traitors all, rather than thus
   be brav'd,
Make England's civil towns huge heaps of
   stones,     30
And ploughs to go about our palace-gates.
*War.* A desperate and unnatural resolution!
Alarum! to the fight!
St. George for England, and the barons' right!
*K. Edw.* Saint George for England, and
   Edward's right!     35
*[Alarums. Exeunt the two parties severally.]*

*Enter Edward with the Barons [and Kent],
   captives*

*K. Edw.* Now, lusty lords, now, not by
   chance of war,
But justice of the quarrel and the cause,
Vail'd is your pride; methinks you hang the
   heads,
But we 'll advance them, traitors. Now 't is time
To be aveng'd on you for all your braves,     40
And for the murther of my dearest friend,
To whom right well you knew our soul was
   knit,
Good Pierce of Gaveston, my sweet favourite.
Ah, rebels! recreants! you made him away.
*Kent.* Brother, in regard of thee, and of thy
   land,     45
Did they remove that flatterer from thy throne.
*K. Edw.* So, sir, you have spoke; away,
   avoid our presence!     *[Exit Kent.]*
Accursed wretches, was 't in regard of us,
When we had sent our messenger to request
He might be spar'd to come to speak with us, 50
And Pembroke undertook for his return,
That thou, proud Warwick, watch'd the pris-
   oner,
Poor Pierce, and headed him 'gainst law of
   arms?
For which thy head shall overlook the rest,
As much as thou in rage outwent'st the rest. 55
*War.* Tyrant, I scorn thy threats and men-
   aces;
It is but temporal that thou canst inflict.
*Lan.* The worst is death, and better die to
   live
Than live in infamy under such a king.
*K. Edw.* Away with them, my lord of Win-
   chester!     60
These lusty leaders, Warwick and Lancaster,
I charge you roundly — off with both their
   heads!
Away!
*War.* Farewell, vain world!
*Lan.*           Sweet Mortimer, farewell.
*Mor.* England, unkind to thy nobility,     65
Groan for this grief, behold how thou art
   maim'd!
*K. Edw.* Go take that haughty Mortimer to
   the Tower.
There see him safe bestow'd; and for the rest,
Do speedy execution on them all.
Begone!     70
*Mor.* What, Mortimer! can ragged stony
   walls
Immure thy virtue that aspires to Heaven?

---

⁴ **countermand:** defy    ⁸ **well near:** almost
**trains:** plots    ³⁰ **civil:** filled with citizens    ³⁹ **advance:** raise (on poles)    ⁵² **watch'd:** ambushed
⁵³ **headed:** beheaded    ⁵⁷ **temporal:** harm in this life    ⁵⁸ **live:** enjoy eternal life    ⁶⁰ **Winchester:**
the elder Spencer    ⁷² **virtue:** driving force
   ¹⁷ **Thou'd . . . them:** ('Th 'ad . . . thee' Qq.)

No, Edward, England's scourge, it may not be;
Mortimer's hope surmounts his fortune far.
          *[The captive Barons are led off.]*
*K. Edw.*  Sound drums and trumpets! March
     with me, my friends,                            75
Edward this day hath crown'd him king anew.
          *Exit [with his retinue]. Manent
               Spencer filius, Levune, & Baldock.*
*Spen.*  Levune, the trust that we repose in
     thee,
Begets the quiet of King Edward's land.
Therefore begone in haste, and with advice
Bestow that treasure on the lords of France,  80
That, therewith all enchanted, like the guard
That suffered Jove to pass in showers of gold
To Danaë, all aid may be denied
To Isabel, the queen, that now in France
Makes friends, to cross the seas with her young
     son,                                            85
And step into his father's regiment.
     *Levune.*  That's it these barons and the
     subtle queen
Long levell'd at.
     *Bald.*            Yea, but, Levune, thou seest,
These barons lay their heads on blocks to-
     gether;
What they intend the hangman frustrates
     clean.                                          90
     *Levune.*  Have you no doubts, my lords, I'll
     clap so close
Among the lords of France with England's gold,
That Isabel shall make her plaints in vain,
And France shall be obdurate with her tears.
     *Spen.*  Then make for France amain;
     Levune, away!                                   95
Proclaim King Edward's wars and victories.
                         *Exeunt omnes.*

### [ACT IV

### SCENE I. — *London, near the Tower.*]

#### *Enter Edmund [Kent]*

*Kent.*  Fair blows the wind for France; blow,
     gentle gale,
Till Edmund be arriv'd for England's good!
Nature, yield to my country's cause in this.
A brother?  No, a butcher of thy friends!
Proud Edward, dost thou banish me thy pres-
     ence?                                            5
But I'll to France, and cheer the wronged
     queen,
And certify what Edward's looseness is.
Unnatural king! to slaughter noblemen
And cherish flatterers! Mortimer, I stay
Thy sweet escape.                                    10
Stand gracious, gloomy night, to his device.

#### *Enter Mortimer, disguised*

*Mor.*  Holla! who walketh there?
Is 't you, my lord?
*Kent.*                   Mortimer, 't is I;
But hath thy potion wrought so happily?
     *Mor.*  It hath, my lord;  the warders all
     asleep,                                         15
I thank them, gave me leave to pass in peace.
But hath your grace got shipping unto France?
*Kent.*  Fear it not.                       *Exeunt.*

### [SCENE II. — *The French court, Paris.*]

#### *Enter the Queen [Isabella] and her son*

*Que.*  Ah, boy! our friends do fail us all in
     France.
The lords are cruel, and the king unkind;
What shall we do?
*Prince.*              Madam, return to England,
And please my father well, and then a fig
For all my uncle's friendship here in France.  5
I warrant you, I'll win his highness quickly;
'A loves me better than a thousand Spencers.
     *Que.*  Ah, boy, thou art deceiv'd, at least in
     this,
To think that we can yet be tun'd together;
No, no, we jar too far.  Unkind Valois!      10
Unhappy Isabel! when France rejects,
Whither, oh! whither dost thou bend thy steps?

#### *Enter Sir John of Hainault*

*Sir J.*  Madam, what cheer?
*Que.*               Ah, good Sir John of Hainault
Never so cheerless, nor so far distress'd.
     *Sir J.*  I hear, sweet lady, of the king's un-
     kindness;                                       15
But droop not, madam; noble minds contemn
Despair.  Will your grace with me to Hainault,
And there stay time's advantage with your
     son?
How say you, my lord, will you go with your
     friends,
And share of all our fortunes equally?        20
     *Prince.*  So pleaseth the queen, my mother,
     me it likes.
The King of England, nor the court of France,
Shall have me from my gracious mother's side,
Till I be strong enough to break a staff;     24
And then have at the proudest Spencer's head.
     *Sir J.*  Well said, my lord.
     *Que.*  O, my sweet heart, how do I moan thy
     wrongs,
Yet triumph in the hope of thee, my joy!
Ah, sweet Sir John! even to the utmost verge
Of Europe, or the shore of Tanais,            30

---

    **86 regiment:** rule    **88 levell'd:** aimed ('leuied' Qq.)    **91 clap so close:** so insinuate ('claps close'
Qq.)    **9 stay:** await    **5 uncle's:** the French king's    **20 share of:** ('shake off' Qq.)    **24 staff:** lance-
shaft    **30 Tanais:** the Don River in South Russia

Will we with thee. To Hainault! — so we will.
The marquis is a noble gentleman;
His grace, I dare presume, will welcome me.
But who are these?

*Enter Edmund [Kent] and Mortimer*

*Kent.*          Madam, long may you live,
Much happier than your friends in England do!
   *Que.* Lord Edmund and Lord Mortimer
      alive!                                              36
Welcome to France! The news was here, my
      lord,
That you were dead, or very near your death.
   *Mor.* Lady, the last was truest of the twain;
But Mortimer, reserv'd for better hap,           40
Hath shaken off the thraldom of the Tower,
And lives t' advance your standard, good my
      lord.
   *Prince.* How mean you, and the king, my
      father, lives?
No, my Lord Mortimer, not I, I trow.
   *Que.* Not, son! why not? I would it were
      no worse.                                          45
But, gentle lords, friendless we are in France.
   *Mor.* Monsieur le Grand, a noble friend of
      yours,
Told us, at our arrival, all the news:
How hard the nobles, how unkind the king
Hath show'd himself; but, madam, right makes
      room                                               50
Where weapons want; and, though a many
      friends
Are made away, as Warwick, Lancaster,
And others of our party and faction;
Yet have we friends, assure your grace, in Eng-
      land
Would cast up caps, and clap their hands for
      joy,                                               55
To see us there, appointed for our foes.
   *Kent.* Would all were well, and Edward well
      reclaim'd,
For England's honour, peace, and quietness.
   *Mor.* But by the sword, my lord, it must be
      deserv'd;
The king will ne'er forsake his flatterers.      60
   *Sir J.* My lords of England, sith the un-
      gentle king
Of France refuseth to give aid of arms
To this distressed queen, his sister here,
Go you with her to Hainault. Doubt ye not,       64
We will find comfort, money, men, and friends
Ere long, to bid the English king a base.
How say, young prince? What think you of
      the match?
   *Prince.* I think King Edward will outrun
      us all.

   *Que.* Nay, son, not so; and you must not
      discourage
Your friends, that are so forward in your aid. 70
   *Kent.* Sir John of Hainault, pardon us, I
      pray;
These comforts that you give our woful queen
Bind us in kindness all at your command.
   *Que.* Yea, gentle brother; and the God of
      heaven
Prosper your happy motion, good Sir John. 75
   *Mor.* This noble gentleman, forward in
      arms,
Was born, I see, to be our anchor-hold.
Sir John of Hainault, be it thy renown,
That England's queen and nobles in distress,
Have been by thee restor'd and comforted.  80
   *Sir J.* Madam, along, and you my lords,
      with me,
That England's peers may Hainault's welcome
      see.                               [*Exeunt.*]

[SCENE III. — *Edward's court.*]

*Enter the King [Edward,] Arundel, the two
      Spencers, with others*

   *K. Edw.* Thus after many threats of wrath-
      ful war,
Triumpheth England's Edward with his friends;
And triumph, Edward, with his friends uncon-
      troll'd!
My lord of Gloucester, do you hear the news?
   *Spen. Jun.* What news, my lord?           5
   *K. Edw.* Why, man, they say there is great
      execution
Done through the realm; my lord of Arundel,
You have the note, have you not?
   *Arun.* From the Lieutenant of the Tower,
      my lord.
   *K. Edw.* I pray let us see it. [*Takes the note.*]
      What have we there?                      10
Read it, Spencer.
      [*Young*] Spencer reads their names.
Why, so; they bark'd apace a month ago:
Now, on my life, they 'll neither bark nor bite.
Now, sirs, the news from France? Gloucester,
      I trow
The lords of France love England's gold so well
As Isabella gets no aid from thence.          16
What now remains? Have you proclaim'd,
      my lord,
Reward for them can bring in Mortimer?
   *Spen. Jun.* My lord, we have; and if he be
      in England,
'A will be had ere long, I doubt it not.      20
   *K. Edw.* If, dost thou say? Spencer, as true
      as death,

⁵¹ **want:** are lacking    ⁵⁶ **appointed:** armed    ⁶⁶ **base:** challenge    ⁶⁷ **match:** game    ⁸¹ **lords:**
('lord' Qq.)        ¹¹ S. D. **reads their names:** (The list of names, written on a separate sheet of **paper,**
**was** not incorporated in the text of the play.)    ¹⁶ **As:** that

He is in England's ground; our portmasters
Are not so careless of their king's command.

*Enter a Post*

How now, what news with thee? From whence
  come these?
*Post.* Letters, my lord, and tidings forth of
  France; —                   25
To you, my lord of Gloucester, from Levune.
        [*Gives letters to Young Spencer.*]
*K. Edw.* Read.
*Spencer reads the letter.*
"My duty to your honour premised, &c., I
have, according to instructions in that behalf,
dealt with the King of France his lords, and [30
effected that the queen, all discontented and
discomforted, is gone: whither, if you ask, with
Sir John of Hainault, brother to the marquis,
into Flanders. With them are gone Lord Edmund, and the Lord Mortimer, having in [35
their company divers of your nation, and
others; and, as constant report goeth, they in-
tend to give King Edward battle in England,
sooner than he can look for them. This is all
the news of import.         40
  Your honour's in all service, Levune."
*K. Edw.* Ah, villains! hath that Mortimer
  escap'd?
With him is Edmund gone associate?
And will Sir John of Hainault lead the round?
Welcome, a' God's name, madam, and your son;
England shall welcome you and all your rout. 46
Gallop apace, bright Phœbus, through the sky,
And dusky night, in rusty iron car:
Between you both shorten the time, I pray,
That I may see that most desired day  50
When we may meet these traitors in the field.
Ah, nothing grieves me but my little boy
Is thus misled to countenance their ills.
Come, friends, to Bristow, there to make us
  strong;
And, winds, as equal be to bring them in,  55
As you injurious were to bear them forth!
        [*Exeunt.*]

[SCENE IV. — *English coast, near Harwich.*]

*Enter the Queen, her son [Prince Edward],
Edmund [Kent], Mortimer, and Sir John
[of Hainault]*

*Que.* Now, lords, our loving friends and
  countrymen,
Welcome to England all, with prosperous
  winds!
Our kindest friends in Belgia have we left,
To cope with friends at home; a heavy case
When force to force is knit, and sword and
  glaive     5

In civil broils make kin and countrymen
Slaughter themselves in others, and their sides
With their own weapons gor'd! But what's the
  help?
Misgovern'd kings are cause of all this wrack;
And, Edward, thou art one among them all, 10
Whose looseness hath betray'd thy land to spoil,
Who made the channels overflow with blood.
Of thine own people patron shouldst thou be,
But thou ——
*Mor.* Nay, madam, if you be a warrior, 15
You must not grow so passionate in speeches.
Lords,
Sith that we are by sufferance of Heaven
Arriv'd and armed in this prince's right,
Here for our country's cause swear we to him 20
All homage, fealty, and forwardness;
And for the open wrongs and injuries
Edward hath done to us, his queen and land,
We come in arms to wreak it with the swords;
That England's queen in peace may repossess
Her dignities and honours; and withal  26
We may remove these flatterers from the king,
That havocs England's wealth and treasury.
*Sir J.* Sound trumpets, my lord, and forward
  let us march.
Edward will think we come to flatter him. 30
*Kent.* I would he never had been flatter'd
  more.       [*Exeunt.*]

[SCENE V. — *Near Bristol.*]

*Enter the King, Baldock, and Spencer the son,
flying about the stage*

*Spen.* Fly, fly, my lord! the queen is over-
  strong;
Her friends do multiply, and yours do fail.
Shape we our course to Ireland, there to
  breathe.
*K. Edw.* What! was I born to fly and run
  away,
And leave the Mortimers conquerors behind? 5
Give me my horse, and let's reinforce our
  troops:
And in this bed of honour die with fame.
*Bald.* O no, my lord, this princely resolution
Fits not the time; away! we are pursu'd.
        [*Exeunt.*]

[*Enter*] *Edmund [Kent] alone with a sword
and target*

*Kent.* This way he fled, but I am come too
  late.      10
Edward, alas! my heart relents for thee.
Proud traitor, Mortimer, why dost thou chase
Thy lawful king, thy sovereign, with thy sword?
Vild wretch! and why hast thou, of all unkind,

---

⁴⁴ round: dance  ⁵³ ills: offenses  ⁵⁴ Bristow: Bristol  ⁵⁵ equal: just  ⁴ cope: contend
⁹ Misgovern'd: intemperate  ²⁸ havocs: ruin

Borne arms against thy brother and thy king?
Rain showers of vengeance on my cursed head,
Thou God, to whom in justice it belongs    17
To punish this unnatural revolt!
Edward, this Mortimer aims at thy life!
O fly him, then! But, Edmund, calm this rage,
Dissemble, or thou diest; for Mortimer    21
And Isabel do kiss, while they conspire;
And yet she bears a face of love forsooth.
Fie on that love that hatcheth death and hate!
Edmund, away! Bristow to Longshanks' blood
Is false. Be not found single for suspect:    26
Proud Mortimer pries near into thy walks.

*Enter the Queen, Mortimer, the young Prince,*
   *and Sir John of Hainault*

*Que.* Successful battles gives the God of
   kings
To them that fight in right and fear his wrath.
Since then successfully we have prevailed,    30
Thanks be Heaven's great architect, and you.
Ere farther we proceed, my noble lords,
We here create our well-beloved son,
Of love and care unto his royal person,
Lord Warden of the realm, and sith the fates 35
Have made his father so infortunate,
Deal you, my lords, in this, my loving lords,
As to your wisdoms fittest seems in all.
  *Kent.* Madam, without offence, if I may ask,
How will you deal with Edward in his fall?   40
  *Prince.* Tell me, good uncle. what Edward
   do you mean?
  *Kent.* Nephew, your father; I dare not call
   him king.
  *Mor.* My lord of Kent, what needs these
   questions?
'T is not in her controlment, nor in ours,
But as the realm and parliament shall please, 45
So shall your brother be disposed of. —
I like not this relenting mood in Edmund.
Madam, 't is good to look to him betimes.
                   *[Aside to the Queen.]*
  *Que.* My lord, the Mayor of Bristow knows
   our mind.
  *Mor.* Yea, madam, and they scape not
   easily    50
That fled the field.
  *Que.*          Baldock is with the king,
A goodly chancellor, is he not, my lord?
  *Sir J.* So are the Spencers, the father and
   the son.
  *Kent.* This Edward is the ruin of the realm.

*Enter Rice ap Howell and the Mayor of Bristow,*
   *with Spencer the father*

  *Rice.* God save Queen Isabel, and her princely
   son!    55
Madam, the mayor and citizens of Bristow,

In sign of love and duty to this presence,
Present by me this traitor to the state,
Spencer, the father to that wanton Spencer,
That, like the lawless Catiline of Rome,    60
Revelled in England's wealth and treasury.
  *Que.* We thank you all.
  *Mor.*              Your loving care in this
Deserveth princely favours and rewards.
But where 's the king and the other Spencer fled?
  *Rice.* Spencer the son, created Earl of Glou-
   cester,    65
Is with that smooth-tongu'd scholar Baldock
   gone,
And shipp'd but late for Ireland with the king.
  *Mor.* *[Aside.]* Some whirlwind fetch them
   back or sink them all! —
They shall be started thence, I doubt it not.
  *Prince.* Shall I not see the king my father
   yet?    70
  *Kent.* *[Aside.]* Unhappy 's Edward, chas'd
   from England's bounds.
  *Sir J.* Madam, what resteth? why stand ye
   in a muse?
  *Que.* I rue my lord's ill-fortune; but alas!
Care of my country call'd me to this war.
  *Mor.* Madam, have done with care and
   sad complaint;    75
Your king hath wrong'd your country and him-
   self,
And we must seek to right it as we may.
Meanwhile, have hence this rebel to the block.
Your lordship cannot privilege your head.
  *Spen. pa.* Rebel is he that fights against his
   prince;    80
So fought not they that fought in Edward's
   right.
  *Mor.* Take him away, he prates.
            *[Exeunt Attendants with the Elder*
            *Spencer.]*
                   You, Rice ap Howell,
Shall do good service to her majesty,
Being of countenance in your country here,
To follow these rebellious runagates.    85
We in meanwhile, madam, must take advice
How Baldock, Spencer, and their 'complices
May in their fall be followed to their end.
                   *Exeunt omnes.*

[SCENE VI. — *Neath Abbey.*]

*Enter the Abbot, Monks, [King] Edward,*
   *Spencer, and Baldock [the three latter dis-*
   *guised]*

  *Abbot.* Have you no doubt, my lord;
   have you no fear;
As silent and as careful will we be,
To keep your royal person safe with us.

---

²⁶ **single:** alone   **for suspect:** lest you arouse suspicion   ³¹ **Thanks:** ('Thankt' Q 2, etc.)
² **resteth:** remains to do   ⁸⁵ **runagates:** vagabonds

Free from suspect and fell invasion
Of such as have your majesty in chase,          5
Yourself, and those your chosen company,
As danger of this stormy time requires.
   *K. Edw.* Father, thy face should harbour no deceit.
O! hadst thou ever been a king, thy heart,
Pierced deeply with sense of my distress,          10
Could not but take compassion of my state.
Stately and proud, in riches and in train,
Whilom I was, powerful, and full of pomp:
But what is he whom rule and empery
Have not in life or death made miserable?          15
Come, Spencer; come, Baldock, come, sit down by me;
Make trial now of that philosophy,
That in our famous nurseries of arts
Thou suck'dst from Plato and from Aristotle.
Father, this life contemplative is Heaven.          20
O that I might this life in quiet lead!
But we, alas! are chas'd; and you, my friends,
Your lives and my dishonour they pursue.
Yet, gentle monks, for treasure, gold, nor fee,
Do you betray us and our company.          25
   *Monks.* Your grace may sit secure, if none but we
Do wot of your abode.
   *Spen.* Not one alive; but shrewdly I suspect
A gloomy fellow in a mead below.
'A gave a long look after us, my lord;          30
And all the land, I know, is up in arms,
Arms that pursue our lives with deadly hate.
   *Bald.* We were embark'd for Ireland, wretched we!
With awkward winds and sore tempests driven
To fall on shore, and here to pine in fear          35
Of Mortimer and his confederates.
   *K. Edw.* Mortimer! who talks of Mortimer?
Who wounds me with the name of Mortimer,
That bloody man? Good father, on thy lap
Lay I this head, laden with mickle care.          40
O might I never open these eyes again!
Never again lift up this drooping head!
O never more lift up this dying heart!
   *Spen.* Look up, my lord. — Baldock, this drowsiness
Betides no good; here even we are betray'd.          45

*Enter, with Welsh hooks, Rice ap Howell, a Mower, and the Earl of Leicester*

   *Mow.* Upon my life, those be the men ye seek.
   *Rice.* Fellow, enough. — My lord, I pray be short.
A fair commission warrants what we do.

   *Leices.* The queen's commission, urg'd by Mortimer;
What cannot gallant Mortimer with the queen?
Alas! see where he sits, and hopes unseen          51
T' escape their hands that seek to reave his life.
Too true it is, *Quem dies vidit veniens superbum,
Hunc dies vidit fugiens jacentem.*
But, Leicester, leave to grow so passionate.          55
Spencer and Baldock, by no other names,
I arrest you of high treason here.
Stand not on titles, but obey th' arrest;
'T is in the name of Isabel the queen.
My lord, why droop you thus?          60
   *K. Edw.* O day, the last of all my bliss on earth!
Centre of all misfortune! O my stars,
Why do you lour unkindly on a king?
Comes Leicester, then, in Isabella's name
To take my life, my company, from me?          65
Here, man, rip up this panting breast of mine,
And take my heart in rescue of my friends!
   *Rice.* Away with them!
   *Spen.*          It may become thee yet
To let us take our farewell of his grace.
   *Abbot.* My heart with pity earns to see this sight. —          70
A king to bear these words and proud commands!
   *K. Edw.* Spencer, ah, sweet Spencer, thus then must we part?
   *Spen.* We must, my lord, so will the angry Heavens.
   *K. Edw.* Nay, so will hell and cruel Mortimer;
The gentle Heavens have not to do in this.          75
   *Bald.* My lord, it is in vain to grieve or storm.
Here humbly of your grace we take our leaves;
Our lots are cast; I fear me, so is thine.
   *K. Edw.* In Heaven we may, in earth never shall we meet:
And, Leicester, say, what shall become of us?          80
   *Leices.* Your majesty must go to Killingworth.
   *K. Edw.* Must! 't is somewhat hard, when kings *must* go.
   *Leices.* Here is a litter ready for your grace,
That waits your pleasure, and the day grows old.
   *Rice.* As good be gone, as stay and be benighted.          85
   *K. Edw.* A litter hast thou? Lay me in a hearse,
And to the gates of hell convey me hence;
Let Pluto's bells ring out my fatal knell,
And hags howl for my death at Charon's shore,
For friends hath Edward none but these and these,          90

---

⁴⁸ commission: authorization in writing          ⁵³⁻⁵⁴ Quem . . . jacentem: "Whom the opening day saw proud, the departing day saw lying low." (From Seneca's *Thyestes.*)          ⁵⁵ leave: cease          ⁶⁷ rescue: quittance          ⁷⁰ earns: pines          ⁸¹ Killingworth: Kenilworth          ⁹⁰ but these: the monks

And these must die under a tyrant's sword.
  *Rice.* My lord, be going; care not for these,
For we shall see them shorter by the heads.
  *K. Edw.* Well, that shall be, shall be; part
    we must!                                94
Sweet Spencer, gentle Baldock, part we must!
Hence, feigned weeds! unfeigned are my woes.
                      [*Throws off his disguise.*]
Father, farewell! Leicester, thou stay'st for
    me,
And go I must. Life, farewell, with my friends.
                      *Exeunt Edward and Leicester.*
  *Spen.* O! is he gone? Is noble Edward
    gone?
Parted from hence, never to see us more?   100
Rent, sphere of Heaven! and, fire, forsake thy
    orb!
Earth, melt to air! gone is my sovereign,
Gone, gone, alas! never to make return.
  *Bald.* Spencer, I see our souls are fleeted
    hence;
We are depriv'd the sunshine of our life:  105
Make for a new life, man; throw up thy eyes,
And heart, and hand to Heaven's immortal
    throne;
Pay nature's debt with cheerful countenance;
Reduce we all our lessons unto this:       109
To die, sweet Spencer, therefore live we all;
Spencer, all live to die, and rise to fall.
  *Rice.* Come, come, keep these preachments
till you come to the place appointed. You,
and such as you are, have made wise work in
England. Will your lordships away?         115
  *Mow.* Your worship, I trust, will remember
    me?
  *Rice.* Remember thee, fellow! what else?
    Follow me to the town.        [*Exeunt.*]

## [ACT V

### Scene I. — *Kenilworth Castle.*]

*Enter the King, Leicester, with a Bishop [of
  Winchester] for the crown [and Sir William
  Trussel]*

  *Leices.* Be patient, good my lord, cease to
    lament.
Imagine Killingworth Castle were your court,
And that you lay for pleasure here a space,
Not of compulsion or necessity.
  *K. Edw.* Leicester, if gentle words might
    comfort me,                             5
Thy speeches long ago had eas'd my sorrows;
For kind and loving hast thou always been.
The griefs of private men are soon allay'd,
But not of kings. The forest deer, being struck,

Runs to an herb that closeth up the wounds; 10
But, when the imperial lion's flesh is gor'd,
He rends and tears it with his wrathful paw,
And highly scorning that the lowly earth
Should drink his blood, mounts up into the air.
And so it fares with me, whose dauntless mind
The ambitious Mortimer would seek to curb, 16
And that unnatural queen, false Isabel,
That thus hath pent and mew'd me in a prison;
For such outrageous passions cloy my soul,
As with the wings of rancour and disdain   20
Full often am I soaring up to Heaven,
To plain me to the gods against them both.
But when I call to mind I am a king,
Methinks I should revenge me of the wrongs
That Mortimer and Isabel have done.        25
But what are kings, when regiment is gone,
But perfect shadows in a sunshine day?
My nobles rule, I bear the name of king;
I wear the crown, but am controll'd by them,
By Mortimer, and my unconstant queen,      30
Who spots my nuptial bed with infamy;
Whilst I am lodg'd within this cave of care,
Where sorrow at my elbow still attends,
To company my heart with sad laments,
That bleeds within me for this strange ex-
    change.                                35
But tell me, must I now resign my crown,
To make usurping Mortimer a king?
  *Bish.* Your grace mistakes; it is for Eng-
    land's good,
And princely Edward's right we crave the
    crown.
  *K. Edw.* No, 't is for Mortimer, not Edward's
    head;                                  40
For he 's a lamb, encompassed by wolves,
Which in a moment will abridge his life.
But if proud Mortimer do wear this crown,
Heavens turn it to a blaze of quenchless fire!
Or like the snaky wreath of Tisiphon       45
Engirt the temples of his hateful head!
So shall not England's vine be perished,
But Edward's name survives, though Edward
    dies.
  *Leices.* My lord, why waste you thus the
    time away?
They stay your answer; will you yield your
    crown?                                 50
  *K. Edw.* Ah, Leicester, weigh how hardly I
    can brook
To lose my crown and kingdom without cause;
To give ambitious Mortimer my right,
That like a mountain overwhelms my bliss!  54
In which extreme my mind here murther'd is.
But what the heavens appoint, I must obey!
Here, take my crown; the life of Edward too!

---

⁹¹ **And these:** Spencer and Baldock    ¹⁰¹ **Rent:** rend    ¹¹⁶ **remember:** *i.e.,* with a gratuity
¹³ **And:** (Not in Qq.)    ²⁷ **sunshine:** sunny    ⁴⁵ **Tisiphon:** Tisiphone, one of the three Furies
⁴⁶ **Engirt:** may it surround    ⁴⁷ **vine:** ('Vines' Qq.)    ⁵¹ **weigh:** consider

Two kings in England cannot reign at once.
                              [*Taking off the crown.*]
But stay awhile, let me be king till night,
That I may gaze upon this glittering crown; 60
So shall my eyes receive their last content,
My head the latest honour due to it,
And jointly both yield up their wished right.
Continue ever thou celestial sun;
Let never silent night possess this clime:      65
Stand still you watches of the element;
All times and seasons, rest you at a stay,
That Edward may be still fair England's
    king!
But day's bright beams doth vanish fast away,
And needs I must resign my wished crown. 70
Inhuman creatures! nurs'd with tiger's milk!
Why gape you for your sovereign's overthrow?
My diadem, I mean, and guiltless life.
See, monsters, see, I 'll wear my crown again!
                              [*He puts on the crown.*]
What, fear you not the fury of your king?    75
But, hapless Edward, thou art fondly led;
They pass not for thy frowns as late they did,
But seeks to make a new-elected king;
Which fills my mind with strange despairing
    thoughts,
Which thoughts are martyr'd with endless
    torments                                   80
And in this torment comfort find I none,
But that I feel the crown upon my head;
And therefore let me wear it yet awhile.
    *Trus.* My lord, the parliament must have
    present news,
And therefore say, will you resign or no?    85
                              *The King rageth.*
    *K. Edw.* I 'll not resign, but whilst I live be
    king.
Traitors, be gone and join you with Mortimer!
Elect, conspire, install, do what you will: —
Their blood and yours shall seal these treach-
    eries!
    *Bish.* This answer we 'll return, and so
    farewell.          [*Going with Trussel.*] 90
    *Leices.* Call them again, my lord, and speak
    them fair;
For if they go, the prince shall lose his right.
    *K. Edw.* Call thou them back, I have no
    power to speak.
    *Leices.* My lord, the king is willing to resign.
    *Bish.* If he be not, let him choose.      95
    *K. Edw.* O would I might, but heavens and
    earth conspire
To make me miserable! Here receive my
    crown.
Receive it? No, these innocent hands of mine

Shall not be guilty of so foul a crime.
He of you all that most desires my blood,   100
And will be call'd the murtherer of a king,
Take it. What, are you mov'd? Pity you me?
Then send for unrelenting Mortimer,
And Isabel, whose eyes, being turn'd to steel,
Will sooner sparkle fire than shed a tear.   105
Yet stay, for rather than I will look on them,
Here, here!                 [*Gives the crown.*]
            Now, sweet God of Heaven,
Make me despise this transitory pomp.
And sit for aye enthronized in Heaven!
Come, death, and with thy fingers close my
    eyes,                                     110
Or if I live, let me forget myself.
    *Bish.* My lord —
    *K. Edw.* Call me not lord; away — out of
    my sight!
Ah, pardon me: grief makes me lunatic!
Let not that Mortimer protect my son;        115
More safety is there in a tiger's jaws
Than his embracements. Bear this to the queen,
Wet with my tears, and dried again with sighs.
                          [*Gives a handkerchief.*]
If with the sight thereof she be not mov'd,
Return it back and dip it in my blood.       120
Commend me to my son, and bid him rule
Better than I. Yet how have I transgress'd,
Unless it be with too much clemency?
    *Trus.* And thus most humbly do we take our
    leave.                                    124
    *K. Edw.* Farewell;      [*Exeunt the Bishop
                        of Winchester and Trussel.*]
        I know the next news that they bring
Will be my death; and welcome shall it be;
To wretched men death is felicity.

*Enter Berkeley* [*who gives a paper to Leicester*]

    *Leices.* Another post! what news brings he?
    *K. Edw.* Such news as I expect — come,
    Berkeley, come,
And tell thy message to my naked breast. 130
    *Berk.* My lord, think not a thought so vil-
    lainous
Can harbour in a man of noble birth.
To do your highness service and devoir,
And save you from your foes, Berkeley would
    die.
    *Leices.* My lord, the council of the queen
    commands                                  135
That I resign my charge.
    *K. Edw.* And who must keep me now? Must
    you, my lord?
    *Berk.* Ay, my most gracious lord; so 't is
    decreed.

---

⁶⁶ **watches:** stars   **element:** sky   ⁶⁷ **at a stay:** immovable   ⁷⁶ **fondly led:** deluded   ⁸⁴ **present:** immediate   ⁸⁶ **be king:** (Not in Qq.)   ¹⁰⁴ **being:** ('beene' Q 1)   ¹¹⁵ **protect:** be guardian of   ¹²⁹ **Berkeley:** (spelled 'Bartley' Qq., which make him enter at line 112)   ¹³⁰ **tell thy message:** *i.e.,* aim thy dagger

*K. Edw.* [*Taking the paper.*] By Mortimer,
whose name is written here! 139
Well may I rent his name that rends my heart!
[*Tears it.*]
This poor revenge hath something eas'd my
mind.
So may his limbs be torn, as is this paper!
Hear me, immortal Jove, and grant it too!
*Berk.* Your grace must hence with me to
Berkeley straight.
*K. Edw.* Whither you will; all places are
alike, 145
And every earth is fit for burial.
*Leices.* Favour him, my lord, as much as lieth
in you.
*Berk.* Even so betide my soul as I use him.
*K. Edw.* Mine enemy hath pitied my estate,
And that 's the cause that I am now remov'd.
*Berk.* And thinks your grace that Berkeley
will be cruel? 151
*K. Edw.* I know not; but of this am I as-
sured,
That death ends all, and I can die but once.
Leicester, farewell!
*Leices.* Not yet, my lord; I 'll bear you on
your way. *Exeunt omnes.* 155

[SCENE II. — *London.*]

*Enter Mortimer and Queen Isabel*

*Mor.* Fair Isabel, now have we our desire:
The proud corrupters of the light-brain'd king
Have done their homage to the lofty gallows,
And he himself lies in captivity.
Be rul'd by me, and we will rule the realm. 5
In any case take heed of childish fear,
For now we hold an old wolf by the ears,
That, if he slip, will seize upon us both,
And gripe the sorer, being gripp'd himself.
Think therefore, madam, that imports us much
To erect your son with all the speed we may, 11
And that I be protector over him;
For our behoof will bear the greater sway
Whenas a king's name shall be under writ.
*Que.* Sweet Mortimer, the life of Isabel,
Be thou persuaded that I love thee well; 16
And therefore, so the prince my son be safe,
Whom I esteem as dear as these mine eyes,
Conclude against his father what thou wilt,
And I myself will willingly subscribe. 20
*Mor.* First would I hear news that he were
depos'd,
And then let me alone to handle him.

*Enter Messenger*

Letters! from whence?
*Mess.* From Killingworth, my lord.

*Que.* How fares my lord the king?
*Mess.* In health, madam, but full of pensive-
ness. 25
*Que.* Alas, poor soul, would I could ease
his grief!
[*Enter the Bishop of Winchester with the crown*]
Thanks, gentle Winchester. [*To the Messenger.*]
Sirrah, be gone. [*Exit Messenger.*]
*Bish.* The king hath willingly resign'd his
crown.
*Que.* O happy news! send for the prince,
my son.
*Bish.* Further, or this letter was seal'd,
Lord Berkeley came, 30
So that he now is gone from Killingworth;
And we have heard that Edmund laid a plot
To set his brother free; no more but so.
The lord of Berkeley is so pitiful
As Leicester that had charge of him before. 35
*Que.* Then let some other be his guardian.
*Mor.* Let me alone, here is the privy seal.
[*Exit Bishop.*]
Who 's there? — Call hither Gurney and Matre-
vis. [*To Attendants within.*]
To dash the heavy-headed Edmund's drift, 39
Berkeley shall be discharg'd, the king remov'd,
And none but we shall know where he lieth.
*Que.* But, Mortimer, as long as he survives,
What safety rests for us, or for my son?
*Mor.* Speak, shall he presently be des-
patch'd and die?
*Que.* I would he were, so 't were not by
my means. 45

*Enter Matrevis and Gurney*

*Mor.* Enough. —
Matrevis, write a letter presently
Unto the lord of Berkeley from ourself,
That he resign the king to thee and Gurney; 49
And when 't is done, we will subscribe our name.
*Mat.* It shall be done, my lord.
*Mor.* Gurney.
*Gur.* My lord.
*Mor.* As thou intendest to rise by Mortimer,
Who now makes Fortune's wheel turn as he
please,
Seek all the means thou canst to make him
droop, 54
And neither give him kind word nor good look.
*Gur.* I warrant you, my lord.
*Mor.* And this above the rest: because we hear
That Edmund casts to work his liberty,
Remove him still from place to place by night,
Till at the last he come to Killingworth, 60
And then from thence to Berkeley back again;
And by the way, to make him fret the more,

141 **something:** somewhat 149 **enemy:** *i.e.,* Leicester 10 **imports:** it concerns **us:** ('as' Q 1–2]
11 **erect:** establish (as king) 13 **behoof:** interest 30 **or:** before 33 **no . . . so:** positively that
34 **so:** equally 37 **Let me alone:** Leave it to me.

Speak curstly to him, and in any case
Let no man comfort him; if he chance to weep,
But amplify his grief with bitter words.      65
   *Mat.* Fear not, my lord, we 'll do as you
   command.
   *Mor.* So now away; post thitherwards
   amain.
   *Que.* Whither goes this letter? To my
   lord the king?
Commend me humbly to his majesty,
And tell him that I labour all in vain      70
To ease his grief, and work his liberty;
And bear him this as witness of my love.
                 *[Gives a token.]*
   *Mat.* I will, madam.
     *Exeunt Matrevis and Gurney. Manent*
     *Isabel and Mortimer.*

*Enter the young Prince and the Earl of Kent*
        *talking with him*

   *Mor.* Finely dissembled. Do so still, sweet
   queen.
Here comes the young prince with Earl of
   Kent.      75
   *Que.* Something he whispers in his childish
   ears.
   *Mor.* If he have such access unto the prince,
Our plots and stratagems will soon be dash'd.
   *Que.* Use Edmund friendly, as if all were
   well.
   *Mor.* How fares my honourable lord of
   Kent?      80
   *Kent.* In health, sweet Mortimer. How
   fares your grace?
   *Que.* Well, if my lord your brother were
   enlarg'd.
   *Kent.* I hear of late he hath depos'd himself.
   *Que.* The more my grief.
   *Mor.*      And mine.
   *Kent.* [*Aside.*]    Ah, they do dissemble!
   *Que.* Sweet son, come hither, I must talk
   with thee.      85
   *Mor.* Thou being his uncle, and the next
   of blood,
Do look to be protector o'er the prince.
   *Kent.* Not I, my lord; who should protect
   the son,
But she that gave him life? I mean the queen.
   *Prince.* Mother, persuade me not to wear
   the crown:      90
Let him be king — I am too young to reign.
   *Que.* But be content, seeing it his highness'
   pleasure.
   *Prince.* Let me but see him first, and then
   I will.
   *Kent.* Ay, do, sweet nephew.
   *Que.* Brother, you know it is impossible.   95

   *Prince.* Why, is he dead?
   *Que.* No, God forbid!
   *Kent.* I would those words proceeded from
   your heart.
   *Mor.* Inconstant Edmund, dost thou favour
   him,
That wast a cause of his imprisonment?   100
   *Kent.* The more cause have I now to make
   amends.
   *Mor.* [*Aside to Que. Isab.*] I tell thee, 't is not
   meet that one so false
Should come about the person of a prince. —
My lord, he hath betray'd the king his brother,
And therefore trust him not.      105
   *Prince.* But he repents, and sorrows for it now.
   *Que.* Come, son, and go with this gentle lord
   and me.
   *Prince.* With you I will, but not with Mor-
   timer.
   *Mor.* Why, youngling, 'sdain'st thou so of
   Mortimer?
Then I will carry thee by force away.   110
   *Prince.* Help, uncle Kent! Mortimer will
   wrong me.
   *Que.* Brother Edmund, strive not; we are
   his friends;
Isabel is nearer than the Earl of Kent.
   *Kent.* Sister, Edward is my charge, redeem
   him.
   *Que.* Edward is my son, and I will keep
   him.      115
   *Kent.* Mortimer shall know that he hath
   wrong'd me! —
[*Aside.*] Hence will I haste to Killingworth
   Castle,
And rescue aged Edward from his foes,
To be reveng'd on Mortimer and thee.
                   *Exeunt omnes.*

[SCENE III. — *Country, near Kenilworth.*]
   *Enter Matrevis and Gurney* [*and Soldiers,*]
           *with the King*

   *Mat.* My lord, be not pensive, we are your
   friends;
Men are ordain'd to live in misery.
Therefore come, — dalliance dangereth our
   lives.
   *K. Edw.* Friends, whither must unhappy
   Edward go?
Will hateful Mortimer appoint no rest?      5
Must I be vexed like the nightly bird,
Whose sight is loathsome to all winged fowls?
When will the fury of his mind assuage?
When will his heart be satisfied with blood?
If mine will serve, unbowel straight this breast,
And give my heart to Isabel and him;      11
It is the chiefest mark they level at.

   [31] **grace:** *i.e.,* the Queen   [82] **enlarg'd:** liberated   [118] **aged:** the elder   [12] **chiefest . . . at:**
mark they chiefly aim at

*Gur.* Not so, my liege: the queen hath given
　this charge
To keep your grace in safety;
Your passions make your dolours to increase.
　*K. Edw.* This usage makes my misery in-
　　crease.　　　　　　　　　　　　　　　　16
But can my air of life continue long
When all my senses are annoy'd with stench?
Within a dungeon England's king is kept,
Where I am starv'd for want of sustenance.　20
My daily diet is heart-breaking sobs,
That almost rents the closet of my heart.
Thus lives old Edward not reliev'd by any,
And so must die, though pitied by many.
O, water, gentle friends, to cool my thirst,　25
And clear my body from foul excrements!
　*Mat.* Here 's channel water, as our charge is
　　given.
Sit down, for we 'll be barbers to your grace.
　*K. Edw.* Traitors, away! What, will you
　　murther me,
Or choke your sovereign with puddle water?　30
　*Gur.* No; but wash your face, and shave
　　away your beard,
Lest you be known and so be rescued.
　*Mat.* Why strive you thus? Your labour is
　　in vain!
　*K. Edw.* The wren may strive against the
　　lion's strength,
But all in vain: so vainly do I strive　　　35
To seek for mercy at a tyrant's hand.
　　　*They wash him with puddle water,*
　　　*and shave his beard away.*
Immortal powers! that knows the painful cares
That waits upon my poor distressed soul,
O level all your looks upon these daring men,
That wrongs their liege and sovereign, Eng-
　　land's king!　　　　　　　　　　　　　40
O Gaveston, it is for thee that I am wrong'd.
For me, both thou and both the Spencers died!
And for your sakes a thousand wrongs I 'll take.
The Spencers' ghosts, wherever they remain,　44
Wish well to mine; then tush, for them I 'll die.
　*Mat.* 'Twixt theirs and yours shall be no en-
　　mity.
Come, come away; now put the torches out,
We 'll enter in by darkness to Killingworth.

　　　*Enter Edmund [Kent]*

　*Gur.* How now, who comes there?
　*Mat.* Guard the king sure: it is the Earl of
　　Kent.　　　　　　　　　　　　　　　　50
　*K. Edw.* O gentle brother, help to rescue me!
　*Mat.* Keep them asunder; thrust in the king.
　*Kent.* Soldiers, let me but talk to him one word.
　*Gur.* Lay hands upon the earl for this assault.
　*Kent.* Lay down your weapons, traitors!
　　Yield the king!　　　　　　　　　　　55

　*Mat.* Edmund, yield thou thyself, or thou
　　shalt die.
　*Kent.* Base villains, wherefore do you gripe
　　me thus?
　*Gur.* Bind him and so convey him to the court.
　*Kent.* Where is the court but here? Here is
　　the king;
And I will visit him; why stay you me?　　60
　*Mat.* The court is where Lord Mortimer re-
　　mains;
Thither shall your honour go; and so farewell.
　　　*Exeunt Matrevis and Gurney, with*
　　　*the king. Manent Edmund and the*
　　　*Soldiers.*
　*Kent.* O miserable is that commonweal,
Where lords keep courts, and kings are lock'd
　　in prison!
　*Sol.* Wherefore stay we? On, sirs, to the
　　court!　　　　　　　　　　　　　　　65
　*Kent.* Ay, lead me whither you will, even to
　　my death,
Seeing that my brother cannot be releas'd.
　　　　　　　　　　　　　*Exeunt omnes.*

　　　[SCENE IV. — *The Court, London.*]

　　　　　*Enter Mortimer, alone*

　*Mor.* The king must die, or Mortimer goes
　　down;
The commons now begin to pity him.
Yet he that is the cause of Edward's death,
Is sure to pay for it when his son 's of age;
And therefore will I do it cunningly.　　　5
This letter, written by a friend of ours,
Contains his death, yet bids them save his life.
　　　　　　　　　　　　　　　　[*Reads.*]
"*Edwardum occidere nolite timere, bonum est:*
Fear not to kill the king, 't is good he die."
But read it thus, and that 's another sense:　10
"*Edwardum occidere nolite, timere bonum est:*
Kill not the king, 't is good to fear the worst."
Unpointed as it is, thus shall it go,
That, being dead, if it chance to be found,
Matrevis and the rest may bear the blame,　15
And we be quit that caus'd it to be done.
Within this room is lock'd the messenger
That shall convey it, and perform the rest;
And by a secret token that he bears,
Shall he be murder'd when the deed is done. —
Lightborn, come forth!　　　　　　　　21

　　　　　[*Enter Lightborn*]

Art thou as resolute as thou wast?
　*Light.* What else, my lord? And far more
　　resolute.
　*Mor.* And hast thou cast how to accomplish
　　it?
　*Light.* Ay, ay, and none shall know which
　　way he died.　　　　　　　　　　　25

---

¹⁷ **air:** breath Sc. IV.　¹³ **Unpointed:** unpunctuated　²⁴ **cast:** plotted

*Mor.* But at his looks, Lightborn, thou wilt relent.

*Light.* Relent! ha, ha! I use much to relent.

*Mor.* Well, do it bravely, and be secret.

*Light.* You shall not need to give instructions; 'Tis not the first time I have kill'd a man. 30
I learn'd in Naples how to poison flowers;
To strangle with a lawn thrust through the throat;
To pierce the windpipe with a needle's point;
Or whilst one is asleep, to take a quill
And blow a little powder in his ears; 35
Or open his mouth and pour quicksilver down.
And yet I have a braver way than these.

*Mor.* What's that?

*Light.* Nay, you shall pardon me; none shall know my tricks.

*Mor.* I care not how it is, so it be not spied. 40
Deliver this to Gurney and Matrevis.
                              [*Gives letter.*]
At every ten miles' end thou hast a horse.
Take this; [*Gives money.*] away! and never see me more.

*Light.* No?

*Mor.* No; 45
Unless thou bring me news of Edward's death.

*Light.* That will I quickly do. Farewell, my lord. [*Exit.*]

*Mor.* The prince I rule, the queen do I command,
And with a lowly congé to the ground,
The proudest lords salute me as I pass; 50
I seal, I cancel, I do what I will.
Fear'd am I more than lov'd; — let me be fear'd,
And when I frown, make all the court look pale.
I view the prince with Aristarchus' eyes,
Whose looks were as a breeching to a boy. 55
They thrust upon me the protectorship,
And sue to me for that that I desire.
While at the council-table, grave enough,
And not unlike a bashful puritan,
First I complain of imbecility, 60
Saying it is *onus quam gravissimum,*
Till being interrupted by my friends,
*Suscepi* that *provinciam* as they term it;
And to conclude, I am Protector now.
Now is all sure: the queen and Mortimer 65
Shall rule the realm, the king; and none rule us.
Mine enemies will I plague, my friends advance;
And what I list command who dare control?
*Major sum quam cui possit fortuna nocere.*
And that this be the coronation-day, 70
It pleaseth me, and Isabel the queen.
                              [*Trumpets within.*]
The trumpets sound, I must go take my place.

*Enter the young King, [Arch]Bishop, Champion, Nobles, Queen*

*Arch.* Long live King Edward, by the grace of God
King of England and Lord of Ireland!

*Cham.* If any Christian, Heathen, Turk, or Jew, 75
Dares but affirm that Edward 's not true king,
And will avouch his saying with the sword,
I am the champion that will combat him.

*Mor.* None comes, sound trumpets.
                              [*Trumpets sound.*]

*King [Edw. III].* Champion, here 's to thee.
                              [*Gives a purse.*]

*Que.* Lord Mortimer, now take him to your charge. 80

*Enter Soldiers, with the Earl of Kent prisoner*

*Mor.* What traitor have we there with blades and bills?

*Sol.* Edmund, the Earl of Kent.

*King [Edw. III].* What hath he done?

*Sol.* 'A would have taken the king away perforce,
As we were bringing him to Killingworth.

*Mor.* Did you attempt his rescue, Edmund? Speak. 85

*Kent.* Mortimer, I did. He is our king,
And thou compell'st this prince to wear the crown.

*Mor.* Strike off his head! he shall have martial law.

*Kent.* Strike off my head! Base traitor, I defy thee!

*King.* My lord, he is my uncle, and shall live. 90

*Mor.* My lord, he is your enemy, and shall die.

*Kent.* Stay, villains!

*King.* Sweet mother, if I cannot pardon him,
Entreat my Lord Protector for his life.

*Que.* Son, be content; I dare not speak a word. 95

*King.* Nor I, and yet methinks I should command;
But, seeing I cannot, I 'll entreat for him. —
My lord, if you will let my uncle live,
I will requite it when I come to age.

*Mor.* 'T is for your highness' good, and for the realm's. — 100
How often shall I bid you bear him hence?

*Kent.* Art thou king? Must I die at thy command?

---

³² **lawn:** filmy cloth    **through:** down    ⁴⁹ **congé:** reverence    ⁵⁴ **Aristarchus:** an Alexandrian grammarian, famed for severity    ⁵⁵ **breeching:** flogging    ⁶⁰ **imbecility:** incompetence    ⁶¹ **onus,** etc.: a most heavy burden    ⁶³ **Suscepi . . . provinciam:** I accepted the duty.    ⁶⁹ "I am too great for fortune to harm me." (Ovid, *Met.* vi. 195)    ⁷⁷ **avouch:** support

*Mor.* At our command — Once more away with him.

*Kent.* Let me but stay and speak; I will not go.
Either my brother or his son is king,          105
And none of both them thirst for Edmund's blood:
And therefore, soldiers, whither will you hale me?

> *They hale Edmund away, and carry him to be beheaded.*

*King.* What safety may I look for at his hands,
If that my uncle shall be murthered thus?

*Que.* Fear not, sweet boy, I 'll guard thee from thy foes;          110
Had Edmund liv'd, he would have sought thy death.
Come, son, we 'll ride a-hunting in the park.

*King.* And shall my uncle Edmund ride with us?

*Que.* He is a traitor; think not on him; come.          *Exeunt omnes.*

[SCENE V. — *Berkeley Castle.*]

*Enter Matrevis and Gurney*

*Mat.* Gurney, I wonder the king dies not,
Being in a vault up to the knees in water,
To which the channels of the castle run,
From whence a damp continually ariseth,
That were enough to poison any man,          5
Much more a king brought up so tenderly.

*Gur.* And so do I, Matrevis: yesternight
I opened but the door to throw him meat,
And I was almost stifled with the savour.

*Mat.* He hath a body able to endure          10
More than we can inflict: and therefore now
Let us assail his mind another while.

*Gur.* Send for him out thence, and I will anger him.

*Mat.* But stay, who 's this?

*Enter Lightborn*

*Light.*          My Lord Protector greets you.
          [*Gives letter.*]

*Gur.* What 's here? I know not how to conster it.          15

*Mat.* Gurney, it was left unpointed for the nonce,
"*Edwardum occidere nolite timere,*"
That 's his meaning.

*Light.* Know you this token? I must have the king.          [*Gives token.*]

*Mat.* Ay. Stay awhile, thou shalt have answer straight. —          20
[*Aside.*] This villain 's sent to make away the king.

*Gur.* [*Aside.*] I thought as much.

*Mat.* [*Aside.*] And when the murder 's done,
See how he must be handled for his labour.
*Pereat iste!* Let him have the king. —          24
What else? Here is the keys, this is the lake.
Do as you are commanded by my lord.

*Light.* I know what I must do. Get you away.
Yet be not far off, I shall need your help;
See that in the next room I have a fire,
And get me a spit, and let it be red-hot.          30

*Mat.* Very well.

*Gur.*          Need you anything besides?

*Light.* What else? A table and a feather-bed.

*Gur.* That 's all?

*Light.* Ay, ay; so, when I call you, bring it in.

*Mat.* Fear not you that.          35

*Gur.* Here 's a light, to go into the dungeon.
          [*Gives a light, and then exit with Matrevis.*]

*Light.* So now
Must I about this gear; ne'er was there any
So finely handled as this king shall be.          39
          [*Draws curtain before rear stage.*]
Foh! here 's a place indeed, with all my heart!

*K. Edw.* Who 's there? What light is that?
Wherefore com'st thou?

*Light.* To comfort you, and bring you joyful news.

*K. Edw.* Small comfort finds poor Edward in thy looks.
Villain, I know thou com'st to murther me.          44

*Light.* To murther you, my most gracious lord!
Far is it from my heart to do you harm.
The queen sent me to see how you were used,
For she relents at this your misery:
And what eyes can refrain from shedding tears,
To see a king in this most piteous state?          50

*K. Edw.* Weep'st thou already? List awhile to me
And then thy heart, were it as Gurney's is,
Or as Matrevis', hewn from the Caucasus,
Yet will it melt, ere I have done my tale.          54
This dungeon where they keep me is the sink
Wherein the filth of all the castle falls.

*Light.* O villains!

*K. Edw.* And there in mire and puddle have I stood
This ten days' space; and, lest that I should sleep,
One plays continually upon a drum.          60
They give me bread and water, being a king;
So that, for want of sleep and sustenance,
My mind 's distemper'd, and my body 's numb'd,
And whether I have limbs or no I know not.          64
O, would my blood dropp'd out from every vein,
As doth this water from my tatter'd robes.
Tell Isabel, the queen, I look'd not thus

---

106 them: ('then' Q 1)          15 conster: construe          16 for the nonce: by chance          24 Pereat iste: "Let this fellow die."          25 lake: dungeon          38 gear: affair          41 com'st: ('comes' Q 1)

When for her sake I ran at tilt in France,
And there unhors'd the Duke of Cleremont.
   *Light.* O speak no more, my lord! this breaks
   my heart. 70
Lie on this bed, and rest yourself awhile.
   *K. Edw.* These looks of thine can harbour
   nought but death:
I see my tragedy written in thy brows.
Yet stay awhile; forbear thy bloody hand,
And let me see the stroke before it comes, 75
That even then when I shall lose my life,
My mind may be more steadfast on my God.
   *Light.* What means your highness to mis-
   trust me thus?
   *K. Edw.* What mean'st thou to dissemble
   with me thus?
   *Light.* These hands were never stain'd with
   innocent blood, 80
Nor shall they now be tainted with a king's.
   *K. Edw.* Forgive my thought. For having
   such a thought —
One jewel have I left — receive thou this.
                   *[Giving jewel.]*
Still fear I, and I know not what 's the cause,
But every joint shakes as I give it thee. 85
O, if thou harbour'st murther in thy heart,
Let this gift change thy mind, and save thy soul!
Know that I am a king: O, at that name
I feel a hell of grief! Where is my crown?
Gone, gone! and do *I* remain alive? 90
   *Light.* You 're overwatch'd, my lord; lie
   down and rest.
   *K. Edw.* But that grief keeps me waking, I
   should sleep;
For not these ten days have these eye-lids clos'd.
Now as I speak they fall, and yet with fear
Open again. O wherefore sitt'st thou here? 95
   *Light.* If you mistrust me, I 'll begone, my
   lord.
   *K. Edw.* No, no, for if thou mean'st to mur-
   ther me,
Thou wilt return again, and therefore stay.
   *Light.* He sleeps.
   *K. Edw.* [*Waking.*] O let me not die yet!
   Stay, O stay a while! 100
   *Light.* How now, my lord?
   *K. Edw.* Something still buzzeth in mine
   ears,
And tells me, if I sleep I never wake.
This fear is that which makes me tremble thus.
And therefore tell me, wherefore art thou come?
   *Light.* To rid thee of thy life. — Matrevis,
   come! 106

       *[Enter Matrevis and Gurney]*

   *K. Edw.* I am too weak and feeble to resist:

Assist me, sweet God, and receive my soul!
   *Light.* Run for the table.
   *K. Edw.* O spare me, or despatch me in a
   trice.    [*Matrevis brings in a table.*] 110
   *Light.* So, lay the table down, and stamp on it,
But not too hard, lest that you bruise his body.
               *[King Edward is murdered.]*
   *Mat.* I fear me that this cry will raise the
   town,
And therefore, let us take horse and away. 114
   *Light.* Tell me, sirs, was it not bravely done?
   *Gur.* Excellent well: take this for thy reward.
          *Then Gurney stabs Lightborn.*
Come, let us cast the body in the moat,
And bear the king's to Mortimer our lord:
Away!                *Exeunt omnes.*

      [SCENE VI. — *London.*]

     *Enter Mortimer and Matrevis*

   *Mor.* Is 't done, Matrevis, and the mur-
   therer dead?
   *Mat.* Ay, my good lord; I would it were
   undone!
   *Mor.* Matrevis, if thou now growest penitent,
I 'll be thy ghostly father; therefore choose,
Whether thou wilt be secret in this, 5
Or else die by the hand of Mortimer.
   *Mat.* Gurney, my lord, is fled, and will, I fear,
Betray us both. Therefore let me fly.
   *Mor.* Fly to the savages!
   *Mat.* I humbly thank your honour. [*Exit.*] 10
   *Mor.* As for myself, I stand as Jove's huge
   tree,
And others are but shrubs compar'd to me.
All tremble at my name, and I fear none;
Let 's see who dare impeach me for his death!

       *Enter the Queen*

   *Que.* Ah, Mortimer, the king, my son, hath
   news 15
His father 's dead, and we have murder'd him!
   *Mor.* What if he have? The king is yet a
   child.
   *Que.* Ay, ay, but he tears his hair, and
   wrings his hands,
And vows to be reveng'd upon us both.
Into the council-chamber he is gone, 20
To crave the aid and succour of his peers.
Ay me! see where he comes, and they with him.
Now, Mortimer, begins our tragedy.

  *Enter the King* [*Edward the Third*] *with the Lords*

   *1 Lord.* Fear not, my lord, know that you
   are a king.
   *King.* Villain! —            25
   *Mor.* How now, my lord!
   *King.* Think not that I am frighted with thy
   words!

---

⁷⁶ **even:** ('and euen' Qq.)    ⁹¹ **overwatch'd:** weak from sleeplessness    ⁹⁵ **sitt'st:** ('sits' Qq.)
²⁴ **1 Lord:** ('Lords' Qq.)

My father 's murdered through thy treachery;
And thou shalt die, and on his mournful hearse
Thy hateful and accursed head shall lie,     30
To witness to the world, that by thy means
His kingly body was too soon interr'd.

*Que.* Weep not, sweet son!

*King.* Forbid not me to weep: he was my
father;
And had you lov'd him half so well as I,     35
You could not bear his death thus patiently.
But you, I fear, conspir'd with Mortimer.

*1 Lord.* Why speak you not unto my lord the
king?

*Mor.* Because I think scorn to be accus'd.
Who is the man dare say I murdered him?     40

*King.* Traitor! in me my loving father
speaks,
And plainly saith, 't was thou that murd'redst
him.

*Mor.* But hath your grace no other proof
than this?

*King.* Yes, if this be the hand of Mortimer.
                    [*Shewing letter.*]

*Mor.* [*Aside.*] False Gurney hath betray'd
me and himself.     45

*Que.* [*Aside.*] I fear'd as much; murther
cannot be hid.

*Mor.* 'T is my hand; what gather you by
this?

*King.* That thither thou didst send a murtherer.

*Mor.* What murtherer? Bring forth the
man I sent.

*King.* Ah, Mortimer, thou knowest that he
is slain;     50
And so shalt thou be too. — Why stays he here?
Bring him unto a hurdle, drag him forth;
Hang him, I say, and set his quarters up;
But bring his head back presently to me.

*Que.* For my sake, sweet son, pity Mortimer!     55

*Mor.* Madam, entreat not, I will rather die,
Than sue for life unto a paltry boy.

*King.* Hence with the traitor! with the
murderer!

*Mor.* Base Fortune, now I see, that in thy
wheel
There is a point, to which when men aspire,     60
They tumble headlong down: that point I
touch'd,
And, seeing there was no place to mount up
higher,
Why should I grieve at my declining fall? —
Farewell, fair queen; weep not for Mortimer,
That scorns the world, and, as a traveller,     65
Goes to discover countries yet unknown.

*King.* What! suffer you the traitor to delay?
                    [*Mortimer is led away.*]

*Que.* As thou receivedest thy life from me,
Spill not the blood of gentle Mortimer!

*King.* This argues that you spilt my father's
blood;     70
Else would you not entreat for Mortimer.

*Que.* I spill his blood? No!

*King.* Ay, madam, you; for so the rumour
runs.

*Que.* That rumour is untrue; for loving
thee,
Is this report rais'd on poor Isabel.     75

*King.* I do not think her so unnatural.

*2 Lord.* My lord, I fear me it will prove too
true.

*King.* Mother, you are suspected for his
death,
And therefore we commit you to the Tower
Till further trial may be made thereof;     80
If you be guilty, though I be your son,
Think not to find me slack or pitiful.

*Que.* Nay, to my death, for too long have
I liv'd,
Whenas my son thinks to abridge my days.

*King.* Away with her, her words enforce
these tears,     85
And I shall pity her if she speak again.

*Que.* Shall I not mourn for my beloved
lord,
And with the rest accompany him to his grave?

*2 Lord.* Thus, madam; 't is the king's will
you shall hence.

*Que.* He hath forgotten me; stay, I am his
mother.     90

*2 Lord.* That boots not; therefore, gentle
madam, go.

*Que.* Then come, sweet death, and rid me
of this grief.                    [*Exit.*]

[*Re-enter 1 Lord, with the head of Mortimer*]

*1 Lord.* My lord, here is the head of Mortimer.

*King.* Go fetch my father's hearse where it
shall lie;
And bring my funeral robes.
                    [*Exeunt Attendants.*]
                    Accursed head,     95
Could I have rul'd thee then, as I do now,
Thou had'st not hatch'd this monstrous treach-
ery! —
Here comes the hearse; help me to mourn, my
lords.

[*Enter Attendants with the hearse and funeral
robes*]

Sweet father, here unto thy murdered ghost
I offer up this wicked traitor's head;     100
And let these tears, distilling from mine eyes,
Be witness of my grief and innocency.
                    [*Exeunt.*]

35, 93 **1 Lord:** ('Lords' Qq.)     77, 89, 91 **2 Lord:** ('Lords' Qq.)     91 **boots:** avails

# THE
# SHOMAKERS
## Holiday.
### OR
## *The Gentle Craft.*

## With the humorous life of Simon
## Eyre, fhoomaker, and Lord Maior
## of London.

As it was aɛted before the Queenes moſt excellent Ma-
ieſtie on New-yeares day at night laſt, by the right
honourable the Earle of Notingham, Lord high Ad-
mirall of England, his feruants.

Printed by Valentine Sims dwelling at the foote of Adling
hill, neere Bainards Caſtle, at the figne of the White
Swanne, and are there to be fold.
**1 6 0 0.**

BIBLIOGRAPHICAL RECORD. Valentine Simmes, a good printer with a rather bad civic record, published the first edition of *The Shoemakers' Holiday* in 1600, prefacing it with the following advertisement to the readers: — *To All Good Fellowes, Professors of the Gentle Craft, of what degree soever. Kinde gentlemen and honest boone companions, I present you here with a merrie-conceited comedie, called The Shoomakers Holyday, acted by my Lorde Admiralls Players this present Christmasse before the Queenes most excellent Maiestie. For the mirth and pleasant matter by her Highnesse graciously accepted, being indeede no way offensive. The Argument of the play I will set downe in this epistle: Sir Hugh Lacie, Earle of Lincolne, had a yong Gentleman of his owne name, his nere kinsman, that loued the Lorde Maiors daughter of London; to preuent and crosse which loue, the earle caused his kinsman to be sent coronell of a companie into France: who resigned his place to another gentleman his friend, and came disguised like a Dutch shoomaker to the house of Symon Eyre in Towerstreete, who serued the Maior and his household with shooes. The merriments that passed in Eyres house, his comming to be Maior of London, Lacies getting his loue, and other accidents, with two merry Three-mens songs. Take all in good worth that is well intended, for nothing is purposed but mirth; mirth lengthneth long life, which, with all other blessings, I heartily wish you. Farewell!*

Simmes, who was having trouble with the authorities at the time, and who did not usually publish the books he printed, seems not to have entered the play on the Stationers' Register, but on April 19, 1610, he transferred his claim to it to John Wright, reserving the right to "haue the workmanship of the printinge thereof for the vse of the sayd John Wrighte during his lyfe." Wright consequently published the second edition in 1610, but employed George Eld, not Simmes, to print it. Other editions were published by Wright in 1618, 1624, and 1631, and a sixth came out in 1657. It is noteworthy that all these quartos are printed in black-letter type, which, even in 1600, was being seldom used except in books that appealed to old-fashioned readers. (The same peculiarity is found in the editions of Marlowe's *Tamburlaine* and *Dr. Faustus*.) All the quartos of *The Shoemakers' Holiday* are anonymous.

DATE AND STAGE PERFORMANCE. The date of the play, as well as its authorship, is determined by an entry in Henslowe's Diary: "Lent vnto Samewell Rowley & Thomas downton the 15 of July 1599 to bye a Boocke of thomas dickers Called the gentle craft the some of iij li." This £3 was doubtless a part payment (being half of what Dekker normally received) and it was paid in behalf of the company of the Earl of Nottingham (Lord Admiral), by whom the Quarto tells us the comedy had been produced. The production at court before the Queen, by the same company, occurred Jan. 1, 1600. An interesting article on "The Players Who Acted in *The Shoemakers' Holiday*" in the *Shakespeare Society Papers*, iv. 110-122 (1849) purports to give, from early manuscript notes in a copy of the 1600 Quarto, the names of the actors who performed the different rôles (Downton having the part of Eyre and Rowley that of Lincoln). The same authority asserts that in this copy the epistle "To all Good Fellowes" quoted above has the signatures, likewise in manuscript, of T. Dekker and R. Wilson; from which he argues that Dekker was assisted in the play by the dramatist Robert Wilson. These things may be true, but the copy of the play with the alleged annotations has not since been heard of, and the tendency is to regard the article as a fraud.

STRUCTURE. The play is of the loose "chronicle" type, suited to the rapid and often vague technique of Henslowe's playhouse. The quartos mark neither acts nor scenes, and the act divisions of modern editions are purely artificial. Dekker probably bothered about the matter only to the extent of inserting an "*Exeunt*," and in verse passages usually a rime-tag, at the close of each episode in his panorama. His main purpose was to present a foreshortened view of the progress up the civic ladder of the legendary Simon Eyre, stated by Stow to have built Leadenhall in 1419, become sheriff of London in 1434, and Lord Mayor in 1445. This serves as stiffening for the rich incrustation of episodes, romantic and realistic, attached to it.

SOURCES. The definite source and inspiration for Dekker's play were a series of prose tales about romantic shoemakers by Thomas Deloney, entitled *The Gentle Craft*, published in the preceding year. Here was found a long account of Eyre; also the tale of Crispine and Crispianus, which suggested the Rose and Lacy plot, and the legend of St. Hugh's bones. In developing his theme Dekker frequently echoes Marlowe, as was his habit, and still more often points to the popular plays by Shakespeare which were filling the rival theatre of the Globe. The King (historically Henry VI) and the wars in France are evidently meant to suggest the hero of the contemporary *Henry V* (who won Agincourt on St. Crispine's Day), and passages in the Hammon story, as Professor R. A. Law has pointed out (*Studies in Philology*, Apr., 1924, p. 356 ff.) echo *Romeo and Juliet*. The name Lacy for the juvenile hero comes from Greene's *Friar Bacon and Friar Bungay*.

# THOMAS DEKKER (1572?–1632)

## THE SHOEMAKERS' HOLIDAY

[DRAMATIS PERSONAE

THE KING (Henry V?)
EARL OF LINCOLN (Sir Hugh Lacy)
EARL OF CORNWALL
ROWLAND LACY, Lincoln's nephew
ASKEW, another relative
LOVELL, a courtier
DODGER, servant to Lincoln

SIR ROGER OTLEY, Lord Mayor of London
Master HAMMON,
Master WARNER, } Citizens of London
Master SCOTT,

SIMON EYRE, the Shoemaker
ROGER (known as HODGE),
FIRK, } EYRE'S workmen
RAFE DAMPORT,

ROSE, daughter of OTLEY
SYBIL, her maid
MARGERY, wife of EYRE
JANE, wife of RAFE

A Dutch Skipper, a Boy, Officers, Soldiers, Shoemakers, and Apprentices.

SCENE: The City of London and the adjacent village of Old Ford.]

## THE PROLOGUE

*As it was pronounced before the Queen's Majesty*

As wretches in a storm, expecting day,
With trembling hands and eyes cast up to heaven,
Make prayers the anchor of their conquer'd hopes,
So we, dear goddess, wonder of all eyes,
Your meanest vassals, through mistrust and fear      5
To sink into the bottom of disgrace
By our imperfect pastimes, prostrate thus
On bended knees, our sails of hope do strike,
Dreading the bitter storms of your dislike.
Since then, unhappy men, our hap is such      10
That to ourselves ourselves no help can bring,
But needs must perish, if your saint-like ears,
Locking the temple where all mercy sits,
Refuse the tribute of our begging tongues;
Oh, grant, bright mirror of true chastity,      15
From those life-breathing stars, your sun-like eyes,
One gracious smile; for your celestial breath
Must send us life, or sentence us to death.

[ACT I

SCENE I. — *A London Street.*]

*Enter Lord Mayor, [and the Earl of] Lincoln*

*Linc.* My lord mayor, you have sundry times
Feasted myself and many courtiers more;
Seldom or never can we be so kind
To make requital of your courtesy.

But, leaving this, I hear my cousin Lacy      5
Is much affected to your daughter Rose.
   *L. Mayor.* True, my good lord, and she loves
      him so well
That I mislike her boldness in the chase.
   *Linc.* Why, my lord mayor, think you it
      then a shame,
To join a Lacy with an Otley's name?      10
   *L. Mayor.* Too mean is my poor girl for his
      high birth;

⁵ cousin: nephew

265

Poor citizens must not with courtiers wed,
Who will in silks and gay apparel spend
More in one year than I am worth, by far:
Therefore your honour need not doubt my
    girl.                                          15
    *Linc.* Take heed, my lord; advise you what
    you do!
A verier unthrift lives not in the world,
Than is my cousin; for I 'll tell you what:
'T is now almost a year since he requested
To travel countries for experience.             20
I furnish'd him with coin, bills of exchange,
Letters of credit, men to wait on him,
Solicited my friends in Italy
Well to respect him. But, to see the end!
Scant had he journey'd through half Germany,
But all his coin was spent, his men cast off, 26
His bills embezzl'd, and my jolly coz,
Asham'd to show his bankrupt presence here,
Became a shoemaker in Wittenberg.
A goodly science for a gentleman               30
Of such descent! Now judge the rest by this.
Suppose your daughter have a thousand pound,
He did consume me more in one half year:
And make him heir to all the wealth you
    have,
One twelvemonth's rioting will waste it all. 35
Then seek, my lord, some honest citizen
To wed your daughter to.
    *L. Mayor.*              I thank your lordship.
[*Aside.*]  Well,  fox,  I  understand  your
    subtlety. —
As for your nephew, let your lordship's eye
But watch his actions, and you need not fear,
For I have sent my daughter far enough.        41
And yet your cousin Rowland might do well,
Now he hath learn'd an occupation:
And yet I scorn to call him son-in-law.
    *Linc.* Ay, but I have a better trade for him.
I thank his grace, he hath appointed him       46
Chief colonel of all those companies
Must'red in London and the shires about,
To serve his highness in those wars of France.
See where he comes! —

*Enter Lovell, Lacy, and Askew*

                Lovell, what news with you?
    *Lovell.* My Lord of Lincoln, 't is his high-
    ness' will,                                     51
That presently your cousin ship for France
With all his powers; he would not for a million,
But they should land at Dieppe within four
    days.
    *Linc.* Go certify his grace, it shall be done.
                              *Exit Lovell.*

Now, cousin Lacy, in what forwardness        56
Are all your companies?
    *Lacy.*                    All well prepar'd.
The men of Hertfordshire lie at Mile-end;
Suffolk and Essex train in Tothill-fields;
The Londoners and those of Middlesex,        60
All gallantly prepar'd in Finsbury,
With frolic spirits long for their parting hour.
    *L. Mayor.* They have their imprest, coats,
    and furniture;
And, if it please your cousin Lacy come
To the Guildhall, he shall receive his pay;   65
And twenty pounds besides my brethren
Will freely give him, to approve our loves
We bear unto my lord, your uncle here.
    *Lacy.* I thank your honour.
    *Linc.*          Thanks, my good lord mayor. 69
    *L. Mayor.* At the Guildhall we will expect
    your coming.                       *Exit.*
    *Linc.* To approve your loves to me! No
    subtlety!
Nephew, that twenty pound he doth bestow
For joy to rid you from his daughter Rose.
But, cousins both, now here are none but
    friends,
I would not have you cast an amorous eye      75
Upon so mean a project as the love
Of a gay, wanton, painted citizen.
I know, this churl even in the height of scorn
Doth hate the mixture of his blood with thine.
I pray thee, do thou so! Remember, coz,       80
What honourable fortunes wait on thee.
Increase the king's love, which so brightly
    shines,
And gilds thy hopes. I have no heir but thee, —
And yet not thee, if with a wayward spirit
Thou start from the true bias of my love.      85
    *Lacy.* My lord, I will for honour, not desire
Of land or livings, or to be your heir,
So guide my actions in pursuit of France,
As shall add glory to the Lacies' name.
    *Linc.* Coz, for those words here 's thirty
    portagues,                                       90
And, nephew Askew, there 's a few for you.
Fair Honour, in her loftiest eminence,
Stays in France for you, till you fetch her
    thence.
Then, nephews, clap swift wings on your de-
    signs.                                            94
Begone, begone, make haste to the Guildhall;
There presently I 'll meet you. Do not stay:
Where honour beckons, shame attends delay.
                              *Exit.*
    *Askew.* How gladly would your uncle have
    you gone!

---

<sup>15</sup> **doubt:** concern yourself about    <sup>27</sup> **embezzl'd:** run through    <sup>41</sup> **sent:** (Not in Q 1)    <sup>46</sup> **grace:**
majesty    <sup>52</sup> **presently:** at once    <sup>63</sup> **imprest:** enlistment pay    **furniture:** equipment    <sup>66</sup> **brethren:**
*i.e.*, the aldermen    <sup>67</sup> **approve:** testify    <sup>85</sup> **bias:** bent, tendency    <sup>90</sup> **portagues:** large gold coins
worth nearly £5    <sup>97</sup> **beckons:** (misprinted 'becomes' Qq )

*Lacy.* True, coz, but I 'll o'erreach his poli-
cies.
I have some serious business for three days, 100
Which nothing but my presence can dispatch.
You, therefore, cousin, with the companies,
Shall haste to Dover; there I 'll meet with
you:
Or, if I stay past my prefixed time,     104
Away for France; we 'll meet in Normandy.
The twenty pounds my lord mayor gives to me
You shall receive, and these ten portagues,
Part of mine uncle's thirty. Gentle coz,
Have care to our great charge; I know your
wisdom
Hath tried itself in higher consequence.    110
    *Askew.* Coz, all myself am yours: yet have
this care,
To lodge in London with all secrecy.
Our uncle Lincoln hath, besides his own,
Many a jealous eye, that in your face
Stares only to watch means for your disgrace.
    *Lacy.* Stay, cousin, who be these?     116

*Enter Simon Eyre, [Margery] his wife, Hodge,*
    *Firk, Jane, and Rafe with a piece*

    *Eyre.* Leave whining, leave whining! Away
with this whimp'ring, this puling, these blub-
b'ring tears, and these wet eyes! I 'll get thy
husband discharg'd, I warrant thee, sweet
Jane. Go to!     121
    *Hodge.* Master, here be the captains.
    *Eyre.* Peace, Hodge; husht, ye knave, husht!
    *Firk.* Here be the cavaliers and the coronels,
master.     125
    *Eyre.* Peace, Firk; peace, my fine Firk!
Stand by with your pishery-pashery; away!
I am a man of the best presence; I 'll speak to
them, and they were Popes. — Gentlemen, captains, colonels, commanders! Brave men, [130
brave leaders, may it please you to give me audience. I am Simon Eyre, the mad shoemaker of
Tower Street; this wench, with the mealy mouth
that will never tire, is my wife, I can tell you;
here 's Hodge, my man and my foreman; [135
here 's Firk, my fine firking journeyman, and
this is blubbered Jane. All we come to be suitors
for this honest Rafe. Keep him at home, and as
I am a true shoemaker and a gentleman of the
gentle craft, buy spurs yourself, and I 'll [140
find ye boots these seven years.
    *Wife.* Seven years, husband?
    *Eyre.* Peace, midriff, peace! I know what
I do. Peace!     144
    *Firk.* Truly, master cormorant, you shall

do God good service to let Rafe and his wife
stay together. She 's a young new-married
woman; if you take her husband away from her
a-night, you undo her. She may beg in the day-
time, for he 's as good a workman at a prick
and an awl as any is in our trade.     151
    *Jane.* O let him stay, else I shall be undone.
    *Firk.* Ay, truly, she shall be laid at one side
like a pair of old shoes else, and be occupied
for no use.     155
    *Lacy.* Truly, my friends, it lies not in my
power:
The Londoners are press'd, paid, and set forth
By the lord mayor; I cannot change a man.
    *Hodge.* Why, then you were as good be a cor-
poral as a colonel, if you cannot discharge [160
one good fellow; and I tell you true, I think
you do more than you can answer, to press a
man within a year and a day of his marriage.
    *Eyre.* Well said, melancholy Hodge; gra-
mercy, my fine foreman.     165
    *Wife.* Truly, gentlemen, it were ill done for
such as you, to stand so stiffly against a poor
young wife, considering her case, she is new-
married; but let that pass. I pray, deal not
roughly with her; her husband is a young man,
and but newly ent'red; but let that pass.   171
    *Eyre.* Away with your pishery-pashery, your
pols and your edipols! Peace, midriff; silence, Cicely Bumtrinket! Let your head
speak.     175
    *Firk.* Yea, and the horns too, master.
    *Eyre.* Too soon, my fine Firk, too soon!
Peace, scoundrels! See you this man? Captains, you will not release him? Well, let him
go; he 's a proper shot; let him vanish! [180
Peace, Jane, dry up thy tears, they 'll make his
powder dankish. Take him, brave men! Hector of Troy was an hackney to him, Hercules
and Termagant scoundrels, Prince Arthur's
Round-table — by the Lord of Ludgate — [185
ne'er fed such a tall, such a dapper swordman;
by the life of Pharaoh, a brave resolute swordman! Peace, Jane! I say no more, mad knaves.
    *Firk.* See, see, Hodge, how my master raves
in commendation of Rafe!     190
    *Hodge.* Rafe, th' art a gull, by this hand,
and thou goest not.
    *Askew.* I am glad, good Master Eyre, it is
my hap
To meet so resolute a soldier.
Trust me, for your report and love to him, 195
A common slight regard shall not respect him.
    *Lacy.* Is thy name Rafe?

---

104 **prefixed:** appointed    116 S. D. **piece:** musket    124 **coronels:** colonels    127 **pishery-pashery:**
nonsense    129 **and:** an, if    136 **firking:** bouncing    143 **midriff:** diaphragm, talking machine
145 **cormorant:** (punning on "colonel")    157 **press'd:** enlisted    164–165 **gramercy:** thanks    173 **pols,**
**edipols:** exclamations    183 **hackney:** spiritless beast    184 **Termagant:** a fictitious Paynim fire-eater
191 **gull:** fool    196 "He shall have uncommon consideration"

*Rafe.*                    Yes, sir.
*Lacy.*                    Give me thy hand;
Thou shalt not want, as I am a gentleman.
Woman, be patient. God, no doubt, will send
Thy husband safe again; but he must go,  200
His country's quarrel says it shall be so.
*Hodge.* Th' art a gull, by my stirrup, if thou
dost not go. I will not have thee strike thy
gimlet into these weak vessels; prick thine
enemies, Rafe.                    205

### Enter Dodger

*Dodger.* My lord, your uncle on the Tower-
hill
Stays with the lord mayor and the aldermen,
And doth request you, with all speed you may,
To hasten thither.
*Askew.*                    Cousin, let 's go.
*Lacy.* Dodger, run you before, tell them we
come. —                    *Exit Dodger.*  210
This Dodger is mine uncle's parasite,
The arrant'st varlet that e'er breath'd on earth.
He sets more discord in a noble house
By one day's broaching of his pickthank tales,
Than can be salv'd again in twenty years;  215
And he, I fear, shall go with us to France,
To pry into our actions.
*Askew.*                    Therefore, coz,
It shall behoove you to be circumspect.
*Lacy.* Fear not, good cousin. — Rafe, hie to
your colours.       [*Exit Lacy and Askew.*]
*Rafe.* I must, because there 's no remedy;
But, gentle master and my loving dame,  221
As you have always been a friend to me,
So in mine absence think upon my wife.
*Jane.* Alas, my Rafe!
*Wife.*       She cannot speak for weeping.  224
*Eyre.* Peace, you crack'd groats, you mus-
tard tokens, disquiet not the brave soldier.
Go thy ways, Rafe!
*Jane.* Ay, ay, you bid him go! what shall I
do
When he is gone?
*Firk.* Why, be doing with me or my fellow
Hodge; be not idle.                    231
*Eyre.* Let me see thy hand, Jane. This fine
hand, this white hand, these pretty fingers must
spin, must card, must work; work, you bombast
cotton-candle-quean; work for your living, [235
with a pox to you. — Hold thee, Rafe, here 's
five sixpences for thee; fight for the honour of
the gentle craft, for the gentlemen shoemakers,
the courageous cordwainers, the flower of St.
Martin's, the mad knaves of Bedlam, Fleet [240
Street, Tower Street and Whitechapel; crack

me the crowns of the French knaves; a pox on
them, crack them; fight, by the Lord of Ludgate; fight, my fine boy!
*Firk.* Here, Rafe, here 's three two- [245
pences; two carry into France, the third shall
wash our souls at parting, for sorrow is dry. For
my sake, firk the *Basa mon cues.*
*Hodge.* Rafe, I am heavy at parting; but
here 's a shilling for thee. God send thee to [250
cram thy slops with French crowns, and thy
enemies' bellies with bullets.
*Rafe.* I thank you, master, and I thank
you all.
Now, gentle wife, my loving lovely Jane,
Rich men, at parting, give their wives rich
gifts,                    255
Jewels and rings, to grace their lily hands.
Thou know'st our trade makes rings for
women's heels:
Here take this pair of shoes, cut out by Hodge,
Stitch'd by my fellow Firk, seam'd by myself,
Made up and pink'd with letters for thy name.
Wear them, my dear Jane, for thy husband's
sake,                    261
And every morning when thou pull'st them on,
Remember me, and pray for my return.
Make much of them; for I have made them so
That I can know them from a thousand mo.  265

*Sound drum. Enter Lord Mayor, Lincoln, Lacy,
Askew, Dodger, and Soldiers. They pass
over the stage; Rafe falls in amongst them;
Firk and the rest cry "Farewell," etc., and
so exeunt.*

## [ACT II

### SCENE I. — *Lord Mayor's Garden, Old Ford.*]

*Enter Rose, alone, making a garland*

Here sit thou down upon this flow'ry bank
And make a garland for thy Lacy's head.
These pinks, these roses, and these violets,
These blushing gilliflowers, these marigolds,
The fair embroidery of his coronet,                    5
Carry not half such beauty in their cheeks,
As the sweet count'nance of my Lacy doth.
O my most unkind father! O my stars,
Why lower'd you so at my nativity,
To make me love, yet live robb'd of my love?
Here as a thief am I imprisoned                    11
For my dear Lacy's sake within those walls,
Which by my father's cost were builded up
For better purposes. Here must I languish
For him that doth as much lament, I know,  15
Mine absence, as for him I pine in woe.

---

[202] **stirrup:** strap that held shoemakers' work in place   [225-226] **groats:** fourpenny bits   **mustard tokens:** substitute currency, issued by shopkeepers   [248] **firk:** trounce   **Basa mon cues:** "baisez mon culs," opprobrious name for the French   [250] **send:** grant   [251] **slops:** loose breeches   [260] **pink'd:** perforated   [265] **mo:** more, others   [1] Compare *Midsummer Night's Dream* IV. i. 1

*Enter Sybil*

*Sybil.* Good morrow, young mistress. I am sure you make that garland for me, against I shall be Lady of the Harvest.

*Rose.* Sybil, what news at London? 20

*Sybil.* None but good: my lord mayor, your father, and master Philpot, your uncle, and Master Scott, your cousin, and Mistress Frigbottom by Doctors' Commons, do all, by my troth, send you most hearty commendations. [25

*Rose.* Did Lacy send kind greetings to his love?

*Sybil.* O yes, out of cry, by my troth. I scant knew him; here 'a wore a scarf; and here a scarf, here a bunch of feathers, and here precious stones and jewels, and a pair [30 of garters, — O, monstrous! like one of our yellow silk curtains at home here in Old Ford House here, in Master Bellymount's chamber. I stood at our door in Cornhill, look'd at him, he at me indeed, spake to him, but he not [35 to me, not a word. Marry gup, thought I, with a wanion! He pass'd by me as proud — Marry foh! are you grown humorous, thought I; and so shut the door, and in I came.

*Rose.* O Sybil, how dost thou my Lacy wrong! 40 My Rowland is as gentle as a lamb, No dove was ever half so mild as he.

*Sybil.* Mild? yea, as a bushel of stamp'd crabs. He look'd upon me as sour as verjuice. Go thy ways, thought I, thou may'st be [45 much in my gaskins, but nothing in my netherstocks. This is your fault, mistress, to love him that loves not you; he thinks scorn to do as he's done to; but if I were as you, I'd cry, "Go by, Jeronimo, go by!" 50

I'd set mine old debts against my new driblets, And the hare's foot against the goose giblets, For if ever I sigh, when sleep I should take, Pray God I may lose my maidenhead when I wake.

*Rose.* Will my love leave me then, and go to France? 55

*Sybil.* I know not that, but I am sure I see him stalk before the soldiers. By my troth, he is a proper man; but he is proper that proper doth. Let him go snick-up, young mistress. 60

*Rose.* Get thee to London, and learn perfectly

Whether my Lacy go to France, or no. Do this, and I will give thee for thy pains My cambric apron and my Romish gloves, My purple stockings and a stomacher. 65 Say, wilt thou do this, Sybil, for my sake?

*Sybil.* Will I, quoth 'a? At whose suit? By my troth, yes, I'll go. A cambric apron, gloves, a pair of purple stockings, and a stomacher! I'll sweat in purple, mistress, for you; [70 I'll take anything that comes a' God's name. O rich! a cambric apron! Faith, then have at 'up tails all.' I'll go jiggy-joggy to London, and be here in a trice, young mistress. *Exit.*

*Rose.* Do so, good Sybil. Meantime wretched I Will sit and sigh for his lost company. *Exit.* 76

[SCENE II. — *Tower Street, London.*]

*Enter Rowland Lacy, like a Dutch Shoemaker*

*Lacy.* How many shapes have gods and kings devis'd, Thereby to compass their desired loves! It is no shame for Rowland Lacy, then, To clothe his cunning with the gentle craft, That, thus disguis'd, I may unknown possess 5 The only happy presence of my Rose. For her have I forsook my charge in France, Incurr'd the king's displeasure, and stirr'd up Rough hatred in mine uncle Lincoln's breast. O love, how powerful art thou, that canst change 10 High birth to baseness, and a noble mind To the mean semblance of a shoemaker! But thus it must be; for her cruel father, Hating the single union of our souls, 14 Hath secretly convey'd my Rose from London, To bar me of her presence; but I trust, Fortune and this disguise will further me Once more to view her beauty, gain her sight. Here in Tower Street with Eyre the shoemaker Mean I a while to work. I know the trade, 20 I learnt it when I was in Wittenberg. Then cheer thy hoping sprites, be not dismay'd, Thou canst not want: do Fortune what she can, The gentle craft is living for a man. *Exit.*

[SCENE III. — *Before Eyre's Shop.*]

*Enter Eyre, making himself ready*

*Eyre.* Where be these boys, these girls, these drabs, these scoundrels? They wallow in the fat brewess of my bounty, and lick up the crumbs of my table, yet will not rise to see my walks

27 **out of cry:** beyond expression (ironic)   36 **Marry gup:** Go your way, forsooth!   37 **wanion:** plague   38 **humorous:** capricious   44 **crabs:** crabapples   **verjuice:** juice of green fruit   46–47 **gaskins:** breeches   **netherstocks:** stockings   50 (Cf. *Spanish Tragedy* III. xii. 30)   52 **hare's . . . giblets:** reconcile one thing with another. Cf. Dekker and Webster, *Westward Ho!* V. iii. (last page but one): 'set the hare's head against the goose-giblets, put all instruments in tune.'   58 **proper:** good-looking   59 **snick-up:** hang   73 **up tails all:** a card game   11 **baseness:** ('barenesse' Qq. 1–3) 22 **sprites:** spirits   Sc. III. s. d. **making . . . ready:** dressing   3 **brewess:** broth

cleansed. Come out, you powder-beef queans! What, Nan! what, Madge Mumble-crust! [6 Come out, you fat midriff, swag-belly-whores, and sweep me these kennels that the noisome stench offend not the noses of my neighbours. What, Firk, I say; what, Hodge! Open my [10 shop windows! What, Firk, I say!

*Enter Firk*

*Firk.* O master, is 't you that speak bandog and Bedlam this morning? I was in a dream, and mused what madman was got into the street so early. Have you drunk this morning that [15 your throat is so clear?

*Eyre.* Ah, well said, Firk; well said, Firk. To work, my fine knave, to work! Wash thy face, and thou 't be more blest.

*Firk.* Let them wash my face that will eat [20 it. Good master, send for a souse-wife, if you 'll have my face cleaner.

*Enter Hodge*

*Eyre.* Away, sloven! avaunt, scoundrel! — Good-morrow, Hodge; good-morrow, my fine foreman. 25

*Hodge.* O master, good-morrow; y' are an early stirrer. Here 's a fair morning. — Good-morrow, Firk, I could have slept this hour. Here 's a brave day towards.

*Eyre.* Oh, haste to work, my fine foreman, [30 haste to work.

*Firk.* Master, I am dry as dust to hear my fellow Roger talk of fair weather; let us pray for good leather, and let clowns and plough-boys and those that work in the fields pray [35 for brave days. We work in a dry shop; what care I if it rain?

*Enter Eyre's wife*

*Eyre.* How now, Dame Margery, can you see to rise? Trip and go, call up the drabs, your maids. 40

*Marg.* See to rise? I hope 't is time enough! 't is early enough for any woman to be seen abroad. I marvel how many wives in Tower Street are up so soon. Gods me, 't is not noon, — here 's a yawling! 45

*Eyre.* Peace, Margery, peace! Where 's Cicely Bumtrinket, your maid? She has a privy fault, she farts in her sleep. Call the quean up; if my men want shoe-thread, I 'll swinge her in a stirrup. 50

*Firk.* Yet, that 's but a dry beating; here 's still a sign of drought.

*Enter Lacy [disguised], singing*

*Lacy.*   *Der was een bore van Gelderland*
            *Frolick si byen;*
      *He was als dronck he cold nyet stand,*
            *Upsolce si byen.* 56
      *Tap eens de canneken,*
      *Drincke, schone mannekin.*

*Firk.* Master, for my life, yonder 's a [59 brother of the gentle craft; if he bear not Saint Hugh's bones, I 'll forfeit my bones. He 's some uplandish workman: hire him, good master, that I may learn some gibble-gabble; 't will make us work the faster. 64

*Eyre.* Peace, Firk! A hard world! Let him pass, let him vanish; we have journeymen enow. Peace, my fine Firk!

*Wife.* Nay, nay, y' are best follow your man's counsel; you shall see what will come on 't. We have not men enow, but we must entertain [70 every butter-box; but let that pass.

*Hodge.* Dame, 'fore God, if my master follow your counsel, he 'll consume little beef. He shall be glad of men, and he can catch them.

*Firk.* Ay, that he shall. 75

*Hodge.* 'Fore God, a proper man, and I warrant, a fine workman. Master, farewell; dame, adieu; if such a man as he cannot find work, Hodge is not for you.           *Offers to go.*

*Eyre.* Stay, my fine Hodge. 80

*Firk.* Faith, and your foreman go, dame, you must take a journey to seek a new journeyman; if Roger remove, Firk follows. If Saint Hugh's bones shall not be set a-work, I may prick mine awl in the walls, and go play. Fare ye well, master; good-bye, dame. 86

*Eyre.* Tarry, my fine Hodge, my brisk foreman! Stay, Firk! Peace, pudding-broth! By the Lord of Ludgate, I love my men as my life. Peace, you gallimaufry! Hodge, if he want [90

---

⁵ **powder-beef:** salt-beef     ⁸ **kennels:** gutters     ¹² **bandog:** chained dog     ¹³ **Bedlam:** madman     ²¹ **souse-wife:** vendor of pickled pigs' ears     ²⁹ **towards:** in prospect     ⁴⁵ **yawling:** howling     ⁵¹ **dry:** one that draws no blood (with pun)     ⁵³⁻⁵⁸ Dubious Dutch, probably meaning:

*There was a boor from Gelderland,*
      *Jolly they be;*
*He was so drunk he could not stand,*
            *Drunken (?) they be:*
*Clink on the cannikin,*
*Drink, pretty little man!*

⁶⁰⁻⁶¹ **Saint Hugh's bones:** bones of the shoemaker-martyr, turned into tools by his followers     ⁶² **uplandish:** provincial     ⁷⁰ **entertain:** hire     ⁷¹ **butter-box:** Dutchman     ⁷⁴, ⁸¹ **and:** if     ⁹⁰ **gallimaufry:** hodge-podge (of left-over meats)

work, I 'll hire him. One of you to him; stay, — he comes to us.

*Lacy.*   *Goeden dach, meester, ende u vro oak.*

*Firk.* Nails! if I should speak after him without drinking, I should choke. And you, [95 friend Oake, are you of the gentle craft?

*Lacy.*   *Yaw, yaw, ik bin den skomawker.*

*Firk.* "Den skomaker," quoth 'a! And hark you, "skomaker," have you all your tools, a good rubbing-pin, a good stopper, a good [100 dresser, your four sorts of awls, and your two balls of wax, your paring knife, your hand-and-thumb-leathers, and good St. Hugh's bones to smooth up your work?         104

*Lacy.*   *Yaw, yaw; be niet vorveard. Ik hab all de dingen voour mack skooes groot and cleane.*

*Firk.* Ha, ha! Good master, hire him; he 'll make me laugh so that I shall work more in mirth than I can in earnest.

*Eyre.* Hear ye, friend, have ye any skill [110 in the mystery of cordwainers?

*Lacy.*   *Ik weet niet wat yow seg; ich verstaw you niet.*

*Firk.* Why, thus, man: [*Imitating by ges-* [114 *ture a shoemaker at work.*] "Ich verste u niet," quoth 'a.

*Lacy.*   *Yaw, yaw, yaw; ick can dat wel doen.*

*Firk.* Yaw, yaw! He speaks yawing like a jackdaw that gapes to be fed with cheese-curds. Oh, he 'll give a villainous pull at a [120 can of double-beer; but Hodge and I have the vantage, we must drink first, because we are the eldest journeymen.

*Eyre.* What is thy name?

*Lacy.* Hans — Hans Meulter.      125

*Eyre.* Give me thy hand; th' art welcome. — Hodge, entertain him; Firk, bid him welcome; come, Hans. Run, wife, bid your maids, your trullibubs, make ready my fine men's breakfasts. To him, Hodge!      130

*Hodge.* Hans, th' art welcome; use thyself friendly, for we are good fellows; if not, thou shalt be fought with, wert thou bigger than a giant.

*Firk.* Yea, and drunk with, wert thou [135 Gargantua. My master keeps no cowards, I tell thee. — Ho, boy, bring him an heel-block, here 's a new journeyman.

*Enter Boy*

*Lacy.*   *O, ich wersto you; ich moet een halve dossen cans betalen; here, boy, nempt dis skill-ing, tap eens freelicke.*      *Exit Boy.* 141

*Eyre.* Quick, snipper-snapper, away! Firk, scour thy throat; thou shalt wash it with Castilian liquor.

*Enter Boy*

Come, my last of the fives, give me a can. Have to thee, Hans; here, Hodge; here, Firk; [146 drink, you mad Greeks, and work like true Trojans, and pray for Simon Eyre, the shoemaker. — Here, Hans, and th' art welcome.

*Firk.* Lo, dame, you would have lost a good fellow that will teach us to laugh. This [151 beer came hopping in well.

*Wife.* Simon, it is almost seven.

*Eyre.* Is 't so, Dame Clapper-dudgeon? Is 't seven o'clock, and my men's breakfast not ready? Trip and go, you sous'd conger, [156 away! Come, you mad hyperboreans; follow me, Hodge; follow me, Hans; come after, my fine Firk; to work, to work a while, and then to breakfast.       *Exit.*

*Firk.* Soft! Yaw, yaw, good Hans, [161 though my master have no more wit but to call you afore me, I am not so foolish to go behind you, I being the elder journeyman.    *Exeunt.*

[SCENE IV. — *Field near Old Ford.*]

*Halloaing within. Enter Warner and Hammon, like Hunters*

*Ham.* Cousin, beat every brake, the game 's
     not far.
This way with winged feet he fled from death,
Whilst the pursuing hounds, scenting his steps,
Find out his highway to destruction.
Besides, the miller's boy told me even now,   5
He saw him take soil, and he halloaed him,
Affirming him to have been so emboss'd
That long he could not hold.

*Warn.*             If it be so,
'T is best we trace these meadows by Old Ford.

*A noise of Hunters within. Enter a Boy*

*Ham.* How now, boy? Where 's the deer?
speak, saw'st thou him?         11

*Boy.* O yea; I saw him leap through a hedge, and then over a ditch, then at my lord mayor's pale: over he skipp'd me, and in he went me, and "Holla" the hunters cried, and "There, [15 boy; there, boy!" But there he is, o' mine honesty.

*Ham.* Boy, Godamercy. Cousin, let 's away; I hope we shall find better sport to-day.     19
                       *Exeunt.*

---

[93] "Good day, sir, and you, lady, too."    [105-106] "Yes, yes; be not fearful. I have all the things to make shoes, great and small."    [111] **mystery:** trade    [112] **verstaw:** understand    [139-141] "O, I understand you; I should like to pay for a half-dozen cans . . . take this shilling, drink gayly."    [145] **last . . . fives:** number five last, diminutive    [154] **Clapper-dudgeon:** beggar    [6] **take soil:** properly, seek refuge in water or marsh    [7] **to . . . been:** (Not in Qq.)    **emboss'd:** foaming    [18] **Godamercy:** many thanks

[SCENE V. — *Lord Mayor's Garden, Old Ford.*]

*Hunting within. Enter Rose and Sybil*

*Rose.* Why, Sybil, wilt thou prove a forester?
*Sybil.* Upon some, no. Forester? Go by;
no, faith, mistress. The deer came running into
the barn through the orchard and over the
pale; I wot well, I look'd as pale as a new cheese
to see him. But whip, says Goodman Pin- [6
close, up with his flail, and our Nick with a
prong, and down he fell, and they upon him,
and I upon them. By my troth, we had such
sport; and in the end we ended him; his throat
we cut, flay'd him, unhorn'd him, and my [11
lord mayor shall eat of him anon, when he
comes.                    *Horns sound within.*
*Rose.* Hark, hark, the hunters come; y' are
best take heed,
They 'll have a saying to you for this deed. 15

*Enter Hammon, Warner, Huntsmen, and
Boy*

*Ham.* God save you, fair ladies.
*Sybil.*                    Ladies! O gross!
*Warn.* Came not a buck this way?
*Rose.*                    No, but two does.
*Ham.* And which way went they? Faith,
we 'll hunt at those.
*Sybil.* At those? Upon some, no. When,
can you tell?
*Warn.* Upon some, ay.
*Sybil.*          Good Lord!
*Warn.*               Wounds! Then farewell! 20
*Ham.* Boy, which way went he?
*Boy.*                    This way, sir, he ran.
*Ham.* This way he ran indeed, fair Mistress
Rose;
Our game was lately in your orchard seen.
*Warn.* Can you advise, which way he took
his flight?
*Sybil.* Follow your nose; his horns will
guide you right.                    25
*Warn.* Th' art a mad wench.
*Sybil.*                    O, rich!
*Rose.*                    Trust me, not I.
It is not like that the wild forest-deer
Would come so near to places of resort;
You are deceiv'd, he fled some other way.
*Warn.* Which way, my sugar-candy, can
you shew?                    30
*Sybil.* Come up, good honeysops! upon some,
no.
*Rose.* Why do you stay, and not pursue your
game?
*Sybil.* I 'll hold my life, their hunting-nags
be lame.

*Ham.* A deer more dear is found within this
place.
*Rose.* But not the deer, sir, which you had
in chase.                    35
*Ham.* I chas'd the deer, but this dear chaseth
me.
*Rose.* The strangest hunting that ever I see.
But where 's your park? *She offers to go away.*
*Ham.* 'T is here: O stay!
*Rose.* Impale me, and then I will not stray.
*Warn.* They wrangle, wench; we are more
kind than they.                    40
*Sybil.* What kind of hart is that dear heart
you seek?
*Warn.* A hart, dear heart.
*Sybil.*                    Who ever saw the like?
*Rose.* To lose your hart, is 't possible you
can?
*Ham.* My heart is lost.
*Rose.*                    Alack, good gentleman!
*Ham.* This poor lost heart would I wish you
might find.                    45
*Rose.* You, by such luck, might prove your
hart a hind.
*Ham.* Why Luck had horns, so have I heard
some say.
*Rose.* Now, God, and 't be his will, send
Luck into your way.

*Enter Lord Mayor and Servants*

*L. Mayor.* What, Master Hammon? Wel-
come to Old Ford!
*Sybil.* Gods pittikins, hands off, sir! Here 's
my lord.                    50
*L. Mayor.* I hear you had ill luck, and lost
your game.
*Ham.* 'T is true, my lord.
*L. Mayor.*                    I am sorry for the same.
What gentleman is this?
*Ham.*                    My brother-in-law.
*L. Mayor.* Y' are welcome both; sith For-
tune offers you
Into my hands, you shall not part from hence,
Until you have refresh'd your wearied limbs. 56
Go, Sybil, cover the board! You shall be guest
To no good cheer, but even a hunter's feast.
*Ham.* I thank your lordship. — Cousin, on
my life,
For our lost venison I shall find a wife.      60
*L. Mayor.* In, gentlemen; I 'll not be ab-
sent long. —          *Exeunt [all but Mayor].*
This Hammon is a proper gentleman,
A citizen by birth, fairly allied;
How fit an husband were he for my girl!
Well, I will in, and do the best I can,      65
To match my daughter to this gentleman. *Exit.*

---

² **Upon some, no:** a finical asseveration      ¹⁵ **have . . . to:** pick a crow with      ¹⁶ **gross:** gross
flattery      ²⁶ **not I:** (in answer to Warner's question, line 24)      ³³ **hold:** wager      ³⁹ **Impale:** put
within a fence

[ACT III

SCENE I. — *Eyre's House.*]

*Enter Lacy [as Hans], Skipper, Hodge, and
Firk*

Skip. *Ick sal yow wat seggen, Hans; dis skip
dat comen from Candy, is all vol, by Got 's sacrament, van sugar, civet, almonds, cambrick, end
alle dingen, towsand towsand ding. Nempt it,
Hans, nempt it vor u meester. Daer be de bils* [5
*van laden. Your meester Simon Eyre sal hae
good copen. Wat seggen yow, Hans?*

Firk. *Wat seggen de reggen de copen, slopen*
— laugh, Hodge, laugh!          9

Hans. *Mine liever broder Firk, bringt Meester
Eyre tot det signe un Swannekin; daer sal yow
finde dis skipper end me. Wat seggen yow, broder
Firk? Doot it, Hodge.* Come, skipper.
                          *Exeunt.*

Firk. Bring him, quod you? Here 's no [14
knavery, to bring my master to buy a ship
worth the lading of two or three hundred
thousand pounds. Alas, that 's nothing; a
trifle, a bauble, Hodge.

Hodge. The truth is, Firk, that the merchant
owner of the ship dares not shew his head, [20
and therefore this skipper that deals for him,
for the love he bears to Hans, offers my master
Eyre a bargain in the commodities. He shall
have a reasonable day of payment; he may [24
sell the wares by that time, and be an huge
gainer himself.

Firk. Yea, but can my fellow Hans lend my
master twenty porpentines as an earnest penny?

Hodge. Portagues, thou wouldst say; here [29
they be, Firk; hark, they jingle in my pocket
like St. Mary Overy's bells.

*Enter Eyre and his Wife*

Firk. Mum! here comes my dame and my
master. She 'll scold, on my life, for loitering
this Monday; but all 's one. Let them all say
what they can, Monday 's our holiday.    35

Wife. You sing, Sir Sauce, but I beshrew your
heart.
I fear, for this your singing we shall smart.

Firk. Smart for me, dame; why, dame, why?

Hodge. Master, I hope you 'll not suffer my
dame to take down your journeymen.    40

Firk. If she take me down, I 'll take her up.
Yea, and take her down too, a button-hole lower.

Eyre. Peace, Firk; not I, Hodge; by the
life of Pharaoh, by the Lord of Ludgate, by
this beard, every hair whereof I value at a [45

king's ransom, she shall not meddle with you. —
Peace, you bombast-cotton-candle-quean; away,
queen of clubs; quarrel not with me and my
men, with me and my fine Firk; I 'll firk you,
if you do.                   50

Wife. Yea, yea, man, you may use me as
you please; but let that pass.

Eyre. Let it pass, let it vanish away; peace!
Am I not Simon Eyre? Are not these my [54
brave men, brave shoemakers, all gentlemen of
the gentle craft? Prince am I none, yet am I
nobly born, as being the sole son of a shoemaker. Away, rubbish! vanish, melt; melt
like kitchen-stuff.              59

Wife. Yea, yea, 't is well; I must be call'd
rubbish, kitchen-stuff, for a sort of knaves.

Firk. Nay, dame, you shall not weep and
wail in woe for me. Master, I 'll stay no
longer; here 's a vennentory of my shop-tools.
Adieu, master; Hodge, farewell.      65

Hodge. Nay, stay, Firk; thou shalt not go
alone.

Wife. I pray, let them go; there be mo
maids than Mawkin, more men than Hodge,
and more fools than Firk.         70

Firk. Fools? Nails! if I tarry now, I would
my guts might be turn'd to shoe-thread.

Hodge. And if I stay, I pray God I may be
turn'd to a Turk, and set in Finsbury for boys
to shoot at. — Come, Firk.         75

Eyre. Stay, my fine knaves, you arms of my
trade, you pillars of my profession. What,
shall a tittle-tattle's words make you forsake
Simon Eyre? — Avaunt, kitchen-stuff! Rip,
you brown-bread Tannikin; out of my sight!
Move me not! Have not I ta'en you from [81
selling tripes in Eastcheap, and set you in my
shop, and made you hail-fellow with Simon
Eyre, the shoemaker? And now do you deal [84
thus with my journeymen? Look, you powder-
beef-quean, on the face of Hodge: here 's a
face for a lord.

Firk. And here 's a face for any lady in
Christendom.               89

Eyre. Rip, you chitterling, avaunt! Boy,
bid the tapster of the Boar's Head fill me a
dozen cans of beer for my journeymen.

Firk. A dozen cans? O, brave! Hodge,
now I 'll stay.

Eyre. [*Aside to Boy.*] And the knave fills [95
any more than two, he pays for them. [*Exit
Boy. Aloud.*] — A dozen cans of beer for my
journeymen. [*Re-enter Boy.*] Here, you mad
Mesopotamians, wash your livers with this
liquor. Where be the odd ten? — No more, [100

---

⁴ **Nempt:** take   ⁷ **copen:** bargain   ³¹ **Overy:** over-the-water (a church on south bank of Thames, near London Bridge)   ⁵⁹ **kitchen-stuff:** grease   ⁶¹ **sort:** crew   ⁶⁴ **vennentory:** inventory   ⁷⁴ **Finsbury:** a practice ground for archers   ⁸⁰ **Tannikin:** nickname for Dutch women   ⁹⁰ **chitterling:** sausage

Madge, no more. — Well said. Drink and to work! — What work dost thou, Hodge? What work?

*Hodge.* I am a-making a pair of shoes for my lord mayor's daughter, Mistress Rose.    105

*Firk.* And I a pair of shoes for Sybil, my lord's maid. I deal with her.

*Eyre.* Sybil? Fie, defile not thy fine work-manly fingers with the feet of kitchenstuff [109 and basting-ladles. Ladies of the court, fine ladies, my lads, commit their feet to our ap-parelling; put gross work to Hans. Yark and seam, yark and seam!

*Firk.* For yarking and seaming let me alone, and I come to 't.    115

*Hodge.* Well, master, all this is from the bias. Do you remember the ship my fellow Hans told you of? The skipper and he are both drinking at the Swan. Here be the porta- [119 gues to give earnest. If you go through with it, you cannot choose but be a lord at least.

*Firk.* Nay, dame, if my master prove not a lord, and you a lady, hang me.

*Wife.* Yea, like enough, if you may loiter and tipple thus.    125

*Firk.* Tipple, dame? No, we have been bar-gaining with Skellum-Skanderbag-can-you-Dutch-spreaken for a ship of silk cypress, laden with sugar-candy.    129

*Enter the Boy with a velvet coat and an Alder-man's gown. Eyre puts it on.*

*Eyre.* Peace, Firk; silence, Tittle-tattle! Hodge, I 'll go through with it. Here 's a sealing-ring, and I have sent for a guarded gown and a damask cassock. See where it comes! look here, Maggy; help me, Firk; apparel me, Hodge: silk and satin, you mad Philistines, [135 silk and satin!

*Firk.* Ha, ha! my master will be as proud as a dog in a doublet, all in beaten damask and velvet.    139

*Eyre.* Softly, Firk, for rearing of the nap, and wearing threadbare my garments. How dost thou like me, Firk? How do I look, my fine Hodge?

*Hodge.* Why, now you look like yourself, master. I warrant you, there 's few in the [145 city but will give you the wall, and come upon you with the "right worshipful."

*Firk.* Nails, my master looks like a thread-bare cloak new turn'd and dress'd. Lord, [149 Lord, to see what good raiment doth! Dame, dame, are you not enamoured?

*Eyre.* How say'st thou, Maggy, am I not brisk? Am I not fine?

*Wife.* Fine? By my troth, sweetheart, very fine! By my troth, I never lik'd thee so well [155 in my life, sweetheart; but let that pass. I war-rant, there be many women in the city have not such handsome husbands, but only for their apparel; but let that pass too.    159

*Enter Hans and Skipper*

Hans. *Godden day, mester. Dis be de skipper dat heb de skip van marchandice; de commodity ben good; nempt it, mester, nempt it.*

*Eyre.* Godamercy, Hans; welcome, skipper. Where lies this ship of merchandise?    164

Skip. *De skip ben in revere; dor be van sugar, civet, almonds, cambrick, and a towsand, tow-sand tings, gotz sacrament; nempt it, mester: ye sal heb good copen.*

*Firk.* To him, master! O sweet master! [169 O sweet wares! Prunes, almonds, sugar-candy, carrot-roots, turnips, O brave fatting meat! Let not a man buy a nutmeg but yourself.

*Eyre.* Peace, Firk! Come, skipper, I 'll go aboard with you. — Hans, have you made him drink?    175

*Skip.* Yaw, yaw, ic heb veale gedrunck.

*Eyre.* Come, Hans, follow me. Skipper, thou shalt have my countenance in the city.
                                        *Exeunt.*

*Firk.* "Yaw, heb veale gedrunck," quoth 'a. They may well be called butter-boxes, when [180 they drink fat veal and thick beer too. But come, dame, I hope you 'll chide us no more.

*Wife.* No, faith, Firk; no, perdy, Hodge. I do feel honour creep upon me, and, which is more, a certain rising in my flesh; but let that pass.    186

*Firk.* Rising in your flesh do you feel, say you? Ay, you may be with child, but why should not my master feel a rising in his flesh, having a gown and a gold ring on? But you are such a shrew, you 'll soon pull him down. [191

*Wife.* Ha, ha! prithee, peace! Thou mak'st my worship laugh; but let that pass. Come, I 'll go in. Hodge, prithee, go before me; Firk, follow me.    195

*Firk.* Firk doth follow: Hodge, pass out in state.                                      *Exeunt.*

[SCENE II. — *Earl of Lincoln's House.*]

*Enter Lincoln and Dodger*

*Linc.* How now, good Dodger, what 's the news in France?

*Dodger.* My lord, upon the eighteenth day of May
The French and English were prepar'd to fight;

---

¹¹² **Yark:** pull (on the needle)   ¹¹⁶⁻¹¹⁷ **from . . . bias:** irrelevant   ¹²⁷ **Skellum:** knave   **Skander-bag:** John Kastriota, hero of a melodramatic play   ¹²⁸ **cypress:** fine cloth   ¹³² **guarded:** richly bor-dered   ¹³⁸ **beaten:** stamped   ¹⁴⁶ **give . . . wall:** yield precedence   ¹⁶⁵ **revere:** river   ¹⁷⁶ **veale:** much

Each side with eager fury gave the sign
Of a most hot encounter. Five long hours 5
Both armies fought together; at the length
The lot of victory fell on our sides.
Twelve thousand of the Frenchmen that day
died,
Four thousand English, and no man of name
But Captain Hyam and young Ardington, 10
Two gallant gentlemen, I knew them well.
   *Linc.* But Dodger, prithee, tell me, in this
fight
How did my cousin Lacy bear himself?
   *Dodger.* My lord, your cousin Lacy was not
there.
   *Linc.* Not there?
   *Dodger.*      No, my good lord.
   *Linc.*      Sure, thou mistakest. 15
I saw him shipp'd, and a thousand eyes beside
Were witnesses of the farewells which he gave,
When I, with weeping eyes, bid him adieu.
Dodger, take heed.
   *Dodger.*      My lord, I am advis'd
That what I spake is true: to prove it so, 20
His cousin Askew, that supplied his place,
Sent me for him from France, that secretly
He might convey himself thither.
   *Linc.*      Is 't even so?
Dares he so carelessly venture his life
Upon the indignation of a king? 25
Has he despis'd my love, and spurn'd those
favours
Which I with prodigal hand pour'd on his head?
He shall repent his rashness with his soul.
Since of my love he makes no estimate,
I 'll make him wish he had not known my
hate. 30
Thou hast no other news?
   *Dodger.*      None else, my lord.
   *Linc.* None worse I know thou hast. — Pro-
cure the king
To crown his giddy brows with ample honours,
Send him chief colonel, and all my hope 34
Thus to be dash'd! But 't is in vain to grieve:
One evil cannot a worse relieve.
Upon my life, I have found out his plot;
That old dog, Love, that fawn'd upon him so,
Love to that puling girl, his fair-cheek'd Rose,
The lord mayor's daughter, hath distracted
him, 40
And in the fire of that love's lunacy
Hath he burnt up himself, consum'd his credit,
Lost the king's love, yea, and, I fear, his life,
Only to get a wanton to his wife,
Dodger, it is so.
   *Dodger.*      I fear so, my good lord. 45
   *Linc.* It is so — nay, sure it cannot be'
I am at my wits' end. — Dodger!

   *Dodger.*      Yea, my lord.
   *Linc.* Thou art acquainted with my neph-
ew's haunts.
Spend this gold for thy pains; go seek him out.
Watch at my lord mayor's — there, if he live, 50
Dodger, thou shalt be sure to meet with him.
Prithee, be diligent. — Lacy, thy name
Liv'd once in honour, now 't is dead in shame. —
Be circumspect.      *Exit.*
   *Dodger.* I warrant you, my lord.      *Exit.*

[SCENE III. — *Lord Mayor's House, London.*]

   *Enter L. Mayor and Master Scott*

   *L. Mayor.* Good Master Scott, I have been
bold with you,
To be a witness to a wedding-knot
Betwixt young Master Hammon and my daugh-
ter.
O, stand aside; see where the lovers come.

   *Enter Hammon and Rose*

   *Rose.* Can it be possible you love me so? 5
No, no, within those eyeballs I espy
Apparent likelihoods of flattery.
Pray now, let go my hand.
   *Ham.*      Sweet Mistress Rose,
Misconstrue not my words, nor misconceive
Of my affection, whose devoted soul 10
Swears that I love thee dearer than my heart.
   *Rose.* As dear as your own heart? I judge
it right,
Men love their hearts best when th' are out of
sight.
   *Ham.* I love you, by this hand.
   *Rose.*      Yet hands off now!
If flesh be frail, how weak and frail 's your vow!
   *Ham.* Then by my life I swear.
   *Rose.*      Then do not brawl; 16
One quarrel loseth wife and life and all.
Is not your meaning thus?
   *Ham.*      In faith, you jest.
   *Rose.* Love loves to sport; therefore leave
love, y' are best.
   *L. Mayor.* What? square they, Master Scott?
   *Scott.* Sir, never doubt. 21
Lovers are quickly in, and quickly out.
   *Ham.* Sweet Rose, be not so strange in
fancying me.
Nay, never turn aside, shun not my sight:
I am not grown so fond, to fond my love
On any that shall quit it with disdain; 26
If you will love me, so; — if not, farewell.
   *L. Mayor.* Why, how now, lovers, are you
both agreed?
   *Ham.* Yes, faith, my lord.
   *L. Mayor.* 'T is well, give me your hand.

Give me yours, daughter. — How now, both
  pull back!                                        30
What means this, girl?
  *Rose.*            I mean to live a maid.
  *Ham.* [*Aside.*] But not to die one; pause, ere
    that be said.
  *L. Mayor.* Will you still cross me, still be
    obstinate?
  *Ham.* Nay, chide her not, my lord, for doing
    well;
If she can live an happy virgin's life,            35
'T is far more blessed than to be a wife.
  *Rose.* Say, sir, I cannot, I have made a vow:
Whoever be my husband, 't is not you.
  *L. Mayor.* Your tongue is quick; but Mas-
    ter Hammon, know,
I bade you welcome to another end.                 40
  *Ham.* What, would you have me pule and
    pine and pray,
With "lovely lady," "mistress of my heart,"
"Pardon your servant," and the rhymer play,
Railing on Cupid and his tyrant's-dart;
Or shall I undertake some martial spoil,          45
Wearing your glove at tourney and at tilt,
And tell how many gallants I unhors'd —
Sweet, will this pleasure you?
  *Rose.*                Yea, when wilt begin?
What, love rhymes, man? Fie on that deadly
    sin!
  *L. Mayor.* If you will have her, I 'll make
    her agree.                                      50
  *Ham.* Enforced love is worse than hate to
    me.
[*Aside.*] There is a wench keeps shop in the
    Old Change,
To her will I — it is not wealth I seek.
I have enough — and will prefer her love
Before the world. — [*Aloud.*] My good lord
    mayor, adieu.                                   55
Old love for me, I have no luck with new. *Exit.*
  *L. Mayor.* Now, mammet, you have well
    behav'd yourself,
But you shall curse your coyness if I live. —
Who 's within there? See you convey your mis-
    tress
Straight to th' Old Ford! I 'll keep you
    straight enough.                                60
Fore God, I would have sworn the puling girl
Would willingly accepted Hammon's love;
But banish him, my thoughts! — Go, minion,
    in!                                *Exit Rose.*
Now tell me, Master Scott, would you have
    thought
That Master Simon Eyre, the shoemaker,            65
Had been of wealth to buy such merchandise?
  *Scott.* 'T was well, my lord, your honour and
    myself

Grew partners with him; for your bills of lading
Shew that Eyre's gains in one commodity
Rise at the least to full three thousand pound
Besides like gain in other merchandise.           70
  *L. Mayor.* Well, he shall spend some of his
    thousands now,
For I have sent for him to the Guildhall.

                    *Enter Eyre*

See, where he comes. — Good morrow, Master
    Eyre.
  *Eyre.* Poor Simon Eyre, my lord, your shoe-
    maker.                                          75
  *L. Mayor.* Well, well, it likes yourself to
    term you so.

                   *Enter Dodger*

Now Master Dodger, what 's the news with
    you?
  *Dodger.* I 'd gladly speak in private to your
    honour.
  *L. Mayor.* You shall, you shall. — Master
    Eyre and Master Scott,
I have some business with this gentleman;          80
I pray, let me entreat you to walk before
To the Guildhall; I 'll follow presently.
Master Eyre, I hope ere noon to call you sheriff.
  *Eyre.* I would not care, my lord, if you
    might call me
King of Spain. — Come, Master Scott.              85
                    *Exeunt* [*Eyre and Scott*].
  *L. Mayor.* Now, Master Dodger, what 's the
    news you bring?
  *Dodger.* The Earl of Lincoln by me greets
    your lordship,
And earnestly requests you, if you can,
Inform him where his nephew Lacy keeps.
  *L. Mayor.* Is not his nephew Lacy now in
    France?                                         90
  *Dodger.* No, I assure your Lordship, but dis-
    guis'd
Lurks here in London.
  *L. Mayor.*          London? Is 't even so?
It may be; but upon my faith and soul,
I know not where he lives, or whether he lives:
So tell my Lord of Lincoln. — Lurch in Lon-
    don?                                            95
Well, Master Dodger, you perhaps may start
    him;
Be but the means to rid him into France,
I 'll give you a dozen angels for your pains:
So much I love his honour, hate his nephew.
And, prithee, so inform thy lord from me.         100
  *Dodger.* I take my leave.        *Exit Dodger.*
  *L. Mayor.* Farewell, good Master Dodger.
Lacy in London? I dare pawn my life,
My daughter knows thereof, and for that cause

---

⁵² **Old Change:** near St. Paul's (predecessor of Sir Thos. Gresham's "New Exchange")    ⁵⁷ **mammet:** puppet    ⁷⁶ **likes:** pleases    ⁹⁵ **Lurch:** lurk

Denied young Master Hammon in his love.
Well, I am glad I sent her to Old Ford.
Gods Lord. 't is late! to Guildhall I must hie;
I know my brethren stay my company. *Exit.* 107

[SCENE IV. — *Eyre's Shop.*]

*Enter Firk, Eyre's wife, [Lacy as] Hans, Roger*

*Wife.* Thou goest too fast for me, Roger.
O, Firk.
*Firk.* Ay, forsooth.
*Wife.* I pray thee, run — do you hear? — run
to Guildhall, and learn if my husband, Mas- [5
ter Eyre, will take that worshipful vocation of
Master Sheriff upon him. Hie thee, good Firk.
*Firk.* Take it? Well, I go; and he should
not take it, Firk swears to forswear him. Yes,
forsooth, I go to Guildhall. 10
*Wife.* Nay, when? Thou art too compendious and tedious.
*Firk.* O rare, your excellence is full of eloquence. How like a new cart-wheel my dame
speaks, and she looks like an old musty ale- [15
bottle going to scalding.
*Wife.* Nay, when? Thou wilt make me melancholy.
*Firk.* God forbid your worship should fall
into that humour; — I run. *Exit.* 20
*Wife.* Let me see now, Roger and Hans.
*Hodge.* Ay, forsooth, dame — mistress, I
should say, but the old term so sticks to the
roof of my mouth, I can hardly lick it off.
*Wife.* Even what thou wilt, good Roger; [25
dame is a fair name for any honest Christian;
but let that pass. How dost thou, Hans?
Hans. *Mee tanck you, vro.*
*Wife.* Well, Hans and Roger, you see, God
hath bless'd your master, and, perdy, if ever [30
he comes to be Master Sheriff of London
— as we are all mortal — you shall see, I will
have some odd thing or other in a corner for
you: I will not be your back-friend; but let
that pass. Hans, pray thee, tie my shoe. 35
Hans. *Yaw, ic sal, vro.*
*Wife.* Roger, thou know'st the length of my
foot; as it is none of the biggest, so I thank
God, it is handsome enough; prithee, let me
have a pair of shoes made: cork, good Roger, [40
wooden heel too.
*Hodge.* You shall.
*Wife.* Art thou acquainted with never a
fardingale-maker, nor a French hood-maker?
I must enlarge my bum, ha, ha! How shall [45
I look in a hood, I wonder! Perdy, oddly, I
think.
*Hodge.* [*Aside.*] As a cat out of a pillory. —
Very well, I warrant you, mistress.
*Wife.* Indeed, all flesh is grass; and, [50

Roger, canst thou tell where I may buy a good
hair?
*Hodge.* Yes, forsooth, at the poulterer's in
Gracious Street.
*Wife.* Thou art an ungracious wag: perdy, [55
I mean a false hair for my periwig.
*Hodge.* Why, mistress, the next time I cut
my beard, you shall have the shavings of it;
but they are all true hairs.
*Wife.* It is very hot. I must get me a fan [60
or else a mask.
*Hodge.* [*Aside.*] So you had need, to hide
your wicked face.
*Wife.* Fie upon it, how costly this world's
calling is; perdy, but that it is one of the [65
wonderful works of God, I would not deal with
it. — Is not Firk come yet? Hans, be not so
sad, let it pass and vanish, as my husband's
worship says.
Hans. *Ick bin vrolicke, lot see yow soo.* 70
*Hodge.* Mistress, will you drink a pipe of
tobacco?
*Wife.* Oh, fie upon it, Roger, perdy! These
filthy tobacco-pipes are the most idle slavering
baubles that ever I felt. Out upon it! God [75
bless us, men look not like men that use them.

*Enter Rafe, being lame*

*Hodge.* What, fellow Rafe? Mistress, look
here, Jane's husband! Why, how now, lame?
Hans, make much of him, he 's a brother of our
trade, a good workman, and a tall soldier. 80
*Hans.* You be welcome, broder.
*Wife.* Perdy, I knew him not. How dost
thou, good Rafe? I am glad to see thee well.
*Rafe.* I would to God you saw me, dame, as
well
As when I went from London into France. 85
*Wife.* Trust me, I am sorry, Rafe, to see
thee impotent. Lord, how the wars have made
him sunburnt! The left leg is not well; 't was
a fair gift of God the infirmity took not hold a
little higher, considering thou camest from [90
France; but let that pass.
*Rafe.* I am glad to see you well, and I rejoice
To hear that God hath bless'd my master so
Since my departure.
*Wife.* Yea, truly, Rafe. I thank my [95
Maker; but let that pass.
*Hodge.* And, sirrah Rafe, what news, what
news in France?
*Rafe.* Tell me, good Roger, first, what news
in England?
How does my Jane? When didst thou see my
wife? 100
Where lives my poor heart? She 'll be poor in-
deed,
Now I want limbs to get whereon to feed.

---

²⁸ **vro**: mistress    ³⁴ **back-friend**: false friend    ⁷¹ **drink**: smoke    ⁸⁴ **to**: (Not in Qq.)

*Hodge.* Limbs? Hast thou not hands, man? Thou shalt never see a shoemaker want bread, though he have but three fingers on a hand. [105

*Rafe.* Yet all this while I hear not of my Jane.

*Wife.* O Rafe, your wife, — perdy, we know not what's become of her. She was here a while, and because she was married, grew more stately than became her; I check'd her, and [110 so forth; away she flung, never returned, nor said bye nor bah; and, Rafe, you know, "ka me, ka thee." And so, as I tell ye —— Roger, is not Firk come yet?

*Hodge.* No, forsooth.                                    115

*Wife.* And so, indeed, we heard not of her, but I hear she lives in London; but let that pass. If she had wanted, she might have opened her case to me or my husband, or to any of my men. I am sure, there's not any of them, [120 perdy, but would have done her good to his power. Hans, look if Firk be come.

*Hans.* Yaw, ik sal, vro.            *Exit Hans.*

*Wife.* And so, as I said — but, Rafe, why dost thou weep? Thou knowest that naked [125 we came out of our mother's womb, and naked we must return; and, therefore, thank God for all things.

*Hodge.* No, faith, Jane is a stranger here; but, Rafe, pull up a good heart. I know [130 thou hast one. Thy wife, man, is in London; one told me, he saw her a while ago very brave and neat; we'll ferret her out, and London hold her.

*Wife.* Alas, poor soul, he's overcome [135 with sorrow; he does but as I do, weep for the loss of any good thing. But, Rafe, get thee in, call for some meat and drink: thou shalt find me worshipful towards thee.

*Rafe.* I thank you, dame; since I want limbs and lands,                          140
I'll trust to God, my good friends, and my hands.                              *Exit.*

*Enter Hans and Firk running*

*Firk.* Run, good Hans! O Hodge, O mistress! Hodge, heave up thine ears; mistress, smug up your looks; on with your best apparel; my master is chosen, my master is called, nay, [145 condemn'd by the cry of the country to be sheriff of the city for this famous year now to come. And, time now being, a great many men in black gowns were ask'd for their voices and their hands, and my master had all their [150 fists about his ears presently, and they cried "Ay, ay, ay, ay," — and so I came away —

Wherefore without all other grieve I do salute you, Mistress Shrieve.

*Hans.* Yaw, my mester is de groot man, de [155 shrieve.

*Hodge.* Did not I tell you, mistress? Now I may boldly say: Good-morrow to your worship.

*Wife.* Good-morrow, good Roger. I [160 thank you, my good people all. — Firk, hold up thy hand: here's a three-penny piece for thy tidings.

*Firk.* 'T is but three-half-pence, I think. Yes, 't is three-pence, I smell the rose.       165

*Hodge.* But, mistress, be rul'd by me, and do not speak so pulingly.

*Firk.* 'T is her worship speaks so, and not she. No, faith, mistress, speak me in the old key: "To it, Firk;" "there, good Firk;" [170 "ply your business, Hodge;" "Hodge; with a full mouth;" "I'll fill your bellies with good cheer, till they cry twang."

*Enter Simon Eyre wearing a gold chain*

*Hans.* See, myn liever broder, heer compt my meester.                              175

*Wife.* Welcome home, Master Shrieve; I pray God continue you in health and wealth.

*Eyre.* See here, my Maggy, a chain, a gold chain for Simon Eyre. I shall make thee a lady; here's a French hood for thee; on [180 with it, on with it! dress thy brows with this flap of a shoulder of mutton, to make thee look lovely. Where be my fine men? Roger, I'll make over my shop and tools to thee; Firk, thou shalt be the foreman; Hans, thou shalt [185 have an hundred for twenty. Be as mad knaves as your master Sim Eyre hath been, and you shall live to be sheriffs of London. — How dost thou like me, Margery? Prince am I none, [189 yet am I princely born. Firk, Hodge, and Hans!

*All Three.* Ay, forsooth, what says your worship, Master Sheriff?

*Eyre.* Worship and honour, you Babylonian knaves, for the gentle craft. But I forgot myself. I am bidden by my lord mayor to din- [195 ner to Old Ford; he's gone before, I must after. Come, Madge, on with your trinkets! Now, my true Trojans, my fine Firk, my dapper Hodge, my honest Hans, some device, some odd crotchets, some morris, or such like, for the [200 honour of the gentle shoemakers. Meet me at Old Ford; you know my mind. Come, Madge, away. Shut up the shop, knaves, and make holiday.                              *Exeunt.*

---

[112-113] **Ka . . . thee:** One good turn deserves another.     [141] **I'll . . . hands:** ('Ile to God, my good friends, and to these my hands' Q 1-2)     [143] **smug:** smarten     [165] **rose:** ( A rose identified some Elizabethan coins.)     [182] **flap . . . mutton:** sheep's fur     [186] **for twenty:** (in return for the 20 portagues mentioned above, III. i. 27)     [192] **Master:** ('mistris' Q 1-4)     [200] **morris:** morris-dance

*Firk.* O rare! O brave! Come, Hodge;
follow me, Hans;                   205
We 'll be with them for a morris-dance.
                                *Exeunt.*

[SCENE V. — *At Old Ford.*]

*Enter Lord Mayor, [Rose,] Eyre, his wife in
a French hood, Sybil, and other Servants*

*L. Mayor.* Trust me, you are as welcome to
  Old Ford
As I myself.
  *Wife.*     Truly, I thank your lordship.
  *L. Mayor.* Would our bad cheer were worth
  the thanks you give.
  *Eyre.* Good cheer, my lord mayor, fine cheer!
A fine house, fine walls, all fine and neat.    5
  *L. Mayor.* Now, by my troth, I 'll tell thee,
  Master Eyre,
It does me good, and all my brethren,
That such a madcap fellow as thyself
Is ent'red into our society.
  *Wife.* Ay, but, my lord, he must learn now
  to put on gravity.                   10
  *Eyre.* Peace, Maggy, a fig for gravity! When
I go to Guildhall in my scarlet gown, I 'll look
as demurely as a saint, and speak as gravely as
a justice of peace; but now I am here at Old
Ford, at my good lord mayor's house, let it [15
go by, vanish, Maggy, I 'll be merry; away with
flip-flap, these fooleries, these gulleries. What,
honey? Prince am I none, yet am I princely
born. What says my lord mayor?
  *L. Mayor.* Ha, ha, ha! I had rather than [20
a thousand pound I had an heart but half so
light as yours.
  *Eyre.* Why, what should I do, my lord? A
pound of care pays not a dram of debt. Hum,
let 's be merry, whiles we are young; old age, [25
sack and sugar will steal upon us ere we be
aware.

THE FIRST THREE-MAN'S SONG

O the month of May, the merry month of May,
  So frolic, so gay, and so green, so green, so
    green!
O, and then did I unto my true love say:    30
  "Sweet Peg, thou shalt be my summer's queen!

"Now the nightingale, the pretty nightingale,
  The sweetest singer in all the forest's choir,
Entreats thee, sweet Peggy, to hear thy true love's
    tale;                                   34
  Lo, yonder she sitteth, her breast against a brier.

"But O, I spy the cuckoo, the cuckoo, the cuckoo;
  See where she sitteth: come away, my joy;
Come away, I prithee: I do not like the cuckoo
  Should sing where my Peggy and I kiss and
    toy."

28–43 **Three-Man's Song**: song for three voices.
without indicating where they were introduced.)

O the month of May, the merry month of May,  40
  So frolic, so gay, and so green, so green, so green!
And then did I unto my true love say:
  "Sweet Peg, thou shalt be my summer's queen!"

  *L. Mayor.* It 's well done. Mistress Eyre,
  pray, give good counsel
To my daughter.                        45
  *Wife.* I hope, Mistress Rose will have the
grace to take nothing that 's bad.
  *L. Mayor.* Pray God she do; for i' faith,
  Mistress Eyre,
I would bestow upon that peevish girl
A thousand marks more than I mean to give her
Upon condition she 'd be rul'd by me.    51
The ape still crosseth me. There came of late
A proper gentleman of fair revénues,
Whom gladly I would call son-in-law:
But my fine cockney would have none of him.
You 'll prove a coxcomb for it, ere you die: 56
A courtier, or no man, must please your eye.
  *Eyre.* Be rul'd, sweet Rose: th' art ripe
for a man. Marry not with a boy that has no
more hair on his face than thou hast on thy [60
cheeks. A courtier! wash, go by, stand not upon
pishery-pashery: those silken fellows are but
painted images, outsides, outsides, Rose; their
inner linings are torn. No, my fine mouse,
marry me with a gentleman grocer like my [65
lord mayor, your father; a grocer is a sweet
trade: plums, plums. Had I a son or daughter
should marry out of the generation and blood
of the shoemakers, he should pack. What, the
gentle trade is a living for a man through
Europe, through the world.                71
       *A noise within of a tabor and a pipe.*
  *L. Mayor.* What noise is this?
  *Eyre.* O my lord mayor, a crew of good fellows that for love to your honour are come
hither with a morris-dance. Come in, my Mesopotamians, cheerily.                  76

*Enter Hodge, Hans, Rafe, Firk, and other Shoe-
  makers, in a morris; after a little dancing,
  the Lord Mayor speaks.*

  *L. Mayor.* Master Eyre, are all these shoe-
  makers?
  *Eyre.* All cordwainers, my good lord mayor.
  *Rose.* [*Aside.*] How like my Lacy looks yond
shoemaker!
  *Hans.* [*Aside.*] O that I durst but speak unto
  my love!                              80
  *L. Mayor.* Sybil, go fetch some wine to
make these drink. You are all welcome.
  *All.* We thank your lordship.
       *Rose takes a cup of wine and goes to Hans.*
  *Rose.* For his sake whose fair shape thou rep-
resent'st,

(Qq. prefix to the play this and the other in V. iv
71 S. D. **tabor**: small drum

Good friend, I drink to thee.      85

*Hans.*   *Ic bedancke, good frister.*

*Wife.*   I see, Mistress Rose, you do not want judgment; you have drunk to the properest man I keep.

*Firk.*   Here be some have done their parts to be as proper as he.      91

*L. Mayor.*   Well, urgent business calls me back to London.

Good fellows, first go in and taste our cheer;
And to make merry as you homeward go,
Spend these two angels in beer at Stratford-Bow.      95

*Eyre.*   To these two, my mad lads, Sim Eyre adds another; then cheerily, Firk; tickle it, Hans, and all for the honour of shoemakers.

           *All go dancing out.*

*L. Mayor.*   Come, Master Eyre, let 's have your company.        *Exeunt.*

*Rose.*   Sybil, what shall I do?      100

*Sybil.*   Why, what 's the matter?

*Rose.*   That Hans the shoemaker is my love Lacy,
Disguis'd in that attire to find me out.      103
How should I find the means to speak with him?

*Sybil.*   What, mistress, never fear; I dare venture my maidenhead to nothing, and that 's great odds, that Hans the Dutchman, when we come to London, shall not only see and speak with you, but in spite of all your father's policies steal you away and marry you. Will not this please you?      111

*Rose.*   Do this, and ever be assured of my love.

*Sybil.*   Away, then, and follow your father to London, lest your absence cause him to suspect something:      115
To-morrow, if my counsel be obey'd,
I 'll bind you prentice to the gentle trade.

           *[Exeunt.]*

## [ACT IV

### SCENE I. — *The "Old Change."*]

*Enter Jane in a Sempster's shop, working; and Hammon, muffled, at another door. He stands aloof.*

*Ham.*   Yonder 's the shop, and there my fair love sits.
She 's fair and lovely, but she is not mine.
O, would she were! Thrice have I courted her,
Thrice hath my hand been moist'ned with her hand,
Whilst my poor famish'd eyes do feed on that   5
Which made them famish. I am infortunate:
I still love one, yet nobody loves me.
I muse in other men what women see
That I so want! Fine Mistress Rose was coy,
And this too curious! Oh, no, she is chaste,   10

And for she thinks me wanton, she denies
To cheer my cold heart with her sunny eyes.
How prettily she works! Oh pretty hand!
Oh happy work! It doth me good to stand
Unseen to see her. Thus I oft have stood   15
In frosty evenings, a light burning by her,
Enduring biting cold, only to eye her.
One only look hath seem'd as rich to me
As a king's crown; such is love's lunacy.
Muffled I 'll pass along, and by that try   20
Whether she know me.

*Jane.*        Sir, what is 't you buy?
What is 't you lack, sir? calico, or lawn,
Fine cambric shirts, or bands? what will you buy?

*Ham.* [*Aside.*]   That which thou wilt not sell.
Faith, yet I 'll try: —
How do you sell this handkercher?

*Jane.*        Good cheap.   25

*Ham.*   And how these ruffs?

*Jane.*        Cheap too.

*Ham.*        And how this band?

*Jane.*   Cheap too.        [hand?

*Ham.*        All cheap; how sell you then this

*Jane.*   My hands are not to be sold.

*Ham.*        To be given then!
Nay, faith, I come to buy.

*Jane.*        But none knows when.

*Ham.*   Good sweet, leave work a little while;
let 's play.      30

*Jane.*   I cannot live by keeping holiday.

*Ham.*   I 'll pay you for the time which shall be lost.

*Jane.*   With me you shall not be at so much cost.

*Ham.*   Look, how you wound this cloth, so you wound me.

*Jane.*   It may be so.

*Ham.*        'T is so.

*Jane.*        What remedy?   35

*Ham.*   Nay, faith, you are too coy.

*Jane.*        Let go my hand.

*Ham.*   I will do any task at your command.
I would let go this beauty, were I not
In mind to disobey you by a power
That controls kings: I love you!

*Jane.*        So, now part.   40

*Ham.*   With hands I may, but never with my heart.
In faith, I love you.

*Jane.*        I believe you do.

*Ham.*   Shall a true love in me breed hate in you?

*Jane.*   I hate you not.

*Ham.*        Then you must love?

*Jane.*        I do
What are you better now? I love not you.   45

---

⁸⁶ **frister:** Miss     Sc. I: **Enter Jane:** (She is discovered by drawing curtain before rear stage. Hammon enters on outer stage.)    ¹⁰ **curious:** squeamish    ²⁶ **Good cheap:** at a bargain

*Ham.*  All this, I hope, is but a woman's fray,
That means, "Come to me," when she cries,
    "Away!"
In earnest, mistress, I do not jest,
A true chaste love hath ent'red in my breast.
I love you dearly, as I love my life,          50
I love you as a husband loves a wife;
That, and no other love, my love requires.
Thy wealth, I know, is little; my desires
Thirst not for gold.  Sweet, beauteous Jane,
    what 's mine          54
Shall, if thou make myself thine, all be thine.
Say, judge, what is thy sentence, life or death?
Mercy or cruelty lies in thy breath.
    *Jane.*  Good sir, I do believe you love me
        well;
For 't is a silly conquest, silly pride,
For one like you — I mean a gentleman —          60
To boast that by his love-tricks he hath brought
Such and such women to his amorous lure;
I think you do not so, yet many do,
And make it even a very trade to woo.
I could be coy, as many women be,          65
Feed you with sunshine smiles and wanton
    looks,
But I detest witchcraft; say that I
Do constantly believe you, constant have ——
    *Ham.*  Why dost thou not believe me?
    *Jane.*                    I believe you;  69
But yet, good sir, because I will not grieve
    you
With hopes to taste fruit which will never fall,
In simple truth this is the sum of all:
My husband lives, — at least, I hope he lives.
Press'd was he to these bitter wars in France;
Bitter they are to me by wanting him.          75
I have but one heart, and that heart 's his due.
How can I then bestow the same on you?
Whilst he lives, his I live, be it ne'er so poor,
And rather be his wife than a king's whore.
    *Ham.*  Chaste and dear woman, I will not
        abuse thee,          80
Although it cost my life, if thou refuse me.
Thy husband, press'd for France, what was his
    name?
    *Jane.*  Rafe Damport.
    *Ham.*          Damport? — Here 's a letter sent
From France to me, from a dear friend of
    mine,
A gentleman of place; here he doth write  85
Their names that have been slain in every
    fight.
    *Jane.*  I hope death's scroll contains not my
        love's name.
    *Ham.*  Cannot you read?
    *Jane.*                    I can.
    *Ham.*                          Peruse the same.
To my remembrance such a name I read
Amongst the rest.  See here.

    *Jane.*                    Ay me, he 's dead!  90
He 's dead!  If this be true, my dear heart 's
    slain!
    *Ham.*  Have patience, dear love.
    *Jane.*                    Hence, hence!
    *Ham.*                          Nay, sweet Jane,
Make not poor sorrow proud with these rich
    tears.
I mourn thy husband's death, because thou
    mourn'st.
    *Jane.*  That bill is forg'd; 't is sign'd by for-
        gery.          95
    *Ham.*  I 'll bring thee letters sent besides to
        many,
Carrying the like report: Jane, 't is too true.
Come, weep not: mourning, though it rise from
    love,
Helps not the mourned, yet hurts them that
    mourn.
    *Jane.*  For God's sake, leave me.
    *Ham.*                    Whither dost thou turn?  100
Forget the dead, love them that are alive;
His love is faded, try how mine will thrive.
    *Jane.*  'T is now no time for me to think on
        love.
    *Ham.*  'T is now best time for you to think
        on love,
Because your love lives not.
    *Jane.*                    Though he be dead,  105
My love to him shall not be buried;
For God's sake, leave me to myself alone.
    *Ham.*  'T would kill my soul, to leave thee
        drown'd in moan.
Answer me to my suit, and I am gone;
Say to me yea or no.
    *Jane.*                    No.
    *Ham.*                          Then farewell!  110
One farewell will not serve, I come again.
Come, dry these wet cheeks; tell me, faith,
    sweet Jane,
Yea or no, once more.
    *Jane.*                    Once more I say no;
Once more be gone, I pray; else will I go.
    *Ham.*  Nay, then I will grow rude, by this
        white hand,          115
Until you change that cold "no"; here I 'll
    stand
Till by your hard heart ——
    *Jane.*                    Nay, for God's love, peace!
My sorrows by your presence more increase.
Not that you thus are present, but all grief
Desires to be alone; therefore in brief          120
Thus much I say, and saying bid adieu:
If ever I wed man, it shall be you.
    *Ham.*  O blessed voice!  Dear Jane, I 'll urge
        no more;
Thy breath hath made me rich.
    *Jane.*                    Death makes me poor.
                                        *Exeunt.*

[SCENE II. — *Hodge's Shop, Tower St.*]

*Enter Hodge, at his shop-board, Rafe, Firk,
Hans, and a Boy at work*

*All.* Hey, down a down, down derry.

*Hodge.* Well said, my hearts; ply your work
to-day, we loit'red yesterday; to it pell-mell,
that we may live to be lord mayors, or aldermen
at least.                                                    5

*Firk.* Hey, down a down, derry.

*Hodge.* Well said, i' faith! How say'st thou,
Hans, doth not Firk tickle it?

*Hans.*  Yaw, mester.

*Firk.* Not so neither; my organ-pipe [10
squeaks this morning for want of liquoring.
Hey, down a down, derry!

*Hans.* Forward, Firk, tow best un jolly yong-
ster.  Hort, I, mester, ic bid yo, cut me un pair
vampres vor Mester Jeffre's boots.                          15

*Hodge.* Thou shalt, Hans.

*Firk.* Master!

*Hodge.* How now, boy?

*Firk.* Pray, now you are in the cutting vein,
cut me out a pair of counterfeits, or else [20
my work will not pass current; hey, down a
down!

*Hodge.* Tell me, sirs, are my cousin Mrs.
Priscilla's shoes done?                                     24

*Firk.* Your cousin?  No, master; one of
your aunts, hang her; let them alone.

*Rafe.* I am in hand with them; she gave
charge that none but I should do them for
her.

*Firk.* Thou do for her?  Then 't will be [30
a lame doing, and that she loves not.  Rafe,
thou might'st have sent her to me, in faith, I
would have yarked and firked your Priscilla.
Hey, down a down, derry.  This gear will not
hold.                                                       35

*Hodge.* How say'st thou, Firk, were we not
merry at Old Ford?

*Firk.* How, merry!  Why, our buttocks went
jiggy-joggy like a quagmire.  Well, Sir Roger
Oatmeal, if I thought all meal of that nature,
I would eat nothing but bagpuddings.                        41

*Rafe.* Of all good fortunes my fellow Hans
had the best.

*Firk.* 'T is true, because Mistress Rose drank
to him.                                                     45

*Hodge.* Well, well, work apace.  They say,
seven of the aldermen be dead, or very sick.

*Firk.* I care not, I 'll be none.

*Rafe.* No, nor I; but then my Master Eyre
will come quickly to be lord mayor.                         50

*Enter Sybil*

*Firk.* Whoop, yonder comes Sybil.

*Hodge.* Sybil, welcome, i' faith; and how
dost thou, mad wench?

*Firk.* Sib-whore, welcome to London.         54

*Sybil.* Godamercy, sweet Firk; good lord,
Hodge, what a delicious shop you have got!
You tickle it, i' faith.

*Rafe.* Godamercy, Sybil, for our good cheer
at Old Ford.

*Sybil.* That you shall have, Rafe.            60

*Firk.* Nay, by the mass, we had tickling
cheer, Sybil; and how the plague dost thou
and Mistress Rose and my lord mayor?  I put
the women in first.

*Sybil.* Well, Godamercy; but God's me, [65
I forget myself, where 's Hans the Fleming?

*Firk.* Hark, butter-box, now you must yelp
out some *spreken.*

*Hans.* Wat begaie you?  Vat vod you, Frister?

*Sybil.* Marry, you must come to my young
mistress, to pull on her shoes you made last. [71

*Hans.* Vare ben your egle fro, vare ben your
mistris?

*Sybil.* Marry, here at our London house in
Cornhill.                                                   75

*Firk.* Will nobody serve her turn but Hans?

*Sybil.* No, sir.  Come, Hans, I stand upon
needles.

*Hodge.* Why then, Sybil, take heed of prick-
ing.                                                        80

*Sybil.* For that let me alone.  I have a trick
in my budget.  Come, Hans.

*Hans.* Yaw, yaw, ic sall meete yo gane.

*Exit Hans and Sybil.*

*Hodge.* Go, Hans, make haste again.  Come,
who lacks work?                                             85

*Firk.* I, master, for I lack my breakfast; 't
is munching-time, and past.

*Hodge.* Is 't so?  Why, then, leave work,
Rafe.  To breakfast!  Boy, look to the tools.
Come, Rafe; come, Firk.          *Exeunt.* 90

[SCENE III. — *The Same.*]

*Enter a Serving-man*

*Serv.* Let me see now! the sign of the Last in
Tower Street.  Mass, yonder 's the house.
What, ho!  Who 's within?

*Enter Rafe*

*Rafe.* Who calls there?  What want you,
sir?                                                         5

*Serv.* Marry, I would have a pair of shoes

---

Sc. II.  s. d. at . . . shop-board: opening the shutters of his shop     13 tow best: thou art     14 Hort:
listen     15 vampres: vamps     20 counterfeits: patterns     26 aunts: slang name for harlots     27 in
hand: at work     40 Oatmeal: (pun on name of Otley, Oatley)     69 begaie: desire     72 egle fro:
noble lady     83 meete yo gane: go with you

made for a gentlewoman against to-morrow morning. What, can you do them?

*Rafe.* Yes, sir, you shall have them. But what length 's her foot?          10

*Serv.* Why you must make them in all parts like this shoe; but, at any hand, fail not to do them, for the gentlewoman is to be married very early in the morning.

*Rafe.* How? by this shoe must it be made? By this? Are you sure, sir, by this?          16

*Serv.* How, by this? Am I sure, by this? Art thou in thy wits? I tell thee, I must have a pair of shoes, — dost thou mark me? A pair of shoes, two shoes, made by this very shoe, this same [20 shoe, against to-morrow morning by four o'clock. Dost understand me? Canst thou do 't?

*Rafe.* Yes, sir, yes — I — I — I can do 't. By this shoe, you say? I should know this shoe. Yes, sir, yes, by this shoe. I can do 't. Four [25 o' clock, well. Whither shall I bring them?

*Serv.* To the sign of the Golden Ball in Watling Street; enquire for one Master Hammon, a gentleman, my master.

*Rafe.* Yea, sir; by this shoe, you say?          30

*Serv.* I say, Master Hammon at the Golden Ball; he 's the bridegroom, and those shoes are for his bride.

*Rafe.* They shall be done by this shoe. Well, well, Master Hammon at the Golden Shoe — I would say, the Golden Ball; very well, very [36 well. But I pray you, sir, where must Master Hammon be married?

*Serv.* At Saint Faith's Church, under Paul's. But what 's that to thee? Prithee, dispatch those shoes, and so farewell.          *Exit.*  41

*Rafe.* By this shoe, said he. How am I amaz'd
At this strange accident! Upon my life,
This was the very shoe I gave my wife,
When I was press'd for France; since when, alas!          45
I never could hear of her. It is the same,
And Hammon's bride no other but my Jane.

### Enter Firk

*Firk.* 'Snails, Rafe, thou hast lost thy part of three pots a countryman of mine gave me to breakfast.          50

*Rafe.* I care not; I have found a better thing.

*Firk.* A thing? Away! Is it a man's thing, or a woman's thing?

*Rafe.* Firk, dost thou know this shoe?

*Firk.* No, by my troth; neither doth that [56 know me! I have no acquaintance with it, 't is a mere stranger to me.

*Rafe.* Why, then, I do; this shoe, I durst be sworn,

Once covered the instep of my Jane.          60
This is her size, her breadth, thus trod my love;
These true-love knots I prick'd. I hold my life,
By this old shoe I shall find out my wife.

*Firk.* Ha, ha! Old shoe, that wert new!
How a murrain came this ague-fit of foolish- [65 ness upon thee?

*Rafe.* Thus, Firk: even now here came a serving-man.
By this shoe would he have a new pair made
Against to-morrow morning for his mistress,
That 's to be married to a gentleman.          70
And why may not this be my sweet Jane?

*Firk.* And why may'st not thou be my sweet ass?
Ha, ha!

*Rafe.* Well, laugh and spare not! But the truth is this:
Against to-morrow morning I 'll provide          75
A lusty crew of honest shoemakers,
To watch the going of the bride to church.
If she prove Jane, I 'll take her in despite
From Hammon and the devil, were he by.
If it be not my Jane, what remedy?          80
Hereof am I sure, I shall live till I die,
Although I never with a woman lie.          *Exit.*

*Firk.* Thou lie with a woman to build nothing but Cripplegates! Well, God sends fools fortune, and it may be, he may light upon [85 his matrimony by such a device; for wedding and hanging goes by destiny.          *Exit.*

### [SCENE IV. — *Sir Roger Otley's House, Cornhill.*]

*Enter [Lacy as] Hans and Rose, arm in arm*

*Hans.* How happy am I by embracing thee!
Oh, I did fear such cross mishaps did reign
That I should never see my Rose again.

*Rose.* Sweet Lacy, since fair opportunity
Offers herself to further our escape,          5
Let not too over-fond esteem of me
Hinder that happy hour. Invent the means,
And Rose will follow thee through all the world.

*Hans.* Oh, how I surfeit with excess of joy,
Made happy by thy rich perfection!          10
But since thou pay'st sweet interest to my hopes,
Redoubling love on love, let me once more
Like to a bold-fac'd debtor crave of thee
This night to steal abroad, and at Eyre's house,
Who now by death of certain aldermen          15
Is mayor of London, and my master once,
Meet thou thy Lacy, where in spite of change,
Your father's anger, and mine uncle's hate,
Our happy nuptials will we consummate.

---

¹³ **at . . . hand:** by all means   ⁶⁵ **murrain:** plague   ⁸⁶ **matrimony:** wife   ⁵ **further:** ('furder' Qq.)

*Enter Sybil*

*Sybil.* Oh God, what will you do, mistress? [20
Shift for yourself, your father is at hand! He 's
coming, he 's coming! Master Lacy, hide yourself in my mistress! For God's sake, shift for
yourselves!

*Hans.* Your father come! Sweet Rose, what
shall I do?                                    25
Where shall I hide me? How shall I escape?

*Rose.* A man, and want wit in extremity?
Come, come, be Hans still, play the shoemaker,
Pull on my shoe.

*Enter Sir Roger Otley*

*Hans.* Mass, and that 's well rememb'red.

*Sybil.* Here comes your father.          31

*Hans.* *Forware, metresse, 't is un good skow,
il sal vel dute, or ye sal neit betallen.*

*Rose.* Oh God, it pincheth me; what will
you do?

*Hans.* [*Aside*]. Your father's presence pincheth, not the shoe.                           35

*Otley.* Well done; fit my daughter well,
and she shall please thee well.

*Hans.* *Yaw, yaw, ick weit dat well; forware,
't is un good skoo, 't is gimait van neits leither:
se euer, mine here.*                          40

*Enter a Prentice*

*Otley.* I do believe it. — What 's the news
with you?

*Prentice.* Please you, the Earl of Lincoln at
the gate
Is newly lighted, and would speak with you.

*Otley.* The Earl of Lincoln come to speak
with me?
Well, well, I know his errand. Daughter Rose,
Send hence your shoemaker, dispatch, have
done!                                        46
Syb, make things handsome! Sir boy, follow
me.                                    *Exit.*

*Hans.* Mine uncle come! Oh, what may
this portend?
Sweet Rose, this of our love threatens an end.

*Rose.* Be not dismay'd at this; whate'er be-
fall,                                        50
Rose is thine own. To witness I speak truth,
Where thou appoints the place, I 'll meet with
thee.
I will not fix a day to follow thee,
But presently steal hence. Do not reply:
Love which gave strength to bear my father's
hate,                                        55
Shall now add wings to further our escape.
                                      *Exeunt.*

[SCENE V. — *The Same.*]

*Enter Sir Roger Otley and Lincoln*

*Otley.* Believe me, on my credit, I speak
truth:
Since first your nephew Lacy went to France,
I have not seen him. It seem'd strange to me,
When Dodger told me that he stay'd behind,
Neglecting the high charge the king imposed. 5

*Lincoln.* Trust me, Sir Roger Otley, I did
think
Your counsel had given head to this attempt,
Drawn to it by the love he bears your child.
Here I did hope to find him in your house;
But now I see mine error, and confess,    10
My judgment wrong'd you by conceiving so.

*Otley.* Lodge in my house, say you?
Trust me, my lord,
I love your nephew Lacy too too dearly,
So much to wrong his honour; and he hath
done so,                                      14
That first gave him advice to stay from France.
To witness I speak truth, I let you know
How careful I have been to keep my daughter
Free from all conference or speech of him;
Not that I scorn your nephew, but in love
I bear your honour, lest your noble blood  20
Should by my mean worth be dishonoured.

*Lincoln.* [*Aside.*] How far the churl's tongue
wanders from his heart! —
Well, well, Sir Roger Otley, I believe you,
With more than many thanks for the kind love
So much you seem to bear me. But, my lord, 25
Let me request your help to seek my nephew,
Whom, if I find, I 'll straight embark for France.
So shall your Rose be free, my thoughts at rest,
And much care die which now lies in my breast.

*Enter Sybil*

*Sybil.* Oh Lord! Help, for God's sake! [30
My mistress; oh, my young mistress!

*Otley.* Where is thy mistress? What 's become of her?

*Sybil.* She 's gone, she 's fled!

*Otley.* Gone! Whither is she fled?        35

*Sybil.* I know not, forsooth; she 's fled out
of doors with Hans the shoemaker; I saw them
scud, scud, scud, apace, apace!

*Otley.* Which way? What, John! Where be
my men? Which way?                           40

*Sybil.* I know not, and it please your worship.

*Otley.* Fled with a shoemaker? Can this
be true?

*Sybil.* Oh Lord, sir, as true as God 's in
Heaven.

*Lincoln.* Her love turn'd shoemaker? I am
glad of this.

---

*Otley.* A Fleming butter-box, a shoe-
maker!                                             45
Will she forget her birth, requite my care
With such ingratitude? Scorn'd she young
Hammon
To love a honnikin, a needy knave?
Well, let her fly, I 'll not fly after her;        49
Let her starve, if she will: she 's none of mine.
*Lincoln.* Be not so cruel, sir.

*Enter Firk with shoes*

*Sybil.*                I am glad, she 's scap'd.
*Otley.* I 'll not account of her as of my
child.
Was there no better object for her eyes,
But a foul drunken lubber, swill-belly,
A shoemaker? That 's brave!                        55
*Firk.* Yea, forsooth; 't is a very brave shoe,
and as fit as a pudding.
*Otley.* How now, what knave is this?
From whence comest thou?
*Firk.* No knave, sir. I am Firk the shoe- [60
maker, lusty Roger's chief lusty journeyman,
and I come hither to take up the pretty leg
of sweet Mistress Rose, and thus hoping your
worship is in as good health, as I was at the
making hereof, I bid you farewell, yours, [65
Firk.
*Otley* Stay, stay, Sir Knave!
*Lincoln.* Come hither, shoemaker!
*Firk.* 'T is happy the knave is put before the
shoemaker, or else I would not have vouch- [70
safed to come back to you. I am moved, for I
stir.
*Otley.* My lord, this villain calls us knaves
by craft.
*Firk.* Then 't is by the gentle craft, and [75
to call one knave gently is no harm. Sit your
worship merry! Syb, your young mistress —
I 'll so bob them, now my master, Master Eyre,
is lord mayor of London.
*Otley.* Tell me, sirrah, whose man are you? 80
*Firk.* I am glad to see your worship so merry.
I have no maw to this gear, no stomach as yet
to a red petticoat.          *Pointing to Sybil.*
*Lincoln.* He means not, sir, to woo you to
his maid,
But only doth demand whose man you are. 85
*Firk.* I sing now to the tune of Rogero.
Roger, my fellow, is now my master.
*Lincoln.* Sirrah, know'st thou one Hans, a
shoemaker?                                         89
*Firk.* Hans, shoemaker? Oh yes, stay, yes,
I have him. I tell you what, I speak it in secret:

Mistress Rose and he are by this time — no, not
so, but shortly are to come over one another
with "Can you dance the shaking of the [94
sheets?" It is that Hans — [*Aside.*] I 'll so
gull these diggers!
*Otley.* Know'st thou, then, where he is?
*Firk.* Yes, forsooth; yea, marry!
*Lincoln.* Canst thou, in sadness ——
*Firk.* No, forsooth, no, marry!                   100
*Otley.* Tell me, good honest fellow, where
he is,
And thou shalt see what I 'll bestow of thee.
*Firk.* Honest fellow? No, sir; not so, sir;
my profession is the gentle craft; I care not [104
for seeing, I love feeling; let me feel it here;
*aurium tenus*, ten pieces of gold; *genuum tenus*,
ten pieces of silver; and then Firk is your man
— [*Aside.*] in a new pair of stretchers.
*Otley.* Here is an angel, part of thy re-
ward,                                              109
Which I will give thee; tell me where he is.
*Firk.* No point! Shall I betray my brother?
No! Shall I prove Judas to Hans? No! Shall
I cry treason to my corporation? No, I shall
be firk'd and yerk'd then. But give me your
angel; your angel shall tell you.                  115
*Lincoln.* Do so, good fellow; 't is no hurt to
thee.
*Firk.* Send simpering Syb away.
*Otley.* Huswife, get you in.                      118
                                       *Exit Sybil.*
*Firk.* Pitchers have ears, and maids have
wide mouths; but for Hans Prauns, upon my
word, to-morrow morning he and young Mistress Rose go to this gear: they shall be married
together, by this rush, or else turn Firk to a
firkin of butter, to tan leather withal.
*Otley.* But art thou sure of this?                125
*Firk.* Am I sure that Paul's steeple is a
handful higher than London Stone, or that
the Pissing-Conduit leaks nothing but pure [128
Mother Bunch? Am I sure I am lusty Firk?
God's nails, do you think I am so base to gull
you?
*Lincoln.* Where are they married? Dost
thou know the church?                              133
*Firk.* I never go to church, but I know the
name of it; it is a swearing church — stay a
while, 't is — ay, by the mass, no, no, — 't is —
ay, by my troth, no, nor that; 't is — ay, by my
faith, that, that, 't is, ay, by my Faith's
Church under Paul's Cross. There they [139
shall be knit like a pair of stockings in matrimony; there they 'll be inconie.

⁴⁸ **honnikin:** Hankin, Dutchman (?)  ⁷⁸ **bob:** outwit  ⁹⁶ **diggers:** crafty questioners  ⁹⁹ **sadness:** earnest  ¹⁰² **of:** on  ¹⁰⁶ **aurium tenus:** up to the ears  **genuum tenus:** up to the knees (Firk
mistranslates.)  ¹⁰⁸ **stretchers:** quibbles  ¹¹¹ **No point:** by no means  ¹²³ **rush:** the rush floor-
covering  ¹²⁷ **London Stone:** a Roman mile-stone in Cannon St.  ¹²⁹ **Mother Bunch:** ale (alluding
to *2 Henry VI.* IV. vi. 1–5?)  ¹⁴¹ **inconie:** a vague adjective of approval, dainty

*Lincoln.* Upon my life, my nephew Lacy walks
In the disguise of this Dutch shoemaker.
*Firk.* Yes, forsooth.
*Lincoln.* Doth he not, honest fellow? 145
*Firk.* No, forsooth; I think Hans is nobody but Hans, no spirit.
*Otley.* My mind misgives me now, 't is so, indeed.
*Lincoln.* My cousin speaks the language, knows the trade. 149
*Otley.* Let me request your company, my lord;
Your honourable presence may, no doubt,
Refrain their headstrong rashness, when myself
Going alone perchance may be o'erborne.
Shall I request this favour?
*Lincoln.* This, or what else. 154
*Firk.* Then you must rise betimes, for they mean to fall to their hey-pass and repass, pindy-pandy, which hand will you have, very early.
*Otley.* My care shall every way equal their haste. 159
This night accept your lodging in my house.
The earlier shall we stir, and at Saint Faith's
Prevent this giddy hare-brain'd nuptial.
This traffic of hot love shall yield cold gains:
They ban our loves, and we 'll forbid their banns. *Exit.*
*Lincoln.* At Saint Faith's Church, thou say'st? 165
*Firk.* Yes, by their troth.
*Lincoln.* Be secret, on thy life. *Exit.*
*Firk.* Yes, when I kiss your wife! Ha, ha, here 's no craft in the gentle craft. I came [169 hither of purpose with shoes to Sir Roger's worship, whilst Rose, his daughter, be concatch'd by Hans. Soft now; these two gulls will be at Saint Faith's Church to-morrow [173 morning, to take Master Bridegroom and Mistress Bride napping, and they, in the mean time, shall chop up the matter at the Savoy. But the best sport is, Sir Roger Otley will find my fellow lame Rafe's wife going to [178 marry a gentleman, and then he 'll stop her instead of his daughter. Oh brave! there will be fine tickling sport. Soft now, what have I to do? Oh, I know; now a mess of shoemakers meet at the Woolsack in Ivy Lane, to cozen my gentleman of lame Rafe's wife: that 's [184 true.

Alack, alack!
Girls, hold out tack!
For now smocks for this jumbling
Shall go to wrack. 189
*Exit.*

[ACT V

SCENE I. — *Eyre's House.*]

*Enter Eyre, his wife,* [*Lacy as*] *Hans, and
Rose*

*Eyre.* This is the morning, then; say, my bully, my honest Hans, is it not?
*Hans.* This is the morning that must make us two happy or miserable; therefore, if you —— 5
*Eyre.* Away with these ifs and ans, Hans, and these et ceteras! By mine honour, Rowland Lacy, none but the king shall wrong thee. Come, fear nothing, am not I Sim Eyre? Is not Sim Eyre lord mayor of London? Fear [10 nothing, Rose: let them all say what they can; dainty, come thou to me — laughest thou?
*Wife.* Good my lord, stand her friend in what thing you may.
*Eyre.* Why, my sweet Lady Madgy, think [15 you Simon Eyre can forget his fine Dutch journeyman? No, vah! Fie, I scorn it. It shall never be cast in my teeth, that I was unthankful. Lady Madgy, thou had'st never cover'd thy Saracen's head with this French flap, nor [20 loaden thy bum with this farthingale, ('t is trash, trumpery, vanity); Simon Eyre had never walk'd in a red petticoat, nor wore a chain of gold, but for my fine journeyman's portagues. — And shall I leave him? No! [25 Prince am I none, yet bear a princely mind.
*Hans.* My lord, 't is time for us to part from hence.
*Eyre.* Lady Madgy, Lady Madgy, take two or three of my pie-crust-eaters, my buff-jerkin varlets, that do walk in black gowns at [30 Simon Eyre's heels; take them, good Lady Madgy; trip and go, my brown queen of periwigs, with my delicate Rose and my jolly Rowland to the Savoy; see them link'd, countenance the marriage; and when it is done, cling, [35 cling together, you Hamborow turtle-doves. I 'll bear you out: come to Simon Eyre; come, dwell with me, Hans, thou shalt eat minc'd-pies and marchpane. Rose, away, cricket; trip and go, my Lady Madgy, to the Savoy; Hans, wed, and to bed; kiss, and away! Go, vanish!
*Wife.* Farewell, my lord. 42
*Rose.* Make haste, sweet love.
*Wife.* She 'd fain the deed were done.
*Hans.* Come, my sweet Rose: faster than deer we 'll run. 45
*They go out.*
*Eyre.* Go, vanish, vanish! Avaunt, I say! By the Lord of Ludgate, it 's a mad life to be

---

¹⁵⁶ **hey-pass, etc.**: (juggling terms) ¹⁶⁴ **ban**: repudiate **banns**: ('baines' Qq., perhaps with pun on "banes") ¹⁷¹⁻¹⁷² **conycatch'd**: taken in ¹⁸² **mess**: party of four ¹⁸⁷ **hold ... tack**: make good resistance ¹ **say**: ('stay' Qo ) ³⁶ **Hamborow**: Hamburg, German ³⁹ **marchpane**: a sweetmeat

a lord mayor; it 's a stirring life, a fine life, a velvet life, a careful life. Well, Simon Eyre, yet set a good face on it, in the honour of Saint [50 Hugh. Soft, the king this day comes to dine with me, to see my new buildings; his majesty is welcome, he shall have good cheer, delicate cheer, princely cheer. This day, my fellow prentices of London come to dine with me too; [55 they shall have fine cheer, gentlemanlike cheer. I promised the mad Cappadocians, when we all served at the Conduit together, that if ever I came to be mayor of London, I would feast them all, and I 'll do 't, I 'll do 't, by the life [60 of Pharaoh; by this beard, Sim Eyre will be no flincher. Besides, I have procur'd that upon every Shrove-Tuesday, at the sound of the pancake bell, my fine dapper Assyrian lads shall clap up their shop windows, and away. [65 This is the day, and this day they shall do 't, they shall do 't.

Boys, that day are you free; let masters care,
And prentices shall pray for Simon Eyre.

*Exit.*

[SCENE II. — *Near St. Faith's Church.*]

*Enter Hodge, Firk, Rafe, and five or six*
*Shoemakers, all with cudgels or such weapons*

*Hodge.* Come, Rafe; stand to it, Firk. My masters, as we are the brave bloods of the shoemakers, heirs apparent to Saint Hugh, and perpetual benefactors to all good fellows, thou shalt have no wrong; were Hammon a king [5 of spades, he should not delve in thy close without thy sufferance. But tell me, Rafe, art thou sure 't is thy wife?

*Rafe.* Am I sure this is Firk? This morning, when I strok'd on her shoes, I look'd upon [10 her, and she upon me, and sighed, ask'd me if ever I knew one Rafe. Yes, said I. For his sake, said she — tears standing in her eyes — and for thou art somewhat like him, spend this piece of gold. I took it; my lame leg and [15 my travel beyond sea made me unknown. All is one for that: I know she 's mine.

*Firk.* Did she give thee this gold? O glorious glittering gold! She 's thine own, 't is thy wife, and she loves thee; for I 'll stand to 't, [20 there 's no woman will give gold to any man, but she thinks better of him that she thinks of them she gives silver to. And for Hammon, neither Hammon nor hangman shall wrong thee in London! Is not our old master Eyre [25 lord mayor? Speak, my hearts.

*All.* Yes, and Hammon shall know it to his cost.

*Enter Hammon, his man, Jane, and others*

*Hodge.* Peace, my bullies; yonder they come.                                            29

*Rafe.* Stand to 't, my hearts. Firk, let me speak first.

*Hodge.* No, Rafe, let me. — Hammon, whither away so early?

*Ham.* Unmannerly, rude slave, what 's that to thee?                                      34

*Firk.* To him, sir? Yes, sir, and to me, and others. Good-morrow, Jane, how dost thou? Good Lord, how the world is changed with you! God be thanked!

*Ham.* Villains, hands off! How dare you touch my love?                                   39

*All.* Villains? Down with them! Cry clubs for prentices!

*Hodge.* Hold, my hearts! Touch her, Hammon? Yea, and more than that: we 'll carry her away with us. My masters and gentlemen, never draw your bird-spits; shoemakers are steel to the back, men every inch of them, [46 all spirit.

*All of Hammon's side.* Well, and what of all this?

*Hodge.* I 'll show you. — Jane, dost thou [50 know this man? 'T is Rafe, I can tell thee; nay, 't is he in faith, though he be lam'd by the wars. Yet look not strange, but run to him, fold him about the neck and kiss him.

*Jane.* Lives then my husband? Oh God, let me go,                                         55
Let me embrace my Rafe.

*Ham.*                          What means my Jane?

*Jane.* Nay, what meant you, to tell me he was slain?

*Ham.* Pardon me, dear love, for being misled.
[*To Rafe.*] 'T was rumour'd here in London, thou wert dead.

*Firk.* Thou seest he lives. Lass, go, pack home with him.                                60
Now, Master Hammon, where 's your mistress, your wife?

*Serv.* 'Swounds, master, fight for her! Will you thus lose her?

*All.* Down with that creature! Clubs! Down with him!                                     65

*Hodge.* Hold, hold!

*Ham.* Hold, fool! Sirs, he shall do no wrong. Will my Jane leave me thus, and break her faith?

*Firk.* Yea, sir! She must, sir! She shall, sir! What then? Mend it!                       70

*Hodge.* Hark, fellow Rafe, follow my counsel: set the wench in the midst, and let her choose her man, and let her be his woman.

---

57–58 **when . . . Conduit:** (Carrying water from the conduit for domestic use was a duty of apprentices. See V. v. 188 ff.)   64 **pancake bell:** (Pancake feasts celebrated the approach of Lent.)   40 **clubs:** the battle cry of London 'prentices

*Jane.* Whom should I choose? Whom should my thoughts affect
But him whom Heaven hath made to be my love?                                    75
Thou art my husband, and these humble weeds
Makes thee more beautiful than all his wealth.
Therefore, I will but put off his attire,
Returning it into the owner's hand,
And after ever be thy constant wife.            80

*Hodge.* Not a rag, Jane! The law 's on our side: he that sows in another man's ground, forfeits his harvest. Get thee home, Rafe; follow him, Jane; he shall not have so much as a busk-point from thee.            85

*Firk.* Stand to that, Rafe; the appurtenances are thine own. Hammon, look not at her!

*Serv.* O, swounds, no!            89

*Firk.* Blue coat, be quiet, we 'll give you a new livery else; we 'll make Shrove Tuesday Saint George's Day for you. Look not, Hammon, leer not! I 'll firk you! For thy head now, one glance, one sheep's eye, anything, at her! Touch not a rag, lest I and my brethren beat you to clouts.            96

*Serv.* Come, Master Hammon, there 's no striving here.

*Ham.* Good fellows, hear me speak; and, honest Rafe,
Whom I have injur'd most by loving Jane,
Mark what I offer thee: here in fair gold       100
Is twenty pound, I 'll give it for thy Jane;
If this content thee not, thou shalt have more.

*Hodge.* Sell not thy wife, Rafe; make her not a whore.

*Ham.* Say, wilt thou freely cease thy claim in her,
And let her be my wife?

*All.*                    No, do not, Rafe.  105

*Rafe.* Sirrah Hammon, Hammon, dost thou think a shoemaker is so base to be a bawd to his own wife for commodity? Take thy gold, choke with it! Were I not lame, I would make thee eat thy words.            110

*Firk.* A shoemaker sell his flesh and blood? Oh indignity!

*Hodge.* Sirrah, take up your pelf, and be packing.

*Ham.* I will not touch one penny, but in lieu
Of that great wrong I offered thy Jane,         116
To Jane and thee I give that twenty pound.
Since I have fail'd of her, during my life,
I vow, no woman else shall be my wife.
Farewell, good fellows of the gentle trade:     120
Your morning mirth my mourning day hath made.                    *Exit.*

*Firk* [*To the Serving-man.*] Touch the gold, creature, if you dare! Y' are best be trudging. Here, Jane, take thou it. Now let 's home, my hearts.            125

*Hodge.* Stay! Who comes here? Jane, on again with thy mask!

*Enter Lincoln, Otley, and Servants*

*Lincoln.* Yonder 's the lying varlet mock'd us so.

*Otley.* Come hither, sirrah!

*Firk.* I, sir? I am sirrah? You mean me, do you not?            130

*Lincoln.* Where is my nephew married?

*Firk.* Is he married? God give him joy, I am glad of it. They have a fair day, and the sign is in a good planet, Mars in Venus.

*Otley.* Villain, thou toldst me that my daughter Rose            135
This morning should be married at Saint Faith's.
We have watch'd there these three hours at the least,
Yet see we no such thing.

*Firk.* Truly, I am sorry for 't; a bride 's a pretty thing.            140

*Hodge.* Come to the purpose. Yonder 's the bride and bridegroom you look for, I hope. Though you be lords, you are not to bar by your authority men from women, are you?

*Otley.* See, see, my daughter 's mask'd.

*Lincoln.*                    True, and my nephew, 145
To hide his guilt, counterfeits him lame.

*Firk.* Yea, truly; God help the poor couple, they are lame and blind.

*Otley.* I 'll ease her blindness.

*Lincoln.*                I 'll his lameness cure.  149

*Firk.* Lie down, sirs, and laugh! My fellow Rafe is taken for Rowland Lacy, and Jane for Mistress Damask Rose. This is all my knavery.

*Otley.* What, have I found you, minion?

*Lincoln.*                O base wretch!
Nay, hide thy face; the horror of thy guilt
Can hardly be wash'd off. Where are thy powers?            155
What battles have you made? O yes, I see,
Thou fought'st with Shame, and Shame hath conquer'd thee.
This lameness will not serve.

*Otley.*                Unmask yourself.

*Lincoln.* Lead home your daughter.

*Otley.*                Take your nephew hence.  159

*Rafe.* Hence! Swounds, what mean you? Are you mad? I hope you cannot enforce my wife from me. Where 's Hammon?

*Otley.* Your wife?

*Lincoln.* What, Hammon?            164

---

**85 busk-point:** corset-string    **90 Blue coat:** common attire of liveried servants    **92 Saint George's Day:** (April 23) the servingman's holiday    **93 For:** on peril of    **121 morning:** ('mornings' Q 1)    **133–134 sign . . . planet:** nonsensical astrology (planets are in signs, not the reverse)

*Rafe.* Yea, my wife; and, therefore, the proudest of you that lay hands on her first, I 'll lay my crutch 'cross his pate.

*Firk.* To him, lame Rafe! Here 's brave sport! 169

*Rafe.* Rose call you her? Why, her name is Jane. Look here else; do you know her now? [*Unmasking Jane.*]

*Lincoln.* Is this your daughter?

*Otley.* No, nor this your nephew. My Lord of Lincoln, we are both abus'd By this base, crafty varlet. 174

*Firk.* Yea, forsooth, no varlet; forsooth, no base; forsooth, I am but mean; no crafty neither, but of the gentle craft.

*Otley.* Where is my daughter Rose? Where is my child?

*Lincoln.* Where is my nephew Lacy married?

*Firk.* Why, here is good lac'd mutton, as I promis'd you. 181

*Lincoln.* Villain, I 'll have thee punish'd for this wrong.

*Firk.* Punish the journeyman villain, but not the journeyman shoemaker.

*Enter Dodger*

*Dodger.* My lord, I come to bring unwelcome news. 185
Your nephew Lacy and your daughter Rose Early this morning wedded at the Savoy, None being present but the lady mayoress. Besides, I learnt among the officers, 189 The lord mayor vows to stand in their defence 'Gainst any that shall seek to cross the match.

*Lincoln.* Dares Eyre the shoemaker uphold the deed?

*Firk.* Yes, sir, shoemakers dare stand in a woman's quarrel, I warrant you, as deep as another, and deeper too. 195

*Dodger.* Besides, his grace to-day dines with the mayor; Who on his knees humbly intends to fall And beg a pardon for your nephew's fault.

*Lincoln.* But I 'll prevent him! Come, Sir Roger Otley; The king will do us justice in this cause. 200 Howe'er their hands have made them man and wife, I will disjoin the match, or lose my life. *Exeunt.*

*Firk.* Adieu, Monsieur Dodger! Farewell, fools! Ha, ha! Oh, if they had stay'd, I [204 would have so lamm'd them with flouts! O heart, my codpiece-point is ready to fly in pieces every time I think upon Mistress Rose. But let that pass, as my lady mayoress says.

*Hodge.* This matter is answer'd. Come, Rafe; home with thy wife. Come, my fine [210 shoemakers, let 's to our master's the new lord mayor, and there swagger this Shrove Tuesday. I 'll promise you wine enough, for Madge keeps the cellar.

*All.* O rare! Madge is a good wench. 215

*Firk.* And I 'll promise you meat enough, for simp'ring Susan keeps the larder. I 'll lead you to victuals, my brave soldiers; follow your captain. O brave! Hark, hark! Bell rings. [219

*All.* The pancake-bell rings, the pancake-bell! Trilill, my hearts!

*Firk.* Oh brave! Oh sweet bell! O delicate pancakes! Open the doors, my hearts, and shut up the windows! keep in the house, let out [224 the pancakes! Oh rare, my hearts! Let 's march together for the honour of Saint Hugh to the great new hall in Gracious Street corner, which our master, the new lord mayor, hath built.

*Rafe.* O the crew of good fellows that will dine at my lord mayor's cost to-day! 230

*Hodge.* By the Lord, my lord mayor is a most brave man. How shall prentices be bound to pray for him and the honour of the gentlemen shoemakers! Let 's feed and be fat with my lord's bounty. 235

*Firk.* O musical bell, still! O Hodge, O my brethren! There 's cheer for the heavens: venison-pasties walk up and down piping hot, like sergeants; beef and brewess comes march- [239 ing in dry-fats, fritters and pancakes comes trowling in in wheel-barrows; hens and oranges hopping in porters' baskets, collops and eggs in scuttles, and tarts and custards comes quavering in in malt-shovels.

*Enter more Prentices*

*All.* Whoop, look here, look here! 245

*Hodge.* How now, mad lads, whither away so fast?

*1 Pren.* Whither? Why, to the great new hall, know you not why? The lord mayor [249 hath bidden all the prentices in London to breakfast this morning.

*All.* Oh brave shoemaker, oh brave lord of incomprehensible good-fellowship! Whoo! Hark you! The pancake-bell rings. 254 *Cast up caps.*

*Firk.* Nay, more, my hearts! Every Shrove-Tuesday is our year of jubilee; and when the pancake-bell rings, we are as free as my lord mayor; we may shut up our shops, and make holiday; I 'll have it call'd Saint Hugh's Holiday. 260

*All.* Agreed, agreed! Saint Hugh's Holiday.

---

[176] **mean:** tenor (punning on "bass" as musical term)    [180] **lac'd mutton:** cant term for a common woman (with gibe at Lacy's name)    [227] **new hall:** Leadenhall (supposed to have been built at **Eyre's** expense)    [239] **brewess:** broth    [240] **dry-fats:** casks    [242] **collops:** slices of meat

*Hodge.* And this shall continue for ever.
*All.* Oh brave! Come, come, my hearts!
Away, away!
*Firk.* O eternal credit to us of the gentle
craft! March fair, my hearts! Oh rare!  265
*Exeunt.*

[SCENE III. — *Street near Leadenhall.*]

*Enter King and his Train over the stage*

*King.* Is our lord mayor of London such a
gallant?
*Nobleman.* One of the merriest madcaps in
your land.
Your grace will think, when you behold the man,
He 's rather a wild ruffian than a mayor.
Yet thus much I 'll ensure your majesty:    5
In all his actions that concern his state
He is as serious, provident, and wise,
As full of gravity amongst the grave,
As any mayor hath been these many years.
*King.* I am with child till I behold this huff-
cap.    10
But all my doubt is, when we come in presence,
His madness will be dash'd clean out of counte-
nance.
*Nobleman.* It may be so, my liege.
*King.*                         Which to prevent,
Let some one give him notice, 't is our pleasure
That he put on his wonted merriment.    15
Set forward!
*All.*         On afore!         *Exeunt.*

[SCENE IV. — *Leadenhall.*]

*Enter Eyre, Hodge, Firk, Rafe, and other
Shoemakers, all with napkins on their shoulders*

*Eyre.* Come, my fine Hodge, my jolly gentlemen shoemakers! soft, where be these cannibals, these varlets, my officers? Let them all
walk and wait upon my brethren; for my meaning is, that none but shoemakers, none but the [5
livery of my company shall in their satin hoods
wait upon the trencher of my sovereign.
*Firk.* O my lord, it will be rare!
*Eyre.* No more, Firk; come, lively! Let your
fellow-prentices want no cheer; let wine be [10
plentiful as beer, and beer as water. Hang these
penny-pinching fathers, that cram wealth in innocent lamb-skins. Rip, knaves, avaunt!
Look to my guests!
*Hodge.* My lord, we are at our wits' end [15
for room; those hundred tables will not feast
the fourth part of them.
*Eyre.* Then cover me those hundred tables
again, and again, till all my jolly prentices be

feasted. Avoid, Hodge! Run, Rafe! Frisk [20
about, my nimble Firk! Carouse me fadom-
healths to the honour of the shoemakers. Do
they drink lively, Hodge? Do they tickle it,
Firk?
*Firk.* Tickle it? Some of them have taken [25
their liquor standing so long that they can stand
no longer; but for meat, they would eat it and
they had it.
*Eyre.* Want they meat? Where 's this swag-
belly, this greasy kitchen-stuff cook? Call [30
the varlet to me! Want meat? Firk, Hodge,
lame Rafe, run, my tall men, beleaguer the
shambles, beggar all Eastcheap, serve me whole
oxen in chargers, and let sheep whine upon the
tables like pigs for want of good fellows to [35
eat them. Want meat? Vanish, Firk! Avaunt,
Hodge!
*Hodge.* Your lordship mistakes my man
Firk; he means, their bellies want meat, not
the boards; for they have drunk so much, [40
they can eat nothing.

THE SECOND THREE-MAN'S SONG

Cold 's the wind, and wet 's the rain,
    Saint Hugh be our good speed:
Ill is the weather that bringeth no gain,
    Nor helps good hearts in need.    45

Trowl the bowl, the jolly nut-brown bowl,
    And here, kind mate, to thee:
Let 's sing a dirge for Saint Hugh's soul,
    And down it merrily.

Down a down, hey down a down,    50
    (*Close with the tenor boy*)
Hey derry derry, down a down!
Ho, well done; to me let come!
    Ring, compass gentle joy

Trowl the bowl, the nut-brown bowl,
    And here, kind mate, to thee: etc.    55
[*Repeat*] *as often as there be men to drink.
At last when all have drunk, this verse:*
Cold 's the wind, and wet 's the rain,
    Saint Hugh be our good speed:
Ill is the weather that bringeth no gain,
    Nor helps good hearts in need.

*Enter Hans, Rose, and Wife*

*Wife.* Where is my lord?    60
*Eyre.* How now, Lady Madgy?
*Wife.* The king's most excellent majesty is
new come; he sends me for thy honour; one of
his most worshipful peers bade me tell thou must
be merry, and so forth; but let that pass. [65
*Eyre.* Is my sovereign come? Vanish, my
tall shoemakers, my nimble brethren; look to
my guests, the prentices. Yet stay a little!
How now, Hans? How looks my little Rose? [69

___
¹⁰ **with child:** filled with longing    **huff-cap:** blusterer    ¹³ **lamb-skins:** parchment bonds (or
purses)    ²¹⁻²² **fadom-healths:** healths a fathom deep    ²⁷ **and:** if    ⁴²⁻⁵⁹ (Printed separately in Qq.
with note: "This is to be sung at the latter end.")    ⁴⁶ **Trowl:** pass around

*Hans.* Let me request you to remember me.
I know, your honour easily may obtain
Free pardon of the king for me and Rose,
And reconcile me to my uncle's grace.

*Eyre.* Have done, my good Hans, my honest
journeyman; look cheerily! I 'll fall upon [75
both my knees, till they be as hard as horn, but
I 'll get thy pardon.

*Wife.* Good my lord, have a care what you
speak to his grace.                                    79

*Eyre.* Away, you Islington whitepot! hence,
you hopper-arse! hence, you barley-pudding,
full of maggots! you broiled carbonado! avaunt,
avaunt, avoid, Mephistophilus! Shall Sim Eyre
learn to speak of you, Lady Madgy? Vanish,
Mother Miniver-cap; vanish, go, trip and [85
go; meddle with your partlets and your pishery-
pashery, your flewes and your whirligigs; go,
rub, out of mine alley! Sim Eyre knows how
to speak to a Pope, to Sultan Soliman, to Tamburlaine, an he were here, and shall I melt, [90
shall I droop before my sovereign? No, come,
my Lady Madgy! Follow me, Hans! About
your business, my frolic free-booters! Firk, frisk
about, and about, and about, for the honour of
mad Simon Eyre, lord mayor of London.      95

*Firk.* Hey, for the honour of the shoemakers!

*Exeunt.*

[SCENE V. — *Outside Leadenhall.*]

*A long flourish, or two. Enter King, Nobles,
Eyre, his Wife, Lacy, Rose. Lacy and Rose
kneel.*

*King.* Well, Lacy, though the fact was very
foul
Of your revolting from our kingly love
And your own duty, yet we pardon you.
Rise both, and, Mistress Lacy, thank my lord
mayor
For your young bridegroom here.       5

*Eyre.* So, my dear liege, Sim Eyre and my
brethren, the gentlemen shoemakers, shall set
your sweet majesty's image cheek by jowl by
Saint Hugh for this honour you have done poor
Simon Eyre. I beseech your grace, pardon [10
my rude behaviour; I am a handicraftsman, yet
my heart is without craft; I would be sorry at
my soul that my boldness should offend my
king.

*King.* Nay, I pray thee, good lord mayor,
be even as merry                                    15
As if thou wert among thy shoemakers;
It does me good to see thee in this humour.

*Eyre.* Say'st thou me so, my sweet Diocle-
sian? Then, hump! Prince am I none, yet am

I princely born. By the Lord of Ludgate, my
liege, I 'll be as merry as a pie.                21

*King.* Tell me, in faith, mad Eyre, how old
thou art.

*Eyre.* My liege, a very boy, a stripling, a
younker; you see not a white hair on my head,
not a gray in this beard. Every hair, I as- [25
sure thy majesty, that sticks in this beard, Sim
Eyre values at the King of Babylon's ransom.
Tamar Cham's beard was a rubbing brush to
't: yet I 'll shave it off, and stuff tennis-balls
with it, to please my bully king.                  30

*King.* But all this while I do not know your
age.

*Eyre.* My liege, I am six-and-fifty year old,
yet I can cry hump! with a sound heart for the
honour of Saint Hugh. Mark this old wench,
my king: I danc'd the shaking of the sheets [35
with her six and thirty years ago, and yet I
hope to get two or three young lord mayors, ere
I die. I am lusty still, Sim Eyre still. Care and
cold lodging brings white hairs. My sweet Majesty, let care vanish, cast it upon thy nobles: [40
it will make thee look always young like Apollo,
and cry hump! Prince am I none, yet am I
princely born.

*King.* Ha, ha!
Say, Cornwall, didst thou ever see his like?   45

*Nobleman.* Not I, my lord.

*Enter Lincoln and Sir Roger Otley*

*King.*          Lincoln, what news with you?

*Lincoln.* My gracious lord, have care unto
yourself,
For there are traitors here.

*All.*               Traitors? Where? Who?

*Eyre.* Traitors in my house? God forbid! [49
Where be my officers? I 'll spend my soul, ere
my king feel harm.

*King.* Where is the traitor, Lincoln?

*Lincoln.*                       Here he stands.

*King.* Cornwall, lay hold on Lacy! — Lincoln, speak,
What canst thou lay unto thy nephew's charge?

*Lincoln.* This, my dear liege: your Grace, to
do me honour,                                       55
Heap'd on the head of this degenerous boy
Desertless favours; you made choice of him
To be commander over powers in France.
But he ——

*King.* Good Lincoln, prithee, pause a while!
Even in thine eyes I read what thou wouldst
speak.                                              60
I know how Lacy did neglect our love,
Ran himself deeply, in the highest degree,
Into vile treason ——

---

⁸⁰ **whitepot:** concoction of milk, eggs, raisins, and sugar   ⁸¹ **hopper-arse:** swag-body   ⁸² **car-**
**bonado:** steak   ⁸⁵ **Miniver-:** fur   ⁸⁶ **partlets:** neckbands   ⁸⁷ **flewes:** flapping skirts   ⁸⁸ **rub:**
obstacle (bowling term)   ²¹ **pie:** magpie   ⁵⁶ **degenerous:** degenerate

*Lincoln.*                     Is he not a traitor?

*King.* Lincoln, he was; now have we pardon'd him.

'T was not a base want of true valour's fire, 65
That held him out of France, but love's desire.

*Lincoln.* I will not bear his shame upon my
back.

*King.* Nor shalt thou, Lincoln; I forgive
you both.

*Lincoln.* Then, good my liege, forbid the boy
to wed
One whose mean birth will much disgrace his
bed.                                                                            70

*King.* Are they not married?

*Lincoln.*                                            No, my liege.

*Both.*                                                     We are.

*King.* Shall I divorce them then? O be it far
That any hand on earth should dare untie
The sacred knot, knit by God's majesty;      74
I would not for my crown disjoin their hands
That are conjoin'd in holy nuptial bands.
How say'st thou, Lacy, wouldst thou lose thy
Rose?

*Lacy.* Not for all India's wealth, my sovereign.

*King.* But Rose, I am sure, her Lacy would
forgo?

*Rose.* If Rose were ask'd that question, she 'd
say no.                                                                        80

*King.* You hear them, Lincoln?

*Lincoln.*                                 Yea, my liege, I do.

*King.* Yet canst thou find i' th' heart to
part these two?
Who seeks, besides you, to divorce these lovers?

*Otley.* I do, my gracious lord. I am her
father.

*King.* Sir Roger Otley, our last mayor, I
think?                                                                          85

*Nobleman.* The same, my liege.

*King.*                          Would you offend Love's laws?
Well, you shall have your wills. You sue to me
To prohibit the match. Soft, let me see —
You both are married, Lacy, art thou not?

*Lacy.* I am, dread sovereign.

*King.*                           Then, upon thy life,      90
I charge thee, not to call this woman wife.

*Otley.* I thank your grace.

*Rose.*                           O my most gracious lord!
                                                                                *Kneel.*

*King.* Nay, Rose, never woo me; I tell you
true,
Although as yet I am a bachelor,
Yet I believe I shall not marry you.          95

*Rose.* Can you divide the body from the soul,
Yet make the body live?

*King.*                           Yea, so profound?
I cannot, Rose, but you I must divide.
This fair maid, bridegroom, cannot be your bride.

Are you pleas'd, Lincoln? Otley, are you
pleas'd?                                                                       100

*Both.* Yes, my lord.

*King.*                           Then must my heart be eas'd;
For, credit me, my conscience lives in pain,
Till these whom I divorc'd, be join'd again.
Lacy, give me thy hand; Rose, lend me thine!
Be what you would be! Kiss now! So, that 's
fine.                                                                           105
At night, lovers, to bed! — Now, let me see,
Which of you all mislikes this harmony.

*Otley.* Will you then take from me my child
perforce?

*King.* Why tell me, Otley: shines not Lacy's
name                                                                            109
As bright in the world's eye as the gay beams
Of any citizen?

*Lincoln.*                           Yea, but, my gracious lord,
I do mislike the match far more than he;
Her blood is too too base.

*King.*                           Lincoln, no more.
Dost thou not know that love respects no blood,
Cares not for difference of birth or state?    115
The maid is young, well born, fair, virtuous,
A worthy bride for any gentleman.
Besides, your nephew for her sake did stoop
To bare necessity, and, as I hear,
Forgetting honours and all courtly pleasures, 120
To gain her love, became a shoemaker.
As for the honour which he lost in France,
Thus I redeem it: Lacy, kneel thee down! —
Arise, Sir Rowland Lacy! Tell me now,       124
Tell me in earnest, Otley, canst thou chide,
Seeing thy Rose a lady and a bride?

*Otley.* I am content with what your grace
hath done.

*Lincoln.* And I, my liege, since there 's no
remedy.

*King.* Come on, then, all shake hands: I 'll
have you friends;
Where there is much love, all discord ends. 130
What says my mad lord mayor to all this love?

*Eyre.* O my liege, this honour you have done
to my fine journeyman here, Rowland Lacy,
and all these favours which you have shown [134
to me this day in my poor house, will make
Simon Eyre live longer by one dozen of warm
summers more than he should.

*King.* Nay, my mad lord mayor, that shall
be thy name;
If any grace of mine can length thy life,
One honour more I 'll do thee: that new build-
ing,                                                                            140
Which at thy cost in Cornhill is erected,
Shall take a name from us; we 'll have it call'd
The Leadenhall, because in digging it
You found the lead that covereth the same. 144

*Eyre.* I thank your majesty.

*Wife.*                God bless your grace!
*King.* Lincoln, a word with you!

*Enter Hodge, Firk, Rafe, and more Shoe-
makers*

*Eyre.* How now, my mad knaves? Peace,
speak softly; yonder is the king.
   *King.* With the old troop, which there we
   keep in pay,
We will incorporate a new supply.          150
Before one summer more pass o'er my head,
France shall repent, England was injured.
What are all those?
   *Lacy.*          All shoemakers, my liege,
Sometimes my fellows; in their companies
I liv'd as merry as an emperor.            155
   *King.* My mad lord mayor, are all these
   shoemakers?
   *Eyre.* All shoemakers, my liege; all gentle-
men of the gentle craft, true Trojans, courageous cordwainers; they all kneel to the shrine
of holy Saint Hugh.                         160
   *All.* God save your majesty, all shoemakers!
   *King.* Mad Simon, would they anything
   with us?
   *Eyre.* Mum, mad knaves! Not a word! I'll
do 't; I warrant you. They are all beggars, my
liege; all for themselves, and I for them [165
all on both my knees do entreat, that for the
honour of poor Simon Eyre and the good of his
brethren, these mad knaves, your grace would
vouchsafe some privilege to my new Leadenhall,
that it may be lawful for us to buy and sell
leather there two days a week.             171
   *King.* Mad Sim, I grant your suit, you shall
   have patent
To hold two market-days in Leadenhall.
Mondays and Fridays, those shall be the times.
Will this content you?
   *All.*             Jesus bless your grace!  175

---

*Eyre.* In the name of these my poor brethren
shoemakers, I most humbly thank your grace.
But before I rise, seeing you are in the giving
vein and we in the begging, grant Sim Eyre one
boon more.                                   180
   *King.* What is it, my lord mayor?
   *Eyre.* Vouchsafe to taste of a poor banquet
that stands sweetly waiting for your sweet pres-
ence.                                        184
   *King.* I shall undo thee, Eyre, only with
   feasts;
Already have I been too troublesome;
Say, have I not?
   *Eyre.* O my dear king, Sim Eyre was taken
unawares upon a day of shroving, which I [189
promis'd long ago to the prentices of London.
For, an 't please your highness, in time past,
I bare the water-tankard, and my coat
Sits not a whit the worse upon my back;
And then, upon a morning, some mad boys
(It was Shrove Tuesday, even as 't is now) [195
gave me my breakfast, and I swore then by the
stopple of my tankard, if ever I came to be
lord mayor of London, I would feast all the
prentices. This day, my liege, I did it, and the
slaves had an hundred tables five times covered.
They are gone home and vanish'd.            201
Yet add more honour to the gentle trade:
Taste of Eyre's banquet, Simon 's happy made.
   *King.* Eyre, I will taste of thy banquet, and
   will say,
I have not met more pleasure on a day.      205
Friends of the gentle craft, thanks to you all.
Thanks, my kind lady mayoress, for our
   cheer. —
Come, lords, a while let 's revel it at home!
When all our sports and banquetings are done,
Wars must right wrongs which Frenchmen
   have begun.             *Exeunt.*  210
                     FINIS

---

154 **Sometimes:** formerly     189 **shroving:** celebration

# A
# WOMAN
## KILDE
# with Kindneſſe.

*As it hath beene oftentimes Aƈted by
the Queenes Maieſt. Seruants.*

*Written by* Tho. Heywood.

The third Edition.

London,
Printed by Iſaac Iaggard, 1617

BIBLIOGRAPHICAL RECORD. The earliest known edition of *A Woman Killed with Kindness* is a Quarto dated 1607. The only other surviving early Quarto, that of 1617, is described on the title-page as the "third edition," so that there was probably another edition of which no copy is known to have been preserved. The Quarto of 1617, here referred to as "Q 2," provides a better text than that of 1607, and forms the basis of the present edition. The play was not entered on the Registers of the Stationers' Co. In neither of the Quartos is it divided into acts and scenes.

DATE AND STAGE PERFORMANCE. The date of composition and performance of this play is fixed with some accuracy by entries in Henslowe's Diary. On Feb. 12 and March 6, 1603, Henslowe paid to Heywood on behalf of Worcester's company of players the sum of £6 for the play itself, and during the same months made payments amounting to more than £8 for a "womones gowne of blacke velluett" and a "blacke satten sewt" for use in the play. The original performance seems to have been by Worcester's Men, and the title-page of the Quarto of 1617 states that the play had been "oftentimes Acted" by Queen Anne's Men, by which title Worcester's company became known soon after the accession of James I. This play, like others of Heywood's, was particularly popular with the bourgeois. An early allusion in Middleton's (?) *Black Book* (1604) speaks of it and *The Merry Devil of Edmonton* as the two current theatrical offerings that could be counted on to tempt an "honest, simple" London servingman. It has shown itself effective also on the modern stage: in 1887 at the Olympic Theatre, London; in 1914 in New York; in 1922 as produced by the Birmingham Repertory Company; and in French translation by J. Copeau at the Théâtre du Vieux Colombier, Paris, 1914.

SOURCES. Some similarities have been noted between Heywood's play and certain novels in Painter's *Palace of Pleasure*, but the material derived from these tales has been very freely used. The three stories from Painter drawn upon are: for the main plot, Bk. I, nos. 43 and 58; for the subplot, Bk. II, no. 30. (See R. G. Martin, "A New Source for *A Woman Killed with Kindness.*" *Englische Studien*, xliii. 229 ff.) The scene has been definitely localized in Heywood's England, and the play represents the type of domestic drama which was his particular contribution to the Elizabethan stage.

# THOMAS HEYWOOD (c. 1574–1641)

# A WOMAN KILLED WITH KINDNESS

[DRAMATIS PERSONAE

SIR FRANCIS ACTON, Brother to Mistress Frankford
SIR CHARLES MOUNTFORD
MASTER JOHN FRANKFORD
MASTER MALBY, friend to Sir Francis
MASTER WENDOLL, friend to Frankford
MASTER CRANWELL
MASTER SHAFTON, false friend to Sir Charles
OLD MOUNTFORD, Uncle to Sir Charles
MASTER SANDY
MASTER RODER
MASTER TIDY, Cousin to Sir Charles

NICHOLAS,
JENKIN, } Household Servants to Frankford
SPIGOT, Butler,

ROGER BRICKBAT, } Country Fellows
JACK SLIME,

MISTRESS ANNE FRANKFORD
SUSAN, Sister to Sir Charles Mountford
CICELY, Maid to Mistress Frankford
JOAN MINIVER,
JANE TRUBKIN, } Country Wenches
ISBELL MOTLEY,

Sheriff; Keeper of the Prison; Officers; Huntsmen; Falconers; Coachmen; Carters; Servants; Musicians; Children.

Scene: — Yorkshire.]

## THE PROLOGUE

I COME but as a harbinger, being sent
To tell you what these preparations mean.
Look for no glorious state; our Muse is bent
Upon a barren subject, a bare scene.
We could afford this twig a timber-tree,                          5
Whose strength might boldly on your favours build;
Our russet, tissue; drone, a honey-bee;
Our barren plot, a large and spacious field;
Our coarse fare, banquets; our thin water, wine;
Our brook, a sea; our bat's eyes, eagle's sight;                 10
Our poet's dull and earthy Muse, divine;
Our ravens, doves; our crow's black feathers, white.
    But gentle thoughts, when they may give the foil,
    Save them that yield, and spare where they may spoil.

[ACT I

SCENE I. — A Room in Frankford's House.]

Enter Master John Frankford, Mistress Anne, Sir Francis Acton, Sir Charles Mountford, Master Malby, Master Wendoll, and Master Cranwell

Francis. Some music, there! None lead the bride a dance?
Charles. Yes, would she dance The Shaking of the Sheets;
But that 's the dance her husband means to lead her.

Wen. That 's not the dance that every man must dance,
According to the ballad.
   Fran.           Music, ho!                5
By your leave, sister, — by your husband's leave,
I should have said, — the hand that but this day
Was given you in the church I 'll borrow. — Sound!
This marriage music hoists me from the ground.
   Frank. Ay, you may caper; you are light and free!          10

Prol. 5 could afford: would fain have    7 russet: homespun cloth    13 foil: defeat    2 Shaking
. . . Sheets: a popular ballad

297

Marriage hath yok'd my heels; pray pardon
me.
*Fran.* I 'll have you dance too, brother!
*Char.* Master Frankford,
Y' are a happy man, sir, and much joy
Succeed your marriage mirth: you have a wife
So qualified, and with such ornaments  15
Both of the mind and body. First, her birth
Is noble, and her education such
As might become the daughter of a prince;
Her own tongue speaks all tongues, and her
own hand
Can teach all strings to speak in their best
grace,  20
From the shrill'st treble to the hoarsest base.
To end her many praises in one word,
She 's Beauty and Perfection's eldest daughter,
Only found by yours, though many a heart hath
sought her.
*Frank.* But that I know your virtues and
chaste thoughts,  25
I should be jealous of your praise, Sir Charles.
*Cran.* He speaks no more than you approve.
*Mal.* Nor flatters he that gives to her her due.
*Anne.* I would your praise could find a fitter
theme
Than my imperfect beauties to speak on!  30
Such as they be, if they my husband please,
They suffice me now I am married.
His sweet content is like a flatt'ring glass,
To make my face seem fairer to mine eye;
But the least wrinkle from his stormy brow  35
Will blast the roses in my cheeks that grow.
*Fran.* A perfect wife already, meek and
patient!
How strangely the word husband fits your
mouth,
Not married three hours since! Sister, 't is
good;  39
You that begin betimes thus must needs prove
Pliant and duteous in your husband's love. —
Gramercies, brother! Wrought her to 't al-
ready,
'Sweet husband,' and a curtsey, the first day?
Mark this, mark this, you that are bachelors,
And never took the grace of honest man;  45
Mark this, against you marry, this one phrase:
'In a good time that man both wins and woos
That takes his wife down in her wedding shoes.'
*Frank.* Your sister takes not after you, Sir
Francis.
All his wild blood your father spent on you;  50
He got her in his age, when he grew civil.
All his mad tricks were to his land entail'd,
And you are heir to all; your sister, she

Hath to her dower her mother's modesty.
*Char.* Lord, sir, in what a happy state live
you!  55
This morning, which to many seems a burthen,
Too heavy to bear, is unto you a pleasure.
This lady is no clog, as many are;
She doth become you like a well-made suit,
In which the tailor hath us'd all his art;  60
Not like a thick coat of unseason'd frieze,
Forc'd on your back in summer. She 's no chain
To tie your neck, and curb ye to the yoke;
But she 's a chain of gold to adorn your neck.
You both adorn each other, and your hands,  65
Methinks, are matches. There 's equality
In this fair combination; y' are both scholars,
Both young, both being descended nobly.
There 's music in this sympathy; it carries
Consort and expectation of much joy,  70
Which God bestow on you from this first day
Until your dissolution, — that 's for aye!
*Fran.* We keep you here too long, good
brother Frankford.
Into the hall; away! Go cheer your guests.
What! Bride and bridegroom both withdrawn
at once?  75
If you be miss'd, the guests will doubt their
welcome,
And charge you with unkindness.
*Frank.* To prevent it,
I 'll leave you here, to see the dance within.
*Anne.* And so will I.
*Exit [with Master Frankford].*
*Fran.* To part you it were sin. —
Now, gallants, while the town musicians  80
Finger their frets within, and the mad lads
And country lasses, every mother's child,
With nosegays and bride-laces in their hats,
Dance all their country measures, rounds, and
jigs,
What shall we do? Hark! They 're all on the
hoigh;  85
They toil like mill-horses, and turn as round, —
Marry, not on the toe! Ay, and they caper,
Not without cutting; you shall see, to-morrow,
The hall-floor peck'd and dinted like a mill-stone,
Made with their high shoes. Though their
skill be small,  90
Yet they tread heavy where their hobnails fall.
*Char.* Well, leave them to their sports! —
Sir Francis Acton,
I 'll make a match with you! Meet me to-
morrow
At Chevy Chase; I 'll fly my hawk with yours.
*Fran.* For what? For what?
*Char.* Why, for a hundred pound.  95

⁴² **Gramercies:** thanks   ⁴⁵ **took the grace:** attained the dignity   ⁴⁶ **against:** in expectation of
the time when   ⁴⁸ **takes . . . down:** reduces to submission (a common proverb)   ⁶¹ **frieze:** coarse
cloth   ⁸¹ **Finger . . . frets:** tune their instruments   ⁸³ **bride-laces:** streamers   ⁸⁵ **on the hoigh·**
in a state of exhilaration   ⁸⁸ **Not:** ('But' Qq.)

*Fran.* Pawn me some gold of that!

*Char.*            Here are ten angels;
I 'll make them good a hundred pound to-mor-
row
Upon my hawk's wing.

*Fran.*           'T is a match; 't is done.
Another hundred pound upon your dogs; —
Dare ye, Sir Charles?

*Char.*          I dare; were I sure to lose,
I durst do more than that. Here 's my hand, 101
The first course for a hundred pound!

*Fran.*              A match.

*Wen.* Ten angels on Sir Francis Acton's
hawk;
As much upon his dogs!

*Cran.* I am for Sir Charles Mountford: I
have seen           105
His hawk and dog both tried. What! Clap ye
hands,
Or is 't no bargain?

*Wen.*          Yes, and stake them down.
Were they five hundred, they were all my own.

*Fran.* Be stirring early with the lark to-
morrow;
I 'll rise into my saddle ere the sun     110
Rise from his bed.

*Char.*       If there you miss me, say
I am no gentleman! I 'll hold my day.

*Fran.* It holds on all sides. — Come, to-
night let 's dance;
Early to-morrow let 's prepare to ride:    114
We 'd need be three hours up before the bride.

                         *Exeunt.*

[SCENE II. — *Yard of the Same.*]

*Enter Nick and Jenkin, Jack Slime, Roger Brick-
bat, with Country Wenches, and two or three
Musicians*

*Jen.* Come, Nick, take you Joan Miniver, to
trace withal; Jack Slime, traverse you with
Cicely Milkpail; I will take Jane Trubkin, and
Roger Brickbat shall have Isbell Motley. And
now that they are busy in the parlour, come, [5
strike up; we 'll have a crash here in the
yard.

*Nich.* My humour is not compendious: dancing I possess not, though I can foot it; yet,
since I am fallen into the hands of Cicely [10
Milkpail, I consent.

*Slime.* Truly, Nick, though we were never
brought up like serving courtiers, yet we have
been brought up with serving creatures, — ay,
and God's creatures, too; for we have been [15
brought up to serve sheep, oxen, horses, hogs,
and such like; and, though we be but country

fellows, it may be in the way of dancing we can
do the horse-trick as well as the serving-men.

*Brick.* Ay, and the cross-point too.      20

*Jen.* O Slime! O Brickbat! Do not you know
that comparisons are odious? Now we are odious ourselves, too; therefore there are no comparisons to be made betwixt us.

*Nich.* I am sudden, and not superfluous: 25
I am quarrelsome, and not seditious;
I am peaceable, and not contentious;
I am brief, and not compendious.

*Slime.* Foot it quickly! If the music overcome
not my melancholy, I shall quarrel; and if [30
they suddenly do not strike up, I shall presently
strike thee down.

*Jen.* No quarrelling, for God's sake! Truly,
if you do, I shall set a knave between ye.

*Slime.* I come to dance, not to quarrel. [35
Come, what shall it be? *Rogero?*

*Jen.* *Rogero?* No; we will dance *The Beginning of the World.*

*Cicely.* I love no dance so well as *John come
kiss me now.*           40

*Nich.* I that have ere now deserv'd a cushion, call for the Cushion-dance.

*Brick.* For my part, I like nothing so well as
*Tom Tyler.*

*Jen.* No; we 'll have *The Hunting of the* [45
*Fox.*

*Slime.* The Hay, the Hay! There 's nothing
like the Hay.

*Nich.* I have said, do say, and will say
again ——           50

*Jen.* Every man agree to have it as Nick says!

*All.* Content.

*Nich.* It hath been, it now is, and it shall
be ——

*Cicely.* What, Master Nicholas? What? 55

*Nich.* *Put on your Smock o' Monday.*

*Jen.* So the dance will come cleanly off! Come,
for God's sake, agree of something: if you like
not that, put it to the musicians; or let me
speak for all, and we 'll have *Sellenger's* [60
*Round.*

*All.* That, that, that!

*Nich.* No, I am resolv'd thus it shall be;
First take hands, then take ye to your heels.

*Jen.* Why, would ye have us run away? 65

*Nich.* No; but I would have you shake your
heels. — Music strike up!

         *They dance; Nick dancing, speaks
         stately and scurvily, the rest after
         the country fashion.*

*Jen.* Hey! Lively, my lasses! Here 's a
turn for thee!           *Exeunt.*

---

**96 angels:** gold coins worth about ten shillings keep my engagement    **2 trace, traverse:** dance
**19, 20 horse-trick, cross-point:** steps in dancing    **6 crash:** frolic    **8 compendious:** all-embracing
tunes.)    **42, 47 Cushion-dance, the Hay:** popular dances    **106 Clap ye hands:** shake on it    **112 hold my day:**    **36–61** (The tunes named here were all familiar dance    **67 S. D. scurvily:** haughtily

[SCENE III. — *Chevy Chase.*]

*Wind horns. Enter Sir Charles [Mountford], Sir Francis [Acton], Malby, Cranwell, Wendoll, Falconer, and Huntsmen*

*Char.* So; well cast off! Aloft, aloft! Well flown!
Oh, now she takes her at the souse, and strikes her
Down to the earth, like a swift thunder-clap.
    *Wen.* She hath struck ten angels out of my way.
    *Fran.* A hundred pound from me.          5
    *Char.* What, falconer!
    *Falc.* At hand, sir!
    *Char.* Now she hath seiz'd the fowl and 'gins to plume her,
Rebeck her not; rather stand still and check her!
So, seize her gets, her jesses, and her bells!  10
Away!
    *Fran.* My hawk kill'd, too.
    *Char.*          Ay, but 't was at the querre,
Not at the mount like mine.
    *Fran.*          Judgment, my masters!
    *Cran.* Yours miss'd her at the ferre.
    *Wen.* Ay, but our merlin first had plum'd the fowl,  15
And twice renew'd her from the river too.
Her bells, Sir Francis, had not both one weight,
Nor was one semi-tune above the other.
Methinks, these Milan bells do sound too full,
And spoil the mounting of your hawk.
    *Char.*          'T is lost.  20
    *Fran.* I grant it not. Mine likewise seiz'd a fowl
Within her talons, and you saw her paws
Full of the feathers; both her petty singles
And her long singles grip'd her more than other;
The terrials of her legs were stain'd with blood,  25
Not of the fowl only; she did discomfit
Some of her feathers; but she brake away.
Come, come; your hawk is but a rifler.
    *Char.*          How!
    *Fran.* Ay, and your dogs are trindle-tails and curs.
    *Char.* You stir my blood.  30
You keep not one good hound in all your kennel,
Nor one good hawk upon your perch.
    *Fran.*          How, knight!
    *Char.* So, knight. You will not swagger, sir?

*Fran.* Why, say I did?
    *Char.*          Why, sir,
I say you would gain as much by swagg'ring  35
As you have got by wagers on your dogs.
You will come short in all things.
    *Fran.*          Not in this!
Now I 'll strike home.  [*Strikes Sir Charles.*]
    *Char.*          Thou shalt to thy long home,
Or I will want my will.
    *Fran.* All they that love Sir Francis, follow me!  40
    *Char.* All that affect Sir Charles, draw on my part!
    *Cran.* On this side heaves my hand.
    *Wen.*          Here goes my heart.
    *They divide themselves. Sir Charles, Cranwell, Falconer, and Huntsman, fight against Sir Francis, Wendoll, his Falconer and Huntsman; and Sir Charles hath the better, and beats them away, killing both of Sir Francis his men. [Exeunt all except Sir Charles.]*
    *Char.* My God, what have I done! What have I done!
My rage hath plung'd into a sea of blood,
In which my soul lies drown'd. Poor innocents,  45
For whom we are to answer! Well, 't is done,
And I remain the victor. A great conquest,
When I would give this right hand, nay, this head,
To breathe in them new life whom I have slain! —
Forgive me, God! 'T was in the heat of blood,  50
And anger quite removes me from myself.
It was not I, but rage, did this vile murther;
Yet I, and not my rage, must answer it.
Sir Francis Acton, he is fled the field;
With him all those that did partake his quarrel;
And I am left alone with sorrow dumb,  56
And in my height of conquest overcome.

*Enter Susan*

*Susan.* O God! My brother wounded 'mong the dead!
Unhappy jest, that in such earnest ends!
The rumour of this fear stretch'd to my ears,  60
And I am come to know if you be wounded.
    *Char.* Oh, sister, sister! Wounded at the heart.
    *Susan.* My God forbid!
    *Char.* In doing that thing which he forbad,
I am wounded, sister.

___

² **souse:** swoop    ⁸ **plume:** pluck    ⁹ **Rebeck:** call back (?)    ¹⁰ **gets, jesses, bells:** parts of the hawk's harness    ¹² **querre:** oblique attack (?)    ¹⁴ **ferre:** further or higher point    ¹⁶ **renew'd:** driven by a fresh attack    ²³ **singles:** toes    ²⁵ **terrials:** talons (?), straps holding bells (?)    ²⁸ **rifler:** bungler    ²⁹ **trindle-tails:** curly-tails    ⁵⁹ **jest:** ('jests' Oq.)

*Susan.*             I hope, not at the heart. 65
*Char.* Yes, at the heart.
*Susan.*                    O God! A surgeon, there!
*Char.* Call me a surgeon, sister, for my soul!
The sin of murther, it hath pierc'd my heart
And made a wide wound there; but for these
    scratches,
They are nothing, nothing.
*Susan.*      Charles, what have you done? 70
Sir Francis hath great friends, and will pursue
    you
Unto the utmost danger of the law.
*Char.* My conscience is become mine enemy,
And will pursue me more than Acton can.
*Susan.* Oh, fly, sweet brother!
*Char.*                Shall I fly from thee? 75
Why, Sue, art weary of my company?
*Susan.* Fly from your foe!
*Char.*                You, sister, are my friend,
And flying you, I shall pursue my end.
*Susan.* Your company is as my eyeball dear;
Being far from you, no comfort can be near. 80
Yet fly to save your life! What would I care
To spend my future age in black despair,
So you were safe? And yet to live one week
Without my brother Charles, through every
    cheek
My streaming tears would downwards run so
    rank, 85
Till they could set on either side a bank,
And in the midst a channel; so my face
For two salt-water brooks shall still find place.
*Char.* Thou shalt not weep so much; for I
    will stay,
In spite of danger's teeth. I 'll live with thee, 90
Or I 'll not live at all. I will not sell
My country and my father's patrimony,
Nor thy sweet sight, for a vain hope of life.

*Enter Sheriff, with Officers*

*Sher.* Sir Charles, I am made the unwilling
    instrument
Of your attach and apprehension. 95
I 'm sorry that the blood of innocent men
Should be of you exacted. It was told me
That you were guarded with a troop of friends,
And therefore I came thus arm'd.
*Char.*                Oh, Master Sheriff!
I came into the field with many friends, 100
But see, they all have left me; only one
Clings to my sad misfortune, my dear sister.
I know you for an honest gentleman;
I yield my weapons, and submit to you.
Convey me where you please!
*Sher.*                To prison, then, 105
To answer for the lives of these dead men.

*Susan.* O God! O God!
*Char.*                Sweet sister, every strain
Of sorrow from your heart augments my pain;
Your grief abounds, and hits against my
    breast.
*Sher.* Sir, will you go?
*Char.*        Even where it likes you best. 110
                    [*Exeunt.*]

## [ACT II

### Scene I. — *Frankford's House.*]

*Enter Master Frankford in a study*

*Frank.* How happy am I amongst other men,
That in my mean estate embrace content!
I am a gentleman, and by my birth
Companion with a king; a king 's no more.
I am possess'd of many fair revenues,       5
Sufficient to maintain a gentleman;
Touching my mind, I am studied in all arts,
The riches of my thoughts, and of my time
Have been a good proficient; but, the chief
Of all the sweet felicities on earth,        10
I have a fair, a chaste, and loving wife, —
Perfection all, all truth, all ornament.
If man on earth may truly happy be,
Of these at once possess'd, sure, I am he.

*Enter Nicholas*

*Nich.* Sir, there 's a gentleman attends with-
    out                                       15
To speak with you.
*Frank.*                On horseback?
*Nich.*                    Yes, on horseback.
*Frank.* Entreat him to alight, and I 'll
    attend him.
Know'st thou him, Nick?
*Nich.* Know him? Yes; his name 's Wendoll.
It seems, he comes in haste: his horse is booted
Up to the flank in mire, himself all spotted 20
And stain'd with plashing. Sure, he rid in
    fear,
Or for a wager. Horse and man both sweat;
I ne'er saw two in such a smoking heat.
*Frank.* Entreat him in: about it instantly!
                    [*Exit Nicholas.*]
This Wendoll I have noted, and his carriage 25
Hath pleas'd me much; by observation
I have noted many good deserts in him.
He 's affable, and seen in many things;
Discourses well; a good companion;
And though of small means, yet a gentleman 3c
Of a good house, somewhat press'd by want.
I have preferr'd him to a second place
In my opinion and my best regard.

---

⁷² **danger:** penalty    ⁸⁵ **rank:** abundantly    ⁹³ **Nor:** ('No ' Q 2)    ⁹⁵ **attach:** arrest    ⁹⁹ **I:** (Not
in Qq.)    ¹⁰⁹ **abounds:** overflows    ¹¹⁰ **likes:** pleases    ⁹ **Have . . . proficient:** have made good use
¹⁹ **booted:** splashed    ²⁸ **seen:** skilled

*Enter Wendoll, Mistress Frankford, and Nick*

*Anne.* Oh, Master Frankford! Master Wen-
doll here
Brings you the strangest news that e'er you
heard.                                                   35
   *Frank.* What news, sweet wife? What news,
good Master Wendoll?
   *Wen.* You knew the match made 'twixt Sir
Francis Acton
And Sir Charles Mountford?
   *Frank.* True; with their hounds and hawks.
   *Wen.* The matches were both play'd.
   *Frank.*               Ha? And which won?
   *Wen.* Sir Francis, your wife's brother, had
the worst,                                               40
And lost the wager.
   *Frank.*           Why, the worse his chance;
Perhaps the fortune of some other day
Will change his luck.
   *Anne.*          Oh, but you hear not all.
Sir Francis lost, and yet was loath to yield.    44
At length the two knights grew to difference,
From words to blows, and so to banding sides;
Where valorous Sir Charles slew, in his spleen,
Two of your brother's men, — his falconer,
And his good huntsman, whom he lov'd so
well.
More men were wounded, no more slain out-
right.                                                   50
   *Frank.* Now, trust me, I am sorry for the
knight.
But is my brother safe?
   *Wen.*                All whole and sound,
His body not being blemish'd with one wound.
But poor Sir Charles is to the prison led,
To answer at th' assize for them that 's dead.
   *Frank.* I thank your pains, sir. Had the
news been better,                                        56
Your will was to have brought it, Master Wen-
doll.
Sir Charles will find hard friends; his case is
heinous
And will be most severely censur'd on.
I 'm sorry for him. Sir, a word with you!    60
I know you, sir, to be a gentleman
In all things; your possibility but mean:
Please you to use my table and my purse;
They are yours.
   *Wen.* O Lord, sir! I shall never deserve
it.
   *Frank.* O sir, disparage not your worth too
much:                                                    65
You are full of quality and fair desert.
Choose of my men which shall attend on
you,

And he is yours. I will allow you, sir,
Your man, your gelding, and your table, all
At my own charge; be my companion!    70
   *Wen.* Master Frankford, I have oft been
bound to you
By many favours; this exceeds them all,
That I shall never merit your least favour;
But when your last remembrance I forget,
Heaven at my soul exact that weighty debt! 75
   *Frank.* There needs no protestation; for I
know you
Virtuous, and therefore grateful. — Prithee,
Nan,
Use him with all thy loving'st courtesy!
   *Anne.* As far as modesty may well ex-
tend,
It is my duty to receive your friend.    80
   *Frank.* To dinner! Come, sir, from this pres-
ent day,
Welcome to me for ever! Come, away!
      *Exit [with Mistress Frankford and
       Wendoll].*
   *Nich.* I do not like this fellow by no means:
I never see him but my heart still earns.
Zounds! I could fight with him, yet know not
why;                                                     85
The devil and he are all one in mine eye.

*Enter Jenkin*

   *Jen.* O Nick! What gentleman is that that
comes to lie at our house? My master allows
him one to wait on him, and I believe it will
fall to thy lot.                                         90
   *Nich.* I love my master; by these hilts, I do;
But rather than I 'll ever come to serve him,
I 'll turn away my master.

*Enter Cicely*

   *Cic.* Nich'las! where are you, Nich'las? You
must come in, Nich'las, and help the gentleman
off with his boots.                                      96
   *Nich.* If I pluck off his boots, I 'll eat the
spurs,
And they shall stick fast in my throat like
burrs.
   *Cic.* Then, Jenkin, come you!
   *Jen.* Nay, 't is no boot for me to deny it. [100
My master hath given me a coat here, but he
takes pains himself to brush it once or twice a
day with a holly wand.
   *Cic.* Come, come, make haste, that you may
wash your hands again, and help to serve [105
in dinner!
   *Jen.* You may see, my masters, though it be
afternoon with you, 't is but early days with
us, for we have not din'd yet. Stay a little;

---

   **⁴⁴ banding:** taking   **⁵⁹ censur'd on:** judged
accomplishments   **⁸⁴ earns:** grieves   **¹⁰⁰ boot:** use
tending an afternoon performance of the play)   **⁶² possibility:** resources   **⁶⁶ quality:** endowments,
   **¹⁰⁷ masters:** (Addressed to the audience at-

I 'll but go in and help to bear up the first [110
course, and come to you again presently.
*Exeunt.*

[SCENE II. — *The Prison.*]

*Enter Malby and Cranwell*

*Mal.* This is the sessions-day; pray can you tell me
How young Sir Charles hath sped? Is he acquit,
Or must he try the law's strict penalty?
   *Cran.* He 's clear'd of all, spite of his enemies,
Whose earnest labour was to take his life.   5
But in this suit of pardon he hath spent
All the revenues that his father left him;
And he is now turn'd a plain countryman,
Reform'd in all things. See, sir, here he comes.

*Enter Sir Charles and his Keeper*

*Keep.* Discharge your fees, and you are then at freedom.   10
   *Char.* Here, Master Keeper, take the poor remainder
Of all the wealth I have! My heavy foes
Have made my purse light; but, alas! to me
'T is wealth enough that you have set me free.
   *Mal.* God give you joy of your delivery!   15
I am glad to see you abroad, Sir Charles.
   *Char.* The poorest knight in England, Master Malby.
My life hath cost me all my patrimony
My father left his son. Well, God forgive them
That are the authors of my penury!   20

*Enter Shafton*

*Shaft.* Sir Charles! A hand, a hand! At liberty?
Now, by the faith I owe, I am glad to see it.
What want you? Wherein may I pleasure you?
   *Char.* Oh me! Oh, most unhappy gentleman!
I am not worthy to have friends stirr'd up,   25
Whose hands may help me in this plunge of want.
I would I were in Heaven, to inherit there
Th' immortal birthright which my Saviour keeps,
And by no unthrift can be bought and sold;
For here on earth what pleasures should we trust!   30
   *Shaft.* To rid you from these contemplations,
Three hundred pounds you shall receive of me;
Nay, five for fail. Come, sir, the sight of gold
Is the most sweet receipt for melancholy,

And will revive your spirits. You shall hold law   35
With your proud adversaries. Tush! let Frank Acton
Wage, with his knighthood, like expense with me,
And a' will sink, he will. — Nay, good Sir Charles,
Applaud your fortune and your fair escape
From all these perils.
   *Char.* Oh, sir! they have undone me.   40
Two thousand and five hundred pound a year
My father at his death possess'd me of;
All which the envious Acton made me spend;
And, notwithstanding all this large expense,
I had much ado to gain my liberty;   45
And I have only now a house of pleasure,
With some five hundred pounds reserv'd,
Both to maintain me and my loving sister.
   *Shaft.* [*Aside.*] That must I have, it lies convenient for me.
If I can fasten but one finger on him,   50
With my full hand I 'll gripe him to the heart.
'T is not for love I proffer'd him this coin,
But for my gain and pleasure. — Come, Sir Charles,
I know you have need of money; take my offer.
   *Char.* Sir, I accept it, and remain indebted
Even to the best of my unable power.   56
Come, gentlemen, and see it tend'red down!
                      [*Exeunt.*]

[SCENE III. — *Frankford's House.*]

*Enter Wendoll, melancholy*

*Wen.* I am a villain, if I apprehend
But such a thought! Then, to attempt the deed,
Slave, thou art damn'd without redemption. —
I 'll drive away this passion with a song.
A song! Ha, ha! A song! As if, fond man,   5
Thy eyes could swim in laughter, when thy soul
Lies drench'd and drowned in red tears of blood!
I 'll pray, and see if God within my heart
Plant better thoughts. Why, prayers are meditations,
And when I meditate (oh, God forgive me!)   10
It is on her divine perfections.
I will forget her; I will arm myself
Not t' entertain a thought of love to her;
And, when I come by chance into her presence,
I 'll hale these balls until my eye-strings crack,   15
From being pull'd and drawn to look that way.

---

   **2 sped:** fared    **6 suit of:** attempt to get    **9 Reform'd:** transformed    **29 unthrift:** spendthrift
**33 for fail:** to prevent failure    **37 with his:** ('with' not in Qq.)    **56 unable:** feeble    **57 tend'red
down:** paid    **1 apprehend:** conceive    **5 fond:** foolish    **15 hale:** hold

*Enter, over the Stage, Frankford, his Wife,*
*and Nick [and exeunt]*

O God, O God! With what a violence
I 'm hurried to mine own destruction!
There goest thou, the most perfect'st man
That ever England bred a gentleman,          20
And shall I wrong his bed? — Thou God of
    thunder!
Stay, in Thy thoughts of vengeance and of
    wrath,
Thy great, almighty, and all-judging hand
From speedy execution on a villain, —
A villain and a traitor to his friend.          25

*Enter Jenkin*

*Jen.* Did your worship call?
*Wen.* He doth maintain me; he allows me
    largely
Money to spend.
*Jen.* [*Aside.*] By my faith, so do not you me:
I cannot get a cross of you.          30
*Wen.* My gelding, and my man.
*Jen.* [*Aside.*] That 's Sorrel and I.
*Wen.* This kindness grows of no alliance
    'twixt us.
*Jen.* [*Aside.*] Nor is my service of any great
    acquaintance.
*Wen.* I never bound him to me by desert.     35
Of a mere stranger, a poor gentleman,
A man by whom in no kind he could gain,
And he hath plac'd me in his highest thoughts,
Made me companion with the best and chiefest
In Yorkshire. He cannot eat without me,     40
Nor laugh without me; I am to his body
As necessary as his digestion,
And equally do make him whole or sick.
And shall I wrong this man? Base man! In-
    grate!
Hast thou the power, straight with thy gory
    hands,          45
To rip thy image from his bleeding heart,
To scratch thy name from out the holy
    book
Of his remembrance, and to wound his name
That holds thy name so dear? Or rend his
    heart
To whom thy heart was knit and join'd to-
    gether? —          50
And yet I must. Then Wendoll, be content!
Thus villains, when they would, cannot repent.
*Jen.* What a strange humour is my new mas-
ter in! Pray God he be not mad; if he should
be so, I should never have any mind to serve [55
him in Bedlam. It may be he 's mad for miss-
ing of me.

*Wen.* What, Jenkin! Where 's your mistress?
*Jen.* Is your worship married?          60
*Wen.* Why dost thou ask?
*Jen.* Because you are my master; and if I
have a mistress, I would be glad, like a good
servant, to do my duty to her.
*Wen.* I mean Mistress Frankford.          65
*Jen.* Marry, sir, her husband is riding out of
town, and she went very lovingly to bring him
on his way to horse. Do you see, sir? Here she
comes, and here I go.
*Wen.* Vanish!          [*Exit Jenkin.*]  70

*Enter Mistress Frankford*

*Anne.* Y' are well met, sir; now, in troth.
    My husband,
Before he took horse, had a great desire
To speak with you; we sought about the house,
Halloo'd into the fields, sent every way,
But could not meet you. Therefore, he enjoin'd
    me
To do unto you his most kind commends, —     75
Nay, more: he wills you, as you prize his love,
Or hold in estimation his kind friendship,
To make bold in his absence, and command
Even as himself were present in the house;     80
For you must keep his table, use his servants,
And be a present Frankford in his absence.
*Wen.* I thank him for his love. —
[*Aside.*] Give me a name, you, whose infec-
    tious tongues
Are tipp'd with gall and poison: as you would
Think on a man that had your father slain,     86
Murd'red your children, made your wives base
    strumpets,
So call me, call me so; print in my face
The most stigmatic title of a villain,
For hatching treason to so true a friend!     90
*Anne.* Sir, you are much beholding to my
    husband;
You are a man most dear in his regard.
*Wen.* I am bound unto your husband, and
    you too.
[*Aside.*] I will not speak to wrong a gentleman
Of that good estimation, my kind friend.     95
I will not; zounds! I will not. I may choose,
And I will choose. Shall I be so misled,
Or shall I purchase to my father's crest
The motto of a villain? If I say
I will not do it, what thing can enforce me? 100
What can compel me? What sad destiny
Hath such command upon my yielding
    thoughts?
I will not; — ha! Some fury pricks me on;
The swift fates drag me at their chariot wheel,

---

³⁰ **cross:** piece of money   ³³ **alliance:** relationship   ³⁷ **kind:** way   ⁴³ **whole:** well   ⁵⁶ **Bedlam:**
the hospital for the insane   ⁸⁹ **stigmatic:** branding with ignomin    ⁹⁵ **estimation:** reputation
⁶⁵ **purchase:** add

And hurry me to mischief. Speak I must: 105
Injure myself, wrong her, deceive his trust!
    *Anne.* Are you not well, sir, that ye seem
    thus troubled?
There is sedition in your countenance.
    *Wen.* And in my heart, fair angel, chaste
    and wise.                          109
I love you! Start not, speak not, answer not;
I love you, — nay, let me speak the rest;
Bid me to swear, and I will call to record
The host of Heaven.
    *Anne.*         The host of Heaven forbid
Wendoll should hatch such a disloyal thought!
    *Wen.* Such is my fate; to this suit was I
    born,                              115
To wear rich pleasure's crown, or fortune's
    scorn.
    *Anne.* My husband loves you.
    *Wen.*             I know it.
    *Anne.*                He esteems you,
Even as his brain, his eye-ball, or his heart.
    *Wen.* I have tried it.
    *Anne.* His purse is your exchequer, and his
    table                              120
Doth freely serve you.
    *Wen.*           So I have found it.
    *Anne.* Oh! With what face of brass, what
    brow of steel,
Can you, unblushing, speak this to the face
Of the espous'd wife of so dear a friend?   124
It is my husband that maintains your state. —
Will you dishonour him? I am his wife,
That in your power hath left his whole affairs.
It is to me you speak.
    *Wen.*          O speak no more;
For more than this I know, and have recorded
Within the red-leav'd table of my heart.   130
Fair, and of all belov'd, I was not fearful
Bluntly to give my life into your hand,
And at one hazard all my earthly means.
Go, tell your husband; he will turn me off,
And I am then undone. I care not, I;   135
'T was for your sake. Perchance, in rage he 'll
    kill me;
I care not, 't was for you. Say I incur
The general name of villain through the world,
Of traitor to my friend; I care not, I.
Beggary, shame, death, scandal, and re-
    proach, —                      140
For you I 'll hazard all. Why, what care I?
For you I 'll live, and in your love I 'll die.
    *Anne.* You move me, sir, to passion and to
    pity.
The love I bear my husband is as precious
As my soul's health.
    *Wen.*         I love your husband too, 145
And for his love I will engage my life.

Mistake me not; the augmentation
Of my sincere affection borne to you
Doth no whit lessen my regard of him.
I will be secret, lady, close as night;   150
And not the light of one small glorious star
Shall shine here in my forehead, to bewray
That act of night.
    *Anne.*         What shall I say?
My soul is wand'ring, hath lost her way.
Oh, Master Wendoll! Oh!
    *Wen.*         Sigh not, sweet saint; 155
For every sigh you breathe draws from my
    heart
A drop of blood.
    *Anne.*        I ne'er offended yet:
My fault, I fear, will in my brow be writ.
Women that fall, not quite bereft of grace,
Have their offences noted in their face.   160
I blush, and am asham'd. Oh, Master Wen-
    doll,
Pray God I be not born to curse your tongue,
That hath enchanted me! This maze I am in
I fear will prove the labyrinth of sin.

            *Enter Nick [behind]*

    *Wen.* The path of pleasure and the gate to
    bliss,                              165
Which on your lips I knock at with a kiss!
    *Nich.* I 'll kill the rogue.
    *Wen.* Your husband is from home, your bed's
    no blab.
Nay, look not down and blush!
            *Exit [with Mistress Frankford]*.
    *Nich.*          Zounds! I 'll stab.
Ay, Nick, was it thy chance to come just in the
    nick?                             170
I love my master, and I hate that slave;
I love my mistress, but these tricks I like not.
My master shall not pocket up this wrong;
I 'll eat my fingers first. What say'st thou,
    metal?
Does not that rascal Wendoll go on legs   175
That thou must cut off? Hath he not ham-
    strings
That thou must hough? Nay, metal, thou shalt
    stand
To all I say. I 'll henceforth turn a spy,
And watch them in their close conveyances.
I never look'd for better of that rascal,   180
Since he came miching first into our house.
It is that Satan hath corrupted her;
For she was fair and chaste. I 'll have an
    eye
In all their gestures. Thus I think of them:
If they proceed as they have done before,   185
Wendoll 's a knave, my mistress is a ——
                             *Exit.*

---

130 **table:** notebook    142 **live:** ('love' Q 2)    143 **passion:** compassion    151 **glorious:** boastful
177 **hough:** cut    179 **close conveyances:** secret doings    181 **miching:** sneaking

[ACT III

SCENE I. — *Sir Charles Mountford's House.*]

*Enter [Sir] Charles and Susan*

*Char.* Sister, you see we are driven to hard shift,
To keep this poor house we have left unsold.
I am now enforc'd to follow husbandry,
And you to milk; and do we not live well?
Well, I thank God.
 *Susan.*   Oh, brother! here 's a change, 5
Since old Sir Charles died in our father's house.
 *Char.* All things on earth thus change, some up, some down;
Content 's a kingdom, and I wear that crown.

*Enter Shafton, with a Sergeant*

*Shaft.* Good morrow, morrow, Sir Charles!
What! With your sister,
Plying your husbandry? — Sergeant, stand off! —        10
You have a pretty house here, and a garden,
And goodly ground about it. Since it lies
So near a lordship that I lately bought,
I would fain buy it of you. I will give you ——
 *Char.* Oh, pardon me; this house successively
Hath long'd to me and my progenitors 16
Three hundred years. My great-great-grand-father,
He in whom first our gentle style began,
Dwelt here, and in this ground increas'd this mole-hill
Unto that mountain which my father left me. 
Where he the first of all our house began, 21
I now the last will end, and keep this house, —
This virgin title, never yet deflower'd
By any unthrift of the Mountfords' line.
In brief, I will not sell it for more gold 25
Than you could hide or pave the ground withal.
 *Shaft.* Ha, ha! a proud mind and a beggar's purse!
Where 's my three hundred pounds, besides the use? —
I have brought it to an execution 29
By course of law. What! Is my monies ready?
 *Char.* An execution, sir, and never tell me
You put my bond in suit? You deal extremely.
 *Shaft.* Sell me the land, and I 'll acquit you straight.
 *Char.* Alas, alas! 'T is all trouble hath left me
To cherish me and my poor sister's life. 35
If this were sold, our names should then be quite
Raz'd from the bead-roll of gentility.
You see what hard shift we have made to keep it

Allied still to our name. This palm you see,
Labour hath glow'd within; her silver brow, 40
That never tasted a rough winter's blast
Without a mask or fan, doth with a grace
Defy cold winter, and his storms outface.
 *Susan.* Sir, we feed sparing, and we labour hard,
We lie uneasy, to reserve to us 45
And our succession this small spot of ground.
 *Char.* I have so bent my thoughts to husbandry,
That I protest I scarcely can remember
What a new fashion is; how silk or satin
Feels in my hand. Why, pride is grown to us 50
A mere, mere stranger. I have quite forgot
The names of all that ever waited on me.
I cannot name ye any of my hounds,
Once from whose echoing mouths I heard all music
That e'er my heart desir'd. What should I say? 55
To keep this place, I have chang'd myself away.
 *Shaft.* Arrest him at my suit! — Actions and actions
Shall keep thee in continual bondage fast;
Nay, more, I 'll sue thee by a late appeal,
And call thy former life in question. 60
The keeper is my friend; thou shalt have irons,
And usage such as I 'll deny to dogs. —
Away with him!
 *Char.*   Ye are too timorous.
But trouble is my master,
And I will serve him truly. — My kind sister,
Thy tears are of no force to mollify 66
This flinty man. Go to my father's brother,
My kinsmen, and allies; entreat them for me,
To ransom me from this injurious man
That seeks my ruin.
 *Shaft.*   Come, irons, irons! Come, away; 70
I 'll see thee lodg'd far from the sight of day.
        [*Exeunt except Susan.*]
 *Susan.* My heart 's so hard'ned with the frost of grief,
Death cannot pierce it through. — Tyrant too fell!
So lead the fiends condemned souls to hell.

*Enter [Sir Francis] Acton and Malby*

 *Fran.* Again to prison! Malby, hast thou seen 75
A poor slave better tortur'd? Shall we hear
The music of his voice cry from the grate,
*Meat, for the Lord's sake?* No, no; yet, I am not
Throughly reveng'd. They say, he hath a pretty wench

To his sister; shall I, in mercy-sake            80
To him and to his kindred, bribe the fool
To shame herself by lewd, dishonest lust?
I 'll proffer largely; but, the deed being done,
I 'll smile to see her base confusion.
    *Mal.* Methinks, Sir Francis, you are full re-
        veng'd            85
For greater wrongs than he can proffer you.
See where the poor sad gentlewoman stands!
    *Fran.* Ha, ha! Now will I flout her poverty,
Deride her fortunes, scoff her base estate;
My very soul the name of Mountford hates.  90
But stay, my heart! Oh, what a look did fly
To strike my soul through with thy piercing eye!
I am enchanted; all my spirits are fled.
And with one glance my envious spleen struck
        dead.
    *Susan.* Acton! That seeks our blood!
                                *Runs away.*
    *Fran.*              O chaste and fair!  95
    *Mal.* Sir Francis! Why, Sir Francis! in a
        trance?
Sir Francis! What cheer, man? Come, come,
        how is 't?
    *Fran.* Was she not fair? Or else this judg-
        ing eye
Cannot distinguish beauty.
    *Mal.*                She was fair.   99
    *Fran.* She was an angel in a mortal's shape,
And ne'er descended from Old Mountford's line.
But soft, soft, let me call my wits together!
A poor, poor wench, to my great adversary
Sister, whose very souls denounce stern war
Each against other! How now, Frank, turn'd
        fool            105
Or madman, whether? But no! Master of
My perfect senses and directest wits.
Then why should I be in this violent humour
Of passion and of love? And with a person
So different every way, and so oppos'd      110
In all contractions and still-warring actions?
Fie, fie! How I dispute against my soul!
Come, come; I 'll gain her, or in her fair quest
Purchase my soul free and immortal rest.
                        *[Exeunt.]*

[SCENE II. — *Frankford's House.*]

*Enter three or four Serving-men, one with a
    voider and a wooden knife, to take away;
    another the salt and bread; another the
    table-cloth and napkins; another the carpet;
    Jenkin with two lights after them*

*Jen.* So; march in order, and retire in
battle array! My master and the guests have

supp'd already; all 's taken away. Here, now,
spread for the serving-men in the hall! — Butler, it belongs to your office.            5
    *But.* I know it, Jenkin. What d' ye call the
gentleman that supp'd there to-night?
    *Jen.* Who? My master?
    *But.* No, no; Master Wendoll, he 's a daily
guest. I mean the gentleman that came [10
but this afternoon.
    *Jen.* His name 's Master Cranwell. God's
light! Hark, within there; my master calls to
lay more billets upon the fire. Come, come!
Lord, how we that are in office here in the [15
house are troubled! One spread the carpet in
the parlour, and stand ready to snuff the lights;
the rest be ready to prepare their stomachs!
More lights in the hall, there! Come, Nicholas.
                *Exeunt [all but Nicholas].*
    *Nich.* I cannot eat; but had I Wendoll's
        heart,            20
I would eat that. The rogue grows impudent,
Oh! I have seen such vild, notorious tricks,
Ready to make my eyes dart from my head.
I 'll tell my master; by this air, I will;
Fall what may fall, I 'll tell him. Here he
        comes.            25

*Enter Master Frankford, as it were brushing
    the crumbs from his clothes with a napkin, as
    newly risen from supper*

    *Frank.* Nicholas, what make you here? Why
        are not you
At supper in the hall, among your fellows?
    *Nich.* Master, I stay'd your rising from the
        board,
To speak with you.
    *Frank.*        Be brief then, gentle Nicholas;
My wife and guests attend me in the parlour. 30
Why dost thou pause? Now, Nicholas, you
        want money,
And, unthrift-like, would eat into your wages
Ere you have earn'd it. Here, sir, 's half-a-
        crown;
Play the good husband, — and away to supper!
    *Nich.* By this hand, an honourable gentle-
        man! I will not see him wrong'd. —   35
Sir, I have serv'd you long; you entertain'd me
Seven years before your beard; you knew me,
        sir,
Before you knew my mistress.
    *Frank.* What of this, good Nicholas?
    *Nich.* I never was a make-bate or a knave;  40
I have no fault but one — I 'm given to quarrel,
But not with women. I will tell you, master,

---

⁸⁰ **mercy-:** ('my mercy' Q 2)    ⁹⁰ **hates:** ('hate' Q 2)    ⁹¹ **Oh:** ('or' Q 2)    ¹⁰⁶ **whether:** which
¹¹¹ **contractions:** legal transactions    Sc. II.  S. D. **voider:** tray or basket for removing the remains of a
meal    **carpet:** table-cloth    ¹⁴ **billets:** logs    ¹⁸ **stomachs:** appetites    ²² **vild:** vile    ²⁶ **make:** do
³⁰ **attend:** await    ³⁴ **husband:** economist    ³⁶ **entertain'd:** took into service    ⁴⁰ **make-bate:** maker
of quarrels

That which will make your heart leap from
   your breast,
Your hair to startle from your head, your ears
   to tingle.
   *Frank.* What preparation 's this to dismal
      news?                                    45
   *Nich.* 'Sblood! sir, I love you better than
      your wife.
I 'll make it good.
   *Frank.* Y' are a knave, and I have much
      ado
With wonted patience to contain my rage,
And not to break thy pate. Th' art a knave. 50
I 'll turn you, with your base comparisons,
Out of my doors.
   *Nich.*            Do, do.
There is not room for Wendoll and me too,
Both in one house. O master, master,
That Wendoll is a villain!
   *Frank.*            Ay, saucy?       55
   *Nich.* Strike, strike, do strike; yet hear me!
      I am no fool;
I know a villain, when I see him act
Deeds of a villain. Master, master, that base
      slave
Enjoys my mistress, and dishonours you.
   *Frank.* Thou hast kill'd me with a weapon,
      whose sharp point                        60
Hath prick'd quite through and through my
      shiv'ring heart.
Drops of cold sweat sit dangling on my hairs,
Like morning's dew upon the golden flowers,
And I am plung'd into strange agonies.
What did'st thou say? If any word that
      touch'd                                   65
His credit, or her reputation,
It is as hard to enter my belief,
As Dives into heaven.
   *Nich.*            I can gain nothing:
They are two that never wrong'd me. I knew
      before
'T was but a thankless office, and perhaps  70
As much as is my service, or my life
Is worth. All this I know; but this, and more,
More by a thousand dangers, could not hire me
To smother such a heinous wrong from you.
I saw, and I have said.                         75
   *Frank.* [*Aside.*] 'T is probable. Though blunt,
      yet he is honest.
Though I durst pawn my life, and on their
      faith
Hazard the dear salvation of my soul,
Yet in my trust I may be too secure.
May this be true? Oh, may it? Can it be?  80
Is it by any wonder possible?
Man, woman, what thing mortal can we trust,

When friends and bosom wives prove so un-
      just? —
What instance hast thou of this strange report?
   *Nich.* Eyes, master, eyes.                 85
   *Frank.* Thy eyes may be deceiv'd, I tell
      thee;
For should an angel from the heavens drop
      down,
And preach this to me that thyself hast told,
He should have much ado to win belief;
In both their loves I am so confident.     90
   *Nich.* Shall I discourse the same by circum-
      stance?
   *Frank.* No more! To supper, and command
      your fellows
To attend us and the strangers! Not a word,
I charge thee, on thy life! Be secret then;
For I know nothing.                         95
   *Nich.* I am dumb; and, now that I have
      eas'd my stomach,
I will go fill my stomach.                 *Exit.*
   *Frank.*            Away! Begone! —
She is well born, descended nobly;
Virtuous her education; her repute
Is in the general voice of all the country  100
Honest and fair; her carriage, her demeanour,
In all her actions that concern the love
To me her husband, modest, chaste, and godly
Is all this seeming gold plain copper?
But he, that Judas that hath borne my purse,
Hath sold me for a sin. O God! O God!  106
Shall I put up these wrongs? No! Shall I trust
The bare report of this suspicious groom,
Before the double-gilt, the well-hatch'd ore
Of their two hearts? No, I will lose these
      thoughts;                             110
Distraction I will banish from my brow,
And from my looks exile sad discontent.
Their wonted favours in my tongue shall
      flow;
Till I know all, I 'll nothing seem to know. —
Lights and a table there! Wife, Master
      Wendoll,                              115
And gentle Master Cranwell!

*Enter Mistress Frankford, Master Wendoll,
   Master Cranwell, Nick, and Jenkin with
   cards, carpets, stools, and other necessaries*

   *Frank.* O! Master Cranwell, you are a
      stranger here,
And often balk my house; faith, y' are a
      churl! —
Now we have supp'd, a table, and to cards!
   *Jen.* A pair of cards, Nicholas, and a carpet
to cover the table! Where 's Cicely, with her [121
counters and her box? Candles and candlesticks,

---

<sup>84</sup> **instance:** evidence   <sup>91</sup> **by circumstance:** in detail   <sup>96</sup> **stomach:** resentment   <sup>107</sup> **put up:**
put up with   <sup>109</sup> **double-gilt:** pure gold   **well-hatch'd:** richly inlaid   <sup>118</sup> **balk:** avoid   <sup>120</sup> **pair:**
pack

there! Fie! We have such a household of serving-creatures! Unless it be Nick and I, there's
not one amongst them all that can say boo to
a goose. — Well said, Nick!                    126

*They spread a carpet: set down
lights and cards.*

*Anne.* Come, Master Frankford, who shall
take my part?

*Frank.* Marry, that will I, sweet wife.      129

*Wen.* No, by my faith, when you are together, I sit out. It must be Mistress Frankford and I, or else it is no match.

*Frank.* I do not like that match.

*Nich.* [*Aside.*] You have no reason, marry,
knowing all.                                   135

*Frank.* 'T is no great matter, neither. —
Come, Master Cranwell, shall you and I take
them up?

*Cran.* At your pleasure, sir.                 139

*Frank.* I must look to you, Master Wendoll,
for you'll be playing false. Nay, so will my
wife, too.

*Nich.* [*Aside.*] I will be sworn she will.

*Anne.* Let them that are taken false,
forfeit the set!                               145

*Frank.* Content; it shall go hard but I'll
take you. Gentlemen, what shall our game be?

*Cran.* Gentlemen, what shall our game be?

*Wen.* Master Frankford, you play best at
noddy.

*Frank.* You shall not find it so; indeed, you
shall not.

*Anne.* I can play at nothing so well as
double-ruff.                                   150

*Frank.* If Master Wendoll and my wife be
together, there's no playing against them at
double-hand.

*Nich.* I can tell you, sir, the game that Master Wendoll is best at.                        155

*Wen.* What game is that, Nick?

*Nich.* Marry, sir, knave out of doors.

*Wen.* She and I will take you at lodam.

*Anne.* Husband, shall we play at saint?

*Frank.* [*Aside.*] My saint's turn'd devil. —
No, we'll none of saint:                       160
You are best at new-cut, wife, you'll play at
that.

*Wen.* If you play at new-cut, I'm soonest
hitter of any here, for a wager.

*Frank.* [*Aside.*] 'T is me they play on. —
Well, you may draw out;                        164
For all your cunning, 't will be to your shame;
I'll teach you, at your new-cut, a new game.
Come, come!

*Cran.* If you cannot agree upon the game,
To post and pair!

*Wen.* We shall be soonest pairs; and my
good host,                                     170
When he comes late home, he must kiss the
post.

*Frank.* Whoever wins, it shall be to thy
cost.

*Cran.* Faith, let it be vide-ruff, and let's
make honours!

*Frank.* If you make honours, one thing let
me crave:
Honour the king and queen, except the
knave.                                         175

*Wen.* Well, as you please for that. — Lift,
who shall deal?

*Anne.* The least in sight. What are you,
Master Wendoll?

*Wen.* I am a knave.

*Nich.* [*Aside.*]          I'll swear it.

*Anne.*                       I am queen.

*Frank.* [*Aside.*] A quean, thou should'st say.
— Well, the cards are mine:
They are the grossest pair that e'er I felt.  180

*Anne.* Shuffle, I'll cut: would I had never
dealt!

*Frank.* I have lost my dealing.

*Wen.*                  Sir, the fault's in me;
This queen I have more than mine own, you
see.
Give me the stock!

*Frank.*            My mind's not on my
game.
Many a deal I've lost; the more's your shame.
You have serv'd me a bad trick, Master Wendoll.                                          186

*Wen.* Sir, you must take your lot. To end
this strife,
I know I have dealt better with your wife.

*Frank.* Thou hast dealt falsely, then.

*Anne.* What's trumps?                         190

*Wen.* Hearts. Partner, I rub.

*Frank.* [*Aside.*] Thou robb'st me of my soul,
of her chaste love;
In thy false dealing thou hast robb'd my
heart. —
Booty you play; I like a loser stand,
Having no heart, or here or in my hand.       195
I will give o'er the set, I am not well.
Come, who will hold my cards?

*Anne.* Not well, sweet Master Frankford?
Alas, what ail you? 'T is some sudden qualm.

*Wen.* How long have you been so, Master
Frankford?                                     200

*Frank.* Sir, I was lusty, and I had my health,
But I grew ill when you began to deal. —
Take hence this table! — Gentle Master Cran-
well.

¹²⁸ **take my part:** be my partner    ¹³⁷⁻¹³⁸ **take . . . up:** play against them    ¹⁶³ **hitter:** winner
¹⁷¹ **kiss the post:** be shut out    ¹⁷⁶ **Lift:** cut    ¹⁷⁹ **quean:** hussy    ¹⁸⁴ **stock:** kitty    ¹⁹¹ **rub:** take
all the cards of one suit    ¹⁹⁴ **Booty you play:** You unite to play false.

Y' are welcome; see your chamber at your
   pleasure!
I am sorry that this megrim takes me so,    205
I cannot sit and bear you company. —
Jenkin, some lights, and show him to his
   chamber!
             [*Exeunt Cranwell and Jenkin.*]
  *Anne.*   A nightgown for my husband;
   quickly, there!
It is some rheum or cold.
  *Wen.*           Now, in good faith,
This illness you have got by sitting late    210
Without your gown.
  *Frank.*       I know it, Master Wendoll.
Go, go to bed, lest you complain like me! —
Wife, prithee, wife, into my bed-chamber!
The night is raw and cold, and rheumatic.
Leave me my gown and light; I 'll walk away
   my fit.                                     215
  *Wen.*  Sweet sir, good night!
  *Frank.* Myself, good night! [*Exit Wendoll.*]
  *Anne.*       Shall I attend you, husband?
  *Frank.*  No, gentle wife, thou 'lt catch cold
   in thy head.
Prithee, begone, sweet; I 'll make haste to bed.
  *Anne.*  No sleep will fasten on mine eyes,
   you know,                                    220
Until you come.                 *Exit.*
  *Frank.*       Sweet Nan, I prithee, go! —
I have bethought me; get me by degrees
The keys of all my doors, which I will mould
In wax, and take their fair impression,
To have by them new keys. This being com-
   pass'd,                                      225
At a set hour a letter shall be brought me,
And when they think they may securely play,
They nearest are to danger. — Nick, I must
   rely
Upon thy trust and faithful secrecy.
  *Nich.*  Build on my faith!
  *Frank.*      To bed, then, not to rest!
Care lodges in my brain, grief in my breast.  231
                     [*Exeunt.*]

[SCENE III. — *Old Mountford's House.*]

*Enter Sir Charles his Sister, Old Mountford,
    Sandy, Roder, and Tidy*

  *Old Mount.*  You say my nephew is in great
   distress;
Who brought it to him but his own lewd life?
I cannot spare a cross. I must confess,
He was my brother's son; why, niece, what
   then?
This is no world in which to pity men.        5
  *Susan.*  I was not born a beggar, though his
   extremes

Enforce this language from me. I protest
No fortune of mine own could lead my tongue
To this base key. I do beseech you, uncle,
For the name's sake, for Christianity, —    10
Nay, for God's sake, to pity his distress.
He is deni'd the freedom of the prison,
And in the hole is laid with men condemn'd;
Plenty he hath of nothing but of irons,
And it remains in you to free him thence.    15
  *Old Mount.*  Money I cannot spare; men
   should take heed.
He lost my kindred when he fell to need. [*Exit.*]
  *Susan.*  Gold is but earth; thou earth enough
   shalt have,
When thou hast once took measure of thy grave.
You know me, Master Sandy, and my suit.   20
  *Sandy.*  I knew you, lady, when the old man
   liv'd;
I knew you ere your brother sold his land.
Then you were Mistress Sue, trick'd up in
   jewels;
Then you sung well, play'd sweetly on the lute;
But now I neither know you nor your suit.   25
                     [*Exit.*]
  *Susan.*  You, Master Roder, was my brother's
   tenant;
Rent-free he plac'd you in that wealthy farm,
Of which you are possess'd.
  *Roder.*         True, he did;
And have I not there dwelt still for his sake?
I have some business now; but, without doubt,
They that have hurl'd him in, will help him
   out.                      *Exit.* 31
  *Susan.*  Cold comfort still. What say you,
   cousin Tidy?
  *Tidy.*  I say this comes of roysting, swag-
   g'ring.
Call me not cousin; each man for himself!
Some men are born to mirth, and some to sor-
   row:                                         35
I am no cousin unto them that borrow.   *Exit.*
  *Susan.*  O Charity, why art thou fled to
   heaven,
And left all things on this earth uneven?
Their scoffing answers I will ne'er return,
But to myself his grief in silence mourn.    40

      *Enter Sir Francis and Malby*

  *Fran.*  She is poor, I 'll therefore tempt her
   with this gold.
Go, Malby, in my name deliver it,
And I will stay thy answer.
  *Mal.*  Fair mistress, as I understand, your
   grief
Doth grow from want, so I have here in store
A means to furnish you, a bag of gold,      46
Which to your hands I freely tender you.

---

²⁰⁸ **nightgown:** dressing-gown    ¹³ **hole:** cell reserved for poorest prisoners    ¹⁷ **my kindred: rela-**
tionship with me    ³³ **roysting:** rioting

*Susan.* I thank you, Heavens! I thank you,
  gentle sir:
God make me able to requite this favour!
  *Mal.* This gold Sir Francis Acton sends by
    me,                                          50
And prays you ——
  *Susan.* Acton? O God! That name I'm
    born to curse.
Hence, bawd; hence, broker! See, I spurn his
  gold.
My honour never shall for gain be sold.
  *Fran.* Stay, lady, stay!
  *Susan.*          From you I'll posting hie,  55
Even as the doves from feather'd eagles fly.
                                         *Exit.*
  *Fran.* She hates my name, my face; how
    should I woo?
I am disgrac'd in everything I do.
The more she hates me, and disdains my love,
The more I am rapt in admiration               60
Of her divine and chaste perfections.
Woo her with gifts I cannot, for all gifts
Sent in my name she spurns; with looks I can-
  not,
For she abhors my sight; nor yet with letters,
For none she will receive. How then? how then?
Well, I will fasten such a kindness on her,    66
As shall o'ercome her hate and conquer it.
Sir Charles, her brother, lies in execution
For a great sum of money; and, besides,
The appeal is sued still for my huntsmen's
  death,                                        70
Which only I have power to reverse.
In her I'll bury all my hate of him. —
Go seek the Keeper, Malby, bring him to me!
To save his body, I his debts will pay;        74
To save his life, I his appeal will stay. [*Exeunt.*]


[ACT IV

SCENE I. — *York Castle.*]

*Enter Sir Charles [Mountford], in prison,
with irons, his feet bare, his garments all
ragged and torn*

  *Char.* Of all on the earth's face most miser-
    able,
Breathe in this hellish dungeon thy laments!
Thus like a slave ragg'd, like a felon gyv'd, —
That hurls thee headlong to this base estate.
Oh, unkind uncle! Oh, my friends ingrate!       5
Unthankful kinsmen! Mountford's all too base,
To let thy name be fetter'd in disgrace.
A thousand deaths here in this grave I die;
Fear, hunger, sorrow, cold, all threat my death,
And join together to deprive my breath.         10
But that which most torments me, my dear
  **sister**

Hath left to visit me, and from my friends
Hath brought no hopeful answer; therefore, I
Divine they will not help my misery.
If it be so, shame, scandal, and contempt      15
Attend their covetous thoughts; need make
  their graves!
Usurers they live, and may they die like slaves!

          *Enter Keeper*

  *Keep.* Knight, be of comfort, for I bring thee
    freedom
From all thy troubles.
  *Char.*          Then, I am doom'd to die:
Death is the end of all calamity.               20
  *Keep.* Live! Your appeal is stay'd; the exe-
    cution
Of all your debts discharg'd; your creditors
Even to the utmost penny satisfied.
In sign whereof your shackles I knock off.
You are not left so much indebted to us        25
As for your fees; all is discharg'd; all paid.
Go freely to your house, or where you please;
After long miseries, embrace your ease.
  *Char.*     Thou grumblest out the sweetest
    music to me
That ever organ play'd. — Is this a dream?     30
Or do my waking senses apprehend
The pleasing taste of these applausive news?
Slave that I was, to wrong such honest friends,
My loving kinsmen, and my near allies!         34
Tongue, I will bite thee for the scandal breath'd
Against such faithful kinsmen; they are all
Compos'd of pity and compassion,
Of melting charity and of moving ruth.
That which I spake before was in my rage;
They are my friends, the mirrors of this age;  40
Bounteous and free. The noble Mountfords'
  race
Ne'er bred a covetous thought, or humour base.

          *Enter Susan*

  *Susan.* I can no longer stay from visiting
My woful brother. While I could, I kept
My hapless tidings from his hopeful ear.        45
  *Char.* Sister, how much am I indebted to
    thee
And to thy travail!
  *Susan.*          What, at liberty?
  *Char.* Thou seest I am, thanks to thy indus-
    try.
Oh! Unto which of all my courteous friends
Am I thus bound? My uncle Mountford, he       50
Even of an infant lov'd me; was it he?
So did my cousin Tidy; was it he?
So Master Roder, Master Sandy, too.
Which of all these did this high kindness do?
  *Susan.* Charles, can you mock me in your
    poverty,                                    55

---

¹² **left:** ceased     ³² **applausive:** joyful     ³⁵ **breath'd:** ('breath' Q 2)

Knowing your friends deride your misery?
Now, I protest I stand so much amaz'd,
To see your bonds free, and your irons knock'd
    off,
That I am rapt into a maze of wonder;
The rather for I know not by what means    60
This happiness hath chanc'd.
    *Char.*              Why, by my uncle,
My cousins, and my friends; who else, I pray,
Would take upon them all my debts to pay?
    *Susan.* Oh, brother! they are men made all
        of flint,
Pictures of marble, and as void of pity    65
As chased bears. I begg'd, I sued, I kneel'd,
Laid open all your griefs and miseries,
Which they derided; more than that, deni'd us
A part in their alliance; but, in pride,
Said that our kindred with our plenty died. 70
    *Char.* Drudges too much, — what did they?
        Oh, known evil!
Rich fly the poor, as good men shun the devil.
Whence should my freedom come? Of whom
    alive,
Saving of those, have I deserv'd so well?
Guess, sister, call to mind, remember me!    75
These have I rais'd, they follow the world's
    guise,
Whom rich they honour, they in woe despise.
    *Susan.* My wits have lost themselves; let's
        ask the keeper!
    *Char.* Jailer!
    *Keep.* At hand, sir.                    80
    *Char.* Of courtesy resolve me one demand!
What was he took the burthen of my debts
From off my back, stay'd my appeal to death,
Discharg'd my fees, and brought me liberty?
    *Keep.* A courteous knight, and call'd Sir
        Francis Acton.                       85
    *Char.* Ha! Acton! Oh me! More distress'd
        in this
Than all my troubles! Hale me back,
Double my irons, and my sparing meals
Put into halves, and lodge me in a dungeon
More deep, more dark, more cold, more com-
    fortless!                               90
By Acton freed! Not all thy manacles
Could fetter so my heels, as this one word
Hath thrall'd my heart; and it must now lie
    bound
In more strict prison than thy stony jail.
I am not free, I go but under bail.          95
    *Keep.* My charge is done, sir, now I have my
        fees.
As we get little, we will nothing leese.
    *Char.* By Acton freed, my dangerous oppo-
        site!

Why, to what end? or what occasion? Ha!
Let me forget the name of enemy,          100
And with indifference balance this high favour!
Ha!
    *Susan.* [*Aside.*] His love to me, upon my
        soul, 't is so!
That is the root from whence these strange
    things grow.
    *Char.* Had this proceeded from my father, he
That by the law of Nature is most bound   106
In offices of love, it had deserv'd
My best employment to requite that grace.
Had it proceeded from my friends, or him, 109
From them this action had deserv'd my life, —
And from a stranger more, because from such
There is less execution of good deeds.
But he, nor father, nor ally, nor friend,
More than a stranger, both remote in blood,
And in his heart oppos'd my enemy,        115
That this high bounty should proceed from
    him, —
Oh! there I lose myself. What should I say,
What think, what do, his bounty to repay?
    *Susan.* You wonder, I am sure, whence this
        strange kindness
Proceeds in Acton; I will tell you, brother. 120
He dotes on me, and oft hath sent me gifts,
Letters, and tokens; I refus'd them all.
    *Char.* I have enough, though poor: my heart
        is set,
In one rich gift to pay back all my debt.
                                    *Exeunt.*

[SCENE II. — *Frankford's House.*]

*Enter Frankford and Nick, with keys and a
        letter in his hand*

    *Frank.* This is the night that I must play my
        part,
To try two seeming angels. — Where's my keys?
    *Nich.* They are made according to your
        mould in wax.
I bade the smith be secret, gave him money,
And here they are. The letter, sir!        5
    *Frank.* True, take it, there it is;
And when thou seest me in my pleasant'st vein,
Ready to sit to supper, bring it me!
    *Nich.* I 'll do 't; make no more question,
        but I 'll do it.                    *Exit.*

*Enter Mistress Frankford, Cranwell, Wendoll,
        and Jenkin*

    *Anne.* Sirrah, 't is six o'clock already
        struck;                            10
Go bid them spread the cloth, and serve in
    supper!

---

⁶⁴ **made:** (Not in Qq.)    ⁷¹ **Drudges too much:** slaves too base    ⁷⁵ **remember:** remind, tell
⁷⁷ **rich they:** ('rich in' Qq.)    ⁸² **What:** who    ⁹⁷ **leese:** lose    ¹⁰¹ **with . . . balance:** weigh impartially    ¹⁰⁸ **employment:** effort

*Jen.* It shall be done, forsooth, mistress.
Where 's Spigot the butler, to give us our salt
and trenchers?                                          14
*Wen.* We that have been a-hunting all the day,
Come   with   prepared   stomachs. — Master
   Frankford,
We wish'd you at our sport.
*Frank.* My heart was with you, and my
   mind was on you. —
Fie, Master Cranwell! You are still thus sad.—
A stool, a stool! Where 's Jenkin, and where 's
   Nick?                                                 20
'T is supper time at least an hour ago.
What 's the best news abroad?
*Wen.* I know none good.
*Frank.* [*Aside.*] But I know too much bad.

*Enter Butler and Jenkin, with a table-cloth,
   bread, trenchers, and salt; [then exeunt]*

*Cran.* Methinks, sir, you might have that
   interest                                              25
In your wife's brother, to be more remiss
In his hard dealing against poor Sir Charles,
Who, as I hear, lies in York Castle, needy
And in great want.
*Frank.*     Did not more weighty business of
   mine own                                              30
Hold me away, I would have labour'd peace
Betwixt them with all care; indeed I would, sir.
*Anne.* I 'll write unto my brother earnestly
In that behalf.
*Wen.*          A charitable deed,
And will beget the good opinion               35
Of all your friends that love you, Mistress
   Frankford.
*Frank.* That 's you, for one; I know you
   love Sir Charles —
[*Aside.*] And my wife too — well.
*Wen.*               He deserves the love
Of all true gentlemen; be yourselves judge!
*Frank.* But supper, ho! — Now, as thou
   lov'st me, Wendoll,                                   40
Which I am sure thou dost, be merry, pleasant,
And frolic it to-night! — Sweet Master Cran-
   well,
Do you the like! — Wife, I protest, my heart
Was ne'er more bent on sweet alacrity.
Where be those lazy knaves to serve in supper?

*Enter Nick*

*Nick.* Here 's a letter, sir.                          46
*Frank.* Whence comes it, and who brought it?
*Nick.* A stripling that below attends your
   answer,
And, as he tells me, it is sent from York.
*Frank.* Have him into the cellar, let him
   taste                                                 50

A cup of our March beer; go, make him
   drink!
*Nich.* I 'll make him drunk, if he be a Tro-
   jan.
*Frank.* [*After reading the letter.*] My boots
   and spurs! Where 's Jenkin? God forgive
   me,
How I neglect my business! — Wife, look here!
I have a matter to be tri'd to-morrow          55
By eight o'clock; and my attorney writes me,
I must be there betimes with evidence,
Or it will go against me. Where 's my boots?

*Enter Jenkin, with boots and spurs*

*Anne.* I hope your business craves no such
   despatch,
That you must ride to-night?
*Wen.* [*Aside.*]               I hope it doth.
*Frank.* God's me! No such despatch?          61
Jenkin, my boots! Where 's Nick? Saddle my
   roan,
And the grey dapple for himself! — Content ye,
It much concerns me. — Gentle Master Cran-
   well,
And Master Wendoll, in my absence use        65
The very ripest pleasures of my house!
*Wen.* Lord! Master Frankford, will you ride
   to-night?
The ways are dangerous.
*Frank.*                   Therefore will I ride
Appointed well; and so shall Nick, my man.
*Anne.* I 'll call you up by five o'clock to-
   morrow.                                               70
*Frank.* No, by my faith, wife, I 'll not trust
   to that:
'T is not such easy rising in a morning
From one I love so dearly. No, by my faith,
I shall not leave so sweet a bedfellow,
But with much pain. You have made me a
   sluggard                                              75
Since I first knew you.
*Anne.*                Then, if you needs will go
This dangerous evening, Master Wendoll,
Let me entreat you bear him company.
*Wen.* With all my heart, sweet mistress. —
   My boots, there!
*Frank.* Fie, fie, that for my private business
I should disease a friend, and be a trouble   81
To the whole house! — Nick!
*Nich.*                    Anon, sir!
*Frank.* Bring forth my gelding! — As you
   love me, sir,
Use no more words: a hand, good Master Cran-
   well!
*Cran.* Sir, God be your good speed!           85
*Frank.* Good night, sweet Nan; nay, nay, a
   kiss, and part!

---

²⁵ **interest:** influence   ²⁶ **more remiss:** less severe   ⁴⁴ **alacrity:** merriment   ⁵² **Trojan: good
fellow**   ⁶⁹ **Appointed:** armed   ⁸¹ **disease:** inconvenience

*[Aside.]* Dissembling lips, you suit not with my
  heart.                    *Exit [with Nick].*
*Wen. [Aside.]* How business, time, and hours,
  all gracious prove,
And are the furtherers to my new-born love!
I am husband now in Master Frankford's place,
And must command the house. — My pleasure is
We will not sup abroad so publicly,       92
But in your private chamber, Mistress Frank-
  ford.
*Anne.* Oh, sir! you are too public in your love,
And Master Frankford's wife ——
*Cran.*                    Might I crave favour,
I would entreat you I might see my chamber.
I am on the sudden grown exceeding ill,     97
And would be spar'd from supper.
*Wen.*                    Light there, ho! —
See you want nothing, sir, for if you do,
You injure that good man, and wrong me too.
*Cran.* I will make bold; good night! *Exit.*
*Wen.*                    How all conspire
To make our bosom sweet, and full entire!  102
Come, Nan, I p'rythee, let us sup within!
*Anne.* Oh! what a clog unto the soul is sin!
We pale offenders are still full of fear;    105
Every suspicious eye brings danger near;
When they, whose clear hearts from offence
  are free,
Despise report, base scandals do outface,
And stand at mere defiance with disgrace.
*Wen.* Fie, fie! You talk too like a puritan.
*Anne.* You have tempted me to mischief,
  Master Wendoll:                  111
I have done I know not what. Well, you plead
  custom;
That which for want of wit I granted erst,
I now must yield through fear. Come, come,
  let 's in;
Once o'er shoes, we are straight o'er head in
  sin.
*Wen.* My jocund soul is joyful beyond meas-
  ure;                        116
I 'll be profuse in Frankford's richest treasure.
                   *Exeunt.*

[SCENE III. — *Another Room in the House.*]

*Enter Cicely, Jenkin, and Butler*

*Jen.* My mistress and Master Wendoll, my
master, sup in her chamber to-night. Cicely,
you are preferr'd, from being the cook, to be
chambermaid. Of all the loves betwixt thee
and me, tell me what thou think'st of this?  5
*Cic.* Mum; there 's an old proverb, — when
the cat 's away, the mouse may play.
*Jen.* Now you talk of a cat, Cicely, I smell a
rat.

*Cic.* Good words, Jenkin, lest you be call'd [10
to answer them!
*Jen.* Why, God make my mistress an honest
woman! Are not these good words? Pray God
my new master play not the knave with my old
master! Is there any hurt in this? God send [15
no villainy intended; and if they do sup together, pray God they do not lie together! God
make my mistress chaste, and make us all His
servants! What harm is there in all this? Nay,
more; here is my hand, thou shalt never have [20
my heart, unless thou say, Amen.
*Cic.* Amen; I pray God, I say.

*Enter Serving-man*

*Serving-man.* My mistress sends that you
should make less noise, to lock up the doors,
and see the household all got to bed! You, [25
Jenkin, for this night are made the porter, to
see the gates shut in.
*Jen.* Thus by little and little I creep into
office. Come, to kennel, my masters, to kennel;
't is eleven o'clock already.                30
*Serving-man.* When you have lock'd the gates
in, you must send up the keys to my mistress.
*Cic.* Quickly, for God's sake, Jenkin; for I
must carry them. I am neither pillow nor bolster, but I know more than both.            35
*Jen.* To bed, good Spigot; to bed, good honest serving-creatures; and let us sleep as snug
as pigs in pease-straw!              *Exeunt.*

[SCENE IV. — *Outside the House.*]

*Enter Frankford and Nick*

*Frank.* Soft, soft! We 've tied our geldings
  to a tree,
Two flight-shoot off, lest by their thundering
  hoofs
They blab our coming. Hear'st thou no noise?
*Nich.* I hear nothing but the owl and you.
*Frank.* So; now my watch's hand points
  upon twelve,                     5
And it is just midnight. Where are my keys?
*Nich.* Here, sir.
*Frank.* This is the key that opes my outward
  gate;
This, the hall-door; this, the withdrawing-
  chamber;                        9
But this, that door that 's bawd unto my shame,
Fountain and spring of all my bleeding thoughts,
Where the most hallowed order and true knot
Of nuptial sanctity hath been profan'd.
It leads to my polluted bed-chamber,
Once my terrestrial heaven, now my earth's hell,
The place where sins in all their ripeness [16
  dwell. —
But I forget myself; now to my gate!

---

¹⁰² **bosom:** intimacy   ¹⁰⁵ **still:** always   Sc. iii. ³ **preferr'd:** promoted   Sc. iv. ² **flight-shoot:**
**bow-shots**

*Nich.* It must ope with far less noise than
Cripplegate, or your plot 's dash'd.
 *Frank.* So; reach me my dark lantern to
  the rest!          20
Tread softly, softly!
 *Nich.*    I will walk on eggs this pace.
 *Frank.* A general silence hath surpris'd the
  house,
And this is the last door. Astonishment,
Fear, and amazement beat upon my heart,
Even as a madman beats upon a drum. 25
Oh, keep my eyes, you Heavens, before I enter,
From any sight that may transfix my soul;
Or, if there be so black a spectacle,
Oh, strike mine eyes stark blind; or if not so,
Lend me such patience to digest my grief, 30
That I may keep this white and virgin hand
From any violent outrage, or red murther! —
And with that prayer I enter.
        *[Exit into the house.]*

[SCENE V. — *Hall of Frankford's House.*]

*Nich.* Here 's a circumstance, indeed! A
man may be made a cuckold in the time he 's
about it. And the case were mine,
As 't is my master's, 'sblood! (that he makes me
 swear!),
I would have plac'd his action, enter'd there; 5
I would, I would!

    *[Enter Frankford]*

*Frank.*    Oh! oh!
 *Nich.* Master! 'Sblood! Master, master!
 *Frank.* Oh me unhappy! I have found them
  lying
Close in each other's arms, and fast asleep. 9
But that I would not damn two precious
 souls,
Bought with my Saviour's blood, and send
 them, laden
With all their scarlet sins upon their backs,
Unto a fearful judgment, their two lives
Had met upon my rapier.
 *Nich.* Master, what, have you left them
  sleeping still?        15
Let me go wake 'em!
 *Frank.*    Stay, let me pause awhile! —
Oh, God! Oh, God! That it were possible
To undo things done; to call back yesterday,
That Time could turn up his swift sandy glass,
To untell the days, and to redeem these hours!
Or that the sun         21
Could, rising from the west, draw his coach
 backward:

Take from th' account of time so many minutes,
Till he had all these seasons call'd again,
Those minutes, and those actions done in them,
Even from her first offence; that I might take
 her               26
As spotless as an angel in my arms!
But, oh! I talk of things impossible,
And cast beyond the moon. God give me
 patience;
For I will in, and wake them.   *Exit.*
 *Nich.*    Here 's patience perforce! 30
He needs must trot afoot that tires his horse.
             *[Exit.]*

*Enter Wendoll, running over the stage in a
 night-gown, he [Frankford] after him with
 his sword drawn; the maid in her smock
 stays his hand, and clasps hold on him.
 He pauses for a while.*

 *Frank.* I thank thee, maid; thou, like an
  angel's hand,
Hast stay'd me from a bloody sacrifice. —
Go, villain; and my wrongs sit on thy soul
As heavy as this grief doth upon mine! 35
When thou record'st my many courtesies,
And shalt compare them with thy treacherous
 heart,
Lay them together, weigh them equally, —
'T will be revenge enough. Go, to thy friend
A Judas; pray, pray, lest I live to see 40
Thee, Judas-like, hang'd on an elder-tree!

*Enter Mistress Frankford in her smock, night-
 gown, and night-attire*

 *Anne.* Oh, by what word, what title, or
  what name,
Shall I entreat your pardon? Pardon! Oh!
I am as far from hoping such sweet grace,
As Lucifer from Heaven. To call you hus-
 band, —          45
(Oh me, most wretched!) I have lost that name;
I am no more your wife.
 *Nich.*    'Sblood, sir, she sounds.
 *Frank.* Spare thou thy tears, for I will weep
  for thee;
And keep thy count'nance, for I 'll blush for
 thee.
Now, I protest, I think 't is I am tainted, 50
For I am most asham'd; and 't is more hard
For me to look upon thy guilty face
Than on the sun's clear brow. What! Would'st
 thou speak?
 *Anne.* I would I had no tongue, no ears, no
  eyes,
No apprehension, no capacity.   55

---

¹⁹ **Cripplegate:** a gate to London near the theatrical district ²⁰ **rest:** (*i.e.,* in addition to the keys,
etc.) Sc. v. (The scene is supposed to shift to the interior of the house, while Nick remains on the stage.)
¹ **circumstance:** pottering ³ **And:** if ⁵ **plac'd his action:** established his case ²⁰ **untell:** count
backwards ²⁹ **cast . . . moon:** talk or think wildly ³²˒³³ Cf. Genesis, xxii, 10, 11 ⁴⁷ **sounds:** swoons

When do you spurn me like a dog? When tread
    me
Under feet? When drag me by the hair?
Though I deserve a thousand, thousand fold,
More than you can inflict — yet, once my hus-
    band,
For womanhood, to which I am a shame,    60
Though once an ornament — even for His sake,
That hath redeem'd our souls, mark not my face,
Nor hack me with your sword; but let me go
Perfect and undeformed to my tomb!
I am not worthy that I should prevail    65
In the least suit; no, not to speak to you,
Nor look on you, nor to be in your presence;
Yet, as an abject, this one suit I crave; —
This granted, I am ready for my grave.
    *Frank.* My God, with patience arm me! —
    Rise, nay, rise,    70
And I 'll debate with thee. Was it for want
Thou play'dst the strumpet? Wast thou not
    suppli'd
With every pleasure, fashion, and new toy, —
Nay, even beyond my calling?
    *Anne.*                      I was.
    *Frank.* Was it, then, disability in me;    75
Or in thine eye seem'd he a properer man?
    *Anne.* Oh, no!
    *Frank.* Did not I lodge thee in my bosom?
Wear thee in my heart?
    *Anne.*             You did.
    *Frank.* I did, indeed; witness my tears, I
    did —
Go, bring my infants hither! —

    [*Two Children are brought in.*]

                    Oh, Nan! Oh, Nan!
If neither fear of shame, regard of honour,    81
The blemish of my house, nor my dear love,
Could have withheld thee from so lewd a fact;
Yet for these infants, these young, harmless
    souls,    84
On whose white brows thy shame is character'd,
And grows in greatness as they wax in years, —
Look but on them, and melt away in tears! —
Away with them; lest, as her spotted body
Hath stain'd their names with stripe of bas-
    tardy,
So her adulterous breath may blast their spirits
With her infectious thoughts! Away with
    them!      [*Exeunt Children.*] 91
    *Anne.* In this one life, I die ten thousand
    deaths.
    *Frank.* Stand up, stand up! I will do noth-
    ing rashly.
I will retire awhile into my study,
And thou shalt hear thy sentence presently.
                                    *Exit.*

    *Anne.* 'T is welcome, be it death. Oh me,
    base strumpet,    96
That, having such a husband, such sweet chil-
    dren,
Must enjoy neither! Oh, to redeem mine hon-
    our,
I 'd have this hand cut off, these my breasts
    sear'd;
Be rack'd, strappado'd, put to any torment: 100
Nay, to whip but this scandal out, I 'd hazard
The rich and dear redemption of my soul!
He cannot be so base as to forgive me,
Nor I so shameless to accept his pardon.
Oh, women, women, you that yet have kept 105
Your holy matrimonial vow unstain'd,
Make me your instance; when you tread awry,
Your sins, like mine, will on your conscience
    lie.

*Enter Cicely, Spigot, all the Serving-men, and
    Jenkin, as newly come out of bed*

    *All.* Oh, mistress, mistress! What have you
    done, mistress?
    *Nich.* 'Sblood, what a caterwauling keep you
    here!    110
    *Jen.* O Lord, mistress, how comes this to
pass? My master is run away in his shirt, and
never so much as call'd me to bring his clothes
after him.
    *Anne.* See what guilt is! Here stand I in
    this place,    115
Asham'd to look my servants in the face.

*Enter Master Frankford and Cranwell; whom
    seeing, she falls on her knees*

    *Frank.* My words are regist'red in Heaven
    already.
With patience hear me! I 'll not martyr thee,
Nor mark thee for a strumpet; but with usage
Of more humility torment thy soul,    120
And kill thee even with kindness.
    *Cran.* Master Frankford ——
    *Frank.* Good Master Cranwell! — Woman,
    hear thy judgment!
Go make thee ready in thy best attire;    124
Take with thee all thy gowns, all thy apparel;
Leave nothing that did ever call thee mistress,
Or by whose sight, being left here in the house,
I may remember such a woman by.
Choose thee a bed and hangings for thy cham-
    ber;
Take with thee everything which hath thy
    mark,    130
And get thee to my manor seven mile off,
Where live; — 't is thine; I freely give it thee.
My tenants by shall furnish thee with wains
To carry all thy stuff within two hours:

---

⁷⁴ **calling:** station in life    ⁷⁶ **properer:** handsomer    ⁸³ **fact:** deed    ¹⁰⁰ **strappado'd: tortured**
¹³³ **by:** near by

No longer will I limit thee my sight.          135
Choose which of all my servants thou lik'st
     best,
And they are thine to attend thee.
     *Anne.*          A mild sentence.
     *Frank.* But, as thou hop'st for Heaven, as
          thou believ'st
Thy name's recorded in the book of life,
I charge thee never after this sad day          140
To see me, or to meet me; or to send,
By word or writing, gift or otherwise,
To move me, by thyself, or by thy friends;
Nor challenge any part in my two children.
So farewell, Nan; for we will henceforth be          145
As we had never seen, ne'er more shall see.
     *Anne.* How full my heart is, in mine eyes
          appears;
What wants in words, I will supply in tears.
     *Frank.* Come, take your coach, your stuff;
          all must along.
Servants and all make ready; all begone!          150
It was thy hand cut two hearts out of one.
                              [*Exeunt.*]

[ACT V

SCENE I. — *Before Sir Francis Acton's House.*]

*Enter Sir Charles [Mountford], gentlemanlike,
     and his Sister, gentlewoman-like*

     *Susan.* Brother, why have you trick'd me
          like a bride,
Bought me this gay attire, these ornaments?
Forget you our estate, our poverty?
     *Char.* Call me not brother, but imagine me
Some barbarous outlaw, or uncivil kern;          5
For if thou shutt'st thy eye, and only hear'st
The words that I shall utter, thou shalt judge me
Some staring ruffian, not thy brother Charles.
Oh, sister! ——
     *Susan.* Oh, brother! what doth this strange
          language mean?          10
     *Char.* Dost love me, sister? Wouldst thou
          see me live
A bankrupt beggar in the world's disgrace,
And die indebted to mine enemies?
Wouldst thou behold me stand like a huge beam
In the world's eye, a bye-word and a scorn?          15
It lies in thee of these to acquit me free,
And all my debt I may outstrip by thee.
     *Susan.* By me? Why, I have nothing, noth-
          ing left;
I owe even for the clothes upon my back;
I am not worth ——
     *Char.*          O sister, say not so!          20
It lies in you my downcast state to raise;
To make me stand on even points with the
     world.

Come, sister, you are rich; indeed you are.
And in your power you have, without delay
Acton's five hundred pound back to repay.          25
     *Susan.* Till now I had thought y' had lov'd
          me. By my honour
(Which I have kept as spotless as the moon),
I ne'er was mistress of that single doit
Which I reserv'd not to supply your wants;
And do ye think that I would hoard from
     you?          30
Now, by my hopes in Heaven, knew I the
     means
To buy you from the slavery of your debts
(Especially from Acton, whom I hate),
I would redeem it with my life or blood!          34
     *Char.* I challenge it, and, kindred set apart,
Thus, ruffian-like, I lay siege to thy heart.
What do I owe to Acton?
     *Susan.* Why, some five hundred pounds; to-
          wards which, I swear,
In all the world I have not one denier.
     *Char.* It will not prove so. Sister, now re-
          solve me:          40
What do you think (and speak your conscience)
Would Acton give, might he enjoy your bed?
     *Susan.* He would not shrink to spend a
          thousand pound
To give the Mountfords' name so deep a wound.
     *Char.* A thousand pound! I but five hundred
          owe:          45
Grant him your bed; he 's paid with interest so.
     *Susan.* Oh, brother!
     *Char.*          Oh, sister! only this one way,
With that rich jewel you my debts may pay.
In speaking this my cold heart shakes with
     shame;
Nor do I woo you in a brother's name,          50
But in a stranger's. Shall I die in debt
To Acton, my grand foe, and you still wear
The precious jewel that he holds so dear?
     *Susan.* My honour I esteem as dear and pre-
          cious
As my redemption.
     *Char.*          I esteem you, sister,          55
As dear, for so dear prizing it.
     *Susan.*          Will Charles
Have me cut off my hands, and send them
     Acton?
Rip up my breast, and with my bleeding heart
Present him as a token?
     *Char.*          Neither, sister;
But hear me in my strange assertion!          60
Thy honour and my soul are equal in my re-
     gard;
Nor will thy brother Charles survive thy shame.
His kindness, like a burthen, hath surcharg'd
     me,

---

135 **limit:** allow     143 **move:** appeal to     1 **trick'd:** dressed     5 **kern:** Irish foot-soldier, peasant
28 **doit:** coin worth half a farthing     39 **denier:** penny     40 **resolve:** tell

And under his good deeds I stooping go,
Not with an upright soul.  Had I remain'd  65
In prison still, there doubtless I had died.
Then, unto him that freed me from that prison,
Still do I owe this life.  What mov'd my foe
To enfranchise me?  'T was, sister, for your
  love;
With full five hundred pounds he bought your
  love; —                                        70
And shall he not enjoy it?  Shall the weight
Of all this heavy burthen lean on me,
And will not you bear part?  You did partake
The joy of my release; will you not stand
In joint-bond bound to satisfy the debt?        75
Shall I be only charg'd?
  *Susan.*                    But that I know
These arguments come from an honour'd mind,
As in your most extremity of need
Scorning to stand in debt to one you hate, —
Nay, rather would engage your unstain'd
  honour,                                        80
Than to be held ingrate, — I should condemn
  you.
I see your resolution, and assent;
So Charles will have me, and I am content.
  *Char.*  For this I trick'd you up.
  *Susan.*                But here 's a knife,
To save mine honour, shall slice out my life.   85
  *Char.*  I know thou pleasest me a thousand
  times
More in thy resolution than thy grant. —
Observe her love; to soothe it to my suit,
Her honour she will hazard, though not lose;
To bring me out of debt, her rigorous hand      90
Will pierce her heart, — O wonder! — that will
  choose,
Rather than stain her blood, her life to lose.
Come, you sad sister to a woful brother,
This is the gate.  I 'll bear him such a present,
Such an acquittance for the knight to seal,     95
As will amaze his senses, and surprise
With admiration all his fantasies.

  *Enter [Sir Francis] Acton and Malby*

  *Susan.*  Before his unchaste thoughts shall
  seize on me,
'T is here shall my imprison'd soul set free.
  *Fran.*  How! Mountford with his sister, hand
  in hand!                                       100
What miracle 's afoot?
  *Mal.*              It is a sight
Begets in me much admiration.
  *Char.*  Stand not amaz'd to see me thus at-
  tended!
Acton, I owe thee money, and, being unable
To bring thee the full sum in ready coin,       105
Lo! for thy more assurance, here 's a pawn, —
My sister, my dear sister, whose chaste honour

⁹⁷ admiration: wonder     ¹²¹ wrested: extreme

I prize above a million.  Here! Nay, take her:
She 's worth your money, man; do not forsake
  her.
  *Fran.*  I would he were in earnest!          110
  *Susan.*  Impute it not to my immodesty.
My brother, being rich in nothing else
But in his interest that he hath in me,
According to his poverty hath brought you       114
Me, all his store; whom, howsoe'er you prize,
As forfeit to your hand, he values highly,
And would not sell, but to acquit your debt,
For any emperor's ransom.
  *Fran. [Aside.]*            Stern heart, relent,
Thy former cruelty at length repent!
Was ever known, in any former age,              120
Such honourable, wrested courtesy?
Lands, honours, life, and all the world forgo,
Rather than stand engag'd to such a foe!
  *Char.*  Acton, she is too poor to be thy bride,
And I too much oppos'd to be thy brother.       125
There, take her to thee; if thou hast the heart
To seize her as a rape, or lustful prey,
To blur our house, that never yet was stain'd;
To murther her that never meant thee harm;
To kill me now, whom once thou sav'dst from
  death: —                                      130
Do them at once; on her all these rely,
And perish with her spotted chastity.
  *Fran.*  You overcome me in your love, Sir
  Charles.
I cannot be so cruel to a lady
I love so dearly.  Since you have not spar'd     135
To engage your reputation to the world,
Your sister's honour, which you prize so dear,
Nay, all the comfort which you hold on earth,
To grow out of my debt, being your foe, —
Your honour'd thoughts, lo! thus I recompense.
Your metamorphos'd foe receives your gift       141
In satisfaction of all former wrongs.
This jewel I will wear here in my heart;
And where before I thought her, for her wants,
Too base to be my bride, to end all strife,     145
I seal you my dear brother, her my wife.
  *Susan.*  You still exceed us.  I will yield to
  fate,
And learn to love, where I till now did hate.
  *Char.*  With that enchantment you have
  charm'd my soul
And made me rich even in those very words! 150
I pay no debt, but am indebted more;
Rich in your love, I never can be poor.
  *Fran.*  All 's mine is yours; we are alike in
  state;
Let 's knit in love what was oppos'd in hate!
Come, for our nuptials we will straight pro-
  vide,
Blest only in our brother and fair bride.       156
                                          *[Exeunt.]*

¹³² with ... chastity: when her chastity is spotted

[SCENE II. — *Frankford's House.*]

*Enter Cranwell, Frankford, and Nick*

*Cran.* Why do you search each room about
  your house,
Now that you have despatch'd your wife away?
  *Frank.* Oh, sir! To see that nothing may be
    left
That ever was my wife's. I lov'd her dearly;
And when I do but think of her unkindness,  5
My thoughts are all in hell; to avoid which
    torment,
I would not have a bodkin or a cuff,
A bracelet, necklace, or rabato wire,
Nor anything that ever was call'd hers,
Left me, by which I might remember her. — 10
Seek round about.
  *Nich.* 'Sblood! master, here's her lute flung
    in a corner.
  *Frank.* Her lute! Oh, God! Upon this in-
    strument
Her fingers have ran quick division,
Sweeter than that which now divides our
    hearts.                                  15
These frets have made me pleasant, that have
    now
Frets of my heart-strings made. Oh, Master
    Cranwell,
Oft hath she made this melancholy wood
(Now mute and dumb for her disastrous chance)
Speak sweetly many a note, sound many a
    strain                                   20
To her own ravishing voice; which being well
    strung,
What pleasant strange airs have they jointly
    rung! —
Post with it after her! — Now nothing's left;
Of her and hers I am at once bereft.
  *Nich.* I'll ride and overtake her; do my
    message,                                 25
And come back again.              [*Exit.*]
  *Cran.*          Meantime, sir, if you please,
I'll to Sir Francis Acton, and inform him
Of what hath pass'd betwixt you and his sister.
  *Frank.* Do as you please. — How ill am I
    bested,
To be a widower ere my wife be dead!        30
                                   [*Exeunt.*]

[SCENE III. — *A Country Road.*]

*Enter Mistress Frankford; with Jenkin, her maid
    Cicely, her Coachman, and three Carters*

  *Anne.* Bid my coach stay! Why should I
    ride in state,
Being hurl'd so low down by the hand of fate?

A seat like to my fortunes let me have, —
Earth for my chair, and for my bed a grave!
  *Jen.* Comfort, good mistress; you have [5
watered your coach with tears already. You
have but two mile now to go to your manor.
A man cannot say by my old master Frankford
as he may say by me, that he wants manors;
for he hath three or four, of which this is one
that we are going to now.                    11
  *Cic.* Good mistress, be of good cheer! Sorrow,
you see, hurts you, but helps you not; we all
mourn to see you so sad.
  *Carter.* Mistress, I see some of my landlord's
    men                                      15
Come riding post: 't is like he brings some news.
  *Anne.* Comes he from Master Frankford, he
    is welcome;
So is his news, because they come from him.

*Enter Nick*

  *Nich.* There!
  *Anne.* I know the lute. Oft have I sung to
    thee;                                    20
We both are out of tune, both out of time.
  *Nich.* Would that had been the worst instrument that e'er you played on! My master com-
mends him unto ye; there's all he can find that
was ever yours; he hath nothing left that ever
you could lay claim to but his own heart, — [26
and he could afford you that! All that I have to
deliver you is this: he prays you to forget him;
and so he bids you farewell.                 29
  *Anne.* I thank him; he is kind, and ever was.
All you that have true feeling of my grief,
That know my loss, and have relenting hearts,
Gird me about, and help me with your tears
To wash my spotted sins! My lute shall groan;
It cannot weep, but shall lament my moan.  35
                              [*She plays.*]

*Enter Wendoll* [*behind*]

  *Wen.* Pursu'd with horror of a guilty soul,
And with the sharp scourge of repentance
    lash'd,
I fly from mine own shadow. O my stars!
What have my parents in their lives deserv'd, 39
That you should lay this penance on their son?
When I but think of Master Frankford's love,
And lay it to my treason, or compare
My murthering him for his relieving me,
It strikes a terror like a lightning's flash,
To scorch my blood up. Thus I, like the owl, 45
Asham'd of day, live in these shadowy woods,
Afraid of every leaf or murmuring blast,
Yet longing to receive some perfect knowledge
How he hath dealt with her. [*Seeing Mistress
    Frankford.*] O my sad fate!

---

⁸ **rabato wire:** wire used to support a ruff    ¹⁴ **division:** melodic variations    ¹⁶ **pleasant:** merry
¹⁹ **for:** because *of*

Here, and so far from home, and thus attended!
Oh, God! I have divorc'd the truest turtles 51
That ever liv'd together, and, being divided,
In several places make their several moan;
She in the fields laments, and he at home;
So poets write that Orpheus made the trees 55
And stones to dance to his melodious harp,
Meaning the rustic and the barbarous hinds,
That had no understanding part in them:
So she from these rude carters tears extracts,
Making their flinty hearts with grief to rise, 60
And draw down rivers from their rocky eyes.
   *Anne.* [*To Nicholas.*] If you return unto
   my master, say
(Though not from me, for I am all unworthy
To blast his name so with a strumpet's tongue)
That you have seen me weep, wish myself
   dead! 65
Nay, you may say, too (for my vow is past),
Last night you saw me eat and drink my
   last.
This to your master you may say and swear;
For it is writ in heaven, and decreed here.
   *Nich.* I 'll say you wept; I 'll swear you
   made me sad. 70
Why, how now, eyes? What now? What 's
   here to do?
I 'm gone, or I shall straight turn baby too.
   *Wen.* [*Aside.*] I cannot weep, my heart is all
   on fire.
Curs'd be the fruits of my unchaste desire!
   *Anne.* Go, break this lute upon my coach's
   wheel, 75
As the last music that I e'er shall make, —
Not as my husband's gift, but my farewell
To all earth's joy; and so your master tell!
   *Nich.* If I can for crying.
   *Wen.* [*Aside.*]       Grief, have done,
Or, like a madman, I shall frantic run. 80
   *Anne.* You have beheld the wofull'st wretch
   on earth, —
A woman made of tears; would you had words
To express but what you see! My inward grief
No tongue can utter; yet unto your power
You may describe my sorrow, and disclose 85
To thy sad master my abundant woes.
   *Nich.* I 'll do your commendations.
   *Anne.*          Oh, no!
I dare not so presume; nor to my children!
I am disclaim'd in both; alas! I am.
Oh, never teach them, when they come to
   speak, 90
To name the name of mother: chide their
   tongue,
If they by chance light on that hated word;
Tell them 't is naught; for when that word
   they name,

Poor, pretty souls! they harp on their own
   shame.
   *Wen.* [*Aside.*] To recompense her wrongs,
   what canst thou do? 95
Thou hast made her husbandless, and childless
   too.
   *Anne.* I have no more to say. — Speak not
   for me;
Yet you may tell your master what you see.
   *Nich.* I 'll do 't.          *Exit.*
   *Wen.* [*Aside.*] I 'll speak to her, and comfort
   her in grief. 100
Oh, but her wound cannot be cur'd with words!
No matter, though; I 'll do my best good
   will
To work a cure on her whom I did kill.
   *Anne.* So, now unto my coach, then to my
   home,
So to my death-bed; for from this sad hour, 105
I never will nor eat, nor drink, nor taste
Of any cates that may preserve my life.
I never will nor smile, nor sleep, nor rest;
But when my tears have wash'd my black soul
   white,
Sweet Saviour, to thy hands I yield my sprite.
   *Wen.* [*Coming forward.*] Oh, Mistress Frank-
   ford!
   *Anne.*     Oh, for God's sake, fly! 111
The devil doth come to tempt me, ere I die.
My coach! — This sin, that with an angel's
   face
Conjur'd mine honour, till he sought my
   wrack,
In my repentant eye seems ugly black. 115
   *Exeunt all* [*except Wendoll and*
   *Jenkin*]; *the Carters whistling.*
   *Jen.* What, my young master, that fled
in his shirt! How come you by your clothes
again? You have made our house in a sweet
pickle, ha' ye not, think you? What, shall I
serve you still, or cleave to the old house? 120
   *Wen.* Hence, slave! Away, with thy unsea-
son'd mirth!
Unless thou canst shed tears, and sigh, and
   howl,
Curse thy sad fortunes, and exclaim on fate,
Thou art not for my turn.
   *Jen.* Marry, an you will not, another will;
farewell, and be hang'd! Would you had [126
never come to have kept this coil within our
doors! We shall ha' you run away like a sprite
again.          [*Exit.*]
   *Wen.* She 's gone to death; I live to want
   and woe, 130
Her life, her sins, and all upon my head.
And I must now go wander, like a Cain,
In foreign countries and remoted climes,

---

     ⁵¹ **turtles:** turtle doves   ⁶⁶ **past:** made   ⁸⁷ **commendations:** greetings   ¹⁰⁷ **cates:** food   ¹¹⁴ **Con-
jur'd:** enchanted   ¹²¹ **unseason'd:** unseasonable   ¹²⁷ **coil:** uproar   ¹³³ **remoted:** distant

Where the report of my ingratitude
Cannot be heard.  I 'll over first to France, 135
And so to Germany and Italy;
Where, when I have recovered, and by travel
Gotten those perfect tongues, and that these
    rumours
May in their height abate, I will return:
And I divine (however now dejected),        140
My worth and parts being by some great man
    prais'd,
At my return I may in court be rais'd.  *Exit.*

[SCENE IV. — *Before the Manor House.*]

*Enter Sir Francis [Acton], Sir Charles [Mount-
ford], Cranwell, [Malby,] and Susan*

*Fran.*  Brother, and now my wife, I think
    these troubles,
Fall on my head by justice of the heavens,
For being so strict to you in your extremities;
But we are now aton'd.  I would my sister
Could with like happiness o'ercome her griefs 5
As we have ours.
    *Susan.*  You tell us, Master Cranwell, won-
        drous things
Touching the patience of that gentleman,
With what strange virtue he demeans his grief.
    *Cran.*  I told you what I was witness of; 10
It was my fortune to lodge there that night.
    *Fran.*  Oh, that same villain, Wendoll!
    'T was his tongue
That did corrupt her; she was of herself
Chaste and devoted well.  Is this the house?
    *Cran.*  Yes, sir; I take it, here your sister
        lies.        15
    *Fran.*  My brother Frankford show'd too
        mild a spirit
In the revenge of such a loathed crime.
Less than he did, no man of spirit could do.
I am so far from blaming his revenge,
That I commend it.  Had it been my case, 20
Their souls at once had from their breasts been
    freed;
Death to such deeds of shame is the due meed.

*Enter Jenkin [and Cicely]*

    *Jen.*  Oh, my mistress, mistress! my poor
mistress!
    *Cicely.*  Alas! that ever I was born; what [25
shall I do for my poor mistress?
    *Sir C.*  Why, what of her?
    *Jen.*  Oh, Lord, sir! she no sooner heard that
her brother and her friends were come to see
how she did, but she, for very shame of her [30
guilty conscience, fell into such a swoon, that
we had much ado to get life in her.

*Susan.*  Alas, that she should bear so hard **a**
fate!
Pity it is repentance comes too late.
    *Fran.*  Is she so weak in body?        35
    *Jen.*  Oh, sir! I can assure you there 's no hope
of life in her; for she will take no sust'nance: she
hath plainly starv'd herself, and now she 's as
lean as a lath.  She ever looks for the good hour.
Many gentlemen and gentlewomen of the [40
country are come to comfort her.        [*Exeunt.*]

[SCENE V. — *In the Manor House.*]

[*Sir Charles Mountford, Sir Francis Acton,
    Malby, Cranwell, and Susan*]

*Enter Mistress Frankford in her bed*

    *Mal.*  How fare you, Mistress Frankford?
    *Anne.*  Sick, sick, oh, sick!  Give me some
        air, I pray!
Tell me, oh, tell me, where is Master Frank-
    ford?
Will not he deign to see me ere I die?
    *Mal.*  Yes, Mistress Frankford; divers gen-
        tlemen,        5
Your loving neighbours, with that just request
Have mov'd, and told him of your weak estate:
Who, though with much ado to get belief,
Examining of the general circumstance,
Seeing your sorrow and your penitence,        10
And hearing therewithal the great desire
You have to see him, ere you left the world,
He gave to us his faith to follow us,
And sure he will be here immediately.
    *Anne.*  You have half reviv'd me with the
        pleasing news,        15
Raise me a little higher in my bed. —
Blush I not, brother Acton?  Blush I not, Sir
    Charles?
Can you not read my fault writ in my cheek?
Is not my crime there?  Tell me, gentlemen.
    *Char.*  Alas, good mistress, sickness hath not
        left you        20
Blood in your face enough to make you blush.
    *Anne.*  Then, sickness, like a friend, my
        fault would hide. —
Is my husband come?  My soul but tarries
His arrive; then I am fit for heaven.
    *Fran.*  I came to chide you, but my words of
        hate        25
Are turn'd to pity and compassionate grief.
I came to rate you, but my brawls, you see,
Melt into tears, and I must weep by thee. —
Here 's Master Frankford now.

*Enter Frankford*

    *Frank.*  Good morrow, brother; morrow,
        gentlemen!        30

God, that hath laid this cross upon our heads,
Might (had He pleas'd) have made our cause
  of meeting
On a more fair and more contented ground;
But He that made us made us to this woe.

  *Anne.* And is he come? Methinks, that
  voice I know.                                        35
  *Frank.* How do you, woman?
  *Anne.* Well, Master Frankford, well; but
  shall be better,
I hope, within this hour. Will you vouchsafe,
Out of your grace and your humanity,
To take a spotted strumpet by the hand?   40
  *Frank.* This hand once held my heart in
  faster bonds,
Than now 't is gripp'd by me. God pardon
  them
That made us first break hold!
  *Anne.*                            Amen, amen!
Out of my zeal to Heaven, whither I'm now
  bound,
I was so impudent to wish you here;        45
And once more beg your pardon. O, good
  man,
And father to my children, pardon me.
Pardon, oh, pardon me: my fault so heinous
  is,
That if you in this world forgive it not,
Heaven will not clear it in the world to come. 50
Faintness hath so usurp'd upon my knees,
That kneel I cannot; but on my heart's knees
My prostrate soul lies thrown down at your
  feet,
To beg your gracious pardon. Pardon, oh,
  pardon me!
  *Frank.* As freely, from the low depth of my
  soul,                                               55
As my Redeemer hath forgiven His death,
I pardon thee. I will shed tears for thee;
Pray with thee; and, in mere pity of thy weak
  estate,
I 'll wish to die with thee.
  *All.*                        So do we all.
  *Nich.*                        So will not I;
I 'll sigh and sob, but, by my faith, not die.  60
  *Fran.* Oh, Master Frankford, all the near
  alliance
I lose by her, shall be suppli'd in thee.
You are my brother by the nearest way,
Her kindred hath fall'n off, but yours doth
  stay.
  *Frank.* Even as I hope for pardon, at that
  day                                                 65
When the Great Judge of heaven in scarlet sits,
So be thou pardon'd! Though thy rash offence
Divorc'd our bodies, thy repentant tears
Unite our souls.

  *Char.* Then comfort, Mistress Frankford!
You see your husband hath forgiven your fall; 70
Then rouse your spirits, and cheer your fainting
  soul!
  *Susan.* How is it with you?
  *Fran.*                        How d'ye feel yourself?
  *Anne.* Not of this world.
  *Frank.* I see you are not, and I weep to see it.
My wife, the mother to my pretty babes!   75
Both those lost names I do restore thee back,
And with this kiss I wed thee once again.
Though thou art wounded in thy honour'd
  name,
And with that grief upon thy death-bed liest,
Honest in heart, upon my soul, thou diest.  80
  *Anne.* Pardon'd on earth, soul, thou in
  heaven art free;
Once more thy wife, dies thus embracing
  thee.                                *[Dies.]*
  *Frank.* New-married, and new-widow'd. —
  Oh! she 's dead,
And a cold grave must be her nuptial bed.
  *Char.* Sir, be of good comfort, and your
  heavy sorrow                                        85
Part equally amongst us; storms divided
Abate their force, and with less rage are guided.
  *Cran.* Do, Master Frankford; he that hath
  least part,
Will find enough to drown one troubled heart.
  *Fran.* Peace with thee, Nan! — Brothers
  and gentlemen,                                      90
All we that can plead interest in her grief,
Bestow upon her body funeral tears!
Brother, had you with threats and usage bad
Punish'd her sin, the grief of her offence
Had not with such true sorrow touch'd her
  heart.                                              95
  *Frank.* I see it had not; therefore, on her
  grave
Will I bestow this funeral epitaph,
Which on her marble tomb shall be engrav'd.
In golden letters shall these words be fill'd:
*Here lies she whom her husband's kindness
kill'd.*                                          100

FINIS

## THE EPILOGUE

AN honest crew, disposed to be merry,
  Came to a tavern by, and call'd for wine.
The drawer brought it, smiling like a cherry,
  And told them it was pleasant, neat and
  fine.
'Taste it,' quoth one. He did so. 'Fie!'
  quoth he,                                            5
'This wine was good; now 't runs too near the
  lee.'

<hr>

[80] **Honest:** chaste    [82] (Verity suggests a colon after *more; i.e.,* Frankford kisses her again.)
[99] **In . . . fill'd:** the engraved letters filled in with gold    [2] **by:** near by    [4] **neat:** pure

Another sipp'd, to give the wine his due,
  And said unto the rest, it drunk too flat;
The third said, it was old; the fourth, too new;
  'Nay,' quoth the fift, 'the sharpness likes
    me not.'                10
Thus, gentlemen, you see how, in one hour,
The wine was new, old, flat, sharp, sweet, and
  sour.

Unto this wine we do allude our play,
  Which some will judge too trivial, some too
    grave:
You as our guests we entertain this day,   15
  And bid you welcome to the best we have.
Excuse us, then; good wine may be disgrac'd,
When every several mouth hath sundry taste.

10 **fift:** fifth   13 **allude:** compare   18 **several:** separate   **sundry:** different, peculiar to itself

*Bussy D'Ambois:*

# A TRAGEDIE:

As
*it hath been often presented
at Paules.*

LONDON,
Printed for *William Aspley.*
1607.

BIBLIOGRAPHICAL RECORD. *Bussy d'Ambois* exists in two texts, each the careful and apparently unaided work of Chapman. The first is that of the first quarto, printed "As it hath been often presented at Paules" in 1607 and reissued in 1608. The other is that of 1641 (reissued in 1646 and 1657), which is described on the title-page as "Being much corrected and amended by the Author before his death." This later edition, which shows many excisions from the text of 1607 and yet more additions to it, besides much verbal revision, is in truth the better and has here been followed. Important passages found only in the earlier quarto are included in square brackets and referred to in the footnotes.

DATE AND STAGE PERFORMANCE. *Bussy d'Ambois* was entered on the Stationers' Register by its first publisher, June 3, 1607: — *William Aspley Entred for his copie vnder thandes [the hands] of Sir George Bucke knight and the Warden Master White The tragedie of Busye D'Amboise made by George Chapman.*

A date of composition shortly after Queen Elizabeth's death in 1603 is probable, and the references to her and her court strengthen the likelihood of this date. Like many of Chapman's other plays, this was written for the boy actors and the aristocratic patrons who attended their productions. Both the boy companies — of St. Paul's and of the Queen's Revels at Blackfriars — appear to have performed it. The former (not otherwise known to have been employed by Chapman) is mentioned on the title-page of the first quarto (see facsimile); and the second is indicated by the statement of the prologue (line 16) in the 1641 edition that Field, the leading actor of the Queen's Revels, first made the part of Bussy famous. When Field joined the King's Men, he is conjectured to have carried *Bussy d'Ambois* with him. It was later played by them, on Easter Monday (April 7), 1634, at the Cockpit-in-Court, and again on March 27, 1638; and it was probably for one of these revivals, with Ilyard Swanston in the title-part, that the extant prologue and epilogue were written by another hand than Chapman's.

The boy actors specialized in ranting parts, in melodramatic and supernatural action, and in learned language fitted to the ears of the gentry. Chapman gave them these things in superabundance, and *Bussy d'Ambois* came nearer than any other play of the early seventeenth century to recapturing the fine excess of Marlowe's *Tamburlaine*. The indebtedness of the incantation scene (IV. ii) to Marlowe's *Faustus* is also obvious. On the other hand, the grandiose, if misguided, exaggeration of the love-and-honor theme makes *Bussy* the most influential, as it is the most impressive poetically, of the precursors of the heroic drama of Dryden's age. This accounts for the great esteem which the play enjoyed after the Restoration. With the famous Charles Hart (Shakespeare's grandnephew) in the chief rôle it continued to hold the stage. Pepys praised it and bought a copy; Dryden, whose sober judgment came to abhor what he regarded as the fustian of Chapman's language, admitted the earlier attractiveness of "those glaring colours which amazed me in *Bussy d'Ambois* upon the theatre." After Hart's death Thomas D'Urfey altered it for the Theatre Royal and the actor Mountford, under the title of *Bussy d'Ambois, or the Husband's Revenge.*

STRUCTURE. In the early editions the acts, but not scenes, are divided. The action all occurs at, or in the neighborhood of, the French Court, within a few days. The influence of Seneca — *e.g.*, in the employment of the Nuntius to introduce epic declamations, in the long psychologizing speeches, and in the profusion of lurid and supernatural incident — is very strong. Many passages, moreover, are intentional imitations of admired lines in Seneca's tragedies or in other classical authors with whom Chapman was peculiarly familiar. On these points the reader will find much help in Professor A. S. Ferguson's article, "The Plays of George Chapman," *Modern Language Review,* Jan., 1918.

SOURCE. No printed account of the career of Louis de Clermont, Sieur de Bussy d'Amboise (1549–1579), available at the time Chapman wrote his play, appears to be known, and it is possible that the dramatist got his information by word of mouth, as Marlowe seems sometimes to have done. The historical d'Amboise had nearly as spectacular a life as Chapman gives him, and (apart from the supernatural heightening) the accepted account of his last love affair and assassination differs from Chapman's mainly in ascribing responsibility for his death to the king himself rather than the king's brother, Monsieur (the duc d'Alençon), who was actually in England at the time. Professor Parrott notes that Dumas, in his novel on the same subject, *La Dame de Monsoreau,* makes the same alteration, and conjectures from this coincidence the existence of some common source.

# GEORGE CHAPMAN (1559--1634)

## BUSSY D'AMBOIS

[DRAMATIS PERSONAE

HENRY III, King of France
Monsieur, his brother (Duke of Alençon)
THE DUKE OF GUISE
COUNT OF MONTSURRY
BUSSY d'AMBOIS
BARRISOR, ⎤
L'ANOU, ⎬ Courtiers; enemies of d'Ambois
PYRHOT, ⎦
BRISAC, ⎤
MELYNELL, ⎬ Courtiers; friends of d'Ambois
FRIAR COMOLET

MAFFÉ, steward to Monsieur
BEHEMOTH, ⎤
CARTOPHYLAX, ⎬ Spirits

ELENOR, Duchess of Guise
TAMYRA, Countess of Montsurry
BEAUPRÉ, niece to Elenor
PERO, maid to Tamyra
CHARLOTTE, maid to Beaupré
PYRA, a court lady
ANNABEL, maid to Elenor

Nuntius; Murderers; Ghost of Friar; Lords, Ladies, Pages, Servants, &c.]

[SCENE. — Paris]

[PROLOGUE

NOT out of confidence that none but we
Are able to present this tragedy,
Not out of envy at the grace of late
It did receive, nor yet to derogate
From their deserts who give out boldly that   5
They move with equal feet on the same flat;
Neither for all nor any of such ends
We offer it, gracious and noble friends,
To your review; we, far from emulation
And (charitably judge) from imitation,   10
With this work entertain you, a piece known
And still believ'd in Court to be our own.
To quit our claim, doubting our right or
    merit,
Would argue in us poverty of spirit
Which we must not subscribe to.    Field is
    gone,   15
Whose action first did give it name, and one
Who came the nearest to him, is denied
By his gray beard to show the height and
    pride
Of d'Ambois' youth and bravery; yet to
    hold
Our title still a-foot, and not grow cold   20
By giving it o'er, a third man with his best
Of care and pains defends our interest;
As Richard he was lik'd, nor do we fear
In personating d'Ambois he'll appear
To faint, or go less, so your free consent,   25
As heretofore, give him encouragement.]

## Actus primi Scena prima

[Open place near the Court.]

Enter Bussy d'Ambois, poor

*Bu.* Fortune, not Reason, rules the state of
    things,
Reward goes backwards, Honour on his head;
Who is not poor, is monstrous; only need
Gives form and worth to every human seed.
As cedars beaten with continual storms,   5
So great men flourish; and do imitate
Unskilful statuaries, who suppose,
In forming a Colossus, if they make him
Straddle enough, strut, and look big, and gape,
Their work is goodly: so men merely great   10
In their affected gravity of voice,
Sourness of countenance, manners' cruelty,
Authority, wealth, and all the spawn of fortune,
Think they bear all the kingdom's worth before
    them;
Yet differ not from those colossic statues,   15
Which, with heroic forms without o'erspread,
Within are nought but mortar, flint, and lead.
Man is a torch borne in the wind, a dream
But of a shadow, summ'd with all his substance.
And as great seamen, using all their wealth   20
And skills in Neptune's deep invisible paths,
In tall ships richly built and ribb'd with brass,
To put a girdle round about the world,
When they have done it (coming near their
    haven)

Prologue: (From the 1641 quarto. Not by Chapman)   ⁷ **statuaries:** sculptors   ¹⁶ **without:**
externally   ¹⁹ **But:** only   **summ'd . . . substance:** when he and all he owns are estimated
²⁰ **wealth:** ('powers' Q 1)

327

Are fain to give a warning-piece, and call   25
A poor, staid fisherman, that never past
His country's sight, to waft and guide them in:
So when we wander furthest through the waves
Of glassy Glory, and the gulfs of State,   29
Topp'd with all titles, spreading all our reaches,
As if each private arm would sphere the earth,
We must to Virtue for her guide resort,
Or we shall shipwrack in our safest port.
                                *Procumbit.*

*[Enter] Monsieur, with two Pages*

[*Mons.*] There is no second place in numer-
   ous state
That holds more than a cipher; in a king   35
All places are contain'd. His words and looks
Are like the flashes and the bolts of Jove;
His deeds inimitable, like the sea   38
That shuts still as it opes, and leaves no tracts
Nor prints of precedent for mean men's facts.
There's but a thread betwixt me and a crown:
I would not wish it cut, unless by nature;
Yet to prepare me for that possible fortune,
'T is good to get resolved spirits about me.
I follow'd d'Ambois to this green retreat;   45
A man of spirit beyond the reach of fear,
Who (discontent with his neglected worth)
Neglects the light, and loves obscure abodes.
But he is young and haughty, apt to take   49
Fire at advancement, to bear state and flourish;
In his rise therefore shall my bounties shine.
None loathes the world so much, nor loves to
   scoff it,
But gold and grace will make him surfeit of it.
What, d'Ambois?
    *Bu.*         He, sir.
    *Mons.*          Turn'd to earth, alive?
Up, man; the sun shines on thee.
    *Bu.*              Let it shine:
I am no mote to play in 't, as great men are.   56
    *Mons.* Call'st thou men great in state
   motes in the sun?
They say so that would have thee freeze in
   shades,
They (like the gross Sicilian gourmandist)
Empty their noses in the cates they love,   60
That none may eat but they. Do thou but
   bring
Light to the banquet Fortune sets before thee,
And thou wilt loathe lean darkness like thy
   death.
Who would believe thy mettle could let sloth
Rust and consume it? If Themistocles   65
Had liv'd obscur'd thus in th' Athenian state,
Xerxes had made both him and it his slaves.

If brave Camillus had lurk'd so in Rome,
He had not five times been Dictator there,
Nor four times triumph'd. If Epaminondas   *1*
(Who liv'd twice twenty years obscur'd in
   Thebes)
Had liv'd so still, he had been still unnam'd,
And paid his country nor himself their right;
But putting forth his strength, he rescu'd both
From imminent ruin; and, like burnish'd steel,
After long use he shin'd; for as the light   76
Not only serves to show, but renders us
Mutually profitable, so our lives
In acts exemplary, not only win
Ourselves good names, but do to others give   80
Matter for virtuous deeds, by which we live.
    *Bu.* What would you wish me?
    *Mons.*         Leave the troubled streams,
And live, where thrivers do, at the well-head.
    *Bu.* At the well-head? Alas, what should I
   do
With that enchanted glass? See devils there?
Or, like a strumpet, learn to set my looks   86
In an eternal brake, or practise juggling,
To keep my face still fast, my heart still loose;
Or bear (like dame schoolmistresses their rid-
   dles)
Two tongues, and be good only for a shift;   90
Flatter great lords, to put them still in mind
Why they were made lords; or please humor-
   ous ladies
With a good carriage, tell them idle tales
To make their physic work; spend a man's life
In sights and visitations, that will make   95
His eyes as hollow as his mistress' heart:
To do none good, but those that have no need;
To gain being forward, though you break for
   haste
All the commandments ere you break your fast;
But believe backwards, make your period   100
And creed's last article, "I believe in God";
And (hearing villainies preach'd) t' unfold their
   art,
Learn to commit them. 'T is a great man's
   part.
Shall I learn this there?
    *Mons.*       No, thou need'st not learn,
Thou hast the theory; now go there and prac-
   tice.   105
    *Bu.* Ay, in a threadbare suit! when men
   come there,
They must have high naps, and go from thence
   bare:
A man may drown the parts of ten rich men
In one poor suit; brave barks and outward
   gloss

---

    25 **fain:** ('glad' Q 1)     **warning-piece:** signal gun     31 **sphere:** encircle     32 **guide:** guidance
33 S. D. **Procumbit:** lies down     40 **facts:** deeds     53 **surfeit:** eat greedily     59 **gourmandist:** glutton
(Gnatho)     60 **cates:** delicacies     87 **brake:** carpenter's vise     92 **humorous:** fastidious     108 **parts:**
incomes     109 **brave barks:** gorgeous clothes

Attract Court loves, be in-parts ne'er so gross.
　*Mons.* Thou shalt have gloss enough, and
　　all things fit　　　　　　　　　　　111
T'enchase in all show thy long-smother'd spirit.
Be rul'd by me, then. The old Scythians
Painted blind Fortune's powerful hands with
　wings,
To show her gifts come swift and suddenly, 115
Which, if her favourite be not swift to take,
He loses them for ever. Then be wise:
Stay but awhile here, and I'll send to thee.
　　*Exit Monsieur [with Pages.] Manet Bussy.*
　*Bu.* What will he send? Some crowns? It
　　is to sow them
Upon my spirit, and make them spring a crown
Worth millions of the seed-crowns he will send.
Like to disparking noble husbandmen,
He'll put his plow into me, plow me up.
But his unsweating thrift is policy,
And learning-hating policy is ignorant　125
To fit his seed-land soil; a smooth plain ground
Will never nourish any politic seed.
I am for honest actions, not for great.
If I may bring up a new fashion,
And rise in Court for virtue, speed his plow! 130
The King hath known me long as well as he,
Yet could my fortune never fit the length
Of both their understandings till this hour.
There is a deep nick in Time's restless wheel
For each man's good, when which nick comes,
　it strikes;　　　　　　　　　　　135
As rhetoric yet works not persuasion,
But only is a mean to make it work,
So no man riseth by his real merit,
But when it cries "clink" in his raiser's spirit.
Many will say, that cannot rise at all,　140
Man's first hour's rise is first step to his fall.
I'll venture that; men that fall low must die,
As well as men cast headlong from the sky.

　　　　　*Enter Maffé*

　*Ma.* Humour of princes! Is this wretch
　　endu'd
With any merit worth a thousand crowns? 145
Will my lord have me be so ill a steward
Of his revénue, to dispose a sum
So great with so small cause as shows in
　him?
I must examine this. *[To Bussy.]* Is your name
　d'Ambois?
　*Bu.* Sir?
　*Ma.* Is your name d'Ambois?
　*Bu.*　　　　　　　Who have we here? 150
Serve you the Monsieur?

　*Ma.*　　　　　How?
　*Bu.*　　　　　　　Serve you the Monsieur?
　*Ma.* Sir, y'are very hot. I do serve the
　　Monsieur;
But in such place as gives me *Table, chessboard,*
　the command　　　　*and tapers behind*
Of all his other servants. *the arras.*
　And because
His grace's pleasure is to give your good　155
His pass through my command, methinks you
　might
Use me with more respect.
　*Bu.*　　　　　Cry you mercy!
Now you have open'd my dull eyes, I see
　you,
And would be glad to see the good you speak of.
What might I call your name?
　*Ma.*　　　　　　Monsieur Maffé.
　*Bu.* Monsieur Maffé? Then, good Monsieur
　　Maffé,　　　　　　　　　　　161
Pray let me know you better.
　*Ma.*　　　　　Pray do so,
That you may use me better. For yourself,
By your no better outside, I would judge you
To be some poet. Have you given my lord 165
Some pamphlet?
　*Bu.*　　Pamphlet?
　*Ma.*　　　　Pamphlet, sir, I say.
　*Bu.* Did your great master's goodness leave
　　the good,
That is to pass your charge to my poor use,
To your discretion?
　*Ma.*　　　Though he did not, sir,
I hope 't is no rude office to ask reason　170
How that his grace gives me in charge goes
　from me?
　*Bu.* That's very perfect, sir.
　*Ma.*　　　　　Why, very good, sir.
I pray, then, give me leave: if for no pam-
　phlet,
May I not know what other merit in you 174
Makes his compunction willing to relieve you?
　*Bu.* No merit in the world, sir.
　*Ma.*　　　　　That is strange.
Y'are a poor soldier, are you?
　*Bu.*　　　　　That I am, sir.
　*Ma.* And have commanded?
　*Bu.*　　　　Ay, and gone without, sir.
　*Ma. [Aside.]* I see the man; a hundred
　　crowns will make him　　　179
Swagger and drink healths to his grace's bounty,
And swear he could not be more bountiful.
So there's nine hundred crowns sav'd. — Here,
　tall soldier,

His grace hath sent you a whole hundred
crowns.
  *Bu.*  A hundred, sir?  Nay, do his highness
right;
I know his hand is larger, and perhaps    185
I may deserve more than my outside shows.
I am a poet, as I am a soldier,
And I can poetise; and (being well encourag'd)
May sing his fame for giving; yours for deliv-
ering    189
(Like a most faithful steward) what he gives.
  *Ma.*  What shall your subject be?
  *Bu.*          I care not much
If to his bounteous grace I sing the praise
Of fair great noses, and to you of long ones.
What qualities have you, sir, beside your
chain
And velvet jacket?  Can your worship dance?
  *Ma.* [*Aside.*]  A pleasant fellow, 'faith; it
seems my lord    196
Will have him for his jester; and by 'r lady,
Such men are now no fools; 't is a knight's
place.
If I (to save his grace some crowns) should urge
him
T'abate his bounty, I should not be heard.  200
I would to heaven I were an errant ass,
For then I should be sure to have the ears
Of these great men, where now their jesters
have them.
'T is good to please him, yet I 'll take no notice
Of his preferment, but in policy    205
Will still be grave and serious, lest he think
I fear his wooden dagger.  Here, sir Ambo!
  *Bu.*  How, Ambo, sir?
  *Ma.*        Ay, is not your name Ambo?
  *Bu.*  You call'd me lately d'Ambois; has
your worship
So short a head?
  *Ma.*        I cry thee mercy, d'Ambois.
A thousand crowns I bring you from my lord.
Serve God, play the good husband, you may
make    212
This a good standing living: 't is a bounty
His highness might perhaps have bestow'd
better.
  *Bu.*  Go, y'are a rascal; hence, away, you
rogue!    215
  *Ma.*  What mean you, sir?
  *Bu.*        Hence! prate no more!
Or, by thy villain's blood, thou prat'st thy last!
A barbarous groom grudge at his master's
bounty!
But since I know he would as much abhor  219

His hind should argue what he gives his friend,
Take that, sir, for your aptness to dispute.
                [*Strikes him.*] *Exit.*
  *Ma.*  These crowns are set in blood; blood
be their fruit!             *Exit.*

[SCENE II. — *The Court.*]

*Henry, Guise, Montsurry, Elenor, Tamyra,*
  *Beaupré, Pero, Charlotte, Pyra, Annabel*

  *Hen.*  Duchess of Guise, your grace is much
enrich'd
In the attendance of that English virgin,
That will initiate her prime of youth
(Dispos'd to Court conditions) under the hand
Of your preferr'd instructions and command,  5
Rather than any in the English Court,
Whose ladies are not match'd in Christendom
For graceful and confirm'd behaviours
More than the Court, where they are bred, is
equall'd.
  *Gui.*  I like not their Court fashion; it is too
crestfall'n    10
In all observance, making demigods
Of their great nobles; and of their old queen,
An ever-young and most immortal goddess.
  *Mons.*  No question she's the rarest queen
in Europe.
  *Gui.*  But what's that to her immortality?  15
  *Hen.*  Assure you, cousin Guise, so great a
courtier,
So full of majesty and royal parts,
No queen in Christendom may vaunt herself.
Her Court approves it: that's a Court indeed!
Not mix'd with clowneries us'd in common
houses,    20
But, as Courts should be, th' abstracts of their
kingdoms,
In all the beauty, state, and worth they hold;
So is hers, amply, and by her inform'd.
The world is not contracted in a man
With more proportion and expression,    25
Than in her Court her kingdom.  Our French
Court
Is a mere mirror of confusion to it:
The king and subject, lord and every slave,
Dance a continual hay; our rooms of state
Kept like our stables; no place more observ'd
Than a rude market-place: and though our
custom    31
Keep this assur'd confusion from our eyes,
'T is ne'er the less essentially unsightly,
Which they would soon see, would they change
their form    34

---

¹⁹³ **great noses:** (Alençon's nose was disfigured by smallpox.)  **long ones:** (symbolizing crafty
rogues)   ²¹³ **standing:** permanent   ⁴ **Dispos'd, etc.:** wishing to acquire courtly breeding   ⁸ **confirm'd:** discreet   ¹⁰ **crestfall'n:** servile   ¹⁴⁻¹⁵ (These lines omitted in earliest Quartos)   ¹⁹ **approves:**
proves   ²⁴ (Playing on the idea that man is a little world)   ²⁶ *I.e.,* her court is a perfect microcosm
**of her** kingdom.   ²⁹ **hay:** a rude, violent dance   ³⁰ **observ'd:** decorous

To this of ours, and then compare them both;
Which we must not affect, because in kingdoms
Where the king's change doth breed the sub-
    ject's terror,
Pure innovation is more gross than error.

*Mont.* No question we shall see them imitate
(Though afar off) the fashions of our Courts, 40
As they have ever ap'd us in attire.
Never were men so weary of their skins,
And apt to leap out of themselves as they;
Who, when they travel to bring forth rare men,
Come home, deliver'd of a fine French suit. 45
Their brains lie with their tailors, and get babies
For their most complete issue; he's sole heir
To all the moral virtues that first greets
The light with a new fashion, which becomes
    them
Like apes, disfigur'd with the attires of men. 50

*Hen.* No question they much wrong their
    real worth
In affectation of outlandish scum;
But they have faults, and we more; they fool-
    ish-proud
To jet in others' plumes so haughtily;
We proud, that they are proud of foolery, 55
Holding our worths more complete for their
    vaunts.

*Enter Monsieur, d'Ambois*

*Mons.* Come, mine own sweetheart, I will
    enter thee.—
Sir, I have brought a gentleman to Court,
And pray you would vouchsafe to do him grace.

*Hen.* D'Ambois, I think?

*Bu.* That's still my name, my lord, 60
Though I be something alter'd in attire.

*Hen.* We like your alteration, and must tell
    you
We have expected th' offer of your service;
For we (in fear to make mild virtue proud)
Use not to seek her out in any man. 65

*Bu.* Nor doth she use to seek out any man:
They that will win must woo her.

*Mons.* I urg'd her modesty in him, my lord,
And gave her those rites that he says she
    merits.

*Hen.* If you have woo'd and won, then,
    brother, wear him. 70

*Mons.* Th'art mine, sweetheart. See, here's
    the Guise's Duchess,
The Countess of Mountsurreau, Beaupré.
Come, I'll enseam thee. Ladies, y'are too
    many
To be in council; I have here a friend
That I would gladly enter in your graces. 75

*Bu.* Save you, ladies.

*Du.* If you enter him in our graces, my lord,
methinks by his blunt behaviour he should
come out of himself.

*Ta.* Has he never been courtier, my lord?

*Mons.* Never, my lady. 81

*Beau.* And why did the toy take him in
th' head now?

*Bu.* 'T is leap-year, lady, and therefore very
good to enter a courtier. 85

*Hen.* Mark, Duchess of Guise, there is one
    is not bashful.

*Du.* No, my lord, he is much guilty of the
    bold extremity.

*Ta.* The man's a courtier at first sight.

*Bu.* I can sing pricksong, lady, at first sight;
and why not be a courtier as suddenly? 90

*Beau.* Here's a courtier rotten before he be
    ripe.

*Bu.* Think me not impudent, lady; I am
yet no courtier; I desire to be one, and would
gladly take entrance, madam, under your
princely colours. 95

*Enter Barrisor, l'Anou, Pyrhot*

*Du.* Soft, sir, you must rise by degrees: first
being the servant of some common lady, or
knight's wife; then a little higher to a lord's
wife; next a little higher to a countess; yet a
little higher to a duchess, and then turn the ladder. 101

*Bu.* Do you allow a man, then, four mistresses when the greatest mistress is allowed
but three servants?

*Du.* Where find you that statute, sir? 105

*Bu.* Why, be judged by the groom-porters.

*Du.* The groom-porters?

*Bu.* Ay, madam; must not they judge of all
gamings i' th' Court?

*Du.* You talk like a gamester. 110

*Gui.* Sir, know you me?

*Bu.* My lord?

*Gui.* I know not you. Whom do you serve?

*Bu.* Serve, my lord?

*Gui.* Go to, companion, your courtship's too
saucy. 116

*Bu.* [*Aside.*] Saucy! Companion! 'T is the
Guise, but yet those terms might have been
spared of the guiserd. Companion! He's jealous, by this light. Are you blind of that side,
duke? I'll to her again for that. — Forth, [121
princely mistress, for the honour of courtship.
Another riddle!

*Gui.* Cease your courtship, or by heaven I'll
cut your throat. 125

---

³⁶ **affect:** wish     ³⁸ **Pure:** intrinsically good     ⁴⁴ **travel:** (with pun on "travail")     ⁴⁶ **babies:** dolls     ⁵⁴ **jet:** strut     ⁷³ **enseam:** introduce     ⁸² **toy:** whim     ⁸⁹ **pricksong:** written music     ⁹⁷ **servant:** lover     ¹⁰⁰ **turn the ladder:** start backwards     ¹⁰⁶ **groom-porters:** court functionaries in charge of gaming     ¹¹⁵ **companion:** fellow     ¹¹⁹ **guiserd:** masquerader with a terrifying false face

*Bu.* Cut my throat? Cut a whetstone, young
Accius Nævius. Do as much with your tongue,
as he did with a razor. Cut my throat!

*Bar.* What new-come gallant have we here,
that dares mate the Guise thus?                    130

*L'A.* 'Sfoot, 't is d'Ambois. The duke mistakes him, on my life, for some knight of the
new edition.

*Bu.* Cut my throat! I would the king fear'd
thy cutting of his throat no more than I fear thy
cutting of mine.                    136

*Gui.* I 'll do 't, by this hand.

*Bu.* That hand dares not do 't. Y' ave cut
too many throats already, Guise; and robb'd
the realm of many thousand souls, more precious
than thine own. — Come madam, talk on. [141
'Sfoot, can you not talk? Talk on, I say!
Another riddle.

*Pyr.* Here 's some strange distemper

*Bar.* Here 's a sudden transmigration with
d'Ambois, — out of the knight's ward into the
duchess' bed.

*L'A.* See what a metamorphosis a brave suit
can work.                    149

*Pyr.* 'Slight, step to the Guise and discover
him.

*Bar.* By no means; let the new suit work.
We 'll see the issue.

*Gui.* Leave your courting.                    154

*Bu.* I will not. — I say, mistress, and I will
stand unto it, that if a woman may have three
servants, a man may have three-score mistresses.

*Gui.* Sirrah, I 'll have you whipp'd out of
the Court for this insolence.                    160

*Bu.* Whipp'd? Such another syllable out o'
th' presence, if thou dar'st, for thy dukedom.

*Gui.* Remember, poltroon.

*Mons.* Pray thee, forbear.                    164

*Bu.* Passion of death! Were not the king
here, he should strow the chamber like a rush.

*Mons.* But leave courting his wife, then.

*Bu.* I will not. I 'll court her in despite of
him. Not court her! Come, madam, talk on,
fear me nothing. [*To Guise.*] Well may'st thou
drive thy master from the Court, but never [171
d'Ambois.

*Mons.* His great heart will not down; 't is
like the sea,
That partly by his own internal heat,
Partly the stars' daily and nightly motion,    175
Their heat and light, and partly of the place
The divers frames, but chiefly by the moon,
Bristled with surges, never will be won

(No, not when th' hearts of all those powers
are burst)
To make retreat into his settled home,    180
Till he be crown'd with his own quiet foam.

*Hen.* [*Moving a chess-piece.*] You have the
mate. Another?

*Gui.* No more.                    *Flourish short.*
                    *Exit Guise, after him the King,*
                    *Monsieur whispering.*

*Bar.* Why, here 's the lion, scar'd with the
throat of a dunghill cock, a fellow that has [185
newly shak'd off his shackles. Now does he
crow for that victory.

*L'A.* 'T is one of the best jigs that ever was
acted.                    189

*Pyr.* Whom does the Guise suppose him to
be, trow?

*L'A.* Out of doubt, some new denizen'd lord,
and thinks that suit newly drawn out o' th'
mercer's books.                    194

*Bar.* I have heard of a fellow, that by a fix'd
imagination, looking upon a bull-baiting, had a
visible pair of horns grew out of his forehead;
and I believe this gallant, overjoyed with the
conceit of Monsieur's cast suit, imagines himself to be the Monsieur.                    200

*L'A.* And why not; as well as the ass, stalk-
ing in the lion's case, bare himself like a lion,
braying all the huger beasts out of the forest?

*Pyr.* Peace, he looks this way.                    204

*Bar.* Marry, let him look, sir. What will you
say now if the Guise be gone to fetch a blanket
for him?

*L'A.* Faith, I believe it for his honour sake.

*Pyr.* But, if d'Ambois carry it clean?
                    *Exeunt Ladies.*

*Bar.* True, when he curvets in the blanket.

*Pyr.* Ay, marry, sir.                    211

*L'A.* 'Sfoot, see how he stares on 's.

*Bar.* Lord bless us, let 's away.

*Bu.* Now, sir, take your full view: how
does the object please ye?                    215

*Bar.* If you ask my opinion, sir, I think your
suit sits as well as if 't had been made for you.

*Bu.* So, sir, and was that the subject of your
ridiculous jollity?

*L'A.* What 's that to you, sir?                    220

*Bu.* Sir, I have observ'd all your fleerings;
and resolve yourselves ye shall give a strict account for 't.

*Enter Brisac, Melynell*

*Bar.* Oh, miraculous jealousy! Do you think
yourself such a singular subject for laughter [225

---

¹²⁷ **Nævius:** (according to Livy he cut a whetstone with a razor)    ¹³⁰ **mate:** put down    ¹³³ **new edition:** (alluding to James I's new knights)    ¹⁴⁶ **knight's ward:** debtor's prison (in the Counter, London)
¹⁵⁰ **discover:** make known    ¹⁶⁶ **rush:** the floor covering of the day    ¹⁷⁷ **frames:** conformations    ¹⁸² **the
mate:** defeat (at chess)    ¹⁹¹ **trow:** do you think?    ¹⁹² **denizen'd:** naturalized (alluding to the immigrant
Scots)    ¹⁹⁹ **cast:** discarded    ²⁰² **case:** skin    ²⁰⁹ **carry it clean:** come off with credit    ²²⁵ **singular: unique**

that none can fall into the matter of our merriment but you?

*L'A.* This jealousy of yours, sir, confesses some close defect in yourself, that we never dream'd of.                                        230

*Pyr.* We held discourse of a perfum'd ass, that being disguis'd in a lion's case, imagin'd himself a lion. I hope that touch'd not you.

*Bu.* So, sir; your descants do marvellous well fit this ground. We shall meet where [235 your buffoonly laughters will cost ye the best blood in your bodies.

*Bar.* For life's sake let 's be gone; he 'll kill 's outright else.

*Bu.* Go, at your pleasures. I 'll be your ghost to haunt you. And ye sleep on 't, hang me. [241

*L'A.* Go, go, sir; court your mistress.

*Pyr.* And be advis'd; we shall have odds against you.

*Bu.* Tush! valour stands not in number; I 'll maintain it, that one man may beat three [246 boys.

*Bri.* Nay, you shall have no odds of him in number, sir. He 's a gentleman as good as the proudest of you, and ye shall not wrong him.

*Bar.* Not, sir?                               251

*Mel.* Not, sir! though he be not so rich, he 's a better man than the best of you; and I will not endure it.

*L'A.* Not you, sir?                           255

*Bri.* No, sir, not I.

*Bu.* I should thank you for this kindness, if I thought these perfum'd musk-cats (being out of this privilege) durst but once mew at us.

*Bar.* Does your confident spirit doubt that, sir? Follow us and try.                        261

*L'A.* Come, sir, we 'll lead you a dance.
                                        *Exeunt.*
                                *Finis Actus primi.*

## Actus secundi Scena prima

*Henry, Guise, Montsurry, and Attendants*

*Hen.* This desperate quarrel sprung out of their envies
To d'Ambois' sudden bravery, and great spirit.

*Gui.* Neither is worth their envy.

*Hen.*                      Less than either
Will make the gall of envy overflow.
She feeds on outcast entrails like a kite;     5
In which foul heap, if any ill lies hid,
She sticks her beak into it, shakes it up,
And hurls it all abroad, that all may view it.
Corruption is her nutriment; but touch her
With any precious ointment, and you kill her.
Where she finds any filth in men, she feasts, 11

And with her black throat bruits it through the world
(Being sound and healthful). But if she but taste
The slenderest pittance of commended virtue,
She surfeits of it, and is like a fly          15
That passes all the body's soundest parts,
And dwells upon the sores; or if her squint eye
Have power to find none there, she forges some.
She makes that crooked ever which is straight;
Calls valour giddiness, justice tyranny.       20
A wise man may shun her, she not herself;
Whithersoever she flies from her harms,
She bears her foe still clasp'd in her own arms:
And therefore, Cousin Guise, let us avoid her.

*Enter Nuntius*

*Nu.* What Atlas or Olympus lifts his head   25
So far past covert, that with air enough
My words may be inform'd, and from their height
I may be seen, and heard through all the world?
A tale so worthy, and so fraught with wonder
Sticks in my jaws, and labours with event.    30

*Hen.* Comest thou from d'Ambois?

*Nu.*                      From him, and the rest,
His friends and enemies; whose stern fight I saw,
And heard their words before and in the fray.

*Hen.* Relate at large what thou hast seen and heard.

*Nu.* I saw fierce d'Ambois and his two brave friends                                      35
Enter the field, and at their heels their foes:
Which were the famous soldiers, Barrisor,
L'Anou, and Pyrhot, great in deeds of arms.
All which arriv'd at the evenest piece of earth
The field afforded, the three challengers     40
Turn'd head, drew all their rapiers, and stood rank'd:
When face to face the three defendants met them,
Alike prepar'd, and resolute alike.
Like bonfires of contributory wood
Every man's look show'd, fed with either's spirit;                                       45
As one had been a mirror to another,
Like forms of life and death, each took from other;
And so were life and death mix'd at their heights,
That you could see no fear of death, for life,
Nor love of life, for death; but in their brows  50
Pyrrho's opinion in great letters shone:
That life and death in all respects are one.

---

²²⁹ **close:** secret    ²³⁴ **descants:** flourishes    ²⁴¹ **And:** if    ²⁵⁹ **privilege:** privileged ground
² **bravery:** fine clothes    ¹² **bruits:** shouts    ²⁶ **covert:** wooded growth    ³⁰ **event:** utterance
³⁹ **arriv'd:** being arrived    ⁵¹ **Pyrrho:** a Greek skeptic, 3rd century B.C.

*Hen.*   Pass'd there no sort of words at their
   encounter?
*Nu.*   As Hector, 'twixt the hosts of Greece
   and Troy,                                         54
(When Paris and the Spartan king should end
The nine years' war) held up his brazen lance
For signal that both hosts should cease from
   arms,
And hear him speak: so Barrisor, advis'd,
Advanc'd his naked rapier 'twixt both sides,
Ripp'd up the quarrel, and compar'd six lives 60
Then laid in balance with six idle words;
Offer'd remission and contrition too;
Or else that he and d'Ambois might conclude
The others' dangers.  D'Ambois lik'd the last;
But Barrisor's friends (being equally engag'd 65
In the main quarrel) never would expose
His life alone to that they all deserv'd.
And, for the other offer of remission,
D'Ambois (that like a laurel put in fire
Sparkled and spit) did much much more than
   scorn                                             70
That his wrong should incense him so like chaff
To go so soon out; and like lighted paper
Approve his spirit at once both fire and ashes.
So drew they lots, and in them fates appointed
That Barrisor should fight with fiery d'Am-
   bois;                                             75
Pyrhot with Melynell; with Brisac L'Anou:
And then like flame and powder they commix'd,
So spritely, that I wish'd they had been spirits,
That the ne'er-shutting wounds they needs
   must open
Might as they open'd shut, and never kill.  80
But d'Ambois' sword (that light'ned as it flew)
Shot like a pointed comet at the face
Of manly Barrisor; and there it stuck.
Thrice pluck'd he at it, and thrice drew on
   thrusts.
From him that of himself was free as fire;   85
Who thrust still as he pluck'd, yet (past belief)
He with his subtle eye, hand, body, scap'd.
At last, the deadly bitten point tugg'd off,
On fell his yet undaunted foe so fiercely
That (only made more horrid with his wound) 90
Great d'Ambois shrunk, and gave a little
   ground;
But soon return'd, redoubled in his danger,
And at the heart of Barrisor seal'd his anger.
Then, as in Arden I have seen an oak
Long shook with tempests, and his lofty top  95
Bent to his root, which being at length made
   loose
(Even groaning with his weight) he 'gan to nod

This way and that, as loath his curled brows
(Which he had oft wrapp'd in the sky with
   storms)                                           99
Should stoop: and yet, his radical fibres burst,
Storm-like he fell, and hid the fear-cold earth:
So fell stout Barrisor, that had stood the shocks
Of ten set battles in your highness' war,
'Gainst the sole soldier of the world, Navarre.
*Gui.*   Oh, piteous and horrid murther!
*Mont.*                               Such a life
Methinks had metal in it to survive          106
An age of men.
   *Hen.*            Such often soonest end.
Thy felt report calls on, we long to know
On what events the other have arriv'd.
   *Nu.*   Sorrow and fury, like two opposite
   fumes
Met in the upper region of a cloud,          111
At the report made by this worthy's fall,
Brake from the earth, and with them rose Re-
   venge,
Ent'ring with fresh powers his two noble friends;
And under that odds fell surcharg'd Brisac,  115
The friend of d'Ambois, before fierce L'Anou;
Which d'Ambois seeing, as I once did see,
In my young travels through Armenia,
An angry unicorn in his full career
Charge with too swift a foot a jeweller      120
That watch'd him for the treasure of his brow,
And, ere he could get shelter of a tree,
Nail him with his rich antler to the earth:
So d'Ambois ran upon reveng'd L'Anou,
Who eying th' eager point borne in his face, 125
And giving back, fell back, and in his fall
His foe's uncurbed sword stopp'd in his heart;
By which time all the life-strings of the tw'
   other
Were cut, and both fell as their spirits flew
Upwards; and still hunt honour at the view: 130
And now, of all the six, sole d'Ambois stood
Untouch'd, save only with the others' blood.
   *Hen.*   All slain outright?
   *Nu.*                     All slain outright but he,
Who kneeling in the warm life of his friends,
(All freckled with the blood his rapier rain'd) 135
He kiss'd their pale lips, and bade both fare-
   well. —
And see the bravest man the French earth
   bears!

   *Enter Monsieur, d'Ambois bare*

*Bu.*   Now is the time; y' are princely vow'd
   my friend;
Perform it princely, and obtain my pardon.

---

⁵⁸ **advis'd:** having taken thought   ⁶⁰ **Ripp'd up:** laid open, explained   ⁸⁴ **he:** Bussy   ⁸⁵ **him:**
Barrisor   ¹⁰⁵ **Mont.** (This speech is assigned in Qq. to Beaumond, who appears instead of Montsurry
in the opening s. D. of the act.  Similarly both texts note the exit of "Beau." instead of Montsurry at
line 206.)   ¹⁰⁸ **calls on:** calls for more   ¹⁰⁹ **other:** others   ¹¹⁵ **surcharg'd:** overstrained   ¹²¹ **treasure:** the unicorn's horn   ¹²⁸ **tw' other:** two others   ¹³⁷ s. D. **bare:** without his hat

*Mons.* Else heaven forgive not me! Come
    on, brave friend! —                                   140
If ever nature held herself her own,
When the great trial of a king and subject
Met in one blood, both from one belly springing;
Now prove her virtue and her greatness one,
Or make the t' one the greater with the t' other,
(As true kings should) and for your brother's love,
(Which is a special species of true virtue)    147
Do that you could not do, not being a king.
    *Hen.* Brother, I know your suit; these wil-
    ful murthers
Are ever past our pardon.
    *Mons.*                         Manly slaughter   150
Should never bear th' account of wilful murther;
It being a spice of justice, where with life
Offending past law, equal life is laid
In equal balance, to scourge that offence
By law of reputation, which to men             155
Exceeds all positive law, and what that leaves
To true men's valours (not prefixing rights
Of satisfaction, suited to their wrongs)
A free man's eminence may supply and take.
    *Hen.* This would make every man that
    thinks him wrong'd                                   160
Or is offended, or in wrong or right,
Lay on this violence, and all vaunt themselves
Law-menders and suppliers, though mere
    butchers, —
Should this fact (though of justice) be forgiven.
    *Mons.* Oh, no, my lord; it would make
    cowards fear                                         165
To touch the reputations of true men
When only they are left to imp the law.
Justice will soon distinguish murtherous minds
From just revengers. Had my friend been slain,
(His enemy surviving) he should die,           170
Since he had added to a murther'd fame
(Which was in his intent) a murther'd man,
And this had worthily been wilful murther;
But my friend only sav'd his fame's dear life,
Which is above life, taking th' under-value,   175
Which in the wrong it did was forfeit to him;
And in this fact only preserves a man
In his uprightness; worthy to survive
Millions of such as murther men alive.
    *Hen.* Well, brother, rise, and raise your
    friend withal                                        180
From death to life; and d'Ambois, let your life
(Refin'd by passing through this merited death)
Be purg'd from more such foul pollution;
Nor on your scape nor valour more presuming
To be again so daring.
    *Bu.*                     My lord,               185

I loathe as much a deed of unjust death
As law itself doth; and to tyrannize,
Because I have a little spirit to dare
And power to do, as to be tyranniz'd.
This is a grace that (on my knees redoubled)
I crave to double this, my short life's gift,  191
And shall your royal bounty centuple,
That I may so make good what God and nature
Have given me for my good: since I am free,
(Offending no just law), let no law make,      195
By any wrong it does, my life her slave:
When I am wrong'd, and that law fails to right
    me,
Let me be king myself (as man was made),
And do a justice that exceeds the law.
If my wrong pass the power of single valour 200
To right and expiate, then be you my king,
And do a right, exceeding law and nature.
Who to himself is law, no law doth need,
Offends no law, and is a king indeed.
    *Hen.* Enjoy what thou entreat'st; we give
    but ours.                                            205
    *Bu.* What you have given, my lord, is ever
    yours.                     *Exit Rex cum Montsurry.*
    *Gui. Mort dieu!* who would have pardon'd
    such a murther?                              *Exit.*
    *Mons.* Now vanish horrors into court attrac-
    tions,
For which let this balm make thee fresh and fair.
And now forth with thy service to the duch-
    ess,                                                 210
As my long love will to Montsurry's countess.
                             *Exit.*
    *Bu.* To whom my love hath long been vow'd
    in heart,
Although in hand for show I held the duchess.
And now through blood and vengeance, deeds
    of height
And hard to be achiev'd, 't is fit I make      215
Attempt of her perfection. I need fear
No check in his rivality, since her virtues
Are so renown'd, and he of all dames hated.
                             *Exit.*

[SCENE II. — *Montsurry's House.*]

[*Montsurry, Tamyra, Beaupré, Pero, Charlotte,*
    *Pyra*

*Mont.* He will have pardon, sure.
    *Ta.*                     'T were pity, else:
For though his great spirit something overflow,
All faults are still borne that from greatness
    grow;
But such a sudden courtier saw I never.

    ¹⁵² **spice:** species   ¹⁵³ **past law:** beyond the scope of regular law   ¹⁵⁶ **that:** *i.e.*, positive law (to
which the following parenthesis also refers)   ¹⁶¹ **or . . . right:** either wrongly or rightly   ¹⁶³ **suppliers:** deputies   ¹⁶⁷ **imp:** graft   ¹⁷⁵ **under-value:** less precious thing   ¹⁹⁰ **grace:** boon  **on . . . redoubled:** twice kneeling   ²¹³ **in hand . . . held:** used as a decoy   Sc. II: (The opening S. D. and
lines 1–50 are omitted in Q 1641.)   ³ **still:** ever

*Be.* He was too sudden, which indeed was
rudeness.                                                        5
*Ta.* True, for it argued his no due conceit
Both of the place and greatness of the persons,
Nor of our sex: all which (we all being
strangers
To his encounter) should have made more
manners                                                          9
Deserve more welcome.
*Mont.*                         All this fault is found
Because he lov'd the duchess and left you.
*Ta.* Alas, love give her joy; I am so far
From envy of her honour, that I swear,
Had he encounter'd me with such proud slight,
I would have put that project face of his          15
To a more test than did her duchesship.
*Be.* Why (by your leave, my lord) I 'll speak
it here,
Although she be my aunt, she scarce was
modest,
When she perceiv'd the duke her husband take
Those late exceptions to her servant's court-
ship,                                                            20
To entertain him.
*Ta.*                       Ay, and stand him still,
Letting her husband give her servant place.
Though he did manly, she should be a woman.

### Enter Guise

[*Gui.*] D'Ambois is pardon'd! Where 's a
king? Where law?
See how it runs, much like a turbulent sea,      25
Here high and glorious as it did contend
To wash the heavens and make the stars more
pure,
And here so low, it leaves the mud of hell
To every common view; come, Count Mont-
surry,                                                           29
We must consult of this.
*Ta.*                        Stay not, sweet lord.
*Mont.* Be pleas'd, I 'll straight return.
                                *Exit cum Guise.*
*Ta.*             Would that would please me!
*Be.* I 'll leave you, madam, to your passions;
I see there 's change of weather in your looks.
                                *Exit cum suis.*
*Ta.* I cannot cloak it; but, as when a fume,
Hot, dry, and gross, within the womb of earth
Or in her superficies begot,                          36
When extreme cold hath struck it to her heart,
The more it is compress'd, the more it rageth;
Exceeds his prison's strength that should con-
tain it,
And then it tosseth temples in the air,              40
All bars made engines to his insolent fury;
So, of a sudden, my licentious fancy

Riots within me: not my name and house
Nor my religion, to this hour observ'd,
Can stand above it. I must utter that               45
That will in parting break more strings in me
Than death when life parts; and that holy man
That, from my cradle, counsell'd for my soul,
I now must make an agent for my blood.              49

### Enter Monsieur

*Mons.* Yet, is my mistress gracious?
*Ta.*                        Yet unanswer'd?]
*Mons.* Pray thee regard thine own good, if
not mine,                                                        51
And cheer my love for that; you do not know
What you may be by me, nor what without me.
I may have power t'advance and pull down
any.
*Ta.* That 's not my study. One way I am
sure                                                             55
You shall not pull down me; my husband's
height
Is crown to all my hopes; and his retiring
To any mean state, shall be my aspiring;
Mine honour 's in mine own hands, spite of
kings.
*Mons.* Honour, what 's that? Your second
maidenhead!                                                      60
And what is that? A word. The word is gone,
The thing remains: the rose is pluck'd, the
stalk
Abides; an easy loss where no lack 's found.
Believe it, there 's as small lack in the loss
As there is pain i' th' losing. Archers ever        65
Have two strings to a bow; and shall great
Cupid
(Archer of archers both in men and women,)
Be worse provided than a common archer?
A husband and a friend all wise wives have.
*Ta.* Wise wives they are that on such strings
depend,                                                          70
With a firm husband joining a loose friend!
*Mons.* Still you stand on your husband! so
do all
The common sex of you, when y' are en-
counter'd
With one ye cannot fancy. All men know         74
You live in Court here by your own election,
Frequenting all our common sports and tri-
umphs,
All the most youthful company of men:
And wherefore do you this? To please your
husband?
'T is gross and fulsome: if your husband's
pleasure
Be all your object, and you aim at honour         80
In living close to him, get you from Court;

---

⁶ no . . . conceit: inadequate appreciation    ¹⁵ project: forward    ³⁶ superficies: outside    ³⁹ his:
its    ⁴⁹ blood: passion    ⁵¹ (Q 1641 begins the scene with this line, prefixing the S. D., "Enter Monsieur, Tamyra, and Pero with a Booke.")

You may have him at home.   These common
    put-offs
For common women serve: "My honour!
    Husband!"
Dames maritorious ne'er were meritorious.
Speak plain, and say, "I do not like you, sir,   85
Y' are an ill-favour'd fellow in my eye;"
And I am answer'd.
    *Ta.*                 Then, I pray, be answer'd:
For in good faith, my lord, I do not like you
In that sort you like.
    *Mons.*               Then have at you, here!
Take (with a politic hand) this rope of pearl,   90
And though you be not amorous, yet be wise:
Take me for wisdom; he that you can love
Is ne'er the further from you.
    *Ta.*                         Now it comes
So ill prepar'd, that I may take a poison
Under a medicine as good cheap as it;         95
I will not have it were it worth the world.
    *Mons.*   Horror of death! could I but please
    your eye,
You would give me the like, ere you would lose
    me.
"Honour and husband!"
    *Ta.*                 By this light, my lord,
Y' are a vile fellow, and I'll tell the king   100
Your occupation of dishonouring ladies,
And of his Court.   A lady cannot live
As she was born, and with that sort of pleasure
That fits her state, but she must be defam'd
With an infámous lord's detraction.           105
Who would endure the Court if these attempts
Of open and profess'd lust must be borne?
Who's there?   Come on, dame; you are at
    your book
When men are at your mistress; have I taught
    you
Any such waiting-woman's quality?             110
    *Mons.*   Farewell, "good husband."
                          *Exit Monsieur.*
    *Mont.*               Farewell, wicked lord.

                    *Enter Montsurry*

    *Mont.*   Was not the Monsieur here?
    *Ta.*                 Yes, to good purpose;
And your cause is as good to seek him too,
And haunt his company.
    *Mont.*               Why, what's the matter?
    *Ta.*   Matter of death, were I some husbands'
    wife.                                     115
I cannot live at quiet in my chamber,
For opportunities almost to rapes
Offer'd me by him.

    *Mont.*               Pray thee, bear with him.
Thou know'st he is a bachelor and a courtier,
Ay, and a prince; and their prerogatives   120
Are to their laws, as to their pardons are
Their reservations, after Parliaments —
One quits another; form gives all their essence.
That prince doth high in virtue's reckoning
    stand
That will entreat a vice, and not command.  125
So far bear with him; should another man
Trust to his privilege, he should trust to death.
Take comfort, then, my comfort, nay, triumph
And crown thyself, thou part'st with victory;
My presence is so only dear to thee          130
That other men's appear worse than they be.
For this night yet, bear with my forced ab-
    sence;
Thou know'st my business; and with how
    much weight
My vow hath charg'd it.
    *Ta.*                 True, my lord, and never
My fruitless love shall let your serious honour;
Yet, sweet lord, do not stay; you know my
    soul                                      136
Is so long time without me, and I dead,
As you are absent.
    *Mont.*               By this kiss, receive
My soul for hostage, till I see my love.
    *Ta.*   The morn shall let me see you?
    *Mont.*                         With the sun
I'll visit thy more comfortable beauties.   141
    *Ta.*   This is my comfort, that the sun hath
    left
The whole world's beauty ere my sun leaves me.
    *Mont.*   'T is late night now indeed; farewell,
    my light.                           *Exit.*
    *Ta.*   Farewell, my light and life; — but not
    in him.                                   145
In mine own dark love and light bent to
    another.
Alas that in the wane of our affections
We should supply it with a full dissembling,
In which each youngest maid is grown a mother.
Frailty is fruitful, one sin gets another.   150
Our loves like sparkles are that brightest shine
When they go out: most vice shows most
    divine. —
Go, maid, to bed; lend me your book, I pray;
Not, like yourself, for form; I'll this night
    trouble
None of your services.   Make sure the doors,
And call your other fellows to their rest.   156
    *Pe.*   I will, — [*Aside.*] yet I will watch to
    know why you watch.                  *Exit.*

---

⁸⁴ **maritorious:** husband-mad    ⁹⁵ **Under:** in guise of    **good cheap:** profitably    ¹¹⁷ **opportunities:** importunings    ¹²⁹ **part'st . . . victory:** come off victorious    ¹³⁵ **let:** obstruct    ¹⁴¹ **comfortable:** (more comforting than the sun's)    ¹⁴⁶ (This unmetrical and difficult line is not in Q 1.)    ¹⁴⁸ **supply it:** supplement the waning love    ¹⁵² **most . . . divine:** The greatest sin is most attractive.    ¹⁵⁴ **like yourself:** as you read it

*Ta.* Now all ye peaceful regents of the night,
Silently-gliding exhalations,
Languishing winds, and murmuring falls of
    waters,                     160
Sadness of heart and ominous secureness,
Enchantments, dead sleeps, all the friends of
    rest,
That ever wrought upon the life of man,
Extend your utmost strengths; and this
    charm'd hour               164
Fix like the centre; make the violent wheels
Of Time and Fortune stand; and great Ex-
    istence
(The Maker's treasury) now not seem to be,
To all but my approaching friends and me.
They come, alas, they come! Fear, fear and hope
Of one thing, at one instant fight in me;   170
I love what most I loathe, and cannot live
Unless I compass that which holds my death;
For life's mere death, loving one that loathes me,
And he I love will loathe me, when he sees
I fly my sex, my virtue, my renown,   175
To run so madly on a man unknown.
                  *The vault opens.*
See, see, a vault is opening that was never
Known to my lord and husband, nor to any
But him that brings the man I love, and me.
How shall I look on him? How shall I live,
And not consume in blushes? I will in,   181
And cast myself off, as I ne'er had been.   *Exit.*

    *Ascendit Friar and d'Ambois*

  *Fr.* Come, worthiest son, I am past measure
    glad,
That you (whose worth I have approv'd so
    long)
Should be the object of her fearful love;   185
Since both your wit and spirit can adapt
Their full force to supply her utmost weakness.
You know her worths and virtues, for report
Of all that know is to a man a knowledge:   189
You know besides, that our affections' storm,
Rais'd in our blood, no reason can reform.
Though she seek then their satisfaction
(Which she must needs, or rest unsatisfied)
Your judgment will esteem her peace, thus
    wrought,              194
Nothing less dear than if yourself had sought;
And (with another colour, which my art
Shall teach you to lay on) yourself must seem
The only agent, and the first orb move
In this our set and cunning world of love.
  *Bu.* Give me the colour, my most honour'd
    father,              200
And trust my cunning then to lay it on.

  *Fr.* 'T is this, good son; Lord Barrisor
    (whom you slew)
Did love her dearly; and with all fit means
Hath urg'd his acceptation, of all which
She keeps one letter written in his blood.   205
You must say thus, then: that you heard from
    me
How much herself was touch'd in conscience
With a report (which is in truth dispers'd)
That your main quarrel grew about her love,
Lord Barrisor imagining your courtship   210
Of the great Guise's Duchess in the presence
Was by you made to his elected mistress;
And so made me your mean now to resolve
    her,
Choosing (by my direction) this night's depth
For the more clear avoiding of all note   215
Of your presumed presence: and with this
(To clear her hands of such a lover's blood)
She will so kindly thank and entertain you,
(Methinks I see how), ay, and ten to one,
Show you the confirmation in his blood,   220
Lest you should think report and she did feign,
That you shall so have circumstantial means
To come to the direct, which must be used:
For the direct is crooked; love comes flying;
The height of love is still won with denying.  225
  *Bu.* Thanks, honour'd father.
  *Fr.*                 She must never know
That you know anything of any love
Sustain'd on her part: for, learn this of me,
In anything a woman does alone,
If she dissemble, she thinks 't is not done.  230
If not dissemble, nor a little chide,
Give her her wish, she is not satisfi'd;
To have a man think that she never seeks,
Does her more good than to have all she
    likes.
This frailty sticks in them beyond their sex,
Which to reform, reason is too perplex:   236
Urge reason to them, it will do no good;
Humour (that is the chariot of our blood
In everybody) must in them be fed,
To carry their affections by it bred.   240
Stand close.

    *Enter Tamyra with a book*

  *Ta.* [*Aside.*] Alas, I fear my strangeness
    will retire him.
If he go back, I die; I must prevent it,
And cheer his onset with my sight at least,
And that's the most. Though every step he
    takes              245
Goes to my heart, I'll rather die than seem
Not to be strange to that I most esteem.

---

   **165 centre:** centre of the planetary system   **182** *I.e.,* slough off my instincts as if I had never had
them.   **198 first . . . move:** supply the original motion, be the *primum mobile*   **215 note:** notice
**216 presumed:** presumptuous   **231 If:** if she do   **236 perplex:** involved   **238 blood:** ('food' Qq. etc.)
**242 strangeness:** aloofness

*Fr.* Madam.
*Ta.*          Ah!
*Fr.*                    You will pardon me, I hope,
That so beyond your expectation,
And at a time for visitants so unfit,          250
I (with my noble friend here) visit you.
You know that my access at any time
Hath ever been admitted; and that friend
That my care will presume to bring with me
Shall have all circumstance of worth in him   255
To merit as free welcome as myself.
     *Ta.* Oh, father, but at this suspicious hour!
You know how apt best men are to suspect us,
In any cause that makes suspicious shadow
No greater than the shadow of a hair:          260
And y' are to blame.  What though my lord
     and husband
Lie forth to-night, and, since I cannot sleep
When he is absent, I sit up to-night;
Though all the doors are sure, and all our
     servants
As sure bound with their sleeps; yet there is
     One                                       265
That wakes above, whose eye no sleep can
     bind.
He sees through doors, and darkness, and our
     thoughts;
And therefore as we should avoid with fear
To think amiss ourselves before his search,
So should we be as curious to shun            270
All cause that other think not ill of us.
     *Bu.* Madam, 't is far from that; I only
     heard
By this my honour'd father, that your con-
     science
Made some deep scruple with a false report
That Barrisor's blood should something touch
     your honour,                              275
Since he imagin'd I was courting you,
When I was bold to change words with the
     duchess,
And therefore made his quarrel; his long love
And service, as I hear, being deeply vowed    279
To your perfections: which my ready presence,
Presum'd on with my father at this season
For the more care of your so curious honour,
Can well resolve your conscience is most false.
     *Ta.* And is it therefore that you come, good
     sir?                                      284
Then crave I now your pardon and my father's,
And swear your presence does me so much
     good,
That all I have it binds to your requital.
Indeed, sir, 't is most true that a report
Is spread, alleging that his love to me
Was reason of your quarrel, and because       290

You shall not think I feign it for my glory
That he importun'd me for his court service,
I 'll show you his own hand, set down in blood
To that vain purpose.  Good sir, then come in.
Father, I thank you now a thousand-fold.   295
               *Exit Tamyra and d'Ambois.*
     *Fr.* May it be worth it to you, honour'd
     daughter.                    *Descendit Friar.*

          *Finis Actus secundi.*

## Actus Tertii Scena Prima

[*The Same.*]

*Enter d'Ambois, Tamyra, with a chain of pearl*

     *Bu.* Sweet mistress, cease!  Your conscience
     is too nice,
And bites too hotly of the Puritan spice.
     *Ta.* Oh, my dear servant, in thy close em-
     braces
I have set open all the doors of danger
To my encompass'd honour, and my life.     5
Before I was secure against death and hell,
But now am subject to the heartless fear
Of every shadow and of every breath,
And would change firmness with an aspen
     leaf:
So confident a spotless conscience is,      10
So weak a guilty.  Oh, the dangerous siege
Sin lays about us, and the tyranny
He exercises when he hath expugn'd!
Like to the horror of a winter's thunder,
Mix'd with a gushing storm, that suffer nothing
To stir abroad on earth but their own rages, 16
Is sin, when it hath gather'd head above us:
No roof, no shelter can secure us so,
But he will drown our cheeks in fear or woe.
     *Bu.* Sin is a coward, madam, and insults  20
But on our weakness, in his truest valour;
And so our ignorance tames us, that we let
His shadows fright us: and like empty clouds,
In which our faulty apprehensions forge
The forms of dragons, lions, elephants,     25
When they hold no proportion, the sly charms
Of the witch, Policy, makes him like a monster
Kept only to show men for servile money.
That false hag often paints him in her cloth
Ten times more monstrous than he is in troth.
In three of us the secret of our meeting     31
Is only guarded, and three friends as one
Have ever been esteem'd: as our three powers
That in our one soul are as one united.
Why should we fear then?  For myself I swear
Sooner shall torture be the sire to pleasure, 36
And health be grievous to one long time sick,
Than the dear jewel of your fame in me

     **281 father:** the friar   **282 curious:** nice   **5 encompass'd:** beleaguered   **13 expugn'd:** conquered
**20 insults:** triumphs   **26 proportion:** resemblance   **29 cloth:** painted cloth, substitute for tapestry
**33 three powers:** of body, mind, spirit   **34 our:** (not in Q 1641)

Be made an outcast to your infamy;
Nor shall my value (sacred to your virtues)  40
Only give free course to it, from myself:
But make it fly out of the mouths of kings
In golden vapours and with awful wings.
*Ta.*  It rests as all kings' seals were set in
  thee.
Now let us call my father, whom I swear  45
I could extremely chide, but that I fear
To make him so suspicious of my love,
Of which, sweet servant, do not let him know
For all the world.
  *Bu.*            Alas! he will not think it.  49
  *Ta.*  Come, then — ho! Father, ope, and
    take your friend.            *Ascendit Friar.*
  *Fr.*  Now, honour'd daughter, is your doubt
    resolv'd?
  *Ta.*  Ay, father, but you went away too soon.
  *Fr.*  Too soon?
  *Ta.*  Indeed you did, you should have stay'd;
Had not your worthy friend been of your bring-
  ing,
And that contains all laws to temper me,  55
Not all the fearful danger that besieg'd us
Had aw'd my throat from exclamation.
  *Fr.*  I know your serious disposition well.
Come, son, the morn comes on.
  *Bu.*            Now, honour'd mistress,
Till farther service call, all bliss supply you.  60
  *Ta.*  And you this chain of pearl, and my
    love only.
          *Descendit Friar and d'Ambois.*
It is not I, but urgent destiny,
That (as great statesmen, for their general end
In politic justice, make poor men offend)
Enforceth my offence to make it just.  65
What shall weak dames do, when th' whole
  work of nature
Hath a strong finger in each one of us?
Needs must that sweep away the silly cobweb
Of our still-undone labours; that lays still
Our powers to it: as to the line, the stone,  70
Not to the stone the line, should be oppos'd.
We cannot keep our constant course in virtue:
What is alike at all parts? Every day
Differs from other: every hour and minute,
Ay, every thought in our false clock of life  75
Ofttimes inverts the whole circumference:
We must be sometimes one, sometimes another.
Our bodies are but thick clouds to our souls,
Through which they cannot shine when they
  desire.
When all the stars, and even the sun himself,  80
Must stay the vapours' times that he exhales,
Before he can make good his beams to us;
Oh, how can we, that are but motes to him,

Wand'ring at randon in his order'd rays,
Disperse our passions' fumes, with our weak
  labours,  85
That are more thick and black than all earth's
  vapours?

          *Enter Montsurry*

  *Mont.*  Good day, my love; what, up and
    ready too!
  *Ta.*  Both, my dear lord; not all this night
    made I
Myself unready, or could sleep a wink.
  *Mont.*  Alas! what troubled my true love,
    my peace,  90
From being at peace within her better self?
Or how could sleep forbear to seize thine eyes
When he might challenge them as his just
    prize?
  *Ta.*  I am in no power earthly, but in yours;
To what end should I go to bed, my lord,  95
That wholly miss'd the comfort of my bed?
Or how should sleep possess my faculties,
Wanting the proper closer of mine eyes?
  *Mont.*  Then will I never more sleep night
    from thee.
All mine own business, all the king's affairs,  100
Shall take the day to serve them; every night
I 'll ever dedicate to thy delight.
  *Ta.*  Nay, good my lord, esteem not my de-
    sires
Such doters on their humours that my judg-
    ment
Cannot subdue them to your worthier pleasure:
A wife's pleas'd husband must her object be  106
In all her acts, not her sooth'd fantasy.
  *Mont.*  Then come, my love, now pay those
    rites to sleep
Thy fair eyes owe him; shall we now to bed?
  *Ta.*  Oh, no, my lord; your holy friar says
All couplings in the day that touch the bed  111
Adulterous are, even in the married;
Whose grave and worthy doctrine, well I know,
Your faith in him will liberally allow.  114
  *Mont.*  He 's a most learned and religious man.
Come to the presence then, and see great
    d'Ambois
(Fortune's proud mushroom shot up in a night)
Stand like an Atlas under our King's arm;
Which greatness with him Monsieur now envies
As bitterly and deadly as the Guise.  120
  *Ta.*  What, he that was but yesterday his
    maker,
His raiser and preserver?
  *Mont.*            Even the same.
Each natural agent works but to this end,
To render that it works on like itself;

⁴⁰ **value:** valor   ⁴⁴ **rests as:** holds firm as if   ⁵⁵ **temper:** control   ⁶⁸ **that:** destiny   ⁷¹ **op-**
**pos'd:** brought into conformity   ⁸¹ **stay . . . times:** await the patience of the mists   ⁸⁴ **random:**
randon   ⁸⁷ **ready:** dressed   ¹¹⁴ **allow:** approve   ¹¹⁹ **greatness:** favor

Which since the Monsieur in his act on d'Am-
    bois                              125
Cannot to his ambitious end effect,
But that (quite opposite) the King hath power,
In his love borne to d'Ambois, to convert
The point of Monsieur's aim on his own breast,
He turns his outward love to inward hate.   130
A prince's love is like the lightning's fume,
Which no man can embrace, but must consume.
                                 *Exeunt.*

### [SCENE II. — *The Court.*]

*Henry, d'Ambois, Monsieur, Guise, Duchess,*
    *Annabel, Charlotte, Attendants*

   *Hen.* Speak home, Bussy; thy impartial
    words
Are like brave falcons that dare truss a fowl
Much greater than themselves; flatterers are
    kites
That check at sparrows; thou shalt be my
    eagle,
And bear my thunder underneath thy wings;
Truth's words like jewels hang in th' ears of
    kings.                               6
   *Bu.* Would I might live to see no Jews hang
    there
Instead of jewels; sycophants, I mean,
Who use truth like the devil, his true foe,
Cast by the angel to the pit of fears,    10
And bound in chains; truth seldom decks
    kings' ears.
Slave Flattery (like a rippier's legs roll'd up
In boots of hay ropes) with kings' soothed guts
Swaddl'd and strappl'd, now lives only free.
Oh, 't is a subtle knave; how like the plague   15
Unfelt he strikes into the brain of man.
And rageth in his entrails, when he can,
Worse than the poison of a red-hair'd man!
   *Hen.* Fly at him and his brood; I cast thee
    off,
And once more give thee surname of mine
    eagle.    20
   *Bu.* I 'll make you sport enough, then; let
    me have
My lucerns too, or dogs inur'd to hunt
Beasts of most rapine, but to put them up,
And if I truss not, let me not be trusted.
Show me a great man (by the people's voice,   25
Which is the voice of God) that by his greatness
Bombasts his private roofs with public riches;
That affects royalty, rising from a clapdish;

That rules so much more by his suffering king,
That he makes kings of his subordinate
    slaves:                               30
Himself and them graduate like woodmongers,
Piling a stack of billets from the earth,
Raising each other into steeples' heights.
Let him convey this on the turning props
Of Protean law, and, his own counsel keeping,
Keep all upright; let me but hawk at him,   36
I 'll play the vulture, and so thump his liver,
That, like a huge unlading argosy,
He shall confess all, and you then may hang
    him.
Show me a clergyman, that is in voice    40
A lark of heaven, in heart a mole of earth;
That hath good living, and a wicked life;
A temperate look, and a luxurious gut;
Turning the rents of his superfluous cures
Into your pheasants and your partridges;    45
Venting their quintessence as men read He-
    brew;
Let me but hawk at him, and, like the other,
He shall confess all, and you then may hang
    him.
Show me a lawyer that turns sacred law
(The equal rend'rer of each man his own,    50
The scourge of rapine and extortion,
The sanctuary and impregnable defence
Of retir'd learning and besieged virtue)
Into a harpy, that eats all but 's own,
Into the damned sins it punisheth;    55
Into the synagogue of thieves and atheists,
Blood into gold, and justice into lust;
Let me but hawk at him, as at the rest,
He shall confess all, and you then may hang
    him.

   *Enter Montsurry, Tamyra, and Pero*

   *Gui.* Where will you find such game as you
    would hawk at?    60
   *Bu.* I 'll hawk about your house for one of
    them.
   *Gui.* Come, y' are a glorious ruffian, and run
    proud
Of the King's headlong graces. Hold your
    breath,
Or, by that poison'd vapour, not the King
Shall back your murtherous valour against
    me.
   *Bu.* I would the King would make his pres-
    ence free    66
But for one bout betwixt us: by the reverence

---

   ² **truss:** overpower    ⁴ **check at:** leave the real prey to follow    ¹² **rippier's:** vendors of fish
¹⁴ **strappl'd:** swathed    ¹⁸ **red-hair'd:** *i.e.*, treacherous (Judas, and later Shylock, wore red wigs on
the stage.)    ²² **lucerns:** lynxes (dogs so called)    ²³ **put . . . up:** rouse from cover    ²⁷ **Bombasts:**
stuffs    ²⁸ **clapdish:** beggar's alms-dish    ²⁹ **by . . . suffering:** by sufferance of    ³¹ **graduate:** rise
by degrees    ³⁴ **convey:** filch   **turning props:** inconstant support    ⁴⁴ **cures:** church livings
⁴⁴, ⁴⁵ (Expending his surplus income on gluttony)    ⁴⁶ **as . . . Hebrew:** *i.e.*, backwards    ⁶² **glorious:**
**braggart**

Due to the sacred space 'twixt kings and sub-
　　jects,
Here would I make thee cast that popular
　　purple,
In which thy proud soul sits and braves thy
　　sovereign.                                          70
　　*Mons.*  Peace, peace, I pray thee peace.
　　*Bu.*                  Let him peace first
That made the first war.
　　*Mons.*              He's the better man.
　　*Bu.*  And therefore may do worst?
　　*Mons.*              He has more titles.
　　*Bu.*  So Hydra had more heads.
　　*Mons.*              He's greater known.
　　*Bu.*  His greatness is the people's; mine's
　　mine own.                                           75
　　*Mons.*  He's nobler born.
　　*Bu.*                  He is not, I am noble;
And noblesse in his blood hath no gradation,
But in his merit.
　　*Gui.*          Th' art not nobly born,
But bastard to the Cardinal of Ambois.
　　*Bu.*  Thou liest, proud Guiserd. Let me fly,
　　my lord.                                            80
　　*Hen.*  Not in my face, my eagle; violence
　　flies
The sanctuaries of a prince's eyes.
　　*Bu.*  Still shall we chide and foam upon this
　　bit?
Is the Guise only great in faction?
Stands he not by himself? Proves he th' opin-
　　ion                                                 85
That men's souls are without them? Be a duke,
And lead me to the field.
　　*Gui.*              Come, follow me.
　　*Hen.*  Stay them! Stay, d'Ambois. Cousin
　　Guise, I wonder
Your honour'd disposition brooks so ill
A man so good, that only would uphold        90
Man in his native noblesse, from whose fall
All our dissensions rise; that in himself
(Without the outward patches of our frailty,
Riches and honour) knows he comprehends
Worth with the greatest. Kings had never
　　borne                                              95
Such boundless empire over other men,
Had all maintain'd the spirit and state of
　　d'Ambois;
Nor had the full impartial hand of nature,
That all things gave in her original        99
Without these definite terms of "mine" and
　　"thine,"
Been turn'd unjustly to the hand of Fortune,
Had all preserv'd her in her prime, like d'Am-
　　bois.
No envy, no disjunction had dissolv'd,

Or pluck'd one stick out of the golden faggot
In which the world of Saturn bound our lives.
Had all been held together with the nerves, 106
The genius, and th' ingenious soul of d'Ambois.
Let my hand therefore be the Hermean rod
To part and reconcile, and so conserve you,
As my combin'd embracers and supporters. 110
　　*Bu.*  'T is our king's motion, and we shall
　　not seem
To worst eyes womanish, though we change
　　thus soon
Never so great grudge for his greater pleasure.
　　*Gui.*  I seal to that; and, so the manly free-
　　dom
That you so much profess hereafter prove not
A bold and glorious license to deprave,      116
To me his hand shall hold the Hermean virtue
His grace affects, in which submissive sign
On this his sacred right hand I lay mine.
　　*Bu.*  'T is well, my lord, and so your worthy
　　greatness                                         120
Decline not to the greater insolence,
Nor make you think it a prerogative
To rack men's freedoms with the ruder wrongs;
My hand (stuck full of laurel, in true sign
'T is wholly dedicate to righteous peace)    125
In all submission kisseth th' other side.
　　*Hen.*  Thanks to ye both; and kindly I in-
　　vite ye
Both to a banquet, where we'll sacrifice
Full cups to confirmation of your loves;     129
At which, fair ladies, I entreat your presence;
And hope you, madam, will take one carouse
For reconcilement of your lord and servant.
　　*Du.*  If I should fail, my lord, some other
　　lady
Would be found there to do that for my servant.
　　*Mons.*  Any of these here?
　　*Du.*              Nay, I know not that.
　　*Bu.*  Think your thoughts like my mistress',
　　honour'd lady?                                     136
　　*Ta.*  I think not on you, sir; y' are one I
　　know not.
　　*Bu.*  Cry you mercy, madam.
　　*Mont.*              Oh, sir, has she met you?
　　　　　　　*Exeunt Henry, d'Ambois, Ladies.*
　　*Mons.*  What had my bounty drunk when
　　it rais'd him?
　　*Gui.*  Y'ave stuck us up a very worthy flag,
That takes more wind than we with all our
　　sails.                                             141
　　*Mons.*  Oh, so he spreads and flourishes.
　　*Gui.*                  He must down;
Upstarts should never perch too near a crown.
　　*Mons.*  'T is true, my lord; and as this dot-
　　ing hand,                                          144

---

<sup>69</sup> **popular purple:** factious dignity    <sup>76</sup> **nobler:** ('nobly' Qq.)    <sup>77</sup> **his:** its    <sup>87</sup> **lead:** (punning on etymology of "duke," from "ducere")    <sup>99</sup> **original:** beginning    <sup>105</sup> **world of Saturn:** golden age    <sup>107</sup> **ingenious:** ingenuous    <sup>108</sup> **Hermean rod:** Hermes' caduceus    <sup>114</sup> **so:** provided

Even out of earth, like Juno, struck this giant,
So Jove's great ordnance shall be here impli'd
To strike him under th' Etna of his pride:
To which work lend your hands, and let us cast
Where we may set snares for his ranging greatness.     149
I think it best, amongst our greatest women;
For there is no such trap to catch an upstart
As a loose downfall; for you know their falls
Are th' ends of all men's rising. If great men
And wise make scapes to please advantages,
'T is with a woman: women, that worst may,
Still hold men's candles. They direct and know     156
All things amiss in all men, and their women
All things amiss in them; through whose charm'd mouths
We may see all the close scapes of the Court.
When the most royal beast of chase, the hart,
(Being old and cunning in his lairs and haunts)
Can never be discovered to the bow,     162
The piece, or hound; yet where, behind some queich,
He breaks his gall, and rutteth with his hind,
The place is mark'd, and by his venery     165
He still is taken. Shall we then attempt
The chiefest mean to that discovery here,
And court our greatest ladies' chiefest women
With shows of love and liberal promises?     169
'T is but our breath. If something given in hand
Sharpen their hopes of more, 't will be well ventur'd.
  *Gui.* No doubt of that; and 't is the cunning'st point
Of our devis'd investigation.
  *Mons.*          I have broken
The ice to it already with the woman
Of your chaste lady, and conceive good hope 175
I shall wade thorow to some wished shore
At our next meeting.
  *Mont.*      Nay, there's small hope there.
  *Gui.* Take say of her, my lord, she comes most fitly.
  *Mons.* Starting back?

    *Enter Charlotte, Annabel, Pero*

  *Gui.* Y' are engag'd, indeed.     180
  *Ch.* Nay, pray, my lord, forbear.
  *Mont.* What, skittish, servant?
  *An.* No, my lord, I am not so fit for your service.

  *Ch.* Pray pardon me now, my lord; my lady
expects me.     186
  *Gui.* I 'll satisfy her expectation, as far as an uncle may.
  *Mons.* Well said; a spirit of courtship of all hands. Now mine own Pero, hast thou re- [190
memb'red me for the discovery I entreated thee to make of thy mistress? Speak boldly, and be sure of all things I have sworn to thee.
  *Pe.* Building on that assurance, my lord, I may speak; and much the rather, because [195
my lady hath not trusted me with that I can tell you; for now I cannot be said to betray her.
  *Mons.* That 's all one, so we reach our objects. Forth, I beseech thee.
  *Pe.* To tell you truth, my lord, I have made a strange discovery.     201
  *Mons.* Excellent, Pero, thou reviv'st me. May I sink quick to perdition if my tongue discover it.
  *Pe.* 'T is thus, then: this last night my lord lay forth, and I, watching my lady's sitting [206
up, stole up at midnight from my pallet; and (having before made a hole both through the wall and arras to her inmost chamber) I saw d'Ambois and herself reading a letter.     210
  *Mons.* D'Ambois?
  *Pe.* Even he, my lord.
  *Mons.* Dost thou not dream, wench?
  *Pe.* I swear he is the man.
  *Mons.* The devil he is, and thy lady his [215
dam! Why, this was the happiest shot that ever flew! The just plague of hypocrisy levell'd it. Oh, the infinite regions betwixt a woman's tongue and her heart! Is this our goddess of [219
chastity? I thought I could not be so slighted if she had not her fraught besides, and therefore plotted this with her woman, never dreaming of d'Ambois. — Dear Pero, I will advance thee for ever; but tell me now, — God's precious, it transforms me with admiration — [225
sweet Pero, whom should she trust with this conveyance? Or, all the doors being made sure, how should his conveyance be made?
  *Pe.* Nay, my lord, that amazes me; I cannot by any study so much as guess at it.     230
  *Mons.* Well, let 's favour our apprehensions with forbearing that a little; for if my heart were not hoop'd with adamant, the conceit of this would have burst it. But hark thee, —
                              *Whispers.*
  [*Ch.* I swear to your grace, all that I can [235
conjecture touching my lady your niece, is a

---

¹⁴⁶ **impli'd:** employed     ¹⁴⁸ **cast:** consider     ¹⁵⁴ **scapes:** escapades    **please advantages:** play into the hands of their opponents ('advantage' Qq.)     ¹⁵⁶ **hold . . . candles:** light men on their way to sin    ¹⁵⁷ **women:** waiting maids    ¹⁶³ **piece:** musket    **queich:** thicket    ¹⁶⁵ **venery:** lust    ¹⁷⁶ **thorow:** through     ¹⁷⁸ **Take say of:** examine     ²¹⁷ **levell'd:** aimed     ²²¹ **fraught:** cargo     ²²⁵ **admiration:** wonder     ²²⁷ **conveyance:** trickery (In the next line it has the usual modern sense.)     ²³³ **conceit:** thought     ²³⁵⁻²⁴⁰ (Omitted by Q 1641)

strong affection she bears to the English
Mylor.

*Gui.* All, quod you? 'T is enough, I assure
you, but tell me.]                                             240

*Mont.* I pray thee, resolve me: the duke
will never imagine that I am busy about 's
wife: hath d'Ambois any privy access to her?

*An.* No, my lord; d'Ambois neglects her, as
she takes it, and is therefore suspicious that
either your lady, or the Lady Beaupré [246
hath closely entertain'd him.

*Mont.* By 'r lady, a likely suspicion, and
very near the life, especially of my wife.

*Mons.* Come, we 'll disguise all with seeming only to have courted. — Away, dry [251
palm! sh'as a liver as dry as a biscuit. A
man may go a whole voyage with her, and
get nothing but tempests from her wind-pipe.

*Gui.* Here 's one, I think, has swallowed a [255
porcupine, she casts pricks from her tongue so.

*Mont.* And here 's a peacock seems to have
devour'd one of the Alps, she has so swelling a
spirit, and is so cold of her kindness.        259

*Ch.* We are no windfalls, my lord; ye must
gather us with the ladder of matrimony, or
we 'll hang till we be rotten.

*Mons.* Indeed, that 's the way to make ye
right openarses. But, alas! ye have no portions
fit for such husbands as we wish you.       265

*Pe.* Portions, my lord? Yes, and such portions as your principality cannot purchase.

*Mons.* What, woman? what are those portions?

*Pe.* Riddle my riddle, my lord.

*Mons.* Ay, marry, wench, I think thy [270
portion is a right riddle, a man shall never find
it out. But let 's hear it.

*Pe.* You shall, my lord.

*What 's that, that being most rare 's most cheap?*
*That when you sow, you never reap?*              275
*That when it grows most, most you in it?*
*And still you lose it when you win it:*
*That when 't is commonest, 't is dearest,*
*And when 't is farthest off, 't is nearest?*

*Mons.* Is this your great portion?            280

*Pe.* Even this, my lord.

*Mons.* Believe me, I cannot riddle it.

*Pe.* No, my lord: 't is my chastity, which
you shall neither riddle nor fiddle.

*Mons.* Your chastity? Let me begin with
the end of it; how is a woman's chastity [286
nearest a man when 't is furthest off?

*Pe.* Why, my lord, when you cannot get it,

it goes to th' heart on you: and that, I think,
comes most near you: and I am sure it [290
shall be far enough off. And so we leave you to
our mercies.                                *Exeunt Women.*

*Mons.* Farewell, riddle.

*Gui.* Farewell, medlar.

*Mont.* Farewell, winter plum.               295

*Mons.* Now, my lords, what fruit of our inquisition? Feel you nothing budding yet?
Speak, good my Lord Montsurry.

*Mont.* Nothing but this: d'Ambois is
thought negligent in observing the duchess, [300
and therefore she is suspicious that your niece
or my wife closely entertains him.

*Mons.* Your wife, my lord? Think you that
possible?

*Mont.* Alas, I know she flies him like her
last hour.                                        306

*Mons.* Her last hour? Why, that comes
upon her the more she flies it. Does d'Ambois
so, think you?

*Mont.* That's not worth the answering. 'T is
miraculous to think with what monsters [311
women's imaginations engross them when they
are once enamour'd, and what wonders they
will work for their satisfaction. They will
make a sheep valiant, a lion fearful.         315

*Mons.* [*Aside.*] And an ass confident. —
Well, my lord, more will come forth shortly;
get you to the banquet.

*Gui.* Come, my lord; I have the blind side
of one of them. *Exit Guise cum Montsurry.* 320

*Mons.* Oh, the unsounded sea of women's
      bloods,
That when 't is calmest, is most dangerous!
Not any wrinkle creaming in their faces
When in their hearts are Scylla and Charybdis,
Which still are hid in dark and standing fogs, 325
Where never day shines, nothing ever grows
But weeds and poisons, that no statesman
      knows:
Not Cerberus ever saw the damned nooks
Hid with the veils of women's virtuous looks.
[But what a cloud of sulphur have I drawn  330
Up to my bosom in this dangerous secret!
Which if my haste with any spark should light,
Ere d'Ambois were engag'd in some sure plot,
I were blown up; he would be sure my death.
Would I had never known it, for before     335
I shall persuade th' importance to Montsurry,
And make him with some studied stratagem
Train d'Ambois to his wreak, his maid may
      tell it,
Or I (out of my fiery thirst to play

²³⁸ **Mylor:** lord    ²⁴⁷ **closely:** secretly    ²⁵⁰ **disguise:** ('put off' Q 1)    ²⁵¹⁻²⁵² **dry palm:** mark of
frigidity    ²⁵² **dry:** ('hard' Q 1)    ²⁵⁴ **from:** ('at' Q 1)    ²⁷⁶ **in:** gather    ³⁰⁰ **observing:** paying
court to    ³²⁵ **standing:** stagnant    ³³⁰⁻⁴⁰⁰ (Added by Q 1641, replacing eight lines in first Qq. In the
addition the scene is thought of as in Monsieur's house, not the king's court as at the opening.)
³³³ **engag'd:** caught

With the fell tiger, up in darkness tied,   340
And give it some light) make it quite break
    loose.
I fear it, afore heaven, and will not see
D'Ambois again, till I have told Montsurry
And set a snare with him to free my fears:
Who 's there?

*Enter Maffé*

*Ma.*      My lord?
*Mons.*          Go call the Count Montsurry,
And make the doors fast; I will speak with
    none                                    346
Till he come to me.
*Ma.*              Well, my lord.   *Exiturus.*
*Mons.*                            Or else
Send you some other, and see all the doors
Made safe yourself, I pray; haste, fly about it.
*Ma.*  You 'll speak with none but with the
Count Montsurry?                            351
*Mons.*  With none but he, except it be the
    Guise.
*Ma.*  See even by this, there 's one exception
    more!
Your grace must be more firm in the command,
Or else shall I as weakly execute.          355
The Guise shall speak with you?
*Mons.*                    He shall, I say.
*Ma.*  And Count Montsurry?
*Mons.*              Ay, and Count Montsurry.
*Ma.*  Your grace must pardon me, that I am
    bold
To urge the clear and full sense of your pleasure:
Which whensoever I have known, I hope   360
Your grace will say, I hit it to a hair.
*Mons.*  You have.
*Ma.*          I hope so, or I would be glad —
*Mons.*  I pray thee, get thee gone! Thou art
    so tedious
In the strict form of all thy services
That I had better have one negligent.      365
You hit my pleasure well, when d'Ambois hit
    you;
Did you not, think you?
*Ma.*          D'Ambois? Why, my lord —
*Mons.*  I pray thee, talk no more, but shut
    the doors:
Do what I charge thee.
*Ma.*              I will, my lord, and yet
I would be glad the wrong I had of d'Ambois —
*Mons.*  Precious! then it is a fate that
    plagues me                              371
In this man's foolery; I may be murthered
While he stands on protection of his folly.
Avaunt! about thy charge!

*Ma.*                  I go, my lord. —
I had my head broke in his faithful service; 375
I had no suit the more, nor any thanks,
And yet my teeth must still be hit with d'Am-
    bois. —
D'Ambois, my lord, shall know —
*Mons.*          The devil and d'Ambois!
                              *Exit Maffé.*
How am I tortur'd with this trusty fool!
Never was any curious in his place         380
To do things justly, but he was an ass.
We cannot find one trusty that is witty,
And therefore bear their disproportion.
Grant thou, great star and angel of my life,
A sure lease of it but for some few days,  385
That I may clear my bosom of the snake
I cherish'd there, and I will then defy
All check to it but Nature's, and her altars
Shall crack with vessels crown'd with every
    liquor
Drawn from her highest and most bloody hu-
    mours.                                  390
I fear him strangely, his advanced valour
Is like a spirit rais'd without a circle,
Endangering him that ignorantly rais'd him,
And for whose fury he hath learnt no limit.

*Enter Maffé hastily*

*Ma.*  I cannot help it: what should I do
    more?                                   395
As I was gathering a fit guard to make
My passage to the doors, and the doors,
    sure,
The man of blood is enter'd.
*Mons.*              Rage of death!
If I had told the secret, and he knew it,
Thus had I been endanger'd.]

*Enter d'Ambois*

                          My sweet heart!
How now, what leap'st thou at?
*Bu.*              O royal object!
*Mons.*  Thou dream'st, awake. Object in
    th' empty air?                          402
*Bu.*  Worthy the brows of Titan, worth his
    chair.
*Mons.*  Pray thee, what mean'st thou?
*Bu.*                  See you not a crown
Impale the forehead of the great King Mon-
    sieur?                                  405
*Mons.*  Oh, fie upon thee!
*Bu.*              Prince, that is the subject
Of all these your retir'd and sole discourses.
*Mons.*  Wilt thou not leave that wrongful
    supposition?

---

347 s. d. **Exiturus**: *i.e.*, Maffé makes a motion to withdraw   380 **curious**: meticulous   382 **witty**:
intelligent   383 **disproportion**: incompatibility   392 **circle**: (within which the magician stood for protection)   403 **Titan**: the sun-god   **chair**: chariot   405 **Impale**: surround   407 **sole discourses**: solitary speculations

*Bu.* Why wrongful, to suppose the doubtless
right
To the succession worth the thinking on? 410
*Mons.* Well, leave these jests. How I am
overjoyed
With thy wish'd presence, and how fit thou
com'st!
For of mine honour I was sending for thee.
*Bu.* To what end?
*Mons.*                    Only for thy company,
Which I have still in thought; but that 's no
payment                                      415
On thy part made with personal appearance.
Thy absence so long suffer'd, oftentimes
Put me in some little doubt thou dost not love
me.
Wilt thou do one thing therefore now sincerely?
*Bu.* Ay, anything, but killing of the King.
*Mons.* Still in that discord, and ill-taken
note?
How most unseasonable thou play'st the
cuckoo,                                      422
In this thy fall of friendship!
*Bu.*                        Then do not doubt,
That there is any act within my nerves
But killing of the King, that is not yours. 425
*Mons.* I will not, then; to prove which by
my love
Shown to thy virtues, and by all fruits else
Already sprung from that still-flourishing tree,
With whatsoever may hereafter spring,
I charge thee utter (even with all the freedom
Both of thy noble nature and thy friendship) 431
The full and plain state of me in thy thoughts.
*Bu.* What, utter plainly what I think of you?
*Mons.* Plain as truth.
*Bu.* Why, this swims quite against the
stream of greatness;                         435
Great men would rather hear their flatteries,
And if they be not made fools, are not wise.
*Mons.* I am no such great fool, and therefore
charge thee,
Even from the root of thy free heart, display me.
*Bu.* Since you affect it in such serious terms,
If yourself first will tell me what you think 441
As freely and as heartily of me,
I 'll be as open in my thoughts of you.
*Mons.* A bargain, of mine honour; and
make this,
That prove we in our full dissection         445
Never so foul, live still the sounder friends.
*Bu.* What else, sir? Come, pay me home;
I 'll bide it bravely.
*Mons.* I will, I swear. I think thee then a
man

That dares as much as a wild horse or tiger;
As headstrong and as bloody; and to feed 450
The ravenous wolf of thy most cannibal valour,
(Rather than not employ it) thou wouldst turn
Hackster to any whore, slave to a Jew
Or English usurer, to force possessions
(And cut men's throats) of mortgaged estates;
Or thou wouldst 'tire thee like a tinker's
strumpet,                                    456
And murther market-folks, quarrel with sheep,
And run as mad as Ajax; serve a butcher,
Do anything but killing of the King:
That in thy valour th' art like other naturals
That have strange gifts in nature, but no soul
Diffus'd quite through, to make them of a
piece,                                       462
But stop at humours that are more absurd,
Childish and villainous than that hackster,
whore,
Slave, cut-throat, tinker's bitch, compar'd
before;                                      465
And in those humours wouldst envy, betray,
Slander, blaspheme, change each hour a reli-
gion;
Do anything but killing of the King:
That in thy valour (which is still the dung-hill,
To which hath reference all filth in thy house)
Th' art more ridiculous and vain-glorious 471
Than any mountebank, and impudent
Than any painted bawd; which, not to soothe
And glorify thee like a Jupiter Hammon,
Thou eat'st thy heart in vinegar; and thy gall
Turns all thy blood to poison, which is cause 476
Of that toad-pool that stands in thy complex-
ion,
And makes thee (with a cold and earthy
moisture,
Which is the dam of putrefaction,
As plague to thy damn'd pride) rot as thou
liv'st:                                      480
To study calumnies and treacheries;
To thy friends' slaughters like a screech-owl
sing,
And do all mischiefs, but to kill the King.
*Bu.* So! have you said?
*Mons.* How think'st thou? Do I flatter?
Speak I not like a trusty friend to thee? 485
*Bu.* That ever any man was blest withal.
So here 's for me. I think you are (at worst)
No devil, since y' are like to be no king;
Of which, with any friend of yours, I 'll lay
This poor stillado here, 'gainst all the stars,
Ay, and 'gainst all your treacheries, which are
more:                                        491
That you did never good, but to do ill;

---

⁴⁰⁹ **doubtless:** undoubted   ⁴¹⁵ **that:** *i.e.*, my thought   ⁴²³ **fall:** autumn, waning (The cuckoo
sings only in spring.)   ⁴²⁴ **nerves:** strength   ⁴⁴⁰ **affect:** crave   ⁴⁴⁴ **this:** this further bargain   ⁴⁴⁶ **live:**
we shall live   ⁴⁵³ **Hackster:** bully   ⁴⁶⁰ **naturals:** idiots   ⁴⁷³ **soothe:** flatter   ⁴⁸³ **do:** ('to' Qq.)
⁴⁹⁰ **stillado:** stiletto

But ill of all sorts, free and for itself:
That (like a murthering piece, making lanes in
    armies,
The first man of a rank, the whole rank falling)
If you have wrong'd one man, you are so far    496
From making him amends that all his race,
Friends, and associates, fall into your chase:
That y' are for perjuries the very prince
Of all intelligencers; and your voice    500
Is like an eastern wind, that where it flies
Knits nets of caterpillars, with which you
    catch
The prime of all the fruits the kingdom yields:
That your political head is the curst fount
Of all the violence, rapine, cruelty,    505
Tyranny, and atheism flowing through the
    realm:
That y'ave a tongue so scandalous, 't will cut
The purest crystal; and a breath that will
Kill to that wall a spider. You will jest
With God, and your soul to the devil tender    510
For lust; kiss horror, and with death engender.
That your foul body is a Lernean fen
Of all the maladies breeding in all men:
That you are utterly without a soul;    514
And, for your life, the thread of that was spun
When Clotho slept, and let her breathing rock
Fall in the dirt; and Lachesis still draws it,
Dipping her twisting fingers in a bowl
Defil'd, and crown'd with virtue's forced soul.
And lastly (which I must for gratitude    520
Ever remember) that of all my height
And dearest life, you are the only spring,
Only in royal hope to kill the King.
   *Mons.* Why, now I see thou lov'st me. Come
   to the banquet.                        *Exeunt.*

         *Finis Actus tertii.*

## Actus Quarti Scena Prima

### [*The Court.*]

*Henry, Monsieur, with a letter; Guise, Mont-*
*surry, Bussy, Elenor, Tamyra, Beaupré,*
*Pero, Charlotte, Annabel, Pyra, with four*
*Pages*

   *Hen.* Ladies, ye have not done our banquet
    right,
Nor look'd upon it with those cheerful rays
That lately turn'd your breaths to floods of
    gold.
Your looks, methinks, are not drawn out with
    thoughts
So clear and free as heretofore, but fare    5
As if the thick complexions of men
Govern'd within them.

   *Bu.*                        'T is not like, my lord,
That men in women rule, but contrary;
For as the moon (of all things God created)
Not only is the most appropriate image    10
Or glass to show them how they wax and
    wane,
But in her height and motion likewise bears
Imperial influences that command
In all their powers, and make them wax and
    wane:    14
So women, that (of all things made of nothing)
Are the most perfect idols of the moon,
Or still-unwean'd sweet moon-calves with white
    faces,
Not only are patterns of change to men,
But as the tender moonshine of their beauties
Clears or is cloudy, make men glad or sad;    20
So then they rule in men, not men in them.
   *Mons.* But here the moons are chang'd, (as
    the King notes)
And either men rule in them, or some power
Beyond their voluntary faculty,
For nothing can recover their lost faces.    25
   *Mont.* None can be always one: our griefs
    and joys
Hold several sceptres in us, and have times
For their divided empires: which grief now in
    them
Doth prove as proper to his diadem.
   *Bu.* And grief's a natural sickness of the
    blood,    30
That time to part asks, as his coming had;
Only slight fools, griev'd, suddenly are glad.
A man may say t' a dead man, "Be reviv'd,"
As well as to one sorrowful, "Be not griev'd,"
And therefore, princely mistress, in all wars    35
Against these base foes that insult on weak-
    ness,
And still fight hous'd behind the shield of Na-
    ture,
Of privilege, law, treachery, or beastly need,
Your servant cannot help; authority here
Goes with corruption: something like some
    states,    40
That back worst men: valour to them must
    creep
That, to themselves left, would fear him asleep.
   *Du.* Ye all take that for granted that doth
    rest
Yet to be prov'd; we all are as we were,
As merry and as free in thought as ever.    45
   *Gui.* And why then can ye not disclose your
    thoughts?
   *Ta.* Methinks the man hath answer'd for us
    well.
   *Mons.* The man? Why, madam, d' ye not
    know his name?

---

**498 chase:** persecution    **500 intelligencers:** informers    **509 to:** as far as    **516 breathing rock:**
distaff, on which the thread of life was spun    **5 fare:** ('foul' Q 1641)    **28 which:** *i.e.*, times

*Ta.* Man is a name of honour for a king: 49
Additions take away from each chief thing:
The school of modesty not to learn learns dames:
They sit in high forms there, that know men's
    names.
    *Mons.* [*To Bussy.*] Hark! sweetheart, here 's
    a bar set to your valour;
It cannot enter here; no, not to notice          54
Of what your name is. Your great eagle's beak
(Should you fly at her) had as good encounter
An Albion cliff, as her more craggy liver.
    *Bu.* I 'll not attempt her, sir; her sight and
    name
(By which I only know her) doth deter me. 59
    *Hen.* So do they all men else.
    *Mons.*             You would say so
If you knew all.
    *Ta.*   Knew all, my lord?  What mean you?
    *Mons.*  All that I know, madam.
    *Ta.*             That you know? Speak it.
    *Mons.*  No, 't is enough, I feel it.
    *Hen.*            But, methinks
Her courtship is more pure than heretofore;
True courtiers should be modest, but not nice;
Bold, but not impudent; pleasure love, not vice.
    *Mons.* Sweetheart, come hither! what if one
    should make
Horns at Montsurry?  Would it not strike him
    jealous
Through all the proofs of his chaste lady's vir-
    tues?
    *Bu.* If he be wise, not.                   70
    *Mons.* What?  Not if I should name the
    gardener
That I would have him think hath grafted him?
    *Bu.* So the large licence that your greatness
    uses
To jest at all men may be taught indeed
To make a difference of the grounds you play
    on,                                      75
Both in the men you scandal, and the matter.
    *Mons.* As how? as how?
    *Bu.*           Perhaps led with a train,
Where you may have your nose made less and
    slit,
Your eyes thrust out.
    *Mons.*     Peace, peace, I pray thee, peace. 79
Who dares do that? The brother of his king?
    *Bu.* Were your king brother in you; all your
    powers
(Stretch'd in the arms of great men and their
    bawds),
Set close down by you; all your stormy laws
Spouted with lawyers' mouths, and gushing
    blood

Like to so many torrents; all your glories  85
(Making you terrible, like enchanted flames)
Fed with bare coxcombs and with crooked
    hams;
All your prerogatives, your shames, and tor-
    tures;
All daring heaven, and opening hell about
    you; —                                    89
Were I the man ye wrong'd so and provok'd,
Though ne'er so much beneath you, like a box-
    tree
I would out of the roughness of my root
Ram hardness, in my lowness, and like death
Mounted on earthquakes, I would trot through
    all
Honours and horrors, thorow foul and fair, 95
And from your whole strength toss you into the
    air.
    *Mons.* Go, th' art a devil; such another spirit
Could not be still'd from all th' Armenian drag-
    ons.
O my love's glory!  Heir to all I have,
(That 's all I can say, and that all I swear) 100
If thou outlive me, as I know thou must,
Or else hath nature no proportion'd end
To her great labours. She hath breath'd a mind
Into thy entrails, of desert to swell
Into another great Augustus Cæsar;         105
Organs and faculties fitted to her greatness;
And should that perish like a common spirit,
Nature 's a courtier and regards no merit.
    *Hen.* Here 's nought but whispering with us;
    like a calm
Before a tempest, when the silent air        110
Lays her soft ear close to the earth to hearken
For that she fears steals on to ravish her;
Some fate doth join our ears to hear it coming.
Come, my brave eagle, let 's to covert fly;
I see almighty Æther in the smoke           115
Of all his clouds descending; and the sky
Hid in the dim ostents of tragedy.
           *Exit Henry with d'Ambois and Ladies.*
    *Gui.* Now stir the humour, and begin the
    brawl.
    *Mont.* The King and d'Ambois now are
    grown all one.                            119
    *Mons.* Nay, they are two, my lord.
                   *[Making horns at Mont.]*
    *Mont.*            How 's that?
    *Mons.*               No more.
    *Mont.* I must have more, my lord.
    *Mons.*          What, more than two?
    *Mont.* How monstrous is this!
    *Mons.*            Why?
    *Mont.*          You make me horns.

---

⁵⁰ **Additions:** titles of honor  ⁵¹ **not . . . dames:** teaches ladies not to learn  ⁵² **high forms:** dunces' seats  ⁵⁷ **liver:** seat of passion (with reference to legend of Prometheus)  ⁷⁰⁻⁷⁹ (Briefer version in Q 1)  ⁷⁷ **train:** stratagem  ⁸⁷ **coxcombs:** heads  **crooked hams:** legs bent in obeisance ⁹⁸ **still'd:** distilled  ¹¹⁷ **ostents:** omens

*Mons.* Not I; it is a work without my power.
Married men's ensigns are not made with fin-
gers;
Of divine fabric they are, not men's hands. 125
Your wife, you know, is a mere Cynthia,
And she must fashion horns out of her nature.
   *Mont.* But doth she? dare you charge her?
Speak, false prince.
   *Mons.* I must not speak, my lord; but if
you 'll use
The learning of a nobleman, and read,   130
Here 's something to those points; — soft, you
must pawn
Your honour, having read it to return it.
             *Enter Tamyra & Pero.*
   *Mont.* Not I. I pawn my honour for a
paper!
   *Mons.* You must not buy it under.
         *Exeunt Guise and Monsieur.*
   *Mont.*                 Keep it then,
And keep fire in your bosom.
   *Ta.*            What says he?
   *Mont.* You must make good the rest.
   *Ta.*           How fares my lord?
Takes my love anything to heart he says? 137
   *Mont.* Come y' are a ——
   *Ta.*          What, my lord?
   *Mont.*        The plague of Herod
Feast in his rotten entrails.
   *Ta.*         Will you wreak
Your anger's just cause, given by him, on me?
   *Mont.* By him?
   *Ta.*    By him, my lord. I have admir'd
You could all this time be at concord with
him,
That still hath play'd such discords on your
honour.              143
   *Mont.* Perhaps 't is with some proud string
of my wife's.
   *Ta.* How 's that, my lord?
   *Mont.* Your tongue will still admire, 145
Till my head be the miracle of the world.
   *Ta.* Oh, woe is me!   *She seems to sound.*
   *Pe.*       What does your lordship mean?
Madam, be comforted; my lord but tries you.
Madam! Help, good my lord, are you not
mov'd?
Do your set looks print in your words your
thoughts?              150
Sweet lord, clear up those eyes, for love of
noblesse!
Unbend that masking forehead; whence is it
You rush upon her with these Irish wars,
More full of sound than hurt? But it is enough;

You have shot home, your words are in her
heart;             155
She has not liv'd to bear a trial now.
   *Mont.* Look up, my love, and by this kiss
receive
My soul amongst thy spirits for supply
To thine, chas'd with my fury.
   *Ta.*              Oh, my lord,
I have too long liv'd to hear this from you. 160
   *Mont.* 'T was from my troubled blood, and
not from me. —
I know not how I fare; a sudden night
Flows through my entrails, and a headlong
chaos
Murmurs within me, which I must digest,
And not drown her in my confusions,   165
That was my life's joy, being best inform'd.
Sweet, you must needs forgive me, that my love
(Like to a fire disdaining his suppression)
Rag'd being discourag'd; my whole heart is
wounded            169
When any least thought in you is but touch'd,
And shall be till I know your former merits,
Your name and memory altogether crave
In just oblivion their eternal grave;
And then you must hear from me: there 's no
mean
In any passion I shall feel for you.    175
Love is a razor, cleansing being well us'd,
But fetcheth blood still being the least abus'd.
To tell you briefly all: the man that left me
When you appear'd, did turn me worse than
woman,
And stabb'd me to the heart thus, with his
fingers.           180
   *Ta.* Oh, happy woman! Comes my stain
from him,
It is my beauty, and that innocence proves
That slew Chimæra, rescued Peleus
From all the savage beasts in Pelion;
And rais'd the chaste Athenian prince from
hell:            185
All suffering with me, they for women's lusts,
I for a man's, that the Augean stable
Of his foul sin would empty in my lap.
How his guilt shunn'd me! sacred innocence,
That, where thou fear'st, art dreadful, and his
face           190
Turn'd in flight from thee, that had thee in
chase!
Come, bring me to him; I will tell the serpent
Even to his venom'd teeth (from whose curst
seed
A pitch'd field starts up 'twixt my lord and me)

---

   **126 mere:** pure    **127** *I.e.*, the nature of Cynthia, the moon-goddess, is to be horned.    **134 under:**
for less    **141 admir'd:** wondered    **147 S. D. sound:** swoon    **151 for . . . noblesse:** (not in Q 1641)
**152 masking:** play-acting    **158 supply:** substitute    **166 being . . . inform'd:** when I was most normal
**185 prince:** Hippolytus    **194 pitch'd field:** field of battle (with allusion to the warriors sprung of dragon's
teeth)

That his throat lies, and he shall curse his fin-
    gers,                                                    195
For being so govern'd by his filthy soul.
  *Mont.*  I know not if himself will vaunt t'
    have been
The princely author of the slavish sin,
Or any other; he would have resolv'd me,
Had you not come; not by his word, but writing,
Would I have sworn to give it him again,    201
And pawn'd mine honour to him for a paper.
  *Ta.*  See how he flies me still; 't is a foul heart
That fears his own hand.  Good my lord, make
    haste
To see the dangerous paper; papers hold    205
Oft-times the forms and copies of our souls,
And (though the world despise them) are the
    prizes
Of all our honours; make your honour then
A hostage for it, and with it confer
My nearest woman here, in all she knows;    210
Who (if the sun or Cerberus could have seen
Any stain in me) might as well as they;
And, Pero, here I charge thee by my love,
And all proofs of it (which I might call boun-
    ties),
By all that thou hast seen seem good in me,   215
And all the ill which thou shouldst spit from
    thee,
By pity of the wound this touch hath given
    me,
Not as thy mistress now, but a poor woman,
To death given over, rid me of my pains,    219
Pour on thy powder; clear thy breast of me.
My lord is only here; here speak thy worst,
Thy best will do me mischief.  If thou spar'st
    me,
Never shine good thought on thy memory!
Resolve my lord, and leave me desperate.
  *Pe.*  My lord!  My lord hath play'd a prodi-
    gal's part,                                               225
To break his stock for nothing; and an inso-
    lent,
To cut a Gordian when he could not loose it.
What violence is this, to put true fire
To a false train? to blow up long-crown'd
    peace
With sudden outrage, and believe a man,    230
Sworn to the shame of women, 'gainst a woman,
Born to their honours!  But I will to him.
  *Ta.*  No, I will write (for I shall never more
Meet with the fugitive) where I will defy
    him,
Were he ten times the brother of my king.   235
To him, my lord, and I 'll to cursing him.
                             *Exeunt.*

[SCENE II. — *Montsurry's House.*]

*Enter d'Ambois and Friar*

  *Bu.*  I am suspicious, my most honour'd
    father,
By some of Monsieur's cunning passages,
That his still ranging and contentious nostrils
To scent the haunts of mischief have so us'd
The vicious virtue of his busy sense,    5
That he trails hotly of him, and will rouse him,
Driving him all enrag'd and foaming on us;
And therefore have entreated your deep skill
In the command of good aërial spirits,
To assume these magic rites, and call up one  10
To know if any have reveal'd unto him
Anything touching my dear love and me.
  *Fr.*  Good son, you have amaz'd me but to
    make
The least doubt of it, it concerns so nearly
The faith and reverence of my name and order.
Yet will I justify upon my soul    16
All I have done.
If any spirit i' the earth or air
Can give you the resolve, do not despair.

*Music: and Tamyra enters with Pero, her
    maid, bearing a letter*

  *Ta.*  Away, deliver it:    *Exit Pero.*
                   O may my lines
Fill'd with the poison of a woman's hate    21
When he shall open them, shrink up his curst
    eyes
With torturous darkness, such as stands in hell,
Stuck full of inward horrors, never lighted;
With which are all things to be fear'd af-
    frighted.    25
  *Bu.*  How is it with my honour'd mistress?
  *Ta.*  O servant, help, and save me from the
    gripes
Of shame and infamy.  Our love is known:
Your Monsieur hath a paper where is writ
Some secret tokens that decipher it.    30
  *Bu.*  What cold dull northern brain, what
    fool but he
Durst take into his Epimethean breast
A box of such plagues as the danger yields
Incurr'd in this discovery?  He had better
Ventur'd his breast in the consuming reach  35
Of the hot surfeits cast out of the clouds,
Or stood the bullets that (to wreak the sky)
The Cyclops ram in Jove's artillery.
  *Fr.*  We soon will take the darkness from his
    face
That did that deed of darkness; we will know  40

---

²⁰⁹ **confer:** compare    ²²⁶ **break his stock:** bankrupt himself    ²²⁷ **Gordian:** Gordian knot
²²⁹ **train:** powder-train, fuse    ⁵ **virtue:** power (with pun)    **busy sense:** meddling shrewdness    ⁶ **hotly
of him:** hot on mischief's track    ¹⁹ **resolve:** assurance    ²⁵ **to be fear'd:** fearful    ³² **Epimethean:**
like that of Epimetheus, who foolishly accepted Pandora and her box    ³⁷ **wreak:** wreck

What now the Monsieur and your husband do;
What is contain'd within the secret paper
Offer'd by Monsieur, and your love's events:
To which ends, honour'd daughter, at your mo-
   tion,
I have put on these exorcising rites,                    45
And, by my power of learned holiness
Vouchsaf'd me from above, I will command
Our resolution of a raised spirit.
   *Ta.*  Good father, raise him in some beaute-
   ous form
That with least terror I may brook his sight.  50
   *Fr.*  Stand sure together, then, whate'er you
   see,
And stir not, as ye tender all our lives.
                   *He puts on his robes.*
*Occidentalium legionum spiritualium impera-*
*tor (magnus ille Behemoth) veni, veni, comitatus*
*cum Astaroth locotenente invicto. Adjuro te* [55
*per Stygis inscrutabilia arcana, per ipsos irre-*
*meabiles anfractus Averni: adesto O Behemoth,*
*tu cui pervia sunt Magnatum scrinia; veni, per*
*Noctis & tenebrarum abdita profundissima; per*
*labentia sidera; per ipsos motus horarum* [60
*furtivos, Hecatesque altum silentium.  Appare*
*in forma spirituali, lucente, splendida & amabili.*
      *Thunder.  Ascendit* [*Behemoth with*
       *Cartophylax and other spirits.*]
   *Beh.*  What would the holy Friar?
   *Fr.*                    I would see
What now the Monsieur and Montsurry do;
And see the secret paper that the Monsieur  65
Offer'd to Count Montsurry, longing much
To know on what events the secret loves
Of these two honour'd persons shall arrive.
   *Beh.*  Why call'dst thou me to this accursed
   light
To these light purposes?  I am emperor  70
Of that inscrutable darkness where are hid
All deepest truths, and secrets never seen,
All which I know; and command legions
Of knowing spirits that can do more than these.
Any of this my guard that circle me  75
In these blue fires, and out of whose dim fumes
Vast murmurs use to break, and from their
   sounds
Articulate voices, can do ten parts more
Than open such slight truths as you require.
   *Fr.*  From the last night's black depth I
   call'd up one                    80

Of the inferior ablest ministers,
And he could not resolve me.  Send one then
Out of thine own command, to fetch the paper
That Monsieur hath to show to Count Mont-
   surry.
   *Beh.*  I will.  Cartophylax, thou that properly
Hast in thy power all papers so inscrib'd,  86
Glide through all bars to it and fetch that paper.
   *Cartoph.*  I will.                    *A torch removes.*
   *Fr.*  Till he returns, great prince of darkness,
Tell me if Monsieur and the Count Montsurry
Are yet encounter'd?
   *Beh.*                    Both them and the Guise
Are now together.
   *Fr.*                    Show us all their persons, 91
And represent the place, with all their actions.
   *Beh.*  The spirit will straight return; and
   then I 'll show thee.
See, he is come;  why brought'st thou not the
   paper?
   *Cartoph.*  He hath prevented me, and got a
   spirit                    95
Rais'd by another, great in our command,
To take the guard of it before I came.
   *Beh.*  This is your slackness, not t' invoke
   our powers
When first your acts set forth to their effects;
Yet shall you see it and themselves.  Behold!
They come here, and the Earl now holds the
   paper.                    101

   *Enter Monsieur, Guise, Montsurry, with a*
              *paper*

   *Bu.*  May we not hear them?
   *Fr.*                    No, be still and see.
   *Bu.*  I will go fetch the paper.
   *Fr.*                    Do not stir.
There 's too much distance and too many locks
'Twixt you and them, how near soe'er they
   seem,
For any man to interrupt their secrets.  106
   *Ta.*  O honour'd spirit, fly into the fancy
Of my offended lord, and do not let him
Believe what there the wicked man hath written.
   *Beh.*  Persuasion hath already enter'd him 110
Beyond reflection; peace till their departure!

   *Mons.*  There is a glass of ink where you
   may see
How to make ready black-fac'd tragedy.

---

  **43** events: outcomes    **48** resolution: information    of: from    **53-62** "Ruler of the western spirit-
bands (thou great Behemoth) come, come! accompanied by Astaroth, thy unconquerable lieutenant.
1 invoke thee by the undiscoverable secrets of Styx, by the irretraceable windings of Avernus:  be at
hand, O Behemoth, thou to whom are accessible the repositories of the mighty.  Come, by the deepest
mysteries of Night and Darkness, by the falling stars, even by the secret motion of the Hours and
Hecate's lofty silence!  Appear in a form spirit-like, luminous, beautiful and lovely."    **85** Cartophylax:
guardian of papers    **88** S. D. torch: *i.e.*, a sp... bearing a torch    **90** encounter'd: met    **95** prevented: anticipated    **101** S. D. (These characters appear on balcony or, possibly, rear stage.)
**112** glass of ink: black mirror

You now discern, I hope, through all her paint-
ings,
Her gasping wrinkles, and fame's sepulchres. 115
*Gui.* Think you he feigns, my lord? What
hold you now?
Do we malign your wife, or honour you?
*Mons.* What, stricken dumb! Nay fie, lord,
be not daunted;
Your case is common; were it ne'er so rare,
Bear it as rarely. Now to laugh were manly. 120
A worthy man should imitate the weather
That sings in tempests, and being clear is silent.
*Gui.* Go home, my lord, and force your wife
to write
Such loving lines to d'Ambois as she us'd,
When she desir'd his presence.
*Mons.*       Do, my lord, 125
And make her name her conceal'd messenger,
That close and most inenarrable pandar,
That passeth all our studies to exquire;
By whom convey the letter to her love:
And so you shall be sure to have him come 130
Within the thirsty reach of your revenge;
Before which, lodge an ambush in her chamber,
Behind the arras, of your stoutest men
All close and soundly arm'd; and let them
share
A spirit amongst them that would serve a thou-
sand.       135

*Enter Pero with a letter*

*Gui.* Yet stay a little; see, she sends for you.
*Mons.* Poor, loving lady; she 'll make all
good yet.
Think you not so, my lord?
      *Exit Montsurry, and stabs Pero.*
*Gui.*       Alas, poor soul!
*Mons.* This was cruelly done, i' faith.
*Pe.*       'T was nobly done.
And I forgive his lordship from my soul. 140
*Mons.* Then much good do 't thee, Pero!
Hast a letter?
*Pe.* I hope it rather be a bitter volume
Of worthy curses for your perjury.
*Gui.* To you, my lord.
*Mons.*       To me? Now, out upon her.
*Gui.* Let me see, my lord.       145
*Mons.* You shall presently. How fares my
Pero?
Who 's there?

*Enter Servant*

Take in this maid, sh'as caught a clap,
And fetch my surgeon to her. Come, my lord,
We 'll now peruse our letter.
      *Exeunt Monsieur, Guise.*

*Pe.*       Furies rise
Out of the black lines, and torment his soul. 150
      *Lead her out.*

*Ta.* Hath my lord slain my woman?
*Beh.*       No, she lives.
*Fr.* What shall become of us?
*Beh.*       All I can say,
Being call'd thus late, is brief, and darkly this:
If d'Ambois' mistress dye not her white hand
In her forc'd blood, he shall remain untouch'd:
So, father, shall yourself, but by yourself. 156
To make this augury plainer: when the voice
Of d'Ambois shall invoke me, I will rise,
Shining in greater light: and show him all
That will betide ye all. Meantime be wise,
And curb his valour with your policies.       161
      *Descendit cum suis.*
*Bu.* Will he appear to me when I invoke
him?
*Fr.* He will, be sure.
*Bu.*       It must be shortly then:
For his dark words have tied my thoughts on
knots,
Till he dissolve, and free them.
*Ta.*       In meantime, 165
Dear servant, till your powerful voice revoke
him,
Be sure to use the policy he advis'd;
Lest fury in your too quick knowledge taken
Of our abuse, and your defence of me,
Accuse me more than any enemy;       170
And, father, you must on my lord impose
Your holiest charges, and the Church's power
To temper his hot spirit and disperse
The cruelty and the blood I know his hand
Will shower upon our heads, if you put not 175
Your finger to the storm, and hold it up,
As my dear servant here must do with Monsieur.
*Bu.* I 'll soothe his plots, and strow my
hate with smiles,
Till all at once the close mines of my heart
Rise at full date, and rush into his blood. 180
I 'll bind his arm in silk, and rub his flesh,
To make the vein swell, that his soul may gush
Into some kennel, where it longs to lie,
And policy shall be flank'd with policy.
Yet shall the feeling centre where we meet 185
Groan with the weight of my approaching feet;
I 'll make th' inspired thresholds of his court
Sweat with the weather of my horrid steps,
Before I enter; yet will I appear
Like calm security before a ruin.       190
A politician must, like lightning, melt
The very marrow, and not taint the skin:

---

[127] **inenarrable:** unutterable    [128] **exquire:** search out    [134] **close:** in hiding    [154] **dye:** ('stay' Q 1)
[155] **her:** ('his' Qq.)    [164] **on:** in    [165] **dissolve:** untie    [178] **soothe:** beguile with flattery    [183] **kennel:**
gutter    [184] **flank'd:** outwitted    [185] **feeling centre:** conscious earth    [187] **inspired:** sentient
[188] **weather:** stormy air (which makes walls "sweat")

His ways must not be seen; the superficies
Of the green centre must not taste his feet,
When hell is plow'd up with his wounding
    tracts;
And all his harvest reap'd by hellish facts.  196
                            *Exeunt.*

        *Finis Actus Quarti.*

## Actus Quinti Scena Prima

### [*The Same.*]

*Montsurry bare, unbraced, pulling Tamyra in by*
*the hair; Friar. One bearing light, a stand-*
*ish and paper, which sets a table*

*Ta.*   Oh, help me, father.
*Fr.*               Impious earl, forbear.
Take violent hand from her, or by mine order
The King shall force thee.
*Mont.*            'T is not violent;
Come you not willingly?
*Ta.*            Yes, good my lord.
*Fr.*   My lord, remember that your soul must
    seek                                5
Her peace as well as your revengeful blood.
You ever to this hour have prov'd yourself
A noble, zealous, and obedient son
T' our holy mother; be not an apostate.
Your wife's offence serves not, (were it the
    worst                             10
You can imagine) without greater proofs,
To sever your eternal bonds and hearts;
Much less to touch her with a bloody hand;
Nor is it manly, much less husbandly,
To expiate any frailty in your wife       15
With churlish strokes or beastly odds of
    strength.
The stony birth of clouds will touch no laurel,
Nor any sleeper; your wife is your laurel,
And sweetest sleeper; do not touch her then;
Be not more rude than the wild seed of vapour
To her that is more gentle than that rude;   21
In whom kind nature suffer'd one offence
But to set off her other excellence.
*Mont.*   Good father, leave us; interrupt no
    more
The course I must run for mine honour sake.  25
Rely on my love to her, which her fault
Cannot extinguish. Will she but disclose
Who was the secret minister of her love,
And through what maze he serv'd it, we are
    friends.
*Fr.*   It is a damn'd work to pursue those
    secrets                          30

That would ope more sin, and prove springs of
    slaughter;
Nor is 't a path for Christian feet to tread,
But out of all way to the health of souls;
A sin impossible to be forgiven;
Which he that dares commit ——        35
    *Mont.*   Good father, cease your terrors;
Tempt not a man distracted; I am apt
To outrages that I shall ever rue.
I will not pass the verge that bounds a Christian,
Nor break the limits of a man nor husband.  40
    *Fr.*   Then God inspire you both with thoughts
    and deeds
Worthy his high respect, and your own souls.
    *Ta.*   Father!
    *Fr.*       I warrant thee, my dearest daughter,
He will not touch thee; think'st thou him a
    pagan?
His honour and his soul lies for thy safety.  45
                               *Exit.*
    *Mont.*   Who shall remove the mountain from
    my breast?
Stand the opening furnace of my thoughts,
And set fit outcries for a soul in hell?
                     *Montsurry turns a key.*
For now it nothing fits my woes to speak
But thunder, or to take into my throat   50
The trump of heaven, with whose determinate
    blasts
The winds shall burst, and the devouring seas
Be drunk up in his sounds; that my hot woes
(Vented enough) I might convert to vapour,
Ascending from my infamy unseen;     55
Shorten the world, preventing the last breath
That kills the living and regenerates death.
    *Ta.*   My lord, my fault (as you may censure
    it
With too strong arguments) is past your par-
    don:
But how the circumstances may excuse me  60
God knows, and your more temperate mind
    hereafter
May let my penitent miseries make you know.
    *Mont.*   Hereafter? 'T is a suppos'd infinite,
That from this point will rise eternally.
Fame grows in going; in the scapes of virtue  65
Excuses damn her: they be fires in cities
Enrag'd with those winds that less lights ex-
    tinguish.
Come, siren, sing, and dash against my rocks
Thy ruffian galley, rigg'd with quench for lust;
Sing, and put all the nets into thy voice   70
With which thou drew'st into thy strumpet's
    lap
The spawn of Venus; and in which ye danc'd;

---

<sup>195</sup> **tracts:** footprints   s. d. **unbraced:** not fully dressed   **standish:** ink stand   **which:** who
<sup>1</sup> **revengeful blood:** passion for revenge   <sup>17</sup> **stony birth:** thunderbolt   <sup>21</sup> **than that:** than the
thunderbolt is   <sup>33</sup> **health:** salvation   <sup>41, 61</sup> **God:** ('heaven' Q 1641)   <sup>56</sup> **preventing . . . breath:**
anticipating the last trump   <sup>57</sup> **regenerates death:** raises the dead

That, in thy lap's stead, I may dig his tomb,
And quit his manhood with a woman's sleight,
Who never is deceiv'd in her deceit.          75
Sing (that is, write), and then take from mine
       eyes
The mists that hide the most inscrutable pandar
That ever lapp'd up an adulterous vomit,
That I may see the devil, and survive
To be a devil, and then learn to wive;          80
That I may hang him, and then cut him down,
Then cut him up, and with my soul's beams
       search
The cranks and caverns of his brain, and study
The errant wilderness of a woman's face,
Where men cannot get out, for all the comets 85
That have been lighted at it; though they know
That adders lie a-sunning in their smiles,
That basilisks drink their poison from their eyes,
And no way there to coast out to their hearts;
Yet still they wander there, and are not stay'd
Till they be fetter'd, nor secure before          91
All cares devour them; nor in human consort
Till they embrace within their wife's two breasts
All Pelion and Cythæron with their beasts.  94
Why write you not?
       *Ta.*                    O good my lord, forbear
In wreak of great faults to engender greater,
And make my love's corruption generate mur-
       ther.
       *Mont.*  It follows needfully as child and
       parent;
The chain-shot of thy lust is yet aloft,
And it must murther; 't is thine own dear
       twin:                                     100
No man can add height to a woman's sin.
Vice never doth her just hate so provoke,
As when she rageth under virtue's cloak.
Write! for it must be — by this ruthless steel,
By this impartial torture, and the death     105
Thy tyrannies have invented in my entrails.
To quicken life in dying, and hold up
The spirits in fainting, teaching to preserve
Torments in ashes, that will ever last.          109
Speak!  Will you write?
       *Ta.*                   Sweet lord, enjoin my sin
Some other penance than what makes it worse;
Hide in some gloomy dungeon my loath'd face,
And let condemned murtherers let me down
(Stopping their noses) my abhorred food·
Hang me in chains, and let me eat these arms
That have offended; bind me face to face  116
To some dead woman, taken from the cart
Of execution, till death and time
In grains of dust dissolve me; I 'll endure:
Or any torture that your wrath's invention 120
Can fright all pity from the world withal;
But to betray a friend with show of friendship,

That is too common for the rare revenge
Your rage affecteth.  Here then are my breasts,
Last night your pillows; here my wretched
       arms,                                     125
As late the wished confines of your life:
Now break them as you please, and all the
       bounds
Of manhood, noblesse, and religion.
       *Mont.*  Where all these have been broken,
       they are kept,
In doing their justice there with any show 130
Of the like cruel cruelty; thine arms have lost
Their privilege in lust, and in their torture
Thus they must pay it.          *Stabs her.*
       *Ta.*                    O Lord!
       *Mont.*                    Till thou writ'st,
I 'll write in wounds (my wrong's fit characters)
Thy right of sufferance.  Write.
       *Ta.*                    Oh, kill me, kill me;  135
Dear husband, be not crueller than death.
You have beheld some Gorgon; feel, oh, feel
How you are turn'd to stone.  With my heart-
       blood
Dissolve yourself again, or you will grow
Into the image of all tyranny.                    140
       *Mont.*  As thou art of adultery; I will ever
Prove thee my parallel, being most a monster.
Thus I express thee yet.          *Stabs her again.*
       *Ta.*                    And yet I live.
       *Mont.*  Ay, for thy monstrous idol is not
       done yet;
This tool hath wrought enough; now, torture,
       use                                       145

*Enter Servants [with an instrument of torture]*

This other engine on th' habituate powers
Of her thrice-damn'd and whorish fortitude.
Use the most madding pains in her that ever
Thy venoms soak'd through, making most of
       death;
That she may weigh her wrongs with them,
       and then                                  150
Stand, vengeance, on thy steepest rock, a victor.
       *Ta.*  Oh, who is turn'd into my lord and hus-
       band?
Husband!  My lord!  None but my lord and
       husband!
Heaven, I ask thee remission of my sins,
Not of my pains; husband, oh, help me, hus-
       band!                                     155

*Ascendit Friar with a sword drawn*

       *Fr.*  What rape of honour and religion —
Oh, wrack of nature!          *Falls and dies.*
       *Ta.*                    Poor man; oh, my father.
Father, look up; oh, let me down, my lord,
And I will write.

---

       ³³ cranks: windings     ⁹⁶ **wreak:** revenge     ¹⁴³ **express . . . yet:** further illustrate your deprav-
ity     ¹⁴⁶ **habituate:** confirmed by habit

*Mont.* Author of prodigies!
What new flame breaks out of the firmament, 160
That turns up counsels never known before?
Now is it true, earth moves, and heaven stands
  still;
Even heaven itself must see and suffer ill.
The too huge bias of the world hath sway'd
Her back part upwards, and with that she
  braves 165
This hemisphere, that long her mouth hath
  mock'd;
The gravity of her religious face,
(Now grown too weighty with her sacrilege,
And here discern'd sophisticate enough)
Turns to th' antipodes; and all the forms 170
That her illusions have impress'd in her
Have eaten through her back; and now all
  see
How she is riveted with hypocrisy.
Was this the way? Was he the mean betwixt
  you?
  *Ta.* He was, he was: kind worthy man, he
    was. 175
  *Mont.* Write, write a word or two.
  *Ta.* I will, I will.
I 'll write, but with my blood, that he may
  see
These lines come from my wounds, and not
  from me. *Writes.*
  *Mont.* Well might he die for thought; me-
    thinks the frame
And shaken joints of the whole world should
  crack 180
To see her parts so disproportionate;
And that his general beauty cannot stand
Without these stains in the particular man.
Why wander I so far? Here, here was she
That was a whole world without spot to
  me,
Though now a world of spots. Oh, what a
  lightning 186
Is man's delight in women! What a bubble
He builds his state, fame, life on, when he
  marries!
Since all earth's pleasures are so short and
  small,
The way t' enjoy it, is t' abjure it all. 190
Enough! I must be messenger myself,
Disguis'd like this strange creature. In, I 'll
  after,
To see what guilty light gives this cave eyes,
And to the world sing new impieties.
  *Exeunt. He puts the Friar in the
  vault and follows. She wraps
  herself in the arras.*

[SCENE II. — *Location indefinite.*]

*Enter Monsieur and Guise*

  *Mons.* Now shall we see that Nature hath
    no end
In her great works responsive to their worths,
That she, that makes so many eyes and souls
To see and foresee, is stark blind herself;
And as illiterate men say Latin prayers 5
By rote of heart and daily iteration,
[In whose hot zeal a man would think they knew
What they ran so away with, and were sure
To have rewards proportion'd to their labours;
Yet may implore their own confusions 10
For anything they know, which often times
It falls out they incur.] So Nature lays
A deal of stuff together, and by use,
Or by the mere necessity of matter,
Ends such a work, fills it, or leaves it empty 15
Of strength or virtue, error or clear truth,
Not knowing what she does; but usually
Gives that which she calls merit to a man,
And believes must arrive him on huge riches,
Honour, and happiness, that effects his ruin. 20
Even as in ships of war, whole lasts of powder
Are laid, (methinks) to make them last, and
  guard them,
When a disorder'd spark, that powder taking,
Blows up with sudden violence and horror
Ships that, kept empty, had sail'd long with
  terror. 25
  *Gui.* He that observes, but like a worldly
    man,
That which doth oft succeed, and by th' events
Values the worth of things, will think it true
That Nature works at random, just with you;
But with as much proportion she may make 30
A thing that from the feet up to the throat
Hath all the wondrous fabric man should have,
And leave it, headless, for a perfect man,
As give a full man valour, virtue, learning,
Without an end more excellent than those 35
On whom she no such worthy part bestows.
  *Mons.* Yet shall you see it here; here will
    be one,
Young, learned, valiant, virtuous, and full
  mann'd;
One on whom Nature spent so rich a hand
That with an ominous eye she wept to see 40
So much consum'd her virtuous treasury.
Yet, as the winds sing through a hollow tree,
And (since it lets them pass through) lets it
  stand;
But a tree solid (since it gives no way

To their wild rage) they rend up by the root; 45
So this whole man,
(That will not wind with every crooked way,
Trod by the servile world) shall reel and fall
Before the frantic puffs of blind-born chance,
That pipes through empty men, and makes
them dance. 50
Not so the sea raves on the Lybian sands,
Tumbling her billows in each other's neck;
Not so the surges of the Euxine sea
(Near to the frosty pole, where free Boötes
From those dark deep waves turns his radiant
team) 55
Swell, being enrag'd even from their inmost drop,
As Fortune swings about the restless state
Of virtue, now thrown into all men's hate.

*Enter Montsurry, disguis'd [as Friar],
with the murtherers*

Away, my lord, you are perfectly disguis'd.
Leave us to lodge your ambush.
    *Mont.*    Speed me, vengeance! *Exit.* 60
    *Mons.* Resolve, my masters: you shall meet
with one
Will try what proofs your privy coats are made
on;
When he is ent'red, and you hear us stamp,
Approach, and make all sure.
    *Mur.*    We will, my lord. *Exeunt.*

[SCENE III. — *Bussy's House.*]

*D'Ambois with two Pages with tapers*

    *Bu.* Sit up to-night, and watch; I'll speak
with none
But the old Friar, who bring to me.
    *Pa.*    We will, sir. *Exeunt.*
    *Bu.* What violent heat is this? Methinks
the fire
Of twenty lives doth on a sudden flash
Through all my faculties; the air goes high 5
In this close chamber, and the frighted earth
                    *Thunder.*
Trembles, and shrinks beneath me; the whole
house
Nods with his shaken burthen.

*Enter Umbra Friar*

                    Bless me, heaven!
    *Um.* Note what I want, dear son, and be
forewarn'd;
O there are bloody deeds past and to come. 10
I cannot stay; a fate doth ravish me:
I'll meet thee in the chamber of thy love. *Exit.*
    *Bu.* What dismal change is here; the good
old Friar

Is murther'd, being made known to serve my
love; 14
And now his restless spirit would forewarn me
Of some plot dangerous and imminent.
Note what he wants? He wants his upper weed,
He wants his life and body; which of these
Should be the want he means, and may supply
me 19
With any fit forewarning? This strange vision
(Together with the dark prediction
Us'd by the Prince of Darkness that was rais'd
By this embodied shadow) stir my thoughts
With reminiscion of the spirit's promise,
Who told me that by any invocation 25
I should have power to raise him, though it
wanted
The powerful words and decent rights of art.
Never had my set brain such need of spirit
T' instruct and cheer it; now, then, I will claim
Performance of his free and gentle vow 30
T' appear in greater light, and make more plain
His rugged oracle. I long to know
How my dear mistress fares, and be inform'd
What hand she now holds on the troubled blood
Of her incensed lord. Methought the spirit 35
(When he had utter'd his perplex'd presage)
Threw his chang'd countenance headlong into
clouds.
His forehead bent, as it would hide his face,
He knock'd his chin against his dark'ned breast,
And struck a churlish silence through his
powers. 40
Terror of darkness! O, thou king of flames!
That with thy music-footed horse dost strike
The clear light out of crystal on dark earth,
And hurl'st instructive fire about the world, 44
Wake, wake the drowsy and enchanted night,
That sleeps with dead eyes in this heavy riddle!
Or thou great prince of shades, where never
sun
Sticks his far-darted beams, whose eyes are
made
To shine in darkness, and see ever best
Where men are blindest, open now the heart 50
Of thy abashed oracle, that, for fear
Of some ill it includes, would fain lie hid,
And rise thou with it in thy greater light.
        *Thunders. Surgit Spiritus cum suis.*
    *Sp.* Thus to observe my vow of apparition
In greater light, and explicate thy fate, 55
I come; and tell thee that if thou obey
The summons that thy mistress next will send
thee,
Her hand shall be thy death.
    *Bu.*             When will she send?
    *Sp.* Soon as I set again, where late I rose. 59

---

⁶¹ **Resolve:** be resolute    ⁶² **privy coats:** concealed coats of mail    ² **who:** whom    ⁸ S. D. **Umbra
Friar:** the friar's ghost    ¹⁷ **weed:** garment    ²³ **embodied:** while still living    ²⁴ **reminiscion:**
memory    ⁴¹ **king of flames:** Apollo

*Bu.* Is the old Friar slain?
*Sp.*                     No, and yet lives not.
*Bu.* Died he a natural death?
*Sp.*                     He did.
*Bu.*                     Who then
Will my dear mistress send?
*Sp.*               I must not tell thee.
*Bu.* Who lets thee?
*Sp.*               Fate.
*Bu.*               Who are fate's ministers?
*Sp.* The Guise and Monsieur.
*Bu.*               A fit pair of shears
To cut the threads of kings and kingly spirits,
And consorts fit to sound forth harmony,   66
Set to the falls of kingdoms: shall the hand
Of my kind mistress kill me?
*Sp.*                     If thou yield
To her next summons. Y' are fair-warn'd: fare-
    well!               *Thunders. Exit.*
*Bu.* I must fare well, however, though I die,
My death consenting with his augury.   71
Should not my powers obey when she com-
    mands,
My motion must be rebel to my will,
My will to life: if, when I have obey'd,
Her hand should so reward me, they must arm it,
Bind me or force it: or, I lay my life,   76
She rather would convert it many times
On her own bosom, even to many deaths.
But were there danger of such violence,
I know 't is far from her intent to send;   80
And who she should send is as far from thought,
Since he is dead, whose only mean she us'd.
                              *Knocks.*
Who 's there! Look to the door, and let him in,
Though politic Monsieur or the violent Guise.

*Enter Montsurry, like the Friar, with a letter
    written in blood*

*Mont.* Hail to my worthy son.
*Bu.*               Oh, lying spirit!
To say the Friar was dead; I 'll now believe  86
Nothing of all his forg'd predictions.
My kind and honour'd father, well reviv'd!
I have been frighted with your death and mine,
And told my mistress' hand should be my death
If I obeyed this summons.
*Mont.*               I believ'd   91
Your love had been much clearer than to give
Any such doubt a thought, for she is clear,
And having freed her husband's jealousy
(Of which her much abus'd hand here is witness)
She prays, for urgent cause, your instant pres-
    ence.                         96

*Bu.* Why, then your prince of spirits may
    be call'd
The prince of liars.
*Mont.*               Holy Writ so calls him.
*Bu.* What, writ in blood?
*Mont.*               Ay, 't is the ink of lovers.
*Bu.* O, 't is a sacred witness of her love. 100
So much elixir of her blood as this
Dropp'd in the lightest dame, would make her
    firm
As heat to fire; and, like to all the signs,
Commands the life confin'd in all my veins.
O, how it multiplies my blood with spirit,  105
And makes me apt t' encounter death and hell.
But come, kind father, you fetch me to heaven,
And to that end your holy weed was given.
                              *Exeunt.*

[SCENE IV]

*Thunder.  Intrat Umbra Friar, and discovers
    Tamyra*

*Um.* Up with these stupid thoughts, still
    loved daughter,
And strike away this heartless trance of an-
    guish.
Be like the sun, and labour in eclipses;
Look to the end of woes: oh, can you sit
Mustering the horrors of your servant's slaughter
Before your contemplation, and not study   6
How to prevent?  Watch when he shall rise,
And with a sudden outcry of his murther,
Blow his retreat before he be revenged.
*Ta.* O father, have my dumb woes wak'd
    your death?                         10
When will our human griefs be at their height?
Man is a tree that hath no top in cares,
No root in comforts; all his power to live
Is given to no end, but t' have power to grieve.
*Um.* It is the misery of our creation.   15
Your true friend,
Led by your husband, shadowed in my weed,
Now enters the dark vault.
*Ta.*               But, my dearest father,
Why will not you appear to him yourself,
And see that none of these deceits annoy him?
*Um.* My power is limited; alas! I cannot.  21
All that I can do — See, the cave opens.
                    *Exit. D'Ambois at the gulf.*
*Ta.* Away, my love, away; thou wilt be
    murther'd!

*Enter Monsieur and Guise above*

*Bu.* Murther'd; I know not what that He-
    brew means:

That word had ne'er been nam'd had all been
   d'Ambois.                                                25
Murther'd? By heaven, he is my murtherer
That shows me not a murtherer; what such bug
Abhorreth not the very sleep of d'Ambois?
Murther'd? Who dares give all the room I see
To d'Ambois' reach? or look with any odds 30
His fight i' th' face, upon whose hand sits
   death;
Whose sword hath wings, and every feather
   pierceth?
If I scape Monsieur's 'pothecary shops,
Foutre for Guise's shambles! 'T was ill
   plotted;
They should have maul'd me here,            35
When I was rising. I am up and ready.
Let in my politic visitants, let them in,
Though ent'ring like so many moving armours.
Fate is more strong than arms and sly than
   treason,
And I at all parts buckl'd in my fate.       40

*Mons.* }
*Gui.*  } Why enter not the coward villains?

*Bu.* Dare they not come?

*Enter Murtherers, with Friar at the other door*

*Ta.*                          They come.
*1 Mur.*                    Come, all at once.
*Um.* Back, coward murtherers, back.
*Omnes.*                    Defend us, heaven.
                   *Exeunt all but the first.*
*1 Mur.* Come ye not on?
*Bu.*               No, slave, nor goest thou off.
                    *[Strikes at him.]*
Stand you so firm? Will it not enter here?  45
You have a face yet! *[Stabs him in the face.]*
           So in thy life's flame
I burn the first rites to my mistress' fame.
*Um.* Breathe thee, brave son, against the
   other charge.
*Bu.* Oh, is it true then that my sense first
   told me?
Is my kind father dead?
*Ta.*                          He is, my love.   50
'T was the Earl, my husband, in his weed that
   brought thee.
*Bu.* That was a speeding sleight, and well
   resembled.
Where is that angry Earl? My lord, come
   forth
And show your own face in your own affair;
Take not into your noble veins the blood    55
Of these base villains, nor the light reports
Of blister'd tongues for clear and weighty
   truth:
But me against the world, in pure defence

Of your rare lady, to whose spotless name
I stand here as a bulwark, and project     60
A life to her renown, that ever yet
Hath been untainted, even in envy's eye,
And, where it would protect, a sanctuary.
Brave Earl, come forth, and keep your scandal
   in;
'T is not our fault if you enforce the spot  65
Nor the wreak yours if you perform it not.

*Enter Montsurry, with all the Murtherers*

*Mont.* Cowards, a fiend or spirit beat ye off?
They are your own faint spirits that have forg'd
The fearful shadows that your eyes deluded. 69
The fiend was in you; cast him out then, thus.
           *D'Ambois hath Mont. down.*
*Ta.* Favour my lord, my love, O, favour him!
*Bu.* I will not touch him: take your life,
   my lord,
And be appeas'd.         *Pistols shot within.*
         O, then the coward Fates
Have maim'd themselves, and ever lost their
   honour.
*Um.* What have ye done, slaves? Irreligious
   lord!                                       75
*Bu.* Forbear them, father; 't is enough for
   me
That Guise and Monsieur, death and destiny,
Come behind d'Ambois. Is my body, then,
But penetrable flesh? And must my mind
Follow my blood? Can my divine part add
No aid to th' earthly in extremity?         81
Then these divines are but for form, not fact.
Man is of two sweet courtly friends compact,
A mistress and a servant; let my death
Define life nothing but a courtier's breath.  85
Nothing is made of nought, of all things made,
Their abstract being a dream but of a shade.
I 'll not complain to earth yet, but to heaven,
And, like a man, look upwards even in death.
And if Vespasian thought in majesty        90
An emperor might die standing, why not I?
          *She offers to help him.*
Nay, without help, in which I will exceed him;
For he died splinted with his chamber grooms.
Prop me, true sword, as thou hast ever done:
The equal thought I bear of life and death  95
Shall make me faint on no side; I am up.
Here like a Roman statue I will stand
Till death hath made me marble. Oh, my fame,
Live in despite of murther; take thy wings
And haste thee where the grey-ey'd morn per-
   fumes                                     100
Her rosy chariot with Sabæan spices;
Fly where the evening from th' Iberian vales,
Takes on her swarthy shoulders Hecate,

---

**27 bug:** bugbear   **34 Foutre:** (word of obscene contempt)   **42 s. D.** (As the murderers enter by
one door, the friar's ghost appears at the other.)   **52 speeding:** successful   **65 spot:** blot on your
honor   **66 wreak:** revenge   **84 mistress:** soul   **servant:** body

Crown'd with a grove of oaks; fly where men
    feel
The burning axletree; and those that suffer 105
Beneath the chariot of the snowy Bear;
And tell them all that d'Ambois now is hasting
To the eternal dwellers; that a thunder
Of all their sighs together (for their frailties
Beheld in me) may quit my worthless fall  110
With a fit volley for my funeral.
  *Um.*  Forgive thy murtherers.
  *Bu.*                    I forgive them all;
And you, my lord, their fautor; for true sign
Of which unfeign'd remission, take my sword;
Take it, and only give it motion,            115
And it shall find the way to victory
By his own brightness, and th' inherent valour
My fight hath 'still'd into 't, with charms of
    spirit.
Now let me pray you that my weighty blood
Laid in one scale of your impartial spleen,  120
May sway the forfeit of my worthy love
Weigh'd in the other; and be reconcil'd
With all forgiveness to your matchless wife.
  *Ta.*  Forgive thou me, dear servant, and this
    hand
That led thy life to this unworthy end;      125
Forgive it, for the blood with which 't is stain'd,
In which I writ the summons of thy death;
The forced summons, by this bleeding wound,
By this here in my bosom; and by this
That makes me hold up both my hands im-
    bru'd                                  130
For thy dear pardon.
  *Bu.*                 O, my heart is broken.
Fate, nor these murtherers, Monsieur, nor the
    Guise,
Have any glory in my death, but this,
This killing spectacle, this prodigy.
My sun is turn'd to blood, in whose red beams
Pindus and Ossa, hid in drifts of snow,      136
Laid on my heart and liver, from their veins
Melt like two hungry torrents, eating rocks,
Into the ocean of all human life,
And make it bitter, only with my blood.      140
O frail condition of strength, valour, virtue,
In me (like warning fire upon the top
Of some steep beacon on a steeper hill)
Made to express it: like a falling star
Silently glanc'd, that like a thunderbolt    145
Look'd to have stuck and shook the firmament.
                      *Moritur.*
  *Um.*  [My terrors are struck inward, and no
    more
My penance will allow they shall enforce
Earthly afflictions but upon myself.]
Farewell, brave relics of a complete man!    150

Look up and see thy spirit made a star.
Join flames with Hercules, and when thou
    sett'st
Thy radiant forehead in the firmament,
Make the vast crystal crack with thy receipt;
Spread to a world of fire; and th' aged sky  155
Cheer with new sparks of old humanity.
  [*To Mont.*]  Son of the earth, whom my un-
    rested soul,
Rues t' have begotten in the faith of heaven;
[Since thy revengeful spirit hath rejected
The charity it commands, and the remission  160
To serve and worship the blind rage of blood]
Assay to gratulate and pacify
The soul fled from this worthy by performing
The Christian reconcilement he besought      164
Betwixt thee and thy lady.  Let her wounds
Manlessly digg'd in her, be eas'd and cur'd
With balm of thine own tears; or be assur'd
Never to rest free from my haunt and horror.
  *Mont.*  See how she merits this, still kneeling
    by,                                    169
And mourning his fall more than her own fault.
  *Um.*  Remove, dear daughter, and content
    thy husband;
So piety wills thee, and thy servant's peace.
  *Ta.*  O wretched piety, that art so distract
In thine own constancy, and in thy right
Must be unrighteous.  If I right my friend, 175
I wrong my husband: if his wrong I shun,
The duty of my friend I leave undone.
Ill plays on both sides; here and there it riseth;
No place, no good, so good but ill compriseth.
[My soul more scruple breeds, than my blood
    sin.                                   180
Virtue imposeth more than any stepdame;]
O had I never married but for form,
Never vow'd faith but purpos'd to deceive,
Never made conscience of any sin,
But cloak'd it privately and made it common;
Nor never honour'd been in blood or mind,   186
Happy had I been then, as others are
Of the like licence; I had then been honour'd;
Liv'd without envy; custom had benumb'd
All sense of scruple, and all note of frailty; 190
My fame had been untouch'd, my heart un-
    broken:
But (shunning all) I strike on all offence.
O husband!  Dear friend!  O my conscience!
  *Mons.*  Come, let 's away; my senses are not
    proof                                  194
Against those plaints.
          *Exeunt Guise, Monsieur; d'Am-
           bois is borne off.*
  *Mont.*  I must not yield to pity, nor to love
So servile and so traitorous.  Cease, my blood,

104–105 **where . . . axletree:** to the tropics    113 **fautor:** patron    130 **imbru'd:** blood-stained
147–149 (Omitted in Q 1641)    154 **vast crystal:** crystalline sphere    **receipt:** reception    159–161 (Not in
Q 1641)    162 **gratulate:** gratify    166 **Manlessly:** unmanly    180, 181 (Not in Q 1641)

To wrastle with my honour, fame, and judg-
    ment. —
Away! Forsake my house; forbear complaints
Where thou hast bred them: here all things
    full                       200
Of their own shame and sorrow; leave my
    house.
    *Ta.*   Sweet lord, forgive me, and I will be
    gone,
And till these wounds, that never balm shall
    close
Till death hath enter'd at them (so I love them,
Being open'd by your hands) by death be cur'd,
I never more will grieve you with my sight, 206
Never endure that any roof shall part
Mine eyes and heaven; but to the open deserts
(Like to a hunted tigress) I will fly,
Eating my heart, shunning the steps of men,
And look on no side till I be arriv'd.     211
    *Mont.*   I do forgive thee, and upon my knees,
With hands held up to heaven, wish that mine
    honour
Would suffer reconcilement to my love;
But since it will not, honour never serve   215
My love with flourishing object till it sterve:
And as this taper, though it upwards look,
Downwards must needs consume, so let our
    love;
As having lost his honey, the sweet taste

Runs into savour, and will needs retain   220
A spice of his first parents, till, like life,
It sees and dies; so let our love; and lastly,
As when the flame is suffer'd to look up,
It keeps his lustre, but, being thus turn'd down,
(His natural course of useful light inverted), 225
His own stuff puts it out; so let our love.
Now turn from me, as here I turn from thee,
And may both points of heaven's straight axle-
    tree
Conjoin in one, before thyself and me.
                        *Exeunt severally.*

    *Finis Actus quinti & ultimi.*

## EPILOGUE

WITH many hands you have seen d'Ambois
    slain,
Yet by your grace he may revive again,
And every day grow stronger in his skill
To please, as we presume he is in will.
The best deserving actors of the time     5
Had their ascents, and by degrees did climb
To their full height, a place to study due.
To make him tread in their path lies in you;
He 'll not forget his makers, but still prove
His thankfulness as you increase your love. 10

                    FINIS

²¹⁶ **sterve:** die

# THE MALCONTENT.

By Iohn Marston.

1 6 o 4.

Printed at London by *v.s.* for *William Aspley*, and are to be solde at his shop in Paules Church-yard,

# THE MALCONTENT.

Augmented by *Marston*.

With the Additions played by the Kings Maiesties seruants.

Written by *Ihon Webster*.

1 6 o 4.

AT LONDON
Printed by V.S. for William Aspley, and are to be sold at his shop in Paules Church-yard.

BIBLIOGRAPHICAL RECORD. *The Malcontent* was entered on the Register of the Stationers' Co. to William Aspley and Thomas Thorpe on July 5, 1604: — *Entred for their Copie vnder the handes of Master Pasfeild and Master Norton warden an Enterlude called the Malecontent, Tragiecomedia . . . vj d.* It appeared in print three times in the same year, the first two quartos being partly from the same setting of type, and the third (here referred to as 'Q 2' since it is a distinct edition) adding the Induction and amplifying the main text in about a dozen places (see footnotes). The wording of the title-page of this quarto, and the heading to the Induction, have led to some confusion as to the part taken by Webster in the revision of the play. Modern opinion inclines to the view that the additions are by Marston, as the title-page seems to state explicitly, and that Webster is responsible only for the Induction. (For new facts on Marston's life see R. E. Brettle, *Modern Language Review*, Jan., July, 1927.)

DATE AND STAGE PERFORMANCE. It is clear from the Induction (lines 54, 55, 100, 101) that *The Malcontent* was first performed by the Children of the Queen's Revels at the Blackfriars Theatre. The book of the play then seems to have been lost and recovered by the King's Men, who acted the play, to which they had no legal right, in retaliation for a piratical production of *Jeronimo* by the boys' company. As Marston seems not to have been connected with the company of the Queen's Revels until 1604, the composition of the play and its original performance may probably be assigned to that date. Some confirmation of this view may be found in the several references to *Hamlet* in the play. Stoll and others, however, have suggested 1600 as a probable date, chiefly because of the reference to the horn "growing in the woman's forehead twelve years since." (I. viii. 23. Cf. E. E. Stoll, "Shakespere, Marston, and the Malcontent Type," *Mod. Phil.*, 3 [1906] 281.) The later date is now regarded as more probable.

STRUCTURE. *The Malcontent* is, as the entry on the Stationers' Register declares, a tragicomedy. The extravagant complications of the plot might easily have ended in violence and death, but Marston chose otherwise. His gift for dramatically effective scenes was far greater than his power of dramatic construction, and the happy ending of the play, although consonant with its mood of bitter cynicism, is not entirely satisfactory. The closing masque suggests the use of similar devices in such Senecan tragedies as *The Spanish Tragedy*, and the conception of the character of Malevole is based on Jonson's theory of humors.

# JOHN MARSTON (*c.* 1575–1634)

## THE MALCONTENT

BENIAMINO IONSONIO, POETÆ ELEGANTISSIMO, GRAVISSIMO, AMICO SVO, CANDIDO ET CORDATO, IOHANNES MARSTON, MVSARVM ALVMNVS, ASPERAM HANC SVAM THALIAM D. D.

[Members of the Company of His Majesty's Servants appearing in the INDUCTION

| | | |
|---|---|---|
| WILLIAM SLY | RICHARD BURBAGE | JOHN LOWIN |
| JOHN SINKLO | HENRY CONDELL | A Tire-man] |

### DRAMATIS PERSONÆ

GIOVANNI ALTOFRONTO, disguised MALEVOLE, sometime Duke of Genoa
PIETRO JACOMO, Duke of Genoa
MENDOZA, a minion to the Duchess of Pietro Jacomo
CELSO, a friend to Altofront
BILIOSO, an old choleric marshal
PREPASSO, a gentleman-usher
FERNEZE, a young courtier, and enamoured on the Duchess
FERRARDO, a minion to Duke Pietro Jacomo

EQUATO ⎫ two courtiers
GUERRINO ⎭
PASSARELLO, fool to Bilioso

AURELIA, Duchess to Duke Pietro Jacomo
MARIA, Duchess to Duke Altofront
EMILIA, ⎫ two ladies attending the Duchess
BIANCA, ⎭ [Aurelia]
MAQUERELLE, an old panderess

THE SCENE. — Genoa.

### TO THE READER

I AM an ill orator; and, in truth, use to indite more honestly than eloquently, for it is my custom to speak as I think, and write as I speak.

In plainness, therefore, understand that in some things I have willingly erred, as in supposing a Duke of Genoa, and in taking names different from that city's families: for which some may wittily accuse me: but my defence shall be as honest as many reproofs unto me have been most [5 malicious; since, I heartily protest, it was my care to write so far from reasonable offence, that even strangers, in whose state I laid my scene, should not from thence draw any disgrace to any, dead or living. Yet, in despite of my endeavours, I understand some have been most unadvisedly over-cunning in misinterpreting me, and with subtlety as deep as hell have maliciously spread ill rumours, which, springing from themselves, might to themselves have heavily returned. Surely [10 I desire to satisfy every firm spirit, who, in all his actions, proposeth to himself no more ends than God and virtue do, whose intentions are always simple: to such I protest that, with my free understanding, I have not glanced at disgrace of any, but of those whose unquiet studies labour innovation, contempt of holy policy, reverend, comely superiority, and establish'd unity. For the rest of my supposed tartness, I fear not but unto every worthy mind it will be approved so gen- [15 eral and honest as may modestly pass with the freedom of a satire. I would fain leave the paper; only one thing afflicts me, to think that scenes, invented merely to be spoken, should be enforcively published to be read, and that the least hurt I can receive is to do myself the wrong. But, since others otherwise would do me more, the least inconvenience is to be accepted. I have myself, therefore, set forth this comedy; but so, that my enforced absence must much rely upon the [20 printer's discretion: but I shall entreat slight errors in orthography may be as slightly overpassed, and that the unhandsome shape, which this trifle in reading presents, may be pardoned for the pleasure it once afforded you, when it was presented with the soul of lively action.

*Sine aliqua dementia nullus Phœbus.*                    I. M.

Ded. To Benjamin Jonson, the most choice and weighty poet, his sincere and judicious friend, John Marston, foster-child of the Muses, gives and dedicates this his rough comedy.    5 **wittily:** cleverly    13–14 **innovation:** disturbance, revolution    21 **slightly:** heedlessly    24 No brilliance without some madness (some copies of Q 1 read, *Me mea sequentur fata*, "My fates will follow me").

[THE INDUCTION TO THE MALCONTENT, AND
The Additions Acted by the King's Majesty's Servants
Written by John Webster

*Enter W. Sly, a Tire-man following him
with a stool*

*Tire-man.* Sir, the gentlemen will be angry
if you sit here.

*Sly.* Why, we may sit upon the stage at the
private house. Thou dost not take me for a
country gentleman, dost? Dost think I fear [5
hissing? I 'll hold my life, thou took'st me for
one of the players.

*Tire-man.* No, sir.

*Sly.* By God's lid, if you had, I would have
given you but sixpence for your stool. Let [10
them that have stale suits sit in the galleries.
Hiss at me! He that will be laugh'd out of a
tavern or an ordinary, shall seldom feed well,
or be drunk in good company. — Where 's
Harry Condell, Dick Burbage, and Will Sly? [15
Let me speak with some of them.

*Tire-man.* An 't please you to go in, sir, you
may.

*Sly.* I tell you, no. I am one that hath seen
this play often, and can give them intelli- [20
gence for their action. I have most of the jests
here in my table-book.

*Enter Sinklo*

*Sinklo.* Save you coz!

*Sly.* O, cousin, come! you shall sit between
my legs here.                                        25

*Sinklo.* No, indeed, cousin: the audience
then will take me for a viol-de-gambo, and think
that you play upon me.

*Sly.* Nay, rather that I work upon you, coz.

*Sinklo.* We stayed for you at supper last [30
night at my cousin Honeymoon's, the woollen-
draper. After supper we drew cuts for a score
of apricocks, the longest cut still to draw an
apricock. By this light, 't was Mistress Frank
Honeymoon's fortune still to have the long- [35
est cut. I did measure for the women. — What
be these, coz?

*Enter D. Burbage, H. Condell, and
J. Lowin*

*Sly.* The players. — God save you!

*Burbage.* You are very welcome.

*Sly.* I pray you, know this gentleman, [40

my cousin; 't is Master Doomsday's son, the
usurer.

*Condell.* I beseech you, sir, be cover'd.

*Sly.* No, in good faith: for mine ease. Look
you, my hat 's the handle to this fan. God 's [45
so, what a beast was I, I did not leave my
feather at home! Well, but I 'll take an order
with you.                *Puts his feather in his pocket.*

*Burbage.* Why do you conceal your feather,
sir?                                                 50

*Sly.* Why, do you think I 'll have jests
broken upon me in the play, to be laugh'd at?
This play hath beaten all your gallants out of
the feathers. Blackfriars hath almost spoil'd
Blackfriars for feathers.                             55

*Sinklo.* God 's so, I thought 't was for somewhat our gentlewomen at home counsell'd me
to wear my feather to the play: yet I am loath
to spoil it.

*Sly.* Why, coz?                                      60

*Sinklo.* Because I got it in the tilt-yard.
There was a herald broke my pate for taking it
up: but I have worn it up and down the Strand,
and met him forty times since, and yet he dares
not challenge it.                                     65

*Sly.* Do you hear, sir? This play is a bitter
play.

*Condell.* Why, sir, 't is neither satire nor
moral, but the mean passage of a history: yet
there are a sort of discontented creatures [70
that bear a stingless envy to great ones, and
these will wrest the doings of any man to their
base, malicious applyment. But should their
interpretation come to the test, like your mar-
moset, they presently turn their teeth to [75
their tail and eat it.

*Sly.* I will not go so far with you; but I say,
any man that hath wit may censure, if he sit
in the twelve-penny room; and I say again,
the play is bitter.                                   80

*Burbage.* Sir, you are like a patron that,
presenting a poor scholar to a benefice, enjoins
him not to rail against anything that stands
within compass of his patron's folly. Why
should not we enjoy the ancient freedom of [85
poesy? Shall we protest to the ladies that their
painting makes them angels? or to my young
gallant that his expense in the brothel shall gain

Induction (Not in Q 1)   S. D. **Tire-man:** dresser or property man   ⁴ **private house:** Blackfriars
Theatre   ¹⁵ **Dick:** ('D:' Q 2)   **Will:** ('W:' Q 2)   ²⁰⁻²¹ **intelligence:** information   ²² **table-book:**
notebook   ³⁰ **stayed:** waited   ⁴³ **be cover'd:** put on your hat   ⁵⁴, ⁵⁵ **Blackfriars:** the theatre and the
district, where feathers were sold (cf. V. ii. 46–47)   ⁵⁵⁻⁵⁷ **somewhat:** some good reason   ⁶⁹ **mean . . .
history:** an ordinary history   ⁷³ **applyment:** application, interpretation   ⁷⁸ **censure:** judge
⁷⁹ **twelve-penny room:** box

him reputation? No, sir, such vices as stand not accountable to law should be cured as [90 men heal tetters, by casting ink upon them. Would you be satisfied in anything else, sir?

*Sly.* Ay, marry, would I: I would know how you came by this play?

*Condell.* Faith, sir, the book was lost; [95 and because 't was pity so good a play should be lost, we found it, and play it.

*Sly.* I wonder you would play it, another company having interest in it.

*Condell.* Why not Malevole in folio with [100 us, as Jeronimo in decimo-sexto with them? They taught us a name for our play; we call it *One for Another.*

*Sly.* What are your additions?

*Burbage.* Sooth, not greatly needful; [105 only as your sallet to your great feast, to entertain a little more time, and to abridge the not-received custom of music in our theatre. I must leave you, sir.                    *Exit Burbage.*

*Sinklo.* Doth he play the Malcontent?    110

*Condell.* Yes, sir.

*Sinklo.* I durst lay four of mine ears the play is not so well acted as it hath been.

*Condell.* O, no, sir, nothing *ad Parmenonis suem.*                                    115

*Lowin.* Have you lost your ears, sir, that you are so prodigal of laying them?

*Sinklo.* Why did you ask that, friend?

*Lowin.* Marry, sir, because I have heard of a fellow would offer to lay a hundred-pound [120 wager, that was not worth five baubees: and in this kind you might venter four of your elbows. Yet God defend your coat should have so many!

*Sinklo.* Nay, truly, I am no great censu- [125 rer; and yet I might have been one of the college of critics once. My cousin here hath an excellent memory, indeed, sir.

*Sly.* Who? I? I 'll tell you a strange thing of myself; and I can tell you, for one that [130 never studied the art of memory, 't is very strange too.

*Condell.* What 's that, sir?

*Sly.* Why, I 'll lay a hundred pound, I 'll walk but once down by the Goldsmith's [135 Row in Cheap, take notice of the signs, and tell you them with a breath instantly.

*Lowin.* 'T is very strange.

*Sly.* They begin as the world did, with Adam and Eve. There 's in all just five and fifty. [140 I do use to meditate much when I come to plays too. What do you think might come into a man's head now, seeing all this company?

*Condell.* I know not, sir.

*Sly.* I have an excellent thought. If [145 some fifty of the Grecians that were cramm'd in the horse-belly had eaten garlic, do you not think the Trojans might have smelt out their knavery?

*Condell.* Very likely.                    150

*Sly.* By God, I would they had, for I love Hector horribly.

*Sinklo.* O, but, coz, coz!
"Great Alexander, when he came to the tomb
    of Achilles,
Spake with a big loud voice, O thou thrice
    blessed and happy!"                    155

*Sly.* Alexander was an ass to speak so well of a filthy cullion.

*Lowin.* Good sir, will you leave the stage? I 'll help you to a private room.

*Sly.* Come, coz, let 's take some tobacco. — Have you never a prologue?            161

*Lowin.* Not any, sir.

*Sly.* Let me see, I will make one extempore. Come to them, and fencing of a congee with arms and legs, be round with them.            165

Gentlemen, I could wish for the women's sakes you had all soft cushions; and gentlewomen, I could wish that for the men's sakes you had all more easy standings.

What would they wish more but the play now? and that they shall have instantly.    171

                            *[Exeunt.]*]

## ACTUS PRIMUS. SCE[NA] PRIMA

*[Palace of the Duke of Genoa]*

*The vilest out-of-tune music being heard, enter Bilioso and Prepasso*

*Bil.* Why, how now! Are ye mad, or drunk, or both, or what?

*Pre.* Are ye building Babylon there?

*Bil.* Here 's a noise in court? You think you are in a tavern, do you not?            5

---

91 **tetters:** skin eruptions    100–101 **Why . . . them:** Why should not we (the King's Men) play this play, which belongs to the Children of the Queen's Revels, since they have appropriated *Jeronimo*, which belongs to us? ("Folio" and "decimo-sexto" refer to the large and diminutive stature, respectively, of the two companies.)    106 **sallet:** salad    106–107 **entertain:** while away (The children introduced musical interludes.)    114–115 **ad . . . suem:** (Parmeno was famous for imitating the sound of a pig. Rivals brought in a pig, which the audience declared to be inferior to Parmeno in grunting.)    117 **laying:** betting    121 **baubees:** halfpennies    122 **venter:** venture    123 **defend:** forbid    151 **they:** ('he' Q 2)    154–155 (Petrarch, Sonnet 153, trans. by John Harvey)    157 **cullion:** rogue    164 **congee:** salute    165 **round:** plain-spoken, severe    Actus Primus (in margin of Qq.: Vexat censura columbas, 'Censorship troubles the doves.')

*Pre.* You think you are in a brothel-house, do you not? — This room is ill-scented.

*Enter one with a perfume*

So, perfume, perfume: some upon me, I pray thee.
The duke is upon instant entrance; so, make place there!

### SCENA SECUNDA

*Enter the Duke Pietro, Ferrardo, Count Equato, Count Celso before, and Guerrino*

*Pietro.* Where breathes that music?
*Bil.* The discord rather than the music is heard from the malcontent Malevole's chamber.
*Fer.* [*Calling.*] Malevole!                      [5
*Mal.* (*Out of his chamber.*) Yaugh, god-a-man, what dost thou there? Duke's Ganymede, Juno 's jealous of thy long stockings. Shadow of a woman, what wouldst, weasel? Thou lamb o' court, what dost thou bleat for? Ah, you smooth chinn'd catamite!       11
*Pietro.* Come down, thou rugged cur, and snarl here; I give thy dogged sullenness free liberty; trot about and bespurtle whom thou pleasest.
*Mal.* I 'll come among you, you goat-  [16
ish-blooded toderers, as gum into taffeta, to fret, to fret. I 'll fall like a sponge into water, to suck up, to suck up. Howl again; I 'll go to church and come to you.       [*Exit above.*]
*Pietro.* This Malevole is one of the most [21
prodigious affections that ever convers'd with nature: a man, or rather a monster, more discontent than Lucifer when he was thrust out of the presence. His appetite is unsatiable as the grave; as far from any content as from [26
heaven. His highest delight is to procure others vexation, and therein he thinks he truly serves heaven; for 't is his position, whosoever in this earth can be contented is a slave and damned; therefore does he afflict all in [31
that to which they are most affected. Th' elements struggle within him; his own soul is at variance within herself; his speech is halter-worthy at all hours. I like him, faith: he gives good intelligence to my spirit, makes [36
me understand those weaknesses which others' flattery palliates. Hark! they sing.

*[A Song]*

### SCENA TERTIA

*Enter Malevole after the song*

[*Pietro.*] See, he comes. Now shall you hear the extremity of a malcontent: he is as free as air; he blows over every man. — And, sir, whence come you now?                        4
*Mal.* From the public place of much dissimulation, the church.
*Pietro.* What didst there?
*Mal.* Talk with a usurer; take up at interest.                                              9
*Pietro.* I wonder what religion thou art of?
*Mal.* Of a soldier's religion.
*Pietro.* And what dost think makes most infidels now?                                      14
*Mal.* Sects, sects. I have seen seeming Piety change her robe so oft, that sure none but some arch-devil can shape her a petticoat.
*Pietro.* O, a religious policy.
*Mal.* But, damnation on a politic religion! I am weary: would I were one of the duke's hounds now!                                       21
*Pietro.* But what 's the common news abroad, Malevole? Thou dogg'st rumour still.
*Mal.* Common news? Why, common words are, "God save ye," "Fare ye well"; com- [25
mon actions, flattery and cozenage; common things, women and cuckolds. — And how does my little Ferrard? Ah, ye lecherous animal! — my little ferret, he goes sucking up and down the palace into every hen's nest, like a weasel: [30
— and to what dost thou addict thy time to now more than to those antique painted drabs that are still affected of young courtiers, Flattery, Pride, and Venery?                        34
*Fer.* I study languages. Who dost think to be the best linguist of our age?
*Mal.* Phew! the devil: let him possess thee; he 'll teach thee to speak all languages most readily and strangely; and great reason, marry, he 's travel'd greatly i' the world, and is everywhere.                                            41
*Fer.* Save i' th' court.
*Mal.* Ay, save i' th' court. — *To Bilioso.* And how does my old muckhill, overspread with fresh snow? Thou half a man, half a [45
goat, all a beast! how does thy young wife, old huddle?
*Bil.* Out, you improvident rascal!
*Mal.* Do, kick, thou hugely-horn'd old duke's ox, good Master Make-please.       50

---

⁹ **upon . . . entrance:** about to enter  Sc. II. ¹¹ **catamite:** male prostitute   ¹² **rugged:** shaggy ('ragged' Q 2)    ¹⁴ **bespurtle:** bespatter   ¹⁷ **toderers:** spewers of slime   ²² **affections:** affected persons   ²⁹ **position:** thesis   ³² **to . . . affected:** which they most like   ³⁴⁻³⁵ **halter-worthy:** worthy of hanging   Sc. III. ⁸ **take up:** borrow   ²⁶ **cozenage:** swindling   ⁴³ **of:** by   ⁴⁷ **huddle:** decrepit old man

*Pietro.* How dost thou live nowadays, Malevole?

*Mal.* Why, like the knight, Sir Patrick Penlolians, with killing o' spiders for my lady's monkey.                                                         55

*Pietro.* How dost spend the night? I hear thou never sleep'st.

*Mal.* O, no; but dream the most fantastical! O heaven! O fubbery, fubbery!

*Pietro.* Dream! What dream'st?                     60

*Mal.* Why, methinks I see that signior pawn his footcloth, that metreza her plate: this madam takes physic that t' other monsieur may minister to her: here is a pander jewel'd; there is a fellow in shift of satin this day, that [65 could not shift a shirt t' other night: here a Paris supports that Helen; there 's a Lady Guinever bears up that Sir Lancelot. Dreams, dreams, visions, fantasies, chimeras, imaginations, tricks, conceits! — (*To Prepasso.*) Sir [70 Tristram Trimtram! come aloft, Jack-an-apes, with a whim-wham: here 's a knight of the land of Catito shall play at trap with any page in Europe; do the sword-dance with any morris-dancer in Christendom; ride at the ring till [75 the fin of his eyes look as blue as the welkin; and run the wildgoose-chase even with Pompey the Huge.

*Pietro.* You run!                                          79

*Mal.* To the devil. Now, signior Guerrino, that thou from a most pitied prisoner shouldst grow a most loath'd flatterer! — Alas, poor Celso, thy star 's oppress'd: thou art an honest lord: 't is pity.

*Equato.* Is 't pity?                                       85

*Mal.* Ay, marry is 't, philosophical Equato; and 't is pity that thou, being so excellent a scholar by art, should'st be so ridiculous a fool by nature. — I have a thing to tell you, duke: bid 'em avaunt, bid 'em avaunt.        90

*Pietro.* Leave us, leave us.

*Exeunt all saving Pietro and Malevole.*

Now, sir, what is 't?

*Mal.* Duke, thou art a becco, a cornuto.

*Pietro.* How!

*Mal.* Thou art a cuckold.                             95

*Pietro.* Speak, unshale him quick.

*Mal.* With most tumbler-like nimbleness.

*Pietro.* Who? By whom? I burst with desire.                                                              99

*Mal.* Mendoza is the man makes thee a horn'd beast; duke, 't is Mendoza cornutes thee.

*Pietro.* What conformance? Relate; short, short.

*Mal.* As a lawyer's beard.     [*Sings.*] 105
*There is an old crone in the court; her name is*
    *Maquerelle.*
*She is my mistress, sooth to say, and she doth*
    *ever tell me.*

Blirt o' rhyme, blirt o' rhyme! Maquerelle is a cunning bawd; I am an honest villain; thy wife is a close drab; and thou art a notorious cuckold. Farewell, duke.                       111

*Pietro.* Stay, stay.

*Mal.* Dull, dull duke, can lazy patience make lame revenge? O God, for a woman to make a man that which God never created, never [115 made!

*Pietro.* What did God never make?

*Mal.* A cuckold: to be made a thing that 's hoodwink'd with kindness, whilst every rascal fillips his brows; to have a coxcomb with [120 egregious horns pinn'd to a lord's back, every page sporting himself with delightful laughter, whilst he must be the last must know it. Pistols and poniards! pistols and poniards!

*Pietro.* Death and damnation!                   125

*Mal.* Lightning and thunder!

*Pietro.* Vengeance and torture!

*Mal.* Catso!

*Pietro.* O, revenge!

*Mal.* Nay, to select among ten thousand
    fairs                                                        130
A lady far inferior to the most,
In fair proportion both of limb and soul;
To take her from austerer check of parents,
To make her his by most devoutful rites,
Make her commandress of a better essence 135
Than is the gorgeous world, even, of a man;
To hug her with as rais'd an appetite
As usurers do their delv'd-up treasury
(Thinking none tells it but his private self);
To meet her spirit in a nimble kiss,         140
Distilling panting ardour to her heart;
True to her sheets, nay, diets strong his blood,
To give her height of hymeneal sweets, —

*Pietro.* O God!

*Mal.* Whilst she lisps, and gives him some
    court-*quelquechose*,                                145
Made only to provoke, not satiate:
And yet, even then, the thaw of her delight
Flows from lewd heat of apprehension,
Only from strange imagination's rankness,
That forms the adulterer's presence in her
    soul,                                                        150

---

⁵⁹ **fubbery:** deceit    ⁶² **footcloth:** trappings of a horse    **metreza:** mistress (Ital.)    ⁶⁶ **shift:** change
⁷¹ **come aloft:** (the cry of the keeper to his trained apes)    ⁷² **whim-wham:** whimsy    ⁷³ **trap:** a ball game
⁷⁶ **fin:** lid    ⁸³ **oppress'd:** in the decline    ⁹³ **becco, cornuto:** cuckold (Ital.)    ⁹⁶ **unshale:** unshell
¹⁰³ **conformance:** corroboration    ¹⁰⁸ **Blirt:** outburst    ¹¹⁰ **close:** secret    ¹¹⁹ **hoodwink'd:** blinded
¹²⁰ **coxcomb:** fool's cap    ¹²⁸ **Catso:** (an Italian term of contempt)    ¹³⁰⁻¹⁷⁵ **Nay . . . it:** (not in Q 1)
¹³⁹ **tells:** counts    ¹⁴⁵ **quelquechose:** delicacy, 'kickshaw'

And makes her think she clips the foul knave's
    loins.
*Pietro.* Affliction to my blood's root!
*Mal.* Nay, think, but think, what may proceed of this; adultery is often the mother of
incest.                                             155
*Pietro.* Incest!
*Mal.* Yes, incest! mark: — Mendoza of his
wife begets perchance a daughter: Mendoza
dies, his son marries this daughter: say you?
nay, 't is frequent, not only probable, but no [160
question often acted, whilst ignorance, fearless
ignorance, clasps his own seed.
*Pietro.* Hideous imagination!
*Mal.* Adultery! Why, next to the sin of
simony, 't is the most horrid transgression under the cope of salvation.                          166
*Pietro.* Next to simony!
*Mal.* Ay, next to simony, in which our men
in next age shall not sin.
*Pietro.* Not sin! why?                             170
*Mal.* Because (thanks to some churchmen)
our age will leave them nothing to sin with.
But adultery, O dullness! should show exemplary punishment, that intemperate bloods may
freeze but to think it. I would damn him [175
and all his generation: my own hands should
do it; ha, I would not trust heaven with my
vengeance, anything.
*Pietro.* Anything, anything, Malevole: thou
shalt see instantly what temper my spirit [180
holds. Farewell; remember I forget thee not;
farewell.                              *Exit Pietro.*
*Mal.* Farewell.
Lean thoughtfulness, a sallow meditation
Suck thy veins dry! Distemperance rob thy
    sleep!                                          185
The heart's disquiet is revenge most deep:
He that gets blood, the life of flesh but spills;
But he that breaks heart's peace, the dear soul
    kills.
Well, this disguise doth yet afford me that 189
Which kings do seldom hear, or great men use, —
Free speech: and though my state 's usurp'd,
Yet this affected strain gives me a tongue
As fetterless as is an emperor's.
I may speak foolishly, ay, knavishly,               194
Always carelessly; yet no one thinks it fashion
To poise my breath; for he that laughs and strikes
Is lightly felt, or seldom struck again.
Duke, I 'll torment thee now: my just revenge
From thee than crown a richer gem shall part:
Beneath God naught 's so dear as a calm
    heart.                                          200

## SCENA QUARTA

*Enter Celso*

*Celso.* My honour'd lord, —
*Mal.* Peace, speak low, peace! O Celso,
    constant lord,
(Thou to whose faith I only rest discover'd,
Thou, one of full ten millions of men,
That lovest virtue only for itself;                  5
Thou in whose hands old Ops may put her soul)
Behold forever-banish'd Altofront,
This Genoa's last year's duke. O truly noble!
I wanted those old instruments of state,
Dissemblance and suspect: I could not time it,
    Celso;                                          10
My throne stood like a point in midst of a circle,
To all of equal nearness; bore with none;
Reign'd all alike; so slept in fearless virtue,
Suspectless, too suspectless; till the crowd,
(Still likerous of untried novelties)               15
Impatient with severer government,
Made strong with Florence, banish'd Altofront.
*Celso.* Strong with Florence! ay, thence your
    mischief rose;
For when the daughter of the Florentine
Was match'd once with this Pietro, now duke,
No stratagem of state untri'd was left,             21
Till you of all —
*Mal.*         Of all was quite bereft:
Alas, Maria too, close prisoned,
My true faith'd duchess, i' the citadel!            24
*Celso.* I 'll still adhere: let 's mutiny and die.
*Mal.* O, no, climb not a falling tower, Celso;
'T is well held desperation, no zeal,
Hopeless to strive with fate. Peace! Tem-
    porize!
Hope, hope, that never forsak'st the wretch-
    ed'st man,                                      29
Yet bidd'st me live, and lurk in this disguise!
What, play I well the free-breath'd discontent?
Why, man, we are all philosophical monarchs
Or natural fools. Celso, the court 's a-fire;
The duchess' sheets will smoke for 't ere it
    be long:
Impure Mendoza, that sharp-nos'd lord, that
    made                                            35
The cursed match link'd Genoa with Florence,
Now broad-horns the duke, which he now
    knows.
Discord to malcontents is very manna:
When the ranks are burst, then scuffle, Alto-
    front.
*Celso.* Ay, but durst, —                           40

---

¹⁵¹ **clips:** embraces    ¹⁶⁰⁻¹⁶¹ **no question:** unquestionably    ¹⁶⁶ **cope of salvation:** heaven
¹⁸³⁻²⁰⁰ **Farewell . . . heart:** (not in Q 1)    ¹⁸⁵ **Distemperance:** physical or mental disorder    ¹⁹⁶ **poise:**
weigh    ¹⁹⁷ **again:** in return    ²⁰⁰ **Beneath God:** under heaven    ³ **faith:** trustworthiness    **dis-**
**covered:** revealed    ⁶ **Ops:** goddess of plenty    ⁹ **wanted:** lacked    ¹⁴ **Suspectless:** without sus·
picion    ¹⁵ **likerous of:** avid for    ¹⁷ **strong:** *i.e.,* an alliance    ²⁰ **this:** ('his' Q 2)

*Mal.* 'T is gone; 't is swallow'd like a mineral:
Some say 't will work; pheut, I 'll not shrink:
He 's resolute who can no lower sink:

*Bilioso entering, Malevole shifteth his speech*

O the father of May-poles! did you never see a fellow whose strength consisted in his breath, [45 respect in his office, religion in his lord, and love in himself? why, then, behold!

*Bil.* Signior, —

*Mal.* My right worshipful lord, your court night-cap makes you have a passing high forehead.   51

*Bil.* I can tell you strange news, but I am sure you know them already: the duke speaks much good of you.

*Mal.* Go to, then: and shall you and I now enter into a strict friendship?   56

*Bil.* Second one another?

*Mal.* Yes.

*Bil.* Do one another good offices?   59

*Mal.* Just: what though I call'd thee old ox, egregious wittol, broken-bellied coward, rotten mummy? yet, since I am in favour —

*Bil.* Words of course, terms of disport. His grace presents you by me a chain, as his grateful remembrance for — I am ignorant for [65 what. Marry, ye may impart: yet howsoever — come — dear friend. Dost know my son?

*Mal.* Your son!

*Bil.* He shall eat woodcocks, dance jigs, make possets, and play at shuttle-cock with [70 any young lord about the court: he has as sweet a lady, too; dost know her little bitch?

*Mal.* 'T is a dog, man.

*Bil.* Believe me, a she-bitch. O, 't is a good creature! thou shalt be her servant. I 'll [75 make thee acquainted with my young wife too. What! I keep her not at court for nothing. 'T is grown to supper-time; come to my table: that, anything I have, stands open to thee.

*Mal.* (*To Celso.*) How smooth to him that is in state of grace,   80
How servile is the rugged'st courtier's face!
What profit, nay, what nature would keep down,
Are heav'd to them are minions to a crown.
Envious ambition never sates his thirst,   84
Till, sucking all, he swells and swells, and bursts.

*Bil.* I shall now leave you with my always-best wishes. Only let 's hold betwixt us a firm correspondence, a mutual friendly-reciprocal kind of steady-unanimous-heartily leagued ——   90

*Mal.* Did your signiorship ne'er see a pigeon-house that was smooth, round, and white without, and full of holes and stink within? Ha' ye not, old courtier?   94

*Bil.* O, yes: 't is the form, the fashion of them all.

*Mal.* Adieu, my true court-friend; farewell, my dear Castilio.   *Exit Bilioso.*

*Celso.* Yonder 's Mendoza.
     *Descries Mendoza.*

*Mal.*      True, the privy-key. 99

*Celso.* I take my leave, sweet lord.

*Mal.*     'T is fit; away! *Exit Celso.*

## SCENA QUINTA

*Enter Mendoza with three or four Suitors*

*Men.* Leave your suits with me; I can and will. Attend my secretary; leave me.
    [*Exeunt Suitors.*]

*Mal.* Mendoza, hark ye, hark ye. You are a treacherous villain: God b' wi' ye!

*Men.* Out, you base-born rascal!   5

*Mal.* We are all the sons of heaven, though a tripe-wife were our mother: ah, you whoreson, hot-rein'd he-marmoset! Ægisthus! didst ever hear of one Ægisthus?

*Men.* Gisthus?   10

*Mal.* Ay, Ægisthus: he was a filthy incontinent flesh-monger, such a one as thou art.

*Men.* Out, grumbling rogue!

*Mal.* Orestes, beware Orestes!

*Men.* Out, beggar!   15

*Mal.* I once shall rise!

*Men.* Thou rise!

*Mal.* Ay, at the resurrection.
*No vulgar seed but once may rise and shall;*
*No king so huge but 'fore he die may fall.*   20
    *Exit.*

*Men.* Now, good Elysium! what a delicious heaven is it for a man to be in a prince's favour! O sweet God! O pleasure! O fortune! O all thou best of life! What should I think, what say, what do? To be a favourite, a minion! to have a general timorous respect observe a [26 man, a stateful silence in his presence, solitariness in his absence, a confused hum and busy murmur of obsequious suitors training him; the cloth held up, and way proclaimed before [30 him; petitionary vassals licking the pavement with their slavish knees, whilst some odd palace-lampreels that engender with snakes, and are full of eyes on both sides, with a kind of insinuated humbleness, fix all [35

44–98 (Not in Q 1)   61 **wittol:** contented cuckold   66 **impart:** tell   70 **possets:** hot drinks of milk, wine, etc.   83 **are:** who are   88 **correspondence:** agreement, unity   98 **Castilio:** (an allusion to Castiglione, author of *The Courtier*, a famous book of manners)   7 **tripe-wife:** seller of tripe   8 **hot-rein'd:** lascivious   26 **observe:** pay obsequious court to   29 **training:** following   33 **lampreels:** lamprey eels

their delights upon his brow. O blessed state!
what a ravishing prospect doth the Olympus of
favour yield! Death, I cornute the duke!
Sweet women! most sweet ladies! nay, angels!
by heaven, he is more accursed than a devil [40
that hates you, or is hated by you; and happier
than a god that loves you, or is beloved by
you. You preservers of mankind, life-blood of
society, who would live, nay, who can live without you? O paradise! how majestical is your [45
austerer presence! how imperiously chaste is
your more modest face! but, O, how full of
ravishing attraction is your pretty, petulant,
languishing, lasciviously-composed countenance! these amorous smiles, those soul- [50
warming sparkling glances, ardent as those
flames that sing'd the world by heedless Phaeton! in body how delicate, in soul how witty, in
discourse how pregnant, in life how wary, in favours how judicious, in day how sociable, and [55
in night how — O pleasure unutterable! indeed, it is most certain, one man cannot deserve
only to enjoy a beauteous woman: but a
duchess! In despite of Phœbus, I 'll write a
sonnet instantly in praise of her.     *Exit.* [60

## SCENA SEXTA

### [*The Same*]

*Enter Ferneze ushering Aurelia, Emilia and
Maquerelle bearing up her train, Bianca attending: all go out but Aurelia, Maquerelle,
and Ferneze.*

*Aurel.*  And is 't possible?  Mendoza slight
me!  Possible?
*Fer.*  Possible!
What can be strange in him that 's drunk with
  favour,
Grows insolent with grace? — Speak, Maquerelle, speak.                                 5
*Maq.*  To speak feelingly, more, more richly
in solid sense than worthless words, give me
those jewels of your ears to receive my enforced
duty. As for my part, 't is well known I can
put up anything (*Ferneze privately feeds Ma-* [10
*querelle's hands with jewels during this speech*);
can bear patiently with any man: but when I
heard he wronged your precious sweetness, I
was enforced to take deep offence. 'T is most
certain he loves Emilia with high appetite: [15
and, as she told me (as you know we women
impart our secrets one to another), when she
repulsed his suit, in that he was possessed with
your endeared grace, Mendoza most ingrate-
fully renounced all faith to you.            20

*Fer.*  Nay, call'd you — Speak, Maquerelle,
  speak.
*Maq.*  By heaven, witch, dri'd biscuit; and
contested blushlessly he lov'd you but for a
spurt or so.
*Fer.*  For maintenance.                      25
*Maq.*  Advancement and regard.
*Aurel.*  O villain! O impudent Mendoza!
*Maq.*  Nay, he is the rustiest jade, the foul-
est-mouth'd knave in railing against our sex:
he will rail against women —               30
*Aurel.*  How? how?
*Maq.*  I am asham'd to speak 't, I.
*Aurel.*  I love to hate him: speak.
*Maq.*  Why, when Emilia scorn'd his base un-
steadiness, the black-throated rascal scolded,
and said —                                    36
*Aurel.*  What?
*Maq.*  Troth, 't is too shameless.
*Aurel.*  What said he?
*Maq.*  Why, that, at four, women were [40
fools; at fourteen, drabs; at forty, bawds; at
fourscore, witches; and at a hundred, cats.
*Aurel.*  O unlimitable impudency!
*Fer.*  But as for poor Ferneze's fixed heart,
Was never shadeless meadow drier parch'd  45
Under the scorching heat of heaven's dog,
Than is my heart with your enforcing eyes.
*Maq.*  A hot simile.
*Fer.*  Your smiles have been my heaven, your
  frowns my hell:
O, pity, then! grace should with beauty dwell. 50
*Maq.*  Reasonable perfect, by 'r lady.
*Aurel.*  I will love thee, be it but in de-
  spite
Of that Mendoza: — witch!    Ferneze, —
  witch! —
Ferneze, thou art the duchess' favourite:
Be faithful, private: but 't is dangerous.    55
*Fer.*  His love is lifeless that for love fears
  breath:
The worst that 's due to sin, O, would 't were
  death!
*Aurel.*  Enjoy my favour. I will be sick in-
stantly and take physic: therefore in depth of
night visit —                                  60
*Maq.*  Visit her chamber, but conditionally
you shall not offend her bed: by this diamond!
*Fer.*  By this diamond.     *Gives it to Maq.*
*Maq.*  Nor tarry longer than you please:
by this ruby!                                  65
*Fer.*  By this ruby.          *Gives again.*
*Maq.*  And that the door shall not creak.
*Fer.*  And that the door shall not creak.
*Maq.*  Nay, but swear.
*Fer.*  By this purse.       *Gives her his purse.*

---

**38 cornute:** make cuckold   **10 up:** (not in Q 2)   **10–11** S. D. (Marginal note in Qq.)   **28 rustiest:**
roughest, foulest   **42 at:** (not in Qq.)   **46 heaven's dog:** the dog star   **47 enforcing:** compelling
**61 conditionally:** on condition that

*Maq.* Go to, I 'll keep your oaths for you: [71 remember, visit.

*Enter Mendoza, reading a sonnet*

*Aurel.* Dried biscuit! — Look where the base wretch comes.                               74
*Men.* "Beauty's life, heaven's model, love's queen," —
*Maq.* That 's his Emilia.
*Men.* "Nature's triumph, best on earth," —
*Maq.* Meaning Emilia.                          79
*Men.* "Thou only wonder that the world hath seen." —
*Maq.* That 's Emilia.
*Aurel.* Must I, then, hear her prais'd? — Mendoza!
*Men.* Madam, your excellency is gra- [85 ciously encount'red: I have been writing passionate flashes in honour of —      *Exit Ferneze.*
*Aurel.* Out, villain, villain!
O judgment, where have been my eyes? what Bewitch'd election made me dote on thee?  90
What sorcery made me love thee? But, be gone; Bury thy head. O, that I could do more Than loathe thee! hence, worst of ill! No reason ask, our reason is our will.
                                   *Exit with Maquerelle.*
*Men.* Women! nay, Furies; nay, worse; [95 for they torment only the bad, but women good and bad. Damnation of mankind! Breath, hast thou prais'd them for this? and is 't you, Ferneze, are wriggled into smock-grace? Sit sure. O, that I could rail against these [100 monsters in nature, models of hell, curse of the earth, women! that dare attempt anything, and what they attempt they care not how they accomplish; without all premeditation or prevention; rash in asking, desperate in working, [105 impatient in suffering, extreme in desiring, slaves unto appetite, mistresses in dissembling, only constant in unconstancy, only perfect in counterfeiting; their words are feigned, their eyes forged, their sighs dissembled, their [110 looks counterfeit, their hair false, their given hopes deceitful, their very breath artificial; their blood is their only god; bad clothes and old age are only the devils they tremble at. That I could rail now!                          115

## SCENA SEPTIMA

*Enter Pietro, his sword drawn*

*Pietro.* A mischief fill thy throat, thou foul-jaw'd slave!
Say thy prayers.

*Men.*           I ha' forgot 'em.
*Pietro.*                        Thou shalt die.
*Men.* So shalt thou. I am heart-mad.
*Pietro.*                        I am horn-mad.
*Men.* Extreme mad.
*Pietro.*           Monstrously mad.
*Men.*                                Why?
*Pietro.* Why! thou, thou hast dishonoured my bed.                                         5
*Men.* I! Come, come, sit; here 's my bare heart to thee,
As steady as is the centre to this glorious world:
And yet, hark, thou art a cornuto, — but by me?
*Pietro.* Yes, slave, by thee.
*Men.* Do not, do not with tart and spleenful breath                                       10
Lose him can loose thee. I offend my duke!
Bear record, O ye dumb and raw-air'd nights,
How vigilant my sleepless eyes have been
To watch the traitor! Record, thou spirit of truth,
With what debasement I ha' thrown myself  15
To under offices, only to learn
The truth, the party, time, the means, the place,
By whom, and when, and where thou wert disgrac'd!
And am I paid with "slave"? Hath my intrusion
To places private and prohibited,           20
Only to observe the closer passages, —
Heaven knows with vows of revelation, —
Made me suspected, made me deem'd a villain?
What rogue hath wrong'd us?
*Pietro.*                   Mendoza, I may err.
*Men.* Err! 't is too mild a name: but err and err,                                        25
Run giddy with suspect, 'fore through me thou know
That which most creatures, save thyself, do know:
Nay, since my service hath so loath'd reject,
'Fore I 'll reveal, shalt find them clipp'd together.                                      29
*Pietro.* Mendoza, thou know'st I am a most plain-breasted man.
*Men.* The fitter to make a cuckold: would your brows were most plain too!
*Pietro.* Tell me: indeed, I heard thee rail —
*Men.* At women, true: why, what cold phlegm could choose,                                 35
Knowing a lord so honest, virtuous,
So boundless-loving, bounteous, fair-shap'd, sweet,

---

**87 flashes:** brief outbursts   **90 election:** choice   **99 smock-grace:** intimate favor   **104-105 prevention:** anticipation   **7 the, this:** ('this,' 'the' Qq.)   **10 spleenful:** angry   **16 under offices:** low tasks   **11 closer passages:** more secret incidents   **26 suspect:** suspicion   **28 reject:** rejection   **35 phlegm:** apathy

To be contemn'd, abus'd, defam'd, made cuckold?
Heart! I hate all women for 't: sweet sheets, [39
wax lights, antique bedposts, cambric smocks,
villainous curtains, arras pictures, oil'd hinges,
and all the tongue-tied lascivious witnesses of
great creatures' wantonness, — what salvation
can you expect?
*Pietro.* Wilt thou tell me?                     45
*Men.* Why, you may find it yourself; ob-
serve, observe.
*Pietro.* I ha' not the patience. Wilt thou
deserve me, tell — give it.
*Men.* Take 't: why, Ferneze is the man, [50
Ferneze: I 'll prove 't; this night you shall take
him in your sheets. Will 't serve?
*Pietro.* It will; my bosom 's in some peace:
till night —
*Men.* What?
*Pietro.* Farewell.
*Men.*            God! how weak a lord are you!
Why, do you think there is no more but so? 55
*Pietro.* Why!
*Men.* Nay, then, will I presume to counsel
you:
It should be thus. You with some guard upon
the sudden
Break into the princess' chamber: I stay be-
hind,
Without the door, through which he needs must
pass:                                            60
Ferneze flies; let him: to me he comes; he 's
kill'd
By me, observe, by me: you follow: I rail,
And seem to save the body. Duchess comes,
On whom (respecting her advanced birth,   64
And your fair nature), I know, nay, I do know,
No violence must be us'd; she comes: I storm,
I praise, excuse Ferneze, and still maintain
The duchess' honour; she for this loves me.
I honour you; shall know her soul, you mine:
Then naught shall she contrive in vengeance 70
(As women are most thoughtful in revenge)
Of her Ferneze, but you shall sooner know 't
Than she can think 't. Thus shall his death
come sure,
Your duchess brain-caught: so your life secure.
*Pietro.* It is too well: my bosom and my
heart.                                           75
When nothing helps, cut off the rotten part.
                                          *Exit.*
*Men.* Who cannot feign friendship can ne'er
produce the effects of hatred. Honest fool duke!

subtle lascivious duchess! silly novice Ferneze!
I do laugh at ye. My brain is in labour till it [80
produce mischief, and I feel sudden throes,
proofs sensible, the issue is at hand.
As bears shape young, so I 'll form my device,
Which grown proves horrid: vengeance makes
    men wise.                              [*Exit.*]

[SCENE VIII. — *The Same*]

*Enter Malevole and Passarello*

*Mal.* Fool, most happily encount'red: canst
sing, fool?
*Pass.* Yes, I can sing, fool, if you 'll bear the
burden; and I can play upon instruments. scurvily, as gentlemen do. O, that I had been [5
gelded! I should then have been a fat fool for
a chamber, a squeaking fool for a tavern, and
a private fool for all the ladies.
*Mal.* You are in good case since you came to
court, fool: what, guarded, guarded!        10
*Pass.* Yes, faith, even as footmen and bawds
wear velvet, not for an ornament of honour,
but for a badge of drudgery; for, now the duke
is discontented, I am fain to fool him asleep
every night.                                15
*Mal.* What are his griefs?
*Pass.* He hath sore eyes.
*Mal.* I never observed so much.
*Pass.* Horrible sore eyes; and so hath every
cuckold, for the roots of the horns spring in [20
the eyeballs, and that 's the reason the horn of
a cuckold is as tender as his eye, or as that
growing in the woman's forehead, twelve years
since, that could not endure to be touch'd. The
duke hangs down his head like a columbine. 25
*Mal.* Passarello, why do great men beg
fools?
*Pass.* As the Welshman stole rushes when
there was nothing else to filch: only to keep
begging in fashion.                          30
*Mal.* Pooh, thou givest no good reason;
thou speakest like a fool.
*Pass.* Faith, I utter small fragments, as your
knight courts your city widow with jingling of
his gilt spurs, advancing his bush-coloured [35
beard, and taking tobacco: this is all the mirror of their knightly complements. Nay, I shall
talk when my tongue is a-going once; 't is like
a citizen on horseback, evermore in a false
gallop.                                      40
*Mal.* And how doth Maquerelle fare now a
days?

---

⁴¹ **arras:** tapestry    ⁴⁹ **deserve me:** earn my favor    ⁷⁴ **brain-caught:** betrayed by deception
⁸² **sensible:** which can be felt    Sc. VIII: (Not in Q 1)    ⁹ **case:** condition    ¹⁰ **guarded:** with facings
on his fool's coat    ²³ **woman:** (described in a pamphlet printed in 1588)    ²⁶⁻²⁷ **beg fools:** sue for the
guardianship of idiots in order to get use of their revenues    ³⁴⁻³⁶ **with . . . beard:** ('with something
of his guilt: some aduauncing his high-coloured beard' some copies of Q 2)    ³⁷ **complements:** accomplishments

*Pass.* Faith, I was wont to salute her as our English women are at their first landing in Flushing; I would call her whore: but now [45 that antiquity leaves her as an old piece of plastic t' work by, I only ask her how her rotten teeth fare every morning, and so leave her. She was the first that ever invented perfum'd smocks for the gentlewomen, and [50 woollen shoes, for fear of creaking, for the visitant. She were an excellent lady, but that her face peeleth like Muscovy glass.

*Mal.* And how doth thy old lord, that hath wit enough to be a flatterer, and conscience enough to be a knave?        56

*Pass.* O, excellent: he keeps beside me fifteen jesters, to instruct him in the art of fooling, and utters their jests in private to the duke and duchess. He 'll lie like to your Switzer or [60 lawyer; he 'll be of any side for most money.

*Mal.* I am in haste, be brief.

*Pass.* As your fiddler when he is paid. — He 'll thrive, I warrant you, while your young courtier stands like Good Friday in Lent; [65 men long to see it, because more fatting days come after it; else he 's the leanest and pitiful'st actor in the whole pageant. Adieu, Malevole.

*Mal.* O world most vild, when thy loose vanities,        70
Taught by this fool, do make the fool seem wise!

*Pass.* You 'll know me again, Malevole.

*Mal.* O, ay, by that velvet.

*Pass.* Ay, as a pettifogger by his buckram bag. I am as common in the court as an [75 hostess's lips in the country; knights, and clowns, and knaves, and all share me; the court cannot possibly be without me. Adieu, Malevole.        [*Exeunt.*]

## ACTUS II. SCENA I

### [*The Duke's Palace*]

*Enter Mendoza, with a sconce, to observe Ferneze's entrance, who, whilst the act is playing, enter unbraced, two Pages before him with lights; is met by Maquerelle and conveyed in; the Pages are sent away.*

*Men.* He 's caught, the woodcock's head is i' th' noose.
Now treads Ferneze in dangerous path of lust,
Swearing his sense is merely deified:
The fool grasps clouds, and shall beget Centaurs;

And now, in strength of panting faint delight, 5
The goat bids heaven envy him. — Good goose,
I can afford thee nothing
But the poor comfort of calamity, pity.
Lust 's like the plummets hanging on clock-
lines,
Will ne'er ha' done till all is quite undone; 10
Such is the course salt, sallow lust doth run;
Which thou shalt try. I 'll be reveng'd. Duke,
thy suspect;
Duchess, thy disgrace; Ferneze, thy rivalship;
Shall have swift vengeance. Nothing so holy,
No band of nature so strong,        15
No law of friendship so sacred,
But I 'll profane, burst, violate, 'fore I 'll
Endure disgrace, contempt, and poverty.
Shall I, whose very "Hum" struck all heads
bare,
Whose face made silence, creaking of whose
shoe        20
Forc'd the most private passages fly ope,
Scrape like a servile dog at some latch'd door?
Learn now to make a leg, and cry "Beseech ye,
Pray ye, is such a lord within?" be aw'd
At some odd usher's scoff'd formality?        25
First sear my brains! *Unde cadis, non quo, re-
fert;*
My heart cries, "Perish all!" How! how! what
fate
Can once avoid revenge, that 's desperate? 28
I 'll to the duke; if all should ope — If! tush.
Fortune still dotes on those who cannot blush.
       [*Exit.*]

### SCENA SECUNDA

#### [*The Same*]

*Enter Malevole at one door; Bianca, Emilia, and Maquerelle at the other door*

*Mal.* Bless ye, cast o' ladies! — Ha, Dipsas! how dost thou, old coal?

*Maq.* Old coal!

*Mal.* Ay, old coal; methinks thou liest like a brand under billets of green wood. He [5 that will inflame a young wench's heart, let him lay close to her an old coal that hath first been fired, a panderess, my half-burnt lint, who though thou canst not flame thyself, yet art able to set a thousand virgins' tapers afire. [10 — And how doth Janivere thy husband, my little periwinkle? Is he troubled with the cough of the lungs still? Does he hawk o' nights still? He will not bite.

---

⁴⁵ **Flushing:** (in the hands of the English as security for a loan)    ⁴⁷ **plastic:** model in wax or clay
⁵³ **Muscovy glass:** talc (which peels off in flakes)    ⁷⁴ **pettifogger:** dishonest or inferior lawyer    **Sc. I**
s. d. **sconce:** lantern    **act:** music between the acts    ³ **merely:** absolutely    ⁹ **plummets:** weights
²³ **leg:** bow    ²⁵ **scoff'd:** derisive    ²⁶ **Unde . . . refert:** Whence you fall, not whither, is the thing
that matters.    ¹ **cast:** pair    **Dipsas:** cf. Lyly's *Endymion*    ¹¹ **Janivere:** January (with reference
to Chaucer's Merchant's Tale)

*Bian.*  No, by my troth, I took him with [15
his mouth empty of old teeth.

*Mal.*  And he took thee with thy belly full of
young bones: marry, he took his maim by the
stroke of his enemy.                                    19

*Bian.*  And I mine by the stroke of my friend.

*Mal.*  The close stock! O mortal wench!
Lady, ha' ye now no restoratives for your decayed Jasons? Look ye, crab's guts bak'd, distill'd ox-pith, the pulverized hairs of a lion's
upper-lip, jelly of cock-sparrows, he-mon- [25
key's marrow, or powder of fox-stones? — And
whither are you ambling now?

*Bian.*  To bed, to bed.

*Mal.*  Do your husbands lie with ye?

*Bian.*  That were country fashion, i' faith. 30

*Mal.*  Ha' ye no foregoers about you? Come,
whither in good deed, la now?

*Maq.*  In good indeed, la now, to eat the most
miraculously, admirably, astonishable-com-
pos'd posset with three curds, without any [35
drink. Will ye help me with a he-fox? — Here 's
the duke.                          *The Ladies go out.*

*Mal.* (*to Bianca.*)  Fri'd frogs are very good,
and Frenchlike too.

## SCENA TERTIA

### [*The Same*]

*Enter Duke Pietro, Count Celso, Count Equato,
Bilioso, Ferrard, and Mendoza*

*Pietro.*  The night grows deep and foul:
what hour is 't?

*Celso.*  Upon the stroke of twelve.

*Mal.*  Save ye, Duke!

*Pietro.*  From thee: begone, I do not love [5
thee! Let me see thee no more; we are displeas'd.

*Mal.*  Why, God be with thee! Heaven hear
my curse, — may thy wife and thee live long
together!                                              10

*Pietro.*  Begone, sirrah!

*Mal.*  "When Arthur first in court began,"
— Agamemnon — Menelaus — was ever any
duke a cornuto?

*Pietro.*  Begone, hence!                               15

*Mal.*  What religion wilt thou be of next?

*Men.*  Out with him!

*Mal.*  With most servile patience. — Time
will come
When wonder of thy error will strike dumb
Thy bezzled sense. —                                   20
Slaves! ay, favour: ay, marry, shall he rise:

Good God! how subtle hell doth flatter vice!
Mounts him aloft, and makes him seem to fly,
As fowl the tortoise mock'd, who to the sky
Th' ambitious shell-fish rais'd! The end of all
Is only, that from height he might dead fall. 26

*Bil.*  Why, when? Out, ye rogue! begone,
ye rascal!

*Mal.*  I shall now leave ye with all my best
wishes.                                                30

*Bil.*  Out, ye cur!

*Mal.*  Only let 's hold together a firm correspondence.

*Bil.*  Out!

*Mal.*  A mutual, friendly-reciprocal, per- [35
petual kind of steady-unanimous-heartily-
leagued —

*Bil.*  Hence, ye gross-jaw'd, peasantly — out,
go!

*Mal.*  Adieu, pigeon-house; thou burr, [40
that only stickest to nappy fortunes. The ser-
pigo, the strangury, an eternal uneffectual
priapism seize thee!

*Bil.*  Out, rogue!

*Mal.*  May'st thou be a notorious wittolly [45
pandar to thine own wife, and yet get no office,
but live to be the utmost misery of mankind, a
beggarly cuckold!                            *Exit.*

*Pietro.*  It shall be so.

*Men.*  It must be so, for where great states
revenge,                                               50
'T is requisite the parts be closely dogg'd,
(Which piety and soft respect forbears).
Lay one into his breast shall sleep with him,
Feed in the same dish, run in self-faction,
Who may discover any shape of danger;          55
For once disgrac'd, displayed in offence,
It makes man blushless, and man is (all confess)
More prone to vengeance than to gratefulness.
Favours are writ in dust; but stripes we feel
Depraved nature stamps in lasting steel.        60

*Pietro.*  You shall be leagued with the duchess.

*Equato.*  The plot is very good.

*Men.*  You shall both kill, and seem the corse
to save.

*Fer.*  A most fine brain-trick.                       65

*Celso.* (*tacite*)  Of a most cunning knave.

*Pietro.*  My lords, the heavy action we intend
Is death and shame, two of the ugliest shapes
That can confound a soul; think, think of it.
I strike, but yet, like him that 'gainst stone
walls                                                  70
Directs, his shafts rebound in his own face;

---

²¹ **stock:** stoccado (a thrust in fencing)   ²³⁻²⁶ **crab's . . . stones:** aphrodisiacs   ³¹ **foregoers:**
ushers (?)   ³³⁻³⁷ (Assigned to Bianca, Q 2)   ³⁸⁻³⁹ (Not in Q 1)   ¹² **When . . . began:** (the first line
of an old ballad; cf. *II Henry IV*, II. iv. 36)   ²⁰ **bezzled:** drunken   ²⁷⁻⁴⁸ (Not in Q 1)   ⁴¹⁻⁴² **ser-
pigo:** skin eruption   ⁵¹⁻⁵² **parts . . . forbears:** ('parts with piety and soft respect forbears, be closely
dogd' Qq.; some copies read "loft" or "lost" for "soft"; emended by Bullen)   ⁶⁶ **tacite:** aside
⁷¹ **Directs:** aims   **shafts:** arrows

My lady's shame is mine, O God, 't is mine!
Therefore I do conjure all secrecy:
Let it be as very little as may be,
Pray ye, as may be.                                    75
Make frightless entrance, salute her with soft
    eyes,
Stain naught with blood; only Ferneze dies,
But not before her brows. O gentlemen,
God knows I love her! Nothing else, but this:—
I am not well: if grief, that sucks veins dry, 80
Rivels the skin, casts ashes in men's faces,
Be-dulls the eye, unstrengthens all the blood,
Chance to remove me to another world,
As sure I once must die, let him succeed:
I have no child; all that my youth begot    85
Hath been your loves, which shall inherit me:
Which as it ever shall, I do conjure it,
Mendoza may succeed: he 's noble born;
With me of much desert.
    *Celso.* (*tacite*)  Much!                         90
    *Pietro.*  Your silence answers, "Ay."
I thank you.  Come on now.  O, that I might die
Before her shame 's display'd!  Would I were
    forc'd
To burn my father's tomb, unheal his bones,
And dash them in the dirt, rather than this! 95
This both the living and the dead offends:
Sharp surgery where naught but death amends.
                          *Exit with the others.*

## SCENA QUARTA

*[Maquerelle's Apartment]*

*Enter Maquerelle, Emilia, and Bianca with
        the posset*

*Maq.*  Even here it is, three curds in three regions individually distinct, most methodical,
according to art compos'd, without any drink.
    *Bian.*  Without any drink!
    *Maq.*  Upon my honour.  Will you sit and [5
eat?
    *Emil.*  Good; the composure, the receipt,
how is 't?
    *Maq.*  'T is a pretty pearl; by this pearl (how
does 't with me?) thus it is: seven and thirty [10
yolks of Barbary hens' eggs; eighteen spoonfuls
and a half of the juice of cock-sparrow bones;
one ounce, three drams, four scruples, and one
quarter of the syrup of Ethiopian dates;
sweetened with three quarters of a pound [15
of pure candied Indian eringoes; strewed over
with the powder of pearl of America, amber
of Cataia, and lamb-stones of Muscovia.
    *Bian.*  Trust me, the ingredients are very

cordial, and, no question, good, and most [20
powerful in restoration.
    *Maq.*  I know not what you mean by res-
toration; but this it doth,—it purifieth the
blood, smootheth the skin, enliveneth the eye,
strengtheneth the veins, mundifieth the teeth,
comforteth the stomach, fortifieth the back, [26
and quickeneth the wit; that 's all.
    *Emil.*  By my troth, I have eaten but two
spoonfuls, and methinks I could discourse most
swiftly and wittily already.                           30
    *Maq.*  Have you the art to seem honest?
    *Bian.*  Ay, thank advice and practice.
    *Maq.*  Why, then, eat me of this posset,
quicken your blood, and preserve your beauty.
Do you know Doctor Plaster-face? by this curd,
he is the most exquisite in forging of veins, [36
spright'ning of eyes, dying of hair, sleeking of
skins, blushing of cheeks, surphling of breasts,
blanching and bleaching of teeth, that ever
made an old lady gracious by torchlight; by
this curd, la.                                         41
    *Bian.*  Well, we are resolved, what God has
given us we 'll cherish.
    *Maq.*  Cherish anything saving your hus-
band; keep him not too high, lest he leap [45
the pale: but, for your beauty, let it be your
saint; bequeath two hours to it every morning
in your closet.  I ha' been young, and yet, in my
conscience, I am not above five-and-twenty:
but, believe me, preserve and use your beauty;
for youth and beauty once gone, we are like [51
beehives without honey, out-o'-fashion apparel
that no man will wear: therefore use me your
beauty.
    *Emil.*  Ay, but men say—                           55
    *Maq.*  Men say! let men say what they will:
life o' woman! they are ignorant of your wants.
The more in years, the more in perfection
they grow; if they lose youth and beauty, they
gain wisdom and discretion: but when our [60
beauty fades, good-night with us.  There cannot
be an uglier thing to see than an old woman:
from which, O pruning, pinching, and painting,
deliver all sweet beauties!     *[Music within.]*
    *Bian.*  Hark! music!                               65
    *Maq.*  Peace, 't is in the duchess' bed-cham-
ber.  Good rest, most prosperously-grac'd ladies.
    *Emil.*  Good-night, sentinel.
    *Bian.*  Night, dear Maquerelle.
                              *Exeunt all but Maq.*
    *Maq.*  May my posset's operation send you
my wit and honesty; and me, your youth [71
and beauty; the pleasing'st rest!     *Exit Maq.*

---

⁷³ conjure: appeal for     ⁷⁸ before her brows: in her sight     ⁸¹ Rivels: wrinkles     ⁹⁴ unheal:
uncover     ⁷ composure: composition     ⁹⁻¹⁰ how . . . me: how does it become me     ¹⁶ eringoes:
roots of sea holly     ²⁰ cordial: restorative     ²⁵ mundifieth: cleanseth     ³⁷ spright'ning: making bright
³⁸ surphling: treating with sulphur water or other cosmetics     ⁴² Well: ('We' Q 2)     ⁵⁰ use: invest,
put out at interest

## SCENA QUINTA

### [A Hall in the Palace]

#### A Song [within]

*Whilst the song is singing, enter Mendoza with
his sword drawn, standing ready to murder
Ferneze as he flies from the Duchess' chamber.*

*All.* [*within.*] Strike, strike!

*Aur.* [*within.*] Save my Ferneze! O, save
my Ferneze!

*Enter Ferneze in his shirt, and is received
upon Mendoza's sword.*

*All.* [*within.*] Follow, pursue!

*Aur.* [*within.*]        O, save Ferneze!

*Men.* Pierce, pierce! — Thou shallow fool,
drop there!

He that attempts a princess' lawless love    5

Must have broad hands, close heart, with
Argus' eyes,

And back of Hercules, or else he dies.

               *Thrusts his rapier in Fer.*

*Enter Aurelia, Duke Pietro, Ferrard, Bilioso,
Celso, and Equato*

*All.* Follow, follow!

*Men.* Stand off, forbear, ye most uncivil
lords!

*Pietro.* Strike!

*Men.* Do not; tempt not a man resolv'd: 10
     [*Mendoza bestrides the wounded body
         of Ferneze, and seems to save him.*]

Would you, inhuman murtherers, more than
death?

*Aur.* O poor Ferneze!

*Men.* Alas, now all defence too late!

*Aur.* He 's dead.

*Pietro.* I am sorry for our shame. — Go to
your bed:                    15

Weep not too much, but leave some tears to
shed

When I am dead.

*Aur.* What, weep for thee! my soul no tears
shall find.

*Pietro.* Alas, alas, that women's souls are
blind!

*Men.* Betray such beauty!           20

Murther such youth! Contemn civility!

He loves him not that rails not at him.

*Pietro.* Thou canst not move us: we have
blood enough. —

And please you, lady, we have quite forgot

All your defects: if not, why, then —     25

*Aur.* Not.

*Pietro.* Not: the best of rest: good-night.

       *Exit Pietro, with other Courtiers.*

*Aur.* Despite go with thee!

*Men.* Madam, you ha' done me foul disgrace; you have wrong'd him much loves [30
you too much: go to, your soul knows you have.

*Aur.* I think I have.

*Men.* Do you but think so?

*Aur.* Nay, sure, I have: my eyes have witnessed thy love: thou hast stood too firm for [35
me.

*Men.* Why, tell me, fair-cheek'd lady, who
even in tears art powerfully beauteous, what
unadvised passion struck ye into such a violent heat against me? Speak, what mis- [40
chief wrong'd us? What devil injur'd us?
Speak.

*Aur.* That thing ne'er worthy of the name of
man, Ferneze;

Ferneze swore thou lov'st Emilia;

Which to advance, with most reproachful
breath                        45

Thou both didst blemish and denounce my love.

*Men.* Ignoble villain! did I for this bestride

Thy wounded limbs? for this, rank opposite

Even to my sovereign? for this, O God, for this,

Sunk all my hopes, and with my hopes my
life?                          50

Ripp'd bare my throat unto the hangman's
axe? —

Thou most dishonour'd trunk! — Emilia!

By life, I know her not — Emilia —!

Did you believe him?

*Aur.*             Pardon me, I did.

*Men.* Did you? And thereupon you graced
him?                         55

*Aur.* I did.

*Men.* Took him to favour, nay even clasp'd
With him?

*Aur.*      Alas, I did!

*Men.*              This night?

*Aur.*                        This night.

*Men.* And in your lustful twines the duke
took you?

*Aur.* A most sad truth.

*Men.* O God, O God! how we dull honest
souls,                          60

Heavy-brain'd men, are swallow'd in the bogs

Of a deceitful ground, whilst nimble bloods,

Light-jointed spirits, speed; cut good men's
throats,

And scape! Alas, I am too honest for this age,

Too full of phlegm and heavy steadiness;    65

Stood still whilst this slave cast a noose about
me;

Nay, then to stand in honour of him and her,

Who had even slic'd my heart!

*Aur.*           Come, I did err,

And am most sorry I did err.

---

⁴⁸⁻⁴⁹ **for . . . sovereign:** (not in Q 2)
**'spent'** Q 2)         ⁴⁸ **rank:** take a stand        ⁶³ **speed:** ('pent' Q 1;

*Men.* Why, we are both but dead: the duke
 hates us;            70
And those whom princes do once groundly hate,
Let them provide to die, as sure as fate.
Prevention is the heart of policy.
 *Aur.* Shall we murder him?
 *Men.* Instantly?         75
 *Aur.* Instantly; before he casts a plot,
Or further blaze my honour's much-known blot,
Let 's murther him.
 *Men.* I would do much for you: will ye
 marry me?
 *Aur.* I 'll make thee duke. We are of Med-
 icis;             80
Florence our friend; in court my faction
Not meanly strengthful; the duke then dead;
We well prepar'd for change; the multitude
Irresolutely reeling; we in force;
Our party seconded; the kingdom maz'd;   85
No doubt of swift success all shall be grac'd.
 *Men.* You do confirm me, we are resolute:
To-morrow look for change: rest confident.
'T is now about the immodest waist of night:
The mother of moist dew with pallid light   90
Spreads gloomy shades about the numbed
 earth.
Sleep, sleep, whilst we contrive our mischief's
 birth.
This man I 'll get inhum'd. Farewell: to bed;
I kiss the pillow, dream the duke is dead.
So, so, good night.      *Exit Aurelia.*
  How fortune dotes on impudence!   95
I am in private the adopted son
Of yon good prince:
I must be duke: why, if I must, I must.
Most silly lord, name me! O heaven! I see
God made honest fools to maintain crafty
 knaves.           100
The duchess is wholly mine too; must kill her
 husband
To quit her shame. Much then marry her, I!
O, I grow proud in prosperous treachery!
As wrestlers clip, so I 'll embrace you all,
Not to support, but to procure your fall.   105

*Enter Malevole*

 *Mal.* God arrest thee!
 *Men.* At whose suit?
 *Mal.* At the devil's. Ah, you treacherous,
damnable monster, how dost? how dost, thou
treacherous rogue? Ah, ye rascal! I am [110
banish'd the court, sirrah.
 *Men.* Prithee, let 's be acquainted; I do
love thee, faith.

 *Mal.* At your service, by the Lord, la: shall 's
go to supper? Let 's be once drunk together, [115
and so unite a most virtuously-strengthened
friendship: shall 's, Huguenot? shall 's?
 *Men.* Wilt fall upon my chamber to-morrow morn?
 *Mal.* As a raven to a dunghill. They [120
say there 's one dead here: prick'd for the pride
of the flesh.
 *Men.* Ferneze: there he is; prithee, bury
him.
 *Mal.* O, most willingly: I mean to turn [125
pure Rochelle churchman, I.
 *Men.* Thou churchman! Why, why?
 *Mal.* Because I 'll live lazily, rail upon authority, deny kings' supremacy in things indifferent, and be a pope in mine own parish.   130
 *Men.* Wherefore dost thou think churches
were made?
 *Mal.* To scour plough-shares: I have seen
oxen plough up altars; *et nunc seges ubi Sion fuit.*
 *Men.* Strange!         135
 *Mal.* Nay, monstrous! I ha' seen a sumptuous steeple turned to a stinking privy; more
beastly, the sacred'st place made a dogs' kennel; nay, most inhuman, the stoned coffins of
long-dead Christians burst up, and made hogs'
troughs: *hic finis Priami.* Shall I ha' some [141
sack and cheese at thy chamber? Good night,
good mischievous incarnate devil; good night,
Mendoza; ah, you inhuman villain, good night!
night, fub.          145
 *Men.* Good night: to-morrow morn.
          *Exit Mendoza.*
 *Mal.* Ay, I will come, friendly damnation, I
will come. I do descry cross-points; honesty
and courtship straddle as far asunder as a true
Frenchman's legs.        150
 *Fer.* O!
 *Mal.* Proclamations! more proclamations!
 *Fer.* O! a surgeon!
 *Mal.* Hark! lust cries for a surgeon. What
news from Limbo? How doth the grand [155
cuckold, Lucifer?
 *Fer.* O, help, help! conceal and save me.
  *Ferneze stirs, and Malevole helps him*
    *up and conveys him away.*
 *Mal.* Thy shame more than thy wounds do
grieve me far:
Thy wounds but leave upon thy flesh some scar;
But fame ne'er heals, still rankles worse and
 worse;          160
Such is of uncontrolled lust the curse.
Think what it is in lawless sheets to lie;

---

71 **groundly:** thoroughly   72 **provide:** prepare   76 **casts:** devises   77 **blaze:** proclaim   82 **Not . . .**
**strengthful:** very strong   85 **maz'd:** confused   86 **of:** by   93 **inhum'd:** buried   102 **quit:** rid herself of   126 **Rochelle:** place of exile for persecuted Protestants   134 **et . . . fuit:** And now there is
corn where Sion was (Ovid).   141 **hic . . . Priami:** This is the end of Priam (*Æneid*, II, 554)
142 **sack:** sweet wine   145 **fub:** cheat   148 **cross-points:** tricks (*lit.,* a step in dancing)

But, O, Ferneze, what in lust to die!
Then thou that shame respects, O, fly converse
With women's eyes and lisping wantonness! 165
Stick candles 'gainst a virgin wall's white back,
If they not burn, yet at the least they 'll black.
Come, I 'll convey thee to a private port,
Where thou shalt live (O happy man!) from
    court.
The beauty of the day begins to rise,
From whose bright form night's heavy shadow
    flies.                                      171
Now 'gins close plots to work; the scene grows
    full,
And craves his eyes who hath a solid skull.
                                        *Exeunt.*

## ACTUS III.  SCENA I

*[The Duke's Palace]*

*Enter Pietro the Duke, Mendoza, Count Equato,
    and Bilioso*

*Pietro.*  'T is grown to youth of day: how
    shall we waste this light?
My heart 's more heavy than a tyrant's crown.
Shall we go hunt?  Prepare for field.
                                  *Exit Equato.*
*Men.*  Would ye could be merry!
*Pietro.*  Would God I could!  Mendoza, bid
    'em haste.              *Exit Mendoza.*  5
I would fain shift place; O vain relief!
Sad souls may well change place, but not change
    grief:
As deer, being struck, fly thorough many soils,
Yet still the shaft sticks fast, so ——
*Bil.*  A good old simile, my honest lord.  10
*Pietro.*  I am not much unlike to some sick
    man
That long desired hurtful drink; at last
Swills in and drinks his last, ending at once
Both life and thirst.  O, would I ne'er had
    known
My own dishonour!  Good God, that men
    should desire                               15
To search out that, which, being found, kills all
Their joy of life! to taste the tree of knowledge,
And then be driven from out paradise! ——
Canst give me some comfort?
*Bil.*  My lord, I have some books which [20
have been dedicated to my honour, and I ne'er
read 'em, and yet they had very fine names,
*Physic for Fortune, Lozenges of Sanctified Sin-
cerity;* very pretty works of curates, scriveners,
and schoolmasters.  Marry, I remember one [25
Seneca, Lucius Annæus Seneca ——
*Pietro.*  Out upon him! he writ of temperance

and fortitude, yet lived like a voluptuous epi-
cure, and died like an effeminate coward. —
Haste thee to Florence:                         30
Here, take our letters; see 'em seal'd; away!
Report in private to the honour'd duke
His daughter's forc'd disgrace; tell him at
    length
We know too much: due compliments advance:
There 's naught that 's safe and sweet but ig-
    norance.              *Exit Duke.*  35

*Enter Bilioso and Bianca*

*Bil.*  Madam, I am going ambassador for
Florence; 't will be great charges to me.
*Bian.*  No matter, my lord, you have the
lease of two manors come out next Christmas;
you may lay your tenants on the greater rack [40
for it: and when you come home again, I 'll
teach you how you shall get two hundred
pounds a-year by your teeth
*Bil.*  How, madam?
*Bian.*  Cut off so much from house-keep- [45
ing: that which is saved by the teeth, you know,
is got by the teeth.
*Bil.*  'Fore God, and so I may; I am in wondrous credit, lady.
*Bian.*  See the use of flattery: I did ever [50
counsel you to flatter greatness, and you have
profited well: any man that will do so shall be
sure to be like your Scotch barnacle, now a
block, instantly a worm, and presently a great
goose: this it is to rot and putrefy in the bosom
of greatness.                                   56
*Bil.*  Thou art ever my politician.  O, how
happy is that old lord that hath a politician in
his young lady!  I 'll have fifty gentlemen shall
attend upon me: marry, the most of them [60
shall be farmers' sons, because they shall bear
their own charges; and they shall go apparelled
thus, — in sea-water-green suits, ash-colour
cloaks, watchet stockings, and popinjay-green
feathers: will not the colours do excellent?  65
*Bian.*  Out upon 't! they 'll look like citizens
riding to their friends at Whitsuntide; their
apparel just so many several parishes.
*Bil.*  I 'll have it so; and Passarello, my fool,
shall go along with me; marry, he shall be in [70
velvet.
*Bian.*  A fool in velvet!
*Bil.*  Ay, 't is common for your fool to wear
satin; I 'll have mine in velvet.
*Bian.*  What will you wear, then, my lord? [75
*Bil.*  Velvet too; marry, it shall be embroidered, because I 'll differ from the fool somewhat.
I am horribly troubled with the gout: nothing
grieves me, but that my doctor hath forbidden

163 **port:** place of retreat    169 **from:** away from    8 **soils:** streams    24 **scriveners:** professional
**scribes**    33 **forc'd:** serious    36—176 (Not in Q 1)    37 **charges:** expense    39 **come out:** expire    53 **barnacle:** (This shell-fish was believed to turn into a wild goose.)    64 **watchet:** pale blue

me wine, and you know your ambassador |80 must drink. Didst thou ask thy doctor what was good for the gout?

*Bian.* Yes; he said, ease, wine, and women, were good for it.

*Bil.* Nay, thou hast such a wit! What was good to cure it, said he? 86

*Bian.* Why, the rack. All your empirics could never do the like cure upon the gout the rack did in England, or your Scotch boot. The French harlequin will instruct you. 90

*Bil.* Surely, I do wonder how thou, having for the most part of thy lifetime been a country body, shouldst have so good a wit.

*Bian.* Who, I? why, I have been a courtier thrice two months. 95

*Bil.* So have I this twenty year, and yet there was a gentleman-usher called me coxcomb t' other day, and to my face too: was 't not a backbiting rascal? I would I were better travell'd, that I might have been better acquainted with the fashions of several countrymen: |101 but my secretary, I think, he hath sufficiently instructed me.

*Bian.* How, my lord?

*Bil.* "Marry, my good lord," quoth he, |105 "your lordship shall ever find amongst a hundred Frenchmen forty hot-shots; amongst a hundred Spaniards, three-score braggarts; amongst a hundred Dutchmen, four-score drunkards; amongst a hundred Englishmen, four-score |110 and ten madmen; and amongst an hundred Welshmen" ——

*Bian.* What, my lord?

*Bil.* "Four-score and nineteen gentlemen."

*Bian.* But since you go about a sad embassy, I would have you go in black, my lord. 116

*Bil.* Why, dost think I cannot mourn, unless I wear my hat in cypress, like an alderman's heir? That 's vile, very old, in faith. 119

*Bian.* I 'll learn of you shortly: O, we should have a fine gallant of you, should not I instruct you! How will you bear yourself when you come into the Duke of Florence' court?

*Bil.* Proud enough, and 't will do well enough. As I walk up and down the chamber, I 'll |125 spit frowns about me, have a strong perfume in my jerkin, let my beard grow to make me look terrible, salute no man beneath the fourth button; and 't will do excellent.

*Bian.* But there is a very beautiful lady |130 there; how will you entertain her?

*Bil.* I 'll tell you that, when the lady hath

entertain'd me: but to satisfy thee, here comes the fool.

*Enter Passarello*

Fool, thou shalt stand for the fair lady. 135

*Pass.* Your fool will stand for your lady most willingly and most uprightly.

*Bil.* I 'll salute her in Latin.

*Pass.* O, your fool can understand no Latin.

*Bil.* Ay, but your lady can. 140

*Pass.* Why, then, if your lady take down your fool, your fool will stand no longer for your lady.

*Bil.* A pestilent fool! 'fore God, I think the world be turned upside down too. 145

*Pass.* O, no, sir; for then your lady and all the ladies in the palace should go with their heels upward, and that were a strange sight, you know. 149

*Bil.* There be many will repine at my preferment.

*Pass.* O, ay, like the envy of an elder sister, that hath her younger made a lady before her.

*Bil.* The duke is wondrous discontented.

*Pass.* Ay, and more melancholic than a |155 usurer having all his money out at the death of a prince.

*Bil.* Didst thou see Madam Floria to-day?

*Pass.* Yes, I found her repairing her face to-day; the red upon the white showed as if |160 her cheeks should have been served in for two dishes of barberries in stewed broth, and the flesh to them a woodcock.

*Bil.* A bitter fool! Come, madam, this night thou shalt enjoy me freely, and tomorrow |165 for Florence.

*Pass.* What a natural fool is he that would be a pair of bodies to a woman's petticoat, to be truss'd and pointed to them! Well, I 'll dog my lord; and the word is proper: for when I |170 fawn upon him, he feeds me; when I snap him by the fingers, he spits in my mouth. If a dog's death were not strangling, I had rather be one than a serving-man; for the corruption of coin is either the generation of a usurer or a lousy |175 beggar. [*Exeunt Bianca and Passarello.*]

## SCENA SECUNDA

### [*The Same*]

*Enter Malevole in some frieze gown, whilst Bilioso reads his patent*

*Mal.* I cannot sleep; my eyes' ill-neighbouring lids

87 empirics: a sect of physicians who drew their rules exclusively from experience    89 Scotch boot: an instrument of torture    90 harlequin: ('Herlakeene' Q 2)    101 several countrymen: men of different countries    107 hot-shots: reckless, hot-headed fellows    114 gentlemen: (The Welsh were inordinately proud of their pedigrees.)    118 cypress: crape    150–151 preferment: advancement (as ambassador)    163 ('Exit' Q 2)    164 fool: ('fowle' Q 2)    168 pair of bodies: bodice    169 truss'd and pointed: tied with "points" or laces    Sc. ii. S. D. frieze: coarse woollen cloth

Will hold no fellowship. O thou pale sober
  night,
Thou that in sluggish fumes all sense dost
  steep;
Thou that gives all the world full leave to
  play,
Unbend'st the feebled veins of sweaty labour!
The galley-slave, that all the toilsome day  6
Tugs at his oar against the stubborn wave,
Straining his rugged veins, snores fast;
The stooping scythe-man, that doth barb the
  field,
Thou mak'st wink sure: in night all creatures
  sleep;                                    10
Only the malcontent, that 'gainst his fate
Repines and quarrels, — alas, he 's goodman
  tell-clock!
His sallow jaw-bones sink with wasting moan;
Whilst others' beds are down, his pillow 's
  stone.
  *Bil.*  Malevole!                         15
  *Mal.*  Elder of Israel, thou honest defect of
wicked nature and obstinate ignorance, when
did thy wife let thee lie with her?
                              *To Bilioso.*
  *Bil.*  I am going ambassador to Florence.
  *Mal.*  Ambassador! Now, for thy country's
honour, prithee, do not put up mutton and [21
porridge in thy cloak-bag. Thy young lady
wife goes to Florence with thee too, does she
not?
  *Bil.*  No, I leave her at the palace.    25
  *Mal.*  At the palace! Now, discretion shield,
man! For God's love, let 's ha' no more cuckolds! Hymen begins to put off his saffron robe:
keep thy wife i' the state of grace. Heart o'
truth, I would sooner leave my lady singled [30
in a bordello than in the Genoa palace.
Sin there appearing in her sluttish shape,
Would soon grow loathsome, even to blushes'
  sense;
Surfeit would choke intemperate appetite,
Make the soul scent the rotten breath of lust: 35
When in an Italian lascivious palace,
A lady guardianless,
Left to the push of all allurement,
The strongest incitements to immodesty,
To have her bound, incens'd with wanton
  sweets,                                   40
Her veins fill'd high with heating delicates,
Soft rest, sweet music, amorous masquerers,
Lascivious banquets, sin itself gilt o'er,
Strong fantasy tricking up strange delights,
Presenting it dress'd pleasingly to sense,  45
Sense leading it unto the soul, confirm'd

With potent example, impudent custom,
Entic'd by that great bawd, Opportunity:
Thus being prepar'd, clap to her easy ear
Youth in good clothes, well-shap'd, rich,   50
Fair-spoken, promising, noble, ardent, blood-
  full,
Witty, flattering, — Ulysses absent,
O Ithaca, can chastest Penelope hold out?
  *Bil.*  Mass, I 'll think on 't. Farewell.
  *Mal.*  Farewell. Take thy wife with thee. 55
    Farewell.                     *Exit Bilioso.*
To Florence; um! it may prove good, it may!
And we may once unmask our brows.

### SCENA TERTIA

#### [*The Same*]

##### *Enter Count Celso*

  *Celso.*  My honour'd lord, —
  *Mal.*  Celso, peace! how is 't? Speak low:
  pale fears
Suspect that hedges, walls, and trees, have ears:
Speak, how runs all?
  *Celso.*  I' faith, my lord, that beast with
  many heads,                               5
The staggering multitude, recoils apace:
Though thorough great men's envy, most men's
  malice,
Their much-intemperate heat hath banish'd
  you,
Yet now they find envy and malice ne'er
Produce faint reformation.                  10
The duke, the too soft duke, lies as a block,
For which two tugging factions seem to saw;
But still the iron through the ribs they draw.
  *Mal.*  I tell thee, Celso, I have ever found
Thy breast most far from shifting cowardice 15
And fearful baseness: therefore I 'll tell thee,
  Celso,
I find the wind begins to come about;
I 'll shift my suit of fortune.
I know the Florentine, whose only force,
By marrying his proud daughter to this
  prince,                                   20
Both banish'd me and made this weak lord
  duke,
Will now forsake them all; be sure he will.
I 'll lie in ambush for conveniency,
Upon their severance to confirm myself.
  *Celso.*  Is Ferneze interr'd?             25
  *Mal.*  Of that at leisure: he lives.
  *Celso.*  But how stands Mendoza? How is 't
with him?
  *Mal.*  Faith, like a pair of snuffers, snibs filth
in other men, and retains it in himself.    30

---

⁹ **barb:** shave, mow   ²⁶ **shield:** forbid   ²⁸ **saffron:** (the usual color of Hymen's robe in masques)
³⁰ **singled:** alone   ³¹ **bordello:** brothel   ³² **there:** in the brothel   ³⁴ **choke:** ('cloke' Q 2)   ³⁸ **push:**
attack   ⁵³ **Ithaca, can:** ('Ithacan' Q 2)   ¹⁶ **fearful:** cowardly   ¹⁹ **only force:** power alone   ²⁴ **con-**
**firm:** strengthen (my position)   ²⁹ **snibs:** rebukes   ³⁰ **himself:** ('itself' Q 2)

*Celso.* He does fly from public notice, methinks, as a hare does from hounds; the feet
whereon he flies betrays him.

*Mal.* I can track him, Celso.
O, my disguise fools him most powerfully!    35
For that I seem a desperate malcontent,
He fain would clasp with me: he 's the true
    slave
That will put on the most affected grace
For some vilde second cause.            39

### *Enter Mendoza*

*Celso.* He 's here.
*Mal.* Give place.            *Exit Celso.*
Illo, ho, ho, ho! art there, old truepenny?
Where hast thou spent thyself this morning?
I see flattery in thine eyes, and damnation in
thy soul. Ha, thou huge rascal!        45
*Men.* Thou art very merry.
*Mal.* As a scholar, *futuens gratis.* How doth
the devil go with thee now?
*Men.* Malevole, thou art an arrant knave.
*Mal.* Who, I? I have been a sergeant, [50
man.
*Men.* Thou art very poor.
*Mal.* As Job, an alchemist, or a poet.
*Men.* The duke hates thee.
*Mal.* As Irishmen do bum-cracks.      55
*Men.* Thou hast lost his amity.
*Mal.* As pleasing as maids lose their virgin-
ity.
*Men.* Would thou wert of a lusty spirit!
Would thou wert noble!           60
*Mal.* Why, sure my blood gives me I am
noble, sure I am of noble kind; for I find myself possessed with all their qualities; — love
dogs, dice, and drabs, scorn wit in stuff-clothes;
have beat my shoemaker, knock'd my seam- [65
stress, cuckolded my 'pothecary, and undone
my tailor. Noble! why not? since the Stoic
said, *Neminem servum non ex regibus, neminem
regem non ex servis esse oriundum;* only busy
Fortune touses, and the provident Chances [70
blends them together. I 'll give you a simile:
did you e'er see a well with two buckets,
whilst one comes up full to be emptied, another
goes down empty to be filled? Such is the
state of all humanity. Why, look you, I [75
may be the son of some duke; for, believe
me, intemperate lascivious bastardy makes nobility doubtful: I have a lusty daring heart,
Mendoza.            79

*Men.* Let 's grasp; I do like thee infinitely.
Wilt enact one thing for me?
*Mal.* Shall I get it? [*Men.*] *gives him
his purse.* Command me; I am thy slave,
beyond death and hell.
*Men.* Murther the duke.        85
*Mal.* My heart's wish, my soul's desire, my
fantasy's dream, my blood's longing, the only
height of my hopes! How, O God, how! O,
how my united spirits throng together, to
strengthen my resolve!           90
*Men.* The duke is now a-hunting.
*Mal.* Excellent, admirable, as the devil
would have it! Lend me, lend me, rapier,
pistol, cross-bow: so, so, I 'll do it.
*Men.* Then we agree.           95
*Mal.* As Lent and fishmongers. Come, a-cap-
a-pe, how? Inform.
*Men.* Know that this weak-brain'd duke,
    who only stands
On Florence' stilts, hath out of witless zeal
Made me his heir, and secretly confirm'd    100
The wreath to me after his life's full point.
*Mal.* Upon what merit?
*Men.*        Merit! by heaven, I horn him.
Only Ferneze's death gave me state's life.
Tut, we are politic, he must not live now.   104
*Mal.* No reason, marry: but how must he
die now?
*Men.* My utmost project is to murder the
duke, that I might have his state, because he
makes me his heir; to banish the duchess, that
I might be rid of a cunning Lacedæmon- [110
ian, because I know Florence will forsake her;
and then to marry Maria, the banished Duke
Altofront's wife, that her friends might
strengthen me and my faction. This is all
law.            115
*Mal.* Do you love Maria?
*Men.* Faith, no great affection, but as wise
men do love great women, to ennoble their blood
and augment their revenue. To accomplish
this now, thus now. The duke is in the [120
forest, next the sea: single him, kill him, hurl
him in the main, and proclaim thou sawest
wolves eat him.
*Mal.* Um! Not so good. Methinks when
    he is slain,
To get some hypocrite, some dangerous
    wretch           125
That 's muffled o'er with feigned holiness,
To swear he heard the duke on some steep cliff

---

<sup>39</sup> **vilde:** vile    **second:** ulterior, subordinate
having sexual relations without pay    <sup>50</sup> **sergeant:** sheriff's officer    <sup>61</sup> **gives:** tells    <sup>64</sup> **stuff:** cloth
(not silk like those of courtiers)    <sup>66</sup> **cuckolded:** ('cuckold' Qq.)    <sup>67</sup> **Stoic:** Seneca (Epistle 45)
<sup>68–69</sup> **Neminem . . . oriundum:** There is no slave who is not descended from kings, no king who is not
descended from slaves.    <sup>70</sup> **touses:** pulls roughly about, maltreats    <sup>82</sup> **get:** gain    <sup>89</sup> **to:** ('so' Qq.)
<sup>96–97</sup> **a-cap . . . pe:** from head to foot    <sup>101</sup> **point:** conclusion    <sup>110–111</sup> **Lacedæmonian:** (slang for
"strumpet")    <sup>115</sup> **law:** positive    <sup>122</sup> **main:** sea

Lament his wife's dishonour, and, in an agony
Of his heart's torture, hurl'd his groaning sides
Into the swollen sea, — this circumstance   130
Well made sounds probable: and hereupon
The duchess ——
*Men.*      May well be banish'd:
O unpeerable invention! rare!
Thou god of policy! it honeys me.
*Mal.*   Then fear not for the wife of Alto-
front;                                      135
I 'll close to her.
*Men.*   Thou shalt, thou shalt.   Our excel-
lency is pleas'd:
Why wert not thou an emperor?   When we
Are duke, I 'll make thee some great man, sure.
*Mal.*   Nay.   Make me some rich knave, and
I 'll make myself                           140
Some great man.
*Men.*            In thee be all my spirit:
Retain ten souls, unite thy virtual powers:
Resolve; ha, remember greatness!   Heart, fare-
well;
The fate of all my hopes in thee doth dwell.
                                   [*Exit.*]

*Enter Celso*

*Mal.*   Celso, didst hear? — O heaven, didst
hear                                        145
Such devilish mischief?   Suffer'st thou the
world
Carouse damnation even with greedy swallow,
And still dost wink, still does thy vengeance
slumber?
If now thy brows are clear, when will they
thunder?                      *Exit* [*with Celso*].


SCENA QUARTA

[*A Forest near the Sea*]

*Enter Pietro, Ferrard, Prepasso,* **and**
*Three Pages*

*Fer.*   The dogs are at a fault.
                              *Cornets like horns.*
*Pietro.*   Would God nothing but the dogs
were at it!   Let the deer pursue safety, the
dogs follow the game, and do you follow the
dogs: as for me, 't is unfit one beast should [5
hunt another; I ha' one chaseth me.   An 't
please you, I would be rid of you a little.
*Fer.*   Would your grief would as soon leave
you as we to quietness!
*Pietro.*   I thank you.                    10
         *Exeunt* [*Ferrardo and Prepasso*].
Boy, what dost thou dream of now?

1 *Page.*   Of a dry summer, my lord; for
here 's a hot world towards: but, my lord, I
had a strange dream last night.
*Pietro.*   What strange dream?             15
1 *Page.*   Why, methought I pleased you with
singing, and then I dreamt you gave me that
short sword.
*Pietro.*   Prettily begg'd: hold thee, I 'll prove
thy dream true; take 't.   [*Giving sword.*] 20
1 *Page.*   My duty: but still I dreamt on, my
lord; and methought, an 't shall please your
excellency, you would needs out of your royal
bounty give me that jewel in your hat.
*Pietro.*   O, thou didst but dream, boy; do [25
not believe it: dreams prove not always true;
they may hold in a short sword, but not in a
jewel.   But now, sir, you dreamt you had
pleased me with singing; make that true, as
I have made the other.                      30
1 *Page.*   Faith, my lord, I did but dream,
and dreams, you say, prove not always true;
they may hold in a good sword, but not in a
good song.   The truth is, I ha' lost my voice.
*Pietro.*   Lost thy voice!   How?          35
1 *Page.*   With dreaming, faith: but here 's
a couple of sirenical rascals shall enchant ye.
What shall they sing, my good lord?
*Pietro.*   Sing of the nature of women: and
then the song shall be surely full of variety, [40
old crotchets, and most sweet closes; it shall
be humorous, grave, fantastic, amorous, melancholy, sprightly, one in all, and all in one.
1 *Page.*   All in one!
*Pietro.*   By 'r lady, too many.   Sing: my [45
speech grows culpable of unthrifty idleness:
sing.

*Song* [*by 2 and 3 Pages*]


SCENA QUINTA

[*The Same*]

*Enter Malevole, with cross-bow and pistol*

*Pietro.*   Ah, so, so, sing.   I am heavy: walk
off; I shall talk in my sleep: walk off.
                              *Exeunt Pages.*
*Mal.*   Brief, brief: who?   The Duke!   Good
heaven, that fools
Should stumble upon greatness! — Do not
sleep, duke;                                4
Give ye good-morrow.   I must be brief, duke;
I am fee'd to murther thee: — start not: —
Mendoza,
Mendoza hir'd me; here 's his gold, his pistol,
Cross-bow, and sword: 't is all as firm as earth.

---

**130** circumstance: detailed narration   **134** honeys: delights   **136** close to: come to terms with
**142** virtual: morally virtuous, powerful   **3** safety: ('safely' Qq.)   **21** duty: thanks   **37** sirenical:
siren-like, alluring   **41** crotchets: quarter-notes   closes: conclusions   **46** idleness: frivolity
Sc. V.   **5** I: ('You' Q 2)

O fool, fool, chok'd with the common maze
Of easy idiots, credulity! 10
Make him thine heir! What, thy sworn mur-
therer!
*Pietro.* O, can it be?
*Mal.* Can!
*Pietro.* Discover'd he not Ferneze?
*Mal.* Yes, but why? but why? For love to
thee? 15
Much, much! To be reveng'd upon his rival,
Who had thrust his jaws awry;
Who being slain, suppos'd by thine own hands,
Defended by his sword, made thee most loath-
some,
Him most gracious with thy loose princess: 20
Thou, closely yielding egress and regress to her,
Madest him heir; whose hot unquiet lust
Straight tous'd thy sheets, and now would seize
thy state.
Politician! Wise man! Death! to be
Led to the stake like a bull by the horns; 25
To make even kindness cut a gentle throat!
Life, why art thou numb'd? Thou foggy dul-
ness, speak:
Lives not more faith in a home-thrusting tongue
Than in these fencing tip-tap courtiers?

*Enter Celso, with a hermit's gown and beard*

*Pietro.* Lord Malevole, if this be true —
*Mal.* If! Come, shade thee with this dis- [31
guise. If! Thou shalt handle it; he shall
thank thee for killing thyself. Come, follow my
directions, and thou shalt see strange sleights.
*Pietro.* World, whither wilt thou? 35
*Mal.* Why, to the devil. Come, the morn
grows late:
A steady quickness is the soul of state.
*Exeunt.*

## ACTUS QUARTUS. SCE[NA] PRIMA

[*The Duke's Palace*]

*Enter Maquerelle, knocking at the ladies' door*

*Maq.* Medam, medam, are you stirring, medam? If you be stirring, medam, — if I
thought I should disturb ye —

[*Enter Page*]

*Page.* My lady is up, forsooth.
*Maq.* A pretty boy, faith: how old art thou?
*Page.* I think, fourteen. 6
*Maq.* Nay, an ye be in the teens — are ye
a gentleman born? Do you know me? My
name is Medam Maquerelle; I lie in the old
Cunnycourt. 10

*Enter Bianca and Emilia*

[*Page.*] See, here the ladies.
*Bian.* A fair day to ye, Maquerelle.
*Emil.* Is the duchess up yet, sentinel?
*Maq.* O ladies, the most abominable mischance! O dear ladies, the most piteous dis- [15
aster! Ferneze was taken last night in the
duchess' chamber. Alas, the duke catch'd him
and kill'd him!
*Bian.* Was he found in bed?
*Maq.* O, no; but the villainous certainty [20
is, the door was not bolted, the tongue-tied
hatch held his peace: so the naked troth is,
he was found in his shirt, whilst I, like an
arrant beast, lay in the outward chamber,
heard nothing; and yet they came by me in [25
the dark, and yet I felt them not, like a senseless creature as I was. O beauties, look to
your busk-points; if not chastely, yet charily:
be sure the door be bolted. — Is your lord gone
to Florence? 30
*Bian.* Yes, Maquerelle.
*Maq.* I hope you 'll find the discretion to
purchase a fresh gown for his return. — Now,
by my troth, beauties, I would ha' ye once
wise. He loves ye; pish! He is witty; bub- [35
ble! Fair-proportioned; mew! Nobly-born!
wind! Let this be still your fix'd position:
esteem me every man according to his good
gifts, and so ye shall ever remain most dear,
and most worthy to be most dear ladies. 40
*Emil.* Is the duke return'd from hunting
yet?
*Maq.* They say not yet.
*Bian.* 'T is now in midst of day.
*Emil.* How bears the duchess with this blemish now?
*Maq.* Faith, boldly; strongly defies defame,
as one that has a duke to her father. And [46
there 's a note to you: be sure of a stout friend
in a corner, that may always awe your husband. Mark the haviour of the duchess now:
she dares defame; cries, "Duke, do what thou
canst, I 'll quit mine honour:" nay, as one [51
confirmed in her own virtue against ten thousand mouths that mutter her disgrace, she 's
presently for dances.

*Enter Ferrard*

*Bian.* For dances! 55
*Maq.* Most true.
*Emil.* Most strange. See, here 's my servant, young Ferrard. How many servants
think'st thou I have, Maquerelle?

---

²¹ **closely:** secretly   ²³ **tous'd:** rumpled   ³⁰ **Pietro:** ('Cel.' Qq.)   ³⁴ **sleights:** tricks   ⁹ **lie:**
lodge, live   ²⁶⁻²⁷ **senseless:** without feeling   ²⁸ **busk-points:** laces fastening the stays   ³⁹⁻⁴⁰ **most . . .**
**ladies:** (Quoted from Sidney's Dedication of the *Arcadia*.)   ⁴⁵ **defame:** infamy   ⁴⁷ **note:** piece of
advice   ⁵⁰ **dares:** defies   ⁵¹ **quit:** clear   ⁵⁷⁻⁵⁸ **servant:** lover

*Maq.* The more, the merrier. 'T was well [60
said, use your servants as you do your smocks;
have many, use one, and change often; for
that 's most sweet and courtlike.

*Fer.* Save ye, fair ladies! Is the duke return'd?

*Bian.* Sweet sir, no voice of him as yet in
court.    65

*Fer.* 'T is very strange.

*Bian.* And how like you my servant, Maquerelle?

*Maq.* I think he could hardly draw Ulysses'
bow; but, by my fidelity, were his nose nar-
rower, his eyes broader, his hands thinner, [70
his lips thicker, his legs bigger, his feet lesser,
his hair blacker, and his teeth whiter, he were
a tolerable sweet youth, i' faith. And he will
come to my chamber, I will read him the fortune of his beard.    *Cornets sound.*  75

*Fer.* Not yet return'd! I fear — but the
duchess approacheth.

## SCENA SECUNDA

### [*The Same*]

*Enter Mendoza supporting the Duchess, Guer-
rino: the ladies that are on the stage rise:
Ferrard ushers in the Duchess, and then
takes a lady to tread a measure.*

*Aur.* We will dance: music! — we will dance.

*Guer.* *Les quanto*, lady, *Pensez bien, Passa
regis*, or *Bianca's brawl?*

*Aur.* We have forgot the brawl.

*Fer.* So soon? 'T is wonder.    5

*Guer.* Why, 't is but two singles on the left,
two on the right, three doubles forward, a traverse of six round: do this twice, three singles
side, galliard trick-of-twenty, coranto-pace; a
figure of eight, three singles broken down, [10
come up, meet, two doubles, fall back, and then
honour.

*Aur.* O Dædalus, thy maze! I have quite
forgot it.

*Maq.* Trust me, so have I, saving the falling-
back, and then honour.    16

#### Enter Prepasso

*Aur.* Music, music!

*Prep.* Who saw the duke? the duke?

#### Enter Equato

*Aur.* Music!

*Equato.* The duke? is the duke returned? 20

*Aur.* Music!

#### Enter Celso

*Celso.* The duke is either quite invisible, or
else is not.

Sc. II. s. d. **measure:** slow dance

*Aur.* We are not pleased with your intrusion
upon our private retirement; we are not [25
pleased: you have forgot yourselves.

#### Enter a Page

*Celso.* Boy, thy master? Where 's the duke?

*Page.* Alas, I left him burying the earth with
his spread joyless limbs: he told me he was
heavy, would sleep; bid me walk off, for [30
that the strength of fantasy oft made him talk
in his dreams. I straight obeyed, nor ever saw
him since: but whereso'er he is, he 's sad.

*Aur.* Music, sound high, as is our heart!
Sound high!    35

## SCENA TERTIA

### [*The Same*]

*Enter Malevole, and Pietro disguised like an
hermit*

*Mal.* The duke, — peace! — the duke is dead.

*Aur.* Music!

*Mal.* Is 't music?

*Men.* Give proof.

*Fer.* How?    5

*Celso.* Where?

*Prep.* When?

*Mal.* Rest in peace, as the duke does:
quietly sit: for my own part, I beheld him but
dead; that 's all. Marry, here 's one can [10
give you a more particular account of him.

*Men.* Speak, holy father, nor let any brow
Within this presence fright thee from the truth.
Speak confidently and freely.

*Aur.*                    We attend.

*Pietro.* Now had the mounting sun's all-
ripening wings    15
Swept the cold sweat of night from earth's dank
breast,
When I, whom men call Hermit of the Rock,
Forsook my cell, and clamber'd up a cliff,
Against whose base the heady Neptune dash'd
His high-curl'd brows; there 't was I eas'd my
limbs:    20
When, lo! my entrails melted with the moan
Some one, who far 'bove me was climb'd, did
make —
I shall offend.

*Men.* Not.

*Aur.* On.    25

*Pietro.* Methinks I hear him yet: — "O fe-
male faith!
Go sow the ingrateful sand, and love a woman!
And do I live to be the scoff of men?
To be the wittol-cuckold, even to hug
My poison? Thou knowest, O truth!    30
Sooner hard steel will melt with southern wind,
A seaman's whistle calm the ocean,

²⁻³ **Les . . . brawl:** names of dances

A town on fire be extinct with tears,
Than women, vow'd to blushless impudence,
With sweet behaviour and soft minioning      35
Will turn from that where appetite is fix'd.
O powerful blood! how thou dost slave their
     soul!
I wash'd an Ethiop, who, for recompense,
Sullied my name: and must I, then, be forc'd   39
To walk, to live thus black? Must! must! fie!
He that can bear with 'must,' he cannot die."
With that he sigh'd so passionately deep,
That the dull air even groan'd: at last he cries,
"Sink shame in seas, sink deep enough!" So
     dies;
For then I view'd his body fall, and souse    45
Into the foamy main. O, then I saw,
That which methinks I see! it was the duke;
Whom straight the nicer-stomach'd sea belch'd
     up:
But then ——
     *Mal.* Then came I in; but, 'las, all was too
     late!                                     50
For even straight he sunk.
     *Pietro.*          Such was the duke's sad fate.
     *Celso.* A better fortune to our Duke Men-
     doza!
     *Omnes.* Mendoza!          *Cornets flourish.*
     *Men.* A guard, a guard!

                    *Enter a Guard*
                         We, full of hearty tears,
For our good father's loss,                    55
(For so we well may call him
Who did beseech your loves for our succession),
Cannot so lightly over-jump his death
As leave his woes revengeless. — *To Aurelia.*
     Woman of shame,
We banish thee for ever to the place          60
From whence this good man comes; nor permit,
On death, unto thy body any ornament;
But, base as was thy life, depart away.
     *Aur.* Ungrateful!
     *Men.* Away!                              65
     *Aur.* Villain, hear me!

*Prepasso and Guerrino lead away the Duchess.*

     *Men.* Begone! My lords,
Address to public council; 't is most fit:
The train of fortune is borne up by wit.
Away! our presence shall be sudden; haste.    70
          *All depart saving Mendoza, Malevole,*
               *and Pietro.*
     *Mal.* Now, you egregious devil! Ha, ye
murthering politician! How dost, duke? How
dost look now? Brave duke, i' faith.

     *Men.* How did you kill him?
     *Mal.* Slatted his brains out, then sous'd
him in the briny sea.                          76
     *Men.* Brain'd him, and drown'd him too?
     *Mal.* O 't was best, sure work; for he that
strikes a great man, let him strike home, or
else 'ware, he 'll prove no man. Shoulder [80
not a huge fellow, unless you may be sure to
lay him in the kennel.
     *Men.* A most sound brain-pan! I 'll make
you both emperors.
     *Mal.* Make us Christians, make us Chris-
tians.                                         86
     *Men.* I 'll hoist ye, ye shall mount.
     *Mal.* To the gallows, say ye? Come: *præ-*
*mium incertum petit, certum scelus.* How stands
the progress?                                  90
     *Men.* Here, take my ring unto the citadel;
                              [*Giving ring.*]
Have entrance to Maria, the grave duchess
Of banish'd Altofront. Tell her we love her;
Omit no circumstance to grace our person:
     do 't.
     *Mal.* I 'll make an excellent pandar: duke,
farewell; 'dieu, adieu, duke.                  96
     *Men.* Take Maquerelle with thee; for 't is
     found
None cuts a diamond but a diamond.
                         *Exit Malevole.*
                              Hermit,
Thou art a man for me, my cónfessor:
O thou selected spirit, born for my good,     100
Sure thou wouldst make
An excellent elder in a deform'd church.
Come, we must be inward, thou and I all
     one.
     *Pietro.* I am glad I was ordained for ye.
     *Men.* Go to, then; thou must know that [105
Malevole is a strange villain; dangerous, very
dangerous: you see how broad 'a speaks; a
gross-jaw'd rogue: I would have thee poison
him: he 's like a corn upon my great toe, I
cannot go for him; he must be cored out, [110
he must. Wilt do 't, ha?
     *Pietro.* Anything, anything.
     *Men.* Heart of my life! thus, then, to the
     citadel
Thou shalt consort with this Malevole;
There being at supper, poison him. It shall
     be laid                                   115
Upon Maria, who yields love or dies.
Scud quick.
     *Pietro.* Like lightning: good deeds crawl,
     but mischief flies.          *Exit Pietro.*

---

³³ **extinct:** extinguished    ⁴² **so:** ('too' Q 2)    ⁴⁵ **souse:** fall (as a hawk on its prey)    ⁵⁸ **over-**
jump: pass over    ⁶² **thy:** ('the' Qq.)    ⁶⁸ **Address to:** prepare for    ⁷⁵ **Slatted:** dashed    ⁸² **kennel:**
gutter    ⁸⁸⁻⁸⁹ **præmium . . . scelus:** He seeks an uncertain reward, but certain guilt.    ⁹⁴ **circum-**
**stance:** detail    ¹⁰³ **inward:** intimate    ¹⁰⁷ **broad:** without restraint    ¹¹⁸ **Like lightning:** (in line
117, Q 2)

*Enter Malevole*

*Mal.* Your devilship's ring has no virtue: the buff-captain, the sallow Westphalian [120 gammon-faced zaza cries, "Stand out!" Must have a stiffer warrant, or no pass into the castle of comfort.

*Men.* Command our sudden letter. — Not enter, sha't? what place is there in Genoa [125 but thou shalt? Into my heart, into my very heart: come, let 's love: we must love, we two, soul and body.

*Mal.* How didst like the hermit? A strange hermit, sirrah. 130

*Men.* A dangerous fellow, very perilous. He must die.

*Mal.* Ay, he must die.

*Men.* Thou 'st kill him. We are wise; we must be wise. 135

*Mal.* And provident.

*Men.* Yea, provident: beware an hypocrite; A churchman once corrupted, O, avoid! A fellow that makes religion his stalking-horse. He breeds a plague. Thou shalt poison him. 140

*Mal.* Ho, 't is wondrous necessary: how?

*Men.* You both go jointly to the citadel; There sup, there poison him: and Maria, Because she is our opposite, shall bear The sad suspect; on which she dies or loves us. 145

*Mal.* I run. *Exit Malevole.*

*Men.* We that are great, our sole self-good still moves us. They shall die both, for their deserts craves more Than we can recompense: their presence still Imbraids our fortunes with beholdingness, 150 Which we abhor; like deed, not doer: then conclude, They live not to cry out "Ingratitude!" One stick burns t' other, steel cuts steel alone: 'T is good trust few; but, O, 't is best trust none! *Exit Mendoza.*

## SCENA QUARTA

### [*Court of the Palace*]

*Enter Malevole and Pietro, still disguised, at several doors*

*Mal.* How do you? How dost, duke?

*Pietro.* O, let The last day fall! drop, drop on our curs'd heads! Let heaven unclasp itself, vomit forth flames.

*Mal.* O, do not rant, do not turn player; [5 there 's more of them than can well live one by another already. What, art an infidel still?

*Pietro.* I am amaz'd, struck in a swoon with wonder. I am commanded to poison thee —

*Mal.* I am commanded to poison thee at [10 supper —

*Pietro.* At supper.

*Mal.* In the citadel —

*Pietro.* In the citadel.

*Mal.* Cross capers! tricks! Truth o' [15 heaven! he would discharge us as boys do eldern guns, one pellet to strike out another. Of what faith art now?

*Pietro.* All is damnation; wickedness extreme: There is no faith in man. 20

*Mal.* In none but usurers and brokers; they deceive no man: men take 'em for bloodsuckers, and so they are. Now, God deliver me from my friends!

*Pietro.* Thy friends! 25

*Mal.* Yes, from my friends; for from mine enemies I 'll deliver myself. O, cut-throat friendship is the rankest villainy! Mark this Mendoza; mark him for a villain: but heaven will send a plague upon him for a rogue. 30

*Pietro.* O world!

*Mal.* World! 't is the only region of death, the greatest shop of the devil; the cruel'st prison of men, out of the which none pass without paying their dearest breath for a fee; [35 there 's nothing perfect in it but extreme, extreme calamity, such as comes yonder.

## SCENA QUINTA

### [*The Same*]

*Enter Aurelia, two halberts before and two after, supported by Celso and Ferrard; Aurelia in base mourning attire*

*Aur.* To banishment! led on to banishment!

*Pietro.* Lady, the blessedness of repentance to you!

*Aur.* Why, why, I can desire nothing but death, Nor deserve anything but hell. 5 If heaven should give sufficiency of grace To clear my soul, it would make heaven graceless: My sins would make the stock of mercy poor; O, they would tire heaven's goodness to reclaim them! Judgment is just, yet from that vast villain! 10

---

¹²⁰ **buff-:** leather (from the material of his jerkin)   ¹²¹ **zaza:** bully   ¹²⁴ **sudden:** immediate
¹²⁵ **sha't:** shalt thou   ¹³⁴ **Thou'st:** thou must   ¹³⁹ ('Shoots under his belly' marginal note in Qq.)
¹⁴⁴ **opposite:** opponent   ¹⁵⁰ **Imbraids:** upbraids   **beholdingness:** indebtedness   ⁵ **rant:** ('rand'
**Q 2)**   ¹⁷ **eldern guns:** popguns of elder wood   Sc. V. s. D. **halberts:** guards armed with halberts

But, sure, he shall not miss sad punishment
'Fore he shall rule. — On to my cell of shame!
   *Pietro.* My cell 't is, lady; where, instead of
     masks,
Music, tilts, tourneys, and such court-like
     shows,
The hollow murmur of the checkless winds  15
Shall groan again; whilst the unquiet sea
Shakes the whole rock with foamy battery.
There usherless the air comes in and out:
The rheumy vault will force your eyes to weep,
Whilst you behold true desolation.     20
A rocky barrenness shall pierce your eyes,
Where all at once one reaches where he stands,
With brows the roof, both walls with both his
     hands.
   *Aur.* It is too good. — Bless'd spirit of my
     lord,
O, in what orb soe'er thy soul is thron'd,   25
Behold me worthily most miserable!
O, let the anguish of my contrite spirit
Entreat some reconciliation!
If not, O, joy, triumph in my just grief!
Death is the end of woes and tears' relief.   30
   *Pietro.* Belike your lord not lov'd you, was
     unkind.
   *Aur.* O heaven!
As the soul loves the body, so lov'd he:
'T was death to him to part my presence, heaven
To see me pleas'd.     35
Yet I, like to a wretch given o'er to hell,
Brake all the sacred rites of marriage,
To clip a base ungentle faithless villain;
O God! a very pagan reprobate —
What should I say? ungrateful, throws me out, 40
For whom I lost soul, body, fame, and honour.
But 't is most fit: why should a better fate
Attend on any who forsake chaste sheets;
Fly the embrace of a devoted heart,
Join'd by a solemn vow 'fore God and man,  45
To taste the brackish flood of beastly lust
In an adulterous touch? O ravenous immodesty!
Insatiate impudence of appetite!
Look, here 's your end; for mark, what sap in
     dust,
What good in sin, even so much love in lust.  50
Joy to thy ghost, sweet lord! pardon to me!
   *Celso.* 'T is the duke's pleasure this night
you rest in court.
   *Aur.* Soul, lurk in shades; run, shame, from
     brightsome skies;
In night the blind man misseth not his eyes.  55
     *Exit [with Celso, Ferrardo, and halberts].*
   *Mal.* Do not weep, kind cuckold: take
comfort, man; thy betters have been beccos:

Agamemnon, emperor of all the merry Greeks,
that tickled all the true Trojans, was a cornuto; Prince Arthur, that cut off twelve [60
kings' beards, was a cornuto; Hercules, whose
back bore up heaven, and got forty wenches
with child in one night, —
   *Pietro.* Nay, 't was fifty.
   *Mal.* Faith, forty 's enow, o' conscience, [65
— yet was a cornuto. Patience; mischief
grows proud: be wise.
   *Pietro.* Thou pinchest too deep; art too
keen upon me.
   *Mal.* Tut, a pitiful surgeon makes a dan- [70
gerous sore; I 'll tent thee to the ground.
Thinkest I 'll sustain myself by flattering thee,
because thou art a prince? I had rather follow
a drunkard, and live by licking up his vomit,
than by servile flattery.     75
   *Pietro.* Yet great men ha' done 't.
   *Mal.* Great slaves fear better than love:
born naturally for a coal-basket; though the
common usher of princes' presence, Fortune,
hath blindly given them better place. I am [80
vowed to be thy affliction.
   *Pietro.* Prithee, be:
I love much misery, and be thou son to me.
   *Mal.* Because you are an usurping duke. —

      *Enter Bilioso*

Your lordship 's well returned from Florence.
                       *To Bilioso.*
   *Bil.* Well return'd, I praise my horse.   86
   *Mal.* What news from the Florentines?
   *Bil.* I will conceal the great duke's pleasure;
only this was his charge: his pleasure is, that
his daughter die; Duke Pietro be banished [90
for publishing his blood's dishonour; and that
Duke Altofront be re-accepted. This is all:
but I hear Duke Pietro is dead.
   *Mal.* Ay, and Mendoza is duke: what will
you do?     95
   *Bil.* Is Mendoza strongest?
   *Mal.* Yet he is.
   *Bil.* Then yet I 'll hold with him.
   *Mal.* But if that Altofront should turn
straight again?     100
   *Bil.* Why, then, I would turn straight again.
'T is good run still with him that has most
     might:
I had rather stand with wrong, than fall with
     right.
   *Mal.* What religion will you be of now?
   *Bil.* Of the Duke's religion, when I know
what it is.     106
   *Mal.* O Hercules!

---

<sup></sup>**17 battery:** battering     **19 rheumy:** inducing rheum or tears   **33 loves:** ('lov'd' Qq.)   **34 part:**
leave   **46 brackish:** salt, licentious   **flood:** ('bloud' Qq.)   **48 impudence:** shamelessness   **50 good**
**in sin:** ('sinne in good' Qq.)   **71 tent:** probe   **78 for . . . basket:** for menial employment   **91 pub-**
**lishing:** ('banishing' Qq.)

*Bil.* Hercules! Hercules was the son of Jupiter and Alcmena.

*Mal.* Your lordship is a very wit-all.    110

*Bil.* Wittal!

*Mal.* Aye, all-wit.

*Bil.* Amphitryo was a cuckold.

*Mal.* Your lordship sweats; your young lady will get you a cloth for your old wor- [115 ship's brows. (*Exit Bilioso.*) Here 's a fellow to be damned: this is his inviolable maxim, — flatter the greatest and oppress the least: a whoreson flesh-fly, that still gnaws upon the lean gall'd backs.    120

*Pietro.* Why dost, then, salute him?

*Mal.* I 'faith, as bawds go to church, for fashion sake. Come, be not confounded; thou art but in danger to lose a dukedom. Think this: — this earth is the only grave and [125 Golgotha wherein all things that live must rot; 't is but the draught wherein the heavenly bodies discharge their corruption; the very muck-hill on which the sublunary orbs cast their excrements: man is the slime of this [130 dung pit, and princes are the governors of these men; for, for our souls, they are as free as emperors, all of one piece; there goes but a pair of sheers betwixt an emperor and the son of a bagpiper; only the dyeing, [135 dressing, pressing, glossing, makes the difference.

Now, what art thou like to lose?

A jailer's office to keep men in bonds,

Whilst toil and treason all life's good confounds.    140

*Pietro.* I here renounce for ever regency:

O Altofront, I wrong thee to supplant thy right,

To trip thy heels up with a devilish sleight!

For which I now from throne am thrown: world-tricks abjure;

For vengeance, though 't comes slow, yet it comes sure.    145

O, I am chang'd! for here, 'fore the dread power,

In true contrition, I do dedicate

My breath to solitary holiness,

My lips to prayer, and my breast's care shall be,

Restoring Altofront to regency.    150

*Mal.* Thy vows are heard, and we accept thy faith.    *Undisguiseth himself.*

#### Enter Ferneze and Celso

Banish amazement: come, we four must stand

Full shock of fortune: be not so wonderstricken.

*Pietro.* Doth Ferneze live?

*Fer.* For your pardon.    155

*Pietro.* Pardon and love. Give leave to recollect

My thoughts dispers'd in wild astonishment.

My vows stand fix'd in heaven, and from hence

I crave all love and pardon.

*Mal.* Who doubts of providence,    160

That sees this change? A hearty faith to all!

He needs must rise who can no lower fall:

For still impetuous vicissitude

Touseth the world; then let no maze intrude

Upon your spirits: wonder not I rise;    165

For who can sink that close can temporize?

The time grows ripe for action: I 'll detect

My privat'st plot, lest ignorance fear suspect.

Let 's close to counsel, leave the rest to fate:    169

Mature discretion is the life of state.    *Exeunt.*

## ACTUS V.  SCENA I

### [*The Duke's Palace*]

#### Enter Bilioso and Passarello

*Bil.* Fool, how dost thou like my calf in a long stocking?

*Pass.* An excellent calf, my lord.

*Bil.* This calf hath been a reveller this twenty year. When Monsieur Gundi lay [5 here ambassador, I could have carried a lady up and down at arm's end in a platter; and I can tell you, there were those at that time who, to try the strength of a man's back and his arm, would be coistered. I have meas- [10 ured calves with most of the palace, and they come nothing near me; besides, I think there be not many armours in the arsenal will fit me, especially for the headpiece. I 'll tell thee —

*Pass.* What, my lord?    15

*Bil.* I can eat stew'd broth as it comes seething off the fire; or a custard as it comes reeking out of the oven; and I think there are not many lords can do it. A good pomander, a little decayed in the scent; but [20 six grains of musk, ground with rose-water, and temper'd with a little civet, shall fetch her again presently.

*Pass.* O, ay, as a bawd with aqua-vitae.

*Bil.* And, what, dost thou rail upon the [25 ladies as thou wert wont?

*Pass.* I were better roast a live cat, and might do it with more safety. I am as secret to the thieves as their painting. There 's Maquerelle, oldest bawd and a perpetual [30 beggar — did you never hear of her trick to be known in the city?

---

*Bil.* Never.

*Pass.* Why, she gets all the picture-makers to draw her picture; when they have done, [35 she most courtly finds fault with them one after another, and never fetcheth them. They, in revenge of this, execute her in pictures as they do in Germany, and hang her in their shops. By this means is she better known [40 to the stinkards than if she had been five times carted.

*Bil.* 'Fore God, an excellent policy.

*Pass.* Are there any revels to-night, my lord?

*Bil.* Yes.                                        45

*Pass.* Good my lord, give me leave to break a fellow's pate that hath abused me.

*Bil.* Whose pate?

*Pass.* Young Ferrard, my lord.

*Bil.* Take heed, he 's very valiant; I [50 have known him fight eight quarrels in five days, believe it.

*Pass.* O, is he so great a quarreller? Why, then, he 's an arrant coward.

*Bil.* How prove you that?                         55

*Pass.* Why, thus. He that quarrels seeks to fight; and he that seeks to fight seeks to die; and he that seeks to die seeks never to fight more; and he that will quarrel, and seeks means never to answer a man more, I think [60 he 's a coward.

*Bil.* Thou canst prove anything.

*Pass.* Anything but a rich knave; for I can flatter no man.

*Bil.* Well, be not drunk, good fool: I [65 shall see you anon in the presence.    *Exeunt.*

### [SCENE I.ᴬ   *The Same*]

*Enter Malevole and Maquerelle at several doors, opposite, singing*

*Mal.* "The Dutchman for a drunkard," —
*Maq.* "The Dane for golden locks," —
*Mal.* "The Irishman for usquebaugh," —
*Maq.* "The Frenchman for the (   )."
*Mal.* O, thou art a blessed creature! Had [5 I a modest woman to conceal, I would put her to thy custody; for no reasonable creature would ever suspect her to be in thy company. Ha, thou art a melodious Maquerelle, — thou picture of a woman, and substance of a beast!

#### *Enter Passarello*

*Maq.* O fool, will ye be ready anon to go [11 with me to the revels? The hall will be so pester'd anon.

*Pass.* Ay, as the country is with attorneys.

*Mal.* What hast thou there, fool?          15

*Pass.* Wine; I have learn'd to drink since I went with my lord ambassador: I 'll drink to the health of Madam Maquerelle.

*Mal.* Why, thou wast wont to rail upon her.

*Pass.* Ay; but since I borrow'd money of [20 her, I 'll drink to her health now; as gentlemen visit brokers, or as knights send venison to the city, either to take up more money, or to procure longer forbearance.

*Mal.* Give me the bowl. I drink a health [25 to Altofront, our deposed duke.    [*Drinks.*]

*Pass.* I 'll take it [*drinks*]: — so. Now I 'll begin a health to Madam Maquerelle.
[*Drinks.*]

*Mal.* Pew! I will not pledge her.

*Pass.* Why, I pledg'd your lord.          30

*Mal.* I care not.

*Pass.* Not pledge Madam Maquerelle! Why, then, will I spew up your lord again with this fool's finger.

*Mal.* Hold; I 'll take it.       [*Drinks.*]

*Maq.* Now thou hast drunk my health, [36 fool, I am friends with thee.

*Pass.* Art? art?

When Griffon saw the reconciled quean
Offering about his neck her arms to cast,      40
He threw off sword and heart's malignant spleen,
And lovely her below the loins embrac'd. —

Adieu, Madam Maquerelle.     *Exit Passarello.*

*Mal.* And how dost thou think o' this transformation of state now?             [45

*Maq.* Verily, very well; for we women always note, the falling of the one is the rising of the other; some must be fat, some must be lean; some must be fools, and some must be lords; some must be knaves, and some [50 must be officers; some must be beggars, some must be knights; some must be cuckolds, and some must be citizens. As for example, I have two court-dogs, the most fawning curs, the one called Watch, th' other Catch: now [55 I, like Lady Fortune, sometimes love this dog, sometimes raise that dog, sometimes favour Watch, most commonly fancy Catch. Now, that dog which I favour I feed; and he 's so ravenous, that what I give he never [60 chaws it, gulps it down whole, without any relish of what he has, but with a greedy expectation of what he shall have. The other dog now —

*Mal.* No more dog, sweet Maquerelle, [65 no more dog. And what hope hast thou of the Duchess Maria? Will she stoop to the duke's lure? Will she come, think'st?

⁴¹ **stinkards:** mob    ⁴² **carted:** the punishment for bawds    Sc. I.ᴬ (Not marked in Qq.)    ³ **us-quebaugh:** whiskey    ¹¹⁻⁴³ (Not in Q 1)    ¹³ **pester'd:** crowded    ³⁹ **Griffon:** a hero in Ariosto's *Orlando Furioso*    **quean:** hussy    ⁴¹ **spleen:** ('stream' Qq.)    ⁶⁸ **come:** yield ('cowe' Q 2)

*Maq.* Let me see, where's the sign now? Ha' ye e'er a calendar? Where's the sign, [70 trow you?

*Mal.* Sign! why, is there any moment in that?

*Maq.* O, believe me, a most secret power: look ye, a Chaldean or an Assyrian, I am [75 sure 't was a most sweet Jew, told me, court any woman in the right sign, you shall not miss. But you must take her in the right vein then; as, when the sign is in Pisces, a fishmonger's wife is very sociable; in Can- [80 cer, a precisian's wife is very flexible; in Capricorn, a merchant's wife hardly holds out; in Libra, a lawyer's wife is very tractable, especially if her husband be at the term; only in Scorpio 't is very dangerous meddling. Has [85 the duke sent any jewel, any rich stones?

*Enter Captain*

*Mal.* Ay, I think those are the best signs to take a lady in. By your favour, signior, I must discourse with the Lady Maria, Altofront's duchess; I must enter for the duke.   90

*Capt.* She here shall give you interview. I received the guardship of this citadel from the good Altofront, and for his use I 'll keep 't, till I am of no use.

*Mal.* Wilt thou? O heavens, that a [95 Christian should be found in a buff-jerkin! Captain Conscience, I love thee, captain. (*Exit Captain.*) We attend. And what hope hast thou of this duchess' easiness?

*Maq.* 'T will go hard, she was a cold [100 creature ever; she hated monkeys, fools, jesters, and gentlemen-ushers extremely; she had the vilde trick on 't, not only to be truly modestly honourable in her own conscience, but she would avoid the least wanton [105 carriage that might incur suspect; as, God bless me, she had almost brought bed-pressing out of fashion; I could scarce get a fine for the lease of a lady's favour once in a fortnight.   109

*Mal.* Now, in the name of immodesty, how many maidenheads hast thou brought to the block?

*Maq.* Let me see: heaven forgive us our misdeeds! — Here's the duchess.   114

## SCENA SECUNDA

*[Before the Citadel]*

*Enter Maria and Captain*

*Mal.* God bless thee, lady!

*Maria.* Out of thy company!

*Mal.* We have brought thee tender of a husband.

*Maria.* I hope I have one already.   5

*Maq.* Nay, by mine honour, madam, as good ha' ne'er a husband as a banish'd husband; he 's in another world now. I 'll tell ye, lady, I have heard of a sect that maintained, when the husband was asleep the [10 wife might lawfully entertain another man, for then her husband was as dead: much more when he is banished.

*Maria.* Unhonest creature!   14

*Maq.* Pish, honesty is but an art to seem so: Pray ye, what's honesty, what's constancy, But fables feign'd, odd old fools' chat, devis'd By jealous fools to wrong our liberty?

*Mal.* Molly, he that loves thee is a duke, Mendoza; he will maintain thee royally, [20 love thee ardently, defend thee powerfully, marry thee sumptuously, and keep thee in despite of Rosicleer or Donzel del Phœbo. There 's jewels: if thou wilt, so; if not, so.

*Maria.* Captain, for God's sake, save poor wretchedness   25
From tyranny of lustful insolence!
Enforce me in the deepest dungeon dwell,
Rather than here; here round about is hell. —
O my dear'st Altofront! where'er thou breathe,
Let my soul sink into the shades beneath,   30
Before I stain thine honour! This thou hast,
And long as I can die, I will live chaste.

*Mal.* 'Gainst him that can enforce how vain is strife!

*Maria.* She that can be enforc'd has ne'er a knife:
She that through force her limbs with lust enrolls,   35
Wants Cleopatra's asps and Portia's coals.
God amend you!   *Exit with Captain.*

*Mal.* Now, the fear of the devil for ever go with thee! — Maquerelle, I tell thee, I have found an honest woman: faith, I perceive, [40 when all is done, there is of women, as of all other things, some good, most bad; some saints, some sinners: for as nowadays no courtier but has his mistress, no captain but has his cockatrice, no cuckold but has his [45 horns, and no fool but has his feather; even so, no woman but has her weakness and feather too, no sex but has his — I can hunt the letter no farther. — [*Aside.*] O God, how [49 loathsome this toying is to me! That a duke should be forc'd to fool it! Well, *stultorum plena sunt omnia:* better play the fool lord

---

⁶⁹ **sign:** *i.e.*, astrological sign of the zodiac   ⁷¹ **trow:** think   ⁸¹ **precisian's:** Puritan's   ⁸⁴ **term:** session of courts of law   ⁸⁶ S. D. **Enter Captain:** (The scene is supposed to have shifted to the Citadel.)   ⁹⁸ **attend:** wait   ¹⁰⁶ **carriage:** behavior   ¹⁰⁸ **fine:** fee   ³ **tender:** offer   ²³ **Rosicleer, Donzel del Phœbo:** heroes in *The Mirror of Knighthood*   ⁴⁵ **cockatrice:** mistress   ⁵¹⁻⁵² **stultorum . . . omnia:** All places are full of fools.

than be the fool lord. — Now, where 's your sleights, Madam Maquerelle?

*Maq.* Why, are ye ignorant that 't is [55 said a squeamish affected niceness is natural to women, and that the excuse of their yielding is only, forsooth, the difficult obtaining? You must put her to 't: women are flax, and will fire in a moment.                                      60

*Mal.* Why, was the flax put into thy mouth, and yet thou —
Thou set fire, thou inflame her!

*Maq.* Marry, but I 'll tell ye now, you were too hot.

*Mal.* The fitter to have inflamed the [65 flax-woman.

*Maq.* You were too boisterous, spleeny, for, indeed —

*Mal.* Go, go, thou art a weak pandress; now I see,
Sooner earth's fire heaven itself shall waste, 70 Than all with heat can melt a mind that 's chaste.
Go; thou the duke's lime-twig! I 'll make the duke turn thee out of thine office: what, not get one touch of hope, and had her at such advantage!                                        75

*Maq.* Now, o' my conscience, now I think in my discretion, we did not take her in the right sign; the blood was not in the true vein, sure.                                           *Exit.*

### [SCENE II. A]

### [The Court]

#### Enter Bilioso

*Bil.* Make way there! The duke returns from the enthronement. — Malevole —

*Mal.* Out, rogue!

*Bil.* Malevole, —

*Mal.* "Hence, ye gross-jawed, peasantly [5 — out, go!"

*Bil.* Nay, sweet Malevole, since my return I hear you are become the thing I always prophesied would be, — an advanced virtue, a worthily-employed faithfulness, a man o' [10 grace, dear friend. Come; what! *Si quoties peccant homines* — if as often as courtiers play the knaves, honest men should be angry — why, look ye, we must collogue sometimes, forswear sometimes.                                 15

*Mal.* Be damn'd sometimes.

*Bil.* Right: *nemo omnibus horis sapit;* "no

man can be honest at all hours:" necessity often depraves virtue.

*Mal.* I will commend thee to the duke.    20

*Bil.* Do: let us be friends, man.

*Mal.* And knaves, man.

*Bil.* Right: let us prosper and purchase: our lordships shall live, and our knavery be forgotten.                                        25

*Mal.* He that by any ways gets riches, his means never shames him.

*Bil.* True.

*Mal.* For impudency and faithlessness are the main stays to greatness.                      30

*Bil.* By the Lord, thou art a profound lad.

*Mal.* By the Lord, thou art a perfect knave: out, ye ancient damnation!

*Bil.* Peace, peace! and thou wilt not be a friend to me as I am a knave, be not a knave to me as I am thy friend, and disclose me. Peace! cornets!                                    37

### SCENA TERTIA

### [The Same]

*Enter Prepasso and Ferrard, two Pages with lights, Celso and Equato, Mendoza in duke's robes, and Guerrino.*

*Men.* On, on; leave us, leave us.
    *Exeunt all saving Malevole [and Mendoza].*
Stay, where is the hermit?

*Mal.* With Duke Pietro, with Duke Pietro.

*Men.* Is he dead? Is he poisoned?

*Mal.* Dead, as the duke is.                     5

*Men.* Good, excellent: he will not blab; secureness lives in secrecy. Come hither, come hither.

*Mal.* Thou hast a certain strong villainous scent about thee my nature cannot endure. 10

*Men.* Scent, man! What returns Maria, what answer to our suit?

*Mal.* Cold, frosty; she is obstinate.

*Men.* Then she 's but dead; 't is resolute, she dies:
"Black deed only through black deed safely flies."                                          15

*Mal.* Pew! *per scelera semper sceleribus tutum est iter.*

*Men.* What, art a scholar? Art a politician? Sure, thou art an arrant knave.

*Mal.* Who, I? I have been twice an [20 under-sheriff, man.

⁵⁶ **niceness:** fastidiousness    ⁷² **lime-twig:** trap (for Maria)    Sc. II ᴬ (Not in Q 1)    ⁵,⁶ (Cf. II. iii. 38)    ¹⁴ **collogue:** have private conversation and understanding    ²³ **purchase:** acquire wealth ³⁰ **stays:** supports    ¹¹ **returns:** answers    ¹⁶⁻¹⁷ **per . . . iter:** The safe way to crimes is always through crimes (Seneca).    ²¹ ff. (Q 2 here inserts these lines: 'Mend. Hast been with Maria? | Mal. As your scrivener to your usurer, I have dealt about taking of this commodity, but she's cold-frosty.' They were probably meant to replace lines 11–21. Lines 22–37 are not in Q 1.)

Well, I will go rail upon some great man, that
I may purchase the bastinado, or else go marry
some rich Genoan lady, and instantly go travel.

*Men.*  Travel, when thou art married?    25

*Mal.*  Ay, 't is your young lord's fashion
to do so, though he was so lazy, being a
bachelor, that he would never travel so far
as the university: yet, when he married her,
tales off, and, Catso, for England!    30

*Men.*  And why for England?

*Mal.*  Because there is no brothel-houses
there.

*Men.*  Nor courtesans?

*Mal.*  Neither; your whore went down [35
with the stews, and your punk came up with
your puritan.

*Men.*  Canst thou empoison? Canst thou
empoison?

*Mal.*  Excellently; no Jew, 'pothecary, or [40
politician better. Look ye, here 's a box:
whom wouldst thou empoison? Here 's a box
[*giving it*], which, opened and the fume taken
up in conduits thorough which the brain purges
itself, doth instantly for twelve hours' space [45
bind up all show of life in a deep senseless
sleep: here 's another [*giving it*], which, being
opened under the sleeper's nose, chokes all
the power of life, kills him suddenly.

*Men.*  I 'll try experiments; 't is good [50
not to be deceived. — So, so; catso!

*Seems to poison Malevole [who falls].*

Who would fear that may destroy?
    Death hath no teeth or tongue;
And he that 's great, to him are slaves,
    Shame, murder, fame, and wrong. —    55

Celso!

*Enter Celso*

*Celso.*  My honoured lord?

*Men.*  The good Malevole, that plain-tongu'd
man,

Alas, is dead on sudden, wondrous strangely!
He held in our esteem good place. Celso,    60
See him buried, see him buried.

*Celso.*  I shall observe ye.

*Men.*  And, Celso, prithee, let it be thy care
to-night
To have some pretty show, to solemnize
Our high instalment; some music, masquery. 65
We 'll give fair entertain unto Maria,
The duchess to the banish'd Altofront:
Thou shalt conduct her from the citadel
Unto the palace. Think on some masquery.

*Celso.*  Of what shape, sweet lord?    70

*Men.*  What shape! Why, any quick-done
fiction;

As some brave spirits of the Genoan dukes
To come out of Elysium, forsooth,
Led in by Mercury, to gratulate
Our happy fortune; some such anything,    75
Some far-fet trick good for ladies, some stale toy
Or other, no matter, so 't be of our devising.
Do thou prepare 't; 't is but for fashion sake.
Fear not, it shall be grac'd, man, it shall take.

*Celso.*  All service.    80

*Men.*  All thanks; our hand shall not be
close to thee; farewell.

[*Aside.*]  Now is my treachery secure, nor can
    we fall:
Mischief that prospers, men do virtue call.
I 'll trust no man: he that by tricks gets
    wreaths
Keeps them with steel; no man securely
    breathes    85
Out of deserved ranks; the crowd will mutter.
    Fool!
Who cannot bear with spite, he cannot rule.
The chiefest secret for a man of state
Is, to live senseless of a strengthless hate.
                                    [*Exit.*]

*Mal.*  Death of    *Starts up and speaks.* [90
the damn'd thief! I 'll make one i' the masque;
thou shalt ha' some brave spirits of the antique
dukes.

*Celso.*  My lord, what strange delusion?

*Mal.*  Most happy, dear Celso, poison'd [95
with an empty box! I 'll give thee all, anon.
My lady comes to court; there is a whirl of
fate comes tumbling on; the castle's captain
stands for me, the people pray for me, and
the great leader of the just stands for me: [100
then courage, Celso;
For no disastrous chance can ever move him
That leaveth nothing but a God above him.
                                    [*Exeunt.*]

[SCENE IV. — *The Presence Chamber.*]

*Enter Prepasso and Bilioso, two Pages before
    them; Maquerelle, Bianca, and Emilia*

*Bil.*  Make room there, room for the ladies!
Why, gentlemen, will not ye suffer the ladies
to be entered in the great chamber? Why,
gallants! and you, sir, to drop your torch
where the beauties must sit too?    5

*Pre.*  And there 's a great fellow plays the
knave; why dost not strike him?

*Bil.*  Let him play the knave, o' God's name;
think'st thou i have no more wit than to
strike a great fellow? — The music! more [10
lights! revelling, scaffolds! do you hear? Let
there be oaths enow ready at the door, swear

---

²³ **bastinado:** a beating    ³⁶ **stews:** brothels
⁷⁶ **far-fet:** cunningly devised (*lit.* "far-fetched")
niggardly    ⁸⁹ **senseless:** oblivious    Sc. IV: (Not marked, Q 2)

⁷¹ **What:** ('Why' Qq.)    ⁷⁴ **gratulate:** greet, salute
**toy:** trifle, fancy    ⁷⁸ **for:** ('for a' Qq.)    ⁸¹ **close:**

out the devil himself. Let 's leave the ladies, and go see if the lords be ready for them.

*All save the ladies depart.*

*Maq.* And, by my troth, beauties, why [15 do you not put you into the fashion? This is a stale cut; you must come in fashion: look ye, you must be all felt, felt and feather, a felt upon your bare hair. Look ye, these tiring things are justly out of request now: [20 and, do ye hear? you must wear falling-bands, you must come into the falling fashion: there is such a deal o' pinning these ruffs, when the fine clean fall is worth all: and again, if ye should chance to take a nap in the [25 afternoon, your falling-band requires no pot-ing-stick to recover his form: believe me, no fashion to the falling, I say.

*Bian.* And is not Signior St. Andrew a gallant fellow now?           30

*Maq.* By my maidenhead, la, honour and he agrees as well together as a satin suit and woollen stockings.

*Emilia.* But is not Marshal Make-room, my servant in reversion, a proper gentleman?   35

*Maq.* Yes, in reversion, as he had his office; as, in truth, he hath all things in reversion: he has his mistress in reversion, his clothes in reversion, his wit in reversion; and, indeed, is a suitor to me for my dog in reversion: [40 but, in good verity, la, he is as proper a gentle-man in reversion as — and, indeed, as fine a man as may be, having a red beard and a pair of warp'd legs.

*Bian.* But, i' faith, I am most mon- [45 strously in love with Count Quidlibet-in-quodli-bet: is he not a pretty, dapper, unidle gallant?

*Maq.* He is even one of the most busy-fingered lords: he will put the beauties to the squeak most hideously.          50

[*Enter Bilioso*]

*Bil.* Room! make a lane there! The duke is entering: stand handsomely for beauty's sake. Take up the ladies there! So, cornets, cornets!

## SCENA QUINTA

*Enter Prepasso, joins to Bilioso, two Pages and lights; Ferrard, Mendoza; at the other door, two Pages with lights, and the Captain lead-ing in Maria; the Duke meets Maria and closeth with her; the rest fall back*

*Men.* Madam, with gentle ear receive my suit;

A kingdom's safety should o'er-peise slight rites;

Marriage is merely nature's policy:
Then, since unless our royal beds be join'd,
Danger and civil tumults frights the state,   5
Be wise as you are fair, give way to fate.

*Maria.* What wouldst thou, thou affliction
   to our house?
Thou ever-devil, 't was thou that banished'st
My truly noble lord!

*Men.* I!                      10

*Maria.* Ay, by thy plots, by thy black strat-
   agems:
Twelve moons have suffer'd change since I
   beheld
The loved presence of my dearest lord.
O thou far worse than Death! he parts but soul
From a weak body; but thou soul from soul 15
Disseverest, that which God's own hand did
   knit;
Thou scant of honour, full of devilish wit!

*Men.* We 'll check your too-intemperate lav-
   ishness:
I can and will.

*Maria.* What canst?          20

*Men.* Go to; in banishment thy husband
   dies.

*Maria.* He ever is at home that 's ever wise.

*Men.* You 'st ne'er meet more: reason
   should love control.

*Maria.* Not meet!           24
She that dear loves, her love 's still in her soul.

*Men.* You are but a woman, lady, you
   must yield.

*Maria.* O, save me, thou innated bashfulness,
Thou only ornament of woman's modesty!

*Men.* Modesty! death! I 'll torment thee. 29

*Maria.* Do, urge all torments, all afflictions
   try;
I 'll die my lord's as long as I can die.

*Men.* Thou obstinate, thou shalt die. —
   Captain, that lady's life
Is forfeited to justice: we have examin'd her,
And we do find she hath empoisoned    34
The reverend hermit; therefore we command
Severest custody. — Nay, if you 'll do 's no
   good,
You 'st do 's no harm: a tyrant's peace is
   blood.

*Maria.* O, thou art merciful; O gracious
   devil,
Rather by much let me condemned be    39
For seeming murder than be damn'd for thee!
I 'll mourn no more; come, girt my brows with
   flowers:
Revel and dance, soul, now thy wish thou hast;

---

²⁰ **tiring things:** head-dresses ·   **request:** demand, fashion     ²¹ **falling-bands:** collars which fell flat from the neck    ²⁶⁻²⁷ **poting-stick:** stick for setting the plaits of a ruff    ⁴⁴ **warp'd:** ('wrapt' Q 2) **Scena Quinta:** ('Scena Quarta' Q 2)    ² **o'er-peise:** outweigh    ²⁷ **innated:** innate    ³³ **forfeited:** ('forteified' Q 2)

Die like a bride, poor heart, thou shalt die
chaste.

*Enter Aurelia in mourning habit*

*Aur.*  "Life is a frost of cold felicity,
And death the thaw of all our vanity:"          45
Was 't not an honest priest that wrote so?
*Men.*  Who let her in?
*Bil.*  Forbear!
*Pre.*  Forbear!
*Aur.*  Alas, calamity is everywhere:          50
Sad misery, despite your double doors,
Will enter even in court.
*Bil.*  Peace!
*Aur.*  I ha' done.
*Bil.*  One word, — take heed!          55
*Aur.*  I ha' done.

*Enter Mercury with loud music*

*Mer.*  Cyllenian Mercury, the god of ghosts,
From gloomy shades that spread the lower
coasts,
Calls four high-famed Genoan dukes to come,
And make this presence their Elysium,          60
To pass away this high triumphal night
With song and dances, court's more soft de-
light.
*Aur.*  Are you god of ghosts? I have a suit
depending in hell betwixt me and my con-
science; I would fain have thee help me to [65
an advocate.
*Bil.*  Mercury shall be your lawyer, lady.
*Aur.*  Nay, faith, Mercury has too good a
face to be a right lawyer.
*Pre.*  Peace, forbear! Mercury presents the
masque.          70

*Cornets: the song to the cornets, which playing,
the masque enters; Malevole, Pietro, Ferneze, and Celso, in white robes, with dukes'
crowns upon laurel wreaths, pistolets and
short swords under their robes*

*Men.*  Celso, Celso, court Maria for our
love. — Lady, be gracious yet, grace.
*Maria.*  With me, sir?     *Malevole takes his
wife [Maria] to dance.*
*Mal.*          Yes, more loved than my breath;
With you I 'll dance.
*Maria.*  Why, then, you dance with death.
But, come, sir, I was ne'er more apt to mirth. 75
Death gives eternity a glorious breath:
O, to die honour'd, who would fear to die?
*Mal.*  They die in fear who live in villainy.
*Men.*  Yes, believe him, lady, and be rul'd
by him.

*Pietro.*  Madam, with me.     *Pietro takes* 80
          *his wife Aurelia to dance.*
*Aur.*  Wouldst, then, be miserable?
*Pietro.*  I need not wish.
*Aur.*  O, yet forbear my hand! away! fly!
fly!
O, seek not her that only seeks to die!
*Pietro.*  Poor loved soul!          85
*Aur.*  What, wouldst court misery?
*Pietro.*  Yes.
*Aur.*  She 'll come too soon: — O my grieved
heart!
*Pietro.*  Lady, ha' done, ha' done:
Come, let 's dance: be once from sorrow free. 90
*Aur.*  Art a sad man?
*Pietro.*  Yes, sweet.
*Aur.*  Then we 'll agree.

*Ferneze takes Maquerelle and Celso,
Bianca: then the cornets sound the
measure, one change and rest.*

*Fer.* (*to Bianca.*)  Believe it, lady; shall I
swear? Let me enjoy you in private, and 195
I 'll marry you, by my soul.
*Bian.*  I had rather you would swear by your
body: I think that would prove the more regarded oath with you.
*Fer.*  I 'll swear by them both, to please [100
you.
*Bian.*  O, damn them not both to please
me, for God's sake!
*Fer.*  Faith, sweet creature, let me enjoy
you to-night, and I 'll marry you to-morrow [105
fortnight, by my troth, la.
*Maq.*  On his troth, la! believe him not;
that kind of cony-catching is as stale as Sir
Oliver Anchovy's perfum'd jerkin: promise of
matrimony by a young gallant, to bring a [110
virgin lady into a fool's paradise; make her
a great woman, and then cast her off; — 't is
as common, as natural to a courtier, as jealousy
to a citizen, gluttony to a puritan, wisdom to an
alderman, pride to a tailor, or an empty [115
hand-basket to one of these six-penny damna-
tions: of his troth, la! believe him not; traps
to catch pole-cats.
*Mal.*  Keep your face constant,     *To Maria.*
let no sudden passion
Speak in your eyes.          120
*Maria.*  O my Altofront!
*Pietro.* [*to Aurelia.*]  A tyrant's jealousies
Are very nimble: you receive it all?
*Aur.*  My heart, though     *Aurelia to Pietro.*
not my knees, doth humbly fall
Low as the earth, to thee.          125
*Mal.*  Peace! next change; no words.

---

44, 45 (From Thomas Bastard's *Chrestoleros*, 1598)     55 (Assigned to Aurelia in Qq.)     57 **Cyllenian:**
(Mercury was said to have been born on Mt. Cyllene.)     58 **coasts:** regions     61 **triumphal:** festive
64 **depending:** pending     69 **right:** true     75 **apt:** inclined     108 **cony-catching:** deceiving     126 (Assigned to Pietro, Qq.)

*Maria.* Speech to such, ay, O, what will
  affords!
    *Cornets sound the measure over again;*
      *which danced, they unmask.*
*Men.* Malevole!
    *They environ Mendoza, bending their*
      *pistols on him.*
*Mal.* No.
*Men.* Altofront! Duke Pietro! Ferneze!
  ha!                            130
*All.* Duke Altofront! Duke Altofront!
    *Cornets, a flourish.*
*Men.* Are we surpris'd? What strange de-
lusions mock
Our senses? Do I dream? or have I dreamt
This two days' space? Where am I?
    *They seize upon Mendoza.*
*Mal.* Where an arch-villain is.     135
*Men.* O, lend me breath till I am fit to die!
For peace with heaven, for your own souls' sake,
Vouchsafe me life!
*Pietro.* Ignoble villain! whom neither heaven
  nor hell,
Goodness of God or man, could once make
  good!                           140
*Mal.* Base, treacherous wretch! what grace
  canst thou expect,
That hast grown impudent in gracelessness?
*Men.* O, life!
*Mal.* Slave, take thy life.
Wert thou defenced, through blood and
  wounds,                      145
The sternest horror of a civil fight,
Would I achieve thee; but prostrate at my feet,
I scorn to hurt thee: 't is the heart of slaves
That deigns to triumph over peasants' graves;
For such thou art, since birth doth ne'er
  enroll                    150
A man 'mong monarchs, but a glorious soul.
O, I have seen strange accidents of state!
The flatterer, like the ivy, clip the oak,
And waste it to the heart; lust so confirm'd,
That the black act of sin itself not sham'd   155
To be term'd courtship.
O, they that are as great as be their sins,
Let them remember that th' inconstant people
Love many princes merely for their faces
And outward shows; and they do covet
  more                      160
To have a sight of these than of their virtues.
Yet thus much let the great ones still conceive,
When they observe not heaven's impos'd con-
  ditions,
They are no kings, but forfeit their commis-
  sions.
*Maq.* O good my lord, I have lived in [165

the court this twenty year: they that have
been old courtiers, and come to live in the
city, they are spited at, and thrust to the walls
like apricocks, good my lord.
*Bil.* My lord, I did know your lordship [170
in this disguise; you heard me ever say, if
Altofront did return, I would stand for him:
besides, 't was your lordship's pleasure to call
me wittol and cuckold: you must not think,
but that I knew you, I would have put it up [175
so patiently.
*Mal.* You o'er-joy'd spirits, wipe your long-
  wet eyes.     *To Pietro and Aurelia.*
Hence with this man!   *Kicks out Mendoza.*
  An eagle takes not flies.
You to your vows!     *To Pietro and Aurelia.*
  And thou unto the suburbs.
                  *To Maquerelle.*
You to my worst friend I would hardly give; 180
Thou art a perfect old knave.   *To Bilioso.*
  All-pleased live!
You two unto my breast:
          *To Celso and the Captain.*
  thou to my heart.     *To Maria.*
The rest of idle actors idly part:
And as for me, I here assume my right,
To which I hope all 's pleas'd: to all, good-
  night.                     185
    *Cornets, a flourish. Exeunt omnes.*

FINIS

An imperfect Ode, being but one staff,
spoken by the Prologue

*To wrest each hurtless thought to private sense*
*Is the foul use of ill-bred impudence:*
  *Immodest censure now grows wild,*
    *All over-running.*
*Let innocence be ne'er so chaste,*     5
  *Yet to the last*
    *She is defil'd*
*With too nice-brained cunning.*
  *O you of fairer soul,*
    *Control*           10
*With an Herculean arm*
  *This harm;*
*And once teach all old freedom of a pen,*
*Which still must write of fools, whiles 't writes of*
*men!*

Epilogus

*Your modest silence, full of heedy stillness,*
*Makes me thus speak: a voluntary illness*
*Is merely senseless; but unwilling error,*
*Such as proceeds from too rash youthful fervour,*

---

128 s. d. **bending:** aiming   152–176 (Not in Q 1)   162 **conceive:** understand ('conceale' Qq.)   175 **put**
**it up:** put up with it   179 **suburbs:** (where the brothels were located)   Ode **staff:** stanza   Epilogus ³ **merely:** wholly

*May well be call'd a fault, but not a sin:*   5
*Rivers take names from founts where they begin.*
*Then let not too severe an eye peruse*
*The slighter brakes of our reformed Muse,*
*Who could herself herself of faults detect,*
*But that she knows 't is easy to correct,*   10
*Though some men's labour: troth, to err is fit,*
*As long as wisdom 's not profess'd, but wit.*
*Then till another's happier Muse appears,*

*Till his Thalia feast your learned ears,*
*To whose desertful lamps pleas'd Fates impart*
*Art above nature, judgment above art,*   16
*Receive this piece, which hope nor fear yet*
*daunteth:*
*He that knows most knows most how much he*
*wanteth.*

FINIS

8 **brakes:** bushy retreats   13 **another's:** Ben Jonson's   14 **Thalia:** comic Muse

# EASTVVARD HOE.

As

It was playd in the
*Black-friers.*

*By*

The Children of her Maiesties Reuels.

*Made by.*

GEO: CHAPMAN. BEN: IONSON. IOH: MARSTON.

AT LONDON
Printed for *William Aspley.*
1 6 0 5.

BIBLIOGRAPHICAL RECORD. On September 4, 1605, William Aspley and Thomas Thorpe (who the year before had likewise registered Marston's *Malcontent* in conjunction) were assigned the copyright of *Eastward Ho!*:

*iiij° Sept 1605*

*Willm Aspley Thomas Thorp Entred for their Copies vnder the hands of Mr Wilson and Mr ffeild warden A Comedie called Eastward Ho*   *vj^d*

Three Quarto editions (the only early texts) appeared in 1605, all printed for Aspley alone, and all naming the authors in alphabetical sequence: Geo. Chapman, Ben Jonson, Joh. Marston. (See facsimile.) Of the first Quarto there were two issues, since the witty but dangerous satire on the Scots in III. iii was cancelled during the printing, and the two leaves concerned (E3, E4) reset. Only two known copies now contain this offending matter. In three other places (mentioned in our notes) Q 1 offers bibliographical evidence that a part of the text has been deleted by the printers. See R. E. Brettle and W. W. Greg, *The Library*, Dec., 1928, 287–304; and the Oxford Jonson, Vol. IV. 489 ff.

DATE AND STAGE PERFORMANCE. *Eastward Ho!* was acted at the Blackfriars Theatre, probably between January and March, 1605, by the Children of the Queen's Revels. It was produced in friendly rivalry (see the Prologue) with *Westward Ho!* by Dekker and Webster, which had been written in the latter half of 1604 and produced by the other boys' company of Paul's. The play, Chapman told the Lord Chamberlain afterwards, was 'much importuned,' and for that or a less innocent reason was produced without license from the censors. King James was naturally incensed by the satire against his Scottish subjects and himself, and the offending authors were promptly sent to prison. Drummond of Hawthornden recorded the following story as told to him years after (1619) by Jonson: 'He was delated (accused) by Sir James Murray to the King for writing something against the Scots in a play, *Eastward Ho!*, and voluntarily imprisoned himself with Chapman and Marston, who had written it amongst them. The report was that they should then (have) had their ears cut and noses . . .' Seven letters by Jonson and three by Chapman have been preserved, written during their incarceration, in which they assure the King, a lady of the court, the Lord Chamberlain, and several other noblemen of their innocence of the two offending passages — which indeed seem, in phrasing at least, to have been the work of Marston. Despite Drummond's testimony, it is not certain that Marston himself was arrested. All three authors escaped in the end without serious penalty. Nor did the King's wrath pursue the play: nine years later (Jan. 25, 1614) it was acted before him at Whitehall by the Lady Elizabeth's Men. See J. Q. Adams: '*Eastward Hoe* and its Satire against the Scots,' *Studies in Philology*, 1931, 689–701.

*Eastward Ho!* was combined with Jonson's *Devil Is an Ass* by Nahum Tate to produce a farce called *Cuckold's Haven* (1685). In 1751 the original was produced by Garrick, and in 1775 a revision by Mrs. Charlotte Lennox under the title *Old City Manners*. The comedy was reprinted in Dodsley's collection of old plays, 1744, and supplied Hogarth with the hint for his series of drawings, the Idle and Industrious Apprentices (1747). It furnished Sir Walter Scott also with realistic background for his *Fortunes of Nigel*.

SOURCES. *Eastward Ho!* revived the old tradition of school plays dramatizing the parable of the Prodigal. In Latin the earliest of these is Wimpheling's *Stylpho* (Heidelberg, 1480), the best perhaps the *Rebelles* of Macropedius and the famous *Acolastus* of Gnaphaeus. In English, Gascoigne's *Glass of Government* is a striking example (1575). This old dramatic theme, familiar to all schoolboys, was well suited to performance by a company of children; and it has been developed to tickle the fancies of London citizens and apprentices, who at this date were very theatre-conscious, though not normally patrons of the aristocratic Blackfriars. The subplot, dealing with Winifred, uses situations in two Italian stories in Masuccio's collection, especially No. 40. For the references to Virginia the authors are indebted both to More's *Utopia* and to Hakluyt's *Voyages*.

DIVISION OF AUTHORSHIP. The play was evidently written hastily and in close collaboration; moreover, it is mainly in fluent prose, which offers fewer criteria of style than verse would do. Marston's vivacious manner is the most easily and largely discernible, especially in the scenes which contrast the two apprentices or satirize the Virginian adventurers. Chapman seems primarily responsible for the Italianate subplot involving Winifred (II. ii, III. iii, IV. i), and his epic manner appears in other places. Jonson's hand is most clearly seen in the Prologue, in III. i, the discussion of alchemy in IV. i, and in many parts of Act V. But the style of this tripartite performance is, like the plot, surprisingly well unified.

# GEORGE CHAPMAN
# BEN JONSON
# JOHN MARSTON

## EASTWARD HO!

[DRAMATIS PERSONAE

WILLIAM TOUCHSTONE, a Goldsmith
FRANCIS QUICKSILVER, } his
GOLDING, } Apprentices
SIR PETRONEL FLASH, a new-made Knight
SECURITY, an old Usurer
BRAMBLE, a Lawyer
POLDAVY, a Tailor

SEAGULL, a Sea-captain
SCAPETHRIFT, } Gentlemen-
SPENDALL, } Adventurers
WOLF, } Officers of
HOLDFAST, } Counter Prison
SLITGUT, a butcher's servant
HAMLET, a Footman
POTKIN, a Tankard-bearer

MISTRESS TOUCHSTONE
GERTRUDE, } her
MILDRED, } Daughters
BETTRICE, her Maid
WINIFRED, Security's Wife
SINDEFY, Quicksilver's Mistress
MISTRESS FOND, } Neigh-
MISTRESS GAZER, } bours

Sir Petronel's Page, Messenger, Coachman, Scrivener, Drawer at Blue Anchor Tavern, Constable, Prisoners, Gentlemen, etc.

SCENE: Touchstone's house and shop, Goldsmith's Row, Cheapside; Sir Petronel's Lodging; Security's House; Blue Anchor Tavern, Billingsgate; Cuckold's Haven on the Thames; one of the Counter Prisons.]

### PROLOGUS

NOT out of envy, for there 's no effect
Where there 's no cause; nor out of imitation,
For we have evermore been imitated;
Nor out of our contention to do better
Than that which is oppos'd to ours in title,   5
For that was good; and better cannot be:
And for the title, if it seem affected,
We might as well have called it, ' God you good even,'
Only that Eastward Westwards still exceeds —
Honour the sun's fair rising, not his setting.  10
Nor is our title utterly enforc'd,
As by the points we touch at you shall see.
Bear with our willing pains, if dull or witty;
We only dedicate it to the City.

### Actus primi Scena prima

[*Goldsmith's Row, Cheapside*]

*Enter Master Touchstone and Quicksilver at several doors; Quicksilver with his hat, pumps, short sword and dagger, and a racket trussed up under his cloak. At the middle door, enter Golding, discovering a goldsmith's shop, and walking short turns before it.*

*Touch.* And whither with you now? What loose action are you bound for?

Come, what comrades are you to meet withal? Where 's the supper? Where 's the rendevous?

*Quick.* Indeed, and in every good sober [5 truth, sir —

*Touch.* ' Indeed, and in very good sober truth, sir '! Behind my back thou wilt swear faster than a French footboy, and talk more bawdily than a common midwife; and now [10 ' indeed and in very good sober truth, sir '! But if a privy search should be made, with what furniture are you rigged now? Sirrah, I tell thee, I am thy master, William Touch-stone, goldsmith, and thou my prentice, [15 Francis Quicksilver; and I will see whither you are running. Work upon that now!

*Quick.* Why, sir, I hope a man may use his recreation with his master's profit.

*Touch.* Prentices' recreations are seldom [20 with their masters' profit. Work upon that now! You shall give up your cloak, though you be no alderman. Heyday, Ruffians' Hall! Sword, pumps, here 's a racket indeed!

*Touchstone uncloaks Quicksilver*

*Quick.* Work upon that now!   25
*Touch.* Thou shameless varlet, dost thou jest at thy lawful master contrary to thy indentures?

*Quick.* Why, 'sblood, sir, my mother 's a

---

⁵ (*Westward Ho!* by Dekker and Webster, produced by the children of Paul's, 1604)   ⁸ **God . . . even:** a conventional salutation (alluding to the fashion of nondescript play-titles like *What You Will, As You Like It*)   ¹¹ **enforc'd:** strained   Sc. I. s. d. **several:** different   ¹⁹ **with:** in harmony with
²²–²³ **though . . . alderman:** (Aldermen wore silken gowns instead of wool cloaks; see *Shoemakers' Holiday*, III. i.)   ²³–²⁴ **Ruffians' Hall:** nickname of a field in West Smithfield, a duelling resort
²⁸ **indentures:** articles of apprenticeship

gentlewoman, and my father a Justice of [30 Peace and of Quorum! And though I am a younger brother and a prentice, yet I hope I am my father's son; and, by God's lid, 't is for your worship and for your commodity that I keep company. I am entertained among [35 gallants, true! They call me cousin Frank, right! I lend them moneys, good! They spend it, well! But when they are spent, must not they strive to get more, must not their land fly? And to whom? Shall not [40 your worship ha' the refusal? Well, I am a good member of the City, if I were well considered. How would merchants thrive, if gentlemen would not be unthrifts? How could gentlemen be unthrifts, if their humours were [45 not fed? How should their humours be fed but by white-meat and cunning secondings? Well, the city might consider us. I am going to an ordinary now: the gallants fall to play; I carry light gold with me; the gallants call, 'Cousin [50 Frank, some gold for silver!'; I change, gain by it; the gallants lose the gold, and then call, 'Cousin Frank, lend me some silver!' Why —

*Touch.* Why? I cannot tell. Seven-score pound art thou out in the cash; but look [55 to it, I will not be gallanted out of my moneys. And as for my rising by other men's fall, God shield me! Did I gain my wealth by ordinaries? No! By exchanging of gold? No! By keeping of gallants' company? No! I [60 hired me a little shop, fought low, took small gain, kept no debt-book, garnished my shop, for want of plate, with good wholesome thrifty sentences, as 'Touchstone, keep thy shop, and thy shop will keep thee.' 'Light gains [65 makes heavy purses.' ''T is good to be merry and wise.' And when I was wived, having something to stick to, I had the horn of suretyship ever before my eyes. You all know the device of the horn, where the [70 young fellow slips in at the butt-end, and comes squeezed out at the buckle. And I grew up, and, I praise Providence, I bear my brows now as high as the best of my neighbours: but thou — well, look to the accounts; [75 your father's bond lies for you; seven-score pound is yet in the rear.

*Quick.* Why, 'slid, sir, I have as good, as proper, gallants' words for it as any are in London; gentlemen of good phrase, perfect [80

language, passingly behaved; gallants that wear socks and clean linen, and call me 'kind cousin Frank,' 'good cousin Frank,' for they know my father: and, by God's lid, shall I not trust 'em? Not trust! 85

*Enter a Page, as inquiring for Touchstone's shop*

*Gold.* What do ye lack, sir? What is 't you 'll buy, sir?
*Touch.* Ay, marry, sir; there 's a youth of another piece. There 's thy fellow-prentice, as good a gentleman born as thou art; nay, [90 and better meaned. But does he pump it, or racket it? Well, if he thrive not, if he outlast not a hundred such crackling bavins as thou art, God and men neglect industry!
*Gold.* It is his shop, and here my master [95 walks.                               *To the Page.*
*Touch.* With me, boy?
*Page.* My master, Sir Petronel Flash, recommends his love to you, and will instantly visit you. 100
*Touch.* To make up the match with my eldest daughter, my wife's dilling, whom she longs to call madam. He shall find me unwillingly ready, boy.             *Exit Page.*
There 's another affliction too. As I have [105 two prentices, the one of a boundless prodigality, the other of a most hopeful industry, so have I only two daughters: the eldest of a proud ambition and nice wantonness, the other of a modest humility and comely sober- [110 ness. The one must be ladyfied, forsooth, and be attired just to the court cut-and-long-tail. So far is she ill natured to the place and means of my preferment and fortune, that she throws all the contempt and despite [115 hatred itself can cast upon it. Well, a piece of land she has, — 't was her grandmother's gift: let her, and her Sir Petronel, flash out that! But as for my substance, she that scorns me, as I am a citizen and tradesman, [120 shall never pamper her pride with my industry, shall never use me as men do foxes: keep themselves warm in the skin, and throw the body that bare it to the dunghill. I must go entertain this Sir Petronel. Golding, [125 my utmost care 's for thee, and only trust in thee; look to the shop. As for you, Master Quicksilver, think of husks, for thy course is

running directly to the Prodigal's hog's-trough. Husks, sirrah! Work upon that now. 130

*Exit Touchstone.*

*Quick.* Marry faugh, goodman flat-cap! 'Sfoot! though I am a prentice, I can give arms; and my father's a Justice-o'-Peace by descent, and 'sblood —

*Gold.* Fie, how you swear! 135

*Quick.* 'Sfoot, man, I am a gentleman, and may swear by my pedigree, God's my life! Sirrah Golding, wilt be ruled by a fool? Turn good fellow, turn swaggering gallant, and let the welkin roar, and Erebus also. [140 Look not westward to the fall of Don Phœbus, but to the East. Eastward Ho!

Where radiant beams of lusty Sol appear,
And bright Eoüs makes the welkin clear.

We are both gentlemen, and therefore [145 should be no coxcombs; let 's be no longer fools to this flat-cap Touchstone. Eastward, bully! This satin belly and canvas-backed Touchstone! 'slife, man, his father was a malt-man, and his mother sold ginger-bread [150 in Christ-church!

*Gold.* What would ye ha' me do?

*Quick.* Why, do nothing, be like a gentleman, be idle; the curse of man is labour. Wipe thy bum with testons, and make [155 ducks and drakes with shillings. What, Eastward Ho! Wilt thou cry, 'What is 't ye lack?', stand with a bare pate and a dropping nose under a wooden pent-house, and art a gentleman? Wilt thou bear tankards, and may'st [160 bear arms? Be ruled, turn gallant, Eastward Ho! Ta, lirra, lirra, ro! 'Who calls Jeronimo? Speak, here I am!' God's so, how like a sheep thou look'st! O' my conscience some cowherd begot thee, thou Golding of Golding Hall! [165 Ha, boy?

*Gold.* Go, ye are a prodigal coxcomb! I a cowherd's son, because I turn not a drunken whore-hunting rake-hell like thyself!

*Quick.* Rake-hell! Rake-hell! 170

*Offers to draw, and Golding trips up his heels and holds him.*

*Gold.* Pish, in soft terms ye are a cowardly bragging boy! I 'll ha' you whipped!

*Quick.* Whipped? That 's good, i' faith! Untruss me?

*Gold.* No, thou wilt undo thyself. Alas, [175

I behold thee with pity, not with anger, thou common shot-clog, gull of all companies; methinks I see thee already walking in Moorfields without a cloak, with half a hat, without a band, a doublet with three buttons, with- [180 out a girdle, a hose with one point and no garter, with a cudgel under thine arm, borrowing and begging threepence.

*Quick.* Nay, 'slife, take this and take all! As I am a gentleman born, I 'll be drunk, [185 grow valiant, and beat thee. *Exit.*

*Gold.* Go, thou most madly vain, whom nothing can recover but that which reclaims atheists, and makes great persons sometimes religious: calamity. As for my place and [190 life, thus I have read: —

Whate'er some vainer youth may term disgrace,
The gain of honest pains is never base;
From trades, from arts, from valour, honour
   springs; 194
These three are founts of gentry, yea, of kings.

*[Exit.]*

[SCENE II.

*A Room in Touchstone's House]*

*Enter Gertrude, Mildred, Bettrice, and Poldavy a tailor; Poldavy with a fair gown, Scotch farthingale, and French fall in his arms; Gertrude in a French head-attire and citizen's gown; Mildred sewing, and Bettrice leading a monkey after her*

*Ger.* For the passion of patience, look if Sir Petronel approach, that sweet, that fine, that delicate, that — for love's sake, tell me if he come. O sister Mill, though my father be a low-capped tradesman, yet I must be a [5 lady; and, I praise God, my mother must call me Medam. Does he come? Off with this gown, for shame's sake, off with this gown; let not my knight take me in the city-cut in any hand. Tear 't, pax on 't!— [10 does he come? — tear 't off. *[Sings.]* 'Thus whilst she sleeps, I sorrow for her sake,' &c.

*Mil.* Lord, sister, with what an immodest impatiency and disgraceful scorn do you put off your City tire; I am sorry to think you [15 imagine to right yourself in wronging that which hath made both you and us.

*Ger.* I tell you I cannot endure it, I must

---

131 goodman flat-cap: Mister Merchant 132-133 give arms: claim gentry 140 let . . . also: (Pistol's rant in 2 *Henry IV*, II. iv) 141 Don Phœbus: the sun 144 Eoüs: the dawn welkin: sky 148 satin . . . backed: pretentious before and cheap behind 155 testons: sixpenny-pieces 159 wooden pent-house: shutter of the shop 161 ruled: advised 162-163 Who . . . am: (*Spanish Tragedy*, II. v. 4) 169 rake-hell: rascal 174 Untruss: prepare for spanking 177 shot-clog: dupe 178-179 Moorfields: unsavory section beyond the north wall of London 180 band: collar 181 point: tape fastening 188 recover: cure s. d. farthingale: hooped skirt fall: flat collar 7 Medam: (an affected pronunciation) 10 -cut: fashion in . . . hand: by any means 11-12 Thus . . . sake: (from one of John Dowland's 'ayres,' 1597) 15 tire: attire

be a lady: do you wear your coif with a London licket, your stammel petticoat with [20 two guards, the buffin gown with the tuf-taffety cape, and the velvet lace. I must be a lady, and I will be a lady. I like some humours of the city dames well: to eat cherries only at an angel a pound, good! [25 To dye rich scarlet black, pretty! To line a grogram gown clean thorough with velvet, tolerable! Their pure linen, their smocks of three pounds a smock, are to be borne withal! But your mincing niceries, taffata pipkins, [30 durance petticoats, and silver bodkins — God 's my life, as I shall be a lady, I cannot endure it! Is he come yet? Lord, what a long knight 't is! — [*Sings.*] 'And ever she cried, Shoot home!' — and yet I knew one longer. [35 'And ever she cried, Shoot home!' Fa, la, ly, re, lo, la!

*Mil.* Well, sister, those that scorn their nest, oft fly with a sick wing.

*Ger.* Bow-bell!     40

*Mil.* Where titles presume to thrust before fit means to second them, wealth and respect often grow sullen, and will not follow. For sure in this I would for your sake I spake not truth: Where ambition of place [45 goes before fitness of birth, contempt and disgrace follow. I heard a scholar once say that Ulysses, when he counterfeited himself mad, yoked cats and foxes and dogs together to draw his plough, whilst he followed and [50 sowed salt; but sure I judge them truly mad that yoke citizens and courtiers, tradesmen and soldiers, a goldsmith's daughter and a knight. Well, sister, pray God my father sow not salt too.     55

*Ger.* Alas! Poor Mill, when I am a lady, I 'll pray for thee yet, i' faith; nay, and I 'll vouchsafe to call thee Sister Mill still; for though thou art not like to be a lady as I am, yet sure thou art a creature of God's [60 making, and mayest peradventure to be saved as soon as I — does he come? — [*Sings.*] 'And ever and anon she doubled in her song.' Now, lady 's my comfort, what a profane ape 's here! Tailor, Poldavis, prithee, fit it, fit it! Is [65 this a right Scot? Does it clip close, and bear up round?

*Pol.* Fine and stiffly, i' faith! 'T will keep your thighs so cool, and make your waist so small; here was a fault in your body, but [70 I have supplied the defect with the effect of my steel instrument, which, though it have but one eye, can see to rectify the imperfection of the proportion.

*Ger.* Most edifying tailor! I protest you [75 tailors are most sanctified members, and make many crooked things go upright. How must I bear my hands? Light, light?

*Pol.* O, ay, now you are in the lady-fashion, you must do all things light. Tread [80 light, light. Ay, and fall so: that 's the court-amble.     *She trips about the stage.*

*Ger.* Has the court ne'er a trot?

*Pol.* No, but a false gallop, lady.

*Ger.* 'And if she will not go to bed, —' 85
     *Cantat.*

*Bet.* The knight 's come, forsooth.

*Enter Sir Petronel, Master Touchstone, and Mistress Touchstone*

*Ger.* Is my knight come? O the Lord, my band! Sister, do my cheeks look well? Give me a little box o' the ear that I may seem to blush; now, now! So, there, there, [90 there! Here he is. O my dearest delight! Lord, Lord, and how does my knight?

*Touch.* Fie, with more modesty!

*Ger.* Modesty! Why, I am no citizen now — modesty! Am I not to be married? [95 Y' are best to keep me modest, now I am to be a lady.

*Sir Pet.* Boldness is good fashion and court-like.

*Ger.* Ay, in a country lady I hope it is, [100 as I shall be. And how chance ye came no sooner, knight?

*Sir Pet.* 'Faith, I was so entertained in the Progress with one Count Epernoum, a Welsh knight; we had a match at balloon [105 too with my Lord Whatchum for four crowns.

*Ger.* At baboon? Jesu! You and I will play at baboon in the country, knight.

*Sir Pet.* O, sweet lady, 't is a strong play with the arm.     110

*Ger.* With arm or leg or any other member, if it be a Court sport. And when shall 's be married, my knight?

*Sir Pet.* I come now to consummate it, and your father may call a poor knight [115 son-in-law.

---

¹⁹ **coif:** linen cap     ²⁰ **licket:** flap (?)     **stammel:** worsted     ²¹ **guards:** trimmings     **buffin:** coarse cloth     ²¹⁻²² **tuf-taffety:** tufted silk     ²⁵ **angel:** about ten shillings     ²⁷ **grogram:** heavy silk ³⁰ **pipkins:** hats     ³¹ **durance:** stout cloth     ³⁴⁻³⁵ **And . . . home:** (from an old ballad)     ³⁵, ³⁶ **Shoot:** ('shoute' Qq.)     ³⁸⁻⁶⁷ (The appearance of the page in Q 1 indicates that about nine lines have been cancelled.)     ⁴⁰ **Bow-bell:** cockney     ⁶³ **doubled:** repeated a note in a higher or lower octave     ⁶⁵ **fit it:** do your fitting     ⁶⁶ **Scot:** Scotch farthingale     ⁷² **instrument:** needle     ⁷⁷ **things:** ('thing' Q 1) ¹⁰⁰ **country:** belonging to the county aristocracy     ¹⁰⁴ **Progress:** royal itinerary     ¹⁰⁵ **balloon:** a game somewhat like football, played with the arms

*Touch.* Sir, ye are come. What is not mine to keep, I must not be sorry to forgo. A hundred pounds land her grandmother left her; 't is yours; herself (as her mother's [120 gift) is yours. But if you expect aught from me, know my hand and mine eyes open together: I do not give blindly. Work upon that now!

*Sir Pet.* Sir, you mistrust not my means? [125 I am a knight.

*Touch.* Sir, sir, what I know not, you will give me leave to say I am ignorant of.

*Mist. Touch.* Yes, that he is, a knight; I know where he had money to pay the [130 gentlemen-ushers and heralds their fees. Ay, that he is, a knight; and so might you have been too, if you had been aught else than an ass, as well as some of your neighbours. And I thought you would not ha' been [135 knighted (as I am an honest woman) I would ha' dubbed you myself. I praise God, I have wherewithal. But as for you, daughter —

*Ger.* Ay, mother, I must be a lady tomorrow; and by your leave, mother (I speak [140 it not without my duty, but only in the right of my husband) I must take place of you, mother.

*Mist. Touch.* That you shall, lady-daughter, and have a coach as well as I too.     145

*Ger.* Yes, mother. But by your leave, mother (I speak it not without my duty, but only in my husband's right) my coach-horses must take the wall of your coach-horses.

*Touch.* Come, come, the day grows low: [150 't is supper-time. Use my house; the wedding solemnity is at my wife's cost; thank me for nothing but my willing blessing, for, (I cannot feign) my hopes are faint. And, sir, respect my daughter; she has refused for [155 you wealthy and honest matches, known good men, well-moneyed, better traded, best reputed.

*Ger.* Body o' truth! Chitizens, chitizens! Sweet knight, as soon as ever we are mar- [160 ried, take me to thy mercy out of this miserable Chity; presently carry me out of the scent of Newcastle coal, and the hearing of Bow-bell; I beseech thee, down with me, for God's sake!     165

*Touch.* Well, daughter, I have read that old wit sings:

'The greatest rivers flow from little springs.
Though thou art full, scorn not thy means at first;
He that 's most drunk may soonest be athirst.'

Work upon that now!     171
> *All but Touchstone, Mildred, and Golding depart.*

No, no! Yond' stand my hopes. Mildred, come hither, daughter! And how approve you your sister's fashion? How do you fancy her choice? What dost thou think?     175

*Mil.* I hope, as a sister, well.

*Touch.* Nay but, nay but, how dost thou like her behaviour and humour? Speak freely.

*Mil.* I am loath to speak ill; and yet, I am sorry, of this I cannot speak well.     180

*Touch.* Well! very good, as I would wish; a modest answer! Golding, come hither; hither, Golding! How dost thou like the knight, Sir Flash? Does he not look big? How lik'st thou the elephant? He says he [185 has a castle in the country.

*Gold.* Pray heaven, the elephant carry not his castle on his back.

*Touch.* 'Fore heaven, very well! But, seriously, how dost repute him?     190

*Gold.* The best I can say of him is, I know him not.

*Touch.* Ha, Golding! I commend thee, I approve thee, and will make it appear my affection is strong to thee. My wife has [195 her humour, and I will ha' mine. Dost thou see my daughter here? She is not fair: well-favoured or so, indifferent, which modest measure of beauty shall not make it thy only work to watch her, nor sufficient mischance [200 to suspect her. Thou art towardly, she is modest; thou art provident, she is careful. She 's now mine; give me thy hand. She 's now thine. Work upon that now!

*Gold.* Sir, as your son, I honour you; [205 and as your servant, obey you.

*Touch.* Sayest thou so? Come hither, Mildred. Do you see yond' fellow? He is a gentleman, though my prentice, and has somewhat to take to; a youth of good hope, [210 well friended, well parted. Are you mine? You are his. Work you upon that now!

*Mil.* Sir, I am all yours. Your body gave me life; your care and love, happiness of life; let your virtue still direct it, for to your [215 wisdom I wholly dispose myself.

*Touch.* Say'st thou so? Be you two better acquainted. Lip her, lip her, knave! So, shut up shop, in! We must make holiday.
> *Exeunt Golding and Mildred.*

This match shall on, for I intend to prove 220
Which thrives the best, the mean or lofty love:

---

¹¹⁹ **A . . . land:** land worth £ 100 a year    ¹³¹ **gentlemen-ushers:** court flunkies    ¹³⁵ **And:** if, an
¹⁴² **place:** precedence    ¹⁵⁶ **known:** approved    ¹⁵⁷ **traded:** established in business    ¹⁵⁹ **Chitizens:**
(a cockney pronunciation)    ¹⁶³ **Newcastle coal:** (London burned "sea-coal," brought by water from
Newcastle.)    ¹⁶⁴ **down:** into the country    ¹⁶⁷ **sings:** who sings    ¹⁹⁸ **indifferent:** tolerably
²⁰¹ **towardly:** promising    ²¹⁰ **take to:** build **on**    ²¹¹ **parted:** endowed

Whether fit wedlock vow'd 'twixt like and like,
Or prouder hopes, which daringly o'erstrike
Their place and means. 'T is honest time's
    expense,
When seeming lightness bears a moral sense. 225
Work upon that now.                      *Exit.*

## Actus secundi Scena prima

*[Goldsmith's Row]*

*Touchstone, Golding, and Mildred, sitting on
either side of the stall*

*Touch.* Quicksilver! Master Francis Quicksilver! Master Quicksilver!

*Enter Quicksilver*

*Quick.* Here, sir — ump!
*Touch.* So, sir; nothing but flat Master
Quicksilver (without any familiar addition) [5
will fetch you! Will you truss my points,
sir?
*Quick.* Ay, forsooth — ump!
*Touch.* How now, sir? The drunken hiccup so soon this morning?                      10
*Quick.* 'T is but the coldness of my stomach, forsooth!
*Touch.* What, have you the cause natural
for it? Y' are a very learned drunkard; I
believe I shall miss some of my silver spoons [15
with your learning. The nuptial night will
not moisten your throat sufficiently, but the
morning likewise must rain her dews into your
gluttonous weasand.
*Quick.* An 't please you, sir, we did but [20
drink — ump! — to the coming off of the
knightly bridegroom.
*Touch.* To the coming off on him?
*Quick.* Ay, forsooth! We drunk to his
coming on — ump! — when we went to bed; [25
and now we are up, we must drink to his
coming off; for that 's the chief honour of a
soldier, sir; and therefore we must drink
so much the more to it, forsooth — ump!
*Touch.* A very capital reason! So that [30
you go to bed late, and rise early to commit
drunkenness; you fulfill the Scripture very
sufficient wickedly, forsooth!
*Quick.* The knight's men, forsooth, be still
o' their knees at it — ump! — and because [35
't is for your credit, sir, I would be loath to
flinch.
*Touch.* I pray, sir, e'en to 'em again,
then; y' are one of the separated crew, one

of my wife's faction, and my young lady's, [40
with whom, and with their great match, I will
have nothing to do.
*Quick.* So, sir; now I will go keep my —
ump! — credit with 'em, an 't please you, sir!
*Touch.* In any case, sir, lay one cup of [45
sack more o' your cold stomach, I beseech
you!
*Quick.* Yes, forsooth!        *Exit Quicksilver.*
*Touch.* This is for my credit; servants
ever maintain drunkenness in their mas- [50
ter's house for their master's credit: a good
idle serving-man's reason. I thank Time,
the night is past! I ne'er waked to such cost;
I think we have stowed more sorts of flesh in
our bellies than ever Noah's ark received; [55
and for wine, why, my house turns giddy with
it, and more noise in it than at a conduit.
Ay me, even beasts condemn our gluttony!
Well, 't is our city's fault, which, because we
commit seldom, we commit the more sin- [60
fully; we lose no time in our sensuality, but
we make amends for it. O that we would do
so in virtue and religious negligences! But
see, here are all the sober parcels my house
can show. I 'll eavesdrop, hear what thoughts [65
they utter this morning.        *[He retires.]*

*Enter Golding*

*Gold.* But is it possible that you, seeing
your sister preferred to the bed of a knight,
should contain your affections in the arms of
a prentice?                      70
*Mil.* I had rather make up the garment of
my affections in some of the same piece, than,
like a fool, wear gowns of two colours, or mix
sackcloth with satin.
*Gold.* And do the costly garments — the [75
title and fame of a lady, the fashion, observation, and reverence proper to such preferment
— no more inflame you than such convenience
as my poor means and industry can offer to
your virtues?                      80
*Mil.* I have observed that the bridle given
to those violent flatteries of fortune is seldom
recovered; they bear one headlong in desire
from one novelty to another, and where those
ranging appetites reign, there is ever more [85
passion than reason: no stay, and so no happiness. These hasty advancements are not
natural. Nature hath given us legs to go to our
objects, not wings to fly to them.
*Gold.* How dear an object you are to my [90
desires I cannot express; whose fruition would

---

²²⁴ **honest . . . expense:** time well spent        ²²⁵ **lightness:** triviality        **bears . . . sense:** has a
good purpose        **II. i. s. d.** (Qq. add 'Quicksilver')        ⁶ **truss my points:** tie the laces of my hose
³² **Scripture:** (Isaiah V. 11)        ⁵³ **waked:** kept awake        ⁵⁷ **conduit:** public hydrant (gossiping-place
for servants)        ⁶⁶ **s. d.** (*I.e.,* Golding comes forward, with Mildred.)        ⁶⁸ **preferred:** advanced        ⁶⁹ **contain:** confine        ⁷⁸ **convenience:** comforts        ⁸⁶ **stay:** support

my master's absolute consent and yours vouchsafe me, I should be absolutely happy. And
though it were a grace so far beyond my merit
that I should blush with unworthiness to re- [95
ceive it, yet thus far both my love and my
means shall assure your requital: you shall
want nothing fit for your birth and education;
what increase of wealth and advancement the
honest and orderly industry and skill of our [100
trade will afford in any, I doubt not will be
aspired by me. I will ever make your contentment the end of my endeavours; I will love
you above all; and only your grief shall be my
misery, and your delight my felicity.        105

*Touch.* Work upon that now! By my
hopes, he wooes honestly and orderly; he shall
be anchor of my hopes! Look, see the ill-
yoked monster, his fellow!

*Enter Quicksilver unlaced, a towel about his
neck, in his flat-cap, drunk*

*Quick.* Eastward Ho! Holla, ye pam- [110
pered jades of Asia!

*Touch.* Drunk now downright, o' my
fidelity!

*Quick.* Ump! Pulldo, pulldo! Showse,
quoth the caliver.                            115

*Gold.* Fie, fellow Quicksilver, what a pickle
are you in!

*Quick.* Pickle? Pickle in thy throat;
zounds, pickle! Wa, ha, ho! Good-morrow,
knight Petronel; morrow, lady Goldsmith; [120
come off, knight, with a counter-buff, for the
honour of knighthood.

*Gold.* Why, how now, sir? Do ye know
where you are?

*Quick.* Where I am? Why, 'sblood, you [125
jolthead, where I am.

*Gold.* Go to, go to, for shame! Go to bed
and sleep out this immodesty: thou sham'st
both my master and his house.

*Quick.* Shame? What shame? I thought [130
thou wouldst show thy bringing-up; and thou
wert a gentleman as I am, thou wouldst think
it no shame to be drunk. Lend me some
money, save my credit; I must dine with the
serving-men and their wives — and their [135
wives, sirrah!

*Gold.* E'en who you will; I 'll not lend thee
threepence.

*Quick.* 'Sfoot, lend me some money! 'Hast
thou not Hiren here?'                         140

*Touch.* Why, how now, sirrah? What
vein 's this, ha?

*Quick.* 'Who cries on murther? Lady, was
it you?' How does our master? Pray thee
cry, Eastward Ho!                             145

*Touch.* Sirrah, sirrah, y' are past your hiccup now; I see y' are drunk —

*Quick.* 'T is for your credit, master.

*Touch.* And hear you keep a whore in
town —                                        150

*Quick.* 'T is for your credit, master.

*Touch.* And what you are out in cash, I
know.

*Quick.* So do I; my father 's a gentleman.
Work upon that now! Eastward Ho!             155

*Touch.* Sir, Eastward Ho will make you
go Westward Ho. I will no longer dishonest
my house, nor endanger my stock with your
license. There, sir, there 's your indenture;
all your apparel (that I must know) is on [160
your back, and from this time my door is shut
to you: from me be free; but for other freedom,
and the moneys you have wasted, Eastward Ho
shall not serve you.

*Quick.* Am I free o' my fetters? Rent, [165
fly with a duck in thy mouth! And now I tell
thee, Touchstone —

*Touch.* Good sir —

*Quick.* 'When this eternal substance of
    my soul' —

*Touch.* Well said; change your gold-ends [170
for your play-ends.

*Quick.* 'Did live imprison'd in my wanton
    flesh'—

*Touch.* What then, sir?

*Quick.* 'I was a courtier in the Spanish
    Court,
And Don Andrea was my name.'               175

*Touch.* Good Master Don Andrea, will you
march?

*Quick.* Sweet Touchstone, will you lend me
two shillings?

*Touch.* Not a penny!                       180

*Quick.* Not a penny? I have friends, and
I have acquaintance; I will piss at thy shop-
posts, and throw rotten eggs at thy sign.
Work upon that now!         *Exit staggering.*

*Touch.* Now, sirrah, you; hear you? [185
You shall serve me no more neither — not an
hour longer.

*Gold.* What mean you, sir?

*Touch.* I mean to give thee thy freedom,

110–111 **Holla . . . Asia:** (from Marlowe's *Tamburlaine*, part II)    114, 115 **Pulldo:** sound of belching
**Showse . . . caliver:** "Bang," said the gun.    126 **jolthead:** blockhead    131 **and:** if    139–140 **Hast . . .
here:** (apparently from a lost play by Peele; quoted also by Pistol in *2 Henry IV*)    143–144 **Who . . .
you:** (mimicking a line in Chapman's *Blind Beggar of Alexandria*, ix. 49, 'Who calls out murther?
Lady, was it you?' Repeated also in Jonson's *Poetaster*, III. iv. 259)    157 **Westward Ho:** (*i.e.*, to
the gallows at Tyburn)    **dishonest:** corrupt    158 **stock:** property    169–175 (Cf. *Spanish Tragedy*,
I. i)

and with thy freedom my daughter, and [190
with my daughter a father's love. And with
all these such a portion as shall make Knight
Petronel himself envy thee! Y' are both agreed,
are ye not?

*Ambo.* With all submission, both of [195
thanks and duty.

*Touch.* Well, then, the great Power of
heaven bless and confirm you! And, Golding, that my love to thee may not show less
than my wife's love to my eldest daughter, [200
thy marriage-feast shall equal the knight's
and hers.

*Gold.* Let me beseech you, no, sir; the
superfluity and cold meat left at their nuptials
will with bounty furnish ours. The grossest [205
prodigality is superfluous cost of the belly;
nor would I wish any invitement of states or
friends, only your reverent presence and witness shall sufficiently grace and confirm us.

*Touch.* Son to mine own bosom, take her [210
and my blessing. The nice fondling, my
lady, sir-reverence, that I must not now
presume to call daughter, is so ravished with
desire to hansel her new coach, and see her
knight's Eastward Castle, that the next [215
morning will sweat with her busy setting forth.
Away will she and her mother, and while their
preparation is making, ourselves, with some
two or three other friends, will consummate
the humble match we have in God's name [220
concluded.

'T is to my wish; for I have often read
Fit birth, fit age, keeps long a quiet bed.
'T is to my wish; for tradesmen (well 't is known)
Get with more ease than gentry keeps his own. 225

*Exit [following Golding and Mildred].*

### [SCENE II. — *Security's House*]

*Security solus*

*Sec.* My privy guest, lusty Quicksilver, has
drunk too deep of the bride-bowl; but with a
little sleep, he is much recovered; and, I think,
is making himself ready to be drunk in a
gallanter likeness. My house is, as 't were, [5
the cave where the young outlaw hoards the
stolen vails of his occupation; and here, when
he will revel it in his prodigal similitude, he
retires to his trunks, and (I may say softly) his
punks: he dares trust me with the keeping [10
of both; for I am Security itself; my name is
Security, the famous usurer.

*Enter Quicksilver in his prentice's coat and
cap, his gallant breeches and stockings,
gartering himself, Security following*

*Quick.* Come, old Security, thou father of
destruction! Th' indented sheepskin is burned
wherein I was wrapped; and I am now loose [15
to get more children of perdition into thy usurous bonds. Thou feed'st my lechery, and I thy
covetousness; thou art pandar to me for my
wench, and I to thee for thy cozenages. Ka
me, ka thee, runs through court and country. [20

*Sec.* Well said, my subtle Quicksilver!
These k's ope the doors to all this world's
felicity; the dullest forehead sees it. Let not
master courtier think he carries all the knavery
on his shoulders. I have known poor Hob [25
in the country, that has worn hob-nails on 's
shoes, have as much villainy in 's head as he
that wears gold buttons in 's cap.

*Quick.* Why, man, 't is the London highway to thrift; if virtue be used, 't is but as [30
a scrap to the net of villainy. They that
use it simply, thrive simply, I warrant. Weight
and fashion makes goldsmiths cuckolds.

*Enter Sindefy, with Quicksilver's doublet, cloak,
rapier, and dagger*

*Sin.* Here, sir, put off the other half of
your prenticeship.                          35

*Quick.* Well said, sweet Sin! Bring forth
    my bravery.
Now let my trunks shoot forth their silks
    conceal'd.
I now am free, and now will justify
My trunks and punks. Avaunt, dull flat-cap,
    then!
Via, the curtain that shadow'd Borgia!    40
There lie, thou husk of my envassal'd state,
I, Samson, now have burst the Philistines'
    bands,
And in thy lap, my lovely Dalida,
I 'll lie and snore out my enfranchis'd state.

> 'When Samson was a tall young man,    45
> His power and strength increas'd than;
> He sold no more nor cup nor can;
> But did them all despise.
> Old Touchstone, now write to thy friends
> For one to sell thy base gold-ends;    50
> Quicksilver now no more attends
> Thee, Touchstone.'

But, Dad, hast thou seen my running gelding
dressed to-day?

---

[207] **states:** dignified persons    [208] **reverent:** reverend    [211] **nice fondling:** spoiled darling    [212] **sir-reverence:** all respect to her!    [214] **hansel:** get the first taste of    [5] **gallanter likeness:** courtlier cos-tume    [7] **vails:** profits    [8] **in . . . similitude:** like the Prodigal    [10] **punks:** harlots    [19] **cozenages:** frauds    [19-20] **Ka . . . thee:** One good turn deserves another    [22] **k's:** (pun on "keys," similarly pronounced)    [40] **Via:** begone    **curtain:** the apprentice costume    **Borgia:** symbol of riotous splen-dor    [42] **bands:** bonds    [43] **Dalida:** Delilah    [45-52] (Parody of an old ballad)    [54] **dressed:** groomed

*Sec.* That I have, Frank. The ostler [55 o' th' Cock dressed him for a breakfast.

*Quick.* What, did he eat him?

*Sec.* No, but he eat his breakfast for dressing him; and so dressed him for breakfast.

*Quick.* O witty age, where age is young in wit,                                            60
And all youth's words have gray beards full of it!

*Sin.* But alas, Frank, how will all this be maintained now? Your place maintained it before.

*Quick.* Why, and I maintained my [65 place. I 'll to the Court, another manner of place for maintenance, I hope, than the silly City! 'I heard my father say, I heard my mother sing, an old song and a true!' Thou art a she-fool, and know'st not what be- [70 longs to our male wisdom. I shall be a merchant, forsooth, trust my estate in a wooden trough as he does! What are these ships but tennis-balls for the winds to play withal? Tossed from one wave to another; now [75 under line, now over the house: sometimes brick-walled against a rock, so that the guts fly out again; sometimes strook under the wide hazard, and farewell, master merchant!

*Sin.* Well, Frank, well! The seas, you [80 say, are uncertain; but he that sails in your court seas shall find 'em ten times fuller of hazard; wherein to see what is to be seen is torment more than a free spirit can endure. But when you come to suffer, how many [85 injuries swallow you! What care and devotion must you use to humour an imperious lord, proportion your looks to his looks, smiles to his smiles, fit your sails to the wind of his breath!

*Quick.* Tush, he 's no journeyman in his [90 craft that cannot do that!

*Sin.* But he 's worse than a prentice that does it; not only humouring the lord, but every trencher-bearer, every groom, that by indulgence and intelligence crept into his [95 favour, and by pandarism into his chamber: he rules the roast; and when my honourable lord says it shall be thus, my worshipful rascal, the groom of his close-stool, says it shall not be thus, claps the door after him, [100 and who dares enter? A prentice, quoth you? 'T is but to learn to live; and does that disgrace a man? He that rises hardly stands firmly; but he that rises with ease, alas, falls as easily!

*Quick.* A pox on you! Who taught you [105 this morality?

*Sec.* 'T is 'long of this witty age, Master Francis. But, indeed, Mistress Sindefy, all trades complain of inconvenience, and therefore 't is best to have none. The merchant, [110 he complains and says, 'Traffic is subject to much uncertainty and loss.' Let 'em keep their goods on dry land, with a vengeance, and not expose other men's substances to the mercy of the winds, under protection of a [115 wooden wall (as Master Francis says); and all for greedy desire to enrich themselves with unconscionable gain, two for one, or so; where I, and such other honest men as live by lending money, are content with moderate profit; [120 thirty or forty i' th' hundred, so we may have it with quietness, and out of peril of wind and weather, rather than run those dangerous courses of trading, as they do.

*Quick.* Ay, Dad, thou mayst well be [125 called Security, for thou takest the safest course.

*Sec.* Faith, the quieter, and the more contented, and, out of doubt, the more godly. For merchants, in their courses, are never [130 pleased, but ever repining against heaven: one prays for a westerly wind to carry his ship forth; another for an easterly to bring his ship home; and at every shaking of a leaf he falls into an agony to think what danger his ship [135 is in on such a coast, and so forth. The farmer, he is ever at odds with the weather: sometimes the clouds have been too barren; sometimes the heavens forget themselves, their harvests answer not their hopes; sometimes the [140 season falls out too fruitful, corn will bear no price, and so forth. Th' artificer, he 's all for a stirring world; if his trade be too dull, and fall short of his expectation, then falls he out of joint. Where we that trade nothing but [145 money are free from all this; we are pleased with all weathers, let it rain or hold up, be calm or windy; let the season be whatsoever, let trade go how it will, we take all in good part, e'en what please the heavens to send us, so [150 the sun stand not still, and the moon keep her usual returns, and make up days, months, and years —

*Quick.* And you have good security!

*Sec.* Ay, marry, Frank, that 's the [155 special point.

*Quick.* And yet, forsooth, we must have trades to live withal; for we cannot stand without legs, nor fly without wings, and a number of such scurvy phrases. No, I say [160 still, he that has wit, let him live by his wit; he that has none, let him be a tradesman.

---

⁵⁶ **Cock:** Cock Tavern     ⁶⁵ (Something has been cancelled here.)     ⁷⁶ **under line:** (tennis term)
⁷⁵⁻⁷⁹ **wide hazard:** (tennis term)     ⁹⁵ **intelligence:** tale-bearing     ¹⁰⁷ **'long of:** on account of
¹²⁵ (Something cancelled here in Q 1)     ¹³⁶ **such:** such and such     ¹⁴³ **dull:** (P. Simpson's emendation: 'full' Qq.)

*Sec.* Witty Master Francis! 'T is pity any trade should dull that quick brain of yours! Do but bring Knight Petronel into my [165 parchment toils once, and you shall never need to toil in any trade, o' my credit. You know his wife's land?

*Quick.* Even to a foot, sir; I have been often there; a pretty fine seat, good land, [170 all entire within itself.

*Sec.* Well wooded?

*Quick.* Two hundred pounds' worth of wood ready to fell. And a fine sweet house, that stands just in the midst on 't, like a [175 prick in the midst of a circle; would I were your farmer, for a hundred pound a year!

*Sec.* Excellent Master Francis, how I do long to do thee good! How I do hunger and thirst to have the honour to enrich thee! [180 Ay, even to die that thou mightest inherit my living; even hunger and thirst! For o' my religion, Master Francis — and so tell Knight Petronel — I do it to do him a pleasure.

*Quick.* Marry, Dad, his horses are now [185 coming up to bear down his lady; wilt thou lend him thy stable to set 'em in?

*Sec.* Faith, Master Francis, I would be loath to lend my stable out of doors; in a greater matter I will pleasure him, but not [190 in this.

*Quick.* A pox of your hunger and thirst! Well, Dad, let him have money; all he could any way get is bestowed on a ship now bound for Virginia; the frame of which voyage is [195 so closely conveyed that his new lady nor any of her friends know it. Notwithstanding, as soon as his lady's hand is gotten to the sale of her inheritance, and you have furnished him with money, he will instantly hoist sail [200 and away.

*Sec.* Now, a frank gale of wind go with him, Master Frank. We have too few such knight adventurers. Who would not sell away competent certainties to purchase, [205 with any danger, excellent uncertainties? Your true knight venturer ever does it. Let his wife seal to-day; he shall have his money to-day.

*Quick.* To-morrow she shall, Dad, before [210 she goes into the country; to work her to which action with the more engines, I purpose presently to prefer my sweet Sin here to the place of her gentlewoman; whom you (for the more credit) shall present as your [215 friend's daughter, a gentlewoman of the country, new come up with a will for awhile to learn fashions, forsooth, and be toward some lady; and she shall buzz pretty devices into her lady's ear, feeding her humours so serv- [220 iceably, as the manner of such as she is, you know —

*Sec.* True, good Master Francis!

*Quick.* That she shall keep her port open to anything she commends to her. 225

*Sec.* O' my religion, a most fashionable project; as good she spoil the lady, as the lady spoil her, for ' t is three to one of one side. Sweet Mistress Sin, how are you bound to Master Francis! I do not doubt to see you [230 shortly wed one of the head men of our city.

*Sin.* But, sweet Frank, when shall my father Security present me?

*Quick.* With all festination; I have broken the ice to it already; and will presently to [235 the knight's house, whither, my good old Dad, let me pray thee with all formality to man her.

*Sec.* Command me, Master Francis; I do hunger and thirst to do thee service. Come, sweet Mistress Sin, take leave of my Wini- [240 fred, and we will instantly meet frank Master Francis at your lady's.

*Enter Winifred above*

*Win.* Where is my Cu there? Cu?

*Sec.* Ay, Winnie!

*Win.* Wilt thou come in, sweet Cu? 245

*Sec.* Ay, Winnie, presently!

*Exeunt [all but Quicksilver].*

*Quick.* Ay, Winnie, quod he! That 's all he can do, poor man, he may well cut off her name at Winnie. O 't is an egregious pandar! What will not an usurous knave be, so he [250 may be rich? O 'tis a notable Jew's trump! I hope to live to see dogs' meat made of the old usurer's flesh, dice of his bones, and indentures of his skin; and yet his skin is too thick to make parchment, 't would make good [255 boots for a peterman to catch salmon in. Your only smooth skin to make fine vellum is your Puritan's skin; they be the smoothest and slickest knaves in a country. *[Exit.]*

## [SCENE III. — *Before Sir Petronel's Lodging*]

*Enter Sir Petronel in boots, with a riding wan [followed by Quicksilver]*

*Pet.* I 'll out of this wicked town as fast as my horse can trot. Here 's now no good action for a man to spend his time in. Taverns

---

¹⁷⁷ **farmer:** tenant　　¹⁸⁹ **out of doors:** to strangers　　¹⁹⁵ **frame:** plan　　²¹² **engines:** contrivances　　²¹⁸ **toward:** expecting service with　　²³⁴ **festination:** haste　　²³⁷ **man:** escort　　²⁴³ **Cu:** (Security's pet name)　　²⁴⁷ **quod:** said　　²⁵¹ **Jew's trump:** Jew's harp, *i.e.*, Jew　　²⁵⁶ **peterman:** fisherman
Sc. III. s. d. **wan:** wand, stick　(The scene clearly changes, but the original stage directions show that Quicksilver remained on the stage and Sir Petronel entered to him.)

grow dead; ordinaries are blown up; plays are at a stand; houses of hospitality at a fall; [5 not a feather waving, not a spur jingling anywhere. I 'll away instantly.

*Quick.* Y'ad best take some crowns in your purse, knight, or else your Eastward Castle will smoke but miserably. 10

*Pet.* O, Frank, my castle! Alas, all the castles I have are built with air, thou know'st!

*Quick.* I know it, knight, and therefore wonder whither your lady is going.

*Pet.* Faith, to seek her fortune, I think. [15 I said I had a castle and land eastward, and eastward she will, without contradiction; her coach and the coach of the sun must meet full butt. And the sun being out-shined with her ladyship's glory, she fears he goes westward [20 to hang himself.

*Quick.* And I fear, when her enchanted castle becomes invisible, her ladyship will return and follow his example.

*Pet.* O that she would have the grace, [25 for I shall never be able to pacify her, when she sees herself deceived so.

*Quick.* As easily as can be. Tell her she mistook your directions, and that shortly yourself will down with her to approve it; [30 and then clothe but her crupper in a new gown, and you may drive her any way you list. For these women, sir, are like Essex calves, you must wriggle 'em on by the tail still, or they will never drive orderly. 35

*Pet.* But, alas, sweet Frank, thou know'st my hability will not furnish her blood with those costly humours.

*Quick.* Cast that cost on me, sir. I have spoken to my old pandar, Security, for [40 money or commodity; and commodity (if you will) I know he will procure you.

*Pet.* Commodity! Alas, what commodity?

*Quick.* Why, sir, what say you to figs and raisins? 45

*Pet.* A plague of figs and raisins, and all such frail commodities! We shall make nothing of 'em.

*Quick.* Why then, sir, what say you to forty pound in roasted beef? 50

*Pet.* Out upon 't! I have less stomach to that than to the figs and raisins. I 'll out of town, though I sojourn with a friend of mine; for stay here I must not; my creditors have laid to arrest me, and I have no friend under [55 heaven but my sword to bail me.

*Quick.* God's me, knight, put 'em in sufficient sureties, rather than let your sword bail you! Let 'em take their choice, either the King's Bench or the Fleet, or which of the [60 two Counters they like best, for, by the Lord, I like none of 'em.

*Pet.* Well, Frank, there is no jesting with my earnest necessity; thou know'st if I make not present money to further my voyage [65 begun, all 's lost, and all I have laid out about it.

*Quick.* Why, then, sir, in earnest, if you can get your wise lady to set her hand to the sale of her inheritance, the bloodhound, [70 Security, will smell out ready money for you instantly.

*Pet.* There spake an angel! To bring her to which conformity, I must feign myself extremely amorous; and alleging urgent [75 excuses for my stay behind, part with her as passionately as she would from her foisting hound.

*Quick.* You have the sow by the right ear, sir. I warrant there was never child longed [80 more to ride a-cock-horse or wear his new coat, than she longs to ride in her new coach. She would long for everything when she was a maid, and now she will run mad for 'em. I lay my life, she will have every year four [85 children; and what charge and change of humour you must endure while she is with child, and how she will tie you to your tackling till she be with child, a dog would not endure. Nay, there is no turnspit dog bound to his [90 wheel more servilely than you shall be to her wheel; for as that dog can never climb the top of his wheel but when the top comes under him, so shall you never climb the top of her contentment but when she is under you. 95

*Pet.* 'Slight, how thou terrifiest me!

*Quick.* Nay, hark you, sir; what nurses, what midwives, what fools, what physicians, what cunning women must be sought for (fearing sometimes she is bewitched, some- [100 times in a consumption) to tell her tales, to talk bawdy to her, to make her laugh, to give her glisters, to let her blood under the tongue and betwixt the toes; how she will revile and kiss you, spit in your face, and lick it off [105 again; how she will vaunt you are her creature, she made you of nothing; how she could have had thousand-mark jointures; she could have been made a lady by a Scotch knight, and

---

<sup>18-19</sup> **full butt:** in full career   <sup>30</sup> **approve:** prove   <sup>34</sup> **still:** constantly   <sup>37</sup> **hability:** ability, means   **blood:** temper   <sup>41</sup> **commodity:** dubiously marketable ware, to be turned into cash by the borrower   <sup>50</sup> **pound:** pounds sterling   <sup>55</sup> **laid:** set ambushes   <sup>58</sup> **sureties:** guarantees (with pun on "places of safe keeping")   <sup>60-61</sup> **King's Bench . . . Counters:** London prisons   <sup>65</sup> **present:** immediate   <sup>77</sup> **foisting:** ill-smelling   <sup>86</sup> **charge:** expense   **change:** inconstancy   <sup>90</sup> **turnspit dog:** dog harnessed to turn the spit on which meat was roasted   <sup>103</sup> **glisters:** clysters, enemas

never ha' married him; she could have had [110 poynados in her bed every morning; how she set you up, and how she will pull you down: you 'll never be able to stand of your legs to endure it.

*Pet.* Out of my fortune! what a death [115 is my life bound face to face to! The best is, a large time-fitted conscience is bound to nothing; marriage is but a form in the school of policy, to which scholars sit fastened only with painted chains. Old Security's young [120 wife is ne'er the further off with me.

*Quick.* Thereby lies a tale, sir. The old usurer will be here instantly with my punk Sindefy, whom you know your lady has promised me to entertain for her gentlewoman; [125 and he (with a purpose to feed on you) invites you most solemnly by me to supper.

*Pet.* It falls out excellently fitly: I see desire of gain makes jealousy venturous.

*Enter Gertrude*

See, Frank, here comes my lady. Lord, [130 how she views thee! She knows thee not, I think, in this bravery.

*Ger.* How now? Who be you, I pray?

*Quick.* One Master Francis Quicksilver, an 't please your ladyship.     135

*Ger.* God 's my dignity! As I am a lady, if he did not make me blush so that mine eyes stood a-water, would I were unmarried again! Where 's my woman, I pray?

*Enter Security and Sindefy*

*Quick.* See, madam, she now comes to [140 attend you.

*Sec.* God save my honourable knight and his worshipful lady!

*Ger.* Y' are very welcome! you must not put on your hat yet.     145

*Sec.* No, madam; till I know your ladyship's further pleasure, I will not presume.

*Ger.* And is this a gentleman's daughter new come out of the country?

*Sec.* She is, madam; and one that her [150 father hath a special care to bestow in some honourable lady's service, to put her out of her honest humours, forsooth; for she had a great desire to be a nun, an 't please you.

*Ger.* A nun? What nun? A nun sub- [155 stantive, or a nun adjective?

*Sec.* A nun substantive, madam, I hope, if a nun be a noun. But I mean, lady, a vowed maid of that order.

*Ger.* I 'll teach her to be a maid of the [160

order, I warrant you! And can you do any work belongs to a lady's chamber?

*Sin.* What I cannot do, madam, I would be glad to learn.

*Ger.* Well said, hold up, then; hold up [165 your head, I say! Come hither a little.

*Sin.* I thank your ladyship.

*Ger.* And hark you — good man, you may put on your hat now; I do not look on you — I must have you of my faction now; not of [170 my knight's, maid!

*Sin.* No, forsooth, madam, of yours.

*Ger.* And draw all my servants in my bow, and keep my counsel, and tell me tales, and put me riddles, and read on a book some- [175 times when I am busy, and laugh at country gentlewomen, and command anything in the house for my retainers; and care not what you spend, for it is all mine; and in any case be still a maid, whatsoever you do, or whatsoever any man can do unto you.     181

*Sec.* I warrant your ladyship for that.

*Ger.* Very well; you shall ride in my coach with me into the country to-morrow morning. Come, knight, pray thee, let 's make a short [185 supper, and to bed presently.

*Sec.* Nay, good madam, this night I have a short supper at home waits on his worship's acceptation.

*Ger.* By my faith, but he shall not go, [190 sir; I shall swoon and he sup from me.

*Pet.* Pray thee, forbear; shall he lose his provision?

*Ger.* Ay, by lady, sir, rather than I lose my longing. Come in, I say; as I am a lady, [195 you shall not go.

*Quick.* [*aside to Security.*] I told him what a burr he had gotten.

*Sec.* If you will not sup from your knight, madam, let me entreat your ladyship to sup [200 at my house with him.

*Ger.* No, by my faith, sir; then we cannot be abed soon enough after supper.

*Pet.* What a med'cine is this! — Well, Master Security, you are new married as [205 well as I; I hope you are bound as well. We must honour our young wives, you know.

*Quick.* [*aside to Security.*] In policy, Dad, till to-morrow he has sealed.

*Sec.* I hope in the morning, yet, your [210 knighthood will breakfast with me?

*Pet.* As early as you will, sir.

*Sec.* Thank your good worship; I do hunger and thirst to do you good, sir.     [214

*Ger.* Come, sweet knight, come; I do hunger and thirst to be abed with thee.     *Exeunt.*

---

¹¹¹ **poynados:** panadas, bread puddings     ¹¹⁵ **Out of:** Out upon!     ¹¹⁷ **large:** liberal     **time-fitted:** up to date, modern     ¹²⁵ **entertain:** employ     ¹³² **bravery:** finery     ¹⁶² **belongs:** which belongs ¹⁷³ **in my bow:** to my faction     ¹⁸⁵ **pray:** ('I pray' Q 3)     ¹⁹¹ **and:** if     **from:** apart from

## Actus tertii Scena prima

*[Security's House]*

*Enter Petronel, Quicksilver, Security, Bramble, and Winifred*

*Pet.* Thanks for your feast-like breakfast, good Master Security; I am sorry (by reason of my instant haste to so long a voyage as Virginia) I am without means by any kind amends to show how affectionately I take [5 your kindness, and to confirm by some worthy ceremony a perpetual league of friendship betwixt us.

*Sec.* Excellent knight, let this be a token betwixt us of inviolable friendship: I am [10 new married to this fair gentlewoman, you know, and by my hope to make her fruitful, though I be something in years, I vow faithfully unto you to make you godfather (though in your absence) to the first child I am [15 bless'd withal; and henceforth call me gossip, I beseech you, if you please to accept it.

*Pet.* In the highest degree of gratitude, my most worthy gossip; for confirmation [20 of which friendly title, let me entreat my fair gossip, your wife here, to accept this diamond, and keep it as my gift to her first child, wheresoever my fortune, in event of my voyage, shall bestow me.            25

*Sec.* How now, my coy wedlock, make you strange of so noble a favour? Take it, I charge you, with all affection, and, by way of taking your leave, present boldly your lips to our honourable gossip.            30

*Quick.* *[aside.]* How venturous he is to him, and how jealous to others!

*Pet.* Long may this kind touch of our lips print in our hearts all the forms of affection. And now, my good gossip, if the writings [35 be ready to which my wife should seal, let them be brought this morning before she takes coach into the country, and my kindness shall work her to dispatch it.

*Sec.* The writings are ready, sir. My [40 learned counsel here, Master Bramble the lawyer, hath perused them; and within this hour I will bring the scrivener with them to your worshipful lady.

*Pet.* Good Master Bramble, I will here [45 take my leave of you, then. God send you fortunate pleas, sir, and contentious clients!

*Bram.* And you foreright winds, sir, and a fortunate voyage!            *Exit.*

*Enter a Messenger*

*Mes.* Sir Petronel, here are three or four [50 gentlemen desire to speak with you.

*Pet.* What are they?

*Quick.* They are your followers in this voyage, Knight, Captain Seagull and his associates; I met them this morning, and told them [55 you would be here.

*Pet.* Let them enter, I pray you; I know they long to be gone, for their stay is dangerous.

*Enter Seagull, Scapethrift, and Spendall*

*Sea.* God save my honourable Colonel!   60

*Pet.* Welcome, good Captain Seagull and worthy gentlemen. If you will meet my friend Frank here and me, at the Blue Anchor Tavern by Billingsgate this evening, we will there drink to our happy voyage, be merry, and take [65 boat to our ship with all expedition.

*Spen.* Defer it no longer, I beseech you, sir; but as your voyage is hitherto carried closely, and in another knight's name, so for your own safety and ours, let it be continued, [70 — our meeting and speedy purpose of departing known to as few as is possible, lest your ship and goods be attached.

*Quick.* Well advised, Captain! Our colonel shall have money this morning to dispatch [75 all our departures. Bring those gentlemen at night to the place appointed, and with our skins full of vintage we 'll take occasion by the vantage, and away.

*Spen.* We will not fail but be there, sir. [80

*Pet.* Good morrow, good Captain and my worthy associates. Health and all sovereignty to my beautiful gossip; for you, sir, we shall see you presently with the writings.

*Sec.* With writings and crowns to my [85 honourable gossip. I do hunger and thirst to do you good, sir!            *Exeunt.*

## Actus tertii Scena secunda

*[An inn-yard]*

*Enter a Coachman in haste, in 's frock, feeding*

*Coach.* Here 's a stir when citizens ride out of town, indeed, as if all the house were afire! 'Slight, they will not give a man leave to eat 's breakfast afore he rises!

*Enter Hamlet, a footman, in haste*

*Ham.* What, coachman! My lady's coach [5 for shame! Her ladyship 's ready to come down.

*Enter Potkin, a tankard-bearer*

---

⁵ **amends:** requital   ¹⁶⁻¹⁷ **gossip:** one related by the sacrament of baptism   ²⁴ **event:** outcome   ²⁶⁻²⁷ **make . . . strange:** are you hesitant   ⁴⁸ **foreright:** favorable   ⁶⁸⁻⁶⁹ **carried closely:** prepared secretly   Sc. II. ⁷ **s. d. tankard-bearer:** water-carrier

*Pot.* 'Sfoot, Hamlet, are you mad? Whither run you now? You should brush up my old mistress!    [*Exit Hamlet.*] 10

*Enter Sindefy*

*Sin.* What, Potkin? You must put off your tankard, and put on your blue coat and wait upon Mistress Touchstone into the country.    *Exit.*
*Pot.* I will, forsooth, presently.    *Exit.*

*Enter Mistress Fond and Mistress Gazer*

*Fond.* Come, sweet Mistress Gazer, let 's [15 watch here, and see my Lady Flash take coach.
*Gaz.* O' my word, here 's a most fine place to stand in. Did you see the new ship launched last day, Mistress Fond?
*Fond.* O God, and we citizens should lose [20 such a sight!
*Gaz.* I warrant here will be double as many people to see her take coach as there were to see it take water.
*Fond.* O she 's married to a most fine [25 castle i' th' country, they say.
*Gaz.* But there are no giants in the castle, are there?
*Fond.* O no; they say her knight killed 'em all, and therefore he was knighted.    30
*Gaz.* Would to God her ladyship would come away!

*Enter Gertrude, Mistress Touchstone, Sindefy, Hamlet, Potkin*

*Fond.* She comes, she comes, she comes!
*Gaz.* }
*Fond.* } Pray heaven bless your ladyship!
*Ger.* Thank you, good people! My [35 coach! for the love of heaven, my coach! In good truth I shall swoon else.
*Ham.* Coach, coach, my lady's coach!    *Exit.*
*Ger.* As I am a lady, I think I am with child already, I long for a coach so. May [40 one be with child afore they are married, mother?
*Mist. Touch.* Ay, by 'r lady, madam; a little thing does that. I have seen a little prick no bigger than a pin's head swell bigger and [45 bigger till it has come to an ancome; and e'en so 't is in these cases.

*Enter Hamlet*

*Ham.* Your coach is coming, madam.
*Ger.* That 's well said. Now, heaven, me-

thinks I am e'en up to the knees in prefer- [50 ment!  [*sings.*]

*But a little higher, but a little higher, but a little higher:*
*There, there, there lies Cupid's fire!*

*Mist. Touch.* But must this young man, an 't please you, madam, run by your coach all the way a-foot?    56
*Ger.* Ay, by my faith, I warrant him! He gives no other milk, as I have another servant does.    59
*Mist. Touch.* Alas, 't is e'en pity, methinks! For God's sake, madam, buy him but a hobby-horse; let the poor youth have something be-twixt his legs to ease 'em. Alas, we must do as we would be done to!    64
*Ger.* Go to, hold your peace, dame; you talk like an old fool, I tell you!

*Enter [Sir] Petronel and Quicksilver*

*Pet.* Wilt thou be gone, sweet honeysuckle, before I can go with thee?
*Ger.* I pray thee, sweet knight, let me; [69 I do so long to dress up thy castle afore thou com'st. But I marle how my modest sister occupies herself this morning, that she cannot wait on me to my coach, as well as her mother.
*Quick.* Marry, madam, she 's married by this time to prentice Golding. Your father, [75 and some one more, stole to church with 'em in all the haste, that the cold meat left at your wedding might serve to furnish their nuptial table.    79
*Ger.* There 's no base fellow, my father, now! But he 's e'en fit to father such a daughter: he must call me daughter no more now; but 'madam,' and, 'please you, madam,' and 'please your worship, madam,' indeed. Out [84 upon him! marry his daughter to a base prentice!
*Mist. Touch.* What should one do? Is there no law for one that marries a woman's daughter against her will? How shall we punish him, madam?    90
*Ger.* As I am a lady, an 't would snow, we 'd so pebble 'em with snow-balls as they come from church! But, sirrah, Frank Quick-silver!
*Quick.* Ay, madam.    95
*Ger.* Dost remember since thou and I clapped what-d 'ye-call-'ts in the garret?
*Quick.* I know not what you mean, madam.

---

⁸ **Hamlet . . . mad:** (jest at Shakespeare's Hamlet; the part was probably played by Robert Hamlett, an adult actor in 1611)    ¹⁰ **old mistress:** Mistress Touchstone    ¹² **blue coat:** footman's uniform    ³² **come away:** make her appearance    ⁴⁶ **ancome:** inflammation, felon    ⁵⁰⁻⁵¹ **preferment:** prosperity    ⁵²⁻⁵³ (From a song by Thos. Campion)    ⁵⁸ **gives . . . milk:** has no other use    ⁷¹ **marle:** marvel

*Ger.* [*sings.*] *His head as white as milk,*
*All flaxen was his hair;*                                          100
*But now he is dead, and laid in his bed,*
*And never will come again.*
*God be at your labour!*

*Enter Touchstone, Golding, Mildred with rose-*
*mary*

*Pet.* [*aside.*] Was there ever such a lady?
*Quick.* See, madam, the bride and bride- [105
groom!
*Ger.* God's my precious! God give you
joy, Mistress What-lack-you! Now out upon
thee, baggage! My sister married in a taffeta
hat! Marry, hang you! Westward with a [110
wanion t' ye! Nay, I have done wi' ye, minion, then, i' faith; never look to have my
count'nance any more, nor anything I can
do for thee. Thou ride in my coach? or come
down to my castle? Fie upon thee! I [115
charge thee in my ladyship's name, call me
sister no more.
*Touch.* An 't please your worship, this is
not your sister; this is my daughter, and
she calls me father, and so does not your [120
ladyship, an 't please your worship, madam.
*Mist. Touch.* No, nor she must not call
thee father by heraldry, because thou mak'st
thy prentice thy son as well as she. Ah,
thou misproud prentice, dar'st thou pre- [125
sume to marry a lady's sister?
*Gold.* It pleased my master, forsooth, to
embolden me with his favour; and though I
confess myself far unworthy so worthy a wife
(being in part her servant, as I am your [130
prentice) yet since (I may say it without
boasting) I am born a gentleman, and by the
trade I have learned of my master (which
I trust taints not my blood) able with mine
own industry and portion to maintain your [135
daughter, my hope is heaven will so bless
our humble beginning that in the end I shall
be no disgrace to the grace with which my
master hath bound me his double prentice.
*Touch.* Master me no more, son, if thou [140
think'st me worthy to be thy father.
*Ger.* Son? Now, good Lord, how he shines,
an you mark him! He's a gentleman!
*Gold.* Ay, indeed, madam, a gentleman
born.                                                          145
*Pet.* Never stand o' your gentry, Master
Bridegroom; if your legs be no better than
your arms, you'll be able to stand upon
neither shortly.

*Touch.* An 't please your good worship, [150
sir, there are two sorts of gentlemen.
[*Doffs his hat.*]
*Pet.* What mean you, sir?
*Touch.* Bold to put off my hat to your
worship.
*Pet.* Nay, pray forbear, sir, and then [155
forth with your two sorts of gentlemen.
*Touch.* If your worship will have it so. I
say there are two sorts of gentlemen. There
is a gentleman artificial, and a gentleman
natural. Now though your worship be a [160
gentleman natural — work upon that now!
*Quick.* Well said, old Touchstone; I am
proud to hear thee enter a set speech, i' faith!
Forth, I beseech thee!
*Touch.* Cry you mercy, sir, your wor- [165
ship's a gentleman I do not know. If you
be one of my acquaintance, y' are very much
disguised, sir.
*Quick.* Go to, old quipper! Forth with
thy speech, I say!                                            170
*Touch.* What, sir, my speeches were ever
in vain to your gracious worship; and therefore, till I speak to you gallantry indeed,
I will save my breath for my broth anon.
Come, my poor son and daughter, let us [175
hide ourselves in our poor humility, and live
safe. Ambition consumes itself with the very
show. Work upon that now!
[*Exeunt Touchstone, Golding and Mildred.*]
*Ger.* Let him go, let him go, for God's
sake! Let him make his prentice his son, [180
for God's sake! Give away his daughter, for
God's sake! And when they come a-begging
to us for God's sake, let's laugh at their
good husbandry, for God's sake! Farewell,
sweet knight, pray thee make haste after. 185
*Pet.* What shall I say? I would not have
thee go.
*Quick.*
*Now, O now, I must depart;*
*Parting though it absence move —*

This ditty, knight, do I see in thy looks in [190
capital letters.
*What a grief 't is to depart,*
*And leave the flower that has my heart!*
*My sweet lady, and alack for woe,*
*Why should we part so?*                                      195

Tell truth, knight, and shame all dissembling
lovers: does not your pain lie on that side?
*Pet.* If it do, canst thou tell me how I
may cure it?

99–102 (Variation of Ophelia's song in *Hamlet*, IV, v, 190–200)    103 S. D. **rosemary**: flower, symbolic
of remembrance, used at weddings (and funerals)    140 **Master me**: call me master    143 **an**: ('and'
Qq.)    148 **arms**: *i.e.*, heraldic arms    161 **natural**: (punning on meaning, "fool")    165 **Cry . . .**
**mercy**: I beg pardon    173 **gallantry indeed**: the real language of fops    188–195 (Based on a song in
John Dowland's *First Book of Ayres*, 1597)

*Quick.* Excellent easily! Divide your- [200 self in two halves, just by the girdlestead; send one half with your lady, and keep the tother yourself. Or else do as all true lovers do: part with your heart, and leave your body behind. I have seen 't done a hundred [205 times: 't is as easy a matter for a lover to part without a heart from his sweetheart, and he ne'er the worse, as for a mouse to get from a trap and leave her tail behind her. See, here comes the writings.     210

*Enter Security with a Scrivener*

*Sec.* Good morrow to my worshipful lady! I present your ladyship with this writing, to which if you please to set your hand with your knight's, a velvet gown shall attend your journey, o' my credit.     215
*Ger.* What writing is it, knight?
*Pet.* The sale, sweetheart, of the poor tenement I told thee of, only to make a little money to send thee down furniture for my castle, to which my hand shall lead thee.     220
*Ger.* Very well! Now give me your pen, I pray.
*Quick.* [*aside.*] It goes down without chewing, i' faith!
*Scriv.* Your worships deliver this as [225 your deed?
*Ambo.* We do.
*Ger.* So now, knight, farewell till I see thee!
*Pet.* All farewell to my sweetheart!
*Mist. Touch.* Good-bye, son knight!     230
*Pet.* Farewell, my good mother!
*Ger.* Farewell, Frank; I would fain take thee down if I could.
*Quick.* I thank your good ladyship. Farewell, Mistress Sindefy.     235

*Exeunt [Gertrude and her party].*

*Pet.* O tedious voyage, whereof there is no end! What will they think of me?
*Quick.* Think what they list. They longed for a vagary into the country and now they are fitted. So a woman marry to ride in a [240 coach, she cares not if she ride to her ruin. 'T is the great end of many of their marriages. This is not first time a lady has rid a false journey in her coach, I hope.
*Pet.* Nay, 't is no matter. I care little [245 what they think; he that weighs men's thoughts has his hands full of nothing. A man, in the course of this world, should be like a surgeon's instrument — work in the wounds of others, and feel nothing himself. [250 The sharper and subtler, the better.
*Quick.* As it falls out now, knight, you shall not need to devise excuses, or endure

her outcries, when she returns. We shall now be gone before, where they cannot reach us. [255
*Pet.* Well, my kind compeer, you have now th' assurance
We both can make you. Let me now entreat you,
The money we agreed on may be brought
To the Blue Anchor, near to Billingsgate,     260
By six o'clock; where I and my chief friends,
Bound for this voyage, will with feasts attend you.
*Sec.* The money, my most honourable compeer, shall without fail observe your appointed hour.     265
*Pet.* Thanks, my dear gossip. I must now impart
To your approved love a loving secret,
As one on whom my life doth more rely
In friendly trust than any man alive.
Nor shall you be the chosen secretary     270
Of my affections for affection only:
For I protest (if God bless my return)
To make you partner in my actions' gain
As deeply as if you had ventur'd with me
Half my expenses. Know then, honest gossip, 275
I have enjoy'd with such divine contentment
A gentlewoman's bed, whom you well know,
That I shall ne'er enjoy this tedious voyage,
Nor live the least part of the time it asketh,
Without her presence; so I thirst and hunger
To taste the dear feast of her company.     281
And if the hunger and the thirst you vow,
As my sworn gossip, to my wished good
Be (as I know it is) unfeign'd and firm,
Do me an easy favour in your power.     285
*Sec.* Be sure, brave gossip, all that I can do,
To my best nerve, is wholly at your service:
Who is the woman, first, that is your friend?
*Pet.* The woman is your learned counsel's wife,     289
The lawyer, Master Bramble; whom would you
Bring out this even in honest neighbourhood,
To take his leave with you of me your gossip,
I, in the mean time, will send this my friend
Home to his house, to bring his wife disguis'd,
Before his face, into our company;     295
For love hath made her look for such a wile
To free her from his tyrannous jealousy.
And I would take this course before another,
In stealing her away to make us sport
And gull his circumspection the more grossly.
And I am sure that no man like yourself     301
Hath credit with him to entice his jealousy
To so long stay abroad as may give time
To her enlargement in such safe disguise.
*Sec.* A pretty, pithy, and most pleasant project!     305

---

Who would not strain a point of neighbourhood
For such a point-device, that, as the ship
Of famous Draco went about the world,
Will wind about the lawyer, compassing
The world himself; he hath it in his arms, 310
And that 's enough for him without his wife.
A lawyer is ambitious, and his head
Cannot be prais'd nor rais'd too high,
With any fork of highest knavery.
I 'll go fetch him straight.     *Exit Security.* 315
  *Pet.* So, so. Now, Frank, go thou home to
    his house,
Stead of his lawyer's, and bring his wife hither,
Who, just like to the lawyer's wife, is
  prison'd
With his stern usurous jealousy, which could
  never                                            319
Be over-reach'd thus but with over-reaching.

*Enter Security*

  *Sec.* And, Master Francis, watch you th'
    instant time
To enter with his exit: 't will be rare,
Two fine horn'd beasts — a camel and a law-
  yer!                              [*Exit.*]
  *Quick.* How the old villain joys in villainy!

*Enter Security*

  *Sec.* And hark you, gossip, when you have
    her here,                                     325
Have your boat ready, ship her to your ship
With utmost haste, lest Master Bramble stay
  you.
To o'er-reach that head that out-reacheth all
  heads,
'T is a trick rampant! 'T is a very quiblin! 329
I hope this harvest to pitch cart with lawyers,
Their heads will be so forked. This sly touch
Will get apes to invent a number such.   *Exit.*
  *Quick.* Was ever rascal honey'd so with
    poison?
He that delights in slavish avarice,
Is apt to joy in every sort of vice.            335
Well, I 'll go fetch his wife, whilst he the lawyer.
  *Pet.* But stay, Frank, let 's think how we
    may disguise her
Upon this sudden.
  *Quick.* God 's me, there 's the mischief!
But hark you, here 's an excellent device;   340
'Fore God, a rare one! I will carry her
A sailor's gown and cap, and cover her,
And a player's beard.
  *Pet.* And what upon her head?

  *Quick.* I tell you; a sailor's cap! 'Slight,
    God forgive me,                               345
What kind of figent memory have you?
  *Pet.* Nay, then, what kind of figent wit
    hast thou?
A sailor's cap? How shall she put it off
When thou present'st her to our company?
  *Quick.* Tush, man, for that, make her a
    saucy sailor.                                 350
  *Pet.* Tush, tush, 't is no fit sauce for such
    sweet mutton!
I know not what t' advise.

*Enter Security, with his wife's gown*

  *Sec.*      Knight, knight, a rare device!
  *Pet.* 'Swounds, yet again!
  *Quick.* What stratagem have you now?
  *Sec.* The best that ever! You talk'd of dis-
    guising?                                      355
  *Pet.* Ay, marry, gossip, that 's our present
    care.
  *Sec.* Cast care away, then; here 's the best
    device
For plain security (for I am no better)
I think, that ever liv'd: here 's my wife's
  gown,
Which you may put upon the lawyer's wife,
And which I brought you, sir, for two great
  reasons:                                        361
One is, that Master Bramble may take hold
Of some suspicion that it is my wife,
And gird me so, perhaps, with his law-
  wit;
The other (which is policy indeed)             365
Is that my wife may now be tied at home,
Having no more but her old gown abroad,
And not show me a quirk, while I firk others.
Is not this rare?
  *Ambo.*      The best that ever was.
  *Sec.* Am I not born to furnish gentlemen?
  *Pet.* O my dear gossip!                       371
  *Sec.* Well, hold, Master Francis!
Watch when the lawyer 's out, and put it in.
And now I will go fetch him.          *Exit.*
  *Quick.* O my Dad!                            375
He goes, as 't were the devil, to fetch the
  lawyer;
And devil shall he be, if horns will make him.

[*Re-enter Security*]

  *Pet.* Why, how now, gossip? Why stay you
    there musing?
  *Sec.* A toy, a toy runs in my head, i' faith!

---

  **307 point-device:** master stroke (with pun on "point of vice")   **308 Draco:** Sir Francis Drake
**315 him:** ('her' Qq., emended by R. H. Case)   **323 Two fine:** ('To finde' uncorrected copies of Q 1,
Qq. 2–3)   **camel:** proverbially stupid beast, who desired horns in a fable   **329 rampant:** full of fire
**quiblin:** trick   **330 pitch cart:** load a cart with a pitchfork   **332 apes:** imitators   **346 figent:**
fidgety   **365 policy:** strategy   **367 abroad:** current, available   **368 quirk:** trick   **firk:** bedevil
**370 furnish:** provide for

*Quick.* A pox of that head! Is there more
toys yet?                                              380
*Pet.* What is it, pray thee, gossip?
*Sec.* Why, sir, what if you
Should slip away now with my wife's best gown,
I having no security for it?
    *Quick.* For that, I hope, Dad, you will take
our words.                                             385
    *Sec.* Ay, by th' mass, your word! That's
a proper staff
For wise Security to lean upon!
But 't is no matter, once I'll trust my name
On your crack'd credits; let it take no shame.
Fetch the wench, Frank.                      *Exit.*
    *Quick.*        I'll wait upon you, sir. 390
And fetch you over, you were ne'er so fetch'd.
Go to the tavern, knight; your followers
Dare not be drunk, I think, before their cap-
tain.                                            *Exit.*
    *Pet.* Would I might lead them to no hotter
service
Till our Virginian gold were in our purses! 395
                         *Exit.*

[SCENE III. — *Blue Anchor Tavern,*
*Billingsgate*]

*Enter Seagull, Spendall, and Scapethrift, in the*
*Tavern, with a Drawer*

*Sea.* Come, drawer, pierce your neatest
hogsheads, and let's have cheer, not fit for
your Billingsgate tavern, but for our Virginian
colonel; he will be here instantly.
    *Draw.* You shall have all things fit, sir; [5
please you have any more wine?
    *Spen.* More wine, slave? Whether we drink
it or no, spill it, and draw more.
    *Scape.* Fill all the pots in your house with
all sorts of liquor, and let 'em wait on us [10
here like soldiers in their pewter coats; and
though we do not employ them now, yet we
will maintain 'em till we do.
    *Draw.* Said like an honourable captain; you
shall have all you can command, sir.        15
                        *Exit Drawer.*
    *Sea.* Come, boys, Virginia longs till we
share the rest of her maidenhead.
    *Spen.* Why, is she inhabited already with
any English?
    *Sea.* A whole country of English is [20
there, man, bred of those that were left there
in '79. They have married with the Indians,

and make 'em bring forth as beautiful faces
as any we have in England; and therefore
the Indians are so in love with 'em, that [25
all the treasure they have they lay at their
feet.
    *Scape.* But is there such treasure there,
captain, as I have heard?
    *Sea.* I tell thee, gold is more plentiful [30
there than copper is with us; and for as much
red copper as I can bring, I'll have thrice the
weight in gold. Why, man, all their dripping-
pans and their chamber-pots are pure gold;
and all the chains with which they chain [35
up their streets are massy gold; all the prisoners they take are fettered in gold; and for rubies
and diamonds, they go forth on holidays and
gather 'em by the sea-shore to hang on their
children's coats and stick in their caps, as [40
commonly as our children wear saffron-gilt
brooches and groats with holes in 'em.
    *Scape.* And is it a pleasant country withal?
    *Sea.* As ever the sun shined on; temperate
and full of all sorts of excellent viands: [45
wild boar is as common there as our tamest
bacon is here; venison, as mutton. And then
you shall live freely there, without sergeants,
or courtiers, or lawyers, or intelligencers; only
a few industrious Scots, perhaps, who, in- [50
deed, are dispersed over the face of the whole
earth. But as for them, there are no greater
friends to Englishmen and England, when they
are out on 't, in the world than they are.
And for my part, I would a hundred thou- [55
sand of 'em were there, for we are all one-
countrymen now, ye know; and we should
find ten times more comfort of them there
than we do here. Then for your means to
advancement there, it is simple, and not [60
preposterously mixed. You may be an alderman there, and never be scavenger: you may
be a nobleman, and never be a slave. You
may come to preferment enough, and never
be a pandar; to riches and fortune enough, [65
and have never the more villainy nor the less
wit.
    *Spen.* God's me! And how far is it
thither?
    *Sea.* Some six weeks' sail, no more, with [70
any indifferent good wind. And if I get to
any part of the coast of Africa, I'll sail
thither with any wind; or when I come to
Cape Finisterre, there's a foreright wind con-

³⁹¹ **fetch'd:** victimized    ²² **in '79:** (The "lost colony" was left on Roanoke Island in 1587.)
³³⁻⁴² (Closely imitated from More's *Utopia*)    ⁴¹ **saffron-gilt:** false gold    ⁴² **groats:** fourpenny pieces
⁴⁹ **intelligencers:** spies    ⁴⁹⁻⁵⁹ **only . . . here:** (This passage survives in only two known copies of
Q 1; in the rest and in the later Qq. it is cancelled.)    ⁶³ **a nobleman:** (changed to 'any other officer'
in cancelled copies of Q 1 and in Qq. 2–3)    ⁶⁷ **wit:** (To fill space, cancelled copies of Q 1, followed by
Qq. 2–3, add: "Besides, there we shall have no more law than conscience, and not too much of either;
serve God enough, eat and drink enough, and enough is as good as a feast ")    ⁷¹ **indifferent:** moderately

tinually wafts us till we come at Virginia. [75
See, our colonel 's come.

*Enter Sir Petronel, with his followers*

*Pet.* Well met, good Captain Seagull, and
my noble gentlemen! Now the sweet hour of
our freedom is at hand. Come, drawer, fill
us some carouses, and prepare us for the [80
mirth that will be occasioned presently. Here
will be a pretty wench, gentlemen, that will
bear us company all our voyage.

*Sea.* Whatsoever she be, here 's to her health,
noble Colonel, both with cap and knee.        85

*Pet.* Thanks, kind Captain Seagull! She 's
one I love dearly, and must not be known till
we be free from all that know us. And so,
gentlemen, here 's to her health!

*Ambo.* Let it come, worthy Colonel. We [90
do hunger and thirst for it.

*Pet.* Afore heaven, you have hit the phrase
of one that her presence will touch from the
foot to the forehead, if ye knew it.

*Spen.* Well, then, we will join his fore- [95
head with her health, sir; and, Captain Scapethrift, here 's to 'em both!

[*All kneel and drink.*]

*Enter Security and Bramble*

*Sec.* See, see, Master Bramble, 'fore heaven,
their voyage cannot but prosper! They are
o' their knees for success to it.        100

*Bram.* And they pray to god Bacchus.

*Sec.* God save my brave colonel, with all
his tall captains and corporals. See, sir, my
worshipful learned counsel, Master Bramble,
is come to take his leave of you.        105

*Pet.* Worshipful Master Bramble, how far
do you draw us into the sweet-brier of your
kindness! Come, Captain Seagull, another
health to this rare Bramble, that hath never
a prick about him.        110

*Sea.* I pledge his most smooth disposition,
sir. Come, Master Security, bend your supporters, and pledge this notorious health here.

*Sec.* Bend you yours likewise, Master Bramble; for it is you shall pledge me.        115

*Sea.* Not so, Master Security; he must not
pledge his own health.

*Sec.* No, Master Captain?

*Enter Quicksilver, with Winnie disguised*

Why, then, here 's one is fitly come to do
him that honour.        120

*Quick.* Here 's the gentlewoman your cousin,
sir, whom, with much entreaty, I have

brought to take her leave of you in a tavern;
ashamed whereof, you must pardon her if she
put not off her mask.        125

*Pet.* Pardon me, sweet cousin; my kind
desire to see you before I went, made me so
importunate to entreat your presence here.

*Sec.* How now, Master Francis, have you
honoured this presence with a fair gentle- [130
woman?

*Quick.* Pray, sir, take you no notice of her,
for she will not be known to you.

*Sec.* But my learned counsel, Master Bramble here, I hope may know her.        135

*Quick.* No more than you, sir, at this time;
his learning must pardon her.

*Sec.* Well, God pardon her for my part,
and I do, I 'll be sworn; and so, Master Francis,
here 's to all that are going eastward to- [140
night towards Cuckold's Haven; and so to
the health of Master Bramble.

*Quick.* I pledge it, sir. Hath it gone round,
Captains?

*Sea.* It has, sweet Frank; and the round [145
closes with thee.

*Quick.* Well, sir, here 's to all eastward and
toward cuckolds, and so to famous Cuckold's
Haven, so fatally remembered.        *Surgit.*

*Pet.* [*to Winifred.*]    Nay, pray thee, [150
coz, weep not. Gossip Security!

*Sec.* Ay, my brave gossip!

*Pet.* A word, I beseech you, sir! Our friend,
Mistress Bramble here, is so dissolved in tears
that she drowns the whole mirth of our [155
meeting. Sweet gossip, take her aside and
comfort her.

*Sec.* [*aside to Winifred.*]    Pity of all true
love, Mistress Bramble! What, weep you to
enjoy your love? What 's the cause, lady? [160
Is 't because your husband is so near, and
your heart earns to have a little abused him?
Alas, alas, the offence is too common to be
respected! So great a grace hath seldom
chanced to so unthankful a woman: to be [165
rid of an old jealous dotard, to enjoy the arms
of a loving young knight, that, when your
prickless Bramble is withered with grief of
your loss, will make you flourish afresh in the
bed of a lady.        170

*Enter Drawer*

*Draw.* Sir Petronel, here 's one of your
watermen come to tell you it will be flood
these three hours; and that 't will be dangerous
going against the tide, for the sky is overcast,
and there was a porcpisce even now seen at [175

---

⁷⁶ S. D. **with . . . followers:** (added in cancel sheet of Q 1)    ¹¹²⁻¹¹³ **supporters:** legs    ¹³³ **will not:**
desires not to    ¹⁴¹ **Cuckold's Haven:** a point on the Thames a mile below London Bridge    ¹⁴⁵ **round:**
circuit of the cup    ¹⁴⁹ **fatally:** ominously    ¹⁴⁹ S. D. **Surgit:** rises from his knees    ¹⁶² **earns:** grieves
¹⁶⁴ **respected:** regarded    ¹⁷² **flood:** incoming tide    ¹⁷⁵ **porcpisce:** porpoise

London Bridge, which is always the messenger
of tempests, he says.

*Pet.* A porcpisce! What 's that to th' purpose? Charge him, if he love his life, to
attend us; can we not reach Blackwall [180
(where my ship lies) against the tide, and
in spite of tempests? Captains and gentlemen, we 'll begin a new ceremony at the
beginning of our voyage, which I believe will
be followed of all future adventurers.          185

*Sea.* What 's that, good Colonel?

*Pet.* This, Captain Seagull. We 'll have
our provided supper brought aboard Sir Francis
Drake's ship, that hath compassed the world;
where, with full cups and banquets, we will [190
do sacrifice for a prosperous voyage. My mind
gives me that some good spirits of the waters
should haunt the desert ribs of her, and be auspicious to all that honour her memory, and will
with like orgies enter their voyages.          195

*Sea.* Rarely conceited! One health more to
this motion, and aboard to perform it. He that
will not this night be drunk, may he never be
sober.

> *They compass in Winifred, dance
> the drunken round, and drink
> carouses.*

*Bram.* Sir Petronel and his honourable [200
Captains, in these young services we old servitors may be spared. We only came to take
our leaves, and with one health to you all,
I 'll be bold to do so. Here, neighbour Security,
to the health of Sir Petronel and all his [205
captains.

*Sec.* You must bend, then, Master Bramble. [*They kneel.*] So, now I am for you.
I have one corner of my brain, I hope, fit
to bear one carouse more. Here, lady, to [210
you that are encompassed there, and are
ashamed of our company. Ha ha, ha! By
my troth, my learned counsel, Master Bramble, my mind runs so of Cuckold's Haven
to-night, that my head runs over with [215
admiration.

*Bram.* [*aside.*] But is not that your wife,
neighbour?

*Sec.* [*aside.*] No, by my troth, Master Bramble. Ha, ha, ha! A pox of all Cuckold's [220
Havens, I say!

*Bram.* [*aside.*] O' my faith, her garments
are exceeding like your wife's.

*Sec.* [*aside.*] *Cucullus non facit monachum,*
my learned counsel; all are not cuckolds [225

that seem so, nor all seem not that are so.
Give me your hand, my learned counsel; you
and I will sup somewhere else than at Sir
Francis Drake's ship to-night. — Adieu, my
noble gossip!          230

*Bram.* Good fortune, brave captains; fair
skies God send ye!

*Omnes.* Farewell, my hearts, farewell!

*Pet.* Gossip, laugh no more at Cuckold's
Haven, gossip.          235

*Sec.* I have done, I have done, sir; will
you lead, Master Bramble? Ha, ha, ha!
                              *Exit [with Bramble].*

*Pet.* Captain Seagull, charge a boat!

*Omnes.* A boat, a boat, a boat!     *Exeunt.*

*Draw.* Y' are in a proper taking, indeed, [240
to take a boat, especially at this time of night,
and against tide and tempest. They say yet,
'drunken men never take harm.' This night
will try the truth of that proverb.     *Exit.*

<br>

[SCENE IV. — *Outside Security's House*]

*Enter Security*

*Sec.* What, Winnie! Wife, I say! Out
doors at this time! Where should I seek the
gad-fly? Billingsgate, Billingsgate, Billingsgate! She 's gone with the knight, she 's gone
with the knight! Woe be to thee, Billingsgate!
A boat, a boat, a boat! A full hundred marks
for a boat!          *Exit.*

## Actus quartus   Scena prima

[*Cuckold's Haven, Surrey*]

*Enter Slitgut, with a pair of ox-horns, dis-
covering Cuckold's Haven, above*

*Slit.* All hail, fair haven of married men
only, for there are none but married men
cuckolds! For my part, I presume not to
arrive here, but in my master's behalf (a poor
butcher of Eastcheap) who sends me to set [5
up (in honour of Saint Luke) these necessary
ensigns of his homage. And up I got this
morning, thus early, to get up to the top of this
famous tree, that is all fruit and no leaves, to
advance this crest of my master's occupa- [10
tion. Up then; heaven and Saint Luke bless
me, that I be not blown into the Thames as I
climb, with this furious tempest. 'Slight, I
think the devil be abroad, in likeness of a
storm, to rob me of my horns! Hark how he [15
roars! Lord, what a coil the Thames keeps!

---

180 **attend:** wait for     192 **gives:** presages     196 **conceited:** imagined     207 **bend:** kneel     216 **admiration:** wonder     224 **Cucullus . . . monachum:** The cowl does not make the monk (with the pun
on "cuckold").     238 **charge:** order     240 **taking:** state     IV, i. s. d. **discovering:** typifying     **above:**
on the upper stage     5 **butcher:** (The London butchers provided the horns set up at Cuckold's Haven.)
1 **St. Luke:** (St. Luke's Day, Oct. 18, was commemorated by a horn-fair.)     9 **tree:** (a bare pole)
16 **coil:** turmoil

She bears some unjust burthen, I believe, that she kicks and curvets thus to cast it. Heaven bless all honest passengers that are upon her back now; for the bit is out of her mouth, [20 I see, and she will run away with 'em! So, so, I think I have made it look the right way; it runs against London Bridge, as it were, even full butt. And now let me discover from this lofty prospect, what pranks the rude [25 Thames plays in her desperate lunacy. O me, here's a boat has been cast away hard by! Alas, alas, see one of her passengers labouring for his life to land at this haven here! Pray heaven he may recover it! His next land [30 is even just under me; hold out yet a little, whatsoever thou art; pray, and take a good heart to thee. 'T is a man; take a man's heart to thee; yet a little further, get up o' thy legs, man; now 't is shallow enough. [35 So, so, so! Alas, he's down again! Hold thy wind, father! 't is a man in a night-cap. So! Now he's got up again; now he's past the worst; yet, thanks be to heaven, he comes toward me pretty and strongly. 40

*Enter Security without his hat, in a night-cap, wet band, &c.*

*Sec.* Heaven, I beseech thee, how have I offended thee! Where am I cast ashore now, that I may go a righter way home by land? Let me see. O, I am scarce able to look about me! Where is there any sea-mark that I am [45 acquainted withal?

*Slit.* Look up, father; are you acquainted with this mark?

*Sec.* What! Landed at Cuckold's Haven! Hell and damnation! I will run back and [50 drown myself. *He falls down.*

*Slit.* Poor man, how weak he is! The weak water has washed away his strength.

*Sec.* Landed at Cuckold's Haven! If it had not been to die twenty times alive, I [55 should never have scaped death! I will never arise more; I will grovel here and eat dirt till I be choked; I will make the gentle earth do that which the cruel water has denied me!

*Slit.* Alas, good father, be not so des- [60 perate! Rise, man; if you will, I'll come presently and lead you home.

*Sec.* Home! Shall I make any know my home, that has known me thus abroad? How low shall I crouch away, that no eye may [65 see me? I will creep on the earth while I live, and never look heaven in the face more.

*Exit creeping.*

*Slit.* What young planet reigns now, trow,

that old men are so foolish? What desperate young swaggerer would have been abroad [70 such a weather as this upon the water? Ay me, see another remnant of this unfortunate ship-wrack, or some other! A woman, i' faith, a woman! Though it be almost at St. Katherine's, I discern it to be a woman, for all her body [75 is above the water, and her clothes swim about her most handsomely. O, they bear her up most bravely! Has not a woman reason to love the taking up of her clothes the better while she lives, for this? Alas, how busy [80 the rude Thames is about her! A pox o' that wave! It will drown her, i' faith, 't will drown her! Cry God mercy, she has scaped it, I thank heaven she has scaped it! O how she swims, like a mermaid! Some vigilant body [85 look out and save her. That's well said; just where the priest fell in, there's one sets down a ladder, and goes to take her up. God's blessing o' thy heart, boy! Now take her up in thy arms and to bed with her. She's up, she's [90 up! She's a beautiful woman, I warrant her; the billows durst not devour her.

*Enter the Drawer in the Tavern before, with Winifred*

*Draw.* How fare you now, lady?

*Win.* Much better, my good friend, than I wish: as one desperate of her fame, now my [95 life is preserved.

*Draw.* Comfort yourself: that Power that preserved you from death can likewise defend you from infamy, howsoever you deserve it. Were not you one that took boat late this [100 night with a knight and other gentlemen at Billingsgate?

*Win.* Unhappy that I am, I was.

*Draw.* I am glad it was my good hap to come down thus far after you, to a house of [105 my friend's here in St. Katherine's, since I am now happily made a mean to your rescue from the ruthless tempest, which (when you took boat) was so extreme, and the gentleman that brought you forth so desperate and un- [110 sober, that I feared long ere this I should hear of your shipwrack, and therefore (with little other reason) made thus far this way. And this I must tell you, since perhaps you may make use of it: there was left behind you [115 at our tavern, brought by a porter (hired by the young gentleman that brought you) a gentlewoman's gown, hat, stockings, and shoes; which, if they be yours, and you please to shift you, taking a hard bed here in this [120 house of my friend, I will presently go fetch you.

---

**²⁵ prospect:** viewpoint  **³⁰ recover:** gain  **next:** nearest  **⁴⁵ sea-mark:** landmark  **⁶⁷ S. D.**
**creeping:** ('creep' Qq.)  **⁶⁸ trow:** pray  **⁷⁴ St. Katherine's:** a home for fallen women  **⁸⁶ well**
**said:** well done

*Win.* Thanks, my good friend, for your more than good news. The gown with all things bound with it are mine; which if you please to fetch as you have promised, I will [125 boldly receive the kind favour you have offered till your return; entreating you, by all the good you have done in preserving me hitherto, to let none take knowledge of what favour you do me, or where such a one as I am bestowed, [130 lest you incur me much more damage in my fame than you have done me pleasure in preserving my life.

*Draw.* Come in, lady, and shift yourself; resolve that nothing but your own pleasure [135 shall be used in your discovery.

*Win.* Thank you, good friend; the time may come, I shall requite you.        *Exeunt.*

*Slit.* See, see, see! I hold my life, there's some other a-taking up at Wapping now! [140 Look, what a sort of people cluster about the gallows there! In good troth it is so. O me, a fine young gentleman! What, and taken up at the gallows! Heaven grant he be not one day taken down there! A' my life, it is [145 ominous! Well, he is delivered for the time. I see the people have all left him; yet will I keep my prospect awhile, to see if any more have been shipwracked.

### Enter Quicksilver, barehead

*Quick.* Accurs'd that ever I was sav'd or born!        150
How fatal is my sad arrival here!
As if the stars and Providence spake to me,
And said, 'The drift of all unlawful courses
(Whatever end they dare propose themselves
In frame of their licentious policies)        155
In the firm order of just Destiny
They are the ready highways to our ruins.'
I know not what to do; my wicked hopes
Are, with this tempest, torn up by the roots.
O, which way shall I bend my desperate steps,        160
In which unsufferable shame and misery
Will not attend them? I will walk this bank,
And see if I can meet the other relics
Of our poor shipwrack'd crew, or hear of them.
The knight — alas! — was so far gone with wine,        165
And th' other three, that I refus'd their boat,
And took the hapless woman in another,
Who cannot but be sunk, whatever Fortune
Hath wrought upon the others' desperate lives.        [*Exit.*]

### Enter Petronel, and Seagull, bareheaded

*Pet.* Zounds, Captain, I tell thee, we [170 are cast up o' the coast of France! 'Sfoot, I am not drunk still, I hope! Dost remember where we were last night?

*Sea.* No, by my troth, knight, not I; but methinks we have been a horrible while [175 upon the water and in the water.

*Pet.* Ay me, we are undone for ever! Hast any money about thee?

*Sea.* Not a penny, by heaven!

*Pet.* Not a penny betwixt us, and cast [180 ashore in France!

*Sea.* Faith, I cannot tell that; my brains nor mine eyes are not mine own yet.

### Enter two Gentlemen

*Pet.* 'Sfoot, wilt not believe me? I know 't by th' elevation of the pole, and by the [185 altitude and latitude of the climate. See, here comes a couple of French gentlemen; I knew we were in France; dost thou think our Englishmen are so Frenchified that a man knows not whether he be in France or in England, [190 when he sees 'em? What shall we do? We must e'en to 'em, and entreat some relief of 'em. Life is sweet, and we have no other means to relieve our lives now but their charities.        [195

*Sea.* Pray you, do you beg on 'em then; you can speak French.

*Pet.* Monsieur, plaist-il d'avoir pitié de nostre grande infortune. Je suis un povre chevalier d'Angleterre qui a souffri l'infor- [200 tune de naufrage.

*1 Gent.* Un povre chevalier d'Angleterre?

*Pet.* Oui, monsieur, il est trop vraye; mais vous scavés bien nous sommes toutes subject à fortune.        205

*2 Gent.* A poor knight of England? A poor knight of Windsor, are you not? Why speak you this broken French, when y' are a whole Englishman? On what coast are you, think you?        210

*Pet.* On the coast of France, sir.

*1 Gent.* On the coast of Dogs, sir; y' are i' th' Isle o' Dogs, I tell you. I see y' ave been washed in the Thames here, and I believe ye were drowned in a tavern before, or else you [215 would never have took boat in such a dawning as this was. Farewell, farewell; we will not know you for shaming of you. — I ken the man weel; he 's one of my thirty-pound knights.        220

---

[134] **shift:** reclothe    [139] **hold:** wager    [140] **a-taking:** being taken    [141] **sort:** crowd    [155] **frame:** planning    [186] **climate:** region    [199] **infortune:** ('infortunes' Qq.)    [204] **scavés:** *i.e.,* savez    [206-207] **poor . . . Windsor:** slang for 'pauper'; properly, 'pensioner'    [213] **Isle o' Dogs:** a small peninsula in the Thames near Greenwich    [218-219] **ken, weel:** (Scotch-English)    [219-220] **he 's . . . knights:** (referring to James I's traffic in knighthoods)

*2 Gent.* No, no, this is he that stole his knighthood o' the grand day for four pound, giving to a page all the money in 's purse, I wot well. *Exeunt [Gentlemen].*

*Sea.* Death, Colonel, I knew you were [225 overshot!

*Pet.* Sure, I think now, indeed, Captain Seagull, we were something overshot.

*Enter Quicksilver*

What, my sweet Frank Quicksilver! Dost thou survive to rejoice me? But what! [230 Nobody at thy heels, Frank? Ay me, what is become of poor Mistress Security?

*Quick.* Faith, gone quite from her name, as she is from her fame, I think; I left her to the mercy of the water. 235

*Sea.* Let her go, let her go! Let us go to our ship at Blackwall, and shift us.

*Pet.* Nay, by my troth, let our clothes rot upon us, and let us rot in them; twenty to one our ship is attached by this time! If we set [240 her not under sail this last tide, I never looked for any other. Woe, woe is me! what shall become of us? The last money we could make, the greedy Thames has devoured; and if our ship be attached, there is no hope can relieve [245 us.

*Quick.* 'Sfoot, knight, what an unknightly faintness transports thee! Let our ship sink, and all the world that 's without us be taken from us, I hope I have some tricks in this [250 brain of mine shall not let us perish.

*Sea.* Well said, Frank, i' faith! O my nimble-spirited Quicksilver! 'Fore God, would thou hadst been our colonel!

*Pet.* I like his spirit rarely; but I see [255 no means he has to support that spirit.

*Quick.* Go to, knight! I have more means than thou art aware of. I have not lived amongst goldsmiths and goldmakers all this while, but I have learned something worthy [260 of my time with 'em. And not to let thee stink where thou stand'st, knight, I 'll let thee know some of my skill presently.

*Sea.* Do, good Frank, I beseech thee!

*Quick.* I will blanch copper so cunningly [265 that it shall endure all proofs but the test: it shall endure malleation, it shall have the ponderosity of Luna, and the tenacity of Luna, by no means friable.

*Pet.* 'Slight, where learnt'st thou these [270 terms, trow?

*Quick.* Tush, knight, the terms of this art

every ignorant quack-salver is perfect in. But I 'll tell you how yourself shall blanch copper thus cunningly. Take arsenic, otherwise [275 called realga (which, indeed, is plain ratsbane); sublime 'em three or four times, then take the sublime of this realga, and put 'em into a glass, into chymia, and let 'em have a convenient decoction natural, four-and-twenty [280 hours, and he will become perfectly fixed; then take this fixed powder, and project him upon well-purged copper, et habebis magisterium.

*Ambo.* Excellent Frank, let us hug thee! [285

*Quick.* Nay, this I will do besides: I 'll take you off twelvepence from every angel, with a kind of aqua-fortis, and never deface any part of the image.

*Pet.* But then it will want weight? 290

*Quick.* You shall restore that thus: take your sal achyme prepared and your distilled urine, and let your angels lie in it but four-and-twenty hours, and they shall have their perfect weight again. Come on, now; I hope this [295 is enough to put some spirit into the livers of you. I 'll infuse more another time. We have saluted the proud air long enough with our bare sconces. Now will I have you to a wench's house of mine at London; there make shift [300 to shift us, and, after, take such fortunes as the stars shall assign us.

*Ambo.* Notable Frank, we will ever adore thee! *Exeunt.*

*Enter Drawer, with Winifred new-attired*

*Win.* Now, sweet friend, you have [305 brought me near enough your tavern, which I desired that I might with some colour be seen near, inquiring for my husband; who, I must tell you, stale thither last night with my wet gown we have left at your friend's — [310 which, to continue your former honest kindness, let me pray you to keep close from the knowledge of any; and so, with all vow of your requital, let me now entreat you to leave me to my woman's wit and fortune. 315

*Draw.* All shall be done you desire; and so, all the fortune you can wish for attend you! *Exit Drawer.*

*Enter Security*

*Sec.* I will once more to this unhappy tavern before I shift one rag of me more, [320 that I may there know what is left behind,

²²⁶ **overshot:** mistaken  ²⁴² **any other:** anything else  ²⁴⁸ **faintness:** faint-heartedness  ²⁶⁵ **blanch:** whiten, turn silvery  ²⁶⁷ **malleation:** hammering  ²⁶⁸ **Luna:** silver  ²⁷⁶ **realga:** realgar, arsenic disulphide  ²⁷⁷ **sublime:** vaporize and then resolidify  ²⁷⁹ **chymia:** kemia, vessel for distillation ²⁸³⁻²⁸⁴ **et . . . magisterium:** and you will have the philosopher's stone  ²⁸⁸ **aqua-fortis:** sulphuric acid  ²⁹² **sal achyme:** chemical salt  ²⁹⁹ **sconces:** skulls  ³⁰⁷ **colour:** plausibility  ³⁰⁹ **stale:** stole

and what news of their passengers. I have
bought me a hat and band with the little
money I had about me, and made the streets
a little leave staring at my night-cap.        325
*Win.* O my dear husband! Where have
you been to-night? All night abroad at
taverns! Rob me of my garments, and fare
as one run away from me! Alas, is this seemly
for a man of your credit, of your age, and [330
affection to your wife?
*Sec.* What should I say? How miraculously
sorts this! Was not I at home, and called thee
last night?
*Win.* Yes, sir, the harmless sleep you [335
broke; and my answer to you would have witnessed it, if you had had the patience to have
stayed and answered me: but your so sudden
retreat made me imagine you were gone to
Master Bramble's, and so rested patient and [340
hopeful of your coming again, till this your un-
believed absence brought me abroad with no
less than wonder, to seek you where the false
knight had carried you.
*Sec.* Villain and monster that I was, how [345
have I abused thee! I was suddenly gone indeed; for my sudden jealousy transferred me.
I will say no more but this, dear wife: I suspected thee.
*Win.* Did you suspect me?        350
*Sec.* Talk not of it, I beseech thee; I am
ashamed to imagine it. I will home, I will
home; and every morning on my knees ask
thee heartily forgiveness.        *Exeunt.*
[*Slit.*] Now will I descend my honourable [355
prospect, the farthest seeing sea-mark of the
world; no marvel, then, if I could see two miles
about me. I hope the red tempest's anger be
now over-blown, which sure, I think, heaven
sent as a punishment for profaning holy [360
Saint Luke's memory with so ridiculous a custom. Thou dishonest satire, farewell to honest
married men. Farewell to all sorts and degrees
of thee! Farewell, thou horn of hunger, that
call'st th' Inns o' Court to their manger! [365
Farewell, thou horn of abundance, that
adornest the headsmen of the commonwealth!
Farewell, thou horn of direction, that is the city
lanthorn! Farewell, thou horn of pleasure,
the ensign of the huntsman; Farewell, thou [370
horn of destiny, th' ensign of the married man!
Farewell, thou horn tree, that bearest nothing
but stone-fruit!        *Exit.*

[SCENE II. — *Touchstone's House*]

*Enter Touchstone*

*Touch.* Ha, sirrah! Thinks my knight ad-
venturer we can no point of our compass?
Do we not know north-north-east, north-east-
and-by-east, east-and-by-north, nor plain eastward? Ha! Have we never heard of Vir- [5
ginia? Nor the Cavallaria? Nor the Colonoria? Can we discover no discoveries? Well,
mine errant Sir Flash, and my runagate Quicksilver, you may drink drunk, crack cans, hurl
away a brown dozen of Monmouth caps [10
or so, in sea ceremony to your *bon voyage;*
but for reaching any coast, save the coast of
Kent or Essex, with this tide, or with this fleet,
I 'll be your warrant for a Gravesend toast.
There 's that gone afore will stay your [15
admiral and vice-admiral and rear-admiral,
were they all (as they are) but one pinnace and
under sail, as well as a remora, doubt it not,
and from this sconce, without either powder
or shot. Work upon that now! Nay, and [20
you 'll show tricks, we 'll vie with you a little.
My daughter, his lady, was sent eastward by
land, to a castle of his i' the air (in what
region I know not) and, as I hear, was glad
to take up her lodging in her coach, she [25
and her two waiting-women (her maid and her
mother), like three snails in a shell, and the
coachman a-top on 'em, I think. Since they
have all found the way back again by Weeping
Cross; but I 'll not see 'em. And for two [30
on 'em, madam and her malkin, they are like
to bite o' the bridle for William, as the poor
horses have done all this while that hurried
'em; or else go graze o' the common. So
should my Dame Touchstone, too; but she [35
has been my cross these thirty years, and I 'll
now keep her to fright away sprites, i' faith. I
wonder I hear no news of my son Golding.
He was sent for to the Guildhall this morning
betimes, and I marvel at the matter. If [40
I had not laid up comfort and hope in him,
I should grow desperate of all. *Enter Golding.*
See, he is come i' my thought! How now,
son? What news at the Court of Aldermen?

*Gold.* Troth, sir, an accident somewhat [45
strange, else it hath little in it worth the re-
porting.

*Touch.* What? It is not borrowing of
money, then?

---

³³³ **sorts:** turns out        ³⁴⁷ **transferred:** transported        ³⁶² **satire:** (*i.e.*, the horn on the pole)
³⁶³⁻³⁶⁴ **all . . . thee:** all kinds of horns        ³⁶⁸ **horn of direction:** sign-post        ² **can:** know        ⁶ **Cavallaria,**
**Colonoria:** the dream-lands of cavaliers and colonists        ⁸ **runagate:** vagrant        ¹⁰ **brown:** round
**Monmouth caps:** (worn by soldiers and sailors)        ¹⁴ **be . . . for:** bet you        **Gravesend toast:** a
proverbially thin potation        ¹⁶ **admiral:** flagship        ¹⁸ **remora:** sucking-fish of fabulous powers
¹⁹ **sconce:** entrenchment (also, head)        ²⁰ **and:** if        ²⁸ **Since:** since then        ³¹ **malkin:** slut        ³² **bite**
**. . . William:** go unfed for all I care        ⁴³ **i':** in the moment of

*Gold.*  No, sir; it hath pleased the wor- [50
shipful commoners of the city to take me one
i' their number at presentation of the in-
quest —

*Touch.*  Ha!

*Gold.*  And the alderman of the ward [55
wherein I dwell to appoint me his deputy —

*Touch.*  How?

*Gold.*  In which place I have had an oath
ministered me, since I went.

*Touch.*  Now, my dear and happy son, [60
let me kiss thy new worship, and a little
boast mine own happiness in thee.  What a
fortune was it (or rather my judgment, indeed) for me, first to see that in his disposition
which a whole city so conspires to second! [65
Ta'en into the livery of his company the first
day of his freedom!  Now (not a week married)
chosen commoner and alderman's deputy in a
day!  Note but the reward of a thrifty course.
The wonder of his time!  Well, I will [70
honour Master Alderman for this act (as becomes me) and shall think the better of the
Common Council's wisdom and worship while
I live, for thus meeting, or but coming after,
me in the opinion of his desert.  For- [75
ward, my sufficient son, and as this is the
first, so esteem it the least step to that high
and prime honour that expects thee.

*Gold.*  Sir, as I was not ambitious of this,
so I covet no higher place; it hath dignity [80
enough, if it will but save me from contempt;
and I had rather my bearing in this or any other
office should add worth to it, than the place
give the least opinion to me.

*Touch.*  Excellently spoken!  This mod- [85
est answer of thine blushes, as if it said, I will
wear scarlet shortly.  Worshipful son!  I cannot contain myself, I must tell thee: I hope
to see thee one o' the monuments of our city,
and reckoned among her worthies to be [90
remembered the same day with the Lady
Ramsey and grave Gresham, when the famous
fable of Whittington and his puss shall be forgotten, and thou and thy acts become the
posies for hospitals; when thy name shall [95
be written upon conduits, and thy deeds played
i' thy lifetime by the best companies of actors,
and be called their get-penny.  This I divine;
this I prophesy.

*Gold.*  Sir, engage not your expectation [100
farder than my abilities will answer.  I, that

know mine own strengths, fear 'em; and there
is so seldom a loss in promising the least,
that commonly it brings with it a welcome
deceit.  I have other news for you, sir.     105

*Touch.*  None more welcome, I am sure!

*Gold.*  They have their degree of welcome,
I dare affirm.  The Colonel and all his company, this morning putting forth drunk from
Billingsgate, had like to have been cast [110
away o' this side Greenwich; and (as I have
intelligence by a false brother) are come dropping to town like so many masterless men,
i' their doublets and hose, without hat, or
cloak, or any other —                        115

*Touch.*  A miracle!  The justice of heaven!
Where are they?  Let 's go presently and lay
for 'em.

*Gold.*  I have done that already, sir, both
by constables and other officers, who shall [120
take 'em at their old Anchor, and with less
tumult or suspicion than if yourself were seen
in 't, under colour of a great press that is now
abroad, and they shall here be brought afore
me.                                          125

*Touch.*  Prudent and politic son!  Disgrace
'em all that ever thou canst; their ship I
have already arrested.  How to my wish it
falls out, that thou hast the place of a justicer
upon 'em!  I am partly glad of the injury [130
done to me, that thou mayst punish it.  Be
severe i' thy place, like a new officer o' the
first quarter, unreflected.  You hear how our
lady is come back with her train from the invisible castle?                              135

*Gold.*  No; where is she?

*Touch.*  Within; but I ha' not seen her
yet, nor her mother, who now begins to wish
her daughter undubbed, they say, and that
she had walked a foot-pace with her sister. [140
Here they come; stand back.

*[Enter] Mistress Touchstone, Gertrude, Mildred,
Sindefy*

God save your ladyship, 'save your good ladyship!  Your ladyship is welcome from your
enchanted castle; so are your beauteous reti-
nue.  I hear your knight errant is travelled [145
on strange adventures.  Surely, in my mind,
your ladyship hath fished fair and caught a
frog, as the saying is.

*Mist. Touch.*  Speak to your father, madam,
and kneel down.                              150

---

<sup>51–53</sup> **take . . . inquest:** make me a member of their committee     <sup>66</sup> **Ta'en . . . livery:** made
a member     <sup>67</sup> **freedom:** (from apprenticeship)     <sup>76</sup> **sufficient:** able     <sup>78</sup> **expects:** awaits     <sup>84</sup> **opinion:**
fame     <sup>87</sup> **wear scarlet:** be an alderman (with pun)     <sup>91–92</sup> **Lady Ramsey:** widow of a Lord Mayor, ben-
efactress of Christ's Hospital     <sup>92</sup> **Gresham:** Sir Thomas, builder of the Royal Exchange     <sup>95</sup> **posies:**
mottoes     <sup>98</sup> **get-penny:** box-office triumph     <sup>112</sup> **false brother:** traitor     <sup>117</sup> **lay:** employ sergeants
to watch     <sup>121</sup> **Anchor:** the inn     <sup>123</sup> **colour:** pretext     **press:** impressment of troops     <sup>133</sup> **unreflected:** dark, like the moon in the first quarter     <sup>140</sup> **a foot-pace:** slowly and sure

*Ger.* Kneel? I hope I am not brought so low yet; though my knight be run away, and has sold my land, I am a lady still.

*Touch.* Your ladyship says true, madam; and it is fitter and a greater decorum, that [155 I should curtsy to you that are a knight's wife, and a lady, than you be brought o' your knees to me, who am a poor cullion and your father.

*Ger.* La! My father knows his duty.    160

*Mist. Touch.* O child!

*Touch.* And therefore I do desire your ladyship, my good Lady Flash, in all humility, to depart my obscure cottage, and return in quest of your bright and most transparent [165 castle, however presently concealed to mortal eyes. And as for one poor woman of your train here, I will take that order, she shall no longer be a charge unto you, nor help to spend your ladyship; she shall stay at home [170 with me, and not go abroad; not put you to the pawning of an odd coach-horse or three wheels, but take part with the Touchstone. If we lack, we will not complain to your ladyship. And so, good madam, with your [175 damosel here, please you to let us see your straight backs in equipage; for truly here is no roost for such chickens as you are, or birds o' your feather, if it like your ladyship.

*Ger.* Marry, fist o' your kindness! I [180 thought as much. Come away, Sin, we shall as soon get a fart from a dead man, as a farthing of courtesy here.

*Mil.* O good sister!

*Ger.* Sister, sir-reverence! Come away, [185 I say, hunger drops out at his nose.

*Gold.* O madam, fair words never hurt the tongue.

*Ger.* How say you by that? You come out with your gold-ends now!    190

*Mist. Touch.* Stay, lady-daughter! Good husband!

*Touch.* Wife, no man loves his fetters, be they made of gold. I list not ha' my head fastened under my child's girdle: as she has [195 brewed, so let her drink, o' God's name! She went witless to wedding, now she may go wisely a-begging. It 's but honeymoon yet with her ladyship; she has coach-horses, apparel, jewels, yet left; she needs care for [200 no friends, nor take knowledge of father, mother, brother, sister, or anybody. When those are pawned or spent, perhaps we shall return into the list of her acquaintance.

*Ger.* I scorn it, i' faith! Come, Sin.    205

*Mist. Touch.* O madam, why do you provoke your father thus?

*Exit Gertrude [with Sindefy]*

*Touch.* Nay, nay; e'en let pride go afore, shame will follow after, I warrant you. Come, why dost thou weep now? Thou art not [210 the first good cow hast had an ill calf, I trust.

[*Exit Mistress Touchstone.*]

What 's the news with that fellow?

*Enter Constable*

*Gold.* Sir, the knight and your man Quicksilver are without; will you ha' 'em brought in?    215

*Touch.* O by any means! [*Exit Constable.*] And, son, here 's a chair; appear terrible unto 'em on the first interview. Let them behold the melancholy of a magistrate, and taste the fury of a citizen in office.    220

*Gold.* Why, sir, I can do nothing to 'em, except you charge 'em with somewhat.

*Touch.* I will charge 'em and recharge 'em, rather than authority should want foil to set it off.    [*Offers Golding a chair.*] 225

*Gold.* No, good sir, I will not.

*Touch.* Son, it is your place; by any means!

*Gold.* Believe it, I will not, sir.

*Enter Knight Petronel, Quicksilver, Constable, Officers*

*Pet.* How misfortune pursues us still [230 in our misery!

*Quick.* Would it had been my fortune to have been trussed up at Wapping, rather than ever ha' come here!

*Pet.* Or mine to have famished in the [235 island!

*Quick.* Must Golding sit upon us?

*Con.* You might carry an M. under your girdle to Master Deputy's worship.

*Gold.* What are those, Master Constable? 240

*Con.* An 't please your worship, a couple of masterless men I pressed for the Low Countries, sir.

*Gold.* Why do you not carry 'em to Bridewell, according to your order, they may be [245 shipped away?

*Con.* An 't please your worship, one of 'em says he is a knight; and we thought good to shew him to your worship, for our discharge.

*Gold.* Which is he?    250

*Con.* This, sir!

*Gold.* And what 's the other?

*Con.* A knight's fellow, sir, an 't please you.

*Gold.* What! A knight and his fellow thus

---

¹⁵⁸ **cullion:** rogue    ¹⁷⁷ **in equipage:** retreating side by side    ¹⁸⁰ **fist:** expression of contempt
¹⁸⁶ **hunger . . . nose:** proverbial saying of misers    ²¹⁶ **by any means:** by all means    ²³³ **trussed**
**. . . Wapping:** hanged    ²³⁶ **island:** Isle of Dogs    ²³⁸⁻²³⁹ **carry . . . girdle:** use the title of respect
²⁴² **masterless:** vagrant    ²⁴⁵ **they:** that they    ²⁴⁹ **discharge:** immunity

accoutred? Where are their hats and [255 feathers, their rapiers and their cloaks?

*Quick.* O, they mock us!

*Con.* Nay, truly, sir, they had cast both their feathers and hats too, before we see 'em. Here 's all their furniture, an 't please [260 you, that we found. They say knights are now to be known without feathers, like cockerels, by their spurs, sir.

*Gold.* What are their names, say they?

*Touch.* [*aside.*] Very well, this! He [265 should not take knowledge of 'em in his place, indeed.

*Con.* This is Sir Petronel Flash.

*Touch.* How!

*Con.* And this, Francis Quicksilver.    270

*Touch.* Is 't possible? I thought your worship had been gone for Virginia, sir. You are welcome home, sir. Your worship has made a quick return, it seems, and no doubt a good voyage. Nay, pray you be covered, [275 sir. How did your biscuit hold out, sir? Methought I had seen this gentleman afore. Good Master Quicksilver, how a degree to the southward has changed you!

*Gold.* Do you know 'em, father? — [280 Forbear your offers a little, you shall be heard anon.

*Touch.* Yes, Master Deputy; I had a small venture with them in the voyage — a thing called a son-in-law, or so. Officers, you [285 may let 'em stand alone, they will not run away; I 'll give my word for them. A couple of very honest gentlemen. One of 'em was my prentice, Master Quicksilver here; and when he had two year to serve, kept his [290 whore and his hunting nag, would play his hundred pound at gresco, or primero, as familiarly (and all o' my purse) as any bright piece of crimson on 'em all; had his changeable trunks of apparel standing at livery, with [295 his mare, his chest of perfumed linen, and his bathing-tubs: which when I told him of, why he — he was a gentleman, and I a poor Cheapside groom! The remedy was, we must part. Since when, he hath had the gift of gath- [300 ering up some small parcels of mine, to the value of five hundred pound, dispersed among my customers, to furnish this his Virginian venture; wherein this knight was the chief, Sir Flash — one that married a daughter [305 of mine, ladyfied her, turned two thousand pounds' worth of good land of hers into cash within the first week, bought her a new gown and a coach, sent her to seek her fortune by land, whilst himself prepared for his [310

fortune by sea; took in fresh flesh at Billingsgate, for his own diet, to serve him the whole voyage — the wife of a certain usurer called Security, who hath been the broker for 'em in all this business. Please, Master Deputy, [315 work upon that now!

*Gold.* If my worshipful father have ended.

*Touch.* I have, it shall please Master Deputy.

*Gold.* Well then, under correction —

*Touch.* [*aside to Golding.*] Now, son, [320 come over 'em with some fine gird, as thus: 'Knight, you shall be encountered,' that is, had to the Counter, or, 'Quicksilver, I will put you into a crucible,' or so.

*Gold.* Sir Petronel Flash, I am sorry to [325 see such flashes as these proceed from a gentleman of your quality and rank; for mine own part, I could wish I could say I could not see them; but such is the misery of magistrates and men in place, that they must not wink [330 at offenders. Take him aside — I will hear you anon, sir.

*Touch.* I like this well, yet; there 's some grace i' the knight left — he cries.

*Gold.* Francis Quicksilver, would God [335 thou hadst turned quacksalver, rather than run into these dissolute and lewd courses! It is great pity; thou art a proper young man, of an honest and clean face, somewhat near a good one (God hath done his part in thee); [340 but thou hast made too much and been too proud of that face, with the rest of thy body; for maintenance of which in neat and garish attire (only to be looked upon by some light housewives) thou hast prodigally consumed [345 much of thy master's estate; and being by him gently admonished at several times, hast returned thyself haughty and rebellious in thine answers, thund'ring out uncivil comparisons, requiting all his kindness with a [350 coarse and harsh behaviour, never returning thanks for any one benefit, but receiving all as if they had been debts to thee and no courtesies. I must tell thee, Francis, these are manifest signs of an ill nature; and [355 God doth often punish such pride and outrecuidance with scorn and infamy, which is the worst of misfortune. My worshipful father, what do you please to charge them withal? From the press I will free 'em, Master Con-[360 stable.

*Con.* Then I 'll leave your worship, sir.

*Gold.* No, you may stay; there will be other matters against 'em.

*Touch.* Sir, I do charge this gallant, [365 Master Quicksilver, on suspicion of felony;

²⁶⁶ place: seat of justice    ²⁷⁵ be covered: put on your hat    ²⁷⁸⁻²⁷⁹ degree . . . southward: southern latitude    ²⁸¹ offers: gestures    ²⁹² gresco, primero: card games    ³³⁰ wink: close their eyes    ³⁴⁶ returned: expressed    ³⁵⁶⁻³⁵⁷ outrecuidance: conceit

and the knight as being accessory in the receipt of my goods.

*Quick.* O God, sir!

*Touch.* Hold thy peace, impudent var- [370 let, hold thy peace! With what forehead or face dost thou offer to chop logic with me, having run such a race of riot as thou hast done? Does not the sight of this worshipful man's fortune and temper confound thee, [375 that was thy younger fellow in household, and now come to have the place of a judge upon thee? Dost not observe this? Which of all thy gallants and gamesters, thy swearers and thy swaggerers, will come now to moan thy [380 misfortune, or pity thy penury? They 'll look out at a window, as thou rid'st in triumph to Tyburn, and cry, 'Yonder goes honest Frank, mad Quicksilver!' 'He was a free boon companion, when he had money,' says one; [385 'Hang him, fool!' says another, 'he could not keep it when he had it!' 'A pox o' the cullion, his master,' says a third, 'he has brought him to this'; when their pox of pleasure and their piles of perdition would have been better [390 bestowed upon thee, that hast ventured for 'em with the best, and by the clew of thy knavery brought thyself weeping to the cart of calamity.

*Quick.* Worshipful master! 395

*Touch.* Offer not to speak, crocodile; I will not hear a sound come from thee. Thou hast learnt to whine at the play yonder. Master Deputy, pray you commit 'em both to safe custody, till I be able farther to charge 'em. 400

*Quick.* O me, what an infortunate thing am I!

*Pet.* Will you not take security, sir?

*Touch.* Yes, marry, will I, Sir Flash, if I can find him, and charge him as deep as [405 the best on you. He has been the plotter of all this; he is your enginer, I hear. Master Deputy, you 'll dispose of these? In the mean time, I 'll to my Lord Mayor, and get his warrant to seize that serpent Security into [410 my hands, and seal up both house and goods to the King's use or my satisfaction.

*Gold.* Officers, take 'em to the Counter.

*Quick.*
*Pet.* } O God!

*Touch.* Nay, on, on! You see the issue of [415 your sloth. Of sloth cometh pleasure, of pleasure cometh riot, of riot comes whoring, of whoring comes spending, of spending comes want, of want comes theft, of theft comes hanging; and there is my Quicksilver fixed. 420

*Exeunt.*

## Actus quintus Scena prima

[*Gertrude's Lodging*]

*Gertrude. Sindefy*

*Ger.* Ah, Sin! hast thou ever read i' the chronicle of any lady and her waiting-woman driven to that extremity that we are, Sin?

*Sin.* Not I, truly, madam; and if I had, it were but cold comfort should come out [5 of books now.

*Ger.* Why, good faith, Sin, I could dine with a lamentable story now. 'O hone, hone, o no nera,' &c.! Canst thou tell ne'er a one, Sin? 10

*Sin.* None but mine own, madam, which is lamentable enough: first to be stolen from my friends, which were worshipful and of good accompt, by a prentice in the habit and disguise of a gentleman, and here brought up [15 to London and promised marriage, and now likely to be forsaken, for he is in possibility to be hanged!

*Ger.* Nay, weep not, good Sin; my Petronel is in as good possibility as he. Thy miseries [20 are nothing to mine, Sin: I was more than promised marriage, Sin; I had it, Sin, and was made a lady; and by a knight, Sin, which is now as good as no knight, Sin. And I was born in London, which is more than [25 brought up, Sin; and already forsaken, which is past likelihood, Sin; and instead of land i' the country, all my knight's living lies i' the Counter, Sin: there 's his castle now!

*Sin.* Which he cannot be forced out of, [30 madam.

*Ger.* Yes, if he would live hungry a week or two. 'Hunger,' they say, 'breaks stone walls.' But he is e'en well enough served, Sin, that so soon as ever he had got my [35 hand to the sale of my inheritance, run away from me, and I had been his punk, God bless us! Would the Knight o' the Sun, or Palmerin of England, have used their ladies so, Sin? Or Sir Lancelot, or Sir Tristram? 40

*Sin.* I do not know, madam.

*Ger.* Then thou know'st nothing, Sin. Thou art a fool, Sin. The knighthood nowadays are nothing like the knighthood of old time. They rid a-horseback; ours go a-foot. [45 They were attended by their squires; ours by their lackeys. They went buckled in their armour; ours muffled in their cloaks. They travelled wildernesses and deserts; ours dare scarce walk the streets. They were still [50

---

³⁷² **chop logic:** bicker  ³⁹² **clew:** ball of thread  ⁴⁰⁷ **enginer:** schemer  ³⁷ **and:** as if
³⁸⁻³⁹ **Knight . . . England:** heroes of popular Spanish romances (see *Knight of the Burning Pestle*)
⁴³ **knighthood:** knights  ⁵⁰⁻⁵¹ **still prest:** always ready

prest to engage their honour; ours still ready
to pawn their clothes. They would gallop on
at sight of a monster; ours run away at sight
of a sergeant. They would help poor ladies;
ours make poor ladies.                          55
*Sin.* Ay, madam, they were knights of the
Round Table at Winchester, that sought adventures; but these of the Square Table at
ordinaries, that sit at hazard.
*Ger.* True, Sin, let him vanish. And tell [60
me, what shall we pawn next?
*Sin.* Ay, marry, madam, a timely consideration; for our hostess (profane woman!) has
sworn by bread and salt, she will not trust
us another meal.                                65
*Ger.* Let it stink in her hand then. I 'll
not be beholding to her. Let me see: my
jewels be gone, and my gowns, and my red
velvet petticoat that I was married in, and
my wedding silk stockings, and all thy [70
best apparel, poor Sin! Good faith, rather
than thou shouldst pawn a rag more, I 'd lay
my ladyship in lavender — if I knew where.
*Sin.* Alas, madam, your ladyship?
*Ger.* Ay, why? You do not scorn my [75
ladyship, though it is in a waistcoat? God 's
my life, you are a peat indeed! Do I offer
to mortgage my ladyship for you and for
your avail, and do you turn the lip and the
alas to my ladyship?                            80
*Sin.* No, madam; but I make question
who will lend anything upon it?
*Ger.* Who? Marry, enow, I warrant you,
if you 'll seek 'em out. I 'm sure I remember the time when I would ha' given a [85
thousand pound (if I had had it) to have been
a lady; and I hope I was not bred and born
with that appetite alone: some other gentle-
born o' the City have the same longing, I
trust. And for my part, I would afford [90
'em a penny'rth; my ladyship is little the
worse for the wearing, and yet I would bate
a good deal of the sum. I would lend it
(let me see) for forty pound in hand, Sin
— that would apparel us — and ten pound [95
a year. That would keep me and you, Sin
(with our needles), and we should never need
to be beholding to our scurvy parents. Good
Lord, that there are no fairies nowadays,
Sin!                                           100
*Sin.* Why, madam?
*Ger.* To do miracles, and bring ladies money.
Sure, if we lay in a cleanly house, they would
haunt it, Sin. I 'll try. I 'll sweep the chamber soon at night, and set a dish of water [105
o' the hearth. A fairy may come, and bring

a pearl or a diamond. We do not know, Sin.
Or, there may be a pot of gold hid o' the
backside, if we had tools to dig for 't? Why
may not we two rise early i' the morning, [110
Sin, afore anybody is up, and find a jewel i'
the streets worth a hundred pound? May not
some great court-lady, as she comes from revels
at midnight, look out of her coach as 't is
running, and lose such a jewel, and we find [115
it? Ha?
*Sin.* They are pretty waking dreams, these.
*Ger.* Or may not some old usurer be drunk
overnight, with a bag of money, and leave it
behind him on a stall? For God-sake, [120
Sin, let 's rise to-morrow by break of day,
and see. I protest, la! if I had as much
money as an alderman, I would scatter some
on 't i' th' streets for poor ladies to find,
when their knights were laid up. And, [125
now I remember my song o' the Golden
Shower, why may not I have such a fortune?
I 'll sing it, and try what luck I shall have
after it.                                      129

  '*Fond fables tell of old*
      *How Jove in Danaë's lap*
  *Fell in a shower of gold,*
      *By which she caught a clap;*
      *O had it been my hap*
  (*How ere the blow doth threaten*)        135
      *So well I like the play,*
      *That I could wish all day*
  *And night to be so beaten.*'

*Enter Mistress Touchstone*

O here 's my mother! Good luck, I hope.
Ha' you brought any money, mother? [140
Pray you, mother, your blessing. Nay, sweet
mother, do not weep.
*Mist. Touch.* God bless you! I would I
were in my grave!
*Ger.* Nay, dear mother, can you steal [145
no more money from my father? Dry your
eyes, and comfort me. Alas, it is my knight's
fault, and not mine, that I am in a waistcoat,
and attired thus simply.
*Mist. Touch.* Simply? 'T is better than [150
thou deserv'st. Never whimper for the matter.
Thou shouldst have looked before thou hadst
leaped. Thou wert afire to be a lady, and
now your ladyship and you may both blow
at the coal, for aught I know. Self do, [155
self have. 'The hasty person never wants woe,'
they say.
*Ger.* Nay, then, mother, you should ha'
looked to it. A body would think you were

---

**67 Winchester:** (where Arthur's Round Table was reputedly preserved)   **69 hazard:** dice-game
**67 beholding:** obliged   **73 in lavender:** in pawn   **76 waistcoat:** under-garment   **77 peat:** saucy
wench   **91 penny'rth:** pennyworth, bargain   **92 bate:** remit

the older; I did but my kind, I. He [160 was a knight, and I was fit to be a lady. 'T is not lack of liking, but lack of living, that severs us. And you talk like yourself and a cittiner in this, i' faith. You show what husband you come on, iwis. You smell [165 the Touchstone — he that will do more for his daughter that has married a scurvy gold-end man and his prentice, than he will for his tother daughter, that has wedded a knight and his customer. By this light, I think [170 he is not my legitimate father.

*Sin.* O good madam, do not take up your mother so!

*Mist. Touch.* Nay, nay, let her e'en alone! Let her ladyship grieve me still, with her [175 bitter taunts and terms. I have not dole enough to see her in this miserable case, I, without her velvet gowns, without ribands, without jewels, without French wires, or cheat-bread, or quails, or a little dog, or a gentle- [180 man-usher, or anything, indeed, that 's fit for a lady —

*Sin.* [*aside.*] Except her tongue.

*Mist. Touch.* And I not able to relieve her, neither, being kept so short by my hus- [185 band. Well, God knows my heart. I did little think that ever she should have had need of her sister Golding.

*Ger.* Why, mother, I ha' not yet. Alas, good mother, be not intoxicate for me! I [190 am well enough; I would not change husbands with my sister, I. The leg of a lark is better than the body of a kite.

*Mist. Touch.* I know that, but —

*Ger.* What, sweet mother, what?    195

*Mist. Touch.* It 's but ill food when nothing 's left but the claw.

*Ger.* That 's true, mother. Ay me!

*Mist. Touch.* Nay, sweet lady-bird, sigh not. Child, madam, why do you weep [200 thus? Be of good cheer; I shall die, if you cry and mar your complexion thus.

*Ger.* Alas, mother, what should I do?

*Mist. Touch.* Go to thy sister's, child; she 'll be proud thy ladyship will come [205 under her roof. She 'll win thy father to release thy knight, and redeem thy gowns and thy coach and thy horses, and set thee up again.

*Ger.* But will she get him to set my [210 knight up, too?

*Mist. Touch.* That she will, or anything else thou 'lt ask her.

*Ger.* I will begin to love her, if I thought she would do this.    [215

*Mist. Touch.* Try her, good chuck, I warrant thee.

*Ger.* Dost thou think she 'll do 't?

*Sin.* Ay, madam, and be glad you will receive it.    [220

*Mist. Touch.* That 's a good maiden; she tells you true. Come, I 'll take order for your debts i' the ale-house.

*Ger.* Go, Sin, and pray for thy Frank, as I will for my Pet.    [*Exeunt.*]

[SCENE II. — *Goldsmith's Row*]

*Enter Touchstone, Golding, Wolf*

*Touch.* I will receive no letters, Master Wolf; you shall pardon me.

*Gold.* Good father, let me entreat you.

*Touch.* Son Golding, I will not be tempted; I find mine own easy nature, and I know [5 not what a well-penned subtle letter may work upon it; there may be tricks, packing, do you see? Return with your packet, sir.

*Wolf.* Believe it, sir, you need fear no packing here. These are but letters of sub- [10 mission all.

*Touch.* Sir, I do look for no submission. I will bear myself in this like blind Justice. Work upon that now! When the Sessions come, they shall hear from me.    15

*Gold.* From whom come your letters, Master Wolf?

*Wolf.* An 't please you, sir, one from Sir Petronel, another from Francis Quicksilver, and a third from old Security, who is al- [20 most mad in prison. There are two to your worship, one from Master Francis, sir, another from the knight.

*Touch.* I do wonder, Master Wolf, why you should travail thus in a business so [25 contrary to kind or the nature o' your place! that you, being the keeper of a prison, should labour the release of your prisoners! Whereas, methinks, it were far more natural and kindly in you to be ranging about for more, and [30 not let these scape you have already under the tooth. But they say, you wolves, when you ha' sucked the blood once, that they are dry, you ha' done.

*Wolf.* Sir, your worship may descant as [35 you please o' my name; but I protest I was never so mortified with any men's discourse or behaviour in prison; yet I have had of

---

¹⁶⁰ **my kind:** according to my nature    ¹⁶⁴ **cittiner:** cockney    ¹⁶⁵ **iwis:** forsooth    ¹⁶⁷ **has:** ('he has' Qq.)    ¹⁷⁶ **dole:** sorrow    ¹⁷⁹⁻¹⁸⁰ **cheat-bread:** bread of fine flour    ¹⁹⁰ **intoxicate:** (perhaps for "exasperate" or "intemperate")    ²¹⁶ **chuck:** term of endearment    ²²² **take order:** arrange    ⁵ **find:** recognize    ⁷ **packing:** scheming    ²⁶ **kind:** natural disposition    ²⁹ **kindly:** normal    ³³ **that:** so that

all sorts of men i' the kingdom under my keys, and almost of all religions i' the land, as [40 Papist, Protestant, Puritan, Brownist, Anabaptist, Millenary, Family-o'-Love, Jew, Turk, Infidel, Atheist, Good-Fellow, &c.

*Gold.* And which of all these, thinks Master Wolf, was the best religion?                    45

*Wolf.* Troth, Master Deputy, they that pay fees best: we never examine their consciences farder.

*Gold.* I believe you, Master Wolf. Good faith, sir, here 's a great deal of humility [50 i' these letters.

*Wolf.* Humility, sir? Ay, were your worship an eye-witness of it, you would say so. The knight will i' the Knight's Ward, do what we can, sir; and Master Quicksilver would [55 be i' the Hole if we would let him. I never knew or saw prisoners more penitent, or more devout. They will sit you up all night singing of psalms and edifying the whole prison; only Security sings a note too high some- [60 times, because he lies i' the twopenny ward, far off, and cannot take his tune. The neighbours cannot rest for him, but come every morning to ask what godly prisoners we have.

*Touch.* Which on 'em is 't is so devout [65 — the knight or the t'other?

*Wolf.* Both, sir; but the young man especially. I never heard his like. He has cut his hair too. He is so well given, and has such good gifts. He can tell you almost all [70 the stories of the Book of Martyrs, and speak you all the Sick Man's Salve, without book.

*Touch.* Ay, if he had had grace, he was brought up where it grew, iwis. On, Master Wolf!                    [75

*Wolf.* And he has converted one Fangs, a sergeant, a fellow could neither write nor read: he was called the Bandog o' the Counter; and he has brought him already to pare his nails and say his prayers; and 't is hoped [80 he will sell his place shortly, and become an intelligencer.

*Touch.* No more; I am coming already. If I should give any farder ear I were taken. Adieu, good Master Wolf! Son, I do feel [85 mine own weaknesses; do not importune me. Pity is a rheum, that I am subject to; but I will resist it. Master Wolf, fish is cast away that is cast in dry pools. Tell hypocrisy it will not do; I have touched and tried too [90 often; I am yet proof, and I will remain so; when the Sessions come they shall hear from me. In the mean time, to all suits, to all entreaties, to

all letters, to all tricks, I will be deaf as an adder, and blind as a beetle, lay mine ear to [95 the ground, and lock mine eyes i' my hand against all temptations.                    *Exit*

*Gold.* You see, Master Wolf, how inexorable he is. There is no hope to recover him. Pray you commend me to my brother [100 knight, and to my fellow Francis; present 'em with this small token of my love [*giving money*]. Tell 'em, I wish I could do 'em any worthier office; but in this, 't is desperate; yet I will not fail to try the uttermost of my power [105 for 'em. And, sir, as far as I have any credit with you, pray you let 'em want nothing; though I am not ambitious they should know so much.

*Wolf.* Sir, both your actions and words [110 speak you to be a true gentleman. They shall know only what is fit, and no more.    *Exeunt.*

[SCENE III. — *The Counter*]

*Holdfast, Bramble;* [*later*] *Security*

*Hold.* Who would you speak with, sir?

*Bram.* I would speak with one Security, that is prisoner here.

*Hold.* You are welcome, sir! Stay there, I 'll call him to you. Master Security!    5

*Sec.* [*at the grate.*] Who calls?

*Hold.* Here 's a gentleman would speak with you.

*Sec.* What is he? Is 't one that grafts my forehead now I am in prison, and comes [10 to see how the horns shoot up and prosper?

*Hold.* You must pardon him, sir. The old man is a little crazed with his imprisonment.

*Sec.* What say you to me, sir? Look you here. My learned counsel, Master Bramble! [15 Cry you mercy, sir! When saw you my wife?

*Bram.* She is now at my house, sir; and desired me that I would come to visit you, and inquire of you your case, that we might work some means to get you forth.    20

*Sec.* My case, Master Bramble, is stone walls and iron grates; you see it, this is the weakest part on 't. And for getting me forth, no means but hang myself, and so to be carried forth, from which they have here bound [25 me in intolerable bands.

*Bram.* Why, but what is 't you are in for, sir?

*Sec.* For my sins, for my sins, sir, whereof marriage is the greatest! O, had I never [30 married, I had never known this purgatory, to which hell is a kind of cool bath in respect.

---

⁴⁸ **farder:** farther    ⁵⁴,⁵⁶ **Knight's Ward, Hole:** inferior parts of the prison    ⁷¹ **Book of Martyrs:** John Fox's Protestant classic, the "Acts and Monuments"    ⁷² **Sick Man's Salve:** popular devotional work by Thomas Becon    ⁸³ **coming:** yielding    ²¹ **case:** container (pun)    ³² **respect:** comparison

My wife's confederacy, sir, with old Touchstone, that she might keep her jubilee and the feast of her new moon. Do you [35 understand me, sir?

*Enter Quicksilver*

*Quick.* Good sir, go in and talk with him. The light does him harm, and his example will be hurtful to the weak prisoners. Fie, Father Security, that you'll be still so [40 profane! Will nothing humble you?

*[Exeunt.]*

*Enter two prisoners with a friend*

*Friend.* What's he?
*1 Pris.* O he is a rare young man! Do you not know him?
*Friend.* Not I! I never saw him, I can [45 remember.
*2 Pris.* Why, it is he that was the gallant prentice of London — Master Touchstone's man.
*Friend.* Who? Quicksilver?          50
*1 Pris.* Ay, this is he.
*Friend.* Is this he? They say he has been a gallant indeed.
*2 Pris.* O the royalest fellow that ever was bred up i' the City! He would play [55 you his thousand pound a night at dice; keep knights and lords company; go with them to bawdy-houses; had his six men in a livery; kept a stable of hunting-horses, and his wench in her velvet gown and her cloth of silver. [60 Here's one knight with him here in prison.
*Friend.* And how miserably he is changed!
*1 Pris.* O that's voluntary in him: he gave away all his rich clothes, as soon as ever he came in here, among the prisoners; and [65 will eat o' the basket, for humility.
*Friend.* Why will he do so?
*1 Pris.* Alas, he has no hope of life. He mortifies himself. He does but linger on till the Sessions.          70
*2 Pris.* O, he has penned the best thing, that he calls his Repentance or his Last Farewell, that ever you heard. He is a pretty poet, and for prose — you would wonder how many prisoners he has helped out, with [75 penning petitions for 'em, and not take a penny. Look! This is the knight, in the rug gown. Stand by!

*Enter Petronel, Bramble, Quicksilver*

*Bram.* Sir, for Security's case, I have told him. Say he should be condemned to be [80 carted or whipped for a bawd, or so, why,

I'll lay an execution on him o' two hundred pound; let him acknowledge a judgment, he shall do it in half an hour; they shall not all fetch him out without paying the exe- [85 cution, o' my word.
*Pet.* But can we not be bailed, Master Bramble?
*Bram.* Hardly; there are none of the judges in town, else you should remove yourself [90 (in spite of him) with a *habeas corpus.* But if you have a friend to deliver your tale sensibly to some justice o' the town, that he may have feeling of it (do you see) you may be bailed; for as I understand the case, [95 'tis only done *in terrorem;* and you shall have an action of false imprisonment against him when you come out, and perhaps a thousand pound costs.

*Enter Master Wolf*

*Quick.* How now, Master Wolf? What [100 news? What return?
*Wolf.* Faith, bad all! Yonder will be no letters received. He says the Sessions shall determine it. Only Master Deputy Golding commends him to you, and with this [105 token wishes he could do you other good.

*[Gives money.]*

*Quick.* I thank him. Good Master Bramble, trouble our quiet no more; do not molest us in prison thus with your winding devices. Pray you, depart. For my part, I commit [110 my cause to him that can succour me; let God work his will. Master Wolf, I pray you, let this be distributed among the prisoners, and desire 'em to pray for us.
*Wolf.* It shall be done, Master Francis. [115

*[Exit Quicksilver.]*

*1 Pris.* An excellent temper!
*2 Pris.* Now God send him good luck!

*Exeunt (Bramble, two Prisoners and Friend).*

*Pet.* But what said my father-in-law, Master Wolf?

*Enter Holdfast*

*Hold.* Here's one would speak with [120 you, sir.
*Wolf.* I'll tell you anon, Sir Petronel. Who is 't?
*Hold.* A gentleman, sir, that will not be seen.          125

*Enter Golding*

*Wolf.* Where is he? Master Deputy! Your worship is welcome —
*Gold.* Peace!

---

³⁵ **feast . . . moon:** orgies of dancing    ⁵⁴ **2 Pris.:** ('Pris.' Qq.)    ⁶⁶ **basket:** alms-basket, refuse food contributed by charity    ⁶⁸ **1 Pris.:** ('Pris. 2' Qq.)    ⁷⁴ **wonder:** be surprised    ⁷⁷ **rug:** coarse wool    ⁹²⁻⁹³ **sensibly:** appealingly    ¹⁰¹ **return:** reply

*Wolf.* Away, sirrah!

     [*Exit Holdfast with Sir Petronel.*]

*Gold.* Good faith, Master Wolf, the es- [130 tate of these gentlemen, for whom you were so late and willing a suitor, doth much affect me; and because I am desirous to do them some fair office, and find there is no means to make my father relent so likely as to [135 bring him to be a spectator of their miseries, I have ventured on a device, which is, to make myself your prisoner, entreating you will presently go report it to my father, and (feigning an action at suit of some third [140 person) pray him by this token [*giving a ring*] that he will presently, and with all secrecy, come hither for my bail; which train, if any, I know will bring him abroad; and then, having him here, I doubt not but we shall [145 be all fortunate in the event.

*Wolf.* Sir, I will put on my best speed to effect it. Please you, come in.

*Gold.* Yes; and let me rest concealed, I pray you.      150

*Wolf.* See here a benefit truly done, when it is done timely, freely, and to no ambition.

               *Exit* [*with Golding*].

### [SCENE IV. — *Touchstone's House*]

*Enter Touchstone, Wife, Daughters,*
         *Sindefy, Winifred*

*Touch.* I will sail by you and not hear you, like the wise Ulysses.

*Mil.* Dear father!

*Mist. Touch.* Husband!

*Ger.* Father.      5

*Win. and Sin.* Master Touchstone!

*Touch.* Away, sirens, I will immure myself against your cries, and lock myself up to your lamentations.

*Mist. Touch.* Gentle husband, hear me! [10

*Ger.* Father, it is I, father, my Lady Flash. My sister and I am friends.

*Mil.* Good father!

*Win.* Be not hardened, good Master Touchstone!      15

*Sin.* I pray you, sir, be merciful!

*Touch.* I am deaf, I do not hear you; I have stopped mine ears with shoemakers' wax, and drunk Lethe and mandragora to forget you. All you speak to me I commit to the [20 air.

           *Enter Wolf*

*Mil.* How now, Master Wolf?

*Wolf.* Where 's Master Touchstone? I must speak with him presently; I have lost my breath for haste.      25

*Mil.* What 's the matter, sir? Pray all be well!

*Wolf.* Master Deputy Golding is arrested upon an execution, and desires him presently to come to him, forthwith.      30

*Mil.* Ay me! Do you hear, father?

*Touch.* Tricks, tricks, confederacy, tricks! I have 'em in my nose — I scent 'em!

*Wolf.* Who 's that? Master Touchstone?

*Mist. Touch.* Why, it is Master Wolf [35 himself, husband.

*Mil.* Father!

*Touch.* I am deaf still, I say, I will neither yield to the song of the siren, nor the voice of the hyena, the tears of the crocodile, [40 nor the howling o' the wolf. Avoid my habitation, monsters!

*Wolf.* Why, you are not mad, sir? I pray you, look forth, and see the token I have brought you, sir.      45

*Touch.* Ha! What token is it?

*Wolf.* Do you know it, sir?

*Touch.* My son Golding's ring! Are you in earnest, Master Wolf?

*Wolf.* Ay, by my faith, sir! He is in [50 prison, and required me to use all speed and secrecy to you.

*Touch.* My cloak, there! — pray you be patient. I am plagued for my austerity. My cloak! At whose suit, Master Wolf?      55

*Wolf.* I 'll tell you as we go, sir.    *Exeunt.*

### [SCENE V. — *The Counter*]

     *Enter Friend, Prisoners*

*Friend.* Why, but is his offence such as he cannot hope of life?

*1 Pris.* Troth, it should seem so; and 't is great pity, for he is exceeding penitent.

*Friend.* They say he is charged but on [5 suspicion of felony yet.

*2 Pris.* Ay, but his master is a shrewd fellow; he 'll prove great matter against him.

*Friend.* I 'd as lief as anything I could see his Farewell.      10

*1 Pris.* O 't is rarely written; why, Toby may get him to sing it to you; he 's not curious to anybody.

*2 Pris.* O no! He would that all the world should take knowledge of his repentance, [15 and thinks he merits in 't, the more shame he suffers.

*1 Pris.* Pray thee, try what thou canst do.

*2 Pris.* I warrant you, he will not deny

---

¹³⁰⁻¹³¹ **estate:** situation    ¹⁴³ **train:** device    ¹⁴⁶ **event:** outcome    ⁹ **your:** ('our' Qq. 2–3)
¹⁹ **Lethe:** river of forgetfulness    **mandragora:** mandrake, a narcotic    ⁵¹ **required:** requested
**Sc. V.** ¹² **curious:** capricious    ¹⁶ **merits:** acquires merit

it, if he be not hoarse with the often re- [20 peating of it.                              *Exit.*

*1 Pris.* You never saw a more courteous creature than he is, and the knight too: the poorest prisoner of the house may command 'em. You shall hear a thing admirably [25 penned.

*Friend.* Is the knight any scholar too?

*1 Pris.* No, but he will speak very well, and discourse admirably of running horses and White-Friars, and against bawds, and [30 of cocks; and talk as loud as a hunter, but is none.

*Enter Wolf and Touchstone*

*Wolf.* Please you, stay here, sir: I 'll call his worship down to you.          [*Exit.*]

*Enter [2nd Prisoner with] Quicksilver, Petronel, [and, at another door, Wolf with Golding].*

*1 Pris.* See, he has brought him, and the [35 knight too. Salute him, I pray. Sir, this gentleman, upon our report, is very desirous to hear some piece of your Repentance.

*Quick.* Sir, with all my heart; and, as I told Master Toby, I shall be glad to have [40 any man a witness of it. And the more openly I profess it, I hope it will appear the heartier and the more unfeigned.

*Touch.* [*aside.*] Who is this? My man Francis, and my son-in-law?          45

*Quick.* Sir, it is all the testimony I shall leave behind me to the world and my master that I have so offended.

*Friend.* Good sir!

*Quick.* I writ it when my spirits were [50 oppressed.

*Pet.* Ay, I 'll be sworn for you, Francis!

*Quick.* It is in imitation of Mannington's: he that was hanged at Cambridge, that cut off the horse's head at a blow.          55

*Friend.* So, sir!

*Quick.* To the tune of 'I wail in woe, I plunge in pain.'

*Pet.* An excellent ditty it is, and worthy of a new tune.          60

Quick. *In Cheapside, famous for gold and plate,*
*Quicksilver, I did dwell of late;*
*I had a master good and kind,*
*That would have wrought me to his mind.*
*He bade me still, Work upon that,*          65
*But, alas, I wrought I knew not what!*
*He was a Touchstone black, but true,*
*And told me still what would ensue;*

*Yet, woe is me! I would not learn:*
*I saw, alas, but could not discern!*          70

*Friend.* Excellent, excellent well!

*Gold.* [*aside to Wolf.*] O let him alone; he is taken already.

Quick. *I cast my coat and cap away,*
*I went in silks and satins gay;*          75
*False metal of good manners I*
*Did daily coin unlawfully.*
*I scorn'd my master, being drunk;*
*I kept my gelding and my punk;*
*And with a knight, Sir Flash by name,*          80
*(Who now is sorry for the same) —*

*Pet.* I thank you, Francis.

[*Quick.*] *I thought by sea to run away,*
*But Thames and tempest did me stay.*

*Touch.* [*aside.*] This cannot be feigned, [85 sure. Heaven pardon my severity. The ragged colt may prove a good horse.

*Gold.* [*aside.*] How he listens, and is transported! He has forgot me.

Quick. *Still Eastward Ho was all my*
          *word;*          90
*But westward I had no regard,*
*Nor never thought what would come after,*
*As did, alas, his youngest daughter!*
*At last the black ox trod o' my foot,*
*And I saw then what long'd unto 't;*          95
*Now cry I, ' Touchstone, touch me still,*
*And make me current by thy skill.'*

*Touch.* [*aside.*] And I will do it, Francis.

*Wolf.* [*aside to Golding.*] Stay him, Master Deputy; now is the time; we shall lose [100 the song else.

*Friend.* I protest it is the best that ever I heard.

*Quick.* How like you it, gentlemen?

*All.* O admirable, sir!          105

*Quick.* This stanze now following alludes to the story of Mannington, from whence I took my project for my invention.

*Friend.* Pray you, go on, sir.

Quick. *O Mannington, thy stories show,*   110
*Thou cut'st a horse-head off at a blow,*
*But I confess, I have not the force*
*For to cut off the head of a horse;*
*Yet I desire this grace to win,*
*That I may cut off the horse-head of Sin,*   115
*And leave his body in the dust*
*Of Sin's highway and bogs of lust,*
*Whereby I may take Virtue's purse,*
*And live with her for better, for worse.*

*Friend.* Admirable, sir, and excellently [120 conceited.

---

[30] **White-Friars:** a sanctuary for ruffians, later called "Alsatia"   [34] S. D. **and . . . Golding:** ('&c.' Qq.)   [53] **Mannington's:** (entered for publication, Nov. 7, 1576, printed in *A Handful of Pleasant Delights,* 1584)   [57] **I . . . pain:** (first line of Mannington's ballad, hence the name of its tune)   [92,93] **after, daughter:** (pronounce "arter," "darter")   [94] **black ox:** symbolic of adversity   [95] **what . . . 't:** what it all meant   [97] **current:** true gold

*Quick.* Alas, Sir!

*Touch.* Son Golding and Master Wolf, I thank you: the deceit is welcome, especially from thee, whose charitable soul in this hath [125 shown a high point of wisdom and honesty. Listen. I am ravished with his Repentance, and could stand here a whole prenticeship to hear him.

*Friend.* Forth, good sir!                          130

*Quick.* This is the last, and the Farewell.

*Farewell, Cheapside, farewell, sweet trade*
*Of Goldsmiths all, that never shall fade!*
*Farewell, dear fellow prentices all,*
*And be you warned by my fall:*                          135
*Shun usurers, bawds, and dice, and drabs;*
*Avoid them as you would French scabs.*
*Seek not to go beyond your tether,*
*But cut your thongs unto your leather;*
*So shall you thrive by little and little,*                          140
*Scape Tyburn, Counters, and the Spital!*

*Touch.* And scape them shalt thou, my penitent and dear Francis.

*Quick.* Master!

*Pet.* Father!                          145

*Touch.* I can no longer forbear to do your humility right. Arise, and let me honour your repentance with the hearty and joyful embraces of a father and friend's love. Quick- [150 silver, thou hast eat into my breast, Quicksilver, with the drops of thy sorrow, and killed the desperate opinion I had of thy reclaim.

*Quick.* O sir, I am not worthy to see your worshipful face!                          155

*Pet.* Forgive me, father!

*Touch.* Speak no more; all former passages are forgotten, and here my word shall release you. Thank this worthy brother and kind friend, Francis. — Master Wolf, I [160 am their bail.                *A shout in the prison.*

[*Security appears at the grate.*]

*Sec.* Master Touchstone! Master Touchstone!

*Touch.* Who 's that?

*Wolf.* Security, sir.                          165

*Sec.* Pray you, sir, if you 'll be won with a song, hear my lamentable tune, too:

SONG

*O Master Touchstone,*
    *My heart is full of woe!*
*Alas, I am a cuckold;*                          170
    *And why it should be so?*
*Because I was a usurer*
*And bawd, as all you know,*
*For which, again I tell you,*
    *My heart is full of woe.*                          175

*Touch.* Bring him forth, Master Wolf, and release his bands. This day shall be sacred to mercy and the mirth of this encounter in the Counter. See, we are encountered with more suitors!                          180

*Enter Mistress Touchstone, Gertrude, Mildred, Sindefy, Winifred, &c.*

Save your breath, save your breath! All things have succeeded to your wishes; and we are heartily satisfied in their events.

*Ger.* Ah, runaway, runaway! Have I caught you? And how has my poor knight done [185 all this while?

*Pet.* Dear lady-wife, forgive me!

*Ger.* As heartily as I would be forgiven, knight. Dear father, give me your blessing and forgive me too; I ha' been proud [190 and lascivious, father, and a fool, father; and being raised to the state of a wanton coy thing, called a lady, father, have scorned you, father, and my sister, and my sister's velvet cap too; and would make a mouth at the [195 City as I rid through it; and stop mine ears at Bow-bell. I have said your beard was a base one, father; and that you looked like Twierpipe the taborer; and that my mother was but my midwife.                          200

*Mist. Touch.* Now God forgi' you, child madam!

*Touch.* No more repetitions! What is else wanting to make our harmony full?                          204

*Gold.* Only this, sir, that my fellow Francis make amends to Mistress Sindefy with marriage.

*Quick.* With all my heart!

*Gold.* And Security give her a dower, which shall be all the restitution he shall make [210 of that huge mass he hath so unlawfully gotten.

*Touch.* Excellently devised! A good motion! What says Master Security?

*Sec.* I say anything, sir, what you 'll ha' [215 me say. Would I were no cuckold!

*Win.* Cuckold, husband? Why, I think this wearing of yellow has infected you.

*Touch.* Why, Master Security, that should rather be a comfort to you than a corasive. [220 If you be a cuckold, it 's an argument you have a beautiful woman to your wife; then you shall be much made of; you shall have store of friends, never want money; you shall be eased of much o' your wedlock pain: [225 others will take it for you. Besides, you being a usurer and likely to go to hell, the devils will never torment you, they 'll take you for one o' their own race. Again, if

---

[130] **Forth:** go on    [152-153] **thy . . . reclaim:** my despair of your cure    [199] **taborer:** drummer
[210] **yellow:** color betokening jealousy; also that worn by prisoners    [220] **corasive:** corrosive, irritant

you be a cuckold, and know it not, you are [230
an innocent; if you know it and endure it,
a true martyr.

*Sec.*    I am resolved, sir.   Come hither,
Winnie!

*Touch.*    Well, then, all are pleased, or [235
shall be anon.   Master Wolf, you look hungry, methinks; have you no apparel to lend
Francis to shift him?

*Quick.*    No, sir, nor I desire none; but
here make it my suit, that I may go home [240
through the streets in these, as a spectacle,
or rather an example, to the children of Cheapside.

*Touch.*    Thou hast thy wish.   Now, Lon-
  don, look about,
And in this moral see thy glass run out:   245
Behold the careful father, thrifty son,

The solemn deeds which each of us have done;
The usurer punish'd, and from fall so steep
The prodigal child reclaim'd, and the lost sheep.

### EPILOGUS

[*Quick.*]  Stay, sir, I perceive the multitude are gathered together to view our coming out at the Counter.   See, if the streets
and the fronts of the houses be not stuck
with people, and the windows filled with  5
ladies, as on the solemn day of the Pageant!

*O may you find in this our pageant, here,*
   *The same contentment which you came to seek;*
*And as that show but draws you once a year,*
   *May this attract you hither once a week.*   10

[*Exeunt.*]

FINIS

---

²⁴⁵ **glass:** (quibble on looking-glass and hour-glass)    ⁶ **Pageant:** the annual Lord Mayor's show
¹⁰ **once a week:** (the maximum frequency of performance to be expected for a Jacobean play)

# EVERY MAN IN
## his Humor.

As it hath beene fundry times
*publickly acted by the right*
Honorable the Lord Cham-
berlaine his feruants.

———— ———— ———— ———— ————

Written by B ᴇɴ. Iᴏʜɴsᴏɴ.

———— ———— ———— ————

*Quod non dant proceres, dabit Hiſtrio.*

*Haud tamen inuidias vati, quem pulpita paſcunt.*

———— ———— ———— ————

Imprinted at London for *Walter Burre*, and are to
be ſould at his ſhoppe in Paules Church-yarde.
**1601.**

BIBLIOGRAPHICAL RECORD. This play is extant in two forms, the Quarto issued in 1601, in which the scene is Florence, and the characters bear Italian names, and the revised version which appeared in the Folio of 1616. In this latter text the action is transferred to London, and the characters are given English names. On Aug. 4, 1600, the play was mentioned on the Registers of the Stationers' Company together with *As You Like It, Henry V,* and *Much Ado about Nothing,* the publication of all these plays being ordered "to be staied." This entry was probably made by the Lord Chamberlain's Company to secure the copyright and checkmate a possible pirate. Yet on Aug. 14 (ten days later) the following entry was made for Cuthbert Burby and Walter Burre: — *Entred for yeir copie vnder the handes of Master Pasvill* [i.e., Pasfield] *and ye wardens, a booke called Euery man in his humour . . . vjd.* The Quarto appeared the following year, under Burre's imprint, bearing the statement on its title-page that the play had "beene sundry times publickly acted by the right Honorable the Lord Chamberlaine his servants."

DEDICATION. When he issued the revised and definitive version of his play in 1616, Jonson added the following dedication to his old schoolmaster at Westminster, the famous antiquary, William Camden, Clarenceux king-of-arms:

"To the most learned, and my honor'd friend, Mr. Cambden, Clarentiaux.

"Sir, There are, no doubt, a supercilious race in the world, who will esteeme all office, done you in this kind, an iniurie; so solemne a vice it is with them to vse the authoritie of their ignorance, to the crying downe of Poetry, or the Professors: But my gratitude must not leaue (*i.e.,* omit) to correct their error; since I am none of those, that can suffer the benefits confer'd vpon my youth, to perish with my age. It is a fraile memorie, that remembers but present things: And, had the fauour of the times so conspir'd with my disposition, as it could haue brought forth other, or better, you had had the same proportion, & number of the fruits, the first. Now, I pray you, to accept this, such, wherein neither the confession of my manners shall make you blush; nor of my studies repent you to haue beene the instructer: And, for the profession of my thankefulnesse, I am sure, it will, with good men, find either praise, or excuse. Your true louer,

BEN. IONSON."

DATE AND STAGE PERFORMANCE. The title-page of the folio version of the play states that it had been "acted in the yeere 1598, By the then Lord Chamberlaine his seruants." As it is not mentioned by Meres in his *Palladis Tamia* (1598), and as it is definitely referred to as a new play in a letter from Tobie Matthew to Dudley Carleton, dated Sept. 20, 1598, it may be definitely assumed that the date given in the folio is the date of the first performance. There is also appended to the folio text a list of the principal actors in the play in 1598, at the head of which appears the name of William Shakespeare. The other actors were Augustine Phillips, Henry Condell, William Sly, William Kempe, Richard Burbage, John Heminges, Thomas Pope, Christopher Beeston, and John Duke. There is an old tradition that *Every Man in his Humour* was acted only as a result of Shakespeare's intercession, but there is no direct proof to support the story. The comedy was acted at court before James I, Feb. 2, 1605, and the original text may have undergone revision at this time; but the very careful rewriting that the 1616 text presents is probably later, perhaps as late as 1612 when the folio collection of Jonson's plays was first projected. Garrick produced the play in 1751 and Kean in 1816. A famous revival took place in 1845, for Leigh Hunt's benefit, Charles Dickens acting the part of Bobadill.

STRUCTURE. The division into acts and scenes is moulded on Latin precedent, and the stage directions are of the classical pattern employed also by Lyly in *Endymion* and by Marlowe in *Tamburlaine.* A new scene is indicated whenever a new character or group of characters appears. At the head of each scene are listed the characters who take part in it in the order in which they speak or appear. Jonson is careful to observe the unities demanded by the renaissance interpretation of classical dramatic theory; but it was the richness of his appreciation of contemporary life, his theory of humours, and his penetrating observation that made the play a great force in English comedy.

# BEN JONSON (1572–1637)

## EVERY MAN IN HIS HUMOUR

### (Version of 1616)

#### THE PERSONS OF THE PLAY

KNOWELL, an old Gentleman
EDWARD KNOWELL, his Son
BRAINWORM, the Father's Man
MASTER STEPHEN, a Country Gull
[GEORGE] DOWNRIGHT, a plain Squire
WELLBRED, his Half-Brother
JUSTICE CLEMENT, an old merry Magistrate
ROGER FORMAL, his Clerk
KITELY, a Merchant

MASTER MATHEW, the Town Gull
[THOMAS] CASH, Kitely's Man
[OLIVER] COB, a Water-bearer
CAPTAIN BOBADILL, a Paul's Man

DAME KITELY, Kitely's Wife
MISTRESS BRIDGET, his Sister
TIB, Cob's Wife
[Servants, etc.]

THE SCENE. — London.

### PROLOGUE

THOUGH need make many poets, and some such
As art and nature have not better'd much;
Yet ours for want hath not so lov'd the stage,
As he dare serve th' ill customs of the age,
Or purchase your delight at such a rate,
As, for it, he himself must justly hate:
To make a child, now swaddled, to proceed
Man, and then shoot up, in one beard and weed,
Past threescore years; or, with three rusty swords,
And help of some few foot-and-half-foot words,                10
Fight over York and Lancaster's long jars,
And in the tiring-house bring wounds to scars.
He rather prays you will be pleas'd to see
One such to-day, as other plays should be:
Where neither chorus wafts you o'er the seas,                 15
Nor creaking throne comes down, the boys to please;
Nor nimble squib is seen, to make afeard
The gentlewomen; nor roll'd bullet heard
To say, it thunders; nor tempestuous drum
Rumbles, to tell you when the storm doth come;               20
But deeds, and language, such as men do use,
And persons, such as Comedy would choose,
When she would show an image of the times,
And sport with human follies, not with crimes;
Except we make 'em such, by loving still                      25
Our popular errors, when we know th' are ill.
I mean such errors as you 'll all confess,
By laughing at them, they deserve no less:
Which when you heartily do, there 's hope left then,
You, that have so grac'd monsters, may like men.            30

---

D. P. **Gull:** fool    **Paul's Man:** one who frequents the aisle of St. Paul's Cathedral, a loafer    **Prologue:** (not in 1601 version)    10 **foot-and-half-foot:** sesquipedalian, very long    11 **York . . . jars:**
probably a reference to the three Henry VI plays    12 **tiring-house:** dressing room    15 (Allusion to
Shakespeare's *Henry V* and *Pericles*)    16–18 **Nor . . . gentlewomen:** (allusion to *Dr. Faustus*)
18–20 **nor . . . come:** (allusion to *King Lear*)    21–30 (These lines define the theory of humors which
Jonson's classical mind opposed to the romantic stage methods indicated in ll. 7–20, which broke all
ancient dramatic laws. Cf. III. iv, 20–25)

## Act I. Scene I

[*Before Knowell's House, Hogsden.*]

*Knowell, [later] Brainworm, Master Stephen*

[*Know.*]  A goodly day toward, and a fresh
    morning. —
Brainworm!

[*Enter Brainworm*]

Call up your young master: bid him rise, sir.
Tell him, I have some business to employ him.
    *Brai.*  I will, sir, presently.
    *Know.*                    But hear you, sirrah,
If he be at his book, disturb him not.      6
    *Brai.*  Well, sir.              [*Exit.*]
    *Know.*  How happy yet should I esteem my-
    self,
Could I, by any practice, wean the boy
From one vain course of study he affects.   10
He is a scholar, if a man may trust
The liberal voice of fame in her report,
Of good account in both our Universities,
Either of which hath favour'd him with graces:
But their indulgence must not spring in me 15
A fond opinion that he cannot err.
Myself was once a student, and, indeed,
Fed with the self-same humour he is now,
Dreaming on nought but idle poetry,
That fruitless and unprofitable art,        20
Good unto none, but least to the professors;
Which then I thought the mistress of all knowl-
    edge;
But since, time and the truth have wak'd my
    judgment,
And reason taught me better to distinguish
The vain from th' useful learnings.

[*Enter Master Stephen*]

               Cousin Stephen,   25
What news with you, that you are here so
    early?
    *Step.*  Nothing, but e'en come to see how you
do, uncle.
    *Know.*  That 's kindly done; you are wel-
come, coz.                                   30
    *Step.*  Ay, I know that, sir; I would not ha'
come else.  How do my cousin Edward, uncle?
    *Know.*  O, well, coz; go in and see; I doubt
he be scarce stirring yet.
    *Step.*  Uncle, afore I go in, can you tell me, [35
an he have e'er a book of the sciences of hawking and hunting; I would fain borrow it.

    *Know.*  Why, I hope you will not a-hawking
now, will you?
    *Step.*  No, wusse; but I 'll practise against [40
next year, uncle.  I have bought me a hawk, and
a hood, and bells, and all; I lack nothing but a
book to keep it by.
    *Know.*  Oh, most ridiculous!
    *Step.*  Nay, look you now, you are angry, [45
uncle. — Why, you know an a man have not
skill in the hawking and hunting languages now-
a-days, I 'll not give a rush for him: they are
more studied than the Greek, or the Latin.
He is for no gallant's company without 'em; [50
and by gadslid I scorn it, I, so I do, to be a consort for every humdrum: hang 'em, scroyles!
there 's nothing in 'em i' the world.  What do
you talk on it?  Because I dwell at Hogsden,
I shall keep company with none but the [55
archers of Finsbury, or the citizens that come a
ducking to Islington ponds!  A fine jest, i'
faith!  'Slid, a gentleman mun show himself
like a gentleman.  Uncle, I pray you be not
angry; I know what I have to do, I trow, I [60
am no novice.
    *Know.*  You are a prodigal, absurd coxcomb:
    go to!
Nay, never look at me, it 's I that speak;
Take 't as you will, sir, I 'll not flatter you.
Ha' you not yet found means enow to waste  65
That which your friends have left you, but you
    must
Go cast away your money on a kite,
And know not how to keep it, when you ha'
    done?
O, it 's comely!  This will make you a gentle-
    man!
Well, cousin, well, I see you are e'en past
    hope                                  70
Of all reclaim. — Ay, so, now you are told on it,
You look another way.
    *Step.*                    What would you ha' me do?
    *Know.*  What would I have you do?  I 'll
tell you, kinsman;
Learn to be wise, and practise how to thrive;
That would I have you do: and not to spend  75
Your coin on every bauble that you fancy,
Or every foolish brain that humours you.
I would not have you to invade each place,
Nor thrust yourself on all societies,
Till men's affections, or your own desert,    80
Should worthily invite you to your rank.
He that is so respectless in his courses,
Oft sells his reputation at cheap market.

---

    ⁵ **presently**: at once    ¹² **fame**: reputation    ¹⁶ **fond**: foolish    ²¹ **professors**: practitioner.
(Lines 19–21 are borrowed from Kyd's *Spanish Tragedy*, IV, i, 68–71.)    ³⁰ **coz**: cousin (here, "nephew")
⁴⁰ **wusse**: ywis, indeed    ⁵¹ **gadslid**: by God's eyelid (a common oath)    ⁵² **scroyles**: scoundrels
⁵⁴ **Hogsden**: Hoxton, a suburb of London    ⁵⁶, ⁵⁷ **Finsbury, Islington**: open tracts north of London
⁵⁸ **'Slid**: cf. n. on l. 51   **mun**: must   ⁶⁷ **kite**: hawk   ⁸² **respectless**: heedless, reckless   **courses**:
behavior

Nor would I you should melt away yourself
In flashing bravery, lest, while you affect     85
To make a blaze of gentry to the world,
A little puff of scorn extinguish it,
And you be left like an unsavoury snuff,
Whose property is only to offend.
I 'd ha' you sober, and contain yourself,     90
Not that your sail be bigger than your boat;
But moderate your expenses now, at first,
As you may keep the same proportion still:
Nor stand so much on your gentility,
Which is an airy and mere borrow'd thing,     95
From dead men's dust and bones; and none of
     yours,
Except you make, or hold it.   Who comes here?

### Act I.   Scene II

[*The Same.*]

*Servant, Master Stephen, Knowell, [later]*

*Brainworm*

[*Serv.*]  Save you, gentlemen!
*Step.*  Nay, we do not stand much on our gentility, friend; yet you are welcome: and I assure you mine uncle here is a man of a thousand
a year, Middlesex land.  He has but one son in [5
all the world, I am his next heir, at the common law, master Stephen, as simple as I stand
here, if my cousin die, as there 's hope he will.  I
have a pretty living o' mine own too, beside,
hard by here.                              10
*Serv.*  In good time, sir.
*Step.*  In good time, sir!  Why, and in very
good time, sir!  You do not flout, friend, do you?
*Serv.*  Not I, sir.
*Step.*  Not you, sir! you were not best, [15
sir; an you should, here be them can perceive it,
and that quickly too: go to: and they can give
it again soundly too, an need be.
*Serv.*  Why, sit, let this satisfy you; good
faith, I had no such intent.               20
*Step.*  Sir, an I thought you had, I would
talk with you, and that presently.
*Serv.*  Good master Stephen, so you may,
sir, at your pleasure.
*Step.*  And so I would, sir, good my saucy [25
companion!  An you were out o' mine uncle's
ground, I can tell you; though I do not stand
upon my gentility, neither, in 't.
*Know.*  Cousin, cousin, will this ne'er be left?
*Step.*  Whoreson, base fellow! a mechani- [30
cal serving-man!  By this cudgel, an 't were not
for shame, I would ——

*Know.*  What would you do, you peremptory
     gull?
If you cannot be quiet, get you hence.
You see the honest man demeans himself     35
Modestly tow'rds you, giving no reply
To your unseason'd, quarrelling, rude fashion;
And still you huff it, with a kind of carriage
As void of wit, as of humanity.
Go, get you in; 'fore heaven, I am asham'd 40
Thou hast a kinsman's interest in me.
               [*Exit Master Stephen.*]
*Serv.*  I pray you, sir, is this master Know-
ell's house?
*Know.*  Yes, marry, is it, sir.           44
*Serv.*  I should inquire for a gentleman here,
one master Edward Knowell; do you know any
such, sir, I pray you?
*Know.*  I should forget myself else, sir.
*Serv.*  Are you the gentleman?  Cry you
mercy, sir: I was requir'd by a gentleman i' [50
the city, as I rode out at this end o' the town, to
deliver you this letter, sir.
*Know.*  To me, sir!  What do you mean? pray
you remember your court'sy. [*Reads.*]   "To
his most selected friend, master Edward [55
Knowell."  What might the gentleman's name
be, sir, that sent it?  Nay, pray you be cover'd.
*Serv.*  One master Wellbred, sir.
*Know.*  Master Wellbred! a young gentleman, is he not?                            60
*Serv.*  The same, sir; master Kitely married
his sister; the rich merchant i' the Old Jewry.
*Know.*  You say very true. — Brainworm!

[*Enter Brainworm*]

*Brai.*  Sir.                              64
*Know.*  Make this honest friend drink here:
pray you, go in.
            [*Exeunt Brainworm and Servant.*]
This letter is directed to my son;
Yet I am Edward Knowell too, and may,
With the safe conscience of good manners, use
The fellow's error to my satisfaction.     70
Well, I will break it ope (old men are curious),
Be it but for the style's sake and the phrase,
To see if both do answer my son's praises,
Who is, almost, grown the idolater         74
Of this young Wellbred.  What have we here?
     What 's this?                *The letter.*
[*Reads.*]  "Why, Ned, I beseech thee, hast
thou forsworn all thy friends i' the Old Jewry?
or dost thou think us all Jews that inhabit there
yet?  If thou dost, come over, and but see our
frippery; change an old shirt for a whole smock [80
with us: do not conceive that antipathy between

us and Hogsden, as was between Jews and hogs-
flesh. Leave thy vigilant father alone, to number over his green apricots, evening and morning, o' the north-west wall. An I had been [85
his son, I had sav'd him the labour long since,
if taking in all the young wenches that pass by
at the back-door, and coddling every kernel of
the fruit for 'em, would ha' serv'd. But prithee,
come over to me quickly this morning; [90
I have such a present for thee! — our Turkey
company never sent the like to the Grand Signior. One is a rhymer, sir, o' your own batch,
your own leaven; but doth think himself poet-
major o' the town, willing to be shown, and [95
worthy to be seen. The other — I will not venter his description with you, till you come, because I would ha' you make hither with an
appetite. If the worst of 'em be not worth your
journey, draw your bill of charges, as un- [100
conscionable as any Guildhall verdict will give
it you, and you shall be allow'd your viaticum.
                                        *From the Windmill."*
From the Bordello it might come as well,
The Spittle, or Pict-hatch. Is this the man
My son hath sung so, for the happiest wit, 105
The choicest brain, the times have sent us forth!
I know not what he may be in the arts,
Nor what in schools; but, surely, for his man-
    ners,
I judge him a profane and dissolute wretch;
Worse by possession of such great good gifts, 110
Being the master of so loose a spirit.
Why, what unhallow'd ruffian would have writ
In such a scurrilous manner to a friend!
Why should he think I tell my apricots,
Or play th' Hesperian dragon with my fruit, 115
To watch it? Well, my son, I 'd thought
Y' had had more judgment t' have made elec-
    tion
Of your companions, than t' have ta'en on trust
Such petulant, jeering gamesters, that can spare
No argument or subject from their jest. 120
But I perceive affection makes a fool
Of any man too much the father. — Brainworm!

*[Enter Brainworm]*

*Brai.* Sir.
*Know.*           Is the fellow gone that brought
this letter?
*Brai.* Yes, sir, a pretty while since.
*Know.* And where 's your young master? 125
*Brai.* In his chamber, sir.
*Know.* He spake not with the fellow, did he?
*Brai.* No, sir, he saw him not.
*Know.* Take you this letter, and deliver it

my son; but with no notice that I have [130
open'd it, on your life.
*Brai.* O Lord, sir! that were a jest indeed.
                                                *[Exit.]*
*Know.* I am resolv'd I will not stop his
    journey,
Nor practise any violent mean to stay      134
The unbridled course of youth in him; for that
Restrain'd grows more impatient; and in kind
Like to the eager, but the generous greyhound,
Who ne'er so little from his game withheld,
Turns head, and leaps up at his holder's throat.
There is a way of winning more by love      140
And urging of the modesty, than fear:
Force works on servile natures, not the free.
He that 's compell'd to goodness, may be good,
But 't is but for that fit; where others, drawn
By softness and example, get a habit.      145
Then, if they stray, but warn 'em, and the same
They should for virtue 've done, they 'll do for
    shame.                                    *[Exit.]*

### Act I.  Scene III

*[A Room in Knowell's House.]*

*Edward Knowell, Brainworm, [later] Master
Stephen*

*[E. Know.]* Did he open it, sayest thou?
*Brai.* Yes, o' my word, sir, and read the
contents.
*E. Know.* That scarce contents me. What
countenance, prithee, made he i' the reading [5
of it? Was he angry or pleas'd?
*Brai.* Nay, sir, I saw him not read it, nor
open it, I assure your worship.
*E. Know.* No! How know'st thou, then,
that he did either?                         10
*Brai.* Marry, sir, because he charg'd me, on
my life, to tell nobody that he open'd it;
which, unless he had done, he would never fear
to have it reveal'd.
*E. Know.* That 's true: well, I thank [15
thee, Brainworm.

*[Enter Stephen]*

*Step.* O, Brainworm, didst thou not see a fellow here in a what-sha'-call-him doublet? He
brought mine uncle a letter e'en now.
*Brai.* Yes, master Stephen; what of him? 20
*Step.* O, I ha' such a mind to beat him ——
where is he? canst thou tell?
*Brai.* Faith, he is not of that mind: he is
gone, master Stephen.
*Step.* Gone! which way? When went [25
he? How long since?

⁸⁸ **coddling:** stewing     ⁹¹⁻⁹² **Turkey company:** (chartered 1581 for trade in the Levant)     ⁹³ **batch:**
a "baking" of bread     ¹⁰² **viaticum:** traveling expenses     **Windmill:** a tavern     ¹⁰³ **Bordello:** brothel
¹⁰⁴ **Spittle:** a hospital for venereal diseases     **Pict-hatch:** a notorious haunt of prostitutes     ¹¹⁴ **tell:**
count     ¹¹⁷ **election:** selection     ¹²⁴ **pretty:** considerable     ¹³⁷ **generous:** well-bred

*Brai.* He is rid hence; he took horse at the street-door.

*Step.* And I stay'd i' the fields! Whoreson Scanderbag rogue! O that I had but a horse [30 to fetch him back again!

*Brai.* Why, you may ha' my master's gelding, to save your longing, sir.

*Step.* But I ha' no boots, that 's the spite on 't.

*Brai.* Why, a fine wisp of hay, roll'd hard, [35 master Stephen.

*Step.* No, faith, it 's no boot to follow him now: let him e'en go and hang. Prithee, help to truss me a little: he does so vex me ——

*Brai.* You 'll be worse vex'd when you are [40 truss'd, master Stephen. Best keep unbrac'd, and walk yourself till you be cold; your choler may founder you else.

*Step.* By my faith, and so I will, now thou tell'st me on 't. How dost thou like my leg, [45 Brainworm?

*Brai.* A very good leg, master Stephen; but the woollen stocking does not commend it so well.

*Step.* Foh! the stockings be good enough, [50 now summer is coming on, for the dust: I 'll have a pair of silk again' winter, that I go to dwell i' the town. I think my leg would show in a silk hose ——

*Brai.* Believe me, master Stephen, rarely well.

*Step.* In sadness, I think it would; I have [56 a reasonable good leg.

*Brai.* You have an excellent good leg, master Stephen: but I cannot stay to praise it longer now, and I am very sorry for 't. [*Exit.*] 60

*Step.* Another time will serve, Brainworm. Gramercy for this.

*E. Know.* Ha, ha, ha! *Knowell laughs, having read the letter.*

*Step.* 'Slid, I hope he laughs not at me; an he do —— 65

*E. Know.* Here was a letter indeed, to be intercepted by a man's father, and do him good with him! He cannot but think most virtuously, both of me, and the sender, sure, that make the careful costermonger of him in our familiar [70 epistles. Well, if he read this with patience I 'll be gelt, and troll ballads for Master John Trundle yonder, the rest of my mortality. It is true, and likely, my father may have as much patience as another man, for he takes much [75 physic; and oft taking physic makes a man very patient. But would your packet, Master

Wellbred, had arriv'd at him in such a minute of his patience! then we had known the end of it, which now is doubtful, and threatens —— [*sees Master Stephen.*] What, my wise [81 cousin! Nay, then, I 'll furnish our feast with one gull more toward the mess. He writes to me of a brace, and here 's one, that 's three: oh, for a fourth! Fortune, if ever thou 'lt use thine eyes, I entreat thee ——    86

*Step.* Oh, now I see who he laughed at: he laughed at somebody in that letter. By this good light, an he had laughed at me ——

*E. Know.* How now, cousin Stephen, [90 melancholy?

*Step.* Yes, a little: I thought you had laughed at me, cousin.

*E. Know.* Why, what an I had, coz? What would you ha' done?    95

*Step.* By this light, I would ha' told mine uncle.

*E. Know.* Nay, if you would ha' told your uncle, I did laugh at you, coz.

*Step.* Did you, indeed?    100

*E. Know.* Yes, indeed.

*Step.* Why then ——

*E. Know.* What then?

*Step.* I am satisfied; it is sufficient.

*E. Know.* Why, be so, gentle coz: and, [105 I pray you, let me entreat a courtesy of you. I am sent for this morning by a friend i' the Old Jewry, to come to him; it 's but crossing over the fields to Moorgate. Will you bear me company? I protest it is not to draw you [110 into bond or any plot against the state, coz.

*Step.* Sir, that 's all one an 't were; you shall command me twice so far as Moorgate, to do you good in such a matter. Do you think I would leave you? I protest ——    115

*E. Know.* No, no, you shall not protest, coz.

*Step.* By my fackins, but I will, by your leave: — I 'll protest more to my friend, than I 'll speak of at this time.

*E. Know.* You speak very well, coz.    120

*Step.* Nay, not so neither, you shall pardon me: but I speak to serve my turn.

*E. Know.* Your turn, coz? Do you know what you say? A gentleman of your sort, parts, carriage, and estimation, to talk o' your turn [125 i' this company, and to me alone, like a tankard-bearer at a conduit! fie! A wight that, hitherto, his every step hath left the stamp of a great foot behind him, as every word the

[30] **Scanderbag:** the Albanian patriot, Castriot, also known as Iskander Bey    [37] **boot:** use, avail   [39] **truss:** tie the laces which held the clothing    [52] **again':** against, in preparation for    [56] **In sadness:** seriously    [62] **Gramercy:** thanks    [70] **costermonger:** dealer in fruit (a term of contempt)   [73] **Trundle:** a publisher of ballads, etc.; in business, 1603–1626    [83] **mess:** group of four at dinner   [96,100] **Step.:** ('Serv.' F)    [117] **fackins:** faith    [124] **sort:** rank    [125] **turn:** (Water-carriers, called "cobs," carried water in large "tankards" from the public cisterns, or "conduits," to private houses. **They** were paid a fixed sum per "turn," or journey from the conduit. Cf. 1. 122)

savour of a strong spirit, and he! this man! [130
so grac'd, gilded, or, to use a more fit metaphor,
so tin-foil'd by nature, as not ten housewives'
pewter, again' a good time, shows more bright
to the world than he! and he! (as I said last,
so I say again, and still shall say it) this [135
man! to conceal such real ornaments as these,
and shadow their glory, as a milliner's wife does
her wrought stomacher, with a smoky lawn, or a
black cypress! O, coz! it cannot be answer'd;
go not about it. Drake's old ship at Dept- [140
ford may sooner circle the world again. Come,
wrong not the quality of your desert, with looking downward, coz; but hold up your head, so:
and let the idea of what you are be portray'd i'
your face, that men may read i' your phys- [145
nomy, *Here within this place is to be seen the true,
rare, and accomplish'd monster, or miracle of nature,* which is all one. What think you of this,
coz?

*Step.* Why, I do think of it: and I will [150
be more proud, and melancholy, and gentleman-
like, than I have been, I'll insure you.

*E. Know.* Why, that's resolute master
Stephen! — [*Aside.*] Now, if I can but hold him
up to his height, as it is happily begun, it [155
will do well for a suburb humour: we may hap
have a match with the city, and play him for
forty pound. — Come, coz.

*Step.* I'll follow you.

*E. Know.* Follow me! You must go before.

*Step.* Nay, an I must, I will. Pray you
show me, good cousin. [*Exeunt.*] 162

## Act I. Scene IIII

*[The Lane before Cob's House.]*

*Master Mathew, Cob*

[*Mat.*] I think this be the house. What, ho!

*[Enter Cob]*

*Cob.* Who's there? O, master Mathew! gi'
your worship good morrow.

*Mat.* What, Cob! how dost thou, good Cob?
Dost thou inhabit here, Cob? 5

*Cob.* Ay, sir, I and my lineage ha' kept a
poor house here, in our days.

*Mat.* Thy lineage, monsieur Cobb! What
lineage, what lineage?

*Cob.* Why, sir, an ancient lineage, and a [10
princely. Mine ance'try came from a king's belly,
no worse man; and yet no man neither (by your
worship's leave, I did lie in that) but herring,

the king of fish (from his belly I proceed), one
o' the monarchs o' the world, I assure you. [15
The first red herring that was broil'd in Adam
and Eve's kitchen do I fetch my pedigree from,
by the harrot's books. His cob was my great,
great, mighty-great grandfather.

*Mat.* Why mighty, why mighty, I pray [20
thee?

*Cob.* O, it was a mighty while ago, sir, and
a mighty great cob.

*Mat.* How know'st thou that?

*Cob.* How know I! why, I smell his ghost
ever and anon. 26

*Mat.* Smell a ghost! O unsavoury jest! and
the ghost of a herring cob?

*Cob.* Ay, sir. With favour of your worship's
nose, master Mathew, why not the ghost of [30
a herring cob, as well as the ghost of Rasher
Bacon?

*Mat.* Roger Bacon, thou would'st say.

*Cob.* I say Rasher Bacon. They were both
broil'd o' the coals; and a man may smell [35
broil'd meat, I hope! You are a scholar; upsolve me that now.

*Mat.* O raw ignorance! — Cob, canst thou
show me of a gentleman, one captain Bobadill,
where his lodging is? 40

*Cob.* O, my guest, sir, you mean.

*Mat.* Thy guest! alas, ha, ha!

*Cob.* Why do you laugh, sir? Do you not
mean captain Bobadill?

*Mat.* Cob, pray thee advise thyself well; [45
do not wrong the gentleman, and thyself too. I
dare be sworn he scorns thy house; he! he
lodge in such a base obscure place as thy house!
Tut, I know his disposition so well, he would
not lie in thy bed if thou 'dst gi' it him. 50

*Cob.* I will not give it him though, sir. Mass,
I thought somewhat was in 't, we could not
get him to bed all night. Well, sir, though he
lie not o' my bed, he lies o' my bench; an 't
please you to go up, sir, you shall find him with
two cushions under his head, and his cloak [56
wrapp'd about him, as though he had neither
won nor lost, and yet, I warrant, he ne'er cast
better in his life, than he has done to-night.

*Mat.* Why, was he drunk? 60

*Cob.* Drunk, sir! you hear not me say so.
Perhaps he swallow'd a tavern-token, or some
such device, sir; I have nothing to do withal.
I deal with water and not with wine. — Gi' me
my tankard there, ho! — God b' wi' you, sir. [65
It 's six o'clock: I should ha' carried two turns
by this. What ho! my stopple! come.

---

133 **again'** . . . **time:** in preparation for a holiday    137 **milliner:** seller of fancy wares or notions
139 **cypress:** crape    140 **Drake's old ship:** the *Golden Hind*, kept on exhibition at Deptford    152 **insure:** promise    18 **harrot's:** herald's    **cob:** red herring    36–37 **upsolve:** *i.e.,* resolve    58 **cast:** to
throw dice or to vomit    62 **swallow'd . . . token:** got drunk (slang)    Taverns issued metal tokens
because of the scarcity of currency.    67 **stopple:** stopper

*[Enter Tib with a water-tankard]*

*Mat.* Lie in a water-bearer's house! a gentleman of his havings! Well, I 'll tell him my mind.                                                      70

*Cob.* What, Tib; show this gentleman up to the captain. *[Exit Tib with Master Mathew.]* Oh, an my house were the Brazen-head now! faith it would e'en speak *Mo fools yet.* You should ha' some now would take this Mas- [75 ter Mathew to be a gentleman, at the least. His father's an honest man, a worshipful fishmonger, and so forth; and now does he creep and wriggle into acquaintance with all the brave gallants about the town, such as my guest is (O, my guest is a fine man!), and they flout him [81 invincibly. He useth every day to a merchant's house where I serve water, one master Kitely's, i' the Old Jewry; and here's the jest, he is in love with my master's sister, Mrs. Bridget, and calls her "Mistress"; and there he will sit [86 you a whole afternoon sometimes, reading o' these same abominable, vile (a pox on 'em! I cannot abide them), rascally verses, poyetry, poyetry, and speaking of interludes; 't will [90 make a man burst to hear him. And the wenches, they do so jeer, and ti-he at him. — Well, should they do so much to me, I 'd forswear them all, by the foot of Pharaoh! There's an oath! How many water-bearers shall you [95 hear swear such an oath? O, I have a guest — he teaches me — he does swear the legiblest of any man christ'ned: *By St. George! The foot of Pharaoh! The body of me! As I am a gentleman and a soldier!* such dainty oaths! and withal [100 he does take this same filthy roguish tobacco, the finest and cleanliest! It would do a man good to see the fume come forth at 's tonnels. — Well, he owes me forty shillings, my wife lent him out of her purse, by sixpence a time, besides his lodging: I would I had it! I shall ha' [106 it, he says, the next action. Helter skelter, hang sorrow, care 'll kill a cat, up-tails all, and a louse for the hangman!                            *[Exit.]*

## Act I.  Scene V

*[A Room in Cob's House.]*

*Bobadill, [later] Tib, Mathew*

*[Bob.]* Hostess, hostess!     *Bobadill is dis-*
                               *covered lying*
          *[Enter Tib]*        *on his bench.*

*Tib.* What say you, sir?

*Bob.* A cup o' thy small beer, sweet hostess.

*Tib.* Sir, there 's a gentleman below would speak with you.                                     5

*Bob.* A gentleman! 'odso, I am not within.

*Tib.* My husband told him you were, sir.

*Bob.* What a plague — what meant he?

*Mat. (below.)* Captain Bobadill!

*Bob.* Who 's there! — Take away the basin, good hostess; — Come up, sir.                        11

*Tib.* He would desire you to come up, sir. You come into a cleanly house, here!

*[Enter Mathew]*

*Mat.* Save you, sir; save you, captain!

*Bob.* Gentle master Mathew! Is it you, sir? Please you sit down.                               16

*Mat.* Thank you, good captain; you may see I am somewhat audacious.

*Bob.* Not so, sir. I was requested to supper last night by a sort of gallants, where you [20 were wish'd for, and drunk to, I assure you.

*Mat.* Vouchsafe me, by whom, good captain?

*Bob.* Marry, by young Wellbred, and others. — Why, hostess, a stool here for this gentleman.

*Mat.* No haste, sir, 't is very well.          25

*Bob.* Body of me! it was so late ere we parted last night, I can scarce open my eyes yet; I was but new risen, as you came. How passes the day abroad, sir? you can tell.

*Mat.* Faith, some half hour to seven. [30 Now, trust me, you have an exceeding fine lodging here, very neat, and private.

*Bob.* Ay, sir: sit down, I pray you. Master Mathew, in any case possess no gentlemen of our acquaintance with notice of my lodging. [35

*Mat.* Who? I, sir? No.

*Bob.* Not that I need to care who know it, for the cabin is convenient; but in regard I would not be too popular, and generally visited, as some are.                                      40

*Mat.* True, captain, I conceive you.

*Bob.* For, do you see, sir, by the heart of valour in me, except it be to some peculiar and choice spirits, to whom I am extraordinarily en-gag'd, as yourself, or so, I could not extend [45 thus far.

*Mat.* O Lord, sir! I resolve so.

*Bob.* I confess I love a cleanly and quiet privacy, above all the tumult and roar of fortune. What new book ha' you there? What! "Go [50 by, Hieronymo?"

*Mat.* Ay: did you ever see it acted? Is 't not well penn'd?

*Bob.* Well penn'd! I would fain see all the poets of these times pen such another play [55 as that was: they 'll prate and swagger, and

**69** havings: wealth     **73** Brazen-head: (See Greene's *Friar Bacon and Friar Bungay.*)     **74** Mo: more     **82** useth . . . to: is accustomed to go to     **103** tonnels: nostrils     **108** up-tails all: refrain of a popular song     **6** 'odso: God's so (an oath)     **20** sort: company     **47** I . . . so: I am sure of it.
**50-51** Go by, Hieronymo: (Cf. *The Spanish Tragedy*, III, xii, 30.)

keep a stir of art and devices, when, as I am a gentleman, read 'em, they are the most shallow, pitiful, barren fellows that live upon the face of the earth again.                           60

*Mat.* Indeed here are a number of fine speeches in this book. *O eyes, no eyes, but fountains fraught with tears!* There 's a conceit! Fountains fraught with tears! *O life, no life, but lively form of death!* — another. *O world, no* [65 *world, but mass of public wrongs!* — a third. *Confus'd and fill'd with murder and misdeeds!* — a fourth. O, the muses! Is 't not excellent? Is 't not simply the best that ever you heard, captain? Ha! how do you like it?            70

*Bob.* 'T is good.

Mat. *To thee, the purest object to my sense,*
*The most refined essence heaven covers,*
*Send I these lines, wherein I do commence*
*The happy state of turtle-billing lovers.*        75
*If they prove rough, unpolish'd, harsh, and rude,*
*Haste made the waste: thus mildly I conclude.*

*Bob.* Nay, proceed, proceed. Where 's this?

*Bobadill is making him ready all this while.*

*Mat.* This, sir! a toy o' mine own, in my nonage; the infancy of my muses. But [80 when will you come and see my study? Good faith, I can show you some very good things I have done of late. — That boot becomes your leg passing well, captain, methinks.

*Bob.* So, so; it 's the fashion gentlemen [85 now use.

*Mat.* Troth, captain, and now you speak o' the fashion, master Wellbred's elder brother and I are fall'n out exceedingly. This other day, I happ'ned to enter into some discourse [90 of a hanger, which, I assure you, both for fashion and workmanship, was most peremptory beautiful and gentlemanlike: yet he condemn'd, and cri'd it down for the most pied and ridiculous that he ever saw.            95

*Bob.* Squire Downright, the half-brother, was 't not?

*Mat.* Ay, sir, he.

*Bob.* Hang him, rook! he! why he has no more judgment than a malt-horse. By St. [100 George, I wonder you 'd lose a thought upon such an animal; the most peremptory absurd clown of Christendom, this day, he is holden. I protest to you, as I am a gentleman and a soldier, I ne'er chang'd words with his like. [105 By his discourse, he should eat nothing but hay; he was born for the manger, pannier, or packsaddle. He has not so much as a good phrase in his belly, but all old iron and rusty proverbs: a

good commodity for some smith to make [110 hob-nails of.

*Mat.* Ay, and he thinks to carry it away with his manhood still, where he comes: he brags he will gi' me the bastinado, as I hear.

*Bob.* How! he the bastinado! How came [115 he by that word, trow?

*Mat.* Nay, indeed, he said cudgel me; I term'd it so, for my more grace.

*Bob.* That may be; for I was sure it was none of his word: but when, when said he so?    120

*Mat.* Faith, yesterday, they say; a young gallant, a friend of mine, told me so.

*Bob.* By the foot of Pharaoh, an 't were my case now, I should send him a chartel presently. The bastinado! a most proper and sufficient [125 dependence, warranted by the great Caranza. Come hither, you shall chartel him. I 'll show you a trick or two you shall kill him with at pleasure; the first stoccata, if you will, by this air.                                           130

*Mat.* Indeed, you have absolute knowledge i' the mystery, I have heard, sir.

*Bob.* Of whom, of whom, ha' you heard it, I beseech you?

*Mat.* Troth, I have heard it spoken of di- [135 vers, that you have very rare, and un-in-one-breath-utterable skill, sir.

*Bob.* By heaven, no, not I; no skill i' the earth; some small rudiments i' the science, as to know my time, distance, or so. I have pro- [140 fess'd it more for noblemen and gentlemen's use, than mine own practice, I assure you. — Hostess, accommodate us with another bed-staff here quickly. [*Enter Tib.*] Lend us another bed-staff — the woman does not understand the words [145 of action. — Look you, sir: exalt not your point above this state, at any hand, and let your poniard maintain your defence, thus: — give it the gentleman, and leave us. [*Exit Tib.*] So, sir. Come on! O, twine your body more about, [150 that you may fall to a more sweet, comely, gentleman-like guard; so! Indifferent. Hollow your body more, sir, thus: now, stand fast o' your left leg, note your distance, keep your due proportion of time. — Oh, you disorder your [155 point most irregularly!

*Mat.* How is the bearing of it now, sir?

*Bob.* O, out of measure ill. A well experienc'd hand would pass upon you at pleasure.

*Mat.* How mean you, sir, pass upon me? [160

*Bob.* Why, thus, sir, — make a thrust at me — [*Master Mathew pushes at Bobadill.*] come in upon the answer, control your point, and

---

**62 O eyes, etc.:** (Cf. *Spanish Tragedy*, III, ii, 1–4.)   **91 hanger:** strap by which a sword hung from the belt   **92–93 peremptory:** exceedingly   **94 pied:** variegated   **99 rook:** fool   **105 chang'd:** exchanged   **112 carry it away:** domineer   **113 still:** always   **116 trow:** do you suppose?   **124 chartel:** challenge   **126 dependence:** quarrel awaiting settlement   **Caranza:** author of the *Philosophy of Arms,* 1569   **129 stoccata:** thrust   **132 mystery:** art, profession

make a full career at the body. The best-
practis'd gallants of the time name it the passada; a most desperate thrust, believe it. [166

*Mat.* Well, come, sir.

*Bob.* Why, you do not manage your weapon
with any facility or grace to invite me. I have
no spirit to play with you; your dearth of [170
judgment renders you tedious.

*Mat.* But one venue, sir.

*Bob.* "Venue!" fie; most gross denomination as ever I heard. O, the "stoccata," while
you live, sir; note that. — Come put on [175
your cloak, and we 'll go to some private
place where you are acquainted; some tavern,
or so — and have a bit. I 'll send for one of
these fencers, and he shall breathe you, by my
direction; and then I will teach you your [180
trick: you shall kill him with it at the first, if
you please. Why, I will learn you, by the true
judgment of the eye, hand, and foot, to control
any enemy's point i' the world. Should your
adversary confront you with a pistol, 't were [185
nothing, by this hand! You should, by the
same rule, control his bullet, in a line, except it
were hail shot, and spread. What money ha'
you about you, master Mathew?

*Mat.* Faith, I ha' not past a two shillings [190
or so.

*Bob.* 'T is somewhat with the least; but
come; we will have a bunch of radish and salt
to taste our wine, and a pipe of tobacco to close
the orifice of the stomach: and then we 'll [195
call upon young Wellbred. Perhaps we shall
meet the Corydon his brother there, and put
him to the question.     [*Exeunt.*]

## Act II. Scene I

[*The Old Jewry. Garden of Kitely's House.*]

*Kitely, Cash, Downright*

[*Kit.*] Thomas, come hither.
There lies a note within upon my desk;
Here take my key: it is no matter, neither. —
Where is the boy?

*Cash.*     Within, sir, i' the warehouse.

*Kit.* Let him tell over straight that Spanish
gold,     5
And weigh it, with th' pieces of eight. Do you
See the delivery of those silver stuffs
To Master Lucar: tell him, if he will,
He shall ha' the grograns at the rate I told him,
And I will meet him on the Exchange anon. 10

*Cash.* Good, sir.     [*Exit.*]

*Kit.* Do you see that fellow, brother Downright?

*Dow.* Ay, what of him?

*Kit.*     He is a jewel, brother.
I took him of a child up at my door,
And christ'ned him, gave him mine own name,
Thomas:     15
Since bred him at the Hospital; where proving
A toward imp, I call'd him home, and taught
him
So much, as I have made him my cashier,
And giv'n him, who had none, a surname, Cash:
And find him in his place so full of faith,    20
That I durst trust my life into his hands.

*Dow.* So would not I in any bastard's,
brother,
As it is like he is, although I knew
Myself his father. But you said you 'd some-
what
To tell me, gentle brother: what is 't? what is 't?

*Kit.* Faith, I am very loath to utter it,    26
As fearing it may hurt your patience;
But that I know your judgment is of strength,
Against the nearness of affection ——

*Dow.* What need this circumstance? Pray
you, be direct.     30

*Kit.* I will not say how much I do ascribe
Unto your friendship, nor in what regard
I hold your love; but let my past behaviour,
And usage of your sister, but confirm
How well I 've been affected to your ——    35

*Dow.* You are too tedious; come to the matter, the matter.

*Kit.* Then, without further ceremony, thus.
My brother Wellbred, sir, I know not how,
Of late is much declin'd in what he was,
And greatly alter'd in his disposition.     40
When he came first to lodge here in my house,
Ne'er trust me if I were not proud of him:
Methought he bare himself in such a fashion,
So full of man, and sweetness in his carriage,
And what was chief, it show'd not borrow'd in
him,     45
But all he did became him as his own,
And seem'd as perfect, proper, and possess'd
As breath with life, or colour with the blood.
But now, his course is so irregular,
So loose, affected, and depriv'd of grace,    50
And he himself withal so far fall'n off
From that first place, as scarce no note re-
mains,
To tell men's judgments where he lately stood.
He 's grown a stranger to all due respect,
Forgetful of his friends; and, not content    55
To stale himself in all societies,

---

172 **venue:** bout, thrust    179 **breathe:** exercise    197 **Corydon:** rustic    6 **pieces of eight:** coins
worth eight reals (about two dollars)    9 **grograns:** stuff of silk and wool    14 **of:** as    16 **Hospital:**
Christ's Hospital, a famous London school (where Peele was educated)    17 **imp:** child    30 **circum-**
**stance:** beating about the bush    52 **as:** that    56 **stale:** make cheap

He makes my house here common as a mart,
A theatre, a public receptacle
For giddy humour, and diseased riot;
And here, as in a tavern or a stews,             60
He and his wild associates spend their hours,
In repetition of lascivious jests,
Swear, leap, drink, dance, and revel night by
    night,
Control my servants; and, indeed, what not?
    *Dow.* 'Sdeins, I know not what I should [65
say to him, i' the whole world! He values me
at a crack'd three-farthings, for aught I see. It
will never out o' the flesh that 's bred i' the bone.
I have told him enough, one would think, if that
would serve; but counsel to him is as good [70
as a shoulder of mutton to a sick horse. Well!
he knows what to trust to, for George: let him
spend, and spend, and domineer, till his heart
ache; an he think to be reliev'd by me, when
he is got into one o' your city pounds, the [75
Counters, he has the wrong sow by the ear, i'
faith; and claps his dish at the wrong man's
door. I 'll lay my hand o' my halfpenny, ere I
part with 't to fetch him out, I 'll assure him.
    *Kit.* Nay, good brother, let it not trouble
    you thus.                                     80
    *Dow.* 'Sdeath! he mads me; I could eat my
very spur-leathers for anger! But, why are you
so tame? Why do you not speak to him, and
tell him how he disquiets your house?
    *Kit.* O, there are divers reasons to dissuade,
    brother.                                      85
But, would yourself vouchsafe to travail in it
(Though but with plain and easy circumstance),
It would both come much better to his sense,
And savour less of stomach, or of passion.
You are his elder brother, and that title        90
Both gives and warrants you authority,
Which, by your presence seconded, must breed
A kind of duty in him, and regard;
Whereas, if I should intimate the least,
It would but add contempt to his neglect,        95
Heap worse on ill, make up a pile of hatred,
That in the rearing would come tott'ring down,
And in the ruin bury all our love.
Nay, more than this, brother; if I should speak,
He would be ready, from his heat of humour,
And overflowing of the vapour in him,            101
To blow the ears of his familiars
With the false breath of telling what disgraces
And low disparagements I had put upon him:
Whilst they, sir, to relieve him in the fable,   105
Make their loose comments upon every word,
Gesture, or look, I use; mock me all over,
From my flat cap unto my shining shoes;

And, out of their impetuous rioting phant'sies,
Beget some slander that shall dwell with me. 110
And what would that be, think you? **Marry,**
    this:
They would give out, because my wife is **fair,**
Myself but lately married, and my sister
Here sojourning a virgin in my house,
That I were jealous! — nay, as sure as death, 115
That they would say; and, how that I had
    quarrell'd
My brother purposely, thereby to find
An apt pretext to banish them my house.
    *Dow.* Mass, perhaps so; they 're like enough
    to do it.
    *Kit.* Brother, they would, believe it; so
    should I,                                     120
Like one of these penurious quack-salvers,
But set the bills up to mine own disgrace,
And try experiments upon myself;
Lend scorn and envy opportunity
To stab my reputation and good name —— 125

## *Act II. Scene II*

### [*The Same.*]

#### *Mathew, Bobadill, Downright, Kitely*

[*Mat.*] I will speak to him.
    *Bob.* Speak to him! away! By the foot of
Pharaoh, you shall not! you shall not do him
that grace. — The time of day to you, gentle-
man o' the house. Is master Wellbred stirring?
    *Dow.* How then? What should he do?   6
    *Bob.* Gentleman of the house, it is to you.
Is he within, sir?
    *Kit.* He came not to his lodging to-night, sir,
I assure you.                                     10
    *Dow.* Why, do you hear? You!
    *Bob.* The gentleman-citizen hath satisfied
    me;
I 'll talk to no scavenger. [*Exeunt Bob. and
    Mat.*]
    *Dow.* How! scavenger! Stay, sir, stay!
    *Kit.* Nay, brother Downright.            15
    *Dow.* 'Heart! stand you away, an you love
    me.
    *Kit.* You shall not follow him now, I pray
you, brother, good faith you shall not; I will
overrule you.
    *Dow.* Ha! scavenger! Well, go to, I say [20
little; but, by this good day (God forgive me I
should swear), if I put it up so, say I am the
rankest cow that ever piss'd. 'Sdeins, an I swallow this, I 'll ne'er draw my sword in the sight of
Fleet-street again while I live; I 'll sit in a [25

---

⁶⁰ **stews:** brothel    ⁶⁵ **'Sdeins:** God's dignity    ⁷² **for George:** *i.e.,* so far as I am concerned
⁷⁶ **Counters:** debtors' prisons    ⁷⁷ **claps his dish:** comes begging    ⁸¹ **'Sdeath:** God's death
⁸⁹ **stomach:** anger    ¹⁰⁵ **fable:** narrative    ¹⁰⁸ **flat . . . shoes:** features of a tradesman's dress
¹²² **set bills up:** advertise    ⁹ **to-night:** last night    ²² **put it up:** endure it

barn with madge-howlet, and catch mice first.
Scavenger! heart! — and I 'll go near to fill that
huge tumbrel-slop of yours with somewhat, an
I have good luck: your Garagantua breech can-
not carry it away so.                                    30

*Kit.* Oh, do not fret yourself thus; never
think on 't.

*Dow.* These are my brother's consorts, these!
These are his comrades, his walking mates!
He 's a gallant, a cavaliero too, right hangman
cut! Let me not live, an I could not find in [35
my heart to swinge the whole ging of 'em, one
after another, and begin with him first. I am
griev'd it should be said he is my brother, and
take these courses. Well, as he brews, so he
shall drink, for George, again. Yet he shall [40
hear on 't, and that tightly too, an I live, i' faith.

*Kit.* But, brother, let your reprehension, then,
Run in an easy current, not o'er high
Carried with rashness, or devouring choler;
But rather use the soft persuading way,     45
Whose powers will work more gently, and com-
    pose
Th' imperfect thoughts you labour to reclaim;
More winning than enforcing the consent.

*Dow.* Ay, ay, let me alone for that, I warrant you.                                *Bell rings.*

*Kit.* How now! Oh, the bell rings to [50
breakfast. Brother, I pray you go in, and bear
my wife company till I come; I 'll but give
order for some despatch of business to my servants.                                *[Exit Downright.]*

## Act II. Scene III

### [The Same.]

### *Kitely, Cob, [later] Dame Kitely*

[*Kit.*] What, Cob! our maids will have you by
the back, i' faith, for coming so late this morning.

*Cob.* Perhaps so, sir; take heed somebody
have not them by the belly, for walking so [5
late in the evening.
            *He passes by with his tankard.*

*Kit.* Well; yet my troubled spirit 's some-
what eas'd,
Though not repos'd in that security
As I could wish: but I must be content,
Howe'er I set a face on 't to the world.     10
Would I had lost this finger at a venter,
So Wellbred had ne'er lodg'd within my house.
Why 't cannot be, where there is such resort
Of wanton gallants and young revellers,

That any woman should be honest long.     15
Is 't like that factious beauty will preserve
The public weal of chastity unshaken,
When such strong motives muster and make
    head
Against her single peace? No, no: beware.
When mutual appetite doth meet to treat,  20
And spirits of one kind and quality
Come once to parley in the pride of blood,
It is no slow conspiracy that follows.
Well, to be plain, if I but thought the time
Had answer'd their affections, all the world 25
Should not persuade me but I were a cuckold.
Marry, I hope they ha' not got that start;
For opportunity hath balk'd 'em yet,
And shall do still, while I have eyes and ears
To attend the impositions of my heart.     30
My presence shall be as an iron bar
'Twixt the conspiring motions of desire:
Yea, every look or glance mine eye ejects
Shall check occasion, as one doth his slave,
When he forgets the limits of prescription. 35

### [Enter Dame Kitely]

*Dame K.* Sister Bridget, pray you fetch down
the rose-water, above in the closet. — Sweetheart, will you come in to breakfast?

*Kit.* An she have overheard me now! ——

*Dame Kit.* I pray thee, good muss, we [40
stay for you.

*Kit.* By heaven, I would not for a thousand
angels.

*Dame K.* What ail you, sweet-heart? are you
not well? Speak, good muss.                   45

*Kit.* Troth, my head aches extremely on a
sudden.

*Dame K. [putting her hand to his forehead.]* O,
the Lord!

*Kit.* How now! What?                         50

*Dame K.* Alas, how it burns! Muss, keep
you warm; good truth, it is this new disease!
there 's a number are troubled withal. For love's
sake, sweet-heart, come in out of the air.

*Kit.* How simple, and how subtle are her
    answers!                                   55
A new disease, and many troubled with it?
Why true; she heard me, all the world to
    nothing.

*Dame K.* I pray thee, good sweet-heart,
come in; the air will do you harm, in troth.

*Kit.* The air! she has me i' the wind. —     60
Sweet-heart, I 'll come to you presently; 't will
away, I hope.

*Dame K.* Pray Heaven it do.        *[Exit.]*

---

²⁶ **madge-howlet:** the barn owl     ²⁸ **tumbrel-slop:** large puffed breeches     ³⁴⁻³⁵ **hangman cut:**
born to be hanged or having the bearing of a hangman     ³⁶ **ging:** gang     ¹⁸ **make head:** gather their
forces     ²⁵ **answer'd . . . affections:** suited their desires     ⁴⁰ **muss:** mouse (a term of endearment)
⁴¹ **stay:** wait     ⁴³ **angels:** coins worth about ten shillings     ⁵² **new disease:** a kind of fever     ⁶⁰ **has
. . . wind:** suspects my thoughts

*Kit.*  A new disease!  I know not, new or old,
But it may well be call'd poor mortals' plague;
For, like a pestilence, it doth infect          66
The houses of the brain.  First it begins
Solely to work upon the phantasy,
Filling her seat with such pestiferous air
As soon corrupts the judgment; and from thence
Sends like contagion to the memory:            71
Still each to other giving the infection,
Which as a subtle vapour spreads itself
Confusedly through every sensive part,
Till not a thought or motion in the mind        75
Be free from the black poison of suspect.
Ah! but what misery is it to know this?
Or, knowing it, to want the mind's erection
In such extremes?  Well, I will once more strive,
In spite of this black cloud, myself to be,     80
And shake the fever off that thus shakes me.
                                        [*Exit.*]

## Act II.   Scene IIII

### [*Moorfields.*]

*Brainworm,* [*later*] *Edward Knowell, Master*
*Stephen*

[*Brai.*]  'Slid, I cannot choose but laugh to see
myself translated thus, from a poor creature to
a creator; for now must I create an intolerable
sort of lies, or my present profession loses the
grace: and yet the lie, to a man of my coat, is [5
as ominous a fruit as the fico.  O, sir, it holds
for good polity ever, to have that outwardly in
vilest estimation, that inwardly is most dear to
us.  So much for my borrowed shape.  Well, the
troth is, my old master intends to follow my [10
young, dry-foot, over Moorfields to London,
this morning; now, I knowing of this hunting-
match, or rather conspiracy, and to insinuate
with my young master (for so must we that
are blue waiters, and men of hope and serv- [15
ice do, or perhaps we may wear motley at
the year's end, and who wears motley, — you
know), have got me afore in this disguise, de-
termining here to lie in ambuscado, and intercept him in the mid-way.  If I can but get his [20
cloak, his purse, his hat, nay, anything to
cut him off, that is, to stay his journey, *Veni,*
*vidi, vici,* I may say with Captain Cæsar, I am
made for ever, i' faith.  Well, now must I practise to get the true garb of one of these lance- [25
knights: my arm here, and —— My young
master, and his cousin, master Stephen, as
I am true counterfeit man of war, and no
soldier!                               [*Exit.*]

### [*Enter E. Knowell and Stephen*]

*E. Know.*  So, sir! and how then, coz?     30
*Step.*  'Sfoot!  I have lost my purse, I think.
*E. Know.*  How! lost your purse?  Where?
When had you it?
*Step.*  I cannot tell; stay.
*Brai.* [*aside.*]  'Slid, I am afeard they will
know me: would I could get by them! [*Retires.*]
*E. Know.*  What, ha' you it?               37
*Step.*  No;  I think I was bewitch'd, I ——
                                        [*Weeps.*]
*E. Know.*  Nay, do not weep the loss: hang
it, let it go.                              40
*Step.*  Oh, it 's here.  No, an it had been lost,
I had not car'd, but for a jet ring mistress Mary
sent me.
*E. Know.*  A jet ring!  O the posy, the posy?
*Step.*  Fine, i' faith. ——                45
            Though Fancy sleep,
            My love is deep.
Meaning, that though I did not fancy her, yet
she loved me dearly.
*E. Know.*  Most excellent!                 50
*Step.*  And then I sent her another, and my
posy was,
            The deeper the sweeter,
            I 'll be judg'd by St. Peter.
*E. Know.*  How, by St. Peter?  I do not [55
conceive that.
*Step.*  Marry, St. Peter, to make up the metre.
*E. Know.*  Well, there the saint was your
good patron, he help'd you at your need; thank
him, thank him.                           60
*Brai.* (*He is come back.*)  I cannot take leave
on 'em so; I will venture, come what will. ——
Gentlemen, please you change a few crowns
for a very excellent good blade here?  I am a
poor gentleman, a soldier, one that, in the [65
better state of my fortunes, scorn'd so mean a
refuge; but now it is the humour of necessity
to have it so.  You seem to be gentlemen well
affected to martial men, else I should rather
die with silence, than live with shame: how- [70
ever, vouchsafe to remember it is my want
speaks, not myself; this condition agrees not
with my spirit ——
*E. Know.*  Where hast thou serv'd?
*Brai.*  May it please you, sir, in all the [75
late wars of Bohemia, Hungary, Dalmatia, Poland, — where not, sir?  I have been a poor
servitor by sea and land any time this fourteen
years, and follow'd the fortunes of the best commanders in Christendom.  I was twice shot [80

---

⁷⁴ **sensive:** sensitive    ⁷⁶ **suspect:** suspicion       ⁶ **fico:** poisoned fig, also an insulting gesture
³ **borrowed shape:** (Brainworm is disguised as a maimed soldier.)      ¹¹ **dry-foot:** by scentless foot-
prints    ¹⁵ **blue waiters:** (Servants then wore blue coats.)    ¹⁶ **motley:** the dress of the Fool    ¹⁹ **ambuscado:** ambush    ²⁵⁻²⁶ **lance-knights:** mercenary foot soldiers    ⁴⁴ **posy:** motto inscribed in a ring
⁷⁶⁻⁷⁷ **Bohemia . . . Poland:** the theatres of recent warfare

at the taking of Aleppo, once at the relief of
Vienna; I have been at Marseilles, Naples, and
the Adriatic gulf, a gentleman-slave in the galleys, thrice; where I was most dangerously shot
in the head, through both the thighs; and [85
yet, being thus maim'd, I am void of maintenance, nothing left me but my scars, the noted
marks of my resolution.

*Step.* How will you sell this rapier, friend?

*Brai.* Generous sir, I refer it to your own
judgment; you are a gentleman, give me [91
what you please.

*Step.* True, I am a gentleman, I know that,
friend; but what though? I pray you say, what
would you ask?       95

*Brai.* I assure you, the blade may become
the side or thigh of the best prince in Europe.

*E. Know.* Ay, with a velvet scabbard, I think.

*Step.* Nay, an 't be mine, it shall have a velvet scabbard, coz, that 's flat; I 'd not wear [100
it, as 't is, an you would give me an angel.

*Brai.* At your worship's pleasure, sir.
[*Stephen examines the blade.*] Nay, 't is a most
pure Toledo.

*Step.* I had rather it were a Spaniard. [105
But tell me, what shall I give you for it? An it
had a silver hilt ——

*E. Know.* Come, come, you shall not buy it.
Hold, there 's a shilling, fellow; take thy rapier.

*Step.* Why, but I will buy it now, because
you say so; and there 's another shilling, [111
fellow; I scorn to be out-bidden. What, shall I
walk with a cudgel, like Higginbottom, and may
have a rapier for money!

*E. Know.* You may buy one in the city. [115

*Step.* Tut! I 'll buy this i' the field, so I will:
I have a mind to 't, because 't is a field rapier.
Tell me your lowest price.

*E. Know.* You shall not buy it, I say.

*Step.* By this money, but I will, though I
give more than 't is worth.      121

*E. Know.* Come away, you are a fool.

*Step.* Friend, I am a fool, that 's granted;
but I 'll have it, for that word's sake. Follow
me for your money.

*Brai.* At your service, sir. [*Exeunt.*] 126

## Act II. Scene V

[*Another Part of Moorfields.*]

*Knowell, [later] Brainworm*

[*Know.*] I cannot lose the thought yet of this
letter
Sent to my son; nor leave t' admire the change
Of manners, and the breeding of our youth

Within the kingdom, since myself was one. ——
When I was young, he liv'd not in the stews 5
Durst have conceiv'd a scorn, and utter'd it,
On a gray head; age was authority
Against a buffoon, and a man had then
A certain reverence paid unto his years,
That had none due unto his life: so much 10
The sanctity of some prevail'd for others.
But now we all are fall'n; youth, from their
fear,
And age, from that which bred it, good example.
Nay, would ourselves were not the first, even
parents,      14
That did destroy the hopes in our own children;
Or they not learn'd our vices in their cradles,
And suck'd in our ill customs with their milk!
Ere all their teeth be born, or they can speak,
We make their palates cunning; the first words
We form their tongues with. are licentious
jests:      20
Can it call "whore"? cry "bastard"? O, then,
kiss it!
A witty child! Can 't swear? The father's
darling!
Give it two plums. Nay, rather than 't shall
learn
No bawdy song, the mother herself will teach it!
But this is in the infancy, the days      25
Of the long coat; when it puts on the breeches,
It will put off all this. Ay, it is like,
When it is gone into the bone already!
No, no; this dye goes deeper than the coat,
Or shirt, or skin; it stains unto the liver 30
And heart, in some: and, rather than it should
not,
Note what we fathers do! Look how we live!
What mistresses we keep! at what expense!
In our sons' eyes, where they may handle our
gifts,
Hear our lascivious courtships, see our dalli-
ance,      35
Taste of the same provoking meats with us,
To ruin of our states! Nay, when our own
Portion is fled, to prey on their remainder,
We call them into fellowship of vice;
Bait 'em with the young chamber-maid, to
seal,      40
And teach 'em all bad ways to buy affliction.
This is one path; but there are millions more,
In which we spoil our own, with leading them.
Well, I thank heaven, I never yet was he
That travell'd with my son, before sixteen, 45
To show him the Venetian courtesans;
Nor read the grammar of cheating I had made,
To my sharp boy, at twelve; repeating still
The rule, *Get money; still, get money, boy;*

---

[113] **Higginbottom:** a contemporary ruffian not certainly identified    [2] **leave t' admire:** desist from
wondering at    [30] **liver:** the seat of the passions    [31] **heart:** seat of knowledge    [40] **seal:** to agree to
the sale of family lands (?)

*No matter by what means; money will do*    50
*More, boy, than my lord's letter.* Neither have I
Dress'd snails or mushrooms curiously before
   him,
Perfum'd my sauces, and taught him how to
   make 'em;
Preceding still, with my gray gluttony,
At all the ord'naries, and only fear'd    55
His palate should degenerate, not his manners.
These are the trade of fathers now; however,
My son, I hope, hath met within my threshold
None of these household precedents, which are
   strong
And swift to rape youth to their precipice.    60
But let the house at home be ne'er so clean-
Swept, or kept sweet from filth, nay dust and
   cobwebs,
If he will live abroad with his companions,
In dung and leystals, it is worth a fear;
Nor is the danger of conversing less    65
Than all that I have mention'd of example.

*[Enter Brainworm, disguised as before]*

*Brai.* [*aside.*] My master! nay, faith, have
at you; I am flesh'd now, I have sped so well. —
Worshipful sir, I beseech you, respect the estate
of a poor soldier; I am asham'd of this base [70
course of life, — God 's my comfort — but extremity provokes me to 't: what remedy?
*Know.* I have not for you, now.
*Brai.* By the faith I bear unto truth, gentleman, it is no ordinary custom in me, but [75
only to preserve manhood. I protest to you, a
man I have been; a man I may be, by your
sweet bounty.
*Know.* Pray thee, good friend, be satisfied.
*Brai.* Good sir, by that hand, you may do [80
the part of a kind gentleman, in lending a poor
soldier the price of two cans of beer, a matter
of small value: the king of heaven shall pay you,
and I shall rest thankful. Sweet worship ——
*Know.* Nay, an you be so importunate — [85
*Brai.* Oh, tender sir! need will have his
course; I was not made to this vile use. Well,
the edge of the enemy could not have abated
me so much: it 's hard when a man hath serv'd
in his prince's cause, and be thus — *He weeps.*
Honourable worship, let me derive a small piece
of silver from you, it shall not be given in the
course of time. By this good ground, I was fain
to pawn my rapier last night for a poor supper;
I had suck'd the hilts long before, I am a [95
pagan else. Sweet honour ——
*Know.* Believe me, I am taken with some
   wonder,
To think a fellow of thy outward presence,

Should, in the frame and fashion of his mind,
Be so degenerate, and sordid-base.    100
Art thou a man, and sham'st thou not to beg?
To practise such a servile kind of life?
Why, were thy education ne'er so mean,
Having thy limbs, a thousand fairer courses
Offer themselves to thy election.    105
Either the wars might still supply thy wants,
Or service of some virtuous gentleman,
Or honest labour; nay, what can I name,
But would become thee better than to beg:
But men of thy condition feed on sloth,    110
As doth the beetle on the dung she breeds in;
Not caring how the metal of your minds
Is eaten with the rust of idleness.
Now, afore me, whate'er he be, that should
Relieve a person of thy quality,    115
While thou insist'st in this loose desperate
   course,
I would esteem the sin not thine, but his.
*Brai.* Faith, sir, I would gladly find some
other course, if so ——
*Know.* Ay, you 'd gladly find it, but you
will not seek it.    121
*Brai.* Alas, sir, where should a man seek?
In the wars, there 's no ascent by desert in these
days; but —— and for service, would it were as
soon purchas'd, as wish'd for! The air 's my [125
comfort. — I know what I would say.
*Know.* What 's thy name?
*Brai.* Please you, Fitz-Sword, sir.
*Know.* Fitz-Sword!
Say that a man should entertain thee now, 130
Wouldst thou be honest, humble, just, and true?
*Brai.* Sir, by the place and honour of a sol-
   dier ——
*Know.* Nay, nay, I like not those affected
oaths. Speak plainly, man, what think'st thou
of my words?    135
*Brai.* Nothing, sir, but wish my fortunes
were as happy as my service should be honest.
*Know.* Well, follow me. I 'll prove thee, if
   thy deeds
Will carry a proportion to thy words. [*Exit.*]
*Brai.* Yes, sir, straight; I 'll but garter [140
my hose. — Oh that my belly were hoop'd now,
for I am ready to burst with laughing! never
was bottle or bagpipe fuller. 'Slid, was there
ever seen a fox in years to betray himself thus!
Now shall I be possess'd of all his counsels; [145
and, by that conduit, my young master. Well,
he is resolv'd to prove my honesty; faith, and
I 'm resolv'd to prove his patience: oh, I shall
abuse him intolerably. This small piece of service will bring him clean out of love with [150
the soldier for ever. He will never come within

---

⁵⁵ **ord'naries:** taverns    ⁶⁴ **leystals:** dung-heaps    ⁶⁸ **flesh'd:** eager, started    ⁹²⁻⁹³ **it . . . time:**
*i.e.,* you will be repaid some day    ¹²⁵ **purchas'd:** obtained    ¹³⁰ **entertain:** give a position to
¹⁴⁷ **prove:** test

the sign of it, the sight of a cassock, or a mus-
ket-rest again.  He will hate the musters at
Mile-end for it, to his dying day.  It 's no matter, let the world think me a bad counterfeit, [155
if I cannot give him the slip at an instant.
Why, this is better than to have stay'd his
journey.  Well, I 'll follow him.  Oh, how I long
to be employed!                              [*Exit.*]

## Act III.  Scene I

*[The Old Jewry.  A Room in the Windmill
Tavern.]*

*Mathew, Wellbred, Bobadill, Edward Knowell,
Stephen*

[*Mat.*]  Yes, faith, sir, we were at your lodging to seek you too.
*Wel.*  Oh, I came not there to-night.
*Bob.*  Your brother delivered us as much.
*Wel.*  Who, my brother Downright?          5
*Bob.*  He.  Master Wellbred, I know not in
what kind you hold me; but let me say to you
this: as sure as honour, I esteem it so much out
of the sunshine of reputation, to throw the
least beam of regard upon such a ——          10
*Wel.*  Sir, I must hear no ill words of my
brother.
*Bob.*  I protest to you, as I have a thing to be
sav'd about me, I never saw any gentleman-like
part ——                                      15
*Wel.*  Good captain, faces about to some
other discourse.
*Bob.*  With your leave, sir, an there were no
more men living upon the face of the earth, I
should not fancy him, by St. George!          20
*Mat.*  Troth, nor I;  he is of a rustical cut, I
know not how: he doth not carry himself like
a gentleman of fashion.
*Wel.*  Oh, master Mathew, that 's a grace peculiar but to a few, *quos æquus amavit Jupiter.* [25
*Mat.*  I understand you, sir.
*Wel.*  No question, you do, — [*aside.*] or
you do not, sir.

*Young Knowell enters.*

Ned Knowell! by my soul, welcome: how dost
thou, sweet spirit, my genius?  'Slid, I shall love
Apollo and the mad Thespian girls the better, [31
while I live, for this, my dear Fury;  now I see
there 's some love in thee.  Sirrah, these be the
two I writ to thee of: nay, what a drowsy humour is this now!  Why dost thou not speak? [35

*E. Know.*  Oh, you are a fine gallant; you
sent me a rare letter.
*Wel.*  Why, was 't not rare?
*E. Know.*  Yes, I 'll be sworn! I was ne'er
guilty of reading the like;  match it in all [40
Pliny, or Symmachus' epistles, and I 'll have
my judgment burn'd in the ear for a rogue:
make much of thy vein, for it is inimitable.  But
I marle what camel it was, that had the carriage of it;  for, doubtless, he was no ordinary
beast that brought it.                        46
*Wel.*  Why?
*E. Know.*  "Why?" say'st thou!  Why, dost
thou think that any reasonable creature, especially in the morning, the sober time of the day
too, could have mista'en my father for me? [51
*Wel.*  'Slid, you jest, I hope.
*E. Know.*  Indeed, the best use we can turn it
to, is to make a jest on 't, now: but I 'll assure
you, my father had the full view o' your [55
flourishing style some hour before I saw it.
*Wel.*  What a dull slave was this! But, sirrah, what said he to it, i' faith?
*E. Know.*  Nay, I know not what he said.
but I have a shrewd guess what he thought.  60
*Wel.*  What, what?
*E. Know.*  Marry, that thou art some strange,
dissolute young fellow, and I — a grain or two
better, for keeping thee company.
*Wel.*  Tut! that thought is like the moon [65
in her last quarter, 't will change shortly.  But,
sirrah, I pray thee be acquainted with my two
hang-by's here;  thou wilt take exceeding pleasure in 'em if thou hear'st 'em once go;  my [69
wind-instruments;  I 'll wind 'em up —— But
what strange piece of silence is this?  The sign
of the Dumb Man?
*E. Know.*  Oh, sir, a kinsman of mine, one
that may make your music the fuller, an he
please;  he has his humour, sir.              75
*Wel.*  Oh, what is 't, what is 't?
*E. Know.*  Nay, I 'll neither do your judgment nor his folly that wrong, as to prepare
your apprehension;  I 'll leave him to the mercy
o' your search;  if you can take him, so!     80
*Wel.*  Well, captain Bobadill, master Mathew,
pray you know this gentleman here;  he is a
friend of mine, and one that will deserve your
affection. — I know not your name, sir (*to* [84
*Master Stephen*), but I shall be glad of any occasion to render me more familiar to you.
*Step.*  My name is master Stephen, sir; I am
this gentleman's own cousin, sir;  his father is

---

¹⁵² **cassock:** soldier's loose cloak or coat    ¹⁵⁴ **Mile-end:** training ground for militia outside London
¹⁵⁶ **slip:** pun on "slip" meaning counterfeit coin    ⁴ **delivered:** told    ¹⁶ **faces about:** about face
²⁵ **quos . . . Jupiter:** whom the impartial Jupiter has loved    ³¹ **Thespian girls:** the Muses    ⁴¹ **Sym-**
**machus:** a Roman scholar, statesman, and orator (4th cent., A.D.), the florid style of whose epistles,
modeled on those of Pliny, was much admired    ⁴⁴ **marle:** marvel    **camel:** proverbially dull
beast

mine uncle, sir. I am somewhat melancholy, [89
but you shall command me, sir, in whatsoever
is incident to a gentleman.

*Bob.* (*to E. Knowell.*) Sir, I must tell you
this, I am no general man; but for master
Wellbred's sake (you may embrace it at what
height of favour you please), I do communi- [95
cate with you, and conceive you to be a gentleman of some parts; I love few words.

*E. Know.* And I fewer, sir; I have scarce
enow to thank you.                                      99

*Mat.* (*to Master Stephen.*) But are you, indeed, sir, so given to it?

*Step.* Ay, truly, sir, I am mightily given to
melancholy.

*Mat.* Oh, it's your only fine humour, sir;
your true melancholy breeds your perfect fine
wit, sir. I am melancholy myself divers [106
times, sir, and then do I no more but take pen
and paper presently, and overflow you half a
score, or a dozen of sonnets at a sitting.

*E. Know.* (*aside.*) Sure he utters them [110
then by the gross.

*Step.* Truly, sir, and I love such things out
of measure.

*E. Know.* I' faith, better than in measure,
I'll undertake.                                        115

*Mat.* Why, I pray you, sir, make use of my
study; it's at your service.

*Step.* I thank you, sir. I shall be bold, I warrant you; have you a stool there to be melancholy upon?                                            120

*Mat.* That I have, sir, and some papers there
of mine own doing, at idle hours, that you'll say
there's some sparks of wit in 'em, when you see
them.

*Wel.* [*aside.*] Would the sparks would kindle once, and become a fire amongst 'em! I [126
might see self-love burnt for her heresy.

*Step.* Cousin, is it well? Am I melancholy
enough?

*E. Know.* Oh ay, excellent.                           130

*Wel.* Captain Bobadill, why muse you so?

*E. Know.* He is melancholy too.

*Bob.* Faith, sir, I was thinking of a most
honourable piece of service, was perform'd to-
morrow, being St. Mark's day, shall be some
ten years now.                                         136

*E. Know.* In what place, captain?

*Bob.* Why, at the beleag'ring of Strigonium,
where, in less than two hours, seven hundred
resolute gentlemen, as any were in Europe, lost
their lives upon the breach. I'll tell you, [141
gentlemen, it was the first, but the best leaguer

that ever I beheld with these eyes, except the
taking in of — what do you call it? last year,
by the Genoways; but that, of all other, was the
most fatal and dangerous exploit that ever [146
I was rang'd in, since I first bore arms before
the face of the enemy, as I am a gentleman and
soldier!

*Step.* So! I had as lief as an angel I could
swear as well as that gentleman.                       151

*E. Know.* Then, you were a servitor at both,
it seems; at Strigonium, and what do you call 't?

*Bob.* O lord, sir! By St. George, I was the
first man that ent'red the breach; and had
I not effected it with resolution, I had been
slain if I had had a million of lives.                 157

*E. Know.* 'T was pity you had not ten; a cat's
and your own, i' faith. But, was it possible?

*Mat.* Pray you mark this discourse, sir.

*Step.* So I do.                                       161

*Bob.* I assure you, upon my reputation, 't is
true, and yourself shall confess.

*E. Know.* [*aside.*] You must bring me to
the rack, first.                                       165

*Bob.* Observe me judicially, sweet sir: they
had planted me three demi-culverins just in
the mouth of the breach; now, sir, as we were
to give on, their master-gunner (a man of no
mean skill and mark, you must think), con- [170
fronts me with his linstock, ready to give fire;
I, spying his intendment, discharg'd my petronel in his bosom, and with these single arms,
my poor rapier, ran violently upon the Moors
that guarded the ordnance, and put 'em pell-
mell to the sword.                                     176

*Wel.* To the sword! To the rapier, captain.

*E. Know.* Oh, it was a good figure observ'd,
sir. But did you all this, captain, without hurt-
ing your blade?

*Bob.* Without any impeach o' the earth: [181
you shall perceive, sir. [*Shows his rapier.*] It
is the most fortunate weapon that ever rid on
poor gentleman's thigh. Shall I tell you, sir?
You talk of Morglay, Excalibur, Durindana, or
so; tut! I lend no credit to that is fabled of [186
'em. I know the virtue of mine own, and therefore I dare the boldlier maintain it.

*Step.* I marle whether it be a Toledo or no.

*Bob.* A most perfect Toledo, I assure you,
sir.                                                   191

*Step.* I have a countryman of his here.

*Mat.* Pray you, let's see, sir; yes, faith, it is.

*Bob.* This a Toledo? Pish!

*Step.* Why do you pish, captain?                      195

*Bob.* A Fleming, by heaven! I'll buy them

---

⁹³ **general:** of easy friendship    ¹³⁸ **Strigonium:** Graan, in Hungary, retaken from the Turks in 1595
¹⁴² **leaguer:** siege    ¹⁴⁴ **taking in:** capture    ¹⁴⁵ **Genoways:** Genoese    ¹⁶⁷ **demi-culverins:** small
cannon    ¹⁶⁹ **give on:** charge    ¹⁷¹ **linstock:** device for firing cannon    ¹⁷²⁻¹⁷³ **petronel:** carbine or
horse-pistol    ¹⁸¹ **o' the earth:** at all    ¹⁸⁵ **Morglay . . . Durindana:** the swords of Bevis, Arthur,
and Orlando in the romances

for a guilder a-piece, an I would have a thousand of them.

*E. Know.* How say you, cousin? I told you
thus much.                                        200

*Wel.* Where bought you it, master Stephen?

*Step.* Of a scurvy rogue soldier: a hundred
of lice go with him! He swore it was a Toledo.

*Bob.* A poor provant rapier, no better.

*Mat.* Mass, I think it be indeed, now I look
on 't better.                                     206

*E. Know.* Nay, the longer you look on 't, the
worse. Put it up, put it up.

*Step.* Well, I will put it up; but by — I ha'
forgot the captain's oath, I thought to ha'
sworn by it — an e'er I meet him ——      211

*Wel.* O, it is past help now, sir; you must
have patience.

*Step.* Whoreson, coney-catching rascal! I
could eat the very hilts for anger.               215

*E. Know.* A sign of good digestion; you
have an ostrich stomach, cousin.

*Step.* A stomach! Would I had him here,
you should see an I had a stomach.

*Wel.* It 's better as 't is. — Come, gentlemen, shall we go?                                 221

## Act III.  Scene II

### [The Same.]

*E. Knowell, Brainworm, Stephen, Wellbred,
Bobadill, Mathew*

[*E. Know.*] A miracle, cousin; look here,
look here!

*Step.* Oh — God's lid. By your leave, do
you know me, sir?

*Brai.* Ay, sir, I know you by sight.        5

*Step.* You sold me a rapier, did you not?

*Brai.* Yes, marry, did I, sir.

*Step.* You said it was a Toledo, ha?

*Brai.* True, I did so.

*Step.* But it is none.                          10

*Brai.* No, sir, I confess it; it is none.

*Step.* Do you confess it? Gentlemen, bear
witness, he has confess'd it: — By God's will,
an you had not confess'd it ——

*E. Know.* Oh, cousin, forbear, forbear!     15

*Step.* Nay, I have done, cousin.

*Wel.* Why, you have done like a gentleman;
he has confess'd it, what would you more?

*Step.* Yet, by his leave, he is a rascal, under
his favour, do you see.                           20

*E. Know.* Ay, by his leave, he is, and under
favour: a pretty piece of civility! Sirrah, how
dost thou like him?

*Wel.* Oh, it 's a most precious fool, make
much on him. I can compare him to nothing [25
more happily than a drum; for every one may
play upon him.

*E. Know.* No, no, a child's whistle were far
the fitter.

*Brai.* Sir, shall I entreat a word with you? 30

*E. Know.* With me, sir? You have not another Toledo to sell, ha' you?

*Brai.* You are conceited, sir. Your name is
Master Knowell, as I take it?

*E. Know.* You are i' the right; you mean [35
not to proceed in the catechism, do you?

*Brai.* No, sir; I am none of that coat.

*E. Know.* Of as bare a coat, though. Well,
say, sir.                                         39

*Brai.* [*taking E. Know. aside.*] Faith, sir, I
am but servant to the drum extraordinary,
and indeed, this smoky varnish being wash'd
off, and three or four patches remov'd, I appear
your worship's in reversion, after the decease
of your good father, — Brainworm.             45

*E. Know.* Brainworm! 'Slight, what breath
of a conjurer hath blown thee hither in this
shape?

*Brai.* The breath o' your letter, sir, this
morning; the same that blew you to the [50
Windmill, and your father after you.

*E. Know.* My father!

*Brai.* Nay, never start, 't is true; he has
follow'd you over the fields by the foot, as you
would do a hare i' the snow.                      55

*E. Know.* Sirrah Wellbred, what shall we
do, sirrah? My father is come over after me.

*Wel.* Thy father! Where is he?

*Brai.* At justice Clement's house here, in
Coleman-street, where he but stays my return;
and then ——                                      61

*Wel.* Who 's this? Brainworm!

*Brai.* The same, sir.

*Wel.* Why how, i' the name of wit, com'st
thou transmuted thus?                            65

*Brai.* Faith, a device, a device; nay, for the
love of reason, gentlemen, and avoiding the
danger, stand not here; withdraw, and I 'll tell
you all.                                          69

*Wel.* But art thou sure he will stay thy return?

*Brai.* Do I live, sir? What a question is that!

*Wel.* We 'll prorogue his expectation, then,
a little: Brainworm, thou shalt go with us. —
Come on, gentlemen. — Nay, I pray thee, [75
sweet Ned, droop not; 'heart, an our wits be so
wretchedly dull, that one old plodding brain
can outstrip us all, would we were e'en press'd

---

¹⁹⁷ **guilder:** a Dutch coin worth less than a dollar     ²⁰⁴ **provant:** of kind issued to common soldiers
²¹⁴ **coney-catching:** swindling     ²¹⁹ **stomach:** courage     ¹⁹⁻²⁰ **under his favour:** with all submission
³³ **conceited:** witty     ³⁷ **none . . . coat:** not a clergyman     ⁴¹ **extraordinary:** for a special occasion
⁷⁸ **press'd:** impressed

to make porters of, and serve out the remnant
of our days in Thames-street, or at Custom- [80
house quay, in a civil war against the carmen!

*Brai.* Amen, amen, amen, say I. [*Exeunt.*]

## Act III. Scene III

[*Kitely's Warehouse.*]

*Kitely, Cash*

[*Kit.*] What says he, Thomas? Did you
    speak with him?

*Cash.* He will expect you, sir, within this
    half hour.

*Kit.* Has he the money ready, can you tell?

*Cash.* Yes, sir, the money was brought in
    last night.

*Kit.* O, that 's well; fetch me my cloak, my
    cloak! —                          [*Exit Cash.*] 5
Stay, let me see, an hour to go and come;
Ay, that will be the least; and then 't will be
An hour before I can dispatch with him,
Or very near; well, I will say two hours.
Two hours! ha! things never dreamt of yet, 10
May be contriv'd, ay, and effected too,
In two hours' absence; well, I will not go.
Two hours! No, fleering Opportunity,
I will not give your subtilty that scope.
Who will not judge him worthy to be robb'd, 15
That sets his doors wide open to a thief,
And shows the felon where his treasure lies?
Again, what earthy spirit but will attempt
To taste the fruit of beauty's golden tree,
When leaden sleep seals up the dragon's
    eyes?
I will not go. Business, go by for once. 21
No, beauty, no; you are of too good caract
To be left so, without a guard, or open.
Your lustre, too, 'll inflame at any distance,
Draw courtship to you, as a jet doth straws; 25
Put motion in a stone, strike fire from ice,
Nay, make a porter leap you with his burden.
You must be then kept up, close, and well
    watch'd,
For, give you opportunity, no quicksand
Devours or swallows swifter! He that lends 30
His wife, if she be fair, or time or place,
Compels her to be false. I will not go!
The dangers are too many: — and then the
    dressing
Is a most main attractive! Our great heads
Within the city never were in safety 35
Since our wives wore these little caps. I 'll
    change 'em;
I 'll change 'em straight in mine: mine shall no
    more

Wear three-pil'd acorns, to make my horns
    ache,
Nor will I go; I am resolv'd for that.

[*Re-enter Cash with a cloak*]

Carry in my cloak again. Yet stay. Yet do,
    too:                                     40
I will defer going, on all occasions.

*Cash.* Sir, Snare, your scrivener, will be
    there with th' bonds.

*Kit.* That 's true: fool on me! I had clean
    forgot it;
I must go. What 's o'clock?

*Cash.*                          Exchange-time, sir.

*Kit.* 'Heart! then will Wellbred presently be
    here too,                                 45
With one or other of his loose consorts.
I am a knave if I know what to say,
What course to take, or which way to resolve.
My brain, methinks, is like an hour-glass,
Wherein my imaginations run like sands, 50
Filling up time; but then are turn'd and turn'd:
So that I know not what to stay upon,
And less, to put in act. — It shall be so.
Nay, I dare build upon his secrecy,
He knows not to deceive me. — Thomas!

*Cash.*                                        Sir. 55

*Kit.* Yet now I have bethought me, too, I
    will not. —
Thomas, is Cob within?

*Cash.*                          I think he be, sir.

*Kit.* But he 'll prate too, there 's no speech
    of him.
No, there were no man o' the earth to Thomas,
If I durst trust him; there is all the doubt. 60
But should he have a chink in him, I were
    gone.
Lost i' my fame for ever, talk for th' Exchange!
The manner he hath stood with, till this present,
Doth promise no such change: what should I
    fear then?
Well, come what will, I 'll tempt my fortune
    once.                                     65
Thomas — you may deceive me, but, I hope —
Your love to me is more —

*Cash.*                          Sir, if a servant's
Duty, with faith, may be call'd love, you are
More than in hope, you are possess'd of it.

*Kit.* I thank you heartily, Thomas: gi' me
    your hand:                                70
With all my heart, good Thomas. I have,
    Thomas,
A secret to impart unto you — but,
When once you have it, I must seal your lips
    up;
So far I tell you, Thomas.

*Cash.*                          Sir, for that ——

---

⁸¹⁻⁸² **carmen:** carters    ²² **caract:** carat, value
velvet of the best quality    ⁴⁴ **Exchange-time:** ten o'clock    ⁵⁹ **to:** compared to
³¹ **or . . . or:** either . . . or    ³⁸ **three-pil'd:** of

*Kit.* Nay, hear me out. Think I esteem
you, Thomas,    75
When I will let you in thus to my private.
It is a thing sits nearer to my crest,
Than thou art 'ware of, Thomas; if thou
should'st
Reveal it, but ——
   *Cash.*       How, I reveal it?
   *Kit.*             Nay,
I do not think thou would'st; but if thou
should'st,    80
'T were a great weakness.
   *Cash.*       A great treachery:
Give it no other name.
   *Kit.*      Thou wilt not do 't, then?
   *Cash.* Sir, if I do, mankind disclaim me ever!
   *Kit.* He will not swear, he has some reserva-
tion,    84
Some conceal'd purpose, and close meaning sure;
Else, being urg'd so much, how should he choose
But lend an oath to all this protestation?
He 's no precisian, that I am certain of,
Nor rigid Roman Catholic: he 'll play
At fayles, and tick-tack; I have heard him
swear.    90
What should I think of it? Urge him again,
And by some other way? I will do so.
Well, Thomas, thou hast sworn not to dis-
close: —
Yes, you did swear?
   *Cash.*      Not yet, sir, but I will,
Please you ——    95
   *Kit.*     No, Thomas, I dare take thy word,
But, if thou wilt swear, do as thou think'st good;
I am resolv'd without it; at thy pleasure.
   *Cash.* By my soul's safety then, sir, I protest,
My tongue shall ne'er take knowledge of a word
Deliver'd me in nature of your trust.    100
   *Kit.* It 's too much; these ceremonies need
not;
I know thy faith to be as firm as rock.
Thomas, come hither, near; we cannot be
Too private in this business. So it is, —
[*Aside.*] Now he has sworn, I dare the safelier
venter.    105
I have of late, by divers observations ——
[*Aside.*] But whether his oath can bind him,
yea, or no,
Being not taken lawfully? Ha! say you?
I will ask counsel ere I do proceed: —
Thomas, it will be now too long to stay,    110
I 'll spy some fitter time soon, or to-morrow.
   *Cash.* Sir, at your pleasure.
   *Kit.*      I will think: — and, Thomas,
I pray you search the books 'gainst my return,
For the receipts 'twixt me and Traps.

   *Cash.*            I will, sir.
   *Kit.* And hear you, if your mistress' brother,
Wellbred,    115
Chance to bring hither any gentlemen
Ere I come back, let one straight bring me word.
   *Cash.* Very well, sir.
   *Kit.*     To the Exchange, do you hear?
Or here in Coleman-street, to justice Clement's.
Forget it not, nor be not out of the way.    120
   *Cash.* I will not, sir.
   *Kit.*      I pray you have a care on 't.
Or, whether he come or no, if any other,
Stranger, or else, fail not to send me word.
   *Cash.* I shall not, sir.
   *Kit.*      Be 't your special business
Now to remember it.
   *Cash.*      Sir, I warrant you.    125
   *Kit.* But, Thomas, this is not the secret,
Thomas,
I told you of.
   *Cash.*     No, sir; I do suppose it.
   *Kit.* Believe me, it is not.
   *Cash.*      Sir, I do believe you.
   *Kit.* By heaven it is not, that 's enough.
But, Thomas,
I would not you should utter it, do you see?    130
To any creature living; yet I care not.
Well, I must hence. Thomas, conceive thus
much;
It was a trial of you, when I meant
So deep a secret to you; I mean not this,    134
But that I have to tell you: this is nothing,
this.
But, Thomas, keep this from my wife, I charge
you,
Lock'd up in silence, midnight, buried here. —
No greater hell than to be slave to fear. [*Exit.*]
   *Cash.* *Lock'd up in silence, midnight, buried
here!*
Whence should this flood of passion, trow, take
head? ha!    140
Best dream no longer of this running humour,
For fear I sink; the violence of the stream
Already hath transported me so far,
That I can feel no ground at all. But soft —
Oh, 't is our water-bearer: somewhat has cross'd
him now.    145

### *Act III. Scene IIII*

#### [*The Same.*]

#### *Cob, Cash*

   [*Cob.*] Fasting-days! what tell you me of
fasting-days? 'Slid, would they were all on a
light fire for me! They say the whole world shall

---

<sup>76</sup> **private:** privacy, private thoughts    <sup>85</sup> **close:** secret    <sup>88</sup> **precisian:** Puritan    <sup>90</sup> **fayles, tick-
tack:** varieties of backgammon    <sup>97</sup> **resolv'd:** convinced    <sup>101</sup> **need not:** are not necessary    <sup>108</sup> **lawfully:** before a magistrate    <sup>2–3</sup> **on . . . fire:** ablaze

be consum'd with fire one day, but would I had these Ember-weeks and villainous Fridays [5 burnt in the mean time, and then ——

*Cash.* Why, how now, Cob? What moves thee to this choler, ha?

*Cob.* Collar, master Thomas! I scorn your collar, I, sir; I am none o' your cart-horse, [10 though I carry and draw water. An you offer to ride me with your collar or halter either, I may hap show you a jade's trick, sir.

*Cash.* O, you 'll slip your head out of the collar? Why, goodman Cob, you mistake me. 15

*Cob.* Nay, I have my rheum, and I can be angry as well as another, sir.

*Cash.* Thy rheum, Cob! Thy humour, thy humour — thou mistak'st.

*Cob.* Humour! mack, I think it be so in- [20 deed. What is that humour? Some rare thing, I warrant.

*Cash.* Marry I 'll tell thee, Cob: it is a gentleman-like monster, bred in the special gallantry of our time by affectation, and fed by folly. 25

*Cob.* How! must it be fed?

*Cash.* Oh ay, humour is nothing if it be not fed; didst thou never hear that? It 's a common phrase, *Feed my humour.*

*Cob.* I 'll none on it: humour, avaunt! I know you not, be gone! Let who will make [31 hungry meals for your monstership, it shall not be I. Feed you, quoth he! 'Slid, I ha' much ado to feed myself; especially on these lean rascally days too; an 't had been any other day [35 but a fasting-day — a plague on them all for me! By this light, one might have done the commonwealth good service, and have drown'd them all i' the flood, two or three hundred thousand years ago. O, I do stomach them [40 hugely. I have a maw now, an 't were for sir Bevis his horse against 'em.

*Cash.* I pray thee, good Cob, what makes thee so out of love with fasting-days?

*Cob.* Marry, that which will make any [45 man out of love with 'em, I think; their bad conditions, an you will needs know. First, they are of a Flemish breed, I am sure on 't, for they raven up more butter than all the days of the week beside; next, they stink of fish and leek-porridge miserably; thirdly, they 'll [51 keep a man devoutly hungry all day, and at night send him supperless to bed.

*Cash.* Indeed, these are faults, Cob.        54

*Cob.* Nay, an this were all, 't were something;

but they are the only known enemies to my generation. A fasting-day no sooner comes, but my lineage goes to wrack; poor cobs! they smoke for it, they are made martyrs o' the gridiron, they melt in passion: and your maids [60 too know this, and yet would have me turn Hannibal, and eat my own fish and blood. My princely coz (*he pulls out a red herring*), fear nothing; I have not the heart to devour you, an I might be made as rich as king Cophetua. O that I had room for my tears, I could weep [66 salt-water enough now to preserve the lives of ten thousand of my kin! But I may curse none but these filthy almanacs; for an 't were not for them, these days of persecution would ne'er [70 be known. I 'll be hang'd an some fishmonger's son do not make of 'em, and puts in more fasting-days than he should do, because he would utter his father's dried stock-fish and stinking conger.                                75

*Cash.* 'Slight, peace! Thou 'lt be beaten like a stock-fish else. Here is master Mathew. Now must I look out for a messenger to my master.
                                        [*Exeunt.*]

## Act III.   Scene V

### [*The Same.*]

*Wellbred, Ed. Knowell, Brainworm, Bobadill, Mathew, Stephen, [later] Thomas, Cob*

[*Wel.*] Beshrew me, but it was an absolute good jest, and exceedingly well carried!

*E. Know.* Ay, and our ignorance maintain'd it as well, did it not?

*Wel.* Yes, faith; but was 't possible thou [5 shouldst not know him? I forgive master Stephen, for he is stupidity itself.

*E. Know.* 'Fore God, not I, an I might have been join'd patten with one of the seven wise masters for knowing him. He had so writhen himself into the habit of one of your poor [11 infantry, your decay'd, ruinous, worm-eaten gentlemen of the round; such as have vowed to sit on the skirts of the city, let your provost and his half-dozen of halberdiers do what [15 they can; and have translated begging out of the old hackney-pace to a fine easy amble, and made it run as smooth off the tongue as a shove-groat shilling. Into the likeness of one of these reformados had he moulded himself so per- [20 fectly, observing every trick of their action, as,

---

<sup>18</sup> **humour:** *Humour,* but not *rheum,* was the fashionable word for affectation or whim.   <sup>20</sup> **mack:** (by the) mass   <sup>40</sup> **do stomach:** am angry with   <sup>41</sup> **maw:** appetite   <sup>49</sup> **raven:** devour   <sup>61–62</sup> **Hannibal:** *i.e.,* cannibal   <sup>62</sup> **fish:** (' Flesh' F 1692)   <sup>74</sup> **utter:** sell, put into circulation   **stock-fish:** salt fish   <sup>75</sup> **conger:** eels   <sup>9</sup> **patten:** by a patent   <sup>10</sup> **writhen:** twisted   <sup>13</sup> **gentlemen of the round:** minor officers who went the rounds of inspection   <sup>14</sup> **sit . . . of:** press hard upon, punish   **provost:** a police officer   <sup>18–19</sup> **shove-groat shilling:** smooth shilling used at shovel-board   <sup>20</sup> **reformados:** officers of disbanded companies

varying the accent, swearing with an emphasis, indeed, all with so special and exquisite a grace, that, hadst thou seen him, thou wouldst have sworn he might have been sergeant-major, if not lieutenant-coronel to the regiment.   26

*Wel.* Why, Brainworm, who would have thought thou hadst been such an artificer?

*E. Know.* An artificer! an architect. Except a man had studied begging all his life time, [30 and been a weaver of language from his infancy for the clothing of it, I never saw his rival.

*Wel.* Where got'st thou this coat, I marle?

*Brai.* Of a Houndsditch man, sir, one of the devil's near kinsmen, a broker.   35

*Wel.* That cannot be, if the proverb hold; for *A crafty knave needs no broker.*

*Brai.* True, sir; but I did need a broker, *ergo* ——

*Wel.* Well put off: — *no crafty knave*, you 'll say.   41

*E. Know.* Tut, he has more of these shifts.

*Brai.* And yet, where I have one the broker has ten, sir.

*[Enter Cash]*

*Cash.* Francis! Martin! Ne'er a one to be found now? What a spite 's this!   46

*Wel.* How now, Thomas? Is my brother Kite'y within?

*Cash.* No, sir, my master went forth e'en now; but master Downright is within. — Cob! what, Cob! Is he gone too?   51

*Wel.* Whither went your master, Thomas, canst thou tell?

*Cash.* I know not: to justice Clement's, I think, sir. — Cob!

*E. Know.* Justice Clement! what 's he? 56

*Wel.* Why, dost thou not know him? He is a city-magistrate, a justice here, an excellent good lawyer, and a great scholar; but the only mad, merry old fellow in Europe. I show'd him you the other day.   61

*E. Know.* Oh, is that he? I remember him now. Good faith, and he has a very strange presence, methinks; it shows as if he stood out of the rank from other men: I have heard many [65 of his jests i' the University. They say he will commit a man for taking the wall of his horse.

*Wel.* Ay, or wearing his cloak of one shoulder, or serving of God; anything indeed, if it come in the way of his humour.   70

*Cash goes in and out calling.*

*Cash.* Gasper! Martin! Cob! 'Heart, where should they be, trow?

*Bob.* Master Kitely's man, pray thee vouchsafe us the lighting of this match.   74

*Cash.* Fire on your match! No time but now to *vouchsafe?* — Francis! Cob!   *[Exit.]*

*Bob.* Body of me! here 's the remainder of seven pound since yesterday was seven-night. 'T is your right Trinidado: did you never take any, master Stephen?   80

*Step.* No, truly, sir; but I 'll learn to take it now, since you commend it so.

*Bob.* Sir, believe me upon my relation, for what I tell you, the world shall not reprove. I have been in the Indies, where this herb grows, where neither myself, nor a dozen gentlemen [86 more of my knowledge, have received the taste of any other nutriment in the world, for the space of one-and-twenty weeks, but the fume of this simple only; therefore it cannot be but 't is most divine. Further, take it in the na- [91 ture, in the true kind; so, it makes an antidote, that, had you taken the most deadly poisonous plant in all Italy, it should expel it, and clarify you, with as much ease as I speak. And for [95 your green wound, your Balsamum and your St. John's wort are all mere gulleries and trash to it, especially your Trinidado: your Nicotian is good too. I could say what I know of the virtue of it, for the expulsion of rheums, [100 raw humours, crudities, obstructions, with a thousand of this kind; but I profess myself no quacksalver. Only thus much; by Hercules, I do hold it, and will affirm it before any prince in Europe, to be the most sovereign and pre- [105 cious weed that ever the earth tend'red to the use of man.

*E. Know.* This speech would ha' done decently in a tobacco-trader's mouth.

*[Re-enter Cash with Cob]*

*Cash.* At justice Clement's he is, in the [110 middle of Coleman-street.

*Cob.* Oh, oh!

*Bob.* Where 's the match I gave thee, master Kitely's man?   114

*Cash.* Would his match and he, and pipe and all, were at Sancto Domingo! I had forgot it.
                     *[Exit.]*

*Cob.* By God's me, I marle what pleasure or felicity they have in taking this roguish tobacco. It 's good for nothing but to choke a man, and fill him full of smoke and embers. [120 There were four died out of one house last week with taking of it, and two more the

---

25 **sergeant-major:** major    26 **coronel:** colonel    34 **Houndsditch:** a part of London where dealers in old clothes congregated    42. **shifts:** devices, suits of clothes    66 **the:** (not in F 1)   67 **taking . . . horse:** (In Elizabethan London streets the position next the wall was safest and cleanest. It was yielded to the superior in rank and demanded by the braggart.)    79 **Trinidado:** The best tobacco came from Trinidad.    81 **reprove:** disprove    90 **simple:** herb    97 **gulleries:** hoaxes    98 **Nicotian:** named from Nicot, who introduced tobacco into France in 1560

bell went for yesternight; one of them, they
say, will ne'er scape it; he voided a bushel of
soot yesterday, upward and downward. By [125
the stocks, an there were no wiser men than I,
I 'd have it present whipping, man or woman,
that should but deal with a tobacco pipe. Why,
it will stifle them all in the end, as many as use
it; it 's little better than ratsbane or rosaker.

*Bobadill beats him with a cudgel.*
*All.*  Oh, good captain, hold, hold!          131
*Bob.*  You base cullion, you!

*[Re-enter Cash]*
*Cash.*  Sir, here 's your match. — Come, thou
must needs be talking too, thou 'rt well enough
serv'd.                                                    135
*Cob.*  Nay, he will not meddle with his match,
I warrant you. Well, it shall be a dear beating,
an I live.
*Bob.*  Do you prate? do you murmur?          139
*E. Know.*  Nay, good captain, will you re-
gard the humour of a fool? Away, knave.
*Wel.*  Thomas, get him away.
*[Exit Cash with Cob.]*
*Bob.*  A whoreson filthy slave, a dung-worm,
an excrement! Body o' Cæsar, but that I scorn
to let forth so mean a spirit, I 'd ha' stabb'd
him to the earth.                                          146
*Wel.*  Marry, the law forbid, sir!
*Bob.*  By Pharaoh's foot, I would have done it.
*Step.*  Oh, he swears admirably! By Pha-
raoh's foot! Body o' Cæsar! — I shall never [150
do it, sure. Upon mine honour, and by St.
George! — No, I ha' not the right grace.
*Mat.*  Master Stephen, will you any? By this
air, the most divine tobacco that ever I drunk.
*Step.*  None, I thank you, sir. O, this [155
gentleman does it rarely too: but nothing like
the other. By this air! As I am a gentleman!
By ——                        *[Exeunt Bob. and Mat.]*
*Brai.*  Master, glance, glance! master Well-
bred! *Master Stephen is practising to the post.*
*Step.*  As I have somewhat to be saved, I pro-
test ——                                                    161
*Wel.*  You are a fool; it needs no affidavit.
*E. Know.*  Cousin, will you any tobacco?
*Step.*  I, sir! Upon my reputation ——
*E. Know.*  How now, cousin!                   165
*Step.*  I protest, as I am a gentleman, but no
soldier, indeed ——
*Wel.*  No, master Stephen! As I remember,
your name is ent'red in the artillery-garden. [169
*Step.*  Ay, sir, that 's true. Cousin, may I
swear "as I am a soldier" by that?
*E. Know.*  O yes, that you may. It 's all
you have for your money.
*Step.*  Then, as I am a gentleman and a sol-
dier, it is divine tobacco!                              175

*Wel.*  But soft, where 's master Mathew?
Gone?
*Brai.*  No, sir; they went in here.
*Wel.*  O let 's follow them. Master Mathew is
gone to salute his mistress in verse; we shall [180
ha' the happiness to hear some of his poetry
now; he never comes unfurnish'd. — Brainworm!
*Step.*  Brainworm! Where? Is this Brain-
worm?
*E. Know.*  Ay, cousin; no words of it, upon
your gentility.                                           186
*Step.*  Not I, body of me! By this air!
St. George! and the foot of Pharaoh!
*Wel.*  Rare! Your cousin's discourse is
simply drawn out with oaths.                          190
*E. Know.*  'T is larded with 'em; a kind of
French dressing, if you love it.        *[Exeunt.]*

## Act III.  Scene VI

*[Coleman-street.  A Room in Justice Clement's
House.]*

*Kitely, Cob*

*[Kit.]*  Ha! how many are there, sayest thou?
*Cob.*  Marry, sir, your brother, master Well-
bred ——
*Kit.*  Tut, beside him: what strangers are
there, man?
*Cob.*  Strangers? let me see, one, two; mass,
I know not well, there are so many.          5
*Kit.*  How! so many?
*Cob.*  Ay, there 's some five or six of them at
the most.
*Kit. [aside.]*  A swarm, a swarm!
Spite of the devil, how they sting my head
With forked stings, thus wide and large! — But,
Cob,                                                       10
How long hast thou been coming hither, Cob?
*Cob.*  A little while, sir.
*Kit.*  Didst thou come running?
*Cob.*  No, sir.
*Kit. [aside.]*  Nay, then I am familiar with
thy haste.                                                15
Bane to my fortunes! what meant I to marry?
I, that before was rank'd in such content,
My mind at rest too, in so soft a peace,
Being free master of mine own free thoughts, 19
And now become a slave? What! never sigh,
Be of good cheer, man; for thou art a cuckold:
'T is done, 't is done! Nay, when such flowing
store,
Plenty itself, falls in my wife's lap,
The cornucopiæ will be mine, I know. —
But, Cob,                                                 25
What entertainment had they? I am sure
My sister and my wife would bid them wel-
come: ha?

---

¹³⁰ **rosaker:** arsenic poison      ¹³² **cullion:** rascal      ¹⁵⁴ **drunk:** smoked      ²⁴ **cornucopiæ:** horns of
plenty, and cuckold's horns

*Cob.* Like enough, sir; yet I heard not a word of it.

*Kit.* No; —

[*Aside.*] Their lips were seal'd with kisses, and the voice,     30
Drown'd in a flood of joy at their arrival,
Had lost her motion, state, and faculty. —
Cob, which of them was 't that first kiss'd my wife,
My sister, I should say? My wife, alas!
I fear not her; ha! who was it, say'st thou? 35

*Cob.* By my troth, sir, will you have the truth of it?

*Kit.* Oh, ay, good Cob, I pray thee heartily.

*Cob.* Then I am a vagabond, and fitter for Bridewell than your worship's company, if I saw any body to be kiss'd, unless they would [40 have kiss'd the post in the middle of the warehouse; for there I left them all at their tobacco, with a pox!

*Kit.* How! were they not gone in then ere thou cam'st!

*Cob.* O no, sir.      45

*Kit.* Spite of the devil! what do I stay here then?
Cob, follow me.      [*Exit.*]

*Cob.* Nay, soft and fair; I have eggs on the spit; I cannot go yet, sir. Now am I, for some five-and-fifty reasons, hammering, hammer- [50 ing revenge: oh for three or four gallons of vinegar, to sharpen my wits! Revenge, vinegar revenge, vinegar and mustard revenge! Nay, an he had not lien in my house, 't would never have griev'd me; but being my guest, one [55 that I 'll be sworn, my wife has lent him her smock off her back, while his one shirt has been at washing; pawn'd her neckerchers for clean bands for him; sold almost all my platters, to buy him tobacco; and he to turn monster of [60 ingratitude, and strike his lawful host! Well, I hope to raise up an host of fury for 't: here comes justice Clement.

## *Act III. Scene VII*

### [*A Tavern.*]

#### *Clement, Knowell, Formal, Cob*

[*Clem.*] What 's master Kitely gone, Roger?

*Form.* Ay, sir.

*Clem.* 'Heart of me! what made him leave us so abruptly? — How now, sirrah! what make you here? What would you have, ha?     5

*Cob.* An 't please your worship, I am a poor neighbour of your worship's ——

*Clem.* A poor neighbour of mine! Why, speak, poor neighbour.

*Cob.* I dwell, sir, at the sign of the Water- [10 tankard, hard by the Green Lattice: I have paid scot and lot there any time this eighteen years.

*Clem.* To the Green Lattice?

*Cob.* No, sir, to the parish. Marry, I [15 have seldom scap'd scot-free at the Lattice.

*Clem.* O, well; what business has my poor neighbour with me?

*Cob.* An 't like your worship, I am come to crave the peace of your worship.     20

*Clem.* Of me, knave! Peace of me, knave! Did I e'er hurt thee, or threaten thee, or wrong thee, ha?

*Cob.* No, sir; but your worship's warrant for one that has wrong'd me, sir. His arms are [25 at too much liberty; I would fain have them bound to a treaty of peace, an my credit could compass it with your worship.

*Clem.* Thou goest far enough about for 't, I am sure.     30

*Know.* Why, dost thou go in danger of thy life for him, friend?

*Cob.* No, sir; but I go in danger of my death every hour, by his means; an I die within a twelve-month and a day, I may swear by the law of the land that he kill'd me.     36

*Clem.* How, how, knave? swear he kill'd thee, and by the law? What pretence, what colour, hast thou for that?

*Cob.* Marry, an 't please your worship, both black and blue; colour enough, I warrant [41 you. I have it here to show your worship.
               [*Shows his bruises.*]

*Clem.* What is he that gave you this, sirrah?

*Cob.* A gentleman and a soldier, he says he is, o' the city here.     45

*Clem.* A soldier o' the city! What call you him?

*Cob.* Captain Bobadill.

*Clem.* Bobadill! and why did he bob and beat you, sirrah? How began the quarrel betwixt you, ha? Speak truly, knave, I advise you. 50

*Cob.* Marry, indeed, an 't please your worship, only because I spake against their vagrant tobacco, as I came by 'em when they were taking on 't; for nothing else.

*Clem.* Ha! you speak against tobacco? For- mal, his name.     56

*Form.* What 's your name, sirrah?

*Cob.* Oliver, sir, Oliver Cob, sir.

*Clem.* Tell Oliver Cob he shall go to the jail, Formal.      60

---

*Form.* Oliver Cob, my master, justice Clement, says you shall go to the jail.

*Cob.* O, I beseech your worship, for God's sake, dear master justice!                    64

*Clem.* Nay, God's precious! an such drunkards and tankards as you are come to dispute of tobacco once, I have done. Away with him!

*Cob.* O, good master justice! — Sweet old gentleman!                    [*To Knowell.*]

*Know.* Sweet Oliver, would I could do [70 thee any good! — Justice Clement, let me intreat you, sir.

*Clem.* What! a thread-bare rascal, a beggar, a slave that never drunk out of better than piss-pot metal in his life! and he to deprave and [75 abuse the virtue of an herb so generally receiv'd in the courts of princes, the chambers of nobles, the bowers of sweet ladies, the cabins of soldiers! — Roger, away with him! By God's precious —— I say, go to.                    80

*Cob.* Dear master justice, let me be beaten again, I have deserv'd it: but not the prison, I beseech you.

*Know.* Alas, poor Oliver!

*Clem.* Roger, make him a warrant: — he shall not go, I but fear the knave.                    86

*Form.* Do not stink, sweet Oliver, you shall not go; my master will give you a warrant.

*Cob.* O, the Lord maintain his worship, his worthy worship!                    90

*Clem.* Away, dispatch him.

                    [*Exeunt Formal and Cob.*]
— How now, master Knowell, in dumps, in dumps! Come, this becomes not.

*Know.* Sir, would I could not feel my cares.

*Clem.* Your cares are nothing: they are [95 like my cap, soon put on, and as soon put off. What! your son is old enough to govern himself; let him run his course, it 's the only way to make him a staid man. If he were an unthrift, a ruffian, a drunkard, or a licentious liver, [100 then you had reason; you had reason to take care: but, being none of these, mirth 's my witness, an I had twice so many cares as you have, I 'd drown them all in a cup of sack. Come, come, let 's try it: I muse your parcel of a [105 soldier returns not all this while.     *Exeunt.*


## Act IIII. Scene I

### [*A Room in Kitely's House.*]

#### *Downright, Dame Kitely*

[*Dow.*] Well, sister, I tell you true; and you 'll find it so in the end.

*Dame K.* Alas, brother, what would you

have me to do? I cannot help it; you see my brother brings 'em in here; they are his [5 friends.

*Dow.* His friends! his fiends. 'Slud! they do nothing but haunt him up and down like a sort of unlucky sprites, and tempt him to all manner of villainy that can be thought of. Well, by this light, a little thing would make me play [11 the devil with some of 'em: an 't were not more for your husband's sake than anything else, I 'd make the house too hot for the best on 'em; they should say, and swear, hell were broken loose, ere they went hence. But, by God's will, 't is nobody's fault but yours; for an you had [17 done as you might have done, they should have been parboil'd, and bak'd too, every mother's son, ere they should ha' come in, e'er a one of 'em.                    21

*Dame K.* God 's my life! did you ever hear the like? What a strange man is this! Could I keep out all them, think you? I should put myself against half a dozen men, should I? Good faith, you 'd mad the patient'st body in the [26 world, to hear you talk so, without any sense or reason.


## Act IIII. Scene II

### [*The Same.*]

#### *Mrs. Bridget, Master Mathew, Dame Kitely, Downright, Wellbred, Stephen, Ed. Knowell, Bobadill, Brainworm, Cash*

[*Brid.*] Servant, in troth you are too prodigal Of your wit's treasure, thus to pour it forth Upon so mean a subject as my worth.

*Mat.* You say well, mistress, and I mean as well.

*Dow.* Hoy-day, here is stuff!                    5

*Wel.* O, now stand close; pray Heaven, she can get him to read! He should do it of his own natural impudency.

*Brid.* Servant, what is this same, I pray you?

*Mat.* Marry, an elegy, an elegy, an odd toy ——                    10

*Dow.* To mock an ape withal! O, I could sew up his mouth, now.

*Dame K.* Sister, I pray you let 's hear it.

*Dow.* Are you rhyme-given too?

*Mat.* Mistress, I 'll read it, if you please. 15

*Brid.* Pray you do, servant.

*Dow.* O, here 's no foppery! Death! I can endure the stocks better.                    [*Exit.*]

*E. Know.* What ails thy brother? Can he not hold his water at reading of a ballad? [20

*Wel.* O, no; a rhyme to him is worse than

---

74-75 **piss-pot metal:** pewter     86 **fear:** frighten
Sc. I. 7 **'Slud:** God's lid (?)   Sc. II. 1 **Servant:** lover
simpleton with (proverbial)

99 **unthrift:** prodigal     105 **muse:** wonder
6 **close:** aside   11 **To . . . withal:** to dupe a

cheese, or a bag-pipe; but mark; you lose the protestation.

*Mat.* Faith, I did it in an humour; I know not how it is; but please you come near, sir. [25 This gentleman has judgment, he knows how to censure of a —— pray you, sir, you can judge?

*Step.* Not I, sir; upon my reputation, and by the foot of Pharaoh!

*Wel.* O, chide your cousin for swearing. 30

*E. Know.* Not I, so long as he does not forswear himself.

*Bob.* Master Mathew, you abuse the expectation of your dear mistress, and her fair sister. Fie! while you live, avoid this prolixity.

*Mat.* I shall, sir, well; *incipere dulce.* 36

*E. Know.* How, *insipere dulce!* "A sweet thing to be a fool," indeed!

*Wel.* What, do you take *incipere* in that sense? 40

*E. Know.* You do not, you! This was your villainy, to gull him with a mot.

*Wel.* O, the benchers' phrase: *pauca verba, pauca verba!*

*Mat.* [*reads.*] *Rare creature, let me speak without offence,* 45
*Would God my rude words had the influence*
*To rule thy thoughts, as thy fair looks do mine,*
*Then shouldst thou be his prisoner, who is thine.*

*E. Know.* This is in "Hero and Leander." [49

*Wel.* O, ay: peace, we shall have more of this.

*Mat.* *Be not unkind and fair: misshapen stuff*
*Is of behaviour boisterous and rough.*

*Wel.* How like you that, sir?
    *Master Stephen answers with shaking his head.*

*E. Know.* 'Slight, he shakes his head like a bottle, to feel an there be any brain in it. [55

*Mat.* But observe the catastrophe, now:
*And I in duty will exceed all other,*
*As you in beauty do excel Love's mother.*

*E. Know.* Well, I 'll have him free of the [59 wit-brokers, for he utters nothing but stol'n remnants.

*Wel.* O, forgive it him.

*E. Know.* A filching rogue, hang him! — and from the dead! It 's worse than sacrilege. [64
    [*Wellbred, E. Knowell, and Master Stephen come forward.*]

*Wel.* Sister, what ha' you here? Verses? Pray you, let 's see. Who made these verses? They are excellent good.

*Mat.* O, Master Wellbred, 't is your disposition to say so, sir. They were good i' the morning: I made 'em *ex tempore* this morning. 70

*Wel.* How! *ex tempore?*

*Mat.* Ay, would I might be hang'd else; ask Captain Bobadill; he saw me write them, at the —— pox on it! — the Star, yonder. 74

*Brai.* Can he find in his heart to curse the stars so?

*E. Know.* Faith, his are even with him; they ha' curs'd him enough already.

*Step.* Cousin, how do you like this gentleman's verses? 80

*E. Know.* O, admirable! the best that ever I heard, coz.

*Step.* Body o' Cæsar, they are admirable! the best that ever I heard, as I am a soldier! [84

*[Re-enter Downright]*

*Dow.* I am vex'd, I can hold ne'er a bone of me still. 'Heart, I think they mean to build and breed here.

*Wel.* Sister, you have a simple servant here, that crowns your beauty with such encomi- [89 ons and devices; you may see what it is to be the mistress of a wit that can make your perfections so transparent, that every blear eye may look through them, and see him drown'd over head and ears in the deep well of desire. [94 Sister Kitely, I marvel you get you not a servant that can rhyme, and do tricks too.

*Dow.* O monster! impudence itself! tricks!

*Dame K.* Tricks, brother! what tricks?

*Brid.* Nay, speak, I pray you, what tricks?

*Dame K.* Ay, never spare any body here; [100 but say, what tricks?

*Brid.* Passion of my heart, do tricks!

*Wel.* 'Slight, here 's a trick vied and revied! Why, you monkeys, you, what a caterwauling do you keep! Has he not given you rhymes [105 and verses and tricks?

*Dow.* O, the fiend!

*Wel.* Nay, you lamp of virginity, that take it in snuff so, come, and cherish this tame poetical fury in your servant; you 'll be begg'd [110 else shortly for a concealment: go to, reward his muse. You cannot give him less than a shilling in conscience, for the book he had it out of cost him a teston at least. How now, gallants! [114 Master Mathew! Captain! what, all sons of silence? No spirit?

*Dow.* Come, you might practise your ruffian

---

³⁶ **incipere dulce:** it is sweet to begin    ⁴³ **benchers:** loungers on tavern benches    **pauca verba:** few words    ⁴⁹ **Hero and Leander:** by Christopher Marlowe (lines 199–202 slightly misquoted; lines 203–204 and 221–222 are repeated below)    ⁶³ **filching:** thieving    ¹⁰³ **vied and revied:** bet on, in cards, and then covered with a larger bet    ¹⁰⁸⁻¹⁰⁹ **take . . . snuff:** take offense (at it)    ¹¹¹ **concealment:** (When the monasteries were dissolved some of the sequestered properties remained in private hands. Queen Elizabeth appointed commissions to search for such holdings, or "concealments." Her courtiers often begged for these lands.)    ¹¹⁴ **teston:** sixpence

tricks somewhere else, and not here, I wuss;
this is no tavern nor drinking-school, to vent [119
your exploits in.

*Wel.* How now; whose cow has calv'd?

*Dow.* Marry, that has mine, sir. Nay, boy,
never look askance at me for the matter; I 'll
tell you of it, I, sir; you and your compan- [124
ions mend yourselves when I ha' done.

*Wel.* My companions!

*Dow.* Yes, sir, your companions, so I say; I
am not afraid of you, nor them neither; your
hangbyes here. You must have your poets [129
and your potlings, your soldados and foolados to
follow you up and down the city; and here they
must come to domineer and swagger. — Sirrah,
you ballad-singer, and Slops your fellow there,
get you out, get you home; or by this steel, [134
I 'll cut off your ears, and that presently.

*Wel.* 'Slight, stay, let 's see what he dare do;
cut off his ears! cut a whetstone. You are an
ass, do you see? Touch any man here, and by
this hand I 'll run my rapier to the hilts [139
in you.

*Dow.* Yea, that would I fain see, boy.

*They all draw, and they of the house
make out to part them.*

*Dame K.* O Jesu! murder! Thomas! Gasper!

*Brid.* Help, help! Thomas!

*E. Know.* Gentlemen, forbear, I pray you. 144

*Bob.* Well, sirrah, you Holofernes; by my
hand, I will pink your flesh full of holes with
my rapier for this; I will, by this good heaven!
Nay, let him come, let him come, gentlemen;
by the body of St. George, I 'll not kill him. [149

*They offer to fight again, and are parted.*

*Cash.* Hold, hold, good gentlemen.

*Dow.* You whoreson, bragging coystril!

## Act IIII.  Scene III

[*The Same.*]

*To them, Kitely*

*Kit.* Why, how now! what 's the matter,
what 's the stir here?
Whence springs the quarrel? Thomas! where
is he?
Put up your weapons, and put off this rage.
My wife and sister, they are cause of this.
What, Thomas! where is this knave?        5

*Cash.* Here, sir.

*Wel.* Come, let 's go; this is one of my
brother's ancient humours, this.

*Step.* I am glad nobody was hurt by his
ancient humour.        10

[*Exeunt Wellbred, Stephen, E. Knowell, Bobadill, and Brainworm.*]

*Kit.* Why, how now, brother, who enforc'd
this brawl?

*Dow.* A sort of lewd rake-hells, that care
neither for God nor the devil. And they must
come here to read ballads, and roguery, and [14
trash! I 'll mar the knot of 'em ere I sleep, perhaps; especially Bob there, he that 's all manner of shapes: and Songs and Sonnets, his
fellow.

*Brid.* Brother, indeed you are too violent,
Too sudden in your humour: and you know 20
My brother Wellbred's temper will not bear
Any reproof, chiefly in such a presence,
Where every slight disgrace he should re-
ceive
Might wound him in opinion and respect.    24

*Dow.* Respect! what talk you of respect
'mong such as ha' nor spark of manhood nor
good manners? 'Sdeins, I am asham'd to hear
you! respect!                              [*Exit.*]

*Brid.* Yes, there was one a civil gentleman,
And very worthily demean'd himself.        30

*Kit.* O, that was some love of yours, sister.

*Brid.* A love of mine! I would it were no
worse, brother;
You'd pay my portion sooner than you think
for.

*Dame K.* Indeed he seem'd to be a gentleman
of an exceeding fair disposition, and of very [35
excellent good parts.

[*Exeunt Dame Kitely and Bridget.*]

*Kit.* Her love, by heaven! my wife's minion.
*Fair disposition! excellent good parts!*
Death! these phrases are intolerable.
Good parts! how should she know his parts? 40
His parts! Well, well, well, well, well, well;
It is too plain, too clear: Thomas, come
hither.
What, are they gone?

*Cash.*                        Ay, sir, they went in.
My mistress and your sister ——

*Kit.* Are any of the gallants within?       45

*Cash.* No, sir, they are all gone.

*Kit.*                        Art thou sure of it?

*Cash.* I can assure you, sir.

*Kit.* What gentleman was that they prais'd
so, Thomas?

*Cash.* One, they call him Master Knowell, [50
a handsome young gentleman, sir.

*Kit.* Ay, I thought so; my mind gave me as
much.
I 'll die, but they have hid him i' the house
Somewhere; I 'll go and search; go with me,
Thomas:                                    54
Be true to me, and thou shalt find me a master.
                                        [*Exeunt.*]

---

¹¹⁹ **whose . . . calv'd:** What's the matter?    ¹³⁰ **potlings:** topers    ¹³³ **Slops:** stuffed breeches.
**Bobadill;** cf. II, ii, 28–30    ¹⁵¹ **coystril:** groom, knave    ²⁴ **opinion:** reputation    ⁵³ **but:** if not

## Act IIII. Scene IIII

*[The Lane before Cob's House.]*

*Cob, Tib*

*[Cob knocks at the door.]* What, Tib! Tib, I say!

*Tib. [within.]* How now, what cuckold is that knocks so hard?

*[Enter Tib]*

O, husband! is 't you? What 's the news?　5

*Cob.* Nay, you have stunn'd me, i' faith; you ha' giv'n me a knock o' the forehead will stick by me. Cuckold! 'Slid, cuckold!

*Tib.* Away, you fool! did I know it was you that knock'd? Come, come, you may call me [10 as bad when you list.

*Cob.* May I? Tib, you are a whore.

*Tib.* You lie in your throat, husband.

*Cob.* How, the lie! and in my throat too! do you long to be stabb'd, ha?　15

*Tib.* Why, you are no soldier, I hope.

*Cob.* O, must you be stabb'd by a soldier? Mass, that 's true! When was Bobadill here, your captain? that rogue, that foist, that fencing Burgullion? I 'll tickle him, i' faith.　20

*Tib.* Why, what 's the matter, trow?

*Cob.* O, he has basted me rarely, sumptuously! but I have it here in black and white *[pulls out the warrant]*, for his black and blue shall pay him. O, the justice, the honestest old brave [25 Trojan in London; I do honour the very flea of his dog. A plague on him, though, he put me once in a villainous filthy fear; marry, it vanish'd away like the smoke of tobacco; but I was smok'd soundly first. I thank the devil, [30 and his good angel, my guest. Well, wife, or Tib, which you will, get you in, and lock the door; I charge you let nobody in to you, wife; nobody in to you; those are my words: not Captain Bob himself, nor the fiend in his [35 likeness. You are a woman, you have flesh and blood enough in you to be tempted; therefore keep the door shut upon all comers.

*Tib.* I warrant you, there shall nobody enter here without my consent.　40

*Cob.* Nor with your consent, sweet Tib; and so I leave you.

*Tib.* It 's more than you know, whether you leave me so.

*Cob.* How?　45

*Tib.* Why, sweet.

*Cob.* Tut, sweet or sour, thou art a flower. Keep close thy door, I ask no more. *[Exeunt.]*

## Act IIII. Scene V

*[A Room in the Windmill Tavern.]*

*Ed. Knowell, Wellbred, Stephen, Brainworm*

*[E. Know.]* Well, Brainworm, perform this business happily, and thou makest a purchase of my love for ever.

*Wel.* I' faith, now let thy spirits use their best faculties: but, at any hand, remember [5 the message to my brother; for there 's no other means to start him.

*Brai.* I warrant you, sir; fear nothing: I have a nimble soul has wak'd all forces of my phant'sie by this time, and put 'em in true [10 motion. What you have possess'd me withal, I 'll discharge it amply, sir; make it no question.　*[Exit.]*

*Wel.* Forth, and prosper, Brainworm. Faith, Ned, how dost thou approve of my abilities in this device?　16

*E. Know.* Troth, well, howsoever; but it will come excellent if it take.

*Wel.* Take, man! why it cannot choose but take, if the circumstances miscarry not: [20 but, tell me ingenuously, dost thou affect my sister Bridget as thou pretend'st?

*E. Know.* Friend, am I worth belief?

*Wel.* Come, do not protest. In faith, she is a maid of good ornament, and much mod- [25 esty; and, except I conceiv'd very worthily of her, thou should'st not have her.

*E. Know.* Nay, that, I am afraid, will be a question yet, whether I shall have her, or no.

*Wel.* 'Slid, thou shalt have her; by this light thou shalt.　31

*E. Know.* Nay, do not swear.

*Wel.* By this hand thou shalt have her; I 'll go fetch her presently. 'Point but where to meet, and as I am an honest man I 'll bring her.

*E. Know.* Hold, hold, be temperate.　36

*Wel.* Why, by —— what shall I swear by? Thou shalt have her, as I am ——

*E. Know.* Pray thee, be at peace, I am satisfied; and do believe thou wilt omit no [40 offered occasion to make my desires complete.

*Wel.* Thou shalt see, and know, I will not.　*[Exeunt.]*

## Act IIII. Scene VI

*[The Old Jewry. A Street.]*

*Formal, Knowell, [followed by] Brainworm*

*[Form.]* Was your man a soldier, sir?

*Know.*　Ay, a knave;

I took him begging o' the way, this morning,
As I came over Moorfields.

*[Enter Brainworm, disguised as before]*

O, here he is! — you 've made fair speed, believe
me.
Where, i' the name of sloth, could you be thus?  5
  *Brai.*  Marry, peace be my comfort, where I
thought I should have had little comfort of
your worship's service.
  *Know.*  How so?                                    9
  *Brai.*  O, sir, your coming to the city, your
entertainment of me, and your sending me to
watch —— indeed all the circumstances either
of your charge, or my employment, are as open
to your son, as to yourself.
  *Know.*  How should that be, unless that
    villain, Brainworm,                               15
Have told him of the letter, and discover'd
All that I strictly charg'd him to conceal?
'T is so.
  *Brai.*  I am partly o' the faith, 't is so,
    indeed.
  *Know.*  But, how should he know thee to be
my man?                                               20
  *Brai.*  Nay, sir, I cannot tell; unless it be by
the black art.  Is not your son a scholar, sir?
  *Know.*  Yes, but I hope his soul is not allied
Unto such hellish practice: if it were,
I had just cause to weep my part in him,              25
And curse the time of his creation.
But, where didst thou find them, Fitz-Sword?
  *Brai.*  You should rather ask where they
found me, sir; for I 'll be sworn, I was going
along in the street, thinking nothing, when, [30
of a sudden, a voice calls, "Master Knowell's
man!"  Another cries, "Soldier!" and thus
half a dozen of 'em, till they had call'd me
within a house, where I no sooner came, but
they seem'd men, and out flew all their [35
rapiers at my bosom, with some three or four
score oaths to accompany 'em; and all to tell
me, I was but a dead man, if I did not confess
where you were, and how I was employed, and
about what; which when they could not get [40
out of me (as, I protest, they must ha' dissected,
and made an anatomy o' me first, and so I
told 'em), they lock'd me up into a room i' the
top of a high house, whence by great miracle
(having a light heart) I slid down by a [45
bottom of packthread into the street, and so
scap'd.  But, sir, thus much I can assure you,
for I heard it while I was lock'd up, there were
a great many rich merchants and brave citizens'
wives with 'em at a feast; and your son, [50
master Edward, withdrew with one of 'em, and
has 'pointed to meet her anon at one Cob's

house, a water-bearer that dwells by the Wall.
Now, there your worship shall be sure to take
him, for there he preys, and fail he will not. 55
  *Know.*  Nor will I fail to break his match, I
    doubt not.
Go thou along with justice Clement's man,
And stay there for me.  At one Cob's house,
    say'st thou?
  *Brai.*  Ay, sir, there you shall have him. [59
*[Exit Knowell.]* Yes — invisible!  Much wench,
or much son!  'Slight, when he has stay'd there
three or four hours, travailing with the expectation of wonders, and at length be deliver'd of air!  O the sport that I should then
take to look on him, if I durst!  But now, I [65
mean to appear no more afore him in this
shape: I have another trick to act yet.  O
that I were so happy as to light on a nupson
now of this justice's novice! — Sir, I make you
stay somewhat long.                                   70
  *Form.*  Not a whit, sir.  Pray you what do
you mean, sir?
  *Brai.*  I was putting up some papers.
  *Form.*  You ha' been lately in the wars, sir,
it seems.                                             75
  *Brai.*  Marry have I, sir, to my loss, and expense of all, almost.
  *Form.*  Troth, sir, I would be glad to bestow a pottle of wine o' you, if it please you to
accept it —                                          80
  *Brai.*  O, sir ——
  *Form.*  But to hear the manner of your
services, and your devices in the wars.  They
say they be very strange, and not like those a
man reads in the Roman histories, or sees at [85
Mile-end.
  *Brai.*  No, I assure you, sir; why at any time
when it please you, I shall be ready to discourse to you all I know; *[aside.]* — and more
too, somewhat.                                        90
  *Form.*  No better time than now, sir; we 'll
go to the Windmill; there we shall have a cup
of neat grist, we call it.  I pray you, sir, let me
request you to the Windmill.
  *Brai.*  I 'll follow you, sir; *[aside.]* — and
make grist o' you, if I have good luck.               96
                                          *[Exeunt.]*

## Act IIII.  Scene VII

*[Moorfields.]*

*Mathew, Ed. Knowell, Bobadill, Stephen,
    [later] Downright*

*[Mat.]*  Sir, did your eyes ever taste the like
clown of him where we were to-day, master
Wellbred's half-brother?  I think the whole earth
cannot show his parallel, by this daylight.

---

¹⁶ **discover'd:** made known   ⁴² **anatomy:** skeleton   ⁴⁶ **bottom:** skein   ⁴⁹ **brave:** richly dressed
⁶⁸ **nupson:** simpleton   ⁷⁹ **pottle:** two quarts   ⁸⁶ **Mile-end:** training ground for militia

*E. Know.* We were now speaking of him: [5 captain Bobadill tells me he is fall'n foul o' you too.

*Mat.* O, ay, sir, he threat'ned me with the bastinado.

*Bob.* Ay, but I think, I taught you pre- [10 vention this morning, for that. You shall kill him beyond question, if you be so generously minded.

*Mat.* Indeed, it is a most excellent trick.

*He practises at a post.*

*Bob.* O, you do not give spirit enough to [15 your motion; you are too tardy, too heavy! O, it must be done like lightning, hay!

*Mat.* Rare, captain!

*Bob.* Tut! 't is nothing, an 't be not done in a —— punto.     20

*E. Know.* Captain, did you ever prove your-self upon any of our masters of defence here?

*Mat.* O good sir! yes, I hope he has.

*Bob.* I will tell you, sir. Upon my first com-ing to the city, after my long travel for knowl- [25 edge in that mystery only, there came three or four of 'em to me, at a gentleman's house, where it was my chance to be resident at that time, to intreat my presence at their schools: and withal so much importun'd me that, [30 I protest to you as I am a gentleman, I was asham'd of their rude demeanour out of all measure. Well, I told 'em that to come to a public school, they should pardon me, it was opposite, in diameter, to my humour; but if [35 so be they would give their attendance at my lodging, I protested to do them what right or favour I could, as I was a gentleman, and so forth.

*E. Know.* So, sir! then you tried their skill?

*Bob.* Alas, soon tried: you shall hear, sir. [41 Within two or three days after, they came; and, by honesty, fair sir, believe me, I grac'd them exceedingly, show'd them some two or three tricks of prevention have purchas'd [45 'em since a credit to admiration. They cannot deny this; and yet now they hate me; and why? Because I am excellent; and for no other vile reason on the earth.

*E. Know.* This is strange and barbarous, [50 as ever I heard.

*Bob.* Nay, for a more instance of their pre-posterous natures, but note, sir. They have assaulted me some three, four, five, six of them together, as I have walk'd alone in divers skirts i' the town, as Turnbull, Whitechapel, [56 Shoreditch, which were then my quarters; and since, upon the Exchange, at my lodging, and

at my ordinary: where I have driven them afore me the whole length of a street, in the [60 open view of all our gallants, pitying to hurt them, believe me. Yet all this lenity will not o'ercome their spleen; they will be doing with the pismire, raising a hill a man may spurn abroad with his foot at pleasure. By myself, [65 I could have slain them all, but I delight not in murder. I am loath to bear any other than this bastinado for 'em: yet I hold it good polity not to go disarm'd, for though I be skilful, I may be oppress'd with multitudes.     70

*E. Know.* Ay, believe me, may you, sir: and in my conceit, our whole nation should sustain the loss by it, if it were so.

*Bob.* Alas, no? what 's a peculiar man to a nation? Not seen.     75

*E. Know.* O, but your skill, sir.

*Bob.* Indeed, that might be some loss; but who respects it? I will tell you, sir, by the way of private, and under seal; I am a gentleman, and live here obscure, and to myself; but [80 were I known to her majesty and the lords, — observe me, — I would undertake, upon this poor head and life, for the public benefit of the state, not only to spare the entire lives of her subjects in general; but to save the one half, [85 nay, three parts of her yearly charge in holding war, and against what enemy soever. And how would I do it, think you?

*E. Know.* Nay, I know not, nor can I con-ceive.     90

*Bob.* Why thus, sir. I would select nineteen more, to myself, throughout the land; gentle-men they should be of good spirit, strong and able constitution; I would choose them by an instinct, a character that I have: and I would teach these nineteen the special rules, as your [96 *punto,* your *reverso,* your *stoccata,* your *imbroc-cata,* your *passada,* your *montanto;* till they could all play very near, or altogether, as well as myself. This done, say the enemy were forty thousand strong, we twenty would come [101 into the field the tenth of March, or thereabouts; and we would challenge twenty of the enemy; they could not in their honour refuse us: well, we would kill them; challenge twenty more, [105 kill them; twenty more, kill them; twenty more, kill them too; and thus would we kill every man his twenty a day, that 's twenty score; twenty score, that 's two hundreth; two hundreth a day, five days a thousand: forty thousand; forty times five, five times forty, [111 two hundred days kills them all up by compu-tation. And this will I venture my poor gentle-

---

¹⁷ **hay:** an exclamation on hitting an opponent in fencing    ²⁰ **punto:** instant    ²⁵ **travel:** *travel,* and also *travail*    ³⁶ **be:** (not in F 1 or Q)    ⁵⁵ **skirts:** outskirts    ⁵⁶⁻⁵⁷ **Turnbull . . . Shoreditch:** all disreputable quarters of London    ⁶⁴ **pismire:** ant    ⁷⁴ **peculiar:** individual    ⁹⁷⁻⁹⁸ **punto . . . mon-tanto:** technical terms in fencing

man-like carcase to perform, provided there be no treason practis'd upon us, by fair and [115 discreet manhood; that is, civilly by the sword.

*E. Know.* Why, are you so sure of your hand, captain, at all times?

*Bob.* Tut! never miss thrust, upon my reputation with you.    120

*E. Know.* I would not stand in Downright's state then, an you meet him, for the wealth of any one street in London.

*Bob.* Why, sir, you mistake me: if he were here now, by this welkin, I would not draw my weapon on him. Let this gentleman do his [126 mind; but I will bastinado him, by the bright sun, wherever I meet him.

*Mat.* Faith, and I 'll have a fling at him, at my distance.    130

*E. Know.* 'God's so, look where he is! yonder he goes.

*Downright walks over the stage.*

*Dow.* What peevish luck have I, I cannot meet with these bragging rascals?

*Bob.* It 's not he, is it?    135

*E. Know.* Yes, faith, it is he.

*Mat.* I 'll be hang'd, then, if that were he.

*E. Know.* Sir, keep your hanging good for some greater matter, for I assure you that was he.    140

*Step.* Upon my reputation, it was he.

*Bob.* Had I thought it had been he, he must not have gone so: but I can hardly be induc'd to believe it was he yet.

*E. Know.* That I think, sir.    145

*[Re-enter Downright]*

But see, he is come again.

*Dow.* O, Pharaoh's foot, have I found you? Come, draw, to your tools; draw, gipsy, or I 'll thresh you.

*Bob.* Gentleman of valour, I do believe in thee; hear me ——    151

*Dow.* Draw your weapon then.

*Bob.* Tall man, I never thought on it till now —— body of me, I had a warrant of the peace served on me, even now as I came along, by a water-bearer; this gentleman saw it, [156 master Mathew.

*Dow.* 'Sdeath! you will not draw then?

*He beats him, and disarms him.*
*Mathew runs away.*

*Bob.* Hold, hold! under thy favour forbear!

*Dow.* Prate again, as you like this, you [160 whoreson foist you! You 'll "control the point," you! Your consort is gone; had he stay'd, he had shar'd with you, sir.    *[Exit.]*

*Bob.* Well, gentlemen, bear witness, I was bound to the peace, by this good day.    165

*E. Know.* No, faith, it 's an ill day, captain,

never reckon it other: but, say you were bound to the peace, the law allows you to defend yourself: that 'll prove but a poor excuse.

*Bob.* I cannot tell, sir; I desire good con- [170 struction in fair sort. I never sustain'd the like disgrace, by heaven! Sure I was struck with a planet thence, for I had no power to touch my weapon.

*E. Know.* Ay, like enough; I have heard of many that have been beaten under a planet: [176 go, get you to a surgeon. 'Slid! an these be your tricks, your *passadas*, and your *montan-tos*, I 'll none of them. *[Exit Bobadill.]* O, manners! that this age should bring forth [180 such creatures! that nature should be at leisure to make 'em! Come, coz.

*Step.* Mass, I 'll ha' this cloak.

*E. Know.* God's will, 't is Downright's.

*Step.* Nay, it 's mine now, another might [185 have ta'en up as well as I: I 'll wear it, so I will.

*E. Know.* How an he see it? He 'll challenge it, assure yourself.

*Step.* Ay, but he shall not ha' it; I 'll say I bought it.    190

*E. Know.* Take heed you buy it not too dear, coz.    *[Exeunt.]*

## *Act IIII. Scene VIII*

*[A Room in Kitely's House.]*

*Kitely, Wellbred, Dame Kitely, Bridget,*
*[later] Brainworm, Cash*

*[Kit.]* Now, trust me, brother, you were much to blame,
T' incense his anger, and disturb the peace
Of my poor house, where there are sentinels
That every minute watch to give alarms
Of civil war, without adjection    5
Of your assistance or occasion.

*Wel.* No harm done, brother, I warrant you, since there is no harm done. Anger costs a man nothing; and a tall man is never his own man till he be angry. To keep his valour in ob- [10 scurity, is to keep himself as it were in a cloak-bag. What 's a musician, unless he play? What 's a tall man unless he fight? For, indeed, all this my wise brother stands upon absolutely; and that made me fall in with him so resolutely. [15

*Dame K.* Ay, but what harm might have come of it, brother!

*Wel.* Might, sister? So might the good warm clothes your husband wears be poison'd, for anything he knows: or the wholesome wine [20 he drunk, even now, at the table.

*Kit. [aside.]* Now, God forbid! O me! now I remember
My wife drunk to me last, and chang'd the cup,
And bade me wear this cursed suit to-day.

---

¹⁴⁸ tools: weapons    ¹⁵³ **Tall**: bold    ⁵ **adjection**: addition

See, if Heaven suffer murder undiscover'd! —
I feel me ill; give me some mithridate,          26
Some mithridate and oil, good sister, fetch me;
O, I am sick at heart, I burn, I burn.
If you will save my life, go fetch it me.
*Wel.*  O strange humour! my very breath [30
has poison'd him.
*Brid.*  Good brother, be content, what do
you mean?
The strength of these extreme conceits will kill
you.
*Dame K.*  Beshrew your heart-blood, brother
Wellbred, now,
For putting such a toy into his head!          35
*Wel.*  Is a fit simile a toy? Will he be poison'd
with a simile?  Brother Kitely, what a strange
and idle imagination is this!  For shame, be
wiser.  O' my soul, there's no such matter. 39
*Kit.*  Am I not sick?  How?  am I then not
poison'd?
Am I not poison'd?  How am I then so sick?
*Dame K.*  If you be sick, your own thoughts
make you sick.
*Wel.*  His jealousy is the poison he has taken.
          [*Brainworm*] *comes, disguised like*
                    *Justice Clement's man.*
*Brai.*  Master Kitely, my master, justice [44
Clement, salutes you; and desires to speak with
you with all possible speed.
*Kit.*  No time but now, when I think I am
sick, very sick!  Well, I will wait upon his worship.  Thomas!  Cob!  I must seek them out,
and set 'em sentinels till I return.  Thomas! [50
Cob!  Thomas!          [*Exit.*]
*Wel.*  This is perfectly rare, Brainworm;
[*takes him aside.*] but how got'st thou this apparel of the justice's man?          54
*Brai.*  Marry, sir, my proper fine pen-man
would needs bestow the grist o' me, at the
Windmill, to hear some martial discourse;
where so I marshall'd him, that I made him
drunk with admiration: and, because too much
heat was the cause of his distemper, I stripp'd
him stark naked as he lay along asleep, and [61
borrowed his suit to deliver this counterfeit
message in, leaving a rusty armour, and an old
brown bill to watch him till my return; which
shall be, when I ha' pawn'd his apparel, and [65
spent the better part o' the money, perhaps.
*Wel.*  Well, thou art a successful merry knave,
Brainworm: his absence will be a good subject
for more mirth.  I pray thee return to thy young
master, and will him to meet me and my [70
sister Bridget at the Tower instantly; for here,
tell him, the house is so stor'd with jealousy,
there is no room for love to stand upright in.
We must get our fortunes committed to some

larger prison, say; and than the Tower, I [75
know no better air, nor where the liberty of the
house may do us more present service.  Away!
          [*Exit Brainworm.*]

[*Re-enter Kitely, talking aside to Cash*]

*Kit.*  Come hither, Thomas.  Now my secret's
ripe,
And thou shalt have it: lay to both thine ears.
Hark what I say to thee.  I must go forth,
Thomas;          80
Be careful of thy promise, keep good watch,
Note every gallant, and observe him well,
That enters in my absence to thy mistress:
If she would show him rooms, the jest is stale,
Follow 'em, Thomas, or else hang on him,  85
And let him not go after; mark their looks;
Note if she offer but to see his band,
Or any other amorous toy about him;
But praise his leg, or foot: or if she say
The day is hot, and bid him feel her hand,  90
How hot it is; O that's a monstrous thing!
Note me all this, good Thomas, mark their
sighs,
And if they do but whisper, break 'em off:
I'll bear thee out in it.  Wilt thou do this?
Wilt thou be true, my Thomas?
*Cash.*          As truth's self, sir.  95
*Kit.*  Why, I believe thee.  Where is Cob,
now?  Cob!          [*Exit.*]
*Dame K.*  He's ever calling for Cob: I won-
der how he employs Cob so.
*Wel.*  Indeed, sister, to ask how he employs
Cob, is a necessary question for you that are [100
his wife, and a thing not very easy for you to be
satisfied in; but this I'll assure you, Cob's wife
is an excellent bawd, sister, and oftentimes your
husband haunts her house; marry, to what end?
I cannot altogether accuse him; imagine [105
you what you think convenient: but I have
known fair hides have foul hearts ere now, sister.
*Dame K.*  Never said you truer than that,
brother, so much I can tell you for your learning.
Thomas, fetch your cloak and go with me. [110
          [*Exit Cash.*]
I'll after him presently: I would to fortune I
could take him there, i' faith.  I'd return him
his own, I warrant him!          [*Exit.*]
*Wel.*  So, let 'em go;  this may make sport
anon.  Now, my fair sister-in-law, that you [115
knew but how happy a thing it were to be fair
and beautiful.
*Brid.*  That touches not me, brother.
*Wel.*  That's true; that's even the fault of
it; for indeed, beauty stands a woman in no [120
stead, unless it procure her touching. — But,
sister, whether it touch you or no, it touches

---

⁲⁶ **mithridate:** antidote     ³³ **conceits:** fancies     ³⁵ **toy:** foolish idea     ⁶⁴ **brown bill:** pike
⁷¹ **Tower:** (They could be married at once in the Tower, which was extra-parochial.)

your beauties; and I am sure they will abide
the touch; an they do not, a plague of all ce-
ruse, say I! and it touches me too in part, [125
though not in the —— Well, there 's a dear and
respected friend of mine, sister, stands very
strongly and worthily affected toward you, and
hath vow'd to inflame whole bonfires of zeal at
his heart, in honour of your perfections.  I [130
have already engag'd my promise to bring you
where you shall hear him confirm much more.
Ned Knowell is the man, sister·  there 's no exception against the party.  You are ripe for a
husband; and a minute's loss to such an [135
occasion is a great trespass in a wise beauty.
What say you, sister?  On my soul he loves
you; will you give him the meeting?

*Brid.*  Faith, I had very little confidence in
mine own constancy, brother, if I durst not [140
meet a man: but this motion of yours savours of
an old knight-adventurer's servant a little too
much, methinks.

*Wel.*  What 's that, sister?

*Brid.*  Marry, of the squire.                      145

*Wel.*  No matter if it did, I would be such an
one for my friend.  But see, who is return'd
to hinder us!

*[Re-enter Kitely]*

*Kit.*  What villainy is this?  Call'd out on a
false message!
This was some plot; I was not sent for. —
     Bridget,                                                       150
Where 's your sister?

*Brid.*                    I think she be gone forth, sir.

*Kit.*  How! is my wife gone forth?  Whither,
for God's sake?

*Brid.*  She 's gone abroad with Thomas.

*Kit.*  Abroad with Thomas! oh, that villain
     dors me:
He hath discover'd all unto my wife.              155
Beast that I was, to trust him!  Whither, I
     pray you,
Went she?

*Brid.*            I know not, sir.

*Wel.*                      I 'll tell you, brother,
Whither I suspect she 's gone.

*Kit.*                                Whither, good brother?

*Wel.*  To Cob's house, I believe: but, keep
my counsel.

*Kit.*  I will, I will: to Cob's house!  Doth
she haunt Cob's?                                           160
She 's gone a' purpose now to cuckold me
With that lewd rascal, who, to win her favour,
Hath told her all.                              *[Exit.]*

*Wel.*              Come, he 's once more gone.
Sister, let 's lose no time; th' affair is worth it.
                                                   *[Exeunt.]*

## Act IIII.  Scene IX

*[A Street.]*

*Mathew, Bobadill, Brainworm*

*[Mat.]*  I wonder, captain, what they will
say of my going away, ha?

*Bob.*  Why, what should they say, but as of a
discreet gentleman; quick, wary, respectful of
nature's fair lineaments? and that 's all.      5

*Mat.*  Why so! but what can they say of
your beating?

*Bob.*  A rude part, a touch with soft wood, a
kind of gross battery us'd, laid on strongly,
borne most patiently; and that 's all.          10

*Mat.*  Ay, but would any man have offered
it in Venice, as you say?

*Bob.*  Tut!  I assure you, no; you shall have
there your *nobilis*, your *gentilezza*, come in
bravely upon your reverse, stand you close, [15
stand you firm, stand you fair, save your *retricato* with his left leg, come to the *assalto* with the
right, thrust with brave steel, defy your base
wood!  But wherefore do I awake this remembrance?  I was fascinated, by Jupiter, fascinated;
but I will be unwitch'd and reveng'd by law. 21

*Mat.*  Do you hear?  Is 't not best to get a
warrant, and have him arrested and brought
before justice Clement?

*Bob.*  It were not amiss?  Would we had it! 25

*[Enter Brainworm disguised as Formal]*

*Mat.*  Why, here comes his man; let 's speak
to him.

*Bob.*  Agreed, do you speak.

*Mat.*  Save you, sir.

*Brai.*  With all my heart, sir.                    30

*Mat.*  Sir, there is one Downright hath abus'd
this gentleman and myself, and we determine
to make our amends by law.  Now, if you would
do us the favour to procure a warrant to [34
bring him afore your master, you shall be well
considered, I assure you, sir.

*Brai.*  Sir, you know my service is my living;
such favours as these gotten of my master is
his only preferment, and therefore you must [39
consider me as I may make benefit of my place.

*Mat.*  How is that, sir?

*Brai.*  Faith, sir, the thing is extraordinary,
and the gentleman may be of great accompt;
yet, be he what he will, if you will lay me
down a brace of angels in my hand you shall [45
have it, otherwise not.

*Mat.*  How shall we do, captain?  He asks a
brace of angels; you have no money?

---

<sup></sup>124–125 **ceruse:** white lead, a cosmetic      145 **squire:** pandar      154 **dors:** fools      14 **nobilis, genti-**
**lezza:** gentry      16–17 **retricato:** retreat (?)      17 **assalto:** attack      20 **fascinated:** bewitched      39 **his**
**only preferment:** the only salary he gives me      40 **as:** in order that      44 **be he:** ("he' F 1 and Q)

*Bob.* Not a cross, by fortune.

*Mat.* Nor I, as I am a gentleman, but two- [50 pence left of my two shillings in the morning for wine and radish: let 's find him some pawn.

*Bob.* Pawn! we have none to the value of his demand.

*Mat.* O, yes; I 'll pawn this jewel in my [55 ear, and you may pawn your silk stockings, and pull up your boots. They will ne'er be miss'd. It must be done now.

*Bob.* Well, an there be no remedy, I 'll step aside and pull 'em off. [*Withdraws.*] 60

*Mat.* Do you hear, sir? We have no store of money at this time, but you shall have good pawns; look you, sir, this jewel, and that gentleman's silk stockings; because we would have it dispatch'd ere we went to our chambers. 65

*Brai.* I am content, sir; I will get you the warrant presently. What 's his name, say you? Downright?

*Mat.* Ay, ay, George Downright.

*Brai.* What manner of man is he? 70

*Mat.* A tall big man, sir; he goes in a cloak most commonly of silk-russet, laid about with russet lace.

*Brai.* 'T is very good, sir.

*Mat.* Here, sir, here 's my jewel. 75

*Bob.* [*returning.*] And here are stockings.

*Brai.* Well, gentlemen, I 'll procure you this warrant presently; but who will you have to serve it?

*Mat.* That 's true, captain: that must [80 be consider'd.

*Bob.* Body o' me, I know not; 't is service of danger.

*Brai.* Why, you were best get one o' the varlets o' the city, a sergeant: I 'll appoint you one, if you please. 86

*Mat.* Will you, sir? Why, we can wish no better.

*Bob.* We 'll leave it to you, sir.

[*Exeunt Bob. and Mat.*]

*Brai.* This is rare! Now will I go pawn [90 this cloak of the justice's man's at the broker's for a varlet's suit, and be the varlet myself; and get either more pawns, or more money of Downright, for the arrest. [*Exit.*]

## Act IIII.   Scene X

[*The Lane before Cob's House.*]

*Knowell, [followed successively by] Tib, Cash, Dame Kitely, Kitely, Cob*

[*Know.*] Oh, here it is; I am glad I have found it now;
Ho! who is within here?

*Tib.* [*within.*] I am within, sir. What 's your pleasure?

*Know.* To know who is within besides yourself.

*Tib.* Why, sir, you are no constable, I hope?

*Know.* O, fear you the constable? Then I doubt not 6
You have some guests within deserve that fear.
I 'll fetch him straight.

[*Enter Tib*]

*Tib.* O' God's name, sir!

*Know.* Go to; come tell me, is not young Knowell here?

*Tib.* Young Knowell! I know none such, sir, o' mine honesty. 10

*Know.* Your honesty, dame! It flies too lightly from you.
There is no way but fetch the constable.

*Tib.* The constable! the man is mad, I think.

[*Exit, and claps to the door.*]

[*Enter Dame Kitely and Cash*]

*Cash.* Ho! who keeps house here?

*Know.* O, this is the female copesmate of my son: 15
Now shall I meet him straight.

*Dame K.* Knock, Thomas, hard.

*Cash.* Ho, goodwife!

[*Re-enter Tib*]

*Tib.* Why, what 's the matter with you?

*Dame K.* Why, woman, grieves it you to ope your door?
Belike you get something to keep it shut.

*Tib.* What mean these questions, pray ye?

*Dame K.* So strange you make it! Is not my husband here? 21

*Know.* Her husband!

*Dame K.* My tried husband, master Kitely?

*Tib.* I hope he needs not to be tried here.

*Dame K.* No, dame, he does it not for need, but pleasure. 24

*Tib.* Neither for need nor pleasure is he here.

*Know.* This is but a device to balk me withal:

[*Enter Kitely, muffled in his cloak*]

Soft, who is this? 'T is not my son disguis'd?

*Dame K.* (*She spies her husband come, and runs to him.*) O, sir, have I forestall'd your honest market?
Found your close walks? You stand amaz'd now, do you? 29
I' faith, I am glad I have smok'd you yet at last.
What is your jewel, trow? In, come, let 's see her;
Fetch forth your huswife, dame; if she be fairer,

In any honest judgment, than myself,
I 'll be content with it: but she is change,
She feeds you fat, she soothes your appetite, 35
And you are well! Your wife, an honest woman,
Is meat twice sod to you, sir! O, you treachour!
   *Know.* She cannot counterfeit thus palpa-
   bly.
   *Kit.* Out on thy more than strumpet's im-
   pudence!
Steal'st thou thus to thy haunts? and have I
   taken                                            40
Thy bawd and thee, and thy companion,
              *Pointing to old Knowell.*
This hoary-headed lecher, this old goat,
Close at your villainy, and would'st thou 'scuse
   it
With this stale harlot's jest, accusing me?
O, old incontinent, dost thou     *To him.*
   not shame,                                       45
When all thy powers in chastity is spent,
To have a mind so hot, and to entice,
And feed th' enticements of a lustful woman?
   *Dame K.* Out, I defy thee, I, dissembling
   wretch!
   *Kit.* Defy me, strumpet! Ask thy pandar
   here,                                            50
Can he deny it? or that wicked elder?
   *Know.* Why, hear you, sir.
   *Kit.*            Tut, tut, tut; never speak:
Thy guilty conscience will discover thee.
   *Know.* What lunacy is this, that haunts this
   man?
   *Kit.* Well, good wife BA'D, Cob's wife, and
   you,                                             55
That make your husband such a hoddy-doddy;
And you, young apple-squire, and old cuckold-
   maker;
I 'll ha' you every one before a justice:
Nay, you shall answer it, I charge you go.
   *Know.* Marry, with all my heart, sir, I go
   willingly;                                       60
Though I do taste this as a trick put on me,
To punish my impertinent search, and justly,
And half forgive my son for the device.
   *Kit.* Come, will you go?
   *Dame K.*      Go! to thy shame, believe it.

              *[Enter Cob]*

   *Cob.* Why, what 's the matter here? what 's
   here to do?                                      65
   *Kit.* O, Cob, art thou come? I have been
   abus'd,
And i' thy house. Never was man so wrong'd!
   *Cob.* 'Slid, in my house, my master Kitely!
Who wrongs you in my house?

   *Kit.* Marry, young lust in old, and old in
   young here:                                      70
Thy wife 's their bawd, here have I taken 'em.
   *Cob.* How, bawd! is my house come to that?
Am I preferr'd thither? Did I charge you to
keep your doors shut, Isbel? and do you let
'em lie open for all comers?                        75
      *He falls upon his wife and beats her.*
   *Know.* Friend, know some cause, before thou
   beat'st thy wife.
This 's madness in thee.
   *Cob.*         Why, is there no cause?
   *Kit.* Yes, I 'll show cause before the justice,
   Cob:
Come, let her go with me.
   *Cob.*          Nay, she shall go.
   *Tib.* Nay, I will go. I 'll see an you may [80
be allow'd to make a bundle o' hemp o' your
right and lawful wife thus, at every cuckoldly
knave's pleasure. Why do you not go?
   *Kit.* A bitter quean! Come, we 'll ha' you
   tam'd.                     *[Exeunt.]*

## Act IIII.  Scene XI

### [A Street.]

*Brainworm, [later] Mathew, Bobadill,*
*Stephen, Downright*

[*Brai.*] Well, of all my disguises yet, now am
I most like myself, being in this sergeant's gown.
A man of my present profession never counterfeits, till he lays hold upon a debtor and says
he 'rests him; for then he brings him to all [5
manner of unrest. A kind of little kings we
are, bearing the diminutive of a mace, made
like a young artichoke, that always carries
pepper and salt in itself. Well, I know not what
danger I undergo by this exploit; pray [10
Heaven I come well off!

### [Enter Mathew and Bobadill]

   *Mat.* See, I think, yonder is the varlet, by
   his gown.
   *Bob.* Let 's go in quest of him.
   *Mat.* 'Save you, friend! Are not you here
by appointment of justice Clement's man?  15
   *Brai.* Yes, an 't please you, sir; he told me
two gentlemen had will'd him to procure a
warrant from his master, which I have about
me, to be serv'd on one Downright.
   *Mat.* It is honestly done of you both; and [20
see where the party comes you must arrest:
serve it upon him quickly, afore he be aware.
   *Bob.* Bear back, master Mathew.

---

   ⁳⁷ **sod:** boiled    **treachour:** traitor    ⁵⁰ **pandar:** (F has in the margin, "*By* [*i.e.*, referring to]
*Thomas.*")    ⁵⁶ **hoddy-doddy:** fool, dupe    ⁵⁷ **apple-squire:** harlot's attendant    ⁸¹ **hemp:** Hemp is
prepared by beating.    ⁸⁴ **quean:** hussy    Sc. XI. s. D. Brainworm is disguised as a City Sergeant
⁷ **mace:** the City Sergeant's badge of office

*[Enter Stephen in Downright's cloak]*

*Brai.* Master Downright, I arrest you i' the queen's name, and must carry you afore a [25 justice by virtue of this warrant.

*Step.* Me, friend! I am no Downright, I; I am master Stephen. You do not well to arrest me, I tell you, truly; I am in nobody's bonds nor books, I would you should know it. A [30 plague on you heartily, for making me thus afraid afore my time!

*Brai.* Why, now, are you deceived, gentlemen?

*Bob.* He wears such a cloak, and that deceived us: but see, here 'a comes indeed; [35 this is he, officer.

*[Enter Downright]*

*Dow.* Why how now, signior gull! Are you turn'd filcher of late! Come, deliver my cloak.

*Step.* Your cloak, sir! I bought it even now, in open market.                                40

*Brai.* Master Downright, I have a warrant I must serve upon you, procur'd by these two gentlemen.

*Dow.* These gentlemen! These rascals!

*[Offers to beat them.]*

*Brai.·* Keep the peace, I charge you, in her majesty's name.                          46

*Dow.* I obey thee. What must I do, officer?

*Brai.* Go before master justice Clement, to answer what they can object against you, sir. I will use you kindly, sir.                50

*Mat.* Come, let 's before, and make the justice, captain.

*Bob.* The varlet 's a tall man, afore heaven!

*[Exeunt Bob. and Mat.]*

*Dow.* Gull, you 'll gi' me my cloak.

*Step.* Sir, I bought it, and I 'll keep it.   55

*Dow.* You will?

*Step.* Ay, that I will.

*Dow.* Officer, there 's thy fee, arrest him.

*Brai.* Master Stephen, I must arrest you.

*Step.* Arrest me! I scorn it. There, take your cloak, I 'll none on 't.            61

*Dow.* Nay, that shall not serve your turn now, sir. Officer, I 'll go with thee to the justice's; bring him along.

*Step.* Why, is not here your cloak? What would you have?                          66

*Dow.* I 'll ha' you answer it, sir.

*Brai.* Sir, I 'll take your word, and this gentleman's too, for his appearance.

*Dow.* I 'll ha' no words taken: bring him along.                                71

*Brai.* Sir, I may choose to do that: I may take bail.

*Dow.* 'T is true, you may take bail, and choose at another time; but you shall not [75 now, varlet. Bring him along, or I 'll swinge you.

*Brai.* Sir, I pity the gentleman's case; here 's your money again.

*Dow.* 'Sdeins, tell not me of my money; bring him away, I say.                     80

*Brai.* I warrant you, he will go with you of himself, sir.

*Dow.* Yet more ado?

*Brai.* *[aside.]* I have made a fair mash on 't.

*Step.* Must I go?                               85

*Brai.* I know no remedy, master Stephen.

*Dow.* Come along afore me here; I do not love your hanging look behind.

*Step.* Why, sir, I hope you cannot hang me for it: can he, fellow?                  90

*Brai.* I think not, sir; it is but a whipping matter, sure.

*Step.* Why then let him do his worst, I am resolute.                        *[Exeunt.]*

## Act V.   Scene I

*[Coleman-street   A Hall in Justice Clement's House.]*

*Clement, Knowell, Kitely, Dame Kitely, Tib, Cash, Cob, Servants*

*[Clem.]* Nay, but stay, stay, give me leave: my chair, sirrah. — You, master Knowell, say you went thither to meet your son?

*Know.* Ay, sir.

*Clem.* But who directed you thither?    5

*Know.* That did mine own man, sir.

*Clem.* Where is he?

*Know.* Nay, I know not now; I left him with your clerk, and appointed him to stay here for me.                               10

*Clem.* My clerk! about what time was this?

*Know.* Marry, between one and two, as I take it.

*Clem.* And what time came my man with the false message to you, master Kitely?  15

*Kit.* After two, sir.

*Clem.* Very good: but, mistress Kitely, how chance that you were at Cob's, ha?

*Dame K.* An 't please you, sir, I 'll tell you: my brother Wellbred told me that Cob's house was a suspected place ——            21

*Clem.* So it appears, methinks: but on.

*Dame K.* And that my husband us'd thither daily.

*Clem.* No matter, so he us'd himself well, mistress.                                26

*Dame K.* True, sir: but you know what grows by such haunts oftentimes.

*Clem.* I see rank fruits of a jealous brain, mistress Kitely: but did you find your hus- [30 band there, in that case as you suspected?

---

⁵¹ **make:** prepare   ⁸⁴ **mash:** muddle   ¹⁸ **chance:** (not in F 1)   ³¹ **case:** situation

*Kit.* I found her there, sir.

*Clem.* Did you so? That alters the case. Who gave you knowledge of your wife's being there?                                                    35

*Kit.* Marry, that did my brother Wellbred.

*Clem.* How? Wellbred first tell her; then tell you after! Where is Wellbred?

*Kit.* Gone with my sister, sir, I know not whither.                                                    40

*Clem.* Why this is a mere trick, a device; you are gull'd in this most grossly, all. Alas, poor wench! wert thou beaten for this?

*Tib.* Yes, most pitifully, an 't please you.

*Cob.* And worthily, I hope, if it shall [45 prove so.

*Clem.* Ay, that 's like, and a piece of a sentence. —

### [*Enter a Servant*]

How now, sir! what 's the matter?

*Serv.* Sir, there 's a gentleman i' the court [50 without, desires to speak with your worship.

*Clem.* A gentleman! what 's he?

*Serv.* A soldier, sir, he says.

*Clem.* A soldier! Take down my armour, my sword quickly. A soldier speak with me! Why, when, knaves! Come on, come on. (*He arms* [56 *himself.*) Hold my cap there, so; give me my gorget, my sword: stand by, I will end your matters anon. —— Let the soldier enter.

[*Exit Servant.*]

## Act V.  Scene II

### [*The Same.*]

### *Bobadill, Mathew [to the rest]*

Now, sir, what ha' you to say to me?

[*Bob.*] By your worship's favour ——

*Clem.* Nay, keep out, sir; I know not your pretence. — You send me word, sir, you are a soldier; why, sir, you shall be answer'd here: [5 here be them have been amongst soldiers. Sir, your pleasure.

*Bob.* Faith, sir, so it is, this gentleman and myself have been most uncivilly wrong'd and beaten by one Downright, a coarse fellow [10 about the town here; and for mine own part, I protest, being a man in no sort given to this filthy humour of quarrelling, he hath assaulted me in the way of my peace, despoil'd me of mine honour, disarm'd me of my weapons, [15 and rudely laid me along in the open streets, when I not so much as once offer'd to resist him.

*Clem.* O, God's precious! is this the soldier? Here, take my armour off quickly, 't will make him swoon, I fear; he is not fit to look on 't, [21 that will put up a blow.

*Mat.* An 't please your worship, he was bound to the peace.

*Clem.* Why, an he were, sir, his hands were not bound, were they?                                      26

### [*Re-enter Servant*]

*Serv.* There 's one of the varlets of the city, sir, has brought two gentlemen here; one, upon your worship's warrant.

*Clem.* My warrant!                                      30

*Serv.* Yes, sir; the officer says, procur'd by these two.

*Clem.* Bid him come in. [*Exit Servant.*] Set by this picture.

## Act V.  Scene III

### [*The Same.*]

### *Downright, Stephen, Brainworm [to the rest]*

What, master Downright! Are you brought at master Freshwater's suit here?

[*Dow.*] I' faith, sir, and here 's another brought at my suit.

*Clem.* What are you, sir?                                5

*Step.* A gentleman, sir. O, uncle!

*Clem.* Uncle! Who? Master Knowell?

*Know.* Ay, sir; this is a wise kinsman of mine.                                                    9

*Step.* God 's my witness, uncle, I am wrong'd here monstrously; he charges me with stealing of his cloak, and would I might never stir, if I did not find it in the street by chance.

*Dow.* O, did you find it now? You said you bought it ere-while.                                        15

*Step.* And you said, I stole it. Nay, now my uncle is here, I 'll do well enough with you.

*Clem.* Well, let this breathe awhile. You that have cause to complain there, stand forth. Had you my warrant for this gentleman's [20 apprehension?

*Bob.* Ay, an 't please your worship.

*Clem.* Nay, do not speak in passion so. Where had you it?

*Bob.* Of your clerk, sir.                                25

*Clem.* That 's well! an my clerk can make warrants, and my hand not at 'em! Where is the warrant? — Officer, have you it?

*Brai.* No, sir. Your worship's man, Master Formal, bid me do it for these gentlemen, [30 and he would be my discharge.

---

⁵² **what:** what kind of man    ⁵⁸ **gorget:** armor for the throat    Sc. II. ¹ (This line is at the end of Sc. I in F.)    ⁴ **pretence:** intention    ¹⁶ **laid me along:** laid me low    ³⁴ **picture:** *i.e.,* mere picture of a soldier    Sc. III. ² **master Freshwater:** *i.e.,* a soldier who has never crossed the sea on service **(This speech is at the end of Sc. II in F.)**    ¹⁸ **breathe:** rest

*Clem.* Why, Master Downright, are you such a novice, to be serv'd and never see the warrant?

*Dow.* Sir, he did not serve it on me. 35

*Clem.* No! how then?

*Dow.* Marry, sir, he came to me, and said he must serve it, and he would use me kindly, and so —— 39

*Clem.* O, God's pity, was it so, sir? He *must* serve it! Give me my long sword there, and help me off, so. Come on, sir varlet, I *must* cut off your legs, sirrah [*Brainworm kneels.*]; nay, stand up, *I'll use you kindly;* I *must* cut off your legs, I say. 45

*He flourishes over him with his long sword.*

*Brai.* O, good sir, I beseech you; nay, good master justice!

*Clem.* I *must* do it, there is no remedy; I *must* cut off your legs, sirrah, I *must* cut off your ears, you rascal, I *must* do it: I *must* [50 cut off your nose, I *must* cut off your head.

*Brai.* O, good your worship!

*Clem.* Well, rise; how dost thou do now? Dost thou feel thyself well? Hast thou no harm? 55

*Brai.* No, I thank your good worship, sir.

*Clem.* Why so! I said I must cut off thy legs, and I must cut off thy arms, and I must cut off thy head; but I did not do it: so you said you must serve this gentleman with my [60 warrant, but you did not serve him. You knave, you slave, you rogue, do you say you *must,* sirrah! Away with him to the jail; I'll teach you a trick for your *must,* sir.

*Brai.* Good sir, I beseech you, be good to [65 me.

*Clem.* Tell him he shall to the jail; away with him, I say.

*Brai.* Nay, sir, if you will commit me, it shall be for committing more than this: I will [70 not lose by my travail any grain of my fame, certain.

[*Throws off his sergeant's gown.*]

*Clem.* How is this?

*Know.* My man Brainworm!

*Step.* O, yes, uncle; Brainworm has been with my cousin Edward and I all this day. 76

*Clem.* I told you all there was some device.

*Brai.* Nay, excellent justice, since I have laid myself thus open to you, now stand strong for me; both with your sword and your balance. [80

*Clem.* Body o' me, a merry knave! give me a bowl of sack. If he belong to you, Master Knowell, I bespeak your patience.

*Brai.* That is it I have most need of. Sir, if you'll pardon me only, I'll glory in all the [85 rest of my exploits.

*Know.* Sir, you know I love not to have my favours come hard from me. You have your pardon, though I suspect you shrewdly for being of counsel with my son against me. 90

*Brai.* Yes, faith, I have, sir, though you retain'd me doubly this morning for yourself: first, as Brainworm; after, as Fitz-Sword. I was your reform'd soldier, sir. 'T was I sent you to Cob's upon the errand without end. 95

*Know.* Is it possible? or that thou should'st disguise thy language so as I should not know thee?

*Brai.* O, sir, this has been the day of my metamorphosis. It is not that shape alone [100 that I have run through to-day. I brought this gentleman, master Kitely, a message too, in the form of master Justice's man here, to draw him out o' the way, as well as your worship, while master Wellbred might make a con- [105 veyance of mistress Bridget to my young master.

*Kit.* How! my sister stol'n away?

*Know.* My son is not married, I hope.

*Brai.* Faith, sir, they are both as sure as love, a priest, and three thousand pound, which [110 is her portion, can make 'em; and by this time are ready to bespeak their wedding-supper at the Windmill, except some friend here prevent 'em, and invite 'em home.

*Clem.* Marry, that will I; I thank thee [115 for putting me in mind on 't. Sirrah, go you and fetch 'em hither upon my warrant. [*Exit Servant.*] Neither's friends have cause to be sorry, if I know the young couple aright. Here, I drink to thee for thy good news. But I pray [120 thee, what hast thou done with my man, Formal?

*Brai.* Faith, sir, after some ceremony past, as making him drunk, first with story, and then with wine, (but all in kindness,) and strip- [125 ping him to his shirt, I left him in that cool vein; departed, sold your worship's warrant to these two, pawn'd his livery for that varlet's gown, to serve it in; and thus have brought myself by my activity to your worship's consideration. 131

*Clem.* And I will consider thee in another cup of sack. Here's to thee, which having drunk of, this is my sentence: Pledge me. Thou hast done, or assisted to nothing, in my [135 judgment, but deserves to be pardon'd for the wit o' the offence. If thy master, or any man here, be angry with thee, I shall suspect his ingine, while I know him, for 't. How now, what noise is that? 140

*[Enter Servant]*

*Serv.* Sir, it is Roger is come home.

*Clem.* Bring him in, bring him in.

---

¹¹³ **prevent:** anticipate      ¹³⁹ **ingine:** wit

## Act V.  Scene IIII

*[The Same.]*

*To them, Formal*

What! drunk?  In arms against me?  Your reason, your reason for this?

[*Form.*]  I beseech your worship to pardon me; I happen'd into ill company by chance, that cast me into a sleep, and stripp'd me of all [5 my clothes.

*Clem.*  Well, tell him I am Justice Clement, and do pardon him: but what is this to your armour?  What may that signify?

*Form.*  An 't please you, sir, it hung up i' [10 the room where I was stripp'd; and I borrow'd it of one o' the drawers to come home in, because I was loath to do penance through the street i' my shirt.

*Clem.*  Well, stand by a while.          15

## Act V.  Scene V

*[The Same.]*

*To them, Ed. Knowell, Wellbred, Bridget*

Who be these?  O, the young company; welcome, welcome!  Gi' you joy.  Nay, mistress Bridget, blush not; you are not so fresh a bride, but the news of it is come hither afore you. Master bridegroom, I ha' made your peace, [5 give me your hand: so will I for all the rest ere you forsake my roof.

[*E. Know.*]  We are the more bound to your humanity, sir.

*Clem.*  Only these two have so little of man in 'em, they are no part of my care.      11

*Wel.*  Yes, sir, let me pray you for this gentleman: he belongs to my sister the bride.

*Clem.*  In what place, sir?

*Wel.*  Of her delight, sir, below the stairs, [15 and in public: her poet, sir.

*Clem.*  A poet!  I will challenge him myself presently at extempore,

*Mount up thy Phlegon, Muse, and testify*
 *How Saturn, sitting in an ebon cloud,*          20
*Disrob'd his podex, white as ivory,*
 *And through the welkin thund'red all aloud.*

*Wel.*  He is not for extempore, sir: he is all for the pocket muse; please you command a sight of it.          25

*Clem.*  Yes, yes, search him for a taste of his vein.          [*They search Mathew's pockets.*]

*Wel.*  You must not deny the queen's justice, sir, under a writ o' rebellion.          29

*Clem.*  What! all this verse?  Body o' me, he carries a whole realm, a commonwealth of paper in 's hose.  Let 's see some of his subjects.
          [*Reads.*]
*Unto the boundless ocean of thy face,*
*Runs this poor river, charg'd with streams of eyes.*
How! this is stol'n.          35

*E. Know.*  A parody! a parody! with a kind of miraculous gift, to make it absurder than it was.

*Clem.*  Is all the rest of this batch?  Bring me a torch; lay it together, and give fire. [40 Cleanse the air.  [*Sets the papers on fire.*]  Here was enough to have infected the whole city, if it had not been taken in time.  See, see, how our poet's glory shines! brighter and brighter! still it increases!  O, now it 's at the highest; [45 and now it declines as fast.  You may see, *sic transit gloria mundi!*

*Know.*  There 's an emblem for you, son, and your studies.          49

*Clem.*  Nay, no speech or act of mine be drawn against such as profess it worthily.  They are not born every year, as an alderman.  There goes more to the making of a good poet than a sheriff, master Kitely.  You look upon me! — though I live i' the city here, amongst you, I [55 will do more reverence to him, when I meet him, than I will to the mayor out of his year. But these paper-pedlars! these ink-dabblers! they cannot expect reprehension or reproach; they have it with the fact.          60

*E. Know.*  Sir, you have sav'd me the labour of a defence.

*Clem.*  It shall be discourse for supper between your father and me, if he dare under- [64 take me.  But to dispatch away these: you sign o' the soldier, and picture o' the poet, (but both so false, I will not ha' you hang'd out at my door till midnight,) while we are at supper, you two shall penitently fast it out in my court without; and, if you will, you may pray there [70 that we may be so merry within as to forgive or forget you when we come out.  Here 's a third, because we tender your safety, shall watch you: he is provided for the purpose. — Look to your charge, sir.          75

*Step.*  And what shall I do?

*Clem.*  O! I had lost a sheep an he had not bleated: why, sir, you shall give master Downright his cloak; and I will entreat him to

---

Sc. IIII.  ¹⁻² (At end of Sc. III in F)        ¹² **drawers:** waiters        Sc. V.  ¹⁻⁷ (At end of Sc. IV in F)
¹⁹ **Phlegon:** one of the horses of the sun  (The passage is a parody of Marston.)        ²¹ **podex:** fundament
³¹ **realm:** ream (with pun on realm, kingdom; cf. *Jew of Malta* IV, iv, 132)        ³³⁻³⁴ Parodied from
Daniel's first Sonnet to Delia        ⁴⁶⁻⁴⁷ **sic . . . mundi:** So passes worldly glory.        ⁵⁷ **out . . . year:**
when his year of office is over        ⁶¹⁻⁶² (In Q, E. Knowell's prototype indulges in a long laudation of
poetry at this point.)        ⁷³ **third:** *i.e.,* Formal

take it.  A trencher and a napkin you shall [80
have i' the buttery, and keep Cob and his wife
company here; whom I will entreat first to be
reconcil'd; and you to endeavour with your wit
to keep 'em so.

*Step.*  I 'll do my best.       85

*Cob.*  Why, now I see thou art honest, Tib,
I receive thee as my dear and mortal wife
again.

*Tib.*  And I you, as my loving and obedient
husband.       90

*Clem.*  Good compliment!  It will be their
bridal night too.  They are married anew.
Come, I conjure the rest to put off all discontent.  You, master Downright, your anger;
you, master Knowell, your cares; Master Kitely
and his wife, their jealousy.       96
For, I must tell you both, while that is fed,
Horns i' the mind are worse than o' the head.

*Kit.*  Sir, thus they go from me; kiss me,
sweetheart.       100

*See what a drove of horns fly in the air,*
*Wing'd with my cleansed and my credulous*
    *breath!*
*Watch 'em, suspicious eyes, watch where they fall.*
*See, see! on heads that think they 've none at all!*
*O, what a plenteous world of this will come!*  105
*When air rains horns, all may be sure of some.*
I ha' learn'd so much verse out of a jealous
man's part in a play.

*Clem.*  'T is well, 't is well!  This night we 'll
dedicate to friendship, love, and laughter.  110
Master bridegroom, take your bride and lead;
every one, a fellow.  Here is my mistress, Brainworm! to whom all my addresses of courtship
shall have their reference: whose adventures
this day, when our grandchildren shall hear [115
to be made a fable, I doubt not but it shall find
both spectators and applause.    *[Exeunt.]*

THE END

106 **some:** ('fame' F)

# BEN: IONSON

## his

## VOLPONE

### Or

## THE FOXE.

*—Simul & iucunda, & idonea dicere vita.*

Printed for *Thomas Thorppe.*
1607.

BIBLIOGRAPHICAL RECORD. *Volpone* was first printed for Thomas Thorpe, the famous publisher of Shakespeare's *Sonnets*, without entry on the Stationers' books. The title-page of this first Quarto (see facsimile) bears the date 1607, but as the author's Epistle Dedicatory is dated February 11, 1607, the volume was probably issued in February or March of 1608, which would be 1607 by the usual Elizabethan reckoning. It was next printed in the Folio of 1616. The play first appears on the Register of the Stationers' Co. on Oct. 3, 1610: — *Walter Burre. Entred for his Copyes by assignemente from Thomas Thorpe and with the consente of Th'wardens vnder their handes, 2 bookes thone called Seianus his fall thother, Vulpone or the ffoxe . . . xij^d.* The quarto text is preceded by a group of ten poems by various hands in commendation of the author, and both folio and quarto texts are dedicated to the two universities of Oxford and Cambridge. The folio text is followed by a list of the principal comedians who took part in the original performance. They were Richard Burbage, Henry Condell, William Sly, John Heminges, John Lowin, and Alexander Cooke. The part taken by each is not specified.

DATE AND STAGE PERFORMANCE. Jonson declares in the prologue to *Volpone* that the play was "fully penned" in five weeks. References to explicit contemporary events in the play indicate that these weeks must have been early in 1606. The folio title-page states that the play was "acted in the yeere 1605 by the K. Maiesties Servants," and this information is repeated at the end of the play. This performance must have been about the middle of March, for the play was certainly composed about February–March, 1606, and had it been played later than March 24 of that year, the date would have been given as 1606. Later in the year it seems to have been acted at both the universities, an honor seldom accorded a play from the London theatres. Two court performances at Whitehall are recorded, on December 27, 1624, and November 8, 1638, respectively. *Volpone* maintained its place on the stage until the closing of the theatres, was revived soon after the Restoration, and was occasionally acted during the eighteenth century. In a debased version it was revived in New York in 1928.

SOURCES. The best treatment yet available of this complex subject will be found in the edition of the play by the late Professor J. D. Rea (1919), where special emphasis is laid upon Jonson's use of Erasmus's *Praise of Folly*. Professor Rea advances the new and clever idea that Sir Politic Would-Be is a caricature of Sir Henry Wotton (1568–1639). The classic sources which have been noted are too numerous to be dealt with here; they include Lucian's dialogues, Libanius, and Horace's fifth satire of his second book. The essential point to note is that, though Jonson shows adequate knowledge of the Venice of his day, he is still drawing his ideas chiefly from the decadent life of imperial Rome, which had been the theme of *Sejanus* (1603). One cannot find in brief space a better characterization of the milieu of *Volpone* than is given in the passages from Ammianus Marcellinus which Gibbon paraphrases in the thirty-first chapter of his *Decline and Fall*.

STRUCTURE. In the list of the Persons of the Play Jonson makes use of a device which he had already employed in *Every Man in his Humour* — that of making the names of the characters suggest their natures, or "humours." Volpone is the fox; Voltore, the vulture; Corbaccio, the raven; Corvino, the crow; Nano, a dwarf; Castrone, an eunuch; Androgyno, a hermaphrodite; Bonario, an honest, good man. Mosca's name, which means "the fly," was often applied to the parasite of Latin comedy. The unities are observed, and the arrangement of scenes is rigidly classic.

# BEN JONSON

## VOLPONE; OR, THE FOX

To The

Most Noble and Most Equal Sisters,

THE TWO FAMOUS UNIVERSITIES,

For Their

Love and Acceptance Shown To His Poem

In The Presentation;

BEN JONSON

The Grateful Acknowledger,

DEDICATES BOTH IT AND HIMSELF

*There follows an Epistle, if you dare venture on the length.*

Never, most equal Sisters, had any man a wit so presently excellent, as that it could raise itself; but there must come both matter, occasion, commenders, and favourers to it. If this be true, and that the fortune of all [5 writers doth daily prove it, it behooves the careful to provide well toward these accidents; and, having acquired them, to preserve that part of reputation most tenderly, wherein the benefit of a friend is also defended. Hence [10 is it, that I now render myself grateful, and am studious to justify the bounty of your act; to which, though your mere authority were satisfying, yet, it being an age wherein poetry and the professors of it hear so ill on all sides, [15 there will a reason be looked for in the subject. It is certain, nor can it with any forehead be opposed, that the too much license of poetasters in this time hath much deformed their mistress; that, every day, their mani- [20 fold and manifest ignorance doth stick unnatural reproaches upon her: but for their petulancy, it were an act of the greatest injustice, either to let the learned suffer, or so divine a skill (which indeed should not be [25 attempted with unclean hands) to fall under the least contempt. For, if men will impartially, and not asquint, look toward the offices and function of a poet, they will easily conclude to themselves the impossibility of any man's [30 being the good poet, without first being a good man. He that is said to be able to inform young men to all good disciplines, inflame grown men to all great virtues, keep old men in their best and supreme state, or, as they [35 decline to childhood, recover them to their first strength; that comes forth the interpreter and arbiter of nature, a teacher of things divine no less than human, a master in manners; and can alone, or with a few, effect the business [40 of mankind: this, I take him, is no subject for pride and ignorance to exercise their railing rhetoric upon. But it will here be hastily answered, that the writers of these days are other things; that not only their manners, [45 but their natures, are inverted, and nothing remaining with them of the dignity of poet, but the abused name, which every scribe usurps; that now, especially in dramatic, or, as they term it, stage-poetry, nothing but [50 ribaldry, profanation, blasphemy, all license of offence to God and man is practised. I dare not deny a great part of this, and am sorry I dare not, because in some men's abortive features (and would they had never boasted [55 the light) it is over true: but that all are embarked in this bold adventure for hell, is a most uncharitable thought, and, uttered, a more malicious slander. For my particular, I can, and from a most clear conscience, affirm, [60 that I have ever trembled to think toward the least profaneness; have loathed the use of such foul and unwashed bawdry, as is now made the food of the scene: and, howsoever I cannot escape, from some, the imputation of sharp- [65 ness, but that they will say, I have taken a pride, or lust, to be bitter, and not my youngest infant but hath come into the world with all his teeth; I would ask of these supercilious politics, what nation, society, or general [70 order or state, I have provoked? what public person? whether I have not in all these preserved their dignity, as mine own person, safe? My works are read, allowed, (I speak of those that are entirely mine,) look into them. [75 What broad reproofs have I used? where have I been particular? where personal? except to a mimic, cheater, bawd, or buffoon, creatures, for their insolencies, worthy to be taxed? Yet to which of these so pointingly, as he might [80

---

Ded. **There . . . length:** (in margin of Q; not in F)    15 **hear so ill:** are so ill spoken of    70 **politics:** politicians, worldly-wise men    74 **allowed:** licensed, approved    79 **taxed:** taken to task

not either ingenuously have confess'd, or wisely dissembled his disease? But it is not rumour can make men guilty, much less entitle me to other men's crimes. I know, that nothing can be so innocently writ or carried, but may be [85 made obnoxious to construction; marry, whilst I bear mine innocence about me, I fear it not. Application is now grown a trade with many; and there are that profess to have a key for the deciphering of everything: but let wise and [90 noble persons take heed how they be too credulous, or give leave to these invading interpreters to be over-familiar with their fames, who cunningly, and often, utter their own virulent malice, under other men's simplest mean- [95 ings. As for those that will (by faults which charity hath raked up, or common honesty concealed) make themselves a name with the multitude, or (to draw their rude and beastly claps) care not whose living faces they in- [100 trench with their petulent styles, may they do it without a rival, for me! I choose rather to live graved in obscurity, than share with them in so preposterous a fame. Nor can I blame the wishes of those severe and wiser patriots, [105 who providing the hurts these licentious spirits may do in a state, desire rather to see fools and devils, and those antique relics of barbarism retrieved, with all other ridiculous and exploded follies, than behold the wounds of private [110 men, of princes and nations: for, as Horace makes Trebatius speak among these,

— *Sibi quisque timet, quanquam est intactus, et odit.*

And men may justly impute such rages, if [114 continued, to the writer, as his sports. The increase of which lust in liberty, together with the present trade of the stage, in all their misc'line interludes, what learned or liberal soul doth not already abhor? where nothing [119 but the filth of the time is uttered, and that with such impropriety of phrase, such plenty of solecisms, such dearth of sense, so bold prolepses, so racked metaphors, with brothelry, able to violate the ear of a pagan, and [124 blasphemy, to turn the blood of a Christian to water.

I cannot but be serious in a cause of this nature, wherein my fame and the reputations of divers honest and learned are the question; when a name so full of authority, antiquity, [130 and all great mark, is (through their insolence) become the lowest scorn of the age;

and those men subject to the petulancy of every vernaculous orator, that were wont to be the care of kings and happiest monarchs. [135 This it is that hath not only rapt me to present indignation, but made me studious heretofore, and by all my actions, to stand off from them; which may most appear in this my latest work, which you, most learned Arbitresses, have [140 seen, judged, and, to my crown, approved; wherein I have laboured for their instruction and amendment, to reduce not only the ancient forms, but manners of the scene, the easiness, the propriety, the innocence, and last, the [145 doctrine, which is the principal end of poesie, to inform men in the best reason of living. And though my catastrophe may, in the strict rigour of comic law, meet with censure, as turning back to my promise; I desire the [150 learned and charitable critic, to have so much faith in me, to think it was done of industry: for with what ease I could have varied it nearer his scale (but that I fear to boast my own faculty) I could here insert. But my special [155 aim being to put the snaffle in their mouths, that cry out, We never punish vice in our interludes, &c. I took the more liberty: though not without some lines of example, drawn even in the ancients themselves, the goings out [160 of whose comedies are not always joyful, but oft times the bawds, the servants, the rivals, yea, and the masters are mulcted; and fitly, it being the office of a comic poet to imitate justice, and instruct to life, as well as purity [165 of language, or stir up gentle affections: to which I shall take the occasion elsewhere to speak.

For the present, most reverenced Sisters, as I have cared to be thankful for your affec- [170 tions past, and here made the understanding acquainted with some ground of your favours; let me not despair their continuance, to the maturing of some worthier fruits: wherein, if my muses be true to me, I shall raise the [175 despised head of poetry again, and stripping her out of those rotten and base rags wherewith the times have adulterated her form, restore her to her primitive habit, feature, and majesty, and render her worthy to be embraced and [180 kiss'd of all the great and master-spirits of our world. As for the vile and slothful, who never affected an act worthy of celebration, or are so inward with their own vicious natures, as they worthily fear her, and think it a [185 high point of policy to keep her in contempt,

---

**85 carried:** managed      **86 obnoxious to construction:** liable to misinterpretation      **88 Application:** explanation of personal satire      **93 fames:** reputations      **97 raked up:** hidden      **102 for me:** for all I care      **106 providing:** foreseeing      **113 Sibi . . . odit:** Every one fears for himself, although he is uninjured, and is angry. (Horace, *Satires*, 2, 1. 23)      **118 misc'line:** mixed      **122–123 prolepses:** anachronisms      **134 vernaculous:** scurrilous      **160 goings out:** dénouements      **184 inward:** familiar

with their declamatory and windy invectives; she shall out of just rage incite her servants (who are *genus irritabile*) to spout ink in their faces, that shall eat farder than their mar- [190 row into their fames; and not Cinnamus the barber, with his art, shall be able to take out the brands; but they shall live, and be read, till the wretches die, as things worst deserving of themselves in chief, and then of all mankind. [195

From my House in the Black-Friars,
   this 11th day of February, 1607

## THE PERSONS OF THE PLAY

VOLPONE, a Magnifico
MOSCA, his Parasite
VOLTORE, an Advocate
CORBACCIO, an old Gentleman
CORVINO, a Merchant
BONARIO, a young Gentleman, [son to Corbaccio]
[SIR] POLITIC WOULD-BE, a Knight
PEREGRINE, a Gentleman Traveller
NANO, a Dwarf
CASTRONE, an Eunuch
ANDROGYNO, a Hermaphrodite

Grege [or Mob]
Commandadori, Officers [of Justice]
Mercatori, three Merchants
Avocatori, four Magistrates
Notario, the Register
Servitore, a Servant

Fine Madame WOULD-BE, the Knight's Wife
CELIA, [Corvino] the Merchant's Wife
[Two Waiting-] Women

THE SCENE: — VENICE

## THE ARGUMENT

V olpone, childless, rich, feigns sick, despairs,
O ffers his state to hopes of several heirs,
L ies languishing: his parasite receives
P resents of all, assures, deludes; then weaves
O ther cross-plots, which ope themselves, are told.     5
N ew tricks for safety are sought; they thrive: when, bold,
E ach tempts th' other again, and all are sold.

## PROLOGUE

Now, luck yet send us, and a little wit
   Will serve to make our play hit;
According to the palates of the season,
   Here is rhyme, not empty of reason.
This we were bid to credit from our poet,     5
   Whose true scope, if you would know it,
In all his poems still hath been this measure,
   To mix profit with your pleasure;
And not as some, whose throats their envy failing,
   Cry hoarsely, "All he writes is railing:"     10
And when his plays come forth, think they can flout them,
   With saying, he was a year about them.
To these there needs no lie, but this his creature,
   Which was two months since no feature:
And though he dares give them five lives to mend it,     15
   'T is known, five weeks fully penn'd it,
From his own hand, without a coadjutor,
   Novice, journeyman, or tutor.
Yet thus much I can give you as a token
   Of his play's worth, no eggs are broken,     20
Nor quaking custards with fierce teeth affrighted,
   Wherewith your rout are so delighted;
Nor hales he in a gull, old ends reciting,
   To stop gaps in his loose writing;

[191] **Cinnamus:** a barber referred to in this vein by Martial     **Argument:** synopsis (The comedies of Plautus were provided with similar acrostical summaries of plot.)     [23] **old ends:** scraps of old plays

With such a deal of monstrous and forc'd action,                    25
    As might make Bethlem a faction:
Nor made he his play for jests stol'n from each table,
    But makes jests to fit his fable;
And so presents quick comedy refin'd,
    As best critics have design'd;                    30
The laws of time, place, persons he observeth,
    From no needful rule he swerveth.
All gall and copperas from his ink he draineth,
    Only a little salt remaineth,
Wherewith he 'll rub your cheeks, till, red with laughter,         35
    They shall look fresh a week after.

## Act I.  Scene I

*[A Room in Volpone's House.]*

*Volpone, Mosca*

[*Volp.*]  Good morning to the day; and next, my gold!
Open the shrine, that I may see my saint.
    [*Mosca withdraws the rear-stage curtain, and discovers piles of gold, plate, jewels, etc.*]
Hail the world's soul, and mine!  More glad than is
The teeming earth to see the long'd-for sun
Peep through the horns of the celestial Ram,            5
Am I, to view thy splendour dark'ning his;
That lying here, amongst my other hoards,
Show'st like a flame by night, or like the day
Struck out of chaos, when all darkness fled
Unto the centre.  O thou son of Sol,                   10
But brighter than thy father, let me kiss,
With adoration, thee, and every relic
Of sacred treasure in this blessed room.
Well did wise poets, by thy glorious name,
Title that age which they would have the best;
Thou being the best of things, and far transcending   16
All style of joy, in children, parents, friends,
Or any other waking dream on earth.
Thy looks when they to Venus did ascribe,
They should have given her twenty thousand Cupids;     20
Such are thy beauties and our loves!  Dear saint,
Riches, the dumb god, that giv'st all men tongues,
That canst do nought, and yet mak'st men do all things;
The price of souls; even hell, with thee to boot,      24
Is made worth heaven.  Thou art virtue, fame,
Honour, and all things else.  Who can get thee,
He shall be noble, valiant, honest, wise ——
    *Mos.*  And what he will, sir.  Riches are in fortune
A greater good than wisdom is in nature.
    *Volp.*  True, my beloved Mosca.  Yet I glory
More in the cunning purchase of my wealth,             31
Than in the glad possession, since I gain
No common way; I use no trade, no venter;
I wound no earth with ploughshares, fat no beasts
To feed the shambles; have no mills for iron,          35
Oil, corn, or men, to grind 'em into powder;
I blow no subtle glass, expose no ships
To threat'nings of the furrow-faced sea;
I turn no moneys in the public bank,
No usure private.
    *Mos.*                    No, sir, nor devour          40
Soft prodigals.  You shall ha' some will swallow
A melting heir as glibly as your Dutch
Will pills of butter, and ne'er purge for it;
Tear forth the fathers of poor families
Out of their beds, and coffin them alive               45
In some kind clasping prison, where their bones
May be forthcoming, when the flesh is rotten:
But your sweet nature doth abhor these courses;
You loathe the widow's or the orphan's tears
Should wash your pavements, or their piteous cries     50
Ring in your roofs, and beat the air for vengeance.
    *Volp.*  Right, Mosca; I do loathe it.
    *Mos.*                    And, besides, sir,
You are not like the thresher that doth stand
With a huge flail, watching a heap of corn,            54
And, hungry, dares not taste the smallest grain,
But feeds on mallows, and such bitter herbs;
Nor like the merchant, who hath fill'd his vaults
With Romagnía, and rich Candian wines,
Yet drinks the lees of Lombard's vinegar:

---

²⁶ **Bethlem:** Bedlam, the hospital for the insane    ³³ **copperas:** vitriol    ¹⁰ **centre:** *i.e.,* of the earth    ³¹ **purchase:** acquisition    ³³ **venter:** investment, speculation    ⁴⁹ **loathe:** *i.e.,* loathe that    ⁵⁸ **Romagnía:** Rumney, Greek

You will not lie in straw, whilst moths and
   worms                          60
Feed on your sumptuous hangings and soft
   beds;
You know the use of riches, and dare give now
From that bright heap, to me, your poor ob-
   server,
Or to your dwarf, or your hermaphrodite,
Your eunuch, or what other household trifle 65
Your pleasure allows maint'nance —
   *Volp.*             Hold thee, Mosca,
Take of my hand; thou strik'st on truth in all,
And they are envious term thee parasite.
Call forth my dwarf, my enunch, and my fool,
And let 'em make me sport.    [*Exit Mos.*]
                 What should I do, 70
But cocker up my genius, and live free
To all delights my fortune calls me to?
I have no wife, no parent, child, ally,
To give my substance to; but whom I make
Must be my heir; and this makes men observe
   me:                         75
This draws new clients daily to my house,
Women and men of every sex and age,
That bring me presents, send me plate, coin,
   jewels,
With hope that when I die (which they expect
Each greedy minute) it shall then return    80
Tenfold upon them; whilst some, covetous
Above the rest, seek to engross me whole,
And counter-work the one unto the other,
Contend in gifts, as they would seem in love:
All which I suffer, playing with their hopes, 85
And am content to coin 'em into profit,
And look upon their kindness, and take more,
And look on that; still bearing them in hand,
Letting the cherry knock against their lips,
And draw it by their mouths, and back again. —
How now!                      91

## *Act I.  Scene II*

### [*The Same.*]

*Nano, Androgyno, Castrone, Volpone, Mosca*

   [*Nan.*]   Now, room for fresh gamesters, who
   do will you to know,
They do bring you neither play nor university
   show;
And therefore do intreat you that whatsoever
   they rehearse,

May not fare a whit the worse, for the false
   pace of the verse.
If you wonder at this, you will wonder more ere
   we pass,                     5
For know, here is inclos'd the soul of Pythag-
   oras,
That juggler divine, as hereafter shall follow;
Which soul, fast and loose, sir, came first from
   Apollo,
And was breath'd into Æthalides, Mercurius
   his son,
Where it had the gift to remember all that ever
   was done.                  10
From thence it fled forth, and made quick
   transmigration
To goldy-lock'd Euphorbus, who was kill'd in
   good fashion,
At the siege of old Troy, by the cuckold of
   Sparta.
Hermotimus was next (I find it in my charta),
To whom it did pass, where no sooner it was
   missing,                 15
But with one Pyrrhus of Delos it learn'd to go
   a-fishing;
And thence did it enter the sophist of Greece.
From Pythagore, she went into a beautiful
   piece,
Hight Aspasia, the meretrix; and the next toss
   of her
Was again of a whore she became a philosopher,
Crates the cynic, as itself doth relate it:   21
Since kings, knights, and beggars, knaves, lords,
   and fools gat it,
Besides ox and ass, camel, mule, goat, and
   brock,
In all which it hath spoke, as in the cobbler's
   cock.                  24
But I come not here to discourse of that matter,
Or his one, two, or three, or his great oath,
   By quater!
His musics, his trigon, his golden thigh,
Or his telling how elements shift; but I
Would ask, how of late thou hast suffer'd
   translation,
And shifted thy coat in these days of reforma-
   tion.                  30
   *And.*   Like one of the reform'd, a fool, as you
   see,
Counting all old doctrine heresy.
   *Nan.*   But not on thine own forbid meats
   hast thou venter'd?

---

    ⁶³ **observer**: servant, obsequious follower    ⁶⁸ **term**: *i.e.*, who call    ⁷¹ **cocker up**: pamper    ⁷⁵ **ob-serve**: be obsequious to    ⁸² **engross**: monopolize    ⁸⁸ **bearing . . . hand**: deceiving them    ⁶ **here**: *i.e.*, in Androgyno    ⁹ **Æthalides**: one of the Argonauts    ¹³ **cuckold**: Menelaus    ¹⁴ **charta**: paper    ¹⁹ **Hight**: called    **meretrix**: harlot    ²³ **brock**: badger    ²⁴ **cobbler's cock**: This interlude, dealing with the Pythagorean transmigrations of the soul, is based on Lucian's dialogue of the Cobbler and the Cock.  The verse, with its "false pace," is the measure which preceded blank verse on the stage.  ²⁶ **Quater**: the tetractys, a geometrical figure which represented the number 10 as the triangle of 4, by which the Pythagoreans swore    ²⁷ **trigon**: triangular lyre    ³¹ **one . . . reform'd**: a Protestant

*And.* On fish, when first a Carthusian I enter'd.

*Nan.* Why, then thy dogmatical silence hath left thee? 35

*And.* Of that an obstreperous lawyer bereft me.

*Nan.* O wonderful change, when sir lawyer forsook thee!
For Pythagore's sake, what body then took thee?

*And.* A good dull moyle.

*Nan.* And how! by that means
Thou wert brought to allow of the eating of beans? 40

*And.* Yes. [thou pass?

*Nan.* But from the moyle into whom didst

*And.* Into a very strange beast, by some writers call'd an ass;
By others a precise, pure, illuminate brother
Of those devour flesh, and sometimes one another;
And will drop you forth a libel, or a sanctifi'd lie,
Betwixt every spoonful of a nativity-pie. 46

*Nan.* Now quit thee, for heaven, of that profane nation,
And gently report thy next transmigration.

*And.* To the same that I am.

*Nan.* A creature of delight,
And, what is more than a fool, an hermaphrodite! 50
Now, pray thee, sweet soul, in all thy variation,
Which body wouldst thou choose to take up thy station?

*And.* Troth, this I am in: even here would I tarry.

*Nan.* 'Cause here the delight of each sex thou canst vary?

*And.* Alas, those pleasures be stale and forsaken; 55
No, 't is your fool wherewith I am so taken,
The only one creature that I can call blessed;
For all other forms I have prov'd most distressed.

*Nan.* Spoke true, as thou wert in Pythagoras still.
This learned opinion we celebrate will, 60
Fellow eunuch, as behooves us, with all our wit and art,
To dignify that whereof ourselves are so great and special a part.

*Volp.* Now, very, very pretty! Mosca, this
Was thy invention?

*Mos.* If it please my patron,
Not else.

*Volp.* It doth, good Mosca.

*Mos.* Then it was, sir. 65
[*Nano and Castrone sing.*]

SONG

Fools, they are the only nation
Worth men's envy or admiration;
Free from care or sorrow-taking,
Selves and others merry making:
All they speak or do is sterling. 70
Your fool he is your great man's dearling,
And your ladies' sport and pleasure;
Tongue and bauble are his treasure.
E'en his face begetteth laughter,
And he speaks truth free from slaughter; 75
He 's the grace of every feast,
And sometimes the chiefest guest;
Hath his trencher and his stool,
When wit waits upon the fool.
O, who would not be 80
He, he, he?
*One knocks without.*

*Volp.* Who 's that? Away! Look, Mosca.

*Mos.* Fool, begone!
[*Exeunt Nano, Cast., and Andro.*]
'T is Signior Voltore, the advocate;
I know him by his knock.

*Volp.* Fetch me my gown,
My furs and night-caps; say my couch is changing 85
And let him entertain himself awhile
Without i' th' gallery. [*Exit Mosca.*] Now,
now my clients
Begin their visitation! Vulture, kite,
Raven, and gorcrow, all my birds of prey, 89
That think me turning carcase, now they come:
I am not for 'em yet.

[*Re-enter Mosca, with the gown, etc.*]
How now! the news?

*Mos.* A piece of plate, sir.

*Volp.* Of what bigness?

*Mos.* Huge,
Massy, and antique, with your name inscrib'd,
And arms engraven.

*Volp.* Good! and not a fox 94
Stretch'd on the earth, with fine delusive sleights,
Mocking a gaping crow? ha, Mosca!

*Mos.* Sharp, sir.

*Volp.* Give me my furs.
[*Puts on his sick dress.*]
Why dost thou laugh so, man?

*Mos.* I cannot choose, sir, when I apprehend
What thoughts he has without now, as he walks: 99
That this might be the last gift he should give,
That this would fetch you; if you died to-day,
And gave him all, what he should be to-morrow;

³⁹ **moyle:** mule  ⁴³ **precise . . . brother:** a Puritan  ⁴⁴ **those:** those who  ⁴⁶ **nativity-pie:** Christmas pie  ⁷⁵ **free from slaughter:** with impunity  ⁸⁹ **gorcrow:** carrion crow

What large return would come of all his venters;   
How he should worshipp'd be, and reverenc'd;
Ride with his furs, and foot cloths; waited on  105
By herds of fools and clients; have clear way
Made for his moyle, as letter'd as himself;
Be call'd the great and learned advocate:  108
And then concludes, there 's nought impossible.
  *Volp.* Yes, to be learned, Mosca.
  *Mos.*             O, no: rich
Implies it. Hood an ass with reverend purple,
So you can hide his two ambitious ears,
And he shall pass for a cathedral doctor.
  *Volp.* My caps, my caps, good Mosca.
Fetch him in.  114
  *Mos.* Stay, sir; your ointment for your eyes.
  *Volp.*            That 's true;
Dispatch, dispatch: I long to have possession
Of my new present.
  *Mos.*         That, and thousands more,
I hope to see you lord of.
  *Volp.*          Thanks, kind Mosca.
  *Mos.* And that, when I am lost in blended
    dust,
And hundred such as I am, in succession —  120
  *Volp.* Nay, that were too much, Mosca.
  *Mos.*          You shall live
Still to delude these harpies.
  *Volp.*         Loving Mosca!
'T is well: my pillow now, and let him enter.
                     [*Exit Mosca.*]
Now, my feign'd cough, my phthisic, and my
    gout,
My apoplexy, palsy, and catarrhs,  125
Help, with your forced functions, this my pos-
    ture,
Wherein, this three year, I have milk'd their
    hopes.
He comes; I hear him — Uh! [*coughing*] uh!
  uh! uh! O ——

### Act I. Scene III

#### [*The Same.*]

##### *Mosca, Voltore, Volpone*

  [*Mos.*] You still are what you were, sir.
  Only you,
Of all the rest, are he commands his love,
And you do wisely to preserve it thus,
With early visitation, and kind notes
Of your good meaning to him, which, I know,  5
Cannot but come most grateful. Patron! sir!
Here 's Signior Voltore is come ——
  *Volp.* [*Faintly.*]        What say you?
  *Mos.* Sir, Signior Voltore is come this morn-
    ing
To visit you.

  *Volp.*         I thank him.
  *Mos.*              And hath brought
A piece of antique plate, bought of St. Mark,
With which he here presents you.
  *Volp.*           He is welcome.  11
Pray him to come more often.
  *Mos.*            Yes.
  *Volt.*            What says he?
  *Mos.* He thanks you, and desires you see
    him often.
  *Volp.* Mosca.
  *Mos.*        My patron!
  *Volp.*        Bring him near, where is he?
I long to feel his hand.
  *Mos.*          The plate is here, sir.  15
  *Volt.* How fare you, sir?
  *Volp.*        I thank you, Signior Voltore;
Where is the plate? mine eyes are bad.
  *Volt.* [*Putting it into his hands.*] I 'm sorry
To see you still thus weak.
  *Mos.* [*Aside.*]       That he is not weaker,
  *Volp.* You are too munificent.
  *Volt.*          No, sir; would to heaven
I could as well give health to you, as that
    plate!  20
  *Volp.* You give, sir, what you can; I thank
    you. Your love
Hath taste in this, and shall not be unanswer'd:
I pray you see me often.
  *Volt.*          Yes, I shall, sir.
  *Volp.* Be not far from me.
  *Mos.*          Do you observe that, sir?
  *Volp.* Hearken unto me still; it will concern
    you.  25
  *Mos.* You are a happy man, sir; know your
    good.
  *Volp.* I cannot now last long ——
  *Mos.* [*Aside.*]       You are his heir, sir.
  *Volt.* [*Aside.*] Am I?
  *Volp.*      I feel me going: Uh! uh! uh! uh!
I am sailing to my port. Uh! uh! uh! uh!
And I am glad I am so near my haven.  30
  *Mos.* Alas, kind gentleman! Well, we must
    all go ——
  *Volt.* But, Mosca ——
  *Mos.*         Age will conquer.
  *Volt.*         Pray thee, hear me;
Am I inscrib'd his heir for certain?
  *Mos.*          Are you!
I do beseech you, sir, you will vouchsafe
To write me i' your family. All my hopes  35
Depend upon your worship: I am lost
Except the rising sun do shine on me.
  *Volt.* It shall both shine, and warm thee,
    Mosca.
  *Mos.* Sir,
I am a man that have not done your love

---

112 **ambitious:** mobile    2 **he:** the one who    10 **of St. Mark:** at a goldsmith's in St. Mark's Square
35 **write . . . family:** enroll me among your servants

All the worst offices: here I wear your keys, 40
See all your coffers and your caskets lock'd,
Keep the poor inventory of your jewels,
Your plate, and moneys; am your steward,
    sir,
Husband your goods here.
    *Volt.*             But am I sole heir?
    *Mos.* Without a partner, sir: confirm'd this
    morning:                    45
The wax is warm yet, and the ink scarce dry
Upon the parchment.
    *Volt.*          Happy, happy me!
By what good chance, sweet Mosca?
    *Mos.*          Your desert, sir;
I know no second cause.
    *Volt.*          Thy modesty
Is loath to know it; well, we shall requite it. 50
    *Mos.* He ever lik'd your course, sir; that
    first took him.
I oft have heard him say how he admir'd
Men of your large profession, that could speak
To every cause, and things mere contraries,
Till they were hoarse again, yet all be law; 55
That, with most quick agility, could turn,
And return; make knots, and undo them;
Give forked counsel; take provoking gold
On either hand, and put it up; these men,
He knew, would thrive with their humility. 60
And, for his part, he thought he should be blest
To have his heir of such a suff'ring spirit,
So wise, so grave, of so perplex'd a tongue,
And loud withal, that would not wag, nor
    scarce
Lie still, without a fee; when every word 65
Your worship but lets fall, is a cecchine! —
                    *Another knocks.*
Who 's that? one knocks; I would not have
    you seen, sir.
And yet — pretend you came and went in
    haste;
I 'll fashion an excuse — and, gentle sir,
When you do come to swim in golden lard, 70
Up to the arms in honey, that your chin
Is borne up stiff with fatness of the flood,
Think on your vassal; but remember me:
I ha' not been your worst of clients.
    *Volt.*          Mosca! ——
    *Mos.* When will you have your inventory
    brought, sir?                    75
Or see a copy of the will? — Anon!
I 'll bring 'em to you, sir. Away, begone,
Put business i' your face.    [*Exit Voltore.*]
    *Volp.* Excellent Mosca!
Come hither, let me kiss thee.
    *Mos.*          Keep you still, sir.
Here is Corbaccio.
    *Volp.*          Set the plate away: 80
The vulture 's gone, and the old raven 's come.

## Act I. Scene IIII

### [*The Same.*]

*Mosca, Corbaccio, Volpone*

[*Mos.*] Betake you to your silence, and your
    sleep.
Stand there and multiply. [*Putting the plate to
    the rest.*] Now shall we see
A wretch who is indeed more impotent
Than this can feign to be; yet hopes to hop
Over his grave.
    [*Enter Corbaccio*]
              Signior Corbaccio!     5
You 're very welcome, sir.
    *Corb.*          How does your patron?
    *Mos.* Troth, as he did, sir; no amends.
    *Corb.*          What! mends he?
    *Mos.* No, sir: he is rather worse.
    *Corb.*         That 's well. Where is he?
    *Mos.* Upon his couch, sir, newly fall'n asleep.
    *Corb.* Does he sleep well?
    *Mos.*         No wink, sir, all this night, 10
Nor yesterday; but slumbers.
    *Corb.*         Good! he should take
Some counsel of physicians: I have brought
    him
An opiate here, from mine own doctor.
    *Mos.* He will not hear of drugs.
    *Corb.*         Why? I myself
Stood by while 't was made, saw all th' ingre-
    dients;                    15
And know it cannot but most gently work:
My life for his, 't is but to make him sleep.
    *Volp.* [*Aside.*] Ay, his last sleep, if he would
    take it.
    *Mos.*     Sir,
He has no faith in physic.
    *Corb.*         Say you, say you?
    *Mos.* He has no faith in physic: he does
    think                     20
Most of your doctors are the greater danger,
And worse disease, t' escape. I often have
Heard him protest that your physician
Should never be his heir.
    *Corb.*         Nor I his heir?
    *Mos.* Not your physician, sir.
    *Corb.*         O, no, no, no, 25
I do not mean it.
    *Mos.*        No, sir, nor their fees
He cannot brook: he says they flay a man
Before they kill him.
    *Corb.*        Right, I do conceive you.
    *Mos.* And then they do it by experiment;
For which the law not only doth absolve 'em,
But gives them great reward: and he is loath 31
To hire his death so.

---

⁵⁹ **put it up:** pocket it    ⁶⁶ **cecchine:** a Venetian gold coin (sequin) worth over two dollars

*Corb.*                    It is true, they kill
With as much license as a judge.
*Mos.*                            Nay, more;
For he but kills, sir, where the law condemns,
And these can kill him too.
*Corb.*                        Ay, or me;   35
Or any man.  How does his apoplex?
Is that strong on him still?
*Mos.*                        Most violent.
His speech is broken, and his eyes are set,
His face drawn longer than 't was wont ——
*Corb.*                          How! how!
Stronger than he was wont?
*Mos.*                  No, sir;  his face   40
Drawn longer than 't was wont.
*Corb.*                          O, good!
*Mos.*                          His mouth
Is ever gaping, and his eyelids hang.
*Corb.*                            Good.
*Mos.*   A freezing numbness stiffens all his
  joints,
And makes the colour of his flesh like lead.
*Corb.*                          'T is good.
*Mos.*   His pulse beats slow, and dull.
*Corb.*                  Good symptoms still.   45
*Mos.*   And from his brain ——
*Corb.*   Ha?  How?  Not from his brain?
*Mos.*   Yes, sir, and from his brain —
*Corb.*              I conceive you;  good.
*Mos.*   Flows a cold sweat, with a continual
  rheum,
Forth the resolved corners of his eyes.
*Corb.*   Is 't possible?  Yet I am better, ha!  50
How does he with the swimming of his head?
*Mos.*   O, sir, 't is past the scotomy;  he now
Hath lost his feeling, and hath left to snort:
You hardly can perceive him, that he breathes.
*Corb.*   Excellent, excellent!  sure I shall out-
  last him:                                55
This makes me young again, a score of years.
*Mos.*   I was a-coming for you, sir.
*Corb.*              Has he made his will?
What has he giv'n me?
*Mos.*                          No, sir.
*Corb.*                      Nothing!  ha?
*Mos.*   He has not made his will, sir.
*Corb.*                        Oh, oh, oh!
What then did Voltore, the lawyer, here?   60
*Mos.*   He smelt a carcase, sir, when he but
  heard
My master was about his testament;
As I did urge him to it for your good ——
*Corb.*   He came unto him, did he?  I thought
so.
*Mos.*   Yes, and presented him this piece of
  plate.                                65

*Corb.*   To be his heir?
*Mos.*                  I do not know, sir.
*Corb.*                        True:
I know it too.
*Mos. [Aside.]*  By your own scale, sir.
*Corb.*                          Well,
I shall prevent him yet.  See, Mosca, look,
Here I have brought a bag of bright cecchines,
Will quite weigh down his plate.
*Mos. [Taking the bag.]*      Yea, marry, sir.  70
This is true physic, this your sacred medicine;
No talk of opiates to this great elixir!
*Corb.*   'T is *aurum palpabile*, if not *potabile*.
*Mos.*   It shall be minister'd to him in his
  bowl.
*Corb.*   Ay, do, do, do.
*Mos.*              Most blessed cordial!   75
This will recover him.
*Corb.*              Yes, do, do, do.
*Mos.*   I think it were not best, sir.
*Corb.*                        What?
*Mos.*                  To recover him.
*Corb.*   O, no, no, no;  by no means.
*Mos.*                  Why, sir, this
Will work some strange effect, if he but feel it.
*Corb.*   'T is true, therefore forbear;  I 'll take
  my venter:                              80
Give me 't again.
*Mos.*          At no hand:  pardon me:
You shall not do yourself that wrong, sir.  I
Will so advise you, you shall have it all.
*Corb.*   How?                        [no man
*Mos.*   All, sir;  't is your right, your own;
Can claim a part:  't is yours without a rival,  85
Decreed by destiny.
*Corb.*          How, how, good Mosca?
*Mos.*   I 'll tell you, sir.  This fit he shall re-
  cover, —
*Corb.*   I do conceive you.
*Mos.*              And on first advantage
Of his gain'd sense, will I re-importune him
Unto the making of his testament:            90
And show him this.   [*Pointing to the money.*]
*Corb.*              Good, good.
*Mos.*                  'T is better yet,
If you will hear, sir.
*Corb.*              Yes, with all my heart.
*Mos.*   Now would I counsel you, make home
  with speed;
There, frame a will;  whereto you shall inscribe
My master your sole heir.
*Corb.*              And disinherit   95
My son?
*Mos.*   O, sir, the better:  for that colour
Shall make it much more taking.
*Corb.*                  O, but colour?

    ⁴⁹ **resolved:** weeping    ⁵² **scotomy:** dizziness    ⁵³ **left:** ceased    ⁶⁷ **scale:** standard    ⁷³ **aurum:**
*Aurum palpabile* is gold which can be felt; *aurum potabile* (drinkable gold) was regarded as a sovereign
remedy of great efficacy.    ⁸¹ **At no hand:** by no means    ⁹⁶ **colour:** pretence

*Mos.* This will, sir, you shall send it unto me.
Now, when I come to enforce, as I will do,
Your cares, your watchings, and your many
    prayers,                    100
Your more than many gifts, your this day's
    present,
And last, produce your will; where, without
    thought,
Or least regard, unto your proper issue,
A son so brave, and highly meriting,
The stream of your diverted love hath thrown
    you                     105
Upon my master, and made him your heir;
He cannot be so stupid, or stone-dead,
But out of conscience and mere gratitude ——
    *Corb.* He must pronounce me his?
    *Mos.*                  'T is true.
    *Corb.*                   This plot
Did I think on before.
    *Mos.*         I do believe it.    110
    *Corb.* Do you not believe it?
    *Mos.*                  Yes, sir.
    *Corb.*              Mine own project.
    *Mos.* Which, when he hath done, sir ——
    *Corb.*           Publish'd me his heir?
    *Mos.* And you so certain to survive him ——
    *Corb.*                    Ay.
    *Mos.* Being so lusty a man ——
    *Corb.*                'T is true.
    *Mos.*                Yes, sir ——
    *Corb.* I thought on that too. See, how he
    should be                115
The very organ to express my thoughts!
    *Mos.* You have not only done yourself a
    good ——
    *Corb.* But multipli'd it on my son.
    *Mos.*             'T is right, sir.
    *Corb.* Still, my invention.
    *Mos.*          'Las, sir! heaven knows,
It hath been all my study, all my care,    120
(I e'en grow gray withal,) how to work
    things ——
    *Corb.* I do conceive, sweet Mosca.
    *Mos.*             You are he
For whom I labour here.
    *Corb.*         Ay, do, do, do:
I 'll straight about it.        [*Going.*]
    *Mos.* [*Aside.*]    Rook go with you, raven!
    *Corb.* I know thee honest.
    *Mos.*             You do lie, sir!
    *Corb.*              And —— 125
    *Mos.* Your knowledge is no better than your
    ears, sir.
    *Corb.* I do not doubt to be a father to thee.
    *Mos.* Nor I to gull my brother of his blessing.
    *Corb.* I may ha' my youth restor'd to me;
    why not?

    *Mos.* Your worship is a precious ass!
    *Corb.*             What sayst thou?
    *Mos.* I do desire your worship to make
    haste, sir.                131
    *Corb.* 'T is done, 't is done; I go.  [*Exit.*]
    *Volp.*             O, I shall burst!
Let out my sides, let out my sides ——
    *Mos.*                  Contain
Your flux of laughter, sir: you know this hope
Is such a bait, it covers any hook.    135
    *Volp.* O, but thy working, and thy placing
    it!
I cannot hold; good rascal, let me kiss thee:
I never knew thee in so rare a humour.
    *Mos.* Alas, sir, I but do as I am taught;
Follow your grave instructions; give 'em
    words;                140
Pour oil into their ears, and send them hence.
    *Volp.* 'T is true, 't is true. What a rare
    punishment
Is avarice to itself!
    *Mos.*          Ay, with our help, sir.
    *Volp.* So many cares, so many maladies,
So many fears attending on old age.    145
Yea, death so often call'd on, as no wish
Can be more frequent with 'em, their limbs
    faint,
Their senses dull, their seeing, hearing, going,
All dead before them; yea, their very teeth,
Their instruments of eating, failing them:  150
Yet this is reckon'd life! Nay, here was one,
Is now gone home, that wishes to live longer!
Feels not his gout, nor palsy; feigns himself
Younger by scores of years, flatters his age
With confident belying it, hopes he may    155
With charms like Æson, have his youth re-
    stor'd;
And with these thoughts so battens, as if fate
Would be as easily cheated on as he,
And all turns air! Who 's that there, now? a
    third!              *Another knocks.*
    *Mos.* Close, to your couch again; I hear his
    voice.                160
It is Corvino, our spruce merchant.
    *Volp.*    [*Lies down as before.*]  Dead.
    *Mos.* Another bout, sir, with your eyes
    [*anointing them*]. Who 's there?

## *Act I.  Scene V*

[*The Same.*]

*Mosca, Corvino, Volpone*

Signior Corvino! come most wish'd for! O,
How happy were you, if you knew it, now!
    *Corv.* Why? what? wherein?
    *Mos.*        The tardy hour is come, sir.

---

[103] **proper issue:** own child    [124] **Rook . . . you:** May you be rooked, or cheated.    [128] **gull:** cheat    [140] **give 'em words:** deceive them    [146] **as:** that    [148] **going:** faculty of walking

*Corv.* He is not dead?

*Mos.*                    Not dead, sir, but as good;
He knows no man.

*Corv.*                    How shall I do then?

*Mos.*                    Why, sir? 5

*Corv.* I have brought him here a pearl.

*Mos.*                    Perhaps he has
So much remembrance left as to know you,
sir:
He still calls on you; nothing but your name
Is in his mouth. Is your pearl orient, sir?

*Corv.* Venice was never owner of the like. 10

*Volp.* [*Faintly.*] Signior Corvino!

*Mos.*                    Hark!

*Volp.*                    Signior Corvino.

*Mos.* He calls you; step and give it him. —
He 's here, sir.
And he has brought you a rich pearl.

*Corv.*                    How do you, sir?
Tell him it doubles the twelfth carat.

*Mos.*                    Sir,
He cannot understand, his hearing 's gone; 15
And yet it comforts him to see you ——

*Corv.*                    Say
I have a diamond for him, too.

*Mos.*                    Best show 't, sir;
Put it into his hand: 't is only there
He apprehends: he has his feeling yet.
See how he grasps it!

*Corv.*                    'Las, good gentleman! 20
How pitiful the sight is!

*Mos.*                    Tut, forget, sir.
The weeping of an heir should still be laughter
Under a visor.

*Corv.*                    Why, am I his heir?

*Mos.* Sir, I am sworn, I may not show the
will
Till he be dead; but here has been Corbaccio,
Here has been Voltore, here were others too, 26
I cannot number 'em, they were so many;
All gaping here for legacies: but I,
Taking the vantage of his naming you,
(Signior Corvino! Signior Corvino!) took 30
Paper, and pen, and ink, and there I ask'd
him
Whom he would have his heir? Corvino. Who
Should be executor? Corvino. And
To any question he was silent to,
I still interpreted the nods he made, 35
Through weakness, for consent: and sent home
th' others,
Nothing bequeath'd them, but to cry and curse.

*Corv.* O, my dear Mosca. *They embrace.*
Does he not perceive us?

*Mos.* No more than a blind harper. He
knows no man,
No face of friend, nor name of any servant, 40

Who 't was that fed him last, or gave him
drink:
Not those he hath begotten, or brought up,
Can he remember.

*Corv.*                    Has he children?

*Mos.*                    Bastards,
Some dozen, or more, that he begot on beggars,
Gypsies, and Jews, and black-moors, when he
was drunk. 45
Knew you not that, sir? 't is the common
fable,
The dwarf, the fool, the eunuch, are all his;
He 's the true father of his family,
In all save me: — but he has giv'n 'em nothing.

*Corv.* That 's well, that 's well! Art sure he
does not hear us? 50

*Mos.* Sure, sir! why, look you, credit your
own sense. [*Shouts in Volp.'s ear.*]
The pox approach, and add to your diseases,
If it would send you hence the sooner, sir,
For your incontinence, it hath deserv'd it
Throughly and throughly, and the plague to
boot! — 55
You may come near, sir. — Would you would
once close
Those filthy eyes of yours, that flow with slime
Like two frog-pits; and those same hanging
cheeks,
Cover'd with hide instead of skin — Nay, help,
sir ——
That look like frozen dish-clouts set on end! 60

*Corv.* Or like an old smok'd wall, on which
the rain
Ran down in streaks!

*Mos.*                    Excellent, sir! speak out:
You may be louder yet; a culverin
Discharged in his ear would hardly bore it.

*Corv.* His nose is like a common sewer, still
running. 65

*Mos.* 'T is good! And what his mouth?

*Corv.*                    A very draught.

*Mos.* O, stop it up ——

*Corv.*                    By no means.

*Mos.*                    Pray you, let me:
Faith I could stifle him rarely with a pillow
As well as any woman that should keep him.

*Corv.* Do as you will; but I 'll begone.

*Mos.*                    Be so; 70
It is your presence makes him last so long.

*Corv.* I pray you use no violence.

*Mos.*                    No, sir! why?
Why should you be thus scrupulous, pray you,
sir?

*Corv.* Nay, at your discretion.

*Mos.*                    Well, good sir, be gone.

*Corv.* I will not trouble him now to take my
pearl. 75

---

⁸ **still:** continually    ⁹ **orient:** of the finest quality    ⁵⁹ **sir:** (to Corvino)    ⁶³ **culverin:** small
cannon    ⁶⁹ **keep:** nurse

*Mos.* Pooh! nor your diamond. What a
    needless care
Is this afflicts you? Is not all here yours?
Am not I here, whom you have made? your
    creature,
That owe my being to you?
    *Corv.*              Grateful Mosca!  79
Thou art my friend, my fellow, my companion,
My partner, and shalt share in all my fortunes.
    *Mos.* Excepting one.
    *Corv.*             What 's that?
    *Mos.*      Your gallant wife, sir. [*Exit Corv.*]
Now is he gone: we had no other means
To shoot him hence but this.
    *Volp.*          My divine Mosca!  84
Thou hast to-day outgone thyself. Who 's
    there?              *Another knocks.*
I will be troubled with no more. Prepare
Me music, dances, banquets, all delights;
The Turk is not more sensual in his pleas-
    ures
Than will Volpone. [*Exit Mos.*] Let me see; a
    pearl!
A diamond! plate! cecchines! Good morning's
    purchase.  90
Why, this is better than rob churches, yet;
Or fat, by eating, once a month, a man ——

              [*Re-enter Mosca*]

Who is 't?
    *Mos.*      The beauteous Lady Would-be, sir,
Wife to the English knight, Sir Politic Would-
    be,
(This is the style, sir, is directed me,)  95
Hath sent to know how you have slept to-night,
And if you would be visited?
    *Volp.*            Not now:
Some three hours hence.
    *Mos.*        I told the squire so much.
    *Volp.* When I am high with mirth and wine;
    then, then:  99
'Fore heaven, I wonder at the desperate valour
Of the bold English, that they dare let loose
Their wives to all encounters!
    *Mos.*          Sir, this knight
Had not his name for nothing, he is *politic,*
And knows, howe'er his wife affect strange
    airs,
She hath not yet the face to be dishonest: 105
But had she Signior Corvino's wife's face ——
    *Volp.* Has she so rare a face?
    *Mos.*         O, sir, the wonder,
The blazing star of Italy! a wench
O' the first year, a beauty ripe as harvest!
Whose skin is whiter than a swan all over, 110
Than silver, snow, or lilies; a soft lip,

Would tempt you to eternity of kissing!
And flesh that melteth in the touch to blood!
Bright as your gold, and lovely as your gold!
    *Volp.* Why had not I known this before?
    *Mos.*           Alas, sir, 115
Myself but yesterday discover'd it.
    *Volp.* How might I see her?
    *Mos.*          O, not possible;
She 's kept as warily as is your gold;
Never does come abroad, never takes air
But at a windore. All her looks are sweet, 120
As the first grapes or cherries, and are watch'd
As near as they are.
    *Volp.*         I must see her.
    *Mos.*                Sir,
There is a guard of ten spies thick upon her,
All his whole household; each of which is set
Upon his fellow, and have all their charge, 125
When he goes out, when he comes in, examin'd.
    *Volp.* I will go see her, though but at her
    windore.
    *Mos.* In some disguise then.
    *Volp.*          That is true; I must
Maintain mine own shape still the same: we 'll
    think.              [*Exeunt.*]

## *Act II.  Scene I*

[*St. Mark's Place, before Corvino's House.*]

[*Sir*] *Politic Would-be, Peregrine*

[*Sir P.*] Sir, to a wise man, all the world 's
    his soil:
It is not Italy, nor France, nor Europe,
That must bound me, if my fates call me forth.
Yet I protest, it is no salt desire
Of seeing countries, shifting a religion,  5
Nor any disaffection to the state
Where I was bred, and unto which I owe
My dearest plots, hath brought me out, much
    less
That idle, antique, stale, grey-headed project
Of knowing men's minds and manners, with
    Ulysses!  10
But a peculiar humour of my wife's
Laid for this height of Venice, to observe,
To quote, to learn the language, and so
    forth ——
I hope you travel, sir, with license?
    *Per.*               Yes.
    *Sir P.* I dare the safelier converse —— How
    long, sir,  15
Since you left England?
    *Per.*          Seven weeks.
    *Sir P.*                 So lately!
You ha' not been with my lord ambassador?
    *Per.* Not yet, sir.

---

⁹⁰ **purchase:** booty   ⁹² **fat:** fatten   ⁹⁸ **squire:** messenger   ¹²⁰ **windore:** window   ¹²² **near:**
closely   ⁴ **salt:** inordinate   ¹² **height:** meridian   ¹³ **quote:** make note of   ¹⁴ **license:** Englishmen
of rank required a royal license to leave the country.

*Sir P.* Pray you, what news, sir, vents our
climate?
I heard last night a most strange thing reported
By some of my lord's followers, and I long   20
To hear how 't will be seconded.
    *Per.*                     What was 't, sir?
    *Sir P.* Marry, sir, of a raven that should
build
In a ship royal of the king's.
    *Per.* [*Aside.*]                This fellow,
Does he gull me, trow? or is gull'd? Your
name, sir?
    *Sir P.* My name is Politic Would-be.
    *Per.* [*Aside.*]           O, that speaks him.   25
A knight, sir?
    *Sir P.*        A poor knight, sir.
    *Per.*                      Your lady
Lies here in Venice, for intelligence
Of tires and fashions, and behaviour,
Among the courtesans? The fine Lady Would-
be?
    *Sir P.* Yes, sir; the spider and the bee oft-
times                                        30
Suck from one flower.
    *Per.*              Good Sir Politic,
I cry you mercy; I have heard much of you:
'T is true, sir, of your raven.
    *Sir P.*             On your knowledge?
    *Per.* Yes, and your lion's whelping in the
Tower.
    *Sir P.* Another whelp!
    *Per.*                   Another, sir.
    *Sir P.*                     Now heaven!   35
What prodigies be these? The fires at Berwick!
And the new star! These things concurring,
strange,
And full of omen! Saw you those meteors?
    *Per.* I did, sir.
    *Sir P.* Fearful! Pray you, sir, confirm me,
Were there three porcpisces seen above the
bridge,                                      40
As they give out?
    *Per.*         Six, and a sturgeon, sir.
    *Sir P.* I am astonish'd.
    *Per.*                Nay, sir, be not so;
I 'll tell you a greater prodigy than these.
    *Sir P.* What should these things portend?
    *Per.*                   The very day
(Let me be sure) that I put forth from London,
There was a whale discover'd in the river,   46
As high as Woolwich, that had waited there,
Few know how many months, for the subversion
Of the Stode fleet.
    *Sir P.*      Is 't possible? Believe it,

'T was either sent from Spain, or the arch-
duke's:                                      50
Spinola's whale, upon my life, my credit!
Will they not leave these projects? Worthy sir,
Some other news.
    *Per.*         Faith, Stone the fool is dead,
And they do lack a tavern fool extremely.
    *Sir P.* Is Mass Stone dead?
    *Per.*         He 's dead, sir; why, I hope   55
You thought him not immortal? — [*Aside.*] O,
this knight,
Were he well known, would be a precious thing
To fit our English stage: he that should write
But such a fellow, should be thought to feign
Extremely, if not maliciously.
    *Sir P.*              Stone dead!   60
    *Per.* Dead. — Lord! how deeply, sir, you
apprehend it!
He was no kinsman to you?
    *Sir P.*             That I know of.
Well! that same fellow was an unknown fool.
    *Per.* And yet you knew him, it seems?
    *Sir P.*                  I did so. Sir,
I knew him one of the most dangerous heads   65
Living within the state, and so I held him.
    *Per.* Indeed, sir?
    *Sir P.*       While he liv'd, in action.
He has receiv'd weekly intelligence,
Upon my knowledge, out of the Low Countries,
For all parts of the world, in cabbages;      70
And those dispens'd again to ambassadors,
In oranges, musk-mellons, apricots,
Lemons, pome-citrons, and such-like; some-
times
In Colchester oysters, and your Selsey cockles.
    *Per.* You make me wonder.
    *Sir P.*           Sir, upon my knowledge.   75
Nay, I've observ'd him, at your public ordinary,
Take his advertisement from a traveller,
A conceal'd statesman, in a trencher of meat;
And instantly, before the meal was done,
Convey an answer in a tooth-pick.
    *Per.*                   Strange!   80
How could this be, sir?
    *Sir P.*            Why, the meat was cut
So like his character, and so laid as he
Must easily read the cipher.
    *Per.*                I have heard,
He could not read, sir.
    *Sir P.*         So 't was given out,
In policy, by those that did employ him:     85
But he could read, and had your languages.
And to 't, as sound a noddle ——
    *Per.*               I have heard, sir,

---

¹⁸ **our climate:** England   ²¹ **seconded:** confirmed   ²⁷ **Lies:** stays   ³⁵ **whelp:** A lion was born
in the Tower of London, Aug. 5, 1604, and another on Feb. 26, 1606.   ⁴⁰ **porcpisces:** porpoises
⁴⁹ **Stode:** Hanseatic town near Hamburg   ⁵¹ **Spinola:** a contemporary Spanish general, known as the
inventor of fantastic military engines   ⁵² **leave . . . projects:** give up these plots   ⁵⁵ **Mass:** master
⁶² **That:** not that   ⁷⁶ **ordinary:** tavern   ⁷⁷ **advertisement:** information   ⁸⁷ **to 't:** in addition

That your baboons were spies, and that they were
A kind of subtle nation near to China.
  *Sir P.* Ay, ay, your Mamaluchi. Faith,
    they had              90
Their hand in a French plot or two; but they
Were so extremely giv'n to women, as
They made discovery of all: yet I
Had my advices here, on Wednesday last,
From one of their own coat, they were return'd,
Made their relations, as the fashion is,   96
And now stand fair for fresh employment.
  *Per.* [*Aside.*]           Heart!
This Sir Pol will be ignorant of nothing. ——
It seems, sir, you know all.
  *Sir P.*         Not all, sir; but
I have some general notions. I do love   100
To note and to observe: though I live out,
Free from the active torrent, yet I 'd mark
The currents and the passages of things
For mine own private use; and know the ebbs
And flows of state.
  *Per.*      Believe it, sir, I hold  105
Myself in no small tie unto my fortunes,
For casting me thus luckily upon you,
Whose knowledge, if your bounty equal it,
May do me great assistance, in instruction
For my behaviour, and my bearing, which  110
Is yet so rude and raw.
  *Sir P.*      Why? came you forth
Empty of rules for travel?
  *Per.*         Faith, I had
Some common ones, from out that vulgar
    grammar,
Which he that cri'd Italian to me, taught me.
  *Sir P.* Why, this it is that spoils all our
    brave bloods,       115
Trusting our hopeful gentry unto pedants,
Fellows of outside, and mere bark. You seem
To be a gentleman of ingenuous race: ——
I not profess it, but my fate hath been
To be, where I have been consulted with,  120
In this high kind, touching some great men's sons,
Persons of blood and honour. ——
  *Per.*      Who be these, sir?

## *Act II.  Scene II*

[*The Same.*]

*Mosca, Politic, Peregrine, Volpone, Nano, Grege*

  [*Mos.*] Under that windore, there 't must
  be. The same.
  *Sir P.* Fellows, to mount a bank. Did your
  instructor

In the dear tongues never discourse to you
Of the Italian mountebanks?
  *Per.*          Yes, sir.
  *Sir P.*               Why,
Here shall you see one.
  *Per.*       They are quacksalvers,
Fellows that live by venting oils and drugs.  6
  *Sir P.* Was that the character he gave you
  of them?
  *Per.* As I remember.
  *Sir P.*       Pity his ignorance.
They are the only knowing men of Europe!
Great general scholars, excellent physicians,  10
Most admir'd statesmen, profess'd favourites
And cabinet counsellors to the greatest princes;
The only languag'd men of all the world!
  *Per.* And, I have heard, they are most lewd
  impostors;
Made all of terms and shreds; no less beliers  15
Of great men's favours, than their own vile
  medicines;
Which they will utter upon monstrous oaths;
Selling that drug for twopence, ere they part,
Which they have valu'd at twelve crowns be-
  fore.
  *Sir P.* Sir, calumnies are answer'd best with
  silence.       20
Yourself shall judge. — Who is it mounts, my
  friends?
  *Mos.* Scoto of Mantua, sir.
  *Sir P.*      Is 't he? Nay, then
I 'll proudly promise, sir, you shall behold
Another man than has been phant'sied to you.
I wonder yet, that he should mount his bank,  25
Here in this nook, that has been wont t' appear
In face of the Piazza! — Here he comes.

[*Enter Volpone, disguised as a mountebank
  Doctor, and followed by a crowd of people*]

  *Volp.* Mount, zany. [*To Nano.*]
  *Grege.* Follow, follow, follow, follow, follow.
  *Sir P.* See how the people follow him! he 's
  a man      30
May write ten thousand crowns in bank here.
  Note,
                [*Volpone mounts the stage.*]
Mark but his gesture: — I do use to observe
The state he keeps in getting up.
  *Per.*         'T is worth it, sir.
  *Volp.* "Most noble gentlemen, and my [34
worthy patrons! It may seem strange that I,
your Scoto Mantuano, who was ever wont to fix
my bank in face of the public Piazza, near
the shelter of the Portico to the Procuratia,

---

  ⁹⁰ **coat:** kind   ⁹⁶ **relations:** reports   ¹⁰⁶ **tie:** obligation   ¹¹⁴ **cri'd:** spoke   Sc. II. s. d. **Grege:**
a mob of people   ² **bank:** platform, bench   ³ **dear tongues:** difficult languages   ⁶ **venting:** dispensing   ¹⁴ **lewd:** ignorant   ¹⁷ **utter:** sell   ²² **Scoto:** an Italian juggler, then in England
²⁴ **phant'sied:** represented   ²⁸ **zany:** buffoon   ³⁴ ff. **Most noble, etc.:** (Volpone's speeches to the
mob, here set in quotation marks, are printed in italic in F.)

should now, after eight months' absence from this illustrious city of Venice, humbly retire [40 myself into an obscure nook of the Piazza."

*Sir P.* Did not I now object the same?

*Per.*                                              Peace, sir.

*Volp.* "Let me tell you: I am not, as your Lombard proverb saith, cold on my feet; or content to part with my commodities at a [45 cheaper rate than I accustom'd: look not for it. Nor that the calumnious reports of that impudent detractor, and shame to our profession (Alessandro Buttone, I mean), who gave out, in public, I was condemn'd *a' sforzato* [50 to the galleys, for poisoning the Cardinal Bembo's cook, hath at all attach'd, much less dejected me. No, no, worthy gentlemen; to tell you true, I cannot endure to see the rabble of these ground *ciarlitani*, that spread their [55 cloaks on the pavement, as if they meant to do feats of activity, and then come in lamely, with their mouldy tales out of Boccaccio, like stale Tabarin, the fabulist: some of them discoursing their travels, and of their tedious cap- [60 tivity in the Turks' galleys, when, indeed, were the truth known, they were the Christians' galleys, where very temporately they eat bread, and drunk water, as a wholesome penance, enjoin'd them by their confessors, for base pil- [65 feries."

*Sir P.* Note but his bearing, and contempt of these.

*Volp.* "These turdy-facy-nasty-paty-lousy-fartical rogues, with one poor groat's-worth [69 of unprepar'd antimony, finely wrapp'd up in several *scartoccios*, are able, very well, to kill their twenty a week, and play; yet these meagre, starv'd spirits, who have half stopp'd the organs of their minds with earthy oppila- [74 tions, want not their favourers among your shrivell'd salad-eating artisans, who are overjoy'd that they may have their half-pe'rth of physic; though it purge 'em into another world, 't makes no matter."

*Sir P.* Excellent! ha' you heard better language, sir?                                         80

*Volp.* "Well, let 'em go. And, gentlemen, honourable gentlemen, know, that for this time, our bank, being thus remov'd from the clamours of the *canaglia* shall be the scene of pleasure and delight; for I have nothing to sell, [85 little or nothing to sell."

*Sir P.* I told you, sir, his end.

*Per.*                                       You did so, sir.

*Volp.* "I protest, I, and my six servants, are not able to make of this precious liquor so fast as it is fetch'd away from my lodging by [90 gentlemen of your city; strangers of the terra firma; worshipful merchants; ay, and senators too: who, ever since my arrival, have detained me to their uses, by their splendidous liberalities. And worthily; for, what avails your [95 rich man to have his magazines stuff'd with *moscadelli*, or of the purest grape, when his physicians prescribe him, on pain of death, to drink nothing but water cocted with anise-seeds? O [99 health! health! the blessing of the rich! the riches of the poor! who can buy thee at too dear a rate, since there is no enjoying this world without thee? Be not then so sparing of your purses, honourable gentlemen, as to abridge the natural course of life ——"                          105

*Per.* You see his end?

*Sir P.*                              Ay, is 't not good?

*Volp.* "For when a humid flux, or catarrh, by the mutability of air, falls from your head into an arm or shoulder, or any other part; take you a ducat, or your cecchine of gold, and [110 apply to the place affected: see what good effect it can work. No, no, 't is this blessed *unguento*, this rare extraction, that hath only power to disperse all malignant humours, that proceed either of hot, cold, moist, or windy causes ——"                                          116

*Per.* I would he had put in dry too.

*Sir P.*                              Pray you observe.

*Volp.* "To fortify the most indigest and crude stomach, ay, were it of one that, through extreme weakness, vomited blood, applying [120 only a warm napkin to the place, after the unction and fricace; — for the *vertigine* in the head, putting but a drop into your nostrils, likewise behind the ears; a most sovereign and ap- [124 proved remedy; the *mal caduco*, cramps, convulsions, paralyses, epilepsies, *tremorcordia*, retired nerves, ill vapours of the spleen, stoppings of the liver, the stone, the strangury, *hernia ventosa, iliaca passio;* stops a *dysenteria* immediately; easeth the torsion of the small [130 guts; and cures *melancholia hypocondriaca*, being taken and applied, according to my printed receipt. For *Pointing to his bill and his glass.* this is the physician, this the medicine; this counsels, this cures; this gives the direction, [135 this works the effect; and, in sum, both together may be term'd an abstract of the theoric and practic in the Æsculapian art. 'T will cost

⁵⁰ **a' sforzato**: with hard labor (Ital.)   ⁵⁵ **ciarlitani**: petty impostors   ⁵⁹ **Tabarin**: member of an Italian strolling company that visited France in 1570     **fabulist**: professional story teller   ⁷¹ **scartoccios**: waste papers   ⁷⁴⁻⁷⁵ **oppilations**: obstructions   ⁸⁴ **canaglia**: rabble   ⁹¹⁻⁹² **terra firma**: main land   ⁹⁶⁻⁹⁷ **moscadelli**: sweet wines   ⁹⁹ **cocted**: boiled   ¹¹³ **unguento**: ointment   ¹²² **fricace**: rubbing   **vertigine**: giddiness. This speech gives a list of diseases which could be cured by Scoto's Oil. Jonson often used strings of technical words to give an air of authenticity to a particular scene.

you eight crowns. And, — Zan Fritada, pray
thee sing a verse extempore in honour of it." [140
*Sir P.*  How do you like him, sir?
*Per.*                              Most strangely, I!
*Sir P.*  Is not his language rare?
*Per.*                              But alchemy,
I never heard the like; or Broughton's books.

[*Nano sings.*]

SONG

Had old Hippocrates, or Galen,
That to their books put med'cines all in, 145
But known this secret, they had never
(Of which they will be guilty ever)
Been murderers of so much paper,
Or wasted many a hurtless taper;
No Indian drug had e'er been famed,     150
Tobacco, sassafras not named;
Ne yet of guacum one small stick, sir,
Nor Raymund Lully's great elixir.
Ne had been known the Danish Gonswart,
Or Paracelsus, with his long sword.    155

*Per.*  All this, yet, will not do; eight crowns
is high.
*Volp.*  "No more. — Gentlemen, if I had but
time to discourse to you the miraculous effects
of this my oil, surnamed *oglio del Scoto;* with
the countless catalogue of those I have [160
cured of th' aforesaid, and many more diseases;
the patents and privileges of all the princes and
commonwealths of Christendom; or but the
depositions of those that appear'd on my part,
before the signiory of the Sanitá and most [165
learned College of Physicians; where I was
authorized, upon notice taken of the admirable
virtues of my medicaments, and mine own excellency in matter of rare and unknown secrets,
not only to disperse them publicly in this [170
famous city, but in all the territories, that happily joy under the government of the most pious
and magnificent states of Italy. But may
some other gallant fellow say, 'O, there be
divers that make profession to have as good, [175
and as experimented receipts as yours.' Indeed,
very many have assay'd, like apes, in imitation
of that, which is really and essentially in me,
to make of this oil; bestow'd great cost in [179
furnaces, stills, alembics, continual fires, and
preparation of the ingredients (as indeed there
goes to it six hundred several simples, besides
some quantity of human fat, for the conglutina-
tion, which we buy of the anatomists), but when
these practitioners come to the last decoc- [185
tion, blow, blow, puff, puff, and all flies in

fumo: ha, ha, ha! Poor wretches! I rather
pity their folly and indiscretion, than their
loss of time and money; for those may be recovered by industry: but to be a fool born, is a
disease incurable.                           191
"For myself, I always from my youth have
endeavour'd to get the rarest secrets, and book
them, either in exchange, or for money; I
spared nor cost nor labour, where anything [195
was worthy to be learned. And, gentlemen,
honourable gentlemen, I will undertake, by
virtue of chymical art, out of the honourable
hat that covers your head, to extract the four
elements; that is to say, the fire, air, water, [200
and earth, and return you your felt without burn
or stain. For, whilst others have been at the
*ballo,* I have been at my book; and am now
past the craggy paths of study, and come to
the flowery plains of honour and reputation." [205
*Sir P.*  I do assure you, sir, that is his aim.
*Volp.*  "But to our price ——"
*Per.*                              And that withal, Sir Pol.
*Volp.*  "You all know, honourable gentle-
men, I never valu'd this *ampulla,* or vial, at less
than eight crowns; but for this time, I am [210
content to be depriv'd of it for six; six crowns is
the price, and less in courtesy I know you cannot offer me; take it or leave it, howsoever,
both it and I am at your service. I ask you not
as the value of the thing, for then I should [215
demand of you a thousand crowns, so the Cardinals Montalto, Fernese, the great Duke of Tus-
cany, my gossip, with divers other princes,
have given me; but I despise money. Only to
show my affection to you, honourable [220
gentlemen, and your illustrous state here, I
have neglected the messages of these princes,
mine own offices, fram'd my journey hither,
only to present you with the fruits of my [224
travels. — Tune your voices once more to the
touch of your instruments, and give the honourable assembly some delightful recreation."
*Per.*  What monstrous and most painful circumstance
Is here, to get some three or four gazettes,
Some threepence i' the whole! for that 't will
come to.                                     230

[*Nano sings.*]

SONG

You that would last long, list to my song,
Make no more coil, but buy of this oil.
Would you be ever fair and young?
Stout of teeth, and strong of tongue?

---

142 **But:** except (in)     143 **Broughton:** an eccentric theologian of the time (cf. *The Alchemist,* II, iii,
242 and IV, v, 1 ff.)     152 **guacum:** a resinous drug     153 **Lully:** a famous mediæval alchemist
154 **Gonswart:** Gansfort, a Westphalian scholar of the 15th century     182 **simples:** herbs     187 **fumo:**
smoke     203 **ballo:** an Italian game of ball     218 **gossip:** familiar friend     223 **offices:** duties     228 **circumstance:** beating about the bush     229 **gazettes:** small Venetian coins     232 **coil:** disturbance

Tart of palate? quick of ear?        235  
Sharp of sight? of nostril clear?  
Moist of hand? and light of foot?  
Or, I will come nearer to 't,  
Would you live free from all diseases?  
Do the act your mistress pleases,     240  
Yet fright all aches from your bones?  
Here 's a med'cine for the nones.

*Volp.* "Well, I am in a humour at this time
to make a present of the small quantity my
coffer contains; to the rich in courtesy, and [245
to the poor for God's sake. Wherefore now
mark: I ask'd you six crowns; and six crowns,
at other times, you have paid me; you shall not
give me six crowns, nor five, nor four, nor three,
nor two, nor one; nor half a ducat; no, nor [250
a *moccinigo.* Sixpence it will cost you, or six
hundred pound — expect no lower price, for, by
the banner of my front, I will not bate a *bagatine.*
— That I will have, only, a pledge of your loves,
to carry something from amongst you, to [255
show I am not contemn'd by you. Therefore,
now, toss your handkerchiefs, cheerfully, cheerfully; and be advertised, that the first heroic
spirit that deigns to grace me with a handkerchief, I will give it a little remembrance of [260
something beside, shall please it better than if
I had presented it with a double pistolet."

*Per.* Will you be that heroic spark, Sir Pol?
    *Celia, at the window, throws down
        her handkerchief.*

O, see! the windore has prevented you.

*Volp.* "Lady, I kiss your bounty; and [265
for this timely grace you have done your poor
Scoto of Mantua, I will return you, over and
above my oil, a secret of that high and inestimable nature, shall make you forever enamour'd
on that minute, wherein your eye first de- [270
scended on so mean, yet not altogether to be
despis'd, an object. Here is a powder conceal'd
in this paper, of which, if I should speak to the
worth, nine thousand volumes were but as one
page, that page as a line, that line as a word; [275
so short is this pilgrimage of man (which some
call life) to the expressing of it. Would I reflect
on the price? Why, the whole world were but as
an empire, that empire as a province, that province as a bank, that bank as a private purse [280
to the purchase of it. I will only tell you; it is
the powder that made Venus a goddess (given
her by Apollo), that kept her perpetually young,

clear'd her wrinkles, firm'd her gums, fill'd
her skin, colour'd her hair; from her de- [285
riv'd to Helen, and at the sack of Troy unfor-
tunately lost: till now, in this our age, it was
as happily recover'd, by a studious antiquary,
out of some ruins of Asia, who sent a moiety
of it to the court of France (but much [290
sophisticated), wherewith the ladies there now
colour their hair. The rest, at this present, remains with me; extracted to a quintessence: so
that, wherever it but touches, in youth it perpetually preserves, in age restores the com- [295
plexion; seats your teeth, did they dance like
virginal jacks, firm as a wall: makes them
white as ivory, that were black as ——"

## Act II.  Scene III

### [*The Same.*]

#### *Corvino, Politic, Peregrine*

[*Corv.*] Spite o' the devil, and my shame!
    come down here;  
Come down! — No house but mine to make
    your scene?  
Signior Flaminio, will you down, sir? down?  
What, is my wife your Franciscina, sir?  
No windores on the whole Piazza, here,    5  
To make your properties, but mine? but
    mine?  
      *He beats away the mountebank, &c.*  
Heart! ere to-morrow I shall be new christen'd,  
And called the Pantalone di Besogniosi,  
About the town.  
    *Per.*      What should this mean, Sir Pol?  
    *Sir P.* Some trick of state, believe it; I will
      home.            10  
    *Per.* It may be some design on you.  
    *Sir P.*                  I know not.  
I 'll stand upon my guard.  
    *Per.*           It is your best, sir.  
    *Sir P.* This three weeks, all my advices, all
      my letters,  
They have been intercepted.  
    *Per.*             Indeed, sir!  
Best have a care.  
    *Sir P.*    Nay, so I will.  
    *Per.*             This knight,  15  
I may not lose him, for my mirth, till night.  
                       *[Exeunt.]*

---

241 **aches:** pronounced aitches   242 **nones:** occasion   251 **moccinigo:** a Venetian coin worth less than
twenty cents   253 **bagatine:** a small Italian coin   262 **pistolet:** a Spanish gold coin   264 **prevented:**
anticipated   297 **virginal jacks:** pieces of wood which made the quills pluck the strings of a virginal
3 **Flaminio:** Corvino ironically pretends that he is taking part in one of the contemporary Italian
comedies in which the dialogue was largely extemporaneous.  The name probably refers to
Flaminio Scala, leader of a famous company of actors.  4 **Franciscina:** a stock character, a
flirtatious servant-girl   8 **Pantalone di Besogniosi:** a stock humorous character (lit. "fool of
beggars")

## Act II.  Scene IIII

*[A Room in Volpone's House.]*

*Volpone, Mosca*

[*Volp.*]  O, I am wounded!

*Mos.*              Where, sir?

*Volp.*          Not without;

Those blows were nothing: I could bear them
    ever.

But angry Cupid, bolting from her eyes,

Hath shot himself into me like a flame;

Where now he flings about his burning heat, 5

As in a furnace an ambitious fire

Whose vent is stopp'd.  The fight is all within
    me.

I cannot live, except thou help me, Mosca;

My liver melts, and I, without the hope

Of some soft air from her refreshing breath, 10

Am but a heap of cinders.

*Mos.*          'Las, good sir,

Would you had never seen her!

*Volp.*         Nay, would thou

Hadst never told me of her!

*Mos.*         Sir, 't is true;

I do confess I was unfortunate,

And you unhappy; but I 'm bound in con-
    science,                 15

No less than duty, to effect my best

To your release of torment, and I will, sir.

*Volp.* Dear Mosca, shall I hope?

*Mos.*         Sir, more than dear,

I will not bid you to despair of aught

Within a human compass.

*Volp.*         O, there spoke 20

My better angel.  Mosca, take my keys,

Gold, plate, and jewels, all 's at thy devotion;

Employ them how thou wilt: nay, coin me
    too:

So thou in this but crown my longings, Mosca.

*Mos.*  Use but your patience.

*Volp.*         So I have.

*Mos.*         I doubt not 25

To bring success to your desires.

*Volp.*         Nay, then,

I not repent me of my late disguise.

*Mos.*  If you can horn him, sir, you need not.

*Volp.*         True:

Besides, I never meant him for my heir.

Is not the colour o' my beard and eyebrows 30

To make me known?

*Mos.*         No jot.

*Volp.*         I did it well.

*Mos.*  So well, would I could follow you in
    mine,

With half the happiness! and yet I would

Escape your epilogue.

*Volp.*         But were they gull'd

With a belief that I was Scoto?

*Mos.*         Sir,    35

Scoto himself could hardly have distinguish'd!

I have not time to flatter you now; we 'll
    part:

And as I prosper, so applaud my art.  *[Exeunt.]*

## Act II.  Scene V

*[A Room in Corvino's House.]*

*Corvino, Celia, Servitore*

[*Corv.*]  Death of mine honour, with the city's
    fool!

A juggling, tooth-drawing, prating mounte-
    bank!

And at a public windore! where, whilst he,

With his strain'd action, and his dole of faces,

To his drug-lecture draws your itching ears, 5

A crew of old, unmarri'd, noted lechers,

Stood leering up like satyrs: and you smile

Most graciously, and fan your favours forth,

To give your hot spectators satisfaction!

What, was your mountebank their call? their
    whistle?                 10

Or were you enamour'd on his copper rings,

His saffron jewel, with the toad-stone in 't,

Or his embroid'red suit, with the cope-stitch,

Made of a hearse cloth? or his old tilt-feather?

Or his starch'd beard!  Well, you shall have
    him, yes!            15

He shall come home, and minister unto you

The fricace for the mother.  Or, let me see,

I think you 'd rather mount; would you not
    mount?

Why, if you 'll mount, you may; yes, truly,
    you may!

And so you may be seen, down to the foot. 20

Get you a cittern, Lady Vanity,

And be a dealer with the virtuous man;

Make one.  I 'll but protest myself a cuckold,

And save your dowry.  I 'm a Dutchman, I!

For if you thought me an Italian,      25

You would be damn'd ere you did this, you
    whore!

Thou 'dst tremble to imagine that the murder

Of father, mother, brother, all thy race,

Should follow, as the subject of my justice.

*Cel.*  Good sir, have patience.

*Corv.*        What couldst thou propose 30

Less to thyself, than in this heat of wrath,

And stung with my dishonour, I should strike

---

²⁸ **horn him:** make him a cuckold    ³⁴ **epilogue:** *i.e.,* the beating from Corvino    ⁴ **dole of faces:** grimaces    ¹² **toad-stone:** the jewel supposed to be found in the toad's head    ¹⁴ **tilt-feather:** discarded plume from the tilt-yard (cf. *The Malcontent*, Induction, 61 ff.)    ¹⁷ **mother:** hysteria    ¹⁸ **mount:** join the mountebanks    ²¹ **cittern:** guitar    ³⁰ **propose:** expect

This steel unto thee, with as many stabs
As thou wert gaz'd upon with goatish eyes?
   *Cel.* Alas, sir, be appeas'd! I could not
    think                           35
My being at the windore should more now
Move your impatience than at other times.
   *Corv.* No! not to seek and entertain a parley
With a known knave, before a multitude!
You were an actor with your handkerchief,  40
Which he most sweetly kiss'd in the receipt,
And might, no doubt, return it with a letter,
And point the place where you might meet;
    your sister's,
Your mother's, or your aunt's might serve the
    turn.
   *Cel.* Why, dear sir, when do I make these
    excuses,                      45
Or ever stir abroad, but to the church?
And that so seldom ——
   *Corv.*          Well, it shall be less;
And thy restraint before was liberty,
To what I now decree: and therefore mark
    me.
First, I will have this bawdy light damm'd
    up;                       50
And till 't be done, some two or three yards
    off,
I 'll chalk a line; o'er which if thou but chance
To set thy desp'rate foot, more hell, more
    horror,
More wild remorseless rage shall seize on
    thee,
Than on a conjuror that had heedless left   55
His circle's safety ere his devil was laid.
Then here 's a lock which I will hang upon
    thee,
And, now I think on 't, I will keep thee back-
    wards;
Thy lodging shall be backwards: thy walks
    backwards;
Thy prospect, all be backwards; and no pleas-
    ure,                    60
That thou shalt know but backwards: nay,
    since you force
My honest nature, know, it is your own,
Being too open, makes me use you thus:
Since you will not contain your subtle nos-
    trils
In a sweet room, but they must snuff the air   65
Of rank and sweaty passengers. *Knock within.*
    One knocks.
Away, and be not seen, pain of thy life;
Nor look toward the windore; if thou dost ——
Nay, stay, hear this —— let me not prosper,
    whore,
But I will make thee an anatomy,         70
Dissect thee mine own self, and read a lecture

Upon thee to the city, and in public.
Away! —                      *[Exit Celia.]*

       *[Enter Servant]*
     Who 's there?
   *Ser.*           'T is Signior Mosca, sir.

### *Act II.  Scene VI*

       *[The Same.]*

     *Corvino, Mosca*

   *[Corv.]* Let him come in. His master 's
    dead; there 's yet
Some good to help the bad. —— My Mosca,
    welcome!
I guess your news.
   *Mos.*         I fear you cannot, sir.
   *Corv.* Is 't not his death?
   *Mos.*           Rather the contrary.
   *Corv.* Not his recovery?
   *Mos.*            Yes, sir.
   *Corv.*            I am curs'd,   5
I am bewitch'd, my crosses meet to vex me.
How? how? how? how?
   *Mos.*         Why, sir, with Scoto's oil;
Corbaccio and Voltore brought of it,
Whilst I was busy in an inner room ——
   *Corv.* Death! that damn'd mountebank! but
    for the law                   10
Now, I could kill the rascal: 't cannot be
His oil should have that virtue. Ha' not I
Known him a common rogue, come fiddling in
To th' *osteria*, with a tumbling whore,
And, when he has done all his forc'd tricks,
    been glad                 15
Of a poor spoonful of dead wine, with flies
    in 't?
It cannot be. All his ingredients
Are a sheep's gall, a roasted bitch's marrow,
Some few sod earwigs, pounded caterpillars,
A little capon's grease, and fasting spittle:   20
I know 'em to a dram.
   *Mos.*           I know not, sir;
But some on 't, there, they pour'd into his ears,
Some in his nostrils, and recover'd him;
Applying but the fricace.
   *Corv.*         Pox o' that fricace!
   *Mos.* And since, to seem the more officious
And flatt'ring of his health, there, they have
    had,                    26
At extreme fees, the college of physicians
Consulting on him, how they might restore
    him;
Where one would have a cataplasm of spices,
Another a flay'd ape clapp'd to his breast,   30
A third would ha' it a dog, a fourth an oil,

---

  **58 backwards:** in the back of the house    **65 passengers:** passers-by    **70 anatomy:** corpse for dis
section    **14 osteria:** inn    **19 sod:** boiled    **29 cataplasm:** poultice

With wild cats' skins: at last, they all resolv'd
That to preserve him, was no other means
But some young woman must be straight sought
    out,
Lusty, and full of juice, to sleep by him;   35
And to this service most unhappily,
And most unwillingly am I now employ'd,
Which here I thought to pre-acquaint you with,
For your advice, since it concerns you most;
Because I would not do that thing might cross
Your ends, on whom I have my whole depend-
    ence, sir;            41
Yet, if I do it not they may delate
My slackness to my patron, work me out
Of his opinion; and there all your hopes,
Venters, or whatsoever, are all frustrate!   45
I do but tell you, sir. Besides, they are all
Now striving who shall first present him; there-
    fore ——
I could entreat you, briefly conclude somewhat;
Prevent 'em if you can.
    *Corv.*           Death to my hopes,
This is my villainous fortune! Best to hire   50
Some common courtesan.
    *Mos.*         Ay. I thought on that, sir;
But they are all so subtle, full of art —
And age again doting and flexible,
So as — I cannot tell — we may, perchance,
Light on a quean may cheat us all.
    *Corv.*          'T is true.   55
    *Mos.* No, no: it must be one that has no
    tricks, sir,
Some simple thing, a creature made unto it;
Some wench you may command. Ha' you no
    kinswoman?
Gods so — Think, think, think, think, think,
    think, think, sir.
One o' the doctors offer'd there his daughter.
    *Corv.* How!
    *Mos.*       Yes, Signior Lupo, the physician.  61
    *Corv.* His daughter!
    *Mos.*       And a virgin, sir. Why, alas,
He knows the state of 's body, what it is:
That nought can warm his blood, sir, but a fe-
    ver;
Nor any incantation raise his spirit:     65
A long forgetfulness hath seiz'd that part.
Besides, sir, who shall know it? Some one or
    two —
    *Corv.* I pray thee give me leave. [*Walks
    aside.*] If any man
But I had had this luck — The thing in 't self,
I know, is nothing. — Wherefore should not
    I                 70
As well command my blood and my affections
As this dull doctor? In the point of honour,
The cases are all one of wife and daughter.

    *Mos.* [*Aside.*] I hear him coming.
    *Corv.*            She shall do 't: 't is done.
Slight! if this doctor, who is not engag'd,   75
Unless 't be for his counsel, which is nothing,
Offer his daughter, what should I, that am
So deeply in? I will prevent him. Wretch!
Covetous wretch! — Mosca, I have determin'd.
    *Mos.* How, sir?          [wot of  80
    *Corv.*     We 'll make all sure. The party you
Shall be mine own wife, Mosca.
    *Mos.*              Sir, the thing,
But that I would not seem to counsel you,
I should have motion'd to you, at the first:
And make your count, you have cut all their
    throats.
Why, 't is directly taking a possession!   85
And in his next fit, we may let him go.
'T is but to pull the pillow from his head,
And he is throttled: 't had been done before
But for your scrupulous doubts.
    *Corv.*          Ay, a plague on 't,
My conscience fools my wit! Well, I 'll be
    brief,          90
And so be thou, lest they should be before us.
Go home, prepare him, tell him with what
    zeal
And willingness I do it: swear it was
On the first hearing, as thou mayst do, truly,
Mine own free motion.
    *Mos.*        Sir, I warrant you,  95
I 'll so possess him with it, that the rest
Of his starv'd clients shall be banish'd all;
And only you receiv'd. But come not, sir,
Until I send, for I have something else
To ripen for your good, you must not know 't.
    *Corv.* But do not you forget to send now.
    *Mos.*          Fear not. [*Exit.*]  101

### Act II. Scene VII

*[The Same.]*

*Corvino, Celia*

[*Corv.*] Where are you, wife? My Celia!
    wife!

*[Enter Celia]*

                — What, blubbering?
Come, dry those tears. I think thou thought'st
    me in earnest;
Ha! by this light I talk'd so but to try thee:
Methinks, the lightness of the occasion
Should ha' confirm'd thee. Come, I am not
    jealous.         5
    *Cel.* No?
    *Corv.*     Faith I am not, I, nor never was;
It is a poor unprofitable humour.

---

  ⁴² **delate**: report (an evil action)   ⁵⁵ **quean**: jade, hussy   ⁵⁷ **made**: prepared   ⁷⁴ **coming**: *i.e.*, into
my trap   ⁸³ **motion'd**: proposed   ⁸⁴ **make your count**: be sure   cut . . . throats: outdone them all

Do not I know, if women have a will,
They 'll do 'gainst all the watches o' the
    world,
And that the fiercest spies are tam'd with gold?
Tut, I am confident in thee, thou shalt see 't; 11
And see, I 'll give thee cause too, to believe it.
Come kiss me.   Go, and make thee ready
    straight,
In all thy best attire, thy choicest jewels,
Put 'em all on, and, with 'em, thy best look: 15
We are invited to a solemn feast,
At old Volpone's, where it shall appear
How far I am free from jealousy or fear.
                                        [*Exeunt.*]

## Act III.   Scene I

### [*A Street.*]

### *Mosca*

*Mos.*   I fear I shall begin to grow in love
With my dear self, and my most prosp'rous
    parts,
They do so spring and burgeon; I can feel
A whimsy i' my blood: I know not how,
Success hath made me wanton.   I could skip 5
Out of my skin now, like a subtle snake,
I am so limber.   O! your parasite
Is a most precious thing, dropp'd from above,
Not bred 'mongst clods and clodpoles, here on
    earth.
I muse, the mystery was not made a science, 10
It is so liberally profess'd!   Almost
All the wise world is little else, in nature,
But parasites or sub-parasites.   And yet
I mean not those that have your bare town-art,
To know who 's fit to feed 'em; have no house,
No family, no care, and therefore mould 16
Tales for men's ears, to bait that sense; or get
Kitchen-invention, and some stale receipts
To please the belly, and the groin; nor those,
With their court dog-tricks, that can fawn and
    fleer,                                          20
Make their revénue out of legs and faces,
Echo my lord, and lick away a moth:
But your fine elegant rascal, that can rise
And stoop, almost together, like an arrow;
Shoot through the air as nimbly as a star; 25
Turn short as doth a swallow; and be here,
And there, and here, and yonder, all at once;
Present to any humour, all occasion;
And change a visor swifter than a thought! 29
This is the creature had the art born with him;
Toils not to learn it, but doth practise it
Out of most excellent nature: and such sparks
Are the true parasites, others but their zanies.

## Act III.   Scene II

### [*The Same.*]

### *Mosca, Bonario*

Who 's this?   Bonario, old Corbaccio's son?
The person I was bound to seek.   Fair sir,
You are happ'ly met.
    *Bon.*                    That cannot be by thee.
    *Mos.*   Why, sir?                    [leave me:
    *Bon.*        Nay, pray thee know thy way, and
I would be loath to interchange discourse      5
With such a mate as thou art.
    *Mos.*                    Courteous sir,
Scorn not my poverty.
    *Bon.*                    Not I, by heaven;
But thou shalt give me leave to hate thy base-
    ness.
    *Mos.*   Baseness!
    *Bon.*        Ay; answer me, is not thy sloth
Sufficient argument? thy flattery?            10
Thy means of feeding?
    *Mos.*                    Heaven be good to me!
These imputations are too common, sir,
And eas'ly stuck on virtue when she 's poor.
You are unequal to me, and howe'er
Your sentence may be righteous, yet you are
    not,                                          15
That, ere you know me, thus proceed in cen-
    sure:
St. Mark bear witness 'gainst you, 't is inhuman.
                                        [*Weeps.*]
    *Bon.* [*Aside.*]   What! does he weep? the sign
    is soft and good:
I do repent me that I was so harsh.
    *Mos.*   'T is true, that, sway'd by strong
    necessity,                                    20
I am enforc'd to eat my careful bread
With too much obsequy; 't is true, beside,
That I am fain to spin mine own poor raiment
Out of my mere observance, being not born
To a free fortune: but that I have done     25
Base offices, in rending friends asunder,
Dividing families, betraying counsels,
Whisp'ring false lies, or mining men with
    praises,
Train'd their credulity with perjuries,
Corrupted chastity, or am in love            30
With mine own tender ease, but would not
    rather
Prove the most rugged and laborious course,
That might redeem my present estimation,
Let me here perish, in all hope of goodness.
    *Bon.* [*Aside.*]   This cannot be a personated
    passion. —                                    35

---

¹⁰ **mystery:** profession      ¹⁷ **sense:** *i.e.,* love of gossip      ²¹ **legs and faces:** bows and smirks
²⁹ **visor:** expression      ⁶ **mate:** fellow      ¹⁴ **unequal:** unjust      ²² **obsequy:** obsequiousness      ²⁴ **observ-**
**ance:** service      ²⁹ **Train'd:** lured      ³³ **estimation:** reputation

I was to blame, so to mistake thy nature;
Pray thee forgive me: and speak out thy busi-
   ness.
  *Mos.*   Sir, it concerns you; and though I
   may seem
At first to make a main offence in manners,
And in my gratitude unto my master,    40
Yet for the pure love which I bear all right,
And hatred of the wrong, I must reveal it.
This very hour your father is in purpose
To disinherit you —
  *Bon.*          How!
  *Mos.*             And thrust you forth,
As a mere stranger to his blood: 't is true, sir.
The work no way engageth me, but as    46
I claim an interest in the general state
Of goodness and true virtue, which I hear
T' abound in you; and for which mere respect,
Without a second aim, sir, I have done it.   50
  *Bon.*   This tale hath lost thee much of the
   late trust
Thou hadst with me; it is impossible.
I know not how to lend it any thought,
My father should be so unnatural.
  *Mos.*   It is a confidence that well becomes   55
Your piety; and form'd, no doubt, it is
From your own simple innocence: which makes
Your wrong more monstrous and abhorr'd.
    But, sir,
I now will tell you more. This very minute,
It is, or will be doing; and if you    60
Shall be but pleas'd to go with me, I 'll bring
  you,
I dare not say where you shall see, but where
Your ear shall be a witness of the deed;
Hear yourself written bastard, and profess'd
The common issue of the earth.
  *Bon.*          I 'm maz'd!   65
  *Mos.*   Sir, if I do it not, draw your just sword,
And score your vengeance on my front and
  face;
Mark me your villain: you have too much
  wrong,
And I do suffer for you, sir. My heart   69
Weeps blood in anguish ——
  *Bon.*       Lead; I follow thee. [*Exeunt.*]

## Act III.   Scene III

[*A Room in Volpone's House.*]

*Volpone, Nano, Androgyno, Castrone*

[*Volp.*]   Mosca stays long, methinks. —
  Bring forth your sports,
And help to make the wretched time more
  sweet.
  *Nan.*   "Dwarf, fool, and eunuch, well met
  here we be.

A question it were now, whether of us three,
Being all the known delicates of a rich man,   5
In pleasing him, claim the precedency can?"
  *Cas.*   "I claim for myself."
  *And.*          "And so doth the fool."
  *Nan.*   "'T is foolish indeed: let me set you
  both to school.
First for your dwarf, he 's little and witty,
And everything, as it is little, is pretty;   10
Else why do men say to a creature of my shape,
So soon as they see him, 'It 's a pretty little
  ape'?
And why a pretty ape, but for pleasing imita-
  tion
Of greater men's action, in a ridiculous fash-
  ion?   14
Beside, this feat body of mine doth not crave
Half the meat, drink, and cloth, one of your
  bulks will have.
Admit your fool's face be the mother of laughter,
Yet, for his brain, it must always come after:
And though that do feed him, it 's a pitiful case,
His body is beholding to such a bad face."   20
                     *One knocks.*
  *Volp.*   Who 's there? My couch; away! look,
  Nano, see!       [*Exeunt And. and Cas.*]
Give me my caps first — go, inquire. [*Exit
  Nano.*] Now, Cupid
Send it be Mosca, and with fair return!
  *Nan.* [*Within.*]   It is the beauteous madam —
  *Volp.*          Would-be — is it?
  *Nan.*   The same.
  *Volp.*   Now torment on me! Squire her
  in:   25
For she will enter, or dwell here for ever.
Nay, quickly, that my fit were past! [*Retires
  to his couch.*] I fear
A second hell too, that my loathing this
Will quite expel my appetite to the other:
Would she were taking now her tedious leave.
Lord, how it threats me what I am to suffer!   31

## Act III.   Scene IIII

[*The Same.*]

*Lady [Politic Would-be], Volpone, Nano,
2 Women*

[*Lady P.*]   I thank you, good sir. Pray you
  signify
Unto your patron I am here. — This band
Shows not my neck enough. — I trouble you
  sir;
Let me request you bid one of my women
Come hither to me. In good faith, I am
  dress'd   5
Most favourably to-day! It is no matter:
'T is well enough.

<sup></sup>⁴ **whether:** which   ⁵ **delicates:** favorites, pets   ¹⁵ **feat:** neatly formed

*[Enter 1 Waiting-woman]*

               Look, see these petulant things,
How they have done this!
*Volp.*       *[Aside.]* I do feel the fever
Ent'ring in at mine ears; O, for a charm,
To fright it hence!
*Lady P.*        Come nearer: is this curl 10
In his right place, or this? Why is this higher
Than all the rest? You ha' not wash'd your
   eyes yet!
Or do they not stand even i' your head?
Where 's your fellow? call her. *[Exit 1 Woman.]*
*Nan.*              Now, St. Mark
Deliver us! anon she 'll beat her women, 15
Because her nose is red.

*[Re-enter 1 with 2 Woman]*

*Lady P.*          I pray you view
This tire, forsooth: are all things apt, or no?
  *1 Wom.* One hair a little here sticks out, for-
    sooth.
*Lady P.* Does 't so, forsooth! and where was
  your dear sight,
When it did so, forsooth! What now! bird-
  ey'd?                         20
And you, too? Pray you, both approach and
  mend it.
Now, by that light I muse you 're not asham'd!
I, that have preach'd these things so oft unto
  you,
Read you the principles, argu'd all the grounds,
Disputed every fitness, every grace,    25
Call'd you to counsel of so frequent dressings —
  *Nan.* (*Aside.*) More carefully than of your
  fame or honour.
*Lady P.* Made you acquainted what an
  ample dowry
The knowledge of these things would be unto
  you,
Able alone to get you noble husbands    30
At your return: and you thus to neglect it!
Besides, you seeing what a curious nation
Th' Italians are, what will they say of me?
"The English lady cannot dress herself."
Here 's a fine imputation to our country!  35
Well, go your ways, and stay i' the next room.
This fucus was too coarse too; it 's no matter. —
Good sir, you 'll give 'em entertainment?
          *[Exeunt Nano and Waiting-women.]*
*Volp.* The storm comes toward me.
*Lady P. [Goes to the couch.]* How does my
  Volpone!
*Volp.* Troubl'd with noise, I cannot sleep;
  I dreamt                        40

That a strange fury ent'red now my house,
And, with the dreadful tempest of her breath,
Did cleave my roof asunder.
*Lady P.*           Believe me, and I
Had the most fearful dream, could I remem-
  ber 't ——
*Volp.* *[Aside.]* Out on my fate! I have
  given her the occasion          45
How to torment me: she will tell me hers.
*Lady P.* Methought the golden mediocrity,
Polite, and delicate ——
*Volp.*          O, if you do love me,
No more: I sweat, and suffer, at the mention
Of any dream; feel how I tremble yet.  50
*Lady P.* Alas, good soul! the passion of the
  heart.
Seed-pearl were good now, boil'd with syrup of
  apples,
Tincture of gold, and coral, citron-pills,
Your elecampane root, myrobalanes ——
*Volp.* Ay me, I have ta'en a grasshopper by
  the wing!                       55
*Lady P.* Burnt silk and amber. You have
  muscadel
Good i' the house ——
*Volp.*       You will not drink, and part?
*Lady P.* No, fear not that. I doubt we shall
  not get
Some English saffron, half a dram would
  serve;                        59
Your sixteen cloves, a little musk, dried mints;
Bugloss, and barley-meal ——
*Volp.*         *[Aside.]* She 's in again!
Before I feign'd diseases, now I have one.
*Lady P.* And these appli'd with a right
  scarlet cloth.
*Volp.* *[Aside.]* Another flood of words! a
  very torrent!
*Lady P.* Shall I, sir, make you a poultice?
*Volp.*            No, no, no. 65
I 'm very well, you need prescribe no more.
*Lady P.* I have a little studied physic; but
  now
I 'm all for music, save, i' the forenoons,
An hour or two for painting. I would have
A lady, indeed, t' have all letters and arts, 70
Be able to discourse, to write, to paint,
But principal, as Plato holds, your music
(And so does wise Pythagoras, I take it,)
Is your true rapture: when there is concent
In face, in voice, and clothes: and is, indeed, 75
Our sex's chiefest ornament.
*Volp.*           The poet
As old in time as Plato, and as knowing,
Says that your highest female grace is silence.

---

   <sup>17</sup> **tire**: headdress    <sup>20</sup> **bird-ey'd**: short-sighted or keen-eyed (in derision)    <sup>32</sup> **curious**: fastidious
<sup>37</sup> **fucus**: rouge   <sup>39</sup> **Volpone**: ('Volp?' F)   <sup>52-54</sup> **Seed-pearl . . . myrobalanes**: remedies for melan-
choly   <sup>55</sup> **grasshopper**: An ancient proverb holds that the faster grasshoppers are held by the wings
the louder they scream.   <sup>74</sup> **concent**: harmony

*Lady P.* Which o' your poets? Petrarch, or
Tasso, or Dante?
Guarini? Ariosto? Aretine?                              80
Cieco di Hadria? I have read them all.
   *Volp.* [*Aside.*] Is everything a cause to my
destruction?
   *Lady P.* I think I ha' two or three of 'em
about me.
   *Volp.* [*Aside.*] The sun, the sea, will sooner
both stand still                                        84
Than her eternal tongue! nothing can scape it.
   *Lady P.* Here 's *Pastor Fido* ——
   *Volp.* [*Aside.*] Profess obstinate silence;
That 's now my safest.
   *Lady P.*                   All our English writers,
I mean such as are happy in th' Italian,
Will deign to steal out of this author, mainly;
Almost as much as from Montagnié:          90
He has so modern and facile a vein,
Fitting the time, and catching the court-ear!
Your Petrarch is more passionate, yet he,
In days of sonnetting, trusted 'em with much:
Dante is hard, and few can understand him.   95
But for a desperate wit, there 's Aretine;
Only his pictures are a little obscene ——
You mark me not.
   *Volp.*              Alas, my mind 's perturb'd.
   *Lady P.* Why, in such cases, we must cure
ourselves,
Make use of our philosophy ——
   *Volp.*                          Oh me!     100
   *Lady P.* And as we find our passions do
rebel,
Encounter 'em with reason, or divert 'em.
By giving scope unto some other humour
Of lesser danger: as, in politic bodies,
There 's nothing more doth overwhelm the
judgment,                                            105
And clouds the understanding, than too much
Settling and fixing, and, as 't were, subsiding
Upon one object. For the incorporating
Of these same outward things, into that part
Which we call mental, leaves some certain
faeces                                               110
That stop the organs, and, as Plato says,
Assassinates our knowledge.
   *Volp.*               [*Aside.*] Now, the spirit
Of patience help me!
   *Lady P.*               Come, in faith, I must
Visit you more a days; and make you well:
Laugh and be lusty.
   *Volp.* [*Aside.*] My good angel save me!  115
   *Lady P.* There was but one sole man in all
the world
With whom I e'er could sympathize; and he
Would lie you, often, three, four hours to-
gether

To hear me speak; and be sometime so rapt,
As he would answer me quite from the pur-
pose,                                                120
Like you, and you are like him, just. I 'll dis-
course,
An 't be but only, sir, to bring you asleep,
How we did spend our time and loves together,
For some six years.
   *Volp.*              Oh, oh, oh, oh, oh, oh!
   *Lady P.* For we were *coætanei*, and brought
up ——                                               125
   *Volp.* Some power, some fate, some fortune
rescue me!


## Act III.  Scene V

### [*The Same.*]

*Mosca, Lady* [*Politic Would-be*], *Volpone*

[*Mos.*] God save you, madam!
   *Lady P.*                    Good sir.
   *Volp.*                             Mosca! welcome,
Welcome to my redemption.
   *Mos.*                           Why, sir?
   *Volp.*                                      Oh,
Rid me of this my torture, quickly, there;
My madam with the everlasting voice:
The bells, in time of pestilence, ne'er made   5
Like noise or were in that perpetual motion!
The Cock-pit comes not near it. All my house,
But now, steam'd like a bath with her thick
breath,
A lawyer could not have been heard; nor scarce
Another woman, such a hail of words            10
She has let fall. For hell's sake, rid her hence.
   *Mos.* Has she presented?
   *Volp.*                        Oh, I do not care;
I 'll take her absence upon any price,
With any loss.
   *Mos.*          Madam ——
   *Lady P.*              I ha' brought your patron
A toy, a cap here, of mine own work.
   *Mos.*                          'T is well.    15
I had forgot to tell you I saw your knight
Where you would little think it. ——
   *Lady P.*                           Where?
   *Mos.*                                   Marry,
Where yet, if you make haste, you may appre-
hend him,
Rowing upon the water in a gondole,
With the most cunning courtesan of Venice.   20
   *Lady P.* Is 't true?
   *Mos.*          Pursue 'em, and believe your eyes:
Leave me to make your gift.
                           [*Exit Lady P. hastily.*]
                           I knew 't would take:

---

⁸⁶ **Pastor Fido:** *The Faithful Shepherd,* Guarini's pastoral drama    ¹¹⁰ **faeces:** dregs    ¹¹⁴ **more
a days:** more frequently    ¹²⁵ **coætanei:** equals in age    ¹² **presented:** made a present

For, lightly, they that use themselves most
    license,
Are still most jealous.
*Volp.*                    Mosca, hearty thanks
For thy quick fiction, and delivery of me.    25
Now to my hopes, what sayst thou?

    [*Re-enter Lady P. Would-be*]

*Lady P.*          But do you hear, sir? ——
*Volp.* Again! I fear a paroxysm.
*Lady P.*                    Which way
Row'd they together?
*Mos.*                Toward the Rialto.
*Lady P.* I pray you lend me your dwarf.    29
*Mos.* I pray you take him. [*Exit Lady P.*]
Your hopes, sir, are like happy blossoms, fair,
And promise timely fruit, if you will stay
But the maturing; keep you at your couch,
Corbaccio will arrive straight, with the will;
When he is gone, I 'll tell you more.    [*Exit.*]
*Volp.*                    My blood,    35
My spirits are return'd; I am alive:
And, like your wanton gamester at primero,
Whose thought had whisper'd to him, not go
    less,
Methinks I lie, and draw —— for an encounter.

## Act III.  Scene VI

### [*The Same.*]

#### Mosca, Bonario

[*Mos.*] Sir, here conceal'd [*opening a door*]
    you may hear all.  But, pray you,
Have patience, sir;          *One knocks.*
    the same 's your father knocks:
I am compell'd to leave you.    [*Exit.*]
*Bon.*          Do so. — Yet
Cannot my thought imagine this a truth.
                    [*Goes in.*]

## Act III.  Scene VII

### [*The Same.*]

#### Mosca, Corvino, Celia, Bonario, Volpone

[*Mos.*] Death on me! you are come too
    soon! what meant you?
Did not I say I would send?
*Corv.*              Yes, but I fear'd
You might forget it, and then they prevent us.
*Mos.* Prevent! [*Aside.*] Did e'er man
    haste so for his horns?
A courtier would not ply it so for a place.    5
— Well, now there is no helping it, stay here;
I 'll presently return.          [*Exit.*]

*Corv.*              Where are you, Celia?
You know not wherefore I have brought you
    hither?
*Cel.* Not well, except you told me.
*Corv.*                    Now I will:
Hark hither.          [*They retire to one side.*]

    [*Re-enter Mosca*]

*Mos.* Sir, your father hath sent word,    10
                    *To Bonario.*
It will be half an hour ere he come;
And therefore, if you please to walk the while
Into that gallery — at the upper end,
There are some books to entertain the time:
And I 'll take care no man shall come unto you,
    sir.                        15
*Bon.* Yes, I will stay there. — [*Aside.*] I do
    doubt this fellow.          [*Exit.*]
*Mos.* There; he is far enough; he can hear
    nothing:
And for his father, I can keep him off.

    [*Draws the curtains before Volpone's couch*]

*Corv.* Nay, now, there is no starting back,
    and therefore,
Resolve upon it:  I have so decreed.    20
It must be done.  Nor would I move 't afore,
Because I would avoid all shifts and tricks,
That might deny me.
*Cel.*          Sir, let me beseech you,
Affect not these strange trials; if you doubt
My chastity, why, lock me up for ever;    25
Make me the heir of darkness.  Let me live
Where I may please your fears, if not your trust.
*Corv.* Believe it, I have no such humour, I.
All that I speak I mean; yet I am not mad;    29
Not horn-mad, see you?  Go to, show yourself
Obedient, and a wife.
*Cel.*          O heaven!
*Corv.*              I say it,
Do so.
*Cel.* Was this the train?
*Corv.*          I 've told you reasons;
What the physicians have set down; how much
It may concern me; what my engagements are;
My means, and the necessity of those means    35
For my recovery: wherefore, if you be
Loyal and mine, be won, respect my venture.
*Cel.* Before your honour?
*Corv.*          Honour! tut, a breath:
There 's no such thing in nature; a mere term
Invented to awe fools.  What is my gold    40
The worse for touching, clothes for being look'd
    on?
Why, this 's no more.  An old decrepit wretch,
That has no sense, no sinew; takes his meat

---

²³ **lightly**: commonly    ³⁷ **primero**: a card game    ³⁸ **go**: wager    ³⁹ **draw**: "Draw" and "encounter" are terms in primero, but Volpone also plays on his position.  His couch is on the inner stage,
and the curtain is drawn before him as the scene closes.  Sc. vii.  ³² **train**: plot

With others' fingers: only knows to gape
When you do scald his gums; a voice, a shadow;
And what can this man hurt you?
 *Cel.*    [*Aside.*] Lord! what spirit  46
Is this hath ent'red him?
 *Corv.*    And for your fame,
That 's such a jig; as if I would go tell it,
Cry it on the Piazza! Who shall know it
But he that cannot speak it, and this fellow,  50
Whose lips are i' my pocket? Save yourself,
(If you 'll proclaim 't, you may,) I know no other
Should come to know it.
 *Cel.* Are heaven and saints then nothing?
Will they be blind or stupid?
 *Corv.*    How!
 *Cel.*    Good sir,
Be jealous still, emulate them; and think  55
What hate they burn with toward every sin.
 *Corv.* I grant you: if I thought it were a sin
I would not urge you. Should I offer this
To some young Frenchman, or hot Tuscan
blood
That had read Aretine, conn'd all his prints,  60
Knew every quirk within lust's labyrinth,
And were profess'd critic in lechery;
And I would look upon him, and applaud him,
This were a sin: but here, 't is contrary,
A pious work, mere charity for physic,  65
And honest polity, to assure mine own.
 *Cel.* O heaven! canst thou suffer such a
change?
 *Volp.* Thou art mine honour, Mosca, and
my pride,
My joy, my tickling, my delight! Go bring
'em.
 *Mos.* [*Advancing.*] Please you draw near,
sir.
 *Corv.*    Come on, what ——  70
You will not be rebellious? By that light ——
 *Mos.* Sir, Signior Corvino, here, is come to
see you.
 *Volp.* Oh!
 *Mos.* And hearing of the consultation had,
So lately, for your health, is come to offer,
Or rather, sir, to prostitute ——
 *Corv.*    Thanks, sweet Mosca.  75
 *Mos.* Freely, unask'd, or unintreated ——
 *Corv.*    Well.
 *Mos.* As the true fervent instance of his love,
His own most fair and proper wife; the beauty
Only of price in Venice ——
 *Corv.*    'T is well urg'd.
 *Mos.* To be your comfortress, and to pre-
serve you.  80
 *Volp.* Alas, I am past, already! Pray you,
thank him
For his good care and promptness; but for that,

'T is a vain labour e'en to fight 'gainst heaven;
Applying fire to a stone — uh, uh, uh, uh!
          [*Coughing.*]
Making a dead leaf grow again. I take  85
His wishes gently, though; and you may tell
him
What I have done for him: marry, my state is
hopeless.
Will him to pray for me; and t' use his fortune
With reverence when he comes to 't.
 *Mos.*    Do you hear, sir?
Go to him with your wife.
 *Corv.*    Heart of my father!  90
Wilt thou persist thus? Come, I pray thee,
come.
Thou seest 't is nothing, Celia. By this hand
I shall grow violent. Come, do 't, I say.
 *Cel.* Sir, kill me, rather: I will take down
poison,
Eat burning coals, do anything ——
 *Corv.*    Be damn'd!  95
Heart, I will drag thee hence home by the hair;
Cry thee a strumpet through the streets; rip up
Thy mouth unto thine ears; and slit thy nose,
Like a raw rochet! — Do not tempt me; come,
Yield, I am loath — Death! I will buy some
slave  100
Whom I will kill, and bind thee to him alive;
And at my windore hang you forth, devising
Some monstrous crime, which I, in capital letters,
Will eat into thy flesh with aquafortis,  104
And burning cor'sives, on this stubborn breast.
Now, by the blood thou hast incens'd, I 'll do 't!
 *Cel.* Sir, what you please, you may; I am
your martyr.
 *Corv.* Be not thus obstinate, I ha' not de-
serv'd it:
Think who it is intreats you. Pray thee,
sweet; —
Good faith, thou shalt have jewels, gowns, at-
tires,  110
What thou wilt think, and ask. Do but go kiss
him.
Or touch him but. For my sake. At my suit —
This once. No! not! I shall remember this.
Will you disgrace me thus? Do you thirst my
undoing?
 *Mos.* Nay, gentle lady, be advis'd.
 *Corv.*    No, no.  115
She has watch'd her time. God's precious, this
is scurvy,
'T is very scurvy; and you are ——
 *Mos.*    Nay, good sir.
 *Corv.* An arrant locust — by heaven, a
locust! —
Whore, crocodile, that hast thy tears prepar'd,
Expecting how thou 'lt bid 'em flow ——

---

 ⁴⁸ **jig:** farce  ⁷⁹ **Only of price:** unparalleled  ⁹⁹ **rochet:** a fish of a red color  ¹⁰⁴ **aquafortis:**
nitric acid  ¹⁰⁵ **cor'sives:** corrosives

*Mos.*                    Nay, pray you, sir! 120
She will consider.
*Cel.*              Would my life would serve
To satisfy ——
*Corv.* 'Sdeath! if she would but speak to him,
And save my reputation, 't were somewhat;
But spitefully to affect my utter ruin!
*Mos.* Ay, now you have put your fortune in
     her hands.                            125
Why i' faith, it is her modesty, I must quit
     her.
If you were absent, she would be more coming;
I know it: and dare undertake for her.
What woman can before her husband? Pray
     you,
Let us depart and leave her here.
*Corv.*                  Sweet Celia, 130
Thou may'st redeem all yet; I 'll say no more:
If not, esteem yourself as lost. Nay, stay there.
                         [*Exit with Mosca.*]
*Cel.* O God, and his good angels! whither,
     whither,
Is shame fled human breasts? that with such
     ease,                                134
Men dare put off your honours, and their own?
Is that, which ever was a cause of life,
Now plac'd beneath the basest circumstance,
And modesty an exile made, for money?
*Volp.* Ay, in Corvino, and such earth-fed
     minds,          *He leaps off from his couch.*
That never tasted the true heaven of love. 140
Assure thee, Celia, he that would sell thee,
Only for hope of gain, and that uncertain,
He would have sold his part of Paradise
For ready money, had he met a cope-man.
Why art thou maz'd to see me thus riviv'd?
Rather applaud thy beauty's miracle;      146
'T is thy great work, that hath, not now alone,
But sundry times rais'd me, in several shapes,
And, but this morning, like a mountebank,
To see thee at thy windore: ay, before    150
I would have left my practice, for thy love,
In varying figures, I would have contended
With the blue Proteus, or the horned flood.
Now art thou welcome.
*Cel.*               Sir!
*Volp.*                    Nay, fly me not,
Nor let thy false imagination            155
That I was bed-rid, make thee think I am so:
Thou shalt not find it. I am now as fresh,
As hot, as high, and in as jovial plight
As, when, in that so celebrated scene,
At recitation of our comedy,             160
For entertainment of the great Valois,
I acted young Antinous; and attracted

The eyes and ears of all the ladies present,
T' admire each graceful gesture, note, and
     footing.                    [*Sings.*]
                 SONG
Come, my Celia, let us prove            165
While we can, the sports of love,
Time will not be ours for ever,
He, at length, our good will sever;
Spend not then his gifts in vain:
Suns that set may rise again;           170
But if once we lose this light,
'T is with us perpetual night.
Why should we defer our joys?
Fame and rumour are but toys.
Cannot we delude the eyes              175
Of a few poor household spies?
Or his easier ears beguile,
Thus removed by our wile?
'T is no sin love's fruits to steal,
But the sweet thefts to reveal:         180
To be taken, to be seen,
These have crimes accounted been.

*Cel.* Some serene blast me, or dire lightning
     strike
This my offending face!
*Volp.*                  Why droops my Celia?
Thou hast, in place of a base husband found 185
A worthy lover: use thy fortune well,
With secrecy and pleasure. See, behold,
What thou art queen of; not in expectation,
As I feed others: but possess'd and crown'd.
See, here, a rope of pearl; and each more
     orient                              190
Than that the brave Ægyptian queen carous'd:
Dissolve and drink 'em. See, a carbuncle,
May put out both the eyes of our St. Mark;
A diamond would have bought Lollia Paulina,
When she came in like star-light, hid with
     jewels                              195
That were the spoils of provinces; take these
And wear, and lose 'em; yet remains an ear-
     ring
To purchase them again, and this whole state.
A gem but worth a private patrimony
Is nothing; we will eat such at a meal.   200
The heads of parrots, tongues of nightingales,
The brains of peacocks, and of estriches,
Shall be our food, and, could we get the phœnix,
Though nature lost her kind, she were our dish.
*Cel.* Good sir, these things might move a
     mind affected                       205
With such delights; but I, whose innocence
Is all I can think wealthy, or worth th' enjoy-
     ing,

---

¹²⁶ **quit:** excuse, acquit    ¹²⁸ **undertake:** promise    ¹⁴⁴ **cope-man:** chapman, merchant    ¹⁵¹ **practice:** plotting    ¹⁵³ **horned flood:** the ocean    ¹⁶¹ **entertainment:** for Henri III of France at Venice in
1574    ¹⁸³ **serene:** mildew    ¹⁹⁴ **Lollia Paulina:** a Roman heiress    ²⁰⁴ **Though . . . kind:** though
this unique bird became thereby extinct

And which, once lost, I have nought to lose be-
    yond it,
Cannot be taken with these sensual baits:
If you have conscience ——
    *Volp.*             'T is the beggar's virtue;
If thou hast wisdom, hear me, Celia.    211
Thy baths shall be the juice of July-flowers,
Spirit of roses, and of violets,
The milk of unicorns, and panthers' breath  214
Gather'd in bags, and mix'd with Cretan wines.
Our drink shall be prepared gold and amber;
Which we will take until my roof whirl round
With the vertigo: and my dwarf shall dance,
My eunuch sing, my fool make up the antic,  219
Whilst we, in changed shapes, act Ovid's
    tales,
Thou, like Europa now, and I like Jove,
Then I like Mars, and thou like Erycine:
So of the rest, till we have quite run through,
And wearied all the fables of the gods.    224
Then will I have thee in more modern forms,
Attired like some sprightly dame of France,
Brave Tuscan lady, or proud Spanish beauty;
Sometimes unto the Persian sophy's wife;
Or the grand signior's mistress; and for change,
To one of our most artful courtesans,    230
Or some quick Negro, or cold Russian;
And I will meet thee in as many shapes:
Where we may so transfuse our wand'ring souls
Out at our lips, and score up sums of pleasures,
                              *[Sings.]*

    That the curious shall not know    235
    How to tell them as they flow;
    And the envious, when they find
    What their number is, be pin'd.

  *Cel.*  If you have ears that will be pierc'd —
    or eyes
That can be open'd — a heart may be touch'd —
Or any part that yet sounds man about
    you —    241
If you have touch of holy saints — or heaven —
Do me the grace to let me scape: — if not,
Be bountiful and kill me. You do know,
I am a creature, hither ill betray'd,    245
By one whose shame I would forget it were:
If you will deign me neither of these graces,
Yet feed your wrath, sir, rather than your lust,
(It is a vice comes nearer manliness,)
And punish that unhappy crime of nature,  250
Which you miscall my beauty: flay my face,
Or poison it with ointments for seducing
Your blood to this rebellion. Rub these hands
With what may cause an eating leprosy,
E'en to my bones and marrow: anything  255
That may disfavour me, save in my honour —
And I will kneel to you, pray for you, pay down

A thousand hourly vows, sir, for your health,
Report, and think you virtuous ——
  *Volp.*             Think me cold,
Frozen, and impotent, and so report me?  260
That I had Nestor's hernia, thou wouldst think.
I do degenerate, and abuse my nation,
To play with opportunity thus long;
I should have done the act, and then have par-
    ley'd.
Yield, or I 'll force thee.        *[Seizes her.]*
  *Cel.*             O! just God!
  *Volp.*             In vain ——  265
  *Bon.*  Forbear, foul ravisher! libidinous
    swine!
             *He leaps out from where Mosca*
                   *had plac'd him.*
Free the forc'd lady, or thou diest, impostor.
But that I 'm loath to snatch thy punishment
Out of the hand of justice, thou shouldst yet
Be made the timely sacrifice of vengeance,  270
Before this altar and this dross, thy idol. ——
Lady, let 's quit the place, it is the den
Of villainy; fear nought, you have a guard:
And he ere long shall meet his just reward.  274
                  *[Exeunt Bon. and Cel.]*
  *Volp.*  Fall on me, roof, and bury me in
    ruin!
Become my grave, that wert my shelter! O!
I am unmask'd, unspirited, undone,
Betray'd to beggary, to infamy ——

## Act III.  Scene VIII

### [The Same.]

#### Mosca, Volpone

  *[Mos.]*  Where shall I run, most wretched
    shame of men,
To beat out my unlucky brains?
  *Volp.*             Here, here.
What! dost thou bleed?
  *Mos.*         O, that his well-driv'n sword
Had been so courteous to have cleft me down
Unto the navel, ere I liv'd to see    5
My life, my hopes, my spirits, my patron, all
Thus desperately engaged by my error!
  *Volp.*  Woe on thy fortune!
  *Mos.*           And my follies, sir.
  *Volp.*  Th' hast made me miserable.
  *Mos.*           And myself, sir.
Who would have thought he would have heark-
    en'd so?    10
  *Volp.*  What shall we do?
  *Mos.*         I know not; if my heart
Could expiate the mischance, I 'd pluck it out.
Will you be pleas'd to hang me, or cut my
    throat?

    **219 antic:** grotesque pageant    **222 Erycine:** Venus    **228 sophy:** Shah    **229 grand signior:** Sultan
    **240 may:** that may

And I 'll requite you, sir. Let 's die like
    Romans,
Since we have liv'd like Grecians.
                        *They knock without.*
*Volp.*             Hark! who 's there?  15
I hear some footing; officers, the saffi,
Come to apprehend us! I do feel the brand
Hissing already at my forehead; now
Mine ears are boring.
*Mos.*            To your couch, sir, you.
Make that place good, however. [*Volpone lies
    down as before.*]  Guilty men    20
Suspect what they deserve still. Signior Cor-
    baccio!

### *Act III.  Scene IX*

[*The Same.*]

*Corbaccio, Mosca, [later] Voltore, Volpone
[on his couch]*

[*Corb.*]  Why, how now, Mosca?
*Mos.*           O, undone, amaz'd, sir.
Your son, I know not by what accident,
Acquainted with your purpose to my patron,
Touching your will, and making him your heir,
Ent'red our house with violence, his sword
    drawn,    5
Sought for you, call'd you wretch, unnatural,
Vow'd he would kill you.
*Corb.*           Me!
*Mos.*           Yes, and my patron.
*Corb.*  This act shall disinherit him indeed:
Here is the will.
*Mos.*        'T is well, sir.
*Corb.*           Right and well:
Be you as careful now for me.

[*Enter Voltore behind*]

*Mos.*           My life, sir,  10
Is not more tender'd; I am only yours.
*Corb.*  How does he?  Will he die shortly,
    think'st thou?
*Mos.*           I fear
He 'll outlast May.
*Corb.*         To-day?
*Mos.*           No, last out May, sir.
*Corb.*  Couldst thou not gi' him a dram?
*Mos.*           O, by no means, sir.
*Corb.*  Nay, I 'll not bid you.
*Volt.* [*Coming forward.*]  This is a knave, I
    see.    15
*Mos.* [*Aside, seeing Volt.*]  How! Signior Vol-
    tore! did he hear me?
*Volt.*           Parasite!
*Mos.*  Who 's that? — O, sir, most timely
    welcome —

*Volt.*           Scarce,
To the discovery of your tricks, I fear.
You are his, *only?*  And mine also, are you *not?*
*Mos.*  Who?  I, sir!
*Volt.*      You, sir.  What device is this  20
About a will?
*Mos.*        A plot for you, sir.
*Volt.*           Come,
Put not your foists upon me; I shall scent 'em.
*Mos.*  Did you not hear it?
*Volt.*         Yes, I hear Corbaccio
Hath made your patron there his heir.
*Mos.*           'T is true,
By my device, drawn to it by my plot,  25
With hope ——
*Volt.*     Your patron should reciprocate?
And you have promis'd?
*Mos.*          For your good I did, sir.
Nay, more, I told his son, brought, hid him
    here,
Where he might hear his father pass the deed;
Being persuaded to it by this thought, sir,  30
That the unnaturalness, first, of the act,
And then his father's oft disclaiming in him,
(Which I did mean t' help on), would sure en-
    rage him
To do some violence upon his parent,  34
On which the law should take sufficient hold,
And you be stated in a double hope.
Truth be my comfort, and my conscience,
My only aim was to dig you a fortune
Out of these two old rotten sepulchres ——
*Volt.*  I cry thee mercy, Mosca.
*Mos.*       — Worth your patience,  40
And your great merit, sir.  And see the change!
*Volt.*  Why, what success?
*Mos.*       Most hapless! you must help, sir.
Whilst we expected th' old raven, in comes
Corvino's wife, sent hither by her husband ——
*Volt.*  What, with a present?
*Mos.*       No, sir, on visitation;  45
(I 'll tell you how anon;) and staying long,
The youth he grows impatient, rushes forth,
Seizeth the lady, wounds me, makes her swear
(Or he would murder her, that was his vow)
T' affirm my patron to have done her rape:  50
Which how unlike it is, you see! and hence,
With that pretext he 's gone, t' accuse his
    father,
Defame my patron, defeat you ——
*Volt.*        Where 's her husband?
Let him be sent for straight.
*Mos.*       Sir, I 'll go fetch him.
*Volt.*  Bring him to the Scrutineo.
*Mos.*         Sir, I will.  55
*Volt.*  This must be stopp'd.
*Mos.*         O you do nobly, sir.

---

¹⁴ **like Romans:** *i.e.*, by suicide    ¹⁵ **like Grecians:** luxuriously    ¹⁶ **saffi:** bailiffs    ¹¹ **tender'd:**
cared for    ²² **foists:** deceits    ⁴⁰ **cry . . . mercy:** beg your pardon    ⁵⁵ **Scrutineo:** Senate House

Alas, 't was labour'd all, sir, for your good;
Nor was there want of counsel in the plot:
But Fortune can, at any time, o'erthrow
The projects of a hundred learned clerks, sir.   60
   *Corb.* [*Listening.*]   What 's that?
   *Volt.*   Wilt please you, sir, to go along?
        [*Exit Corbaccio, followed by Voltore.*]
   *Mos.*   Patron, go in, and pray for our success.
   *Volp.* [*Rising from his couch.*]   Need makes
    devotion: heaven your labour bless'
                    [*Exeunt.*]

## Act IIII.  Scene I

### [A Street.]

### Politic, Peregrine

[*Sir P.*]   I told you, sir, it was a plot; you
  see
What observation is!  You mention'd me
For some instructions: I will tell you, sir,
(Since we are met here in this height of Venice,)
Some few particulars I have set down,          5
Only for this meridian, fit to be known
Of your crude traveller; and they are these.
I will not touch, sir, at your phrase, or clothes,
For they are old.
   *Per.*                Sir, I have better.
   *Sir P.*                        Pardon,
I meant, as they are themes.
   *Per.*                O, sir, proceed:   10
I 'll slander you no more of wit, good sir.
   *Sir P.*   First, for your garb, it must be grave
   and serious,
Very reserv'd and lock'd; not tell a secret
On any terms, not to your father; scarce
A fable, but with caution: make sure choice   15
Both of your company and discourse; beware
You never speak a truth ——
   *Per.*                How!
   *Sir P.*                Not to strangers,
For those be they you must converse with
   most;
Others I would not know, sir, but at distance
So as I still might be a saver in 'em:          20
You shall have tricks else pass'd upon you hourly.
And then, for your religion, profess none,
But wonder at the diversity of all;
And, for your part, protest, were there no other
But simply the laws o' th' land, you could con-
   tent you.                                    25
Nick Machiavel and Monsieur Bodin, both
Were of this mind.  Then must you learn the use
And handling of your silver fork at meals,
The metal of your glass; (these are main mat-
   ters

With your Italian;) and to know the hour   30
When you must eat your melons and your figs.
   *Per.*   Is that a point of state too?
   *Sir P.*                        Here it is:
For your Venetian, if he see a man
Preposterous in the least, he has him straight;
He has; he strips him.  I 'll acquaint you, sir.   35
I now have liv'd here 't is some fourteen
   months:
Within the first week of my landing here,
All took me for a citizen of Venice,
I knew the forms so well ——
   *Per.* [*Aside.*]          And nothing else.
   *Sir P.*   I had read Contarene, took me a
   house,                                      40
Dealt with my Jews to furnish it with mov-
   ables ——
Well, if I could but find one man, one man
To mine own heart, whom I durst trust, I
   would ——
   *Per.*   What, what, sir?
   *Sir P.*   Make him rich; make him a fortune:
He should not think again.  I would command
   it.                                          45
   *Per.*   As how?
   *Sir P.*        With certain projects that I have;
Which I may not discover.
   *Per.* [*Aside.*]          If I had
But one to wager with, I would lay odds now,
He tells me instantly.
   *Sir P.*          One is, and that
I care not greatly who knows, to serve the state
Of Venice with red herrings for three years,   51
And at a certain rate, from Rotterdam,
Where I have correspondence.  There 's a letter,
Sent me from one o' th' states, and to that pur-
   pose:
He cannot write his name, but that 's his
   mark.                                        55
   *Per.*   He is a chandler?
   *Sir P.*                No, a cheesemonger.
There are some other too with whom I treat
About the same negotiation;
And I will undertake it: for 't is thus.
I 'll do 't with ease, I have cast it all.  Your
   hoy                                          60
Carries but three men in her, and a boy;
And she shall make me three returns a year:
So if there come but one of three, I save;
If two, I can defalk: — but this is now,
If my main project fail.
   *Per.*                Then you have others?   65
   *Sir P.*   I should be loath to draw the subtle
   air
Of such a place, without my thousand aims.
I 'll not dissemble, sir: where'er I come,

---

<sup>10</sup> **themes:** subjects to discuss   <sup>13</sup> **lock'd:** reticent   <sup>26</sup> **Bodin:** a French writer on politics (1530–
1596)   <sup>40</sup> **Contarene:** Gasparo Contarini (1483-1542), cardinal, diplomatist, and writer on Venice
<sup>42</sup> **think:** *i.e.,* about money   <sup>60</sup> **cast:** calculated   **hoy:** small sloop   <sup>64</sup> **defalk:** make a reduction

I love to be considerative; and 't is true,
I have at my free hours thought upon          70
Some certain goods unto the state of Venice,
Which I do call my Cautions; and, sir, which
I mean, in hope of pension, to propound
To the Great Council, then unto the Forty,          74
So to the Ten. My means are made already ——
   *Per.*          By whom?          [be obscure,
   *Sir P.*          Sir, one that though his place
Yet he can sway, and they will hear him. He 's
A *commandadore.*
   *Per.*          What! a common sergeant?
   *Sir P.* Sir, such as they are, put it in their
   mouths,
What they should say, sometimes; as well as
   greater:          80
I think I have my notes to show you ——
              *[Searching his pockets.]*
   *Per.*          Good sir.
   *Sir P.* But you shall swear unto me, on your
   gentry,
Not to anticipate ——
   *Per.*          I, sir!
   *Sir P.*          Nor reveal
A circumstance —— My paper is not with me.
   *Per.* O, but you can remember, sir.
   *Sir P.*          My first is          85
Concerning tinder-boxes. You must know,
No family is here without its box.
Now, sir, it being so portable a thing,
Put case, that you or I were ill affected
Unto the state, sir; with it in our pockets,          90
Might not I go into the Arsenal,
Or you? come out again, and none the wiser?
   *Per.* Except yourself, sir.
   *Sir P.* Go to, then. I therefore
Advertise to the state, how fit it were
That none but such as were known patriots,          95
Sound lovers of their country, should be suf-
   fer'd
T' enjoy them in their houses; and even those
Seal'd at some office, and at such a bigness
As might not lurk in pockets.
   *Per.*          Admirable!
   *Sir P.* My next is, how t' inquire, and be
   resolv'd          100
By present demonstration, whether a ship,
Newly arriv'd from Soria, or from
Any suspected part of all the Levant,
Be guilty of the plague: and where they use
To lie out forty, fifty days, sometimes,          105
About the Lazaretto, for their trial;
I'll save that charge and loss unto the merchant,
And in an hour clear the doubt.
   *Per.*          Indeed, sir!
   *Sir P.* Or —— I will lose my labour.

   *Per.*          My faith, that 's much.
   *Sir P.* Nay, sir, conceive me. 'T will cost
   me, in onions,          110
Some thirty livres ——
   *Per.*          Which is one pound sterling.
   *Sir P.* Beside my waterworks: for this I do,
   sir.
First, I bring in your ship 'twixt two brick
   walls;
But those the state shall venter. On the one
I strain me a fair tarpaulin, and in that          115
I stick my onions, cut in halves; the other
Is full of loopholes, out at which I thrust
The noses of my bellows; and those bellows
I keep, with waterworks, in perpetual motion,
Which is the easiest matter of a hundred.          120
Now, sir, your onion, which doth naturally
Attract th' infection, and your bellows blowing
The air upon him, will show instantly,
By his chang'd colour, if there be contagion;
Or else remain as fair as at the first.          125
Now 't is known, 't is nothing.
   *Per.*          You are right, sir.
   *Sir P.* I would I had my note.
   *Per.*          Faith, so would I:
But you ha' done well for once, sir.
   *Sir P.*          Were I false,
Or would be made so, I could show you reasons
How I could sell this state now to the Turk,          130
Spite of their galleys, or their ——
              *[Examining his papers.]*
   *Per.*          Pray you, Sir Pol.
   *Sir P.* I have 'em not about me.
   *Per.*          That I fear'd.
They are there, sir?
   *Sir P.*          No, this is my diary,
Wherein I note my actions of the day.          134
   *Per.* Pray you, let 's see, sir. What is here?
   "*Notandum:*          [*Reads.*]
A rat had gnawn my spur-leathers; notwith-
   standing,
I put on new, and did go forth; but first
I threw three beans over the threshold. *Item,*
I went and bought two toothpicks, whereof
   one
I burst immediately, in a discourse          140
With a Dutch merchant, 'bout *ragion' del stato.*
From him I went and paid a *moccinigo*
For piecing my silk stockings; by the way
I cheapen'd sprats; and at St. Mark's I
   urin'd."
'Faith these are politic notes!
   *Sir P.*          Sir, I do slip          145
No action of my life, thus, but I quote it.
   *Per.* Believe me, it is wise!
   *Sir P.*          Nay, sir, read forth.

**69** considerative: thoughtful    **76** be obscure: ('b' obscure' F)    **89** Put case: suppose    **102** Soria: Syria    **106** Lazaretto: building or ship used for quarantine    **111** livres: French coins    **114** venter: invest in    **115** strain: stretch    **141** ragion' del stato: politics    **144** cheapen'd: bargained for

## Act IIII.   Scene II

*[The Same.]*

*Lady [Politic Would-be], Nano, Women,*
*[Sir] Politic, Peregrine*

*[Lady P.]*   Where should this loose knight
be, trow?  Sure he 's hous'd.
*Nan.*   Why, then he 's fast.
*Lady P.*                       Ay, he plays both with me.
I pray you stay.  This heat will do more harm
To my complexion than his heart is worth.
(I do not care to hinder, but to take him.)   5
How it comes off!        *[Rubbing her cheeks.]*
1 *Wom.*        My master 's yonder.
*Lady P.*                                      Where?
2 *Wom.*   With a young gentleman.
*Lady P.*                         That same 's the party:
In man's apparel!  Pray you, sir, jog my
knight:
I will be tender to his reputation,
However he demerit.
*Sir P. [Seeing her.]*   My lady!
*Per.*                                    Where?   10
*Sir P.*   'T is she indeed, sir; you shall know
her.  She is,
Were she not mine, a lady of that merit,
For fashion and behaviour; and for beauty
I durst compare ——
*Per.*            It seems you are not jealous,
That dare commend her.
*Sir P.*         Nay, and for discourse ——   15
*Per.*   Being your wife, she cannot miss that.
*Sir P. [Introducing Per.]*                Madam,
Here is a gentleman, pray you, use him fairly;
He seems a youth, but he is ——
*Lady P.*                            None?
*Sir P.*                                Yes, one
Has put his face as soon into the world ——
*Lady P.*   You mean, as early?  But to-day?
*Sir P.*                              How 's this?   20
*Lady P.*   Why, in this habit, sir; you appre-
hend me.
Well, Master Would-be, this doth not become
you;
I had thought the odour, sir, of your good
name
Had been more precious to you; that you would
not
Have done this dire massácre on your honour;
One of your gravity, and rank besides!   26
But knights, I see, care little for the oath
They make to ladies; chiefly their own ladies.
*Sir P.*   Now, by my spurs, the symbol of my
knighthood ——

*Per. [Aside.]*  Lord, how his brain is humbled
for an oath!                                      30
*Sir P.*   I reach you not.
*Lady P.*                      Right, sir, your polity
May bear it through thus.  Sir, a word with you.
                                              *[To Per.]*
I would be loath to contest publicly
With any gentlewoman, or to seem
Froward, or violent, as the courtier says;   35
It comes too near rusticity in a lady,
Which I would shun by all means: and how-
ever
I may deserve from Master Would-be, yet
T' have one fair gentlewoman thus be made
The unkind instrument to wrong another,   40
And one she knows not, ay, and to perséver;
In my poor judgment, is not warranted
From being a solecism in our sex,
If not in manners.
*Per.*               How is this!
*Sir P.*                            Sweet madam,
Come nearer to your aim.
*Lady P.*             Marry, and will, sir.   45
Since you provoke me with your impudence,
And laughter of your light land-siren here,
Your Sporus, your hermaphrodite ——
*Per.*                                What 's here?
Poetic fury and historic storms!   49
*Sir P.*   The gentleman, believe it, is of worth
And of our nation.
*Lady P.*          Ay, your Whitefriars nation.
Come, I blush for you, Master Would-be, I;
And am asham'd you should ha' no more fore-
head
Than thus to be the patron, or St. George,
To a lewd harlot, a base fricatrice,   55
A female devil, in a male outside.
*Sir P.*                                   Nay,
An you be such a one, I must bid adieu
To your delights.  The case appears too liquid.
                                              *[Exit.]*
*Lady P.*   Ay, you may carry 't clear, with
your state-face!
But for your carnival concupiscence,   60
Who here is fled for liberty of conscience,
From furious persecution of the marshal,
Her will I disc'ple.
*Per.*           This is fine, i' faith!
And do you use this often?  Is this part   64
Of your wit's exercise, 'gainst you have occasion?
Madam ——
*Lady P.*   Go to, sir.
*Per.*                Do you hear me, lady?
Why, if your knight have set you to beg shirts,
Or to invite me home, you might have done it
A nearer way by far.

---

² **both:** *i.e.,* fast and loose   ²⁸ **chiefly:** particularly   ³¹ **reach:** understand   ⁵¹ **Whitefriars:** a
part of London where malefactors were immune from arrest   ⁵³ **forehead:** sense of shame   ⁵⁵ **fricatrice:**
prostitute   ⁵⁸ **liquid:** clear   ⁶³ **disc'ple:** discipline, punish

*Lady P.*          This cannot work you
Out of my snare.
*Per.*          Why, am I in it, then?     70
Indeed your husband told me you were fair,
And so you are; only your nose inclines,
That side that 's next the sun, to the queen-
          apple.
*Lady P.*   This cannot be endur'd by any pa-
          tience.

## Act IIII.   Scene III

### [*The Same.*]

*Mosca, Lady* [*Politic Would-be*], *Peregrine*

[*Mos.*]   What 's the matter, madam?
*Lady P.*          If the senate
Right not my quest in this, I will protest 'em
To all the world no aristocracy.
*Mos.*   What is the injury, lady?
*Lady P.*          Why, the callet
You told me of, here I have ta'en disguis'd.   5
*Mos.*   Who? this! what means your lady-
          ship?   The creature
I mention'd to you is apprehended now,
Before the senate; you shall see her ——
*Lady P.*          Where?
*Mos.*   I 'll bring you to her.   This young
          gentleman,
I saw him land this morning at the port.   10
*Lady P.*   Is 't possible! how has my judg-
          ment wander'd?
Sir, I must, blushing, say to you, I have err'd;
And plead your pardon.
*Per.*          What, more changes yet!
*Lady P.*   I hope you ha' not the malice to
          remember
A gentlewoman 's passion.   If you stay   15
In Venice here, please you to use me, sir ——
*Mos.*   Will you go, madam?
*Lady P.*          Pray you, sir, use me; in faith,
The more you see me the more I shall conceive
You have forgot our quarrel.

[*Exeunt Lady Would-be, Mosca, Nano, and
          Waiting-women*]

*Per.*          This is rare!
Sir Politic Would-be?   No, Sir Politic Bawd,   20
To bring me thus acquainted with his wife!
Well, wise Sir Pol, since you have practis'd
          thus
Upon my freshman-ship, I 'll try your salt-head,
What proof it is against a counter-plot.
          [*Exit.*]

## Act IIII.   Scene IIII

### [*The Scrutineo.*]

*Voltore, Corbaccio, Corvino, Mosca*

[*Volt.*]   Well, now you know the carriage of
          the business,
Your constancy is all that is requir'd
Unto the safety of it.
*Mos.*          Is the lie
Safely convey'd amongst us?   Is that sure?
Knows every man his burden?
*Corv.*          Yes.
*Mos.*          Then shrink not.   5
*Corv.*   But knows the advocate the truth?
*Mos.*          O, sir,
By no means; I devis'd a formal tale,
That salv'd your reputation.   But be valiant, sir.
*Corv.*   I fear no one but him, that this his
          pleading
Should make him stand for a co-heir ——
*Mos.*          Co-halter!   10
Hang him; we will but use his tongue, his noise,
As we do croaker's here.
*Corv.*          Ay, what shall he do?
*Mos.*   When we ha' done, you mean?
*Corv.*          Yes.
*Mos.*          Why, we 'll think;
Sell him for mummia: he 's half dust al-
          ready. ——
Do not you smile, to see this buffalo,   15
          *To Voltore.*
How he doth sport it with his head?   [*Aside.*]
          I should,
If all were well and past. — Sir, only you
          *To Corbaccio.*
Are he that shall enjoy the crop of all,
And these not know for whom they toil.
*Corb.*          Ay, peace.
*Mos.*   But you shall eat it.   [*Aside.*]   Much!
          — Worshipful sir,   20
          *To Corvino, then to Voltore again.*
Mercury sit upon your thund'ring tongue,
Or the French Hercules, and make your lan-
          guage
As conquering as his club, to beat along,
As with a tempest, flat, our adversaries;
But much more yours, sir.
*Volt.*          Here they come, ha' done.   25
*Mos.*   I have another witness, if you need, sir,
I can produce.
*Volt.*          Who is it?
*Mos.*          Sir, I have her.

---

⁷³ **queen-apple:** This apple is red on the side toward the sun.   ⁴ **callet:** wanton   ²³ **salt-head:**
(the opposite of "freshman")   ¹ **carriage:** purpose, conduct   ⁴ **convey'd:** communicated   ⁵ **burden:** the refrain he has to sing   ¹² **croaker's:** Corbaccio's   ¹⁴ **mummia:** a drug supposed to be
derived from mummies   ¹⁵ **buffalo:** horned beast   ²⁰ **Much:** *i.e.,* Much chance you have of doing
so!   ²² **French Hercules:** Ogmius, a symbol of eloquence

## Act IIII.  Scene V

[*The Same.*]

4 *Avocatori, Bonario, Celia, Voltore, Corbaccio,
Corvino, Mosca, Notario, Commandadori*

[1 *Avoc.*]  The like of this the senate never
  heard of.
2 *Avoc.*  'T will come most strange to them
  when we report it.
4 *Avoc.*  The gentlewoman has been ever held
Of unreproved name.
3 *Avoc.*                So the young man.
4 *Avoc.*  The more unnatural part that of his
  father.                                              5
2 *Avoc.*  More of the husband.
1 *Avoc.*                I not know to give
His act a name, it is so monstrous!
  4 *Avoc.*  But the impostor, he is a thing
  created
T' exceed example!
1 *Avoc.*          And all after-times!
2 *Avoc.*  I never heard a true voluptuary     10
Describ'd but him.
  3 *Avoc.*        Appear yet those were cited?
*Not.*  All but the old magnifico, Volpone.
1 *Avoc.*  Why is not he here?
*Mos.*              Please your fatherhoods,
Here is his advocate: himself 's so weak,
So feeble ——
  4 *Avoc.*  Who are you?
*Bon.*              His parasite,     15
His knave, his pandar.  I beseech the court
He may be forc'd to come, that your grave eyes
May bear strong witness of his strange impos-
  tures.
*Volt.*  Upon my faith and credit with your
  virtues,
He is not able to endure the air.           20
2 *Avoc.*  Bring him, however.
3 *Avoc.*            We will see him.
4 *Avoc.*                  Fetch him.
*Volt.*  Your fatherhoods' fit pleasures be
  obey'd;                  [*Exeunt Officers.*]
But sure, the sight will rather move your pities
Than indignation.  May it please the court,
In the mean time, he may be heard in me.    25
I know this place most void of prejudice,
And therefore crave it, since we have no reason
To fear our truth should hurt our cause.
  3 *Avoc.*                  Speak free.
*Volt.*  Then know, most honour'd fathers, I
  must now
Discover to your strangely abused ears,      30
The most prodigious and most frontless piece
Of solid impudence, and treachery,

That ever vicious nature yet brought forth
To shame the state of Venice.  This lewd
  woman,
That wants no artificial looks or tears       35
To help the vizor she has now put on,
Hath long been known a close adulteress
To that lascivious youth there; not suspected,
I say, but known, and taken in the act        39
With him; and by this man, the easy husband,
Pardon'd; whose timeless bounty makes him
  now
Stand here, the most unhappy, innocent person,
That ever man's own goodness made accus'd.
For these, not knowing how to owe a gift
Of that dear grace, but with their shame; be-
  ing plac'd                                  45
So above all powers of their gratitude,
Began to hate the benefit; and in place
Of thanks, devise t' extirp the memory
Of such an act: wherein I pray your father-
  hoods
To observe the malice, yea, the rage of crea-
  tures                                       50
Discover'd in their evils: and what heart
Such take, ev'n from their crimes: — but that
  anon
Will more appear. — This gentleman, the
  father,
Hearing of this foul fact, with many others,
Which daily struck at his too tender ears,    55
And griev'd in nothing more than that he could
  not
Preserve himself a parent (his son's ills
Growing to that strange flood), at last decreed
To disinherit him.
  1 *Avoc.*          These be strange turns!
  2 *Avoc.*  The young man's fame was ever
  fair and honest.                            60
*Volt.*  So much more full of danger is his vice,
That can beguile so, under shade of virtue.
But, as I said, my honour'd sires, his father
Having this settled purpose, by what means
To him betray'd, we know not, and this day   65
Appointed for the deed; that parricide,
I cannot style him better, by confederacy
Preparing this his paramour to be there,
Ent'red Volpone's house (who was the man,
Your fatherhoods must understand, design'd   70
For the inheritance), there sought his father: —
But with what purpose sought he him, my lords?
I tremble to pronounce it, that a son
Unto a father, and to such a father,
Should have so foul, felonious intent!        75
It was to murder him: when being prevented
By his more happy absence, what then did he?
Not check his wicked thoughts; no, now new
  deeds;

⁴ **So . . . man:** ('So has the youth' Q)  ³¹ **frontless:** shameless  ⁴¹ **timeless:** untimely  ⁴³ **goodness:** ('vertue' Q)  ⁴⁴ **owe:** own  ⁵⁴ **fact:** deed

(Mischief doth ever end where it begins)
An act of horror, fathers! He dragg'd forth 80
The aged gentleman that had there lien bed-rid
Three years and more, out of his innocent couch,
Naked upon the floor; there left him; wounded
His servant in the face; and with this strumpet,
The stale to his forg'd practice, who was glad
To be so active, — (I shall here desire    86
Your fatherhoods to note but my collections,
As most remarkable, —) thought at once to stop
His father's ends, discredit his free choice
In the old gentleman, redeem themselves,   90
By laying infamy upon this man,
To whom, with blushing, they should owe
   their lives.
1 *Avoc.*   What proofs have you of this?
*Bon.*          Most honour'd fathers,
I humbly crave there be no credit given
To this man's mercenary tongue.
   2 *Avoc.*           Forbear.   95
*Bon.*   His soul moves in his fee.
   3 *Avoc.*            O, sir.
*Bon.*          This fellow,
For six sols more would plead against his
   Maker.
1 *Avoc.*   You do forget yourself.
*Volt.*         Nay, nay, grave fathers,
Let him have scope: can any man imagine   99
That he will spare his accuser, that would not
Have spar'd his parent?
   1 *Avoc.*       Well, produce your proofs.
*Cel.*   I would I could forget I were a creature.
*Volt.*   Signior Corbaccio!
          [*Corbaccio comes forward.*]
4 *Avoc.*       What is he?
*Volt.*         The father.
2 *Avoc.*   Has he had an oath?
*Not.*       Yes.
*Corb.*       What must I do now? 104
*Not.*   Your testimony 's crav'd.
*Corb.*        Speak to the knave?
I 'll ha' my mouth first stopp'd with earth; my
   heart
Abhors his knowledge: I disclaim in him.
   1 *Avoc.*   But for what cause?
*Corb.*        The mere portent of nature!
He is an utter stranger to my loins.     109
   *Bon.*   Have they made you to this?
*Corb.*        I will not hear thee,
Monster of men, swine, goat, wolf, parricide!
Speak not, thou viper.
   *Bon.*       Sir, I will sit down,
And rather wish my innocence should suffer
Than I resist the authority of a father.    114
   *Volt.*   Signior Corvino!
         [*Corvino comes forward.*]

2 *Avoc.*        This is strange.
1 *Avoc.*         Who 's this?
*Not.*   The husband.
4 *Avoc.*        Is he sworn?
*Not.*        He is.
3 *Avoc.*        Speak then.
*Corv.*   This woman, please your fatherhoods,
   is a whore,
Of most hot exercise, more than a partridge,
Upon record ——
   1 *Avoc.*       No more.
*Corv.*       Neighs like a jennet.   119
*Not.*   Preserve the honour of the court.
*Corv.*        I shall,
And modesty of your most reverend ears.
And yet I hope that I may say, these eyes
Have seen her glu'd unto that piece of cedar,
That fine well timber'd gallant: and that
   here
The letters may be read, thorough the horn, 125
That make the story perfect.
   *Mos.*       Excellent! sir.
*Corv.* [*Aside to Mosca.*]   There is no shame
   in this now, is there?
*Mos.*        None.
*Corv.*   Or if I said, I hop'd that she were on-
   ward
To her damnation, if there be a hell
Greater than whore and woman, a good Catho-
   lic                     130
May make the doubt.
   3 *Avoc.*   His grief hath made him frantic.
1 *Avoc.*   Remove him hence.
2 *Avoc.*       Look to the woman.
                    *She swoons.*
*Corv.*           Rare
Prettily feign'd again!
   4 *Avoc.*      Stand from about her.
1 *Avoc.*   Give her the air.
3 *Avoc.*   What can you say?   [*To Mosca.*]
*Mos.*        My wound,
May 't please your wisdoms, speaks for me, re-
   ceiv'd                  135
In aid of my good patron, when he miss'd
His sought-for father, when that well-taught
   dame
Had her cue giv'n her to cry out, "A rape!"
   *Bon.*   O most laid impudence! Fathers —
3 *Avoc.*       Sir, be silent;   139
You had your hearing free, so must they theirs.
   2 *Avoc.*   I do begin to doubt th' imposture
   here.
4 *Avoc.*   This woman has too many moods.
*Volt.*        Grave fathers,
She is a creature of a most profess'd
And prostituted lewdness.

*Corv.*                              Most impetuous, 144
Unsatisfi'd, grave fathers!
*Volt.*                               May her feignings
Not take your wisdoms: but this day she baited
A stranger, a grave knight, with her loose eyes,
And more lascivious kisses.  This man saw 'em
Together on the water, in a gondola.
*Mos.*   Here is the lady herself, that saw 'em
    too,                                                    150
Without; who then had in the open streets
Pursu'd them, but for saving her knight's hon-
    our.
1 *Avoc.*   Produce that lady.
2 *Avoc.*            Let her come.  [*Exit Mosca.*]
4 *Avoc.*                          These things,
They strike with wonder.
3 *Avoc.*            I am turn'd a stone.

## Act IIII.  Scene VI

*[The Same.]*

*Mosca, Lady [Politic Would-be],*
*Avocatori, &c.*

*Mos.*   Be resolute, madam.
*Lady P.*                      Ay, this same is she.
                              [*Pointing to Celia.*]
Out, thou chameleon harlot! now thine eyes
Vie tears with the hyena.  Dar'st thou look
Upon my wronged face?  I cry your pardons,
I fear I have forgettingly trangress'd        5
Against the dignity of the court ——
2 *Avoc.*                        No, madam.
*Lady P.*   And been exorbitant ——
1 *Avoc.*               You have not, lady.
4 *Avoc.*   These proofs are strong.
*Lady P.*               Surely, I had no purpose
To scandalize your honours, or my sex's.
3 *Avoc.*   We do believe it.
*Lady P.*        Surely you may believe it.   10
2 *Avoc.*   Madam, we do.
*Lady P.*        Indeed you may; my breeding
Is not so coarse ——
4 *Avoc.*                We know it.
*Lady P.*                        To offend
With pertinacy ——
3 *Avoc.*        Lady ——
*Lady P.*                   Such a presence!
No surely.
1 *Avoc.*   We well think it.
*Lady P.*                   You may think it.
1 *Avoc.*   Let her o'ercome.  What witnesses
    have you,                                               15
To make good your report?
*Bon.*                       Our consciences.
*Cel.*   And heaven, that never fails the inno-
    cent.
4 *Avoc.*   These are no testimonies.

*Bon.*                        Not in your courts,
Where multitude and clamour overcomes.
1 *Avoc.*   Nay, then you do wax insolent.

*Volpone is brought in, as impotent*

*Volt.*                          Here, here,   20
The testimony comes that will convince,
And put to utter dumbness their bold tongues!
See here, grave fathers, here 's the ravisher,
The rider on men's wives, the great impostor,
The grand voluptuary!  Do you not think   25
These limbs should affect venery? or these
    eyes
Covet a concubine?  Pray you, mark these
    hands;
Are they not fit to stroke a lady's breasts?
Perhaps he doth dissemble!
*Bon.*                    So he does.
*Volt.*   Would you ha' him tortur'd?
*Bon.*                   I would have him prov'd.   30
*Volt.*   Best try him then with goads, or burn-
    ing irons;
Put him to the strappado: I have heard
The rack hath cur'd the gout; faith, give it
    him,
And help him of a malady; be courteous.   34
I 'll undertake, before these honour'd fathers,
He shall have yet as many left diseases,
As she has known adulterers, or thou strumpets.
O, my most equal hearers, if these deeds,
Acts of this bold and most exorbitant strain,
May pass with suff'rance, what one citizen   40
But owes the forfeit of his life, yea, fame,
To him that dares traduce him?  Which of you
Are safe, my honour'd fathers?  I would ask,
With leave of your grave fatherhoods, if their
    plot
Have any face or colour like to truth?   45
Or if, unto the dullest nostril here,
It smell not rank, and most abhorred slander?
I crave your care of this good gentleman,
Whose life is much endanger'd by their fable;
And as for them, I will conclude with this,   50
That vicious persons, when they 're hot, and
    flesh'd
In impious acts, their constancy abounds:
Damn'd deeds are done with greatest confi-
    dence.
1 *Avoc.*   Take 'em to custody, and sever
    them.
2 *Avoc.*   'T is pity two such prodigies should
    live.                                                   55
1 *Avoc.*   Let the old gentleman be return'd
    with care.
                  [*Exeunt Officers with Volpone.*]
I 'm sorry our credulity wrong'd him.
4 *Avoc.*   These are two creatures!
3 *Avoc.*            I have an earthquake in me.

---

³² **strappado**: a cruel form of torture   ³⁸ **equal**: impartial

2 *Avoc.* Their shame, ev'n in their cradles,
    fled their faces.
4 *Avoc.*  You 've done a worthy service to
    the state, sir,              60
In their discovery.              [*To Volt.*]
1 *Avoc.*         You shall hear, ere night,
What punishment the court decrees upon 'em.
*Volt.* We thank your fatherhoods.
        [*Exeunt Avocat., Not., and Officers*
            *with Bonario and Celia.*]
            How like you it?
*Mos.*                   Rare.
I 'd ha' your tongue, sir, tipp'd with gold for
    this;
I 'd ha' you be the heir to the whole city;  65
The earth I 'd have want men ere you want
    living:
They 're bound to erect your statue in St.
    Mark's.
Signior Corvino, I would have you go
And show yourself that you have conquer'd.
  *Corv.*                  Yes.
  *Mos.* It was much better that you should
    profess                  70
Yourself a cuckold thus, than that the other
Should have been prov'd.
  *Corv.*        Nay, I consider'd that:
Now it is her fault.
  *Mos.*        Then it had been yours.
  *Corv.* True; I do doubt this advocate still.
  *Mos.*               I' faith,
You need not, I dare ease you of that care.  75
  *Corv.* I trust thee, Mosca.      [*Exit.*]
  *Mos.*          As your own soul, sir.
  *Corb.*                 Mosca!
  *Mos.* Now for your business, sir.
  *Corb.*          How! ha' you business?
  *Mos.* Yes, yours, sir.
  *Corb.*          O, none else?
  *Mos.*           None else, not I.
  *Corb.* Be careful, then.
  *Mos.*      Rest you with both your eyes, sir.
  *Corb.* Dispatch it.
  *Mos.*          Instantly.
  *Corb.*         And look that all,  80
Whatever, be put in, jewels, plate, moneys,
Household stuff, bedding, curtains.
  *Mos.*        Curtain-rings, sir:
Only the advocate's fee must be deducted.
  *Corb.* I 'll pay him now; you 'll be too prod-
    igal.
  *Mos.* Sir, I must tender it.
  *Corb.*        Two cecchines is well.  85
  *Mos.* No, six, sir.
  *Corb.*       'T is too much.
  *Mos.*        He talk'd a great while;
You must consider that, sir.
  *Corb.*       Well, there 's three ——

*Mos.* I 'll give it him.
  *Corb.* Do so, and there 's for thee.  [*Exit.*]
  *Mos.* [*Aside.*]  Bountiful bones!  What hor-
    rid strange offence
Did he commit 'gainst nature, in his youth,  90
Worthy this age? — You see, sir, [*to Volt.*] how
    I work
Unto your ends; take you no notice.
  *Volt.*                 No,
I 'll leave you.
  *Mos.*     All is yours, the devil and all,
Good advocate! — Madam, I 'll bring you home.
  *Lady P.* No, I 'll go see your patron.
  *Mos.*          That you shall not:  95
I 'll tell you why.  My purpose is to urge
My patron to reform his will, and for
The zeal you 've shown to-day, whereas before
You were but third or fourth, you shall be now  99
Put in the first; which would appear as begg'd
If you were present.  Therefore ——
  *Lady P.*    You shall sway me.  [*Exeunt.*]

## Act V.  Scene I

### [*Volpone's House.*]

#### *Volpone*

Well, I am here, and all this brunt is past.
I ne'er was in dislike with my disguise
Till this fled moment: here 't was good, in pri-
    vate;
But in your public, — *cave* whilst I breathe.  4
'Fore God, my left leg 'gan to have the cramp,
And I apprehended straight some power had
    struck me
With a dead palsy.  Well!  I must be merry,
And shake it off.  A many of these fears
Would put me into some villainous disease,
Should they come thick upon me: I 'll prevent
    'em.                      10
Give me a bowl of lusty wine, to fright
This humour from my heart.  *He drinks.*
    Hum, hum, hum!
'T is almost gone already; I shall conquer.
Any device now of rare ingenious knavery,  14
That would possess me with a violent laughter,
Would make me up again.
    So, so, so, so!          *Drinks again.*
This heat is life; 't is blood by this time: —·
    Mosca!

## Act V.  Scene II

### [*The Same.*]

*Mosca, Volpone, [and later] Nano, Castrone*

[*Mos.*]  How now, sir?  Does the day look
    clear again?
Are we recover'd, and wrought out of error,

---

79 **Rest . . . eyes:** Leave the matter to me.    1 **brunt:** crisis    4 **cave:** beware

Into our way, to see our path before us?
Is our trade free once more?
   *Volp.*                Exquisite Mosca!
   *Mos.*  Was it not carri'd learnedly?
   *Volp.*          And stoutly:  5
Good wits are greatest in extremities.
   *Mos.*  It were a folly beyond thought to trust
Any grand act unto a cowardly spirit.
You are not taken with it enough, methinks.
   *Volp.*  O, more than if I had enjoy'd the
    wench:  10
The pleasure of all woman-kind 's not like it.
   *Mos.*  Why, now you speak, sir.  We must
here be fix'd;
Here we must rest; this is our masterpiece;
We cannot think to go beyond this.
   *Volp.*                True,
Thou hast play'd thy prize, my precious Mosca.
   *Mos.*           Nay, sir,  15
To gull the court ——
   *Volp.*      And quite divert the torrent
Upon the innocent.
   *Mos.*        Yes, and to make
So rare a music out of discords ——
   *Volp.*            Right.
That yet to me 's the strangest, how th' hast
    borne it!
That these, being so divided 'mongst them-
    selves,  20
Should not scent somewhat, or in me or thee,
Or doubt their own side.
   *Mos.*       True, they will not see 't.
Too much light blinds' em, I think.  Each of 'em
Is so possess'd and stuff'd with his own hopes
That anything unto the contrary,  25
Never so true, or never so apparent,
Never so palpable, they will resist it ——
   *Volp.*  Like a temptation of the devil.
   *Mos.*           Right, sir.
Merchants may talk of trade, and your great
    signiors
Of land that yields well; but if Italy  30
Have any glebe more fruitful than these fellows,
I am deceiv'd.  Did not your advocate rare?
   *Volp.*  O — "My most honour'd fathers, my
    grave fathers,
Under correction of your fatherhoods,
What face of truth is here?  If these strange
    deeds  35
May pass, most honour'd fathers" — I had
    much ado
To forbear laughing.
   *Mos.*      'T seem'd to me, you sweat, sir.
   *Volp.*  In troth, I did a little.
   *Mos.*         But confess, sir,
Were you not daunted?
   *Volp.*         In good faith, I was

A little in a mist, but not dejected:  40
Never but still myself.
   *Mos.*        I think it, sir.
Now, so truth help me, I must needs say this, sir,
And out of conscience for your advocate,
He has taken pains, in faith, sir, and deserv'd,
(In my poor judgment, I speak it under favour,
Not to contrary you, sir,) very richly —  46
Well — to be cozen'd.
   *Volp.*       Troth, and I think so too,
By that I heard him in the latter end.
   *Mos.*  O, but before, sir: had you heard him
    first
Draw it to certain heads, then aggravate,  50
Then use his vehement figures — I look'd still
When he would shift a shirt; and doing this
Out of pure love, no hope of gain ——
   *Volp.*           'T is right.
I cannot answer him, Mosca, as I would,
Not yet; but for thy sake, at thy entreaty,  55
I will begin, e'en now — to vex 'em all,
This very instant.
   *Mos.*       Good sir.
   *Volp.*           Call the dwarf
And eunuch forth.
   *Mos.*        Castrone, Nano!

       *[Enter Castrone and Nano]*

   *Nano.*                 Here.
   *Volp.*  Shall we have a jig now?
   *Mos.*        What you please, sir.
   *Volp.*                Go,
Straight give out about the streets, you two,  60
That I am dead; do it with constancy,
Sadly, do you hear?  Impute it to the grief
Of this late slander.
               *[Exeunt Cast. and Nano.]*
   *Mos.*        What do you mean, sir?
   *Volp.*                O,
I shall have instantly my Vulture, Crow,
Raven, come flying hither, on the news,  65
To peck for carrion, my she-wolf, and all,
Greedy, and full of expectation ——
   *Mos.*  And then to have it ravish'd from
    their mouths!
   *Volp.*  'T is true.  I will ha' thee put on a
    gown,  69
And take upon thee, as thou wert mine heir;
Show 'em a will.  Open that chest, and reach
Forth one of those that has the blanks; I 'll
    straight
Put in thy name.
   *Mos.*        It will be rare, sir.
                *[Gives him a paper.]*
   *Volp.*                Ay,
When they e'en gape, and find themselves de-
    luded ——  74

---

³¹ **glebe:** soil   ³² **rare:** finely   ⁴⁸ **latter end:** conclusion of his speech   ⁵⁰ **aggravate:** emphasize
⁵² **shift a shirt:** because of the violence of his gestures   ⁶² **Sadly:** seriously

*Mos.* Yes.　　　　　　　　　　　[patch,
*Volp.* And thou use them scurvily! Dis-
Get on thy gown.
*Mos.* [*Putting on a gown.*] But what, sir, if
they ask
After the body?
*Volp.*　　　　Say, it was corrupted.
*Mos.* I 'll say it stunk, sir; and was fain to
have it
Coffin'd up instantly, and sent away.
*Volp.* Anything; what thou wilt. Hold,
here 's my will.　　　　　　　　　80
Get thee a cap, a count-book, pen and ink,
Papers afore thee; sit as thou wert taking
An inventory of parcels. I 'll get up
Behind the curtain, on a stool, and hearken:
Sometime peep over, see how they do look, 85
With what degrees their blood doth leave their
faces.
O, 't will afford me a rare meal of laughter!
*Mos.* Your advocate will turn stark dull upon
it.
*Volp.* It will take off his oratory's edge. 89
*Mos.* But your clarissimo, old roundback, he
Will crump you like a hog-louse, with the touch.
*Volp.* And what Corvino?
*Mos.*　　　　　　　O, sir, look for him,
To-morrow morning, with a rope and a dagger,
To visit all the streets; he must run mad.
My lady too, that came into the court,　95
To bear false witness for your worship ——
*Volp.*　　　　　　　　　　　　　Yes,
And kiss'd me 'fore the fathers, when my face
Flow'd all with oils ——
*Mos.*　　　　And sweat, sir. Why, your gold
Is such another med'cine, it dries up　100
All those offensive savours: it transforms
The most deformed, and restores 'em lovely,
As 't were the strange poetical girdle. Jove
Could not invent t' himself a shroud more subtle
To pass Acrisius' guards. It is the thing
Makes all the world her grace, her youth, her
beauty.　　　　　　　　　　105
*Volp.* I think she loves me.
*Mos.*　　　　　　Who? The lady, sir?
She 's jealous of you.
*Volp.*　　　　Dost thou say so?
　　　　　　　　　　　[*Knocking within.*]
*Mos.*　　　　　　　　　　　Hark.
There 's some already.
*Volp.*　　　　Look.
*Mos.*　　　　　　　It is the Vulture;
He has the quickest scent.
*Volp.*　　　　　I 'll to my place,
Thou to thy posture.　[*Goes to upper stage.*]

*Mos.*　　　　　　　　I am set.
*Volp.*　　　　　　　But, Mosca, 110
Play the artificer now, torture 'em rarely.

## Act V.　Scene III

[*The Same.*]

*Voltore, Mosca, Corbaccio, Corvino, Lady
[Politic Would-be], Volpone*

[*Volt.*] How now, my Mosca?
*Mos.* [*Writing.*] "Turkey carpets, nine ——"
*Volt.* Taking an inventory! that is well.
*Mos.* "Two suits of bedding, tissue ——"
*Volt.*　　　　　Where 's the will?
Let me read that the while.

[*Enter Servants with Corbaccio in a chair*]

*Corb.*　　　　　So, set me down, 5
And get you home.　　[*Exeunt Servants.*]
*Volt.*　　　Is he come now, to trouble us?
*Mos.* "Of cloth of gold, two more ——"
*Corb.*　　　　　Is it done, Mosca?
*Mos.* "Of several vellets, eight ——"
*Volt.*　　　　　I like his care.
*Corb.* Dost thou not hear?

[*Enter Corvino*]

*Corv.*　　　Ha! is the hour come, Mosca?
*Volp.* Ay, now they muster.
　　*Volpone peeps from behind a traverse.*
*Corv.* What does the advocate here, 10
Or this Corbaccio?
*Corb.*　　　What do these here?

[*Enter Lady Pol. Would-be*]

*Lady P.*　　　　　　　　Mosca!
Is his thread spun?
*Mos.*　　　"Eight chests of linen ——"
*Volp.*　　　　　　　　　　O,
My fine Dame Would-be, too!
*Corv.*　　　　Mosca, the will,
That I may show it these, and rid 'em hence.
*Mos.* "Six chests of diaper, four of dam-
ask." — There.　　　　　　　15
　　[*Gives them the will carelessly, over
　　his shoulder.*]
*Corb.* Is that the will?
*Mos.*　　"Down-beds, and bolsters ——"
*Volp.*　　　　　　　　　Rare!
Be busy still. Now they begin to flutter:
They never think of me. Look, see, see, see!
How their swift eyes run over the long deed,
Unto the name, and to the legacies,　20
What is bequeath'd them there ——

---

⁹⁰ **clarissimo:** Corbaccio　⁹¹ **crump you:** curl up　⁹³,⁹⁴ (This alludes to *The Spanish Tragedy*, III.
xii; see page 121 above.)　¹⁰² **girdle:** "cestus" (Jonson's note), the girdle of Venus　¹⁰⁴ **Acrisius:**
father of Danaë　¹¹¹ **artificer:** artist　³ **tissue:** of rich fabric　⁸ **vellets:** velvets　¹⁰ s. D. **traverse:**
curtain　¹⁵ **diaper:** a fabric with a woven pattern

*Mos.*          "Ten suits of hangings ——"
*Volp.*  Ay, i' their garters, Mosca.  Now their hopes
Are at the gasp.
*Volt.*          Mosca the heir!
*Corb.*                    What 's that?
*Volp.*  My advocate is dumb; look to my merchant,
He 's heard of some strange storm, a ship is lost,                                   25
He faints; my lady will swoon.  Old glazen-eyes,
He hath not reach'd his despair yet.
*Corb.*                    All these
Are out of hope; I 'm, sure, the man.
                         [*Takes the will.*]
*Corv.*                    But, Mosca ——
*Mos.*  "Two cabinets ——"
*Corv.*              Is this in earnest?
*Mos.*                    "One
Of ebony ——"
*Corv.*          Or do you but delude me?   30
*Mos.*  "The other, mother of pearl." — I am very busy,
Good faith, it is a fortune thrown upon me —
"Item, one salt of agate" — not my seeking.
*Lady P.*  Do you hear, sir?          [bear,
*Mos.*  "A perfum'd box" — Pray you, for-
You see I am troubled — "made of an onyx ——"
*Lady P.*                    How!   35
*Mos.*  To-morrow or next day, I shall be at leisure
To talk with you all.
*Corv.*          Is this my large hope's issue?
*Lady P.*  Sir, I must have a fairer answer.
*Mos.*                    Madam!
Marry, and shall: pray you, fairly quit my house.
Nay, raise no tempest with your looks; but hark you,                               40
Remember what your ladyship off'red me
To put you in an heir; go to, think on 't:
And what you said e'en your best madams did
For maintenance; and why not you?  Enough.
Go home, and use the poor Sir Pol, your knight, well,                              45
For fear I tell some riddles; go, be melancholic.
                         [*Exit Lady Would-be.*]
*Volp.*  O, my fine devil!
*Corv.*          Mosca, pray you a word.
*Mos.*  Lord! will not you take your dispatch hence yet?
Methinks, of all, you should have been th' example.
Why should you stay here?  With what thought, what promise?                        50

Hear you; do not you know, I know you an ass,
And that you would most fain have been a wit-tol,
If fortune would have let you? that you are
A declar'd cuckold, on good terms?  This pearl,
You 'll say, was yours? right: this diamond?  55
I 'll not deny 't, but thank you.  Much here else?
It may be so.  Why, think that these good works
May help to hide your bad.  I 'll not betray you;
Although you be but extraordinary,
And have it only in title, it sufficeth:       60
Go home, be melancholic too, or mad.
                         [*Exit Corvino.*]
*Volp.*  Rare Mosca! how his villainy becomes him!
*Volt.*  Certain he doth delude all these for me.
*Corb.*  Mosca the heir!
*Volp.*          O, his four eyes have found it.
*Corb.*  I 'm cozen'd, cheated, by a parasite-slave;                               65
Harlot, th' hast gull'd me.
*Mos.*                    Yes, sir.  Stop your mouth,
Or I shall draw the only tooth is left.
Are not you he, that filthy covetous wretch,
With the three legs, that here, in hope of prey,
Have, any time this three year, snuff'd about,
With your most grov'ling nose, and would have hir'd                                71
Me to the pois'ning of my patron, sir?
Are not you he that have to-day in court
Profess'd the disinheriting of your son?
Perjur'd yourself?  Go home, and die, and stink;                                   75
If you but croak a syllable, all comes out:
Away, and call your porters! [*Exit Corbaccio.*]
     Go, go, stink.
*Volp.*  Excellent varlet!
*Volt.*                    Now, my faithful Mosca,
I find thy constancy ——
*Mos.*              Sir!
*Volt.*                    Sincere.
*Mos.* [*Writing.*]                    "A table
Of porphyry" — I marle you 'll be thus troublesome.                               80
*Volt.*  Nay, leave off now, they are gone.
*Mos.*              Why, who are you?
What! who did send for you?  O, cry you mercy,
Reverend sir!  Good faith, I am griev'd for you,
That any chance of mine should thus defeat
Your (I must needs say) most deserving trav-ails:                                  85

---

²² **Ay . . . garters:** (playing on "hangings")
⁶⁴ **Harlot:** fellow (originally used only of males)
³³ **salt:** salt cellar     ⁵² **wittol:** a willing cuckold
⁸⁰ **marle:** marvel

But I protest, sir, it was cast upon me,
And I could almost wish to be without it,
But that the will o' th' dead must be observ'd.
Marry, my joy is that you need it not;
You have a gift, sir, (thank your education),      90
Will never let you want, while there are men,
And malice, to breed causes.  Would I had
But half the like, for all my fortune, sir!
If I have any suits, as I do hope,
Things being so easy and direct, I shall not,      95
I will make bold with your obstreperous aid, —
Conceive me, for your fee, sir.  In mean time,
You that have so much law, I know ha' the
      conscience
Not to be covetous of what is mine.
Good sir, I thank you for my plate; 't will
      help                                          100
To set up a young man.  Good faith, you look
As you were costive; best go home and purge,
      sir.                              [_Exit Voltore._]
   _Volp._ [_Comes down._] Bid him eat lettuce
      well.  My witty mischief,
Let me embrace thee.  O that I could now
Transform thee to a Venus! — Mosca, go,           105
Straight take my habit of clarissimo,
And walk the streets; be seen, torment 'em
      more:
We must pursue, as well as plot.  Who would
Have lost this feast?
   _Mos._              I doubt it will lose them.
   _Volp._  O, my recovery shall recover all.      110
That I could now but think on some disguise
To meet 'em in, and ask 'em questions:
How I would vex 'em still at every turn!
   _Mos._  Sir, I can fit you.
   _Volp._                     Canst thou?
   _Mos._                                  Yes, I know
One o' the _commandadori_, sir, so like you;       115
Him will I straight make drunk, and bring
      you his habit.
   _Volp._  A rare disguise, and answering thy
      brain!
O, I will be a sharp disease unto 'em.
   _Mos._  Sir, you must look for curses ——
   _Volp._                          Till they burst;
The Fox fares ever best when he is curs'd.         120
                                    [_Exeunt._]

## Act V.  Scene IIII

[_A Hall in Sir Politic's House._]

_Peregrine, 3 Mercatori, [later] Woman, Politic_

   [_Per._]  Am I enough disguis'd?
   _1 Mer._                         I warrant you.
   _Per._  All my ambition is to fright him only.

   _2 Mer._  If you could ship him away, 't were
      excellent.
   _3 Mer._  To Zant, or to Aleppo!
   _Per._                          Yes, and ha' his
Adventures put i' th' Book of Voyages,              5
And his gull'd story regist'red for truth.
Well, gentlemen, when I am in a while,
And that you think us warm in our discourse,
Know your approaches.
   _1 Mer._             Trust it to our care.      9
                              [_Exeunt Merchants._]

[_Enter Waiting-woman_]

   _Per._  Save you, fair lady! Is Sir Pol within?
   _Wom._  I do not know, sir.
   _Per._                      Pray you, say unto him,
Here is a merchant, upon earnest business,
Desires to speak with him.
   _Wom._                   I will see, sir.  [_Exit._]
   _Per._                                    Pray you.
I see the family is all female here.

[_Re-enter Waiting-woman_]

   _Wom._  He says, sir, he has weighty affairs of
      state,                                        15
That now require him whole; some other time
You may possess him.
   _Per._              Pray you, say again,
If those require him whole, these will exact him,
Whereof I bring him tidings.  [_Exit Woman._]
   What might be
His grave affair of state now!  How to make      20
Bolognian sausages here in Venice, sparing
One o' th' ingredients?

[_Re-enter Waiting-woman_]

   _Wom._                  Sir, he says, he knows
By your word "tidings," that you are no
      statesman,
And therefore wills you stay.
   _Per._                      Sweet, pray you, return him,
I have not read so many proclamations,            25
And studied them for words, as he has done ——
But — here he deigns to come.  [_Exit Woman._]

[_Enter Sir Politic_]

   _Sir P._                     Sir, I must crave
Your courteous pardon.  There hath chanc'd
      to-day
Unkind disaster 'twixt my lady and me;
And I was penning my apology,                     30
To give her satisfaction, as you came now.
   _Per._  Sir, I am griev'd I bring you worse dis-
      aster:
The gentleman you met at th' port to-day,
That told you he was newly arriv'd ——

⁹² **causes:** law-suits   ¹⁰² **costive:** constipated   ¹⁰³ **eat lettuce:** to cure his complexion   ⁴ **Zant:**
Zacynthus, a Greek island   ⁵ **Book of Voyages:** Hakluyt's _Principal Navigations, Voyages, etc._ (2nd.
ed. 1598–1600)   ¹⁸ **exact:** bring to an end, finish utterly (Latinism)   ²⁴ **return:** answer

*Sir P.*                                      Ay, was
A fugitive punk?
*Per.*                        No, sir, a spy set on you: 35
And he has made relation to the senate,
That you profess'd to him to have a plot
To sell the State of Venice to the Turk.
*Sir P.* O me!                              [this time,
*Per.*   For which warrants are sign'd by
To apprehend you, and to search your study 40
For papers ——
*Sir P.*          Alas, sir, I have none, but notes
Drawn out of play-books ——
*Per.*                        All the better, sir.
*Sir P.* And some essays. What shall I do?
*Per.*                        Sir, best
Convey yourself into a sugar-chest;
Or, if you could lie round, a frail were rare; 45
And I could send you aboard.
*Sir P.*                       Sir, I but talk'd so,
For discourse sake merely. *They knock without.*
*Per.*                        Hark! they are there.
*Sir P.* I am a wretch, a wretch!
*Per.*             What will you do, sir?
Ha' you ne'er a currant-butt to leap into?
They 'll put you to the rack; you must be
     sudden.                                  50
*Sir P.* Sir, I have an ingine ——
3 *Mer.* [*Within.*]        Sir Politic Would-be!
2 *Mer.* [*Within.*]   Where is he?
*Sir P.*  That I have thought upon before time.
*Per.* What is it?
*Sir P.*        I shall ne'er endure the torture.
Marry, it is, sir, of a tortoise-shell,
Fitted for these extremities: pray you, sir, help
     me.                                       55
Here I 've a place, sir, to put back my legs,
Please you to lay it on, sir, [*Lies down while
     Per. places the shell upon him.*] — with
     this cap,
And my black gloves. I 'll lie, sir, like a
     tortoise,
Till they are gone.
*Per.*            And call you this an ingine?
*Sir P.* Mine own device. —— Good sir, bid
     my wife's women                           60
To burn my papers.

### They rush in.

1 *Mer.*                      Where 's he hid?
3 *Mer.*                      We must,
And will sure find him.
2 *Mer.*                  Which is his study?
1 *Mer.*                                    What
Are you, sir?
*Per.*        I 'm a merchant, that came here
To look upon this tortoise.
3 *Mer.*          How!

1 *Mer.*                      St. Mark!
What beast is this?
*Per.*            It is a fish.
2 *Mer.*                      Come out here! 65
*Per.* Nay, you may strike him, sir, and tread
     upon him;
He 'll bear a cart.
1 *Mer.*          What, to run over him?
*Per.*                                    Yes.
3 *Mer.* Let 's jump upon him.
2 *Mer.*                      Can he not go?
*Per.*                                    He creeps.
1 *Mer.* Let 's see him creep.
*Per.*     No, good sir, you will hurt him.  69
2 *Mer.* Heart, I 'll see him creep, or prick
     his guts.
3 *Mer.* Come out here!
*Per.*               Pray you, sir, creep a little.
1 *Mer.*                                    Forth.
2 *Mer.* Yet further.
*Per.*              Good sir! — Creep.
2 *Mer.* We 'll see his legs.
     *They pull off the shell and discover him.*
3 *Mer.* Gods so, he has garters!
1 *Mer.*                    Ay, and gloves!
2 *Mer.*                                Is this
Your fearful tortoise?
*Per.* [*Discovering himself.*]  Now, Sir Pol,
we are even;
For your next project I shall be prepar'd: 75
I am sorry for the funeral of your notes, sir.
1 *Mer.* 'T were a rare motion to be seen in
     Fleet-street.
2 *Mer.* Ay, i' the Term.
1 *Mer.*              Or Smithfield, in the fair.
3 *Mer.* Methinks 't is but a melancholic
     sight.
*Per.* Farewell, most politic tortoise!
               [*Exeunt Per. and Merchants.*

### Re-enter Waiting-woman]

*Sir P.*                      Where 's my lady? 80
Knows she of this?
*Wom.*            I know not, sir.
*Sir P.*                        Enquire. —
O, I shall be the fable of all feasts,
The freight of the gazetti, ship-boys' tale;
And, which is worst, even talk for ordinaries.
*Wom.* My lady 's come most melancholic
     home,                                     85
And says, sir, she will straight to sea, for
     physic.
*Sir P.* And I, to shun this place and clime
     for ever,
Creeping with house on back, and think it well
To shrink my poor head in my politic shell.
                                   [*Exeunt.*]

---

<sup>35</sup> **punk**: prostitute   <sup>45</sup> **frail**: rush basket   <sup>49</sup> **currant-butt**: wine-cask   <sup>51</sup> **ingine**: contrivance
<sup>72</sup> **further** ('furder' F)   <sup>77</sup> **motion**: exhibition   <sup>78</sup> **fair**: Bartholomew Fair   <sup>83</sup> **gazetti**: newspapers

## Act V. Scene V

*[A Room in Volpone's House.]*

*Volpone, Mosca. The first in the habit of a
Commandadore: the other, of a Clarissimo*

[*Volp.*] Am I then like him?
*Mos.*                           O, sir, you are he;
No man can sever you.
*Volp.*                           Good.
*Mos.*                           But what am I?
*Voip.* 'Fore heaven, a brave clarissimo;
thou becom'st it!
Pity thou wert not born one.
*Mos. [Aside.]*                           If I hold
My made one, 't will be well.
*Volp.*                           I 'll go and see  5
What news first at the court.         [*Exit.*]
*Mos.*                           Do so. My Fox
Is out on his hole, and ere he shall re-enter,
I 'll make him languish in his borrow'd case,
Except he come to composition with me. —
Androgyno, Castrone, Nano!

*[Enter Androgyno, Castrone, and Nano]*

*All.*                           Here.         10
*Mos.*  Go, recreate yourselves abroad; go,
sport. —                           [*Exeunt.*]
So, now I have the keys, and am possess'd.
Since he will needs be dead afore his time,
I 'll bury him, or gain by him: I 'm his heir,
And so will keep me, till he share at least.  15
To cozen him of all, were but a cheat
Well plac'd; no man would construe it a sin:
Let his sport pay for 't. This is call'd the Fox-
trap.                           [*Exit.*]

## Act V.  Scene VI

*[A Street.]*

*Corbaccio, Corvino, [later] Volpone*

[*Corb.*]  They say the court is set.
*Corv.*                           We must maintain
Our first tale good, for both our reputations.
*Corb.*  Why, mine 's no tale: my son would
there have kill'd me.
*Corv.*  That 's true, I had forgot: — mine is,
I 'm sure.
But for your will, sir.
*Corb.*                           Ay, I 'll come upon him  5
For that hereafter, now his patron 's dead.

*[Enter Volpone]*

*Volp.*  Signior Corvino! and Corbaccio! sir,
Much joy unto you.

*Corv.*                           Of what?
*Volp.*                           The sudden good
Dropp'd down upon you ——
*Corb.*                           Where?
*Volp.*                           And none knows how,
From old Volpone, sir.
*Corb.*                           Out, arrant knave!  10
*Volp.*  Let not your too much wealth, sir,
make you furious.
*Corb.*  Away, thou varlet.
*Volp.*                           Why, sir?
*Corb.*                           Dost thou mock me?
*Volp.*  You mock the world, sir; did you not
change wills?
*Corb.*  Out, harlot!
*Volp.*                           O! belike you are the man,
Signior Corvino? Faith, you carry it well;  15
You grow not mad withal; I love your spirit:
You are not over-leaven'd with your fortune.
You should ha' some would swell now, like a
wine-fat,
With such an autumn. — Did he gi' you all,
sir?
*Corb.*  Avoid, you rascal!
*Volp.*                           Troth, your wife has shown  20
Herself a very woman; but you are well,
You need not care, you have a good estate,
To bear it out, sir, better by this chance:
Except Corbaccio have a share.
*Corb.*                           Hence, varlet.
*Volp.*  You will not be a'known, sir; why,
't is wise.                           25
Thus do all gamesters, at all games, dissem-
ble:
No man will seem to win. [*Exeunt Corvino and
Corbaccio.*] Here comes my Vulture,
Heaving his beak i' the air, and snuffing.

## Act V.  Scene VII

*[The Same.]*

*Voltore, Volpone*

[*Volt.*]  Outstripp'd thus, by a parasite! a
slave,
Would run on errands, and make legs for
crumbs!
Well, what I 'll do ——
*Volp.*                           The court stays for your worship.
I e'en rejoice, sir, at your worship's happiness,
And that it fell into so learned hands,         5
That understand the fing'ring ——
*Volt.*                           What do you mean?
*Volp.*  I mean to be a suitor to your wor-
ship,
For the small tenement, out of reparations,

---

Sc. v. ² **sever**: distinguish   ⁸ **case**: skin   ⁹ **composition**: terms, agreement   Sc. vi. ¹⁸ **wine-fat**:
wine-vat   ¹⁹ **autumn**: harvest   ²⁵ **a'known**: acknow (will not confess it)   Sc. vii. ³ **your**:
('you' F)   ⁸ **reparations**: repair

That, at the end of your long row of houses,
By the Piscaria: it was, in Volpone's time,     10
Your predecessor, ere he grew diseas'd,
A handsome, pretty, custom'd bawdy-house
As any was in Venice, none disprais'd;
But fell with him: his body and that house
Decay'd together.
   *Volt.*       Come, sir, leave your prating.     15
   *Volp.*   Why, if your worship give me but
     your hand
That I may ha' the refusal, I have done.
'T is a mere toy to you, sir; candle-rents;
As your learn'd worship knows ——
   *Volt.*         What do I know?
   *Volp.*   Marry, no end of your wealth, sir;
     God decrease it!     20
   *Volt.*   Mistaking knave! what, mock'st thou
     my misfortune?       [*Exit.*]
   *Volp.*   His blessing on your heart, sir; would
     't were more! ——
Now to my first again, at the next corner.
                       [*Exit.*]

## Act V.  Scene VIII

### [*Another Street.*]

*Corbaccio, Corvino (Mosca passant), [later]*
*Volpone*

   [*Corb.*]   See, in our habit! see the impudent
     varlet!
   *Corv.*   That I could shoot mine eyes at him,
     like gun-stones!

           [*Enter Volpone*]

   *Volp.*   But is this true, sir, of the parasite?
   *Corb.*   Again, t' afflict us! monster!
   *Volp.*            In good faith, sir,
I 'm heartily griev'd, a beard of your grave
     length     5
Should be so over-reach'd.  I never brook'd
That parasite's hair; methought his nose should
     cozen:
There still was somewhat in his look, did prom-
     ise
The bane of a clarissimo.
   *Corb.*        Knave ——
   *Volp.*              Methinks
Yet you, that are so traded i' the world,     10
A witty merchant, the fine bird, Corvino,
That have such moral emblems on your name,
Should not have sung your shame, and dropp'd
     your cheese,
To let the Fox laugh at your emptiness.
   *Corv.*   Sirrah, you think the privilege of the
     place,     15

And your red saucy cap, that seems to me
Nail'd to your jolt-head with those two cecchines,
Can warrant your abuses; come you hither:
You shall perceive, sir, I dare beat you; ap-
     proach.
   *Volp.*   No haste, sir, I do know your valour
     well,     20
Since you durst publish what you are, sir.
   *Corv.*                   Tarry,
I 'd speak with you.
   *Volp.*          Sir, sir, another time ——
   *Corv.*   Nay, now.
   *Volp.*        O God, sir!  I were a wise man,
Would stand the fury of a distracted cuckold.
                *Mosca walks by 'em.*
   *Corb.*   What, come again!
   *Volp.*       Upon 'em, Mosca; save me.     25
   *Corb.*   The air 's infected where he breathes.
   *Corv.*                Let 's fly him.
          [*Exeunt Corv. and Corb.*]
   *Volp.*   Excellent basilisk! turn upon the Vul-
     ture.

## Act V.  Scene IX

### [*The Same.*]

*Voltore, Mosca, Volpone*

   [*Volt.*]   Well, flesh-fly, it is summer with you
     now;
Your winter will come on.
   *Mos.*            Good advocate,
'Pray thee not rail, nor threaten out of place,
     thus;
Thou 'lt make a solecism, as madam says.
Get you a biggin more; your brain breaks
     loose.          [*Exit.*]     5
   *Volt.*   Well sir.            [slave,
   *Volp.*   Would you ha' me beat the insolent
Throw dirt upon his first good clothes?
   *Volt.*               This same
Is doubtless some familiar.
   *Volp.*          Sir, the court,
In troth, stays for you.  I am mad, a mule,
That never read Justinian, should get up,     10
And ride an advocate.  Had you no quirk
To avoid gullage, sir, by such a creature?
I hope you do but jest; he has not done 't:
This 's but confederacy to blind the rest.
You are the heir?
   *Volt.*        A strange, officious,     15
Troublesome knave! thou dost torment me.
   *Volp.*             I know ——
It cannot be, sir, that you should be cozen'd;
'T is not within the wit of man to do it;

---

[10] **Piscaria:** fish-market    [12] **custom'd:** well-frequented    Sc. viii.  S. D. **passant:** walking across
the stage   [1] **habit:** that of clarissimo    [2] **gun-stones:** cannon-balls    [13] **sung your:** ('sung you' F)
[17] **jolt-head:** blockhead    [27] **basilisk:** a mythical beast who killed by a look    Sc. ix.  [5] **biggin:**
lawyer's cap   [8] **familiar:** demon

You are so wise, so prudent; and 't is fit    19
That wealth and wisdom still should go together.                                *[Exeunt.]*

## Act V.  Scene X

*[The Scrutineo.]*

*4 Avocatori, Notario, Commandadori, Bonario,
Celia, Corbaccio, Corvino, [later] Voltore, Volpone*

[*1 Avoc.*]  Are all the parties here?
*Not.*                         All but the advocate.
*2 Avoc.*  And here he comes.

*[Enter Voltore and Volpone]*

*1 Avoc.*  Then bring 'em forth to sentence.
*Volt.*   O, my most honour'd fathers, let your
  mercy
Once win upon your justice, to forgive —
I am distracted ——
  *Volp.*    (*Aside.*)  What will he do now?
*Volt.*                              O, 5
I know not which t' address myself to first;
Whether your fatherhoods, or these innocents —
  *Corv.* (*Aside.*)  Will he betray himself?
*Volt.*                            Whom equally
I have abus'd, out of most covetous ends ——
  *Corv.* (*Aside.*) The man is mad!
  *Corb.* (*Aside.*)       What 's that?
  *Corv.* (*Aside.*)          He is possess'd. 10
*Volt.*  For which, now struck in conscience,
  here I prostrate
Myself at your offended feet, for pardon.
  *1, 2 Avoc.*  Arise.
  *Cel.*        O heaven, how just thou art!
  *Volp.*                      I 'm caught
I' mine own noose ——
  *Corv.* [*To Corbaccio.*]  Be constant, sir;
  nought now                                14
Can help but impudence.
  *1 Avoc.*         Speak forward.
  *Com.*                    Silence!
*Volt.*  It is not passion in me, reverend
  fathers,
But only conscience, conscience, my good sires,
That makes me now tell truth.  That parasite,
That knave, hath been the instrument of all. 19
  *1 Avoc.*  Where is that knave?  Fetch him.
  *Volp.*              I go.   [*Exit.*]
  *Corv.*                   Grave fathers,
This man 's distracted; he confess'd it now:
For, hoping to be old Volpone's heir,
Who now is dead ——
  *3 Avoc.*  How!
  *2 Avoc.*            Is Volpone dead?
  *Corv.*  Dead since, grave fathers —
  *Bon.*              O sure vengeance!

*1 Avoc.*                          Stay,
Then he was no deceiver?
  *Volt.*           O no, none:    25
The parasite, grave fathers.
  *Corv.*           He does speak
Out of mere envy, 'cause the servant 's made
The thing he gap'd for.  Please your father-
  hoods,
This is the truth, though I 'll not justify
The other, but he may be some-deal faulty. 30
  *Volt.*  Ay, to your hopes, as well as mine,
  Corvino:
But I 'll use modesty.  Pleaseth your wisdoms,
To view these certain notes, and but confer
  them;
As I hope favour, they shall speak clear truth.
  *Corv.*  The devil has ent'red him!
  *Bon.*              Or bides in you. 35
  *4 Avoc.*  We have done ill, by a public officer
To send for him, if he be heir.
  *2 Avoc.*                For whom?
  *4 Avoc.*  Him that they call the parasite.
  *3 Avoc.*                'T is true,
He is a man of great estate, now left.
  *4 Avoc.*  Go you, and learn his name, and say
  the court                                40
Entreats his presence here, but to the clearing
Of some few doubts.        [*Exit Notary.*]
  *2 Avoc.*        This same 's a labyrinth!
  *1 Avoc.*  Stand you unto your first report?
  *Corv.*                    My state,
My life, my fame ——
  *Bon.* (*Aside.*)      Where is 't?
  *Corv.*              Are at the stake.
  *1 Avoc.*  Is yours so too?
  *Corb.*        The advocate 's a knave,  45
And has a forked tongue ——
  *2 Avoc.*          Speak to the point.
  *Corb.*  So is the parasite too.
  *1 Avoc.*            This is confusion.
  *Volt.*  I do beseech your fatherhoods, read
  but those —        [*Giving them papers.*]
  *Corv.*  And credit nothing the false spirit
  hath writ:                             49
It cannot be but he is possess'd, grave fathers.
                                   [*Exeunt.*]

## Act V.   Scene XI

*[A Street.]*

*Volpone, [later] Nano, Androgyno, Castrone*

[*Volp.*]  To make a snare for mine own neck
  and run
My head into it, wilfully! with laughter!
When I had newly scap'd, was free and clear,
Out of mere wantonness!  O, the dull devil
Was in this brain of mine when I devis'd it, 5

---

³² **modesty:** moderation    ³³ **confer:** compare

And Mosca gave it second; he must now
Help to sear up this vein, or we bleed dead.

*[Enter Nano, Androgyno, and Castrone]*

How now! Who let you loose? Whither go
   you now?
What, to buy gingerbread, or to drown kitlings?
*Nan.* Sir, Master Mosca call'd us out of doors,
And bid us all go play, and took the keys.   11
*And.* Yes.            [Why, so!
*Volp.*     Did Master Mosca take the keys?
I 'm farther in. These are my fine conceits!
I must be merry, with a mischief to me!   14
What a vile wretch was I, that could not bear
My fortune soberly? I must ha' my crochets,
And my conundrums! Well, go you, and seek
   him:
His meaning may be truer than my fear.
Bid him, he straight come to me to the court;
Thither will I, and, if 't be possible,   20
Unscrew my advocate, upon new hopes:
When I provok'd him, then I lost myself.

## Act V. Scene XII

### [The Scrutineo.]

### Avocatori, &c.

[*1 Avoc.*] These things can ne'er be recon-
   cil'd. He here     [*Showing the papers.*]
Professeth that the gentleman was wrong'd,
And that the gentlewoman was brought thither,
Forc'd by her husband, and there left.
*Volt.*                 Most true.
*Cel.* How ready is heaven to those that
   pray!
*1 Avoc.* But that             5
Volpone would have ravish'd her, he holds
Utterly false, knowing his impotence.
*Corv.* Grave fathers, he 's possess'd; again,
   I say,
Possess'd: nay, if there be possession, and
Obsession, he has both.
*3 Avoc.*       Here comes our officer.   10

### [Enter Volpone]

*Volp.* The parasite will straight be here,
   grave fathers.
*4 Avoc.* You might invent some other name,
   sir varlet.
*3 Avoc.* Did not the notary meet him?
*Volp.*              Not that I know.
*4 Avoc.* His coming will clear all.
*2 Avoc.*            Yet it is misty.
*Volt.* May 't please your fatherhoods ——
      *Volpone whispers the Advocate.*
*Volp.*          Sir, the parasite   15
Will'd me to tell you that his master lives;

That you are still the man; your hopes the
   same;
And this was only a jest ——
   *Volt.*                 How?
   *Volp.*               Sir, to try
If you were firm, and how you stood affected.
*Volt.* Art sure he lives?
*Volp.*               Do I live, sir?
*Volt.*                     O me!
I was too violent.
*Volp.*       Sir, you may redeem it.   21
They said you were possess'd; fall down, and
   seem so:
I 'll help to make it good.     *Voltore falls.*
   God bless the man! ——
Stop your wind hard, and swell — See, see, see,
   see!
He vomits crooked pins! His eyes are set,   25
Like a dead hare's hung in a poulter's shop!
His mouth 's running away! Do you see,
   signior?
Now 't is in his belly.
   *Corv. (Aside.)*      Ay, the devil!
*Volp.* Now in his throat.
*Corv. (Aside.)*    Ay, I perceive it plain.
*Volp.* 'T will out, 't will out! stand clear.
   See where it flies,            30
In shape of a blue toad, with a bat's wings!
Do not you see it, sir?
   *Corb.*         What? I think I do.
*Corv.* 'T is too manifest.
*Volp.*       Look! he comes t' himself!
*Volt.* Where am I?
*Volp.* Take good heart, the worst is past, sir.
You 're dispossess'd.
*1 Avoc.*      What accident is this!   35
*2 Avoc.* Sudden and full of wonder!
*3 Avoc.*              If he were
Possess'd, as it appears, all this is nothing.
   *Corv.* He has been often subject to these fits.
*1 Avoc.* Show him that writing: — do you
   know it, sir?
*Volp. [Whispers Volt.]* Deny it, sir, for-
   swear it; know it not.        40
*Volt.* Yes, I do know it well, it is my hand;
But all that it contains is false.
*Bon.*               O practice!
*2 Avoc.* What maze is this!
*1 Avoc.*         Is he not guilty then,
Whom you there name the parasite?
*Volt.*              Grave fathers,
No more than his good patron, old Volpone.   45
*4 Avoc.* Why, he is dead.
*Volt.*         O no, my honour'd fathers,
He lives ——
*1 Avoc.*    How! lives?
*Volt.*        Lives.
*2 Avoc.*            This is subtler yet!

Sc. xi. ¹³ **farther:** ('farder' F)   ¹⁶ **crochets:** whimsical fancies   Sc. xii. ⁴² **practice:** conspiracy

*3 Avoc.* You said he was dead.
*Volt.* Never.
*3 Avoc.* You said so.
*Corv.* I heard so.
*4 Avoc.* Here comes the gentleman; make him way.

*[Enter Mosca]*

*3 Avoc.* A stool.
*4 Avoc. [Aside.]* A proper man; and were Volpone dead, 50
A fit match for my daughter.
*3 Avoc.* Give him way.
*Volp. [Aside to Mos.]* Mosca, I was a'most lost; the advocate
Had betray'd all; but now it is recover'd;
All 's o' the hinge again —— Say I am living.
*Mos.* What busy knave is this! — Most reverend fathers, 55
I sooner had attended your grave pleasures,
But that my order for the funeral
Of my dear patron did require me ——
*Volp. [Aside.]* Mosca!
*Mos* Whom I intend to bury like a gentleman.
*Volp. [Aside.]* Ay, quick, and cozen me of all.
*2 Avoc.* Still stranger! 60
More intricate!
*1 Avoc.* And come about again!
*4 Avoc. [Aside.]* It is a match, my daughter is bestow'd.
*Mos. [Aside to Volp.]* Will you gi' me half?
*Volp.* First I 'll be hang'd.
*Mos.* I know
Your voice is good, cry not so loud.
*1 Avoc.* Demand
The advocate. — Sir, did not you affirm 65
Volpone was alive?
*Volp.* Yes, and he is;
This gent'man told me so. — *[Aside to Mos.]* Thou shalt have half.
*Mos.* Whose drunkard is this same? Speak, some that know him:
I never saw his face. — *[Aside to Volp.]* I cannot now
Afford it you so cheap.
*Volp.* No!
*1 Avoc.* What say you? 70
*Volt.* The officer told me.
*Volp.* I did, grave fathers,
And will maintain he lives, with mine own life,
And that this creature *[points to Mos.]* told me. *[Aside.]* — I was born
With all good stars my enemies.
*Mos.* Most grave fathers,
If such an insolence as this must pass 75

<sup></sup>⁶⁰ **quick:** alive    ⁸⁵ **uncase:** remove his skin
various animals

Upon me, I am silent: 't was not this
For which you sent, I hope.
*2 Avoc.* Take him away.
*Volp.* Mosca!
*3 Avoc.* Let him be whipp'd.
*Volp. [Aside.]* Wilt thou betray me?
Cozen me?
*3 Avoc.* And taught to bear himself
Toward a person of his rank.
*4 Avoc.* Away. 80
*[The Officers seize Volpone.]*
*Mos.* I humbly thank your fatherhoods.
*Volp.* Soft, soft: *[Aside.]* Whipp'd!
And lose all that I have! If I confess,
It cannot be much more.
*4 Avoc.* Sir, are you married?
*Volp. [Aside.]* They 'll be alli'd anon; I must be resolute; 84
The Fox shall here uncase.
*He puts off his disguise.*
*Mos. [Aside.]* Patron!
*Volp.* Nay, now
My ruins shall not come alone; your match
I 'll hinder sure: my substance shall not glue you,
Nor screw you into a family.
*Mos. [Aside.]* Why, patron!
*Volp.* I am Volpone, and this is my knave;
*[Pointing to Mosca.]*
This *[To Volt.]*, his own knave; this *[to Corb.]*, avarice's fool; 90
This *[To Corv.]*, a chimera of wittol, fool, and knave:
And, reverend fathers, since we all can hope
Nought but a sentence, let 's not now despair it.
You hear me brief.
*Corv.* May it please your fatherhoods ——
*Com.* Silence. 94
*1 Avoc.* The knot is now undone by miracle.
*2 Avoc.* Nothing can be more clear.
*3 Avoc.* Or can more prove
These innocent.
*1 Avoc.* Give 'em their liberty.
*Bon.* Heaven could not long let such gross crimes be hid.
*2 Avoc.* If this be held the highway to get riches, 99
May I be poor!
*3 Avoc.* This 's not the gain, but torment.
*1 Avoc.* These possess wealth, as sick men possess fevers,
Which trulier may be said to possess them.
*2 Avoc.* Disrobe that parasite.
*Corv. [and] Mos.* Most honour'd fathers ——
*1 Avoc.* Can you plead aught to stay the course of justice? 104
If you can, speak.

<sup></sup>⁹¹ **chimera:** a monster composed of the parts of

*Corv.* [*and*] *Volt.*        We beg favour.
*Cel.*                                                    And mercy.
1 *Avoc.* You hurt your innocence, suing for
the guilty.
Stand forth; and first the parasite. You appear
T' have been the chiefest minister, if not plot-
ter,
In all these lewd impostures, and now, lastly,
Have with your impudence abus'd the court,
And habit of a gentleman of Venice,        111
Being a fellow of no birth or blood:
For which our sentence is, first, thou be
whipp'd;
Then live perpetual prisoner in our galleys.   114
*Volp.* I thank you for him.
*Mos.*                    Bane to thy wolfish nature!
1 *Avoc.* Deliver him to the saffi. [*Mosca is
carried out.*] Thou, Volpone,
By blood and rank a gentleman, canst not fall
Under like censure; but our judgment on thee
Is, that thy substance all be straight confiscate
To the hospital of the *Incurabili:*        120
And since the most was gotten by imposture,
By feigning lame, gout, palsy, and such dis-
eases,
Thou art to lie in prison, cramp'd with irons,
Till thou be'st sick and lame indeed. Remove
him.                    [*He is taken from the Bar.*]
*Volp.* This is called mortifying of a Fox.   125
1 *Avoc.* Thou, Voltore, to take away the
scandal
Thou hast giv'n all worthy men of thy profes-
sion,
Art banish'd from their fellowship, and our
state.
Corbaccio! — bring him near. We here possess
Thy son of all thy state, and confine thee   130
To the monastery of San Spirito;
Where, since thou knew'st not how to live well
here,
Thou shalt be learn'd to die well.
*Corb.*                    Ha! what said he?

*Com.* You shall know anon, sir.
1 *Avoc.*                    Thou, Corvino, shalt
Be straight embark'd from thine own house,
and row'd                                        135
Round about Venice, through the Grand Canal.
Wearing a cap, with fair long ass's ears,
Instead of horns! and so to mount, a paper
Pinn'd on thy breast, to the *berlina.*
*Corv.*                                        Yes.   139
And have mine eyes beat out with stinking fish,
Bruis'd fruit, and rotten eggs — 't is well. I 'm
glad
I shall not see my shame yet.
1 *Avoc.*                    And to expiate
Thy wrongs done to thy wife, thou art to send
her
Home to her father, with her dowry trebled:
And these are all your judgments.
*All.*                    Honour'd fathers —— 145
1 *Avoc.* Which may not be revok'd. Now
you begin,
When crimes are done and past, and to be
punish'd,
To think what your crimes are. Away with
them!
Let all that see these vices thus rewarded,
Take heart, and love to study 'em. Mischiefs
feed                                            150
Like beasts, till they be fat, and then they
bleed.                                [*Exeunt.*]

*Volpone* [*comes forward*]

"The seasoning of a play is the applause.
Now, though the Fox be punish'd by the
laws,
He yet doth hope, there is no suff'ring due, 154
For any fact which he hath done 'gainst you;
If there be, censure him; here he doubtful
stands.
If not, fare jovially, and clap your hands."
                                        [*Exit.*]

THE END

---

¹¹⁰ **abus'd:** imposed upon        ¹³⁰ **state:** estate        ¹³⁹ **berlina:** pillory ('berlino' F)

# EPICOENE,

## OR

## The silent VVoman.

*A Comœdie.*

Acted in the yeere 1609. By
the Children of her Maiesties
REVELLS.

## The Author B. I.

HORAT.

*Vt sis tu similis Cæli, Byrrhiꞯ latronum,*
*Non ego sim Capri, neꞯ Sulci. Cur metuas me?*

LONDON,
Printed by WILLIAM STANSBY.

M. DC. XVI.

BIBLIOGRAPHICAL RECORD. The earliest record of the text of *Epicœne* is to be found in two entries on the Register of the Stationers' Company. On September 20, 1610, the following entry was made on behalf of John Browne and John Busby, Junior: *Entred for their Copye vnder th[e h]andes of Sir George Bucke and master Waterson for master warden Leake, a booke called, Epicœne or the silent woman by Ben: Johnson . . . vj d.* The second entry, transferring the copyright to Walter Burre, was made on September 28, 1612: *Entred for his copie by assignement from John Browne and consent of the Wardens in full Court holden this Day. A booke called the Commodye of the silent Woman . . . vj d.* The first surviving text of the play is that in the First Folio of Jonson's works, published in 1616, and the first extant separate edition is a Quarto dated 1620. Baker, in his *Biographia Dramatica* (1812), records an edition of the play in 1609, and Gifford (1816) refers to one of 1612. No trace of either has since been found. An edition in 1609 is unlikely in view of the entry in the Stationers' Register, and if Gifford actually saw an edition dated 1612, the volume is no longer known to exist.

DATE AND STAGE PERFORMANCE. The title-page of the folio text states that *Epicœne* had been "acted in the yeere 1609. By the Children of her Maiesties Revells," and this information is repeated at the end of the play. The Whitefriars Theatre, where the original performance seems to have been given (cf. Prol., line 24), became the home of the Children of the Queen's Revels on or after January 4, 1610, so that the play may be assumed to have been first produced between that date and March 25, when the new year began according to the reckoning of the time. It was doubtless written toward the end of 1609. After the folio text is a page containing a list of the principal comedians. They were: Nathan Field, Giles Carie, Hugh Attwell, John Smith, William Barksted, William Penn, Richard Alleyn (or Allen), and John Blaney. *Epicœne* seems to have become popular at once, in spite of Jonson's somewhat facetious remark to Drummond that "when his play of a Silent Woman was first acted, ther was found verses after on the stage against him, concluding that the play was well named the Silent Woman, ther never was one man to say *Plaudite* to it." Against this statement may be set the anonymous contemporary jingle:

> The Fox, the Alchemist, and Silent Woman,
> Done by Ben Jonson, and outdone by no man.

The play was revived at court twice in 1636 (Feb. 18, Apr. 4), and was frequently acted after the Restoration. Dryden selected it for special analysis and praise in his *Essay of Dramatic Poesy* (1668). It held the stage during the eighteenth century, and has had occasional performances ever since.

STRUCTURE. Jonson created this plot with his usual meticulous care. The classical unities, as interpreted by the stagecraft of his time, are accurately observed, and there is a continuity of scenes that is unusual even in Jonson. New scenes are indicated whenever a new character appears, and the names of the characters appearing in each scene are grouped at its head. Some stage directions are here added in square brackets for the sake of clarity.

SOURCES. The main plot is derived from two chief sources. The conception of Morose suffering from the talkativeness of his bride is taken from the *Sixth Declamation* of Libanius, a Greek sophist of the fourth century, A.D., a folio edition of whose works had been published in Paris in 1606 with both Greek and Latin texts. For the *dénouement* in which the sex of Epicœne is revealed, Jonson is indebted to the *Casina* of Plautus. The gulling of Daw and La-Foole by Truewit (IV. v) resembles very closely the fourth scene of Act III of *Twelfth Night*. The dialogue, as is usual with Jonson, reflects his familiarity with the classical writers and his extraordinary power of assimilation. There are reminiscences, translations, or adaptations of passages from Vergil, Terence, Cicero, and Horace, but the two works to which Jonson is particularly indebted for his dialogue are the *Ars Amatoria* of Ovid and the *Sixth Satire* of Juvenal, the greater part of which is put to use in Act II, Sc. ii. See also O. J. Campbell, "The Relation of *Epicœne* to Aretino's *Il Marescalco*," PMLA, 1931, pp. 752–762.

PERSONAL ALLUSIONS. The exact significance of Jonson's protests against the interpretation of the play as personal satire is no longer certain, but is probably to be found in a dispatch from the Venetian ambassador dated February 8, 1610. He reported that Lady Arabella Stuart "complains that in a certain comedy the playwright introduced an allusion to her person and the part played by the Prince of Moldavia. The play was suppressed." (Cf. V. i. 17.) The Prince of Moldavia visited London in 1607 and was said to have been a suitor for this lady's hand. (See T. S. Graves, "Jonson's *Epicœne* and Lady Arabella Stuart," *Mod. Phil.*, Jan., 1917.) Fleay also suggested that Sir John Daw was intended as a caricature of Sir John Harington.

# BEN JONSON

## EPICŒNE; OR, THE SILENT WOMAN

### TO THE TRULY NOBLE BY ALL TITLES

### SIR FRANCIS STUART

SIR, — My hope is not so nourish'd by example, as it will conclude, this dumb piece should please you, by cause it hath pleas'd others before; but by trust, that when you have read it, you will find it worthy to have displeas'd none. This makes that I now number you, not only in the names of favour, but the names of justice to what I write; and do presently call you to the exercise of that noblest, and manliest virtue; as coveting rather to be freed in my fame, by the authority of a judge, than the [5 credit of an undertaker. Read, therefore, I pray you, and censure. There is not a line, or syllable in it, changed from the simplicity of the first copy. And, when you shall consider, through the certain hatred of some, how much a man's innocency may be endanger'd by an uncertain accusation; you will, I doubt not, so begin to hate the iniquity of such natures, as I shall love the contumely done me, whose end was so honourable as to be wip'd off by your sentence. Your unprofitable, but true Lover, 10

BEN JONSON.

### THE PERSONS OF THE PLAY

MOROSE, a Gentleman that loves no noise
[SIR] DAUPHINE EUGENIE, a Knight, his nephew
[NED] CLERIMONT, a Gentleman, his friend
TRUEWIT, another friend
EPICŒNE, a young gentleman, suppos'd the Silent Woman
[SIR] JOHN DAW, a Knight, her servant
[SIR] AMOROUS LA-FOOLE, a Knight also
THOMAS OTTER, a land and sea Captain
CUTBEARD, a Barber

MUTE, one of MOROSE his servants
MADAME HAUGHTY,
MADAME CENTAURE, } Ladies Colle-
MISTRESS [DOL.] } giates
MAVIS,
MISTRESS TRUSTY,
the LADY HAUGHTY'S woman,
MISTRESS OTTER, the Captain's wife,
} Pretenders

Parson, Pages, Servants

THE SCENE: LONDON

### PROLOGUE

TRUTH says, of old the art of making plays
Was to content the people; and their praise
Was to the poet money, wine, and bays.
But in this age, a sect of writers are,
That, only, for particular likings care, 5
And will taste nothing that is populare.
With such we mingle neither brains nor breasts;
Our wishes, like to those make public feasts,
Are not to please the cook's taste but the guests'.
Yet, if those cunning palates hither come, 10
They shall find guests' entreaty, and good room;
And though all relish not, sure there will be some,

That, when they leave their seats, shall make 'em say,
Who wrote that piece, could so have wrote a play,
But that he knew this was the better way. 15
For, to present all custard, or all tart,
And have no other meats to bear a part,
Or to want bread, and salt, were but coarse art.
The poet prays you then, with better thought
To sit; and, when his cates are all in brought,
Though there be none far-fet, there will dear-bought, 21
Be fit for ladies: some for lords, knights, squires;
Some for your waiting-wench, and city-wires;
Some for your men, and daughters of White-friars.

Ded. ³⁻⁴ **This . . . write:** For this reason I now include you not only as a patron but as a vindicator of my work. ⁵ **fame:** reputation ⁶ **undertaker:** one who attempts to affect judgment by personal influence **censure:** judge ⁸ **accusation:** (Jonson was accused of bitter personal satire in his earlier plays.) Persons, Epicœne: "of either gender" or "promiscuous" (Greek) Prol. ¹ **of old:** (in Terence's *Andria*) ⁸ **those:** those who ¹¹ **entreaty:** entertainment ¹³ **'em:** (spelled ''hem' regularly in F) ²⁰ **cates:** dainties ²¹ **far-fet:** brought from distant lands ²³ **city-wires:** women of fashion

Nor is it, only, while you keep your seat    25
　Here, that his feast will last; but you shall
　　eat
　A week at ord'naries, on his broken meat:
　　If his muse be true,
　　Who commends her to you.

## Another

*Occasion'd by some person's impertinent
exception*

The ends of all, who for the scene do write,
　Are, or should be, to profit and delight.
And still 't hath been the praise of all best times,
　So persons were not touch'd, to tax the
　　crimes.
Then, in this play, which we present tonight, 5
　And make the object of your ear and sight,
On forfeit of yourselves, think nothing true:
　Lest so you make the maker to judge you.
For he knows, poet never credit gain'd
　By writing truths, but things, like truths,
　　well feign'd.                                10
If any yet will, with particular sleight
Of application, wrest what he doth write;
And that he meant, or him, or her, will say:
　They make a libel, which he made a play.

## Act I.  Scene I

*[A Room in Clerimont's House]*

*Clerimont, Boy, [later] Truewit*

*[Cler.]*  Ha' you got the song yet perfect, I
ga' you, boy?
　*Boy.*  Yes, sir.
　　　　*He comes out making himself ready.*
　*Cler.*  Let me hear it.
　*Boy.*  You shall, sir; but i' faith let no- [5
body else.
　*Cler.*  Why, I pray?
　*Boy.*  It will get you the dangerous name
of a poet in town, sir; besides me a perfect
deal of ill-will at the mansion you wot of, [10
whose lady is the argument of it; where now
I am the welcom'st thing under a man that
comes there.
　*Cler.*  I think; and above a man too, if the
truth were rack'd out of you.                    15
　*Boy.*  No, faith, I 'll confess before, sir.  The
gentlewomen play with me, and throw me o'
the bed, and carry me in to my lady: and she
kisses me with her oil'd face, and puts a peruke
o' my head; and asks me an I will wear her [20

gown? and I say no: and then she hits me
a blow o' the ear, and calls me innocent, and
lets me go.
　*Cler.*  No marvel if the door be kept shut
against your master, when the entrance is [25
so easy to you —— well, sir, you shall go there
no more, lest I be fain to seek your voice in my
lady's rushes, a fortnight hence.  Sing, sir.
　　　　　　　　　　　　　　　　　*Boy sings.*
　　　　　*[Enter Truewit]*
　*True.*  Why, here 's the man that can melt
away his time and never feels it!  What [30
between his mistress abroad and his ingle at
home, high fare, soft lodging, fine clothes, and
his fiddle; he thinks the hours ha' no wings,
or the day no post-horse.  Well, sir gallant,
were you struck with the plague this minute, [35
or condemn'd to any capital punishment to-
morrow, you would begin then to think, and
value every article o' your time, esteem it at the
true rate, and give all for 't.
　*Cler.*  Why, what should a man do?    40
　*True.*  Why, nothing; or that which, when
'tis done, is as idle.  Hearken after the next
horse-race, or hunting-match, lay wagers, praise
Puppy, or Peppercorn, White-foot, Franklin;
swear upon Whitemane's party; speak aloud, [45
that my lords may hear you; visit my ladies
at night, and be able to give 'em the character
of every bowler or better o' the green.  These
be the things wherein your fashionable men
exercise themselves, and I for company.    50
　*Cler.*  Nay, if I have thy authority, I 'll not
leave yet.  Come, the other are considerations,
when we come to have gray heads and weak
hams, moist eyes and shrunk members.  We 'll
think on 'em then; then we 'll pray and fast. [55
　*True.*  Ay, and destine only that time of
age to goodness, which our want of ability
will not let us employ in evil!
　*Cler.*  Why, then 't is time enough.
　*True.*  Yes; as if a man should sleep all [60
the term, and think to effect his business the
last day.  O, Clerimont, this time, because it
is an incorporeal thing, and not subject to
sense, we mock ourselves the fineliest out of it,
with vanity and misery indeed! not seeking [65
an end of wretchedness, but only changing the
matter still.
　*Cler.*  Nay, thou 'lt not leave now —
　*True.*  See but our common disease! with
what justice can we complain, that great [70
men will not look upon us, nor be at leisure to
give our affairs such dispatch as we expect,

---

　²⁷ **ord'naries:** taverns    ⁴ **tax the crimes:** censure abuses, not the persons who commit them
⁸ **maker:** poet    ¹¹ **sleight:** trick    ¹² **application:** *i.e.,* to particular persons    ¹¹ **argument:** theme
²⁸ **rushes:** floor covering    ³¹ **ingle:** boy-favorite    ⁴⁴⁻⁴⁵ **Puppy . . . Whitemane:** ('Horses o' the
time,' marginal note, F 1)    ⁴⁵ **speak:** ('spend' F 1, Q)    ⁶¹ **term:** term of court    ⁶⁹ **disease:**
fault

when we will never do it to ourselves? nor hear, nor regard ourselves?

*Cler.* Foh! thou hast read Plutarch's [75 *Morals*, now, or some such tedious fellow; and it shows so vilely with thee! 'fore God, 't will spoil thy wit utterly. Talk me of pins, and feathers, and ladies, and rushes, and such things: and leave this Stoicity alone, till [80 thou mak'st sermons.

*True.* Well, sir; if it will not take, I have learn'd to lose as little of my kindness as I can; I 'll do good to no man against his will, certainly. When were you at the college?  85

*Cler.* What college?

*True.* As if you knew not!

*Cler.* No, faith, I came but from court yesterday.

*True.* Why, is it not arriv'd there yet, [90 the news? A new foundation, sir, here i' the town, of ladies, that call themselves the Collegiates, an order between courtiers and country-madams, that live from their husbands; and give entertainment to all the wits, and brav- [95 eries o' the time, as they call 'em: cry down, or up, what they like or dislike in a brain or a fashion, with most masculine, or rather hermaphroditical authority; and every day gain to their college some new probationer.  100

*Cler.* Who is the president?

*True.* The grave and youthful matron, the lady Haughty.

*Cler.* A pox of her autumnal face, her piec'd beauty! there 's no man can be admitted [105 till she be ready, now-a-days, till she has painted, and perfum'd, and wash'd, and scour'd, but the boy, here; and him she wipes her oil'd lips upon, like a sponge. I have made a song (I pray thee hear it) o' the subject.  110

[*Boy sings.*]

SONG

Still to be neat, still to be dress'd,
As you were going to a feast;
Still to be powder'd, still perfum'd;
Lady, it is to be presumed,
Though art's hid causes are not found,  115
All is not sweet, all is not sound.

Give me a look, give me a face,
That makes simplicity a grace;
Robes loosely flowing, hair as free:
Such sweet neglect more taketh me,  120
Than all th' adulteries of art;
They strike mine eyes, but not my heart.

*True.* And I am clearly o' the other side: I love a good dressing before any beauty o' the world. O, a woman is then like a deli- [125

cate garden; nor is there one kind of it; she may vary every hour; take often counsel of her glass, and choose the best. If she have good ears, show 'em; good hair, lay it out; good legs, wear short clothes; a good hand, [130 discover it often: practise any art to mend breath, cleanse teeth, repair eye-brows; paint, and profess it.

*Cler.* How! publicly?

*True.* The doing of it, not the manner: [135 that must be private. Many things that seem foul i' the doing, do please done. A lady should, indeed, study her face, when we think she sleeps; nor, when the doors are shut, should men be enquiring; all is sacred within, [140 then. Is it for us to see their perukes put on, their false teeth, their complexion, their eye-brows, their nails? You see gilders will not work, but inclos'd. They must not discover how little serves, with the help of art, to [145 adorn a great deal. How long did the canvas hang afore Aldgate? Were the people suffer'd to see the city's Love and Charity, while they were rude stone, before they were painted and burnish'd? No. No more should servants [150 approach their mistresses, but when they are complete and finish'd.

*Cler.* Well said, my Truewit.

*True.* And a wise lady will keep a guard always upon the place, that she may do [155 things securely. I once followed a rude fellow into a chamber, where the poor madam, for haste, and troubled, snatch'd at her peruke to cover her baldness; and put it on the wrong way.  160

*Cler.* O prodigy!

*True.* And the unconscionable knave held her in compliment an hour with that revers'd face, when I still look'd when she should talk from the t'other side.  165

*Cler.* Why, thou shouldst ha' reliev'd her.

*True.* No, faith, I let her alone, as we 'll let this argument, if you please, and pass to another. When saw you Dauphine Eugenie?

*Cler.* Not these three days. Shall we go [170 to him this morning? he is very melancholic, I hear.

*True.* Sick o' the uncle, is he? I met that stiff piece of formality, his uncle, yesterday, with a huge turban of night-caps on his [175 head, buckled over his ears.

*Cler.* O, that 's his custom when he walks abroad. He can endure no noise, man.

*True.* So I have heard. But is the disease so ridiculous in him as it is made? They [180

---

[79] **rushes:** *i.e.,* trifles  [80] **Stoicity:** stoical indifference  [95–96] **braveries:** gallants  [121] **adulteries:** adulterations  [126] **it:** dressing  [131] **discover:** reveal  [147] **Aldgate:** a gate in the old London wall, rebuilt, with gilded figures, in 1609  [150] **servants:** lovers  [163] **compliment:** fashionable small-talk  [164] **still:** always, continually  [171] **melancholic:** afflicted with the fashionable disease of melancholy

say he has been upon divers treaties with the fish-wives and orange-women; and articles propounded between them: marry, the chim-\ney-sweepers will not be drawn in.

*Cler.* No, nor the broom-men: they [185 stand out stiffly. He cannot endure a costard-monger, he swoons if he hear one.

*True.* Methinks a smith should be ominous.

*Cler.* Or any hammer-man. A brasier is not suffer'd to dwell in the parish, nor an [190 armourer. He would have hang'd a pewterer's prentice once upon a Shrove-Tuesday's riot, for being o' that trade, when the rest were quit.

*True.* A trumpet should fright him terribly, or the hautboys.                                          195

*Cler.* Out of his senses. The waights of the city have a pension of him not to come near that ward. This youth practis'd on him one night like the bell-man; and never left till he had brought him down to the door with a [200 long sword; and there left him flourishing with the air.

*Boy.* Why, sir, he hath chosen a street to lie in so narrow at both ends, that it will receive no coaches, nor carts, nor any of these com- [205 mon noises: and therefore we that love him devise to bring him in such as we may, now and then, for his exercise, to breathe him. He would grow resty else in his ease: his virtue would rust without action. I entreated a [210 bearward, one day, to come down with the dogs of some four parishes that way, and I thank him he did; and cried his games under master Morose's windore: till he was sent crying away, with his head made a most [215 bleeding spectacle to the multitude. And, another time, a fencer, marching to his prize, had his drum most tragically run through, for taking that street in his way at my request.

*True.* A good wag! How does he for the [220 bells?

*Cler.* O, i' the Queen's time, he was wont to go out of town every Saturday at ten o'clock, or on holy day eves. But now, by reason of the sickness, the perpetuity of ringing has made him devise a room, with double [226 walls and treble ceilings; the windores close shut and caulk'd: and there he lives by candle-light. He turn'd away a man, last week, for having a pair of new shoes that creak'd. And this fellow waits on him now in tennis-court [231

socks, or slippers sol'd with wool: and they talk each to other in a trunk. See, who comes here!

### Act I.  Scene II

#### Dauphine, Truewit, Clerimont

[*Daup.*] How now! what ail you, sirs? dumb?

*True.* Struck into stone, almost, I am here, with tales o' thine uncle. There was never such a prodigy heard of.                                          5

*Daup.* I would you would once lose this subject, my masters, for my sake. They are such as you are, that have brought me into that predicament I am with him.

*True.* How is that?                                          10

*Daup.* Marry, that he will disinherit me; no more. He thinks, I and my company are authors of all the ridiculous Acts and Monuments are told of him.

*True.* 'Slid, I would be the author of [15 more to vex him; that purpose deserves it: it gives thee law of plaguing him. I 'll tell thee what I would do. I would make a false almanack, get it printed; and then ha' him drawn out on a coronation day to the Tower- [20 wharf, and kill him with the noise of the ordnance. Disinherit thee! he cannot, man. Art not thou next of blood, and his sister's son?

*Daup.* Ay, but he will thrust me out of it, he vows, and marry.                                          25

*True.* How! that 's a more portent. Can he endure no noise, and will venter on a wife?

*Cler.* Yes: why thou art a stranger, it seems, to his best trick, yet. He has employ'd a fellow this half year all over England to hearken [30 him out a dumb woman; be she of any form, or any quality, so she be able to bear children: her silence is dowry enough, he says.

*True.* But I trust to God he has found none.

*Cler.* No; but he has heard of one that 's [35 lodg'd i' the next street to him, who is exceedingly soft-spoken; thrifty of her speech; that spends but six words a day. And her he 's about now, and shall have her.

*True.* Is 't possible! who is his agent i' [40 the business?

*Cler.* Marry, a barber, one Cutbeard; an honest fellow, one that tells Dauphine all here.

*True.* Why you oppress me with wonder: a woman, and a barber, and love no noise! [45

---

¹⁸² **fish-wives, etc.:** (London peddlers of all sorts cried their wares in the streets.)     ¹⁸⁶⁻¹⁸⁷ **costard-monger:** itinerant vender of fruit (from "costard," a kind of apple)     ¹⁹² **Shrove-Tuesday's riot:** The festival of the apprentices on Shrove-Tuesday often led to disorders (cf. *Shoemakers' Holiday* V, i). ¹⁹³ **quit:** acquitted     ¹⁹⁵ **hautboys:** oboes (or players of them)     ¹⁹⁶ **waights:** bands of musicians (usually, "waits")     ¹⁹⁹ **bell-man:** night watchman (who rang a bell as he walked)     ²⁰⁹ **resty:** sluggish     **virtue:** strength     ²¹¹ **bearward:** keeper of a trained bear     ²¹⁴ **windore:** window     ²¹⁷ **prize:** contest     ²²⁵ **sickness:** plague     ²³³ **trunk:** speaking-tube     ¹³⁻¹⁴ **Acts and Monuments:** (a reference to Fox's "Book of Martyrs")     ²⁰⁻²¹ **Tower-wharf:** where the cannon were kept     ²⁶ **more:** greater ³² **quality:** rank in society

*Cler.* Yes, faith. The fellow trims him silently, and has not the knack with his shears or his fingers: and that continence in a barber he thinks so eminent a virtue, as it has made him chief of his counsel.                                    50

*True.* Is the barber to be seen, or the wench?

*Cler.* Yes, that they are.

*True.* I prithee, Dauphine, let 's go thither.

*Daup.* I have some business now: I cannot, i' faith.                                    55

*True.* You shall have no business shall make you neglect this, sir: we 'll make her talk, believe it; or, if she will not, we can give out at least so much as shall interrupt the treaty; we will break it. Thou art bound in con- [60 science, when he suspects thee without cause, to torment him.

*Daup.* Not I, by any means. I 'll give no suffrage to 't. He shall never ha' that plea against me, that I oppos'd the least phant'sy [65 of his. Let it lie upon my stars to be guilty, I 'll be innocent.

*True.* Yes, and be poor, and beg; do, innocent: when some groom of his has got him an heir, or this barber, if he himself [70 cannot. Innocent! — I pray thee, Ned, where lies she? let him be innocent still.

*Cler.* Why, right over against the barber's; in the house where Sir John Daw lies.

*True.* You do not mean to confound me! [75

*Cler.* Why?

*True.* Does he that would marry her know so much?

*Cler.* I cannot tell.

*True.* T' were enough of imputation to [80 her with him.

*Cler.* Why?

*True.* The only talking sir i' th' town! Jack Daw! and he teach her not to speak! — God be wi' you. I have some business too. [85

*Cler.* Will you not go thither, then?

*True.* Not with the danger to meet Daw, for mine ears.

*Cler.* Why, I thought you two had been upon very good terms.                                    90

*True.* Yes, of keeping distance.

*Cler.* They say, he is a very good scholar.

*True.* Ay, and he says it first. A pox on him, a fellow that pretends only to learning, buys titles, and nothing else of books in [95 him!

*Cler.* The world reports him to be very learned.

*True.* I am sorry the world should so con- spire to belie him.                                    100

*Cler.* Good faith, I have heard very good things come from him.

*True.* You may; there 's none so des- perately ignorant to deny that: would they were his own! God be wi' you, gentlemen. [105
*[Exit hastily.]*

*Cler.* This is very abrupt!

### Act I. Scene III

#### Dauphine, Clerimont, Boy

*[Daup.]* Come, you are a strange open man, to tell everything thus.

*Cler.* Why, believe it, Dauphine, Truewit 's a very honest fellow.

*Daup.* I think no other: but this frank [5 nature of his is not for secrets.

*Cler.* Nay, then, you are mistaken, Dau- phine: I know where he has been well trusted, and discharg'd the trust very truly, and heartily.

*Daup.* I contend not, Ned; but with the [10 fewer a business is carried, it is ever the safer. Now we are alone, if you 'll go thither, I am for you.

*Cler.* When were you there?

*Daup.* Last night: and such a Decam- [15 eron of sport fallen out! Boccace never thought of the like. Daw does nothing but court her; and the wrong way. He would lie with her, and praises her modesty; desires that she would talk and be free, and commends her [20 silence in verses; which he reads, and swears are the best that ever man made. Then rails at his fortunes, stamps, and mutines, why he is not made a counsellor, and call'd to affairs of state.                                    25

*Cler.* I pray thee, let 's go. I would fain partake this. — Some water, boy. *[Exit Boy.]*

*Daup.* We are invited to dinner together, he and I, by one that came thither to him, Sir La-Foole.                                    30

*Cler.* O, that 's a precious mannikin!

*Daup.* Do you know him?

*Cler.* Ay, and he will know you too, if e'er he saw you but once, though you should meet him at church in the midst of prayers. He [35 is one of the braveries, though he be none o' the wits. He will salute a judge upon the bench, and a bishop in the pulpit, a lawyer when he is pleading at the bar, and a lady when she is dancing in a masque, and put her out. He [40 does give plays, and suppers, and invites his guests to 'em, aloud, out of his windore, as they ride by in coaches. He has a lodging in the Strand for the purpose. Or to watch when

---

**48 fingers:** (Barbers were supposed to be proficient in snapping their fingers.)   **66 Let . . . stars:** even though I am destined   **69 innocent:** fool   **75 confound:** defeat my plan   **80 imputation:** imputing a fault   **85 God . . . you:** ('God b' w' you' F)   **1 open:** frank   **11 carried:** managed   **23 muti- nes:** rebels   **why:** that, because   **44 Strand:** a fashionable place of lodging

ladies are gone to the china-houses, or the [45
Exchange, that he may meet 'em by chance,
and give 'em presents, some two or three
hundred pounds' worth of toys, to be laugh'd
at. He is never without a spare banquet, or
sweet-meats in his chamber, for their [50
women to alight at, and come up to for a bait.

*Daup.* Excellent! he was a fine youth last
night; but now he is much finer! what is his
christen-name? I ha' forgot.

*[Enter Boy]*

*Cler.* Sir Amorous La-Foole.                          55
*Boy.* The gentleman is here below that owns
that name.
*Cler.* 'Heart, he 's come to invite me to
dinner, I hold my life.
*Daup.* Like enough: pray thee, let 's ha'
him up.                                                  61
*Cler.* Boy, marshal him.
*Boy.* With a truncheon, sir?
*Cler.* Away, I beseech you. *[Exit Boy.]* —
I 'll make him tell us his pedigree now; and
what meat he has to dinner; and who are [66
his guests; and the whole course of his fortunes;
with a breath.

## Act I. Scene IIII

### La-Foole, Clerimont, Dauphine

*[La-F.]* 'Save, dear Sir Dauphine! honour'd master Clerimont!
*Cler.* Sir Amorous! you have very much
honested my lodging with your presence.
*La-F.* Good faith, it is a fine lodging: [5
almost as delicate a lodging as mine.
*Cler.* Not so, sir.
*La-F.* Excuse me, sir, if it were i' the Strand,
I assure you. I am come, master Clerimont,
to entreat you wait upon two or three ladies, [10
to dinner, to-day.
*Cler.* How, sir! wait upon 'em? did you
ever see me carry dishes?
*La-F.* No, sir, dispense with me; I meant,
to bear 'em company.                                    15
*Cler.* O, that I will, sir: the doubtfulness
o' your phrase, believe it, sir, would breed you
a quarrel once an hour, with the terrible boys,
if you should but keep 'em fellowship a day.
*La-F.* It should be extremely against [20
my will, sir, if I contested with any man.

*Cler.* I believe it, sir. Where hold you your
feast?
*La-F.* At Tom Otter's, sir.
*Daup.* Tom Otter! what 's he?                          25
*La-F.* Captain Otter, sir; he is a kind of
gamester, but he has had command both by
sea and by land.
*Daup.* O, then he is *animal amphibium?*
*La-F.* Ay, sir: his wife was the rich [30
china-woman, that the courtiers visited so
often; that gave the rare entertainment. She
commands all at home.
*Cler.* Then she is Captain Otter.
*La-F.* You say very well, sir; she is my [35
kinswoman, a La-Foole by the mother-side, and
will invite any great ladies for my sake.
*Daup.* Not of the La-Fooles of Essex?
*La-F.* No, sir, the La-Fooles of London.
*Cler. [Aside.]* Now, h' is in.                         40
*La-F.* They all come out of our house, the
La-Fooles o' the north, the La-Fooles of the
west, the La-Fooles of the east and south — we
are as ancient a family as any is in Europe —
but I myself am descended lineally of the [45
French La-Fooles — and, we do bear for our
coat yellow, or *or*, checker'd *azure*, and *gules*,
and some three or four colours more, which is
a very noted coat, and has, sometimes, been
solemnly worn by divers nobility of our [50
house — but let that go, antiquity is not
respected now. — I had a brace of fat does
sent me, gentlemen, and half a dozen of pheasants, a dozen or two of godwits, and some other
fowl, which I would have eaten, while they [55
are good, and in good company: — there will
be a great lady or two, my lady Haughty, my
lady Centaure, mistress Dol Mavis — and they
come o' purpose to see the silent gentlewoman,
mistress Epicœne, that honest Sir John [60
Daw has promis'd to bring thither — and then,
mistress Trusty, my lady's woman, will be
there too, and this honourable knight, Sir Dauphine, with yourself, master Clerimont — and
we 'll be very merry, and have fiddlers, and [65
dance. — I have been a mad wag in my time,
and have spent some crowns since I was a page
in court, to my lord Lofty, and after, my lady's
gentleman-usher, who got me knighted in Ireland, since it pleas'd my elder brother to [70
die. — I had as fair a gold jerkin on that day,
as any was worn in the Island Voyage, or at
Caliz, none disprais'd; and I came over in it

---

⁴⁵ **china-houses:** places for the display of oriental merchandise      ⁴⁶ **Exchange:** a new shopping
centre in the Strand      ⁵¹ **bait:** light repast      ⁶³ **truncheon:** staff of authority      ¹ **'Save:** God save
you      ⁴ **honested:** honored      ¹⁴ **dispense with:** pardon      ¹⁸ **terrible boys:** roisterers      ²⁵ **what 's:**
what kind of man is      ³¹ **china-woman:** proprietress of a china-house      ⁴⁷ **coat:** coat of arms (with
suggestion of the garb of the court fool)      **azure:** blue      **gules:** red      ⁵⁴ **godwits:** marsh birds
⁶⁷ **crowns:** coins worth five shillings      ⁷² **Island Voyage:** expedition of Ralegh and Essex to the
Azores, 1597      ⁷³ **Caliz:** Cadiz, captured by the English under the leadership of Howard, Essex, and
Ralegh in 1596      **disprais'd:** depreciated

hither, show'd myself to my friends in court, and after went down to my tenants in the [75 country, and survey'd my lands, let new leases, took their money, spent it in the eye o' the land here, upon ladies: — and now I can take up at my pleasure.

*Daup.* Can you take up ladies, sir?    80

*Cler.* O, let him breathe, he has not recover'd.

*Daup.* Would I were your half in that commodity!

*La-F.* No, sir, excuse me: I meant [85 money, which can take up anything. I have another guest or two, to invite, and say as much to, gentlemen. I 'll take my leave abruptly, in hope you will not fail —— Your servant.                [*Exit.*] 90

*Daup.* We will not fail you, sir precious La-Foole; but she shall, that your ladies come to see, if I have credit afore Sir Daw.

*Cler.* Did you ever hear such a wind-sucker, as this?    95

*Daup.* Or such a rook as the other, that will betray his mistress to be seen! Come, 't is time we prevented it.

*Cler.* Go.               [*Exeunt.*]

## Act II. Scene I

[*A Room in Morose's House*]

*Morose, Mute*

[*Mor.*] Cannot I, yet, find out a more compendious method, than by this trunk, to save my servants the labour of speech, and mine ears the discord of sounds? Let me see: all discourses but mine own afflict me; they seem [5 harsh, impertinent, and irksome. Is it not possible, that thou should'st answer me by signs, and I apprehend thee, fellow? Speak not, though I question you. You have taken the ring off from the street door, as I bade [10 you? Answer me not by speech, but by silence; unless it be otherwise [*Mute makes a leg.*] — Very good. And you have fastened on a thick quilt, or flock-bed, on the outside of the door; that if they knock with their daggers, or [15 with brick-bats, they can make no noise? — But with your leg, your answer, unless it be otherwise [*makes a leg.*] — Very good. This is not only fit modesty in a servant, but good state and discretion in a master. And you [20 have been with Cutbeard the barber, to have

him come to me? [*makes a leg.*] — Good. And, he will come presently? Answer me not but with your leg, unless it be otherwise; if it be otherwise, shake your head, or shrug [*makes* [25 *a leg.*] — So! Your Italian and Spaniard are wise in these: and it is a frugal and comely gravity. How long will it be ere Cutbeard come? Stay; if an hour, hold up your whole hand, if half an hour, two fingers; if a quar- [30 ter, one; [*holds up a finger bent.*] — Good: half a quarter? 'tis well. And have you given him a key, to come in without knocking? [*makes a leg.*] — Good. And is the lock oil'd, and the hinges, to-day? [*makes a leg.*] — Good. And [35 the quilting of the stairs no where worn out and bare? [*makes a leg.*] — Very good. I see, by much doctrine, and impulsion, it may be effected; stand by. The Turk, in this divine discipline, is admirable, exceeding all the [40 potentates of the earth; still waited on by mutes; and all his commands so executed; yea, even in the war, as I have heard, and in his marches, most of his charges and directions given by signs, and with silence: an exquisite [45 art! and I am heartily asham'd, and angry oftentimes, that the princes of Christendom should suffer a barbarian to transcend 'em in so high a point of felicity. I will practise it hereafter. (*One winds a horn without.*) — [50 How now? oh! oh! what villain, what prodigy of mankind is that? look. [*Exit Mute.*] (*Again.*) — Oh! cut his throat, cut his throat! what murderer, hell-hound, devil can this be?

[*Enter Mute*]

*Mute.* It is a post from the court —    55

*Mor.* Out, rogue! and must thou blow thy horn too?

*Mute.* Alas, it is a post from the court, sir, that says, he must speak with you, pain of death —    60

*Mor.* Pain of thy life, be silent!

## Act II. Scene II

*Truewit, Morose,* [*later*] *Cutbeard*

[*True.*] By your leave, sir; — I am a stranger here: — Is your name master Morose? is your name master Morose? Fishes! Pythagoreans all! This is strange. What say you, sir? nothing! Has Harpocrates [5 been here with his club, among you? Well,

---

⁷⁷⁻⁷⁸ **eye . . . land:** London    ⁷⁸⁻⁷⁹ **take up:** borrow    ⁸³⁻⁸⁴ **commodity:** merchandise obtained from the usurer in lieu of cash    ⁹⁴ **wind-sucker:** an unserviceable kind of hawk    ⁹⁶ **rook:** fool ¹⁰ **ring:** knocker    ¹² S. D. **leg:** bow (In place of stage directions in this speech F has dashes and a marginal note: 'At the breaches still the fellow makes legs or signs.')    ¹⁴ **flock-bed:** mattress ²⁰ **state:** mode of living    ³⁸ **doctrine:** discipline    **impulsion:** force    ⁵⁰ S. D. **winds:** blows    ⁴ **Pythagoreans:** (who observed strict silence with regard to their beliefs and practices)    ⁵ **Harpocrates:** the Egyptian Horus, god of silence

sir, I will believe you to be the man at this time.
I will venter upon you, sir. Your friends at
court commend 'em to you, sir —

*Mor.* [*Aside.*]  O men! O manners! was [10
there ever such an impudence?

*True.*  And are extremely solicitous for you,
sir.

*Mor.*  Whose knave are you?

*True.*  Mine own knave, and your com- [15
peer, sir.

*Mor.*  Fetch me my sword —

*True.*  You shall taste the one half of my
dagger, if you do, groom; and you the other,
if you stir, sir: Be patient, I charge you, in [20
the king's name, and hear me without insurrection. They say, you are to marry; to marry!
do you mark, sir?

*Mor.*  How then, rude companion!

*True.*  Marry, your friends do wonder, [25
sir, the Thames being so near, wherein you
may drown so handsomely; or London-bridge,
at a low fall, with a fine leap, to hurry you
down the stream; or, such a delicate steeple
i' the town, as Bow, to vault from; or a [30
braver height, as Paul's. Or, if you affected
to do it nearer home, and a shorter way, an
excellent garret-windore into the street; or,
a beam in the said garret, with this halter
(*He shows him a halter.*) — which they have [35
sent, and desire, that you would sooner commit your grave head to this knot, than to the
wedlock noose; or, take a little sublimate, and
go out of the world like a rat; or a fly, as one
said, with a straw i' your arse: any way, [40
rather than to follow this goblin Matrimony.
Alas, sir, do you ever think to find a chaste
wife in these times? now? when there are so
many masques, plays, Puritan preachings, mad
folks, and other strange sights to be seen [45
daily, private and public? If you had liv'd in
King Etheldred's time, sir, or Edward the
Confessor's, you might, perhaps, have found
in some cold country hamlet, then, a dull
frosty wench, would have been contented [50
with one man: now, they will as soon be
pleas'd with one leg, or one eye. I 'll tell you,
sir, the monstrous hazards you shall run with a
wife.

*Mor.*  Good sir, have I ever cozen'd any [55
friends of yours of their land? bought their
possessions? taken forfeit of their mortgage?
begg'd a reversion from 'em? bastarded their

issue? What have I done, that may deserve
this?                                                       60

*True.*  Nothing, sir, that I know, but your
itch of marriage.

*Mor.*  Why, if I had made an assassinate
upon your father, vitiated your mother, ravished your sisters —                                    65

*True.*  I would kill you, sir, I would kill you,
if you had.

*Mor.*  Why, you do more in this, sir: it
were a vengeance centuple, for all facinorous
acts that could be nam'd, to do that you do. [70

*True.*  Alas, sir, I am but a messenger: I
but tell you, what you must hear. It seems
your friends are careful after your soul's health,
sir, and would have you know the danger:
(but you may do your pleasure for all them, [75
I persuade not, sir.) If, after you are married,
your wife do run away with a vaulter, or the
Frenchman that walks upon ropes, or him that
dances the jig, or a fencer for his skill at his
weapon; why it is not their fault, they have [80
discharged their consciences, when you know
what may happen. Nay, suffer valiantly, sir,
for I must tell you all the perils that you
are obnoxious to. If she be fair, young and
vegetous, no sweetmeats ever drew more [85
flies; all the yellow doublets and great roses
i' the town will be there. If foul and crooked,
she 'll be with them, and buy those doublets
and roses, sir. If rich, and that you marry
her dowry, not her, she 'll reign in your [90
house as imperious as a widow. If noble, all
her kindred will be your tyrants. If fruitful,
as proud as May, and humorous as April; she
must have her doctors, her midwives, her
nurses, her longings every hour; though [95
it be for the dearest morsel of man. If learned,
there was never such a parrot; all your patrimony will be too little for the guests that must
be invited to hear her speak Latin and Greek;
and you must lie with her in those languages [100
too, if you will please her. If precise, you must
feast all the silenc'd brethren, once in three
days; salute the sisters; entertain the whole
family, or wood of 'em; and hear long-winded
exercises, singings and catechizings, which [105
you are not given to, and yet must give for;
to please the zealous matron your wife, who
for the holy cause, will cozen you over and
above. You begin to sweat, sir! but this is
not half, i' faith: you may do your pleas- [110

---

[14] **knave:** servant      [21-22] **insurrection:** resistance      [24] **companion:** fellow      [28] **low fall:** rapid
ebb-tide through the arches of the bridge      [30] **Bow:** the church of St. Mary-le-Bow      [31] **Paul's:** St.
Paul's      [50] **would:** who would      [55] **cozen'd:** cheated      [58] **reversion:** the promise of an office or estate after the death of the holder of it      **from:** away from, to the disappointment of      [63] **assassinate:**
murderous assault      [69] **facinorous:** infamous      [84] **obnoxious:** liable      [85] **vegetous:** vigorous
[86] **roses:** (on the shoes)      [93] **humorous:** capricious      [101] **precise:** a Puritan      [102] **silenc'd:** (Puritans
were forbidden to worship independently.)

ure, notwithstanding, as I said before: I come not to persuade you. (*The Mute is stealing away.*) — Upon my faith, master serving-man, if you do stir, I will beat you.

*Mor.* O, what is my sin! what is my sin! [115

*True.* Then, if you love your wife, or rather dote on her, sir; O, how she 'll torture you, and take pleasure i' your torments! you shall lie with her but when she lists; she will not hurt her beauty, her complexion; or it must be [120 for that jewel, or that pearl, when she does: every half hour's pleasure must be bought anew, and with the same pain and charge you woo'd her at first. Then you must keep what servants she please; what company she will; that [125 friend must not visit you without her license; and him she loves most, she will seem to hate eagerliest, to decline your jealousy; or feign to be jealous of you first; and for that cause go live with her she-friend, or cousin at the [130 college, that can instruct her in all the mysteries of writing letters, corrupting servants, taming spies; where she must have that rich gown for such a great day; a new one for the next; a richer for the third; be serv'd in silver; [135 have the chamber fill'd with a succession of grooms, footmen, ushers, and other messengers; besides embroiderers, jewellers, tire-women, sempsters, feathermen, perfumers; while she feels not how the land drops away, nor the [140 acres melt; nor foresees the change when the mercer has your woods for her velvets; never weighs what her pride costs, sir; so she may kiss a page, or a smooth chin, that has the [144 despair of a beard: be a stateswoman, know all the news, what was done at Salisbury, what at the Bath, what at court, what in progress; or, so she may censure poets, and authors, and styles, and compare 'em; Daniel with Spen- [149 ser, Jonson with the t' other youth, and so forth; or be thought cunning in controversies, or the very knots of divinity; and have often in her mouth the state of the question; and then skip to the mathematics, and demon- [154 stration: and answer in religion to one, in state to another, in bawdry to a third.

*Mor.* O, O!

*True.* All this is very true, sir. And then her going in disguise to that conjurer, and [159 this cunning woman: where the first question is, how soon you shall die? next, if her present servant love her? next that, if she shall have a new servant? and how many? which of her

family would make the best bawd, male or [164 female? what precedence she shall have by her next match? and sets down the answers, and believes 'em above the scriptures. Nay, perhaps she 'll study the art.

*Mor.* Gentle sir, ha' you done? ha' you [169 had your pleasure o' me? I 'll think of these things.

*True.* Yes, sir: and then comes reeking home of vapour and sweat, with going afoot, and lies in a month of a new face, all oil [174 and birdlime; and rises in asses' milk, and is cleans'd with a new fucus: God be wi' you, sir. One thing more, which I had almost forgot. This too, with whom you are to marry, may have made a conveyance of her virginity [179 aforehand, as your wise widows do of their states, before they marry, in trust to some friend, sir. Who can tell? Or if she have not done it yet, she may do, upon the wedding-day, or the night before, and antedate you cuck- [184 old. The like has been heard of in nature. 'T is no devis'd, impossible thing, sir. God be wi' you: I 'll be bold to leave this rope with you, sir, for a remembrance. — Farewell, Mute! [*Exit.*]

*Mor.* Come, ha' me to my chamber: [189 but first shut the door. (*The horn again.*) O, shut the door, shut the door! is he come again?

[*Enter Cutbeard*]

*Cut.* 'T is I, sir, your barber.

*Mor.* O, Cutbeard, Cutbeard, Cutbeard! here has been a cutthroat with me: help [194 me in to my bed, and give me physic with thy counsel.          [*Exeunt.*]

## Act II.   Scene III

*[A Room in Sir John Daw's House]*

*Daw, Clerimont, Dauphine, Epicœne*

[*Daw.*] Nay, and she will, let her refuse at her own charges; 't is nothing to me, gentlemen: but she will not be invited to the like feasts or guests every day.

*Cler.* O, by no means, she may not refuse [5 — to stay at home, if you love your reputation. 'Slight, you are invited thither o' purpose to be seen, and laugh'd at by the lady of the college, and her shadows. This trumpeter hath proclaim'd you. (*They dissuade her privately.*) [10

*Daup.* You shall not go; let him be laugh'd at in your stead, for not bringing you: and

119 **lists:** pleases    123 **charge:** expense    128 **decline:** avert    138 **tire-women:** dressmakers
139 **sempsters:** tailors    142 **mercer:** dealer in cloth    146 **Salisbury:** a centre for horse-racing
147 **Bath:** already a popular watering-place    **in progress:** on the king's journeys    150 **t' other youth:**
possibly Marston    155 **answer:** do her lesson    160 **cunning woman:** fortune-teller    176 **fucus:** rouge
or other cosmetic    181 **states:** property    186 **devis'd:** invented    2 **charges:** risk    9 **shadows:** un-
invited guests brought to a dinner

put him to his extemporal faculty of fooling
and talking loud, to satisfy the company.

*[Aside to Epi.]*

*Cler.* He will suspect us; talk aloud. — [15
Pray, mistress Epicœne, let 's see your verses;
we have Sir John Daw's leave; do not conceal
your servant's merit, and your own glories.

*Epi.* They 'll prove my servant's glories, if
you have his leave so soon.    20

*Daup.* His vain-glories, lady!

*Daw.* Show 'em, show 'em, mistress; I dare
own 'em.

*Epi.* Judge you, what glories.

*Daw.* Nay, I 'll read 'em myself too: an [25
author must recite his own works. It is a
madrigal of Modesty.

> *Modest and fair, for fair and good are near*
>       *Neighbours, howe'er.* —

*Daup.* Very good.    30

*Cler.* Ay, is 't not?

Daw.    *No noble virtue ever was alone,*
>       *But two in one.*

*Daup.* Excellent!

*Cler.* That again, I pray, Sir John.    35

*Daup.* It has something in 't like rare wit
and sense.

*Cler.* Peace.

Daw.    *No noble virtue ever was alone,*
>       *But two in one.*    40
>     *Then, when I praise sweet modesty, I*
>       *praise*
>     *Bright beauty's rays:*
>     *And having prais'd both beauty and*
>       *modestee,*
>       *I have prais'd thee.*

*Daup.* Admirable!    45

*Cler.* How it chimes, and cries tink i' the
close, divinely!

*Daup.* Ay, 't is Seneca.

*Cler.* No, I think 't is Plutarch.

*Daw.* The dor on Plutarch and Seneca! [50
I hate it: they are mine own imaginations, by
that light. I wonder those fellows have such
credit with gentlemen.

*Cler.* They are very grave authors.

*Daw.* Grave asses! mere essayists: a few [55
loose sentences, and that 's all. A man would
talk so his whole age: I do utter as good things
every hour, if they were collected and observ'd,
as either of 'em.

*Daup.* Indeed, Sir John!    60

*Cler.* He must needs; living among the wits
and braveries too.

*Daup.* Ay, and being president of 'em, as
he is.

*Daw.* There 's Aristotle, a mere common- [65
place fellow; Plato, a discourser; Thucydides
and Livy, tedious and dry; Tacitus, an entire
knot; sometimes worth the untying, very seldom.

*Cler.* What do you think of the poets, Sir [70
John?

*Daw.* Not worthy to be nam'd for authors.
Homer, an old tedious, prolix ass, talks of
curriers, and chines of beef; Vergil of dunging
of land, and bees; Horace, of I know not [75
what.

*Cler.* I think so.

*Daw.* And so, Pindarus, Lycophron, Anacreon, Catullus, Seneca the tragedian, Lucan,
Propertius, Tibullus, Martial, Juvenal, Au- [80
sonius, Statius, Politian, Valerius Flaccus, and
the rest —

*Cler.* What a sackfull of their names he has
got!

*Daup.* And how he pours 'em out! Poli- [85
tian with Valerius Flaccus!

*Cler.* Was not the character right of him?

*Daup.* As could be made, i' faith.

*Daw.* And Persius, a crabbed coxcomb, not
to be endur'd.    90

*Daup.* Why, whom do you account for
authors, Sir John Daw?

Daw.    *Syntagma juris civilis; Corpus juris
civilis; Corpus juris canonici;* the King of
Spain's Bible —    95

*Daup.* Is the king of Spain's Bible an author?

*Cler.* Yes, and Syntagma.

*Daup.* What was that Syntagma, sir?

*Daw.* A civil lawyer, a Spaniard.

*Daup.* Sure, Corpus was a Dutchman.    100

*Cler.* Ay, both the Corpuses, I knew 'em:
they were very corpulent authors.

*Daw.* And then there 's Vatablus, Pom-
ponatius, Symancha: the other are not to
be receiv'd, within the thought of a scholar. [105

*Daup.* 'Fore God, you have a simple learn'd
servant, lady, — in titles.    *[Aside.]*

*Cler.* I wonder that he is not called to the
helm, and made a counsellor.

*Daup.* He is one extraordinary.    110

*Cler.* Nay, but in ordinary: to say truth,
the state wants such.

*Daup.* Why, that will follow.

*Cler.* I muse a mistress can be so silent to
the dotes of such a servant.    115

---

¹³ **extemporal:** extemporaneous    ²³ **own:** acknowledge authorship of    ⁵⁰ **dor on:** deuce with (a
mock imprecation)    ⁷⁴ **curriers:** tanners    ⁸¹ **Politian:** a Florentine humanist (1454–1494), introduced to show the confusion in Daw's mind    ⁸⁷ **character:** description    ⁹³ **Syntagma:** corpus, com-
pilation    ⁹⁴ **juris canonici:** canon, or ecclesiastical, law    ⁹⁴⁻⁹⁵ **King . . . Bible:** a polyglot Bible
published at Antwerp, 1569–1572, with the sanction of Philip II    ¹⁰³⁻¹⁰⁴ **Vatablus . . . Symancha:**
European scholars of the 16th century    ¹¹⁵ **dotes:** natural endowments

*Daw.* 'T is her virtue, sir. I have written somewhat of her silence too.

*Daup.* In verse, Sir John?

*Cler.* What else?

*Daup.* Why, how can you justify your [120 own being of a poet, that so slight all the old poets?

*Daw.* Why, every man that writes in verse is not a poet; you have of the wits that write verses, and yet are no poets: they are poets [125 that live by it, the poor fellows that live by it.

*Daup.* Why, would not you live by your verses, Sir John?

*Cler.* No, 't were pity he should. A knight live by his verses! he did not make 'em to [130 that end, I hope.

*Daup.* And yet the noble Sidney lives by his, and the noble family not asham'd.

*Cler.* Ay, he profess'd himself; but Sir John Daw has more caution: he 'll not hinder [135 his own rising i' the state so much. Do you think he will? Your verses, good Sir John, and no poems.

*Daw.*    *Silence in woman, is like speech in man;*
       *Deny 't who can.*           140

*Daup.* Not I, believe it: your reason, sir.

*Daw.*      *Nor is 't a tale,*
     *That female vice should be a virtue male,*
     *Or masculine vice a female virtue be:*
       *You shall it see*         145
     *Prov'd with increase;*
     *I know to speak, and she to hold her*
       *peace.*

Do you conceive me, gentlemen?

*Daup.* No, faith; how mean you "with increase," Sir John?        150

*Daw.* Why, with increase is, when I court her for the common cause of mankind, and she says nothing, but *consentire videtur;* and in time is *gravida.*

*Daup.* Then this is a ballad of procreation?

*Cler.* A madrigal of procreation; you [156 mistake.

*Epi.* Pray give me my verses again, servant.

*Daw.* If you 'll ask 'em aloud, you shall.

*Cler.* See, here 's Truewit again!      160

     [*Walks aside with the papers.*]

## Act II. Scene IIII

*Clerimont, Truewit, Dauphine, [later] Cutbeard,*
*Daw, Epicœne*

[*Cler.*] Where hast thou been, in the name of madness, thus accoutred with thy horn?

*True.* Where the sound of it might have pierc'd your senses with gladness, had you been in ear-reach of it. Dauphine, fall down [5 and worship me; I have forbid the bans, lad: I have been with thy virtuous uncle, and have broke the match.

*Daup.* You ha' not, I hope.

*True.* Yes, faith; and thou shouldst [10 hope otherwise, I should repent me: this horn got me entrance; kiss it. I had no other way to get in, but by feigning to be a post; but when I got in once, I prov'd none, but rather the contrary, turn'd him into a post, or a [15 stone, or what is stiffer, with thund'ring into him the incommodities of a wife, and the miseries of marriage. If ever Gorgon were seen in the shape of a woman, he hath seen her in my description: I have put him off o' that scent [20 for ever. — Why do you not applaud and adore me, sirs? Why stand you mute? Are you stupid? You are not worthy o' the benefit.

*Daup.* Did not I tell you? Mischief! —

*Cler.* I would you had plac'd this benefit [25 somewhere else.

*True.* Why so?

*Cler.* 'Slight, you have done the most inconsiderate, rash, weak thing, that ever man did to his friend.        30

*Daup.* Friend! if the most malicious enemy I have had studied to inflict an injury upon me, it could not be a greater.

*True.* Wherein, for God's sake? Gentlemen, come to yourselves again.        35

*Daup.* But I presag'd thus much afore to you.

*Cler.* Would my lips had been solder'd when I spake on 't! 'Slight, what mov'd you to be thus impertinent?        40

*True.* My masters, do not put on this strange face to pay my courtesy; off with this vizor. Have good turns done you, and thank 'em this way!

*Daup.* 'Fore heaven, you have undone [45 me. That which I have plotted for, and been maturing now these four months, you have blasted in a minute. Now I am lost, I may speak. This gentlewoman was lodg'd here by me o' purpose, and, to be put upon my uncle, [50 hath profess'd this obstinate silence for my sake; being my entire friend, and one that for the requital of such a fortune as to marry him, would have made me very ample conditions; where now, all my hopes are utterly mis- [55 carried by this unlucky accident.

*Cler.* Thus 't is when a man will be ignorantly officious, do services, and not know his why; I wonder what courteous itch possess'd

<sup>138</sup> **and:** ('are' F 2)     <sup>148</sup> **conceive:** understand     <sup>153</sup> **consentire videtur:** seems to consent
<sup>12</sup> **post:** messenger    <sup>17</sup> **incommodities:** inconveniences    <sup>23</sup> **benefit:** kindness    <sup>43</sup> **vizor:** pretens[
<sup>59</sup> **why:** reasons

you. You never did absurder part i' your [60
life, nor a greater trespass to friendship, to
humanity.

*Daup.* Faith, you may forgive it best; 't was
your cause principally.

*Cler.* I know it; would it had not.          65

### [Enter Cutbeard]

*Daup.* How now, Cutbeard! what news?

*Cut.* The best, the happiest that ever was,
sir. There has been a mad gentleman with
your uncle this morning, [*seeing Truewit.*] — I
think this be the gentleman — that has al- [70
most talk'd him out of his wits, with threat'ning
him from marriage —

*Daup.* On, I pray thee.

*Cut.* And your uncle, sir, he thinks 't was
done by your procurement; therefore he [75
will see the party you wot of presently; and
if he like her, he says, and that she be so inclining to dumb as I have told him, he swears
he will marry her to-day, instantly, and not
defer it a minute longer.          80

*Daup.* Excellent! beyond our expectation!

*True.* Beyond your expectation! By this
light, I knew it would be thus.

*Daup.* Nay, sweet Truewit, forgive me.

*True.* No, I was "ignorantly officious, im- [85
pertinent;" this was the "absurd, weak part."

*Cler.* Wilt thou ascribe that to merit now,
was mere fortune!

*True.* Fortune! mere providence. Fortune
had not a finger in 't. I saw it must neces- [90
sarily in nature fall out so: my genius is never
false to me in these things. Show me how it
could be otherwise.

*Daup.* Nay, gentlemen, contend not; 't is
well now.          95

*True.* Alas, I let him go on with "inconsiderate," and "rash," and what he pleas'd.

*Cler.* Away, thou strange justifier of thyself, to be wiser than thou wert, by the event!

*True.* Event! by this light, thou shalt [100
never persuade me, but I foresaw it as well as
the stars themselves.

*Daup.* Nay, gentlemen, 't is well now. Do
you two entertain Sir John Daw with discourse,
while I send her away with instructions.          105

*True.* I 'll be acquainted with her first, by
your favour.

*Cler.* Master Truewit, lady, a friend of ours.

*True.* I am sorry I have not known you
sooner, lady, to celebrate this rare virtue [110
of your silence.

[*Exeunt Daup. Epi., and Cutbeard.*]

*Cler.* Faith, an you had come sooner, you
should ha' seen and heard her well celebrated
in Sir John Daw's madrigals.

*True.* [*Advances to Daw.*] Jack Daw, [115
God save you! when saw you La-Foole?

*Daw.* Not since last night, master Truewit.

*True.* That 's a miracle! I thought you two
had been inseparable.

*Daw.* He 's gone to invite his guests.          120

*True.* Gods so! 't is true! What a false
memory have I towards that man! I am one:
I met him e'en now, upon that he calls his
delicate, fine, black horse, rid into a foam, with
posting from place to place, and person to [125
person, to give 'em the cue —

*Cler.* Lest they should forget?

*True.* Yes: there was never poor captain
took more pains at a muster to show men, than
he, at this meal, to show friends.          130

*Daw.* It is his quarter-feast, sir.

*Cler.* What! do you say so, Sir John?

*True.* Nay, Jack Daw will not be out, at
the best friends he has, to the talent of his wit.
Where 's his mistress, to hear and applaud [135
him? Is she gone?

*Daw.* Is mistress Epicœne gone?

*Cler.* Gone afore, with Sir Dauphine, I warrant, to the place.

*True.* Gone afore! That were a mani- [140
fest injury, a disgrace and a half; to refuse him
at such a festival-time as this, being a bravery,
and a wit too!

*Cler.* Tut, he 'll swallow it like cream: he 's
better read in *Jure civili*, than to esteem [145
anything a disgrace, is offer'd him from a
mistress.

*Daw.* Nay, let her e'en go; she shall sit
alone, and be dumb in her chamber a week
together, for John Daw, I warrant her. [150
Does she refuse me?

*Cler.* No, sir, do not take it so to heart;
she does not refuse you, but a little neglect you.
Good faith, Truewit, you were to blame, to put
it into his head, that she does refuse him.          155

*True.* She does refuse him, sir, palpably,
however you mince it. An I were as he, I
would swear to speak ne'er a word to her to-day
for 't.

*Daw.* By this light, no more I will not.          160

*True.* Nor to anybody else, sir.

*Daw.* Nay, I will not say so, gentlemen.

*Cler.* [*Aside.*] It had been an excellent
happy condition for the company, if you could
have drawn him to it.          165

*Daw.* I 'll be very melancholic, i' faith.

---

⁶⁰ **part:** action          ⁶³⁻⁶⁴ **'t was . . . cause:** you were the cause of it          ⁷⁵ **procurement:** arrangement          ¹¹⁸ **a:** (not in F 1)          ¹²² **one:** *i.e.*, of his guests          ¹³¹ **quarter-feast:** feast celebrating the beginning of one of the quarters of the business year          ¹³³⁻¹³⁴ **Nay . . . wit:** *i.e.*, will sacrifice a good
friend for a joke

*Cler.* As a dog, if I were as you, Sir John.

*True.* Or a snail, or a hog-louse: I would roll myself up for this day; in troth, they should not unwind me.                    171

*Daw.* By this pick-tooth, so I will.

*Cler.* 'T is well done. He begins already to be angry with his teeth.

*Daw.* Will you go, gentlemen?

*Cler.* Nay, you must walk alone, if you [176 be right melancholic, Sir John.

*True.* Yes, sir, we 'll dog you, we 'll follow you afar off.                    [*Exit Daw.*]

*Cler.* Was there ever such a two yards of knighthood measur'd out by time, to be [181 sold to laughter?

*True.* A mere talking mole, hang him! no mushroom was ever so fresh. A fellow so utterly nothing, as he knows not what he would be.                    186

*Cler.* Let 's follow him: but first let 's go to Dauphine, he 's hovering about the house to hear what news.

*True.* Content.                    [*Exeunt.*]


## Act II. Scene V

[*A Room in Morose's House*]

*Morose, Epicœne, Cutbeard, Mute*

[*Mor.*] Welcome, Cutbeard! draw near with your fair charge: and in her ear softly entreat her to unmask. [*Epi. takes off her mask.*] — So! Is the door shut? [*Mute makes a leg.*] — Enough. Now, Cutbeard, with the same [5 discipline I use to my family, I will question you. As I conceive, Cutbeard, this gentle-woman is she you have provided, and brought, in hope she will fit me in the place and person of a wife? Answer me not but with your [10 leg, unless it be otherwise. [*Cut. makes a leg.*] — Very well done, Cutbeard. I conceive, be-sides, Cutbeard, you have been pre-acquainted with her birth, education, and qualities, or else you would not prefer her to my acceptance, [15 in the weighty consequence of marriage. This I conceive, Cutbeard. Answer me not but with your leg, unless it be otherwise. [*Cut-beard bows again.*] — Very well done, Cutbeard. Give aside now a little, and leave me to [20 examine her condition, and aptitude to my affection. (*He goes about her and views her.*) — She is exceeding fair, and of a special good

favour; a sweet composition or harmony of limbs; her temper of beauty has the true [25 height of my blood. The knave hath exceed-ingly well fitted me without: I will now try her within. — Come near, fair gentlewoman; let not my behaviour seem rude, though unto you, being rare, it may haply appear strange. [30 (*She curtsies.*) Nay, lady, you may speak, though Cutbeard and my man might not; for of all sounds, only the sweet voice of a fair lady has the just length of mine ears. I beseech you, say, lady; out of the first fire [35 of meeting eyes, they say, love is stricken: do you feel any such motion suddenly shot into you, from any part you see in me? ha, lady? (*Curtsy.*) — Alas, lady, these answers by silent curtsies from you are too courtless [40 and simple. I have ever had my breeding in court; and she that shall be my wife, must be accomplished with courtly and audacious ornaments. Can you speak, lady?

*Epi.* Judge you, forsooth.                    45

*She speaks softly.*

*Mor.* What say you, lady? Speak out, I beseech you.

*Epi.* Judge you, forsooth.

*Mor.* O' my judgment, a divine softness! But can you naturally, lady, as I enjoin [50 these by doctrine and industry, refer yourself to the search of my judgment, and, not taking pleasure in your tongue, which is a woman's chiefest pleasure, think it plausible to answer me by silent gestures, so long as my speeches [55 jump right with what you conceive? (*Curtsy.*) — Excellent! divine! if it were possible she should hold out thus! — Peace, Cutbeard, thou art made for ever, as thou hast made me, if this felicity have lasting: but I will try her [60 further. Dear lady, I am courtly, I tell you, and I must have mine ears banqueted with pleasant and witty conferences, pretty girds, scoffs, and dalliance in her that I mean to choose for my bed-pheere. The ladies in [65 court think it a most desperate impair to their quickness of wit, and good carriage, if they cannot give occasion for a man to court 'em; and when an amorous discourse is set on foot, minister as good matter to continue it, as [70 himself. And do you alone so much differ from all them, that what they, with so much circumstance, affect and toil for, to seem learn'd, to seem judicious, to seem sharp and conceited, you can bury in yourself with [75 silence, and rather trust your graces to the

---

[172] **pick-tooth:** toothpick (a fashionable implement)     [15] **prefer:** recommend     [24] **favour:** appear-ance     [25] **temper:** character, quality     [37] **motion:** influence, impulse     [43] **audacious:** spirited     [52] **search:** examination, attempt to understand     [56] **jump right:** agree     [60] **lasting:** endurance     [63] **conferences:** conversations     **girds:** gibes     [65] **bed-pheere:** bedfellow     [66] **impair:** impairment     [67] **carriage:** manner in society     [73] **circumstance:** effort, ceremony     [75] **conceited:** clever

fair conscience of virtue, than to the world's
or your own proclamation?

*Epi.* [*Softly.*] I should be sorry else.

*Mor.* What say you, lady? good lady, [80
speak out.

*Epi.* I should be sorry else.

*Mor.* That sorrow doth fill me with gladness.
O Morose, thou art happy above mankind!
Pray that thou mayest contain thyself. I [85
will only put her to it once more, and it
shall be with the utmost touch and test of
their sex. But hear me, fair lady; I do also
love to see her whom I shall choose for my
heifer, to be the first and principal in all [90
fashions, precede all the dames at court by a
fortnight, have her council of tailors, lineners,
lace-women, embroiderers: and sit with 'em
sometimes twice a day upon French intelligences, and then come forth varied like [95
nature, or oftener than she, and better by the
help of art, her emulous servant. This do I
affect: and how will you be able, lady, with
this frugality of speech, to give the manifold
but necessary instructions, for that bodice, [100
these sleeves, those skirts, this cut, that stitch,
this embroidery, that lace, this wire, those
knots, that ruff, those roses, this girdle, that
fan, the t' other scarf, these gloves? Ha! what
say you, lady?                                105

*Epi.* [*Softly.*] I 'll leave it to you, sir.

*Mor.* How, lady? pray you, rise a note.

*Epi.* I leave it to wisdom and you, sir.

*Mor.* Admirable creature! I will trouble
you no more: I will not sin against so sweet [110
a simplicity. Let me now be bold to print
on those divine lips the seal of being mine. —
Cutbeard, I give thee the lease of thy house
free; thank me not but with thy leg. [*Cutbeard makes a leg.*] — I know what thou [115
wouldst say: she 's poor, and her friends deceased. She has brought a wealthy dowry in
her silence, Cutbeard; and in respect of her
poverty, Cutbeard, I shall have her more loving
and obedient, Cutbeard. Go thy ways, and [120
get me a minister presently, with a soft low
voice, to marry us; and pray him he will
not be impertinent, but brief as he can; away:
softly, Cutbeard. [*Exit Cut.*] — Sirrah, conduct your mistress into the dining-room, [125
your now-mistress. [*Exit Mute, followed by
Epi.*] — O my felicity! how I shall be reveng'd
on mine insolent kinsman, and his plots to

fright me from marrying! This night I will get
an heir, and thrust him out of my blood, [130
like a stranger. He would be knighted, forsooth, and thought by that means to reign
over me; his title must do it: No, kinsman,
I will now make you bring me the tenth lord's
and the sixteenth lady's letter, kinsman; [135
and it shall do you no good, kinsman. Your
knighthood itself shall come on its knees, and
it shall be rejected; it shall be sued for its
fees to execution, and not be redeem'd; it shall
cheat at the twelvepenny ordinary, it [140
knighthood, for its diet, all the term-time, and
tell tales for it in the vacation to the hostess;
or it knighthood shall do worse, take sanctuary
in Cole-harbour, and fast. It shall fright all
it friends with borrowing letters; and when [145
one of the fourscore hath brought it knighthood ten shillings, it knighthood shall go to
the Cranes, or the Bear at the Bridge-foot,
and be drunk in fear; it shall not have money
to discharge one tavern-reckoning, to invite [150
the old creditors to forbear it knighthood, or
the new, that should be, to trust it knighthood.
It shall be the tenth name in the bond to take
up the commodity of pipkins and stone-jugs:
and the part thereof shall not furnish it [155
knighthood forth for the attempting of a
baker's widow, a brown baker's widow. It
shall give it knighthood's name for a stallion,
to all gamesome citizens' wives, and be refus'd,
when the master of a dancing-school, or [160
How-do-you-call-him, the worst reveller in the
town, is taken: it shall want clothes, and by
reason of that, wit, to fool to lawyers. It shall
not have hope to repair itself by Constantinople, Ireland, or Virginia; but the best and [165
last fortune to it knighthood shall be to make
Dol Tear-sheet, or Kate Common a lady, and
so it knighthood may eat.          [*Exit.*]

## Act II.   Scene VI

[*A Lane, near Morose's House*]

*Truewit, Dauphine, Clerimont,* [*later*] *Cutbeard*

[*True.*] Are you sure he is not gone by?

*Daup.* No, I stay'd in the shop ever since.

*Cler.* But he may take the other end of the
lane.

*Daup.* No, I told him I would be here [5
at this end: I appointed him hither.

---

[77] **conscience:** consciousness    [87] **touch:** trial    [90] **heifer:** ('heicfar' F 1)    [94-95] **intelligences:**
news    [98] **affect:** aim at, like    [107] **rise:** raise your voice    [123] **impertinent:** irrelevant    [130] **him:**
Dauphine    [139] **to execution:** to the limit of the law    [140] **it:** its    [142] **tell tales:** (Taverns sometimes
gave free board to a good talker.)    [144] **Cole-harbour:** Cold-Harbour, a sanctuary for debtors, etc.
[148] **Cranes, Bear:** well-known taverns    [154] **commodity:** cf. I. iv. 83-84 and note    [157] **brown baker:**
baker of coarse bread    [164-165] **Constantinople, etc.:** by emigration, and, possibly, by investment in the
Turkey Company    [167] **Dol Tear-sheet:** (cf. *Henry IV*, Pt. II)

*True.* What a barbarian it is to stay, then!

*Daup.* Yonder he comes.

*Cler.* And his charge left behind him, which is a very good sign, Dauphine. 10

*[Enter Cutbeard]*

*Daup.* How now, Cutbeard! succeeds it, or no?

*Cut.* Past imagination, sir, *omnia secunda;* you could not have pray'd to have had it so well. *Saltat senex,* as it is i' the proverb; [15 he does triumph in his felicity, admires the party! He has given me the lease of my house too! and I am now going for a silent minister to marry 'em, and away.

*True.* 'Slight! get one o' the silenc'd [20 ministers; a zealous brother would torment him purely.

*Cut. Cum privilegio,* sir.

*Daup.* O, by no means; let 's do nothing to hinder it now: when 't is done and [25 finished, I am for you, for any device of vexation.

*Cut.* And that shall be within this half hour, upon my dexterity, gentlemen. Contrive what you can in the mean time, *bonis avibus.* [30
*[Exit.]*

*Cler.* How the slave doth Latin it!

*True.* It would be made a jest to posterity, sirs, this day's mirth, if ye will.

*Cler.* Beshrew his heart that will not, I pronounce. 35

*Daup.* And for my part. What is 't?

*True.* To translate all La-Foole's company, and his feast hither, to-day, to celebrate this bride-ale.

*Daup.* Ay, marry; but how will 't be [40 done?

*True.* I 'll undertake the directing of all the lady-guests thither, and then the meat must follow.

*Cler.* For God's sake, let 's effect it; it [45 will be an excellent comedy of affliction, so many several noises.

*Daup.* But are they not at the other place, already, think you?

*True.* I 'll warrant you for the college- [50 honours: one o' their faces has not the priming colour laid on yet, nor the other her smock sleek'd.

*Cler.* O, but they 'll rise earlier than ordinary to a feast. 55

*True.* Best go see, and assure ourselves.

*Cler.* Who knows the house?

*True.* I 'll lead you. Were you never there yet?

*Daup.* Not I. 60

*Cler.* Nor I.

*True.* Where ha' you liv'd then? not know Tom Otter!

*Cler.* No: for God's sake, what is he?

*True.* An excellent animal, equal with [65 your Daw or La-Foole, if not transcendent; and does Latin it as much as your barber. He is his wife's subject; he calls her princess, and at such times as these follows her up and down the house like a page, with his hat off, partly [70 for heat, partly for reverence. At this instant he is marshalling of his bull, bear, and horse.

*Daup.* What be those, in the name of Sphinx?

*True.* Why, sir, he has been a great man [75 at the Bear-garden in his time; and from that subtle sport has ta'en the witty denomination of his chief carousing cups. One he calls his bull, another his bear, another his horse. And then he has his lesser glasses, that [80 he calls his deer and his ape; and several degrees of 'em too; and never is well, nor thinks any entertainment perfect, till these be brought out, and set o' the cupboard.

*Cler.* For God's love! — we should miss [85 this, if we should not go.

*True.* Nay, he has a thousand things as good, that will speak him all day. He will rail on his wife, with certain commonplaces, behind her back; and to her face — 90

*Daup.* No more of him. Let 's go see him, I petition you. *[Exeunt.]*

## Act III.  Scene I

*[A Room in Otter's House]*

Otter, Mrs. Otter, [*later*] Truewit, Clerimont, Dauphine

*[Ott.]* Nay, good princess, hear me *pauca verba.*

*Mrs. Ott.* By that light, I 'll ha' you chain'd up, with your bull-dogs and bear-dogs, if you be not civil the sooner. I 'll send you to [5 kennel, i' faith. You were best bait me with your bull, bear, and horse. Never a time that the courtiers or collegiates come to the house, but you make it a Shrove-Tuesday! I would have you get your Whitsuntide velvet cap, [10 and your staff i' your hand, to entertain 'em: yes, in troth, do.

---

⁷ it: he    stay: delay    ¹³ omnia secunda: everything favorable    ¹⁵ Saltat senex: The old man dances.    ²³ Cum privilegio: with authority    ³⁰ bonis avibus: with good omens    ³⁵ pronounce: declare    ³⁹ bride-ale: bridal feast    ⁵³ sleek'd: ironed    ⁷⁶ Bear-garden: an amphitheatre used for baiting bulls and bears    ⁸² well: happy    ⁸⁸ speak him: show his character or humor    ¹⁻² pauca verba: a few words    ⁹⁻¹⁰ Shrove-Tuesday, Whitsuntide: occasions of celebration; cf. I. i. 192

*Ott.* Not so, princess, neither; but under correction, sweet princess, gi' me leave. — These things I am known to the courtiers [15 by. It is reported to them for my humour, and they receive it so, and do expect it. Tom Otter's bull, bear, and horse is known all over England, *in rerum natura.*

*Mrs. Ott.* 'Fore me, I will *na-ture* 'em [20 over to Paris-garden, and *na-ture* you thither too, if you pronounce 'em again. Is a bear a fit beast, or a bull, to mix in society with great ladies? think, i' your discretion, in any good polity?                                         25

*Ott.* The horse then, good princess.

*Mrs. Ott.* Well, I am contented for the horse; they love to be well hors'd, I know. I love it myself.

*Ott.* And it is a delicate fine horse this: [30 *Poetarum Pegasus.* Under correction, princess, Jupiter did turn himself into a — *taurus,* or bull, under correction, good princess.

*[Enter Truewit, Clerimont, and Dauphine, behind]*

*Mrs. Ott.* By my integrity, I 'll send you over to the Bank-side; I 'll commit you [35 to the master of the Garden, if I hear but a syllable more. Must my house or my roof be polluted with the scent of bears and bulls, when it is perfum'd for great ladies? Is this according to the instrument, when I married [40 you? that I would be princess, and reign in mine own house; and you would be my subject, and obey me? What did you bring me, should make you thus peremptory? Do I allow you your half-crown a day, to spend where [45 you will, among your gamesters, to vex and torment me at such times as these? Who gives you your maintenance, I pray you? who allows you your horse-meat and man's meat? your three suits of apparel a year? your four [50 pair of stockings, one silk, three worsted? your clean linen, your bands and cuffs, when I can get you to wear 'em? — 't is marle you ha' 'em on now. — Who graces you with courtiers or great personages, to speak to you out of [55 their coaches, and come home to your house? Were you ever so much as look'd upon by a lord or a lady, before I married you, but on the Easter or Whitsun-holidays? and then out at the banqueting-house windore, when [60

Ned Whiting or George Stone were at the stake?

*True.* [*Aside.*] For God's sake, let 's go stave her off him.

*Mrs. Ott.* Answer me to that. And did [65 not I take you up from thence, in an old greasy buff-doublet, with points, and green vellet sleeves, out at the elbows? You forget this.

*True.* [*Aside.*] She 'll worry him, if we help not in time.              [*They come forward.*]

*Mrs. Ott.* O, here are some o' the gallants! [71 Go to, behave yourself distinctly, and with good morality; or, I protest, I 'll take away your exhibition.

## *Act III. Scene II*

*Truewit, Mrs. Otter, Cap. Otter, Clerimont, Dauphine, [later] Cutbeard*

*[True.]* By your leave, fair mistress Otter, I 'll be bold to enter these gentlemen in your acquaintance.

*Mrs. Ott.* It shall not be obnoxious, or difficil, sir.                                         5

*True.* How does my noble captain? Is the bull, bear, and horse in *rerum natura* still?

*Ott.* Sir, *sic visum superis.*

*Mrs. Ott.* I would you would but intimate 'em, do. Go your ways in, and get toasts [10 and butter made for the woodcocks: that 's a fit province for you.          [*Drives him off.*]

*Cler.* Alas, what a tyranny is this poor fellow married to!

*True.* O, but the sport will be anon, [15 when we get him loose.

*Daup.* Dares he ever speak?

*True.* No Anabaptist ever rail'd with the like license: but mark her language in the mean time, I beseech you.                        20

*Mrs. Ott.* Gentlemen, you are very aptly come. My cousin, Sir Amorous, will be here briefly.

*True.* In good time, lady. Was not Sir John Daw here, to ask for him, and the company? [25

*Mrs. Ott.* I cannot assure you, master Truewit. Here was a very melancholy knight in a ruff, that demanded my subject for somebody, a gentleman, I think.

*Cler.* Ay, that was he, lady.                        30

*Mrs. Ott.* But he departed straight, I can resolve you.

---

[16] **humour:** eccentricity, distinguishing mark  [19] **in . . . natura:** in the nature of things  [21] **Paris-garden:** a bear-garden on the Bankside in Southwark  [25] **polity:** government  [40] **instrument:** legal agreement  [49] **horse-meat:** food for horses  [53] **marle:** a marvel  [60] **out . . . windore:** (Bears were sometimes baited in the courtyard of Whitehall on holidays.)  [61] **Ned . . . Stone:** famous bears, who bore their masters' names  [67] **points:** laces which held clothing together  [69] **worry:** as the bear did the dog  [74] **exhibition:** allowance  [4-5] **difficil:** difficult  [8] **sic . . . superis:** So it has pleased the gods.  [9] **intimate:** refer to  [11] **woodcocks:** simpletons  [18] **Anabaptist:** dissenter  [12] **resolve:** inform

*Daup.* What an excellent choice phrase this lady expresses in.

*True.* O, sir, she is the only authentical [35 courtier, that is not naturally bred one, in the city.

*Mrs. Ott.* You have taken that report upon trust, gentlemen.

*True.* No, I assure you, the court governs [40 it so, lady, in your behalf.

*Mrs. Ott.* I am the servant of the court and courtiers, sir.

*True.* They are rather your idolaters.

*Mrs. Ott.* Not so, sir.                    45

[*Enter Cutbeard*]

*Daup.* How now, Cutbeard! any cross?

*Cut.* O no, sir, *omnia bene*. 'T was never better o' the hinges; all 's sure. I have so pleas'd him with a curate, that he 's gone to 't almost with the delight he hopes for soon. 50

*Daup.* What is he for a vicar?

*Cut.* One that has catch'd a cold, sir, and can scarce be heard six inches off; as if he spoke out of a bulrush that were not pick'd, or his throat were full of pith: a fine quick [55 fellow, and an excellent barber of prayers. I came to tell you, sir, that you might *omnem movere lapidem*, as they say, be ready with your vexation.

*Daup.* Gramercy, honest Cutbeard! be [60 thereabouts with thy key, to let us in.

*Cut.* I will not fail you, sir; *ad manum*.
                                        [*Exit.*]

*True.* Well, I 'll go watch my coaches.

*Cler.* Do; and we 'll send Daw to you, if you meet him not.       [*Exit Truewit.*] 65

*Mrs. Ott.* Is master Truewit gone?

*Daup.* Yes, lady, there is some unfortunate business fallen out.

*Mrs. Ott.* So I judged by the physiognomy of the fellow that came in; and I had a [70 dream last night too of the new pageant, and my lady mayoress, which is always very ominous to me. I told it my lady Haughty t' other day, when her honour came hither to see some China stuffs; and she expounded it out of [75 Artemidorus, and I have found it since very true. It has done me many affronts.

*Cler.* Your dream, lady?

*Mrs. Ott.* Yes, sir, anything I do but dream o' the city. It stain'd me a damask table- [80 cloth, cost me eighteen pound, at one time; and burnt me a black satin gown, as I stood by the fire, at my lady Centaure's chamber in the college, another time. A third time,

at the lords' masque, it dropp'd all my wire [85 and my ruff with wax candle, that I could not go up to the banquet. A fourth time, as I was taking coach to go to Ware, to meet a friend, it dash'd me a new suit all over (a crimson satin doublet, and black velvet [90 skirts) with a brewer's horse, that I was fain to go in and shift me, and kept my chamber a leash of days for the anguish of it.

*Daup.* These were dire mischances, lady.

*Cler.* I would not dwell in the city, an [95 't were so fatal to me.

*Mrs. Ott.* Yes, sir; but I do take advice of my doctor to dream of it as little as I can.

*Daup.* You do well, mistress Otter.

[*Enter Sir John Daw, and is taken aside by Clerimont*]

*Mrs. Ott.* Will it please you to enter [100 the house farther, gentlemen?

*Daup.* And your favour, lady: but we stay to speak with a knight, Sir John Daw, who is here come. We shall follow you, lady.

*Mrs. Ott.* At your own time, sir. It is [105 my cousin Sir Amorous his feast —

*Daup.* I know it, lady.

*Mrs. Ott.* And mine together. But it is for his honour, and therefore I take no name of it, more than of the place.           110

*Daup.* You are a bounteous kinswoman.

*Mrs. Ott.* Your servant, sir.        [*Exit.*]

## Act III.  Scene III

*Clerimont, Daw, La-Foole, Dauphine, Otter*

[*Cler. coming forward with Daw.*] Why, do not you know it, Sir John Daw?

*Daw.* No, I am a rook if I do.

*Cler.* I 'll tell you, then; she 's married by this time. And, whereas you were put i' [5 the head, that she was gone with Sir Dauphine, I assure you, Sir Dauphine has been the noblest, honestest friend to you, that ever gentleman of your quality could boast of. He has discover'd the whole plot, and made your mis- [10 tress so acknowledging, and indeed so ashamed of her injury to you, that she desires you to forgive her, and but grace her wedding with your presence to-day. — She is to be married to a very good fortune, she says, his uncle, [15 old Morose; and she will'd me in private to tell you, that she shall be able to do you more favours, and with more security now than before.

---

⁴⁶ **cross:** difficulty     ⁴⁷ **omnia bene:** All (goes) well.     ⁵⁷⁻⁵⁸ **omnem . . . lapidem:** move every stone     ⁶⁰ **Gramercy:** thanks     ⁶² **ad manum:** at hand     ⁶⁸ **fallen out:** that has happened     ⁷⁶ **Artemidorus:** Greek writer on the interpretation of dreams     ⁸⁵ **wire:** fabric supporting the coiffure     ⁹² **shift me:** change my clothes     ⁹³ **leash:** three     ¹¹ **acknowledging:** grateful

*Daw.* Did she say so, i' faith?

*Cler.* Why, what do you think of me, [20 Sir John? ask Sir Dauphine.

*Daw.* Nay, I believe you. — Good Sir Dauphine, did she desire me to forgive her?

*Daup.* I assure you, Sir John, she did.

*Daw.* Nay, then, I do with all my heart, [25 and I 'll be jovial.

*Cler.* Yes, for look you, sir, this was the injury to you. La-Foole intended this feast to honour her bridal day, and made you the property to invite the college ladies, and [30 promise to bring her; and then at the time she should have appear'd, as his friend, to have given you the dor. Whereas now, Sir Dauphine has brought her to a feeling of it, with this kind of satisfaction, that you shall [35 bring all the ladies to the place where she is, and be very jovial; and there, she will have a dinner, which shall be in your name: and so disappoint La-Foole, to make you good again, and, as it were, a saver i' the main. 40

*Daw.* As I am a knight, I honour her; and forgive her heartily.

*Cler.* About it then presently. Truewit is gone before to confront the coaches, and to acquaint you with so much, if he meet you. [45 Join with him, and 't is well. —

*[Enter Sir Amorous La-Foole]*

See; here comes your antagonist; but take you no notice, but be very jovial.

*La-F.* Are the ladies come, Sir John Daw, and your mistress? *[Exit Daw.]* — Sir Dau- [50 phine! you are exceeding welcome, and honest master Clerimont. Where 's my cousin? did you see no collegiates, gentlemen?

*Daup.* Collegiates! do you not hear, Sir Amorous, how you are abus'd? 55

*La-F.* How, sir!

*Cler.* Will you speak so kindly to Sir John Daw, that has done you such an affront?

*La-F.* Wherein, gentlemen? Let me be a suitor to you to know, I beseech you. 60

*Cler.* Why, sir, his mistress is married to-day to Sir Dauphine's uncle, your cousin's neighbour, and he has diverted all the ladies, and all your company thither, to frustrate your provision, and stick a disgrace upon you. [65 He was here now to have entic'd us away from you too: but we told him his own, I think.

*La-F.* Has Sir John Daw wrong'd me so inhumanely?

*Daup.* He has done it, Sir Amorous, [70

most maliciously and treacherously: but, if you 'll be rul'd by us, you shall quit him, i' faith.

*La-F.* Good gentlemen, I 'll make one, believe it. How, I pray? 75

*Daup.* Marry, sir, get me your pheasants, and your godwits, and your best meat, and dish it in silver dishes of your cousin's presently; and say nothing, but clap me a clean towel about you, like a sewer; and, bare-headed, [80 march afore it with a good confidence, ('t is but over the way, hard by,) and we 'll second you, where you shall set it o' the board, and bid 'em welcome to 't, which shall show 't is yours, and disgrace his preparation utterly: [85 and for your cousin, whereas she should be troubled here at home with care of making and giving welcome, she shall transfer all that labour thither, and be a principal guest herself; sit rank'd with the college-honours, and [90 be honour'd, and have her health drunk as often, as bare and as loud as the best of 'em.

*La-F.* I 'll go tell her presently. It shall be done, that 's resolv'd. *[Exit.]*

*Cler.* I thought he would not hear it [95 out, but 't would take him.

*Daup.* Well, there be guests and meat now; how shall we do for music?

*Cler.* The smell of the venison, going through the street, will invite one noise of fiddlers [100 or other.

*Daup.* I would it would call the trumpeters thither!

*Cler.* Faith, there is hope: they have intelligence of all feasts. There 's good cor- [105 respondence betwixt them and the London cooks: 't is twenty to one but we have 'em.

*Daup.* 'T will be a most solemn day for my uncle, and an excellent fit of mirth for us.

*Cler.* Ay, if we can hold up the emula- [110 tion betwixt Foole and Daw, and never bring them to expostulate.

*Daup.* Tut, flatter 'em both, as Truewit says, and you may take their understandings in a purse-net. They 'll believe themselves [115 to be just such men as we make 'em, neither more nor less. They have nothing, not the use of their senses, but by tradition.

*Cler.* See! Sir Amorous has his towel on already. *He enters like a sewer.* 120 Have you persuaded your cousin?

*La-F.* Yes, 't is very feasible: she 'll do any thing, she says, rather than the La-Fooles shall be disgrac'd.

---

[30] **property:** tool    [33] **given . . . dor:** made game of    [40] **saver:** one who escapes loss (in gaming), though without gain    **main:** ('man' F, Q)    [44] **confront:** meet    [64] **frustrate:** make useless    [65] **provision:** preparations    [67] **told . . . own:** put him in his place    [72] **quit:** requite    [74] **make one:** join in your plan    [80] **sewer:** waiter    [82] **second:** support    [92] **bare:** bareheaded    [100] **noise:** company [104-106] **correspondence:** friendly relation    [112] **expostulate:** explain

*Daup.* She is a noble kinswoman. It [125] will be such a pestling device, Sir Amorous; it will pound all your enemy's practices to powder, and blow him up with his own mine, his own train.

*La-F.* Nay, we 'll give fire, I warrant [130] you.

*Cler.* But you must carry it privately, without any noise, and take no notice by any means —

### [*Enter Captain Otter*]

*Ott.* Gentlemen, my princess says you [135] shall have all her silver dishes, *festinate:* and she 's gone to alter her tire a little, and go with you —

*Cler.* And yourself too, Captain Otter?

*Daup.* By any means, sir.          140

*Ott.* Yes, sir, I do mean it: but I would entreat my cousin Sir Amorous, and you, gentlemen, to be suitors to my princess, that I may carry my bull and my bear, as well as my horse.          145

*Cler.* That you shall do, Captain Otter.

*La-F.* My cousin will never consent, gentlemen.

*Daup.* She must consent, Sir Amorous, to reason.          150

*La-F.* Why, she says they are no decorum among ladies.

*Ott.* But they are *decora,* and that 's better, sir.

*Cler.* Ay, she must hear argument. Did [155] not Pasiphaë, who was a queen, love a bull? and was not Calisto, the mother of Arcas, turn'd into a bear, and made a star, mistress Ursula, i' the heavens?

*Ott.* O God! that I could ha' said as [160] much! I will have these stories painted i' the Bear-garden, *ex Ovidii Metamorphosi.*

*Daup.* Where is your princess, captain? pray, be our leader.

*Ott.* That I shall, sir.          165

*Cler.* Make haste, good Sir Amorous.

[*Exeunt.*]

## Act III.  Scene IIII

### [*A Room in Morose's House*]

*Morose, Epicœne, Parson, Cutbeard*

[*Mor.*] Sir, there 's an angel for yourself, and a brace of angels for your cold. Muse not at this manage of my bounty. It is fit we should thank fortune, double to nature, for any benefit she confers upon us; besides, [5] it is your imperfection, but my solace.

*Par.* I thank your worship; so is it mine, now.          *The Parson speaks as having a cold.*

*Mor.* What says he, Cutbeard?

*Cut.* He says, *præsto,* sir, whensoever [10] your worship needs him, he can be ready with the like. He got this cold with sitting up late, and singing catches with cloth-workers.

*Mor.* No more. I thank him.

*Par.* God keep your worship, and give [15] you much joy with your fair spouse! — umh, umh.          *He coughs.*

*Mor.* O, O! stay, Cutbeard! let him give me five shillings of my money back. As it is bounty to reward benefits, so is it equity to [20] mulct injuries. I will have it. What says he?

*Cler.* He cannot change it, sir.

*Mor.* It must be changed.

*Cut.* [*Aside to Parson.*] Cough again.

*Mor.* What says he?          25

*Cut.* He will cough out the rest, sir.

*Par.* Umh, umh, umh.          *Again.*

*Mor.* Away, away with him! stop his mouth! away! I forgive it. —

[*Exit Cut. thrusting out the Par.*]

*Epi.* Fie, master Morose, that you will [30] use this violence to a man of the church.

*Mor.* How!

*Epi.* It does not become your gravity, or breeding, as you pretend, in court, to have offer'd this outrage on a waterman, or any [35] more boisterous creature, much less on a man of his civil coat.

*Mor.* You can speak then!

*Epi.* Yes, sir.

*Mor.* Speak out, I mean.          40

*Epi.* Ay, sir. Why, did you think you had married a statue, or a motion only? one of the French puppets, with the eyes turn'd with a wire? or some innocent out of the hospital, that would stand with her hands thus, and [45] a plaise mouth, and look upon you?

*Mor.* O immodesty! a manifest woman! What, Cutbeard!

*Epi.* Nay, never quarrel with Cutbeard, sir; it is too late now. I confess it doth bate [50] somewhat of the modesty I had, when I writ simply maid: but I hope I shall make it a stock still competent to the estate and dignity of your wife.

*Mor.* She can talk!          55

*Epi.* Yes, indeed, sir.

---

[125] **pestling:** pulverizing     [136] **festinate:** immediately     [137] **tire:** headdress     [153] **decora:** beautiful     [3] **manage:** handling     [4] **double to:** *i.e.,* twice as much as we thank     [10] **præsto:** here     [13] **cloth-workers:** (who sang psalms and hymns as they worked)     [21] **mulct:** punish     [35] **waterman:** boatman on the Thames     [42] **motion:** puppet     [44] **innocent:** idiot     [46] **plaise:** pursed, like a fish     [53] **competent:** suited

*[Enter Mute]*

*Mor.* What sirrah! None of my knaves there? Where is this impostor Cutbeard?

*[Mute makes signs.]*

*Epi.* Speak to him, fellow, speak to him! I 'll have none of this coacted, unnatural [60 dumbness in my house, in a family where I govern. *[Exit Mute.]*

*Mor.* She is my regent already! I have married a Penthesilea, a Semiramis; sold my liberty to a distaff. 65

## Act III. Scene V

*Truewit, Morose, Epicœne*

*[True.]* Where 's master Morose?

*Mor.* Is he come again! Lord have mercy upon me!

*True.* I wish you all joy, mistress Epicœne, with your grave and honourable match. 5

*Epi.* I return you the thanks, master Truewit, so friendly a wish deserves.

*Mor.* She has acquaintance, too!

*True.* God save you, sir, and give you all contentment in your fair choice, here! Be- [10 fore, I was the bird of night to you, the owl; but now I am the messenger of peace, a dove, and bring you the glad wishes of many friends to the celebration of this good hour.

*Mor.* What hour, sir? 15

*True.* Your marriage hour, sir. I commend your resolution, that, notwithstanding all the dangers I laid afore you, in the voice of a night-crow, would yet go on, and be yourself. It shows you are a man constant to your [20 own ends, and upright to your purposes, that would not be put off with left-handed cries.

*Mor.* How should you arrive at the knowledge of so much?

*True.* Why, did you ever hope, sir, com- [25 mitting the secrecy of it to a barber, that less than the whole town should know it? You might as well ha' told it the conduit, or the bake-house, or the infantry that follow the court, and with more security. Could your [30 gravity forget so old and noted a remnant, as, *lippis et tonsoribus notum?* Well, sir, forgive it yourself now, the fault, and be communicable with your friends. Here will be three or four fashionable ladies from the college to visit [35 you presently, and their train of minions and followers.

*Mor.* Bar my doors! bar my doors! Where are all my eaters? my mouths, now? —

*[Enter Servants]*

Bar up my doors, you varlets! 40

*Epi.* He is a varlet that stirs to such an office. Let 'em stand open. I would see them that dares move his eyes toward it. Shall I have a barricado made against my friends, to be barr'd of any pleasure they can bring in [45 to me with honourable visitation? *[Exeunt Ser.]*

*Mor.* O Amazonian impudence!

*True.* Nay, faith, in this, sir, she speaks but reason; and, methinks, is more continent than you. Would you go to bed so presently, [50 sir, afore noon? A man of your head and hair should owe more to that reverend ceremony, and not mount the marriage-bed like a town-bull, or a mountain-goat; but stay the due season; and ascend it then with religion [55 and fear. Those delights are to be steep'd in the humour and silence of the night; and give the day to other open pleasures, and jollities of feast, of music, of revels, of discourse. We 'll have all, sir, that may make your Hymen [60 high and happy.

*Mor.* O my torment, my torment!

*True.* Nay, if you endure the first half hour, sir, so tediously, and with this irksomeness; what comfort or hope can this fair gentle- [65 woman make to herself hereafter, in the consideration of so many years as are to come —

*Mor.* Of my affliction. Good sir, depart, and let her do it alone.

*True.* I have done, sir. 70

*Mor.* That cursed barber!

*True.* Yes, faith, a cursed wretch indeed, sir.

*Mor.* I have married his cittern, that 's common to all men. Some plague above the plague — 75

*True.* All Egypt's ten plagues.

*Mor.* Revenge me on him!

*True.* 'T is very well, sir. If you laid on a curse or two more, I 'll assure you he 'll bear 'em. As, that he may get the pox with [80 seeking to cure it, sir; or, that while he is curling another man's hair, his own may drop off; or, for burning some male-bawd's lock, he may have his brain beat out with the curling iron.

*Mor.* No, let the wretch live wretched. 85 May he get the itch, and his shop so lousy, as no man dare come at him, nor he come at no man!

*True.* Ay, and if he would swallow all his balls for pills, let not them purge him. 90

*Mor.* Let his warming-pan be ever cold.

*True.* A perpetual frost underneath it, sir.

*Mor.* Let him never hope to see fire again.

*True.* But in hell, sir.                    94

*Mor.* His chairs be always empty, his scissors rust, and his combs mould in their cases.

*True.* Very dreadful that! And may he lose the invention, sir, of carving lanterns in paper.

*Mor.* Let there be no bawd carted that year, to employ a basin of his: but let him [100 be glad to eat his sponge for bread.

*True.* And drink lotium to it, and much good do him.

*Mor.* Or, for want of bread —

*True.* Eat ear-wax, sir. I'll help you. [105 Or, draw his own teeth, and add them to the lute-string.

*Mor.* No, beat the old ones to powder, and make bread of them.

*True.* Yes, make meal o' the mill-stones. [110

*Mor.* May all the botches and burns that he has cur'd on others break out upon him.

*True.* And he now forget the cure of 'em in himself, sir; or, if he do remember it, let him ha' scrap'd all his linen into lint for 't, [115 and have not a rag left him to set up with.

*Mor.* Let him never set up again, but have the gout in his hands for ever! — Now, no more, sir.

*True.* O, that last was too high set; you [120 might go less with him, i' faith, and be reveng'd enough: as, that he be never able to new-paint his pole —

*Mor.* Good sir, no more, I forgot myself.

*True.* Or, want credit to take up with a [125 comb-maker —

*Mor.* No more, sir.

*True.* Or, having broken his glass in a former despair, fall now into a much greater, of ever getting another —                    130

*Mor.* I beseech you, no more.

*True.* Or, that he never be trusted with trimming of any but chimney-sweepers —

*Mor.* Sir —

*True.* Or, may he cut a collier's throat [135 with his razor, by chance-medley, and yet hang for 't.

*Mor.* I will forgive him, rather than hear any more. I beseech you, sir.

## Act III. Scene VI

*Daw, Morose, Truewit, Haughty, Centaure, Mavis, Trusty*

[*Daw.*] This way, madam.

*Mor.* O, the sea breaks in upon me! an-

other flood! an inundation! I shall be o'erwhelmed with noise. It beats already at my shores. I feel an earthquake in myself [5 for 't.

*Daw.* 'Give you joy, mistress.

*Mor.* Has she servants too!

*Daw.* I have brought some ladies here to see and know you. My lady Haughty — [10 (*She kisses them severally as he presents them.*) this my lady Centaure — mistress Dol Mavis — mistress Trusty, my lady Haughty's woman. Where 's your husband? Let 's see him: can he endure no noise? Let me come to him.

*Mor.* What nomenclator is this!            15

*True.* Sir John Daw, sir, your wife's servant, this.

*Mor.* A Daw, and her servant! O, 't is decreed, 't is decreed of me, and she have such servants.            [*Going.*] 20

*True.* Nay, sir, you must kiss the ladies; you must not go away, now: they come toward you to seek you out.

*Hau.* I' faith, master Morose, would you steal a marriage thus, in the midst of so [25 many friends, and not acquaint us? Well, I'll kiss you, notwithstanding the justice of my quarrel. You shall give me leave, mistress, to use a becoming familiarity with your husband.            30

*Epi.* Your ladyship does me an honour in it, to let me know he is so worthy your favour: as you have done both him and me grace to visit so unprepar'd a pair to entertain you.

*Mor.* Compliment! compliment!            35

*Epi.* But I must lay the burden of that upon my servant here.

*Hau.* It shall not need, mistress Morose; we will all bear, rather than one shall be oppress'd.            40

*Mor.* I know it: and you will teach her the faculty, if she be to learn it.

[*Walks aside while the rest talk apart.*]

*Hau.* Is this the Silent Woman?

*Cen.* Nay, she has found her tongue since she was married, master Truewit says.            45

*Hau.* O, master Truewit! 'save you. What kind of creature is your bride here? She speaks, methinks!

*True.* Yes, madam, believe it, she is a gentlewoman of very absolute behaviour, and [50 of a good race.

*Hau.* And Jack Daw told us she could not speak!

*True.* So it was carried in plot, madam, to

---

100 **basin:** (Barbers rented metal basins to spectators who wished to increase the din as a bawd was carted through the streets.)    102 **lotium:** lotion    106 **draw . . . teeth:** (The barber was also the dentist and letter of blood.)    106–107 **add . . . -string:** (Barber-surgeons' rooms were decorated with strings of extracted teeth.)    136 **chance-medley:** accident    15 **nomenclator:** a servant who announces the names of guests    19 **decreed:** fated **and:** if    50 **absolute:** perfect    54 **carried:** arranged, managed

put her upon this old fellow, by Sir Dau- [55
phine, his nephew, and one or two more of
us: but she is a woman of an excellent assurance, and an extraordinary happy wit and
tongue. You shall see her make rare sport
with Daw ere night.                               60

*Hau.* And he brought us to laugh at her!

*True.* That falls out often, madam, that
he that thinks himself the master-wit, is the
master-fool. I assure your ladyship, ye cannot
laugh at her.                                     65

*Hau.* No, we 'll have her to the college.
And she have wit, she shall be one of us, shall
she not, Centaure? We 'll make her a collegiate.

*Cen.* Yes, faith, madam, and Mavis and
she will set up a side.                           70

*True.* Believe it, madam, and mistress Mavis,
she will sustain her part.

*Mav.* I 'll tell you that, when I have talk'd
with her, and tried her.

*Hau.* Use her very civilly, Mavis.               75

*Mav.* So I will, madam.   [*Whispers her.*]

*Mor.* [*Aside.*] Blessed minute! that they
would whisper thus ever!

*True.* In the mean time, madam, would but
your ladyship help to vex him a little: you [80
know his disease, talk to him about the wedding
ceremonies, or call for your gloves, or —

*Hau.* Let me alone. Centaure, help me. —
Master bridegroom, where are you?

*Mor.* [*Aside.*] O, it was too miracu- [85
lously good to last!

*Hau.* We see no ensigns of a wedding here;
no character of a bride-ale: where be our
scarves and our gloves? I pray you, give 'em
us. Let 's know your bride's colours, and [90
yours at least.

*Cen.* Alas, madam, he has provided none.

*Mor.* Had I known your ladyship's painter,
I would.

*Hau.* He has given it you, Centaure, [95
i' faith. But do you hear, master Morose? a
jest will not absolve you in this manner. You
that have suck'd the milk of the court, and
from thence have been brought up to the very
strong meats and wine of it; been a courtier [100
from the biggen to the night-cap, as we may say,
and you to offend in such a high point of ceremony as this, and let your nuptials want all
marks of solemnity! How much plate have you
lost to-day, (if you had but regarded your [105
profit,) what gifts, what friends, through your
mere rusticity!

*Mor.* Madam—

*Hau.* Pardon me, sir, I must insinuate your
errors to you; no gloves? no garters? no [110
scarves? no epithalamium? no masque?

*Daw.* Yes, madam, I 'll make an epithalamium, I promis'd my mistress; I have begun
it already: will your ladyship hear it?

*Hau.* Ay, good Jack Daw.                         115

*Mor.* Will it please your ladyship command
a chamber, and be private with your friend?
You shall have your choice of rooms to retire
to after: my whole house is yours. I know it
hath been your ladyship's errand into the [120
city at other times, however now you have
been unhappily diverted upon me; but I shall
be loath to break any honourable custom of
your ladyship's. And therefore, good madam —

*Epi.* Come, you are a rude bridegroom, [125
to entertain ladies of honour in this fashion.

*Cen.* He is a rude groom indeed.

*True.* By that light, you deserve to be
grafted, and have your horns reach from one side
of the island to the other. — Do not mis- [130
take me, sir; I but speak this to give the ladies
some heart again, not for any malice to you.

*Mor.* Is this your bravo, ladies?

*True.* As God help me, if you utter such [134
another word, I 'll take mistress bride in, and
begin to you in a very sad cup; do you see?
Go to, know your friends, and such as love
you.

## Act III.   Scene VII

*Clerimont, Morose, Truewit, Dauphine,*
*La-Foole, Otter, Mrs. Otter, &c.*

[*Cler.*] By your leave, ladies. Do you want
any music? I have brought you variety of
noises. Play, sirs, all of you. *Music of all sorts.*

*Mor.* O, a plot, a plot, a plot, a plot, upon
me! This day I shall be their anvil to work [5
on, they will grate me asunder. 'T is worse
than the noise of a saw.

*Cler.* No, they are hair, rosin, and guts:
I can give you the receipt.

*True.* Peace, boys!                              10

*Cler.* Play! I say.

*True.* Peace, rascals! You see who 's your
friend now, sir: take courage, put on a martyr's
resolution. Mock down all their attemptings
with patience. 'T is but a day, and I would [15
suffer heroically. Should an ass exceed me
in fortitude? No. You betray your infirmity

---

⁷⁰ **set . . . side:** be partners     ⁸² **gloves:** (It was customary to give gloves and scarves to wedding-
guests.)     ⁸⁷ **ensigns:** signs     ⁹⁰ **colours:** (The bride and groom had different colors which were worn
by their respective friends.)     ¹⁰¹ **biggen:** infant's cap     ¹¹⁰ **garters:** (It was the custom for the attendants to try to get the bride's garters.)     ¹¹¹ **masque:** (A wedding masque was often performed in
the evening.)     ¹²⁹ **horns:** (of a cuckold)     ¹³³ **bravo:** swaggering fellow     ¹³⁴ **As:** so     ¹³⁷ **Go to:**
Come, come!     ²⁻³ **variety of noises:** groups of different sorts of musicians

with your hanging dull ears, and make them insult: bear up bravely, and constantly.    20

*La-Foole passes over sewing the meat.*

Look you here, sir, what honour is done you unexpected, by your nephew; a wedding-dinner come, and a knight-sewer before it, for the more reputation: and fine mistress Otter, your neighbour, in the rump or tail of it.    25

*Mor.* Is that Gorgon, that Medusa come! hide me, hide me.

*True.* I warrant you, sir, she will not transform you. Look upon her with a good courage. Pray you, entertain her, and conduct your [30 guests in. No? — Mistress bride, will you entreat in the ladies? your bridegroom is so shame-fac'd, here.

*Epi.* Will it please your ladyship, madam?

*Hau.* With the benefit of your company, [35 mistress.

*Epi.* Servant, pray you perform your duties.

*Daw.* And glad to be commanded, mistress.

*Cen.* How like you her wit, Mavis?

*Mav.* Very prettily, absolutely well.    40

*Mrs. Ott.* 'T is my place.

*[Trying to take precedence.]*

*Mav.* You shall pardon me, mistress Otter.

*Mrs. Ott.* Why, I am a collegiate.

*Mav.* But not in ordinary.

*Mrs. Ott.* But I am.    45

*Mav.* We 'll dispute that within.

*[Exeunt Ladies.]*

*Cler.* Would this had lasted a little longer.

*True.* And that they had sent for the heralds.

*[Enter Captain Otter]*

— Captain Otter! what news?    50

*Ott.* I have brought my bull, bear, and horse, in private, and yonder are the trumpeters without, and the drum, gentlemen.

*The drum and trumpets sound.*

*Mor.* O, O, O!

*Ott.* And we will have a rouse in each of [55 'em, anon, for bold Britons, i' faith.

*[They sound again.]*

*Mor.* O, O, O!      *[Exit hastily.]*

*All.* Follow, follow, follow!     *[Exeunt.]*

## Act IIII. Scene I

*[A Room in Morose's House]*

*Truewit, Clerimont, Dauphine*

*[True.]* Was there ever poor bridegroom so tormented? or man, indeed?

*Cler.* I have not read of the like in the chronicles of the land.

*True.* Sure, he cannot but go to a place [5 of rest, after all this purgatory.

*Cler.* He may presume it, I think.

*True.* The spitting, the coughing, the laughter, the neezing, the farting, dancing, noise of the music, and her masculine and loud [10 commanding, and urging the whole family, makes him think he has married a fury.

*Cler.* And she carries it up bravely.

*True.* Ay, she takes any occasion to speak: that 's the height on 't.    15

*Cler.* And how soberly Dauphine labours to satisfy him, that it was none of his plot!

*True.* And has almost brought him to the faith, i' the article. Here he comes. —

*[Enter Sir Dauphine]*

Where is he now? what 's become of him, [20 Dauphine?

*Daup.* O, hold me up a little, I shall go away i' the jest else. He has got on his whole nest of night-caps, and lock'd himself up i' the top o' the house, as high as ever he can [25 climb from the noise. I peep'd in at a cranny, and saw him sitting over a cross-beam o' the roof, like him o' the saddler's horse in Fleet-street, upright: and he will sleep there.

*Cler.* But where are your collegiates?    30

*Daup.* Withdrawn with the bride in private.

*True.* O, they are instructing her i' the college-grammar. If she have grace with them, she knows all their secrets instantly.

*Cler.* Methinks the lady Haughty looks [35 well to-day, for all my dispraise of her i' the morning. I think, I shall come about to thee again, Truewit.

*True.* Believe it, I told you right. Women ought to repair the losses time and years [40 have made i' their features, with dressings. And an intelligent woman, if she know by herself the least defect, will be most curious to hide it: and it becomes her. If she be short, let her sit much, lest, when she stands, she [45 be thought to sit. If she have an ill foot, let her wear her gown the longer, and her shoe the thinner. If a fat hand, and scald nails, let her carve the less, and act in gloves. If a sour breath, let her never discourse fasting, and [50 always talk at her distance. If she have black and rugged teeth, let her offer the less at laughter, especially if she laugh wide and open.

*Cler.* O, you shall have some women, when

---

they laugh, you would think they bray'd, [55
it is so rude and —

*True.* Ay, and others, that will stalk i' their
gait like an estrich, and take huge strides.
I cannot endure such a sight. I love measure
i' the feet, and number i' the voice: they [60
are gentlenesses, that oft-times draw no less
than the face.

*Daup.* How cam'st thou to study these
creatures so exactly? I would thou wouldst
make me a proficient.                          65

*True.* Yes, but you must leave to live i'
your chamber, then, a month together upon
*Amadis de Gaul,* or *Don Quixote,* as you are
wont; and come abroad where the matter is
frequent, to court, to tiltings, public shows [70
and feasts, to plays, and church sometimes:
thither they come to show their new tires too,
to see, and to be seen. In these places a man
shall find whom to love, whom to play with, [75
whom to touch once, whom to hold ever. The
variety arrests his judgment. A wench to
please a man comes not down dropping from
the ceiling, as he lies on his back droning a
tobacco-pipe. He must go where she is.     80

*Daup.* Yes, and be never the near.

*True.* Out, heretic! That diffidence makes
thee worthy it should be so.

*Cler.* He says true to you, Dauphine.

*Daup.* Why?                                   85

*True.* A man should not doubt to overcome
any woman. Think he can vanquish 'em, and
he shall: for though they deny, their desire is
to be tempted. Penelope herself cannot hold
out long. Ostend, you saw, was taken at [90
last. You must perséver, and hold to your
purpose. They would solicit us, but that they
are afraid. Howsoever, they wish in their
hearts we should solicit them. Praise 'em,
flatter 'em, you shall never want eloquence [95
or trust: even the chastest delight to feel themselves that way rubb'd. With praises you must
mix kisses too. If they take them, they 'll take
more — though they strive, they would be overcome.                                          100

*Cler.* O, but a man must beware of force.

*True.* It is to them an acceptable violence,
and has oft-times the place of the greatest
courtesy. She that might have been forc'd,
and you let her go free without touching, [105
though she then seem to thank you, will ever
hate you after; and glad i' the face, is assuredly
sad at the heart.

*Cler.* But all women are not to be taken all
ways.                                          110

*True.* 'T is true; no more than all birds,
or all fishes. If you appear learned to an
ignorant wench, or jocund to a sad, or witty
to a foolish, why she presently begins to mistrust herself. You must approach them i' [115
their own height, their own line; for the contrary makes many, that fear to commit themselves to noble and worthy fellows, run into
the embraces of a rascal. If she love wit, give
verses, though you borrow 'em of a friend, [120
or buy 'em to have good. If valour, talk of
your sword, and be frequent in the mention
of quarrels, though you be staunch in fighting.
If activity, be seen o' your barbary often, or
leaping over stools, for the credit of your [125
back. If she love good clothes or dressing,
have your learned council about you every
morning, your French tailor, barber, linener,
&c. Let your powder, your glass, and your
comb be your dearest acquaintance. Take [130
more care for the ornament of your head, than
the safety; and wish the commonwealth rather
troubled, than a hair about you. That will
take her. Then, if she be covetous and craving,
do you promise anything, and perform [135
sparingly; so shall you keep her in appetite
still. Seem as you would give, but be like a
barren field, that yields little; or unlucky dice
to foolish and hoping gamesters. Let your
gifts be slight and dainty, rather than pre- [140
cious. Let cunning be above cost. Give
cherries at time of year, or apricots; and say,
they were sent you out o' the country, though
you bought 'em in Cheapside. Admire her
tires: like her in all fashions; compare her [145
in every habit to some deity; invent excellent
dreams to flatter her, and riddles; or, if she be
a great one, perform always the second parts
to her: like what she likes, praise whom she
praises, and fail not to make the household [150
and servants yours, yea the whole family, and
salute 'em by their names, ('t is but light cost,
if you can purchase 'em so,) and make her
physician your pensioner, and her chief woman.
Nor will it be out of your gain to make love [155
to her too, so she follow, not usher her lady's
pleasure. All blabbing is taken away, when
she comes to be a part of the crime.

*Daup.* On what courtly lap hast thou late
slept, to come forth so sudden and absolute [160
a courtling?

---

⁵⁸ **estrich:** ostrich     ⁵⁹ **measure:** moderation     ⁶⁰ **number:** rhythm     ⁶¹ **draw:** attract
⁶⁸ **Amadis de Gaul:** a popular romance which originated in Spain     ⁶⁹ **matter:** material for study
⁷⁹ **droning:** smoking     ⁸¹ **near:** nearer (comparative of 'nigh')     ⁹⁰⁻⁹¹ **Ostend . . . last:** (by
Spinola in 1604, after a siege of more than three years)     ¹⁰⁹⁻¹¹⁰ **all ways:** ('alwaies' F)
¹²³ **staunch:** reserved, niggardly     ¹²⁴ **barbary:** Barbary horse     ¹⁴⁶ **habit:** dress     ¹⁶¹ **courtling:**
courtier

*True.* Good faith, I should rather question you. that are so heark'ning after these mysteries. I begin to suspect your diligence, Dauphine. Speak, art thou in love in earnest? 165
*Daup.* Yes, by my troth, am I; 't were ill dissembling before thee.
*True.* With which of 'em, I pray thee?
*Daup.* With all the collegiates.
*Cler.* Out on thee! We 'll keep you at [170 home, believe it, i' the stable, and you be such a stallion.
*True.* No; I like him well. Men should love wisely, and all women; some one for the face, and let her please the eye; another [175 for the skin, and let her please the touch; a third for the voice, and let her please the ear; and where the objects mix, let the senses so too. Thou would'st think it strange, if I should make 'em all in love with thee afore night! [180
*Daup.* I would say, thou hadst the best philtre i' the world, and couldst do more than madam Medea, or doctor Foreman.
*True.* If I do not, let me play the mountebank for my meat, while I live, and the [185 bawd for my drink.
*Daup.* So be it, I say.

## Act IIII.  Scene II

*Otter, Clerimont, Daw, Dauphine, Morose, Truewit, La-Foole, Mrs. Otter*

[*Ott.*] O lord, gentlemen, how my knights and I have miss'd you here!
*Cler.* Why, captain, what service, what service?
*Ott.* To see me bring up my bull, bear, [5 and horse to fight.
*Daw.* Yes, faith, the captain says we shall be his dogs to bait 'em.
*Daup.* A good employment.
*True.* Come on, let 's see a course, then. [10
*La-F.* I am afraid my cousin will be offended, if she come.
*Ott.* Be afraid of nothing. — Gentlemen, I have plac'd the drum and the trumpets, and one to give 'em the sign when you are ready. [15 Here 's my bull for myself, and my bear for Sir John Daw, and my horse for Sir Amorous. Now set your foot to mine, and yours to his, and —
*La-F.* Pray God my cousin come not. 20
*Ott.* St. George, and St. Andrew, fear no cousins. Come, sound, sound! [*Drum and*

*trumpets sound.*] *Et rauco strepuerunt cornua cantu.*                    [*They drink.*]
*True.* Well said, captain, i' faith; well [25 fought at the bull.
*Cler.* Well held at the bear.
*True.* Low, low! captain.
*Daup.* O, the horse has kick'd off his dog already. 30
*La-F.* I cannot drink it, as I am a knight.
*True.* Gods so! off with his spurs, somebody.
*La-F.* It goes again my conscience. My cousin will be angry with it. 35
*Daw.* I ha' done mine.
*True.* You fought high and fair, Sir John.
*Cler.* At the head.
*Daup.* Like an excellent bear-dog.
*Cler.* You take no notice of the business, [40 I hope?
*Daw.* Not a word, sir; you see we are jovial.
*Ott.* Sir Amorous, you must not equivocate. It must be pull'd down for all my cousin.
*Cler.* 'Sfoot, if you take not your drink, [45 they 'll think you are discontented with something; you 'll betray all, if you take the least notice.
*La-F.* Not I; I 'll both drink and talk then.
*Ott.* You must pull the horse on his knees, [50 Sir Amorous; fear no cousins. *Jacta est alea.*
*True.* O, now he 's in his vein, and bold. The least hint given him of his wife now, will make him rail desperately.
*Cler.* Speak to him of her. 55
*True.* Do you, and I 'll fetch her to the hearing of it.                    [*Exit.*]
*Daup.* Captain He-Otter, your She-Otter is coming, your wife.
*Ott.* Wife! buz? *titivilitium!* There 's no [60 such thing in nature. I confess, gentlemen, I have a cook, a laundress, a house-drudge, that serves my necessary turns, and goes under that title; but he 's an ass that will be so uxorious to tie his affections to one circle. [65 Come, the name dulls appetite. Here, replenish again; another bout. [*Fills the cups again.*] Wives are nasty, sluttish animals.
*Daup.* O, captain.
*Ott.* As ever the earth bare, *tribus verbis.* [70 — Where 's master Truewit?
*Daw.* He 's slipp'd aside, sir.
*Cler.* But you must drink and be jovial.
*Daw.* Yes, give it me.
*La-F.* And me too. 75
*Daw.* Let 's be jovial.

163 **heark'ning:** eager    182 **philtre:** love-potion    183 **Foreman:** Dr. Simon Forman (1552–1611), a famous London quack, medium, and conjurer    10 **course:** encounter at bear-baiting    23–24 **Et . . . cantu:** And the trumpets resounded with a hoarse noise.    32 **spurs:** symbols of knighthood    51 **Jacta est alea:** The die is cast.    60 **titivilitium:** "good for nothing" (Titivillus was a common name for the Devil in morality plays.)    70 **tribus verbis:** in three words

*La-F.*  As jovial as you will.

*Ott.*  Agreed. Now you shall ha' the bear, cousin, and Sir John Daw the horse, and I 'll ha' the bull still. Sound, Tritons o' the [80 Thames! [*Drum and trumpets sound again.*] *Nunc est bibendum, nunc pede libero —*

*Mor.*  Villains, murderers, sons of the earth, and traitors, what do you there?

*Morose speaks from above: the trumpets sounding.*

*Cler.*  O, now the trumpets have wak'd [85 him, we shall have his company.

*Ott.*  A wife is a scurvy clogdogdo, an unlucky thing, a very foresaid bear-whelp, without any good fashion or breeding, *mala bestia.*

*His wife is brought out to hear him.*

*Daup.*  Why did you marry one then, [90 captain?

*Ott.*  A pox! — I married with six thousand pound, I. I was in love with that. I ha' not kissed my Fury these forty weeks.

*Cler.*  The more to blame you, captain.  95

*True.*  Nay, mistress Otter, hear him a little first.

*Ott.*  She has a breath worse than my grandmother's, *profecto.*

*Mrs. Ott.*  O treacherous liar! Kiss me, [100 sweet master Truewit, and prove him a slandering knave.

*True.*  I 'll rather believe you, lady.

*Ott.*  And she has a peruke that 's like a pound of hemp, made up in shoe-threads.  105

*Mrs. Ott.*  O viper, mandrake!

*Ott.*  O most vile face! and yet she spends me forty pound a year in mercury and hogs-bones. All her teeth were made i' the Blackfriars, both her eyebrows i' the Strand, and her hair in [110 Silverstreet. Every part o' the town owns a piece of her.

*Mrs. Ott.* [*Comes forward.*] I cannot hold.

*Ott.*  She takes herself asunder still when she goes to bed, into some twenty boxes; and [115 about next day noon is put together again, like a great German clock: and so comes forth, and rings a tedious larum to the whole house, and then is quiet again for an hour, but for her quarters — Ha' you done me right, gentle- [120 men?

*Mrs. Ott.*  No, sir, I 'll do you right with my quarters, with my quarters.

*She falls upon him and beats him.*

*Ott.*  O, hold, good princess.

*True.*  Sound, sound!                         125

[*Drum and trumpets sound.*]

*Cler.*  A battle, a battle!

*Mrs. Ott.*  You notorious stinkardly bearward, does my breath smell?

*Ott.*  Under correction, dear princess. — Look to my bear and my horse, gentlemen. [130

*Mrs. Ott.*  Do I want teeth, and eyebrows, thou bull-dog?

*True.*  Sound, sound still.

[*They sound again.*]

*Ott.*  No, I protest, under correction —

*Mrs. Ott.*  Ay, now you are under cor- [135 rection, you protest: but you did not protest before correction, sir. Thou Judas, to offer to betray thy princess! I 'll make thee an example —                                  [*Beats him.*]

*Morose descends with a long sword.*

*Mor.*  I will have no such examples in my [140 house, lady Otter.

*Mrs. Ott.*  Ah! —

[*Mrs. Otter, Daw, and La-Foole, run off.*]

*Mor.*  Mistress Mary Ambree, your examples are dangerous. — Rogues, hell-hounds, Stentors! out of my doors, you sons of noise [145 and tumult, begot on an ill May-day, or when the galley-foist is afloat to Westminster! [*Drives out the musicians.*] A trumpeter could not be conceiv'd but then.

*Daup.*  What ails you, sir?                   150

*Mor.*  They have rent my roof, walls, and all my windores asunder, with their brazen throats.                                       [*Exit.*]

*True.*  Best follow him, Dauphine.

*Daup.*  So I will.                [*Exit.*]  155

*Cler.*  Where 's Daw and La-Foole?

*Ott.*  They are both run away, sir. Good gentlemen, help to pacify my princess, and speak to the great ladies for me. Now must I go lie with the bears this fortnight, and [160 keep out o' the way, till my peace be made, for this scandal she has taken. Did you not see my bull-head, gentlemen?

*Cler.*  Is 't not on, captain?

*True.*  No; but he may make a new one, [165 by that is on.

*Ott.*  O, here 'tis. And you come over, gentlemen, and ask for Tom Otter, we 'll go down to Ratcliff, and have a course i' faith, for all these disasters. There 's *bona spes* left. [170

---

⁸²  **Nunc . . . libero:** Now one must drink, now with free foot — (Horace, Ode I. 37)      ⁸⁷  **clogdogdo:** clog suitable for a dog      ⁸⁹  **mala bestia:** evil beast      ⁹⁹  **profecto:** truly      ¹⁰⁸  **mercury, hogsbones:** ingredients used in cosmetics      ¹¹⁸  **larum:** alarm      ¹²⁰  **done me right:** drunk with me      ¹⁴³  **Mary Ambree:** a female soldier at the siege of Ghent in 1584; subject of a ballad      ¹⁴⁶  **ill May-day:** day of the great riot in 1517 (hence proverbial)      ¹⁴⁷  **galley-foist:** state barge used when a new Lord Mayor took office      ¹⁶²  **scandal:** offence      ¹⁶⁷  **And:** an, if      ¹⁶⁹  **Ratcliff:** a suburb east of London, on the Thames      ¹⁷⁰  **bona spes:** good hope

*True.* Away, captain, get off while you are well.                              [*Exit Otter.*]

*Cler.* I am glad we are rid of him.

*True.* You had never been, unless we had put his wife upon him. His humour is as [175 tedious at last, as it was ridiculous at first.

                                   [*Exeunt.*]

## Act IIII.  Scene III

### [*A Gallery in the same*]

*Haughty, Mrs. Otter, Mavis, Daw, La-Foole, Centaure, Epicœne, Truewit, Clerimont*

[*Hau.*] We wonder'd why you shriek'd so, mistress Otter.

*Mrs. Ott.* O God, madam, he came down with a huge long naked weapon in both his hands, and look'd so dreadfully! Sure he 's [5 beside himself.

*Mav.* Why, what made you there, mistress Otter?

*Mrs. Ott.* Alas, mistress Mavis, I was chastising my subject, and thought nothing of [10 him.

*Daw.* Faith, mistress, you must do so too: learn to chastise. Mistress Otter corrects her husband so, he dares not speak but under correction.                              15

*La-F.* And with his hat off to her: 't would do you good to see.

*Hau.* In sadness, 't is good and mature counsel; practise it, Morose. I 'll call you Morose still now, as I call Centaure and [20 Mavis; we four will be all one.

*Cen.* And you 'll come to the college, and live with us?

*Hau.* Make him give milk and honey.

*Mav.* Look how you manage him at first, [25 you shall have him ever after.

*Cen.* Let him allow you your coach, and four horses, your woman, your chamber-maid, your page, your gentleman-usher, your French cook, and four grooms.                       30

*Hau.* And go with us to Bedlam, to the china-houses, and to the Exchange.

*Cen.* It will open the gate to your fame.

*Hau.* Here 's Centaure has immortaliz'd herself, with taming her wild male.          35

*Mav.* Ay, she has done the miracle of the kingdom.

*Epi.* But, ladies, do you count it lawful to have such plurality of servants, and do 'em all graces?                                40

*Hau.* Why not? why should women deny their favours to men? are they the poorer or the worse?

*Daw.* Is the Thames the less for the dyers' water, mistress?                         45

*La-F.* Or a torch for lighting many torches?

*True.* Well said, La-Foole; what a new one he has got!

*Cen.* They are empty losses women fear in this kind.                               50

*Hau.* Besides, ladies should be mindful of the approach of age, and let no time want his due use. The best of our days pass first.

*Mav.* We are rivers, that cannot be call'd back, madam: she that now excludes her [55 lovers, may live to lie a forsaken beldame, in a frozen bed.

*Cen.* 'T is true, Mavis: and who will wait on us to coach then? or write, or tell us the news then? make anagrams of our names, and [60 invite us to the Cockpit, and kiss our hands all the play-time, and draw their weapons for our honours?

*Hau.* Not one.

*Daw.* Nay, my mistress is not altogether [65 unintelligent of these things; here be in presence have tasted of her favours.

*Cler.* What a neighing hobby-horse is this!

*Epi.* But not with intent to boast 'em again, servant. — And have you those ex- [70 cellent receipts, madam, to keep yourselves from bearing of children?

*Hau.* O yes, Morose: how should we maintain our youth and beauty else? Many births of a woman make her old, as many crops [75 make the earth barren.

## Act IIII.  Scene IIII

*Morose, Dauphine, Truewit, Epicœne, Clerimont, Daw, Haughty, La-Foole, Centaure, Mavis, Mrs. Otter, [later] Trusty*

[*Mor.*] O my cursed angel, that instructed me to this fate!

*Daup.* Why, sir?

*Mor.* That I should be seduc'd by so foolish a devil as a barber will make!          5

*Daup.* I would I had been worthy, sir, to have partaken your counsel; you should never have trusted it to such a minister.

*Mor.* Would I could redeem it with the loss of an eye, nephew, a hand, or any other member.                                 11

*Daup.* Marry, God forbid, sir, that you should geld yourself, to anger your wife.

*Mor.* So it would rid me of her! — and, that

---

⁷ **made:** did    ¹⁸ **sadness:** seriousness    ³¹ **Bedlam:** Bethlehem Hospital, for the insane
⁵¹ **Cockpit:** the small court theatre at Whitehall known as the Cockpit-in-Court    ⁶⁶ **unintelligent:**
**unaware**    ⁶⁸ **hobby-horse:** fool

I did supererogatory penance in a belfry, at Westminster-hall, i' the Cockpit, at the fall [15 of a stag, the Tower-wharf — what place is there else? — London-bridge, Paris-garden, Billingsgate, when the noises are at their height and loudest. Nay, I would sit out a play, that were nothing but fights at sea, drum, trum- [20 pet, and target.

*Daup.* I hope there shall be no such need, sir. Take patience, good uncle. This is but a day, and 't is well worn too now.

*Mor.* O, 't will be so for ever, nephew, I [25 foresee it, for ever. Strife and tumult are the dowry that comes with a wife.

*True.* I told you so, sir, and you would not believe me.

*Mor.* Alas, do not rub those wounds, [30 master Truewit, to blood again: 't was my negligence. Add not affliction to affliction. I have perceiv'd the effect of it, too late, in madam Otter.

*Epi.* How do you, sir?                          35

*Mor.* Did you ever hear a more unnecessary question? as if she did not see! Why, I do as you see, empress, empress.

*Epi.* You are not well, sir; you look very ill: something has distemper'd you.        40

*Mor.* O horrible, monstrous impertinencies! Would not one of these have serv'd, do you think, sir? would not one of these have serv'd?

*True.* Yes, sir; but these are but notes of female kindness, sir; certain tokens that [45 she has a voice, sir.

*Mor.* O, is 't so! Come, and 't be no otherwise —— What say you?

*Epi.* How do you feel yourself, sir?

*Mor.* Again that!                          50

*True.* Nay, look you, sir, you would be friends with your wife upon unconscionable terms; her silence.

*Epi.* They say you are run mad, sir.

*Mor.* Not for love, I assure you, of you; [55 do you see?

*Epi.* O lord, gentlemen! lay hold on him, for God's sake. What shall I do? Who 's his physician, can you tell, that knows the state of his body best, that I might send for him? [60 Good sir, speak; I 'll send for one of my doctors else.

*Mor.* What, to poison me, that I might die intestate, and leave you possess'd of all!

*Epi.* Lord, how idly he talks, and how [65 his eyes sparkle! He looks green about the temples! do you see what blue spots he has!

*Cler.* Ay, it 's melancholy.

*Epi.* Gentlemen, for Heaven's sake, counsel me. Ladies! — Servant, you have read Pliny [70 and Paracelsus; ne'er a word now to comfort a poor gentlewoman? Ay me, what fortune had I, to marry a distracted man!

*Daw.* I 'll tell you, mistress —

*True.* How rarely she holds it up!        75
                          [*Aside to Cler.*]

*Mor.* What mean you, gentlemen?

*Epi.* What will you tell me, servant?

*Daw.* The disease in Greek is called μανία, in Latin *insania, furor, vel ecstasis melancholica,* that is, *egressio,* when a man *ex melancholico* [80 *evadit fanaticus.*

*Mor.* Shall I have a lecture read upon me alive?

*Daw.* But he may be but *phreneticus* yet, mistress; and *phrenetis* is only *delirium,* [85 or so.

*Epi.* Ay, that is for the disease, servant; but what is this to the cure? We are sure enough of the disease.

*Mor.* Let me go.                          90

*True.* Why, we 'll entreat her to hold her peace, sir.

*Mor.* O no, labour not to stop her. She is like a conduit-pipe, that will gush out with more force when she opens again.        95

*Hau.* I 'll tell you, Morose, you must talk divinity to him altogether, or moral philosophy.

*La-F.* Ay, and there 's an excellent book of moral philosophy, madam, of Reynard the Fox, and all the beasts, call'd *Doni's Phi-* [100 *losophy.*

*Cen.* There is indeed, Sir Amorous La-Foole.

*Mor.* O misery!

*La-F.* I have read it, my lady Centaure, all over, to my cousin here.                          105

*Mrs. Ott.* Ay, and 't is a very good book as any is, of the moderns.

*Daw.* Tut, he must have Seneca read to him, and Plutarch, and the ancients; the moderns are not for this disease.        110

*Cler.* Why, you discommended them too, to-day, Sir John.

*Daw.* Ay, in some cases: but in these they are best, and Aristotle's *Ethics.*

*Mav.* Say you so, Sir John? I think [115 you are deceiv'd; you took it upon trust.

*Hau.* Where 's Trusty, my woman? I 'll end this difference. I prithee, Otter, call her. Her father and mother were both mad, when they put her to me.                          120

---

<sup>21</sup> **target:** shield    <sup>40</sup> **distemper'd:** upset    <sup>70</sup> **Pliny:** (mentioned here because of his studies in natural history)    <sup>71</sup> **Paracelsus:** physician and lecturer on medicine (1493–1541)    <sup>80–81</sup> **ex . . . fanaticus:** A melancholy man ends as a madman.    <sup>82</sup> **lecture:** *i.e.,* an anatomical lecture    <sup>84</sup> **phreneticus:** insane    <sup>100–101</sup> **Doni's Philosophy:** Doni's Italian version of the Fables of Bidpai, translated by Sir Thomas North in 1570 (here confused with the ancient story of Reynard the Fox)    <sup>120</sup> **to me:** in my service

*Mor.* I think so. — Nay, gentlemen, I am tame. This is but an exercise, I know, a marriage ceremony, which I must endure.

*Hau.* And one of 'em, I know not which, was cur'd with the Sick Man's Salve, and [125 the other with Greene's Groat's-worth of Wit.

*True.* A very cheap cure, madam.

[*Enter Trusty*]

*Hau.* Ay, it 's very feasible.

*Mrs. Ott.* My lady call'd for you, mistress Trusty: you must decide a controversy.   130

*Hau.* O, Trusty, which was it you said, your father, or your mother, that was cur'd with the Sick Man's Salve?

*Trus.* My mother, madam, with the Salve.

*True.* Then it was the sick woman's [135 salve?

*Trus.* And my father with the Groat's-worth of Wit. But there was other means us'd: we had a preacher that would preach folk asleep still; and so they were prescrib'd [140 to go to church, by an old woman that was their physician, thrice a week —

*Epi.* To sleep?

*Trus.* Yes, forsooth: and every night they read themselves asleep on those books.   145

*Epi.* Good faith, it stands with great reason. I would I knew where to procure those books.

*Mor.* Oh!

*La-F.* I can help you with one of 'em, [150 mistress Morose, the Groat's-worth of Wit.

*Epi.* But I shall disfurnish you, Sir Amorous: can you spare it?

*La-F.* O yes, for a week, or so; I 'll read it myself to him.   155

*Epi.* No, I must do that, sir; that must be my office.

*Mor.* Oh, oh!

*Epi.* Sure he would do well enough, if he could sleep.   160

*Mor.* No, I should do well enough, if you could sleep. Have I no friend that will make her drunk, or give her a little laudanum, or opium?

*True.* Why, sir, she talks ten times worse [165 in her sleep.

*Mor.* How!

*Cler.* Do you not know that, sir? never ceases all night.

*True.* And snores like a porcpisce.   170

*Mor.* O redeem me, fate; redeem me, fate! For how many causes may a man be divorc'd, nephew?

*Daup.* I know not, truly, sir.

*True.* Some divine must resolve you in [175 that, sir, or canon-lawyer.

*Mor.* I will not rest, I will not think of any other hope or comfort, till I know.
         [*Exit with Dauphine.*]

*Cler.* Alas, poor man!

*True.* You 'll make him mad indeed, [180 ladies, if you pursue this.

*Hau.* No, we 'll let him breathe now, a quarter of an hour or so.

*Cler.* By my faith, a large truce!

*Hau.* Is that his keeper, that is gone [185 with him?

*Daw.* It is his nephew, madam.

*La-F.* Sir Dauphine Eugenie.

*Cen.* He looks like a very pitiful knight —

*Daw.* As can be. This marriage has put [190 him out of all.

*La-F.* He has not a penny in his purse, madam.

*Daw.* He is ready to cry all this day.

*La-F.* A very shark; he set me i' the [195 nick t' other night at primero.

*True.* How these swabbers talk!

*Cler.* Ay, Otter's wine has swell'd their humours above a springtide.

*Hau.* Good Morose, let 's go in again. [200 I like your couches exceeding well; we 'll go lie and talk there. [*Exeunt Hau., Cen., Mav.,                 Trus., La-Foole, and Daw.*]

*Epi.* [*Following them.*] I wait on you, madam.

*True.* [*Stopping her.*] 'Slight, I will have 'em as silent as signs, and their posts too, ere I [205 ha' done. Do you hear, lady-bride? I pray thee now, as thou art a noble wench, continue this discourse of Dauphine within; but praise him exceedingly: magnify him with all the height of affection thou canst; — I have [210 some purpose in 't: and but beat off these two rooks, Jack Daw and his fellow, with any discontentment hither, and I 'll honour thee for ever.

*Epi.* I was about it here. It angered [215 me to the soul, to hear 'em begin to talk so malapert.

*True.* Pray thee perform it, and thou winn'st me an idolater to thee everlasting.

*Epi.* Will you go in and hear me do it? 220

*True.* No, I 'll stay here. Drive 'em out of your company, 'tis all I ask; which cannot be any way better done, than by extolling Dauphine, whom they have so slighted.   224

*Epi.* I warrant you; you shall expect one of 'em presently.          [*Exit.*]

---

[125] **Sick Man's Salve**: a tract by the Rev. Thomas Becon, published in 1561    [126] **Groat's-worth of Wit**: by Robert Greene, published in 1592    [152] **disfurnish**: deprive    [170] **porcpisce**: porpoise [195] **shark**: card-sharper   [195–196] **set . . . nick**: defeated me   [196] **primero**: a card game   [197] **swabbers**: base fellows   [199] **humours**: eccentricities   [213] **discontentment**: vexation   [217] **malapert**: rudely

*Cler.* What a cast of kastrils are these, to hawk after ladies, thus!

*True.* Ay, and strike at such an eagle as [229 Dauphine.

*Cler.* He will be mad when we tell him. Here he comes.

## Act IIII. Scene V

### Clerimont, Truewit, Dauphine,
#### [later] Daw, La-Foole

[*Cler to Daup.*] O sir, you are welcome.

*True.* Where 's thine uncle?

*Daup.* Run out o' doors in his night-caps, to talk with a casuist about his divorce. It works admirably. 5

*True.* Thou wouldst ha' said so, and thou hadst been here! The ladies have laugh'd at thee most comically, since thou went'st, Dauphine.

*Cler.* And ask'd, if thou wert thine uncle's [10 keeper.

*True.* And the brace of baboons answer'd, "Yes;" and said thou wert a pitiful poor fellow, and didst live upon posts, and hadst nothing but three suits of apparel, and some [15 few benevolences that the lords ga' thee to fool to 'em, and swagger.

*Daup.* Let me not live, I 'll beat 'em: I 'll bind 'em both to grand-madam's bed-posts, and have 'em baited with monkeys. 20

*True.* Thou shalt not need, they shall be beaten to thy hand, Dauphine. I have an execution to serve upon 'em, I warrant thee, shall serve; trust my plot.

*Daup.* Ay, you have many plots! so you [25 had one to make all the wenches in love with me.

*True.* Why, if I do not yet afore night, as near as 't is, and that they do not every one invite thee, and be ready to scratch for [30 thee, take the mortgage of my wit.

*Cler.* 'Fore God, I 'll be his witness thou shalt have it, Dauphine: thou [*to True.*] shalt be his fool for ever, if thou dost not.

*True.* Agreed. Perhaps 't will be the [35 better estate. Do you observe this gallery, or rather lobby, indeed? Here are a couple of studies, at each end one: here will I act such a tragi-comedy between the Guelphs and the Ghibellines, Daw and La-Foole — which [40

of 'em comes out first, will I seize on; — you two shall be the chorus behind the arras, and whip out between the acts and speak. — If I do not make 'em keep the peace for this remnant of the day, if not of the year, I have [45 fail'd once. —— I hear Daw coming: hide, [*they withdraw*] and do not laugh, for God's sake.

#### [*Enter Daw*]

*Daw.* Which is the way into the garden, trow? 50

*True.* O, Jack Daw! I am glad I have met with you. In good faith, I must have this matter go no furder between you: I must ha' it taken up.

*Daw.* What matter, sir? between whom? [55

*True.* Come, you disguise it: Sir Amorous and you. If you love me, Jack, you shall make use of your philosophy now, for this once, and deliver me your sword. This is not the wedding the Centaurs were at, though there be a she [60 one here. [*Takes his sword.*] The bride has entreated me I will see no blood shed at her bridal: you saw her whisper me erewhile.

*Daw.* As I hope to finish Tacitus, I intend no murder. 65

*True.* Do you not wait for Sir Amorous?

*Daw.* Not I, by my knighthood.

*True.* And your scholarship too?

*Daw.* And my scholarship too.

*True.* Go to, then I return you your [70 sword, and ask you mercy; but put it not up, for you will be assaulted. I understood that you had apprehended it, and walk'd here to brave him; and that you had held your life contemptible, in regard of your honour. 75

*Daw.* No, no; no such thing, I assure you. He and I parted now, as good friends as could be.

*True.* Trust not you to that vizor. I saw him since dinner with another face. I have [80 known many men in my time vex'd with losses, with deaths, and with abuses; but so offended a wight as Sir Amorous did I never see or read of. For taking away his guests, sir, to-day, that 's the cause; and he declares it behind [85 your back with such threatenings and contempts. He said to Dauphine, you were the arrant'st ass —

*Daw.* Ay, he may say his pleasure.

*True.* And swears you are so protested [90

[227] **cast:** couple   **kastrils:** degenerate hawks   [4] **casuist:** theologian   [14] **posts:** sheriff's posts upon which public notices were displayed   (Pun on the term 'knight of the post,' professional false witness)   [23] **execution:** legal writ or warrant   [39-40] **Guelphs, Ghibellines:** the rival parties in Italy during the Middle Ages   [42] **arras:** tapestry wall-hanging   [54] **taken up:** stopped   [56] **disguise:** i.e., pretend not to know   [59-60] **wedding . . . at:** that of Hippodamia and Pirithous   [71] **ask you mercy:** beg your pardon   [74] **brave:** defy   [75] **in . . . of:** in comparison with   [79] **vizor:** pretense, mask   [86-87] **contempts:** expressions of contempt   [88] **arrant'st:** ('errandst' F)   [90] **protested:** notorious

a coward, that he knows you will never do him any manly or single right; and therefore he will take his course.

*Daw.* I 'll give him any satisfaction, sir — but fighting.                                                     95

*True.* Ay, sir: but who knows what satisfaction he 'll take? Blood he thirsts for, and blood he will have; and whereabouts on you he will have it, who knows but himself?

*Daw.* I pray you, master Truewit, be [100 you a mediator.

*True.* Well, sir, conceal yourself then in this study till I return. (*He puts him up.*) Nay, you must be content to be lock'd in; for, for mine own reputation, I would not have you [105 seen to receive a public disgrace, while I have the matter in managing. Gods so, here he comes; keep your breath close, that he do not hear you sigh. — In good faith, Sir Amorous, he is not this way; I pray you be merciful, [110 do not murder him; he is a Christian, as good as you: you are arm'd as if you sought a revenge on all his race. Good Dauphine, get him away from this place. I never knew a man's choler so high, but he would speak to his friends, [115 he would hear reason. — Jack Daw, Jack Daw! asleep?

*Daw.* [*Within.*] Is he gone, master Truewit?

*True.* Ay; did you hear him?

*Daw.* O God! yes.                                          120

*True.* What a quick ear fear has!

*Daw.* [*Comes out of the closet.*] But is he so arm'd, as you say?

*True.* Arm'd! did you ever see a fellow set out to take possession?                                         125

*Daw.* Ay, sir.

*True.* That may give you some light to conceive of him; but 't is nothing to the principal. Some false brother i' the house has furnish'd him strangely; or, if it were out [130 o' the house, it was Tom Otter.

*Daw.* Indeed he 's a captain, and his wife is his kinswoman.

*True.* He has got some body's old two-hand sword, to mow you off at the knees; and [135 that sword hath spawn'd such a dagger! — But then he is so hung with pikes, halberds, petronels, calivers and muskets, that he looks like a justice of peace's hall; a man of two thousand a year is not cess'd at so many [140 weapons as he has on. There was never fencer challeng'd at so many several foils. You would think he meant to murder all St. Pulchre's parish. If he could but victual himself

for half a-year in his breeches, he is suf- [145 ficiently arm'd to over-run a country.

*Daw.* Good lord! what means he, sir? I pray you, master Truewit, be you a mediator.

*True.* Well, I 'll try if he will be appeas'd with a leg or an arm; if not, you must die [150 once.

*Daw.* I would be loath to lose my right arm, for writing madrigals.

*True.* Why, if he will be satisfied with a thumb or a little finger, all 's one to me. [155 You must think, I 'll do my best.

*Daw.* Good sir, do.

*He puts him up again and then comes forth.*

*Cler.* What hast thou done?

*True.* He will let me do nothing, man; he does all afore me; he offers his left arm.      160

*Cler.* His left wing for a Jack Daw.

*Daup.* Take it by all means.

*True.* How! maim a man for ever, for a jest? What a conscience hast thou!

*Daup.* 'T is no loss to him; he has no [165 employment for his arms, but to eat spoon-meat. Beside, as good maim his body as his reputation.

*True.* He is a scholar and a wit, and yet he does not think so. But he loses no repu- [170 tation with us; for we all resolv'd him an ass before. To your places again.

*Cler.* I pray thee, let me be in at the other a little.

*True.* Look, you 'll spoil all; these be [175 ever your tricks.

*Cler.* No, but I could hit of some things that thou wilt miss, and thou wilt say are good ones.

*True.* I warrant you. I pray forbear, [180 I 'll leave it off, else.

*Daup.* Come away, Clerimont.

[*Daup. and Cler. withdraw as before. Enter La-Foole.*]

*True.* Sir Amorous!

*La-F.* Master Truewit.

*True.* Whither were you going?                          185

*La-F.* Down into the court to make water.

*True.* By no means, sir; you shall rather tempt your breeches.

*La-F.* Why, sir?

*True.* Enter here, if you love your life. [190 [*Opening the door of the other study.*]

*La-F.* Why? why?

*True.* Question till your throat be cut, do: dally till the enraged soul find you.

---

114 **choler:** anger      125 **possession:** (of an estate which must be taken by force)      129 **principal:** original, *i.e.*, Sir Amorous      138 **petronels:** horse-pistols      **calivers:** light muskets      140 **cess'd:** assessed      142 **foils:** weapons      143–144 **St. Pulchre's:** St. Sepulchre's, in the outskirts of London      145 **breeches:** (which were very large and stuffed)      151 **once:** one time or another      171 **resolv'd him:** determined him to be      177 **of:** on

*La-F.* Who 's that?

*True.* Daw it is: will you in?                      195

*La-F.* Ay, ay, I 'll in: what 's the matter?

*True.* Nay, if he had been cool enough to tell us that, there had been some hope to atone you; but he seems so implacably enrag'd!

*La-F.* 'Slight, let him rage! I 'll hide [200 myself.

*True.* Do, good sir. But what have you done to him within, that should provoke him thus? You have broke some jest upon him afore the ladies.                              205

*La-F.* Not I, never in my life, broke jest upon any man. The bride was praising Sir Dauphine, and he went away in snuff, and I followed him; unless he took offence at me in his drink erewhile, that I would not [210 pledge all the horse full.

*True.* By my faith, and that may be; you remember well: but he walks the round up and down, through every room o' the house, with a towel in his hand, crying "Where 's [215 La-Foole? Who saw La-Foole?" And when Dauphine and I demanded the cause, we can force no answer from him, but — "O revenge, how sweet art thou! I will strangle him in this towel" — which leads us to conjecture that [220 the main cause of his fury is, for bringing your meat to-day, with a towel about you, to his discredit.

*La-F.* Like enough. Why, and he be angry for that, I 'll stay here till his anger be [225 blown over.

*True.* A good becoming resolution, sir; if you can put it on o' the sudden.

*La-F.* Yes, I can put it on: or, I 'll away into the country presently.                    230

*True.* How will you get out o' the house, sir? He knows you are i' the house, and he 'll watch you this se'ennight, but he 'll have you: he 'll outwait a sergeant for you.

*La-F.* Why, then I 'll stay here.           235

*True.* You must think how to victual yourself in time then.

*La-F.* Why, sweet master Truewit, will you entreat my cousin Otter to send me a cold venison pasty, a bottle or two of wine, and [240 a chamber-pot?

*True.* A stool were better, sir, of Sir Ajax his invention.

*La-F.* Ay, that will be better, indeed; and a pallat to lie on.                              245

*True.* O, I would not advise you to sleep by any means.

*La-F.* Would you not, sir? Why, then I will not.

*True.* Yet there 's another fear —        250

*La-F.* Is there, sir! What is 't?

*True.* No, he cannot break open this door with his foot, sure.

*La-F.* I 'll set my back against it, sir. I have a good back.                               255

*True.* But then if he should batter.

*La-F.* Batter! if he dare, I 'll have an action of batt'ry against him.

*True.* Cast you the worst. He has sent for powder already, and what he will do with [260 it, no man knows: perhaps blow up the corner o' the house where he suspects you are. Here he comes; in quickly. *He feigns as if one were present, to fright the other, who is run in to hide himself.* [265 I protest, Sir John Daw, he is not this way: what will you do? Before God, you shall hang no petard here. I 'll die rather. Will you not take my word? I never knew one but would be satisfied. — Sir Amorous, [*speaks through the key-hole,*] there 's no standing [270 out: he has made a petard of an old brass pot, to force your door. Think upon some satisfaction, or terms to offer him.

*La-F.* [*Within.*] Sir, I 'll give him any satisfaction. I dare give any terms.          [275

*True.* You 'll leave it to me then?

*La-F.* Ay, sir: I 'll stand to any conditions.

*True.* How now, what think *He calls forth* you, sirs? Were 't *Clerimont and Dauphine.* not a difficult thing to determine which of these two fear'd most?

*Cler.* Yes, but this fears the bravest: the other a whiniling dastard, Jack Daw! But La-Foole, a brave heroic coward! and is afraid [285 in a great look and a stout accent; I like him rarely.

*True.* Had it not been pity these two should ha' been conceal'd?

*Cler.* Shall I make a motion?            290

*True.* Briefly: for I must strike while 't is hot.

*Cler.* Shall I go fetch the ladies to the catastrophe?

*True.* Umph! ay, by my troth.            295

*Daup.* By no mortal means. Let them continue in the state of ignorance, and err still; think 'em wits and fine fellows, as they have done. 'T were sin to reform them.

*True.* Well, I will have 'em fetch'd, now [300 I think on 't, for a private purpose of mine:

¹⁹⁸ **atone:** set at one   ²⁰⁸ **went . . . snuff:** became angry   ²¹³ **walks the round:** (like a sentinel) ²³⁴ **sergeant:** sheriff's officer   ²⁴² **Sir Ajax:** (Sir John Harington published, in 1596, the *Metamorphosis of Ajax,* a facetious work on the sanitary conditions of the time, punning on the word "jakes," meaning "privy.")   ²⁴⁵ **pallat:** cot   ²⁵⁹ **Cast:** anticipate   ²⁶⁷ **petard:** an early form of bomb ²⁸⁴ **whiniling:** whining   ²⁹⁰ **motion:** proposal

do, Clerimont, fetch 'em, and discourse to 'em all that's past, and bring 'em into the gallery here.

*Daup.* This is thy extreme vanity, now: [305 thou think'st thou wert undone, if every jest thou mak'st were not publish'd.

*True.* Thou shalt see how unjust thou art presently. Clerimont, say it was Dauphine's plot. [*Exit Clerimont.*] Trust me not, if [310 the whole drift be not for thy good. There's a carpet i' the next room, put it on, with this scarf over thy face, and a cushion o' thy head, and be ready when I call Amorous. Away! [*Exit Daup.*] John Daw!          315

[*Goes to Daw's closet and brings him out.*]

*Daw.* What good news, sir?

*True.* Faith, I have followed and argued with him hard for you. I told him you were a knight, and a scholar, and that you knew fortitude did consist *magis patiendo quam* [320 *faciendo, magis ferendo quam feriendo.*

*Daw.* It doth so indeed, sir.

*True.* And that you would suffer, I told him: so at first he demanded by my troth, in my conceit, too much.          325

*Daw.* What was it, sir?

*True.* Your upper lip, and six o' your fore-teeth.

*Daw.* 'T was unreasonable.

*True.* Nay, I told him plainly, you could [330 not spare 'em all. So after long argument *pro et con.* as you know, I brought him down to your two butter-teeth, and them he would have.

*Daw.* O, did you so? Why, he shall have 'em.          335

*True.* But he shall not, sir, by your leave. The conclusion is this, sir: because you shall be very good friends hereafter, and this never to be remembered or upbraided; besides, that he may not boast he has done any [340 such thing in his own person; he is to come here in disguise, give you five kicks in private, sir, take your sword from you, and lock you up in that study during pleasure: which will be but a little while, we'll get it re- [345 leas'd presently.

*Daw.* Five kicks! he shall have six, sir, to be friends.

*True.* Believe me, you shall not over-shoot yourself, to send him that word by me.          350

*Daw.* Deliver it, sir; he shall have it with all my heart, to be friends.

*True.* Friends! Nay, and he should not be

so, and heartily too, upon these terms, he shall have me to enemy while I live. Come, [355 sir, bear it bravely.

*Daw.* O God, sir, 't is nothing.

*True.* True: what's six kicks to a man that reads Seneca?

*Daw.* I have had a hundred, sir.          360

*True.* Sir Amorous! — No speaking one to another, or rehearsing old matters.

*Dauphine comes forth and kicks him*

*Daw.* One, two, three, four, five. I protest, Sir Amorous, you shall have six.          365

*True.* Nay, I told you, you should not talk. Come give him six, and he will needs. [*Dauphine kicks him again.*] — Your sword. [*Takes his sword.*] Now return to your safe custody; you shall presently meet afore the ladies, [370 and be the dearest friends one to another. [*Puts Daw into the study.*] — Give me the scarf now, thou shalt beat the other bare-fac'd. Stand by. [*Dauphine retires, and Truewit releases La-Foole.*] — Sir Amorous!          375

*La-F.* What's here! A sword?

*True.* I cannot help it, without I should take the quarrel upon myself. Here he has sent you his sword —

*La-F.* I'll receive none on't.          380

*True.* And he wills you to fasten it against a wall, and break your head in some few several places against the hilts.

*La-F.* I will not: tell him roundly. I cannot endure to shed my own blood.          385

*True.* Will you not?

*La-F.* No. I'll beat it against a fair flat wall, if that will satisfy him: if not, he shall beat it himself, for Amorous.

*True.* Why, this is strange starting off, [390 when a man undertakes for you! I offer'd him another condition; will you stand to that?

*La-F.* Ay, what is 't?

*True.* That you will be beaten in private.

*La-F.* Yes, I am content, at the blunt. 395

[*Enter, above, Haughty, Centaure, Mavis, Mistress Otter, Epicœne, and Trusty*]

*True.* Then you must submit yourself to be hoodwink'd in this scarf, and be led to him, where he will take your sword from you, and make you bear a blow over the mouth, gules, and tweaks by the nose *sans nombre.*          400

*La-F.* I am content. But why must I be blinded?

---

³⁰² **discourse:** narrate     ³¹¹ **drift:** scheme     ³¹² **carpet:** table-cover     ³²⁰⁻³²¹ **magis . . . feriendo:** more in enduring than in doing, more in bearing than in striking     ³²³ **suffer:** endure punishment     ³³³ **butter-teeth:** incisors     ³³⁷ **because:** in order that     ³³⁹ **upbraided:** brought up as a subject for argument     ³⁶⁶ **you, you:** ('you' Ff, Q)     ³⁸⁹ **for Amorous:** as far as Amorous is concerned     ³⁹¹ **undertakes:** assumes responsibility     ³⁹⁵ **at the blunt:** with the flat of the sword     ³⁹⁷ **hoodwink'd:** blindfolded     ⁴⁰⁰ **sans nombre:** without number

*True.* That 's for your good, sir; because, if he should grow insolent upon this, and publish it hereafter to your disgrace, (which I [405 hope he will not do,) you might swear safely, and protest, he never beat you, to your knowledge.

*La-F.*  O, I conceive.

*True.*  I do not doubt but you 'll be per- [410 fect good friends upon 't, and not dare to utter an ill thought one of another in future.

*La-F.*  Not I, as God help me, of him.

*True.*  Nor he of you, sir.  If he should,— [*binds his eyes.*] — Come, sir [*leads him* [415 *forward.*] — *All hid,* Sir John!

### *Dauphine enters to tweak him*

*La-F.*  O, Sir John, Sir John!  Oh, o-o-o-o-o-Oh —

*True.*  Good Sir John, leave tweaking, you 'll blow his nose off. — 'T is Sir John's pleas- [420 ure, you should retire into the study.  [*Puts him up again.*] — Why, now you are friends. All bitterness between you, I hope, is buried; you shall come forth by and by, Damon and Pythias upon 't, and embrace with all the [425 rankness of friendship that can be. — I trust, we shall have 'em tamer i' their language hereafter.  Dauphine, I worship thee. — God's will, the ladies have surpris'd us!

## *Act IIII.  Scene VI*

*Haughty, Centaure, Mavis, Mrs. Otter, Epicœne, Trusty (having discover'd part of the past scene above); Dauphine, Truewit, &c.*

[*Hau.*]  Centaure, how our judgments were impos'd on by these adulterate knights!

*Cen.*  Nay, madam, Mavis was more deceiv'd than we; 'twas her commendation utter'd 'em in the college.                                  5

*Mav.*  I commended but their wits, madam, and their braveries.  I never look'd toward their valours.

*Hau.*  Sir Dauphine is valiant, and a wit too, it seems.                                          10

*Mav.*  And a bravery too.

*Hau.*  Was this his project?

*Mrs. Ott.*  So master Clerimont intimates, madam.

*Hau.*  Good Morose, when you come to [15 the college, will you bring him with you? He seems a very perfect gentleman.

*Epi.*  He is so, madam, believe it.

*Cen.*  But when will you come, Morose?

*Epi.*  Three or four days hence, madam, [20 when I have got me a coach and horses.

*Hau.*  No, to-morrow, good Morose; Centaure shall send you her coach.

*Mav.*  Yes faith, do, and bring Sir Dauphine with you.                                            25

*Hau.*  She has promis'd that, Mavis.

*Mav.*  He is a very worthy gentleman in his exteriors, madam.

*Hau.*  Ay, he shows he is judicial in his clothes.                                               30

*Cen.*  And yet not so superlatively neat as some, madam, that have their faces set in a brake.

*Hau.*  Ay, and have every hair in form.

*Mav.*  That wear purer linen than our- [35 selves, and profess more neatness than the French hermaphrodite!

*Epi.*  Ay, ladies, they, what they tell one of us, have told a thousand; and are the only thieves of our fame, that think to take us [40 with that perfume, or with that lace, and laugh at us unconscionably when they have done.

*Hau.*  But Sir Dauphine's carelessness becomes him.                                             45

*Cen.*  I could love a man for such a nose.

*Mav.*  Or such a leg.

*Cen.*  He has an exceeding good eye, madam.

*Mav.*  And a very good lock.

*Cen.*  Good Morose, bring him to my [50 chamber first.

*Mrs. Ott.*  Please your honours to meet at my house, madam.

*True.*  See how they eye thee, man! they are taken, I warrant thee.                               55

[*Haughty comes forward.*]

*Hau.*  You have unbrac'd our brace of knights here, master Truewit.

*True.*  Not I, madam; it was Sir Dauphine's ingine: who, if he have disfurnish'd your ladyship of any guard or service by it, is able [60 to make the place good again in himself.

*Hau.*  There 's no suspicion of that, sir.

*Cen.*  God so, Mavis, Haughty is kissing.

*Mav.*  Let us go too, and take part.

[*They come forward.*]

*Hau.*  But I am glad of the fortune (be- [65 side the discovery of two such empty caskets) to gain the knowledge of so rich a mine of virtue as Sir Dauphine.

*Cen.*  We would be all glad to style him of our friendship, and see him at the college.    70

*Mav.*  He cannot mix with a sweeter society, I 'll prophesy; and I hope he himself will think so.

---

⁴¹⁶ **All hid:** a signal in a child's game    ⁴²⁶ **rankness:** extravagance    S. D. **Having . . . above:** (marginal note in F)    ⁴⁻⁵ **utter'd:** made (them) acceptable    ⁷ **braveries:** finery    ³²⁻³³ **set . . . brake:** fixed, as a horse held for shoeing    ⁴⁹ **lock:** love-lock    ⁵⁶ **unbrac'd:** disarmed    ⁵⁹ **ingine:** plot

*Daup.* I should be rude to imagine otherwise, lady.                                              75

*True.* Did not I tell thee, Dauphine! Why, all their actions are governed by crude opinion, without reason or cause; they know not why they do anything; but, as they are inform'd, believe, judge, praise, condemn, love, hate, [80 and in emulation one of another, do all these things alike. Only they have a natural inclination sways 'em generally to the worst, when they are left to themselves. But pursue it, now thou hast 'em.                                    85

*Hau.* Shall we go in again, Morose?

*Epi.* Yes, madam.

*Cen.* We 'll entreat Sir Dauphine's company.

*True.* Stay, good madam, the inter- [90 view of the two friends, Pylades and Orestes: I 'll fetch 'em out to you straight.

*Hau.* Will you, master Truewit?

*Daup.* Ay, but, noble ladies, do not confess in your countenance, or outward bearing to [95 'em, any discovery of their follies, that we may see how they will bear up again, with what assurance and erection.

*Hau.* We will not, Sir Dauphine.

*Cen. Mav.* Upon our honours, Sir Dau- [100 phine.

*True.* [*Goes to the first closet.*] Sir Amorous, Sir Amorous! The ladies are here.

*La-F.* [*Within.*] Are they?

*True.* Yes; but slip out by and by, as [105 their backs are turn'd, and meet Sir John here, as by chance, when I call you. [*Goes to the other.*] — Jack Daw.

*Daw.* [*Within.*] What say you, sir?

*True.* Whip out behind me suddenly, [110 and no anger i' your looks to your adversary. Now, now!

[*La-Foole and Daw slip out of their respective closets, and salute each other.*]

*La-F.* Noble Sir John Daw, where have you been?

*Daw.* To seek you, Sir Amorous.                       115

*La-F.* Me! I honour you.

*Daw.* I prevent you, sir.

*Cler.* They have forgot their rapiers.

*True.* O, they meet in peace, man.

*Daup.* Where 's your sword, Sir John?     120

*Cler.* And yours, Sir Amorous?

*Daw.* Mine! my boy had it forth to mend the handle, e'en now.

*La-F.* And my gold handle was broke too, and my boy had it forth.                            125

*Daup.* Indeed, sir! — How their excuses meet!

*Cler.* What a consent there is i' the handles!

*True.* Nay, there is so i' the points too, I warrant you.                                      130

*Mrs. Ott.* O me! madam, he comes again, the madman! Away!

[*Ladies, Daw, and La-Foole, run off.*]

## Act IIII.   Scene VII

### Morose, Truewit, Clerimont, Dauphine

[*Mor.*] What make these naked weapons here, gentlemen?   *He had found the two swords drawn within.*

*True.* O sir! here hath like to been murder since you went; a couple of knights fallen [5 out about the bride's favours! We were fain to take away their weapons; your house had been begg'd by this time else.

*Mor.* For what?

*Cler.* For manslaughter, sir, as being [10 accessary.

*Mor.* And for her favours?

*True.* Ay, sir, heretofore, not present. — Clerimont, carry 'em their swords now. They have done all the hurt they will do.            15

[*Exit Cler. with the two swords.*]

*Daup.* Ha' you spoke with a lawyer, sir?

*Mor.* O no! there is such a noise i' the court, that they have frighted me home with more violence than I went! such speaking and counter-speaking, with their several voices [20 of citations, appellations, allegations, certificates, attachments, intergatories, references, convictions, and afflictions indeed, among the doctors and proctors, that the noise here is silence to 't, a kind of calm midnight!        25

*True.* Why, sir, if you would be resolv'd indeed, I can bring you hither a very sufficient lawyer, and a learned divine, that shall inquire into every least scruple for you.

*Mor.* Can you, master Truewit?            30

*True.* Yes, and are very sober, grave persons, that will dispatch it in a chamber, with a whisper or two.

*Mor.* Good sir, shall I hope this benefit from you, and trust myself into your hands? [35

*True.* Alas, sir! your nephew and I have been asham'd and oft-times mad, since you went, to think how you are abus'd. Go in, good sir, and lock yourself up till we call you; we 'll tell you more anon, sir.                    40

*Mor.* Do your pleasure with me, gentlemen; I believe in you, and that deserves no delusion.                                      [*Exit.*]

*True.* You shall find none, sir; — but heap'd, heap'd plenty of vexation.                       45

---

**98 erection:** exaltation   **128 consent:** agreement   **8 begg'd:** confiscated and given to some suitor at court   **22 intergatories:** interrogatories, questions to be answered under oath   **24 proctors:** court officers   **27 sufficient:** competent

*Daup.* What wilt thou do now, Wit?

*True.* Recover me hither Otter and the barber, if you can, by any means, presently.

*Daup.* Why? to what purpose?

*True.* O, I 'll make the deepest divine, [50 and gravest lawyer, out o' them two for him —

*Daup.* Thou canst not, man; these are waking dreams.

*True.* Do not fear me. Clap but a civil gown with a welt o' the one, and a canonical [55 cloak with sleeves o' the other, and give 'em a few terms i' their mouths, if there come not forth as able a doctor and complete a parson, for this turn, as may be wish'd, trust not my election: and I hope, without wronging the [60 dignity of either profession, since they are but persons put on, and for mirth's sake, to torment him. The barber smatters Latin, I remember.

*Daup.* Yes, and Otter too.

*True.* Well then, if I make 'em not [65 wrangle out this case to his no comfort, let me be thought a Jack Daw or La-Foole or anything worse. Go you to your ladies, but first send for them.

*Daup.* I will.                    [*Exeunt.*] 70

## Act V.  Scene I

### [*A Room in Morose's House*]

*La-Foole, Clerimont, Daw,* [*later*] *Mavis*

[*La-F.*] Where had you our swords, master Clerimont?

*Cler.* Why, Dauphine took 'em from the madman.

*La-F.* And he took 'em from our boys, [5 I warrant you.

*Cler.* Very like, sir.

*La-F.* Thank you, good master Clerimont. Sir John Daw and I are both beholden to you.

*Cler.* Would I knew how to make you [10 so, gentlemen!

*Daw.* Sir Amorous and I are your servants, sir.                    [*Enter Mavis*]

*Mav.* Gentlemen, have any of you a pen and ink? I would fain write out a riddle [15 in Italian, for Sir Dauphine to translate.

*Cler.* Not I, in troth, lady; I am no scrivener.

*Daw.* I can furnish you, I think, lady.
                    [*Exeunt Daw and Mavis.*]

*Cler.* He has it in the haft of a knife, I [20 believe.

*La-F.* No, he has his box of instruments.

*Cler.* Like a surgeon!

*La-F.* For the mathematics: his squire, his compasses, his brass pens, and black-lead, [25 to draw maps of every place and person where he comes.

*Cler.* How, maps of persons!

*La-F.* Yes, sir, of Nomentack when he was here, and of the Prince of Moldavia, and [30 of his mistress, mistress Epicœne.

### [*Enter Daw*]

*Cler.* Away! he has not found out her latitude, I hope.

*La-F.* You are a pleasant gentleman, sir.

*Cler.* Faith, now we are in private, let 's [35 wanton it a little, and talk waggishly. — Sir John, I am telling Sir Amorous here, that you two govern the ladies where'er you come; you carry the feminine gender afore you.

*Daw.* They shall rather carry us afore [40 them, if they will, sir.

*Cler.* Nay, I believe that they do, withal — but that you are the prime men in their affections, and direct all their actions —

*Daw.* Not I; Sir Amorous is.              45

*La-F.* I protest, Sir John is.

*Daw.* As I hope to rise i' the state, Sir Amorous, you ha' the person.

*La-F.* Sir John, you ha' the person, and the discourse too.              50

*Daw.* Not I, sir. I have no discourse — and then you have activity beside.

*La-F.* I protest, Sir John, you come as high from Tripoly as I do, every whit: and lift as many join'd stools, and leap over 'em, if [55 you would use it.

*Cler.* Well, agree on 't together, knights: for between you, you divide the kingdom or commonwealth of ladies' affections: I see it, and can perceive a little how they observe [60 you, and fear you, indeed. You could tell strange stories, my masters, if you would, I know.

*Daw.* Faith, we have seen somewhat, sir.

*La-F.* That we have — vellet petticoats, [65 and wrought smocks, or so.

*Daw.* Ay, and —

*Cler.* Nay, out with it, Sir John; do not envy your friend the pleasure of hearing, when you have had the delight of tasting.              70

*Daw.* Why — a —— Do you speak, Sir Amorous.

---

**54 fear:** doubt **civil:** of a civil lawyer      **55 welt:** border of fur or velvet      **59 turn:** occasion **60 election:** discrimination      **62 put on:** assumed, pretended      **1 had you:** did you get      **18 scrivener:** professional scribe      **24 squire:** square      **29 Nomentack:** an Indian who had been brought to London from Virginia      **30 Moldavia:** now part of Roumania      **36 wanton it:** be frivolous      **53–54 come . . . Tripoly:** a common phrase apparently referring to some feat of jumping      **56 use:** practise      **60 observe:** show respectful attention to

*La-F.*  No, do you, Sir John Daw.

*Daw.*  I' faith, you shall.

*La-F.*  I' faith, you shall.                    75

*Daw.*  Why, we have been —

*La-F.*  In the great bed at Ware together in our time. On, Sir John.

*Daw.*  Nay, do you, Sir Amorous.

*Cler.*  And these ladies with you, knights?  80

*La-F.*  No, excuse us, sir.

*Daw.*  We must not wound reputation.

*La-F.*  No matter — they were these, or others. Our bath cost us fifteen pound when we came home.                    85

*Cler.*  Do you hear, Sir John? You shall tell me but one thing truly, as you love me.

*Daw.*  If I can, I will, sir.

*Cler.*  You lay in the same house with the bride here?                    90

*Daw.*  Yes, and convers'd with her hourly, sir.

*Cler.*  And what humour is she of? Is she coming and open, free?

*Daw.*  O, exceeding open, sir. I was her [95 servant, and Sir Amorous was to be.

*Cler.*  Come, you have both had favours from her: I know, and have heard so much.

*Daw.*  O no, sir.

*La-F.*  You shall excuse us, sir; we must [100 not wound reputation.

*Cler.*  Tut, she is married now, and you cannot hurt her with any report; and therefore speak plainly: how many times, i' faith? which of you led first? ha!                    105

*La-F.*  Sir John had her maidenhead, indeed.

*Daw.*  O, it pleases him to say so, sir; but Sir Amorous knows what 's what, as well.

*Cler.*  Dost thou, i' faith, Amorous?  110

*La-F.*  In a manner, sir.

*Cler.*  Why, I commend you, lads. Little knows Don Bridegroom of this; nor shall he, for me.

*Daw.*  Hang him, mad ox!                    115

*Cler.*  Speak softly; here comes his nephew, with the lady Haughty: he 'll get the ladies from you, sirs, if you look not to him in time.

*La-F.*  Why, if he do, we 'll fetch 'em home again, I warrant you.                    120

[*Exit with Daw. Cler. walks aside.*]

## Act V.  Scene II

*Haughty, Dauphine, Centaure, Mavis, Clerimont*

[*Hau.*]  I assure you, Sir Dauphine, it is the price and estimation of your virtue only, that hath embark'd me to this adventure; and I could not but make out to tell you so: nor can I repent me of the act, since it is [5 always an argument of some virtue in our selves, that we love and affect it so in others.

*Daup.*  Your ladyship sets too high a price on my weakness.

*Hau.*  Sir, I can distinguish gems from [10 pebbles —

*Daup.*  [*Aside.*] Are you so skilful in stones?

*Hau.*  And howsoever I may suffer in such a judgment as yours, by admitting equality of rank or society with Centaure or Mavis — [15

*Daup.*  You do not, madam; I perceive they are your mere foils.

*Hau.*  Then are you a friend to truth, sir; it makes me love you the more. It is not the outward, but the inward man that I affect. [20 They are not apprehensive of an eminent perfection, but love flat and dully.

*Cen.*  [*Within.*]  Where are you, my lady Haughty?

*Hau.*  I come presently, Centaure. — My [25 chamber, sir, my page shall show you; and Trusty, my woman, shall be ever awake for you: you need not fear to communicate any thing with her, for she is a Fidelia. I pray you, wear this jewel for my sake, Sir Dau- [30 phine —          [*Enter Centaure*]

Where 's Mavis, Centaure?

*Cen.*  Within, madam, a-writing. I 'll follow you presently. [*Exit Hau.*] I 'll but speak a word with Sir Dauphine.                    35

*Daup.*  With me, madam?

*Cen.*  Good Sir Dauphine, do not trust Haughty, nor make any credit to her whatever you do besides. Sir Dauphine, I give you this caution, she is a perfect courtier, and [40 loves nobody but for her uses; and for her uses she loves all. Besides, her physicians give her out to be none o' the clearest; whether she pay 'em or no, heaven knows; and she 's above fifty too, and pargets! See her in [45 a forenoon. Here comes Mavis, a worse face than she! you would not like this by candle-light.          [*Enter Mavis*]

If you 'll come to my chamber one o' these mornings early, or late in an evening, I 'll [50 tell you more. Where 's Haughty, Mavis?

*Mav.*  Within, Centaure.

*Cen.*  What ha' you there?

*Mav.*  An Italian riddle for Sir Dauphine, — you shall not see it, i' faith, Centaure. — [55 [*Exit Cen.*] Good Sir Dauphine, solve it for me: I 'll call for it anon.          [*Exit.*]

---

77 **great . . . Ware:** a famous bed twelve feet square; cf. *Twelfth Night*, III. ii    93 **humour:** disposition    94 **coming:** complaisant    **open:** frank    115 **ox:** *i.e.*, cuckold    21 **apprehensive of:** quick to perceive    38 **make . . . her:** believe what she says    45 **pargets:** paints

*Cler.* [*Coming forward.*] How now, Dauphine! how dost thou quit thyself of these females?                                                          60

*Daup.* 'Slight, they haunt me like fairies, and give me jewels here; I cannot be rid of 'em.

*Cler.* O, you must not tell though.

*Daup.* Mass, I forgot that: I was never [65 so assaulted. One loves for virtue, and bribes me with this; [*shows the jewel.*] — another loves me with caution, and so would possess me; a third brings me a riddle here: and all are jealous, and rail each at other.        70

*Cler.* A riddle! pray le' me see 't.

*He reads the paper.*

Sir Dauphine, I chose this way of intimation for privacy. The ladies here, I know, have both hope and purpose to make a collegiate and servant of you. If I might be so honour'd, as to appear [75 at any end of so noble a work, I would enter into a fame of taking physic to-morrow, and continue it four or five days, or longer, for your visitation.

MAVIS

By my faith, a subtle one! Call you [80 this a riddle? what 's their plain-dealing, trow?

*Daup.* We lack Truewit to tell us that.

*Cler.* We lack him for somewhat else too: his knights reformados are wound up as high and insolent as ever they were.              85

*Daup.* You jest.

*Cler.* No drunkards, either with wine or vanity, ever confess'd such stories of themselves. I would not give a fly's leg in balance against all the women's reputations here, if [90 they could be but thought to speak truth: and for the bride, they have made their affidavit against her directly —

*Daup.* What, that they have lien with her?

*Cler.* Yes; and tell times and circum- [95 stances, with the cause why, and the place where. I had almost brought 'em to affirm that they had done it to-day.

*Daup.* Not both of 'em?

*Cler.* Yes, faith; with a sooth or two [100 more I had effected it. They would ha' set it down under their hands.

*Daup.* Why, they will be our sport, I see, still, whether we will or no.

## Act V. Scene III

*Truewit, Morose, Otter, Cutbeard, Clerimont, Dauphine*

[*True.*] O, are you here? Come, Dauphine; go call your uncle presently: I have fitted my divine and my canonist, dyed their beards and all. The knaves do not know themselves, they are so exalted and alter'd. Perferment [5 changes any man. Thou shalt keep one door and I another, and then Clerimont in the midst, that he may have no means of escape from their cavilling, when they grow hot once. And then the women, as I have given the bride [10 her instructions, to break in upon him i' the l'envoy. O, 't will be full and twanging! Away! fetch him.                                        [*Exit Dauphine.*]

[*Enter Otter disguised as a divine, and Cutbeard as a canon lawyer*]

Come, master doctor, and master parson, look to your parts now, and discharge 'em [15 bravely; you are well set forth, perform it as well. If you chance to be out, do not confess it with standing still, or humming, or gaping one at another; but go on, and talk aloud and eagerly; use vehement action, and only [20 remember your terms, and you are safe. Let the matter go where it will: you have many will do so. But at first be very solemn and grave, like your garments, though you loose your selves after, and skip out like a brace [25 of jugglers on a table. Here he comes: set your faces, and look superciliously, while I present you.

[*Enter Dauphine with Morose*]

*Mor.* Are these the two learned men?

*True.* Yes, sir; please you salute 'em.        30

*Mor.* Salute 'em! I had rather do any thing, than wear out time so unfruitfully, sir. I wonder how these common forms, as "God save you," and "You are welcome," are come to be a habit in our lives: or, "I am glad [35 to see you!" when I cannot see what the profit can be of these words, so long as it is no whit better with him whose affairs are sad and grievous, that he hears this salutation.

*True.* 'T is true, sir; we 'll go to the [40 matter then. — Gentlemen, master doctor, and master parson, I have acquainted you sufficiently with the business for which you are come hither; and you are not now to inform yourselves in the state of the question, I [45 know. This is the gentleman who expects your resolution, and therefore, when you please, begin.

*Ott.* Please you, master doctor.

*Cut.* Please you, good master parson.

*Ott.* I would hear the canon-law speak [50 first.

*Cut.* It must give place to positive divinity, sir.

*Mor.* Nay, good gentlemen, do not throw

---

**59** quit: free    **64** you . . . tell: (since this would anger the fairies)    **77** fame: public report
**84** reformados: ostensibly reformed    **100** sooth: flattery    **12** l'envoy: conclusion    **twanging: fine**
**47** resolution: decision, judgment

me into circumstances. Let your comforts [55
arrive quickly at me, those that are. Be swift
in affording me my peace, if so I shall hope
any. I love not your disputations, or your
court-tumults. And that it be not strange
to you, I will tell you. My father, in my [60
education, was wont to advise me, that I should
always collect and contain my mind, not suffering it to flow loosely; that I should look to
what things were necessary to the carriage
of my life, and what not; embracing the [65
one and eschewing the other: in short, that
I should endear myself to rest, and avoid turmoil; which now is grown to be another nature
to me. So that I come not to your public
pleadings, or your places of noise; not that [70
I neglect those things that make for the dignity
of the commonwealth; but for the mere avoiding of clamours and impertinencies of orators,
that know not how to be silent. And for the
cause of noise, am I now a suitor to you. [75
You do not know in what a misery I have been
exercis'd this day, what a torrent of evil! my
very house turns round with the tumult! I
dwell in a windmill: the perpetual motion is
here, and not at Eltham.       80
*True.* Well, good master doctor, will you
break the ice? master parson will wade after.
*Cut.* Sir, though unworthy, and the weaker,
I will presume.
*Ott.* 'T is no presumption, *domine* doctor. 85
*Mor.* Yet again!
*Cut.* Your question is, For how many causes
a man may have *divortium legitimum,* a lawful
divorce? First, you must understand the nature of the word, divorce, *a divertendo* —       90
*Mor.* No excursions upon words, good doctor; to the question briefly.
*Cut.* I answer then, the canon law affords
divorce but in few cases; and the principal
is in the common case, the adulterous case. [95
But there are *duodecim impedimenta,* twelve
impediments, as we call 'em, all which do not
*dirimere contractum,* but *irritum reddere matrimonium,* as we say in the canon law, *not take
away the bond, but cause a nullity therein.*       100
*Mor.* I understood you before: good sir,
avoid your impertinency of translation.
*Ott.* He cannot open this too much, sir,
by your favour.
*Mor.* Yet more!       105
*True.* O, you must give the learned men
leave, sir. — To your impediments, master doctor.

*Cut.* The first is *impedimentum errorts.*
*Ott.* Of which there are several species. 110
*Cut.* Ay, as *error personæ.*
*Ott.* If you contract yourself to one person,
thinking her another.
*Cut.* Then, *error fortunæ.*
*Ott.* If she be a beggar, and you thought [115
her rich.
*Cut.* Then, *error qualitatis.*
*Ott.* If she prove stubborn or headstrong,
that you thought obedient.
*Mor.* How! is that, sir, a lawful im- [120
pediment? One at once, I pray you, gentlemen.
*Ott.* Ay, *ante copulam,* but not *post copulam,*
sir.
*Cut.* Master parson says right. *Nec post
nuptiarum benedictionem.* It doth indeed [125
but *irrita reddere sponsalia,* annul the contract;
after marriage it is no obstancy.
*True.* Alas, sir, what a hope are we fall'n
from by this time!
*Cut.* The next is *conditio:* if you thought [130
her free born, and she prove a bond-woman,
there is impediment of estate and condition.
*Ott.* Ay, but, master doctor, those servi-
tudes are *sublatæ* now, among us Christians.
*Cut.* By your favour, master parson — 135
*Ott.* You shall give me leave, master doctor.
*Mor.* Nay, gentlemen, quarrel not in that
question; it concerns not my case: pass to the
third.
*Cut.* Well then, the third is *votum:* if [140
either party have made a vow of chastity.
But that practice, as master parson said of the
other, is taken away among us, thanks be to
discipline. The fourth is *cognatio;* if the persons
be of kin within the degrees.       145
*Ott.* Ay: do you know what the degrees
are, sir?
*Mor.* No, nor I care not, sir; they offer
me no comfort in the question, I am sure.
*Cut.* But there is a branch of this im- [150
pediment may, which is *cognatio spiritualis:*
if you were her godfather, sir, then the marriage
is incestuous.
*Ott.* That comment is absurd and superstitious, master doctor: I cannot endure it. [155
Are we not all brothers and sisters, and as
much akin in that, as godfathers and god-
daughters?
*Mor.* O me! to end the controversy, I never
was a godfather, I never was a godfather [160
in my life, sir. Pass to the next.
*Cut.* The fift is *crimen adulterii;* the known

---

⁵⁵ **circumstances:** details    ⁸⁰ **Eltham:** (where there was a famous puppet-show or 'motion')
⁹⁰ **a divertendo:** etymologically from "divertere," to separate    ¹⁰³ **open:** expound    ¹²⁴⁻¹²⁵ **Nec, etc.:**
nor after the marriage benediction    ¹²⁶ **contract:** of betrothal, not marriage    ¹²⁷ **obstancy:** legal impediment    ¹³⁴ **sublatæ:** abolished    ¹⁴⁴ **discipline:** (of the church)    ¹⁴⁵ **degrees:** prescribed degrees of
relationship within which marriage is forbidden    ¹⁶²⁻¹⁶³ **fift, sixt:** (correct older forms; so 'eight' in 178)

case. The sixt, *cultus disparitas,* difference of
religion: Have you ever examin'd her, what
religion she is of?                                    165
*Mor.* No, I would rather she were of none,
than be put to the trouble of it.
*Ott.* You may have it done for you, sir.
*Mor.* By no means, good sir; on to the
rest! Shall you ever come to an end, think [170
you?
*True.* Yes, he has done half, sir. — On to
the rest. — Be patient, and expect, sir.
*Cut.* The seventh is, *vis:* if it were upon
compulsion or force.                                  175
*Mor.* O no, it was too voluntary, mine;
too voluntary.
*Cut.* The eight is, *ordo;* if ever she have
taken holy orders.
*Ott.* That 's superstitious too.        180
*Mor.* No matter, master parson. Would
she would go into a nunnery yet.
*Cut.* The ninth is, *ligamen;* if you were
bound, sir, to any other before.
*Mor.* I thrust myself too soon into these [185
fetters.
*Cut.* The tenth is, *publica honestas;* which
is *inchoata quædam affinitas.*
*Ott.* Ay, or *affinitas orta ex sponsalibus;* and
is but *leve impedimentum.*                        190
*Mor.* I feel no air of comfort blowing to
me, in all this.
*Cut.* The eleventh is, *affinitas ex fornicatione.*
*Ott.* Which is no less *vera affinitas,* than the
other, master doctor.                                 195
*Cut.* True, *quæ oritur ex legitimo matrimonio.*
*Ott.* You say right, venerable doctor: and,
*nascitur ex eo, quod per conjugium duæ personæ
efficiuntur una caro —*
*Mor.* Hey-day, now they begin!          200
*Cut.* I conceive you, master parson: *ita
per fornicationem æque est verus pater, qui sic
generat —*
*Ott.* *Et vere filius qui sic generatur —*
*Mor.* What 's all this to me?            205
*Cler.* Now it grows warm.
*Cut.* The twelfth and last is, *si forte coire
nequibis.*

*Ott.* Ay, that is *impedimentum gravissimum:*
it doth utterly annul, and annihilate, that. [210
If you have *manifestam frigiditatem,* you are
well, sir.
*True.* Why, there is comfort come at length,
sir. Confess yourself but a man unable, and
she will sue to be divorc'd first.        215
*Ott.* Ay, or if there be *morbus perpetuus, et
insanabilis;* as *paralysis, elephantiasis,* or so —
*Daup.* O, but *frigiditas* is the fairer way,
gentlemen.
*Ott.* You say troth, sir, and as it is in [220
the canon, master doctor —
*Cut.* I conceive you, sir.
*Cler.* Before he speaks!
*Ott.* That a boy, or child, under years, is
not fit for marriage, because he cannot [225
*reddere debitum.* So your *omnipotentes —*
*True.* Your *impotentes,* you whoreson lobster!                           [*Aside to Ott.*]
*Ott.* Your *impotentes,* I should say, are
*minime apti ad contrahenda matrimonium.*   230
*True.* *Matrimonium!* we shall have most
unmatrimonial Latin with you: *matrimonia,*
and be hang'd!
*Daup.* You put 'em out, man.
*Cut.* But then there will arise a doubt, [235
master parson, in our case, *post matrimonium:*
that *frigiditate præditus* — do you conceive me,
sir?
*Ott.* Very well, sir.
*Cut.* Who cannot *uti uxore pro uxore,* [240
may *habere eam pro sorore.*
*Ott.* Absurd, absurd, absurd, and merely
apostatical!
*Cut.* You shall pardon me, master parson,
I can prove it.                               245
*Ott.* You can prove a will, master doctor;
you can prove nothing else. Does not the
verse of your own canon say,

*Hæc socianda vetant connubia, facta retractant?*

*Cut.* I grant you; but how do they [250
*retractare,* master parson?
*Mor.* O, this was it I feared.
*Ott.* *In æternum,* sir.

---

[173] **expect:** wait     [187] **publica** ('publice' F) **honestas:** public reputation (*i.e.,* previous marriage or
engagement)     [188] **inchoata . . . affinitas:** some incomplete relationship by marriage     [189] **orta ex
sponsalibus:** arising from betrothal     [190] **leve impedimentum:** slight impediment     [193] **affinitas ex fornicatione:** (An illegitimate relation made man or woman subject to the laws governing the degrees of con-
sanguinity.)     [196] **quæ . . . matrimonio:** which arises from legitimate marriage     [198–199] **nascitur . . .
caro:** arises from this, that through marriage two persons are made one flesh     [201–203] **ita . . . generat:**
so by fornication he in like manner is the true father who thus begets —     [204] **Et . . . generatur:** and
truly the son who is thus begotten     [207–208] **si . . . nequibis:** if you shall be unable to beget children
[216–217] **morbus . . . insanabilis:** permanent and incurable disease     [226] **reddere debitum:** pay his
(connubial) debt     [230] **minime . . . matrimonium:** least fitted for contracting marriage     [232] **unmatrimonial:** (because discordant grammatically)     [237] **præditus:** a man possessed of     [240] **uti . . .
uxore:** use his wife as a wife     [241] **habere . . . sorore:** have her as a sister     [243] **apostatical:** heretical
[249] **Hæc . . . retractant:** These things forbid marriages to be made; if they have been made, revoke them.
(From St. Thomas Aquinas, *Summa Theologiæ*)

*Cut.* That 's false in divinity, by your favour.    255

*Ott.* 'T is false in humanity to say so. Is he not *prorsus inutilis ad thorum?* Can he *præstare fidem datam?* I would fain know.

*Cut.* Yes; how if he do *convalere?*

*Ott.* He cannot *convalere,* it is impossible. 260

*True.* Nay, good sir, attend the learned men; they 'll think you neglect 'em else.

*Cut.* Or, if he do *simulare* himself *frigidum, odio uxoris,* or so?

*Ott.* I say, he is *adulter manifestus* then. 265

*Daup.* They dispute it very learnedly, i' faith.

*Ott.* And *prostitutor uxoris;* and this is positive.

*Mor.* Good sir, let me escape.    270

*True.* You will not do me that wrong, sir?

*Ott.* And, therefore, if he be *manifeste frigidus,* sir —

*Cut.* Ay, if he be *manifeste frigidus,* I grant you —    275

*Ott.* Why, that was my conclusion.

*Cut.* And mine too.

*True.* Nay, hear the conclusion, sir.

*Ott.* Then, *frigiditatis causa* —

*Cut.* Yes, *causa frigiditatis* —    280

*Mor.* O, mine ears!

*Ott.* She may have *libellum divortii* against you.

*Cut.* Ay, *divortii libellum* she will sure have.

*Mor.* Good echoes, forbear.    285

*Ott.* If you confess it. —

*Cut.* Which I would do, sir —

*Mor.* I will do anything.

*Ott.* And clear myself *in foro conscientiæ* —

*Cut.* Because you want indeed —    290

*Mor.* Yet more!

*Ott.* *Exercendi potestate.*

## Act V. Scene IIII

*Epicœne, Morose, Haughty, Centaure, Mavis, Mrs. Otter, Daw, Truewit, Dauphine, Clerimont, La-Foole, Otter, Cutbeard*

[*Epi.*] I will not endure it any longer. Ladies, I beseech you, help me. This is such a wrong as never was offer'd to poor bride before: upon her marriage-day to have her husband conspire against her, and a couple [5 of mercenary companions to be brought in for form's sake, to persuade a separation! If you had blood or virtue in you, gentlemen, you

would not suffer such earwigs about a husband, or scorpions to creep between man and wife. 10

*Mor.* O the variety and changes of my torment!

*Hau.* Let 'em be cudgell'd out of doors by our grooms.

*Cen.* I 'll lend you my footman.    15

*Mav.* We 'll have our men blanket 'em i' the hall.

*Mrs. Ott.* As there was one at our house, madam, for peeping in at the door.

*Daw.* Content, i' faith.    20

*True.* Stay, ladies and gentlemen; you 'll hear before you proceed?

*Mav.* I 'd ha' the bridegroom blanketed too.

*Cen.* Begin with him first.

*Hau.* Yes, by my troth.    25

*Mor.* O mankind generation!

*Daup.* Ladies, for my sake forbear.

*Hau.* Yes, for Sir Dauphine's sake.

*Cen.* He shall command us.

*La-F.* He is as fine a gentleman of his [30 inches, madam, as any is about the town, and wears as good colours when he list.

*True.* Be brief, sir, and confess your infirmity; she 'll be a-fire to be quit of you, if she but hear that nam'd once; you shall [35 not entreat her to stay. She 'll fly you like one that had the marks upon him.

*Mor.* Ladies, I must crave all your pardons —

*True.* Silence, ladies.    40

*Mor.* For a wrong I have done to your whole sex, in marrying this fair and virtuous gentlewoman —

*Cler.* Hear him, good ladies.

*Mor.* Being guilty of an infirmity, which, [45 before I conferr'd with these learned men, I thought I might have conceal'd —

*True.* But now being better inform'd in his conscience by them, he is to declare it, and give satisfaction, by asking your public [50 forgiveness.

*Mor.* I am no man, ladies.

*All.* How!

*Mor.* Utterly unabled in nature, by reason of frigidity, to perform the duties, or any [55 the least office of a husband.

*Mav.* Now out upon him, prodigious creature!

*Cen.* Bridegroom uncarnate!

*Hau.* And would you offer it to a young [60 gentlewoman?

*Mrs. Ott.* A lady of her longings?

---

²⁵⁷ **prorsus . . . thorum:** utterly useless in his bed    ²⁵⁸ **præstare . . . datam:** perform the pledge which he has given    ²⁵⁹ **convalere:** regain strength or health    ²⁶⁴ **odio:** from hatred    ²⁸² **libellum:** writ    ²⁸⁹ **in . . . conscientiæ:** in the court of my own conscience    ²⁹² **Exercendi potestate:** the power of achieving    ¹⁶ **blanket:** toss in a blanket    ²⁶ **mankind:** masculine, violent    ³² **list:** pleases    ³⁷ **marks:** of the plague    ⁵⁹ **uncarnate:** without flesh and blood

*Epi.* Tut, a device, a device, this! It smells rankly, ladies. A mere comment of his own.

*True.* Why, if you suspect that, ladies, [65 you may have him search'd —

*Daw.* As the custom is, by a jury of physicians.

*La-F.* Yes, faith, 't will be brave.

*Mor.* O me, must I undergo that?    70

*Mrs. Ott.* No, let women search him, madam; we can do it ourselves.

*Mor.* Out on me! worse.

*Epi.* No, ladies, you shall not need, I 'll take him with all his faults.    75

*Mor.* Worst of all!

*Cler.* Why then, 't is no divorce, doctor, if she consent not?

*Cut.* No, if the man be *frigidus*, it is *de parte uxoris*, that we grant *libellum divortii*, [80 in the law.

*Ott.* Ay, it is the same in theology.

*Mor.* Worse, worse than worst!

*True.* Nay, sir, be not utterly dishearten'd; we have yet a small relic of hope left, as [85 near as our comfort is blown out. Clerimont, produce your brace of knights. What was that, master parson, you told me *in errore qualitatis*, e'en now? — Dauphine, whisper the bride, that she carry it as if she were guilty, and [90 asham'd.    [*Aside.*]

*Ott.* Marry, sir, *in errore qualitatis*, (which master doctor did forbear to urge,) if she be found *corrupta*, that is, vitiated or broken up, that was *pro virgine desponsa*, espous'd for a [95 maid —

*Mor.* What then, sir?

*Ott.* It doth *dirimere contractum*, and *irritum reddere* too.

*True.* If this be true, we are happy again, [100 sir, once more. Here are an honourable brace of knights, that shall affirm so much.

*Daw.* Pardon us, good master Clerimont.

*La-F.* You shall excuse us, master Clerimont.    105

*Cler.* Nay, you must make it good now, knights, there is no remedy; I 'll eat no words for you, nor no men: you know you spoke it to me.

*Daw.* Is this gentleman-like, sir?    110

*True.* Jack Daw, he 's worse than Sir Amorous; fiercer a great deal. [*Aside to Daw.*] — Sir Amorous, beware, there be ten Daws in this Clerimont.    [*Aside to La-Foole.*]

*La-F.* I 'll confess it, sir.    115

*Daw.* Will you, Sir Amorous, will you wound reputation?

*La-F.* I am resolv'd.

*True.* So should you be too, Jack Daw: what should keep you off? She is but a [120 woman, and in disgrace: he 'll be glad on 't.

*Daw.* Will he? I thought he would ha' been angry.

*Cler.* You will dispatch, knights; it must be done, i' faith.    125

*True.* Why, an it must, it shall, sir, they say: they 'll ne'er go back. — Do not tempt his patience.    [*Aside to them.*]

*Daw.* It is true indeed, sir.

*La-F.* Yes, I assure you, sir.    130

*Mor.* What is true, gentlemen? what do you assure me?

*Daw.* That we have known your bride, sir —

*La-F.* In good fashion. She was our mistress, or so —    135

*Cler.* Nay, you must be plain, knights, as you were to me.

*Ott.* Ay, the question is, if you have *carnaliter*, or no?

*La-F.* *Carnaliter!* what else, sir?    140

*Ott.* It is enough; a plain nullity.

*Epi.* I am undone, I am undone!

*Mor.* O let me worship and adore you, gentlemen!

*Epi.* I am undone.    [*Weeps.*]    145

*Mor.* Yes, to my hand, I thank these knights. Master parson, let me thank you otherwise.    [*Gives him money.*]

*Cen.* And ha' they confess'd?

*Mav.* Now out upon 'em, informers!    150

*True.* You see what creatures you may bestow your favours on, madams.

*Hau.* I would except against 'em as beaten knights, wench, and not good witnesses in law.

*Mrs. Ott.* Poor gentlewoman, how she [155 takes it!

*Hau.* Be comforted, Morose, I love you the better for 't.

*Cen.* So do I, I protest.

*Cut.* But, gentlemen, you have not [160 known her since *matrimonium*?

*Daw.* Not to-day, master doctor.

*La-F.* No, sir, not to-day.

*Cut.* Why, then I say, for any act before, the *matrimonium* is good and perfect; un- [165 less the worshipful bridegroom did precisely, before witness, demand, if she were *virgo ante nuptias*.

*Epi.* No, that he did not, I assure you, master doctor.    170

*Cut.* If he cannot prove that, it is *ratum conjugium*, notwithstanding the premises; and they do no way *impedire*. And this is my sentence, this I pronounce.

---

[64] **comment:** quibble    [66] **search'd:** examined    [79–80] **de parte:** on behalf of    [88] **in . . . qualitatis:** (cf. sc. iii. 117)    [153] **except against:** take exception to    **beaten:** (Recreant knights were debarred as witnesses.)    [171] **ratum:** valid

*Ott.* I am of master doctor's resolution [175 too, sir; if you made not that demand *ante nuptias.*

*Mor.* O my heart! wilt thou break? wilt thou break? this is worst of all worst worsts that hell could have devis'd! Marry a [180 whore, and so much noise!

*Daup.* Come, I see now plain confederacy in this doctor and this parson, to abuse a gentleman. You study his affliction. I pray be gone, companions. — And, gentlemen, I [185 begin to suspect you for having parts with 'em. — Sir, will it please you hear me?

*Mor.* O do not talk to me; take not from me the pleasure of dying in silence, nephew.

*Daup.* Sir, I must speak to you. I have [190 been long your poor despis'd kinsman, and many a hard thought has strengthen'd you against me: but now it shall appear if either I love you or your peace, and prefer them to all the world beside. I will not be long or [195 grievous to you, sir. If I free you of this unhappy match absolutely, and instantly, after all this trouble, and almost in your despair, now —

*Mor.* It cannot be.        200

*Daup.* Sir, that you be never troubled with a murmur of it more, what shall I hope for, or deserve of you?

*Mor.* O, what thou wilt, nephew! thou shalt deserve me, and have me.        205

*Daup.* Shall I have your favour perfect to me, and love hereafter?

*Mor.* That, and anything beside. Make thine own conditions. My whole estate is thine; manage it, I will become thy ward. 210

*Daup.* Nay, sir, I will not be so unreasonable.

*Epi.* Will Sir Dauphine be mine enemy too?

*Daup.* You know I have been long a suitor to you, uncle, that out of your estate, which [216 is fifteen hundred a-year, you would allow me but five hundred during life, and assure the rest upon me after; to which I have often, by myself and friends, tendered you a writ- [220 ing to sign, which you would never consent or incline to. If you please but to effect it now —

*Mor.* Thou shalt have it, nephew: I will do it, and more.

*Daup.* If I quit you not presently, and [225 for ever, of this cumber, you shall have power instantly, afore all these, to revoke your act, and I will become whose slave you will give me to, for ever.

*Mor.* Where is the writing? I will seal [230 to it, that, or to a blank, and write thine own conditions.

*Epi.* O me, most unfortunate, wretched gentlewoman!

*Hau.* Will Sir Dauphine do this?        235

*Epi.* Good sir, have some compassion on me.

*Mor.* O, my nephew knows you, belike; away, crocodile!

*Cen.* He does it not, sure, without good ground.        240

*Daup.* Here, sir.

*[Gives him the parchments.]*

*Mor.* Come, nephew, give me the pen; I will subscribe to anything, and seal to what thou wilt, for my deliverance. Thou art my restorer. Here, I deliver it thee as my [245 deed. If there be a word in it lacking, or writ with false orthography, I protest before heaven I will not take the advantage.

*[Returns the writings.]*

*Daup.* Then here is your    *He takes off Epi-* release, sir. — You have mar-    *cœne's peruke.* ried a boy, a gentleman's son, that I have brought up this half year at my great charges, and for this composition, which I have now made with you. — What say you, master doctor? This is *justum impedimentum*, I hope, [255 *error personæ?*

*Ott.* Yes, sir, *in primo gradu.*

*Cut.* *In primo gradu.*

*Daup.* I thank you, good doctor Cutbeard, and parson Otter. — You are    *He pulls off their* beholden to 'em, sir,    *beards and disguises.* that have taken this pains for you; and my friend, master Truewit, who enabled 'em for the business. Now you may go in and rest; be as private as you will, sir. *[Exit Morose.]* [265 I 'll not trouble you, till you trouble me with your funeral, which I care not how soon it come. — Cutbeard, I 'll make your lease good. "Thank me not, but with your leg, Cutbeard." And Tom Otter, your princess shall be [270 reconcil'd to you. — How now, gentlemen, do you look at me?

*Cler.* A boy!

*Daup.* Yes, mistress Epicœne.

*True.* Well, Dauphine, you have lurch'd [275 your friends of the better half of the garland, by concealing this part of the plot: but much good do it thee, thou deserv'st it, lad. And, Clerimont, for thy unexpected bringing in these two to confession, wear my part of it freely. [280 Nay, Sir Daw and Sir La-Foole, you see the gentlewoman that has done you the favours! we are all thankful to you, and so should the woman-kind here, specially for lying on her,

---

¹⁸⁴ **study:** (with the idea of augmenting)    ²¹⁸ **assure:** settle    ²²⁶ **cumber:** trouble    ²³⁸ **crocodile:** hypocrite    ²⁴⁷ **heaven:** (dash in F)    ²⁵³ **composition:** agreement    ²⁶³ **enabled:** qualified    ²⁷⁵ **lurch'd:** swindled    ²⁷⁶ **garland:** symbol of victory    ²⁸⁴ **on:** about

though not with her! you meant so, I am [285 sure. But that we have stuck it upon you to-day, in your own imagin'd persons, and so lately, this Amazon, the champion of the sex, should beat you now thriftily, for the common slanders which ladies receive from such [290 cuckoos as you are. You are they that, when no merit or fortune can make you hope to enjoy their bodies, will yet lie with their reputations, and make their fame suffer. Away, you common moths of these, and all ladies' [295 honours. Go, travel to make legs and faces, and come home with some new matter to be laugh'd at; you deserve to live in an air as corrupted as that wherewith you feed rumour. [*Exeunt Daw and La-Foole.*] — Madams, [300

you are mute, upon this new metamorphosis! But here stands she that has vindicated your fames. Take heed of such *insectæ* hereafter. And let it not trouble you, that you have discover'd any mysteries to this young gentle- [305 man. He is almost of years, and will make a good visitant within this twelvemonth. In the mean time, we 'll all undertake for his secrecy, that can speak so well of his silence. [*Coming forward.*] — Spectators, if you like this [310 comedy, rise cheerfully, and now Morose is gone in, clap your hands. It may be, that noise will cure him, at least please him.      [*Exeunt.*]

**THE END**

289 **thriftily:** punctiliously

# THE ALCHEMIST.

VVritten

by

BEN. IONSON.

———*Neque, me vt miretur turba, laboro:*
*Contentus paucis lectoribus.*

LONDON,
Printed by *Thomas Snodham*, for *Walter Burre*,
and are to be sold by *Iohn Stepneth*, at the
West-end of Paules.
1612.

BIBLIOGRAPHICAL RECORD. *The Alchemist* was first printed in a Quarto which appeared in 1612, and four years later was included in the Folio of 1616. It was entered on the Registers of the Stationers' Co. on Oct. 3, 1610: — *Walter Burre Entred for his Copy vnder the[e h]andes of Sir George Bucke and Th'wardens a Comœdy called,* The Alchymist *made by Ben: Johnson* . . . vjd. The texts of both Quarto and Folio are preceded by a dedication to Lady Mary Wroth, the niece of Sir Philip Sidney, and the Quarto also contains a commendatory poem by George Lucy. The Folio text is followed by a list of the principal comedians (of the King's Company) who took part in the original performance. They were Richard Burbage, John Lowin, Henry Condell, Alexander Cooke, Robert Armin, John Heminges, William Ostler, John Underwood, Nicholas Tooley, and William Ecclestone.

DATE AND STAGE PERFORMANCE. The title-page and final page of the Folio state that *The Alchemist* was first acted by the King's Majesty's Servants in the year 1610. The date is confirmed by internal evidence (e.g., Dame Pliant, who is nineteen years old, II. vi. 32, was born three years after 1588, IV. iv. 29 ff.), and the first performance undoubtedly took place in that year, either before the theatres were closed by plague in July, or, more probably, after they reopened in November. The plague references are so vivid as to convey the impression that Jonson was writing during the visitation, and the notes of time are clearly to the autumn season. The play was given at court before James I in 1612, and again at Whitehall on New Year's night, 1623. It was many times adapted for the later theatres, Garrick's version (which made Abel Drugger the star part) being long famous. The most recent production was that at the Malvern Festival in August, 1932.

SOURCES. The play draws upon the profundity of Jonson's reading and observation of contemporary life. Contemporary alchemists like Dee and Kelly and theologians, such as Hugh Broughton, are brought in to vivify the author's enormous learning in these subjects. For the conception of the "deserted" house Jonson took some hints from the *Mostellaria* of Plautus, and he got other suggestions from the same poet's *Pœnulus.* There is little reason for supposing that he was acquainted with Giordano Bruno's farce, *Il Candelaio* (1582), which has some similarities of theme.

STRUCTURE. The division into acts and scenes is rigidly classical, and all the unities are observed with particular care. Coleridge's praise of the plot as one of the three most perfect ever planned, is well known. The place of action throughout is a house in the Blackfriars, in the immediate neighborhood of the Blackfriars Theatre, and the time a single day in the autumn of 1610.

# BEN JONSON

## THE ALCHEMIST

THE PERSONS OF THE PLAY

SUBTLE, the ALCHEMIST
FACE, the House-keeper
DOL COMMON, their colleague
DAPPER, a [Lawyer's] clerk
DRUGGER, a Tobacco-man
LOVEWIT, Master of the House
[Sir] EPICURE MAMMON, a Knight

[PERTINAX] SURLY, a Gamester
TRIBULATION [WHOLESOME], a Pastor of Amsterdam
ANANIAS, a Deacon there
KASTRIL, the angry boy
DAME PLIANT, his sister, a Widow
Neighbours
Officers, Mutes

THE SCENE: LONDON

## [TO THE READER

IF thou beest more, thou art an understander, and then I trust thee. If thou art one that tak'st up, and but a pretender, beware at what hands thou receiv'st thy commodity; for thou wert never more fair in the way to be coz'ned than in this age in poetry, especially in plays: wherein now the concupiscence of jigs and dances so reigneth, as to run away from nature and be afraid of her is the only point of art that tickles the spectators. But how out of purpose and place do I [5 name art, when the professors are grown so obstinate contemners of it, and presumers on their own naturals, as they are deriders of all diligence that way, and, by simple mocking at the terms when they understand not the things, think to get off wittily with their ignorance! Nay, they are esteem'd the more learned and sufficient for this by the multitude, through their excellent vice of judgment. For they commend writers as they do fencers or wrastlers; who, if they come [10 in robustiously and put for it with a great deal of violence, are receiv'd for the braver fellows; when many times their own rudeness is the cause of their disgrace, and a little touch of their adversary gives all that boisterous force the foil. I deny not but that these men who always seek to do more than enough may some time happen on some thing that is good and great; but very seldom: and when it comes, it doth not recompense the rest of their ill. It sticks out, per- [15 haps, and is more eminent, because all is sordid and vile about it; as lights are more discern'd in a thick darkness than a faint shadow. I speak not this out of a hope to do good on any man against his will; for I know, if it were put to the question of theirs and mine, the worse would find more suffrages, because the most favour common errors. But I give thee this warning, that there is a great difference between those that (to gain the opinion of copy) utter all they [20 can, however unfitly, and those that use election and a mean. For it is only the disease of the un-skillful to think rude things greater than polish'd, or scatter'd more numerous than compos'd.]

## THE ARGUMENT

T HE sickness hot, a master quit, for fear,
H is house in town, and left one servant there.
E ase him corrupted, and gave means to know
A Cheater and his punk; who now brought low,
L eaving their narrow practice, were become      5
C oz'ners at large; and only wanting some
H ouse to set up, with him they here contract,
E ach for a share, and all begin to act.

---

**To the Reader:** (This epistle is found in the Quarto only.)    ⁴ **jigs and dances:** (Some copies of Q read 'daunces and antikes.')   ⁶ **professors:** practitioners   ⁷ **naturals:** natural gifts   ⁹ **multitude:** (Some copies read 'many.')   **excellent:** surpassing   ¹⁰ **vice:** defect   ¹³ **foil:** defeat   ²⁰ **opinion:** reputation   **copy:** copiousness   **utter:** publish   ²¹ **election:** judicious selection   ¹ **hot:** raging ⁴ **punk:** mistress, harlot   ⁶ **Coz'ners:** swindlers

M uch company they draw, and much abuse,  
I n casting figures, telling fortunes, news,                          10  
S elling of flies, flat bawdry, with the stone,  
T ill it, and they, and all in fume are gone.

## PROLOGUE

FORTUNE, that favours fools, these two short hours  
    We wish away, both for your sakes and ours,  
Judging spectators; and desire in place,  
    To th' author justice, to ourselves but grace.  
Our scene is London, 'cause we would make known,              5  
    No country's mirth is better than our own.  
No clime breeds better matter for your whore,  
    Bawd, squire, imposter, many persons more,  
Whose manners, now call'd humours, feed the stage;  
    And which have still been subject for the rage         10  
Or spleen of comic writers: though this pen  
    Did never aim to grieve, but better men;  
Howe'er the age he lives in doth endure  
    The vices that she breeds, above their cure.  
But when the wholesome remedies are sweet,                    15  
    And, in their working gain and profit meet,  
He hopes to find no spirit so much diseas'd,  
    But will with such fair correctives be pleas'd.  
For here he doth not fear who can apply.  
    If there be any that will sit so nigh                  20  
Unto the stream, to look what it doth run,  
    They shall find things, they'd think, or wish, were done;  
They are so natural follies, but so shown,  
    As even the doers may see, and yet not own.

## Act I.  Scene I

*[A Room in Lovewit's House]*

*Face, Subtle, Dol Common*

*Face.*  Believe 't, I will.  
*Sub.*                           Thy worst.  I fart at thee.  
*Dol.*  Ha' you your wits?  Why, gentlemen!  
for love ——  
*Face.*  Sirrah, I 'll strip you ——  
*Sub.*                           What to do?  Lick figs  
Out at my ——                           [sleights.  
*Face.*             Rogue, rogue! — out of all your  
*Dol.*  Nay, look ye, sovereign, general, are  
you madmen?                                          5  
*Sub.*  O, let the wild sheep loose.  I 'll gum  
your silks  
With good strong water, an you come.  
*Dol.*                           Will you have  
The neighbours hear you?  Will you betray  
all?  
Hark!  I hear somebody.

*Face.*                           Sirrah ——  
*Sub.*                           I shall mar  
All that the tailor has made, if you approach.   10  
*Face.*  You most notorious whelp, you inso-  
lent slave,  
Dare you do this?  
*Sub.*                           Yes, faith; yes, faith.  
*Face.*                           Why, who  
Am I, my mongrel, who am I?  
*Sub.*                           I 'll tell you,  
Since you know not yourself.  
*Face.*                           Speak lower, rogue.  
*Sub.*  Yes.  You were once (time 's not long  
past) the good,                                      15  
Honest, plain, livery-three-pound-thrum, that  
kept  
Your master's worship's house here in the  
Friars,  
For the vacations ——  
*Face.*                           Will you be so loud?  
*Sub.*  Since, by my means, translated suburb-  
captain.  
*Face.*  By your means, doctor dog!

---

<sup>9</sup> **abuse:** cheat   <sup>10</sup> **casting figures:** calculating horoscopes   <sup>11</sup> **flies:** familiar spirits   **stone:** philosopher's stone   <sup>12</sup> **fume:** smoke   <sup>3</sup> **Lick figs:** (*see* Rabelais, Bk. IV, Ch. 45)   <sup>4</sup> **sleights:** tricks   <sup>7</sup> **strong water:** (Subtle has a vial of chemical in his hand.)   <sup>16</sup> **livery ... thrum:** poorly paid servant   <sup>17</sup> **Friars:** Blackfriars, fashionable section of London   <sup>19</sup> **captain:** Face wears a captain's uniform.

*Sub.*                    Within man's memory,   20
All this I speak of.

*Face.*                    Why, I pray you, have I
Been countenanc'd by you, or you by me?
Do but collect, sir, where I met you first.

*Sub.*    I do not hear well.

*Face.*                    Not of this, I think it.
But I shall put you in mind, sir; — at Pie-cor-
ner,                                                    25
Taking your meal of steam in, from cooks' stalls,
Where, like the father of hunger, you did walk
Piteously costive, with your pinch'd-horn-nose,
And your complexion of the Roman wash,
Stuck full of black and melancholic worms,  30
Like powder-corns shot at th' artillery-yard.

*Sub.*    I wish you could advance your voice a
little.

*Face.*    When you went pinn'd up in the
several rags
Y' had rak'd and pick'd from dunghills, be-
fore day;
Your feet in mouldy slippers, for your kibes;
A felt of rug, and a thin threaden cloak,     36
That scarce would cover your no-buttocks ——

*Sub.*                    So, sir!

*Face.*    When all your alchemy, and your alge-
bra,
Your minerals, vegetals, and animals,
Your conjuring, coz'ning; and your dozen of
trades,                                                 40
Could not relieve your corpse with so much
linen
Would make you tinder, but to see a fire;
I ga' you count'nance, credit for your coals,
Your stills, your glasses, your materials;
Built you a furnace, drew you customers,   45
Advanc'd all your black arts; lent you, beside,
A house to practise in ——

*Sub.*                    Your master's house!

*Face.*    Where you have studied the more
thriving skill
Of bawdry, since.

*Sub.*                    Yes, in your master's house.
You and the rats here kept possession.        50
Make it not strange.  I know you were one
could keep
The buttery-hatch still lock'd, and save the
chippings,
Sell the dole beer to aqua-vitæ men,
The which, together with your Christmas vails
At post-and-pair, your letting out of counters,

Made you a pretty stock, some twenty marks, 56
And gave you credit to converse with cobwebs,
Here, since your mistress' death hath broke up
house.

*Face.*    You might talk softlier, rascal.

*Sub.*                    No, you scarab,
I 'll thunder you in pieces.  I will teach you   60
How to beware to tempt a Fury again
That carries tempest in his hand and voice.

*Face.*    The place has made you valiant.

*Sub.*                    No, your clothes.
Thou vermin, have I ta'en thee out of dung,
So poor, so wretched, when no living thing    65
Would keep thee company, but a spider or
worse?
Rais'd thee from brooms, and dust, and wat'r-
ing-pots,
Sublim'd thee, and exalted thee, and fix'd thee
I' the third region, call'd our state of grace?
Wrought thee to spirit, to quintessence, with
pains                                                   70
Would twice have won me the philosopher's
work?
Put thee in words and fashion? made thee fit
For more than ordinary fellowships?
Giv'n thee thy oaths, thy quarrelling dimen-
sions?
Thy rules to cheat at horse-race, cock-pit, cards,
Dice, or whatever gallant tincture else?       76
Made thee a second in mine own great art?
And have I this for thank!  Do you rebel?
Do you fly out i' the projection?
Would you be gone now?

*Dol.*                    Gentlemen, what mean you?   80
Will you mar all?

*Sub.*    Slave, thou hadst had no name ——

*Dol.*    Will you undo yourselves with civil
war?

*Sub.*    Never been known, past *equi clibanum*,
The heat of horse-dung, under ground, in cel-
lars,
Or an ale-house darker than deaf John's; been
lost                                                     85
To all mankind, but laundresses and tapsters,
Had not I been.

*Dol.*    D' you know who hears you, sovereign?

*Face.*    Sirrah ——                      [were civil.

*Dol.*                    Nay, general, I thought you

*Face.*    I shall turn desperate, if you grow
thus loud.

*Sub.*    And hang thyself, I care not.

---

²³ **collect:** recollect      ²⁵ **Pie-corner:** in West Smithfield, noted for cookery shops      ²⁹ **Roman wash:** a wash of alum water(?)      ³¹ **powder-corns:** grains of powder      ³⁵ **kibes:** chilblains      ³⁶ **felt of rug:** hat of coarse material      ⁴² **but . . . fire:** *i.e.*, for enough fire to be visible      ⁴⁸ **skill:** art, trade      ⁵¹ **Make . . . strange:** Do not assume ignorance.      ⁵²⁻⁵³ **chippings . . . men:** (Doles of broken bread, or "chippings," and beer were distributed to the poor from great houses.  Face is ac-cused of selling such beer to the liquor-dealers.)      ⁵⁴ **vails:** tips      ⁵⁵ **post-and-pair:** a card game      **letting . . . counters:** supplying chips      ⁵⁹ **scarab:** beetle (a term of abuse)      ⁶⁸⁻⁷⁰ **technical terms in alchemy**      ⁷⁶ **tincture:** quality, accomplishment      ⁷⁹ **i' the projection:** when success is near      ⁸³ **equi clibanum:** (translated in next line)

*Face.*                    Hang thee, collier,
And all thy pots and pans, in picture I will, 91
Since thou hast mov'd me ——
  *Dol.*        [*Aside.*]  O, this 'll o'erthrow all.
  *Face.*  Write thee up bawd in Paul's; have
    all thy tricks
Of coz'ning with a hollow coal, dust, scrapings.
Searching for things lost, with a sieve and
    shears, 95
Erecting figures in your rows of houses,
And taking in of shadows with a glass,
Told in red letters; and a face cut for thee,
Worse than Gamaliel Ratsey's.
  *Dol.*                    Are you sound?
Ha' you your senses, masters?
  *Face.*                  I will have 100
A book, but rarely reckoning thy impostures,
Shall prove a true philosopher's stone to
    printers.
  *Sub.*  Away, you trencher-rascal!
  *Face.*                  Out, you dog-leech!
The vomit of all prisons ——
  *Dol.*                  Will you be
Your own destructions, gentlemen?
  *Face.*                  Still spew'd out 105
For lying too heavy o' the basket.
  *Sub.*                      Cheater!
  *Face.*  Bawd!
  *Sub.*          Cow-herd!
  *Face.*              Conjurer!
  *Sub.*                  Cutpurse!
  *Face.*                      Witch!
  *Dol.*                        O me!
We are ruin'd, lost!  Ha' you no more regard
To your reputations?  Where 's your judgment?
  'Slight, 109
Have yet some care of me, o' your republic ——
  *Face.*  Away, this brach!  I 'll bring thee,
    rogue, within
The statute of sorcery, tricesimo tertio
Of Harry the Eight: ay, and perhaps thy neck
Within a noose, for laund'ring gold and barbing
    it.
  *Dol.*  You 'll bring your head within a cox-
    comb, will you? 115
      *She catcheth out Face his sword,*
        *and breaks Subtle's glass.*
And you, sir, with your menstrue! — Gather
    it up.
'Sdeath, you abominable pair of stinkards,
Leave off your barking, and grow one again,

Or, by the light that shines, I 'll cut your
    throats.
I 'll not be made a prey unto the marshal 120
For ne'er a snarling dog-bolt o' you both.
Ha' you together cozen'd all this while,
And all the world, and shall it now be said,
You've made most courteous shift to cozen
    yourselves?
  [*To Face.*]  You will accuse him!  You will
    "bring him in 125
Within the statute!"  Who shall take your word?
A whoreson, upstart, apocryphal captain,
Whom not a Puritan in Blackfriars will trust
So much as for a feather: and you, too,
                          [*To Subtle*]
Will give the cause, forsooth!  You will insult,
And claim a primacy in the divisions! 131
You must be chief!  As if you, only, had
The powder to project with, and the work
Were not begun out of equality! 134
The venter tripartite!  All things in common!
Without priority!  'Sdeath! you perpetual curs,
Fall to your couples again, and cozen kindly,
And heartily, and lovingly, as you should,
And lose not the beginning of a term,
Or, by this hand, I shall grow factious too, 140
And take my part, and quit you.
  *Face.*                  'T is his fault;
He ever murmurs, and objects his pains,
And says, the weight of all lies upon him.
  *Sub.*  Why, so it does.
  *Dol.*                How does it?  Do not we
Sustain our parts?
  *Sub.*      Yes, but they are not equal. 145
  *Dol.*  Why, if your part exceed to-day, I hope
Ours may to-morrow match it.
  *Sub.*              Ay, they *may.*
  *Dol.*  May, murmuring mastiff!  Ay, and do.
    Death on me!
Help me to throttle him.
                  [*Seizes Sub. by the throat.*]
  *Sub.*          Dorothy!  Mistress Dorothy!
'Ods precious, I 'll do anything.  What do you
    mean? 150
  *Dol.*  Because o' your fermentation and ciba-
    tion?
  *Sub.*  Not I, by heaven ——
  *Dol.*          Your Sol and Luna —— help me.
                            [*To Face.*]
  *Sub.*  Would I were hang'd then!  I 'll con-
    form myself.

---

⁹³ **Paul's:** St. Paul's Church, a place of resort for business and pleasure    ⁹⁴⁻⁹⁸ Tricks of alchemy or astrology    ⁹⁹ **Ratsey:** a notorious highwayman who wore a hideous mask    ¹⁰⁶ **lying . . . basket:** eating more than his share of prison rations    ¹¹¹ **brach:** bitch    ¹¹², ¹¹³ **tricesimo . . . Eight:** 33 Henry VIII (1541), the first law against witchcraft    ¹¹⁴ **laund'ring:** washing in acid    **barbing:** chipping coins    ¹¹⁵ **coxcomb:** fool's cap    ¹¹⁶ **menstrue:** a liquid which dissolves solids    ¹²¹ **dog-bolt:** scoundrel    ¹³⁰ **insult:** boast    ¹³¹ **primacy:** first choice    ¹³³ **powder:** (spelled 'poulder' here and elsewhere)    **project:** transmute metals    ¹³⁵ **venter tripartite:** threefold agreement    ¹³⁹ **term:** *i.e.,* a term of the law courts    ¹⁵¹ **fermentation and cibation:** processes in alchemy    ¹⁵² **Sol:** gold    **Luna:** silver

*Dol.* Will you, sir? Do so then, and quickly:
swear.
*Sub.* What should I swear?
*Dol.*                      To leave your faction, sir,
And labour kindly in the common work.    156
  *Sub.* Let me not breathe if I meant aught
    beside.
I only us'd those speeches as a spur
To him.
  *Dol.* I hope we need no spurs, sir. Do we?
  *Face.* 'Slid, prove to-day who shall shark
    best.
  *Sub.* Agreed.                                 160
  *Dol.* Yes, and work close and friendly.
  *Sub.*                      'Slight, the knot
Shall grow the stronger for this breach, with
    me.                      [*They shake hands.*]
  *Dol.* Why, so, my good baboons! Shall we
    go make
A sort of sober, scurvy, precise neighbours,
That scarce have smil'd twice sin' the king
    came in,                               165
A feast of laughter at our follies? Rascals,
Would run themselves from breath, to see me
    ride,
Or you t' have but a hole to thrust your heads
    in,
For which you should pay ear-rent? No, agree.
And may Don Provost ride a-feasting long, 170
In his old velvet jerkin and stain'd scarfs,
My noble sovereign, and worthy general,
Ere we contribute a new crewel garter
To his most worsted worship.
  *Sub.*                      Royal Dol!
Spoken like Claridiana, and thyself.       175
  *Face.* For which at supper, thou shalt sit in
    triumph,
And not be styl'd Dol Common, but Dol
    Proper,
Dol Singular: the longest cut at night
Shall draw thee for his Dol Particular.
                            [*Bell rings without.*]
  *Sub.* Who 's that? One rings. To the win-
    do', Dol! [*Exit Dol.*] — Pray heav'n, 180
The master do not trouble us this quarter.
  *Face.* O, fear not him. While there dies one
    a week
O' the plague, he 's safe from thinking toward
    London.
Beside, he 's busy at his hop-yards now;
I had a letter from him. If he do,       185
He 'll send such word, for airing o' the house,
As you shall have sufficient time to quit it:

Though we break up a fortnight, 't is no mat-
    ter.
                            [*Re-enter Dol*]
  *Sub.* Who is it, Dol?
  *Dol.*                      A fine young quodling.
  *Face.*                                    O,
My lawyer's clerk, I lighted on last night,   190
In Holborn, at the Dagger. He would have
(I told you of him) a familiar,
To rifle with at horses, and win cups.
  *Dol.* O, let him in.
  *Sub.*                Stay. Who shall do 't?
  *Face.*                              Get you   194
Your robes on; I will meet him, as going out.
  *Dol.* And what shall I do?
  *Face.*                      Not be seen; away! [*Exit Dol.*]
Seem you very reserv'd.
  *Sub.*                Enough.          [*Exit.*]
  *Face.* [*Aloud and retiring.*]   God be wi' you,
    sir,
I pray you, let him know that I was here:
His name is Dapper. I would gladly have
    stay'd, but ——

## *Act I.  Scene II*

### [*The Same*]

*Dapper, Face, Subtle*

[*Dap. within.*]   Captain, I am here.
  *Face.* Who 's that? — He 's come, I think,
    doctor.
                            [*Enter Dapper*]
Good faith, sir, I was going away.
  *Dap.*                              In truth,
I 'm very sorry, captain.
  *Face.*                But I thought
Sure I should meet you.
  *Dap.*                Ay, I 'm very glad.
I had a scurvy writ or two to make,           5
And I had lent my watch last night to one
That dines to-day at the shrieve's, and so was
    robb'd
Of my pass-time.
      [*Re-enter Subtle in his velvet cap and gown*]
                    Is this the cunning-man?
  *Face.* This is his worship.
  *Dap.*                      Is he a doctor?
  *Face.*                                    Yes.
  *Dap.* And ha' you broke with him, captain?
  *Face.*       Ay.
  *Dap.*                            And how?   10

---

¹⁵⁵ **faction:** quarreling       ¹⁶⁴ **sort:** group       ¹⁶⁵ **sin'** . . . **in:** 1603, seven years before the play
¹⁶⁷ **ride:** *i.e.*, on a cart as a bawd       ¹⁶⁸ **hole** . . . **in:** the pillory       ¹⁶⁹ **pay ear-rent:** have your ears
cut off       ¹⁷⁰ **Don Provost:** the hangman       ¹⁷⁵ **Claridiana:** the heroine of a popular romance, *The
Mirror of Knighthood*       ¹⁸⁹ **quodling:** green apple, youth       ¹⁹¹ **Dagger:** a tavern       ¹⁹² **familiar:**
familiar spirit, "fly"       ¹⁹³ **rifle:** gamble       ¹⁹⁷ **God** . . . **you:** ('God b' w' you' F)       ⁷ **shrieve's:**
sheriff's       ⁸ **pass-time:** watch       ¹⁰ **broke:** introduced the subject

*Face.* Faith, he does make the matter, sir so dainty,
I know not what to say.
    *Dap.* Not so, good captain.
    *Face.* Would I were fairly rid on 't, believe me.
    *Dap.* Nay, now you grieve me, sir. Why should you wish so?
I dare assure you, I 'll not be ungrateful.  15
    *Face.* I cannot think you will, sir. But the law
Is such a thing —— and then he says, Read's matter
Falling so lately ——
    *Dap.* Read! he was an ass,
And dealt, sir, with a fool.
    *Face.* It was a clerk, sir.  19
    *Dap.* A clerk!
    *Face.* Nay, hear me, sir. You know the law
Better, I think ——
    *Dap.* I should, sir, and the danger:
You know, I show'd the statute to you.
    *Face.* You did so.
    *Dap.* And will I tell then! By this hand of flesh,
Would it might never write good courthand more,
If I discover. What do you think of me,  25
That I am a chiaus?
    *Face.* What 's that?
    *Dap.* The Turk was here.
As one would say, do you think I am a Turk?
    *Face.* I 'll tell the doctor so.
    *Dap.* Do, good sweet captain.
    *Face.* Come, noble doctor, pray thee, let 's prevail;
This is the gentleman, and he is no chiaus.  30
    *Sub.* Captain, I have return'd you all my answer.
I would do much, sir, for your love —— But this
I neither may, nor can.
    *Face.* Tut, do not say so.
You deal now with a noble fellow, doctor,
One that will thank you richly; and he 's no chiaus:  35
Let that, sir, move you.
    *Sub.* Pray you, forbear ——
    *Face.* He has
Four angels here.
    *Sub.* You do me wrong, good sir.
    *Face.* Doctor, wherein? To tempt you with these spirits?

    *Sub.* To tempt my art and love, sir, to my peril.
'Fore heav'n, I scarce can think you are my friend,  40
That so would draw me to apparent danger.
    *Face.* I draw you! A horse draw you, and a halter,
You, and your flies together ——
    *Dap.* Nay, good captain.
    *Face.* That know no difference of men.
    *Sub.* Good words, sir.
    *Face.* Good deeds, sir, doctor dogs'-meat.
'Slight, I bring you  45
No cheating Clim o' the Cloughs or Claribels,
That look as big as five-and-fifty, and flush;
And spit out secrets like hot custard ——
    *Dap.* Captain!
    *Face.* Nor any melancholic underscribe,
Shall tell the vicar; but a special gentle,  50
That is the heir to forty marks a year,
Consorts with the small poets of the time,
Is the sole hope of his old grandmother;
That knows the law, and writes you six fair hands,
Is a fine clerk, and has his ciph'ring perfect;  55
Will take his oath o' the Greek Xenophon,
If need be, in his pocket; and can court
His mistress out of Ovid.
    *Dap.* Nay, dear captain ——
    *Face.* Did you, not tell me so?
    *Dap.* Yes; but I 'd ha' you
Use master doctor with some more respect.  60
    *Face.* Hang him, proud stag, with his broad velvet head! —
But for your sake, I 'd choke ere I would change
An article of breath with such a puck-fist!
Come, let 's be gone.     [*Going.*]
    *Sub.* Pray you, le' me speak with you.
    *Dap.* His worship calls you, captain.
    *Face.* I am sorry
I e'er embark'd myself in such a business.  66
    *Dap.* Nay, good sir; he did call you.
    *Face.* Will he take then?
    *Sub.* First, hear me ——
    *Face.* Not a syllable, 'less you take.
    *Sub.* Pray ye, sir ——
    *Face* Upon no terms but an *assumpsit.*
    *Sub.* Your humour must be law.
    *He takes the money.*
    *Face.* Why now, sir, talk.  70
Now I dare hear you with mine honour. Speak.
So may this gentleman too.

---

[11] **make . . . dainty:** has such scruples   [17] **Read:** a magician indicted in 1608   [24] **courthand:** law-court script   [25] **discover:** reveal   [26] **chiaus:** (literally a Turkish envoy or agent. Gifford reports that one had swindled London merchants in 1609, and the word came to mean 'a cheat.')   [37] **angels:** gold coins worth about 10s.   [46] **Clim . . . Claribels:** heroes of ballad and romance   [47] **five . . . flush:** winning hands in the game of primero   [50] **gentle:** gentleman   [56] **Xenophon:** ('Testament' Q)   [63] **puck-fist:** niggardly person (literally, puff-ball)   [69] **assumpsit:** He has taken the money and undertaken the affair (legal term).

*Sub.*          Why, sir ——
       [*Offering to whisper Face.*]
*Face.*          No whisp'ring.
*Sub.* 'Fore heav'n, you do not apprehend
the loss
You do yourself in this.
*Face.*          Wherein? for what?
*Sub.* Marry, to be so importunate for one   75
That, when he has it, will undo you all:
He 'll win up all the money i' the town.
*Face.* How!
*Sub.*        Yes, and blow up gamester after
    gamester,
As they do crackers in a puppet-play.
If I do give him a familiar,          80
Give you him all you play for; never set
    him:
For he will have it.
*Face.*       You 're mistaken, doctor.
Why, he does ask one but for cups and horses,
A rifling fly; none o' your great familiars.
*Dap.* Yes, captain, I would have it for all
    games.          85
*Sub.* I told you so.
*Face.* [*Taking Dap. aside.*] 'Slight, that 's a
    new business!
I understood you, a tame bird, to fly
Twice in a term, or so, on Friday nights,
When you had left the office; for a nag
Of forty or fifty shillings.
*Dap.*        Ay, 't is true, sir;   90
But I do think, now, I shall leave the law,
And therefore ——
*Face.*     Why, this changes quite the case.
D' you think that I dare move him?
*Dap.*        If you please, sir;
All 's one to him, I see.
*Face.*        What! for that money?   94
I cannot with my conscience; nor should you
Make the request, methinks.
*Dap.*          No, sir, I mean
To add consideration.
*Face.*        Why, then, sir,
I 'll try. [*Goes to Subtle.*] Say that it were for
all games, doctor?
*Sub.* I say then, not a mouth shall eat for
    him
At any ordinary, but o' the score,      100
That is a gaming mouth, conceive me.
*Face.*          Indeed!
*Sub.* He 'll draw you all the treasure of the
    realm,
If it be set him.
*Face.*       Speak you this from art?
*Sub.* Ay, sir, and reason too, the ground of
    art.

He 's o' the only best complexion,    105
The queen of Faery loves.
*Face.*          What! Is he?
*Sub.*               Peace.
He 'll overhear you. Sir, should she but see
    him ——
*Face.* What?
*Sub.*        Do not you tell him.
*Face.*        Will he win at cards too?
*Sub.* The spirits of dead Holland, living
    Isaac,          109
You 'd swear, were in him; such a vigorous luck
As cannot be resisted. 'Slight, he 'll put
Six o' your gallants to a cloak, indeed.
*Face.* A strange success, that some man shall
    be born to!
*Sub.* He hears you, man ——
*Dap.*        Sir, I 'll not be ingrateful.
*Face.* Faith, I have a confidence in his good
    nature:          115
You hear, he says he will not be ingrateful.
*Sub.* Why, as you please; my venture fol-
    lows yours.
*Face.* Troth, do it, doctor; think him trusty,
    and make him.
He may make us both happy in an hour;
Win some five thousand pound, and send us
    two on 't.          120
*Dap.* Believe it, and I will, sir.
*Face.*        And you shall, sir.
You have heard all?    *Face takes him aside.*
*Dap.*    No, what was 't? Nothing, I, sir.
*Face.* Nothing?
*Dap.*       A little, sir.
*Face.*          Well, a rare star
Reign'd at your birth.
*Dap.*        At mine, sir! No.
*Face.*          The doctor
Swears that you are ——
*Sub.* Nay, captain, you 'll tell all now. 125
*Face.* Allied to the queen of Faery.
*Dap.*        Who! That I am?
Believe it, no such matter ——
*Face.*        Yes, and that
You were born with a caul o' your head.
*Dap.*        Who says so?
*Face.*          Come,
You know it well enough, though you dissemble
    it.          129
*Dap.* I' fac, I do not; you are mistaken.
*Face.*          How!
Swear by your fac, and in a thing so known
Unto the doctor? How shall we, sir, trust you
I' the other matter? Can we ever think,
When you have won five or six thousand pound,
You 'll send us shares in 't, by this rate?

---

⁷⁹ **crackers:** fire-crackers    ⁸¹ **set:** bet against
**o' the score:** on credit    ¹⁰⁹ **Holland . . . Isaac:** two alchemists(?)    ¹¹¹⁻¹¹² **put . . . cloak:** reduce
them to one cloak among them all    ¹³¹ **fac:** faith

*Dap.*                    By Jove, sir, 135
I 'll win ten thousand pound, and send you
  half.
I' fac 's no oath.
  *Sub.*          No, no, he did but jest.
  *Face.* Go to. Go thank the doctor. He 's
  your friend,
To take it so.
  *Dap.*        I thank his worship.
  *Face.*                          So!
Another angel.
  *Dap.*        Must I?
  *Face.*              Must you! 'Slight, 140
What else is thanks? Will you be trivial? —
  Doctor,    [*Dapper gives him the money.*]
When must he come for his familiar?
  *Dap.* Shall I not ha' it with me?
  *Sub.*                          O, good sir!
There must a world of ceremonies pass;
You must be bath'd and fumigated first: 145
Besides, the queen of Faery does not rise
Till it be noon.
  *Face.*        Not if she danc'd to-night.
  *Sub.* And she must bless it.
  *Face.*                    Did you never see
Her royal grace yet?
  *Dap.*        Whom?
  *Face.*              Your aunt of Faery?
  *Sub.* Not since she kiss'd him in the cradle,
  captain;                              150
I can resolve you that.
  *Face.*        Well, see her grace,
Whate'er it cost you, for a thing that I know.
It will be somewhat hard to compass; but
However, see her. You are made, believe it, 154
If you can see her. Her grace is a lone woman,
And very rich; and if she take a fancy,
She will do strange things. See her, at any
  hand.
'Slid, she may hap to leave you all she has!
It is the doctor's fear.
  *Dap.*        How will 't be done, then?
  *Face.* Let me alone, take you no thought.
  Do you                              160
But say to me, "Captain, I 'll see her grace."
  *Dap.* "Captain, I 'll see her grace."
  *Face.* Enough.        *One knocks without.*
  *Sub.*                    Who 's there?
Anon. — [*Aside to Face.*] Conduct him forth
  by the back way. —
Sir, against one o'clock prepare yourself;
Till when you must be fasting; only take 165
Three drops of vinegar in at your nose,
Two at your mouth, and one at either ear;
Then bathe your fingers' ends and wash your
  eyes,

To sharpen your five senses, and cry "hum" 169
Thrice, and then "buz" as often; and then
  come.                              [*Exit.*]
  *Face.* Can you remember this?
  *Dap.*                    I warrant you.
  *Face.* Well then, away. 'Tis but your be-
  stowing
Some twenty nobles 'mong her grace's servants,
And put on a clean shirt. You do not know 174
What grace her grace may do you in clean
  linen.

*[Exeunt Face and Dapper.]*

## Act I.  Scene III

*[The Same]*

*Subtle, Drugger, Face*

[*Sub. within.*] Come in! Good wives, I
  pray you, forbear me now;
Troth, I can do you no good till afternoon. —

*[Enter Subtle, followed by Drugger]*

What is your name, say you? Abel Drugger?
  *Drug.*        Yes, sir.
  *Sub.* A seller of tobacco?
  *Drug.*                    Yes, sir.
  *Sub.*                          Umph!
Free of the grocers?
  *Drug.*        Ay, an 't please you.
  *Sub.*                    Well —— 5
Your business, Abel?
  *Drug.*        This, an 't please your worship;
I am a young beginner, and am building
Of a new shop, an 't like your worship, just
At corner of a street. — Here 's the plot on
  't ——                              9
And I would know by art, sir, of your worship,
Which way I should make my door, by necro-
  mancy,
And where my shelves; and which should be
  for boxes,
And which for pots. I would be glad to thrive,
  sir:
And I was wish'd to your worship by a gentle-
  man,
One Captain Face, that says you know men's
  planets,                              15
And their good angels, and their bad.
  *Sub.*                          I do,
If I do see 'em ——

*[Enter Face]*

  *Face.*        What! my honest Abel?
Thou art well met here.

---

147 **to-night:** last night    151 **resolve:** tell    169, 170 **hum, buz:** cabalistic words used in witchcraft
173 **nobles:** coins worth 6s. 8d    1 **forbear:** spare    5 **Free . . . grocers:** a member of the Grocers'
Company    9 **plot:** plan    14 **wish'd:** recommended

*Drug.*                Troth, sir, I was speaking,
Just as your worship came here, of your wor-
    ship.
I pray you, speak for me to master doctor.   20
    *Face.* He shall do anything.  Doctor, do
    you hear?
This is my friend, Abel, an honest fellow;
He lets me have good tobacco, and he does
    not
Sophisticate it with sack-lees or oil,
Nor washes it in muscadel and grains,        25
Nor buries it in gravel, under ground,
Wrapp'd up in greasy leather, or piss'd clouts:
But keeps it in fine lily pots, that, open'd,
Smell like conserve of roses, or French beans.
He has his maple block, his silver tongs,    30
Winchester pipes, and fire of juniper:
A neat, spruce, honest fellow, and no gold-
    smith.
    *Sub.* He 's a fortunate fellow, that I am
    sure on.
    *Face.* Already, sir, ha' you found it?  Lo
    thee, Abel!
    *Sub.* And in right way toward riches ——
    *Face.*                Sir!
    *Sub.*                This summer, 35
He will be of the clothing of his company,
And next spring call'd to the scarlet; spend
    what he can.
    *Face.* What, and so little beard?
    *Sub.*                Sir, you must think,
He may have a receipt to make hair come:
But he 'll be wise, preserve his youth, and fine
    for 't;                                     40
His fortune looks for him another way.
    *Face.* 'Slid, doctor, how canst thou know
    this so soon?
I am amus'd at that.
    *Sub.*                By a rule, captain,
In metoposcopy, which I do work by;           44
A certain star i' the forehead, which you see
    not.
Your chestnut or your olive-colour'd face
Does never fail: and your long ear doth prom-
    ise.
I knew 't, by certain spots, too, in his teeth,
And on the nail of his mercurial finger.
    *Face.* Which finger 's that?
    *Sub.*                His little finger.  Look. 50
You were born upon a Wednesday?
    *Drug.*                Yes, indeed, sir.

    *Sub.* The thumb, in chiromancy, we give
    Venus;
The forefinger to Jove; the midst to Saturn;
The ring to Sol; the least to Mercury,
Who was the lord, sir, of his horoscope,      55
His house of life being Libra; which foreshow'd
He should be a merchant, and should trade with
    balance.
    *Face.* Why, this is strange!  Is 't not, honest
    Nab?
    *Sub.* There is a ship now coming from Or-
    mus,
That shall yield him such a commodity         60
Of drugs —— This is the west, and this the
    south?          [*Pointing to the plan.*]
    *Drug.* Yes, sir.
    *Sub.*                And those are your two sides?
    *Drug.*                Ay, sir.
    *Sub.* Make me your door then, south; your
    broad side, west:
And on the east side of your shop, aloft,
Write Mathlai, Tarmiel, and Baraborat;        65
Upon the north part, Rael, Velel, Thiel.
They are the names of those Mercurial spirits
That do fright flies from boxes.
    *Drug.*                Yes, sir.
    *Sub.*                And
Beneath your threshold, bury me a loadstone   69
To draw in gallants that wear spurs: the rest,
They 'll seem to follow.
    *Face.*                That 's a secret, Nab!
    *Sub.* And, on your stall, a puppet, with a
    vice
And a court-fucus, to call city-dames:
You shall deal much with minerals.
    *Drug.*                Sir, I have,
At home, already ——
    *Sub.*                Ay, I know, you 've arsenic, 75
Vitriol, sal-tartar, argaile, alkali,
Cinoper: I know all. — This fellow, captain,
Will come, in time, to be a great distiller,
And give a say — I will not say directly,
But very fair — at the philosopher's stone.   80
    *Face.* Why, how now, Abel! is this true?
    *Drug.* [*Aside to Face.*]        Good captain,
What must I give?
    *Face.*                Nay, I 'll not counsel thee.
Thou hear'st what wealth (he says, spend what
    thou canst),
Th' art like to come to.
    *Drug.*                I would gi' him a crown.

---

²⁴ **Sophisticate:** adulterate        ²⁵ **grains:** a kind of spice        ²⁸ **lily pots:** ornamental jars
³⁰⁻³¹ **maple . . . juniper:** (Tobacconists provided facilities for smoking in their shops.  The tobacco
was shredded on a maple block, and pipes were lighted from coals of juniper wood held in silver tongs.)
³² **goldsmith:** usurer     ³⁶ **clothing:** livery     ³⁷ **call'd . . . scarlet:** made sheriff     ⁴⁰ **fine:** pay the fine
for refusing to serve     ⁴³ **amus'd:** amazed, made to muse     ⁴⁴ **metoposcopy:** a branch of physiognomy
⁶⁰ **commodity:** bargain     ⁶⁵⁻⁶⁶ **Mathlai . . . Thiel:** names of spirits in Pietro d'Abano's *Elementa
Magica*     ⁷¹ **seem:** think it seemly     ⁷² **puppet . . . vice:** mechanical doll     ⁷³ **court-fucus:** cosmetic
⁷⁹ **give a say:** make an attempt

*Face.* A crown! and toward such a fortune?
Heart,    85
Thou shalt rather gi' him thy shop. No gold
about thee?
*Drug.* Yes, I have a portague, I ha' kept
this half-year.
*Face.* Out on thee, Nab! 'Slight, there was
such an offer —
Shalt keep 't no longer, I 'll gi' it him for thee.
Doctor,
Nab prays your worship to drink this, and
swears    90
He will appear more grateful, as your skill
Does raise him in the world.
*Drug.*    I would entreat
Another favour of his worship.
*Face.*    What is 't, Nab?
*Drug.* But to look over, sir, my almanac,
And cross out my ill-days, that I may neither
Bargain, nor trust upon them.
*Face.*    That he shall, Nab:    96
Leave it, it shall be done, 'gainst afternoon.
*Sub.* And a direction for his shelves.
*Face.*    Now, Nab,
Art thou well pleas'd, Nab?
*Drug.* 'Thank, sir, both your worships.    99
*Face.* Away.    [*Exit Drugger.*]
Why, now, you smoky persecutor of nature!
Now do you see, that something 's to be done,
Beside your beech-coal, and your cor'sive
waters,
Your crosslets, crucibles, and cucurbites?
You must have stuff brought home to you, to
work on:    105
And yet you think, I am at no expense
In searching out these veins, then following 'em,
Then trying 'em out. 'Fore God, my intelli-
gence
Costs me more money than my share oft comes
to,
In these rare works.
*Sub.* You 're pleasant, sir. — How now! 110

## Act I. Scene IIII

*[The Same]*

*Face, Dol, Subtle*

[*Sub.*] What says my dainty Dolkin?
*Dol.*    Yonder fish-wife
Will not away. And there 's your giantess,
The bawd of Lambeth.
*Sub.*    Heart, I cannot speak with 'em.

*Dol.* Not afore night, I have told 'em in a
voice,
Thorough the trunk, like one of your familiars.
But I have spied Sir Epicure Mammon ——
*Sub.*    Where?    6
*Dol.* Coming along, at far end of the lane,
Slow of his feet, but earnest of his tongue
To one that 's with him.
*Sub.*    Face, go you and shift.
Dol, you must presently make ready too.    10
    [*Exit Face.*]
*Dol.* Why, what 's the matter?
*Sub.*    O, I did look for him
With the sun's rising: marvel he could sleep!
This is the day I am to perfect for him
The magisterium, our great work, the stone;
And yield it, made, into his hands; of which    15
He has, this month, talk'd as he were possess'd.
And now he 's dealing pieces on 't away.
Methinks I see him ent'ring ordinaries,
Dispensing for the pox, and plaguy houses,
Reaching his dose, walking Moorfields for
lepers,    20
And off'ring citizens' wives pomander-bracelets,
As his preservative, made of the elixir;
Searching the 'spital, to make old bawds young;
And the highways, for beggars to make rich.
I see no end of his labours. He will make    25
Nature asham'd of her long sleep; when art,
Who 's but a step-dame, shall do more than she,
In her best love to mankind, ever could.
If his dream last, he 'll turn the age to gold.
    [*Exeunt.*]

## Act II.  Scene I

*[A Room in Lovewit's House]*

*[Sir Epicure] Mammon, Surly*

[*Mam.*] Come on, sir. Now you set your
foot on shore
In *Novo Orbe;* here 's the rich Peru:
And there within, sir, are the golden mines,
Great Solomon's Ophir! He was sailing to 't
Three years, but we have reach'd it in ten
months.    5
This is the day wherein, to all my friends,
I will pronounce the happy word, *Be rich;*
*This day you shall be spectatissimi.*
You shall no more deal with the hollow die,    9
Or the frail card; no more be at charge of keep-
ing
The livery-punk for the young heir, that must

---

87 **portague:** a gold coin worth about $18    95 **ill-days:** unlucky days    97 **'gainst:** by, before
103 **cor'sive:** corrosive    104 **crosslets, cucurbites:** glass vessels used in alchemy    3 **Heart:** a petty
oath    5 **trunk:** speaking-tube    21 **pomander:** a perfume ball thought to protect the wearer from infection    22 **elixir:** philosopher's stone    23 **'spital:** hospital    2 **Novo Orbe:** the New World
8 **spectatissimi:** most gazed at    9 **hollow die:** loaded dice    11 **livery-punk:** female accomplice of a
swindler

Seal, at all hours, in his shirt: no more,
If he deny, ha' him beaten to 't, as he is
That brings him the commodity; no more
Shall thirst of satin, or the covetous hunger    15
Of velvet entrails for a rude-spun cloak,
To be display'd at Madam Augusta's, make
The sons of Sword and Hazard fall before
The golden calf, and on their knees, whole
    nights,
Commit idolatry with wine and trumpets:    20
Or go a-feasting after drum and ensign.
No more of this. You shall start up young vice-
    roys,
And have your punks and punkettees, my
    Surly.
And unto thee I speak it first, *be rich.*
Where is my Subtle there? Within, ho!
    [*Face within.*]                                    Sir,    25
He 'll come to you by and by.
    *Mam.*                          That 's his fire-drake,
His Lungs, his Zephyrus, he that puffs his coals,
Till he firk nature up, in her own centre.
You are not faithful, sir. This night I 'll change
All that is metal in my house to gold:    30
And, early in the morning, will I send
To all the plumbers and the pewterers,
And buy their tin and lead up; and to Lothbury
For all the copper.
    *Sur.*                          What, and turn that, too?
    *Mam.* Yes, and I 'll purchase Devonshire
    and Cornwall,                                    35
And make them perfect Indies! You admire
    now?
    *Sur.* No, faith.
    *Mam.* But when you see th' effects of the
    Great Med'cine,
Of which one part projected on a hundred
Of Mercury, or Venus, or the Moon,    40
Shall turn it to as many of the Sun;
Nay, to a thousand, so *ad infinitum:*
You will believe me.
    *Sur.*                          Yes, when I see 't, I will.
But if my eyes do cozen me so, and I
Giving 'em no occasion, sure I 'll have    45
A whore, shall piss 'em out next day.
    *Mam.*                                    Ha! why?
Do you think I fable with you? I assure you,
He that has once the flower of the sun,
The perfect ruby, which we call elixir,
Not only can do that, but by its virtue,    50

Can confer honour, love, respect, long life;
Give safety, valour, yea, and victory,
To whom he will. In eight-and-twenty days,
I 'll make an old man of fourscore a child.
    *Sur.* No doubt: he 's that already.
    *Mam.*                          Nay, I mean,    55
Restore his years, renew him, like an eagle,
To the fifth age; make him get sons and daugh-
    ters,
Young giants; as our philosophers have done,
The ancient patriarchs, afore the flood,
But taking, once a week, on a knife's point,    60
The quantity of a grain of mustard of it;
Become stout Marses, and beget young Cu-
    pids.
    *Sur.* The decay'd vestals of Pickt-hatch
    would thank you,
That keep the fire alive there.
    *Mam.*                          'T is the secret
Of nature naturiz'd 'gainst all infections,    65
Cures all diseases coming of all causes;
A month's grief in a day, a year's in twelve;
And, of what age soever, in a month,
Past all the doses of your drugging doctors.
I 'll undertake, withal, to fright the plague    70
Out o' the kingdom in three months.
    *Sur.*                          And I 'll
Be bound, the players shall sing your praises
    then,
Without their poets.
    *Mam.*                          Sir, I 'll do 't. Meantime,
I 'll give away so much unto my man,
Shall serve th' whole city with preservative    75
Weekly; each house his dose, and at the
    rate ——
    *Sur.* As he that built the Water-work does
    with water?
    *Mam.* You are incredulous.
    *Sur.*                          Faith, I have a humour,
I would not willingly be gull'd. Your stone
Cannot transmute me.
    *Mam.*                          Pertinax Surly,    80
Will you believe antiquity? Records?
I 'll show you a book where Moses, and his
    sister,
And Solomon have written of the art;
Ay, and a treatise penn'd by Adam ——
    *Sur.*                                    How!
    *Mam.* O' the philosopher's stone, and in
    High Dutch.                                    85

---

[12] **Seal:** seal a bond, in favor of the swindlers
borrowers merchandise, or "commodity," instead of cash. The borrower was obliged to sell the goods
for what they would bring.)    [16] **entrails:** lining    [17] **Madam Augusta:** mistress of a brothel(?)
[26] **fire-drake:** dragon    [27] **Lungs:** blower of bellows    [28] **firk:** stir    [29] **faithful:** a believer    [30] **my:**
(so Q; 'thy' F)    [33] **Lothbury:** a street in London inhabited largely by coppersmiths    [35] **Devonshire, Cornwall:** counties noted for tin and copper mines    [36] **admire:** wonder    [40] **Venus:** copper
**Moon:** silver    [41] **Sun:** gold    [52] **valour:** ('valure' Q, F)    [63] **Pickt-hatch:** a resort of prostitutes and
pick-pockets    [72] **players:** (The theatres were closed by law during visitations of the plague, so that
the players lost their livelihood during these periods.)    [77] **Water-work:** built in 1594 to supply water
from the Thames

*Sur.* Did Adam write, sir, in High Dutch?
*Mam.*                                    He did;
Which proves it was the primitive tongue.
*Sur.*                                    What paper?
*Mam.* On cedar board.
*Sur.*                                    O that, indeed, they say,
Will last 'gainst worms.
*Mam.*                                    'T is like your Irish wood
'Gainst cobwebs.  I have a piece of Jason's
    fleece too,                                                        90
Which was no other than a book of alchemy,
Writ in large sheepskin, a good fat ram-vellum.
Such was Pythagoras' thigh, Pandora's tub,
And all that fable of Medea's charms,               94
The manner of our work; the bulls, our furnace,
Still breathing fire; our *argent-vive*, the dragon:
The dragon's teeth, mercury sublimate,
That keeps the whiteness, hardness, and the
    biting;
And they are gather'd into Jason's helm,          99
Th' alembic, and then sow'd in Mars his field,
And thence sublim'd so often, till they 're fix'd.
Both this, th' Hesperian garden, Cadmus' story,
Jove's shower, the boon of Midas, Argus' eyes,
Boccace his Demogorgon, thousands more, 104
All abstract riddles of our stone. — How now!

## Act II.  Scene II

### [*The Same*]

### [*Sir Epicure*] *Mammon, Face, Surly*

[*Mam.*]  Do we succeed?  Is our day come?
    And holds it?
*Face.*  The evening will set red upon you, sir;
You have colour for it, crimson: the red fer-
    ment
Has done his office; three hours hence prepare
    you
To see projection.
*Mam.*                                    Pertinax, my Surly,          5
Again I say to thee, aloud, *be rich.*
This day thou shalt have ingots; and to-
    morrow
Give lords th' affront. — Is it, my Zephyrus,
    right?
Blushes the bolt's-head?
*Face.*                                    Like a wench with child, sir,
That were but now discover'd to her master. 10
*Mam.* Excellent witty Lungs! — My only
    care is
Where to get stuff enough now, to project on;
This town will not half serve me.
*Face.*                                    No, sir?  Buy
The covering off o' churches.

*Mam.*                                    That 's true.
*Face.*                                    Yes.
Let 'em stand bare, as do their auditory;        15
Or cap 'em new with shingles.
*Mam.*                                    No, good thatch.
Thatch will lie light upo' the rafters, Lungs.
Lungs, I will manumit thee from the furnace;
I will restore thee thy complexion, Puff,
Lost in the embers; and repair this brain,     20
Hurt wi' the fume o' the metals.
*Face.*                                    I have blown, sir,
Hard, for your worship; thrown by many a
    coal,
When 't was not beech; weigh'd those I put in,
    just,
To keep your heat still even.  These blear'd
    eyes
Have wak'd to read your several colours, sir, 25
Of the pale citron, the green lion, the crow,
The peacock's tail, the plumed swan.
*Mam.*                                    And lastly,
Thou hast descried the flower, the *sanguis agni?*
*Face.* Yes, sir.
*Mam.*                          Where's master?
*Face.*                                    At 's prayers, sir, he;
Good man, he 's doing his devotions          30
For the success.
*Mam.*          Lungs, I will set a period
To all thy labours; thou shalt be the master
Of my seraglio.
*Face.*          Good, sir.
*Mam.*                                    But do you hear?
I 'll geld you, Lungs.
*Face.*                          Yes, sir.
*Mam.*                                    For I do mean
To have a list of wives and concubines          35
Equal with Solomon, who had the stone
Alike with me; and I will make me a back
With the elixir, that shall be as tough
As Hercules, to encounter fifty a night. —
Th' art sure thou saw'st it blood?
*Face.*                          Both blood and spirit, sir. 40
*Mam.*  I will have all my beds blown up, not
    stuff'd;
Down is too hard: and then, mine oval room
Fill'd with such pictures as Tiberius took
From Elephantis, and dull Aretine
But coldly imitated.  Then, my glasses          45
Cut in more subtle angles, to disperse
And multiply the figures, as I walk
Naked between my succubæ.  My mists
I 'll have of perfume, vapour'd 'bout the room,
To lose our selves in; and my baths, like
    pits                                                              50
To fall into; from whence we will come forth,

---

**96 argent-vive:** quicksilver     **104 Demogorgon:** the ancestor of all the gods in Boccaccio's *Genealo-
gia Deorum*      **9 bolt's-head:** a kind of flask     **15 auditory:** congregation     **23 just:** precisely
**25 colours:** indications of the progress of the operation     **44 Elephantis, Aretine:** both wrote verses to
accompany lewd pictures     **48 succubæ:** mistresses

And roll us dry in gossamer and roses. —
Is it arrived at ruby? —— Where I spy
A wealthy citizen, or rich lawyer,
Have a sublim'd pure wife, unto that fellow    55
I 'll send a thousand pound to be my cuckold.
   *Face.*  And I shall carry it?
   *Mam.*    No, I 'll ha' no bawds
But fathers and mothers: they will do it best,
Best of all others.  And my flatterers
Shall be the pure, and gravest of divines    60
That I can get for money.  My mere fools,
Eloquent burgesses, and then my poets
The same that writ so subtly of the fart,
Whom I will entertain still for that subject.
The few that would give out themselves to be    65
Court- and town-stallions, and, each-where, bely
Ladies who are known most innocent, for
   them, —
Those will I beg, to make me eunuchs of:
And they shall fan me with ten estrich tails
Apiece, made in a plume to gather wind.    70
We will be brave, Puff, now we ha' the med'-
   cine.
My meat shall all come in, in Indian shells,
Dishes of agate set in gold, and studded
With emeralds, sapphires, hyacinths, and ru-
   bies.
The tongues of carps, dormice, and camels'
   heels,    75
Boil'd i' the spirit of Sol, and dissolv'd pearl
(Apicius' diet, 'gainst the epilepsy):
And I will eat these broths with spoons of am-
   ber,
Headed with diamond and carbuncle.
My foot-boy shall eat pheasants, calver'd sal-
   mons,    80
Knots, godwits, lampreys:  I myself will have
The beards of barbels serv'd, instead of salads;
Oil'd mushrooms;  and the swelling unctuous
   paps
Of a fat pregnant sow, newly cut off,    84
Dress'd with an exquisite and poignant sauce;
For which, I 'll say unto my cook, *There's gold;
Go forth, and be a knight.*
   *Face.*    Sir, I 'll go look
A little, how it heightens.    [*Exit.*]
   *Mam.*    Do. — My shirts
I 'll have of taffeta-sarsnet, soft and light    90
As cobwebs;  and for all my other raiment,
It shall be such as might provoke the Persian,
Were he to teach the world riot anew.
My gloves of fishes and birds' skins, perfum'd
With gums of paradise, and Eastern air ——
   *Sur.*  And do you think to have the stone
   with this?    95

   *Mam.*  No, I do think t' have all this with
   the stone.
   *Sur.*  Why, I have heard he must be *homo
frugi,*
A pious, holy, and religious man,
One free from mortal sin, a very virgin.
   *Mam.*  That makes it, sir;  he is so.  But I
   buy it;    100
My venter brings it me.  He, honest wretch,
A notable, superstitious, good soul,
Has worn his knees bare, and his slippers bald,
With prayer and fasting for it: and, sir, let him
Do it alone, for me, still.  Here he comes.    105
Not a profane word afore him;  't is poison. —

## Act II.  Scene III

### [*The Same*]

#### *Mammon, Subtle, Surly, [later] Face*

[*Mam.*]  Good morrow, father.
   *Sub.*    Gentle son, good morrow,
And to your friend there.  What is he is with
   you?
   *Mam.*  An heretic, that I did bring along,
In hope, sir, to convert him.
   *Sub.*    Son, I doubt
You 're covetous, that thus you meet your time
I' the just point, prevent your day at morn-
   ing.    6
This argues something worthy of a fear
Of importune and carnal appetite.
Take heed you do not cause the blessing leave
   you,
With your ungovern'd haste.  I should be sorry
To see my labours, now e'en at perfection,    11
Got by long watching and large patience,
Not prosper where my love and zeal hath plac'd
   'em:
Which (heaven I call to witness, with your self,
To whom I have pour'd my thoughts) in all my
   ends,    15
Have look'd no way, but unto public good,
To pious uses, and dear charity,
Now grown a prodigy with men.  Wherein
If you, my son, should now prevaricate,
And to your own particular lusts employ    20
So great and catholic a bliss, be sure
A curse will follow, yea, and overtake
Your subtle and most secret ways.
   *Mam.*    I know, sir;
You shall not need to fear me;  I but come
To ha' you confute this gentleman.
   *Sur.*    Who is,    25

---

⁷⁶ **spirit of Sol:** gold    ⁷⁵, ⁷⁷ From Lampridius's life of Heliogabalus    ⁸⁰ **calver'd:** elaborately dressed    ⁸¹ **Knots:** a kind of snipe    **godwits:** marsh birds    ⁸² **barbels:** fresh-water fish    ⁸⁹ **taffeta-sarsnet:** fine silk    ⁹⁷ **homo frugi:** a temperate man    ¹⁰¹ **venter:** investment, speculation    ⁴ **doubt:** fear    ⁶ **just:** exact    **prevent:** anticipate    ¹⁴ **Which:** I who

Indeed, sir, somewhat costive of belief
Toward your stone; would not be gull'd.
   *Sub.*                  Well, son,
All that I can convince him in, is this,
The work is done, bright Sol is in his robe.
We have a med'cine of the triple soul,    30
The glorified spirit. Thanks be to heaven,
And make us worthy of it! — Ulen Spiegel!
   *Face.* [*Within.*] Anon, sir.
   *Sub.*          Look well to the register,
And let your heat still lessen by degrees,
To the aludels.                   35
   *Face.* [*Within.*] Yes, sir.
   *Sub.*               Did you look
O' the bolt's-head yet?
   *Face.* [*Within.*] Which? On D, sir?
   *Sub.*                     Ay;
What 's the complexion?
   *Face.* [*Within.*] Whitish.
   *Sub.*              Infuse vinegar,  40
To draw his volatile substance and his tincture:
And let the water in glass E be filt'red,
And put into the gripe's egg. Lute him well;
And leave him clos'd *in balneo.*
   *Face.* [*Within.*]         I will, sir.
   *Sur.* What a brave language here is! next to
canting.                     45
   *Sub.* I have another work you never saw,
son,
That three days since past the philosopher's
wheel,
In the lent heat of Athanor; and 's become
Sulphur o' Nature.
   *Mam.*        But 't is for me?
   *Sub.*             What need you?
You have enough, in that is, perfect.
   *Mam.*            O, but ——   50
   *Sub.* Why, this is covetise!
   *Mam.*           No, I assure you,
I shall employ it all in pious uses,
Founding of colleges and grammar schools,
Marrying young virgins, building hospitals,
And, now and then, a church.

         *[Re-enter Face]*

   *Sub.*              How now!
   *Face.*        Sir, please you,   55
Shall I not change the filter?
   *Sub.*              Marry, yes;
And bring me the complexion of glass B.
                      *[Exit Face.]*
   *Mam.* Ha' you another?

   *Sub.*           Yes, son; were I assur'd
Your piety were firm, we would not want
The means to glorify it: but I hope the best.  60
I mean to tinct C in sand-heat to-morrow,
And give him imbibition.
   *Mam.*          Of white oil?
   *Sub.* No, sir, of red. F is come over the
helm too,
I thank my maker, in St. Mary's bath,
And shows *lac virginis.* Blessed be heaven!  65
I sent you of his fæces there calcin'd:
Out of that calx, I ha' won the salt of mercury.
   *Mam.* By pouring on your rectified water?
   *Sub.* Yes, and reverberating in Athanor.

         *[Re-enter Face]*

How now! what colour says it?
   *Face.*         The ground black, sir.   70
   *Mam.* That 's your crow's head?
   *Sur.*       Your cock's comb's, is it not?
   *Sub.* No, 't is not perfect. Would it were
the crow!
That work wants something.
   *Sur.* [*Aside.*]      O, I look'd for this,
The hay is a-pitching.
   *Sub.*       Are you sure you loos'd 'em
I' their own menstrue?
   *Face.* Yes, sir, and then married 'em,  75
And put 'em in a bolt's-head nipp'd to diges-
tion,
According as you bade me, when I set
The liquor of Mars to circulation
In the same heat.
   *Sub.*     The process then was right.   79
   *Face.* Yes, by the token, sir, the retort brake,
And what was sav'd was put into the pelican,
And sign'd with Hermes' seal.
   *Sub.*          I think 't was so.
We should have a new amalgama.
   *Sur.* [*Aside.*]        O, this ferret
Is rank as any polecat.
   *Sub.*         But I care not;
Let him e'en die; we have enough beside,   85
In embrion. H has his white shirt on?
   *Face.*              Yes, sir,
He 's ripe for inceration, he stands warm,
In his ash-fire. I would not you should let
Any die now, if I might counsel, sir,
For luck's sake to the rest: it is not good.   90
   *Mam.* He says right.
   *Sur.* (*Aside.*)        Ay, are you bolted?
   *Face.*            Nay, I know 't, sir,

---

30 **med'cine . . . soul:** the philosopher's stone    32 **Ulen Spiegel:** Owl Glass, the hero of an early
German jest-book    33 ff. (Jonson here uses the highly technical jargon of the alchemists to give the
effect of authenticity. The original audience probably understood it little better than does the modern
reader. Cf. *Volpone,* II. ii. 122 ff. "Aludels," "gripe's egg," "Athanor," etc. are vessels or implements
used in alchemy; "lute," "imbibition," "calx," etc., are processes or materials employed in the science.)
45 **canting:** thieves' slang    48 **lent:** slow, moderate    51 **covetise:** covetousness    71 **cock's comb's:**
*i.e.,* coxcomb's, fool's    74 **hay:** net for catching rabbits    91 **bolted:** driven out by the ferret

I 've seen th' ill fortune. What is some three
 ounces
Of fresh materials?
 *Mam.*    Is 't no more?
 *Face.*      No more, sir,
Of gold, t' amalgam with some six of mercury.
 *Mam.* Away, here 's money. What will
 serve?
 *Face.*    Ask him, sir. 95
 *Mam.* How much?
 *Sub.* Give him nine pound: you may gi' him
 ten.
 *Sur.* Yes, twenty, and be cozen'd; do.
 *Mam.* There 't is. [*Gives Face the money.*]
 *Sub.* This needs not; but that you will have
 it so,
To see conclusions of all: for two
Of our inferior works are at fixation, 100
A third is in ascension. Go your ways.
Ha' you set the oil of Luna in kemia?
 *Face.* Yes, sir.
 *Sub.*   And the philosopher's vinegar?
 *Face.*     Ay. [*Exit.*]
 *Sur.* We shall have a salad!
 *Mam.*   When do you make projection?
 *Sub.* Son, be not hasty, I exalt our med'cine,
By hanging him *in balneo vaporoso*, 106
And giving him solution; then congeal him;
And then dissolve him; then again congeal
 him;
For look, how oft I iterate the work,
So many times I add unto his virtue. 110
As, if at first one ounce convert a hundred,
After his second loose, he 'll turn a thousand;
His third solution, ten; his fourth, a hun-
 dred;
After his fifth, a thousand thousand ounces
Of any imperfect metal, into pure 115
Silver or gold, in all examinations
As good as any of the natural mine.
Get you your stuff here against afternoon,
Your brass, your pewter, and your andirons.
 *Mam.* Not those of iron?
 *Sub.*   Yes, you may bring them too; 120
We 'll change all metals.
 *Sur.*    I believe you in that.
 *Mam.* Then I may send my spits?
 *Sub.*    Yes, and your racks.
 *Sur.* And dripping-pans, and pot-hangers,
 and hooks?
Shall he not?
 *Sub.* If he please.
 *Sur.*   — To be an ass. 124
 *Sub.* How, sir!
 *Mam.* This gent'man you must bear withal.
I told you he had no faith.
 *Sur.*   And little hope, sir;
But much less charity, should I gull myself.

 *Sub.* Why, what have you observ'd, sir, in
 our art,
Seems so impossible?
 *Sur.*   But your whole work, no more,
That you should hatch gold in a furnace, sir,
As they do eggs in Egypt!
 *Sub.*    Sir, do you 131
Believe that eggs are hatch'd so?
 *Sur.*    If I should?
 *Sub.* Why, I think that the greater miracle.
No egg but differs from a chicken more
Than metals in themselves.
 *Sur.*   That cannot be. 135
The egg 's ordain'd by nature to that end,
And is a chicken *in potentia*.
 *Sub.* The same we say of lead and other
 metals,
Which would be gold if they had time.
 *Mam.*     And that
Our art doth furder.
 *Sub.*   Ay, for 't were absurd 140
To think that nature in the earth bred gold
Perfect i' the instant: something went before.
There must be remote matter.
 *Sur.*   Ay, what is that?
 *Sub.* Marry, we say ——
 *Mam.*   Ay, now it heats: stand, father,
Pound him to dust.
 *Sub.*   It is, of the one part, 145
A humid exhalation, which we call
*Materia liquida*, or the unctuous water;
On th' other part, a certain crass and viscous
Portion of earth; both which, concorporate,
Do make the elementary matter of gold; 150
Which is not yet *propria materia*,
But common to all metals and all stones;
For, where it is forsaken of that moisture,
And hath more dryness, it becomes a stone:
Where it retains more of the humid fatness, 155
It turns to sulphur, or to quicksilver,
Who are the parents of all other metals.
Nor can this remote matter suddenly
Progress so from extreme unto extreme, 159
As to grow gold, and leap o'er all the means.
Nature doth first beget th' imperfect, then
Proceeds she to the perfect. Of that airy
And oily water, mercury is engend'red;
Sulphur o' the fat and earthy part; the one, 164
Which is the last, supplying the place of
 male,
The other of the female, in all metals.
Some do believe hermaphrodeity,
That both do act and suffer. But these two
Make the rest ductile, malleable, extensive.
And even in gold they are; for we do find 170
Seeds of them by our fire, and gold in them;
And can produce the species of each metal
More perfect thence, than nature doth in earth.

---

102 **kemia:** vessel for distillation  160 **means:** intermediate stages

Beside, who doth not see in daily practice
Art can beget bees, hornets, beetles, wasps, 175
Out of the carcases and dung of creatures;
Yea, scorpions of an herb, being rightly plac'd;
And these are living creatures, far more perfect
And excellent than metals.
    *Mam.*              Well said, father!
Nay, if he take you in hand, sir, with an argu-
    ment,                           180
He 'll bray you in a mortar.
    *Sur.*             Pray you, sir, stay.
Rather than I 'll be bray'd, sir, I 'll believe
That Alchemy is a pretty kind of game,
Somewhat like tricks o' the cards, to cheat a
    man
With charming.
    *Sub.*      Sir?
    *Sur.*     What else are all your terms, 185
Whereon no one o' your writers 'grees with
    other?
Of your elixir, your *lac virginis,*
Your stone, your med'cine, and your chryso-
    sperm,
Your sal, your sulphur, and your mercury, 189
Your oil of height, your tree of life, your blood,
Your marchesite, your tutie, your magnesia,
Your toad, your crow, your dragon, and your
    panther;
Your sun, your moon, your firmament, your
    adrop,
Your lato, azoch, zernich, chibrit, heautarit, 194
And then your red man, and your white woman,
With all your broths, your menstrues, and ma-
    terials
Of piss and egg-shells, women's terms, man's
    blood,
Hair o' the head, burnt clouts, chalk, merds,
    and clay,
Powder of bones, scalings of iron, glass,
And worlds of other strange ingredients, 200
Would burst a man to name?
    *Sub.*           And all these, nam'd,
Intending but one thing; which art our writers
Us'd to obscure their art.
    *Mam.*              Sir, so I told him —
Because the simple idiot should not learn it,
And make it vulgar.
    *Sub.*       Was not all the knowledge 205
Of the Egyptians writ in mystic symbols?
Speak not the Scriptures oft in parables?
Are not the choicest fables of the poets,
That were the fountains and first springs of
    wisdom,
Wrapp'd in perplexed allegories?
    *Mam.*           I urg'd that, 210
And clear'd to him, that Sisyphus was damn'd
To roll the ceaseless stone, only because

He would have made ours common.   *Dol is*
    Who is this?                     *seen.*
    *Sub.*   God's precious! — What do you mean?
    Go in, good lady,
Let me entreat you. [*Dol retires.*] — Where 's
    this varlet?

                  *[Re-enter Face]*

    *Face.*         Sir.                 215
    *Sub.*   You very knave! do you use me thus?
    *Face.*               Wherein, sir?
    *Sub.*   Go in and see, you traitor.  Go!
                             *[Exit Face.]*
    *Mam.*              Who is it, sir?
    *Sub.*   Nothing, sir; nothing.
    *Mam.*          What 's the matter, good sir?
I have not seen you thus distemp'red: who is 't?
    *Sub.*   All arts have still had, sir, their adver-
    saries;                           220
But ours the most ignorant. —

                  *Face returns.*

                           What now?
    *Face.*  'T was not my fault, sir; she would
    speak with you.
    *Sub.*   Would she, sir! Follow me. [*Exit.*]
    *Mam.* [*Stopping him.*]  Stay, Lungs.
    *Face.*              I dare not, sir.
    *Mam.*   How! pray thee, stay.
    *Face.*   She 's mad, sir, and sent hither — 225
    *Mam.*   Stay, man; what is she?
    *Face.*          A lord's sister, sir.
He 'll be mad too. —
    *Mam.*   I warrant thee. — Why sent hither?
    *Face.*   Sir, to be cur'd.
    *Sub.* [*Within.*]  Why, rascal!
    *Face.*           Lo you! — Here, sir!
                         *He goes out.*
    *Mam.*   'Fore God, a Bradamante, a brave
    piece.
    *Sur.*   Heart, this is a bawdy-house!  I 'll be
    burnt else.                      230
    *Mam.*   O, by this light, no: do not wrong
    him.  He 's
Too scrupulous that way: it is his vice.
No, he 's a rare physician, do him right,
An excellent Paracelsian, and has done
Strange cures with mineral physic.  He deals all
With spirits, he; he will not hear a word 236
Of Galen; or his tedious recipes. —

                  *Face again*

                     How now, Lungs!
    *Face.*  Softly, sir; speak softly.  I meant
To ha' told your worship all.  This must not
    hear.
    *Mam.*   No, he will not be gull'd; let him
    alone.

---

   **197 terms:** menstrual discharge    **199 merds:** excrement    **204 Because:** so that    **229 Brada-**
**mante:** a heroine in Ariosto's *Orlando Furioso*    **239 This:** Surly

*Face.* Y' are very right, sir; she is a most
rare scholar, 241
And is gone mad with studying Broughton's
works.
If you but name a word touching the Hebrew,
She falls into her fit, and will discourse
So learnedly of genealogies, 245
As you would run mad too, to hear her, sir.
*Mam.* How might one do t' have conference
with her, Lungs?
*Face.* O, divers have run mad upon the con-
ference.
I do not know, sir: I am sent in haste
To fetch a vial.
*Sur.* Be not gull'd, Sir Mammon. 250
*Mam.* Wherein? Pray ye, be patient.
*Sur.* Yes, as you are,
And trust confederate knaves and bawds and
whores.
*Mam.* You are too foul, believe it. — Come
here, Ulen,
One word.
*Face.* I dare not, in good faith. [*Going.*]
*Mam.* Stay, knave.
*Face.* He 's extreme angry that you saw her,
sir. 255
*Mam.* Drink that. [*Gives him money.*]
What is she when she 's out of her fit?
*Face.* O, the most affablest creature, sir! so
merry!
So pleasant! She 'll mount you up, like quick-
silver,
Over the helm; and circulate like oil,
A very vegetal: discourse of state, 260
Of mathematics, bawdry, anything —
*Mam.* Is she no way accessible? no means,
No trick to give a man a taste of her — wit
Or so, Ulen?
*Face.* I 'll come to you again, sir. [*Exit.*]
*Mam.* Surly, I did not think one o' your
breeding 266
Would traduce personages of worth.
*Sur.* Sir Epicure,
Your friend to use; yet still loath to be gull'd:
I do not like your philosophical bawds.
Their stone is lechery enough to pay for, 270
Without this bait.
*Mam.* Heart, you abuse yourself.
I know the lady, and her friends, and means,
The original of this disaster. Her brother
Has told me all.
*Sur.* And yet you ne'er saw her
Till now! 275
*Mam.* O yes, but I forgot. I have, believe
it,

One o' the treacherous'st memories, I do think,
Of all mankind.
*Sur.* What call you her brother?
*Mam.* My lord —
He wi' not have his name known, now I think
on 't.
*Sur.* A very treacherous memory!
*Mam.* O' my faith — 280
*Sur.* Tut, if you ha' it not about you, pass it
Till we meet next.
*Mam.* Nay, by this hand, 't is true.
He 's one I honour, and my noble friend;
And I respect his house.
*Sur.* Heart! can it be
That a grave sir, a rich, that has no need, 285
A wise sir, too, at other times, should thus,
With his own oaths, and arguments, make hard
means
To gull himself? An this be your elixir,
Your *lapis mineralis*, and your lunary,
Give me your honest trick yet at primero, 290
Or gleek, and take your *lutum sapientis*,
Your *menstruum simplex!* I 'll have gold before
you,
And with less danger of the quicksilver,
Or the hot sulphur.

[*Re-enter Face*]

*Face.* Here 's one from Captain Face, sir, 295
To Surly.
Desires you meet him i' the Temple-church,
Some half-hour hence, and upon earnest busi-
ness. — He whispers Mammon.
Sir, if you please to quit us now, and come
Again within two hours, you shall have
My master busy examining o' the works; 300
And I will steal you in unto the party,
That you may see her converse. — Sir, shall I
say
You 'll meet the captain's worship?
*Sur.* Sir, I will. — [*Walks aside.*]
But, by attorney, and to a second purpose.
Now I am sure it is a bawdy-house; 305
I 'll swear it, were the marshal here to thank me:
The naming this commander doth confirm it.
Don Face! why he 's the most authentic dealer
I' these commodities, the superintendent
To all the quainter traffickers in town! 310
He is the visitor, and does appoint
Who lies with whom, and at what hour; what
price;
Which gown, and in what smock; what fall,
what tire.
Him will I prove, by a third person, to find
The subtleties of this dark labyrinth: 315

242 **Broughton:** an eccentric theologian (d. 1612) 260 **vegetal:** animated person 289 **lapis minera-**
lis' philosopher's stone **lunary:** a medicinal plant used by alchemists 290, 291 **primero, gleek:** card
games 291 **lutum sapientis:** philosopher's clay 292 **menstruum simplex:** simple dissolvent 313 **fall:**
veil or band for the neck **tire:** headdress

Which if I do discover, dear Sir Mammon,
You 'll give your poor friend leave, though no
    philosopher,
To laugh; for you that are, 't is thought, shall
    weep.
    *Face.*   Sir, he does pray you 'll not forget.
    *Sur.*                     I will not, sir.
Sir Epicure, I shall leave you?     [*Exit.*]
    *Mam.*          I follow you straight.   320
    *Face.*   But do so, good sir, to avoid suspicion.
This gent'man has a parlous head.
    *Mam.*              But wilt thou, Ulen,
Be constant to thy promise?
    *Face.*               As my life, sir.
    *Mam.*   And wilt thou insinuate what I am,
    and praise me,
And say I am a noble fellow?
    *Face.*           O, what else, sir?   325
And that you 'll make her royal with the stone,
An empress; you yourself king of Bantam.
    *Mam.*   Wilt thou do this?
    *Face.*            Will I, sir!
    *Mam.*           Lungs, my Lungs!
I love thee.
    *Face.*   Send your stuff, sir, that my master
May busy himself about projection.   330
    *Mam.*   Thou 'st witch'd me, rogue: take, go.
              [*Gives him money.*]
    *Face.*          Your jack, and all, sir.
    *Mam.*   Thou art a villain — I will send my
    jack,
And the weights too. Slave, I could bite thine
    ear.
Away, thou dost not care for me.
    *Face.*              Not I, sir?
    *Mam.*   Come, I was born to make thee, my
    good weasel,   335
Set thee on a bench, and ha' thee twirl a chain
With the best lord's vermin of 'em all.
    *Face.*              Away, sir.
    *Mam.*   A count, nay, a count palatine ——
    *Face.*             Good sir, go.
    *Mam.*   Shall not advance thee better: no,
    nor faster.                  [*Exit.*]

## Act II.   Scene IIII

### [*The Same*]

### Subtle, Face, Dol

[*Sub.*]   Has he bit? has he bit?
    *Face.*           And swallow'd, too, my
    Subtle.
I ha' given him line, and now he plays, i' faith.
    *Sub.*   And shall we twitch him?
    *Face.*           Thorough both the gills.

A wench is a rare bait, with which a man
No sooner 's taken, but he straight firks mad.  5
    *Sub.*   Dol, my Lord What's-hum's sister,
    you must now
Bear yourself ſtateliſ).
    *Dol.*           O, let me alone,
I 'll not forget my race, I warrant you.
I 'll keep my distance, laugh and talk aloud;
Have all the tricks of a proud scurvy lady,   10
And be as rude 's her woman.
    *Face.*           Well said, sanguine!
    *Sub.*   But will he send his andirons?
    *Face.*              His jack too,
And 's iron shoeing-horn; I ha' spoke to him.
    Well,
I must not lose my wary gamester yonder.
    *Sub.*   O, Monsieur Caution, that will not be
    gull'd?   15
    *Face.*   Ay,
If I can strike a fine hook into him, now! —
The Temple-church, there I have cast mine an-
    gle.
Well, pray for me. I 'll about it.   *One knocks.*
    *Sub.*   What, more gudgeons!   20
Dol, scout, scout!  [*Dol goes to the window.*]
    Stay, Face, you must go to the door;
'Pray God it be my Anabaptist — Who is 't,
    Dol?
    *Dol.*   I know him not: he looks like a gold-
    end-man.
    *Sub.*   Gods so! 't is he, he said he would send
    — what call you him?
The sanctified elder, that should deal   25
For Mammon's jack and andirons. Let him in.
Stay, help me off, first, with my gown.  [*Exit
    Face with the gown.*]   Away,
Madam, to your withdrawing chamber. Now,
                      [*Exit Dol.*]
In a new tune, new gesture, but old language. —
This fellow is sent from one negotiates with me
About the stone too, for the holy brethren   31
Of Amsterdam, the exil'd saints, that hope
To raise their discipline by it. I must use him
In some strange fashion now, to make him ad-
    mire me.

## Act II.   Scene V

### [*The Same*]

### Subtle, Face, Ananias

Where is my drudge?
                    [*Enter Face*]
    *Face.*   Sir!
    *Sub.*       Take away the recipient,
And rectify your menstrue from the phlegma.

---

<sup>331</sup> **jack:** machine for turning a spit   <sup>5</sup> **firks:** becomes rapidly   <sup>7</sup> **ſtateliſ):** with dignity   <sup>11</sup> **san-
guine:** red cheeks   <sup>18</sup> **angle:** fish-hook   <sup>20</sup> **gudgeons:** dupes   <sup>23</sup> **gold-end-man:** one who buys
odds and ends of gold   <sup>33</sup> **discipline:** Puritan form of church government

Then pour it o' the Sol, in the cucurbite,
And let 'em macerate together.
*Face.*               Yes, sir.
And save the ground?
*Sub.*          No: *terra damnata* 5
Must not have entrance in the work. — Who
are you?
*Ana.* A faithful brother, if it please you.
*Sub.*             What 's that?
A Lullianist? a Ripley? *Filius artis?*
Can you sublime and dulcify? Calcine?
Know you the sapor pontic? Sapor stiptic? 10
Or what is homogene, or heterogene?
*Ana.* I understand no heathen language,
truly.
*Sub.* Heathen! You Knipperdoling? Is
Ars sacra,
Or chrysopoeia, or spagyrica,
Or the pamphysic, or panarchic knowledge, 15
A heathen language?
*Ana.*          Heathen Greek, I take it.
*Sub.* How! Heathen Greek?
*Ana.*        All 's heathen but the Hebrew.
*Sub.* Sirrah my varlet, stand you forth and
speak to him
Like a philosopher: answer i' the language.
Name the vexations, and the martyrizations 20
Of metals in the work.
*Face.*          Sir, putrefaction,
Solution, ablution, sublimation,
Cohobation, calcination, ceration, and
Fixation.
*Sub.* This is heathen Greek, to you, now! —
And when comes vivification?
*Face.*         After mortification. 25
*Sub.* What 's cohobation?
*Face.*        'T is the pouring on
Your *aqua regis*, and then drawing him off,
To the trine circle of the seven spheres.
*Sub.* What 's the proper passion of metals?
*Face.*             Malleation.
*Sub.* What 's your *ultimum supplicium auri?*
*Face.*            Antimonium. 30
*Sub.* This 's heathen Greek to you! — And
what 's your mercury?
*Face.* A very fugitive, he will be gone,
sir.
*Sub.* How know you him?
*Face.*         By his viscosity,
His oleosity, and his suscitability.
*Sub.* How do you sublime him?
*Face.*    With the calce of egg-shells, 35
White marble, talc.
*Sub.*        Your magisterium now,
What 's that?
*Face.*      Shifting, sir, your elements,

Dry into cold, cold into moist, moist into hot,
Hot into dry.
*Sub.*      This 's heathen Greek to you still!
Your *lapis philosophicus?*
*Face.*           'T is a stone, 40
And not a stone; a spirit, a soul, and a body:
Which if you do dissolve, it is dissolv'd;
If you coagulate, it is coagulated;
If you make it to fly, it flieth.
*Sub.*          Enough. [*Exit Face.*]
This 's heathen Greek to you! What are you,
sir?                      45
*Ana.* Please you, a servant of the exil'd
brethren,
That deal with widows' and with orphans'
goods,
And make a just account unto the saints:
A deacon.
*Sub.* O, you are sent from Master Whole-
some,
Your teacher?
*Ana.*      From Tribulation Wholesome, 51
Our very zealous pastor.
*Sub.*        Good! I have
Some orphans' goods to come here.
*Ana.*        Of what kind, sir?
*Sub.* Pewter and brass, andirons and kitchen-
ware;
Metals, that we must use our med'cine on: 55
Wherein the brethren may have a penn'orth
For ready money.
*Ana.*       Were the orphans' parents
Sincere professors?
*Sub.*       Why do you ask?
*Ana.*           Because
We then are to deal justly, and give, in truth,
Their utmost value.
*Sub.*      'Slid, you 'd cozen else, 60
An if their parents were not of the faithful! —
I will not trust you, now I think on 't,
Till I ha' talk'd with your pastor. Ha' you
brought money
To buy more coals?
*Ana.*     No, surely.
*Sub.*        No? How so?
*Ana.* The brethren bid me say unto you,
sir,
Surely, they will not venter any more    66
Till they may see projection.
*Sub.*        How!
*Ana.*        You 've had
For the instruments, as bricks, and loam, and
glasses,
Already thirty pound; and for materials,
They say, some ninety more: and they have
heard since,           70

---

⁷ **brother:** Puritan      ⁸ **Lullianist, Ripley:** follower of Raymond Lully or George Ripley, both
famous alchemists    **Filius artis:** son of the art      ¹³ **Knipperdoling:** a leader of the Anabaptists
⁶⁸ **ioam:** clay

That one, at Heidelberg, made it of an egg,
And a small paper of pin-dust.
   *Sub.*             What 's your name?
   *Ana.*  My name is Ananias.
   *Sub.*              Out, the varlet
That cozen'd the apostles! Hence, away!
Flee, mischief! had your holy consistory   75
No name to send me, of another sound
Than wicked Ananias?  Send your elders
Hither, to make atonement for you, quickly,
And gi' me satisfaction; or out goes
The fire; and down th' alembics, and the fur-
   nace,                          80
*Piger Henricus*, or what not.  Thou wretch!
Both *sericon* and *bufo* shall be lost,
Tell 'em.  All hope of rooting out the bishops,
Or th' anti-Christian hierarchy shall perish,
If they stay threescore minutes: the aqueity,
Terreity, and sulphureity            86
Shall run together again, and all be annull'd,
Thou wicked Ananias! [*Exit Ananias.*] This
   will fetch 'em,
And make 'em haste towards their gulling
   more.
A man must deal like a rough nurse, and fright
Those that are froward to an appetite.     91

## *Act II.  Scene VI*

### [*The Same*]

*Face, Subtle, Drugger*

   [*Face.*]  He 's busy with his spirits, but we 'll
   upon him.
   *Sub.*  How now!  What mates, what Bayards
   ha' we here?
   *Face.*  I told you he would be furious. — Sir,
   here 's Nab
Has brought you another piece of gold to look
   on;
— We must appease him.  Give it me, — and
   prays you,                    5
You would devise — what is it, Nab?
   *Drug.*                A sign, sir.
   *Face.*  Ay, a good lucky one, a thriving sign,
   doctor.
   *Sub.*  I was devising now.
   *Face.* [*Aside to Subtle.*]  'Slight, do not say
   so,
He will repent he ga' you any more. —
What say you to his constellation, doctor,   10
The Balance?
   *Sub.*    No, that way is stale and common.

A townsman born in Taurus, gives the bull,
Or the bull's head: in Aries, the ram, —
A poor device!  No, I will have his name   14
Form'd in some mystic character; whose *radii*,
Striking the senses of the passers-by,
Shall, by a virtual influence, breed affections,
That may result upon the party owns it:
As thus ——                      19
   *Face.*  Nab!
   *Sub.*  He first shall have *a bell*, that 's *Abel;*
And by it standing one whose name is *Dee*,
In a *rug* gown, there 's *D*, and *Rug*, that 's
   *drug*
And right anenst him a dog snarling *er;*
There 's Drugger, Abel Drugger.  That 's his
   sign.
And here 's now mystery and hieroglyphic!   25
   *Face.*  Abel, thou art made.
   *Drug.*          Sir, I do thank his worship.
   *Face.*  Six o' thy legs more will not do it,
   Nab.
He has brought you a pipe of tobacco, doctor.
   *Drug.*                   Yes, sir:
I have another thing I would impart ——   29
   *Face.*  Out with it, Nab.
   *Drug.*         Sir, there is lodg'd, hard by me,
A rich young widow ——
   *Face.*           Good! a bona roba?
   *Drug.*  But nineteen at the most.
   *Face.*             Very good, Abel.
   *Drug.*  Marry, she 's not in fashion yet; she
   wears
A hood, but 't stands a cop.
   *Face.*           No matter, Abel.
   *Drug.*  And I do now and then give her a fu-
   cus ——                   35
   *Face.*  What! dost thou deal, Nab?
   *Sub.*          I did tell you, captain.
   *Drug.*  And physic too, sometime, sir: for
   which she trusts me
With all her mind.  She 's come up here of
   purpose
To learn the fashion.
   *Face.*    Good (his match too!) — On, Nab.
   *Drug.*  And she does strangely long to know
   her fortune.                  40
   *Face.*  God's lid, Nab, send her to the doctor,
   hither.
   *Drug.*  Yes, I have spoke to her of his worship
   already;
But she 's afraid it will be blown abroad,
And hurt her marriage.
   *Face.*        Hurt it! 't is the way
To heal it, if 't were hurt; to make it more  45

---

⁷² pin-dust: fine metallic dust    ² Bayards: blind horses (from the legendary horse given by Charlemagne to the sons of Aymon.  His name came to mean both "a blind horse" and "a chivalrous person.")    ¹⁷ virtual: from the virtue of the device    affections: inclinations    ²¹ Dee: Dr. John Dee, a famous astrologer (d. 1608)    ²² rug: of coarse frieze    ²⁷ legs: bows    ³¹ bona roba: handsome wanton    ³⁴ a cop: on the peak of her head, unbecomingly

Follow'd and sought. Nab, thou shalt tell her
    this.
She 'll be more known, more talk'd of; and your
    widows
Are ne'er of any price till they be famous;
Their honour is their multitude of suitors.   49
Send her! it may be thy good fortune. What!
Thou dost not know?
    *Drug.*          No, sir, she 'll never marry
Under a knight: her brother has made a vow.
    *Face.* What! and dost thou despair, my little
    Nab,
Knowing what the doctor has set down for thee,
And seeing so many o' the city dubb'd?   55
One glass o' thy water, with a madam I know,
Will have it done, Nab. What 's her brother? a
    knight?
    *Drug.* No, sir, a gentleman newly warm in 's
    land, sir,
Scarce cold in his one-and-twenty, that does
    govern
His sister here; and is a man himself   60
Of some three thousand a year, and is come
    up
To learn to quarrel, and to live by his wits,
And will go down again, and die i' the country.
    *Face.* How! to quarrel?
    *Drug.*        Yes, sir, to carry quarrels,
As gallants do; to manage 'em by line.   65
    *Face.* 'Slid, Nab, the doctor is the only
    man
In Christendom for him. He has made a table,
With mathematical demonstrations,
Touching the art of quarrels: he will give him
An instrument to quarrel by. Go, bring 'em
    both,   70
Him and his sister. And, for thee, with her
The doctor happ'ly may persuade. Go to:
'Shalt give his worship a new damask suit
Upon the premises.
    *Sub.*         O, good captain!
    *Face.*             He shall;
He is the honestest fellow, doctor. Stay not,  75
No offers; bring the damask, and the parties.
    *Drug.* I 'll try my power, sir.
    *Face.*           And thy will too, Nab.
    *Sub.* 'T is good tobacco, this! What is 't an
    ounce?
    *Face.* He 'll send you a pound, doctor.
    *Sub.*           O no.
    *Face.*            He will do 't.
It is the goodest soul! — Abel, about it.   80
Thou shalt know more anon. Away, be gone.
                              *[Exit Abel.]*
A miserable rogue, and lives with cheese,
And has the worms. That was the cause, in-
    deed,

Why he came now: he dealt with me in pri-
    vate,   84
To get a med'cine for 'em.
    *Sub.*         And shall, sir. This works.
    *Face.* A wife, a wife for one on 's, my dear
    Subtle!
We 'll e'en draw lots, and he that fails, shall
    have
The more in goods, the other has in tail.
    *Sub.* Rather the less; for she may be so
    light
She may want grains.
    *Face.*       Ay; or be such a burden,   90
A man would scarce endure her for the whole.
    *Sub.* Faith, best let 's see her first, and then
    determine.
    *Face.* Content: but Dol must ha' no breath
    on 't.
    *Sub.* Mum.
Away you, to your Surly yonder, catch him.
    *Face.* Pray God I ha' not stay'd too long.  95
    *Sub.*           I fear it. *[Exeunt.]*

## Act III.   Scene I

*[The Lane before Lovewit's House]*

*Tribulation [Wholesome], Ananias*

*[Tri.]* These chastisements are common to
    the saints,
And such rebukes we of the separation
Must bear with willing shoulders, as the trials
Sent forth to tempt our frailties.
    *Ana.*          In pure zeal,
I do not like the man; he is a heathen,   5
And speaks the language of Canaan, truly.
    *Tri.* I think him a profane person indeed.
    *Ana.*             He bears
The visible mark of the beast in his forehead.
And for his stone, it is a work of darkness,
And with philosophy blinds the eyes of man.  10
    *Tri.* Good brother, we must bend unto all
    means
That may give furtherance to the holy cause.
    *Ana.* Which his cannot: the sanctified cause
Should have a sanctified course.
    *Tri.*         Not always necessary:
The children of perdition are oft times   15
Made instruments even of the greatest works.
Besides, we should give somewhat to man's
    nature,
The place he lives in, still about the fire,
And fume of metals, that intoxicate
The brain of man, and make him prone to
    passion.   20
Where have you greater atheists than your
    cooks?

---

Or more profane, or choleric, than your glass-
      men?
More anti-Christian than your bell-founders?
What makes the devil so devilish, I would ask
      you,
Sathan, our common enemy, but his being   25
Perpetually about the fire, and boiling
Brimstone and arsenic? We must give, I say,
Unto the motives, and the stirrers up
Of humours in the blood. It may be so,
Whenas the work is done, the stone is made,   30
This heat of his may turn into a zeal,
And stand up for the beauteous discipline
Against the menstruous cloth and rag of Rome.
We must await his calling, and the coming
Of the good spirit. You did fault, t' upbraid
      him                                                    35
With the brethren's blessing of Heidelberg,
      weighing
What need we have to hasten on the work,
For the restoring of the silenc'd saints,
Which ne'er will be but by the philosopher's
      stone.
And so a learned elder, one of Scotland,   40
Assur'd me; *aurum potabile* being
The only med'cine for the civil magistrate,
T' incline him to a feeling of the cause;
And must be daily us'd in the disease.
   *Ana.* I have not edified more, truly, by man;
Not since the beautiful light first shone on
      me:                                                    46
And I am sad my zeal hath so offended.
   *Tri.* Let us call on him then.
   *Ana.*                        The motion 's good,
And of the spirit; I will knock first. [*Knocks.*]
      Peace be within! [*The door is opened,
      and they enter.*]

## *Act III. Scene II*

[*A Room in Lovewit's House*]

*Subtle, Tribulation, Ananias*

[*Sub.*] O, are you come? 'T was time. Your
      threescore minutes
Were at the last thread, you see; and down had
      gone
*Furnus acediæ, turris circulatorius:*
Limbec, bolt's-head, retort, and pelican
Had all been cinders. Wicked Ananias!   5
Art thou return'd? Nay, then, it goes down
      yet.
   *Tri.* Sir, be appeased; he is come to humble
Himself in spirit, and to ask your patience,

If too much zeal hath carried him aside
From the due path.
   *Sub.*                        Why, this doth qualify!   10
   *Tri.* The brethren had no purpose, verily,
To give you the least grievance; but are ready
To lend their willing hands to any project
The spirit and you direct.
   *Sub.*                        This qualifies more!
   *Tri.* And for the orphans' goods, let them
      be valu'd,                                           15
Or what is needful else to the holy work,
It shall be numb'red; here, by me, the saints
Throw down their purse before you.
   *Sub.*                        This qualifies most!
Why, thus it should be, now you understand.
Have I discours'd so unto you of our stone,   20
And of the good that it shall bring your cause?
Show'd you (beside the main of hiring forces
Abroad, drawing the Hollanders, your friends,
From th' Indies, to serve you, with all their
      fleet)
That even the med'cinal use shall make you a
      faction                                              25
And party in the realm? As, put the case,
That some great man in state, he have the
      gout,
Why, you but send three drops of your elixir,
You help him straight: there you have made a
      friend.
Another has the palsy or the dropsy,   30
He takes of your incombustible stuff,
He 's young again: there you have made a
      friend.
A lady that is past the feat of body,
Though not of mind, and hath her face decay'd
Beyond all cure of paintings, you restore   35
With the oil of talc: there you have made a
      friend;
And all her friends. A lord that is a leper,
A knight that has the bone-ache, or a squire
That hath both these, you make 'em smooth
      and sound
With a bare fricace of your med'cine; still   40
You increase your friends.
   *Tri.*                        Ay, 't is very pregnant.
   *Sub.* And then the turning of this lawyer's
      pewter
To plate at Christmas ——
   *Ana.*                        Christ-tide, I pray you.
   *Sub.* Yet, Ananias!
   *Ana.*                        I have done.
   *Sub.*                        Or changing
His parcel gilt to massy gold. You cannot   45
But raise you friends withal, to be of power

---

³³ **menstruous:** filthy, polluted   ³⁸ **silenc'd:** non-conformist ministers were not allowed to preach
⁴¹ **aurum potabile:** a sovereign remedy (here bribery)   ⁴⁸ **motion:** suggestion   ³ The compound
furnace and glass still   ¹⁰ **qualify:** soothe, appease   ⁴⁰ **fricace:** rubbing, massage   ⁴³ **Christ-tide:**
the Puritans avoided *mass* as a Popish word   ⁴⁵ **parcel gilt:** partly gilded silverware   ⁴⁶ **withal·**
(' With all' F)

To pay an army in the field, to buy
The King of France out of his realms, or Spain
Out of his Indies. What can you not do
Against lords spiritual or temporal,          50
That shall oppone you?
   *Tri.*           Verily, 't is true.
We may be temporal lords ourselves, I take it.
   *Sub.* You may be anything, and leave off to
   make
Long-winded exercises; or suck up
Your *ha!* and *hum!* in a tune. I not deny,   55
But such as are not graced in a state,
May, for their ends, be adverse in religion,
And get a tune to call the flock together:
For, to say sooth, a tune does much with women
And other phlegmatic people; it is your bell.  60
   *Ana.* Bells are profane; a tune may be re-
   ligious.
   *Sub.* No warning with you? Then farewell
   my patience.
'Slight, it shall down; I will not be thus tortur'd.
   *Tri.* I pray you, sir.
   *Sub.*      All shall perish. I have spoke it.
   *Tri.* Let me find grace, sir, in your eyes; the
   man,                                      65
He stands corrected: neither did his zeal,
But as yourself, allow a tune somewhere,
Which now, being tow'rd the stone, we shall
   not need.
   *Sub.* No, nor your holy vizard, to win widows
To give you legacies; or make zealous wives  70
To rob their husbands for the common cause:
Nor take the start of bonds broke but one day,
And say they were forfeited by providence.
Nor shall you need o'er night to eat huge meals,
To celebrate your next day's fast the better;  75
The whilst the brethren and the sisters hum-
   bled,
Abate the stiffness of the flesh. Nor cast
Before your hungry hearers scrupulous bones;
As whether a Christian may hawk or hunt,
Or whether matrons of the holy assembly     80
May lay their hair out, or wear doublets,
Or have that idol, starch, about their linen.
   *Ana.* It is indeed an idol.
   *Tri.*          Mind him not, sir.
I do command thee, spirit (of zeal, but trouble),
To peace within him! Pray you, sir, go on.   85
   *Sub.* Nor shall you need to libel 'gainst the
   prelates,
And shorten so your ears against the hearing
Of the next wire-drawn grace. Nor of necessity
Rail against plays, to please the alderman
Whose daily custard you devour; nor lie      90
With zealous rage till you are hoarse. Not one

Of these so singular arts. Nor call yourselves
By names of Tribulation, Persecution,
Restraint, Long-patience, and such like, af-
   fected
By the whole family or wood of you,          95
Only for glory, and to catch the ear
Of the disciple.
   *Tri.*       Truly, sir, they are
Ways that the godly brethren have invented,
For propagation of the glorious cause,
As very notable means, and whereby also     100
Themselves grow soon, and profitably, famous.
   *Sub.* O, but the stone, all 's idle to 't! No-
   thing!
The art of angels, nature's miracle,
The divine secret that doth fly in clouds
From east to west: and whose tradition       105
Is not from men, but spirits.
   *Ana.*          I hate traditions;
I do not trust them ——
   *Tri.*           Peace!
   *Ana.*        They are popish all.
I will not peace: I will not ——
   *Tri.*          Ananias!
   *Ana.* Please the profane, to grieve the godly!
   I may not.
   *Sub.* Well, Ananias, thou shalt overcome. 110
   *Tri.* It is an ignorant zeal that haunts him,
   sir:
But truly else a very faithful brother,
A botcher, and a man by revelation
That hath a competent knowledge of the truth.
   *Sub.* Has he a competent sum there i' the
   bag                                       115
To buy the goods within? I am made guardian,
And must, for charity and conscience' sake,
Now see the most be made for my poor orphan;
Though I desire the brethren, too, good gainers:
There they are within. When you have view'd
   and bought 'em,                            120
And ta'en the inventory of what they are,
They are ready for projection; there 's no more
To do: cast on the med'cine, so much silver
As there is tin there, so much gold as brass,
I 'll gi' it you in by weight.
   *Tri.*       But how long time,   125
Sir, must the saints expect yet?
   *Sub.*         Let me see,
How 's the moon now? Eight, nine, ten days
   hence,
He will be silver potate; then three days
Before he citronize. Some fifteen days,
The magisterium will be perfected.           130
   *Ana.* About the second day of the third week,
In the ninth month?

---

<sup>51</sup> **oppone:** oppose   <sup>68</sup> **tow'rd:** near possession of   <sup>69</sup> **vizard:** face, expression   <sup>78</sup> **scrupulous bones:** *i.e.,* discussion of such scruples as are given in ll. 79–82   <sup>87</sup> **shorten:** have cut off in the pillory   <sup>95</sup> **wood:** assemblage   <sup>113</sup> **botcher:** mender, petty tailor   <sup>126</sup> **expect:** wait   <sup>129</sup> **citronize:** turn yellow   <sup>130</sup> **magisterium:** process of transmutation

*Sub.*                          Yes, my good Ananias.

*Tri.*  What will the orphans' goods arise to,
think you?

*Sub.*  Some hundred marks, as much as fill'd
three cars,
Unladed now: you 'll make six millions of
'em ——                                          135
But I must ha' more coals laid in.

*Tri.*                          How?

*Sub.*                          Another load,
And then we ha' finish'd. We must now in-
crease
Our fire to *ignis ardens;* we are past
*Fimus equinus, balnei, cineris,*
And all those lenter heats. If the holy purse
Should with this draught fall low, and that the
saints                                          141
Do need a present sum, I have a trick
To melt the pewter, you shall buy now in-
stantly,
And with a tincture make you as good Dutch
dollars
As any are in Holland.

*Tri.*                          Can you so?      145

*Sub.*  Ay, and shall bide the third examination.

*Ana.*  It will be joyful tidings to the brethren.

*Sub.*  But you must carry it secret.

*Tri.*                          Ay; but stay,
This act of coining, is it lawful?

*Ana.*                          Lawful!
We know no magistrate: or, if we did,      150
This 's foreign coin.

*Sub.*                          It is no coining, sir.
It is but casting.

*Tri.*          Ha! you distinguish well:
Casting of money may be lawful.

*Ana.*                          'T is, sir.

*Tri.*  Truly, I take it so.

*Sub.*                          There is no scruple,
Sir, to be made of it; believe Ananias;      155
This case of conscience he is studied in.

*Tri.*  I 'll make a question of it to the brethren.

*Ana.*  The brethren shall approve it lawful,
doubt not.
Where shall 't be done?

*Sub.*  For that we 'll talk anon.
                              *Knock without.*
There 's some to speak with me. Go in, I pray
you,                                            160
And view the parcels. That 's the inventory.
I 'll come to you straight. [*Exeunt Trib. and
Ana.*] Who is it? — Face! appear.

## *Act III. Scene III*

[*The Same*]

*Subtle, Face, [later] Dol*

[*Sub.*]  How now! good prize?

*Face.*          Good pox! Yond' costive cheater
Never came on.

*Sub.*          How then?

*Face.*                          I ha' walk'd the round
Till now, and no such thing.

*Sub.*                          And ha' you quit him?

*Face.*  Quit him! An hell would quit him
too, he were happy.
'Slight! would you have me stalk like a mill-
jade,                                            5
All day, for one that will not yield us grains?
I know him of old.

*Sub.*          O, but to ha' gull'd him,
Had been a mastery.

*Face.*          Let him go, black boy!
And turn thee, that some fresh news may pos-
sess thee.
A noble count, a don of Spain (my dear      10
Delicious compeer, and my party-bawd),
Who is come hither private for his conscience
And brought munition with him, six great
slops,
Bigger than three Dutch hoys, beside round
trunks,                                          14
Furnish'd with pistolets, and pieces of eight,
Will straight be here, my rogue, to have thy
bath,
(That is the colour,) and to make his batt'ry
Upon our Dol, our castle, our cinqueport,
Our Dover pier, our what thou wilt. Where is
she?
She must prepare perfumes, delicate linen,   20
The bath in chief, a banquet, and her wit,
For she must milk his epididymis.
Where is the doxy?

*Sub.*          I 'll send her to thee:
And but despatch my brace of little John Ley-
dens
And come again myself.

*Face.*                          Are they within then?

*Sub.*  Numb'ring the sum.

*Face.*          How much?

*Sub.*          A hundred marks, boy. [*Exit.*]  26

*Face.*  Why, this 's a lucky day. Ten pounds
of Mammon!
Three o' my clerk! A portague o' my grocer!
This o' the brethren! Beside reversions

---

[139] Three gradations of heat: from horse-dung, hot water, ashes    [142] a trick: ('trick' Q, F)
[150] know: recognize    [1] cheater: Surly    [2] round: at the Temple-church    [11] party-: partner
[13] slops: stuffed breeches    [14] hoys: small sloops    trunks: hose    [15] pistolets: Spanish gold coins
worth about $4    pieces of eight: coins worth about $1    [17] colour: pretext    [18, 19] cinqueport,
Dover pier: English strongholds on the Channel    [23] doxy: wench    [24] John Leydens: Puritans

And states to come, i' the widow, and my
count!    30
My share to-day will not be bought for forty —

*[Enter Dol]*

*Dol.*                          What?
*Face.* Pounds, dainty Dorothy! Art thou
so near?
*Dol.* Yes; say, lord general, how fares our
camp?
*Face.* As with the few that had entrench'd
themselves
Safe, by their discipline, against a world, Dol, 35
And laugh'd within those trenches, and grew
fat
With thinking on the booties, Dol, brought in
Daily by their small parties. This dear hour,
A doughty don is taken with my Dol;
And thou mayst make his ransom what thou
wilt,    40
My Dowsabel; he shall be brought here, fet-
ter'd
With thy fair looks, before he sees thee; and
thrown
In a down-bed, as dark as any dungeon;
Where thou shalt keep him waking with thy
drum;
Thy drum, my Dol, thy drum; till he be
tame    45
As the poor blackbirds were i' the great frost,
Or bees are with a basin; and so hive him
I' the swan-skin coverlid and cambric sheets,
Till he work honey and wax, my little God's-
gift.
*Dol.* What is he, general?
*Face.*               An *adalantado*,   50
A grandee, girl. Was not my Dapper here yet?
*Dol.* No.
*Face.*     Nor my Drugger?
*Dol.*                 Neither.
*Face.*                   A pox on 'em,
They are so long a furnishing! such stinkards
Would not be seen upon these festival days. —

*[Re-enter Subtle]*

How now! ha' you done?
*Sub.* Done. They are gone: the sum   55
Is here in bank, my Face. I would we knew
Another chapman now would buy 'em out-
right.
*Face.* 'Slid, Nab shall do 't against he ha' the
widow,
To furnish household.
*Sub.*          Excellent, well thought on:
Pray God he come.

*Face.*          I pray he keep away   60
Till our new business be o'erpast.
*Sub.*                 But, Face,
How cam'st thou by this secret don?
*Face.*                A spirit
Brought me th' intelligence in a paper here,
As I was conjuring yonder in my circle
For Surly; I ha' my flies abroad. Your bath 65
Is famous, Subtle, by my means. Sweet Dol,
You must go tune your virginal, no losing
O' the least time. And — do you hear? — good
action!
Firk like a flounder; kiss like a scallop, close;
And tickle him with thy mother-tongue. His
great   70
Verdugoship has not a jot of language;
So much the easier to be cozen'd, my Dolly.
He will come here in a hir'd coach, obscure,
And our own coachman, whom I have sent as
guide,
No creature else. — Who 's that?
                    *One knocks.* *[Exit Dol.]*
*Sub.*                  It is not he?
*Face.* O no, not yet this hour.

*[Re-enter Dol]*

*Sub.*                 Who is 't?
*Dol.*                 Dapper,   76
Your clerk.
*Face.*     God's will then, Queen of Faery,
On with your tire; *[Exit Dol.]* and, doctor, with
your robes.
Let 's despatch him for God's sake.
*Sub.*               'T will be long.
*Face.* I warrant you, take but the cues I
give you,   80
It shall be brief enough. *[Goes to the window.]*
    'Slight, here are more!
Abel, and, I think, the angry boy, the heir,
That fain would quarrel.
*Sub.*            And the widow?
*Face.*                    No,
Not that I see. Away!    *[Exit Sub.]*  84

## Act III. Scene IIII

*[The Same]*

*Face, Dapper, [later] Drugger, Kastril*

*[Face.]*         O, sir, you are welcome.
The doctor is within a-moving for you;
I have had the most ado to win him to it! —
He swears you 'll be the darling o' the dice:
He never heard her highness dote till now, he
says.   5

---

41 **Dowsabel:** English form of name Dulcibella   46 **great frost:** of 1608   49 **God's-gift:** literal meaning of Dorothea   50 **adalantado:** a Spanish governor (of a province)   67 **virginal:** spinet   69 **Firk:**
move briskly   71 **Verdugoship:** (The Spanish word means "executioner.")   **language:** *i.e.,* English
1 **O . . . welcome:** (at end of Sc. iii. in F)

Your aunt has giv'n you the most gracious
 words
That can be thought on.
   *Dap.*            Shall I see her grace?
   *Face.*   See her, and kiss her too. —

        *[Enter Abel, followed by Kastril]*
                   What, honest Nab!
Hast brought the damask?
   *Nab.*        No, sir; here 's tobacco.
   *Face.*  'T is well done, Nab; thou 'lt bring
    the damask too?                    10
   *Drug.*  Yes. Here 's the gentleman, captain,
    Master Kastril,
I have brought to see the doctor.
   *Face.*            Where 's the widow?
   *Drug.*  Sir, as he likes, his sister, he says,
    shall come.
   *Face.*  O, is it so? Good time. Is your name
Kastril, sir?
   *Kas.*  Ay, and the best o' the Kastrils, I 'd
    be sorry else,                       15
By fifteen hundred a year. Where is this
  doctor?
My mad tobacco-boy here tells me of one
That can do things. Has he any skill?
   *Face.*                Wherein, sir?
   *Kas.*  To carry a business, manage a quarrel
    fairly,
Upon fit terms.
   *Face.*     It seems, sir, y' are but young   20
About the town, that can make that a question.
   *Kas.*  Sir, not so young but I have heard
    some speech
Of the angry boys, and seen 'em take tobacco;
And in his shop; and I can take it too.
And I would fain be one of 'em, and go down
And practise i' the country.
   *Face.*           Sir, for the duello,   26
The doctor, I assure you, shall inform you,
To the least shadow of a hair; and show you
An instrument he has of his own making,
Wherewith, no sooner shall you make report   30
Of any quarrel, but he will take the height on 't
Most instantly, and tell in what degree
Of safety it lies in, or mortality.
And how it may be borne, whether in a right
  line,
Or a half circle; or may else be cast        35
Into an angle blunt, if not acute:
All this he will demonstrate. And then, rules
To give and take the lie by.
   *Kas.*            How! to take it?
   *Face.*  Yes, in oblique he 'll show you, or in
    circle;

But never in diameter. The whole town   40
Study his theorems, and dispute them ordinarily
At the eating academies.
   *Kas.*            But does he teach
Living by the wits too?
   *Face.*           Anything whatever.
You cannot think that subtlety but he reads it.
He made me a captain. I was a stark pimp,   45
Just o' your standing, 'fore I met with him;
It 's not two months since. I 'll tell you his
  method:
First, he will enter you at some ordinary.
   *Kas.*  No, I 'll not come there: you shall par-
    don me.
   *Face.*  For why, sir?
   *Kas.*  There 's gaming there, and tricks.
   *Face.*            Why, would you be   50
A gallant, and not game?
   *Kas.*           Ay, 't will spend a man.
   *Face.*  Spend you! It will repair you when
    you are spent.
How do they live by their wits there, that have
  vented
Six times your fortunes?
   *Kas.*         What, three thousand a year!
   *Face.*  Ay, forty thousand.
   *Kas.*            Are there such?
   *Face.*               Ay, sir,   55
And gallants yet. Here 's a young gentleman
Is born to nothing, — *[points to Dapper.]* forty
  marks a year
Which I count nothing: — he 's to be initiated,
And have a fly o' the doctor. He will win you
By unresistible luck, within this fortnight,   60
Enough to buy a barony. They will set him
Upmost, at the groom porter's, all the Christ-
  mas:
And for the whole year through at every place
Where there is play, present him with the
  chair,              64
The best attendance, the best drink, sometimes
Two glasses of Canary, and pay nothing;
The purest linen and the sharpest knife;
The partridge next his trencher: and somewhere
The dainty bed, in private, with the dainty.
You shall ha' your ordinaries bid for him,   70
As playhouses for a poet; and the master
Pray him aloud to name what dish he affects,
Which must be butter'd shrimps: and those
  that drink
To no mouth else, will drink to his, as being
The goodly president mouth of all the board.   75
   *Kas.*  Do you not gull one?
   *Face.*        'Ods my life! Do you think it?
You shall have a cast commander, (can but get

---

   **15 best:** *i.e.,* richest    **19 business:** affair of honor    **23 angry boys:** riotous youths    **39 oblique,
circle:** the lie circumstantial    **40 diameter:** the lie direct    **53 vented:** spent    **62 groom porter:** an
officer of the royal household in charge of gaming   (He provided materials, settled disputes, and had
the privilege of keeping a free table at Christmas.)    **77 cast:** cashiered

in credit with a glover, or a spurrier,
For some two pair of either's ware aforehand,)
Will, by most swift posts, dealing with him,   80
Arrive at competent means to keep himself,
His punk, and naked boy, in excellent fashion,
And be admir'd for 't.
    *Kas.*              Will the doctor teach this?
    *Face.*   He will do more, sir: when your land
      is gone,
(As men of spirit hate to keep earth long),   85
In a vacation, when small money is stirring,
And ordinaries suspended till the term,
He 'll show a perspective, where on one side
You shall behold the faces and the persons
Of all sufficient young heirs in town,     90
Whose bonds are current for commodity;
On th' other side, the merchants' forms, and
     others,
That without help of any second broker,
Who would expect a share, will trust such par-
     cels:
In the third square, the very street and sign   95
Where the commodity dwells, and does but wait
To be deliver'd, be it pepper, soap,
Hops, or tobacco, oatmeal, woad, or cheeses.
All which you may so handle, to enjoy
To your own use, and never stand oblig'd.   100
    *Kas.*   I' faith! is he such a fellow?
    *Face.*           Why, Nab here knows him.
And then for making matches for rich widows,
Young gentlewomen, heirs, the fortunat'st man!
He 's sent to, far and near, all over England, 104
To have his counsel, and to know their fortunes.
    *Kas.*   God's will, my suster shall see him.
    *Face.*           I 'll tell you, sir,
What he did tell me of Nab. It 's a strange
     thing —
(By the way, you must eat no cheese, Nab, it
     breeds melancholy,
And that same melancholy breeds worms) but
     pass it : —                     109
He told me, honest Nab here was ne'er at tavern
But once in 's life.
    *Drug.*      Truth, and no more I was not.
    *Face.*   And then he was so sick ——
    *Drug.*         Could he tell you that too?
    *Face.*   How should I know it?
    *Drug.*        In troth, we had been a-shooting,
And had a piece of fat ram-mutton to supper,
That lay so heavy o' my stomach ——
    *Face.*         And he has no head   115
To bear any wine; for what with the noise o'
     the fiddlers,

And care of his shop, for he dares keep no serv-
     ants ——
    *Drug.*   My head did so ache ——
    *Face.*     As he was fain to be brought home.
The doctor told me: and then a good old
     woman ——
    *Drug.*   Yes, faith, she dwells in Seacoal-lane,
     — did cure me,                 120
With sodden ale, and pellitory o' the wall;
Cost me but twopence. I had another sickness
Was worse than that.
    *Face.*           Ay, that was with the grief
Thou took'st for being 'cess'd at eighteen-
     pence,
For the waterwork.
    *Drug.*        In truth, and it was like   125
T' have cost me almost my life.
    *Face.*              Thy hair went off?
    *Drug.*   Yes, sir; 't was done for spite.
    *Face.*          Nay, so says the doctor.
    *Kas.*   Pray thee, tobacco-boy, go fetch my
     suster;
I 'll see this learned boy before I go;
And so shall she.
    *Face.*          Sir, he is busy now:     130
But if you have a sister to fetch hither,
Perhaps your own pains may command her
     sooner;
And he by that time will be free.
    *Kas.*                  I go. [*Exit.*]
    *Face.*   Drugger, she 's thine: the damask! —
     [*Exit Abel.*]   Subtle and I
Must wrastle for her. [*Aside.*] — Come on,
     Master Dapper,             135
You see how I turn clients here away,
To give your cause dispatch; ha' you perform'd
The ceremonies were enjoin'd you?
    *Dap.*           Yes, o' the vinegar,
And the clean shirt.
    *Face.*     'T is well: that shirt may do you
More worship than you think. Your aunt 's a-
     fire,                        140
But that she will not show it, t' have a sight on
     you.
Ha' you provided for her grace's servants?
    *Dap.*   Yes, here are six score Edward shil-
     lings.
    *Face.*   Good!
    *Dap.*         And an old Harry's sovereign.
    *Face.*               Very good!
    *Dap.*   And three James shillings, and an
     Elizabeth groat,            145
Just twenty nobles.

---

    [86] **vacation:** *i.e.*, when the law courts are not sitting       [88] **perspective:** an ingeniously made pic-
ture, the appearance of which changes with the spectator's point of view or which looks distorted unless
seen from a certain angle. Another form could be properly seen only through a small hole in a piece
of paper.     [91] **commodity:** (cf. note on II. i. 14)     [98] **woad:** a plant from which blue dye was made
[121] **pellitory:** an herb    [124] **'cess'd:** assessed, taxed     [143] **Edward:** coined in the reign of Edward VI
[144] **Harry's:** Henry VII or Henry VIII     [146] **twenty nobles:** about $33

*Face.*                    O, you are too just.
I would you had had the other noble in Maries.
*Dap.*    I have some Philip and Maries.
*Face.*                              Ay, those same
Are best of all: where are they?  Hark, the
doctor.

## Act III.  Scene V

### [*The Same*]

*Subtle, Face, Dapper,* [*and later*] *Dol. Subtle
disguis'd like a Priest of Faery*

[*Sub. in a feigned voice.*]   Is yet her grace's
cousin come?
*Face.*                He is come.
*Sub.*    And is he fasting?
*Face.*              Yes.
*Sub.*                      And hath cried "hum"?
*Face.*    Thrice, you must answer.
*Dap.*                          Thrice.
*Sub.*    And as oft "buz"?
*Face.*    If you have, say.
*Dap.*                    I have.
*Sub.*                      Then, to her cuz,
Hoping that he hath vinegar'd his senses,    5
As he was bid, the Faery Queen dispenses,
By me, this robe, the petticoat of Fortune;
Which that he straight put on, she doth impor-
tune.
And though to Fortune near be her petticoat,  9
Yet nearer is her smock, the queen doth
note:
And therefore, even of that a piece she hath
sent,
Which, being a child, to wrap him in was
rent;
And prays him for a scarf he now will wear it,
With as much love as then her grace did tear
it,
About his eyes, to show he is fortunate;    15
                *They blind him with a rag.*
And, trusting unto her to make his state,
He 'll throw away all worldly pelf about him;
Which that he will perform, she doth not doubt
him.
  *Face.*    She need not doubt him, sir. Alas, he
  has nothing
But what he will part withal as willingly,    20
Upon her grace's word — throw away your
purse —
As she would ask it: — handkerchiefs and all —
She cannot bid that thing but he 'll obey. —
If you have a ring about you, cast it off,    24
Or a silver seal at your wrist; her grace will
send    *He throws away, as they bid him.*

Her fairies here to search you, therefore deal
Directly with her highness: if they find
That you conceal a mite, you are undone.
*Dap.*    Truly, there 's all.
*Face.*                      All what?
*Dap.*                      My money; truly.
*Face.*    Keep nothing that is transitory about
you.                                    30
[*Aside to Subtle.*]  Bid Dol play music. — Look,
the elves are come
                  *Dol. enters with a cittern.*
To pinch you, if you tell not truth.  Advise you.
                              *They pinch him.*
*Dap.*    O!  I have a paper with a spur-ryal
in 't.
*Face.*    *Ti, ti.*
They knew 't, they say.
*Sub.*              *Ti, ti, ti, ti.*  He has more yet.
*Face.  Ti, ti-ti-ti.*  I' the other pocket?
*Sub.*              *Titi, titi, titi, titi.*  35
They must pinch him or he will never confess,
they say.              [*They pinch him again.*]
*Dap.*    O, O!
*Face.*    Nay, pray you, hold: he is her grace's
nephew.
*Ti, ti, ti?*  What care you?  Good faith, you
shall care. —                            39
Dea! plainly, sir, and shame the fairies.  Show
You are an innocent.
*Dap.*        By this good light, I ha' nothing.
*Sub.  Titi, tititota.*  He does equivocate, she
says:
*Ti, ti do ti, ti ti do, ti da;* and swears by the
light when he is blinded.
*Dap.*    By this good dark, I ha' nothing but a
half-crown                              44
Of gold about my wrist, that my love gave me;
And a leaden heart I wore sin' she forsook
me.
*Face.*    I thought 't was something.  And
would you incur
Your aunt's displeasure for these trifles?  Come,
I had rather you had thrown away twenty half-
crowns.
You may wear your leaden heart still. — How
now!                                    50
*Sub.*    What news, Dol?
*Dol.*    Yonder 's your knight, Sir Mam-
mon.
*Face.*    God's lid, we never thought of him till
now!
Where is he?
*Dol.*        Here hard by.  He 's at the door.
*Sub.*    And you are not ready now!  Dol, get
his suit.                      [*Exit Dol.*]
He must not be sent back.

---

¹⁴⁷ **Maries:** coins of the reign of Queen Mary.  Some bore her head and that of Philip II.    ²⁷ **Directly:** honestly    ³³ **spur-ryal:** a gold coin worth about $4    ⁵⁴ **his suit:** *i.e.,* Face's servant
livery

*Face.*            O, by no means.  55
What shall we do with this same puffin here,
Now he 's o' the spit?
   *Sub.*         Why, lay him back awhile,
With some device.

     *[Re-enter Dol with Face's clothes]*

         — Ti, titi, tititi. Would her grace
speak with me?
I come. — Help, Dol!
   *Face.*        — Who 's there? Sir Epicure,
     *He speaks through the keyhole, the*
         *other knocking.*
My master 's i' the way. Please you to walk 60
Three or four turns, but till his back be turn'd,
And I am for you. — Quickly, Dol!
   *Sub.*             Her grace
Commends her kindly to you, master Dapper.
   *Dap.*  I long to see her grace.
   *Sub.*          She now is set
At dinner in her bed, and she has sent you  65
From her own private trencher, a dead mouse,
And a piece of gingerbread, to be merry withal,
And stay your stomach, lest you faint with
   fasting:
Yet if you could hold out till she saw you, she
   says,
It would be better for you.
   *Face.*       Sir, he shall    70
Hold out, an 't were this two hours, for her
   highness;
I can assure you that. We will not lose
All we ha' done. ——
   *Sub.*       He must not see, nor speak
To anybody, till then.
   *Face.*       For that we 'll put, sir,
A stay in 's mouth.
   *Sub.*     Of what?
   *Face.*        Of gingerbread.  75
Make you it fit. He that hath pleas'd her grace
Thus far, shall not now crinkle for a little. ——
Gape, sir, and let him fit you.
     *[They thrust a gag of gingerbread*
         *into his mouth.]*
   *Sub.*       —— Where shall we now
Bestow him?
   *Dol.*    I' the privy. ——
   *Sub.*        Come along, sir,  80
I now must show you Fortune's privy lodgings.
   *Face.*  Are they perfum'd, and his bath
   ready?
   *Sub.*               All:
Only the fumigation 's somewhat strong.
   *Face. [Speaking through the keyhole.]*  Sir Epi-
cure, I am yours, sir, by and by.
         *[Exeunt with Dapper.]*

## Act IIII.  Scene I

*[A Room in Lovewit's House]*
*Face, Mammon, [and later] Dol*

   *[Face.]*  O, sir, y' are come i' the only finest
   time. ——
   *Mam.*  Where 's master?
   *Face.*     Now preparing for projection, sir.
Your stuff will be all chang'd shortly.
   *Mam.*             Into gold?
   *Face.*  To gold and silver, sir.
   *Mam.*          Silver I care not for.
   *Face.*  Yes, sir, a little to give beggars.
   *Mam.*          Where 's the lady?  5
   *Face.*  At hand here. I ha' told her such
   brave things o' you,
Touching your bounty and your noble spirit ——
   *Mam.*            Hast thou?
   *Face.*  As she is almost in her fit to see you.
But, good sir, no divinity i' your conference,
For fear of putting her in rage.
   *Mam.*        I warrant thee.  10
   *Face.*  Six men will not hold her down.
   And then,
If the old man should hear or see you ——
   *Mam.*           Fear not.
   *Face.*  The very house, sir, would run mad.
   You know it,
How scrupulous he is, and violent,
'Gainst the least act of sin. Physic or mathe-
   matics,         15
Poetry, state, or bawdry, as I told you,
She will endure, and never startle; but
No word of controversy.
   *Mam.*       I am school'd, good Ulen.
   *Face.*  And you must praise her house, re-
   member that,
And her nobility.
   *Mam.*       Let me alone:    20
No herald, no, nor antiquary, Lungs,
Shall do it better. Go.
   *Face. [Aside.]*     Why, this is yet
A kind of modern happiness, to have
Dol Common for a great lady.     *[Exit.]*
   *Mam.*         Now, Epicure,
Heighten thyself, talk to her all in gold;  25
Rain her as many showers as Jove did drops
Unto his Danaë; show the god a miser,
Compar'd with Mammon. What! the stone will
   do 't.
She shall feel gold, taste gold, hear gold, sleep
   gold;
Nay, we will *concumbere* gold: I will be puis-
   sant,
And mighty in my talk to her. —

---

   55 **puffin:** a sea-bird (term of derision)    77 **crinkie:** turn aside from his purpose    3 **be all:** ('b' all'
F)   16 **state:** politics   18 **Ulen:** ('Lungs' Q)   23 **modern:** common, moderate    **happiness:** ap-
propriateness   30 **concumbere:** fornicate

*[Re-enter Face with Dol richly dressed]*

Here she comes.  31

*Face.*  To him, Dol, suckle him. — This is
the noble knight
I told your ladyship ——
*Mam.*                    Madam, with your pardon,
I kiss your vesture.
*Dol.*                    Sir, I were uncivil
If I would suffer that; my lip to you, sir.  35
*Mam.*  I hope my lord your brother be in
health, lady.
*Dol.*  My lord my brother is, though I no
lady, sir.
*Face. [Aside.]*  Well said, my Guinea bird.
*Mam.*                    Right noble madam ——
*Face. [Aside.]*  O, we shall have most fierce
idolatry.
*Mam.*  'T is your prerogative.
*Dol.*                    Rather your courtesy.  40
*Mam.*  Were there nought else t' enlarge
your virtues to me,
These answers speak your breeding and your
blood.
*Dol.*  Blood we boast none, sir; a poor
baron's daughter.
*Mam.*  Poor! and gat you? Profane not.
Had your father
Slept all the happy remnant of his life  45
After that act, lien but there still, and panted,
He 'd done enough to make himself, his issue,
And his posterity noble.
*Dol.*                    Sir, although
We may be said to want the gilt and trappings,
The dress of honour, yet we strive to keep  50
The seeds and the materials.
*Mam.*                    I do see
The old ingredient, virtue, was not lost,
Nor the drug money us'd to make your com-
pound.
There is a strange nobility i' your eye,
This lip, that chin! Methinks you do resemble
One o' the Austriac princes.
*Face. [Aside.]*           Very like!  56
Her father was an Irish costermonger.
*Mam.*  The house of Valois, just, had such a
nose,
And such a forehead yet the Medici
Of Florence boast.
*Dol.*           Troth, and I have been lik'ned  60
To all these princes.
*Face. [Aside.]*       I 'll be sworn, I heard it.
*Mam.*  I know not how! it is not any one,
But e'en the very choice of all their features.
*Face. [Aside.]*  I 'll in, and laugh.  *[Exit.]*
*Mam.*                    A certain touch, or air,

That sparkles a divinity beyond  65
An earthly beauty!
*Dol.*           O, you play the courtier.
*Mam.*  Good lady, gi' me leave ——
*Dol.*                    In faith, I may not,
To mock me, sir.
*Mam.*           To burn i' this sweet flame;
The phœnix never knew a nobler death.
*Dol.*  Nay, now you court the courtier, and
destroy  70
What you would build. This art, sir, i' your
words,
Calls your whole faith in question.
*Mam.*                    By my soul ——
*Dol.*  Nay, oaths are made o' the same air, sir.
*Mam.*                    Nature
Never bestow'd upon mortality
A more unblam'd, a more harmonious feature;
She play'd the step-dame in all faces else:  76
Sweet madam, le' me be particular ——
*Dol.*  Particular, sir! I pray you, know your
distance.
*Mam.*  In no ill sense, sweet lady: but to ask
How your fair graces pass the hours? I see  80
Y' are lodg'd here, i' the house of a rare man,
An excellent artist: but what 's that to you?
*Dol.*  Yes, sir; I study here the mathematics,
And distillation.
*Mam.*           O, I cry your pardon.
He 's a divine instructor! can extract  85
The souls of all things by his art; call all
The virtues, and the miracles of the sun,
Into a temperate furnace; teach dull nature
What her own forces are. A man, the emp'ror
Has courted above Kelly; sent his medals  90
And chains, t' invite him.
*Dol.*           Ay, and for his physic, sir ——
*Mam.*  Above the art of Æsculapius,
That drew the envy of the thunderer!
I know all this, and more.
*Dol.*                    Troth, I am taken, sir,
Whole with these studies that contemplate na-
ture.  95
*Mam.*  It is a noble humour; but this form
Was not intended to so dark a use.
Had you been crooked, foul, of some coarse
mould,
A cloister had done well; but such a feature,
That might stand up the glory of a kingdom,
To live recluse is a mere solecism,  101
Though in a nunnery. It must not be.
I muse, my lord your brother will permit it:
You should spend half my land first, were I he.
Does not this diamond better on my finger  105
Than i' the quarry?
*Dol.*           Yes.

___

38  **Guinea bird:** slang for prostitute    41  **enlarge:** set forth    46  **lien:** lain    83  **mathematics:**
astrology    84  **distillation:** chemistry    90  **Kelly:** an alchemist (d. 1595), patronized by **Rudolph II**
of Germany, an associate of Dr. Dee

*Mam.* Why, you are like it.
You were created, lady, for the light.
Here, you shall wear it; take it, the first pledge
Of what I speak, to bind you to believe me.
*Dol.* In chains of adamant?
*Mam.* Yes, the strongest bands. 110
And take a secret too. — Here, by your side,
Doth stand this hour the happiest man in
    Europe.
*Dol.* You are contented, sir?
*Mam.* Nay, in true being,
The envy of princes and the fear of states.
*Dol.* Say you so, Sir Epicure?
*Mam.* Yes, and thou shalt prove it, 115
Daughter of honour. I have cast mine eye
Upon thy form, and I will rear this beauty
Above all styles.
*Dol.* You mean no treason, sir?
*Mam.* No, I will take away that jealousy.
I am the lord of the philosopher's stone, 120
And thou the lady.
*Dol.* How, sir! ha' you that?
*Mam.* I am the master of the mastery.
This day the good old wretch here o' the house
Has made it for us: now he's at projection.
Think therefore thy first wish now, let me hear
    it; 125
And it shall rain into thy lap, no shower,
But floods of gold, whole cataracts, a deluge,
To get a nation on thee.
*Dol.* You are pleas'd, sir,
To work on the ambition of our sex.
*Mam.* I 'm pleas'd the glory of her sex
    should know, 130
This nook here of the Friars is no climate
For her to live obscurely in, to learn
Physic and surgery, for the constable's wife
Of some odd hundred in Essex; but come forth,
And taste the air of palaces; eat, drink 135
The toils of emp'rics, and their boasted practice;
Tincture of pearl, and coral, gold, and amber;
Be seen at feasts and triumphs; have it ask'd,
What miracle she is; set all the eyes
Of court a-fire, like a burning glass, 140
And work 'em into cinders, when the jewels
Of twenty states adorn thee, and the light
Strikes out the stars; that, when thy name is
    mention'd,
Queens may look pale; and, we but showing our
    love,
Nero's Poppæa may be lost in story! 145
Thus will we have it.
*Dol.* I could well consent, sir.
But in a monarchy, how will this be?
The prince will soon take notice, and both seize
You and your stone, it being a wealth unfit
For any private subject.

*Mam.* If he knew it. 150
*Dol.* Yourself do boast it, sir.
*Mam.* To thee, my life.
*Dol.* O, but beware, sir! You may come to
    end
The remnant of your days in a loath'd prison,
By speaking of it.
*Mam.* 'T is no idle fear. 154
We 'll therefore go with all, my girl, and live
In a free state, where we will eat our mullets,
Sous'd in high-country wines, sup pheasants'
    eggs,
And have our cockles boil'd in silver shells;
Our shrimps to swim again, as when they liv'd,
In a rare butter made of dolphins' milk, 160
Whose cream does look like opals; and with
    these
Delicate meats set ourselves high for pleasure,
And take us down again, and then renew
Our youth and strength with drinking the
    elixir,
And so enjoy a perpetuity 165
Of life and lust! And thou shalt ha' thy ward-
    robe
Richer than Nature's, still to change thyself,
And vary oft'ner, for thy pride, than she,
Or Art, her wise and almost-equal servant.

*[Re-enter Face]*

*Face.* Sir, you are too loud. I hear you
    every word 170
Into the laboratory. Some fitter place;
The garden, or great chamber above. How like
    you her?
*Mam.* Excellent! Lungs. There's for thee.
    *[Gives him money.]*
*Face.* But do you hear?
Good sir, beware, no mention of the rabbins.
*Mam.* We think not on 'em.
    *[Exeunt Mam. and Dol.]*
*Face.* O, it is well, sir. — Subtle! 175

## Act IIII. Scene II

*[The Same]*

*Face, Subtle, [and later] Kastril, Dame Pliant*

Dost thou not laugh?
*Sub.* Yes; are they gone?
*Face.* All 's clear.
*Sub.* The widow is come.
*Face.* And your quarreling disciple?
*Sub.* Ay.
*Face.* I must to my captainship again then.
*Sub.* Stay, bring 'em in first.
*Face.* So I meant. What is she?
A bonnibel?

---

¹¹⁹ **jealousy:** suspicion    ¹²² **mastery:** art of transmutation, magisterium    ¹³⁴ **hundred:** subdivi-
sion of a county    ³ **captainship:** *i.e.,* his captain's uniform    ⁵ **bonnibel:** pretty girl

*Sub.*          I know not.
*Face.*                    We 'll draw lots:  5
You 'll stand to that?
*Sub.*                What else?
*Face.*                        O, for a suit,
To fall now like a curtain, flap!
*Sub.*                        To th' door, man.
*Face.*  You 'll ha' the first kiss, 'cause I am
     not ready.                              [*Exit.*]
*Sub.*  Yes, and perhaps hit you through both
     the nostrils.                               9
*Face.* [*Within.*]  Who would you speak with?
*Kas.* [*Within.*]          Where 's the captain?
*Face.* [*Within.*]                  Gone, sir,
About some business.
*Kas.* [*Within.*]  Gone!
*Face.* [*Within.*]          He 'll return straight.
But, master doctor, his lieutenant, is here.

[*Enter Kastril, followed by Dame Pliant*]

*Sub.*  Come near, my worshipful boy, my
     *terræ fili,*
That is, my boy of land; make thy approaches:
Welcome;  I know thy lusts and thy desires,  15
And I will serve and satisfy 'em.  Begin,
Charge me from thence, or thence, or in this
     line;
Here is my centre: ground thy quarrel.
*Kas.*                        You lie.
*Sub.*  How, child of wrath and anger! the
     loud lie?
For what, my sudden boy?
*Kas.*              Nay, that look you to, 20
I am aforehand.
*Sub.*          O, this 's no true grammar,
And as ill logic!  You must render causes,
     child,
Your first and second intentions, know your
     canons
And your divisions, moods, degrees, and differ-
     ences,
Your predicaments, substance, and accident, 25
Series extern and intern, with their causes,
Efficient, material, formal, final,
And ha' your elements perfect —
*Kas.*                    What is this?
The angry tongue he talks in?
*Sub.*              That false precept,
Of being aforehand, has deceiv'd a number, 30
And made 'em enter quarrels oftentimes
Before they were aware; and afterward,
Against their wills.
*Kas.*          How must I do then, sir?
*Sub.*  I cry this lady mercy; she should first
Have been saluted.  I do call you lady,  35

Because you are to be one ere 't be long,
My soft and buxom widow.      *He kisses her.*
*Kas.*                    Is she, i' faith?
*Sub.*  Yes, or my art is an egregious liar.
*Kas.*  How know you?
*Sub.*          By inspection on her forehead,  39
And subtlety of her lip, which must be tasted
Often to make a judgment.      *He kisses her*
'Slight, she melts                *again.*
Like a myrobolane.  Here is yet a line,
In *rivo frontis,* tells me he is no knight.
*Dame P.*  What is he then, sir?
*Sub.*              Let me see your hand.
O, your *linea fortunæ* makes it plain;      45
And *stella* here *in monte Veneris.*
But, most of all, *junctura annularis.*
He is a soldier, or a man of art, lady,
But shall have some great honour shortly.
*Dame P.*                    Brother,
He 's a rare man, believe me!

[*Re-enter Face, in his uniform*]

*Kas.*                Hold your peace.  50
Here comes the tother rare man. — 'Save you,
     captain.
*Face.*  Good master Kastril!  Is this your
     sister?
*Kas.*      Ay, sir.
Please you to kuss her, and be proud to know
     her.
*Face.*  I shall be proud to know you, lady.
                              [*Kisses her.*]
*Dame P.*                    Brother,
He calls me lady, too.
*Kas.*              Ay, peace: I heard it.  55
                              [*Takes her aside.*]
*Face.*  The count is come.
*Sub.*                Where is he?
*Face.*                        At the door.
*Sub.*  Why, you must entertain him.
*Face.*                    What 'll you do
With these the while?
*Sub.*          Why, have 'em up, and show 'em
Some fustian book, or the dark glass.
*Face.*                      'Fore God,
She is a delicate dabchick!  I must have her.
                              [*Exit.*]
*Sub.* [*Aside.*]  Must you!  Ay, if your for-
     tune will, you must. —                   61
Come, sir, the captain will come to us presently:
I 'll ha' you to my chamber of demonstrations,
Where I 'll show you both the grammar and
     logic,
And rhetoric of quarreling; my whole method
Drawn out in tables; and my instrument,  66

---

9 **hit . . . nostrils:** put your nose out of joint   13 **terræ fili:** person of low birth   21 ff. (Subtle's
language, derived from scholastic logic and philosophy, is designed to confuse Kastril.)   29 **angry:**
swaggering   42 **myrobolane:** sugar plum   43 **rivo frontis:** frontal vein   45-47 **linea . . . annularis:**
terms in palmistry   59 **fustian:** dull, bombastic   **dark glass:** magic crystal

That hath the several scale upon 't shall make
you
Able to quarrel at a straw's-breadth by moon-
light.
And, lady, I 'll have you look in a glass,   69
Some half an hour, but to clear your eyesight,
Against you see your fortune; which is greater
Than I may judge upon the sudden, trust me.
                              [*Exeunt.*]

## Act IIII.   Scene III

[*The Same*]

*Face, Subtle,* [*later*] *Surly*

[*Face.*]   Where are you, doctor?
*Sub.* [*Within.*]   I 'll come to you presently.
*Face.*   I will ha' this same widow, now I ha'
seen her,
On any composition.

[*Enter Subtle*]

*Sub.*                What do you say?
*Face.*   Ha' you dispos'd of them?
*Sub.*              I ha' sent 'em up.
*Face.*   Subtle, in troth, I needs must have
this widow.                      5
*Sub.*   Is that the matter?
*Face.*            Nay, but hear me.
*Sub.*                       Go to.
If you rebel once, Dol shall know it all:
Therefore be quiet, and obey your chance.
*Face.*   Nay, thou art so violent now. Do but
conceive,
Thou art old, and canst not serve ——
*Sub.*            Who cannot? I? I?  10
'Slight, I will serve her with thee, for a ——
*Face.*                      Nay,
But understand: I 'll gi' you composition.
*Sub.*   I will not treat with thee. What! sell
my fortune?
'T is better than my birthright. Do not mur-
mur:
Win her, and carry her. If you grumble, Dol 15
Knows it directly.
*Face.*         Well, sir, I am silent.
Will you go help to fetch in Don in state?
                              [*Exit.*]
*Sub.*   I follow you, sir. We must keep Face
in awe,
Or he will overlook us like a tyrant.

[*Re-enter Face, introducing*] *Surly like a Spaniard*

Brain of a tailor! who comes here? Don
John!

*Sur.*   *Señores, beso las manos a vuestras merce-
des.*                                21
*Sub.*   Would you had stoop'd a little, and
kiss'd our *anos.*
*Face.*   Peace, Subtle!
*Sub.*        Stab me; I shall never hold, man.
He looks in that deep ruff like a head in a plat-
ter,
Serv'd in by a short cloak upon two trestles. 25
*Face.*   Or what do you say to a collar of
brawn, cut down
Beneath the souse, and wriggled with a knife?
*Sub.*   'Slud, he does look too fat to be a Span-
iard.
*Face.*   Perhaps some Fleming or some Hol-
lander got him
In d'Alva's time; Count Egmont's bastard.
*Sub.*                            Don,  30
Your scurvy, yellow, Madrid face is welcome.
*Sur.*   *Gratia.*
*Sub.*         He speaks out of a fortification.
Pray God he ha' no squibs in those deep sets.
*Sur.*   *Por dios, señores, muy linda casa!*
*Sub.*   What says he?
*Face.*          Praises the house, I think;  35
I know no more but 's action.
*Sub.*                 Yes, the *casa,*
My precious Diego, will prove fair enough
To cozen you in. Do you mark? You shall
Be cozened, Diego.
*Face.*          Cozened, do you see,
My worthy Donzel, cozened.
*Sur.*                *Entiendo.*  40
*Sub.*   Do you intend it? So do we, dear Don.
Have you brought pistolets or portagues,
My solemn Don? [*To Face.*]   Dost thou feel
any?                  *He feels his pockets.*
*Face.*                      Full.
*Sub.*   You shall be emptied, Don, pumped
and drawn
Dry, as they say.
*Face.*       Milked, in troth, sweet Don.  45
*Sub.*   See all the monsters; the great lion of
all, Don.
*Sur.*   *Con licencia, se puede ver a esta se-
ñora?*
*Sub.*   What talks he now?
*Face.*                O' the señora.
*Sub.*                       O, Don,
That is the lioness, which you shall see
Also, my Don.
*Face.*    'Slid, Subtle, how shall we do?  50
*Sub.*   For what?
*Face.*         Why, Dol's employ'd, you know.

---

<sup></sup> **71 Against you see:** in preparation for seeing    **3 composition:** terms, agreement    **12 composition:**
recompense   **19 overlook:** dominate   **21** Gentlemen, I kiss your hands (Spanish).   **26 brawn:** boar's
flesh  **27 souse:** ear   **30 d'Alva:** governor of the Netherlands, 1567–1573  **Egmont:** a patriot executed by Alva   **32 Gratia:** thanks   **33 sets:** plaits of his ruff   **34** Indeed, sirs, a very pretty house.
**39 Diego:** Spaniard   **40 Donzel:** little don  **Entiendo:** I understand.   **47** If you please, may I see the lady?

*Sub.*                                          That 's true.
'Fore heav'n 1 know not: he must stay, that 's
  all.
*Face.*   Stay! that he must not by no means.
*Sub.*                                          No! why?
*Face.*   Unless you 'll mar all. 'Slight, he 'll
  suspect it;
And then he will not pay, not half so well.   55
This is a travell'd punk-master, and does know
All the delays; a notable hot rascal,
And looks already rampant.
*Sub.*                          'Sdeath, and Mammon
Must not be troubled.
*Face.*                   Mammon! in no case.
*Sub.*   What shall we do then?
*Face.*                   Think: you must be sudden.   60
*Sur.*   *Entiendo que la señora es tan hermosa,*
*que codicio tan a verla como la bien aventuranza*
*de mi vida.*
*Face.*   *Mi vida!* 'Slid, Subtle, he puts me in
  mind o' the widow.
What dost thou say to draw her to 't, ha!   65
And tell her it is her fortune?  All our venter
Now lies upon 't.  It is but one man more,
Which on 's chance to have her: and beside,
There is no maidenhead to be fear'd or lost.
What dost thou think on 't, Subtle?
*Sub.*                   Who, I? why ——   70
*Face.*   The credit of our house, too, is en-
  gag'd.
*Sub.*   You made me an offer for my share ere-
  while.
What wilt thou gi' me, i' faith?
*Face.*                   O, by that light,
I 'll not buy now.  You know your doom to
  me.
E'en take your lot, obey your chance, sir; win
  her,                                          75
And wear her — out for me.
*Sub.*                   'Slight, I 'll not work her then.
*Face.*   It is the common cause; therefore be-
  think you.
Dol else must know it, as you said.
*Sub.*                                          I care not.
*Sur.*   *Señores, porque se tarda tanto?*
*Sub.*   Faith, I am not fit, I am old.
*Face.*                   That 's now no reason, sir.   80
*Sur.*   *Puede ser de hazer burla de mi amor?*
*Face.*   You hear the Don too?  By this air,
  I call,
And loose the hinges.  Dol!
*Sub.*                   A plague of hell ——
*Face.*   Will you then do?

*Sub.*                   Y' are a terrible rogue!
I 'll think of this.  Will you, sir, call the widow?
*Face.*   Yes, and I 'll take her, too, with all
  her faults,                                   86
Now I do think on 't better.
*Sub.*                   With all my heart, sir;
Am I discharg'd o' the lot?
*Face.*                   As you please.
*Sub.*   Hands.  [*They shake hands.*]
*Face.*   Remember now, that upon any change
You never claim her.
*Sub.*   Much good joy and health to you,
  sir.                                          90
Marry a whore!  Fate, let me wed a witch first.
*Sur.*   *Por estas honradas barbas ——*
*Sub.*                   He swears by his beard.
Dispatch, and call the brother too.  [*Exit Face.*]
*Sur.*   *Tengo duda, señores, que no me hagan*
*alguna traycion.*                              95
*Sub.*   How, issue on?  Yes, *præsto, señor.*
  Please you
*Enthratha* the *chambratha*, worthy don:
Where if you please the fates, in your *bathada*,
You shall be soak'd, and strok'd, and tubb'd,
  and rubb'd,
And scrubb'd, and fubb'd, dear don, before
  you go.                                       100
You shall in faith, my scurvy baboon don,
Be curried, claw'd, and flaw'd, and taw'd,
  indeed.
I will the heartilier go about it now,
And make the widow a punk so much the
  sooner,
To be reveng'd on this impetuous Face:   105
The quickly doing of it is the grace.
                        [*Exeunt Sub. and Surly.*]

## Act IIII.   Scene IIII

[*Another Room in Lovewit's House*]

*Face, Kastril, Dame Pliant, [later] Subtle,*
*Surly*

[*Face.*]   Come, lady: I knew the doctor
  would not leave
Till he had found the very nick of her fortune.
*Kas.*   To be a countess, say you?
*Face.*                   A Spanish countess, sir.
*Dame P.*   Why, is that better than an Eng-
  lish countess?
*Face.*   Better!  'Slight, make you that a ques-
  tion, lady?                                   5

---

⁶⁰ **sudden:** quick   ⁶¹⁻⁶³ **Entiendo . . . vida:** I understand that the lady is so beautiful that I am as anxious about seeing her as about the good fortune of my life.   ⁷¹ **engag'd:** involved   ⁷⁴ **doom:** stated decision   ⁷⁹ Sirs, why this long delay? ('tanta' in Q F)   ⁸¹ Can it be to make fun of my love?   ⁸⁸ **lot:** lottery   ⁹² **Por . . . barbas:** by this honored beard   ⁹⁴⁻⁹⁵ I fear, sirs, you are play-ing me some foul trick.   ⁹⁶ **præsto, señor:** immediately, sir   ¹⁰⁰ **fubb'd:** cheated   ¹⁰² **flaw'd** cracked, damaged   **taw'd:** soaked   ³ **A . . . sir:** (given to Kastril in F)

*Kas.* Nay, she is a fool, captain, you must
    pardon her.
*Face.* Ask from your courtier to your inns-
    of-court-man,
To your mere milliner; they will tell you all,
Your Spanish jennet is the best horse; your
    Spanish
Stoop is the best garb; your Spanish beard 10
Is the best cut; your Spanish ruffs are the best
Wear; your Spanish pavin the best dance;
Your Spanish titillation in a glove
The best perfume: and for your Spanish pike,
And Spanish blade, let your poor captain
    speak. —                                         15
Here comes the doctor.

    *[Enter Subtle with a paper]*

*Sub.*                    My most honour'd lady,
For so I am now to style you, having found
By this my scheme, you are to undergo
An honourable fortune very shortly,           19
What will you say now, if some ——
    *Face.*                    I ha' told her all, sir,
And her right worshipful brother here, that she
    shall be
A countess; do not delay 'em sir; a Spanish
    countess.
    *Sub.* Still, my scarce-worshipful captain,
    you can keep
No secret! Well, since he has told you, madam
Do you forgive him, and I do.
    *Kas.*                    She shall do that, sir; 25
I 'll look to 't; 't is my charge.
    *Sub.*                    Well then: nought rests
But that she fit her love now to her fortune.
    *Dame P.* Truly I shall never brook a Span-
    iard.
    *Sub.* No?
    *Dame P.* Never sin' eighty-eight could I
    abide 'em,
And that was some three year afore I was born,
    in truth.                                        30
    *Sub.* Come, you must love him, or be miser-
    able;
Choose which you will.
    *Face.*         By this good rush, persuade her.
She will cry strawberries else within this
    twelvemonth.
    *Sub.* Nay, shads and mackerel, which is
    worse.
    *Face.* Indeed, sir!
    *Kas.* God's lid, you shall love him, or I 'll
    kick you.

*Dame P.* Why,                                       35
I 'll do as you will ha' me, brother.
    *Kas.*                    Do,
Or by this hand I 'll maul you.
    *Face.*                    Nay, good sir,
Be not so fierce.
    *Sub.*         No, my enraged child;
She will be rul'd. What, when she comes to taste
The pleasures of a countess! to be courted ——
    *Face.* And kiss'd and ruffled!                  41
    *Sub.*                    Ay, behind the hangings.
    *Face.* And then come forth in pomp!
    *Sub.*                    And know her state!
    *Face.* Of keeping all th' idolators o' the
    chamber
Barer to her, than at their prayers!
    *Sub.*                    Is serv'd
Upon the knee!
    *Face.*         And has her pages, ushers, 45
Footmen, and coaches ——
    *Sub.*                    Her six mares ——
    *Face.*                    Nay, eight!
    *Sub.* To hurry her through London, to th'
    Exchange,
Bet'lem, the China-houses ——
    *Face.*                    Yes and have
The citizens gape at her, and praise her tires,
And my lord's goose-turd bands, that rides
    with her!                                        50
    *Kas.* Most brave! By this hand, you are
    not my suster
If you refuse.
    *Dame P.* I will not refuse, brother.

    *[Enter Surly]*

*Sur.* *Que es esto, señores, que non se venga?*
*Esta tardanza me mata!*
    *Face.*                    It is the count come:
The doctor knew he would be here, by his art.
    *Sub.* *En gallanta madama, Don! gallantis-
    sima!*                                           56
    *Sur.* *Por todos los dioses, la mas acabada*
*Hermosura, que he visto en ma vida!*
    *Face.* Is 't not a gallant language that they
    speak?
    *Kas.* An admirable language! Is 't not
    French?                                          60
    *Face.* No, Spanish, sir.
    *Kas.*                    It goes like law French,
And that, they say, is the courtliest language.
    *Face.*                    List, sir.
    *Sur.* *El sol ha perdido su lumbre, con el*
*Resplandor que trae esta dama! Valga me dios!*

---

⁸ **milliner:** seller of fancy wares    ¹⁰ **garb:** bodily carriage    ¹⁸ **scheme:** horoscope    ²⁹ **eighty-
eight:** the year of the Armada    ³³ **cry:** sell on the street    ⁴⁵ **ushers:** ('huishers' F)    ⁴⁷ **Exchange:** a
shopping center    ⁴⁸ **Bet'lem:** Bethlehem Hospital, for the insane    **China-houses:** shops for the
sale of goods from China and the East Indies    ⁵⁰ **goose-turd:** greenish-yellow    ⁵⁵⁻⁵⁴ **Que . . .
mata:** Why does she not come, sirs? This delay is killing me.    ⁵⁷⁻⁵⁸ By all the gods, the most perfect
beauty that I have seen in my life!    ⁶¹ **law French:** the official language of the courts for several cen-
turies    ⁶³⁻⁶⁴ The sun has lost his light with the splendor this lady brings, so help me God.

*Face.* H' admires your sister.
*Kas.*                Must not she make curt'sy? 65
*Sub.* 'Ods will, she must go to him, man,
   and kiss him!
It is the Spanish fashion, for the women
To make first court.
*Face.*                'T is true he tells you, sir:
His art knows all.
*Sur.*                *Porque no se acude?*
*Kas.* He speaks to her, I think.
*Face.*                          That he does, sir. 70
*Sur. Por el amor de dios, que es esto que se
   tarda?*
*Kas.* Nay, see: she will not understand
   him! Gull, noddy!
*Dame P.* What say you, brother?
*Kas.*                          Ass, my suster,
Go kuss him, as the cunning man would ha'
   you;
I 'll thrust a pin i' your buttocks else.
*Face.*                O no, sir. 75
*Sur. Señora mia, mi persona muy indigna
   esta*
*Allegar a tanta hermosura.*
*Face.* Does he not use her bravely?
*Kas.*                          Bravely, i' faith!
*Face.* Nay, he will use her better.
*Kas.*                          Do you think so?
*Sur. Señora, si sera servida, entremos.* 80
                    [*Exit with Dame Pliant.*]
*Kas.* Where does he carry her?
*Face.*                          Into the garden, sir;
Take you no thought: I must interpret for
   her.
*Sub.* Give Dol the word.
                    [*Aside to Face, who goes out.*]
                — Come, my fierce child, advance,
We 'll to our quarrelling lesson again.
*Kas.*                          Agreed.
I love a Spanish boy with all my heart.        85
*Sub.* Nay, and by this means, sir, you shall
   be brother
To a great count.
*Kas.*                Ay, I knew that at first.
This match will advance the house of the Kas-
   trils.
*Sub.* 'Pray God your sister prove but pliant!
*Kas.*                          Why,
Her name is so, by her other husband.
*Sub.*                          How! 90
*Kas.* The Widow Pliant. Knew you not
   that?
*Sub.*                          No, faith, sir;

Yet, by the erection of her figure, I guess'd it.
Come, let 's go practise.
*Kas.*                Yes, but do you think, doctor,
I e'er shall quarrel well?
*Sub.*                          I warrant you. [*Exeunt.*]

## *Act IIII. Scene V*

### [*Another Room*]

*Dol, Mammon,* [*later*] *Face, Subtle*

[*Dol.*]                          In her fit of talking.
*For after Alexander's death* ——
*Mam.*                Good lady ——
*Dol. That Perdiccas and Antigonus were slain,
The two that stood, Seleuc' and Ptolemy* ——
*Mam.*                          Madam —
*Dol. Make up the two legs, and the fourth beast,
That was Gog-north and Egypt-south: which
   after*                                          5
*Was call'd Gog-iron-leg and South-iron-leg* ——
*Mam.*                          Lady ——
*Dol. And then Gog-horned. So was Egypt,
   too:
Then Egypt-clay-leg, and Gog-clay-leg* ——
*Mam.*                          Sweet madam ——
*Dol. And last Gog-dust, and Egypt-dust, which
   fall
In the last link of the fourth chain. And these* 10
*Be stars in story, which none see, or look at* ——
*Mam.* What shall I do?
*Dol.*                *For,* as he says, *except
We call the rabbins, and the heathen Greeks* ——
*Mam.* Dear lady ——
*Dol. To come from Salem, and from Athens,
And teach the people of Great Britain* ——

[*Enter Face hastily, in his servant's dress*]

*Face.*                What 's the matter, sir? 15
*Dol. To speak the tongue of Eber and Ja-
   van* ——
*Mam.*                O,
She 's in her fit.
*Dol.*                *We shall know nothing* ——
*Face.*                          Death, sir,
We are undone!
*Dol.*                *Where then a learned linguist
Shall see the ancient us'd communion
Of vowels and consonants* ——
*Face.*                My master will hear! 20
*Dol. A wisdom, which Pythagoras held most
   high* ——
*Mam.* Sweet honourable lady!

---

⁶⁹ **Porque . . . acude:** Why does she not draw near?          ⁷¹ For the love of God, why does she delay?          ⁷⁶⁻⁷⁷ My lady, my person is unworthy to approach such beauty.          ⁸⁰ Madam, if you please, let
us go in.          ⁹² **figure:** horoscope (with pun on her bearing)          ¹ ff. (Dol's raving is taken from Hugh
Broughton's *Concent of Scripture,* somewhat garbled for comic effect.          The empire of Alexander played
an important part in Broughton's interpretation of the Bible.)          ¹² **he:** Broughton (cf II. iii. 242)
¹⁶ **Eber:** Hebrew          **Javan:** Greek

*Dol.*                                         *To comprise*
*All sounds of voices, in few marks of letters.*
  *Face.*   Nay, you must never hope to lay her
    now.                          *They speak together.*
  *Dol.*   *And so we may arrive by Talmud skill,*
*And profane Greek, to raise the building up*    26
*Of Helen's house against the Ismaelite,*
*King of Thogarma, and his habergions*
*Brimstony, blue, and fiery; and the force*
*Of king Abaddon, and the beast of Cittim:*      30
*Which rabbi David Kimchi, Onkelos,*
*And Aben Ezra do interpret Rome.*
  *Face.*   How did you put her into 't?
  *Mam.*                         Alas, I talk'd
Of a fift monarchy I would erect                 34
With the philosopher's stone, by chance, and
    she
Falls on the other four straight.
  *Face.*                  Out of Broughton!
I told you so. 'Slid, stop her mouth.
  *Mam.*                          Is 't best?
  *Face.*   She 'll never leave else. If the old
    man hear her,
We are but *fæces*, ashes.
  *Sub.* [*Within.*]  What 's to do there?
  *Face.*   O, we are lost!  Now she hears him,
    she is quiet.                             40

          [*Enter Subtle.*]  *Upon Subtle's entry they*
                         *disperse*

  *Mam.*   Where shall I hide me!
  *Sub.*                 How!  What sight is here?
Close deeds of darkness, and that shun the
    light!
Bring him again.  Who is he?  What, my son!
O, I have liv'd too long.
  *Mam.*            Nay, good, dear father,
There was no unchaste purpose.
  *Sub.*                      Not? and flee me   45
When I come in?
  *Mam.*             That was my error.
  *Sub.*                          Error?
Guilt, guilt, my son; give it the right name.
    No marvel
If I found check in our great work within,
When such affairs as these were managing!   49
  *Mam.*   Why, have you so?
  *Sub.*        It has stood still this half hour:
And all the rest of our less works gone back.
Where is the instrument of wickedness,
My lewd false drudge?
  *Mam.*            Nay, good sir, blame not him;
Believe me, 't was against his will or knowl-
    edge:                                     54
I saw her by chance.

  *Sub.*                 Will you commit more sin,
T' excuse a varlet?
  *Mam.*             By my hope, 't is true, sir.
  *Sub.*   Nay, then I wonder less, if you, for
    whom
The blessing was prepar'd, would so tempt
    heaven,
And lose your fortunes.
  *Mam.*              Why, sir?
  *Sub.*                       This 'll retard
The work a month at least.
  *Mam.*                 Why, if it do,   60
What remedy?  But think it not, good father:
Our purposes were honest.
  *Sub.*                 As they were,
So the reward will prove.   *A great crack and*
    How now! ay me!         *noise within.*
God and all saints be good to us. ——

                [*Re-enter Face*]
                            What 's that?  64
  *Face.*   O, sir, we are defeated!  All the works
Are flown *in fumo*, every glass is burst;
Furnace and all rent down, as if a bolt
Of thunder had been driven through the house.
Retorts, receivers, pelicans, bolt-heads,   69
All struck in shivers!  Help, good sir! alas,
            *Subtle falls down, as in a swoon.*
Coldness and death invades him.  Nay, Sir
    Mammon,
Do the fair offices of a man!  You stand,
As you were readier to depart than he.
                            *One knocks.*
Who 's there?  My lord her brother is come.
  *Mam.*                          Ha, Lungs!
  *Face.*   His coach is at the door.  Avoid his
    sight,                                    75
For he 's as furious as his sister is mad.
  *Mam.*   Alas!
  *Face.*          My brain is quite undone with
    the fume, sir,
I ne'er must hope to be mine own man again.
  *Mam.*   Is all lost, Lungs?  Will nothing be
    preserv'd
Of all our cost?
  *Face.*          Faith, very little, sir;    80
A peck of coals or so, which is cold comfort,
    sir.
  *Mam.*   O, my voluptuous mind! I am justly
    punish'd.
  *Face.*   And so am I, sir.
  *Mam.*              Cast from all my hopes ——
  *Face.*   Nay, certainties, sir.
  *Mam.*              By mine own base affections.
                   *Subtle seems come to himself.*

────────────────────────────────

²⁵⁻⁴⁰ (In the early editions these lines are printed in parallel columns to indicate that all the characters speak at once.)    ²⁸ **habergions:** coats of armor, armed men    ³² **Aben Ezra:** Browning's Rabbi
Ben Ezra    ³⁹ **fæces:** sediment, dregs    ⁴² **Close:** secret    ⁶² **honest:** chaste    ⁶⁶ **in fumo:** in smoke
⁷⁰ **shivers:** splinters

*Sub.* ' O, the curst fruits of vice and lust!
*Mam.*                              Good father,  85
It was my sin. Forgive it.
*Sub.*                              Hangs my roof
Over us still, and will not fall, O justice,
Upon us, for this wicked man!
*Face.*                            Nay, look, sir,
You grieve him now with staying in his sight.
Good sir, the nobleman will come too, and take
    you,                                     90
And that may breed a tragedy.
*Mam.*                              I 'll go.
*Face.* Ay, and repent at home, sir. It may be,
For some good penance you may ha' it yet;
A hundred pound to the box at Bet'lem ——
*Mam.*                              Yes.
*Face.* For the restoring such as — ha' their
    wits.
*Mam.* I 'll do 't.                          95
*Face.* I 'll send one to you to receive it.
*Mam.*                              Do.
Is no projection left?
*Face.*                   All flown, or stinks, sir.
*Mam.* Will nought be sav'd that 's good for
    med'cine, think'st thou?
*Face.* I cannot tell, sir. There will be per-
    haps
Something about the scraping of the shards, 100
Will cure the itch, — though not your itch of
    mind, sir. [*Aside.*]
It shall be sav'd for you, and sent home. Good
    sir,
This way, for fear the lord should meet you.
                          [*Exit Mammon.*]
*Sub.* [*Raising his head.*]                 Face!
*Face.* Ay.
*Sub.*               Is he gone?
*Face.*                    Yes, and as heavily
As all the gold he hop'd for were in his blood. 105
Let us be light though.
*Sub.* [*Leaping up.*] Ay, as balls, and bound
And hit our heads against the roof for joy:
There 's so much of our care now cast away.
*Face.* Now to our don.
*Sub.* Yes, your young widow by this time
Is made a countess, Face; she 's been in travail
Of a young heir for you.
*Face.*                   Good, sir.
*Sub.*                    Off with your case, 111
And greet her kindly, as a bridegroom should,
After these common hazards.
*Face.*                     Very well, sir.
Will you go fetch Don Diego off the while?
*Sub.* And fetch him over too, if you 'll be
    pleas'd, sir.                            115
Would Dol were in her place, to pick his pock-
    ets now!

*Face.* Why, you can do it as well, if you
    would set to 't.
I pray you prove your virtue.
*Sub.*                For your sake, sir. [*Exeunt.*]

## Act IIII.  Scene VI

*Surly, Dame Pliant, [later] Subtle, Face*

[*Sur.*]  Lady, you see into what hands you
    are fall'n;
'Mongst what a nest of villains! and how near
Your honour was t' have catch'd a certain clap,
Through your credulity, had I but been
So punctually forward, as place, time,       5
And other circumstance would ha' made a man;
For y' are a handsome woman: would you
    were wise too!
I am a gentleman come here disguis'd,
Only to find the knaveries of this citadel;
And where I might have wrong'd your honour,
    and have not,                            10
I claim some interest in your love. You are,
They say, a widow, rich; and I 'm a bachelor,
Worth nought: your fortunes may make me a
    man,
As mine ha' preserv'd you a woman. Think
    upon it,
And whether I have deserv'd you or no.
*Dame P.*                    I will, sir.  15
*Sur.* And for these household-rogues, let me
    alone
To treat with them.

                    [*Enter Subtle*]

*Sub.*                How doth my noble Diego,
And my dear madam countess? Hath the count
Been courteous, lady? liberal and open?
Donzel, methinks you look meláncholic,       20
After your *coitum*, and scurvy! Truly,
I do not like the dulness of your eye;
It hath a heavy cast, 't is upsee Dutch,
And says you are a lumpish whore-master.
Be lighter, I will make your pockets so.      25
                    *He falls to picking of them.*
*Sur.* Will you, don bawd and pick-purse?
    [*Strikes him down.*] How now! Reel you?
Stand up, sir, you shall find, since I am so heavy,
I 'll gi' you equal weight.
*Sub.*                     Help! murder!
*Sur.*                               No, sir.
There 's no such thing intended. A good cart
And a clean whip shall ease you of that fear. 30
I am the Spanish don that should be cozened,
Do you see? Cozened? Where 's your Captain
    Face,
That parcel-broker, and whole-bawd, all rascal?

---

¹¹¹ **case:** his costume as Lungs    ¹¹⁸ **virtue:** power, ability    ²³ **upsee Dutch:** like a Dutch
drunkard's    ³⁰ **whip:** Bawds were whipped at the tail of a cart.    ³³ **parcel-:** part

*[Enter Face in his uniform]*

*Face.*　How, Surly!

*Sur.*　O, make your approach, good cap-
　　tain.　　　　　　　　　　　　　　　　35
I 've found from whence your copper rings and
　　spoons
Come now, wherewith you cheat abroad in tav-
　　erns.
'T was here you learn'd t' anoint your boot with
　　brimstone,
Then rub men's gold on 't for a kind of touch,
And say, 't was naught, when you had chang'd
　　the colour,　　　　　　　　　　　　　40
That you might ha 't for nothing. And this doc-
　　tor,
Your sooty, smoky-bearded compeer, he
Will close you so much gold, in a bolt's-head,
And, on a turn, convey i' the stead another
With sublim'd mercury, that shall burst i' the
　　heat,　　　　　　　　　　　　　　　45
And fly out all *in fumo!* Then weeps Mammon;
Then swoons his worship. Or, *[Face slips out.]*
　　he is the Faustus,
That casteth figures and can conjure, cures
Plagues, piles, and pox, by the ephemerides,
And holds intelligence with all the bawds　50
And midwives of three shires: while you send
　　in ——
Captain! — what! is he gone? — damsels with
　　child,
Wives that are barren, or the waiting-maid
With the green sickness. *[Seizes Subtle as he
　　is retiring.]* — Nay, sir, you must tarry,
Though he be scap'd; and answer by the ears,
　　sir.　　　　　　　　　　　　　　　　55

## Act IIII.　Scene VII

### *[The Same]*

*Face, Kastril, Surly, Subtle, [later] Drugger,
　　Ananias, Dame Pliant, Dol*

*[Face.]*　Why, now 's the time, if ever you will
　　quarrel
Well, as they say, and be a true-born child:
The doctor and your sister both are abus'd.

*Kas.*　Where is he? Which is he? He is a
　　slave,
Whate'er he is, and the son of a whore. — Are
　　you　　　　　　　　　　　　　　　　5
The man, sir, I would know?

*Sur.*　　　　　　　I should be loath, sir,
To confess so much.

*Kas.*　　　　　Then you lie i' your throat.

*Sur.*　　　　　　　　　　　　How!

*Face.* *[To Kastril.]*　A very arrant rogue, sir,
　　and a cheater,
Employ'd here by another conjurer
That does not love the doctor, and would cross
　　him,　　　　　　　　　　　　　　　1'
If he knew how.

*Sur.*　　　　Sir, you are abus'd.

*Kas.*　　　　　　　　　　　You lie:
And 't is no matter.

*Face.*　　　　Well said, sir! He is
The impudent'st rascal ——

*Sur.*　You are indeed. Will you hear me, sir?

*Face.*　By no means: bid him be gone.

*Kas.*　　　　　　Begone, sir, quickly.

*Sur.*　This 's strange! — Lady, do you in-
　　form your brother.　　　　　　　　15

*Face.*　There is not such a foist in all the
　　town.
The doctor had him presently; and finds yet
The Spanish count will come here. — Bear up,
Subtle.　　　　　　　　　*[Aside.]*

*Sub.*　Yes, sir, he must appear within this
　　hour.

*Face.*　And yet this rogue would come in a
　　disguise,　　　　　　　　　　　　20
By the temptation of another spirit,
To trouble our art, though he could not hurt it!

*Kas.*　　　　　　　　　　　　Ay,
I know — Away, *[to his sister.]* you talk like a
　　foolish mauther.

*Sur.*　Sir, all is truth she says.

*Face.*　　　　　Do not believe him, sir.　24
He is the lying'st swabber! Come your ways,
　　sir.

*Sur.*　You are valiant out of company!

*Kas.*　　　　　　Yes, how then, sir?

*[Enter Drugger with a piece of damask]*

*Face.*　Nay, here 's an honest fellow too that
　　knows him,
And all his tricks.　(Make good what I say,
　　Abel.
This cheater would ha' cozen'd thee o' the
　　widow.) —　　　　　*[Aside to Drug.]*
He owes this honest Drugger here seven pound,
He has had on him in twopenny'orths of to-
　　bacco.　　　　　　　　　　　　31

*Drug.*　Yes, sir. And 's damn'd himself three
　　terms to pay me.

*Face.*　And what does he owe for lotium?

*Drug.*　　　　　　Thirty shillings, sir;
And for six syringes.

*Sur.*　　　　　Hydra of villainy!

*Face.*　Nay, sir, you must quarrel him out o'
　　the house.

*Kas.*　I will:　　　　　　　　　　　35

---

⁴⁵ **sublim'd:** sublimated, refined　⁴⁹ **ephemerides:** astrological almanacs　⁸ **arrant:** ('errant' Q, F)
¹⁶ **foist:** cheat　²³ **mauther:** girl　²⁵ **swabber:** rogue　**Come . . . ways:** Be on your way.
¹⁸ **out of company:** when you are alone　³³ **lotium:** lotion

— Sir, if you get not out o' doors, you lie;
And you are a pimp.
 *Sur.*      Why, this is madness, sir,
Not valour in you; I must laugh at this.
 *Kas.*  It is my humour; you are a pimp and
a trig,
And an Amadis de Gaul, or a Don Quixote. 40
 *Drug.*  Or a knight o' the curious coxcomb,
do you see?

    *[Enter Ananias]*

 *Ana.*  Peace to the household!
 *Kas.*      I 'll keep peace for no man.
 *Ana.*  Casting of dollars is concluded lawful.
 *Kas.*  Is he the constable?
 *Sub.*      Peace, Ananias.
 *Face.*      No, sir.
 *Kas.*  Then you are an otter, and a shad, a
whit,         45
A very tim.
 *Sur.*    You 'll hear me, sir?
 *Kas.*      I will not.
 *Ana.*  What is the motive?
 *Sub.*     Zeal in the young gentleman,
Against his Spanish slops.
 *Ana.*      They are profane,
Lewd, superstitious, and idolatrous breeches.
 *Sur.*  New rascals!
 *Kas.*     Will you be gone, sir?
 *Ana.*      Avoid, Sathan! 50
Thou art not of the light! That ruff of pride
About thy neck betrays thee; and is the same
With that which the unclean birds, in seventy-
seven,
Were seen to prank it with on divers coasts:
Thou look'st like Antichrist, in that lewd hat. 55
 *Sur.*  I must give way.
 *Kas.*      Be gone, sir.
 *Sur.*      But I 'll take
A course with you ——
 *Ana.*     Depart, proud Spanish fiend!
 *Sur.*  Captain and doctor ——
 *Ana.*     Child of perdition!
 *Kas.*      Hence, sir! — *[Exit Surly.]*
Did I not quarrel bravely?
 *Face.*      Yes, indeed, sir.
 *Kas.*  Nay, an I give my mind to 't, I shall
do 't.          60
 *Face.*  O, you must follow, sir, and threaten
him tame:
He 'll turn again else.
 *Kas.*     I 'll re-turn him then. *[Exit.]*
 *Face.*  Drugger, this rogue prevented us, for
thee:
We had determin'd that thou should'st ha'
come

In a Spanish suit, and ha' carried her so; and
he,             65
A brokerly slave, goes, puts it on himself
Hast brought the damask?
 *Drug.*      Yes, sir.
 *Face.*      Thou must borrow
A Spanish suit. Hast thou no credit with the
players?
 *Drug.*  Yes, sir; did you never see me play
the Fool?
 *Face.*  I know not, Nab; — thou shalt, if I
can help it. —      *[Aside.]* 70
Hieronimo's old cloak, ruff, and hat will serve;
I 'll tell thee more when thou bring'st 'em.
        *[Exit Drugger.]*
 *Ana.*      Sir, I know.
 *Subtle hath whisper'd with him this while.*
The Spaniard hates the brethren, and hath
spies
Upon their actions: and that this was one
I make no scruple. — But the holy synod   75
Have been in prayer and meditation for it;
And 't is reveal'd no less to them than me,
That casting of money is most lawful.
 *Sub.*      True.
But here I cannot do it: if the house
Should chance to be suspected, all would out, 80
And we be lock'd up in the Tower for ever,
To make gold there for th' state, never come
out;
And then are you defeated.
 *Ana.*      I will tell
This to the elders and the weaker brethren,
That the whole company of the separation   85
May join in humble prayer again.
 *Sub.*      And fasting.
 *Ana.*  Yea, for some fitter place. The peace
of mind
Rest with these walls!      *[Exit.]*
 *Sub.*     Thanks, courteous Ananias.
 *Face.*  What did he come for?
 *Sub.*     About casting dollars,
Presently, out of hand. And so I told him, 90
A Spanish minister came here to spy,
Against the faithful ——
 *Face.*     I conceive. Come, Subtle,
Thou art so down upon the least disaster!
How wouldst thou ha' done, if I had not help'd
thee out?
 *Sub.*  I thank thee, Face, for the angry boy,
i' faith.          95
 *Face.*  Who would ha' look'd it should ha'
been that rascal
Surly? He had dy'd his beard and all. Well,
sir,
Here 's damask come to make you a suit.

---

 **39** trig: coxcomb   **40 Amadis de Gaul:** the hero of an old romance of chivalry   45, 46 **whit, tim:**
of uncertain meaning, but intended only to show Kastril's bravado   53 **unclean . . . seven:** unexplained
allusion   **71 Hieronimo:** in Kyd's *Spanish Tragedy*   92 **conceive:** understand   96 **look'd:** expected

*Sub.*                    Where 's Drugger?
*Face.*  He is gone to borrow me a Spanish
   habit:                                    99
I 'll be the count now.
   *Sub.*              But where 's the widow?
*Face.*  Within, with my lord's sister; Madam
   Dol
Is entertaining her.
   *Sub.*              By your favour, Face,
Now she is honest, I will stand again.
   *Face.*  You will not offer it?
   *Sub.*  Why?
   *Face.*              Stand to your word,
Or — here comes Dol! — she knows ——
   *Sub.*         Y' are tyrannous still.   105

[*Enter Dol hastily*]

*Face.*  — Strict for my right. — How now,
   Dol! Hast told her,
The Spanish count will come?
   *Dol.*          Yes; but another is come,
You little look'd for!
   *Face.*          Who 's that?
   *Dol.*                  Your master;
The master of the house.
   *Sub.*              How, Dol!
   *Face.*                  She lies,
This is some trick.  Come, leave your quiblins,
   Dorothy.                                  110
*Dol.*  Look out and see.
                [*Face goes to the window.*]
   *Sub.*          Art thou in earnest?
   *Dol.*                  'Slight,
Forty o' the neighbours are about him, talking.
   *Face.*  'T is he, by this good day.
   *Dol.*              'T will prove ill day
For some on us.
   *Face.*          We are undone, and taken.
   *Dol.*  Lost, I 'm afraid.
   *Sub.*          You said he would not come,  115
While there died one a week within the liber-
   ties.
*Face.*  No: 't was within the walls.
   *Sub.*          Was 't so?  Cry you mercy.
I thought the liberties.  What shall we do now,
   Face?
*Face.*  Be silent: not a word, if he call or
   knock.                                    119
I 'll into mine old shape again and meet him,
Of Jeremy, the butler.  I' the meantime,
Do you two pack up all the goods and pur-
   chase
That we can carry i' the two trunks.  I 'll keep
   him
Off for to-day, if I cannot longer: and then 124
At night, I 'll ship you both away to Ratcliff,

Where we will meet to-morrow, and there we 'll
   share.
Let Mammon's brass and pewter keep the cel-
   lar;
We 'll have another time for that.  But, Dol,
'Pray thee go heat a little water quickly;  129
Subtle must shave me.  All my captain's beard
Must off, to make me appear smooth Jeremy.
You 'll do 't?
   *Sub.*  Yes, I 'll shave you as well as I can.
   *Face.*  And not cut my throat, but trim me?
   *Sub.*          You shall see, sir.  [*Exeunt.*]

*Act V.  Scene I*

[*Before Lovewit's House*]

*Lovewit, Neighbours*

[*Love.*]  Has there been such resort, say you?
*1 Nei.*                          Daily, Sir.
*2 Nei.*  And nightly, too.
*3 Nei.*          Ay, some as brave as lords.
*4 Nei.*  Ladies and gentlewomen.
*5 Nei.*                  Citizens' wives.
*1 Nei.*  And knights.
*6 Nei.*          In coaches.
*2 Nei.*          Yes, and oyster-women.
*1 Nei.*  Beside other gallants.
*3 Nei.*                  Sailors' wives.
*4 Nei.*                  Tobacco men.  5
*5 Nei.*  Another Pimlico.
*Love.*          What should my knave advance,
To draw this company?  He hung out no banners
Of a strange calf with five legs to be seen,
Or a huge lobster with six claws?
*6 Nei.*                      No, sir.
*3 Nei.*  We had gone in then, sir.
*Love.*          He has no gift  10
Of teaching i' the nose that e'er I knew of.
You saw no bills set up that promis'd cure
Of agues or the tooth-ache?
*2 Nei.*              No such thing, sir!
*Love.*  Nor heard a drum struck for baboons
   or puppets?
*5 Nei.*  Neither, sir.
*Love.*          What device should he bring forth
   now?                                      15
I love a teeming wit as I love my nourishment:
'Pray God he ha' not kept such open house,
That he hath sold my hangings, and my bed-
   ding!
I left him nothing else.  If he have eat 'em,
A plague o' the moth, say I!  Sure he has got 20
Some bawdy pictures to call all this ging:
The Friar and the Nun; or the new motion

---

¹¹⁰ **quiblins:** quibbles   ¹¹⁶ **liberties:** outlying districts of London   ¹²² **purchase:** booty   ⁶ **Pim-**
**lico:** a popular summer resort, near Hogsden   ¹¹ **teaching . . . nose:** *i.e.,* preaching like a Puritan
¹² **bills:** posters   ²¹ **ging:** gang   ²² **motion:** puppet show

Of the knight's courser covering the parson's
   mare;
The boy of six year old, with the great thing: 24
Or 't may be, he has the fleas that run at tilt
Upon a table, or some dog to dance.
When saw you him?
   *1 Nei.*                Who, sir, Jeremy?
   *2 Nei.*                Jeremy butler?
We saw him not this month.
   *Love.*        How!
   *4 Nei.*               Not these five weeks, sir.
   [6] *Nei.*    These six weeks, at the least.
   *Love.*         You amaze me, neighbours!
   *5 Nei.*   Sure, if your worship know not where
   he is,                                        30
He 's slipp'd away.
   *6 Nei.*      Pray God he be not made away.
                                     *He knocks.*
   *Love.* Ha! it 's no time to question, then.
   *6 Nei.*                                About
Some three weeks since I heard a doleful cry,
As I sat up a-mending my wife's stockings.
   *Love.*  This 's strange that none will answer!
   Did'st thou hear                              35
A cry, sayst thou?
   *6 Nei.*              Yes, sir, like unto a man
That had been strangled an hour, and could not
   speak.
   *2 Nei.*  I heard it, too, just this day three
   weeks, at two o'clock
Next morning.
   *Love.*  These be miracles, or you make 'em so!
A man an hour strangled, and could not speak,
And both you heard him cry?
   *3 Nei.*            Yes, downward, sir.  41
   *Love.*  Thou art a wise fellow.  Give me thy
   hand, I pray thee.
What trade art thou on?
   *3 Nei.*   A smith, an 't please your worship.
   *Love.*  A smith! Then lend me thy help to
   get this door open.
   *3 Nei.*   That I will presently, sir, but fetch
   my tools —                  [*Exit.*]  45
   *1 Nei.*  Sir, best to knock again afore you
   break it.

## Act V.  Scene II

### [*The Same*]

*Lovewit, Face, Neighbours*

[*Love. knocks again.*] I will.

   [*Enter Face in his butler's livery*]

*Face.*                    What mean you, sir?
*1, 2, 4 Nei.*              O, here 's Jeremy!
*Face.*  Good sir, come from the door.

   *Love.*             Why, what 's the matter?
   *Face.*  Yet farder, you are too near yet.
   *Love.*             I' the name of wonder,
What means the fellow!
   *Face.*         The house, sir, has been visited.
   *Love.*  What, with the plague?  Stand thou
   then farder.
   *Face.*            No, sir,                   5
I had it not.
   *Love.*        Who had it then?  I left
None else but thee i' the house.
   *Face.*                Yes, sir, my fellow,
The cat that kept the buttery, had it on her
A week before I spied it; but I got her
Convey'd away i' the night: and so I shut  10
The house up for a month ——
   *Love.*                    How!
   *Face.*                Purposing then, sir,
T' have burnt rose-vinegar, treacle, and tar,
And ha' made it sweet, that you should ne'er
   ha' known it;
Because I knew the news would but afflict you,
   sir.
   *Love.*  Breathe less, and farder off!  Why
   this is stranger:                            15
The neighbours tell me all here that the doors
Have still been open ——
   *Face.*         How, sir!
   *Love.*               Gallants, men and women,
And of all sorts, tag-rag, been seen to flock here
In threaves, these ten weeks, as to a second
   Hogsden,
In days of Pimlico and Eye-bright.
   *Face.*                    Sir,          20
Their wisdoms will not say so.
   *Love.*                  To-day they speak
Of coaches and gallants; one in a French hood
Went in, they tell me; and another was seen
In a velvet gown at the windore: divers more
Pass in and out.                      [then,
   *Face.*          They did pass through the doors
Or walls, I assure their eye-sights, and their
   spectacles;                                  26
For here, sir, are the keys, and here have been,
In this my pocket, now above twenty days!
And for before, I kept the fort alone there.
But that 't is yet not deep i' the afternoon,  30
I should believe my neighbours had seen double
Through the black pot, and made these ap-
   paritions!
For, on my faith to your worship, for these
   three weeks
And upwards, the door has not been open'd.
   *Love.*                        Strange!
   *1 Nei.*  Good faith, I think I saw a coach.
   *2 Nei.*                  And I too,      35
I 'd ha' been sworn.

*Love.*               Do you but think it now?
And but one coach?
    4 *Nei.*          We cannot tell, sir: Jeremy
Is a very honest fellow.
    *Face.*           Did you see me at all?
    1 *Nei.*   No; that we are sure on.
    2 *Nei.*          I 'll be sworn o' that.
    *Love.*   Fine rogues to have your testimonies
        built on!                              40

*[Re-enter third Neighbour, with his tools]*

    3 *Nei.*   Is Jeremy come!
    1 *Nei.*   O yes; you may leave your tools;
We were deceiv'd, he says.
    2 *Nei.*                 He 's had the keys;
And the door has been shut these three weeks.
    3 *Nei.*                 Like enough.
    *Love.*   Peace, and get hence, you changelings.

*[Enter Surly and Mammon]*

    *Face. [Aside.]*           Surly come!
And Mammon made acquainted! They 'll tell
        all.                                   45
How shall I beat them off? What shall I do?
Nothing 's more wretched than a guilty con-
science.

## Act V.  Scene III

### [The Same]

*Surly, Mammon, Lovewit, Face, Neighbours,
    [later] Kastril, Ananias, Tribulation, Dap-
    per, Subtle*

*[Sur.]* No, sir, he was a great physician. This,
It was no bawdy-house, but a mere chancel!
You knew the lord and his sister.
    *Mam.*               Nay, good Surly.
    *Sur.* The happy word, *be rich* ——
    *Mam.*               Play not the tyrant.
    *Sur.* Should be to-day pronounc'd to all
        your friends.                          5
And where be your andirons now?  And your
        brass pots,
That should ha' been golden flagons, and great
        wedges?
    *Mam.* Let me but breathe.  What, they ha'
        shut their doors,
Methinks!        *Mammon and Surly knock.*
    *Sur.*   Ay, now 't is holiday with them.
    *Mam.*                 Rogues,
Cozeners, impostors, bawds!
    *Face.*           What mean you, sir?   10
    *Mam.* To enter if we can.
    *Face.*                 Another man's house!
Here is the owner, sir; turn you to him,
And speak your business.
    *Mam.*           Are you, sir, the owner?
    *Love*   Yes, sir.

    *Mam.*   And are those knaves, within, your
        cheaters?
    *Love.*  What knaves, what cheaters?
    *Mam.*               Subtle and his Lungs.   15
    *Face.* The gentleman is distracted, sir!  No
        lungs
Nor lights ha' been seen here these three weeks,
        sir,
Within these doors upon my word.
    *Sur.*               Your word,
Groom arrogant!
    *Face.*   Yes, sir.  I am the housekeeper,
And know the keys ha' not been out o' my hands.
    *Sur.* This 's a new Face.
    *Face.*   You do mistake the house, sir:   21
What sign was 't at?
    *Sur.*             You rascal!  This is one
O' the confederacy.  Come, let 's get officers,
And force the door.
    *Love.*           Pray you, stay, gentlemen.
    *Sur.* No, sir, we 'll come with warrant.
    *Mam.*               Ay, and then   25
We shall ha' your doors open.
                *[Exeunt Mam. and Sur.]*
    *Love.*           What means this?
    *Face.* I cannot tell, sir.
    1 *Nei.*           These are two o' the gallants
That we do think we saw.
    *Face.*           Two o' the fools!
You talk as idly as they.  Good faith, sir,
I think the moon has craz'd 'em all. — *[Aside.]*
        O me,                                  30

### [Enter Kastril]

The angry boy come too!  He 'll make a noise,
And ne'er away till he have betray'd us all.
                        *Kastril knocks.*
    *Kas.* What, rogues, bawds, slaves, you 'll
        open the door anon!
Punk, cockatrice, my suster!  By this light,   34
I 'll fetch the marshal to you.  You are a whore
To keep your castle ——
    *Face.*   Who would you speak with, sir?
    *Kas.* The bawdy doctor, and the cozening
        captain,
And puss my suster.
    *Love.*           This is something, sure.
    *Face.* Upon my trust, the doors were never
        open, sir.
    *Kas.* I have heard all their tricks told me
        twice over,                            40
By the fat knight and the lean gentleman.
    *Love.* Here comes another.

### [Enter Ananias and Tribulation]

    *Face.*               Ananias too!
And his pastor!
    *Tri.*   The doors are shut against us.
                *They beat, too, at the door.*

34 **cockatrice:** harlot

*Ana.* Come forth, you seed of sulphur, sons
of fire!
Your stench it is broke forth; abomination 45
Is in the house.
  *Kas.*        Ay, my suster 's there.
  *Ana.*        The place,
It is become a cage of unclean birds.
  *Kas.* Yes, I will fetch the scavenger, and the
constable.
  *Tri.* You shall do well.
  *Ana.*        We 'll join to weed them out.
  *Kas.* You will not come then, punk devise,
my suster!    50
  *Ana.* Call her not sister; she is a harlot
verily.
  *Kas.* I 'll raise the street.
  *Love.*        Good gentlemen, a word.
  *Ana.* Sathan, avoid, and hinder not our zeal!
         [*Exeunt Ana., Tri., and Kas.*]
  *Love.* The world 's turn'd Bet'lem.
  *Face.*        These are all broke loose,
Out of St. Katherine's, where they use to keep
The better sort of mad-folks.
  *1 Nei.*        All these persons 56
We saw go in and out here.
  *2 Nei.*        Yes, indeed, sir.
  *3 Nei.* These were the parties.
  *Face.*        Peace, you drunkards! Sir,
I wonder at it. Please you to give me leave
To touch the door; I 'll try an the lock be
chang'd.    60
  *Love.* It mazes me!
  *Face.* [*Goes to the door.*]    Good faith, sir, I
believe
There 's no such thing: 't is all *deceptio visus.* —
[*Aside.*] Would I could get him away.
         *Dapper cries out within.*
  *Dap.* Master captain! Master doctor!
  *Love.* Who 's that?
  *Face.* [*Aside.*] Our clerk within, that I for-
got! — I know not, sir.    65
  *Dap.* [*Within.*] For God's sake, when will
her grace be at leisure?
  *Face.*        Ha!
Illusions, some spirit o' the air! — [*Aside.*] His
gag is melted,
And now he sets out the throat.
  *Dap.* [*Within.*]    I am almost stifled ——
  *Face.* [*Aside.*] Would you were altogether.
  *Love.*        'T is i' the house.
Ha! list.
  *Face.* Believe it, sir, i' the air.
  *Love.*        Peace, you. 70
  *Dap.* [*Within.*] Mine aunt's grace does not
use me well.
  *Sub.* [*Within.*] You fool,
Peace, you 'll mar all.
  *Face.* [*Speaks through the keyhole, while Love-*

*wit advances to the door unobserved.*] Or
you will else, you rogue.
  *Love.* O, is it so? Then you converse with
spirits! —
Come, sir. No more o' your tricks, good
Jeremy.
The truth, the shortest way.
  *Face.*        Dismiss this rabble, sir. — 75
[*Aside.*] What shall I do? I am catch'd.
  *Love.*        Good neighbours,
I thank you all. You may depart. [*Exeunt
Neighbours.*] — Come, sir,
You know that I am an indulgent master;
And therefore conceal nothing. What 's your
med'cine,
To draw so many several sorts of wild fowl? 80
  *Face.* Sir, you were wont to affect mirth
and wit —
But here 's no place to talk on 't i' the street.
Give me but leave to make the best of my for-
tune,
And only pardon me th' abuse of your house:
It 's all I beg. I 'll help you to a widow, 85
In recompense, that you shall gi' me thanks for,
Will make you seven years younger, and a rich
one.
'T is but your putting on a Spanish cloak:
I have her within. You need not fear the house;
It was not visited.
  *Love.*        But by me, who came 90
Sooner than you expected.
  *Face.*        It is true, sir.
'Pray you forgive me.
  *Love.* Well: let's see your widow. [*Exeunt.*]

## *Act V. Scene IIII*

[*A Room in Lovewit's House*]

*Subtle, Dapper, [later] Face, Dol*

[*Sub.*] How! ha' you eaten your gag?
  *Dap.*        Yes, faith, it crumbled
Away i' my mouth.
  *Sub.*        You ha' spoil'd all then.
  *Dap.*        No!
I hope my aunt of Faery will forgive me.
  *Sub.* Your aunt 's a gracious lady; but in
troth
You were to blame.
  *Dap.*        The fume did overcome me, 5
And I did do 't to stay my stomach. 'Pray you
So satisfy her grace.

       [*Enter Face in his uniform*]

       Here comes the captain.
  *Face.* How now! Is his mouth down?
  *Sub.*        Ay, he has spoken!

---

⁵⁰ **punk devise:** perfect harlot    ⁶² **deceptio visus:** optical illusion    ⁷ **satisfy:** explain it to

*Face.* [*Aside.*] A pox, I heard him, and you
  too. [*Aloud.*] He 's undone then. —
[*Aside to Subtle.*] I have been fain to say, the
  house is haunted              10
With spirits, to keep churl back.
  *Sub.*            And hast thou done it?
*Face.* Sure, for this night.
  *Sub.*         Why, then triumph and sing
Of Face so famous, the precious king
Of present wits.
  *Face.*        Did you not hear the coil   14
About the door?
  *Sub.*       Yes, and I dwindled with it.
*Face.* Show him his aunt, and let him be dis-
  patch'd:
I 'll send her to you.           [*Exit Face.*]
  *Sub.*       Well, sir, your aunt her grace
Will give you audience presently, on my suit,
And the captain's word that you did not eat
  your gag
In any contempt of her highness.
                        [*Unbinds his eyes.*]
  *Dap.*           Not I, in troth, sir.   20

    [*Enter*] *Dol like the Queen of Faery*

  *Sub.* Here she is come. Down o' your knees
  and wriggle:
She has a stately presence. [*Dapper kneels and
  shuffles toward her.*] Good! Yet nearer,
And bid, God save you!
  *Dap.*           Madam!
  *Sub.*              And your aunt.
  *Dap.* And my most gracious aunt, God save
  your grace.
  *Dol.* Nephew, we thought to have been
  angry with you;             25
But that sweet face of yours hath turn'd the tide,
And made it flow with joy, that ebb'd of love.
Arise, and touch our velvet gown.
  *Sub.*             The skirts,
And kiss 'em. So!
  *Dol.*      Let me now stroke that head.
*Much, nephew, shalt thou win, much shalt thou
  spend;*             30
*Much shalt thou give away, much shalt thou lend.*
  *Sub.* [*Aside.*] Ay, much! indeed. — Why do
  you not thank her grace?
  *Dap.* I cannot speak for joy.
  *Sub.*         See, the kind wretch!
Your grace's kinsman right.
  *Dol.*       Give me the bird. ——
Here is your fly in a purse, about your neck,
  cousin;            35
Wear it, and feed it about this day sev'n-night,
On your right wrist ——

*Sub.*          Open a vein with a pin
And let it suck but once a week; till then,
You must not look on 't.
  *Dol.*          No: and, kinsman,
Bear yourself worthy of the blood you come on.
  *Sub.* Her grace would ha' you eat no more
  Woolsack pies,            41
Nor Dagger frume'ty.
  *Dol.*         Nor break his fast
In Heaven and Hell.
  *Sub.*       She 's with you everywhere!
Nor play with costermongers, at mumchance,
  traytrip,
God-make-you-rich (when as your aunt has
  done it); but keep         45
The   gallant'st   company,   and   the   best
  games ——
  *Dap.*         Yes, sir.
  *Sub.* Gleek and primero; and what you
  get, be true to us.
  *Dap.* By this hand, I will.
  *Sub.*      You may bring 's a thousand pound
Before to-morrow night, if but three thousand
Be stirring, an you will.
  *Dap.*        I swear I will then.   50
  *Sub.* Your fly will learn you all games.
  *Face.* [*Within.*]     Ha' you done there?
  *Sub.* Your grace will command him no more
  duties?
  *Dol.*     No:
But come and see me often. I may chance
To leave him three or four hundred chests of
  treasure,           54
And some twelve thousand acres of fairy land,
If he game well and comely with good game-
  sters.
  *Sub.* There 's a kind aunt: kiss her departing
  part. —
But you must sell your forty mark a year now.
  *Dap.* Ay, sir, I mean.
  *Sub.*      Or, gi' 't away; pox on 't!
  *Dap.* I 'll gi' 't mine aunt. I 'll go and fetch
  the writings.         60
  *Sub.* 'T is well; away.    [*Exit Dapper.*]

    [*Re-enter Face*]

  *Face.*         Where 's Subtle?
  *Sub.*         Here: what news?
  *Face.* Drugger is at the door; go take his
  suit,
And bid him fetch a parson presently.
Say he shall marry the widow. Thou shalt
  spend          64
A hundred pound by the service!
                      [*Exit Subtle.*]

---

10–15 (Marked as spoken aside in F. Dapper does not hear.)   14 **coil:** disturbance   15 **dwindled:**
shrank with fear   41 **Woolsack:** a tavern   42 **Dagger:** a tavern   **frume'ty:** wheat boiled in milk
('Frumenty' Q)   43 **Heaven, Hell:** taverns   44–45 **mumchance . . . rich:** games of chance   47 **Gleek,**
**primero:** card games

Now, Queen Dol,
Have you pack'd up all?
 *Dol.*     Yes.
 *Face.*    And how do you like
The Lady Pliant?
 *Dol.*   A good dull innocent.

[Re-enter Subtle]

 *Sub.* Here's your Hieronimo's cloak and hat.
 *Face.*    Give me 'em.
 *Sub.* And the ruff too?
 *Face.* Yes; I 'll come to you presently.
            [*Exit.*]
 *Sub.* Now he is gone about his project, Dol,
I told you of, for the widow.
 *Dol.*     'T is direct 71
Against our articles.
 *Sub.*   Well, we 'll fit him, wench.
Hast thou gull'd her of her jewels or her brace-
 lets?
 *Dol.* No; but I will do 't.
 *Sub.*   Soon at night, my Dolly,
When we are shipp'd, and all our goods aboard,
Eastward for Ratcliff, we will turn our course 76
To Brainford, westward, if thou sayst the word,
And take our leaves of this o'erweening rascal,
This peremptory Face.
 *Dol.*   Content; I 'm weary of him.
 *Sub.* Thou 'st cause, when the slave will run
  a-wiving, Dol, 80
Against the instrument that was drawn be-
 tween us.
 *Dol.* I 'll pluck his bird as bare as I can.
 *Sub.*    Yes, tell her
She must by any means address some present
To th' cunning man, make him amends for
 wronging
His art with her suspicion; send a ring, 85
Or chain of pearl; she will be tortur'd else
Extremely in her sleep, say, and ha' strange
 things
Come to her. Wilt thou?
 *Dol.*   Yes.
 *Sub.*   My fine flitter-mouse,
My bird o' the night! We 'll tickle it at the
 Pigeons, 89
When we have all, and may unlock the trunks,
And say, this 's mine, and thine; and thine,
 and mine.     *They kiss.*

[Re-enter Face]

 *Face.* What now! a-billing?
 *Sub.*  Yes, a little exalted
In the good passage of our stock-affairs.
 *Face.* Drugger has brought his parson; take
 him in, Subtle,
And send Nab back again to wash his face. 95

 *Sub.* I will: and shave himself? [*Exit.*]
 *Face.*    If you can get him.
 *Dol.* You are hot upon it, Face, whate'er it
 is!
 *Face.* A trick that Dol shall spend ten pound
 a month by.

[Re-enter Subtle]

Is he gone?
 *Sub.* The chaplain waits you i' the hall, sir.
 *Face.* I 'll go bestow him. [*Exit.*]
 *Dol.*  He 'll now marry her instantly.
 *Sub.* He cannot yet, he is not ready. Dear
 Dol, 101
Cozen her of all thou canst. To deceive him
Is no deceit, but justice, that would break
Such an inextricable tie as ours was.
 *Dol.* Let me alone to fit him.

[Re-enter Face]

 *Face.*   Come, my venturers,
You ha' pack'd up all? Where be the trunks?
 Bring forth. 106
 *Sub.* Here.
 *Face.* Let 's see 'em. Where 's the money?
 *Sub.*    Here,
In this.
 *Face.* Mammon's ten pound; eight score
 before:
The brethren's money this. Drugger's and
 Dapper's.
What paper 's that?
 *Dol.* The jewel of the waiting maid's, 110
That stole it from her lady, to know cer-
 tain ——
 *Face.* If she should have precedence of her
 mistress?
 *Dol.* Yes.
 *Face.* What box is that?
 *Sub.*  The fish-wives' rings, I think,
And th' ale-wives' single money. Is 't not, Dol?
 *Dol.* Yes; and the whistle that the sailor's
 wife 115
Brought you to know an her husband were with
 Ward.
 *Face.* We 'll wet it to-morrow; and our silver
 beakers
And tavern cups. Where be the French petti-
 coats
And girdles and hangers?
 *Sub.*   Here, i' the trunk,
And the bolts of lawn.
 *Face.*   Is Drugger's damask there,
And the tobacco?
 *Sub.* Yes.
 *Face.*   Give me the keys. 121
 *Dol.* Why you the keys?

---

⁸⁸ **flitter-mouse:** bat ⁸⁹ **Pigeons:** a tavern at Brainford ¹¹⁴ **single money:** small change
¹¹⁶ **Ward:** a famous pirate, subject of a prose narrative, 1609, and a play by Daborne

*Sub.*        No matter, Dol; because
We shall not open 'em before he comes.
  *Face.* 'T is true, you shall not open them, indeed;
Nor have 'em forth, do you see? Not forth, Dol.
  *Dol.* No!                      125
  *Face.* No, my smock-rampant. The right is, my master
Knows all, has pardon'd me, and he will keep 'em.
Doctor, 't is true — you look — for all your figures:
I sent for him, indeed. Wherefore, good partners,
Both he and she, be satisfied: for here    130
Determines the indenture tripartite
'Twixt Subtle, Dol, and Face. All I can do
Is to help you over the wall, o' the back-side,
Or lend you a sheet to save your velvet gown, Dol.
Here will be officers presently, bethink you 135
Of some course suddenly to scape the dock;
For thither you 'll come else. *Some knock.*
  Hark you, thunder.
  *Sub.* You are a precious fiend!
  *Offi.* [*Without.*]        Open the door.
  *Face.* Dol, I am sorry for thee, i' faith; but hear'st thou?
It shall go hard but I will place thee somewhere:           140
Thou shalt ha' my letter to Mistress Amo ——
  *Dol.*               Hang you!
  *Face.* Or Madam Cæsarean.
  *Dol.*          Pox upon you, rogue,
Would I had but time to beat thee!
  *Face.*            Subtle,
Let 's know where you set up next; I 'll send you        144
A customer now and then, for old acquaintance.
What new course ha' you?
  *Sub.*        Rogue, I 'll hang myself;
That I may walk a greater devil than thou,
And haunt thee i' the flock-bed and the buttery.          [*Exeunt.*]

## Act V. Scene V

[*Another Room in Lovewit's House*]

*Lovewit, Officers, Mammon, Surly, Face, Kastril, Ananias, Tribulation, Drugger, Dame Pliant*

  [*Love.*] What do you mean, my masters?
  *Mam.* [*Without.*]        Open your door,
Cheaters, bawds, conjurers.

  *Offi.* [*Without.*]     Or we 'll break it open.
  *Love.* What warrant have you?
  *Offi.* [*Without.*]        Warrant enough, sir, doubt not,
If you 'll not open it.
  *Love.*        Is there an officer there?
  *Offi.* [*Without.*] Yes, two or three for failing.
  *Love.*         Have but patience,   5
And I will open it straight.

         [*Enter Face, as butler*]

  *Face.*         Sir, ha' you done?
Is it a marriage? Perfect?
  *Love.*         Yes, my brain.
  *Face.* Off with your ruff and cloak then; be yourself, sir.
  *Sur.* [*Without.*] Down with the door.
  *Kas.* [*Without.*]     'Slight, ding it open.
  *Love.* [*Opening the door.*]         Hold,
Hold, gentlemen, what means this violence? 10

  [*Mammon, Surly, Kastril, Ananias, Tribulation and Officers rush in*]

  *Mam.* Where is this collier?
  *Sur.*        And my Captain Face?
  *Mam.* These day-owls.
  *Sur.*    That are birding in men's purses.
  *Mam.* Madam Suppository.
  *Kas.*        Doxy, my suster.
  *Ana.*            Locusts,
Of the foul pit.
  *Tri.*    Profane as Bel and the Dragon.
  *Ana.* Worse than the grasshoppers, or the lice of Egypt.        15
  *Love.* Good gentlemen, hear me. Are you officers,
And cannot stay this violence?
  *Offi.*        Keep the peace.
  *Love.* Gentlemen, what is the matter? Whom do you seek?
  *Mam.* The chemical cozener.
  *Sur.*       And the captain pandar.
  *Kas.* The nun my suster.
  *Mam.*        Madam Rabbi.
  *Ana.*        Scorpions,   20
And caterpillars.
  *Love.*     Fewer at once, I pray you.
  *Offi.* One after another, gentlemen, I charge you,
By virtue of my staff.
  *Ana.*       They are the vessels
Of pride, lust, and the cart.
  *Love.*       Good zeal, lie still
A little while.
  *Tri.*     Peace, Deacon Ananias.   25
  *Love.* The house is mine here, and the doors are open;

---

<sup>126</sup> **right:** fact    <sup>131</sup> **Determines:** ends    <sup>141, 142</sup> **Mistress Amo, Madam Cæsarean:** mistresses of brothels    <sup>148</sup> **flock-bed . . . buttery:** at bed and board    <sup>5</sup> **for failing:** lest there should not be enough    <sup>9</sup> **ding:** break    <sup>12</sup> **birding:** stealing

If there be any such persons as you seek for,
Use your authority, search on o' God's name.
I am but newly come to town, and finding
This tumult 'bout my door, to tell you true, 30
It somewhat maz'd me; till my man here, fear-
    ing
My more displeasure, told me he had done
Somewhat an insolent part, let out my house
(Belike presuming on my known aversion
From any air o' the town while there was sick-
    ness),                                          35
To a doctor and a captain: who, what they are
Or where they be, he knows not.
  *Mam.*                              Are they gone?
  *Love.*  You may go in and search, sir.  *They*
    Here, I find                            *enter.*
The empty walls worse than I left 'em, smok'd,
A few crack'd pots, and glasses, and a furnace;
The ceiling fill'd with poesies of the candle, 41
And "Madam with a dildo" writ o' the walls.
Only one gentlewoman I met here,
That is within, that said she was a widow ——
  *Kas.*  Ay, that 's my suster; I 'll go thump
    her.  Where is she?        [*Goes in.*]  45
  *Love.*  And should ha' married a Spanish
    count, but he,
When he came to 't, neglected her so grossly,
That I, a widower, am gone through with her.
  *Sur.*  How! have I lost her, then?
  *Love.*                          Were you the don, sir?
Good faith, now, she does blame you extremely,
    and says                                       50
You swore, and told her you had ta'en the pains
To dye your beard, and umber o'er your face,
Borrow'd a suit, and ruff, all for her love:
And then did nothing.  What an oversight
And want of putting forward, sir, was this! 55
Well fare an old harquebusier yet,
Could prime his powder, and give fire, and hit,
All in a twinkling!          *Mammon comes forth.*
  *Mam.*                        The whole nest are fled!
  *Love.*  What sort of birds were they?
  *Mam.*                          A kind of choughs,
Or thievish daws, sir, that have pick'd my
    purse                                          60
Of eight score and ten pounds within these five
    weeks,
Beside my first materials; and my goods,
That lie i' the cellar, which I am glad they ha'
    left,
I may have home yet.
  *Love.*                  Think you so, sir?
  *Mam.*                                    Ay.
  *Love.*  By order of law, sir, but not otherwise.
  *Mam.*  Not mine own stuff!
  *Love.*          Sir, I can take no knowledge  66
That they are yours, but by public means.

If you can bring certificate that you were gull'd
    of 'em,
Or any formal writ out of a court,
That you did cozen yourself, I will not hold
    them.                                          70
  *Mam.*  I 'll rather lose 'em.
  *Love.*                      That you shall not, sir,
By me, in troth; upon these terms, they 're
    yours.
What, should they ha' been, sir, turn'd into
    gold, all?
  *Mam.*          No.
I cannot tell. — It may be they should. — What
    then?
  *Love.*  What a great loss in hope have you
    sustain'd!                                     75
  *Mam.*  Not I; the commonwealth has.
  *Face.*                  Ay, he would ha' built
The city new; and made a ditch about it
Of silver, should have run with cream from
    Hogsden;
That every Sunday in Moorfields the youn-
    kers,
And tits and tom-boys should have fed on,
    gratis.                                        80
  *Mam.*  I will go mount a turnip-cart, and
    preach
The end o' the world within these two months.
    Surly,
What! in a dream?
  *Sur.*              Must I needs cheat myself
With that same foolish vice of honesty!
Come, let us go and hearken out the rogues: 85
That Face I 'll mark for mine, if e'er I meet him.
  *Face.*  If I can hear of him, sir, I 'll bring you
    word
Unto your lodging; for in troth, they were
    strangers
To me; I thought 'em honest as myself, sir.
                                  *They come forth.*

[*Re-enter Ananias and Tribulation*]

  *Tri.*  'T is well, the saints shall not lose all
    yet.  Go                                       90
And get some carts ——
  *Love.*          For what, my zealous friends?
  *Ana.*  To bear away the portion of the right-
    eous
Out of this den of thieves.
  *Love.*                  What is that portion?
  *Ana.*  The goods, sometimes the orphans',
    that the brethren
Bought with their silver pence.
  *Love.*              What, those i' the cellar,  95
The knight Sir Mammon claims?
  *Ana.*                      I do defy
The wicked Mammon, so do all the brethren.

---

⁴² **Madam . . . dildo:** refrain of popular ballad   ⁵⁶ **harquebusier:** musketeer   ⁵⁹ **choughs: crows**
⁷⁹ **younkers:** young men    ⁸⁰ **tits: girls**    ⁸⁵ **hearken:** search    ⁹⁴ **sometimes:** formerly

Thou profane man! I ask thee with what con-
science
Thou canst advance that idol against us,
That have the seal? Were not the shillings
numb'red     100
That made the pounds; were not the pounds
told out
Upon the second day of the fourth week,
In the eight month, upon the table dormant,
The year of the last patience of the saints,
Six hundred and ten?
   *Love.* Mine earnest vehement botcher,    105
And deacon also, I cannot dispute with you:
But if you get you not away the sooner,
I shall confute you with a cudgel.
   *Ana.*                        Sir!
   *Tri.* Be patient, Ananias.
   *Ana.*            I am strong,
And will stand up, well girt, against an host 110
That threaten Gad in exile.
   *Love.*          I shall send you
To Amsterdam, to your cellar.
   *Ana.*         I will pray there,
Against thy house. May dogs defile thy walls,
And wasps and hornets breed beneath thy roof,
This seat of falsehood, and this cave of coz'-
nage!      [*Exeunt Ana. and Trib.*]

        *Drugger enters*

   *Love.* Another too?
   *Drug.*    Not I, sir, I am no brother.   116
   *Love.* Away, you Harry Nicholas! do you
talk?            *He beats him away.*
   *Face.* No, this was Abel Drugger. Good sir,
go,                (*To the Parson*)
And satisfy him; tell him all is done:
He stay'd too long a-washing of his face.   120
The doctor, he shall hear of him at Westches-
ter:
And of the captain, tell him, at Yarmouth, or
Some good port-town else, lying for a wind.
                 [*Exit Parson.*]
If you get off the angry child now, sir ——

     [*Enter Kastril, dragging in his sister*]

   *Kas.* Come on, you ewe, you have match'd
most sweetly, ha' you not?     125
Did not I say, I would never ha' you tupp'd
But by a dubb'd boy, to make you a lady-tom?
'Slight, you are a mammet! O, I could touse
you now.
Death, mun you marry with a pox!
   *Love.*          You lie, boy;
As sound as you; and I 'm aforehand with you.

   *Kas.*                    Anon? 130
   *Love.* Come, will you quarrel? I will feize
you, sirrah;
Why do you not buckle to your tools?
   *Kas.*                God's light,
This is a fine old boy as e'er I saw!
   *Love.* What, do you change your copy now?
Proceed;                 134
Here stands my dove: stoop at her if you dare.
   *Kas.* 'Slight, I must love him! I cannot
choose, i' faith,
An I should be hang'd for 't! Suster, I protest,
I honour thee for this match.
   *Love.*          O, do you so, sir?
   *Kas.* Yes, an thou canst take tobacco and
drink, old boy,
I 'll give her five hundred pound more to her
marriage,             140
Than her own state.
   *Love.*       Fill a pipe full, Jeremy.
   *Face.* Yes; but go in and take it, sir.
   *Love.*               We will.
I will be rul'd by thee in anything, Jeremy.
   *Kas.* 'Slight, thou art not hide-bound, thou
art a jovy boy!        144
Come, let 's in, I pray thee, and take our whiffs.
   *Love.* Whiff in with your sister, brother boy.
         [*Exeunt Kas. and Dame P.*]
               That master
That had receiv'd such happiness by a servant,
In such a widow, and with so much wealth,
Were very ungrateful, if he would not be
A little indulgent to that servant's wit,    150
And help his fortune, though with some small
strain
Of his own candour. [*Advancing.*] Therefore,
gentlemen,
And kind spectators, if I have outstripp'd
An old man's gravity, or strict canon, think 154
What a young wife and a good brain may do;
Stretch age's truth sometimes, and crack it too.
Speak for thyself, knave.
   *Face.* So I will, sir. [*Advancing to the front
of the stage.*] Gentlemen,
My part a little fell in this last scene,
Yet 't was decorum. And though I am clean
Got off from Subtle, Surly, Mammon, Dol, 160
Hot Ananias, Dapper, Drugger, all
With whom I traded; yet I put myself
On you, that are my country: and this pelf
Which I have got, if you do quit me, rests,
To feast you often, and invite new guests.   165
                    [*Exeunt.*]

              THE END

[100] **have the seal:** are sealed as God's people    [103] **table dormant:** permanent table    [117] **Harry Nicholas:** a religious fanatic    [121] **Westchester:** Chester    [127] **dubb'd boy:** knight    [128] **mammet:** doll, puppet    **touse:** handle roughly    [129] **mun:** must    [131] **feize:** beat    [134] **copy:** tune, manners    [135] **stoop:** swoop (a term in falconry)    [144] **jovy:** jovial    [152] **candour:** integrity    [159] **decorum:** dramatic propriety    [163] **country:** jury (legal term)

# A MASQUE OF
THE
# METAMORPHOSD
## GYPSIES.

AS

# IT WAS THRICE
## PRESENTED TO
### KING IAMES.

FIRST,

## AT BVRLEIGH
### on the Hill.

NEXT,

## AT BELVOYR.

AND LASTLY,

## AT WINDSOR.

AVGVST,
1621.

BIBLIOGRAPHICAL RECORD. Jonson's most elaborate and most popular masque, *The Gipsies Metamorphosed*, exists in four different texts, of which the best is, on the whole, a contemporary manuscript (referred to as 'MS' in our notes). This was prepared subsequently to the last performance, at Windsor, in September, 1621. It is now in the Huntington Library, and has been reproduced in excellent facsimile in Dr. George Watson Cole's standard edition of the masque, published for the Modern Language Association of America in 1931. The poem was entered for publication on the Stationers' Register, Feb. 20, 1639–1640, the record reading: *John Benson. Entred for his Copie vnder the hands of doctor Wykes and Master Bourne warden a booke called The Masque of the Gypsies by Benjamin Johnson vi*ᵃ.

Benson accordingly printed the masque in a small duodecimo volume containing other short works by Jonson (D); and another printed text appeared in the same year in the second volume of the 1640 Jonson Folio (F). The textual situation is extraordinarily intricate, owing primarily to the confusion created in the original version when Jonson found occasion to adapt it to a different local setting and group of masquers from those for which it had been first designed. Benson's duodecimo itself represents, in its varying copies, two distinct texts, on account of the fact that Benson originally set up a short early version of the masque, and then undertook to work in the additions by means of extensive 'cancels.' No complete copy of the duodecimo in its early form exists; that in the Cambridge University Library contains the greatest number of uncanceled leaves. Dr. Cole's edition deals admirably with this difficult bibliographical problem. We have attempted in our text and notes to give adequate account of all four versions.

DATE. The masque was first performed, August 3, 1621, when James I and his court were entertained at the Marquess of Buckingham's house, Burleigh-on-the-Hill, in Rutlandshire. It was repeated by royal request two days later at Belvoir Castle in Leicestershire, and again at Windsor during the week beginning September 4 (see facsimile of the Folio title-page). For the last performance considerable changes were made, the most essential being the substitution of a new set of fortunes, to fit the lords of the king's official circle, in place of those addressed to the ladies of Buckingham's family. The coarse antimasque in Part II also shows by its local allusions that it was fitted to the latitude of Windsor.

SOURCE. Jonson's chief source was doubtless Dekker's *Lanthorne and Candle-light* (1608), which contains a "Canters' Dictionary" of vagabond slang explaining nearly all the "Gipsy" terms employed in the masque. This is probably the "third volume of Reports, set forth by the learned in the laws of canting," to which Jonson playfully alludes (I. 60. 61), the earlier works on vagabondage by Harman and Greene respectively being possibly thought of as volumes one and two. (*Beggars' Bush* by Fletcher and Massinger probably owes a debt to this masque as well as to Dekker; see the introduction to that play.)

STRUCTURE. Like other masques, this consists essentially of five formal masqued dances, separated by songs and dramatic interludes. The second, or main, dance has six different 'strains' or movements, between which fortunes are told by the Gipsies. A distinguishing feature is the large part taken by the noble participants, not in the dancing alone (which was their normal assignment), but in the dramatic dialogue. The difficult rôles of Jackman and Patrico were doubtless supported by professional singers; but the Gipsies otherwise were all nobles, the Captain and Second Gipsy being Buckingham himself and his brother, Viscount Purbeck; the peasants of the antimasque were all knights, and the wenches court pages. The antimasque, or humorous background, has been inordinately developed, and causes the work to fall as a dramatic piece into three sections, indicated by our numbering of lines. In its blending of grossly robust humor and ethereal delicacy this masque illustrates admirably both the spirit of James I's court and the genius of Ben Jonson.

# BEN JONSON

## THE GIPSIES METAMORPHOSED

### [DRAMATIS PERSONAE

GIPSIES
  Jackman, } (Professional
  Patrico, } Singers)
  Captain (Marquess of Buckingham)
  2nd. Gipsy (Viscount Purbeck, his brother)
  Four Others (unidentified noblemen)

WENCHES (played by Pages)
  Prudence
  Frances Addlebreech
  Meg
  Christian

CLOWNS (played by Knights)
  Jack Cockrell
  Tom Clod
  Townshead
  Paul Puppy
  Tom Ticklefoot, a minstrel

SPECTATORS, whose fortunes are told
  At Burleigh (and Belvoir?): King James, Prince Charles, Marchioness of Buckingham, Countess of
  Rutland, Countess of Exeter, Viscountess Purbeck, Lady Elizabeth Hatton (-Coke)
  At Windsor: King James, Prince Charles, the Lord Keeper of the Great Seal, Lord Treasurer, Lord
  Privy Seal, Earl Marshal, Lord High Steward, Marquess of Hamilton, Lord Chamberlain]

## [PROLOGUE]

### At the King's Entrance at Burleigh

IF for our thoughts there could but speech be
  found,
And all that speech be utter'd in one sound —
So that some Power above us would afford
The means to make a language of a word:
It should be, *Welcome*. In that only voice      5
We would receive, retain, enjoy, rejoice,
And all effects of love and life dispense,
Till it were call'd a copious eloquence.
For should we vent our spirits, now you are
  come,
In other syllables, were as to be dumb.      10
Welcome, oh, welcome, then! and enter here
The house your bounty hath built, and still
  doth rear
With those high favours and those heap'd in-
  creases
As shows a hand not griev'd but when it ceases.
The master is your creature, as the place,      15
And every good about him is your grace;
Whom, though he stand by silent, think not
  rude,
But as a man turn'd all to gratitude
For what he ne'er can hope how to restore,
Since while he meditates one, you pour on more.
Vouchsafe to think he only is oppress'd      21
With their abundance, not that in his breast
His powers are stupid grown; for, please you
  enter
Him and his house, and search him to the
  centre,
You 'll find within no thanks or vows there
  shorter      25
For having trusted thus much to his Porter.

### Prologue at Windsor

As many blessings as there be bones
In Ptolemy's fingers, and all at ones
Held up in an Andrew's cross for the nones,
  Light on you, good Master!
  I dare be no waster      5
Of time or of speech,
  Where you are in place.
I only beseech
  You take in good grace
Our following the court,      10
Since 't is for your sport,
To have you still merry,
And not make you weary.
We may strive to please
So long, some will say, till we grow a disease.  15
But you, Sir, that twice
Have grac'd us already, encourage to thrice:
Wherein if our boldness your patience invade,
Forgive us the fault that your favour hath
  made.

Prologue. **Burleigh:** in Rutlandshire, the home of George Villiers, Marquess (later Duke) of
Buckingham      **9 vent:** utter      **10 were:** it would signify as much      **12 hath built:** ('built' D)
**rear:** raise      **14 As shows:** which show ('which' DF)      **ceases:** *i.e.*, to confer benefits      **16 grace:**
bounty      **20 one:** one honor or benefaction      Prol. at Windsor **1–19:** (Not in D; in F precedes the
Prol. at Burleigh.)      **2 ones:** once      **3 nones:** nonce      **15 disease:** nuisance      **17 thrice:** a third
venture      **18 invade:** affront

627

## [PART I.]

*Enter a Gipsy leading a horse laden with five little children, bound in a trace of scarfs upon him; a second leading another horse laden with stolen poultry &c. The first, leading, Gipsy speaks, being the*

*Jackman.* Room for the five Princes of Egypt, mounted all upon one horse like the four sons of Aymon, to make the miracle the more by a head, if it may be. Gaze upon them as on the offspring of Ptolemy, begotten upon several [5 Cleopatras in their several counties, especially on this brave spark struck out of Flintshire upon Justice Jugg's daughter, then sheriff of the county; who running away with a kinsman of our Captain's, and her father pursu- [10 ing her to the marches — he great with justice, she great with Juggling — they were both for the time turn'd stone upon the sight of each other in Chester. Till at last (see the wonder!) a jug of the town ale reconciling [15 them, the memorial of both their gravities — his in beard and hers in belly — hath remain'd ever since preserv'd in picture upon the most stone jugs of the kingdom. The famous imp yet grew a wretchock, and though for seven [20 years together he were carefully carried at his mother's back, rock'd in a cradle of Welsh cheese like a maggot, and there fed with broken beer and blown wine of the best daily, yet looks he as if he never saw his *quinquennium.* [25 'T is true he can thread needles on horseback, or draw a yard of inkle through his nose; but what is that to a grown Gipsy, one o' the blood and of his time, if he had thriv'd? Therefore (till with his painful progenitors [30 he be able to beat it on the hard hoof to the *ben bowse* or the *stauling ken,* to nip a *jan* and *cly the jarke*) 't is thought fit he march in the infants' equipage                                    34

With the convoy cheats and peckage
Out of clutch of Harman-beckage,
To their Libkens at the Crackmans
Or some skipper of the Blackman's.

2 *Gipsy.* Where the cacklers, but no grunt-ers,
Shall uncas'd be for the hunters.                                    40
Those we still must keep alive,
Ay, and put them forth to thrive
In the parks and in the chases,
And the finer walled places,
As St. James's, Greenwich, Tiballs;                                    45
Where the acorns plump as chibals
Soon shall change both kind and name,
And proclaim them the King's game.
So the act no harm may be
Unto their keeper Barnabe,                                    50
It will prove as good a service
As did ever Gipsy Jervis,
Or our captain Charles, the tall man,
And a part too of our salmon.

*Jackman.* If here we be a little obscure, [55 it is our pleasure; for rather than we will offer to be our own interpreters, we are resolved not to be understood. Yet if any man doubt of the significancy of the language, we refer him to the third volume of Reports, [60 set forth by the learned in the laws of canting, and published in the Gipsy tongue. Give me my guittara, and room for our Chief!

*Dance 1, being the entrance of the Captain, with six more to a stand. After which the Jackman sings.*

### Song 1

From the famous Peak of Darby,
And the Devil's-arse there hard by,                                    65
Where we yearly keep our musters,
Thus th' Egyptians throng in clusters.

Be not frighted with our fashion!
Though we seem a tatter'd nation,
We account our rags our riches,                                    70
So our tricks exceed our stitches.

Give us bacon, rinds of walnuts,
Shells of cockles and of small-nuts,
Ribands, bells, and saffron'd linen:
All the world is ours to win in.                                    75

S. D. **trace:** harness    [1] **Jackman:** (properly, jarkman), an educated Gipsy, employed at counterfeiting licenses, etc.    [2-3] **four . . . Aymon:** peers of Charlemagne in a popular romance, who all rode on one horse    [11] **marches:** border (of Wales)    [13] **time:** ('same time' D)    [13-14] **of each:** ('each of' F)    [19] **of:** ('in' D)    **imp:** scion    [20] **wretchock:** stunted fowl    [21] **were:** ('was' D; 'were very' F)    [23] **broken:** opened, stale    [25] **quinquennium:** fifth year    [27] **inkle:** linen tape    [31] **beat . . . hoof:** foot it briskly    [32] **ben bowse:** good drink    **stauling ken:** depository of stolen goods    **nip a jan:** pick a purse    [33] **cly the jarke:** be whipped    [35] **convoy cheats:** baggage    **peckage:** victuals    [36] **Harman-beckage:** the constabulary    [37] **their:** ('the' D)    **Libkens:** lodging    **Crackmans:** hedge    [38] **skipper:** barn    **Blackman's:** night    [39] **2. Gipsy:** (probably the Patrico; cf. line 88)    **cacklers:** poultry    **grunters:** pigs    [40] **uncas'd:** plucked or skinned    [43] **chases:** hunting-grounds    [45] **Tiballs:** Theobalds, a favorite residence of James I    [46] **chibals:** onions    [47] **kind:** nature (*i.e.,* shall make them wild boars)    [54] **salmon:** beggars' oath    [61] **canting:** vagrancy    S. D. **stand:** conclusion of the dance    [55] **Devil's-arse:** a place-name in Derbyshire    [67] **Egyptians:** Gipsies    [71] **So:** so greatly    [74] **saffron'd:** yellow-colored

Knacks we have that will delight you,
Sleights of hand that will invite you
To endure our tawny faces,
And not cause you cut your laces.

All your fortunes we can tell ye,     80
Be they for your back or belly;
In the moods, too, and the tenses
That may fit your fine five senses.

Draw but then your gloves, we pray you,
And sit still: we will not fray you;     85
For though we be here at Burly,
We 'd be loath to make a hurly.

*Patrico.*   Stay, my sweet singer,
The touch of thy finger
A little, and linger     90
For me that am bringer
Of bound to the border,
The rule and recorder
And mouth of your order,
As priest of the game     95
And prelate of the same.

There 's a gentry-cove here
Is the top of the shire,
Of the *Beaver-ken*,
A man among men.     100
Ye need not to fear:
I 've an eye and an ear
That turns here and there
To look to our gear.
Some say that there be     105
One or two, if not three,
That are greater than he.

And for the *Roome morts*,
I know by their ports
And their jolly resorts,     110
They are of the sorts
That love the true sports
Of King Ptolemæus,
Our great coryphæus,
And Queen Cleopatra,     115
The Gipsies' grand-matra.
Then if we shall shark it,
Here fair is and market.

Leave pig by and goose,
And play fast and loose,     120
A short cut and long,
With (ever and among)
Some inch of a song —
Pythagoras' lot,
Drawn out of a pot —     125
With what says Alchindus
And Pharaotes Indus,
John de Indagine,
With all their *paginæ*
Treating of palmistry:     130
And this is all mystery.

Lay by your wimbles,
Your boring for thimbles,
Or using your nimbles
In diving the pockets     135
And sounding the sockets
Of *simper the Cockets*,
Or angling the purses
Of such as will curse us.
But in the strict duel     140
Be merry and cruel:
Strike fair at some jewel,
That mint may accrue well;
For that is the fuel
To make the tun brew well,     145
And the pot ring well,
And the brain sing well, —
Which we may bring well
About by a string well,
And do the thing well.     150
    It is but a strain
    Of true leger-de-main:
    Once, twice, and again.

Or what will you say now,
If with our fine play now,     155
Our knackets and dances,
We work on the fancies
Of some of these Nancies,
These Trickets and Tripsies,
And make 'em turn Gipsies?     160
Here 's no Justice Lippus
Will seek for to nip us
In cramp-ring or cippus,

<hr>

[79] **cut your laces:** (altered at the Windsor performance to 'quit your places')    [80] **tell ye:** ('tell you' MS)    [84] **Draw:** take off    [85] **fray:** frighten    [89] **touch:** (*i.e.*, on the guitar)    [97] **gentry-cove:** gentleman    [98] **top:** head, lord lieutenant    [99] **Beaver-ken:** Belvoir Castle, residence of Earl of Rutland    [100] **among:** ('amongst' D)    [101] **Ye:** ('You' MS F)    [102] **I 've:** ('I have' MS F)    [104] **gear:** business    [108] **Roome morts:** great ladies    [109] **ports:** manners    [110] **resorts:** attendance, presence    [114] **coryphæus:** leader of a chorus    [116] **grand-matra:** grandmother    [117] **shark it:** use our tricks    [122] **ever and among:** meantime    [126] **Alchindus:** Arabian philosopher, 9th century A.D.    [127] **Pharaotes Indus:** (unknown)    [128] **John de Indagine:** a Carthusian monk of Erfurt (d. 1475), author of a book on palmistry    [129] **paginæ:** pages    [130] **Treating of:** ('Faces and' D; 'Of faces and' F)    [132] **wimbles:** gimlets    [134] **nimbles:** fingers    [137] **simper the Cockets:** Cockney belles    [143] **mint:** money    [156-160] (Replaced at Windsor performance by "Our feats and our fingering, | Here without lingering, | Cozening the sights | Of the lords and the knights, | Some one of their Georges | Come off to save charges.")    [156] **knackets:** ('knackes' MS)    **and:** ('and our' F)    [163] **cramp-ring:** fetter    **cippus:** stocks

And then for to strip us,
And after to whip us,                             165
(His justice to vary),
While here we do tarry.
But be wise and wary,
And we may both carry
The Kate and the Mary,                            170
And all the bright aery,
Away to the quarry,
If our brave Ptolemy
Will but say, "Follow me."

3. *Gipsy.* Captain, if ever at the *bowsing
ken*                                              175
You have in drafts of Darby drill'd your
    men,
And we have serv'd there armed all in ale,
With the brown bowl, and charg'd in braggat
    stale:
If muster'd thus and disciplin'd in drink,
In our long watches we did never wink,            180
But so, commanded by you, kept our sta-
    tion
As we preserv'd ourselves a loyal nation;
And never yet did branch of statute break,
Made in your famous palace of the Peak:
If we have deem'd that mutton, lamb, or
    veal,                                         185
Chick, capon, turkey sweetest we did steal
As being by our Magna Charta taught
To judge no viands wholesome that are bought:
If for our linen we still us'd the lift,
And with the hedge (our *Trade's Increase*)
    made shift;                                   190
And ever at your solemn feasts and calls
We have been ready with th' Egyptian brawls,
To set Kit Callot forth in prose or rime,
Or who was Cleopatra for the time:
If we have done this, that, more, such, or so, 195
Now lend your ear but to the Patrico.
    *Captain.* Well, dance another strain, and
we 'll think how.
*1 Gipsy.* Meantime in song do you conceive
    some vow.

DANCE 2.  1. STRAIN  SONG 2
*Patrico.*
    The faery beam upon you,
    The stars to-glister on you,                  200
        A moon of light
        In the noon of night,
    Till the fire-drake hath o'ergone you!

    The wheel of fortune guide you,
    The boy with the bow beside you               205
        Run aye in the way,
        Till the bird of day
    And the luckier lot betide you!

*Captain.* Bless my sweet masters, the old and
    the young,
From the gall of the heart and the stroke of
    the tongue.                                   210
With you, lucky bird, I begin.  Let me see.
                    *Goes up to the King.*
I aim at the best, and I trow you are he.
Here 's some luck already, if I understand
The grounds of my art.  Here 's a gentleman's
    hand: —
I 'll kiss it for luck's sake.  You should by this
    line                                          215
Love a horse and a hound, but no part of a
    swine;
To hunt the brave stag, not so much for your
    food,
As the weal of your body and the health of your
    blood.
Y' are a man of good means, and have terri-
    tories store,
Both by sea and by land; and were born, Sir,
    to more,                                      220
Which you, like a lord and a prince of your
    peace,
Content with your havings, despise to increase.
You are no great wencher, I see by your table.
Although your *Mons Veneris* says you are able
You live chaste and single, and have buried
    your wife,                                    225
And mean not to marry, by the line of your life:

---

¹⁶⁶ **vary:** (alluding to the varied punishments listed in 162–165)   ¹⁶⁶,¹⁶⁷ (Given in reverse order, MS.)
¹⁷⁰⁻¹⁷² (For these lines Jonson substituted at the Windsor performance: "The George and the Garter |
Into our own quarter; | Or durst I go farder | In method and order, | There 's a purse and a seal | I have
a great mind to steal, | That when our tricks are done, | We might seal our own pardon. | All this we
may do, And a great deal more too.")   ¹⁷⁰ **Kate, Mary:** (Christian names of the Marchioness of
Buckingham and of her mother-in-law, the Countess, respectively)   ¹⁷¹ **aery:** the group of maids of
honor   ¹⁷⁵ **bowsing ken:** alehouse   ¹⁷⁶ **Darby:** Derbyshire ale   ¹⁷⁸ **braggat:** a drink made from
honey and ale   ¹⁸⁰ **long:** ('strict' D)   **wink:** close our eyes   ¹⁸² **As:** that   ¹⁸³ **yet did:** ('did
yet' D)   ¹⁸⁴ **Peak:** the Peak of Derbyshire   ¹⁸⁶ **we:** which we   ¹⁸⁹ **lift:** conveyance by theft
¹⁹⁰ **hedge:** used for drying linen   **Trade's Increase:** name of a large vessel built in 1609 by the East
India Co.   ¹⁹² **brawls:** a dance   ¹⁹³ **Kit Callot:** Kate Harlot   ¹⁹⁴ **Cleopatra:** Gipsy queen   ¹⁹⁸ (Not
in MS or F)   S. D. **Strain:** movement (The second, or main, dance is divided into six 'strains,' between which the Gipsies tell the masquers' fortunes.)   ²⁰⁰ **to-glister:** glitter brightly   ²⁰³ **fire-drake:**
fiery meteor   ²⁰⁵ **boy . . . bow:** Cupid   ²¹¹ S. D. (Not in MS F)   ²¹⁷ **To hunt:** love to hunt
²¹⁷⁻²¹⁸ **your . . . your . . . your:** ('the . . . the . . . the' D; 'the . . . your . . . your' F)   ²¹⁹ **store:**
plenty   ²²⁰ **born . . . more:** (referring to his heraldic claim to France)   ²²³ **table:** central part of
the palm   ²²⁵ **wife:** Anne of Denmark, d. 1619

Whence he that conjectures your quality learns
You 're an honest good man and have care of
    your bairns.
Your Mercury's hill too a wit doth betoken;
Some book-craft you have, and are pretty
    well spoken.                                        230
But stay!  In your Jupiter's mount what 's
    here?
A king? a monarch?  What wonders appear!
High, bountiful, just; a Jove for your parts,
A master of men, and that reign in their hearts.

        I 'll tell it my train,                     235
        And come to you again.
                    [*Withdraws.*]

### SONG 3

To the old, long life and treasure;
To the young, all health and pleasure;
    To the fair, their face,
    With eternal grace;                               240
And the foul, to be lov'd at leisure.

To the witty, all clear mirrors;
To the foolish, their dark errors;
    To the loving sprite,
    A secure delight;                                 245
To the jealous, his own false terrors.

*After which the King's fortune is pursued by the*
*              Captain*

Could any doubt that saw this hand,
Or who you are, or what command
    You have upon the fate of things;
Or would not say you were let down                      250
From heaven on earth, to be the crown
    And top of all your neighbour kings.

To see the ways of truth you take,
To balance business and to make
    All Christian differences cease;                  255
Or till the quarrel and the cause
You can compose, to give them laws
    As Arbiter of war and peace:

For this of all the world you shall
Be styled James the Just, and all                       260
    Their states dispose, their sons and daugh-
    ters;
And for your fortune you alone,
Amongst them all, shall work your own
    By peace and not by human slaughters.

But why do I presume, though true,                      265
To tell a fortune, Sir, to you,
    Who are the maker here of all:
Where none do stand or sit in view
But owe their fortunes unto you —
    At least what they good fortune call.             270

Myself a Gipsy here do shine,
Yet are you maker, Sir, of mine.
    Oh, that confession would content
So high a bounty that doth know
No part of motion but to flow,                           275
    And, giving, never to repent.

May still the matter wait your hand,
That it not feel or stay or stand,
    But all desert still overcharge.
And may your goodness ever find                         280
In me, whom you have made, a mind
    As thankful as your own is large.

### DANCE 2.  2. STRAIN

*After which the Prince's fortune is offer'd at by the*
*                2. Gipsy*

As my Captain hath begun
With the sire, I take the son.
    Your hand, Sir. —                                 285
Of your fortune be secure,
Love and she are both at your
    Command, Sir.

See what states are here at strife,
Who shall tender you a wife,                             290
    A brave one;
And a fitter for a man
Than is offer'd here you can-
    Not have one.

She is sister of a star,                                 295
One the noblest now that are,
    Bright Hesper;
Whom the Indians in the East
Phosphor call, and in the West
    Hight Vesper.                                     300

Courses even with the Sun
Doth her mighty brother run
    For splendour.
What can to the marriage night,
More than morn and evening light,                       305
    Attend her?

---

²⁴¹ **foul:** ugly     **at leisure:** in the course of time     ²⁴⁶ S. D. **pursued:** continued     ²⁴⁸ **Or:** either
²⁵⁵⁻²⁵⁸ (Referring to James's vain efforts as peacemaker in the opening of the Thirty Years' War)     ²⁶² **fortune:** ('fortunes' D)     ²⁶³ **Amongst:⁹⁄** ('Among' DF)     ²⁶⁵⁻²⁸² (The Cambridge Univ. copy of D sub-
stitutes for this: "This little from so short a view | I tell, and as a teller true | Of fortunes, but their
maker, Sir, are you.")     ²⁶⁹⁻²⁷⁰ **fortunes . . . fortune:** (transposed DF)     ²⁷² **mine:** my good fortune
²⁷³ **would:** ('could' DF)     ²⁷⁵ (*I.e.*, knows no ebb)     ²⁷⁸ **or . . . stand:** either obstacle or stoppage
²⁷⁹ **overcharge:** overload with favors     ²⁸⁶ **secure:** confident     ²⁸⁷ **she:** fortune     ²⁸⁹ **states:**
('Starres' D)     ²⁹⁵ **She:** the Infanta Maria, sister of Philip IV of Spain     ²⁹⁶ **One:** one of     ²⁹⁷ **Hes-
per:** evening star, star of the west (alluding to Spanish America)     ³⁰¹⁻³⁰³ (The sun never sets on the
Spanish domain.)

Save the promise before day
Of a little James to play
   Hereafter
'Twixt his Grandsire's knees, and move 310
All the pretty ways of love
   And laughter.

Whilst with care you strive to please
In your giving his cares ease
   And labours,                         315
And, by being long the aid
Of the empire, make afraid
   Ill neighbours;

Till yourself shall come to see
What we wish, yet far, to be            320
   Attending.
For it skills not when or where
That begins which cannot fear
   An ending;

Since your name in peace or wars        325
Naught shall bound, until the stars
   Up-take you,
And to all succeeding view
Heaven a constellation new
   Shall make you.                     330

### Dance 2. 3. Strain

*After which the Lady Marquess
Buckingham's by the
3. Gipsy*

Hurl after an old shoe:
I 'll be merry whate'er I do.
Though I keep no time,
My words shall chime:
I 'll overtake the sense with a rime.   335
   Face of a rose,
   I prithee, dispose
Some small piece of silver. It shall be no loss,
But only to make the sign of the cross.
If your hand you hallow,                340
Good fortune will follow.
   I swear by these ten,
   You shall have it again: —
   I do not say when.
But, Lady, either I am tipsy,           345
Or you are to fall in love with a Gipsy.
   Blush not, Dame Kate,
   For early or late,

I do assure you, it will be your fate.  349
Nor need you be once asham'd of it, Madam:
He 's as handsome a man as ever was Adam;
   A man out of wax,
   As a lady would aks.
   Yet he is not to wed ye:
   H'as enjoyed you already,            355
   And I hope he has sped ye
   A dainty young fellow.
   And though he look yellow,
   He ne'er will be jealous,
   But love you most zealous:          360
There 's never a line in your hand but doth tell
   us.
And you are a soul so white and so chaste,
A table so smooth and so newly ras'd,
   As nothing call'd foul
   Dares approach with a blot,         365
   Or any least spot;
   But still you control
   Or make your own lot,
Preserving love pure as it first was begot.
   But, Dame, I must tell ye,          370
   The fruit of your belly
   Is that you must tender,
   And care so to render,
   That as yourself came,
   In blood and in name,               375
   From one house of fame,
   So that may remain
   The glory of twain.

### Dance 2. 4. Strain

*After which the Countess of Rutland's by the
3. Gipsy*

   You, sweet Lady, have a hand too,
   And a fortune you may stand to.     380
   Both your bravery and your bounty
   Style you mistress of the county.
   You will find it from this night,
   Fortune will forget her spite,
   And heap all the blessings on you   385
   That she can pour out upon you.
   To be lov'd where most you love
   Is the worst that you shall prove;
   And by him to be embrac'd
   Who so long hath known you chaste,  390
   Wise, and fair, whilst you renew
   Joys to him, and he to you;

307–330 (Not in Cambridge Univ. copy of D)    314–315 giving . . . labours: alleviating James's cares
and labors    318 Ill: evil    320 What we wish: Charles's accession    yet far: (because it implies the
death of King James)    321 Attending: in prospect    322 skills: matters    328–330 (Not in DF)    337 dispose: lay out    340 hallow: bless (with silver)    342 ten: fingers    352 out of wax: perfectly formed,
like an image    353 aks: (older form of 'ask')    354 (Because they had already been married, May 16,
1620)    358 yellow: color betokening jealousy; also that of the false Gipsies' complexion    363 table:
wax tablet    newly ras'd: freshly prepared for writing    372 tender: consider heedfully    378 S. D.
Countess of Rutland: stepmother of the Marchioness of Buckingham    380 stand to: depend on
381 bravery: noble appearance    382 mistress . . . county: (i.e., wife of the lord lieutenant)    384 will:
('shall' DF)    forget her spite: (Her two sons had both died in infancy.)

And when both your years are told,
Neither think the other old.

*And the Countess of Exeter's by the
Patrico*

Madam, we knew of your coming so late,   395
We could not well fit you a nobler fate
  Than what you have ready-made.
    An old man's wife
    Is the light of his life;
A young one is but his shade.   400
    You will not importune
    The change of your fortune;
For if you dare trust to my forecasting,
'T is presently good, and it will be lasting.

### DANCE 2.   5. STRAIN

*After which the Countess of
Buckingham's by the
4. Gipsy*

Your pardon, Lady! Here you stand,   405
If some should judge you by your hand,
  The greatest felon in the land
    Detected.

I cannot tell you by what arts,
But you have stol'n so many hearts,   410
  As they would make you at all parts
    Suspected.

Your very face, first, such a one
As, being viewed, it was alone
  Too slippery to be look'd upon,   415
    And threw men.

But then your graces, they were such
As none could e'er behold too much:
  Both every taste and every touch
    So drew men.   420

Still bless'd in all you think or do:
Two of your sons are Gipsies too.
You shall our Queen be, and see who
  Importunes

The hurt of either yours or you,   425
And doth not wish both George and Sue,
And every bairn besides, all new
  Good fortunes.

*The Lady Purbeck's by the
2. Gipsy*

Help me, wonder! Here 's a book,
Where I would for ever look.   430
Never yet did Gipsy trace
Smoother lines in hand or face.
Venus here doth Saturn move
That you should be Queen of Love,
And the other stars consent.   435
Only Cupid 's not content,
For, though you the theft disguise,
You have robb'd him of his eyes;
And to show his envy further,
Here he chargeth you with murther:   440
Says, although that at your sight
He must all his torches light,
Though your either cheek discloses
Mingled baths of milk and roses,
Though your lips be banks of blisses   445
Where he plants and gathers kisses,
And yourself the reason why
Wisest men for love may die:
  You will turn all hearts to tinder,
  And shall make the world one cinder.   450

*And the Lady Elizabeth Hatton's by the
5. Gipsy*

Mistress of a fairer table
Hath no history nor fable.
Others' fortunes may be shown:
You are builder of your own;
And whatever heaven hath gi'n you,   455
You preserve the state still in you.
That which time would have depart,
Youth, without the help of art
You do keep still, and the glory
Of your sex is but your story.   460

*[Passage substituted at Windsor
for lines 331–460]*

*At Windsor in place of the Ladies' fortunes were
spoken these following of the Lords.*

### DANCE 2.   3. STRAIN

*The Lord Keeper's by the
Patrico*

*As happy a palm, Sir, as most in the land!
It should be a pure and an innocent hand,*

---

³⁹⁵ **knew:** ('know' DF)    ³⁹⁸ **old man's wife:** (Her husband was forty years her senior.)    ⁴⁰⁴ **presently:** at present   **it:** (not in DF)   S. D. **Countess of Buckingham:** (mother of the Marquess)    ⁴¹¹ **parts:** places    ⁴¹⁵ **slippery:** shining with beauty     ⁴²² (Marquess of Buckingham and Lord Purbeck) ⁴²³ **see:** ('he' D)    ⁴²⁵ **hurt:** ('heart' DF)    ⁴²⁶ **George:** the Marquess    **Sue:** his sister, Countess of Denbigh    ⁴²⁸ S. D. **Lady Purbeck:** a noted court beauty, daughter of Sir Edward Coke, wife of Buckingham's eldest brother (the second Gipsy)    ⁴³³ **move:** urge    ⁴³⁸ **robb'd** ('told' DF)    ⁴⁵⁰ S. D. **Lady Elizabeth Hatton:** (widow of Sir William Hatton, formerly aspired to by Francis Bacon; at this time wife of Sir Edward Coke; mother of Lady Purbeck)    ⁴⁵¹ **table:** in palmistry (cf. line 223), with pun on Lady Hatton's famous hospitality    ⁴⁶⁰ S. D. **At . . . Lords:** (only in MS)   **Lord Keeper:** Bishop of Lincoln, keeper of the great seal, or chancellor

*And worthy the trust;*
*For it says you 'll be just,*
*And carry that purse*                                    465
*Without any curse*
*Of the public weal.*
*When you take out the seal,*
*You do not appear*
*A judge of a year.*                                      470
*I 'll venter my life,*
*You never had wife;*
*But I 'll venter my skill,*
*You may when you will.*
*You have the King's conscience, too, in your*
*    breast,*                                             475
*And that 's a good guest,*
*Which you 'll have true touch of,*
*And yet not make much of,*
*More than by truth yourself forth to bring,*
*The man that you are for God and the King.* 480

### The Lord Treasurer's by the
### 3. Gipsy

*I come, Sir, to borrow, and you 'll grant my de-*
*    mand, Sir,*
*Sin' 't is not for money: pray, lend me your*
*    hand, Sir. —*
*And yet this good hand, if you please to stretch it,*
*Had the errand been money, could easily fetch it.*
*You command the King's treasure; and yet, o'*
*    my soul,*                                            485
*You handle not much, for your palm is not*
*    foul.*
*Your fortune is good, and will be to set*
*The office upright and the King out of debt,*
*To put all that have pensions soon out of their*
*    pain*
*By bringing th' Exchequer in credit again.*    490

### The Lord Privy Seal's by the
### 2. Gipsy

*Honest and old:*
*In those the good part of a fortune is told.*
*    God send you health!*
*The rest is provided: honour and wealth;*
*    All which you possess*                               495
*Without the making of any man less.*
*Nor need you my warrant enjoy it you shall,*
*For you have a good privy seal for it all.*

### The Earl Marshal's by the
### 3. Gipsy

*Next the great master, who is the doncr,*
*I read you here the preserver of honour,*        500
*And spy it in all your singular parts.*
*What a father you are and nurse of the arts!*
*By cherishing which a way you have found,*
*How they, free to all, to one may be bound;*
*And they again love their bonds, for to be*      505
*Obliged to you, is the way to be free.*
*But this is their fortune. Hark to your own!*
*Yours shall be to make true gentry known*
*From the fictitious; not to prize blood*
*So much by the greatness as by the good;*        510
*To show and to open clear Virtue the way,*
*Both whither she should and how far she may;*
*And whilst you do judge twixt valour and noise,*
*To extinguish the race of the Roaring Boys.*

### The Lord Steward's by the
### 4. Gipsy

*I find by this hand,*                                   515
*You have the command*
*Of the very best man's house in the land.*
*Our Captain and we*
*Ere long will see*
*If you keep a good table.*                              520
*Your master is able;*
*And here be bountiful lines that say,*
*You 'll keep no part of his bounty away.*
*There 's written "frank"*
*On your Venus' bank.*                                   525
*To prove a false Steward you 'll find much ado,*
*Being a true one by blood and by office too.*

### DANCE 2.  4. STRAIN
### The Lord Marquess Hamilton's by the
### 3. Gipsy

*Only your hand, Sir, and you 're welcome to court!*
*Here is a man both for earnest and sport.*
*You were lately employed,*                              530
*And your master is joyed*
*To have such in his train,*
*So well can sustain*
*His person abroad,*
*And not shrink for the load.*                           535
*But had you been here,*
*You should have been a Gipsy, I swear.*

**465** that: ('the' D)   **471–474** (Not in MS)   **471** venter: venture   **475** the . . . too: (alluding to
the Keeper's clerical position and chaplaincy to the King)   **480** S. D. Lord Treasurer: Lord Cranfield,
later Earl of Middlesex, impeached and disgraced in 1624   **482** Sin': since   **489** all . . . pensions:
(Jonson had one, which was trebled in 1621.)   **490** S. D. Lord Privy Seal: Earl of Worcester, last sur-
vivor of the great Elizabethan nobles   **493** you: ('you your' DF)   **498** S. D. Earl Marshal: Earl of
Arundel, by his office arbiter in questions of rank and precedence   **499** master: the king   **502** (Arundel
formed the first great art collection in England, later given to Oxford.)   and: ('and a' DF)   **514** Roaring Boys: 'Mohocks,' ruffianly young men of wealth   **514** S. D Lord Steward: Lodowick Stuart, Duke
of Lenox   **521** master is: ('Masters' MS DF)   **524** There 's written: ('Thus written to' DF)
**525** Venus' bank: mons Veneris   **527** S. D. Marquess Hamilton: recently employed as the king's representative at the Scottish Parliament   **528** you 're: ('your' MS; not in DF)

*Our Captain had summon'd you by a doxy,*
*To whom you would not have answer'd by proxy;*
*One, had she come in the way of your sceptre,*    540
*'T is odds you had laid it by to have leapt her.*

### The Lord Chamberlain's by the
### Jackman

*Though you, Sir, be chamberlain, I have a key*
*To open your fortune a little by the way.*
    *You are a good man,*
    *Deny it that can;*    545
    *And faithful you are,*
    *Deny it that dare.*
*You know how to use your sword and your pen,*
*And you love not alone the arts but the men.*
*The Graces and Muses everywhere follow*    550
*You, as you were their second Apollo.*
*Only your hand here tells you to your face,*
    *You have wanted one grace,*
*To perform what hath been a right of your place:*
*For by this line, which is Mars his trench,*    555
*You never yet help'd your master to a wench.*
    *'T is well for your honour he's pious and*
    *chaste,*
    *Or you had most certainly been displac'd.*

## [PART II.]

DANCE 2.  6. STRAIN, WHICH LEADS
INTO DANCE 3

### Dance 3

*During which enter the Clowns, Cockrell, Clod,*
*Townshead, Puppy, whilst the Patrico and*
*Jackman sing this song.*

### SONG

*Patr.*   Why, this is a sport —
    See it north, see it south —
For the taste of the court.

*Jack.*   For the court's own mouth!
    Come Windsor the towne    5
    With the mayor and oppose,
We'll put 'em all down.

*Patr.*   Do-do-down like my hose!
    A Gipsy in his shape
      More calls the beholder    10
    Than the fellow with the ape.

*Jack.*   Or the ape on his shoulder.
    He's a sight that will take
      An old judge from his wench,
    Ay, and keep him awake.    15

*Patr.*   Yes, awake o' the bench.
    And has so much worth,
      Though he sit i' the stocks,
    He will draw the girls forth.

*Jack.*   Ay, forth i' their smocks.    20
    Tut, a man's a man:
      Let the clowns with their sluts
    Come mend us if they can.

*Patr.*   If they can for their guts.
    Come mend us, come lend us their shouts
      and their noise.    25

*Both.*   Like thunder, and wonder at Ptolemy's
    boys!
*Cock.*   O the Lord! What be these, Tom,
dost thou know? Come hither, come hither,
Dick. Didst thou ever see such? The finest
olive-colour'd sprites! They have so danc'd [30
and jingled here as if they had been a set of
overgrown fairies.
*Clod.*   They should be morris-dancers by
their jingle, but they have no napkins.
*Cock.*   No, nor a hobby-horse.    35
*Clod.*   O, he is often forgotten: that's no
rule. But there is no Maid Marian nor friar
amongst them, which is the surer mark.
*Cock.*   Nor a fool, that I see.
*Clod.*   Unless they be all fools.    40
*Town.*   Well said, Tom Fool! Why, thou
simple parish-ass, thou! Didst thou never see
any Gipsies? These are a covey of Gipsies,
and the bravest new covey that ever constable
flew at: goodly game. Gipsies! They are [45
Gipsies of this year, o' this moon, in my conscience.

---

⁵³⁸ **doxy:** Gipsy wench    ⁵⁴⁰ **sceptre:** the badge of his viceregal employment    ⁵⁴¹ S. D. **Lord Chamberlain:** Earl of Pembroke, elder of the "two imcomparable brethren" to whom the Shakespeare Folio was dedicated in 1623    ⁵⁴²⁻⁵⁵⁸ (In the printed editions the Lord Chamberlain's fortune is placed first, preceding the Lord Keeper's, ll. 461 ff. These editions add a set of doggerel verses on the Earl of Buc-cleugh, not in MS and of dubious authenticity.)    ⁵⁴² **chamberlain:** functionary in charge of accommodations, at court and also in inns    **key:** (pronounce "kay")    ⁵⁵⁵ **Mars his trench:** line of palm on "mountain of Mars"    **Dance 3:** (The dividing point in the masque: the comic two-part song that follows introduces the antimasque.)    ¹⁻²⁵ (Not in Cambridge Univ. copy of D. In other printed texts, Dance 3 and the entrance of the Clowns follow this song.)    ⁸ **Do-do-down:** (imitating a stammer)    ¹¹ **fellow . . . ape:** man with a performing ape    ³⁴ **jingle:** (Morris-dancers had small bells attached to their costumes.)    **napkins:** kerchiefs of bright color    ³⁵ **hobby-horse:** performer impersonating a horse    ³⁶ **he . . . forgotten:** (alluding to proverbial saying, "The hobby-horse is forgot")    ³⁷ **friar:** Friar Tuck    ⁴⁶ **o' . . . moon:** of the newest coinage    **moon:** month

*Clod.* O, they are call'd the moon-men, I remember now.

*Cock.* One shall hardly see such gentle- [50 manlike Gipsies, though, under a hedge in a whole summer's day, — if they be Gipsies.

*Town.* Male Gipsies all; not a mort amongst them.

*Pup.* Where? where? I could never en- [55 dure the sight of one of these rogue-Gipsies. Which be they? I would fain see 'em.

*Clod.* Yonder they are.

*Pup.* Can they cant or mill? Are they masters in their arts?                                60

*Town.* No, bachelors these: they cannot have proceeded so far. They have scarce had their time to be lousy yet.

*Pup.* All the better. I would be acquainted with them while they are in clean life: they [65 will do their tricks the cleanlier.

*Cock.* We must have some music, then, and take out the wenches.

*Pup.* Music! we'll have a whole poverty of pipers. Call Cheeks upon the bagpipe [70 and Tom Ticklefoot with his tabor. Clod, will you gather the pipe money?

*Clod.* I'll gather it an you will, but I'll give none.

*Pup.* Why, well said. Claw a churl by [75 the arse, and he'll shit in your fist.

*Cock.* Ay, or whistle to a jade, and he'll pay you with a fart.

*Clod.* Fart? It's an ill wind blows no man to profit. See, where the minstrel's come [80 i' the mouth on 't.

*Cock.* Ay, and all the good wenches of Windsor after him. Yonder's Prue o' the Park.

*Town.* And Frances o' the Castle.      85

*Pup.* And long Meg of Eton.

*Clod.* And Christian o' Dorney.

*Town.* See the miracle of a minstrel!

*Cock.* He's able to muster up the smocks o' the two shires.                                90

*Pup.* And set the codpieces and they by the ears at pleasure.

*Town.* I cannot hold now. There's my groat: let's have a fit for mirth's sake.

*Cock.* Yes, and they'll come about us [95 for luck sake.

*Pup.* But look to our pockets and purses for our own sake.

*Clod.* Ay. I have the greatest charge, if I gather the money.                                100

*Cock.* Come, girls; here be Gipsies come to town. If we can, let's dance them down.

*Minstrel [plays a] country dance, during which the Gipsies come about them, prying, and after the*

### Patrico

Sweet doxies and dells,
My Roses and Nells,
Scarce out of the shells:                       105
Your hands! Nothing else.
We ring you no knells
With our Ptolemy's bells,
Though we come from the fells,
But bring you good spells;                       110
And tell you some chances,
In midst of your dances,
That fortune advances
To Prudence or Francis,
To Sisley or Harry,                              115
To Roger or Mary,
Or Peg of the dairy,
To Maudlin or Thomas:
Then do not run from us.
Although we look tawny,                          120
We are healthy and brawny;
Whate'er your demand is,
We'll give you no jaundice.

*Pup.* Say you so, old Gipsy? 'Slid, these go to 't in rime that is better than canting [125 by t' one half.

*Town.* Nay, you shall hear 'em. Peace! They begin with Prudence: mark that.

*Pup.* The wiser Gipsies they, marry!

*Town.* Are you advis'd?                         130

*Pup.* Yes, and I'll stand to 't that a wise Gipsy (take him at time o' year) is as politic a piece of flesh as most justices in the county where he stalks.

*3. Gipsy.*

To love a keeper your fortune will be,          135
But the doucets better than him or his fee.

*Town.* Ho, Prue, has he hit you in the teeth with the sweetbit?

*Pup.* Let it alone; she'll swallow it well enough. A learned Gipsy!                          140

*Town.* You'll hear more hereafter.

---

⁴⁸ **moon-men:** a name for Gipsies   ⁵³ **mort:** female   ⁵⁹ **cant:** beg   **mill:** steal   ⁶¹ **bachelors:** very recent graduates   ⁶³ **their:** ('the' D)   ⁶⁶ **cleanlier:** more neatly (with pun)   ⁶⁸ **take out:** dance with   **and . . . wenches:** (not in D)   ⁶⁹ **poverty:** ragged company   ⁷¹ **tabor:** small drum   ⁷³⁻¹⁰² (As in MS. Printed texts differ.)   ⁸⁴ **Park:** Windsor Park   ⁸⁵ **Castle:** Windsor Castle   ⁸⁷ **Dorney:** like Eton, a village near Windsor   ⁹¹ **codpieces:** males (from a suggestive piece of male apparel)   ⁹³ **hold:** hold back   ⁹⁴ **groat:** fourpence   **fit:** piece of minstrelsy   ⁹⁹ **charge:** money in trust   ¹⁰³ **dells:** Gipsy virgins   ¹⁰⁵ (Not in D)   ¹⁰⁷ **knells:** sounds of foreboding   ¹¹⁰ **But:** ('And' D)   ¹¹⁷ **Peg:** ('Meg' D)   ¹²⁶ **t' one:** the one   ¹³⁰ **advis'd:** sure of it   ¹³² **at . . . year:** when he is in season ('i' th' time o' th' eare' D)   ¹³⁴ **stalks:** ('maunds' D)   ¹³⁶ **doucets:** testes of deer   ¹³⁷ **hit . . . teeth:** spoken a home truth

*Pup.* Marry, and I 'll listen. Who stands next? Jack Cockrell.

  *2. Gipsy.*
You 'll steal yourself drunk, I find here true:
As you rob the pot, the pot will rob you.    145

*Pup.* A prophet! a prophet! No Gipsy; or if he be a Gipsy, a divine Gipsy!

*Town.* Mark Frances now; she 's going to 't: the virginity o' the parish.

  *Patr.*
Fear not: in hell you 'll never lead apes,    150
A mortified maiden of five 'scapes.

*Pup.* By 'r lady, he touch'd the virgin string there a little too hard. They are arrant learn'd men all, I see. What say they upon Tom Clod? List.    155

  *4. Gipsy.*
Clod's feet will in Christmas go near to be bare,
When he has lost all his hobnails at post and at pair.

*Pup.* H' as hit the right nail o' the head: his own game.

*Town.* And the very metal he deals in at [160 play, if you mark it.

*Pup.* Peace. Who 's this? Long Meg!

*Town.* Long and foul Meg, if she be a Meg, as ever I saw of her inches. Pray God they fit her with a fair fortune. She hangs an [165 arse terribly.

  *Patr.*
She 'll have a tailor take measure of her breech,
And ever after be troubled with a stitch.

*Town.* That 's as homely as she.

*Pup.* The better: a turd 's as good for [170 a sow as a pancake.

*Town.* Hark, now they treat upon Tickle-foot.

  *4. Gipsy.*
On Sundays you rob the poor's box with your tabor.
The collectors would do it: you save 'em a labour.    175

*Pup.* Faith, but little. They do it *non upstante.*

*Town.* Here 's my little Christian forgot! Ha' you any fortune left for her, a strait-lac'd Christian of sixteen?    180

  *Patr.*
Christian shall get her a loose-bodied gown
In trying how a gentleman differs from a clown.

*Pup.* Is that a fortune for a Christian? A Turk with a Gipsy could not have told her a worse.    185

*Town.* Come, I 'll stand myself, and once venter the poor head o' the town. Do your worst. My name 's Townshead, and here 's my hand I 'll not be angry.

  *3. Gipsy.*
A cuckold you must be, and that for three lives:    190
Your own, the parson's, and your wives.

*Town.* I swear I 'll never marry for that, an 't be but to give fortune my foe the lie. Come, Paul Puppy, you must in too.

*Pup.* No, I am well enough. I would [195 ha' no good fortune, an I might.

  *Patr.*
Yet look to yourself: you 'll ha' some ill luck;
And shortly — [*aside.*] for I have his purse with a pluck.
        Away, birds, mum!
        I hear by the hum,    200
        If Beck-Harman come,
        He 'll strike us all dumb,
        With a noise like a drum.
        Let 's give him our room.
        Here, this way some,    205
        And that way others:
        We are not all brothers.
        Leave me to the cheats;
        I 'll show 'em some feats.

*Pup.* What, are they gone? flown all of [210 a sudden? This is fine, i' faith. A covey, call ye 'em? They are a covey soon scattered, methinks. Who sprung 'em, I marle?

*Town.* Marry, yourself, Puppy, for aught I know. You quested last.    215

*Clod.* Would he had quested first for me, and sprung 'em an hour ago!

*Town.* Why, what 's the matter, man?

*Clod.* 'Slid, they ha' sprung my purse and all I had about me.    220

*Town.* They ha' not, ha' they?

*Clod.* As I am true Clod, ha' they, and ransacked me of every penny. Outcept I were with child of an owl (as they say), I

---

[142] **Who stands:** ('who 's' D)    [144-145] (F substitutes: 'You 'll ha' good luck to horse-flesh, o' my life; You plow'd so late with the vicar's wife.')    [147] **be:** ('must be' D)    **divine:** (punning on 'divine,' prophesy)    [150] **lead apes:** (the proverbial lot of unmarried maids)    [151] **mortified:** null and void    **'scapes:** escapades    [156] **will . . . go:** ('in Christmas will goe' D)    [157] **post . . . pair:** a card game    [158] **H' as:** he has    **right nail:** ('Hobnaile' D)    [165-171] **She . . . pancake:** (not in F)    [172] **Hark . . . they:** ('They slip her, and' F)    [176-177] **treat upon:** deal with    **non upstante:** non obstante, nevertheless ('notwithstanding' D)    [184] **with a:** (not in D; 'or a' F)    [189] **hand:** (given in pledge that)    [191] **wives:** wife's    [193] **fortune my foe:** (name and opening words of a popular song)    [201] **Beck-Harman:** the constable    [213] **sprung:** put to flight (of birds)    **marle:** marvel    [215] **quested:** gave tongue (of dogs)    [216] **for me:** (follows 'ago' in DF)    [222] **Clod:** ('Tom Clod' D)    [223] **Outcept:** except

never saw such luck. It is enough to make [225
a man a whore.

*Pup.* Hold thy peace. Thou talk'st as if
thou hadst a license to lose thy purse alone
in this company. 'Slid, here be them can
lose a purse in honour of the Gipsies as well [230
as thou for thy heart, and never make word
of it. I ha' lost my purse too.

*Cock.* What was there i' thy purse, thou
keepest such a whimpering? Was the lease
of thy house in it?                                       235

*Pup.* Or thy grannam's silver ring?

*Clod.* No, but a mill sixpence I lov'd as
dearly; and twopence I had to spend over
and above, beside the harper that was gather'd
amongst us to pay the piper.                              240

*Town.* Our whole stock, is that gone? how
will Tom Ticklefoot do to wet his whistle, then?

*Pup.* Marry, a new collection: there 's no
music else. He can ill pipe that wants his
upper lip.                                                245

*Prue.* They have robb'd me too of a race
of ginger and a jet ring I had to draw Jack
Straw hither o' holidays.

*Town.* Is 't possible? fine-finger'd Gipsies,
faith!                                                    250

*Meg.* And I have lost an enchanted nutmeg, all gilded-over — enchanted at Oxford —
I had to put i' my sweetheart's ale o' mornings; with a row of white pins that prick me to
the very heart, the loss of 'em.                          255

*Clod.* And I ha' lost, beside my purse, my
best bridelace I had at Joan Turnup's wedding,
and a halp'orth of hobnails; and Frances
Addlebreech has lost somewhat too.

*Fran.* Ay, I ha' lost my thimble, and a [260
skein of Coventry blue I had to work Gregory
Lichfield a handkerchief.

*Chri.* And I — unhappy Christian as I am!
— have lost my "Practice of Piety," with a
bowed groat and the ballet of "Whoop, [265
Barnabe," which grieves me ten times worse.

*Clod.* And Ticklefoot has lost his clout,
he says, with a threepence and four tokens
in it, besides his taboring-stick, even now.

*Cock.* And I my knife and sheath, and [270
my fine dog's leather gloves.

*Town.* Have we lost ne'er a dog amongst
us? where 's Puppy?

*Pup.* Here, goodman Townshead: you ha'
nothing to lose, it seems, but the town's [275
brains you are trusted with.

*Patrico.*

    O my dear marrows,
    No shooting of arrows,
    Or shafts of your wit,
    Each other to hit                                 280
    In your skirmishing fit.
    Your store is but small:
    Then venter not all.
    Remember, each mock
    Doth spend o' the stock:                          285
    And what was here done,
    Being under the moon,
    And at afternoon,
    Will prove right soon
    *Deceptio visus*,                                 290
    Done *gratia risus*.
    There 's no such thing
    As the loss of a ring,
    Or, what you count worse,
    The miss of a purse.                              295
    But hey for the main!
    And pass of the strain!
    Here 's both come again.
    And there 's an old twinger,
    Can show you the ginger.                          300
    The pins and the nutmeg
    Are safe here with slut Meg.
    Then strike up your tabor,
    And there 's for your labour.
    The sheath and the knife, —                       305
    I 'll venter my life,
    Shall breed you no strife;
    But like man and wife,
    Or sister and brother,
    Keep one with another;                            310
    And, light as a feather,
    Make haste to come hether.
    The Coventry blue
    Hangs there upon Prue;
    And here 's one opens                             315
    The clout and the tokens.
    Deny the bow'd groat,

---

**229 them:** ('those' D)    **231 for thy heart:** for all you can do    **232 purse too:** (three lines of gag added
in D)    **233-234 thou . . . whimpering:** (not in D; 'thou . . . whining' F)    **237 mill:** with milled edges
**sixpence:** (D adds 'of my Mothers')    **239 harper:** coin marked with a harp, depreciated shilling (?)
**244 He:** ('Masters he' DF)    **245 lip:** (followed in D by the speech: 'Town. Yes, a Bag-piper may
want both'; 'lippe; Money' F)    **246-263 Prue . . . Chri:** (In D the wenches do not speak, their words
being given, with slight variation, by the clowns.)    **246 race:** root    **247-248 jet . . . Straw:** (The joke is
that jet, black lignite, has electrical qualities and will attract straws.)    **251 enchanted:** (*i.e.*, to be used as
a love-charm)    **257 I had . . . wedding:** (not in D)    **258 halp'orth:** halfpenny-worth    **261 Coventry
blue:** blue thread, for which Coventry was famed    **Gregory:** ('Will' D)    **264 Practice of Piety:**
a popular book of devotion by Bishop Bayly    **265 bow'd:** bent    **267 clout:** handkerchief    **271 my fine:**
('a pair of' D)    **272 lost:** ('left' D)    **273 Puppy:** ('Puppy gone' D)    **277 marrows:** intimate friends
**286 here:** (not in MS)    **290 Deceptio visus:** optical illusion    **291 gratia risus:** for the sake of sport
**299 twinger:** snatcher    **300 you:** (not in MS)    **312 hether:** hither    **315 here 's:** ('here' D)

And you lie in your throat;
Or the taborer's ninepence,
Or the six fine pence.                              320
As for the ballet,
Or book, what-you-call-it,
Alas, our society
Mells not with piety:
Himself hath forsook it,                            325
That first undertook it.
For thimble or bridelace,
Search yonder side, lass.
All 's to be found,
If you look yourselves round.                       330
We scorn to take from ye;
We had rather spend on ye.
If any man wrong ye,
The thief 's among ye.

*Town.* Excellent, i' faith: a most re- [335
storative Gipsy! All 's here again; and yet
by his learning of leger-de-main he would make
us believe we had robb'd ourselves, for the hob-
nails are come to me.

*Cock.* May be he knew whose shoes [340
lack'd clouting.

*Pup.* Ay, he knows more than that; or
I 'll never trust my judgment in a Gipsy again.

*Cock.* A Gipsy of quality, believe it, and
one of the King's Gipsies, this: a Drink- [345
alian, or a Drink-bragatan. Ask him. The
King has a noise of Gipsies as well as bearwards.

*Pup.* What sort or order of Gipsy, I pray,
Sir? A flagonfleakian?                              350

*Patrico.*

A devil's-arse-a-peakian:
Born first at Niglington,
Bred up at Filchington,
Boarded at Tappington,
Bedded at Wappington.                               355

*Town.* 'Fore me, a dainty-derived Gipsy!

*Pup.* But I pray, Sir, if a man might ask
you: how came your Captain's place first
to be called the Devil's Arse?

*Patrico.*

For that, take my word,                             360
We have a record
That doth it afford,
And says our first lord —
Cock-Lorell he hight —
On a time did invite                                365
The Devil to a feast.

The tail of the jest
(Though since it be long)
Lives yet in a song;
Which if you would hear,                            370
Shall plainly appear,
Like a chime in your ear.
I 'll call in my clark,
Shall sing 't like a lark.

*Cock.* O, ay! The song, the song, in any [375
case! If you want music, we 'll lend him our
minstrel.

*Patrico.*

Come in, my long shark,
With thy face brown and dark;
With thy tricks and thy toys                        380
Make a merry, merry noise
To these mad country boys,
And chant out the farce
Of the grand Devil's Arse.

SONG

Cock-Lorell would needs have the Devil his
          guest,                                    385
And bade him into the Peak to dinner,
Where never the fiend had such a feast
Provided him yet at the charge of a sinner.

His stomach was queasy (he came thither
          coach'd):
The jogging had made some crudities rise. 390
To help it he call'd for a Puritan poach'd,
That used to turn up the eggs of his eyes.

And so, recovered to his wish,
He sate him down, and he fell to eat.
*Promoter in plum-broth* was his first dish: 395
His own privy kitchen had no such meat.

Yet (though with this he much were taken)
Upon a sudden he shifted his trencher,
As soon as he spies the *Bawd-and-Bacon,*
By which you may note the Devil 's a wencher.

Six pickled tailors, slic'd and cut;               401
Sempsters, tirewomen, fit for his palate,
With feather-men and perfumers put
Some twelve in a charger, to make a grand
          sallet.

A rich fat usurer stewed in his marrow,            405
And by him a lawyer's head and green sauce;
Both which his belly took in like a barrow,
As if till then he had never seen sauce.

---

324 **Mells:** meddles    341 **clouting:** mending    345–346 **Drinkalian:** drinker of ale    **-bragatan:** (See
note on I. 178.)    347 **noise:** band of musicians    347–348 **bearwards:** bear-keepers    350 **flagonfleakian:**
drunkard (D adds this to Patrico's speech.)    351 (A native of Devil's-arse in the Peak of Derbyshire)
356 **dainty-derived:** of excellent origin    362 **it:** (not in MS.)    372,375–377 (Not in DF)    378 **shark:**
thief (probably the Jackman)    385 **Cock-Lorell:** a mythical rogue, hero of *Cock Lorell's Boat*    386 **into:**
('once into' DF)    389 **he . . . thither:** ('for coming there' DF)    390 **made:** ('caus'd' DF)    392 **eggs:**
whites    393 **to his wish:** perfectly    395 **Promoter:** informer    399 **spies:** ('spy'd' DF)    402 **Semp-**
**sters:** seamstresses    **tirewomen:** milliners, wigmakers    403 **feather-men:** plume-sellers    404 **charger:**
dish    **sallet:** salad    408 **had never:** ('neuer had' MS)

Then, carbonado'd and cook'd with pains,
  Was brought up a cloven serjeant's face;  410
The sauce was made of his yeoman's brains,
  That had been beaten out with his own mace.

Two roasted sheriffs came whole to the board:
  The feast had nothing been without 'em.
Both living and dead they were fox'd and
  furr'd;                                    415
  Their chains like sausages hung about 'em.

The next dish was the mayor of a town,
  With a pudding of maintenance thrust in
    his belly:
Like a goose in the feathers, dress'd in his gown;
  And his couple of hinch-boys boil'd to a
    jelly.                                   420

A London cuckold, hot from the spit:
  And when the carver up had broke him,
The Devil chopp'd up his head at a bit,
  But the horns were very near like to choke
    him.

The chine of a lecher, too, there was, roasted,
  With a plump harlot's haunch and garlic;  426
A pandar's pettitoes, that had boasted
  Himself for a captain, yet never was warlike.

A large fat pasty of midwife hot;
  And, for a cold bak'd-meat, into the story  430
A reverend painted lady was brought,
  Was coffin'd in crust, till now she was hoary.

To these an overgrown justice of peace,
  With a clerk, like a gizzard, truss'd under
    each arm,
And warrants, for sippets, laid in his own
  grease,                                    435
  Set over a chafing-dish to be kept warm.

The jowl of a jailer serv'd for fish,
  A constable sous'd with vinegar by;
Two aldermen-lobsters asleep in a dish;
  A deputy-tart, a churchwarden-pie.         440

All which devour'd, he then, for a close,
  Did for a full draught of Darby call.
He heav'd the huge vessel up to his nose,
  And left not till he had drunk up all.

Then from the table he gave a start,         445
  Where banquet and wine were nothing scarce·
All which he blew away with a fart,
  From whence it was call'd the Devil's-arse.

And there he made such a breach with the wind,
  The hole too standing open the while,      450
That the scent of the vapour, before and be-
  hind,
  Hath foully perfumed most part of the isle.

And this was tobacco, the learned suppose;
  Which since, in country, court, and town,
In the Devil's glister-pipe smokes at the nose 455
  Of polecat, and madam, of gallant and clown.

From which wicked weed, with swine's flesh and
  ling,
  Or anything else that 's feast for the fiend,
Our Captain and we cry: God save the King,
  And send him good meat, and mirth without
    end!                                     460

*Pup.* An excellent song, and a sweet song-
ster; and would ha' done rarely in a cage with
a dish of water and hempseed. A fine breast
of his own! Sir, you are a prelate of the order,
I understood, and I have a terrible grudg- [465
ing now upon me to be one of your company.
Will your Captain take a prentice, Sir? I
would bind myself to him, body and soul,
either for one-and-twenty years or as many
lives as he would.                           470
  *Clod.* Ay, and put in my life for one, for
I am come about too. I am sorry I had no
more money in my purse when you came first
upon me, Sir. If I had known you would have
pick'd my pocket so like a gentleman, I [475
would ha' been better provided. I shall be
glad to venter a purse with your worship at
any time you 'll appoint, so you would prefer
me to your Captain. I 'll put in security for
my truth, and serve out my time, though [480
I die to-morrow.
  *Cock.* Ay, upon those terms, Sir, and in
hope your Captain keeps better cheer than he
made the Devil (for my stomach will never
agree with that diet), we 'll be all his fol- [485
lowers. I 'll go home and fetch a little money,
Sir: all I have; and you shall pick my pocket

---

⁴⁰⁹ **carbonado'd:** broiled      ⁴¹⁰ **serjeant:** police constable      ⁴¹¹ **yeoman:** serjeant's attendant
⁴¹⁵ **fox'd and furr'd:** dressed in ceremonial robes      ⁴¹⁶ **chains:** gold chains of office      ⁴¹⁸ **maintenance:**
bribery      ⁴²⁰ **hinch-boys:** foot-pages      ⁴²³ **chopp'd:** gobbled      **bit:** mouthful      ⁴²⁴ **choke:** ('have
choakt' DF)      ⁴²⁷ **pettitoes:** pig's feet      ⁴³² **Was:** ('And' DF)      **coffin'd in crust:** enclosed in pastry
**hoary:** mouldy      ⁴⁴⁴ **left:** stopped      ⁴⁴⁷ **blew:** ('flirted' DF)      ⁴⁴⁹⁻⁴⁶⁰ (Not in MS)      ⁴⁵⁷ **ling:** a fish
resembling cod (like tobacco and pork, loathed by King James)      ⁴⁶³ **breast:** singing voice      ⁴⁶⁵ **understood:** ('understand' DF)      ⁴⁶⁶ **now:** (not in D)      ⁴⁶⁹⁻⁴⁷⁰ **either . . . lives:** (terms for which land
was leased)      ⁴⁷⁷ **at:** (not in D)      ⁴⁷⁸ **prefer:** commend      ⁴⁸⁰ **truth:** honesty      ⁴⁸⁴ **made:** ('made
for' D)

to my face, and I 'll avouch it.  A man would
not desire to have his purse pick'd in better
company.                                    490
*Pup.*  Tut, they have other manner of gifts
than telling of fortunes or picking of pockets.
*Cock.*  Ay, an if they please to show them,
or thought us poor country folks worthy of
them.                                        495
*Pup.*  What might a man do to be a gentleman of your company, Sir?
*Cock.*  Ay, a Gipsy in ordinary or nothing.
*Patrico.*

 Friends, not to refell ye,
 Or any way quell ye,                   500
 To buy or to sell ye, —
 I only must tell ye:
 Ye aim at a mystery
 Worthy a history.
 There 's much to be done,              505
 Ere you can be a son,
 Or a brother, o' the moon.
 'T is not so soon
 Acquir'd as desir'd.
 You must be ben-bowsy,                 510
 And sleepy and drowsy,
 And lazy and lousy,
 Before ye can rouse ye
 In shape that avows ye.
 And then ye may stalk                  515
 The Gipsies' walk,
 To the coops and the pens,
 And bring in the hens.
 Though the cock be left sullen
 For loss o' the pullen,                520
 Take turkey and capon,
 And gammons of bacon:
 Let naught be forsaken.
 We 'll let you go loose,
 Like a fox to a goose,                 525
 And show you the sty
 Where the little pigs lie;
 Whence if you can take
 One or two, and not wake
 The sow in her dreams,                 530
 But by the moon-beams
 So warily hie
 As neither do cry,
 You shall the next day
 Have a license to play                 535
 At the hedge a flirt
 For a sheet or a shirt.
 If your hand be light,
 I 'll show ye the sleight

 Of our Ptolemy's knot:                 540
 It is and 't is not.
 To change your complexion
 With the noble confection
 Of walnuts and hog's grease,
 Better than dog's grease;              545
 And to milk the kine,
 Ere the milkmaid fine
 Have open'd her eyne;
 Or if you desire,
 To spit or fart fire.                  550
 I 'll teach you the knacks
 Of eating of flax,
 And out of your noses
 Draw ribbons for posies.
 As for example,                        555
 Mine own is as ample
 And fruitful a nose
 As a wit can suppose.
 Yet it shall go hard
 But there will be spar'd              560
 Each of you a yard,
 And worth your regard,
 When the colour and size
 Arrive at your eyes.
 And if you incline                     565
 To a cup of good wine,
 When you sup or dine;
 If you chance it to lack,
 Be it claret or sack,
 I 'll make this snout                  570
 To deal it about,
 Or this to run out,
 As 't were from a spout.
*Town.*  Admirable tricks! and he does 'em
all *se defendendo*, as if he would not be taken [575
in the trap of authority by a frail fleshly con-
stable.
*Pup.*  Without the aid of a cheese.
*Clod.*  Or help of a flitch of bacon.
*Cock.*  O, he would chirp in a pair of [580
stocks sumptuously.  I 'ld give anything to
see him play loose with his hands, when his
feet are fast.
*Pup.*  O' my conscience, he fears not that,
an the marshal himself were here.  I pro- [585
test, I admire him.

*Patrico.*

 Is this worth your wonder?
 Nay, then, you shall under-
 Stand more of my skill.
 I can, for I will,                     590

---

**488 avouch:** uphold **491–497** (One speech in F) **493 an . . . please:** ('and they would be
pleased' D) **494 poor:** ('poor mortall' D) **folks:** ('mortalls' F) **499 refell:** repulse **500 quell:**
dishearten **503 mystery:** profession **510 ben-bowsy:** bibulous **514 avows ye:** shows what you are
**519 left:** (not in MS F) **520 pullen:** poultry **529 or:** (not in D) **536 flirt:** bout, trial of skill
**546 to:** (not in D) **580** (This may originally have followed lines 463–464, 'a fine breast of his own'.)
**590 I can:** ('For I can' D)

Here at Burleigh o' th' hill,
Give you all your fill,
Each Jack with his Jill;
And show ye the King,
And Prince, too, and bring  595
The Gipsies were here
Like lords to appear;
With such their attenders
As you thought offenders,
Who now become new men.  600
You 'll know 'em for true men:
For he we call Chief
(I 'll tell 't you in brief)
Is so far from a thief
As he gives ye relief  605
With his bread, beer, and beef.
And 't is not long syne
Ye drank of his wine,
And it made ye fine,
Both claret and sherry.  610
Then let us be merry,
And help with your call
For a hall, a hall!
Stand up to the wall,
Both good men and tall:  615
We are one man's all.
Make it a jolly night,
If not a holy night,
Spite o' the constable,
Or Dean of Dunstable.  620
*All.* A hall! a hall! a hall!

# [PART III.]

THE GIPSIES CHANG'D. DANCE
*Patrico.*
 Why, now ye behold
'T was truth that I told,
And no device:
They 're chang'd in a trice;
And so will I  5
Be myself by and by.
I only now
Must study how
To come off with a grace
By my Patrico's place:  10
Some short kind of blessing,
Itself addressing

Unto my good Master, —
Which light on him faster
Than wishes can fly!  15
And you that stand by,
Be as jocund as I.
Each man with his voice
Give his heart to rejoice;
Which I 'll requite,  20
If my art hit right,
Though late now at night:
Each clown here in sight,
Before day-light,
Shall prove a good knight;  25
And your lasses pages,
Worthy their wages,
Where fancy engages
Girls to their ages.
 *Clowns.* O, anything for the Patrico! [30
What is 't? what is 't?
 *Patrico.* Nothing but bear the bob of the
  close;
It will be no burthen, you well may sup-
  pose,
But bless the Sovereign and his senses,
And to wish away offences.  35
 *Clowns.* Let us alone: "Bless the Sovereign
and his senses!"
 *Patrico.* We 'll take 'em in order, as they
  have being;
And first of *seeing.*
From a Gipsy in the morning,  40
Or a pair of squint eyes turning;
From the goblin and the spectre,
Or a drunkard, though with nectar;
From a woman true to no man,
And is ugly beside common;  45
A smock rampant, and that itches
To be putting on the breeches:
Wheresoe'er they have their being,
Bless the Sovereign and his *seeing!*

From a fool and serious toys;  50
From a lawyer three parts noise;
From impertinence, like a drum
Beat at dinner in his room;
From a tongue without a file
(Heaps of phrases and no style);  55
From a fiddle out of tune,
As the cuckoo is in June;

---

⁵⁹⁴ **ye:** ('you' DF) ⁵⁹⁶ **were:** who were ⁶⁰²⁻⁶¹⁶ (Replaced at the Belvoir performance by: 'The fift of August | Will not let sawdust | Lie in your throats | Or cobwebs or oats | But help to scour ye. | This is no Gowrie | Hath drawn James hether | But the good man of Bever | Our Buckingham's father | Then so much the rather.') ⁶⁰² **Chief:** Captain of Gipsies, Buckingham (the host at Burleigh) ⁶⁰⁵ **As . . . ye:** ('He gives you' D) ⁶⁰⁶ **bread . . . and:** ('Beere and his' D) ⁶¹³ **a hall:** cry that the room be cleared for dancing ⁶¹⁸ **If not:** (at Belvoir, 'for 'tis') ⁶²⁰ **Dean of Dunstable:** an imaginary official Part III. S. D. **Chang'd:** in new costumes ³ **device:** fiction ⁹ **come off:** conclude ¹⁰ **By:** as regards ('With' DF) ²¹ **art:** ('heart' D) ³² **bob:** refrain ³³ **burthen:** (punning on two senses) ³⁶ **Let us alone:** Leave it to us. ³⁸ **in . . . being:** in their natural order ⁴³ **though:** though drunk ⁴⁵ **And:** ('which'DF) ⁴⁶ **smock rampant:** virago **that:** ('the' DF) ⁵⁰ **serious toys:** dull trifling ⁵⁴ **without a file:** unpolished

From the candlesticks of Lothbury,
And the loud pure wives of Banbury;
Or a long pretended fit,                                         60
Meant for mirth, but is not it,
Only time and ears outwearing:
Bless the Sovereign and his *hearing!*

From a strolling tinker's sheet,
And a pair of carrier's feet;                                    65
From a lady that doth breathe
Worse above than underneath;
From the diet and the knowledge
Of the students in Bears' College;
From tobacco with the type                                       70
Of the Devil's glister-pipe;
Or a stink all stinks excelling,
A fishmonger's dwelling:
Bless the Sovereign and his *smelling!*

From an oyster and fried fish,                                   75
A sow's baby in a dish,
Any portion of a swine;
From bad venison and worse wine;
Ling, what cook soe'er it boil,
Though with mustard sauc'd and oil;                              80
Or what else would keep man fasting:
Bless the Sovereign and his *tasting!*

Both from birdlime and from pitch;
From a doxy and her itch;
From the bristles of a hog;                                      85
Or the ring-worm of a dog;
From the courtship of a briar;
From St. Anthony's old fire;
From a needle or a thorn,
In the bed at even or morn;                                      90
Or from any gout's least grouching:
Bless the Sovereign and his *touching!*

Bless him, too, from all offences
In his sports as in his senses:
From a boy to cross his way,                                     95
From a fall or a foul day.

Bless him, O bless him, Heaven, and lend him
    long,
To be the sacred burthen of all song;
The acts and years of all our kings to outgo,
And while he 's mortal, we not think him so! 100

*After which, ascending up, the Jackman sings*

SONG 1

The sports are done, yet do not let
Your joys in sudden silence set.
Delight and dumbness never met
    In one self subject yet.
If things oppos'd must mix'd appear,            105
Then add a boldness to your fear,
    And speak a hymn
    To him,
Where all your duties do of right belong,
Which I will sweeten with an undersong.   110

*Captain.*  Glory of ours, and grace of all the
    earth,
How well your figure doth become your birth!
As if your form and fortune equal stood,
And only virtue got above your blood.

SONG 2

Virtue! His kingly virtue, which did merit   115
This isle entire, and you are to inherit.

*4. Gipsy.*  How right he doth confess him in
    his face:
His brow, his eye, and every mark of state;
As if he were the issue of each Grace,
And bore about him both his fame and fate.  120

SONG 3

    Look, look!  Is he not fair,
        And fresh and fragrant too,
    As summer's sky or purged air!
        And looks as lilies do,
    That were this morning blown!           125

*4. Gipsy.*  O, more! that more of him were
    known.
*3. Gipsy.*  Look how the winds upon the
    waves, grown tame,
Take up land sounds upon their purple wings;
And, catching each from other, bear the same
    To every angle of their sacred springs.  130

So will we take his praise, and hurl his name
    About the globe in thousand airy rings,
If his great virtue be in love with fame:
    For, that contemn'd, both are neglected
    things.

---

⁵⁸ **Lothbury:** street in London occupied by brass-grinders; cf. *1 Henry IV*, III. i. 131    ⁵⁹ **pure:** Puritan    **Banbury:** in Oxfordshire, a hotbed of Puritanism    ⁶⁰⁻⁶¹ (Not in MS)    ⁶⁰ **pretended fit:** pretentious tale    ⁶⁸ **knowledge:** acquaintance    ⁶⁹ **Bears' College:** Paris Garden, the bear-baiting arena    ⁷⁷ **Any:** ('From any' DF)    ⁸⁶ **of:** ('in' DF)    ⁸⁸ **St. Anthony's fire:** erysipelas    ⁹¹ **grouching:** grumbling    ⁹⁹ **outgo:** excel    ¹⁰⁴ **self subject:** the same person    ¹⁰⁵ **things oppos'd:** (*i.e.*, the Gipsies and royalty)    ¹⁰⁶ **fear:** diffidence    ¹¹⁰ **undersong:** supporting refrain    ¹¹³ **if your:** ('in you' MS)    ¹¹⁶ **isle entire:** England and Scotland    **you . . . inherit:** (Suggests, like l. 53, Part I, that the Captain's part was originally written for Prince Charles.)    ¹¹⁷ **confess him:** express himself    ¹²² **purged:** purified (by rain)    ¹²⁶ **that . . . known:** that we may know more of him    ¹³⁴ **that:** fame

### SONG 4

Good princes soar above their fame,                       135
  And in their worth
  Come greater forth
Than in their name.
Such, such the Father is,
Whom every title strives to kiss;                          140
Who on his royal grounds unto himself doth
    raise
The work to trouble fame and to astonish
    praise.

    *4. Gipsy.*   Indeed, he is not lord alone of the
estate,
But of the love of men and of the empire's fate.
The muses, arts, the schools, commerce, our
    honour's laws,                                      145
And virtues hang on him as on their working
    cause.
    *2. Gipsy.*   His handmaid, Justice is.
    *3. Gipsy.*   Wisdom, his wife.
    *4. Gipsy.*   His mistress, Mercy.
    *5. Gipsy.*   Temperance, his life.              150
    *2. Gipsy.*   His pages, Bounty and Grace,
which many prove.
    *3. Gipsy.*   His guards are Magnanimity and
Love.
    *4. Gipsy.*   His ushers, Counsel, Truth, and
Piety.
    *5. Gipsy.*   And all that follows him, Felicity.

### SONG 5

O that we understood                                       155
  Our good!
There 's happiness, indeed, in blood
  And store;
But how much more,
When virtue's flood                                        160

In the same stream doth hit:
As that grows high with years, so happiness
  with it.
    *Captain.*   Love, love, his fortune, then,
      And virtues known,
      Who is the top of men,                      165
      But make the happiness our own;
Since where the prince for goodness is renown'd,
The subject with felicity is crown'd.

THE END

### THE EPILOGUE

At Burleigh, Belvoir, and now last at Windsor,
Which shows we are Gipsies of no common
  kind, Sir,
You have beheld, and with delight, their
  change;
And how they came transform'd may think it
  strange,
If being a thing not touch'd at by our poet.   5
Good Ben slept there, or else forgot to show it.
But lest it prove like wonder to the sight
To see a Gipsy as an Æthiop white:
Know that what dyed our faces was an oint-
  ment,
Made and laid on by Mr. Wolf's appoint-
  ment,                                                  10
The court's *lycanthropos;* yet without spells,
By a mere barber and no magic else.
It was fetch'd off with water and a ball;
And to our transformation this was all,
Save what the Master Fashioner calls his:      15
For to a Gipsy's metamorphosis
(Who doth disguise his habit and his face,
And takes on a false person by his place)
The power of poesy can never fail her,
Assisted by a barber and a tailor.              20

---

<sup>137</sup> **Come . . . forth:** appear greater    <sup>141</sup> **royal grounds:** regal personality    <sup>143</sup> **the estate:** ('all
the State' DF)    <sup>153</sup> **ushers:** court attendants    <sup>158</sup> **store:** wealth    <sup>161</sup> **doth hit:** converges
<sup>162</sup> **that:** virtue's flood    <sup>166</sup> **make:** esteem ('makes' DF)    <sup>6</sup> **slept:** nodded, erred    <sup>7</sup> **like:** equal
<sup>10</sup> **Wolf:** John Wolfgang Rumler, the king's apothecary    <sup>11</sup> **lycanthropos:** wolf-man    <sup>13</sup> **ball:** ball
of soap    <sup>14</sup> **was:** ('is' DF)    <sup>15</sup> **Fashioner:** costumer (perhaps a gibe at Inigo Jones)    <sup>19</sup> **poesy:**
('Poetry' DF)

# THE
# TRAGEDY
## OF THE DVTCHESSE
## Of Malfy.

*As it was Presented priuatly, at the Black-Friers; and publiquely at the Globe, By the Kings Maiesties Seruants.*

The perfect and exact Coppy, with diuerse things Printed, that the length of the Play would not beare in the Presentment.

VVritten by *John Webster.*

Hora.——— *Si quid*-----
———*Candidus Impertì sì non bis vtere mecum.*

*LONDON:*

Printed by NICHOLAS OKES, for IOHN
WATERSON, and are to be sold at the
signe of the Crowne, in *Paules*
Church-yard, 1623.

BIBLIOGRAPHICAL RECORD. *The Tragedy of the Duchess of Malfi*, second and last of Webster's great plays, first appeared in 1623 in an excellent text from the press of the veteran printer Nicholas Okes, for sale by John Waterson. No entry has been found in the Stationers' Register. Three commendatory poems, by the dramatists Middleton, Rowley, and Ford, are prefixed. Middleton's, the longest, is headed: "In the just Worth of that well Deserver, Mr JOHN WEBSTER, and upon this Maister-peece of Tragoedy." The following letter of the author to Lord Berkeley prefaces the play: — *My Noble Lord, That I may present my excuse, why (being a stranger to your Lordshippe) I offer this Poem to your Patronage, I plead this warrant; Men (who never saw the Sea, yet desire to behold that regiment of waters,) choose some eminent River, to guide them thither; and make that, as it were, their Conduct, or Postilion: By the like ingenious meanes has your fame arrived at my knowledge, receiving it from some of worth, who both in contemplation, and practise, owe to your Honor their clearest service. I do not altogether looke up at your Title: The ancien'st Nobility being but a rellique of time past, and the truest Honor indeede beeing for a man to conferre Honor on himselfe, which your Learning strives to propagate, and shall make you arrive at the Dignity of a great Example. I am confident this worke is not unworthy your Honors perusal for by such Poems as this Poets have kist the hands of Great Princes, and drawne their gentle eyes to looke downe upon their sheetes of paper, when the Poets themselves were bound up in their winding-sheetes. The like curtesie from your Lordship shall make you live in your grave, and laurell spring out of it; when the ignorant scorners of the Muses (that, like wormes in Libraries, seeme to live onely to destroy learning) shall wither, neglected, and forgotten. This worke and my selfe I humbly present to your approved censure. It being the utmost of my wishes, to have your Honorable selfe my weighty and perspicuous Comment: which grace so done me, shall ever be acknowledged By your Lordships in all duty and Observance, JOHN WEBSTER.*

A second quarto appeared in 1640, a third in 1678, and another in 1708, without material improvement or alteration of the text.

DATE AND STAGE PERFORMANCE. The list of actors supplied by Q1 gives important evidence for the date and early history of the play. Since the first performer of Antonio's part, William Ostler, is now known (from papers discovered by the late C. W. Wallace in 1909) to have died on Dec. 16, 1614, the earliest production of the piece must have preceded that date. Mr. W. J. Lawrence (London *Athenaeum*, Nov. 21, 1919) argues that it occurred about Easter, 1613. Indication of a revival in 1617 is found in lines 5–15 of the first scene, which apparently refer to the assassination by the French King's guard of the dissolute favorite Concini, Apr. 24, 1617. This implies that Antonio's first speech in the play was added or rewritten several years after the death of the original Antonio. The actor-names marked "2" in the Q1 list point to a re-casting in connection with another revival subsequent to Burbage's death in 1619. There is no record of court performance before the Restoration. The tragedy was revived, about 1664, at Lincoln's Inn Fields, and, says Genest, "filled the house 8 days successively." The edition of 1678 presents it "As it is now acted at the Duke's Theater," and gives a list of actors showing that Betterton played Bosola and his wife the Duchess. The 1708 text, entitled "The Unfortunate Dutchess of Malfy, or the Unnatural Brothers," gives it as "Now acted at the Queen's Theatre in the Hay-Market."

STRUCTURE. In structure, as in tone, the play is highly romantic. About a year elapses between Acts I and II, and a number of years between II and III. The scene shifts from Amalfi to various distant parts of Italy, and in the last two acts it is not always clear where the action is supposed to occur. The stage directions at the opening of scenes follow the pseudo-classic principle of "massed entrances," that is, all characters ultimately appearing in a scene are listed at its opening, though actually only one or two of them may be on the stage when it begins.

SOURCES. The historical story of Giovanna, Duchess of Amalfi, covering the years from about 1504 till 1513, is told by Bandello (*Novelle* I. 26), who seems himself to have been an eye-witness of Antonio's assassination (Oct. 6, 1513) and to be the prototype of Delio in Webster's play. Webster drew his information chiefly from Painter's *Palace of Pleasure* (1567), which represents an adaptation of Bandello through the medium of Belleforest's French translation. Webster handles the story with great freedom, especially in the fourth and fifth acts, where the circumstances of all the deaths are mainly his own invention. A remarkable feature of the play is Webster's adroit introduction into his dialogue of admired passages in Sidney's *Arcadia*, Montaigne's Essays, and Donne's *Anatomy of the World* (1611), which Mr. Charles Crawford pointed out (*Collectanea*, 1906–1907). The scene of the wax figures is taken from the *Arcadia*, and the masque of madmen perhaps from Campion's *Lords' Masque*, February, 1613.

# JOHN WEBSTER (1580?–c. 1630)

## THE DUCHESS OF MALFI

THE ACTORS' NAMES

BOSOLA, *J. Lowin*
FERDINAND [Duke of Calabria], *1 R. Burbidge.*
*2 J. Taylor*
CARDINAL [his Brother],
*1 H. Cundaile. 2 R. Robinson*
ANTONIO [BOLOGNA, Steward to the Duchess],
*1 W. Ostler. 2 R. Benfeild*
DELIO, *J. Underwood*
FOROBOSCO, *N. Towley* [A mute character in the
existing text; perhaps the same as RODERIGO or
GRISOLAN]
MALATESTE
MARQUESSE OF PESCARA, *J. Rice*
SILVIO, *T. Pollard*
[CASTRUCHIO, an Old Lord, Husband of Julia]

[RODERIGO and GRISOLAN, Gentlemen attending
the Duke]
The Several Madmen, *N. Towley, J. Underwood,
&c.*

THE DUCHESS, *R. Sharpe*
The Cardinal's Mistress [JULIA], *J. Tomson*

The Doctor, ⎫
CARIOLA, ⎬ *R. Pallant*
Court Officers, ⎭

[Old Lady]

Three Young Children; Two Pilgrims; [Executioners, and Other Attendants]

(SCENE: The Duchess's palace, Amalfi; Cardinal's palace, Rome; Loretto and neighboring country;
Milan.)

### Actus Primus. Scena Prima

[*The Duchess's Palace, Amalfi.*]

*Antonio and Delio, [later] Bosola, Cardinal*

*Delio.* You are welcome to your country,
dear Antonio;
You have been long in France, and you return
A very formal Frenchman in your habit.
How do you like the French court?
*Ant.*                    I admire it.
In seeking to reduce both state and people  5
To a fix'd order, their judicious king
Begins at home; quits first his royal palace
Of flatt'ring sycophants, of dissolute
And infamous persons, — which he  sweetly
terms
His Master's masterpiece, the work of heaven;
Considering duly that a prince's court  11
Is like a common fountain, whence should flow
Pure silver drops in general, but if 't chance
Some curs'd example poison 't near the head,
Death and diseases through the whole land
spread.  15
And what is 't makes this blessed government
But a most provident council, who dare freely

Inform him the corruption of the times?
Though some o' th' court hold it presump-
tion
To instruct princes what they ought to do,  20
It is a noble duty to inform them
What they ought to foresee. — Here comes Bo-
sola,
The only court-gall; yet I observe his railing
Is not for simple love of piety:
Indeed, he rails at those things which he
wants;  25
Would be as lecherous, covetous, or proud,
Bloody, or envious, as any man,
If he had means to be so. — Here 's the cardi-
nal.

[*Enter Cardinal and Bosola*]

*Bos.* I do haunt you still.
*Card.* So.  30
*Bos.* I have done you better service than to
be slighted thus.  Miserable age, where only the
reward of doing well is the doing of it!
*Card.* You enforce your merit too much.
*Bos.* I fell into the galleys in your serv- [35
ice; where, for two years together, I wore two
towels instead of a shirt, with a knot on the
shoulder, after the fashion of a Roman mantle.

---

³ **habit:** dress   ⁷ **quits:** rids   ⁹ **which:** which ridding   ¹⁰ **Master's masterpiece:** alluding to
Christ's ridding the Temple of moneychangers   ¹³ **in general:** invariably   ²² **foresee:** provide against
²³ **court-gall:** courtly cynic   ³⁵ **galleys:** penal servitude

647

Slighted thus! I will thrive some way. Blackbirds fatten best in hard weather; why not [40
I in these dog-days?

*Card.* Would you could become honest!

*Bos.* With all your divinity do but direct me
the way to it. I have known many travel far
for it, and yet return as arrant knaves as [45
they went forth, because they carried themselves always along with them. [*Exit Cardinal.*]
Are you gone? Some fellows, they say, are possessed with the devil, but this great fellow
were able to possess the greatest devil, and [50
make him worse.

*Ant.* He hath denied thee some suit?

*Bos.* He and his brother are like plum-trees
that grow crooked over standing-pools; they
are rich and o'erladen with fruit, but none but
crows, pies, and caterpillars feed on them. 56
Could I be one of their flattering pandars, I
would hang on their ears like a horseleech, till
I were full, and then drop off. I pray, leave me.
Who would rely upon these miserable depend-
ances, in expectation to be advanc'd to- 61
morrow? What creature ever fed worse than
hoping Tantalus? Nor ever died any man more
fearfully than he that hop'd for a pardon.
There are rewards for hawks and dogs when 65
they have done us service; but for a soldier
that hazards his limbs in a battle, nothing but
a kind of geometry is his last supportation.

*Delio.* Geometry?

*Bos.* Ay, to hang in a fair pair of slings, take
his latter swing in the world upon an hon- 71
ourable pair of crutches, from hospital to hospital. Fare ye well, sir: and yet do not you scorn
us; for places in the court are but like beds in
the hospital, where this man's head lies at that
man's foot, and so lower and lower. [*Exit.*] 76

*Del.* I knew this fellow seven years in the
   galleys
For a notorious murther; and 't was thought
The cardinal suborn'd it: he was releas'd
By the French general, Gaston de Foix,       80
When he recover'd Naples.

*Ant.*                        'T is great pity
He should be thus neglected: I have heard
He 's very valiant. This foul melancholy
Will poison all his goodness; for, I 'll tell
   you,
If too immoderate sleep be truly said        85
To be an inward rust unto the soul,
It then doth follow want of action

Breeds all black malcontents; and their close
   rearing,
Like moths in cloth, do hurt for want of wearing.

### SCENA II. — [*The same.*]

*Antonio, Delio.* [*Enter to them*] *Silvio, Castruchio, Julia, Roderigo, and Grisolan*

*Delio.* The presence 'gins to fill; you prom-
   is'd me
To make me the partaker of the natures
Of some of your great courtiers.

*Ant.*                    The lord cardinal's
And other strangers' that are now in court?
I shall. — Here comes the great Calabrian duke.

[*Enter Ferdinand and Attendants*]

*Ferd.* Who took the ring oft'nest?          6

*Sil.* Antonio Bologna, my lord.

*Ferd.* Our sister duchess' great master of her
household? Give him the jewel. — When shall
we leave this sportive action, and fall to action
indeed?                                       11

*Cast.* Methinks, my lord, you should not desire to go to war in person.

*Ferd.* Now for some gravity. — Why, my
lord?                                         15

*Cast.* It is fitting a soldier arise to be a prince,
but not necessary a prince descend to be a captain.

*Ferd.* No?

*Cast.* No, my lord; he were far better do it
by a deputy.                                  21

*Ferd.* Why should he not as well sleep or eat
by a deputy? This might take idle, offensive,
and base office from him, whereas the other de-
prives him of honour.                        25

*Cast.* Believe my experience: that realm is
never long in quiet where the ruler is a soldier.

*Ferd.* Thou told'st me thy wife could not endure fighting.

*Cast.* True, my lord.                       30

*Ferd.* And of a jest she broke of a captain
she met full of wounds: I have forgot it.

*Cast.* She told him, my lord, he was a pitiful
fellow, to lie, like the children of Ismael, all in
tents.                                        35

*Ferd.* Why, there 's a wit were able to undo
all the chirurgeons o' the city; for although
gallants should quarrel, and had drawn their
weapons, and were ready to go to it, yet her
persuasions would make them put up.          40

---

⁵⁴ **standing-pools:** stagnant ponds    ⁵⁶ **pies:** magpies    ⁶³ **died:** ('did' Q 1)    ⁶⁴ **pardon:**
('pleadon' Q 1)    ⁶⁸ **supportation:** support    ⁸⁰ **Gaston de Foix:** slain in victory at Ravenna, 1512
⁸¹ **recover'd:** conquered (The French captured Naples, 1501, but not under Gaston de Foix.)    ⁸⁸ **close:**
secluded    Scene II, s. D. (Q 1 lists all the characters appearing during the scene: 'Antonio, Delio,
Ferdinand, Cardinall, Dutchesse, Castruchio, Siluio, Rodocico [*sic*], Grisolan, Bosola, Iulia, Cariola.')
¹ **presence:** presence-chamber    ² **the partaker:** informed    ⁶ **ring:** the target in 'riding at the ring'
³¹ **broke:** 'cracked'    ³⁵ **tents:** linen surgical dressings    ³⁷ **chirurgeons:** surgeons

*Cast.* That she would, my lord. — How do you like my Spanish jennet?

*Rod.* He is all fire.

*Ferd.* I am of Pliny's opinion: I think he was begot by the wind; he runs as if he were ballass'd with quicksilver. 46

*Sil.* True, my lord, he reels from the tilt often.

*Rod., Gris.* Ha, ha, ha!

*Ferd.* Why do you laugh? Methinks you that are courtiers should be my touch-wood, [51 take fire when I give fire; that is, laugh when I laugh, were the subject never so witty.

*Cast.* True, my lord: I myself have heard a very good jest, and have scorn'd to seem to have so silly a wit as to understand it. 56

*Ferd.* But I can laugh at your fool, my lord.

*Cast.* He cannot speak, you know, but he makes faces; my lady cannot abide him.

*Ferd.* No? 60

*Cast.* Nor endure to be in merry company; for she says too much laughing, and too much company, fills her too full of the wrinkle.

*Ferd.* I would, then, have a mathematical instrument made for her face, that she might not laugh out of compass. — I shall shortly visit [66 you at Milan, Lord Silvio.

*Sil.* Your grace shall arrive most welcome.

*Ferd.* You are a good horseman, Antonio: you have excellent riders in France. What do you think of good horsemanship? 71

*Ant.* Nobly, my lord: as out of the Grecian horse issued many famous princes, so out of brave horsemanship arise the first sparks of growing resolution, that raise the mind to noble action. 76

*Ferd.* You have bespoke it worthily.

*Sil.* Your brother, the lord cardinal, and sister duchess.

[*Enter Cardinal, with Duchess, and Cariola*]

*Card.* Are the galleys come about?

*Gris.*         They are, my lord. 80

*Ferd.* Here 's the Lord Silvio is come to take his leave.

*Delio.* Now, sir, your promise: what 's that cardinal?

I mean his temper. They say he 's a brave fellow,

Will play his five thousand crowns at tennis, dance,

Court ladies, and one that hath fought single combats. 85

*Ant.* Some such flashes superficially hang

on him for form; but observe his inward character: he is a melancholy churchman. The spring in his face is nothing but the engend'ring of toads; where he is jealous of any man, he lays worse plots for them than ever was im- 91 pos'd on Hercules, for he strews in his way flatterers, pandars, intelligencers, atheists, and a thousand such political monsters. He should have been Pope; but instead of coming to it by the primitive decency of the church, he did 96 bestow bribes so largely and so impudently as if he would have carried it away without heaven's knowledge. Some good he hath done ——

*Delio.* You have given too much of him. What 's his brother? 100

*Ant.* The duke there? A most perverse and turbulent nature.

What appears in him mirth is merely outside;

If he laugh heartily, it is to laugh

All honesty out of fashion.

*Delio.*                     Twins?

*Ant.*                          In quality.

He speaks with others' tongues, and hears men's suits 105

With others' ears; will seem to sleep o' th' bench

Only to entrap offenders in their answers;

Dooms men to death by information;

Rewards by hearsay.

*Delio.*         Then the law to him

Is like a foul, black cobweb to a spider, — 110

He makes it his dwelling and a prison

To entangle those shall feed him.

*Ant.*                     Most true:

He never pays debts unless they be shrewd turns,

And those he will confess that he doth owe.

Last, for his brother there, the cardinal, 115

They that do flatter him most say oracles

Hang at his lips; and verily I believe them,

For the devil speaks in them.

But for their sister, the right noble duchess,

You never fix'd your eye on three fair medals

Cast in one figure, of so different temper. 121

For her discourse, it is so full of rapture,

You only will begin then to be sorry

When she doth end her speech, and wish, in wonder,

She held it less vain-glory to talk much, 125

Than your penance to hear her. Whilst she speaks,

She throws upon a man so sweet a look

That it were able raise one to a galliard

That lay in a dead palsy, and to dote

---

⁴² **jennet:** small Spanish horse   ⁴⁵⁻⁴⁶ **ballass'd:** ballasted   ⁸⁹⁻⁹⁰ **spring . . . toads:** (compare *Bussy D' Ambois*, III. ii. 477, 'that toad-pool that stands in thy complexion,' and *The Changeling*, II. i. 59.)   ⁹³ **intelligencers:** informers   ⁹⁴ **should:** was expected to   ¹⁰⁸ **information:** testimony of spies   ¹⁰⁹ **hearsay:** random report   ¹¹³ **shrewd:** ill ('shewed' Q 1)   ¹²⁵⁻¹²⁶ **held . . . her:** were less convinced that much talk is vanity than she is that her auditors are not interested   ¹²⁸ **galliard:** quick dance

On that sweet countenance; but in that look 130
There speaketh so divine a continence
As cuts off all lascivious and vain hope.
Her days are practis'd in such noble virtue,
That sure her nights, nay, more, her very
sleeps,
Are more in heaven than other ladies' shrifts. 135
Let all sweet ladies break their flatt'ring glasses,
And dress themselves in her.
  *Delio.*                     Fie, Antonio,
You play the wire-drawer with her commenda-
tions.
  *Ant.*  I 'll case the picture up: only thus
much;
All her particular worth grows to this sum, —
She stains the time past, lights the time to
come.                                         141
  *Cari.*  You must attend my lady in the gal-
lery,
Some half an hour hence.
  *Ant.*  I shall. [*Exeunt Antonio and Delio.*]
  *Ferd.*  Sister, I have a suit to you.
  *Duch.*                     To me, sir?
  *Ferd.*  A gentleman here, Daniel de Bosola,
One that was in the galleys ——
  *Duch.*              Yes, I know him. 146
  *Ferd.*  A worthy fellow he 's: pray, let me en-
treat for
The provisorship of your horse.
  *Duch.*              Your knowledge of him
Commends him and prefers him.
  *Ferd.*     Call him hither. [*Exit Attendants.*]
We are now upon parting.  Good Lord Silvio,
Do us commend to all our noble friends 151
At the leaguer.
  *Sil.*        Sir, I shall.
  *Duch.*              You are for Milan?
  *Sil.*  I am.
  *Duch.*  Bring the caroches. — We 'll bring
you down
To the haven.
        [*Exeunt Duchess, Silvio, Castruchio,
        Roderigo, Grisolan, Cariola, Julia,
        and Attendants.*]
  *Card.*  Be sure you entertain that Bosola 154
For your intelligence.  I would not be seen in 't;
And therefore many times I have slighted him,
When he did court our furtherance, as this
morning.
  *Ferd.*  Antonio, the great master of her house-
hold,
Had been far fitter.
  *Card.*              You are deceiv'd in him. 159
His nature is too honest for such business. —
He comes: I 'll leave you.          [*Exit.*]

[*Re-enter Bosola*]

  *Bos.*                  I was lur'd to you.
  *Ferd.*  My brother here, the cardinal. could
never
Abide you.
  *Bos.*     Never since he was in my debt.
  *Ferd.*  May be some oblique character in
your face
Made him suspect you.
  *Bos.*        Doth he study physiognomy? 165
There 's no more credit to be given to th' face
Than to a sick man's urine, which some call
The physician's whore, because she cozens him.
He did suspect me wrongfully.
  *Ferd.*              For that
You must give great men leave to take their
times.                                        170
Distrust doth cause us seldom be deceiv'd.
You see, the oft shaking of the cedar-tree
Fastens it more at root.
  *Bos.*              Yet take heed;
For to suspect a friend unworthily
Instructs him the next way to suspect you, 175
And prompts him to deceive you.
  *Ferd.*              There 's gold.
  *Bos.*                          So:
What follows? — [*Aside.*] Never rain'd such
showers as these
Without thunderbolts i' th' tail of them. —
Whose throat must I cut?
  *Ferd.*  Your inclination to shed blood rides
post
Before my occasion to use you.  I give you that
To live i' th' court here, and observe the
duchess;                                      181
To note all the particulars of her haviour,
What suitors do solicit her for marriage,
And whom she best affects.  She 's a young
widow:
I would not have her marry again.
  *Bos.*                  No, sir? 185
  *Ferd.*  Do not you ask the reason; but be
satisfied.
I say I would not.
  *Bos.*        It seems you would create me
One of your familiars.
  *Ferd.*        Familiar! What 's that?
  *Bos.*  Why, a very quaint invisible devil in
flesh, —
An intelligencer.
  *Ferd.*     Such a kind of thriving thing 190
I would wish thee; and ere long thou mayst
arrive
At a higher place by 't.

¹³⁹ **case . . . up:** remove from view   ¹⁴¹ **stains:** dims   ¹⁴⁸ **provisorship:** office of purveyor
¹⁵⁰ **are:** (not in Qq. 1–3)  **upon:** on the point of   ¹⁵² **leaguer:** camp  **Duch.** (Qq. assign her speech to
Ferdinand.)   ¹⁵³ **caroches:** coaches   ¹⁵⁴ **entertain:** employ   ¹⁵⁵ **intelligence:** secret service   ¹⁶⁸ **cozens:**
cheats   ¹⁷⁵ **next:** shortest   ¹⁷⁹ **post:** posthaste   ¹⁸² **haviour:** behavior   ¹⁸⁴ **affects:** cares for

*Bos.*                    Take your devils,
Which hell calls angels! These curs'd gifts would make
You a corrupter, me an impudent traitor;
And should I take these, they 'd take me to hell.                                                    195
*Ferd.* Sir, I 'll take nothing from you that I have given.
There is a place that I procur'd for you
This morning, the provisorship o' th' horse.
Have you heard on 't?
*Bos.*                    No.
*Ferd.* 'T is yours: is 't not worth thanks?
*Bos.* I would have you curse yourself now, that your bounty                                          200
(Which makes men truly noble) e'er should make me
A villain. O, that to avoid ingratitude
For the good deed you have done me, I must do
All the ill man can invent! Thus the devil
Candies all sins o'er: and what heaven terms vild,                                                    205
That names he complimental.
*Ferd.*                    Be yourself;
Keep your old garb of melancholy; 't will express
You envy those that stand above your reach,
Yet strive not to come near 'em. This will gain
Access to private lodgings, where yourself     210
May, like a politic dormouse ——
*Bos.*                    As I have seen some
Feed in a lord's dish, half asleep, not seeming
To listen to any talk; and yet these rogues
Have cut his throat in a dream. What 's my place?
The provisorship o' th' horse? Say, then, my corruption                                               215
Grew out of horse-dung: I am your creature.
*Ferd.*                    Away! [*Exit.*]
*Bos.* Let good men, for good deeds, covet good fame,
Since place and riches oft are bribes of shame.
Sometimes the devil doth preach. *Exit Bosola.*

[SCENE III]

*[Enter Ferdinand, Duchess, Cardinal, and Cariola]*

*Card.* We are to part from you; and your own discretion
Must now be your director.
*Ferd.*                    You are a widow:

You know already what man is; and therefore
Let not youth, high promotion, eloquence ——
*Card.* No,                                                5
Nor anything without the addition, honour,
Sway your high blood.
*Ferd.*                    Marry! They are most luxurious
Will wed twice.
*Card.*          O, fie!
*Ferd.*                    Their livers are more spotted
Than Laban's sheep.
*Duch.*                    Diamonds are of most value,
They say, that have pass'd through most jewellers' hands.                                             10
*Ferd.* Whores by that rule are precious.
*Duch.*                    Will you hear me?
I 'll never marry.
*Card.*          So most widows say;
But commonly that motion lasts no longer
Than the turning of an hour-glass: the funeral sermon
And it end both together.
*Ferd.*                    Now hear me:     15
You live in a rank pasture, here, i' th' court;
There is a kind of honey-dew that 's deadly;
'T will poison your fame; look to 't. Be not cunning;
For they whose faces do belie their hearts
Are witches ere they arrive at twenty years, 20
Ay, and give the devil suck.
*Duch.* This is terrible good counsel.
*Ferd.* Hypocrisy is woven of a fine small thread,
Subtler than Vulcan's engine: yet, believe 't,
Your darkest actions, nay, your privat'st thoughts,                                                   25
Will come to light.
*Card.*                    You may flatter yourself,
And take your own choice; privately be married
Under the eaves of night ——
*Ferd.*                    Think 't the best voyage
That e'er you made; like the irregular crab,
Which, though 't goes backward, thinks that it goes right                                             30
Because it goes its own way: but observe,
Such weddings may more properly be said
To be executed than celebrated.
*Card.*                    The marriage night
Is the entrance into some prison.
*Ferd.*                    And those joys,
Those lustful pleasures, are like heavy sleeps 35
Which do fore-run man's mischief.
*Card.*                    Fare you well.
Wisdom begins at the end: remember it.
                                          [*Exit.*]

---

¹⁹³ **angels:** gold coins     ¹⁹⁵ **to:** (not in Qq. 1-3)     ²⁰⁵ **vild:** vile     ²⁰⁶ **complimental:** gracious
Scene III: (No indication of new scene in Qq.)     ⁷ **luxurious:** lustful     ⁸ **Will:** who will     **livers:**
supposed seat of passions     ⁹ **Laban's sheep:** (cf. *Genesis*, ch. 30; *Merchant of Venice*, I. iii. 72 ff.)
¹³ **motion:** resolution     ²⁴ **engine:** the fine net in which he entrapped Mars     ²⁸ **Under . . . night·**
skulkingly     ³⁷ **Wisdom . . . end:** (cf. Solon's advice to Crœsus)

*Duch.* I think this speech between you both
    was studied,
It came so roundly off.
    *Ferd.*                    You are my sister;
This was my father's poniard, do you see?    40
I 'd be loath to see 't look rusty, 'cause 't was
    his.
I would have you to give o'er these chargeable
    revels:
A vizor and a mask are whispering-rooms
That were never built for goodness. Fare ye
    well —
And women like that part which, like the
    lamprey,                                    45
Hath never a bone in 't.
    *Duch.*                    Fie, sir!
    *Ferd.*                    Nay,
I mean the tongue: variety of courtship.
What cannot a neat knave with a smooth
    tale
Make a woman believe? Farewell, lusty widow.
                                    [*Exit.*]
    *Duch.* Shall this move me? If all my royal
        kindred                                50
Lay in my way unto this marriage,
I 'd make them my low footsteps. And even
    now,
Even in this hate, as men in some great battles,
By apprehending danger, have achiev'd
Almost impossible actions (I have heard
    soldiers say so),                          55
So I through frights and threat'nings will assay
This dangerous venture. Let old wives re-
    port
I wink'd and chose a husband. — Cariola,
To thy known secrecy I have given up
More than my life, — my fame.
    *Cari.*                    Both shall be safe;  60
For I 'll conceal this secret from the world
As warily as those that trade in poison
Keep poison from their children.
    *Duch.*                    Thy protestation
Is ingenious and hearty; I believe it.
Is Antonio come?
    *Cari.*                    He attends you.
    *Duch.*                    Good dear soul,  65
Leave me; but place thyself behind the
    arras,
Where thou may'st overhear us. Wish me good
    speed;
For I am going into a wilderness,
Where I shall find nor path nor friendly clue
To be my guide.
            [*Cariola goes behind the arras.*]

        [*Enter Antonio*]

            I sent for you: sit down;  70
Take pen and ink, and write. Are you ready?
    *Ant.*                    Yes.
    *Duch.* What did I say?
    *Ant.*        That I should write somewhat.
    *Duch.*                    O, I remember.
After these triumphs and this large expense
It 's fit, like thrifty husbands, we inquire   75
What 's laid up for to-morrow.
    *Ant.* So please your beauteous excellence.
    *Duch.*                    Beauteous!
Indeed, I thank you. I look young for your
    sake;
You have ta'en my cares upon you.
    *Ant.*                    I 'll fetch your grace
The particulars of your revenue and expense.  80
    *Duch.*                    O, you are
An upright treasurer, but you mistook;
For when I said I meant to make inquiry
What 's laid up for to-morrow, I did mean
What 's laid up yonder for me.
    *Ant.*                    Where?
    *Duch.*                    In heaven.  85
I am making my will (as 't is fit princes should,
In perfect memory), and, I pray, sir, tell me,
Were not one better make it smiling, thus,
Than in deep groans and terrible ghastly looks,
As if the gifts we parted with procur'd       90
That violent distraction?
    *Ant.*                    O, much better.
    *Duch.* If I had a husband now, this care were
        quit:
But I intend to make you overseer.
What good deed shall we first remember?
    Say.
    *Ant.* Begin with that first good deed began
        i' th' world.                          95
After man's creation, the sacrament of mar-
    riage.
I 'd have you first provide for a good husband:
Give him all.
    *Duch.*        All!
    *Ant.*                    Yes, your excellent self.
    *Duch.* In a winding-sheet?
    *Ant.*                    In a couple.
    *Duch.* Saint Winfrid, that were a strange
        will!                                 100
    *Ant.* 'T were stranger if there were no will
        in you
To marry again.
    *Duch.*        What do you think of marriage?
    *Ant.* I take 't, as those that deny purgatory:

---

⁴² **to:** (not in Qq. 2–3)    **chargeable:** expensive    ⁴⁵ **lamprey:** eel-like fish    ⁵² **footsteps:** stepping stones    ⁵⁸ **wink'd:** closed both eyes    ⁶⁴ **ingenious:** ingenuous    ⁷³ **somewhat:** something
⁷⁴ **triumphs:** celebrations    ⁷⁵ **husbands:** economists    ⁹⁰ **procur'd:** were the cause of    ⁹² **quit:** removed    ⁹⁵ **began:** which began **first . . . began:** ('good deed that first began' Qq. 2–3)    ¹⁰⁰ **Win-
frid:** Boniface, an English saint (There was also a lady-saint, Winifred.)    ¹⁰¹ **stranger:** ('strange' Qq.)

It locally contains or heaven or hell;
There 's no third place in 't.
    *Duch.*            How do you affect it? 105
    *Ant.* My banishment, feeding my melancholy,
Would often reason thus: —
    *Duch.*            Pray, let 's hear it.
    *Ant.* Say a man never marry, nor have
children,
What takes that from him? Only the bare
name
Of being a father, or the weak delight     110
To see the little wanton ride a-cock-horse
Upon a painted stick, or hear him chatter
Like a taught starling.
    *Duch.*        Fie, fie, what 's all this?
One of your eyes is blood-shot; use my ring
to 't.
They say 't is very sovereign. 'T was my wed-
ding-ring,     115
And I did vow never to part with it
But to my second husband.
    *Ant.* You have parted with it now.
    *Duch.* Yes, to help your eye-sight.
    *Ant.* You have made me stark blind.
    *Duch.*             How? 120
    *Ant.* There is a saucy and ambitious devil
Is dancing in this circle.
    *Duch.*           Remove him.
    *Ant.*               How?
    *Duch.* There needs small conjuration, when
your finger
May do it: thus. Is it fit?
        [*She puts the ring upon his finger;*]
        *he kneels.*
    *Ant.*           What said you?
    *Duch.*               Sir,
This goodly roof of yours is too low built;   125
I cannot stand upright in 't nor discourse,
Without I raise it higher. Raise yourself;
Or, if you please my hand to help you: so!
            [*Raises him.*]
    *Ant.* Ambition, madam, is a great man's
madness,
That is not kept in chains and close-pent rooms,
But in fair lightsome lodgings, and is girt   131
With the wild noise of prattling visitants,
Which makes it lunatic beyond all cure.
Conceive not I am so stupid but I aim
Whereto your favours tend: but he 's a fool 135
That, being a-cold, would thrust his hands i'
th' fire
To warm them.
    *Duch.*       So, now the ground 's broke,
You may discover what a wealthy mine
I make you lord of.

    *Ant.*           O my unworthiness!
    *Duch.* You were ill to sell yourself:   140
This dark'ning of your worth is not like that
Which tradesmen use i' th' city; their false
lights
Are to rid bad wares off: and I must tell you,
If you will know where breathes a complete
man
(I speak it without flattery), turn your eyes, 145
And progress through yourself.
    *Ant.* Were there nor heaven nor hell,
I should be honest: I have long serv'd virtue,
And never ta'en wages of her.
    *Duch.*         Now she pays it.
The misery of us that are born great!   150
We are forc'd to woo, because none dare woo us;
And as a tyrant doubles with his words
And fearfully equivocates, so we
Are forc'd to express our violent passions
In riddles and in dreams, and leave the path 155
Of simple virtue, which was never made
To seem the thing it is not. Go, go brag
You have left me heartless; mine is in your
bosom:
I hope 't will multiply love there. You do
tremble:
Make not your heart so dead a piece of flesh, 160
To fear more than to love me. Sir, be confi-
dent:
What is 't distracts you? This is flesh and
blood, sir;
'T is not the figure cut in alablaster
Kneels at my husband's tomb. Awake, awake,
man!
I do here put off all vain ceremony,   165
And only do appear to you a young widow
That claims you for her husband, and, like a
widow,
I use but half a blush in 't.
    *Ant.*         Truth speak for me:
I will remain the constant sanctuary
Of your good name.
    *Duch.*      I thank you, gentle love: 170
And 'cause you shall not come to me in debt,
(Being now my steward) here upon your lips
I sign your *Quietus est.* This you should have
begg'd now.
I have seen children oft eat sweetmeats thus,
As fearful to devour them too soon.   175
    *Ant.* But for your brothers?
    *Duch.*       Do not think of them:
All discord without this circumference
Is only to be pitied, and not fear'd:
Yet, should they know it, time will easily
Scatter the tempest.

---

    [104] **locally:** within itself    **or . . . or:** either . . . or    [115] **sovereign:** efficacious    [122] **circle: the ring**    [134] **but I aim:** as not to guess    [140] **were ill:** would be ill-fitted    [146] **progress:** make a royal journey    [152] **doubles:** speaks ambiguously    [163] **alablaster:** alabaster (used for funeral monuments)    [173] **Quietus est:** acquittance    [177] **without . . . circumference:** outside this room

*Ant.* These words should be mine, 180
And all the parts you have spoke, if some part
of it
Would not have savour'd flattery.
*Duch.* Kneel.
[*Cariola comes from behind the arras.*]
*Ant.* Ha!
*Duch.* Be not amaz'd: this woman 's of my
counsel.
I have heard lawyers say, a contract in a cham-
ber
*Per verba [de] presenti* is absolute marriage. 185
[*She and Antonio kneel.*]
Bless, heaven, this sacred Gordian, which let
violence
Never untwine.
*Ant.* And may our sweet affections, like the
spheres,
Be still in motion!
*Duch.* Quick'ning, and make
The like soft music! 190
*Ant.* That we may imitate the loving palms,
Best emblem of a peaceful marriage,
That never bore fruit, divided!
*Duch.* What can the church force more?
*Ant.* That fortune may not know an acci-
dent, 195
Either of joy or sorrow, to divide
Our fixed wishes!
*Duch.* How can the church build faster?
We now are man and wife, and 't is the church
That must but echo this. — Maid, stand apart:
I now am blind.
*Ant.* What 's your conceit in this? 200
*Duch.* I would have you lead your fortune
by the hand
Unto your marriage-bed:
(You speak in me this, for we now are one).
We 'll only lie and talk together, and plot
T' appease my humorous kindred; and if you
please, 205
Like the old tale in *Alexander and Lodowick*,
Lay a naked sword between us, keep us chaste.
O, let me shroud my blushes in your bosom,
Since 't is the treasury of all my secrets!
[*Exeunt Duchess and Antonio.*]
*Cari.* Whether the spirit of greatness or of
woman 210
Reign most in her, I know not; but it shows
A fearful madness. I owe her much of pity.
*Exit.*

ACTUS II. SCENA I

[*The Palace, Amalfi.*]

[*Enter*] Bosola and Castruchio

*Bos.* You say you would fain be taken for an
eminent courtier?
*Cast.* 'T is the very main of my ambition.
*Bos.* Let me see: you have a reasonable good
face for 't already, and your night-cap expresses
your ears sufficient largely. I would have you [5
learn to twirl the strings of your band with a
good grace, and in a set speech, at th' end of
every sentence, to hum three or four times, or
blow your nose till it smart again, to recover
your memory. When you come to be a presi- [10
dent in criminal causes, if you smile upon a
prisoner, hang him; but if you frown upon him
and threaten him, let him be sure to scape the
gallows.
*Cast.* I would be a very merry president. 15
*Bos.* Do not sup o' nights; 't will beget you
an admirable wit.
*Cast.* Rather it would make me have a good
stomach to quarrel; for they say, your roaring
boys eat meat seldom, and that makes them so
valiant. But how shall I know whether the [20
people take me for an eminent fellow?
*Bos.* I will teach a trick to know it: give out
you lie a-dying, and if you hear the common
people curse you, be sure you are taken for one
of the prime night-caps. 25

[*Enter an Old Lady*]

You come from painting now.
*Old Lady.* From what?
*Bos.* Why, from your scurvy face-physic. To
behold thee not painted inclines somewhat near
a miracle. These in thy face here were deep ruts
and foul sloughs the last progress. There was [31
a lady in France that, having had the small-pox,
flayed the skin off her face to make it more level;
and whereas before she looked like a nutmeg-
grater, after she resembled an abortive hedge-
hog.
*Old Lady.* Do you call this painting? 36
*Bos.* No, no, but I call it careening of an old
morphew'd lady, to make her disembogue again:
there 's rough-cast phrase to your plastic.
*Old Lady.* It seems you are well acquainted [40
with my closet.
*Bos.* One would suspect it for a shop of witch-

---

¹⁸² **savour'd:** smacked of    ¹⁸⁵ **Per . . . presenti:** (using the present tense, not the future)
¹⁸⁶ **Gordian:** knot    ¹⁸⁹ **still:** constantly    **Quick'ning:** giving life    ¹⁹⁷ **faster:** more solidly
²⁰⁰ **conceit:** idea    ²⁰⁵ **humorous:** hard to please    ²⁰⁶ **Alexander and Lodowick:** a ballad version of
the mediæval romance of Amis and Amiloun    ²⁰⁸ **shrowd:** cover    ²¹² S. D. **Exit:** ('Exeunt' Qq.)
S. D. (Qq. list: 'Bosola, Castruchio, an Old Lady, Antonio, Delio, Dutchesse, Rodorico, Grisolan.')
² **main:** object    ⁴ **night-cap:** the coif, or lawn cap, worn by lawyers    ¹⁸ **stomach:** disposition
¹⁸–¹⁹ **roaring boys:** bullies    ²⁵ **night-caps:** lawyers    ³⁷ **I:** ('you' Qq).    **it:** (not in Q 1–2)    **careening:** turning (a ship) on its side for scraping    ³⁸ **morphew'd:** covered with scurf    **disembogue:** put
out to sea    ³⁹ **plastic:** facial surgery

craft, to find in it the fat of serpents, spawn of
snakes, Jews' spittle, and their young children's
ordure: and all these for the face. I would [45
sooner eat a dead pigeon taken from the soles
of the feet of one sick of the plague, than kiss
one of you fasting. Here are two of you, whose
sin of your youth is the very patrimony of the
physician; makes him renew his foot-cloth [50
with the spring, and change his high-pric'd
courtesan with the fall of the leaf. I do wonder
you do not loathe yourselves. Observe my meditation now:

What thing is in this outward form of man  55
To be belov'd? We account it ominous,
If nature do produce a colt, or lamb,
A fawn, or goat, in any limb resembling
A man, and fly from 't as a prodigy.
Man stands amaz'd to see his deformity     60
In any other creature but himself.
But in our own flesh though we bear diseases
Which have their true names only ta'en from
    beasts, —
As the most ulcerous wolf and swinish measle,—
Though we are eaten up of lice and worms,  65
And though continually we bear about us
A rotten and dead body, we delight
To hide it in rich tissue: all our fear,
Nay, all our terror, is, lest our physician  69
Should put us in the ground to be made sweet.—
Your wife 's gone to Rome: you two couple,
and get you to the wells at Lucca to recover
your aches. I have other work on foot.

*[Exeunt Castruchio and Old Lady]*

I observe our duchess                         74
Is sick a-days, she pukes, her stomach seethes,
The fins of her eye-lids look most teeming blue,
She wanes i' th' cheek, and waxes fat i' th'
    flank,
And, contrary to our Italian fashion,
Wears a loose-bodied gown: there 's somewhat
    in 't.
I have a trick may chance discover it,       80
A pretty one: I have bought some apricocks,
The first our spring yields.

*[Enter Antonio and Delio, talking together
apart]*

*Delio.*          And so long since married?
You amaze me.
    *Ant.*          Let me seal your lips for ever:
For, did I think that anything but th' air
Could carry these words from you, I should
    wish                                      85

You had no breath at all. — Now, sir, in your
    contemplation?
You are studying to become a great wise fellow.
    *Bos.* O, sir, the opinion of wisdom is a foul
tetter that runs all over a man's body: if simplicity direct us to have no evil, it directs us [90
to a happy being; for the subtlest folly proceeds
from the subtlest wisdom. Let me be simply
honest.
    *Ant.* I do understand your inside.
    *Bos.*                              Do you so?
    *Ant.* Because you would not seem to appear
    to th' world                             95
Puff'd up with your preferment, you continue
This out-of-fashion melancholy: leave it, leave
    it.
    *Bos.* Give me leave to be honest in any
phrase, in any compliment whatsoever. Shall I
confess myself to you? I look no higher than [100
I can reach: they are the gods that must ride
on winged horses. A lawyer's mule of a slow
pace will both suit my disposition and business;
for, mark me, when a man's mind rides faster
than his horse can gallop, they quickly both [105
tire.
    *Ant.* You would look up to heaven, but I
    think
The devil, that rules i' th' air, stands in your
    light.
    *Bos.* O, sir, you are lord of the ascendant,
chief man with the duchess: a duke was your [110
cousin-german remov'd. Say you were lineally
descended from King Pepin, or he himself, what
of this? Search the heads of the greatest rivers
in the world, you shall find them but bubbles of
water. Some would think the souls of princes [115
were brought forth by some more weighty cause
than those of meaner persons: they are deceiv'd,
there 's the same hand to them; the like
passions sway them; the same reason that
makes a vicar go to law for a tithe-pig, and [120
undo his neighbours, makes them spoil a whole
province, and batter down goodly cities with
the cannon.

*[Enter Duchess and Ladies]*

    *Duch.* Your arm, Antonio: do I not grow fat?
I am exceeding short-winded. — Bosola,     125
I would have you, sir, provide me a litter;
Such a one as the Duchess of Florence rode in.
    *Bos.* The duchess us'd one when she was
    great with child.
    *Duch.* I think she did. — Come hither, mend
    my ruff:                                 129

---

⁵⁰ **foot-cloth:** ornamental trappings for saddle-animal    ⁶⁴ **wolf:** a tubercular affection of the nose,
known as "lupus"    **measle:** a disease of hogs    ⁷² **recover:** cure    ⁷⁶ **teeming:** as in pregnancy
⁸⁸ **opinion:** repute    ⁸⁹ **tetter:** eruption    ⁸⁹⁻⁹⁰ **simplicity:** foolishness    ¹⁰⁹ **ascendant:** the first
astrological "house," controlling destiny    ¹¹¹ **cousin . . . remov'd:** first cousin once removed
¹²⁹ **mend:** arrange

Here, when? thou art such a tedious lady; and
Thy breath smells of lemon-peels: would thou
   hadst done!
Shall I sound under thy fingers? I am
So troubled with the mother!
   *Bos.* [*Aside.*]           I fear, too much.
   *Duch.* I have heard you say that the French
   courtiers
Wear their hats on 'fore the king.     135
   *Ant.* I have seen it.
   *Duch.*          In the presence?
   *Ant.*                Yes.
   *Duch.* Why should not we bring up that
   fashion?
'T is ceremony more than duty that consists
In the removing of a piece of felt.
Be you the example to the rest o' th' court; 140
Put on your hat first.
   *Ant.*          You must pardon me:
I have seen, in colder countries than in France,
Nobles stand bare to th' prince; and the distinc-
   tion
Methought show'd reverently.
   *Bos.* I have a present for your grace.
   *Duch.*          For me, sir? 145
   *Bos.* Apricocks, madam.
   *Duch.*       O, sir, where are they?
I have heard of none to-year.
   *Bos.* [*Aside.*]   Good; her colour rises.
   *Duch.* Indeed, I thank you: they are won-
   drous fair ones.
What an unskilful fellow is our gardener!
We shall have none this month.     150
   *Bos.* Will not your grace pare them?
   *Duch.* No: they taste of musk, methinks;
   indeed they do.
   *Bos.* I know not: yet I wish your grace had
   par'd 'em.
   *Duch.* Why?
   *Bos.* I forgot to tell you, the knave gardener,
(Only to raise his profit by them the sooner) 156
Did ripen them in horse-dung.
   *Duch.*         O, you jest. —
You shall judge: pray, taste one.
   *Ant.*            Indeed, madam,
I do not love the fruit.
   *Duch.*        Sir, you are loath
To rob us of our dainties. 'T is a delicate fruit;
They say they are restorative.
   *Bos.*          'T is a pretty art, 161
This grafting.
   *Duch.* 'T is so; a bettering of nature.
   *Bos.* To make a pippin grow upon a crab,

A damson on a black-thorn. — [*Aside.*] How
   greedily she eats them!
A whirlwind strike off these bawd-farthingales!
For, but for that and the loose-bodied gown, 166
I should have discover'd apparently
The young springal cutting a caper in her belly.
   *Duch.* I thank you, Bosola: they were right
   good ones,
If they do not make me sick.
   *Ant.*          How now, madam! 170
   *Duch.* This green fruit and my stomach are
   not friends:
How they swell me!
   *Bos.* [*Aside.*] Nay, you are too much swell'd
   already.
   *Duch.* O, I am in an extreme cold sweat!
   *Bos.*         I am very sorry. [*Exit.*]
   *Duch.* Lights to my chamber! — O good An-
   tonio,                175
I fear I am undone!
   *Delio.*        Lights there, lights!
               *Exit Duchess* [*with Ladies*].
   *Ant.* O my most trusty Delio, we are lost!
I fear she 's fall'n in labour; and there 's left
No time for her remove.
   *Delio.*        Have you prepar'd
Those ladies to attend her; and procur'd  180
That politic safe conveyance for the midwife
Your duchess plotted?
   *Ant.*          I have.
   *Delio.* Make use, then, of this forc'd occa-
   sion.
Give out that Bosola hath poison'd her
With these apricocks; that will give some
   colour                 185
For her keeping close.
   *Ant.*        Fie, fie, the physicians
Will then flock to her.
   *Delio.* For that you may pretend
She 'll use some prepar'd antidote of her own,
Lest the physicians should re-poison her.  190
   *Ant.* I am lost in amazement: I know not
what to think on 't.            *Exeunt.*

SCENA II. — [*A gallery in the same.*]

*Bosola* [*and a little later*] *Old Lady*

   *Bos.* So, so, there 's no question but her techiness and most vulturous eating of the apricocks are apparent signs of breeding. — Now?
   *Old Lady.* I am in haste, sir.
   *Bos.* There was a young waiting-woman had
a monstrous desire to see the glass-house —— 6

---

  **130 when:** impatient expletive    **131 lemon-peels:** chewed to counteract bad breath    **132 sound:**
swoon   **133 mother:** hysteria   **144 Methought:** ('My thought' Qq.)   **147 to-year:** this year   **163 crab:**
crab-apple   **165 farthingales:** hooped skirts   **167 apparently:** manifestly   **168 springal:** youth
Scene ii. s. d. (Qq. list: 'Bosola, old Lady, Antonio, Roderigo, Grisolan: seruants, Delio, Cariola.')
**1-2 techiness:** irritability   **6 glass-house:** (A glass-factory near Blackfriars was one of the sights of
London.)

*Old Lady.* Nay, pray, let me go.

*Bos.* And it was only to know what strange instrument it was should swell up a glass to the fashion of a woman's belly. 10

*Old Lady.* I will hear no more of the glass-house. You are still abusing women!

*Bos.* Who? I? No; only (by the way now and then) mention your frailties. The orange-tree bears ripe and green fruit and blossoms all [15 together; and some of you give entertainment for pure love, but more for more precious reward. The lusty spring smells well; but drooping autumn tastes well. If we have the same golden showers that rained in the time of [20 Jupiter the thunderer, you have the same Danaës still, to hold up their laps to receive them. Didst thou never study the mathematics?

*Old Lady.* What 's that, sir? 25

*Bos.* Why, to know the trick how to make a many lines meet in one centre. Go, go, give your foster-daughters good counsel: tell them, that the devil takes delight to hang at a woman's girdle, like a false rusty watch, that [30 she cannot discern how the time passes.

[*Exit Old Lady.*]

[*Enter Antonio, Roderigo, and Grisolan*]

*Ant.* Shut up the court-gates.

*Rod.*            Why, sir? What 's the danger?

*Ant.* Shut up the posterns presently, and call
All the officers o' th' court.

*Gris.*            I shall instantly. [*Exit.*]

*Ant.* Who keeps the key o' th' park-gate?

*Rod.*            Forobosco. 35

*Ant.* Let him bring 't presently.

[*Re-enter Grisolan with Servants*]

1 *Serv.* O, gentlemen o' th' court, the foulest treason!

*Bos.* [*Aside.*] If that these apricocks should be poison'd now,
Without my knowledge!

1 *Serv.* There was taken even now a Switzer in the duchess' bed-chamber —— 40

2 *Serv.* A Switzer!

1 *Serv.* With a pistol in his great codpiece.

*Bos.* Ha, ha, ha!

1 *Serv.* The codpiece was the case for 't.

2 *Serv.* There was a cunning traitor. Who would have search'd his codpiece? 46

1 *Serv.* True; if he had kept out of the ladies' chambers. And all the moulds of his buttons were leaden bullets.

2 *Serv.* O wicked cannibal! A fire-lock in 's codpiece! 50

1 *Serv.* 'T was a French plot, upon my life.

2 *Serv.* To see what the devil can do!

*Ant.* All the officers here?

*Servants.* We are.

*Ant.* Gentlemen, 55
We have lost much plate, you know; and but this evening
Jewels, to the value of four thousand ducats,
Are missing in the duchess' cabinet.
Are the gates shut?

*Serv.*            Yes.

*Ant.*            'T is the duchess' pleasure
Each officer be lock'd into his chamber 60
Till the sun-rising; and to send the keys
Of all their chests and of their outward doors
Into her bed-chamber. She is very sick.

*Rod.* At her pleasure.

*Ant.* She entreats you take 't not ill: the innocent 65
Shall be the more approv'd by it.

*Bos.* Gentleman o' th' wood-yard, where 's your Switzer now?

1 *Serv.* By this hand, 't was credibly reported by one o' th' black guard. 70

[*Exeunt all except Antonio and Delio.*]

*Delio.* How fares it with the duchess?

*Ant.* She 's expos'd
Unto the worst of torture, pain and fear.

*Delio.* Speak to her all happy comfort.

*Ant.* How I do play the fool with mine own danger!
You are this night, dear friend, to post to Rome: 75
My life lies in your service.

*Delio.*            Do not doubt me.

*Ant.* O, 't is far from me: and yet fear presents me
Somewhat that looks like danger.

*Delio.*            Believe it,
'T is but the shadow of your fear, no more.
How superstitiously we mind our evils! 80
The throwing down salt, or crossing of a hare,
Bleeding at nose, the stumbling of a horse,
Or singing of a cricket, are of power
To daunt whole man in us. Sir, fare you well:
I wish you all the joys of a bless'd father; 85
And (for my faith) lay this unto your breast:
Old friends, like old swords, still are trusted best.            [*Exit.*]

[*Enter Cariola*]

*Cari.* Sir, you are the happy father of a son:
Your wife commends him to you.

*Ant.*            Blessed comfort! —
For heaven' sake, tend her well: I 'll presently
Go set a figure for 's nativity.            *Exeunt.* 91

⁵³ officers: ('Offices' Q 1)      ⁶⁶ approv'd: vindicated      ⁷⁰ black guard: scullions      ⁸⁴ whole
man: all manhood      ⁹¹ set a figure: cast a horoscope

SCENA III. — [*The same.*]

*Bosola,* [*with a dark lantern, and later*] *Antonio*

*Bos.* Sure I did hear a woman shriek: list, ha!
And the sound came, if I receiv'd it right,
From the duchess' lodgings. There's some stratagem
In the confining all our courtiers
To their several wards: I must have part of it;
My intelligence will freeze else. List, again! 6
It may be 't was the melancholy bird,
Best friend of silence and of solitariness,
The owl, that scream'd so. — Ha! Antonio!

[*Enter Antonio with a candle, his sword drawn*]

*Ant.* I heard some noise. — Who's there?
What art thou? Speak. 10
*Bos.* Antonio? put not your face nor body
To such a forc'd expression of fear:
I am Bosola, your friend.
*Ant.* Bosola? —
[*Aside.*] This mole does undermine me. —
Heard you not
A noise even now?
*Bos.* From whence?
*Ant.* From the duchess' lodging. 15
*Bos.* Not I: did you?
*Ant.* I did, or else I dream'd.
*Bos.* Let's walk towards it.
*Ant.* No: it may be 't was
But the rising of the wind.
*Bos.* Very likely.
Methinks 't is very cold, and yet you sweat:
You look wildly.
*Ant.* I have been setting a figure 20
For the duchess' jewels.
*Bos.* Ah, and how falls your question?
Do you find it radical?
*Ant.* What's that to you?
'T is rather to be question'd what design,
When all men were commanded to their lodgings,
Makes you a night-walker.
*Bos.* In sooth, I'll tell you: 25
Now all the court's asleep, I thought the devil
Had least to do here. I came to say my prayers;
And if it do offend you I do so,
You are a fine courtier.
*Ant.* [*Aside.*] This fellow will undo me! —

You gave the duchess apricocks to-day: 30
Pray heaven they were not poison'd!
*Bos.* Poison'd! a Spanish fig
For the imputation!
*Ant.* Traitors are ever confident
Till they are discover'd. There were jewels stol'n too:
In my conceit, none are to be suspected 35
More than yourself.
*Bos.* You are a false steward.
*Ant.* Saucy slave, I'll pull thee up by the roots.
*Bos.* May be the ruin will crush you to pieces.
*Ant.* You are an impudent snake indeed, sir:
Are you scarce warm, and do you show your sting? 40
You libel well, sir?
*Bos.* No, sir: copy it out,
And I will set my hand to 't.
*Ant.* [*Aside.*] My nose bleeds.
One that were superstitious would count
This ominous, when it merely comes by chance.
Two letters, that are wrought here for my name, 45
Are drown'd in blood!
Mere accident. — For you, sir, I'll take order.
I' th' morn you shall be safe. — [*Aside.*] 'T is that must colour
Her lying-in. — Sir, this door you pass not:
I do not hold it fit that you come near 50
The duchess' lodgings, till you have quit yourself. —
[*Aside.*] The great are like the base; nay, they are the same,
When they seek shameful ways to avoid shame.
*Exit.*

*Bos.* Antonio hereabout did drop a paper: —
Some of your help, false friend. — O, here it is.
What's here? a child's nativity calculated! 56
[*Reads.*]
'*The duchess was deliver'd of a son, 'tween the hours twelve and one in the night, Anno Dom. 1504.*' — that's this year — '*decimo nono Decembris,*' — that's this night — '*taken ac-* [60 *cording to the meridian of Malfi,*' — that's our duchess: happy discovery! — '*The lord of the first house being combust in the ascendant signifies short life; and Mars being in a human sign, joined to the tail of the Dragon, in the eight* [65 *house, doth threaten a violent death. Cætera non scrutantur.*'

---

⁵ **have part:** be informed    ²² **radical:** capable of astrological solution    ²⁸ **I:** that I    ³⁵ **conceit:** opinion    ⁴¹ **libel:** write out charges(?)    (Possibly a speech by Bosola following line 40 has been lost.)
⁴⁵ **letters:** embroidered initials on his handkerchief    ⁴⁸ **safe:** under guard    ⁵¹ **quit:** exonerated
⁵⁵ **false friend:** the lantern    ⁶²⁻⁶³ **lord . . . house:** planet controlling birth    ⁶³ **combust:** so near the sun as to lose its beneficent effect    ⁶⁴ **human sign:** sign of the Zodiac called by a human name (Aquarius, Gemini, Virgo, Sagittarius)    ⁶⁵ **tail . . . Dragon:** where the descending moon crossed the Ecliptic    **eight:** eighth    ⁶⁶ **Cætera, etc.:** the other omens are not examined

Why now 't is most apparent; this precise fel-
    low
Is the duchess' bawd: — I have it to my wish!
This is a parcel of intelligency                    70
Our courtiers were cas'd up for.  It needs must
    follow
That I must be committed on pretence
Of poisoning her; which I 'll endure, and laugh
    at.
If one could find the father now! but that
Time will discover.  Old Castruchio                    75
I' th' morning posts to Rome: by him I 'll send
A letter that shall make her brothers' galls
O'erflow their livers.  This was a thrifty way!
Though Lust do mask in ne'er so strange dis-
    guise,
She 's oft found witty, but is never wise.                    80
                                 *[Exit.]*


SCENA IIII. — [*Rome: the Cardinal's Palace.*]

*Cardinal and Julia, [later] Servant, and Delio*

    *Card.*  Sit: thou art my best of wishes.  Pri-
    thee, tell me
What trick didst thou invent to come to Rome
Without thy husband?
    *Julia.*                    Why, my lord, I told him
I came to visit an old anchorite
Here for devotion.
    *Card.*          Thou art a witty false one, — 5
I mean, to him.
    *Julia.*                    You have prevail'd with me
Beyond my strongest thoughts; I would not
    now
Find you inconstant.
    *Card.*                    Do not put thyself
To such a voluntary torture, which proceeds
Out of your own guilt.
    *Julia.*                    How, my lord!
    *Card.*                    You fear 10
My constancy, because you have approv'd
Those giddy and wild turnings in yourself.
    *Julia.*  Did you e'er find them?
    *Card.*                    Sooth, generally for women,
A man might strive to make glass malleable,
Ere he should make them fixed.
    *Julia.*                    So, my lord. 15
    *Card.*  We had need go borrow that fantastic
    glass
Invented by Galileo, the Florentine,
To view another spacious world i' th' moon,
And look to find a constant woman there.
    *Julia.*  This is very well, my lord.
    *Card.*                    Why do you weep? 20

Are tears your justification?  The self-same
    tears
Will fall into your husband's bosom, lady,
With a loud protestation that you love him
Above the world.  Come, I 'll love you wisely,
That 's jealously; since I am very certain                    25
You cannot make me cuckold.
    *Julia.*                    I 'll go home
To my husband.
    *Card.*          You may thank me, lady.
I have taken you off your melancholy perch,
Bore you upon my fist, and show'd you game,
And let you fly at it. — I pray thee, kiss
    me. —                    30
When thou wast with thy husband, thou wast
    watch'd
Like a tame elephant: — still you are to thank
    me: —
Thou hadst only kisses from him and high
    feeding;
But what delight was that?  'T was just like one
That hath a little fing'ring on the lute,                    35
Yet cannot tune it: — still you are to thank
    me.
    *Julia.*  You told me of a piteous wound i' th'
    heart,
And a sick liver, when you woo'd me first,
And spake like one in physic.
    *Card.*                    Who 's that? ——
                 *[Enter Servant]*
Rest firm! for my affection to thee,                    40
Lightning moves slow to 't.
    *Serv.*                    Madam, a gentleman
That 's comes post from Malfi, desires to see
    you.
    *Card.*  Let him enter: I 'll withdraw.  *Exit.*
    *Serv.*                    He says
Your husband, old Castruchio, is come to
    Rome,
Most pitifully tir'd with riding post.  *[Exit.]* 45
               *[Enter Delio]*
    *Julia.* [*Aside.*]  Signior Delio! 't is one of
    my old suitors.
    *Delio.*  I was bold to come and see you.
    *Julia.*                    Sir, you are welcome.
    *Delio.*  Do you lie here?
    *Julia.*                    Sure, your own experience
Will satisfy you no: our Roman prelates
Do not keep lodging for ladies.
    *Delio.*                    Very well:                    50
I have brought you no commendations from
    your husband,
For I know none by him.
    *Julia.*                    I hear he 's come to Rome.

---

    **70 parcel:** piece    **78 thrifty:** shrewd    **4 anchorite:** hermit    **11 approv'd:** experienced    **16 fan-**
tastic glass: (anachronism: Galileo's telescope was invented in 1609.)    **26 make me:** ('me make' Q 1)
**28 perch, etc.:** figures from falconry    **35 hath:** has learned    **39 in physic:** under medical care
**40 Rest firm:** be assured    **48 lie:** lodge

*Delio.*  I never knew man and beast, of a
  horse and a knight,
So weary of each other.  If he had had a good
  back,
He would have undertook to have borne his
  horse,                                              55
His breech was so pitifully sore.
*Julia.*                            Your laughter
Is my pity.
*Delio.*  Lady, I know not whether
You want money, but I have brought you
  some.
*Julia.*  From my husband?
*Delio.*      No, from mine own allowance.    60
*Julia.*  I must hear the condition, ere I be
  bound to take it.
*Delio.*  Look on 't, 't is gold; hath it not a
  fine colour?
*Julia.*  I have a bird more beautiful.
*Delio.*                         Try the sound on 't.
*Julia.*  A lute-string far exceeds it.
It hath no smell, like cassia or civet;          65
Nor is it physical, though some fond doctors
Persuade us seethe 't in cullises.  I 'll tell you,
This is a creature bred by ——

                    [*Re-enter Servant*]

*Serv.*                Your husband 's come,
Hath deliver'd a letter to the Duke of Calabria
That, to my thinking, hath put him out of his
  wits.                                   [*Exit.*]  70
*Julia.*  Sir, you hear:
Pray, let me know your business and your suit
As briefly as can be.
*Delio.*  With good speed:  I would wish you
(At such time as you are non-resident        75
With your husband) my mistress.
*Julia.*  Sir, I 'll go ask my husband if I shall,
And straight return your answer.        *Exit.*
*Delio.*                                Very fine!
Is this her wit, or honesty, that speaks thus?
I heard one say the duke was highly mov'd    80
With a letter sent from Malfi.  I do fear
Antonio is betray'd.  How fearfully
Shows his ambition now!  Unfortunate fortune!
They pass through whirl-pools, and deep woes
  do shun,
Who the event weigh ere the action 's done.  85
                                           *Exit.*

           Scena V. — [*The Same.*]

      *Cardinal and Ferdinand with a letter*

*Ferd.*  I have this night digg'd up a mandrake.

*Card.*          Say you?
*Ferd.*  And I am grown mad with 't.
*Card.*                   What 's the prodigy?
*Ferd.*  Read there, — a sister damn'd: she 's
  loose i' th' hilts;
Grown a notorious strumpet.
*Card.*                     Speak lower.
*Ferd.*                                  Lower!
Rogues do not whisper 't now, but seek to pub-
  lish 't                                                5
(As servants do the bounty of their lords)
Aloud; and with a covetous searching eye,
To mark who note them.  O, confusion seize
  her!
She hath had most cunning bawds to serve her
  turn,
And more secure conveyances for lust        10
Than towns of garrison for service.
*Card.*                         Is 't possible?
Can this be certain?
*Ferd.*              Rhubarb!  O, for rhubarb
To purge this choler!  Here 's the cursed day
To prompt my memory; and here 't shall stick
Till of her bleeding heart I make a sponge    15
To wipe it out.
*Card.*           Why do you make yourself
So wild a tempest?
*Ferd.*            Would I could be one,
That I might toss her palace 'bout her ears,
Root up her goodly forests, blast her meads,
And lay her general territory as waste        20
As she hath done her honours.
*Card.*                    Shall our blood,
The royal blood of Arragon and Castile,
Be thus attainted?
*Ferd.*            Apply desperate physic:
We must not now use balsamum, but fire,
The smarting cupping-glass, for that 's the mean
To purge infected blood, such blood as hers. 26
There is a kind of pity in mine eye, —
I 'll give it to my handkercher; and now 't is
  here.
I 'll bequeath this to her bastard.
*Card.*                         What to do?
*Ferd.*  Why, to make soft lint for his moth-
  er's wounds,                                     30
When I have hew'd her to pieces.
*Card.*                       Curs'd creature!
Unequal nature, to place women's hearts
So far upon the left side!
*Ferd.*                 Foolish men,
That e'er will trust their honour in a bark
Made of so slight weak bulrush as is woman, 35
Apt every minute to sink it!

---

⁵³ **of:** namely    ⁶⁰ **allowance:** bounty    ⁶⁶ **physical:** curative    **fond:** foolish    ⁶⁷ **seethe 't:**
('seeth's' Q 1–2; 'seeth'd' Q 3)    **cullises:** broths    ¹ **mandrake:** poisonous root. supposed to have
supernatural powers    ⁷ **covetous:** ('coueteous' Q 1)    ¹² **Rhubarb:** supposed to alleviate the choleri.
'humour'    ¹⁶ **yourself:** for yourself    ²⁴ **balsamum:** balm    ²⁵ **cupping-glass:** receptacle for blood
³² **Unequal:** unjust    ³³ **left:** *i.e.,* the gauche or sinister side

*Card.* Thus ignorance, when it hath pur-
chas'd honour,
It cannot wield it.
    *Ferd.*      Methinks I see her laughing, —
Excellent hyena! Talk to me somewhat,
quickly,
Or my imagination will carry me      40
To see her in the shameful act of sin.
    *Card.* With whom?      [bargeman,
    *Ferd.*      Happily with some strong-thigh'd
Or one o' th' wood-yard that can quoit the
sledge
Or toss the bar, or else some lovely squire
That carries coals up to her privy lodgings. 45
    *Card.* You fly beyond your reason.
    *Ferd.*      Go to, mistress!
'T is not your whore's milk that shall quench
my wild-fire,
But your whore's blood.
    *Card.* How idly shows this rage, which
carries you,
As men convey'd by witches through the air, 50
On violent whirlwinds! This intemperate noise
Fitly resembles deaf men's shrill discourse,
Who talk aloud, thinking all other men
To have their imperfection.
    *Ferd.*      Have not you
My palsy?
    *Card.* Yes, yet I can be angry      55
Without this rupture. There is not in nature
A thing that makes man so deform'd, so beastly,
As doth intemperate anger. Chide yourself.
You have divers men who have not yet express'd
Their strong desire of rest but by unrest,      60
By vexing of themselves. Come, put yourself
In tune.
    *Ferd.* So I will only study to seem
The thing I am not. I could kill her now,
In you, or in myself; for I do think
It is some sin in us heaven doth revenge      65
By her.
    *Card.* Are you stark mad?
    *Ferd.*      I would have their bodies
Burnt in a coal-pit with the ventage stopp'd,
That their curs'd smoke might not ascend to
heaven;
Or dip the sheets they lie in in pitch or sulphur, 70
Wrap them in 't, and then light them like a
match;
Or else to boil their bastard to a cullis,
And give 't his lecherous father to renew
The sin of his back.
    *Card.*      I 'll leave you.
    *Ferd.*      Nay, I have done.
I am confident, had I been damn'd in hell,      75

And should have heard of this, it would have
put me
Into a cold sweat. In, in; I 'll go sleep.
Till I know who leaps my sister, I 'll not stir:
That known, I 'll find scorpions to string my
whips,
And fix her in a general eclipse.      *Exeunt.* 80

## ACTUS III. SCENA I

*[Amalfi: the Duchess's Palace.]*

*Antonio and Delio, [later,] Duchess, Ferdinand,
Bosola*

    *Ant.* Our noble friend, my most beloved
Delio!
O, you have been a stranger long at court.
Came you along with the Lord Ferdinand?
    *Delio.* I did, sir: and how fares your noble
duchess?
    *Ant.* Right fortunately well: she 's an excel-
lent      5
Feeder of pedigrees; since you last saw her,
She hath had two children more, a son and
daughter.
    *Delio.* Methinks 't was yesterday. Let me
but wink,
And not behold your face, which to mine eye
Is somewhat leaner, verily I should dream      10
It were within this half hour.
    *Ant.* You have not been in law, friend Delio,
Nor in prison, nor a suitor at the court,
Nor begg'd the reversion of some great man's
place,      14
Nor troubled with an old wife, which doth make
Your time so insensibly hasten.
    *Delio.*      Pray, sir, tell me,
Hath not this news arriv'd yet to the ear
Of the lord cardinal?
    *Ant.*      I fear it hath:
The Lord Ferdinand, that 's newly come to
court,
Doth bear himself right dangerously.
    *Delio.*      Pray, why? 20
    *Ant.* He is so quiet that he seems to sleep
The tempest out, as dormice do in winter.
Those houses that are haunted are most still,
Till the devil be up.
    *Delio.*      What say the common people?
    *Ant.* The common rabble do directly say 25
She is a strumpet.
    *Delio.*      And your graver heads
Which would be politic, what censure they?
    *Ant.* They do observe I grow to infinite pur-
chase,

---

⁴² **Happily:** perhaps    ⁴³ **o':** (not in Qq. 1–2)    **quoit the sledge:** throw the hammer    ⁵⁵ **yet:** (conj.
Brereton; not in Qq.)    ⁵⁶ **rupture:** flying to pieces    ⁶⁸ **ventage:** chimney    ⁷² **to boil:** (perhaps for
'to-boil,' boil down)    ⁸ **wink:** close my eyes    ¹⁵ **which:** (*i.e.,* the absence of these troubles)
⁹ **politic:** statesmanlike    **censure:** opine    ²⁶ **purchase:** wealth

The left-hand way; and all suppose the duchess
Would amend it, if she could; for, say they, 30
Great princes, though they grudge their officers
Should have such large and unconfined means
To get wealth under them, will not complain,
Lest thereby they should make them odious
Unto the people. For other obligation, 35
Of love or marriage between her and me,
They never dream of.
   *Delio.*           The Lord Ferdinand
Is going to bed.

*[Enter Duchess, Ferdinand, and Attendants]*

   *Ferd.*          I 'll instantly to bed,
For I am weary. — I am to bespeak
A husband for you.
   *Duch.*     For me, sir! Pray, who is 't? 40
   *Ferd.* The great Count Malateste.
   *Duch.*          Fie upon him!
A count! He's a mere stick of sugar-candy;
You may look quite thorough him. When I
  choose
A husband, I will marry for your honour.
   *Ferd.* You shall do well in 't. — How is 't,
  worthy Antonio? 45
   *Duch.* But, sir, I am to have private confer-
  ence with you
About a scandalous report is spread
Touching mine honour.
   *Ferd.*      Let me be ever deaf to 't:
One of Pasquil's paper-bullets, court-calumny,
A pestilent air, which princes' palaces 50
Are seldom purg'd of. Yet, say that it were
  true,
I pour it in your bosom, my fix'd love
Would strongly excuse, extenuate, nay, deny
Faults, were they apparent in you. Go, be safe
In your own innocency.
   *Duch. [Aside].*     O bless'd comfort! 55
This deadly air is purg'd.
   *Exeunt [Duchess, Antonio, Delio, and*
       *Attendants].*
   *Ferd.*        Her guilt treads on
Hot-burning coulters.

*[Enter Bosola]*

             Now, Bosola,
How thrives our intelligence?
   *Bos.*         Sir, uncertainly:
'T is rumour'd she hath had three bastards, but
By whom we may go read i' th' stars.
   *Ferd.*         Why, some 60
Hold opinion all things are written there.
   *Bos.* Yes, if we could find spectacles to read
them.

I do suspect there hath been some sorcery
Us d on the duchess.
   *Ferd.*        Sorcery! to what purpose?
   *Bos.* To make her dote on some desertless
  fellow 65
She shames to acknowledge.
   *Ferd.*      Can your faith give way
To think there 's power in potions or in charms,
To make us love whether we will or no?
   *Bos.* Most certainly.
   *Ferd.* Away! these are mere gulleries, hor-
  rid things, 70
Invented by some cheating mountebanks
To abuse us. Do you think that herbs or charms
Can force the will? Some trials have been made
In this foolish practice, but the ingredients
Were lenitive poisons, such as are of force 75
To make the patient mad; and straight the
  witch
Swears by equivocation they are in love.
The witchcraft lies in her rank blood. This
  night
I will force confession from her. You told me
You had got, within these two days, a false
  key 80
Into her bed-chamber.
   *Bos.*         I have.
   *Ferd.*          As I would wish.
   *Bos.* What do you intend to do?
   *Ferd.*         Can you guess?
   *Bos.*            No.
   *Ferd.*        Do not ask, then:
He that can compass me, and know my drifts,
May say he hath put a girdle 'bout the world,
And sounded all her quick-sands.
   *Bos.*        I do not 85
Think so.
   *Ferd.* What do you think, then, pray?
   *Bos.*           That you
Are your own chronicle too much, and grossly
Flatter yourself.
   *Ferd.*    Give me thy hand; I thank thee:
I never gave pension but to flatterers,
Till I entertained thee. Farewell. 90
That friend a great man's ruin strongly checks,
Who rails into his belief all his defects.
                *Exeunt.*

SCENA II. — *[The Duchess's Bed-chamber.]*

*Duchess, Antonio, Cariola, [and later]*
*Ferdinand, Bosola, Officers*

   *Duch.* Bring me the casket hither, and the
  glass. —
You get no lodging here to-night, my lord.

---

⁴⁹ **Pasquil**: nickname of a mutilated statue in Rome, to which invective verses were affixed
**paper-bullets**: lampoons  ⁵⁷ **coulters**: plow-blades  ⁵⁸ **intelligence**: detective work  ⁷⁰ **gulleries**:
deceits  ⁷⁵ **lenitive**: softening, reducing will-power  ⁷⁸ **rank**: wanton  ⁸³ **compass**: comprehend
**drifts**: purposes

*Ant.*  Indeed, I must persuade one.
*Duch.*                                           Very good:
I hope in time 't will grow into a custom,
That noblemen shall come with cap and knee  5
To purchase a night's lodging of their wives.
  *Ant.*  I must lie here.
  *Duch.*  Must! You are a lord of mis-rule.
  *Ant.*  Indeed, my rule is only in the night.
  *Duch.*  To what use will you put me?
  *Ant.*                           We 'll sleep together.
  *Duch.*  Alas, what pleasure can two lovers
    find in sleep?                               10
  *Cari.*  My lord, I lie with her often, and I
    know
She 'll much disquiet you.
  *Ant.*                  See, you are complain'd of.
  *Cari.*  For she 's the sprawling'st bedfellow.
  *Ant.*  I shall like her the better for that.
  *Cari.*  Sir, shall I ask you a question?       15
  *Ant.*  I pray thee, Cariola.
  *Cari.*  Wherefore still when you lie with my
    lady
Do you rise so early?
  *Ant.*               Labouring men
Count the clock oft'nest, Cariola,
Are glad when their task 's ended.
  *Duch.*  I 'll stop your mouth. [*Kisses him.*]  20
  *Ant.*  Nay, that 's but one; Venus had two
    soft doves
To draw her chariot: I must have another. —
                        [*She kisses him again.*]
When wilt thou marry, Cariola?
  *Cari.*                         Never, my lord.
  *Ant.*  O, fie upon this single life! forgo it.
We read how Daphne, for her peevish slight,
Became a fruitless bay-tree; Syrinx turn'd  26
To the pale empty reed; Anaxarete
Was frozen into marble: whereas those
Which married, or prov'd kind unto their
    friends,
Were by a gracious influence trans-shap'd  30
Into the olive, pomegranate, mulberry,
Became flowers, precious stones, or eminent
    stars.
  *Cari.*  This is a vain poetry: but I pray you,
    tell me,
If there were propos'd me wisdom, riches, and
    beauty,
In three several young men, which should I
    choose?                                      35
  *Ant.*  'T is a hard question. This was Paris'
    case,
And he was blind in 't, and there was great
    cause;
For how was 't possible he could judge right,
Having three amorous goddesses in view,

And they stark naked? 'T was a motion       40
Were able to benight the apprehension
Of the severest counsellor of Europe.
Now I look on both your faces so well form'd,
It puts me in mind of a question I would ask.
  *Cari.*  What is 't?
  *Ant.*  I do wonder why hard-favour'd ladies,
For the most part, keep worse-favour'd waiting-
    women                                        46
To attend them, and cannot endure fair ones.
  *Duch.*  O, that 's soon answer'd.
Did you ever in your life know an ill painter
Desire to have his dwelling next door to the
    shop                                         50
Of an excellent picture-maker? 'T would dis-
    grace
His face-making, and undo him. I prithee,
When were we so merry? My hair tangles.
  *Ant.*  Pray thee, Cariola, let 's steal forth
    the room,
And let her talk to herself. I have divers times
Serv'd her the like, when she hath chaf'd ex-
    tremely.                                     56
I love to see her angry. Softly, Cariola.
                *Exeunt* [*Antonio and Cariola*].
  *Duch.*  Doth not the colour of my hair 'gin to
    change?
When I wax gray, I shall have all the court
Powder their hair with arras, to be like me.  60
You have cause to love me; I ent'red you into
    my heart

           [*Enter Ferdinand unseen*]

Before you would vouchsafe to call for the keys.
We shall one day have my brothers take you
    napping.
Methinks his presence, being now in court,
Should make you keep your own bed; but
    you 'll say                                  65
Love mix'd with fear is sweetest. I 'll assure
    you,
You shall get no more children till my brothers
Consent to be your gossips. Have you lost your
    tongue?
'T is welcome:                                   69
For know, whether I am doom'd to live or die,
I can do both like a prince.
  *Ferd.*                      Die, then, quickly.
              *Ferdinand gives her a poniard.*
Virtue, where art thou hid? What hideous
    thing
Is it that doth eclipse thee?
  *Duch.*                        Pray, sir, hear me.
  *Ferd.*  Or is it true thou art but a bare name,
And no essential thing?
  *Duch.*                   Sir ——

⁷ **lord of mis-rule:** officer of license (title of the purveyor of amusement at court revels)    ²⁵ **peevish slight:** perverse contempt of Apollo    ³⁴ **propos'd:** offered    ⁴⁰ **motion:** puppet show    ⁶⁰ **arras:**
white powder of iris-root    ⁶⁸ **gossips:** sponsors

*Ferd.*                           Do not speak. 75
*Duch.*   No, sir:
I will plant my soul in mine ears, to hear you.
   *Ferd.*   O most imperfect light of human
    reason,
That mak'st us so unhappy to foresee
What we can least prevent! Pursue thy wishes,
And glory in them: there 's in shame no com-
    fort                                       81
But to be past all bounds and sense of shame.
   *Duch.*   I pray, sir, hear me: I am married.
   *Ferd.*                                        So!
   *Duch.*   Happily, not to your liking: but for
    that,
Alas, your shears do come untimely now      85
To clip the bird's wings that 's already flown!
Will you see my husband?
   *Ferd.*                   Yes, if I could change
Eyes with a basilisk.
   *Duch.*                Sure, you came hither
By his confederacy.
   *Ferd.*             The howling of a wolf 89
Is music to thee, screech-owl: prithee, peace. —
Whate'er thou art that hast enjoy'd my sister,
For I am sure thou hear'st me, for thine own
    sake
Let me not know thee.  I came hither prepar'd
To work thy discovery; yet am now persuaded
It would beget such violent effects           95
As would damn us both.  I would not for ten
    millions
I had beheld thee: therefore use all means
I never may have knowledge of thy name.
Enjoy thy lust still, and a wretched life,
On that condition. — And for thee, vild woman,
If thou do wish thy lecher may grow old      101
In thy embracements, I would have thee build
Such a room for him as our anchorites
To holier use inhabit.  Let not the sun
Shine on him till he 's dead; let dogs and mon-
    keys                                      105
Only converse with him, and such dumb things
To whom nature denies use to sound his name;
Do not keep a paraquito, lest she learn it.
If thou do love him, cut out thine own tongue,
Lest it bewray him.
   *Duch.*            Why might not I marry? 110
I have not gone about in this to create
Any new world or custom.
   *Ferd.*                   Thou art undone;
And thou hast ta'en that massy sheet of lead
That hid thy husband's bones, and folded it
About my heart.
   *Duch.*           Mine bleeds for 't.
   *Ferd.*                       Thine! thy heart! 115
What should I name 't, unless a hollow bullet
Fill'd with unquenchable wild-fire?

*Duch.*                            You are in this
Too strict; and were you not my princely
    brother,
I would say, too wilful: my reputation
Is safe.
   *Ferd.*   Dost thou know what reputation is?
I 'll tell thee, — to small purpose, since th' in-
    struction                                 121
Comes now too late.
Upon a time Reputation, Love, and Death
Would travel o'er the world; and it was con-
    cluded
That they should part, and take three several
    ways.                                       125
Death told them, they should find him in great
    battles,
Or cities plagu'd with plagues; Love gives
    them counsel
To inquire for him 'mongst unambitious shep-
    herds,
Where dowries were not talk'd of, and some-
    times
'Mongst quiet kindred that had nothing left 130
By their dead parents. 'Stay,' quoth Reputa-
    tion,
'Do not forsake me; for it is my nature,
If once I part from any man I meet,
I am never found again.' And so for you:
You have shook hands with Reputation,     135
And made him invisible.  So, fare you well:
I will never see you more.
   *Duch.*               Why should only I,
Of all the other princes of the world,
Be cas'd up, like a holy relic?  I have youth
And a little beauty.
   *Ferd.*      So you have some virgins 140
That are witches.  I will never see thee more.
                          *Exit.*

*Enter Antonio with a pistol [and Cariola]*

   *Duch.*   You saw this apparition?
   *Ant.*                              Yes: we are
Betray'd.  How came he hither?  I should turn
This to thee, for that.
   *Cari.*            Pray, sir, do; and when
That you have cleft my heart, you shall read
    there                                       145
Mine innocence.
   *Duch.*          That gallery gave him entrance.
   *Ant.*   I would this terrible thing would come
    again,
That, standing on my guard, I might relate
My warrantable love. —   *She shows the poniard.*
              Ha! what means this?
   *Duch.*   He left this with me.
   *Ant.*              And it seems did wish 150
You would use it on yourself?

---

<sup>79</sup> **us:** (not in Qq. 1–3)     <sup>88</sup> **basilisk:** fabulous monster whose look was death     <sup>135</sup> **shook hands:**
parted

*Duch.* His action seem'd
To intend so much.
*Ant.* This hath a handle to 't,
As well as a point: turn it towards him, and
So fasten the keen edge in his rank gall.
[*Knocking within.*]
How now! who knocks? More earthquakes?
*Duch.* I stand 155
As if a mine beneath my feet were ready
To be blown up.
*Cari.* 'T is Bosola.
*Duch.* Away!
O misery! methinks unjust actions
Should wear these masks and curtains, and not
we.
You must instantly part hence: I have fash-
ion'd it already. *Exit Antonio.* 160

[*Enter Bosola*]

*Bos.* The duke your brother is ta'en up in a
whirlwind;
Hath took horse, and 's rid post to Rome.
*Duch.* So late?
*Bos.* He told me, as he mounted into th'
saddle,
You were undone.
*Duch.* Indeed, I am very near it.
*Bos.* What 's the matter? 165
*Duch.* Antonio, the master of our household,
Hath dealt so falsely with me in 's accounts.
My brother stood engag'd with me for money
Ta'en up of certain Neapolitan Jews,
And Antonio lets the bonds be forfeit. 170
*Bos.* Strange! — [*Aside.*] This is cunning.
*Duch.* And hereupon
My brother's bills at Naples are protested
Against. — Call up our officers.
*Bos.* I shall. *Exit.*

[*Re-enter Antonio*]

*Duch.* The place that you must fly to is
Ancona:
Hire a house there. I 'll send after you 175
My treasure and my jewels. Our weak safety
Runs upon enginous wheels: short syllables
Must stand for periods. I must now accuse you
Of such a feigned crime as Tasso calls
*Magnanima menzogna,* a noble lie, 180
'Cause it must shield our honours. — Hark!
they are coming.

[*Re-enter Bosola and Officers*]

*Ant.* Will your grace hear me?
*Duch.* I have got well by you; you have
yielded me
A million of loss: I am like to inherit
The people's curses for your stewardship. 185

You had the trick in audit-time to be sick,
Till I had sign'd your quietus; and that cur'd
you
Without help of a doctor. — Gentlemen,
I would have this man be an example to you
all;
So shall you hold my favour; I pray, let him;
For h'as done that, alas, you would not think
of, 191
And (because I intend to be rid of him)
I mean not to publish. — Use your fortune else-
where.
*Ant.* I am strongly arm'd to brook my over-
throw,
As commonly men bear with a hard year. 195
I will not blame the cause on 't; but do think
The necessity of my malevolent star
Procures this, not her humour. O, the incon-
stant
And rotten ground of service! You may see,
'T is e'en like him, that in a winter night, 200
Takes a long slumber o'er a dying fire,
As loath to part from 't; yet parts thence as cold
As when he first sat down.
*Duch.* We do confiscate,
Towards the satisfying of your accounts,
All that you have.
*Ant.* I am all yours; and 't is very fit 205
All mine should be so.
*Duch.* So, sir, you have your pass.
*Ant.* You may see, gentlemen, what 't is to
serve
A prince with body and soul. *Exit.*
*Bos.* Here 's an example for extortion: what
moisture is drawn out of the sea, when foul [210
weather comes, pours down, and runs into the
sea again.
*Duch.* I would know what are your opinions
Of this Antonio. 214
2 *Off.* He could not abide to see a pig's
head gaping: I thought your grace would find
him a Jew.
3 *Off.* I would you had been his officer,
for your own sake.
4 *Off.* You would have had more money. 220
1 *Off.* He stopp'd his ears with black wool,
and to those came to him for money said he was
thick of hearing.
2 *Off.* Some said he was an hermaphrodite,
for he could not abide a woman. 225
4 *Off.* How scurvy proud he would look
when the treasury was full! Well, let him go.
1 *Off.* Yes, and the chippings of the buttery
fly after him, to scour his gold chain. 229
*Duch.* Leave us. —— *Exeunt [Officers].*
What do you think of these?

169 **Ta'en up:** borrowed 177 **enginous:** wit-driven (all depends on speed and cleverness) 202 **As loath:** (Some copies of Q 1 read 'A-loth.') 228 **chippings:** bread crumbs (used for cleaning gold) 229 **chain:** steward's badge of office

*Bos.* That these are rogues that in 's prosperity,
But to have waited on his fortune, could have wish'd
His dirty stirrup riveted through their noses,
And follow'd after 's mule, like a bear in a ring;
Would have prostituted their daughters to his lust;                                        236
Made their first-born intelligencers; thought none happy
But such as were born under his blest planet.
And wore his livery: and do these lice drop off now?
Well, never look to have the like again:     240
He hath left a sort of flatt'ring rogues behind him;
Their doom must follow. Princes pay flatterers
In their own money: flatterers dissemble their vices,
And they dissemble their lies; that 's justice.
Alas, poor gentleman!                         245
  *Duch.* Poor! he hath amply fill'd his coffers.
  *Bos.* Sure, he was too honest. Pluto, the god of riches,
When he 's sent by Jupiter to any man,
He goes limping, to signify that wealth
That comes on God's name comes slowly; but when he 's sent                             250
On the devil's errand, he rides post and comes in by scuttles.
Let me show you what a most unvalu'd jewel
You have in a wanton humour thrown away,
To bless the man shall find him. He was an excellent
Courtier and most faithful; a soldier that thought it                                      255
As beastly to know his own value too little
As devilish to acknowledge it too much.
Both his virtue and form deserv'd a far better fortune:
His discourse rather delighted to judge itself than show itself:
His breast was fill'd with all perfection,     260
And yet it seem'd a private whisp'ring-room,
It made so little noise of 't.
  *Duch.* But he was basely descended.
  *Bos.* Will you make yourself a mercenary herald,
Rather to examine men's pedigrees than virtues?                                          265
You shall want him:
For know, an honest statesman to a prince
Is like a cedar planted by a spring;
The spring bathes the tree's root, the grateful tree

Rewards it with his shadow: you have not done so.                                       270
I would sooner swim to the Bermoothes on
Two politicians' rotten bladders, tied
Together with an intelligencer's heart-string,
Than depend on so changeable a prince's favour.
Fare thee well, Antonio! Since the malice of the world                                   275
Would needs down with thee, it cannot be said yet
That any ill happen'd unto thee, considering thy fall
Was accompanied with virtue.
  *Duch.* O, you render me excellent music!
  *Bos.*                                   Say you?
  *Duch.* This good one that you speak of is my husband.                                  280
  *Bos.* Do I not dream? Can this ambitious age
Have so much goodness in 't as to prefer
A man merely for worth, without these shadows
Of wealth and painted honours? Possible?
  *Duch.* I have had three children by him.
  *Bos.*                              Fortunate lady! 285
For you have made your private nuptial bed
The humble and fair seminary of peace,
No question but: many an unbenefic'd scholar
Shall pray for you for this deed, and rejoice
That some preferment in the world can yet    290
Arise from merit. The virgins of your land
That have no dowries shall hope your example
Will raise them to rich husbands. Should you want
Soldiers, 't would make the very Turks and Moors
Turn Christians, and serve you for this act. 295
Last, the neglected poets of your time,
In honour of this trophy of a man,
Rais'd by that curious engine, your white hand,
Shall thank you in your grave for 't, and make that
More reverend than all the cabinets         300
Of living princes. For Antonio,
His fame shall likewise flow from many a pen,
When heralds shall want coats to sell to men.
  *Duch.* As I taste comfort in this friendly speech,
So would I find concealment.                 305
  *Bos.* O, the secret of my prince,
Which I will wear on th' inside of my heart!
  *Duch.* You shall take charge of all my coin and jewels,
And follow him; for he retires himself
To Ancona.
  *Bos.*        So.

---

²³⁷ **intelligencers:** spies   ²⁴¹ **sort:** crew   ²⁴⁷ **Pluto:** properly, Plutus   ²⁵¹ **scuttles:** leaps and hounds   ²⁵² **unvalu'd:** invaluable   ²⁵⁴ **shall:** who shall   ²⁷¹ **Bermoothes:** Bermudas   ²⁹⁷ **trophy:** *i.e.,* monument of virtue   ²⁹⁸ **curious:** worthy of regard   ³⁰³ **shall . . . men:** no longer traffic in coats of arms

*Duch.*         Whither, within few days, 310
I mean to follow thee.
   *Bos.*         Let me think:
I would wish your grace to feign a pilgrimage
To our Lady of Loretto, scarce seven leagues
From fair Ancona; so may you depart
Your country with more honour, and your flight
Will seem a princely progress, retaining    316
Your usual train about you.
   *Duch.*        Sir, your direction
Shall lead me by the hand.
   *Cari.*        In my opinion,
She were better progress to the baths at Lucca,
Or go visit the Spa        320
In Germany; for, if you will believe me,
I do not like this jesting with religion,
This feigned pilgrimage.
   *Duch.*   Thou art a superstitious fool!
Prepare us instantly for our departure.    325
Past sorrows, let us moderately lament them,
For those to come, seek wisely to prevent them.
                 *Exit [Duchess with Cariola].*
   *Bos.*  A politician is the devil's quilted anvil;
He fashions all sins on him, and the blows
Are never heard: he may work in a lady's
   chamber        330
(As here for proof). What rests but I reveal
All to my lord? O, this base quality
Of intelligencer! Why, every quality i' th'
   world
Prefers but gain or commendation:
Now, for this act I am certain to be rais'd, 335
And men that paint weeds to the life are prais'd.
                          *Exit.*

SCENA III.—*[Rome: the Cardinal's Palace.]*

*Cardinal, Ferdinand, Malateste, Pescara, Silvio,*
   *Delio, [and later] Bosola*

   *Card.*  Must we turn soldier, then?
   *Mal.*         The emperor,
Hearing your worth that way (ere you attain'd
This reverend garment), joins you in commis-
   sion
With the right fortunate soldier, the Marquis of
   Pescara,
And the famous Lannoy.
   *Card.*      He that had the honour 5
Of taking the French king prisoner?
   *Mal.*         The same.
Here 's a plot drawn for a new fortification
At Naples.
   *Ferd.*  This great Count Malateste, I per-
   ceive,
Hath got employment?

   *Delio.*       No employment, my lord;
A marginal note in the muster-book that he is 10
A voluntary lord.
   *Ferd.*       He 's no soldier?
   *Delio.*  He has worn gun-powder in 's hollow
   tooth for the tooth-ache.
   *Sil.*  He comes to the leaguer with a full in-
   tent
To eat fresh beef and garlic, means to stay
Till the scent be gone, and straight return to
   court.        15
   *Delio.*  He hath read all the late service
As the City Chronicle relates it;
And keeps two pewterers going, only to express
Battles in model.
   *Sil.*       Then he 'll fight by the book.
   *Delio.*  By the almanac, I think,    20
To choose good days and shun the critical.
That 's his mistress' scarf.
   *Sil.*         Yes, he protests
He would do much for that taffeta.
   *Delio.*  I think he would run away from a
   battle,
To save it from taking prisoner.
   *Sil.*         He is horribly afraid 25
Gun-powder will spoil the perfume on 't.
   *Delio.*  I saw a Dutchman break his pate
   once
For calling him a pot-gun; he made his head
Have a bore in 't like a musket.
   *Sil.*  I would he had made a touch-hole to 't. 30
He is indeed a guarded sumpter-cloth,
Only for the remove of the court.

                 *[Enter Bosola]*

   *Pes.*  Bosola arriv'd! What should be the
   business?
Some falling-out amongst the cardinals.
These factions amongst great men, they are like
Foxes: when their heads are divided,    36
They carry fire in their tails, and all the country
About them goes to wrack for 't.
   *Sil.*        What 's that Bosola?
   *Delio.*  I knew him in Padua, — a fantastical
scholar, like such who study to know how many
knots was in Hercules' club, of what colour [41
Achilles' beard was, or whether Hector were
not troubled with the tooth-ache. He hath
studied himself half blear-ey'd to know the
true symmetry of Cæsar's nose by a shoeing- [45
horn; and this he did to gain the name of a
speculative man.
   *Pes.*  Mark Prince Ferdinand:
A very salamander lives in 's eye,
To mock the eager violence of fire.    50

³²⁸ **quilted:** covered with wool to deaden sound    ³³² **quality:** profession    ³³⁴ **Prefers:** offers
¹ **emperor:** Charles V   ⁴·⁵ **Pescara . . . Lannoy:** commanders under the Emperor at the battle of
Pavia (1525)   ⁶ **French king:** Francis I   ¹⁹ **in model:** illustrated by pewter soldiers   ²⁵ **taking:**
being taken   ²⁸ **pot-gun:** pop-gun   ³¹ **guarded:** ornamental   **sumpter-cloth:** saddle blanket

*Sil.* That cardinal hath made more bad
faces with his oppression than ever Michael
Angelo made good ones. He lifts up 's nose,
like a foul porpoise before a storm.
*Pes.* The Lord Ferdinand laughs.
*Delio.*                              Like a deadly cannon 55
That lightens ere it smokes.
*Pes.* These are your true pangs of death,
The pangs of life, that struggle with great
  statesmen.
*Delio.* In such a deformed silence witches
  whisper their charms.
*Card.* Doth she make religion her riding-
  hood                                                    60
To keep her from the sun and tempest?
*Ferd.* That, that damns her. Methinks her
  fault and beauty,
Blended together, show like leprosy,
The whiter the fouler. I make it a question
Whether her beggarly brats were ever chris-
  t'n'd.                                                    65
*Card.* I will instantly solicit the state of
  Ancona
To have them banish'd.
*Ferd.*                              You are for Loretto?
I shall not be at your ceremony, fare you well. —
Write to the Duke of Malfi, my young nephew,
She had by her first husband, and acquaint
  him                                                       70
With 's mother's honesty.
*Bos.*                    I will.
*Ferd.*                              Antonio!
A slave that only smell'd of ink and counters,
And nev'r in 's life look'd like a gentleman,
But in the audit-time. — Go, go presently,
Draw me out an hundreth and fifty of our
  horse,                                                    75
And meet me at the fort-bridge.        *Exeunt.*

### Scena IIII

*Two Pilgrims to the Shrine of our Lady of
Loretto*

*1 Pil.* I have not seen a goodlier shrine than
  this;
Yet I have visited many.
*2 Pil.*                    The Cardinal of Arragon
Is this day to resign his cardinal's hat;
His sister duchess likewise is arriv'd
To pay her vow of pilgrimage. I expect      5
A noble ceremony.
*1 Pil.*                No question. — They come.
  *Here the ceremony of the Cardinal's
    instalment in the habit of a sol-
    dier: perform'd in delivering up
    his cross, hat, robes and ring at
    the shrine, and investing him with*

*sword, helmet, shield, and spurs.
Then Antonio, the Duchess and
their children, having presented
themselves at the shrine, are (by a
form of banishment in dumb show
expressed towards them by the
Cardinal and the state of Ancona)
banished. During all which ceremony, this ditty is sung, to very
solemn music, by divers churchmen; and then exeunt [all except
the two Pilgrims].*

Arms and honours deck thy story,
To thy fame's eternal glory!          *The Author*
Adverse fortune ever fly thee;        *disclaims*
No disastrous fate come nigh thee!    *this ditty* 10
I alone will sing thy praises,        *to be his*
Whom to honour virtue raises,
And thy study, that divine is,
Bent to martial discipline is.
Lay aside all those robes lie by thee;             15
Crown thy arts with arms, they 'll beautify thee.

O worthy of worthiest name, adorn'd in this
  manner,
Lead bravely thy forces on under war's warlike
  banner!
O, mayst thou prove fortunate in all martial
  courses!
Guide thou still by skill in arts and forces! 20
Victory attend thee nigh, whilst fame sings
  loud thy powers;
Triumphant conquest crown thy head, and
  blessings pour down showers!

*1 Pil.* Here 's a strange turn of state! who
  would have thought
So great a lady would have match'd herself
Unto so mean a person? Yet the cardinal   25
Bears himself much too cruel.
*2 Pil.*                    They are banish'd.
*1 Pil.* But I would ask what power hath this
  state
Of Ancona to determine of a free prince?
*2 Pil.* They are a free state, sir, and her
  brother show'd
How that the Pope, fore-hearing of her looseness,                                                    30
Hath seiz'd into th' protection of the church
The dukedom which she held as dowager.
*1 Pil.* But by what justice?
*2 Pil.*                    Sure, I think by none,
Only her brother's instigation.
*1 Pil.* What was it with such violence he
  took                                                      35
Off from her finger?

---

**⁷⁶ fort-bridge:** drawbridge    **⁸⁻¹¹ s. d. The Author . . . his:** (in Q 1 only)    **²⁸ determine: pass**
judgment

2 *Pil.*          'T was her wedding-ring;
Which he vow'd shortly he would sacrifice
To his revenge.
   1 *Pil.*         Alas, Antonio!
If that a man be thrust into a well,      39
No matter who sets hand to 't, his own weight
Will bring him sooner to th' bottom. Come,
   let 's hence.
Fortune makes this conclusion general:
All things do help th' unhappy man to fall.
                     *Exeunt.*

SCENA V.—[*A road near Loretto.*]

*Antonio, Duchess, Children, Cariola, Servants,*
*[and later] Bosola, Soldiers, with Vizards*

   *Duch.*   Banish'd Ancona!
   *Ant.*           Yes, you see what power
Lightens in great men's breath.
   *Duch.*          Is all our train
Shrunk to this poor remainder?
   *Ant.*          These poor men,
Which have got little in your service, vow
To take your fortune: but your wiser bunt-
   ings,                          5
Now they are fledg'd, are gone.
   *Duch.*        They have done wisely.
This puts me in mind of death: physicians thus,
With their hands full of money, use to give o'er
Their patients.
   *Ant.*       Right the fashion of the world: 9
From decay'd fortunes every flatterer shrinks;
Men cease to build where the foundation sinks.
   *Duch.*   I had a very strange dream to-night.
   *Ant.*           What was 't?
   *Duch.*   Methought I wore my coronet of
   state,
And on a sudden all the diamonds
Were chang'd to pearls.
   *Ant.*          My interpretation 15
Is, you 'll weep shortly; for to me the pearls
Do signify your tears.
   *Duch.*        The birds, that live i' th' field
On the wild benefit of nature, live
Happier than we: for they may choose their
   mates,
And carol their sweet pleasures to the spring. 20

       [*Enter Bosola with a letter*]

   *Bos.*   You are happily o'erta'en.
   *Duch.*          From my brother?
   *Bos.*   Yes, from the Lord Ferdinand, your
   brother,
All love and safety.
   *Duch.*       Thou dost blanch mischief,
Would'st make it white. See, see, like to calm
   weather

At sea before a tempest, false hearts speak fair 25
To those they intend most mischief.    [*Reads.*]
                         *A Letter.*
" Send Antonio to me; I want his head in a
   business."
A politic equivocation!
He doth not want your counsel, but your head;
That is, he cannot sleep till you be dead.    30
And here 's another pitfall that 's strew'd o'er
With roses; mark it. 't is a cunning one:
                         [*Reads.*]
" I stand engaged for your husband for several
debts at Naples: let not that trouble him; I
had rather have his heart than his money." —
And I believe so too.
   *Bos.*          What do you believe? 36
   *Duch.*   That he so much distrusts my hus-
   band's love,
He will by no means believe his heart is with
   him
Until he see it. The devil is not cunning enough
To circumvent us in riddles.          40
   *Bos.*   Will you reject that noble and free
   league
Of amity and love which I present you?
   *Duch.*   Their league is like that of some poli-
   tic kings,
Only to make themselves of strength and power
To be our after-ruin: tell them so.      45
   *Bos.*   And what from you?
   *Ant.*          Thus tell him: I will not come.
   *Bos.*   And what of this?
   *Ant.*          My brothers have dispers'd
Bloodhounds abroad; which till I hear are
   muzzl'd,
No truce, though hatch'd with ne'er such poli-
   tic skill,
Is safe, that hangs upon our enemies' will.    50
I 'll not come at them.
   *Bos.*        This proclaims your breeding.
Every small thing draws a base mind to fear
As the adamant draws iron. Fare you well, sir;
You shall shortly hear from 's.          *Exit.*
   *Duch.*       I suspect some ambush;
Therefore by all my love I do conjure you    55
To take your eldest son, and fly towards Milan,
Let us not venture all this poor remainder
In one unlucky bottom.
   *Ant.*          You counsel safely.
Best of my life, farewell. Since we must part,
Heaven hath a hand in 't; but no otherwise 60
Than as some curious artist takes in sunder
A clock or watch, when it is out of frame,
To bring 't in better order.
   *Duch.*   I know not which is best,
To see you dead, or part with you. Farewell,
   boy:                          65

Scene v. s. d. **Vizards:** masks    ⁵ **buntings:** small birds resembling finches    ¹² **to-night:** last
night    ⁵³ **adamant:** loadstone

Thou art happy that thou hast not understand-
  ing
To know thy misery; for all our wit
And reading brings us to a truer sense
Of sorrow. — In the eternal church, sir,
I do hope we shall not part thus.
    *Ant.*                 O, be of comfort! 70
Make patience a noble fortitude,
And think not how unkindly we are us'd:
Man, like to cassia, is prov'd best, being bruis'd.
    *Duch.* Must I, like to a slave-born Russian,
Account it praise to suffer tyranny?      75
And yet, O heaven, thy heavy hand is in 't!
I have seen my little boy oft scourge his top,
And compar'd myself to 't: naught made me
  e'er
Go right but heaven's scourge-stick.
    *Ant.*                Do not weep:
Heaven fashion'd us of nothing; and we strive
To bring ourselves to nothing. — Farewell,
  Cariola,                            81
And thy sweet armful. — If I do never see thee
  more,
Be a good mother to your little ones,
And save them from the tiger: fare you well.
    *Duch.* Let me look upon you once more, for
  that speech                     85
Came from a dying father. Your kiss is colder
Than that I have seen an holy anchorite
Give to a dead man's skull.
    *Ant.* My heart is turn'd to a heavy lump of
  lead,
With which I sound my danger: fare you well.
                         *Exit* [*with his son.*]
    *Duch.* My laurel is all withered.       91
    *Cari.* Look, madam, what a troop of armed
  men
Make toward us!

    *Enter Bosola* [*vizarded,*] *with a Guard*

    *Duch.*          O, they are very welcome:
When Fortune's wheel is over-charg'd with
  princes,
The weight makes it move swift: I would have
  my ruin                         95
Be sudden. — I am your adventure, am I not?
    *Bos.* You are: you must see your husband
  no more.
    *Duch.* What devil art thou that counterfeits
  heaven's thunder?
    *Bos.* Is that terrible? I would have you tell
  me whether
Is that note worse that frights the silly birds 100
Out of the corn, or that which doth allure
  them
To the nets? You have heark'ned to the last
  too much.

    *Duch.* O misery! like to a rusty o'ercharg'd
  cannon,
Shall I never fly in pieces? Come, to what
  prison?
    *Bos.* To none.
    *Duch.*          Whither, then?
    *Bos.*                To your palace.
    *Duch.*              I have heard 105
That Charon's boat serves to convey all o'er
The dismal lake, but brings none back again.
    *Bos.* Your brothers mean you safety and
  pity.
    *Duch.*                     Pity!
With such a pity men preserve alive
Pheasants and quails, when they are not fat
  enough                        110
To be eaten.
    *Bos.*         These are your children?
    *Duch.*                 Yes.
    *Bos.*               Can they prattle?
    *Duch.* No:
But I intend, since they were born accurs'd,
Curses shall be their first language.
    *Bos.*                  Fie, madam!
Forget this base, low fellow.
    *Duch.*            Were I a man, 115
I 'd beat that counterfeit face into thy other.
    *Bos.* One of no birth.
    *Duch.*         Say that he was born mean,
Man is most happy when 's own actions
Be arguments and examples of his virtue.
    *Bos.* A barren, beggarly virtue.      120
    *Duch.* I prithee, who is greatest? Can you
  tell?
Sad tales befit my woe: I 'll tell you one.
A salmon, as she swam unto the sea,
Met with a dog-fish, who encounters her
With this rough language: 'Why art thou so
  bold                            125
To mix thyself with our high state of floods,
Being no eminent courtier, but one
That for the calmest and fresh time o' th' year
Dost live in shallow rivers, rank'st thyself
With silly smelts and shrimps? And darest
  thou                         130
Pass by our dog-ship without reverence?'
'O,' quoth the salmon, 'sister, be at peace:
Thank Jupiter we both have pass'd the net!
Our value never can be truly known,
Till in the fisher's basket we be shown:    135
I' th' market then my price may be the higher,
Even when I am nearest to the cook and fire.'
So to great men the moral may be stretched;
Men oft are valu'd high, when th' are most
  wretched.
But come, whither you please. I am arm'd
  'gainst misery;                     140

---

    ⁸⁹ **lump of lead:** such as sailors use in taking soundings     ⁹⁶ **your adventure:** object of your
journey    ¹¹⁶ **counterfeit face:** mask

Bent to all sways of the oppressor's will.
There's no deep valley but near some great
    hill.                                *Exeunt.*

### ACTUS IIII. SCENA I

*[Scene uncertain.]*

*Ferdinand, Bosola, [and later,] Duchess, Cariola,
    Servants*

    *Ferd.*  How doth our sister duchess bear her-
        self
In her imprisonment?
    *Bos.*                    Nobly: I 'll describe her.
She 's sad as one long us'd to 't, and she seems
Rather to welcome the end of misery
Than shun it; a behaviour so noble              5
As gives a majesty to adversity.
You may discern the shape of loveliness
More perfect in her tears than in her smiles:
She will muse four hours together; and her
    silence,
Methinks, expresseth more than if she spake. 10
    *Ferd.*  Her melancholy seems to be fortified
With a strange disdain.
    *Bos.*                    'T is so; and this restraint,
(Like English mastiffs that grow fierce with
    tying)
Makes her too passionately apprehend
Those pleasures she 's kept from.
    *Ferd.*                    Curse upon her! 15
I will no longer study in the book
Of another's heart.  Inform her what I told
    you.                                *Exit.*

    *[Enter Duchess and Attendants]*

    *Bos.*  All comfort to your grace!
    *Duch.*                    I will have none.
Pray thee, why dost thou wrap thy poison'd
    pills
In gold and sugar?                             20
    *Bos.*  Your elder brother, the Lord Ferdi-
    nand,
Is come to visit you, and sends you word,
'Cause once he rashly made a solemn vow
Never to see you more, he comes i' th' night;
And prays you gently neither torch nor taper 25
Shine in your chamber.  He will kiss your hand,
And reconcile himself; but for his vow
He dares not see you.
    *Duch.*                    At his pleasure. —
Take hence the lights. — He 's come.
    *[Exeunt Attendants with lights.]*

    *[Enter Ferdinand]*

    *Ferd.*                    Where are you?
    *Duch.*                    Here, sir.
    *Ferd.*  This darkness suits you well.

    *Duch.*          I would ask you pardon. 30
    *Ferd.*  You have it;
For I account it the honourabl'st revenge,
Where I may kill, to pardon. — Where are your
    cubs?
    *Duch.*  Whom?
    *Ferd.*          Call them your children;
For though our national law distinguish bas-
    tards                                      35
From true legitimate issue, compassionate na-
    ture
Makes them all equal.
    *Duch.*          Do you visit me for this?
You violate a sacrament o' th' church
Shall make you howl in hell for 't.
    *Ferd.*                    It had been well, 39
Could you have liv'd thus always; for, indeed,
You were too much i' th' light. — But no more;
I come to seal my peace with you.  Here 's a
    hand          *Gives her a dead man's hand.*
To which you have vow'd much love; the ring
    upon 't
You gave.
    *Duch.*          I affectionately kiss it.
    *Ferd.*  Pray, do, and bury the print of it in
    your heart.                               45
I will leave this ring with you for a love-token;
And the hand as sure as the ring: and do not
    doubt
But you shall have the heart too.  When you
    need a friend,
Send it to him that ow'd it; you shall see
Whether he can aid you.
    *Duch.*          You are very cold: 50
I fear you are not well after your travel. —
Ha! lights! —— O, horrible!
    *Ferd.*  Let her have lights enough.  *Exit.*
    *Duch.*  What witchcraft doth he practise,
    that he hath left
A dead man's hand here?
    *Here is discover'd, behind a traverse,
        the artificial figures of Antonio
        and his children, appearing as if
        they were dead.*
    *Bos.*  Look you, here 's the piece from which
    't was ta'en.                             55
He doth present you this sad spectacle,
That, now you know directly they are dead,
Hereafter you may wisely cease to grieve
For that which cannot be recovered.
    *Duch.*  There is not between heaven and
    earth one wish                            60
I stay for after this.  It wastes me more
Than were 't my picture, fashion'd out of wax,
Stuck with a magical needle, and then buried
In some foul dung-hill; and yond 's an excellent
    property
For a tyrant, which I would account mercy.

---

⁴⁹ ow'd: owned    ⁵⁴ S. D. **traverse:** curtain    ⁶⁴ **property:** appropriate act

*Bos.*                    What 's that? 65
*Duch.*   If they would bind me to that liveless
    trunk,
And let me freeze to death.
*Bos.*                    Come, you must live.
*Duch.*   That 's the greatest torture souls feel
    in hell:
In hell that they must live, and cannot die.
Portia, I 'll new-kindle thy coals again,      70
And revive the rare and almost dead example
Of a loving wife.
*Bos.*                 O, fie! despair?   Remember
You are a Christian.
*Duch.*          The church enjoins fasting:
I 'll starve myself to death.
*Bos.*                 Leave this vain sorrow.
Things being at the worst begin to mend: the
    bee                                        75
When he hath shot his sting into your hand,
May then play with your eye-lid.
*Duch.*              Good comfortable fellow,
Persuade a wretch that 's broke upon the wheel
To have all his bones new set; entreat him live
To be executed again.   Who must despatch me?
I account this world a tedious theatre,       81
For I do play a part in 't 'gainst my will.
*Bos.*   Come, be of comfort; I will save your
    life.
*Duch.*   Indeed, I have not leisure to tend
    so small a business.
*Bos.*   Now, by my life, I pity you.
*Duch.*              Thou art a fool, then,   85
To waste thy pity on a thing so wretched
As cannot pity itself.   I am full of daggers.
Puff, let me blow these vipers from me.

*[Enter Servant]*

What are you?
*Serv.*          One that wishes you long life.
*Duch.*   I would thou wert hang'd for the hor-
    rible curse                                90
Thou hast given me: I shall shortly grow one
Of the miracles of pity.   I 'll go pray! —
                              *[Exit Serv.]*
No, I 'll go curse.
*Bos.*          O, fie!
*Duch.*              I could curse the stars —
*Bos.*                 O, fearful!
*Duch.*   And those three smiling seasons of
    the year
Into a Russian winter; nay, the world   95
To its first chaos.
*Bos.*          Look you, the stars shine still.
*Duch.*   O, but you must
Remember, my curse hath a great way to go. —
Plagues, that make lanes through largest families,
Consume them! —

*Bos.*                    Fie, lady!
*Duch.*          Let them, like tyrants,   190
Never be remember'd but for the ill they have
    done;
Let all the zealous prayers of mortified
Churchmen forget them! —
*Bos.*                 O, uncharitable!
*Duch.*   Let heaven a little while cease crown-
    ing martyrs,
To punish them! —                          105
Go, howl them this, and say, I long to bleed:
It is some mercy when men kill with speed.
                                          *Exit.*

*[Re-enter Ferdinand]*

*Ferd.*   Excellent, as I would wish; she 's
    plagu'd in art.
These presentations are but fram'd in wax
By the curious master in that quality,   110
Vincentio Lauriola, and she takes them
For true substantial bodies.
*Bos.*              Why do you do this?
*Ferd.*   To bring her to despair.
*Bos.*                 Faith, end here,
And go no farther in your cruelty.
Send her a penitential garment to put on   115
Next to her delicate skin, and furnish her
With beads and prayer-books.
*Ferd.*          Damn her! that body of hers,
While that my blood ran pure in 't, was more
    worth
Than that which thou wouldst comfort, call'd
    a soul.                                  119
I will send her masques of common courtesans,
Have her meat serv'd up by bawds and ruffians,
And, 'cause she 'll needs be mad, I am resolv'd
To remove forth the common hospital
All the mad-folk, and place them near her
    lodging;                                 124
There let them practise together, sing and dance,
And act their gambols to the full o' th' moon:
If she can sleep the better for it, let her.
Your work is almost ended.
*Bos.*              Must I see her again?
*Ferd.*   Yes.
*Bos.*          Never.
*Ferd.*          You must.
*Bos.*              Never in mine own shape;
That 's forfeited by my intelligence      130
And this last cruel lie: when you send me next,
The business shall be comfort.
*Ferd.*              Very likely!
Thy pity is nothing of kin to thee.   Antonio
Lurks about Milan: thou shalt shortly thither,
To feed a fire as great as my revenge,   135
Which never will slack till it hath spent his fuel:
Intemperate agues make physicians cruel.
                                        *Exeunt.*

⁷⁰ **Portia:** who died by swallowing burning coals   ¹⁰⁸ **art:** artifice   ¹²¹ **ruffians:** pandars
¹²³ **forth:** out of   ¹³⁰ **intelligence:** betrayal

SCENA II

*Duchess, Cariola, [and later] Servant, Madmen,*
*Bosola, Executioners, Ferdinand*

*Duch.* What hideous noise was that?
*Cari.*           'T is the wild consort
Of madmen, lady, which your tyrant brother
Hath plac'd about your lodging. This tyranny,
I think, was never practis'd till this hour.
  *Duch.* Indeed, I thank him. Nothing but
    noise and folly           5
Can keep me in my right wits; whereas reason
And silence make me stark mad. Sit down;
Discourse to me some dismal tragedy.
  *Cari.* O, 't will increase your melancholy!
  *Duch.*           Thou art deceiv'd:
To hear of greater grief would lessen mine. 10
This is a prison?
  *Cari.*        Yes, but you shall live
To shake this durance off.
  *Duch.*          Thou art a fool:
The robin-red-breast and the nightingale
Never live long in cages.
  *Cari.*       Pray, dry your eyes.
What think you of, madam?
  *Duch.*         Of nothing;    15
When I muse thus, I sleep.
  *Cari.* Like a madman, with your eyes open?
  *Duch.* Dost thou think we shall know one
    another
In th' other world?
  *Cari.*       Yes, out of question.
  *Duch.* O, that it were possible we might 20
But hold some two days' conference with the
    dead!
From them I should learn somewhat, I am sure,
I never shall know here. I 'll tell thee a mir-
    acle:
I am not mad yet, to my cause of sorrow:
Th' heaven o'er my head seems made of molten
    brass,         25
The earth of flaming sulphur, yet I am not mad.
I am acquainted with sad misery
As the tann'd galley-slave is with his oar;
Necessity makes me suffer constantly,
And custom makes it easy. Who do I look like
    now?         30
  *Cari.* Like to your picture in the gallery,
A deal of life in show, but none in practice;
Or rather like some reverend monument
Whose ruins are even pitied.
  *Duch.*         Very proper;
And Fortune seems only to have her eye-sight
To behold my tragedy. — How now!    36
What noise is that?

*[Enter Servant]*

  *Serv.*          I am come to tell you,
Your brother hath intended you some sport.
A great physician, when the Pope was sick
Of a deep melancholy, presented him   40
With several sorts of madmen, which wild ob-
    ject
(Being full of change and sport) forc'd him to
    laugh,
And so th' imposthume broke: the self-same
    cure
The duke intends on you.
  *Duch.*         Let them come in.
  *Serv.* There 's a mad lawyer; and a secular
    priest;         45
A doctor that hath forfeited his wits
By jealousy; an astrologian
That in his works said such a day o' th' month
Should be the day of doom, and, failing of 't,
Ran mad; an English tailor, craz'd i' th' brain
With the study of new fashions; a gentleman-
    usher        51
Quite beside himself with care to keep in mind
The number of his lady's salutations,
Or ' How do you,' she employ'd him in each
    morning;
A farmer, too, an excellent knave in grain, 55
Mad 'cause he was hinder'd transportation:
And let one broker that 's mad loose to these,
You 'd think the devil were among them.
  *Duch.* Sit, Cariola. — Let them loose when
    you please,
For I am chain'd to endure all your tyranny. 60

*[Enter Madmen]*

*Here by a Madman this song is sung to a dismal*
*kind of music.*

  *O, let us howl some heavy note,*
    *Some deadly dogged howl,*
  *Sounding as from the threat'ning throat*
    *Of beasts and fatal fowl!*
  *As ravens, screech-owls, bulls, and bears,*   65
    *We 'll bell, and bawl our parts,*
  *Till irksome noise have cloy'd your ears*
    *And corrosiv'd your hearts.*
  *At last, when as our choir wants breath,*
    *Our bodies being blest,*     70
  *We 'll sing, like swans, to welcome death,*
    *And die in love and rest.*

  1 *Madman.* Doom's-day not come yet! I 'll
draw it nearer by a perspective, or make a [74
glass that shall set all the world on fire upon an
instant. I cannot sleep; my pillow is stuff'd
with a litter of porcupines.

    ¹ consort: band    ⁴³ imposthume: ulcer    ⁵¹ fashions: ('fashion' Q 1)    ⁵⁵ in grain: fast-dyed
⟨ ...th pun on the grain trade)    ⁵⁶ hinder'd transportation: forbidden to export (his grain)    ⁶⁶ bell:
...ter the cry of stags, etc. ('bill' in Q 1)    ⁶⁸ corrosiv'd: corroded    ⁷⁴ perspective: telescope

*2 Madman.* Hell is a mere glass-house, where the devils are continually blowing up women's souls on hollow irons, and the fire [80 never goes out.

*3 Madman.* I will lie with every woman in my parish the tenth night. I will tithe them over like hay-cocks.                              84

*4 Madman.* Shall my 'pothecary out-go me, because I am a cuckold? I have found out his roguery: he makes alum of his wife's urine, and sells it to Puritans that have sore throats with over-straining.

*1 Madman.* I have skill in heraldry.        90

*2 Madman.* Hast?

*1 Madman.* You do give for your crest a woodcock's head with the brains pick'd out on 't; you are a very ancient gentleman.    94

*3 Madman.* Greek is turn'd Turk: we are only to be sav'd by the Helvetian translation.

*1 Madman.* Come on, sir, I will lay the law to you.

*2 Madman.* O, rather lay a corrosive: the law will eat to the bone.                      100

*3 Madman.* He that drinks but to satisfy nature is damn'd.

*4 Madman.* If I had my glass here, I would show a sight should make all the women here call me mad doctor.                        105

*1 Madman.* What 's he? A rope-maker?

*2 Madman.* No, no, no; a snuffling knave that while he shows the tombs, will have his hand in a wench's placket.              109

*3 Madman.* Woe to the caroche that brought home my wife from the masque at three o'clock in the morning! It had a large feather-bed in it.

*4 Madman.* I have pared the devil's nails forty times, roasted them in raven's eggs, [115 and cur'd agues with them.

*3 Madman.* Get me three hundred milch-bats, to make possets to procure sleep.

*4 Madman.* All the college may throw their caps at me: I have made a soap-boiler cos- [120 tive; it was my masterpiece.

*Here the dance, consisting of Eight Madmen, with music answerable thereunto; after which, Bosola (like an old man) enters.*

*Duch.* Is he mad too?

*Serv.*        Pray, question him. I 'll leave you.

            *[Exeunt Servant and Madmen.]*

*Bos.* I am come to make thy tomb.

*Duch.*                            Ha! my tomb!

Thou speak'st as if I lay upon my death-bed, Gasping for breath. Dost thou perceive me sick?                                      125

*Bos.* Yes, and the more dangerously, since thy sickness is insensible.

*Duch.* Thou art not mad, sure: dost know me?

*Bos.*              Yes.

*Duch.*                    Who am I?

*Bos.* Thou art a box of worm-seed, at best but a salvatory of green mummy. What 's this flesh? A little crudded milk, fantasti- [131 cal puff-paste. Our bodies are weaker than those paper-prisons boys use to keep flies in; more contemptible, since ours is to preserve earth-worms. Didst thou ever see a lark in [135 a cage? Such is the soul in the body: this world is like her little turf of grass, and the heaven o'er our heads, like her looking-glass, only gives us a miserable knowledge of the small compass of our prison.             140

*Duch.* Am not I thy duchess?

*Bos.* Thou art some great woman, sure, for riot begins to sit on thy forehead (clad in gray hairs) twenty years sooner than on a merry milk-maid's. Thou sleep'st worse than if a [145 mouse should be forc'd to take up her lodging in a cat's ear: a little infant that breeds its teeth, should it lie with thee, would cry out, as if thou wert the more unquiet bedfellow.

*Duch.* I am Duchess of Malfi still.     150

*Bos.* That makes thy sleeps so broken: Glories, like glow-worms, afar off shine bright, But, look'd to near, have neither heat nor light.

*Duch.* Thou art very plain.

*Bos.* My trade is to flatter the dead, not [155 the living; I am a tomb-maker.

*Duch.* And thou com'st to make my tomb?

*Bos.* Yes.

*Duch.* Let me be a little merry: — of what stuff wilt thou make it?                    160

*Bos.* Nay, resolve me first of what fashion?

*Duch.* Why, do we grow fantastical in our deathbed?

Do we affect fashion in the grave?

*Bos.* Most ambitiously. Princes' images on their tombs do not lie, as they were wont, [165 seeming to pray up to heaven; but with their hands under their cheeks, as if they died of the tooth-ache. They are not carved with their eyes fix'd upon the stars; but, as their minds were wholly bent upon the world, the self- [170 same way they seem to turn their faces.

*Duch.* Let me know fully therefore the effect

---

[93] **woodcock:** a proverbially stupid bird    [96] **Helvetian:** Genevan    [118] **possets:** sedative drafts, of spiced wine and milk    [119–120] **throw . . . caps:** despair of emulating    [120–121] **costive:** constipated    [130] **salvatory:** ointment-box    **green:** fresh    **mummy:** drug, supposed to come from embalmed bodies    [131] **crudded:** curdled    [161] **resolve:** inform    [162] **fantastical:** fastidious    [164] **Princes' images, etc.:** (Semi-recumbent statues, resting on their elbows, became popular in the 16th century.)

Of this thy dismal preparation,
This talk fit for a charnel.
   *Bos.*            Now I shall: —

*[Enter Executioners, with] A coffin, cords, and*
*a bell*

Here is a present from your princely brothers;
And may it arrive welcome, for it brings  176
Last benefit, last sorrow.
   *Duch.*         Let me see it:
I have so much obedience in my blood,
I wish it in their veins to do them good.
   *Bos.*  This is your last presence-chamber. 180
   *Cari.*  O my sweet lady!
   *Duch.*        Peace; it affrights not me.
   *Bos.*  I am the common bellman
That usually is sent to condemn'd persons
The night before they suffer.
   *Duch.*       Even now thou said'st
Thou wast a tomb-maker.
   *Bos.*       'T was to bring you 185
By degrees to mortification.  Listen.

*Hark, now everything is still,*
*The screech-owl and the whistler shrill*
*Call upon our dame aloud,*
*And bid her quickly don her shroud!*  190
*Much you had of land and rent;*
*Your length in clay 's now competent:*
*A long war disturb'd your mind;*
*Here your perfect peace is sign'd.*
*Of what is 't fools make such vain keeping?*  195
*Sin their conception, their birth weeping,*
*Their life a general mist of error,*
*Their death a hideous storm of terror.*
*Strew your hair with powders sweet,*
*Don clean linen, bathe your feet,*  200
*And (the foul fiend more to check)*
*A crucifix let bless your neck.*
*'T is now full tide 'tween night and day;*
*End your groan, and come away.*

   *Cari.*  Hence, villains, tyrants, murderers!
   Alas!  205
What will you do with my lady? — Call for
   help!
   *Duch.*  To whom?  To our next neighbours?
   They are mad-folks.
   *Bos.*  Remove that noise.
   *Duch.*        Farewell, Cariola.
In my last will I have not much to give:
A many hungry guests have fed upon me; 210
Thine will be a poor reversion.
   *Cari.*       I will die with her.
   *Duch.*  I pray thee, look thou giv'st my little
   boy

Some syrup for his cold, and let the girl
Say her prayers ere she sleep.
     *[Cariola is forced out by the Executioners.]*
          Now what you please!
What death?
   *Bos.*  Strangling: here are your executioners.
   *Duch.*  I forgive them:  216
The apoplexy, catarrh, or cough o' th' lungs,
Would do as much as they do.
   *Bos.*  Doth not death fright you?
   *Duch.*       Who would be afraid on 't,
Knowing to meet such excellent company 220
In th' other world?
   *Bos.*  Yet, methinks,
The manner of your death should much afflict
   you:
This cord should terrify you.
   *Duch.*        Not a whit:
What would it pleasure me to have my throat
   cut  225
With diamonds? or to be smothered
With cassia? or to be shot to death with pearls?
I know death hath ten thousand several doors
For men to take their exits; and 't is found
They go on such strange geometrical hinges, 230
You may open them both ways: any way, for
   heaven-sake,
So I were out of your whispering.  Tell **my**
   brothers
That I perceive death, now I am well awake,
Best gift is they can give or I can take.
I would fain put off my last woman's-fault: 235
I 'd not be tedious to you.
   *Execut.*      We are ready.
   *Duch.*  Dispose my breath how please you;
   but my body
Bestow upon my women, will you?
   *Execut.*      Yes.
   *Duch.*  Pull, and pull strongly, for your able
   strength
Must pull down heaven upon me: —  240
Yet stay; heaven-gates are not so highly arch'd
As princes' palaces; they that enter there
Must go upon their knees *[kneels]*. — Come,
   violent death,
Serve for mandragora to make me sleep! —
Go tell my brothers, when I am laid out,  245
They then may feed in quiet.  *They strangle*
   *Bos.*  Where 's the waiting-woman?  *her.*
Fetch her: some other strangle the children.

     *[Enter Cariola]*

Look you, there sleeps your mistress.
   *Cari.*       O, you are damn'd
Perpetually for this!  My turn is next; —  250
Is 't not so order'd?

---

182–184 An endowment for this purpose was made by Robert Dowe of London in 1605.  188 **whistler:** a nocturnal bird of ill omen, perhaps the whimbrel or curlew  192 **competent:** sufficient  227 **cassia:** cinnamon  236 **tedious:** dilatory

*Bos.*              Yes, and I am glad
You are so well prepar'd for 't.
    *Cari.*              You are deceiv'd, sir,
I am not prepar'd for 't, I will not die;
I will first come to my answer, and know
How I have offended.
    *Bos.*           Come, despatch her. — 255
You kept her counsel; now you shall keep
ours.
    *Cari.*   I will not die, I must not; I am con-
tracted
To a young gentleman.
    *Execut.*        Here 's your wedding-ring.
    *Cari.*   Let me but speak with the duke. I 'll
discover
Treason to his person.
    *Bos.*         Delays: — throttle her. 260
    *Execut.*   She bites and scratches.
    *Cari.*           If you kill me now,
I am damn'd; I have not been at confession
This two years.
    *Bos.* [*To Executioners.*] When!
    *Cari.*          I am quick with child.
    *Bos.*              Why, then,
Your credit 's sav'd.
           [*Executioners strangle Cariola.*]
           Bear her into th' next room; 265
Let this lie still.
      [*Exeunt Executioners with body of
      Cariola.*

          *Enter Ferdinand*]

    *Ferd.*           Is she dead?
    *Bos.*           She is what
You 'd have her. But here begin your pity:
          *Shows the Children strangled.*
Alas, how have these offended?
    *Ferd.*           The death
Of young wolves is never to be pitied.
    *Bos.*   Fix your eye here.
    *Ferd.*          Constantly.
    *Bos.*          Do you not weep? 270
Other sins only speak; murther shrieks out.
The element of water moistens the earth,
But blood flies upwards and bedews the heavens.
    *Ferd.*   Cover her face; mine eyes dazzle: she
     died young.
    *Bos.*   I think not so; her infelicity     275
Seem 'd to have years too many.
    *Ferd.*   She and I were twins;
And should I die this instant, I had liv'd
Her time to a minute.
    *Bos.*       It seems she was born first:
You have bloodily approv'd the ancient truth,
That kindred commonly do worse agree    281
Than remote strangers.
    *Ferd.*        Let me see her face
Again. Why didst not thou pity her? What

An excellent honest man mightst thou have
     been,
If thou hadst borne her to some sanctuary! 285
Or, bold in a good cause, oppos'd thyself,
With thy advanced sword above thy head,
Between her innocence and my revenge!
I bade thee, when I was distracted of my wits,
Go kill my dearest friend, and thou hast done 't.
For let me but examine well the cause:    291
What was the meanness of her match to me?
Only I must confess I had a hope,
Had she continu'd widow, to have gain'd
An infinite mass of treasure by her death: 295
And that was the main cause, — her marriage,
That drew a stream of gall quite through my
     heart.
For thee (as we observe in tragedies
That a good actor many times is curs'd
For playing a villain's part) I hate thee for 't.
And, for my sake, say, thou hast done much
     ill well.                         301
    *Bos.*   Let me quicken your memory, for I
     perceive
You are falling into ingratitude: I challenge
The reward due to my service.
    *Ferd.*           I 'll tell thee
What I 'll give thee.
    *Bos.*   Do.
    *Ferd.*          I 'll give thee a pardon 305
For this murther.
    *Bos.*       Ha!
    *Ferd.*          Yes, and 't is
The largest bounty I can study to do thee.
By what authority didst thou execute
This bloody sentence?
    *Bos.*          By yours.
    *Ferd.*   Mine! Was I her judge?        310
Did any ceremonial form of law
Doom her to not-being? Did a complete jury
Deliver her conviction up i' th' court?
Where shalt thou find this judgment register'd,
Unless in hell? See, like a bloody fool,    315
Thou 'st forfeited thy life, and thou shalt die
     for 't.
    *Bos.*   The office of justice is perverted quite
When one thief hangs another. Who shall dare
To reveal this?
    *Ferd.*       O, I 'll tell thee;
The wolf shall find her grave, and scrape it up,
Not to devour the corpse, but to discover    321
The horrid murther.
    *Bos.*        You, not I, shall quake for 't.
    *Ferd.*   Leave me.
    *Bos.*        I will first receive my pension.
    *Ferd.*   You are a villain.
    *Bos.*         When your ingratitude
Is judge, I am so.
    *Ferd.*        O horror,       325

---

²⁵⁴ **answer:** trial    ²⁶³ **When!:** expression of impatience    ²⁶⁶ **this:** the Duchess's body

That not the fear of him which binds the devils
Can prescribe man obedience! —
Never look upon me more.
   *Bos.*                            Why, fare thee well.
Your brother and yourself are worthy men!
You have a pair of hearts are hollow graves, 330
Rotten, and rotting others; and your vengeance,
Like two chain'd bullets, still goes arm in arm.
You may be brothers; for treason, like the
   plague,
Doth take much in a blood. I stand like one
That long hath ta'en a sweet and golden
   dream:                                      335
I am angry with myself, now, that I wake.
   *Ferd.* Get thee into some unknown part o'
   th' world,
That I may never see thee.
   *Bos.*                        Let me know
Wherefore I should be thus neglected. Sir,
I serv'd your tyranny, and rather strove   340
To satisfy yourself than all the world:
And though I loath'd the evil, yet I lov'd
You that did counsel it; and rather sought
To appear a true servant than an honest man.
   *Ferd.* I 'll go hunt the badger by owl-light: 345
'T is a deed of darkness.                  *Exit.*
   *Bos.* He 's much distracted. Off, my painted
   honour!
While with vain hopes our faculties we tire,
We seem to sweat in ice and freeze in fire.
What would I do, were this to do again?    350
I would not change my peace of conscience
For all the wealth of Europe. — She stirs;
   here 's life: —
Return, fair soul, from darkness, and lead
   mine
Out of this sensible hell! — she 's warm, she
   breathes: —
Upon thy pale lips I will melt my heart,   355
To store them with fresh colour. — Who 's
   there?
Some cordial drink! — Alas! I dare not call:
So pity would destroy pity. — Her eye opes,
And heaven in it seems to ope, that late was
   shut,
To take me up to mercy.                    360
   *Duch.* Antonio!
   *Bos.*            Yes, madam, he is living;
The dead bodies you saw were but feign'd
   statues.
He 's reconcil'd to your brothers; the Pope
   hath wrought
The atonement.
   *Duch.*      Mercy!              *She dies.*
   *Bos.* O, she 's gone again! there the cords of
life broke.                                365

O sacred innocence, that sweetly sleeps
On turtles' feathers, whilst a guilty conscience
Is a black register wherein is writ
All our good deeds and bad, a perspective
That shows us hell! That we cannot be suffer'd
To do good when we have a mind to it!      371
This is manly sorrow!
These tears, I am very certain, never grew
In my mother's milk. My estate is sunk
Below the degree of fear: where were       375
These penitent fountains while she was living?
O, they were frozen up! Here is a sight
As direful to my soul as is the sword
Unto a wretch hath slain his father.
Come, I 'll bear thee hence,                380
And execute thy last will; that 's deliver
Thy body to the reverend dispose
Of some good women: that the cruel tyrant
Shall not deny me. Then I 'll post to Milan,
Where somewhat I will speedily enact       385
Worth my dejection.         *Exit [with the body].*

### ACTUS V. SCENA I

*[Milan: A Public Place.]*

*Antonio, Delio, [and later] Pescara, Julia*

   *Ant.* What think you of my hope of recon-
   cilement
To the Arragonian brethren?
   *Delio.*                    I misdoubt it;
For though they have sent their letters of safe-
   conduct
For your repair to Milan, they appear
But nets to entrap you. The Marquis of
   Pescara,                                  5
Under whom you hold certain land in cheat,
Much 'gainst his noble nature hath been mov'd
To seize those lands; and some of his dependants
Are at this instant making it their suit
To be invested in your revenues.           10
I cannot think they mean well to your life
That do deprive you of your means of life,
Your living.
   *Ant.*     You are still an heretic
To any safety I can shape myself.
   *Delio.* Here comes the marquis: I will make
   myself                                    15
Petitioner for some part of your land,
To know whether it is flying.
   *Ant.*              I pray, do. *[Withdraws.]*

*[Enter Pescara]*

   *Delio.* Sir, I have a suit to you.
   *Pes.*                        To me?
   *Delio.*                          An easy one:

---

<sup>334</sup> **Doth . . . blood:** affects members of the same family   <sup>382</sup> **dispose:** care   <sup>386</sup> **Worth my de-
jection:** suitable to my distress   <sup>6</sup> **in cheat:** subject to forfeiture   <sup>13</sup> **heretic:** skeptic   <sup>17</sup> **whether:**
('whither' Qq. 2-3)

There is the Citadel of Saint Bennet,
With some demesnes, of late in the possession
Of Antonio Bologna, — please you bestow them
    on me.                                                                21
    *Pes.*   You are my friend; but this is such a
    suit,
Nor fit for me to give, nor you to take.
    *Delio.*  No, sir?
    *Pes.*      I will give you ample reason for 't
Soon in private.  Here 's the cardinal's mis-
    tress.                                                              25

### [*Enter Julia*]

    *Julia.*  My lord, I am grown your poor peti-
    tioner,
And should be an ill beggar, had I not
A great man's letter here (the cardinal's)
To court you in my favour.      [*Gives a letter.*]
    *Pes.*                            He entreats for you
The Citadel of Saint Bennet, that belong'd   30
To the banish'd Bologna.
    *Julia.*                     Yes.
    *Pes.*  I could not have thought of a friend I
    could rather
Pleasure with it: 't is yours.
    *Julia.*                  Sir, I thank you;
And he shall know how doubly I am engag'd,
Both in your gift, and speediness of giving,  35
Which makes your grant the greater.      *Exit.*
    *Ant.* [*Aside.*]               How they fortify
Themselves with my ruin!
    *Delio.*                  Sir, I am
Little bound to you.
    *Pes.*           Why?
    *Delio.*  Because you denied this suit to me,
    and gave 't
To such a creature.
    *Pes.*           Do you know what it was?
It was Antonio's land: not forfeited           41
By course of law, but ravish'd from his throat
By the cardinal's entreaty.  It were not fit
I should bestow so main a piece of wrong
Upon my friend: 't is a gratification         45
Only due to a strumpet, for it is injustice.
Shall I sprinkle the pure blood of innocents
To make those followers I call my friends
Look ruddier upon me?  I am glad
This land, ta'en from the owner by such wrong,
Returns again unto so foul an use            51
As salary for his lust.  Learn, good Delio,
To ask noble things of me, and you shall find
I 'll be a noble giver.
    *Delio.*          You instruct me well.
    *Ant.* [*Aside.*] Why, here 's a man now would
    fright impudence                             55
From sauciest beggars.
    *Pes.*        Prince Ferdinand 's come to Milan,
Sick, as they give out, of an apoplexy;

But some say 't is a frenzy.  I am going
To visit him.                                    *Exit.*
    *Ant.*          'T is a noble old fellow.
    *Delio.*  What course do you mean to take,
    Antonio?                                       60
    *Ant.*  This night I mean to venture all my
    fortune,
Which is no more than a poor ling'ring life,
To the cardinal's worst of malice.  I have got
Private access to his chamber; and intend
To visit him about the mid of night,          65
As once his brother did our noble duchess.
It may be that the sudden apprehension
Of danger, — for I 'll go in mine own shape, —
When he shall see it fraight with love and duty,
May draw the poison out of him, and work   70
A friendly reconcilement.  If it fail,
Yet it shall rid me of this infamous calling;
For better fall once than be ever falling.
    *Delio.*  I 'll second you in all danger; and,
    howe'er,
My life keeps rank with yours.                 75
    *Ant.*  You are still my lov'd and best friend.
                               *Exeunt.*

### SCENA II

*Pescara, a Doctor, [later] Ferdinand, Cardinal,*
*Malateste, Bosola, Julia*

    *Pes.*  Now, doctor, may I visit your patient?
    *Doc.*  If 't please your lordship; but he 's
    instantly
To take the air here in the gallery
By my direction.
    *Pes.*          Pray thee, what 's his disease?
    *Doc.*  A very pestilent disease, my lord,      5
They call lycanthropia.
    *Pes.*                What 's that?
I need a dictionary to 't.
    *Doc.*               I 'll tell you.
In those that are possess'd with 't there o'er-
flows
Such melancholy humour they imagine
Themselves to be transformed into wolves;   10
Steal forth to church-yards in the dead of night,
And dig dead bodies up: as two nights since
One met the duke 'bout midnight in a lane
Behind Saint Mark's church, with the leg of a
    man
Upon his shoulder; and he howl'd fearfully; 15
Said he was a wolf, only the difference
Was, a wolf's skin was hairy on the outside,
His on the inside; bade them take their swords,
Rip up his flesh, and try. Straight I was sent for,
And, having minister'd to him, found his grace
Very well recovered.                           21
    *Pes.*  I am glad on 't.
    *Doc.*              Yet not without some fear

----
    **44 main:** egregious     **69 fraight:** fraught     **74 howe'er:** whatever happens

Of a relapse. If he grow to his fit again,
I 'll go a nearer way to work with him
Than ever Paracelsus dream'd of; if     25
They 'll give me leave, I 'll buffet his madness
   out of him.
Stand aside; he comes.

   [*Enter Ferdinand, Cardinal, Malateste, and
             Bosola*]

*Ferd.* Leave me.
*Mal.* Why doth your lordship love this soli-
   tariness?
*Ferd.* Eagles commonly fly alone: they are [30
crows, daws, and starlings that flock together.
Look, what 's that follows me?
*Mal.* Nothing, my lord.
*Ferd.* Yes.
*Mal.* 'T is your shadow.     35
*Ferd.* Stay it; let it not haunt me.
*Mal.* Impossible, if you move, and the sun
   shine.
*Ferd.* I will throttle it.
     [*Throws himself down on his shadow.*]
*Mal.* O, my lord, you are angry with nothing.
*Ferd.* You are a fool: how is 't possible I [40
should catch my shadow, unless I fall upon 't?
When I go to hell, I mean to carry a bribe; for,
look you, good gifts evermore make way for the
worst persons.
*Pes.* Rise, good my lord.     45
*Ferd.* I am studying the art of patience.
*Pes.* 'T is a noble virtue.
*Ferd.* To drive six snails before me from this
town to Moscow; neither use goad nor whip to
them, but let them take their own time; — [50
the patient'st man i' th' world match me for an
experiment! And I 'll crawl after like a sheepbiter.
*Card.* Force him up.     [*They raise him.*]
*Ferd.* Use me well, you were best. What I [55
have done, I have done: I 'll confess nothing.
*Doc.* Now let me come to him. — Are you
mad, my lord?
Are you out of your princely wits?
*Ferd.*              What 's he?
*Pes.*              Your doctor.
*Ferd.* Let me have his beard saw'd off, and
his eye-brows fil'd more civil.     60
*Doc.* I must do mad tricks with him, for that
's the only way on 't. — I have brought your
grace a salamander's skin to keep you from sun-
burning.
*Ferd.* I have cruel sore eyes.     65
*Doc.* The white of a cockatrix's egg is pres-
ent remedy.

*Ferd.* Let it be a new-laid one, you were best.
Hide me from him: physicians are like kings, —
They brook no contradiction.     70
*Doc.* Now he begins to fear me: now let me
alone with him.
   [*Puts off his four cloaks, one after
          another.*]
*Card.* How now! put off your gown?
*Doc.* Let me have some forty urinals filled
with rose-water: he and I 'll go pelt one [75
another with them. — Now he begins to fear me.
— Can you fetch a frisk, sir? — Let him go,
let him go, upon my peril. I find by his eye he
stands in awe of me: I 'll make him as tame as
a dormouse.     80
*Ferd.* Can you fetch your frisks, sir! — I will
stamp him into a cullis, flay off his skin to
cover one of the anatomies this rogue hath
set i' th' cold yonder in Barber-Chirurgeon's-
hall. — Hence, hence! you are all of you like [85
beasts for sacrifice. [*Throws the Doctor down
and beats him.*] There 's nothing left of you but
tongue and belly, flattery and lechery. [*Exit.*]
*Pes.* Doctor, he did not fear you throughly.
*Doc.* True; I was somewhat too forward. 90
*Bos.* Mercy upon me, what a fatal judgment
Hath fall'n upon this Ferdinand!
*Pes.*             Knows your grace
What accident hath brought unto the prince
This strange distraction?
*Card.* [*Aside.*] I must feign somewhat. —
   Thus they say it grew.     95
You have heard it rumour'd, for these many
   years,
None of our family dies but there is seen
The shape of an old woman, which is given
By tradition to us to have been murther'd  99
By her nephews for her riches. Such a figure
One night, as the prince sat up late at 's book,
Appear'd to him; when crying out for help,
The gentlemen of 's chamber found his grace
All on a cold sweat, alter'd much in face
And language: since which apparition,     105
He hath grown worse and worse, and I much
   fear
He cannot live.
*Bos.*            Sir, I would speak with you.
*Pes.* We 'll leave your grace,
Wishing to the sick prince, our noble lord,
All health of mind and body.
*Card.*            You are most welcome.
   [*Exeunt Pescara, Malateste, and Doctor.*]
Are you come? so. — [*Aside.*] This fellow must
   not know     111
By any means I had intelligence

---

⁵²⁻⁵³ **sheepbiter:** sheep-stealing dog   ⁶⁰ **civil:** becomingly   ⁶⁶ **cockatrix:** a fabulous monster
⁷² S. D. (Added in ed. of 1708. A piece of late clownage, perhaps borrowed from the grave-diggers'
scene in *Hamlet*.)   ⁷⁷ **fetch a frisk:** cut a caper   ⁸² **cullis:** broth, made of bruised flesh   ⁸³ **anatomies:** skeletons   ⁸⁹ **throughly:** thoroughly   ¹¹² **had intelligence:** was accessory

In our duchess' death; for, though I counsell'd
it,
The full of all th' engagement seem'd to grow
From Ferdinand. — Now, sir, how fares our
sister?                                                                            115
I do not think but sorrow makes her look
Like to an oft-dy'd garment: she shall now
Taste comfort from me. Why do you look so
wildly?
O, the fortune of your master here, the prince,
Dejects you; but be you of happy comfort: 120
If you 'll do one thing for me I 'll entreat,
Though he had a cold tomb-stone o'er his bones,
I 'd make you what you would be.
   *Bos.*                                                 Anything!
Give it me in a breath, and let me fly to 't.
They that think long small expedition win, 125
For musing much o' th' end cannot begin.

### [Enter Julia]

*Julia.* Sir, will you come in to supper?
*Card.*                              I am busy; leave me.
*Julia.* [Aside.] What an excellent shape hath
   that fellow!                                                  *Exit.*
*Card.* 'T is thus. Antonio lurks here in Milan:
Inquire him out, and kill him. While he lives,
Our sister cannot marry; and I have thought
Of an excellent match for her. Do this, and
style me                                                                      132
Thy advancement.
   *Bos.* But by what means shall I find him
   out?
*Card.* There is a gentleman call'd Delio 135
Here in the camp, that hath been long approv'd
His loyal friend. Set eye upon that fellow;
Follow him to mass; may be Antonio,
Although he do account religion
But a school-name, for fashion of the world 140
May accompany him; or else go inquire out
Delio's confessor, and see if you can bribe
Him to reveal it. There are a thousand ways
A man might find to trace him: as to know
What fellows haunt the Jews for taking up 145
Great sums of money, for sure he 's in want;
Or else to go to th' picture-makers, and learn
Who bought her picture lately: some of these
Happily may take.
   *Bos.*            Well, I 'll not freeze i' th' business:
I would see that wretched thing, Antonio,  150
Above all sights i' th' world.
   *Card.*                     Do, and be happy. *Exit.*
   *Bos.* This fellow doth breed basilisks in 's
   eyes,
He 's nothing else but murder; yet he seems
Not to have notice of the duchess' death.
'T is his cunning: I must follow his example;
There cannot be a surer way to trace       156
Than that of an old fox.

### [Re-enter Julia, with a pistol]

*Julia.* So, sir, you are well met.
*Bos.*                                    How now!
*Julia.* Nay, the doors are fast enough:
Now, sir, I will make you confess your treach-
   ery.                                                                        160
*Bos.* Treachery!
*Julia.*                  Yes, confess to me
Which of my women 't was you hir'd to put
Love-powder into my drink?
   *Bos.* Love-powder!
*Julia.*                    Yes, when I was at Malfi.
Why should I fall in love with such a face else?
I have already suffer'd for thee so much pain,
The only remedy to do me good            167
Is to kill my longing.
   *Bos.*                Sure, your pistol holds
Nothing but perfumes or kissing-comfits.
Excellent lady!                                                        170
You have a pretty way on 't to discover
Your longing. Come, come, I 'll disarm you,
And arm you thus: yet this is wondrous
   strange.
*Julia.* Compare thy form and my eyes to-
   gether,
You 'll find my love no such great miracle. 175
Now you 'll say
I am wanton. This nice modesty in ladies
Is but a troublesome familiar
That haunts them.
   *Bos.* Know you me: I am a blunt soldier.
*Julia.*                                        The better:
Sure, there wants fire where there are no lively
   sparks                                                                    181
Of roughness.
   *Bos.*            And I want compliment.
*Julia.*                                      Why, ignorance
In courtship cannot make you do amiss,
If you have a heart to do well.
   *Bos.*                          You are very fair.
*Julia.* Nay, if you lay beauty to my charge,
I must plead unguilty.
   *Bos.*                    Your bright eyes   186
Carry a quiver of darts in them, sharper
Than sun-beams.                                           [tion,
*Julia.*      You will mar me with commenda-
Put yourself to the charge of courting me,
Whereas now I woo you.                                 190
*Bos.* [Aside.] I have it, I will work upon this
   creature. —
Let us grow most amorously familiar.
If the great cardinal now should see me thus,
Would he not count me a villain?
*Julia.* No; he might count me a wanton, 195
Not lay a scruple of offence on you;
For if I see and steal a diamond,
The fault is not i' th' stone, but in me the thief

---

**148 bought:** ('brought' Qq.)   **169 kissing-comfits:** breath-sweetening confections

That purloins it. I am sudden with you.
We that are great women of pleasure use to cut
    off                                                           200
These uncertain wishes and unquiet longings,
And in an instant join the sweet delight
And the pretty excuse together. Had you been
    i' th' street,
Under my chamber-window, even there
I should have courted you.                                      205
    *Bos.* O, you are an excellent lady!
    *Julia.* Bid me do somewhat for you presently
To express I love you.
    *Bos.*        I will; and if you love me,
Fail not to effect it.
The cardinal is grown wondrous melancholy:
Demand the cause, let him not put you off      211
With feign'd excuse; discover the main ground
    on 't.
    *Julia.* Why would you know this?
    *Bos.*        I have depended on him,
And I hear that he is fall'n in some disgrace
With the emperor: if he be, like the mice    215
That forsake falling houses, I would shift
To other dependance.
    *Julia.*        You shall not need
Follow the wars: I 'll be your maintenance.
    *Bos.* And I your loyal servant: but I cannot
Leave my calling.
    *Julia.*        Not leave an ungrateful    220
General for the love of a sweet lady!
You are like some cannot sleep in feather-beds,
But must have blocks for their pillows.
    *Bos.*        Will you do this?
    *Julia.* Cunningly.
    *Bos.* To-morrow I 'll expect th' intelligence.
    *Julia.* To-morrow! Get you into my cabi-
    net;                                                      226
You shall have it with you. Do not delay me,
No more than I do you: I am like one
That is condemn'd; I have my pardon prom-
    is'd,
But I would see it seal'd. Go, get you in:    230
You shall see me wind my tongue about his
    heart
Like a skein of silk.        [*Exit Bosola.*]

          [*Re-enter Cardinal*]

    *Card.*        Where are you?

          [*Enter Servants*]

    *Servants.*        Here.
    *Card.* Let none, upon your lives, have con-
ference
With the Prince Ferdinand, unless I know
    it. —
[*Aside.*] In this distraction he may reveal 235
The murther.        [*Exeunt Servants.*]

Yond 's my lingering consumption:
I am weary of her, and by any means
Would be quit of.
    *Julia.*      How now, my lord! what ails you?
    *Card.* Nothing.
    *Julia.*        O, you are much alter'd:
Come, I must be your secretary, and remove
This lead from off your bosom: what 's the
    matter?                                                   241
    *Card.* I may not tell you.
    *Julia.* Are you so far in love with sorrow
You cannot part with part of it? Or think
    you
I cannot love your grace when you are sad 245
As well as merry? Or do you suspect
I, that have been a secret to your heart
These many winters, cannot be the same
Unto your tongue?
    *Card.*        Satisfy thy longing. —
The only way to make thee keep my counsel
Is, not to tell thee.
    *Julia.*        Tell your echo this,      251
Or flatterers, that like echoes still report
What they hear, though most imperfect, and
    not me;
For if that you be true unto yourself,
I 'll know.
    *Card.* Will you rack me?
    *Julia.*        No, judgment shall
Draw it from you: it is an equal fault,      256
To tell one's secrets unto all or none.
    *Card.* The first argues folly.
    *Julia.* But the last tyranny.
    *Card.* Very well: why, imagine I have com-
    mitted                                                    260
Some secret deed which I desire the world
May never hear of.
    *Julia.*        Therefore may not I know it?
You have conceal'd for me as great a sin
As adultery. Sir, never was occasion
For perfect trial of my constancy            265
Till now; sir, I beseech you ——
    *Card.*        You 'll repent it.
    *Julia.* Never.
    *Card.* It hurries thee to ruin: I 'll not tell
    thee.
Be well advis'd, and think what danger 't is
To receive a prince's secrets. They that do, 270
Had need have their breasts hoop'd with ada-
    mant
To contain them. I pray thee, yet be satisfi'd;
Examine thine own frailty; 't is more easy
To tie knots than unloose them. 'T is a secret
That, like a ling'ring poison, many chance lie
Spread in thy veins, and kill thee seven year
    hence.                                                    276
    *Julia.* Now you dally with me.

---

²⁰⁸ **express:** make known    ²³⁸ **of:** ('off' Q 1–2; 'off her' Q 3)    ²⁴⁰ **secretary:** confidante
²⁴⁹ **Satisfy:** calm    ²⁵⁵ **judgment:** discretion

*Card.*                 No more; thou shalt know it.
By my appointment, the great Duchess of
     Malfi
And two of her young children, four nights
     since,
Were strangled.
*Julia.*         O heaven! sir, what have you done!
*Card.* How now? How settles this? Think
     you your bosom                                    281
Will be a grave dark and obscure enough
For such a secret?
*Julia.*              You have undone yourself, sir.
*Card.* Why?
*Julia.*                  It lies not in me to conceal it.
*Card.*                                              No?
Come, I will swear you to 't upon this book.
*Julia.* Most religiously.
*Card.*         Kiss it. [*She kisses the book.*] 286
Now you shall never utter it; thy curiosity
Hath undone thee: thou 'rt poison'd with that
     book.
Because I knew thou couldst not keep my
     counsel,
I have bound thee to 't by death.            290

          [*Re-enter Bosola*]

*Bos.* For pity sake, hold!
*Card.*                        Ha, Bosola!
*Julia.*                          I forgive you
This equal piece of justice you have done,
For I betray'd your counsel to that fellow.
He overheard it: that was the cause I said
It lay not in me to conceal it.              295
*Bos.* O foolish woman,
Couldst not thou have poison'd him?
*Julia.*                            'T is weakness
Too much to think what should have been
     done. I go,
I know not whither.                    [*Dies.*]
*Card.*          Wherefore com'st thou hither?
*Bos.* That I might find a great man like
     yourself,                                        300
Not out of his wits, as the Lord Ferdinand,
To remember my service.
*Card.* I 'll have thee hew'd in pieces.
*Bos.* Make not yourself such a promise of
     that life
Which is not yours to dispose of.
*Card.*                        Who plac'd thee here?
*Bos.* Her lust, as she intended.
*Card.*                          Very well: 306
Now you know me for your fellow-murderer.
*Bos.* And wherefore should you lay fair
     marble colours
Upon your rotten purposes to me?
Unless you imitate some that do plot great
     treasons,                                        310

And when they have done, go hide themselves
     i' th' graves
Of those were actors in 't?
*Card.*                        No more; there is
A fortune attends thee.
*Bos.* Shall I go sue to Fortune any longer?
'T is the fool's pilgrimage.                  315
*Card.* I have honours in store for thee.
*Bos.* There are a many ways that conduct to
     seeming
Honour, and some of them very dirty ones.
*Card.* Throw to the devil
Thy melancholy. The fire burns well;         320
What need we keep a-stirring of 't, and make
A greater smother? Thou wilt kill Antonio?
*Bos.* Yes.
*Card.* Take up that body.
*Bos.*                          I think I shall
Shortly grow the common bier for church-yards.
*Card.* I will allow thee some dozen of attend-
     ants                                             325
To aid thee in the murther.
*Bos.* O, by no means. Physicians that apply
horse-leeches to any rank swelling use to cut off
their tails, that the blood may run through them
the faster: let me have no train when I go [330
to shed blood, less it make me have a greater
when I ride to the gallows.
*Card.* Come to me after midnight, to help to
     remove
That body to her own lodging. I 'll give out
She died o' th' plague; 't will breed the less
     inquiry                                          335
After her death.
*Bos.* Where 's Castruchio her husband?
*Card.* He 's rode to Naples, to take posses-
     sion
Of Antonio's citadel.
*Bos.* Believe me, you have done a very happy
     turn.                                            340
*Card.* Fail not to come. There is the master-
     key
Of our lodgings; and by that you may conceive
What trust I plant in you.                *Exit.*
*Bos.*                Υou shall find me ready.
O poor Antonio, though nothing be so needful
To thy estate as pity, yet I find             345
Nothing so dangerous! I must look to my foot-
     ing.
In such slippery ice-pavements men had need
To be frost-nail'd well: they may break their
     necks else.
The precedent 's here afore me. How this man
Bears up in blood! seems fearless! Why, 't is
     well:                                            350
Security some men call the suburbs of hell,
Only a dead wall between. Well, good Antonio,

---

308 **marble colours:** paint applied to wood to make it resemble marble          322 **smother:** smoke
348 **frost-nail'd:** wearing boots provided with hobnails

I 'll seek thee out; and all my care shall be
To put thee into safety from the reach
Of these most cruel biters that have got   355
Some of thy blood already.  It may be,
I 'll join with thee in a most just revenge.
The weakest arm is strong enough that strikes
With the sword of justice.  Still methinks the duchess
Haunts me: there, there! — 'T is nothing but
   my melancholy.   360
O Penitence, let me truly taste thy cup,
That throws men down only to raise them up!
                      *Exit.*

### Scena III

*Antonio, Delio, Echo (from the Duchess' Grave)*

   *Delio.*  Yond 's the cardinal's window.  This
   fortification
Grew from the ruins of an ancient abbey;
And to yond side o' th' river lies a wall,
Piece of a cloister, which in my opinion
Gives the best echo that you ever heard,   5
So hollow and so dismal, and withal
So plain in the distinction of our words,
That many have suppos'd it is a spirit
That answers.
    *Ant.*       I do love these ancient ruins.
We never tread upon them but we set   10
Our foot upon some reverend history;
And, questionless, here in this open court,
Which now lies naked to the injuries
Of stormy weather, some men lie interr'd
Lov'd the church so well, and gave so largely
   to 't,   15
They thought it should have canopied their
   bones
Till dooms-day.  But all things have their
   end;
Churches and cities, which have diseases like
   to men,
Must have like death that we have.
   *Echo.*        *Like death that we have.*
   *Delio.*  Now the echo hath caught you.   20
   *Ant.*  It groan'd, methought, and gave
A very deadly accent.
   *Echo.*        *Deadly accent.*
   *Delio.*  I told you 't was a pretty one.  You
   may make it
A huntsman, or a falconer, a musician,
Or a thing of sorrow.
   *Echo.*      *A thing of sorrow.*   25
   *Ant.*  Ay, sure, that suits it best.
   *Echo.*        *That suits it best.*
   *Ant.*  'T is very like my wife's voice.
   *Echo.*        *Ay, wife's voice.*
   *Delio.*  Come, let 's us walk farther from 't.

I would not have you go to th' cardinal's to-
   night:
Do not.   30
   *Echo.*  *Do not.*
   *Delio.*  Wisdom doth not more moderate
   wasting sorrow
Than time.  Take time for 't; be mindful of
   thy safety.
   *Echo.*  *Be mindful of thy safety.*
   *Ant.*  Necessity compels me.   35
Make scrutiny throughout the passages
Of your own life, you 'll find it impossible
To fly your fate.
   *Echo.*      *O, fly your fate!*
   *Delio.*  Hark! the dead stones seem to have
   pity on you,
And give you good counsel.   40
   *Ant.*  Echo, I will not talk with thee,
For thou art a dead thing.
   *Echo.*      *Thou art a dead thing.*
   *Ant.*  My duchess is asleep now,
And her little ones, I hope sweetly.  O heaven,
Shall I never see her more?
   *Echo.*      *Never see her more.* 45
   *Ant.*  I mark'd not one repetition of the echo
But that; and on the sudden a clear light
Presented me a face folded in sorrow.
   *Delio.*  Your fancy merely.
   *Ant.*      Come, I 'll be out of this ague.
For to live thus is not indeed to live:   50
It is a mockery and abuse of life.
I will not henceforth save myself by halves;
Lose all, or nothing.
   *Delio.*      Your own virtue save you!
I 'll fetch your eldest son, and second you.
It may be that the sight of his own blood,   55
Spread in so sweet a figure, may beget
The more compassion.  However, fare you
   well.
Though in our miseries Fortune have a part,
Yet in our noble suff'rings she hath none.
Contempt of pain, that we may call our own. 60
                      *Exeunt.*

### Scena IIII

*Cardinal, Pescara, Malateste, Roderigo, Grisolan.
[later] Bosola, Ferdinand, Antonio, Servant*

   *Card.*  You shall not watch to-night by the
   sick prince;
His grace is very well recover'd.
   *Mal.*  Good my lord, suffer us.
   *Card.*      O, by no means;
The noise, and change of object in his eye,
Doth more distract him.  I pray, all to bed; 5
And though you hear him in his violent fit,
Do not rise, I entreat you.
   *Pes.*  So, sir; we shall not.

*Card.*                    Nay, I must have you promise
Upon your honours, for I was enjoin'd to 't
By himself; and he seem'd to urge it sensibly.
    *Pes.* Let our honours bind this trifle!          11
    *Card.* Nor any of your followers.
    *Mal.* Neither.
    *Card.* It may be, to make trial of your prom-
ise,
When he 's asleep, myself will rise and feign 15
Some of his mad tricks, and cry out for help,
And feign myself in danger.
    *Mal.* If your throat were cutting,
I 'd not come at you, now I have protested
    against it.
    *Card.* Why, I thank you.
    *Gris.*           'T was a foul storm to-night. 20
    *Rod.* The Lord Ferdinand's chamber shook
    like an osier.
    *Mal.* 'T was nothing but pure kindness in
    the devil
To rock his own child.
                    *Exeunt [all except the Cardinal].*
    *Card.* The reason why I would not suffer
    these
About my brother, is, because at midnight  25
I may with better privacy convey
Julia's body to her own lodging.  O, my con-
    science!
I would pray now; but the devil takes away
    my heart
For having any confidence in prayer.
About this hour I appointed Bosola          30
To fetch the body.  When he hath serv'd my
    turn,
He dies.                                      *Exit.*
                    *[Enter Bosola]*
    *Bos.* Ha! 't was the cardinal's voice; I heard
him name Bosola and my death.  Listen; I hear
one's footing.                                35
                    *[Enter Ferdinand]*
    *Ferd.* Strangling is a very quiet death.
    *Bos.* [*Aside.*] Nay, then, I see I must stand
    upon my guard.
    *Ferd.* What say to that? Whisper softly: do
you agree to 't? So; it must be done i' th'
dark: the cardinal would not for a thousand [40
pounds the doctor should see it.            *Exit.*
    *Bos.* My death is plotted; here 's the con-
sequence of murther.
We value not desert nor Christian breath,
When we know black deeds must be cur'd with
    death.
                *[Enter Antonio and Servant]*
    *Serv.* Here stay, sir, and be confident, I pray;
I 'll fetch you a dark lantern.             *Exit.* 46

    *Ant.* Could I take him at his prayers,
There were hope of pardon.
    *Bos.* Fall right, my sword! — [*Stabs him.*]
I 'll not give thee so much leisure as to pray. 50
    *Ant.* O, I am gone! Thou hast ended a long
    suit
In a minute.
    *Bos.*           What art thou?
    *Ant.*                    A most wretched thing,
That only have thy benefit in death,
To appear myself.
                *[Re-enter Servant with a lantern]*
    *Serv.* Where are you, sir?                 55
    *Ant.* Very near my home. — Bosola!
    *Serv.* O, misfortune!
    *Bos.* Smother thy pity, thou art dead else. —
    Antonio!
The man I would have sav'd 'bove mine own
    life!
We are merely the stars' tennis-balls, struck
    and bandied                                 60
Which way please them. — O good Antonio,
I 'll whisper one thing in thy dying ear
Shall make thy heart break quickly! Thy fair
    duchess
And two sweet children ——
    *Ant.*                    Their very names
Kindle a little life in me.
    *Bos.*                Are murder'd. 65
    *Ant.* Some men have wish'd to die
At the hearing of sad tidings; I am glad
That I shall do 't in sadness. I would not now
Wish my wounds balm'd nor heal'd, for I have
    no use                                      69
To put my life to. In all our quest of greatness,
Like wanton boys whose pastime is their care,
We follow after bubbles blown in th' air.
Pleasure of life, what is 't? Only the good hours
Of an ague; merely a preparative to rest,
To endure vexation. I do not ask            75
The process of my death; only commend me
To Delio.
    *Bos.*      Break, heart!
    *Ant.* And let my son fly the courts of princes.
                                              *[Dies.]*
    *Bos.* Thou seem'st to have lov'd Antonio.
    *Serv.* I brought him hither,             80
To have reconcil'd him to the cardinal.
    *Bos.* I do not ask thee that.
Take him up, if thou tender thine own life,
And bear him where the lady Julia
Was wont to lodge. — O, my fate moves swift!
I have this cardinal in the forge already;   86
Now I 'll bring him to th' hammer. O direful
    misprision!
I will not imitate things glorious,

---

⁶⁰ **bandied:** ('banded' Qq.)    ⁶⁸ **sadness:** actuality    ⁷³ **good:** free from pain    ⁷⁴ **ague: inter-**
mittent fever    ⁷⁶ **process:** circumstances, reason    ⁸⁷ **misprision:** misunderstanding

No more than base: I 'll be mine own example.—
On, on, and look thou represent, for silence, 90
The thing thou bear'st.                    *Exeunt.*

SCENA V

*Cardinal, with a book.* [*Later,*] *Bosola, Pescara,*
*Malateste, Roderigo, Ferdinand, Delio, Serv-*
*ant with Antonio's body*

*Card.* I am puzzl'd in a question about hell;
He says, in hell there 's one material fire,
And yet it shall not burn all men alike.
Lay him by. How tedious is a guilty conscience!
When I look into the fish-ponds in my garden, 5
Methinks I see a thing arm'd with a rake,
That seems to strike at me.

[*Enter Bosola and Servant bearing Antonio's*
*body*]
                              Now, art thou come?
Thou look'st ghastly;
There sits in thy face some great determination,
Mix'd with some fear.
  *Bos.*           Thus it lightens into action: 10
I am come to kill thee.
  *Card.*                    Ha! — Help! our guard!
  *Bos.* Thou art deceiv'd: they are out of thy
howling.
  *Card.* Hold; and I will faithfully divide
Revenues with thee.
  *Bos.*                    Thy prayers and proffers
Are both unseasonable.
  *Card.*                    Raise the watch!   15
We are betray'd!
  *Bos.*           I have confin'd your flight:
I 'll suffer your retreat to Julia's chamber,
But no further.
  *Card.*           Help! we are betray'd!

[*Enter, above, Pescara, Malateste, Roderigo, and*
*Grisolan*]

  *Mal.* Listen.
  *Card.* My dukedom for rescue!              20
  *Rod.* Fie upon his counterfeiting!
  *Mal.* Why, 't is not the cardinal.
  *Rod.* Yes, yes, 't is he:
But I 'll see him hang'd ere I 'll go down to him.
  *Card.* Here 's a plot upon me; I am as-
saulted! I am lost,                          25
Unless some rescue!
  *Gris.*           He doth this pretty well;
But it will not serve to laugh me out of mine
honour.
  *Card.* The sword 's at my throat!
  *Rod.*           You would not bawl so loud then.
  *Mal.* Come, come, let 's go to bed: he told
us thus much aforehand.                      30

  *Pes.* He wish'd you should not come at him;
but, believe 't,
The accent of the voice sounds not in jest.
I 'll down to him, howsoever, and with engines
Force ope the doors.                    [*Exit above.*]
  *Rod.*           Let 's follow him aloof,
And note how the cardinal will laugh at him.
          [*Exeunt, above, Malateste, Roderigo,*
                    *and Grisolan*]
  *Bos.* There 's for you first,              36
'Cause you shall not unbarricade the door
To let in rescue.           *He kills the Servant.*
  *Card.*           What cause hast thou to pursue
my life?
  *Bos.*           Look there.
  *Card.* Antonio!
  *Bos.*           Slain by my hand unwittingly.
Pray, and be sudden. When thou kill'd'st thy
sister,                                      40
Thou took'st from Justice her most equal bal-
ance,
And left her naught but her sword.
  *Card.*                    O, mercy!
  *Bos.* Now it seems thy greatness was only
outward;
For thou fall'st faster of thyself than calamity
Can drive thee. I 'll not waste longer time;
there!                              [*Stabs him.*]
  *Card.* Thou hast hurt me.
  *Bos.*           Again!
  *Card.*           Shall I die like a leveret, 46
Without any resistance? — Help, help, help!
I am slain!

[*Enter Ferdinand*]

  *Ferd.* Th' alarum! Give me a fresh horse!
Rally the vaunt-guard, or the day is lost!
Yield, yield! I give you the honour of arms, 50
Shake my sword over you; will you yield?
  *Card.* Help me; I am your brother!
  *Ferd.*                    The devil!
My brother fight upon the adverse party!
          *He wounds the Cardinal, and* (*in the*
                    *scuffle*) *gives Bosola his death-*
                    *wound.*
There flies your ransom.
  *Card.* O justice!                         55
I suffer now for what hath former bin:
Sorrow is held the eldest child of sin.
  *Ferd.* Now you 're brave fellows. Cæsar's
fortune was harder than Pompey's: Cæsar died
in the arms of prosperity, Pompey at the [60
feet of disgrace. You both died in the field.
The pain 's nothing; pain many times is taken
away with the apprehension of greater, as the
tooth-ache with the sight of a barber that comes
to pull it out. There 's philosophy for you. 65

---

⁹⁰ **represent:** imitate   ⁴⁶ **leveret:** young hare   ⁵⁰ **honour of arms:** honorable terms of surrender
⁵⁶ **former:** earlier   **bin:** been   ⁶⁴ **barber:** *i.e.,* barber-surgeon-dentist

*Bos.*  Now my revenge is perfect. — Sink,
  thou main cause            *He kills Ferdinand.*
Of my undoing! — The last part of my life
Hath done me best service.
      *Ferd.*  Give me some wet hay; I am broken-
        winded.
I do account this world but a dog-kennel:    70
I will vault credit and affect high pleasures
Beyond death.
      *Bos.*            He seems to come to himself,
Now he 's so near the bottom.
      *Ferd.*  My sister, O my sister! there 's the
        cause on 't.
Whether we fall by ambition, blood, or lust,    75
Like diamonds, we are cut with our own dust.
                                        [*Dies.*]
      *Card.*  Thou hast thy payment too.
      *Bos.*  Yes, I hold my weary soul in my teeth;
'T is ready to part from me.  I do glory    79
That thou, which stood'st like a huge pyramid
Begun upon a large and ample base,
Shalt end in a little point, a kind of nothing.

[*Enter, below, Pescara, Malateste, Roderigo, and
                  Grisolan*]

      *Pes.*  How now, my lord!
      *Mal.*            O sad disaster!
      *Rod.*                        How comes this?
      *Bos.*  Revenge for the Duchess of Malfi mur-
        dered
By th' Arragonian brethren; for Antonio    85
Slain by this hand; for lustful Julia
Poison'd by this man; and lastly for myself,
That was an actor in the main of all
Much 'gainst mine own good nature, yet i' th'
        end
Neglected.
      *Pes.*      How now, my lord!
      *Card.*            Look to my brother:
He gave us these large wounds, as we were
        struggling                                91
Here i' th' rushes.  And now, I pray, let me
Be laid by and never thought of.      [*Dies.*]

      *Pes.*  How fatally, it seems, he did withstand
His own rescue!
      *Mal.*          Thou wretched thing of blood,    95
How came Antonio by his death?
      *Bos.*  In a mist; I know not how.
Such a mistake as I have often seen
In a play.  O, I am gone!                        99
We are only like dead walls or vaulted graves,
That, ruin'd, yields no echo.  Fare you well!
It may be pain, but no harm, to me to die
In so good a quarrel.  O, this gloomy world!
In what a shadow, or deep pit of darkness,
Doth womanish and fearful mankind live!    105
Let worthy minds ne'er stagger in distrust
To suffer death or shame for what is just:
Mine is another voyage.                [*Dies.*]
      *Pes.*  The noble Delio, as I came to th' palace,
Told me of Antonio's being here, and show'd
        me                                        110
A pretty gentleman, his son and heir.

[*Enter Delio, and Antonio's Son*]

      *Mal.*  O sir, you come too late!
      *Delio.*                      I heard so, and
Was arm'd for 't, ere I came.  Let us make
        noble use
Of this great ruin; and join all our force
To establish this young hopeful gentleman    115
In 's mother's right.  These wretched eminent
        things
Leave no more fame behind 'em, than should
        one
Fall in a frost, and leave his print in snow:
As soon as the sun shines, it ever melts,
Both form and matter.  I have ever thought    120
Nature doth nothing so great for great men
As when she 's pleas'd to make them lords of
        truth:
Integrity of life is fame's best friend,
Which nobly, beyond death, shall crown the
        end.                            *Exeunt.*

                        FINIS

⁸⁶ **this:** ('his' Qq.)    ⁸⁸ **main:** chief part    ⁹² **rushes:** (used as floor covering by the great)

# THE
# KNIGHT OF
## the Burning Peſtle.

——— ——— ——— *Quod ſi*
*Iudicium ſubtile, videndis artibus illud*
*Ad libros & ad hæc Muſarum dona vocares:*
*Bœotum in craſſo iurares aëre natos.*
Horat. in Epiſt. ad Oct. Aug.

*LONDON,*
Printed for *Walter Burre*, and are to be ſold at the
ſigne of the Crane in Paules Church-yard.
**1613.**

BIBLIOGRAPHICAL RECORD. No entry of copyright for *The Knight of the Burning Pestle* has been found. It was, however, the second of the Beaumont-Fletcher plays to appear in print (the first being *The Woman-Hater*, 1607), and was published in 1613 by Walter Burre, without indication of authorship. Burre appended the following important dedication to Robert Keysar, who had been manager of the Children of the Queen's Revels between 1607 and 1610.

*To his many waies endeered friend Maister Robert Keysar. Sir, this unfortunate child, who in eight daies (as lately I have learned) was begot and borne, soone after, was by his parents (perhaps because hee was so unlike his brethren) exposed to the wide world, who for want of judgement, or not understanding the privy marke of Ironie about it (which shewed it was no of-spring of any vulgar braine) utterly rejected it: so that for want of acceptance it was even ready to give up the Ghost, and was in danger to have bene smothered in perpetuall oblivion, if you (out of your direct antipathy to ingratitude) had not bene moved both to relieve and cherish it: wherein I must needs commend both your judgement, understanding, and singular love to good wits; you afterwards sent it to mee, yet being an infant and somewhat ragged, I have fostred it privately in my bosome these two yeares, and now to shew my love returne it to you, clad in good lasting cloaths, which scarce memory will weare out, and able to speake for it selfe; and withall, as it telleth mee, desirous to try his fortune in the world, where if yet it be welcome, father, foster-father, nurse and child, all have their desired end. If it be slighted or traduced, it hopes his father will beget him a yonger brother, who shall revenge his quarrell, and challenge the world either of fond and meerely literall interpretation, or illiterate misprision. Perhaps it will be thought to bee of the race of Don Quixote: we both may confidently sweare, it is his elder above a yeare; and therefore may (by vertue of his birth-right) challenge the wall of him. I doubt not but they will meet in their adventures, and I hope the breaking of one staffe will make them friends; and perhaps they will combine themselves, and travell through the world to seeke their adventures. So I commit him to his good fortune, and my selfe to your love. Your assured friend W. B.*

The second and third Quartos both appeared in 1635. The title-page of each of these names Beaumont and Fletcher as the authors and characterizes the play 'as it is now acted by Her Majesties Servants at the Private house in Drury lane' (*i.e*, Queen Henrietta's Men at the Phœnix or Cockpit). The texts of these editions and of the Folio of 1679 (F) vary only in minor points from that of Q 1.

DATE AND STAGE HISTORY. The date of composition cannot be earlier than 1607 or later than 1610. There has been much argument for both dates. The earlier seems to us the more likely, chiefly because (1) the extremely small evidence of Fletcher's hand in the play points to the time before Beaumont and he had formed the habit of working together, and the burlesque tone of the play indicates that it belongs, like *The Woman-Hater*, to Beaumont's earliest period; and (2) the Grocer's remark in the Induction (line 6), "This seven years there hath been plays at this house," etc., precisely fits the Blackfriars theatre in 1607 (where the boys had commenced acting in 1600), but not the Whitefriars in 1610 (to which Keysar had transferred the boys in 1609, when Shakespeare's adult company secured the use of Blackfriars). It is clear from the text that the play was written to be acted by boys at a private theatre, and (unlike the later plays of Beaumont and Fletcher) it did not come into the repertory of the King's Company till after the Restoration. As Burre's letter, quoted above, indicates, it was a failure when first produced. The revival by the Queen's Men a quarter-century later met with more favor, evidenced by the two editions in 1635 and a court performance at St. James's Palace, Feb. 28, 1635–1636. The King's Men produced it on May 5, 1662, and a few years later with "a new Prologue [instead of the old one in prose] being spoken by Mrs. Ellen Guin" (Nell Gwynn); but not even in the days of Charles II does this magnificent satire seem to have received the approbation which it deserved, and which was so lavished upon other plays of Beaumont and Fletcher.

SOURCES. The chief problem concerns the relation of *The Knight of the Burning Pestle* to the *Don Quixote* of Cervantes, of which the first part was printed in Spain in 1605, made more available for English readers through an edition printed at Brussels in 1607, translated into English (from the Brussels text) about 1608 by Thomas Shelton, and published in Shelton's version in 1612. The plot of the play suggests that the author had a general notion of the scheme of Cervantes, but the only detail which is closely similar is that of Ralph's interview with the host at the opening of III, ii. Beaumont has drawn very heavily upon the popular Spanish romances like *Palmerin de Oliva* and *Knight of the Sun*, and for Merrythought's songs has introduced scraps from current ballads.

STRUCTURE. The old editions divide the acts, but not the scenes. The play illustrates very vividly the mode of performance at a private theatre, where favored auditors sat on the stage, and the act-intervals were filled with music, dancing, comment, and refreshment.

# FRANCIS BEAUMONT (1584–1616) [and JOHN FLETCHER?]

## THE KNIGHT OF THE BURNING PESTLE

### To the Readers of this COMEDY

Gentlemen, the world is so nice in these our times, that for apparel there is no fashion; for music, which is a rare art (though now slighted), no instrument; for diet none but the French kickshaws that are delicate; and for plays no invention but that which now runneth an invective way, touching some particular persons, or else it is contemned before it is throughly understood. This is all that I have to say: that the author had no intent to wrong any one in this comedy, but as a merry passage here and there interlaced it with delight, which he hopes will please all and be hurtful to none.

#### THE ACTORS' NAMES

THE PROLOGUE [a boy actor]
Then a CITIZEN [George, a Grocer]
The Citizen's WIFE [Nell], and RALPH, her man, sitting below amidst the Spectators
A rich Merchant [VENTUREWELL]
JASPER [MERRYTHOUGHT], his Apprentice
Master HUMPHREY, a Friend to the Merchant

MICHAEL, a second Son of Mistress Merrythought
Old Master MERRYTHOUGHT
[TIM] A Squire, \ [Apprentices to the Grocer,
[GEORGE] A Dwarf, / serving Ralph]
LUCE, the Merchant's Daughter
Mistress MERRYTHOUGHT, Jasper's Mother
[POMPIONA, Daughter of the King of Moldavia]

A Tapster; A Boy that danceth and singeth; An Host; A Barber; Two Knights [i.e., Travellers, also a Man and Woman, all Prisoners to the Barber]; A Sergeant [and] Soldiers [in a militia company]

[SCENE: Various parts of London, Waltham and Waltham Forest; Moldavia]

### [INDUCTION

*Several Gentlemen sitting on Stools upon the
    Stage. The Citizen, his Wife, and Ralph
    sitting below among the Audience]*

#### Enter Prologue

*Prol.* "From all that 's near the court, from
    all that 's great,
Within the compass of the city-walls,
We now have brought our scene ——"

*Citizen [leaps on the stage.]*

*Cit.* Hold your peace, goodman boy!
*Prol.* What do you mean, sir?                    5
*Cit.* That you have no good meaning: this
seven years there hath been plays at this house,
I have observed it, you have still girds at citizens; and now you call your play "The London

Merchant." Down with your title, boy! down
with your title!                                    11
*Prol.* Are you a member of the noble city?
*Cit.* I am.
*Prol.* And a freeman?
*Cit.* Yea, and a grocer.                          15
*Prol.* So, grocer, then, by your sweet favour,
we intend no abuse to the city.
*Cit.* No, sir! yes, sir. If you were not resolv'd
to play the jacks, what need you study for
new subjects, purposely to abuse your bet- [20
ters? Why could not you be contented, as well
as others, with "The legend of Whittington,"
or "The Life and Death of Sir Thomas
Gresham, with the building of the Royal Exchange," or "The story of Queen Eleanor, [25
with the rearing of London Bridge upon woolsacks?"

---

To the Readers, etc.: (This Epistle is not in Q 1. Q 2–F append to it a prologue, which is merely that
of Lyly's *Sapho and Phao*, slightly amplified.)    **The Actors' Names:** (As in F, with slight changes)
⁴ **goodman:** sirrah    ⁷ **this house:** probably Blackfriars    ⁸ **still:** continually    **girds:** sneers
¹⁰ **title:** the title-board giving name of the piece to be presented    ¹⁹ **play the jacks:** make mischief
²³ **The Life, etc.:** Heywood's *If You Know Not Me*, Part II    ²⁵ **The story, etc.:** perhaps Peele's *Edward I*

*Prol.* You seem to be an understanding man: what would you have us do, sir? 29

*Cit.* Why, present something notably in honour of the commons of the city.

*Prol.* Why, what do you say to "The Life and Death of fat Drake, or the Repairing of Fleet-privies?" 34

*Cit.* I do not like that; but I will have a citizen, and he shall be of my own trade.

*Prol.* Oh, you should have told us your mind a month since; our play is ready to begin now.

*Cit.* 'T is all one for that; I will have a grocer, and he shall do admirable things. 40

*Prol.* What will you have him do?

*Cit.* Marry, I will have him ——

*Wife. below.* Husband, husband!

*Ralph. below.* Peace, mistress. 44

*Wife. [below.]* Hold thy peace, Ralph; I know what I do, I warrant ye. — Husband, husband!

*Cit.* What sayst thou, cony?

*Wife. [below.]* Let him kill a lion with a [49 pestle, husband! Let him kill a lion with a pestle!

*Cit.* So he shall. I 'll have him kill a lion with a pestle.

*Wife. [below.]* Husband! shall I come up, husband? 55

*Cit.* Ay, cony. — Ralph, help your mistress this way. — Pray, gentlemen, make her a little room. — I pray you, sir, lend me your hand to help up my wife: I thank you, sir. — So.

*[Wife comes on the stage.]*

*Wife.* By your leave, gentlemen all; I 'm [60 something troublesome. I 'm a stranger here; I was ne'er at one of these plays, as they say, before; but I should have seen "Jane Shore" once; and my husband hath promised me, any time this twelvemonth, to carry me [65 to "The Bold Beauchamps," but in truth he did not. I pray you, bear with me.

*Cit.* Boy, let my wife and I have a couple of stools and then begin; and let the grocer do rare things. *[Stools are brought.]* 70

*Prol.* But, sir, we have never a boy to play him: every one hath a part already.

*Wife.* Husband, husband, for God's sake, let Ralph play him! Beshrew me, if I do not think he will go beyond them all. 75

*Cit.* Well rememb'red, wife. — Come up, Ralph. — I 'll tell you, gentlemen; let them but

lend him a suit of reparel and necessaries, and, by gad, if any of them all blow wind in the tail on him, I 'll be hang'd. 80

*[Ralph comes on the stage.]*

*Wife.* I pray you, youth, let him have a suit of reparel! — I 'll be sworn, gentlemen, my husband tells you true. He will act you sometimes at our house, that all the neighbours [84 cry out on him; he will fetch you up a couraging part so in the garret, that we are all as fear'd, I warrant you, that we quake again: we 'll fear our children with him; if they be never so unruly, do but cry, "Ralph comes, Ralph comes!" to them, and they 'll be as [90 quiet as lambs. — Hold up thy head, Ralph; show the gentlemen what thou canst do; speak a huffing part; I warrant you, the gentlemen will accept of it.

*Cit.* Do, Ralph, do. 95

*Ralph.* "By Heaven, methinks, it were an easy leap
To pluck bright honour from the pale-fac'd moon;
Or dive into the bottom of the sea,
Where never fathom-line touch'd any ground,
And pluck up drowned honour from the lake of hell." 100

*Cit.* How say you, gentlemen, is it not as I told you?

*Wife.* Nay, gentlemen, he hath play'd before, my husband says, "Mucedorus," before the wardens of our company. 105

*Cit.* Ay, and he should have play'd Jeronimo with a shoemaker for a wager.

*Prol.* He shall have a suit of apparel, if he will go in.

*Cit.* In, Ralph, in, Ralph; and set out the grocery in their kind, if thou lov'st me. 111
*[Exit Ralph.]*

*Wife.* I warrant, our Ralph will look finely when he 's dress'd.

*Prol.* But what will you have it call'd?

*Cit.* "The Grocer's Honour." 115

*Prol.* Methinks "The Knight of the Burning Pestle" were better.

*Wife.* I 'll be sworn, husband, that 's as good a name as can be.

*Cit.* Let it be so. — Begin, begin; my wife and I will sit down. 121

*Prol.* I pray you, do.

*Cit.* What stately music have you? You have shawms?

²⁸ **understanding:** (with pun on "groundling") ³³ **fat Drake:** perhaps a local scavenger (cf. *Times Lit. Sup.*, Sept. 20, 1928) ⁴⁵ **Ralph:** ('Rafe' or 'Raph' throughout in Qq. and so pronounced) ⁴⁸ **cony:** rabbit ⁶³ **should:** was to ⁶³⁻⁶⁴ **Jane Shore:** probably Heywood's *Edward IV* ⁶⁶ **The Bold Beauchamps:** a lost play ⁷⁸ **reparel:** apparel ⁷⁹⁻⁸⁰ **blow . . . on:** come near (horse-racing term) ⁸⁵⁻⁸⁶ **couraging:** boisterous ⁹³ **huffing:** swaggering ⁹⁶⁻¹⁰⁰ (A slightly exaggerated version of Hotspur's rant, *I Henry IV*, I. iii. 201–205) ¹⁰⁴ **Mucedorus:** an absurdly popular play, falsely ascribed to Shakespeare ¹⁰⁶⁻¹⁰⁷ **Jeronimo:** *The Spanish Tragedy* ¹²⁴ **shawms:** reed instruments

*Prol.* Shawms? No.

*Cit.* No! I 'm a thief if my mind did not [126
give me so. Ralph plays a stately part, and he
must needs have shawms. I 'll be at the charge
of them myself, rather than we 'll be without
them.     130

*Prol.* So you are like to be.

*Cit.* Why, and so I will be: there 's two shillings; — [*gives money.*] — let 's have the waits
of Southwark; they are as rare fellows as any
are in England; and that will fetch them all
o 'er the water with a vengeance, as if they [136
were mad.

*Prol.* You shall have them. Will you sit
down then?

*Cit.* Ay. — Come, wife.     140

*Wife.* Sit you merry all, gentlemen; I 'm
bold to sit amongst you for my ease.

            [*Citizen and Wife sit down.*]

*Prol.* "From all that 's near the court, from
    all that 's great,
Within the compass of the city-walls,
We now have brought our scene. Fly far from
    hence     145
All private taxes, immodest phrases,
Whatever may but show like vicious!
For wicked mirth never true pleasure brings,
But honest minds are pleas'd with honest
    things." —
Thus much for that we do; but for Ralph's
part you must answer for yourself.     151

*Cit.* Take you no care for Ralph; he 'll discharge himself, I warrant you.

            [*Exit Prologue.*]

*Wife.* I' faith, gentlemen, I 'll give my word
for Ralph.     155

## Actus Primus.
## Scæna Prima.

[*Venturewell's House.*]

*Enter Merchant [Venturewell] and Jasper,
his Prentice*

*Vent.* Sirrah, I 'll make you know you are
    my prentice,
And whom my charitable love redeem'd
Even from the fall of fortune; gave thee heat
And growth, to be what now thou art; new-cast
    thee,
Adding the trust of all I have, at home,     5
In foreign staples, or upon the sea,
To thy direction; tied the good opinions
Both of myself and friends to thy endeavours,

So fair were thy beginnings. But with these,
As I remember, you had never charge     10
To love your master's daughter, and even then
When I had found a wealthy husband for her.
I take it, sir, you had not: but, however,
I 'll break the neck of that commission,
And make you know you are but a merchant's
    factor.     15

*Jasp.* Sir, I do liberally confess I am yours,
Bound both by love and duty to your service,
In which my labour hath been all my profit:
I have not lost in bargain, nor delighted
To wear your honest gains upon my back;     20
Nor have I given a pension to my blood,
Or lavishly in play consum'd your stock.
These, and the miseries that do attend them,
I dare with innocence proclaim are strangers 24
To all my temperate actions. For your daughter,
If there be any love to my deservings
Borne by her virtuous self, I cannot stop it;
Nor am I able to refrain her wishes.
She 's private to herself, and best of knowledge
Whom she will make so happy as to sigh for: 30
Besides, I cannot think you mean to match her
Unto a fellow of so lame a presence,
One that hath little left of nature in him.

*Vent.* 'T is very well, sir: I can tell your
    wisdom
How all this shall be cur'd.

*Jasp.*          Your care becomes you.   35

*Vent.* And thus it must be, sir: I here dis-
    charge you
My house and service; take your liberty;
And when I want a son, I 'll send for you. *Exit.*

*Jasp.* These be the fair rewards of them
    that love!
Oh, you that live in freedom, never prove   40
The travail of a mind led by desire!

*Enter Luce*

*Luce.* Why, how now, friend? Struck with
    my father's thunder!

*Jasp.* Struck, and struck dead, unless the
    remedy
Be full of speed and virtue; I am now,
What I expected long, no more your father's. 45

*Luce.* But mine.

*Jasp.*        But yours, and only yours, I am;
That 's all I have to keep me from the statute.
You dare be constant still?

*Luce.*           Oh, fear me not!
In this I dare be better than a woman:
Nor shall his anger nor his offers move me,   50
Were they both equal to a prince's power.

---

¹²⁷ **give:** misgive    ¹³³ **waits:** street musicians
remade    ⁶ **staples:** market towns    ¹³ **however:**
even though you had    ¹⁵ **factor:** agent    ²¹ **pen-**
**sion . . . blood:** spent money on my pleasures    ²⁸ **refrain:** bridle    ²⁹ **private . . . knowledge:** a
free individual and the best judge    ³² **lame presence:** poor appearance    ³⁶ **must:** ('shall' F)
⁴⁴ **virtue:** efficacy    ⁴⁷ **statute:** law against vagrants

*Jasp.*  You know my rival!
*Luce.*                    Yes, and love him dearly,
Even as I love an ague or foul weather.
I prithee, Jasper, fear him not.
    *Jasp.*                        Oh, no!
I do not mean to do him so much kindness. 55
But to our own desires: you know the plot
We both agreed on?
    *Luce.*            Yes, and will perform
My part exactly.
    *Jasp.*        I desire no more.
Farewell, and keep my heart; 't is yours.
    *Luce.*                        I take it;
He must do miracles makes me forsake it. 60
                        *Exeunt [severally].*

*Cit.*  Fie upon 'em, little infidels! what a
matter 's here now! Well, I 'll be hang'd for a
halfpenny, if there be not some abomination
knavery in this play. Well; let 'em look to 't;
Ralph must come, and if there be any tricks [65
a-brewing ——
    *Wife.*  Let 'em brew and bake too, husband,
a' God's name; Ralph will find all out, I warrant you, and they were older than they are. —
[*Enter Boy.*] — I pray, my pretty youth, is [70
Ralph ready?
    *Boy.*  He will be presently.
    *Wife.*  Now, I pray you, make my commen-
dations unto him, and withal carry him this stick
of liquorice. Tell him his mistress sent it [75
him; and bid him bite a piece; 't will open his
pipes the better, say.            [*Exit Boy.*]

### [SCENE II. — *The Same.*]

*Enter Merchant [Venturewell] and
Master Humphrey*

*Vent.*  Come, sir, she 's yours; upon my faith,
    she 's yours;
You have my hand: for other idle lets
Between your hopes and her, thus with a wind
They are scatter'd and no more. My wanton
    prentice,
That like a bladder blew himself with love, 5
I have let out, and sent him to discover
New masters yet unknown.
    *Hum.*            I thank you, sir;
Indeed, I thank you, sir; and, ere I stir,
It shall be known, however you do deem,
I am of gentle blood and gentle seem. 10
    *Vent.*  Oh, sir, I know it certain.
    *Hum.*                Sir, my friend,
Although, as writers say, all things have end,
And that we call a pudding hath his two,
Oh, let it not seem strange, I pray, to you,

If in this bloody simile I put            15
My love, more endless than frail things or gut!
    *Wife.*  Husband, I prithee, sweet lamb, tell
me one thing; but tell me truly. — Stay, youths,
I beseech you, till I question my husband.
    *Cit.*  What is it, mouse?            20
    *Wife.*  Sirrah, didst thou ever see a prettier
child? how it behaves itself, I warrant ye, and
speaks and looks, and perts up the head! — I
pray you, brother, with your favour, were you
never none of Master Moncaster's scholars? [25
    *Cit.*  Chicken, I prithee heartily, contain thy-
self: the childer are pretty childer; but when
Ralph comes, lamb ——
    *Wife.*  Ay, when Ralph comes, cony! — Well,
my youth, you may proceed.            30

*Vent.*  Well, sir, you know my love, and rest,
    I hope,
Assur'd of my consent; get but my daughter's,
And wed her when you please. You must be
    bold,
And clap in close unto her: come, I know
You have language good enough to win a
    wench.            35

*Wife.*  A whoreson tyrant! h'as been an old
stringer in 's days, I warrant him.

*Hum.*  I take your gentle offer, and withal
Yield love again for love reciprocal.
    *Vent.*  What, Luce! within there!

*Enter Luce*

*Luce.*                    Call'd you, sir?
    *Vent.*                        I did: 40
Give entertainment to this gentleman;
And see you be not froward. — To her, sir:
My presence will but be an eye-sore to you.
                        *Exit.*
    *Hum.*  Fair Mistress Luce, how do you?
    Are you well?
Give me your hand, and then I pray you tell 45
How doth your little sister and your brother;
And whether you love me or any other.
    *Luce.*  Sir, these are quickly answer'd.
    *Hum.*                So they are,
Where women are not cruel. But how far
Is it now distant, from the place we are in, 50
Unto that blessed place, your father's warren?
    *Luce.*  What makes you think of that, sir?
    *Hum.*                Even that face;
For, stealing rabbits whilom in that place,
God Cupid, or the keeper, I know not whether,
Unto my cost and charges brought you thither,
And there began ——

---

⁶⁰ **makes**: who makes    ⁶⁹ **and**: an, if (as frequently later)    ² **lets**: obstacles    ¹³ **two**: two ends
¹⁵ **bloody**: (alluding to blood-puddings)    ²³ **perts**: tosses    ²⁵ **Moncaster**: Richard Mulcaster. Head-
master of St. Paul's school, 1596–1608    ³⁷ **stringer**: roué    ⁵⁴ **whether**: which

*Luce.*                Your game, sir.
*Hum.*                        Let no game, 56
Or anything that tendeth to the same,
Be evermore rememb'red, thou fair killer,
For whom I sat me down, and brake my
    tiller.

*Wife.* There 's a kind gentleman, I war- [60
rant you; when will you do as much for me,
George?

*Luce.* Beshrew me, sir, I am sorry for your
    losses,
But, as the proverb says, I cannot cry.
I would you had not seen me!
*Hum.*                        So would I, 65
Unless you had more maw to do me good.
*Luce.* Why, cannot this strange passion be
    withstood?
Send for a constable, and raise the town.
*Hum.* Oh, no! my valiant love will batter
    down
Millions of constables, and put to flight 70
Even that great watch of Midsummer-day at
    night.
*Luce.* Beshrew me, sir, 't were good I yielded,
    then;
Weak women cannot hope, where valiant men
Have no resistance.
*Hum.*                        Yield, then; I am full
Of pity, though I say it, and can pull 75
Out of my pocket thus a pair of gloves.
Look, Lucy, look; the dog's tooth nor the
    dove's
Are not so white as these; and sweet they be,
And whipp'd about with silk, as you may see.
If you desire the price, shoot from your eye 80
A beam to this place, and you shall espy
*F S*, which is to say, my sweetest honey,
They cost me three and twopence, or no money.
*Luce.* Well, sir, I take them kindly, and I
    thank you:
What would you more?
*Hum.*                Nothing.
*Luce.*                    Why, then, farewell. 85
*Hum.* Nor so, nor so; for, lady, I must tell,
Before we part, for what we met together:
God grant me time and patience and fair
    weather!
*Luce.* Speak, and declare your mind in terms
    so brief.
*Hum.* I shall: then, first and foremost, for
    relief 90
I call to you, if that you can afford it;
I care not at what price, for, on my word, it
Shall be repaid again, although it cost me
More than I 'll speak of now; for love hath tost
    me

In furious blanket like a tennis-ball, 95
And now I rise aloft, and now I fall.
*Luce.* Alas, good gentleman, alas the day!
*Hum.* I thank you heartily; and, as I say,
Thus do I still continue without rest,
I' th' morning like a man, at night a beast, 100
Roaring and bellowing mine own disquiet,
That much I fear, forsaking of my diet
Will bring me presently to that quandary,
I shall bid all adieu.
*Luce.*                Now, by St. Mary,
That were great pity!
*Hum.*                So it were, beshrew me! 105
Then, ease me, lusty Luce, and pity show me.
*Luce.* Why, sir, you know my will is nothing
    worth
Without my father's grant; get his consent,
And then you may with assurance try me.
*Hum.* The worshipful your sire will not
    deny me; 110
For I have ask'd him, and he hath replied,
"Sweet Master Humphrey, Luce shall be thy
    bride."
*Luce.* Sweet Master Humphrey, then I am
    content.
*Hum.* And so am I, in truth.
*Luce.*                Yet take me with you;
There is another clause must be annex'd, 115
And this it is: I swore, and will perform it,
No man shall ever joy me as his wife
But he that stole me hence. If you dare ven-
    ture,
I am yours (you need not fear; my father loves
    you);
If not, farewell for ever!
*Hum.*                Stay, nymph, stay: 120
I have a double gelding, colour'd bay,
Sprung by his father from Barbarian kind;
Another for myself, though somewhat blind,
Yet true as trusty tree.
*Luce.*                I am satisfied;
And so I give my hand. Our course must
    lie 125
Through Waltham Forest, where I have a
    friend
Will entertain us. So, farewell, sir Humphrey,
And think upon your business.            *Exit.*
*Hum.*                        Though I die,
I am resolv'd to venture life and limb
For one so young, so fair, so kind, so trim. 130
                                    *Exit.*

*Wife.* By my faith and troth, George, and as
I am virtuous, it is e'en the kindest young man
that ever trod on shoe-leather. — Well, go thy
ways; if thou hast her not, 't is not thy fault,
'faith.                                135

---

⁵⁹ **tiller:** part of crossbow    ⁶⁶ **maw:** craving    ⁷¹ **great watch:** annual gathering of city militia
⁸² **F S:** a dealer's mark    ¹¹⁴ **take . . . you:** understand me

*Cit.* I prithee, mouse, be patient; 'a shall have her, or I 'll make some of 'em smoke for 't.

*Wife.* That 's my good lamb, George. — Fie, this stinking tobacco kills me! would there [140 were none in England! — Now, I pray, gentlemen, what good does this stinking tobacco do you? Nothing, I warrant you: make chimneys o' your faces! — Oh, husband, husband, now, now! there 's Ralph, there 's Ralph.        145

[SCENE III. — *The Grocer's Shop.*]

*Enter Ralph, like a Grocer in 's shop with two Prentices [Tim and George], reading "Palmerin of England"*

*Cit.* Peace, fool! let Ralph alone. — Hark you, Ralph; do not strain yourself too much at the first. — Peace! — Begin, Ralph.

*Ralph.* [*reads.*] Then Palmerin and Trineus, snatching their lances from their dwarfs, [5 and clasping their helmets, gallop'd amain after the giant; and Palmerin, having gotten a sight of him, came posting amain, saying, "Stay, traitorous thief! for thou mayst not so carry away her, that is worth the greatest lord in [10 the world;" and, with these words, gave him a blow on the shoulder, that he struck him besides his elephant. And Trineus, coming to the knight that had Agricola behind him, set him soon besides his horse, with his neck [15 broken in the fall; so that the princess, getting out of the throng, between joy and grief, said, "All happy knight, the mirror of all such as follow arms, now may I be well assured of the love thou bearest me." I wonder why the [20 kings do not raise an army of fourteen or fifteen hundred thousand men, as big as the army that the Prince of Portigo brought against Rosicleer, and destroy these giants; they do much hurt to wandering damsels, that go in [25 quest of their knights.

*Wife.* Faith, husband, and Ralph says true; for they say the King of Portugal cannot sit at his meat, but the giants and the ettins will come and snatch it from him.        30

*Cit.* Hold thy tongue. — On, Ralph!

*Ralph.* And certainly those knights are much to be commended, who, neglecting their possessions, wander with a squire and a dwarf through the deserts to relieve poor ladies.        35

*Wife.* Ay, by my faith, are they, Ralph; let 'em say what they will, they are indeed. Our knights neglect their possessions well enough, but they do not the rest.

*Ralph.* There are no such courteous and [40 fair well-spoken knights in this age: they will call one the son of a whore, that Palmerin of England would have called "fair sir;" and one that Rosicleer would have call'd "right beauteous damsel," they will call "damn'd [45 bitch."

*Wife.* I 'll be sworn will they, Ralph; they have call'd me so an hundred times about a scurvy pipe of tobacco.

*Ralph.* But what brave spirit could be [50 content to sit in his shop, with a flappet of wood, and a blue apron before him, selling mithridatum and dragon's-water to visited houses, that might pursue feats of arms, and, through his noble achievements, procure such a fa- [55 mous history to be written of his heroic prowess?

*Cit.* Well said, Ralph; some more of those words, Ralph!

*Wife.* They go finely, by my troth.

*Ralph.* Why should not I, then, pursue [60 this course, both for the credit of myself and our company? for amongst all the worthy books of achievements, I do not call to mind that I yet read of a grocer-errant. I will be the said knight. — Have you heard of any that hath [65 wandered unfurnished of his squire and dwarf? My elder prentice Tim shall be my trusty squire, and little George my dwarf. Hence, my blue apron! Yet, in remembrance of my former trade, upon my shield shall be portray'd a [70 Burning Pestle, and I will be call'd the Knight of the Burning Pestle.

*Wife.* Nay, I dare swear thou wilt not forget thy old trade; thou wert ever meek.

*Ralph.* Tim!        75
*Tim.* Anon.
*Ralph.* My beloved squire, and George, my dwarf, I charge you that from henceforth you never call me by any other name but "the right courteous and valiant Knight of the Burning [80 Pestle;" and that you never call any female by the name of a woman or wench, but "fair lady," if she have her desires, if not, "distressed dam-

137 **smoke:** suffer        140 **me:** ('men' Qq. F) Scene iii. S. D. **"Palmerin of England"**: (a popular romance of Spanish origin; but the passage below is from *Palmerin de Oliva*)        12–13 **besides:** down from        13 **elephant:** (a ludicrous heightening: "horse" in the romance)        14 **Agricola:** an English princess        29 **ettins:** Germanic giants        51 **flappet:** small flap (the shop shutter?)        52–53 **mithridatum:** antidote against poison        53 **dragon's-water:** plague remedy        **visited:** plague-smitten

sel;" that you call all forests and heaths "deserts," and all horses "palfreys." 85

*Wife.* This is very fine, faith. — Do the gentlemen like Ralph, think you, husband?

*Cit.* Ay, I warrant thee; the players would give all the shoes in their shop for him.

*Ralph.* My beloved squire Tim, stand [90 out. Admit this were a desert, and over it a knight-errant pricking, and I should bid you inquire of his intents: what would you say?

*Tim.* Sir, my master sent me to know whither you are riding? 95

*Ralph.* No, thus: "Fair sir, the right courteous and valiant Knight of the Burning Pestle commanded me to inquire upon what adventure you are bound, whether to relieve some distressed damsel, or otherwise." 100

*Cit.* Whoreson blockhead, cannot remember!

*Wife.* I' faith, and Ralph told him on 't before: all the gentlemen heard him. — Did he not, gentlemen? Did not Ralph tell him on 't?

*George.* Right courteous and valiant [105 Knight of the Burning Pestle, here is a distressed damsel to have a halfpenny-worth of pepper.

*Wife.* That's a good boy! See, the little boy can hit it; by my troth, it 's a fine child. 110

*Ralph.* Relieve her, with all courteous language. Now shut up shop; no more my prentice, but my trusty squire and dwarf. I must bespeak my shield and arming pestle.

[*Exeunt Tim and George.*]

*Cit.* Go thy ways, Ralph! As I 'm a true [115 man, thou art the best on 'em all.

*Wife.* Ralph, Ralph!

*Ralph.* What say you, mistress?

*Wife.* I prithee, come again quickly, sweet Ralph. 120

*Ralph.* By and by.           *Exit.*

[SCENE IV. — *Merrythought's House.*]

*Enter Jasper and his mother, Mistress Merry-thought*

*Mist. Mer.* Give thee my blessing? No, I 'll ne 'er give thee my blessing; I 'll see thee hang'd first; it shall ne'er be said I gave thee my blessing. Th' art thy father's own son, of the right blood of the Merrythoughts. I may [5 curse the time that e'er I knew thy father; he hath spent all his own and mine too; and when

I tell him of it, he laughs, and dances, and sings, and cries, "A merry heart lives long-a." And thou art a wastethrift, and art run [10 away from thy master that lov'd thee well, and art come to me; and I have laid up a little for my younger son Michael, and thou think'st to bezzle that, but thou shalt never be able to do it. — Come hither, Michael! 15

*Enter Michael*

Come, Michael, down on thy knees: thou shalt have my blessing.

*Mich.* [*kneels.*] I pray you, mother, pray to God to bless me.

*Mist. Mer.* God bless thee! but Jasper shall [20 never have my blessing; he shall be hang'd first; shall he not, Michael? How sayst thou?

*Mich.* Yes, forsooth, mother, and grace of God.

*Mist. Mer.* That 's a good boy! 25

*Wife.* I' faith, it 's a fine spoken child.

*Jasp.* Mother, though you forget a parent's love,
I must preserve the duty of a child.
I ran not from my master, nor return
To have your stock maintain my idleness. 30

*Wife.* Ungracious child, I warrant him; hark, how he chops logic with his mother! — Thou hadst best tell her she lies; do, tell her she lies.

*Cit.* If he were my son, I would hang him [35 up by the heels, and flay him, and salt him, whoreson haltersack.

*Jasp.* My coming only is to beg your love,
Which I must ever, though I never gain it;
And, howsoever you esteem of me, 40
There is no drop of blood hid in these veins
But, I remember well, belongs to you
That brought me forth, and would be glad for you
To rip them all again, and let it out.

*Mist. Mer.* I' faith, I had sorrow enough [45 for thee, God knows; but I 'll hamper thee well enough. Get thee in, thou vagabond, get thee in, and learn of thy brother Michael.

[*Exeunt Jasper and Michael.*]

*Old Mer. within.*

Nose, nose, jolly red nose,
And who gave thee this jolly red nose? 50

*Mist. Mer.* Hark, my husband! he 's singing and hoiting; and I 'm fain to cark and care, and all little enough. — Husband! Charles! Charles Merrythought!

---

114 **arming:** armorial     14 **bezzle:** waste on drink     32 **chops logic:** quibbles     37 **haltersack:** gallows-bird     52 **hoiting:** rejoicing noisily

*Enter old Merrythought*

*Mer.* [*sings.*]

Nutmegs and ginger, cinnamon and cloves;    55
And they gave me this jolly red nose.

*Mist. Mer.* If you would consider your estate,
you would have list to sing, i-wis.
*Mer.* It should never be considered, while it
were an estate, if I thought it would spoil [60
my singing.
*Mist. Mer.* But how wilt thou do, Charles?
Thou art an old man, and thou canst not work,
and thou hast not forty shillings left, and thou
eatest good meat, and drinkest good drink, [65
and laughest.
*Mer.* And will do.
*Mist. Mer.* But how wilt thou come by it,
Charles?
*Mer.* How! why, how have I done hitherto [70
this forty years? I never came into my dining
room, but, at eleven and six o'clock, I found
excellent meat and drink o' th' table: my
clothes were never worn out, but next morning
a tailor brought me a new suit: and with- [75
out question it will be so ever; use makes per-
fectness. If all should fail, it is but a little
straining myself extraordinary, and laugh myself to death.

*Wife.* It 's a foolish old man this; is not [80
he, George?
*Cit.* Yes, cony.
*Wife.* Give me a penny i' th' purse while I
live, George.
*Cit.* Ay, by lady, cony, hold thee there.    85

*Mist. Mer.* Well, Charles, you promis'd to
provide for Jasper, and I have laid up for Michael. I pray you, pay Jasper his portion: he 's
come home, and he shall not consume Michael's
stock. He says his master turn'd him away, [90
but, I promise you truly, I think he ran away.

*Wife.* No, indeed, Mistress Merrythought;
though he be a notable gallows, yet I 'll assure
you his master did turn him away, even in this
place. 'T was, i' faith, within this half- [95
hour, about his daughter; my husband was
by.
*Cit.* Hang him, rogue! he serv'd him well
enough: love his master's daughter! By my
troth, cony, if there were a thousand boys, [100
thou wouldst spoil them all with taking their
parts; let his mother alone with him.
*Wife.* Ay, George; but yet truth is truth.

*Mer.* Where is Jasper? He 's welcome, however. Call him in; he shall have his portion. [105
Is he merry?
*Mist. Mer.* Ah, foul chive him, he is too
merry! — Jasper! Michael!

*Enter Jasper and Michael*

*Mer.* Welcome, Jasper! though thou run'st
away, welcome! God bless thee! 'T is thy [110
mother's mind thou shouldst receive thy portion; thou hast been abroad, and I hope hast
learn'd experience enough to govern it; thou
art of sufficient years. Hold thy hand: — one,
two, three, four, five, six, seven, eight, nine, [115
there 's ten shillings for thee. [*Gives money.*]
Thrust thyself into the world with that, and
take some settled course. If fortune cross thee,
thou hast a retiring place; come home to me; I
have twenty shillings left. Be a good hus- [120
band; that is, wear ordinary clothes, eat the
best meat, and drink the best drink; be merry,
and give to the poor, and, believe me, thou hast
no end of thy goods.
*Jasp.* Long may you live free from all
    thought of ill,                              125
And long have cause to be thus merry still!
But, father ——
*Mer.* No more words, Jasper; get thee gone.
Thou hast my blessing; thy father's spirit upon
    thee!
Farewell, Jasper!                [*Sings.*]  130

    But yet, or ere you part (oh cruel?)
    Kiss me, kiss me, sweeting, mine own dear
        jewel!

So, now begone; no words.        *Exit Jasper.*
*Mist. Mer.* So, Michael, now get thee gone
too.                                            135
*Mich.* Yes, forsooth, mother; but I 'll have
my father's blessing first.
*Mist. Mer.* No, Michael; 't is no matter for
his blessing. Thou hast my blessing; begone.
I 'll fetch my money and jewels, and follow [140
thee; I 'll stay no longer with him, I warrant
thee. [*Exit Michael.*] — Truly, Charles, I 'll
be gone too.
*Mer.* What! you will not?
*Mist. Mer.* Yes, indeed will I.                145
*Mer.* [*sings.*]

    Heigh-ho, farewell, Nan!
    I 'll never trust wench more again, if I can.

*Mist. Mer.* You shall not think, when all
your own is gone, to spend that I have been
scraping up for Michael.                        150
*Mer.* Farewell, good wife; I expect it not:
all I have to do in this world is to be merry;

---

⁵⁷ **estate:** ('state' Q 1–2)    ⁵⁸ **list:** desire    **i-wis:** forsooth    ⁸⁵ **hold . . . there:** stick to that
⁹³ **gallows:** hangdog    ¹⁰⁴⁻¹⁰⁵ **however:** in any case    ¹⁰⁷ **foul chive:** ill betide    ¹²⁰⁻¹²¹ **husband:**
economist

which I shall, if the ground be not taken from me; and if it be,          [*Sings.*]

When earth and seas from me are reft,          155
The skies aloft for me are left.
                         *Exeunt [severally].*
          *Boy danceth. Music*
          *Finis Actus Primi*

*Wife.* I 'll be sworn he 's a merry old gentleman for all that. Hark, hark, husband, hark! fiddles, fiddles! now surely they go finely. They say 't is present death for these fid- [160 dlers to tune their rebecks before the great Turk's grace; is 't not, George? But, look, look! here 's a youth dances! — Now, good youth, do a turn o' th' toe. — Sweetheart, i' faith, I 'll have Ralph come and do some [165 of his gambols. — He 'll ride the wild mare, gentlemen, 't would do your hearts good to see him. — I thank you, kind youth; pray, bid Ralph come.          169

*Cit.* Peace, cony! — Sirrah, you scurvy boy, bid the players send Ralph; or, by God's —— and they do not, I 'll tear some of their periwigs beside their heads: this is all riff-raff.
                         [*Exit Boy.*]

## Actus Secundus.
## Scæna Prima.

[*Venturewell's House.*]

*Enter Merchant [Venturewell] and*
*Humphrey*

*Vent.* And how, faith, how goes it now, son Humphrey?

*Hum.* Right worshipful, and my beloved friend,
And father dear, this matter 's at an end.

*Vent.* 'T is well; it should be so. I 'm glad the girl
Is found so tractable.

*Hum.*          Nay, she must whirl   5
From hence (and you must wink; for so, I say,
The story tells,) to-morrow before day.

*Wife.* George, dost thou think in thy conscience now 't will be a match? Tell me but what thou think'st, sweet rogue. Thou seest [10 the poor gentleman, dear heart, how it labours and throbs, I warrant you, to be at rest! I 'll go move the father for 't.

*Cit.* No, no; I prithee, sit still, honeysuckle; thou 'lt spoil all. If he deny him, I 'll bring [15 half-a-dozen good fellows myself, and in the shutting of an evening, knock 't up, and there 's an end.

*Wife.* I 'll buss thee for that, i' faith, boy. Well, George, well, you have been a wag in [20 your days, I warrant you; but God forgive you, and I do with all my heart.

*Vent.* How was it, son? You told me that to-morrow
Before day break, you must convey her hence.

*Hum.* I must, I must; and thus it is agreed:
Your daughter rides upon a brown-bay steed, 26
I on a sorrel, which I bought of Brian,
The honest host of the Red roaring Lion,
In Waltham situate. Then, if you may,
Consent in seemly sort; lest, by delay,          30
The Fatal Sisters come, and do the office,
And then you 'll sing another song.

*Vent.*                              Alas,
Why should you be thus full of grief to me,
That do as willing as yourself agree
To anything, so it be good and fair?          35
Then, steal her when you will, if such a pleasure
Content you both; I 'll sleep and never see it,
To make your joys more full. But tell me why
You may not here perform your marriage?

*Wife.* God's blessing o' thy soul, old man! 40
I' faith, thou art loath to part true hearts. I see
'a has her, George; and I 'm as glad on 't —
Well, go thy ways, Humphrey, for a fair-spoken man; I believe thou hast not thy fellow within the walls of London; and I should say the [45 suburbs too, I should not lie. — Why dost not rejoice with me, George?

*Cit.* If I could but see Ralph again, I were as merry as mine host, i' faith.

*Hum.* The cause you seem to ask, I thus declare —          5c
Help me, O Muses nine! Your daughter sware
A foolish oath, the more it was the pity;
Yet none but myself within this city
Shall dare to say so, but a bold defiance          54
Shall meet him, were he of the noble science;
And yet she sware, and yet why did she swear?
Truly, I cannot tell, unless it were
For her own ease; for, sure, sometimes an oath,
Being sworn, thereafter is like cordial broth;
And this it was she swore, never to marry          60
But such a one whose mighty arm could carry
(As meaning me, for I am such a one)
Her bodily away, through stick and stone,
Till both of us arrive, at her request,          64
Some ten miles off, in the wild Waltham Forest.

*Vent.* If this be all, you shall not need to fear
Any denial in your love: proceed;
I 'll neither follow, nor repent the deed.

---

¹⁶¹ **rebecks:** three-stringed violins          ¹⁶⁶ **wild mare:** seesaw          ¹⁷ **evening:** (Query: 'eyelid'?)
¹⁹ **buss:** kiss          ⁵⁵ **science:** of fencing          ⁶⁰ **this:** ('thus' Q 1)          ⁶⁵ **wild:** ('wide' F)

*Hum.* Good night, twenty good nights, and twenty more,
And twenty more good nights, — that makes three-score!    *Exeunt [severally].*  70

[SCENE II. — *Waltham Forest.*]

*Enter Mistress Merrythought and her son Michael*

*Mist. Mer.* Come, Michael; art thou not weary, boy?

*Mich.* No, forsooth, mother, not I.

*Mist. Mer.* Where be we now, child?

*Mich.* Indeed, forsooth, mother, I cannot [5 tell, unless we be at Mile-End. Is not all the world Mile-End, mother?

*Mist. Mer.* No, Michael, not all the world, boy; but I can assure thee, Michael, Mile-End is a goodly matter: there has been a pitch- [10 field, my child, between the naughty Spaniels and the Englishmen; and the Spaniels ran away, Michael, and the Englishmen followed. My neighbour Coxstone was there, boy, and kill'd them all with a birding-piece.   15

*Mich.* Mother, forsooth —

*Mist. Mer.* What says my white boy?

*Mich.* Shall not my father go with us too?

*Mist. Mer.* No, Michael, let thy father go snick-up; he shall never come between a [20 pair of sheets with me again while he lives; let him stay at home, and sing for his supper, boy. Come, child, sit down, and I 'll show my boy fine knacks indeed. [*They sit down: and she takes out a casket.*] Look here, Michael; here 's a ring, and here 's a brooch, and here 's a [26 bracelet, and here 's two rings more, and here 's money and gold by th' eye, my boy.

*Mich.* Shall I have all this, mother?

*Mist. Mer.* Ay, Michael, thou shalt have [30 all, Michael.

*Cit.* How lik'st thou this, wench?

*Wife.* I cannot tell; I would have Ralph, George; I 'll see no more else, indeed, la; and I pray you, let the youths understand so [35 much by word of mouth; for, I tell you truly, I 'm afraid o' my boy. Come, come, George, let 's be merry and wise: the child 's a fatherless child; and say they should put him into a strait pair of gaskins, 't were worse than [40 knot-grass; he would never grow after it.

*Enter Ralph, Squire [Tim], and Dwarf [George]*

*Cit.* Here 's Ralph, here 's Ralph!

*Wife.* How do you, Ralph? you are welcome, Ralph, as I may say. It 's a good boy, hold up thy head, and be not afraid; we are thy

friends, Ralph; the gentlemen will praise thee, Ralph, if thou play'st thy part with audac- [47 ity. Begin, Ralph, o' God's name!

*Ralph.* My trusty squire, unlace my helm; give me my hat.
Where are we, or what desert may this be?   50

*George.* Mirror of knighthood, this is, as I take it, the perilous Waltham-down, in whose bottom stands the enchanted valley.

*Mist. Mer.* Oh, Michael, we are betray'd, we are betray'd! Here be giants! Fly, boy! fly, boy, fly!   56

*Exeunt Mother and Michael [leaving the casket]*

*Ralph.* Lace on my helm again. What noise is this?
A gentle lady, flying the embrace
Of some uncourteous knight! I will relieve her.
Go, squire, and say, the Knight that wears this Pestle   60
In honour of all ladies, swears revenge
Upon that recreant coward that pursues her.
Go, comfort her, and that same gentle squire
That bears her company.

*Tim.*              I go, brave knight. [*Exit.*]

*Ralph.* My trusty dwarf and friend, reach me my shield,   65
And hold it while I swear. First, by my knighthood;
Then by the soul of Amadis de Gaul,
My famous ancestor; then by my sword
The beauteous Brionella girt about me;
By this bright burning Pestle, of mine honour
The living trophy; and by all respect   71
Due to distressed damsels: here I vow
Never to end the quest of this fair lady
And that forsaken squire till by my valour
I gain their liberty!

*George.*         Heaven bless the knight   75
That thus relieves poor errant gentlewomen!

*Exeunt.*

*Wife.* Ay, marry, Ralph, this has some savour in 't; I would see the proudest of them all offer to carry his books after him. But, George, I will not have him go away so soon; I shall be sick if he go away, that I shall. Call Ralph [81 again, George, call Ralph again; I prithee, sweetheart, let him come fight before me, and let 's ha' some drums and some trumpets, and let him kill all that comes near him, and thou lov'st me, George!   86

*Cit.* Peace a little, bird: he shall kill them all, and they were twenty more on 'em than there are.

---

⁶ **Mile-End:** suburban district one mile from Aldgate   ¹⁰⁻¹¹ **pitch-field:** (reference to some sham battle)   ¹¹ **Spaniels:** *i.e.,* Spaniaras   ¹⁷ **white:** darling   ²⁰ **snick-up:** hang   ²⁸ **by th' eye:** in profusion   ⁴⁰ **strait:** tight   **gaskins:** breeches   ⁴¹ **knot-grass:** (supposed to retard growth)   ⁶⁹ **Brionella:** a lady in *Palmerin de Oliva*   ⁷⁹ **carry . . . books:** follow obsequiously

*Enter Jasper*

*Jasp.* Now, Fortune, if thou be'st not only
ill,                                               90
Show me thy better face, and bring about
Thy desperate wheel, that I may climb at length,
And stand. This is our place of meeting,
If love have any constancy. Oh age,
Where only wealthy men are counted happy! 95
How shall I please thee, how deserve thy smiles,
When I am only rich in misery?
My father's blessing and this little coin
Is my inheritance, a strong revénue!
From earth thou art, and to the earth I give
thee:          [*Throws away the money.*]
There grow and multiply, whilst fresher air 101
Breeds me a fresher fortune. — How! illusion?
                            *Spies the casket.*
What, hath the devil coin'd himself before me?
'T is metal good, it rings well; I am waking,
And taking too, I hope. Now, God's dear bless-
ing                                                105
Upon his heart that left it here! 'T is mine;
These pearls, I take it, were not left for swine.
                            *Exit [with the casket].*

*Wife.* I do not like that this unthrifty youth
should embezzle away the money; the poor
gentlewoman his mother will have a heavy [110
heart for it, God knows.
*Cit.* And reason good, sweetheart.
*Wife.* But let him go; I 'll tell Ralph a tale
in 's ear shall fetch him again with a wanion; I
warrant him, if he be above ground; and besides, George, here are a number of suffi- [116
cient gentlemen can witness, and myself, and
yourself, and the musicians, if we be call'd in
question. But here comes Ralph, George; thou
shalt hear him speak as he were an emperal.

[SCENE III. — *The Same.*]

*Enter Ralph and Dwarf [George]*

*Ralph.* Comes not sir squire again?
*George.*          Right courteous knight,
Your squire doth come, and with him comes the
lady,

*Enter Mistress Merrythought, Michael,
and Squire [Tim]*

For and the Squire of Damsels, as I take it.
*Ralph.* Madam, if any service or devoir   4
Of a poor errant knight may right your wrongs,
Command it; I am prest to give you succour,
For to that holy end I bear my armour.
*Mist. Mer.* Alas, sir, I am a poor gentle-
woman, and I have lost my money in this forest!

*Ralph.* Desert, you would say, lady; and
not lost                                           10
Whilst I have sword and lance. Dry up your
tears,
Which ill befits the beauty of that face,
And tell the story, if I may request it,
Of your disastrous fortune.
*Mist. Mer.* Out, alas! I left a thousand [15
pound, a thousand pound, e'en all the money I
had laid up for this youth, upon the sight of
your mastership, you look'd so grim, and, as I
may say it, saving your presence, more like a
giant than a mortal man.                           20
*Ralph.* I am as you are, lady; so are they;
All mortal. But why weeps this gentle squire?
*Mist. Mer.* Has he not cause to weep, do you
think, when he hath lost his inheritance?
*Ralph.* Young hope of valour, weep not; I
am here                                            25
That will confound thy foe, and pay it dear
Upon his coward head, that dares deny
Distressed squires and ladies equity.
I have but one horse, on which shall ride
This fair lady behind me, and before,             30
This courteous squire: fortune will give us more
Upon our next adventure. Fairly speed
Beside us, squire and dwarf, to do us need!
                            *Exeunt.*

*Cit.* Did not I tell you, Nell, what your man
would do? By the faith of my body, wench, [35
for clean action and good delivery, they may all
cast their caps at him.
*Wife.* And so they may, i' faith; for I dare
speak it boldly, the twelve companies of London cannot match him, timber for timber.
Well, George, and he be not inveigled by [41
some of these paltry players, I ha' much marvel:
but, George, we ha' done our parts, if the boy
have any grace to be thankful.
*Cit.* Yes, I warrant thee, duckling.          45

[SCENE IV. — *The Same.*]

*Enter Humphrey and Luce*

*Hum.* Good Mistress Luce, however I in
fault am
For your lame horse, you 're welcome unto
Waltham;
But which way now to go, or what to say,
I know not truly, till it be broad day.
*Luce.* Oh, fear not, Master Humphrey; I
am guide                                           5
For this place good enough.
*Hum.*                Then, up and ride;
Or, if it please you, walk, for your repose;

---

¹¹⁴ **wanion:** vengeance      ¹²⁰ **as:** ('an' Q 1–2)      **emperal:** emperor      ³ **For and:** as well as
⁶ **prest:** prepared      ³⁷ **cast . . . caps:** despair of imitating; cf. *Duchess of Malfi,* IV. ii. 120, 121
³⁹ **companies:** incorporated guilds

Or sit, or, if you will, go pluck a rose;
Either of which shall be indifferent
To your good friend and Humphrey, whose con-
    sent                               10
Is so entangled ever to your will,
As the poor harmless horse is to the mill.
  *Luce.* Faith, and you say the word, we 'll
    e'en sit down,
And take a nap.
  *Hum.*           'T is better in the town,
Where we may nap together; for, believe me,
To sleep without a snatch would mickle grieve
  me.                                  16
  *Luce.* You 're merry, Master Humphrey.
  *Hum.*                  So I am,
And have been ever merry from my dam.
  *Luce.* Your nurse had the less labour.
  *Hum.*             Faith, it may be,
Unless it were by chance I did beray me.   20

*Enter Jasper*

  *Jasp.* Luce! dear friend Luce!
  *Luce.*             Here, Jasper.
  *Jasp.*             You are mine.
  *Hum.* If it be so, my friend, you use me fine.
What do you think I am?
  *Jasp.*            An arrant noddy.
  *Hum.* A word of obloquy! Now, by God's
  body,
I 'll tell thy master; for I know thee well.   25
  *Jasp.* Nay, and you be so forward for to tell,
Take that, and that; and tell him, sir, I gave it:
And say, I paid you well.    [*Beats him.*]
  *Hum.*          Oh, sir, I have it,
And do confess the payment! Pray, be quiet.
  *Jasp.* Go, get you to your night-cap and the
  diet,                             30
To cure your beaten bones.
  *Luce.*           Alas, poor Humphrey;
Get thee some wholesome broth, with sage and
  comfrey;
A little oil of roses and a feather
To 'noint thy back withal.
  *Hum.*         When I came hither,
Would I had gone to Paris with John Dory!
  *Luce.* Farewell, my pretty Nump; I am
  very sorry                        36
I cannot bear thee company.
  *Hum.*           Farewell:
The devil's dam was ne'er so bang'd in hell.
                 *Exeunt Luce and Jasper.*
                 *Manet Humphrey.*
  *Wife.* This young Jasper will prove me an-
other thing, o' my conscience, and he may be

suffered. George, dost not see, George, how 'a
swaggers, and flies at the very heads o' folks, [42
as he were a dragon? Well, if I do not do his
lesson for wronging the poor gentleman, I am
no true woman. His friends that brought him
up might have been better occupied, i-wis, than
ha' taught him these fegaries: he 's e'en in [47
the high way to the gallows, God bless him!
  *Cit.* You 're too bitter, cony; the young
man may do well enough for all this.   50
  *Wife.* Come hither, Master Humphrey; has
he hurt you? Now, beshrew his fingers for
't! Here, sweetheart, here 's some green ginger for thee. Now, beshrew my heart, but 'a
has peppernel in 's head, as big as a pullet's
egg! Alas, sweet lamb, how thy temples [56
beat! Take the peace on him, sweetheart, take
the peace on him.
  *Cit.* No, no; you talk like a foolish woman:
I 'll ha' Ralph fight with him, and swinge him
up well-favour'dly. *Enter a Boy.* — Sirrah boy,
come hither. Let Ralph come in and fight [62
with Jasper.
  *Wife.* Ay, and beat him well; he 's an unhappy boy.   65
  *Boy.* Sir, you must pardon us; the plot of
our play lies contrary; and 't will hazard the
spoiling of our play.
  *Cit.* Plot me no plots! I 'll ha' Ralph come
out; I 'll make your house too hot for you else.
  *Boy.* Why, sir, he shall; but if anything fall
out of order, the gentlemen must pardon us. [72
  *Cit.* Go your ways, goodman boy! [*Exit
Boy.*] I 'll hold him a penny, he shall have his
bellyful of fighting now. Ho, here comes
Ralph! No more!   76

*Enter Ralph, Mistress Merrythought, Michael,*
    *Squire [Tim], and Dwarf [George]*

  *Ralph.* What knight is that, squire? Ask
  him if he keep
The passage, bound by love of lady fair,
Or else but prickant.
  *Hum.*         Sir, I am no knight,
But a poor gentleman, that this same night  80
Had stol'n from me, on yonder green,
My lovely wife, and suffer'd (to be seen
Yet extant on my shoulders) such a greeting,
That whilst I live I shall think of that meeting.

  *Wife.* Ay, Ralph, he beat him unmercifully,
Ralph; and thou spar'st him, Ralph, I would [86
thou wert hang'd.
  *Cit.* No more, wife, no more.

---

    **16 snatch:** bit of refreshment    **20 beray me:** soil myself    **32 comfrey:** medicinal weed of the
borage family    **35 John Dory:** the discomfited French hero of a comic ballad    **36 Nump:** pet-name
for Humphrey    **38 S. D. Manet:** remains on the stage    **43-44 do his lesson:** teach him    **47 fegaries:**
vagaries    **55 peppernel:** a lump    **57 peace:** surety for good behavior    **64-65 unhappy:** good-for-
naught    **74 hold:** bet    **79 prickant:** casually, en route

*Ralph*   Where is the caitiff-wretch hath done
this deed?
Lady, your pardon, that I may proceed          90
Upon the quest of this injurious knight. —
And thou, fair squire, repute me not the worse,
In leaving the great venture of the purse
And the rich casket, till some better leisure.

*Enter Jasper and Luce*

*Hum.*   Here comes the broker hath pur-
loin'd my treasure.          95
*Ralph.*   Go, squire, and tell him I am here,
An errant knight-at-arms, to crave delivery
Of that fair lady to her own knight's arms.
If he deny, bid him take choice of ground,
And so defy him.
*Tim.*          From the Knight that bears 100
The Golden Pestle, I defy thee, knight,
Unless thou make fair restitution
Of that bright lady.
*Jasp.*          Tell the knight that sent thee,
He is an ass; and I will keep the wench,
And knock his head-piece.
*Ralph.*          Knight, thou art but dead   105
If thou recall not thy uncourteous terms.

*Wife.*   Break 's pate, Ralph; break 's pate,
Ralph, soundly!

*Jasp.*   Come, knight; I am ready for you.
Now your Pestle (*Snatches away his pestle.*)
Shall try what temper, sir, your mortar 's of.
"With that he stood upright in his stirrups, [111
and gave the Knight of the calf-skin such a
knock [*knocks Ralph down.*] that he forsook
his horse, and down he fell; and then he leaped
upon him, and plucking off his helmet ——" [115
*Hum.*   Nay, and my noble knight be down so
soon,
Though I can scarcely go, so I needs must run.
          *Exeunt Humphrey and Ralph.*

*Wife.*   Run, Ralph, run, Ralph; run for thy
life, boy!
Jasper comes, Jasper comes!

*Jasp.*   Come Luce, we must have other arms
for you:          120
Humphrey, and Golden Pestle, both adieu!
          *Exeunt.*

*Wife.*   Sure the devil (God bless us!) is in this
springald! Why, George, didst ever see such
a fire-drake? I am afraid my boy 's miscarried:
if he be, though he were Master Merrythought's
son a thousand times, if there be any law in [126
England, I 'll make some of them smart for 't.
*Cit.*   No, no; I have found out the matter,

sweetheart; Jasper is enchanted; as sure as we
are here, he is enchanted: he could no more [130
have stood in Ralph's hands than I can stand in
my lord mayor's. I 'll have a ring to discover
all enchantments, and Ralph shall beat him yet.
Be no more vex'd, for it shall be so.

[SCENE V. — *Near the Bell Inn, Waltham.*]

*Enter Ralph, Squire [Tim], Dwarf [George],*
*Mistress Merrythought, and Michael*

*Wife.*   Oh, husband, here 's Ralph again! —
Stay, Ralph, let me speak with thee. How
dost thou, Ralph? Art thou not shrewdly
hurt? — The foul great lungies laid unmercifully on thee: there 's some sugar-candy for [5
thee. Proceed; thou shalt have another bout
with him.
*Cit.*   If Ralph had him at the fencing-school,
if he did not make a puppy of him, and drive
him up and down the school, he should ne'er [10
come in my shop more.

*Mist. Mer.*   Truly, Master Knight of the
Burning Pestle, I am weary.
*Mich.*   Indeed, la, mother, and I am very
hungry.          15
*Ralph.*   Take comfort, gentle dame, and you,
fair squire;
For in this desert there must needs be plac'd
Many strong castles held by courteous knights;
And till I bring you safe to one of those,
I swear by this my order ne'er to leave you.   20

*Wife.*   Well said, Ralph! — George, Ralph
was ever comfortable, was he not?
*Cit.*   Yes, duck.
*Wife.*   I shall ne'er forget him. When we had
lost our child, (you know it was stray'd al- [25
most, alone, to Puddle-Wharf, and the criers
were abroad for it, and there it had drown'd
itself but for a sculler,) Ralph was the most
comfortablest to me: "Peace, mistress," says
he, "let it go; I 'll get you another as good." [30
Did he not, George, did he not say so?
*Cit.*   Yes, indeed did he, mouse.

*George.*   I would we had a mess of pottage and
a pot of drink, squire, and were going to bed!
*Tim.*   Why, we are at Waltham town's [35
end, and that 's the Bell Inn.
*George.*   Take courage, valiant knight, dam-
sel, and squire!
I have discovered, not a stone cast off,
An ancient castle, held by the old knight
Of the most holy order of the Bell,          40
Who gives to all knights-errant entertain.
There plenty is of food, and all prepar'd

---

[117] **go:** walk   [123] **springald:** young one   [124] **-drake:** dragon   **miscarried:** ruined   [3] **shrewdly:**
seriously   [4] **lungies:** tall lout   [22] **comfortable:** helpful   [41] **entertain:** hospitality

By the white hands of his own lady dear.
He hath three squires that welcome all his
    guests:
The first, hight Chamberlino, who will see        45
Our beds prepar'd, and bring us snowy sheets,
Where never footman stretch'd his butter'd
    hams;
The second, hight Tapstero, who will see
Our pots full fill'd, and no froth therein;
The third, a gentle squire, Ostlero hight,        50
Who will our palfreys slick with wisps of straw,
And in the manger put them oats enough,
And never grease their teeth with candle-snuff.

*Wife.* That same dwarf 's a pretty boy, but
the squire 's a groutnol.        55
*Ralph.* Knock at the gates, my squire, with
        stately lance.        [*Tim knocks at the door.*]

*Enter Tapster*

*Tap.* Who 's there? — You 're welcome, gen-
tlemen: will you see a room?
*George.* Right courteous and valiant Knight
of the Burning Pestle, this is the Squire [60
Tapstero.
*Ralph.* Fair Squire Tapstero, I a wandering
    knight,
Hight of the Burning Pestle, in the quest
Of this fair lady's casket and wrought purse,
Losing myself in this vast wilderness,        65
Am to this castle well by fortune brought;
Where, hearing of the goodly entertain
Your knight of holy order of the Bell
Gives to all damsels and all errant knights,
I thought to knock, and now am bold to en-
    ter.        70
*Tap.* An 't please you see a chamber, you
are very welcome.        *Exeunt.*

*Wife.* George, I would have something done,
and I cannot tell what it is.
*Cit.* What is it, Nell?        75
*Wife.* Why, George, shall Ralph beat nobody again? Prithee, sweetheart, let him.
*Cit.* So he shall, Nell; and if I join with him,
we 'll knock them all.

[SCENE VI. — *Venturewell's House.*]

*Enter Humphrey and Merchant [Venturewell]*

*Wife.* Oh, George, here 's Master Humphrey
again now, that lost Mistress Luce, and Mistress Luce's father. Master Humphrey will do
somebody's errand, I warrant him.

*Hum.* Father, it 's true in arms I ne'er shall
    clasp her;        5
For she is stol'n away by your man Jasper.

*Wife.* I thought he would tell him.

*Vent.* Unhappy that I am, to lose my child!
Now I begin to think on Jasper's words,
Who oft hath urg'd to me thy foolishness.        10
Why didst thou let her go? Thou lov'st her not,
That wouldst bring home thy life, and not
    bring her.
*Hum.* Father, forgive me. Shall I tell you
    true?
Look on my shoulders, they are black and blue.
Whilst to and fro fair Luce and I were wind-
    ing,        15
He came and basted me with a hedge-binding.
*Vent.* Get men and horses straight: we will
    be there
Within this hour. You know the place again?
*Hum.* I know the place where he my loins
    did swaddle;
I 'll get six horses, and to each a saddle.        20
*Vent.* Meantime I 'll go talk with Jasper's
    father.        *Exeunt [severally].*

*Wife.* George, what wilt thou lay with me
now, that Master Humphrey has not Mistress
Luce yet? Speak, George, what wilt thou lay
with me?        25
*Cit.* No, Nell; I warrant thee Jasper is at
Puckeridge with her by this.
*Wife.* Nay, George, you must consider Mistress Luce's feet are tender; and besides 't is
dark; and, I promise you truly, I do not see [30
how he should get out of Waltham Forest with
her yet.
*Cit.* Nay, cony, what wilt thou lay with me,
that Ralph has her not yet?
*Wife.* I will not lay against Ralph, honey, [35
because I have not spoken with him. But look,
George, peace! here comes the merry old
gentleman again.

[SCENE VII. — *Merrythought's House.*]

*Enter old Merrythought*

*Mer. [sings.]*

When it was grown to dark midnight,
    And all were fast asleep,
In came Margaret's grimly ghost,
    And stood at William's feet.

I have money, and meat, and drink before- [5
hand, till to-morrow at noon; why should I be
sad? Methinks I have half-a-dozen jovial spirits
within me!        [*Sings.*]
    I am three merry men, and three merry men!

---

<sup>47</sup> footman: running courier, whose legs were greased to prevent cramp        <sup>53</sup> candle-snuff: tallow-
drippings, applied to prevent horses from eating        <sup>55</sup> groutnol: blockhead        <sup>13</sup> Shall I: ('I shall'
Q 2-F)        <sup>27</sup> Puckeridge: village in Hertfordshire (25 miles from London)

To what end should any man be sad in this [10
world? Give me a man who when he goes to
hanging cries,

        Trowl the black bowl to me!

and a woman that will sing a catch in her travail! I have seen a man come by my door [15
with a serious face, in a black cloak, without a
hatband, carrying his head as if he look'd for
pins in the street; I have look'd out of my window half a year after, and have spied that man's
head upon London-bridge. 'T is vile: never [20
trust a tailor that does not sing at his work; his
mind is of nothing but filching.

*Wife.* Mark this, George; 't is worth noting:
Godfrey my tailor, you know, never sings, and
he had fourteen yards to make this gown: [25
and I 'll be sworn, Mistress Pennistone, the
draper's wife, had one made with twelve.

*Mer.* [*sings.*]

     'T is mirth that fills the veins with blood,
     More than wine, or sleep, or food;
     Let each man keep his heart at ease,     30
     No man dies of that disease.
     He that would his body keep
     From diseases, must not weep;
     But whoever laughs and sings,
     Never he his body brings     35
     Into fevers, gouts, or rheums,
     Or ling'ringly his lungs consumes,
     Or meets with achés in the bone,
     Or catarrhs or griping stone;
     But contented lives for aye:     40
     The more he laughs, the more he may.

*Wife.* Look, George; how saist thou by
this, George? Is 't not a fine old man? — Now,
God's blessing o' thy sweet lips! — When wilt
thou be so merry, George? Faith, thou art [45
the frowning'st little thing, when thou art
angry, in a country.

       *Enter Merchant* [*Venturewell*]

*Cit.* Peace, cony; thou shalt see him taken
down too, I warrant thee. Here 's Luce's
father come now.     50

*Mer.* [*sings.*]

     As you came from Walsingham,
       From that holy land,
     There met you not with my true love
       By the way as you came?

*Vent.* Oh, Master Merrythought, my daughter 's gone!     55
This mirth becomes you not; my daughter 's
gone!

*Mer.* [*sings.*]

     Why, an if she be, what care I?
     Or let her come, or go, or tarry.

*Vent.* Mock not my misery; it is your son
(Whom I have made my own, when all forsook
    him)     60
Has stol'n my only joy, my child away.

*Mer.* [*sings.*]

     He set her on a milk-white steed,
       And himself upon a grey;
     He never turn'd his face again,
       But he bore her quite away.     65

*Vent.* Unworthy of the kindness I have
    shown
To thee and thine! too late I well perceive
Thou art consenting to my daughter's loss.

*Mer.* Your daughter! what a stir 's here wi'
your daughter? Let her go, think no more [70
on her, but sing loud. If both my sons were on
the gallows, I would sing,

     Down, down, down they fall;
     Down, and arise they never shall.

*Vent.* Oh, might I behold her once again,     75
And she once more embrace her aged sire!

*Mer.* Fie, how scurvily this goes! "And she
once more embrace her aged sire"? You 'll
make a dog on her, will ye? She cares much
for her aged sire, I warrant you.     [*Sings.*]

     She cares not for her daddy, nor     81
       She cares not for her mammy,
     For she is, she is, she is, she is
       My lord of Lowgave's lassy.

*Vent.* For this thy scorn I will pursue that
    son     85
Of thine to death.

*Mer.*     Do; and when you ha' kill'd him,
                             [*Sings.*]
Give him flowers enow, palmer, give him flowers
    enow;
Give him red, and white, and blue, green, and
    yellow.

*Vent.* I 'll fetch my daughter ——

*Mer.* I 'll hear no more o' your daughter; it
spoils my mirth.     91

*Vent.* I say, I 'll fetch my daughter.

*Mer.* [*sings.*]

     Was never man for lady's sake,
       Down, down,
     Tormented as I, poor Sir Guy,     95
       De derry down,
     For Lucy's sake, that lady bright,
       Down, down,
     As ever men beheld with eye
       De derry down.     100

*Vent.* I 'll be reveng'd, by Heaven!
                     *Exeunt* [*severally*].

    *Music. Finis Actus secundi*

---

¹³ **Trowl:** pass round    ²⁰ **London-bridge:** where decapitated traitors' heads were placed    ⁴⁷ country: countryside    ⁷⁹ **dog:** ("sire" being a dog-fancier's term)

*Wife.* How dost thou like this, George?

*Cit.* Why, this is well, cony; but if Ralph were hot once, thou shouldst see more.

*Wife.* The fiddlers go again, husband.     105

*Cit.* Ay, Nell; but this is scurvy music. I gave the whoreson gallows money, and I think he has not got me the waits of Southwark. If I hear 'em not anon, I 'll twinge him by the ears. — You musicians, play *Baloo!*     110

*Wife.* No, good George, let 's ha' *Lachrymæ!*

*Cit.* Why, this is it, cony.

*Wife.* It 's all the better, George. Now, sweet lamb, what story is that painted upon the cloth? The Confutation of St. Paul?     115

*Cit.* No, lamb; that 's Ralph and Lucrece.

*Wife.* Ralph and Lucrece! Which Ralph? Our Ralph?

*Cit.* No, mouse; that was a Tartarian.

*Wife.* A Tartarian! Well, I would the [120 fiddlers had done, that we might see our Ralph again!

### Actus Tertius.
### Scæna Prima.

*[Waltham Forest.]*

*Enter Jasper and Luce*

*Jasp.* Come, my dear dear; though we have lost our way,

We have not lost ourselves. Are you not weary
With this night's wand'ring, broken from your rest,
And frighted with the terror that attends
The darkness of this wild unpeopled place?     5

*Luce.* No, my best friend; I cannot either fear,
Or entertain a weary thought, whilst you
(The end of all my full desires) stand by me.
Let them that lose their hopes, and live to languish
Amongst the number of forsaken lovers,     10
Tell the long weary steps, and number time,
Start at a shadow, and shrink up their blood,
Whilst I (possess'd with all content and quiet)
Thus take my pretty love, and thus embrace him.

*Jasp.* You have caught me, Luce, so fast, that, whilst I live,     15
I shall become your faithful prisoner,
And wear these chains for ever. Come, sit down,
And rest your body, too, too delicate
For these disturbances. — *[They sit down.]* So: will you sleep?

Come, do not be more able than you are;     20
I know you are not skilful in these watches,
For women are no soldiers. Be not nice,
But take it; sleep, I say.

*Luce.*                              I cannot sleep;
Indeed, I cannot, friend.

*Jasp.*                              Why, then we 'll sing,
And try how that will work upon our senses.     25

*Luce.* I 'll sing, or say, or anything but sleep.

*Jasp.* Come, little mermaid, rob me of my heart
With that enchanting voice.

*Luce.* You mock me, Jasper. *[They sing.]*

SONG

*Jasp.* Tell me, dearest, what is love?
*Luce.* 'T is a lightning from above;     30
   'T is an arrow, 't is a fire,
   'T is a boy they call Desire;
         'T is a smile
         Doth beguile
*Jasp.* The poor hearts of men that prove.     35

   Tell me more, are women true?
*Luce.* Some love change, and so do you.
*Jasp.* Are they fair and never kind?
*Luce.* Yes, when men turn with the wind.
*Jasp.*       Are they froward?     40
*Luce.*       Ever toward
   Those that love, to love anew.

*Jasp.* Dissemble it no more; I see the god
Of heavy sleep lay on his heavy mace     44
Upon your eyelids.

*Luce.*              I am very heavy. *[Sleeps.]*

*Jasp.* Sleep, sleep; and quiet rest crown thy sweet thoughts!
Keep from her fair blood distempers, startings,
Horrors, and fearful shapes! Let all her dreams
Be joys, and chaste delights, embraces, wishes,
And such new pleasures as the ravish'd soul     50
Gives to the senses! — So; my charms have took. —
Keep her, you powers divine, whilst I contemplate
Upon the wealth and beauty of her mind!
She is only fair and constant, only kind,
And only to thee, Jasper. Oh, my joys!     55
Whither will you transport me? Let not fulness
Of my poor buried hopes come up together
And overcharge my spirits! I am weak.
Some say (however ill) the sea and women

---

¹⁰⁷ **gallows:** hangdog, cheat     ¹⁰⁹ **'em:** ('him' in Qq.–F)     ¹¹⁰ **Baloo:** a ballad tune     ¹¹¹ **Lachry-mæ:** a tune for the lute, composed by John Dowland (1563?–1626?)     ¹¹⁵ **cloth:** painted cloths were sparingly used for stage scenery     **Confutation:** *i.e.,* conversion     ¹¹⁶ **Ralph** ('Raph' in Q 1) **and Lucrece:** *i.e.,* Rape of Lucrece     ¹¹⁹ **Tartarian:** thief     ¹¹ **number:** count     ²¹ **watches:** wakings     ²² **nice:** fastidious     ²³ **take it:** yield     ³⁵ **prove:** experience

Are govern'd by the moon; both ebb and
flow,                                          60
Both full of changes; yet to them that know,
And truly judge, these but opinions are,
And heresies, to bring on pleasing war
Between our tempers, that without these were
Both void of after-love and present fear;     65
Which are the best of Cupid. Oh, thou child
Bred from despair, I dare not entertain thee,
Having a love without the faults of women,
And greater in her perfect goods than men!
Which to make good, and please myself the
stronger,                                      70
Though certainly I am certain of her love,
I 'll try her, that the world and memory
May sing to after-times her constancy. —
                            [Draws his sword.]
Luce! Luce! awake!
*Luce.*              Why do you fright me, friend,
With those distemper'd looks? What makes
your sword                                     75
Drawn in your hand? Who hath offended
you?
I prithee, Jasper, sleep; thou art wild with
watching.
*Jasp.* Come, make your way to Heaven, and
bid the world,
With all the villainies that stick upon it,
Farewell; you 're for another life.
*Luce.*                    Oh, Jasper,          80
How have my tender years committed evil,
(Especially against the man I love)
Thus to be cropp'd untimely?
*Jasp.*                     Foolish girl,
Canst thou imagine I could love his daughter,
That flung me from my fortune into nothing? 85
Discharged me his service, shut the doors
Upon my poverty, and scorn'd my prayers,
Sending me, like a boat without a mast,
To sink or swim? Come; by this hand you
die;
I must have life and blood, to satisfy         90
Your father's wrongs.

*Wife.* Away, George, away! raise the watch
at Ludgate, and bring a mittimus from the
justice for this desperate villain! — Now, I
charge you, gentlemen, see the king's peace [95
kept! — Oh, my heart, what a varlet 's this
to offer manslaughter upon the harmless gentlewoman!
*Cit.* I warrant thee, sweetheart, we 'll have
him hampered.

*Luce.* Oh, Jasper, be not cruel!             100
If thou wilt kill me, smile, and do it quickly,
And let not many deaths appear before me.
I am a woman, made of fear and love,
A weak, weak woman; kill not with thy eyes,
They shoot me through and through. Strike, I
am ready;                                      105
And, dying, still I love thee.

*Enter Merchant [Venturewell], Humphrey,
and his men*

*Vent.*                         Whereabouts?
*Jasp.* No more of this; now to myself again.
                                  [Aside.]
*Hum.* There, there he stands, with sword,
like martial knight,
Drawn in his hand; therefore beware the fight,
You that be wise; for, were I good Sir Bevis,
I would not stay his coming, by your leaves. 111
*Vent.* Sirrah, restore my daughter!
*Jasp.*                         Sirrah, no.
*Vent.* Upon him, then!
    [They attack Jasper, and force Luce
    from him.]

*Wife.* So; down with him, down with him,
down with him!
Cut him i' th' leg, boys, cut him i' th' leg!  116

*Vent.* Come your ways, minion: I 'll provide
a cage
For you, you 're grown so tame. — Horse her
away.
*Hum.* Truly, I 'm glad your forces have the
day.            *Exeunt. Manet Jasper.*
*Jasp.* They are gone, and I am hurt; my
love is lost,                                  120
Never to get again. Oh, me unhappy!
Bleed, bleed and die! I cannot. Oh, my
folly,
Thou hast betray'd me! Hope, where art thou
fled?
Tell me, if thou be'st anywhere remaining,
Shall I but see my love again? Oh, no!        125
She will not deign to look upon her butcher,
Nor is it fit she should; yet I must venter.
Oh, Chance, or Fortune, or whate'er thou
art,
That men adore for powerful, hear my cry,
And let me loving live, or losing die!    *Exit.*

*Wife.* Is 'a gone, George?                   131
*Cit.* Ay, cony.
*Wife.* Marry, and let him go, sweetheart. By
the faith o' my body, 'a has put me into such
a fright, that I tremble (as they say) as [135
't were an aspen-leaf. Look o' my little finger,
George, how it shakes. Now, i' truth, every
member of my body is the worse for 't.
*Cit.* Come, hug in mine arms, sweet mouse;
he shall not fright thee any more. Alas. mine
own dear heart, how it quivers!               141

**93** mittimus: order for arrest

[SCENE II. — *The Bell Inn.*]

*Enter Mistress Merrythought, Ralph, Michael,*
*Squire [Tim], Dwarf [George], Host, and*
*a Tapster*

*Wife.* Oh, Ralph! how dost thou, Ralph?
How hast thou slept to-night? Has the knight
us'd thee well?

*Cit.* Peace, Nell; let Ralph alone.

*Tap.* Master, the reckoning is not paid. 5
*Ralph.* Right courteous knight, who, for the
    order's sake
Which thou hast ta'en, hang'st out the holy
    Bell,
As I this flaming Pestle bear about,
We render thanks to your puissant self,
Your beauteous lady, and your gentle squires,
For thus refreshing of our wearied limbs, 11
Stiff'ned with hard achievements in wild desert.

*Tap.* Sir, there is twelve shillings to pay.
*Ralph.* Thou merry Squire Tapstero, thanks
    to thee
For comforting our souls with double jug: 15
And, if advent'rous fortune prick thee forth,
Thou jovial squire, to follow feats of arms,
Take heed thou tender every lady's cause,
Every true knight, and every damsel fair;
But spill the blood of treacherous Saracens, 20
And false enchanters that with magic spells
Have done to death full many a noble knight.

*Host.* Thou valiant Knight of the Burning
Pestle, give ear to me; there is twelve shillings
to pay, and, as I am a true knight, I will not [25
bate a penny.

*Wife.* George, I prithee, tell me, must Ralph
pay twelve shillings now?

*Cit.* No, Nell, no; nothing but the old knight
is merry with Ralph. 30

*Wife.* Oh, is 't nothing else? Ralph will be
as merry as he.

*Ralph.* Sir Knight, this mirth of yours be-
    comes you well;
But to requite this liberal courtesy,
If any of your squires will follow arms, 35
He shall receive from my heroic hand
A knighthood, by the virtue of this Pestle.

*Host.* Fair knight, I thank you for your
    noble offer:
Therefore, gentle knight,
Twelve shillings you must pay, or I must cap
    you. 40

*Wife.* Look, George! did not I tell thee as
much? The knight of the Bell is in earnest.

Ralph shall not be beholding to him: give him
his money, George, and let him go snick up.

*Cit.* Cap Ralph? No. — Hold your hand, [45
Sir Knight of the Bell; there 's your money
[*gives money.*]: have you anything to say to
Ralph now? Cap Ralph!

*Wife.* I would you should know it, Ralph has
friends that will not suffer him to be capp'd [50
for ten times so much, and ten times to the end
of that. — Now take thy course, Ralph.

*Mist. Mer.* Come, Michael; thou and I will
go home to thy father; he hath enough left to
keep us a day or two, and we 'll set fellows [55
abroad to cry our purse and our casket: shall
we, Michael?

*Mich.* Ay, I pray, mother; in truth my feet
are full of chilblains with travelling.

*Wife.* Faith, and those chilblains are a [60
foul trouble. Mistress Merrythought, when
your youth comes home, let him rub all the
soles of his feet, and his heels, and his ankles,
with a mouse-skin; or, if none of your people
can catch a mouse, when he goes to bed, let [65
him roll his feet in the warm embers, and, I
warrant you, he shall be well; and you may
make him put his fingers between his toes, and
smell to them: it 's very sovereign for his head,
if he be costive. 70

*Mist. Mer.* Master Knight of the Burning
Pestle, my son Michael and I bid you farewell:
I thank your worship heartily for your kind-
ness.

*Ralph.* Farewell, fair lady, and your tender
    squire. 75
If pricking through these deserts, I do hear
Of any traitorous knight, who through his
    guile
Hath light upon your casket and your purse,
I will despoil him of them, and restore them.

*Mist. Mer.* I thank your worship. 80
                                        *Exit with Michael.*

*Ralph.* Dwarf, bear my shield; squire, ele-
    vate my lance: —
And now farewell, you Knight of holy Bell.

*Cit.* Ay, ay, Ralph, all is paid.

*Ralph.* But yet, before I go, speak, worthy
    knight,
If aught you do of sad adventures know, 85
Where errant knight may through his prowess
    win
Eternal fame, and free some gentle souls
From endless bonds of steel and ling'ring pain.

*Host.* Sirrah, go to Nick the barber, and bid

---

² **to-night:** last night    ¹⁵ **double jug:** extra strong ale    ²⁶ **bate:** rebate    ⁴⁰ **cap:** arrest (from
writ of "capias")    ⁶⁹ **sovereign:** efficacious    ⁷⁰ **costive:** constipated    ⁸⁵ **sad:** arduous    ⁸⁶ **knight:**
('Knights' Qq., F)

him prepare himself, as I told you before, [90 quickly.

*Tap.* I am gone, sir.                    *Exit.*

*Host.* Sir Knight, this wilderness affordeth none
But the great venture, where full many a knight
Hath tried his prowess, and come off with shame;                                      95
And where I would not have you lose your life,
Against no man, but furious fiend of hell.

*Ralph.* Speak on, Sir Knight; tell what he is and where:
For here I vow, upon my blazing badge,
Never to blaze a day in quietness,        100
But bread and water will I only eat,
And the green herb and rock shall be my couch,
Till I have quell'd that man, or beast, or fiend,
That works such damage to all errant knights.

*Host.* Not far from hence, near to a craggy cliff,                                    105
At the north end of this distressed town,
There doth stand a lowly house,
Ruggedly builded, and in it a cave
In which an ugly giant now doth won,
Ycleped Barbaroso: in his hand          110
He shakes a naked lance of purest steel,
With sleeves turn'd up; and him before he wears
A motley garment, to preserve his clothes
From blood of those knights which he massacres,
And ladies gent: without his door doth hang
A copper basin on a prickant spear;      116
At which no sooner gentle knights can knock,
But the shrill sound fierce Barbaroso hears,
And rushing forth, brings in the errant knight
And sets him down in an enchanted chair; 120
Then with an engine, which he hath prepar'd,
With forty teeth, he claws his courtly crown;
Next makes him wink, and underneath his chin
He plants a brazen piece of mighty bord.
And knocks his bullets round about his cheeks;
Whilst with his fingers, and an instrument 126
With which he snaps his hair off, he doth fill
The wretch's ears with a most hideous noise.
Thus every knight-adventurer he doth trim,
And now no creature dares encounter him. 130

*Ralph.* In God's name, I will fight him. Kind sir,
Go but before me to this dismal cave,

Where this huge giant Barbaroso dwells,
And, by that virtue that brave Rosicleer
That damned brood of ugly giants slew,    135
And Palmerin Franarco overthrew,
I doubt not but to curb this traitor foul,
And to the devil send his guilty soul.

*Host.* Brave-sprighted knight, thus far I will perform
This your request: I 'll bring you within sight
Of this most loathsome place, inhabited    141
By a more loathsome man; but dare not stay,
For his main force swoops all he sees away.

*Ralph.* Saint George, set on before! March, squire and page!                   *Exeunt.*

*Wife.* George, dost think Ralph will confound the giant?                       [145
*Cit.* I hold my cap to a farthing he does. Why, Nell, I saw him wrastle with the great Dutchman, and hurl him.
*Wife.* Faith, and that Dutchman was a goodly man, if all things were answerable to his [151 bigness. And yet they say there was a Scotchman higher than he, and that they two and a knight met, and saw one another for nothing. But of all the sights that ever were in London, since I was married, methinks the little [155 child that was so fair grown about the members was the prettiest; that and the hermaphrodite.
*Cit.* Nay, by your leave, Nell, Ninivie was better.                            160
*Wife.* Ninivie! Oh, that was the story of Jone and the wall, was it not, George?
*Cit.* Yes, lamb.

*Enter Mistress Merrythought*

*Wife.* Look, George, here comes Mistress Merrythought again! and I would have Ralph come and fight with the giant. I tell you [166 true, I long to see 't.
*Cit.* Good Mistress Merrythought, begone, I pray you, for my sake; I pray you, forbear a little; you shall have audience presently. [170 I have a little business.
*Wife.* Mistress Merrythought, if it please you to refrain your passion a little, till Ralph have despatch'd the giant out of the way, we shall think ourselves much bound to you. [175 I thank you, good Mistress Merrythought.

*Exit Mistress Merrythought.*

*Enter a Boy*

*Cit.* Boy, come hither. Send away Ralph and this whoreson giant quickly.

---

[103] **quell'd:** killed    [109] **won:** dwell    [115] **gent:** gentle    [116] (The sign of the barber-surgeons) **prickant:** pointing upward    [121] **engine:** *i.e.,* comb    [123] **wink:** shut the eyes    [124] **piece:** barber's bowl    **bord:** rim    [125] **bullets:** pellets of soap    [134] **Rosicleer:** hero of *The Mirror of Knighthood* [136] **Franarco:** the giant mentioned above, I. iii. 7    [143] **swoops:** ('soopes' Q 1)    [150–158] (Compare *Tempest*, II. ii. 30 ff., *Alchemist*, V. i. 20 ff.)    [159] **Ninivie:** a popular puppet play or "motion" [162] **Jone . . . wall:** Jonah and the Whale    [177] **away:** *i.e.,* upon the stage

*Boy.* In good faith, sir, we cannot; you 'll [179
utterly spoil our play, and make it to be hiss'd;
and it cost money. You will not suffer us to go
on with our plot. — I pray, gentlemen, rule him.
*Cit.* Let him come now and despatch this,
and I 'll trouble you no more.
*Boy.* Will you give me your hand of that? 185
*Wife.* Give him thy hand, George, do; and
I 'll kiss him. I warrant thee, the youth means
plainly.
*Boy.* I 'll send him to you presently. 189
*Wife.* [*kissing him.*] I thank you, little youth.
(*Exit Boy.*) Faith, the child hath a sweet breath,
George; but I think it be troubled with the
worms; *carduus benedictus* and mare's milk
were the only thing in the world for 't. Oh,
Ralph 's here, George! — God send thee good
luck, Ralph! 196

[SCENE III. — *Before the Barber's Shop,
Waltham.*]

*Enter Ralph, Host, Squire [Tim], and
Dwarf [George]*

*Host.* Puissant knight, yonder his mansion is.
Lo, where the spear and copper basin are!
Behold that string, on which hangs many a
tooth,
Drawn from the gentle jaw of wand'ring
knights!
I dare not stay to sound; he will appear. 5
*Exit.*
*Ralph.* O faint not, heart! Susan, my lady
dear,
The cobbler's maid in Milk-street, for whose
sake
I take these arms, O, let the thought of thee
Carry thy knight through all adventurous
deeds;
And, in the honour of thy beauteous self, 10
May I destroy this monster Barbaroso! —
Knock, squire, upon the basin, till it break
With the shrill strokes, or till the giant speak.
[*Tim knocks upon the basin.*]

*Enter Barber*

*Wife.* O, George, the giant, the giant! —
Now, Ralph for thy life! 15

*Bar.* What fond, unknowing wight is this,
that dares
So rudely knock at Barbaroso's cell,
Where no man comes but leaves his fleece be-
hind?
*Ralph.* I, traitorous caitiff, who am sent by
fate
To punish all the sad enormities 20

Thou hast committed against ladies gent
And errant knights. Traitor to God and men,
Prepare thyself! This is the dismal hour
Appointed for thee to give strict account
Of all thy beastly treacherous villainies. 25
*Bar.* Fool-hardy knight, full soon thou shalt
aby
This fond reproach: thy body will I bang;
*He takes down his pole.*
And, lo, upon that string thy teeth shall hang!
Prepare thyself, for dead soon shalt thou be.
*Ralph.* Saint George for me! *They fight.*
*Bar.* Gargantua for me! 31

*Wife.* To him, Ralph, to him! hold up the
giant; set out thy leg before, Ralph!
*Cit.* Falsify a blow, Ralph, falsify a blow!
The giant lies open on the left side. 35
*Wife.* Bear 't off, bear 't off still! there,
boy! —
Oh, Ralph 's almost down, Ralph 's almost
down!

*Ralph.* Susan, inspire me! Now have up
again.

*Wife.* Up, up, up, up, up! so, Ralph! down
with him, down with him, Ralph! 40
*Cit.* Fetch him o'er the hip, boy!
[*Ralph knocks down the Barber.*]
*Wife.* There, boy! kill, kill, kill, kill, kill,
Ralph!
*Cit.* No, Ralph; get all out of him first.

*Ralph.* Presumptuous man, see to what des-
perate end
Thy treachery hath brought thee! The just
gods, 45
Who never prosper those that do despise them,
For all the villainies which thou hast done
To knights and ladies, now have paid thee
home
By my stiff arm, a knight adventurous.
But say, vile wretch, before I send thy soul 50
To sad Avernus, whither it must go,
What captives holdst thou in thy sable cave?
*Bar.* Go in, and free them all; thou hast the
day. 53
*Ralph.* Go, squire and dwarf, search in this
dreadful cave,
And free the wretched prisoners from their
bonds. *Exeunt Squire and Dwarf.*
*Bar.* I crave for mercy, as thou art a knight,
And scorn'st to spill the blood of those that
beg.
*Ralph.* Thou show'd'st no mercy, nor shalt
thou have any;
Prepare thyself, for thou shalt surely die.

**188 plainly:** sincerely **189 presently:** at once
**pay for 34 falsify:** aim deceptively

**5 sound:** blow horn **16 fond:** foolish **26 aby:**

*Enter Squire [Tim], leading one winking,*
*with a basin under his chin*

*Tim.* Behold, brave knight, here is one
   prisoner,        60
Whom this wild man hath used as you see.

*Wife.* This is the first wise word I heard the
squire speak.

*Ralph.* Speak what thou art, and how thou
   hast been us'd,
That I may give him condign punishment.  65
*1 Kn.* I am a knight that took my journey
   post
Northward from London; and in courteous
   wise
This giant train'd me to his loathsome den,
Under pretence of killing of the itch;
And all my body with a powder strew'd,   70
That smarts and stings; and cut away my
   beard,
And my curl'd locks wherein were ribands tied;
And with a water wash'd my tender eyes,
(Whilst up and down about me still he skipp'd,)
Whose virtue is, that, till mine eyes be wip'd
With a dry cloth, for this my foul disgrace,  76
I shall not dare to look a dog i' th' face.

*Wife.* Alas, poor knight! — Relieve him,
Ralph; relieve poor knights, whilst you live.

*Ralph.* My trusty squire, convey him to the
   town,        80
Where he may find relief. — Adieu, fair knight.
       *Exit Knight.*

*Enter Dwarf [George], leading one with a*
*patch o'er his nose*

*George.* Puissant Knight, of the Burning Pes-
   tle hight,
See here another wretch, whom this foul beast
Hath scorch'd and scor'd in this inhuman wise.
*Ralph.* Speak me thy name, and eke thy
   place of birth,      85
And what hath been thy usage in this cave.
*2 Kn.* I am a knight, Sir Pockhole is my
   name,
And by my birth I am a Londoner,
Free by my copy, but my ancestors
Were Frenchmen all; and riding hard this
   way       90
Upon a trotting horse, my bones did ache;
And I, faint knight, to ease my weary limbs,
Light at this cave; when straight this furious
   fiend,
With sharpest instrument of purest steel,
Did cut the gristle of my nose away,   95

And in the place this velvet plaster stands.
Relieve me, gentle knight, out of his hands!

*Wife.* Good Ralph, relieve Sir Pockhole, and
send him away; for in truth his breath stinks.

*Ralph.* Convey him straight after the other
   knight. —      100
Sir Pockhole, fare you well.
*2 Kn.*          Kind sir, good night. *Exit.*
*Man. [within.]* Deliver us!   *Cries within.*
*Woman. [within.]* Deliver us!

*Wife.* Hark, George, what a woeful cry there
is! I think some woman lies in there.   105

*Man. [within.]* Deliver us!
*Woman. [within.]* Deliver us!
*Ralph.* What ghastly noise is this? Speak,
   Barbaroso,
Or, by this blazing steel, thy head goes off!
*Bar.* Prisoners of mine, whom I in diet keep.
Send lower down into the cave,    111
And in a tub that 's heated smoking hot,
There may they find them, and deliver them.
*Ralph.* Run, squire and dwarf; deliver them
   with speed.    *Exeunt Squire and Dwarf.*

*Wife.* But will not Ralph kill this giant?
Surely I am afeard, if he let him go, he will do
as much hurt as ever he did.    117
*Cit.* Not so, mouse, neither, if he could convert him.
*Wife.* Ay, George, if he could convert him;
but a giant is not so soon converted as one of us
ordinary people. There 's a pretty tale of a
witch, that had the devil's mark about her,
(God bless us!) that had a giant to her son, [124
that was call'd Lob-lie-by-the-fire; didst never
hear it, George?

*Enter Squire [Tim], leading a Man, with a glass*
*of lotion in his hand, and Dwarf [George],*
*leading a Woman, with diet-bread and drink*

*Cit.* Peace, Nell, here comes the prisoners.

*George.* Here be these pined wretches, man-
   ful knight,
That for this six weeks have not seen a wight.
*Ralph.* Deliver what you are, and how you
   came      130
To this sad cave, and what your usage was?
*Man.* I am an errant knight that followed
   arms
With spear and shield; and in my tender years
I stricken was with Cupid's fiery shaft,
And fell in love with this my lady dear,   135
And stole her from her friends in Turnbull-
   street,

---

[66] **post**: in haste    [84] **scorch'd**: (probably) scotch'd, cut    [89] **Free . . . copy**: enrolled as freeman
[90] **Frenchmen**: (syphilis being supposed to come from France)    [129] **this**: ('these' Q 1)    [136] **Turnbull-street**: notorious for prostitutes

And bore her up and down from town to
town,
Where we did eat and drink, and music hear;
Till at the length at this unhappy town
We did arrive, and coming to this cave,        140
This beast us caught, and put us in a tub,
Where we this two months sweat, and should
have done
Another month, if you had not reliev'd us.
   *Woman.*  This bread and water hath our diet
been,
Together with a rib cut from a neck        145
Of burned mutton: hard hath been our fare.
Release us from this ugly giant's snare!
   *Man.*  This hath been all the food we have
receiv'd;
But only twice a-day, for novelty,
He gave a spoonful of this hearty broth        150
To each of us, through this same slender quill.
          *Pulls out a syringe.*
   *Ralph.*  From this infernal monster you shall
go,
That useth knights and gentle ladies so! —
Convey them hence.
          *Exeunt Man and Woman.*

   *Cit.*  Cony, I can tell thee, the gentlemen like
Ralph.        156
   *Wife.*  Ay, George, I see it well enough. —
Gentlemen, I thank you all heartily for grac-
ing my man Ralph; and I promise you, you
shall see him oft'ner.        160

   *Bar.*  Mercy, great knight! I do recant my
ill,
And henceforth never gentle blood will spill.
   *Ralph.*  I give thee mercy; but yet shalt thou
swear
Upon my Burning Pestle, to perform
Thy promise utter'd.        165
   *Bar.*  I swear and kiss.  *[Kisses the Pestle.]*
   *Ralph.*        Depart, then, and amend. —
          *[Exit Barber.]*
Come, squire and dwarf; the sun grows towards
his set,
And we have many more adventures yet.
          *Exeunt.*

   *Cit.*  Now Ralph is in this humour, I know he
would ha' beaten all the boys in the house, if
they had been set on him.        171
   *Wife.*  Ay, George, but it is well as it is. I
warrant you, the gentlemen do consider what
it is to overthrow a giant. But, look, [174
George; here comes Mistress Merrythought,
and her son Michael. — Now you are welcome,
Mistress Merrythought; now Ralph has done,
you may go on.

   [SCENE IV. — *Before Merrythought's House.*]

   *Enter Mistress Merrythought and Michael*

   *Mist. Mer.*  Mick, my boy —
   *Mich.*  Ay, forsooth, mother.
   *Mist. Mer.*  Be merry, Mick; we are at home
now; where, I warrant you, you shall find the
house flung out at the windows.  [*Music* [5
*within.*]  Hark! hey, dogs, hey! this is the old
world, i' faith, with my husband. If I get in
among 'em I 'll play 'em such a lesson, that they
shall have little list to come scraping hither
again. — Why, Master Merrythought! husband! Charles Merrythought!        11
   *Mer. within [appearing above, and singing.]*

If you will sing, and dance, and laugh,
  And hollo, and laugh again,
And then cry, "There, boys, there!" why, then,
  One, two, three, and four,        15
We shall be merry within this hour.

   *Mist. Mer.*  Why, Charles, do you not know
your own natural wife? I say, open the door,
and turn me out those mangy companions; 't is
more than time that they were fellow and [20
fellow-like with you. You are a gentleman,
Charles, and an old man, and father of two
children; and I myself, (though I say it) by my
mother's side niece to a worshipful gentleman
and a conductor; he has been three times [25
in his majesty's service at Chester, and is now
the fourth time, God bless him and his charge,
upon his journey.
   *Mer. [sings.]*

     Go from my window, love, go;
     Go from my window, my dear!        30
       The wind and the rain
       Will drive you back again;
     You cannot be lodged here.

Hark you, Mistress Merrythought, you that
walk upon adventures, and forsake your hus- [35
band, because he sings with never a penny
in his purse; what, shall I think myself the
worse? Faith, no, I 'll be merry. You come not
here; here 's none but lads of mettle, lives of
a hundred years and upwards; care never [40
drunk their bloods, nor want made 'em warble
"Heigh-ho, my heart is heavy."
   *Mist. Mer.*  Why, Master Merrythought,
what am I, that you should laugh me to scorn
thus abruptly? Am I not your fellow-feeler, [45
as we may say, in all our miseries? your comforter
in health and sickness? Have I not brought
you children? Are they not like you, Charles?
look upon thine own image, hard-hearted man!
and yet for all this ——        50

*Mer.* [*sings.*] *within.*

> Begone, begone, my juggy, my puggy,
> Begone, my love, my dear!
> The weather is warm,
> 'T will do thee no harm:
> Thou canst not be lodged here. —                    55

Be merry, boys! some light music, and more
wine!                              [*Exit above.*]

*Wife.* He 's not in earnest, I hope, George,
is he?
*Cit.* What if he be, sweetheart?          60
*Wife.* Marry, if he be, George, I 'll make
bold to tell him he 's an ingrant old man to use
his bed-fellow so scurvily.
*Cit.* What! how does he use her, honey?
*Wife.* Marry, come up, sir saucebox! I think
you 'll take his part, will you not? Lord, how [66
hot you are grown! You are a fine man, an
you had a fine dog; it becomes you sweetly!
*Cit.* Nay, prithee, Nell, chide not; for, as I
am an honest man and a true Christian [70
grocer, I do not like his doings.
*Wife.* I cry you mercy, then, George! you
know we are all frail and full of infirmities. —
D' ye hear, Master Merrythought? May I
crave a word with you?                     75
*Mer. within* [*appearing above.*] Strike up
lively, lads!
*Wife.* I had not thought, in truth, Master
Merrythought, that a man of your age and discretion (as I may say) being a gentleman, [80
and therefore known by your gentle conditions,
could have used so little respect to the weakness
of his wife; for your wife is your own flesh,
the staff of your age, your yoke-fellow, with
whose help you draw through the mire of [85
this transitory world. Nay, she 's your own rib:
and again ——
*Mer.* [*sings.*]

> I come not hither for thee to teach,
> I have no pulpit for thee to preach,
> I would thou hadst kiss'd me under the breech,  90
> As thou art a lady gay.

*Wife.* Marry, with a vengeance! I am heartily sorry for the poor gentlewoman: but if I
were thy wife, i' faith, greybeard, i' faith ——
*Cit.* I prithee, sweet honeysuckle, be [95
content.
*Wife.* Give me such words, that am a gentlewoman born! Hang him, hoary rascal! Get me
some drink, George; I am almost molten with
fretting: now, beshrew his knave's heart [100
for it!                            [*Exit Citizen.*]

*Mer.* Play me a light lavolta. Come, be
frolic. Fill the good fellows wine.
*Mist. Mer.* Why, Master Merrythought, are
you disposed to make me wait here? You 'll [105
open, I hope; I 'll fetch them that shall open
else.
*Mer.* Good woman, if you will sing, I 'll
give you something; if not —— [*Sings.*]

> You are no love for me, Margaret,      110
> I am no love for you. —

Come aloft, boys, aloft!          [*Exit above.*]
*Mist. Mer.* Now a churl's fart in your teeth,
sir! — Come, Mick, we 'll not trouble him; 'a
shall not ding us i' th' teeth with his bread [115
and his broth, that he shall not. Come, boy;
I 'll provide for thee, I warrant thee. We 'll go
to Master Venturewell's, the merchant: I 'll
get his letter to mine host of the Bell in Waltham; there I 'll place thee with the tapster: [120
will not that do well for thee, Mick? And let
me alone for that old cuckoldly knave your
father; I 'll use him in his kind, I warrant ye.
[*Exeunt.*]

[*Re-enter Citizen with Beer*]

*Wife.* Come, George, where 's the beer?
*Cit.* Here, love.                       125
*Wife.* This old fornicating fellow will not out
of my mind yet. — Gentlemen, I 'll begin to
you all; and I desire more of your acquaintance
with all my heart. [*Drinks.*] Fill the gentlemen some beer, George.          *Music.* 130

*Finis Actus tertii.*

## Actus Quartus.
### Scæna Prima.

#### *Boy danceth*

*Wife.* Look, George, the little boy 's come
again: methinks he looks something like the
Prince of Orange in his long stocking, if he had a
little harness about his neck. George, I will
have him dance *Fading. — Fading* is a fine jig, [5
I 'll assure you, gentlemen. — Begin, brother.
— Now 'a capers, sweetheart! — Now a turn o'
th' toe, and then tumble! cannot you tumble,
youth?
*Boy.* No, indeed, forsooth.             10
*Wife.* Nor eat fire?
*Boy.* Neither.
*Wife.* Why, then, I thank you heartily;
there 's twopence to buy you points withal.

---

*Enter Jasper and Boy*

*Jasp.* There, boy, deliver this; but do it
well.                    [*Gives a letter.*] 15
Hast thou provided me four lusty fellows,
Able to carry me? and art thou perfect
In all thy business?
  *Boy.*                    Sir, you need not fear;
I have my lesson here, and cannot miss it:
The men are ready for you, and what else    20
Pertains to this employment.
  *Jasp.*                    There, my boy;
Take it, but buy no land.    [*Gives money.*]
  *Boy.*                    Faith, sir, 't were rare
To see so young a purchaser. I fly,
And on my wings carry your destiny.
  *Jasp.* Go and be happy! [*Exit Boy.*] Now,
my latest hope,                    25
Forsake me not, but fling thy anchor out,
And let it hold! Stand fix'd, thou rolling stone,
Till I enjoy my dearest! Hear me, all
You powers, that rule in men, celestial! *Exit.*

  *Wife.* Go thy ways; thou art as crooked a [30
sprig as ever grew in London. I warrant him,
he 'll come to some naughty end or other; for
his looks say no less: besides, his father (you
know, George) is none of the best; you heard
him take me up like a flirt-gill, and sing [35
bawdy songs upon me; but i' faith, if I live,
George ——
  *Cit.* Let me alone, sweetheart: I have a trick
in my head shall lodge him in the Arches
for one year, and make him sing *peccavi* ere [40
I leave him; and yet he shall never know who
hurt him neither.
  *Wife.* Do, my good George, do!
  *Cit.* What shall we have Ralph do now,
boy?                    45
  *Boy.* You shall have what you will, sir.
  *Cit.* Why, so, sir; go and fetch me him then,
and let the Sophy of Persia come and christen
him a child.                    49
  *Boy.* Believe me, sir, that will not do so well;
't is stale; it has been had before at the Red
Bull.
  *Wife.* George, let Ralph travel over great
hills, and let him be very weary, and come to
the King of Cracovia's house, covered with [55
velvet; and there let the king's daughter stand
in her window, all in beaten gold, combing her
golden locks with a comb of ivory; and let her
spy Ralph, and fall in love with him, and come

down to him, and carry him into her fa- [60
ther's house; and then let Ralph talk with her.
  *Cit.* Well said, Nell; it shall be so. — Boy,
let 's ha 't done quickly.
  *Boy.* Sir, if you will imagine all this to be
done already, you shall hear them talk to- [65
gether; but we cannot present a house covered
with black velvet, and a lady in beaten gold.
  *Cit.* Sir boy, let 's ha 't as you can, then.
  *Boy.* Besides, it will show ill-favouredly to
have a grocer's prentice to court a king's [70
daughter.
  *Cit.* Will it so, sir? You are well read in histories! I pray you, what was Sir Dagonet?
Was not he prentice to a grocer in London?
Read the play of "The Four Prentices of [75
London," where they toss their pikes so. I pray
you, fetch him in, sir, fetch him in.
  *Boy.* It shall be done. — It is not our fault,
gentlemen.                    *Exit.*
  *Wife.* Now we shall see fine doings, I war- [80
rant 'ee, George.

[SCENE II. — *King of Moldavia's Palace.*]

*Enter Ralph and the Lady [Pompiona],
Squire, and Dwarf*

  *Wife.* Oh, here they come, how prettily the
King of Cracovia's daughter is dress'd!
  *Cit.* Ay, Nell, it is the fashion of that coun-
try, I warrant 'ee.

  *Lady.* Welcome, Sir Knight, unto my father's
court,                    5
King of Moldavia: unto me Pompiona,
His daughter dear! But, sure, you do not like
Your entertainment, that will stay with us
No longer but a night.
  *Ralph.*                    Damsel right fair,
I am on many sad adventures bound,    10
That call me forth into the wilderness;
Besides, my horse's back is something gall'd,
Which will enforce me ride a sober pace.
But many thanks, fair lady, be to you
For using errant knight with courtesy!    15
  *Lady.* But say, brave knight, what is your
name and birth?
  *Ralph.* My name is Ralph; I am an English-
man,
As true as steel, a hearty Englishman,
And prentice to a grocer in the Strand
By deed indent, of which I have one part:    20
But fortune calling me to follow arms,

---

³⁵ **flirt-gill:** hussy    ³⁹ **Arches:** ecclesiastical court in London    ⁴⁸⁻⁴⁹ **Sophy . . . child:** This incident occurs at close of *The Travels of Three English Brothers* by Day, Rowley, and Wilkins (1607).
⁵¹⁻⁵² **Red Bull:** a plebeian playhouse, used by the Queen's Company.    ⁵⁵ **Cracovia:** Poland (apparently identified with Moldavia in modern Rumania)    ⁷³ **Sir Dagonet:** the fool at King Arthur's
court    ⁷⁵⁻⁷⁶ **"The . . . London":** by Thomas Heywood    ²⁰ **deed indent:** contract, made out in du-
plicate

On me this holy order I did take
Of Burning Pestle, which in all men's eyes
I bear, confounding ladies' enemies.
   *Lady.* Oft have I heard of your brave coun-
     trymen,                25
And fertile soil, and store of wholesome food.
My father oft will tell me of a drink
In England found, and nipitato call'd,
Which driveth all the sorrow from your hearts.
   *Ralph.* Lady, 't is true; you need not lay
     your lips              30
To better nipitato than there is.
   *Lady.* And of a wild fowl he will often
     speak,
Which powd'red-beef-and-mustard called is:
For there have been great wars 'twixt us and
   you;
But truly, Ralph, it was not 'long of me.  35
Tell me then, Ralph, could you contented be
To wear a lady's favour in your shield?
   *Ralph.* I am a knight of religious order,
And will not wear a favour of a lady's   39
That trusts in Antichrist and false traditions.
   *Cit.* Well said, Ralph! convert her, if thou
canst.
   *Ralph.* Besides, I have a lady of my own
In merry England, for whose virtuous sake
I took these arms; and Susan is her name,  45
A cobbler's maid in Milk-street; whom I vow
Ne'er to forsake whilst life and Pestle last.
   *Lady.* Happy that cobbling dame, whoe'er
     she be,
That for her own, dear Ralph, hath gotten
   thee!
Unhappy I, that ne'er shall see the day  50
To see thee more, that bear'st my heart away!
   *Ralph.* Lady, farewell; I needs must take
     my leave.
   *Lady.* Hard-hearted Ralph, that ladies dost
     deceive!
   *Cit.* Hark thee, Ralph: there 's money for
thee [*gives money*]: give something in the King of
Cracovia's house; be not beholding to him. [56
   *Ralph.* Lady, before I go, I must remember
Your father's officers, who truth to tell,
Have been about me very diligent.
Hold up thy snowy hand, thou princely maid!
There 's twelve-pence for your father's cham-
   berlain;         61
And another shilling for his cook,
For, by my troth, the goose was roasted well;
And twelve-pence for your father's horse-
   keeper,
For 'nointing my horse' back, and for his but-
   ter       65

There is another shilling. To the maid
That wash'd my boot-hose there 's an English
   groat,
And two-pence to the boy that wip'd my boots;
And last, fair lady, there is for yourself
Three-pence, to buy you pins at Bumbo Fair.
   *Lady.* Full many thanks; and I will keep
     them safe       71
Till all the heads be off, for thy sake, Ralph.
   *Ralph.* Advance, my squire and dwarf! I
     cannot stay.
   *Lady.* Thou kill'st my heart in parting thus
     away.        *Exeunt.*

   *Wife.* I commend Ralph yet, that he will [75
not stoop to a Cracovian; there 's properer
women in London than any are there, I-wis.
But here comes Master Humphrey and his love
again now, George.
   *Cit.* Ay, cony; peace.       80

   [SCENE III. — *Venturewell's House.*]

   *Enter Merchant* [*Venturewell*], *Humphrey,*
     *Luce, and a Boy*

   *Vent.* Go, get you up; I will not be en-
     treated;
And, gossip mine, I 'll keep you sure hereafter
From gadding out again with boys and un-
   thrifts.
Come, they are women's tears; I know your
   fashion, —
Go, sirrah, lock her in, and keep the key  5
Safe as you love your life.
           *Exeunt Luce and Boy.*
          Now, my son Humphrey,
You may both rest assured of my love
In this, and reap your own desire.
   *Hum.* I see this love you speak of, through
     your daughter,
Although the hole be little; and hereafter  10
Will yield the like in all I may or can,
Fitting a Christian and a gentleman.
   *Vent.* I do believe you, my good son, and
     thank you;
For 't were an impudence to think you flat-
   tered.
   *Hum.* It were, indeed: but shall I tell you
     why?       15
I have been beaten twice about the lie.
   *Vent.* Well, son, no more of compliment.
     My daughter
Is yours again: appoint the time and take her.
We 'll have no stealing for it; I myself  19
And some few of our friends will see you married.
   *Hum.* I would you would, i' faith! for, be it
     known,
I ever was afraid to lie alone.

*Vent.* Some three days hence, then.
*Hum.*                           Three days! let me see:
'T is somewhat of the most; yet I agree,
Because I mean against the appointed day        25
To visit all my friends in new array.

*Enter Servant*

*Serv.* Sir, there 's a gentlewoman without
would speak with your worship.
*Vent.* What is she?
*Serv.* Sir, I ask'd her not.                    30
*Vent.* Bid her come in.        [*Exit Servant.*]

*Enter Mistress Merrythought and Michael*

*Mist. Mer.* Peace be to your worship! I
come as a poor suitor to you, sir, in the behalf
of this child.
*Vent.* Are you not wife to Merrythought?
*Mist. Mer.* Yes, truly. Would I had ne'er [36
seen his eyes! He has undone me and himself
and his children; and there he lives at home,
and sings and hoits and revels among his
drunken companions! but, I warrant you, [40
where to get a penny to put bread in his mouth
he knows not: and therefore, if it like your
worship, I would entreat your letter to the
honest host of the Bell in Waltham, that I
may place my child under the protection of his
tapster, in some settled course of life.        46
*Vent.* I 'm glad the heavens have heard my
prayers. Thy husband,
When I was ripe in sorrows, laugh'd at me;
Thy son, like an unthankful wretch, I having
Redeem'd him from his fall, and made him
mine,                                            50
To show his love again, first stole my daugh-
ter,
Then wrong'd this gentleman, and, last of all,
Gave me that grief had almost brought me
down
Unto my grave, had not a stronger hand
Reliev'd my sorrows. Go, and weep as I did,
And be unpitied: for I here profess           56
An everlasting hate to all thy name.
*Mist. Mer.* Will you so, sir? how say you by
that? — Come, Mick; let him keep his wind to
cool his porridge. We 'll go to thy nurse's, [60
Mick: she knits silk stockings, boy; and we 'll
knit too, boy, and be beholding to none of
them all.        *Exeunt Michael and Mother.*

*Enter a Boy with a letter*

*Boy.* Sir, I take it you are the master of this
house.                                           65
*Vent.* How then, boy?
*Boy.* Then to yourself, sir, comes this letter.

*Vent.* From whom, my pretty boy?
*Boy.* From him that was your servant; but
no more
Shall that name ever be, for he is dead:        70
Grief of your purchas'd anger broke his heart.
I saw him die, and from his hand receiv'd
This paper, with a charge to bring it hither:
Read it, and satisfy yourself in all.

*Letter*

Vent. [*reads.*] *Sir, that I have wronged your
love I must confess; in which I have pur-* [76
*chas'd to myself, besides mine own undoing,
the ill opinion of my friends. Let not your
anger, good sir, outlive me, but suffer me to
rest in peace with your forgiveness: let my* [80
*body (if a dying man may so much prevail with
you) be brought to your daughter, that she may
truly know my hot flames are now buried, and
withal receive a testimony of the zeal I bore
her virtue. Farewell for ever, and be ever* [85
*happy!*
                                    *Jasper.*

God's hand is great in this. I do forgive him;
Yet I am glad he 's quiet, where I hope
He will not bite again. — Boy, bring the body,
And let him have his will, if that be all.       90
*Boy.* 'T is here without, sir.
*Vent.*                   So, sir; if you please,
You may conduct it in; I do not fear it.
*Hum.* I 'll be your usher, boy; for, though
I say it,
He ow'd me something once, and well did pay
it.                                  *Exeunt.*

[SCENE IV. — *Luce's Chamber.*]

*Enter Luce alone*

*Luce.* If there be any punishment inflicted
Upon the miserable, more than yet I feel,
Let it together seize me, and at once
Press down my soul! I cannot bear the pain
Of these delaying tortures. — Thou that art   5
The end of all, and the sweet rest of all,
Come, come, oh, Death! bring me to thy peace,
And blot out all the memory I nourish
Both of my father and my cruel friend! —       9
Oh, wretched maid, still living to be wretch'd,
To be a say to Fortune in her changes,
And grow to number times and woes together!
How happy had I been, if, being born,
My grave had been my cradle!

*Enter Servant*

*Serv.*                      By your leave,
Young mistress; here 's a boy hath brought a
coffin:                                          15

²⁴ **of . . . most:** over-long    ³⁹ **hoits:** plays the fool    ⁷¹ **your purchas'd:** that which he had
aroused in you    ¹¹ **say:** testing material

What 'a would say, I know not; but your
    father
Charg'd me to give you notice. Here they come.
                              *[Exit.]*

*Enter two bearing a Coffin, Jasper in it*

*Luce.*    For me I hope 't is come, and 't is
    most welcome.
*Boy.*    Fair mistress, let me not add greater
    grief
To that great store you have already. Jasper 20
(That whilst he liv'd was yours, now dead
And here enclos'd) commanded me to bring
His body hither, and to crave a tear
From those fair eyes, (though he deserv'd not
    pity,)
To deck his funeral; for so he bid me      25
Tell her for whom he died.
    *Luce.*             He shall have many. —
Good friends, depart a little, whilst I take
My leave of this dead man, that once I lov'd.
            *Exeunt Coffin-carrier and Boy.*
Hold yet a little, life! and then I give thee
To thy first heavenly being. Oh, my friend! 30
Hast thou deceiv'd me thus, and got before me?
I shall not long be after. But, believe me,
Thou wert too cruel, Jasper, 'gainst thyself,
In punishing the fault I could have pardon'd
With so untimely death: thou didst not wrong
    me,      35
But ever wert most kind, most true, most lov-
    ing;
And I the most unkind, most false, most cruel!
Didst thou but ask a tear? I 'll give thee all,
Even all my eyes can pour down, all my sighs,
And all myself, before thou goest from me.    40
These are but sparing rites; but if thy soul
Be yet about this place, and can behold
And see what I prepare to deck thee with,
It shall go up, borne on the wings of peace,
And satisfied. First will I sing thy dirge,    45
Then kiss thy pale lips, and then die myself,
And fill one coffin and one grave together.

              SONG

    Come, you whose loves are dead,
        And, whiles I sing,
           Weep, and wring      50
    Every hand, and every head
    Bind with cypress and sad yew;
    Ribands black and candles blue
    For him that was of men most true!

    Come with heavy moaning,      55
        And on his grave
        Let him have
    Sacrifice of sighs and groaning;

    Let him have fair flowers enow,
    White and purple, green and yellow,    60
    For him that was of men most true!

Thou sable cloth, sad cover of my joys,
I lift thee up, and thus I meet with death.
         *[Removes the cloth, and Jasper rises*
               *out of the coffin.]*
*Jasp.*    And thus you meet the living.
*Luce.*                Save me, Heaven!
*Jasp.*    Nay, do not fly me, fair; I am no
    spirit:      65
Look better on me; do you know me yet?
    *Luce.*    Oh, thou dear shadow of my friend!
    *Jasp.*                Dear substance!
I swear I am no shadow; feel my hand.
It is the same it was; I am your Jasper,
Your Jasper that 's yet living, and yet loving.
Pardon my rash attempt, my foolish proof    71
I put in practice of your constancy;
For sooner should my sword have drunk my
    blood,
And set my soul at liberty, than drawn
The least drop from that body: for which bold-
    ness      75
Doom me to anything; if death, I take it,
And willingly.
    *Luce.*           This death I 'll give you for it.
                                     *[Kisses him.]*
So, now I am satisfied you are no spirit,
But my own truest, truest, truest friend.
Why do you come thus to me?
    *Jasp.*             First, to see you;    80
Then to convey you hence.
    *Luce.*             It cannot be;
For I am lock'd up here, and watch'd at all
    hours,
That 't is impossible for me to 'scape.
    *Jasp.*    Nothing more possible. Within this
    coffin
Do you convey yourself. Let me alone:      85
I have the wits of twenty men about me.
Only I crave the shelter of your closet
A little, and then fear me not. Creep in,
That they may presently convey you hence: 89
Fear nothing, dearest love; I 'll be your second;
         *[Luce lies down in the coffin, and*
           *Jasper covers her with the cloth.]*
Lie close: so; all goes well yet. — Boy!

        *[Re-enter Boy and Man]*
*Boy.*                  At hand, sir.
*Jasp.*    Convey away the coffin, and be wary.
*Boy.*    'T is done already.
               *[Exeunt with the coffin.]*
*Jasp.*          Now must I go conjure.
                   *Exit [into a closet].*

---

[17] S. D. **two:** (*i.e.*, the Boy and another)    [41] **These:** ('There' Qq., F)    [55] **moaning:** ('mourning'
Qq., F)      [78] **satisfied:** convinced      [88] **fear me not:** have no fear for me      [90] **second:** helper
[91] **close:** concealed

*Enter Merchant [Venturewell]*

*Vent.*  Boy, boy!

*Boy.*  Your servant, sir.    95

*Vent.*  Do me this kindness, boy: — (hold, here's a crown:) — Before thou bury the body of this fellow, carry it to his old merry father, and salute him from me, and bid him sing. He hath cause.    100

*Boy.*  I will, sir.

*Vent.*  And then bring me word what tune he is in,
And have another crown; but do it truly.    103
I have fitted him a bargain now will vex him.

*Boy.*  God bless your worship's health, sir!

*Vent.*  Farewell, boy! *Exeunt [severally].*

[SCENE V. — *Merrythought's House.*]

*Enter Master Merrythought*

*Wife.*  Ah, old Merrythought, art thou there again? Let's hear some of thy songs.

*Mer. [sings.]*

> Who can sing a merrier note
> Than he that cannot change a groat?

Not a denier left, and yet my heart leaps.  I [5 do wonder yet, as old as I am, that any man will follow a trade, or serve, that may sing and laugh, and walk the streets.  My wife and both my sons are I know not where; I have nothing left, nor know I how to come by meat to sup- [10 per; yet am I merry still, for I know I shall find it upon the table at six o'clock.  Therefore, hang thought!    [*Sings.*]

> I would not be a serving-man
>     To carry the cloak-bag still,    15
> Nor would I be a falconer
>     The greedy hawks to fill;
> But I would be in a good house,
>     And have a good master too;
> But I would eat and drink of the best,    20
>     And no work would I do.

This is it that keeps life and soul together, — mirth; this is the philosopher's stone that they write so much on, that keeps a man ever young.    25

*Enter a Boy*

*Boy.*  Sir, they say they know all your money is gone, and they will trust you for no more drink.

*Mer.*  Will they not? let 'em choose!  The best is, I have mirth at home, and need not [30 send abroad for that; let them keep their drink to themselves.    [*Sings.*]

> For Jillian of Berry, she dwells on a hill,
> And she hath good beer and ale to sell,
> And of good fellows she thinks no ill;    35
>     And thither will we go now, now now,
>     And thither will we go now.
>
> And when you have made a little stay,
> You need not ask what is to pay,
> But kiss your hostess, and go your way;    40
>     And thither will we go now, now now,
>     And thither will we go now.

*Enter another Boy*

*2 Boy.*  Sir, I can get no bread for supper.

*Mer.*  Hang bread and supper!  Let's pre-serve our mirth, and we shall never feel [45 hunger, I'll warrant you.  Let's have a catch; boy, follow me, come sing this catch.

> Ho, ho, nobody at home!
> Meat, nor drink, nor money ha' we none.
>     Fill the pot, Eedy,    50
>     Never more need I.

*Mer.*  So, boys; enough.  Follow me: let's change our place, and we shall laugh afresh.
    *Exeunt.*

*Wife.*  Let him go, George; 'a shall not have any countenance from us, nor a good word from any i' th' company, if I may strike stroke in 't.

*Cit.*  No more 'a sha'not, love.  But, Nell, [57 I will have Ralph do a very notable matter now, to the eternal honour and glory of all grocers. — Sirrah! you there, boy!  Can none of you hear?    61

[*Enter Boy*]

*Boy.*  Sir, your pleasure?

*Cit.*  Let Ralph come out on May-day in the morning, and speak upon a conduit, with all his scarfs about him, and his feathers, and his rings, and his knacks.    66

*Boy.*  Why, sir, you do not think of our plot. What will become of that, then?

*Cit.*  Why, sir, I care not what become on 't: I'll have him come out, or I'll fetch him [70 out myself; I'll have something done in honour of the city.  Besides, he hath been long enough upon adventures.  Bring him out quickly; or, if I come in amongst you ——

*Boy.*  Well, sir, he shall come out, but if our play miscarry, sir, you are like to pay for 't. [76

*Cit.*  Bring him away then!
    *Exit Boy.*

*Wife.*  This will be brave, i' faith!  George, shall not he dance the morris too, for the credit of the Strand?    80

*Cit.*  No, sweetheart, it will be too much for the boy.  Oh, there he is, Nell! he's reason-

---

⁶ **denier:** penny    ¹⁶ **cloak-bag:** traveling-bag    ¹⁷ **fill:** feed    ⁵⁰ **Eedy:** Edith    ⁵⁶ **strike**
**stroke:** have a hand    ⁶⁴ **upon a conduit:** standing on a hydrant

able well in reparel: but he has not rings enough.

*Enter Ralph [dressed as a May-lord]*

Ralph.  London, to thee I do present the
    merry month of May;                         85
*Let each true subject be content to hear me what
    I say:*
*For from the top of conduit-head, as plainly may
    appear,*
*I will both tell my name to you, and wherefore
    I came here.*
*My name is Ralph, by due descent though not
    ignoble I,*
*Yet far inferior to the flock of gracious grocery;* 90
*And by the common counsel of my fellows in
    the Strand,*
*With gilded staff and crossed scarf, the May-
    lord here I stand.*
*Rejoice, oh, English hearts, rejoice! rejoice, oh,
    lovers dear!*
*Rejoice, oh, city, town, and country! rejoice,
    eke every shire!*
*For now the fragrant flowers do spring and
    sprout in seemly sort,*                      95
*The little birds do sit and sing, the lambs do
    make fine sport;*
*And now the birchen-tree doth bud, that makes
    the schoolboy cry;*
*The morris rings, while hobby-horse doth foot
    it feateously;*
*The lords and ladies now abroad, for their dis-
    port and play,*
*Do kiss sometimes upon the grass, and some-
    times in the hay;*                           100
*Now butter with a leaf of sage is good to purge
    the blood;*
*Fly Venus and phlebotomy, for they are neither
    good.*
*Now little fish on tender stone begin to cast their
    bellies,*
*And sluggish snails, that erst were mew'd, do
    creep out of their shellies;*
*The rumbling rivers now do warm, for little boys
    to paddle;*                                  105
*The sturdy steed now goes to grass, and up they
    hang his saddle;*
*The heavy hart, the bellowing buck, the rascal,
    and the pricket,*
*Are now among the yeoman's peas, and leave
    the fearful thicket:*
*And be like them, oh, you, I say, of this same
    noble town,*
*And lift aloft your velvet heads, and slipping
    off your gown,*                              110

*With bells on legs, and napkins clean unto your
    shoulders tied,*
*With scarfs and garters as you please, and
    "Hey for our town!" cried,*
*March out, and show your willing minds, by
    twenty and by twenty,*
*To Hogsden or to Newington, where ale and
    cakes are plenty;*
*And let it ne'er be said for shame, that we the
    youths of London*                           115
*Lay thrumming of our caps at home, and left
    our custom undone.*
*Up, then, I say, both young and old, both man
    and maid a-maying,*
*With drums, and guns that bounce aloud, and
    merry tabor playing!*
*Which to prolong, God save our king, and send
    his country peace,*
*And root out treason from the land! and so, my
    friends, I cease.*            *Exit.* 120

*Finis Act. 4*

## Actus Quintus.
## Scæna Prima.

[*Venturewell's House.*]

*Enter Merchant [Venturewell], solus*

Vent.  I will have no great store of company
at the wedding; a couple of neighbours and
their wives; and we will have a capon in stewed
broth, with marrow, and a good piece of beef
stuck with rosemary.                             5

*Enter Jasper, his face mealed*

Jasp.  Forbear thy pains, fond man! it is
too late.
Vent.  Heaven bless me!  Jasper!
Jasp.                    Ay, I am his ghost,
Whom thou hast injur'd for his constant love,
Fond worldly wretch! who dost not understand
In death that true hearts cannot parted be.  10
First know, thy daughter is quite borne away
On wings of angels, through the liquid air,
To far out of thy reach, and never more
Shalt thou behold her face: but she and I
Will in another world enjoy our loves;       15
Where neither father's anger, poverty,
Nor any cross that troubles earthly men,
Shall make us sever our united hearts.
And never shalt thou sit or be alone
In any place, but I will visit thee           20
With ghastly looks, and put into thy mind
The great offences which thou didst to me.

---

**89–90** (Parody of *Spanish Tragedy*, I. i. 5–7)    **98 feateously:** nimbly    **103 bellies:** *i.e.* spawn
**104 mew'd:** confined ('mute' Qq.–F)    **107 rascal:** lean deer    **pricket:** two-year-old buck    **116 thrum-**
**ming:** affixing tufts or thrums of wool    **118 bounce:** make a report    **tabor:** small drum
**5** s. d. **mealed:** whitened with flour    **13 To:** ('Too' Q 2, F)

When thou art at thy table with thy friends,
Merry in heart, and fill'd with swelling wine,
I 'll come in midst of all thy pride and mirth, 25
Invisible to all men but thyself,
And whisper such a sad tale in thine ear
Shall make thee let the cup fall from thy hand,
And stand as mute and pale as death itself.
*Vent.* Forgive me, Jasper! Oh, what might
   I do, 30
Tell me, to satisfy thy troubled ghost?
*Jasp.* There is no means; too late thou
   think'st of this.
*Vent.* But tell me what were best for me to
   do?
*Jasp.* Repent thy deed, and satisfy my
·   father,
And beat fond Humphrey out of thy doors. 35
                              *Exit.*

*Wife.* Look, George; his very ghost would
have folks beaten.

#### Enter Humphrey

*Hum.* Father, my bride is gone, fair Mistress
Luce:
My soul 's the fount of vengeance, mischief's
   sluice.
*Vent.* Hence, fool, out of my sight with thy
   fond passion! 40
Thou hast undone me. [*Beats him.*]
*Hum.*                    Hold, my father dear,
For Luce thy daughter's sake, that had no
   peer!
*Vent.* Thy father, fool! There 's some blows
   more; begone. — [*Beats him.*]
Jasper, I hope thy ghost be well appeas'd
To see thy will perform'd. Now will I go 45
To satisfy thy father for thy wrongs. *Exit.*
*Hum.* What shall I do? I have been beaten
   twice,
And Mistress Luce is gone. Help me, device!
Since my true love is gone, I never more,
Whilst I do live, upon the sky will pore; 50
But in the dark will wear out my shoe-soles
In passion in Saint Faith's church under Paul's.
                              *Exit.*

*Wife.* George, call Ralph hither; if you love
me, call Ralph hither: I have the bravest thing
for him to do, George; prithee, call him quickly.
*Cit.* Ralph! why, Ralph, boy! 56

#### Enter Ralph

*Ralph.* Here, sir.
*Cit.* Come hither, Ralph; come to thy mistress, boy.

*Wife.* Ralph, I would have thee call all [60
the youths together in battle-ray, with drums,
and guns, and flags, and march to Mile-End in
pompous fashion, and there exhort your soldiers to be merry and wise, and to keep their
beards from burning, Ralph; and then skir- [65
mish, and let your flags fly, and cry, "Kill,
kill, kill!" My husband shall lend you his jerkin, Ralph, and there 's a scarf; for the rest,
the house shall furnish you, and we 'll pay for 't.
Do it bravely, Ralph; and think before [70
whom you perform, and what person you represent.
*Ralph.* I warrant you, mistress; if I do it
not for the honour of the city and the credit
of my master, let me never hope for free- [75
dom!
*Wife.* 'T is well spoken, i' faith. Go thy
ways; thou art a spark indeed.
*Cit.* Ralph, Ralph, double your files bravely,
Ralph! 80
*Ralph.* I warrant you, sir. *Exit.*
*Cit.* Let him look narrowly to his service; I
shall take him else. I was there myself a pike-
man once, in the hottest of the day, wench;
had my feather shot sheer away, the fringe of
my pike burnt off with powder, my pate [86
broken with a scouring-stick, and yet, I thank
God, I am here. *Drum within.*
*Wife.* Hark, George, the drums!
*Cit.* Ran, tan, tan, tan; ran, tan! Oh, wench,
an thou hadst but seen little Ned of Aldgate, [91
Drum Ned, how he made it roar again, and
laid on like a tyrant, and then struck softly till
the ward came up, and then thund'red again,
and together we go! "Sa, sa, sa, bounce!" [95
quoth the guns; "Courage, my hearts!"
quoth the captains; "Saint George!" quoth
the pikemen; and withal, here they lay, and
there they lay: and yet for all this I am here,
wench. 100
*Wife.* Be thankful for it, George; for indeed
't is wonderful.

#### [SCENE II. — *A Street.*]

#### Enter Ralph and his Company, with drums and colours

*Ralph.* March fair, my hearts! Lieutenant,
beat the rear up. — Ancient, let your colours
fly; but have a great care of the butchers'
hooks at Whitechapel; they have been the
death of many a fair ancient. — Open your [5
files, that I may take a view both of your persons and munition. — Sergeant, call a muster.

---

²⁶ Reminiscence of Banquo's ghost  ⁵² **passion:** grief  **Saint Faith's:** a parish church built under
the choir of old St. Paul's  ⁷⁵⁻⁷⁶ **freedom:** *i.e.*, rank of freeman in the Grocers' guild  ⁸² **service:** drill
⁸³ **take:** detect his errors  ⁸⁷ **scouring-stick:** ramrod  ⁹⁴ **ward:** detachment of militia  ² **Ancient:**
ensign-bearer  ⁵ **ancient:** ensign

*Serg.* A stand! — William Hammerton, pewterer!

*Ham.* Here, captain!                                    10

*Ralph.* A corselet and a Spanish pike; 't is well: can you shake it with a terror?

*Ham.* I hope so, captain.

*Ralph.* Charge upon me. [*He charges on Ralph.*] — 'T is with the weakest: put more [15 strength, William Hammerton, more strength. As you were again! — Proceed, Sergeant.

*Serg.* George Greengoose, poulterer!

*Green.* Here!

*Ralph.* Let me see your piece, neighbour [20 Greengoose: when was she shot in?

*Green.* An 't like you, master captain, I made a shot even now, partly to scour her, and partly for audacity.

*Ralph.* It should seem so certainly, for her [25 breath is yet inflamed; besides, there is a main-fault in the touch-hole, it runs and stinketh; and I tell you moreover, and believe it, ten such touch-holes would breed the pox in the army. Get you a feather, neighbour, get you [30 a feather, sweet oil, and paper, and your piece may do well enough yet. Where 's your powder?

*Green.* Here.

*Ralph.* What, in a paper! As I am a soldier and a gentleman, it craves a martial court! [35 You ought to die for 't. Where 's your horn? Answer me to that.

*Green.* An 't like you, sir, I was oblivious.

*Ralph.* It likes me not you should be so; 't is a shame for you, and a scandal to all our [40 neighbours, being a man of worth and estimation, to leave your horn behind you: I am afraid 't will breed example. But let me tell you no more on 't. — Stand, till I view you all. What 's become o' th' nose of your flask?     45

*1 Sold.* Indeed, la, captain, 't was blown away with powder.

*Ralph.* Put on a new one at the city's charge. — Where 's the stone of this piece?

*2 Sold.* The drummer took it out to light [50 tobacco.

*Ralph.* 'T is a fault, my friend; put it in again. — You want a nose, — and you a stone. — Sergeant, take a note on 't, for I mean to stop it in the pay. — Remove, and march! [*They [55 march.*] Soft and fair, gentlemen, soft and fair! Double your files! As you were! Faces about! Now, you with the sodden face, keep in there! Look to your match, sirrah, it will be in your fellow's flask anon. So; make a crescent now: [60 advance your pikes: stand and give ear! — Gentlemen, countrymen, friends, and my fellow-soldiers, I have brought you this day, from the shops of security and the counters of content, to measure out in these furious fields honour by [65 the ell, and prowess by the pound. Let it not, oh, let it not, I say, be told hereafter, the noble issue of this city fainted; but bear yourselves in this fair action like men, valiant men, and free men! Fear not the face of the enemy, [70 nor the noise of the guns, for, believe me, brethren, the rude rumbling of a brewer's car is far more terrible, of which you have a daily experience. Neither let the stink of powder offend you, since a more valiant stink is nightly with you.                                          76

To a resolved mind his home is everywhere:
I speak not this to take away
The hope of your return; for you shall see
(I do not doubt it) and that very shortly     80
Your loving wives again and your sweet children,
Whose care doth bear you company in baskets.
Remember, then, whose cause you have in hand,
And, like a sort of true-born scavengers,
Scour me this famous realm of enemies.     85
I have no more to say but this: stand to your
tacklings, lads, and show to the world you can
as well brandish a sword as shake an apron.
Saint George, and on, my hearts!

*Omnes.* Saint George, Saint George!     90
                                      *Exeunt.*

*Wife.* 'T was well done, Ralph! I 'll send thee a cold capon a-field and a bottle of March beer; and, it may be, come myself to see thee.

*Cit.* Nell, the boy has deceived me much; I did not think it had been in him. He has [95 performed such a matter, wench, that, if I live, next year I 'll have him captain of the galley-foist or I 'll want my will.

[SCENE III. — *Merrythought's House.*]

*Enter Old Merrythought*

*Mer.* Yet, I thank God, I break not a wrinkle more than I had. Not a stoop, boys! Care, live with cats; I defy thee! My heart is as sound as an oak; and though I want drink to wet my whistle, I can sing;          [*Sings.*]  5

Come no more there, boys, come no more there;
For we shall never whilst we live come any more
  there.

*Enter a Boy, [and two Men] with a Coffin*

*Boy.* God save you, sir!

*Mer.* It 's a brave boy. Canst thou sing?

*Boy.* Yes, sir, I can sing; but 't is not so [10 necessary at this time.

*Mer.* [*sings.*]

Sing we, and chant it;
Whilst love doth grant it.

---

²⁰ **piece:** musket    ²² **An 't:** ('And' Qq., F) ⁴⁹ **stone:** flint    ⁸⁴ **sort:** crew    ⁹⁷⁻⁹⁸ **galley-foist:** state barge

*Boy.* Sir, sir, if you knew what I have brought you, you would have little list to [15 sing.

*Mer.* [*sings.*]

> Oh, the Mimon round,
> Full long, long I have thee sought,
> And now I have thee found,
> And what hast thou here brought?        20

*Boy.* A coffin, sir, and your dead son Jasper in it.        [*Exit with Men.*]
*Mer.* Dead!        [*Sings.*]

> Why, farewell he!
> Thou wast a bonny boy,        25
> And I did love thee.

*Enter Jasper*

*Jasp.* Then, I pray you, sir, do so still.
*Mer.* Jasper's ghost!        [*Sings.*]

> Thou art welcome from Stygian lake so soon;
> Declare to me what wondrous things in Pluto's
> court are done.        30

*Jasp.* By my troth, sir, I ne'er came there; 't is too hot for me, sir.
*Mer.* A merry ghost, a very merry ghost!        [*Sings.*]

> And where is your true love? Oh, where is yours?

*Jasp.* Marry, look you, sir!        35
        *Heaves up the coffin.*
*Mer.* Ah, ha! art thou good at that, i' faith?        [*Sings.*]

> With hey, trixy, terlery-whiskin,
> The world it runs on wheels:
> When the young man's ——,
> Up goes the maiden's heels.        40

*Mistress Merrythought and Michael within*

*Mist. Mer.* [*within.*] What, Master Merrythought! will you not let 's in? What do you think shall become of us?
*Mer.* [*sings.*]

> What voice is that, that calleth at our door?

*Mist. Mer.* [*within.*] You know me well [45 enough; I am sure I have not been such a stranger to you.
*Mer.* [*sings.*]

> And some they whistled, and some they sung,
>         Hey, down, down!
> And some did loudly say,        50
> Ever as the Lord Barnet's horn blew,
>         Away, Musgrave, away!

*Mist. Mer.* [*within.*] You will not have us starve here, will you, Master Merrythought?
*Jasp.* Nay, good sir, be persuaded; she is my mother.        55

If her offences have been great against you,
Let your own love remember she is yours,
And so forgive her.
*Luce.*        Good Master Merrythought,
Let me entreat you; I will not be denied.
*Mist. Mer.* [*within.*] Why, Master Merry- [60 thought, will you be a vext thing still?
*Mer.* Woman, I take you to my love again; but you shall sing before you enter; therefore despatch your song and so come in.
*Mist. Mer.* [*within.*] Well, you must [65 have your will, when all 's done. — Mick, what song canst thou sing, boy?
*Mich.* [*within.*] I can sing none, forsooth, but *A Lady's Daughter, of Paris properly.*
*Mist. Mer.* Song.

> It was a lady's daughter, &c.        70

[*Merrythought opens the door. Enter Mistress Merrythought and Michael*]

*Mer.* Come, you 're welcome home again.        [*Sings.*]

> If such danger be in playing,
>         And jest must to earnest turn,
> You shall go no more a-maying —

*Vent. within.* Are you within, sir? Mas- [75 ter Merrythought!
*Jasp.* It is my master's voice! Good sir, go hold him
In talk, whilst we convey ourselves into
Some inward room.        [*Exit with Luce.*]
*Mer.*        What are you? Are you merry?
You must be very merry, if you enter.        80
*Vent.* [*within.*] I am, sir.
*Mer.* Sing, then.
*Vent.* [*within.*] Nay, good sir, open to me.
*Mer.* Sing, I say, or, by the merry heart, you come not in!        85
*Vent.* [*within.*] Well, sir, I 'll sing. [*Sings.*]

> Fortune, my foe, &c.

[*Merrythought opens the door. Enter Venturewell*]

*Mer.* You are welcome, sir, you are welcome: you see your entertainment; pray you, be merry.        90
*Vent.* Oh, Master Merrythought, I am come to ask you
Forgiveness for the wrongs I offer'd you
And your most virtuous son! They 're infinite;
Yet my contrition shall be more than they:
I do confess my hardness broke his heart,        95
For which just Heaven hath given me punishment
More than my age can carry. His wand'ring spirit,

---

**39** man's —: (so in all texts)        **61** vext: cantankerous        **69** A . . . properly: (an anti-papal ballad)

Not yet at rest, pursues me everywhere,
Crying, "I 'll haunt thee for thy cruelty."
My daughter, she is gone, I know not how, 100
Taken invisible, and whether living
Or in grave, 't is yet uncertain to me.
Oh, Master Merrythought, these are the
    weights
Will sink me to my grave! Forgive me, sir.
    *Mer.*   Why, sir, I do forgive you; and be
    merry.   105
And if the wag in 's lifetime play'd the knave,
Can you forgive him too?
    *Vent.*           With all my heart, sir.
    *Mer.*   Speak it again, and heartily.
    *Vent.*               I do, sir;
Now, by my soul, I do.

       *Enter Luce and Jasper*

    *Mer.* [*sings.*]

    With that came out his paramour;   110
    She was as white as the lily flower:
        Hey, troul, troly, loly!
    With that came out her own dear knight;
    He was as true as ever did fight, &c.

Sir, if you will forgive him, clap their hands [115
together; there 's no more to be said i' th'
matter.
    *Vent.*   I do, I do.

    *Cit.*   I do not like this. Peace, boys! Hear
me, one of you! Everybody's part is come to
an end but Ralph's, and he 's left out.   121
    *Boy.*   'T is 'long of yourself, sir; we have
nothing to do with his part.
    *Cit.*   Ralph, come away! — Make an end on
him, as you have done of the rest, boys;
come.   126
    *Wife.*   Now, good husband, let him come out
and die.
    *Cit.*   He shall, Nell. — Ralph, come away
quickly, and die, boy!   130
    *Boy.*   'T will be very unfit he should die, sir,
upon no occasion, and in a comedy too.
    *Cit.*   Take you no care of that, sir boy; is
not his part at an end, think you, when he 's
dead? — Come away, Ralph!   135

  *Enter Ralph, with a forked arrow through his
        head*

    *Ralph.*   When I was mortal, this my costive
    corpse
Did lap up figs and raisins in the Strand;
Where sitting, I espi'd a lovely dame,
Whose master wrought with lingel and with
    awl,
And underground he vamped many a boot. 140

Straight did her love prick forth me, tender
    sprig,
To follow feats of arms in warlike wise
Through Waltham Desert; where I did per-
    form
Many achievements, and did lay on ground
Huge Barbaroso, that insulting giant,   145
And all his captives soon set at liberty.
Then honour prick'd me from my native soil
Into Moldavia, where I gain'd the love
Of Pompiona, his beloved daughter;
But yet prov'd constant to the black thumb'd
    maid,   150
Susan, and scorned Pompiona's love.
Yet liberal I was, and gave her pins,
And money for her father's officers.
I then returned home, and thrust myself
In action, and by all men chosen was   155
Lord of the May, where I did flourish it,
With scarfs and rings, and posy in my hand.
After this action I preferred was,
And chosen city-captain at Mile-End,   159
With hat and feather, and with leading-staff,
And train'd my men, and brought them all off
    clear,
Save one man that beray'd him with the noise.
But all these things I Ralph did undertake
Only for my beloved Susan's sake.
Then coming home, and sitting in my shop   165
With apron blue, Death came unto my stall
To cheapen *aqua vitæ;* but ere I
Could take the bottle down and fill a taste,
Death caught a pound of pepper in his hand,
And sprinkled all my face and body o'er,   170
And in an instant vanished away.

    *Cit.*   'T is a pretty fiction, i' faith.

    *Ralph.*   Then took I up my bow and shaft in
    hand,
And walk'd into Moorfields to cool myself;
But there grim cruel Death met me again, 175
And shot this forked arrow through my head;
And now I faint; therefore be warn'd by me,
My fellows every one, of forked heads!
Farewell, all you good boys in merry Lon-
    don!
Ne'er shall we more upon Shrove-Tuesday
    meet,   180
And pluck down houses of iniquity; —
My pain increaseth — I shall never more
Hold open, whilst another pumps both legs,
Nor daub a satin gown with rotten eggs;
Set up a stake, oh, never more I shall!   185
I die! fly, fly, my soul, to Grocers' Hall!
Oh, oh, oh, &c.

     116 **said:** ('sad' Q 1)   124 **an end:** (not in Qq., F)   139 **lingel:** waxed thread   146 **all his:** (pronounce "all 's")   160 **leading-staff:** baton   167 **cheapen:** bargain for   181 A traditional liberty of the apprentices on Shrove-Tuesday

*Wife.* Well said, Ralph! do your obeisance to the gentlemen, and go your ways: well said, Ralph! 190

*Exit Ralph.*

*Mer.* Methinks all we, thus kindly and unexpectedly reconciled, should not depart without a song.

*Vent.* A good motion.

*Mer.* Strike up, then! 195

SONG

Better music ne'er was known
Than a choir of hearts in one.
Let each other, that hath been
Troubled with the gall or spleen,
Learn of us to keep his brow 200
Smooth and plain, as ours are now.
Sing, though before the hour of dying;
He shall rise, and then be crying,
"Hey, ho, 't is nought but mirth
That keeps the body from the earth!" 205

*Exeunt omnes.*

EPILOGUS

*Cit.* Come, Nell, shall we go? The play 's done.

*Wife.* Nay, by my faith, George, I have more manners than so; I 'll speak to these gentlemen first. — I thank you all, gentlemen, [210 for your patience and countenance to Ralph, a poor fatherless child; and if I might see you at my house, it should go hard but I would have a pottle of wine and a pipe of tobacco for you: for, truly, I hope you do like the youth, but [215 I would be glad to know the truth. I refer it to your own discretions, whether you will applaud him or no; for I will wink, and whilst you shall do what you will. I thank you with all my heart. God give you good night! — Come, [220 George. [*Exeunt.*]

192 **depart:** separate  218 **whilst:** meanwhile

# PHYLASTER.

### Or, Loue lyes a Bleeding.

*Acted at the Globe by his Maiesties Seruants.*

Written by ⎰ *Francis Baymont* ⎱ Gent.
⎱ and ⎰
⎰ *Iohn Fletcher.* ⎱

The Princes.    A Cuntrie Gentellman.

Phielaster.

Printed at *London* for *Thomas Walkley*, and are to be sold at his
shop at the *Eagle and Child* in Brittaines Bursse. 1620.

BIBLIOGRAPHICAL RECORD. The Stationers' Register contains the following entry: — *10 Januari⟩ 1619 [i.e., 1620]. Thomas Walkley. Entred for his copie vnder the handes of Master Tauernor and Master Jaggard warden A Play Called Philaster. vjd.* In the same year Walkley issued the earliest edition, noting on the title-page that the play had been "Acted at the Globe by his Maiesties Seruants" and "Written by Francis Baymont and Iohn Fletcher, Gent[lemen]." This first Quarto varies greatly from all others. For the first 130 lines of Act I and the last two scenes of Act V it offers an altogether different and inferior text. Elsewhere we have followed it in a large number of passages where the later editions seem to present misprints or actors' sophistication, and we have cited in the footnotes numerous readings of Q 1 which may illustrate authors' revision.

Two years later (1622) Walkley published the "Second Impression, corrected and amended," to which he appended the following note: — *To the Reader. Courteous Reader. Philaster, and Arethusa his love, have laine so long a bleeding, by reason of some dangerous and gaping wounds, which they received in the first Impression, that it is wondered how they could goe abroad so long, or travaile so farre as they have done. Although they were hurt neither by me, nor the Printer; yet I knowing and finding by experience, how many well-wishers they have abroad, have adventured to bind up their wounds, & to enable them to visite upon better tearmes such friends of theirs as were pleased to take knowledge of them, so maimed and deformed as they at the first were; and if they were then gracious in your sight, assuredly they will now finde double favour, being reformed, and set forth suteable to their birth and breeding. By your serviceable Friend, Thomas Walkley.*

Other editions were published in 1628 (Q3) and 1634 (Q4) by Richard Hawkins, to whom Walkley assigned his right, March 1, 1628. After Hawkins' death the copyright passed to William Leake (S. R., May 29, 1638, Jan. 25, 1639), who published the fifth Quarto in 1639, brought out two new editions in 1652, and a final one, without date, about 1660. *Philaster* is one of the plays excluded from the first Beaumont-Fletcher Folio, but was reprinted from the last Quarto in the Folio of 1679 (F).

DATE AND STAGE PERFORMANCE. Dryden, speaking of Beaumont in his *Essay of Dramatic Poesy*, says: — "The first play that brought Fletcher and him in esteem was their *Philaster*: for before that they had written two or three very unsuccessfully, as the like is reported of Ben Johnson before he writ *Every Man in his Humour*." We have no precise criteria for the date of composition or production, but the indications point to 1608–1610. Many striking echoes of *Hamlet* and *Othello* show it to be later than those plays, and a couple of lines in IV. iii. (106–107) are so close to *Cymbeline* V. ii. 1–6 that we must suppose it also earlier than *Philaster*, unless we accept the less probable alternative that Shakespeare here borrowed from Beaumont.

In the list of fourteen plays produced before Prince Charles and the Court in the season of 1612–1613 *Philaster* is mentioned twice. Under its normal title it heads the list, and at the end is again named, "And one other called *Love Lies a bleeding*." Since the sum disbursed shows that fourteen, and not thirteen, performances were paid for, it is to be assumed that *Philaster* was given twice; and it is a reasonable conjecture that the alterations evidenced by Q1 (where the conclusion is sweetened by providing husbands for Euphrasia and Galatea) had their origin at this time. The play was acted at St. James's Palace, Feb. 21, 1637, before the King and Queen. During the period when the theatres were closed (1642–1660), the farcical scene, V. iv, was presented surreptitiously as a "droll" under the title of "The Club Men." At some time in the same period Samuel Pepys, still a boy, learned the part of Arethusa for a production at Sir Robert Cooke's, which for some reason never occurred (cf. *Diary*, May 30, 1668). After the Restoration *Philaster* remained in the repertory of the King's Company, Nell Gwyn playing Bellario and Hart, Philaster; but it seems to have been regarded as rather outmoded. Pepys first saw it acted Nov. 18, 1661, and found it "far short" of his expectations. An adaptation, ascribed to the Duke of Buckingham, and entitled *The Restauration*, was not printed till 1714. Another, with "the two last acts new written" by Elkanah Settle, was produced at the Theatre Royal and printed in 1695.

AUTHORSHIP. The major portion of the play is undoubtedly Beaumont's in style, and probably in conception. Fletcher wrote the effective, if melodramatic, scenes iii and iv of Act V; also the greater part of the opening scene in its approved form (from about I. i. 100), and of II. ii (from about line 64), as well as the latter half of II. iv (from about line 110) and part of III. ii (lines 36–128).

SOURCES. Essentially the plot of *Philaster* is the invention of the authors, who were, however, strongly influenced by themes that Shakespeare had made popular: the melancholy and sensitive prince, deprived of his heritage and prone to suspicion; the amorous girl disguised as a boy; the falsely suspected heroine, etc. *Cymbeline* is the play that most resembles *Philaster* in tone as in date. Professor T. P. Harrison has suggested (PMLA, June, 1926) that the continuation of Montemayor's *Diana* by Alonzo Perez may have provided numerous hints for the plot.

# FRANCIS BEAUMONT (1584–1616) AND JOHN FLETCHER (1579–1625)

## PHILASTER

OR

## LOVE LIES A–BLEEDING

THE ACTORS' NAMES

KING of Sicily [and Calabria]
PHILASTER, Heir to the Crown [of Sicily]
PHARAMOND, a Spanish Prince
DION, a Lord
CLEREMONT, ⎫ Noble Gentlemen,
THRASILINE, ⎭ his Associates

ARETHUSA, the King's Daughter
EUPHRASIA, Daughter of Dion, but disguised like a page and called Bellario
GALATEA, a wise modest Lady attending the Princess
MEGRA, a lascivious Lady

An old Captain; five Citizens; a Country Fellow; two Woodmen; the King's Guard and Train; Messenger; two Ladies.

SCENE: Sicily. The Court and a neighboring Forest.

### Actus Primus. Scena Prima.

*[The Palace.]*

*Enter Dion, Cleremont, and Thrasiline*

*Cle.* Here 's nor lords nor ladies.

*Dion.* Credit me, gentlemen, I wonder at it. They receiv'd strict charge from the King to attend here; besides, it was boldly published that no officer should forbid any gentleman [5 that desired to attend and hear.

*Cle.* Can you guess the cause?

*Dion.* Sir, it is plain, about the Spanish Prince that 's come to marry our kingdom's heir and be our sovereign. 10

*Thra.* Many that will seem to know much say she looks not on him like a maid in love.

*Dion.* Faith, sir, the multitude, that seldom know anything but their own opinions, speak that they would have; but the prince, be- [15 fore his own approach, receiv'd so many confident messages from the state, that I think she 's resolv'd to be rul'd.

*Cle.* Sir, it is thought, with her he shall enjoy both these kingdoms of Sicily and Calabria.

*Dion.* Sir, it is without controversy so [21 meant. But 't will be a troublesome labour for him to enjoy both these kingdoms with safety, the right heir to one of them living, and living so virtuously: especially, the people admir- [25 ing the bravery of his mind and lamenting his injuries.

*Cle.* Who? Philaster?

*Dion.* Yes; whose father, we all know, was by our late King of Calabria unrighteously [30 deposed from his fruitful Sicily. Myself drew some blood in those wars, which I would give my hand to be washed from.

*Cle.* Sir, my ignorance in state-policy will not let me know why, Philaster being heir to one [35 of these kingdoms, the King should suffer him to walk abroad with such free liberty.

*Dion.* Sir, it seems your nature is more constant than to inquire after state-news. But the King, of late, made a hazard of both the [40 kingdoms, of Sicily and his own, with offering but to imprison Philaster; at which the city was in arms, not to be charm'd down by any state-order or proclamation, till they saw Philaster ride through the streets pleas'd and [45 without a guard: at which they threw their hats and their arms from them; some to make bonfires, some to drink, all for his deliverance: which wise men say is the cause the King labours to bring in the power of a foreign nation to awe his own with. 51

*Enter Galatea, Megra, and a Lady*

*Thra.* See, the ladies! What 's the first?

*Dion.* A wise and modest gentlewoman that attends the princess.

---

1–130 (Q 1 offers a very different and inferior version of these lines.)    21 **controversy**: doubt
33 **washed**: cleansed

725

*Cle.* The second?                                                    55

*Dion.* She is one that may stand still discreetly enough and ill-favour'dly dance her measure; simper when she is courted by her friend, and slight her husband.

*Cle.* The last?                                                     60

*Dion.* Faith, I think she is one whom the state keeps for the agents of our confederate princes; she 'll cog and lie with a whole army, before the league shall break. Her name is common through the kingdom, and the tro- [65 phies of her dishonour advanced beyond Hercules' Pillars. She loves to try the several constitutions of men's bodies; and, indeed, has destroyed the worth of her own body by making experiment upon it for the good of the com- [70 monwealth.

*Cle.* She 's a profitable member.

*La.* Peace, if you love me! You shall see these gentlemen stand their ground and not court us.

*Gal.* What if they should?                                          75

*Meg.* What if they should!

*La.* Nay, let her alone. — What if they should! Why, if they should, I say they were never abroad. What foreigner would do so? [79 It writes them directly untravell'd.

*Gal.* Why, what if they be?

*Meg.* What if they be!

*La.* Good madam, let her go on. — What if they be! Why, if they be, I will justify, [84 they cannot maintain discourse with a judicious lady, nor make a leg nor say "Excuse me."

*Gal.* Ha, ha, ha!

*La.* Do you laugh, madam?

*Dion.* Your desires upon you, ladies!

*La.* Then you must sit beside us.                                   90

*Dion.* I shall sit near you then, lady.

*La.* Near me, perhaps; but there 's a lady endures no stranger; and to me you appear a very strange fellow.                                            94

*Meg.* Methinks he 's not so strange; he would quickly be acquainted.

*Thra.* Peace, the King!

*Enter King, Pharamond, Arethusa, and Train*

*King.* To give a stronger testimony of love Than sickly promises (which commonly In princes find both birth and burial        100 In one breath) we have drawn you, worthy sir,
To make your fair endearments to our daughter
And worthy services known to our subjects,
Now lov'd and wondered at; next, our intent
To plant you deeply our immediate heir      105
Both to our blood and kingdoms. For this lady,
(The best part of your life, as you confirm me,

And I believe,) though her few years and sex
Yet teach her nothing but her fears and blushes,
Desires without desire, discourse and knowledge        110
Only of what herself is to herself,
Make her feel moderate health; and when she sleeps,
In making no ill day, knows no ill dreams.
Think not, dear sir, these undivided parts,
That must mould up a virgin, are put on   115
To show her so, as borrow'd ornaments
To speak her perfect love to you, or add
An artificial shadow to her nature, —
No, sir; I boldly dare proclaim her yet
No woman. But woo her still, and think her modesty        120
A sweeter mistress than the offer'd language
Of any dame, were she a queen, whose eye
Speaks common loves and comforts to her servants.
Last, noble son (for so I now must call you),
What I have done thus public, is not only   125
To add a comfort in particular
To you or me, but all; and to confirm
The nobles and the gentry of these kingdoms
By oath to your succession, which shall be
Within this month at most.                                   130

*Thra.* This will be hardly done.

*Cle.* It must be ill done, if it be done.

*Dion.* When 't is at best, 't will be but half done, whilst
So brave a gentleman 's wrong'd and flung off.

*Thra.* I fear.                                                      135

*Cle.* Who does not?

*Dion.* I fear not for myself, and yet I fear too.
Well, we shall see, we shall see. No more.

*Pha.* Kissing your white hand, mistress, I take leave
To thank your royal father; and thus far   140
To be my own free trumpet. Understand,
Great King, and these your subjects, mine that must be,
(For so deserving you have spoke me, sir,
And so deserving I dare speak myself,)
To what a person, of what eminence,        145
Ripe expectation, of what faculties,
Manners and virtues, you would wed your kingdoms:
You in me have your wishes. Oh, this country!
By more than all the gods, I hold it happy; 149
Happy in their dear memories that have been
Kings great and good; happy in yours that is;
And from you (as a chronicle to keep
Your noble name from eating age) do I
Opine myself most happy. Gentlemen,

---

⁶⁰ **The last:** Megra      ⁶³ **cog:** cheat      ⁸⁶ **leg:** bow      ¹²³ **servants:** suitors      ¹⁴⁸ **You:** ('And· Q 1)
¹⁴⁹ **all . . . gods:** ('all my hopes' Q 4–F)      ¹⁵³ **eating:** ('rotting' Q 1)      ¹⁵⁴ **Opine** ('Open' Qq.)

Believe me in a word, a prince's word, 155
There shall be nothing to make up a kingdom
Mighty and flourishing, defenced, fear'd,
Equal to be commanded and obeyed,
But through the travails of my life I 'll find it,
And tie it to this country. By all the gods, 160
My reign shall be so easy to the subject,
That every man shall be his prince himself,
And his own law — yet I his prince and law.
And, dearest lady, to your dearest self
(Dear in the choice of him whose name and
    lustre 165
Must make you more and mightier) let me say,
You are the blessed'st living; for, sweet prin-
    cess,
You shall enjoy a man of men to be
Your servant; you shall make him yours, for
    whom
Great queens must die. 170
    *Thra.* Miraculous!
    *Cle.* This speech calls him Spaniard, being
nothing but a large inventory of his own com-
mendations.
    *Dion.* I wonder what 's his price; for cer-
    tainly 175
He 'll sell himself, he has so prais'd his shape.

    *Enter Philaster*

But here comes one more worthy those large
    speeches
Than the large speaker of them.
Let me be swallow'd quick, if I can find,
In all the anatomy of yon man's virtues, 180
One sinew sound enough to promise for him,
He shall be constable. By this sun,
He 'll ne'er make king unless it be of trifles,
In my poor judgment.
    *Phi.* [*kneeling.*] Right noble sir, as low as
    my obedience, 185
And with a heart as loyal as my knee,
I beg your favour.
    *King.*    Rise; you have it, sir.
        [*Philaster rises.*]
    *Dion.* Mark but the king, how pale he looks
    with fear!
Oh, this same whoreson conscience, how it jades
    us!
    *King.* Speak your intents, sir.
    *Phi.*    Shall I speak 'em freely? 190
Be still my royal sovereign.
    *King.*    As a subject,
We give you freedom.
    *Dion.*    Now it heats.
    *Phi.*    Then thus I turn

My language to you, prince, you foreign man!
Ne'er stare nor put on wonder, for you must
Endure me, and you shall. This earth you
    tread upon 195
(A dowry, as you hope, with this fair princess),
By my dead father (oh, I had a father,
Whose memory I bow to!) was not left
To your inheritance, and I up and living —
Having myself about me and my sword, 200
The souls of all my name and memories,
These arms and some few friends besides the
    gods —
To part so calmly with it, and sit still
And say, "I might have been." I tell thee,
    Pharamond, 204
When thou art king, look I be dead and rotten,
And my name ashes: for, hear me, Pharamond!
This very ground thou goest on, this fat earth,
My father's friends made fertile with their
    faiths,
Before that day of shame shall gape and swallow
Thee and thy nation, like a hungry grave, 210
Into her hidden bowels. Prince, it shall:
By the just gods, it shall!
    *Pha.*    He 's mad beyond cure, mad.
    *Dion.* Here is a fellow has some fire in 's
    veins:
The outlandish prince looks like a tooth-drawer.
    *Phi.* Sir Prince of popinjays, I 'll make it
    well 215
Appear to you I am not mad.
    *King.*    You displease us:
You are too bold.
    *Phi.*    No, sir, I am too tame,
Too much a turtle, a thing born without pas-
    sion,
A faint shadow, that every drunken cloud
Sails over, and makes nothing.
    *King.*    I do not fancy this. 220
Call our physicians; sure, he 's somewhat
    tainted.
    *Thra.* I do not think 't will prove so.
    *Dion.* H'as given him a general purge al-
    ready,
For all the right he has; and now he means
To let him blood. Be constant, gentlemen: 225
By heaven, I 'll run his hazard, although I run
My name out of the kingdom!
    *Cle.*    Peace, we are all one soul.
    *Pha.* What you have seen in me to stir offence
I cannot find, unless it be this lady,
Offer'd into mine arms with the succession; 230
Which I must keep, (though it hath pleas'd
    your fury

160 **By . . . gods:** ('And I vow' Q 4–F)
('praises' Q 1)    180–181 (Misprinted in Q 1)
('he fears' Q 1–3)    197–198 (Lines transposed in Qq., F)
('Nemesis' Q 4–F)    214 **outlandish:** foreign
('this choller' Q 1)    221 **tainted:** insane
171 **Miraculous:** ('Miracles' Q 1)    177 **speeches:**
182 **shall be:** will make an adequate    188 **with fear:**
208 **My:** which my    212 **the . . . gods:**
218 **turtle:** *i.e.,* dove    220–221 **this . . . physicians:**

To mutiny within you,) without disputing
Your genealogies, or taking knowledge
Whose branch you are.  The king will leave it
    me,
And I dare make it mine.  You have your an-
    swer.                                        235
   *Phi.*  If thou wert sole inheritor to him
That made the world his, and couldst see no
    sun
Shine upon anything but thine; were Phara-
    mond
As truly valiant as I feel him cold,            239
And ring'd among the choicest of his friends,
(Such as would blush to talk such serious follies,
Or back such bellied commendations),
And from this presence, spite of all these bugs,
You should hear further from me.
   *King.*  Sir, you wrong the prince; I gave
    you not this freedom                         245
To brave our best friends.  You deserve our
    frown.
Go to; be better temper'd.
   *Phi.*  It must be, sir, when I am nobler us'd.
   *Gal.*  Ladies,                               249
This would have been a pattern of succession,
Had he ne'er met this mischief.  By my life,
He is the worthiest the true name of man
This day within my knowledge.
   *Meg.*  I cannot tell what you may call your
    knowledge;
But the other is the man set in mine eye.       255
Oh, 't is a prince of wax!
   *Gal.*                       A dog it is.
   *King.*  Philaster, tell me
The injuries you aim at in your riddles.
   *Phi.*  If you had my eyes, sir, and sufferance,
My griefs upon you, and my broken fortunes,
My wants great, and now-nothing hopes and
    fears,                                       261
My wrongs would make ill riddles to be laugh'd
    at.
Dare you be still my king, and right me not?
   *King.*  Give me your wrongs in private.
   *Phi.*                       Take them,       264
And ease me of a load would bow strong Atlas.
                                 *They whisper.*
   *Cle.*  He dares not stand the shock.
   *Dion.*  I cannot blame him; there 's danger
in 't.  Every man in this age has not a soul of
crystal, for all men to read their actions [269
through: men's hearts and faces are so far asunder, that they hold no intelligence.  Do but view
yon stranger well, and you shall see a fever
through all his bravery, and feel him shake
like a true tyrant.  If he give not back his [274

crown again upon the report of an elder-gun, I
have no augury.
   *King.*  Go to;
Be more yourself, as you respect our favour;    278
You 'll stir us else.  Sir, I must have you know,
That y' are and shall be, at our pleasure, what
Fashion we will put upon you.  Smooth your
    brow,
Or by the gods ——
   *Phi.*  I am dead, sir; y' are my fate.  It was
    not I
Said I was wrong'd: I carry all about me
My weak stars lead me to, all my weak for-
    tunes.                                       285
Who dares in all this presence speak, (that is
But man of flesh, and may be mortal,) tell me
I do not most entirely love this prince,
And honour his full virtues!
   *King.*                       Sure, he 's possess'd.
   *Phi.*  Yes, with my father's spirit.  It 's here,
O King,                                          290
A dangerous spirit!  Now he tells me, King,
I was a king's heir, bids me be a king,
And whispers to me, these are all my subjects.
'T is strange he will not let me sleep, but dives
Into my fancy, and there gives me shapes  295
That kneel and do me service, cry me king.
But I 'll suppress him; he 's a factious spirit,
And will undo me. — [*To Phar.*]  Noble sir,
    your hand;
I am your servant.
   *King.*               Away!  I do not like this:
I 'll make you tamer, or I'll dispossess you  300
Both of your life and spirit.  For this time
I pardon your wild speech, without so much
As your imprisonment.
              *Exeunt King, Pharamond, Arethusa.*
   *Dion.*  I thank you, sir; you dare not for the
    people.
   *Gal.*  Ladies, what think you now of this
    brave fellow?                                305
   *Meg.*  A pretty talking fellow, hot at hand.
But eye yon stranger: is he not a fine complete
gentleman?  Oh, these strangers, I do affect
them strangely!  They do the rarest home- [309
things, and please the fullest!  As I live, I could
love all the nation over and over for his sake.
   *Gal.*  Gods comfort your poor head-piece,
lady!  'T is a weak one, and had need of a
night-cap.                         *Exeunt Ladies.*  314
   *Dion.*  See, how his fancy labours!  Has he
    not
Spoke home and bravely?  What a dangerous
    train
Did he give fire to!  How he shook the king,

242 **bellied:** inflated    243 **bugs:** bugbears    246 (Not in Q 1)    250 **pattern of succession:** model
heir    256 **of wax:** incomparable    259 **sufferance:** suffering    261 **now-nothing:** extinguished ('now
nought but' Q 4–F)    273 **bravery:** insolence    274 **tyrant:** ('truant' Q 1; 'tenant' Q 2–F)    308 **affect:**
incline to    312 **Gods:** ('Pride' Q 4–F)

Made his soul melt within him, and his blood
Run into whey! It stood upon his brow
Like a cold winter dew.
   *Phi.*             Gentlemen,   320
You have no suit to me? I am no minion.
You stand, methinks, like men that would be
   courtiers,
If you could well be flatter'd at a price
Not to undo your children. Y' are all honest:
Go, get you home again, and make your coun-
   try   325
A virtuous court, to which your great ones
   may,
In their diseased age, retire and live recluse.
   *Cle.* How do you, worthy sir?
   *Phi.*             Well, very well;
And so well that, if the king please, I find
I may live many years.
   *Dion.*         The king must please,   330
Whilst we know what you are and who you are,
Your wrongs and virtues. Shrink not, worthy
   sir,
But add your father to you; in whose name
We 'll waken all the gods, and conjure up
The rods of vengeance, the abused people,   335
Who, like to raging torrents, shall swell high,
And so begirt the dens of these male-dragons,
That, through the strongest safety, they shall
   beg
For mercy at your sword's point.
   *Phi.*           Friends, no more;
Our ears may be corrupted; 't is an age   340
We dare not trust our wills to. Do you love
   me?
   *Thra.* Do we love Heaven and honour?
   *Phi.* My Lord Dion, you had
A virtuous gentlewoman call'd you father.
Is she yet alive?
   *Dion.*       Most honour'd sir, she is;   345
And, for the penance but of an idle dream
Has undertook a tedious pilgrimage.

            *Enter a Lady*

   *Phi.* Is it to me, or any of these gentlemen,
   you come?
   *La.* To you, brave lord; the princess would
   entreat
Your present company.   350
   *Phi.* The princess send for me! Y' are mis-
   taken.
   *La.* If you be call'd Philaster, 't is to you.
   *Phi.* Kiss her fair hand, and say I will attend
   her.                   *[Exit Lady.]*
   *Dion.* Do you know what you do?
   *Phi.* Yes; go to see a woman.   355

   *Cle.* But do you weigh the danger you are
   in?
   *Phi.* Danger in a sweet face!
By Jupiter, I must not fear a woman!
   *Thra.* But are you sure it was the princess
   sent?   359
It may be some foul train to catch your life.
   *Phi.* I do not think it, gentlemen; she 's noble.
Her eye may shoot me dead, or those true red
And white friends in her cheeks may steal my
   soul out:
There 's all the danger in 't. But, be what may,
Her single name hath arm'd me.     *Exit.*
   *Dion.*            Go on,   365
And be as truly happy as th' art fearless! —
Come, gentlemen, let 's make our friends ac-
   quainted,
Lest the king prove false.         *Exeunt.*

    [SCENE II. — *Arethusa's Apartment.*]

       *Enter Arethusa and a Lady*

   *Are.* Comes he not?
   *La.*           Madam?
   *Are.*               Will Philaster come?
   *La.* Dear madam, you were wont to credit
   me
At first.
   *Are.* But didst thou tell me so?
I am forgetful, and my woman's strength     5
Is so o'ercharg'd with dangers like to grow
About my marriage, that these under-things
Dare not abide in such a troubled sea.
How look'd he when he told thee he would
   come?
   *La.* Why, well.   10
   *Are.* And not a little fearful?
   *La.* Fear, madam! Sure, he knows not
   what it is.
   *Are.* You all are of his faction; the whole
   court
Is bold in praise of him; whilst I
May live neglected, and do noble things,   15
As fools in strife throw gold into the sea,
Drown'd in the doing. But, I know he fears.
   *La.* Fear, madam! Methought, his looks
   hid more
Of love than fear.
   *Are.*         Of love! To whom? To you?
Did you deliver those plain words I sent   20
With such a winning gesture and quick look
That you have caught him?
   *La.*         Madam, I mean to you.
   *Are.* Of love to me! Alas, thy ignorance
Lets thee not see the crosses of our births!

---

³²¹ **minion:** king's favorite   ³³² **virtues:** ('injuries' Q 2–F)   ³³³ **add:** ('call' Q 1)   ³³⁷ **begirt:**
besiege   ³³⁸ **through . . . safety:** however strongly entrenched   ³³⁹ **Friends:** ('Friend' Q 1)   ³⁴⁰ **ears:**
('years' Q 5–F)   ³⁶⁰ **train:** plot   ³⁶³ **cheeks:** ('face' Q 2–F)   ³⁶⁵ **single:** mere   Scene ii. S. D.
('Enter Princesse and her Gentle-woman' Q 1)   ²¹ **winning:** ('woing' Q 1)

Nature, that loves not to be questioned    25
Why she did this or that, but has her ends,
And knows she does well, never gave the world
Two things so opposite, so contrary,
As he and I am: if a bowl of blood
Drawn from this arm of mine would poison
    thee,    30
A draught of his would cure thee. Of love to me!
*La.*    Madam, I think I hear him.
*Are.*                    Bring him in. [*Exit Lady.*]
You gods, that would not have your dooms
    withstood,
Whose holy wisdoms at this time it is
To make the passion of a feeble maid    35
The way unto your justice, I obey.

*Enter Philaster [with Lady]*

*La.*    Here is my Lord Philaster.
*Are.*                    Oh, 't is well.
Withdraw yourself.                [*Exit Lady.*]
*Phi.*            Madam, your messenger
Made me believe you wish'd to speak with me.
*Are.*    'T is true, Philaster; but the words are
    such    40
I have to say, and do so ill beseem
The mouth of woman, that I wish them said,
And yet am loath to speak them.  Have you
    known
That I have aught detracted from your worth?
Have I in person wrong'd you, or have set    45
My baser instruments to throw disgrace
Upon your virtues?
*Phi.*            Never, madam, you.
*Are.*    Why, then, should you, in such a
    public place,
Injure a princess, and a scandal lay
Upon my fortunes, fam'd to be so great,    50
Calling a great part of my dowry in question?
*Phi.*    Madam, this truth which I shall speak
    will be
Foolish: but, for your fair and virtuous self,
I could afford myself to have no right
To anything you wish'd.
*Are.*            Philaster, know,    55
I must enjoy these kingdoms.
*Phi.*                Madam, both?
*Are.*    Both, or I die: by heaven, I die, Phi-
    laster,
If I not calmly may enjoy them both.
*Phi.*    I would do much to save that noble life;
Yet would be loath to have posterity    60
Find in our stories, that Philaster gave
His right unto a sceptre and a crown
To save a lady's longing.
*Are.*            Nay, then, hear:
I must and will have them, and more ——
*Phi.*                What more?

*Are.*    Or lose that little life the gods prepared
To trouble this poor piece of earth withal.    66
*Phi.*    Madam, what more?
*Are.*                Turn, then, away thy face.
*Phi.*    No.
*Are.*    Do.
*Phi.*    I can endure it.  Turn away my face!    70
I never yet saw enemy that look'd
So dreadfully, but that I thought myself
As great a basilisk as he; or spake
So horrible, but that I thought my tongue
Bore thunder underneath as much as his;    75
Nor beast that I could turn from.  Shall I then
Begin to fear sweet sounds?  A lady's voice,
Whom I do love?  Say you would have my life;
Why, I will give it you; for it is of me
A thing so loath'd, and unto you that ask    80
Of so poor use, that I shall make no price:
If you entreat, I will unmov'dly hear.
*Are.*    Yet, for my sake, a little bend thy
    looks.
*Phi.*    I do.
*Are.*    Then know, I must have them and thee.
*Phi.*    And me?
*Are.*    Thy love; without which, all the land
Discover'd yet will serve me for no use    86
But to be buried in.
*Phi.*            Is 't possible?
*Are.*    With it, it were too little to bestow
On thee.  Now, though thy breath do strike
    me dead,
(Which, now, it may,) I have unripp'd my
    breast.    90
*Phi.*    Madam, you are too full of noble
    thoughts,
To lay a train for this contemned life,
Which you may have for asking.  To suspect
Were base, where I deserve no ill.  Love you!
By all my hopes, I do, above my life!    95
But how this passion should proceed from you
So violently, would amaze a man
That would be jealous.
*Are.*    Another soul into my body shot
Could not have fill'd me with more strength and
    spirit    100
Than this thy breath.  But spend not hasty
    time
In seeking how I came thus: 't is the gods,
The gods, that make me so; and, sure, our love
Will be the nobler and the better blest,
In that the secret justice of the gods    105
Is mingled with it.  Let us leave, and kiss;
Lest some unwelcome guest should fall betwixt
    us,
And we should part without it.
*Phi.*                'T will be ill
I should abide here long.

*Are.*                    'T is true; and worse
You should come often.  How shall we devise
To hold intelligence, that our true loves,        111
On any new occasion, may agree
What path is best to tread?
    *Phi.*                    I have a boy,
Sent by the gods, I hope, to this intent,        114
Not yet seen in the court.  Hunting the buck,
I found him sitting by a fountain's side,
Of which he borrow'd some to quench his thirst,
And paid the nymph again as much in tears.
A garland lay him by, made by himself
Of many several flowers bred in the vale,        120
Stuck in that mystic order that the rareness
Delighted me: but ever when he turn'd
His tender eyes upon 'em, he would weep,
As if he meant to make 'em grow again.
Seeing such pretty helpless innocence            125
Dwell in his face, I ask'd him all his story.
He told me that his parents gentle died,
Leaving him to the mercy of the fields,
Which gave him roots; and of the crystal
    springs,                                     129
Which did not stop their courses; and the sun,
Which still, he thank'd him, yielded him his
    light.
Then took he up his garland, and did show
What every flower, as country-people hold,
Did signify, and how all, order'd thus,
Express'd his grief; and, to my thoughts, did
    read                                         135
The prettiest lecture of his country-art
That could be wish'd: so that methought I
    could
Have studied it.  I gladly entertain'd
Him, who was glad to follow; and have got
The trustiest, loving'st, and the gentlest boy 140
That ever master kept.  Him will I send
To wait on you, and bear our hidden love.

### Enter Lady

*Are.*  'T is well; no more.
*La.*  Madam, the prince is come to do his
    service.
*Are.*  What will you do, Philaster, with your-
    self?                                        145
*Phi.*  Why, that which all the gods have
    pointed out for me.
*Are.*  Dear, hide thyself. —
Bring in the prince.                  [*Exit Lady.*]
    *Phi.*              Hide me from Pharamond!
When thunder speaks, which is the voice of
    Jove,
Though I do reverence, yet I hide me not; 150
And shall a stranger-prince have leave to brag

Unto a foreign nation, that he made
Philaster hide himself?
    *Are.*                    He cannot know it.
    *Phi.*  Though it should sleep for ever to the
        world,
It is a simple sin to hide myself,               155
Which will for ever on my conscience lie.
    *Are.*  Then, good Philaster, give him scope
        and way
In what he says; for he is apt to speak
What you are loath to hear.  For my sake, do.
    *Phi.*  I will.                                160

### Enter Pharamond

*Pha.*  My princely mistress, as true lovers
    ought,
I come to kiss these fair hands, and to show,
In outward ceremonies, the dear love
Writ in my heart.                                164
    *Phi.*  If I shall have an answer no directlier,
I am gone.
    *Pha.*  To what would he have answer?
    *Are.*  To his claim unto the kingdom.
    *Pha.*  Sirrah, I forbare you before the king —
    *Phi.*  Good sir, do so still; I would not talk
        with you.                                170
    *Pha.*  But now the time is fitter.  Do but offer
To make mention of right to any kingdom,
Though it be scarce habitable ——
    *Phi.*                    Good sir, let me go.
    *Pha.*  And by the gods —
    *Phi.*              Peace, Pharamond! if thou ——
    *Are.*  Leave us, Philaster.
    *Phi.*              I have done. [*Going.*] 175
    *Pha.*  You are gone!  by Heaven I 'll fetch
        you back.
    *Phi.*  You shall not need.         [*Returning.*]
    *Pha.*                    What now?
    *Phi.*                    Know, Pharamond,
I loathe to brawl with such a blast as thou,
Who art nought but a valiant voice; but if
Thou shalt provoke me further, men shall say,
Thou wert, and not lament it.
    *Pha.*                    Do you slight 181
My greatness so, and in the chamber of
The princess?
    *Phi.*  It is a place to which I must confess
I owe a reverence; but were 't the church, 185
Ay, at the altar, there 's no place so safe,
Where thou dar'st injure me, but I dare kill
    thee.
And for your greatness, know, sir, I can grasp
You and your greatness thus, thus into nothing.
Give not a word, not a word back! Farewell.
                                          *Exit.*

---

<sup>118</sup> **nymph:** *i.e.,* of the fountain       <sup>120</sup> **vale:** ('bay' Q 2–F)       <sup>121</sup> **in that:** in such       <sup>134</sup> **order'd:**
arranged       <sup>146</sup> **pointed:** ('appointed' Qq., F)       <sup>149</sup> **Jove:** ('God' Q 1)       <sup>164</sup> **Writ in:** ('within' Q 1)
<sup>169</sup> **forbare:** spared       <sup>178</sup> **blast:** windbag       <sup>181</sup> **wert:** *i.e.,* hast died       <sup>186</sup> **Ay . . . altar:** ('at the high
altar' Q 1)

*Pha.* 'T is an odd fellow, madam; we must stop 191
His mouth with some office when we are married.
*Are.* You were best make him your controller.
*Pha.* I think he would discharge it well.
But, madam,
I hope our hearts are knit; but yet so slow 195
The ceremonies of state are, that 't will be long
Before our hands be so. If then you please,
Being agreed in heart, let us not wait
For dreaming form, but take a little stolen
Delights, and so prevent our joys to come. 200
*Are.* If you dare speak such thoughts,
I must withdraw in honour.        *Exit.*
*Pha.* The constitution of my body will never hold out till the wedding; I must seek elsewhere.        *Exit.* 205

### Actus Secundus.  Scena Prima.

[*Philaster's Lodging.*]

*Enter Philaster and his boy, called Bellario*

*Phi.* And thou shalt find her honourable, boy;
Full of regard unto thy tender youth
For thine own modesty; and, for my sake,
Apter to give than thou wilt be to ask,
Ay, or deserve.
*Bel.*        Sir, you did take me up 5
When I was nothing; and only yet am something
By being yours. You trusted me unknown;
And that which you were apt to conster
A simple innocence in me, perhaps
Might have been craft, the cunning of a boy 10
Harden'd in lies and theft: yet ventur'd you
To part my miseries and me: for which,
I never can expect to serve a lady
That bears more honour in her breast than you.
*Phi.* But, boy, it will prefer thee. Thou art young, 15
And bear'st a childish overflowing love
To them that clap thy cheeks and speak thee fair yet;
But when thy judgment comes to rule those passions,
Thou wilt remember best those careful friends
That plac'd thee in the noblest way of life. 20
She is a princess I prefer thee to.
*Bel.* In that small time that I have seen the world,
I never knew a man hasty to part
With a servant he thought trusty. I remember,

My father would prefer the boys he kept 25
To greater men than he; but did it not
Till they were grown too saucy for himself.
*Phi.* Why, gentle boy, I find no fault at all
In thy behaviour.
*Bel.*        Sir, if I have made
A fault of ignorance, instruct my youth: 30
I shall be willing, if not apt, to learn;
Age and experience will adorn my mind
With larger knowledge; and if I have done
A wilful fault, think me not past all hope
For once. What master holds so strict a hand
Over his boy, that he will part with him 36
Without one warning? Let me be corrected
To break my stubbornness, if it be so,
Rather than turn me off; and I shall mend. 39
*Phi.* Thy love doth plead so prettily to stay,
That (trust me) I could weep to part with thee.
Alas, I do not turn thee off! Thou knowest
It is my business that doth call thee hence;
And when thou art with her, thou dwell'st with me,
Think so, and 't is so; and when time is full, 45
That thou hast well discharg'd this heavy trust,
Laid on so weak a one, I will again
With joy receive thee; as I live, I will!
Nay, weep not, gentle boy. 'T is more than time
Thou didst attend the princess.
*Bel.*        I am gone. 50
But since I am to part with you, my lord,
And none knows whether I shall live to do
More service for you, take this little prayer:
Heaven bless your loves, your sighs, all your designs! 54
May sick men, if they have your wish, be well;
And Heaven hate those you curse, though I be one!        *Exit.*
*Phi.* The love of boys unto their lords is strange;
I have read wonders of it: yet this boy
For my sake (if a man may judge by looks
And speech) would out-do story. I may see 60
A day to pay him for his loyalty.        *Exit.*

[Scene II. — *Lobby of the Court.*]

*Enter Pharamond*

*Pha.* Why should these ladies stay so long?
They must come this way. I know the queen
employs 'em not; for the reverend mother
sent me word, they would all be for the garden.
If they should all prove honest now, I were [5
in a fair taking. I was never so long without

sport in my life, and, in my conscience, 't is not my fault. Oh, for our country ladies!

*Enter Galatea*

Here 's one bolted; I 'll hound at her. — Madam!

*Gal.* Your grace!

*Pha.* Shall I not be a trouble?

*Gal.*                    Not to me, sir. [*Going.*]    11

*Pha.* Nay, nay, you are too quick. By this sweet hand ——

*Gal.* You 'll be forsworn, sir; 't is but an old glove.

If you will talk at distance, I am for you:

But, good prince, be not bawdy, nor do not brag.                                                    15

These two I only bar;

And then, I think, I shall have sense enough

To answer all the weighty apophthegms

Your royal blood shall manage.

*Pha.* Dear lady, can you love?                    20

*Gal.* Dear prince! how dear? I ne'er cost you a coach yet, nor put you to the dear repentance of a banquet. Here 's no scarlet, sir, to blush the sin out it was given for. This wire mine own hair covers; and this face has [25 been so far from being dear to any, that it ne'er cost penny painting; and, for the rest of my poor wardrobe, such as you see, it leaves no hand behind it, to make the jealous mercer's wife curse our good doings.                    30

*Pha.* You mistake me, lady.

*Gal.* Lord, I do so; would you or I could help it!

*Pha.* Y' are very dangerous bitter, like a potion.

*Gal.* No, sir, I do not mean to purge you, though

I mean to purge a little time on you.            35

*Pha.* Do ladies of this country use to give No more respect to men of my full being?

*Gal.* Full being! I understand you not, unless your grace means growing to fatness; and then your only remedy (upon my knowledge, [40 prince) is, in a morning, a cup of neat white wine brewed with carduus, then fast till supper; about eight you may eat. Use exercise, and keep a sparrow-hawk; you can shoot in a tiller: but, of all, your grace must fly phle- [45 botomy, fresh pork, conger, and clarified whey; they are all dullers of the vital spirits.

*Pha.* Lady, you talk of nothing all this while.

*Gal.* 'T is very true, sir; I talk of you.    49

*Pha.* [*Aside.*] This is a crafty wench. I like her wit well; 't will be rare to stir up a leaden appetite. She 's a Danaë, and must be courted in a shower of gold. — Madam, look here; all these, and more than ——                    54

*Gal.* What have you there, my lord? Gold! now, as I live, 't is fair gold! You would have silver for it, to play with the pages. You could not have taken me in a worse time; but, if you have present use, my lord, I 'll send my man with silver and keep your gold safe for you.

                                        [*Takes the gold.*]

*Pha.* Lady, lady!                                    61

*Gal.* She 's coming, sir, behind, will take white money. —

[*Aside.*] Yet for all this I 'll match ye.

                        *She slips behind the arras.*

*Pha.* If there be but two such more in this kingdom, and near the court, we may even [65 hang up our harps. Ten such camphor constitutions as this would call the golden age again in question, and teach the old way for every ill-fac'd husband to get his own children; and what a mischief that would breed, let all consider!                                                    71

*Enter Megra*

Here 's another: if she be of the same last, the devil shall pluck her on. — Many fair mornings, lady!

*Meg.* As many mornings bring as many days, Fair, sweet and hopeful to your grace!        76

*Pha.* [*Aside.*] She gives good words yet; sure this wench is free. —

If your more serious business do not call you,

Let me hold quarter with you; we will talk

An hour out quickly.

*Meg.*          What would your grace talk of?  80

*Pha.* Of some such pretty subject as yourself:

I 'll go no further than your eye, or lip;

There 's theme enough for one man for an age.

*Meg.* Sir, they stand right, and my lips are yet even,

Smooth, young enough, ripe enough, and red enough,                                                    85

Or my glass wrongs me.

*Pha.* Oh, they are two twinn'd cherries dy'd in blushes,

Which those fair suns above with their bright beams

---

⁸ **country:** native (*i.e.*, Spanish)    ⁹ **bolted:** broken cover    ¹⁶ **only:** (not in Q 2–F)    ²³ **of:** ('of a play and' Q 1)    ²⁴⁻²⁵ **blush . . . covers:** ('to make you blush, this is my owne hayre' Q 1) ²⁴ **wire:** support for coiffure    ²⁷ **painting:** to have it painted    ²⁹ **hand:** note of hand, evidence of an unpaid bill    **mercer's:** ('silke-mans' Q 1)    ³² **do so:** (pun on "mistake," take amiss)    ³³⁻³⁵ (In Q 1 only)    ³⁷ **full being:** dignity    ⁴² **carduus:** carduus benedictus, a thistle used in medicine ⁴³ **eight:** ('five' Q 1)    ⁴⁵ **tiller:** part of cross-bow in which the arrow lay    ⁴⁵⁻⁴⁶ **phlebotomy:** blood-letting    ⁴⁶ **conger:** eel    ⁶⁰ **safe:** (not in Q 2–F)    ⁶² **white:** silver    ⁶⁶ **camphor:** frigid    ⁷⁰ **would:** ('will' Q 2–F)    ⁷⁹ **quarter:** friendly intercourse

Reflect upon and ripen. Sweetest beauty,
Bow down those branches, that the longing
    taste                                 90
Of the faint looker-on may meet those blessings,
And taste and live.            *They kiss.*
  *Meg.* [*Aside.*]  Oh, delicate sweet prince!
She that hath snow enough about her heart
To take the wanton spring of ten such lines off,
May be a nun without probation. — Sir,   95
You have in such neat poetry gather'd a kiss,
That if I had but five lines of that number,
Such pretty begging blanks, I should com-
    mend
Your forehead or your cheeks, and kiss you
    too.
  *Pha.*  Do it in prose; you cannot miss it,
    madam.                         100
  *Meg.*  I shall, I shall.
  *Pha.*           By my life, but you shall not;
I 'll prompt you first.  [*Kisses her.*]  Can you
    do it now?
  *Meg.*  Methinks 't is easy, now you ha' done
    't before me;
But yet I should stick at it.    [*Kisses him.*]
  *Pha.*                Stick till to-morrow;
I 'll ne'er part you, sweetest. But we lose time:
Can you love me?                     106
  *Meg.*  Love you, my lord! How would you
    have me love you?
  *Pha.*  I 'll teach you in a short sentence,
'cause I will not load your memory; this is all:
love me, and lie with me.             110
  *Meg.*  Was it "lie with you" that you said?
'T is impossible.
  *Pha.*  Not to a willing mind, that will en-
deavour. If I do not teach you to do it as easily
in one night as you 'll go to bed, I 'll lose my
royal blood for 't.                   116
  *Meg.*  Why, prince, you have a lady of your
    own
That yet wants teaching.
  *Pha.*  I 'll sooner teach a mare the old measures than teach her anything belonging to [120
the function. She 's afraid to lie with herself
if she have but any masculine imaginations
about her. I know, when we are married, I
must ravish her.
  *Meg.*  By mine honour, that 's a foul fault,
    indeed;                        125
But time and your good help will wear it out,
    sir.
  *Pha.*  And for any other I see, excepting your
dear self, dearest lady, I had rather be Sir
Tim the schoolmaster, and leap a dairy-maid.
  *Meg.*  Has your grace seen the court-star, [130
Galatea?

  *Pha.*  Out upon her! She 's as cold of her favour as an apoplex; she sail'd by but now.
  *Meg.*  And how do you hold her wit, sir?
  *Pha.*  I hold her wit? The strength of all [135
the guard cannot hold it, if they were tied to it:
she would blow 'em out of the kingdom. They
talk of Jupiter; he 's but a squib-cracker to her.
Look well about you, and you may find a tongue-
bolt. But speak, sweet lady, shall I be [140
freely welcome?
  *Meg.*  Whither?
  *Pha.*  To your bed. If you mistrust my faith,
you do me the unnoblest wrong.
  *Meg.*  I dare not, prince, I dare not.   145
  *Pha.*  Make your own conditions: my purse
shall seal 'em, and what you dare imagine you
can want, I 'll furnish you withal. Give two
hours to your thoughts every morning about it.
Come, I know y' are bashful;          150
Speak in my ear, will you be mine? Keep this,
And with it me: soon I will visit you.
  *Meg.*  My lord, my chamber 's most unsafe;
    but when 't is night,               153
I 'll find some means to slip into your lodging;
Till when ——                   [*thee!*
  *Pha.*  Till when, this and my heart go with
    *Exeunt several ways.*

       *Enter Galatea from behind the hangings*

  *Gal.*  Oh, thou pernicious petticoat prince!
are these your virtues? Well, if I do not lay a
train to blow your sport up, I am no woman:
and, Lady Dowsabel, I 'll fit you for 't. *Exit.* 160

      [Scene III. — *Arethusa's Apartment.*]

        *Enter Arethusa and a Lady*

  *Are.*  Where 's the boy?
  *La.*  Within, madam.
  *Are.*  Gave you him gold to buy him clothes?
  *La.*  I did.
  *Are.*  And has he done 't?            5
  *La.*  Yes, madam.
  *Are.*  'T is a pretty sad-talking boy, is it not?
Ask'd you his name?
  *La.*  No, madam.                9

          *Enter Galatea*

  *Are.*  Oh, you are welcome. What good news?
  *Gal.*  As good as any one can tell your grace,
That says she has done that you would have
    wish'd.
  *Are.*  Hast thou discovered?
  *Gal.*  Of modesty for you I have strain'd a
    point.
  *Are.*  I prithee, how?            15

        ⁹⁷ **number:** metre    ⁹⁸ **blanks:** blank verses    ¹⁰¹ **but:** (not in Q 2–F)    ¹⁰³ **you , . . me:** ('I
ha' don' 't before' Q 2–F)    ¹¹⁹⁻¹²⁰ **measures:** formal dances    ¹³⁸ **squib-cracker:** fire-cracker
¹³⁹⁻¹⁴⁰ **tongue-bolt:** verbal thunderbolt (this sentence not in Q 1)    ¹⁶⁰ **Dowsabel:** ('Towsabel' Q 2–F)

*Gal.* In list'ning after bawdry. I see, let a
lady live never so modestly, she shall be sure
to find a lawful time to hearken after bawdry.
Your prince, brave Pharamond, was so hot
on 't!                                            20
    *Are.* With whom?
    *Gal.* Why, with the lady I suspected. I can
tell the time and place.
    *Are.* Oh, when, and where?
    *Gal.* To-night, his lodging.                25
    *Are.* Run thyself into the presence; mingle
    there again
With other ladies; leave the rest to me.
                  [*Exit Galatea.*]
If destiny (to whom we dare not say,
"Why didst thou this?") have not decreed it so,
In lasting leaves (whose smallest characters   30
Were never alter'd yet), this match shall
    break. —
Where 's the boy?
    *La.* Here, madam.

           *Enter Bellario*

    *Are.* Sir, you are sad to change your service:
    is 't not so?
    *Bel.* Madam, I have not chang'd; I wait on
    you,                                        35
To do him service.
    *Are.*          Thou disclaim'st in me.
Tell me thy name.
    *Bel.* Bellario.
    *Are.* Thou canst sing and play?
    *Bel.* If grief will give me leave, madam, I
    can.                                        40
    *Are.* Alas, what kind of grief can thy years
know?
Hadst thou a curst master when thou went'st
    to school?
Thou art not capable of other grief;
Thy brows and cheeks are smooth as waters be
When no breath troubles them. Believe me,
    boy,                                        45
Care seeks out wrinkled brows and hollow eyes,
And builds himself caves, to abide in them.
Come, sir, tell me truly, does your lord love me?
    *Bel.* Love, madam! I know not what it is.
    *Are.* Canst thou know grief, and never yet
    knew'st love?                               50
Thou art deceiv'd, boy. Does he speak of me
As if he wish'd me well?
    *Bel.*          If it be love
To forget all respect of his own friends
With thinking of your face; if it be love
To sit cross-arm'd and sigh away the day,      55
Mingled with starts, crying your name as loud

And hastily as men i' the streets do fire;
If it be love to weep himself away
When he but hears of any lady dead
Or kill'd, because it might have been your
    chance;                                    60
If, when he goes to rest (which will not be),
'Twixt every prayer he says, to name you once,
As others drop a bead, be to be in love,
Then, madam, I dare swear he loves you.
    *Are.* Oh y' are a cunning boy, and taught
    to lie                                      65
For your lord's credit! But thou know'st a lie
That bears this sound is welcomer to me
Than any truth that says he loves me not.
Lead the way, boy. — [*To Lady.*] Do you at-
    tend me too. —                             69
'T is thy lord's business hastes me thus. Away!
                      *Exeunt.*

[SCENE IV. — *Before Pharamond's Lodging.*]

   *Enter Dion, Cleremont, Thrasiline, Megra,*
              *Galatea*

    *Dion.* Come, ladies, shall we talk a round?
    As men
Do walk a mile, women should talk an hour
After supper: 't is their exercise.
    *Gal.* 'T is late.
    *Meg.* 'T is all                             5
My eyes will do to lead me to my bed.
    *Gal.* I fear, they are so heavy, you 'll scarce
    find
The way to your own lodging with 'em to-night.

          *Enter Pharamond*

    *Thra.* The prince!
    *Pha.* Not a-bed, ladies? Y' are good sit-
    ters-up.                                    10
What think you of a pleasant dream, to last
Till morning?
    *Meg.* I should choose, my lord, a pleasing
    wake before it.

      *Enter Arethusa and Bellario*

    *Are.* 'T is well, my lord; y' are courting of
    these ladies. —
Is 't not late, gentlemen?                       15
    *Cle.* Yes, madam.
    *Are.* Wait you there.          *Exit.*
    *Meg.* [*Aside.*] She 's jealous, as I live. —
    Look you, my lord,
The princess has a Hylas, an Adonis.
    *Pha.* His form is angel-like.                20
    *Meg.* Why this is he that must, when you
    are wed,

    ²⁹ **didst thou:** ('thou didst' Qq., F)    ³⁶ **disclaim'st:** (supply "interest")    ⁴² **curst:** ill-natured
('crosse' Q 1)    ⁵³ **respect:** consideration    ⁵⁵ **sigh:** ('thinke' Q 1–3)    ⁵⁹ **lady:** ('woman' Q 1)
¹¹ **pleasant:** ('pleasing' Q 1)    ¹⁹ **Hylas:** the beautiful boy whom Hercules loved    ²¹ **he . . . must:**
('that must' Q 1, 'he must' Q 2–F)

Sit by your pillow, like young Apollo, with
His hand and voice binding your thoughts in
    sleep.
The princess does provide him for you and for
    herself.
    *Pha.* I find no music in these boys.
    *Meg.*                      Nor I:  25
They can do little, and that small they do,
They have not wit to hide.
    *Dion.*          Serves he the princess?
    *Thra.* Yes.             [keeps him!
    *Dion.*    'T is a sweet boy: how brave she
    *Pha.* Ladies all, good rest; I mean to kill a
    buck
To-morrow morning ere y' have done your
    dreams.                             30
    *Meg.* All happiness attend your grace! [*Exit
    Pharamond.*] Gentlemen, good rest. —
Come, shall we to bed?
    *Gal.*          Yes. — All, good night.
    *Dion.* May your dreams be true to you! —
               *Exeunt Galatea and Megra.*
What shall we do, gallants? 't is late. The
    king
Is up still: see, he comes; a guard along  35
With him.

    *Enter King, Arethusa, and Guard*

    *King.* Look your intelligence be true.
    *Are.* Upon my life, it is; and I do hope
Your highness will not tie me to a man
That in the heat of wooing throws me off,
And takes another.
    *Dion.*          What should this mean?  40
    *King.* If it be true,
That lady had been better have embrac'd
Cureless diseases. Get you to your rest:
You shall be righted.
            *Exeunt Arethusa, Bellario.*
            — Gentlemen, draw near;
We shall employ you. Is young Pharamond  45
Come to his lodging?
    *Dion.*         I saw him enter there.
    *King.* Haste, some of you, and cunningly
    discover
If Megra be in her lodging.     [*Exit Dion.*]
    *Cle.* Sir,
She parted hence but now, with other ladies.  50
    *King.* If she be there, we shall not need to
    make
A vain discovery of our suspicion.
[*Aside.*] You gods, I see that who unrighteously
Holds wealth or state from others shall be curs'd
In that which meaner men are blest withal:  55
Ages to come shall know no male of him
Left to inherit, and his name shall be

Blotted from earth. If he have any child,
It shall be crossly match'd; the gods themselves
Shall sow wild strife betwixt her lord and her.
Yet, if it be your wills, forgive the sin  61
I have committed; let it not fall
Upon this undeserving child of mine!
She has not broke your laws. But how can I
Look to be heard of gods that must be just,  65
Praying upon the ground I hold by wrong?

    *Enter Dion*

    *Dion.* Sir, I have asked, and her women swear
she is within; but they, I think, are bawds.
I told 'em, I must speak with her; they laugh'd,
and said, their lady lay speechless. I said, [70
my business was important; they said, their
lady was about it. I grew hot, and cried, my
business was a matter that concern'd life and
death; they answered, so was sleeping, at which
their lady was. I urg'd again, she had scarce [75
time to be so since last I saw her: they smil'd
again, and seem'd to instruct me that sleeping was nothing but lying down and winking.
Answers more direct I could not get: in short,
sir, I think she is not there.          80
    *King.* 'T is then no time to dally. — You o'
    the guard,
Wait at the back door of the prince's lodging,
And see that none pass thence, upon your lives.
             [*Exeunt Guards.*]
Knock, gentlemen; knock loud; — louder yet.
    [*Dion, Cle., &c. knock at the door
        of Pharamond's Lodging.*]
What, has their pleasure taken off their hear-
    ing? —                           85
I 'll break your meditations. — Knock again. —
Not yet? I do not think he sleeps, having this
'Larum by him. — Once more. — Pharamond!
    prince!       *Pharamond [appears] above.*
    *Pha.* What saucy groom knocks at this dead
    of night?
Where be our waiters? By my vexed soul,  90
He meets his death that meets me, for his bold-
    ness.
    *King.* Prince, prince, you wrong your
    thoughts; we are your friends:
Come down.
    *Pha.*       The king!
    *King.*           The same, sir. Come down:
We have cause of present counsel with you.
    *Pha.* If your grace please          95
To use me, I 'll attend you to your chamber.

    *Enter Pharamond below*

    *King.* No, 't is too late, prince; I 'll make
    bold with yours.

---

<sup>28</sup> **brave:** well-dressed    <sup>58</sup> **child:** daughter    <sup>59</sup> **crossly match'd:** ill married    <sup>63</sup> **undeserving:**
guiltless ('understanding' Q 2–F)   <sup>78</sup> **winking:** shutting the eyes    <sup>85</sup> **their . . . their:** ('your . . .
your' Q 1)   <sup>88</sup> S. D. **above:** appearing on upper stage   <sup>92</sup> **wrong your:** indulge unworthy

*Pha.* I have some private reasons to myself
Makes me unmannerly, and say you cannot. —
*They press to come in.*
Nay, press not forward, gentlemen; he must 100
Come through my life that comes here.
   *King.* Sir, be resolv'd I must and will come.
— Enter.
   *Pha.* I will not be dishonour'd.
He that enters, enters upon his death.
Sir, 't is a sign you make no stranger of me, 105
To bring these renegadoes to my chamber
At these unseason'd hours.
   *King.*        Why do you
Chafe yourself so? You are not wrong'd nor
shall be;
Only I 'll search your lodging, for some cause
To ourself known. — Enter, I say.
   *Pha.*              I say, no. 110

      *[Enter] Megra above*

   *Meg.* Let 'em enter, prince, let 'em enter;
I am up and ready: I know their business;
'T is the poor breaking of a lady's honour
They hunt so hotly after: let 'em enjoy it. —
You have your business, gentlemen; I lay
here.                           115
Oh, my lord the king, this is not noble in you
To make public the weakness of a woman!
   *King.* Come down.
   *Meg.* I dare, my lord. Your hootings and
your clamours,                 119
Your private whispers and your broad fleerings,
Can no more vex my soul than this base car-
riage.
But I have vengeance yet in store for some
Shall, in the most contempt you can have of me,
Be joy and nourishment.
   *King.*        Will you come down?
   *Meg.* Yes, to laugh at your worst; but I shall
wring you,                 125
If my skill fail me not.     *[Exit above.]*
   *King.* Sir, I must dearly chide you for this
looseness;
You have wrong'd a worthy lady; but, no
more. — Conduct him to my lodging and to bed.
    *[Exeunt Pharamond and Attendants.]*
   *Cle.* Get him another wench, and you bring
him to bed indeed.        131
   *Dion.* 'T is strange a man cannot ride a stage
Or two, to breathe himself, without a warrant.
If his gear hold, that lodgings be search'd thus,
Pray God we may lie with our own wives in
safety,               135
That they be not by some trick of state mis-
taken!

    *Enter [Attendants] with Megra [below]*

   *King.* Now, lady of honour, where 's your
honour now?
No man can fit your palate but the prince.
Thou most ill-shrouded rottenness, thou piece
Made by a painter and a 'pothecary,   140
Thou troubled sea of lust, thou wilderness
Inhabited by wild thoughts, thou swoln cloud
Of infection, thou ripe mine of all diseases,
Thou all-sin, all-hell, and last, all-devils, tell me,
Had you none to pull on with your courtesies
But he that must be mine, and wrong my
daughter?             146
By all the gods, all these, and all the pages,
And all the court, shall hoot thee through the
court,
Fling rotten oranges, make ribald rhymes,
And sear thy name with candles upon walls! 150
Do you laugh, Lady Venus?
   *Meg.* Faith, sir, you must pardon me;
I cannot choose but laugh to see you merry.
If you do this, O King! nay, if you dare do it,
By all those gods you swore by, and as many 155
More of my own, I will have fellows, and such
Fellows in it, as shall make noble mirth!
The princess, your dear daughter, shall stand
by me
On walls, and sung in ballads, anything.  159
Urge me no more; I know her and her haunts,
Her lays, leaps, and outlays, and will discover
all;
Nay, will dishonour her. I know the boy
She keeps; a handsome boy, about eighteen;
Know what she does with him, where, and
when.           164
Come, sir, you put me to a woman's madness,
The glory of a fury; and if I do not
Do 't to the height ——
   *King.*      What boy is this she raves at?
   *Meg.* Alas! good-minded prince, you know
not these things!
I am loath to reveal 'em. Keep this fault,
As you would keep your health from the hot
air           170
Of the corrupted people, or, by Heaven,
I will not fall alone. What I have known
Shall be as public as a print; all tongues
Shall speak it as they do the language they
Are born in, as free and commonly; I 'll set it,
Like a prodigious star, for all to gaze at,  176
And so high and glowing, that other kingdoms
far and foreign
Shall read it there, nay, travel with it, till they
find

    ⁹⁹ S. D. (In Q 1 only)   ¹⁰² **be resolv'd:** understand   ¹⁰⁶ **renegadoes:** ('runagates' Q 1)
¹¹² **ready:** dressed   ¹²¹ **carriage:** behavior   ¹²³ **Shall:** which shall   ¹³⁴ **gear:** business   ¹³⁵ **God:**
('heaven' Q 2–F)   ¹⁶¹ **Her . . . outlays:** ('her fayre leaps And out-lying' Q 1)   **lays:** lodging places
**outlays:** remote lairs   ¹⁷² **fall:** ('sinke' Q 1)   ¹⁷³ **a print:** printed ballad ('in print' Q 1)

No tongue to make it more, nor no more peo-
    ple;
And then behold the fall of your fair princess!
  *King.*  Has she a boy?          181
  *Cle.*  So please your grace, I have seen a boy
    wait
On her, a fair boy.
  *King.*          Go, get you to your quarter:
For this time I will study to forget you.
  *Meg.*  Do you study to forget me, and I 'll
    study          185
To forget you.
            *Exeunt King, Megra, Guard.*
  *Cle.*  Why, here 's a male spirit fit for Hercules. If ever there be Nine Worthies of women,
this wench shall ride astride and be their captain.          190
  *Dion.*  Sure, she has a garrison of devils in her
tongue, she uttered such balls of wild-fire. She
has so nettled the king, that all the doctors in
the country will scarce cure him. That boy was
a strange-found-out antidote to cure her [195
infection: that boy, that princess' boy; that
brave, chaste, virtuous lady's boy; and a fair
boy, a well-spoken boy! All these considered,
can make nothing else — but there I leave you,
gentlemen.          200
  *Thra.*  Nay, we 'll go wander with you.
                *Exeunt.*

## *Actus Tertius.  Scena Prima.*

### [*The Court.*]

*Enter Cleremont, Dion, and Thrasiline*

  *Cle.*  Nay, doubtless, 't is true.
  *Dion.*  Ay; and 't is the gods
That rais'd this punishment, to scourge the
    king
With his own issue. Is it not a shame
For us that should write noble in the land,  5
For us that should be freemen, to behold
A man that is the bravery of his age,
Philaster, press'd down from his royal right
By this regardless king? and only look
And see the sceptre ready to be cast    10
Into the hands of that lascivious lady,
That lives in lust with a smooth boy, now to be
    married
To yon strange prince, who, but that people
    please
To let him be a prince, is born a slave
In that which should be his most noble part,  15
His mind?
  *Thra.*  That man that would not stir with you

To aid Philaster, let the gods forget
That such a creature walks upon the earth!
  *Cle.*  Philaster is too backward in 't himself.
The gentry do await it, and the people,  20
Against their nature, are all bent for him,
And like a field of standing corn, that 's mov'd
With a stiff gale, their heads bow all one
    way.
  *Dion.*  The only cause that draws Philaster
    back
From this attempt is the fair princess' love,  25
Which he admires, and we can now confute.
  *Thra.*  Perhaps he 'll not believe it.
  *Dion.*  Why, gentlemen, 't is without ques-
    tion so.
  *Cle.*  Ay, 't is past speech she lives dishon-
    estly.
But how shall we, if he be curious, work  30
Upon his faith?
  *Thra.*  We all are satisfied within ourselves.
  *Dion.*  Since it is true, and tends to his own
    good,
I 'll make this new report to be my knowl-
    edge.
I 'll say I know it; nay, I 'll swear I saw it.  35
  *Cle.*  It will be best.
  *Thra.*          'T will move him.

*Enter Philaster*

  *Dion.*          Here he comes.
Good morrow to your honour: we have spent
Some time in seeking you.
  *Phi.*          My worthy friends,
You that can keep your memories to know
Your friend in miseries, and cannot frown  40
On men disgrac'd for virtue, a good day
Attend you all! What service may I do
Worthy your acceptation?
  *Dion.*          My good lord,
We come to urge that virtue, which we know
Lives in your breast, forth. Rise, and make a
    head;          45
The nobles and the people are all dull'd
With this usurping king; and not a man,
That ever heard the word, knows such a thing
As virtue, but will second your attempts.
  *Phi.*  How honourable is this love in you  50
To me that have deserv'd none! Know, my
    friends,
(You, that were born to shame your poor Phi-
    laster
With too much courtesy,) I could afford
To melt myself in thanks: but my designs
Are not yet ripe. Suffice it, that ere long  55
I shall employ your loves; but yet the time
Is short of what I would.

---

    **5 write noble:** rank as nobles    **13 prince:** ('thing' Q 1)    **19** (Not in Q 1)    **26 Which:** whom
**29 past speech:** fact, not rumor    **30 curious:** skeptical    **31 Upon . . . faith:** ('on his beleefe' Q 1)
**45 make a head:** gather an army    **48 knows:** (as in Q 1; 'or knowne' Q 2; 'or knew' Q 3, etc.)

*Dion.* The time is fuller, sir, than you expect;
That which hereafter will not, perhaps, be reach'd
By violence, may now be caught. As for the king,                                           60
You know the people have long hated him;
But now the princess, whom they lov'd ——
*Phi.* Why, what of her?
*Dion.*                   Is loath'd as much as he.
*Phi.* By what strange means?
*Dion.*                   She 's known a whore.
*Phi.*                   Thou liest.
*Dion.* My lord ——                                      65
*Phi.* Thou liest,
                    *Offers to draw and is held.*
And thou shalt feel it! I had thought thy mind
Had been of honour. Thus to rob a lady
Of her good name is an infectious sin
Not to be pardon'd. Be it false as hell,        70
'T will never be redeem'd, if it be sown
Amongst the people, fruitful to increase
All evil they shall hear. Let me alone
That I may cut off falsehood whilst it springs!
Set hills on hills betwixt me and the man    75
That utters this, and I will scale them all,
And from the utmost top fall on his neck,
Like thunder from a cloud.
*Dion.*                   This is most strange:
Sure, he does love her.
*Phi.*                   I do love fair truth.
She is my mistress, and who injures her        80
Draws vengeance from me. Sirs, let go my arms.
*Thra.* Nay, good my lord, be patient.
*Cle.*                   Sir, remember,
This is your honour'd friend,
That comes to do his service, and will show you
Why he utter'd this.
*Phi.*                   I ask you pardon, sir; 85
My zeal to truth made me unmannerly:
Should I have heard dishonour spoke of you,
Behind your back, untruly, I had been
As much distemper'd and enrag'd as now.
*Dion.* But this, my lord, is truth.
*Phi.*                   Oh, say not so! 90
Good sir, forbear to say so: 't is then truth,
That womankind is false: urge it no more;
It is impossible. Why should you think
The princess light?
*Dion.*                   Why, she was taken at it. 94
*Phi.* 'T is false! by Heaven, 't is false! It cannot be!

Can it? Speak, gentlemen; for God's love, speak!
Is 't possible? Can women all be damn'd?
*Dion.* Why, no, my lord.
*Phi.*                   Why, then, it cannot be.
*Dion.* And she was taken with her boy.
*Phi.*                   What boy? 99
*Dion.* A page, a boy that serves her.
*Phi.*                   Oh, good gods!
A little boy?
*Dion.*                   Ay; know you him, my lord?
*Phi.* [*Aside.*] Hell and sin know him! — Sir, you are deceiv'd;
I 'll reason it a little coldly with you.
If she were lustful, would she take a boy,
That knows not yet desire? She would have one                                            105
Should meet her thoughts and know the sin he acts,
Which is the great delight of wickedness.
You are abus'd, and so is she, and I.
*Dion.* How you, my lord?
*Phi.*                   Why, all the world 's abus'd 109
In an unjust report.
*Dion.*                   Oh, noble sir, your virtues
Cannot look into the subtle thoughts of woman!
In short, my lord, I took them; I myself.
*Phi.* Now, all the devils, thou didst! Fly from my rage!
Would thou hadst ta'en devils engend'ring plagues,
When thou didst take them! Hide thee from mine eyes!                                     115
Would thou hadst taken thunder on thy breast,
When thou didst take them; or been strucken dumb
For ever; that this foul deed might have slept In silence!
*Thra.* Have you known him so ill-temper'd?
*Cle.* Never before.
*Phi.*                   The winds that are let loose 120
From the four several corners of the earth,
And spread themselves all over sea and land,
Kiss not a chaste one. What friend bears a sword
To run me through?
*Dion.*                   Why, my lord, are you
So mov'd at this?
*Phi.*                   When any fall from virtue, 125
I am distracted; I have an interest in 't.
*Dion.* But, good my lord, recall yourself, and think
What 's best to be done.
*Phi.*                   I thank you; I will do it.

---

⁷² fruitful: ('faithfull' Q 1)     ⁷⁴ off . . . springs: ('out falsehood where it grows' Q 1)     ⁸⁵ you: ('your' Q 1)     ⁸⁶ made: ('makes' Q 1)     ⁹² womankind is: ('women all are' Q 1)     ¹⁰³ coldly: ('milder' Q 1)     ¹⁰⁸ abus'd: deceived     ¹¹⁶ thunder on: ('daggers in' Q 1)     ¹²⁶ distracted: ('distract' Q 4–F)

Please you to leave me; I 'll consider of it.
To-morrow I will find your lodging forth,    130
And give you answer.
   *Dion.*              All the gods direct you
The readiest way!
   *Thra.*            He was extreme impatient.
   *Cle.*   It was his virtue and his noble mind.
        *Exeunt Dion, Cleremont, and Thrasi-*
        *line.*
   *Phi.*   I had forgot to ask him where he took
   them;
I 'll follow him.  Oh that I had a sea    135
Within my breast, to quench the fire I feel!
More circumstances will but fan this fire:
It more afflicts me now, to know by whom
This deed is done, than simply that 't is done;
And he that tells me this is honourable,    140
As far from lies as she is far from truth.
Oh, that, like beasts, we could not grieve our-
   selves
With that we see not!  Bulls and rams will
   fight
To keep their females, standing in their sight;
But take 'em from them, and you take at
   once    145
Their spleens away; and they will fall again
Unto their pastures, growing fresh and fat,
And taste the waters of the springs as sweet
As 't was before, finding no start in sleep;    149
But miserable man ——

          *Enter Bellario*

                 See, see, you gods,
He walks still; and the face you let him wear
When he was innocent is still the same,
Not blasted!  Is this justice?  Do you mean
To intrap mortality, that you allow
Treason so smooth a brow?  I cannot now    155
Think he is guilty.
   *Bel.*          Health to you, my lord!
The princess doth commend her love, her life,
And this, unto you.    *He gives him a letter.*
   *Phi.*         Oh, Bellario,
Now I perceive she loves me: she does show it
In loving thee, my boy.  She has made thee
   brave.    160
   *Bel.* My lord, she has attir'd me past my wish,
Past my desert; more fit for her attendant,
Though far unfit for me who do attend.
   *Phi.*   Thou art grown courtly, boy. — Oh,
   let all women,    164
That love black deeds, learn to dissemble here,
Here, by this paper!  She does write to me
As if her heart were mines of adamant

To all the world besides; but, unto me,
A maiden-snow that melted with my looks. —
Tell me, my boy, how doth the princess use
   thee?    170
For I shall guess her love to me by that.
   *Bel.*   Scarce like her servant, but as if I were
Something allied to her, or had preserv'd
Her life three times by my fidelity:
As mothers fond do use their only sons,    175
As I 'd use one that 's left unto my trust,
For whom my life should pay if he met harm,
So she does use me.
   *Phi.*          Why, this is wondrous well
But what kind language does she feed thee
   with?
   *Bel.*   Why, she does tell me she will trust my
   youth    180
With all her loving secrets, and does call me
Her pretty servant; bids me weep no more
For leaving you; she 'll see my services
Regarded: and such words of that soft strain
That I am nearer weeping when she ends    185
Than ere she spake.
   *Phi.*         This is much better still.
   *Bel.*   Are you not ill, my lord?
   *Phi.*          Ill?  No, Bellario.
   *Bel.*   Methinks your words
Fall not from off your tongue so evenly,
Nor is there in your looks that quietness    190
That I was wont to see.
   *Phi.*        Thou art deceiv'd, boy:
And she strokes thy head?
   *Bel.*          Yes.
   *Phi.*   And she does clap thy cheeks?
   *Bel.*          She does, my lord.
   *Phi.*   And she does kiss thee, boy?  ha!
   *Bel.*          How, my lord?    194
   *Phi.*   She kisses thee?
   *Bel.*         Never, my lord, by heaven.
   *Phi.*   That 's strange, I know she does.
   *Bel.*         No, by my life.
   *Phi.*   Why then she does not love me.  Come,
   she does.
I bade her do it; I charg'd her, by all charms
Of love between us, by the hope of peace
We should enjoy, to yield thee all delights    200
Naked as to her bed; I took her oath
Thou shouldst enjoy her.  Tell me, gentle boy,
Is she not parallelless?  Is not her breath
Sweet as Arabian winds when fruits are ripe?
Are not her breasts two liquid ivory balls?    205
Is she not all a lasting mine of joy?
   *Bel.*   Ay, now I see why my disturbed
   thoughts

---

     <sup>182–133</sup> **He . . . mind:** (not in Q 1)    <sup>137</sup> **circumstances:** details    <sup>171</sup> (Not in Q 1)    <sup>181</sup> **loving secrets:** ('maiden store' Q 1)    <sup>184</sup> **Regarded:** rewarded (which Q 1 prints)    <sup>186</sup> **spake:** ('speakes' Q 1)    <sup>187</sup> **not ill:** ('not well' Q 1)    <sup>190</sup> **quietness:** ('quicknesse' Q 1)    <sup>195</sup> **Never . . . heaven:** ('Not so, my Lord' Q 4–F)    <sup>196</sup> **That 's strange:** ('Come, come' Q 4–F)    <sup>201</sup> **bed:** ('Lord' Q 1)    <sup>203</sup> **parallelless:** ('paradise' Q 1)    <sup>207</sup> **disturbed:** ('discurled' Q 1)

Were so perplex'd.  When first I went to her,
My heart held augury.  You are abus'd;
Some villain has abus'd you; I do see          210
Whereto you tend.  Fall rocks upon his head
That put this to you! 'T is some subtle train
To bring that noble frame of yours to nought.
   *Phi.*  Thou think'st I will be angry with
   thee.  Come,                                  214
Thou shalt know all my drift.  I hate her more
Than I love happiness, and plac'd thee there
To pry with narrow eyes into her deeds.
Hast thou discover'd?  Is she fall'n to lust,
As I would wish her?  Speak some comfort to
   me.
   *Bel.*  My lord, you did mistake the boy you
   sent.                                          220
Had she the lust of sparrows or of goats,
Had she a sin that way, hid from the world,
Beyond the name of lust, I would not aid
Her base desires; but what I came to know
As servant to her, I would not reveal,        225
To make my life last ages.
   *Phi.*                              Oh, my heart!
This is a salve worse than the main disease. —
Tell me thy thoughts; for I will know the
   least
That dwells within thee, or will rip thy heart
To know it.  I will see thy thoughts as plain 230
As I do now thy face.
   *Bel.*                           Why, so you do.
She is (for aught I know) by all the gods,
As chaste as ice!  But were she foul as hell,
And I did know it thus, the breath of kings,
The points of swords, tortures, nor bulls of
   brass,                                        235
Should draw it from me.
   *Phi.*                         Then it is no time
To dally with thee; I will take thy life,
For I do hate thee.  I could curse thee now.
   *Bel.*  If you do hate, you could not curse me
   worse;
The gods have not a punishment in store      240
Greater for me than is your hate.
   *Phi.*                                  Fie, fie,
So young and so dissembling!  Tell me when
And where thou didst enjoy her, or let plagues
Fall on me, if I destroy thee not!
                        *Draws his sword.*
   *Bel.*  Heaven knows, I never did; and when I
   lie                                           245
To save my life, may I live long and loath'd!
Hew me asunder, and, whilst I can think,
I 'll love those pieces you have cut away
Better than those that grow, and kiss those
   limbs                                         249
Because you made 'em so.

   *Phi.*                           Fear'st thou not death?
Can boys contemn that?
   *Bel.*                          Oh, what boy is he
Can be content to live to be a man,
That sees the best of men thus passionate,
Thus without reason?
   *Phi.*                      Oh, but thou dost not know
What 't is to die.
   *Bel.*                     Yes, I do know, my lord: 255
'T is less than to be born; a lasting sleep;
A quiet resting from all jealousy,
A thing we all pursue.  I know, besides,
It is but giving over of a game            259
That must be lost.
   *Phi.*                 But there are pains, false boy,
For perjur'd souls.  Think but on those, and
   then
Thy heart will melt, and thou wilt utter all.
   *Bel.*  May they fall all upon me whilst I live,
If I be perjur'd, or have ever thought
Of that you charge me with!  If I be false, 265
Send me to suffer in those punishments
You speak of; kill me!
   *Phi.*                       Oh, what should I do?
Why, who can but believe him?  He does
   swear
So earnestly, that if it were not true,
The gods would not endure him.  Rise, Bel-
   lario:                                        270
Thy protestations are so deep, and thou
Dost look so truly when thou utter'st them,
That, though I know 'em false as were my
   hopes,
I cannot urge thee further.  But thou wert
To blame to injure me, for I must love      275
Thy honest looks, and take no revenge upon
Thy tender youth.  A love from me to thee
Is firm, whate'er thou dost; it troubles me
That I have call'd the blood out of thy cheeks,
That did so well become thee.  But, good boy,
Let me not see thee more: something is
   done                                          281
That will distract me, that will make me mad,
If I behold thee.  If thou tender'st me,
Let me not see thee.
   *Bel.*                       I will fly as far
As there is morning, ere I give distaste    285
To that most honour'd mind.  But through
   these tears,
Shed at my hopeless parting, I can see
A world of treason practis'd upon you,
And her, and me.  Farewell for evermore! 289
If you shall hear that sorrow struck me dead,
And after find me loyal, let there be
A tear shed from you in my memory,
And I shall rest in peace.              *Exit.*

---

   ²¹⁷ **narrow:** ('sparrowes' Q 1)    ²²² **way, hid:** ('weighed' Q 1)    ²³⁶ **draw:** ('wrack' Q 1)
²⁴⁵ **Heaven knows:** ('By heaven' Q 1)   ²⁵² **Can:** ('Could' Q 1)   ²⁸⁶ **mind:** ('frame' Q 1)   ²⁸⁷ **hopeless:** ('haplesse' Q 1)

*Phi.*                                    Blessing be with thee,
Whatever thou deserv'st! Oh, where shall I
Go bathe this body? Nature too unkind; 295
That made no medicine for a troubled mind!
                                              *Exit.*

[SCENE II. — *Arethusa's Apartment.*]

*Enter Arethusa*

*Are.* I marvel my boy comes not back again:
But that I know my love will question him
Over and over, — how I slept, wak'd, talk'd,
How I rememb'red him, when his dear name
Was last spoke, and how, when I sigh'd, wept,
    sung,                                           5
And ten thousand such, — I should be angry at
    his stay.

*Enter King*

*King.* What, at your meditations! Who at-
    tends you?
*Are.* None but my single self. I need no
    guard;
I do no wrong, nor fear none.
*King.* Tell me, have you not a boy?
*Are.*                                    Yes, sir. 10
*King.* What kind of boy?
*Are.*                          A page, a waiting-boy.
*King.* A handsome boy?
*Are.*                          I think he be not ugly:
Well qualified and dutiful I know him;
I took him not for beauty.
*King.* He speaks and sings and plays?
*Are.*                                    Yes, sir. 15
*King.* About eighteen?
*Are.*                          I never ask'd his age.
*King.* Is he full of service?
*Are.* By your pardon, why do you ask?
*King.* Put him away.
*Are.*                          Sir!
*King.*                          Put him away, I say.
H'as done you that good service shames me to
    speak of.                                        20
*Are.* Good sir, let me understand you.
*King.*                                    If you fear me,
Show it in duty; put away that boy.
*Are.* Let me have reason for it, sir, and then
Your will is my command.
*King.* Do not you blush to ask it? Cast him
    off,                                             25
Or I shall do the same to you. Y' are one
Shame with me, and so near unto myself,
That, by my life, I dare not tell myself
What you, myself, have done.
*Are.* What have I done, my lord?              30
*King.* 'T is a new language, that all love to
    learn:

The common people speak it well already;
They need no grammar. Understand me well:
There be foul whispers stirring. Cast him off,
And suddenly. Do it! Farewell. *Exit King.* 35
*Are.* Where may a maiden live securely free,
Keeping her honour fair? Not with the living.
They feed upon opinions, errors, dreams,
And make 'em truths; they draw a nourish-
    ment
Out of defamings, grow upon disgraces,        40
And, when they see a virtue fortified
Strongly above the battery of their tongues,
Oh, how they cast to sink it! and, defeated,
(Soul-sick with poison) strike the monuments
Where noble names lie sleeping, till they sweat,
And the cold marble melt.                       46

*Enter Philaster*

*Phi.* Peace to your fairest thoughts, dearest
    mistress!
*Are.* Oh, my dearest servant, I have a war
    within me!
*Phi.* He must be more than man that makes
    these crystals
Run into rivers. Sweetest fair, the cause? 50
And, as I am your slave, tied to your goodness,
Your creature, made again from what I was
And newly-spirited, I 'll right your honour.
*Are.* Oh, my best love, that boy!
*Phi.*                                    What boy?
*Are.* The pretty boy you gave me ——
*Phi.*                                    What of him? 55
*Are.* Must be no more mine.
*Phi.*          Why?
*Are.*                          They are jealous of him.
*Phi.* Jealous! Who?
*Are.*                          The king.
*Phi.* [*Aside.*]                          Oh, my misfortune!
Then 't is no idle jealousy. — Let him go.
*Are.* Oh, cruel!
Are you hard-hearted too? Who shall now tell
    you                                             60
How much I lov'd you? Who shall swear it to
    you,
And weep the tears I send? Who shall now
    bring you
Letters, rings, bracelets? Lose his health in
    service?
Wake tedious nights in stories of your praise?
Who shall now sing your crying elegies,         65
And strike a sad soul into senseless pictures,
And make them mourn? Who shall take up his
    lute,
And touch it till he crown a silent sleep
Upon my eye-lids, making me dream, and cry,
"Oh, my dear, dear Philaster!"

---

¹⁹ **I say:** (not in Q 3–F)     ²⁶ **the same:** ('that shame' Q 1)     ²⁸ **my life:** ('the gods' Q 1)
³⁷ **fair:** ('safe' Q 4–F)     ⁴³ **cast:** plot ('mind' Q 1)     ⁴⁹ **crystals:** eyes     ⁶⁶ **strike:** implant
⁶⁷ **mourn:** ('warme' Q 1)

*Phi.* [*Aside.*]                         Oh, my heart! 70
Would he had broken thee, that made thee
   know
This lady was not loyal! — Mistress,
Forget the boy; I 'll get thee a far better.
   *Are.* Oh, never, never such a boy again
As my Bellario!
   *Phi.*        'T is but your fond affection. 75
   *Are.* With thee, my boy, farewell for ever
All secrecy in servants! Farewell, faith,
And all desire to do well for itself!
Let all that shall succeed thee for thy wrongs
Sell and betray chaste love!                    80
   *Phi.*   And all this passion for a boy?
   *Are.* He was your boy, and you put him to me,
And the loss of such must have a mourning for.
   *Phi.* Oh, thou forgetful woman!
   *Are.*                      How, my lord?
   *Phi.*   False Arethusa!                      85
Hast thou a medicine to restore my wits,
When I have lost 'em? If not, leave to talk,
And do thus.
   *Are.*        Do what, sir? Would you sleep?
   *Phi.* For ever, Arethusa. Oh, you gods
Give me a worthy patience! Have I stood, 90
Naked, alone, the shock of many fortunes?
Have I seen mischiefs numberless and mighty
Grow like a sea upon me? Have I taken
Danger as stern as death into my bosom,
And laugh'd upon it, made it but a mirth,    95
And flung it by? Do I live now like him,
Under this tyrant king, that languishing
Hears his sad bell and sees his mourners? Do I
Bear all this bravely, and must sink at length
Under a woman's falsehood? Oh, that boy, 100
That cursed boy! None but a villain boy
To ease your lust?
   *Are.*              Nay, then, I am betray'd:
I feel the plot cast for my overthrow.
Oh, I am wretched!
   *Phi.* Now you may take that little right I
      have                                   105
To this poor kingdom. Give it to your joy;
For I have no joy in it. Some far place,
Where never womankind durst set her foot
For bursting with her poisons, must I seek,
And live to curse you;                       110
There dig a cave, and preach to birds and beasts
What woman is, and help to save them from you:
How heaven is in your eyes, but in your hearts
More hell than hell has; how your tongues, like
      scorpions,
Both heal and poison; how your thoughts are
      woven                                  115

With thousand changes in one subtle web,
And worn so by you; how that foolish man,
That reads the story of a woman's face
And dies believing it, is lost for ever;
How all the good you have is but a shadow, 120
I' th' morning with you, and at night behind
      you,
Past and forgotten; how your vows are frosts,
Fast for a night, and with the next sun gone;
How you are, being taken all together,
A mere confusion, and so dead a chaos,       125
That love cannot distinguish. These sad texts,
Till my last hour, I am bound to utter of you.
So, farewell all my woe, all my delight! *Exit.*
   *Are.* Be merciful, ye gods, and strike me
      dead!
What way have I deserv'd this? Make my
      breast                                 130
Transparent as pure crystal, that the world,
Jealous of me, may see the foulest thought
My heart holds. Where shall a woman turn her
      eyes,
To find out constancy?

                  *Enter Bellario*

                               Save me, how black
And guiltily, methinks, that boy looks now! 135
Oh, thou dissembler, that, before thou spak'st,
Wert in thy cradle false, sent to make lies
And betray innocents! Thy lord and thou
May glory in the ashes of a maid
Fool'd by her passion; but the conquest is 140
Nothing so great as wicked. Fly away!
Let my command force thee to that which
      shame
Would do without it. If thou understood'st
The loathed office thou hast undergone,
Why, thou wouldst hide thee under heaps of
      hills,                                 145
Lest men should dig and find thee.
   *Bel.*                          Oh, what god,
Angry with men, hath sent this strange disease
Into the noblest minds! Madam, this grief
You add unto me is no more than drops        149
To seas, for which they are not seen to swell.
My lord hath struck his anger through my
      heart,
And let out all the hope of future joys.
You need not bid me fly; I came to part,
To take my latest leave. Farewell for ever!
I durst not run away in honesty              155
From such a lady, like a boy that stole
Or made some grievous fault. The power of
      gods

---

⁷³ **thee:** ('you' Q 1)   ⁷⁸ **desire . . . itself:** ('desires . . . thy sake' Q 1)   ⁹¹ **alone:** ('above'
O 1)   ⁹⁴ **stern:** ('deepe' Q 1)   ¹⁰⁹ **For:** for fear of   ¹¹⁵ **heal:** (Scorpion bites were thought to be
cured by applying the scorpion to them.)   ¹³³ **a . . . her:** ('women . . . their' Q 1)   ¹³⁵ **guiltily:**
('vile' Q 1; 'guilty' Q 3–F)   ¹⁴¹ **Nothing:** by no means   ¹⁴⁴ **undergone:** ('undertooke' Q 1)
¹⁴⁷ **men:** ('me' Q 1)   ¹⁵⁷ **grievous:** ('greater' Q 1)

Assist you in your sufferings! Hasty time
Reveal the truth to your abused lord
And mine, that he may know your worth;
    whilst I              160
Go seek out some forgotten place to die! *Exit.*
  *Are.* Peace guide thee! Thou hast overthrown
    me once;
Yet, if I had another Troy to lose,
Thou, or another villain with thy looks,    164
Might talk me out of it, and send me naked,
My hair dishevell'd, through the fiery streets.

### Enter a Lady

  *La.* Madam, the king would hunt, and
    calls for you
With earnestness.
  *Are.*          I am in tune to hunt!
Diana, if thou canst rage with a maid
As with a man, let me discover thee    170
Bathing, and turn me to a fearful hind,
That I may die pursued by cruel hounds,
And have my story written in my wounds!
                      *Exeunt.*

## Actus Quartus. Scena Prima.

### [The Court.]

*Enter King, Pharamond, Arethusa, Galatea,
Megra, Dion, Cleremont, Thrasiline, and
Attendants*

  *King.* What, are the hounds before and all
    the woodmen?
Our horses ready and our bows bent?
  *Dion.*             All, sir.
  *King.* [*to Pharamond.*] Y' are cloudy, sir.
    Come, we have forgotten
Your venial trespass; let not that sit heavy
Upon your spirit; here 's none dare utter it.  5
  *Dion.* He looks like an old surfeited stallion
after his leaping, dull as a dormouse. See how
he sinks! The wench has shot him between wind
and water, and, I hope, sprung a leak.
  *Thra.* He needs no teaching, he strikes [10
sure enough. His greatest fault is, he hunts too
much in the purlieus; would he would leave off
poaching!
  *Dion.* And for his horn, h'as left it at the
lodge where he lay late. Oh, he 's a precious [15
limehound! Turn him loose upon the pursuit
of a lady, and if he lose her, hang him up i' the

slip. When my fox-bitch, Beauty, grows proud,
I 'll borrow him.
  *King.* Is your boy turn'd away?    20
  *Are.* You did command, sir, and I obey'd
you.
  *King.* 'T is well done. Hark ye further.
                [*They talk apart.*]
  *Cle.* Is 't possible this fellow should repent?
Methinks, that were not noble in him; and [25
yet he looks like a mortified member, as if he
had a "Sick Man's Salve" in 's mouth. If a
worse man had done this fault now, some
physical justice or other would presently
(without the help of an almanac) have [30
opened the obstructions of his liver, and let
him blood with a dog-whip.
  *Dion.* See, see how modestly yon lady looks,
as if she came from churching with her neighbours! Why, what a devil can a man see in [35
her face but that she 's honest!
  *Thra.* Faith, no great matter to speak of: a
foolish twinkling with the eye, that spoils her
coat: but he must be a cunning herald that
finds it.    40
  *Dion.* See how they muster one another! Oh,
there 's a rank regiment where the devil carries
the colours and his dam drum-major! Now the
world and the flesh come behind with the carriage.    45
  *Cle.* Sure this lady has a good turn done her
against her will; before she was common talk,
now none dare say cantharides can stir her.
Her face looks like a warrant, willing and commanding all tongues, as they will answer it, [50
to be tied up and bolted when this lady means
to let herself loose. As I live, she has got her a
goodly protection and a gracious; and may use
her body discreetly for her health's sake, once
a week, excepting Lent and dog-days. Oh, [55
if they were to be got for money, what a great
sum would come out of the city for these
licences!
  *King.* To horse, to horse! we lose the morning, gentlemen.          *Exeunt.* 60

### [Scene II. — The Forest.]

#### Enter two Woodmen

  *1 Wood.* What, have you lodged the deer?
  *2 Wood.* Yes, they are ready for the bow.
  *1 Wood.* Who shoots?

---

    [163] **Yet . . . Troy:** ('But . . . time' Q 1)    [165] **talk:** ('take' Q 1). The allusion in lines 163–165
is to the story of Sinon.    [3] **cloudy:** moody    [5] **here 's:** (not in Q 4–F)    [12] **purlieus:** open ground
near a forest    [15] **precious:** ('pernitious' Q 1)    [16] **limehound:** dog on leash, blood-hound    [18] **slip:**
dog-leash    **proud:** heated sexually    [27] **"Sick Man's Salve":** a popular work of devotion, by Thomas
Becon    [28] **worse:** inferior in rank    [29] **physical:** curative    [30] **almanac:** used to determine the time
for blood-letting    [33] **yon:** ('your' F)    [39] **coat:** coat of arms (stars inserted in them marked an inferior branch of the family)    [43] **his dam:** the devil's dam acts as    [44-45] **carriage:** baggage    [48] **cantharides:** Spanish flies, used as a stimulant    [1] **lodged:** brought within reach of the shooting
stands

2 *Wood.* The princess.

1 *Wood.* No, she 'll hunt.                                          5

2 *Wood.* She 'll take a stand, I say.

1 *Wood.* Who else?

2 *Wood.* Why, the young stranger-prince.

1 *Wood.* He shall shoot in a stone-bow for
me. I never lov'd his beyond-sea-ship since [10
he forsook the say, for paying ten shillings.
He was there at the fall of a deer, and would
needs (out of his mightiness) give ten groats
for the dowcets; marry, his steward would
have the velvet-head into the bargain, to [15
turf his hat withal. I think he should love
venery; he is an old Sir Tristram; for, if you be
rememb'red, he forsook the stag once to strike a
rascal miching in a meadow, and her he kill'd
in the eye. Who shoots else?                                        20

2 *Wood.* The Lady Galatea.

1 *Wood.* That 's a good wench, and she would
not chide us for tumbling of her women in the
brakes. She 's liberal, and by the gods, they
say she 's honest, and whether that be a [25
fault, I have nothing to do. There 's all?

2 *Wood.* No, one more; Megra.

1 *Wood.* That 's a firker, i' faith, boy.
There 's a wench will ride her haunches as
hard after a kennel of hounds as a hunting [30
saddle, and when she comes home, get 'em
clapp'd, and all is well again. I have known her
lose herself three times in one afternoon (if the
woods have been answerable), and it has been
work enough for one man to find her, and [35
he has sweat for it. She rides well and she pays
well. Hark! let 's go.                        *Exeunt.*

### *Enter Philaster*

*Phi.* Oh, that I had been nourish'd in these
    woods
With milk of goats and acorns, and not known
The right of crowns nor the dissembling trains
Of women's looks; but digg'd myself a cave  41
Where I, my fire, my cattle, and my bed
Might have been shut together in one shed;
And then had taken me some mountain-girl,
Beaten with winds, chaste as the harden'd
    rocks                                                           45
Whereon she dwelt, that might have strew'd
    my bed
With leaves and reeds, and with the skins of
    beasts,
Our neighbours, and have borne at her big
    breasts

My large coarse issue! This had been a life
Free from vexation.

### *Enter Bellario*

*Bel.*                 Oh, wicked men!                               50
An innocent may walk safe ámong beasts;
Nothing assaults me here. See, my griev'd lord
Sits as his soul were searching out a way
To leave his body! — Pardon me, that must
Break thy last commandment; for I must
    speak.                                                          55
You that are griev'd can pity; hear, my lord!

*Phi.* Is there a creature yet so miserable,
That I can pity?

*Bel.*                 Oh, my noble lord,
View my strange fortune, and bestow on me,
According to your bounty (if my service        60
Can merit nothing), so much as may serve
To keep that little piece I hold of life
From cold and hunger!

*Phi.*                 Is it thou? Be gone!
Go, sell those misbeseeming clothes thou wear'st,
And feed thyself with them.                                        65

*Bel.* Alas, my lord, I can get nothing for
    them!
The silly country-people think 't is treason
To touch such gay things.

*Phi.*                 Now, by the gods, this is
Unkindly done, to vex me with thy sight.
Th 'art fallen again to thy dissembling trade;
How shouldst thou think to cozen me again? 71
Remains there yet a plague untried for me?
Even so thou wept'st, and look'd'st, and spok'st
    when first
I took thee up.
Curse on the time! If thy commanding tears 75
Can work on any other, use thy art;
I 'll not betray it. Which way wilt thou take,
That I may shun thee, for thine eyes are
    poison
To mine, and I am loath to grow in rage?
This way, or that way?                                             80

*Bel.* Any will serve; but I will choose to
    have
That path in chase that leads unto my grave.
                                        *Exeunt severally.*

### *Enter [on one side] Dion, and [on the other] the Woodmen*

*Dion.* This is the strangest sudden chance!
    — You, woodmen!

1 *Wood.* My lord Dion?

---

⁵ **hunt:** pursue on horseback     ⁹ **stone-bow:** child's weapon, projecting stones     ¹¹ **say:** assay, test of fatness of a slain deer     **for:** to avoid     ¹³ **groats:** four-penny pieces     ¹⁵ **velvet-head:** head with new, velvety horns     ¹⁶ **turf:** cover     ¹⁹ **rascal:** unseasonable, lean deer     **miching:** skulking ('milking' in Qq., F)     ²² **and:** an, if     ²⁴ **the gods:** ('my Bowe' Q 4–F)     ²⁸ **firker:** frisker ³⁰ **kennel:** pack     ⁴¹ **women's looks:** ('cruell love' Q 1)     ⁴⁶ **dwelt:** ('dwells' Q 2 –F)     ⁵¹ **may:** ('man may' F)     ⁶³⁻⁶⁸ **Phi. . . . gay things:** (not in Q 1)     ⁶⁸ **the gods:** ('my life' Q 4–F)     ⁷³ **and look'd'st:** (not in Q 4–F)

*Dion.* Saw you a lady come this way on a
sable horse studded with stars of white? 85
*2 Wood.* Was she not young and tall?
*Dion.* Yes. Rode she to the wood or to the
plain?
*2 Wood.* Faith, my lord, we saw none.

*Exeunt Woodmen.*

*Dion.* Pox of your questions then!

*Enter Cleremont*

What, is she found?
*Cle.* Nor will be, I think. 90
*Dion.* Let him seek his daughter himself.
She cannot stray about a little necessary natural
business, but the whole court must be in arms.
When she has done, we shall have peace.
*Cle.* There 's already a thousand father- [95
less tales amongst us. Some say, her horse ran
away with her; some, a wolf pursued her;
others, 't was a plot to kill her, and that arm'd
men were seen in the wood: but questionless
she rode away willingly. 100

*Enter King and Thrasiline*

*King.* Where is she?
*Cle.*                    Sir, I cannot tell.
*King.*                    How 's that?
Answer me so again!
*Cle.*          Sir, shall I lie?
*King.* Yes, lie and damn, rather than tell me
that.
I say again, where is she? Mutter not! —
Sir, speak you; where is she?
*Dion.*               Sir, I do not know. 105
*King.* Speak that again so boldly, and, by
Heaven,
It is thy last! — You, fellows, answer me;
Where is she? Mark me, all; I am your
king:
I wish to see my daughter; show her me;
I do command you all, as you are subjects, 110
To show her me! What! am I not your king?
If ay, then am I not to be obeyed?
*Dion.* Yes, if you command things possible
and honest.
*King.* Things possible and honest! Hear me,
thou, ——
Thou traitor, that dar'st confine thy king to
things 115
Possible and honest! Show her me,
Or, let me perish, if I cover not
All Sicily with blood!
*Dion.*          Faith, I cannot,
Unless you tell me where she is.
*King.* You have betray'd me; you have let
me lose 120
The jewel of my life. Go, bring her me,
And set her here before me. 'T is the king

Will have it so; whose breath can still the
winds,
Uncloud the sun, charm down the swelling sea,
And stop the floods of heaven. Speak, can it
not? 125
*Dion.* No.
*King.*          No! cannot the breath of kings do
this?
*Dion.* No; nor smell sweet itself, if once the
lungs
Be but corrupted.
*King.*          Is it so? Take heed!
*Dion.* Sir, take you heed how you dare the
powers
That must be just.
*King.*          Alas! what are we kings? 130
Why do you gods place us above the rest,
To be serv'd, flatter'd, and ador'd, till we
Believe we hold within our hands your thun-
der?
And when we come to try the power we have,
There 's not a leaf shakes at our threatenings.
I have sinn'd, 't is true, and here stand to be
punish'd; 136
Yet would not thus be punish'd. Let me choose
My way, and lay it on!
*Dion.* [*Aside.*] He articles with the gods.
Would somebody would draw bonds for the
performance of covenants betwixt them! 141

*Enter Pharamond, Galatea, and Megra*

*King.* What, is she found?
*Pha.*          No; we have ta'en her horse;
He gallop'd empty by. There is some treason.
You, Galatea, rode with her into
The wood. Why left you her?
*Gal.*          She did command me. 145
*King.* Command! you should not.
*Gal.* 'T would ill become my fortunes and
my birth
To disobey the daughter of my king.
*King.* Y' are all cunning to obey us for our
hurt;
But I will have her.
*Pha.*          If I have her not, 150
By this hand, there shall be no more Sicily.
*Dion.* [*Aside.*] What, will he carry it to Spain
in 's pocket?
*Pha.* I will not leave one man alive, but the
king,
A cook, and a tailor. 154
*Dion.* [*Aside.*] Yes; you may do well to spare
your lady-bedfellow; and her you may keep
for a spawner.
*King.* [*Aside.*] I see the injuries I have done
must be reveng'd.
*Dion.* Sir, this is not the way to find her
out.

*King.* Run all, disperse yourselves.  The
man that finds her,                                    160
Or (if she be kill'd) the traitor, I 'll make him
great.
*Dion.* I know some would give five thousand
pounds to find her.
*Pha.* Come, let us seek.
*King.* Each man a several way; here I my-
self.
*Dion.* Come, gentlemen, we here.            165
*Cle.* Lady, you must go search too.
*Meg.* I had rather be search'd myself.
                                    *Exeunt omnes.*

[SCENE III. — *Another part of the Forest.*]

*Enter Arethusa*

*Are.* Where am I now?  Feet, find me out a
way,
Without the counsel of my troubled head.
I 'll follow you boldly about these woods,
O'er mountains, thorough brambles, pits, and
floods.
Heaven, I hope, will ease me: I am sick.     5
                                    *Sits down.*

*Enter Bellario*

*Bel.* [*Aside.*] Yonder 's my lady.  God knows
I want nothing,
Because I do not wish to live; yet I
Will try her charity. — Oh hear, you that have
plenty!
From that flowing store drop some on dry
ground. — See,
The lively red is gone to guard her heart!   10
I fear she faints. — Madam, look up! — She
breathes not. —
Open once more those rosy twins, and send
Unto my lord your latest farewell! — Oh, she
stirs. —
How is it, Madam?  Speak comfort.
*Are.*                 'T is not gently done,
To put me in a miserable life,               15
And hold me there.  I prithee, let me go;
I shall do best without thee; I am well.

*Enter Philaster*

*Phi.* I am to blame to be so much in rage.
I 'll tell her coolly when and where I heard
This killing truth.  I will be temperate      20
In speaking, and as just in hearing. ——
Oh, monstrous!  Tempt me not, you gods! good
gods,
Tempt not a frail man!  What's he, that has
a heart,
But he must ease it here!
*Bel.* My lord, help, help!  The princess! 25

*Are.* I am well: forbear.
*Phi.* [*Aside.*] Let me love lightning, let me
be embrac'd
And kiss'd by scorpions, or adore the eyes
Of basilisks, rather than trust the tongues
Of hell-bred women!  Some good god look
down,                                          30
And shrink these veins up!  Stick me here a
stone,
Lasting to ages in the memory
Of this damn'd act! — Hear me, you wicked
ones!
You have put hills of fire into this breast,
Not to be quench'd with tears; for which may
guilt                                          35
Sit on your bosoms!  At your meals and beds
Despair await you!  What, before my face?
Poison of asps between your lips!  Diseases
Be your best issues!  Nature make a curse,
And throw it on you!
*Are.*                    Dear Philaster, leave 40
To be enrag'd, and hear me.
*Phi.*                        I have done;
Forgive my passion.  Not the calmed sea,
When Æolus locks up his windy brood,
Is less disturb'd than I.  I 'll make you
know 't.
Dear Arethusa, do but take this sword,        45
                        *Offers his drawn sword.*
And search how temperate a heart I have;
Then you and this your boy may live and
reign
In lust without control. — Wilt thou, Bellario?
I prithee kill me; thou art poor, and may'st 49
Nourish ambitious thoughts; when I am dead,
Thy way were freer.  Am I raging now?
If I were mad, I should desire to live.
Sirs, feel my pulse, whether you have known
A man in a more equal tune to die.
*Bel.* Alas, my lord, your pulse keeps mad-
man's time!                                    55
So does your tongue.
*Phi.*            You will not kill me, then?
*Are.* Kill you!
*Bel.*          Not for the world.
*Phi.*                        I blame not thee,
Bellario; thou hast done but that which gods
Would have transform'd themselves to do.  Be
gone,
Leave me without reply; this is the last       60
Of all our meetings — (*Exit Bellario.*)  Kill
me with this sword;
Be wise, or worse will follow: we are two
Earth cannot bear at once.  Resolve to do,
Or suffer.                                     64
*Are.* If my fortune be so good to let me
fall

Upon thy hand, I shall have peace in death.
Yet tell me this, will there be no slanders,
No jealousy in the other world; no ill there?
  *Phi.*  No.
  *Are.*  Show me, then, the way.  70
  *Phi.*  Then guide my feeble hand,
You that have power to do it, for I must
Perform a piece of justice! — If your youth
Have any way offended Heaven, let prayers
Short and effectual reconcile you to it.  75
  *Are.*  I am prepared.

    *Enter a Country Fellow*

  *C. Fell.*  I 'll see the king, if he be in the
forest; I have hunted him these two hours. If
I should come home and not see him, my sisters would laugh at me. I can see nothing [80
but people better hors'd than myself, that out-
ride me; I can hear nothing but shouting.
These kings had need of good brains; this
whooping is able to put a mean man out of
his wits. There 's a courtier with his sword [85
drawn; by this hand, upon a woman, I think!
  *Phi.*  Are you at peace?
  *Are.*          With heaven and earth.
  *Phi.*  May they divide thy soul and body!
    *Philaster wounds her.*
  *C. Fell.*  Hold, dastard! strike a woman!
Th' art a craven. I warrant thee, thou [90
wouldst be loath to play half a dozen venies at
wasters with a good fellow for a broken head.
  *Phi.*  Leave us, good friend,
  *Are.*  What ill-bred man art thou, to intrude
thyself
Upon our private sports, our recreations?  95
  *C. Fell.*  God 'uds me, I understand you not;
but
I know the rogue has hurt you.
  *Phi.*  Pursue thy own affairs: it will be ill
To multiply blood upon my head; which
thou
Wilt force me to.  100
  *C. Fell.*  I know not your rhetoric; but I
can lay it on, if you touch the woman.
  *Phi.*  Slave, take what thou deservest!
    *They fight.*
  *Are.*        Heaven guard my lord!
  *C. Fell.*  Oh, do you breathe?  104
  *Phi.*  I hear the tread of people. I am hurt.
The gods take part against me: could this
boor
Have held me thus else? I must shift for
life,
Though I do loathe it. I would find a course
To lose it rather by my will than force.
    *Exit.*

  *C. Fell.*  I cannot follow the rogue. I pray
thee, wench, come and kiss me now.  111

    *Enter Pharamond, Dion, Cleremont, Thrasiline,*
    *and Woodmen*

  *Pha.*  What art thou?
  *C. Fell.*  Almost kill'd I am for a foolish
woman; a knave has hurt her.  114
  *Pha.*  The princess, gentlemen! — Where 's
the wound, madam? Is it dangerous?
  *Are.*  He has not hurt me.
  *C. Fell.*  By God, she lies; h'as hurt her in
the breast;
Look else.
  *Pha.*  O sacred spring of innocent blood!
  *Dion.*  'Tis above wonder! Who should dare
this?  120
  *Are.*  I felt it not.
  *Pha.*  Speak, villain, who has hurt the prin-
cess?
  *C. Fell.*  Is it the princess?
  *Dion.*  Ay.
  *C. Fell.*  Then I have seen something yet.  125
  *Pha.*  But who has hurt her?
  *C. Fell.*  I told you, a rogue; I ne'er saw him
before, I.
  *Pha.*  Madam, who did it?
  *Are.*        Some dishonest wretch;
Alas, I know him not, and do forgive him!
  *C. Fell.*  He 's hurt too; he cannot go far; [130
I made my father's old fox fly about his ears.
  *Pha.*  How will you have me kill him?
  *Are.*  Not at all; 't is some distracted fellow.
  *Pha.*  By this hand, I 'll leave ne'er a piece
of him bigger than a nut, and bring him [135
all to you in my hat.
  *Are.*  Nay, good sir,
If you do take him, bring him quick to me,
And I will study for a punishment
Great as his fault.  140
  *Pha.*  I will.
  *Are.*        But swear.
  *Pha.*        By all my love, I will. ——
Woodmen, conduct the princess to the king,
And bear that wounded fellow to dressing. ——
Come, gentlemen, we 'll follow the chase close.
    *Exeunt [on one side] Pharamond,*
    *Dion, Cleremont, and Thrasiline;*
    *[exit on the other] Arethusa [attended*
    *by] 1 Woodman*
  *C. Fell.*  I pray you, friend, let me see [145
the king.
  *2 Wood.*  That you shall, and receive
thanks.
  *C. Fell.*  If I get clear of this, I 'll go see no
more gay sights.      *Exeunt.*  150

---

⁶⁶ **Upon:** at    ⁷⁶ **then, the way:** ('the way to ioy' Q 1)    ⁹¹⁻⁹² **venies . . . wasters:** cudgel-bouts    ⁹⁶ **God . . . me:** ('God iudge me' Q 1)    ¹¹⁸ **By God:** ('I' faith' Q 3–F)    ¹¹⁹ **sacred:** ('secret' Q 1)    ¹²⁶ **hurt her:** ('done it' Q 1)    ¹³¹ **fox:** sword    ¹³⁴ **hand:** ('ayre' Q 1)    ¹³⁸ **quick:** alive

[SCENE IV. — *Another part of the Forest.*]

*Enter Bellario*

*Bel.* A heaviness near death sits on my brow,
And I must sleep. Bear me, thou gentle bank,
For ever, if thou wilt. You sweet ones all,
                              [*Lies down.*]
Let me unworthy press you; I could wish
I rather were a corse strew'd o'er with you    5
Than quick above you. Dulness shuts mine
    eyes,
And I am giddy: oh, that I could take
So sound a sleep that I might never wake!
                              [*Sleeps.*]
*Enter Philaster*

*Phi.* I have done ill; my conscience calls
    me false
To strike at her that would not strike at me.    10
When I did fight, methought I heard her pray
The gods to guard me. She may be abus'd,
And I a loathed villain; if she be,
She will conceal who hurt her. He has wounds
And cannot follow; neither knows he me.    15
Who 's this? Bellario sleeping! If thou be'st
Guilty, there is no justice that thy sleep
Should be so sound, and mine, whom thou hast
    wrong'd,
So broken. (*Cry within.*) Hark! I am pursued.
    You gods,
I 'll take this offer'd means of my escape.    20
They have no mark to know me by my blood,
If she be true; if false, let mischief light
On all the world at once! Sword, print my
    wounds
Upon this sleeping boy! I ha' none, I think,
Are mortal, nor would I lay greater on thee.    25
                    *He wounds him.*
*Bel.* Oh, death, I hope, is come! Blest be
    that hand!
It meant me well. Again, for pity's sake!
*Phi.* I have caught myself;    *Falls.*
The loss of blood hath stay'd my flight. Here,
    here,    29
Is he that struck thee: take thy full revenge;
Use me, as I did mean thee, worse than death;
I 'll teach thee to revenge. This luckless hand
Wounded the princess; tell my followers
Thou didst receive these hurts in staying me,
And I will second thee; get a reward.    35
*Bel.* Fly, fly, my lord, and save yourself!
*Phi.*                    How 's this?
Wouldst thou I should be safe?
*Bel.*                    Else were it vain
For me to live. These little wounds I have
Ha' not bled much. Reach me that noble
    hand;
I 'll help to cover you.

*Phi.*                    Art thou true to me?    40
*Bel.* Or let me perish loath'd! Come, my
    good lord,
Creep in amongst those bushes; who does
    know
But that the gods may save your much-lov'd
    breath?
*Phi.* Then I shall die for grief, if not for
    this,
That I have wounded thee. What wilt thou
    do?    45
*Bel.* Shift for myself well. Peace! I hear 'em
    come.    [*Philaster creeps into a bush.*]
[*Voices*] *within.* Follow, follow, follow! that
    way they went.
*Bel.* With my own wounds I 'll bloody my
    own sword.
I need not counterfeit to fall; Heaven knows
That I can stand no longer.    *Falls.* 50

*Enter Pharamond, Dion, Cleremont, Thrasiline*

*Pha.* To this place we have track'd him by
    his blood.
*Cle.* Yonder, my lord, creeps one away.
*Dion.* Stay, sir! what are you?
*Bel.* A wretched creature, wounded in these
    woods    54
By beasts. Relieve me, if your names be men,
Or I shall perish.
*Dion.*                    This is he, my lord,
Upon my soul, that hurt her. 'T is the boy,
That wicked boy, that serv'd her.
*Pha.*                    Oh, thou damn'd
In thy creation! What cause couldst thou shape
To hurt the princess?
*Bel.*                    Then I am betray'd.    60
*Dion.* Betray'd! No, apprehended.
*Bel.*                    I confess
(Urge it no more) that, big with evil thoughts,
I set upon her, and did make my aim
Her death. For charity let fall at once
The punishment you mean, and do not load    65
This weary flesh with tortures.
*Pha.*                    I will know
Who hir'd thee to this deed.
*Bel.*                    Mine own revenge.
*Pha.* Revenge! for what?
*Bel.*                    It pleas'd her to receive
Me as her page and, when my fortunes ebb'd,
That men strid o'er them careless, she did
    shower    70
Her welcome graces on me, and did swell
My fortunes till they overflow'd their banks,
Threat'ning the men that cross'd 'em; when, as
    swift
As storms arise at sea, she turn'd her eyes
To burning suns upon me, and did dry    75

---

³ **sweet ones:** flowers   ³⁵ **second:** confirm   ³⁶ **Fly, fly:** ('Hide, hide' Q 1)   ⁴⁰ **true:** ('then true'
**Q 1)**   ⁷⁰ **strid:** strode

The streams she had bestow'd, leaving me
    worse
And more contemn'd than other little brooks,
Because I had been great.  In short, I knew
I could not live, and therefore did desire
To die reveng'd.
    *Pha.*        If tortures can be found  80
Long as thy natural life, resolve to feel
The utmost rigour.
                *Philaster creeps out of a bush.*
    *Cle.*        Help to lead him hence.
    *Phi.*  Turn back, you ravishers of innocence!
Know ye the price of that you bear away
So rudely?
    *Pha.*   Who 's that?
    *Dion.*          'T is the Lord Philaster. 85
    *Phi.*  'T is not the treasure of all kings in one,
The wealth of Tagus, nor the rocks of pearl
That pave the court of Neptune, can weigh
    down
That virtue.  It was I that hurt the princess.
Place me, some god, upon a pyramis    90
Higher than hills of earth, and lend a voice
Loud as your thunder to me, that from thence
I may discourse to all the under-world
The worth that dwells in him!
    *Pha.*          How 's this?
    *Bel.*              My lord, some man
Weary of life, that would be glad to die.  95
    *Phi.*  Leave these untimely courtesies, Bel-
    lario.
    *Bel.*  Alas, he 's mad!  Come, will you lead
    me on?
    *Phi.*  By all the oaths that men ought most
    to keep,
And gods to punish most when men do break,
He touch'd her not. — Take heed, Bellario, 100
How thou dost drown the virtues thou hast
    shown
With perjury. — By all that 's good, 't was I!
You know she stood betwixt me and my right.
    *Pha.*  Thy own tongue be thy judge!
    *Cle.*             It was Philaster.
    *Dion.*  Is 't not a brave boy?  105
Well, sirs, I fear me we were all deceived.
    *Phi.*  Have I no friend here?
    *Dion.*        Yes.
    *Phi.*            Then show it: some
Good body lend a hand to draw us nearer.
Would you have tears shed for you when you
    die?
Then lay me gently on his neck, that there  110
I may weep floods and breathe forth my spirit.
'T is not the wealth of Plutus, nor the gold
                *[Embraces Bel.]*

Lock'd in the heart of earth, can buy away
This arm-full from me; this had been a ran-
    som  114
To have redeem'd the great Augustus Cæsar,
Had he been taken.  You hard-hearted men,
More stony than these mountains, can you
    see
Such clear pure blood drop, and not cut your
    flesh
To stop his life, to bind whose bitter wounds,
Queens ought to tear their hair, and with their
    tears  120
Bathe 'em? — Forgive me, thou that art the
    wealth
Of poor Philaster!

       *Enter King, Arethusa, and Guard*

    *King.*             Is the villain ta'en?
    *Pha.*  Sir, here be two confess the deed; but
    sure
It was Philaster.
    *Phi.*        Question it no more;
It was.
    *King.*  The fellow that did fight with him  125
Will tell us that.
    *Are.*        Aye me! I know he will.
    *King.*  Did not you know him?
    *Are.*            Sir, if it was he,
He was disguis'd.
    *Phi.*         I was so. — Oh, my stars,
That I should live still.            *Aside.*
    *King.*         Thou ambitious fool,
Thou that hast laid a train for thy own life! —
Now I do mean to do, I 'll leave to talk.  131
Bear them to prison.
    *Are.*  Sir, they did plot together to take
    hence
This harmless life; should it pass unreveng'd,
I should to earth go weeping.  Grant me, then,
By all the love a father bears his child,  136
Their custodies, and that I may appoint
Their tortures and their deaths.
    *Dion.*  Death! Soft; our law will not reach
    that for this fault.
    *King.*  'T is granted; take 'em to you with
    a guard. —  140
Come, princely Pharamond, this business past,
We may with more security go on
To your intended match.
         *[Exeunt all except Dion, Cleremont,*
                 *and Thrasiline.]*
    *Cle.*  I pray that this action lose not Philaster
the hearts of the people.  145
    *Dion.*  Fear it not; their over-wise heads will
think it but a trick.         *Exeunt.*

---

    **90 pyramis:** obelisk ('pyramades' Q 1)    **97 lead . . . on:** ('beare me hence' Q 1)    **99 to:** ('do' Q 2–F)    **111 forth:** ('out' Q 3–F)    **112 'T is not . . . Plutus:** ('Not all . . . Pluto' Q 1)    **123 sure:** ('sute' Q 1, 'say' Q 2–F)    **126 that:** (not in Q 4–F)    **128 so:** (Quibbling on one sense of " disguis'd," intoxicated, out of my wits)    **131 leave:** cease    **132 them:** ('him' Q 2–F)    **143 To your:** ('With our' Q 1)

*Actus Quintus. Scena Prima.*

*[Front Stage. Location indefinite.]*

*Enter Dion, Cleremont, and Thrasiline*

*Thra.* Has the king sent for him to death?
*Dion.* Yes; but the king must know 't is not in his power to war with Heaven.
*Cle.* We linger time; the king sent for Philaster and the headsman an hour ago.  5
*Thra.* Are all his wounds well?
*Dion.* All; they were but scratches; but the loss of blood made him faint.
*Cle.* We dally, gentlemen.
*Thra.* Away!  10
*Dion.* We 'll scuffle hard before he perish.
*Exeunt.*

*[SCENE II. — A prison.]*

*Enter Philaster, Arethusa, Bellario*

*Are.* Nay, faith, Philaster, grieve not; we are well.
*Bel.* Nay, good my lord, forbear; we 're wondrous well.
*Phi.* Oh, Arethusa, oh, Bellario, Leave to be kind!
I shall be shut from Heaven, as now from earth,
If you continue so.  I am a man  6
False to a pair of the most trusty ones
That ever earth bore; can it bear us all?
Forgive, and leave me.  But the king hath sent
To call me to my death: oh, show it me,  10
And then forget me!  And for thee, my boy,
I shall deliver words will mollify
The hearts of beasts to spare thy innocence.
*Bel.* Alas, my lord, my life is not a thing
Worthy your noble thoughts! 'T is not a life,  15
'T is but a piece of childhood thrown away.
Should I outlive you, I should then outlive
Virtue and honour; and when that day comes,
If ever I shall close these eyes but once,
May I live spotted for my perjury,  20
And waste by time to nothing!
*Are.* And I (the woful'st maid that ever was,
Forc'd with my hands to bring my lord to death)
Do by the honour of a virgin swear
To tell no hours beyond it!
*Phi.*  Make me not hated so.  25
*Are.* Come from this prison all joyful to our deaths!
*Phi.* People will tear me, when they find you true
To such a wretch as I; I shall die loath'd.

Enjoy your kingdoms peaceably, whilst I
For ever sleep forgotten with my faults.  30
Every just servant, every maid in love,
Will have a piece of me, if you be true.
*Are.* My dear lord, say not so.
*Bel.*  A piece of you!
He was not born of woman that can cut
It and look on.  35
*Phi.* Take me in tears betwixt you, for my heart
Will break with shame and sorrow.
*Are.*  Why, 't is well.
*Bel.* Lament no more.
*Phi.*  Why, what would you have done
If you had wrong'd me basely, and had found
My life no price compar'd to yours?  For love, sirs,  40
Deal with me truly.
*Bel.*  'T was mistaken, sir.
*Phi.* Why, if it were?
*Bel.*  Then, sir, we would have ask'd
You pardon.
*Phi.*  And have hope to enjoy it?
*Are.* Enjoy it! ay.
*Phi.*  Would you indeed?  Be plain.
*Bel.* We would, my lord.
*Phi.*  Forgive me, then.
*Are.*  So, so. 45
*Bel.* 'T is as it should be now.
*Phi.*  Lead to my death. *Exeunt.*

*[SCENE III. — The Palace.]*

*Enter King, Dion, Cleremont, Thrasiline [with a guard]*

*King.* Gentlemen, who saw the prince?
*Cle.* So please you, sir, he 's gone to see the city
And the new platform, with some gentlemen
Attending on him.
*King.*  Is the princess ready
To bring her prisoner out?
*Thra.*  She waits your grace. 5
*King.* Tell her we stay. *[Exit Thrasiline.]*
*Dion.* *[Aside.]* King, you may be deceiv'd yet.
The head you aim at cost more setting on
Than to be lost so lightly.  If it must off, —
Like a wild overflow, that swoops before him
A golden stack, and with it shakes down bridges,  10
Cracks the strong hearts of pines, whose cable-roots
Held out a thousand storms, a thousand thunders,

⁵ **shut:** ('shot' Q 2–F)  ²¹ **by time:** ('by limbs' Q 2; 'my limbs' Q 3–F)  ²² **that:** ('as' F)  **was:** ('liv'd' Q 1)  ²⁵ **tell:** count  ³¹ **servant:** lover  ³³ **dear lord:** ('deerest' Q 1)  ³⁵ **look:** (Perhaps 'I look' should be read.)  ⁴⁰ **no price:** invaluable ('no whit' Q 1)  ⁶ **stay:** wait  ⁹ **swoops:** ('soops' Qq., F)

And, so made mightier, takes whole villages
Upon his back, and in that heat of pride　14
Charges strong towns, towers, castles, palaces,
And lays them desolate; so shall thy head,
Thy noble head, bury the lives of thousands,
That must bleed with thee like a sacrifice,
In thy red ruins.

*Enter Philaster, Arethusa, Bellario in a robe
and garland [and Thrasiline]*

　*King.* How now? What masque is this?　20
　*Bel.* Right royal sir, I should
Sing you an epithalamium of these lovers,
But having lost my best airs with my fortunes,
And wanting a celestial harp to strike
This blessed union on, thus in glad story　25
I give you all. These two fair cedar-branches,
The noblest of the mountain where they grew,
Straightest and tallest, under whose still shades
The worthier beasts have made their lairs, and
　　slept
Free from the fervour of the Sirian star　30
And the fell thunder-stroke, free from the
　　clouds
When they were big with humour and deliver'd
In thousand spouts their issues to the earth:
Oh, there was none but silent quiet there!
Till never-pleased Fortune shut up shrubs,　35
Base under-brambles, to divorce these branches;
And for a while they did so, and did reign
Over the mountain, and choke up his beauty
With brakes, rude thorns and thistles, till the
　　sun
Scorch'd them even to the roots and dried them
　　there.　40
And now a gentle gale hath blown again,
That made these branches meet and twine to-
　　gether,
Never to be unarm'd. The god that sings
His holy numbers over marriage-beds
Hath knit their noble hearts; and here they
　　stand　45
Your children, mighty King; and I have done.
　*King.* How, how?
　*Are.*　　　Sir, if you love it in plain truth,
(For now there is no masquing in 't,) this gen-
　　tleman,
The prisoner that you gave me, is become
My keeper, and through all the bitter throes　50
Your jealousies and his ill fate have wrought
　　him,
Thus nobly hath he struggled, and at length
Arriv'd here my dear husband.

　*King.*　　　Your dear husband! —
Call in the captain of the citadel —
There you shall keep your wedding. I 'll pro-
　　vide　55
A masque shall make your Hymen turn his saf-
　　fron
Into a sullen coat, and sing sad requiems
To your departing souls.
Blood shall put out your torches; and, instead
Of gaudy flowers about your wanton necks,　60
An axe shall hang, like a prodigious meteor,
Ready to crop your loves' sweets. Hear, you
　　gods!
From this time do I shake all title off
Of father to this woman, this base woman;
And what there is of vengeance in a lion　65
Chaf'd among dogs or robb'd of his dear young,
The same, enforc'd more terrible, more mighty,
Expect from me!
　*Are.* Sir, by that little life I have left to
　　swear by,　69
There 's nothing that can stir me from myself.
What I have done, I have done without repent-
　　ance,
For death can be no bugbear unto me,
So long as Pharamond is not my headsman.
　*Dion.* [*Aside.*] Sweet peace upon thy soul,
　　thou worthy maid,
Whene'er thou diest! For this time I 'll excuse
　　thee,　75
Or be thy prologue.
　*Phi.*　　　Sir, let me speak next;
And let my dying words be better with you
Than my dull living actions. If you aim
At the dear life of this sweet innocent,
You are a tyrant and a savage monster,　80
That feeds upon the blood you gave a life to;
Your memory shall be as foul behind you,
As you are living; all your better deeds
Shall be in water writ, but this in marble;　84
No chronicle shall speak you, though your own,
But for the shame of men. No monument,
Though high and big as Pelion, shall be able
To cover this base murder: make it rich
With brass, with purest gold, and shining jas-
　　per,
Like the Pyramides; lay on epitaphs　90
Such as make great men gods; my little marble,
That only clothes my ashes, not my faults,
Shall far outshine it. And for after-issues,
Think not so madly of the heavenly wisdoms,
That they will give you more for your mad
　　rage　95

---

¹⁹ S. D. **Bellario . . . garland:** ('Boy, with a garland of flowers on 's head' Q 1)　³⁰ **the . . . of:** (only in Q 1)　³² **humour:** moisture　³⁶ **divorce:** ('devour' Q 1)　⁴³ **unarm'd:** out of each other's arms ('divided' Q 2–F)　⁴⁶ **mighty:** ('worthy' Q 1)　⁵⁰ **throes:** ('threats' Q 1)　⁵⁶ **saffron:** orange-color, symbolic of weddings　⁶¹ **prodigious:** ominous　⁶⁶ **Chaf'd:** heated by chasing ('Chast' or 'Cast' Q 2–F)　⁷⁵ **excuse:** absolve　⁷⁶ **be thy prologue:** precede thee (in death)　⁸¹ **That . . . to:** (only in Q 1)　⁹³ **after-issues:** prospective children

To cut off, unless it be some snake, or something
Like yourself, that in his birth shall strangle
  you.
Remember my father, King! There was a fault.
But I forgive it. Let that sin persuade you
To love this lady; if you have a soul,           100
Think, save her, and be saved. For myself,
I have so long expected this glad hour,
So languish'd under you, and daily wither'd,
That, Heaven knows, it is a joy to die:
I find a recreation in 't.                        105

*Enter a Messenger*

*Mess.* Where 's the king?
*King.*                Here.
*Mess.*                Get to your strength,
And rescue the Prince Pharamond from danger;
He 's taken prisoner by the citizens,
Fearing the Lord Philaster.
*Dion.* [*Aside.*]           Oh, brave fellows!
Mutiny, my fine dear countrymen, mutiny!    110
Now, my brave valiant foremen, show your
  weapons
In honour of your mistresses!

*Enter another Messenger*

2 *Mess.* Arm, arm, arm, arm!
*King.* A thousand devils take these citizens!
*Dion.* [*Aside.*] A thousand blessings on 'em!
2 *Mess.* Arm, O King! The city is in mu-
  tiny,                                            116
Led by an old gray ruffian, who comes on
In rescue of the Lord Philaster.
*King.* Away to the citadel! I 'll see them
  safe,
And then cope with these burghers. Let the
  guard                                           120
And all the gentlemen give strong attendance.
      *Exeunt all except Dion, Cleremont,*
            *and Thrasiline.*
*Cle.* The city up! This was above our wishes.
*Dion.* Ay, and the marriage too. By my life,
This noble lady has deceiv'd us all.
A plague upon myself, a thousand plagues,    125
For having such unworthy thoughts of her dear
  honour!
Oh, I could beat myself! Or do you beat me,
And I 'll beat you; for we had all one thought.
*Cle.* No no, 't will but lose time.            129
*Dion.* You say true. Are your swords sharp?
— Well, my dear countrymen What-ye-lacks,

if you continue, and fall not back upon the first
broken shin, I 'll have ye chronicled and
chronicled, and cut and chronicled, and all-to
be-prais'd and sung in sonnets, and bawled  [135
in new brave ballads, that all tongues shall troll
you in *sæcula sæculorum*, my kind can-carriers.
*Thra.* What, if a toy take 'em i' th' heels
now, and they run all away, and cry, "the
devil take the hindmost"?                       140
*Dion.* Then the same devil take the foremost
too, and souse him for his breakfast! If they
all prove cowards, my curses fly among them,
and be speeding! May they have murrains
reign to keep the gentlemen at home un-  [145
bound in easy frieze! May the moths branch
their velvets, and their silks only be worn before sore eyes! May their false lights undo
'em, and discover presses, holes, stains, and
oldness in their stuffs, and make them shop-  [150
rid! May they keep whores and horses, and
break; and live mewed up with necks of beef
and turnips! May they have many children,
and none like the father! May they know no
language but that gibberish they prattle to  [155
their parcels, unless it be the goatish Latin they
write in their bonds — and may they write that
false, and lose their debts!

*Enter the King*

*King.* Now the vengeance of all the gods confound them! How they swarm together!  [160
What a hum they raise! — Devils choke your
wide throats! — If a man had need to use their
valours, he must pay a brokage for it; and then
bring 'em on, and they will fight like sheep.
'T is Philaster, none but Philaster, must allay
this heat. They will not hear me speak, but  [166
fling dirt at me and call me tyrant. Oh, run,
dear friend, and bring the Lord Philaster! Speak
him fair; call him prince; do him all the courtesy you can; commend me to him. Oh, my  [170
wits, my wits!                    *Exit Cleremont.*
*Dion.* [*Aside.*] Oh, my brave citizens!
as I live, I will not buy a pin out of your walls
for this. Nay, you shall cozen me, and I 'll
thank you, and send you brawn and bacon, and
soil you every long vacation a brace of fore-  [176
men, that at Michaelmas shall come up fat
and kicking.
*King.* What they will do with this poor
prince, the gods know, and I fear.            180

---

    [106] **Get:** ('Get you' Q 2–F)    **strength:** fortress
lowers' Q 2–F)    [114] **these citizens:** (' 'em' Q 2–F)
**ye-lacks:** shopkeepers    [133] **shin:** ('skin' Q 1)
[135] **bawled** (Heath's conjecture, 'bath'd' Qq.–F)
effective    **murrains:** plagues    [146] **branch:** work
bankrupt    [162] **wide:** ('wild' Q 2–F)    [163] **brokage:**
trymen' Q 2–F)    [174] **cozen:** cheat    [176] **soil:** fatten
ing: ('and foule shall come up fat And in brave liking' Q 1)
    [109] **Fearing:** anxious about    **fellows:** ('fol-
    [123] **my life:** ('all the gods' Q 1)    [131] **What-
have ye:** ('see you' Q 1)    [134] **cut:** pictured
[138] **toy:** whim    [142] **souse:** pickle    [144] **speeding:**
patterns in    [149] **presses:** creases    [152] **break:** go
broker's fee, *i.e.*, press-money    [172] **citizens:** ('coun-
    **foremen:** geese (?)    [176–178] **a brace . . . kick-

*Dion.* [*Aside.*] Why, sir, they 'll flay him,
and make church-buckets on 's skin, to quench
rebellion; then clap a rivet in 's sconce, and
hang him up for a sign.

*Enter Cleremont with Philaster*

*King.* Oh, worthy sir, forgive me! Do not
make                                                            185
Your miseries and my faults meet together,
To bring a greater danger. Be yourself,
Still sound amongst diseases. I have wrong'd
you;
And though I find it last, and beaten to it,
Let first your goodness know it. Calm the
people,                                                         190
And be what you were born to. Take your love,
And with her my repentance, all my wishes,
And all my prayers. By the gods, my heart
speaks this;
And if the least fall from me not perform'd,
May I be struck with thunder!
*Phi.*                                Mighty sir, 195
I will not do your greatness so much wrong,
As not to make your word truth. Free the
princess
And the poor boy, and let me stand the shock
Of this mad sea-breach, which I 'll either turn,
Or perish with it.
*King.*        Let your own word free them. 200
*Phi.* Then thus I take my leave, kissing your
hand,
And hanging on your royal word. Be kingly,
And be not mov'd, sir. I shall bring you peace
Or never bring myself back.
*King.* All the gods go with thee.               205
                                        *Exeunt omnes.*

[SCENE IV. — *A Public Place.*]

*Enter an old Captain and Citizens with Phar-
amond*

*Cap.* Come, my brave myrmidons, let us fall
on.
Let your caps swarm, my boys, and your nimble
tongues
Forget your mother-gibberish of "What do you
lack?"
And set your mouths ope, children, till your
palates

Fall frighted half a fathom past the cure      5
Of bay-salt and gross pepper, and then cry
"Philaster, brave Philaster!" Let Philaster
Be deeper in request, my ding-dongs,
My pairs of dear indentures, kings of clubs,   9
Than your cold water-camlets, or your paintings
Spitted with copper. Let not your hasty silks,
Or your branch'd cloth of bodkin, or your
tissues,
Dearly belov'd of spiced cake and custards,
Your Robin Hoods, Scarlets, and Johns, tie
your affections
In darkness to your shops. No, dainty duckers,
Up with your three-pil'd spirits, your wrought
valours;                                                        16
And let your uncut cholers make the king feel
The measure of your mightiness. Philaster!
Cry, my rose-nobles, cry!
*All.*                        Philaster! Philaster!
*Cap.* How do you like this, my Lord Prince?
These are mad boys, I tell you; these are
things                                                            21
That will not strike their top-sails to a foist,
And let a man of war, an argosy,
Hull and cry cockles.
*Pha.* Why, you rude slave, do you know
what you do?                                                    25
*Cap.* My pretty prince of puppets, we do
know;
And give your greatness warning that you talk
No more such bug's-words, or that solder'd
crown
Shall be scratch'd with a musket. Dear prince
Pippin,
Down with your noble blood, or, as I live,    30
I 'll have you coddled. — Let him loose, my
spirits:
Make us a round ring with your bills, my Hec-
tors,
And let us see what this trim man dares do.
Now, sir, have at you! here I lie;
And with this swashing blow (do you see,
sweet prince?)                                                  35
I could hulk your grace, and hang you up
cross-legg'd,
Like a hare at a poulter's, and do this with
this wiper.
*Pha.* You will not see me murder'd, wicked
villains?

¹⁸² **church-buckets:** fire-buckets (stored in the church)   ¹⁹⁰ **Let . . . it:** ('Let me your goodnesse
know.' Q 1)   ¹⁹⁴ **the . . . perform'd:** my slightest promise is not fulfilled   ²⁰³ **mov'd:** excited   **you:**
('your' Q 2–F)   ³ **mother-gibberish:** native language   ⁸ **ding-dongs:** cockneys   ⁹ **indentures:**
bonds of apprenticeship   **clubs:** the apprentices' weapons   ¹⁰ **cold:** ('cut' Q 1)   **water-camlets:** wool-
and-silk cloth with a wavy surface   ¹² **branch'd . . . bodkin:** figured cloth   ¹³ (Q 1 has 'Deerly be-
lovers of Custards & Cheescakes.')   ¹⁵ **darkness:** ('durance' Q 1)   **duckers:** ingratiating salesmen
¹⁶ **three-pil'd:** superlative   **valours:** (pun on "velours")   ¹⁷ **cholers:** (pun on "collars")   ¹⁹ **rose-
nobles:** (1) coins, (2) noble insurgents   ²² **foist:** small boat   ²⁴ **Hull:** drift   **cry cockles:** waste his
time   ²⁸ **bug's-words:** braggadocio   ³¹ **coddled:** boiled   ³⁵ **swashing:** slashing   ³⁶ **hulk:** disembowel
³⁷ **poulter's:** poultryman's   **wiper:** slang for "weapon"   ³⁸ (From this point to the end of the play
Q 1 diverges entirely from the standard text.)

1 *Cit.* Yes, indeed, will we, sir; we have
not seen one
For a great while.
   *Cap.* He would have weapons, would he? 40
Give him a broadside, my brave boys, with
   your pikes;
Branch me his skin in flowers like a satin,
And between every flower a mortal cut. —
Your royalty shall ravel! — Jag him, gentle-
   men;
I 'll have him cut to the kell, then down the
   seams.                                        45
O for a whip to make him galloon-laces!
I 'll have a coach-whip.
   *Pha.*            Oh, spare me, gentlemen!
   *Cap.* Hold, hold;
The man begins to fear and know himself.
He shall for this time only be seel'd up,  50
With a feather through his nose, that he may
   only
See heaven, and think whither he is going.
Nay, my beyond-sea sir, we will proclaim you:
You would be king!
Thou tender heir apparent to a church-ale, 55
Thou slight prince of single sarcenet,
Thou royal ring-tail, fit to fly at nothing
But poor men's poultry, and have every boy
Beat thee from that too with his bread and
   butter!
   *Pha.* Gods keep me from these hell-hounds!
1 *Cit.* Shall 's geld him, captain? 61
   *Cap.* No, you shall spare his dowcets, my
   dear donsels;
As you respect the ladies, let them flourish.
The curses of a longing woman kill
As speedy as a plague, boys.                     65
   1 *Cit.* I 'll have a leg, that 's certain.
   2 *Cit.*                    I 'll have an arm.
   3 *Cit.* I 'll have his nose, and at mine own
   charge build
A college and clap 't upon the gate.
   4 *Cit.* I 'll have his little gut to string a kit
   with;
For certainly a royal gut will sound like silver.
   *Pha.* Would they were in thy belly, and I
   past                                          71
My pain once!
   5 *Cit.* Good captain, let me have his liver
   to feed ferrets.
   *Cap.* Who will have parcels else? Speak.
   *Pha.* Good gods, consider me! I shall be
   tortur'd.                                     75

1 *Cit.* Captain, I 'll give you the trimming
   of your two-hand sword,
And let me have his skin to make false scab-
   bards.
   2 *Cit.* He had no horns, sir, had he?
   *Cap.* No, sir, he 's a pollard.
What wouldst thou do with horns?
   2 *Cit.*              Oh, if he had had, 80
I would have made rare hafts and whistles of
   'em;
But his shin-bones, if they be sound, shall serve
   me.

                *Enter Philaster*

   *All.* Long live Philaster, the brave Prince
   Philaster!
   *Phi.* I thank you, gentlemen. But why are
   these
Rude weapons brought abroad, to teach your
   hands                                         85
Uncivil trades?
   *Cap.*         My royal Rosicleer,
We are thy myrmidons, thy guard, thy roarers;
And when thy noble body is in durance,
Thus do we clap our musty morions on,
And trace the streets in terror. Is it peace, 90
Thou Mars of men? Is the king sociable,
And bids thee live? Art thou above thy foe-
   men,
And free as Phœbus? Speak. If not, this
   stand
Of royal blood shall be abroach, a-tilt,
And run even to the lees of honour.              95
   *Phi.* Hold, and be satisfied. I am myself,
Free as my thoughts are; by the gods, I am!
   *Cap.* Art thou the dainty darling of the
   king?
Art thou the Hylas to our Hercules?
Do the lords bow, and the regarded scarlets
Kiss their gumm'd golls, and cry, "We are
   your servants"?                              101
Is the court navigable and the presence stuck
With flags of friendship? If not, we are thy
   castle,
And this man sleeps.
   *Phi.* I am what I desire to be, your friend;
I am what I was born to be, your prince. 106
   *Pha.* Sir, there is some humanity in you;
You have a noble soul. Forget my name,
And know my misery; set me safe aboard
From these wild cannibals, and as I live, 110
I 'll quit this land for ever. There is nothing,—

⁴² **Branch me:** figure    ⁴⁵ **kell:** caul    **seams:** layers of fat    ⁴⁶ **galloon-laces:** ribbons    ⁵⁰ **seel'd
up:** have his eyelids sewn together    ⁵⁵ **church-ale:** parish supper    ⁵⁶ **single sarcenet:** thin silk
⁵⁷ **ring-tail:** buzzard    ⁶² **donsels:** young gentlemen    ⁶⁷⁻⁶⁸ (Alluding to Brasenose College, Oxford).
⁶⁹ **kit:** lute    ⁷⁴ **parcels:** portions    ⁷⁹ **pollard:** dehorned beast    ⁸⁶ **Rosicleer:** hero of a popular
Spanish romance, *The Mirror of Knighthood*    ⁸⁹ **morions:** open-faced helmets    ⁹³ **stand:** tub
⁹⁴ **a-tilt:** tilted up    ¹⁰⁰ **regarded scarlets:** dignitaries, judges    ¹⁰¹ **gumm'd golls:** perfumed hands
¹⁰² **presence:** king's chamber

Perpetual prisonment, cold, hunger, sickness
Of all sorts, of all dangers, and all together,
The worst company of the worst men, madness,
  age,
To be as many creatures as a woman, 115
And do as all they do, nay, to despair, —
But I would rather make it a new nature,
And live with all these, than endure one hour
Amongst these wild dogs.
  *Phi.* I do pity you. — Friends, discharge
  your fears; 120
Deliver me the prince. I 'll warrant you
I shall be old enough to find my safety.
  *3 Cit.* Good sir, take heed he does not hurt
  you;
He is a fierce man, I can tell you, sir.
                                *He strives.*
  *Cap.* Prince, by your leave, I 'll have a sur-
  cingle, 125
And mail you like a hawk.
  *Phi.* Away, away, there is no danger in
  him:
Alas, he had rather sleep to shake his fit off!
Look you, friends, how gently he leads! Upon
  my word,
He 's tame enough, he needs no further watch-
  ing. 130
Good my friends, go to your houses,
And by me have your pardons and my love;
And know there shall be nothing in my power
You may deserve, but you shall have your
  wishes.
To give you more thanks, were to flatter you:
Continue still your love; and for an earnest, 136
Drink this. [*Gives money.*]
  *All.* Long mayst thou live, brave prince,
  brave prince, brave prince!
                        *Exeunt Phi. and Pha.*
  *Cap.* Go thy ways, thou art the king of
  courtesy!
Fall off again, my sweet youths. Come, 140
And every man trace to his house again,
And hang his pewter up; then to the tavern,
And bring your wives in muffs. We will have
  music;
And the red grape shall make us dance and
  rise, boys. *Exeunt.*

[SCENE V. — *The Palace.*]

*Enter King, Arethusa, Galatea, Megra, Dion,
Cleremont, Thrasiline, Bellario, and Attendants*

  *King.* Is it appeas'd?
  *Dion.* Sir, all is quiet as this dead of
  night,

As peaceable as sleep. My lord Philaster
Brings on the prince himself.
  *King.* Kind gentleman!
I will not break the least word I have given 5
In promise to him. I have heap'd a world
Of grief upon his head, which yet I hope
To wash away.

        *Enter Philaster and Pharamond*

  *Cle.* My lord is come.
  *King.* My son!
Blest be the time that I have leave to call
Such virtue mine! Now thou art in mine arms,
Methinks I have a salve unto my breast 11
For all the stings that dwell there. Streams of
  grief
That I have wrong'd thee, and as much of joy
That I repent it, issue from mine eyes;
Let them appease thee. Take thy right; take
  her; 15
She is thy right too; and forget to urge
My vexed soul with that I did before.
  *Phi.* Sir, it is blotted from my memory,
Past and forgotten. — For you, prince of Spain,
Whom I have thus redeem'd, you have full leave
To make an honourable voyage home. 21
And if you would go furnish'd to your realm
With fair provision, I do see a lady,
Methinks, would gladly bear you company.
How like you this piece?
  *Meg.* Sir, he likes it well, 25
For he hath tried it, and hath found it worth
His princely liking. We were ta'en abed;
I know your meaning. I am not the first
That nature taught to seek a fellow forth.
Can shame remain perpetually in me, 30
And not in others? Or have princes salves
To cure ill names, that meaner people want?
  *Phi.* What mean you?
  *Meg.* You must get another ship,
To bear the princess and her boy together.
  *Dion.* How now! 35
  *Meg.* Others took me, and I took her and him
At that all women may be ta'en sometime.
Ship us all four, my lord; we can endure
Weather and wind alike.
  *King.* Clear thou thyself, or know not me
  for father. 40
  *Are.* This earth, how false it is! What
  means is left for me
To clear myself? It lies in your belief.
My lords, believe me; and let all things else
Struggle together to dishonour me.
  *Bel.* Oh, stop your ears, great King, that I
  may speak 45
As freedom would! Then I will call this lady

124 S. D. **He:** *i.e.*, Pharamond 125 **surcingle:** girdle 126 **mail:** wrap 140 **Fall off:** disband
141 **trace:** move on 142 **pewter:** arms 4 **gentleman:** ('gentlemen' Qq., F) 13 **wrong'd:** ('wrought'
Qq., F)

As base as are her actions.  Hear me, sir;
Believe your heated blood when it rebels
Against your reason, sooner than this lady.
   *Meg.*  By this good light, he bears it hand-
    somely.                                         50
   *Phi.*  This lady!  I will sooner trust the wind
With feathers, or the troubled sea with pearl,
Than her with anything.  Believe her not.
Why, think you, if I did believe her words,
I would outlive 'em?  Honour cannot take  55
Revenge on you;  then what were to be known
But death?
   *King.*  Forget her, sir, since all is knit
Between us.  But I must request of you
One favour, and will sadly be denied.
   *Phi.*  Command, whate'er it be.
   *King.*                          Swear to be true  60
To what you promise.
   *Phi.*                     By the powers above,
Let it not be the death of her or him,
And it is granted!
   *King.*                 Bear away that boy
To torture;  I will have her clear'd or buried.
   *Phi.*  Oh, let me call my word back, worthy
    sir!                                            65
Ask something else:  bury my life and right
In one poor grave;  but do not take away
My life and fame at once.
   *King.*  Away with him!  It stands irrevocable.
   *Phi.*  Turn all your eyes on me.  Here stands
    a man,                                          70
The falsest and the basest of this world.
Set swords against this breast, some honest man,
For I have liv'd till I am pitied!
My former deeds were hateful;  but this last
Is pitiful, for I unwillingly               75
Have given the dear preserver of my life
Unto his torture.  Is it in the power
Of flesh and blood to carry this, and live?
               *Offers to kill himself.*
   *Are.*  Dear sir, be patient yet!  Oh, stay
    that hand!
   *King.*  Sirs, strip that boy.
   *Dion.*               Come, sir;  your tender flesh  80
Will try your constancy.
   *Bel.*                    Oh, kill me, gentlemen!
   *Dion.*  No. — Help, sirs.
   *Bel.*                     Will you torture me?
   *King.*                              Haste there;
Why stay you?
   *Bel.*          Then I shall not break my vow,
You know, just gods, though I discover all.
   *King.*  How 's that?  Will he confess?
   *Dion.*                          Sir, so he says.  85
   *King.*  Speak then.
   *Bel.*               Great King, if you command
This lord to talk with me alone, my tongue

Urg'd by my heart, shall utter all the thoughts
My youth hath known;  and stranger things
   than these
You hear not often.
   *King.*              Walk aside with him.  90
             *[Dion and Bellario walk apart.]*
   *Dion.*  Why speak'st thou not?
   *Bel.*                    Know you this face, my lord?
   *Dion.*  No.
   *Bel.*       Have you not seen it, nor the like?
   *Dion.*  Yes, I have seen the like, but readily
I know not where.
   *Bel.*             I have been often told
In court of one Euphrasia, a lady,         95
And daughter to you;  betwixt whom and me
(They that would flatter my bad face would
   swear)
There was such strange resemblance, that we two
Could not be known asunder, dress'd alike.
   *Dion.*  By Heaven, and so there is!
   *Bel.*                      For her fair sake,  100
Who now doth spend the spring-time of her life
In holy pilgrimage, move to the king,
That I may scape this torture.
   *Dion.*                    But thou speak'st
As like Euphrasia as thou dost look.
How came it to thy knowledge that she lives  105
In pilgrimage?
   *Bel.*           I know it not, my lord;
But I have heard it, and do scarce believe it.
   *Dion.*  Oh, my shame!  is 't possible?  Draw
    near,
That I may gaze upon thee.  Art thou she, 109
Or else her murderer?  Where wert thou born?
   *Bel.*  In Syracusa.
   *Dion.*            What 's thy name?
   *Bel.*                            Euphrasia.
   *Dion.*  Oh, 't is just, 't is she!
Now I do know thee.  Oh, that thou hadst died,
And I had never seen thee nor my shame!
How shall I own thee?  Shall this tongue of
   mine                                        115
E'er call thee daughter more?
   *Bel.*  Would I had died indeed!  I wish it too;
And so I must have done by vow, ere publish'd
What I have told, but that there was no means
To hide it longer.  Yet I joy in this,     120
The princess is all clear.
   *King.*                  What, have you done?
   *Dion.*  All is discover'd.
   *Phi.*                    Why then hold you me?
All is discover'd!  Pray you, let me go.
            *He offers to stab himself.*
   *King.*  Stay him.
   *Are.*            What is discover'd?
   *Dion.*                         Why, my shame.
It is a woman;  let her speak the rest.    125

---

**⁵⁹ sadly:** (perhaps misprint for 'hardly')  **¹¹⁰ murderer:** (alluding to the savage belief that a slayer acquired the characteristics of his victim)

*Phi.* How? That again!

*Dion.*                                    It is a woman.

*Phi.* Blest be you powers that favour innocence!

*King.* Lay hold upon that lady.

[*Megra is seized.*]

*Phi.* It is a woman, sir! — Hark, gentlemen,
It is a woman! — Arethusa, take          130
My soul into thy breast, that would be gone
With joy. It is a woman! Thou art fair,
And virtuous still to ages, in despite
Of malice.

*King.* Speak you, where lies his shame?

*Bel.*                          I am his daughter. 135

*Phi.* The gods are just.

*Dion.* I dare accuse none; but, before you
two,
The virtue of our age, I bend my knee
For mercy.                          [*Kneels.*]

*Phi.*    Take it freely; for I know,
Though what thou didst were undiscreetly
done,                                      140
'T was meant well.

*Are.*                          And for me,
I have a power to pardon sins, as oft
As any man has power to wrong me.

*Cle.* Noble and worthy!

*Phi.*                    But, Bellario,
(For I must call thee still so,) tell me why 145
Thou didst conceal thy sex. It was a fault,
A fault, Bellario, though thy other deeds
Of truth outweigh'd it: all these jealousies
Had flown to nothing if thou hadst discover'd
What now we know.

*Bel.*              My father oft would speak 150
Your worth and virtue; and, as I did grow
More and more apprehensive, I did thirst
To see the man so prais'd. But yet all this
Was but a maiden-longing, to be lost
As soon as found; till, sitting in my window, 155
Printing my thoughts in lawn, I saw a god,
I thought, (but it was you,) enter our gates.
My blood flew out and back again, as fast
As I had puff'd it forth and suck'd it in 159
Like breath. Then was I call'd away in haste
To entertain you. Never was a man,
Heav'd from a sheep-cote to a sceptre, rais'd
So high in thoughts as I. You left a kiss
Upon these lips then, which I mean to keep
From you for ever. I did hear you talk,    165
Far above singing. After you were gone,
I grew acquainted with my heart, and search'd
What stirr'd it so: alas, I found it love!
Yet far from lust; for, could I but have liv'd
In presence of you, I had had my end.      170
For this I did delude my noble father
With a feign'd pilgrimage, and dress'd myself

In habit of a boy; and, for I knew
My birth no match for you, I was past hope
Of having you; and, understanding well    175
That when I made discovery of my sex
I could not stay with you, I made a vow,
By all the most religious things a maid
Could call together, never to be known,
Whilst there was hope to hide me from men's
eyes,                                      180
For other than I seem'd, that I might ever
Abide with you. Then sat I by the fount,
Where first you took me up.

*King.*                    Search out a match
Within our kingdom, where and when thou
wilt,
And I will pay thy dowry; and thyself      185
Wilt well deserve him.

*Bel.*                  Never, sir, will I
Marry; it is a thing within my vow:
But, if I may have leave to serve the princess,
To see the virtues of her lord and her,
I shall have hope to live.

*Are.*                    I, Philaster,       190
Cannot be jealous, though you had a lady
Dress'd like a page to serve you; nor will I
Suspect her living here. — Come, live with me;
Live free as I do. She that loves my lord,
Curs'd be the wife that hates her!         195

*Phi.* I grieve such virtue should be laid in
earth
Without an heir. — Hear me, my royal father:
Wrong not the freedom of our souls so much,
To think to take revenge of that base woman;
Her malice cannot hurt us. Set her free    200
As she was born, saving from shame and sin.

*King.* Set her at liberty. — But leave the
court;
This is no place for such. — You, Pharamond,
Shall have free passage, and a conduct home
Worthy so great a prince. When you come
there,                                     205
Remember 't was your faults that lost you her,
And not my purpos'd will.

*Pha.*                    I do confess,
Renowned sir.

*King.* Last, join your hands in one. Enjoy,
Philaster,
This kingdom, which is yours, and, after me, 210
Whatever I call mine. My blessing on you!
All happy hours be at your marriage-joys,
That you may grow yourselves over all lands,
And live to see your plenteous branches spring
Wherever there is sun! Let princes learn   215
By this to rule the passions of their blood;
For what Heaven wills can never be withstood.

*Exeunt omnes.*

---

[152] **apprehensive:** understanding    [153] **prais'd:** ('rais'd' Qq.,F)    [156] **Printing . . . lawn:** embroidering

# The Maids Tragedie.

## AS IT HATH BEENE

diuers times Acted at the *Black-Friers* by
the Kings Maiesties Seruants.

Newly perufed, augmented, and inlarged, This fecond Impreffion.

ASPATIA.    AMINTOR,

LONDON,
Printed for *Francis Conftable*, and are
to be fold at the White LION in
*Pauls* Church-yard. 1622.

BIBLIOGRAPHICAL RECORD. *The Maid's Tragedy*, like *Philaster*, was not printed till about a decade after its production on the stage, but was thereafter deservedly popular with the reading public. It was registered at Stationers' Hall by Richard Higgenbotham and Francis Constable, the entry reading: — *28° Aprilis 1619. Master Higgenbotham, Master Constable. Entred for their copie vnder the handes of Sir George Buck and both the wardens A play Called The maides tragedy. vj^d.*

The First Quarto was accordingly published in 1619 by Constable, who in 1622 brought out the second, described as *Newly perused, augmented, and inlarged.* The chief difficulty about the text concerns the differences between these two editions. The second introduces nearly a hundred new lines, together with phrasal variants so numerous and often so debatable that only a very elaborate critical apparatus can handle them. Q 2 is in general the most trustworthy text of the play, but it was issued six years after the death of the chief author and cannot claim to give in all respects his authentic final revision. We have included some genuine lines in Q 1 which it omits and have frequently substituted Q 1 readings where Q 2 shows signs of theatrical manipulation.

The Third Quarto was prepared for by the following notice of transfer in the Stationers' Register: — *27° Octobris, 1629. Master Hawkins. Assigned ouer vnto him by Master Heggenbotham and Master Constable All their and either of their estate right title and Interest in the Copie Called The Maides Tragedie, done by Consent of master Bill warden vnder his hand. vj^d.* Richard Hawkins consequently published in 1630 "The Third Impression, Revised and Refined," which for the first time specified the names of the authors, but made only three or four significant changes in the text of Q 2. The Fourth Quarto appeared in 1638, the fifth in 1641, the sixth (claiming falsely to be "Revised and Corrected exactly by the Original") in 1650 and, in a reissue, in 1661. *The Maid's Tragedy* (like the other plays which had already been printed separately) was omitted from the Beaumont-Fletcher Folio of 1647, but in the second Folio of 1679 (referred to as F in our notes) it is given the place of honor as the first play in the volume.

DATE AND STAGE PERFORMANCE. All the quarto editions state that *The Maid's Tragedy* had been acted at the Blackfriars Theatre by the King's Company (Shakespeare's) — which would point to a period not earlier than the autumn of 1609, when the King's men first began using the Blackfriars private theatre. The fact that Sir George Buck, who licensed this play at some unrecorded time, nicknamed another work, presented to him without title in October, 1611, "The *Second* Maiden's Tragedy," implies that our play was then familiar to him. The two years covered by these limits pretty certainly saw the first performance, and the possible dates are still further restricted by the fact that during much of 1609 and 1610 the theatres were closed by plague. With Burbage in the part of Melantius it was performed at Court during the season 1612–1613. It was produced at Hampton Court, Nov. 29, 1636, and revived at the Red Bull playhouse by the King's Company, Nov. 17, 1660, becoming one of the most popular pieces of the Restoration age. "Of all our elder Plays," wrote Edmund Waller of it, "This and *Philaster* have the loudest fame." For Waller's revision of the last act, eliminating the killing of the king, and the general history of the play after 1660, see A. C. Sprague, *Beaumont and Fletcher on the Restoration Stage.*

AUTHORSHIP. *The Maid's Tragedy* is mainly the work of Beaumont. Fletcher's recognizable style appears in only about five hundred lines (Act II. ii, Act IV. i, Act V. i [to Evadne's exit] and ii). One casual inconsistency arising from double authorship is seen in the fact that whereas Beaumont has in III. ii made Amintor reveal to Melantius the king's connection with Evadne, Fletcher makes the next scene (IV. i) focus upon Melantius's effort to secure just this information. It is Beaumont who passionately avows the divinity that doth hedge a king (II. ii. 308 ff., etc.), and Fletcher who asserts (V. ii. 37 ff.) the regicidal rights of the outraged subject.

SOURCES. The plot is the free invention of the dramatists, who may be suspected to have written into the effective characters of the two heroes some reflection of their own famous friendship and of their dissimilar but complementary personalities. One sees much of Beaumont in Amintor and of Fletcher in Melantius. The great quarrel scene in III. ii is no mere copy of the quarrel between Brutus and Cassius in *Julius Cæsar*, but was probably written with a conscious eye upon it. Professor W. D. Briggs has shown (*Modern Language Notes*, Dec., 1916) that the episode of Melantius, Calianax, and the King in IV. ii has a close analogue in Valerius Maximus.

STRUCTURE. The acts, but not scenes, are divided in the old copies. The action occurs in three or four parts of the city of Rhodes, and is limited to two nights and a day. There are few better built plays, whether one considers the variety and vividness of the characters, the skilful meshing and compression of the intricate plot, or the histrionic opportunity offered by the greater scenes. The introduction of a complete court masque, with its social background, at the close of Act I is a *tour de force* that must have added to the novelty of the play.

# FRANCIS BEAUMONT AND JOHN FLETCHER

## THE MAID'S TRAGEDY

### PERSONS REPRESENTED IN THE PLAY

KING
LYSIPPUS, brother to the King
AMINTOR, a noble Gentleman
MELANTIUS, } brothers to Evadne
DIPHILUS,
CALIANAX, an old humorous Lord, and father to
  Aspatia
CLEON, } Gentlemen
STRATO,
DIAGORAS, a servant

EVADNE, wife to Amintor
ASPATIA, troth-plight wife to Amintor
ANTIPHILA, } waiting gentlewomen to Aspatia
OLYMPIAS,
DULA, a Lady, [attendant on Evadne]

MASQUERS

Night, Cynthia, Neptune, Æolus, [Sea Gods,
  Winds]

SCENE: The City of Rhodes

### Actus Primus. Scena Prima

[*The King's Palace.*]

*Enter Cleon, Strato, Lysippus, Diphilus*

*Cle.* The rest are making ready, sir.
*Lys.*                    So let them;
There 's time enough.
  *Diph.* You are the brother to the king, my
    lord;
We 'll take your word.
  *Lys.* Strato, thou hast some skill in poetry; 5
What think'st thou of the masque? Will it be
    well?
  *Stra.* As well as masques can be.
  *Lys.*                    As masques can be!
  *Stra.* Yes; they must commend their king,
    and speak in praise
Of the assembly, bless the bride and bride-
    groom
In person of some god; they 're tied to rules 10
Of flattery.
  *Cle.*      See, good my lord, who is return'd!

*Enter Melantius*

  *Lys.* Noble Melantius, the land by me
Welcomes thy virtues home to Rhodes;
Thou that with blood abroad buyest us our
    peace!
The breath of kings is like the breath of gods;
My brother wish'd thee here, and thou art
    here.                    15
He will be too too kind, and weary thee

With often welcomes; but the time doth give
    thee
A welcome above his or all the world's.
  *Mel.* My lord, my thanks; but these
    scratch'd limbs of mine                20
Have spoke my love and truth unto my friends,
More than my tongue e'er could. My mind 's
    the same
It ever was to you: where I find worth,
I love the keeper till he let it go,
And then I follow it.
  *Diph.*           Hail, worthy brother! 25
He that rejoices not at your return
In safety is mine enemy for ever.
  *Mel.* I thank thee, Diphilus. But thou art
    faulty:
I sent for thee to exercise thine arms
With me at Patria; thou cam'st not, Diphilus;
'T was ill.
  *Diph.* My noble brother, my excuse     31
Is my king's straight command, which you, my
    lord,
Can witness with me.
  *Lys.*           'T is most true, Melantius;
He might not come till the solemnities
Of this great match were past.
  *Diph.*                Have you heard of it? 35
  *Mel.* Yes, and have given cause to those that
    here
Envy my deeds abroad to call me gamesome:
I have no other business here at Rhodes.
  *Lys.* We have a masque to-night, and you
    must tread
A soldier's measure.                    40

---

¹ **Lys.:** (speech assigned to Strato Q 2–F)     ¹³ **to Rhodes:** (not in Q 1)     ¹⁴ **blood . . . peace:**
('blowes abroad bringst us our peace at home' Q 1)     ¹⁷ **too too:** very     ³⁰ **Patria:** Patara, seaport of
Asia Minor, 60 miles east of Rhodes     ³⁶ (Altered in Q 2–F)

*Mel.* These soft and silken wars are not for
        me:
The music must be shrill and all confus'd
That stirs my blood; and then I dance with
        arms.
But is Amintor wed?
        *Diph.*                This day.
*Mel.* All joys upon him! for he is my friend.
Wonder not that I call a man so young my
        friend:                                            46
His worth is great; valiant he is and temper-
        ate;
And one that never thinks his life his own,
If his friend need it.   When he was a boy,
As oft as I return'd (as, without boast,    50
I brought home conquest), he would gaze upon
        me
And view me round, to find in what one limb
The virtue lay to do those things he heard;
Then would he wish to see my sword, and feel
The quickness of the edge, and in his hand   55
Weigh it.   He oft would make me smile at this.
His youth did promise much, and his ripe years
Will see it all perform'd.

                *Enter Aspatia, passing by*

                        Hail, maid and wife!
Thou fair Aspatia, may the holy knot
That thou hast tied to-day last till the hand   60
Of age undo 't!   May'st thou bring a race
Unto Amintor, that may fill the world
Successively with soldiers!
        *Asp.*                My hard fortunes
Deserve not scorn, for I was never proud
When they were good.            *Exit Aspatia.*
        *Mel.*        How 's this?
        *Lys.*                You are mistaken, sir;   65
She is not married.
        *Mel.*        You said Amintor was.
        *Diph.* 'T is true; but ——
        *Mel.*        Pardon me; I did receive
Letters at Patria from my Amintor,
That he should marry her.
        *Diph.*                And so it stood
In all opinion long; but your arrival    70
Made me imagine you had heard the change.
        *Mel.* Who has he taken then?
        *Lys.*                A lady, sir,
That bears the light above her, and strikes dead
With flashes of her eye: the fair Evadne,
Your virtuous sister.
        *Mel.*        Peace of heart betwixt them!   75
But this is strange.
        *Lys.*        The king, my brother, did it
To honour you; and these solemnities
Are at his charge.

*Mel.* 'T is royal, like himself.   But I am sad
My speech bears so infortunate a sound    80
To beautiful Aspatia.   There is rage
Hid in her father's breast, Calianax,
Bent long against me; and he should not think,
Could I but call it back, that I would take
So base revenges, as to scorn the state    85
Of his neglected daughter.   Holds he still
His greatness with the king?
        *Lys.*                Yes.   But this lady
Walks discontented, with her watery eyes
Bent on the earth.   The unfrequented woods
Are her delight; where, when she sees a bank
Stuck full of flowers, she with a sigh will tell   91
Her servants what a pretty place it were
To bury lovers in; and make her maids
Pluck 'em, and strow her over like a corse.
She carries with her an infectious grief,   95
That strikes all her beholders: she will sing
The mournful'st things that ever ear hath heard,
And sigh, and sing again; and when the rest
Of our young ladies, in their wanton blood,
Tell mirthful tales in course, that fill the room
With laughter, she will, with so sad a look,   101
Bring forth a story of the silent death
Of some forsaken virgin, which her grief
Will put in such a phrase that, ere she end,
She 'll send them weeping one by one away.   105
        *Mel.* She has a brother under my command,
Like her; a face as womanish as hers;
But with a spirit that hath much outgrown
The number of his years.

                *Enter Amintor*

        *Cle.*                My lord the bridegroom!
        *Mel.* I might run fiercely, not more hastily,
Upon my foe.   I love thee well, Amintor;   111
My mouth is much too narrow for my heart;
I joy to look upon those eyes of thine;
Thou art my friend, but my disorder'd speech
Cuts off my love.
        *Amin.*        Thou art Melantius:   115
All love is spoke in that.   A sacrifice,
To thank the gods Melantius is return'd
In safety!   Victory sits on his sword,
As she was wont.   May she build there and
        dwell;
And may thy armour be, as it hath been,   120
Only thy valour and thine innocence!
What endless treasures would our enemies give,
That I might hold thee still thus!
        *Mel.*                I am poor
In words; but credit me, young man, thy
        mother   124
Could do no more but weep for joy to see thee
After long absence.   All the wounds I have

⁴³ with arms: (not in Q 1)   ⁴⁶ my friend: (not in Q 1)   ⁴⁷ and temperate: (not in Q 1)   ⁷² has:
('hath' Q 2–F)   ⁷³ bears . . . light: shines   ⁸⁴ Could I but: ('If I could' Q 2–F)   ⁸⁵ So: ('Such'
Q 1)   ⁸⁶⁻⁸⁷ Holds . . . king: (not in Q 1)   ¹⁰⁰ in course: one by one

Fetch'd not so much away, nor all the cries
Of widowed mothers. But this is peace,
And that was war.
    *Amin.*            Pardon, thou holy god
Of marriage-bed, and frown not, I am forc'd,
In answer of such noble tears as those,     131
To weep upon my wedding-day!
    *Mel.* I fear thou art grown too fickle; for I
    hear
A lady mourns for thee, men say, to death;
Forsaken of thee, on what terms I know not.
    *Amin.* She had my promise; but the king
forbade it,     136
And made me make this worthy change, thy
    sister,
Accompanied with graces above her,
With whom I long to lose my lusty youth
And grow old in her arms.
    *Mel.*           Be prosperous!   140

*Enter Messenger*

*Mess.* My lord, the masquers rage for you.
*Lys.* We are gone. Cleon, Strato, Diphilus!
*Amin.* We 'll all attend you. —
          *Exeunt Lysippus, Cleon, Strato,*
          *Diphilus [and Messenger].*
          We shall trouble you
With our solemnities.
    *Mel.*           Not so, Amintor;
But if you laugh at my rude carriage   145
In peace, I 'll do as much for you in war,
When you come thither. Yet I have a mistress
To bring to your delights; rough though I am,
I have a mistress, and she has a heart,   149
She says; but, trust me, it is stone, no better;
There is no place that I can challenge in 't.
But you stand still, and here my way lies.
          *Exeunt [severally].*

[SCENE II. — *The Banqueting Hall.*]

*Enter Calianax with Diagoras*

*Cal.* Diagoras, look to the doors better, for
shame! You let in all the world, and anon the
king will rail at me. Why, very well said. By
Jove, the king will have the show i' th' court!
*Diag.* Why do you swear so, my lord? You
know he 'll have it here.   6
*Cal.* By this light, if he be wise, he will not.
*Diag.* And if he will not be wise, you are for-
sworn.
*Cal.* One must sweat out his heart with swear-
ing, and get thanks on no side. I 'll be gone, [11
look to 't who will.
*Diag.* My lord, I shall never keep them out.
Pray, stay; your looks will terrify them.
*Cal.* My looks terrify them, you coxcom- [15

bly ass, you! I 'll be judged by all the company
whether thou hast not a worse face than I.
*Diag.* I mean, because they know you and
your office.
*Cal.* Office! I would I could put it off! I [20
am sure I sweat quite through my office. I
might have made room at my daughter's wedding; — they ha' near kill'd her among them; —
and now I must do service for him that hath
forsaken her. Serve that will!     *Exit.* 25
*Diag.* He 's so humorous since his daughter
was forsaken! (*Knock within.*) Hark, hark!
there, there! so, so! codes, codes! What now?
*Mel.* Open the door.     *Within.*
*Diag.* Who 's there?   30
*Mel.* [*within.*] Melantius.
*Diag.* I hope your lordship brings no troop
with you; for, if you do, I must return them.
          [*Opens the door.*]

*Enter Melantius and a Lady*

*Mel.* None but this lady, sir.
*Diag.* The ladies are all placed above, save [35
those that come in the king's troop; the best of
Rhodes sit there, and there 's room.
*Mel.* I thank you, sir. —When I have seen you
placed, madam, I must attend the king; but,
the masque done, I 'll wait on you again.   40
*Diag.* [*opening another door.*] Stand back
there! — Room for my Lord Melantius! (*Exeunt Melantius and Lady.*) — Pray, bear
back — this is no place for such youth and
their trulls — let the doors shut again. — No!
— do your heads itch? I 'll scratch them for [46
you. [*Shuts the door.*] — So, now thrust and hang.
[*Knocking within.*] — Again! who is 't now? — I
cannot blame my Lord Calianax for going
away; would he were here! He would run [50
raging amongst them, and break a dozen wiser
heads than his own in the twinkling of an eye.
— What 's the news now?
    [*Voice*] *within.* I pray you, can you help me
to the speech of the master-cook?   55
*Diag.* If I open the door, I 'll cook some of
your calves-heads. Peace, rogues! [*Knocking
within.*] — Again! who is 't?
*Mel.* Melantius.     *Within.*

*Enter Calianax*

*Cal.* Let him not in.   60
*Diag.* O, my lord, a' must. [*Opening the door.*]
— Make room there for my lord. Is your lady
plac'd?

*Enter Melantius*

*Mel.* Yes, sir. I thank you. —
My Lord Calianax, well met.   65
Your causeless hate to me I hope is buried.

*Cal.* Yes, I do service for your sister here,
That brings mine own poor child to timeless
death.
She loves your friend Amintor; such another
False-hearted lord as you.
   *Mel.*            You do me wrong, 70
A most unmanly one, and I am slow
In taking vengeance : but be well advis'd.
   *Cal.* It may be so. — Who plac'd the lady
there
So near the presence of the king?
   *Mel.*                 I did.
   *Cal.* My lord, she must not sit there.
   *Mel.*                 Why? 75
   *Cal.* The place is kept for women of more
worth.
   *Mel.* More worth than she! It misbecomes
your age
And place to be thus womanish : forbear!
What you have spoke, I am content to think
The palsy shook your tongue to.
   *Cal.*           Why, 't is well, 80
If I stand here to place men's wenches.
   *Mel.*                    I
Shall quite forget this place, thy age, my safety,
And, through all, cut that poor sickly week
Thou has to live away from thee.
   *Cal.* Nay, I know you can fight for your
whore.           85
   *Mel.* Bate me the king, and, be he flesh and
blood,
A' lies that says it! Thy mother at fifteen
Was black and sinful to her.
   *Diag.*         Good my lord —
   *Mel.* Some god pluck threescore years from
that fond man,         89
That I may kill him, and not stain mine honour!
It is the curse of soldiers, that in peace
They shall be brav'd by such ignoble men
As, if the land were troubled, would with tears
And knees beg succour from 'em. Would the
blood,
That sea of blood, that I have lost in fight, 95
Were running in thy veins, that it might make
thee
Apt to say less, or able to maintain,
Should'st thou say more! This Rhodes, I see, is
nought
But a place privileg'd to do men wrong.
   *Cal.* Ay, you may say your pleasure.

*Enter Amintor*

   *Amin.*          What vild wrong 100
Has stirr'd my worthy friend, who is as slow
To fight with words as he is quick of hands?
   *Mel.* That heap of age, which I should rever-
ence

If it were temperate, but testy years
Are most contemptible.
   *Amin.*         Good sir, forbear. 105
   *Cal.* There is just such another as yourself.
   *Amin.* He will wrong you, or me, or any man,
And talk as if he had no life to lose,
Since this our match. The king is coming in;
I would not for more wealth than I enjoy 110
He should perceive you raging. He did hear
You were at difference now, which hasten'd him.
                       *Hautboys play within.*
   *Cal.* Make room there!

*Enter King, Evadne, Aspatia, Lords and Ladies*

   *King.* Melantius, thou art welcome, and my
love
Is with thee still; but this is not a place 115
To brabble in. — Calianax, join hands.
   *Cal.* He shall not have mine hand.
   *King.*            This is no time
To force you to 't. I do love you both: —
Calianax, you look well to your office; —
And you, Melantius, are welcome home. 120
Begin the masque.
   *Mel.* Sister, I joy to see you and your choice;
You look'd with my eyes when you took that
man.
Be happy in him!         *Recorders [play].*
   *Evad.*       O, my dearest brother,
Your presence is more joyful than this day 125
Can be unto me.

## THE MASQUE

### Night rises in mists

   *Night.*   *Our reign is come; for in the quenching
sea*
*The sun is drown'd, and with him fell the Day.*
*Bright Cynthia, hear my voice! I am the Night,*
*For whom thou bear'st about thy borrow'd light.*
*Appear! no longer thy pale visage shroud,*   5
*But strike thy silver horns quite through a cloud,*
*And send a beam upon my swarthy face,*
*By which I may discover all the place*
*And persons, and how many longing eyes*
*Are come to wait on our solemnities.*   10

### Enter Cynthia

*How dull and black am I! I could not find*
*This beauty without thee, I am so blind:*
*Methinks they show like to those eastern streaks,*
*That warn us hence before the morning breaks.*
*Back, my pale servant! for these eyes know how* 15
*To shoot far more and quicker rays than thou.*
   *Cynth.*   *Great queen, they be a troop for
whom alone*
*One of my clearest moons I have put on:*

---

  **85 Bate me:** except   **89 fond:** foolish   **100 vild:** vile   **116 brabble:** squabble   **124 S. D. Recorders:** small flutes

*A troop that looks as if thyself and I*
*Had pluck'd our reins in and our whips laid*
      *by,*                                    20
*To gaze upon these mortals, that appear*
*Brighter than we.*
      Night.          *Then let us keep 'em here,*
*And never more our chariots drive away,*
*But hold our places and outshine the Day.*
      Cynth.     *Great queen of shadows, you are*
      *pleas'd to speak*                       25
*Of more than may be done.   We may not break*
*The gods' decrees; but, when our time is come,*
*Must drive away, and give the Day our room.*
*Yet, whilst our reign lasts, let us stretch our*
      *power*
*To give our servants one contented hour,*    30
*With such unwonted solemn grace and state,*
*As may forever after force them hate*
*Our brother's glorious beams, and wish the Night*
*Crown'd with a thousand stars and our cold*
      *light:*
*For almost all the world their service bend*  35
*To Phœbus, and in vain my light I lend,*
*Gaz'd on unto my setting from my rise*
*Almost of none but of unquiet eyes.*
      Night.     *Then shine at full, fair queen, and by*
      *thy power*
*Produce a birth, to crown this happy hour,*  40
*Of nymphs and shepherds; let their songs dis-*
      *cover,*
*Easy and sweet, who is a happy lover;*
*Or, if thou woo 't, thine own Endymion*
*From the sweet flowery bank he lies upon,*
*On Latmus' brow, thy pale beams drawn away,* 45
*And of his long night let him make thy day.*
      Cynth.     *Thou dream'st, dark queen; that fair*
      *boy was not mine,*
*Nor went I down to kiss him.   Ease and wine*
*Have bred these bold tales: poets, when they rage,*
*Turn gods to men, and make an hour an age.*  50
*But I will give a greater state and glory,*
*And raise to time a nobler memory*
*Of what these lovers are. — Rise, rise, I say,*
*Thou power of deeps, thy surges laid away,*
*Neptune, great king of waters, and by me*    55
*Be proud to be commanded!*

                Neptune rises

      Nept.                    *Cynthia, see*
*Thy word hath fetch'd me hither: let me know*
*Why I ascend.*
      Cynth.     *Doth this majestic show*
*Give thee no knowledge yet?*
      Nept.                    *Yes, now I see*
*Something intended, Cynthia, worthy thee.*    60
*Go on;  I 'll be a helper.*

      Cynth.                   *Hie thee, then,*
*And charge the Wind fly from his rocky den,*
*Let loose his subjects; only Boreas,*
*Too foul for our intention as he was,*
*Still keep him fast chain'd: we must have none*
      *here*                                   65
*But vernal blasts and gentle winds appear,*
*Such as blow flowers, and through the glad boughs*
      *sing*
*Many soft welcomes to the lusty spring;*
*These are our music.   Next, thy watery race*
*Bring on in couples we are pleas'd to grace*  70
*This noble night, each in their richest things*
*Your own deeps or the broken vessels brings.*
*Be prodigal, and I shall be as kind*
*And shine at full upon you.*
      Nept.                    *See! the Wind-*
*Commanding Æolus!*

          Enter Æolus out of a Rock

      Æol.                     *Great Neptune!*
      Nept.                          *He.*    75
      Æol.   *What is thy will?*
      Nept.                     *We do command thee free*
*Favonius and thy milder winds, to wait*
*Upon our Cynthia; but tie Boreas straight,*
*He 's too rebellious.*
      Æol.                *I shall do it.*
      Nept.                          *Do.*
                              [Exit Æolus.]
      Æol. [within.]  *Great master of the flood and*
      *all below,*                             80
*Thy full command has taken. —— Ho, the Main!*
*Neptune!*
      Nept.   *Here.*

[Re-enter Æolus, followed by Favonius and
          other Winds]

      Æol.                     *Boreas has broke his chain,*
*And, struggling with the rest, has got away.*
      Nept.   *Let him alone, I 'll take him up at sea;*
*He will not long be thence.   Go once again,*  85
*And call out of the bottoms of the main*
*Blue Proteus and the rest; charge them put on*
*Their greatest pearls, and the most sparkling*
      *stone*
*The beaten rock breeds.   Tell this night is done*
*By me a solemn honour to the Moon:*          90
*Fly, like a full sail.*
      Æol.                *I am gone.*          [Exit.]
      Cynth.                    *Dark Night,*
*Strike a full silence, do a thorough right*
*To this great chorus, that our music may*
*Touch high as Heaven, and make the east break*
      *day*
*At midnight.*                         Music. 95

²⁹⁻³³ (Not in Q 1)   ⁴³ **woo 't:** desire   ⁵⁴ **power of deeps:** sea-god   ⁷³ **we:** whom we   ⁷² (*I.e.,*
jewels either created by the sea or collected from sunken ships)   ⁷⁸ **straight:** straightway   ⁸⁵ **He:**
('**I**' Q 1)   ⁸⁹ **beaten:** wave-worn   **Tell:** say that

## SONG

[During which Proteus and other Sea-deities enter]

*Cynthia, to thy power and thee*
    *We obey.*
*Joy to this great company!*
    *And no day*
*Come to steal this night away,*     100
    *Till the rites of love are ended.*
*And the lusty bridegroom say,*
    *Welcome, light, of all befriended!*

*Pace out, you watery powers below;*
    *Let your feet,*     105
*Like the galleys when they row,*
    *Even beat.*
*Let your unknown measures, set*
    *To the still winds, tell to all,*
*That gods are come, immortal, great,*     110
*To honour this great nuptial.*

The Measure.

## SECOND SONG

*Hold back thy hours, dark Night, till we have done;*
    *The Day will come too soon:*
*Young maids will curse thee, if thou steal'st away,*
*And leav'st their losses open to the day:*     115
    *Stay, stay, and hide*
    *The blushes of the bride.*

*Stay, gentle Night, and with thy darkness cover*
    *The kisses of her lover;*
*Stay, and confound her tears and her shrill cryings,*
*Her weak denials, vows, and often-dyings;*     121
    *Stay, and hide all:*
    *But help not, though she call.*

Nept.   *Great queen of us and Heaven, hear what I bring*
*To make this hour a full one.*
Cynth.         *Speak, sea's king.*  125
Nept.   *The tunes my Amphitrite joys to have,*
*When she will dance upon the rising wave,*
*And court me as she sails. My Tritons, play*
*Music to lay a storm! I'll lead the way.*

A Measure, Neptune leads it.

## SONG

*To bed, to bed! Come, Hymen, lead the bride,*  130
*And lay her by her husband's side;*
    *Bring in the virgins every one,*
    *That grieve to lie alone,*
*That they may kiss while they may say a maid;*

*To-morrow 't will be other kiss'd and said.*   135
*Hesperus, be long a-shining,*
    *Whilst these lovers are a-twining.*

Æol. [within.]  *Ho, Neptune!*
Nept.                    *Æolus!*

[Re-enter Æolus]

Æol.                *The sea goes high,*
*Boreas hath rais'd a storm: go and apply*
*Thy trident; else, I prophesy, ere day*   140
*Many a tall ship will be cast away.*
*Descend with all the gods and all their power,*
*To strike a calm.*
    Cynth.   *We thank you for this hour:*
*My favour to you all. To gratulate*   145
*So great a service, done at my desire,*
*Ye shall have many floods, fuller and higher*
*Than you have wish'd for; and no ebb shall dare*
*To let the Day see where your dwellings are.*
*Now back unto your governments in haste,*   150
*Lest your proud charge should swell above the waste,*
*And win upon the island.*
Nept.               *We obey.*

Neptune descends and the Sea-Gods.
    [Exeunt Favonius and other Winds.]

Cynth.   *Hold up thy head, dead Night; see'st thou not Day?*
*The east begins to lighten. I must down,*
*And give my brother place.*
    Night.         *Oh, I could frown*  155
*To see the Day, the Day that flings his light*
*Upon my kingdom and contemns old Night!*
*Let him go on and flame! I hope to see*
*Another wild-fire in his axle-tree,*
*And all fall drench'd. But I forget; — speak, queen:*   160
*The Day grows on; I must no more be seen.*
    Cynth.   *Heave up thy drowsy head and see*
*A greater light, a greater majesty,*
*Between our set and us! Whip up thy team:*   164
*The Day breaks here, and yon sun-flaring stream*
*Shot from the south. Which way wilt thou go? Say.*
Night.   *I'll vanish into mists.*
Cynth.                *I into Day.*
                  Exeunt.  Finis Masque.

King.   Take lights there! — Ladies, get the
    bride to bed. —
We will not see you laid; good night, Amintor;
We'll ease you of that tedious ceremony.   170
Were it my case, I should think time run slow.

---

¹¹¹ S. D. **Measure:** formal dance   ¹²⁴⁻¹³⁷ (Not in Q 1)   ¹³⁶ **Hesperus:** the evening star   ¹⁵⁹ (*I.e.,* the sun's chariot burned again, as when Phaethon drove it)   ¹⁶⁴ **set:** setting, the west ('sect' in early editions)   ¹⁶⁶ **Which ... go? Say:** ('Say, which ... go' Qq., F)   ¹⁶⁷ **I ... Day:** ('Adew' Q 1)

If thou be'st noble, youth, get me a boy,
That may defend my kingdom from my foes.
  *Amin.*  All happiness to you!
  *King.*    Good night, Melantius. *Exeunt.*

### Actus Secundus

[SCENE I. — *Evadne's Apartment.*]

*Enter Evadne, Aspatia, Dula, and other Ladies*

  *Dula.* Madam, shall we undress you for this
    fight?
The wars are nak'd that you must make to-
  night.
  *Evad.* You are very merry, Dula.
  *Dula.*           I should be
Far merrier, madam, if it were with me
As it is with you.
  *Evad.*      How 's that?
  *Dula.*        That I might go 5
To bed with him wi' th' credit that you do.
  *Evad.* Why, how now, wench?
  *Dula.*      Come, ladies, will you help?
  *Evad.* I am soon undone.
  *Dula.*        And as soon done:
Good store of clothes will trouble you at both.
  *Evad.* Art thou drunk, Dula?
  *Dula.*    Why, here 's none but we. 10
  *Evad.* Thou think'st belike there is no mod-
  esty
When we 're alone.
  *Dula.* Ay, by my troth, you hit my thoughts
  aright.
  *Evad.* You prick me, lady.
  *1 Lady.*      'T is against my will.
  *Dula.* Anon you must endure more and lie
  still;                      15
You 're best to practise.
  *Evad.*      Sure, this wench is mad.
  *Dula.* No, faith, this is a trick that I have
  had
Since I was fourteen.
  *Evad.*      'T is high time to leave it.
  *Dula.* Nay, now I 'll keep it till the trick
  leave me.
A dozen wanton words put in your head    20
Will make you livelier in your husband's bed.
  *Evad.* Nay, faith, then take it.
  *Dula.*      Take it, madam! Where?
We all, I hope, will take it that are here.
  *Evad.* Nay, then I 'll give thee o'er.
  *Dula.*        So will I make
The ablest man in Rhodes, or his heart ache. 25
  *Evad.* Wilt take my place to-night?
  *Dula.*      I 'll hold your cards
Against any two I know.

  *Evad.*          What wilt thou do?
  *Dula.* Madam, we 'll do 't, and make 'em
  leave play too.
  *Evad.* Aspatia, take her part.
  *Dula.*        I will refuse it:
She will pluck down a side; she does not use
  it.                           30
  *Evad.* Why, do, I prithee.
  *Dula.*      You will find the play
Quickly, because your head lies well that way.
  *Evad.* I thank thee, Dula. Would thou
  couldst instil
Some of thy mirth into Aspatia!
Nothing but sad thoughts in her breast do
  dwell:                        35
Methinks, a mean betwixt you would do well.
  *Dula.* She is in love: hang me, if I were so,
But I could run my country. I love too
To do those things that people in love do.
  *Asp.* It were a timeless smile should prove
  my cheek.                     40
It were a fitter hour for me to laugh,
When at the altar the religious priest
Were pacifying the offended powers
With sacrifice, than now. This should have
  been
My rite; and all your hands have been em-
  ploy'd                      45
In giving me a spotless offering
To young Amintor's bed, as we are now
For you. Pardon, Evadne: would my worth
Were great as yours, or that the king, or he,
Or both, thought so! Perhaps he found me
  worthless:                 50
But till he did so, in these ears of mine,
These credulous ears, he pour'd the sweetest
  words
That art or love could frame. If he were false,
Pardon it, Heaven! and if I did want
Virtue, you safely may forgive that too;    55
For I have lost none that I had from you.
  *Evad.* Nay, leave this sad talk, madam.
  *Asp.*        Would I could!
Then I should leave the cause.
  *Evad.* Lo, if you have not spoil'd all Dula's
  mirth!
  *Asp.* Thou think'st thy heart hard; but, if
  thou be'st caught,           60
Remember me; thou shalt perceive a fire
Shot suddenly into thee.
  *Dula.*      That 's not so good;
Let 'em shoot anything but fire, and I fear 'em
  not.
  *Asp.* Well, wench, thou may'st be taken.
  *Evad.* Ladies, good night; I 'll do the rest
  myself.                    65

¹⁷³ **kingdom:** ('kingdomes' Q 1)    ⁵⁻⁶ **How 's . . . do:** (in Q 1 only)    ³⁰ **a side:** pair of partners at cards    ³¹ **I prithee:** (in Q 1 only. The speech refers to Evadne's question, line 26.)    ⁴⁰ **timeless:** untimely    **prove:** make trial of

*Dula.* Nay, let your lord do some.
*Asp.* [*singing.*]

> Lay a garland on my hearse
> Of the dismal yew —

*Evad.* That 's one of your sad songs, madam.
*Asp.* Believe me, 't is a very pretty one. 70
*Evad.* How is it, madam?

SONG

*Asp.* *Lay a garland on my hearse*
> *Of the dismal yew;*
> *Maidens, willow-branches bear;*
> *Say I died true.* 75
> *My love was false, but I was firm*
> *From my hour of birth:*
> *Upon my buried body lie*
> *Lightly, gentle earth!*

*Evad.* Fie on 't, madam! The words are so
strange, they 80
Are able to make one dream of hobgoblins. —
"I could never have the power" — sing that,
Dula.

Dula. *I could never have the power*
> *To love one above an hour,*
> *But my heart would prompt mine eye* 85
> *On some other man to fly.*
> *Venus, fix mine eyes fast,*
> *Or, if not, give me all that I shall see at*
> *last!*

*Evad.* So, leave me now.
*Dula.*          Nay, we must see you laid. 90
*Asp.* Madam, good night. May all the mar-
riage-joys
That longing maids imagine in their beds
Prove so unto you! May no discontent
Grow 'twixt your love and you! but, if there do,
Inquire of me, and I will guide your moan; 95
Teach you an artificial way to grieve,
To keep your sorrow waking. Love your lord
No worse than I; but, if you love so well,
Alas, you may displease him! so did I.
This is the last time you shall look on me. — 100
Ladies, farewell. As soon as I am dead,
Come all and watch one night about my hearse;
Bring each a mournful story and a tear,
To offer at it when I go to earth;
With flattering ivy clasp my coffin round; 105
Write on my brow my fortune; let my bier
Be borne by virgins, that shall sing by course
The truth of maids and perjuries of men.
*Evad.* Alas, I pity thee.
*Omnes.* Madam, good night. *Exit Evadne.*
1 *Lady.* Come, we 'll let in the bridegroom.
*Dula.*          Where 's my lord? 110

*Enter Amintor*

1 *Lady.* Here, take this light.
*Dula.*          He 'll find her in the dark.
1 *Lady.* Your lady 's scarce a-bed yet; you
must help her.
*Asp.* Go, and be happy in your lady's love.
May all the wrongs that you have done to me
Be utterly forgotten in my death! 115
I 'll trouble you no more; yet I will take
A parting kiss, and will not be denied.
[*Kisses Amintor.*]
You 'll come, my lord, and see the virgins
weep
When I am laid in earth, though you yourself
Can know no pity. Thus I wind myself 120
Into this willow-garland, and am prouder
That I was once your love, though now refus'd,
Than to have had another true to me.
So with my prayers I leave you, and must try
Some yet unpractis'd way to grieve and die. 125
*Exit Aspatia.*
*Dula.* Come, ladies, will you go?
*Omnes.*          Good night, my lord.
*Amin.* Much happiness unto you all!
*Exeunt Ladies.*
I did that lady wrong. Methinks, I feel
A grief shoot suddenly through all my veins;
Mine eyes rain: this is strange at such a
time. 130
It was the king first mov'd me to 't; but he
Has not my will in keeping. Why do I
Perplex myself thus? Something whispers me,
Go not to bed. My guilt is not so great
As mine own conscience, too sensible, 135
Would make me think. I only brake a promise,
And 't was the king enforc'd me. Timorous
flesh,
Why shak'st thou so? Away, my idle fears!

*Enter Evadne*

Yonder she is, the lustre of whose eye
Can blot away the sad remembrance 140
Of all these things. — Oh, my Evadne, spare
That tender body; let it not take cold!
The vapours of the night shall not fall here.
To bed, my love: Hymen will punish us
For being slack performers of his rites. 145
Cam'st thou to call me?
*Evad.*          No.
*Amin.*          Come, come, my love,
And let us lose ourselves to one another.
Why art thou up so long?
*Evad.*          I am not well.
*Amin.* To bed then; let me wind thee in
these arms
Till I have banish'd sickness.

*Evad.*          Good my lord, 150
I cannot sleep.
*Amin.*      Evadne, we will watch;
I mean no sleeping.
*Evad.*        I 'll not go to bed.
*Amin.* I prithee, do.
*Evad.*        I will not for the world.
*Amin.* Why, my dear love?
*Evad.*      Why! I have sworn I will not.
*Amin.* Sworn!
*Evad.*     Ay.
*Amin.*      How? Sworn, Evadne! 155
*Evad.* Yes, sworn, Amintor; and will swear
again,
If you will wish to hear me.
*Amin.* To whom have you sworn this?
*Evad.* If I should name him, the matter were
not great.
*Amin.* Come, this is but the coyness of a
bride. 160
*Evad.* The coyness of a bride!
*Amin.*       How prettily
That frown becomes thee!
*Evad.*        Do you like it so?
*Amin.* Thou canst not dress thy face in such
a look
But I shall like it.
*Evad.*      What look likes you best?
*Amin.* Why do you ask? 165
*Evad.* That I may show you one less pleas-
ing to you.
*Amin.* How 's that?
*Evad.* That I may show you one less pleas-
ing to you.
*Amin.* I prithee, put thy jests in milder
looks;
It shows as thou wert angry.
*Evad.*        So perhaps 170
I am indeed.
*Amin.*     Why, who has done thee wrong?
Name me the man, and by thyself I swear,
Thy yet unconquer'd self, I will revenge thee!
*Evad.* Now I shall try thy truth. If thou
dost love me,
Thou weigh'st not anything compar'd with
me: 175
Life, honour, joys eternal, all delights
This world can yield, or hopeful people feign,
Or in the life to come, are light as air
To a true lover when his lady frowns,
And bids him, "Do this." Wilt thou kill this
man? 180
Swear, my Amintor, and I 'll kiss the sin
Off from thy lips.
*Amin.*     I wo' not swear, sweet love,
Till I do know the cause.
*Evad.*      I would thou wouldst.

Why, it is thou that wrong'st me; I hate
thee;
Thou should'st have kill'd thyself. 185
*Amin.* If I should know that, I should
quickly kill
The man you hated.
*Evad.*      Know it, then, and do 't.
*Amin.* Oh, no! what look soe'er thou shalt
put on
To try my faith, I shall not think thee false;
I cannot find one blemish in thy face, 190
Where falsehood should abide. Leave, and to
bed.
If you have sworn to any of the virgins
That were your old companions, to preserve
Your maidenhead a night, it may be done
Without this means.
*Evad.*      A maidenhead, Amintor, 195
At my years!
*Amin.*      Sure she raves; this cannot be
Her natural temper. — Shall I call thy maids?
Either thy healthful sleep hath left thee long,
Or else some fever rages in thy blood.
*Evad.* Neither, Amintor: think you I am
mad, 200
Because I speak the truth?
*Amin.*      Is this the truth?
Will you not lie with me to-night?
*Evad.*        To-night!
You talk as if you thought I would hereafter.
*Amin.* Hereafter! yes, I do.
*Evad.*        You are deceiv'd.
Put off amazement, and with patience mark 205
What I shall utter, for the oracle
Knows nothing truer. 'T is not for a night
Or two that I forbear your bed, but ever.
*Amin.* I dream. Awake, Amintor!
*Evad.*        You hear right:
I sooner will find out the beds of snakes, 210
And with my youthful blood warm their cold
flesh,
Letting them curl themselves about my limbs,
Than sleep one night with thee. This is not
feign'd,
Nor sounds it like the coyness of a bride.
*Amin.* Is flesh so earthly to endure all
this? 215
Are these the joys of marriage? Hymen, keep
This story (that will make succeeding youth
Neglect thy ceremonies) from all ears;
Let it not rise up, for thy shame and mine
To after-ages: we will scorn thy laws, 220
If thou no better bless them. Touch the heart
Of her that thou hast sent me, or the world
Shall know this. Not an altar then will smoke
In praise of thee; we will adopt us sons.
Then virtue shall inherit, and not blood. 225

**164 likes:** pleases ('will like' Q 1)     **197 Her:** ('Thy' Q 1)     **201 Is . . . truth:** (in Q 1 only)
**203 you thought:** (in Q 1 only)    **204 deceiv'd:** mistaken    **215 to:** as to

If we do lust, we 'll take the next we meet,
Serving ourselves as other creatures do;
And never take note of the female more,
Nor of her issue. — I do rage in vain;
She can but jest. — Oh, pardon me, my love! 230
So dear the thoughts are that I hold of thee,
That I must break forth. Satisfy my fear;
It is a pain, beyond the hand of death,
To be in doubt. Confirm it with an oath,
If this be true.
    *Evad.*    Do you invent the form; 235
Let there be in it all the binding words
Devils and conjurers can put together,
And I will take it. I have sworn before,
And here by all things holy do again,
Never to be acquainted with thy bed! 240
Is your doubt over now?
    *Amin.* I know too much; would I had
    doubted still!
Was ever such a marriage-night as this!
You powers above, if you did ever mean
Man should be us'd thus, you have thought a
    way 245
How he may bear himself, and save his honour:
Instruct me in it; for to my dull eyes
There is no mean, no moderate course to run;
I must live scorn'd, or be a murderer.
Is there a third? Why is this night so calm? 250
Why does not Heaven speak in thunder to us,
And drown her voice?
    *Evad.*    This rage will do no good.
    *Amin.* Evadne, hear me. Thou hast ta'en
    an oath,
But such a rash one, that to keep it were
Worse than to swear it. Call it back to thee; 255
Such vows as that never ascend the Heaven;
A tear or two will wash it quite away.
Have mercy on my youth, my hopeful youth,
If thou be pitiful! for, without boast,
This land was proud of me. What lady was
    there, 260
That men call'd fair and virtuous in this isle,
That would have shunn'd my love? It is in
    thee
To make me hold this worth. — Oh, we vain
    men,
That trust out all our reputation
To rest upon the weak and yielding hand 265
Of feeble woman! But thou art not stone;
Thy flesh is soft, and in thine eyes doth dwell
The spirit of love; thy heart cannot be hard.
Come, lead me from the bottom of despair
To all the joys thou hast; I know thou wilt; 270
And make me careful lest the sudden change
O'ercome my spirits.
    *Evad.*    When I call back this oath,
The pains of hell environ me!

*Amin.* I sleep, and am too temperate. Come
    to bed!
Or by those hairs, which, if thou hadst a soul 275
Like to thy locks, were threads for kings to
    wear
About their arms ——
    *Evad.*    Why, so perhaps they are.
    *Amin.* I 'll drag thee to my bed, and make
    thy tongue
Undo this wicked oath, or on thy flesh
I 'll print a thousand wounds to let out life! 280
    *Evad.* I fear thee not: do what thou darest
    to me!
Every ill-sounding word or threatening look
Thou shew'st to me will be reveng'd at full.
    *Amin.* It will not, sure, Evadne?
    *Evad.* Do not you hazard that.
    *Amin.*    Ha' ye your champions? 285
    *Evad.* Alas, Amintor, think'st thou I for-
    bear
To sleep with thee, because I have put on
A maiden's strictness? Look upon these cheeks,
And thou shalt find the hot and rising blood
Unapt for such a vow. No; in this heart 290
There dwells as much desire and as much will
To put that wished act in practice as ever yet
Was known to woman; and they have been
    shown
    Both. But it was the folly of thy youth
To think this beauty, to what hand soe'er 295
It shall be call'd, shall stoop to any second.
I do enjoy the best, and in that height
Have sworn to stand or die. You guess the
    man.
    *Amin.* No; let me know the man that
    wrongs me so,
That I may cut his body into motes, 300
And scatter it before the northern wind.
    *Evad.* You dare not strike him.
    *Amin.*    Do not wrong me so.
Yes, if his body were a poisonous plant
That it were death to touch, I have a soul
Will throw me on him.
    *Evad.*    Why, 't is the King.
    *Amin.*    The King! 305
    *Evad.* What will you do now?
    *Amin.*    It is not the King!
    *Evad.* What did he make this match for,
    dull Amintor?
    *Amin.* Oh, thou hast nam'd a word, that
    wipes away
All thoughts revengeful! In that sacred name,
"The King," there lies a terror: What frail
    man 310
Dares lift his hand against it? Let the gods
Speak to him when they please: till when, let us
Suffer and wait.

    **256** **that:** ('those' Q 2, etc.)   **264** **out:** (not in Q 1-2)   **295** **hand:** falconer's hand (Bullen's conjecture; 'land' in Qq., F)

*Evad.* Why should you fill yourself so full of
heat,
And haste so to my bed? I am no virgin. 315
*Amin.* What devil put it in thy fancy, then.
To marry me?
*Evad.*     Alas, I must have one
To father children, and to bear the name
Of husband to me, that my sin may be
More honourable!
*Amin.*     What strange thing am I! 320
*Evad.* A miserable one; one that myself
Am sorry for.
*Amin.*     Why, show it then in this:
If thou hast pity, though thy love be none,
Kill me; and all true lovers, that shall live
In after ages cross'd in their desires,     325
Shall bless thy memory, and call thee good,
Because such mercy in thy heart was found,
To rid a lingering wretch.
*Evad.*     I must have one
To fill thy room again, if thou wert dead;
Else, by this night, I would! I pity thee. 330
*Amin.* These strange and sudden injuries
have fallen
So thick upon me, that I lose all sense
Of what they are. Methinks, I am not wrong'd;
Nor is it aught, if from the censuring world
I can but hide it. Reputation!     335
Thou art a word, no more! — But thou hast
shown
An impudence so high, that to the world
I fear thou wilt betray or shame thyself.
*Evad.* To cover shame I took thee; never
fear
That I would blaze myself.
*Amin.*     Nor let the king 340
Know I conceive he wrongs me; then mine
honour
Will thrust me into action, that my flesh
Could bear with patience. And it is some ease
To me in these extremes, that I know this
Before I touch'd thee; else, had all the sins 345
Of mankind stood betwixt me and the king,
I had gone through 'em to his heart and thine.
I have left one desire: 't is not his crown
Shall buy me to thy bed, now I resolve
He has dishonour'd thee. Give me thy hand:
Be careful of thy credit, and sin close;   351
'T is all I wish. Upon thy chamber-floor
I 'll rest to-night, that morning visitors
May think we did as married people use:  354
And prithee, smile upon me when they come,
And seem to toy, as if thou hadst been pleased
With what we did.
*Evad.*     Fear not; I will do this.

*Amin.* Come, let us practise; and, as wantonly
As ever longing bride and bridegroom met,
Let 's laugh and enter here.
*Evad.*     I am content. 360
*Amin.* Down all the swellings of my troubled
heart!
When we walk thus intwin'd, let all eyes see
If ever lovers better did agree.     *Exeunt.*

[SCENE II. — *House of Calianax.*]

*Enter Aspatia, Antiphila, Olympias*

*Asp.* Away, you are not sad! force it no fur-
ther.
Good gods, how well you look! Such a full
colour
Young bashful brides put on: sure, you are
new married!
*Ant.* Yes, madam, to your grief.
*Asp.*     Alas, poor wenches!
Go learn to love first; learn to lose yourselves; 5
Learn to be flattered, and believe and bless
The double tongue that did it; make a faith
Out of the miracles of ancient lovers,
Such as spake truth and died in 't; and, like
me,
Believe all faithful, and be miserable.     10
Did you ne'er love yet, wenches? Speak,
Olympias:
Thou hast an easy temper, fit for stamp.
*Olym.* Never.
*Asp.*     Nor you, Antiphila?
*Ant.*     Nor I.
*Asp.* Then, my good girls, be more than
women, wise;
At least be more than I was; and be sure  15
You credit anything the light gives life to,
Before a man. Rather believe the sea
Weeps for the ruin'd merchant, when he roars;
Rather, the wind courts but the pregnant sails,
When the strong cordage cracks; rather, the
sun     20
Comes but to kiss the fruit in wealthy autumn,
When all falls blasted. If you needs must love,
(Forc'd by ill fate,) take to your maiden-bosoms
Two dead-cold aspics, and of them make lovers.
They cannot flatter nor forswear; one kiss 25
Makes a long peace for all. But man —
Oh, that beast man! Come, let 's be sad, my
girls:
That down-cast of thine eye, Olympias,
Shows a fine sorrow. — Mark, Antiphila;
Just such another was the nymph Œnone's, 30
When Paris brought home Helen. — Now, a
tear;

³⁴⁰ **blaze:** expose  ³⁴² **that:** (modern editors alter to 'though')  ³⁴⁴ **extremes:** extremities  ³⁴⁸ **left:** abandoned ('lost' in Q 2, etc.)  ³⁴⁹ **resolve:** am assured  ³⁵¹ **close:** in private  ³⁵⁹ **longing:** ('louing' in Q 2, etc.)  ¹¹ (Follows line 8 in Q 2, etc. Q 1 reduces 7–12 to three lines.)  ¹² **easy:** ('metled' Q 1) ¹⁵⁻²⁷ **and be sure . . . beast man:** (not in Q 1)  ²⁰ **cordage:** rigging  ²⁴ **aspics:** asps

And then thou art a piece expressing fully
The Carthage queen, when from a cold sea-
    rock,
Full with her sorrow, she tied fast her eyes  34
To the fair Trojan ships; and, having lost
    them,
Just as thine does, down stole a tear. — An-
    tiphila,
What would this wench do, if she were Aspatia?
Here she would stand, till some more pitying
    god
Turn'd her to marble! — 'T is enough, my
    wench!
Show me the piece of needlework you wrought.
  *Ant.*  Of Ariadne, madam?
  *Asp.*            Yes, that piece. — 41
This should be Theseus; h'as a cozening face. —
You meant him for a man?
  *Ant.*         He was so, madam.
  *Asp.*  Why, then, 't is well enough. — Never
    look back;
You have a full wind and a false heart, The-
    seus. —                     45
Does not the story say, his keel was split,
Or his masts spent, or some kind rock or
    other
Met with his vessel?
  *Ant.*        Not as I remember.
  *Asp.*  It should ha' been so.  Could the gods
    know this,
And not, of all their number, raise a storm? 50
But they are all as evil.  This false smile
Was well express'd; just such another caught
    me. —
You shall not go so. —
Antiphila, in this place work a quicksand,
And over it a shallow smiling water,     55
And his ship ploughing it; and then a Fear:
Do that Fear bravely, wench.
  *Ant.*       'T will wrong the story.
  *Asp.*  'T will make the story, wrong'd by
    wanton poets,
Live long and be believ'd.  But where's the
    lady?
  *Ant.*  There, madam.              60
  *Asp.*  Fie, you have miss'd it here, Antiph-
    ila;
You are much mistaken, wench.
These colours are not dull and pale enough
To show a soul so full of misery
As this sad lady's was.  Do it by me,    65
Do it again by me, the lost Aspatia;
And you shall find all true but the wild island.
Suppose I stand upon the sea-breach now,

Mine arms thus, and mine hair blown with the
    wind,
Wild as that desert; and let all about me  70
Tell that I am forsaken.  Do my face
(If thou had'st ever feeling of a sorrow)
Thus, thus, Antiphila: strive to make me look
Like Sorrow's monument; and the trees about
    me,
Let them be dry and leafless; let the rocks  75
Groan with continual surges; and behind me,
Make all a desolation.  See, see, wenches,
A miserable life of this poor picture!
  *Olym.*  Dear madam!
  *Asp.*        I have done.  Sit down; and let us
Upon that point fix all our eyes, that point
    there.                         80
Make a dull silence, till you feel a sudden sad-
    ness
Give us new souls.

          *Enter Calianax*

  *Cal.*  The king may do this, and he may not
    do it:
My child is wrong'd, disgrac'd. — Well, how
    now, huswives?                 84
What, at your ease!  Is this time to sit still?
Up, you young lazy whores, up, or I'll swinge
    you!
  *Olym.*  Nay, good my lord —
  *Cal.*  You'll lie down shortly.  Get you in,
    and work!
What, are you grown so resty you want heats?
We shall have some of the court-boys heat you
    shortly.                     90
  *Ant.*  My lord, we do no more than we are
    charg'd:
It is the lady's pleasure we be thus
In grief she is forsaken.
  *Cal.*         There's a rogue too,
A young dissembling slave! — Well, get you
    in. —
I'll have a bout with that boy.  'T is high time
Now to be valiant: I confess my youth  96
Was never prone that way.  What, made an
    ass!
A court-stale!  Well, I will be valiant,
And beat some dozen of these whelps; I will!
And there's another of 'em, a trim cheating
    soldier;                    100
I'll maul that rascal; h'as out-brav'd me
    twice;
But now, I thank the gods, I am valiant. —
Go, get you in. — I'll take a course withal.
                       *Exeunt omnes.*

---

  ⁴² **cozening:** beguiling   ⁵¹ **evil:** (so Dyce; 'ill' in Qq., F)   ⁵³ **You:** (*i.e.,* Theseus)   ⁵⁷ **bravely:**
finely (Q 2, etc., substitute 'to the life')   ⁶⁵ **by:** on the model of   ⁶⁸ ('I stand upon the sea-breach
now, and think' Q 2-F)   ⁷¹ **Tell . . . forsaken:** ('Be teares of my story' Q 1)   ⁷⁸ **life:** living image
⁸¹ **dull:** ('dumbe' Q 1-2)   ⁸⁹ **resty:** restive ('rusty' Q 1)   ⁹⁰ **heat . . . shortly:** ('do that office'
Q 2-F)   ⁹¹ **charg'd:** commanded   ⁹³ **she:** because she   ⁹⁸ **-stale:** laughing-stock

## Actus Tertius

[SCENE I. — *Evadne's Apartment.*]

*Enter Cleon, Strato, Diphilus*

*Cle.* Your sister is not up yet.

*Diph.* Oh, brides must take their morning's
rest; the night is troublesome.

*Stra.* But not tedious.

*Diph.* What odds, he has not my sister's [5
maidenhead to-night.

*Stra.* None; it 's odds against any bridegroom living, he ne'er gets it while he lives.

*Diph.* Y' are merry with my sister; you 'll
please to allow me the same freedom with [10
your mother.

*Stra.* She 's at your service.

*Diph.* Then she 's merry enough of herself;
she needs no tickling. Knock at the door.

*Stra.* We shall interrupt them.     15

*Diph.* No matter; they have the year before
them.        [*Strato knocks at the door.*]
Good morrow, sister. Spare yourself to-day;
The night will come again.

*Enter Amintor*

*Amin.* Who 's there? My brother! I 'm no
   readier yet.     20
Your sister is but now up.

*Diph.* You look as you had lost your eyes to-
night:
I think you ha' not slept.

*Amin.*          I' faith I have not.

*Diph.* You have done better, then.

*Amin.* We ventur'd for a boy; when he is
   twelve,     25
'A shall command against the foes of Rhodes.
Shall we be merry?

*Stra.* You cannot; you want sleep.

*Amin.* 'T is true. — (*Aside.*) But she,
As if she had drunk Lethe, or had made
Even with Heaven, did fetch so still a sleep,  30
So sweet and sound ——

*Diph.*         What 's that?

*Amin.*          Your sister frets
This morning; and does turn her eyes upon me,
As people on the headsman. She does chafe,
And kiss, and chafe again, and clap my cheeks:
She 's in another world.     35

*Diph.* Then I had lost: I was about to lay
You had not got her maidenhead to-night.

*Amin.* [*Aside.*] Ha! does he not mock me? —
Y'ad lost indeed;
I do not use to bungle.

*Cle.*       You do deserve her.

*Amin.* (*Aside.*) I laid my lips to hers, and
   that wild breath,     40
That was so rude and rough to me last night,
Was sweet as April. I 'll be guilty too,
If these be the effects.

*Enter Melantius*

*Mel.* Good day, Amintor; for to me the name
Of brother is too distant: we are friends,   45
And that is nearer.

*Amin.*       Dear Melantius!
Let me behold thee. Is it possible?

*Mel.* What sudden gaze is this?

*Amin.*       'T is wondrous strange!

*Mel.* Why does thine eye desire so strict a
   view
Of that it knows so well? There 's nothing
   here     50
That is not thine.

*Amin.*     I wonder much, Melantius,
To see those noble looks, that make me think
How virtuous thou art: and, on this sudden,
'T is strange to me thou shouldst have worth
   and honour;
Or not be base, and false, and treacherous,  55
And every ill. But ——

*Mel.*       Stay, stay, my friend;
I fear this sound will not become our loves.
No more; embrace me.

*Amin.*       Oh, mistake me not!
I know thee to be full of all those deeds   59
That we frail men call good; but by the course
Of nature thou shouldst be as quickly chang'd
As are the winds; dissembling as the sea,
That now wears brows as smooth as virgins' be,
Tempting the merchant to invade his face,
And in an hour calls his billows up,     65
And shoots 'em at the sun, destroying all
A' carries on him. — (*Aside.*) Oh, how near
   am I
To utter my sick thoughts.

*Mel.* But why, my friend, should I be so by
   nature?

*Amin.* I have wed thy sister, who hath vir-
   tuous thoughts     70
Enough for one whole family; and it is strange
That you should feel no want.

*Mel.* Believe me, this is compliment too
   cunning for me.

*Diph.* What should I be then by the course
   of nature,     74
They having both robb'd me of so much virtue?

*Stra.* Oh, call the bride, my Lord Amintor,
That we may see her blush, and turn her eyes
   down.
It is the prettiest sport!

---

⁷ **None:** ('No' Q 2–F)   ²⁰ **readier:** more completely dressed   ²² **to-night:** last night   ³³ **the:**
('their' Q 2)   **headsman:** state executioner   ⁵³ **on this sudden:** abruptly, at this moment (Q 2, etc.,
weaken by altering 'this' to 'the')

*Amin.* Evadne!

*Evad.*          My lord?          *Within.*

*Amin.*          Come forth, my love;
Your brothers do attend to wish you joy.          80

*Evad.* [*within.*] I am not ready yet.

*Amin.*          Enough, enough.

*Evad.* [*within.*] They 'll mock me.

*Amin.*          Faith, thou shalt come in.

*Enter Evadne*

*Mel.* Good morrow, sister. He that under-
stands
Whom you have wed, need not to wish you joy;
You have enough: take heed you be not proud.

*Diph.* Oh, sister, what have you done?          86

*Evad.* I done! why, what have I done?

*Stra.* My Lord Amintor swears you are no
maid now.

*Evad.* Pish!

*Stra.* I' faith, he does.

*Evad.*          I knew I should be mock'd. 90

*Diph.* With a truth.

*Evad.*          If 't were to do again,
In faith I would not marry.

*Amin.* Nor I, by Heaven!          *Aside.*

*Diph.*          Sister, Dula swears
She heard you cry two rooms off.

*Evad.*          Fie, how you talk!

*Diph.* Let 's see you walk, Evadne. By my
troth,          95
Y' are spoil'd.

*Mel.* Amintor. —

*Amin.* Ha!

*Mel.*          Thou art sad.

*Amin.*          Who, I? I thank you for that.
Shall Diphilus, thou, and I, sing a catch?

*Mel.* How!          100

*Amin.* Prithee, let 's.

*Mel.* Nay, that 's too much the other way.

*Amin.* I am so lighten'd with my happiness!
How dost thou, love? Kiss me.

*Evad.* I cannot love you, you tell tales of
me.          105

*Amin.* Nothing but what becomes us. —
Gentlemen,
Would you had all such wives! — [*Aside.*] and
all the world,
That I might be no wonder! — Y' are all sad:
What, do you envy me? I walk, methinks,
On water, and ne'er sink, I am so light.          110

*Mel.* 'T is well you are so.

*Amin.*          Well! how can I be other,
When she looks thus? — Is there no music
there?
Let 's dance.

*Mel.*          Why, this is strange, Amintor!

*Amin.* I do not know myself; yet I could
wish
My joy were less.          115

*Diph.* I 'll marry too, if it will make one
thus.

*Evad.* Amintor, hark.

*Amin.* What says my love? I must obey.

*Evad.* [*Aside.*] You do it scurvily, 't will be
perceiv'd.

*Cle.* My lord, the king is here.          120

*Amin.* Where?

*Stra.* And his brother.

*Enter King and Lysippus*

*King.* Good morrow, all! —
Amintor, joy on joy fall thick upon thee! —
And, madam, you are alter'd since I saw you. —
I must salute you [*Kisses her.*] — You are
now another's.          126
How lik'd you your night's rest?

*Evad.*          Ill, sir.

*Amin.*          Indeed,
She took but little.

*Lys.*          You 'll let her take more,
And thank her too, shortly.

*King.* Amintor, wert thou truly honest till
Thou wert married?

*Amin.* Yes, sir.

*King.*          Tell me how, then, shows 131
The sport to thee?

*Amin.* Why, well.

*King.*          What did you do?

*Amin.* No more, nor less, than other couples
use;
You know what 't is; it has but a coarse name.

*King.* But, prithee, I should think, by her
black eye,          135
And her red cheek, she should be quick and
stirring
In this same business; ha?

*Amin.*          I cannot tell;
I ne'er tried other, sir; but I perceive
She is as quick as you delivered.

*King.* Well, you 'll trust me then, Amintor,
to choose          140
A wife for you again?

*Amin.*          No, never, sir.

*King.* Why, like you this so ill?

*Amin.*          So well I like her.
For this I bow my knee in thanks to you,
And unto Heaven will pay my grateful tribute
Hourly; and do hope we shall draw out          145
A long contented life together here,
And die both, full of grey hairs, in one day:
For which the thanks is yours. But if the
powers
That rule us please to call her first away,

Without pride spoke, this world holds not a
wife 150
Worthy to take her room.
*King.* [*Aside.*] I do not like this. —
All forbear the room, but you, Amintor,
And your lady. I have some speech with you,
That may concern your after living well. 155
[*Exeunt all but the King, Amintor,
and Evadne.*]
*Amin.* [*Aside.*] A' will not tell me that he
lies with her!
If he do, something heavenly stay my heart,
For it is apt to thrust this arm of mine
To acts unlawful!
*King.* You will suffer me
To talk with her, Amintor, and not have 160
A jealous pang?
*Amin.* Sir, I dare trust my wife
With whom she dares to talk, and not be jeal-
ous. [*Retires.*]
*King.* How do you like Amintor?
*Evad.* As I did, sir.
*King.* How 's that?
*Evad.* As one that, to fulfil your pleasure, 165
I have given leave to call me wife and love.
*King.* I see there is no lasting faith in sin;
They that break word with Heaven will break
again
With all the world, and so dost thou with me.
*Evad.* How, sir?
*King.* This subtle woman's ignorance 170
Will not excuse you: thou hast taken oaths,
So great that, methought, they did misbecome
A woman's mouth, that thou wouldst ne'er en-
joy
A man but me.
*Evad.* I never did swear so;
You do me wrong.
*King.* Day and night have heard it. 175
*Evad.* I swore indeed that I would never
love
A man of lower place; but, if your fortune
Should throw you from this height, I bade you
trust
I would forsake you, and would bend to him
That won your throne. I love with my ambi-
tion, 180
Not with my eyes. But, if I ever yet
Touch'd any other, leprosy light here
Upon my face! which for your royalty
I would not stain!
*King.* Why, thou dissemblest, and it is in
me 185
To punish thee.
*Evad.* Why, it is in me, then,

Not to love you, which will more afflict
Your body than your punishment can mine.
*King.* But thou hast let Amintor lie with
thee.
*Evad.* I ha' not.
*King.* Impudence! he says himself so.
*Evad.* A' lies.
*King.* A' does not.
*Evad.* By this light, he does, 191
Strangely and basely! and I 'll prove it so.
I did not only shun him for a night,
But told him I would never close with him.
*King.* Speak lower; 't is false.
*Evad.* I am no man
To answer with a blow; or, if I were, 196
You are the king. But urge me not; 't is most
true.
*King.* Do not I know the uncontrolled
thoughts
That youth brings with him, when his blood is
high
With expectation and desire of that 200
He long hath waited for? Is not his spirit,
Though he be temperate, of a valiant strain
As this our age hath known? What could he do,
If such a sudden speech had met his blood,
But ruin thee for ever, if he had not kill'd
thee?
He could not bear it thus: he is as we, 206
Or any other wrong'd man.
*Evad.* This is dissembling.
*King.* Take him! farewell: henceforth I am
thy foe;
And what disgraces I can blot thee with, look
for.
*Evad.* Stay, sir! — Amintor! — You shall
hear. — Amintor! 210
*Amin.* [*coming forward.*] What, my love.
*Evad.* Amintor, thou hast an ingenious
look,
And shouldst be virtuous: it amazeth me
That thou canst make such base malicious lies!
*Amin.* What, my dear wife?
*Evad.* Dear wife! I do despise thee.
Why, nothing can be baser than to sow 216
Dissension amongst lovers.
*Amin.* Lovers! Who?
*Evad.* The king and me —
*Amin.* Oh, God!
*Evad.* Who should live long, and love with-
out distaste,
Were it not for such pickthanks as thyself. 220
Did you lie with me? Swear now, and be pun-
ish'd
In hell for this!

*Amin.*            The faithless sin I made
To fair Aspatia is not yet reveng'd;
It follows me. — I will not lose a word
To this vile woman: but to you, my King,  225
The anguish of my soul thrusts out this truth:
Y' are a tyrant! and not so much to wrong
An honest man thus, as to take a pride
In talking with him of it.
*Evad.*                  Now, sir, see
How loud this fellow lied!                 230
*Amin.*  You that can know to wrong, should
     know how men
Must right themselves. What punishment is due
From me to him that shall abuse my bed?
Is it not death?  Nor can that satisfy,
Unless I send your limbs through all the land,
To show how nobly I have freed myself.  236
     *King.*  Draw not thy sword; thou know'st I
          cannot fear
A subject's hand; but thou shalt feel the
     weight
Of this, if thou dost rage.
     *Amin.*            The weight of that!
If you have any worth, for Heaven's sake, think
I fear not swords; for, as you are mere man,  241
I dare as easily kill you for this deed,
As you dare think to do it.  But there is
Divinity about you that strikes dead
My rising passions: as you are my king,  245
I fall before you, and present my sword
To cut mine own flesh, if it be your will.
Alas, I am nothing but a multitude
Of walking griefs!  Yet, should I murder you,
I might before the world take the excuse  250
Of madness: for, compare my injuries,
And they will well appear too sad a weight
For reason to endure.  But, fall I first
Amongst my sorrows, ere my treacherous sword
Touch holy things! But why (I know not what
I have to say), why did you choose out me  256
To make thus wretched? There were thousands,
     fools
Easy to work on, and of state enough,
Within the island.
     *Evad.*            I would not have a fool;
It were no credit for me.
     *Amin.*            Worse and worse!  260
Thou, that dar'st talk unto thy husband thus,
Profess thyself a whore, and, more than so,
Resolve to be so still! —— It is my fate
To bear and bow beneath a thousand griefs,
To keep that little credit with the world! —
But there were wise ones too; you might have
     ta'en                                 266
Another.

*King.*  No: for I believ'd thee honest,
As thou wert valiant.
     *Amin.*            All the happiness
Bestow'd upon me turns into disgrace.      270
Gods, take your honesty again, for I
Am loaden with it! — Good my lord the King,
Be private in it.
     *King.*            Thou mayst live, Amintor,
Free as thy king, if thou wilt wink at this,
And be a means that we may meet in secret.
     *Amin.*  A bawd! Hold, hold, my breast! A
          bitter curse                     276
Seize me, if I forget not all respects
That are religious, on another word
Sounded like that; and through a sea of sins
Will wade to my revenge, though I should call
Pains here and after life upon my soul!  281
     *King.*  Well, I am resolute you lay not with
          her;
And so I leave you.            *Exit King.*
     *Evad.*            You must needs be prating;
And see what follows!
     *Amin.*            Prithee, vex me not.
Leave me; I am afraid some sudden start
Will pull a murther on me.
     *Evad.*            I am gone;      286
I love my life well.            *Exit Evadne.*
     *Amin.*            I hate mine as much.
This 't is to break a troth!  I should be glad,
If all this tide of grief would make me mad.
                              *Exit.*

[SCENE II. — *The Palace.*]

*Enter Melantius*

*Mel.*  I 'll know the cause of all Amintor's
     griefs,
Or friendship shall be idle.

*Enter Calianax*

*Cal.*                  Oh, Melantius,
My daughter will die!
     *Mel.*            Trust me, I am sorry:
Would thou hadst ta'en her room!
     *Cal.*            Thou art a slave,
A cut-throat slave, a bloody treacherous slave!
     *Mel.*  Take heed, old man; thou wilt be
          heard to rave,                    6
And lose thine offices.
     *Cal.*            I am valiant grown
At all these years, and thou art but a slave!
     *Mel.*  Leave!
Some company will come, and I respect  10
Thy years, not thee, so much, that I could wish
To laugh at thee alone.
     *Cal.*            I 'll spoil your mirth:

---

²²² **faithless sin:** sin of infidelity   ²²⁵ **vile:** ('wild' Qq., F)   ²³⁴ **Is it:** ('It is' Qq., F)   ²³⁵⁻²³⁶ **send
. . . To:** (not in Q 1)   **limbs:** ('lives' Q 2, etc.)   ²⁵⁴ **sword:** ('hand' Q 2, etc.)   ²⁵⁹ **island:**
('Land' Q 1)   ²⁶³ **fate:** ('fault' Q 1)   ²⁸² **resolute:** certain   ² **idle:** vain   ⁴ **ta'en . . . room:** died
in her place

I mean to fight with thee. There lie, my cloak.
This was my father's sword, and he durst fight.
Are you prepar'd?
*Mel.*                Why wilt thou dote thyself 15
Out of thy life? Hence, get thee to bed,
Have careful looking-to, and eat warm things,
And trouble not me: my head is full of thoughts
More weighty than thy life or death can be.
*Cal.* You have a name in war, where you
    stand safe        20
Amongst a multitude; but I will try
What you dare do unto a weak old man
In single fight. You will give ground, I fear.
Come, draw.
*Mel.* I will not draw, unless thou pull'st thy
    death        25
Upon thee with a stroke. There 's no one blow,
That thou canst give hath strength enough to
    kill me.
Tempt me not so far, then: the power of earth
Shall not redeem thee.
*Cal.* [*Aside.*]        I must let him alone;
He 's stout and able; and, to say the truth, 30
However I may set a face and talk,
I am not valiant. When I was a youth,
I kept my credit with a testy trick
I had 'mongst cowards, but durst never fight.
*Mel.* I will not promise to preserve your life,
If you do stay.
*Cal.* [*Aside.*] I would give half my land 36
That I durst fight with that proud man a
    little.
If I had men to hold him, I would beat him
Till he ask'd me mercy.
*Mel.*                Sir, will you be gone?
*Cal.* [*Aside.*] I dare not stay; but I will go
    home, and beat        40
My servants all over for this.        *Exit.*
*Mel.* This old fellow haunts me.
But the distracted carriage of mine Amintor
Takes deeply on me. I will find the cause: 44
I fear his conscience cries, he wrong'd Aspatia.

*Enter Amintor*

*Amin.* [*Aside.*] Men's eyes are not so subtle
    to perceive
My inward misery: I bear my grief
Hid from the world. How art thou wretched
    then?
For aught I know, all husbands are like me;
And every one I talk with of his wife        50
Is but a well-dissembler of his woes,
As I am. Would I knew it! for the rareness
Afflicts me now.
*Mel.* Amintor, we have nòt enjoy'd our [54
friendship of late, for we were wont to change
our souls in talk.

*Amin.* Melantius, I can tell thee a good jest
of Strato and a lady the last day.
*Mel.* How was 't?
*Amin.* Why, such an odd one!        60
*Mel.* I have long'd to speak with you; not of
an idle jest that 's forc'd, but of matter you are
bound to utter to me.
*Amin.* What is that, my friend?
*Mel.* I have observ'd your words fall from
    your tongue        65
Wildly; and all your carriage
Like one that strives to show his merry mood,
When he were ill dispos'd. You were not wont
To put such scorn into your speech, or wear
Upon your face ridiculous jollity.        70
Some sadness sits here, which your cunning
    would
Cover o'er with smiles, and 't will not be. What
    is it?
*Amin.* A sadness here! What cause
Can fate provide for me to make me so?        74
Am I not lov'd through all this isle? The king
Rains greatness on me. Have I not received
A lady to my bed, that in her eye
Keeps mounting fire, and on her tender cheeks
Inevitable colour, in her heart
A prison for all virtue? Are not you,        80
Which is above all joys, my constant friend?
What sadness can I have? No; I am light,
And feel the courses of my blood more warm
And stirring than they were. Faith, marry too;
And you will feel so unexpress'd a joy        85
In chaste embraces, that you will indeed
Appear another.
*Mel.*                You may shape, Amintor,
Causes to cozen the whole world withal,
And yourself too; but 't is not like a friend
To hide your soul from me. 'T is not your
    nature        90
To be thus idle. I have seen you stand
As you were blasted 'midst of all your mirth;
Call thrice aloud, and then start, feigning joy
So coldly! — World, what do I here? A friend
Is nothing. Heaven, I would ha' told that man
My secret sins! I 'll search an unknown land, 96
And there plant friendship; all is wither'd here.
Come with a compliment! I would have fought,
Or told my friend a' lied, ere sooth'd him so. —
Out of my bosom!        100
*Amin.* But there is nothing.
*Mel.*                Worse and worse! farewell:
From this time have acquaintance, but no
    friend.
*Amin.* Melantius, stay: you shall know what
    that is.
*Mel.* See how you play'd with friendship! Be
    advis'd

---

⁴⁴ **Takes:** impresses itself        ⁵⁵ **change:** ('charge' Qq., F)        ⁶⁷ **strives:** ('stroue' Q 2, etc.)        ⁷⁹ **Inevitable:** irresistible ('Immutable' Q 1)        ⁸⁵ **unexpress'd:** inexpressible

How you give cause unto yourself to say     105
You ha' lost a friend.
   *Amin.*               Forgive what I ha' done;
For I am so o'ergone with miseries
Unheard of, that I lose consideration
Of what I ought to do. Oh, oh!
   *Mel.*               Do not weep.
What is 't? May I once but know the man 110
Hath turn'd my friend thus!
   *Amin.*             I had spoke at first,
But that ——
   *Mel.*     But what?
   *Amin.*           I held it most unfit
For you to know. Faith, do not know it yet.
   *Mel.* Thou see'st my love, that will keep
    company     114
With thee in tears; hide nothing, then, from me;
For when I know the cause of thy distemper,
With mine old armour I 'll adorn myself,
My resolution, and cut through thy foes,
Unto thy quiet, till I place thy heart
As peaceable as spotless innocence.     120
What is it?
   *Amin.* Why, 't is this —— it is too big
To get out —— let my tears make way awhile.
   *Mel.* Punish me strangely, Heaven, if he
    'scape
Of life or fame, that brought this youth to this!
   *Amin.* Your sister ——
   *Mel.*     Well said.
   *Amin.*     You 'll wish 't unknown, 125
When you have heard it.
   *Mel.*     No.
   *Amin.*     Is much to blame,
And to the king has given her honour up,
And lives in whoredom with him.
   *Mel.*          How 's this?
Thou art run mad with injury indeed;
Thou couldst not utter this else. Speak again;
For I forgive it freely; tell thy griefs.     131
   *Amin.* She 's wanton: I am loath to say, a
   whore,
Though it be true.
   *Mel.* Speak yet again, before mine anger grow
Up beyond throwing down. What are thy
   griefs?     135
   *Amin.* By all our friendship, these.
   *Mel.*       What, am I tame?
After mine actions, shall the name of friend
Blot all our family, and strike the brand
Of whore upon my sister, unrevenged?
My shaking flesh, be thou a witness for me, 140
With what unwillingness I go to scourge
This railer, whom my folly hath call'd friend!
I will not take thee basely: thy sword     143
               [*Draws his sword.*]

Hangs near thy hand: draw it, that I may
   whip
Thy rashness to repentance; draw thy sword!
   *Amin.* Not on thee, did thine anger go as high
As troubled waters. Thou shouldst do me ease
Here and eternally, if thy noble hand
Would cut me from my sorrows.
   *Mel.*       This is base
And fearful. They that use to utter lies     150
Provide not blows but words to qualify
The men they wrong'd. Thou hast a guilty
   cause.
   *Amin.* Thou pleasest me: for so much more
   like this
Will raise my anger up above my griefs,
(Which is a passion easier to be borne,)     155
And I shall then be happy.
   *Mel.*      Take, then, more
To raise thine anger: 't is mere cowardice
Makes thee not draw; and I will leave thee
   dead,
However. But if thou art so much press'd
With guilt and fear as not to dare to fight, 160
I 'll make thy memory loath'd, and fix a scandal
Upon thy name forever.
   *Amin.* [*drawing his sword.*] Then I draw,
As justly as our magistrates their swords
To cut offenders off. I knew before
'T would grate your ears; but it was base in you
To urge a weighty secret from your friend, 166
And then rage at it. I shall be at ease,
If I be kill'd; and if you fall by me,
I shall not long outlive you.
   *Mel.*      Stay awhile. —
The name of friend is more than family,     170
Or all the world besides: I was a fool.
Thou searching human nature, that didst wake
To do me wrong, thou art inquisitive,     173
And thrusts me upon questions that will take
My sleep away! Would I had died, ere known
This sad dishonour! — Pardon me, my friend!
               [*Sheaths his sword.*]
If thou wilt strike, here is a faithful heart;
Pierce it, for I will never heave my hand
To thine. Behold the power thou hast in me!
I do believe my sister is a whore,     180
A leprous one. Put up thy sword, young man.
   *Amin.* How should I bear it, then, she being
   so?
I fear, my friend, that you will lose me shortly;
               [*Sheaths his sword.*]
And I shall do a foul act on myself,
Through these disgraces.
   *Mel.*     Better half the land 185
Were buried quick together. No, Amintor;
Thou shalt have ease. Oh, this adulterous king,

---

<sup>107</sup> **miseries:** ('iniuries' Q 2, etc.)   <sup>108</sup> **consideration:** power to discriminate   <sup>117</sup> **old:** ('own' Q 3–F)
<sup>138</sup> **strike:** ('stick' Q 1)   <sup>146–147</sup> **go . . . waters:** ('swell as hie As the wilde surges' Q 2, etc.)   <sup>151</sup> **qualify:**
appease   <sup>172</sup> **searching:** spying   <sup>174</sup> **thrusts:** thrustest   <sup>186</sup> **quick:** alive   <sup>187</sup> **ease. Oh:** ('ease of' Q 1)

That drew her to 't! Where got he the spirit
To wrong me so?
   *Amin.*            What is it, then, to me,
If it be wrong to you?
   *Mel.*            Why, not so much.   190
The credit of our house is thrown away.
But from his iron den I 'll waken Death,
And hurl him on this king. My honesty
Shall steel my sword; and on its horrid point
I 'll wear my cause, that shall amaze the eyes
Of this proud man, and be too glittering   196
For him to look on.
   *Amin.* I have quite undone my fame.
   *Mel.* Dry up thy watery eyes,
And cast a manly look upon my face;   200
For nothing is so wild as I, thy friend,
Till I have freed thee. Still this swelling breast.
I go thus from thee, and will never cease
My vengeance till I find thy heart at peace.
   *Amin.* It must not be so. Stay. Mine eyes
    would tell   205
How loath I am to this; but, love and tears,
Leave me awhile! for I have hazarded
All that this world calls happy. — Thou hast
    wrought
A secret from me, under name of friend,
Which art could ne'er have found, nor torture
    wrung   210
From out this bosom. Give it me again;
For I will find it, wheresoe'er it lies,
Hid in the mortal'st part. Invent a way
To give it back.
   *Mel.*            Why would you have it back?
I will to death pursue him with revenge.   215
   *Amin.* Therefore I call it back from thee; for
    I know
Thy blood so high, that thou wilt stir in this,
And shame me to posterity. Take to thy
    weapon!          [*Draws his sword.*]
   *Mel.* Hear thy friend, that bears more years
    than thou.
   *Amin.* I will not hear: but draw, or I ——
   *Mel.*            Amintor!   220
   *Amin.* Draw, then; for I am full as resolute
As fame and honour can enforce me be:
I cannot linger. Draw!
   *Mel.*            I do. But is not
My share of credit equal with thine,
If I do stir?
   *Amin.* No; for it will be call'd   225
Honour in thee to spill thy sister's blood,
If she her birth abuse; and on the king
A brave revenge: but on me, that have walk'd
With patience in it, it will fix the name
Of fearful cuckold. Oh, that word! Be quick.
   *Mel.* Then, join with me.

   *Amin.*            I dare not do a sin,   231
Or else I would. Be speedy.
   *Mel.* Then, dare not fight with me; for that 's
    a sin. —
His grief distracts him. — Call thy thoughts
    again,   234
And to thyself pronounce the name of friend,
And see what that will work. I will not fight.
   *Amin.* You must.
   *Mel.* [*sheathing his sword.*] I will be kill'd
    first. Though my passions
Offer'd the like to you, 't is not this earth
Shall buy my reason to it. Think awhile,   240
For you are (I must weep when I speak that)
Almost besides yourself.
   *Amin.* [*sheathing his sword.*] Oh, my soft
    temper!
So many sweet words from thy sister's mouth,
I am afraid, would make me take her to   245
Embrace, and pardon her. I am mad indeed,
And know not what I do. Yet, have a care
Of me in what thou dost.
   *Mel.*            Why, thinks my friend
I will forget his honour? or, to save
The bravery of our house, will lose his fame,   250
And fear to touch the throne of majesty?
   *Amin.* A curse will follow that; but rather
    live
And suffer with me.
   *Mel.*            I will do what worth
Shall bid me, and no more.
   *Amin.*            Faith, I am sick,
And desperately, I hope; yet, leaning thus,   255
I feel a kind of ease.
   *Mel.*            Come, take again
Your mirth about you.
   *Amin.*            I shall never do 't.
   *Mel.* I warrant you; look up; we 'll walk to-
    gether;
Put thine arm here; all shall be well again.
   *Amin.* Thy love (oh, wretched!) ay, thy love,
    Melantius;   260
Why, I have nothing else.
   *Mel.*            Be merry, then. *Exeunt.*

              *Enter Melantius again*

   *Mel.* This worthy young man may do violence
Upon himself; but I have cherish'd him
To my best power, and sent him smiling from
    me,
To counterfeit again. Sword, hold thine edge;
My heart will never fail me.

              *Enter Diphilus*
                           Diphilus!   266
Thou com'st as sent.
   *Diph.* Yonder has been such laughing.
   *Mel.* Betwixt whom?

    **211 this:** ('my' Q 2, etc.)    **218 And . . . posterity:** (not in Q 1)    **241 that:** ('it' Q 1)    **247 Yet:**
('But' Q 1)    **254 and no more:** (not in Q 1)    **264 To . . . power:** ('As well as I could' Q 1)    **267 as
sent:** as if providentially sent

*Diph.*        Why, our sister and the king.
I thought their spleens would break; they
        laugh'd us all
Out of the room.        270
    *Mel.* They must weep, Diphilus.
    *Diph.*        Must they?
    *Mel.*        They must.
Thou art my brother; and, if I did believe
Thou hadst a base thought, I would rip it out,
Lie where it durst.
    *Diph.*        You should not; I would first
Mangle myself and find it.
    *Mel.*        That was spoke    275
According to our strain. Come, join thy hands,
And swear a firmness to what project I
Shall lay before thee.
    *Diph.*        You do wrong us both.
People hereafter shall not say there pass'd
A bond, more than our loves, to tie our lives
And deaths together.        281
    *Mel.* It is as nobly said as I would wish.
Anon I 'll tell you wonders: we are wrong'd.
    *Diph.* But I will tell you now, we 'll right
        ourselves.
    *Mel.* Stay not: prepare the armour in my
        house;        285
And what friends you can draw unto our side,
Not knowing of the cause, make ready too.
Haste, Diphilus, the time requires it, haste! —
                    *Exit Diphilus.*
I hope my cause is just; I know my blood
Tells me it is; and I will credit it.        290
To take revenge, and lose myself withal,
Were idle; and to 'scape impossible,
Without I had the fort, which (misery!)
Remaining in the hands of my old enemy
Calianax —— but I must have it. See    295

                *Enter Calianax*

Where he comes shaking by me! — Good my
        lord,
Forget your spleen to me. I never wrong'd you,
But would have peace with every man.
    *Cal.*        'T is well;
If I durst fight, your tongue would lie at quiet.
    *Mel.* Y' are touchy without all cause.
    *Cal.*        Do! mock me.    300
    *Mel.* By mine honour, I speak truth.
    *Cal.*        Honour! where is 't?
    *Mel.* See, what starts you make
Into your idle hatred, to my love
And freedom to you. I come with resolution
To obtain a suit of you.
    *Cal.*        A suit of me!    305
'T is very like it should be granted, sir.
    *Mel.* Nay, go not hence.

'T is this; you have the keeping of the fort,
And I would wish you, by the love you ought
To bear unto me, to deliver it        310
Into my hands.
    *Cal.*        I am in hope thou art mad,
To talk to me thus.
    *Mel.*        But there is a reason
To move you to it: I would kill the king,
That wrong'd you and your daughter.
    *Cal.*        Out, traitor!
    *Mel.* Nay, but stay: I cannot 'scape, the
        deed once done,        315
Without I have this fort.
    *Cal.*        And should I help thee?
Now thy treacherous mind betrays itself.
    *Mel.* Come, delay me not;
Give me a sudden answer, or already
Thy last is spoke! Refuse not offer'd love    320
When it comes clad in secrets.
    *Cal.* [*Aside.*]        If I say
I will not, he will kill me; I do see 't
Writ in his looks; and should I say I will,
He 'll run and tell the king. — I do not shun
Your friendship, dear Melantius; but this cause
Is weighty: give me but an hour to think.    326
    *Mel.* Take it. — [*Aside.*] I know this goes
        unto the king;
But I am arm'd.        *Exit Melantius.*
    *Cal.*        Methinks I feel myself
But twenty now again. This fighting fool
Wants policy: I shall revenge my girl,    330
And make her red again. I pray my legs
Will last that pace that I will carry them:
I shall want breath before I find the king.
                    *Exit.*

## Actus Quartus

[SCENE I. — *Evadne's Apartment.*]

*Enter Melantius, Evadne, and Ladies*

    *Mel.* Save you!
    *Evad.*        Save you, sweet brother.
    *Mel.* In my blunt eye, methinks, you look
        Evadne —
    *Evad.* Come, you would make me blush.
    *Mel.*        I would, Evadne;
I shall displease my ends else.
    *Evad.* You shall, if you commend me; I am
        bashful.        5
Come, sir, how do I look?
    *Mel.* I would not have your women hear me
        break
Into commendation of you; 't is not seemly.
    *Evad.* Go wait me in the gallery.
                    *Exeunt Ladies.*
Now speak.

*Mel.*        I 'll lock the door first.
*Evad.*                        Why?   10
*Mel.*  I will not have your gilded things, that
    dance
In visitation with their Milan skins,
Choke up my business.
    *Evad.*        You are strangely dispos'd, sir.
*Mel.*  Good madam, not to make you merry.
*Evad.*  No; if you praise me, 't will make me
    sad.                                    15
*Mel.*  Such a sad commendation I have for
    you.
*Evad.*  Brother,
The court has made you witty, and learn to
    riddle.
*Mel.*  I praise the court for 't: has it learn'd
    you nothing?
*Evad.*  Me!
*Mel.*        Ay, Evadne; thou art young and
    handsome,
A lady of a sweet complexion,            20
And such a flowing carriage, that it cannot
Choose but inflame a kingdom.
    *Evad.*                Gentle brother!
*Mel.*  'T is yet in thy repentance, foolish
    woman,
To make me gentle.
    *Evad.*        How is this?
*Mel.*                        'T is base;   24
And I could blush, at these years, through all
My honour'd scars, to come to such a parley.
    *Evad.*  I understand ye not.
*Mel.*                You dare not, fool!
They that commit thy faults fly the remem-
    brance.
*Evad.*  My faults, sir! I would have you
    know, I care not                        29
If they were written here, here in my forehead.
    *Mel.*  Thy body is too little for the story;
The lusts of which would fill another woman,
Though she had twins within her.
    *Evad.*                This is saucy:
Look you intrude no more! There lies your way.
    *Mel.*  Thou art my way, and I will tread upon
    thee,                                   35
Till I find truth out.
    *Evad.*        What truth is that you look for?
*Mel.*  Thy long-lost honour. Would the gods
    had set me
Rather to grapple with the plague, or stand
One of their loudest bolts!  Come, tell me
    quickly,
Do it without enforcement, and take heed   40
You swell me not above my temper.
    *Evad.*                How, sir!
Where got you this report?

*Mel.*                Where there was people,
In every place.
    *Evad.*        They and the seconds of it
Are base people: believe them not, they lied.  44
    *Mel.*  Do not play with mine anger; do not,
    wretch!                        [*Seizes her.*]
I come to know that desperate fool that drew
    thee
From thy fair life. Be wise, and lay him open.
    *Evad.*  Unhand me, and learn manners! Such
    another
Forgetfulness forfeits your life.
    *Mel.*  Quench me this mighty humour, and
    then tell me                            50
Whose whore you are; for you are one, I know it.
Let all mine honours perish but I 'll find him,
Though he lie lock'd up in thy blood! Be sud-
    den;
There is no facing it; and be not flatter'd.
The burnt air, when the Dog reigns, is not
    fouler                                  55
Than thy contagious name, till thy repentance
(If the gods grant thee any) purge thy sickness.
    *Evad.*  Begone! you are my brother; that 's
    your safety.
*Mel.*  I 'll be a wolf first. 'T is, to be thy
    brother,
An infamy below the sin of coward.       60
I am as far from being part of thee
As thou art from thy virtue. Seek a kindred
'Mongst sensual beasts, and make a goat thy
    brother;
A goat is cooler. Will you tell me yet?
    *Evad.*  If you stay here and rail thus, I shall
    tell you                                65
I 'll ha' you whipp'd! Get you to your com-
    mand,
And there preach to your sentinels, and tell
    them
What a brave man you are: I shall laugh at you.
    *Mel.*  Y' are grown a glorious whore! Where
    be your fighters?                       69
What mortal fool durst raise thee to this daring,
And I alive! By my just sword, he 'd safer
Bestrid a billow when the angry North
Ploughs up the sea, or made Heaven's fire his
    foe!
Work me no higher. Will you discover yet?
    *Evad.*  The fellow 's mad. Sleep, and speak
    sense.                                  75
*Mel.*  Force my swol'n heart no further; I
    would save thee.
Your great maintainers are not here, they dare
    not.
Would they were all, and arm'd! I would speak
    loud;

¹² **Milan skins:** milliners' gloves    ¹⁸ **learn'd:** taught    ³⁴ **There lies:** ('theres' Q 1)    ³⁸ **stand:**
withstand    ⁴³ **seconds:** supporters    ⁵⁵ **Dog:** Sirius, the dog-star    ⁶³ **brother:** ('father' Q 1)
⁶⁹ **glorious:** bragging    ⁷³ **foe:** ('food' Q 2, etc.)

Here 's one should thunder to 'em! Will you
   tell me? —
Thou hast no hope to 'scape. He that dares
   most,     80
And damns away his soul to do thee service,
Will sooner snatch meat from a hungry lion
Than come to rescue thee. Thou hast death
   about thee; —
H'as undone thine honour, poison'd thy virtue,
And, of a lovely rose, left thee a canker.     85
   *Evad.* Let me consider.
   *Mel.*        Do, whose child thou wert,
Whose honour thou hast murder'd, whose grave
   open'd,
And so pull'd on the gods that in their justice
They must restore him flesh again and life,    89
And raise his dry bones to revenge this scandal.
   *Evad.* The gods are not of my mind; they
   had better
Let 'em iie sweet still in the earth; they 'll stink
   here.
   *Mel.* Do you raise mirth out of my easiness?
Forsake me, then, all weaknesses of nature,
                 [*Draws his sword.*]
That make men women! Speak, you whore,
   speak truth,     95
Or, by the dear soul of thy sleeping father,
This sword shall be thy lover! Tell, or I 'll kill
   thee;
And, when thou hast told all, thou wilt deserve
   it.
   *Evad.* You will not murder me?
   *Mel.* No; 't is a justice, and a noble one,    100
To put the light out of such base offenders.
   *Evad.* Help!
   *Mel.* By thy foul self, no human help shall
   help thee,
If thou criest! When I have kill'd thee, as I
Have vow'd to do, if thou confess not, naked   105
As thou hast left thine honour will I leave thee,
That on thy branded flesh the world may read
Thy black shame and my justice. Wilt thou
   bend yet?
   *Evad.* Yes.
   *Mel.* Up, and begin your story.     110
   *Evad.* Oh, I am miserable!
   *Mel.* 'T is true, thou art. Speak truth still.
   *Evad.* I have offended: noble sir, forgive me!
   *Mel.* With what secure slave?
   *Evad.*          Do not ask me, sir;
Mine own remembrance is a misery     115
Too mighty for me.
   *Mel.*        Do not fall back again;
My sword 's unsheathed yet.
   *Evad.*        What shall I do?

   *Mel.* Be true, and make your fault less.
   *Evad.*           I dare not tell,
   *Mel.* Tell, or I 'll be this day a-killing thee.
   *Evad.* Will you forgive me, then?     120
   *Mel.* Stay; I must ask mine honour first.
I have too much foolish nature in me: speak.
   *Evad.* Is there none else here?
   *Mel.* None but a fearful conscience; that 's
   too many.
Who is 't?
   *Evad.* Oh, hear me gently! It was the king.
   *Mel.* No more. My worthy father's and my
   services     126
Are liberally rewarded! King, I thank thee!
For all my dangers and my wounds thou hast
   paid me
In my own metal: these are soldiers' thanks! —
How long have you liv'd thus, Evadne?
   *Evad.*          Too long.    130
   *Mel.* Too late you find it. Can you be sorry?
   *Evad.* Would I were half as blameless!
   *Mel.* Evadne, thou wilt to thy trade again.
   *Evad.* First to my grave.
   *Mel.*        Would gods th'adst been so blest!
Dost thou not hate this king now? Prithee,
   hate him:     135
H'as sunk thy fair soul: I command thee,
   curse him;
Curse till the gods hear, and deliver him
To thy just wishes. Yet I fear, Evadne,
You had rather play your game out.
   *Evad.*          No; I feel
Too many sad confusions here, to let in     140
Any loose flame hereafter.
   *Mel.* Dost thou not feel, 'mongst all those,
   one brave anger,
That breaks out nobly, and directs thine arm
To kill this base king?
   *Evad.*        All the gods forbid it!
   *Mel.* No, all the gods require it;     145
They are dishonour'd in him.
   *Evad.*          'T is too fearful.
   *Mel.* Y' are valiant in his bed, and bold
   enough
To be a stale whore, and have your madam's
   name
Discourse for grooms and pages; and hereafter,
When his cool majesty hath laid you by,     150
To be at pension with some needy sir
For meat and coarser clothes; thus far you
   knew
No fear. Come, you shall kill him.
   *Evad.*          Good sir!
   *Mel.* An 't were to kiss him dead, thou 'dst
   smother him:

---

80—85 (Not in Q 1)     85 **canker:** weed     88 **pull'd on:** provoked     114 **secure:** self-confident
123 **none else:** ('no more' Q 1)     125 **Oh . . . was:** (not in Q 1)     126 **No more:** (not in Q 1)     131 (As
in Q 2, etc.; Q 1 differs.)     133 **Evadne . . . wilt:** ('Woman, thou wilt not' Q 1)     136 **H'as . . . soul:**
('Could'st thou not curse him' Q 2, etc.)     152 **knew:** ('had' Q 1)

Be wise, and kill him.  Canst thou live, and
   know                                                    155
What noble minds shall make thee, see thy-
   self
Found out with every finger, made the shame
Of all successions, and in this great ruin
Thy brother and thy noble husband broken?
Thou shalt not live thus.  Kneel, and swear to
   help me,                                                160
When I shall call thee to it; or, by all
Holy in Heaven and earth, thou shalt not live
To breathe a full hour longer; not a thought!
Come, 't is a righteous oath.  Give me thy hands,
And, both to Heaven held up, swear, by that
   wealth                                                   165
This lustful thief stole from thee, when I say it,
To let his foul soul out.
    *Evad.*                    Here I swear it;  [*Kneels.*]
And, all you spirits of abused ladies,
Help me in this performance!
    *Mel.* [*raising her.*]  Enough.  This must be
   known to none                                          170
But you and I, Evadne; not to your lord,
Though he be wise and noble, and a fellow
Dares step as far into a worthy action
As the most daring, ay, as far as justice.
Ask me not why.  Farewell.      *Exit Mel.*   175
    *Evad.*  Would I could say so to my black dis-
   grace!
Oh, where have I been all this time?  How
   friended,
That I should lose myself thus desperately,
And none for pity show me how I wander'd?
There is not in the compass of the light      180
A more unhappy creature: sure, I am mon-
   strous;
For I have done those follies, those mad mis-
   chiefs,
Would dare a woman.  Oh, my loaden soul,
Be not so cruel to me; choke not up
The way to my repentance!

            *Enter Amintor*

                 Oh, my lord!   185
    *Amin.*  How now?
    *Evad.*             My much abused lord!  *Kneel.*
    *Amin.*                          This cannot be!
    *Evad.*  I do not kneel to live; I dare not hope
   it;
The wrongs I did are greater.  Look upon me,
Though I appear with all my faults.
    *Amin.*                          Stand up.
This is a new way to beget more sorrows;    190
Heaven knows I have too many.  Do not mock
   me:

Though I am tame, and bred up with my
   wrongs,
Which are my foster-brothers, I may leap,
Like a hand-wolf, into my natural wildness, 194
And do an outrage.  Prithee, do not mock me.
    *Evad.*  My whole life is so leprous, it infects
All my repentance.  I would buy your pardon,
Though at the highest set, even with my life:
That 's slight contrition, that, no sacrifice  199
For what I have committed.
    *Amin.*                    Sure, I dazzle;
There cannot be a faith in that foul woman,
That knows no god more mighty than her mis-
   chiefs.
Thou dost still worse, still number on thy
   faults,
To press my poor heart thus.  Can I believe
There 's any seed of virtue in that woman  205
Left to shoot up, that dares go on in sin
Known, and so known as thine is?  Oh, Evadne!
Would there were any safety in thy sex,
That I might put a thousand sorrows off,
And credit thy repentance! but I must not.   210
Thou hast brought me to that dull calamity,
To that strange misbelief of all the world
And all things that are in it, that I fear
I shall fall like a tree, and find my grave,
Only rememb'ring that I grieve.
    *Evad.*                     My lord,   215
Give me your griefs: you are an innocent,
A soul as white as Heaven; let not my sins
Perish your noble youth.  I do not fall here
To shadow my dissembling with my tears,
(As all say women can,) or to make less   220
What my hot will hath done, which Heaven
   and you
Knows to be tougher than the hand of time
Can cut from man's remembrance; no, I do not;
I do appear the same, the same Evadne,
Dress'd in the shames I liv'd in, the same mon-
   ster.                                                   225
But these are names of honour to what I am;
I do present myself the foulest creature,
Most poisonous, dangerous, and despis'd of men,
Lerna e'er bred or Nilus.  I am hell,      229
Till you, my dear lord, shoot your light into me,
The beams of your forgiveness; I am soul-sick,
And wither with the fear of one condemn'd,
Till I have got your pardon.
    *Amin.*                    Rise, Evadne.
Those heavenly powers that put this good into
   thee
Grant a continuance of it!  I forgive thee:  235
Make thyself worthy of it; and take heed,
Take heed, Evadne, this be serious.

164 **hands:** ('hand' Qq., F)      183 **dare:** cow
194 **hand-:** tame    **wildness:** ('wilderness' F)      198 **set:** stake      199 **That's . . . that:** ('That . . .
that Q 1; 'That . . . that 's' Q 2, etc.)      203 **number on:** add to the count of      219 **my:** ('by' in
all previous texts)      227 **present:** declare      229 **Lerna . . .    Nilus:** Lernæan hydra or Egyptian asp

Mock not the powers above, that can and
   dare
Give thee a great example of their justice
To all ensuing ages, if thou play'st        240
With thy repentance, the best sacrifice.
   *Evad.* I have done nothing good to win be-
      lief,
My life hath been so faithless.  All the crea-
   tures,
Made for Heaven's honours, have their ends,
   and good ones, —
All but the cozening crocodiles, false women.
They reign here like those plagues, those killing
   sores,                                    246
Men pray against; and when they die, like
   tales
Ill told and unbeliev'd, they pass away,
And go to dust forgotten.  But, my lord,
Those short days I shall number to my rest  250
(As many must not see me) shall, though too
   late,
Though in my evening, yet perceive a will, —
Since I can do no good, because a woman, —
Reach constantly at something that is near it.
I will redeem one minute of my age,         255
Or, like another Niobe, I 'll weep
Till I am water.
   *Amin.*          I am now dissolved:
My frozen soul melts.  May each sin thou
   hast
Find a new mercy!  Rise; I am at peace.
Hadst thou been thus, thus excellently good, 260
Before that devil-king tempted thy frailty,
Sure thou hadst made a star.  Give me thy
   hand:
From this time I will know thee; and, as far
As honour gives me leave, be thy Amintor.
When we meet next, I will salute thee fairly, 265
And pray the gods to give thee happy days:
My charity shall go along with thee,
Though my embraces must be far from thee.
I should ha' kill'd thee, but this sweet repent-
   ance
Locks up my vengeance: for which thus I kiss
   thee —                                    270
The last kiss we must take: and would to
   Heaven
The holy priest that gave our hands together
Had given us equal virtues!  Go, Evadne;
The gods thus part our bodies.  Have a care
My honour falls no farther: I am well, then.
   *Evad.*  All the dear joys here, and above
      hereafter,                            276
Crown thy fair soul!  Thus I take leave, my
   lord;
And never shall you see the foul Evadne,

Till she have tried all honour'd means, that
   may
Set her in rest and wash her stains away.   280
                       *Exeunt [severally].*

[SCENE II. — *The Palace.*]

*Banquet.  Enter King, Calianax.  Hautboys play
                     within.*

   *King.*  I cannot tell how I should credit this
From you, that are his enemy.
   *Cal.*                    I am sure
He said it to me; and I 'll justify it
What way he dares oppose — but with my
   sword.
   *King.*  But did he break, without all circum-
      stance,                                5
To you, his foe, that he would have the fort,
To kill me, and then 'scape?
   *Cal.*                    If he deny it,
I 'll make him blush.
   *King.*            It sounds incredibly.
   *Cal.*  Ay, so does everything I say of late.
   *King.*  Not so, Calianax.
   *Cal.*                    Yes, I should sit  10
Mute, whilst a rogue with strong arms cuts your
   throat.
   *King.*  Well, I will try him; and, if this be
      true,
I 'll pawn my life I 'll find it; if 't be false,
And that you clothe your hate in such a lie,
You shall hereafter dote in your own house, 15
Not in the court.
   *Cal.*          Why, if it be a lie,
Mine ears are false, for I 'll be sworn I heard
   it.
Old men are good for nothing; you were best
Put me to death for hearing, and free him
For meaning it.  You would ha' trusted me  20
Once, but the time is alter'd.
   *King.*                    And will still,
Where I may do with justice to the world.
You have no witness.
   *Cal.*            Yes, myself.
   *King.*                      No more,
I mean, there were that heard it.
   *Cal.*                        How? no more!
Would you have more?  Why, am not I
   enough                                    25
To hang a thousand rogues?
   *King.*                  But so you may
Hang honest men too, if you please.
   *Cal.*                           I may!
'T is like I will do so: there are a hundred
Will swear it for a need too, if I say it ——
   *King.*  Such witnesses we need not.

239 **Give:** render     240 **ages:** ('eyes' Qq., F)     242 **win:** ('get' Q 1)     251 **many:** many days
254 **Reach:** to reach   257 **now:** (not in Q 1)   5 **break:** impart   **circumstance:** explanatory detail
22 **do:** do so

*Cal.* And 't is hard 30
If my word cannot hang a boisterous knave.
*King.* Enough. — Where 's Strato?

*Enter Strato*

*Strato.* Sir?
*King.* Why, where 's all the company? Call
Amintor in;
Evadne. Where 's my brother, and Melantius?
Bid him come too; and Diphilus. Call all 35
That are without there. *Exit Strato.*
If he should desire
The combat of you, 't is not in the power
Of all our laws to hinder it, unless
We mean to quit 'em.
*Cal.* Why, if you do think
'T is fit an old man and a councillor 40
To fight for what he says, then you may grant
it.

*Enter Amintor, Evadne, Melantius, Diphilus,
Lysippus, Cleon, Strato, Diagoras*

*King.* Come, sirs! — Amintor, thou art yet
a bridegroom,
And I will use thee so; thou shalt sit down. —
Evadne, sit; — and you, Amintor, too;
This banquet is for you, sir. — Who has brought
A merry tale about him, to raise laughter 46
Amongst our wine? Why, Strato, where art
thou?
Thou wilt chop out with them unseasonably,
When I desire 'em not.
*Stra.* 'T is my ill luck, sir, so to spend them,
then. 50
*King.* Reach me a bowl of wine. — Melan-
tius, thou
Art sad.
*Mel.* I should be, sir, the merriest here,
But I ha' ne'er a story of mine own
Worth telling at this time.
*King.* Give me the wine. — 55
Melantius, I am now considering
How easy 't were for any man we trust
To poison one of us in such a bowl.
*Mel.* I think it were not hard, sir, for a
knave.
*Cal.* [*Aside.*] Such as you are. 60
*King.* I' faith, 't were easy. It becomes us
well
To get plain-dealing men about ourselves,
Such as you all are here. — Amintor, to thee;
And to thy fair Evadne. [*Drinks.*]
*Mel.* Have you thought
Of this, Calianax? *Aside.*
*Cal.* Yes, marry, have I. 65
*Mel.* And what 's your resolution?
*Cal.* Ye shall have it, —
[*Aside.*] Soundly, I warrant you.

*King.* Reach to Amintor, Strato.
*Amin.* Here, my love;
[*Drinks and then hands the cup to
Evadne.*]
This wine will do thee wrong, for it will set
Blushes upon thy cheeks; and, till thou dost 70
A fault, 't were pity.
*King.* Yet I wonder much
Of the strange desperation of these men,
That dare attempt such acts here in our state:
He could not 'scape that did it.
*Mel.* Were he known,
Unpossible.
*King.* It would be known, Melantius. 75
*Mel.* It ought to be. If he got then away,
He must wear all our lives upon his sword:
He need not fly the island; he must leave
No one alive.
*King.* No; I should think no man
Could kill me, and 'scape clear, but that old
man. 80
*Cal.* But I! Heaven bless me! I! should I,
my liege?
*King.* I do not think thou wouldst; but yet
thou mightst,
For thou hast in thy hands the means to 'scape,
By keeping of the fort. — He has, Melantius,
And he has kept it well.
*Mel.* From cobwebs, sir, 85
'T is clean swept; I can find no other art
In keeping of it now. 'T was ne'er besieg'd
Since he commanded.
*Cal.* I shall be sure
Of your good word; but I have kept it safe
From such as you.
*Mel.* Keep your ill temper in: 90
I speak no malice; had my brother kept it,
I should ha' said as much.
*King.* You are not merry.
Brother, drink wine. Sit you all still: — (*Aside.*)
Calianax,
I cannot trust this. I have thrown out words,
That would have fetch'd warm blood upon the
cheeks 95
Of guilty men, and he is never mov'd;
He knows no such thing.
*Cal.* Impudence may 'scape,
When feeble virtue is accus'd.
*King.* A' must,
If he were guilty, feel an alteration
At this our whisper, whilst we point at him:
You see he does not.
*Cal.* Let him hang himself; 101
What care I what he does? This he did say.
*King.* Melantius, you can easily conceive
What I have meant; for men that are in fault
Can subtly apprehend when others aim 105
At what they do amiss: but I forgive

---

³⁹ **quit:** prorogue   ⁶⁸ **Reach:** pass the cup   ⁷² **Of:** at   ⁹⁴ **this:** ('thus' Qq., F)

Freely before this man, — Heaven do so too!
I will not touch thee, so much as with shame
Of telling it.  Let it be so no more.
   *Cal.*  Why, this is very fine!
   *Mel.*                  I cannot tell   110
What 't is you mean; but I am apt enough
Rudely to thrust into an ignorant fault.
But let me know it.  Happily 't is nought
But misconstruction; and, where I am clear,
I will not take forgiveness of the gods,   115
Much less of you.
   *King.*         Nay, if you stand so stiff,
I shall call back my mercy.
   *Mel.*             I want smoothness
To thank a man for pardoning of a crime
I never knew.
   *King.*  Not to instruct your knowledge, but
    to show you   120
My ears are everywhere: you meant to kill me,
And get the fort to 'scape.
   *Mel.*            Pardon me, sir;
My bluntness will be pardon'd.  You preserve
A race of idle people here about you,
Facers and talkers, to defame the worth   125
Of those that do things worthy.  The man that
    utter'd this
Had perish'd without food, be 't who it will,
But for this arm, that fenc'd him from the foe;
And if I thought you gave a faith to this,
The plainness of my nature would speak more.
Give me a pardon (for you ought to do 't)   131
To kill him that spake this.
   *Cal.* [*Aside.*]        Ay, that will be
The end of all; then I am fairly paid
For all my care and service.
   *Mel.*            That old man,
Who calls me enemy, and of whom I   135
(Though I will never match my hate so low)
Have no good thought, would yet, I think, ex-
    cuse me,
And swear he thought me wrong'd in this,
   *Cal.*            Who, I?
Thou shameless fellow! didst thou not speak
    to me
Of it thyself?
   *Mel.*    Oh, then it came from him!   140
   *Cal.* From me! who should it come from but
    from me?
   *Mel.* Nay, I believe your malice is enough;
But I ha' lost my anger. — Sir, I hope
You are well satisfied.
   *King.*         Lysippus, cheer
Amintor and his lady. — There 's no sound  145
Comes from you;  I will come and do 't my-
    self.
   *Amin.* [*Aside.*] You have done already, sir,
    for me, I thank you.

   *King.*  Melantius, I do credit this from him,
How slight soe'er you make 't.
   *Mel.*          'T is strange you should.
   *Cal.* 'T is strange a' should believe an old
    man's word   150
That never lied in 's life!
   *Mel.*         I talk not to thee. —
Shall the wild words of this distemper'd man,
Frantic with age and sorrow, make a breach
Betwixt your majesty and me? 'T was wrong
To hearken to him; but to credit him,   155
As much at least as I have power to bear.
But pardon me — whilst I speak only truth,
I may commend myself — I have bestow'd
My careless blood with you, and should be loath
To think an action that would make me lose
That and my thanks too.  When I was a boy,
I thrust myself into my country's cause,   162
And did a deed that pluck'd five years from
    time,
And styl'd me man then.  And for you, my
    King,
Your subjects all have fed by virtue of   165
My arm.  This sword of mine hath plough'd
    the ground,
And reap'd the fruit in peace;
And you yourself have liv'd at home in ease.
So terrible I grew, that without swords
My name hath fetch'd you conquest: and my
    heart   170
And limbs are still the same; my will as great
To do you service.  Let me not be paid
With such a strange distrust.
   *King.*          Melantius,
I held it great injustice to believe
Thine enemy, and did not; if I did,   175
I do not; let that satisfy. — What, struck
With sadness all? More wine!
   *Cal.*         A few fine words
Have overthrown my truth.  Ah, th' art a
    villain!
   *Mel.*    Why, thou wert better    *Aside.*
    let me have the fort:
Dotard, I will disgrace thee thus for ever;  180
There shall no credit lie upon thy words.
Think better, and deliver it.
   *Cal.*        My liege,
He 's at me now again to do it. — Speak;
Deny it, if thou canst. — Examine him
Whilst he is hot; for, if he cool again,   185
He will forswear it.
   *King.*        This is lunacy,
I hope, Melantius.
   *Mel.*         He hath lost himself
Much, since his daughter miss'd the happiness
My sister gain'd; and, though he call me foe,
I pity him.

---

[113] **Happily:** perhaps   [114] **misconstruction:** slander   [125] **Facers:** impudent hypocrites ('Eaters' Q 2, etc.)   **worth:** ('world' Q 1)   [156] **As much:** Is as much   [166-167] **This . . . peace:** (not in Q 1)

*Cal.*     Pity! A pox upon you!     190
*Mel*     Mark his disorder'd words: and at the masque
Diagoras knows he rag'd and rail'd at me,
And call'd a lady "whore," so innocent
She understood him not. But it becomes
Both you and me too to forgive distraction: 195
Pardon him, as I do.
*Cal.*     I 'll not speak for thee,
For all thy cunning. — If you will be safe,
Chop off his head; for there was never known
So impudent a rascal.
*King.*     Some, that love him,
Get him to bed. Why, pity should not let     200
Age make itself contemptible; we must be
All old. Have him away.
*Mel.*     Calianax,
The king believes you; come, you shall go home,
And rest; you ha' done well. [*Aside.*] You 'll give it up,
When I have us'd you thus a month, I hope. 205
*Cal.*     Now, now, 't is plain, sir; he does move me still.
He says, he knows I 'll give him up the fort,
When he has us'd me thus a month. I am mad,
Am I not, still?
*Omnes.*     Ha, ha, ha!
*Cal.*     I shall be mad indeed, if you do thus.
Why should you trust a sturdy fellow there, 211
That has no virtue in him, (all 's in his sword)
Before me? Do but take his weapons from him,
And he 's an ass; and I am a very fool,
Both with 'em and without 'em, as you use me.     215
*Omnes.*     Ha, ha, ha!
*King.*     'T is well, Calianax: but if you use
This once again, I shall entreat some other
To see your offices be well discharg'd. —
Be merry, gentlemen. — It grows somewhat late. —     220
Amintor, thou wouldst be a-bed again.
*Amin.*     Yes, sir.
*King.*     And you, Evadne. — Let me take
Thee in my arms, Melantius, and believe
Thou art, as thou deserv'st to be, my friend
Still and for ever. — Good Calianax,     225
Sleep soundly; it will bring thee to thyself.
          *Exeunt omnes. Manent Mel. and Cal.*
*Cal.*     Sleep soundly! I sleep soundly now, I hope;
I could not be thus else. — How dar'st thou stay
Alone with me, knowing how thou hast us'd me?

*Mel.*     You cannot blast me with your tongue, and that 's     230
The strongest part you have about you.
*Cal.*     I
Do look for some great punishment for this;
For I begin to forget all my hate,
And take 't unkindly that mine enemy
Should use me so extremely scurvily.     235
*Mel.*     I shall melt too, if you begin to take
Unkindnesses: I never meant you hurt.
*Cal.* Thou 'lt anger me again. Thou wretched rogue,
Meant me no hurt! Disgrace me with the king!
Lose all my offices! This is no hurt,     240
Is it? I prithee, what dost thou call hurt?
*Mel.* To poison men, because they love me not;
To call the credit of men's wives in question;
To murder children betwixt me and land:     244
This I call hurt.
*Cal.*     All this thou think'st is sport,
For mine is worse: but use thy will with me;
For betwixt grief and anger I could cry.
*Mel.* Be wise, then, and be safe; thou may'st revenge.
*Cal.* Ay, o' the king: I would revenge of thee.
*Mel.* That you must plot yourself.
*Cal.*     I 'm a fine plotter!
*Mel.* The short is, I will hold thee with the king     251
In this perplexity, till peevishness
And thy disgrace have laid thee in thy grave.
But if thou wilt deliver up the fort,
I 'll take thy trembling body in my arms,     255
And bear thee over dangers. Thou shalt hold
Thy wonted state.
*Cal.*     If I should tell the king,
Canst thou deny 't again?
*Mel.*     Try, and believe.
*Cal.* Nay, then, thou canst bring anything about.
Melantius, thou shalt have the fort.
*Mel.*     Why, well.
Here let our hate be buried; and this hand 261
Shall right us both. Give me thy aged breast
To compass.
*Cal.*     Nay, I do not love thee yet;
I cannot well endure to look on thee;
And if I thought it were a courtesy,     265
Thou shouldst not have it. But I am disgrac'd;
My offices are to be ta'en away;
And, if I did but hold this fort a day,
I do believe the king would take it from me,

---

²¹⁵ **'em . . . 'em:** ('him . . him' Qq., F)     ²²³ **and believe:** (not in Q 1)     ²²⁶ S. D. **Manent:** remain on the stage     ²³¹⁻²³² **I . . . look:** ('Dost not thou look' Q 1)     ²³³ **For I:** ('I feele myself' Q 1)
²³⁵ **extremely:** ('extraordinarily' Q 2, etc.)     ²⁴⁴ **land:** *i.e.,* an inheritance     ²⁴⁵ **I call:** ('is all' Q 2, etc.)
²⁶³ **compass:** embrace

And give it thee, things are so strangely car-
  ried.                                            270
Ne'er thank me for't; but yet the king shall
  know
There was some such thing in 't I told him of,
And that I was an honest man.
  *Mel.*                      He 'll buy
That knowledge very dearly.

#### Enter Diphilus

                    Diphilus,
What news with thee?
  *Diph.*              This were a night indeed
To do it in: the king hath sent for her.    276
  *Mel.* She shall perform it, then. — Go, Diph-
  ilus,
And take from this good man, my worthy
  friend,
The fort; he 'll give it thee.
  *Diph.*                Ha' you got that?
  *Cal.* Art thou of the same breed? Canst
  thou deny                                    280
This to the king too?
  *Diph.*                With a confidence
As great as his.
  *Cal.*          Faith, like enough.
  *Mel.* Away, and use him kindly.
  *Cal.*                    Touch not me;
I hate the whole strain. If thou follow me
A great way off, I 'll give thee up the fort; 285
And hang yourselves.
  *Mel.*                Begone.
  *Diph.*            He 's finely wrought.
                    *Exeunt Calianax, Diphilus.*
  *Mel.* This is a night, spite of astronomers,
To do the deed in. I will wash the stain
That rests upon our house off with his blood.

#### Enter Amintor

  *Amin.* Melantius, now assist me: if thou
  be'st                                          290
That which thou say'st, assist me. I have lost
All my distempers, and have found a rage
So pleasing! Help me.
  *Mel.* [*Aside.*]      Who can see him thus,
And not swear vengeance? — What 's the mat-
  ter, friend?
  *Amin.* Out with thy sword; and, hand in
  hand with me,                                 295
Rush to the chamber of this hated king,
And sink him with the weight of all his sins
To hell for ever.
  *Mel.*            'T were a rash attempt,
Not to be done with safety. Let your reason
Plot your revenge, and not your passion.    300
  *Amin.* If thou refusest me in these extremes,
Thou art no friend. He sent for her to me;
By Heaven, to me, myself! and, I must tell ye,

I love her as a stranger: there is worth
In that vild woman, worthy things, Melantius;
And she repents. I 'll do 't myself alone, 306
Though I be slain. Farewell.
  *Mel.* [*Aside.*]          He 'll overthrow
My whole design with madness. — Amintor,
Think what thou dost: I dare as much as
  valour;
But 't is the King, the King, the King, Amin-
  tor,                                          310
With whom thou fightest! — I know he 's
  honest,                          *Aside.*
And this will work with him.
  *Amin.*                  I cannot tell
What thou hast said; but thou hast charm'd
  my sword
Out of my hand, and left me shaking here,
Defenceless.
  *Mel.*        I will take it up for thee.   315
  *Amin.* What a wild beast is uncollected
  man!
The thing that we call honour bears us all
Headlong unto sin, and yet itself is nothing.
  *Mel.* Alas, how variable are thy thoughts!
  *Amin.* Just like my fortunes. I was run to
  that                                          320
I purpos'd to have chid thee for. Some plot,
I did distrust, thou hadst against the king,
By that old fellow's carriage. But take heed;
There 's not the least limb growing to a king
But carries thunder in it.
  *Mel.*                  I have none        325
Against him.
  *Amin.* Why, come, then; and still remember
We may not think revenge.
  *Mel.*                  I will remember. *Exeunt.*

## Actus Quintus

### [SCENE I. — *The Palace.*]

*Enter Evadne and a Gentleman [of the Bed-
  chamber]*

  *Evad.* Sir, is the king a-bed?
  *Gent.*                  Madam, an hour ago.
  *Evad.* Give me the key, then, and let none
  be near;
'T is the king's pleasure.
  *Gent.* I understand you, madam; would
  't were mine!
I must not wish good rest unto your ladyship. 5
  *Evad.* You talk, you talk.
  *Gent.* 'T is all I dare do, madam; but the
  king
Will wake, and then, methinks —
  *Evad.* Saving your imagination, pray, good
  night, sir.

*Gent.* A good night be it, then, and a long
  one. madam.                                      10
I am gone.                                   *Exit.*
  *Evad.* The night grows horrible; and all
    about me                          *King abed.*
Like my black purpose. Oh, the conscience
Of a lost virtue, whither wilt thou pull me?
To what things dismal as the depth of hell  15
Wilt thou provoke me? Let no woman dare
From this hour be disloyal, if her heart be flesh,
If she have blood, and can fear. 'T is a daring
Above that desperate fool's that left his peace,
And went to sea to fight: 't is so many sins,  20
An age cannot repent 'em; and so great,
The gods want mercy for. Yet I must through
  'em:
I have begun a slaughter on my honour,
And I must end it there.—A' sleeps. O God!  24
Why give you peace to this untemperate beast,
That has so long transgress'd you? I must kill
  him,
And I will do it bravely: the mere joy
Tells me, I merit in it. Yet I must not
Thus tamely do it as he sleeps—that were  29
To rock him to another world: my vengeance
Shall take him waking, and then lay before
  him
The number of his wrongs and punishments.
I 'll shape his sins like Furies, till I waken
His evil angel, his sick conscience,
And then I 'll strike him dead. — King, by
  your leave; —                             35
              *Ties his arms to the bed.*
I dare not trust your strength; your grace and I
Must grapple upon even terms no more.
So, if he rail me not from my resolution,
I shall be strong enough. — My lord the King!
My lord! — A' sleeps, as if he meant to wake  40
No more. — My lord! — Is he not dead al-
  ready? —
Sir! My lord!
  *King.* Who 's that?
  *Evad.*            Oh, you sleep soundly sir!
  *King.*                My dear Evadne,
I have been dreaming of thee; come to bed.
  *Evad.* I am come at length, sir; but how
    welcome?                              45
  *King.* What pretty new device is this,
    Evadne?
What, do you tie me to you? By my love,
This is a quaint one. Come, my dear, and kiss
  me;
I 'll be thy Mars; to bed, my queen of love.
Let us be caught together, that the gods  50
May see and envy our embraces.

  *Evad.*                  Stay, sir, stay;
You are too hot, and I have brought you physic
To temper your high veins.
  *King.* Prithee, to bed, then; let me take it
    warm;
There thou shalt know the state of my body
  better.                                 55
  *Evad.* I know you have a surfeited foul
    body;
And you must bleed.           [*Draws a knife.*]
  *King.*              Bleed!
  *Evad.* Ay, you shall bleed. Lie still; and, if
    the devil,
Your lust, will give you leave, repent. This
  steel
Comes to redeem the honour that you stole,  60
King, my fair name; which nothing but thy
  death
Can answer to the world.
  *King.*              How 's this, Evadne?
  *Evad.* I am not she; nor bear I in this breast
So much cold spirit to be call'd a woman:
I am a tiger; I am anything              65
That knows not pity. Stir not! If thou dost,
I 'll take thee unprepar'd, thy fears upon thee,
That make thy sins look double, and so send
  thee
(By my revenge, I will!) to look those torments
Prepar'd for such black souls.             70
  *King.* Thou dost not mean this; 't is impos-
    sible;
Thou art too sweet and gentle.
  *Evad.*                No, I am not:
I am as foul as thou art, and can number
As many such hells here. I was once fair,
Once I was lovely; not a blowing rose     75
More chastely sweet, till thou, thou, thou, foul
  canker,
(Stir not!) didst poison me. I was a world of
  virtue,
Till your curs'd court and you (Hell bless you
  for 't!)
With your temptations on temptations
Made me give up mine honour; for which,
  King,                                   80
I am come to kill thee.
  *King.*            No!
  *Evad.*                I am.
  *King.*                    Thou art not!
I prithee speak not these things. Thou art
  gentle,
And wert not meant thus rugged.
  *Evad.*                Peace, and hear me.
Stir nothing but your tongue, and that for
  mercy

---

¹² s. d. **King abed:** (Prompter's note. The king's bed on rear stage is discovered when Evadne draws the curtain at line 24.) ¹⁴ **virtue:** ('virgin' Q 2, etc.) ¹⁸ **daring:** ('madnesse' Q 1) ²¹ **repent:** ('prevent' Q 2, etc.) ²⁴ **O God:** ('Good Heavens' Q 2, etc.) ³⁹ **I . . . enough:** ('As I believe he shall not, I shall fit him' Q 1) ⁶⁹ **look:** look for ⁷⁶ **canker:** caterpillar

To those above us; by whose lights I vow, 85
Those blessed fires that shot to see our sin,
If thy hot soul had substance with thy blood,
I would kill that too; which, being past my
    steel,
My tongue shall reach. Thou art a shameless
    villain;
A thing out of the overcharge of nature   90
Sent, like a thick cloud, to disperse a plague
Upon weak catching women; such a tyrant,
That for his lust would sell away his subjects,
Ay, all his Heaven hereafter!
    *King.*                Hear, Evadne,
Thou soul of sweetness, hear! I am thy king.
    *Evad.* Thou art my shame! Lie still; there 's
    none about you,   96
Within your cries; all promises of safety
Are but deluding dreams. Thus, thus, thou
    foul man,
Thus I begin my vengeance!    *Stabs him.*
    *King.*             Hold, Evadne!
I do command thee hold.
    *Evad.*           I do not mean, sir, 100
To part so fairly with you; we must change
More of these love-tricks yet.
    *King.*          What bloody villain
Provok'd thee to this murther?
    *Evad.*          Thou, thou monster!
    *King.* Oh!
    *Evad.* Thou kept'st me brave at court, and
    whor'd me, King;   105
Then married me to a young noble gentleman,
And whor'd me still.
    *King.*          Evadne, pity me!
    *Evad.* Hell take me, then! This for my lord
    Amintor.
This for my noble brother! And this stroke
For the most wrong'd of women!    *Kills him.*
    *King.*          Oh! I die. 110
    *Evad.* Die all our faults together! I forgive
    thee.                      *Exit.*

*Enter two [Gentlemen] of the bed-chamber*

    *1 Gent.* Come, now she 's gone, let 's enter;
the king expects it, and will be angry.
    *2 Gent.* 'T is a fine wench; we 'll have a snap
at her one of these nights, as she goes from 115
him.
    *1 Gent.* Content. How quickly he had done
with her! I see kings can do no more that way
than other mortal people.
    *2 Gent.* How fast he is! I cannot hear him
    breathe.   120
    *1 Gent.* Either the tapers give a feeble light,
Or he looks very pale.
    *2 Gent.*          And so he does:
Pray Heaven he be well; let 's look. — Alas!

He 's stiff, wounded, and dead!    Treason,
    treason!
    *1 Gent.* Run forth and call.    125
    *2 Gent.* Treason, treason!    *Exit.*
    *1 Gent.*          This will be laid on us:
Who can believe a woman could do this?

*Enter Cleon and Lysippus*

    *Cleon.* How now! where 's the traitor?
    *1 Gent.* Fled, fled away; but there her woe-
    ful act
Lies still.    130
    *Cleon.* Her act! a woman!
    *Lys.*             Where 's the body?
    *1 Gent.* There.
    *Lys.* Farewell, thou worthy man! There were
    two bonds
That tied our loves, a brother and a king,
The least of which might fetch a flood of tears;
But such the misery of greatness is,   135
They have no time to mourn; then, pardon me!

*Enter Strato*

Sirs, which way went she?
    *Stra.*           Never follow her;
For she, alas! was but the instrument.
News is now brought in that Melantius   140
Has got the fort, and stands upon the wall,
And with a loud voice calls those few that
    pass
At this dead time of night, delivering
The innocence of this act.
    *Lys.*           Gentlemen,
I am your king.
    *Stra.*         We do acknowledge it.   145
    *Lys.* I would I were not! Follow, all; for this
Must have a sudden stop.    *Exeunt.*

[SCENE II. — *Before the Fort.*]

*Enter Melantius, Diphilus, Calianax, on the
Walls*

    *Mel.* If the dull people can believe I am
    arm'd,
(Be constant, Diphilus) now we have time
Either to bring our banish'd honours home,
Or create new ones in our ends.
    *Diph.*           I fear not;
My spirit lies not that way. — Courage, Cali-
    anax!   5
    *Cal.* Would I had any! you should quickly
    know it.
    *Mel.* Speak to the people; thou art eloquent.
    *Cal.* 'T is a fine eloquence to come to the gal-
    lows:
You were born to be my end; the devil take
    you!

---

    **86 fires . . . shot:** meteors    **90 overcharge:** superfluity    **92 catching:** susceptible    **120 fast:**
fast asleep    Scene II s. d. **Walls:** *i.e.,* the upper stage

Now must I hang for company. 'T is strange, 10
I should be old, and neither wise nor valiant.

*Enter Lysippus, Diagoras, Cleon, Strato, Guard*

*Lys.* See where he stands, as boldly confident
As if he had his full command about him.
*Stra.* He looks as if he had the better cause,
sir;
Under your gracious pardon, let me speak it! 15
Though he be mighty-spirited, and forward
To all great things, to all things of that dan-
ger
Worse men shake at the telling of, yet certainly
I do believe him noble, and this action
Rather pull'd on than sought: his mind was
ever 20
As worthy as his hand.
*Lys.* 'T is my fear, too.
Heaven forgive all! — Summon him, Lord
Cleon.
*Cleon.* Ho, from the walls there!
*Mel.* Worthy Cleon, welcome:
We could ha' wish'd you here, lord; you are
honest.
*Cal. (Aside.)* Well, thou art as flattering a
knave, though 25
I dare not tell thee so ——
*Lys.* Melantius!
*Mel.* Sir?
*Lys.* I am sorry that we meet thus; our old
love
Never requir'd such distance. Pray to Heaven,
You have not left yourself, and sought this
safety
More out of fear than honour! You have lost 30
A noble master, which your faith, Melantius,
Some think might have preserv'd: yet you
know best.
*Cal. [Aside.]* When time was, I was mad:
some that dares fight,
I hope will pay this rascal.
*Mel.* Royal young man, those tears look
lovely on thee: 35
Had they been shed for a deserving one,
They had been lasting monuments. Thy
brother,
Whilst he was good, I call'd him King, and
serv'd him
With that strong faith, that most unwearied
valour,
Pull'd people from the farthest sun to seek
him, 40
And beg his friendship. I was then his soldier.
But since his hot pride drew him to disgrace
me,
And brand my noble actions with his lust,
(That never-cur'd dishonour of my sister,

Base stain of whore, and, which is worse, the
joy 45
To make it still so,) like myself, thus I
Have flung him off with my allegiance;
And stand here, mine own justice, to revenge
What I have suffer'd in him, and this old man
Wrong'd almost to lunacy.
*Cal.* Who, I? 50
You would draw me in. I have had no wrong;
I do disclaim ye all.
*Mel.* The short is this.
'T is no ambition to lift up myself
Urgeth me thus; I do desire again
To be a subject, so I may be free: 55
If not, I know my strength, and will unbuild
This goodly town. Be speedy, and be wise,
In a reply.
*Stra.* Be sudden, sir, to tie
All up again. What 's done is past recall,
And past you to revenge; and there are
thousands 60
That wait for such a troubled hour as this.
Throw him the blank.
*Lys.* Melantius, write in that
Thy choice: my seal is at it.
*[Throws a paper to Melantius.]*
*Mel.* It was our honours drew us to this act,
Not gain; and we will only work our pardons. 65
*Cal.* Put my name in too.
*Diph.* You disclaim'd us all
But now, Calianax.
*Cal.* That 's all one;
I 'll not be hang'd hereafter by a trick:
I 'll have it in.
*Mel.* You shall, you shall. —
Come to the back gate, and we 'll call you
King, 70
And give you up the fort.
*Lys.* Away, away. *Exeunt omnes.*

[SCENE III. — *Amintor's Apartment.*]

*Enter Aspatia, in man's apparel [with arti-
ficial scars on her face]*

*Asp.* This is my fatal hour. Heaven may
forgive
My rash attempt, that causelessly hath laid
Griefs on me that will never let me rest,
And put a woman's heart into my breast,
It is more honour for you that I die; 5
For she that can endure the misery
That I have on me, and be patient too,
May live and laugh at all that you can do.

*Enter Servant*

God save you, sir!
*Ser.* And you, sir! What 's your business?

*Asp.* With you, sir, now, to do me the fair
   office                                           10
To help me to your lord.
   *Ser.*                What, would you serve him?
*Asp.* I 'll do him any service; but, to haste,
For my affairs are earnest, I desire
To speak with him.
   *Ser.* Sir, because you are in such haste, I
      would                                         15
Be loath delay you longer: you can not.
   *Asp.* It shall become you, though, to tell
      your lord.
   *Ser.* Sir, he will speak with nobody;
But in particular, I have in charge,
About no weighty matters.
   *Asp.*                This is most strange.   20
Art thou gold-proof? There 's for thee; help
   me to him.                      [*Gives money.*]
   *Ser.* Pray be not angry, sir: I 'll do my best.
                                              *Exit.*
   *Asp.* How stubbornly this fellow answer'd
   me!
There is a vild dishonest trick in man,
More than in women. All the men I meet    25
Appear thus to me, are harsh and rude,
And have a subtilty in everything,
Which love could never know; but we fond
   women
Harbour the easiest and the smoothest thoughts,
And think all shall go so. It is unjust    30
That men and women should be match'd to-
   gether.

*Enter Amintor and his man*

*Amin.* Where is he?
   *Ser.*                There, my lord.
   *Amin.*                What would you, sir?
   *Asp.* Please it your lordship to command
      your man
Out of the room, I shall deliver things
Worthy your hearing.
   *Amin.*      Leave us.   [*Exit Servant.*]
   *Asp.*                Oh, that that shape   35
Should bury falsehood in it!            *Aside.*
   *Amin.*                Now your will, sir.
   *Asp.* When you know me, my lord, you needs
   · must guess
My business; and I am not hard to know;
For, till the chance of war mark'd this smooth
   face
With these few blemishes, people would call
   me                                              40
My sister's picture, and her mine. In short,
I am the brother to the wrong'd Aspatia.
   *Amin.* The wrong'd Aspatia! Would thou
   wert so too
Unto the wrong'd Amintor! Let me kiss

That hand of thine, in honour that I bear    45
Unto the wrong'd Aspatia. Here I stand
That did it. Would he could not! Gentle youth,
Leave me; for there is something in thy looks
That calls my sins in a most hideous form
Into my mind; and I have grief enough    50
Without thy help.
   *Asp.*          I would I could with credit!
Since I was twelve years old, I had not seen
My sister till this hour I now arriv'd:
She sent for me to see her marriage, —
A woeful one! but they that are above    55
Have ends in everything. She us'd few words,
But yet enough to make me understand
The baseness of the injuries you did her.
That little training I have had is war:
I may behave myself rudely in peace;    60
I would not, though. I shall not need to tell
   you
I am but young, and would be loath to lose
Honour, that is not easily gain'd again.
Fairly I mean to deal: the age is strict
For single combats; and we shall be stopp'd,  65
If it be publish'd. If you like your sword,
Use it; if mine appear a better to you,
Change; for the ground is this, and this the
   time,
To end our difference.            [*Draws.*]
   *Amin.*                Charitable youth,
If thou be'st such, think not I will maintain  70
So strange a wrong: and, for thy sister's sake,
Know, that I could not think that desperate
   thing
I durst not do; yet, to enjoy this world,
I would not see her; for, beholding thee,
I am I know not what. If I have aught    75
That may content thee, take it, and begone,
For death is not so terrible as thou:
Thine eyes shoot guilt into me.
   *Asp.*                Thus, she swore,
Thou wouldst behave thyself, and give me
   words
That would fetch tears into my eyes; and so   80
Thou dost indeed. But yet she bade me watch
Lest I were cozen'd; and be sure to fight
Ere I return'd.
   *Amin.*      That must not be with me.
For her I 'll die directly; but against her
Will never hazard it.
   *Asp.*          You must be urg'd.    85
I do not deal uncivilly with those
That dare to fight; but such a one as you
Must be us'd thus.            *She strikes him.*
   *Amin.* I prithee, youth, take heed.
Thy sister is a thing to me so much    90
Above mine honour, that I can endure
All this — Good gods! a blow I can endure. —

But stay not, lest thou draw a timeless death
Upon thyself.
    *Asp.*       Thou art some prating fellow —
One that has studied out a trick to talk,  95
And move soft-hearted people — to be kick'd.
                    *She kicks him.*
Thus to be kick'd. — Why should he be so slow
In giving me my death?         *Aside.*
    *Amin.*       A man can bear
No more, and keep his flesh.  Forgive me,
    then!
I would endure yet, if I could.  Now show  100
                      *[Draws.]*
The spirit thou pretend'st, and understand
Thou hast no hour to live.
       *They fight. [Aspatia is wounded.]*
                What dost thou mean?
Thou canst not fight: the blows thou mak'st at
    me
Are quite besides; and those I offer at thee.
Thou spread'st thine arms, and tak'st upon thy
    breast,  105
Alas, defenceless!
    *Asp.*        I have got enough,
And my desire.  There is no place so fit
For me to die as here.        *[Falls.]*

*Enter Evadne, her hands bloody, with a knife*

    *Evad.*  Amintor, I am loaden with events,
That fly to make thee happy; I have joys,  110
That in a moment can call back thy wrongs,
And settle thee in thy free state again.
It is Evadne still that follows thee,
But not her mischiefs.  114
    *Amin.*  Thou canst not fool me to believe
    again;
But thou hast looks and things so full of news,
That I am stay'd.
    *Evad.*  Noble Amintor, put off thy amaze,
Let thine eyes loose, and speak.  Am I not fair?
Looks not Evadne beauteous with these rites
    now?  120
Were those hours half so lovely in thine eyes
When our hands met before the holy man?
I was too foul within to look fair then:
Since I knew ill, I was not free till now.
    *Amin.*  There is presage of some important
    thing  125
About thee, which, it seems, thy tongue hath
    lost.
Thy hands are bloody, and thou hast a knife.
    *Evad.*  In this consists thy happiness and
    mine.
Joy to Amintor! for the king is dead.
    *Amin.*  Those have most power to hurt us,
    that we love;  130
We lay our sleeping lives within their arms.

Why, thou hast rais'd up mischief to his height,
And found one to out-name thy other faults;
Thou hast no intermission of thy sins
But all thy life is a continued ill.  135
Black is thy colour now, disease thy nature.
Joy to Amintor!  Thou hast touch'd a life,
The very name of which had power to chain
Up all my rage, and calm my wildest wrongs.
    *Evad.*  'T is done; and, since I could not find
    a way  140
To meet thy love so clear as through his life,
I cannot now repent it.
    *Amin.*  Couldst thou procure the gods to
    speak to me,
To bid me love this woman and forgive,  144
I think I should fall out with them.  Behold,
Here lies a youth whose wounds bleed in my
    breast,
Sent by his violent fate to fetch his death
From my slow hand!  And, to augment my woe,
You now are present, stain'd with a king's
    blood
Violently shed.  This keeps night here,  150
And throws an unknown wilderness about me.
    *Asp.*  Oh, oh, oh!
    *Amin.*  No more; pursue me not.
    *Evad.*             Forgive me, then,
And take me to thy bed: we may not part.
                      *[Kneels.]*
    *Amin.*  Forbear, be wise, and let my rage go
    this way.  155
    *Evad.*  'T is you that I would stay, not it.
    *Amin.*            Take heed;
It will return with me.
    *Evad.*           If it must be,
I shall not fear to meet it.  Take me home.
    *Amin.*  Thou monster of cruelty, forbear!
    *Evad.*  For Heaven's sake look more calm!
    Thine eyes are sharper  160
Than thou canst make thy sword.
    *Amin.*          Away, away!
Thy knees are more to me than violence.
I am worse than sick to see knees follow me
For that I must not grant.  For God's sake,
    stand.
    *Evad.*  Receive me, then.
    *Amin.*    I dare not stay thy language.  165
In midst of all my anger and my grief,
Thou dost awake something that troubles me,
And says, I lov'd thee once.  I dare not stay;
There is no end of woman's reasoning.
                      *Leaves her.*
    *Evad.* [*rising.*]  Amintor, thou shalt love me
    now again.  170
Go; I am calm.  Farewell, and peace for ever!
Evadne, whom thou hat'st, will die for thee.
                      *Stabs herself.*

---

⁹³ **timeless:** untimely    ¹⁰⁴ **besides:** random
**shed:** (not in Q 1)    ¹⁶⁰ **sharper:** ('crueller' Q 1)

¹³³ **out-name:** excel in fame    ¹⁴⁸⁻¹⁵⁰ **And . . .**
¹⁶⁵ **stay:** abide

*Amin.* I have a little human nature yet,
That 's left for thee, that bids me stay thy
    hand.                                  *Returns.*
*Evad.* Thy hand was welcome, but it came
    too late.                                    175
Oh, I am lost! the heavy sleep makes haste.
                                        *She dies.*
*Asp.* Oh, oh, oh!
*Amin.* This earth of mine doth tremble, and
    I feel
A stark affrighted motion in my blood.
My soul grows weary of her house, and I    180
All over am a trouble to myself.
There is some hidden power in these dead things,
That calls my flesh unto 'em; I am cold.
Be resolute and bear 'em company.
There 's something yet, which I am loath to
    leave:                                      185
There 's man enough in me to meet the fears
That death can bring; and yet would it were
    done!
I can find nothing in the whole discourse
Of death, I durst not meet the boldest way;
Yet still, betwixt the reason and the act,    190
The wrong I to Aspatia did stands up;
I have not such another fault to answer.
Though she may justly arm herself with scorn
And hate of me, my soul will part less troubled,
When I have paid to her in tears my sorrow.  195
I will not leave this act unsatisfied,
If all that 's left in me can answer it.
*Asp.* Was it a dream? There stands Amin-
    tor still;
Or I dream still.
*Amin.* How dost thou? speak; receive my
    love and help.                              200
Thy blood climbs up to his old place again;
There 's hope of thy recovery.
*Asp.* Did you not name Aspatia?
*Amin.*                            I did.
*Asp.* And talk'd of tears and sorrow unto
    her?
*Amin.* 'T is true; and, till these happy signs
    in thee                                     205
Stay'd my course, 't was thither I was going.
*Asp.* Thou art there already, and these
    wounds are hers.
Those threats I brought with me sought not re-
    venge,
But came to fetch this blessing from thy hand:
I am Aspatia yet.                              210
*Amin.* Dare my soul ever look abroad again?
*Asp.* I shall sure live, Amintor; I am well;
A kind of healthful joy wanders within me.
*Amin.* The world wants lives ·to excuse thy
    loss;                                       214
Come, let me bear thee to some place of help.

*Asp.* Amintor, thou must stay; I must rest
    here;
My strength begins to disobey my will.
How dost thou, my best soul? I would fain
    live
Now, if I could. Wouldst thou have lov'd me,
    then?
*Amin.* Alas,                                  220
All that I am 's not worth a hair from thee!
*Asp.* Give me thy hand; mine hands grope
    up and down,
And cannot find thee; I am wondrous sick.
Have I thy hand, Amintor?
*Amin.* Thou greatest blessing of the world,
    thou hast.                                  225
*Asp.* I do believe thee better than my sense.
Oh, I must go! farewell!            *Dies.*
*Amin.* She sounds. — Aspatia! — Help! for
    God's sake, water,
Such as may chain life ever to this frame! —
Aspatia, speak! — What, no help yet? I fool!
I 'll chafe her temples. Yet there 's nothing
    stirs.                                      231
Some hidden power tell her, Amintor calls,
And let her answer me! — Aspatia, speak! —
I have heard, if there be any life, but bow
The body thus, and it will show itself.        235
Oh, she is gone! I will not leave her yet.
Since out of justice we must challenge nothing,
I 'll call it mercy, if you 'll pity me,
You heavenly powers, and lend for some few
    years
The blessed soul to this fair seat again!      240
No comfort comes; the gods deny me too.
I 'll bow the body once again. — Aspatia! —
The soul is fled for ever; and I wrong
Myself, so long to lose her company.           244
Must I talk now? Here 's to be with thee, love!
                                        *Kills himself.*

*Enter Servant*

*Ser.* This is a great grace to my lord, to
have the new king come to him. I must tell
him he is entering. — Oh, God! — Help, help!

*Enter Lysippus, Melantius, Calianax, Cleon,
    Diphilus, Strato*

*Lys.* Where 's Amintor?
*Stra.*                    Oh, there, there!
*Lys.* How strange is this!
*Cal.*                    What should we do here? 250
*Mel.* These deaths are such acquainted
    things with me,
That yet my heart dissolves not. May I stand
Stiff here for ever! — Eyes, call up your
    tears!
This is Amintor. Heart, he was my friend;

Melt! now it flows. — Amintor, give a word    255
To call me to thee.
   *Amin.* Oh!
   *Mel.* Melantius calls his friend Amintor. Oh,
Thy arms are kinder to me than thy tongue!
Speak, speak!                        260
   *Amin.* What?
   *Mel.*      That little word was worth all the
     sounds
That ever I shall hear again.
   *Diph.*             Oh, brother,
Here lies your sister slain! You lose yourself
In sorrow there.
   *Mel.*        Why, Diphilus, it is     265
A thing to laugh at, in respect of this.
Here was my sister, father, brother, son:
All that I had. — Speak once again; what
    youth
Lies slain there by thee?
   *Amin.*          'T is Aspatia.
My last is said. Let me give up my soul    270
Into thy bosom.                  [*Dies.*]
   *Cal.* What's that? What's that? Aspatia!
   *Mel.*               I never did
Repent the greatness of my heart till now;
It will not burst at need.            274
   *Cal.* My daughter dead here too! And you
have all fine new tricks to grieve; but I ne'er
knew any but direct crying.

      [289] **good:** ('sharp' Q 1–3)

   *Mel.* I am a prattler: but no more.
                 [*Offers to stab himself.*]
   *Diph.*             Hold, brother!
   *Lys.* Stop him.
   *Diph.* Fie, how unmanly was this offer in
    you!                          280
Does this become our strain?
   *Cal.* I know not what the matter is, but I am
grown very kind, and am friends with you
all now. You have given me that among you
will kill me quickly; but I'll go home, and live
as long as I can.            *Exit.* 286
   *Mel.* His spirit is but poor that can be kept
From death for want of weapons.
Is not my hands a weapon good enough
To stop my breath? or, if you tie down
    those,
I vow, Amintor, I will never eat,     291
Or drink, or sleep, or have to do with that
That may preserve life! This I swear to
    keep.
   *Lys.* Look to him, though, and bear those
    bodies in.
May this a fair example be to me     295
To rule with temper; for on lustful kings
Unlook'd-for sudden deaths from God are
    sent;
But curs'd is he that is their instrument.
                      [*Exeunt.*]

      [296] **temper:** self-restraint

# THE
# ISLAND PRINCESS:
## OR THE
# Generous Portugal.

---

# A Comedy.

---

As it is Acted at the *Theatre Royal* by
His *MAJESTIES* Servants.

## With the Alterations and New
### Additional Scenes.

---

Licensed *May* 31. 1669.

Roger *L'Estrange.*

---

### LONDON,
Printed for *H. R.* and *A. M.* and are to be Sold by
*William Cademan* at the *Popes Head* in the Lower walk of the
*New Exchange,* and *Robert Pask* at the Stationers Arms
and Ink-bottle under *Pinners Hall* in *Winchester-
Street* by *Gresham-Colledge.* 1669.

BIBLIOGRAPHICAL RECORD. *The Island Princess* first appeared in print in the Folio edition of the plays of Beaumont and Fletcher in 1647, and was reprinted, with minor changes, in the second Folio in 1679. Its first separate publication was in 1669, when it was issued in a Quarto "with the Alterations and New Additional Scenes," both of which, however, were relatively slight (see facsimile of title-page). A further revision of the play by Nahum Tate was acted and printed in 1687, and an operatic version by Pierre Motteux, with music by Purcell and others, was issued in 1699. For interesting details see A. C. Sprague, *Beaumont and Fletcher on the Restoration Stage* (1926).

DATE AND STAGE PERFORMANCE. This play was acted at the court during the Christmas festivities in 1621 (December 26). The list of the principal actors indicates that the play belonged to the King's Men, in whose repertory it was listed in 1641. It was revived, in a revised form, as indicated above, shortly after the reopening of the theatres in 1660, and belongs to the group (which includes also *Philaster*, *The Maid's Tragedy*, and *Beggars' Bush*) of the ten Beaumont-Fletcher plays most popular on the Restoration stage.

SOURCES. *The Island Princess* may owe something to a French version of the story by De Bellan appended to a translation of the novels of Cervantes and published in 1614–1615, but it is much closer to a Spanish work by Bartolome Leonardo de Argensola, published in Madrid in 1609 under the title *La Conquista de las Islas Malucas*. Five pages in Argensola's book (ed. 1609, Book IV, pp. 148 ff.) give the story, which Fletcher follows closely in his first three acts. In the Spanish original Armusia, called Salama, is a native islander and a Mohammedan. The change in the hero's nationality and religion motivates Acts IV and V, which are the dramatist's free invention. Since Fletcher is not certainly known to have read Spanish, it has been suggested that there may have been a translation of the *Conquista* in French or English. If so, it no longer survives.

AUTHORSHIP. *The Island Princess* is by all the evidences Fletcher's unassisted work, done at the height of his powers and in the exotic style in which his fancy was at its best. As Mr. Oliphant has well said, "It is perhaps not possible to find a play that is more characteristically Fletcher's from start to finish." It would not be easy to find one that better illustrates that charm about the plays of the Beaumont-Fletcher canon which J. R. Lowell has expressed in a notable essay (*The Old English Dramatists*, 1892): "Of the later dramatists, I think Beaumont and Fletcher rank next to Shakespeare in the amount of pleasure they give, though not in the quality of it, and in fanciful charm of expression. In spite of all their coarseness, there is a delicacy, a sensibility, an air of romance, and above all a grace, in their best work that make them forever attractive to the young, and to all those who have learned to grow old amiably." Milton's allusion to the fleet

> "Close sailing from Bengala, or the isles
> Of Ternate and Tidore, whence merchants bring
> Their spicy drugs," (*Par. Lost*, II. 636 ff.)

is doubtless reminiscent of this play and particularly of Armusia's languorous description (1 iii. 16 ff.)

> "We are arriv'd among the blessed islands,
> Where every wind that rises blows perfumes," etc.

# JOHN FLETCHER (1579–1625)

## THE ISLAND PRINCESS:

## A Tragi-Comedy

### The Persons represented in the Play

KING OF TIDORE, *an Island*
KING OF BAKAM, } *Suitors to the*
KING OF SYANA, } *Princess Quisara*
GOVERNOR OF TERNATA, *an Island. An ill man*
RUY DIAS, *a Captain of Portugal, also suitor to the Princess*
PYNIERO, *Nephew to Ruy Dias, a merry Captain*

CHRISTOPHERO, } *Soldiers and Friends*
PEDRO, } *to Pyniero*
ARMUSIA, *a noble daring Portuguese, in love with the Princess*
SOZA, } *Companions to Armusia, and his*
EMANUEL, } *valiant followers*
Keeper, Moors, Guard, Captain, Citizens, Townsmen

### Women

QUISARA, *the Island Princess, Sister to the King of Tidore*
QUISANA, *Aunt to the Princess*

PANURA, *Waiting-woman to the Princess Quisara*
Citizens' Wives

## The Scene India

### The Principal Actors were

John Lowin
John Underwood
William Eglestone
Rich. Sharpe

Joseph Tailor
Robert Benfield
George Birch
Tho. Polard

### Actus Primus. Scæna Prima.

*[Tidore.—The Ramparts of the Portuguese Fort]*
*A Bell Rings*

*Enter Pyniero, Christophero, and Pedro*

*Pyniero.* Open the ports, and see the watch reliev'd,
And let the guards be careful of their business,
Their vigilant eyes fix'd on these islanders.
They are false and desperate people, when they find
The least occasion open to encouragement,    5
Cruel, and crafty souls. Believe me, gentlemen,
Their late attempt, which is too fresh amongst us,
In which, against all arms and honesty,
The Governor of Ternata made surprise
Of our confederate, the King of Tidore,    10

As for his recreation he was rowing
Between both lands, bids us be wise and circumspect.
*Chr.* It was a mischief suddenly imagin'd,
And as soon done; that governor 's a fierce knave,
Unfaithful as he is fierce, too: there 's no trusting.    15
But I wonder much, how such poor and base pleasures,
As tugging at an oar, or skill in steerage,
Should become princes.
*Py.*        Base breedings love base pleasure:
They take as much delight in a baratto,
A little, scurvy boat to row her tithly,    20
And have the art to turn and wind her nimbly,—
Think it as noble, too, though it be slavish,
And a dull labour that declines a gentleman,—
As we Portugals or the Spaniards do in riding,
In managing a great-horse, which is princely,    25

Persons represented: (From F 2; not in F 1)    9–10 Ternata, Tidore: two of the Molucca Islands
19 baratto: native boat    20 scurvy: mean    tithly: dexterously ('tightly' F 2)    21 wind: turn (a term in horsemanship)    23 declines: degrades    25 great-horse: war-horse

The French in courtship, or the dancing English
In carrying a fair presence.
   *Ped.*          He was strangely taken;
But where no faith is, there 's no trust: he has
    paid for 't.
His sister yet, the fair and great Quisara,
Has show'd a noble mind, and much love in 't 30
To her afflicted brother, and the nobler
Still it appears, and seasons of more tenderness,
Because his ruin styles her absolute
And his imprisonment adds to her profit.
Feeling all this, which makes all men admire
    her,                      35
The warm beams of this fortune that fall on her,
Yet has she made divers and noble treaties,
And propositions for her brother's freedom,
If wealth or honour —
   *Py.*        Peace, peace, you are fool'd, sir;
Things of these natures have strange outsides,
    Pedro,                     40
And cunning shadows, set 'em far from us; —
Draw 'em but near, they are gross, — and they
    abuse us;
They that observe her close, shall find her na-
    ture,
Which I doubt mainly will not prove so ex-
    cellent;
She is a princess, and she must be fair,   45
That 's the prerogative of being royal:
Let her want eyes and nose, she must be beau-
    teous,
And she must know it, too, and the use of it,
And people must believe it, they are damn'd
    else:
Why, all our neighbour princes are mad for
    her.                     50
   *Chr.*  Is she not fair, then?
   *Py.*          But her hopes are fairer,
And there 's a haughty master, the King of
    Bakam,
That lofty sir, that speaks far more and louder
In his own commendations, than a cannon:
He is strucken dumb with her.
   *Ped.*  Beshrew me, she is a sweet one.  55
   *Py.*  And there 's that hopeful man of Syana,
That sprightly fellow, he that 's wise and
    temperate,
He is a lover, too.
   *Chr.*         Would I were worth her looking,
For, by my life, I hold her a complete one.
The very sun, I think, affects her sweetness,  60
And dares not, as he does to all else, dye it
Into his tawny livery.

   *Py.*           She dares not see him,
But keeps herself at distance from his kisses,
And wears her complexion in a case, let him
    but like it
A week, or two, or three, she would look like a
    lion.                     65
But the main sport on 't is, or rather wonder,
The Governor of Ternata, her mortal enemy,
He that has catch'd her brother-king, is struck,
    too,
And is arriv'd under safe conduct also,
And hostages of worth deliver'd for him;   70
And he brought a letter from his prisoner,
Whether compell'd, or willingly deliver'd
From the poor king, or what else dare be in 't.
   *Chr.*  So it be honourable, anything, 't is all
    one,
For I dare think she 'll do the best.
   *Py.*              'T is certain  75
He has admittance, and solicits hourly.
Now if he have the trick —
   *Ped.*            What trick?
   *Py.*               The true one,
To take her, too, if he be but skill'd in bat-
    fowling,
And lime his bush right.
   *Chr.*        I 'll be hang'd when that hits,
For 't is not a compell'd, or forc'd affection  80
That must take her; I guess her stout and vir-
    tuous.
But where 's your uncle, sir, our valiant captain,
The brave Ruy Dias, all this while?
   *Py.*               Ay, marry.
He is amongst 'em, too.
   *Ped.*        A lover?
   *Py.*                   Nay,
I know not that, but, sure, he stands in favour,
Or would stand stiffly, he is no Portugal else.  86
   *Chr.*  The voice says in good favour, in the
    list, too,
Of the privy wooers.  How cunningly of late,
I have observ'd him, and how privately
He has stol'n at all hours from us, and how
    readily                  90
He has feign'd a business to bid the fort fare-
    well
For five or six days, or a month together.
Sure there is something —
   *Py.*  Yes, yes, there is a thing in 't,
A thing would make the best on 's all dance
    after it;
A dainty thing.  Lord, how this uncle of mine 95
Has read to me, and rated me for wenching,

---

    ²⁶ **courtship**: courtly behavior   ³² **seasons**: savors   ³³ **absolute**: an absolute ruler   ⁴¹ **cunning . . . us**: beguiling appearances, when seen from a distance   ⁴² **abuse**: deceive   ⁴⁴ **mainly**: earnestly   ⁴⁷ **want**: lack   ⁵², ⁵⁶ **Bakam, Syana**: other Molucca Islands   ⁶⁰ **affects**: loves   ⁶⁴ **wears·** (not in F 2)   **case**: mask   ⁷⁸ **bat-fowling**: bird-hunting at night   ⁷⁹ **lime**: smear with cement (as was done to catch birds)   ⁸¹ **stout**: brave   ⁸⁵ **sure**: ('since' F 2)   ⁸⁷ **voice**: rumor   ⁹⁶ **read**: lectured

And told me m what desperate case 't would
    leave me,
And how 't would stew my bones.
    *Ped.*            You car'd not for it.
    *Py.* I' faith, not much; I ventur'd on still
    easily,
And took my chance; danger is a soldier's
    honour;                       100
But that this man, this herb of grace, Ruy
    Dias,
This father of our faculties, should slip thus!—
For sure he is a-ferreting; that he     103
That would drink nothing, to depress the spirit,
But milk and water, eat nothing but thin air
To make his blood obedient, that his youth,
In spite of all his temperance, should tickle,
And have a love-mange on him!
    *Chr.*           'T is in him, sir,
But honourable courtship, and becomes his
    rank, too.
    *Py.* In me 't were abominable lechery, or
    would be,                      110
For when our thoughts are on 't, and miss their
    level,
We must hit something.
    *Ped.*       Well, he 's a noble gentleman,
And if he be a suitor, may he speed in 't.
    *Py.* Let him alone, our family ne'er fail'd
    yet.
    *Chr.* Our mad lieutenant still, merry Py-
    niero!                      115
Thus would he do, if the surgeon were searching
    of him.
    *Ped.* Especially if a warm wench had shot
    him.
    *Py.* But hark, Christophero; come hither,
    Pedro;
When saw you our brave countryman, Ar-
    musia?
He that 's arriv'd here lately, and his gallants?
A goodly fellow, and a brave companion     121
Methinks he is, and no doubt, truly valiant,
For he that dares come hither, dares fight any-
    where.
    *Chr.* I saw him not of late. A sober gentle-
    man
I am sure he is, and no doubt bravely sprung,  125
And promises much nobleness.
    *Py.*                I love him,
And by my troth would fain be inward with
    him;
Pray let 's go seek him.
    *Ped.*          We 'll attend you, sir.
    *Py.* By that time we shall hear the burst of
    business.                    *Exeunt.*

[SCENE II. — *The Same. The House
of Quisana*]

*Enter Ruy Dias, Quisara, Quisana, and Panura*

    *Quisar.* Aunt, I much thank you for your
    courtesy,
And the fair liberty you still allow me,
Both of your house and service. Though I be
A princess, and by that prerogative stand free
From the poor malice of opinion,     5
And no ways bound to render up my actions,
Because no power above me can examine me,
Yet, my dear brother being still a prisoner,
And many wand'ring eyes upon my ways,
Being left alone a sea-mark, it behooves me  10
To use a little caution, and be circumspect.
    *Quisan.* You 're wise and noble, lady.
    *Quisar.*              Often, aunt,
I resort hither, and privately, to see you;
It may be to converse with some I favour;  14
I would not have it known as oft, nor cónstru'd:
It stands not with my care.
    *Quisan.*        You speak most fairly,
For even our pure devotions are examin'd.
    *Quisar.* So mad are men's minds now.
    *Ruy.*            Or rather monstrous;
They are thick dreams, bred in fogs, that know
    no fairness.
    *Quisan.* Madam, the house is yours, I am
    yours, pray use me,           20
And at your service all I have lies prostrate;
My care shall ever be to yield ye honour,
And when your fame falls here, 't is my fault,
    lady;
A poor and simple banquet I have provided,
Which if you please to honour with your pres-
    ence —                      25
    *Quisar.* I thank ye, aunt, I shall be with you
    instantly:
A few words with this gentleman.
    *Quisan.*               I 'll leave ye,
And when you please retire, I 'll wait upon you.
               *Exeunt Quisana & Panura.*
    *Quisar.* Why, how now, captain, what,
    afraid to speak to me?
A man of arms, and danted with a lady?     30
Commanders have the power to parle with
    princes.
    *Ruy.* Madam, the favours you have still
    show'r'd on me,
Which are so high above my means of merit,
So infinite, that nought can value 'em
But their own goodness, no eyes look up to 'em
But those that are of equal light, and lustre,  36

---

    103 **a-ferreting:** wenching   111 **level:** aim   116 **searching:** probing   125 **bravely sprung:** well
born   127 **inward:** intimate   6 **render up:** account for   10 **sea-mark:** *i.e.*, a conspicuous figure
15 **cónstru'd:** interpreted, discussed   16 **stands:** is consistent   28 **please:** please to   30 **danted**
**with:** daunted or frightened by   31 **parle:** converse   32 **still:** always

Strike me thus mute.  You are my royal mis-
   tress,
And all my services that aim at honour
Take life from you, the saint of my devotions;
Pardon my wish, it is a fair ambition,         40
And well becomes the man that honours you;
I would I were of worth, of something near you,
Of such a royal piece, a king I would be,      43
A mighty king that might command affection,
And bring a youth upon me might bewitch ye,
And you a sweet soul'd Christian.
   *Quisar.*              Now you talk, sir!
You Portugals, though you be rugged soldiers,
Yet, when you list to flatter, you are plain
   courtiers;
And could you wish me Christian, brave Ruy
   Dias?
   *Ruy.*  At all the danger of my life, great
   lady,                                       50
At all my hopes, at all —
   *Quisar.*           Pray ye, stay a little.
To what end runs your wish?
   *Ruy.*                   O glorious lady,
That I might — but I dare not speak.
   *Quisar.*              I dare, then. —
That you might hope to marry me; nay, blush
   not,
An honourable end needs no excuse;             55
And would you love me then?
   *Ruy.*              My soul not dearer.
   *Quisar.*  Do some brave thing that may en-
   tice me that way,
Something of such a meritorious goodness,
Of such an unmatch'd nobleness, that I may
   know
You have a power beyond ours that preserves
   you:                                        60
'T is not the person, nor the royal title,
Nor wealth, nor glory, that I look upon;
That inward man I love that 's lin'd with virtue,
That well deserving soul works out a favour.
I have many princes suitors, many great ones,
Yet above these I love you; you are valiant,   66
An active man, able to build a fortune.
I do not say I dote, nor mean to marry,
Only the hope is, something may be done,
That may compel my faith, and ask my free-
   dom,                                        70
And leave opinion fair.
   *Ruy.*            Command, dear lady,
And let the danger be as deep as hell,
As direful to attempt —
   *Quisar.*           Y' are too sudden:
I must be rul'd by you.  Find out a fortune
Wisely, and handsomely; examine time          75
And court occasion that she may be ready;
A thousand uses for your forward spirit

Ye may find daily; be sure ye take a good
   one,
A brave and worthy one that may advance ye;
Forc'd smiles reward poor dangers.  You are a
   soldier,                                    80
I would not talk so else, and I love a soldier,
And that that speaks him true and great, his
   valour.
Yet for all these, which are but women's follies,
You may do what you please;  I shall still
   know ye,
And though ye wear no sword.
   *Ruy.*              Excellent lady,       85
When I grow so cold, and disgrace my nation,
That from their hardy nurses suck adventures,
'T were fit I wore a tombstone.  You have read
   to me
The story of your favour;  if I mistake it,
Or grow a truant in the study of it,           90
A great correction, lady —
   *Quisar.*              Let 's to th' banquet,
And have some merrier talk, and then to
   court,
Where I give audience to my general suitors;
Pray heaven my woman's wit hold!  There,
   brave captain,
You may perchance meet something that may
   startle ye;                                 95
I 'll say no more, come, be not sad —
I love ye.                           *Exeunt.*

[SCENE III. — *The Same.  A Hall in the
                  Palace*]

*Enter Pyniero, Armusia, Soza, Christophero,
                  and Emanuel*

*Py.*  You are welcome, gentlemen, most
   worthy welcome,
And know, there 's nothing in our power may
   serve ye,
But you may freely challenge.
   *Arm.*              Sir, we thank ye,
And rest your servants, too.
   *Py.*              Ye are worthy Portugals.
You show the bravery of your minds and
   spirits,                                    5
The nature of our country, too, that brings
   forth
Stirring, unwearied souls to seek adventures,
Minds never satisfied with search of honour.
Where time is, and the sun gives light, brave
   countrymen,
Our names are known; new worlds disclose
   their riches,                               10
Their beauties, and their prides to our em-
   braces;
And we the first of nations find these wonders.

---

⁴³ **royal piece:** piece of royalty   ⁶³ **lin'd:** fortified   ⁶⁴ **works out:** which creates or forces   ⁷¹ **opinion:** reputation   ⁷⁷ **forward:** ardent, zealous   ⁹⁰ **truant:** ('tenant' F 1)

*Arm.* These noble thoughts, sir, have en-
tic'd us forward,
And minds unapt for ease, to see these miracles,
In which we find report a poor relater.   15
We are arriv'd among the blessed islands,
Where every wind that rises blows perfumes,
And every breath of air is like an incense.
The treasure of the sun dwells here, each tree,
As if it envied the old Paradise,   20
Strives to bring forth immortal fruit; the spices
Renewing nature, though not deifying,
And when that falls by time, scorning the
earth,
The sullen earth, should taint or suck their
beauties,
But as we dreamt, for ever so preserve us.   25
Nothing we see, but breeds an admiration;
The very rivers, as we float along,
Throw up their pearls, and curl their heads to
court us;
The bowels of the earth swell with the births
Of thousand unknown gems, and thousand
riches;   30
Nothing that bears a life, but brings a treasure.
The people they show brave, too, civil-
manner'd,
Proportion'd like the masters of great minds;
The women, which I wonder at —
*Py.*                   Ye speak well.
*Arm.* Of delicate aspécts, fair, clearly beau-
teous,   35
And, to that admiration, sweet and courteous.
*Py.* And is not that a good thing? Brave
Armusia,
You never saw the court before?
*Arm.*              No, certain;
But that I see a wonder, too, all excellent,
The government exact.
*Chr.*           Ye shall see, anon,   40
That that will make ye start indeed, such
beauties,
Such riches, and such form.

*Enter Bakam, Syana, Governor*

*Soz.*             We are fire already;
The wealthy magazine of nature sure
Inhabits here.
*Arm.*      These, sure, are all islanders.
*Py.* Yes, and great princes, too, and lusty
lovers.   45
*Arm.* They are goodly persons. What might
he be, signior,
That bears so proud a state?
*Py.*             King of Bakam,
A fellow that farts terror.

*Em.*             He looks highly;
Sure, he was begot o' th' top of a steeple.
*Chr.* It may well be,
For you shall hear him ring anon.
*Py.*                That is Syana,   50
And a brave-temper'd fellow, and more valiant.
*Soz.* What rugged face is that?
*Py.*           That 's the great governor,
The man surpris'd our friend; I told ye of
him.
*Arm.* 'Has dangerous eyes.
*Py.*          A perilous thief, and subtile.
*Chr.* And to that subtilty a heart of iron. 55
*Py.* Yet the young lady makes it melt.
*Arm.*            They start all,
And thunder in the eyes.
*Ba.*         Away, ye poor ones!
Am I in competition with such bubbles?
My virtue and my name rank'd with such
trifles?
*Sy.* Ye speak loud.
*Ba.*     Young man, I will speak louder;   60
Can any man but I deserve her favour,
           *Princes fly at one another.*
You petty princes.
*Py.*       He will put 'em all in 's pocket.
*Sy.* Thou proud mad thing, be not so full of
glory,
So full of vanity.
*Ba.*        How? I contemn thee,
And that fort-keeping fellow.
*Py.*       How the dog looks,   65
The bandog governor!
*Gov.*         Ha! Why —
*Ba.*            Away, thing,
And keep your rank with those that fit your
royalty.
Call out the princess.
*Gov.*       Dost thou know me, bladder,
Thou insolent imposthume?
*Ba.*        I despise thee;
*Gov.* Art thou acquainted with my nature,
baby?   70
With my revenge for injuries? dar'st thou
hold me
So far behind thy file, I cannot reach thee?
What canst thou merit?
*Ba.*       Merit? I am above it;
I am equal with all honours, all achievements,
And what is great and worthy; the best doer 75
I keep at my command, fortune 's my servant,
'T is in my power now to despise such wretches,
To look upon ye slightly, and neglect ye;
And, but she deigns at some hours to remember
ye,

---

$^{20}$ **envied:** vied with, emulated    $^{25}$ **as:** as if    **preserve:** embalm    $^{26}$ **admiration:** wonder
$^{48}$ **highly:** arrogantly    $^{53}$ **surpris'd:** *i.e.*, who captured    $^{55}$ **to:** in addition to    $^{57}$ **thunder** . . .
**eyes:** look threateningly    $^{61}$ s. d.: (not in F 2)    $^{63}$ **glory:** boastful spirit    $^{66}$ **bandog:** mastiff-like
$^{69}$ **imposthume:** abscess    $^{71}$ **With:** ('Let' F 1)    **injuries:** insults    $^{72}$ **file:** rank

And people have bestow'd some titles on ye, 80
I should forget your names —
    *Sy.*                        Mercy of me;
What a blown fool has self-affection
Made of this fellow! did not the queen your
    mother
Long for bellows and bagpipes, when she was
    great with ye,
She brought forth such a windy birth?
    *Gov.*               'T is ten to one 85
She eat a drum, and was deliver'd of a 'larum,
Or else he was swaddl'd in an old sail when he
    was young.
    *Sy.*  He swells too mainly with his medita-
tions.
Faith, talk a little handsomer, ride softly
That we may be able to hold way with ye. We
    are princes, 90
But those are but poor things to you: talk
    wiser,
'T will well become your mightiness; talk less,
That men may think ye can do more.
    *Gov.*                  Talk truth,
That men may think ye are honest, and be-
    lieve ye,
Or talk yourself asleep, for I am weary of
    you. 95
    *Ba.*  Why, I can talk and do.
    *Gov.*           That would do excellent.
    *Ba.*  And tell you, only I deserve the prin-
    cess,
And make good "only I," if you dare, — you,
    sir,
Or you, Syana's prince.
    *Py.*          Here 's a storm toward,
Methinks it sings already. To him, governor.
    *Gov.*  Here lies my proof.
    *Sy.*           And mine.
    *Gov.*           I 'll be short with ye, 101
For these long arguments I was never good
    at.
    *Py.*  How white the boaster looks!

*Enter Ruy Dias, Quisara, Quisana, Panura*

    *Arm.*          I see he lacks faith.
    *Ruy.*  For shame, forbear, great princes, rule
    your angers.
You violate the freedom of this place, 105
The state and royalty —
    *Gov.*          He 's well contented,
It seems, and so I have done.
    *Arm.*         Is this she, signior?
    *Py.*  This is the princess, sir.

    *Arm.*          She is sweet and goodly,
An admirable form; they have cause to justle.
    *Quisar.*  Ye wrong me and my court, ye
    forward princes! 110
Comes your love wrapp'd in violence to seek
    us?
Is 't fit, though you be great, my presence
    should be
Stain'd and polluted with your bloody rages?
My privacies affrighted with your swords?
He that loves me, loves my command; be
    temper'd, 115
Or be no more what ye profess, my servants.
    *Omnes.*  We are calm as peace.
    *Arm.*         What command she carries!
And what a sparkling majesty flies from her!
    *Quisar.*  Is it ye love to do? Ye shall find
    danger,
And danger that shall start your resolutions, 120
But not this way. 'T is not contention,
Who loves me to my face best, or who can flatter
    most
Can carry me: he that deserves my favour,
And will enjoy what I bring, love and majesty,
Must win me with his worth, must travail for
    me; 125
Must put his hasty rage off, and put on
A well-confirm'd, a temperate, and true valour.
    *Omnes.*  But show the way.
    *Quisar.*         And will; and then show you
A will to tread the way, I 'll say ye are worthy.
    *Py.*  What task now will she turn 'em to?
    These hot youths, 130
I fear, will find a cooling-card; I read in her
    eyes
Something that has some swinge must fly
    amongst 'em.
By this hand I love her a little now.
    *Quisar.*  'T is not unknown to you
I had a royal brother, now miserable, 135
And prisoner to that man. If I were ambi-
    tious,
Gap'd for that glory was ne'er born with me,
There he should lie, his miseries upon him;
If I were covetous, and my heart set
On riches, and those base effects that follow 140
On pleasures uncontroll'd, or safe revenges,
There he should die; his death would give me
    all these;
For then stood I up absolute to do all;
Yet all these flattering shows of dignity,
These golden dreams of greatness, cannot force
    me 145

---

    ⁸² **blown:** swollen (with pride)    **self-affection:** self-love    ⁸⁶ **'larum:** loud noise, call to arms
⁸⁸ **mainly:** violently    ⁸⁹ **handsomer:** more properly    ⁹⁷ **only I:** I alone    ⁹⁹ **toward:** forthcoming
¹⁰⁹ **justle:** quarrel    ¹¹⁵ **temper'd:** under control    ¹¹⁹ **Is ... do:** Is action what you desire?    ¹²³ **carry:**
win    ¹²⁵ **travail:** ('travel' Ff)    ¹²⁸ **show you:** if or when you show    ¹³¹ **cooling-card:** something
to cool their ardor    ¹³² **swinge:** power, driving force    ¹³⁸ **There ... miseries:** ('There they should
lye as miseries' F 1)    ¹⁴⁰ **effects:** results    ¹⁴² **would:** ('will' F 2)    ¹⁴⁵ **me:** (not in Ff)

To forget nature and my fair affection.
Therefore that man that would be known my
  lover,
Must be known his redeemer, and must bring
  him,
Either alive or dead, to my embraces,
(For even his bones I scorn shall feel such
  slavery,)                                    150
Or seek another mistress. 'T will be hard
To do this, wondrous hard, a great adventure,
Fit for a spirit of an equal greatness;
But, being done, the reward is worthy of it.
  *Chr.*  How they stand gaping all!
  *Quisar.* [*Aside.*]     Ruy Dias cold?  155
Not fly like fire into it?—May be you doubt me:
He that shall do this is my husband-prince;
By the bright heavens, he is, by whose justice
I openly proclaim it; if I lie,
Or seek to set you on with subtilty,          160
Let that meet with me, and reward my false-
  hood! —              [*To Ruy Dias.*]
No stirring yet, no start into a bravery?
  *Ruy.*  Madam, it may be, but being a main
  danger,
Your grace must give me leave to look about
  me,
And take a little time: the cause will ask it. 165
Great acts require great counsels.
  *Quisar.*            Take your pleasure. —
I fear the Portugal. [*Aside.*]
  *Ba.*            I 'll raise an army
That shall bring back his island, fort and all,
And fix it here.
  *Gov.*           How long will this be doing?
You should have begun in your grandfather's
  days.                                        170
  *Sy.*   What may be,
And what my power can promise, noblest lady,
My will, I am sure, stands fair.
  *Quisar.*          Fair be your fortune,
Few promises are best, and fair performance.
  *Gov.*  These cannot do;
Their power and arts are weak ones.            175
'T is in my will, I have this king your brother,
He is my prisoner. I accept your proffer,
And bless the fair occasion that achiev'd him.
I love ye, and I honour ye; but speak,
Whether alive or dead he shall be render'd, 180
And see how readily, how in an instant,
Quick as your wishes, lady —
  *Quisar.*            No, I scorn ye,
You and your courtesy; I hate your love, sir;
And ere I would so basely win his liberty,
I would study to forget he was my brother. 185
By force he was taken; he that shall enjoy me,
Shall fetch him back by force, or never know me.

  *Py.*  As I live, a rare wench.
  *Arm.*             She has a noble spirit.
  *Gov.*                     By force?
  *Quisar.*  Yes, sir, by force, and make you
  glad, too,
To let him go.
  *Gov.*  How? You may look nobler on me, 190
And think me no such boy: by force he must
  not,
For your love much may be.
  *Quisar.*          Put up your passion,
And pack ye home; I say, by force, and sud-
  denly.
He lies there till he rots else, although I love him
Most tenderly and dearly, as a brother,     195
And out of these respects would joy to see him;
Yet to receive him as thy courtesy,
With all the honour thou couldst add unto him,
From his hands that most hates him, I had
  rather,
Though no condition were propounded for him,
See him far sunk i' th' earth, and there forget
  him.                                          201
  *Py.*  Your hopes are gelt, good governor.
  *Arm.*                     A rare woman.
  *Gov.*                        Lady,
I 'll pull this pride, I 'll quench this bravery,
And turn your glorious scorn to tears and
  howlings;
I will, proud princess; this neglect of me  205
Shall make thy brother-king most miserable;
Shall turn him into curses 'gainst thy cruelty;
For where before I us'd him like a king,
And did those royal offices unto him,
Now he shall lie a sad lump in a dungeon,  210
Loaden with chains and fetters; colds and hun-
  ger,
Darkness, and ling'ring death for his com-
  panions;
And let me see who dare attempt his rescue,
What desperate fool look toward it. Farewell,
And when thou know'st him thus, lament thy
  follies!                                      215
Nay, I will make thee kneel to take my offer:
Once more farewell, and put thy trust in
  puppets.                            *Exit.*
  *Quisar.*  If none dare undertake it, I 'll live a
  mourner.
  *Ba.*  You cannot want.
  *Sy.*              You must not.
  *Ruy.*              'T is most dangerous,
And wise men would proceed with care and
  counsel,                                      220
Yet some way would I knew. —       *Exeunt.*
               Walk with me, gentlemen.
        *Manent Armusia and his Companions.*

---

167 **fear:** doubt    168 **his:** ('this' F 2)    177 **proffer:** ('prisoner' F 1)    178 **achiev'd:** gained,
put in my power    180 **render'd:** returned    196 **out . . . respects:** for these reasons    199 **hates:**
('hate' Ff)    203 **pull:** humble    208 **where:** whereas    209 **offices:** services

*Arm.* How do you like her spirit?

*Soz.*                              'T is a clear one,
Clogg'd with no dirty stuff, she is all pure
honour.

*Em.* The bravest wench I ever look'd upon,
And of the strongest parts: she is most fair, 225
Yet her mind such a mirror —

*Arm.*                              What an action
Would this be to put forward on, what a glory,
And what an everlasting wealth to end it!
Methinks my soul is strangely rais'd.

*Soz.*                              To step into it,
Just while they think, and ere they have
determin'd                                                230
To bring the king off.

*Arm.* Things have been done as dangerous.

*Em.* And prosper'd best when they were
least consider'd.

*Arm.* Bless me, my hopes, and you, my
friends, assist me.
None but our companions. —

*Soz.*                              You deal wisely,
And if we shrink, the name of slaves die with us.

*Em.* Stay not for second thoughts.

*Arm.*                              I am determin'd; 236
And though I lose, it shall be sung I was valiant,
And my brave offer shall be turn'd to story,
Worthy the princess' tongue. A boat, that 's
all
That 's unprovided, and habits like to mer-
chants,                                                      240
The rest we 'll counsel as we go.

*Soz.*                              Away, then!
Fortune looks fair on those make haste to win
her.                                                    *Exeunt.*

## Actus Secundus. Scæna Prima.

[*Ternata. — A Prison*]

*Enter Keeper, and 2 or 3 Moors*

*Kee.* I have kept many a man, and many a
great one,
Yet, I confess, I ne'er saw before
A man of such a sufferance: he lies now
Where I would not lay my dog, for sure 't would
kill him;
Where neither light or comfort can come near
him,                                                          5
Nor air, nor earth that 's wholesome: it
grieves me
To see a mighty king, with all his glory,
Sunk o' th' sudden to the bottom of a dungeon.
Whether should we descend that are poor
rascals,
If we had our deserts?

*1 Mo.*                              'T is a strange wonder, 10
Load him with irons, oppress him with con-
tempts,
Which are the governor's commands, give him
nothing,
Or so little, to sustain life, 't is next nothing,
They stir not him; he smiles upon his miseries,
And bears 'em with such strength, as if his
nature                                                        15
Had been nurs'd up, and foster'd with calami-
ties.

*2 Mo.* He gives no ill words, curses, nor
repines not,
Blames nothing, hopes in nothing we can
hear of;
And in the midst of all these frights, fears
nothing.

*Kee.* I 'll be sworn                                      20
He fears not, for even when I shake for him,
As many times my pity will compel me,
When other souls, that bear not half his bur-
then,
Shrink in their powers, and burst with their
oppressions;
Then will he sing, woo his afflictions,            25
And court 'em in sad airs, as if he would wed
'em.

*1 Mo.* That 's more than we have heard yet;
we are only
Appointed for his guard, but not so near him.
If we could hear that wonder —

*Kee.*                              Many times
I fear the governor should come to know it; 30
For his voice so affects me, so delights me,
That when I find his hour, I have music ready,
And it stirs me infinitely. Be but still and pri-
vate,
And you may chance to hear.

*King appears loaden with chains, his head
and arms only above.*

*2 Mo.*                              We will not stir, sir;
This is a sudden change, but who dares blame
it?                                                           35

*Kee.* Now hark and melt, for I am sure I
shall;
Stand silent. What stubborn weight of chains —

*1 Mo.* Yet he looks temperately.

*2 Mo.* His eyes not sunk, and his complexion
firm still,
No wildness, no distemper'd touch upon him. 40
How constantly he smiles, and how undaunted!
With what a majesty he heaves his head up!
                                                       *Music.*

*Kee.* Now mark, I know he will sing; do
not disturb him. —                              [*To King.*]

---

Your allowance from the governor. Would it
    were more, sir,              [*Gives him food.*]
Or in my power to make it handsomer.        45
    *King.* Do not transgress thy charge; I take
        his bounty
And fortune, whilst I bear a mind contented,
Not leaven'd with the glory I am fallen from,
Nor hang upon vain hopes, that may corrupt me.

*Enter Governor*

    *Gov.* Thou art my slave, and I appear above
        thee.                                          50
    *Kee.* The governor himself.
    *Gov.*                        What, at your banquet?
And in such state, and with such change of
        service?
    *King.* Nature's no glutton, sir; a little
        serves her.
    *Gov.* This diet's wholesome, then.
    *King.*                      I beg no better.
    *Gov.* A calm contented mind! Give him less
        next;                                          55
These full meals will oppress his health. His
        grace
Is of a tender and pure constitution,
And such repletions —
    *King.* Mock, mock, it moves not me, sir,
Thy mirths, as do thy mischiefs, fly behind
        me.
    *Gov.* Ye carry it handsomely; but tell me,
        patience,                                      60
Do not you curse the brave and royal lady,
Your gracious sister? Do not you damn her
        pity,
Damn twenty times a day, and damn it seri-
        ously?
Do not you swear aloud, too, cry and kick?
The very soul sweat in thee with the agony   65
Of her contempt of me? Couldst not thou eat
        her
For being so injurious to thy fortune,
Thy fair and happy fortune? Couldst not thou
        wish her
A bastard or a whore? Fame might proclaim
        her,
Black, ugly fame? Or that thou hadst had no
        sister, —                                      70
Spitting the general name out, and the nature;
Blaspheming heaven for making such a mis-
        chief;
For giving power to pride, and will to woman?
    *King.* No, tyrant, no, I bless and love her
        for it;
And though her scorn of thee had laid up for me
As many plagues as the corrupted air breeds, 76
As many mischiefs as the hours have minutes,
As many forms of death, as doubt can figure;

Yet I should love her more still, and more
    honour her.
All thou canst lay upon me, cannot bend me; 80
No, not the stroke of death, that I despise, too:
For if fear could possess me, thou hadst won me.
As little from this hour I prize thy flatteries,
And less than those thy prayers, though thou
    wouldst kneel to me;
And if she be not mistress of this nature,      85
She is none of mine, no kin, and I contemn her.
    *Gov.* Are you so valiant, sir?
    *King.*                      Yes, and so fortunate;
For he that holds his constancy still conquers.
Hadst thou preserv'd me as a noble enemy,
And, as at first, made my restraint seem to me
But only as the shadow of captivity,            91
I had still spoke thee noble, still declar'd thee
A valiant, great, and worthy man, still lov'd
    thee,
And still preferr'd thy fair love to my sister;
But to compel this from me with a misery,      95
A most inhuman and unhandsome slavery —
    *Gov.* You will relent, for all this talk, I fear
        not,
And put your wits a-work again.
    *King.*                      You are cozen'd;
Or, if I were so weak to be wrought to it,
So fearful to give way to so much poverty,     100
How I should curse her heart if she consented!
    *Gov.* You shall write and entreat, or —
    *King.*                      Do thy utmost,
And e'en in all thy tortures I 'll laugh at thee,
I 'll think thee no more valiant, but a villain;
Nothing thou hast done brave, but, like a thief,
Achiev'd by craft and kept by cruelty;         106
Nothing thou canst deserve, thou art unhonest;
Nor no way live to build a name, thou art
        barbarous.
    *Gov.* Down with him low enough! There
        let him murmur,
And see his diet be so light and little,        110
He grow not thus high-hearted on 't. I will
        cool ye,
And make ye cry for mercy, and be ready
To work my ends, and willingly; and your
        sister taken down,
Your scornful, cruel sister shall repent, too,
And sue to me for grace. — Give him no
        liberty,                                       115
But let his bands be doubled, his ease lessen'd;
Nothing his heart desires, but vex and torture
        him:
Let him not sleep; nothing that 's dear to
        nature
Let him enjoy; yet take heed that he die not;
Keep him as near death, and as willing to em-
        brace it,                                      120

⁷⁸ **figure:** imagine    ⁷⁹ **her:** (not in F 2)    ⁸³ **prize:** regard    ⁸⁸ **his:** ('my' F 1)    ⁹⁴ **preferr'd:**
commended    ⁹⁷ **for:** in spite of    ¹⁰⁰ **fearful:** afraid    **to:** as to    ¹¹⁶ **bands:** bonds

But see he arrive not at it; I will humble him,
And her stout heart that stands on such de-
     fiance.
And let me see her champions that dare venture,
Her high and mighty wooers! Keep your
     guards close,
And, as you love your lives, be diligent.   125
And what I charge, observe.
     *Omnes.*                    We shall be dutiful.
     *Gov.* I 'll pull your courage, king, and all
          your bravery.          *Exit Governor.*
                              [*King disappears.*]
     *1 Mo.* Most certain he is resolv'd, nothing
          can stir him;
For if he had but any part about him
Gave way to fear or hope, he durst not talk
     thus,                                        130
And do thus stoutly, too. As willingly,
And quietly he sunk down to his sorrows,
As some men to their sleeps.
     *Kee.*          Yes, and sleeps with 'em;
So little he regards them, there 's the wonder,
And often soundly sleeps. Would I durst pity
     him,                                          135
Or would it were in my will, but we are servants,
And tied unto command.
     *2 Mo.*               I wish him better,
But much I fear h'as found his tomb already.
We must observe our guards.
     *1 Mo.*               He cannot last long,
And when he is dead, he is free.
     *Kee.*          That 's the most cruelty,   140
That we must keep him living.
     *2 Mo.*               That 's as he please;
For that man that resolves, needs no physician.
                              *Exeunt.*

[SCENE II. — *The Same.   A Street*]

*Enter Armusia, Soza, Emanuel like Merchants,*
          *arm'd underneath*

     *Arm.* Our prosperous passage was an omen
          to us,
A lucky and a fair omen.
     *Omnes.*               We believe it.
     *Arm.* The sea and wind strove who should
          most befriend us,
And as they favour'd our design, and lov'd us,
So led us forth. Where lies the boat that
     brought us?                                    5
     *Soz.* Safe lodg'd within the reeds, close by
          the castle,
That no eye can suspect, nor thought come
     near it.
     *Em.* But where have you been, brave sir?
     *Arm.*          I have broke the ice, boys;

I have begun the game; fair fortune guide it!
Suspectless have I travell'd all the town
          through,                                  10
And in this merchant's shape won much ac-
     quaintance,
Survey'd each strength and place that may be-
     friend us,
View'd all his magazines, got perfect knowledge
Of where the prison is, and what power guards
     it.
     *Soz.* These will be strong attempts.
     *Arm.*               Courage is strong.   15
What we began with policy, my dear friends,
Let 's end with manly force; there 's no retiring,
Unless it be with shame.
     *Em.*               Shame his that hopes it!
     *Arm.* Better a few, and clearer fame will
          follow us,
However, lose or win, and speak our memories,
Than if we led our armies. Things done thus,   21
And of this noble weight, will style us worthies.
     *Soz.* Direct, and we have done; bring us to
          execute,
And if we flinch or fail —
     *Arm.*               I am sure ye dare not.
Then farther know, and let no ear be near us,   25
That may be false —
     *Em.*               Speak boldly on; we are honest,
Our lives and fortunes yours.
     *Arm.*               Hard by the place, then,
Where all his treasure lies, his arms, his women,
Close by the prison, too, where he keeps the
     king,
I have hir'd a lodging, as a trading merchant,   30
A cellar to that, too, to stow my wares in,
The very wall of which, joins to his storehouse.
     *Soz.* What of all this?
     *Arm.*          Ye are dull, if ye apprehend not:
Into that cellar, elected friends, I have con-
     vey'd,
And unsuspected, too, that that will do it;   35
That that will make all shake, and smoke, too.
     *Em.*                                   Ha?
     *Arm.* My thoughts have not been idle, nor
          my practice.
The fire I brought here with me shall do some-
     thing,
Shall burst into material flames, and bright ones,
That all the island shall stand wond'ring at it,
As if they had been stricken with a comet.   41
Powder is ready, and enough, to work it,
The match is left afire, all, all hush'd, and lock'd
     close,
No man suspecting what l am but merchant.
An hour hence, my brave friends, look for the
     fury,                                          45

The fire to light us to our honour'd purpose,
For by that time 't will take.
 *Soz.*      What are our duties?
 *Arm.*   When all are full of fear and fright, the governor
Out of his wits, to see the flames so imperious,
Ready to turn to ashes all he worships,    50
And all the people there to stop these ruins,
No man regarding any private office;
Then fly we to the prison suddenly,
Here 's one has found the way, and dares direct us.
 *Em.*   Then to our swords and good hearts!
I long for it.           55
 *Arm.*   Certain we shall not find much opposition,
But what is must be forc'd.
 *Soz.*       'T is bravely cast, sir,
And surely, too, I hope.
 *Arm.*      If the fire fail not,
And powder hold his nature. Some must presently,
Upon the first cry of th' amazed people,   60
(For nothing will be mark'd then but the misery,)
Be ready with the boat upon an instant,
And then all 's right and fair.
 *Em.*      Bless us, dear Fortune!
 *Arm.*   Let us be worthy of it in our courage,
And fortune must befriend us. Come, all sever,          65
But keep still within sight. When the flame rises
Let 's meet, and either do or die.
 *Soz.*        So be it.
              *Exeunt.*

[SCENE III. — *The Same. Another Street*]

*Enter Governor and Captain*

 *Gov.*   No, captain, for those troops, we need 'em not;
The town is strong enough to stand their furies;
I would see 'em come and offer to do something.
They are high in words.
 *Cap.*     'T is safer, sir, than doing.
 *Gov.*   Dost think they dare attempt?
 *Cap.*      May be by treaty,   5
But sure by force they will not prove so froward.
 *Gov.*   No faith, I warrant thee, they know me well enough
And know they have no child in hand to play with:
They know my nature, too, I have bit some of 'em,
And to the bones; they have reason to remember me.         10

It makes me laugh to think how glorious
The fools are in their promises, and how pregnant
Their wits and powers are to bring things to pass.
Am I not grown lean with loss of sleep and care
To prevent these threat'nings, captain?
 *Cap.*      You look well, sir:   15
Upon my conscience, you are not like to sicken
Upon any such conceit.
 *Gov.*      I hope I shall not:
Well, would I had this wench, for I must have her,
She must be mine: and there 's another charge, captain;
What betwixt love and brawling I get nothing,          20
All goes in maintenance —   *The train takes.*
        Hark, what was that,
That noise there? it went with a violence.
 *Cap.*   Some old wall belike, sir,
That had no neighbour help to hold it up,
Is fallen suddenly.
 *Gov.*   I must discard these rascals,   25
That are not able to maintain their buildings.
They blur the beauty of the town.
 *Within.*        Fire! Fire!
 *Gov.*   I hear another tune, good captain,
It comes on fresher still, 't is loud and fearful.
Look up into the town; how bright the air shows!          30
Upon my life some sudden fire. *Exit Captain.*
       The bell, too? *Bell rings.*
I hear the noise more clear.

*Enter Citizen*

 *Cit.*        Fire! Fire!
 *Gov.*        Where? where?
 *Cit.*   Suddenly taken in a merchant's house, sir,
Fearful and high it blazes; help, good people.
            [*Exit.*]
 *Gov.*   Pox o' their paper-houses, how they smother!          35
They light like candles! how the roar still rises!

*Enter Captain*

 *Cap.*   Your magazine 's afire, sir! help, help, suddenly!
The castle, too, is in danger, in much danger:
All will be lost. Get the people presently,
And all that are your guard, and all help! all hands, sir.         40
Your wealth, your strength, is burnt else, the town perish'd;
The castle now begins to flame.
 *Gov.*        My soul shakes.

---

<sup>52</sup> **office:** duty   <sup>57</sup> **cast:** contrived   <sup>65</sup> **sever:** separate   <sup>67</sup> **and:** ('or' Ff)   <sup>11</sup> **glorious:** boastful
<sup>17</sup> **conceit:** fancy, idea   <sup>20</sup> **get:** ('got' Ff)   <sup>21</sup> S. D. **train takes:** mine explodes

*Cap.* A merchant's house next joining?
shame light on him,
That ever such a neighbour, such a villain —
*Gov.* Raise all the garrison, and bring 'em
up; 45

*Enter other Citizens*

And beat the people forward. — Oh, I have lost
all:
In one house, all my hopes. Good worthy
citizens,
Follow me all, and all your powers give to me.
I will reward you all. Oh, cursed fortune —
The flame 's more violent: arise still, help, help,
citizens, 50
Freedom and wealth to him that helps: follow,
oh, follow!
Fling wine, or anything, I 'll see 't recompens'd.
Buckets, more buckets! fire, fire, fire!
*Exeunt omnes.*

*Enter Armusia, and his company*

*Arm.* Let it flame on, a comely light it
gives up
To our discovery.
*Soz.* Hark, what a merry cry 55
These hounds make! Forward fairly.
We are not seen in the mist, we are not noted.
Away, away! Now if we lose our fortune —
*Exeunt.*

[SCENE IV. — *The Same. Another Street*]

*Enter Captain and Citizens*

*Cap.* Up, soldiers, up, and deal like men.
*Cit.* More water, more water, all is con-
sumed else.
*Cap.* All 's gone, unless you undertake it
straight; your wealth, too,
That must preserve and pay your labour
bravely.
Up, up, away!
*Exeunt Captain and Citizens. Then,*

[SCENE V. — *The Prison*]

*Enter Armusia and his company breaking open
a door*

*Arm.* So, thou art open. — Keep the way
clear behind still.
Now for the place.

*Sold.* 'T is here, sir.
*Arm.* Sure, this is it.
Force ope the door. — A miserable creature!
Yet by his manly face —
*The king discover'd.*
*King.* Why stare ye on me? 5
You cannot put on faces to affright me:
In death I am a king still, and contemn ye.
Where is that governor? Methinks his man-
hood
Should be well pleas'd to see my tragedy,
And come to bathe his stern eyes in my sorrows:
I dare him to the sight, bring his scorns with
him, 10
And all his rugged threats. Here 's a throat,
soldiers;
Come, see who can strike deepest.
*Em.* Break the chain, there.
*King.* What does this mean?
*Arm.* Come, talk of no more governors,
He has other business, sir. Put your legs for-
ward,
And gather up your courage like a man, 15
We 'll carry off your head else. We are friends,
And come to give your sorrows ease.
*Soz.* On bravely;
Delays may lose again.

*Enter Guard*

*Arm.* The guard.
*Soz.* Upon 'em.
*Arm.* Make speedy and sure work.
*[They fight.]*
*Em.* They fly.
*Arm.* Up with him, and to the boat; stand
fast, now be speedy; 20
When this heat 's past, we 'll sing our history.
Away like thoughts, sudden as desires, friends;
Now sacred chance be ours.
*Soz.* Pray when we have done, sir.
*Exeunt.*

[SCENE VI. — *The Same. A Street*]

*Enter 3 or 4 Citizens severally*

*1 Cit.* What, is the fire allay'd?
*2 Cit.* 'T is out, 't is out,
Or past the worst. I never did so stoutly,
I 'll assure you, neighbours, since I was a man.
I have been burnt at both ends like a squib;
I liv'd two hours in the fire. 'T was a hideous
matter; 5

⁵⁷ **mist:** haze, smoke   Sc. IV ¹ **deal:** act   Sc. V ²¹ **heat:** action, quarrel   Sc. VI. This
scene has been rewritten in the edition of 1669 to exploit the recent Fire of London (1666), such topical allusions as the following being added: — "*Sec. Neighbour.* . . . how many thousands were there
that pretended to help people to remove their goods, and ran quite away with 'em. If I had but
Commission to search for those Rogues, and to hang 'em when I had done, I should make the Gallowes
groan more than forty Sessions would do. *Third Neigh.* Neighbour, there were Country Rogues that
came in with their Carts, but were as bad Rogues as the others. *Sec. Neigh.* I [Ay], for they pretended
to come in Charity, but for all that would not carry a load of Goods under five or ten pound. Damn'd
Rogues, the more distress people were in, the more they exacted, and the higher they set their price."

But when men of understanding come about it,
Men that judge of things, — my wife gave me
   over,
And took her leave a hundred times; I bore up
   still,
And toss'd the buckets, boys.

*3 Cit.*         We are all mere martins.
*1 Cit.*  I heard a voice at latter end o' th'
   hurry,                    10
Or else I dreamt I heard it, that said "treason."
*2 Cit.*  'T is like enough, it might cry "murder," too,
For there was many without a joint; but
   what 's that to us?
Let 's home and fright our wives, for we look
   like devils.

*Enter 3 Women*

*3 Cit.*  Here come some of 'em to fright us. 15
*1 Wo.*  Mine 's alive, neighbour! — Oh, sweet
   honey husband!
*2 Cit.*  Thou liest, I think, abominably: and
   thou hadst been
In my place, thou wouldst have stunk at both
   ends.
Get me some drink, give me whole tuns of
   drink,
Whole cisterns, for I have four dozen of fine
   firebrands                   20
In my belly; I have more smoke in my mouth,
   than would
Bloat a hundred herrings.
*2 Wo.*         Art thou come safe again?
*3 Wo.*  I pray you, what became of my man,
   is he well?
*2 Cit.*  At heart's ease in a well; is very well,
   neighbour.
We left him drinking of a new dozen of buckets:                      25
Thy husband 's happy; he was thorough roasted,
And now he 's basting of himself at all points:
The clerk and he are cooling their pericraniums.
Body o' me, neighbours, there 's fire in my codpiece.
*1 Wo.*  Bless my husband!        30
*2 Cit.*  Blow it out, wife! blow, blow! the
   gable end o' th' store-house.
*Women.*  Some water! water, water!
*3 Cit.*         Peace, 't is but a sparkle;
Raise not the town again; 't will be a great
   hindrance,
I 'm glad 't is out, and 't had ta'en in my hay-
   loft —
What frights are these? marry, heaven bless thy
   modicum.                35

*3 Wo.*  But is 'a drown'd outright? pray put
   me out of fear, neighbour.
*2 Cit.*  Thou wouldst have it so,
But, after a hundred fires more, he 'll live
To see thee burnt for brewing musty liquor.
*1 Cit.*       Come, let 's go, neighbour, 40
For I would very fain turn down this liquor.
*2 Cit.*  Come, come, I fry like a burnt mary-
   bone:
Women, get you afore, and draw upon us;
Run, wenches, run, and let your taps run with
   ye;
Run as the fire were in your tails; cry "Ale,
   Ale!"                  45
*Wom.*  Away, let 's nourish the poor
   wretches.
*2 Cit.*  We 'll rally up the rest of the burnt
   regiment.            [*Exeunt.*]

[SCENE VII. — *The Same.  Before the*
            *Governor's Castle*]

*Enter Governor, Captain, Soldier, and Guard*

*Gov.*  The fire 's quench'd, captain, but the
   mischief hangs still;
The king 's redeem'd and gone, too; a trick,
   a damn'd one:
Oh, I am overtaken poorly, tamely.
*Cap.*  Where were the guard that waited
   upon the prison?
*Sold.*  Most of 'em slain, yet some scap'd, sir,
   and they deliver,             5
They saw a little boat ready to receive him
And those redeem'd him, making such haste
   and fighting;
Fighting beyond the force of men.
*Gov.*           I am lost, captain,
And all the world will laugh at this, and scorn
   me,
Count me a heavy, sleepy fool, a coward,  10
A coward past recovery, a confirm'd coward,
One without carriage or common sense.
*Sold.*           He 's gone, sir,
And put to sea amain, past our recovery,
Not a boat ready to pursue: if there were any,
The people stand amaz'd so at their valour, 16
And the sudden fright of fire, none knows to
   execute.
*Gov.*  Oh, I could tear my limbs, and knock
   my boy's brains
'Gainst every post I meet! Fool'd with a fire?
*Cap.*  It was a crafty trick.
*Gov.*          No, I was lazy, 20
Confident, sluggish, lazy. Had I but met 'em
And chang'd a dozen blows, I had forgiv'n 'em.

---

⁹ **martins:** *i.e.*, chimney-swallows, which live amid smoke    ¹⁷ **and:** an, if    ²² **Bloat:** cure
²³ **well:** ('in a Well' Ff)    ⁴¹ **For . . . liquor:** (given to 2 Cit. Ff)    ⁴² **mary-bone:** marrow bone
³ **overtaken:** outwitted    ⁵ **deliver:** report    ¹² **carriage:** capacity    ¹⁴ **amain:** without delay
¹⁷ **to execute:** how to act    ²² **chang'd:** exchanged

By both these hands held up, and by that
   brightness
That gilds the world with light, by all our wor-
   ships,
The hidden ebbs and flows of the blue ocean, 25
I will not rest; no mirth shall dwell upon me,
Wine touch my mouth, nor anything refresh
   me,
Till I be wholly quit of this dishonour!
Make ready my barratoes instantly,
And what I shall intend —
   *Cap.*      We are your servants. *Exeunt.* 30

[Scene VIII. — *Tidore.  Before the Palace*]

*Enter Quisara, Ruy Dias*

*Quisar.*  Never tell me!  You never car'd to
   win me;
Never for my sake to attempt a deed
Might draw me to a thought you sought my
   favour.
If not for love of me, for love of arms, sir,
For that cause you profess, for love of honour, 5
Of which you style yourself the mighty master,
You might have stepp'd out nobly, and made
   an offer,
As if you had intended something excellent,
Put on a forward face —
   *Ruy.*         Dear lady, hold me —
   *Quisar.*  I hold ye, as I find ye, a faint serv-
   ant.                               10
   *Ruy.*  By heaven, I dare do —
   *Quisar.*         In a lady's chamber,
I dare believe ye; there 's no mortal danger.
Give me the man that dares do to deserve that!
I thought you Portugals had been rare wonders,
Men of those haughty courages and credits, 15
That all things were confin'd within your
   promises;
The lords of fate and fortune I believ'd ye,
But well I see I am deceiv'd, Ruy Dias,
And blame, too late, my much belief.
   *Ruy.*         I am asham'd, lady, 20
I was so dull, so stupid to your offer:
Now you have once more school'd me, I am
   right,
And something shall be thought on suddenly,
And put in act as soon, some preparation —
   *Quisar.*  And give it out?
   *Ruy.*      Yes, lady, and so great, too; 25
In which the noise of all my countrymen —
   *Quisar.*  Those will do well, for they are all
   approv'd ones,
And though he be restor'd alive.
   *Ruy.*               I have ye.

*Quisar.*  For then we are both servants.
*Ruy.*                  I conceive ye.
Good madam, give me leave to turn my fancies.
   *Quisar.*  Do, and make all things fit, and then
   I 'll visit you.                 *Exit.* 31
   *Ruy.*  Myself, the cousin, and the garrison,
The neighbours of the out-isles of our nation,
Syana's strength, for I can humour him;
And proud Bakamus, I shall deceive his glory.
                         *A shout.*
What ringing sound of joy is this? whence
   comes it?                            36
May be the princes are in sport.

*Enter Pyniero, Christophero*

   *Py.*                     Where are ye?
   *Ruy.*  Now, Pyniero, what 's the haste you
   seek me?
   *Py.*  Do you know this sign, sir?
   *Ruy.*      Ha!
   *Py.*          Do you know this emblem?
Your nose is bor'd.
   *Ruy.*         Bor'd?  What 's that?
   *Py.*           Y' are topp'd, sir: 40
The king 's come home again, the king.
   *Ruy.*              The devil!
   *Py.*  Nay, sure, he came o' God's name
   home:
He 's return'd, sir.
   *Chr.*       And all this joy ye hear —
   *Ruy.*  Who durst attempt him?  The princes
   are all here.
   *Chr.*  They are worthy princes,      44
They are special princes, all; they love by
   ounces.
Believe it, sir, 't is done, and done most bravely
And easily.  What fortune have ye lost, sir?
What justice have ye now unto this lady?
   *Py.*  How stands your claim?  That ever
   man should be fool'd so,         49
When he should do and prosper; stand pro-
   testing,
Kissing the hand, and farting for a favour,
When he should be about his business sweating.
She bid you go, and pick'd you out a purpose,
To make yourself a fortune by, a lady,
A lady, and a lusty one, a lovely,      55
That now you may go look; she pointed ye,
Knowing you were a man of worth and merit,
And bid you fly: you have made a fair flight
   on 't,
You have caught a goose.
   *Ruy.*  How dare you thus molest me? *A shout.*
It cannot be.
   *Chr.*      Hark how the general joy rings! 61

---

²⁴ **worships:** objects of worship    ⁸ **intended:** intended to do    ¹⁰ **servant:** lover    ¹¹ **heaven:**
(represented by a dash in Ff)    ²⁶ **noise:** report, fame    ³⁰ **turn my fancies:** turn over my thoughts
⁴⁰ **topp'd:** defeated    ⁴³ **justice:** claim    ⁵⁶ **look:** *i.e.*, seek in vain    **pointed:** appointed, chose
⁶⁰ **molest:** annoy

*Py.* Have you your hearing left? Is not
  that drunk, too?
For if you had been sober, you had been wise,
  sure.
*Ruy.* Done? Who dares do?
*Py.*                     It seems, an honest fellow,
That has ended his market before you be up. 65
*Chr.* The shame on 't, 's a stranger, too.
*Py.*                               'T is no shame;
He took her at her word, and tied the bargain,
Dealt like a man, indeed, stood not demurring,
But clapp'd close to the cause, as he will do to
  the lady.
'Is a fellow of that speed and handsomeness, 70
He will get her with child, too, ere you shall
  come to know him.
Is it not brave, a gentleman scarce landed,
Scarce eating of the air here, not acquainted,
No circumstance of love depending on him,
Nor no command to show him, must start forth,
At the first sight, too —
*Ruy.*                    I am undone.
*Py.*                    Like an oyster! — 76
She neither taking view, nor value of him,
Unto such deeds as these — Pox o' these,
These wise delayings; they make men cowards.
You are undone as a man would undo an egg, 80
A hundred shames about ye.

*Enter Quisara, Panura, and train*

*Quisar.*                     Can it be possible,
A stranger that I have not known, not seen yet,
A man I never grac'd; oh, captain, captain,
What shall I do? I am betray'd by fortune:
It cannot be, it must not be.
*Py.*                     It is, lady, 85
And, by my faith, a handsome gentleman;
'T is his poor scholar's prize.
*Quisar.*               Must I be given
Unto a man I never saw, ne'er spoke with,
I know not of what nation?
*Py.*                     'Is a Portugal,
And of as good a pitch — He will be giv'n to
  you, lady,                                   90
For he 's given much to handsome flesh.
*Quisar.*               Oh, Ruy Dias,
This was your sloth, your sloth, your sloth,
  Ruy Dias.
*Py.* Your love-sloth, uncle; do you find it
  now?
You should have done at first, and faithfully,
                                      *A shout.*
And then th' other had lied ready for ye; 95
Madam, the general joy comes.
*Quisar.*               We must meet it —
But with what comfort?

*Enter Citizens carrying boughs, boys singing after
  'em; then King, Armusia, Soza, Emanuel;
  the Princes and train following*

*Quisar.* Oh, my dear brother, what a joy
  runs through me,
To see you safe again, yourself, and mighty,
What a blest day is this!
*King.*                    Rise up, fair sister, 100
I am not welcome till you have embrac'd me.
*Ruy.* A general gladness, sir, flies through
  the city,
And mirth possesses all to see your grace ar-
  rive,
Thus happily arriv'd again, and fairly.
'T was a brave venture whosoe'er put for it, 105
A high and noble one, worthy much honour;
And had it fail'd, we had not fail'd, great sir,
And in short time, too, to have forc'd the
  governor,
In spite of all his threats, —
*King.*                    I thank ye, gentleman.
*Ruy.* And all his subtilties, to set you free,
With all his heart and will, too.
*King.*                    I know ye love me. 111
*Py.* [*Aside.*] This had been good with
  something done before it,
Something set off to beautify it.
Now it sounds empty, like a barber's basin;
Pox, there 's no metal in 't, no noble marrow.
*Ba.* I have an army, sir, (but that the gov-
  ernor,                                       115
The foolish fellow, was a little provident,
And wise in letting slip no time; became him,
  too,)
That would have scour'd him else, and all his
  confines;
That would have rung him such a peal —
*Py.* [*Aside.*]               Yes, backward, 120
To make dogs howl. I know thee to a farthing.
Thy army 's good for hawks, there 's nothing
But sheep's hearts in it.
*Sy.* I have done nothing, sir, therefore I
  think it
Convenient I say little what I purpos'd, 125
And what my love intended.
*King.*                    I like your modesty,
And thank ye, royal friends. I know it griev'd
  ye
To know my misery; but this man, princes,
I must thank heartily, indeed, and truly,
For this man saw me in 't, and redeem'd me:
He look'd upon me sinking, and then caught
  me.                                          131
This, sister, this, this all-man, this all-valour,
This pious man.

---

⁷³ **eating:** breathing    ⁷⁴ **circumstance:** state, detail    ⁸⁰ **undo:** break    ⁸⁷ **scholar's prize:** one
of the prizes offered at the fencing school    ⁹⁰ **pitch:** degree    **giv'n:** devoted    ¹⁰⁵ **put for:** undertook    ¹²⁵ **Convenient:** fitting    ¹²⁸ **princes:** ('Princess' F 2)

*Ruy.* [*Aside.*] My countenance! it shames me.
One scarce arriv'd, not harden'd yet, not read
In dangers and great deeds, seasick, not
   season'd —                                      135
Oh, I have boy'd myself.
   *King.*                     This noble bulwark,
This lance and honour of our age and kingdom,
This that I never can reward, nor hope
To be once worthy of the name of friend to:
This, this man from the bowels of my sorrows
Has new-begot my name, and once more made
   me.                                            141
Oh, sister, if there may be thanks for this,
Or anything near recompense invented —
   *Arm.* You are too noble, sir; there is re-
      ward,
Above my action, too, by millions;               145
A recompense so rich and glorious,
I durst not dream it mine, but that 't was
   promis'd;
But that it was propounded, sworn, and seal'd
Before the face of heaven, I durst not hope it;
For nothing in the life of man or merit,          150
It is so truly great, can else embrace it.
   *King.* O speak it, speak it, bless mine ears
      to hear it;
Make me a happy man, to know it may be;
For still methinks I am a prisoner,
And feel no liberty before I find it.             155
   *Arm.* Then know it is your sister; she is
      mine, sir.
I claim her by her own word and her honour;
It was her open promise to that man
That durst redeem ye. Beauty set me on,
And fortune crowns me fair, if she receive me.
   *King.* Receive ye, sir — why, sister — Ha!
      so backward,                                161
Stand as you knew me not? nor what he has
   ventur'd?
My dearest sister —
   *Arm.*                     Good sir, pardon me:
There is a blushing modesty becomes her,
That holds her back. Women are nice to woo,
   sir;                                           165
I would not have her forc'd. Give her fair
   liberty;
For things compell'd and frighted, of soft
   natures.
Turn into fears, and fly from their own wishes.
   *King.* Look on him, my Quisara, such
      another,
Oh, all ye powers, so excellent in nature,        170
In honour so abundant! —
   *Quisar.*                     I confess, sir;

Confess my word is pass'd, too, he has pur-
   chas'd;
Yet, good sir, give me leave to think; but time
To be acquainted with his worth and person,
To make me fit to know it. We are both
   strangers,                                     175
And how we should believe so suddenly,
Or come to fasten our affections —
Alas, love has his complements.
   *King.*                     Be sudden
And certain in your way, no woman's doubles,
Nor coy delays; you are his, and so assure it,
Or cast from me and my remembrance ever. 181
Respect your word; I know you will: come,
   sister,
Let 's see what welcome you can give a pris-
   oner,
And what fair looks a friend. — Oh, my most
   noble
Princes, no discontents, but all be lusty!        185
He that frowns this day is an open enemy. —
Thus in my arms, my dear.
   *Arm.*                     You make me blush, sir.
   *King.* And now lead on, our whole court
      crown'd with pleasure.
   *Ruy.* [*To Quisara.*] Madam, despair not,
      something shall be done yet,
And suddenly, and wisely.
   *Quisar.*                     O, Ruy Dias!     190
            *Exeunt* [*all except Pyniero, Soza,
                  and Christophero*].

   *Py.* Well, he 's a brave fellow, and he has
      deserv'd her richly;
And you have had your hands full, I dare
   swear, gentlemen.
   *Soz.* We have done something, sir, if it hit
      right.
   *Chr.* The woman has no eyes else, nor no
      honesty:
So much I think.
   *Py.* Come, let 's go bounce amongst 'em,
To the king's health and my brave country-
   man's.                                         196
My uncle looks as though he were sick o' th'
   worms, friends.                                *Exeunt*


### Actus Tertius. Scæna Prima.

#### [*Tidore. — The Palace*]

#### *Enter Pyniero*

[*Py.*] Mine uncle haunts me up and down,
      looks melancholy,
Wondrous proof-melancholy, sometimes swears.

---

¹³⁴ **read**: learned, experienced   ¹³⁶ **boy'd**: disgraced by acting like a boy   ¹⁶⁵ **nice**: difficult, fastidious   ¹⁶⁹ **him**: (not in F 1)   ¹⁷² **purchas'd**: gained the prize   ¹⁷⁸ **complements**: formal courtesies
¹⁷⁹ **doubles**: tricks ('woman doubles' F 2)   ¹⁸⁰ **assure**: feel certain of   ¹⁸¹ **cast**: dismissed
¹⁸⁵ **lusty**: merry   ¹⁹³ **hit right**: succeed   ² **proof-**: strong

Then whistles, starts, cries, and groans, as if
  he had the bots,
As, to say truth, I think h'as little better,
And would fain speak; bids me good morrow
  at midnight,                                               5
And good night when 't is noon, has something
  hovers
About his brains, that would fain find an issue,
But cannot out, or dares not. Still he follows.

*Enter Ruy Dias*

How he looks still, and how he beats about,
Like an old dog at a dead scent! Ay, marry, 10
There was a sigh would 'a set a ship a-sailing:
These winds of love and honour blow at all
  ends.
Now speak and 't be thy will. Good morrow,
  uncle.
  *Ruy.* Good morrow, sir.
  *Py.* [*Aside.*]      This is a new salute:
Sure h'as forgot me: — this is purblind Cupid.
  *Ruy.* My nephew?
  *Py.*      Yes, sir, if I be not chang'd. 16
  *Ruy.* I would fain speak with you.
  *Py.*      I would fain have ye, sir,
For to that end I stay.
  *Ruy.*      You know I love ye,
And I have lov'd ye long, my dear Pyniero,
Bred and supplied you.
  *Py.* [*Aside.*] Whither walks this pre-
  amble?                                                    20
  *Ruy.* You may remember, though I am but
  your uncle,
I sure had a father's care, a father's tenderness.
  *Py.* [*Aside.*] Sure he would wrap me into
  something now suddenly
He doubts my nature in, for mine is honest,
He winds about me so.
  *Ruy.*      A father's diligence.  25
My private benefits I have forgot, sir,
But those you might lay claim to as my fol-
  lower;
Yet some men would remember —
  *Py.*      I do daily.
  *Ruy.* The place which I have put ye in,
  which is no weak one.
Next to myself you stand in all employments,
Your counsels, cares, assignments with me
  equal;                                                     31
So is my study still to plant your person:
These are small testimonies I have not forgot
  ye,
Nor would not be forgotten.
  *Py.*      Sure, you cannot.
  *Ruy.* Oh, Pyniero —
  *Py.*      Sir, what hangs upon you, 35

What heavy weight oppresses ye? Ye have
  lost,
(I must confess) in those that understand ye,
Some little of your credit, but time will cure
  that;
The best may slip sometimes.
  *Ruy.*      Oh, my best nephew —
  *Py.* It may be ye fear her, too; that dis-
  turbs ye,                                                 40
That she may fall herself, or be forc'd from ye.
  *Ruy.* She is ever true, but I undone for ever.
Oh, that Armusia, that new thing, that
  stranger,
That flag stuck up to rob me of mine honour,
That murd'ring chain-shot at me from my
  country:                                                   45
That goodly plague that I must court to kill me.
  *Py.* [*Aside.*] Now it comes flowing from
  him. I fear'd this,
Knew, he that durst be idle, durst be ill, too. —
Has he not done a brave thing?
  *Ruy.* I must confess it, nephew, must allow
  it;                                                        50
But that brave thing has undone me, has sunk
  me,
Has trod me like a name in sand, to nothing,
Hangs betwixt hope and me, and threatens
  my ruin;
And if he rise and blaze, farewell my fortune;
And when that 's set, where 's thy advance-
  ment, cousin?                                             55
That were a friend, that were a noble kinsman,
That would consider these; that man were
  grateful;
And he that durst do something here, durst
  love me.
  *Py.* You say true. 'T is worth consideration;
Your reasons are of weight, and, mark me,
  uncle,                                                     60
For I 'll be sudden, and to th' purpose with you.
Say this Armusia, then, were taken off,
As it may be easily done, how stands the
  woman?
  *Ruy.* She is mine for ever;
For she contemns his deed and him.
  *Py.* [*Aside.*]      Pox on him. 65
Or if the single pox be not sufficient,
The hog's, the dog's, the devil's pox possess
  him! —
'Faith, this Armusia stumbles me. 'T is a brave
  fellow;
And if he could be spar'd, uncle —
  *Ruy.*      I must perish. 70
Had he set up at any rest but this,
Done anything but what concern'd my credit.
The everlasting losing of my worth —

---

³ **bots:** a disease of horses    ²⁰ **Bred:** brought up    **supplied:** supported    ²³ **wrap:** involve, im-
plicate    ⁴⁸ **ill:** wicked    ⁶⁸ **stumbles me:** causes me to hesitate    ⁷⁰ **set . . . rest:** played for any
other stakes

*Py.* [*Aside.*] I understand you now, who set you on, too.
I had a reasonable good opinion of the devil
Till this hour; and I see he is a knave, indeed,
An arrant, stinking knave, for now I smell him. — 76
I 'll see what may be done, then; you shall know
You have a kinsman, — but no villain, uncle,
Nor no betrayer of fair fame, I scorn it;
I love and honour virtue. [*Aside.*] — I must have 80
Access unto the lady to know her mind, too;
A good word from her mouth, you know, may stir me;
A lady's look at setting on —
*Ruy.*                                    You say well,
Here, cousin, here 's a letter ready for you,
                              [*Gives letter.*]
And you shall see how nobly she 'll receive you, 85
And with what care direct.
*Py.*                                    Farewell, then, uncle.
After I have talk'd with her, I am your servant, —
To make you honest if I can, else hate you.
[*Aside.*] —
Pray ye, no more compliments, my head is busy.                              [*Exit Ruy Dias.*]
Heaven bless me, 90
What a malicious soul does this man carry!
And to what scurvy things this love converts us!
What stinking things, and how sweetly they become us!
Murther's a moral virtue with these lovers,
A special piece of divinity, I take it. 95
I may be mad, or violently drunk,
Which is a whelp of that litter; or I may be covetous,
And learn to murther men's estates, that 's base, too;
Or proud, but that 's a paradise to this;
Or envious, and sit eating of myself 100
At others' fortunes; I may lie, and damnably,
Beyond the patience of an honest hearer;
Cozen cutpurses, sit i' th' stocks for apples:
But when I am a lover, Lord have mercy!
These are poor pelting sins, or rather plagues:
Love and ambition draw the devil's coach. 106

#### Enter Quisana and Panura

How now! who are these? Oh, my great lady's followers,
Her riddle-founders, and her fortune-tellers.
Her readers of her love-lectures, her inflamers:

These doors I must pass through, I hope they are wide. [*Aside.*] — 110
Good day to your beauties. — How they take it to 'em!
As if they were fair indeed. [*Aside.*]
*Quisan.*                          Good morrow to you, sir.
*Py.* [*Aside.*] That 's the old hen, the brood-bird! how she bustles!
How like an inventory of lechery she looks!
Many a good piece of iniquity 115
Has pass'd her hands, I warrant her. — I beseech you,
Is the fair princess stirring?
*Pan.*                          Yes, marry, is she, sir,
But somewhat private: have you a business with her?
*Py.* Yes, forsooth, have I, and a serious business.
*Pan.* May not we know?
*Py.* Yes, when you can keep counsel. 120
*Pan.* How prettily he looks! he 's a soldier, sure,
His rudeness sits so handsomely upon him.
*Quisan.* A good, blunt gentleman.
*Py.*                          Yes, marry, am I:
Yet for a push or two at sharp, and 't please you —
*Pan.* My honest friend, you know not who you speak to: 125
This is the princess's aunt.
*Py.*                          I like her the better.
And she were her mother, lady, or her grandmother,
I am not so bashful, but I can buckle with her.
*Pan.* Of what size is your business?
*Py.*                          Of the long sixteens,
And will make way, I warrant ye.
*Pan.*                          How fine he talks! 130
*Py.* Nay, in troth, I talk but coarsely, lady,
But I hold it comfortable for the understanding. —                              [*Aside.*]
How fain they would draw me into ribaldry!
These wenches that live easily, live high,
And love these broad discourses, as they love possets; 135
These dry delights serve for preparatives.
*Pan.* Why do you look so on me?
*Py.*                          I am guessing
By the cast of your face, what the property of your place should be,
For I presume you turn a key, sweet beauty,
And you another, gravity, under the princess,
And by my soul I warrant ye good places, 141
Comely commodious seats.

---

⁷⁶ **care:** ('dare' F 2)   ¹⁰³ **for:** for stealing   ¹⁰⁵ **pelting:** paltry   ¹¹⁸ **have you:** ('you have' F 2)
¹²⁴ **push:** thrust   **at sharp:** with sharp weapons   ¹²⁷ **And:** if   ¹²⁸ **buckle:** cope   ¹²⁹ **long sixteens:**
large size (of shoes)   ¹³⁰ **make way:** travel far   ¹³⁵ **possets:** sweet drinks of milk, wine, etc.   ¹³⁸ **property:** nature   ¹⁴¹ **soul:** (represented by a dash in Ff)   ¹⁴² **seats:** ('feates' F 1)

*Quisan.*           Prithee, let him talk still.
For methinks he talks handsomely.
*Py.*                    And truly,
As near as my understanding shall enable me.
You look as if you kept my lady's secrets: 145
Nay, do not laugh, for I mean honestly. —
How these young things tattle, when they get
     a toy by th' end!
And how their hearts go pit-a-pat, and look
     for it!
Would it not dance, too, if it had a fiddle?
     [*Aside.*] —
Your gravity, I guess, to take the petitions, 150
And hear the ling'ring suits in love dispos'd,
Their sighs and sorrows in their proper place,
You keep the "Ay, me!" office.
*Quisan.*           Prithee, suffer him,
For, as I live, he is a pretty fellow;
I love to hear sometimes what men think of
     us:                            155
And thus deliver'd freely, 't is no malice.
Proceed, good, honest man.
*Py.*            I will, good madam.
According to men's states and dignities,
Moneys and moveables, you rate their dreams,
And cast the nativity of their desires.     160
If he reward well, all he thinks is prosperous,
And if he promise place, his dreams are oracles;
Your ancient, practique art, too, in these dis-
     coveries, —
Who loves at such a length, who a span farther,
And who draws home, — yields you no little
     profit,                     165
For these ye milk by circumstance.
*Quisan.*           Ye are cunning.
*Py.*   And as they oil ye, and advance your
     spindle,
So you draw out the lines of love. Your doors,
     too,
The doors of destiny, that men must pass
     through;
These are fair places.
*Pan.*            He knows all.
*Py.*               Your trap-doors, 170
To pop fools in at, that have no providence;
Your little wickets, to work wise men, like
     wires, through at,
And draw their states and bodies into cobwebs;
Your postern-doors, to catch those that are
     cautelous,
And would not have the world's eye find their
     knaveries;                  175
Your doors of danger, (some men hate a
     pleasure,
Unless that may be full of fears); your hope-
     doors,

And those are fine commodities, where fools
     pay
For every new encouragement a new custom.
You have your doors of honour and of pleasure;
But those are for great princes, glorious
     vanities,                  181
That travail to be famous through diseases.
There be the doors of poverty and death, too:
But these you do the best you can to dam up,
For then your gain goes out.
*Quisan.*          This is a rare lecture. 185
*Py.*   Read to them that understand.
*Pan.*                Beshrew me,
I dare not venture on ye; ye cut too keen, sir.
*Quisan.*   We thank you, sir, for your good
     mirth,
You are a good companion.
Here comes the princess now, attend your busi-
     ness.                        190

             *Enter Quisara*

*Quisar.*   Is there no remedy, no hopes can
     help me?
No wit to set me free? Who 's there, ho?
*Quisan.*   Troubled?
Her looks are almost wild: what ails the prin-
     cess?
I know nothing she wants.
*Quisar.*   Who 's that there with you?    195
Oh, Signior Pyniero? you are most welcome.
How does your noble uncle?
*Py.*           Sad as you are, madam:
But he commends his service, and this letter.
                      [*Gives letter.*]
*Quisar.*   [*To Quisan. and Pan.*]   Go off;
     attend within. — Fair sir, I thank ye,
Pray be no stranger, for indeed you are wel-
     come,                     200
For your own virtues, welcome.
*Quisan.*         We are mistaken,
This is some brave fellow, sure.
*Pan.*       I 'm sure he 's a bold fellow:
But if she hold him so, we must believe it.
            *Exeunt* [*Quisana and Panura*].
*Quisar.*   Do you know of this, fair sir?
*Py.*           I guess it, madam,
And whither it intends: I had not brought it
     else.                     205
*Quisar.*   It is a business of no common reck-
     oning.
*Py.*   The handsomer for him that goes about
     it.
Slight actions are rewarded with slight thanks:
Give me a matter of some weight to wade in.
*Quisar.*   And can you love your uncle so
     directly,                  210

---

146 **honestly:** decently    147 **toy:** trifle    153 **suffer:** allow freedom to    160 **nativity:** horoscope
163 **practique:** cunning    171 **at:** ('it' Ff)   **providence:** foresight    173 **states:** estates    174 **cautelous:**
cautious    182 **travail:** ('travel' Ff)    205 **intends:** tends

So seriously, and so full, to undertake this?
Can there be such a faith?
*Py.*                  Dare you say "ay" to it,
And set me on? 'T is no matter for my uncle,
Or what I owe to him, dare you but wish it.
*Quisar.* I would fain —
*Py.*      Have it done; say but so, lady. 215
*Quisar.* Conceive it so.
*Py.*            I will, 't is that I am bound to:
Your will that must command me, and your
    pleasure,
The fair aspects of those eyes that must direct
    me.
I am no uncle's agent, I am mine own, lady;
I scorn my able youth should plough for others,
Or my ambition serve for pay.  I aim,     221
Although I never hit, as high as any man,
And the reward I reach at shall be equal,
And what love spurs me on to.  This desire
Makes me forget an honest man, a brave man,
A valiant, and a virtuous man, my country-
    man,                                      226
Armusia, the delight of all, the minion.
This love of you, doting upon your beauty,
The admiration of your excellence,
Make me but servant to the poorest smile,  230
Or the least grace you have bestow'd on others,
And see how suddenly I 'll work your safety,
And set your thoughts at peace.  I am no
    flatterer,
To promise infinitely, and out-dream dangers;
To lie abed, and swear men into fevers,   235
Like some of your trim suitors; when I
    promise,
The light is not more constant to the world,
Than I am to my word. — She turns, for mil-
    lions.                        [*Aside.*]
*Quisar.* [*Aside.*] I have not seen a braver
    confirm'd courage.
*Py.* [*Aside.*] For a tun of crowns she turns:
    she is a woman,                       240
And much I fear, a worse than I expected. —
You are the object, lady, you are the eye
In which all excellence appears, all wonder,
From which all hearts take fire, all hands their
    valour:
And when he stands disputing, when you bid
    him,                                 245
Or but thinks of his estate, father, mother,
Friends, wife, and children, h' is a fool, and I
    scorn him, —
And 't be but to make clean his sword, a
    coward.
Men have forgot their fealty to beauty.
Had I the place in your affections      250
My most unworthy uncle is fit to fall from,
Liv'd in those blessed eyes, and read the stories

Of everlasting pleasures figur'd there,
I would find out your commands before you
    thought 'em,
And bring 'em to you done, ere you dreamt of
    'em.                                    255
*Quisar.* [*Aside.*] I admire his boldness.
*Py.*                This, or anything;
Your brother's death, mine uncle's, any man's,
No state that stands secure, if you frown on it.
Look on my youth, I bring no blastings to you
The first flower of my strength, my faith.
*Quisar.*              No more, sir.   260
I am too willing to believe; rest satisfi'd,
If you dare do for me, I shall be thankful.
You are a handsome gentleman, a fair one,
My servant, if you please; I seal it thus, sir.
                              [*Kisses him.*]
No more, till you deserve more.
*Py.*                I am rewarded. —   265
                        *Exit* [*Quisara*].
This woman 's cunning, but she 's bloody, too;
Although she pulls her talons in, she 's mis-
    chievous;
Form'd like the face of heaven, clear and trans-
    parent.
I must pretend still, bear 'em both in hopes,
For fear some bloody slave thrust in, indeed,
Fashion'd and flesh'd to what they wish.
    Well, uncle,                          271
What will become of this, and what dishonour
Follow this fatal shaft, if shot, let time tell.
I can but only fear, and strive to cross it.  *Exit.*

[SCENE II. — *The Same.  Another Room in the
    Palace*]

*Enter Armusia, Emanuel, and Soza*

*Em.*  Why are you thus sad?  What can
    grieve or vex you
That have the pleasures of the world, the
    profits,
The honour, and the loves at your disposes?
Why should a man that wants nothing, want
    his quiet?
*Arm.*  I want what beggars are above me in,
    content;                               5
I want the grace I have merited, the favour,
The due respect.
*Soz.*          Does not the king allow it?
*Arm.*      Yes, and all honours else, all I can
    ask,
That he has power to give; but from his sister,
The scornful cruelty, — forgive me, beauty, 10
That I transgress! — from her that should
    look on me,
That should a little smile upon my service,
And foster my deserts for her own faith's sake:

That should at least acknowledge me, speak to
    me.
*Soz.*  And you go whining up and down for
    this, sir?                               15
Lamenting and disputing of your grievances?
Sighing and sobbing like a sullen schoolboy,
And cursing good-wife fortune for this favour?
    *Arm.*  What would you have me do?
    *Soz.*               Do what you should do,
What a man would do in this case, a wise man,
An understanding man that knows a woman, 21
Knows her and all her tricks, her scorns, and all
    her trifles:
Go to her, and take her in your arms, and
    shake her,
Take her and toss her like a bar.
    *Em.*  But be sure you pitch her upon a
    feather-bed,                       25
Shake her between a pair of sheets, sir; there
    shake
These sullen fits out of her, spare her not there;
There you may break her will, and bruise no
    bone, sir.
    *Soz.*  Go to her —
    *Em.*           That 's the way.
    *Soz.*              And tell her, and boldly,
And do not mince the matter, nor mock your-
    self,                                  30
With being too indulgent to her pride:
Let her hear roundly from ye what ye are,
And what ye have deserv'd, and what she
    must be.
    *Em.*  And be not put off like a common
    fellow,
With "The princess would be private,"    35
Or that she has taken physic, and admits none:
I would talk to her anywhere.
    *Arm.*               It makes me smile.
    *Em.*  Now you look handsomely.
Had I a wench to win, I would so flutter her!
They love a man that crushes 'em to ver-
    juice;                             40
A woman held at hard meat is your spaniel.
    *Soz.*  Pray take our council, sir.
    *Arm.*            I shall do something,
But not your way; it shows too boisterous,
For my affections are as fair and gentle,
As her they serve.

*Enter King*

    *Soz.*          The king.
    *King.*          Why, how now, friend? 45
Why do you rob me of the company
I love so dearly, sir? I have been seeking you;
For when I want you, I want all my pleasure.
Why sad? thus sad still, man? I will not have it;
I must not see the face I love thus shadow'd. 50

    *Em.*  And 't please your grace, methinks it
    ill becomes him:
A soldier should be jovial, high and lusty.
    *King.*  He shall be so. Come, come, I know
    your reason,
It shall be none to cross you, ye shall have her;
Take my word, ('t is a king's word) ye shall
    have her;                           55
She shall be yours or nothing, pray be merry.
    *Arm.*  Your grace has given me cause; I
    shall be, sir,
And ever your poor servant.
    *King.*            Me, myself, sir,
My better self. I shall find time, and suddenly,
To gratify your loves, too, gentlemen,      60
And make you know how much I stand bound
    to you.
Nay, 't is not worth your thanks, no further
    compliment.
Will you go with me, friend?
    *Arm.*           I beseech your grace,
Spare me an hour or two, I shall wait on you;
Some little private business with myself, sir, 65
For such a time.
    *King.*         I 'll hinder no devotion,
For I know you are regular. I 'll take you,
    gentlemen,
Because he shall have nothing to disturb him.
I shall look for you, friend.
    *Arm.*          I dare not fail, sir. —
                  *Exeunt. Manet Armusia.*
What shall I do to make her know my misery? 70

*Enter Panura*

To make her sensible? This is her woman:
I have a toy come to me suddenly.
It may work for the best, she can but scorn me,
And lower than I am, I cannot tumble.
I 'll try, whate'er my fate be.    [*Aside.*]
    — Good even, fair one.                   75
    *Pan.*  [*Aside.*] 'T is the brave stranger. — A
good night to you, sir, —
Now by my lady's hand, a goodly gentleman!
How happy shall she be in such a husband!
Would I were so provided, too. [*Aside.*]
    *Arm.*               Good pretty one,
Shall I keep you company for an hour or two?
I want employment for this evening.      81
I am an honest man.
    *Pan.*          I dare believe ye;
Or if ye were not, sir, that 's no great matter;
We take men's promises. Would ye stay with
    me, sir?
    *Arm.*  So it please you, pray let 's be better
    acquainted,                       85
I know you are the princess's gentlewoman,
And wait upon her near.

---

¹⁶ **disputing of:** discussing    ²² **trifles:** whims
**pliment:** formal politeness    ⁶⁸ **Because:** so that
⁶⁹ **you, friend:** ('your friend' Ff)    ⁷² **toy:** fancy
³² **roundly:** plainly    ⁴³ **shows:** seems    ⁶² **com-**

*Pan.*                          'T is like I do so.

*Arm.*   And may befriend a man, do him fair
   courtesies,
If he have business your way.

*Pan.*                          I understand ye.

*Arm.*   So kind an office, that you may bind
   a gentleman,                                        90
Hereafter to be yours, and your way, too;
And ye may bless the hour you did this bene-
   fit:
Sweet, handsome faces should have courteous
   minds,
And ready faculties.

*Pan.*                          Tell me your business,
Yet if I think it be to her, yourself, sir, — 95
For I know what you are, and what we hold
   ye,
And in what grace ye stand, — without a
   second,
For that but darkens, you would do it better.
The princess must be pleas'd with your ac-
   cesses;
I 'm sure I should.

*Arm.*   I want a courtier's boldness,   100
And am yet but a stranger: I would fain speak
   with her.

*Pan.*   'T is very late, and upon her hour of
   sleep, sir.

*Arm.*   Pray ye wear this,   [*Gives a*] *Jewel.*
and believe my meaning civil,
My business of that fair respect and carriage:
This for our more acquaintance. [*Kisses her.*]

*Pan.* [*Aside.*] How close he kisses! And
   how sensible                                        106
The passings of his lips are! I must do it,
And I were to be hang'd now, and I will do it.
He may do as much for me, that 's all I aim at;
And come what will on 't, life or death, I 'll
   do it,                                              110
For ten such kisses more, and 't were high trea-
   son.

*Arm.*   I would be private with her.

*Pan.*                          So you shall;
'T is not worth thanks else. You must dispatch
   quick.

*Arm.*   Suddenly.

*Pan.*   And I must leave you in my chamber,
   sir,                                                115
Where you must lock yourself that none may
   see you;
'T is close to her, you cannot miss the entrance,
When she comes down to bed.

*Arm.*                          I understand ye,
And once more thank ye, lady.

*Pan.*                          Thank me but thus.

*Arm.*   If I fail thee —
                     Come, close, then. *Exeunt.* 120

[SCENE III. — *The Same.   A Bed-chamber
in the Palace*]

*Enter Quisara and Quisana*

*Quisar.*   'T is late; good aunt, to bed; I am
   ev'n unready,
My woman will not be long away.

*Quisan.*                          I would have you
A little merrier first. Let me sit by ye,
And read or discourse something that ye fancy,
Or take my instrument.

*Quisar.*                          No, no, I thank you,  5
I shall sleep without these. I wrong your age,
   aunt,
To make ye wait thus; pray let me intreat
   ye.
To-morrow I 'll see ye; I know y' are sleepy,
And rest will be a welcome guest. You shall
   not,
Indeed, you shall not stay. Oh, here 's my
   woman.                                              10

*Enter Panura*

Good night, good night, and good rest, aunt,
   attend you.

*Quisan.*   Sleep dwell upon your eyes, and
   fair dreams court ye.            [*Exit.*]

*Quisar.*   Come, where have you been, wench?
   make me unready;
I slept but ill last night.

*Pan.*                          You 'll sleep the better
I hope to-night, madam.

*Quisar.*   A little rest contents me;              15
Thou lovest thy bed, Panura.

*Pan.*                          I am not in love, lady,
Nor seldom dream of devils; I sleep soundly.

*Quisar.*   I 'll swear thou dost: thy husband
   would not take it so well,
If thou wert married, wench.

*Pan.*                          Let him take, madam,
The way to waken me; I am no dormouse. 20
Husbands have 'larum bells, if they but ring
   once.

*Quisar.*   Thou art a merry wench.

*Pan.*                          I shall live the longer.

*Quisar.*   Prithee fetch my book.

*Pan.* [*Aside.*]               I am glad of that.

*Quisar.*   I 'll read awhile before I sleep.

*Pan.*                          I will, madam.

*Quisar.*   And if Ruy Dias meet you, and be
   importunate,                                        25
He may come in.

*Pan.* [*Aside.*] I have a better fare for you;
Now least in sight play I.                  *Exit.*

*Quisar.*   Why should I love him?
Why should I dote upon a man deserves not,

⁸⁷ **like:** probable   ¹⁰⁴ **respect:** quality   **carriage:** import   ¹⁰⁶ **sensible:** capable of stirring
emotion   ¹ **unready:** undressed   ¹⁵ **to-night:** ('too night' F 1; 'no night' F 2)

*Enter Armusia, locks the door*

Nor has no will to work it? Who 's there,
   wench?
What are you? or whence come you?
  *Arm.*           Ye may know me,  30
I bring not such amazement, noble lady.
  *Quisar.*   Who let you in?
  *Arm.*       My restless love that serves ye.
  *Quisar.*   This is an impudence I have not
   heard of,
A rudeness that becomes a thief or ruffian;
Nor shall my brother's love protect this bold-
   ness,                  35
You build so strongly on. My rooms are
   sanctuaries,
And with that reverence, they that seek my
   favours,
And humble fears, shall render their approaches.
  *Arm.*   Mine are no less.
  *Quisar.*       I am mistress of myself, sir,
And will be so; I will not be thus visited:  40
These fears and dangers thrust into my privacy.
Stand further off, I 'll cry out else.
  *Arm.*             Oh, dear lady!
  *Quisar.*   I see dishonour in your eyes.
  *Arm.*             There is none:
By all that beauty, they are innocent!
Pray ye, tremble not; you have no cause.  45
  *Quisar.*   I 'll die first;
Before you have your will, be torn in pieces;
The little strength I have left me to resist
   you,
The gods will give me more, before I am forc'd
To that I hate, or suffer —
  *Arm.*         You wrong my duty.  50
  *Quisar.*   So base a violation of my liberty?
I know you are bent unnobly; I 'll take to me
The spirit of a man, borrow his boldness,
And force my woman's fears into a madness,
And ere you arrive at what you aim at —
  *Arm.*           Lady, [*Kneels.*]  55
If there be in you any woman's pity,
And if your fears have not proclaim'd me mon-
   strous;
Look on me, and believe me. Is this violence?
Is it to fall thus prostrate to your beauty,
A ruffian's boldness? Is humility a rudeness?  60
The griefs and sorrows that grow here an im-
   pudence?
These forcings, and these fears I bring along
   with me,
These impudent abuses offer'd ye?
And thus high has your brother's favour
   blown me:
Alas, dear lady of my life, I came not     65
With any purpose, rough or desperate,

With any thought that was not smooth and
   gentle
As your fair hand, with any doubt or danger!
Far be it from my heart to fright your quiet;
A heavy curse light on it, when I intend it!  70
  *Quisar.*   Now I dare hear you.
  *Arm.*          If I had been mischievous,
As then I must be mad, or were a monster,
If any such base thought had harbour'd here,
Or any violence that became not man,
You have a thousand bulwarks to assure
   you.                  75
The holy powers bear shields to defend chastity;
Your honour and your virtues are such ar-
   mours,
Your clear thoughts such defences. If you mis-
   doubt still
And yet retain a fear I am not honest,
Come with impure thoughts to this place,  80
              [*Offers his sword.*]
Take this, and sheath it here; be your own
   safety;
Be wise, and rid your fears, and let me perish:
How willing shall I sleep to satisfy you!
  *Quisar.*   No; I believe now, you speak
   worthily;
What came you, then, for?
  *Arm.*        To complain me, beauty,  85
But modestly.
  *Quisar.*   Of what?
  *Arm.*          Of your fierce cruelty,
For though I die, I will not blame the doer;
Humbly to tell your grace, ye had forgot me;
A little to have touch'd at, not accus'd,
For that I dare not do, your scorns, — pray
   pardon me            90
And be not angry that I use the liberty
To urge that word; a little to have show'd you
What I have been, and what done to deserve ye;
If anything that love commands may reach
   ye,
To have remember'd ye, but I am unworthy,  95
And to that misery falls all my fortunes,
To have told ye, and, by my life, ye may be-
   lieve me,
That I am honest, and will only marry
You, or your memory: pray be not angry.
  *Quisar.*   I thank you, sir, and let me tell you
   seriously,            100
Ye have taken now the right way to befriend ye,
And to beget a fair and clear opinion;
Yet, to try your obedience —
  *Arm.*          I stand ready, lady
Without presuming to ask anything.
  *Quisar.*   Or at this time to hope for further
   favour;            105
Or to remember services or smiles,

---

⁵⁰ **duty:** reverence    ⁷⁴ **any:** (not in Ff)    ⁸¹ **here:** *i.e., in his breast*    ⁸² **rid: remove, destroy**
⁹⁵ **remember'd:** reminded

Dangers you have pass'd through, and rewards
    due to 'em;
Loves or despairs, but leaving all to me,
Quit this place presently.
    *Arm.*                I shall obey ye.

              *Enter Ruy Dias*

  *Ruy.*  Ha?
  *Arm.*  Who 's this? — What art thou?
  *Ruy.*            A gentleman. 110
  *Arm.*  Thou art no more, I 'm sure. — Oh,
    't is Ruy Dias;
How high he looks, and harsh! [*Aside.*]
  *Ruy.*         Is there not door enough,
You take such elbow room?
  *Arm.*       If I take it, I 'll carry it.
  *Ruy.*  Does this become you, princess?
  *Arm.*         The captain 's jealous,
Jealous of that he never durst deserve yet. 115
Go freely, go; I 'll give thee leave.
  *Ruy.*           Your leave, sir?
  *Arm.*  Yes, my leave, sir. I 'll not be
    troubled neither,
Nor shall my heart ache, or my head be jealous,
Nor strange suspicious thoughts reign in my
    memory;
Go on, and do thy worst; I 'll smile at thee. —120
I kiss your fair hand first, then farewell, cap-
    tain.                     *Exit.*
  *Quisar.* [*Aside.*] What a pure soul inherits
    here! what innocence!
Sure I was blind when I first lov'd this fellow,
And long'd to live in that fog still: how he
    blusters!
  *Ruy.*  Am I your property? or those your
    flatteries, 125
The banquets that ye bid me to, the trust
I build my goodly hopes on?
  *Quisar.*          Be more temperate.
  *Ruy.*  Are these the shows of your respect and
    favour?
What did he here, what language had he with ye?
Did ye invite him? could ye stay no longer? 130
Is he so gracious in your eye?
  *Quisar.*        You are too forward.
  *Ruy.*  Why, at these private hours? —
  *Quisar.*        You are too saucy,
Too impudent, to task me with those errors.
Do ye know what I am, sir, and my prerogative?
Though you be a thing I have call'd by th'
    name of friend, 135
I never taught you to dispose my liberty;
How durst you touch mine honour? blot my
    meanings?

And name an action, and of mine, but noble?
Thou poor unworthy thing, how have I grac'd
    thee!
How have I nourish'd thee, and rais'd thee
    hourly! 140
Are these the gratitudes you bring, Ruy Dias?
The thanks? the services? I am fairly paid.
Was 't not enough I saw thou wert a coward,
And shadow'd thee? no noble sparkle in thee?
Daily provok'd thee, and still found thee cow-
    ard? 145
Rais'd noble causes for thee, strangers started at,
Yet still, still, still a coward, ever coward;
And with those taints, dost thou upbraid my
    virtues?
  *Ruy.*  I was to blame, lady.
  *Quisar.*  So blindly bold to touch at my be-
    haviour? 150
Durst thou but look amiss at my allowance?
If thou hadst been a brave fellow, thou hadst
    had some license,
Some liberty I might have then allow'd thee
For thy good face, some scope to have argued
    with me;
But being nothing but a sound, a shape, 155
The mere sign of a soldier, of a lover,
The dregs and draffy part, disgrace and jealousy,
I scorn thee, and contemn thee.
  *Ruy.*            Dearest lady.
If I have been too free —
  *Quisar.*      Thou hast been too foolish,
And go on still; I 'll study to forget thee. 160
I would I could, and yet I pity thee.    *Exit.*
  *Ruy.*  I am not worth it; if I were, that 's
    misery.
The next door is but death, I must aim at it.
                             *Exit.*

## *Actus Quartus. — Scæna Prima.*

*[The Same. — A Room in the Palace]*

*Enter King and Governor, like a Moor-Priest*

  *King.*  So far and truly you have discover'd
    to me
The former currents of my life and fortune,
That I am bound to acknowledge ye most holy,
And certainly to credit your predictions,
Of what are yet to come.
  *Gov.*           I am no liar. — 5
'T is strange I should, and live so near a neigh-
    bour;
But these are not my ends. [*Aside.*]

---

¹²⁴ **long'd:** ('long' Ff)   ¹²⁸ **respect:** esteem   ¹³⁰ **him:** (not in Ff)   **stay:** wait   ¹³³ **task:** tax
¹³⁶ **dispose:** control   ¹³⁷ **blot:** tarnish   **meanings:** intents, purposes   ¹⁴⁴ **shadow'd:** protected
¹⁴⁵ **provok'd:** incited   ¹⁵¹ **allowance:** approbation   ¹⁵⁷ **draffy part:** lees   S. D. **Moor-:** Moorish   ¹ **discover'd:** revealed   ⁶ **'T is . . . should:** *i.e.*, it would be strange if I did not know these
facts

*King.*　　　　　Pray ye, sit, good father. —
Certain a reverend man, and most religious.
　　　　　　　　　　　　　　　　[*Aside.*]
*Gov.* [*Aside.*] Ay, that belief 's well now,
　　and let me work, then;
I 'll make ye curse religion ere I leave ye. — 10
I have liv'd a long time, son, a mew'd-up man,
Sequester'd by the special hand of heaven
From the world's vanities, bid farewell to
　　follies,
And shook hands with all heats of youth and
　　pleasures.
As in a dream these twenty years I have
　　slumber'd,　　　　　　　　　　　　　15
Many a cold moon have I, in meditation
And searching out the hidden wills of heaven,
Lain shaking under; many a burning sun
Has sear'd my body, and boil'd up my blood,
Feebl'd my knees, and stamp'd a meagreness 20
Upon my figure, all to find out knowledge,
Which I have now attain'd to, thanks to
　　heaven,
All for my country's good, too: and many a
　　vision,
Many a mystic vision have I seen, son.
And many a sight from heaven, which has been
　　terrible,　　　　　　　　　　　　　　25
Wherein the goods and evils of these islands
Were lively shadow'd; many a charge I have
　　had, too,
Still as the time grew ripe to reveal these,
To travel and discover: now I am come, son,
The hour is now appointed, my tongue is
　　touch'd,　　　　　　　　　　　　　　30
And now I speak.
　　*King.*　　　　　Do, holy man, I 'll hear ye.
　　*Gov.* Beware these Portugals; I say be-
　　ware 'em,
These smooth-fac'd strangers; have an eye
　　upon 'em.
The cause is now the God's; hear, and believe,
　　king.
　　*King.* I do hear, but before I give rash
　　credit,　　　　　　　　　　　　　　35
Or hang too light on belief, which is a sin,
　　father,
Know I have found 'em gentle, faithful, valiant,
And am in my particular bound to 'em,
I mean to some, for my most strange deliver-
　　ance.
　　*Gov.* Oh, son, the future aims of men, ob-
　　serve me,　　　　　　　　　　　　　40
Above their present actions, and their glory,
Are to be look'd at. The stars show many
　　turnings,
If you could see; mark but with my eyes, pupil.

These men came hither, as my vision tells me,
Poor, weather-beaten, almost lost, starv'd,
　　feebled,　　　　　　　　　　　　　　45
Their vessels like themselves, most miserable;
Made a long suit for traffic, and for comfort,
To vent their children's toys, cure their dis-
　　eases:
They had their suit, they landed, and to th' rate
Grew rich and powerful, suck'd the fat and
　　freedom　　　　　　　　　　　　　50
Of this most blessed isle, taught her to tremble.
Witness the castle here, the citadel,
They have clapp'd upon the neck of your Ti-
　　dore,
This happy town, till that she knew these
　　strangers,
To check her when she 's jolly.
　　*King.*　　　They have so, indeed, father. 55
　　*Gov.* Take heed, take heed, I find your fair
　　delivery,
Though you be pleas'd to glorify that fortune,
And think these strangers gods, take heed, I
　　say,
I find it but a handsome preparation,
A fair-fac'd prologue to a further mischief: 60
Mark but the end, good king, the pin he
　　shoots at,
That was the man deliver'd ye, the mirror!
Your sister is his due; what 's she? your heir,
　　sir.
And what 's he akin, then, to the kingdom?
But heirs are not ambitious; who then suffers?
What reverence shall the gods have? and what
　　justice　　　　　　　　　　　　　　66
The miserable people? what shall they do?
　　*King.* [*Aside.*] He points at truth directly.
　　*Gov.*　　　　　Think of these, son:
The person, nor the manner I mislike not
Of your preserver, nor the whole man to-
　　gether,　　　　　　　　　　　　　70
Were he but season'd in the faith we are,
In our devotions learn'd.
　　*King.*　　　　You say right, father.
　　*Gov.* To change our worships now, and our
　　religion?
To be traitor to our God?
　　*King.*　　　You have well advis'd me,
And I will seriously consider, father.　　75
In the mean time you shall have your fair access
Unto my sister: advise her to your purpose,
And let me still know how the gods determine.
　　*Gov.* I will. — But my main end is to ad-
　　vise
The destruction of you all, a general ruin; 80
And when I am reveng'd, let the gods whistle.
　　　　　　　　　　　[*Aside.*] *Exeunt.*

¹¹ **mew'd-:** shut　　²⁷ **lively:** vividly　　³⁸ **in . . . particular:** personally　　⁴⁰ **observe:** give heed
to　　⁴⁹ **to th' rate:** according to the standard　　⁶¹ **pin:** mark in centre of a target　　⁸¹ **when:**
('then' F 1)

[Scene II. — *The Same. Before the Palace*]

*Enter Ruy Dias and Pyniero*

*Ruy.* Indeed, I am right glad ye were not greedy,
And sudden in performing what I will'd you
Upon the person of Armusia.
I was afraid, for I well knew your valour,
And love to me.
*Py.* 'T was not a fair thing, uncle, 5
It show'd not handsome, carried no man in it.
*Ruy.* I must confess 't was ill; and I abhor it;
Only this good has risen from this evil,
I have tried your honesty, and find it proof,
A constancy that will not be corrupted, 10
And I much honour it.
*Py.* This bell sounds better.
*Ruy.* My anger now, and that disgrace I
have suffer'd,
Shall be more manly vented, and wip'd off,
And my sick honour cur'd the right and straight way;
My sword 's in my hand now, nephew, my cause upon it, 15
And man to man, one valour to another,
My hope to his.
*Py.* Why, this is like Ruy Dias!
This carries something of some substance in it;
Some mettle and some man, this sounds a gentleman;
And now methinks ye utter what becomes ye. 20
To kill men scurvily, 't is such a dog-trick,
Such a rat-catcher's occupation —
*Ruy.* It is no better. But, Pyniero, now —
*Py.* Now you do bravely.
*Ruy.* The difference of our states flung by, forgotten,
The full opinion I have won in service, 25
And such respects that may not show us equal,
Laid handsomely aside, only our fortunes,
And single manhoods —
*Py.* In a service, sir,
Of this most noble nature, all I am,
If I had ten lives more, those and my fortunes 30
Are ready for ye. I had thought ye had
Forsworn fighting, or banish'd those brave thoughts
Were wont to wait upon you; I am glad
To see 'em call'd home again.
*Ruy.* They are, nephew,
And thou shalt see what fire they carry in them. 35
Here, you guess what this means?
*Shows a challenge.*

*Py.* Yes, very well, sir;
A portion of Scripture that puzzles many an interpreter.
*Ruy.* As soon as you can find him —
*Py.* That will not be long, uncle,
And o' my conscience he 'll be ready as quickly.
*Ruy.* I make no doubt, good nephew. Carry it so, 40
If you can possible, that we may fight —
*Py.* Nay you shall fight, assure yourself.
*Ruy.* Pray ye, hear me —
In some such place where it may be possible
The princess may behold us.
*Py.* I conceive ye;
Upon the sand behind the castle, sir, 45
A place remote enough, and there be windows
Out of her lodgings, too, or I am mistaken.
*Ruy.* Y' are i' th' right. If ye can work that handsomely —
*Py.* Let me alone, and pray, be you prepar'd
Some three hours hence.
*Ruy.* I will not fail.
*Py.* Get you home, 50
And if you have any things to dispose of,
Or a few light prayers
That may befriend you, run 'em over quickly.
I warrant I 'll bring him on.
*Ruy.* Farewell, nephew,
And when we meet again —
*Py.* Ay, ay, fight handsomely; 55
Take a good draught or two of wine to settle ye,
*[Exit Ruy Dias.]*
'T is an excellent armour for an ill conscience, uncle.
I am glad to see this man's conversion;
I was afraid fair honour had been bed-rid,
Or beaten out o' th' island, soldiers, and good ones, 60
Intended such base courses. He will fight now;
And, I believe, too, bravely; I have seen him
Curry a fellow's carcass handsomely;
And, in the head of a troop, stand as if he had been rooted there,
Dealing large doles of death. What a rascal was I, 65
I did not see his will drawn!

*Enter Quisara*

What does she here?
If there be any mischief towards, a woman makes one still. —
Now what new business is for me?
*Quisar.* I was sending for ye,
But since we have met so fair, you have sav'd that labour:
I must intreat you, sir —

---

⁶ **man:** manliness   ⁹ **it:** (not in Ff)   **proof:** of proved strength   ²³ **you:** ('I' F 1)   ⁶³ **Curry:** cut up (a technical hunting term)   ⁶⁷ **makes one:** is present

*I'y.*　　　　　Anything, madam, 70
Your wills are my commands.
*Quisar.*　　　　　Y' are nobly courteous.
Upon my better thoughts, Signior Pyniero,
And my more peaceable considerations,
Which now I find the richer ornaments,
I would desire you to attempt no farther　75
Against the person of the noble stranger, —
In truth, I am asham'd of my share in 't;
Nor be incited farther by your uncle.
I see it will sit ill upon your person;
I have consider'd, and it will show ugly,　80
Carried at best, a most unheard-of cruelty;
Good sir, desist —
　*Py.*　　　　　You speak now like a woman,
And wondrous well this tenderness becomes ye;
But this you must remember, — your command
Was laid on with a kiss, and seriously　85
It must be taken off the same way, madam,
Or I stand bound still.
　*Quisar.*　　　That shall not endanger ye.
Look ye, fair sir, thus I take off that duty.
　　　　　　　　[*Kisses him.*]
　*Py.* [*Aside.*] By th' mass 't was soft and
　sweet! Some bloods would bound now,
And run a-tilt. — Do not you think, bright
　beauty,　90
You have done me in this kiss a mighty favour,
And that I stand bound, by virtue of this
　honour,
To do whatever you command me?
　*Quisar.*　　　　　I think, sir,
From me these are unusual courtesies,
And ought to be respected so. There are
　some,　95
And men of no mean rank, would hold them-
　selves
Not poorly bless'd to taste of such a bounty.
　*Py.* I know there are, that would do many
　unjust things
For such a kiss (and yet I hold this modest) —
All villainies, body and soul, dispense with,　100
For such a provocation, kill their kindred,
Demolish the fair credits of their parents;
Those kisses I am not acquainted with. Most
　certain, madam,
The appurtenance of this kiss would not pro-
　voke me
To do a mischief; 't is the devil's own dance, 105
To be kiss'd into cruelty.
　*Quisar.* I am glad you make that use, sir.
　*Py.*　　　　　I am gladder
That you made me believe you were cruel,
For, by this hand, I know I am so honest,
However I deceiv'd ye, ('t was high time, too, 110
Some common slave might have been set upon
　it else.)

That willingly I would not kill a dog
That could but fetch and carry for a woman.
She must be a good woman made me kick him,
And that will be hard to find, to kill a man,　115
If you will give me leave to get another,
Or any she that play'd the best game at it,
And 'fore a woman's anger, prefer her fancy.
　*Quisar.* I take it in you well.
　*Py.*　　　　　I thank ye, lady,
And I shall study to confirm it.
　*Quisar.*　　　　　Do, sir,　120
For this time, and this present cause, I allow it.
　　　　　　　　[*Exit Pyniero.*]

*Enter Governor, Quisana, and Panura*

Most holy sir.
　*Gov.* Bless ye, my royal daughter,
And in you, bless this island, heaven.
　*Quisar.*　　　　　Good aunt,
What think ye of this man?
　*Quisan.*　　　Sure, h 'is a wise man,
And a religious. He tells us things have
　happen'd　125
So many years ago, almost forgotten,
As readily as if they were done this hour.
　*Quisar.* Does he not meet with your sharp
　tongue?
　*Pan.*　　　　　He tells me, madam,
Marriage, and mouldy cheese will make me
　tamer.
　*Gov.* A stubborn keeper, and worse fare, 130
An open stable, and cold care,
Will tame a jade, may be your share.
　*Pan.* By 'r lady, a sharp prophet! When
　this proves good,
I 'll bequeath you a skin to make ye a hood.
　*Gov.* Lady, I would talk with you.
　*Quisar.*　　　Do, reverend sir. 135
　*Gov.* And for your good, for that that must
　concern ye;
And give ear wisely to me.
　*Quisar.*　　　I shall, father.
　*Gov.* You are a princess of that excellence,
Sweetness, and grace, that angel-like fair fea-
　ture, —
Nay, do not blush, I do not flatter you,　140
Nor do I dote in telling this, — I am amaz'd,
　lady,
And as I think the gods bestow'd these on ye,
The gods that love ye.
　*Quisar.*　　　I confess their bounty.
　*Gov.* Apply it, then, to their use, to their
　honour.
To them and to their service give this sweet-
　ness;　145
They have an instant great use of your good-
　ness;

⁸² I stand: ('Island' F 2)　¹⁰⁰ dispense with: consent to　¹⁰⁷ use: interpretation　¹¹⁵⁻¹¹⁸ ('These lines are apparently corrupt.)

You are a saint esteem'd here for your beauty,
And many a longing heart —
   *Quisar.*               I seek no fealty,
Nor will I blemish that heaven has seal'd on
  me.
I know my worth. Indeed the Portugals   150
I have at those commands, and their last serv-
  ices,
Nay, even their lives, so much I think my hand-
  someness,
That what I shall enjoin —
   *Gov.*             Use it discreetly.
For I perceive ye understand me rightly,
For here the gods regard your help, and
  suddenly;           155
The Portugals, like sharp thorns (mark me,
  lady)
Stick in our sides, like razors wound religion,
Draw deep; they wound till the life-blood
  follows.
Our gods they spurn at, and their worships
  scorn,
A mighty hand they bear upon our govern-
  ment:           160
These are the men your miracle must work on,
Your heavenly form, either to root them out,
(Which, as you may endeavour, will be easy;
Remember whose great cause you have to ex-
  ecute,)
To nip their memory, that may not spring
  more,           165
Or fairly bring 'em home to our devotions,
Which will be blessed, and, for which, you
  sainted, —
But cannot be; and they go, let me bustle.
                                [*Aside.*]
   *Quisar.* Go up with me,
Where we 'll converse more privately;
I 'll show ye shortly how I hold their temper;
And in what chain their souls.
   *Gov.*        Keep fast that hold still, 171
And either bring that chain, and those bound
  in it,
And link it to our gods and their fair worships,
Or, daughter, pinch their hearts apieces with it.
I 'll wait upon your grace.
   *Quisar.*    Come, reverend father. —   175
Wait you below. *Exeunt Quisara and Governor.*
   *Pan.*   If this prophet were a young thing,
I should suspect him now, he cleaves so close
  to her;
These holy coats are long, and hide iniquities.
   *Quisan.* Away, away, fool, a poor wretch.
   *Pan.*          These poor ones,
Warm but their stomachs once —
   *Quisan.* Come in, thou art foolish.   180
          *Exeunt Quisana and Panura.*

[SCENE III. — *The Same. The Beach*]

*Enter Armusia, Emanuel, and Pyniero*

   *Arm.* I am sorry, sir, my fortune is so
  stubborn,
To court my sword against my countryman.
I love my nation well, and where I find
A Portugal of noble name and virtue,
I am his humble servant. Signior Pyniero,   5
Your person, nor your uncle's, am I angry with;
You are both fair gentlemen in my opinion,
And, I protest, I had rather use my sword
In your defences than against your safeties.
'T is, methinks, a strange dearth of enemies,   10
When we seek foes among ourselves.
   *Em.*           You are injur'd,
And you must make the best on 't now, and
  readiest —
   *Arm.* You see I am ready in the place, and
  arm'd
To his desire that call'd me.
   *Py.*          Ye speak honestly,
And I could wish ye had met on terms more
  friendly;           15
But it cannot now be so.

*Enter Ruy Dias*

   *Em.*           Turn, sir, and see.
   *Py.* I have kept my word with ye, uncle;
The gentleman is ready.

*Enter Governor and Quisara, above*

   *Arm.*          Ye are welcome.
   *Ruy.* Bid those fools welcome, that affect
  your courtesy;
I come not to use compliment. Ye have
  wrong'd me,         20
And ye shall feel, proud man, ere I part from ye,
The effects of that. If fortune do not fool me,
Thy life is mine, and no hope shall redeem thee.
   *Arm.* That 's a proud word,
More than your faith can justify.
   *Quisar.*       Sure, they will fight.
   *Ruy.* [*Aside.*] She 's there; I am happy.   25
   *Gov.* Let 'em alone; let 'em kill one an-
  other. —
These are the main posts; if they fall, the
  buildings
Will tumble quickly.         [*Aside.*]
   *Quisar.*     How temperate Armusia!
No more, be quiet yet.
   *Arm.*         I am not bloody,
Nor do not feel such mortal malice in me,   30
But since we cannot both enjoy the princess,
I am resolv'd to fight.
   *Ruy.*          Fight home, Armusia,
For if thou faint'st or fall'st —

---

*Arm.* Do ye make all vantages?
*Ruy.* Always, unto thy life; I will not spare thee,
Nor look not for thy mercy.
*Arm.* I am arm'd, then. 35
*Ruy.* Stand still, I charge ye, nephew, as ye honour me.
*Arm.* And, good Emanuel, stir not —
*Py.* Ye speak fitly,
For we had not stood idle else.
*Gov.* [*Aside.*] I am sorry for 't.
*Em.* But since you will have it so —
*Ruy.* Come, sir.
*Arm.* I wait ye.
[*They fight.*]
*Py.* Ay, marry, this looks handsomely, 40
This is warm work!
*Gov.* [*Aside.*] Both fall, and 't be thy will.
*Ruy falls.*
*Py.* My uncle dead? [*Draws.*]
*Em.* Stand still, or my sword 's in —
*Arm.* Now, brave Ruy Dias,
Now where 's your confidence, your prayers? Quickly
Your own spite has condemn'd ye.
*Quisar.* Hold, Armusia. 45
*Arm.* Most happy lady!
*Quisar.* Hold, and let him rise,
Spare him for me.
*Arm.* A long life may he enjoy, lady.
*Gov.* What ha' you done? 't is better they had all perish'd.
*Quisar.* Peace, father; I work for the best. Armusia,
Be in the garden an hour hence.
*Exeunt Quisara and Governor.*
*Arm.* I shall, madam. 50
*Py.* Now, as I live, a gentleman at all inches!
So brave a mingled temper saw I never.
*Arm.* Why are ye sad, sir? how would this have griev'd you,
If ye had fall'n under a profess'd enemy?
Under one had taken vantage of your shame, too? 55
Pray ye, be at peace; I am so far from wronging ye,
Or glorying in the pride of such a victory,
That I desire to serve ye. Pray look cheerfully.
*Py.* Do you hear this, sir? this love, sir? do you see this gentleman,
How he courts ye? why do you hold your head down? 60
'T is no high treason, I take it, to be equall'd;
To have a slip i' th' field, no sin that 's mortal.
Come, come, thank fortune and your friend.
*Arm.* It may be

You think my tongue may prove your enemy;
And, though restrain'd, sometime, out of a bravery, 65
May take a license to disable ye:
Believe me, sir, so much I hate that liberty,
That in a stranger's tongue 't will prove an injury,
And I shall right you in 't.
*Py.* Can you have more, uncle?
*Ruy.* Sir, you have beat me both ways, yet so nobly, 70
That I shall ever love the hand that did it.
Fortune may make me worthy of some title
That may be near your friend.
*Arm.* Sir, I must leave ye,
But with so hearty love — and, pray, be confident,
I carry nothing from this place shall wrong ye. 75
*Exeunt Armusia & Emanuel.*
*Py.* Come, come, you are right again, sir; love your honour,
And love your friend; take heed of bloody purposes,
And unjust ends; good heaven is angry with ye;
Make your fair virtues and your fame your mistress,
And let these trinkets go.
*Ruy.* You teach well, nephew. 80
Now to be honourably even with this gentleman,
Shall be my business, and my ends his.
[*Exeunt.*]

[SCENE IV. — *The Same. A Room in the Palace*]

*Enter Governor and King*

*Gov.* Sir, sir, you must do something suddenly,
To stop his pride, so great and high he is shot up;
Upon his person, too; your state is sunk else.
You must not stand now upon terms of gratitude,
And let a simple tenderness besot ye. 5
I 'll bring ye suddenly where you shall see him
Attempting your brave sister privately.
Mark but his high behaviour then.
*King.* I will, father.
*Gov.* And with scorn, I fear, contempt, too.
*King.* I hope not.
*Gov.* I will not name a lust; it may be that also. 10
A little force must be applied upon him,
Now, now applied, a little force to humble him.
These sweet entreaties do but make him wanton.

*King.* Take heed ye wrong him not.

*Gov.*                    Take heed to your safety,
I but forewarn ye, king; if you mistrust me, 15
Or think I come unsent —

*King.*                    No, I 'll go with you.

*Exeunt.*

[SCENE V. — *The Same. A Garden near
the Palace*]

*Enter Armusia, Quisara*

*Arm.* Madam, you see there 's nothing I
can reach at,
Either in my obedience or my service,
That may deserve your love, or win a liking,
Not a poor thought, but I pursue it seriously,
Take pleasure in your will, even in your anger,
Which other men would grudge at, and grow
stormy.                                                        6
I study new humility to please ye,
And take a kind of joy in my afflictions;
Because they come from ye, I love my sorrows:
Pray, madam, but consider —

*Quisar.*                    Yes, I do, sir, 10
And to that honest end I drew thee hither.
I know ye have deserv'd as much as man
can,
And know it is a justice to requite you:
I know ye love.

*Arm.*                    If ever love was mortal,
And dwelt in man, and for that love command
me,                                                            15
So strong I find it, and so true, here, lady,
Something of such a greatness to allow me,
Those things I have done already may seem
foils to.
'T is equity that man aspires to heaven
Should win it by his worth, and not sleep to
it.                                                            20

*Enter Governor, and King [behind]*

*Gov.* Now stand close, king, and hear, and
as you find him,
Believe me right, or let religion suffer.

*Quisar.* I dare believe your worth without
additions,
But since you are so liberal of your love, sir,
And would be farther tried, I do intend it, 25
Because you shall not, or you would not, win
me
At such an easy rate.

*Arm.*                    I am prepar'd still,
And if I shrink —

*Quisar.*                    I know ye are no coward:
This is the utmost trial of your constancy,
And if you stand fast now, I am yours, your
wife, sir.                                                     30

You hold there 's nothing dear that may
achieve me,
Doubted or dangerous.

*Arm.*                    There 's nothing, nothing:
Let me but know, that I may straight fly to it.

*Quisar.* I 'll tell you, then: change your
religion,
And be of one belief with me.

*Arm.*                    How?

*Quisar.*                    Mark.   35
Worship our gods, renounce that faith ye are
bred in.
'T is easily done, I 'll teach ye suddenly,
And humbly on your knees —

*Arm.*                    Ha! I 'll be hang'd first.

*Quisar.* Offer as we do.

*Arm.*                    To the devil, lady?
Offer to him I hate? I know the devil.         40
To dogs and cats? you make offer to them;
To every bird that flies, and every worm.
How terribly I shake! Is this the venture,
The trial that you talk'd of? Where have I
been?
And how forgot myself? how lost my memory?
When did I pray, or look up steadfastly,   46
Had any goodness in my heart to guide me,
That I should give this vantage to mine enemy,
The enemy to my peace? Forsake my faith?

*Quisar.* Come, come, I know ye love me.

*Arm.*                    Love ye this way? 50
This most destroying way? sure, you but jest,
lady.

*Quisar.* My love and life are one way.

*Arm.*                    Love alone then —
And mine another way. I 'll love diseases first,
Dote on a villain that would cut my throat,
Woo all afflictions of all sorts, kiss cruelty! 55
Have mercy, heaven! how have I been wan-
d'ring!
Wand'ring the way of lust, and left my Maker!
How have I slept like cork upon a water,
And had no feeling of the storm that toss'd me!
Trod the blind paths of death! forsook assur-
ance,                                                          60
Eternity of blessedness, for a woman!
For a young handsome face hazard my being!

*Quisar.* Are not our powers eternal, so their
comforts?
As great and full of hopes as yours?

*Arm.*                    They are puppets.

*Gov.* Now mark him, sir, and but observe
him nearly.                                                    65

*Arm.* Their comforts like themselves, cold,
senseless outsides;
You make 'em sick, as we are, peevish, mad,
Subject to age; and how can they cure us,
That are not able to refine themselves?

---

**Not:** ('But' Ff)   **⁶ grudge:** grumble   **¹⁷ allow:** prove (me) worthy   **²¹ close:** hidden   **²³ additions:** marks of distinction   **³² Doubted:** fearful, uncertain   **⁴¹ offer:** offerings   **⁶⁵ nearly:** closely

*Quisar.* The Sun and Moon we worship,
those are heavenly,      70
And their bright influences we believe.
   *Arm.*                  Away, fool,
I adore the Maker of that sun and moon,
That gives those bodies light and influence,
That pointed out their paths, and taught their
motions;
They are not so great as we, they are our serv-
ants,      75
Plac'd there to teach us time, to give us knowl-
edge
Of when and how the swellings of the main are,
And their returns again; they are but our
stewards
To make the earth fat with their influence,
That she may bring forth her increase, and
feed us.      80
Shall I fall from this faith to please a woman?
For her embraces bring my soul to ruin?
I look'd you should have said, "Make me a
Christian;
Work that great cure," for 't is a great one,
woman;
That labour truly to perform, that venture, 85
The crown of all great trial, and the fairest.
I look'd ye should have wept and kneel'd to
beg it,
Wash'd off your mist of ignorance with waters,
Pure and repentant, from those eyes; I look'd
You should have brought me your chief god
ye worship,      90
He that you offer human blood and life to,
And made a sacrifice of him to memory,
Beat down his altars, ruin'd his false temples.
   *Gov.* Now you may see.
   *Quisar.* Take heed; you go too far, sir. —
And yet I love to hear him. [*Aside.*] — I must
have ye,      95
And to that end I let you storm a little.
I know there must be some strife in your bosom
To cool and quiet ye, ere you can come back.
I know old friends cannot part suddenly,    99
There will be some let still; yet I must have ye,
Have ye of my faith, too, and so enjoy ye.
   *Arm.* Now I contemn ye, and I hate my-
self
For looking on that face lasciviously;
And it looks ugly now, methinks.
   *Quisar.*             How, Portugal?
   *Arm.* It looks like death itself, to which
't would lead me;      105
Your eyes resemble pale despair; they fright
me,
And in their rounds a thousand horrid ruins
Methinks I see; and in your tongue hear fear-
fully

The hideous murmurs of weak souls have
suffer'd.
Get from me, I despise ye; and know, woman,
That for all this trap you have laid to catch
my life in,      111
To catch my immortal life, I hate and curse ye,
Contemn your deities, spurn at their powers,
And where I meet your Mahumet gods, I 'll
swing 'em
Thus o'er my head, and kick 'em into puddles;
Nay, I will out of vengeance search your tem-
ples,      116
And with those hearts that serve my God
demolish
Your shambles of wild worships.
   *Gov.*           Now, now you hear, sir.
   *Arm.* I will have my faith, since you are so
crafty,
The glorious Cross, although I love your
brother;      120
Let him frown, too, I will have my devotion,
And let your whole state storm.
   *King.* Enter and take him; [*Guards seize
Armusia.*]
I am sorry, friend, that I am forc'd to do this.
   *Gov.* Be sure you bind him fast.
   *Quisar.*           But use him nobly.
   *King.* Had it to me been done, I had for-
given it,      125
And still preserv'd you fair, but to our gods,
sir —
   *Quisar.* [*Aside.*] Methinks I hate 'em now.
   *King.*            To our religion;
To these to be thus stubborn, thus rebellious,
To threaten them —
   *Arm.*          Use all your violence.
I ask no mercy, nor repent my words:     130
I spit at your best powers. I serve One,
Will give me strength to scourge your gods —
   *Gov.*            Away with him.
   *Arm.* To grind 'em into base dust, and dis-
perse 'em,
That never more their bloody memories —
   *Gov.* Clap him close up.
   *King.*          Good friend, be cooler.
   *Arm.*             Never; 135
Your painted sister I despise, too —
   *King.*            Softly.
   *Arm.* And all her devilish arts laugh and
scorn at,
Mock her blind purposes.
   *King.*        You must be temperate.
Offer him no violence, I command you strictly.
   *Gov.* [*Aside.*] Now thou art up, I shall
have time to speak, too. —      140
   *Quisar.* [*Aside.*] Oh, how I love this man,
how truly honour him.      *Exeunt.*

---

⁹² **made:** ('make' Ff)    ¹⁰⁰ **let:** hindrance
**been damned**    ¹¹⁴ **Mahumet:** idolatrous    ¹⁴⁰ **up:** imprisoned    ¹⁰⁷ **rounds:** orbs    ¹⁰⁹ **have suffer'd:** which have

*Actus Quintus. Scæna Prima.*

[*Tidore. — Before the Portuguese Fort*]

*Enter Christophero and Pedro (at one door),
Emanuel and Soza (at another)*

*Chr.*  Do you know the news, gentlemen?
*Em.*            Would we knew as well, sir,
How to prevent it.
*Soz.*                  Is this the love they bear us
For our late benefit? taken so maliciously,
And clapp'd up close?  Is that the thanks they
render?                                                    5
*Chr.*  It must not be put up thus, smother'd
slightly;
'T is such a base, unnatural wrong!
*Ped.*                          I know,
They may think to do wonders, aim at all,
And to blow us with a vengeance out o' th'
Islands;
But if we be ourselves, honest and resolute,   10
And continue but masters of our ancient
courages,
Stick close, and give no vantage to their vil-
lainies —
*Soz.*  Nay, if we faint or fall apieces now,
We are fools, and worthy to be mark'd for
misery.
Begin to strike at him they are all bound to!  15
To cancel his deserts! what must we look for
If they can carry this?
*Em.*                  I 'll carry coals, then.
I have but one life and one fortune, gentlemen,
But I 'll so husband it to vex these rascals,
These barbarous slaves —
*Chr.*  Shall we go charge 'em presently?     20
*Soz.*  No, that will be too weak, and too fool-
hardy;
We must have grounds that promise safety,
friends,
And sure offence; we lose our angers else,
And, worse than that, venture our lives too
lightly.

*Enter Pyniero*

*Py.*  Did you see mine uncle? — Plague o'
these barbarians,                                          25
How the rogues stick in my teeth! — I know
ye are angry;
So I am, too, monstrous angry, gentlemen;
I am angry, that I choke again.
You hear Armusia 's up, honest Armusia,
Clapp'd up in prison, friends, the brave
Armusia!                                                   30
Here are fine boys.
*Em.*  We hope he shall not stay there.

*Py.*  Stay?  No, he must not stay, no talk
of staying;
These are no times to stay.  Are not these ras-
cals?
Speak, I beseech ye, speak, are they not
rogues?
Think some abominable names — are they not
devils?                                                    35
But the devil 's a great deal too good for 'em
— fusty villains.
*Chr.*  They are a kind of hounds.
*Py.*              Hounds were their fathers;
Old, blear-ey'd, bob-tail'd hounds. — Lord,
where 's my uncle?
*Soz.*  But what shall be done, sir?
*Py.*                            Done?
*Soz.*                    Yes, to relieve him?
If it be not sudden, they may take his life, too.
*Py.*  They dare as soon take fire and swallow
it,                                                        41
Take stakes and thrust into their tails for
glisters.
His life, why 't is a thing worth all the islands,
And they know will be rated at that value.
His very imprisonment will make the town
stink,                                                     45
And shake and stink.  I have physic in my
hand for 'em
Shall give the goblins such a purge —

*Enter Ruy Dias*

*Ped.*                            Your uncle.
*Ruy.*  I hear strange news, and have been
seeking ye;
They say Armusia 's prisoner.
*Py.*                        'T is most certain.
*Ruy.*  Upon what cause?
*Py.*              He has deserv'd too much, sir;   50
The old heathen policy has light upon him,
And paid him home.
*Ruy.*            A most unnoble dealing.
*Py.*  You are the next, if you can carry it
tamely.
He has deserv'd of all.
*Ruy.*                I must confess it,
Of me so nobly, too.
*Py.*                I am glad to hear it.           55
You have a time now to make good your con-
fession,
Your faith will show but cold else, and for
fashion.
Now to redeem all, now to thank his courtesy,
Now to make those believe that held you back-
ward,
And an ill instrument, you are a gentleman,    60
An honest man, and you dare love your Nation,
Dare stick to virtue, though she be oppress'd,

And, for her own fair sake, step to her rescue.
If you live ages, sir, and lose this hour,
Not now redeem and vindicate your honour, 65
Your life will be a murmur, and no man in 't.
   *Ruy.* I thank ye, nephew. — Come along
   with me, gentlemen,
We 'll make 'em dancing sport immediately:
We are masters of the fort yet; we shall see
What that can do.
   *Py.*        Let it but spit fire finely, 70
And play their turrets, and their painted
   palaces,
A frisking round or two, that they may trip it,
And caper in the air.
   *Ruy.*      Come, we 'll do something
Shall make 'em look about; we 'll send 'em
   plums,
If they be not too hard for their teeth.
   *Py.*        And fine potatoes 75
Roasted in gunpowder; such a banquet, sir,
Will prepare their unmannerly stomachs —
   *Ruy.*        They shall see
There is no safe retreat in villainy.
Come, be high-hearted all.
   *Omnes.*    We are all on fire, sir. *Exeunt.*

[SCENE II. — *The Same. A Hall in
the Palace*]

*Enter King and Governor [with Attendants]*

   *King.* I am ungrateful, and a wretch, per-
   suade me not;
Forgetful of the mercy he show'd me,
The timely noble pity. Why should I
See him fast bound and fetter'd, whose true
   courtesy,
Whose manhood, and whose mighty hand set
   me free?                      5
Why should it come from me? why I command
   this?
Shall not all tongues and truths call me un-
   thankful?
   *Gov.* Had the offence been thrown on you,
   't is certain
It had been in your power and your discretion
To have turn'd it into mercy, and forgiven it,
And then it had show'd a virtuous point of
   gratitude,                   11
Timely and nobly taken; but since the cause
Concerns the honour of our gods and their
   title,
And so transcends your power and your com-
   passion, —
A little your own safety, if you saw it, too, 15
If your too-fond indulgence did not dazzle
   you, —

It cannot now admit a private pity;
'T is in their wills, their mercies or revenges,
And these revolts in you show mere rebellions.
   *King.* They are mild and pitiful.
   *Gov.*           To those repent. 20
   *King.* Their nature 's soft and tender.
   *Gov.*           To true hearts,
That feel compunction for their trespasses.
This man defies 'em still, threatens destruc-
   tion
And demolition of their arms and worship,
Spits at their powers. Take heed ye be not
   found, sir,                   25
And mark'd a favourer of their dishonour;
They use no common justice.
   *King.*         What shall I do
To deserve of this man?
   *Gov.*       If ye more bemoan him,
Or mitigate your power to preserve him,
I 'll curse ye from the gods, call up their ven-
   geance,                   30

*Enter Quisara with her hands bound, Quisana,
Panura*

And fling it on your land and you: I have
   charge for 't. —
I hope to wrack you all. [*Aside.*]
   *King.*        What ails my sister?
Why is she bound? why looks she so dis-
   tractedly?
Who does do this?
   *Quisan.*      We did it, — pardon, sir, —
And for her preservation. She is grown wild, 35
And raving on the stranger's love and honour,
Sometimes crying out, "Help, help, they will
   torture him,
They will take his life, they will murder him
   presently!"
If we had not prevented, violently
Have laid hands on her own life.
   *Gov.*        These are tokens 40
The gods' displeasure is gone out. Be quick,
And, ere it fall, do something to appease 'em.
You know the sacrifice. — I am glad it works
   thus.                  [*Aside.*]
   *Quisar.* How low and base thou look'st
   now, that wert noble!
No figure of a king, methinks, shows on you, 45
No face of majesty; foul, swarth ingratitude
Has taken off thy sweetness; base forgetful-
   ness
Of mighty benefits has turn'd thee devil.
Thou hast persecuted goodness, innocence,
And laid a hard and violent hand on virtue, 50
On that fair virtue that should teach and guide
   us.

   ⁷² **round:** dance tune    ¹⁸ *I.e.,* mercy or punishment now rests with the gods    ¹⁹ **mere:** absolute
²⁹ **mitigate . . . power:** exercise clemency    ³¹ **for 't:** (not in F 2)    ³² **wrack:** wreck    ⁴⁰ **Have:** she
would have    ⁴⁶ **swarth:** black

Thou hast wrong'd thine own preserver, whose
    least merit,
Pois'd with thy main estate, thou canst not
    satisfy;
Nay, put thy life in, too, 't will be too light still.
What hast thou done?
    *Gov.* Go for him presently, [*Exit Guard.*]
And once more we 'll try if we can win him
    fairly:                  56
If not, let nothing she says hinder ye, or stir ye;
She speaks distractedly. Do that the gods
    command ye.
Do you know what ye say, lady?
    *Quisar.*          I could curse thee, too.
Religion and severity has steel'd thee,    60
Has turn'd thy heart to stone; thou hast made
    the gods hard, too,
Against their sweet and patient natures, cruel.
None of ye feel what bravery ye tread on,
What innocence, what beauty!
    *King.*             Pray, be patient.
    *Quisar.* What honourable things ye cast
    behind ye,              65
What monuments of man!

*Enter Armusia and Guard*

    *King.*            Once more, Armusia,
Because I love ye tenderly and dearly,
And would be glad to win ye mine, I wish ye,
Even from my heart I wish and woo ye —
    *Arm.*               What, sir?
Take heed how ye persuade me falsely; then
    ye hate me:            70
Take heed how ye entrap me.
    *King.*            I advise ye,
And tenderly and truly I advise ye,
Both for your soul's health, and your safety —
    *Arm.*                 Stay,
And name my soul no more; she is too precious,
Too glorious for your flatteries, too secure, too.
    *Gov.* Consider the reward, sir, and the
    honour             76
That is prepar'd, the glory you shall grow to.
    *Arm.* They are not to be consider'd in
    these cases,
Not to be nam'd, when souls are questioned;
They are vain and flying vapours. Touch my
    life,                 80
'T is ready for ye; put it to what test
It shall please ye, I am patient; but for the
    rest,
You may remove rocks with your little fingers,
Or blow a mountain out o' th' way with bel-
    lows,
As soon as stir my faith: use no more argu-
    ments.             85
    *Gov.* We must use tortures, then.

    *Arm.*           Your worst and painfull'st
I am joyful to accept.
    *Gov.*           You must the sharpest.
For such has been your hate against our deities
Deliver'd openly, your threats and scornings,
And either your repentance must be mighty,  90
Which is your free conversion to our customs,
Or equal punishment, which is your life, sir.
    *Arm.* I am glad I have it for ye; take it,
    priest,
And all the miseries that shall attend it.
Let the gods glut themselves with Christian
    blood,             95
It will be ask'd again, and so far follow'd,
So far reveng'd, and with such holy justice,
Your gods of gold shall melt and sink before it;
Your altars and your temples shake to nothing;
And you false worshippers, blind fools of cere-
    mony,             100
Shall seek for holes to hide your heads and fears
    in,
For seas to swallow you from this destruction,
Darkness to dwell about ye, and conceal ye;
Your mothers' womb again —
    *Gov.*          Make the fires ready,
And bring the several tortures out!
    *Quisar.*          Stand fast, sir,  105
And fear 'em not. You that have stepp'd so
    nobly
Into this pious trial, start not now.
Keep on your way, a virgin will assist ye,
A virgin won by your fair constancy,    109
And, glorying that she is won so, will die by ye.
I have touch'd ye every way, tried ye most
    honest,
Perfect, and good, chaste, blushing-chaste,
    and temperate,
Valiant without vain-glory, modest, staid,
No rage, or light affection ruling in you;
Indeed, the perfect school of worth I find ye,
The temple of true honour.
    *Arm.* [*Aside.*]    Whether will she? — 116
What do you infer by this fair argument, lady?
    *Quisar.* Your faith and your religion must
    be like ye,
They that can show you these must be pure
    mirrors:
When the streams flow clear and fair, what
    are the fountains?         120
I do embrace your faith, sir, and your fortune.
Go on; I will assist ye; I feel a sparkle here,
A lively spark that kindles my affection,
And tells me it will rise to flames of glory.
Let 'em put on their angers; suffer nobly,  125
Show me the way, and, when I faint, instruct
    me;
And if I follow not —

*Arm.*                 Oh, blessed lady,
Since thou art won, let me begin my triumph!
Come clap your terrors on.
    *Quisar.*                 All your fell tortures;
For there is nothing he shall suffer, brother, 130
(I swear by a new faith, which is most sacred,
And I will keep it so,) but I will follow in,
And follow to a scruple of affliction,
In spite of all your gods, without prevention.
    *Gov.* [*Aside.*] Death! she amazes me.
    *King.*             What shall be done now?  135
    *Gov.* They must die both,
And suddenly; they will corrupt all else. —
This woman makes me weary of my mischief,
She shakes me, and she staggers me. [*Aside.*]
    — Go in, sir;
I 'll see the execution.
    *King.*             Not so sudden:        140
If they go, all my friends and sisters perish.
    *Gov.* [*Aside.*] Would I were safe at home
again.

                *Enter Messenger*

*Mes.*                 Arm, arm, sir!
Seek for defence; the castle plays and thunders,
The town rocks, and the houses fly i' th' air,
The people die for fear.  Captain Ruy Dias 145
Has made an oath he will not leave a stone
here,
No, not the memory, here has stood a city,
Unless Armusia be deliver'd fairly.
    *King.* I have my fears: what can our gods
        do now for us?
    *Gov.* Be patient, but keep him still: he is a
        cure, sir,                         150
Against both rage and cannon.  Go and fortify;
Call in the princess, make the palace sure,
And let 'em know you are a king; look nobly,
And take your courage to ye.  Keep close the
        prisoner,
And under command, we are betray'd else.  155
    *Arm.* How joyfully I go!
    *Quisar.*             Take my heart with thee.
    *Gov.* [*Aside.*] I hold a wolf by the ear now:
Fortune free me!                     *Exeunt.*

[SCENE III. — *The Same.  A Street*]

            *Enter four Townsmen*

*1.* Heaven bless us, what a thund'ring 's
    here! what fire-spitting!
We cannot drink, but our cans are maul'd
    amongst us.
*2.* I would they would maul our scores, too!
    Shame o' their guns!
i thought they had been bird-pots, or great
    candle-cases.

How devilishly they bounce, and how the
    bullets                               5
Borrow a piece of a house here, there another,
And mend those up again with another parish!
Here flies a powd'ring-tub, the meat ready
    roasted,
And there a barrel pissing vinegar;
And they two, over-taking the top of a high
    steeple,                              10
Newly slic'd off for a sallet.
    *3.*                 A vengeance fire 'em.
    *2.* Nay, they fire fast enough; you need
        not help 'em.
    *4.* Are these the Portugal bulls?  How
        loud they bellow!
    *2.* Their horns are plaguey strong, they
        push down palaces;
They toss our little habitations like whelps,  15
Like grindle-tails, with their heels upward;
All the windows i' th' town dance a new trench-
        more, —
'T is like to prove a blessed age for glaziers.
I met a hand, and a letter in 't, in great haste,
And by and by a single leg running after it,  20
As if the arm had forgot part of his errand;
Heads fly like footballs everywhere.
    *1.* What shall we do?
    *2.*             I care not; my shop 's cancell'd,
And all the pots and earthen pans in 't
    vanish'd.
There was a single bullet and they together
    by the ears;                         25
You would have thought Tom Tumbler had
    been there,
And all his troop of devils.
    *3.*             Let 's to the king,
And get this gentleman deliver'd handsomely:
By this hand, there 's no walking above ground
    else.
    *2.* By this leg — let me swear nimbly by it,
For I know not how long I shall owe it, —  31
If I were out o' th' town once, if I came in
    again to
Fetch my breakfast, I will give 'em leave to
    cram me
With a Portugal pudding.  Come; let 's do
    anything
To appease this thunder.             *Exeunt.*

    [SCENE IV. — *The Same.  Before the
            Portuguese Fort*]

        *Enter Pyniero and Panura*

*Py.* Art sure it was that blind priest?
*Pan.*                 Yes, most certain,
He has provok'd all this.  The king is merciful,

---

¹³³ **scruple:** minute particle   ¹⁵⁴ **your:** ('you' F 2)   ³ **scores:** tavern reckonings   ⁸ **powd'ring-tub:** tub for salting meat   ¹¹ **sallet:** salad   ¹⁶ **grindle-tails:** a kind of dog   ¹⁷ **trenchmore:** a lively dance   ³¹ **owe:** own

And wond'rous loving; but he fires him on still,
And, when he cools, enrages him; I know it;
Threatens new vengeance and the gods' fierce justice,                                                    5
When he but looks with fair eyes on Armusia,
Will lend him no time to relent.  My royal mistress,
She has entertain'd a Christian hope.
*Py.*                                    Speak truly.
*Pan.*  Nay, 't is most true, but Lord! how he lies at her,
And threatens her, and flatters her, and damns her;                                                      10
And I fear, if not speedily prevented,
If she continue stout, both shall be executed.
*Py.*  I 'll kiss thee for this news; nay, more, Panura,
If thou wilt give me leave, I 'll get thee with Christian,
The best way to convert thee.
*Pan.*                      Make me believe so?  15
*Py.*  I will, i' faith.  But which way cam'st thou hither?
The palace is close guarded, and barricado'd.
*Pan.*  I came through a private vault, which few there know of;
It rises in a temple not far hence,
Close by the castle here.
*Py.*                     How!  To what end?  20
*Pan.*  A good one;
To give ye knowledge of my new-born mistress;
And in what doubt Armusia stands:
Think any present means or hope to stop 'em
From their fell ends.  The princes are come in, too,                                                     25
And they are harden'd, also.
*Py.*                       The damn'd priest —
*Pan.*  Sure, he 's a cruel man.  Methinks religion
Should teach more temperate lessons.
*Py.*                       He the fire-brand!
He dare to touch at such fair lives as theirs are!
Well, prophet, I shall prophesy I shall catch ye,
When all your prophecies will not redeem ye. —
Wilt thou do one thing bravely?
*Pa.*         Any good I am able.  32
*Py.*  And by thine own white hand, I 'll swear thou art virtuous,
And a brave wench.  Durst thou but guide me presently,
Through the same vault thou cam'st, into the palace,                                                      35
And those I shall appoint, such as I think fit?
*Pa.*  Yes, I will do it, and suddenly, and truly.

*Py.*  I would fain behold this prophet.
*Pa.*                          Now I have ye,
And shall bring ye where ye shall behold him,
Alone, too, and unfurnish'd of defences.   40
That shall be my care; but you must not betray me.
*Py.*  Dost thou think we are so base, such slaves, rogues?
*Pa.*                          I do not;
And you shall see how fairly I 'll work for ye.
*Py.*  I must needs steal that priest, steal him, and hang him.
*Pa.*  Do anything to remove his mischief; strangle him —                                           45
*Py.*  Come, prithee, love.
*Pa.*          You 'll offer me no foul play?
The vault is dark.
*Py.*               'T was well remember'd.
*Pa.*                          And ye may —
But I hold ye honest.
*Py.*          Honest enough, I warrant thee.
*Pa.*  I am but a poor, weak wench; and what with the place,
And your persuasions, sir — but I hope you will not —                                                 50
You know we are often cozen'd.
*Py.*               If thou dost fear me,
Why dost thou put me in mind?
*Pa.*               To let you know, sir,
Though it be in your power, and things fitting to it,
Yet a true gentleman —
*Py.*          I know what he 'll do.  54
Come and remember me, and I 'll answer thee,
I 'll answer thee to the full.  We 'll call at th' castle,
And then, my good guide, do thy will; sha't find me
A very tractable man.
*Pa.*          I hope I shall, sir.          *Exeunt.*

[SCENE V. — *The Same.  Before the Palace*]

*Enter Bakam, Syana, and Soldiers*

*Ba.*  Let my men guard the gates.
*Sy.*                   And mine the temple,
For fear the honour of our gods should suffer,
And on your lives be watchful.
*Ba.*               And be valiant;
And let 's see, if these Portugals dare enter,
What their high hearts dare do.  Let 's see how readily                                               5
The great Ruy Dias will redeem his country-man.
He speaks proud words, and threatens.
*Sy.*               He is approv'd, sir,
And will put fair for what he promises.

---

¹² **stout:** firm       Sc. V ⁶ **countryman:** ('countrymen' Ff)       ⁷ **approv'd:** of proved prowess
⁸ **put fair:** make a strong effort

I could wish friendlier terms; yet for our
   liberties
And for our gods, we are bound in our best
   service                                                              10
Even in the hazard of our lives.

            *Enter the King above*

*King.*                Come up, princes,
And give your counsels, and your helps. The
   fort still
Plays fearfully upon us, beats our buildings,
And turns our people wild with fears.
  *Ba.*           Send for the prisoner,
And give us leave to argue.

      *Exeunt Bakam and Syana; then,*

 *Enter Ruy Dias, Emanuel, Christophero,*
      *Pedro, with Soldiers*

  *Ruy.*            Come on nobly, 15
And let the fort play still. We are strong
   enough
To look upon 'em, and return at pleasure.
It may be on our view they will return him.
  *Chr.* We will return 'em such thanks else,
   shall make 'em
Scratch where it itches not.
  *Em.*        How the people stare! 20
And some cry, some pray, and some curse
   heartily:
But it is the king —

  *Enter Syana, Bakam, Quisara, Armusia,*
      *with Soldiers, above*

  *Ruy.*     I cannot blame their wisdoms.
They are all above, Armusia chain'd and
   bound, too!
Oh, these are thankful squires.
  *Ba.*          Hear us, Ruy Dias,
Be wise and hear us, and give speedy answer,
Command thy cannon presently to cease, 26
No more to trouble the afflicted people,
Or suddenly Armusia's head goes off,
As suddenly as said.
  *Em.*          Stay, sir; be moderate.
  *Arm.* Do nothing that's dishonourable,
   Ruy Dias;                                                         30
Let not the fear of me master thy valour;
Pursue 'em still; they are base malicious
   people.
  *King.* Friend, be not desperate.
  *Arm.*       I scorn your courtesies,
Strike when you dare! A fair arm guide the
   gunner,
And may he let fly still with fortune! Friend,
Do me the honour of a soldier's funerals, 36
The last fair Christian rite; see me i' th'
   ground,
And let the palace burn first, then the temples,

And on their scorned gods, erect my monument:
Touch not the princess, as you are a soldier. 40
  *Quisar.* Which way you go, sir, I must fol-
   low necessary.
One life, and one death.
  *King.*         Will you take a truce yet?

  *Enter Pyniero, Soza, and Soldiers, with*
      *the Governor*

  *Py.* No, no, go on! Look here, your god,
   your prophet.
  *King.* How came he taken?
  *Py.*          I conjur'd for him, king.
I am a sure cur at an old blind prophet.    45
I'll hunt ye such a false knave admirably.
A terrier, I; I earth'd him, and then snapp'd
   him.
  *Soz.* Saving the reverence of your grace,
   we stole him,
E'en out of the next chamber to ye.
  *Py.*        Come, come, begin, king;
Begin this bloody matter when you dare;   50
And yet I scorn my sword should touch the
   rascal;
I'll tear him thus before ye. Ha! What art
   thou?        *Pulls his beard and hair off.*
  *King.* How's this! Art thou a prophet?
  *Ruy.*        Come down, princes.
  *King.* We are abus'd. — Oh, my most dear
   Armusia —
Off with his chains. — And now, my noble
   sister,                                                                55
Rejoice with me; I know ye are pleas'd as I am.
            [*Exeunt from above.*]
  *Py.* This is a precious prophet. Why,
   Don Governor,
What make you here? how long have you taken
   orders?
  *Ruy.* Why, what a wretch art thou to work
   this mischief?
To assume this holy shape to ruin honour, 60
Honour and chastity?

      *Enter King, and all from above*

  *Gov.*         I had paid you all,
But fortune play'd the slut. Come, give me my
   doom.
  *King.* I cannot speak for wonder.
  *Gov.*         Nay, 't is I, sir,
And here I stay your sentence.
  *King.*        Take her, friend
You have half persuaded me to be a Chris-
   tian,                                                                65
And with her all the joys, and all the blessings.
Why, what dream have we dwelt in?
  *Ruy.*        All peace to ye,
And all the happiness of heart dwell with ye!
Children as sweet and noble as their parents —

---

³⁴ **arm:** (Query, "aim"?)    ⁴⁶ **hunt:** ('haunt' Ff)    ⁴⁷ **snapp'd:** captured    ⁵⁴ **abus'd:** deceived
⁶³ **make:** do    ⁶⁴ **stay:** await

*Py.*  And kings at least.

*Arm.*        Good sir, forget my rashness.   70
And, noble princess, for I was once angry,
And out of that might utter some distemper,
Think not 't is my nature.

*Sy.*              Your joy is ours, sir,
And nothing we find in ye but most noble.

*King.*  To prison with this dog! There let
him howl,                                   75
And, if he can repent, sigh out his villainies!
His island we shall seize into our hands,
His father and himself have both usurp'd it,
And kept it by oppression.  The town and
castle,
In which I lay myself most miserable,        80
Till my most honourable friend redeem'd me,
Signior Pyniero, I bestow on you;

The rest of next command upon these gentlemen;
Upon ye all, my love.

*Arm.*              Oh, brave Ruy Dias,
You have started now beyond me.  I must
thank ye,                                   85
And thank ye for my life, my wife, and honour.

*Ruy.*  I am glad I had her for you, sir.

*King.*              Come, princes;
Come, friends and lovers all; come, noble
gentlemen;
No more guns now, nor hates, but joys and
triumphs!
An universal gladness fly about us;          90
And know, however subtle men dare cast,
And promise wrack, the gods give peace at last.
                                        *Exeunt*

⁹¹ **cast:** plot

POETARUM INGENIOSISSIMUS
IOANNES FLETCHERUS
ANGLUS, EPISCOPI LOND: FILI

TRAGŒDIA.                                    COMEDIA.

Obyt 1625                                    Ætat. 49

Felicis ævi ac Præsulis Natus; comes
Beaumontio; sic, quippe Parnassus, biceps;
FLETCHERUS unam in Pyramida furcas agens,
Struxit chorum plus simplicem Vates Duplex;
Plus duplicem solus: nec ullum transtulit;
Nec transferendus: Dramatum æterni sales,
Anglo Theatro, Orbi, Sibi, superstites.
FLETCHERE, facies absq; vultu pingitur;
Quantus! vel umbram circuit nemo tuam

Gulielᵒ
Marshall
Fecit.

J. Berkenhead.

BIBLIOGRAPHICAL RECORD. *Beggars' Bush* first appeared in print as the seventh play in the first Folio of Beaumont and Fletcher, published in 1647. In 1661 appeared a Quarto (in two issues) which was printed from the folio text, and in 1679 the play was again printed as the ninth item in the second Folio. The editors of the second Folio took some care with their texts. "And we were very opportunely informed," they said, "of a Copy which an ingenious and worthy Gentleman had taken the pains (or rather the pleasure) to read over; wherein he had all along Corrected several faults (some very gross) which had crept in by the frequent imprinting of them. His Corrections were the more to be valued, because he had an intimacy with both our Authors, and had been a Spectator of most of them when they were Acted in their life-time. This therefore we resolved to purchase at any Rate; and accordingly with no small cost obtain'd it." The result of their labors is a text which corrects many errors from the first Folio but introduces many new ones. The stage directions in F 2 usually give the assumed names of the characters, *e.g.*, Goswin for Florez, Clause for Gerrard, Gertrude for Bertha, whereas F 1 usually gives their real names. This edition takes account of both texts, giving significant variants in the notes. A manuscript text of the play in contemporary handwriting is now in private ownership, but has not been made available for study (see F. Marcham, *The King's Office of the Revels, 1610–1622*, 1925, p. 6, and W. W. Greg, *Elizabethan Dramatic Documents*, 1931, p. 367).

AUTHORSHIP. Critical opinion at present inclines to the view, first advanced by Fleay (*New Shakspere Society's Transactions*, 1874, p. 51 ff.), that *Beggars' Bush* is the combined work of Fletcher and Massinger. Mr. E. H. C. Oliphant, however, conjectures that the play in its present form is a revision of an earlier version in which Beaumont had a share (*Plays of Beaumont and Fletcher*, 1927, pp. 256–265). Massinger was probably responsible for Act I and portions of Act V, but the assignment of other parts of the play to him is uncertain.

DATE AND STAGE PERFORMANCE. The title of this play appears under date of December 27, in a list of "Revels and Playes performed and acted at Christmas in the court at Whitehall, 1622," by the King's Men. The dependence of the play on Dekker's *Lanthorne and Candlelight* (1608) for its Gipsy language has been thought to imply an earlier date; but there is no record which would indicate the existence of *Beggars' Bush* in any form before 1622, and it is very likely that Fletcher and Massinger got their hint from the success of Jonson's masque of the *Metamorphosed Gipsies* in the previous year. That the play was still the property of the King's Men in 1641 appears from a list of plays belonging to the company at that time, and there is a record of a performance at Hampton Court on Nov. 19, 1636, and another at Richmond on New Year's Day, 1639. Under the title of *The Lame Commonwealth*, the farcical first scene of Act II was surreptitiously acted during the period of dramatic prohibition, 1642–1660, and the complete comedy again took the stage immediately after the Restoration, being seen by Pepys in 1660, 1661, and 1668. During the eighteenth century it was often performed, and two alterations were made: *The Royal Merchant, or Beggars' Bush*, by H. N. (perhaps the comedian, Henry Norris), in 1705, and *The Royal Merchant: an Opera*, by Thomas Hull, in 1768. In 1815 *The Merchant of Bruges: or, Beggar's Bush*, by the Hon. Douglas Kinnaird, was produced at the Drury-lane Theatre, with Edmund Kean in the part of Florez, and had a long run. The most appropriate comment upon this lastingly popular play is that of Coleridge (*Table Talk*, February 17, 1833): "I could read the *Beggars' Bush* from morning to night. How sylvan and sunshiny it is!" The pleasant reminiscences of Shakespeare's *Merchant of Venice* and *As You Like It* will not escape the reader.

# JOHN FLETCHER (1579–1625)

# PHILIP MASSINGER (1583–1640)

## BEGGARS' BUSH

### PERSONS REPRESENTED IN THE PLAY

WOLFORT, an usurper of the earldom of Flanders
HEMSKIRK, a captain under him
HUBERT, an honest lord
HERMAN, a courtier
FLOREZ, rightful Earl of Flanders; a merchant of Bruges, falsely called Goswin
GERRARD, falsely called Clause, King of the Beggars, father to Florez
ARNOLD, a nobleman, disguised as a beggar, under the name of Ginks
COSTIN, a nobleman disguised as a beggar; a mute personage

HIGGEN,
FERRET,
PRIG, } Beggars
SNAP,
and others
VANDUNK, burgomaster of Bruges
VANLOCK, a merchant
BERTHA, called Gertrude, daughter to the Duke of Brabant
JACQUELINE, daughter to Gerrard, disguised as a beggar under the name of Minche
MARGARET, wife to Vandunk
FRANCES, daughter to Vanlock

Merchants, Boors, a Sailor, Soldiers, Attendants.

### THE SCENE: FLANDERS

### Actus Primus, Scæna Prima.

[*Ghent. — Before the Palace of Wolfort.*]

*Enter a Merchant and Herman*

*Mer.* Is he, then, taken?
*Her.*      And brought back even now, sir.
*Mer.* He was not in disgrace?
*Her.*      No man more lov'd,
Nor more deserv'd it, being the only man
That durst be honest in this court.
*Mer.*      Indeed,
We have heard abroad, sir, that the state hath suffer'd      5
A great change, since the countess' death.
*Her.*      It hath, sir.
*Mer.* My five years' absence hath kept me a stranger
So much to all the occurrents of my country,
As you shall bind me for some short relation,
To make me understand the present times.      10
*Her.* I must begin, then, with a war was made,
And seven years with all cruelty continued,
Upon our Flanders by the Duke of Brabant.
The cause grew thus. During our earl's minority,
Wolfort, who now usurps, was employ'd thither,

To treat about a match between our earl      16
And the daughter and heir of Brabant: during which treaty,
The Brabander pretends, this daughter was
Stol'n from his court by practice of our state;
Though we are all confirm'd 't was a sought quarrel,      20
To lay an unjust gripe upon this earldom,
It being here believ'd the Duke of Brabant
Had no such loss. This war upon 't proclaim'd,
Our earl being then a child, although his father
Good Gerrard liv'd, yet (in respect he was      25
Chosen by the countess' favour for her husband,
And but a gentleman, and Florez holding
His right unto this country from his mother)
The state thought fit in this defensive war,
Wolfort being then the only man of mark,      30
To make him general.
*Mer.*      Which place we have heard
He did discharge with honour.
*Her.*      Ay, so long,
And with so bless'd successes, that the Brabander
Was forc'd (his treasures wasted, and the choice
Of his best men of arms tir'd or cut off)      35
To leave the field, and sound a base retreat
Back to his country: but so broken, both

---

D. P.: (Revised from lists in Q and F 2)   **8 occurrents:** occurrences   **9 bind me for:** oblige me **by**   **11 was:** which was   **19 practice:** stratagem, craft   **20 confirm'd:** convinced   **21 gripe: grip** **25 in respect:** because   **34 choice: élite**   **35 cut off:** killed

In mind and means, e'er to make head again,
That hitherto he sits down by his loss,
Not daring, or for honour or revenge,          40
Again to tempt his fortune.  But this victory
More broke our state, and made a deeper hurt
In Flanders, than the greatest overthrow
She ever receiv'd; for Wolfort, now beholding
Himself and actions in the flattering glass    45
Of self-deservings, and that cherish'd by
The strong assurance of his power, — for then
All captains of the army were his creatures,
The common soldier, too, at his devotion,
Made so by full indulgence to their rapines,   50
And secret bounties;  this strength too well
    known,
And what it could effect soon put in practice,
As further'd by the childhood of the earl,
And their improvidence that might have pierc'd
The heart of his designs, gave him occasion    55
To seize the whole: and in that plight you find
    it.
    *Mer.*  Sir, I receive the knowledge of thus
        much,
As a choice favour from you.
    *Her.*                    Only I must add,
Bruges holds out.
    *Mer.*                Whither, sir, I am going;
For there last night I had a ship put in,      60
And my horse waits me.
    *Her.*  I wish you a good journey.  *Exeunt.*

[SCENE II. — *Wolfort's Palace.*]

*Enter Wolfort, Hubert [and Attendants]*

    *Wol.*  What, Hubert, stealing from me! —
        Who disarm'd him?
It was more than I commanded. — Take your
    sword;
I am best guarded with it in your hand;
I have seen you use it nobly.
    *Hub.*                And will turn it
On my own bosom, ere it shall be drawn      5
Unworthily or rudely.
    *Wol.*                Would you leave me
Without a farewell, Hubert? fly a friend
Unwearied in his study to advance you?
What have I e'er possess'd which was not yours?
Or rather did not court you to command it?  10
Who ever yet arriv'd to any grace,
Reward, or trust from me, but his approaches
Were by your fair reports of him preferr'd?
And what is more, I made myself your servant,
In making you the master of those secrets   15
Which not the rack of conscience could draw
    from me,

Nor I, when I ask'd mercy, trust my prayers
    with:
Yet, after these assurances of love,
These ties and bonds of friendship, to forsake
    me?
Forsake me as an enemy!  Come, you must  20
Give me a reason.
    *Hub.*                Sir, and so I will:
If I may do 't in private, and you hear it.
    *Wol.*  All leave the room.
                            [*Exeunt Attendants.*]
                You have your will: sit down,
And use the liberty of our first friendship.
    *Hub.*  Friendship!  When you prov'd traitor
    first, that vanish'd;                      25
Nor do I owe you any thought but hate.
I know my flight hath forfeited my head;
And, so I may make you first understand
What a strange monster you have made your-
    self,
I welcome it.
    *Wol.*      To me this is strange language.  30
    *Hub.*  To you! why, what are you?
    *Wol.*                Your prince and master,
The Earl of Flanders.
    *Hub.*                By a proper title!
Rais'd to it by cunning, circumvention, force,
Blood, and proscriptions!
    *Wol.*                And in all this, wisdom:
Had I not reason, when by Gerrard's plots,  35
I should have first been call'd to a strict ac-
    compt,
How and which way I had consum'd that mass
Of money, as they term it, in the war;
Who underhand had by his ministers
Detracted my great actions, made my faith   40
And loyalty suspected;  in which failing,
He sought my life by practice?
    *Hub.*                With what forehead
Do you speak this to me, who (as I know 't)
Must and will say 't is false?
    *Wol.*                My guard there!
    *Hub.*                            Sir,
You bade me sit, and promis'd you would
    hear;                                       45
Which I now say you shall: not a sound more!
For I, that am contemner of mine own,
Am master of your life; then here 's a sword
                        [*Draws his sword.*]
Between you and all aids, sir.  Though you
    blind
The credulous beast, the multitude, you pass
    not                                         50
These gross untruths on me.
    *Wol.*                How! gross untruths!

**38 make head:** make war    **39 sits . . . by:** accepts, acquiesces in    **49 at his devotion:** devoted
to him    **50 rapines:** acts of pillage    Sc. II: (Not marked, Ff, Q)    **10 rather:** ('either' Ff, Q)
**13 preferr'd:** promoted, given preference    **33 circumvention:** craft, fraud    **40 Detracted:** belittled,
traduced    **actions:** ('action' Ff, Q)    **42 forehead:** assurance

*Hub.* Ay, and it is favourable language:
They had been in a mean man lies, and foul
    ones.
*Wol.* You take strange licence.
*Hub.*                    Yes; were not those rumours
Of being call'd unto your answer spread    55
By your own followers? and weak Gerrard
    wrought
(But by your cunning practice) to believe
That you were dangerous; yet not to be
Punish'd by any formal course of law,
But first to be made sure, and have your crimes
Laid open after? which your quaint train
    taking,                                    61
You fled unto the camp, and there crav'd
    humbly
Protection for your innocent life, and that,
Since you had scap'd the fury of the war,
You might not fall by treason; and for proof 65
You did not for your own ends make this
    danger,
Some, that had been before by you suborn'd,
Came forth, and took their oaths they had
    been hir'd
By Gerrard to your murther. This once heard,
And easily believ'd, th' enraged soldier,    70
Seeing no further than the outward man,
Snatch'd hastily his arms, ran to the court,
Kill'd all that made resistance, cut in pieces
Such as were servants, or thought friends to
    Gerrard,
Vowing the like to him.
*Wol.*                    Will you yet end?    75
*Hub.* Which he foreseeing, with his son, the
    earl,
Forsook the city, and by secret ways,
As you give out, and we would gladly have it,
Escap'd their fury; though 't is more than
    fear'd
They fell among the rest. Nor stand you
    there,                                      80
To let us only mourn the impious means
By which you got it; but your cruelties since
So far transcend your former bloody ills,
As, if compar'd, they only would appear
Essays of mischief. Do not stop your ears;   85
More are behind yet.
*Wol.*                    Oh, repeat them not!
'T is hell to hear them nam'd.
*Hub.*                    You should have thought,
That hell would be your punishment when
    you did them:
A prince in nothing but your princely lusts
And boundless rapines!
*Wol.*                    No more, I beseech you.  90

*Hub.* Who was the lord of house or land,
    that stood
Within the prospect of your covetous eye?
*Wol.* You are in this to me a greater tyrant
Than e'er I was to any.
*Hub.*                    I end thus
The general grief. Now to my private wrong,
The loss of Gerrard's daughter, Jacqueline: 96
The hop'd-for partner of my lawful bed
Your cruelty hath frighted from mine arms;
And her I now was wandering to recover.
Think you that I had reason now to leave
    you,                                       100
When you are grown so justly odious,
That ev'n my stay here, with your grace and
    favour,
Makes my life irksome? Here, surely take it;
                    [*Offers his sword.*]
And do me but this fruit of all your friend-
    ship,
That I may die by you, and not your hang-
    man.                                       105
*Wol.* Oh, Hubert, these your words and
    reasons have
As well drawn drops of blood from my griev'd
    heart,
As these tears from mine eyes! despise them
    not:
By all that 's sacred, I am serious, Hubert!
You now have made me sensible, what Furies,
Whips, hangmen, and tormentors, a bad
    man                                        111
Does ever bear about him: let the good
That you this day have done be ever number'd
The first of your best actions. Can you think
Where Florez is, or Gerrard, or your love,   115
Or any else, or all, that are proscrib'd?
I will resign what I usurp, or have
Unjustly forc'd: the days I have to live
Are too, too few to make them satisfaction
With any penitence; yet I vow to practise 120
All of a man.
*Hub.* Oh, that your heart and tongue
Did not now differ!
*Wol.*                    By my griefs, they do not!
Take the good pains to search them out; 't is
    worth it.
You have made clean a leper, — trust me, you
    have, —
And made me once more fit for the society, 125
I hope, of good men.
*Hub.*                    Sir, do not abuse
My aptness to believe.
*Wol.*                    Suspect not you
A faith that 's built upon so true a sorrow.

---

⁵⁵ **answer:** defense    ⁵⁶ **wrought:** beguiled    ⁶⁰ **sure:** harmless (by death or capture)    ⁶¹ **quaint:**
clever    **train:** artifice    ⁶⁶ **make:** invent    ⁸⁰ **among:** ('amongst' F 2)    ⁸⁵ **Essays of:** first attempts
at    ¹¹⁰ **sensible:** aware of    ¹¹⁵ **Florez:** ('Goswin' F 2)    ¹¹⁸ **forc'd:** taken by force    ¹²¹ **All . . .**
**man:** all that a man can do    ¹²⁷ **aptness:** readiness

Make your own safeties; ask them all the ties
Humanity can give.  Hemskirk, too, shall  130
Along with you to this so-wish'd discovery,
And in my name profess all that you promise:
And I will give you this help to 't; I have
Of late receiv'd certain intelligence
That some of them are in or about Bruges  135
To be found out; which I did then interpret
The cause of that town's standing out against
   me;
But now am glad it may direct your purpose
Of giving them their safety and me peace.
   *Hub.*  Be constant to your goodness, and
   you have it.        *Exeunt.*  140

### Scæna Tertia.

[*Bruges. — The Exchange.*]

*Enter 3 Merchants*

*1 Mer.*  'T is much that you deliver of this
   Goswin.
*2 Mer.*  But short of what I could, yet have
   the country
Confirm it true, and by a general oath,
And not a man hazard his credit in it.
He bears himself with such a confidence,  5
As if he were the master of the sea,
And not a wind upon the sailors' compass
But from one part or other was his factor,
To bring him in the best commodities
Merchant e'er ventur'd for.
   *1 Mer.*        'T is strange.
   *2 Mer.*        And yet  10
This does in him deserve the least of wonder,
Compar'd with other his peculiar fashions,
Which all admire: he 's young, and rich, at
   least
Thus far reputed so, that, since he liv'd
In Bruges, there was never brought to har-
   bour  15
So rich a bottom but his bill would pass
Unquestion'd for her lading.
   *3 Mer.*        Yet he still
Continues a good man.
   *2 Mer.*        So good, that but
To doubt him would be held an injury,
Or rather malice, with the best that traffic: 20
But this is nothing; a great stock, and fortune
Crowning his judgment in his undertakings,
May keep him upright that way; but that
   wealth

Should want the power to make him dote on it,
Or youth teach him to wrong it, best com-
   mends  25
His constant temper.  For his outward habit,
'T is suitable to his present course of life;
His table furnish'd well, but not with dainties
That please the appetite only for their rareness
Or the dear price; nor given to wine or women,
Beyond his health, or warrant of a man,  31
I mean, a good one; and so loves his state,
He will not hazard it at play, nor lend
Upon the assurance of a well-penn'd letter,
Although a challenge second the denial,  35
From such as make th' opinion of their valour
Their means of feeding.
   *1 Mer.*        These are ways to thrive,
And the means not curs'd.
   *2 Mer.*        What follows, this
Makes many venturers with him in their wishes
For his prosperity; for when desert  40
Or reason leads him to be liberal,
His noble mind and ready hand contend
Which can add most to his free courtesies,
Or in their worth or speed to make them so.
Is there a virgin of good fame wants dower? 45
He is a father to her; or a soldier,
That, in his country's service, from the war
Hath brought home only scars and want? his
   house
Receives him, and relieves him with that care
As if what he possess'd had been laid up  50
For such good uses, and he steward of it.
But I should lose myself to speak him further,
And stale, in my relation, the much good
You may be witness of, if your remove
From Bruges be not speedy.
   *1 Mer.*        This report,  55
I do assure you, will not hasten it;
Nor would I wish a better man to deal with
For what I am to part with.
   *3 Mer.*        Never doubt it,
He is your man and ours; only I wish
His too-much forwardness to embrace all bar-
   gains  60
Sink him not in the end.
   *2 Mer.*        Have better hopes;
For my part, I am confident.  Here he comes.

*Enter Florez [as Goswin] and the Fourth
Merchant*

   *Flo.*  I take it at your own rates, your wine
of Cyprus;

**129** safeties: conditions of security  them: for them  **132** profess: affirm  **134** intelligence: information  Sc. III Tertia: ('Secunda' F 1)  **1** deliver: relate  **3** Confirm: ('Confirm'd' Ff, Q)  **8** factor:
agent  **12** other his: his other  **13** admire: wonder at  **16** bottom: ship  **18** good: of wealth and
credit  **19** injury: insult  **26** habit: clothing  **30** the: ('their' F 2)  **31** warrant: proper allowance
**32** state: estate  **36** opinion: reputation  **43** free: generous  **45** fame: reputation  **wants**: who
lacks  **52** speak: describe  **53** stale: make stale or flat  **59** wish: hope  **60** forwardness: eager-
ness

But, for your Candy sugars, they have met
With such foul weather, and are priz'd so
    high,                                            65
I cannot save in them.
*4 Mer.*                    I am unwilling
To seek another chapman: make me offer
Of something near my price, that may assure
    me
You can deal for them.
    *Flo.*                    I both can and will,
But not with too much loss: your bill of
    lading                                          70
Speaks of two hundred chests, valu'd by you
At thirty thousand guilders; I will have them
At twenty-eight; so, in the payment of
Three thousand sterling, you fall only in
Two hundred pound.
    *4 Mer.*    You know, they are so cheap, — 75
    *Flo.*    Why, look you, I 'll deal fairly.  There's
    in prison,
And at your suit, a pirate, but unable
To make you satisfaction, and past hope
To live a week, if you should prosecute
What you can prove against him: set him
    free                                            80
And you shall have your money to a stiver,
And present payment.
    *4 Mer.*                This is above wonder,
A merchant of your rank, that have at sea
So many bottoms in the danger of
These water-thieves, should be a means to
    save 'em;                                       85
It more importing you, for your own safety,
To be at charge to scour the sea of them,
Than stay the sword of justice, that is ready
To fall on one so conscious of his guilt
That he dares not deny it.
    *Flo.*                    You mistake me,  90
If you think I would cherish in this captain
The wrong he did to you or any man.
I was lately with him (having first, from others'
True testimony, been assur'd a man
Of more desert never put from the shore);   95
I read his letters of mart, from this state
    granted
For the recovery of such losses as
He had receiv'd in Spain; 't was that he aim'd
    at,
Not at three tuns of wine, biscuit, or beef,
Which his necessity made him take from you. 100
If he had pillag'd you near, or sunk your ship,
Or thrown your men o'erboard, then he de-
    serv'd

The law's extremest rigour: but since want
Of what he could not live without compell'd
    him
To that he did (which yet our state calls
    death),                                         105
I pity his misfortune, and, to work you
To some compassion of them, I come up
To your own price: save him, the goods are
    mine;
If not, seek elsewhere, I 'll not deal for them.
    *4 Mer.*    Well, sir, for your love, I will once
    be led                                          110
To change my purpose.
    *Flo.*                For your profit rather.
    *4 Mer.*    I 'll presently make means for his
    discharge;
Till when, I leave you.                  [*Exit.*]
    *2 Mer.*            What do you think of this?
    *1 Mer.*    As of a deed of noble pity, guided
By a strong judgment.
    *2 Mer.*        Save you, Master Goswin!  115
    *Flo.*    Good day to all.
    *2 Mer.*            We bring you the refusal
Of more commodities.
    *Flo.*                Are you the owners
Of the ship that last night put into the har-
    bour?
    *1 Mer.*    Both of the ship and lading.
    *Flo.*                What 's the fraught?
    *1 Mer.*    Indigo, cochineal, choice China
    stuffs.                                         120
    *3 Mer.*    And cloth of gold brought from
    Cambal.
    *Flo.*                        Rich lading;
For which I were your chapman, but I am
Already out of cash.
    *1 Mer.*            I 'll give you day
For the moiety of all.
    *Flo.*                How long?
    *3 Mer.*                        Six months.
    *Flo.*    'T is a fair offer; which, if we agree  125
About the prices, I, with thanks, accept of,
And will make present payment of the rest:
Some two hours hence I 'll come aboard.
    *1 Mer.*                    The gunner
Shall speak you welcome.
    *Flo.*                I 'll not fail.
    *3 Mer.*    Good morrow.    *Exeunt Merchants.*
    *Flo.*    Heaven grant my ships a safe return
    before                                          130
The day of this great payment; as they are
Expected three months sooner; and my credit
Stands good with all the world.

---

⁶⁴ **Candy:** of Candia (Crete)   ⁶⁵ **priz'd:** valued   ⁶⁶ **save:** make a profit   ⁶⁷ **chapman:** merchant   ⁶⁹ **deal:** bargain   ⁷² **guilders:** Dutch coins, worth about 1s. 8d.   ⁸¹ **stiver:** coin of insig-
nificant value   ⁸² **present:** immediate   ⁸⁶ **importing:** behooving   ⁸⁷ **charge:** expense   ⁹⁶ **letters
of mart:** letters of marque, royal license to use a privateer against the shipping of a hostile country
¹⁰¹ **near:** to the bare skin   ¹⁰⁶ **work:** move   ¹¹² **means:** measures   ¹¹⁹ **fraught:** cargo   ¹²¹ **Cam-
bal:** Peking   ¹²³ **day:** credit, time for payment   ¹²⁴ **moiety:** half

*Enter Gerrard [as Clause]*

*Ger.*                            Bless my good master!
The prayers of your poor beadsman ever shall
Be sent up for you.
    *Flo.*                    God 'a mercy, Clause! 135
There 's something to put thee in mind here-
    after
To think of me.                    [*Gives money.*]
    *Ger.*                    May he that gave it you
Reward you for it with increase, good master.
    *Flo.* I thrive the better for thy prayers.
    *Ger.*                            I hope so.
This three years have I fed upon your bounties,
And by the fire of your bless'd charity warm'd
    me;                                    141
And yet, good master, pardon me, that must,
Though I have now receiv'd your alms, pre-
    sume
To make one suit more to you.
    *Flo.*                    What is 't, Clause?
    *Ger.* Yet do not think me impudent, I
    beseech you,                            145
Since hitherto your charity hath prevented
My begging your relief; 't is not for money,
Nor clothes, good master, but your good word
    for me.
    *Flo.* That thou shalt have, Clause; for I
    think thee honest.
    *Ger.* To-morrow, then, dear master, take
    the trouble                            150
Of walking early unto Beggars' Bush;
And, as you see me, among others, brethren
In my affliction, when you are demanded
Which you like best among us, point out me,
And then pass by, as if you knew me not.  155
    *Flo.* But what will that advantage thee?
    *Ger.*                    Oh, much, sir!
'T will give me the pre-eminence of the rest,
Make me a king among 'em, and protect me
From all abuse such as are stronger might
Offer my age. Sir, at your better leisure  160
I will inform you further of the good
It may do to me.
    *Flo.*                    Troth, thou mak'st me wonder:
Have you a king and commonwealth among
    you?
    *Ger.* We have; and there are states are
    govern'd worse.
    *Flo.* Ambition among beggars?
    *Ger.*                    Many great ones 165

Would part with half their states, to have the
    place
And credit to beg in the first file, master.
But shall I be so much bound to your further-
    ance
In my petition?
    *Flo.*                    That thou shalt not miss of,
Nor any worldly care make me forget it:  170
I will be early there.
    *Ger.* Heaven bless my master!    *Exeunt.*

## Actus Secundus, Scæna Prima.

*[The Beggars' Bush, in the Woods near Bruges.]*

*Enter Higgen, Ferret, Prig, [Gerrard as] Clause,
Jacqueline [as Minche], Snap, Ginks, and
other Beggars*

    *Hig.* Come, princes of the ragged regiment;
You o' the blood, Prig, my most upright Lord,
And these, what name or title e'er they bear,
Jarkman, or Patrico, Crank, or Clapper-
    dudgeon,
Frater, or Abram-man; I speak to all      5
That stand in fair election for the title
Of King of Beggars, with the command adjoin-
    ing;
Higgen, your orator, in this inter-regnum,
That whilom was your Dommerer, doth be-
    seech you
All to stand fair, and put yourselves in rank, 10
That the first comer may, at his first view,
Make a free choice, to say up the question.
    *Fer.*  ⎱ 'T is done, Lord Higgen.
    *Prig.* ⎰
    *Hig.* Thanks to Prince Prig, Prince Ferret.
    *Fer.* Well, pray, my masters all, Ferret be
    chosen;
Y' are like to have a merciful mild prince of
    me.                                    15
    *Prig.* A very tyrant, I, an arrant tyrant,
If e'er I come to reign (therefore look to 't,)
Except you do provide me hum enough,
And lour to bouze with: I must have my
    capons
And turkeys brought me in, with my green
    geese,                                    20
And ducklings i' the season; fine fat chickens;
Or, if you chance where an eye of tame pheas-
    ants
Or partridges are kept, see they be mine:

  <sup>134</sup> **beadsman:** one who prays for the soul of another   <sup>146</sup> **prevented:** anticipated   <sup>151</sup> **Beggars'
Bush:** originally, a tree near Huntingdon, a noted rendezvous for beggars   <sup>167</sup> **file:** rank   <sup>168</sup> **furtherance:** aid   <sup>2</sup> **upright:** The "upright-man" was the aristocrat among beggars. For description
of this type and those mentioned below, see Dekker's *Bellman of London*, 1608.   <sup>4</sup> **Jarkman:** counter-
feiter of licenses, etc.   **Patrico:** hedge-priest   **Crank:** beggar who feigned sickness   **Clapper-
dudgeon:** beggar born and bred   <sup>5</sup> **Frater, Abram-man:** spurious solicitors and pretended lunatics who
lived by begging after the dissolution of the monasteries   <sup>9</sup> **Dommerer:** beggar who pretends to be
dumb   <sup>12</sup> **say up:** decide   <sup>18</sup> **hum:** strong ale   <sup>19</sup> **lour:** money   **bouze:** drink   <sup>20</sup> **green:** young
  <sup>22</sup> **eye:** brood

Or straight I seize on all your privilege,
Places, revénues, offices, as forfeit,                          25
Call in your crutches, wooden legs, false bellies,
Forc'd eyes and teeth, with your dead arms;
    not leave you
A dirty clout to beg with o' your heads,
Or an old rag with butter, frankincense,
Brimstone and rosin, birdlime, blood, and
    cream,                                                        30
To make you an old sore; not so much soap
As you may foam with i' the falling-sickness;
The very bag you bear, and the brown dish,
Shall be escheated; all your daintiest dells, too,
I will deflower, and take your dearest doxies 35
From your warm sides; and then, some one
    cold night,
I 'll watch you what old barn you go to roost in,
And there I 'll smother you all i' th' musty hay.
    *Hig.* This is tyrant-like, indeed. But what
        would Ginks
Or Clause be here, if either of them should
    reign?                                                        40
    *Ger.* Best ask an ass, if he were made a
        camel,
What he would be; or a dog, and he were a
    lion.
    *Ginks.* I care not what you are, sirs: I shall
        be
A beggar still, I am sure; I find myself there.

                    *Enter Florez*

    *Snap.* Oh, here a judge comes!
    *Hig.*                    Cry, a judge, a judge! 45
    *Flo.* What ail you, sirs? what means this
        outcry?
    *Hig.*                                      Master,
A sort of poor souls met, God's fools, good
    master,
Have had some little variance amongst our-
    selves
Who should be honestest of us, and which lives
Uprightest in his call: now, 'cause we thought
We ne'er should 'gree on 't ourselves, because,
    indeed,                                                       51
'T is hard to say, we all dissolv'd to put it
To him that should come next, and that 's your
    mastership,
Who, I hope, will 'termine it as your mind
    serves you,
Right, and no otherwise we ask it. Which,     55
Which does your worship think is he? Sweet
    master,
Look over us all, and tell us: we are seven of us,
Like to the Seven Wise Masters, or the planets.

    *Flo.* I should judge this the man, with the
        grave beard;
And, if he be not —
    *Ger.* Bless you, good master, bless you!    60
    *Flo.* I would he were. There 's something,
        too, amongst you,
To keep you all honest.
                            *[Gives money, and] Exit.*
    *Snap.* King of Heaven go with you!
    *Omnes.*                    Now good reward him! —
May he never want it! — to comfort still the
    poor! —
In a good hour!
    *Fer.* What is 't? see: Snap has got it.     65
    *Snap.* A good crown, marry.
    *Prig.* A crown of gold.
    *Fer.* For our new king; good luck.
    *Ginks.* To the common treasury with it;
        if 't be gold,
Thither it must.
    *Prig.*         Spoke like a patriot, Ginks! — 70
King Clause, I bid God save thee first, first,
    Clause,
After this golden token of a crown. —
Where 's orator Higgen with his gratuling
    speech now,
In all our names?
    *Fer.*         Here he is, pumping for it.
    *Ginks.* H'as cough'd the second time; 't is
        but once more                                            75
And then it comes.
    *Fer.*         So, out with all. — Expect now!
    *Hig.* That thou art chosen, venerable
        Clause,
Our king and sovereign, monarch o' the maund-
    ers,
Thus we throw up our nab-cheats first, for
    joy,
And then our filches; last, we clap our fam-
    bles;                                                         80
Three subject signs we do it without envy;
For who is he here did not wish thee chosen,
Now thou art chosen? ask 'em; all will say so,
Nay, swear 't; 't is for the king; but let that
    pass.
When last in conference at the bouzing-ken, 85
This other day, we sate about our dead prince
Of famous memory (rest go with his rags!),
And that I saw thee at the table's end
Rise mov'd, and, gravely leaning on one crutch,
Lift the other like a sceptre at my head,     90
I then presag'd thou shortly wouldst be king;
And now thou art so. But what need presage
To us, that might have read it in thy beard,

---

²⁷ **Forc'd:** artificial   ²⁸ **clout:** rag   ³⁴ **escheated:** confiscated   **dells:** maidens   ³⁵ **doxies:**
mistresses   ⁴² **and:** an, if   ⁴⁴ **still:** always   ⁴⁷ **sort:** group, company   ⁵⁰ **call:** calling ('calling'
F 2)   ⁵² **dissolv'd:** *i.e.,* resolved   ⁷⁰ **Ginks:** ('Ferret' Ff, Q)   ⁷³ **gratuling:** congratulatory   ⁷⁶ **Ex-**
**pect:** wait   ⁷⁸ **maunders:** beggars   ⁷⁹ **nab-cheats:** hats   ⁸⁰ **filches:** staffs, fitted with hooks
**fambles:** hands   ⁸⁵ **bouzing-ken:** ale-house

As well as he that chose thee? by that beard
Thou wert found out, and mark'd for sover-
    eignty:    95
Oh, happy beard! but happier prince, whose
    beard
Was so remark'd as marked out our prince,
Not bating us a hair! long may it grow,
And thick and fair, that who lives under it
May live as safe as under Beggars' Bush,  100
Of which this is the thing, that but the type!
   *Omnes.*  Excellent, excellent orator! for-
    ward, good Higgen! —
Give him leave to spit. — The fine, well-spoken
    Higgen!
   *Hig.*  This is the beard, the bush, or bushy
    beard,
Under whose gold and silver reign, 't was
    said,  105
So many ages since, we all should smile.
No impositions, taxes, grievances,
Knots in a state, and whips unto a subject,
Lie lurking in this beard, but all kemb'd out.
If now the beard be such, what is the prince
That owes the beard? a father? no, a grand-
    father,  111
Nay, the great-grandfather of you his people:
He will not force away your hens, your bacon,
When you have ventur'd hard for 't, nor take
    from you
The fattest of your puddings: under him,  115
Each man shall eat his own stol'n eggs and
    butter,
In his own shade or sun-shine, and enjoy
His own dear dell, doxy, or mort, at night,
In his own straw, with his own shirt or sheet
That he hath filch'd that day; ay, and pos-
    sess  120
What he can purchase, back or belly-cheats,
To his own prop: he will have no purveyors
For pigs and poultry.
   *Ger.*  That we must have, my learned orator;
It is our will; and every man to keep  125
In his own path and circuit.
   *Hig.*             Do you hear?
You must hereafter maund on your own pads,
    he says.
   *Ger.*  And what they get there is their own:
    besides,
To give good words.
   *Hig.*      Do you mark? to cut bene whids;
That is the second law.
   *Ger.*          And keep afoot  130

The humble and the common phrase of begging,
Lest men discover us.
   *Hig.*            Yes, and cry sometimes,
To move compassion. Sir, there is a table,
That doth command all these things. and en-
    joins 'em
Be perfect in their crutches, their feign'd
    plasters,  135
And their torn passports, with the ways to
    stammer,
And to be dumb, and deaf, and blind, and lame:
There all the halting paces are set down
I' th' learned language.
   *Ger.*          Thither I refer them;
Those you at leisure shall interpret to them: 140
We love no heaps of laws, where few will serve.
   *Omnes.*  Oh, gracious prince! Save, save
    the good King Clause!
   *Hig.*  A song to crown him!
   *Fer.*            Set a sentinel out first.
   *Snap.*  The word?
   *Hig.*  "A cove comes," and "fumbumbis"
    to it. —          *Strike.* [*Exit Snap.*]

### THE SONG

Cast our caps and cares away!  145
This is beggars' holiday:
At the crowning of our king,
Thus we ever dance and sing.
In the world look out and see,
Where so happy a prince as he?  150
Where the nation live so free,
And so merry as do we?
Be it peace or be it war,
Here at liberty we are,
And enjoy our ease and rest:  155
To the field we are not press'd;
Nor are call'd into the town,
To be troubled with the gown:
Hang all officers, we cry,
And the magistrate, too, by!  160
When the subsidy's increas'd,
We are not a penny sess'd;
Nor will any go to law
With the beggar for a straw.
All which happiness, he brags,  165
He doth owe unto his rags.

*Enter Snap, Hubert, and Hemskirk*

   *Snap.*  A cove! fumbumbis!
   *Prig.*          To your postures! arm!
   *Hub.*  Yonder 's the town: I see it.

---

⁹⁸ **bating:** deducting  ¹⁰⁷ **No:** ('On' Ff, Q)  ¹⁰⁹ **kemb'd:** combed  ¹¹¹ **owes:** owns  ¹¹⁸ **mort:**
girl, wench  ¹²¹ **purchase:** obtain (not necessarily by buying)  **back . . . cheats:** things for back
or belly, clothing or food  ¹²² **To . . . prop:** for his own property  **purveyors:** officers who exacted
contributions of food, etc., for royal progresses  ¹²⁷ **maund . . . pads:** beg on your own roads
¹²⁹ **cut . . . whids:** give good words  ¹³⁶ **torn:** ('true' F 1, Q)  ¹⁴⁴ **cove:** fellow  **fumbumbis:** a
watchword (?)  ¹⁴⁴ S. D. **Strike:** strike up, sing or play (?)  ¹⁴⁵⁻¹⁶⁶ (For a source of this song in Erasmus,
see W. D. Briggs, *Mod. Lang. Notes,* 1924, p. 379.)  ¹⁵⁰ **Where:** ('where 's' F 2)  ¹⁵⁸ **gown:** judicial business  ¹⁶² **sess'd:** assessed  ¹⁶⁶ S. D.: (Hubert and Hemskirk are in disguise.)  ¹⁶⁷ **cove:** ('cove comes' F 2)

*Hem.*                    There 's our danger,
Indeed, afore us, if our shadows save not.
*Hig.*  Bless your good worships! —
*Fer.*                    One small piece of money — 170
*Prig.*  Amongst us all poor wretches —
*Ger.*                    Blind and lame —
*Ginks.*  For his sake that gives all —
*Hig.*                    Pitiful worships! —
*Snap.*  One little doit —

*Enter Jacqueline*

*Jac.*  King, by your leave, where are you?
*Fer.*  To buy a little bread —
*Hig.*                    To feed so many
Mouths, as will ever pray for you.
*Prig.*                    Here be seven of us. 175
*Hig.*  Seven, good master; oh, remember
    seven.
Seven blessings —
*Fer.*                    Remember, gentle worship —
*Hig.*  'Gainst seven deadly sins —
*Prig.*                    And seven sleepers.
*Hig.*  If they be hard of heart, and will give
    nothing —
Alas, we had not a charity this three days. 180
*Hub.* There 's amongst you all. [*Gives money.*]
*Fer.*                    Heaven reward you!
*Prig.*  Lord reward you!
*Hig.*                    The prince of pity bless thee!
*Hub.* [*Aside.*] Do I see? or is 't my fancy
    that would have it so?
Ha! 't is her face. — Come hither, maid.
*Jac.*                    What, ha' you
Bells for my squirrel? I ha' giv'n Bun meat.
You do not love me, do you? Catch me a
    butterfly,                    186
And I 'll love you again: when? can you tell?
Peace, we go a-birding: I shall have a fine
    thing.                    *Exit.*
*Hub.* [*Aside.*] Her voice, too, says the same;
    but, for my head,
I would not that her manners were so
    chang'd. —                    190
Hear me, thou honest fellow; what 's this
    maiden,
That lives amongst you here?
*Ginks.*                    Ao, ao, ao, ao.
*Hub.*  How! nothing but signs?
*Ginks.*                    Ao, ao, ao, ao.
*Hub.* [*Aside.*]                    This is strange:
I would fain have it her, but not her thus.
*Hig.*  He is de-de-de-de-de-de-deaf, and du-
    du-dude-dumb, sir.                    195
    [*Exeunt all the Beggars except Snap.*]
*Hub.*  'Slid, they did all speak plain ev'n
    now, methought. —
Dost thou know this same maid?

*Snap.*  Whi-whi-whi-whi-which, Gu-Gu-Gu-
    Gu-God's fool?
She was bo-bo-bo-bo-born at the barn yonder,
    by Be-Be-Be-Be-Beggars' Bush Bo-Bo-
    Bush:
Her name is Mi-Mi-Mi-Mi-Mi-Minche; so was
    her mo-mo-mo-mother's, too-too.
*Hub.*  I understand no word he says. —
    How long                    200
Has she been here?
*Snap.*  Lo-lo-long enough to be ni-ni-niggl'd,
    and she ha' go-go-go-good luck.
*Hub.* [*Aside.*] I must be better inform'd
    than by this way:
Here was another face, too, that I mark'd —
Oh, the old man's: but they are vanish'd
    all                    205
Most suddenly. I will come here again:
Oh, that I were so happy as to find it,
What I yet hope it is, put on!
*Hem.*                    What mean you, sir,
To stay there with that stammerer?
*Hub.*                    Farewell, friend. — [*Exit Snap.*]
It will be worth return to search. [*Aside.*] —
    Come;                    210
Protect us our disguise now! Prithee, Hems-
    kirk,
If we be taken, how dost thou imagine
This town will use us, that hath stood so
    long
Out against Wolfort?
*Hem.*                    Even to hang us forth
Upon their walls a-sunning, to make crow's
    meat.                    215
If I were not assur'd o' the burgomaster,
And had a pretty 'scuse to see a niece there,
I should scarce venture.
*Hub.*                    Come, 't is now too late
To look back at the ports. Good luck, and
    enter!                    *Exeunt.*

## *Scæna Secunda.*

[*Bruges. — The Exchange.*]

*Enter Florez*

*Flo.*  Still blow'st thou there? and from all
    other parts,
Do all my agents sleep, that nothing comes?
There 's a conspiracy of winds and servants,
If not of elements, to ha' me break.
What should I think? unless the seas and
    sands                    5
Had swallow'd up my ships, or fire had spoil'd
My warehouses, or death devour'd my factors,
I must ha' had some returns.

---

169 **shadows:** disguises    173 **doit:** small coin    185 **meat:** food    199 **Minche:** ('match' Ff, Q)
202 **niggl'd:** mated    205 **Oh:** ('Of' F 2)    206 **put on:** assumed    219 **ports:** harbors of safety

*Enter Merchant*

*Mer.*                              Save you, sir!
*Flo.*                              Save you!
*Mer.* No news yet o' your ships?
*Flo.*                              Not any yet, sir.
*Mer.* 'T is strange.
*Flo.*          'T is true, sir. *Exit* [*Merchant*].
What a voice was here now! 10
This was one passing-bell; a thousand ravens
Sung in that man now, to presage my ruins.

[*Enter Second Merchant*]

*2 Mer.* Goswin, good day.  These winds
are very constant.
*Flo.* They are so, sir, — to hurt.
*2 Mer.*                    Ha' you had no letters
Lately from England, nor from Denmark?
*Flo.*                              Neither. 15
*2 Mer.* This wind brings them.  Nor no
news over land,
Through Spain, from the Straits?
*Flo.*                              Not any.
*2 Mer.* I am sorry, sir. *Exit.*
*Flo.* They talk me down; and as 't is said of
vultures,
They scent a field fought, and do smell the
carcasses
By many hundred miles, so do these my
wracks                                    20
At greater distances.  Why, thy will, Heaven,
Come on, and be! yet, if thou please preserve
me
But in my own adventure here at home,
Of my chaste love, to keep me worthy of her,
It shall be put in scale 'gainst all ill fortunes: 25
I am not broken yet; nor should I fall,
Methinks, with less than that: that ruins all.
                                        *Exit.*

## Scæna Tertia.

[*The Same. — The House of Vandunk.*]

*Enter Vandunk, Hubert, Hemskirk, and
Margaret*

*Vand.* Captain, you are welcome; so is this
your friend,
Most safely welcome; though our town stand
out
Against your master, you shall find good quarter:
The troth is, we not love him.  Meg, some
wine. —

[*Exit Margaret, who presently re-enters
with wine.*]

Let 's talk a little treason, if we can       5
Talk treason 'gainst the traitors: by your leave,
gentlemen,
We here in Bruges think he does usurp,
And therefore I am bold with him.
*Hub.*                    Sir, your boldness
Haply becomes your mouth, but not our ears,
While we are his servants; and, as we come
here,                                        10
Not to ask questions, walk forth on your walls,
Visit your courts of guard, view your munition,
Ask of your corn-provisions, nor inquire
Into the least, as spies upon your strengths;
So let 's entreat, we may receive from you   15
Nothing in passage or discourse, but what
We may with gladness, and our honesties, hear;
And that shall seal our welcome.
*Vand.*          Good: let 's drink, then. —
Meg, fill out. — I keep mine old pearl still,
captain.
*Marg.* I hang fast, man.
*Hem.* Old jewels commend their keeper, sir.
*Vand.* Here 's to you with a heart, my
captain's friend,                            21
With a good heart! and, if this make us speak
Bold words anon, 't is all under the rose,
Forgotten: drown all memory, when we drink!
*Hub.* 'T is freely spoken, noble burgomas-
ter:                                         25
I 'll do you right.
*Hem.*              Nay, sir, Mynheer Vandunk
Is a true statesman.
*Vand.* Fill my captain's cup there. — Oh,
that your master Wolfort
Had been an honest man!
*Hub.*              Sir?
*Vand.*                    Under the rose.
*Hem.* Here 's to you, Marget.
*Marg.*          Welcome, welcome, captain. 30
*Vand.* Well said, my pearl, still!
*Hem.*                    And how does my niece?
Almost a woman, I think.  This friend of
mine
I drew along with me, through so much hazard,
Only to see her: she was my errand.
*Vand.* Ay, a kind uncle you are, — fill him
his glass, —                                 35
That in seven years could not find leisure —
*Hem.*                                        No,
It 's not so much.
*Vand.*          I 'll bate you ne'er an hour on 't:
It was before the Brabander 'gan his war
For moonshine i' the water there, his daughter
That never was lost; yet you could not find
time                                         40

---

**8** S. D. **Merchant:** ('Merchants' Ff, Q)    **20 wracks:** ruins, shipwrecks    Sc. III. s. D.: (Ff, Q add
*Boors*, by mistake)    **3 quarter:** treatment    **16 passage:** casual remark    **19 Meg:** ('Mage' F 1, Q;
not in F 2)    **pearl:** (alluding to the etymology of 'Margaret')    **39 For . . . water:** for a false or
pretended cause

To see a kinswoman: but she is worth the
    seeing, sir,
Now you are come. You ask if she were a
    woman?
She is a woman, sir, — fetch her forth,
    Marget, —
And a fine woman, and has suitors.

                          *Exit Margaret.*
*Hem.*                        How!
What suitors are they?
    *Vand.*        Bachelors, young burghers;  45
And one a gallant; the young prince of mer-
    chants
We call him here in Bruges.
    *Hem.*            How! a merchant!
I thought, Vandunk, you had understood me
    better,
And my niece, too, so trusted to you by me,
Than to admit of such in name of suitors.  50
    *Vand.*   Such! he is such a such, as, were she
    mine,
I 'd give him thirty thousand crowns with her.
    *Hem.*   But the same things, sir, fit not you
    and me.                         *Exit.*
    *Vand.*   Why, give 's some wine, then; this
    will fit us all.
Here 's to you still, my captain's friend, all
    out!                                55
And still would Wolfort were an honest man!
Under the rose I speak it. — But this merchant
Is a brave boy: he lives so, i' the town here,
We know not what to think on him: at some
    times
We fear he will be bankrupt; he does stretch,  60
Tenter his credit so; embraces all;
And, to 't, the winds have been contrary long:
But then, if he should have all his returns,
We think he would be a king, and are half sure
    on 't. —
Your master is a traitor, for all this,       65
Under the rose, — here 's to you, — and usurps
The earldom from a better man.
    *Hub.*                Ay, marry, sir,
Where is that man?
    *Vand.*       Nay, soft: and I could tell you,
'T is ten to one I would not. Here 's my hand;
I love not Wolfort: sit you still with that.   70
Here comes my captain again, and his fine niece;
And there 's my merchant; view him well. —
    Fill wine here!

    *Enter Hemskirk, [Margaret], Bertha, and*
                 *Florez*

    *Hem.*   You must not only know me for your
    uncle
Now, but obey me: you, go cast yourself

Away, upon a dunghill here! a merchant!   75
A petty fellow! one that makes his trade
With oaths and perjuries!
    *Flo.*           What is that you say, sir?
If it be me you speak of, as your eye
Seems to direct, I wish you would speak to
    me, sir.
    *Hem.*   Sir, I do say, she is no merchan-
    dise:                             80
Will that suffice you?
    *Flo.*             Merchandise, good sir!
Though you be kinsman to her, take no leave
    thence
To use me with contempt: I ever thought
Your niece above all price.
    *Hem.*           And do so still, sir:
I assure you, her rate 's at more than you are
    worth.                            85
    *Flo.*   You do not know what a gentleman 's
    worth, sir,
Nor can you value him.
    *Hub.*           Well said, merchant!
    *Vand.*                   Nay,
Let him alone, and ply your matter.
    *Hem.*             A gentleman!
What, o' the wool-pack? or the sugar-chest?
Or lists of velvet? which is 't, pound or yard,  90
You vent your gentry by?
    *Hub.*           Oh, Hemskirk, fie!
    *Vand.*   Come, do not mind 'em; drink. —
    He is no Wolfort,
Captain, I advise you.
    *Hem.*         Alas, my pretty man,
I think 't be angry, by its look! come hither,
Turn this way a little: if it were the blood   95
Of Charlemagne, as 't may, for aught I know,
Be some good botcher's issue, here in Bruges —
    *Flo.*                    How!
    *Hem.*   Nay, I 'm not certain of that; of this
    I am,
If it once buy and sell, its gentry is gone.
    *Flo.*   Ha, ha!
    *Hem.*     You are angry, though ye laugh.
    *Flo.*           No, now 't is pity  100
Of your poor argument. Do not you, the lords
Of land, (if you be any,) sell the grass,
The corn, the straw, the milk, the cheese —
    *Vand.*              And butter.
Remember butter; do not leave out butter.
    *Flo.*   The beefs and muttons, that your
    grounds are stored with?            105
Swine, with the very mast, beside the woods?
    *Hem.*   No; for those sordid uses we have
    tenants,
Or else our bailiffs.
    *Flo.*         Have not we, sir, chapmen

---

    ⁴³ **Marget:** ('Margee' F 1)   ⁵⁵ **all out:** bottoms up    ⁶¹ **Tenter:** stretch (as cloth is stretched on
tenter-hooks)   ⁶² **to 't:** besides   ⁷⁶ **his:** ('this' F 1)   ⁹⁰ **lists:** strips   ⁹¹ **vent:** sell   ⁹⁷ **botcher:**
mender of old clothes   ¹⁰⁶ **mast:** acorns, etc., used as food for swine

And factors, then, to answer these? Your
　honour,
Fetch'd from the heralds' A B C, and said
　over,　　　　　　　　　　　　　　　　110
With your court-faces, once an hour, shall never
Make me mistake myself.　Do not your lawyers
Sell all their practice, as your priests their
　prayers?
What is not bought and sold? the company
That you had last, what had you for 't, i'
　faith?　　　　　　　　　　　　　　　115
　*Hem.*　You now grow saucy.
　*Flo.*　　　　　　　　　Sure, I have been bred
Still with my honest liberty, and must use it.
　*Hem.*　Upon your equals, then.
　*Flo.*　　　　　　　　　　Sir, he that will
Provoke me first doth make himself my equal.
　*Hem.*　Do ye hear? no more!
　*Flo.*　　　　　　　Yes, sir, this little, I pray you, 120
And 't shall be aside; then, after, as you please.
You appear the uncle, sir, to her I love
More than mine eyes; and I have heard your
　scorns
With so much scoffing, and with so much shame,
As each strives which is greater: but, believe me,
I suck'd not in this patience with my milk. 126
Do not presume, because you see me young;
Or cast despites on my profession,
For the civility and tameness of it:
A good man bears a contumely worse　　　130
Than he would do an injury.　Proceed not
To my offence: wrong is not still successful;
Indeed, it is not.　I would approach your
　kinswoman
With all respect done to yourself and her.
　　　　　　　　　　　*[Takes Bertha's hand.]*
　*Hem.*　Away, companion! handling her?
　take that!　　　　　　　*Strikes him.* 135
　*Flo.*　Nay, I do love no blows, sir: there 's
　exchange!
　　　*He gets Hemskirk's sword and cuts him
　　　　　　　　on the head.*
　*Hub.*　Hold, sir!
　*Marg.*　　　　　Oh, murther!
　*Ber.*　　　　　　　　　Help my Goswin!
　*Marg.*　　　　　　　　　　　Man! —
　*Vand.*　Let 'em alone.　My life for one!
　*Flo.*　　　　　　　　　　　Nay, come,
If you have will.
　*Hub.*　　　　　None to offend you I, sir.
　*Flo.*　He that had, thank himself! — Not
　hand her? yes, sir,　　　　　　　　140
And clasp her, and embrace her; and (would
　she

Now go with me) bear her through all her race,
Her father, brethren, and her uncles, arm'd,
And all their nephews, though they stood a
　wood
Of pikes, and wall of cannon. — Kiss me,
　Gertrude;　　　　　　　　　　　145
Quake not, but kiss me.
　*Vand.*　　　　　Kiss him, girl; I bid you. —
My merchant royal!　Fear no uncles: hang
　'em,
Hang up all uncles!　Are we not in Bruges,
Under the rose here?
　*Flo.*　　　　　　In this circle, love,
Thou art as safe as in a tower of brass.　　150
Let such as do wrong, fear.
　*Vand.*　　　　　　　Ay, that 's good:
Let Wolfort look to that.
　*Flo.*　　　　　　　Sir, here she stands,
Your niece, and my beloved.　One of these titles
She must apply to: if unto the last,
Not all the anger can be sent unto her,　　155
In frown or voice, or other art, shall force her,
Had Hercules a hand in 't. — Come, my joy,
Say thou art mine aloud, love, and profess it.
　*Vand.*　Do: and I drink to it.
　*Flo.*　　　　　　Prithee, say so, love.
　*Ber.*　'T would take away the honour from
　my blushes; —　　　　　　　　　160
Do not you play the tyrant, sweet; — they
　speak it.
　*Hem.*　I thank you, niece.
　*Flo.*　　　　　Sir, thank her for your life;
And fetch your sword within.
　*Hem.*　　　　　　You insult too much
With your good fortune, sir.
　　　　　　　　　　*Exeunt Florez and Bertha.*
　*Hub.*　　　　　　A brave clear spirit! —
Hemskirk, you were to blame: a civil habit 165
Oft covers a good man; and you may meet,
In person of a merchant, with a soul
As resolute and free, and all ways worthy,
As else in any file of mankind.　Pray you,
What meant you so to slight him?
　*Hem.*　　　　　　　'T is done now; 170
Ask no more of it; I must suffer.
　　　　　　　　　　　　*Exit Hemskirk.*
　*Hub.*　　　　　　This
Is still the punishment of rashness — sorrow.
Well, I must to the woods, for nothing here
Will be got out.　There I may chance to learn
Somewhat to help my inquiries further. —
　*Vand.*　　　　　　　Ha! 175
A looking-glass!
　*Hub.*　　　　　How now, brave burgomaster?

109 **honour:** ('errour' F 1, Q)　114 **company:** (alluding to the sale of military offices)　124 **with:**
(not in Ff, Q)　125 **strives:** ('strive' Ff, Q)　128 **despites:** scorn　129 **civility:** quality appropriate
to the citizen rather than to the gentleman　135 **companion:** fellow　137 **Man:** husband　148 **we
not:** ('not we' F 2)　154 **apply:** conform　163 **within:** (Florez had thrown away Hemskirk's sword.)
**insult:** vaunt, are arrogant　164 ('**Exit Florez**' F 1)　176 **looking-glass:** chamber-pot

*Vand.* I love no Wolforts, and my name 's
Vandunk.
*Hub.* Van-drunk it 's rather. Come, go
sleep within.
*Vand.* Earl Florez is right heir; and this
same Wolfort, —
Under the rose I speak it —
*Hub.*                          Very hardly.  180
*Vand.* Usurps; and a rank traitor, as ever
breath'd,
And all that do uphold him. Let me go;
No man shall hold me up, that upholds him.
Do you uphold him?
*Hub.*                No.
*Vand.*            Then hold me up.
*Exeunt.*

[SCENE IV. — *Before the House of Vandunk.*]

*Enter Florez and Hemskirk*

*Hem.* Sir, I presume you have a sword of
your own,
That can so handle another's.
*Flo.*                       Faith, you may, sir.
*Hem.* And ye have made me have so much
better thoughts of you,
As I am bound to call you forth.
*Flo.*                          For what, sir?
*Hem.* To the repairing of mine honour and
hurt here.                                   5
*Flo.* Express your way.
*Hem.*              By fight, and speedily.
*Flo.* You have your will. Require you any
more?
*Hem.* That you be secret, and come single.
*Flo.*                                I will.
*Hem.* As you are the gentleman you would
be thought!
*Flo.* Without the conjuration, and I 'll bring
Only my sword, which I will fit to yours.   11
I 'll take his length within.
*Hem.*              Your place now, sir?
*Flo.* By the sand-hills.
*Hem.*              Sir, nearer to the woods,
If you thought so, were fitter.
*Flo.*                       There, then.
*Hem.*                              Good.
Your time?
*Flo.* 'Twixt seven and eight.
*Hem.*              You 'll give me, sir,   15
Cause to report you worthy of my niece,
If you come like your promise.
*Flo.*                       If I do not,
Let no man think to call me unworthy first:
I 'll do 't myself, and justly wish to want her.
*Exeunt.*

## Actus Tertius, Scæna Prima.

[*Before a Tavern in the Outskirts of Bruges.*]

*Enter three or four Boors*

*1 Boor.* Come, English beer, hostess, English beer by th' belly!
*2 Boor.* Stark beer, boy, stout and strong
beer! — So; sit down, lads,
And drink me upsey-Dutch: frolic, and fear
not.

*Enter Higgen like a sow-gelder, singing*

Have ye any work for the sow-gelder, ho?
My horn goes to high, to low, to high, to low!
    Have ye any pigs, calves, or colts,       6
    Have ye any lambs in your holts,
       To cut for the stone?
       Here comes a cunning one.
Have ye any braches to spade,               10
    Or e'er a fair maid
    That would be a nun?
    Come, kiss me, 't is done.
Hark, how my merry horn doth blow
To high, to low, to high, to low!           15

*1 Boor.* Oh, excellent! — Two-pence apiece,
boys, two-pence apiece! —
Give the boy some drink there! — Piper, wet
your whistle.
Canst tell me a way now how to cut off my
wife's concupiscence?
*Hig.* I 'll sing ye a song for 't.

THE SONG

    Take her, and hug her,                   20
    And turn her, and tug her,
And turn her again, boy, again:
    Then, if she mumble,
    Or if her tail tumble,
Kiss her amain, boy, amain!                 25

    Do thy endeavour
    To take off her fever,
Then her disease no longer will reign.
    If nothing will serve her,
    Then thus, to preserve her,              30
Swinge her amain, boy, amain!

    Give her cold jelly,
    To take up her belly,
And once a day swinge her again.
    If she stand all these pains,            35
    Then knock out her brains;
Her disease no longer will reign.

---

180 **Very hardly**: with great difficulty   183 **up**: (not in Ff, Q)   Sc. IV: (Not marked, Ff, Q)
10 **conjuration**: formal oath   3 **upsey-Dutch**: in the Dutch fashion, to excess   7 **holts**: pastures (usually
"woods")   10 **braches**: bitches   17 **boy**: ('boys' Ff, Q)   25 **amain**: vehemently   31 **Swinge**: beat

*1 Boor.* More excellent, more excellent, sweet sow-gelder!

*2 Boor.* Three-pence apiece, three-pence apiece!

*Hig.* Will you hear a song how the devil was gelded? 40

*3 Boor.* Ay, ay; let 's hear the devil roar, sow-gelder.

### SONG

#### 1.

He ran at me first in the shape of a ram,
And over and over the sow-gelder came:
I rise, and I halter'd him fast by the horn;
I pluck'd out his stones, as you'd pick out a corn. 45
Baa! quoth the devil, and forth he slunk,
And left us a carcass of mutton that stunk.

#### 2.

The next time I rode a good mile and a half,
Where I heard he did live in disguise of a calf:
I bound and I gelt him, ere he did any evil; 50
He was here at his best but a sucking devil.
Maa! yet he cried, and forth he did steal,
And this was sold after for excellent veal.

#### 3.

Some half a year after, in the form of a pig,
I met with the rogue, and he look'd very big: 55
I catch'd at his leg, laid him down on a log;
Ere a man could fart twice, I had made him a hog.
Owgh! quoth the devil, and forth gave a jerk,
That a Jew was converted, and eat of the perk.

*1 Boor.* Groats apiece, groats apiece, groats apiece! — 60
There, sweet sow-gelder. [*Gives money.*]

*Enter Prig [disguised as a juggler,] and Ferret [as his man]*

*Prig.* Will ye see any feats of activity,
Some sleight of hand, legerdemain? hey, pass,
Presto, be gone there?

*2 Boor.*                    Sit down, juggler.

*Prig.* Sirrah, play you your art well [*aside to Ferret.*] — Draw near, piper. 65
                              [*To Higgen.*]
Look you, my honest friends, you see my hands;
Plain-dealing is no devil. Lend me some money;
Twelve-pence apiece will serve.

*1 and 2 Boor.* There, there. [*Giving money.*]

*Prig.*                              I thank you,
Thank ye heartily. When shall I pay ye?

*All Boors.* Ha, ha, ha! by th' mass, this was a fine trick. 70

*Prig.* A merry slight toy. But now I 'll show your worships
A trick indeed.

*Hig.*            Mark him well now, my masters.

*Prig.* Here are three balls: these balls shall be three bullets.
One, two, and three! *ascentibus, malentibus!*
Presto, be gone! They are vanish'd: fair play, gentlemen. 75
Now, these three, like three bullets, from your three noses
Will I pluck presently. Fear not; no harm, boys.
*Tityre, tu patulæ.*
          [*Pulls the Boors' noses, while Higgen
          and Ferret pick their pockets, and
          remove some of their cloaks.*]

*1 Boor.* Oh, oh, oh!

*Prig.* *Recubans sub tegmine fagi.* 80

*2 Boor.* Ye pull too hard; ye pull too hard!

*Prig.*                              Stand fair, then
*Silvertram trim-tram.*

*3 Boor.* Hold, hold, hold!

*Prig.* Come aloft, bullets three, with a whim-wham! —
Have ye their moneys?
                    [*Aside to Higgen and Ferret.*]

*Hig.*                    Yes, yes.

*1 Boor.*                    Oh, rare juggler! 85

*2 Boor.* Oh, admirable juggler!

*Prig.*                    One trick more yet.
Hey, come aloft! *sa, sa, flim, flum, taradumbis!*
East, west, north, south, now fly like Jack with a *bumbis!*
Now all your money 's gone: pray, search your pockets.

*1 Boor.* Humh! 90

*2 Boor.* He!

*3 Boor.* The devil a penny's here!

*Prig.*                    This was a rare trick.

*1 Boor.* But 't would be a far rarer to restore it.

*Prig.* I 'll do ye that, too. Look upon me earnestly,
And move not any ways your eyes from this place, 95
This button here.
          [*While the Boors look at Prig counters
          are put into their pockets by Higgen
          and Ferret.*]
Pow, whir, whiss! Shake your pockets.

---

⁴²⁻⁵⁹ **Song:** (not in F 1, Q)    ⁴⁴ **rise:** (past tense, pronounce "riz")    ⁵⁷ **hog:** castrated swine
⁵⁹ **perk:** *i.e.,* pork    ⁶⁰ **groats:** coins worth fourpence    ⁷¹ **toy:** trifle    ⁷⁴ **ascentibus, etc.:** (nonsense intended to confuse the Boors)    ⁷⁸⁻⁸⁰ **Tityre . . . fagi:** (Line 1 of Vergil's first eclogue)    ⁸⁰ **tegmine:** ('jermine' Ff, Q)    ⁹⁶ S. D. **counters:** imitation coins, tokens

*1 Boor.* By th' mass, 't is here again, boys.
*Prig.*              Rest ye merry:
My first trick has paid me.
*All Boors.*          Ay, take it, take it,
And take some drink, too.
    *Prig.*     Not a drop now, I thank you. —
Away! we are discover'd else.         100
         *Exit [with Higgen and Ferret].*

*Enter Gerrard like a blind aquavitæ-man,*
*and a Boy singing the Song*

Bring out your cony-skins, fair maids, to me,
And hold 'em fair, that I may see;
Grey, black, and blue: for your smaller skins,
I 'll give ye looking-glasses, pins;
And for your whole cony,           105
Here 's ready, ready money.
Come, gentle Joan, do thou begin
With thy black, black, black cony-skin;
And Mary then, and Jane will follow,
With their silver-hair'd skins and their yellow.
The white cony-skin I will not lay by,    111
For, though it be faint, 't is fair to the eye;
The grey, it is warm; but yet, for my money,
Give me the bonny, bonny black cony.
Come away, fair maids; your skins will de-
     cay:                       115
Come and take money, maids; put your ware
     away.
Cony-skins, cony-skins! have ye any cony-
     skins?
I have fine bracelets, and fine silver pins.

*Ger.* Buy any brand-wine, buy any brand-
     wine?
*Boy.* Have ye any cony-skins?      120
*2 Boor.* My fine canary-bird, there 's a
     cake for thy worship.
*1 Boor.* Come, fill, fill, fill, fill, suddenly.
Let 's see, sir;
What 's this?
    *Ger.*     A penny, sir.
*1 Boor.*          Fill till 't be six-pence,
And there 's my pig.
    *Boy.*      This is a counter, sir.
*1 Boor.* A counter! Stay ye: what are
these, then? —              125
Oh, execrable juggler! oh, damn'd juggler! —
Look in your hose, ho! this comes of looking
     forward.
*3 Boor.* Devil o' Dunkirk! what a rogue 's
     this juggler,
This hey-pass, re-pass! h'as repass'd us sweetly.
*2 Boor.* Do ye call these tricks?     130

*Enter Higgen [disguised as a gold-end-man]*

*Hig.* Have ye any ends of gold or silver?
*2 Boor.* This fellow comes to mock us. —
     Gold or silver! cry copper!
*1 Boor.*         Yes, my good friend,
We have e'en an end of all we have.
*Hig.*                  'T is well, sir;
You have the less to care for. — Gold and
     silver!            *Exit.* 135

*Enter Prig [disguised as an old-clothes man]*

*Prig.* Have ye any old cloaks to sell, have
     ye any old cloaks to sell?      *Exit.*
*1 Boor.* Cloaks! — Look about ye, boys;
     mine 's gone!
*2 Boor.*        A pox juggle 'em!
Pox o' their prestoes! mine 's gone, too!
*3 Boor.*          Here 's mine yet.
*1 Boor.* Come, come, let 's drink, then. —
More brand-wine!
*Boy.*           Here, sir.
*1 Boor.* If e'er I catch your sow-gelder, by
     this hand, I 'll strip him.       140
Were ever fools so ferk'd? We have two cloaks
     yet,
And all our caps: the devil take the flincher!
*All Boors.* Yaw, yaw, yaw, yaw!

*Enter Hemskirk*

*Hem.*         Good den, my honest fellows:
You are merry here, I see.
*3 Boor.*      'T is all we have left, sir.
*Hem.* What hast thou? aquavitæ?
*Boy.*                 Yes.
*Hem.*        Fill out, then; 145
And give these honest fellows round.
*All Boors.*          We thank ye.
*Hem.* May I speak a word in private to ye?
*All Boors.*            Yes, sir.
*Hem.* I have a business for you, honest
     friends,
If you dare lend your help, shall get you
     crowns.
*Ger.*                 Ha!
Lead me a little nearer, boy. *[Aside to Boy.]*
*1 Boor.*         What is 't, sir? 150
If it be anything to purchase money (which is
our want), command us.
*All Boors.* All, all, all, sir.
*Hem.* You know the young spruce merchant
     in Bruges?
*2 Boor.* Who, Master Goswin?
*Hem.*         That: he owes me money,
And here in town there is no stirring of him. 155

---

⁹⁷ **Rest ye merry:** be content    ¹⁰⁰ S. D. **aquavitæ-man:** seller of brandy    ¹⁰¹ **cony-skins:** rabbit-
skins    ¹¹⁹ **brand-wine:** brandy    ¹²³ **What 's this:** What is the price of the brandy you have poured
out?    ¹²⁴ **pig:** sixpence    ¹²⁷ **hose:** breeches    ¹³⁰ S. D. **gold-end-man:** itinerant buyer of old gold
¹³⁷⁻¹³⁸ **pox:** (represented by dash, Ff, Q)    ¹⁴¹ **ferk'd:** cheated    ¹⁴² **flincher:** one who flinches while
drinking    ¹⁴³ **den:** evening ('do'n' Ff, Q)

*Ger.* [*Aside.*] Say ye so?

*Hem.*    This day, upon a sure appointment,
He meets me a mile hence, by the chase-side,
Under the row of oaks: do you know it?

*All Boors.*                     Yes, sir.

*Hem.*    Give 'em more drink. — There, if
you dare but venture,
When I shall give the word, to seize upon
him,   160
Here 's twenty pound.

*3 Boor.*            Beware the juggler!

*Hem.*    If he resist, down with him, have no
mercy.

*1 Boor.*    I warrant you, we 'll hamper him.

*Hem.*              To discharge you,
I have a warrant here about me.

*3 Boor.*          Here 's our warrant;
This carries fire i' th' tail. [*Showing his cudgel.*]

*Hem.*         Away with me, then!  165
[*Aside.*] The time draws on.
I must remove so insolent a suitor,
And, if he be so rich, make him pay ransom
Ere he sees Bruges' towers again.  Thus wise
men
Repair the hurts they take by a disgrace,  170
And piece the lion's skin with the fox's case.

*Ger.* [*Aside.*]  I am glad I have heard this
sport yet.

*Hem.*    There 's for thy drink. — Come, pay
the house within, boys,
And lose no time.

*Ger.*         Away with all our haste, too!
                            *Exeunt.*

## Scæna Secunda.

[*A Chase bordering on the Woods near Bruges.*]

*Enter Florez*

*Flo.*  No wind blow fair yet? no return of
moneys,
Letters, nor anything to hold my hopes up?
Why, then, 't is destin'd that I fall, fall miser-
ably,
My credit I was built on sinking with me.
Thou boist'rous North-wind, blowing my mis-
fortunes,  5
And frosting all my hopes to cakes of coldness,
Yet stay thy fury! give the gentle South
Yet leave to court those sails that bring me
safety!
And you, auspicious fires; bright twins in
heaven,
Dance on the shrouds! He blows still stub-
bornly,  10

And on his boist'rous rack rides my sad ruin.
There is no help, there can be now no comfort;
To-morrow, with the sun-set, sets my credit.
Oh, misery! thou curse of man, thou plague,
In the midst of all our strength, thou strikest
us!  15
My virtuous love is lost, too: all, what I have
been,
No more hereafter to be seen than shadow.
To prison now! Well, yet there 's this hope
left me;
I may sink fairly under this day's venture,
And so to-morrow 's cross'd, and all those
curses.  20
Yet manly I 'll invite my fate: base Fortune
Shall never say, she has cut my throat in fear.
This is the place his challenge call'd me to,
And was a happy one at this time for me;
For let me fall before my foe i' the field,  25
And not at bar before my creditors! —

*Enter Hemskirk*

H'as kept his word. — Now, sir, your sword's
tongue only,
Loud as you dare; all other language —

*Hem.*                Well, sir,
You shall not be long troubl'd.  Draw.

*Flo.*               'T is done, sir;
And now, have at ye!

*Hem.*          Now!

*Enter Boors* [*who attempt to seize Florez*]

*Flo.*         Betray'd to villains! —  30
Slaves, ye shall buy me bravely! —
And thou, base coward —

*Enter Gerrard and Beggars* [*disguised*]

*Ger.*         Now upon 'em bravely!
Conjure 'em soundly, boys!

*Boors.*            Hold, hold!

*Ger.*            Lay on still!
Down with that gentleman-rogue, swinge him
to syrup! —      [*Hemskirk runs off.*]
Retire, sir, and take breath. — Follow, and
take him;  35
Take all; 't is lawful prize.
             [*Exeunt some of the Beggars.*]

*Boors.*            We yield.

*Ger.*            Down with 'em!
Into the wood, and rifle 'em, tew 'em, swinge
'em!
Knock me their brains into their breeches!

*Boors.*            Hold, hold!
                *Exeunt* [*all except Florez*].

---

[157] **chase:** forest preserve   [163] **hamper:** bind, overcome   **discharge:** free from charges   [171] **case:** skin   [7] **South:** south wind   [9] **bright twins:** constellation of the Gemini (Castor and Pollux), sup- posed to produce electrical effects which were regarded as good omens   [11] **rack:** mass of driving clouds   [16] **lost:** ('toss'd' F 1, Q)   [20] **cross'd:** cancelled   [37] **tew:** beat

*Flo.* What these men are I know not; nor
for what cause
They should thus thrust themselves into my
danger                                                    40
Can I imagine — but, sure, heaven's hand was
in 't —
Nor why this coward knave should deal so
basely,
To eat me up with slaves: but, Heaven, I thank
thee!
I hope thou hast reserv'd me to an end
Fit for thy creature, and worthy of thine
honour.                                                   45
Would all my other dangers here had suffer'd!
With what a joyful heart should I go home,
then!
Where now, Heaven knows, like him that waits
his sentence,
Or hears his passing-bell; but there 's my hope
still.

*Enter Gerrard [as Clause]*

*Ger.* Blessing upon you, master!
*Flo.*                          Thank ye. Leave me;   50
For, by my troth, I have nothing now to give
thee.
*Ger.* Indeed, I do not ask, sir; only it
grieves me
To see ye look so sad.  Now, goodness keep ye
From troubles in your mind!
*Flo.*                          If I were troubl'd,
What could thy comfort do? prithee, Clause,
leave me.                                                 55
*Ger.* Good master, be not angry; for what
I say
Is out of true love to ye.
*Flo.*                          I know thou lov'st me.
*Ger.* Good master, blame that love, then,
if I prove so saucy
To ask ye why ye are sad.
*Flo.*                          Most true, I am so;
And such a sadness I have got will sink me.   60
*Ger.* Heaven shield it, sir!
*Flo.*          Faith, thou must lose thy master.
*Ger.* I had rather lose my neck, sir.  Would
I knew —
*Flo.* What would the knowledge do thee
good (so miserable
Thou canst not help thyself), when all my ways,
Nor all the friends I have —
*Ger.*                          You do not know, sir,   65
What I can do: cures, sometimes, for men's
cares,
Flow where they least expect 'em.
*Flo.*                          I know thou wouldst do:
But farewell, Clause, and pray for thy poor
master.

*Ger.* I will not leave ye.
*Flo.*                          How!
*Ger.* I dare not leave ye, sir, I must not
leave ye,                                                 70
And, till ye beat me dead, I will not leave ye.
By what ye hold most precious, by Heaven's
goodness,
As your fair youth may prosper, good sir, tell
me!
My mind believes yet something 's in my power
May ease you of this trouble.
*Flo.*                          I will tell thee.   75
For a hundred thousand crowns, upon my
credit,
Taken up of merchants to supply my traffics,
The winds and weather envying of my fortune,
And no return to help me off yet showing,
To-morrow, Clause, to-morrow, which must
come,                                                     80
In prison thou shalt find me poor and broken.
*Ger.* I cannot blame your grief, sir.
*Flo.*                          Now, what say'st thou?
*Ger.* I say, you should not shrink; for he
that gave ye,
Can give you more; his power can bring ye off,
sir;
When friends and all forsake ye, yet he sees
you.                                                      85
*Flo.* There 's all my hope.
*Ger.*                          Hope still, sir.  Are you tied
Within the compass of a day, good master,
To pay this mass of money?
*Flo.*                          Even to-morrow.
But why do I stand mocking of my misery?
Is 't not enough the floods and friends forget
me?                                                       90
*Ger.* Will no less serve?
*Flo.*                          What if it would?
*Ger.*                          Your patience:
I do not ask to mock ye.  'T is a great sum,
A sum for mighty men to start and stick at;
But not for honest.  Have ye no friends left ye,
None that have felt your bounty, worth this
duty?                                                     95
*Flo.* Duty! thou know'st it not.
*Ger.*                          It is a duty,
And, as a duty, from those men have felt ye,
Should be return'd again.  I have gain'd by ye;
A daily alms these seven years you have
shower'd on me.
Will half supply your want?
*Flo.*                          Why dost thou fool me?  100
Canst thou work miracles?
*Ger.*                          To save my master,
I can work this.
*Flo.*          Thou wilt make me angry with thee.
*Ger.* For doing good?

⁴⁹ **there:** in heaven   ⁶¹ **shield:** forbid   ⁷⁶ **crowns:** coins worth five shillings   ⁷⁷ **traffics:** business affairs   ⁸¹ **broken:** bankrupt   ⁸⁴ **bring ye off:** save you   ⁸⁶ **There 's:** ('That 's' F 1, Q)

*Flo.*                    What power hast thou?
*Ger.*                    Inquire not,
So I can do it, to preserve my master.
Nay, if it be three parts —
   *Flo.*                Oh, that I had it!  105
But, good Clause, talk no more; I feel thy
   charity,
As thou hast felt mine: but alas —
   *Ger.*                Distrust not;
'T is that that quenches ye: pull up your spirit,
Your good, your honest, and your noble spirit;
For if the fortunes of ten thousand people  110
Can save ye, rest assur'd.  You have forgot,
   sir,
The good ye did, which was the power you gave
   me:
Ye shall now know the King of Beggars' treas-
   ure;
And let the winds blow as they list, the seas
   roar,
Yet here to-morrow you shall find your har-
   bour.                                  115
Here fail me not, for, if I live, I 'll fit ye.
   *Flo.*  How fain I would believe thee!
   *Ger.*                If I lie, master,
Believe no man hereafter.
   *Flo.*                I will try thee:
But He knows, that knows all.
   *Ger.*                Know me to-morrow,
And, if I know not how to cure ye, kill me.  120
So, pass in peace, my best, my worthiest master!
                           *Exeunt.*

## *Scæna Tertia.*

### [*The Woods near Bruges.*]

#### *Enter Hubert like a huntsman*

*Hub.*  Thus have I stol'n away disguis'd
   from Hemskirk,
To try these people; for my heart yet tells me
Some of these beggars are the men I look for.
Appearing like myself, they have no reason
(Though my intent is fair, my main end
   honest)                                 5
But to avoid me narrowly.  That face, too,
That woman's face, how near it is!  Oh, may it
But prove the same, and, Fortune, how I 'll
   bless thee!
Thus, sure, they cannot know me, or suspect
   me,
If to my habit I but change my nature,    10
As I must do.  This is the wood they live in;
A place fit for concealment; where, till for-
   tune
Crown me with that I seek, I 'll live amongst
   'em.                                  *Exit.*

[SCENE IV. — *Another Part of the Woods.*]

*Enter Higgen, Prig, Ferret, Ginks, [and other
   Beggars], and the rest of the Boors*

   *Hig.*  Come, bring 'em out, for here we sit
   in justice.
Give to each one a cudgel, a good cudgel: —
And now attend your sentence.  That you are
   rogues,
And mischievous base rascals, — there 's the
   point now, —
I take it, is confess'd.                   5
   *Prig.*  Deny it if you dare, knaves!
   *Boors.*                We are rogues, sir.
   *Hig.*  To amplify the matter, then; rogues
   as ye are,
(And lamb'd ye shall be ere we leave ye) —
   *Boors.*                        Yes, sir.
   *Hig.*  And to the open handling of our jus-
   tice, —
Why did ye this upon the proper person  10
Of our good master? were you drunk when you
   did it?
   *Boors.*  Yes, indeed, were we.
   *Prig.*              You shall be beaten sober.
   *Hig.*  Was it for want you undertook it?
   *Boors.*                        Yes, sir.
   *Hig.*  You shall be swing'd abundantly.
   *Prig.*                And yet for all that,
You shall be poor rogues still.
   *Hig.*              Has not the gentleman, —  15
Pray, mark this point, brother Prig, — that
   noble gentleman,
Reliev'd ye often, found ye means to live by,
By employing some at sea, some here, some
   there,
According to your callings?
   *Boors.*                'T is most true, sir.
   *Hig.*  Is not the man an honest man?
   *Boors.*                Yes, truly.  20
   *Hig.*  A liberal gentleman? and, as ye are
   true rascals
Tell me but this, — have ye not been drunk,
   and often,
At his charge?
   *Boors.*      Often, often.
   *Hig.*                There 's the point, then:
They have cast themselves, brother Prig.
   *Prig.*              A shrewd point, brother.
   *Hig.*  Brother, proceed you now; the cause
   is open;                                 25
I am somewhat weary.
   *Prig.*          Can you do these things
You most abominable, stinking rascals,
You turnip-eating rogues?
   *Boors.*              We are truly sorry.

114 **list:** ('please' F 1, Q)    116 **fit:** provide    Sc. IV: (Not marked, Ff, Q)    8 **lamb'd:** beaten
soundly    24 **cast:** thrown (as in wrestling), convicted

*Prig.* Knock at your hard hearts, rogues,
and presently
Give us a sign you feel compunction: 30
Every man up with 's cudgel, and on his neigh-
bour
Bestow such alms, till we shall say sufficient,
(For there your sentence lies) without partiality
Either of head or hide, rogues, without sparing,
Or we shall take the pains to beat you dead
else. 35
You know your doom.
    *Hig.* One, two, and three! about it!
                       *Beat one another.*
    *Prig.* That fellow in the blue has true com-
punction;
He beats his fellows bravely. — Oh, well struck,
boys!

        *Enter Gerrard*

    *Hig.* Up with that blue breech! now plays
he the devil!
So; get ye home, drink small beer, and be
honest.       [*Exeunt Boors.*] 40
Call in the gentleman.
    *Ger.* Do, bring him presently;
His cause I 'll hear myself.
          [*Exeunt some of the Beggars.*]
*Hig.* }
*Prig.* }     With all due reverence,
We do resign, sir.

      *Enter Hemskirk*

    *Ger.* Now, huffing sir, what 's your name?
    *Hem.* What 's that to you, sir?
    *Ger.* It shall be, ere we part.
    *Hem.* My name is Hemskirk. 45
I follow the earl, which you shall feel.
    *Ger.* No threatening,
For we shall cool you, sir. Why didst thou
basely
Attempt the murder of the merchant Goswin?
    *Hem.* What power hast thou to ask me?
    *Ger.* I will know it,
Or flay thee till thy pain discover it. 50
    *Hem.* He did me wrong, base wrong.
    *Ger.* That cannot save ye.
Who sent ye hither? and what further villainies
Have ye in hand?
    *Hem.* Why wouldst thou know?
what profit,
If I had any private way, could rise
Out of my knowledge, to do thee commodity?
Be sorry for what thou hast done, and make
amends, fool: 56
I 'll talk no further to thee, nor these rascals.
    *Ger.* Tie him to that tree.
          [*They tie him to a tree.*]

    *Hem.* I have told you whom I follow.
    *Ger.* The devil you should do, by your
villainies. —
Now he that has the best way, wring it from
him. 60
    *Hig.* I undertake it. Turn him to the sun,
boys:
Give me a fine sharp rush. — Will ye confess
yet?
    *Hem.* Ye have robb'd me already; now
you 'll murder me.
    *Hig.* Murder your nose a little. Does your
head purge, sir?
To it again; 't will do ye good.
    *Hem.* Oh, 65
I cannot tell you anything!
    *Ger.* Proceed, then. [*To Higgen.*]
    *Hig.* There 's maggots in your nose; I 'll
fetch 'em out, sir.
    *Hem.* Oh, my head breaks!
    *Hig.* The best thing for the rheum, sir,
That falls into your worship's eyes.
    *Hem.* Hold, hold!
    *Ger.* Speak, then.
    *Hem.* I know not what.
    *Hig.* It lies in 's brain yet; 70
In lumps it lies: I 'll fetch it out the finest!
What pretty faces the fool makes! heigh!
    *Hem.* Hold,
Hold, and I 'll tell ye all! Look in my doublet,
And there, within the lining, in a paper,
You shall find all.
    *Ger.* Go fetch that paper hither, 75
And let him loose for this time.
        [*They untie him. Exit Ferret.*]

   *Enter Hubert* [*disguised as before*]

    *Hub.* Good ev'n, my honest friends.
    *Ger.* Good ev'n, good fellow.
    *Hub.* May a poor huntsman, with a merry
heart,
A voice shall make the forest ring about him,
Get leave to live amongst ye? true as steel,
boys; 80
That knows all chases, and can watch all hours,
And with my quarter-staff, though the devil
bid stand,
Deal such an alms shall make him roar again;
Prick ye the fearful hare through cross-ways,
sheep-walks,
And force the crafty Reynard climb the quick-
sets; 85
Rouse ye the lofty stag, and with my bell-horn
Ring him a knell, that all the woods shall
mourn him,
Till, in his funeral tears, he fall before me?

---

³⁶ **You:** ('You shall' Ff, Q)   **doom:** judgment, sentence   ⁴⁴ **huffing:** blustering   ⁵⁰ **discover:**
reveal   ⁵⁵ **commodity:** benefit   ⁷⁶ **for . . . time:** for the present   ⁸¹ **watch:** stay awake
⁸⁴ **Prick:** track   ⁸⁵ **quicksets:** hedges, thickets

The pole-cat, martern, and the rich-skinn'd
   lucern,
I know to chase; the roe, the wind outstrip-
   ping;                          90
Isgrin himself, in all his bloody anger,
I can beat from the bay; and the wild sounder
Single, and with my arm'd staff turn the boar,
Spite of his foamy tushes, and thus strike him,
Till he fall down my feast.
   *Ger.*           A goodly fellow! 95
   *Hub.* (*Aside.*) What mak'st thou here,
   ha? —
   *Ger.*     We accept thy fellowship.
   *Hub.* (*Aside.*) Hemskirk, thou art not right,
   I fear; I fear thee. —

*Enter Ferret, with a letter*

   *Fer.*  Here is the paper; and, as he said, we
   found it.
   *Ger.*  Give me it. — I shall make a shift yet,
   old as I am,
To find your knavery. [*Reads.*] You are sent
   here, sirrah,                        100
To discover certain gentlemen, a spy-knave,
And, if ye find 'em, if not by persuasion
To bring 'em back, by poison to despatch 'em.
   *Hub.* [*Aside.*] By poison! ha! —
   *Ger.*         Here is another, Hubert:
What is that Hubert, sir?
   *Hem.*        You may perceive there. 105
   *Ger.*  I may perceive a villainy, and a rank
   one.
Was he join'd partner of thy knavery?
   *Hem.*                 No;
He had an honest end (would I had had so!);
Which makes him scape such cut-throats.
   *Ger.*           So it seems;
For here thou art commanded, when that Hu-
   bert                           110
Has done his best and worthiest service this
   way,
To cut his throat; for here he's set down
   dangerous.
   *Hub.* [*Aside.*] This is most impious. —
   *Ger.*       I am glad we have found ye.
Is not this true?
   *Hem.*      Yes; what are you the better?
   *Ger.*  You shall perceive, sir, ere you get
   your freedom. —                115
Take him aside. — And, friend, we take thee
   to us,
Into our company. Thou dar'st be true unto
   us?

   *Hig.*  Ay, and obedient too?
   *Hub.*           As you had bred me.
   *Ger.*  Then, take our hand; thou art now a
   servant to us. —
Welcome him, all.
   *Hig.*  Stand off, stand off: I'll do it. — 120
We bid ye welcome three ways; first, for your
   person,
Which is a promising person; next, for your
   quality,
Which is a decent and a gentle quality;
Last, for the frequent means you have to feed
   us:
You can steal, 't is to be presum'd?
   *Hub.*             Yes, venison, 125
Or, if I want —
   *Hig.*      'T is well; you understand right,
And shall practise daily. You can drink, too?
   *Hub.*                 Soundly.
   *Hig.*  And ye dare know a woman from a
   weather-cock?
   *Hub.*  Yes, if I handle her.
   *Ger.*             Now swear him.
   *Hig.*  I crown thy nab with a gag of bene-
   bowse,                       130
And stall thee by the salmon into the clowes;
To maund on the pad, and strike all the cheats,
To mill from the ruffmans commission and
   slates,
Twang dells i' the strommel, and let the queer-
   cuffin
And harmanbecks trine, and trine to the
   ruffin!                     135
   *Ger.*  Now interpret this unto him.
   *Hig.*  I pour on thy pate a pot of good ale,
And by the rogues' oath a rogue thee instal;
To beg on the way, to rob all thou meets,
To steal from the hedge both the shirt and the
   sheets,                      140
And lie with thy wench in the straw till she
   twang,
Let the constable, justice, and devil go hang! —
You are welcome, brother!
   *All.*       Welcome, welcome, welcome! —
But who shall have the keeping of this fellow?
   *Hub.*  Thank ye, friends:        145
And I beseech ye, if you dare but trust me
(For I have kept wild dogs and beasts for
   wonder
And made 'em tame, too), give into my custody
This roaring rascal: I shall hamper him,
With all his knacks and knaveries, and, I
   fear me,                    150

---

⁸⁹ **pole-cat, martern:** varieties of weasel  **lucern:** lynx  ⁹¹ **Isgrin:** the wolf in the romance of Reynard the Fox   ⁹² **sounder:** herd of wild swine   ⁹³ **Single:** separate  ⁹⁶ **mak'st:** dost   ¹⁰⁵ **What:**
what sort of person   ¹¹⁴ **what:** in what way   ¹¹⁸ **As:** as if   ¹²² **quality:** occupation   ¹²⁶ **Or** . . .
**I:** ('and . . . you' F 2)   ¹²⁷ **practise:** ('learn' F 1, Q)   ¹²⁹⁻¹³⁶ (These lines, much confused in F 1 and
Q, corrected in F 2)   ¹²⁹ **Yes:** (not in F 2)   ¹³⁰⁻¹³⁵ (Translated in lines 137–142)   ¹⁴⁵⁻¹⁴⁶ **Thank** . . .
**beseech ye:** ('Sir' F 2)   ¹⁴⁷ **I:** ('if I' Ff, Q)   ¹⁵⁰ **knacks:** tricks

Discover yet a further villainy in him:
Oh, he smells rank o' th' rascal!
*Ger.*                              Take him to thee;
But, if he scape —
*Hub.*      Let me be ev'n hang'd for him. —
Come, sir, I 'll tie ye to my leash.
*Hem.*                              Away, rascal!
*Hub.*   Be not so stubborn: I shall swinge
   ye soundly,                                        155
And ye play tricks with me.
*Ger.*                           So, now come in:
But ever have an eye, sir, to your prisoner.
*Hub.*   He must blind both mine eyes, if he
   get from me.
*Ger.*   Go, get some victuals and some drink,
   some good drink;
For this day we 'll keep holy to good fortune.
Come, and be frolic with us.                          161
*Hig.*   You are a stranger, brother; I pray,
   lead;
You must, you must, brother.      *Exeunt.*

## Scæna Quinta.

*[Bruges. — The House of Vandunk.]*

*Enter Florez and Bertha*

*Ber.*   Indeed y' are welcome: I have heard
   your scape;
And therefore give her leave, that only loves
   you,
Truly and dearly loves ye, give her joy leave
To bid ye welcome. What is 't makes you sad,
   man?
Why do you look so wild? is 't I offend ye?      5
Beshrew my heart, not willingly.
*Flo.*                              No, Gertrude.
*Ber.*   Is 't the delay of that ye long have
   look'd for, —
A happy marriage? Now I come to urge it;
Now when you please to finish it.
*Flo.* [*Aside.*]                  No news yet? —
*Ber.*   Do you hear, sir?
*Flo.*                                      Yes.
*Ber.*                          Do you love me?
*Flo.* [*Aside.*]                  Have I liv'd      10
In all the happiness fortune could seat me,
In all men's fair opinions —
*Ber.*                        I have provided
A priest, that 's ready for us.
*Flo.* [*Aside.*]                And can the devil,
In one ten days, that devil Chance, devour
   me? —
*Ber.*   We 'll fly to what place you please.
*Flo.* [*Aside.*]              No star prosperous?      15
All at a swoop? —

*Ber.*                    You do not love me, Goswin;
You will not look upon me.
*Flo.* [*Aside.*]                Can men's prayers,
Shot up to Heaven with such a zeal as mine
   are,
Fall back like lazy mists, and never prosper?
Gyves I must wear, and cold must be my
   comfort;                                            20
Darkness, and want of meat. Alas, she weeps
   too!
Which is the top of all my sorrows. — Ger-
   trude.
*Ber.*   No, no, you will not know me; my
   poor beauty,
Which has been worth your eyes —
*Flo.* [*Aside.*]              The time grows on still;
And, like a tumbling wave, I see my ruin      25
Come rolling over me. —
*Ber.*                        Yet will ye know me?
*Flo.* [*Aside.*]   For a hundred thousand
   crowns —
*Ber.*                        Yet will ye love me?
Tell me but how I have deserv'd your slight-
   ing?
*Flo.* [*Aside.*]   For a hundred thousand
   crowns —
*Ber.*                    Farewell, dissembler! —
*Flo.* [*Aside.*]   Of which I have scarce ten.
Oh, how it starts me! —                                30
*Ber.*   And may the next you love, hearing
   my ruin —
*Flo.*   I had forgot myself. Oh, my best
Gertrude,
Crown of my joys and comforts!
*Ber.*                        Sweet, what ail ye?
I thought you had been vex'd with me.
*Flo.*                          My mind, wench,
My mind, o'erflow'd with sorrow, sunk my
   memory.                                             35
*Ber.*   Am I not worthy of the knowledge of
   it?
And cannot I as well affect your sorrows
As your delights? You love no other woman?
*Flo.*   No, I protest.
*Ber.*                    You have no ships lost lately?
*Flo.*   None that I know of.                          40
*Ber.*   I hope you have spilt no blood whose
   innocence
May lay this on your conscience.
*Flo.*                            Clear, by Heaven!
*Ber.*   Why should you be thus, then?
*Flo.*                        Good Gertrude, ask not;
Even by the love you bear me.
*Ber.*                        I am obedient.
*Flo.*   Go in, my fair; I will not be long
   from ye. —                                          45

¹⁵⁴ **Come:** ('Roome' F 1, Q)   ¹⁶²⁻¹⁶³ ('Ye are a stranger' F 1, Q)   **Sc. V Quinta:** ('Quarta' F 1; 'IV'
F 2)   ¹ **scape:** escape   ¹¹ **seat:** settle on   ³⁰ **starts:** causes me to start or flinch   ³⁷ **affect:**
feel

[*Aside.*] Nor long, I fear me, with thee. —
    At my return,
Dispose me as you please.
    *Ber.*        The good gods guide ye! *Exit.*
    *Flo.* Now for myself, which is the least I
        hope for,
And, when that fails, for man's worst fortune,
        pity!                        *Exit.*

## *Actus Quartus, Scæna Prima.*

[*Bruges. — The Exchange.*]

*Enter Florez and 4 Merchants*

*Flo.* Why, gentlemen, 't is but a week more
    I entreat you,
But seven short days; I am not running from
    ye;
Nor, if you give me patience, is it possible
All my adventures fail. You have ships
    abroad                                   4
Endure the beating both of wind and weather:
I am sure 't would vex your hearts to be pro-
    tested:
Ye are all fair merchants.
    *1 Mer.*        Yes, and must have fair play;
There is no living here else: one hour's failing
Fails us of all our friends, of all our credits.
For my part, I would stay, but my wants tell
    me,                                     10
I must wrong others in 't.
    *Flo.*                No mercy in ye?
    *2 Mer.* 'T is foolish to depend on others'
        mercy:
Keep yourself right, and even cut your cloth,
    sir,
According to your calling. You have liv'd
    here
In lord-like prodigality, high, and open,      15
And now ye find what 't is: the liberal spending
The summer of your youth, which you should
    glean in,
And, like the labouring ant, make use and gain
    of,
Has brought this bitter stormy winter on ye,
And now you cry.
    *3 Mer.*        Alas, before your poverty,    20
We were no men, of no mark, no endeavour!
You stood alone, took up all trade, all business
Running through your hands, scarce a sail at
    sea
But loaden with your goods: we, poor weak
    pedlars,
When by your leave, and much entreaty to
    it,                                      25

We could have stowage for a little cloth
Or a few wines, put off, and thank'd your wor-
    ship.
Lord, how the world 's chang'd with ye! Now,
    I hope, sir,
We shall have sea-room.
    *Flo.*            Is my misery
Become my scorn, too? have ye no humanity?
No part of men left? are all the bounties in
    me                                      31
To you, and to the town, turn'd my reproaches?
    *4 Mer.* Well, get your moneys ready: 't is
        but two hours;
We shall protest ye else, and suddenly.
    *Flo.* But two days!
    *1 Mer.*                Not an hour. Ye know
        the hazard.        *Exeunt* [*Merchants*].  35
    *Flo.* How soon my light 's put out! Hard-
        hearted Bruges!
Within thy walls may never honest merchant
Venture his fortunes more! Oh, my poor
    wench too!

*Enter Gerrard*

    *Ger.* Good fortune, master!
    *Flo.*            Thou mistak'st me, Clause;
I am not worth thy blessing.
    *Ger.*                Still a sad man?   40
No belief, gentle master? — Come, bring it in,
    then. —

*Enter Higgen and Prig, like porters,*
    [*bringing in bags of money*]

And now believe your beadsman.
    *Flo.*            Is this certain?
Or dost thou work upon my troubled sense?
    *Ger.*                'T is gold, sir.
Take it, and try it.
    *Flo.*            Certainly, 't is treasure.
Can there be yet this blessing?
    *Ger.*                Cease your wonder:   45
You shall not sink for ne'er a sous'd flap-
    dragon,
For ne'er a pickled pilcher of 'em all, sir.
'T is there; your full sum, a hundred thousand
    crowns:
And, good sweet master, now be merry. Pay
    'em,
Pay the poor pelting knaves that know no
    goodness;                               50
And cheer your heart up handsomely.
    *Flo.*                Good Clause,
How cam'st thou by this mighty sum? if
    naughtily,
I must not take it of thee; 't will undo me.

---

⁴⁷ **Dispose:** ('Despise' F 1)   ⁶ **protested:** publicly proclaimed for non-payment of debts   ⁸ **liv-ing:** ('lying' F 1, Q)   ²¹ **endeavour:** enterprise   ²⁷ **put off:** took off our hats   **thank'd:** ('thank' Ff)   ³¹ **part of men:** human feelings   ⁴⁶ **flap-dragon:** raisin in dish of flaming liquor from which it must be snatched with the mouth   ⁴⁷ **pilcher:** pilchard, herring-like fish   ⁵⁰ **pelting:** paltry

*Ger.* Fear not; you have it by as honest
    means
As though your father gave it. Sir, you know
    not                                                                            55
To what a mass the little we get daily
Mounts in seven years: we beg it for Heaven's
    charity
And to the same good we are bound to render it.
    *Flo.* What great security?
    *Ger.*                                    Away with that, sir!
Were not ye more than all the men in Bruges,
And all the money, in my thoughts —
    *Flo.*                            But, good Clause,        61
I may die presently.
    *Ger.*                        Then this dies with ye.
Pay when you can, good master; I 'll no parch-
    ments:
Only this charity I shall entreat ye, —
Leave me this ring.
    *Flo.*        Alas, it is too poor, Clause!        65
    *Ger.* 'T is all I ask; and this withal, that
    when
I shall deliver this back, you shall grant me
Freely one poor petition.
    *Flo.*                                    There; I confirm it;
                                            *Gives the ring.*
And may my faith forsake me when I shun it!
    *Ger.* Away! your time draws on. Take up
    the money,                                                            70
And follow this young gentleman.
    *Flo.*                                    Farewell, Clause,
And may thy honest memory live ever.
    *Ger.* Heaven bless ye, and still keep ye!
    farewell, master.                                        *Exeunt.*

### Scæna Secunda.

*[The Woods near Bruges.]*

*Enter Hubert [disguised as before]*

*Hub.* I have lock'd my youth up, close
    enough for gadding,
In an old tree, and set watch over him.

#### Enter Jacqueline

Now for my love, for sure this wench must be
    she;
She follows me. — Come hither, pretty Minche.
    *Jac.* No, no, you 'll kiss.
    *Hub.*                        So I will.
    *Jac.*                                    I'deed, la!        5
How will ye kiss me, pray you?
    *Hub.*                        Thus. — *[Aside.]* Soft as
    my love's lips! —
    *Jac.* Oh!
    *Hub.* What 's your father's name?
    *Jac.*                            He 's gone to heaven.

*Hub.* Is it not Gerrard, sweet?
    *Jac.* *[Aside.]*                    I 'll stay no longer. —
My mother 's an old woman, and my brother
Was drown'd at sea with catching cockles. —
    *[Aside.]* Oh, love!                                        10
Oh, how my heart melts in me! how thou firest
    me! —
    *Hub.* *[Aside.]* 'T is certain she. — Pray let
    me see your hand, sweet.
    *Jac.* No, no, you 'll bite it.
    *Hub.*            Sure, I should know that gimmal.
    *Jac.* *[Aside.]* 'T is certain he: I had forgot
    my ring, too.
Oh, Hubert, Hubert! —
    *Hub.* *[Aside.]* Ha! Methought she nam'd
    me. —                                                            15
Do you know me, chick?
    *Jac.*                        No, indeed; I never saw ye;
But, methinks, you kiss finely.
    *Hub.*                        Kiss again, then. —
*[Aside.]* By heaven, 't is she! —
    *Jac.* *[Aside.]*                    Oh, what a joy
    he brings me! —
    *Hub.* You are not Minche?
    *Jac.*                        Yes, pretty gentleman;
And I must be married to-morrow to a cap-
    per.                                                                20
    *Hub.* Must ye, my sweet? and does the
    capper love ye?
    *Jac.* Yes, yes; he 'll give me pie, and look
    in mine eyes, thus. —
*[Aside.]* 'T is he; 't is my dear love! oh, blest
    fortune!
    *Hub.* *[Aside.]* How fain she would conceal
    herself, yet shows it! —
Will ye love me, and leave that man? I 'll
    serve —                                                            25
    *Jac.* *[Aside.]* Oh, I shall lose myself! —
    *Hub.*                        I 'll wait upon ye,
And make ye dainty nosegays.
    *Jac.*                        And where will ye stick 'em?
    *Hub.* Here in thy bosom; and make a
    crown of lilies
For your fair head.
    *Jac.*                    And will ye love me, 'deed la?
    *Hub.* With all my heart.
    *Jac.*                        Call me to-morrow, then,    30
And we 'll have brave cheer, and go to church
    together.
Give you good ev'n, sir.
    *Hub.*                    But one word, fair Minche!
    *Jac.* I must be gone a-milking.
    *Hub.*                        Ye shall presently
Did you never hear of a young maid call'd Jac-
    queline?
    *Jac.* *[Aside.]* I am discover'd. — Hark in
    your ear; I 'll tell ye:                                    35

You must not know me; kiss, and be constant
ever.

*Hub.* Heaven curse me else! — [*Aside.*]
'T is she; and now I am certain
They are all here. Now for my other project!
          *Exeunt.*

## Scæna Tertia.

[*Bruges. — The Exchange.*]

*Enter Florez, 4 Merchants; Higgen and Prig,
[disguised as before, with bags of money]*

*1 Mer.* Nay, if 't would do you courtesy —
*Flo.*       None at all, sir:
Take it, 't is yours; there 's your ten thousand
for ye;
Give in my bills. — Your sixteen.
 *3 Mer.*     Pray, be pleas'd, sir,
To make a further use.
 *Flo.*      No.
 *3 Mer.*     What I have, sir,
You may command. Pray, let me be your
 servant.           5
 *Flo.* Put your hats on: I care not for your
 courtesies;
They are most untimely done, and no truth in
 'em.
 *2 Mer.* I have a fraught of pepper —
 *Flo.*       Rot your pepper!
Shall I trust you again? There 's your seven
 thousand.
 *4 Mer.* Or, if you want fine sugar, 't is but
 sending.           10
 *Flo.* No, I can send to Barbary; those
 people,
That never yet knew faith, have nobler freedoms. —
These carry to Vanlock, and take my bills in;
To Peter Zuten these; bring back my jewels. —
Why are these pieces?    [*Guns fired.*]

*Enter Sailor*

 *Sail.*   Health to the noble merchant! 15
The *Susan* is return'd.
 *Flo.*     Well?
 *Sail.*       Well, and rich, sir,
And now put in.
 *Flo.* Heaven, thou hast heard my prayers!
 *Sail.* The brave *Rebecca*, too, bound from
 the Straits,
With the next tide is ready to put after.
 *Flo.* What news o' th' fly-boat?
 *Sail.*    If this wind hold till midnight, 20
She will be here, and wealthy; escap'd fairly.
 *Flo.* How, prithee, sailor?
 *Sail.*     Thus, sir: she had fight,

Seven hours together, with six Turkish galleys,
And she fought bravely, but at length was
 boarded,
And overlaid with strength; when presently 25
Comes boring up the wind Captain Vannoke,
That valiant gentleman you redeem'd from
 prison:
He knew the boat, set in, and fought it bravely;
Beat all the galleys off, sunk three, redeem'd
 her,
And, as a service to ye, sent her home, sir. 30
 *Flo.* An honest, noble captain, and a thank-
 ful.
There 's for thy news: go, drink the merchant's
 health, sailor.     [*Gives money.*]
 *Sail.* I thank your bounty, and I 'll do it
 to a doit, sir.     *Exit Sailor.*
 *1 Mer.* What miracles are pour'd upon this
 fellow!
 *Flo.* This year, I hope, my friends, I shall
 scape prison,         35
For all your cares to catch me.
 *2 Mer.*    You may please, sir,
To think of your poor servants in displeasure,
Whose all they have, goods, moneys, are at
 your service.
 *Flo.* I thank you;
When I have need of you, I shall forget you. 40
You are paid, I hope?
 *All.*    We joy in your good fortunes.
           [*Exeunt.*]

*Enter Vandunk*

 *Vand.* Come, sir, come, take your ease; you
 must go home with me;
Yonder is one weeps and howls.
 *Flo.*      Alas, how does she?
 *Vand.* She will be better soon, I hope.
 *Flo.*        Why soon, sir?
 *Vand.* Why, when you have her in your
 arms: this night, my boy,     45
She is thy wife.
 *Flo.*    With all my heart I take her.
 *Vand.* We have prepar'd; all thy friends
 will be there,
And all my rooms shall smoke to see the revel.
Thou hast been wrong'd, and no more shall my
 service
Wait on the knave her uncle: I have heard
 all,             50
All his baits for my boy; but thou shalt have
 her.
Hast thou despatch'd thy business?
 *Flo.*       Most.
 *Vand.*       By the mass, boy,
Thou tumblest now in wealth, and I joy in it;

---

 **4 use:** loan  **12 freedoms:** habits of generosity  **20 fly-boat:** fast-sailing vessel  **25 overlaid:**
overpowered  **35 This year:** ('This ye are' F 1; 'This here' F 2)  **51 baits:** traps  **52 despatch'd:**
finished

Thou art the best boy that Bruges ever
  nourish'd.                   54
Thou hast been sad: I 'll cheer thee up with sack,
And, when thou art lusty, I 'll fling thee to thy
  mistress:
She 'll hug thee, sirrah.
    *Flo.*              I long to see it. —
I had forgot you: there 's for you, my friends;
  [*To Higgen and Prig, giving them money.*]
You had but heavy burthens. Commend my
  love
To Clause; my best love, all the love I have,   60
To honest Clause; shortly I will thank him
  better.          *Exit* [*with Vandunk*].
  *Hig.* By the mass, a royal merchant! gold
  by the handful!
Here will be sport soon, Prig.
  *Prig.*          It partly seems so;
And here will I be in a trice.
  *Hig.*           And I, boy.
Away apace! we are look'd for.
  *Prig.*       Oh, these bak'd meats!   65
Methinks I smell them hither.
  *Hig.*      Thy mouth waters. *Exeunt.*

## Scæna Quarta.

### [*The Woods near Bruges.*]

*Enter Hubert [disguised as before], and*
*Hemskirk*

  *Hub.* I must not.
  *Hem.*     Why? 't is in thy power to do it,
And in mine to reward thee to thy wishes.
  *Hub.* I dare not, nor I will not.
  *Hem.*          Gentle huntsman,
Though thou hast kept me hard, though in thy
  duty,
Which is requir'd to do it, th' hast used me
  stubbornly,                5
I can forgive thee freely.
  *Hub.*       You the earl's servant?
  *Hem.* I swear, I am near as his own thoughts
  to him;
Able to do thee —
  *Hub.*     Come, come, leave your prating.
  *Hem.* If thou dar'st but try —
  *Hub.*     I thank you heartily; you will be
The first man that will hang me; a sweet recom-
  pense!                10
I could do 't (but I do not say I will)
To any honest fellow that would think on 't,
And be a benefactor.
  *Hem.* If it be not recompens'd, and to thy
  own desires;
If, within these ten days, I do not make thee —

  *Hub.* What? a false knave?       16
  *Hem.* Prithee, prithee, conceive me rightly;
  anything
Of profit or of place that may advance thee —
  *Hub.* Why, what a goosecap wouldst thou
  make me! do not I know
That men in misery will promise anything,   20
More than their lives can reach at?
  *Hem.*       Believe me, huntsman,
There shall not one short syllable that comes
  from me pass
Without its full performance.
  *Hub.*          Say you so, sir?
Have ye e'er a good place for my quality?
  *Hem.* A thousand; chases, forests, parks;
  I 'll make thee               25
Chief ranger over all the games.
  *Hub.*          When?
  *Hem.*              Presently.
  *Hub.* This may provoke me: and yet, to
  prove a knave, too —
  *Hem.* 'T is to prove honest; 't is to do good
  service,
Service for him thou art sworn to, for thy
  prince:
Then, for thyself that good. What fool would
  live here                30
Poor, and in misery, subject to all dangers
Law and lewd people can inflict, when bravely,
And to himself, he may be law and credit?
  *Hub.* Shall I believe thee?
  *Hem.*     As that thou hold'st most holy.
  *Hub.* Ye may play tricks.
  *Hem.*     Then let me never live more.   35
  *Hub.* Then you shall see, sir, I will do a
  service
That shall deserve, indeed.
  *Hem.*       'T is well said, huntsman.
And thou shalt be well thought of.
  *Hub.*         I will do it:
'T is not your setting free, for that 's mere
  nothing,
But such a service, if the earl be noble,   40
He shall for ever love me.
  *Hem.*       What is 't, huntsman?
  *Hub.* Do you know any of these people
  live here?
  *Hem.* No.
  *Hub.* You are a fool, then: here be those,
  to have 'em,
I know the earl so well, would make him
  caper.
  *Hem.* Any of the old lords that rebell'd?
  *Hub.*           Peace! all:   45
I know 'em every one, and can betray 'em.
  *Hem.* But wilt thou do this service?

---

**55** sack: sweet Spanish wine   **60** Clause: (not in Ff, Q)   **2** to thy: according to thy   **5** stubbornly: harshly   **11** do 't: ('do' Ff, Q)   **17** conceive: understand   **19** goosecap: fool   **26** Presently:
immediately   **32** lewd: worthless, rude   **39** setting: ('letting' F 1, Q)

*Hub.*                               If you 'll keep
Your faith and free word to me.
*Hem.*                        Wilt thou swear me?
*Hub.*  No, no, I will believe ye. More than
   that, too,
Here 's the right heir.
*Hem.*        Oh, honest, honest huntsman! 50
*Hub.*  Now, how to get these gallants,
   there 's the matter.
You will be constant? 't is no work for me else.
*Hem.*  Will the sun shine again?
*Hub.*                        The way to get 'em!
*Hem.*  Propound it, and it shall be done.
*Hub.*                            No sleight
(For they are devilish crafty, it concerns 'em),
Nor reconcilement (for they dare not trust,
   neither),                                     56
Must do this trick.
*Hem.*            By force?
*Hub.*                    Ay, that must do it;
And with the person of the earl himself:
Authority, and mighty, must come on 'em, 59
Or else in vain: and thus I would have ye do it.
To-morrow night be here; a hundred men will
   bear 'em,
So he be there, for he 's both wise and valiant,
And with his terror will strike dead their forces:
The hour be twelve o'clock: now, for a guide
To draw ye without danger on these persons, 65
The woods being thick and hard to hit, myself,
With some few with me, made unto our purpose,
Beyond the wood, upon the plain, will wait ye
By the great oak.
*Hem.*        I know it. Keep thy faith,
   huntsman,
And such a shower of wealth —
*Hub.*              I warrant ye: 70
Miss nothing that I tell ye.
*Hem.*                No.
*Hub.*                    Farewell.
You have your liberty; now use it wisely,
And keep your hour. Go closer about the
   wood there,
For fear they spy you.
*Hem.*        Well.
*Hub.*            And bring no noise with ye.
*Hem.*  All shall be done to th' purpose.
   Farewell, huntsman.        *Exeunt.* 75

[SCENE V. — *Another Part of the Woods.*]

*Enter Gerrard, Higgin, Prig, Ginks, Snap, Ferret*

*Ger.*  Now, what 's the news in town?
*Ginks.*                No news, but joy, sir;

Every man wooing of the noble merchant,
Who has his hearty commendations to ye.
*Fer.*  Yes, this is news; this night he 's to
   be married.
*Ginks.*  By th' mass, that 's true; he marries
   Vandunk's daughter,                          5
The dainty black-eyed belle.
*Hig.*              I would my clapper
Hung in his baldrick! what a peal could I ring!
*Ger.*  Married!
*Ginks.*        'T is very true, sir. Oh, the pies,
The piping-hot mince-pies!
*Prig.*                Oh, the plum-pottage!
*Hig.*  For one leg of a goose, now, would I
   venture a limb, boys:                         10
I love a fat goose, as I love allegiance;
And, pox upon the boors, too well they know
   it,
And therefore starve their poultry.
*Ger.*                    To be married
To Vandunk's daughter!
*Hig.*            Oh, this precious merchant!
What sport he will have! But, hark ye, brother
   Prig;                                        15
Shall we do nothing in the foresaid wedding?
There 's money to be got, and meat, I take it:
What think ye of a morris?
*Prig.*            No, by no means;
That goes no further than the street, there
   leaves us:
Now, we must think of something that must
   draw us                                       20
Into the bowels of it, into th' buttery,
Into the kitchen, into the cellar; something
That that old drunken burgomaster loves:
What think ye of a wassail?
*Hig.*                I think worthily.
*Prig.*  And very fit it should be: thou, and
   Ferret,                                       25
And Ginks, to sing the song; I for the structure,
Which is the bowl.
*Hig.*            Which must be upsey-English,
Strong, lusty, London beer. Let 's think more
   of it.
*Ger.* [*Aside.*]  He must not marry. —

*Enter Hubert*

*Hub.*                  By your leave, in private,
One word, sir, with ye. Gerrard! do not start
   me:                                           30
I know ye, and he knows ye, that best loves ye:
Hubert speaks to ye, and you must be Gerrard:
The time invites you to it.
*Ger.*                Make no show, then.

---

⁵⁴ **sleight:** trick    ⁶⁷ **made:** persuaded, converted    ⁷³ **keep . . . hour:** be on time    **closer:** more secretly    Sc. V: (Not marked, Ff, Q)    ⁶ **belle:** The first recorded instance of this word; ('bell' Ff, Q)    ⁷ **baldrick:** belt, bell-rope    ¹² **pox:** (represented by a dash, Ff, Q)    ¹⁸ **morris:** grotesque dance    ²¹ **buttery:** storage room for provisions    ²⁴ **wassail:** revel    ²⁷ **upsey-English:** in the English manner    ³⁰ **me:** (the so-called "ethical dative")

I am glad to see you, sir; and I am Gerrard.
How stand affairs?

*Hub.*       Fair, if ye dare now follow. 35
Hemskirk, I have let go, and these my causes
I 'll tell ye privately, and how I have wrought
  him:
And then, to prove me honest to my friends,
Look upon these directions; you have seen his.
                     [*Gives a paper.*]

*Hig.* Then will I speak a speech, and a
  brave speech,          40
In praise of merchants. Where 's the ape?

*Prig.*          Pox take him!
A gouty bear-ward stole him the other day.

*Hig.* May his bears worry him! That ape
  had paid it:
What dainty tricks, — (pox o' that whoreson
  bear-ward!)
In his French doublet, with his blister'd bul-
  lions,                    45
In a long stock tied up. Oh, how daintily
Would I have made him wait, and change a
  trencher,
Carry a cup of wine! Ten thousand stinks
Wait on thy mangy hide, thou lousy bear-ward!

*Ger.* [*To Hubert.*] 'T is passing well; I both
  believe and joy in 't,         50
And will be ready. Keep you here the mean
  while,
And keep this in. — I must a while forsake
  ye:
Upon mine anger, no man stir this two hours.

*Hig.* Not to the wedding, sir?

*Ger.*          Not any whither.

*Hig.* The wedding must be seen, sir: we
  want meat, too;         55
We be monstrous out of meat.

*Prig.*          Shall it be spoken,
Fat capons shak'd their tails at 's in defiance?
And turkey-tombs, such honourable monu-
  ments?
Shall pigs, sir, that the parson's self would envy,
And dainty ducks —

*Ger.*        Not a word more! obey me. 60
                        *Exit Ger.*

*Hig.* Why, then, come doleful death! This
  is flat tyranny,
And, by this hand —

*Hub.* What?

*Hig.* I 'll go sleep upon 't. *Exit Hig.*

*Prig.* Nay, and there be a wedding, and we
  wanting,
Farewell, our happy days! — We do obey, sir.
                        *Exeunt.*

## Scæna Sexta.

[*Bruges. — Before the House of Vandunk.*]

### Enter two young Merchants

*1 Mer.* Well met, sir: you are for this lusty
  wedding?

*2 Mer.* I am so; so are you, I take it.

*1 Mer.*                  Yes;
And it much glads me, that to do him service,
Who is the honour of our trade, and lustre,
We meet thus happily.

*2 Mer.*        He 's a noble fellow, 5
And well becomes a bride of such a beauty.

*1 Mer.* She is passing fair, indeed. Long
  may their loves
Continue like their youths, in spring of sweet-
  ness!
All the young merchants will be here, no doubt
  on 't;
For he that comes not to attend this wedding,
The curse of a most blind one fall upon him, 11
A loud wife, and a lazy! — Here 's Vanlock.

### Enter Vanlock and Frances

*Vanl.* Well overtaken, gentlemen: save ye!

*1 Mer.* The same to you, sir. — Save ye,
  fair Mistress Frances!
I would this happy night might make you
  blush, too.              15

*Vanl.* She dreams apace.

*Fran.*         That 's but a drowsy fortune.

*2 Mer.* Nay, take us with ye, too; we come
  to that end:
I am sure ye are for the wedding.

*Vanl.*           Hand and heart, man,
And what these feet can do; I could have
  tripp'd it
Before this whoreson gout.

### Enter Gerrard

*Ger.*           Bless ye, masters! 20

*Vanl.* Clause! how now, Clause? thou art
  come to see thy master
(And a good master he is to all poor people)
In all his joy; 't is honestly done of thee.

*Ger.* Long may he live, sir! but my business
  now is,
If you would please to do it, and to him
  too —                    25

### Enter Florez

*Vanl.* He 's here himself.

*Flo.*         Stand at the door, my friends!

---

³⁷ **wrought:** worked on (him) for my own purposes      ⁴¹, ⁴⁴ **Pox:** (represented by a dash, Ff, Q)
⁴² **bear-ward:** keeper of a trained bear    ⁴⁴ **whoreson:** rascally    ⁴⁵ **bullions:** trunk hose, puffed out
at the top    ⁴⁶ **stock:** stockings    ⁴⁷ **change:** ('shift' F 2)    **trencher:** wooden dish    ⁵⁶ **be mon-**
**strous:** ('are horrible' F 2)    ⁵⁸ **tombs:** pies    Sc. VI **Sexta:** ('Quinta' Ff, Q)    ¹⁹ **these:** ('their'
Ff, Q)

I pray, walk in. Welcome, fair Mistress
　　Frances;
See what the house affords: there 's a young
　　lady
Will bid you welcome.
　*Vanl.*　　　　　　We joy your happiness.
　*Flo.* I hope it will be so.
　　　　*Exeunt [all except Florez and Gerrard].*
　　　　　　Clause, nobly welcome!　30
My honest, my best friend, I have been careful
To see thy moneys —
　*Ger.*　　　　　Sir, that brought not me.
Do you know this ring again?
　*Flo.*　　　　　　Thou hadst it of me.
　*Ger.* And do you well remember yet the
　　boon you gave me,
Upon return of this?
　*Flo.*　　　　　Yes, and I grant it,　35
Be it what it will: ask what thou canst, I 'll
　do it,
Within my power.
　*Ger.*　　　　Ye are not married yet?
　*Flo.*　　　　　　　　　　No.
　*Ger.* Faith, I shall ask you that that will
　　disturb ye;
But I must put ye to your promise.
　*Flo.*　　　　　　　　　Do;
And, if I faint and flinch in 't —
　*Ger.*　　　　　　Well said, master!　40
And yet it grieves me, too; and yet it must be.
　*Flo.* Prithee, distrust me not.
　*Ger.*　　　　　　You must not marry:
That 's part of the power you gave me; which
　to make up,
You must presently depart, and follow me.
　*Flo.* Not marry, Clause!
　*Ger.*　　　Not if you keep your promise,　45
And give me power to ask.
　*Flo.*　　　　　Prithee, think better:
I will obey, by Heaven!
　*Ger.*　　　　I have thought the best, sir.
　*Flo.* Give me thy reason: dost thou fear
　　her honesty?
　*Ger.* Chaste as the ice, for anything I know,
　sir.
　*Flo.* Why shouldst thou light on that, then?
　　to what purpose?　50
　*Ger.* I must not now discover.
　*Flo.*　　　　　　Must not marry.
Shall I break now, when my poor heart is
　pawn'd?
When all the preparation —
　*Ger.*　　　　　　Now, or never.
　*Flo.* Come, 't is not that thou wouldst; thou
　　dost but fright me.
　*Ger.* Upon my soul, it is, sir; and I bind
　ye.　55
　*Flo.* Clause, canst thou be so cruel?

　*Ger.*　　　　　　You may break, sir;
But never more in my thoughts appear honest.
　*Flo.* Didst ever see her?
　*Ger.*　　　　No.
　*Flo.*　　　　　She is such a thing, —
Oh, Clause, she is such a wonder! such a mirror.
For beauty and fair virtue, Europe has not!　6u
Why hast thou made me happy to undo me?
But look upon her; then, if thy heart relent not,
I 'll quit her presently. — Who waits there?
　*Serv. (Within.)*　　　　　　　Sir?
　*Flo.* Bid my fair love come hither, and the
　　company. —
Prithee, be good unto me: take a man's
　heart,　65
And look upon her truly; take a friend's heart,
And feel what misery must follow this.
　*Ger.* Take you a noble heart, and keep your
　　promise:
I forsook all I had, to make you happy.
Can that thing, call'd a woman, stop your
　goodness?　70

　　　*Enter Bertha, Vandunk, and the rest*
　　　　　　　*Merchants*

　*Flo.* Look, there she is: deal with me as
　　thou wilt now:
Didst ever see a fairer?
　*Ger.*　　　　She is most goodly.
　*Flo.* Pray ye, stand still.
　*Ber.*　　　　　What ails my love?
　*Flo.*　　　　　　Didst thou ever,
By the fair light of Heaven, behold a sweeter?
Oh, that thou knew'st but love, or ever felt
　him!　75
Look well, look narrowly upon her beauties.
　*1 Mer.* Sure, h'as some strange design in
　　hand, he starts so.
　*2 Mer.* This beggar has a strong power over
　　his pleasure.
　*Flo.* View all her body.
　*Ger.*　　　　'T is exact and excellent.
　*Flo.* Is she a thing, then, to be lost thus
　　lightly?　80
Her mind is ten times sweeter, ten times
　nobler;
And but to hear her speak, a paradise;
And such a love she bears to me, a chaste love,
A virtuous, fair, and fruitful love! 't is now, too,
I am ready to enjoy it; the priest ready,
　Clause,　85
To say the holy words shall make us happy:
This is a cruelty beyond man's study:
All these are ready, all our joys are ready,
And all the expectation of our friends:
'T will be her death to do it.
　*Ger.*　　　　Let her die, then.　90
　*Flo.* Thou canst not; 't is impossible.

────────────────────────────

²⁹ **joy:** rejoice in　⁴⁸ **honesty:** chastity

*Ger.*                 It must be.
*Flo.* 'T will kill me, too; 't will murder me.
By Heaven, Clause,
I 'll give thee half I have! come, thou shalt
save me.
*Ger.* Then you must go with me, — I can
stay no longer, —
If ye be true and noble.
*Flo.*          Hard heart, I 'll follow. 95
                 [*Exit Gerrard.*]
Pray ye, all go in again, and, pray, be merry:
I have a weighty business — Give my cloak
there! —

      *Enter Servant, with a cloak*

Concerns my life and state — make no in-
quiry —
This present hour befall'n me: with the soonest
I shall be here again. Nay, pray, go in, sir, 100
And take them with you. — 'T is but a night
lost, gentlemen.
*Vand.* Come, come in; we will not lose our
meat yet,
Nor our good mirth; he cannot stay long from
her,
I am sure of that.
*Flo.*       I will not stay, believe sir. —
    *Exit [Vandunk with Merchants and
           Servant].*
Gertrude, a word with you.
*Ber.*         Why is this stop, sir? 105
*Flo.* I have no more time left me, but to
kiss thee,
And tell thee this, — I am ever thine: farewell,
wench.                  *Exit.*
*Ber.* And is that all your ceremony? is this
a wedding?
Are all my hopes and prayers turn'd to nothing?
Well, I will say no more, nor sigh, nor sorrow —
Oh me! — till to thy face I prove thee false. 111
                     *Exit.*


*Actus Quintus, Scæna Prima.*

[*A Plain by the Woods near Bruges.*]

    *Enter Bertha [masked], and a Boor
           [with a torch]*

*Ber.* Lead, if thou think'st we are right.
Why dost thou make
These often stands? thou said'st thou knew'st
the way.
*Boor.* Fear nothing; I do know it. —
[*Aside.*] Would 't were homeward! —
*Ber.* [*Aside.*] Wrought from me by a beg-
gar! at the time

That most should tie him! 'T is some other
love,                            5
That hath a more command on his affections;
And he that fetch'd him a disguised agent,
Not what he personated, for his fashion
Was more familiar with him, and more power-
ful,
Than one that ask'd an alms: I must find out
One, if not both. Kind darkness, be my
shroud,                        11
And cover love's too-curious search in me!
For yet, suspicion, I would not name thee. —
*Boor.* Mistress, it grows somewhat pretty
and dark.
*Ber.*        What then?
*Boor.* Nay, nothing. Do not think I am
afraid,                          15
Although perhaps you are.
*Ber.*        I am not. Forward!
*Boor.* Sure, but you are. Give me your
hand; fear nothing.
There 's one leg in the wood: do not pull back-
ward.
What a sweat one on 's are in, you or I!
Pray God it do not prove the plague! yet,
sure,                        20
It has infected me; for I sweat, too;
It runs out at my knees: feel, feel, I pray you.
*Ber.* What ails the fellow?
*Boor.*       Hark, hark, I beseech you!
Do you hear nothing?
*Ber.*       No.
*Boor.*            List! a wild hog;
He grunts: now 't is a bear; this wood is full
of 'em:                        25
And now a wolf, mistress; a wolf, a wolf;
It is the howling of a wolf.
*Ber.*           The braying
Of an ass, is it not?
*Boor.*        Oh, now one has me.
Oh, my left ham! — Farewell.
*Ber.*          Look to your shanks;
Your breech is safe enough; the wolf 's a fern-
brake.                        30
*Boor.* But see, see, see! there is a serpent
in it;
It has eyes as broad as platters; it spits fire;
Now it creeps towards us: help me to say my
prayers:
It hath swallow'd me almost; my breath is
stopp'd;
I cannot speak: do I speak, mistress? tell
me.                        35
*Ber.* Why, thou strange timorous sot, canst
thou perceive
Anything i' th' bush but a poor glow-worm?

**99** with the soonest: immediately    ¹¹¹ **Oh me:** ('Ah me' F 2, removed to end of line)    ⁵ **often:**
**frequent**    ⁶ **more:** greater    ⁸ **fashion:** manner    ¹⁸ **pull:** ('pull me' F 2)    ²⁹ **ham:** ('haunch' F 2)
**36 strange:** (not in F 1, Q)

*Boor.* It may be 't is but a glow-worm now;
but 't will
Grow to a fire-drake presently.
   *Ber.*               Come thou from it.
I have a precious guide of you, and a courte-
ous,                                 40
That gives me leave to lead myself the way
thus.
   *Within.*  Holla!
   *Boor.* It thunders: you hear that now?
   *Ber.*                 I hear one holla.
   *Boor.* 'T is thunder, thunder: see, a flash of
lightning!
Are you not blasted, mistress? pull your mask
off:                                  45
It has play'd the barber with me here; I have
lost
My beard, my beard: pray God you be not
shaven!
'T will spoil your marriage, mistress.
   *Ber.*             What strange wonders
Fear fancies in a coward!
   *Boor.*        Now the earth opens.
   *Ber.* Prithee, hold thy peace.
   *Boor.*          Will you on, then?  50
   *Ber.* Both love and jealousy have made
me bold:
Where my fate leads me I must go.
   *Boor.*          God be with you, then!
                       *Exit* [*Bertha*].

*Enter Wolfort, Hemskirk, and Attendants*

   *Hem.* It was the fellow, sure, he that should
guide me,
The huntsman, that did holla us.
   *Wol.*              Best make a stand,
And listen to his next. — Ha!
   *Hem.*           Who goes there?  55
   *Boor.* Mistress, I am taken.
   *Hem.*        Mistress! — Look forth, soldiers.
                    [*Exeunt Soldiers.*]
   *Wol.* What are you, sirrah?
   *Boor.*             Truly, all is left
Of a poor boor by daylight; by night, nobody.
You might have spar'd your drum, and guns,
and pikes, too,
For I am none that will stand out, sir, I:   60
You may take me in with a walking-stick,
Even when you please, and hold me with a
pack-thread.
   *Hem.* What woman was 't you call'd to?
   *Boor.*            Woman! none, sir.
   *Wol.* None! did you not name mistress?
   *Boor.*            Yes, but she 's
No woman yet: she should have been this
night,                            65

But that a beggar stole away her bridegroom,
Whom we were going to make hue and cry
after.
I tell you true, sir; she should ha' been married
to-day,
And was the bride and all; but in came Clause,
The old lame beggar, and whips up Master
Goswin                            70
Under his arm, away with him; as a kite,
Or an old fox, would swoop away a gosling.

       [*Enter Soldiers with Bertha*]

   *Hem.* 'T is she, 't is she, 't is she! Niece!
   *Ber.*                       Ha!
   *Hem.*                      She, sir!
This was a noble entrance to your fortune,
That, being on the point thus to be married,  75
Upon her venture here, you should surprise her.
   *Wol.* I begin, Hemskirk, to believe my fate
Works to my ends.
   *Hem.*           Yes, sir; and this adds trust
Unto the fellow our guide, who assur'd me
Florez
Liv'd in some merchant's shape, as Gerrard did
I' the old beggar's, and that he would use   81
Him for the train to call the other forth;
All which we find is done.     *Holla again.*
   *Hem.*           That 's he again.
   *Wol.* Good we sent out to meet him.
   *Hem.*              Here 's the oak.
   *Ber.* Oh, I am miserably lost, thus fall'n  85
Into my uncle's hands from all my hopes!
No matter now, whe'r thou be false or no,
Goswin; whether thou love another better,
Or me alone; or whe'r thou keep thy vow
And word, or that thou come or stay; for I  90
To thee from henceforth must be ever absent,
And thou to me. No more shall we come near,
To tell ourselves how bright each other's eyes
were,
How soft our language, and how sweet our
kisses,
Whilst we made one our food, th' other our
feast;                               95
Not mix our souls by sight, or by a letter,
Hereafter; but as small relation have,
As two new gone to inhabiting a grave.
Can I not think away myself and die?

*Enter Hubert* [*disguised as before*], *Higgen,
   Prig, Ferret, Snap, Ginks, like Boors*

   *Hub.* I like your habits well: they are safe;
stand close.                             100
   *Hig.* But what 's the action we are for now,
ha?
Robbing a ripper of his fish?

³⁹ **fire-drake:** fiery dragon    ⁶¹ **take me in:** conquer me    ⁸⁰ **shape:** ('shop' F 1, Q)    ⁸² **train:**
artifice    ⁸⁵ᵇ⁻⁹⁹ (Corruptly printed in F 1, Q; reduced to three lines in F 2)    ⁸⁷ **whe'r:** whether
¹⁰⁰ **close:** hidden    ¹⁰² **ripper:** rippier, itinerant fishmonger

*Prig.*                   Or taking
A poulterer prisoner, without ransom, bullies?
   *Hig.*    Or cutting off a convoy of butter?
   *Fer.*    Or surprising a boor's ken, for grunting-
cheats?                          105
   *Prig.*    Or cackling-cheats?
   *Hig.*         Or Margery-praters, Rogers,
And Tibs o' th' buttery?
   *Prig.*        Oh, I could drive a regiment
Of geese afore me, such a night as this,
Ten leagues, with my hat and staff, and not a
hiss
Heard, nor a wing of my troops disorder'd!
   *Hig.*                  Tell us,    110
If it be milling of a lag of duds,
The fetching of a buck of clothes, or so?
We are horribly out of linen.
   *Hub.*             No such matter.
   *Hig.*    Let me alone for any farmer's dog,
If you have a mind to the cheese-loft; 't is but
thus —                          115
And he is a silenc'd mastiff, during pleasure.
   *Hub.*    Would it would please you to be
silent!
   *Hig.*    Mum.
   *Wol.*    Who 's there?
   *Hub.*           A friend; the huntsman.
   *Hem.*                  Oh, 't is he.
   *Hub.*    I have kept touch, sir. Which is the
earl, of these?
Will ye know a man now?
   *Hem.*          This, my lord, 's the friend    120
Hath undertook the service.
   *Hub.*           If 't be worth
His lordship's thanks, anon, when 't is done,
Lording, I 'll look for 't. A rude woodman, I
Know how to pitch my toils, drive in my game;
And I have done 't; both Florez and his
father                          125
Old Gerrard, with Lord Arnold of Benthuisen,
Costin, and Jacqueline, young Florez' sister:
I have 'em all.
   *Wol.*    Thou speak'st too much, too happy,
To carry faith with it.
   *Hub.*           I can bring you
Where you shall see, and find 'em.
   *Wol.*          We will double    130
Whatever Hemskirk then hath promis'd thee.
   *Hub.*    And I 'll deserve it treble. What
horse ha' you?
   *Wol.*    A hundred.
   *Hub.*          That 's well. Ready to take
Upon surprise of 'em?

   *Hem.*         Yes.
   *Hub.*                 Divide, then,
Your force into five squadrons; for there
are                          135
So many outlets, ways thorough the wood,
That issue from the place where they are
lodg'd;
Five several ways; of all which passages
We must possess ourselves, to round 'em in;
For by one starting-hole they 'll all escape
else.                         140
I, and four boors here to me, will be guides:
The squadron where you are myself will lead;
And, that they may be more secure, I 'll use
My wonted whoops and hollas, as I were
A hunting for 'em; which will make them
rest                         145
Careless of any noise, and be a direction
To the other guides how we approach 'em still.
   *Wol.*    'T is order'd well, and relisheth the
soldier.
Make the division, Hemskirk. — You are my
charge,
Fair one; I 'll look to you.
   *Boor.*            Shall nobody need    150
To look to me. I 'll look unto myself.
                   [*Aside, and then runs off.*]
   *Hub.*    'T is but this, remember.
   *Hig.*          Say, 't is done, boy. *Exeunt.*

### Scæna Secunda.

*[Woods near Bruges.]*

*Enter Gerrard and Florez*

   *Ger.*    By this time, sir, I hope you want no
reasons
Why I broke off your marriage; for, though I
Should as a subject study you my prince
In things indifferent, it will not therefore
Discredit you to acknowledge me your father, 5
By hearkening to my necessary counsels.
   *Flo.*    Acknowledge you my father! sir, I do;
                         [*Kneels.*]
And may impiety, conspiring with
My other sins, sink me, and suddenly,
When I forget to pay you a son's duty    10
In my obedience, and that help'd forth
With all the cheerfulness —
   *Ger.*         I pray you, rise; [*Florez rises.*]
And may those powers that see and love this
in you
Reward you for it! Taught by your example,

---

[105] **ken:** house    **grunting-cheats:** pigs    [106] **cackling-cheats:** fowls    **Margery-praters:** hens
**Rogers:** geese    [107] **Tibs . . . buttery:** geese    [111] **milling . . . duds:** stealing a tubful of clothes
[112] **buck:** washtub ('back' Ff, Q)    [119] **kept touch:** kept my promise    [120] **ye:** ('he' F 2)    [124] **pitch**
**my toils:** set my traps    [127] **Costin:** ('Cozen' Ff, Q)    [129] **faith:** belief    [132] **What horse:** how many
horsemen    [133–134] **take Upon:** undertake    [138] **several:** separate    [139] **round:** surround    [141] **to me:**
in addition to me    [143] **relisheth:** savors of

Having receiv'd the rights due to a father, 15
I tender you th' allegiance of a subject;
Which, as my prince, accept of.        [*Kneels.*]
    *Flo.*            Kneel to me!  [*Raises him.*]
May mountains first fall down beneath their
        valleys,
And fire no more mount upwards, when I suffer
An act in nature so preposterous!        20
I must o'ercome in this; in all things else
The victory be yours.  Could you here read me,
You should perceive how all my faculties
Triumph in my bless'd fate, to be found yours:
I am your son, your son, sir! and am prouder 25
To be so, to the father to such goodness,
(Which Heaven be pleas'd I may inherit from
        you!)
Than I shall ever of those specious titles
That plead for my succession in the earldom
(Did I possess it now) left by my mother.  30
    *Ger.*   I do believe it: but —
    *Flo.*            Oh, my lov'd father,
Before I knew you were so, by instinct
Nature had taught me to look on your wants,
Not as a stranger's! and, I know not how,
What you call'd charity, I thought the pay-
        ment        35
Of some religious debt Nature stood bound for:
And, last of all, when your magnificent bounty,
In my low ebb of fortune, had brought in
A flood of blessings, though my threatening
        wants,
And fear of their effects, still kept me stupid, 40
I soon found out it was no common pity
That led you to it.
    *Ger.*            Think of this hereafter,
When we with joy may call it to remembrance;
There will be a time more opportune than now,
To end your story, with all circumstances.  45
I add this only: when we fled from Wolfort,
I sent you into England, and there plac'd you
With a brave Flanders merchant, call'd rich
        Goswin,
A man suppli'd by me unto that purpose,
As bound by oath never to discover you;  50
Who, dying, left his name and wealth unto you,
As his reputed son, and yet receiv'd so.
But now, as Florez, and a prince, remember,
The country's and the subject's general good
Must challenge the first part in your affec-
        tion;        55
The fair maid, whom you chose to be your wife,
Being so far beneath you, that your love
Must grant she 's not your equal.
    *Flo.*            In descent,
Or borrow'd glories from dead ancestors;
But for her beauty, chastity, and all virtues 60
Ever remember'd in the best of women,
A monarch might receive from her, not give,

Though she were his crown's purchase: in
        this only
Be an indulgent father: in all else
Use your authority.

    *Enter Hubert [disguised as before], Hem-
    skirk, Wolfort, Bertha, and Soldiers*

    *Hub.*            Sir, here be two of 'em, 65
The father and the son; the rest you shall have
As fast as I can rouse them.        [*Exit.*]
    *Ger.*            Who 's this?  Wolfort?
    *Wol.*   Ay, cripple; your feign'd crutches
        will not help you,
Nor patch'd disguise, that hath so long con-
        ceal'd you;
It 's now no halting: I must here find Ger-
        rard,        70
And in this merchant's habit one call'd Florez,
Who would be an earl.
    *Ger.*            And is, wert thou a subject.
    *Flo.*   Is this that traitor Wolfort?
    *Wol.*            Yes; but you
Are they that are betray'd. — Hemskirk!
    *Ber.*            My Goswin
Turn'd prince! Oh, I am poorer by this great-
        ness        75
Than all my former jealousies or misfortunes!
    *Flo.*   Gertrude!
    *Wol.*   Stay, sir; you were to-day too near
        her:
You must no more aim at those easy accesses,
'Less you can do 't in air, without a head;
Which shall be suddenly tried.
    *Ber.*            Oh, take my heart first! 80
And, since I cannot hope now to enjoy him,
Let me but fall a part of his glad ransom.
    *Wol.*   You know not your own value that
        entreat —
    *Ger.*   So proud a fiend as Wolfort!
    *Wol.*            For so lost
A thing as Florez.
    *Flo.*            And that would be so, 85
Rather than she should stoop again to thee;
There is no death, but 's sweeter than all life,
When Wolfort is to give it. — Oh my Gertrude,
It is not that, nor princedom, that I go from;
It is from thee; that loss includeth all!  90
    *Wol.*   Ay, if my young prince knew his loss,
        he would say so;
Which, that he yet may chew on, I will tell him.
This is no Gertrude, nor no Hemskirk's niece,
Nor Vandunk's daughter: this is Bertha,
        Bertha!
The heir of Brabant, she that caus'd the war, 95
Whom I did steal, during my treaty there,
In your minority, to raise myself;
I then foreseeing 't would beget a quarrel;
That, a necessity of my employment;

---

⁴⁵ **circumstances:** details    ⁴⁹ **suppli'd:** furnished with money    ⁶⁶ **your:** ('my' F 1, Q)

The same employment make me master of
    strength;                                     100
That strength, the lord of Flanders; so of
    Brabant,
By marrying her: which had not been to do, sir,
She come of years, but that the expectation,
First, of her father's death, retarded it;    104
And since, the standing-out of Bruges; where
Hemskirk had hid her, till she was near lost:
But, sir, we have recover'd her: your merchant-
    ship
May break; for this was one of your best
    bottoms,
I think.
    *Ger.*   Insolent devil!

*Enter Hubert, with Jacqueline, Ginks, and*
*Costin*

    *Wol.*             Who are these, Hemskirk?
    *Hem.*   More, more, sir.
    *Flo.*   How they triumph in their treachery!
    *Hem.*   Lord Arnold of Benthuisen, this Lord
    Costin,                                  111
This Jacqueline, the sister unto Florez.
    *Wol.*   All found! Why, here 's brave game;
    this was sport royal,
And puts me in thought of a new kind of death
    for 'em.
Huntsman, your horn: first, wind me Florez'
    fall;                                    115
Next, Gerrard's; then, his daughter Jacque-
    line's.
Those rascals, they shall die without their rites:
Hang 'em, Hemskirk, on these trees. I 'll take
The assay of these myself.
    *Hub.*            Not here, my lord:
Let 'em be broken up upon a scaffold;    120
'T will show the better when their arbour 's
    made.
    *Ger.*   Wretch, art thou not content thou
    hast betray'd us,
But mock us, too?
    *Ginks.*     False Hubert, this is monstrous!
    *Wol.*   Hubert!
    *Hem.*   Who? this?
    *Ger.*            Yes, this is Hubert, Wolfort;
I hope he has help'd himself to a tree.
    *Wol.*           The first,    125
The first of any, — and most glad I have you,
    sir:
I let you go before, but for a train.
Is 't you have done this service?
    *Hub.*          As your huntsman;
But now as Hubert — save yourselves — I
    will —
The wolf 's afoot! let slip! kill, kill, kill, kill! 130

*Enter, with a drum, Vandunk, Merchants,*
*Higgen, Prig, Ferret, Snap*

    *Wol.*   Betray'd!
    *Hub.*         No, but well catch'd; and I the
    huntsman.
    *Vand.*   How do you, Wolfort? rascal! good
    knave, Wolfort!
I speak it now without the rose! — and Hem-
    skirk,
Rogue, Hemskirk! you that have no niece:
    this lady
Was stolen by you, and ta'en by you, and
    now    135
Resign'd by me to the right owner here. —
Take her, my prince!
    *Flo.*            Can this be possible? —
Welcome, my love, my sweet, my worthy love!
    *Vand.*   I ha' given you her twice: now keep
    her better: and thank
Lord Hubert, that came to me in Gerrard's
    name,    140
And got me out, with my brave boys, to march
Like Cæsar, when he bred his Commentaries;
So I, to breed my chronicle, came forth
Cæsar Vandunk, *et veni, vidi, vici.* —
Give me my bottle, and set down the drum. —
You had your tricks, sir, had you? we ha'
    tricks, too:    146
You stole the lady?
    *Hig.*         And we led your squadrons
Where they ha' scratch'd their legs a little
    with brambles,
If not their faces.
    *Prig.*       Yes, and run their heads
Against trees.
    *Hig.*       'T is Captain Prig, sir.
    *Prig.*          And Coronel Higgen.    150
    *Hig.*   We have fill'd a pit with your people,
    some with legs,
Some with arms broken, and a neck or two
I think be loose.
    *Prig.*      The rest, too, that escap'd,
Are not yet out o' the briars.
    *Hig.*         And your horses, sir,
Are well set up in Bruges all by this time.    155
You look as you were not well, sir, and would
    be
Shortly let blood: do you want a scarf?
    *Vand.*          A halter!
    *Ger.*   'T was like yourself, honest and noble
    Hubert! —
Canst thou behold these mirrors all together
Of thy long, false, and bloody usurpation,    160
Thy tyrannous proscription, and fresh treason;
And not so see thyself as to fall down,

---

¹⁰² **to do:** left undone    ¹¹⁷ **rites:** ('rights' Ff, Q)    ¹¹⁹ **assay:** ceremony of cutting up the deer,
usually performed by the chief person at the hunt    ¹²¹ **arbour:** part of process of cutting up the game
¹³³ **without the rose:** not *sub rosa*, openly    ¹⁴³ **breed:** ('end' F 1, Q)

And, sinking, force a grave, with thine own
  guilt,
As deep as hell, to cover thee and it?
  *Wol.*   No, I can stand, and praise the toils
    that took me;                                    165
And laughing in them die: they were brave
  snares.
  *Flo.*   'T were truer valour, if thou durst re-
  pent
The wrongs th' hast done, and live.
  *Wol.*                          Who? I repent,
And say I am sorry? Yes, 't is the fool's lan-
  guage,
And not for Wolfort.
  *Vand.*        Wolfort, thou art a devil, 170
And speak'st his language. — Oh, that I had
  my longing!
Under this row of trees now would I hang him.
  *Flo.*   No, let him live until he can repent;
But banish'd from our state: — that is thy
  doom.
  *Vand.*   Then hang his worthy captain here,
    this Hemskirk,                                  175
For profit of th' example.
  *Flo.*              No; let him
Enjoy his shame, too, with his conscious life
To show how much our innocence contemns
All practice, from the guiltiest, to molest us.
  *Vand.*   A noble prince!
  *Ger.*        Sir, you must help to join    180
A pair of hands, as they have done their hearts
  here,
And to their loves wish joy.
  *Flo.*              As to mine own. —
My gracious sister! worthiest brother!
  *Vand.*   I 'll go afore, and have the bonfire
  made,
My fireworks, and flap-dragons, and good
  backrack;                                          185
With a peck of little fishes, to drink down
In healths to this day.
  *Hig.*          'Slight, here be changes!
The bells ha' not so many, nor a dance, Prig.
  *Prig.*   Our company 's grown horrible thin
  by it. —
What think you, Ferret?
  *Fer.*              Marry, I do think    190
That we might all be lords now, if we could
  stand for 't.
  *Hig.*   Not I, if they should offer it: I 'll dis-
  lodge first,
Remove the Bush to another climate.
  *Ger.*   Sir, you must thank this worthy bur-
  gomaster.
Here be friends ask to be look'd on, too,    195

And thank'd; who, though their trade and
  course of life
Be not so perfect but it may be better'd,
Have yet us'd me with courtesy, and been
  true
Subjects unto me, while I was their king;
A place I know not well how to resign,      200
Nor unto whom. But this I will entreat
Your grace; command them follow me to
  Bruges;
Where I will take the care on me to find
Some manly, and more profitable course,
To fit them as a part of the republic.      205
  *Flo.*   Do you hear, sirs? do so.
  *Hig.*        Thanks to your good grace!
  *Prig.*   To your good lordship!
  *Fer.*              May you both live long!
  *Ger.*   Attend me at Vandunk's, the burgo-
  master's.        *Exeunt all but Beggars.*
  *Hig.*   Yes, to beat hemp, and be whipp'd
  twice a week,
Or turn the wheel for Crab, the rope-maker; 210
Or learn to go along with him his course;
That 's a fine course now, i' the commonwealth.
  — Prig,
What say you to it?
  *Prig.*        It is the backward'st course
I know i' the world.
  *Hig.*   Then Higgen will scarce thrive by it,
You do conclude?
  *Prig.*        Faith, hardly, very hardly.    215
  *Hig.*   Troth, I am partly of your mind,
  Prince Prig:
And therefore, farewell, Flanders! Higgen will
  seek
Some safer shelter, in some other climate,
With this his tatter'd colony. Let me see;
Snap, Ferret, Prig, and Higgen, all are left 220
O' the true blood: what, shall we into Eng-
  land?
  *Prig.*   Agreed.
  *Hig.*   Then bear up bravely with your
  Brute, my lads!
Higgen hath prigg'd the prancers in his days,
And sold good penny-worths: we will have a
  course;                                            225
The spirit of Bottom is grown bottomless.
  *Prig.*   I 'll maund no more, nor cant.
  *Hig.*              Yes, your sixpenny-worth
In private, brother: sixpence is a sum
I 'll steal you any man's dog for.
  *Prig.*              For sixpence more
You 'll tell the owner where he is.
  *Hig.*              'T is right:    230
Higgen must practise, so must Prig, to eat;

---

¹⁶⁶ **brave:** fine    ¹⁸² **wish:** ('with' Ff, Q)    ¹⁸⁵ **backrack:** Rhine wine (from Bacharach)    ²²³ **Brute:**
Brutus, the grandson of Æneas, who was supposed to have led the Trojans to England    ²²⁴ **prigg'd:**
stolen    **prancers:** horses    ²²⁶ **Bottom:** (in *Midsummer Night's Dream;* the meaning of the line is
uncertain)    ²²⁷ **cant:** talk like a beggar

And write the letter, and gi' the word. —
                              But now
No more, as either of these —
   *Prig.*                    But as true beggars
As e'er we were —
   *Hig.*          We stand here for an epilogue.
Ladies, your bounties first! the rest will follow;
For women's favours are a leading alms;    236
If you be pleas'd, look cheerly, throw your eyes
Out at your masks.
   *Prig.*          And let your beauties sparkle.
   *Hig.* So may you ne'er want dressings,
    jewels, gowns,
Still i' the fashion!
   *Prig.*          Nor the men you love,    240
Wealth nor discourse to please you!
   *Hig.*                    May you, gentlemen,
Never want good fresh suits, nor liberty!
   *Prig.* May every merchant here see safe
    his ventures!

   *Hig.*  And every honest citizen his debts in!
   *Prig.*  The lawyers gain good clients!
   *Hig.*                    And the clients    245
Good counsel.
   *Prig.*  All the gamesters here, good fortune!
   *Hig.*  The drunkards, too, good wine!
   *Prig.*                    The eaters, meat
Fit for their tastes and palates!
   *Hig.*                    The good wives,
Kind husbands!
   *Prig.*  The young maids, choice of suitors!
   *Hig.*  The midwives, merry hearts!
   *Prig.*                And all, good cheer!    250
   *Hig.*  As you are kind unto us and our Bush!
We are the beggars, and your daily beads-
   men,
And have your money; but the alms we ask,
And live by, is your grace: give that, and then
We 'll boldly say, our word is, Come agen!    255
                    [*Exeunt*].

# A NEW WAY TO PAY

# OLD DEBTS

## A COMOEDIE

*As it hath beene often acted at the Phœnix in Drury-Lane, by the Queenes Maiesties seruants.*

The Author.

## PHILIP MASSINGER.

**LONDON,**
Printed by *E. P.* for *Henry Seyle.*, dwelling in S.
*Pauls* Church-yard, at the signe of the
Tygers head. Anno. **M. DC.**
**XXXIII.**

BIBLIOGRAPHICAL RECORD. On Nov. 10, 1632, there was entered on the Register of the Station-ers' Co., on behalf of Henry Seile and by authority of Sir Henry Herbert and Master Aspley, "A Comedy called *A new way to pay old Debtes* by Phillip Massinger." During the following year appeared the only early Quarto of the play. This Quarto is printed with unusual care. Act and scene divisions are accurately marked in Latin, the names of the characters are grouped at the head of each scene, after the classical manner, and stage directions, usually in English but occasionally in Latin, are given in the margins. The play is preceded by a dedication to the Earl of Carnarvon, who had married a daughter of Philip Herbert, Earl of Montgomery, in the service of whose family Massinger's father had passed his life. There are also prefixed to the play com-plimentary poems from the pens of Sir Henry Moody and Sir Thomas Jay, the latter of whom ranks Massinger with Beaumont and Fletcher and praises him for his command of

> The crafty mazes of the cunning plot;
> The polish'd phrase; the sweet expression; got
> Neither by theft nor violence; the conceit
> Fresh and unsullied . . .

DATE AND STAGE PERFORMANCE. The title-page of the Quarto of 1633 states that *A New Way* had "beene often acted at the Phœnix in Drury-Lane, by the Queenes Maiesties seruants." The reference to the capture of Breda by Spinola in 1625 (I. ii. 27, 28) and an allusion to the play in Act I, sc. iii of Massinger's *Roman Actor* (licensed in 1626) suggest that it appeared late in 1625 or early in 1626. Further evidence for this date is to be found in the fact that the London theatres were closed because of the plague in May of 1625, and the Phœnix was not occupied by the Queen's Men until December of that year, when the theatres reopened. No notice of the play is to be found in the books kept by the Master of the Revels, but his records for this period survive in incomplete form. The subsequent stage history of *A New Way* is unique among Elizabethan and Jacobean plays other than those of Shakespeare. It was revived by David Garrick in 1748, and ever since that time has been acted at frequent intervals. A. H. Cruickshank's edition of the play (Oxford, 1926) gives a very complete and impressive list of performances in England and America (Appendix II, pp. 125–138).

PERSONAL ALLUSIONS. It is probable that the characters of Sir Giles Overreach and Justice Greedy are drawn from life. One Sir Giles Mompessen (1584–1651?) and his legal associate, Sir Francis Michel, had obtained commissions from James I for controlling licenses to inn-keepers and supervising the monopoly for the manufacture of gold and silver thread. Their abuse of these privileges was so flagrant and inhuman that public indignation forced the king, in 1621, to prosecute and punish both offenders. The affair was a notorious scandal. (See also S. R. Gardi-ner: "The Political Element in Massinger," *Transactions New Shakspere Society, 1877–1878*, pp. 314 ff.)

# PHILIP MASSINGER (1583–1640)

## A NEW WAY TO PAY OLD DEBTS

### DRAMATIS PERSONAE

[Lord] Lovell, an English Lord
Sir Giles Overreach, a cruel extortioner
[Frank] Wellborn, a Prodigal
[Tom] Allworth, a young Gentleman, Page to Lord Lovell
Greedy, a hungry Justice of Peace
Marrall, a Term-Driver; a creature of Sir Giles Overreach
Order [Steward],
Amble [Usher],
Furnace [Cook],
Watchall [Porter], } Servants to the Lady Allworth

Willdo, a Parson
Tapwell, an Alehouse Keeper
Three Creditors, [Servants, &c.]

The Lady Allworth, a rich Widow
Margaret, Overreach his daughter
Froth, Tapwell's Wife
Chambermaid
Waiting Woman

[Scene. — *The Country near Nottingham.*]

### *Actus primi, Scena prima*

[*Before Tapwell's Alehouse*]

*Wellborn. Tapwell. Froth*

*Well.* No bouse? nor no tobacco?
*Tap.* Not a suck, sir;
Nor the remainder of a single can
Left by a drunken porter, all night pall'd too.
*Froth.* Not the dropping of the tap for your morning's draught, sir.
'T is verity, I assure you.
*Well.* Verity, you brach! 5
The devil turn'd precisian! Rogue, what am I?
*Tap.* Troth, durst I trust you with a looking-glass,
To let you see your trim shape, you would quit me
And take the name yourself.
*Well.* How, dog!
*Tap.* Even so, sir.
And I must tell you, if you but advance 10
Your Plymouth cloak you shall be soon instructed
There dwells, and within call, if it please your worship,
A potent monarch call'd the constable,
That does command a citadel call'd the stocks;
Whose guards are certain files of rusty billmen
Such as with great dexterity will hale 16
Your tatter'd, lousy ——

*Well.* Rascal! slave!
*Froth.* No rage, sir.
*Tap.* At his own peril. Do not put yourself
In too much heat, there being no water near
To quench your thirst; and sure, for other liquor, 20
As mighty ale, or beer, they are things, I take it,
You must no more remember; not in a dream, sir.
*Well.* Why, thou unthankful villain, dar'st thou talk thus!
Is not thy house, and all thou hast, my gift?
*Tap.* I find it not in chalk; and Timothy Tapwell 25
Does keep no other register.
*Well.* Am not I he
Whose riots fed and cloth'd thee? Wert thou not
Born on my father's land, and proud to be
A drudge in his house?
*Tap.* What I was, sir, it skills not; 29
What you are, is apparent. Now, for a farewell,
Since you talk of father, in my hope it will torment you,
I 'll briefly tell your story. Your dead father,
My quondam master, was a man of worship,
Old Sir John Wellborn, justice of peace and *quorum*,
And stood fair to be *custos rotulorum;* 35
Bore the whole sway of the shire, kept a great house,

---

D. P. **Term-Driver:** one who goes from court to court in hope of gain   ¹ bouse: drink   ³ pall'd: flat from standing   ⁵ **brach:** bitch   ⁶ **precisian:** Puritan   ⁸ **quit:** absolve   ¹¹ **Plymouth cloak:** cudgel ('Plimworth' Q)   ¹⁵ **rusty:** rough, churlish   ²⁹ **skills:** matters   ³⁴ **quorum:** one of the more eminent justices whose presence was necessary to constitute a bench   ³⁵ **custos rotulorum: Keeper of the Rolls**

Reliev'd the poor, and so forth; but he dying
And the twelve hundred a year coming to you,
Late Master Francis, but now forlorn Well-
  born ——
*Well.*  Slave, stop! or I shall lose myself.
*Froth.*                              Very hardly;  40
You cannot out of your way.
*Tap.*                          But to my story.
You were then a lord of acres, the prime gal-
  lant,
And I your under-butler.  Note the change
  now:
You had a merry time of 't; hawks and hounds;
With choice of running horses; mistresses  45
Of all sorts and all sizes, yet so hot,
As their embraces made your lordships melt;
Which your uncle, Sir Giles Overreach, observ-
  ing,
(Resolving not to lose a drop of 'em,)
On foolish mortgages, statutes, and bonds,  50
For a while suppli'd your looseness, and then
  left you.
*Well.*  Some curate hath penn'd this invec-
  tive, mongrel,
And you have studied it.
*Tap.*                    I have not done yet.
Your land gone, and your credit not worth a
  token,
You grew the common borrower; no man
  'scap'd
Your paper-pellets, from the gentleman  56
To the beggars on highways, that sold you
  switches
In your gallantry.
*Well.*            I shall switch your brains out.
*Tap.*  Where poor Tim Tapwell, with a little
  stock,
Some forty pounds or so, bought a small cot-
  tage;                                      60
Humbled myself to marriage with my Froth
  here,
Gave entertainment ——
*Well.*              Yes, to whores and canters,
Clubbers by night.
*Tap.*          True, but they brought in profit,
And had a gift to pay for what they call'd for,
And stuck not like your mastership.  The poor
  income                                    65
I glean'd from them hath made me in my parish
Thought worthy to be scavenger, and in time
May rise to be overseer of the poor;
Which if I do, on your petition, Wellborn,
I may allow you thirteen-pence a quarter,  70
And you shall thank my worship.
*Well.*                Thus, you dog-bolt,
And thus ——              *Beats and kicks him.*

*Tap.*  [*To his wife.*]  Cry out for help!
*Well.*                    Stir, and thou diest:
Your potent prince, the constable, shall not
  save you.
Hear me, ungrateful hell-hound!  Did not I
Make purses for you?  Then you lick'd my
  boots,                                     75
And thought your holiday cloak too coarse to
  clean 'em.
'T was I that, when I heard thee swear if ever
Thou couldst arrive at forty pounds thou
  wouldst
Live like an emperor, 't was I that gave it
In ready gold.  Deny this, wretch!
*Tap.*                        I must, sir;  80
For, from the tavern to the taphouse, all,
On forfeiture of their licenses, stand bound
Ne'er to remember who their best guests were,
If they grew poor like you.
*Well.*              They are well rewarded
That beggar themselves to make such cuckolds
  rich.                                      85
Thou viper, thankless viper! impudent bawd!
But since you are grown forgetful, I will help
Your memory, and tread thee into mortar,
Not leave one bone unbroken.
                        [*Beats him again.*]
*Tap.*  Oh!
*Froth.*                          Ask mercy.

          *Enter Allworth*

*Well.*  'T will not be granted.
*All.*        Hold — for my sake, hold.  90
Deny me, Frank?  They are not worth your
  anger.
*Well.*  For once thou hast redeem'd them
  from this sceptre;              *His Cudgel.*
But let 'em vanish, creeping on their knees,
And, if they grumble, I revoke my pardon.
*Froth.*  This comes of your prating, husband;
  you presum'd                               95
On your ambling wit, and must use your glib
  tongue,
Though you are beaten lame for 't.
*Tap.*                      Patience, Froth;
There 's law to cure our bruises.
          *They go off on their hands and knees.*
*Well.*                Sent to your mother?
*All.*  My lady, Frank, my patroness, my all!
She 's such a mourner for my father's death,
And, in her love to him, so favours me,  101
That I cannot pay too much observance to her.
There are few such stepdames.
*Well.*                  'T is a noble widow,
And keeps her reputation pure, and clear
From the least taint of infamy; her life,  105

---

⁴⁰ **hardly:** with difficulty    ⁴⁷ **As:** that    ⁵⁴ **token:** (issued by tradesmen in lieu of small coins)
⁵⁶ **paper-pellets:** promissory notes    ⁶² **canters:** ruffians who used thieves' slang    ⁶⁵ **stuck:** deferred
**payment**    ⁷¹ **dog-bolt:** blunt arrow, a term of reproach

With the splendour of her actions, leaves no
    tongue
To envy or detraction. Prithee tell me,
Has she no suitors?
    *All.*      Even the best of the shire, Frank,
My lord excepted; such as sue and send,
And send and sue again, but to no purpose; 110
Their frequent visits have not gain'd her pres-
    ence.
Yet she 's so far from sullenness and pride,
That I dare undertake you shall meet from her
A liberal entertainment. I can give you
A catalogue of her suitors' names.
    *Well.*        Forbear it, 115
While I give you good counsel. I am bound to
    it;
Thy father was my friend, and that affection
I bore to him, in right descends to thee;
Thou art a handsome and a hopeful youth, 119
Nor will I have the least affront stick on thee,
If I with any danger can prevent it.
    *All.* I thank your noble care; but, pray
    you, in what
Do I run the hazard?
    *Well.*        Art thou not in love?
Put it not off with wonder.
    *All.*        In love, at my years!
    *Well.* You think you walk in clouds, but
    are transparent. 125
I have heard all, and the choice that you have
    made,
And, with my finger, can point out the north
    star
By which the loadstone of your folly 's guided;
And, to confirm this true, what think you of
Fair Margaret, the only child and heir 130
Of Cormorant Overreach? Does it blush and
    start,
To hear her only nam'd? Blush at your want
Of wit and reason.
    *All.*      You are too bitter, sir.
    *Well.* Wounds of this nature are not to be
    cur'd
With balms, but corrosives. I must be plain: 135
Art thou scarce manumiz'd from the porter's
    lodge
And yet sworn servant to the pantofle,
And dar'st thou dream of marriage? I fear
'T will be concluded for impossible
That there is now, nor e'er shall be hereafter, 140
A handsome page or player's boy of fourteen
But either loves a wench, or drabs love him;
Court-waiters not exempted.
    *All.*        This is madness.
Howe'er you have discover'd my intents,

You know my aims are lawful; and if ever 145
The queen of flowers, the glory of the spring,
The sweetest comfort to our smell, the rose,
Sprang from an envious briar, I may infer
There 's such disparity in their conditions 149
Between the goodness of my soul, the daughter,
And the base churl, her father.
    *Well.*        Grant this true,
As I believe it, canst thou ever hope
To enjoy a quiet bed with her whose father
Ruin'd thy state?
    *All.*        And yours too.
    *Well.*        I confess it; 154
True; I must tell you as a friend, and freely,
That, where impossibilities are apparent,
'T is indiscretion to nourish hopes.
Canst thou imagine (let not self-love blind
    thee)
That Sir Giles Overreach, that, to make her
    great 159
In swelling titles, without touch of conscience
Will cut his neighbour's throat, and I hope his
    own too,
Will e'er consent to make her thine? Give o'er,
And think of some course suitable to thy rank,
And prosper in it.
    *All.*      You have well advis'd me. 164
But in the meantime you that are so studious
Of my affairs wholly neglect your own.
Remember yourself, and in what plight you are.
    *Well.* No matter, no matter.
    *All.*      Yes, 't is much material.
You know my fortune and my means; yet
    something
I can spare from myself to help your wants.
    *Well.*        How 's this? 170
    *All.* Nay, be not angry; there 's eight pieces
To put you in better fashion.
    *Well.*        Money from thee!
From a boy. A stipendary! One that lives
At the devotion of a stepmother
And the uncertain favour of a lord! 175
I 'll eat my arms first. Howsoe'er blind For-
    tune
Hath spent the utmost of her malice on me —
Though I am vomited out of an alehouse,
And thus accoutred — know not where to eat,
Or drink, or sleep, but underneath this can-
    opy — 180
Although I thank thee, I despise thy offer;
And as I in my madness broke my state
Without th' assistance of another's brain,
In my right wits I 'll piece it; at the worst, 184
Die thus and be forgotten.
    *All.*      A strange humour! *Exeunt.*

---

¹²⁴ **wonder:** affected surprise    ¹³⁶ **manumiz'd . . . lodge:** freed from the condition of servitude,
or from that of extreme youth (?)    ¹³⁷ **sworn . . . pantofle:** in love (?)    ¹⁴³ **Court-waiters:** pages
¹⁴⁸ **envious:** malicious    ¹⁶⁸ **much material:** very important    ¹⁷¹ **pieces:** coins worth 22 s. each
¹⁷² **put . . . fashion:** clothe you better    ¹⁷³ **stipendary:** pensioner

## Actus primi, Scena secunda

[*A Room in Lady Allworth's House*]

*Order. Amble. Furnace. Watchall*

*Ord.*  Set all things right, or, as my name is
Order,
And by this staff of office that commands you,
This chain and double ruff, symbols of power,
Whoever misses in his function,
For one whole week makes forfeiture of his
breakfast     5
And privilege in the wine-cellar.
*Amb.*          You are merry,
Good master steward.
*Furn.*        Let him; I 'll be angry.
*Amb.*  Why, fellow Furnace, 't is not twelve
o'clock yet,
Nor dinner taking up; then, 't is allow'd,
Cooks, by their places, may be choleric.   10
*Furn.*  You think you have spoke wisely,
goodman Amble,
My lady's go-before!
*Ord.*        Nay, nay, no wrangling.
*Furn.*  Twit me with the authority of the
kitchen!
At all hours, and all places, I 'll be angry;  14
And thus provok'd, when I am at my prayers
I will be angry.
*Amb.*       There was no hurt meant.
*Furn.*  I am friends with thee; and yet I will
be angry.
*Ord.*  With whom?
*Furn.*       No matter whom: yet, now I
think on 't,
I am angry with my lady.
*Watch.*        Heaven forbid, man!
*Ord.*  What cause has she given thee?
*Furn.*     Cause enough, master steward.  20
I was entertain'd by her to please her palate,
And, till she forswore eating, I perform'd it.
Now, since our master, noble Allworth, died,
Though I crack my brains to find out tempting
sauces,
And raise fortifications in the pastry    25
Such as might serve for models in the Low
Countries,
Which, if they had been practised at Breda,
Spinola might have thrown his cap at it, and
ne'er took it ——
*Amb.*  But you had wanted matter there to
work on.
*Furn.*  Matter! with six eggs, and a strike
of rye meal,    30

I had kept the town till doomsday, perhaps
longer.
*Ord.*  But what 's this to your pet against my
lady?
*Furn.*  What 's this? Marry this: when I
am three parts roasted
And the fourth part parboil'd to prepare her
viands,
She keeps her chamber, dines with a panada  35
Or water-gruel, my sweat never thought on.
*Ord.*  But your art is seen in the dining-room.
*Furn.*           By whom?
By such as pretend love to her, but come
To feed upon her. Yet, of all the harpies
That do devour her, I am out of charity  40
With none so much as the thin-gutted squire
That 's stol'n into commission.
*Ord.*        Justice Greedy?
*Furn.*  The same, the same: meat 's cast
away upon him,
It never thrives; he holds this paradox,
Who eats not well, can ne'er do justice well.  45
His stomach 's as insatiate as the grave,
Or strumpet's ravenous appetites.

*Allworth knocks, and enters*

*Watch.*        One knocks.
*Ord.*  Our late young master!
*Amb.*         Welcome, sir.
*Furn.*         Your hand;
If you have a stomach, a cold bake-meat 's
ready.
*Ord.*  His father's picture in little.
*Furn.*       We are all your servants.  50
*Amb.*  In you he lives.
*All.*        At once, my thanks to all;
This is yet some comfort. Is my lady stirring?

*Enter the Lady Allworth, Waiting Woman,
Chambermaid*

*Ord.*  Her presence answer for us.
*Lady.*       Sort those silks well.
I 'll take the air alone.
*Exeunt Waiting Woman and Chambermaid*
*Furn.*       You air and air;
But will you never taste but spoon-meat more?
To what use serve I?
*Lady.*     Prithee, be not angry;  56
I shall ere long. I' the mean time, there is gold
To buy thee aprons, and a summer suit.
*Furn.*  I am appeas'd, and Furnace now
grows cool.
*Lady.*  And, as I gave directions, if this
morning    60
I am visited by any, entertain 'em

---

⁴ **function:** task, duty  ⁹ **taking up:** being served  ¹⁰ **by . . . places:** ex officio  ²¹ **entertain'd:** employed  ²⁷ **Breda:** in the Netherlands, captured by the Spaniards under Spinola in 1625  ³⁰ **strike:** bushel  ³² **pet:** pique  ³⁵ **panada:** bread cooked in milk  ³⁸ **pretend:** profess  ⁴² **stol'n . . . commission:** gained his commission as justice of the peace by fraud  ⁵⁹ **cool:** ('Cooke' Q)

As heretofore; but say, in my excuse,
I am indispos'd.
   *Ord.*           I shall, madam.
   *Lady.*           Do, and leave me.
Nay, stay you, Allworth.
        *Exeunt Order, Amble, Furnace,*
            *Watch-all.*
   *All.*         I shall gladly grow here,
To wait on your commands.
   *Lady.*      So soon turn'd courtier! 65
   *All.* Style not that courtship, madam, which
   is duty,
Purchas'd on your part.
   *Lady.*      Well, you shall o'ercome;
I 'll not contend in words.  How is it with
Your noble master?
   *All.*        Ever like himself,
No scruple lessen'd in the full weight of hon-
   our.                        70
He did command me (pardon my presumption)
As his unworthy deputy, to kiss
Your ladyship's fair hands.
   *Lady.*      I am honour'd in
His favour to me.  Does he hold his purpose
For the Low Countries?
   *All.*     Constantly, good madam; 75
But he will in person first present his service.
   *Lady.* And how approve you of his course?
   You are yet
Like virgin parchment, capable of any
Inscription, vicious or honourable.
I will not force your will, but leave you free 80
To your own election.
   *All.*        Any form you please
I will put on; but, might I make my choice,
With humble emulation I would follow
The path my lord marks to me.
   *Lady.*        'T is well answer'd,
And I commend your spirit.  You had a father,
Bless'd be his memory! that some few hours 86
Before the will of Heaven took him from me,
Who did commend you, by the dearest ties
Of perfect love between us, to my charge;
And, therefore, what I speak you are bound to
   hear                        90
With such respect as if he liv'd in me.
He was my husband, and howe'er you are not
Son of my womb, you may be of my love,
Provided you deserve it.
   *All.*        I have found you,
Most honour'd madam, the best mother to me;
And, with my utmost strengths of care and
   service,                  96
Will labour that you never may repent
Your bounties shower'd upon me.
   *Lady.*      I much hope it.
These were your father's words: " If e'er my son

Follow the war, tell him it is a school   100
Where all the principles tending to honour
Are taught, if truly followed:  but for such
As repair thither as a place in which
They do presume they may with license practise
Their lusts and riots, they shall never merit 105
The noble name of soldiers.  To dare boldly
In a fair cause, and for their country's safety
To run upon the cannon's mouth undaunted;
To obey their leaders, and shun mutinies;
To bear with patience the winter's cold   110
And summer's scorching heat, and not to faint,
When plenty of provision fails, with hunger;
Are the essential parts make up a soldier,
Not swearing, dice, or drinking."
   *All.*        There 's no syllable
You speak, but is to me an oracle,   115
Which but to doubt were impious.
   *Lady.*        To conclude:
Beware ill company, for often men
Are like to those with whom they do converse;
And, from one man I warn you, and that 's
   Wellborn:
Not 'cause he 's poor, that rather claims your
   pity;                       120
But that he 's in his manners so debauch'd,
And hath to vicious courses sold himself.
'T is true, your father lov'd him, while he was
Worthy the loving; but if he had liv'd
To have seen him as he is, he had cast him off,
As you must do.
   *All.*      I shall obey in all things.   126
   *Lady.*  You follow me to my chamber, you
   shall have gold
To furnish you like my son, and still supplied,
As I hear from you.
   *All.*     I am still your creature.  *Exeunt.*

## Actus primi, Scena tertia

### [A Hall in the Same]

*Overreach.  Greedy.  Order.  Amble.  Furnace.*
       *Watchall.  Marrall*

   *Greedy.*  Not to be seen!
   *Over.*       Still cloister'd up!  Her reason,
I hope, assures her, though she make herself
Close prisoner ever for her husband's loss,
'T will not recover him.
   *Ord.*        Sir, it is her will,
Which we, that are her servants, ought to
   serve it,                  5
And not dispute.  Howe'er, you are nobly wel-
   come;
And, if you please to stay, that you may think
   so,

There came, not six days since, from Hull, a
    pipe
Of rich Canary, which shall spend itself
For my lady's honour.
    *Greedy.*                Is it of the right race? 10
    *Ord.* Yes, Master Greedy.
    *Amb.*                How his mouth runs o'er!
    *Furn.* I 'll make it run, and run. Save your
        good worship!
    *Greedy.* Honest Master Cook, thy hand
        again. How I love thee!
Are the good dishes still in being? Speak,
    boy.
    *Furn.* If you have a mind to feed, there is a
        chine                        15
Of beef, well season'd.
    *Greedy.*                Good!
    *Furn.*                A pheasant, larded.
    *Greedy.* That I might now give thanks for 't!
    *Furn.*                Other kickshaws.
Besides, there came last night, from the forest
    of Sherwood,
The fattest stag I ever cook'd.
    *Greedy.*                A stag, man!
    *Furn.* A stag, sir; part of it prepar'd for
        dinner,                        20
And bak'd in puff-paste.
    *Greedy.*                Puff-paste too! Sir Giles,
A ponderous chine of beef! a pheasant larded!
And red deer too, Sir Giles, and bak'd in puff-
    paste!
All business set aside, let us give thanks here.
    *Furn.* How the lean skeleton's rapt!
    *Over.*                You know we cannot. 25
    *Mar.* Your worships are to sit on a commis-
        sion,
And if you fail to come, you lose the cause.
    *Greedy.* Cause me no causes. I 'll prove 't,
        for such dinner
We may put off a commission: you shall find
    it
*Henrici decimo quarto.*
    *Over.*                Fie, Master Greedy! 30
Will you lose me a thousand pounds for a din-
    ner?
No more, for shame! We must forget the belly
When we think of profit.
    *Greedy.*                Well, you shall o'er-rule me;
I could ev'n cry now. — Do you hear, Master
    Cook,
Send but a corner of that immortal pasty, 35
And I, in thankfulness, will, by your boy,
Send you — a brace of three-pences.
    *Furn.*                Will you be so prodigal?

*Enter Wellborn*

    *Over.* Remember me to your lady. Who
        have we here?
    *Well.* You know me.
    *Over.*                I did once, but now I will not;
Thou art no blood of mine. Avaunt, thou beg-
    gar!                        40
If ever thou presume to own me more,
I 'll have thee cag'd and whipp'd.
    *Greedy.*                I 'll grant the warrant.
Think of Pie-corner, Furnace!

*Exeunt Overreach, Greedy, Marrall*

    *Watch.*                Will you out, sir?
I wonder how you durst creep in.
    *Ord.*                This is rudeness,
And saucy impudence.
    *Amb.*                Cannot you stay 45
To be serv'd, among your fellows, from the
    basket,
But you must press into the hall?
    *Furn.*                Prithee, vanish
Into some outhouse, though it be the pigstye;
My scullion shall come to thee.

*Enter Allworth*

    *Well.*                This is rare.
Oh, here 's Tom Allworth. Tom!
    *All.*                We must be strangers; 50
Nor would I have you seen here for a million.

*Exit Allworth.*

    *Well.* Better and better. He contemns me
        too!

*Enter Woman and Chambermaid*

    *Woman.* Foh, what a smell 's here! What
        thing 's this?
    *Cham.*                A creature
Made out of the privy; let us hence, for love's
    sake,
Or I shall swoon.
    *Woman.*                I begin to feel faint already. 55

*Exeunt Woman and Chambermaid.*

    *Watch.* Will know your way;
    *Amb.*                Or shall we teach it you,
By the head and shoulders?
    *Well.*                No; I will not stir;
Do you mark, I will not: let me see the wretch
That dares attempt to force me. Why, you
    slaves,
Created only to make legs, and cringe; 60
To carry in a dish, and shift a trencher;
That have not souls only to hope a blessing
Beyond black-jacks or flagons; you, that were
    born

---

⁸ **pipe:** cask    ¹⁰ **race:** vintage    ¹⁶ **larded:** stuffed with bacon    ¹⁷ **kickshaws:** trifles ('kuku-
shawes' Q)    ³⁰ **Henrici . . . quarto:** Laws were designated by the year of the reign in which they
were passed.    ⁴³ **Pie-corner:** street in London containing numerous eating houses    ⁴⁶ **basket:** in
which scraps were placed for the poor    ⁵⁶ **Will:** will you    ⁶⁰ **make legs:** bow    ⁶³ **black-jacks:**
leather drinking vessels

Only to consume meat and drink, and batten
Upon reversions! — who advances? Who      65
Shows me the way?
*Ord.*                    My lady!

*Enter Lady [Allworth]. Woman. Chambermaid*

  *Cham.*                Here 's the monster.
  *Woman.*    Sweet madam, keep your glove to
    your nose.
  *Cham.*                Or let me
Fetch some perfumes may be predominant;
You wrong yourself else.
  *Well.*                Madam, my designs
Bear me to you.
  *Lady.*                To me!
  *Well.*            And though I have met with   70
But ragged entertainment from your grooms
    here,
I hope from you to receive that noble usage
As may become the true friend of your husband,
And then I shall forget these.
  *Lady.*                I am amaz'd
To see and hear this rudeness. Dar'st thou
    think,                75
Though sworn, that it can ever find belief,
That I, who to the best men of this country
Deni'd my presence since my husband's death,
Can fall so low as to change words with thee?
Thou son of infamy, forbear my house,       80
And know and keep the distance that 's be-
    tween us;
Or, though it be against my gentler temper,
I shall take order you no more shall be
An eyesore to me.
  *Well.*            Scorn me not, good lady;
But, as in form you are angelical,       85
Imitate the heavenly natures, and vouchsafe
At the least awhile to hear me. You will grant
The blood that runs in this arm is as noble
As that which fills your veins; those costly
    jewels,
And those rich clothes you wear, your men's
    observance       90
And women's flattery, are in you no virtues,
Nor these rags, with my poverty, in me vices.
You have a fair fame, and, I know, deserve it;
Yet, lady, I must say, in nothing more
Than in the pious sorrow you have shown   95
For your late noble husband.
  *Ord.*                How she starts!
  *Furn.*    And hardly can keep finger from the
    eye,
To hear him nam'd.
  *Lady.*        Have you aught else to say?
  *Well.*    That husband, madam, was once in
    his fortune       99
Almost as low as I; want, debts, and quarrels

Lay heavy on him: let it not be thought
A boast in me, though I say I reliev'd him.
'T was I that gave him fashion; mine the sword
That did on all occasions second his;
I brought him on and off with honour, lady; 105
And when in all men's judgments he was sunk,
And, in his own hopes, not to be buoy'd up,
I stepp'd unto him, took him by the hand,
And set him upright.
  *Furn.*            Are not we base rogues,
That could forget this?
  *Well.*            I confess, you made him 110
Master of your estate; nor could your friends,
Though he brought no wealth with him, blame
    you for 't;
For he had a shape, and to that shape a mind
Made up of all parts either great or noble;
So winning a behaviour, not to be       115
Resisted, madam.
  *Lady.*        'T is most true, he had.
  *Well.*  For his sake, then, in that I was his
    friend,
Do not contemn me.
  *Lady.*            For what 's past excuse me,
I will redeem it. Order, give the gentleman
A hundred pounds.
  *Well.*            No, madam, on no terms: 120
I will nor beg nor borrow sixpence of you,
But be suppli'd elsewhere, or want thus ever.
Only one suit I make, which you deny not
To strangers; and 't is this. *Whispers to her.*
  *Lady.*                Fie! nothing else?
  *Well.*  Nothing, unless you please to charge
    your servants       125
To throw away a little respect upon me.
  *Lady.*  What you demand is yours.
  *Well.*                I thank you, lady.
Now what can be wrought out of such a suit
Is yet in supposition: I have said all;
When you please, you may retire. —
                  *[Exit Lady All.]*
    Nay, all 's forgotten; *[to the Servants.]*
And, for a lucky omen to my project,       131
Shake hands, and end all quarrels in the cellar.
  *Ord.*    Agreed, agreed.
  *Furn.*        Still merry Master Wellborn.
                       *Exeunt.*

### Actus secundi, Scena prima

*[A Room in Overreach's House]*

*Overreach. Marrall*

*Over.*  He 's gone, I warrant thee; this com-
    mission crush'd him.
*Mar.*  Your worship have the way on 't, and
    ne'er miss

---

⁶⁴⁻⁶⁵ **batten . . . reversions:** feast upon remains        ⁷⁹ **change:** exchange        ¹⁰⁷ **buoy'd:**
('bung'd' Q)

To squeeze these unthrifts into air; and yet,
The chapfallen justice did his part, returning
For your advantage the certificate,                    5
Against his conscience, and his knowledge too,
With your good favour, to the utter ruin
Of the poor farmer.
   *Over.*           'T was for these good ends
I made him a justice; he that bribes his belly,
Is certain to command his soul.
   *Mar.*                I wonder,    10
Still with your license, why your worship hav-
    ing
The power to put this thin-gut in commission,
You are not in 't yourself?
   *Over.*              Thou art a fool.
In being out of office I am out of danger;
Where, if I were a justice, besides the trouble,
I might, or out of wilfulness or error,                16
Run myself finely into a *præmunire*,
And so become a prey to the informer.
No, I 'll have none of 't; 't is enough I keep
Greedy at my devotion; so he serve              20
My purposes, let him hang or damn, I care
    not;
Friendship is but a word.
   *Mar.*           You are all wisdom.
   *Over.*  I would be worldly wise; for the other
    wisdom,
That does prescribe us a well-govern'd life,
And to do right to others as ourselves,          25
I value not an atom.
   *Mar.*           What course take you,
With your good patience, to hedge in the manor
Of your neighbour, Master Frugal? as 't is said,
He will nor sell, nor borrow, nor exchange;
And his land, lying in the midst of your many
    lordships,                                       30
Is a foul blemish.
   *Over.*       I have thought on 't, Marrall,
And it shall take. I must have all men sellers,
And I the only purchaser.
   *Mar.*          'T is most fit, sir.
   *Over.*  I 'll therefore buy some cottage near
    his manor,
Which done, I 'll make my men break ope his
    fences,                                          35
Ride o'er his standing corn, and in the night
Set fire on his barns, or break his cattle's legs.
These trespasses draw on suits and suits ex-
    penses,
Which I can spare, but will soon beggar him.
When I have harried him thus two or three
    year,                                            40
Though he sue *in forma pauperis*, in spite
Of all his thrift and care, he 'll grow behindhand.

   *Mar.*  The best I ever heard! I could adore
    you.
   *Over.*  Then, with the favour of my man of
    law,
I will pretend some title. Want will force him
To put it to arbitrement; then, if he sell    46
For half the value, he shall have ready money,
And I possess his land.
   *Mar.*          'T is above wonder!
Wellborn was apt to sell, and needed not
These fine arts, sir, to hook him in.
   *Over.*          Well thought on. 50
This varlet, Marrall, lives too long, to upbraid
    me
With my close cheat put upon him. Will nor
    cold
Nor hunger kill him?
   *Mar.*      I know not what to think on 't.
I have us'd all means; and the last night I
    caus'd                                           54
His host, the tapster, to turn him out of doors;
And have been since with all your friends and
    tenants,
And, on the forfeit of your favour, charg'd
    'em,
Though a crust of mouldy bread would keep
    him from starving,
Yet they should not relieve him. This is done,
    sir.
   *Over.*  That was something, Marrall; but
    thou must go further,                          60
And suddenly, Marrall.
   *Mar.*      Where, and when you please, sir.
   *Over.*  I would have thee seek him out, and,
    if thou canst,
Persuade him that 't is better steal than beg;
Then, if I prove he has but robb'd a henroost,
Not all the world shall save him from the gal-
    lows.                                            65
Do anything to work him to despair;
And 't is thy masterpiece.
   *Mar.*         I will do my best, sir.
   *Over.*  I am now on my main work with the
    Lord Lovell,
The gallant-minded, popular Lord Lovell,
The minion of the people's love. I hear    70
He 's come into the country, and my aims are
To insinuate myself into his knowledge,
And then invite him to my house.
   *Mar.*           I have you;
This points at my young mistress.
   *Over.*          She must part with
That humble title, and write honourable,   75
Right honourable, Marrall, my right honour-
    able daughter,

---

   [3] **unthrifts:** spendthrifts   [4] **chapfallen:** thin-faced  **returning:** ruling out   [5] **certificate:** document  [13] **Where:** whereas    [17] **præmunire:** encroachment on rights of the crown   [20] **at my devotion:** devoted to my interests   [36] **corn:** grain   [41] **in . . . pauperis:** in the status of a pauper   [52] **close:** secret  [57] **'em:** ('him' Q)   [70] **minion:** darling

If all I have, or e'er shall get, will do it.
I 'll have her well attended; there are ladies
Of errant knights decay'd and brought so low,
That for cast clothes and meat will gladly serve
   her. 80
And 't is my glory, though I come from the
   city,
To have their issue whom I have undone,
To kneel to mine as bondslaves.
  *Mar.*             'T is fit state, sir.
  *Over.* And therefore, I 'll not have a cham-
  bermaid
That ties her shoes, or any meaner office,   85
But such whose fathers were right worshipful.
'T is a rich man's pride! there having ever
  been
More than a feud, a strange antipathy,
Between us and true gentry.

*Enter Wellborn*

  *Mar.*          See, who 's here, sir.
  *Over.* Hence, monster! prodigy!
  *Well.*         Sir, your wife's nephew; 90
She and my father tumbled in one belly.
  *Over.* Avoid my sight! thy breath 's infec-
  tious, rogue!
I shun thee as a leprosy, or the plague.
Come hither, Marrall — [*aside*] this is the time
  to work him.         *Exit Overreach.*
  *Mar.* I warrant you, sir.
  *Well.* By this light, I think he 's mad. 95
  *Mar.* Mad! had you took compassion on
  yourself,
You long since had been mad.
  *Well.*         You have took a course,
Between you and my venerable uncle,
To make me so.
  *Mar.*      The more pale-spirited you,
That would not be instructed. I swear
  deeply ——               100
  *Well.* By what?
  *Mar.*         By my religion.
  *Well.*             Thy religion!
The devil's creed: — but what would you have
  done?
  *Mar.* Had there been but one tree in all the
  shire,
Nor any hope to compass a penny halter,
Before, like you, I had outliv'd my fortunes, 105
A withe had serv'd my turn to hang myself.
I am zealous in your cause; pray you hang
  yourself,
And presently, as you love your credit.
  *Well.*            I thank you.
  *Mar.* Will you stay till you die in a ditch,
  or lice devour you? ——
Or, if you dare not do the feat yourself,   110

But that you 'll put the state to charge and
  trouble,
Is there no purse to be cut, house to be broken,
Or market-women with eggs, that you may
  murther,
And so dispatch the business?
  *Well.*             Here 's variety,
I must confess; but I 'll accept of none   115
Of all your gentle offers, I assure you.
  *Mar.* Why, have you hope ever to eat again,
Or drink? or be the master of three farthings?
If you like not hanging, drown yourself! Take
  some course
For your reputation.
  *Well.*       'T will not do, dear tempter, 120
With all the rhetoric the fiend hath taught
  you.
I am as far as thou art from despair;
Nay, I have confidence, which is more than
  hope,
To live, and suddenly, better than ever.
  *Mar.* Ha! ha! these castles you build in the
  air                         125
Will not persuade me or to give or lend
A token to you.
  *Well.*        I 'll be more kind to thee:
Come, thou shalt dine with me.
  *Mar.*          With you!
  *Well.*           Nay more, dine gratis.
  *Mar.* Under what hedge, I pray you? or at
  whose cost?
Are they padders or abram-men that are your
  consorts?               130
  *Well.* Thou art incredulous; but thou shalt
  dine
Not alone at her house, but with a gallant
  lady;
With me, and with a lady.
  *Mar.*         Lady! what lady?
With the Lady of the Lake, or Queen of Fairies?
For I know it must be an enchanted dinner. 135
  *Well.* With the Lady Allworth, knave.
  *Mar.*          Nay, now there 's hope
Thy brain is crack'd.
  *Well.*       Mark there, with what respect
I am entertain'd.
  *Mar.* With choice, no doubt, of dog-whips.
Why, dost thou ever hope to pass her porter?
  *Well.* 'T is not far off, go with me; trust
  thine own eyes.             140
  *Mar.* Troth, in my hope, or my assurance
  rather,
To see thee curvet and mount like a dog in a
  blanket,
If ever thou presume to pass her threshold,
I will endure thy company.
  *Well.*       Come along then. *Exeun .*

---

  **80 cast:** cast off     **108 presently:** immediately     **111 charge:** expense     **126 or to:** either to
**130 padders:** footpads    **abram-men:** beggars    **142 curvet:** when tossed like a dog in a blanket

## Actus secundi, Scena secunda

[*A Room in Lady Allworth's House*]

*Allworth. Waiting Woman. Chambermaid.*
*Order. Amble. Furnace. Watchall*

*Woman.*   Could you not command your lei-
sure one hour longer?
*Cham.*   Or half an hour?
*All.*         I have told you what my haste is:
Besides, being now another's, not mine own,
Howe'er I much desire to enjoy you longer,
My duty suffers, if, to please myself,            5
I should neglect my lord.
*Woman.*         Pray you, do me the favour
To put these few quince-cakes into your pocket;
They are of mine own preserving.
*Cham.*               And this marmalade;
'T is comfortable for your stomach.
*Woman.*               And, at parting,
Excuse me if I beg a farewell from you.      10
*Cham.*   You are still before me.   I move the
same suit, sir.
            [*Allworth*] *kisses 'em severally.*
*Furn.*   How greedy these chamberers are of a
beardless chin!
I think the tits will ravish him.
*All.*                     My service
To both.
*Woman.*   Ours waits on you.
*Cham.*               And shall do ever.
*Ord.*   You are my lady's charge, be therefore
careful                                                              15
That you sustain your parts.
*Woman.*         We can bear, I warrant you.
            *Exeunt Woman and Chambermaid.*
*Furn.*   Here, drink it off; the ingredients are
cordial,
And this the true elixir; it hath boil'd
Since midnight for you. 'T is the quintessence
Of five cocks of the game, ten dozen of spar-
rows,                                                               20
Knuckles of veal, potato-roots and marrow,
Coral and ambergris. Were you two years
elder,
And I had a wife, or gamesome mistress,
I durst trust you with neither. You need not
bait
After this, I warrant you, though your jour-
ney 's long;                                                      25
You may ride on the strength of this till to-
morrow morning.
*All.*   Your courtesies overwhelm me: I much
grieve
To part from such true friends; and yet find
comfort,

---

My attendance on my honourable lord,
Whose resolution holds to visit my lady,      30
Will speedily bring me back.
            *Knocking at the gate;  Marrall and*
                        *Wellborn within.*
*Mar.*               Dar'st thou venture further?
*Well.*   Yes, yes, and knock again.
*Ord.*                         'T is he; disperse!
*Amb.*   Perform it bravely.
*Furn.*               I know my cue, ne'er doubt me.
                        *They go off several ways.*

[*Enter Watchall, ceremoniously introducing*
                        *Wellborn and Marrall*]

*Watch.*   Beast that I was, to make you stay!
Most welcome;                                              34
You were long since expected.
*Well.*                     Say so much
To my friend, I pray you.
*Watch.*               For your sake, I will, sir.
*Mar.*   For his sake!
*Well.*               Mum; this is nothing.
*Mar.*                     More than ever
I would have believ'd, though I had found it in
my primer.
*All.*   When I have given you reasons for my
late harshness,
You 'll pardon and excuse me; for, believe
me,                                                                   40
Though now I part abruptly, in my service
I will deserve it.
*Mar.*               Service! with a vengeance!
*Well.*   I am satisfied: farewell, Tom.
*All.*   All joy stay with you!   *Exit Allworth.*

### Enter Amble

*Amb.*   You are happily encounter'd; I yet
never
Presented one so welcome as I know           45
You will be to my lady.
*Mar.*               This is some vision,
Or, sure, these men are mad, to worship a
dunghill;
It cannot be a truth.
*Well.*               Be still a pagan,
An unbelieving infidel; be so, miscreant,
And meditate on "blankets, and on dog-
whips!"                                                           50

### Enter Furnace

*Furn.*   I am glad you are come; until I know
your pleasure
I knew not how to serve up my lady's dinner.
*Mar.*   His pleasure! is it possible?
*Well.*                     What 's thy will?
*Furn.*   Marry, sir, I have some grouse,
and turkey chicken,

---

¹³ tits: wenches   ¹⁸ elixir: prolonger of life
formerly a book of prayers, etc.

²² Coral: lobster eggs   ²⁴ bait: feed   ³⁸ primer:

Some rails and quails, and my lady will'd me
   ask you,                                                   55
What kind of sauces best affect your palate,
That I may use my utmost skill to please it.
   *Mar.* [*Aside.*] The devil 's enter'd this cook.
   Sauce for his palate!
That, on my knowledge, for almost this twelve-
   month,
Durst wish but cheese-parings and brown bread
   on Sundays.                                                60
   *Well.* That way I like 'em best.
   *Furn.*          It shall be done, sir. *Exit Furnace.*
   *Well.* What think you of "the hedge we
   shall dine under"?
Shall we feed gratis?
   *Mar.*          I know not what to think;
Pray you, make me not mad.

### Enter Order

   *Ord.*          This place becomes you not; 64
Pray you, walk, sir, to the dining room.
   *Well.*                    I am well here,
Till her ladyship quits her chamber.
   *Mar.*                Well here, say you?
'T is a rare change! But yesterday you thought
Yourself well in a barn, wrapp'd up in pease-
   straw.

### Enter Woman and Chambermaid

   *Woman.* O! sir, you are wish'd for.
   *Cham.*          My lady dreamt, sir, of you.
   *Woman.* And the first command she gave,
   after she rose,                                            70
Was (her devotions done) to give her notice
When you approach'd here.
   *Cham.*          Which is done, on my virtue.
   *Mar.* I shall be converted; I begin to grow
Into a new belief, which saints nor angels      74
Could have won me to have faith in.
   *Woman.*                    Sir, my lady!

### Enter Lady [Allworth]

   *Lady.* I come to meet you, and languish'd
   till I saw you.
This first kiss is for form; I allow a second
To such a friend.          [*Kisses Wellborn.*]
   *Mar.* To such a friend! Heaven bless me!
   *Well.* I am wholly yours; yet, madam, if you
   please
To grace this gentleman with a salute ——      80
   *Mar.* Salute me at his bidding!
   *Well.*          I shall receive it
As a most high favour.
   *Lady.*          Sir, you may command me.
   [*Advances to kiss Marrall, who re-
   tires.*]
   *Well.* Run backward from a lady! and such
   a lady!

   *Mar.* To kiss her foot is, to poor me, a fa-
   vour
I am unworthy of.          *Offers to kiss her foot.*
   *Lady.*          Nay, pray you, rise;      85
And since you are so humble, I 'll exalt you.
You shall dine with me to-day, at mine own
   table.
   *Mar.* Your ladyship's table! I am not good
   enough
To sit at your steward's board.
   *Lady.*          You are too modest;
I will not be deni'd.

### Enter Furnace

   *Furn.*          Will you still be babbling 90
Till your meat freeze on the table? The old
   trick still;
My art ne'er thought on!
   *Lady.* Your arm, Master Wellborn: ——
Nay, keep us company.          [*To Marrall.*]
   *Mar.*          I was ne'er so grac'd.
   *Exeunt Wellborn, Lady* [*Allworth*],
   *Amble, Marrall, Woman,* [*and
   Chambermaid*].
   *Ord.* So! we have play'd our parts, and are
   come off well;
But if I know the mystery, why my lady      95
Consented to it, or why Master Wellborn
Desir'd it, may I perish!
   *Furn.*          Would I had
The roasting of his heart that cheated him,
And forces the poor gentleman to these shifts!
By fire! (for cooks are Persians, and swear by
   it,)                                                       100
Of all the griping and extorting tyrants
I ever heard or read of, I ne'er met
A match to Sir Giles Overreach.
   *Watch.*          What will you take
To tell him so, fellow Furnace?
   *Furn.*          Just as much
As my throat is worth, for that would be the
   price on 't.                                                105
To have a usurer that starves himself,
And wears a cloak of one-and-twenty years
On a suit of fourteen groats, bought of the
   hangman,
To grow rich, and then purchase, is too com-
   mon;
But this Sir Giles feeds high, keeps many serv-
   ants,                                                      110
Who must at his command do any outrage;
Rich in his habit, vast in his expenses;
Yet he to admiration still increases
In wealth and lordships.
   *Ord.* He frights men out of their estates,
And breaks through all law-nets, made to curb
   ill men,                                                   115

As they were cobwebs.  No man dares reprove
  him.
Such a spirit to dare and power to do were never
Lodg'd so unluckily.

*Enter Amble [laughing]*

*Amb.*                  Ha! ha! I shall burst.
*Ord.*  Contain thyself, man.
*Furn.*                 Or make us partakers
Of your sudden mirth.
  *Amb.*               Ha! ha! my lady has got  120
Such a guest at her table! — this term-driver,
  Marrall,
This snip of an attorney ——
  *Furn.*              What of him, man?
*Amb.*  The knave thinks still he 's at the
  cook's shop in Ram Alley,
Where the clerks divide, and the elder is to
  choose;
And feeds so slovenly!
  *Furn.*              Is this all?
  *Amb.*                     My lady  125
Drank to him for fashion sake, or to please
Master Wellborn;
As I live, he rises, and takes up a dish
In which there were some remnants of a boil'd
  capon,
And pledges her in white broth!
  *Furn.*                    Nay, 't is like
The rest of his tribe.
  *Amb.*    And when I brought him wine,  130
He leaves his stool, and, after a leg or two,
Most humbly thanks my worship.
  *Ord.*                  Rose already!
  *Amb.*  I shall be chid.

*Enter Lady [Allworth], Wellborn, Marrall*

*Furn.*       My lady frowns.
*Lady.*       You wait well! [*To Amble.*]
Let me have no more of this:  I observ'd your
  jeering.
Sirrah, I 'll have you know, whom I  think
  worthy                                   135
To sit at my table, be he ne'er so mean,
When I am present, is not your companion.
  *Ord.* Nay, she 'll preserve what 's due to her.
  *Furn.*                 This refreshing
Follows your flux of laughter.
  *Lady.* [*To Wellborn.*]      You are master
Of your own will.  I know so much of manners,
As not to inquire your purposes;  in a word, 141
To me you are ever welcome, as to a house
That is your own.
  *Well.* [*Aside to Marrall.*] Mark that.
  *Mar.*                With reverence, sir,
An it like your worship.
  *Well.*        Trouble yourself no farther,

Dear madam;  my heart 's full of zeal and serv-
  ice,                                       145
However in my language I am sparing.
Come, Master Marrall.
  *Mar.*            I attend your worship.
                   *Exeunt Wellborn, Marrall.*
*Lady.*  I see in your looks you are sorry,
  and you know me
An easy mistress.  Be merry;  I have forgot all.
Order and Furnace, come with me;  I  must
  give you                                   150
Further directions.
  *Ord.*            What you please.
  *Furn.*        We are ready. [*Exeunt.*]

*Actus secundi, Scena tertia*

[*The Country near Lady Allworth's House*]

*Wellborn.  Marrall*

*Well.*  I think I am in a good way.
*Mar.*           Good!  Sir, the best way,
The certain best way.
  *Well.*       There are casualties
That men are subject to.
  *Mar.*            You are above 'em;
And as you are already worshipful,
I hope ere long you will increase in worship,  5
And be right worshipful.
  *Well.*         Prithee do not flout me:
What I shall be, I shall be.  Is 't for your ease,
You keep your hat off?
  *Mar.*       Ease! an it like your worship,
I hope Jack Marrall shall not live so long,
To prove himself such an unmannerly beast,  10
Though it hail hazel-nuts, as to be cover'd
When your worship 's present.
  *Well.* (*Aside.*)      Is not this a true rogue,
That, out of mere hope of a future coz'nage,
Can turn thus suddenly?  'T is rank already.
  *Mar.* I know your worship 's wise, and needs
  no counsel,                               15
Yet if, in my desire to do you service,
I humbly offer my advice, (but still
Under correction,) I hope I shall not
Incur your high displeasure.
  *Well.*             No;  speak freely.
  *Mar.*  Then, in my judgment, sir, my simple
  judgment,                                 20
(Still with your worship's favour,) I could wish
  you
A better habit, for this cannot be
But much distasteful to the noble lady
(I say no more) that loves you;  for, this morn-
  ing,
To me, and I am but a swine to her,        25

---

¹²³ **Ram Alley:** a London street, famous for cook shops   ¹³¹ **leg:** bow   ² **casualties:** accidents
⁸ **like:** please   ¹³ **coz'nage:** cheating

Before th' assurance of her wealth perfum'd
you,
You savour'd not of amber.
*Well.*                              I do now then!
*Mar.*   This your batoon hath got a touch of
it.—— *Kisses the end of his cudgel.*
Yet, if you please, for change, I have twenty
pounds here,
Which, out of my true love, I presently          30
Lay down at your worship's feet; 't will serve
to buy you
A riding suit.
*Well.*          But where 's the horse?
*Mar.*                              My gelding
Is at your service; nay, you shall ride me,
Before your worship shall be put to the trouble
To walk afoot. Alas, when you are lord          35
Of this lady's manor, as I know you will be,
You may with the lease of glebe land, call'd
Knave's-acre,
A place I would manure, requite your vassal.
*Well.* I thank thy love, but must make no
use of it;
What 's twenty pounds?
*Mar.*          'T is all that I can make, sir. 40
*Well.* Dost thou think, though I want
clothes, I could not have 'em,
For one word to my lady?
*Mar.*          As I know not that!
*Well.* Come, I 'll tell thee a secret, and so
leave thee.
I 'll not give her the advantage, though she be
A gallant-minded lady, after we are married, 45
(There being no woman but is sometimes fro-
ward,)
To hit me in the teeth, and say, she was forc'd
To buy my wedding-clothes, and took me on
With a plain riding-suit, and an ambling nag.
No, I 'll be furnish'd something like myself, 50
And so farewell: for thy suit touching Knave's-
acre,
When it is mine, 't is thine.
*Mar.*          I thank your worship. *Exit Well.*
How was I cozen'd in the calculation
Of this man's fortune! My master cozen'd too,
Whose pupil I am in the art of undoing men; 55
For that is our profession! Well, well, Master
Wellborn,
You are of a sweet nature, and fit again to be
cheated:
Which, if the Fates please, when you are pos-
sess'd
Of the land and lady, you, sans question, shall
be.
I 'll presently think of the means.
                              *Walk by, musing.*

*Enter Overreach [speaking to a Servant within]*
*Over.*                    Sirrah, take my horse. 60
I 'll walk to get me an appetite; 't is but a mile,
And exercise will keep me from being pursy.
Ha! Marrall! Is he conjuring? Perhaps
The knave has wrought the prodigal to do
Some outrage on himself, and now he feels 65
Compunction in his conscience for 't: no matter,
So it be done. Marrall!
*Mar.*                    Sir.
*Over.*                    How succeed we
In our plot on Wellborn?
*Mar.*                    Never better, sir.
*Over.* Has he hang'd or drown'd himself?
*Mar.*                    No, sir, he lives;
Lives once more to be made a prey to you, 70
A greater prey than ever.
*Over.*                    Art thou in thy wits?
If thou art, reveal this miracle, and briefly.
*Mar.* A lady, sir, is fall'n in love with him.
*Over.* With him? What lady?
*Mar.*                    The rich Lady Allworth.
*Over.* Thou dolt! how dar'st thou speak this?
*Mar.*                    I speak truth; 75
And I do so but once a year, unless
It be to you, sir. We din'd with her ladyship,
I thank his worship.
*Over.*                    His worship!
*Mar.*                    As I live, sir,
I din'd with him, at the great lady's table,
Simple as I stand here; and saw when she
kiss'd him,                                   80
And would, at his request, have kiss'd me too:
But I was not so audacious as some youths
are,
That dare do anything, be it ne'er so absurd,
And sad after performance.
*Over.*                    Why, thou rascal!
To tell me these impossibilities.          85
Dine at her table! and kiss him! or thee!——
Impudent varlet, have not I myself,
To whom great countesses' doors have oft flew
open,
Ten times attempted, since her husband's
death,
In vain, to see her, though I came — a suitor?
And yet your good solicitorship, and rogue
Wellborn,                                   91
Were brought into her presence, feasted with
her!——
But that I know thee a dog that cannot blush,
This most incredible lie would call up one
On thy buttermilk cheeks.
*Mar.*          Shall I not trust my eyes, sir, 95
Or taste? I feel her good cheer in my belly.

---

27 **amber:** ambergris     29 **change:** change of dress (?), small change (?)     37 **glebe land:** field
38 **manure:** cultivate     40 **make:** procure, "raise"     53 **I:** (not in Q)     62 **pursy:** short-winded
80 **Simple as:** as sure as     84 **And sad:** and regret it

*Over.* You shall feel me, if you give not over,
sirrah:
Recover your brains again, and be no more
gull'd
With a beggar's plot, assisted by the aids
Of serving-men and chambermaids, (for beyond
these                                              100
Thou never saw'st a woman,) or I 'll quit you
From my employments.
    *Mar.*          Will you credit this yet?
On my confidence of their marriage, I offer'd
Wellborn ——
I would give a crown now I durst say "his
worship" ——                              *Aside.*
My nag and twenty pounds.
    *Over.* Did you so, idiot!  *Strikes him down.*
Was this the way to work him to despair,  106
Or rather to cross me?
    *Mar.*        Will your worship kill me?
    *Over.* No, no; but drive the lying spirit out
of you.
    *Mar.* He 's gone.
    *Over.*    I have done then: now, forgetting
Your late imaginary feast and lady,     110
Know, my Lord Lovell dines with me to-mor-
row.
Be careful nought be wanting to receive him;
And bid my daughter's women trim her up.
Though they paint her, so she catch the lord,
I 'll thank them.
There 's a piece for my late blows.
    *Mar.*        I must yet suffer: 115
But there may be a time ——          *Aside.*
    *Over.*        Do you grumble?
    *Mar.*        No, sir. *[Exeunt.]*

## *Actus tertii, Scena prima*

*[The Country near Overreach's House]*

*[Lord] Lovell. Allworth. Servants*

*Lov.* Walk the horses down the hill: some-
thing in private
I must impart to Allworth.     *Exeunt Servi.*
    *All.*          O, my lord,
What sacrifice of reverence, duty, watching,
Although I could put off the use of sleep,
And ever wait on your commands to serve
'em;                                               5
What dangers, though in ne'er so horrid shapes,
Nay death itself, though I should run to meet
it,
Can I, and with a thankful willingness, suffer!
But still the retribution will fall short
Of your bounties shower'd upon me.
    *Lov.*         Loving youth, 10
Till what I purpose be put into act,

Do not o'erprize it. Since you have trusted me
With your soul's nearest, nay, her dearest
secret,
Rest confident 't is in a cabinet lock'd
Treachery shall never open. I have found you 15
(For so much to your face I must profess,
Howe'er you guard your modesty with a blush
for 't)
More zealous in your love and service to me
Than I have been in my rewards.
    *All.*          Still great ones,
Above my merit.
    *Lov.*    Such your gratitude calls 'em; 20
Nor am I of that harsh and rugged temper
As some great men are tax'd with, who imagine
They part from the respect due to their hon-
ours
If they use not all such as follow 'em,     24
Without distinction of their births, like slaves.
I am not so condition'd; I can make
A fitting difference between my footboy
And a gentleman by want compell'd to serve
me.
    *All.* 'T is thankfully acknowledg'd; you
have been
More like a father to me than a master.     30
Pray you, pardon the comparison.
    *Lov.*          I allow it:
And, to give you assurance I am pleas'd in 't,
My carriage and demeanour to your mistress,
Fair Margaret, shall truly witness for me
I can command my passions.
    *All.*         'T is a conquest 35
Few lords can boast of when they are tempted.
— Oh!
    *Lov.* Why do you sigh? Can you be doubt-
ful of me?
By that fair name I in the wars have pur-
chas 'd,
And all my actions, hitherto untainted,
I will not be more true to mine own honour 40
Than to my Allworth!
    *All.*      As you are the brave Lord Lovell,
Your bare word only given is an assurance
Of more validity and weight to me
Than all the oaths, bound up with impreca-
tions,
Which, when they would deceive, most court-
iers practise;                                    45
Yet being a man, (for, sure, to style you more
Would relish of gross flattery,) I am forc'd,
Against my confidence of your worth and vir-
tues,
To doubt, nay, more, to fear.
    *Lov.*      So young, and jealous!
    *All.* Were you to encounter with a single foe,
The victory were certain; but to stand     51

The charge of two such potent enemies,
At once assaulting you, as wealth and beauty,
And those too seconded with power, is odds
Too great for Hercules.
    *Lov.*          Speak your doubts and fears, 55
Since you will nourish 'em, in plainer language,
That I may understand 'em.
    *All.*          What 's your will,
Though I lend arms against myself, (provided
They may advantage you,) must be obeyed.
My much-lov'd lord, were Margaret only fair, 60
The cannon of her more than earthly form,
Though mounted high, commanding all beneath it,
And ramm'd with bullets of her sparkling eyes,
Of all the bulwarks that defend your senses
Could batter none, but that which guards your
    sight.          65
But when the well-tun'd accents of her tongue
Make music to you, and with numerous sounds
Assault your hearing, (such as if Ulysses
Now liv'd again, howe'er he stood the Sirens,
Could not resist,) the combat must grow doubtful          70
Between your reason and rebellious passions.
Add this too; when you feel her touch, and breath
Like a soft western wind when it glides o'er
Arabia, creating gums and spices;
And, in the van, the nectar of her lips, 75
Which you must taste, bring the battalia on,
Well arm'd, and strongly lin'd with her discourse,
And knowing manners, to give entertainment; —
Hippolytus himself would leave Diana,
To follow such a Venus.
    *Lov.*          Love hath made you 80
Poetical, Allworth.
    *All.*          Grant all these beat off,
Which if it be in man to do, you 'll do it,
Mammon, in Sir Giles Overreach, steps in
With heaps of ill-got gold, and so much land,
To make her more remarkable, as would tire 85
A falcon's wings in one day to fly over.
O my good lord! these powerful aids, which would
Make a mis-shapen negro beautiful,
(Yet are but ornaments to give her lustre,
That in herself is all perfection,) must 90
Prevail for her. I here release your trust;
'T is happiness enough for me to serve you
And sometimes, with chaste eyes, to look upon
    her.
    *Lov.* Why, shall I swear?
    *All.*          O, by no means, my lord;

And wrong not so your judgment to the world
As from your fond indulgence to a boy, 96
Your page, your servant, to refuse a blessing
Divers great men are rivals for.
    *Lov.*          Suspend
Your judgment till the trial. How far is it
T' Overreach-House?
    *All.* At the most, some half hour's riding; 100
You 'll soon be there.
    *Lov.*          And you the sooner freed
From your jealous fears.
    *All.*          O that I durst but hope it! *Exeunt.*


### Actus tertii, Scena secunda

[*A Room in Overreach's House*]

*Overreach. Greedy. Marrall*

    *Over.* Spare for no cost: let my dressers crack with the weight
Of curious viands.
    *Greedy.*          "Store indeed 's no sore," sir.
    *Over.* That proverb fits your stomach, Master Greedy.
And let no plate be seen but what 's pure gold,
Or such whose workmanship exceeds the matter          5
That it is made of; let my choicest linen
Perfume the room, and, when we wash, the water,
With precious powders mix'd, so please my lord
That he may with envy wish to bathe so ever
    *Mar.* 'T will be very chargeable.
    *Over.*          Avaunt, you drudge! 10
Now all my labour'd ends are at the stake,
Is 't a time to think of thrift? Call in my
    daughter.          [*Exit Marrall.*]
And, Master Justice, since you love choice dishes,
And plenty of 'em ——
    *Greedy.*          As I do, indeed, sir,
Almost as much as to give thanks for 'em. 15
    *Over.* I do confer that providence, with my power
Of absolute command to have abundance,
To your best care.
    *Greedy.*          I 'll punctually discharge it,
And give the best directions. Now am I,
In mine own conceit, a monarch; at the least,
Arch-president of the boil'd, the roast, the bak'd;          21
For which I will eat often, and give thanks
When my belly 's brac'd up like a drum, and
    that 's pure justice.          *Exit Greedy.*

---

⁵⁹ **advantage:** help     ⁶⁵ **none:** ('more' Q)     ⁶⁷ **numerous:** rhythmical     ⁷⁷ **lin'd:** strengthened ('liu'd' Q)     ² **Store . . . sore:** It never hurts to have enough     ¹⁰ **chargeable:** expensive     ¹⁶ **providence:** duty of oversight     ²⁰ **conceit:** fancy

*Over.* It must be so. Should the foolish girl
   prove modest,
She may spoil all; she had it not from me,  25
But from her mother; I was ever forward,
As she must be, and therefore I 'll prepare her.

### [*Enter*] *Margaret*

Alone — and let your women wait without.
   *Marg.* Your pleasure, sir?
   *Over.*                     Ha! this is a neat dressing!
These orient pearls and diamonds well plac'd
   too!                                           30
The gown affects me not, it should have been
Embroider'd o'er and o'er with flowers of gold;
But these rich jewels and quaint fashion help
   it.
And how below? since oft the wanton eye
The face observ'd, descends unto the foot,    35
Which being well proportion'd, as yours is,
Invites as much as perfect white and red,
Though without art.  How like you your new
   woman,
The Lady Downfall'n?
   *Marg.*                     Well, for a companion;
Not as a servant.
   *Over.*                     Is she humble, Meg,    40
And careful too, her ladyship forgotten?
   *Marg.* I pity her fortune.
   *Over.*                     Pity her! trample on her.
I took her up in an old tamin gown,
(Even starv'd for want of twopenny chops,) to
   serve thee;
And if I understand she but repines          45
To do thee any duty, though ne'er so servile,
I 'll pack her to her knight, where I have lodg'd
   him,
Into the Counter and there let 'em howl to-
   gether.
   *Marg.* You know your own ways; but for me,
   I blush
When I command her, that was once attended
With persons not inferior to myself          51
In birth.
   *Over.* In birth! why, art thou not my
      daughter,
The blest child of my industry and wealth?
Why, foolish girl, was 't not to make thee great
That I have ran, and still pursue, those ways  55
That hale down curses on me, which I mind
   not?
Part with these humble thoughts, and apt thy-
   self
To the noble state I labour to advance thee;
Or, by my hopes to see thee honourable,
I will adopt a stranger to my heir,          60

And throw thee from my care.  Do not provoke
   me.
   *Marg.* I will not, sir; mould me which way
   you please.

### *Enter Greedy*

   *Over.* How! Interrupted!
   *Greedy.*                     'T is matter of importance.
The cook, sir, is self-will'd, and will not learn
From my experience.  There 's a fawn brought
   in, sir,                                      65
And, for my life, I cannot make him roast it
With a Norfolk dumpling in the belly of it;
And, sir, we wise men know, without the dump-
   ling
'T is not worth three-pence.
   *Over.*                     Would it were whole in thy belly,
To stuff it out! Cook it any way; prithee, leave
   me.                                           70
   *Greedy.* Without order for the dumpling?
   *Over.*                     Let it be dumpl'd
Which way thou wilt; or tell him, I will scald
   him
In his own caldron.
   *Greedy.*                     I had lost my stomach
Had I lost my mistress dumpling; I 'll give
   thanks for 't.                     *Exit Greedy.*
   *Over.* But to our business, Meg; you have
   heard who dines here?                         75
   *Marg.* I have, sir.
   *Over.*                     'T is an honourable man;
A lord, Meg, and commands a regiment
Of soldiers, and, what 's rare, is one himself,
A bold and understanding one; and to be
A lord and a good leader, in one volume,     80
Is granted unto few but such as rise up
The kingdom's glory.

### *Enter Greedy*

   *Greedy.*                     I 'll resign my office,
If I be not better obey'd.
   *Over.*                     'Slight, art thou frantic?
   *Greedy.* Frantic! 'T would make me frantic
   and stark mad,                                84
Were I not a justice of peace and quorum too,
Which this rebellious cook cares not a straw for.
There are a dozen of woodcocks ——
   *Over.*                     Make thyself
Thirteen, the baker's dozen.
   *Greedy.*                     I am contented,
So they may be dress'd to my mind; he has
   found out
A new device for sauce, and will not dish 'em
With toasts and butter.  My father was a
   tailor,                                       91

---

²⁴ It: ('I' Q)     ³⁰ orient: of best quality     ³¹ affects: pleases     ⁴³ tamin: thin woollen cloth
⁴⁵ repines: frets, is unwilling     ⁴⁸ Counter: prison     ⁵⁷ apt: fit     ⁶⁰ to: as, for     ⁷³ stomach: appetite     ⁸⁴ me frantic: ('me a franticke' Q)     ⁸⁵ quorum: ('coram' Q)     ⁸⁷ woodcocks: traditionally
types of stupidity

And my name, though a justice, Greedy Wood-
    cock;
And, ere I 'll see my lineage so abus'd,
I 'll give up my commission.
    *Over.* [*Loudly.*]    Cook! — Rogue, obey him!
I have given the word, pray you, now remove
    yourself                                                95
To a collar of brawn, and trouble me no farther.
    *Greedy.* I will, and meditate what to eat at
    dinner.                               *Exit Greedy.*
    *Over.* And as I said, Meg, when this gull
    disturb'd us,
This honourable lord, this colonel,
I would have thy husband
    *Marg.* There 's too much disparity 100
Between his quality and mine, to hope it.
    *Over.* I more than hope 't, and doubt not
    to effect it.
Be thou no enemy to thyself, my wealth
Shall weight his titles down, and make you
    equals.
Now for the means to assure him thine, ob-
    serve me:                                          105
Remember he 's a courtier and a soldier,
And not to be trifled with; and, therefore,
    when
He comes to woo you, see you do not coy it:
This mincing modesty hath spoil'd many a
    match
By a first refusal, in vain after hop'd for.    110
    *Marg.* You 'll have me, sir, preserve the dis-
    tance that
Confines a virgin?
    *Over.*                      Virgin me no virgins!
I must have you lose that name, or you lose me.
I will have you private — start not — I say,
    private;
If thou art my true daughter, not a bastard, 115
Thou wilt venture alone with one man, though
    he came
Like Jupiter to Semele, and come off, too;
And therefore, when he kisses you, kiss close.
    *Marg.* I have heard this is the strumpet's
    fashion, sir,
Which I must never learn.
    *Over.*                        Learn anything, 120
And from any creature that may make thee
    great;
From the devil himself.
    *Marg.* [*Aside.*]    This is but devilish doc-
    trine!
    *Over.* Or, if his blood grow hot, suppose he
    offer
Beyond this, do not you stay till it cool,
But meet his ardour; if a couch be near,    125
Sit down on 't, and invite him.
    *Marg.*                        In your house,

Your own house, sir! For Heaven's sake, what
    are you then?
Or what shall I be, sir?
    *Over.*                        Stand not on form;
Words are no substances.
    *Marg.*                  Though you could dispense
With your own honour, cast aside religion,    130
The hopes of Heaven, or fear of hell, excuse me,
In worldly policy this is not the way
To make me his wife; his whore, I grant it
    may do.
My maiden honour so soon yielded up,
Nay, prostituted, cannot but assure him    135
I, that am light to him, will not hold weight
When he is tempted by others; so, in judgment,
When to his lust I have given up my honour,
He must and will forsake me.
    *Over.*                        How! forsake thee!
Do I wear a sword for fashion? or is this arm
Shrunk up or wither'd?    Does there live a
    man                                                141
Of that large list I have encounter'd with
Can truly say I e'er gave inch of ground
Not purchas'd with his blood that did oppose
    me?
Forsake thee when the thing is done! He dares
    not.                                               145
Give me but proof he has enjoy'd thy person,
Though all his captains, echoes to his will,
Stood arm'd by his side to justify the wrong,
And he himself in the head of his bold troop,
Spite of his lordship, and his colonelship,    150
Or the judge's favour, I will make him render
A bloody and a strict accompt, and force him,
By marrying thee, to cure thy wounded honour!
I have said it.

*Enter Marrall*

    *Mar.*          Sir, the man of honour 's come,
Newly alighted.
    *Over.*          In, without reply.                155
And do as I command, or thou art lost.
                                        *Exit Margaret.*
Is the loud music I gave order for
Ready to receive him?
    *Mar.*          'T is, sir.
    *Over.*          Let 'em sound
A princely welcome. [*Exit Marrall.*] Rough-
    ness awhile leave me;
For fawning now, a stranger to my nature,    160
Must make way for me.

    *Loud music.    Enter [Lord] Lovell, Greedy,
            Allworth, Marrall*

    *Lov.*          Sir, you meet your trouble.
    *Over.* What you are pleas'd to style so is an
    honour
Above my worth and fortunes.

---

⁹⁸ **collar of brawn:** piece of boar's meat    ⁹⁸ **gull:** fool    ¹⁰¹ **quality:** birth, station    ¹¹⁷ **come off:**
escape unburned (not like Semele)    ¹³⁶ **hold weight:** retain his love

*All.* [*Aside.*]                     Strange, so humble.
*Over.* A justice of peace, my lord.
                              *Presents Greedy to him.*
*Lov.*                        Your hand, good sir.
*Greedy.* [*Aside.*] This is a lord, and some
    think this a favour;                            165
But I had rather have my hand in my dump-
    ling.
*Over.* Room for my lord.
*Lov.*                I miss, sir, your fair daughter
To crown my welcome.
*Over.*                        May it please my lord
To taste a glass of Greek wine first, and sud-
    denly
She shall attend my lord.
*Lov.*                        You 'll be obey'd, sir. 170
                    *Exeunt omnes preter Overreach.*
*Over.* 'T is to my wish: as soon as come, ask
    for her!
Why, Meg!  Meg Overreach. —

              [*Re-enter Margaret*]

                              How! tears in your eyes!
Hah! dry 'em quickly, or I 'll dig 'em out.
Is this a time to whimper?  Meet that great-
    ness
That flies into thy bosom, think what 't is  175
For me to say, "My honourable daughter;"
And thou, when I stand bare, to say, "Put
    on;"
Or, "Father, you forget yourself."  No more:
But be instructed, or expect —— He comes.

*Enter* [*Lord*] *Lovell, Greedy, Allworth, Marrall.*
              *They salute.*

A black-brow'd girl, my lord.
*Lov.*                As I live, a rare one. 180
*All.* [*Aside.*] He 's took already: I am lost.
*Over.* [*Aside.*]                        That kiss
Came twanging off, I like it. — Quit the room.
                              *The rest off.*
A little bashful, my good lord, but you,
I hope, will teach her boldness.
*Lov.*                        I am happy
In such a scholar: but ——
*Over.*                I am past learning, 185
And therefore leave you to yourselves. — Re-
    member — *To his daughter. Exit Overreach.*
*Lov.* You see, fair lady, your father is so-
    licitous
To have you change the barren name of
    virgin
Into a hopeful wife.
*Marg.*                His haste, my lord,
Holds no power o'er my will.
*Lov.*                But o'er your duty. 190

*Marg.* Which, forc'd too much, may break.
*Lov.*                Bend rather, sweetest.'
Think of your years.
*Marg.*                Too few to match with yours:
And choicest fruits too soon pluck'd, rot and
    wither.
*Lov.* Do you think I am old?
*Marg.*                I am sure I am too young.
*Lov.* I can advance you.
*Marg.*                To a hill of sorrow, 195
Where every hour I may expect to fall,
But never hope firm footing.  You are noble,
I of a low descent, however rich;
And tissues match'd with scarlet suit but ill.
O, my good lord, I could say more, but that 200
I dare not trust these walls.
*Lov.*                Pray you, trust my ear then.

    *Enter Overreach* [*behind*], *listening*

*Over.* Close at it! whispering! this is excel-
    lent!
And, by their postures, a consent on both parts.

        *Enter Greedy* [*behind*]

*Greedy.* Sir Giles, Sir Giles!
*Over.*                The great fiend stop that clapper!
*Greedy.* It must ring out, sir, when my belly
    rings noon.                                    205
The bak'd-meats are run out, the roast turn'd
    powder.
*Over.* I shall powder you.
*Greedy.*                Beat me to dust, I care not;
In such a cause as this, I 'll die a martyr.
*Over.* Marry, and shall, you barathrum of
    the shambles!              *Strikes him.*
*Greedy.* How! strike a justice of peace! 'T is
    petty treason,                                 210
*Edwardi quinto:* but that you are my friend,
I could commit you without bail or main-
    prize.
*Over.* Leave your bawling, sir, or I shall
    commit you
Where you shall not dine to-day.  Disturb my
    lord,
When he is in discourse!
*Greedy.*                Is 't a time to talk  215
When we should be munching!
*Lov.*                Hah! I heard some noise.
*Over.* Mum, villain; vanish! Shall we break
    a bargain
Almost made up?              *Thrust Greedy off.*
*Lov.*                Lady, I understand you.
And rest most happy in your choice, believe
    it;
I 'll be a careful pilot to direct            220
Your yet uncertain bark to a port of safety.

───────────────────────

    169 **suddenly:** immediately    170 S. D. **preter:** except    177 **Put on:** Put on your hat.    189 **His haste:**
('He hast' Q)    199 **tissues . . . scarlet:** silk and wool, the court and the city    209 **barathrum:**
glutton (lit. 'consuming pit')    212 **main-prize:** writ commanding the sheriff to take bail

*Marg.* So shall your honour save two lives,
and bind us
Your slaves for ever.
  *Lov.*                    I am in the act rewarded,
Since it is good; howe'er, you must put on
An amorous carriage towards me to delude 225
Your subtle father.
  *Marg.*          I am prone to that.
  *Lov.* Now break we off our conference. —
Sir Giles!
Where is Sir Giles?
                  *Enter Overreach, and the rest.*
  *Over.*              My noble lord; and how
Does your lordship find her?
  *Lov.*              Apt, Sir Giles, and coming;
And I like her the better.
  *Over.*              So do I too.      230
  *Love.* Yet should we take forts at the first
assault,
'T were poor in the defendant; I must confirm
her
With a love-letter or two, which I must have
Deliver'd by my page, and you give way to 't.
  *Over.* With all my soul: — a towardly gen-
tleman!                              235
Your hand, good Master Allworth: know my
house
Is ever open to you.
  *All. (Aside.)*          'T was shut till now.
  *Over.* Well done, well done, my honourable
daughter!
Th' art so already. Know this gentle youth,
And cherish him, my honourable daughter. 240
  *Marg.* I shall, with my best care.
                  *Noise within, as of a coach.*
  *Over.*                    A coach!
  *Greedy.*              More stops
Before we go to dinner! O my guts!

  *Enter Lady [Allworth] and Wellborn*

  *Lady.*              If I find welcome,
You share in it; if not, I 'll back again,
Now I know your ends; for I come arm'd for
all
Can be objected.
  *Lov.*          How! the Lady Allworth! 245
  *Over.* And thus attended!
      *Lovell salutes the Lady, the Lady salutes
                  Margaret.*
  *Mar.*              No, "I am a dolt!
The spirit of lies had ent'red me!"
  *Over.*              Peace, Patch;
'T is more than wonder! an astonishment
That does possess me wholly!
  *Lov.*              Noble lady,
This is a favour, to prevent my visit,      250
The service of my life can never equal.

  *Lady.* My lord, I laid wait for you, and
much hop'd
You would have made my poor house your first
inn:
And therefore doubting that you might forget
me,
Or too long dwell here, having such ample
cause,                              255
In this unequall'd beauty, for your stay,
And fearing to trust any but myself
With the relation of my service to you,
I borrow'd so much from my long restraint
And took the air in person to invite you.   260
  *Lov.* Your bounties are so great, they rob
me, madam,
Of words to give you thanks.
  *Lady.*          Good Sir Giles Overreach.
                              *Salutes him.*
— How dost thou, Marrall? Lik'd you my
meat so ill,
You 'll dine no more with me?
  *Greedy.* I will, when you please, 264
An it like your ladyship.
  *Lady.*          When you please, Master Greedy;
If meat can do it, you shall be satisfied.
And now, my lord, pray take into your knowl-
edge
This gentleman; howe'er his outside 's coarse,
                              *Presents Wellborn.*
His inward linings are as fine and fair      269
As any man's; wonder not I speak at large:
And howsoe'er his humour carries him
To be thus accoutred, or what taint soever,
For his wild life, hath stuck upon his fame,
He may ere long, with boldness, rank himself
With some that have contemn'd him. Sir Giles
Overreach,                          275
If I am welcome, bid him so.
  *Over.*              My nephew!
He has been too long a stranger. Faith you
have,
Pray let it be mended.
                  *Lovell conferring with Wellborn.*
  *Mar.*          Why, sir, what do you mean?
This is "rogue Wellborn, monster, prodigy,
That should hang or drown himself;" no man
of worship,                          280
Much less your nephew.
  *Over.*          Well, sirrah, we shall reckon
For this hereafter.
  *Mar.*          I 'll not lose my jeer,
Though I be beaten dead for 't.
  *Well.*              Let my silence plead
In my excuse, my lord, till better leisure
Offer itself to hear a full relation          285
Of my poor fortunes.
  *Lov.*          I would hear, and help 'em.

---

²²⁵ **carriage:** behavior    ²²⁶ **prone to:** ready to do    ²⁴¹ **stops:** delays    ²⁴⁷ **Patch:** fool    ²⁵⁰ **pre-vent:** anticipate    ²⁷⁰ **at large:** freely    ²⁷³ **fame:** reputation

*Over.* Your dinner waits you.
*Lov.*                          Pray you lead, we follow.
*Lady.* Nay, you are my guest; come, dear
  Master Wellborn. *Exeunt; manet Greedy.*
*Greedy.* "Dear Master Wellborn!" so she
  said: Heaven! Heaven!
If my belly would give me leave, I could rumi-
  nate                                                    290
All day on this. I have granted twenty war-
  rants
To have him committed, from all prisons in the
  shire,
To Nottingham jail; and now "Dear Master
  Wellborn!"
And, "My good nephew!" — but I play the fool
To stand here prating, and forget my dinner. 295

*Enter Marrall*

Are they set, Marrall?
*Mar.*          Long since; pray you a word, sir.
*Greedy.* No wording now.
*Mar.*                    In troth, I must. My master,
Knowing you are his good friend, makes bold
  with you,
And does entreat you, more guests being come
  in
Than he expected, especially his nephew,   300
The table being full too, you would excuse him,
And sup with him on the cold meat.
*Greedy.*                        How! No dinner,
After all my care?
*Mar.*                  'T is but a penance for
A meal; besides, you broke your fast.
*Greedy.*                            That was
But a bit to stay my stomach. A man in com-
  mission                                                 305
Give place to a tatterdemalion!
*Mar.*                      No bug words, sir;
Should his worship hear you ——
*Greedy.*                    Lose my dumpling too,
And butter'd toasts, and woodcocks!
*Mar.*                      Come, have patience.
If you will dispense a little with your worship,
And sit with the waiting women, you 'll have
  dumpling,                                              310
Woodcock, and butter'd toasts too.
*Greedy.*                          This revives me:
I will gorge there sufficiently.
*Mar.*                    This is the way, sir. *Exeunt.*

*Actus tertii, Scena tertia*

[*Another Room in Overreach's House*]

*Overreach, as from dinner*

*Over.* She 's caught! O women! — she neglects my lord,
And all her compliments appli'd to Wellborn!

The garments of her widowhood laid by,
She now appears as glorious as the spring.
Her eyes fix'd on him, in the wine she drinks,  5
He being her pledge, she sends him burning
  kisses,
And sits on thorns, till she be private with
  him.
She leaves my meat to feed upon his looks,
And if in our discourse he be but nam'd,        9
From her a deep sigh follows. But why grieve I
At this? It makes for me; if she prove his,
All that is hers is mine, as I will work him.

*Enter Marrall*

*Mar.* Sir, the whole board is troubled at
  your rising.
*Over.* No matter, I 'll excuse it. Prithee,
  Marrall,
Watch an occasion to invite my nephew       15
To speak with me in private.
*Mar.*                        Who? "The rogue
The lady scorn'd to look on"?
*Over.*                      You are a wag.

*Enter Lady* [*Allworth*] *and Wellborn*

*Mar.* See, sir, she 's come, and cannot be
  without him.
*Lady.* With your favour, sir, after a plente-
  ous dinner,
I shall make bold to walk a turn or two,      20
In your rare garden.
*Over.*              There 's an arbour too,
If your ladyship please to use it.
*Lady.*                    Come, Master Wellborn.
      *Exeunt Lady* [*Allworth*] *and Wellborn.*
*Over.* Grosser and grosser! Now I believe
  the poet
Feign'd not, but was historical, when he wrote
Pasiphae was enamour'd of a bull:            25
This lady's lust 's more monstrous. —

*Enter* [*Lord*] *Lovell, Margaret, and the rest*

                                My good lord,
Excuse my manners.
*Lov.*                There needs none, Sir Giles,
I may ere long say father, when it pleases
My dearest mistress to give warrant to it.
*Over.* She shall seal to it, my lord, and make
  me happy.                                              30

*Enter Wellborn and the Lady*

*Marg.* My lady is return'd.
*Lady.*                      Provide my coach,
I 'll instantly away. My thanks, Sir Giles,
For my entertainment.
*Over.*                'T is your nobleness
To think it such.
*Lady.*            I must do you a further wrong
In taking away your honourable guest.        35

³⁰⁶ **bug:** frightening    ³⁰⁹ **worship:** dignity    ³¹⁰ **you 'll:** ('you' Q)

*Lov.* I wait on you, madam; farewell, good
Sir Giles.
*Lady.*    Good Mistress Margaret!   Nay,
come, Master Wellborn,
I must not leave you behind; in sooth, I must
not.
*Over.*   Rob me not, madam, of all joys at
once;
Let my nephew stay behind.  He shall have my
    coach,                                                    40
And, after some small conference between us,
Soon overtake your ladyship.
*Lady.*                         Stay not long, sir.
*Lov.*  This parting kiss!  [*Kisses Margaret.*]
    You shall every day hear from me
By my faithful page.
*All.*                  'T is a service I am proud of.
    *Exeunt* [*Lord*] *Lovell, Lady* [*Allworth*],
        *Allworth, Marrall*
*Over.*  Daughter, to your chamber. —
                        *Exit Margaret.*
    — You may wonder, nephew,   45
After so long an enmity between us,
I should desire your friendship.
*Well.*                      So I do, sir;
'T is strange to me.
*Over.*           But I 'll make it no wonder;
And what is more, unfold my nature to you.
We worldly men, when we see friends and kins-
    men                                                     50
Past hope sunk in their fortunes, lend no hand
To lift 'em up, but rather set our feet
Upon their heads, to press 'em to the bottom;
As, I must yield, with you I practis'd it:
But, now I see you in a way to rise,   55
I can and will assist you.  This rich lady
(And I am glad of 't) is enamour'd of you;
'T is too apparent, nephew.
*Well.*                     No such thing:
Compassion rather, sir.
*Over.*               Well, in a word,   59
Because your stay is short, I 'll have you seen
No more in this base shape; nor shall she say
She married you like a beggar, or in debt.
*Well.*  He 'll run into the noose, and save
    my labour.                            *Aside.*
*Over.*  You have a trunk of rich clothes, not
    far hence,
In pawn; I will redeem 'em; and that no clam-
    our                                                     65
May taint your credit for your petty debts,
You shall have a thousand pounds to cut 'em
    off,
And go a free man to the wealthy lady.
*Well.*  This done, sir, out of love, and no ends
    else ——
*Over.*  As it is, nephew.
*Well.*            Binds me still your servant.  70

*Over.*  No compliments; you are stay'd for.
    Ere y'ave supp'd
You shall hear from me.  My coach, knaves,
    for my nephew.
To-morrow I will visit you.
*Well.*                    Here 's an uncle
In a man 's extremes!  How much they do belie
    you,
That say you are hard-hearted!
*Over.*                  My deeds, nephew,  75
Shall speak my love; what men report I weigh
    not.                                 *Exeunt.*
            *Finis Actus Tertii.*


## Actus quarti, Scena prima

[*Lady Allworth's House*]

*Lovell.   Allworth*

*Lov.*  'T is well; give me my cloak; I now dis-
    charge you
From further service.  Mind your own affairs;
I hope they will prove successful.
*All.*                   What is blest
With your good wish, my lord, cannot but pros-
    per.
Let aftertimes report, and to your honour,   5
How much I stand engag'd, for I want language
To speak my debt; yet if a tear or two
Of joy, for your much goodness, can supply
My tongue's defects, I could ——
*Lov.*                    Nay, do not melt:
This ceremonial thanks to me 's superfluous. 10
*Over.* (*Within.*)  Is my lord stirring?
*Lov.*  'T is he! oh, here 's your letter.  Let
    him in.

*Enter Overreach, Greedy, Marrall*

*Over.*  A good day to my lord!
*Lov.*                  You are an early riser,
Sir Giles.
*Over.* And reason, to attend your lordship. 15
*Lov.*  And you, too, Master Greedy, up so
    soon!
*Greedy.* In troth, my lord, after the sun is up,
I cannot sleep, for I have a foolish stomach
That croaks for breakfast.  With your lord-
    ship's favour,
I have a serious question to demand   20
Of my worthy friend Sir Giles.
*Lov.*                Pray you, use your pleasure.
*Greedy.*  How far, Sir Giles, and pray you
    answer me
Upon your credit, hold you it to be
From your manor-house, to this of my Lady
    Allworth's?
*Over.*  Why, some four mile.
*Greedy.*  How! four mile, good Sir Giles ——

---

⁵⁴ **yield:** admit   ⁷⁰ **me:** ('my' Q)   ⁷⁴ **extremes:** extremities   ⁷⁶ **weigh:** care   ⁶ **engag'd:** indebted

Upon your reputation, think better; 26
For if you do abate but one half-quarter
Of five, you do yourself the greatest wrong
That can be in the world; for four miles riding
Could not have rais'd so huge an appetite 30
As I feel gnawing on me.
*Mar.* Whether you ride,
Or go afoot, you are that way still provided,
An it please your worship.
*Over.* How now, sirrah? Prating
Before my lord! No deference? Go to my nephew,
See all his debts discharg'd, and help his worship 35
To fit on his rich suit.
*Mar.* [*Aside.*] I may fit you too.
Toss'd like a dog still! *Exit Marrall.*
*Lov.* I have writ this morning
A few lines to my mistress, your fair daughter.
*Over.* 'T will fire her, for she 's wholly yours already. —
Sweet Master Allworth, take my ring; 't will carry you 40
To her presence, I dare warrant you; and there plead
For my good lord, if you shall find occasion.
That done, pray ride to Nottingham, get a license,
Still by this token. I 'll have it dispatch'd,
And suddenly, my lord, that I may say, 45
My honourable, nay, right honourable daughter.
*Greedy.* Take my advice, young gentleman, get your breakfast;
'T is unwholesome to ride fasting. I 'll eat with you,
And eat to purpose.
*Over.* Some Fury 's in that gut;
Hungry again! Did you not devour, this morning, 50
A shield of brawn, and a barrel of Colchester oysters?
*Greedy.* Why, that was, sir, only to scour my stomach,
A kind of a preparative. Come, gentleman,
I will not have you feed like the hangman of Flushing,
Alone, while I am here.
*Lov.* Haste your return. 55
*All.* I will not fail, my lord.
*Greedy.* Nor I, to line
My Christmas coffer.
*Exeunt Greedy and Allworth.*
*Over.* To my wish: we are private.
I come not to make offer with my daughter
A certain portion, — that were poor and trivial:
In one word, I pronounce all that is mine, 60
In lands or leases, ready coin or goods,

With her, my lord, comes to you; nor shall you have
One motive to induce you to believe
I live too long, since every year I 'll add
Something unto the heap, which shall be yours too. 65
*Lov.* You are a right kind father.
*Over.* You shall have reason
To think me such. How do you like this seat?
It is well wooded, and well water'd, the acres
Fertile and rich: would it not serve for change,
To entertain your friends in a summer progress?
What thinks my noble lord?
*Lov.* 'T is a wholesome air, 71
And well-built pile; and she that 's mistress of it,
Worthy the large revénue.
*Over.* She the mistress!
It may be so for a time: but let my lord
Say only that he likes it, and would have it, 75
I say, ere long 't is his.
*Lov.* Impossible.
*Over.* You do conclude too fast, not knowing me,
Nor the engines that I work by. 'T is not alone
The Lady Allworth's lands, for those once Wellborn's 79
(As by her dotage on him I know they will be,)
Shall soon be mine; but point out any man's
In all the shire, and say they lie convenient
And useful for your lordship, and once more
I say aloud, they are yours.
*Lov.* I dare not own
What 's by unjust and cruel means extorted; 85
My fame and credit are more dear to me,
Than so to expose 'em to be censur'd by
The public voice.
*Over.* You run, my lord, no hazard.
Your reputation shall stand as fair,
In all good men's opinions, as now; 90
Nor can my actions, though condemn'd for ill,
Cast any foul aspersion upon yours.
For, though I do contemn report myself
As a mere sound, I still will be so tender 94
Of what concerns you, in all points of honour,
That the immaculate whiteness of your fame,
Nor your unquestion'd integrity,
Shall e'er be sullied with one taint or spot
That may take from your innocence and candour.
All my ambition is to have my daughter 100
Right honourable, which my lord can make her:
And might I live to dance upon my knee
A young Lord Lovell, borne by her unto you,
I write *nil ultra* to my proudest hopes.
As for possessions and annual rents, 105

---

³¹ **Whether:** ('Whither' Q)   ³⁴ **deference:** ('difference' Q)   ⁵¹ **shield:** part of neck   ⁷⁸ **engines:** devices   ⁹⁹ **candour:** purity   ¹⁰⁴ nil ultra: nothing beyond

Equivalent to maintain you in the port
Your noble birth and present state requires,
I do remove that burthen from your shoulders,
And take it on mine own: for, though I ruin
The country to supply your riotous waste, 110
The scourge of prodigals, want, shall never find
     you.
     *Lov.* Are you not frighted with the imprecations
And curses of whole families, made wretched
By your sinister practices?
     *Over.*             Yes, as rocks are,
When foamy billows split themselves against
Their flinty ribs; or as the moon is mov'd 116
When wolves, with hunger pin'd, howl at her
     brightness.
I am of a solid temper, and, like these,
Steer on a constant course. With mine own
     sword,                    119
If call'd into the field, I can make that right,
Which fearful enemies murmur'd at as wrong.
Now, for these other piddling complaints
Breath'd out in bitterness; as when they call me
Extortioner, tyrant, cormorant, or intruder 124
On my poor neighbour's right, or grand incloser
Of what was common, to my private use;
Nay, when my ears are pierc'd with widows'
     cries,
And undone orphans wash with tears my
     threshold,
I only think what 't is to have my daughter 129
Right honourable; and 't is a powerful charm
Makes me insensible of remorse, or pity,
Or the least sting of conscience.
     *Lov.*             I admire
The toughness of your nature.
     *Over.*                 'T is for you,
My lord, and for my daughter, I am marble;
Nay more, if you will have my character 135
In little, I enjoy more true delight
In my arrival to my wealth these dark
And crooked ways, than you shall e'er take
     pleasure
In spending what my industry hath compass'd.
My haste commands me hence; in one word,
     therefore,             140
Is it a match?
     *Lov.*      I hope, that is past doubt now.
     *Over.* Then rest secure; not the hate of all
     mankind here,
Nor fear of what can fall on me hereafter,
Shall make me study aught but your advancement
One story higher: an earl! if gold can do it. 145
Dispute not my religion, nor my faith;
Though I am borne thus headlong by my will,

You may make choice of what belief you please,
To me they are equal; so, my lord, good mor-
     row.                     *Exit.*
     *Lov.* He 's gone.— I wonder how the earth
     can bear             150
Such a portent! I, that have liv'd a soldier,
And stood the enemy's violent charge undaunted,
To hear this blasphemous beast am bath'd all
     over
In a cold sweat: yet, like a mountain, he
(Confirm'd in atheistical assertions)      155
Is no more shaken than Olympus is
When angry Boreas loads his double head
With sudden drifts of snow.

     *Enter Amble, Lady [Allworth], Woman*

     *Lady.*             Save you, my lord!
Disturb I not your privacy?
     *Lov.*             No, good madam;
For your own sake I am glad you came no
     sooner,             160
Since this bold bad man, Sir Giles Overreach,
Made such a plain discovery of himself,
And read this morning such a devilish matins,
That I should think it a sin next to his
But to repeat it.
     *Lady.*      I ne'er press'd, my lord, 165
On others' privacies; yet, against my will,
Walking, for health' sake, in the gallery
Adjoining to your lodgings, I was made
(So vehement and loud he was) partaker
Of his tempting offers.
     *Lov.*          Please you to command 170
Your servants hence, and I shall gladly hear
Your wiser counsel.
     *Lady.*         'T is, my lord, a woman's,
But true and hearty; — wait in the next room,
But be within call; yet not so near to force me
To whisper my intents.
     *Amb.*         We are taught better 175
By you, good madam.
     *Wom.*        And well know our distance.
     *Lady.* Do so, and talk not; 't will become
     your breeding,
                *Exeunt Amble and Woman.*
Now, my good lord; if I may use my freedom,
As to an honour'd friend ——
     *Lov.*            You lessen else
Your favour to me.
     *Lady.*        I dare then say thus: 180
As you are noble (howe'er common men
Make sordid wealth the object and sole end
Of their industrious aims) 't will not agree
With those of eminent blood, who are engag'd
More to prefer their honours than to increase

The state left to 'em by their ancestors,    186
To study large additions to their fortunes,
And quite neglect their births: — though I
    must grant
Riches, well got, to be a useful servant,
But a bad master.
    *Lov.*           Madam, 't is confessed; 190
But what infer you from it?
    *Lady.*           This, my lord;
That as all wrongs, though thrust into one scale,
Slide of themselves off when right fills the other
And cannot bide the trial; so all wealth,
(I mean, if ill-acquir'd,) cemented to honour 195
By virtuous ways achiev'd, and bravely pur-
    chas'd,
Is but as rubbish pour'd into a river,
(Howe'er intended to make good the bank,)
Rendering the water, that was pure before,
Polluted and unwholesome.  I allow      200
The heir of Sir Giles Overreach, Margaret,
A maid well qualified and the richest match
Our north part can make boast of; yet she can-
    not,
With all that she brings with her, fill their
    mouths,
That never will forget who was her father; 205
Or that my husband Allworth's lands, and Well-
    born's,
(How wrung from both needs now no repeti-
    tion,)
Were real motives that more work'd your lord-
    ship
To join your families, than her form and vir-
    tues:
You may conceive the rest.
    *Lov.*           I do, sweet madam, 210
And long since have consider'd it.  I know,
The sum of all that makes a just man happy
Consists in the well choosing of his wife:
And there, well to discharge it, does require
Equality of years, of birth, of fortune;    215
For beauty being poor, and not cried up
By birth or wealth, can truly mix with neither.
And wealth, where there 's such difference in
    years,
And fair descent, must make the yoke un-
    easy: —
But I come nearer.
    *Lady.*           Pray you do, my lord. 220
    *Lov.*  Were Overreach' states thrice centu-
    pl'd, his daughter
Millions of degrees much fairer than she is,
Howe'er I might urge precedents to excuse me,
I would not so adulterate my blood
By marrying Margaret, and so leave my issue
Made up of several pieces, one part scarlet, 226

And the other London blue.  In my own tomb
I will inter my name first.
    *Lady.* (*Aside.*)   I am glad to hear this. ———
Why then, my lord, pretend you marriage to
    her?
Dissimulation but ties false knots      230
On that straight line by which you, hitherto,
Have measur'd all your actions.
    *Lov.*           I make answer,
And aptly, with a question.  Wherefore have
    you,
That, since your husband's death, have liv'd a
    strict
And chaste nun's life, on the sudden given your-
    self                                  235
To visits and entertainments?  Think you,
    madam,
'T is not grown public conference?  Or the fa-
    vours
Which you too prodigally have thrown on Well-
    born,
Being too reserv'd before, incur not censure?
    *Lady.*  I am innocent here; and, on my life,
    I swear                             240
My ends are good.
    *Lov.*           On my soul, so are mine
To Margaret; but leave both to the event:
And since this friendly privacy does serve
But as an offer'd means unto ourselves,
To search each other farther, you having shown
Your care of me, I my respect to you,    246
Deny me not, but still in chaste words, madam,
An afternoon's discourse.
    *Lady.*           So I shall hear you. [*Exeunt.*]


### *Actus quarti, Scena secunda*

[*Before Tapwell's Alehouse*]

*Tapwell.  Froth*

*Tap.*  Undone, undone! this was your coun-
    sel, Froth.
*Froth.*  Mine!  I defy thee.  Did not Master
    Marrall
(He has marr'd all, I am sure) strictly command
    us,
On pain of Sir Giles Overreach' displeasure,
To turn the gentleman out of doors?
    *Tap.*                             'T is true; 5
But now he 's his uncle's darling, and has got
Master Justice Greedy, since he fill'd his belly,
At his commandment, to do anything.
Woe, woe to us!
    *Froth.*           He may prove merciful.      9
*Tap.*  Troth, we do not deserve it at his hands.

    204 **fill . . . mouths:** stop their gossiping    208 **motives:** ('motive' Q)    214 **well . . . it:** properly
to accomplish it    221 **Overreach' states:** ('Overreach, stat 's' Q)    227 **blue:** the color of servants'
liveries    237 **conference:** gossip    242 **event:** outcome    248 **So:** on these conditions

Though he knew all the passages of our house,
As the receiving of stolen goods, and bawdry,
When he was rogue Wellborn no man would be-
    lieve him,
And then his information could not hurt us;
But now he is right worshipful again,          15
Who dares but doubt his testimony? Methinks,
I see thee, Froth, already in a cart,
For a close bawd, thine eyes ev'n pelted out
With dirt and rotten eggs; and my hand hissing
(If I scape the halter) with the letter R          20
Printed upon it.
    *Froth.*          Would that were the worst!
That were but nine days' wonder: as for credit,
We have none to lose, but we shall lose the
    money
He owes us, and his custom; there's the hell on't.
    *Tap.* He has summon'd all his creditors by
        the drum,          25
And they swarm about him like so many soldiers
On the pay day: and has found out such A NEW
    WAY
TO PAY HIS OLD DEBTS, as 't is very likely
He shall be chronicled for it!
    *Froth.*          He deserves it
More than ten pageants. But are you sure his
    worship          30
Comes this way, to my lady's?
*A cry within:* "Brave Master Wellborn!"
    *Tap.*          Yes: — I hear him.
    *Froth.* Be ready with your petition and pre-
        sent it
To his good grace.

*Enter Wellborn in a rich habit,* [Marrall,]
    *Greedy, Order, Furnace, three Creditors;*
    *Tapwell kneeling, delivers his bill of debt.*

    *Well.*          How 's this? Petition'd too?
But note what miracles the payment of
A little trash, and a rich suit of clothes,          35
Can work upon these rascals! I shall be,
I think, Prince Wellborn.
    *Mar.*          When your worship 's married,
You may be — I know what I hope to see you.
    *Well.* Then look thou for advancement.
    *Mar.*          To be known
Your worship's bailiff, is the mark I shoot at.
    *Well.* And thou shalt hit it.
    *Mar.*          Pray you, sir, despatch 41
These needy followers, and for my admittance,
Provided you 'll defend me from Sir Giles,
Whose service I am weary of, I 'll say something
You shall give thanks for.
    *Well.*          Fear me not Sir Giles. 45
    *This interim, Tapwell and Froth flat-*
        *tering and bribing Justice Greedy.*

*Greedy.* Who, Tapwell? I remember thy
    wife brought me,
Last new-year's tide, a couple of fat turkeys.
    *Tap.* And shall do every Christmas, let your
        worship
But stand my friend now.
    *Greedy.*          How! with Master Wellborn?
I can do anything with him on such terms. —
See you this honest couple; they are good
    souls          51
As ever drew out faucet; have they not
A pair of honest faces?
    *Well.*          I o'erheard you,
And the bribe he promis'd. You are cozen'd in
    'em;
For, of all the scum that grew rich by my riots,
This, for a most unthankful knave, and this, 56
For a base bawd and whore, have worst de-
    serv'd me,
And therefore speak not for 'em. By your place
You are rather to do me justice. Lend me your
    ear;
— Forget his turkeys, and call in his license, 60
And, at the next fair, I 'll give you a yoke of
    oxen
Worth all his poultry.
    *Greedy.*          I am chang'd on the sudden
In my opinion! Come near; nearer, rascal.
And, now I view him better, did you e'er see
One look so like an arch-knave? His very coun-
    tenance,          65
Should an understanding judge but look upon
    him,
Would hang him, though he were innocent.
    *Tap. Froth.*          Worshipful sir.
    *Greedy.* No, though the great Turk came, in-
        stead of turkeys,
To beg my favour, I am inexorable.
Thou hast an ill name: besides thy musty ale, 70
That hath destroy'd many of the king's liege
    people,
Thou never hadst in thy house, to stay men's
    stomachs,
A piece of Suffolk cheese or gammon of bacon,
Or any esculent, as the learned call it,
For their emolument, but sheer drink only, 75
For which gross fault I here do damn thy license,
Forbidding thee ever to tap or draw;
For, instantly, I will, in mine own person,
Command the constable to pull down thy sign,
And do it before I eat.
    *Froth.*          No mercy?
    *Greedy.*          Vanish! 80
If I show any, may my promis'd oxen gore me!
    *Tap.* Unthankful knaves are ever so re-
        warded. *Exeunt Greedy, Tapwell, Froth.*

11 **passages:** occurrences, doings    18 **close:** secret    20 **R:** symbol for "rogue" branded on the
hand    42 **admittance:** appointment    45 **Fear me not:** do not fear    46 **I:** (not in Q)    74 **esculent:**
edible thing

*Well.* Speak, what are you?

1 *Cred.*                                      A decay'd vintner, sir,
That might have thriv'd, but that your worship
    broke me
With trusting you with muscadine and eggs,
And five pound suppers, with your after drink-
    ings,                                                                  86
When you lodg'd upon the Bankside.

*Well.*                                                    I remember.

1 *Crd.* I have not been hasty, nor e'er laid
    to arrest you;
And therefore, sir ——

*Well.*                            Thou art an honest fellow,
I 'll set thee up again; see his bill paid. —         90
What are you?

2 *Cred.* A tailor once, but now mere botcher.
I gave you credit for a suit of clothes,
Which was all my stock, but you failing in pay-
    ment,
I was remov'd from the shopboard, and confin'd
Under a stall.

*Well.* See him paid; — and botch no more.   95

2 *Cred.* I ask no interest, sir.

*Well.*                              Such tailors need not;
If their bills are paid in one-and-twenty year,
They are seldom losers. — O, I know thy face,
                                          [*To Creditor.*]
Thou wert my surgeon. You must tell no tales;
Those days are done. I will pay you in private.

*Ord.* A royal gentleman!

*Furn.*                          Royal as an emperor!  101
He 'll prove a brave master; my good lady knew
To choose a man.

*Well.*                        See all men else discharg'd;
And since old debts are clear'd by a new way,
A little bounty will not misbecome me;              105
There 's something, honest cook, for thy good
    breakfasts;
And this, for your respect: [*to Order*] take 't,
    't is good gold,
And I able to spare it.

*Ord.*                            You are too munificent.

*Furn.* He was ever so.

*Well.*                          Pray you, on before.

3 *Cred.*                                  Heaven bless you!

*Mar.* At four o'clock the rest know where
    to meet me.                                                       110
            *Exeunt Order, Furnace, Creditors.*

*Well.* Now, Master Marrall, what 's the
    weighty secret
You promis'd to impart?

*Mar.*                            Sir, time nor place
Allow me to relate each circumstance;
This only, in a word: I know Sir Giles
Will come upon you for security               115

For his thousand pounds, which you must not
    consent to.
As he grows in heat, as I am sure he will,
Be you but rough, and say he 's in your debt
Ten times the sum, upon sale of your land;
I had a hand in 't (I speak it to my shame)   120
When you were defeated of it.

*Well.*                              That 's forgiven.

*Mar.* I shall deserve 't. Then urge him to
    produce
The deed in which you pass'd it over to him,
Which I know he 'll have about him, to deliver
To the Lord Lovell, with many other writ-   125
    ings,
And present moneys. I 'll instruct you further,
As I wait on your worship. If I play not my
    prize
To your full content, and your uncle's much
    vexation,
Hang up Jack Marrall.

*Well.*                          I rely upon thee. *Exeunt.*

## Actus quarti, Scena ultima

[*Overreach's House*]

*Allworth. Margaret*

*All.* Whether to yield the first praise to my
    lord's
Unequall'd temperance or your constant sweet-
    ness
That I yet live, my weak hands fasten'd on
Hope's anchor, spite of all storms of despair,
I yet rest doubtful.

*Marg.*                          Give it to Lord Lovell:  5
For what in him was bounty, in me 's duty.
I make but payment of a debt to which
My vows, in that high office regist'red,
Are faithful witnesses.

*All.*                            'T is true, my dearest:
Yet, when I call to mind how many fair ones  10
Make wilful shipwrack of their faiths, and
    oaths
To God and man, to fill the arms of greatness,
And you rise up no less than a glorious star,
To the amazement of the world, that hold out
Against the stern authority of a father,        15
And spurn at honour when it comes to court
    you;
I am so tender of your good, that faintly,
With your wrong, I can wish myself that right
You yet are pleas'd to do me.

*Marg.*                                Yet, and ever.
To me what 's title, when content is want-
    ing?                                                                20

---

⁸⁵ muscadine: a sweet wine    ⁸⁷ Bankside: Southwark side of the Thames, where several of the
theatres were, and where Massinger was buried    I: (not in Q)    ⁹¹ botcher: mender    ¹²¹ defeated:
robbed    ¹²⁷ prize: part ('price' Q)    ¹ Whether: ('Whither' Q)    ⁸ high office: heaven    ¹³ no:
(not in Q)

Or wealth, rak'd up together with much care,
And to be kept with more, when the heart
    pines
In being dispossess'd of what it longs for
Beyond the Indian mines? or the smooth brow
Of a pleas'd sire, that slaves me to his will,   25
And, so his ravenous humour may be feasted
By my obedience, and he see me great,
Leaves to my soul nor faculties nor power
To make her own election?
    *All.*                    But the dangers
That follow the repulse ——
    *Marg.*          To me they are nothing;  30
Let Allworth love, I cannot be unhappy.
Suppose the worst, that, in his rage, he kill me,
A tear or two, by you dropp'd on my hearse
In sorrow for my fate, will call back life
So far as but to say, that I die yours;   35
I then shall rest in peace: or should he prove
So cruel, as one death would not suffice
His thirst of vengeance, but with ling'ring tor-
    ments
In mind and body I must waste to air,
In poverty join'd with banishment; so you
    share                                        40
In my afflictions, which I dare not wish you,
So high I prize you, I could undergo 'em
With such a patience as should look down
With scorn on his worst malice.
    *All.*                   Heaven avert
Such trials of your true affection to me!    45
Nor will it unto you, that are all mercy,
Show so much rigour: but since we must run
Such desperate hazards, let us do our best
To steer between 'em.
    *Marg.*          Your lord 's ours, and sure:
And, though but a young actor, second me  50
In doing to the life what he has plotted,

*Enter Overreach [behind]*

The end may yet prove happy. Now, my All-
    worth —                *[Seeing her father.]*
    *All.* To your letter, and put on a seeming
    anger.
    *Marg.* I 'll pay my lord all debts due to his
    title;
And when with terms, not taking from his
    honour,                                       55
He does solicit me, I shall gladly hear him.
But in this peremptory, nay, commanding way,
T' appoint a meeting, and without my knowl-
    edge,
A priest to tie the knot can ne'er be undone
Till death unloose it, is a confidence    60
In his lordship will deceive him.
    *All.*                  I hope better,
Good lady.

    *Marg.* Hope, sir, what you please: for me
I must take a safe and secure course; I have
A father, and without his full consent,
Though all lords of the land kneel'd for my
    favour,                                       65
I can grant nothing.
    *Over.* I like this obedience: *[Comes forward.]*
But whatsoe'er my lord writes, must and shall
    be
Accepted and embrac'd. Sweet Master All-
    worth,
You show yourself a true and faithful servant
To your good lord; he has a jewel of you.   70
How! frowning, Meg? Are these looks to re-
    ceive
A messenger from my lord? What 's this?
    Give me it.
    *Marg.* A piece of arrogant paper, like th'
    inscriptions.        *Overreach read the letter.*
    *Over.* "Fair mistress, from your servant
    learn all joys
That we can hope for, if deferr'd, prove toys;
Therefore this instant, and in private, meet  76
A husband, that will gladly at your feet
Lay down his honours, tend'ring them to you
With all content, the church being paid her
    due."
— Is this the arrogant piece of paper? Fool!  80
Will you still be one? In the name of madness
    what
Could his good honour write more to content
    you?
Is there aught else to be wish'd, after these two,
That are already offer'd; marriage first,
And lawful pleasure after: what would you
    more?                                         85
    *Marg.* Why, sir, I would be married like
    your daughter;
Not hurried away i' th' night I know not
    whither,
Without all ceremony; no friends invited
To honour the solemnity.
    *All.*                An 't please your honour,
For so before to-morrow I must style you,   90
My lord desires this privacy, in respect
His honourable kinsmen are far off,
And his desires to have it done brook not
So long delay as to expect their coming;
And yet he stands resolv'd, with all due
    pomp,                                         95
As running at the ring, plays, masques, and
    tilting,
To have his marriage at court celebrated,
When he has brought your honour up to Lon-
    don.
    *Over.* He tells you true: 't is the fashion, on
    my knowledge:

---

²⁰ **election:** choice   ⁶⁰ **is:** ('as' Q)   **confidence:** presumption   ⁷⁵ **toys:** trifles   ⁹¹ **desires:**
('desire' Q)   **in respect:** because   ⁹⁴ **expect:** await

Yet the good lord, to please your peevish-
    ness,                                          100
Must put it off, forsooth! and lose a night,
In which perhaps he might get two boys on
    thee.
Tempt me no farther, if you do, this goad
              [*Points to his sword.*]
Shall prick you to him.
    *Marg.*                    I could be contented,
Were you but by, to do a father's part,    105
And give me in the church.
    *Over.*                    So my lord have you,
What do I care who gives you?  Since my lord
Does purpose to be private, I 'll not cross him.
I know not, Master Allworth, how my lord
May be provided, and therefore there 's a
    purse                                       110
Of gold, 't will serve this night's expense; to-
    morrow
I 'll furnish him with any sums.  In the mean
    time,
Use my ring to my chaplain; he is benefic'd
At my manor of Gotham, and call'd Parson
    Willdo.
'T is no matter for a license, I 'll bear him out
    in 't.                                       115
    *Marg.*  With your favour, sir, what warrant
is your ring?
He may suppose I got that twenty ways,
Without your knowledge; and then to be re-
    fus'd
Were such a stain upon me! — If you pleas'd,
    sir,
Your presence would do better.
    *Over.*                    Still perverse!  120
I say again, I will not cross my lord;
Yet I 'll prevent you too. — Paper and ink,
    there!
    *All.*  I can furnish you.
    *Over.*          I thank you, I can write then.
                *Writes on his book.*
    *All.*  You may, if you please, put out the
name of my lord,
In respect he comes disguis'd, and only write, 125
" Marry her to this gentleman."
    *Over.*                    Well advis'd.
'T is done;  away! —          *Margaret kneels.*
    My blessing, girl?  Thou hast it.
Nay, no reply, be gone. — Good Master All-
    worth,
This shall be the best night's work you ever
    made.
    *All.*  I hope so, sir.                      130
           *Exeunt Allworth and Margaret.*
    *Over.*  Farewell! — Now all 's cocksure:
Methinks I hear already knights and ladies

Say, Sir Giles Overreach, how is it with
Your honourable daughter?  Has her honour
Slept well to-night?  or, will her honour
    please                                       135
To accept this monkey, dog, or paraquit
(This is state in ladies), or my eldest son
To be her page, and wait upon her trencher?
My ends, my ends are compass'd! — then for
    Wellborn
And the lands: were he once married to the
    widow,                                       140
I have him here. — I can scarce contain myself,
I am so full of joy, nay, joy all over.    *Exit.*

        *The end of the fourth Act.*


### Actus quinti, Scena prima

        [*Lady Allworth's House*]

[*Lord*] Lovell.  Lady [*Allworth*].  Amble

    *Lady.*  By this you know how strong the
motives were
That did, my lord, induce me to dispense
A little with my gravity to advance,
In personating some few favours to him,
The plots and projects of the down-trod Well-
    born.                                          5
Nor shall I e'er repent, although I suffer
In some few men's opinions for 't, the action:
For he that ventur'd all for my dear husband
Might justly claim an obligation from me
To pay him such a courtesy; which had I    10
Coyly or over-curiously denied,
It might have argu'd me of little love
To the deceas'd.
    *Lov.*          What you intended, madam
For the poor gentleman hath found good suc-
    cess;
For, as I understand, his debts are paid,    15
And he once more furnish'd for fair employ-
    ment:
But all the arts that I have us'd to raise
The fortunes of your joy and mine, young All-
    worth,
Stand yet in supposition, though I hope well;
For the young lovers are in wit more pregnant
Than their years can promise; and for their
    desires,                                       21
On my knowledge, they are equal.
    *Lady.*              As my wishes
Are with yours, my lord; yet give me leave to
    fear
The building, though well grounded: to deceive
Sir Giles, that 's both a lion and a fox    25
In his proceedings, were a work beyond

---

    ¹⁰³ **goad:** ('good' Q)    ¹¹⁴ **Gotham:** a village near Nottingham (famed for the stupidity of its in-
habitants)    ¹³⁶ **paraquit:** parrot    **Scena prima:** ('Scena quinta' Q)    ¹¹ **over-curiously: fastidiously**
¹⁹ **in supposition:** still unsettled

The strongest undertakers; not the trial
Of two weak innocents.

*Lov.*                    Despair not, madam:
Hard things are compass'd oft by easy means;
And judgment, being a gift deriv'd from
  Heaven,                                          30
Though sometimes lodg'd i' th' hearts of
  worldly men,
That ne'er consider from whom they receive it,
Forsakes such as abuse the giver of it.
Which is the reason that the politic
And cunning statesman, that believes he fath-
  oms                                              35
The counsels of all kingdoms on the earth,
Is by simplicity oft over-reach'd.

*Lady.*  May he be so! Yet, in his name to
  express it,
Is a good omen.

*Lov.*          May it to myself
Prove so, good lady, in my suit to you!           40
What think you of the motion?

*Lady.*                    Troth, my lord,
My own unworthiness may answer for me;
For had you, when that I was in my prime,
My virgin flower uncropp'd, presented me
With this great favour; looking on my low-
  ness
Not in a glass of self-love, but of truth,        46
I could not but have thought it as a blessing
Far, far beyond my merit.

*Lov.*                    You are too modest,
And undervalue that which is above
My title, or whatever I call mine.                 50
I grant, were I a Spaniard, to marry
A widow might disparage me; but being
A true-born Englishman, I cannot find
How it can taint my honour: nay, what 's
  more,
That which you think a blemish is to me           55
The fairest lustre. You already, madam,
Have given sure proofs how dearly you can
  cherish
A husband that deserves you; which confirms
  me
That, if I am not wanting in my care
To do you service, you 'll be still the same      60
That you were to your Allworth: in a word,
Our years, our states, our births are not un-
  equal,
You being descended nobly, and alli'd so;
If then you may be won to make me happy,
But join your lips to mine, and that shall be     65
A solemn contract.

*Lady.*          I were blind to my own good
Should I refuse it; [*kisses him*] yet, my lord,
  receive me
As such a one, the study of whose whole life
Shall know no other object but to please you.

*Lov.*  If I return not, with all tenderness,     70
Equal respect to you, may I die wretched!

*Lady.*  There needs no protestation, my lord,
To her that cannot doubt, —

*Enter Wellborn [handsomely apparelled]*

                    You are welcome, sir.
Now you look like yourself.

*Well.*          And will continue
Such in my free acknowledgment that I am         75
Your creature, madam, and will never hold
My life mine own, when you please to command
  it.

*Lov.*  It is a thankfulness that well becomes
  you.
You could not make choice of a better shape
To dress your mind in.

*Lady.*          For me, I am happy    80
That my endeavours prosper'd. Saw you of
  late
Sir Giles, your uncle?

*Well.*          I heard of him, madam,
By his minister, Marrall; he 's grown into
  strange passions
About his daughter. This last night he look'd
  for
Your lordship at his house, but missing you,     85
And she not yet appearing, his wise head
Is much perplex'd and troubl'd.

*Lov.*                    It may be,
Sweetheart, my project took.

*Lady.*          I strongly hope.

*Over.* [*Within.*] Ha! find her, booby, thou
  huge lump of nothing,
I 'll bore thine eyes out else.

*Well.*          May it please your lordship,   90
For some ends of mine own, but to withdraw
A little out of sight, though not of hearing,
You may, perhaps, have sport.

*Lov.*          You shall direct me. *Steps aside.*

*Enter Overreach, with distracted looks, driving in
  Marrall before him [with a box]*

*Over.*  I shall *sol fa* you, rogue!

*Mar.*                    Sir, for what cause
Do you use me thus?

*Over.*  Cause, slave! Why, I am angry,         95
And thou a subject only fit for beating,
And so to cool my choler. Look to the writing;
Let but the seal be broke upon the box
That has slept in my cabinet these three years,
I 'll rack thy soul for 't.

*Mar.* (*Aside.*) I may yet cry quittance,      100
Though now I suffer, and dare not resist.

*Over.*  Lady, by your leave, did you see my
  daughter lady?
And the lord her husband? Are they in your
  house?

---

³⁷ **over-reach'd:** ('overreach' Q)    ⁴¹ **motion:** proposal    ⁹⁹ **slept:** ('slepp'd' O)

If they are, discover, that I may bid 'em joy;
And, as an entrance to her place of honour, 105
See your ladyship on her left hand, and make
   courtesies
When she nods on you; which you must receive
As a special favour.
   *Lady.*         When I know, Sir Giles,
Her state requires such ceremony, I shall pay
   it;
But in the meantime, as I am myself,     110
I give you to understand, I neither know
Nor care where her honour is.
   *Over.*       When you once see her
Supported, and led by the lord her husband,
You 'll be taught better. —— Nephew.
   *Well.*             Sir.
   *Over.*             No more?
   *Well.*   'T is all I owe you.
   *Over.*       Have your redeem'd rags 115
Made you thus insolent?
   *Well.* (*In scorn.*)    Insolent to you!
Why, what are you, sir, unless in your years,
At the best, more than myself?
   *Over.* [*Aside.*]     His fortune swells him.
'T is rank he 's married.
   *Lady.*          This is excellent!
   *Over.*  Sir, in calm language, though I seldom
   use it,      120
I am familiar with the cause that makes you
Bear up thus bravely; there 's a certain buzz
Of a stol'n marriage, do you hear? of a stol'n
   marriage,
In which, 't is said, there 's somebody hath been
   cozen'd;
I name no parties.
   *Well.*    Well, sir, and what follows? 125
   *Over.*  Marry, this; since you are peremp-
   tory. Remember,
Upon mere hope of your great match, I lent you
A thousand pounds: put me in good security,
And suddenly, by mortgage or by statute,
Of some of your new possessions, or I 'll have
   you     130
Dragg'd in your lavender robes to the jail.
   You know me,
And therefore do not trifle.
   *Well.*         Can you be
So cruel to your nephew, now he 's in
The way to rise? Was this the courtesy
You did me " in pure love, and no ends else " ?
   *Over.*  End me no ends! Engage the whole
   estate,     136
And force your spouse to sign it, you shall have
Three or four thousand more, to roar and swag-
   ger
And revel in bawdy taverns.

   *Well.*          And beg after,
Mean you not so?
   *Over.*  My thoughts are mine, and free.  140
Shall I have security?
   *Well.*         No, indeed, you shall not,
Nor bond, nor bill, nor bare acknowledgment;
Your great looks fright not me.
   *Over.*        But my deeds shall.
Outbrav'd!   *They both draw; the servants enter.*
   *Lady.*  Help, murther! murther!
   *Well.*         Let him come on,
With all his wrongs and injuries about him, 145
Arm'd with his cut-throat practices to guard
   him;
The right that I bring with me will defend me,
And punish his extortion.
   *Over.*         That I had thee
But single in the field!
   *Lady.*        You may; but make not
My house your quarrelling scene.
   *Over.*      Were 't in a church, 150
By Heaven and Hell, I 'll do 't!
   *Mar.*          Now put him to
The showing of the deed.
                   [*Aside to Wellborn.*]
   *Well.*        This rage is vain, sir;
For fighting, fear not, you shall have your
   hands full,
Upon the least incitement; and whereas
You charge me with a debt of a thousand
   pounds     155
If there be law, (howe'er you have no con-
   science,)
Either restore my land or I 'll recover
A debt, that 's truly due to me from you,
In value ten times more than what you chal-
   lenge.
   *Over.*  I in thy debt! O impudence! did I
   not purchase     160
The land left by thy father, that rich land,
That had continued in Wellborn's name
Twenty descents; which, like a riotous fool,
Thou didst make sale of it? Is not here in-
   clos'd
The deed that does confirm it mine?
   *Mar.*         Now, now! 165
   *Well.*  I do acknowledge none; I ne'er pass'd
   o'er
Any such land. I grant for a year or two
You had it in trust; which if you do dis-
   charge,
Surrend'ring the possession, you shall ease
Yourself and me of chargeable suits in law, 170
Which, if you prove not honest, as I doubt
   it,
Must of necessity follow.

---

<sup>104</sup> **discover:** show (them)    <sup>106</sup> **on . . . hand:** in the inferior position    <sup>119</sup> **rank:** obvious
<sup>122</sup> **buzz:** rumor   <sup>129</sup> **by mortgage:** ('my Mortgage' Q)   <sup>131</sup> **lavender robes:** clothes recently in pawn
<sup>159</sup> **challenge:** claim   <sup>163</sup> **descents:** generations   <sup>171</sup> **doubt it:** fear

*Lady.*           In my judgment,
He does advise you well.
*Over.*         Good! good! Conspire
With your new husband, lady; second him
In his dishonest practices; but when    175
This manor is extended to my use,
You 'll speak in humbler key, and sue for
    favour.
*Lady.* Never: do not hope it.
*Well.*        Let despair first seize me.
*Over.* Yet, to shut up thy mouth, and make
    thee give
Thyself the lie, the loud lie, I draw out    180
The precious evidence; if thou canst forswear
Thy hand and seal, and make a forfeit of
        *Opens the box [and displays the bond].*
Thy ears to the pillory, see! here 's that will
    make
My interest clear — ha!
*Lady.*       A fair skin of parchment.
*Well.* Indented, I confess, and labels too; 185
But neither wax nor words. How! thunder-
    struck?
Not a syllable to insult with? My wise uncle,
Is this your precious evidence? Is this that
    makes
Your interest clear?
*Over.*    I am o'erwhelm'd with wonder!
What prodigy is this? What subtle devil    190
Hath raz'd out the inscription, the wax
Turn'd into dust? The rest of my deeds whole
As when they were deliver'd, and this only
Made nothing! Do you deal with witches, ras-
    cal?
There is a statute for you, which will bring 195
Your neck in an hempen circle; yes, there is;
And now 't is better thought for, cheater, know
This juggling shall not save you.
*Well.*         To save thee
Would beggar the stock of mercy.
*Over.*          Marrall!
*Mar.*                   Sir.
*Over.* (*Flattering him.*) Though the witnesses
    are dead, your testimony    200
Help with an oath or two: and for thy master,
Thy liberal master, my good honest servant,
I know you will swear anything, to dash
This cunning sleight: besides, I know thou art
A public notary, and such stand in law    205
For a dozen witnesses: the deed being drawn
    too
By thee, my careful Marrall, and deliver'd
When thou wert present, will make good my
    title.
Wilt thou not swear this?

*Mar.*           I! No, I assure you: 209
I have a conscience not sear'd up like yours:
I know no deeds.
*Over.*      Wilt thou betray me?
*Mar.*               Keep him
From using of his hands, I 'll use my tongue,
To his no little torment.
*Over.*          Mine own varlet
Rebel against me!
*Mar.*        Yes, and uncase you too.
The idiot, the patch, the slave, the booby, 215
The property fit only to be beaten
For your morning exercise, your " football," or
" Th' unprofitable lump of flesh," your
    " drudge,"
Can now anatomize you, and lay open    219
All your black plots, and level with the earth
Your hill of pride, and, with these gabions
    guarded
Unload my great artillery, and shake,
Nay pulverize, the walls you think defend you.
*Lady.* How he foams at the mouth with
    rage!
*Well.* To him again.
*Over.* O that I had thee in my gripe, I would
    tear thee    225
Joint after joint!
*Mar.*        I know you are a tearer,
But I 'll have first your fangs par'd off, and
    then
Come nearer to you; when I have discover'd,
And made it good before the judge, what
    ways
And devilish practices you us'd to cozen    230
With an army of whole families, who yet live,
And, but enroll'd for soldiers, were able
To take in Dunkirk.
*Well.*        All will come out.
*Lady.*          The better.
*Over.* But that I will live, rogue, to torture
    thee,    234
And make thee wish, and kneel in vain, to die,
These swords that keep thee from me should
    fix here,
Although they made my body but one wound,
But I would reach thee.
*Lov.* (*Aside.*)      Heaven's hand is in this:
One bandog worry the other!
*Over.*           I play the fool,
And make my anger but ridiculous;    240
There will be a time and place, there will be,
    cowards,
When you shall feel what I dare do.
*Well.*          I think so:

---

[176] **extended:** seized   [177] **humbler:** ('a humble' Q)   [184] **fair:** not written on   [195] **statute:** the law against witchcraft   [204] **sleight:** trick   [214] **uncase:** strip, expose   [219] **anatomize:** dissect   [221] **gabions:** wicker baskets filled with earth used as defenses in war   [228] **discover'd:** revealed   [233] **take in:** capture   [239] **bandog:** fierce dog

You dare do any ill, yet want true valour
To be honest, and repent.
   *Over.*         They are words I know not,
Nor e'er will learn.  Patience, the beggar's
   virtue,                        245

     *Enter Greedy and Parson Willdo*

Shall find no harbour here: — after these
   storms
At length a calm appears.  Welcome, most wel-
   come!
There 's comfort in thy looks.  Is the deed done?
Is my daughter married?  Say but so, my
   chaplain,
And I am tame.
   *Willdo.*    Married!  Yes, I assure you.  250
   *Over.* Then vanish all sad thoughts!  There 's
more gold for thee.
My doubts and fears are in the titles drown'd
Of my honourable, my right honourable
   daughter.
   *Greedy.*  Here will I be feasting!  At least
   for a month
I am provided: empty guts, croak no more.  255
You shall be stuff'd like bagpipes, not with
   wind,
But bearing dishes.
   *Over.*        Instantly be here?
                *Whispering to Willdo.*
To my wish! to my wish!  Now you that plot
   against me,
And hop'd to trip my heels up, that contemn'd
   me,
Think on 't and tremble. — (*Loud music*) —
   They come!  I hear the music.      260
A lane there for my lord!
   *Well.*          This sudden heat
May yet be cool'd, sir.
   *Over.*        Make way there for my lord!

     *Enter Allworth and Margaret*

   *Marg.*  Sir, first your pardon, then your
   blessing, with
Your full allowance of the choice I have made.
As ever you could make use of your reason,  265
                     *Kneeling.*
Grow not in passion; since you may as well
Call back the day that 's past, as untie the
   knot
Which is too strongly fasten'd.  Not to dwell
Too long on words, this is my husband.
   *Over.*             How!
   *All.*  So I assure you; all the rites of mar-
   riage,                     270
With every circumstance, are past.  Alas! sir,
Although I am no lord, but a lord's page,
Your daughter and my lov'd wife mourns not
   for it;

And, for right honourable son-in-law, you may
   say,
Your dutiful daughter.
   *Over.*        Devil! are they married?  275
   *Willdo.*  Do a father's part, and say, " Heav-
   en give 'em joy!"
   *Over.* Confusion and ruin!  Speak, and speak
   quickly,
Or thou art dead.
   *Willdo.*        They are married.
   *Over.*          Thou hadst better
Have made a contract with the king of fiends,
Then these: — my brain turns!
   *Willdo.*        Why this rage to me?  280
Is not this your letter, sir, and these the words?
" Marry her to this gentleman."
   *Over.*           It cannot —
Nor will I e'er believe it; 'sdeath!  I will not;
That I, that in all passages I touch'd
At worldly profit have not left a print   285
Where I have trod for the most curious search
To trace my footsteps, should be gull'd by
   children,
Baffl'd and fool'd, and all my hopes and labours
Defeated and made void.
   *Well.*         As it appears,
You are so, my grave uncle.
   *Over.*           Village nurses  290
Revenge their wrongs with curses; I 'll not
   waste
A syllable, but thus take the life
Which, wretched, I gave to thee.
                 *Offers to kill Margaret.*
   *Lov.* [*Coming forward.*]  Hold, for your own
   sake!
Though charity to your daughter hath quite
   left you,                   295
Will you do an act, though in your hopes lost
   here,
Can leave no hope for peace or rest hereafter?
Consider; at the best you are but a man,
And cannot so create your aims but that
They may be cross'd.
   *Over.*        Lord! thus I spit at thee, 300
And at thy counsel; and again desire thee,
And as thou art a soldier, if thy valour
Dares show itself where multitude and example
Lead not the way, let 's quit the house, and
   change
Six words in private.
   *Lov.*         I am ready.
   *Lady.*           Stay, sir,  305
Contest with one distracted!
   *Well.*        You 'll grow like him,
Should you answer his vain challenge.
   *Over.*           Are you pale?
Borrow his help, though Hercules call it odds,
I 'll stand against both as I am, hemm'd in thus.

     257 **bearing:** solid    271 **circumstance:** incident, detail

Since, like a Libyan lion in the toil,        310
My fury cannot reach the coward hunters,
And only spends itself, I 'll quit the place.
Alone I can do nothing; but I have servants
And friends to second me; and if I make not
This house a heap of ashes (by my wrongs, 315
What I have spoke I will make good!) or leave
One throat uncut, — if it be possible,
Hell, add to my afflictions!        *Exit Overreach.*
*Mar.*                    Is 't not brave sport?
*Greedy.* Brave sport! I am sure it has ta'en
    away my stomach;
I do not like the sauce.
*All.*                    Nay, weep not, dearest, 320
Though it express your pity; what 's decreed
Above, we cannot alter.
*Lady.*                    His threats move me
No scruple, madam.
*Mar.*                    Was it not a rare trick,
An it please your worship, to make the deed
    nothing?
I can do twenty neater, if you please        325
To purchase and grow rich; for I will be
Such a solicitor and steward for you
As never worshipful had.
*Well.*                    I do believe thee;
But first discover the quaint means you us'd
To raze out the conveyance?
*Mar.*                    They are mysteries 330
Not to be spoke in public: certain minerals
Incorporated in the ink and wax —
Besides, he gave me nothing, but still fed me
With hopes and blows; but that was the in-
    ducement        334
To this conundrum. If it please your worship
To call to memory, this mad beast once caus'd
    me
To urge you or to drown or hang yourself;
I 'll do the like to him, if you command me.
*Well.* You are a rascal! He that dares be
    false        339
To a master, though unjust, will ne'er be true
To any other. Look not for reward
Or favour from me; I will shun thy sight
As I would do a basilisk's. Thank my pity
If thou keep thy ears; howe'er, I will take order
Your practice shall be silenc'd.
*Greedy.*                    I 'll commit him, 345
If you 'll have me, sir.
*Well.*                    That were to little purpose;
His conscience be his prison. Not a word,
But instantly be gone.
*Ord.*                    Take this kick with you.
*Amb.* And this.
*Furn.*                    If that I had my cleaver here,
I would divide your knave's head.

*Mar.*                    This is the haven 350
False servants still arrive at.        *Exit Marrall.*

*Enter Overreach*

*Lady.*                    Come again!
*Lov.* Fear not, I am your guard.
*Well.*                    His looks are ghastly.
*Willdo.* Some little time I have spent, under
    your favours,
In physical studies, and if my judgment err
    not,
He 's mad beyond recovery: but observe him,
And look to yourselves.
*Over.*                    Why, is not the whole world
Included in myself? To what use then        357
Are friends and servants? Say there were a
    squadron
Of pikes, lin'd through with shot, when I am
    mounted
Upon my injuries, shall I fear to charge 'em?
No: I 'll through the battalia, and, that routed,
                    *Flourishing his sword sheathed.*
I 'll fall to execution — Ha! I am feeble:        362
Some undone widow sits upon mine arm,
And takes away the use of 't; and my sword,
Glu'd to my scabbard with wrong'd orphans'
    tears,        365
Will not be drawn. Ha! what are these? Sure,
    hangmen
That come to bind my hands, and then to drag
    me
Before the judgment-seat: now they are new
    shapes,
And do appear like Furies, with steel whips 369
To scourge my ulcerous soul. Shall I then fall
Ingloriously, and yield? No; spite of Fate,
I will be forc'd to hell like to myself,
Though you were legions of accursed spirits,
Thus would I fly among you.
            [*Rushes forward and flings himself on
                the ground.*]
*Well.*                    There 's no help;
Disarm him first, then bind him.
*Greedy.*                    Take a *mittimus,* 375
And carry him to Bedlam.
*Lov.*                    How he foams!
*Well.* And bites the earth!
*Willdo.*                    Carry him to some dark room,
There try what art can do for his recovery.
*Marg.* O my dear father!
                    *They force Overreach off.*
*All.*                    You must be patient, mistress.
*Lov.* Here is a precedent to teach wicked
    men        380
That when they leave religion, and turn athe-
    ists,

---

Their own abilities leave 'em.  Pray you take
    comfort,
I will endeavour you shall be his guardians
In his distractions: and for your land, Master
    Wellborn,
Be it good or ill in law, I 'll be an umpire   385
Between you, and this, th' undoubted heir
Of Sir Giles Overreach.  For me, here 's the
    anchor
That I must fix on.
    *All.*               What you shall determine,
My lord, I will allow of.
    *Well.*            'T is the language   389
That I speak too; but there is something else
Beside the repossession of my land,
And payment of my debts, that I must practise.
I had a reputation, but 't was lost
In my loose course, and till I redeem it
Some noble way, I am but half made up.   395
It is a time of action; if your lordship
Will please to confer a company upon me
In your command, I doubt not in my service

To my king and country but I shall do some-
    thing
That may make me right again.
    *Lov.*            Your suit is granted  400
And you lov'd for the motion.
    *Well.* [*Coming forward.*] Nothing wants then
But your allowance —

## THE EPILOGUE

But your allowance, and in that our all
Is comprehended; it being known, nor we,
Nor he that wrote the comedy, can be free  405
Without your manumission; which if you
Grant willingly, as a fair favour due
To the poet's and our labours, (as you may,
For we despair not, gentlemen, of the play,)
We jointly shall profess your grace hath might
To teach us action, and him how to write.  411
                         [*Exeunt.*]

FINIS

389 **allow of:** agree to    402 **allowance:** approval

# THE
# CHANGELING:

As it was Acted (with great Applause)
at the Privat house in D R U R Y ʃ L A N E,
and *Salisbury Court.*

---

Written by {
THOMAS MIDLETON,
and
WILLIAM ROWLEY.
} Gent'.

---

*Never Printed before.*

---

### LONDON,
Printed for H U M P H R E Y  M O S E L E Y, and are to
be fold at his fhop at the fign of the *Princes-Arms*
in St *Pauls* Church-yard, 1 6 5 3.

BIBLIOGRAPHICAL RECORD. The publication of *The Changeling* was long delayed, for the play did not appear in print until 1653. Copies of this Quarto were issued with two different title-pages. A second Quarto, produced in 1668, seems to be no more than left-over sheets of the original edition issued with a third title-page. The Quartos divide the play into acts, but fail to indicate scene-divisions. The division of verse lines is extremely inaccurate and has been silently corrected in the present edition.

DATE AND STAGE PERFORMANCE. That *The Changeling* was on the stage by the beginning of 1624 is shown by an entry in the Office Book of Sir Henry Herbert, who had recently assumed the office and title of Master of the Revels. What is doubtless an early, if not the original, performance of the play is recorded in "A Note of such Playes as were Acted at Court in 1623 and 1624." "Upon the Sonday after," writes Herbert, "beinge the 4 of January, 1623 [*i.e.*, 1624] by the Queen of Bohemias company, *The Changelinge*, the prince only being there, Att Whitehall." The actors belonged to the company enjoying the patronage of the Princess Elizabeth, who, by her marriage to the Elector Palatine, had become Queen of Bohemia. *The Changeling* seems to have been a popular play for many years. It held the stage until the closing of the theatres and was revived after the Restoration. Pepys saw it with approval on Feb. 23, 1661.

SOURCES. A further indication of date is to be found in the sources used. The main plot of the play is taken from *The Triumphs of God's Revenge against Murther*, by John Reynolds, first published in 1621, and one episode in it from Leonard Digges's translation of the Spanish novel, *Gerardo*, 1622 (see B. Lloyd, "A Minor Source for *The Changeling*," *Modern Language Review*, Jan., 1924). No source for the sub-plot (from which the title is taken) has been discovered.

AUTHORSHIP. The sub-plot of this play and the first and last scenes of the main plot have been convincingly shown to be from the pen of Rowley. The rest of the main plot seems to be by Middleton. (P. G. Wiggin, *An Inquiry into the Authorship of the Middleton-Rowley Plays*, Radcliffe College Monographs, No. 9, 1897.) Important new information, correcting traditional assumptions about Middleton's life, will be found in an article by Dr. Mark Eccles, "Middleton's Birth and Education," *Review of English Studies*, Oct., 1931.

# THOMAS MIDDLETON (1580–1627)

# WILLIAM ROWLEY (c. 1585–1626)

## THE CHANGELING

### DRAMATIS PERSONAE

VERMANDERO, [governor of the castle of Alicante,]
  father to Beatrice
TOMASO DE PIRACQUO, a noble lord
ALONZO DE PIRACQUO, his brother, suitor to Bea-
  trice
ALSEMERO, a nobleman, afterwards married to
  Beatrice
JASPERINO, his friend
ALIBIUS, a jealous doctor
LOLLIO, his man

PEDRO, friend to Antonio
ANTONIO, the changeling
FRANCISCUS, the counterfeit madman
DE FLORES, servant to Vermandero
Madmen, Servants

BEATRICE [–JOANNA], daughter to Vermandero
DIAPHANTA, her waiting-woman
ISABELLA, wife to Alibius

THE SCENE: *Allegant.*

## ACTUS PRIMUS

### [SCENE I. — *A Street.*]

*Enter Alsemero*

[*Als.*] 'T was in the temple where I first be-
  held her,
And now again the same: what omen yet
Follows of that? None but imaginary.
Why should my hopes or fate be timorous?
The place is holy, so is my intent:   5
I love her beauties to the holy purpose;
And that, methinks, admits comparison
With man's first creation, the place blessed,
And is his right home back, if he achieve it.
The church hath first begun our interview,   10
And that 's the place must join us into one;
So there 's beginning and perfection too.

*Enter Jasperino*

*Jas.* O sir, are you here? Come, the wind 's
  fair with you;
Y' are like to have a swift and pleasant passage.
*Als.* Sure, y 'are deceived, friend, 't is con-
  trary,   15
In my best judgment.
*Jas.*         What, for Malta?
If you could buy a gale amongst the witches,
They could not serve you such a lucky penny-
  worth
As comes a' God's name.

*Als.*           Even now I observ'd
The temple's vane to turn full in my face;   20
I know 't is against me.
*Jas.*         Against you? Then,
You know not where you are.
*Als.*         Not well, indeed.
*Jas.* Are you not well, sir?
*Als.*         Yes, Jasperino,
Unless there be some hidden malady
Within me, that I understand not.
*Jas.*         And that   25
I begin to doubt, sir. I never knew
Your inclinations to travels at a pause
With any cause to hinder it, till now.
Ashore you were wont to call your servants
  up,
And help to trap your horses for the speed;   30
At sea I 've seen you weigh the anchor with 'em,
Hoist sails for fear to lose the foremost breath,
Be in continual prayers for fair winds;
And have you chang'd your orisons?
*Als.*         No, friend;
I keep the same church, same devotion.   35
*Jas.* Lover I 'm sure y' are none; the Stoic
  was
Found in you long ago; your mother nor
Best friends, who have set snares of beauty, ay,
And choice ones too, could never trap you that
  way.
What might be the cause?
*Als.*         Lord, how violent   40

---

D. P. **Allegant:** Alicante, a seaport on the east coast of Spain    **8 place blessed:** Paradise
('blest' Q)    ²⁶ **doubt:** fear    ³⁰ **trap:** harness    **for the speed:** to hasten the preparations    ³⁴ **orisons:** prayers (cf. preceding line)

Thou art! I was but meditating of
Somewhat I heard within the temple.
   *Jas.*              Is this
Violence? 'T is but idleness compar'd
With your haste yesterday.
   *Als.*         I 'm all this while
A-going, man.

*Enter Servants*

   *Jas.*     Backwards, I think, sir. Look, 45
Your servants.
   *1 Ser.* The seamen call; shall we board your
trunks?
   *Als.* No, not to-day.
   *Jas.* 'T is the critical day, it seems, and the
sign in Aquarius. 51
   *2 Ser.* We must not to sea to-day; this smoke
will bring forth fire.
   *Als.* Keep all on shore; I do not know the
end,
Which needs I must do, of an affair in hand 55
Ere I can go to sea.
   *1 Ser.*      Well, your pleasure.
   *2 Ser.* Let him e'en take his leisure too; we
are safer on land.      *Exeunt Servants.*

*Enter Beatrice, Diaphanta, and Servants [Alse-*
*mero accosts Beatrice and then kisses her.]*

   *Jas.* [*Aside.*] How now? The laws of the
Medes are chang'd sure; salute a woman! He
kisses too; wonderful! Where learnt he [61
this? and does it perfectly too. In my con-
science, he ne'er rehears'd it before. Nay, go
on; this will be stranger and better news at
Valencia than if he had ransom'd half Greece
from the Turk. 66
   *Beat.* You are a scholar, sir?
   *Als.*        A weak one, lady.
   *Beat.* Which of the sciences is this love you
speak of?
   *Als.* From your tongue I take it to be
music.
   *Beat.* You are skilful in 't, can sing at first
sight. 70
   *Als.* And I have show'd you all my skill at
once;
I want more words to express me further,
And must be forc'd to repetition;
I love you dearly.
   *Beat.*     Be better advis'd, sir:
Our eyes are sentinels unto our judgments, 75
And should give certain judgment what they
see;
But they are rash sometimes, and tell us won-
ders

Of common things, which when our judgments
find,
They can then check the eyes, and call them
blind.
   *Als.* But I am further, lady; yesterday 80
Was mine eyes' employment, and hither now
They brought my judgment, where are both
agreed.
Both houses then consenting, 't is agreed;
Only there wants the confirmation
By the hand royal; that 's your part, lady. 85
   *Beat.* Oh, there 's one above me, sir. —
   [*Aside.*] For five days past
To be recall'd! Sure mine eyes were mistaken;
This was the man was meant me. That he
should come
So near his time, and miss it!
   *Jas.* We might have come by the carriers [90
from Valencia, I see, and sav'd all our sea-
provision; we are at farthest sure. Methinks I
should do something too;
I meant to be a venturer in this voyage.
Yonder 's another vessel, I 'll board her; 95
If she be lawful prize, down goes her topsail.
            [*Accosts Diaphanta.*]

*Enter De Flores*

   *De F.* Lady, your father ——
   *Beat.*       Is in health, I hope,
   *De F.* Your eye shall instantly instruct you,
lady;
He 's coming hitherward.
   *Beat.*      What needed then
Your duteous preface? I had rather 100
He had come unexpected; you must stall
A good presence with unnecessary blabbing;
And how welcome for your part you are,
I 'm sure you know.
   *De F.* [*Aside.*]    Will 't never mend, this
scorn,
One side nor other? Must I be enjoin'd 105
To follow still whilst she flies from me? Well,
Fates, do your worst, I 'll please myself with
sight
Of her at all opportunities,
If but to spite her anger. I know she had
Rather see me dead than living; and yet 110
She knows no cause for 't but a peevish
will.
   *Als.* You seem'd displeas'd, lady, on the sud-
den.
   *Beat.* Your pardon, sir, 't is my infirmity;
Nor can I other reason render you
Than his or hers, of some particular thing 115
They must abandon as a deadly poison,

<hr>

<sup>51</sup> **sign in Aquarius:** *i.e.,* watery vacillation is indicated   <sup>58</sup> S. D. **Enter . . . Servants:** (Q adds the name of "Joanna," as if she were a different character from Beatrice.)   <sup>83</sup> **Both houses:** Lords and Commons  <sup>94</sup> **venturer:** sharer  <sup>96</sup> S. D. **De Flores:** (spelled "Deflores" in Q consistently)  <sup>101</sup> **stall:** forestall  <sup>106</sup> **still:** always  <sup>115</sup> **his or hers:** someone's  **of:** ('or' Q)

Which to a thousand other tastes were whole-
    some;
Such to mine eyes is that same fellow there,
The same that report speaks of the basi-
    lisk.
    *Als.* This is a frequent frailty in our nature;
There 's scarce a man amongst a thousand
    found                                    121
But hath his imperfection: one distastes
The scent of roses, which to infinites
Most pleasing is and odoriferous;
One oil, the enemy of poison;            125
Another wine, the cheerer of the heart
And lively refresher of the countenance.
Indeed this fault, if so it be, is general;
There 's scarce a thing but is both lov'd and
    loath'd:                              129
Myself, I must confess, have the same frailty.
    *Beat.* And what may be your poison, sir?
I am bold with you.
    *Als.* And what might be your desire? per-
    haps, a cherry.
    *Beat.* I am no enemy to any creature
My memory has, but yon gentleman.
    *Als.* He does ill to tempt your sight, if he
    knew it.                              135
    *Beat.* He cannot be ignorant of that, sir,
I have not spar'd to tell him so; and I want
To help myself, since he 's a gentleman
In good respect with my father, and follows
    him.
    *Als.* He 's out of his place then now.    140
                        [*They talk apart.*]
    *Jas.* I am a mad wag, wench.
    *Dia.* So methinks; but for your comfort, I
can tell you, we have a doctor in the city that
undertakes the cure of such.
    *Jas.* Tush, I know what physic is best for
the state of mine own body.               146
    *Dia.* 'T is scarce a well-govern'd state, I be-
lieve.
    *Jas.* I could show thee such a thing with an
ingredient that we two would compound to- [150
gether, and if it did not tame the maddest blood
i' th' town for two hours after, I 'll ne'er profess physic again.
    *Dia.* A little poppy, sir, were good to cause
you sleep.                               155
    *Jas.* Poppy? I 'll give thee a pop i' th' lips
for that first, and begin there. Poppy is one
simple indeed, and cuckoo (what-you-call 't)
another. I 'll discover no more now; another
time I 'll show thee all.        [*Exit.*]  160

*Enter Vermandero and Servants*

    *Beat.* My father, sir.
    *Ver.*            O Joanna, I came to meet thee.
Your devotion 's ended?
    *Beat.*            For this time, sir. —
[*Aside.*] I shall change my saint, I fear me; I
    find
A giddy turning in me. — Sir, this while
I am beholding to this gentleman,         165
Who left his own way to keep me company,
And in discourse I find him much desirous
To see your castle. He hath deserv'd it, sir,
If ye please to grant it.
    *Ver.*            With all my heart, sir.
Yet there 's an article between; I must know
Your country; we use not to give survey   171
Of our chief strengths to strangers; our citadels
Are plac'd conspicuous to outward view,
On promonts' tops, but within are secrets.
    *Als.* A Valencian, sir.
    *Ver.*            A Valencian?          175
That 's native, sir. Of what name, I beseech
    you?
    *Als.* Alsemero, sir.
    *Ver.*            Alsemero? Not the son
Of John de Alsemero?
    *Als.*            The same, sir.
    *Ver.* My best love bids you welcome.
    *Beat.* [*Aside.*]         He was wont
To call me so, and then he speaks a most   180
Unfeigned truth.
    *Ver.*            O sir, I knew your father;
We two were in acquaintance long ago,
Before our chins were worth iulan down,
And so continued till the stamp of time
Had coin'd us into silver. Well, he 's gone; 185
A good soldier went with him.
    *Als.* You went together in that, sir.
    *Ver.* No, by Saint Jacques, I came behind
    him;
Yet I 've done somewhat too: an unhappy day
Swallowed him at last at Gibraltar,        190
In fight with those rebellious Hollanders.
Was it not so?
    *Als.*            Whose death I had reveng'd,
Or follow'd him in fate, had not the late
    league
Prevented me.
    *Ver.*            Ay, ay, 't was time to breathe. —
O Joanna, I should ha' told thee news;     195
I saw Piracquo lately.
    *Beat.* [*Aside.*]         That 's ill news.

---

¹¹⁹ **basilisk:** a fabulous beast whose look was said to kill   ¹²² **distastes:** dislikes   ¹²³ **infinites:** innumerable people   ¹³⁴ **yon:** ('yon'' Q, perhaps for "yonder")   ¹³⁷⁻¹³⁸ **Want . . . myself:** have no means to get out of my difficulty   ¹³⁹ **respect:** repute   ¹⁵⁸ **simple:** herb, remedy   ¹⁵⁹ **discover:** reveal   ¹⁷⁰ **article:** proviso   ¹⁷⁴ **promonts':** promontories'   ¹⁸³ **iulan down:** first growth of the beard   ¹⁹⁰ **Gibraltar:** (Apparently located by the author in the Netherlands. This passage is taken directly out of Reynolds.)   ¹⁹³ **league:** the armistice of 1612

*Ver.* He 's hot preparing for this day of triumph:
Thou must be a bride within this sevennight.
*Als.* [*Aside.*] Ha!
*Beat.* Nay, good sir, be not so violent; with speed    200
I cannot render satisfaction
Unto the dear companion of my soul,
Virginity, whom I thus long have liv'd with,
And part with it so rude and suddenly.
Can such friends divide, never to meet again,
Without a solemn farewell?
*Ver.*       Tush, tush! there 's a toy.   206
*Als.* [*Aside.*] I must now part, and never meet again
With any joy on earth. — Sir, your pardon;
My affairs call on me.
*Ver.*       How, sir? By no means:
Not chang'd so soon, I hope? You must see my castle,    210
And her best entertainment, e'er we part;
I shall think myself unkindly us'd else.
Come, come, let 's on; I had good hope your stay
Had been a while with us in Allegant;
I might have bid you to my daughter's wedding.    215
*Als.* [*Aside.*] He means to feast me, and poisons me beforehand. —
I should be dearly glad to be there, sir,
Did my occasions suit as I could wish.
*Beat.* I shall be sorry if you be not there
When it is done, sir; but not so suddenly.   220
*Ver.* I tell you, sir, the gentleman 's complete,
A courtier and a gallant, enrich'd
With many fair and noble ornaments;
I would not change him for a son-in-law
For any he in Spain, the proudest he,    225
And we have great ones, that you know.
*Als.*       He 's much
Bound to you, sir.
*Ver.*       He shall be bound to me
As fast as this tie can hold him; I 'll want
My will else.
*Beat.* [*Aside.*] I shall want mine, if you do it.
*Ver.* But come, by the way I 'll tell you more of him.    230
*Als.* [*Aside.*] How shall I dare to venture in his castle,
When he discharges murderers at the gate?
But I must on, for back I cannot go.
*Beat.* [*Aside.*] Not this serpent gone yet?
      [*Drops a glove.*]
*Ver.*       Look, girl, thy glove 's fallen.
Stay, stay; De Flores, help a little.    235
     [*Exeunt Vermandero, Alsemero, and Servants.*]

*De F.* Here, lady.     [*Offers her the glove.*]
*Beat.* Mischief on your officious forwardness;
Who bade you stoop? They touch my hand no more:
There! For t' other's sake I part with this,
     [*Takes off and throws down the other glove.*]
Take 'em and draw thine own skin off with 'em!    240
      *Exeunt [Beatrice and Diaphanta].*
*De F.* Here 's a favour come with a mischief.
Now I know
She had rather wear my pelt tann'd in a pair
Of dancing pumps, than I should thrust my fingers
Into her sockets here. I know she hates me,
Yet cannot choose but love her. No matter, 245
If but to vex her, I 'll haunt her still;
Though I get nothing else, I 'll have my will.
      *Exit.*

[SCENE II. — *A Room in the House of Alibius.*]
     *Enter Alibius and Lollio*

*Alib.* Lollio, I must trust thee with a secret,
But thou must keep it.
*Lol.* I was ever close to a secret, sir.
*Alib.* The diligence that I have found in thee,
The care and industry already past,    5
Assures me of thy good continuance.
Lollio, I have a wife.
*Lol.* Fie, sir, 't is too late to keep her secret;
she 's known to be married all the town and country over.    10
*Alib.* Thou goest too fast, my Lollio. That knowledge
I allow no man can be barr'd it;
But there is a knowledge which is nearer,
Deeper, and sweeter, Lollio.
*Lol.* Well, sir, let us handle that between you and I.    15
*Alib.* 'T is that I go about, man. Lollio,
My wife is young.
*Lol.* So much the worse to be kept secret, sir.
*Alib.* Why, now thou meet'st the substance of the point;
I am old, Lollio.    20
*Lol.* No, sir, 't is I am old Lollio.
*Alib.* Yet why may not this concord and sympathize?
Old trees and young plants often grow together,
Well enough agreeing.    24
*Lol.* Ay, sir, but the old trees raise themselves higher and broader than the young plants.
*Alib.* Shrewd application! There 's the fear man;

---

²⁰⁶ **toy:** trifle    ²²³ **ornaments:** qualities    ²²⁸⁻²²⁹ **want my will:** fail in my purpose    ²³² **mur-**
**derers:** cannon

I would wear my ring on my own finger;
Whilst it is borrow'd, it is none of mine,   30
But his that useth it.
   *Lol.* You must keep it on still then, if it but
lie by, one or other will be thrusting into 't.
   *Alib.* Thou conceiv'st me, Lollio; here thy
watchful eye
Must have employment. I cannot always be  35
At home.
   *Lol.* I dare swear you cannot.
   *Alib.* I must look out.
   *Lol.* I know 't, you must look out; 't is every
man's case.
   *Alib.* Here, I do say, must thy employ-
ment be;   40
To watch her treadings, and in my absence
Supply my place.
   *Lol.* I 'll do my best, sir; yet surely I cannot
see who you should have cause to be jealous
of.   45
   *Alib.* Thy reason for that, Lollio? It is
A comfortable question.
   *Lol.* We have but two sorts of people in the
house, and both under the whip, that 's fools
and madmen; the one has not wit enough to  [50
be knaves, and the other not knavery enough
to be fools.
   *Alib.* Ay, those are all my patients, Lollio;
I do profess the cure of either sort;
My trade, my living 't is; I thrive by it;   55
But here 's the care that mixes with my thrift:
The daily visitants, that come to see
My brain-sick patients, I would not have
To see my wife. Gallants I do observe
Of quick enticing eyes, rich in habits,   60
Of stature and proportion very comely:
These are most shrewd temptations, Lollio.
   *Lol.* They may be easily answered, sir; if
they come to see the fools and madmen, you
and I may serve the turn, and let my mis-  [65
tress alone; she 's of neither sort.
   *Alib.* 'T is a good ward; indeed, come they
to see
Our madmen or our fools, let 'em see no more
Than what they come for; by that consequent
They must not see her; I 'm sure she 's no
fool.   70
   *Lol.* And I 'm sure she 's no madman.
   *Alib.* Hold that buckler fast; Lollio, my
trust
Is on thee, and I account it firm and strong.
What hour is 't, Lollio?
   *Lol.*         Towards belly-hour, sir.
   *Alib.* Dinner-time? Thou mean'st twelve
o'clock?   75
   *Lol.* Yes, sir, for every part has his hour: we
wake at six and look about us, that 's eye hour;

at seven we should pray, that 's knee-hour: at
eight walk, that 's leg-hour; at nine gather
flowers and pluck a rose, that 's nose-hour; [80
at ten we drink, that 's mouth-hour; at eleven
lay about us for victuals, that 's hand-hour; at
twelve go to dinner, that 's belly-hour.
   *Alib.* Profoundly, Lollio! It will be long
Ere all thy scholars learn this lesson, and   85
I did look to have a new one ent'red; — stay,
I think my expectation is come home.

*Enter Pedro, and Antonio [disguised] like an idiot*

   *Ped.* Save you, sir; my business speaks itself:
This sight takes off the labour of my tongue.
   *Alib.* Ay, ay, sir, it is plain enough, you
mean   90
Him for my patient.
   *Ped.* And if your pains prove but commodious, to give but some little strength to his sick
and weak part of nature in him, these are
[*gives him money*] but patterns to show you [95
of the whole pieces that will follow to you, beside the charge of diet, washing, and other
necessaries, fully defrayed.
   *Alib.* Believe it, sir, there shall no care be
wanting.
   *Lol.* Sir, an officer in this place may de- [100
serve something. The trouble will pass through
my hands.
   *Ped.* 'T is fit something should come to your
hands then, sir.      [*Gives him money.*]
   *Lol.* Yes, sir, 't is I must keep him sweet, [105
and read to him: what is his name?
   *Ped.* His name is Antonio; marry, we use
but half to him, only Tony.
   *Lol.* Tony, Tony, 't is enough, and a very
good name for a fool. — What 's your name, [110
Tony?
   *Ant.* He, he, he! well, I thank you, cousin;
he, he, he!
   *Lol.* Good boy! hold up your head. — He can
laugh; I perceive by that he is no beast.   115
   *Ped.* Well, sir,
If you can raise him but to any height,
Any degree of wit; might he attain,
As I might say, to creep but on all four
Towards the chair of wit, or walk on crutches,
'T would add an honour to your worthy
pains,   121
And a great family might pray for you,
To which he should be heir, had he discre-
tion
To claim and guide his own. Assure you,
sir,
He is a gentleman.   125
   *Lol.* Nay, there 's nobody doubted that; at

first sight I knew him for a gentleman, he looks no other yet.

*Ped.* Let him have good attendance and sweet lodging.

*Lol.* As good as my mistress lies in, sir; [130 and as you allow us time and means, we can raise him to the higher degree of discretion.

*Ped.* Nay, there shall no cost want, sir.

*Lol.* He will hardly be stretch'd up to the wit of a magnifico.        135

*Ped.* O no, that 's not to be expected; far shorter will be enough.

*Lol.* I 'll warrant you I 'll make him fit to bear office in five weeks; I 'll undertake to wind him up to the wit of constable.        140

*Ped.* If it be lower than that, it might serve turn.

*Lol.* No, fie; to level him with a head-borough, beadle, or watchman, were but little better than he is. Constable I 'll able him; [145 if he do come to be a justice afterwards, let him thank the keeper: or I 'll go further with you; say I do bring him up to my own pitch, say I make him as wise as myself.

*Ped.* Why, there I would have it.        150

*Lol.* Well, go to; either I 'll be as arrant a fool as he, or he shall be as wise as I, and then I think 't will serve his turn.

*Ped.* Nay, I do like thy wit passing well.

*Lol.* Yes, you may; yet if I had not been [155 a fool, I had had more wit than I have, too. Remember what state you find me in.

*Ped.* I will, and so leave you. Your best cares, I beseech you.

*Alib.* Take you none with you, leave 'em [160 all with us.        *Exit Pedro.*

*Ant.* O, my cousin 's gone! cousin, cousin, O!

*Lol.* Peace, peace, Tony; you must not cry, child, you must be whipp'd if you do; your cousin is here still; I am your cousin, Tony. [165

*Ant.* He, he! then I 'll not cry, if thou be'st my cousin; he, he, he!

*Lol.* I were best try his wit a little, that I may know what form to place him in.

*Alib.* Ay, do, Lollio, do.        170

*Lol.* I must ask him easy questions at first. — Tony, how many true fingers has a tailor on his right hand?

*Ant.* As many as on his left, cousin.

*Lol.* Good: and how many on both?        175

*Ant.* Two less than a deuce, cousin.

*Lol.* Very well answered. I come to you again, cousin Tony: how many fools goes to a wise man?

*Ant.* Forty in a day sometimes, cousin.        180

*Lol.* Forty in a day? How prove you that?

*Ant.* All that fall out amongst themselves, and go to a lawyer to be made friends.

*Lol.* A parlous fool! he must sit in the fourth form at least. I perceive that. — I come [185 again, Tony; how many knaves make an honest man?

*Ant.* I know not that, cousin.

*Lol.* No, the question is too hard for you. I 'll tell you, cousin; there 's three knaves [190 may make an honest man, — a sergeant, a jailer, and a beadle; the sergeant catches him, the jailer holds him, and the beadle lashes him; and if he be not honest then, the hangman must cure him.        195

*Ant.* Ha, ha, ha! that 's fine sport, cousin.

*Alib.* This was too deep a question for the fool, Lollio.

*Lol.* Yes, this might have serv'd yourself, though I say 't. — Once more and you shall go play, Tony.        201

*Ant.* Ay, play at push-pin, cousin; ha, ha!

*Lol.* So thou shalt: say how many fools are here ——

*Ant.* Two, cousin; thou and I.        205

*Lol.* Nay, y' are too forward there, Tony. Mark my question; how many fools and knaves are here; a fool before a knave, a fool behind a knave, between every two fools a knave; how many fools, how many knaves?        210

*Ant.* I never learnt so far, cousin.

*Alib.* Thou putt'st too hard questions to him, Lollio.

*Lol.* I 'll make him understand it easily. — Cousin, stand there.        215

*Ant.* Ay, cousin.

*Lol.* Master, stand you next the fool.

*Alib.* Well, Lollio.

*Lol.* Here 's my place. Mark now, Tony, there 's a fool before a knave.        220

*Ant.* That 's I, cousin.

*Lol.* Here 's a fool behind a knave, that 's I; and between us two fools there is a knave, that 's my master, 't is but we three, that 's all.

*Ant.* We three, we three, cousin.        225

*Madmen within.*

1 [*Mad.*] *within.* Put 's head i' th' pillory, the bread 's too little.

2 [*Mad.*] *within.* Fly, fly, and he catches the swallow.

3 [*Mad.*] *within.* Give her more onion, or the devil put the rope about her crag.        231

*Lol.* You may hear what time of day it is, the chimes of Bedlam goes.

*Alib.* Peace, peace, or the wire comes!

---

138 **I 'll make:** ('make' Q)        143–144 **head-borough:** constable of a small town        144 **beadle:** minor parish officer        145 **able:** qualify him for the office of        157 **state:** position        172 **true:** honest        176 **Two . . . deuce:** *i.e.*, none        178 **goes to:** make        184 **parlous:** shrewd        202 **push-pin:** a child's game        220 **there 's:** ('there' Q)        231 **crag:** neck        234 **wire:** whip

3 [*Mad.*] *within.* Cat whore, cat whore! her permasant, her permasant!                      236

*Alib.* Peace, I say! — Their hour 's come, they must be fed, Lollio.

*Lol.* There 's no hope of recovery of that Welsh madman; was undone by a mouse that spoil'd him a permasant; lost his wits for 't. [241]

*Alib.* Go to your charge, Lollio; I 'll to mine.

*Lol.* Go you to your madmen's ward, let me alone with your fools.                      245

*Alib.* And remember my last charge, Lollio.                      *Exit.*

*Lol.* Of which your patients do you think I am? Come, Tony, you must amongst your school-fellows now; there 's pretty scholars [250] amongst 'em, I can tell you; there 's some of 'em at *stultus, stulta, stultum.*

*Ant.* I would see the madmen, cousin, if they would not bite me.

*Lol.* No, they shall not bite thee, Tony. 255

*Ant.* They bite when they are at dinner, do they not, coz?

*Lol.* They bite at dinner, indeed, Tony. Well, I hope to get credit by thee; I like thee the best of all the scholars that ever I [260] brought up, and thou shalt prove a wise man, or I 'll prove a fool myself.                      *Exeunt.*

## ACTUS SECUNDUS

[SCENE I. — *A Room in the Castle.*]

*Enter Beatrice and Jasperino severally*

*Beat.* O sir, I 'm ready now for that fair service

Which makes the name of friend sit glorious on you!

Good angels and this conduct be your guide!
                      [*Giving a paper.*]

Fitness of time and place is there set down, sir.

*Jas.* The joy I shall return rewards my service.                      *Exit.* 5

*Beat.* How wise is Alsemero in his friend!

It is a sign he makes his choice with judgment;

Then I appear in nothing more approv'd

Than making choice of him; for 't is a principle,

He that can choose                      10

That bosom well who of his thoughts partakes,

Proves most discreet in every choice he makes.

Methinks I love now with the eyes of judgment,

And see the way to merit, clearly see it.

A true deserver like a diamond sparkles;      15

In darkness you may see him, that 's in absence,

Which is the greatest darkness falls on love;

Yet is he best discern'd then

With intellectual eyesight. What 's Piracquo,

My father spends his breath for? And his blessing                      20

Is only mine as I regard his name,

Else it goes from me, and turns head against me,

Transform'd into a curse. Some speedy way

Must be rememb'red. He 's so forward too,

So urgent that way, scarce allows me breath 25

To speak to my new comforts.

*Enter De Flores*

*De F.* [*Aside.*]                      Yonder 's she;

Whatever ails me, now a-late especially,

I can as well be hang'd as refrain seeing her;

Some twenty times a day, nay, not so little,

Do I force errands, frame ways and excuses, 30

To come into her sight; and I have small reason for 't,

And less encouragement, for she baits me still

Every time worse than other; does profess herself

The cruellest enemy to my face in town;

At no hand can abide the sight of me,      35

As if danger or ill-luck hung in my looks.

I must confess my face is bad enough,

But I know far worse has better fortune,

And not endur'd alone, but doted on;

And yet such pick-hair'd faces, chins like witches',                      40

Here and there five hairs whispering in a corner,

As if they grew in fear one of another,

Wrinkles like troughs, where swine deformity swills

The tears of perjury, that lie there like wash

Fallen from the slimy and dishonest eye, — 45

Yet such a one plucks sweets without restraint,

And has the grace of beauty to his sweet.

Though my hard fate has thrust me out to servitude,

I tumbled into th' world a gentleman.

She turns her blessed eye upon me now,      50

And I 'll endure all storms before I part with 't.

*Beat.* [*Aside.*] Again?

This ominous ill-fac'd fellow more disturbs me

Than all my other passions.

*De F.* [*Aside.*] Now 't begins again;      55

I 'll stand this storm of hail, though the stones pelt me.

*Beat.* Thy business? What 's thy business?

*De F.* [*Aside.*]                      Soft and fair!

I cannot part so soon now.

²³⁶ **permasant:** Parmesan cheese      ²⁴⁸⁻²⁴⁹ **Of . . . am:** Do you think me fool or madman?      ²⁵² **stultus:** foolish      ²⁴ **rememb'red:** thought of      ³² **baits:** harasses      ⁴⁰ **pick-hair'd:** thin-bearded      ⁴⁶ **plucks:** ('pluckt' Q)      ⁴⁷ **to his sweet:** for his mistress

*Beat.* [*Aside.*]          The villain 's fix'd. —
Thou standing toad-pool ——
*De F.* [*Aside.*] The shower falls amain now.
*Beat.* Who sent thee? What 's thy errand?
Leave my sight!                                           60
*De F.* My lord your father charg'd me to deliver
A message to you.
*Beat.*                What, another since?
Do 't, and be hang'd then; let me be rid of thee.
*De F.* True service merits mercy.
*Beat.*                What 's thy message?
*De F.* Let beauty settle but in patience,   65
You shall hear all.
*Beat.*                A dallying, trifling torment!
*De F.* Signor Alonzo de Piracquo, lady,
Sole brother to Tomaso de Piracquo ——
*Beat.* Slave, when wilt make an end?
*De F.*                Too soon I shall.
*Beat.* What all this while of him?
*De F.*                The said Alonzo,   70
With the foresaid Tomaso ——
*Beat.*                Yet again?
*De F.* Is new alighted.
*Beat.*                Vengeance strike the news!
Thou thing most loath'd, what cause was there in this
To bring thee to my sight?
*De F.*                My lord your father
Charg'd me to seek you out.
*Beat.*                Is there no other   75
To send his errand by?
*De F.*                It seems 't is my luck
To be i' th' way still.
*Beat.*                Get thee from me!
*De F.* So: —
[*Aside.*] Why, am not I an ass to devise ways
Thus to be rail'd at? I must see her still!   80
I shall have a mad qualm within this hour again,
I know 't; and, like a common Garden bull,
I do but take breath to be lugg'd again.
What this may bode I know not; I 'll despair
the less,                                                  84
Because there 's daily precedents of bad faces
Belov'd beyond all reason. These foul chops
May come into favour one day 'mongst their fellows.
Wrangling has prov'd the mistress of good pastime;
As children cry themselves asleep, I ha' seen
Women have chid themselves a-bed to men.   90
                                        *Exit De Flores.*
*Beat.* I never see this fellow but I think
Of some harm towards me; danger 's in my mind still;

I scarce leave trembling of an hour after.
The next good mood I find my father in,
I 'll get him quite discarded. O, I was   95
Lost in this small disturbance, and forgot
Affliction's fiercer torrent that now comes
To bear down all my comforts!

        *Enter Vermandero, Alonzo, Tomaso*

*Ver.*                Y' are both welcome,
But an especial one belongs to you, sir,   99
To whose most noble name our love presents
The addition of a son, our son Alonzo.
*Alon.* The treasury of honour cannot bring forth
A title I should more rejoice in, sir.
*Ver.* You have improv'd it well. — Daughter, prepare;
The day will steal upon thee suddenly.   105
*Beat.* [*Aside.*] Howe'er, I will be sure to keep the night,
If it should come so near me.
        [*Beatrice and Vermandero talk apart.*]
*Tom.*                Alonzo.
*Alon.*                Brother?
*Tom.* In troth I see small welcome in her eye.
*Alon.* Fie, you are too severe a censurer
Of love in all points, there 's no bringing on you.   110
If lovers should mark everything a fault,
Affection would be like an ill-set book,
Whose faults might prove as big as half the volume.
*Beat.* That 's all I do entreat.
*Ver.*                It is but reasonable;   114
I 'll see what my son says to 't. — Son Alonzo,
Here 's a motion made but to reprieve
A maidenhead three days longer; the request
Is not far out of reason, for indeed
The former time is pinching.
*Alon.*                Though my joys
Be set back so much time as I could wish   120
They had been forward, yet since she desires it,
The time is set as pleasing as before,
I find no gladness wanting.
*Ver.*                May I ever
Meet it in that point still! Y' are nobly welcome, sirs.
        *Exeunt Vermandero and Beatrice.*
*Tom.* So; did you mark the dulness of her parting now?   125
*Alon.* What dulness? Thou art so exceptious still!
*Tom.* Why, let it go then; I am but a fool
To mark your harms so heedfully.
*Alon.*                Where 's the oversight?

---

[59] **standing:** stagnant (Compare *Duchess of Malfi,* I. ii. 89, 90, and note.)   **amain:** with full force
[82] **Garden:** Paris Garden, on the Bankside, where bulls were baited   [83] **lugg'd:** dragged by the ear
[87] **their:** ('his' Q)   [101] **addition:** title   [109] **censurer:** judge   [110] **bringing on you:** getting you to concede anything   [116] **motion:** proposal   [126] **exceptious:** captious   [128] **mark:** note

*Tom.* Come, your faith 's cozen'd in her,
   strongly cozen'd.
Unsettle your affection with all speed    130
Wisdom can bring it to; your peace is ruin'd
   else.
Think what a torment 't is to marry one
Whose heart is leapt into another's bosom:
If ever pleasure she receive from thee,
It comes not in thy name, or of thy gift;   135
She lies but with another in thine arms,
He the half-father unto all thy children
In the conception; if he get 'em not,
She helps to get 'em for him; and how dan-
   gerous                139
And shameful her restraint may go in time too,
It is not to be thought on without sufferings.
   *Alon.* You speak as if she lov'd some other,
   then.
   *Tom.* Do you apprehend so slowly?
   *Alon.*             Nay, an that
Be your fear only, I am safe enough.
Preserve your friendship and your counsel,
   brother,               145
For times of more distress; I should depart
An enemy, a dangerous, deadly one,
To any but thyself, that should but think
She knew the meaning of inconstancy,
Much less the use and practice: yet w' are
   friends.               150
Pray, let no more be urg'd; I can endure
Much, till I meet an injury to her,
Then I am not myself. Farewell, sweet brother;
How much w' are bound to Heaven to depart
   lovingly.           *Exit.*
   *Tom.* Why, here is love's tame madness;
   thus a man          155
Quickly steals into his vexation.     *Exit.*

[SCENE II. — *Another Room in the Castle.*]

*Enter Diaphanta and Alsemero*

*Dia.* The place is my charge; you have kept
   your hour,
And the reward of a just meeting bless you!
I hear my lady coming. Complete gentleman,
I dare not be too busy with my praises,
They 're dangerous things to deal with.   *Exit.*
   *Als.*           This goes well; 5
These women are the ladies' cabinets,
Things of most precious trust are lock'd into 'em.

*Enter Beatrice*

*Beat.* I have within mine eye all my desires.
Requests that holy prayers ascend Heaven for,
And brings 'em down to furnish our defects, 10

Come not more sweet to our necessities
Than thou unto my wishes.
   *Als.*              W' are so like
In our expressions, lady, that unless I borrow
The same words, I shall never find their equals.
   *Beat.* How happy were this meeting, this em-
   brace,              15
If it were free from envy! This poor kiss
It has an enemy, a hateful one,
That wishes poison to 't. How well were I now,
If there were none such name known as Pi-
   racquo,
Nor no such tie as the command of parents! 20
I should be but too much bless'd.
   *Als.*            One good service
Would strike off both your fears, and I 'll go
   near it too,
Since you are so distress'd. Remove the cause,
The command ceases; so there 's two fears
   blown out
With one and the same blast.
   *Beat.*        Pray, let me find you, sir: 25
What might that service be, so strangely happy?
   *Als.* The honourablest piece about man,
   valour:
I 'll send a challenge to Piracquo instantly.
   *Beat.* How? Call you that extinguishing of
   fear,
When 't is the only way to keep it flaming? 30
Are not you ventur'd in the action,
That 's all my joys and comforts? Pray, no
   more, sir.
Say you prevail'd, you 're danger's and not
   mine then;
The law would claim you from me, or obscurity
Be made the grave to bury you alive.    35
I 'm glad these thoughts come forth; O, keep
   not one
Of this condition, sir! Here was a course
Found to bring sorrow on her way to death;
The tears would ne'er ha' dried, till dust had
   chok'd 'em.
Blood-guiltiness becomes a fouler visage; — 40
[*Aside.*] And now I think on one; I was to
   blame,
I ha' marr'd so good a market with my scorn;
'T had been done questionless: the ugliest
   creature
Creation fram'd for some use: yet to see   44
I could not mark so much where it should be!
   *Als.* Lady ——
   *Beat.* [*Aside.*] Why, men of art make much
   of poison,
Keep one to expel another. Where was my art?
   *Als.* Lady, you hear not me.

*Beat.*                    I do especially, sir.
The present times are not so sure of our side
As those hereafter may be; we must use 'em
  then                                            50
As thrifty folks their wealth, sparingly now,
Till the time opens.
   *Als.*          You teach wisdom, lady.
   *Beat.* Within there! Diaphanta!

*Enter Diaphanta*

   *Dia.*               Do you call, madam?
   *Beat.* Perfect your service, and conduct this
  gentleman
The private way you brought him.
   *Dia.*               I shall, madam.  55
   *Als.* My love 's as firm as love e'er built upon.
   *Exeunt Diaphanta and Alsemero.*

*Enter De Flores*

   *De F.* [*Aside.*] I 've watch'd this meeting, and
  do wonder much
What shall become of t' other; I 'm sure both
Cannot be serv'd unless she transgress; haply
Then I 'll put in for one; for if a woman  60
Fly from one point, from him she makes a hus-
  band,
She spreads and mounts then like arithmetic;
One, ten, a hundred, a thousand, ten thousand,
Proves in time sutler to an army royal.
Now do I look to be most richly rail'd at,  65
Yet I must see her.
   *Beat.* [*Aside.*] Why, put case I loath'd him
As much as youth and beauty hates a sepulchre,
Must I needs show it? Cannot I keep that
  secret,
And serve my turn upon him? See, he 's here. —
De Flores.
   *De F.* [*Aside.*] Ha, I shall run mad with joy!
She call'd me fairly by my name De Flores, 71
And neither rogue nor rascal.
   *Beat.*                What ha' you done
To your face a' late? You 've met with some
  good physician;
You 've prun'd yourself, methinks: you were
  not wont
To look so amorously.
   *De F.*             Not I; —         75
[*Aside.*] 'T is the same physnomy, to a hair and
  pimple,
Which she call'd scurvy scarce an hour ago:
How is this?
   *Beat.* Come hither; nearer, man.
   *De F.* [*Aside.*] I 'm up to the chin in Heaven!
   *Beat.*                Turn, let me see;
Faugh, 't is but the heat of the liver, I per-
  ceive 't;                                        80
I thought it had been worse.

   *De F.* [*Aside.*]      Her fingers touch'd me!
She smells all amber.
   *Beat.* I 'll make a water for you shall cleanse
  this
Within a fortnight.
   *De F.*          With your own hands, lady? 84
   *Beat.* Yes, mine own, sir; in a work of cure
I 'll trust no other.
   *De F.* [*Aside.*]     'T is half an act of pleasure
To hear her talk thus to me.
   *Beat.*                When w' are us'd
To a hard face, it is not so unpleasing;
It mends still in opinion, hourly mends;
I see it by experience.
   *De F.* [*Aside.*]      I was blest      90
To light upon this minute; I 'll make use on 't.
   *Beat.* Hardness becomes the visage of a man
  well;
It argues service, resolution, manhood,
If cause were of employment.
   *De F.*               'T would be soon seen
If e'er your ladyship had cause to use it;  95
I would but wish the honour of a service
So happy as that mounts to.
   *Beat.*                We shall try you. —
O my De Flores!
   *De F.* [*Aside.*] How 's that? She calls me
  hers
Already! *My* De Flores! — You were about
To sigh out somewhat, madam?
   *Beat.*                No, was I? 100
I forgot, — O! ——
   *De F.* There 't is again, the very fellow
  on 't.
   *Beat.* You are too quick, sir.
   *De F.* There 's no excuse for 't now; I heard
  it twice, madam;
That sigh would fain have utterance: take pity
  on 't,
And lend it a free word. 'Las, how it labours
For liberty! I hear the murmur yet      106
Beat at your bosom.
   *Beat.*             Would creation ——
   *De F.* Ay, well said, that 's it.
   *Beat.*               Had form'd me man!
   *De F.* Nay, that 's not it.
   *Beat.*              O, 't is the soul of freedom!
I should not then be forc'd to marry one  110
I hate beyond all depths; I should have power
Then to oppose my loathings, nay, remove 'em
For ever from my sight.
   *De F.* [*Aside.*]      O bless'd occasion! ——
Without change to your sex you have your
  wishes;
Claim so much man in me.
   *Beat.*               In thee, De Flores? 115
There is small cause for that.

---

⁷⁴ **prun'd:** preened, beautified   ⁷⁵ **amorously:** like a lover   ⁸² **amber:** ambergris   ⁸³ **water.**
lotion   ⁸⁹ **mends:** improves

*De F.*                    Put it not from me,
It is a service that I kneel for it to you. [*Kneels.*]
*Beat.* You are too violent to mean faithfully.
There's horror in my service, blood, and danger;
Can those be things to sue for?
*De F.*                    If you knew 120
How sweet it were to me to be employ'd
In any act of yours, you would say then
I fail'd, and us'd not reverence enough
When I receiv'd the charge on 't.
*Beat.* [*Aside.*]                    This is much,
Methinks; belike his wants are greedy; and 125
To such gold tastes like angel's food. — Rise.
*De F.* I 'll have the work first.
*Beat.* [*Aside.*]                    Possible his need
Is strong upon him. — There 's to encourage
thee;                    [*Gives money.*]
As thou art forward, and thy service dangerous,
Thy reward shall be precious.
*De F.*                    That I have thought on; 130
I have assur'd myself of that beforehand,
And know it will be precious; the thought rav-
ishes!
*Beat.* Then take him to thy fury!
*De F.*                    I thirst for him.
*Beat.* Alonzo de Piracquo.
*De F.* [*Rising.*]                    His end 's upon him;
He shall be seen no more.
*Beat.*                    How lovely now 135
Dost thou appear to me! Never was man
Dearlier rewarded.
*De F.*                    I do think of that.
*Beat.* Be wondrous careful in the execution.
*De F.* Why, are not both our lives upon the
cast?
*Beat.* Then I throw all my fears upon thy
service.                    140
*De F.* They ne'er shall rise to hurt you.
*Beat.*                    When the deed 's done,
I 'll furnish thee with all things for thy flight;
Thou may'st live bravely in another country.
*De F.* Ay, ay;
We 'll talk of that hereafter.
*Beat.* [*Aside.*]                    I shall rid myself 145
Of two inveterate loathings at one time,
Piracquo, and his dog-face.                    *Exit.*
*De F.*                    O my blood!
Methinks I feel her in mine arms already;
Her wanton fingers combing out this beard,
And, being pleased, praising this bad face. 150
Hunger and pleasure, they 'll commend some-
times
Slovenly dishes, and feed heartily on 'em:
Nay, which is stranger, refuse daintier for 'em.
Some women are odd feeders. — I 'm too loud.
Here comes the man goes supperless to bed, 155
Yet shall not rise to-morrow to his dinner.

*Enter Alonzo*

*Alon.* De Flores.
*De F.*                    My kind, honourable lord?
*Alon.* I am glad I ha' met with thee.
*De F.*                    Sir?
*Alon.*                    Thou canst show me
The full strength of the castle?
*De F.*                    That I can, sir.
*Alon.* I much desire it.
*De F.*                    And if the ways and straits 160
Of some of the passages be not too tedious for
you,
I will assure you, worth your time and sight, my
lord.
*Alon.* Pooh, that shall be no hindrance.
*De F.*                    I 'm your servant, then.
'T is now near dinner-time; 'gainst your lord-
ship's rising
I 'll have the keys about me.
*Alon.*                    Thanks, kind De Flores. 165
*De F.* [*Aside.*] He 's safely thrust upon me
beyond hopes.                    *Exeunt.*

## ACTUS TERTIUS

[SCENE I. — *A Narrow Passage in the Castle.*]

*Enter Alonzo and De Flores. In the act-time
De Flores hides a naked rapier* [*behind a
door*].

*De Flores.* Yes, here are all the keys; I was
afraid, my lord,
I 'd wanted for the postern, this is it.
I 've all, I 've all, my lord: this for the sconce.
*Alon.* 'T is a most spacious and impregnable
fort.
*De F.* You 'll tell me more, my lord. This
descent                    5
Is somewhat narrow, we shall never pass
Well with our weapons, they 'll but trouble us.
*Alon.* Thou sayest true.
*De F.*                    Pray, let me help your lordship.
*Alon.* 'T is done: thanks, kind De Flores.
*De F.*                    Here are hooks, my lord,
To hang such things on purpose.                    10
[*Hangs up his own sword and that
of Alonzo.*]
*Alon.* Lead, I 'll follow thee.
*Exeunt at one door and enter at the
other.*

[SCENE II. — *A Vault.*]

[*Enter Alonzo and De Flores*]

*De F.* All this is nothing; you shall see anon
A place you little dream on.
*Alon.*                    I am glad

---

¹⁵¹ **pleasure:** lust     ¹⁶⁴ **'gainst:** in anticipation of     Act III. s. d. **act-time:** interval between acts
⁴ **sconce:** fortification

I have this leisure; all your master's house
Imagine I ha' taken a gondola.
*De F.* All but myself, sir, — [*aside*] which
makes up my safety.                                  5
My lord, I 'll place you at a casement here
Will show you the full strength of all the castle.
Look, spend your eye awhile upon that object.
*Alon.* Here 's rich variety, De Flores.
*De F.*                                    Yes, sir.
*Alon.* Goodly munition.
*De F.*            Ay, there 's ordnance, sir, 10
No bastard metal, will ring you a peal like
bells
At great men's funerals. Keep your eye
straight, my lord;
Take special notice of that sconce before you,
There you may dwell awhile.
        [*Takes the rapier which he had hid
        behind the door.*]
*Alon.*                     I am upon 't.
*De F.* And so am I.        [*Stabs him.*]
*Alon.*        De Flores! O De Flores! 15
Whose malice hast thou put on?
*De F.*                Do you question
A work of secrecy? I must silence you.
                        [*Stabs him.*]
*Alon.* O, O, O!
*De F.*     I must silence you. [*Stabs him.*]
So here 's an undertaking well accomplish'd.
This vault serves to good use now: ha, what 's
that                                                 20
Threw sparkles in my eye? O, 't is a diamond
He wears upon his finger; 't was well found;
This will approve the work. What, so fast on?
Not part in death? I 'll take a speedy course
then.
Finger and all shall off. [*Cuts off the finger.*]
So, now I 'll clear                                  25
The passages from all suspect or fear.
                        *Exit with body.*

[SCENE III. — *A Room in the House of Alibius.*]
    *Enter Isabella and Lollio*

*Isa.* Why, sirrah, whence have you commis-
sion
To fetter the doors against me?
If you keep me in a cage, pray, whistle to me,
Let me be doing something.
*Lol.* You shall be doing, if it please you;  5
I 'll whistle to you, if you 'll pipe after.
*Isa.* Is it your master's pleasure, or your
own,
To keep me in this pinfold?
*Lol.* 'T is for my master's pleasure, lest being
taken in another man's corn, you might be [10
pounded in another place.

*Isa.* 'T is very well, and he 'll prove very wise.
*Lol.* He says you have company enough in
the house, if you please to be sociable, of all
sorts of people.                                     15
*Isa.* Of all sorts? Why, here 's none but
fools and madmen.
*Lol.* Very well: and where will you find any
other, if you should go abroad? There 's my
master and I to boot too.                            20
*Isa.* Of either sort one, a madman and a
fool.
*Lol.* I would ev'n participate of both then if
I were as you; I know y' are half mad already,
be half foolish too.                                 25
*Isa.* Y' are a brave saucy rascal! Come on,
sir,
Afford me then the pleasure of your Bedlam.
You were commending once to-day to me
Your last-come lunatic; what a proper
Body there was without brains to guide it,   30
And what a pitiful delight appear'd
In that defect, as if your wisdom had found
A mirth in madness; pray, sir, let me par-
take,
If there be such a pleasure.
*Lol.* If I do not show you the handsomest, [35
discreetest madman, one that I may call the
understanding madman, then say I am a fool.
*Isa.* Well, a match, I will say so.
*Lol.* When you have a taste of the madman,
you shall, if you please, see Fool's College, [40
o' th' other side. I seldom lock there; 't is
but shooting a bolt or two, and you are amongst
'em.            *Exit. Enter presently.*
Come on, sir; let me see how handsomely
you 'll behave yourself now.                         45

    *Enter Lollio [with] Franciscus*

*Fran.* How sweetly she looks! O, but there 's
a wrinkle in her brow as deep as philosophy.
Anacreon, drink to my mistress' health, I 'll
pledge it. Stay, stay, there 's a spider in the
cup! No, 't is but a grape-stone; swallow it, [50
fear nothing, poet; so, so, lift higher.
*Isa.* Alack, alack, it is too full of pity
To be laugh'd at! How fell he mad? Canst
thou tell?
*Lol.* For love, mistress. He was a pretty
poet, too, and that set him forwards first; [55
the muses then forsook him; he ran mad for a
chambermaid, yet she was but a dwarf neither.
*Fran.* Hail, bright Titania!
Why stand'st thou idle on these flow'ry banks?
Oberon is dancing with his Dryades;          60
I 'll gather daisies, primrose, violets,
And bind them in a verse of poesy.

---

²³ **approve:** prove the performance of    ²⁶ **suspect:** suspicion    ⁸ **pinfold:** sheep-pen, **pound**
²⁷ **Bediam:** lunatic asylum    ²⁹ **proper:** handsome    ³⁸ **a match:** it is agreed    ⁴¹ **other:** (not in Q)
⁴⁴⁻⁴⁵ **Come . . . now:** (This is spoken off-stage.)

*Lol.* [*Holding up a whip.*] Not too near!
You see your danger.
    *Fran.* O, hold thy hand, great Diomede! 65
Thou feed'st thy horses well, they shall obey
thee:
Get up, Bucephalus kneels.    [*Kneels.*]
    *Lol.* You see how I awe my flock; a shepherd
has not his dog at more obedience.
    *Isa.* His conscience is unquiet; sure that was
The cause of this: a proper gentleman!   71
    *Fran.* Come hither, Æsculapius; hide the
poison.
    *Lol.* Well, 't is hid.    [*Hides the whip.*]
    *Fran.* Didst thou ne'er hear of one Tiresias,
A famous poet?
    *Lol.*      Yes, that kept tame wild geese. 75
    *Fran.* That 's he; I am the man.
    *Lol.* No?
    *Fran.* Yes; but make no words on 't. I was
a man
Seven years ago.
    *Lol.*      A stripling, I think, you might.
    *Fran.* Now I 'm a woman, all feminine.  80
    *Lol.* I would I might see that!
    *Fran.* Juno struck me blind.
    *Lol.* I 'll ne'er believe that; for a woman,
they say, has an eye more than a man.
    *Fran.* I say she struck me blind.    85
    *Lol.* And Luna made you mad: you have
two trades to beg with.
    *Fran.* Luna is now big-bellied, and there 's
room
For both of us to ride with Hecate;
I 'll drag thee up into her silver sphere,  90
And there we 'll kick the dog — and beat the
bush —
That barks against the witches of the night;
The swift lycanthropi that walks the round,
We 'll tear their wolvish skins, and save the
sheep.    [*Attempts to seize Lollio.*]
    *Lol.* Is 't come to this? Nay, then, my [95
poison comes forth again. [*Showing the whip.*]
Mad slave, indeed, abuse your keeper!
    *Isa.* I prithee, hence with him, now he grows
dangerous.
    *Fran.*                   *Sing.*

    Sweet love, pity me,
    Give me leave to lie with thee.  100

    *Lol.* No, I 'll see you wiser first. To your
own kennel!
    *Fran.* No noise, she sleeps; draw all the cur-
tains round,
Let no soft sound molest the pretty soul
But love, and love creeps in at a mouse-hole.
    *Lol.* I would you would get into your hole!

(*Exit Franciscus.*) — Now, mistress, I will [106
bring you another sort; you shall be fool'd
another while.    Tony, come hither, Tony:
look who 's yonder, Tony.

             *Enter Antonio*

    *Ant.* Cousin, is it not my aunt?    110
    *Lol.* Yes, 't is one of 'em, Tony.
    *Ant.* He, he! how do you, uncle?
    *Lol.* Fear him not, mistress, 't is a gentle
nigget; you may play with him, as safely with
him as with his bauble.  115
    *Isa.* How long hast thou been a fool?
    *Ant.* Ever since I came hither, cousin.
    *Isa.* Cousin? I 'm none of thy cousins, fool.
    *Lol.* O, mistress, fools have always so much
wit as to claim their kindred.  120
    *Madman within.* Bounce, bounce! he falls,
he falls!
    *Isa.* Hark you, your scholars in the upper
    room
Are out of order.
    *Lol.* Must I come amongst you there? — [125
Keep you the fool, mistress; I 'll go up and
play left-handed Orlando amongst the madmen.                         *Exit.*
    *Isa.* Well, sir.
    *Ant.* 'T is opportuneful now, sweet lady!
nay,  130
Cast no amazing eye upon this change.
    *Isa.* Ha!
    *Ant.* This shape of folly shrouds your dearest
love,
The truest servant to your powerful beauties,
Whose magic had this force thus to transform
me.  135
    *Isa.* You are a fine fool indeed!
    *Ant.*            O, 't is not strange!
Love has an intellect that runs through all
The scrutinous sciences; and, like a cunning
poet,
Catches a quantity of every knowledge,
Yet brings all home into one mystery,  140
Into one secret that he proceeds in.
    *Isa.* Y' are a parlous fool.
    *Ant.* No danger in me; I bring nought but
love
And hiss oft-wounding shafts to strike you with.
Try but one arrow; if it hurt you, I  145
Will stand you twenty back in recompense.
                    [*Kisses her.*]
    *Isa.* A forward fool too!
    *Ant.*        This was love's teaching:
A thousand ways he fashion'd out my way,
And this I found the safest and the nearest,
To tread the galaxia to my star.  150

---

  **93** lycanthropi: werewolves    **110** aunt: bawd (slang)    **114** nigget: idiot    **127** play . . . Orlando: strike terror    **131** amazing: wondering    **138** scrutinous: scrutinizing, speculative    **145–146** I Will: ('I'le' Q)    **148** he: ('she' Q)    **149** the nearest: ('neerest' Q)    **150** galaxia: Milky Way

*Isa.* Profound withal! certain you dream'd
of this,
Love never taught it waking.
    *Ant.*               Take no acquaintance
Of these outward follies, there is within
A gentleman that loves you.
    *Isa.*          When I see him, 154
I 'll speak with him; so, in the meantime, keep
Your habit, it becomes you well enough.
As you are a gentleman, I 'll not discover you;
That 's all the favour that you must expect. 158
When you are weary, you may leave the
school,
For all this while you have but play'd the fool.

*Enter Lollio*

    *Ant.* And must again. — He, he! I thank
you, cousin;
I 'll be your valentine to-morrow morning.
    *Lol.* How do you like the fool, mistress?
    *Isa.* Passing well, sir.         164
    *Lol.* Is he not witty, pretty well, for a fool?
    *Isa.* If he hold on as he begins, he 's like
To come to something.
    *Lol.* Ay, thank a good tutor. You may put
him to 't; he begins to answer pretty hard questions. — Tony, how many is five times six? [170
    *Ant.* Five times six is six times five.
    *Lol.* What arithmetician could have answer'd
better? How many is one hundred and seven?
    *Ant.* One hundred and seven is seven hundred
and one, cousin.         175
    *Lol.* This is no wit to speak on! — Will you
be rid of the fool now?
    *Isa.* By no means; let him stay a little.
    *Madman (Within).* Catch there, catch the
last couple in hell!     180
    *Lol.* Again! must I come amongst you?
Would my master were come home! I am not
able to govern both these wards together. *Exit.*
    *Ant.* Why should a minute of love's hour
be lost?     184
    *Isa.* Fie, out again! I had rather you kept
Your other posture; you become not your
tongue
When you speak from your clothes.
    *Ant.* How can he freeze    188
Lives near so sweet a warmth? Shall I alone
Walk through the orchard of the Hesperides,
And, cowardly, not dare to pull an apple?

*Enter Lollio above*

This with the red cheeks I must venter for.
                  *[Attempts to kiss her.]*
    *Isa.* Take heed, there 's giants keep 'em.

    *Lol. [Aside.]* How now, fool, are you good at
that? Have you read Lipsius? He 's past [195
*Ars Amandi;* I believe I must put harder ques-
tions to him, I perceive that.
    *Isa.* You are bold without fear too.
    *Ant.*          What should I fear,
Having all joys about me? Do you smile,
And love shall play the wanton on your lip,
Meet and retire, retire and meet again;  201
Look you but cheerfully, and in your eyes
I shall behold mine own deformity,
And dress myself up fairer. I know this shape
Becomes me not, but in those bright mirrors
I shall array me handsomely.
    *Lol.*        Cuckoo, cuckoo! *Exit.* 206
    *Madmen above, some as birds, others
      as beasts.*
    *Ant.* What are these?
    *Isa.*         Of fear enough to part us;
Yet are they but our schools of lunatics,
That act their fantasies in any shapes,
Suiting their present thoughts: if sad, they
   cry;    210
If mirth be their conceit, they laugh again:
Sometimes they imitate the beasts and birds,
Singing or howling, braying, barking; all
As their wild fancies prompt 'em.

*Enter Lollio*

    *Ant.*          These are no fears.
    *Isa.* But here 's a large one, my man.  215
    *Ant.* Ha, he! that 's fine sport, indeed,
cousin.
    *Lol.* I would my master were come home!
'T is too much for one shepherd to govern two
of these flocks; nor can I believe that one [220
churchman can instruct two benefices at once;
there will be some incurable mad of the one
side, and very fools on the other. — Come,
Tony.
    *Ant.* Prithee, cousin, let me stay here still. [225
    *Lol.* No, you must to your book now; you
have play'd sufficiently.
    *Isa.* Your fool is grown wondrous witty.
    *Lol.* Well, I 'll say nothing: but I do not think
but he will put you down one of these [230
days.         *Exeunt Lollio and Antonio.*
    *Isa.* Here the restrained current might make
breach,
Spite of the watchful bankers. Would a woman
stray,
She need not gad abroad to seek her sin,
It would be brought home one ways or another:
The needle's point will to the fixed north;  236
Such drawing Articks womens' beauties are.

    179–180 **catch . . . hell:** an allusion to the game of "barley-break"    187 **from:** out of keeping
with  195 **Lipsius:** Lipsius Justus (1547–1606), a popular humanist writer (with pun on "lips")  196 **Ars
Amandi:** Ovid's "Art of Love"  233 **bankers:** dike-tenders  235 **another:** ('other' Q)  237 **Articks:**
poles

*Enter Lollio*

*Lol.* How dost thou, sweet rogue?

*Isa.* How now?

*Lol.* Come, there are degrees; one fool may be better than another.                    241

*Isa.* What 's the matter?

*Lol.* Nay, if thou giv'st thy mind to fool's flesh, have at thee!

*Isa.* You bold slave, you!

*Lol.* I could follow now as t' other fool [246 did:
"What should I fear,
Having all joys about me?  Do you but smile,
And love shall play the wanton on your lip,
Meet and retire, retire and meet again;          251
Look you but cheerfully, and in your eyes
I shall behold my own deformity,
And dress myself up fairer.  I know this shape
Becomes me not —"
And so as it follows: but is not this the [256 more foolish way?  Come, sweet rogue; kiss me, my little Lacedæmonian; let me feel how thy pulses beat.  Thou hast a thing about thee would do a man pleasure, I 'll lay my hand on 't.                    261

*Isa.* Sirrah, no more!  I see you have dis-cover'd
This love's knight errant, who hath made adventure
For purchase of my love: be silent, mute,
Mute as a statue, or his injunction          265
For me enjoying, shall be to cut thy throat;
I 'll do it, though for no other purpose; and
Be sure he 'll not refuse it.

*Lol.*                    My share, that 's all;
I 'll have my fool's part with you.

*Isa.*                    No more!  Your master.

*Enter Alibius*

*Alib.* Sweet, how dost thou?

*Isa.*                    Your bounden servant, sir.

*Alib.* Fie, fie, sweetheart, no more of that. 271

*Isa.* You were best lock me up.

*Alib.* In my arms and bosom, my sweet Isabella,
I'll lock thee up most nearly. — Lollio,
We have employment, we have task in hand.
At noble Vermandero's, our castle captain,  276
There is a nuptial to be solemniz'd —
Beatrice-Joanna, his fair daughter, bride, —
For which the gentleman hath bespoke our pains,
A mixture of our madmen and our fools,  280
To finish, as it were, and make the fag
Of all the revels, the third night from the first;

Only an unexpected passage over,
To make a frightful pleasure, that is all,
But not the all I aim at.  Could we so act it,
To teach it in a wild distracted measure,    286
Though out of form and figure, breaking time's head,
It were no matter, 't would be heal'd again
In one age or other, if not in this:
This, this, Lollio, there 's a good reward begun,
And will beget a bounty, be it known.       291

*Lol.* This is easy, sir, I 'll warrant you: you have about you fools and madmen that can dance very well; and 't is no wonder, your best dancers are not the wisest men; the reason is, with often jumping they jolt their brains [296 down into their feet, that their wits lie more in their heels than in their heads.

*Alib.* Honest Lollio, thou giv'st me a good reason,
And a comfort in it.

*Isa.*                    Y'ave a fine trade on 't.
Madmen and fools are a staple commodity. 301

*Alib.* O wife, we must eat, wear clothes, and live.
Just at the lawyer's haven we arrive,
By madmen and by fools we both do thrive.

*Exeunt.*

[SCENE IV. — *A Room in the Castle.*]

*Enter Vermandero, Alsemero, Jasperino, and Beatrice*

*Ver.* Valencia speaks so nobly of you, sir,
I wish I had a daughter now for you.

*Als.* The fellow of this creature were a part-ner
For a king's love.

*Ver.*                    I had her fellow once, sir,
But Heaven has married her to joys eternal; 5
'T were sin to wish her in this vale again.
Come, sir, your friend and you shall see the pleasures
Which my health chiefly joys in.

*Als.*                    I hear
The beauty of this seat largely commended.

*Ver.* It falls much short of that.

*Exeunt.  Manet Beatrice.*

*Beat.*                    So, here 's one step 10
Into my father's favour; time will fix him;
I 've got him now the liberty of the house.
So wisdom, by degrees, works out her free-dom;
And if that eye be dark'ned that offends me, —
I wait but that eclipse, — this gentleman    15
Shall soon shine glorious in my father's lik-ing,
Through the refulgent virtue of my love.

*Enter De Flores*

*De F.* [*Aside.*] My thoughts are at a ban-
quet; for the deed,
I feel no weight in 't; 't is but light and cheap
For the sweet recompense that I set down for 't.
*Beat.* De Flores?
*De F.* Lady?
*Beat.*        Thy looks promise cheerfully. 21
*De F.* All things are answerable, time, cir-
cumstance,
Your wishes, and my service.
*Beat.*                Is it done, then?
*De F.* Piracquo is no more.
*Beat.* My joys start at mine eyes; our
sweet'st delights        25
Are evermore born weeping.
*De F.*                I 've a token for you.
*Beat.* For me?
*De F.* But it was sent somewhat unwillingly;
I could not get the ring without the finger.
        [*Producing the finger and ring.*]
*Beat.* Bless me, what hast thou done?
*De F.*                Why, is that more 30
Than killing the whole man? I cut his heart-
strings;
A greedy hand thrust in a dish at court,
In a mistake hath had as much as this.
*Beat.* 'T is the first token my father made
me send him.
*De F.* And I have made him send it back
again        35
For his last token. I was loath to leave it,
And I 'm sure dead men have no use of jewels;
He was as loath to part with 't, for it stuck
As if the flesh and it were both one substance.
*Beat.* At the stag's fall, the keeper has his
fees;        40
'T is soon appli'd: all dead men's fees are yours,
sir.
I pray, bury the finger, but the stone
You may make use on shortly; the true value,
Take 't of my truth, is near three hundred
ducats.
*De F.* 'T will hardly buy a capcase for one's
conscience though,        45
To keep it from the worm, as fine as 't is.
Well, being my fees, I 'll take it;
Great men have taught me that, or else my
merit
Would scorn the way on 't.
*Beat.*                It might justly, sir.
Why, thou mistak'st, De Flores; 't is not given
In state of recompense.
*De F.*                No, I hope so, lady; 51
You should soon witness my contempt to 't
then.

*Beat.* Prithee, — thou look'st as if thou wert
offended.
*De F.* That were strange, lady; 't is not
possible        54
My service should draw such a cause from you.
Offended! Could you think so? That were
much
For one of my performance, and so warm
Yet in my service.
*Beat.* 'T were misery in me to give you cause,
sir.
*De F.* I know so much, it were so; misery 60
In her most sharp condition.
*Beat.*                'T is resolv'd then;
Look you, sir, here 's three thousand golden
florins;
I have not meanly thought upon thy merit.
*De F.* What! salary? Now you move me.
*Beat.*                How, De Flores?
*De F.* Do you place me in the rank of ver-
minous fellows,        65
To destroy things for wages? Offer gold
For the life-blood of man? Is anything
Valued too precious for my recompense?
*Beat.* I understand thee not.
*De F.*                I could ha' hir'd
A journeyman in murder at this rate,        70
And mine own conscience might have slept at
ease,
And have had the work brought home.
*Beat.* [*Aside.*]                I 'm in a labyrinth;
What will content him? I would fain be rid of
him.
I 'll double the sum, sir.
*De F.*                You take a course
To double my vexation, that 's the good you do.
*Beat.* [*Aside.*] Bless me, I am now in worse
plight than I was;        76
I know not what will please him. — For my
fear's sake,
I prithee, make away with all speed possible;
And if thou be'st so modest not to name
The sum that will content thee, paper blushes
not:        80
Send thy demand in writing, it shall follow thee;
But, prithee, take thy flight.
*De F.*                You must fly too, then.
*Beat.* I?
*De F.* I 'll not stir a foot else.
*Beat.*                What 's your meaning?
*De F.* Why, are not you as guilty? In, I 'm
sure,
As deep as I; and we should stick together. 85
Come, your fears counsel you but ill; my ab-
sence
Would draw suspect upon you instantly;
There were no rescue for you.

---

**35 have:** (not in Q)    **45 capcase:** band-box    **51 state:** place    **67 For:** (not in Q)    **71 slept
at ease:** (not in Q)    **72 brought home:** (*i.e.*, done by an agent)    **87 suspect:** suspicion

*Beat.* [*Aside.*] He speaks home!
*De F.* Nor is it fit we two, engag'd so jointly,
Should part and live asunder.
*Beat.* How now, sir? 90
This shows not well.
*De F.* What makes your lip so strange?
This must not be betwixt us.
*Beat.* The man talks wildly!
*De F.* Come, kiss me with a zeal now.
*Beat.* [*Aside.*] Heaven, I doubt him!
*De F.* I will not stand so long to beg 'em
shortly. 95
*Beat.* Take heed, De Flores, of forgetfulness,
'T will soon betray us.
*De F.* Take you heed first;
Faith, y' are grown much forgetful, y' are to
blame in 't.
*Beat.* [*Aside.*] He 's bold, and I am blam'd
for 't.
*De F.* I have eas'd you
Of your trouble, think on 't; I 'm in pain, 100
And must be eas'd of you; 't is a charity.
Justice invites your blood to understand me.
*Beat.* I dare not.
*De F.* Quickly!
*Beat.* O, I never shall!
Speak it yet further off, that I may lose
What has been spoken, and no sound remain
on 't;
I would not hear so much offence again 106
For such another deed.
*De F.* Soft, lady, soft!
The last is not yet paid for. O, this act
Has put me into spirit; I was as greedy on 't
As the parch'd earth of moisture, when the
clouds weep. 110
Did you not mark, I wrought myself into 't,
Nay, sued and kneel'd for 't? Why was all
that pains took?
You see I 've thrown contempt upon your gold;
Not that I want it not, for I do piteously. 114
In order I 'll come unto 't, and make use on 't,
But 't was not held so precious to begin with,
For I place wealth after the heels of pleasure;
And were I not resolv'd in my belief
That thy virginity were perfect in thee,
I should but take my recompense with grudg-
ing, 120
As if I had but half my hopes I agreed for.
*Beat.* Why, 't is impossible thou canst be so
wicked,
Or shelter such a cunning cruelty,
To make his death the murderer of my honour!
Thy language is so bold and vicious, 125
I cannot see which way I can forgive it
With any modesty.

*De F.* Pish! you forget yourself;
A woman dipp'd in blood, and talk of modesty!
*Beat.* O misery of sin! would I 'd been bound
Perpetually unto my living hate 130
In that Piracquo, than to hear these words!
Think but upon the distance that creation
Set 'twixt thy blood and mine, and keep thee
there.
*De F.* Look but into your conscience, read
me there;
'T is a true book, you 'll find me there your
equal. 135
Pish! fly not to your birth, but settle you
In what the act has made you; y' are no more
now.
You must forget your parentage to me;
You 're the deed's creature; by that name
You lost your first condition, and I challenge
you, 140
As peace and innocency has turn'd you out,
And made you one with me.
*Beat.* With thee, foul villain!
*De F.* Yes, my fair murd'ress. Do you urge
me,
Though thou writ'st maid, thou whore in thy
affection?
'T was chang'd from thy first love, and that 's
a kind 145
Of whoredom in thy heart; and he 's chang'd
now
To bring thy second on, thy Alsemero,
Whom, by all sweets that ever darkness tasted,
If I enjoy thee not, thou ne'er enjoy'st!
I 'll blast the hopes and joys of marriage, 150
I 'll confess all; my life I rate at nothing.
*Beat.* De Flores!
*De F.* I shall rest from all lover's plagues
then;
I live in pain now; that shooting eye
Will burn my heart to cinders.
*Beat.* O sir, hear me!
*De F.* She that in life and love refuses me, 155
In death and shame my partner she shall be.
*Beat.* [*Kneeling.*] Stay, hear me once for
all; I make thee master
Of all the wealth I have in gold and jewels;
Let me go poor unto my bed with honour,
And I am rich in all things!
*De F.* Let this silence thee:
The wealth of all Valencia shall not buy 161
My pleasure from me;
Can you weep Fate from its determin'd pur-
pose?
So soon may you weep me.
*Beat.* Vengeance begins;
Murder, I see, is followed by more sins. 165

101 of: by    114 it not: ('it' Q)    127, 136 Pish: ('Push' Q)    138 parentage: birth, position    to:
in your relation with    152 lover's: (Dyce omits and reads "love-shooting" in the next line.)    164 you:
(not in Q)

Was my creation in the womb so curst,
It must engender with a viper first?
   *De F.* [*Raising her.*] Come, rise and shroud
    your blushes in my bosom;
Silence is one of pleasure's best receipts:  169
Thy peace is wrought for ever in this yielding.
'Las! how the turtle pants! Thou 'lt love anon
What thou so fear'st and faint'st to venture on.
                  *Exeunt.*

## ACTUS QUARTUS

### [Dumb Show]

*Enter Gentlemen, Vermandero meeting them with
action of wonderment at the flight of Piracquo. Enter Alsemero with Jasperino and
gallants: Vermandero points to him, the
gentlemen seeming to applaud the choice.
Alsemero, Jasperino, and Gentlemen;* [6
*Beatrice the bride following in great state,
accompanied with Diaphanta, Isabella, and
other gentlewomen; De Flores after all,
smiling at the accident: Alonzo's ghost* [10
*appears to De Flores in the midst of his
smile, startles him, showing him the hand
whose finger he had cut off. They pass over
in great solemnity.*

[Scene I. — *Alsemero's Apartment in the
Castle.*]

*Enter Beatrice*

  *Beat.* This fellow has undone me endlessly;
Never was bride so fearfully distress'd.
The more I think upon th' ensuing night,
And whom I am to cope with in embraces,
One who 's ennobled both in blood and mind,
So clear in understanding, — that 's my plague
   now —                  6
Before whose judgment will my fault appear
Like malefactors' crimes before tribunals.
There is no hiding on 't, the more I dive
Into my own distress. How a wise man  10
Stands for a great calamity! There 's no ven-
   turing
Into his bed, what course soe'er I light upon,
Without my shame, which may grow up to
   danger.
He cannot but in justice strangle me
As I lie by him; as a cheater use me;  15
'T is a precious craft to play with a false die
Before a cunning gamester. Here 's his closet;
The key left in 't, and he abroad i' th' park!
Sure 't was forgot; I 'll be so bold as look in 't.
                [*Opens closet.*]

Bless me! a right physician's closet 't is,  20
Set round with vials; every one her mark too.
Sure he does practise physic for his own use,
Which may be safely call'd your great man's
   wisdom.
What manuscript lies here? " The Book of
   Experiment,
Call'd Secrets in Nature." So 't is: 't is so. 25
[*Reads.*] " How to know whether a woman
   be with child or no."
I hope I am not yet; if he should try though!
Let me see [*reads*] " folio forty-five," here 't is,
The leaf tuck'd down upon 't, the place suspi-
   cious.  29
[*Reads.*] " If you would know whether a wo-
man be with child or not, give her two spoonfuls
of the white water in glass C —— "
Where 's that glass C? O yonder, I see 't now —
[*reads*] " and if she be with child, she sleeps
full twelve hours after; if not, not: "  35
None of that water comes into my belly;
I 'll know you from a hundred; I could break
   you now,
Or turn you into milk, and so beguile
The master of the mystery; but I 'll look to
   you.
Ha! that which is next is ten times worse:  40
[*Reads.*] " How to know whether a woman be
a maid or not: "
If that should be appli'd, what would become
   of me?
Belike he has a strong faith of my purity,
That never yet made proof; but this he calls [45
[*reads*] " A merry slight, but true experiment; the author Antonius Mizaldus. Give
the party you suspect the quantity of a spoonful
of the water in the glass M, which, upon her
that is a maid, makes three several effects; [50
't will make her incontinently gape, then fall
into a sudden sneezing, last into a violent
laughing; else, dull, heavy, and lumpish."
Where had I been?
I fear it, yet 't is seven hours to bed-time.  55

*Enter Diaphanta*

  *Dia.* Cuds, madam, are you here?
  *Beat.*          Seeing that wench now,
A trick comes in my mind; 't is a nice piece
Gold cannot purchase. [*Aside.*] — I come
   hither, wench,
To look my lord.
  *Dia.*        Would I had such a cause
To look him too! — Why, he 's i' th' park,
   madam.  60

---

Dumb Show  ¹⁰ **accident:** occasion  Sc. I  ⁵ **who 's:** ('both' Q)  ¹¹ **Stands for:** is open to  ¹⁵ **by:** ('by by' Q)  ⁴⁶ **slight:** trick  ⁴⁷ **Mizaldus:** Antoine Mizauld (1520–1578), author of a work called *De Arcanis Naturæ* (cf. 1. 25). But the test comes from the same author's *Centuriæ IX. Memorabilium* (1613).  ⁵¹ **incontinently:** immediately  ⁵⁶ **Cuds:** a petty oath  ⁵⁷ **piece:** young woman  ⁵⁹ **look:** look for

*Beat.* There let him be.

*Dia.* Ay, madam, let him compass
Whole parks and forests, as great rangers do,
At roosting-time a little lodge can hold 'em.
Earth-conquering Alexander, that thought the
        world
Too narrow for him, in th' end had but his pit-
        hole.                                                       65

*Beat.* I fear thou art not modest, Diaphanta.

*Dia.* Your thoughts are so unwilling to be
        known, madam.
'T is ever the bride's fashion, towards bed-time,
To set light by her joys, as if she ow'd 'em not.

*Beat.* Her joys? Her fears thou wouldst
        say.

*Dia.*                    Fear of what?                          70

*Beat.* Art thou a maid, and talk'st so to a
        maid?
You leave a blushing business behind;
Beshrew your heart for 't!

*Dia.*       Do you mean good sooth, madam?

*Beat.* Well, if I 'd thought upon the fear at
        first,
Man should have been unknown.

*Dia.*                        Is 't possible? 75

*Beat.* I will give a thousand ducats to that
        woman
Would try what my fear were, and tell me true
To-morrow, when she gets from 't; as she likes,
I might perhaps be drawn to 't.

*Dia.*                      Are you in earnest?

*Beat.* Do you get the woman, then challenge
        me,                                                        80
And see if I 'll fly from 't; but I must tell you
This by the way, she must be a true maid.
Else there 's no trial, my fears are not hers else.

*Dia.* Nay, she that I would put into your
        hands, madam,
Shall be a maid.

*Beat.* You know I should be sham'd else, 85
Because she lies for me.

*Dia.*                    'T is a strange humour!
But are you serious still? Would you resign
Your first night's pleasure, and give money too?

*Beat.* As willingly as live. — [*Aside.*] Alas,
        the gold
Is but a by-bet to wedge in the honour!          90

*Dia.* I do not know how the world goes
        abroad
For faith or honesty; there 's both requir'd in
        this.
Madam, what say you to me, and stray no
        further?
I 've a good mind, in troth, to earn your money.

*Beat.* Y' are too quick, I fear, to be a maid. 95

*Dia.* How? Not a maid? Nay, then you
        urge me, madam;

Your honourable self is not a truer,
With all your fears upon you ——

*Beat.* [*Aside.*]                 Bad enough then.

*Dia.* Than I with all my lightsome joys
        about me.

*Beat.* I 'm glad to hear 't. Then you dare
        put your honesty                                          100
Upon an easy trial.

*Dia.*              Easy? Anything.

*Beat.* I 'll come to you straight.
                          [*Goes to the closet.*]

*Dia.*          She will not search me, will she.
Like the forewoman of a female jury?

*Beat.* Glass M: ay, this is it. [*Brings vial.*]
        Look, Diaphanta,
You take no worse than I do.        [*Drinks.*]

*Dia.*                    And in so doing, 105
I will not question what it is, but take it.
                                  [*Drinks.*]

*Beat.* [*Aside.*] Now if th' experiment be
        true, 't will praise itself,
And give me noble ease: begins already;
                          [*Diaphanta gapes.*]
There 's the first symptom; and what haste it
        makes
To fall into the second, there by this time! 110
                        [*Diaphanta sneezes.*]
Most admirable secret! on the contrary,
It stirs not me a whit, which most concerns it.

*Dia.* Ha, ha, ha!

*Beat.* [*Aside.*] Just in all things, and in
        order
As if 't were circumscrib'd; one accident      115
Gives way unto another.

*Dia.* Ha, ha, ha!

*Beat.* How now, wench?

*Dia.*                Ha, ha, ha! I 'm so, so light
At heart — ha, ha, ha! — so pleasurable!
But one swig more, sweet madam.

*Beat.*                    Ay, to-morrow, 120
We shall have time to sit by 't.

*Dia.*                Now I 'm sad again.

*Beat.* [*Aside.*] It lays itself so gently too!
— Come, wench.
Most honest Diaphanta I dare call thee now.

*Dia.* Pray, tell me, madam, what trick call
        you this?

*Beat.* I 'll tell thee all hereafter; we must
        study                                                     125
The carriage of this business.

*Dia.*                    I shall carry 't well,
Because I love the burthen.

*Beat.*                    About midnight
You must not fail to steal forth gently,
That I may use the place.

*Dia.*                  O, fear not, madam,
I shall be cool by that time. The bride's place,

---

⁶² **rangers:** hunting dogs      ⁶⁹ **ow'd:** owned      ⁸⁶ **humour:** whim      ⁹⁰ **by-bet:** supplement
¹⁰⁰ **honesty:** chastity      ¹¹⁵ **accident:** symptom      ¹²² **lays:** allays

And with a thousand ducats! I 'm for a justice
now, 131
I bring a portion with me; I scorn small fools.
*Exeunt.*

[SCENE II. — *Another Room in the Castle.*]

*Enter Vermandero and Servant*

*Ver.* I tell thee, knave, mine honour is in
question,
A thing till now free from suspicion,
Nor ever was there cause. Who of my gentle-
men
Are absent? Tell me, and truly, how many,
and who?
*Ser.* Antonio, sir, and Franciscus. 5
*Ver.* When did they leave the castle?
*Ser.* Some ten days since, sir; the one in-
tending to
Briamata, th' other for Valencia.
*Ver.* The time accuses 'em; a charge of
murder
Is brought within my castle-gate, Piracquo's
murder; 10
I dare not answer faithfully their absence.
A strict command of apprehension
Shall pursue 'em suddenly, and either wipe
The stain off clear, or openly discover it.
Provide me winged warrants for the purpose. 15
*Exit Servant.*
See, I am set on again.

*Enter Tomaso*

*Tom.* I claim a brother of you.
*Ver.* Y' are too hot;
Seek him not here.
*Tom.* Yes, 'mongst your dearest bloods,
If my peace find no fairer satisfaction.
This is the place must yield account for him,
For here I left him; and the hasty tie 21
Of this snatch'd marriage gives strong testi-
mony
Of his most certain ruin.
*Ver.* Certain falsehood!
This is the place indeed; his breach of faith
Has too much marr'd both my abused love, 25
The honourable love I reserv'd for him,
And mock'd my daughter's joy; the prepar'd
morning
Blush'd at his infidelity; he left
Contempt and scorn to throw upon those friends
Whose belief hurt 'em. O, 't was most ignoble
To take his flight so unexpectedly, 31
And throw such public wrongs on those that
lov'd him!

*Tom.* Then this is all your answer?
*Ver.* 'T is too fair
For one of his alliance; and I warn you
That this place no more see you. *Exit.*

*Enter De Flores*

*Tom.* The best is, 36
There is more ground to meet a man's revenge
on. —
Honest De Flores?
*De F.* That 's my name indeed.
Saw you the bride? Good sweet sir, which way
took she?
*Tom.* I 've bless'd mine eyes from seeing
such a false one. 40
*De F.* [*Aside.*] I 'd fain get off, this man 's
not for my company;
I smell his brother's blood when I come near
him.
*Tom.* Come hither, kind and true one; I
remember
My brother lov'd thee well.
*De F.* O, purely. dear sir! —
[*Aside.*] Methinks I 'm now again a-killing
on him, 45
He brings it so fresh to me.
*Tom.* Thou canst guess, sirrah —
An honest friend has an instinct of jealousy —
At some foul guilty person.
*De F.* Alas! sir,
I am so charitable, I think none
Worse than myself! You did not see the bride
then? 50
*Tom.* I prithee, name her not: is she not
wicked?
*De F.* No, no; a pretty, easy, round-pack'd
sinner,
As your most ladies are, else you might think
I flatter'd her; but, sir, at no hand wicked,
Till th' are so old their chins and noses meet,
And they salute witches. I 'm call'd, I think,
sir. — 56
[*Aside.*] His company ev'n o'erlays my con-
science. *Exit.*
*Tom.* That De Flores has a wondrous honest
heart!
He 'll bring it out in time, I 'm assur'd on 't.
O, here 's the glorious master of the day's joy!
'T will not be long till he and I do reckon. — 61

*Enter Alsemero*

Sir.
*Als.* You are most welcome.
*Tom.* You may call that word back;
I do not think I am, nor wish to be.

---

⁸ **Briamata:** Vermandero's house ten leagues from Alicante (mentioned in Reynolds, *Triumphs of God's Revenge against Murther*)   ¹¹ **answer faithfully:** answer for confidently   ¹² **apprehension:** arrest   ³⁴ **alliance:** station, family   ⁴⁷ **An:** ('One' Q)   ⁵³ **your most:** most of your   ⁵⁶ **chins and noses:** ('sins and vices' Q)

*Als.* 'T is strange you found the way to this
house then.
*Tom.* Would I 'd ne'er known the cause!
I 'm none of those, sir,                           65
That come to give you joy, and swill your wine;
'T is a more precious liquor that must lay
The fiery thirst I bring.
*Als.*                    Your words and you
Appear to me great strangers.
*Tom.*                    Time and our swords
May make us more acquainted. This the busi-
ness:                                              70
I should have had a brother in your place;
How treachery and malice have dispos'd of him,
I 'm bound to inquire of him which holds his
right,
Which never could come fairly.
*Als.*                    You must look
To answer for that word, sir.
*Tom.*                    Fear you not,    75
I 'll have it ready drawn at our next meeting.
Keep your day solemn; farewell, I disturb it not;
I 'll bear the smart with patience for a time.
                                        *Exit.*
*Als.* 'T is somewhat ominous this; a quarrel
ent'red
Upon this day; my innocence relieves me,    80

### Enter Jasperino

I should be wondrous sad else. — Jasperino,
I have news to tell thee, strange news.
*Jas.*                    I ha' some too,
I think as strange as yours. Would I might
keep
Mine, so my faith and friendship might be kept
in 't!
Faith, sir, dispense a little with my zeal,    85
And let it cool in this.
*Als.*                    This puts me on,
And blames thee for thy slowness.
*Jas.*                    All may prove nothing,
Only a friendly fear that leapt from me, sir.
*Als.* No question, 't may prove nothing;
let 's partake it though.
*Jas.* 'T was Diaphanta's chance — for to
that wench                                        90
I pretend honest love, and she deserves it —
To leave me in a back part of the house,
A place we chose for private conference,
She was no sooner gone, but instantly
I heard your bride's voice in the next room to
me;                                               95
And lending more attention, found De Flores
Louder than she.
*Als.* De Flores! Thou art out now.
*Jas.* You 'll tell me more anon.

*Als.*                    Still I 'll prevent thee,
The very sight of him is poison to her.
*Jas.* That made me stagger too; but Dia-
phanta                                           100
At her return confirm'd it.
*Als.*                    Diaphanta!
*Jas.* Then fell we both to listen, and words
pass'd
Like those that challenge interest in a woman.
*Als.* Peace: quench thy zeal, 't is dangerous
to thy bosom.
*Jas.* Then truth is full of peril.
*Als.*                    Such truths are.
O, were she the sole glory of the earth,    106
Had eyes that could shoot fire into king's
breasts,
And touch'd, she sleeps not here! Yet I have
time,
Though night be near, to be resolv'd hereof;
And, prithee, do not weigh me by my passions.
*Jas.* I never weigh'd friend so.
*Als.*                    Done charitably! 111
That key will lead thee to a pretty secret,
                                    [*Giving key.*]
By a Chaldean taught me, and I have
My study upon some. Bring from my closet
A glass inscrib'd there with the letter M,    115
And question not my purpose.
*Jas.*                    It shall be done, sir.    *Exit.*
*Als.* How can this hang together? Not an
hour since
Her woman came pleading her lady's fears,
Deliver'd her for the most timorous virgin
That ever shrunk at man's name, and so
modest,                                          120
She charg'd her weep out her request to me,
That she might come obscurely to my bosom.

### Enter Beatrice

*Beat.* [*Aside.*] All things go well; my wom-
an's preparing yonder
For her sweet voyage, which grieves me to lose;
Necessity compels it; I lose all, else.    125
*Als.* [*Aside.*] Pish! modesty's shrine is set
in yonder forehead:
I cannot be too sure though. — My Joanna!
*Beat.* Sir, I was bold to weep a message to
you;
Pardon my modest fears.
*Als.* [*Aside.*]                    The dove's not meeker;
She 's abus'd, questionless.

### Enter Jasperino [*with vial*].

                                    O, are you come, sir?
*Beat.* [*Aside.*] The glass, upon my life! I
see the letter.                                  131

*Jas.* Sir, this is M.    [*Giving vial.*]
*Als.*    'T is it.
*Beat.* [*Aside.*]    I am suspected.
*Als.* How fitly our bride comes to partake
with us!
*Beat.* What is 't, my lord?
*Als.*    No hurt.
*Beat.*    Sir, pardon me,
I seldom taste of any composition.    135
*Als.* But this, upon my warrant, you shall
venture on.
*Beat.* I fear 't will make me ill.
*Als.*    Heaven forbid that.
*Beat.* [*Aside.*] I 'm put now to my cunning:
th' effects I know,
If I can now but feign 'em handsomely.
    [*Drinks.*]
*Als.* It has that secret virtue, it ne'er miss'd
sir,    140
Upon a virgin.
*Jas.*    Treble-qualitied?
    [*Beatrice gapes and sneezes.*]
*Als.* By all that 's virtuous it takes there!
proceeds!
*Jas.* This is the strangest trick to know a
maid by.
*Beat.* Ha, ha, ha!
You have given me joy of heart to drink, my
lord.    145
*Als.* No, thou hast given me such joy of
heart,
That never can be blasted.
*Beat.*    What 's the matter, sir?
*Als.* [*Aside.*] See now 't is settled in a
melancholy;
Keeps both the time and method. — My Jo-
anna,
Chaste as the breath of Heaven, or morning's
womb,    150
That brings the day forth! thus my love en-
closes thee.    *Exeunt.*

[SCENE III. — *A Room in the House of Alibius.*]

*Enter Isabella and Lollio*

*Isa.* O Heaven! is this the waning moon?
Does love turn fool, run mad, and all at
once?
Sirrah, here 's a madman, akin to the fool too,
A lunatic lover.
*Lol.* No, no, not he I brought the letter
from?    5
*Isa.* Compare his inside with his out, and
tell me.
*Lol.* The out 's mad, I 'm sure of that; I
had a taste on 't. [*Reads letter.*] " To the
bright Andromeda, chief chambermaid to the

Knight of the Sun, at the sign of Scorpio, in [10
the middle region, sent by the bellows-mender
of Æolus. Pay the post." This is stark madness!
*Isa.* Now mark the inside. [*Takes the letter
and reads.*] " Sweet lady, having now cast [15
off this counterfeit cover of a madman, I appear
to your best judgment a true and faithful lover
of your beauty."
*Lol.* He is mad still.
*Isa.* [*Reads.*] " If any fault you find, [20
chide those perfections in you which have made
me imperfect; 't is the same sun that causeth
to grow and enforceth to wither —— "
*Lol.* O rogue!
*Isa.* [*Reads.*] " Shapes and transshapes, [25
destroys and builds again. I come in winter to
you, dismantled of my proper ornaments; by
the sweet splendour of your cheerful smiles,
I spring and live a lover."
*Lol.* Mad rascal still!    30
*Isa.* [*Reads.*] " Tread him not under foot,
that shall appear an honour to your bounties.
I remain — mad till I speak with you, from
whom I expect my cure. Yours all, or one
beside himself, *Franciscus.*"    35
*Lol.* You are like to have a fine time on 't.
My master and I may give over our profes-
sions; I do not think but you can cure fools and
madmen faster than we, with little pains too.
*Isa.* Very likely.    40
*Lol.* One thing I must tell you, mistress:
you perceive that I am privy to your skill; if I
find you minister once, and set up the trade, I
put in for my thirds; I shall be mad or fool else.
*Isa.* The first place is thine, believe it, Lollio,
If I do fall, —
*Lol.*    I fall upon you.
*Isa.*    So.    46
*Lol.* Well, I stand to my venture.
*Isa.* But thy counsel now; how shall I deal
with 'em?
*Lol.* Why, do you mean to deal with 'em? [50
*Isa.* Nay, the fair understanding, how to
use 'em.
*Lol.* Abuse 'em! That 's the way to mad
the fool, and make a fool of the madman, and
then you use 'em kindly.
*Isa.* 'T is easy, I 'll practise; do thou ob-
serve it.    55
The key of thy wardrobe.
*Lol.* There [*gives key*]; fit yourself for 'em,
and I 'll fit 'em both for you.
*Isa.* Take thou no further notice than the
outside.    *Exit*
*Lol.* Not an inch; I 'll put you to the inside.    60

¹ **waning**: ('waiting' Q)    ⁵⁰ **Why**: ('We' Q)    ⁵¹ **the . . . understanding**: understand **my**
words in the modest sense    ⁵² **Abuse**: deceive

*Enter Alibius*

*Alib.* Lollio, art there? Will all be perfect, think'st thou?
To-morrow night, as if to close up the
Solemnity, Vermandero expects us.

*Lol.* I mistrust the madmen most; the fools will do well enough; I have taken pains with [65 them.

*Alib.* Tush! they cannot miss; the more absurdity,
The more commends it, so no rough be-
haviours
Affright the ladies; they 're nice things, thou know'st.

*Lol.* You need not fear, sir; so long as we [70 are there with our commanding pizzles, they 'll be as tame as the ladies themselves.

*Alib.* I will see them once more rehearse before they go.

*Lol.* I was about it, sir: look you to the [75 madmen's morris, and let me alone with the other. There is one or two that I mistrust their fooling; I 'll instruct them, and then they shall rehearse the whole measure.

*Alib.* Do so; I 'll see the music prepar'd: but, Lollio,                                            80
By the way, how does my wife brook her re-
straint?
Does she not grudge at it?

*Lol.* So, so; she takes some pleasure in the house, she would abroad else. You must allow her a little more length, she 's kept too short. [85

*Alib.* She shall along to Vermandero's with us,
That will serve her for a month's liberty.

*Lol.* What 's that on your face, sir?

*Alib.* Where, Lollio? I see nothing.

*Lol.* Cry you mercy, sir, 't is your nose; [90 it show'd like the trunk of a young elephant.

*Alib.* Away, rascal! I 'll prepare the music, Lollio.                                            *Exit Alibius.*

*Lol.* Do, sir, and I 'll dance the whilst. —
Tony, where art thou, Tony?

*Enter Antonio*

*Ant.* Here, cousin; where art thou?        95

*Lol.* Come, Tony, the footmanship I taught you.

*Ant.* I had rather ride, cousin.

*Lol.* Ay, a whip take you! but I 'll keep you out; vault in: look you, Tony; fa, la, la, la, la.                                         [*Dances.*] 100

*Ant.* Fa, la, la, la, la.       [*Sings and dances.*]

*Lol.* There, an honour.

*Ant.* Is this an honour, coz?

*Lol.* Yes, and it please your worship.

*Ant.* Does honour bend in the hams, coz? 105

*Lol.* Marry does it, as low as worship, squireship, nay, yeomanry itself sometimes, from whence it first stiffened: there rise, a caper.

*Ant.* Caper after an honour, coz?        110

*Lol.* Very proper, for honour is but a caper, rises as fast and high, has a knee or two, and falls to th' ground again. You can remember your figure, Tony?

*Ant.* Yes, cousin; when I see thy figure, [115 I can remember mine.        *Exit [Lollio].*

*Enter Isabella, [dressed as a madwoman]*

*Isa.* Hey, how he treads the air! Shough, shough, t' other way! he burns his wings else.
Here 's wax enough below, Icarus, more than will be cancelled these eighteen moons. He 's down, he 's down! what a terrible fall he had!        121
Stand up, thou son of Cretan Dædalus,
And let us tread the lower labyrinth;
I 'll bring thee to the clue.

*Ant.* Prithee, coz, let me alone.

*Isa.*                Art thou not drown'd? 125
About thy head I saw a heap of clouds
Wrapp'd like a Turkish turban; on thy back
A crookt chameleon-colour'd rainbow hung
Like a tiara down unto thy hams.
Let me suck out those billows in thy belly; 130
Hark, how they roar and rumble in the straits!
Bless thee from the pirates!

*Ant.* Pox upon you, let me alone!

*Isa.* Why shouldst thou mount so high as Mercury,
Unless thou hadst reversion of his place?    135
Stay in the moon with me, Endymion,
And we will rule these wild rebellious waves,
That would have drown'd my love.

*Ant.*                I 'll kick thee, if
Again thou touch me, thou wild unshapen antic;
I am no fool, you bedlam!        140

*Isa.* But you are, as sure as I am, mad.
Have I put on this habit of a frantic,
With love as full of fury, to beguile
The nimble eye of watchful jealousy,
And am I thus rewarded?

*Ant.*        Ha! dearest beauty! 145

*Isa.* No, I have no beauty now,
Nor never had but what was in my garments.
You a quick-sighted lover! Come not near me:

---

⁶⁸ **so:** provided that    ⁶⁹ **nice:** fastidious    ⁷¹ **pizzles:** whips    ⁷⁶ **morris:** dance    ⁹⁰ **Cry . . . mercy:** I beg your pardon    ⁹¹ **trunk . . . elephant:** a traditional characteristic of the cuckold    ¹⁰² **honour:** bow    ¹¹⁴ **figure:** dance    ¹¹⁷ **he:** ('she' Q)    ¹³¹ **straits:** ('streets' Q)    ¹³² **Bless:** (God) protect

Keep your caparisons, y' are aptly clad;
I came a feigner, to return stark mad. *Exit.* 150
*Ant.* Stay, or I shall change condition,
And become as you are.

### Enter Lollio

*Lol.* Why, Tony, whither now? Why,
fool ——
*Ant.* Whose fool, usher of idiots? You cox-
comb!
I have fool'd too much. 155
*Lol.* You were best be mad another while
then.
*Ant.* So I am, stark mad; I have cause
enough;
And I could throw the full effects on thee,
And beat thee like a fury.
*Lol.* Do not, do not; I shall not forbear [160
the gentleman under the fool, if you do. Alas!
I saw through your fox-skin before now! Come,
I can give you comfort; my mistress loves you;
and there is as arrant a madman i' th' house
as you are a fool, your rival, whom she loves [165
not. If after the masque we can rid her of
him, you earn her love, she says, and the fool
shall ride her.
*Ant.* May I believe thee?
*Lol.* Yes, or you may choose whether you
will or no. 170
*Ant.* She 's eas'd of him; I 've a good quarrel on 't.
*Lol.* Well, keep your old station yet, and
be quiet.
*Ant.* Tell her I will deserve her love. [*Exit.*]
*Lol.* And you are like to have your desire.

### Enter Franciscus

*Fran.* [*Sings.*] "Down, down, down, a-down
a-down,"—and then with a horse-trick
To kick Latona's forehead, and break her bow-
string. 176
*Lol.* [*Aside.*] This is t' other counterfeit; I 'll
put him out of his humour. — [*Takes out a letter
and reads.*] "Sweet lady, having now cast this
counterfeit cover of a madman, I appear to [180
your best judgment a true and faithful lover of
your beauty." This is pretty well for a madman.
*Fran.* Ha! what 's that?
*Lol.* [*Reads.*] "Chide those perfections in you
which have made me imperfect." 185
*Fran.* I am discover'd to the fool.
*Lol.* I hope to discover the fool in you ere
I have done with you. [*Reads.*] "Yours all, or
one beside himself, *Franciscus*." This madman
will mend sure. 190
*Fran.* What do you read, sirrah?

*Lol.* Your destiny, sir; you 'll be hang'd for
this trick, and another that I know.
*Fran.* Art thou of counsel with thy mistress?
*Lol.* Next her apron-strings. 195
*Fran.* Give me thy hand.
*Lol.* Stay, let me put yours in my pocket
first. [*Putting letter into his pocket.*] Your
hand is true, is it not? It will not pick? I
partly fear it, because I think it does lie. 200
*Fran.* Not in a syllable.
*Lol.* So if you love my mistress so well as
you have handled the matter here, you are like
to be cur'd of your madness.
*Fran.* And none but she can cure it. 205
*Lol.* Well, I 'll give you over then, and she
shall cast your water next.
*Fran.* Take for thy pains past.
[*Gives him money.*]
*Lol.* I shall deserve more, sir, I hope. My
mistress loves you, but must have some [210
proof of your love to her.
*Fran.* There I meet my wishes.
*Lol.* That will not serve, you must meet her
enemy and yours.
*Fran.* He 's dead already. 215
*Lol.* Will you tell me that, and I parted but
now with him?
*Fran.* Show me the man.
*Lol.* Ay, that 's a right course now; see him
before you kill him, in any case; and yet it [220
needs not go so far neither. 'T is but a fool that
haunts the house and my mistress in the shape
of an idiot; bang but his fool's coat well-
favouredly, and 't is well.
*Fran.* Soundly, soundly! 225
*Lol.* Only reserve him till the masque be
past; and if you find him not now in the dance
yourself, I 'll show you. In, in! my master!
[*Dancing.*]
*Fran.* He handles him like a feather. Hey!
[*Exit.*]

### Enter Alibius

*Alib.* Well said: in a readiness, Lollio? 230
*Lol.* Yes, sir.
*Alib.* Away then, and guide them in, Lollio:
Entreat your mistress to see this sight.
Hark, is there not one incurable fool
That might be begg'd? I 've friends.
*Lol.*                                I have him for you, 235
One that shall deserve it too.
*Alib.* Good boy, Lollio!
*The madmen and fools dance.*
'T is perfect: well, fit but once these strains,
We shall have coin and credit for our pains.
*Exeunt.*

---

175 **horse-trick:** caper    185 **have:** (not in Q)    199 **true:** honest    207 **cast . . . water:** diag-
nose your disease    234–235 **fool . . . begg'd:** whose guardianship and income might be begged
from the king

## ACTUS QUINTUS

*[SCENE I. - - A Gallery in the Castle.]*

*Enter Beatrice: a clock strikes one*

*Beat.* One struck, and yet she lies by 't!
O my fears!
This strumpet serves her own ends, 't is appar-
ent now,
Devours the pleasure with a greedy appetite,
And never minds my honour or my peace,      5
Makes havoc of my right.  But she pays dearly
for 't;
No trusting of her life with such a secret
That cannot rule her blood to keep her prom-
ise;
Beside, I 've some suspicion of her faith to me,
Because I was suspected of my lord,      10
And it must come from her.           *Strike two.*
                    Hark! by my horrors,
Another clock strikes two!

*Enter De Flores*

*De F.*                    Pist! where are you?
*Beat.* De Flores?
*De F.*   Ay.  Is she not come from him yet?
*Beat.* As I 'm a living soul, not!
*De F.*                    Sure the devil
Hath sow'd his itch within her.  Who would
trust      15
A waiting-woman?
*Beat.*           I must trust somebody.
*De F.*   Pish! they are termagants;
Especially when they fall upon their masters
And have their ladies' first fruits; they 're mad
whelps,
You cannot stave 'em off from game royal:
then      20
You are so rash and hardy, ask no counsel;
And I could have help'd you to a 'pothecary's
daughter
Would have fall'n off before eleven, and thank'd
you too.
*Beat.* O me, not yet! this whore forgets
herself.
*De F.* The rascal fares so well: look, y' are
undone;      25
The day-star, by this hand! see Phosphorus
plain yonder.
*Beat.* Advise me now to fall upon some ruin;
There is no counsel safe else.
*De F.*                    Peace!  I ha 't now,
For we must force a rising, there 's no remedy.
*Beat.* How? take heed of that.      30
*De F.*   Tush! be you quiet, or else give over
all.
*Beat.* Prithee, I ha' done then.

*De F.*                    This is my reach: I 'll set
Some part a-fire of Diaphanta's chamber.
*Beat.* How?  Fire, sir?  That may endanger
the whole house.
*De F.*   You talk of danger when your fame 's
on fire?      35
*Beat.* That 's true; do what thou wilt now.
*De F.*                    Pish!  I aim
At a most rich success strikes all dead sure.
The chimney being a-fire, and some light par-
cels
Of the least danger in her chamber only,
If Diaphanta should be met by chance then      40
Far from her lodging, which is now suspicious,
It would be thought her fears and affrights
then
Drove her to seek for succour; if not seen
Or met at all, as that 's the likeliest,
For her own shame she 'll hasten towards her
lodging;      45
I will be ready with a piece high-charg'd,
As 't were to cleanse the chimney there: 't is
proper now,
But she shall be the mark.
*Beat.*           I 'm forc'd to love thee now,
'Cause thou provid'st so carefully for my hon-
our.
*De F.*   'Slid, it concerns the safety of us
both,      50
Our pleasure and continuance.
*Beat.*                    One word now,
Prithee; how for the servants?
*De F.*                    I 'll despatch them,
Some one way, some another in the hurry,
For buckets, hooks, ladders; fear not you,
The deed shall find its time; and I 've thought
since      55
Upon a safe conveyance for the body too:
How this fire purifies wit!  Watch you your
minute.
*Beat.* Fear keeps my soul upon 't, I cannot
stray from 't.

*Enter Alonzo's Ghost*

*De F.*   Ha! what art thou that tak'st away
the light
'Twixt that star and me?  I dread thee
not. —      60
'T was but a mist of conscience; all 's clear
again.                    *Exit.*
*Beat.* Who 's that, De Flores?  Bless me, it
slides by!           *[Exit Ghost.]*
Some ill thing haunts the house; 't has left behind it
A shivering sweat upon me; I 'm afraid now,
This night hath been so tedious!  O this strumpet!      65

²¹ **rash:** ('harsh' Q)      ²³ **thank'd:** ('thank' Q)      ²⁶ **Phosphorus:** the morning star ('Bos-
phorus' Q)      ³² **reach:** scheme      ⁴⁶ **piece:** gun

Had she a thousand lives, he should not leave
her
Till he had destroy'd the last. List! O my
terrors!                          *Struck three o'clock.*
Three struck by St. Sebastian's!
   *Within.* Fire, fire, fire!                          69
   *Beat.* Already? How rare is that man's speed!
How heartily he serves me! his face loathes one;
But look upon his care, who would not love him?
The east is not more beauteous than his service.
   *Within.* Fire, fire, fire!

*Enter De Flores: Servants pass over: ring a bell.*

   *De F.*   Away, despatch! hooks, buckets, lad-
ders! that 's well said.                          75
The fire-bell rings; the chimney works, my
charge;
The piece is ready.                          *Exit.*
   *Beat.*          Here 's a man worth loving!

*Enter Diaphanta*

O, y' are a jewel!
   *Dia.*          Pardon frailty, madam;
In troth, I was so well, I ev'n forgot myself.
   *Beat.* Y' have made trim work!
   *Dia.*          What?
   *Beat.*   Hie quickly to your chamber;   80
Your reward follows you.
   *Dia.*          I never made
So sweet a bargain.                          *Exit.*

*Enter Alsemero*

   *Als.*          O my dear Joanna,
Alas! art thou risen too? I was coming,
My absolute treasure!
   *Beat.*          When I miss'd you,
I could not choose but follow.
   *Als.*          Th' art all sweetness:   85
The fire is not so dangerous.
   *Beat.*          Think you so, sir?
   *Als.* I prithee, tremble not; believe me, 't is
not.

*Enter Vermandero, Jasperino*

   *Ver.* O bless my house and me!
   *Als.*          My lord your father.

*Enter De Flores with a piece*

   *Ver.* Knave, whither goes that piece?
   *De F.*   To scour the chimney. *Exit.*
   *Ver.* O, well said, well said!          90
That fellow 's good on all occasions.
   *Beat.* A wondrous necessary man, my lord.
   *Ver.* He hath a ready wit; he 's worth 'em
all, sir;
Dog at a house of fire; I ha' seen him singed ere
now. —                          *The piece goes off.*
Ha, there he goes!

   *Beat.*          'T is done!
   *Als.*   Come, sweet, to bed now;   95
Alas! thou wilt get cold.
   *Beat.*          Alas! the fear keeps that out!
My heart will find no quiet till I hear
How Diaphanta, my poor woman, fares;
It is her chamber, sir, her lodging cham-
ber.
   *Ver.* How should the fire come there?   100
   *Beat.* As good a soul as ever lady counte-
nanc'd,
But in her chamber negligent and heavy:
She 'scap'd a mine twice.
   *Ver.*          Twice?
   *Beat.*          Strangely twice, sir.
   *Ver.* Those sleepy sluts are dangerous in a
house,
An they be ne'er so good.

*Enter De Flores*

   *De F.*          O poor virginity,   105
Thou hast paid dearly for 't!
   *Ver.*          Bless us, what 's that?
   *De F.* A thing you all knew once, Dia-
phanta 's burnt.
   *Beat.* My woman! O my woman!
   *De F.*          Now the flames
Are greedy of her; burnt, burnt, burnt to
death, sir!
   *Beat.* O my presaging soul!
   *Als.*          Not a tear more!   110
I charge you by the last embrace I gave you
In bed, before this rais'd us.
   *Beat.*          Now you tie me;
Were it my sister, now she gets no more.

*Enter Servant*

   *Ver.* How now?
   *Ser.* All danger 's past; you may now take   115
Your rests, my lords; the fire is throughly
quench'd.
Ah, poor gentlewoman, how soon was she
stifled!
   *Beat.* De Flores, what is left of her inter,
And we as mourners all will follow her.
I will entreat that honour to my servant   120
Ev'n of my lord himself.
   *Als.*          Command it, sweetness.
   *Beat.* Which of you spied the fire first?
   *De F.*          'T was I, madam.
   *Beat.* And took such pains in 't too? A
double goodness!
'T were well he were rewarded.
   *Ver.*          He shall be. —
De Flores, call upon me.
   *Als.*          And upon me, sir.   125
                          *Exeunt [all except De Flores].*

---

⁷⁵ **well said:** well done   ⁹⁴ **Dog:** keen   ¹⁰¹ **countenanc'd:** had in service   ¹¹⁶ **throughly:**
thoroughly

*De F.*  Rewarded? Precious! here 's a trick
    beyond me.
I see in all bouts, both of sport and wit,
Always a woman strives for the last hit.  *Exit.*

[SCENE II. — *Another Room in the Castle.*]

*Enter Tomaso*

*Tom.*  I cannot taste the benefits of life
With the same relish I was wont to do.
Man I grow weary of, and hold his fellowship
A treacherous bloody friendship; and because
I am ignorant in whom my wrath should settle,
I must think all men villains, and the next    6
I meet, whoe'er he be, the murderer
Of my most worthy brother.   Ha! what 's he?
    *Enter De Flores; passes over the stage.*
O, the fellow that some call honest De Flores;
But methinks honesty was hard bested    10
To come there for a lodging; as if a queen
Should make her palace of a pest-house.
I find a contrariety in nature
Betwixt that face and me; the least occasion
Would give me game upon him; yet he 's so foul
One would scarce touch him with a sword he
    lov'd    16
And made account of; so most deadly venomous,
He would go near to poison any weapon
That should draw blood on him; one must
    resolve
Never to use that sword again in fight    20
In way of honest manhood that strikes him;
Some river must devour it; 't were not fit
That any man should find it.   What, again?

*Enter De Flores*

He walks a' purpose by, sure, to choke me up,
To infect my blood.
*De F.*              My worthy noble lord! 25
*Tom.*  Dost offer to come near and breathe
    upon me?                    [*Strikes him.*]
*De F.*  A blow!                    [*Draws.*]
*Tom.*              Yea, are you so prepar'd?
I 'll rather like a soldier die by th' sword,
Than like a politician by thy poison.  [*Draws.*]
*De F.*  Hold, my lord, as you are honourable!
*Tom.*  All slaves that kill by poison are still
    cowards.                    31
*De F.* [*Aside.*] I cannot strike; I see his
    brother's wounds
Fresh bleeding in his eye, as in a crystal. —
I will not question this, I know y' are noble;
I take my injury with thanks given, sir,    35
Like a wise lawyer, and as a favour
Will wear it for the worthy hand that gave it. —
[*Aside.*] Why this from him that yesterday
    appear'd

So strangely loving to me?
O, but instinct is of a subtler strain!    40
Guilt must not walk so near his lodge again;
He came near me now.                    *Exit.*
*Tom.*  All league with mankind I renounce
    for ever,
Till I find this murderer; not so much
As common courtesy but I 'll lock up;    45
For in the state of ignorance I live in,
A brother may salute his brother's murderer,
And wish good speed to th' villain in a greeting.

*Enter Vermandero, Alibius, and Isabella*

*Ver.*  Noble Piracquo!
*Tom.*              Pray, keep on your way, sir;
I 've nothing to say to you.
*Ver.*              Comforts bless you, sir; 50
*Tom.*  I 've forsworn compliment, in troth I
    have, sir;
As you are merely man, I have not left
A good wish for you, nor any here.
*Ver.*  Unless you be so far in love with grief,
You will not part from 't upon any terms,    55
We bring that news will make a welcome for us.
*Tom.*  What news can that be?
*Ver.*              Throw no scornful smile
Upon the zeal I bring you, 't is worth more, sir.
Two of the chiefest men I kept about me    59
I hide not from the law or your just vengeance.
*Tom.*  Ha!
*Ver.*  To give your peace more ample satis-
    faction,
Thank these discoverers.
*Tom.*              If you bring that calm,
Name but the manner I shall ask forgiveness in
For that contemptuous smile I threw upon you;
I 'll perfect it with reverence that belongs    66
Unto a sacred altar.                    [*Kneels.*]
*Ver.* [*Raising him.*]  Good sir, rise;
Why, now you overdo as much a' this hand
As you fell short a' t' other. — Speak, Alibius.
*Alib.*  'T was my wife's fortune, as she is most
    lucky    70
At a discovery, to find out lately,
Within our hospital of fools and madmen,
Two counterfeits slipp'd into these disguises,
Their names Franciscus and Antonio.
*Ver.*  Both mine, sir, and I ask no favour for
    'em.    75
*Alib.*  Now that which draws suspicion to
    their habits:
The time of their disguisings agrees justly
With the day of the murder.
*Tom.*              O blest revelation!
*Ver.*  Nay, more, nay, more, sir — I 'll not
    spare mine own    79
In way of justice — they both feign'd a journey

To Briamata, and so wrought out their leaves;
My love was so abus'd in 't.
*Tom.*                    Time 's too precious
To run in waste now; you have brought a peace
The riches of five kingdoms could not purchase
Be my most happy conduct; I thirst for 'em: 85
Like subtle lightning will I wind about 'em,
And melt their marrow in 'em.         *Exeunt.*

[SCENE III.—*Alsemero's Apartment in the
                    Castle.*]

*Enter Alsemero and Jasperino*

*Jas.* Your confidence, I 'm sure, is now of
       proof;
The prospect from the garden has show'd
Enough for deep suspicion.
*Als.*                    The black mask
That so continually was worn upon 't
Condemns the face for ugly ere 't be seen,    5
Her despite to him, and so seeming bottomless.
*Jas.* Touch it home then; 't is not a shallow
       probe
Can search this ulcer soundly; I fear you 'll
       find it
Full of corruption. 'T is fit I leave you,
She meets you opportunely from that walk; 10
She took the back door at his parting with her.
                              *Exit Jasperino.*
*Als.* Did my fate wait for this unhappy
       stroke
At my first sight of woman? She is here.

*Enter Beatrice*

*Beat.* Alsemero!
*Als.*                    How do you?
*Beat.*                              How do I?
Alas! how do you? You look not well.    15
   *Als.* You read me well enough; I am not well.
*Beat.* Not well, sir? Is 't in my power to
       better you?
*Als.* Yes.
*Beat.* Nay, then y' are cur'd again.
*Als.* Pray, resolve me one question, lady. 20
*Beat.* If I can.
*Als.* None can so sure: are you honest?
*Beat.* Ha, ha, ha! that 's a broad question,
       my lord.
*Als.* But that 's not a modest answer, my
       lady.
Do you laugh? My doubts are strong upon
       me.                                        25
   *Beat.* 'T is innocence that smiles, and no
rough brow
Can take away the dimple in her cheek.
Say I should strain a tear to fill the vault,
Which would you give the better faith to?  29
   *Als.* 'T were but hypocrisy of a sadder colour,

But the same stuff; neither your smiles nor tears
Shall move or flatter me from my belief:
You are a whore!
   *Beat.*              What a horrid sound it hath!
It blasts a beauty to deformity;
Upon what face soever that breath falls,    35
It strikes it ugly. O, you have ruin'd
What you can ne'er repair again!
   *Als.*                              I 'll all
Demolish, and seek out truth within you,
If there be any left; let your sweet tongue
Prevent your heart's rifling; there I 'll ransack
And tear out my suspicion.
   *Beat.*              You may, sir;    41
'T is an easy passage; yet, if you please,
Show me the ground whereon you lost your
       love;
My spotless virtue may but tread on that
Before I perish.
   *Als.*              Unanswerable;         45
A ground you cannot stand on; you fall down
Beneath all grace and goodness when you set
Your ticklish heel on 't. There was a vizor
O'er that cunning face, and that became you;
Now Impudence in triumph rides upon 't.   50
How comes this tender reconcilement else
'Twixt you and your despite, your rancorous
       loathing,
De Flores? he that your eye was sore at sight of,
He 's now become your arm's supporter, your
Lip's saint!
   *Beat.* Is there the cause?
   *Als.*              Worse, your lust's devil,  55
Your adultery!
   *Beat.*     Would any but yourself say that,
'T would turn him to a villain!
   *Als.*                    It was witness'd
By the counsel of your bosom, Diaphanta.
   *Beat.* Is your witness dead then?
   *Als.*                    'T is to be fear'd
It was the wages of her knowledge; poor soul,
She liv'd not long after the discovery.      61
   *Beat.* Then hear a story of not much less
       horror
Than this your false suspicion is beguil'd with;
To your bed's scandal I stand up innocence,
Which even the guilt of one black other deed 65
Will stand for proof of; your love has made me
A cruel murd'ress.
   *Als.*     Ha!
   *Beat.*          A bloody one:
I have kiss'd poison for it, strok'd a serpent:
That thing of hate, worthy in my esteem
Of no better employment, and him most worthy
To be so employ'd, I caus'd to murder      71
That innocent Piracquo, having no
Better means than that worst to assure
Yourself to me.

---

⁸¹ **wrought out:** obtained      ⁴⁸ vizor: mask      ⁶⁴ **stand up innocence:** am innocent

*Als.*        O, the place itself e'er since
Has crying been for vengeance! The temple, 75
Where blood and beauty first unlawfully
Fir'd their devotion and quench'd the right one;
'T was in my fears at first, 't will have it now:
O, thou art all deform'd!
*Beat.*        Forget not, sir, 79
It for your sake was done. Shall greater dangers
Make the less welcome?
*Als.*        O, thou should'st have gone
A thousand leagues about to have avoided
This dangerous bridge of blood! Here we are
     lost.
*Beat.*   Remember, I am true unto your bed.
*Als.*   The bed itself 's a charnel, the sheets
     shrouds        85
For murder'd carcasses. It must ask pause
What I must do in this; meantime you shall
Be my prisoner only: enter my closet;
                 *Exit Beatrice.*
I 'll be your keeper yet. O, in what part
Of this sad story shall I first begin? Ha!   90
This same fellow has put me in. — De Flores!

### Enter De Flores

*De F.*   Noble Alsemero!
*Als.*        I can tell you
News, sir; my wife has her commended to you.
*De F.*   That 's news indeed, my lord; I think
     she would
Commend me to the gallows if she could,   95
She ever lov'd me so well; I thank her.
*Als.*   What 's this blood upon your band,
     De Flores?
*De F.*   Blood! no, sure 't was wash'd since.
*Als.*        Since when, man?
*De F.*   Since t' other day I got a knock
In a sword-and-dagger school; I think 't is out.
*Als.*   Yes, 't is almost out, but 't is perceiv'd
     though.        101
I had forgot my message; this it is,
What price goes murder?
*De F.*        How, sir?
*Als.*        I ask you, sir;
My wife 's behindhand with you, she tells me,
For a brave bloody blow you gave for her
     sake        105
Upon Piracquo.
*De F.*   Upon? 'T was quite through him
     sure:
Has she confess'd it?
*Als.*        As sure as death to both of you;
And much more than that.
*De F.*        It could not be much more;
'T was but one thing, and that — she is a whore.
*Als.*   It could not choose but follow. O cun-
     ning devils!        110

How should blind men know you from fair-
     fac'd saints?
*Beat.* (*Within.*) He lies! the villain does belie
     me!
*De F.*   Let me go to her, sir.
*Als.*        Nay, you shall to her. —
Peace, crying crocodile, your sounds are heard;
Take your prey to you; — get you in to her, sir:
                 *Exit De Flores.*
I 'll be your pandar now; rehearse again   116
Your scene of lust, that you may be perfect
When you shall come to act it to the black au-
     dience,
Where howls and gnashings shall be music to you.
Clip your adulteress freely, 't is the pilot   120
Will guide you to the *mare mortuum*,
Where you shall sink to fathoms bottomless.

### Enter Vermandero, Alibius, Isabella, Tomaso, Franciscus, and Antonio

*Ver.*   O Alsemero! I have a wonder for you.
*Als.*   No, sir, 't is I, I have a wonder for you.
*Ver.*   I have suspicion near as proof itself 125
For Piracquo's murder.
*Als.*        Sir, I have proof
Beyond suspicion for Piracquo's murder.
*Ver.*   Beseech you, hear me; these two have
     been disguis'd
E'er since the deed was done.
*Als.*        I have two other
That were more close disguis'd than your two
     could be        130
E'er since the deed was done.
*Ver.*   You 'll hear me — these mine own ser-
     vants ——
*Als.*   Hear me — those nearer than your
     servants
That shall acquit them, and prove them guilt-
     less.        134
*Fran.*   That may be done with easy truth, sir.
*Tom.*   How is my cause bandied through
     your delays!
'T is urgent in my blood and calls for haste.
Give me a brother alive or dead;
Alive, a wife with him; if dead, for both
A recompense for murder and adultery.   140
*Beat.* (*Within.*) O, O, O!
*Als.*        Hark! 't is coming to you.
*De F.* (*Within.*) Nay, I 'll along for company.
*Beat.* (*Within.*)        O, O!
*Ver.*   What horrid sounds are these?
*Als.*        Come forth, you twins
Of mischief!

### Enter De Flores, bringing in Beatrice [wounded]

*De F.*   Here we are; if you have any more
To say to us, speak quickly, I shall not   145

⁹¹ **put me in:** given me the cue    ⁹⁷ **band:** collar    ¹⁰⁴ **behindhand with:** in debt to    ¹¹⁸ **black audience:** *i.e.,* of devils    ¹²⁰ **Clip:** embrace    ¹²¹ **mare mortuum:** dead sea    ¹³⁷ **my:** (not in Q)

Give you the hearing else; I am so stout yet,
And so, I think, that broken rib of mankind.
   *Ver.* An host of enemies ent'red my citadel
Could not amaze like this: Joanna! Beatrice!
Joanna!
   *Beat.* O, come not near me, sir, I shall defile
    you!                     150
I am that of your blood was taken from you,
For your better health; look no more upon 't,
But cast it to the ground regardlessly,
Let the common sewer take it from distinction.
Beneath the stars, upon yon meteor     155
             [*Pointing to De Flores.*]
Ever hung my fate 'mongst things corruptible;
I ne'er could pluck it from him; my loathing
Was prophet to the rest, but ne'er believ'd.
Mine honour fell with him, and now my life. —
Alsemero, I 'm a stranger to your bed;    160
Your bed was coz'ned on the nuptial night, —
For which your false bride died.
   *Als.*               Diaphanta?
   *De F.* Yes, and the while I coupled with
    your mate
At barley-break; now we are left in hell.
   *Ver.* We are all there, it circumscribes us
    here.                   165
   *De F.* I lov'd this woman in spite of her heart:
Her love I earn'd out of Piracquo's murder.
   *Tom.* Ha! my brother's murtherer?
   *De F.*         Yes, and her honour's prize
Was my reward; I thank life for nothing
But that pleasure; it was so sweet to me,   170
That I have drunk up all, left none behind
For any man to pledge me.
   *Ver.*              Horrid villain!
Keep life in him for further tortures.
   *De F.*                No!
I can prevent you; here 's my pen-knife still;
It is but one thread more [*stabbing himself*], and
   now 't is cut. —               175
Make haste, Joanna, by that token to thee,
Canst not forget, so lately put in mind;
I would not go to leave thee far behind. *Dies.*
   *Beat.* Forgive me, Alsemero, all forgive!
'T is time to die when 't is a shame to live. 180
                     *Dies.*
   *Ver.* O, my name 's ent'red now in that
    record
Where till this fatal hour 't was never read.
   *Als.* Let it be blotted out; let your heart
    lose it,
And it can never look you in the face,
Nor tell a tale behind the back of life    185
To your dishonour. Justice hath so right
The guilty hit, that innocence is quit
By proclamation, and may joy again. —

Sir, you are sensible of what truth hath done;
'T is the best comfort that your grief can find.
   *Tom.* Sir, I am satisfied; my injuries   191
Lie dead before me; I can exact no more,
Unless my soul were loose, and could o'ertake
Those black fugitives that are fled from hence,
To take a second vengeance; but there are
    wraths                 195
Deeper than mine, 't is to be fear'd, about 'em.
   *Als.* What an opacous body had that moon
That last chang'd on us! Here is beauty
    chang'd
To ugly whoredom; here servant-obedience
To a master-sin, imperious murder;    200
I, a suppos'd husband, chang'd embraces
With wantonness, — but that was paid be-
    fore. —
Your change is come too, from an ignorant
    wrath
To knowing friendship. — Are there any more
    on 's?                 204
   *Ant.* Yes, sir, I was chang'd too from a little
ass as I was to a great fool as I am; and had
like to ha' been chang'd to the gallows, but
that you know my innocence always excuses
me.
   *Fran.* I was chang'd from a little wit to be
    stark mad,             210
Almost for the same purpose.
   *Isa.*          Your change is still behind,
But deserve best your transformation:
You are a jealous coxcomb, keep schools of
    folly,
And teach your scholars how to break your own
    head.
   *Alib.* I see all apparent, wife, and will
    change now            215
Into a better husband, and never keep
Scholars that shall be wiser than myself.
   *Als.* Sir, you have yet a son's duty living,
Please you, accept it; let that your sorrow,
As it goes from your eye, go from your heart,
Man and his sorrow at the grave must part. 221

### EPILOGUE

   *Als.* All we can do to comfort one another,
To stay a brother's sorrow for a brother,
To dry a child from the kind father's eyes,
Is to no purpose, it rather multiplies:    225
Your only smiles have power to cause re-live
The dead again, or in their rooms to give
Brother a new brother, father a child;
If these appear, all griefs are reconcil'd.
                   *Exeunt omnes.*

### FINIS

---

   **151 that . . . you:** that part of your blood which was taken from you    **154 distinction:** separate
existence   **156 hung:** ('hang' Q)    **164** Cf. III. iii. 180   **165 us:** (not in Q)   **194 hence:** ('thence' Q)
**196 take:** receive   **208 innocence:** idiocy

# A Gam(e) at Chæss as it was Acted nine days to gether at the Globe

The Black-House | on the banks side | The White-House.

Black Q: · Black K: · White K: · White Qi

Black D: · White D:

Fatte Bishop · White B:

the Fatte Bishop · the Black Knight · the White Knight

*A letter from his Holynes.*

*Keepe y(our) distance.*

*Check mate by discovery.*

BIBLIOGRAPHICAL RECORD. *A Game at Chess* is unusual among plays of the period in that it exists in five manuscripts and four quartos. The MSS. are as follows: (1) Trinity College, Cambridge; (2) the Henry E. Huntington Library (formerly in the Bridgewater Library); (3) Lansdowne MS. 690 in the British Museum; (4) Malone MS. 25 in the Bodleian; and (5) a MS. sold at Sotheby's on April 4, 1928. The first of these and a portion of the second are in Middleton's handwriting. The four quartos may all be assigned with some certainty to 1625. The earliest has an engraved title-page but no indication of date or printer (see facsimile). A second quarto followed with a new setting for only part of the text. This latter quarto was reissued without the title-page and with a new preliminary half-sheet bearing the date 1625. The fourth quarto appeared without indication of date or printer and with a new engraved title-page. All of the quartos present very imperfect texts. The only edition of the play which takes into account all the sources for the text is that by R. C. Bald (1929). His text is based on the Trinity College MS. (here referred to as 'MS'), with necessary additions from the Bridgewater-Huntington MS., and is here generally followed. (See, however, B. M. Wagner in *Modern Language Notes*, March, 1931, p. 195.)

DATE AND STAGE PERFORMANCE. The composition and original performance of this play belong to 1624. The sentence of impeachment against the Earl of Middlesex (the White Knight's Pawn) was pronounced on May 13, 1624. On June 12 the play was licensed by Sir Henry Herbert, and on August 6 it was acted by the King's Men. It produced an immediate sensation. Two quartos state that it was "Acted nine days together at the Globe on the banks side," although a different play was ordinarily produced every day. It was said to have produced the enormous sum of £ 1500, and a contemporary letter said that the actors took in £ 100 a day. The Spanish ambassador, however, quickly entered a protest, and on August 17 the theatre was closed, ostensibly because of the law forbidding the presentation of a modern Christian king on the public stage. The players appeared before the authorities on the following day, the future performance of the play was forbidden, and the Globe was closed during the King's pleasure. The actors were required to furnish bond, but the King's anger was short-lived, and the theatre shortly reopened on condition that the play should never be acted again. Middleton seems to have been in a place of safety during this period, and probably escaped without punishment, the tradition that he suffered imprisonment resting on no better authority than a manuscript note in an early copy of the play. (See B. M. Wagner, "New Allusions to *A Game at Chess*," *P. M. L. A.*, Sept., 1929.)

HISTORICAL BACKGROUND. *A Game at Chess* gives effective dramatic expression to the current popular feeling and prejudice against Spain and the Roman Church. This feeling reached a focal point at the return of Prince Charles and Buckingham from Madrid in 1623. Their journey, which had been engineered by Gondomar, was for the purpose of arranging a marriage between Charles and the Infanta Maria. When the project fell through there was hysterical rejoicing in England, where it was generally believed that the union would have reduced England to a state of subservience to Spain and to the Pope. The patriotic fears of the English were centered on two figures, Count Gondomar, the Spanish ambassador, and Marco Antonio de Dominis, archbishop of Spalatro, who wavered between Catholicism and Protestantism, received great favors from King James, and was the symbol of Roman Catholic perfidy to the heated English mind. The important figures in the history of the moment are represented in the play as follows: Black Knight — Gondomar; Fat Bishop — de Dominis; White King — King James; White Knight — Prince Charles; White Duke — Buckingham; Black King — Philip IV of Spain; Black Duke — Olivares, his chief minister; White Bishop — Archbishop Abbot of Canterbury; Black Bishop — the Father General of the Jesuits; White Queen — Church of England; Black Queen — Church of Rome; White Knight's Pawn — Lionel Cranfield, Earl of Middlesex. The minor plot deals in a general way with the methods of the Jesuits, and the characters probably represent types rather than individuals. The episode of the gelding of the White Bishop's Pawn seems to refer to the loss of the Palatinate by Frederick, the son-in-law of King James.

SOURCES. Middleton derived much material, particularly for the minor plot, from some of the innumerable anti-Catholic pamphlets. His chief sources were: Thomas Robinson, *The Anatomie of the English Nunnerie at Lisbon* (1622); John Gee, *The Foote out of the Snare* (1624) and *New Shreds of the Old Snare* (1624); Thomas Scott, *Vox Populi* (1620) and *The Second Part of Vox Populi* (1624); and two anonymous pamphlets, *A Declaration of the Variance betweene the Pope and the Segniory of Venice* (1606) and *Newes from Rome: Spalato's Doome* (1624). For a more detailed discussion of sources and historical background, see the introduction to Bald's edition of the play, and the valuable notes in Bullen's (1886).

# THOMAS MIDDLETON (1580–1627)

## A GAME AT CHESS

[DRAMATIS PERSONAE

| | |
|---|---|
| WHITE KING | BLACK KING |
| WHITE KNIGHT | BLACK KNIGHT |
| WHITE DUKE | BLACK DUKE |
| WHITE BISHOP | BLACK BISHOP |
| PAWNS | PAWNS |

FAT BISHOP
HIS PAWN

| | |
|---|---|
| WHITE QUEEN | BLACK QUEEN |
| HER PAWN | HER PAWN |

IN THE INDUCTION

IGNATIUS LOYOLA
ERROR]

### THE PICTURE PLAINLY EXPLAINED AFTER THE MANNER OF THE CHESS-PLAY

A GAME at Chess is here display'd,
Between the Black and White House made,
Wherein crown-thirsting policy
For the Black House, by fallacy,
To the White Knight check often gives,    5
And to some straits him thereby drives;
The Fat Black Bishop helps also,
With faithless heart, to give the blow:
Yet, maugre all their craft, at length
The White Knight, with wit-wondrous strength    10
And circumspective prudency,
Gives check-mate by discovery
To the Black Knight: and so at last,
The Game thus won, the Black House cast
Into the Bag, and therein shut,    15
Find all their plumes and coxcombs cut.
Plain dealing thus, by wisdom's guide,
Defeats the cheats of craft and pride.

### PROLOGUE

WHAT of the game call'd Chess-play can be made
To make a stage-play, shall this day be play'd:
First, you shall see the men in order set,
States and their pawns, when both the sides are met,
The Houses well distinguish'd; in the game    5
Some men entrapp'd and taken, to their shame,
Rewarded by their play; and, in the close,
You shall see check-mate given to virtue's foes:
But the fair'st jewel that our hopes can deck,
Is so to play our game to avoid your check.    10

**The Picture:** (See page 943.)    Prol.  ⁴ **States:** persons of high rank

## The Induction

*Ignatius Loyola appearing, Error at his*
*foot as asleep*

*Ign.* Ha! where? what angle of the world is
   this,
That I can neither see the politic face,
Nor with my refin'd nostrils taste the footsteps
Of any of my disciples, sons and heirs
As well of my designs as institution?            5
I thought they 'd spread over the world by this
   time,
Cover'd the earth's face, and made dark the
   land,
Like the Egyptian grasshoppers.
Here 's too much light appears, shot from the
   eyes
Of Truth and Goodness never yet deflower'd:
Sure they were never here; then is their mon-
   archy                                          11
Unperfect yet; a just reward, I see,
For their ingratitude so long to me,
Their father and their founder.
'T is not five years since I was sainted by 'em: 15
Where slept my honour all the time before?
Could they be so forgetful to canónize
Their prosperous institutor? when they had
   sainted me,
They found no room in all their calendar
To place my name, that should have remov'd
   princes,                                       20
Pull'd the most eminent prelates by the roots
   up
For my dear coming, to make way for me;
Let every petty martyr and saint homily,
Roch, Main, and Petronill, itch- and ague-
   curers,
Your Abbess Aldegund and Cunegund,              25
The widow Marcell, parson Polycarp,
Cecily and Ursula, all take place of me;
And but for the bissextile or leap-year,
And that 's but one in three, I fall by chance
Into the nine-and-twentieth day of February; 30
There were no room else for me: see their
   love,
Their conscience too, to thrust me a lame soldier
Into leap-year! My wrath 's up, and, methinks,
I could with the first syllable of my name
Blow up their colleges. — Up, Error, wake!    35
Father of supererogation, rise!
It is Ignatius calls thee, Loyola.
   *Error.* What have you done? O, I could
   sleep in ignorance

Immortally, the slumber is so pleasing!
I saw the bravest setting for a game now      40
That ever my eye fix'd on.
   *Ign.* Game, what game?
   *Error.* The noblest game of all, a game at
   chess,
Betwixt our side and the White House; the
   men set
In their just order, ready to go to it.         45
   *Ign.* Were any of my sons plac'd for the
   game?
   *Error.* Yes, and a daughter too; a secular
   daughter
That plays the Black Queen's Pawn, he the
   Black Bishop's.
   *Ign.* If ever power could show a mastery
   in thee,
Let it appear in this!
   *Error.*             'Tis but a dream,        50
A vision, you must think.
   *Ign.*                     I care not what,
So I behold the children of my cunning,
And see what rank they keep.
   *Error.*              You have your wish:

*Music. Enter severally, in order of game,*
*the White and Black Houses*

Behold, there 's the full number of the game,
Kings and their Pawns, Queens, Bishops,
   Knights, and Dukes.                           55
   *Ign.* Dukes? they 're call'd Rooks by some.
   *Error.*                        Corruptively;
*Le roc* the word, *custode de la roche,*
The keeper of the forts, in whom both Kings
Repose much confidence; and for their trust-
   sake,
Courage, and worth, do well deserve those
   titles.                                        60
   *Ign.* The answer 's high: I see my son and
   daughter.
   *Error.* Those are two Pawns, the Black
   Queen's and Black Bishop's.
   *Ign.* Pawns argue but poor spirits and slight
   preferments,
Nor worthy of the name of my disciples:
If I had stood so nigh, I would have cut       65
That bishop's throat but I'd have had his place,
And told the Queen a love-tale in her ear
Would make her best pulse dance: there 's no
   elixir
Of brain or spirit amongst 'em.
   *Error.* Why, would you have 'em play
   against themselves?                            70
That 's quite against the rule of game, Ignatius.

---

Induction S. D. **Loyola:** founder of Society of Jesus (1491–1556)     ¹ **angle:** corner     ³ **taste:**
smell, detect     ⁸ **Egyptian grasshoppers:** (a common term for the Jesuits)     ¹⁵ (Loyola was canon-
ized in 1623.)     ¹⁸ **institutor:** founder     ²⁴⁻²⁷ **Roch . . . Ursula:** well-known saints or persons renowned for piety     ³² **lame:** (Loyola limped as the result of a wound received at the siege of Pampeluna
in 1521.)     ⁴⁹ **mastery:** masterly operation     ⁵⁷ **Le roc:** fortress (original form of "rook")

*Ign.*  Pish, I would rule myself, not observe rule.

*Error.*  Why, then, you 'd play a game all by yourself.

*Ign.*  I would do anything to rule alone:
'T is rare to have the world reign'd in by one. 75

*Error.*  See 'em anon, and mark 'em in their play;
Observe, as in a dance, they glide away.
                          [*Exeunt the two Houses.*]

*Ign.*  O, with what longings will this breast be toss'd,
Until I see this great game won and lost.
                                          [*Exeunt.*]

## Actus Primi, Scæna Prima

[*Field between the two Houses*]

*Enter from the Black House, the Black Queen's Pawn, from the White House, the White Queen's Pawn*

*B. Q. Pawn.*  I ne'er see that face but my pity rises;
When I behold so clear a masterpiece
Of heaven's art wrought out of dust and ashes,
And at next thought to give her lost eternally,
In being not ours, but the daughter of heresy, 5
My soul bleeds at mine eyes.

*W. Q. Pawn.*  Where should truth speak,
If not in such a sorrow? they 're tears plainly:
Beshrew me, if she weep not heartily!
What is my peace to her to take such pains in 't?
If I wander to loss, and with broad eyes  10
Yet miss the path she can run blindfold in
Through often exercise, why should my oversight,
Though in the best game that e'er Christian lost,
Raise the least spring of pity in her eye?
'T is doubtless a great charity; and no virtue 15
Could win me surer.

*B. Q. Pawn.*  Blessed things prevail with 't!
If ever goodness made a gracious promise,
It is in yonder look: what little pains
Would build a fort for virtue to all memory
In that sweet creature, were the ground-work firmer!  20

*W. Q. Pawn.*  It has been all my glory to be firm
In what I have profess'd.

*B. Q. Pawn.*  That is the enemy
That steals your strength away, and fights against you,

Disarms your soul e'en in the heat of battle;
Your firmness that way makes you more infirm  25
For the right Christian conflict.  There I spied
A zealous primitive sparkle but now flew
From your devoted eye,
Able to blow up all the heresies
That ever sate in council with your spirit.  30
And here comes he whose sanctimonious breath
Can make that spark a flame.  List to him, virgin,
At whose first entrance princes will fall prostrate;
Women are weaker vessels.

*Enter the Black Bishop's Pawn: a Jesuit*

*W. Q. Pawn.*  By my penitence,
A comely presentation, and the habit  35
To admiration reverend!

*B. Q. Pawn.*  But the heart, the heart, lady,
So meek that as you see good Charity pictur'd still
With young ones in her arms, so will he cherish
All his young, tractable, sweet obedient daughters
E'en in his bosom, in his own dear bosom.  40
I am myself a secular Jesuit,
As many ladies are of wealth and greatness:
A second sort are Jesuits *in voto*,
Giving their vow in to the Father General,
That 's the Black Bishop of our House, whose Pawn  45
This gentleman now stands for, to receive
The college-habit at his holy pleasure.

*W. Q. Pawn.*  But how are those *in voto* employ'd, lady,
Till they receive the habit?

*B. Q. Pawn.*  They 're not idle;
He finds 'em all true labourers in the work  50
Of the universal monarchy, which he
And his disciples principally aim at:
Those are maintain'd in many courts and palaces,
And are induc'd by noble personages
Into great princes' services, and prove  55
Some councillors of state, some secretaries;
All serving in notes of intelligence —
As parish-clerks their mortuary-bills —
To the Father General: so are designs
Oft-times prevented, and important secrets  60
Of states discover'd, yet no author found,
But those suspected oft that are most sound.
This mystery is too deep yet for your entrance;
And I offend to set your zeal so back:

---

⁴ **give her:** regard her as     ¹⁰ **broad:** wide open     ¹² **often:** frequent     ³⁵ **presentation:** appearance     ⁴¹ **Jesuit:** (There was an order of women who preached in the Jesuit habit.)     ⁴³ **in voto:** by vow, as novices     ⁵¹ **universal monarchy:** popularly supposed to be Spain's ambition     ⁵⁴ **induc'd:** introduced     ⁴⁷ **intelligence:** news, information     ⁶⁰ **prevented:** anticipated     ⁶¹ **discover'd:** revealed     ⁶³ **for . . . entrance:** for you to be initiated into

Check'd by obedience with desire to hasten 65
Your progress to perfection, I commit you
To the great worker's hands; to whose grave
worth
I fit my reverence, as to you my wishes.
    B. B. Pawn. [Aside to B. Q. Pawn.] Dost
find her supple?
    B. Q. Pawn.    There 's a little passage made.
                                        [Exit.]
    B. B. Pawn.    Let me contemplate,       70
With holy wonder season my access,
And, by degrees, approach the sanctuary
Of unmatch'd beauty, set in grace and good-
ness.
Amongst the daughters of men I have not found
A more Catholical aspéct: that eye        75
Does promise single life and meek obedience;
Upon those lips, the sweet fresh buds of youth,
The holy dew of prayer lies, like pearl
Dropp'd from the opening eyelids of the morn
Upon the bashful rose. How beauteously   80
A gentle fast, not rigorously impos'd,
Would look upon that cheek! and how delight-
fully
The courteous physic of a tender penance,
Whose utmost cruelty should not exceed
The first fear of a bride, to beat down frailty, 85
Would work to sound health your long-fester'd
judgment,
And make your merit, which, through erring
ignorance,
Appears but spotted righteousness to me,
Far clearer than the innocence of infants!
    W. Q. Pawn.    To that good work I bow, and
will become                                90
Obedience' humblest daughter, since I find
Th' assistance of a sacred strength to aid me:
The labour is as easy to serve virtue
The right way, since 't is she I ever serv'd
In my desire, though I transgress'd in judg-
ment.                                       95
    B. B. Pawn.    That 's easily absolv'd amongst
the rest:
You shall not find the virtue that you serve now
A sharp and cruel mistress; her ear 's open
To all your supplications; you may boldly
And safely let in the most secret sin      100
Into her knowledge, which, like vanish'd man,
Never returns into the world again;
Fate locks not up more trulier.
    W. Q. Pawn.                To the guilty
That may appear some benefit.
    B. B. Pawn.                Who is so innocent
That never stands in need on 't in some kind? 105
If every thought were blabb'd that 's so con-
fess'd,

The very air we breathe would be unblest.
Now to the work indeed, which is to catch
Her inclination; that 's the special use
We make of all our practice in all kingdoms; 110
For by disclosing their most secret frailties,
Things which, once ours, they must not hide
from us
(That 's the first article in the creed we teach
'em),
Finding to what point their blood most inclines,
Know best to apt them then to our designs. 115
                                        [Aside.]
Daughter, the sooner you disperse your errors,
The sooner you make haste to your recovery:
You must part with 'em; to be nice or modest
Toward this good action, is to imitate
The bashfulness of one conceals an ulcer,  120
For the uncomely parts the tumour vexes,
Till 't be past cure. Resolve you thus far,
lady;
The privat'st thought that runs to hide itself
In the most secret corner of your heart now,
Must be of my acquaintance, so familiarly 125
Never she-friend of your night-counsel nearer.
    W. Q. Pawn.    I stand not much in fear of
any action
Guilty of that black time, most noble holiness.
I must confess, as in a sacred temple
Throng'd with an auditory, some come rather
To feed on human object than to taste    131
Of angels' food;
So in the congregation of quick thoughts,
Which are more infinite than such assemblies,
I cannot with truth's safety speak for all:  135
Some have been wanderers, some fond, some
sinful,
But those found ever but poor entertainment,
They 'd small encouragement to come again.
The single life, which strongly I profess now,
Heaven pardon me! I was about to part
from.                                      140
    B. B. Pawn.    Then you have pass'd through
love?
    W. Q. Pawn.    But left no stain
In all my passage, sir, no print of wrong
For the most chaste maid that may trace my
footsteps.
    B. B. Pawn.    How came you off so clear?
    W. Q. Pawn.                I was discharg'd
By an inhuman accident, which modesty   145
Forbids me to put any language to.
    B. B. Pawn.    How you forget yourself! all
actions
Clad in their proper language, though most
sordid,
My ear is bound by duty to let in

---

⁷⁹ Compare Milton's *Lycidas* (1638), line 26: "Under the opening eyelids of the Morn."    ¹¹⁵ **apt:**
fit    ¹¹⁸ **nice:** fastidious    ¹³⁰ **auditory:** congregation    ¹³³ **quick:** living    ¹³⁴ **infinite:** innumerable
¹³⁶ **fond:** foolish

And lock up everlastingly.  Shall I help you?
He was not found to answer his creation:   151
A vestal virgin in a slip of prayer
Could not deliver man's loss modestlier:
'T was the White Bishop's Pawn.
  *W. Q. Pawn.*        The same, blest sir.
  *B. B. Pawn.*  An heretic well pickled.
  *W. Q. Pawn.*       By base treachery, 155
And violence prepar'd by his competitor,
The Black Knight's Pawn, whom I shall ever
    hate for 't.
  *B. B. Pawn.*  'T was of revenges the unman-
    liest way
That ever rival took; a villainy
That, for your sake, I 'll ne'er absolve him of.
  *W. Q. Pawn.*  I wish it not so heavy.
  *B. B. Pawn.*      He must feel it: 161
I never yet gave absolution
To any crime of that unmanning nature.
It seems then you refus'd him for defect;
Therein you stand not pure from the desire 165
That other women have in ends of marriage:
Pardon my boldness, if I sift your goodness
To the last grain.
  *W. Q. Pawn.*  I reverence your pains, sir,
And must acknowledge custom to enjoy
What other women challenge and possess   170
More rul'd me than desire; for my desires
Dwell all in ignorance, and I 'll never wish
To know that fond way may redeem them
    thence.
  *B. B. Pawn.* [*Aside.*]  I never was so taken;
    beset doubly
Now with her judgment: what a strength it
    puts forth! —                              175
I bring work nearer to you: when you have
    seen
A masterpiece of man, compos'd by heaven
For a great prince's favour, kingdom's love;
So exact, envy could not find a place
To stick a blot on person or on fame;      180
Have you not found ambition swell your wish
    then,
And desire stir your blood?
  *W. Q. Pawn.*      By virtue, never!
I have only in the dignity of the creature
Admir'd the maker's glory.
  *B. B. Pawn.* [*Aside.*]  She 's impregnable;
A second siege must not fall off so tamely: 185
She 's one of those must be inform'd to know
A daughter's duty, which some take untaught;
Her modesty brings her behind-hand much;
My old means I must fly to: yes, 't is it.—
Please you, peruse this small tract of obe-
    dience:                                    190
'T will help you forward well.   [*Gives a book.*]

  *W. Q. Pawn.*       Sir, that 's a virtue
I have ever thought on with especial reverence.
  *B. B. Pawn.*  You will conceive by that my
    power, your duty.

*Enter White Bishop's Pawn*

  *W. Q. Pawn.*  The knowledge will be precious
    of both, sir.
  *W. B. Pawn.* [*Aside.*]  What makes yond
    troubler of all Christian waters           195
So near that blessed spring?  But that I know
Her goodness is the rock from whence it issues
Unmoveable as fate, 't would more afflict me
Than all my sufferings for her, which so long
As she holds constant to the House she comes
    of,                                        200
The whiteness of the cause, the side, the quality,
Are sacrifices to her worth and virtue;
And, though confin'd in my religious joys,
I marry her and possess her.

*Enter Black Knight's Pawn*

  *B. B. Pawn.*       Behold, lady,
The two inhuman enemies, the Black Knight's
    Pawn                                       205
And the White Bishop's; the gelder and the
    gelded.
  *W. Q. Pawn.*  There 's my grief, my hate!
  *B. Kt.'s Pawn.* [*Aside.*]  What, in the Jes-
    uit's fingers?  By this hand,
I 'll give my part now for a parrot's feather,
She never returns virtuous, 't is impossible: 210
I 'll undertake more wagers will be laid
Upon a usurer's return from hell
Than upon hers from him now.  Have I been
    guilty
Of such base malice that my very conscience
Shakes at the memory of, and, when I look
To gather fruit, find nothing but the savin-
    tree,                                      216
Too frequent in nuns' orchards, and there
    planted,
By all conjecture, to destroy fruit rather?
I 'll be resolved now.  Most noble virgin —
  *W. Q. Pawn.*  Ignoble villain! dare that un-
    hallow'd tongue                            220
Lay hold upon a sound so gracious?
What 's nobleness to thee, or virgin chastity?
They 're not of thy acquaintance:  talk of
    violence
That shames creation, deeds would make night
    blush,
That 's company for thee.  Hast thou the im-
    pudence                                    225
To court me with a leprosy upon thee
Able t' infect the walls of a great building?

---

<sup>170</sup> **challenge:** claim as a right   <sup>173</sup> **may:** which may   <sup>180</sup> **fame:** reputation   <sup>195</sup> **makes:** does
<sup>216</sup> **savin-tree:** (an infusion of the leaves of which was believed to produce abortions)   <sup>219</sup> **resolved:** satisfied

*B. B. Pawn.*   Son of offence, forbear! go, set
your evil
Before your eyes; a penitential vesture
Would better become you, some shirt of
hair.                                                          230
  *B. Kt.'s Pawn.*   And you a three-pound
smock 'stead of an alb,
An epicœne chasuble. — This holy fellow
Robs safe and close: I feel a sting that's worse,
too.                                           [*Aside.*]
White Pawn, hast so much charity to accept
A reconcilement?   Make thy own conditions,
For I begin to be extremely burden'd.          236
  *W. B. Pawn.* [*Aside.*]   No truth or peace of
that Black House protested
Is to be trusted; but for hope of quittance,
And warn'd by diffidence, I may entrap him
soonest. —
I admit conference.
  *B. Kt.'s Pawn.*   It is a nobleness        240
That makes confusion cleave to all my merits.
    [*Exeunt W. B. Pawn and B. Kt.'s Pawn.*]

*Enter Black Knight*

*B. B. Pawn.* [*To W. Q. Pawn.*]   That treatise
will instruct you fully.
  *B. Knight.* [*Aside.*]        So, so!
The business of the universal monarchy
Goes forward well now! the great college-pot,
That should be always boiling with the fuel 245
Of all intelligences possible
Thorough the Christian kingdoms.   Is this
fellow
Our prime incendiary, one of those
That promis'd the White Kingdom seven years
since
To our Black House?   Put a new daughter to
him,                                                        250
The great work stands; he minds nor monarchy
Nor hierarchy, diviner principality.
I've bragg'd less,
But have done more than all the conclave on
'em,
Take their assistant fathers in all parts,     255
Ay, or their Father General in to boot;
And what I have done, I have done facetiously,
With pleasant subtlety and bewitching court-
ship,
Abus'd all my believers with delight, —
They took a comfort to be cozen'd by me: 260
To many a soul I have let in mortal poison,
Whose cheeks have crack'd with laughter to
receive it;
I could so roll my pills in sugar'd syllables,

And strew such kindly mirth o'er all my mis-
chief,
They took their bane in way of recreation, 265
As pleasure steals corruption into youth.
He spies me now: I must uphold his reverence,
Especially in public, though I know
Priapus, guardian of the cherry-gardens,
Bacchus' and Venus' chit, is not more vicious. 270
  *B. B. Pawn.*   Blessings' accumulation keep
with you, sir!
  *B. Knight.*   Honour's dissimulation be your
due, sir!
  *W. Q. Pawn.* [*Aside.*]   How deep in duty his
observance plunges!
His charge must needs be reverend.
  *B. B. Pawn.*                I am confessor
To this Black Knight too; you see devotion's
fruitful,                                                  275
Sh'as many sons and daughters.
  *B. Knight.* [*Aside.*]        I do this the more
T' amaze our adversaries to behold
The reverence we give these guitonens,
And to beget a sound opinion
Of holiness in them and zeal in us.            280
                              [*Exit W. Q. Pawn.*]
As also to invite the like obedience
In other pusills by our meek example. —
So, is your trifle vanish'd?
  *B. B. Pawn.*   Trifle call you her? 't is a good
Pawn, sir;
Sure she's the second Pawn of the White
House,                                                      285
And to the opening of the game I hold her.
  *B. Knight.*   Ay, you
Hold well for that, I know your play of old:
If there were more Queen's Pawns, you'd ply
the game
A great deal harder.   Now, sir, we're in
private;                                                    290
But what for the main work, the great existence,
The hope monarchal?
  *B. B. Pawn.*        It goes on in this.
  *B. Knight.*   In this! I cannot see 't.
  *B. B. Pawn.*                You may deny so
A dial's motion, 'cause you cannot see
The hand move, or a wind that rends the
cedar.                                                      295
  *B. Knight.*   Where stops the current of
intelligence?
Your Father General, Bishop of the Black
House,
Complains for want of work.
  *B. B. Pawn.*            Here's from all parts,
Sufficient to employ him; I receiv'd

²³² **epicœne:** adapted to, or worn by, both sexes       ²³³ **close:** secretly       ²³⁸ **quittance:** requital
²³⁹ **diffidence:** suspicion    ²⁴⁶ **intelligences:** news, secret reports    ²⁴⁷ **Thorough:** through    ²⁵¹ **minds:**
is mindful of    ²⁵² **hierarchy:** *i.e.*, the ecclesiastical hierarchy    ²⁵³⁻²⁶⁶ (These lines represent the
popular conception of the character and methods of Gondomar.)    ²⁵⁹ **Abus'd:** deceived    ²⁶⁰ **cozen'd:**
cheated    ²⁷⁰ **chit:** child    ²⁷⁸ **guitonens:** lazy beggars    ²⁸² **pusills:** drabs, girls (Fr., "pucelle")

A packet from the Assistant Fathers lately; 300
Look you, there 's Anglica, this Gallica.
                *[Gives letters.]*
  *B. Knight.* Ay, marry, sir, there 's some
    quick flesh in this.
  *B. B. Pawn.* Germanica.   *[Gives letter.]*
  *B. Knight.* I think they 've seal'd this with
    butter.
  *B. B. Pawn.* Italica this. *[Gives letter.]* 305
  *B. Knight.* They put their pens the Hebrew
    way, methinks.
  *B. B. Pawn.* Hispanica here. *[Gives letter.]*
  *B. Knight.* Hispanica! blind work 't is; the
    Jesuit
Has writ this with juice of lemons sure,
It must be held close to the fire of purgatory 310
Ere 't can be read.
  *B. B. Pawn.* You will not lose your jest,
    Knight,
Though it wounded your own fame.
  *B. Knight. Curanda pecunia.*
  *B. B. Pawn.* Take heed, sir; we 're en-
    trapp'd, — the White King's Pawn.

        *Enter White King's Pawn*

  *B. Knight.* He 's made our own, man; half
    *in voto* yours,                 315
His heart 's in the Black House: leave him to
  me. —         *[Exit B. B. Pawn.]*
Most of all friends endear'd, preciously special!
  *W. Kg.'s Pawn.* You see my outside, but
    you know my heart, Knight,
Great difference in the colour. There 's some
  intelligence;        *[Gives letter.]*
And as more ripens, so your knowledge still
Shall prove the richer: there shall nothing
  happen,                 321
Believe it, to extenuate your cause,
Or to oppress her friends, but I will strive
To cross it with my counsel, purse, and power;
Keep all supplies back both in means and men
That may raise strength against you. We
  must part:            326
I dare not longer of this theme discuss;
The ear of state is quick and jealous.
  *B. Knight.* Excellent estimation! thou art
    valu'd
Above the fleet of gold that came short home.
            *[Exit W. Kg.'s Pawn.]*
Poor Jesuit-ridden soul! how art thou fool'd 331
Out of thy faith, from thy allegiance drawn.
Which way soe'er thou tak'st, thou 'rt a lost
  Pawn.               *[Exit.]*

### *Finit Actus Primus.*

## *Incipit Secundus.*

### [ACT II. SCENE I.

*Field between the two Houses]*

*Enter White Queen's Pawn with a book
in her hand*

*W. Q. Pawn.* And here again: *[Reads.]* It is
  the daughter's duty
To obey her cónfessor's command in all things,
Without exception or expostulation:
'T is the most general rule that e'er I read of;
Yet when I think how boundless virtue is,   5
Goodness and grace, 't is gently reconcil'd,
And then it appears well to have the power
Of the dispenser as uncircumscrib'd.

*Enter Black Bishop's Pawn*

  *B. B. Pawn.* She 's hard upon 't; 't was the
    most modest key
That I could use to open my intents:     10
What little or no pains goes to some people!
Hah! a seal'd note! whence this?
          *[Takes up a letter.]*
*[Reads.]* "To the Black Bishop's Pawn,
  these." How? to me?
Strange! who subscribes it? The Black King:
  what would he?

*The Letter*

*[Reads.]* "Pawn sufficiently holy, but un- [15
measurably politic; we had late intelligence
from our most industrious servant, famous in
all parts of Europe, our Knight of the Black
House, that you have at this instant in chase
the White Queen's Pawn, and very likely, [20
by the carriage of your game, to entrap and
take her: these are therefore to require you,
by the burning affection I bear to the rape
of devotion, that speedily, upon the surprisal
of her, by all watchful advantage you make [25
some attempt upon the White Queen's person,
whose fall or prostitution our lust most violently rages for."

Sir, after my desire has took a julep
For its own inflammation, that yet scorches
  me,                30
I shall have cooler time to think of yours.
Sh'as pass'd the general rule, the large extent
Of our prescriptions for obedience;
And yet with what alacrity of soul
Her eyes moves on the letters!

301 **Gallica:** French   304 **I:** (not in MS)   309 **with . . . lemons:** in invisible ink   313 **Curanda pecunia:** Money must be cared for.   320 **still:** always   322 **extenuate:** disparage, injure   324 **cross:** defeat   326 **strength:** (not in MS)   330 **came . . . home:** reached home after suffering losses, or failed to reach home   21 **carriage:** conduct, management   23 **affection:** inclination, desire   29 **julep:** cooling drink

*W. Q. Pawn.*                    Holy sir,    35
Too long I have miss'd you; O, your absence
  starves me!
Hasten for time's redemption: worthy sir,
Lay your commands as thick and fast upon me
As you can speak 'em; how I thirst to hear 'em!
Set me to work upon this spacious virtue,    40
Which the poor span of life 's too narrow for,
Boundless obedience!
The humblest yet the mightiest of all duties,
Well here set down, a universal goodness.
    *B. B. Pawn.* [*Aside.*]  By holiness of gar-
      ment, her safe innocence                45
Has frighted the full meaning from itself;
She 's farder off from understanding now
The language of my intent than at first meeting.
    *W. Q. Pawn.*  For virtue's sake, good sir,
      command me something;
Make trial of my duty in some small service; 50
And as you find the faith of my obedience
  there,
Then trust it with a greater.
    *B. B. Pawn.*              You speak sweetly:
I do command you first then —
    *W. Q. Pawn.*              With what joy
I do prepare my duty!
    *B. B. Pawn*      .  To meet me,
And seal a kiss of love upon my lip.        55
    *W. Q. Pawn.*  Hah!
    *B. B. Pawn.*  At first disobedient! in so
      little too!
How shall I trust you with a greater, then,
Which was your own request?
    *W. Q. Pawn.*        Pray, send not back  59
My innocence to wound me; be more courteous.
I must confess, much like an ignorant plaintiff,
  who,
Presuming on the fair path of his meaning,
Goes rashly on, till on a sudden brought
Into the wilderness of law by words
Dropp'd unadvisedly, hurts his good cause, 65
And gives his adversary advantage by it, —
Apply it you can best, sir.  If my obedience
And your command can find no better way,
Fond men command, and wantons best obey.
    *B. B. Pawn.*  If I can at that distance send
      you a blessing,                        70
Is it not nearer to you in mine arms?
It flies from these lips dealt abroad in parcels;
And I, to honour thee above all daughters,
Invite thee home to the House, where thou
  may'st surfeit
On that which others miserably pine for;   75
A favour which the daughters of great poten-
  tates
Would look on envy's colour but to hear.
    *W. Q. Pawn.*  Good men may err sometimes;
      you are mistaken sure:

If this be virtue's path, 't is a most strange
  one;
I never came this way before.
    *B. B. Pawn.*          That 's your ignorance; 80
And therefore shall that idiot still conduct you
That knows no way but one, nor ever seeks it?
If there be twenty ways to some poor village
'T is strange that virtue should be put to
  one.                                       84
Your fear is wondrous faulty; cast it from you;
'T will gather else in time a disobedience
Too stubborn for my pardon.
    *W. Q. Pawn.*          Have I lock'd myself
At unawares into sin's servitude
With more desire of goodness?  Is this the
  top
Of all strict order, and the holiest        90
Of all societies, the three-vow'd people
For poverty, obedience, chastity, —
The last the most forgot?  When a virgin 's
  ruin'd,
I see the great work of obedience           94
Is better than half finish'd.
    *B. B. Pawn.*          What a stranger
Are you to duty grown!  What distance keep
  you!
Must I bid you come forward to a happiness
Yourself should sue for? 't was never so with me.
I dare not let this stubbornness be known,
'T would bring such fierce hate on you: yet
  presume not                               100
To make that courteous care a privilege
For wilful disobedience; it turns then
Into the blackness of a curse upon you:
Come, come, be nearer.
    *W. Q. Pawn.*          Nearer!
    *B. B. Pawn.*              Was that scorn?
I would not have it prove so for the hopes 105
Of the grand monarchy: if it were like it,
Let it not dare to stir abroad again;
A stronger ill will cope with 't.
    *W. Q. Pawn.*          Bless me, threatens me,
And quite dismays the good strength that
  should help me!
I never was so doubtful of my safety.      110
    *B. B. Pawn.*  'T was but my jealousy; for-
      give me, sweetness:
Yours is the house of meekness, and no venom
  lives
Under that roof.  Be nearer: why so fearful?
Nearer the altar, the more safe and sacred.
    *W. Q. Pawn.*  But nearer to the offerer, oft
      more wicked.                          115
    *B. B. Pawn.*  A plain and most insufferable
      contempt!
My glory I have lost upon this woman,
In freely offering that she should have kneel'd
A year in vain for; my respect is darken'd.

<hr>

⁴⁷ **farder:** further    ⁷⁷ **on:** of

Give me my reverence again thou hast robb'd
   me of                                          120
In thy repulse; thou shalt not carry it hence.
*W. Q. Pawn.* Sir?
*B. B. Pawn.*   Thou 'rt too great a winner
   to depart so,
And I too deep a loser to give way to it.
*W. Q. Pawn.* O heaven!
*B. B. Pawn.*          Lay me down reputation
Before thou stirr'st; thy nice virginity      125
Is recompense too little for my love,
'T is well if I accept of that for both:
Thy loss is but thine own, there 's art to help
   thee,
And fools to pass thee to; in my discovery
The whole Society suffers, and in that        130
The hope of absolute monarchy eclips'd.
Assurance thou canst make none for thy secrecy
But by thy honour's loss; that act must awe
   thee.
*W. Q. Pawn.* O my distress'd condition!
*B. B. Pawn.*            Dost thou weep?
If thou hadst any pity, this necessity        135
Would wring it from thee: I must else destroy
   thee;
We must not trust the policy of Europe
Upon a woman's tongue.
*W. Q. Pawn.*         Then take my life, sir,
And leave mine honour for my guide to heaven!
*B. B. Pawn.* Take heed I take not both,
   which I have vow'd,                         140
Since if longer thou resist me —
*W. Q. Pawn.*             Help! O, help!
*B. B. Pawn.* Art thou so cruel, for an
   honour's bubble
T' undo a whole fraternity, and disperse
The secrets of most nations lock'd in us?     144
*W. Q. Pawn.* For heaven and virtue's sake!
*B. B. Pawn.*         Must force confound —
                                *A noise within.*
Hah! what 's that? — Silence, if fair worth be
   in thee.
*W. Q. Pawn.* I venture my escape upon all
   dangers now.
*B. B. Pawn.* Who comes to take me? Let
   me see that Pawn's face,
Or his proud tympanous master, swell'd with
   state-wind,
Which being once prick'd in the convocation-
   house,                                       150
The corrupt air puffs out, and he falls shrivell'd.
*W. Q. Pawn.* I will discover thee, arch-
   hypocrite,
To all the kindreds of the earth.      *Exit.*
*B. B. Pawn.*            Confusion!

In that voice rings the alarum of my undoing.
How, which way 'scap'd she from me?

*Enter Black Queen's Pawn*

*B. Q. Pawn.*               Are you mad? 155
Can lust infatuate a man so hopeful?
No patience in your blood? the dog-star reigns,
   sure:
Time and fair temper would have wrought her
   pliant.
I spied a Pawn of the White House walk
   near us,
And made that noise o' purpose to give warn-
   ing —                                        160
For mine own turn, which end in all I work for.
                                 *[Aside.]*
*B. B. Pawn.* Methinks I stand over a
   powder-vault,
And the match now a-kindling: what 's to
   be done?
*B. Q. Pawn.* Ask the Black Bishop's coun-
   sel; you 're his pawn;                       164
'T is his own case, he will defend you mainly;
And happily here he comes, with the Black
   Knight too.

*Enter Black Bishop and Black Knight*

*B. Bishop.* O, y'ave made noble work for
   the White House yonder!
This act will fill the adversary's mouth,
And blow the Lutherans' cheek till 't crack
   again.
*B. Knight.* This will advance the great
   monarchal business                          170
In all parts well, and help the agents for-
   ward!
What I in seven years labour'd to accom-
   plish,
One minute sets back by some codpiece college
   still.
*B. B. Pawn.* I dwell not, sir, alone in this
   default,
The Black House yields me partners.
*B. Bishop.*            All more cautelous. 175
*B. Knight. Qui caute, caste;* that 's my
   motto ever;
I have travell'd with that word over most
   kingdoms,
And lain safe with most nations; of a leaking
   bottom,
I have been as often toss'd on Venus' seas
As trimmer, fresher barks, when sounder
   vessels                                      180
Have lain at anchor, that is, kept the door.

---

    [129] **my discovery:** revelation of my plot    [130] **Society:** Society of Jesus    [145] **confound:** ('confound noise' MSS., Qq.)    [149] **tympanous:** puffed-up, empty    [161] **turn:** purposes    [165] **mainly:** forcibly    [173] **codpiece:** lascivious    [174] **default:** fault    [175] **cautelous:** crafty    [176] **Qui . . . caste:** He who acts prudently, acts virtuously.    [177] **word:** motto    [178] **of . . . bottom:** though sickly

*B. Bishop.*   She has no witness then?
*B. B. Pawn.*        None, none.
*B. Knight.*              Gross! witness?
When went a man of his Society
To mischief with a witness?
*B. Bishop.*        I have done 't then:
Away upon the wings of speed! Take post-
horse,                                        185
Cast thirty leagues of earth behind thee sud-
denly;
Leave letters ante-dated with our House
Ten days at least from this.
*B. Knight.*            Bishop, I taste thee;
Good, strong, episcopal counsel! take a bottle
on 't,                                        189
'T will serve thee all the journey.
*B. B. Pawn.*              But, good sir,
How for my getting forth unspied?
*B. Knight.*        There 's check again.
*B. Q. Pawn.*   No, I 'll help that.
*B. Knight.* Well said, my bouncing Jesuitess!
*B. Q. Pawn.*   There lies a secret vault.
*B. Knight.*        Away, make haste then! 193
*B. B. Pawn.*   Run for my cabinet of intelli-
gences,
For fear they search the house.
                    [*Exit B. Q. Pawn.*]
        — Good Bishop, burn 'em rather;
I cannot stand to pick 'em now.
*B. Bishop.*            Begone!
The danger 's all in you.   [*Exit. B. B. Pawn.*]

[*Enter Black Queen's Pawn with cabinet*]

*B. Knight.*        Let me see, Queen's Pawn:
How formally h'as pack'd up his intelli-
gences!                                       198
H'as laid 'em all in truckle-beds, methinks,
And, like court-harbingers, has writ their names
In chalk upon their chambers: Anglica, —
O, this is the English House; what news there,
trow?
Hah, by this hand, most of these are bawdy
epistles!                                     203
Time they were burnt indeed! whole bundles on
'em.
Here 's from his daughter Blanche and daughter
Bridget,
From their safe sanctuary in the Whitefriars;
These from two tender sisters of Compassion
In the bowels of Bloomsbury;                  208
Three from the nunnery in Drury Lane.
A fire, a fire, good Jesuitess, a fire! —
What have you there?
*B. Bishop.*   A note, sir, of state policy,
And one exceeding safe one.

*B. Knight.*        Pray, let 's see it, sir, —
                            [*Reads.*]
"To sell away all the powder in a kingdom,  213
To prevent blowing up:" that 's safe, I 'll
able it.
Here 's a facetious observation now,
And suits my humour better; he writes here
Some wives in England will commit adultery,
And then send to Rome for a bull for their hus-
bands.                                        218
*B. Bishop.*   Have they those shifts?
*B. Knight.*   O, there 's no female breathing
Sweeter and subtler! — Here, wench, take these
papers,
Scorch me 'em soundly, burn 'em to French
russet,
And put 'em in again.
*B. Bishop.*        Why, what 's your mystery?
*B. Knight.*   O, sir, 't will mock the adversary
strangely,                                    223
If e'er the House be search'd: 't was done in
Venice
Upon the Jesuitical expulse there,
When the Inquisitors came all spectacled
To pick out syllables out of the dung of trea-
son,
As children pick out cherry-stones, yet found
none                                          228
But what they made themselves with ends of
letters. —
Do as I bid you, Pawn.
            [*Exeunt B. Knight and B. Bishop.*]
*B. Q. Pawn.*   Fear not: in all,
I love roguery too well to let it fall. —

*Enter Black Knight's Pawn*

How now, what news with you?
*B. Kt.'s Pawn.*        The sting of conscience
Afflicts me so for that inhuman violence  233
On the White Bishop's Pawn, it takes away
My joy, my rest.
*B. Q. Pawn.*   This 't is to make an eunuch!
You made a sport on 't then.
*B. Kt.'s Pawn.*        Cease aggravation:
I come to be absolv'd for 't: where's my con-
fessor?
Why dost thou point to the ground?
*B. Q. Pawn.*   'Cause he went that way.  238
Come, come, help me in with this cabinet;
And after I have sing'd these papers throughly,
I 'll tell thee a strange story.
*B. Kt.'s Pawn.*        If 't be sad,
'T is welcome.
*B. Q. Pawn.*   'T is not troubled with much
mirth, sir.                          *Exeunt.* 242

---

<sup>188</sup> **taste thee:** catch your meaning   <sup>200</sup> **court-harbingers:** officer who provides lodgings   <sup>202</sup> **trow:** think you?   <sup>206–209</sup> **Whitefriars, Bloomsbury, Drury Lane:** centers of Roman Catholicism in London   <sup>214</sup> **able:** warrant, answer for   <sup>218</sup> **bull:** Papal decree   <sup>219</sup> **shifts:** tricks   <sup>222</sup> **mystery: secret pur-pose**   <sup>225</sup> **expulse:** expulsion (of the Jesuits in 1606)   <sup>240</sup> **throughly:** thoroughly

[SCENE II. — *The Same*]

*Enter Fat Bishop with a Pawn*

*F. Bishop.*   Pawn.

*F. B. Pawn.*   I attend at your great holiness'
service.

*F. Bishop.*   For great, I grant you, but for
greatly holy,
There the soil alters: fat cathedral bodies
Have very often but lean little souls,
Much like the lady in the lobster's head,    5
A great deal of shell and garbage of all colours,
But the pure part, that should take wings and
mount,
Is at last gasp; as if a man should gape,
And from this huge bulk let forth a butterfly,
Like those big-bellied mountains, which the
poet                                          10
Delivers, that are brought abed with mouse-
flesh.
Are my books printed, Pawn, my last invectives
Against the Black House?
*F. B. Pawn.*            Ready for publication,
For I saw perfect books this morning, sir.
*F. Bishop.*   Fetch me a few, which I will
instantly                                     15
Distribute 'mongst the White House.
*F. B. Pawn.*            With all speed, sir.
*Exit Fat Bishop's Pawn.*
*F. Bishop.*   'T is a most lordly life to rail at
ease,
Sit, eat and feed upon the fat of one kingdom,
And rail upon another with the juice on 't.
I have writ this book out of the strength and
marrow                                        20
Of six and thirty dishes at a meal,
But most on 't out of cullis of cock-sparrows;
'T will stick and glue the faster to the adversary,
'T will slit the throat of their most calvish cause;
And yet I eat but little butcher's meat       25
In the conception.
Of all things I commend the White House best
For plenty and variety of victuals:
When I was one of the Black side profess'd,
My flesh fell half a cubit; time to turn       30
When mine own ribs revolted. But to say true,
I have no preferment yet that 's suitable
To the greatness of my person and my parts:
I grant I live at ease, for I am made

The master of the beds, the long acre of beds; 35
But there 's no marigolds that shuts and opens,
Flower-gentles, Venus-baths, apples of love,
Pinks, hyacinths, honeysuckles, daffadown-
dillies:
There was a time I had more such drabs than
beds;
Now I 've more beds than drabs;                40
Yet there 's no eminent trader deals in whole-
sale,
But she and I have clapp'd a bargain up,
Let in at water-gate, for which I have rack'd
My tenants' purse-strings that they have
twang'd again.

*Enter Black Knight and Black Bishop*

Yonder Black Knight, the fistula of Europe, 45
Whose disease once I undertook to cure
With a High Holborn halter! When he last
Vouchsaf'd to peep into my privileg'd lodgings,
He saw good store of plate there and rich hang-
ings;
He knew I brought none to the White House
with me:                                       50
I have not lost the use of my profession
Since I turn'd White-House Bishop.

*Enter his Pawn with books*

*B. Knight.*            Look, more books yet!
Yond greasy, turncoat, gormandising prelate
Does work our House more mischief by his
scripts,
His fat and fulsome volumes, than the whole 55
Body of the adverse party.
*B. Bishop.*            O, 't were
A masterpiece of serpent subtlety
To fetch him o' this side again!
*B. Knight.*            And then damn him
Into the bag for ever, or expose him
Against the adverse party, which now he feeds
upon;                                          60
And that would double-damn him.  My re-
venge
Hath prompted me already: I 'll confound him
On both sides for the physic he provided,
And the base surgeon he invented for me.
I 'll tell you what a most uncatholic jest   65
He put upon me once when my pain tortur'd
me:
He told me he had found a present cure for me,

---

² ff. (The Fat Bishop, in this scene, gives a satirical portrait of the appearance, character, and methods of de Dominis. The original actor of this part seems to have been Middleton's collaborator in *The Changeling*, William Rowley, who died in February, 1626. See London *Times Lit. Supplement*, Feb. 6, 1930.)   ⁵ **lady:** (really a formation in the lobster's stomach)   ¹¹ **Delivers:** describes   ²² **cullis:** a strong broth   ³²⁻³³ **I . . . parts:** (De Dominis received several lucrative positions in the English church, including the deanship of Windsor, and wished to be archbishop of York.)   ³⁵ **master . . . beds:** Master of the Hospital of the Savoy   ⁴⁵ **fistula:** (Gondomar suffered from that disease.)   ⁴⁷ **High Holborn:** the scene of executions   ⁶³ **physic:** (De Dominis once told Gondomar that "three turns at Tyburn" [*i.e.*, hanging] was the only way to cure his fistula.)   ⁶⁷ **present:** immediate

Which I grew proud on, and observ'd him
seriously.
What think you 't was? being execution-day,
He show'd the hangman to me out at win-
dow,                                            70
The common hangman!
  *B. Bishop.*              O, insufferable!
  *B. Knight.* I 'll make him the balloon-ball
of the churches,
And both the sides shall toss him: he looks like
one,
A thing swell'd up with mingled drink and
urine,
And will bound well from one side to another. 75
Come, you shall write; our second bishop ab-
sent,
(Which has yet no employment in the game,
Perhaps nor ever shall; it may be won
Without his motion, it rests most in ours,)
He shall be flatter'd with *sede vacante;*      80
Make him believe he comes into his place,
And that will fetch him with a vengeance to us;
For I know powder is not more ambitious
When the match meets it, than his mind, for
mounting;
As covetous and lecherous —
  *B. Bishop.*             No more now, sir; 85

*Enter both Houses*

Both the sides fill.
  *W. King.* This has been look'd for long.
  *F. Bishop.* The stronger sting it shoots into
the blood
Of the Black adversary: I am asham'd now
I was theirs ever; what a lump was I
When I was led in ignorance and blindness! 90
I must confess,
I 've all my lifetime play'd the fool till now.
  *B. Knight.* And now he plays two parts, the
fool and knave.
  *F. Bishop.* There is my recantation in the
last leaf,
Writ, like a Ciceronian, in pure Latin.        95
  *W. Bishop.* Pure honesty, the plainer Latin
serves then.
  *B. Knight.* Plague on those pestilent pam-
phlets! those are they
That wound our cause to the heart.
  *B. Bishop.*          Here comes more anger.

*Enter White Queen's Pawn*

  *B. Knight.* But we come well provided for
this storm.
  *W. Queen.* Is this my Pawn, she that should
guard our person,                              100
Or some pale figure of dejection

Her shape usurping? Sorrow and affrightment
Has prevail'd strangely with her.
  *W. Q. Pawn.*            King of integrity,
Queen of the same, and all the House, pro-
fessors
Of noble candour, uncorrupted justice,         105
And truth of heart, through my alone dis-
covery —
My life and honour wondrously preserv'd —
I bring into your knowledge with my suffer-
ings,
Fearful affrightments, and heart-killing terrors:
The great incendiary of Christendom,           110
The absolut'st abuser of true sanctity,
Fair peace, and holy order, can be found
In any part of the universal globe;
Who, making meek devotion keep the door, —
His lips being full of holy zeal at first, —    115
Would have committed a foul rape upon me.
  *W. Queen.* Ha!
  *W. King.* A rape? that 's foul indeed; the
very sound
To our ear fouler than the offence itself
To some kings of the earth.
  *W. Q. Pawn.* Sir, to proceed, —            120
Gladly I offer'd life to preserve honour,
Which would not be accepted without both,
The chief of his ill aim being at my honour;
Till heaven was pleas'd, by some unlook'd-for
accident,
To give me courage to redeem myself.           125
  *W. King.* When we find desperate sins in ill
men's companies,
We place a charitable sorrow there,
But custom, and their leprous inclination,
Quits us of wonder, for our expectation
Is answer'd in their lives; but to find sin,    130
Ay, and a masterpiece of darkness, shelter'd
Under a robe of sanctity, is able
To draw all wonder to that monster only,
And leave created monsters unadmir'd.
The pride of him that took first fall for pride 135
Is to be angel-shap'd, and imitate
The form from whence he fell; but this of-
fender,
Far baser than sin's master, fix'd by vow
To holy order, which is angels' method,
Takes pride to use that shape to be a devil. 140
It grieves me that my knowledge must be
tainted
With his infected name:
O, rather with thy finger point him out!
  *W. Q. Pawn.* The place which he should fill
is void, my lord,
His guilt hath seiz'd him, — the Black Bishop's
Pawn.                                          145

⁶⁸ **proud:** pleased    **observed:** paid attention to
⁸⁰ **sede vacante:** vacant seat or position in the church
**pandar**    ⁷² **balloon-ball:** leather ball used in a game
¹⁰⁶ **alone:** single    ¹¹⁴ **keep the door:** act as

*B. Bishop.*  Ha! mine? my Pawn? the glory of his order,
The prime and president zealot of the earth?
Impudent Pawn, for thy sake at this minute
Modesty suffers, all that 's virtuous blushes,
And truth's self, like the sun vex'd with a mist,     150
Looks red with anger.
    *W. Bishop.*  Be not you drunk with rage too.
    *B. Bishop.*  Sober sincerity, nor you with a cup
Spic'd with hypocrisy.
    *W. Knight.*  You name there, Bishop,
But your own Christmas-bowl, your morning's draught,
Next your episcopal heart all the twelve days,
Which smack you cannot leave all the year following.     156
    *B. Knight.*  A shrewd retort!
H'as made our Bishop smell of burning too:
Would I stood farder off! were 't no impeachment
To my honour or the game, would they 'd play faster! —     [*Aside.*]     160
White Knight, there is acknowledg'd from our House
A reverence to you, and a respect
To that lov'd Duke stands next you: with the favour
Of the White King and the 'forenam'd respected,
I combat with this cause.  If with all speed, —
Waste not one syllable, unfortunate Pawn,     166
Of what I speak, — thou dost not plead distraction,
A plea which will but faintly take thee off, neither,
From this leviathan-scandal that lies rolling
Upon the crystal waters of devotion;     170
Or, what may quit thee more, though enough nothing,
Fall down and foam, and by that pang discover
The vexing spirit of falsehood strong within thee,
Make thyself ready for perdition;
There 's no remove in all the game to 'scape it;
This Pawn or this, the Bishop or myself,     176
Will take thee in the end, play how thou canst.
    *W. Q. Pawn.*  Spite of sin's glorious ostentation,
And all loud threats, those thunder-cracks of pride,
Ushering a storm of malice; House of impudence,     180

Craft, and equivocation, my true cause
Shall keep the path it treads in.
    *B. Knight.*          I play thus, then:
Now in the hearing of this high assembly
Bring forth the time of this attempt's conception.
    *W. Q. Pawn.*  Conception?  O, how tenderly you handle it!     185
    *W. Bishop.*  It seems, Black Knight, you are afraid to touch it.
    *B. Knight.*  Well, its eruption: will you have it so then?
Or you, White Bishop, for her? the uncleaner,
Vile, and more impious that you urge the strain to,
The greater will her shame's heap show i' th' end,     190
And the wrong'd, meek man's glory. — The time, Pawn?
    *W. Q. Pawn.*  Yesterday's cursed evening.
    *B. Knight.*          O the treasure
Of my revenge!  I cannot spend all on thee,
Ruin to spare for all thy kindred too:
For honour's sake call in more slanderers;     195
I have such plentiful confusion,
I know not how to waste it.  I 'll be nobler yet,
And put her to her own House. — King of meekness,
Take the cause to thee, for our hand 's too heavy;
Our proofs will fall upon her like a tower,     200
And grind her bones to powder.
    *W. Q. Pawn.*          What new engine
Has the devil rais'd in him now?
    *B. Knight.*          Is it he,
And that the time?  Stand firm now to your scandal,
Pray, do not shift your slander.
    *W. Q. Pawn.*          Shift your treacheries;
They 've worn one suit too long.
    *B. Knight.*          That holy man,     205
So wrongfully accus'd by this lost Pawn,
Hath not been seen these ten days in these parts.
    *W. Knight.*  How?
    *B. Knight.*  Nay, at this instant thirty leagues from hence.
    *W. Q. Pawn.*  Fathomless falsehood! will it 'scape unblasted?     210
    *W. King.*  Can you make this appear?
    *B. Knight.*          Light is not clearer;
By his own letters, most impartial monarch.
    *W. Kg.'s Pawn.*  How wrongfully may sacred virtue suffer, sir!
    *B. Knight.*  Bishop, we have a treasure of that false heart.

¹⁴⁷ **president:** chief     ¹⁵² **with:** (not in MS) ficient     ¹⁷⁵ **remove:** move     ¹⁸⁷ **eruption:** breaking out     ¹⁸⁹ **strain:** recital     ¹⁹⁴ **Ruin** (Several texts, including MS, read 'Ruin enough.')     ¹⁷¹ **quit:** acquit     **enough nothing:** not at all sufficient     ¹⁹⁷ **waste:** use, spend     ²⁰¹ **engine:** device

*W. King.* Step forth, and reach those
    proofs.                                          215
    [*Exit B. Kt.'s Pawn, who presently re-*
    *turns with papers.*]
*W. Q. Pawn.*           Amazement covers me!
Can I be so forsaken of a cause
So strong in truth and equity? Will virtue
Send me no aid in this hard time of friendship?
    *B. Knight.*  There 's an infallible staff and a
    red hat                                          220
Reserv'd for you.
    *W. Kg.'s Pawn.*  O, sir endear'd!
    *B. Knight.*                          A staff
That will not easily break; you may trust to it;
And such a one had your corruption need of;
There 's a state-fig for you now.
    *W. King.*                          Behold all,
How they cohere in one! I always held       225
A charity so good to holiness
Profess'd, I ever believ'd rather
The accuser false than the professor vicious.
    *B. Knight.*  A charity, like all your virtues
    else,
Gracious and glorious.
    *W. King.*  Where settles the offence,     230
Let the fault's punishment be deriv'd from
    thence:
We leave her to your censure.
    *B. Knight.*                          Most just majesty!
    [*Exeunt W. King, W. Queen, W. Bishop,*
    *and W. Kg.'s Pawn; F. Bishop and*
    *F. B. Pawn.*]
*W. Q. Pawn.*  Calamity of virtue! my Queen
    leave me too!
Am I cast off as th' olive casts her flower?
Poor harmless innocence, art thou left a
    prey                                             235
To the devourer?
    *W. Knight.*  No, thou art not lost,
Let 'em put on their bloodiest resolutions,
If the fair policy I aim at prospers. —
Thy counsel, noble Duke!
    *W. Duke.*           For that work cheerfully.
    *W. Knight.*  A man for speed now!
    *W. B. Pawn.*  Let it be my honour, sir;      240
Make me that flight, that owes her my life's
    service.
    *Exeunt* [*W. Knight, W. Duke, and*
    *W. B. Pawn.*]
    *B. Knight.*  Was not this brought about well
    for our honours?
    *B. Bishop.*  Pish, that Galician sconce can
    work out wonders.
    *B. Knight.*  Let 's use her as, upon the like
    discovery,

A maid was us'd at Venice; every one     245
Be ready with a penance. — Begin, majesty. —
Vessel of foolish scandal, take thy freight:
Had there been in that cabinet of niceness
Half the virginities of the earth lock'd up,
And all swept at one cast by the dexterity  250
Of a Jesuitical gamester, 't had not valued
The least part of that general worth thou hast
    tainted.
    *B. King.*  First, I enjoin thee to a three days'
    fast for 't.
    *B. Queen.*  You 're too penurious, sir; I 'll
    make it four.
    *B. Bishop.*  I to a twelve hours' kneeling at
    one time.                                        255
    *B. Knight.*  And in a room filled all with
    Aretine's pictures,
More than the twice-twelve labours of luxury:
Thou shalt not see so much as the chaste
    pommel
Of Lucrece' dagger peeping; nay, I 'll punish
    thee
For a discoverer, I 'll torment thy modesty.  260
    *B. Duke.*  After that four days' fast, to the
    Inquisition-house,
Strengthen'd with bread and water for worse
    penance.
    *B. Knight.*  Why, well said, duke of our
    House, nobly aggravated!
    *W. Q. Pawn.*  Virtue, to show her influence
    more strong,
Fits me with patience mightier than my
    wrong.                               *Exeunt.* 265

## Finit Actus Secundus.

## Incipit Tertius.

### [ACT III.  SCENE I. —

*Field between the two Houses*]

*Enter Fat Bishop*

    *F. Bishop.*  I know my pen draws blood of
    the Black House,
There 's never a book I write but their cause
    bleeds;
It hath lost many an ounce of reputation
Since I came of this side; I strike deep in,
And leave the orifex gushing where I come,   5
But where 's my advancement all this while I
    ha' gap'd for?
I 'd have some round preferment, corpulent
    dignity,
That bears some breadth and compass in the
    gift on 't:

---

²²⁰ **red hat:** cardinal's hat    ²²⁴ **state-fig:** diplomatic insult    ²⁴¹ **flight:** swift messenger    ²⁴³ **Gali-**
**cian sconce:** Spanish brain    ²⁵⁶ **Aretine's pictures:** (a reference to a notorious series of scandalous
illustrations by Giulio Romano to a book of obscene verses by Pietro Aretino)    ²⁵⁷ **luxury:** lust
²⁶⁰ **discoverer:** one who reveals a secret    ⁵ **orifex:** wound

I am persuaded that this flesh would fill
The biggest chair ecclesiastical,                10
If it were put to trial.
To be made master of an hospital
Is but a kind of diseas'd bed-rid honour;
Or dean of the poor alms-knights that wear
    badges:
There 's but two lazy, beggarly preferments 15
In the White Kingdom, and I have got 'em
    both:
My merit doth begin to be crop-sick
For want of other titles.

*Enter Black Knight*

   *B. Knight.* [*Aside.*] O, here walks
His fulsome holiness: now for the master-trick
T' undo him everlastingly, that 's put home, 20
And make him hang in hell most seriously
That jested with a halter upon me.
   *F. Bishop.* [*Aside.*] The Black Knight! I
    must look to my play then.
   *B. Knight.* I bring fair greetings to your
    reverend virtues
From Cardinal Paulus, your most princely
    kinsman.            [*Gives a letter.*] 25
   *F. Bishop.* Our princely kinsman, say'st
    thou? we accept 'em.
Pray, keep your side and distance; I am chary
Of my episcopal person:
I know the Knight's walk in this game too well;
He may skip over me, and where am I then? [30
   *B. Knight.* [*Aside.*] There where thou shalt
    be shortly, if art fail not.            *The Letter.*
   *F. Bishop.* [*Reads.*] "Right reverend and
noble, "—meaning ourself,—"our true kinsman
in blood, but alienated in affection, your unkind
disobedience to the mother cause proves as [35
this time the only cause of your ill fortune: my
present remove by election to the papal dignity
had now auspiciously settled you in my *sede
vacante*"—ha! had it so? — "which at my next
remove by death might have prov'd your [40
step to supremacy."
How! all my body's blood mounts to my face
To look upon this letter.
   *B. Knight.* [*Aside.*] The pill works with
    him.
   *F. Bishop.* [*Reads.*] "Think on 't seriously;
it is not yet too late, thorough the submiss [46
acknowledgment of your disobedience, to be
lovingly receiv'd into the brotherly bosom of
the conclave."
This was the chair of ease I ever aim'd at.  50
I 'll make a bonfire of my books immediately;

All that are left against that side I 'll sacrifice;
Pack up my plate and goods, and steal away
By night at water-gate. It is but penning
Another recantation, and inventing        55
Two or three bitter books against the White
    House,
And then I 'm in on t'other side again
As firm as e'er I was, as fat and flourishing. —
                                [*Aside.*]
Black Knight, expect a wonder ere 't be long,
You shall see me one of the Black House
    shortly.                            60
   *B. Knight.* Your holiness is merry with the
    messenger;
Too happy to be true; you speak what should
    be,
If natural compunction touch'd you truly.
O, y'ave drawn blood, life-blood, the blood of
    honour,
From your most dear, your primitive mother's
    heart!                            65
Your sharp invectives have been points of
    spears
In her sweet tender sides! The unkind wounds
Which a son gives, a son of reverence 'specially,
They rankle ten times more than the adver-
    sary's:
I tell you, sir, your reverend revolt        70
Did give the fearfull'st blow to adoration
Our cause e'er felt; it shook the very statues,
The urns and ashes of the sainted sleepers.
   *F. Bishop.* Forbear, or I shall melt in the
    place I stand,
And let forth a fat bishop in sad syrup:    75
Suffices I am yours, when they least dream
    on 't;
Ambition's fodder, power and riches, draws me:
When I smell honour, that 's the lock of hay
That leads me through the world's field every
    way.                            *Exit.*
   *B. Knight.* Here 's a sweet paunch to propa-
    gate belief on,                        80
Like the foundation of a chapel laid
Upon a quagmire! I may number him now
Amongst my inferior policies, and not shame
    'em.
But let me a little solace my designs
With the remembrance of some brave ones
    past,                            85
To cherish the futurity of project,
Whose motion must be restless till that great
    work,
Call'd the possession of the world, be ours.
Was it not I procur'd a precious safeguard

---

¹⁴ **poor alms-knights:** Poor Knights of Windsor    ²⁵ **Cardinal Paulus:** *i.e.*, Pope Paul V    ²⁹ **walk:**
move    ³⁷ **remove:** removal, translation    ³⁹ **at:** ('by' MS)    ⁴⁶ **submiss:** submissive    ⁴⁸ **lovingly**
. . . **brotherly:** ('brotherly . . . loving' Q 2)    ⁸⁹ **precious safeguard:** (Some texts read 'gallant fleet.')
⁸⁹⁻⁹² (Gondomar persuaded the English to fight the Turks in the Mediterranean, to the great advantage
of Spain.)

From the White Kingdom to secure our coasts
'Gainst the infidel pirate, under pretext          91
Of more necessitous expedition?
Who made the jails fly open, without miracle,
And let the locusts out, those dangerous flies,
Whose property is to burn corn with touching?
The heretic granaries feel it to this minute: 96
And now they have got amongst the country
    crops,
They stick so fast to the converted ears,
The loudest tempest that authority rouses
Will hardly shake 'em off: they have their dens
In ladies' couches — there's safe groves and
    fens!                                         101
Nay, were they follow'd and found out by th'
    scent,
Palm-oil will make a pursuivant relent.
Whose policy was 't to put a silenc'd muzzle
On all the barking tongue-men of the time?
Made pictures, that were dumb enough be-
    fore,                                          106
Poor sufferers in that politic restraint?
My light spleen skips and shakes my ribs to
    think on 't.
Whilst our drifts walk'd uncensur'd but in
    thought,
A whistle or a whisper would be question'd
In the most fortunate angle of the world.   111
The court has held the city by the horns
Whilst I have milk'd her: I have had good sops
    too
From country ladies for their liberties,
From some for their most vainly-hop'd pre-
    ferments,                                      115
High offices in the air. I should not live
But for this *mel aerium*, this mirth-manna.

*Enter his Pawn*

My Pawn! — How now, the news?
  *B. Kt.'s Pawn.*    Expect none very pleasing
That comes, sir, of my bringing; I'm for sad
    things.                                        120
  *B. Knight.*    Thy conscience is so tender-
    hoof'd of late,
Every nail pricks it.
  *B. Kt.'s Pawn.*    This may prick yours
    too,
If there be any quick flesh in a yard on 't.
  *B. Knight.*    Mine?
Mischief must find a deep nail, and a driver
Beyond the strength of any Machiavel      126
The politic kingdoms fatten, to reach mine.
Prithee, compunction needle-prick'd, a little
Unbind this sore wound.
  *B. Kt.'s Pawn.*    Sir, your plot 's discover'd.

  *B. Knight.*    Which of the twenty thousand
    and nine hundred                               130
Four score and five? canst tell?
  *B. Kt.'s Pawn.*            Bless us, so many!
How do poor countrymen have but one plot
To keep a cow on, yet in law for that?
You cannot know 'em all, sure, by their names,
    sir.
  *B. Knight.*    Yes, were their number trebled:
    thou hast seen                                 135
A globe stands on the table in my closet?
  *B. Kt.'s Pawn.*    A thing, sir, full of countries
    and hard words?
  *B. Knight.*    True, with lines drawn, some
    tropical, some oblique.
  *B. Kt.'s Pawn.*    I can scarce read, I was
    brought up in blindness.
  *B. Knight.*    Just such a thing, if e'er my
    skull be open'd,                               140
Will my brains look like.
  *B. Kt.'s Pawn.*    Like a globe of countries?
  *B. Knight.*    Ay, and some master-politician,
That has sharp state-eyes, will go near to
    pick out
The plots, and every climate where they fas-
    ten'd;
'T will puzzle 'em too.                            145
  *B. Kt.'s Pawn.*    I'm of your mind for that,
    sir.
  *B. Knight.*    They 'll find 'em to fall thick
    upon some countries;
They 'd need use spectacles: but I turn to you
    now;
What plot is that discover'd?
  *B. Kt.'s Pawn.*            Your last brat, sir,
Begot 'twixt the Black Bishop and yourself, 150
Your ante-dated letters 'bout the Jesuit.
  *B. Knight.*                Discover'd! how?
  *B. Kt.'s Pawn.*    The White Knight's policy
    has outstripp'd yours, it seems,
Join'd with th' assistant counsel of his Duke:
The Bishop's White Pawn undertook the
    journey,
Who, as they say, discharg'd it like a flight, 155
Ay, made him for the business fit and light.
  *B. Knight.*    'T is but a bawdy Pawn out of
    the way a little;
Enow of them in all parts.

*Enter Black Bishop and both the Houses*

  *B. Bishop.*            You have heard all then?
  *B. Knight.*    The wonder 's past with me; but
    some shall down for 't.
  *W. Knight.*    Set free that virtuous Pawn
    from all her wrongs;                           160

---

93–96 (Gondomar procured the release of all priests and Jesuits imprisoned in England.)    103 **Palm-**
**oil:** bribes    **pursuivant:** officer used to enforce ecclesiastical laws    104 **muzzle:** (Preachers were forbidden to discuss Spanish affairs.)    106 **pictures:** (An engraving by the Rev. Samuel Ward had been
suppressed.)    109 **drifts:** purposes    117 **mel aerium:** airy honey    125 **deep:** ('deeper' MS)

Let her be brought with honour to the face
Of her malicious adversaries.
                              [*Exit W. Kg.'s Pawn.*]
*B. Knight.*                              Good.
*W. King.* Noble chaste Knight, a title of
    that candour
The greatest prince on earth without impeach-
    ment
May have the dignity of his worth compris'd in,
This fair delivering act Virtue will register 166
In that white book of the defence of virgins,
Where the clear fames of all preserving knights
Are to eternal memory consecrated;
And we embrace, as partner of that honour,
This worthy Duke, the counsel of the act, 171
Whom we shall ever place in our respect.
*W. Duke.* Most blest of kings, thron'd in all
    royal graces,
Every good deed sends back its own reward
Into the bosom of the enterpriser;         175
But you to express yourself as well to be
King of munificence as integrity,
Adds glory to the gift.
*W. King.*                   Thy deserts claim it,
Zeal, and fidelity. — Appear, thou beauty
Of truth and innocence, best ornament      180
Of patience, thou that mak'st thy sufferings
    glorious!

[*Enter White King's Pawn with White
    Queen's Pawn*]

*B. Knight.* I 'll take no knowledge on 't.
    [*Aside.*] — What makes she here?
How dares yond Pawn unpenanc'd, with a
    cheek                                  184
Fresh as her falsehood yet, where castigation
Has left no pale print of her visiting anguish,
Appear in this assembly? — Let me alone:
Sin must be bold; that 's all the grace 't is
    born to.                          [*Aside.*]
*W. Knight.* What 's this?
*W. King.*                I 'm wonder-struck!
*W. Q. Pawn.* Assist me, goodness!         190
I shall to prison again.
*B. Knight.* At least I have maz'd 'em,
Scatter'd their admiration of her innocence,
As the fir'd ships put in sever'd the fleet
In eighty-eight: I 'll on with 't; impudence 195
Is mischief's patrimony. [*Aside.*] — Is this
    justice?
Is injur'd reverence no sharplier righted?
I ever held that majesty impartial
That, like most equal heaven, looks on the
    manners,
Not on the shapes they shroud in.

*W. King.*                   That Black Knight 200
Will never take an answer; 't is a victory
To make him understand he does amiss,
When he knows in his own clear understanding
That he does nothing else. Show him the
    testimony,
Confirm'd by good men, how that foul at-
    tempter                                205
Got but this morning to the place from
    whence
He dated his forg'd lines for ten days past.
*B. Knight.* Why, may not that corruption
    sleep in this
By some connivance, as you have wak'd in ours
By too rash confidence?
*W. Duke.*                I 'll undertake     210
That Knight shall teach the devil how to lie.
*W. Knight.* If sin were half so wise as im-
    pudent,
She 'd ne'er seek farder for an advocate.

*Enter Black Queen's Pawn*

*B. Q. Pawn.* Now to act treachery with an
    angel's tongue:
Since all 's come out, I 'll bring him strangely in
    again.                      [*Aside.*] 215
Where is this injur'd chastity, this goodness
Whose worth no transitory piece can value?
This rock of constant and invincible virtue,
That made sin's tempest weary of his fury? —
*B. Queen.* What, is my Pawn distracted?
*B. Knight.*                I think rather 220
There is some notable masterprize of roguery
This drum strikes up for.
*B. Q. Pawn.* Let me fall with reverence
Before this blessed altar.
*B. Queen.*                This is madness.
*B. Knight.* Well, mark the end; I stand for
    roguery still,
I will not change my side.
*B. Q. Pawn.* I shall be tax'd, I know; 225
I care not what the Black House thinks of me.
*B. Queen.* What say you now?
*B. Knight.*                I will not be unlaid yet.
*B. Q. Pawn.* How any censure flies, I honour
    sanctity;
That is my object, I intend no other:
I saw this glorious and most valiant virtue 230
Fight the most noblest combat with the devil.
*B. Knight.* If both the Bishops had been
    there for seconds,
'T ad been a complete duel.
*W. King.*                Then thou heard'st
The violence intended?
*B. Q. Pawn.*                'T is a truth

---

¹⁷⁵ **enterpriser:** performer      ¹⁷⁶ **you:** *i.e.*, for you      ¹⁹¹ **maz'd:** bewildered      ¹⁹⁴ **fir'd ships:** the English fire-ships which dislodged the Armada from Calais harbor in 1588      ¹⁹⁹ **equal:** just, impartial      ²¹⁷ **piece . . . value:** ('prize . . . equall' Q 2)      **value:** equal in value      ²²⁵ **tax'd:** rebuked      ²²⁷ **unlaid:** unsettled      ²²⁸ **How any:** ('However' Q 2)      ²³¹ **noblest:** ('noble' Q 2)

I joy to justify: I was an agent, sir,                    235
On virtue's part, and rais'd that confus'd
  noise
That startled his attempt, and gave her liberty.
  *W. Q. Pawn.*  O, 't is a righteous story she
has told, sir!
My life and fame stand mutually engag'd
Both to the truth and goodness of this Pawn.
  *W. King.*  Does it appear to you yet clear
    as the sun?                                           241
  *B. Knight.*  'Las, I believ'd it long before
    't was done!
  *B. King.*  Degenerate —
  *B. Queen.*           Base —
  *B. Bishop.*                   Perfidious —
  *B. Duke.*                           Trait'rous Pawn!
  *B. Q. Pawn.*  What, are you all beside your-
    selves?
  *B. Knight.*  But I;
Remember that, Pawn.
  *B. Q. Pawn.*  May a fearful barrenness     245
Blast both my hopes and pleasures, if I brought
  not
Her ruin in my pity! a new trap
For her more sure confusion.
  *B. Knight.*                       Have I won now?
Did not I say 't was craft and machination?
I smelt conspiracy all the way it went,       250
Although the mess were cover'd; I 'm so us'd
  to it.
  *B. King.*  That Queen would I fain finger.
  *B. Knight.*                   You 're too hot, sir;
If she were took, the game would be ours
  quickly:
My aim 's at that White Knight; entrap him
  first,
The Duke will follow, too.
  *B. Bishop.*                   I would that Bishop
Were in my diocese!  I 'd soon change his
  whiteness.                                              256
  *B. Knight.*  Sir, I could whip you up a Pawn
  immediately;
I know where my game stands.
  *B. King.*                       Do it suddenly;
Advantage least must not be lost in this play.
  *B. Knight.*  Pawn, thou art ours.
                        [*Seizes White King's Pawn.*]
  *W. Knight.*              He 's taken by default,
By wilful negligence.  Guard the sacred per-
  sons;                                                   261
Look well to the White Bishop, for that Pawn
Gave guard to the Queen and him in the third
  place.
  *B. Knight.*  See what sure piece you lock
    your confidence in!
I made this Pawn here by corruption ours,
As soon as honour by creation yours.          266

This whiteness upon him is but the leprosy
Of pure dissimulation: view him now,
His heart and his intents are of our colour.
          *His upper garment taken off, he appears
              black underneath.*
  *W. Knight.*  Most dangerous hypocrite!
  *W. Queen.*              One made against us! 270
  *W. Duke.*  His truth of their complexion!
  *W. King.*                       Has my goodness,
Clemency, love, and favour gracious, rais'd
  thee
From a condition next to popular labour,
Took thee from all the dubitable hazards
Of fortune, her most unsecure adventures,     275
And grafted thee into a branch of honour,
And dost thou fall from the top-bough by the
  rottenness
Of thy alone corruption, like a fruit
That 's over-ripen'd by the beams of favour?
Let thy own weight reward thee;  I have
  forgot thee:                                           280
Integrity of life is so dear to me,
Where I find falsehood or a crying trespass,
Be it in any whom our grace shines most on,
I 'd tear 'em from my heart.
  *W. Bishop.*  Spoke like heaven's substitute!
  *W. King.*  You have him, we can spare him;
    and his shame                                        285
Will make the rest look better to their game.
  *B. Knight.*  The more cunning we must use
    then.
  *B. King.*                       We shall match you,
Play how you can, perhaps and mate you
  too.
  *F. Bishop.*  Is there so much amazement
    spent on him
That 's but half black? there might be hope of
    that man;                                            290
But how will this House wonder if I stand forth
And show a whole one, instantly discover
One that 's all black, where there 's no hope
    at all!
  *W. King.*  I 'll say, thy heart then justifies
    thy books;                                           294
I long for that discovery.
  *F. Bishop.*              Look no farder then:
Bear witness, all the House, I am the man,
And turn myself into the Black House freely;
I am of this side now.
  *W. Knight.*           Monster ne'er match'd him!
  *B. King.*  This is your noble work, Knight.
  *B. Knight.*                   Now I 'll halter him.
  *F. Bishop.*  Next news you hear, expect my
    books against you,                                   300
Printed at Douay, Brussels, or Spalato.
  *W. King.*  See his goods seiz'd on!
  *F. Bishop.*           'Las, they were all convey'd

---

272–276 **rais'd . . . honour:** (The Earl of Middlesex, the probable original of the White King's Pawn,
began as an apprentice and rose to the post of Lord Treasurer of the kingdom.)     299 **halter: hang**

Last night by water to a tailor's house,
A friend of the Black cause.
    *W. Knight.*        A prepar'd hypocrite! 304
    *W. Duke.*  Premeditated turncoat!
        *Exeunt* [*W. King, W. Queen, W.
           Knight, W. Duke, and W. Bishop.*]
    *F. Bishop.*        Yes, rail on;
I 'll reach you in my writings when I 'm gone.
    *B. Knight.*  Flatter him a while with honours
    till we put him
Upon some dangerous service, and then burn
    him.
    *B. King.*  This came unlook'd for.
    *B. Duke.*        How we joy to see you!
    *F. Bishop.*  Now I 'll discover all the White
    House to you.               310
    *B. Duke.*  Indeed, that will both reconcile
    and raise you.
        [*Exeunt B. King, B. Queen, B. Duke,
          B. Bishop, and F. Bishop.*]
    *W. Kg.'s Pawn.*  I rest upon you, Knight,
    for my advancement.
    *B. Knight.*  O, for the staff, the strong staff
    that will hold,
And the red hat, fit for the guilty mazzard?
Into the empty bag know thy first way:    315
Pawns that are lost are ever out of play.
    *W. Kg.'s Pawn.*  How 's this?
    *B. Knight.*    No replications, you know me:
No doubt ere long you 'll have more company;
The bag is big enough, 't will hold us all.  319
        *Exeunt* [*B. Knight, W. Kg.'s Pawn,
          and B. Kt.'s Pawn.*]
    *W. Q. Pawn.*  I sue to thee, prithee be one of
    us!
Let my love win thee: thou hast done truth
    this day
And yesterday my honour noble service;
The best Pawn of our House could not tran-
    scend it.
    *B. Q. Pawn.*  My pity flam'd with zeal,
    especially                324
When I foresaw your marriage, then it mounted.
    *W. Q. Pawn.*  How! marriage?
    *B. Q. Pawn.*        That contaminating act
Would have spoil'd all your fortunes — a rape!
    God bless us!
    *W. Q. Pawn.*  Thou talk'st of marriage!
    *B. Q. Pawn.*       Yes, yes, you do marry;
I saw the man.
    *W. Q. Pawn.*  The man!        329
    *B. Q. Pawn.*  An absolute handsome gentle-
    man, a complete one, —
You 'll say so when you see him, — heir to
    three red hats,

Besides his general hopes in the Black
    House.
    *W. Q. Pawn.*  Why, sure thou 'rt much mis-
    taken for this man;
Why, I have promis'd single life to all my
    affections.               334
    *B. Q. Pawn.*  Promise you what you will, or
    I or all on 's,
There 's a Fate rules and overrules us all, me-
    thinks.
    *W. Q. Pawn.*  Why, how came you to see
    or know this mystery?
    *B. Q. Pawn.*  A magical glass I bought of an
    Egyptian,               338
Whose stone retains that speculative virtue,
Presented the man to me: your name brings
    him
As often as I use it; and methinks
I never have enough, person and postures
Are all so pleasing.
    *W. Q. Pawn.*  This is wondrous strange!
The faculties of soul are still the same;
I can feel no one motion tend that way.    345
    *B. Q. Pawn.*  We do not always feel our
    faith we live by,
Nor ever see our growth, yet both work up-
    ward.
    *W. Q. Pawn.*  'T was well applied; but may
    I see him too?
    *B. Q. Pawn.*  Surely you may, without all
    doubt or fear,
Observing the right use, as I was taught it, 350
Not looking back or questioning the spectre.
    *W. Q. Pawn.*  That 's no hard observation;
    trust it with me:
Is 't possible?  I long to see this man.
    *B. Q. Pawn.*  Pray follow me, then, and I 'll
    ease you instantly.            *Exeunt.*

### [SCENE II]

*Enter a Black Jesting Pawn*

    *B. J. Pawn.*  I would so fain take one of
    these White Pawns now!
I 'd make him do all under-drudgery,
Feed him with asses' milk crumb'd with goats'
    cheese,
And all the whitemeats could be devis'd for him;

*Enter a White Pawn*

So make him my white jennet when I prance it.
After the Black Knight's litter.
    *W. Pawn.*        And you would look then 6
Just like the devil striding o'er a nightmare
Made of a miller's daughter.
    *B. J. Pawn.*        A pox on you,

---

³¹⁴ **mazzard:** head   ³¹⁷ **replications:** replies   ³²⁷ **God . . . us:** ('bless us all' MS)   ³³⁰ **absolute:** perfectly   ³³⁹ **speculative:** having the power of vision   ³⁴⁵ **motion:** impulse   Sc. II (Not definitely located)   ³ **crumb'd:** thickened   ⁴ **whitemeats:** food made of milk, eggs, bread, etc.   ⁵ **So . . . prance it:** ('1 'd . . . pranc'd' MS)   **jennet:** small Spanish horse

Were you so near?  I 'm taken, 'like a black-
    bird
In the great snow, this White Pawn grinning
    over me.                                          10
  *W. Pawn.*  And now because I will not foul
    my clothes
Ever hereafter, for white quickly soils, you
    know —
  *B. J. Pawn.*  I prithee, get thee gone, then;
    I shall smut thee.
  *W. Pawn.*  Nay, I 'll put that to venture;
    now I have snapp'd thee,
Thou shalt do all the dirty drudgery          15
That slavery was e'er put to.
  *B. J. Pawn.*                I shall cozen you:
You may chance come and find your work un-
    done then,
For I 'm too proud to labour, — I 'll starve
    first;
I tell you that beforehand.
  *W. Pawn.*                I will fit you then
With a black whip, that shall not be behind-
    hand.                                           20
  *B. J. Pawn.*  Pugh, I have been us'd to
    whipping; I have whipp'd
Myself three mile out of town in a morning;
    and
I can fast a fortnight, and make all your meat
Stink and lie on your hands.
  *W. Pawn.*                      To prevent that,
Your food shall be blackberries, and upon
    gaudy-days                                     25
A pickled spider, cut out like an anchovis:
I 'm not to learn a monkey's ordinary.
Come, sir, will you frisk?

*Enter a Second Black Pawn*

  *Sec. B. Pawn.*  Soft, soft, you! you have no
Such bargain on 't, if you look well about you.
  *W. Pawn.*  By this hand,                     31
I am snapp'd too, a Black Pawn in the breech
    of me!
We three look like a bird-spit, a white chick
Between two russet woodcocks.
  *B. J. Pawn.*                I 'm glad of this!
  *W. Pawn.*  But you shall have but small
    cause, for I 'll firk you.                     35
  *Sec. B. Pawn.*  Then I 'll firk you again.
  *W. Pawn.*       And I 'll firk him again.
  *B. J. Pawn.*  Mass, here will be old firking!
    I shall have
The worst on 't; I can firk nobody.
We draw together now for all the world
Like three flies with one straw thorough their
    buttocks.                          *Exeunt.* 40

[SCENE III.  *A Chamber, with a large
Mirror*]

*Enter Black Queen's Pawn and White
Queen's Pawn*

  *B. Q. Pawn.*  This is the room he did appear
    to me in;
And, look you, this the magical glass that
    show'd him.
  *W. Q. Pawn.*  I find no motion yet: what
    should I think on 't?
A sudden fear invades me, a faint trembling,
Under this omen,                                    5
As is oft felt the panting of a turtle
Under a stroking hand.
  *B. Q. Pawn.*           That bodes good luck still,
Sign you shall change state speedily; for that
    trembling
Is always the first symptom of a bride.
For any vainer fears that may accompany     10
His apparition, by my truth to friendship,
I quit you of the least; never was object
More gracefully presented; the very air
Conspires to do him honour, and creates
Sweet vocal sounds, as if a bridegroom enter'd;
Which argues the blest harmony of your
    loves.                                         16
  *W. Q. Pawn.*  And will the using of my
    name produce him?
  *B. Q. Pawn.*  Nay, of yours only, else the
    wonder halted:
To clear you of that doubt, I 'll put the dif-
    ference
In practice, the first thing I do, and make    20
His invocation in the name of others.
  *W. Q. Pawn.*  'T will satisfy me much, that.
  *B. Q. Pawn.*                It shall be done. —

*The Invocation*

*Thou, whose gentle form and face
Fill'd lately this Egyptic glass,
By the imperious powerful name                  25
And the universal fame
Of the mighty Black-House Queen,
I conjure thee to be seen! —*

What, see you nothing yet?
  *W. Q. Pawn.*                Not any part:
Pray, try another.
  *B. Q. Pawn.*  You shall have your will. — 30

*I double my command and power,
And at the instant of this hour
Invoke thee in the White Queen's name,
With stay for time, and shape the same. —*

What see you yet?

----

¹⁴ **venture:** trial, chance  ²⁵ **gaudy-days:** days of festival  ²⁶ **anchovis:** anchovy  ²⁷ **ordinary:**
diet (*i.e.*, spiders)  ²⁸ **frisk:** move quickly  ³⁵ **firk:** beat  ³⁷ **old:** abundant  Sc. III. (The suggestion for this scene seems to come from Spenser, *Faerie Queene*, III. ii. 18 ff.)  ⁶ **turtle:** turtle-
dove

*W. Q. Pawn.* There 's nothing shows at all.
*B. Q. Pawn.* My truth reflects the clearer
then: now fix 36
And bless your fair eyes with your own for
ever. —

*Thou well-compos'd, by Fate's hand drawn*
*To enjoy the White Queen's Pawn,*
*Of whom thou shalt, by virtue met,* 40
*Many graceful issues get;*
*By the beauty of her fame,*
*By the whiteness of her name,*
*By her fair and fruitful love,*
*By her truth that mates the dove,* 45
*By the meekness of her mind,*
*By the softness of her kind,*
*By the lustre of her grace, —*
*By all these thou art summon'd to this place! —*

Hark, how the air, enchanted with your
praises 50
And his approach, those words to sweet notes
raises!

*Music: enter the Jesuit in rich attire, like an*
*apparition; presents himself before the glass;*
*then exit.*

*W. Q. Pawn.* O, let him stay a while! a little
longer!
*B. Q. Pawn.* That 's a good hearing.
*W. Q. Pawn.* If he be mine, why should he
part so soon?
*B. Q. Pawn.* Why, this is but the shadow of
yours. How do you? 55
*W. Q. Pawn.* O, I did ill to give consent to
see it!
What certainty is in our blood or state?
What we still write is blotted out by fate;
Our wills are like a cause that is law-toss'd,
What one court orders, is by another cross'd. 60
*B. Q. Pawn.* I find no fit place for this pas-
sion here,
'T is merely an intruder. He is a gentleman
Most wishfully compos'd; honour grows on
him,
And wealth pil'd up for him; h'as youth
enough, too,
And yet in the sobriety of his countenance 65
Grave as a tetrarch, which is gracious
In the eye of modest pleasure. Where 's the
emptiness?
What can you more request?
*W. Q. Pawn.* I do not know
What answer yet to make; it does require
A meeting 'twixt my fear and my desire. 70

*B. Q. Pawn.* [*Aside.*] She 's caught, and,
which is strange, by her most wronger.
*Exeunt.*

### Finit Actus Tertius.

### Incipit Quartus.

[ACT IV. SCENE I

*Field between the two Houses*]

*Enter Black Knight's Pawn meeting the Black*
*Bishop's Pawn richly accoutred*

*B. Kt.'s Pawn.* [*Aside.*] 'T is he, my cónfes-
sor; he might ha' pass'd me
Seven year together, had I not by chance
Advanc'd mine eye upon that letter'd hat-band,
The Jesuitical symbol to be known by,
Worn by the brave collegians with consent: 5
'T is a strange habit for a holy father,
A President of poverty especially;
But we, the sons and daughters of obedience,
Dare not once think awry, but must confess
ourselves
As humbly to the father of that feather, 10
Long spur, and poniard, as to the alb and altar,
And happy we 're so highly grac'd to attain
to 't. —
Holy and reverend!
*B. B. Pawn.* How! hast found me out?
*B. Kt.'s Pawn.* O sir, put on the sparkling'st
trim of glory,
Perfection will shine foremost; and I knew
you 15
By the catholical mark you wear about you,
The mark above your forehead.
*B. B. Pawn.* Are you grown
So ambitious in your observance? Well, your
business?
I have my game to follow.
*B. Kt.'s Pawn.* I have a worm
Follows me so, that I can follow no game: 20
The most faint-hearted pawn, if he could see
his play,
Might snap me up at pleasure. I desire, sir,
To be absolv'd: my conscience being at ease,
I could then with more courage play my game.
*B. B. Pawn.* 'T was a base fact.
*B. Kt.'s Pawn.* 'T was to a schismatic pawn.
sir. 25
*B. B. Pawn.* What 's that to the nobility of
revenge?
Suffices I have neither will nor power
To give you absolution for that violence.

---

**47 kind:** nature **53 hearing:** news **54 part:** depart **60 cross'd:** thwarted, denied **61 passion:**
sorrow, lament **62 merely:** wholly **66 tetrarch:** Roman provincial governor **3 hat-band:** (The
Jesuits were often disguised as gallants, but wore gold hat-bands inscribed with letters as identification
to each other.) **5 with consent:** by mutual agreement ('by consent' MS) **19 worm:** conscience
**24 play:** ('ply' MS)

Make your petition to the Penance-chamber:
If the tax-register relieve you in 't          30
By the Black Bishop's clemency, you have
    wrought out
A singular piece of favour with your money;
That 's all your refuge now.
    *B. Kt.'s Pawn.*          The sting shoots deeper.
                                            *Exit.*

*Enter White Queen's Pawn and Black Queen's
    Pawn*

    *B. B. Pawn.* Yonder 's my game, which, like
    a politic chess-master,
I must not seem to see.
    *W. Q. Pawn.*          O my heart!          35
    *B. Q. Pawn.* That 't is.
    *W. Q. Pawn.* The very self-same that the
    magical mirror
Presented lately to me.
    *B. Q. Pawn.*          And how like
A most regardless stranger he walks by,
Merely ignorant of his fate! You are not
    minded,                                   40
The principall'st part of him. What strange
    mysteries
Inscrutable love works by!
    *W. Q. Pawn.*          The time, you see,
Is not yet come.
    *B. Q. Pawn.* But 't is in our power now
To bring time nearer — knowledge is a mas-
    tery —
And make it observe us, and not we it.       45
    *W. Q. Pawn.* I would force nothing from its
    proper virtue;
Let time have his full course. I 'd rather die
The modest death of undiscover'd love
Than have heaven's least and lowest servant
    suffer,
Or in his motion receive check, for me.      50
How is my soul's growth alter'd! that single life,
The fittest garment that peace ever made for 't,
Is grown too strait, too stubborn, on the sudden.
    *B. Q. Pawn.* He comes this way again.
    *W. Q. Pawn.*          O, there 's a traitor
Leap'd from my heart into my cheek already,  55
That will betray all to his powerful eye,
If it but glance upon me!
    *B. Q. Pawn.*          By my verity,
Look, he 's pass'd by again, drown'd in neglect,
Without the prosperous hint of so much happi-
    ness
To look upon his fortunes! How close fate    60
Seals up the eye of human understanding,
Till, like the sun's flower, time and love un-
    closes it!
'T were pity he should dwell in ignorance longer.

    *W. Q. Pawn.* What will you do?
    *B. Q. Pawn.* Yes, die a bashful death, do,
And let the remedy pass by unus'd still:     65
You are chang'd enough already, an you'd
    look into it. —
Absolute sir, with your most noble pardon
For this my rude intrusion, I am bold
To bring the knowledge of a secret nearer
By many days, sir, than it would arrive      70
In its own proper revelation with you.
Pray, turn and fix: do you know yond noble
    goodness?
    *B. B. Pawn.* 'T is the first minute my eye
    bless'd me with her,
And clearly shows how much my knowledge
    wanted,
Not knowing her till now.
    *B. Q. Pawn.* She 's to be lik'd, then?    75
Pray, view advisedly: there is strong reason
That I 'm so bold to urge it; you must guess
The work concerns you nearer than you think
    for.
    *B. B. Pawn.* Her glory and the wonder of
    this secret
Puts a reciprocal amazement on me.           80
    *B. Q. Pawn.* And 't is not without worth:
    you two must be
Better acquainted.
    *B. B. Pawn.*          Is there cause, affinity,
Or any courteous help creation joys in,
To bring that forward?
    *B. Q. Pawn.*          Yes, yes, I can show you
The nearest way to that perfection           85
Of a most virtuous one that joy e'er found.
Pray, mark her once again, then follow me,
And I will show you her must be your wife, sir.
    *B. B. Pawn.* The mystery extends, or else
    creation
Has set that admirable piece before us       90
To choose our chaste delights by.
    *B. Q. Pawn.*          Please you follow, sir.
    *B. B. Pawn.* What art have you to put me
    on an object
And cannot get me off! 't is pain to part from 't.
                    *Exit [with Black Queen's Pawn].*
    *W. Q. Pawn.* If there prove no check in that
    magical glass,
But my proportion come as fair and full      95
Into his eye as his into mine lately,
Then I 'm confirm'd he is mine own for ever.

*Enter again [Black Queen's Pawn and
    Black Bishop's Pawn]*

    *B. B. Pawn.* The very self-same that the
    mirror bless'd me with,
From head to foot, the beauty and the habit! —

---

³³ **all your:** your only   ³⁴ **chess-master:** ('Chessner' Q 2)   ⁴⁰ **minded:** observed, in his mind
⁴⁴ **mastery:** power   ⁴⁵ **observe:** show attention to, obey   ⁴⁶ **proper:** natural   **virtue: nature,**
power   ⁷² **fix:** look   ⁷⁴ **wanted:** lacked   ⁹⁵ **proportion:** figure, appearance

Kept you this place still? did you not remove,
    lady?                                    100
*W. Q. Pawn.*  Not a foot farder, sir.
*B. B. Pawn.*              Is 't possible?
I would have sworn I 'd seen the substance
    yonder,
'T was to that lustre, to that life presented.
*W. Q. Pawn.*  E'en so was yours to me, sir.
*B. B. Pawn.*           Saw you mine?
*W. Q. Pawn.*  Perfectly clear; no sooner my
    name us'd                           105
But yours appear'd.
*B. B. Pawn.*  Just so did yours at mine now.
*B. Q. Pawn.*  Why stand you idle? will you
    let time cozen you,
Protracting time, of those delicious benefits
That fate hath mark'd to you? You modest pair
Of blushing gamesters, — and you, sir, the
    bashfull'st,                        110
I cannot flatter a foul fault in any, —
Can you be more than man and wife assign'd,
And by a power the most irrevocable?
Others, that be adventurers in delight,
May meet with crosses, shame, or separation,
Their fortunes hid, and the events lock'd
    from 'em:                        116
You know the mind of fate, you must be
    coupled.
*B. B. Pawn.*  She speaks but truth in this:
    I see no reason then
That we should miss the relish of this night,
But that we are both shamefac'd.
*W. Q. Pawn.*  How? this night, sir?  120
Did not I know you must be mine, and therein
Your privilege runs strong, for that loose motion
You never should be. Is it not my fortune
To match with a pure mind, then am I mis-
    erable.
The doves and all chaste-loving winged crea-
    tures                          125
Have their pairs fit, their desires justly mated;
Is woman more unfortunate, a virgin,
The May of woman? Fate, that has ordain'd,
    sir,
We should be man and wife, has not given
    warrant
For any act of knowledge till we are so.    130
*B. B. Pawn.*  Tender-ey'd modesty, how it
    grieves at this! —
I 'm as far off, for all this strange imposture,
As at first interview. Where lies our game
    now?
You know I cannot marry by my order.
*B. Q. Pawn.*  I know you cannot, sir; yet
    you may venture               135
Upon a contract.

*B. B. Pawn.*  Ha!
*B. Q. Pawn.*          Surely you may, sir,
Without all question, so far without danger,
Or any stain to your vow; and that may take
    her:
Nay, do 't with speed; she 'll think you mean
    the better, too.
*B. B. Pawn.*  Be not so lavish of that blessed
    spring;                       140
Y'ave wasted that upon a cold occasion now
Would wash a sinful soul white. By our love-
    joys,
That motion shall ne'er light upon my tongue
    more
Till we 're contracted; then, I hope, y' are mine.
*W. Q. Pawn.*  In all just duty ever.
*B. Q. Pawn.*  Then? do you question it? 145
Pish! then y' are man and wife, all but church-
    ceremony:
Pray, let 's see that done first; she shall do
    reason then. —
Now I 'll enjoy the sport, and cozen you both:
My blood's game is the wages I have work'd for.
                         *Exeunt.* [*Aside.*]

        [SCENE II. *An Apartment in the*
                *Black House*]

    *Enter Black Knight with his Pawn*

*B. Knight.*  Pawn, I have spoke to the Fat
    Bishop for thee;
I 'll get thee absolution from his own mouth.
Reach me my chair of ease, my chair of cozen-
    age;
Seven thousand pound in women, reach me
    that:
I love a' life to sit upon a bank          5
Of heretic gold. O, soft and gently, sirrah!
There 's a foul flaw in the bottom of my drum,
    Pawn:
I ne'er shall make sound soldier, but sound
    treacher
With any he in Europe. How now? qualm?
Thou hast the puking'st soul that e'er I met
    with;                        10
It cannot bear one suckling villainy:
Mine can digest a monster without crudity,
A sin as weighty as an elephant,
And never wamble for 't.
*B. Kt.'s Pawn.*  Ay, you have been us'd to
    it, sir;
That 's a great help. The swallow of my
    conscience                 15
Has but a narrow passage; you must think yet
It lies in the penitent pipe, and will not down:
If I had got seven thousand pound by offices,

---

    102 **yonder:** *i.e.*, in the mirror   108 **Protracting:** delaying   111 **flatter:** condone for purposes of flat-
tery   122 **motion:** proposal   131 **grieves:** ('gives' MS)   149 **blood:** passion   5 **a' life:** as my life, exceedingly   8 **treacher:** deceiver   12 **crudity:** indigestion   14 **wamble:** rumble   15 **swallow:** throat

And gull'd down that, the bore would have been
    bigger.
*B. Knight.*  Nay, if thou prov'st facetious,
    I shall hug thee.                                    20
Can a soft, rear, poor-poach'd iniquity
So ride upon thy conscience? I 'm asham'd of
    thee.
Hadst thou betray'd the White House to the
    Black,
Beggar'd a kingdom by dissimulation,
Unjointed the fair frame of peace and traffic, 25
Poison'd allegiance, set faith back, and wrought
Women's soft souls e'en up to masculine malice
To pursue truth to death, if the cause rous'd
    'em,
That stares and parrots are first taught to
    curse thee —
    *B. Kt.'s Pawn.*  Ay, marry, sir, here 's
    swapping sins indeed!                                30
    *B. Knight.*  All these, and ten times trebled,
    has this brain
Been parent to; they are my offsprings all.
    *B. Kt.'s Pawn.*  A goodly brood!
    *B. Knight.*            Yet I can jest as lightly,
Laugh and tell stirring stories to court-madams,
Daughters of my seducement, with alacrity 35
As high and hearty as youth's time of innocence
That never knew a sin to shape a sorrow by:
I feel no tempest, not a leaf wind-stirring
To shake a fault; my conscience is becalm'd
    rather.
    *B. Kt.'s Pawn.*  I 'm sure there is a whirl-
    wind huffs in mine, sir.                             40
    *B. Knight.*  Sirrah, I have sold the groom-o'-
    the-stool six times,
And receiv'd money of six several ladies
Ambitious to take place of baronets' wives:
To three old mummy matrons I have promis'd
The mothership o' the maids: I have taught
    our friends, too,                                    45
To convey White-House gold to our Black
    Kingdom
In cold bak'd pasties, and so cozen searchers:
For venting hallow'd oil, beads, medals, pardons,
Pictures, Veronica's heads in private presses,
That 's done by one i' th' habit of a pedlar; 50
Letters convey'd in rolls, tobacco-balls:
When a restraint comes, by my politic counsel,
Some of our Jesuits turn gentlemen-ushers,
Some falconers, some park-keepers, and some
    huntsmen;
One took the shape of an old lady's cook
    once,                                                55

And despatch'd two chares on a Sunday
    morning,
The altar and the dresser. Pray, what use
Put I my summer-recreation to,
But more to inform my knowledge in the state
And strength of the White Kingdom?  No
    fortification,                                       60
Haven, creek, landing-place about the White
    coast,
But I got draft and platform; learn'd the depth
Of all their channels, knowledge of all sands,
Shelves, rocks, and rivers for invasion proper'st;
A catalogue of all the navy royal,                      65
The burden of the ships, the brassy murderers,
The number of the men, to what cape bound:
Again, for the discovery of the inlands,
Never a shire but the state better known
To me than to her best inhabitants;                     70
What power of men and horse, gentry's rev-
    énues,
Who well affected to our side, who ill,
Who neither well nor ill, all the neutrality:
Thirty-eight thousand souls have been seduc'd,
    Pawn,
Since the jails vomited with the pill I gave
    'em.                                                 75
    *B. Kt.'s Pawn.*  Sure, you put oil of toad
    into that physic, sir.
    *B. Knight.*  I 'm now about a masterpiece of
    play
To entrap the White Knight, and with false
    allurements
Entice him to the Black House, — more will
    follow, —
Whilst our Fat Bishop sets upon the Queen; 80
Then will our game lie sweetly.

*Enter Fat Bishop [with a book]*

    *B. Kt.'s Pawn.*            He 's come now, sir.
    *F. Bishop.*  Here 's *Taxa Pœnitentiaria*,
    Knight,
The Book of General Pardons, of all prices:
I have been searching for his sin this half hour,
And cannot light upon 't.
    *B. Knight.*  That 's strange; let me see it. 85
    *B. Kt.'s Pawn.*  Pawn wretched that I am!
    has my rage done that
There is no precedent of pardon for?
    *B. Knight.*  [*Reads.*]  "For wilful murder
    thirteen pound four shillings
And sixpence," — that 's reasonable cheap, —
    "For killing,
Killing, killing killing, killing, killing" —           90

---

**19 gull'd:** swallowed    **21 rear:** underdone    **29 stares:** starlings    **30 swapping:** huge    **33 lightly:**
('titelie' MS)        **40 huffs:** blows, puffs        **41 groom . . . stool:** menial officer in royal household
**44 mummy:** ancient, dried-up        **45 mothership . . . maids:** post of supervisor of maids-in-waiting
**48 venting:** selling    **56 chares:** jobs    **62 platform:** plan    **64 Shelves:** reefs    **66 brassy murderers:**
guns    **70 her best:** ('the breast' MS)    **72 affected:** disposed    **82 Taxa:** *Taxæ Sacræ Pœnitentiariæ
Apostolicæ*, which assigned fees for absolution for all varieties of sins

Why, here 's nothing but killing, Bishop, of this
 side.
 *F. Bishop.* Turn the sheet over, and you
 shall find adultery
And other trivial sins.
 *B. Knight.*   Adultery? O,
I 'm in 't now. — [*Reads.*] "For adultery a
 couple
Of shillings, and for fornication fivepence," —
Mass, those are two good pennyworths! I
 cannot        96
See how a man can mend himself. — "For lying
With mother, sister, and daughter," — ay,
 marry, sir, —
"Thirty-three pound three shillings, three-
 pence," —
The sin's gradation right, paid all in threes too.
 *F. Bishop.* You have read the story of that
 monster, sir,      101
That got his daughter, sister, and his wife
Of his own mother?
 *B. Knight.* [*Reads.*] "Simony, nine pound."
 *F. Bishop.* They may thank me for that;
 't was nineteen
Before I came;
   I have mitigated many of the sums. 105
 *B. Knight.* [*Reads.*] "Sodomy, sixpence" —
you should put that sum
Ever on the backside of your book, Bishop.
 *F. Bishop.* There 's few on 's very forward,
 sir.
 *B. Knight.* What 's here, sir? [*Reads.*]
'Two old precedents of encouragement" — 110
 *F. Bishop.* Ay, those are ancient notes.
 *B. Knight.* [*Reads.*] "Given, as a gratuity,
for the killing of an heretical prince with a
poison'd knife, ducats five thousand."
 *F. Bishop.* True, sir; that was paid. 115
 *B. Knight.* [*Reads.*] "Promised also to Doc-·
tor Lopez for poisoning the maiden queen of the
White Kingdom, ducats twenty thousand;
which said sum was afterwards given as a meri-
torious alms to the nunnery at Lisbon, [120
having at this present ten thousand pound more
at use in the town-house of Antwerp."
 *B. Kt.'s Pawn.* What 's all this to my conscience, worthy holiness?
I sue for pardon; I have brought money with
me.
 *F. Bishop.* You must depart; you see there
 is no precedent     125
Of any price or pardon for your fact.
 *B. Kt.'s Pawn.* Most miserable! Are fouler
 sins remitted,
Killing, nay, wilful murder?

 *F. Bishop.*   True, there 's instance:
Were you to kill him, I would pardon you;
There 's precedent for that, and price set
 down,        130
But none for gelding.
 *B. Kt.'s Pawn.* I have pick'd out under-
standing now for ever
Out of that cabalistic bloody riddle:
I 'll make away all my estate, and kill him,
And by that act obtain full absolution. 135
          *Exit.*

    *Enter Black King*

 *B. King.* Why, Bishop, Knight, where 's
 your removes, your traps?
Stand you now idle in the heat of game?
 *B. Knight.* My life for yours, Black sov-
 ereign, the game 's ours;
I have wrought underhand for the White
 Knight
And his brave Duke, and find 'em coming
 both.        140
 *F. Bishop.* Then for their sanctimonious
 Queen's surprisal,
In this state-puzzle and distracted hurry,
Trust my arch-subtlety with.
 *B. King.*   O eagle pride!
Never was game more hopeful of our side.
    [*Exeunt B. King and F. Bishop.*]
 *B. Knight.* If Bishop Bull-beef be not
 snapp'd next bout,    145
As the men stand, I 'll never trust art more.
          *Exit.*

     [SCENE III]

    [*Dumb Show*]

*Enter Black Queen's Pawn, as conducting the
White to a chamber; then, fetching in the
Black Bishop's Pawn, the Jesuit, conveys
him to another, puts out the light, and she
follows.*

[SCENE IV. *Field between the two Houses*]

  *Enter White Knight and White Duke*

 *W. Knight.* True, noble Duke, fair virtue's
 most endear'd one;
Let us prevent their rank insinuation
With truth of cause and courage, meet their
 plots
With confident goodness that shall strike 'em
 grovelling.
 *W. Duke.* Sir, all the gins, traps, and alluring snares,     5

 ⁹⁷ **mend himself:** make a better bargain ¹⁰¹ **the story:** (See the *Heptameron*, novel 30.) ¹¹³ **heretical prince:** Henri III of France ¹¹⁷ **Lopez:** Portuguese physician to Queen Elizabeth, executed (1594)
for accepting a bribe from Spain to kill her ¹²⁶ **fact:** deed ¹²⁸ **instance:** precedent (for that)
² **prevent:** anticipate

The devil has been at work since eighty-eight
on,
Are laid for the great hope of this game only.
   *W. Knight.* Why, the more noble will
   truth's triumph be:
When they have wound about our constant
   courages
The glittering'st serpent that e'er falsehood fash-
ion'd,                                                    10
And glorying most in his resplendent poisons,
Just heaven can find a bolt to bruise his
   head.
   *W. Duke.* Look, would you see destruction
   lie a-sunning?

       *Enter Black Knight*

In yonder smile sit blood and treachery bask-
   ing;
In that perfidious model of face-falsehood     15
Hell is drawn grinning.
   *W. Knight.*               What a pain it is
For truth to feign a little!
   *B. Knight.*               O fair knight,
The rising glory of that House of Candour,
Have I so many protestations lost,
Lost, lost, quite lost? Am I not worth your
   confidence?                                          20
I that have vow'd the faculties of soul,
Life, spirit, and brain, to your sweet game of
   youth,
Your noble, fruitful game? Can you mis-
   trust
Any foul play in me, that have been ever
The most submiss observer of your virtues, 25
And no way tainted with ambition,
Save only to be thought your first admirer?
How often have I chang'd, for your delight,
The royal presentation of my place
Into a mimic jester, and become,              30
For your sake and th' expulsion of sad thoughts,
Of a grave state-sire a light son of pastime,
Made three-score years a tomboy, a mere wan-
   ton!
I 'll tell you what I told a Savoy dame once,
New-wed, high, plump, and lusting for an
   issue:                                                35
Within the year I promis'd her a child,
If she could stride over Saint Rumbant's
   breeches,
A relique kept at Mechlin: the next morning
One of my followers' old hose was convey'd
Into her chamber, where she tried the feat;   40
By that, and a court-friend, after grew great.
   *W. Knight.* Why, who could be without
   thee?

   *B. Knight.*               I will change
To any shape to please you; and my aim
Has been to win your love in all this game.
   *W. Knight.* Thou hast it nobly, and we
   long to see                                           45
The Black-House pleasure, state, and dignity.
   *B. Knight.* Of honour you 'll so surfeit and
   delight,
You 'll ne'er desire again to see the White.
                           *Exeunt.*

       *Enter White Queen*

   *W. Queen.* My love, my hope, my dearest!
   O, he 's gone,
Ensnar'd, entrapp'd, surpris'd amongst the
   Black ones!                                           50
I never felt extremity like this:
Thick darkness dwells upon this hour; integ-
   rity,
Like one of heaven's bright luminaries, now
By error's dullest element interpos'd,
Suffers a black eclipse. I never was           55
More sick of love than now I am of horror:
I shall be taken; the game 's lost, I 'm set
   upon! —

       *Enter Fat Bishop*

O, 't is the turncoat Bishop, having watch'd
The advantage of his play, comes now to seize
   on me!
O, I 'm hard beset, distress'd most miserably! 60
   *F. Bishop.* 'T is vain to stir; remove which
   way you can,
I take you now; this is the time we 've hop'd
   for:
Queen, you must down.
   *W. Queen.*              No rescue, no deliverance!
   *F. Bishop.* The Black King's blood burns
   for thy prostitution,
And nothing but the spring of thy chaste virtue
Can cool his inflammation; instantly           66

       *Enter White Bishop*

He dies upon a pleurisy of luxury,
If he deflower thee not.
   *W. Queen.*              O strait of misery!
   *W. Bishop.* And is your holiness his divine
   procurer?
   *F. Bishop.* The devil 's in 't, I 'm taken by
   a ringdove!                                           70
Where stood this Bishop that I saw him not?
   *W. Bishop.* You were so ambitious you
   look'd over me!
You aim'd at no less person than the Queen,
The glory of the game; if she were won,
The way were open to the master-check.         75

---

   ¹¹ **his:** ('their' MS)   ²⁹ **presentation:** manner of appearing   ³¹ (Not in MS)   ³⁶⁻³⁷ (The relics
of St. Romold were popularly believed to have the power of performing this service.)   ⁴⁹ **he 's gone:**
(a reference to the journey of Prince Charles and Buckingham to Madrid in 1623)   ⁶² **we 've:** ('we
ever' MS)   ⁶⁷ **pleurisy:** excess   ⁷⁵ **master-check:** checkmate

*Enter White King*

Which, look you, he or his lives to give you;
Honour and virtue guide him in his station!
  *W. Queen.* O my safe sanctuary!
  *W. King.*              Let heaven's blessings
Be mine no longer than I am thy sure one!
The dove's house is not safer in the rock    80
Than thou in my firm bosom.
  *W. Queen.*              I am blest in 't.
  *W. King.* Is it that lump of rank ingratitude,
Swell'd with the poison of hypocrisy?
Could he be so malicious, has partaken
Of the sweet fertile blessings of our kingdom? —
Bishop, thou 'st done our White House gra-
  cious service,                            86
And worthy the fair reverence of thy place. —
For thee, Black Holiness, that work'st out thy
  death
As the blind mole, the proper'st son of earth,
Who, in the casting his ambitious hills up,   90
Is often taken and destroy'd i' the midst
Of his advanced work; 't were well with thee
If, like that verminous labourer, which thou
  imitat'st
In hills of pride and malice, when death puts
  thee up,
The silent grave might prove thy bag for ever;
No deeper pit than that: for thy vain hope  96
Of the White Knight and his most firm assistant,
Two princely pieces, which I know thy thoughts
Give lost for ever now, my strong assurance
Of their fix'd virtues, could you let in seas  100
Of populous untruths against that fort,
'T would burst the proudest billows.
  *W. Queen.*          My fear 's past then.
  *W. King.* Fear? you were never guilty of an
  injury
To goodness, but in that.
  *W. Queen.*         It stay'd not with me, sir.
  *W. King.* It was too much if it usurp'd a
  thought:                              105
Place a good guard there.
  *W. Queen.*         Confidence is set, sir.
  *W. King.* Take that prize hence; go, rev-
  erend of men,
Put covetousness into the bag again.
  *F. Bishop.* The bag had need be sound, or
  it goes to wrack;
Sin and my weight will make a strong one
  crack.                     *[Exeunt.]* 110

## *Finit Actus Quartus.*

*Incipit Quintus et Ultimus.*

[ACT V.  SCENE I

*Before the Black House*]

*Music.* [*Black Bishop's Pawn discovered above.*]
  *Enter the Black Knight in his litter: calls*

  *B. Knight.* Hold, hold!
Is the Black Bishop's Pawn, the Jesuit,
Planted above for his concise oration?
  *B. B. Pawn.* Ecce triumphante me fixum
  Cæsaris arce!
  *B. Knight.* Art there, my holy boy? sirrah,
  Bishop Tumbrel                       5
Is snapp'd in the bag by this time.
  *B. B. Pawn.* Hæretici pereant sic!
  *B. Knight.* All Latin! Sure the oration has
  infected him.
Away, make haste, they 're coming.

*Hautboys. Enter Black King, [Black] Queen,*
  [*Black*] *Duke, meeting the White Knight*
  *and Duke: Black Bishop's Pawn from above*
  *entertains him* [*i.e., White Knight*] *with*
  *this Latin oration.*

### *The Oration*

  *B. B. Pawn.* Si quid mortalibus unquam [10
oculis hilarem et gratum aperuit diem, si quid
peramantibus amicorum animis gaudium attu-
lit peperitve lætitiam, Eques Candidissime,
prælucentissime, felicem profecto tuum a [14
Domo Candoris ad Domum Nigritudinis ac-
cessum promisisse, peperisse, attulisse fatemur:
omnes adventus tui conflagrantissimi, omni qua
possumus lætitia, gaudio, congratulatione, ac-
clamatione, animis observantissimis, affecti-
bus devotissimis, obsequiis venerabundis, te [20
sospitem congratulamur!
  *B. King.* Sir, in this short congratulatory
  speech
You may conceive how the whole House affects you.
  *B. Knight.* The colleges and sanctimonious
  seed-plots.
  *W. Knight.* 'T is clear and so acknowledg'd,
  royal sir.                              25
  *B. King.* What honours, pleasures, rarities,
  delights,
Your noble thought can think —
  *B. Queen.*      Your fair eye fix on,

---

**89 proper'st:** most veritable     Sc. I (This scene represents the journey to Madrid; cf. IV. iv,
V. iii.)    **4** Behold me fixed on Cæsar's triumphal arch!    **7** May (all) heretics perish so!    **10–21** If
anything ever to mortal eyes opened a merry and welcome day, if anything ever brought joy to the
most loving souls of friends, or begat happiness, most white and shining Knight, assuredly we confess that your happy arrival from the White House to the Black House has promised, has begotten,
has brought it. All of us, most excited by your coming, with all gladness, joy, congratulation, and
acclamation, with most respectful souls, most devoted feelings, and reverent allegiance, congratulate
your safety.

That 's comprehended in the spacious circle
Of our Black Kingdom, they 're your servants
  all.                                                        30
  *W. Knight.*   How amply you endear us!
  *W. Duke.*                   They are favours
That equally enrich the royal giver,
As the receiver, in the free donation.
       *Music. An altar discovered and stat-*
        *ues, with a song.*
  *B. Knight.*   Hark, to enlarge your welcome,
    from all parts
Is heard sweet-sounding airs! abstruse things
  open                                                       35
Of voluntary freeness; and yond altar,
The seat of adoration, seems to adore
The virtues you bring with you.
  *W. Knight.*                     There 's a taste
Of the old vessel still, the erroneous relish.

Song

*Wonder work some strange delight,*            40
  *(This place was never yet without),*
*To welcome the fair White-House Knight,*
  *And to bring our hopes about!*
*May from the altar flames aspire,*
*Those tapers set themselves afire!*           45
*May senseless things our joys approve,*
*And those brazen statues move,*
*Quicken'd by some power above,*
*Or what more strange, to show our love!*

*The images move in a dance.*

  *B. Knight.*   A happy omen waits upon this
  hour;                                                      50
All move portentously the right-hand way.
  *B. King.*   Come, let 's set free all the most
  choice delights,
That ever adorned days or quicken'd nights.
                    *Exeunt.*

[SCENE II.   *Field between the two Houses*]

*Enter White Queen's Pawn*

  *W. Q. Pawn.*   I see 't was but a trial of my
  love now;
H'as a more modest mind, and in that virtue
Most worthily has fate provided for me.

*Enter Jesuit*

Ha! 't is the bad man in the reverend habit:
Dares he be seen again, traitor to holiness,   5
O marble-fronted impudence! and knows
How much he has wrong'd me?   I 'm asham'd
  he blushes not.
  *B. B. Pawn.*   Are you yet stor'd with any
  woman's pity?
Are you the mistress of so much devotion,

Kindness, and charity, as to bestow           10
An alms of love on your poor sufferer yet
For your sake only?
  *W. Q. Pawn.*   Sir, for the reverence and
  respect you ought
To give to sanctity, though none to me,
In being her servant vow'd and wear her livery,
If I might counsel you, you should ne'er
  speak                                                      16
The language of unchasteness in that habit;
You would not think how ill it does with you.
The world 's a stage on which all parts are
  play'd:
You 'd think it most absurd to have a devil 20
Presented there not in a devil's shape,
Or, wanting one, to send him out in yours;
You 'd rail at that for an absurdity
No college e'er committed. For decorum's sake,
  then,
For pity's cause, for sacred virtue's honour,   25
If you 'll persist still in your devil's part,
Present him as you should do, and let one
That carries up the goodness of the play
Come in that habit, and I 'll speak with him;
Then will the parts be fitted, and the specta-
  tors                                                       30
Know which is which: they must have cunning
  judgments
To find it else, for such a one as you
Is able to deceive a mighty audience;
Nay, those you have seduc'd, if there be any
In the assembly, if they see what manner       35
You play your game with me, they cannot love
  you.
Is there so little hope of you, to smile, sir?
  *B. B. Pawn.*   Yes, at your fears, at the igno-
  rance of your power,
The little use you make of time, youth, fortune,
Knowing you have a husband for lust's shelter,
You dare not yet make bold with a friend's
  comfort;                                                   41
This is the plague of weakness.
  *W. Q. Pawn.*                   So hot burning!
The syllables of sin fly from his lips
As if the letter came new-cast from hell.
  *B. B. Pawn.*   Well, setting aside the dish
  you loathe so much,                                        45
Which has been heartily tasted by your betters,
I come to marry you to the gentleman
That last enjoy'd you: 'hope that pleases you;
There 's no immodest relish in that office.
  *W. Q. Pawn.* [*Aside.*]   Strange of all others
  he should light on him                                     50
To tie that holy knot that sought to undo me! —
Were you requested to perform that business.
  sir?

---

<sup>29</sup> **comprehended:** included   <sup>46</sup> **approve:** put to proof, feel   <sup>48</sup> **Quicken'd:** brought to rife
<sup>49</sup> **what:** something, anything   <sup>18</sup> **does with:** suits   <sup>28</sup> **carries up:** represents   <sup>31</sup> **they . . . judg-
ments:** ('it must be strange cunning' MS)

*B. B. Pawn.* I name you a sure token.
*W. Q. Pawn.*                          As for that, sir,
Now y' are most welcome; and my fair hope 's of you,
You 'll never break the sacred knot you tie once          55
With any lewd solicitings hereafter.
   *B. B. Pawn.* But all the craft 's in getting of it knit:
You 're all on fire to make your cozening market.
I am the marrier and the man — do you know me?
Do you know me, nice iniquity, strict luxury, 60
And holy whoredom? — that would clap on marriage
With all hot speed to solder up your game:
See what a scourge fate hath provided for thee!
You were a maid; swear still, y' are no worse now,
I left you as I found you: have I startled you?
I am quit with you now for my discovery,   66
Your outcries, and your cunnings: farewell, brokage!
   *W. Q. Pawn.* Nay, stay, and hear me but give thanks a little,
If your ear can endure a work so gracious;
Then you may take your pleasure.
   *B. B. Pawn.*          I have done that. 70
   *W. Q. Pawn.* That power, that hath preserv'd me from this devil —
   *B. B. Pawn.* How?
   *W. Q. Pawn.* This that may challenge the chief chair in hell,
And sit above his master —
   *B. B. Pawn.*          Bring in merit.
   *W. Q. Pawn.* That suffered'st him, through blind lust, to be led          75
Last night to the action of some common bed —
   *B. Q. Pawn. (Intus.)* Not over-common, neither.
   *B. B. Pawn.* Ha, what voice is that?
   *W. Q. Pawn.* Of virgins be thou ever honoured! —
Now you may go; you hear I have given thanks, sir.
   *B. B. Pawn.* Here 's a strange game! Did not I lie with you?          81
   *B. Q. Pawn. (Intus.)* No.
   *B. B. Pawn.* What a devil art thou?
   *W. Q. Pawn.* I will not answer you, sir,
After thanksgiving.
   *B. B. Pawn.* Why, you made promise to me          85
After the contract.
   *B. Q. Pawn. (Intus.)* Yes.
   *B. B. Pawn.*          A pox confound thee!

I speak not to thee — and you were prepar'd for 't,
And set your joys more high —
   *B. Q. Pawn. (Intus.)* Than you could reach, sir.
   *B. B. Pawn.* Light, 't is a bawdy voice; I 'll slit the throat on 't!

*Enter Black Queen's Pawn*

   *B. Q. Pawn.* What, offer violence to your bedfellow?          90
To one that works so kindly without rape?
   *B. B. Pawn.*          My bedfellow?
   *B. Q. Pawn.* Do you plant your scorn against me?
Why, when I was probationer at Brussels,
That engine was not known; then adoration
Fill'd up the place, and wonder was in fashion:
Is 't turn'd to the wild seed of contempt so soon?          96
Can five years stamp a bawd? Pray, look upon me,
I have youth enough to take it: 't is no more
Since you were chief agent for the transportation
Of ladies' daughters, if you be remember'd: 100
Some of their portions I could name; who purs'd 'em, too:
They were soon dispossess'd of worldly cares
That came into your fingers.
   *B. B. Pawn.*          Shall I hear her?
   *B. Q. Pawn.* Holy derision, yes, till thy ear swells
With thy own venom, thy profane life's vomit:
Whose niece was she you poison'd, with child twice,          106
Then gave her out possess'd with a foul spirit,
When 't was indeed your bastard?
   *B. B. Pawn.*          I am taken
In mine own toils!

*Enter White Bishop's Pawn and*
*White Queen*

   *W. B. Pawn.* Yes, and 't is just you should be.
   *W. Queen.* And thou, lewd Pawn, the shame of womanhood!          110
   *B. B. Pawn.* I 'm lost of all hands!
   *B. Q. Pawn.*          And I cannot feel
The weight of my perdition; now he 's taken,
'T 'as not the burden of a grasshopper.
   *B. B. Pawn.* Thou whore of order, cockatrice *in voto!*

*Enter Black Knight's Pawn*

   *B. Kt.'s Pawn.* Yond 's the White Bishop's Pawn; have at his heart now.          115
   *W. Q. Pawn.* Hold, monster-impudence! would'st thou heap a murder

---

   ⁶⁷ **brokage:** trickery   ⁷⁷ **Intus:** within   ¹¹³ **burden:** weight   ¹¹⁴ **cockatrice:** harlot

On thy first foul attempt? O merciless blood-
hound,
'T is time that thou wert taken!
   *B. Kt.'s Pawn.*       Death! prevented!
   *W. Q. Pawn.*  For thy sake and yond part-
ner in thy shame,
I 'll never know man farder than by name. 120
                     *Exeunt.*

   [SCENE III.  *In the Black House*]

*Enter Black King, [Black] Queen, [Black]
Duke, Black Knight, [Black Bishop], with
the White Knight and his Duke*

   *W. Knight.*  Y'ave both enrich'd my knowl-
edge, royal sir,
And my content together.
   *B. King.*          'Stead of riot
We set you only welcome: surfeit is
A thing that 's seldom heard of in these parts.
   *W. Knight.*  I hear of the more virtue when
I miss on 't.                   5
   *B. Knight.*  We do not use to bury in our
bellies
Two hundred thousand ducats, and then boast
on 't;
Or exercise the old Roman painful idleness
With care of fetching fishes far from home,
The golden-headed coracine out of Egypt,  10
The salpa from Eleusis, or the pelamis,
Which some call summer-whiting, from Chal-
cedon,
Salmons from Aquitaine, helops from Rhodes,
Cockles from Chios, frank'd and fatted up
With far and sapa, flour and cocted wine;  15
We cram no birds, nor, Epicurean-like,
Enclose some creeks of the sea, as Sergius
Crata did,
He that invented the first stews for oysters
And other sea-fish, who, beside the pleasure of
his
Own throat, got large revénues by th' inven-
tion,                        20
Whose fat example the nobility follow'd;
Nor do we imitate that arch-gormandizer
With two-and-twenty courses at one dinner,
And, betwixt every course, he and his guess
Wash'd and us'd women, then sat down and
strengthen'd,                25
Lust swimming in their dishes, which no sooner
Was tasted but was ready to be vented.
   *W. Knight.*  Most impious epicures!

   *B. Knight.*         We commend rather,
Of two extremes, the parsimony of Pertinax,
Who had half-lettuces set up to serve again; 30
Or his successor Julian, that would make
Three meals of a lean hare, and often sup
With a green fig and wipe his beard, as we can,
The old bewailers of excess in those days
Complain'd there was more coin bid for a cook
Than for a war-horse; but now cooks are
purchas'd                 36
After the rate of triumphs, and some dishes
After the rate of cooks; which must needs make
Some of your White-House gormandizers,
'specially
Your wealthy, plump plebeians, like the hogs
Which Scaliger cites, that could not move for
fat,                       41
So insensible of either prick or goad,
That mice made holes to needle in their but-
tocks,
And they ne'er felt 'em. There was once a
ruler,
Cyrene's governor, chok'd with his own paunch;
Which death fat Sanctius, King of Castile,
fearing,                46
Through his infinite mass of belly, rather chose
To be kill'd suddenly by a pernicious herb
Taken to make him lean, which old Corduba,
King of Morocco, counsell'd his fear to,  50
Than he would hazard to be stunk to death,
As that huge cormorant that was chok'd before
him.
   *W. Knight.*  Well, you 're as sound a spokes-
man, sir, for parsimony,
Clean abstinence, and scarce one meal a day,
As ever spake with tongue.
   *B. King.*         Censure him mildly, sir; 55
'T was but to find discourse.
   *B. Queen.*       He 'll raise 't of any thing.
   *W. Knight.*  I shall be half afraid to feed
hereafter.
   *W. Duke.*  Or I, beshrew my heart, for I fear
fatness,
The fog of fatness, as I fear a dragon:
The comeliness I wish for, that 's as glorious. 60
   *W. Knight.*  Your course is wondrous strict:
I should transgress, sure,
Were I to change my side, as you have
wrought me.
   *B. Knight.*  How you misprize! this is not
meant to you-ward:
You that are wound up to the height of feeding

---

² riot: profligacy    ¹⁴ frank'd: stuffed    ¹⁵ far: flour    sapa: boiled wine    cocted: boiled
¹⁷ Crata: (The proper classical form is "Orata.")    ¹⁸ stews: breeding beds    ²⁴ guess: guests
²⁷ vented: emitted    ³¹ Julian: Didius Julianus, successor to Pertinax, here confused with the abste-
mious Julian the Apostate    ³⁷ triumphs: public shows    ⁴³ needle: nestle    ⁵³⁻⁵⁵ Well . . . tongue:
(a reference to the niggardly entertainment offered to Charles and Buckingham at Madrid)    ⁵⁶ raise 't:
('rayse' MS; 'talke' Q 2)    ⁶² wrought me: impelled me ('much wrought me to it' MS)    ⁶³ misprize:
misunderstand

By clime and custom, are dispens'd withal; 65
You may eat kid, cabrito, calf, and tons,
Eat and eat every day, twice, if you please;
Nay, the frank'd hen, fatten'd with milk and
corn,
A riot which the inhabitants of Delos 69
Were first inventors of, or the cramm'd cockle.
   *W. Knight.* Well, for the food I 'm happily
resolv'd on;
But for the diet of my disposition,
There comes a trouble; you will hardly find
Food to please that.
   *B. Knight.* It must be a strange nature
We cannot find a dish for, having Policy, 75
The master-cook of Christendom, to dress it:
Pray, name your nature's diet.
   *W. Knight.*            The first mess
Is hot ambition.
   *B. Knight.* That 's but serv'd in puff-paste;
Alas, the meanest of our cardinals' cooks
Can dress that dinner: your ambition, sir, 80
Can fetch no farder compass than the world?
   *W. Knight.* That 's certain, sir.
   *B. Knight.*       We 're about that already;
And in the large feast of our vast ambition
We count but the White Kingdom, whence you
come from,
The garden for our cook to pick his salads; 85
The food 's lean France, larded with Ger-
many;
Before which comes the grave, chaste signiory
Of Venice, serv'd in, capon-like, in white broth;
From our chief oven, Italy, the bake-meats;
Savoy the salt, Geneva the chipp'd manchet; 90
Below the salt the Netherlands are plac'd,
A common dish at lower end o' the table,
For meaner pride to fall to: for our second
course,
A spit of Portugals serv'd in for plovers;
Indians and Moors for blackbirds: all this
while 95
Holland stands ready-melted to make sauce
On all occasions: when the voider comes,
And with such cheer our cramm'd hopes we
suffice,
Zealand says grace for fashion; then we rise.
   *W. Knight.* Here 's meat enough, o' con-
science, for ambition! 100
   *B. Knight.* If there be any want, there 's
Switzerland,
Polonia, and such pickled things will serve
To furnish out the table.
   *W. Knight.*        You say well, sir:
But here 's the misery; when I have stopp'd the
mouth
Of one vice, there 's another gapes for food; 105

I am as covetous as a barren womb,
The grave, or what 's more ravenous.
   *B. Knight.*        We are for you, sir:
Call you that heinous, that 's good husbandry?
Why, we make money of our faiths, our prayers;
We make the very deathbed buy her com-
forts, 110
Most dearly pay for all her pious counsels,
Leave rich revénues for a few sale orisons,
Or else they pass unreconcil'd without 'em:
Did you but view the vaults within our mon-
asteries,
You 'd swear then Plutus, which the fiction
calls 115
The lord of riches, were entomb'd within 'em.
   *B. Duke.* You cannot pass for tuns.
   *W. Knight.*         Is 't possible?
   *W. Duke.* But how shall I bestow the vice I
bring, sirs?
You quite forget me; I shall be lock'd out
By your strict key of life.
   *B. Knight.*      Is yours so foul, sir? 120
   *W. Duke.* Some that are pleas'd to make a
wanton on 't,
Call it infirmity of blood, flesh-frailty;
But certain there 's a worse name in your books
for 't.
   *B. Knight.* The trifle of all vices, the mere
innocent,
The very novice of this house of clay, —
venery: 125
If I but hug thee hard, I show the worst on 't;
'T is all the fruit we have here after supper;
Nay, at the ruins of a nunnery once,
Six thousand infants' heads found in a fish-
pond.
   *W. Duke.* How!
   *B. Knight.* How, ay, how? how came they
thither, think you? 130
Huldrick, bishop of Augsburg, in his Epistle
To Nicholas the First, can tell you how;
May be he was at cleansing of the pond:
I can but smile to think how it would puzzle
All mother-maids that ever liv'd in those
parts 135
To know their own child's heads. But is this
all?
   *B. Duke.* Are you ours yet?
   *W. Knight.* One more, and I am silenc'd:
But this that comes now will divide us question-
less;
'T is ten times, ten times worse than the fore-
runners.
   *B. Knight.* Is it so vild there is no name
ordain'd for 't? 140
Toads have their titles, and creation gave

---

**66 cabrito:** lamb    **tons:** tunny-fish    **71 resolv'd:** satisfied    **90 manchet:** small loaf of fine bread    **97 voider:** basket for removing remnants    **98 cheer:** food    **112 sale:** mercenary, insipid **115 fiction:** story    **117 tuns:** wine casks    **138 questionless:** undoubtedly

Serpents and adders those names to be known
by.
*W. Knight.*  This of all others bears the
hidden'st venom.
The smoothest poison; I am an arch-dissem-
bler, sir.
*B. Knight.*  How?
*W. Knight.*  'T is my nature's brand; turn
from me, sir;                                              145
The time is yet to come that e'er I spake
What my heart meant.
*B. Knight.*          And call you that a vice? ¬
Avoid all profanation, I beseech you, —
The only prime state-virtue upon earth,
The policy of empires; O, take heed, sir,      150
For fear it take displeasure and forsake you!
It is a jewel of that precious value,
Whose worth 's not known but to the skilful
lapidary;
The instrument that picks ope princes' hearts,
And locks up ours from them, with the same
motion:                                                      155
You never yet came near our souls till now.
*B. Duke.*  Now y' are a brother to us.
*B. Knight.*                What we have done
Has been dissemblance ever.
*W. Knight.*                     There you lie then,
And the game 's ours; we give thee check-mate
by
Discovery, King, the noblest mate of all!     160
*B. King.*  I 'm lost, I 'm taken!
                    *A great shout and flourish.*
*W. Knight.*                 Ambitious, covetous,
Luxurious falsehood!
*W. Duke.*        Dissembler, that includes all.
*B. King.*  All hopes confounded!
*B. Queen.*                    Miserable condition!

*Enter White King, [White] Queen, [White
Bishop, White Queen's Pawn, and other]
White Pawns*

*W. King.*  O, let me bless mine arms with
this dear treasure,
Truth's glorious masterpiece! See, Queen of
sweetness,                                                  165
He 's in my bosom safe; and yond fair struc-
ture
Of comely honour, his true blest assistant.
          [*Embracing W. Knight and W. Duke.*]
*W. Queen.*  May their integrities ever possess
That peaceful sanctuary!
*W. Knight.*               As 't was a game, sir,
Won with much hazard, so with much more
triumph.                                                    170
We gave him check-mate by discovery, sir.
*W. King.*  Obscurity is now the fittest favour
Falsehood can sue for; it well suits perdition:

'T is their best course that so have lost their
fame
To put their heads into the bag for shame;   175
And there, behold, the bag's mouth, like hell,
opens  *The bag opens, the Black Side in it.*
To take her due, and the lost sons appear
Greedily gaping for increase of fellowship
In infamy, the last desire of wretches,
Advancing their perdition-branded foreheads
Like Envy's issue, or a bed of snakes.         181
*B. B. Pawn.*  [*In the bag.*]  See, all 's con-
founded; the game 's lost, King 's taken.
*F. Bishop.*  [*In the bag.*]  The White House
has given us the bag, I thank 'em.
*B. Jesting Pawn.*  [*In the bag.*]  They had
need have given you a whole bag by your-
self:
'Sfoot, this Fat Bishop has so squelch'd and
squeez'd me,                                               185
So overlaid me, I have no verjuice left in me!
You shall find all my goodness, an you look
for 't,
In the bottom of the bag.
*F. Bishop.*  Thou malapert Pawn.
The Bishop must have room; he will have
room,
And room to lie at pleasure.
*B. Jesting Pawn.*  All the bag, I think,   190
Is room too scant for your Spalato paunch.
*B. B. Pawn.*  Down, viper of our order!
art thou showing
Thy impudent whorish front?
*B. Q. Pawn.*             Yes, monster-holiness!
*W. Knight.*  Contention in the pit! is hell
divided?
*W. King.*  You 'd need have some of majesty
and power                                                   195
To keep good rule amongst you: make room,
Bishop.          [*Puts B. King into the bag.*]
*F. Bishop.*  I am not so easily mov'd; when
I 'm once set,
I scorn to stir for any king on earth.
*W. Queen.*  Here comes the Queen; what
say you then to her?
                    [*Puts B. Queen into the bag.*]
*F. Bishop.*  Indeed a Queen may make a
Bishop stir.                                                200
*W. Knight.*  Room for the mightiest Ma-
chiavel-politician
That e'er the devil hatch'd of a nun's egg!
                    [*Puts B. Knight into the bag.*]
*F. Bishop.*  He 'll peck a hole in the bag and
get out shortly;
But I 'm sure I shall be the last creeps out,
And that 's the misery of greatness ever.    205
Foh, your politician is not sound i' the vent.
I smell him hither.

---

¹⁵⁷ **B. Duke:** (MS incorporates his speech in the Black Knight's.)  ¹⁶² **that:** (not in MS)  ¹⁸³ **given**
· · · **bag:** cheated us

*W. Duke.* Room for a sun-burnt, tansy-
fac'd belov'd,
An olive-colour'd Ganymede! and that 's all
That 's worth the bagging.
*F. Bishop.* Crowd in all you can, 210
The Bishop will be still uppermost man,
Maugre King, Queen, or politician.
*W. King.* So, now let the bag close, the
fittest womb
For treachery, pride, and malice; whilst we,
winner-like,
Destroying, through heaven's power, what
would destroy, 215
Welcome our White Knight with loud peals of
joy. *Exeunt.*
*Finis.*

²⁰⁸ **tansy-fac'd:** yellow-skinned
²¹² **Maugre:** in spite of

## EPILOGUE

*White Queen's Pawn*

My mistress, the White Queen, hath sent me
forth,
And bade me bow thus low to all of worth,
That are true friends of the White House and
cause,
Which she hopes most of this assembly draws:
For any else, by envy's mark denoted, 5
To those night glow-worms in the bag devoted,
Where'er they sit, stand, and in corners lurk,
They 'll be soon known by their depraving work;
But she 's assur'd what they 'd commit to bane,
Her White friends' loves will build up fair
again. 10

²⁰⁹ **olive-colour'd:** (Referring to Olivares, the Black Duke)

# THE
# BROKEN
# HEART.

## A Tragedy.

*ACTED*
By the KING'S Majesties Seruants
at the priuate Houſe in the
BLACK-FRIERS.

*Fide Honor.*

**LONDON:**
Printed by *I. B.* for HVGH BEESTON, and are to
be ſold at his Shop, neere the *Caſtle* in
*Corne-hill* 1 6 3 3.

BIBLIOGRAPHICAL RECORD. The only source of the text of *The Broken Heart* is a Quarto published in 1633, in agreement with the following entry on the Stationers' Register: *28° Martij 1633. Hugh Beeston Entred for his Copy vnder the hands of Sir Henry Herbert and master Aspley Warden a Tragedy called The Broken Heart by John Fford . . . vjᵈ.*

The title-page bears Ford's anagram, *Fide Honor* (Iohn Forde), and the text is prefaced by the following signed letter to the illustrious Lord Craven, a nobleman (as Gifford says of him) "worthy of all praise, and not ill chosen for the patron of a wild, a melancholy, and romantic tale":

'To the most worthy deserver of the noblest titles in honour, William, Lord Craven, Baron of Hamsteed-Marshall.

My Lord: The glory of a *great name*, acquired by a greater glory of *Action*, hath in all ages liu'd the truest chronicle to his owne Memory. In the practise of which Argument, *your grouth* to perfection (even in youth) hath appear'd so sincere, so un-flattering a *Penneman;* that Posterity cannot with more delight read the merit of *Noble endeauours*, then *noble endeauours* merit thankes from Posterity to be read with delight. Many nations, many eyes, have beene witnesses of your *Deserts*, and lou'd Them: Be pleas'd then, with the freedome of your own Nature, to admit ONE amongst All, particularly into the list of such as honour a faire Example of Nobilitie. There is a kinde of humble *Ambition*, not vn-commendable, when the silence of study breaks forth into Discourse, coveting rather encouragement then Applause; yet herein *Censure* commonly is too severe an Auditor, without the moderation of an able *Patronage*. I have ever beene slow in courtship of greatnesse, not ignorant of such defects as are frequent to *Opinion:* but the Iustice of your Inclination to *Industry*, emboldens my weaknesse of confidence to rellish an experience of *your Mercy*, as many brave Dangers have tasted of *your Courage*. Your Lordship stroue to be knowne to the world (when the world knew you least) by voluntary but excellent *Attempts:* Like Allowance I plead of being knowne to your Lordship (in this low presumption) by tendring to a favourable entertainment a *Deuotion* offred from a heart, that can be as truely sensible of any least respect, as ever professe the owner in my best, my readiest services, A Lover of your naturall Love to Vertue,

*Iohn Ford.*'

Though thus evidently published with the poet's sanction, the Quarto is badly printed. It omits many necessary words, and contains some passages so corrupted as to defy satisfactory emendation.

DATE AND STAGE PERFORMANCE. The play was acted by the King's Company at the Blackfriars, but is not mentioned in the extant records of Sir Henry Herbert. Probably its composition did not long precede its publication. Dr. Neilson has noted that *The Garland of Good Will*, mentioned in IV. ii. 15, was published in 1631.

SOURCE. No printed source has been discovered, and the probability that one existed is lessened by lines 15 and 16 of the Prologue:

> "What may be here thought a fiction, when time's youth
> Wanted some riper years, was known a truth."

In an admirable article on "Stella and *The Broken Heart*" (PMLA, 1909, 274–285), the late Stuart P. Sherman pointed out the resemblance of the story of the play to the history of Sir Philip Sidney, Penelope Devereux, and Lord Rich, and also the relation between the Spartan scene and the treatment of Sparta in Sidney's *Arcadia*. It is doubtless only a pretty coincidence that Lord Craven, to whom Ford dedicated his play, became the hero of a similar romance with James I's unfortunate daughter, the Queen of Bohemia.

# JOHN FORD (1586–164–?)

## THE BROKEN HEART

### The Speakers' Names, Fitted to Their Qualities

AMYCLAS, *Common to the Kings of Laconia*
ITHOCLES, *Honour of loveliness*, a Favourite
ORGILUS, *Angry*, son to Crotolon
BASSANES, *Vexation*, a jealous Nobleman
ARMOSTES, *an Appeaser*, a Councillor of State
CROTOLON, *Noise*, another Councillor
PROPHILUS, *Dear*, Friend to Ithocles
NEARCHUS, *Young Prince*, Prince of Argos
TECNICUS, *Artist*, a Philosopher
LEMOPHIL, *Glutton*,
GRONEAS, *Tavern-haunter*, } two Courtiers
AMELUS, *Trusty*, Friend to Nearchus
PHULAS, *Watchful*, Servant to Bassanes

CALANTHA, *Flower of beauty*, the King's Daughter
PENTHEA, *Complaint*, Sister to Ithocles [and Wife
    to Bassanes]
EUPHRANEA, *Joy*, a Maid of honour [Daughter to
    Crotolon]
CHRISTALLA, *Christal*,
PHILEMA, *A Kiss*, } Maids of honour
GRAUSIS, *Old Beldam*, Overseer of Penthea

PERSONS INCLUDED

THRASUS, *Fierceness*, Father of Ithocles
APLOTES, *Simplicity*, Orgilus so disguised

The Scene, SPARTA

## The Prologue

OUR scene is Sparta. He whose best of art
Hath drawn this piece calls it *The Broken Heart*.
The title lends no expectation here
Of apish laughter, or of some lame jeer
At place or persons; no pretended clause          5
Of jests fit for a brothel courts applause
From vulgar admiration: such low songs,
Tun'd to unchaste ears, suit not modest tongues.
The Virgin Sisters then deserv'd fresh bays,
When Innocence and Sweetness crown'd their lays;  10
Then vices gasp'd for breath, whose whole commerce
Was whipp'd to exile by unblushing verse.
This law we keep in our presentment now,
Not to take freedom more than we allow.
What may be here thought a fiction, when time's youth   15
Wanted some riper years, was known a truth:
In which, if words have cloth'd the subject right,
You may partake a pity with delight.

*Actus Primus: Scæna prima*

[*House of Crotolon*]

*Enter Crotolon and Orgilus*

Crot. Dally not further; I will know the
  reason
That speeds thee to this journey.

Org.                              Reason! good sir,
I can yield many.
Crot.                 Give me one, a good one;
Such I expect, and ere we part must have.
Athens! Pray, why to Athens? You intend
  not                                              5
To kick against the world, turn Cynic, Stoic?
Or read the logic lecture? or become
An Areopagite, and judge in causes

Speakers' Names: **Lemophil**: (apparently for "Lenophil," lover of the wine-vat. In the text of Q the name is generally, but not invariably, printed "Hemophil.") **Amelus**: (The name should mean "careless," not "trusty.") Prol. ⁵ **pretended clause**: counterfeit passage ¹⁴ **allow**: approve ⁶ **partake . . . delight**: find pleasure in tragic sympathy ⁷ **read . . . lecture**: take a course in logic ⁸ **Areopagite**: member of the Athenian criminal court

Touching the commonwealth? for, as I take it,
The budding of your chin cannot prognosticate
So grave an honour.
  *Org.*          All this I acknowledge. 11
  *Crot.* You do! Then, son, if books and love
    of knowledge
Inflame you to this travel, here in Sparta
You may as freely study.
  *Org.*        'T is not that, sir.
  *Crot.* Not that, sir! As a father, I command
    thee         15
To acquaint me with the truth.
  *Org.*        Thus I obey ye.
After so many quarrels as dissension,
Fury, and rage had broach'd in blood, and
    sometimes
With death to such confederates as sided
With now-dead Thrasus and yourself, my lord;
Our present king, Amyclas, reconcil'd  21
Your eager swords and seal'd a gentle peace.
Friends you profess'd yourselves; which to con-
    firm,
A resolution for a lasting league
Betwixt your families was entertain'd,  25
By joining in a Hymenean bond
Me and the fair Penthea, only daughter
To Thrasus.
  *Crot.*    What of this?
  *Org.*        Much, much, dear sir.
A freedom of converse, an interchange
Of holy and chaste love, so fix'd our souls  30
In a firm growth of holy union, that no time
Can eat into the pledge. We had enjoy'd
The sweets our vows expected, had not cruelty
Prevented all those triumphs we prepar'd for
By Thrasus his untimely death.
  *Crot.*      Most certain. 35
  *Org.* From this time sprouted up that poison-
    ous stalk
Of aconite, whose ripen'd fruit hath ravish'd
All health, all comfort of a happy life;
For Ithocles, her brother, proud of youth,
And prouder in his power, nourish'd closely 40
The memory of former discontents,
To glory in revenge. By cunning partly,
Partly by threats, 'a woos at once and forces
His virtuous sister to admit a marriage
With Bassanes, a nobleman, in honour  45
And riches, I confess, beyond my fortunes.
  *Crot.* All this is no sound reason to impor-
    tune
My leave for thy departure.
  *Org.*      Now it follows.
Beauteous Penthea, wedded to this torture
By an insulting brother, being secretly  50
Compell'd to yield her virgin freedom up
To him who never can usurp her heart,

Before contracted mine, is now so yok'd
To a most barbarous thraldom, misery,
Affliction, that he savours not humanity,  55
Whose sorrow melts not into more than pity
In hearing but her name.
  *Crot.*     As how, pray?
  *Org.*        Bassanes,
The man that calls her wife, considers truly
What heaven of perfections he is lord of
By thinking fair Penthea his. This thought  60
Begets a kind of monster-love, which love
Is nurse unto a fear so strong and servile
As brands all dotage with a jealousy:
All eyes who gaze upon that shrine of beauty,
He doth resolve, do homage to the miracle;  65
Some one, he is assur'd, may now or then,
If opportunity but sort, prevail.
So much, out of a self-unworthiness,
His fears transport him; not that he finds
    cause
In her obedience, but his own distrust.  70
  *Crot.* You spin out your discourse.
  *Org.*      My griefs are violent:
For knowing how the maid was heretofore
Courted by me, his jealousies grow wild
That I should steal again into her favours,
And undermine her virtues; which the gods  75
Know I nor dare nor dream of. Hence, from
    hence
I undertake a voluntary exile;
First, by my absence to take off the cares
Of jealous Bassanes; but chiefly, sir,
To free Penthea from a hell on earth;  80
Lastly, to lose the memory of something
Her presence makes to live in me afresh.
  *Crot.* Enough, my Orgilus, enough. To
    Athens!
I give a full consent. — Alas, good lady! —
We shall hear from thee often?
  *Org.*      Often.
  *Crot.*      See, 85
Thy sister comes to give a farewell.

*Enter Euphranea*

  *Euph.*      Brother!
  *Org.* Euphranea, thus upon thy cheeks I
    print
A brother's kiss; more careful of thine honour,
Thy health, and thy well-doing, than my life.
Before we part, in presence of our father,  90
I must prefer a suit t' ye.
  *Euph.*     You may style it,
My brother, a command.
  *Org.*     That you will promise
To pass never to any man, however
Worthy, your faith, till, with our father's leave,
I give a free consent.

*Crot.*                    An easy motion!     95
I 'll promise for her, Orgilus.
   *Org.*                    Your pardon;
Euphranea's oath must yield me satisfaction.
   *Euph.*   By Vesta's sacred fires I swear.
   *Crot.*                                And I,
By great Apollo's beams, join in the vow,
Not without thy allowance to bestow her     100
On any living.
   *Org.*          Dear Euphranea,
Mistake me not: far, far 't is from my thought,
As far from any wish of mine, to hinder
Preferment to an honourable bed
Or fitting fortune.   Thou art young and hand-
   some;                                     105
And 't were injustice, — more, a tyranny, —
Not to advance thy merit.   Trust me, sister,
It shall be my first care to see thee match'd
As may become thy choice and our contents. 109
I have your oath.
   *Euph.*   You have.   But mean you, brother,
To leave us, as you say?
   *Crot.*                    Ay, ay, Euphranea.
He has just grounds direct him.   I will prove
A father and a brother to thee.
   *Euph.*                                Heaven
Does look into the secrets of all hearts.
Gods, you have mercy with ye, else —
   *Crot.*                    Doubt nothing;   115
Thy brother will return in safety to us.
   *Org.*   Souls sunk in sorrows never are with-
   out 'em;
They change fresh airs, but bear their griefs
   about 'em.                    *Exeunt omnes.*

## Scene 2

### [*The Court*]

*Flourish.   Enter Amyclas the King, Armos-*
   *tes, Prophilus, and Attendants*

   *Amy.*   The Spartan gods are gracious; our
   humility
Shall bend before their altars, and perfume
Their temples with abundant sacrifice.
See, lords, Amyclas, your old king, is ent'ring
Into his youth again!   I shall shake off      5
This silver badge of age, and change this snow
For hairs as gay as are Apollo's locks.
Our heart leaps in new vigour.
   *Arm.*                    May old time
Run back to double your long life, great sir!
   *Amy.*   It will, it must, Armostes.   Thy bold
   nephew,                                    10
Death-braving Ithocles, brings to our gates
Triumphs and peace upon his conquering
   sword.
Laconia is a monarchy at length;

Hath in this latter war trod under foot
Messene's pride; Messene bows her neck     15
To Lacedæmon's royalty.   O, 't was
A glorious victory, and doth deserve
More than a chronicle — a temple, lords,
A temple to the name of Ithocles. —
Where didst thou leave him, Prophilus?
   *Pro.*                    At Pephon,     20
Most gracious sovereign.   Twenty of the no-
   blest
Of the Messenians there attend your pleasure,
For such conditions as you shall propose
In settling peace, and liberty of life.
   *Amy.*   When comes your friend, the general?
   *Pro.*                    He promis'd    25
To follow with all speed convenient.

*Enter Crotolon, Calantha, Christalla, Philema*
   [*with a garland*] *and Euphranea*

   *Amy.*   Our daughter! — Dear Calantha, the
   happy news,
The conquest of Messene, hath already
Enrich'd thy knowledge.
   *Cal.*                    With the circumstance
And manner of the fight, related faithfully   30
By Prophilus himself. — But, pray, sir, tell me,
How doth the youthful general demean
His actions in these fortunes?
   *Pro.*                    Excellent princess,
Your own fair eyes may soon report a truth
Unto your judgment, with what moderation, 35
Calmness of nature, measure, bounds, and
   limits
Of thankfulness and joy, 'a doth digest
Such amplitude of his success as would
In others, moulded of a spirit less clear,
Advance 'em to comparison with heaven.     40
But Ithocles —
   *Cal.*          Your friend —
   *Pro.*                    He is so, madam,
In which the period of my fate consists:
He, in this firmament of honour, stands
Like a star fix'd, not mov'd with any thunder
Of popular applause or sudden lightning     45
Of self-opinion.   He hath serv'd his country,
And thinks 't was but his duty.
   *Crot.*                    You describe
A miracle of man.
   *Amy.*          Such, Crotolon,
On forfeit of a king's word, thou wilt find
   him. —                    *Flourish.*     49
Hark, warning of his coming!   All attend him.

*Enter Ithocles, Lemophil, and Groneas; the*
   *rest of the Lords ushering him in*

Return into these arms, thy home, thy sanctuary,

---

¹⁰⁰ **allowance:** approval     ¹¹² **direct:** which direct     ⁴² **period:** summation     ⁴⁶ **self-opinion:**
vanity

Delight of Sparta, treasure of my bosom,
Mine own, own Ithocles!
   *Ith.*              Your humblest subject.
   *Arm.* Proud of the blood I claim an interest
in,
As brother to thy mother, I embrace thee,   55
Right noble nephew.
   *Ith.*       Sir, your love 'ᵤ too partial.
   *Crot.* Our country speaks by me, who by thy
valour,
Wisdom, and service, shares in this great ac-
tion;
Returning thee, in part of thy due merits,
A general welcome.
   *Ith.*        You exceed in bounty.   60
   *Cal.* Christalla, Philema, the chaplet. [*Takes
the chaplet from them.*] — Ithocles,
Upon the wings of Fame the singular
And chosen fortune of an high attempt
Is borne so past the view of common sight,
That I myself with mine own hands have
wrought,   65
To crown thy temples, this provincial garland:
Accept, wear, and enjoy it as our gift
Deserv'd, not purchas'd.
   *Ith.*         Y' are a royal maid.
   *Amy.* She is in all our daughter.
   *Ith.*            Let me blush,
Acknowledging how poorly I have serv'd,   70
What nothings I have done, compar'd with th'
honours
Heap'd on the issue of a willing mind.
In that lay mine ability, that only:
For who is he so sluggish from his birth,
So little worthy of a name or country,   75
That owes not out of gratitude for life
A debt of service, in what kind soever
Safety or counsel of the commonwealth
Requires, for payment?
   *Cal.*         'A speaks truth.
   *Ith.*          Whom heaven
Is pleas'd to style victorious, there to such   80
Applause runs madding, like the drunken
priests
In Bacchus' sacrifices, without reason
Voicing the leader-on a demi-god;
Whenas, indeed, each common soldier's blood
Drops down as current coin in that hard pur-
chase   85
As his whose much more delicate condition
Hath suck'd the milk of ease. Judgment com-
mands,
But resolution executes. I use not,
Before this royal presence, these fit slights
As in contempt of such as can direct;   90

My speech hath other end: not to attribute
All praise to one man's fortune, which is
strengthen'd
By many hands. For instance, here is Pro-
philus,
A gentleman — I cannot flatter truth —
Of much desert; and, though in other rank,   95
Both Lemophil and Groneas were not missing
To wish their country's peace; for, in a word,
All there did strive their best, and 't was our
duty.
   *Amy.* Courtiers turn soldiers! — We vouch-
safe our hand.
      [*Lemophil and Groneas kiss his hand.*]
Observe your great example.
   *Lem.*         With all diligence.   100
   *Gron.* Obsequiously and hourly.
   *Amy.*           Some repose
After these toils are needful. We must think
on
Conditions for the conquer'd; they expect 'em.
On! — Come, my Ithocles.
   *Euph.*         Sir, with your favour,
I need not a supporter.
   *Pro.*         Fate instructs me.   105
     *Exeunt. Manent Lemophil, Groneas,
      Christalla, et Philema. Lemophil
      stays Christalla, Groneas Philema.*
   *Chris.* With me?
   *Phil.*       Indeed, I dare not stay.
   *Lem.*          Sweet lady,
Soldiers are blunt, — your lip.
   *Chris.*       Fie, this is rudeness:
You went not hence such creatures.
   *Gro.*       Spirit of valour
Is of a mounting nature.
   *Phil.*        It appears so. —
Pray, in earnest, how many men apiece   110
Have you two been the death of?
   *Gro.*         'Faith, not many;
We were compos'd of mercy.
   *Lem.*       For our daring,
You have heard the general's approbation
Before the king.
   *Chris.* You "wish'd your country's peace":
That show'd your charity. Where are your
spoils,   115
Such as the soldier fights for?
   *Phil.*       They are coming.
   *Chris.* By the next carrier, are they not?
   *Gro.*         Sweet Philema,
When I was in the thickest of mine enemies,
Slashing off one man's head, another's nose,
Another's arms and legs, —
   *Phil.*       And all together.   120

---

   ⁵⁹ **part:** part payment   ⁶³ **attempt:** enterprise   ⁶⁶ **provincial:** worn by the conqueror of a province   ⁶⁸ **purchas'd:** casually acquired   ⁷² **issue:** accomplishment   ⁸⁹ **slights:** underratings ¹⁰⁰ **Observe:** pay homage to   **example:** exemplar (Ithocles)   ¹¹¹ **you:** ('yon' Q)   ¹²⁰ **all to- gether:** ('altogether' Q)

*Gro.* Then would I with a sigh remember
thee,
And cry "Dear Philema, 't is for thy sake
I do these deeds of wonder!" — Dost not love
me
With all thy heart now?
*Phil.*                    Now as heretofore.
I have not put my love to use; the principal 125
Will hardly yield an interest.
*Gro.*                         By Mars,
I 'll marry thee!
*Phil.*          By Vulcan, y' are forsworn,
Except my mind do alter strangely.
*Gro.*                              One word.
*Chris.* You lie beyond all modesty: — for-
bear me.                                     129
*Lem.* I 'll make thee mistress of a city; 't is
Mine own by conquest.
*Chris.*                  By petition; sue for 't
*In forma pauperis.* — City! kennel. — Gallants,
Off with your feathers, put on aprons, gallants;
Learn to reel, thrum, or trim a lady's dog, 131
And be good quiet souls of peace, hobgoblins!
*Lem.* Christalla!
*Chris.*          Practise to drill hogs, in hope
To share in the acorns. — Soldiers! corncutters,
But not so valiant: they ofttimes draw blood,
Which you durst never do. When you have
practis'd
More wit or more civility, we 'll rank ye   140
I' th' list of men: till then, brave things-at-
arms,
Dare not to speak to us, — most potent Gro-
neas! —
*Phil.* And Lemophil the hardy! — at your
services.      *Exeunt Christalla et Philema.*
*Gro.* They scorn us as they did before we
went.
*Lem.* Hang 'em! let us scorn them, and be
reveng'd.                                    145
*Gro.* Shall we?
*Lem.* We will: and when we slight them
thus,
Instead of following them, they 'll follow us.
It is a woman's nature.
*Gro.*          'T is a scurvy one. *Exeunt omnes.*

## Scene 3

⌊*Grove near the palace*⌋

*Enter Tecnicus, a philosopher, and Orgilus
disguised like a Scholar of his*

*Tec.* Tempt not the stars; young man, thou
canst not play
With the severity of fate: this change

Of habit and disguise in outward view
Hides not the secrets of thy soul within thee
From their quick-piercing eyes, which dive at
all times                                      5
Down to thy thoughts. In thy aspect I note
A consequence of danger.
*Org.*                    Give me leave,
Grave Tecnicus, without foredooming destiny,
Under thy roof to ease my silent griefs
By applying to my hidden wounds the balm  10
Of thy oraculous lectures. If my fortune
Run such a crooked by-way as to wrest
My steps to ruin, yet thy learned precepts
Shall call me back and set my footings straight.
I will not court the world.
*Tec.*              Ah, Orgilus,        15
Neglects in young men of delights and life
Run often to extremities; they care not
For harms to others who contemn their own.
*Org.* But I, most learned artist, am not so
much
At odds with nature that I grutch the thrift  20
Of any true deserver; nor doth malice
Of present hopes so check them with despair
As that I yield to thought of more affliction
Than what is incident to frailty: wherefore
Impute not this retired course of living   25
Some little time to any other cause
Than what I justly render, — the information
Of an unsettled mind; as the effect
Must clearly witness.
*Tec.*              Spirit of truth inspire thee!
On these conditions I conceal thy change,  30
And willingly admit thee for an auditor. —
I 'll to my study.
*Org.*          I to contemplations
In these delightful walks.   [*Exit Tecnicus.*]
                    Thus metamorphos'd
I may without suspicion hearken after
Penthea's usage and Euphranea's faith.    35
Love, thou art full of mystery! The deities
Themselves are not secure in searching out
The secrets of those flames, which, hidden,
waste
A breast made tributary to the laws
Of beauty. Physic yet hath never found    40
A remedy to cure a lover's wound. —
Ha! who are those that cross yon private walk
Into the shadowing grove in amorous foldings?

*Prophilus passeth over, supporting Euphra-
nea, and whispering*

My sister! O, my sister! 't is Euphranea
With Prophilus: supported too! I would    45
It were an apparition! Prophilus
Is Ithocles his friend. It strangely puzzles me.

---

¹³² kennel: gutter    ¹³³ feathers: ('Fathers' Q)    ¹³⁴ thrum: weave    ⁷ consequence: augury
¹⁰ grutch: begrudge    ²¹ malice: discouragement    ²⁴ frailty: mortal imperfection    ⁴³ foldings\
embraces

Again! help me, my book; this scholar's habit
Must stand my privilege: my mind is busy,
Mine eyes and ears are open.

*Walks by, reading.*

*Enter again Prophilus and Euphranea*

*Pro.*                              Do not waste   50
The span of this stol'n time, lent by the gods
For precious use, in niceness.  Bright Eu-
     phranea,
Should I repeat old vows, or study new,
For purchase of belief to my desires, —
*Org.* [*Aside.*]  Desires!
*Pro.*            My service, my integrity, —   55
*Org.* [*Aside.*]  That 's better.
*Pro.*            I should but repeat a lesson
Oft conn'd without a prompter but thine eyes.
My love is honourable.
*Org.* [*Aside.*]            So was mine
To my Penthea, chastely honourable.
*Pro.*  Nor wants there more addition to my
     wish                                          60
Of happiness than having thee a wife;
Already sure of Ithocles, a friend
Firm and unalterable.
*Org.* [*Aside.*]            But a brother
More cruel than the grave.
*Euph.*            What can you look for,
In answer to your noble protestations,           65
From an unskilful maid, but language suited
To a divided mind?
*Org.* [*Aside.*]        Hold out, Euphranea!
*Euph.*  Know, Prophilus, I never under-
     valu'd,
From the first time you mention'd worthy love,
Your merit, means, or person.  It had been  70
A fault of judgment in me, and a dulness
In my affections, not to weigh and thank
My better stars that offer'd me the grace
Of so much blissfulness.  For, to speak truth,
The law of my desires kept equal pace       75
With yours; nor have I left that resolution:
But, only in a word, whatever choice
Lives nearest in my heart must first procure
Consent both from my father and my brother,
Ere he can own me his.
*Org.* [*Aside.*]            She is forsworn else.  80
*Pro.*  Leave me that task.
*Euph.*            My brother, ere he parted
To Athens, had my oath.
*Org.* [*Aside.*]            Yes, yes, 'a had, sure.
*Pro.*  I doubt not, with the means the court
     supplies,
But to prevail at pleasure.
*Org.* [*Aside.*]            Very likely!
*Pro.*  Meantime, best, dearest, I may build
     my hopes                                       85

On the foundation of thy constant suff'rance
In any opposition.
*Euph.*            Death shall sooner
Divorce life and the joys I have in living
Than my chaste vows from truth.
*Pro.*            On thy fair hand
I seal the like.                                    90
*Org.* [*Aside.*]  There is no faith in woman.
Passion, O, be contain'd!  My very heart-
     strings
Are on the tenters.
*Euph.*            Sir, we are overheard
Cupid protect us!  'T was a stirring, sir.
Of some one near.
*Pro.*            Your fears are needless, lady.  95
None have access into these private pleas-
     ures
Except some near in court, or bosom-student
From Tecnicus his oratory, granted
By special favour lately from the king
Unto the grave philosopher.
*Euph.*            Methinks      100
I hear one talking to himself, — I see him.
*Pro.*  'T is a poor scholar, as I told you,
     lady.
*Org.* [*Aside.*]  I am discover'd. — [*Half aloud
to himself, as if studying.*]  Say it: is it
     possible,
With a smooth tongue, a leering countenance,
Flattery, or force of reason — I come t' ye,
     sir —                                          105
To turn or to appease the raging sea?
Answer to that. — Your art! what art to catch
And hold fast in a net the sun's small atoms?
No, no; they 'll out, they 'll out: ye may as
     easily
Outrun a cloud driven by a northern blast  110
As fiddle-faddle so!  Peace, or speak sense.
*Euph.*  Call you this thing a scholar?  'Las,
     he 's lunatic.
*Pro.*  Observe him, sweet; 't is but his recrea-
     tion.
*Org.*  But will you hear a little?  You are
     so tetchy,
You keep no rule in argument.  Philosophy  115
Works not upon impossibilities,
But natural conclusions. — Mew! — absurd!
The metaphysics are but speculations
Of the celestial bodies, or such accidents
As not mix'd perfectly, in the air engend'red,
Appear to us unnatural; that 's all.        121
Prove it.  Yet, with a reverence to your gravity,
I 'll balk illiterate sauciness, submitting
My sole opinion to the touch of writers.
*Pro.*  Now let us fall in with him.
                              [*They come forward.*]
*Org.*                         Ha, ha, ha!  125

---

⁵¹ **niceness:** coyness      ⁷⁷ **choice:** chosen lover      ⁹³ **tenters:** tenter-hooks, for stretching cloth
⁹⁶ **pleasures:** pleasure grounds      ⁹⁸ **oratory:** private chapel      ¹¹⁴ **tetchy:** peevish

These apish boys, when they but taste the grammates
And principles of theory, imagine
They can oppose their teachers.  Confidence
Leads many into errors.
*Pro.*                        By your leave, sir.
*Euph.*  Are you a scholar, friend?
*Org.*                  I am, gay creature,  130
With pardon of your deities, a mushroom
On whom the dew of heaven drops now and then.
The sun shines on me too, I thank his beams!
Sometime I feel their warmth, and eat and sleep.
*Pro.*  Does Tecnicus read to thee?
*Org.*                    Yes, forsooth,  135
He is my master surely;  yonder door
Opens upon his study.
*Pro.*                      Happy creatures.
Such people toil not, sweet, in heats of state,
Nor sink in thaws of greatness;  their affections
Keep order with the limits of their modesty; 140
Their love is love of virtue. — What 's thy name?
*Org.*  Aplotes, sumptuous master, a poor wretch.
*Euph.*  Dost thou want anything?
*Org.*                  Books, Venus, books.
*Pro.*  Lady, a new conceit comes in my thought,
And most available for both our comforts.  145
*Euph.*  My lord, —
*Pro.*            Whiles I endeavour to deserve
Your father's blessing to our loves, this scholar
May daily at some certain hours attend
What notice I can write of my success,      149
Here in this grove, and give it to your hands;
The like from you to me:  so can we never,
Barr'd of our mutual speech, want sure intelligence,
And thus our hearts may talk when our tongues cannot.
*Euph.*  Occasion is most favourable;  use it.
*Pro.*  Aplotes, wilt thou wait us twice a day,
At nine i' th' morning and at four at night,  156
Here in this bower, to convey such letters
As each shall send to other?  Do it willingly,
Safely, and secretly, and I will furnish
Thy study, or what else thou canst desire. 160
*Org.*  Jove, make me thankful, thankful, I beseech thee,
Propitious Jove!  I will prove sure and trusty:
You will not fail me books?
*Pro.*                  Nor aught besides
Thy heart can wish.  This lady's name 's Euphranea,
Mine Prophilus.

*Org.*            I have a pretty memory;  165
It must prove my best friend.  I will not miss
One minute of the hours appointed.
*Pro.*                          Write
The books thou wouldst have bought thee in a note,
Or take thyself some money.
*Org.*                        No, no money.
Money to scholars is a spirit invisible,    170
We dare not finger it:  or books, or nothing.
*Pro.*  Books of what sort thou wilt:  do not forget
Our names.
*Org.*      I warrant ye, I warrant ye.
*Pro.*  Smile, Hymen, on the growth of our desires;
We 'll feed thy torches with eternal fires!  175
                    *Exeunt.  Manet Orgilus.*
*Org.*  Put out thy torches, Hymen, or their light
Shall meet a darkness of eternal night!
Inspire me, Mercury, with swift deceits.
Ingenious Fate has leapt into mine arms,    179
Beyond the compass of my brain.  Mortality
Creeps on the dung of earth, and cannot reach
The riddles which are purpos'd by the gods.
Great arts best write themselves in their own stories;
They die too basely who outlive their glories.
                                    *Exit.*

## Actus Secundus: Scæna prima

### [House of Bassanes]

*Enter Bassanes and Phulas*

*Bass.*  I 'll have that window next the street damm'd up.
It gives too full a prospect to temptation,
And courts a gazer's glances.  There 's a lust
Committed by the eye, that sweats and travails,
Plots, wakes, contrives, till the deformed bearwhelp,                                      5
Adultery, be lick'd into the act,
The very act.  That light shall be damm'd up;
D' ye hear, sir?
*Phu.*          I do hear, my lord; a mason
Shall be provided suddenly.
*Bass.*                  Some rogue.
Some rogue of your confederacy, — factor   10
For slaves and strumpets! — to convey close packets
From this spruce springal and the t' other youngster,
That gaudy earwig, or my lord your patron,

¹²⁸ **grammates:** rudiments    ¹³⁵ **read:** lecture    ¹⁴⁴ **conceit:** idea    ¹⁴⁸ **attend:** await    ¹⁵² **intelligence:** information    ⁷ **light:** window    ⁹ **suddenly:** immediately    ¹⁰ **factor:** agent    ¹¹ **close packets:** secret letters    ¹² **springal:** youth

Whose pensioner you are. — I 'll tear thy throat
    out,
Son of a cat, ill-looking hound's-head, rip up 15
Thy ulcerous maw, if I but scent a paper,
A scroll, but half as big as what can cover
A wart upon thy nose, a spot, a pimple,
Directed to my lady. It may prove
A mystical preparative to lewdness.                    20
    *Phu.*  Care shall be had: I will turn every
    thread
About me to an eye. — [*Aside.*] Here 's a sweet
    life!
    *Bass.*  The city housewives, cunning in the
    traffic
Of chamber merchandise, set all at price
By wholesale; yet they wipe their mouths and
    simper,                                             25
Cull, kiss, and cry "sweetheart," and stroke
    the head
Which they have branch'd; and all is well
    again!
Dull clods of dirt, who dare not feel the rubs
Stuck on their foreheads.
    *Phu.*            'T is a villainous world;
One cannot hold his own in 't.
    *Bass.*          Dames at court, 30
Who flaunt in riots, run another bias.
Their pleasure heaves the patient ass that suf-
    fers
Up on the stilts of office, titles, incomes;
Promotion justifies the shame, and sues for 't.
Poor honour, thou art stabb'd, and bleed'st to
    death                                               35
By such unlawful hire! The country mistress
Is yet more wary, and in blushes hides
Whatever trespass draws her troth to guilt.
But all are false. On this truth I am bold:
No woman but can fall, and doth, or would. —
Now for the newest news about the city;       41
What blab the voices, sirrah?
    *Phu.*            O, my lord,
The rarest, quaintest, strangest, tickling news
That ever —
    *Bass.*  Hey-day! up and ride me, rascal!
What is 't?
    *Phu.*  Forsooth, they say the king has
    mew'd                                                45
All his gray beard, instead of which is budded
Another of a pure carnation colour,
Speckled with green and russet.
    *Bass.*            Ignorant block!
    *Phu.*  Yes, truly; and 't is talk'd about the
    streets
That, since Lord Ithocles came home, the lions
Never left roaring, at which noise the bears    51
Have danc'd their very hearts out.

    *Bass.*           Dance out thine too.
    *Phu.*  Besides, Lord Orgilus is fled to Athens
Upon a fiery dragon, and 't is thought
'A never can return.
    *Bass.*         Grant it, Apollo!    55
    *Phu.*  Moreover, please your lordship, 't is
    reported
For certain, that whoever is found jealous,
Without apparent proof that 's wife is wanton,
Shall be divorc'd: but this is but she-news;
I had it from a midwife. I have more yet.   60
    *Bass.*  Antic, no more! Idiots and stupid
    fools
Grate my calamities. Why, to be fair
Should yield presumption of a faulty soul! —
Look to the doors.
    *Phu.* [*Aside.*]  The horn of plenty crest him!
                           *Exit Phulas.*
    *Bass.*  Swarms of confusion huddle in my
    thoughts                                             65
In rare distemper. — Beauty! O, it is
An unmatch'd blessing or a horrid curse.

    *Enter Penthea and Grausis, an old Lady*

She comes, she comes! so shoots the morning
    forth,
Spangled with pearls of transparent dew. —
The way to poverty is to be rich,                  70
As I in her am wealthy; but for her,
In all contents a bankrupt. —
                     Lov'd Penthea!
How fares my heart's best joy?
    *Grau.*          In sooth, not well.
She is so over-sad.
    *Bass.*        Leave chattering, magpie. —
Thy brother is return'd, sweet, safe, and hon-
    our'd                                               75
With a triumphant victory: thou shalt visit
    him.
We will to court, where, if it be thy pleasure,
Thou shalt appear in such a ravishing lustre
Of jewels above value, that the dames
Who brave it there, in rage to be outshin'd,   80
Shall hide them in their closets, and unseen
Fret in their tears; whiles every wond'ring
    eye
Shall crave none other brightness but thy pres-
    ence.
Choose thine own recreations; be a queen
Of what delights thou fanciest best, what com-
    pany,                                               85
What place, what times. Do anything, do all
    things
Youth can command, so thou wilt chase these
    clouds
From the pure firmament of thy fair looks.

---

    [20] **mystical:** disguised    [23] **housewives:** hussies    [24–25] **set . . . wholesale:** are wholly venal
[26] **Cull:** hug   [27] **branch'd:** horned   [28] **rubs:** roughnesses   [29] **their:** ('the' Q)   [31] **bias:** indirect
course   [39] **bold:** firmly assured   [45] **mew'd:** moulted   [58] **that 's:** that his

*Grau.* Now 't is well said, my lord. — What,
   lady! laugh,
Be merry; time is precious.
   *Bass.* [*Aside.*]         Furies whip thee!  90
*Pen.* Alas, my lord, this language to your
   hand-maid
Sounds as would music to the deaf. I need
No braveries nor cost of art to draw
The whiteness of my name into offence.
Let such, if any such there are, who covet  95
A curiosity of admiration,
By laying out their plenty to full view,
Appear in gaudy outsides; my attires
Shall suit the inward fashion of my mind;
From which, if your opinion, nobly plac'd,  100
Change not the livery your words bestow,
My fortunes with my hopes are at the highest.
   *Bass.* This house, methinks, stands some-
      what too much inward,
It is too melancholy; we 'll remove       104
Nearer the court: or what thinks my Penthea
Of the delightful island we command?
Rule me as thou canst wish.
   *Pen.*                  I am no mistress.
Whither you please, I must attend; all ways
Are alike pleasant to me.
   *Grau.*                Island? prison!
A prison is as gaysome: we 'll no islands;  110
Marry, out upon 'em! Whom shall we see
   there?
Sea-gulls, and porpoises, and water-rats,
And crabs, and mews, and dog-fish? goodly
   gear
For a young lady's dealing, — or an old one's!
On no terms islands; I 'll be stew'd first.
   *Bass.* [*Aside to Grausis.*]    Grausis,  115
You are a juggling bawd. — This sadness,
   sweetest,
Becomes not youthful blood. — [*Aside to Grau-
   sis.*] I 'll have you pounded. —
For my sake put on a more cheerful mirth;
Thou 't mar thy cheeks, and make me old in
   griefs. —
[*Aside to Grausis.*] Damnable bitch-fox!
   *Grau.*          I am thick of hearing,  120
Still, when the wind blows southerly. — What
   think ye,
If your fresh lady breed young bones, my
   lord?
Would not a chopping boy d' ye good at heart?
But, as you said —
   *Bass.* [*Aside to Grausis.*] I 'll spit thee on a
      stake,
Or chop thee into collops!

*Grau.*          Pray, speak louder.  125
Sure, sure the wind blows south still.
   *Pen.*          Thou prat'st madly.
*Bass.* 'T is very hot; I sweat extremely.

*Enter Phulas*

                           Now?
*Phu.* A herd of lords, sir.
*Bass.*                Ha!
*Phu.*                A flock of ladies.
*Bass.* Where?
*Phu.*          Shoals of horses.
*Bass.*                Peasant, how?
*Phu.*                Caroches
In drifts; th' one enter, th' other stand with-
   out, sir:                              130
And now I vanish.          *Exit Phulas.*

*Enter Prophilus, Lemophil, Groneas,
   Christalla, and Philema*

*Pro.*          Noble Bassanes!
*Bass.* Most welcome, Prophilus! Ladies,
   gentlemen,
To all my heart is open; you all honour me, —
[*Aside.*] A tympany swells in my head al-
   ready, —
Honour me bountifully. — [*Aside.*] How they
   flutter,                              135
Wagtails and jays together!
*Pro.*                From your brother,
By virtue of your love to him, I require
Your instant presence, fairest.
*Pen.*                He is well, sir?
*Pro.* The gods preserve him ever! Yet, dear
   beauty,
I find some alteration in him lately,       140
Since his return to Sparta. — My good lord,
I pray, use no delay.
*Bass.*          We had not needed
An invitation, if his sister's health
Had not fallen into question. — Haste, Penthea,
Slack not a minute. — Lead the way, good
   Prophilus;                            145
I 'll follow step by step.
*Pro.*          Your arm, fair madam.
   *Exeunt omnes sed Bassanes & Grausis.*
*Bass.* One word with your old bawdship:
   th' hadst been better
Rail'd at the sins thou worshipp'st than have
   thwarted
My will. I 'll use thee cursedly.
*Grau.*                You dote,
You are beside yourself. A politician        150
In jealousy? No, y' are too gross, too vulgar.

---

⁹⁶ Admiration to please their whimsical vanity  ⁹⁸ **outsides:** external trappings  ¹⁰¹ **livery . . . be-**
**stow:** *i.e.*, the state of mind induced by your praise  ¹¹⁰ **gaysome:** pleasant  ¹²¹ **Still:** always
¹²³ **chopping:** lusty  ¹²⁵ **collops:** hunks of flesh  ¹²⁹ **Caroches:** coaches  ¹³⁴ **tympany:** inflation
¹⁴⁶ S. D. **sed:** except  ¹⁴⁷⁻¹⁴⁸ **th' . . . Rail'd:** It would have been better for thee to have blasphemed.
¹⁴⁸ **sins:** evil deities  ¹⁵⁰ **politician:** schemer

Pish, teach not me my trade; I know my cue.
My crossing you sinks me into her trust,
By which I shall know all: my trade 's a sure
   one.
*Bass.*   Forgive me, Grausis, 't was considera-
tion                         155
I relish'd not; but have a care now.
*Grau.*                  Fear not,
I am no new-come-to 't.
*Bass.*            Thy life 's upon it,
And so is mine. My agonies are infinite.
                            *Exeunt omnes.*

## Scene 2

### [*Lodging of Ithocles*]

*Enter Ithocles, alone*

*Ith.*   Ambition! 't is of vipers' breed: it
   gnaws
A passage through the womb that gave it mo-
tion.
Ambition, like a seeled dove, mounts upward,
Higher and higher still, to perch on clouds,
But tumbles headlong down with heavier ruin.
So squibs and crackers fly into the air,      6
Then, only breaking with a noise, they vanish
In stench and smoke. Morality, appli'd
To timely practice, keeps the soul in tune,
At whose sweet music all our actions dance. 10
But this is form of books and school-tradition;
It physics not the sickness of a mind
Broken with griefs: strong fevers are not eas'd
With counsel, but with best receipts and means.
Means, speedy means and certain; that 's the
   cure.                              15

*Enter Armostes and Crotolon*

*Arm.*   You stick. Lord Crotolon, upon a
   point
Too nice and too unnecessary; Prophilus
Is every way desertful. I am confident,
Your wisdom is too ripe to need instruction
From your son's tutelage.
*Crot.*            Yet not so ripe,  20
My Lord Armostes, that it dares to dote
Upon the painted meat of smooth persuasion,
Which tempts me to a breach of faith.
*Ith.*                    Not yet
Resolv'd, my lord? Why, if your son's consent
Be so available, we 'll write to Athens    25
For his repair to Sparta. The king's hand
Will join with our desires; he has been mov'd
to 't.

*Arm.*   Yes, and the king himself impórtun'd
   Crotolon
For a dispatch.
*Crot.*          Kings may command; their wills
Are laws not to be question'd.
*Ith.*            By this marriage  30
You knit an union so devout, so hearty,
Between your loves to me and mine to yours,
As if mine own blood had an interest in it;
For Prophilus is mine, and I am his.
*Crot.*   My lord, my lord! —
*Ith.*   What, good sir? Speak your thought.
*Crot.*   Had this sincerity been real once,  36
My Orgilus had not been now unwiv'd,
Nor your lost sister buried in a bride-bed.
Your uncle here, Armostes, knows this truth;
For had your father Thrasus liv'd, — but peace
Dwell in his grave! I have done.
*Arm.*            Y' are bold and bitter.  41
*Ith.* [*Aside.*] 'A presses home the injury; it
   smarts. —
No reprehensions, uncle; I deserve 'em.
Yet, gentle sir, consider what the heat
Of an unsteady youth, a giddy brain,     45
Green indiscretion, flattery of greatness,
Rawness of judgment, wilfulness in folly,
Thoughts vagrant as the wind and as uncertain,
Might lead a boy in years to: — 't was a fault,
A capital fault; for then I could not dive  50
Into the secrets of commanding love;
Since when, experience, by the extremes (in
   others),
Hath forc'd me to collect. And, trust me,
   Crotolon,
I will redeem those wrongs with any service
Your satisfaction can require for current.  55
*Arm.*   Thy acknowledgment is satisfaction.
— [*To Crot.*] What would you more?
*Crot.*          I 'm conquer'd. If Euphranea
Herself admit the motion, let it be so;
I doubt not my son's liking.
*Ith.*                Use my fortunes,
Life, power, sword, and heart, — all are your
   own.                              60

*Enter Bassanes, Prophilus, Calantha, Penthea,*
*Euphranea, Christalla, Philema, and Grausis*

*Arm.*   The princess, with your sister!
*Cal.*                I present ye
A stranger here in court, my lord; for did not
Desire of seeing you draw her abroad,
We had not been made happy in her com-
pany.

---

¹⁵⁵⁻¹⁵⁶ **'t was . . . not:** This was an aspect I didn't perceive.   ¹⁵⁷ **upon it:** at stake   ³ **seeled:**
blinded (by stitching the eyelids together)   ⁸ **Morality:** philosophy   ⁹ **timely practice:** the business
of the moment   ¹¹ **form:** pedantry   ¹⁴ **receipts:** recipes, formulas for action   ¹⁷ **nice:** fastidious
²² **painted meat:** unsubstantial bait   ²⁵ **available:** advantageous   ⁵⁰ **capital:** deadly   ⁵² **extremes:**
('extremities' Q)   ⁵³ **collect:** comprehend   ⁵⁵ **for current:** to be performed   ⁵⁸ **admit:** accept
⁶¹ **ye:** (' 'ee' Q)

*Ith.* You are a gracious princess. — Sister,
  wedlock                               65
Holds too severe a passion in your nature,
Which can engross all duty to your hus-
  band,
Without attendance on so dear a mistress. —
[*To Bassanes.*] 'T is not my brother's pleasure
  I presume,
T' immure her in a chamber.
  *Bass.*            'T is her will;  70
She governs her own hours. Noble Ithocles,
We thank the gods for your success and wel-
  fare.
Our lady has of late been indispos'd,
Else we had waited on you with the first.
  *Ith.* How does Penthea now?
  *Pen.*           You best know, brother,  75
From whom my health and comforts are de-
  riv'd.
  *Bass.* [*Aside.*] I like the answer well; 't is
  sad and modest.
There may be tricks yet, tricks. — Have an eye,
  Grausis!
  *Cal.* Now, Crotolon, the suit we join'd in
  must not
Fall by too long demur.
  *Crot.*          'T is granted, princess,  80
For my part.
  *Arm.*      With condition, that his son
Favour the contract.
  *Cal.*         Such delay is easy. —
The joys of marriage make thee, Prophilus,
A proud deserver of Euphranea's love,
And her of thy desert!
  *Pro.*         Most sweetly gracious!  85
  *Bass.* The joys of marriage are the heaven
  on earth,
Life's paradise, great princess, the soul's quiet,
Sinews of concord, earthly immortality,
Eternity of pleasures; — no restoratives
Like to a constant woman! — [*Aside.*] But
  where is she?                           90
'T would puzzle all the gods but to create
Such a new monster. — I can speak by proof,
For I rest in Elysium; 't is my happiness.
  *Crot.* Euphranea, how are you resolv'd,
  speak freely,
In your affections to this gentleman?   95
  *Euph.* Nor more nor less than as his love
  assures me;
Which (if your liking with my brother's war-
  rants)
I cannot but approve in all points worthy.
  *Crot.* So, so! — [*To Prophilus.*] I know
  your answer.
  *Ith.*         'T had been pity
To sunder hearts so equally consented.   100

*Enter Lemophil*

  *Lem.* The king, Lord Ithocles, commands
  your presence; —
And, fairest princess, yours.
  *Cal.*            We will attend him.

*Enter Groneas*

  *Gro.* Where are the lords? All must unto
  the king
Without delay: the Prince of Argos —
  *Cal.*                  Well, sir?
  *Gro.* Is coming to the court, sweet lady.
  *Cal.*                  How!  105
The Prince of Argos?
  *Gro.*        'T was my fortune, madam,
T' enjoy the honour of these happy tidings.
  *Ith.* Penthea! —
  *Pen.*           Brother?
  *Ith.*             Let me an hour hence
Meet you alone within the palace-grove;   109
I have some secret with you. — Prithee, friend,
Conduct her thither, and have special care
The walks be clear'd of any to disturb us.
  *Pro.* I shall.
  *Bass.* [*Aside.*] How 's that?
  *Ith.*           Alone, pray be alone. —
I am your creature, princess. — On, my lords!
               *Exeunt.* [*Manet*] *Bassanes.*
  *Bass.* Alone! alone! What means that word
  "alone"?                              115
Why might not I be there? — hum! — he 's
  her brother.
Brothers and sisters are but flesh and blood,
And this same whoreson court ease is tempta-
  tion
To a rebellion in the veins. — Besides,   119
His fine friend Prophilus must be her guardian:
Why may not he dispatch a business nim-
  bly
Before the other come? — or — pand'ring, pan-
  d'ring
For one another, — be 't to sister, mother,
Wife, cousin, anything, — 'mongst youths of
  mettle
Is in request. It is so — stubborn fate!   125
But if I be a cuckold, and can know it,
I will be fell, and fell.

*Enter Groneas*

  *Gro.*        My lord, y' are call'd for.
  *Bass.* Most heartily I thank ye. Where 's
  my wife, pray?
  *Gro.* Retir'd amongst the ladies.
  *Bass.*           Still I thank ye.
There 's an old waiter with her; saw you her
  too?                                130

---

  77 **sad:** sedate    82 **easy:** easily overcome    100 **consented:** in harmony    118 **ease:** unemploy-
ment    125 **in request:** fashionable    127 **fell, and fell:** fierce, and very fierce    130 **waiter:** attendant

*Gro.* She sits i' th' presence-lobby fast asleep, sir.

*Bass.* Asleep! sleep, sir!

*Gro.*                         Is your lordship troubled?
You will not to the king?

*Bass.*                         Your humblest vassal.

*Gro.* Your servant, my good lord.

*Bass.*                         I wait your footsteps.
                                                    *Exeunt.*

## Scene the third

[*The Palace-Grove*]

*Prophilus, Penthea*

*Pro.* In this walk, lady, will your brother
find you:
And, with your favour, give me leave a little
To work a preparation.  In his fashion
I have observ'd of late some kind of slackness
To such alacrity as nature once          5
And custom took delight in.  Sadness grows
Upon his recreations, which he hoards
In such a willing silence, that to question
The grounds will argue little skill in friendship,
And less good manners.

*Pen.*                         Sir, I 'm not inquisitive   10
Of secrecies without an invitation.

*Pro.* With pardon, lady, not a syllable
Of mine implies so rude a sense; the drift —

*Enter Orgilus [disguised as before]*

[*To Org.*]  Do thy best
To make this lady merry for an hour.  *Exit.* 15

*Org.* Your will shall be a law, sir.

*Pen.*                         Prithee, leave me.
I have some private thoughts I would account
with:
Use thou thine own.

*Org.*                         Speak on, fair nymph; our souls
Can dance as well to music of the spheres
As any's who have feasted with the gods.   20

*Pen.* Your school-terms are too troublesome.

*Org.*                         What Heaven
Refines mortality from dross of earth
But such as uncompounded beauty hallows
With glorified perfection?

*Pen.*                         Set thy wits
In a less wild proportion.

*Org.*                         Time can never   25
On the white table of unguilty faith
Write counterfeit dishonour; turn those eyes,
The arrows of pure love, upon that fire,
Which once rose to a flame, perfum'd with
vows
As sweetly scented as the incense smoking  30

On Vesta's altars,  . . . . . . .
. . . the holiest odours, virgin tears,
. . . . like sprinkled dews, to feed 'em
And to increase their fervour.

*Pen.*                         Be not frantic.

*Org.* All pleasures are but mere imagination,
Feeding the hungry appetite with steam    36
And sight of banquet, whilst the body pines,
Not relishing the real taste of food:
Such is the leanness of a heart divided
From intercourse of troth-contracted loves.   40
No horror should deface that precious figure
Seal'd with the lively stamp of equal souls.

*Pen.* Away! some fury hath bewitch'd thy
tongue.
The breath of ignorance, that flies from thence,
Ripens a knowledge in me of afflictions    45
Above all suff'rance. — Thing of talk, begone!
Begone, without reply!

*Org.*                         Be just, Penthea,
In thy commands: when thou send'st forth a
doom
Of banishment, know first on whom it lights.
Thus I take off the shroud, in which my cares 50
Are folded up from view of common eyes.
                    [*Removes his Scholar's gown.*]
What is thy sentence next?

*Pen.*                         Rash man! thou layest
A blemish on mine honour, with the hazard
Of thy too-desperate life.  Yet I profess,
By all the laws of ceremonious wedlock,     55
I have not given admittance to one thought
Of female change since cruelty enforc'd
Divorce betwixt my body and my heart.
Why would you fall from goodness thus?

*Org.*                         O, rather
Examine me, how I could live to say        60
I have been much, much wrong'd.  'T is for thy
sake
I put on this imposture.  Dear Penthea,
If thy soft bosom be not turn'd to marble,
Thou 't pity our calamities; my interest
Confirms me, thou art mine still.

*Pen.*                         Lend your hand.  65
With both of mine I clasp it thus, thus kiss it,
Thus kneel before ye.

*Org.*                         You instruct my duty.

*Pen.* We may stand up. — Have you aught
else to urge
Of new demand?  As for the old, forget it;
'T is buried in an everlasting silence,      70
And shall be, shall be ever.  What more would
ye?

*Org.* I would possess my wife; the equity
Of very reason bids me.

---

**¹³⁴ wait:** attend   **³ fashion:** bearing   **⁵ once:** (not in Q)   **⁸ willing:** resolute   **⁹ little:** (not in Q)   **²¹ school-terms:** scholastic phrases   **²³ uncompounded:** not artificial   **²⁵ proportion:** balance, harmony   **³¹⁻³³** (Text evidently corrupted by printer of Q, which reads: 'The holiest Artars. Virgin teares [like |   On *Vesta's* odours] sprinkled dewes to feed 'em.')   **⁶⁵ Confirms:** assures

*Pen.* Is that all?

*Org.* Why, 't is the all of me, myself.

*Pen.* Remove
Your steps some distance from me: — at this
space 75
A few words I dare change; but first put on
Your borrow'd shape.

*Org.* You are obey'd; 't is done.
[*He resumes his disguise.*]

*Pen.* How, Orgilus, by promise I was thine
The heavens do witness: they can witness too
A rape done on my truth. How I do love
thee 80
Yet, Orgilus, and yet, must best appear
In tendering thy freedom; for I find
The constant preservation of thy merit,
By thy not daring to attempt my fame
With injury of any loose conceit, 85
Which might give deeper wounds to discon-
tents.
Continue this fair race: then, though I cannot
Add to thy comfort, yet I shall more often
Remember from what fortune I am fallen, 89
And pity mine own ruin. — Live, live happy, —
Happy in thy next choice, that thou mayst
people
This barren age with virtues in thy issue!
And O, when thou art married, think on me
With mercy, not contempt! I hope thy wife,
Hearing my story, will not scorn my fall. — 95
Now let us part.

*Org.* Part! yet advise thee better:
Penthea is the wife to Orgilus,
And ever shall be.

*Pen.* Never shall nor will.

*Org.* How!

*Pen.* Hear me; in a word I 'll tell thee
why.
The virgin-dowry which my birth bestow'd 100
Is ravish'd by another; my true love
Abhors to think that Orgilus deserv'd
No better favours than a second bed.

*Org.* I must not take this reason.

*Pen.* To confirm it,
Should I outlive my bondage, let me meet 105
Another worse than this and less desir'd,
If, of all the men alive, thou shouldst but touch
My lip or hand again!

*Org.* Penthea, now
I tell 'ee, you grow wanton in my sufferance.
Come, sweet, th' art mine.

*Pen.* Uncivil sir, forbear! 110
Or I can turn affection into vengeance;
Your reputation, if you value any,
Lies bleeding at my feet. Unworthy man,

If ever henceforth thou appear in language,
Message, or letter, to betray my frailty, 115
I 'll call thy former protestations lust,
And curse my stars for forfeit of my judgment.
Go thou, fit only for disguise and walks,
To hide thy shame: this once I spare thy life.
I laugh at mine own confidence; my sorrows
By thee are made inferior to my fortunes. 121
If ever thou didst harbour worthy love,
Dare not to answer. My good genius guide me,
That I may never see thee more! — Go from
me!

*Org.* I 'll tear my veil of politic frenzy off,
And stand up like a man resolv'd to do: 126
Action, not words, shall show me. — O Penthea!
*Exit Orgilus.*

*Pen.* 'A sigh'd my name, sure, as he parted
from me:
I fear I was too rough. Alas, poor gentleman!
'A look'd not like the ruins of his youth, 130
But like the ruins of those ruins. Honour,
How much we fight with weakness to preserve
thee! [*Walks aside.*]

*Enter Bassanes and Grausis*

*Bass.* Fie on thee! damn thee, rotten maggot, damn thee!
Sleep? sleep at court? and now? Aches, convulsions,
Imposthumes, rheums, gouts, palsies, clog thy
bones 135
A dozen years more yet!

*Grau.* Now y' are in humours.

*Bass.* She 's by herself, there 's hope of that;
she 's sad too;
She 's in strong contemplation; yes, and fix'd:
The signs are wholesome.

*Grau.* Very wholesome, truly,

*Bass.* Hold your chops, nightmare! — Lady,
come; your brother 140
Is carried to his closet; you must thither.

*Pen.* Not well, my lord?

*Bass.* A sudden fit; 't will off!
Some surfeit or disorder. — How dost, dearest?

*Pen.* Your news is none o' the best.

*Enter Prophilus*

*Pro.* The chief of men,
The excellentest Ithocles, desires 145
Your presence, madam.

*Bass.* We are hasting to him.

*Pen.* In vain we labour in this course of life
To piece our journey out at length, or crave
Respite of breath: our home is in the grave.

*Bass.* Perfect philosophy!

---

⁸² tendering: cherishing  ⁸⁷ race: course of action  ¹⁰⁹ **grow . . . sufferance:** abuse my patience  ¹¹⁷ **for . . . judgment:** for the mistake I made in loving you  ¹¹⁸ **walks:** lurking places  ¹²⁶ **frenzy:** (*i.e.*, the pose of mad scholar; 'French' Q)  ¹²⁷ **show:** reveal  ¹³⁴ **Aches:** (Pronounce in two syllables: "atches,")  ¹³⁵ **Imposthumes:** abscesses  ¹³⁸ **fix'd:** quiet  ¹⁴⁰ **chops:** jaws

*Pen.*                        Then let us care   150
To live so, that our reckonings may fall even
When w' are to make account.
    *Pro.*                     He cannot fear
Who builds on noble grounds: sickness or pain
Is the deserver's exercise; and such
Your virtuous brother to the world is known.
Speak comfort to him, lady; be all gentle:   156
Stars fall but in the grossness of our sight;
A good man dying, th' earth doth lose a light.
                              *Exeunt omnes.*

## Actus Tertius: Scæna prima

*[House of Tecnicus]*

*Enter Tecnicus, and Orgilus in his own
shape*

*Tec.*   Be well advis'd; let not a resolution
Of giddy rashness choke the breath of reason.
*Org.*   It shall not, most sage master.
*Tec.*                        I am jealous;
For if the borrow'd shape so late put on
Inferr'd a consequence, we must conclude   5
Some violent design of sudden nature
Hath shook that shadow off, to fly upon
A new-hatch'd execution.  Orgilus,
Take heed thou hast not, under our integrity,
Shrouded unlawful plots; our mortal eyes   10
Pierce not the secrets of your heart, the gods
Are only privy to them.
*Org.*                   Learned Tecnicus,
Such doubts are causeless; and, to clear the
    truth
From misconceit, the present state commands
    me.
The Prince of Argos comes himself in person   15
In quest of great Calantha for his bride,
Our kingdom's heir; besides, mine only sister,
Euphranea, is dispos'd to Prophilus;
Lastly, the king is sending letters for me
To Athens, for my quick repair to court:   20
Please to accept these reasons.
*Tec.*                   Just ones, Orgilus,
Not to be contradicted: yet beware
Of an unsure foundation.  No fair colours
Can fortify a building faintly jointed.
I have observ'd a growth in thy aspect   25
Of dangerous extent, sudden, and — look to
    't —
I might add, certain —
*Org.*                   My aspéct!  Could art
Run through mine inmost thoughts, it should
    not sift

An inclination there more than what suited
With justice of mine honour.
    *Tec.*                   I believe it.   30
But know then, Orgilus, what honour is.
Honour consists not in a bare opinion
By doing any act that feeds content,
Brave in appearance, 'cause we think it brave.
Such honour comes by accident, not nature,   35
Proceeding from the vices of our passion,
Which makes our reason drunk.  But real
    honour
Is the reward of virtue, and acquir'd
By justice, or by valour which for basis
Hath justice to uphold it.  He then fails   40
In honour, who for lucre or revenge
Commits thefts, murthers, treasons, and adul-
    teries,
With suchlike, by intrenching on just laws,
Whose sovereignty is best preserv'd by jus-
    tice.
Thus, as you see how honour must be grounded
On knowledge, not opinion, — for opinion   46
Relies on probability and accident,
But knowledge on necessity and truth, —
I leave thee to the fit consideration
Of what becomes the grace of real honour,   50
Wishing success to all thy virtuous meanings.
    *Org.*   The gods increase thy wisdom, reverend
        oracle,
And in thy precepts make me ever thrifty!
    *Tec.*   I thank thy wish.        *Exit Orgilus.*
                    Much mystery of fate
Lies hid in that man's fortunes.  Curiosity   55
May lead his actions into rare attempts: —
But let the gods be moderators still;
No human power can prevent their will.

*Enter Armostes [with a casket]*

From whence come ye?
    *Arm.*            From King Amyclas, — pardon
My interruption of your studies. — Here,   60
In this seal'd box, he sends a treasure dear
To him as his crown.  'A prays your gravity,
You would examine, ponder, sift, and bolt
The pith and circumstance of every tittle
The scroll within contains.
    *Tec.*            What is 't, Armostes?   65
    *Arm.*   It is the health of Sparta, the king's
        life,
Sinews and safety of the commonwealth;
The sum of what the oracle deliver'd
When last he visited the prophetic temple
At Delphos: what his reasons are, for which,   70
After so long a silence, he requires

---

    ¹⁵⁰ **Pen:** (not in Q, which gives this speech to Bassanes)   ¹⁵⁴ **exercise:** discipline   ³ **jealous:**
suspicious   ⁵ **consequence:** logical purpose   ⁸ **execution:** enterprise   ¹¹ **heart:** ('hearts' Q)
¹⁴ **the . . . state:** immediate public business   ²⁴ **faintly:** weakly   ²⁶ **extent:** intensity   ³³ **feeds
content:** satisfies vanity   ³⁹ **basis:** ('Bases' Q)   ⁴¹ **or:** ('of' Q)   ⁵³ **thrifty:** thriving   ⁵⁵ **Curiosity:** subtlety   ⁶³ **bolt:** winnow

Your counsel now, grave man, his majesty
Will soon himself acquaint you with.
  *Tec.* [*Takes the casket.*]        Apollo
Inspire my intellect! — The Prince of Argos
Is entertain'd?
  *Arm.*      He is; and has demanded   75
Our princess for his wife; which I conceive
One special cause the king importunes you
For resolution of the oracle.
  *Tec.* My duty to the king, good peace to
    Sparta,
And fair day to Armostes!
  *Arm.*     Like to Tecnicus! *Exeunt.*  80

[SCENE II. — *Ithocles' Apartment*]

*Soft Music. A Song*

Can you paint a thought? or number
Every fancy in a slumber?
Can you count soft minutes roving
From a dial's point by moving?
Can you grasp a sigh? or, lastly,     5
Rob a virgin's honour chastely?
  No, O, no! yet you may
Sooner do both that and this,
This and that, and never miss,
Than by any praise display     10
Beauty's beauty; such a glory,
As beyond all fate, all story,
  All arms, all arts,
  All loves, all hearts,
Greater than those or they,     15
Do, shall, and must obey.

*During which time enters Prophilus, Bassanes,
Penthea, Grausis, passing over the stage.
Bassanes and Grausis enter again softly,
stealing to several stands, and listen.*

  *Bass.* All silent, calm, secure.    Grausis, no
    creaking?
No noise?  Dost hear nothing?
  *Grau.*          Not a mouse,
Or whisper of the wind.
  *Bass.*       The floor is matted;
The bedposts sure are steel or marble. — Sol-
    diers    20
Should not affect, methinks, strains so effem-
    inate:
Sounds of such delicacy are but fawnings
Upon the sloth of luxury, they heighten
Cinders of covert lust up to a flame.
  *Grau.* What do you mean, my lord? — speak
    low; that gabbling    25
Of yours will but undo us.

  *Bass.*          Chamber-combats
Are felt, not heard.
  *Pro.* [*Within.*]    'A wakes.
  *Bass.*          What 's that?
  *Ith.* [*Within.*]        Who 's there?
Sister? — All quit the room else.
  *Bass.*         'T is consented!

*Enter Prophilus*

  *Pro.* Lord Bassanes, your brother would be
    private.
We must forbear; his sleep hath newly left
    him.    30
Please ye, withdraw.
  *Bass.*      By any means; 't is fit.
  *Pro.* Pray, gentlewoman, walk too.
  *Grau.*       Yes, I will, sir. *Exeunt omnes.*

*Ithocles discovered in a chair, and Penthea*

  *Ith.* Sit nearer, sister, to me; nearer yet.
We had one father, in one womb took life,   34
Were brought up twins together, yet have liv'd
At distance, like two strangers.  I could wish
That the first pillow whereon I was cradled
Had prov'd to me a grave.
  *Pen.*      You had been happy:
Then had you never known that sin of life,
Which blots all following glories with a ven-
    geance    40
For forfeiting the last will of the dead,
From whom you had your being.
  *Ith.*         Sad Penthea,
Thou canst not be too cruel; my rash spleen
Hath with a violent hand pluck'd from thy
    bosom
A love-bless'd heart, to grind it into dust;   45
For which mine 's now a-breaking.
  *Pen.*        Not yet, Heaven,
I do beseech thee!  First let some wild fires
Scorch, not consume it! may the heat be cher-
    ish'd
With desires infinite, but hopes impossible!
  *Ith.* Wrong'd soul, thy prayers are heard.
  *Pen.*      Here, lo, I breathe,   50
A miserable creature, led to ruin
By an unnatural brother!
  *Ith.*         I consume
In languishing affections for that trespass;
Yet cannot die.
  *Pen.*     The handmaid to the wages  54
Of country toil drinks the untroubled streams
With leaping kids and with the bleating lambs,
And so allays her thirst secure; whiles I
Quench my hot sighs with fleetings of my
    tears.

---

<sup></sup>  **78 resolution:** interpretation    **16 S. D. several stands:** different positions    **22-23 fawnings
Upon:** concessions to    **23 luxury:** lasciviousness    **32 S. D. discovered:** (by drawing the rear-stage
curtain)  **45 love-bless'd:** ('louer-blest' Q)    **54-55 The . . . toil:** the peasant girl    **55** ('The
vntroubled of Country toyle, drinkes streames' Q)    **57 secure:** in peace    **58 fleetings:** drippings

*Ith.* The labourer doth eat his coarsest bread,
Earn'd with his sweat, and lies him down to sleep; 60
While every bit I touch turns in digestion
To gall as bitter as Penthea's curse.
Put me to any penance for my tyranny,
And I will call thee merciful.

*Pen.* Pray kill me,
Rid me from living with a jealous husband; 65
Then we will join in friendship, be again
Brother and sister. — Kill me, pray; nay, will ye?

*Ith.* How does thy lord esteem thee?

*Pen.* Such an one
As only you have made me: a faith-breaker,
A spotted whore. — Forgive me, I am one 70
In act, not in desires, the gods must witness.

*Ith.* Thou dost belie thy friend.

*Pen.* I do not, Ithocles;
For she that 's wife to Orgilus, and lives
In known adultery with Bassanes,
Is at the best a whore. Wilt kill me now? 75
The ashes of our parents will assume
Some dreadful figure, and appear to charge
Thy bloody guilt, that hast betray'd their name
To infamy in this reproachful match.

*Ith.* After my victories abroad, at home 80
I meet despair; ingratitude of nature
Hath made my actions monstrous. Thou shalt stand
A deity, my sister, and be worshipp'd
For thy resolved martyrdom: wrong'd maids
And married wives shall to thy hallow'd shrine
Offer their orisons, and sacrifice 86
Pure turtles, crown'd with myrtle; if thy pity
Unto a yielding brother's pressure lend
One finger but to ease it.

*Pen.* O, no more!

*Ith.* Death waits to waft me to the Stygian banks, 90
And free me from this chaos of my bondage;
And till thou wilt forgive, I must endure.

*Pen.* Who is the saint you serve?

*Ith.* Friendship, or nearness
Of birth to any but my sister, durst not
Have mov'd that question. 'T is a secret, sister, 95
I dare not murmur to myself.

*Pen.* Let me,
By your new protestations, I conjure 'ee,
Partake her name.

*Ith.* Her name? — 't is — 't is — I dare not.

*Pen.* All your respects are forg'd.

*Ith.* They are not. — Peace!
Calantha is — the princess — the king's daughter — 100
Sole heir of Sparta. — Me most miserable!
Do I now love thee? For my injuries
Revenge thyself with bravery, and gossip
My treasons to the king's ears, do. Calantha
Knows it not yet, nor Prophilus, my nearest. 105

*Pen.* Suppose you were contracted to her, would it not
Split even your very soul to see her father
Snatch her out of your arms against her will,
And force her on the Prince of Argos?

*Ith.* Trouble not
The fountains of mine eyes with thine own story; 110
I sweat in blood for 't.

*Pen.* We are reconcil'd.
Alas, sir, being children, but two branches
Of one stock, 't is not fit we should divide.
Have comfort, you may find it.

*Ith.* Yes, in thee;
Only in thee, Penthea mine.

*Pen.* If sorrows 115
Have not too much dull'd my infected brain,
I 'll cheer invention for an active strain.

*Ith.* Mad man! why have I wrong'd a maid so excellent!

*Enter Bassanes with a poniard, Prophilus,
Groneas, Lemophil, and Grausis*

*Bass.* I can forbear no longer; more, I will not.
Keep off your hands, or fall upon my point. —
Patience is tir'd; for, like a slow-pac'd ass, 121
Ye ride my easy nature, and proclaim
My sloth to vengeance a reproach and property.

*Ith.* The meaning of this rudeness?

*Pro.* He 's distracted.

*Pen.* O, my griev'd lord! —

*Grau.* Sweet lady, come not near him; 125
He holds his perilous weapon in his hand
To prick 'a cares not whom nor where, — see, see, see!

*Bass.* My birth is noble. Though the popular blast
Of vanity, as giddy as thy youth,
Hath rear'd thy name up to bestride a cloud,
Or progress in the chariot of the sun, 131
I am no clod of trade, to lackey pride,
Nor, like your slave of expectation, wait
The bawdy hinges of your doors, or whistle
For mystical conveyance to your bed-sports. 135

*Gro.* Fine humours! they become him.

---

⁶¹ **While:** ('Which' Q) **digestion:** ('disgestion' Q) ⁹³ **nearness:** (not in Q) ⁹⁵ **'T is:** ('as' Q)
⁹⁹ **respects:** avowals of affection (to Penthea) ¹¹⁷ **cheer . . . strain:** urge my mind to activity
¹²³ **property:** tool ¹³⁰ **bestride a cloud:** (alluding to the myth of Ixion: compare IV. i. 69–71)
¹³¹ **progress:** travel (like Phaeton) ¹³³ **slave of expectation:** expectant lackey **wait:** attend at
¹³⁵ **mystical:** secret

*Lem.*                                    How 'a stares,
Struts, puffs, and sweats!   Most admirable
lunacy!
*Ith.*   But that I may conceive the spirit of
wine
Has took possession of your soberer custom,
I 'd say you were unmannerly.
*Pen.*                         Dear brother! —   140
*Bass.*           Unmannerly! — mew, kitling! —
smooth Formality
Is usher to the rankness of the blood,
But Impudence bears up the train.   Indeed, sir,
Your fiery mettle, or your springal blaze
Of huge renown, is no sufficient royalty     145
To print upon my forehead the scorn, "cuck-
old."
*Ith.*   His jealousy has robb'd him of his wits;
'A talks 'a knows not what.
*Bass.*                      Yes, and 'a knows
To whom 'a talks; to one that franks his lust
In swine-security of bestial incest.           150
*Ith.*   Ha, devil!
*Bass.*   I will halloo 't; though I blush more
To name the filthiness than thou to act it.
*Ith.*   Monster!            [*Draws his sword.*]
*Pro.*            Sir, by our friendship —
*Pen.*                        By our bloods —
Will you quite both undo us, brother?
*Grau.*                          Out on him!
These are his megrims, firks, and melancho-
lies.                                              155
*Lem.*   Well said, old touch-hole.
*Gro.*                      Kick him out at doors.
*Pen.*   With favour, let me speak. — My lord,
what slackness
In my obedience hath deserv'd this rage?
Except humility and silent duty
Have drawn on your unquiet, my simplicity 160
Ne'er studied your vexation.
*Bass.*                      Light of beauty,
Deal not ungently with a desperate wound!
No breach of reason dares make war with her
Whose looks are sovereignty, whose breath is
balm.
O, that I could preserve thee in fruition      165
As in devotion!
*Pen.*            Sir, may every evil
Lock'd in Pandora's box shower, in your pres-
ence,
On my unhappy head, if, since you made me
A partner in your bed, I have been faulty
In one unseemly thought against your honour!
*Ith.*   Purge not his griefs, Penthea.
*Bass.*                      Yes, say on,   171
Excellent   creature! — [*To   Ithocles.*]   Good,
be not a hindrance
To peace and praise of virtue. — O, my senses

Are charm'd with sounds celestial! — On, dear,
on.
I never gave you one ill word; say, did I?   175
Indeed I did not.
*Pen.*                  Nor, by Juno's forehead,
Was I e'er guilty of a wanton error.
*Bass.*   A goddess! let me kneel.
*Grau.*                      Alas, kind animal!
*Ith.*   No; but for penance.
*Bass.*                    Noble sir, what is it?
With gladness I embrace it; yet, pray let
not
My rashness teach you to be too unmerciful. 181
*Ith.*   When you shall show good proof that
manly wisdom,
Not oversway'd by passion or opinion,
Knows how to lead your judgment, then this
lady,
Your wife, my sister, shall return in safety 185
Home, to be guided by you; but, till first
I can out of clear evidence approve it,
She shall be my care.
*Bass.*                  Rip my bosom up,
I 'll stand the execution with a constancy;
This torture is unsufferable.
*Ith.*                      Well, sir,       190
I dare not trust her to your fury.
*Bass.*                          But
Penthea says not so.
*Pen.*                She needs no tongue
To plead excuse who never purpos'd wrong.
*Lem.* [*To Grausis.*]  Virgin of reverence and
antiquity,
Stay you behind.
*Gro.*          The court wants not your
diligence.                                        195
          *Exeunt omnes sed Bass. & Grau.*
*Grau.*   What will you do, my lord?   My
lady 's gone;
I am denied to follow.
*Bass.*              I may see her,
Or speak to her once more?
*Grau.*                  And feel her too, man.
Be of good cheer, she 's your own flesh and
bone.
*Bass.*   Diseases desperate must find cures
alike.                                            200
She swore she has been true.
*Grau.*              True, on my modesty.
*Bass.*   Let him want truth who credits not
her vows!
Much wrong I did her, but her brother infinite;
Rumour will voice me the contempt of man-
hood,                                             204
Should I run on thus.   Some way I must try
To outdo art, and tie up jealousy.
                              *Exeunt omnes.*

---

<sup>137</sup> **admirable:** wonderful    <sup>144</sup> **springal:** precocious    <sup>145</sup> **royalty:** license    <sup>149</sup> **franks:** gorges
<sup>155</sup> **megrims:** fits of temper    **firks:** pranks    <sup>184</sup> **your:** (not in Q)    <sup>206</sup> **tie up:** ('cry a' Q)

[SCENE III. — *The Court*]

*Flourish. Enter Amyclas, Nearchus, leading Calantha, Armostes, Crotolon, Euphranea, Christalla, Philema, and Amelus*

*Amy.* Cousin of Argos, what the heavens have pleas'd,
In their unchanging counsels, to conclude
For both our kingdoms' weal, we must submit to:
Nor can we be unthankful to their bounties,
Who, when we were even creeping to our grave,                                5
Sent us a daughter, in whose birth our hope
Continues of succession. As you are
In title next, being grandchild to our aunt,
So we in heart desire you may sit nearest
Calantha's love; since we have ever vow'd      10
Not to enforce affection by our will,
But by her own choice to confirm it gladly.
*Near.* You speak the nature of a right just father.
I come not hither roughly to demand
My cousin's thraldom, but to free mine own. 15
Report of great Calantha's beauty, virtue,
Sweetness, and singular perfections, courted
All ears to credit what I find was publish'd
By constant truth; from which, if any service
Of my desert can purchase fair construction, 20
This lady must command it.
*Cal.*                          Princely sir,
So well you know how to profess observance,
That you instruct your hearers to become
Practitioners in duty; of which number
I 'll study to be chief.
*Near.*            Chief, glorious virgin,   25
In my devotions, as in all men's wonder.
*Amy.* Excellent cousin, we deny no liberty;
Use thine own opportunities. — Armostes,
We must consult with the philosophers;
The business is of weight.
*Arm.*            Sir, at your pleasure.  30
*Amy.* You told me, Crotolon, your son 's return'd
From Athens: wherefore comes 'a not to court
As we commanded?
*Crot.*            He shall soon attend
Your royal will, great sir.
*Amy.*            The marriage
Between young Prophilus and Euphranea   35
Tastes of too much delay.
*Crot.*            My lord, —
*Amy.*            Some pleasures
At celebration of it would give life
To th' entertainment of the prince our kinsman.
Our court wears gravity more than we relish.

*Arm.* Yet the heavens smile on all your high attempts,                                40
Without a cloud.
*Crot.*            So may the gods protect us.
*Cal.* A prince a subject?
*Near.*            Yes, to beauty's sceptre:
As all hearts kneel, so mine.
*Cal.*            You are too courtly.

*To them Ithocles, Orgilus, Prophilus*

*Ith.* Your safe return to Sparta is most welcome:
I joy to meet you here, and, as occasion   45
Shall grant us privacy, will yield you reasons
Why I should covet to deserve the title
Of your respected friend; for, without compliment,
Believe it, Orgilus, 't is my ambition.
*Org.* Your lordship may command me, your poor servant.                                50
*Ith.* [*Aside.*] So amorously close! — so soon! — my heart!
*Pro.* What sudden change is next?
*Ith.*            Life to the king!
To whom I here present this noble gentleman,
New come from Athens. Royal sir, vouchsafe
Your gracious hand in favour of his merit.  55
            [*The King gives Orgilus his hand to kiss.*]
*Crot.* [*Aside.*] My son preferr'd by Ithocles!
*Amy.*            Our bounties
Shall open to thee, Orgilus; for instance, —
Hark in thine ear, — if, out of those inventions
Which flow in Athens, thou hast there engross'd
Some rarity of wit, to grace the nuptials   60
Of thy fair sister, and renown our court
In th' eyes of this young prince, we shall be debtor
To thy conceit: think on 't.
*Org.*            Your highness honours me.
*Near.* My tongue and heart are twins.
*Cal.*            A noble birth,
Becoming such a father. — Worthy Orgilus,   65
You are a guest most wish'd for.
*Org.*            May my duty
Still rise in your opinion, sacred princess!
*Ith.* Euphranea's brother, sir; a gentleman
Well worthy of your knowledge.
*Near.*            We embrace him,
Proud of so dear acquaintance.
*Amy.*            All prepare  70
For revels and disport; the joys of Hymen,
Like Phœbus in his lustre, put to flight
All mists of dulness, crown the hours with gladness:
No sounds but music, no discourse but mirth!

---

⁵ **grave:** ('graues' Q)      ²² **observance:** courtly service      ³⁶ **Tastes:** partakes      ⁵⁹ **flow:** abound
**engross'd:** made yours      ⁶³ **conceit:** invention      ⁷² **put:** ('puts' Q)

*Cal.*  Thine arm, I prithee, Ithocles. — Nay, good                                                        75
My lord, keep on your way; I am provided.
*Near.*  I dare not disobey.
*Ith.*                          Most heavenly lady!  *Exeunt.*

[SCENE IV. — *House of Crotolon*]

*Enter Crotolon, Orgilus*

*Crot.*  The king hath spoke his mind.
*Org.*                          His will he hath;
But were it lawful to hold plea against
The power of greatness, not the reason, haply
Such undershrubs as subjects sometimes might
Borrow of nature justice, to inform                       5
That license sovereignty holds without check
Over a meek obedience.
*Crot.*                  How resolve you
Touching your sister's marriage? Prophilus
Is a deserving and a hopeful youth.
*Org.*  I envy not his merit, but applaud it; 10
Could wish him thrift in all his best desires,
And with a willingness inleague our blood
With his, for purchase of full growth in friend-
ship.
He never touch'd on any wrong that malic'd
The honour of our house, nor stirr'd our peace:
Yet, with your favour, let me not forget        16
Under whose wing he gathers warmth and com-
fort,
Whose creature he is bound, made, and must
live so.
*Crot.*  Son, son, I find in thee a harsh condi-
tion;
No courtesy can win it; 't is too rancorous. 20
*Org.*  Good sir, be not severe in your con-
struction.
I am no stranger to such easy calms
As sit in tender bosoms: lordly Ithocles
Hath grac'd my entertainment in abundance,
Too humbly hath descended from that height
Of arrogance and spleen which wrought the
rape                                                      26
On griev'd Penthea's purity; his scorn
Of my untoward fortunes is reclaim'd
Unto a courtship, almost to a fawning: —
I 'll kiss his foot, since you will have it so.   30
*Crot.*  Since I will have it so! Friend, I will
have it so,
Without our ruin by your politic plots,
Or wolf-of-hatred snarling in your breast.
You have a spirit, sir, have ye? A familiar
That posts i' th' air for your intelligence?     35
Some such hobgoblin hurried you from Athens,
For yet you come unsent for.
*Org.*                          If unwelcome,
I might have found a grave there.

*Crot.*                          Sure, your business
Was soon dispatch'd, or your mind alter'd
quickly.
*Org.*  'T was care, sir, of my health cut short
my journey;                                               40
For there a general infection
Threatens a desolation.
*Crot.*                  And I fear
Thou hast brought back a worse infection with
thee, —
Infection of thy mind; which, as thou say'st,
Threatens the desolation of our family.          45
*Org.*  Forbid it, our dear genius! I will
rather
Be made a sacrifice on Thrasus' monument,
Or kneel to Ithocles, his son, in dust,
Than woo a father's curse. My sister's mar-
riage
With Prophilus is from my heart confirm'd. 50
May I live hated, may I die despis'd,
If I omit to further it in all
That can concern me!
*Crot.*              I have been too rough.
My duty to my king made me so earnest;
Excuse it, Orgilus.
*Org.*              Dear sir! —
*Crot.*                          Here comes   55
Euphranea with Prophilus and Ithocles.

*Enter to them Prophilus, Euphranea, Itho-
cles, Groneas, Lemophil*

*Org.*  Most honoured! — ever famous!
*Ith.*                          Your true friend,
On earth not any truer. — With smooth eyes
Look on this worthy couple; your consent
Can only make them one.
*Org.*                  They have it. — Sister,   60
Thou pawn'dst to me an oath, of which engage-
ment
I never will release thee, if thou aim'st
At any other choice than this.
*Euph.*                          Dear brother,
At him, or none.
*Crot.*          To which my blessing 's added.
*Org.*  Which, till a greater ceremony per-
fect, —                                                   65
Euphranea, lend thy hand. — Here, take her,
Prophilus.
Live long a happy man and wife; and further,
That these in presence may conclude an omen,
Thus for a bridal song I close my wishes:

[*Sings.*]

*Comforts lasting, loves increasing,*           70
*Like soft hours never ceasing:*
*Plenty's pleasure, peace complying,*
*Without jars, or tongues envying;*

---

⁵ **inform**: qualify    ¹¹ **wish**: ('with' Q)    **thrift**: success    ¹⁹ **condition**: state of mind    ²⁸ **reclaim'd**: altered for the better    ⁴⁶ **genius**: household divinity    ⁵⁸ **smooth**: gracious

*Hearts by holy union wedded,*
*More than theirs by custom bedded;* 75
*Fruitful issues; life so graced,*
*Not by age to be defaced;*
*Budding, as the year ensu'th,*
*Every spring another youth:*
*All what thought can add beside* 80
*Crown this bridegroom and this bride!*

*Pro.* You have seal'd joy close to my soul. —
Euphranea,
Now I may call thee mine.
*Ith.*      I but exchange
One good friend for another.
*Org.*      If these gallants
Will please to grace a poor invention 85
By joining with me in some slight device,
I 'll venture on a strain my younger days
Have studied for delight.
*Lem.*      With thankful willingness
I offer my attendance.
*Gro.*      No endeavour
Of mine shall fail to show itself.
*Ith.*      We will 90
All join to wait on thy directions, Orgilus.
*Org.* O, my good lord, your favours flow
towards
A too unworthy worm; — but as you please.
I am what you will shape me.
*Ith.*      A fast friend.
*Crot.* I thank thee, son, for this acknowledg-
ment; 95
It is a sight of gladness.
*Org.*      But my duty. *Exeunt omnes.*

[SCENE V. — *Calantha's Apartment*]

*Enter Calantha, Penthea, Christalla,*
*Philema*

*Cal.* Whoe'er would speak with us, deny his
entrance.
Be careful of our charge.
*Chris.*      We shall, madam.
*Cal.* Except the king himself, give none ad-
mittance;
Not any.
*Phil.* Madam, it shall be our care.
*Exeunt [Christalla and Philema].*
*Cal.* Being alone, Penthea, you have granted
The opportunity you sought, and might 6
At all times have commanded.
*Pen.*      'T is a benefit
Which I shall owe your goodness even in death
for.
My glass of life, sweet princess, hath few
minutes

Remaining to run down; the sands are spent;
For by an inward messenger I feel 1:
The summons of departure short and certain.
*Cal.* You feel too much your melancholy.
*Pen.*      Glories
Of human greatness are but pleasing dreams
And shadows soon decaying: on the stage 15
Of my mortality my youth hath acted
Some scenes of vanity, drawn out at length
By varied pleasures, sweet'ned in the mixture,
But tragical in issue. Beauty, pomp,
With every sensuality our giddiness 20
Doth frame an idol, are unconstant friends,
When any troubled passion makes assault
On the unguarded castle of the mind.
*Cal.* Contemn not your condition for the
proof
Of bare opinion only: to what end 25
Reach all these moral texts?
*Pen.*      To place before ye
A perfect mirror, wherein you may see
How weary I am of a ling'ring life,
Who count the best a misery.
*Cal.*      Indeed
You have no little cause; yet none so great 30
As to distrust a remedy.
*Pen.*      That remedy
Must be a winding-sheet, a fold of lead,
And some untrod-on corner in the earth. —
Not to detain your expectation, princess,
I have an humble suit.
*Cal.*      Speak, and enjoy it. 35
*Pen.* Vouchsafe, then, to be my executrix,
And take that trouble on ye to dispose
Such legacies as I bequeath, impartially.
I have not much to give, the pains are easy;
Heaven will reward your piety, and thank it 40
When I am dead; for sure I must not live;
I hope I cannot.
*Cal.*      Now, beshrew thy sadness;
Thou turn'st me too much woman. [*Weeps.*]
*Pen.* [*Aside.*]      Her fair eyes
Melt into passion. Then I have assurance
Encouraging my boldness. — In this paper 45
My will was character'd; which you, with par-
don,
Shall now know from mine own mouth.
*Cal.*      Talk on, prithee;
It is a pretty earnest.
*Pen.*      I have left me
But three poor jewels to bequeath. The first is
My youth; for though I am much old in griefs,
In years I am a child.
*Cal.*      To whom that? 51
*Pen.* To virgin-wives, such as abuse not wed-
lock

87 **strain:** literary effort    96 **But:** only    1 **deny:** forbid    9 **glass:** hour-glass    19 **issue:** outcome    25 **bare opinion:** mere generalities    34 **expectation:** attention    35 **and:** ('I' Q)    46 **character'd:** written

By freedom of desires, but covet chiefly
The pledges of chaste beds for ties of love, 51
Rather than ranging of their blood; and next
To married maids, such as prefer the number
Of honourable issue in their virtues
Before the flattery of delights by marriage:
May those be ever young!
*Cal.* A second jewel
You mean to part with?
*Pen.* 'T is my fame, I trust 60
By scandal yet untouch'd: this I bequeath
To Memory, and Time's old daughter, Truth.
If ever my unhappy name find mention
When I am fall'n to dust, may it deserve
Beseeming charity without dishonour! 65
*Cal.* How handsomely thou play'st with
harmless sport
Of mere imagination! Speak the last.
I strangely like thy will.
*Pen.* This jewel, madam,
Is dearly precious to me; you must use
The best of your discretion to employ 70
This gift as I intend it.
*Cal.* Do not doubt me.
*Pen.* 'T is long agone since first I lost my
heart.
Long I have liv'd without it, else for certain
I should have given that too; but instead
Of it, to great Calantha, Sparta's heir, 75
By service bound and by affection vow'd,
I do bequeath, in holiest rites of love,
Mine only brother, Ithocles.
*Cal.* What saidst thou?
*Pen.* Impute not, heaven-bless'd lady, to
ambition
A faith as humbly perfect as the prayers 80
Of a devoted suppliant can endow it.
Look on him, princess, with an eye of pity;
How like the ghost of what he late appear'd
'A moves before you.
*Cal.* Shall I answer here,
Or lend my ear too grossly?
*Pen.* First his heart 85
Shall fall in cinders, scorch'd by your disdain,
Ere he will dare, poor man, to ope an eye
On these divine looks, but with low-bent
thoughts
Accusing such presumption. As for words,
'A dares not utter any but of service: 90
Yet this lost creature loves ye. — Be a princess
In sweetness as in blood; give him his doom,
Or raise him up to comfort.
*Cal.* What new change
Appears in my behaviour, that thou dar'st
Tempt my displeasure?
*Pen.* I must leave the world 95
To revel in Elysium, and 't is just

To wish my brother some advantage here:
Yet, by my best hopes, Ithocles is ignorant
Of this pursuit. But if you please to kill him,
Lend him one angry look or one harsh word, 100
And you shall soon conclude how strong a
power
Your absolute authority holds over
His life and end.
*Cal.* You have forgot, Penthea,
How still I have a father.
*Pen.* But remember
I am a sister, though to me this brother 105
Hath been, you know, unkind, O, most unkind!
*Cal.* Christalla, Philema, where are ye? —
Lady,
Your check lies in my silence.

*Enter Christalla and Philema*

*Both.* Madam, here.
*Cal.* I think ye sleep, ye drones: wait on
Penthea
Unto her lodging. — [*Aside.*] Ithocles? Wrong'd
lady! 110
*Pen.* My reckonings are made even; death
or fate
Can now nor strike too soon, nor force too late.
*Exeunt.*

## Actus Quartus: Scæna prima

### [A Hall in the Palace]

### Enter Ithocles and Armostes

*Ith.* Forbear your inquisition: curiosity
Is of too subtle and too searching nature,
In fears of love too quick, too slow of credit. —
I am not what you doubt me.
*Arm.* Nephew, be, then,
As I would wish; — all is not right. — Good
heaven 5
Confirm your resolutions for dependence
On worthy ends, which may advance your quiet.
*Ith.* I did the noble Orgilus much injury,
But griev'd Penthea more: I now repent it, —
Now, uncle, now; this "now" is now too late.
So provident is folly in sad issue, 11
That after-wit, like bankrupts' debts, stands
tallied,
Without all possibilities of payment.
Sure, he 's an honest, very honest gentleman;
A man of single meaning.
*Arm.* I believe it: 15
Yet, nephew, 't is the tongue informs our ears;
Our eyes can never pierce into the thoughts,
For they are lodg'd too inward: — but I ques-
tion
No truth in Orgilus. — The princess, sir.

⁹⁶ in: (not in Q)    ¹⁰⁴ check: rebuke    ¹ curiosity: anxiety    ¹¹ provident: productive
¹² after-wit: the wisdom that comes later    tallied: indebted    ¹⁵ single: sincere

*Ith.* The princess! ha!

*Arm.* With her the Prince of Argos. 20

*Enter Nearchus, leading Calantha; Amelus, Christalla, Philema*

*Near.* Great fair one, grace my hopes with any instance
Of livery, from the allowance of your favour.
This little spark —
[*Attempts to take a ring from her finger.*]

*Cal.* A toy!

*Near.* Love feasts on toys,
For Cupid is a child; — vouchsafe this bounty:
It cannot be deni'd.

*Cal.* You shall not value, 25
Sweet cousin, at a price what I count cheap;
So cheap, that let him take it who dares stoop for 't,
And give it at next meeting to a mistress.
She 'll thank him for 't, perhaps.
                              *Casts it to Ithocles.*

*Ame.* The ring, sir, is
The princess's; I could have took it up. 30

*Ith.* Learn manners, prithee. — To the blessed owner,
Upon my knees —
[*Kneels and offers it to Calantha.*]

*Near.* Y' are saucy.

*Cal.* This is pretty!
I am, belike, "a mistress" — wondrous pretty!
Let the man keep his fortune, since he found it.
He 's worthy on 't. — On, cousin!

*Ith.* [*To Amelus.*] Follow. spaniel; 35
I 'll force ye to a fawning else.

*Ame.* You dare not.
                    *Exeunt. Manent Ith. and Arm.*

*Arm.* My lord, you were too forward.

*Ith.* Look 'ee, uncle.
Some such there are whose liberal contents
Swarm without care in every sort of plenty;
Who after full repasts can lay them down 40
To sleep; and they sleep, uncle: in which silence
Their very dreams present 'em choice of pleasures,
Pleasures — observe me, uncle — of rare object;
Here heaps of gold, there increments of honours,
Now change of garments, then the votes of people; 45
Anon varieties of beauties, courting,
In flatteries of the night, exchange of dalliance:
Yet these are still but dreams. Give me felicity
Of which my senses waking are partakers,
A real, visible, material happiness; 50

And then, too, when I stagger in expectance
Of the least comfort that can cherish life. ——
I saw it, sir, I saw it; for it came
From her own hand.

*Arm.* The princess threw it t' ye.

*Ith.* True; and she said — well I remember what. 55
Her cousin prince would beg it.

*Arm.* Yes, and parted
In anger at your taking on 't.

*Ith.* Penthea!
O, thou hast pleaded with a powerful language!
I want a fee to gratify thy merit;
But I will do —

*Arm.* What is 't you say?

*Ith.* In anger! 60
In anger let him part; for could his breath,
Like whirlwinds, toss such servile slaves as lick
The dust his footsteps print into a vapour,
It durst not stir a hair of mine. It should not;
I 'd rend it up by th' roots first. To be anything 65
Calantha smiles on, is to be a blessing
More sacred than a petty prince of Argos
Can wish to equal, or in worth or title.

*Arm.* Contain yourself, my lord. Ixion, aiming
To embrace Juno, bosom'd but a cloud, 70
And begat Centaurs: 't is an useful moral.
Ambition hatch'd in clouds of mere opinion
Proves but in birth a prodigy.

*Ith.* I thank 'ee;
Yet, with your licence, I should seem uncharitable
To gentler fate, if, relishing the dainties 75
Of a soul's settled peace, I were so feeble
Not to digest it.

*Arm.* He deserves small trust
Who is not privy-counsellor to himself.

*Re-enter Nearchus, Orgilus, and Amelus*

*Near.* Brave me!

*Org.* Your excellence mistakes his temper;
For Ithocles in fashion of his mind 80
Is beautiful, soft, gentle, the clear mirror
Of absolute perfection.

*Ame.* Was 't your modesty
Term'd any of the prince his servants "spaniel"?
Your nurse, sure, taught you other language.

*Ith.* Language!

*Near.* A gallant man-at-arms is here, a doctor 85
In feats of chivalry, blunt and rough-spoken,
Vouchsafing not the fustian of civility,
Which rash spirits style good manners!

*Ith.* Manners!

---

²¹ **instance:** mark  ²² **livery:** vassalage  ²⁵ **be deni'd:** ('beny'd' Q)  ³⁸ **liberal contents:** easily satisfied minds  ⁷² **opinion:** fantasy  ⁸³ **rash:** superficial

*Org.* No more, illustrious sir; 't is matchless
  Ithocles.
*Near.* You might have understood who I
  am.
*Ith.*                     Yes.  90
I did; else — but the presence calm'd th' af-
  front —
Y' are cousin to the princess.
*Near.*            To the king, too;
A certain instrument that lent supportance
To your colossic greatness — to that king too,
You might have added.
*Ith.*         There is more divinity
In beauty than in majesty.
*Arm.*           O fie, fie!   96
*Near.* This odd youth's pride turns heretic
  in loyalty.
Sirrah! low mushrooms never rival cedars.
           *Exeunt Nearchus and Amelus.*
*Ith.* Come back! — What pitiful dull thing
  am I
So to be tamely scolded at! come back! —  100
Let him come back, and echo once again
That scornful sound of "mushroom"! painted
  colts —
Like heralds' coats gilt o'er with crowns and
  sceptres —
May bait a muzzled lion.
*Arm.*          Cousin, cousin,
Thy tongue is not thy friend.
*Org.*         In point of honour  105
Discretion knows no bounds. Amelus told me,
'T was all about a little ring.
*Ith.*             A ring
The princess threw away, and I took up.
Admit she threw 't to me, what arm of brass
Can snatch it hence? No; could 'a grind the
  hoop                       110
To powder, 'a might sooner reach my heart
Than steal and wear one dust on 't. — Orgilus,
I am extremely wrong'd.
*Org.*          A lady's favour
Is not to be so slighted.
*Ith.*          Slighted!
*Arm.*               Quiet
These vain unruly passions, which will render
  ye                     115
Into a madness.
*Org.*      Griefs will have their vent.

      *Enter Tecnicus [with a scroll]*

*Arm.* Welcome; thou com'st in season, rev-
  erend man,
To pour the balsam of a suppling patience
Into the festering wound of ill-spent fury.
*Org. [Aside.]* What makes he here?
*Tec.*     The hurts are yet not mortal, 120
Which shortly will prove deadly. To the king,

Armostes, see in safety thou deliver
This seal'd-up counsel; bid him with a con-
  stancy
Peruse the secrets of the gods. — O Sparta,
O Lacedæmon! double-nam'd, but one   125
In fate: when kingdoms reel, — mark well my
  saw, —
Their heads must needs be giddy. Tell the king
That henceforth he no more must inquire after
My aged head; Apollo wills it so.
I am for Delphos.
*Arm.*     Not without some conference  130
With our great master?
*Tec.*       Never more to see him:
A greater prince commands me. — Ithocles,
*When youth is ripe, and age from time doth*
  *part,*
*The lifeless trunk shall wed the broken heart.*
*Ith.* What 's this, if understood?
*Tec.*          List, Orgilus!  135
Remember what I told thee long before.
These tears shall be my witness.
*Arm.*           'Las, good man!
*Tec.* *Let craft with courtesy a while confer,*
  *Revenge proves its own executioner.*
*Org.* Dark sentences are for Apollo's priests;
I am not Œdipus.
*Tec.*       My hour is come.  141
Cheer up the king; farewell to all. — O Sparta,
O Lacedæmon!         *Exit Tecnicus.*
*Arm.*     If prophetic fire
Have warm'd this old man's bosom, we might
  cónstrue
His words to fatal sense.
*Ith.*       Leave to the powers  145
Above us the effects of their decrees;
My burthen lies within me. Servile fears
Prevent no great effects. — Divine Calantha!
*Arm.* The gods be still propitious!
      *Exeunt [Ith. and Arm.]. Manet Org.*
*Org.*       Something oddly
The book-man prated, yet 'a talk'd it weeping;
  *Let craft with courtesy a while confer,*  151
  *Revenge proves its own executioner.*
Con it again; — for what? It shall not puzzle
  me;
'T is dotage of a wither'd brain. — Penthea
Forbade me not her presence; I may see her,
And gaze my fill. Why see her, then, I may, 156
When, if I faint to speak — I must be silent.
                   *Exit Orgilus.*

    [SCENE II. — *House of Bassanes*]

   *Enter Bassanes, Grausis, and Phulas*

*Bass.* Pray, use your recreations. All the
  service
I will expect is quietness amongst ye:

      **102** painted colts: gaudy youths     **118** suppling: ('supplying' Q)     **120** not: ('but' Q)

Take liberty at home, abroad, at all times,
And in your charities appease the gods,
Whom I, with my distractions, have offended. 5
    *Grau.*   Fair blessings on thy heart!
    *Phu.* [*Aside.*]        Here 's a rare change!
My lord, to cure the itch, is surely gelded;
The cuckold in conceit hath cast his horns.
    *Bass.*   Betake ye to your several occasions;
And wherein I have heretofore been faulty, 10
Let your constructions mildly pass it over.
Henceforth I 'll study reformation, — more
I have not for employment.
    *Grau.*           O, sweet man!
Thou art the very "Honeycomb of Honesty."
    *Phu.*   The "Garland of Good-will." — Old
lady, hold up        15
Thy reverend snout, and trot behind me softly,
As it becomes a moil of ancient carriage.
                    *Exeunt. Manet Bass.*
    *Bass.*   Beasts, only capable of sense, enjoy
The benefit of food and ease with thankfulness;
Such silly creatures, with a grudging, kick not
Against the portion nature hath bestow'd: 21
But men, endow'd with reason and the use
Of reason, to distinguish from the chaff
Of abject scarcity the quintessence,
Soul, and elixir of the earth's abundance, 25
The treasures of the sea, the air, nay, heaven,
Repining at these glories of creation
Are verier beasts than beasts; and of those
    beasts
The worst am I. I, who was made a monarch
Of what a heart could wish for, — a chaste
    wife, —        30
Endeavour'd what in me lay to pull down
That temple built for adoration only,
And level 't in the dust of causeless scandal.
But, to redeem a sacrilege so impious,
Humility shall pour, before the deities    35
I have incens'd, a largess of more patience
Than their displeased altars can require.
No tempests of commotion shall disquiet
The calms of my composure.

               *Enter Orgilus*

    *Org.*           I have found thee,
Thou patron of more horrors than the bulk 40
Of manhood, hoop'd about with ribs of iron,
Can cram within thy breast. Penthea, Bas-
    sanes,
Curs'd by thy jealousies, — more, by thy dot-
    age, —
Is left a prey to words.
    *Bass.*          Exercise
Your trials for addition to my penance;    45
I am resolv'd.
    *Org.*      Play not with misery

Past cure. Some angry minister of fate hath
Depos'd the empress of her soul, her reason,
From its most proper throne; but, — what 's
    the miracle
More new, — I, I have seen it, and yet live! 50
    *Bass.*   You may delude my senses, not my
    judgment;
'T is anchor'd into a firm resolution;
Dalliance of mirth or wit can ne'er unfix it.
Practise yet further.
    *Org.*        May thy death of love to her
Damn all thy comforts to a lasting fast    55
From every joy of life! Thou barren rock,
By thee we have been split in ken of harbour.

*Enter Ithocles, Penthea, her hair about her ears;*
    [*Armostes,*] *Philema, Christalla*

    *Ith.*   Sister, look up; your Ithocles, your
    brother,
Speaks t' ye; why do you weep? Dear, turn
    not from me. —
Here is a killing sight; lo, Bassanes,    60
A lamentable object!
    *Org.*          Man, dost see 't?
Sports are more gamesome; am I yet in merri-
    ment?
Why dost not laugh?
    *Bass.*        Divine and best of ladies,
Please to forget my outrage; mercy ever
Cannot but lodge under a roof so excellent. 65
I have cast off that cruelty of frenzy
Which once appear'd, impostor, and then
    juggled
To cheat my sleeps of rest.
    *Org.*           Was I in earnest?
    *Pen.*   Sure, if we were all Sirens, we should
    sing pitifully.
And 't were a comely music, when in parts  70
One sung another's knell. The turtle sighs
When he hath lost his mate; and yet some say
'A must be dead first. 'T is a fine deceit
To pass away in a dream; indeed, I 've slept
With mine eyes open a great while. No false-
    hood    75
Equals a broken faith; there 's not a hair
Sticks on my head but, like a leaden plum-
    met,
It sinks me to the grave. I must creep thither;
The journey is not long.
    *Ith.*        But, thou, Penthea,
Hast many years, I hope, to number yet,    80
Ere thou canst travel that way.
    *Bass.*         Let the sun first
Be wrapp'd up in an everlasting darkness,
Before the light of nature, chiefly form'd
For the whole world's delight, feel an eclipse
So universal!

    ⁸ **in conceit:** imaginary    ¹⁷ **moil:** mule    ⁵⁷ **ken:** sight    ⁶⁵ **roof:** ('root' Q)    ⁶⁷ **impostor:** a
deceiving spirit ('Impostors' Q)    ⁸¹ **sun:** ('Swan' Q)

*Org.*          Wisdom, look 'ee, begins     85
To rave! — Art thou mad too, antiquity?
*Pen.*  Since I was first a wife, I might have been
Mother to many pretty prattling babes.
They would have smil'd when I smil'd, and for certain
I should have cri'd when they cri'd: — truly, brother,     90
My father would have pick'd me out a husband,
And then my little ones had been no bastards.
But 't is too late for me to marry now,
I am past child-bearing; 't is not my fault.
*Bass.*  Fall on me, if there be a burning Ætna,     95
And bury me in flames! Sweats hot as sulphur
Boil through my pores! Affliction hath in store
No torture like to this.
*Org.*                    Behold a patience!
Lay by thy whining gray dissimulation,
Do something worth a chronicle; show justice     100
Upon the author of this mischief; dig out
The jealousies that hatch'd this thraldom first
With thine own poniard. Every antic rapture
Can roar as thine does.
*Ith.*                Orgilus, forbear.
*Bass.*  Disturb him not; it is a talking motion
Provided for my torment. What a fool am I     106
To bandy passion! Ere I 'll speak a word,
I will look on and burst.
*Pen.*          I lov'd you once. [*To Orgilus.*]
*Org.*  Thou didst, wrong'd creature: in despite of malice,
For it I love thee ever.
*Pen.*          Spare your hand;     110
Believe me, I 'll not hurt it.
*Org.*                Pain my heart too!
*Pen.*  Complain not though I wring it hard.
I 'll kiss it;
O, 't is a fine soft palm! — hark, in thine ear:
Like whom do I look, prithee? — Nay, no whispering.
Goodness! we had been happy; too much happiness     115
Will make folk proud, they say — but that is he —                    *Points at Ithocles.*
And yet he paid for 't home; alas, his heart
Is crept into the cabinet of the princess;
We shall have points and bride-laces. Remember,
When we last gather'd roses in the garden,     120
I found my wits; but truly you lost yours.
That 's he, and still 't is he.
                    [*Again pointing at Ithocles.*]

*Ith.*                    Poor soul, how idly
Her fancies guide her tongue!
*Bass.* [*Aside.*]          Keep in, vexation,
And break not into clamour.
*Org.* [*Aside.*]          She has tutor'd me:
Some powerful inspiration checks my laziness. —     125
Now let me kiss your hand, griev'd beauty.
*Pen.*                    Kiss it. —
Alack, alack, his lips be wondrous cold.
Dear soul, h'as lost his colour: have ye seen
A straying heart? All crannies! every drop
Of blood is turned to an amethyst,     130
Which married bachelors hang in their ears.
*Org.*  Peace usher her into Elysium! —
If this be madness, madness is an oracle.
                    *Exit Org.*
*Ith.*  Christalla, Philema, when slept my sister?
Her ravings are so wild.
*Chris.*          Sir, not these ten days.     135
*Phil.*  We watch by her continually; besides,
We can not any way pray her to eat.
*Bass.*  O, misery of miseries!
*Pen.*                Take comfort;
You may live well, and die a good old man.
By yea and nay, an oath not to be broken,     140
If you had join'd our hands once in the temple, —
'T was since my father died, for had he liv'd,
He would have done 't, — I must have call'd you father. —
O, my wrack'd honour! ruin'd by those tyrants,
A cruel brother and a desperate dotage!     145
There is no peace left for a ravish'd wife,
Widow'd by lawless marriage; to all memory
Penthea's, poor Penthea's name is strumpeted:
But since her blood was season'd by the forfeit
Of noble shame with mixtures of pollution,     150
Her blood — 't is just — be henceforth never heighten'd
With taste of sustenance! Starve; let that fulness
Whose pleurisy hath fever'd faith and modesty —
Forgive me; O, I faint!
                    [*Falls into the arms of her Attendants.*]
*Arm.*                Be not so wilful,
Sweet niece, to work thine own destruction.
*Ith.*                    Nature     155
Will call her daughter monster! — What! not eat?
Refuse the only ordinary means
Which are ordain'd for life? Be not, my sister
A murth'ress to thyself. — Hear'st thou this, Bassanes?

---

¹⁰³ **antic rapture**: stage passion     ¹⁰⁵ **motion**: puppet     ¹⁰⁷ **bandy**: ('bawdy' Q)     ¹¹⁰ **Spare**: lend me     ¹¹² **Pen**: (not in Q)     ¹¹⁹ **points . . . -laces**: souvenirs of a wedding     ¹²⁵ **checks**: reproaches
⁵³ **pleurisy**: excess

*Bass.* Foh! I am busy; for I have not thoughts 160
Enow to think: all shall be well anon.
'T is tumbling in my head; there is a mastery
In art to fatten and keep smooth the outside;
Yes, and to comfort up the vital spirits 164
Without the help of food, fumes or perfumes,
Perfumes or fumes. Let her alone; I 'll search out
The trick on 't.
*Pen.* Lead me gently; heavens reward ye.
Griefs are sure friends; they leave without control
Nor cure nor comforts for a leprous soul.
*Exeunt the maids supporting Penthea.*
*Bass.* I grant ye; and will put in practice instantly 170
What you shall still admire: 't is wonderful,
'T is super-singular, not to be match'd;
Yet, when I 've done 't, I 've done 't: — ye shall all thank me. *Exit Bassanes.*
*Arm.* The sight is full of terror.
*Ith.* On my soul
Lies such an infinite clog of massy dulness, 175
As that I have not sense enough to feel it. —
See, uncle, th' angry thing returns again;
Shall 's welcome him with thunder? We are haunted,
And must use exorcism to conjure down
This spirit of malevolence.
*Arm.* Mildly, nephew. 180

*Enter Nearchus and Amelus*

*Near.* I come not, sir, to chide your late disorder,
Admitting that th' inurement to a roughness
In soldiers of your years and fortunes, chiefly,
So lately prosperous, hath not yet shook off
The custom of the war in hours of leisure; 185
Nor shall you need excuse, since y' are to render
Account to that fair excellence, the princess,
Who in her private gallery expects it
From your own mouth alone: I am a messenger
But to her pleasure.
*Ith.* Excellent Nearchus, 190
Be prince still of my services, and conquer
Without the combat of dispute; I honour ye.
*Near.* The king is on a sudden indispos'd,
Physicians are call'd for; 't were fit, Armostes,
You should be near him.
*Arm.* Sir, I kiss your hands. 195
*Exeunt. Manent Nearchus & Amelus.*
*Near.* Amelus, I perceive Calantha's bosom
Is warm'd with other fires than such as can
Take strength from any fuel of the love
I might address to her. Young Ithocles,
Or ever I mistake, is lord ascendant 200

Of her devotions; one, to speak him truly,
In every disposition nobly fashioned.
*Ame.* But can your highness brook to be so rival'd,
Considering th' inequality of the persons? 204
*Near.* I can, Amelus; for affections injur'd
By tyranny or rigour of compulsion,
Like tempest-threaten'd trees unfirmly rooted,
Ne'er spring to timely growth: observe, for instance,
Life-spent Penthea and unhappy Orgilus.
*Ame.* How does your grace determine?
*Near.* To be jealous 210
In public of what privately I 'll further;
And though they shall not know, yet they shall find it. *Exeunt omnes.*

[SCENE III. — *The Palace*]

*Enter Lemophil and Groneas leading Amyclas and placing him in a chair; followed by Armostes [with a box], Crotolon, and Prophilus*

*Amy.* Our daughter is not near?
*Arm.* She is retir'd, sir,
Into her gallery.
*Amy.* Where 's the prince our cousin?
*Pro.* New walk'd into the grove, my lord.
*Amy.* All leave us
Except Armostes, and you, Crotolon;
We would be private.
*Pro.* Health unto your majesty! 5
*Exeunt Prophilus, Lemophil, and Groneas.*
*Amy.* What! Tecnicus is gone?
*Arm.* He is to Delphos.
And to your royal hands presents this box.
*Amy.* Unseal it, good Armostes; therein lies
The secrets of the oracle; out with it:
[*Armostes takes out the scroll.*]
Apollo live our patron! Read, Armostes. 10
*Arm.* [*Reads.*] *The plot in which the vine takes root
Begins to dry from head to foot;
The stock soon withering, want of sap
Doth cause to quail the budding grape;
But from the neighbouring elm a dew 15
Shall drop, and feed the plot anew.*
*Amy.* That is the oracle: what exposition
Makes the philosopher?
*Arm.* This brief one only.
[*Reads.*] *The plot is Sparta, the dri'd vine the king;
The quailing grape his daughter; but the thing 20
Of most importance, not to be reveal'd,
Is a near prince, the elm: the rest conceal'd.*
*Tecnicus.*

177 angry: ('augury' Q)    14 quail: dry up

*Amy.* Enough; although the opening of this riddle
Be but itself a riddle, yet we construe
How near our labouring age draws to a rest.   25
But must Calantha quail too? that young grape
Untimely budded! I could mourn for her;
Her tenderness hath yet deserv'd no rigour
So to be cross'd by fate.
*Arm.*                     You misapply, sir, —
With favour let me speak it, — what Apollo   30
Hath clouded in hid sense. I here conjecture
Her marriage with some neighb'ring prince, the dew
Of which befriending elm shall ever strengthen
Your subjects with a sovereignty of power.
*Crot.* Besides, most gracious lord, the pith of oracles   35
Is to be then digested when th' events
Expound their truth, not brought as soon to light
As utter'd. Truth is child of Time; and herein
I find no scruple, rather cause of comfort,
With unity of kingdoms.
*Amy.*                   May it prove so,   40
For weal of this dear nation! — Where is Ithocles? —
Armostes, Crotolon, when this wither'd vine
Of my frail carcass, on the funeral pile
Is fir'd into its ashes, let that young man
Be hedg'd about still with your cares and loves.   45
Much owe I to his worth, much to his service. —
Let such as wait come in now.
*Arm.*                          All attend here!

*Enter Ithocles, Calantha, Prophilus, Orgilus, Euphranea, Lemophil, and Groneas*

*Cal.* Dear sir! king! father!
*Ith.*                          O my royal master!
*Amy.* Cleave not my heart, sweet twins of my life's solace,
With your forejudging fears; there is no physic   50
So cunningly restorative to cherish
The fall of age, or call back youth and vigour,
As your consents in duty. I will shake off
This languishing disease of time, to quicken
Fresh pleasures in these drooping hours of sadness.   55
Is fair Euphranea married yet to Prophilus?
*Crot.* This morning, gracious lord.
*Org.*                               This very morning;
Which, with your highness' leave, you may observe too.
Our sister looks, methinks, mirthful and sprightly,

As if her chaster fancy could already   60
Expound the riddle of her gain in losing
A trifle maids know only that they know not.
Pish! prithee, blush not; 't is but honest change
Of fashion in the garment, loose for strait,
And so the modest maid is made a wife.   65
Shrewd business — is 't not, sister?
*Euph.*                               You are pleasant.
*Amy.* We thank thee, Orgilus; this mirth becomes thee.
But wherefore sits the court in such a silence?
A wedding without revels is not seemly.
*Cal.* Your late indisposition, sir, forbade it.   70
*Amy.* Be it thy charge, Calantha, to set forward
The bridal sports, to which I will be present;
If not, at least consenting. — Mine own Ithocles,
I have done little for thee yet.
*Ith.*                           Y' have built me
To the full height I stand in.
*Cal. [Aside.]*                Now or never! —   75
May I propose a suit?
*Amy.*                 Demand, and have it.
*Cal.* Pray, sir, give me this young man, and no further
Account him yours than he deserves in all things
To be thought worthy mine: I will esteem him
According to his merit.
*Amy.*                   Still th' art my daughter,   80
Still grow'st upon my heart. — [*To Ithocles.*]
Give me thine hand. —
Calantha, take thine own: in noble actions
Thou 'lt find him firm and absolute. — I would not
Have parted with thee, Ithocles, to any
But to a mistress who is all what I am.   85
*Ith.* A change, great king, most wish'd for, 'cause the same.
*Cal. [To Ithocles.]* Th' art mine. Have I now kept my word?
*Ith.*                    Divinely.
*Org.* Rich fortunes guard, the favour of a princess
Rock thee, brave man, in ever-crowned plenty!
Y' are minion of the time; be thankful for it. —   90
[*Aside.*] Ho! here 's a swing in destiny! Apparent,
The youth is up on tiptoe, yet may stumble.
*Amy.* On to your recreations. — Now convey me
Unto my bed-chamber: none on his forehead
Wear a distemper'd look.
*Omnes.*                   The gods preserve ye!   95

---

²⁵ **opening:** expounding     ³⁹ **scruple:** ill omen     ⁸⁸ **the:** ('to' Q)     ⁹¹ **Apparent:** clearly
⁹⁵ **ye:** (' 'ee' Q)

*Cal.* [*Aside to Ithocles.*] Sweet, be not from
   my sight.
*Ith.*   My whole felicity!
      *Exeunt, carrying out of the king. Orgi-*
         *lus stays Ithocles.*
*Org.*   Shall I be bold, my lord?
*Ith.*                Thou canst not, Orgilus.
Call me thine own; for Prophilus must hence-
   forth
Be all thy sister's: friendship, though it cease
   not                                                    100
In marriage, yet is oft at less command
Than when a single freedom can dispose it.
   *Org.*   Most right, my most good lord, my
      most great lord,
My gracious princely lord, — I might add,
   royal.
   *Ith.*   Royal! A subject royal?
   *Org.*                Why not, pray, sir?   105
The sovereignty of kingdoms in their nonage
Stoop'd to desert, not birth; there 's as much
   merit
In clearness of affection as in puddle
Of generation.  You have conquer'd love
Even in the loveliest; if I greatly err not,   110
The son of Venus hath bequeath'd his quiver
To Ithocles his manage, by whose arrows
Calantha's breast is open'd.
   *Ith.*                Can 't be possible?
   *Org.*   I was myself a piece of suitor once,
And forward in preferment too; so forward  115
That, speaking truth, I may without offence,
   sir,
Presume to whisper that my hopes, and — hark
   'ee —
My certainty of marriage stood assured
With as firm footing — by your leave — as
   any's
Now at this very instant — but —
   *Ith.*                'T is granted:   120
And for a league of privacy between us,
Read o'er my bosom and partake a secret:
The princess is contracted mine.
   *Org.*                Still, why not?
I now applaud her wisdom: when your king-
   dom                                               124
Stands seated in your will, secure and settled,
I dare pronounce you will be a just mon-
   arch:
Greece must admire and tremble.
   *Ith.*                Then the sweetness
Of so imparadis'd a comfort, Orgilus!
It is to banquet with the gods.
   *Org.*                The glory
Of numerous children, potency of nobles,   130
Bent knees, hearts pav'd to tread on!

*Ith.*                With a friendship
So dear, so fast, as thine.
   *Org.*                I am unfitting
For office; but for service —
   *Ith.*                We 'll distinguish
Our fortunes merely in the title; partners
In all respects else but the bed.
   *Org.*                The bed!   135
Forfend it Jove's own jealousy! — till lastly
We slip down in the common earth together.
And there our beds are equal; save some mon-
   ument
To show this was the king, and this the sub-
   ject. —               *Soft sad music.*
List, what sad sounds are these? — extremely
   sad ones.                                          140
*Ith.*   Sure, from Penthea's lodgings.
*Org.*                Hark! a voice too.

### A Song [*within*]

*O, no more, no more! too late*
   *Sighs are spent; the burning tapers*
*Of a life as chaste as fate,*
   *Pure as are unwritten papers,*                   145
*Are burnt out: no heat, no light*
*Now remains; 't is ever night.*

*Love is dead; let lovers' eyes,*
   *Lock'd in endless dreams,*
   *Th' extremes of all extremes,*                   150
*Ope no more, for now Love dies,*
   *Now Love dies, — implying*
*Love's martyrs must be ever, ever dying.*

*Ith.*   O, my misgiving heart!
*Org.*                A horrid stillness
Succeeds this deathful air; let 's know the rea-
   son.                                              155
Tread softly; there is mystery in mourning.
                                    *Exeunt.*

[SCENE IV. — *Penthea's Apartment*]

*Enter Christalla and Philema, bringing in Pen-*
   *thea in a chair, veiled: two other Servants*
   *placing two chairs, one on the one side, and*
   *the other with an engine on the other.  The*
   *Maids sit down at her feet, mourning.  The*
   *Servants go out: meet them Ithocles and*
   *Orgilus.*

1 *Ser.* [*Aside to Orgilus.*] 'T is done; that on
   her right hand.
*Org.*                Good: begone.
                           [*Exeunt Servants.*]
*Ith.*   Soft peace enrich this room!
*Org.*                How fares the lady?

---

108 **clearness of affection:** nobility of disposition
of heredity   112 **manage:** handling   131 **pav'd:** laid
in Q)   Sc. IV. s. d. **engine:** mechanical device
108–109 **puddle Of generation:** the cloudy workings
down like paving-stones   139 s. d. (Follows 141

*Phil.*  Dead!
*Chris.*          Dead!
*Phil.*                  Starv'd!
*Chris.*                          Starv'd!
*Ith.*                                  Me miserable!
*Org.*                                          Tell us,
How parted she from life?
*Phil.*                  She call'd for music,
And begg'd some gentle voice to tune a fare-
well                                            5
To life and griefs.  Christalla touch'd the
lute;
I wept the funeral song.
*Chris.*                  Which scarce was ended
But her last breath seal'd up these hollow
sounds,
"O, cruel Ithocles and injur'd Orgilus!"
So down she drew her veil, so died.
*Ith.*                          So died!  10
*Org.*  Up! you are messengers of death; go
from us.
Here 's woe enough to court without a
prompter.
Away! and — hark ye — till you see us next,
No syllable that she is dead. — Away!
Keep a smooth brow.
                *Exeunt Philema and Christalla.*
                My lord, —
*Ith.*                  Mine only sister!  15
Another is not left me.
*Org.*                  Take that chair;
I 'll seat me here in this.  Between us sits
The object of our sorrows; some few tears
We 'll part among us.  I perhaps can mix
One lamentable story to prepare 'em. —     20
There, there; sit there, my lord.
*Ith.*                  Yes, as you please.
        *Ithocles sits down, and is catch'd in
                the engine.*
What means this treachery?
*Org.*                  Caught! you are caught,
Young master.  'T is thy throne of coronation,
Thou fool of greatness!  See, I take this veil off.
Survey a beauty wither'd by the flames     25
Of an insulting Phaeton, her brother.
*Ith.*  Thou mean'st to kill me basely?
*Org.*                  I foreknew
The last act of her life, and train'd thee hither
To sacrifice a tyrant to a turtle.
You dreamt of kingdoms, did ye?  How to
bosom                                          30
The delicacies of a youngling princess;
How with this nod to grace that subtle courtier,
How with that frown to make this noble trem-
ble,
And so forth; whiles Penthea's groans and tor-
tures,
Her agonies, her miseries, afflictions,        35

Ne'er touch'd upon your thought.  As for my
injuries,
Alas, they were beneath your royal pity;
But yet they liv'd, thou proud man, to con-
found thee.
Behold thy fate, this steel!  [*Draws a dagger.*]
*Ith.*                  Strike home!  A courage
As keen as thy revenge shall give it welcome.
But prithee, faint not; if the wound close up, 41
Tent it with double force, and search it deeply.
Thou look'st that I should whine and beg com-
passion,
As loath to leave the vainness of my glories.
A statelier resolution arms my confidence,     45
To cozen thee of honour.  Neither could I
Wish equal trial of unequal fortune
By hazard of a duel: 't were a bravery
Too mighty for a slave intending murther.
On to the execution, and inherit             50
A conflict with thy horrors.
*Org.*                  By Apollo,
Thou talk'st a goodly language!  For requital
I will report thee to thy mistress richly.
And take this peace along: some few short
minutes
Determin'd, my resolves shall quickly follow 55
Thy wrathful ghost; then, if we tug for mas-
tery,
Penthea's sacred eyes shall lend new courage.
Give me thy hand: be healthful in thy part-
ing
From lost mortality! thus, thus I free it.
                        *Kills him.*
*Ith.*  Yet, yet, I scorn to shrink.
*Org.*                  Keep up thy spirit:  60
I will be gentle even in blood; to linger
Pain, which I strive to cure, were to be cruel.
                        [*Stabs him again.*]
*Ith.*  Nimble in vengeance, I forgive thee.
Follow
Safety, with best success: O, may it prosper! —
Penthea, by thy side thy brother bleeds,     65
The earnest of his wrongs to thy forc'd faith.
Thoughts of ambition, or delicious banquet
With beauty, youth, and love, together perish
In my last breath, which on the sacred altar
Of a long-look'd-for peace — now — moves —
to heaven.                      *Moritur.* 70
*Org.*  Farewell, fair spring of manhood!
Henceforth welcome
Best expectation of a noble suff'rance.
I 'll lock the bodies safe, till what must follow
Shall be approv'd. — Sweet twins, shine stars
for ever! —
In vain they build their hopes whose life is
shame:                                         75
No monument lasts but a happy name.
                        *Exit Orgilus.*

²⁸ **train'd:** decoyed     ⁴² **Tent:** probe     ⁴⁸ **bravery:** distinction     ⁶⁶ **earnest:** payment

## Actus Quintus: Scæna prima

[*The House of Bassanes*]

*Enter Bassanes, alone*

*Bass.*  Athens — to Athens I have sent, the
   nursery
Of Greece for learning and the fount of knowl-
   edge;
For here in Sparta there 's not left amongst us
One wise man to direct; we 're all turn'd mad-
   caps.
'T is said Apollo is the god of herbs,          5
Then certainly he knows the virtue of 'em:
To Delphos I have sent too.  If there can be
A help for nature, we are sure yet.

*Enter Orgilus*

*Org.*                                      Honour
Attend thy counsels ever!
*Bass.*                       I beseech thee
With all my heart, let me go from thee quietly;
I will not aught to do with thee, of all men.   11
The doubles of a hare, — or, in a morning,
Salutes from a splay-footed witch, — to drop
Three drops of blood at th' nose just and no
   more, —
Croaking of ravens, or the screech of owls,   15
Are not so boding mischief as thy crossing
My private meditations.  Shun me, prithee;
And if I cannot love thee heartily,
I 'll love thee as well as I can.
*Org.*                           Noble Bassanes,
Mistake me not.
*Bass.*   Phew! then we shall be troubled.   20
Thou wert ordain'd my plague — heaven make
   me thankful, —
And give me patience too, heaven, I beseech
   thee.
*Org.*  Accept a league of amity; for hence-
   forth,
I vow, by my best genius, in a syllable,
Never to speak vexation.  I will study          25
Service and friendship, with a zealous sorrow
For my past incivility towards ye.
*Bass.*  Hey-day, good words! good words!  I
   must believe 'em,
And be a coxcomb for my labour.
*Org.*                          Use not
So hard a language; your misdoubt is cause-
   less.                                          30
For instance, if you promise to put on
A constancy of patience, — such a patience
As chronicle or history ne'er mentioned,
As follows not example, but shall stand
A wonder and a theme for imitation,             35

The first, the index pointing to a second, —
I will acquaint ye with an unmatch'd secret,
Whose knowledge to your griefs shall set a
   period.
*Bass.*  Thou canst not, Orgilus; 't is in the
   power
Of the gods only: yet, for satisfaction,        40
Because I note an earnest in thine utterance,
Unforc'd and naturally free, be resolute.
The virgin-bays shall not withstand the light-
   ning
With a more careless danger than my constancy
The full of thy relation.  Could it move        45
Distraction in a senseless marble statue,
It should find me a rock: I do expect now
Some truth of unheard moment.
*Org.*                          To your patience
You must add privacy, as strong in silence
As mysteries lock'd up in Jove's own bosom.  50
*Bass.*  A skull hid in the earth a treble age
Shall sooner prate.
*Org.*                Lastly, to such direction
As the severity of a glorious action
Deserves to lead your wisdom and your judg-
   ment,
You ought to yield obedience.
*Bass.*                       With assurance  55
Of will and thankfulness.
*Org.*                    With manly courage
Please, then, to follow me.
*Bass.*                     Where'er, I fear not.
                              *Exeunt omnes.*

## Scene 2

[*The Court*]

*Loud music.  Enter Groneas and Lemophil, lead-
   ing Euphranea; Christalla and Philema,
   leading Prophilus; Nearchus supporting
   Calantha; Crotolon and Amelus.  Cease
   loud music; all make a stand.*

*Cal.*  We miss our servant Ithocles and
   Orgilus;
On whom attend they?
*Crot.*                My son, gracious princess,
Whisper'd some new device, to which these
   revels
Should be but usher: wherein I conceive
Lord Ithocles and he himself are actors.
*Cal.*  A fair excuse for absence: as for Bas-
   sanes,
Delights to him are troublesome.  Armostes
Is with the king?
*Crot.*           He is.
*Cal.*                  On to the dance! —
Dear cousin, hand you the bride; the bride-
   groom must be

---

¹² **doubles**: twistings, crossing one's path; an unlucky omen ('doublers' Q)   ⁴² **resolute**: assured
⁴⁴ **more . . . danger**: more contempt of danger   ⁴⁸ **unheard**: unheard of   ⁵¹ **treble**: threefold

Intrusted to my courtship. Be not jealous, 10
Euphranea; I shall scarcely prove a tempt-
    ress. —
Fall to our dance.

*Music. Nearchus dance with Euphranea, Pro-*
    *philus with Calantha, Christalla with Lem-*
    *ophil, Philema with Groneas.*

*They dance the first change; during which*
    *Enter Armostes*

*Arm.* (*In Calantha's ear.*) The king your
    father 's dead.
*Cal.*    To the other change.
*Arm.*    Is 't possible?        *Dance again.*

*Enter Bassanes*

*Bass.* [*Whispers Calantha.*]    O, madam!
Penthea, poor Penthea 's starv'd.
*Cal.*                Beshrew thee! —
Lead to the next.
*Bass.*        Amazement dulls my senses. 15
                    *Dance again.*

*Enter Orgilus*

*Org.* [*Whispers Calantha.*]  Brave Ithocles is
    murther'd, murther'd cruelly.
*Cal.*  How dull this music sounds! Strike
    up more sprightly;
Our footings are not active like our heart,
Which treads the nimbler measure.
*Org.*            I am thunderstruck.
                *Last change. Cease music.*
*Cal.*  So! let us breathe awhile. — Hath not
    this motion                    20
Rais'd fresher colour on your cheeks?
*Near.*                Sweet princess,
A perfect purity of blood enamels
The beauty of your white.
*Cal.*            We all look cheerfully;
And, cousin, 't is, methinks, a rare presumption
In any who prefer our lawful pleasures    25
Before their own sour censure, to interrupt
The custom of this ceremony bluntly.
*Near.*  None dares, lady.
*Cal.*  Yes, yes; some hollow voice deliver'd
    to me
How that the king was dead.
*Arm.*            The king is dead: 30
That fatal news was mine; for in mine arms
He breath'd his last, and with his crown be-
    queath'd ye
Your mother's wedding ring; which here I ten-
    der.
*Crot.*  Most strange!
*Cal.*  Peace crown his ashes! We are queen,
    then.                        35

*Near.*  Long live Calantha! Sparta's sov-
    ereign queen!
*Omnes.*  Long live the queen!
*Cal.*                What whisper'd Bassanes?
*Bass.*  That my Penthea, miserable soul,
Was starv'd to death.
*Cal.*        She 's happy; she hath finish'd
A long and painful progress. — A third mur-
    mur                        40
Pierc'd mine unwilling ears.
*Org.*                That Ithocles
Was murther'd; — rather butcher'd, had not
    bravery
Of an undaunted spirit, conquering terror,
Proclaim'd his last act triumph over ruin.
*Arm.*  How! murther'd!
*Cal.*            By whose hand?
*Org.*            By mine; this weapon  45
Was instrument to my revenge: the reasons
Are just, and known; quit him of these, and
    then
Never liv'd gentleman of greater merit,
Hope or abiliment to steer a kingdom.
*Crot.*  Fie, Orgilus!
*Euph.*                Fie, brother!
*Cal.*                You have done it?  50
*Bass.*  How it was done let him report, the
    forfeit
Of whose allegiance to our laws doth covet
Rigour of justice; but that done it is,
Mine eyes have been an evidence of credit
Too sure to be convinc'd. Armostes, rent not
Thine arteries with hearing the bare circum-
    stances                    56
Of these calamities. Thou 'st lost a nephew,
A niece, and I a wife: continue man still.
Make me the pattern of digesting evils,
Who can outlive my mighty ones, not shrink-
    ing                        60
At such a pressure as would sink a soul
Into what 's most of death, the worst of hor-
    rors.
But I have seal'd a covenant with sadness,
And enter'd into bonds without condition,
To stand these tempests calmly. Mark me,
    nobles:                    65
I do not shed a tear, not for Penthea!
Excellent misery!
*Cal.*            We begin our reign
With a first act of justice: thy confession,
Unhappy Orgilus, dooms thee a sentence;
But yet thy father's or thy sister's presence 70
Shall be excus'd. — Give, Crotolon, a bless-
    ing
To thy lost son; — Euphranea, take a fare-
    well; —
And both be gone.

¹² s. d. change: figure   ²⁵ prefer: ('prefers' Q)   ⁴⁹ abiliment: mental equipment   ⁵⁵ convinc'd: confuted

*Crot.* [*To Orgilus.*] Confirm thee, noble sor-
row,
In worthy resolution!
*Euph.* Could my tears speak,
My griefs were slight.
*Org.* All goodness dwell amongst ye! 75
Enjoy my sister, Prophilus: my vengeance
Aim'd never at thy prejudice.
*Cal.* Now withdraw.
*Exeunt Crotolon, Prophilus, and Eu-
phranea.*
Bloody relater of thy stains in blood,
For that thou hast reported him, whose for-
tunes
And life by thee are both at once snatch'd
from him, 80
With honourable mention, make thy choice
Of what death likes thee best: there 's all our
bounty. —
But to excuse delays, let me, dear cousin,
Intreat you and these lords see execution
Instant before ye part.
*Near.* Your will commands us. 85
*Org.* One suit, just queen, my last: vouch-
safe your clemency,
That by no common hand I be divided
From this my humble frailty.
*Cal.* To their wisdoms
Who are to be spectators of thine end
I make the reference. Those that are dead 90
Are dead; had they not now died, of necessity
They must have paid the debt they ow'd to
nature
One time or other. — Use dispatch, my lords;
We 'll suddenly prepare our coronation.
*Exeunt Calantha, Philema, Christalla.*
*Arm.* 'T is strange these tragedies should
never touch on 95
Her female pity.
*Bass.* She has a masculine spirit;
And wherefore should I pule, and, like a girl,
Put finger in the eye? Let 's be all toughness,
Without distinction betwixt sex and sex.
*Near.* Now, Orgilus, thy choice?
*Org.* To bleed to death. 100
*Arm.* The executioner?
*Org.* Myself, no surgeon;
I am well skill'd in letting blood. Bind fast
This arm, that so the pipes may from their con-
duits
Convey a full stream; here 's a skilful instru-
ment. [*Shows his dagger.*]
Only I am a beggar to some charity 105
To speed me in this execution
By lending th' other prick to th' tother arm,
When this is bubbling life out.
*Bass.* I am for 'ee;

It most concerns my art, my care, my credit. —
Quick, fillet both his arms.
*Org.* Gramercy, friendship! 110
Such courtesies are real which flow cheerfully
Without an expectation of requital.
Reach me a staff in this hand.
[*They give him a staff.*]
—If a proneness
Or custom in my nature from my cradle
Had been inclin'd to fierce and eager blood-
shed, 115
A coward guilt, hid in a coward quaking,
Would have betray'd fame to ignoble flight
And vagabond pursuit of dreadful safety:
But look upon my steadiness, and scorn not
The sickness of my fortune, which, since Bas-
sanes 120
Was husband to Penthea, had lain bed-rid.
We trifle time in words: — thus I show cunning
In opening of a vein too full, too lively.
[*Pierces the vein with his dagger.*]
*Arm.* Desperate courage!
*Org.* Honourable infamy!
*Lem.* I tremble at the sight.
*Gro.* Would I were loose! 125
*Bass.* It sparkles like a lusty wine new
broach'd;
The vessel must be sound from which it is-
sues. —
Grasp hard this other stick — I 'll be as nim-
ble —
But prithee, look not pale — have at ye! stretch
out
Thine arm with vigour and unshook virtue.
[*Opens the vein.*]
Good! O, I envy not a rival, fitted 131
To conquer in extremities. This pastime
Appears majestical; some high-tun'd poem
Hereafter shall deliver to posterity
The writer's glory and his subject's triumph. 135
How is 't, man? Droop not yet.
*Org.* I feel no palsies.
On a pair-royal do I wait in death;
My sovereign, as his liegeman; on my mis-
tress,
As a devoted servant; and on Ithocles,
As, if no brave, yet no unworthy enemy. 140
Nor did I use an engine to entrap
His life, out of a slavish fear to combat
Youth, strength, or cunning; but for that I
durst not
Engage the goodness of a cause on fortune,
By which his name might have outfac'd my
vengeance. 145
O, Tecnicus, inspir'd with Phœbus' fire!
I call to mind thy augury: 't was perfect;
*Revenge proves its own executioner.*

---

[83] **excuse:** obviate　　[90] **I . . . reference:** I refer your request　　[94] **suddenly:** immediately
[113] **cunning:** skill　　[144] **Engage:** stake

When feeble man is bending to his mother,
The dust 'a was first fram'd on, thus he totters.
   *Bass.*   Life's fountain is dri'd up.
   *Org.*            So falls the standard   151
Of my prerogative in being a creature!
A mist hangs o'er mine eyes, the sun's bright
   splendour
Is clouded in an everlasting shadow:
Welcome, thou ice, that sitt'st about my heart!
No heat can ever thaw thee.          *Dies.*
   *Near.*          Speech hath left him.   156
   *Bass.*   'A has shook hands with time; his
   funeral urn
Shall be my charge: remove the bloodless body.
The coronation must require attendance;
That past, my few days can be but one mourn-
   ing.                 *Exeunt.*   160

[SCENE III. — *A Temple*]

*An altar covered with white; two lights of virgin*
*wax, during which music of recorders; enter*
*four bearing Ithocles on a hearse, or in a*
*chair, in a rich robe, and a crown on his*
*head; place him on one side of the altar.*
*After him enter Calantha in a white robe*
*and crown'd; Euphranea, Philema, Chris-*
*talla, in white; Nearchus, Armostes,*
*Crotolon, Prophilus, Amelus, Bassanes,*
*Lemophil, and Groneas.*

*Calantha goes and kneels before the altar, the*
*rest stand off, the women kneeling behind.*
*Cease recorders, during her devotions. Soft*
*music. Calantha and the rest rise, doing*
*obeisance to the altar.*

   *Cal.*   Our orisons are heard; the gods are
   merciful. —
Now tell me, you whose loyalties pays tribute
To us your lawful sovereign, how unskilful
Your duties or obedience is to render
Subjection to the sceptre of a virgin,      5
Who have been ever fortunate in princes
Of masculine and stirring composition.
A woman has enough to govern wisely
Her own demeanours, passions, and divi-
   sions.
A nation warlike and inur'd to practice    10
Of policy and labour cannot brook
A feminate authority: we therefore
Command your counsel, how you may advise
   us
In choosing of a husband whose abilities
Can better guide this kingdom.
   *Near.*           Royal lady,   15
Your law is in your will.
   *Arm.*         We have seen tokens
Of constancy too lately to mistrust it.
   *Crot.*   Yet, if your highness settle on a choice

By your own judgment both allow'd and lik'd
   of,
Sparta may grow in power, and proceed    20
To an increasing height.
   *Cal.*         Hold you the same mind?
   *Bass.*   Alas, great mistress, reason is so
   clouded
With the thick darkness of my infinite woes,
That I forecast nor dangers, hopes, or safety.
Give me some corner of the world to wear
   out   25
The remnant of the minutes I must number,
Where I may hear no sounds but sad com-
   plaints
Of virgins who have lost contracted partners;
Of husbands howling that their wives were
   ravish'd
By some untimely fate; of friends divided   30
By churlish opposition; or of fathers
Weeping upon their children's slaughter'd car-
   cases;
Or daughters groaning o'er their fathers'
   hearses:
And I can dwell there, and with these keep
   consort
As musical as theirs. What can you look for   35
From an old, foolish, peevish, doting man
But craziness of age?
   *Cal.*   Cousin of Argos, —
   *Near.*           Madam?
   *Cal.*              Were I presently
To choose you for my lord, I 'll open freely
What articles I would propose to treat on    40
Before our marriage.
   *Near.*         Name them, virtuous lady.
   *Cal.*   I would presume you would retain the
   royalty
Of Sparta in her own bounds; then in Argos
Armostes might be viceroy; in Messene
Might Crotolon bear sway; and Bassanes —   45
   *Bass.*   I, queen! alas, what I?
   *Cal.*           Be Sparta's marshal.
The multitudes of high employments could
   not
But set a peace to private griefs. These gentle-
   men,
Groneas and Lemophil, with worthy pensions,
Should wait upon your person in your cham-
   ber. —                 50
I would bestow Christalla on Amelus, —
She 'll prove a constant wife; and Philema
Should into Vesta's Temple.
   *Bass.*           This is a testament!
It sounds not like conditions on a marriage.
   *Near.*   All this should be perform'd.
   *Cal.*          Lastly, for Prophilus,   55
He should be, cousin, solemnly invested
In all those honours, titles, and preferments

_____

¹⁵¹ **standard:** ('Standards' Q)    ⁹ **divisions:** inner doubts    ³⁴ **consort:** harmony

Which his dear friend and my neglected husband
Too short a time enjoy'd.
*Pro.*         I am unworthy
To live in your remembrance.
*Euph.*         Excellent lady! 60
*Near.* Madam, what means that word,
"neglected husband"?
*Cal.* Forgive me: — now I turn to thee, thou shadow
Of my contracted lord! Bear witness all,
I put my mother's wedding-ring upon
His finger; 't was my father's last bequest. 65
    [*Places a ring on the finger of Ithocles.*]
Thus I new-marry him whose wife I am;
Death shall not separate us. O, my lords,
I but deceiv'd your eyes with antic gesture,
When one news straight came huddling on another
Of death, and death, and death! still I danc'd forward; 70
But it struck home, and here, and in an instant.
Be such mere women, who with shrieks and outcries
Can vow a present end to all their sorrows,
Yet live to vow new pleasures, and outlive them?
They are the silent griefs which cut the heart-strings; 75
Let me die smiling.
*Near.*        'T is a truth too ominous.
*Cal.* One kiss on these cold lips, my last!
    [*Kisses Ithocles.*] — Crack, crack! —
Argos now 's Sparta's king. — Command the voices
Which wait at th' altar now to sing the song
I fitted for my end.
*Near.*       Sirs, the song! 80

*A Song*

*All.*   *Glories pleasures, pomps, delights, and ease,*
    *Can but please*
    *Outward senses when the mind*
    *Is not untroubled or by peace refin'd.*
1 [*Voice.*] *Crowns may flourish and decay,* 85
    *Beauties shine, but fade away.*
2 [*Voice.*] *Youth may revel, yet it must*
    *Lie down in a bed of dust.*

105 **counsels:** secret purposes

3 [*Voice.*] *Earthly honours flow and waste,*
    *Time alone doth change and last.* 90
*All.*   *Sorrows mingled with contents prepare*
    *Rest for care;*
    *Love only reigns in death; though art*
    *Can find no comfort for a broken heart.*

    [*Calantha dies.*]

*Arm.* Look to the queen!
*Bass.*     Her heart is broke, indeed. 95
O, royal maid, would thou hadst miss'd this part!
Yet 't was a brave one. I must weep to see
Her smile in death.
*Arm.*       Wise Tecnicus! thus said he.
*When youth is ripe, and age from time doth part,*
*The Lifeless Trunk shall wed the Broken Heart.*
'T is here fulfill'd.
*Near.*     I am your king.
*Omnes.*       Long live 101
Nearchus, King of Sparta!
*Near.*       Her last will
Shall never be digress'd from: wait in order
Upon these faithful lovers, as becomes us. —
The counsels of the gods are never known 105
Till men can call th' effects of them their own.
    [*Exeunt.*]

FINIS

# The Epilogue

WHERE noble judgments and clear eyes are fix'd
To grace endeavour, there sits truth, not mix'd
With ignorance: those censures may command
Belief which talk not till they understand.
Let some say, "This was flat;" some, "Here the scene 5
Fell from its height;" another, that the mean
Was ill observ'd in such a growing passion
As it transcended either state or fashion.
Some few may cry, "'T was pretty well," or so,
"But —" and there shrug in silence; yet we know 10
Our writer's aim was in the whole address'd
Well to deserve of *all*, but please the *best:*
Which granted, by th' allowance of this strain
The BROKEN HEART may be piec'd up again.

Epilogue   6 **mean:** artistic restraint

# THE
# CARDINAL,
## A
# TRAGEDIE,

### AS
It was acted at the private Houſe
### IN
## *BLACK FRYERS,*

### WRITTEN
### By JAMES SHIRLEY.

*Not Printed before.*

***LONDON,***
Printed for *Humphrey Robinſon* at the Three
Pigeons, and *Humphrey Moſeley* at the Prince's
Arms in St. *Paul's* Church-yard.
1652.

BIBLIOGRAPHICAL RECORD. The only early text of *The Cardinal* is to be found in a small octavo volume (here referred to as "Q") which was published in 1653 with the title, *Six New Playes, Viz. The Brothers. Sisters. Doubtfull Heir. Imposture. Cardinall. Court Secret. The Five first were acted at the Private House in Black Fryers with great Applause. The last was never Acted. All Written by James Shirley. Never printed before.* Each play in the volume has a separate title-page, those of *The Cardinal* and four others being dated 1652. *The Cardinal* is preceded by a dedication to "G. B., Esq." in which Shirley ventures the opinion that this is his best play. There is also a commendatory poem, signed "Hall," which makes the following too sanguine prophecy as to Shirley's place in the history of the drama:

> And though I do not tell you, how you dress
> Virtue in gloryes, and bold vice depress;
> Nor celebrate your lovely Dutchess fall,
> Or the just ruine of your Cardinal;
> Yet this I dare assert, when men have nam'd
> Iohnson (the Nations Laureat,) the fam'd
> Beaumont, and Fletcher, he, that wo' not see
> Shirley, the fourth, must forfeit his best ey[e].

DATE AND STAGE PERFORMANCE. *The Cardinal* was licensed by Sir Henry Herbert, the Master of the Revels, on November 25, 1641, and was acted by the King's Men at the Blackfriars Theatre. On the evidence of what remains of Herbert's office books, it was the last of Shirley's plays, except one, to be licensed before the closing of the theatres. *The Sisters* received Herbert's approval, April 26, 1642; and after several other entries irrelevant to Shirley, the Master wound up his accounts with the note, "Here ended my allowance of plaies, for the war began in Aug. 1642."

After the Restoration the tragedy was revived with success. A performance on July 23, 1662, is recorded by Herbert, and Pepys gives a very interesting account of another, on October 2 of the same year, witnessed by Charles II and his Queen. Later productions attended by Pepys were on August 24, 1667, and April 27, 1668.

STRUCTURE AND SOURCES. The play is loosely divided into five acts, without indication of the separate scenes in the original text, and with no concern for the unities. Webster's *Duchess of Malfi* is its closest prototype, and the two tragedies can be profitably compared. The remarkable contemporary figure of Cardinal Richelieu in France must have affected Shirley's general handling of the plot (see Prologue). For specific parallels with other dramas see R. S. Forsythe, *The Relations of Shirley's Plays to the Elizabethan Drama*, 1914, pp. 185–189. (Important new biographical material on Shirley will be found in two papers by Professor A. C. Baugh, *Modern Language Review*, 1922, pp. 228–235; *Review of English Studies*, 1931, pp. 62–66.)

THE CLOSING OF THE THEATRES. On September 2, 1642 (nine months after *The Cardinal* had been licensed), war having broken out between Charles I and his Parliament, the latter passed the following ordinance, which for eighteen years prevented all but the surreptitious production of plays in London:

"*An Order of the Lords and Commons concerning Stage-playes.* Whereas the distressed Estate of Ireland, steeped in her own Blood, and the distracted Estate of England, threatned with a Cloud of Blood by a Civill Warre, call for all possible meanes to appease and avert the Wrath of God appearing in these Judgements; amongst which Fasting and Prayer, having bin often tryed to be very effectuall, have bin lately, and are still enjoyned; and whereas publike Sports doe not well agree with publike Calamities, nor publike Stage-playes with the Seasons of Humiliation, this being an Exercise of sad and pious solemnity, and the others being Spectacles of pleasure, too commonly expressing laciuious Mirth and Levitie: It is therefore thought fit, and Ordeined by the Lords and Commons in this Parliament Assembled, that while these sad Causes and set times of Humiliation doe continue, publike Stage-Playes shall cease, and bee forborne. Instead of which, are recommended to the people of this Land, the profitable and seasonable Considerations of Repentance. Reconciliation, and peace with God, which probably may produce outward peace and prosperity and bring againe Times of Joy and Gladnesse to these Nations."

# JAMES SHIRLEY (1596–1666)

## THE CARDINAL

### PERSONS

KING OF NAVARRE
CARDINAL
COLUMBO, the Cardinal's Nephew
[COUNT D'] ALVAREZ
HERNANDO, a Colonel
ALPHONSO, [a Captain]

[ANTONIO,] Secretary to the Duchess
ANTONELLI, the Cardinal's Servant

DUCHESS ROSAURA
VALERIA, } Ladies
CELINDA, }
PLACENTIA, a Lady that waits upon the Duchess

Lords, Colonels, Gentleman-Usher, Surgeon, Guard, Attendants, &c.

SCENE. — NAVARRE

### Prologue

*THE CARDINAL! 'Cause we express no scene,*
*We do believe most of you, gentlemen,*
*Are at this hour in France, and busy there,*
*Though you vouchsafe to lend your bodies here;*
*But keep your fancy active, till you know,* 5
*By th' progress of our play, 't is nothing so.*
*A poet's art is to lead on your thought*
*Through subtle paths and workings of a plot;*
*And where your expectation does not thrive,*
*If things fall better, yet you may forgive.* 10
*I will say nothing positive; you may*
*Think what you please; we call it but a Play.*
*Whether the comic Muse, or ladies' love,*
*Romance, or direful tragedy it prove,*
*The bill determines not; and would you be* 15
*Persuaded, I would have 't a comedy,*
*For all the purple in the name and state*
*Of him that owns it; but 't is left to fate.*
*Yet I will tell you, ere you see it play'd,*
*What the author, and he blush'd, too, when he said,* 20
*Comparing with his own, (for 't had been pride,*
*He thought, to build his wit a pyramid*
*Upon another's wounded fame,) this play*
*Might rival with his best, and dar'd to say —*
*Troth, I am out: he said no more. You, then,* 25
*When 't 's done, may say your pleasures, gentlemen.*

### ACT I

[SCENE I. *A Room in the Palace*]

*Enter two Lords (at one door); Secretary [Antonio] (at the other)*

1 *Lord.* Who is that?
2 *Lord.* The duchess' secretary.
1 *Lord.* Signior!

*Sec.* Your lordship's servant.
1 *Lord.* How does her grace, since she left her
mourning 5
For the young Duke Mendoza, whose timeless
death
At sea left her a virgin and a widow?
2 *Lord.* She 's now inclining to a second
bride. ——
When is the day of mighty marriage
To our great Cardinal's nephew, Don Columbo?

Prologue ¹ **express:** indicate (by locality boards on the stage, or by "bills"; see line 15) ³ **Are ... France:** (In 1641 Cardinal Richelieu had reached the height of his spectacular power in France; he died the next year.) ⁸ **inclining to:** disposed to become

1017

*Sec.*  When they agree, they wo' not steal to
   church;                                        11
I guess the ceremonies will be loud and public.
Your lordships will excuse me.            *Exit.*
   1 *Lord.*  When they agree! Alas! poor lady,
   she
Dotes not upon Columbo, when she thinks   15
Of the young Count d'Alvarez, divorc'd from
   her
By the king's power.
   2 *Lord.*          And counsel of the Cardinal,
To advance his nephew to the duchess' bed;
'T is not well.
   1 *Lord.*      Take heed; the Cardinal holds
Intelligence with every bird i' th' air.    20
   2 *Lord.*  Death on his purple pride! He gov-
   erns all;
And yet Columbo is a gallant gentleman.
   1 *Lord.*  The darling of the war, whom victory
Hath often courted; a man of daring,
And most exalted spirit.  Pride in him     25
Dwells like an ornament, where so much hon-
   our
Secures his praise.
   2 *Lord.*            This is no argument
He should usurp, and wear Alvarez' title
To the fair duchess.  Men of coarser blood
Would not so tamely give this treasure up.  30
   1 *Lord.*  Although Columbo's name is great
   in war,
Whose glorious art and practice is above
The greatness of Alvarez, yet he cannot
Want soul, in whom alone survives the virtue
Of many noble ancestors, being the last    35
Of his great family.
   2 *Lord.*            'T is not safe, you 'll say,
To wrastle with the king.
   1 *Lord.*  More danger if the Cardinal be dis-
   pleas'd,
Who sits at helm of state.  Count d'Alvarez
Is wiser to obey the stream, than by        40
Insisting on his privilege to her love,
Put both their fates upon a storm.
   2 *Lord.*              If wisdom,
Not inborn fear, make him compose, I like it.
How does the duchess bear herself?
   1 *Lord.*  She moves by the rapture of another
   wheel,                                    45
That must be obey'd; like some sad passenger,
That looks upon the coast his wishes fly to,
But is transported by an adverse wind,
Sometimes a churlish pilot.
   2 *Lord.*  She has a sweet and noble nature.
   1 *Lord.*                        That    50
Commends Alvarez; Hymen cannot tie
A knot of two more equal hearts and blood.

*Enter Alphonso*

   2 *Lord.*  Alphonso!
   *Alph.*              My good lord.
   1 *Lord.*                  What great affair
Hath brought you from the confines?
   *Alph.*                        Such as will
Be worth your counsels, when the king hath
   read                                      55
My letters from the governor.  The Arragonians,
Violating their confederate oath and league,
Are now in arms: they have not yet march'd to-
   wards us;
But 't is not safe to expect, if we may timely
Prevent invasion.
   2 *Lord.*          Dare they be so insolent?  60
   1 *Lord.*  This storm I did foresee.
   2 *Lord.*              What have they, but
The sweetness of the king, to make a crime?
   1 *Lord.*  But how appears the Cardinal at this
   news?
   *Alph.*  Not pale, although
He knows they have no cause to think him in-
   nocent,                                   65
As by whose counsel they were once surpris'd.
   1 *Lord.*  There is more
Than all our present art can fathom in
This story, and I fear I may conclude
This flame has breath at home to cherish it.  70
There 's treason in some hearts, whose faces are
Smooth to the state.
   *Alph.*          My lords, I take my leave.
   2 *Lord.*  Your friends, good captain.
                                    *Exeunt.*

[SCENE II.  *A Room in the Duchess's House*]

*Enter Duchess, Valeria, Celinda*

   *Val.*  Sweet madam, be less thoughtful; this
   obedience
To passion will destroy the noblest frame
Of beauty that this kingdom ever boasted.
   *Cel.*  This sadness might become your other
   habit,
And ceremonious black for him that died.    5
The times of sorrow are expir'd; and all
The joys that wait upon the court, your birth,
And a new Hymen, that is coming towards you,
Invite a change.
   *Duch.*          Ladies, I thank you both.
I pray, excuse a little melancholy           10
That is behind; my year of mourning hath not
So clear'd my account with sorrow, but there
   may
Some dark thoughts stay, with sad reflections
Upon my heart for him I lost.  Even this

---

²⁰ **Intelligence:** communication   ⁴² **upon a storm:** in danger   ⁴³ **compose:** come to agreement
⁴⁵ **rapture:** drawing force, momentum   ⁵⁴ **confines:** frontiers   ⁵⁹ **expect:** wait   ⁶⁰ **Prevent:** forestall   ¹ **obedience:** yielding   ⁸ **Hymen:** marriage

New dress and smiling garment, meant to
show                                          15
A peace concluded 'twixt my grief and me,
Is but a sad remembrance.  But I resolve
To entertain more pleasing thoughts; and if
You wish me heartily to smile, you must
Not mention grief, not in advice to leave it. 20
Such counsels open but afresh the wounds
Ye would close up, and keep alive the cause,
Whose bleeding you would cure.  Let 's talk of
something
That may delight.  You two are read in all
The histories of our court: tell me, Valeria, 25
Who has thy vote for the most handsome
man? —
Thus I must counterfeit a peace, when all
Within me is at mutiny.  [Aside.]
   Val.                    I have examin'd
All that are candidates for the praise of ladies,
But find — may I speak boldly to your grace?
And will you not return it in your mirth,  31
To make me blush?
   Duch.                No, no; speak freely.
   Val.  I wo' not rack your patience, madam;
but
Were I a princess, I should think Count d'Al-
varez
Had sweetness to deserve me from the world. 35
   Duch.  [Aside.]  Alvarez! she 's a spy upon
my heart.
   Val.  He 's young and active, and compos'd
most sweetly.
   Duch.  I have seen a face more tempting.
   Val.                        It had, then,
Too much of woman in 't: his eyes speak mov-
ingly,
Which may excuse his voice, and lead away  40
All female pride his captive; his hair, black,
Which, naturally falling into curls —
   Duch.  Prithee, no more; thou art in love
with him. —
The man in your esteem, Celinda, now?
   Cel.  Alvarez is, I must confess, a gentle-
man                                          45
Of handsome composition; but with
His mind, the greater excellence, I think
Another may delight a lady more,
If man be well consider'd, that 's Columbo,
Now, madam, voted to be yours.
   Duch.  [Aside.]              My torment! 50
   Val.  [Aside.]  She affects him not.
   Cel.  He has a person, and a bravery beyond
All men that I observe.
   Val.                He is a soldier,
A rough-hewn man, and may show well at dis-
tance.
His talk will fright a lady; War, and grim-  55

Fac'd Honour are his mistresses; he raves
To hear a lute; Love meant him not his
priest. —
Again your pardon, madam.  We may talk,
But you have art to choose, and crown affec-
tion.      [Celinda and Valeria walk aside.]
   Duch.  What is it to be born above these
ladies,                                      60
And want their freedom!  They are not con-
strain'd,
Nor slav'd by their own greatness or the king's,
But let their free hearts look abroad, and choose
By their own eyes to love.  I must repair
My poor afflicted bosom, and assume       65
The privilege I was born with, which now
prompts me
To tell the king, he hath no power nor art
To steer a lover's soul. —

*Enter Secretary [Antonio]*

                  What says Count d'Alvarez?
   Sec.  Madam, he 'll attend you.
   Duch.  Wait you, as I directed.  When he
comes,                                       70
Acquaint me privately.
   Sec.              Madam, I have news;
'T is now arriv'd the court: we shall have wars.
   Duch.  [Aside.]  I find an army here of killing
thoughts.
   Sec.  The king has chosen Don Columbo gen-
eral,
Who is immediately to take his leave.     75
   Duch.  [Aside.]  What flood is let into my
heart! — How far
Is he to go?
   Sec.      To Arragon.
   Duch.                That 's well
At first; he should not want a pilgrimage
To the unknown world, if my thoughts might
convey him.
   Sec.  'T is not impossible he may go thither.
   Duch.                        How?  80
   Sec.  To the unknown other world; he goes to
fight,
That 's in his way: such stories are in nature.
   Duch.  Conceal this news.
   Sec.                He wo' not be long absent;
The affair will make him swift
To kiss your grace's hand.            [Exit.]
   Duch.                He cannot fly  85
With too much wing to take his leave. — I
must
Be admitted to your conference; ye have
Enlarg'd my spirits; they shall droop no more.
   Cel.  We are happy, if we may advance one
thought
To your grace's pleasure.                   90

---

³⁵ **deserve:** be worthy of    **from:** in comparison with    ³⁷ **compos'd:** fashioned    ⁵¹ **affects:**
likes    ⁵² **a person:** ('person' Q)

*Val.* Your eye before was in eclipse; these smiles
Become you, madam.

*Duch.* [*Aside.*] I have not skill to contain myself.

*Enter Placentia*

*Pla.* The Cardinal's nephew, madam, Don Columbo.

*Duch.* Already! Attend him.
*Exit Placentia.*

*Val.*                                   Shall we take our leave? 95

*Duch.* He shall not know, Celinda, how you prais'd him.

*Cel.* If he did, madam, I should have the confidence
To tell him my free thoughts.

*Enter Columbo*

*Duch.* My lord, while I 'm in study to requite
The favour you ha' done me, you increase 100
My debt to such a sum, still by a new honour-ing
Your servant, I despair of my own freedom.

*Colum.* Madam, he kisseth your white hand, that must
Not surfeit in this happiness — and, ladies,
I take your smiles for my encouragement! 105
I have not long to practise these court tactics.
[*Kisses them.*]

*Cel.* He has been taught to kiss.

*Duch.*                                   There 's something, sir,
Upon your brow I did not read before.

*Colum.* Does the charácter please you, madam?

*Duch.*                                                    More,
Because it speaks you cheerful.

*Colum.*                                   'T is for such 110
Access of honour, as must make Columbo
Worth all your love; the king is pleas'd to think
Me fit to lead his army.

*Duch.*                                   How! an army?

*Colum.* We must not use the priest, till I bring home
Another triumph that now stays for me, 115
To reap it in the purple field of glory.

*Duch.* But do you mean to leave me, and expose
Yourself to the devouring war? No enemy
Should divide us; the king is not so cruel.

*Colum.* The king is honourable; and this grace 120
More answers my ambition than his gift
Of thee and all thy beauty, which I can
Love, as becomes thy soldier, and fight

To come again, a conqueror of thee.
*She weeps.*
Then I must chide this fondness. 125

*Enter Secretary [Antonio]*

*Sec.* Madam, the king, and my lord Cardi-nal. [*Exit.*]

*Enter King, Cardinal, and Lords*

*King.* Madam, I come to call a servant from you,
And strengthen his excuse; the public cause
Will plead for your consent; at his return
Your marriage shall receive triumphant cere-monies; 130
Till then you must dispense.

*Car.*                                   She appears sad
To part with him. — I like it fairly, nephew.

*Cel.* Is not the general a gallant man?
What lady would deny him a small courtesy?

*Val.* Thou hast converted me, and I begin
To wish it were no sin. 136

*Cel.* Leave that to narrow consciences.

*Val.*                                   You are pleasant.

*Cel.* But he would please one better. Do such men
Lie with their pages?

*Val.*                                   Wouldst thou make a shift?

*Cel.* He is going to a bloody business; 140
'T is pity he should die without some heir.
That lady were hard-hearted, now, that would
Not help posterity, for the mere good
O' th' king and commonwealth.

*Val.* Thou art wild; we may be observ'd.

*Duch.* Your will must guide me; happiness and conquest 146
Be ever waiting on his sword!

*Colum.*                                   Farewell.
*Exeunt King, Columbo, Cardinal, Lords.*

*Duch.* Pray, give me leave to examine a few thoughts;
Expect me in the garden.

*Ladies.*                                   We attend. *Exeunt Ladies.* 149

*Duch.* This is above all expectation happy.
Forgive me, Virtue, that I have dissembled,
And witness with me, I have not a thought
To tempt or to betray him, but secure
The promise I first made to love and hon-our. 154

*Enter Secretary [Antonio]*

*Sec.* The Count d'Alvarez, madam.

*Duch.*                                   Admit him.
And let none interrupt us. [*Exit Antonio.*]
How shall I
Behave my looks? The guilt of my neglect,
Which had no seal from hence, will call up blood

---

⁹⁴ **Celinda:** ('Valeria' Q. The ladies are so confused in speeches and speech-tags throughout the remainder of this scene. Cf. lines 45–57.) ¹¹⁵ **stays:** waits ¹²⁵ **fondness:** foolishness ¹²⁷ **servant:** lover ¹⁴⁸ **me:** (not in Q) ¹⁴⁹ **Expect:** await ¹⁵⁷ **Behave:** control

To write upon my cheeks the shame and story
In some red letter.

*Enter d'Alvarez*

*Alv.*                    Madam, I present     160
One that was glad to obey your grace, and come
To know what your commands are.
*Duch.*                    Where I once
Did promise love, a love that had the power
And office of a priest to chain my heart
To yours, it were injustice to command.     165
*Alv.*  But I can look upon you, madam, as
Becomes a servant; with as much humility,
(In tenderness of your honour and great for-
    tune,)
Give up, when you call back your bounty, all
    that                                    169
Was mine, as I had pride to think them favours.
*Duch.*  Hath love taught thee no more assur-
    ance in
Our mutual vows, thou canst suspect it possible
I should revoke a promise, made to heaven
And thee, so soon? This must arise from some
Distrust of thy own faith.
*Alv.*                    Your grace's pardon; 175
To speak with freedom, I am not so old
In cunning to betray, nor young in time,
Not to see when and where I am at loss,
And how to bear my fortune and my wounds,
Which, if I look for health, must still bleed in-
    ward,                                   180
A hard and desperate condition.
I am not ignorant your birth and greatness
Have plac'd you to grow up with the king's
    grace
And jealousy, which to remove, his power
Hath chosen a fit object for your beauty     185
To shine upon, Columbo, his great favourite.
I am a man on whom but late the king
Has pleas'd to cast a beam, which was not meant
To make me proud, but wisely to direct,     189
And light me to my safety. Oh, dear madam!
I will not call more witness of my love
(If you will let me still give it that name)
Than this, that I dare make myself a loser,
And to your will give all my blessings up.
Preserve your greatness, and forget a trifle, 195
That shall, at best, when you have drawn me up,
But hang about you like a cloud, and dim
The glories you are born to.
*Duch.*                    Misery
Of birth and state! That I could shift into
A meaner blood, or find some art to purge     200
That part which makes my veins unequal! Yet
Those nice distinctions have no place in us;
There 's but a shadow difference, a title:
Thy stock partakes as much of noble sap     204

As that which feeds the root of kings; and he
That writes a lord hath all the essence of
Nobility.
*Alv.*      'T is not a name that makes
Our separation; the king's displeasure
Hangs a portent to fright us, and the matter
That feeds this exhalation is the Cardinal's 210
Plot to advance his nephew; then Columbo,
A man made up for some prodigious act,
Is fit to be consider'd: in all three
There is no character you fix upon
But has a form of ruin to us both.     215
*Duch.*  Then you do look on these with fear?
*Alv.*                    With eyes
That should think tears a duty, to lament
Your least unkind fate; but my youth dares
    boldly
Meet all the tyranny o' th' stars, whose black
Malevolence but shoots my single tragedy.   220
You are above the value of many worlds
Peopled with such as I am.
*Duch.*                    What if Columbo,
Engag'd to war, in his hot thirst of honour,
Find out the way to death?
*Alv.*                    'T is possible.
*Duch.*  Or say, (no matter by what art or
    motive,)                               225
He give his title up, and leave me to
My own election?
*Alv.*              If I then be happy
To have a name within your thought, there
    can                                     228
Be nothing left to crown me with new blessing.
But I dream thus of heaven, and wake to find
My amorous soul a mockery. When the priest
Shall tie you to another, and the joys
Of marriage leave no thought at leisure to
Look back upon Alvarez, that must wither
For loss of you; yet then I cannot lose     235
So much of what I was once in your favour,
But, in a sigh, pray still you may live happy. *Exit.*
*Duch.*  My heart is in a mist; some good star
    smile
Upon my resolution, and direct             239
Two lovers in their chaste embrace to meet!
Columbo's bed contains my winding sheet.
                                        *Exit.*

## ACT II

[SCENE I. *Before the Walls of the frontier
    City. — Columbo's Tent*]

*Enter General Columbo, Hernando, two Colonels,
    Alphonso, two Captains, and other Officers,
    as at a Council of War*

*Colum.*  I see no face in all this council that
Hath one pale fear upon 't, though we arriv'd
    not

---

So timely to secure the town, which gives
Our enemy such triumph.
   *1 Col.*          'T was betray'd.
   *Alph.*  The wealth of that one city     5
Will make the enemy glorious.
   *1 Col.*             They dare
Not plunder it.
   *Alph.*         They give fair quarter yet:
They only seal up men's estates, and keep
Possession for the city's use: they take up
No wares without security; and he,    10
Whose single credit will not pass, puts in
Two lean comrades, upon whose bonds 't is not
Religion to deny 'em.
   *Colum.*         To repair this
With honour, gentlemen?
   *Her.*         My opinion is
To expect awhile.
   *Colum.*      Your reason?
   *Her.*         Till their own  15
Surfeit betray 'em; for their soldiers,
Bred up with coarse and common bread, will
   show
Such appetites on the rich cates they find,
They 'll spare our swords a victory, when their
   own
Riot and luxury destroys 'em.
   *1 Col.*          That    20
Will show our patience too like a fear.
With favour of his excellence, I think
The spoil of cities takes not off the courage,
But doubles it on soldiers; besides,
While we have tameness to expect, the noise  25
Of their success and plenty will increase
Their army.
   *Her.*    'T is considerable; we do not
Exceed in foot or horse, our muster not
'Bove sixteen thousand both; and the infantry
Raw, and not disciplin'd to act.
   *Alph.*         Their hearts,  30
But with a brave thought of their country's
   honour,
Will teach 'em how to fight, had they not
   seen
A sword. But we decline our own too much;
The men are forward in their arms, and take
The use with avarice of fame.
               *They rise, and talk privately.*
   *Colum.*         — Colonel,  35
I do suspect you are a coward.
   *Her.*         Sir!
   *Colum.*  Or else a traitor; take your choice.
No more.
I call'd you to a council, sir, of war;
Yet keep your place.
   *Her.*        I have worn other names.

   *Colum.*  Deserve 'em. Such      40
Another were enough to unsoul an army.
Ignobly talk of patience, till they drink
And reel to death! We came to fight, and force
   'em
To mend their pace! Thou hast no honour in
   thee,
Not enough noble blood to make a blush  45
For thy tame eloquence.
   *Her.*         My lord, I know
My duty to a general; yet there are
Some that have known me here. Sir, I de-
   sire
To quit my regiment.
   *Colum.*        You shall have license. —
Ink and paper!                50

   *Enter [Attendant] with paper and standish*

   *1 Col.*  The general 's displeas'd.
   *2 Col.*         How is 't, Hernando?
   *Her.*  The general has found out employment
   for me;
He is writing letters back.
   *Al. Capt.*        To his mistress?
   *Her.*  Pray do not trouble me; yet, prithee,
   speak,
And flatter not thy friend. Dost think I dare  55
Not draw my sword, and use it, when a cause,
With honour, calls to action?
   *Al. Col.*  With the most valiant man alive.
   *Her.*  You 'll do me some displeasure in your
   loves:
Pray, to your places.             60
   *Colum.*  So; bear those letters to the king;
They speak my resolution, before
Another sun decline, to charge the enemy.
   *Her. [Aside.]*  A pretty court way
Of dismissing an officer. — I obey; success  65
Attend your counsels!           *Exit.*
   *Colum.*  If here be any dare not look on dan-
   ger,
And meet it like a man, with scorn of death,
I beg his absence; and a coward's fear
Consume him to a ghost!
   *1 Col.*        None such are here.  70
   *Colum.*  Or, if in all your regiments you
   find
One man that does not ask to bleed with hon-
   our,
Give him a double pay to leave the army;
There 's service to be done will call the spirits
And aid of men.
   *1 Col.*       You give us all new flame.  75
   *Colum.*  I am confirm'd, and you must lose
   no time.
The soldier that was took last night to me

---

   **6 glorious:** boastful   **18 cates:** dainties   **25 noise:** rumor, report   **33 decline:** depreciate
**34–35 take ... fame:** pursue fame greedily   **44 mend ... pace:** take to their heels   **50 S. D. standish:**
inkstand   **56 a cause:** ('cause' Q)   **62 They speak:** ('It speaks' Q)   **70 are:** (not in Q)

Discover'd their whole strength, and that we have
A party in the town, — the river, that
Opens the city to the west, unguarded.     80
We must this night use art and resolutions.
We cannot fall ingloriously.
    1 *Capt.*        That voice
Is every man's.

    *Enter Soldier and Secretary [Antonio]*
        *with a letter*

*Colum.* What now?
*Sold.* Letters.              85
*Colum.* Whence?
*Sold.* From the duchess. —
*Colum.* They are welcome. —
            [*Takes the letter.*]
Meet at my tent again this evening;
Yet stay, some wine. — The duchess' health! 90
            [*Drinks.*]
See it go round.        [*Opens the letter.*]
    *Sec.* It wo' not please his excellence.
    1 *Col.* The duchess' health!    [*Drinks.*]
    2 *Capt.* To me! more wine.
    *Sec.* The clouds are gathering, and his eyes
     shoot fire;             95
Observe what thunder follows.
    2 *Capt.* The general has but ill news. I suspect
The duchess sick, or else the king.
    1 *Capt.*            May be
The Cardinal.
    2 *Capt.* His soul has long been look'd for.
    *Colum.* [*Aside.*] She dares not be so insolent.
     It is             100
The duchess' hand. How am I shrunk in fame
To be thus play'd withal! She writes, and counsels,
Under my hand to send her back a free
Resign of all my interest to her person,
Promise, or love; that there 's no other way,
With safety of my honour, to revisit her.    106
The woman is possess'd with some bold devil,
And wants an exorcism; or I am grown
A cheap, dull, phlegmatic fool, a post that 's carv'd
I' th' common street, and holding out my forehead            110
To every scurril wit to pin disgrace
And libels on 't. — Did you bring this to me, sir?
My thanks shall warm your heart.
            *Draws a pistol.*
    *Sec.*          Hold, hold! my lord!
I know not what provokes this tempest, but
Her grace ne'er show'd more freedom from a storm            115

When I receiv'd this paper. If you have
A will to do an execution,
Your looks, without that engine, sir, may serve. —
I did not like the employment.
    *Colum.*           Ha! had she
No symptom, in her eye or face, of anger,    120
When she gave this in charge?
    *Sec.*           Serene, as I
Have seen the morning rise upon the spring;
No trouble in her breath, but such a wind
As came to kiss and fan the smiling flowers.
    *Colum.* No poetry.
    *Sec.*        By all the truth in prose,   125
By honesty, and your own honour, sir,
I never saw her look more calm and gentle.
    *Colum.* I am too passionate; you must forgive me. —
I have found it out; the duchess loves me dearly;
She express'd a trouble in her when I took   130
My leave, and chid me with a sullen eye.
'T is a device to hasten my return;
Love has a thousand arts. I 'll answer it
Beyond her expectation, and put
Her soul to a noble test. [*Aside.*] — Your patience, gentlemen;       135
The king's health will deserve a sacrifice
Of wine.    [*Retires to the table and writes.*]
    *Sec.* [*Aside.*] I am glad to see this change,
     and thank my wit
For my redemption.
    1 *Col.*        Sir, the soldiers' curse
On him loves not our master!
    2 *Col.*        And they curse   140
Loud enough to be heard.
    2 *Capt.* Their curse has the nature of gunpowder.
    *Sec.* They do not pray with half the noise.
    1 *Col.* Our general is not well mix'd;
He has too great a portion of fire.       145
    2 *Col.* His mistress cool him, (her complexion
Carries some phlegm,) when they two meet in bed!
    2 *Capt.* A third may follow.
    1 *Capt.*       'T is much pity     149
The young duke liv'd not to take the virgin off.
    1 *Col.* 'T was the king's act, to match two rabbit-suckers.
    2 *Col.* A common trick of state;
The little great man marries, travels then
Till both grow up, and dies when he should do
The feat. These things are still unlucky    155
On the male side.
    *Colum.* This to the duchess' fair hand.
            [*Gives Antonio a letter.*]

---

**78 Discover'd:** revealed    **111 scurril:** vulgar    **112 libels:** defamatory bills    **144 mix'd:** tempered
**146 complexion:** temperament    **151 rabbit-suckers:** children (literally, young rabbits)

*Sec.* She will think
Time hath no wing, till 1 return. [*Exit.*]
*Colum.* Gentlemen,
Now each man to his quarter, and encourage
The soldier. I shall take a pride to know 160
Your diligence, when I visit all your
Several commands.
*Omnes.* We shall expect.
2 *Col.* And move
By your directions.
*Colum.* Y' are all noble. *Exeunt.*

[SCENE II. *A Room in the Duchess's House*]

*Enter Cardinal, Duchess, Placentia*

*Car.* I shall perform a visit daily, madam,
In th' absence of my nephew, and be happy
If you accept my care.
*Duch.* You have honour'd me;
And if your entertainment have not been
Worthy your grace's person, 't is because 5
Nothing can reach it in my power; but where
There is no want of zeal, other defect
Is only a fault to exercise your mercy.
*Car.* You are bounteous in all. I take my
leave.
My fair niece, shortly, when Columbo has 10
Purchas'd more honours to prefer his name
And value to your noble thoughts! — Mean-
time,
Be confident you have a friend, whose office
And favour with the king shall be effectual
To serve your grace.
*Duch.* Your own good deeds reward you, 15
Till mine rise equal to deserve their benefit. —
*Exit Cardinal.*
Leave me awhile. — *Exit Placentia.*
Do not I walk upon the teeth of serpents,
And, as I had a charm against their poison,
Play with their stings? The Cardinal is subtle,
Whom 't is not wisdom to incense, till I 21
Hear to what destiny Columbo leaves me.
May be the greatness of his soul will scorn
To own what comes with murmur. If he can
Interpret me so happily, —

*Enter Secretary [Antonio] with a letter*

Art come? 25
*Sec.* His excellence salutes your grace.
*Duch.* Thou hast
A melancholy brow. How did he take my
letter?
*Sec.* As he would take a blow; with so much
sense
Of anger, his whole soul boil'd in his face,
And such prodigious flame in both his eyes, 30
As they 'd been th' only seat of fire, and at

Each look a salamander leaping forth,
Not able to endure the furnace.
*Duch.* Ha! thou dost
Describe him with some horror.
*Sec.* Soon as he
Had read again, and understood your mean-
ing, 35
His rage had shot me with a pistol, had not
I us'd some soft and penitential language
To charm the bullet.
*Duch.* Wait at some more distance. —
My soul doth bathe itself in a cold dew;
Imagine I am opening of a tomb; 40
[*Opens the letter.*]
Thus I throw off the marble, to discover
What antic posture death presents in this
Pale monument to fright me. — *Reads.*
Ha!
My heart, that call'd my blood and spirits to
Defend it from the invasion of my fears, 45
Must keep a guard about it still, lest this
Strange and too mighty joy crush it to noth-
ing. —
Antonio.
*Sec.* Madam.
*Duch.* Bid my steward give thee
Two thousand ducats. Art sure I am awake?
*Sec.* I shall be able to resolve you, madam,
When he has paid the money. 51
*Duch.* Columbo now is noble.
*Exit Duchess.*
*Sec.* This is better
Than I expected, — if my lady be
Not mad, and live to justify her bounty. *Exit.*

[SCENE III. *A Room in the Palace*]

*Enter King, Alvarez, Hernando, Lords*

*King.* The war is left to him; but we must
have
You reconcil'd, if that be all your difference.
His rage flows like a torrent, when he meets
With opposition; leave to wrastle with him,
And his hot blood retreats into a calm, 5
And then he chides his passion. You shall
back
With letters from us.
*Her.* Your commands are not
To be disputed.
*King.* Alvarez. [*Takes him aside.*]
1 *Lord.* Lose not
Yourself by cool submission; he will find
His error, and the want of such a soldier. 10
2 *Lord.* Have you seen the Cardinal?
*Her.* Not yet.
1 *Lord.* He wants no plot —
*Her.* The king I must obey;

---

11 **prefer:** advance in dignity     50 **resolve:** inform     4 **leave:** cease

But let the purple gownman place his engines
I' th' dark that wounds me.
    *2 Lord.*                Be assur'd
Of what we can to friend you; and the king    15
Cannot forget your service.
    *Her.*               I am sorry
For that poor gentleman.
    *Alv.*           I must confess, sir,
The duchess has been pleas'd to think me
    worthy
Her favours, and in that degree of honour
That has oblig'd my life to make the best    20
Return of service, which is not, with bold
Affiance in her love, to interpose
Against her happiness and your election.
I love so much her honour, I have quitted    24
All my desires; yet would not shrink to bleed
Out my warm stock of life, so the last drop
Might benefit her wishes.
    *King.*          I shall find
A compensation for this act, Alvarez;
It hath much pleas'd us.

*Enter Duchess with a letter; Gentleman-Usher*

    *Duch.*          Sir, you are the king,
And in that sacred title it were sin    30
To doubt a justice. All that does concern
My essence in this world, and a great part
Of the other bliss, lives in your breath.
    *King.*    What intends the duchess?
    *Duch.*    That will instruct you, sir. [*Gives the*
    *letter.*] — Columbo has,    35
Upon some better choice or discontent,
Set my poor soul at freedom.
    *King.*         'T is his charácter. *Reads.*
*Madam, I easily discharge all my pretensions*
*to your love and person. I leave you to your own*
*choice; and in what you have obliged yourself to*
*me, resume a power to cancel, if you please.* [41
                           *Columbo.*
This is strange!
    *Duch.*        Now do an act to make
Your chronicle belov'd and read for ever.
    *King.*    Express yourself.
    *Duch.*        Since by divine infusion, —    45
For 't is no art could force the general to
This change, — second this justice, and bestow
The heart you would have given from me, by
Your strict commands to love Columbo, where
'T was meant by heaven; and let your breath
    return    50
Whom you divorc'd, Alvarez, mine.
    *Lords.*             This is
But justice, sir.
    *King.*          It was decreed above;
And since Columbo has releas'd his interest,

Which we had wrought him, not without some
    force
Upon your will, I give you your own wishes:    55
Receive your own Alvarez. When you please
To celebrate your nuptial, I invite
Myself your guest.
    *Duch.*         Eternal blessings crown you!
    *Omnes.*    And every joy your marriage!
          *Exit King, who meets the Cardinal; they*
                 *confer.*
    *Alv.*    I know not whether I shall wonder
    most    60
Or joy to meet this happiness.
    *Duch.*         Now the king
Hath planted us, methinks we grow already,
And twist our loving souls, above the wrath
Of thunder to divide us.
    *Alv.*           Ha! the Cardinal
Has met the king! I do not like this confer-
    ence;
He looks with anger this way. I expect    66
A tempest.
    *Duch.*      Take no notice of his presence;
Leave me to meet, and answer it. If the king
Be firm in 's royal word, I fear no lightning.
Expect me in the garden.
    *Alv.*           I obey;    70
But fear a shipwrack on the coast.    *Exit.*
    *Car.*               Madam.
    *Duch.*    My lord.
    *Car.*    The king speaks of a letter that has
    brought
A riddle in 't.
    *Duch.*        'T is easy to interpret.    74
    *Car.*    From my nephew? May I deserve the
    favour?    [*Duchess gives him the letter.*]
    *Duch.* [*Aside.*] He looks as though his eyes
    would fire the paper.
They are a pair of burning glasses, and
His envious blood doth give 'em flame.
    *Car.* [*Aside.*] What lethargy could thus un-
    spirit him?
I am all wonder. — Do not believe, madam,    80
But that Columbo's love is yet more sacred
To honour and yourself than thus to forfeit
What I have heard him call the glorious wreath
To all his merits, given him by the king,
From whom he took you with more pride than
    ever    85
He came from victory: his kisses hang
Yet panting on your lips; and he but now
Exchang'd religious farewell to return,
But with more triumph, to be yours.
    *Duch.*           My lord,
You do believe your nephew's hand was not    90
Surpris'd or strain'd to this?

    ¹³⁻¹⁴ **But . . . me:** (*i.e.*, let me not detect him plotting my injury)    ¹³ **purple gownman:** the
Cardinal    ²² **Affiance:** confidence    ³³ **other:** that of heaven    ³⁷ **charácter:** handwriting    ⁴⁵ **in-**
**fusion:** influence    ⁵⁰ **let . . . return:** let your voice once more pronounce    ⁹¹ **strain'd:** forced

*Car.* Strange arts and windings in the world! most dark
And subtle progresses! Who brought this letter?
*Duch.* I enquir'd not his name; I thought it not
Considerable to take such narrow knowledge.
*Car.* Desert and honour urg'd it here, nor can                                            96
I blame you to be angry; yet his person
Oblig'd you should have given a nobler pause,
Before you made your faith and change so violent,
From his known worth into the arms of one,
However fashion'd to your amorous wish,    101
Not equal to his cheapest fame, with all
The gloss of love and merit.
*Duch.*                    This comparison,
My good lord Cardinal, I cannot think
Flows from an even justice; it betrays    105
You partial where your blood runs.
*Car.*                    I fear, madam,
Your own takes too much license, and will soon
Fall to the censure of unruly tongues.
Because Alvarez has a softer cheek,
Can, like a woman, trim his wanton hair,    110
Spend half a day with looking in the glass
To find a posture to present himself,
And bring more effeminacy than man
Or honour to your bed, must he supplant him?
Take heed, the common murmur, when it catches    115
The scent of a lost fame —
*Duch.*                    My fame, lord Cardinal?
It stands upon an innocence as clear
As the devotions you pay to heaven.
I shall not urge, my lord, your soft indulgence
At my next shrift.
*Car.*                    You are a fine court lady!    120
*Duch.* And you should be a reverend churchman.
*Car.*                                        One
That, if you have not thrown off modesty,
Would counsel you to leave Alvarez.
*Duch.*                                    'Cause
You dare do worse than marriage, must not I
Be admitted what the church and law allows me?    125
*Car.* Insolent! Then you dare marry him?
*Duch.*                                        Dare!
Let your contracted flame and malice, with
Columbo's rage, higher than that, meet us
When we approach the holy place, clasp'd hand
In hand: we 'll break through all your force, and fix    130
Our sacred vows together there.

*Car.*                                        I knew
When, with as chaste a brow, you promis'd fair
To another. You are no dissembling lady!
*Duch.* Would all your actions had no falser lights
About 'em!                                        135
*Car.* Ha!
*Duch.* The people would not talk, and curse so loud.
*Car.* I 'll have you chid into a blush for this.
*Duch.* Begin at home, great man, there 's cause enough.
You turn the wrong end of the pérspective    140
Upon your crimes, to drive them to a far
And lesser sight; but let your eyes look right,
What giants would your pride and surfeit seem!
How gross your avarice, eating up whole families!
How vast are your corruptions and abuse    145
Of the king's ear! at which you hang, a pendant,
Not to adorn, but ulcerate, while the honest
Nobility, like pictures in the arras,
Serve only for court ornament. If they speak,
'T is when you set their tongues, which you wind up    150
Like clocks, to strike at the just hour you please.
Leave, leave, my lord, these usurpations,
And be what you were meant, a man to cure,
Not let in agues to religion:
Look on the church's wounds.
*Car.*                    You dare presume,    155
In your rude spleen to me, to abuse the church?
*Duch.* Alas, you give false aim, my lord;
't is your
Ambition and scarlet sins, that rob
Her altar of the glory, and leave wounds
Upon her brow; which fetches grief and paleness    160
Into her cheeks, making her troubled bosom
Pant with her groans, and shroud her holy blushes
Within your reverend purples.
*Car.*                    Will you now take breath?
*Duch.* In hope, my lord, you will behold yourself
In a true glass, and see those injust acts    165
That so deform you, and by timely cure
Prevent a shame, before the short-hair'd men
Do crowd and call for justice; I take leave.
                                        *Exit.*

*Car.* This woman has a spirit that may rise
To tame the devil's. There 's no dealing with
Her angry tongue; 't is action and revenge    17:
Must calm her fury. Were Columbo here,

---

⁹⁵ **Considerable:** important    ⁹⁸ **Oblig'd . . . given:** put you under obligation to give    ¹⁰² **cheapest fame:** meanest reputation    ¹⁴⁰ **pérspective:** telescope    ¹⁵¹ **just:** exact    ¹⁶⁷ **short-hair'd men:** Puritans

I could resolve; but letters shall be sent
To th' army, which may wake him into sense
Of his rash folly, or direct his spirit          175
Some way to snatch his honour from this flame.
All great men know the soul of life is fame.
                                        *Exit.*

### ACT III

[SCENE I.   *A Room in the Palace*]

*Enter Valeria, Celinda*

*Val.*  I did not think, Celinda, when I prais'd
Alvarez to the duchess, that things thus
Would come about.  What does your ladyship
Think of Columbo now?  It staggers all
The court, he should forsake his mistress; I   5
Am lost with wonder yet.
   *Cel.*                    'T is very strange,
Without a spell; but there 's a fate in love; —
I like him ne'er the worse.

*Enter two Lords*

   *1 Lord.*  Nothing but marriages and triumph
now!
   *Val.*  What new access of joy makes you, my
lord,                                           10
So pleasant?
   *1 Lord.*             There 's a packet come to court
Makes the king merry; we are all concern'd in 't.
Columbo hath given the enemy a great
And glorious defeat, and is already
Preparing to march home.                        15
   *Cel.*  He thriv'd the better for my prayers.
   *2 Lord.*                    You have been
His great admirer, madam.
   *1 Lord.*                    The king longs
To see him.
   *Val.*         This news exalts the Cardinal.

*Enter Cardinal*

   *1 Lord.*  He 's here!
He appears with discontent; the marriage   20
With Count d'Alvarez hath a bitter taste,
And not worn off his palate: but let us leave
him.
   *Ladies.*  We 'll to the duchess.
                    *Exeunt.  Manet Cardinal.*
   *Car.*  He has not won so much upon the Ar-
ragon
As he has lost at home; and his neglect   25
Of what my studies had contriv'd, to add
More lustre to our family by the access
Of the great duchess' fortune, cools his triumph,
And makes me wild.

*Enter Hernando*

   *Her.*                    My good lord Cardinal!
   *Car.*  You made complaint to th' king about
your general.                                   30

*Her.*  Not a complaint, my lord; I did but
satisfy
Some questions o' the king's.
   *Car.*                    You see he thrives
Without your personal valour or advice,
Most grave and learned in the wars.
   *Her.*                                My lord,
I envy not his fortune.
   *Car.*                    'T is above         35
Your malice, and your noise not worth his
anger;
'T is barking 'gainst the moon.
   *Her.*                    More temper would
Become that habit.
   *Car.*  The military thing would show some
spleen.
I 'll blow an army of such wasps about   40
The world. — Go look your sting you left i' th'
camp, sir.

*Enter King and Lords*

   *Her.*  The king! — This may be one day
counted for.                                *Exit.*
   *King.*  All things conspire, my lord, to make
you fortunate.
Your nephew's glory —
   *Car.*                    'T was your cause and justice
Made him victorious; had he been so valiant   45
At home, he had had another conquest to
Invite, and bid her welcome to new wars.
   *King.*  You must be reconcil'd to Providence,
my lord.
I heard you had a controversy with
The duchess; I will have you friends.         50
   *Car.*  I am not angry.
   *King.*                    For my sake, then,
You shall be pleas'd, and with me grace the
marriage.
A churchman must show charity, and shine
With first example: she 's a woman.
   *Car.*  You shall prescribe in all things, sir.
You cannot                                      55
Accuse my love, if I still wish my nephew
Had been so happy to be constant to
Your own and my election.  Yet my brain
Cannot reach how this comes about; I know
My nephew lov'd her with a near affection   60

*Enter Hernando*

   *King.*  He 'll give you fair account at his re-
turn. —
Colonel, your letters may be spar'd; the gen-
eral
Has finish'd, and is coming home.      [*Exit.*]
   *Her.*  I am glad on 't, sir. — My good lord
Cardinal,                                       64
'T is not impossible but some man provok'd
May have a precious mind to cut your throat.

---

*Car.* You shall command me, noble Colonel;
I know you wo' not fail to be at th' wedding.

*Her.* 'T is not Columbo that is married, sir.

*Car.* Go teach the postures of the pike and musket; 70
Then drill your myrmidons into a ditch,
Where sterve, and stink in pickle. — You shall find
Me reasonable; you see the king expects me.
[*Exit.*]

*Her.* So does the devil. — 74
Some desperate hand may help you on your journey. *Exit.*

[SCENE II. *A Room in the Duchess's House*]

*Enter Secretary [Antonio] and Servants [with masques, dresses, etc.]*

*Sec.* Here, this; ay, this will fit your part: you shall wear the slashes, because you are a soldier. Here 's for the blue mute.

*1 Serv.* This doublet will never fit me; pox on 't! Are these breeches good enough for a [5 prince too? Pedro plays but a lord, and he has two laces more in a seam.

*Sec.* You must consider Pedro is a foolish lord; he may wear what lace he please.

*2 Serv.* Does my beard fit my clothes well, [10 gentlemen?

*Sec.* Pox o' your beard!

*3 Serv.* That will fright away the hair.

*1 Serv.* This fellow plays but a mute, and he is so troublesome, and talks. 15

*3 Serv.* Master Secretary might have let Jaques play the soldier; he has a black patch already.

*2 Serv.* By your favour, Master Secretary, I was ask'd who writ this play for us? 20

*Sec.* For us? Why, art thou any more than a blue mute?

*2 Serv.* And, by my troth, I said, I thought it was all your own.

*Sec.* Away, you coxcomb! 25

*4 Serv.* Dost think he has no more wit than to write a comedy? My lady's chaplain made the play, though he is content, for the honour and trouble of the business, to be seen in 't.

*5 Serv.* Did anybody see my head, gentle- [30 men? 'T was here but now. — I shall have never a head to play my part in.

*Sec.* Is thy head gone? 'T was well thy part was not in 't. Look, look about; has not Jaques it? 35

*4 Serv.* I his head? 'T wo' not come on upon my shoulders.

*Sec.* Make haste, gentlemen; I 'll see whether the king has supp'd. Look every man to his wardrobe and his part. *Exit.* 40

*2 Serv.* Is he gone? In my mind, a masque had been fitter for a marriage.

*4 Serv.* Why, mute? There was no time for 't, and the scenes are troublesome.

*2 Serv.* Half a score deal tack'd together [45 in the clouds, what 's that? A throne, to come down and dance; all the properties have been paid forty times over, and are in the court stock: — but the secretary must have a play, to show his wit. 50

*4 Serv.* Did not I tell thee 't was the chaplain's? Hold your tongue, mute.

*1 Serv.* Under the rose, and would this cloth-of-silver doublet might never come off again, if there be any more plot than you see in the [55 back of my hand.

*2 Serv.* You talk of a plot! I 'll not give this for the best poet's plot in the world, an if it be not well carried.

*4 Serv.* Well said, mute. 60

*3 Serv.* Ha, ha! Pedro, since he put on his doublet, has repeated but three lines, and he has broke five buttons.

*2 Serv.* I know not; but by this false beard, and here 's hair enough to hang a reasonable [65 honest man, I do not remember to say a strong line indeed in the whole comedy, but when the chambermaid kisses the captain.

*3 Serv.* Excellent, mute!

*5 Serv.* They have almost supp'd, and I [70 cannot find my head yet.

*4 Serv.* Play in thine own.

*5 Serv.* Thank you for that! so I may have it made a property. If I have not a head found me, let Master Secretary play my part him- [75 self without it.

*Enter Secretary [Antonio]*

*Sec.* Are you all ready, my masters? The king is coming through the gallery. Are the women dress'd?

*1 Serv.* Rogero wants a head. 80

*Sec.* Here, with a pox to you! take mine. You a player! you a puppy-dog. Is the music ready?

*Enter Gentleman-Usher*

*Gent.* Gentlemen, it is my lady's pleasure that you expect till she call for you. There [85 are a company of cavaliers in gallant equipage, newly alighted, have offer'd to present their Revels in honour of this Hymen; and 't is her grace's command, that you be silent till their entertainment be over. 90

*1 Serv.* Gentlemen?

---

**72 sterve:** die　　**2 blue mute:** mute who was to play the servant's part　　**45 deal:** boards
**46 clouds:** roof of the stage　　**66 to say:** if I may say so

*2 Serv.* Affronted?

*5 Serv.* Master Secretary, there 's your head again; a man 's a man. Have I broken my sleep to study fifteen lines for an ambassa- [95 dor, and after that a constable, and is it come to this?

*Sec.* Patience, gentlemen, be not so hot; 't is but deferr'd, and the play may do well enough cold.        100

*4 Serv.* If it be not presented, the chaplain will have the greatest loss; he loses his wits.

                             *Hautboys.*

*Sec.* This music speaks the king upon entrance. Retire, retire, and grumble not.

                *Exeunt [all but Antonio].*

*Enter King, Cardinal, Alvarez, Duchess, Celinda, Valeria, Placentia, Lords, Hernando. They being set, enter Columbo and five more, in rich habits, vizarded; between every two a torch-bearer. They dance, and after beckon to Alvarez, as desirous to speak with him.*

*Alv.* With me!    *They embrace and whisper.*

*King.* Do you know the masquers, madam?

*Duch.*               Not I, sir.   106

*Car.* There 's one, — but that my nephew is abroad,
And has more soul than thus to jig upon
Their hymeneal night, I should suspect
'T were he.    *The Masquers lead in Alvarez.*

*Duch.* Where 's my Lord d'Alvarez?

                           *Recorders.*

*King.*          Call in the bridegroom.   111

*Enter Columbo. Four Masquers bring in Alvarez dead, in one of their habits, and having laid him down, exeunt.*

*Duch.* What mystery is this?

*Car.* We want the bridegroom still.

*King.*             Where is Alvarez?

    *Columbo points to the body; they unvizard it, & find Alvarez bleeding.*

*Duch.* Oh, 't is my lord! He 's murder'd!

*King.* Who durst commit this horrid act?

*Colum.*                I, sir.   115

            *[Throws off his disguise.]*

*King.* Columbo? Ha!

*Colum.* Yes; Columbo, that dares stay
To justify that act.

*Her.*          Most barbarous!

*Duch.* Oh, my dearest lord!

*King.*        Our guard seize on them all.
This sight doth shake all that is man within me.
Poor Alvarez, is this thy wedding day?   121

              *Enter Guard*

*Duch.* If you do think there is a heaven, or pains

To punish such black crimes i' th' other world,
Let me have swift, and such exemplar justice
As shall become this great assassinate;    125
You will take off our faith else: and, if here
Such innocence must bleed, and you look on,
Poor men, that call you gods on earth, will doubt
To obey your laws, nay, practise to be devils,
As fearing, if such monstrous sins go on,    130
The saints will not be safe in heaven.

*King.*                      You shall,
You shall have justice.

*Car. [Aside.]*    Now to come off were brave.

                *Enter Servant*

*Serv.* The masquers, sir, are fled; their horse, prepar'd
At gate, expected to receive 'em, where
They quickly mounted: coming so like friends,
None could suspect their haste, which is secur'd    136
By advantage of the night.

*Colum.* I answer for 'em all; 't is stake enough
For many lives: but if that poniard
Had voice, it would convince they were but all
Spectators of my act. And now, if you    141
Will give your judgments leave, though at the first
Face of this object your cool bloods were frighted,
I can excuse this deed, and call it justice;
An act your honours and your office, sir,    145
Is bound to build a law upon, for others
To imitate. I have but took his life,
And punish'd her with mercy, who had both
Conspir'd to kill the soul of all my fame.
Read there; and read an injury as deep    150
In my dishonour as the devil knew
A woman had capacity or malice
To execute: read there, how you were cozen'd, sir, —

    *[Gives the Duchess's letter to the king.]*
Your power affronted, and my faith; her smiles,
A juggling witchcraft to betray and make    155
My love her horse to stalk withal, and catch
Her curled minion.

*Car.*          Is it possible
The duchess could dissemble so, and forfeit
Her modesty with you and to us all?
Yet I must pity her. My nephew has    160
Been too severe; though this affront would call
A dying man from prayers, and turn him tiger;
There being nothing dearer than our fame,
Which, if a common man, whose blood has no
Ingredient of honour, labour to    165

---

Preserve, a soldier (by his nearest tie
To glory) is, above all others, bound
To vindicate: — and yet it might have been
Less bloody.
　　*Her.*　　　　Charitable devil!
　　King reads.　*I pray, my lord, release* [170
*under your hand what you dare challenge in my
love or person, as a just forfeit to myself; this act
will speak you honourable to my thoughts; and
when you have conquered thus yourself, you may
proceed to many victories, and after, with* [175
*safety of your fame, visit again.*
　　　　　　　　　　　　*The lost Rosaura.*
To this your answer was a free resign?
　　*Colum.*　Flatter'd with great opinion of her
　　　faith,　　　　　　　　　　　　　　　179
And my desert of her (with thought that she,
Who seem'd to weep and chide my easy will
To part with her, could not be guilty of
A treason or apostasy so soon,
Bur rather meant this a device to make
Me expedite the affairs of war), I sent　　185
That paper, which her wickedness, not jus-
　　tice,
Applied (what I meant trial,) her divorce.
I lov'd her so, I dare call heaven to witness,
I knew not whether I lov'd most; while she,
With him, whose crimson penitence I pro-
　　vok'd,　　　　　　　　　　　　　　　190
Conspir'd my everlasting infamy:
Examine but the circumstance.
　　*Car.*　　　　　　　　'T is clear;
This match was made at home, before she sent
That cunning writ, in hope to take him off,
As knowing his impatient soul would scorn　195
To own a blessing came on crutches to him.
It was not well to raise his expectation,
(Had you, sir, no affront?) to ruin him
With so much scandal and contempt.
　　*King.*　　　　　　　　We have
Too plentiful a circumstance to accuse　　200
You, madam, as the cause of your own sorrows;
But not without an accessory more
Than young Alvarez.
　　*Car.*　　　　　　Any other instrument?
　　*King.*　Yes; I am guilty, with herself, and
　　Don
Columbo, though our acts look'd several ways,
That thought a lover might so soon be ran-
　　som'd;　　　　　　　　　　　　　　206
And did exceed the office of a king
To exercise dominion over hearts,
That owe to the prerogative of heaven
Their choice or separation: you must, there-
　　fore,　　　　　　　　　　　　　　210
When you do kneel for justice and revenge,

Madam, consider me a lateral agent
In poor Alvarez' tragedy.
　　*1 Lord.*　It was your love to Don Columbo,
　　sir.
　　*Her.*　So, so! the king is charm'd.　Do you
　　observe　　　　　　　　　　　　　　215
How, to acquit Columbo, he would draw
Himself into the plot?　Heaven, is this justice?
　　*Car.*　Your judgment is divine in this.
　　*King.*　　　　　　　　　And yet
Columbo cannot be secure, and we
Just in his pardon, that durst make so great　220
And insolent a breach of law and duty.
　　*2 Lord.*　Ha! will he turn again?
　　*King.*　　　　　　And should we leave
This guilt of blood to heaven, which cries and
　　strikes
With loud appeals the palace of eternity;
Yet here is more to charge Columbo than　225
Alvarez' blood, and bids me punish it
Or be no king.
　　*Her.*　'T is come about, my lords.
　　*King.*　And if I should forgive
His timeless death, I cannot the offence,
That with such boldness struck at me.　Has
　　my　　　　　　　　　　　　　　230
Indulgence to your merits, which are great,
Made me so cheap, your rage could meet no
　　time
Nor place for your revenge, but where my eyes
Must be affrighted, and affronted with
The bloody execution?　This contempt　235
Of majesty transcends my power to pardon,
And you shall feel my anger, sir.
　　*Her.*　　　　　　　　Thou shalt
Have one short prayer more for that.
　　*Colum.*　　　　　　　　Have I,
I' th' progress of my life,
No actions to plead me up deserving　　240
Against this ceremony?
　　*Car.*　　　　　　Contain yourself.
　　*Colum.*　I must be dumb then.　Where is
　　honour
And gratitude of kings, when they forget
Whose hand secur'd their greatness?　Take my
　　head off;
Examine then which of your silken lords,　245
As I have done, will throw himself on dangers;
Like to a floating island move in blood;
And where your great defence calls him to
　　stand
A bulwark, upon his bold breast to take
In death, that you may live: — but soldiers
　　are　　　　　　　　　　　　　　250
Your valiant fools, whom, when your own se-
　　curities

<hr>

　　[187] **Applied:** interpreted as　　　[189] **whether:** which (heaven or Rosaura)　　　[190] **provok'd:** brought
about　　　[192] **circumstance:** details　　　[196] **came on crutches:** which came grudgingly　　　[206] **ransom'd:**
transferred　　　[212] **lateral agent:** accessory　　　[229] **timeless:** untimely　　　[241] **ceremony:** formal justice

Are bleeding, you can cherish; but when once
Your state and nerves are knit, not thinking
   when
To use their surgery again, you cast
Them off, and let them hang in dusty armor-
   ies,      255
Or make it death to ask for pay.
   *King.*              No more;
We thought to have put your victory and merits
In balance with Alvarez' death, which, while
Our mercy was to judge, had been your safety;
But the affront to us, made greater by    260
This boldness to upbraid our royal bounty,
Shall tame or make you nothing.
   *Lord.*              Excellent!
   *Her.* The Cardinal is not pleas'd.
   *Car.*             Humble yourself
To th' king.
   *Colum.*    And beg my life? Let cowards
   do 't
That dare not die; I 'll rather have no head  265
Than owe it to his charity.
   *King.*         To th' castle with him! —
       [*Columbo is led off by the Guard.*]
Madam, I leave you to your grief, and what
The king can recompense to your tears, or
   honour
Of your dead lord, expect.
   *Duch.* This shows like justice. *Exeunt.*

## ACT IV

[SCENE I.   *A Room in the Palace*]

*Enter two Lords, Hernando*

   *1 Lord.* This is the age of wonders.
   *2 Lord.*             Wondrous mischiefs.
   *Her.* Among those guards, which some call
   tutelar angels,
Whose office is to govern provinces,
Is there not one will undertake Navarre?
Hath Heaven forsook us quite?
   *1 Lord.*          Columbo at large!  5
   *2 Lord.* And grac'd now more than ever.
   *1 Lord.*          He was not pardon'd;
That word was prejudicial to his fame.
   *Her.* But, as the murder done had been a
   dream
Vanish'd to memory, he 's courted as
Preserver of his country. With what chains  10
Of magic does this Cardinal hold the king?
   *2 Lord.* What will you say, my lord, if they
   enchant
The duchess now, and by some impudent art
Advance a marriage to Columbo yet?
   *Her.* Say!                      15
I 'll say no woman can be sav'd; nor is 't
Fit, indeed, any should pretend to heaven
After one such impiety in their sex:

And yet my faith has been so stagger'd, since
The king restor'd Columbo, I 'll be now   20
Of no religion.
   *1 Lord.*         'T is not possible
She can forgive the murder; I observ'd
Her tears.
   *Her.*      Why, so did I, my lord;
And if they be not honest, 't is to be
Half damn'd, to look upon a woman weeping.  25
When do you think the Cardinal said his pray-
   ers?
   *2 Lord.* I know not.
   *Her.*     Heaven forgive my want of charity!
But if I were to kill him, he should have
No time to pray; his life could be no sacrifice,
Unless his soul went, too.
   *1 Lord.*         That were too much.  30
   *Her.* When you mean to dispatch him, you
   may give
Time for confession: they have injur'd me
After another rate.
   *2 Lord.* You are too passionate, cousin.

*Enter Columbo, Colonels, Alphonso, Cour-*
*tiers. They pass over the stage.*

   *Her.* How the gay men do flutter to con-
   gratulate          35
His jail delivery! There 's one honest man:
What pity 't is a gallant fellow should
Depend on knaves for his preferment!
   *1 Lord.* Except this cruelty upon Alvarez,
Columbo has no mighty stain upon him;   40
But for his uncle —
   *Her.*          If I had a son
Of twelve years old that would not fight with
   him,
And stake his soul against his cardinal's cap,
I would disinherit him. Time has took a lease
But for three lives, I hope; a fourth may see
Honesty walk without a crutch.
   *2 Lord.*                This is   46
But air and wildness.
   *Her.*       I will see the duchess.
   *1 Lord.* You may do well to comfort her;
   we must
Attend the king.
   *Her.*       Your pleasures.
                        *Exit Hernando.*

*Enter King and Cardinal*

   *1 Lord.* A man of a brave soul.
   *2 Lord.*          The less his safety. —  50
The king and Cardinal in consult!
   *King.* Commend us to the duchess, and
   employ
What language you think fit and powerful
To reconcile her to some peace. — My lords.
   *Car.* Sir, I possess all for your sacred uses.  55
                   *Exeunt severally.*

<hr/>

48 **You . . . her:** (given to Hernando, Q)

[SCENE II. *A Room in the Duchess's
House*]

*Enter Secretary [Antonio] and Celinda*

*Sec.* Madam, you are the welcom'st lady
living.
*Cel.* To whom, Master Secretary?
*Sec.*                    If you have mercy
To pardon so much boldness, I durst say,
To me — I am a gentleman.
*Cel.*                    And handsome.
*Sec.* But my lady has                    5
Much wanted you.
*Cel.*                    Why, Master Secretary?
*Sec.* You are the prettiest, —
*Cel.* So!
*Sec.* The wittiest, —
*Cel.* So!                    10
*Sec.* The merriest lady i' th' court.
*Cel.* And I was wish'd, to make the duchess
pleasant?
*Sec.* She never had so deep a cause of sor-
row;
Her chamber 's but a coffin of a larger
Volume, wherein she walks so like a ghost,    15
'T would make you pale to see her.
*Cel.*                    Tell her grace
I attend here.
*Sec.*          I shall most willingly. —
A spirited lady! would I had her in my closet!
She is excellent company among the lords.
Sure, she has an admirable treble. [*Aside.*] —
Madam.                    *Exit.*    20
*Cel.* I do suspect this fellow would be nib-
bling,
Like some, whose narrow fortunes will not rise
To wear things when the invention 's rare and
new,
But, treading on the heel of pride, they hunt
The fashion when 't is crippled, like fell tyrants.
I hope I am not old yet; I had the honour    26
To be saluted by our Cardinal's nephew
This morning: there 's a man!

*Enter Secretary [Antonio]*

*Sec.*                    I have prevail'd.
Sweet madam, use what eloquence you can
Upon her; and if ever I be useful    30
To your ladyship's service, your least breath
commands me.                    [*Exit.*]

*Enter Duchess*

*Duch.* Madam, I come to ask you but one
question:
If you were in my state, my state of grief,
I mean, an exile from all happiness
Of this world, and almost of heaven, (for my    35

Affliction is finding out despair,)
What would you think of Don Columbo?
*Cel.*                    Madam?
*Duch.* Whose bloody hand wrought all this
misery.
Would you not weep, as I do, and wish rather
An everlasting spring of tears to drown    40
Your sight, than let your eyes be curs'd to see
The murderer again, and glorious?
So careless of his sin that he is made
Fit for new parricide, even while his soul    44
Is purpled o'er, and reeks with innocent blood?
But do not, do not answer me; I know
You have so great a spirit, (which I want,
The horror of his fact surprising all
My faculties), you would not let him live:
But I, poor I, must suffer more. There 's not    50
One little star in heaven will look on me,
Unless to choose me out the mark, on whom
It may shoot down some angry influence.

*Enter Placentia*

*Pla.* Madam, here 's Don Columbo says he
must
Speak with your grace.
*Duch.*          But he must not, I charge you.    55
                    [*Exit Placentia.*]
None else wait? — Is this well done,
To triumph in his tyranny? Speak, madam,
Speak but your conscience.

*Enter Columbo and Secretary [Antonio]*

*Sec.*                    Sir, you must not see her.
*Colum.* Not see her? Were she cabled up
above
The search of bullet or of fire, were she    60
Within her grave, and that the toughest mine
That ever nature teem'd and groan'd withal,
I would force some way to see her. — Do not
fear    63
I come to court you, madam; y' are not worth
The humblest of my kinder thoughts. I come
To show the man you have provok'd and lost,
And tell you what remains of my revenge. —
Live, but never presume again to marry;
I 'll kill the next at th' altar, and quench all
The smiling tapers with his blood: if after,    70
You dare provoke the priest and heaven so
much
To take another, in thy bed I 'll cut him from
Thy warm embrace, and throw his heart to
ravens.
*Cel.* This will appear an unexampled cruelty.
*Colum.* Your pardon, madam; rage and my
revenge,    75
Not perfect, took away my eyes. You are
A noble lady, this not worth your eye-beam;
One of so slight a making, and so thin,

An autumn leaf is of too great a value
To play, which shall be soonest lost i' th' air.    80
Be pleas'd to own me by some name in your
Assurance, I despise to be receiv'd
There; let her witness that I call you mis-
    tress.
Honour me to make these pearls your carcanet.
                        [*Gives her a necklace.*]
    *Cel.*  My lord, you are too humble in your
        thoughts.                        85
    *Colum.* [*Aside.*]  There's no vexation too
        great to punish her.            *Exit.*
    *Sec.*  Now, madam.
    *Cel.*  Away, you saucy fellow! — Madam, I
Must be excus'd, if I do think more honoura-
    bly
Than you have cause of this great lord.
    *Duch.*                    Why, is not    90
All womankind concern'd to hate what's im-
    pious?
    *Cel.*  For my part —
    *Duch.*            Antonio, is this a woman?
    *Sec.*  I know not whether she be man or
        woman;
I should be nimble to find out the experiment.
She look'd with less state when Columbo came.
    *Duch.*  Let me entreat your absence. — I
        am cozen'd in her. [*Aside.*] —        96
I took you for a modest, honest lady.
    *Cel.*  Madam, I scorn any accuser; and
Deducting the great title of a duchess,
I shall not need one grain of your dear honour
To make me full weight: if your grace be jeal-
    ous,                            101
I can remove.                    *Exit.*
    *Sec.*        She is gone.
    *Duch.*                    Prithee remove
My fears of her return.  (*Exit Secretary.*) —
        She is not worth
Considering; my anger's mounted higher.
He need not put in caution for my next    105
Marriage. — Alvarez, I must come to thee,
Thy virgin wife, and widow; but not till
I ha' paid those tragic duties to thy hearse
Become my piety and love.  But how?
Who shall instruct a way?

                *Enter Placentia*

    *Pla.*                    Madam, Don    110
Hernando much desires to speak with you.
    *Duch.*  Will not thy own discretion think I
        am
Unfit for visit?
    *Pla.*        Please your grace, he brings
Something, he says, imports your ear, and love
Of the dead lord, Alvarez.
    *Duch.*  Then admit him. [*Exit Placentia.*]115

        *Enter* [*Placentia with*] *Hernando*

    *Her.*  I would speak, madam, to yourself.
    *Duch.*        Your absence.  [*Exit Placentia.*]
    *Her.*  I know not how your grace will cen-
        sure so
Much boldness, when you know the affairs I
    come for.
    *Duch.*  My servant has prepar'd me to re-
        ceive it,
If it concern my dead lord.
    *Her.*                    Can you name    120
So much of your Alvarez in a breath,
Without one word of your revenge?    Oh,
    madam,
I come to chide you, and repent my great
Opinion of your virtue, that can walk,
And spend so many hours in naked solitude;  125
As if you thought that no arrears were due
To his death, when you had paid his funeral
    charges,
Made your eyes red, and wept a handkercher.
I come to tell you that I saw him bleed;
I, that can challenge nothing in his name    130
And honour, saw his murder'd body warm,
And panting with the labour of his spirits,
Till my amaz'd soul shrunk and hid itself;
While barbarous Columbo grinning stood,
And mock'd the weeping wounds.  It is too
    much,                            135
That you should keep your heart alive so long
After this spectacle, and not revenge it.
    *Duch.*  You do not know the business of my
        heart,
That censure me so rashly; yet I thank you;
And, if you be Alvarez' friend, dare tell    140
Your confidence that I despise my life,
But know not how to use it in a service
To speak me his revenger:  this will need
No other proof than that to you, who may
Be sent with cunning to betray me, I        145
Have made this bold confession.  I so much
Desire to sacrifice to that hovering ghost
Columbo's life, that I am not ambitious
To keep my own two minutes after it.
    *Her.*  If you will call me coward, which is
        equal                        150
To think I am a traitor, I forgive it
For this brave resolution, which time
And all the destinies must aid.  I beg
That I may kiss your hand for this; and may
The soul of angry honour guide it —
    *Duch.*                    Whither?  155
    *Her.*  To Don Columbo's heart.
    *Duch.*  It is too weak, I fear, alone.
    *Her.*  Alone?  Are you in earnest?  Why,
        will it not

⁸⁴ **carcanet**: necklace    ⁸⁶ ('Enter Secretary' Q; but he has been present during this scene)    ¹⁰² **re-**
**move**: go away    ¹¹⁴ **imports**: which concerns

Be a dishonour to your justice, madam,
Another arm should interpose? But that   160
It were a saucy act to mingle with you,
I durst, nay, I am bound in the revenge
Of him that 's dead, (since the whole world has interest
In every good man's loss,) to offer it.
Dare you command me, madam?
*Duch.*                    Not command;   165
But I should more than honour such a truth
In man, that durst, against so mighty odds,
Appear Alvarez' friend, and mine. The Cardinal —
*Her.*  Is for the second course. Columbo must
Be 'first cut up; his ghost must lead the dance:
Let him die first.                          171
*Duch.*          But how?
*Her.*  How! with a sword; and, if I undertake it,
I wo' not lose so much of my own honour
To kill him basely.
*Duch.*              How shall I reward
This infinite service? 'T is not modesty,   175
While now my husband groans beneath his tomb,
And calls me to his marble bed, to promise
What this great act might well deserve, myself,
If you survive the victor; but if thus
Alvarez' ashes be appeas'd, it must         180
Deserve an honourable memory;
And though Columbo (as he had all power,
And grasp'd the fates) has vow'd to kill the man
That shall succeed Alvarez —
*Her.*                  Tyranny!
*Duch.*  Yet, if ever                       185
I entertain a thought of love hereafter,
Hernando from the world shall challenge it;
Till when, my prayers and fortune shall wait on you.
*Her.*  This is too mighty recompense.
*Duch.*                    'T is all just.
*Her.*  If I outlive Columbo, I must not   190
Expect security at home.
*Duch.*              Thou canst
Not fly where all my fortunes and my love
Shall not attend to guard thee.
*Her.*  If I die —
*Duch.*          Thy memory            194
Shall have a shrine, the next within my heart
To my Alvarez.
*Her.*            Once again your hand.
Your cause is so religious, you need not
Strengthen it with your prayers; trust it to me.

*Enter Placentia, and Cardinal*

*Pla.*  Madam, the Cardinal.
*Duch.*                    Will you appear?
*Her.*  And he had all the horror of the devil
In 's face, I would not balk him.           201
*He stares upon the Cardinal in his exit.*
*Car.* [*Aside.*]  What makes Hernando here?
    I do not like
They should consult; I 'll take no note. — The king
Fairly salutes your grace; by whose command
I am to tell you, though his will and actions  205
Illimited stoop not to satisfy
The vulgar inquisition, he is
Yet willing to retain a just opinion
With those that are plac'd near him; and although
You look with nature's eye upon yourself,   210
Which needs no perspective to reach, nor art
Of any optic to make greater, what
Your narrow sense applies an injury,
(Ourselves still nearest to ourselves,) but there 's
Another eye that looks abroad, and walks   215
In search of reason, and the weight of things,
With which, if you look on him, you will find
His pardon to Columbo cannot be
So much against his justice as your erring
Faith would persuade your anger.
*Duch.*              Good my lord,   220
Your phrase has too much landscape, and I cannot
Distinguish at this distance you present
The figure perfect; but indeed my eyes
May pray your lordship find excuse, for tears
Have almost made them blind.
*Car.*              Fair peace restore 'em!   225
To bring the object nearer, the king says,
He could not be severe to Don Columbo
Without injustice to his other merits,
Which call more loud for their reward and honour
Than you for your revenge; the kingdom made   230
Happy by those; you only, by the last,
Unfortunate: — nor was it rational,
(I speak the king's own language,) he should die
For taking one man's breath, without whose valour   234
None now had been alive without dishonour.
*Duch.*  In my poor understanding, 't is the crown
Of virtue to proceed in its own tract,
Not deviate from honour. If you acquit
A man of murder, 'cause he has done brave

---

²⁰¹ **balk:** shun, avoid   ²⁰² **makes:** does   ²⁰⁶ **Illimited:** not subject to control   ²⁰⁷ **inquisition:** inquiry   ²¹² **optic:** lens, telescope   ²¹³ **applies:** regards as   ²²² **you present:** whether you present   ²³⁷ **tract:** path

Things in the war, you will bring down his
  valour                                                      240
To a crime, nay, to a bawd, if it secure
A rape, and but teach those that deserve well
To sin with greater license.  But dispute
Is now too late, my lord; 't is done; and you
By the good king, in tender of my sorrows,    245
Sent to persuade me 't is unreasonable
That justice should repair me.
  *Car.*                              You mistake;
For if Columbo's death could make Alvarez
Live, the king had given him up to law,
Your bleeding sacrifice; but when his life    250
Was but another treasure thrown away,
To obey a clamorous statute, it was wisdom
To himself, and common safety, to take off
This killing edge of law, and keep Columbo
To recompense the crime by noble acts,    255
And sorrow, that in time might draw your pity.
  *Duch.*  This is a greater tyranny than that
Columbo exercis'd;  he kill'd my lord;
And you have not the charity to let
Me think it worth a punishment.
  *Car.*                           To that,    260
In my own name, I answer.  I condemn,
And urge the bloody guilt against my nephew;
'T was violent and cruel, a black deed;
A deed whose memory doth make me shudder;
An act that did betray a tyrannous nature,    265
Which he took up in war, the school of ven-
  geance;
And though the king's compassion spare him
  here,
Unless his heart
Weep itself out in penitent tears, hereafter —
  *Duch.*                          This sounds
As you were now a good man.
  *Car.*                        Does your grace    270
Think I have conscience to allow the murder?
Although, when it was done, I did obey
The stream of nature, as he was my kinsman,
To plead he might not pay his forfeit life,
Could I do less for one so near my blood?    275
Consider, madam, and be charitable;
Let not this wild injustice make me lose
The character I bear and reverend habit.
To make you full acquainted with my inno-
  cence,
I challenge here my soul and heaven to witness,
If I had any thought or knowledge with    281
My nephew's plot, or person, when he came,
Under the smooth pretence of friend, to violate
Your hospitable laws, and do that act,
Whose frequent mention draws this tear, a
  whirlwind                                                285
Snatch me to endless flames!

  *Duch.*                              I must believe,
And ask your grace's pardon.  I confess
I ha' not lov'd you since Alvarez' death,
Though we were reconcil'd.
  *Car.*                    I do not blame
Your jealousy, nor any zeal you had    290
To prosecute revenge against me, madam,
As I then stood suspected, nor can yet
Implore your mercy to Columbo.  All
I have to say is, to retain my first
Opinion and credit with your grace;    295
Which you may think I urge not out of fear,
Or ends upon you, (since, I thank the king,
I stand firm on the base of royal favour,)
But for your own sake, and to show I have
Compassion of your sufferings.
  *Duch.*                        You have clear'd    300
A doubt, my lord; and by this fair remon-
  strance
Given my sorrow so much truce to think
That we may meet again, and yet be friends. —
But be not angry, if I still remember    304
By whom Alvarez died, and weep, and wake
Another justice with my prayers.
  *Car.*                          All thoughts
That may advance a better peace dwell with
  you!                                      *Exit.*
  *Duch.*  How would this cozening statesman
  bribe my faith
With flatteries to think him innocent!
No; if his nephew die, this Cardinal must
  not                                              310
Be long-liv'd.  All the prayers of a wrong'd
  widow
Make firm Hernando's sword! and my own
  hand
Shall have some glory in the next revenge.
I will pretend my brain with grief distracted.
It may gain easy credit; and beside    315
The taking off examination
For great Columbo's death, it makes what act
I do in that believ'd want of my reason
Appear no crime, but my defence. — Look
  down,
Soul of my lord, from thy eternal shade,    320
And unto all thy blest companions boast
Thy duchess busy to revenge thy ghost!  *Exit.*

[SCENE III.  *Outside the City*]

*Enter Columbo, Hernando, Alfonso, Colonel*

  *Colum.*  Hernando, now I love thee, and do
  half
Repent the affront my passion threw upon thee.
  *Her.*  You wo' not be too prodigal o' your
  penitence.

---

²⁴⁵ **tender:** consideration     ²⁴⁷ **repair me:** remedy the wrong done me     ²⁶⁶ **took up:** acquired
²⁷¹ **allow:** approve     ²⁹⁰ **jealousy:** mistrust     ²⁹⁷ **ends:** designs     ³¹⁶ **examination:** trial     ³¹⁸ **believ'd:**
supposed

*Colum.* This makes good thy nobility of birth;
Thou may'st be worth my anger and my sword, 5
If thou dost execute as daringly
As thou provok'st a quarrel. I did think
Thy soul a starveling, or asleep.
*Her.* You 'll find it
Active enough to keep your spirit waking;
Which to exasperate, for yet I think 10
It is not high enough to meet my rage —
D' ye smile?
*Colum.* This noise is worth it. — Gentlemen,
I 'm sorry this great soldier has engag'd
Your travail; all his business is to talk.
*Her.* A little of your lordship's patience: 15
You shall have other sport, and swords that will
Be as nimble 'bout your heart as you can wish.
'T is pity more than our two single lives
Should be at stake.
*Colom.* Make that no scruple, sir.
*Her.* To him, then, that survives, if fate allow 20
That difference, I speak, that he may tell
The world, I came not hither on slight anger,
But to revenge my honour, stain'd and trampled on
By this proud man; when general, he commanded
My absence from the field.
*Colum.* I do remember, 25
And I 'll give your soul now a discharge.
*Her.* I come
To meet it, if your courage be so fortunate.
But there is more than my own injury
You must account for, sir, if my sword prosper; 29
Whose point and every edge is made more keen
With young Alvarez' blood, in which I had
A noble interest. Does not that sin benumb
Thy arteries, and turn the guilty flowings
To trembling jelly in thy veins? Canst hear
Me name that murder, and thy spirits not 35
Struck into air, as thou wert shot by some
Engine from heaven?
*Colum.* You are the duchess' champion!
Thou hast given me a quarrel now. I grieve
It is determin'd all must fight, and I
Shall lose much honour in his fall.
*Her.* That duchess, 40
(Whom but to mention with thy breath is sacrilege,)
An orphan of thy making, and condemn'd
By thee to eternal solitude, I come
To vindicate; and while I am killing thee,
By virtue of her prayers sent up for justice 45

At the same time, in heaven I am pardon'd for 't.
*Colum.* I cannot hear the bravo.
*Her.* Two words more,
And take your chance. Before you all I must
Pronounce that noble lady without knowledge
Or thought of what I undertake for her. 50
Poor soul! she 's now at her devotions,
Busy with heaven, and wearing out the earth
With her stiff knees, and bribing her good angel
With treasures of her eyes, to tell her lord
How much she longs to see him. My attempt 55
Needs no commission from her: were I
A stranger in Navarre, the inborn right
Of every gentleman to Alvarez' loss
Is reason to engage their swords and lives
Against the common enemy of virtue. 60
*Colum.* Now have you finish'd? I have an instrument
Shall cure this noise, and fly up to thy tongue,
To murder all thy words.
*Her.* One little knot
Of phlegm that clogs my stomach, and I ha' done: —
You have an uncle, call'd a Cardinal. 65
Would he were lurking now about thy heart,
That the same wounds might reach you both, and send
Your reeling souls together! Now have at you.
*Alph.* We must not, sir, be idle.
*They fight; Columbo's second [Alphonso] slain.*
*Her.* What think you now of praying?
*Colum.* Time enough. 70
*He kills Hernando's second.*
Commend me to my friend; the scales are even.
I would be merciful, and give you time
Now to consider of the other world;
You 'll find your soul benighted presently.
*Her.* I 'll find my way i' the dark.
*They fight, and close; Columbo gets both the swords, and Hernando takes up the second's weapon.*
*Colum.* A stumble 's dangerous. 75
Now ask thy life. — Ha!
*Her.* I despise to wear it,
A gift from any but the first bestower.
*Colum.* I scorn a base advantage. —
*Columbo throws away one of the swords. They fight; Hernando wounds Columbo. —*
Ha!
*Her.* I am now
Out of your debt.

---

¹² **D' ye:** ('D' ee' Q)   ¹⁸⁻¹⁹ (The seconds, as well as the principals, fought in seventeenth-century duels.)   ³³ **flowings: blood**

*Colum.* Th'ast don 't, and I forgive thee.
Give me thy hand; when shall we meet again?
   *Her.* Never, I hope.          81
   *Colum.* I feel life ebb apace: yet I 'll look
     upwards,
And show my face to heaven.     *[Dies.]*
   *Her.*         The matter 's done;
I must not stay to bury him.     *Exit.*

## ACT V

### [Scene I. *A Garden*]

*Enter two Lords*

   1 *Lord.* Columbo's death doth much afflict
     the king.
   2 *Lord.* I thought the Cardinal would have
     lost his wits
At first, for 's nephew; it drowns all the talk
Of the other that were slain.
   1 *Lord.*         We are friends.
I do suspect Hernando had some interest,   5
And knew how their wounds came.
   2 *Lord.*        His flight confirms it,
For whom the Cardinal has spread his nets.
   1 *Lord.* He is not so weak to trust himself
     at home
To his enemy's gripe.
   2 *Lord.*       All strikes not me so much
As that the duchess, most oppressed lady,   10
Should be distracted, and before Columbo
Was slain.
   1 *Lord.* But that the Cardinal should be
     made
Her guardian, is to me above that wonder.
   2 *Lord.* So it pleas'd the king; and she, with
     that small stock
Of reason left her, is so kind and smooth   15
Upon him.
   1 *Lord.* She 's turn'd a child again: a mad-
     ness,
That would ha' made her brain and blood boil
     high,
In which distemper she might ha' wrought
     something —
   2 *Lord.* Had been to purpose.
   1 *Lord.* The Cardinal is cunning; and how-
     e'er   20
His brow does smile, he does suspect Hernando
Took fire from her, and waits a time to punish
     it.
   2 *Lord.* But what a subject of disgrace and
     mirth
Hath poor Celinda made herself by pride,
In her belief Columbo was her servant!   25
Her head hath stoop'd much since he died, and
     she
Almost ridiculous at court.

*Enter Cardinal, Antonelli, Servant*

   1 *Lord.*         The Cardinal
Is come into the garden, now —
   *Car.*       Walk off. — *[Exeunt Lords.]*
It troubles me the duchess by her loss
Of brain is now beneath my great revenge.   30
She is not capable to feel my anger,
Which, like to unregarded thunder spent
In woods, and lightning aim'd at senseless
     trees,
Must idly fall, and hurt her not, not to
That sense her guilt deserves: a fatal stroke,   35
Without the knowledge for what crime, to
     fright her
When she takes leave, and make her tug with
     death,
Until her soul sweat, is a pigeon's torment,
And she is sent a babe to the other world.
Columbo's death will not be satisfied,   40
An I but wound her with a two-edg'd feather.
I must do more: I have all opportunity,
(She by the king now made my charge,) but
     she 's
So much a turtle, I shall lose by killing her,
Perhaps do her a pleasure and preferment.   45
That must not be.

*Enter Celinda with a parchment*

   *Anton.* [*Stopping her.*] — Is not this she that
     would be thought to have been
Columbo's mistress? — Madam, his grace is
     private,
And would not be disturb'd; you may dis-
     please him.
   *Cel.* What will your worship wager that he
     shall   50
Be pleas'd again before we part?
   *Anton.* I 'll lay this diamond, madam, 'gainst
     a kiss,
And trust yourself to keep the stakes.
   *Cel.*       'T is done. [*Comes forward.*]
   *Anton.* I have long had an appetite to this
     lady;
But the lords keep her up so high — this toy   55
May bring her on.
   *Car.* This interruption tastes not of good
     manners.
   *Cel.* But where necessity, my lord, compels,
The boldness may meet pardon, and when you
Have found my purpose, I may less appear   60
Unmannerly.
   *Car.*      To th' business.
   *Cel.*         It did please
Your nephew, sir, before his death, to credit me
With so much honourable favour, I
Am come to tender to his near'st of blood,
Yourself, what does remain a debt to him.   65

      ⁴ **other:** others   ⁴⁴ **turtle:** turtle-dove   ⁵⁵ **toy:** trifle

Not to delay your grace with circumstance,
That deed, if you accept, makes you my heir
Of no contemptible estate. — This way
                                        *He reads.*
Is only left to tie up scurril tongues
And saucy men, that since Columbo's death 70
Venture to libel on my pride and folly;
His greatness and this gift, which I enjoy
Still for my life, (beyond which term a king-
        dom 's
Nothing,) will curb the giddy spleens of men
That live on impudent rhyme, and railing at 75
Each wandering fame they catch.    [*Aside.*]
    *Car.*              Madam, this bounty
Will bind my gratitude and care to serve you.
    *Cel.*  I am your grace's servant.
    *Car.*                Antonelli! — *Whisper.*
And when this noble lady visits me,
Let her not wait.                        80
    *Cel.*  What think you, my officious sir? His
        grace
Is pleas'd, you may conjecture. I may keep
Your gem; the kiss was never yours.
    *Anton.*              Sweet madam —
    *Cel.*  Talk if you dare; you know I must not
        wait;
And so, farewell for this time.    [*Exit.*] 85
    *Car.*  'T is in my brain already, and it forms
Apace — good, excellent revenge, and pleasant!
She 's now within my talons. 'T is too cheap
A satisfaction for Columbo's death,
Only to kill her by soft charm or force.    90
I 'll rifle first her darling chastity;
'T will be after time enough to poison her,
And she to th' world be thought her own de-
        stroyer.
As I will frame the circumstance, this night
All may be finish'd: for the colonel,    95
Her agent in my nephew's death, (whom I
Disturb'd at counsel with her,) I may reach him
Hereafter, and be master of his fate.
We starve our conscience when we thrive in
        state.                        *Exeunt.*

        [SCENE II.    *A Room in the Duchess's
                House*]

    *Enter Secretary [Antonio] and Placentia*

    *Sec.*  Placentia, we two are only left
Of all my lady's servants; let us be true
To her and one another; and be sure,
When we are at prayers, to curse the Cardinal.
    *Pla.*  I pity my sweet lady.    5
    *Sec.*  I pity her, too, but am a little angry;
She might have found another time to lose
Her wits.
    *Pla.*  That I were a man!
    *Sec.*  What would'st thou do, Placentia? 10

    *Pla.*  I would revenge my lady.
    *Sec.*  'T is better being a woman; thou
        may'st do
Things that may prosper better, and the fruit
Be thy own another day.
    *Pla.*              Your wit still loves
To play the wanton.
    *Sec.*          'T is a sad time, Placentia; 15
Some pleasure would do well. The truth is, I
Am weary of my life, and I would have
One fit of mirth before I leave the world.
    *Pla.*  Do not you blush to talk thus wildly?
    *Sec.*  'T is good manners            20
To be a little mad after my lady;
But I ha' done. Who is with her now?
    *Pla.*  Madam Valeria.
    *Sec.*  Not Celinda? There 's a lady for my
        humour!
A pretty book of flesh and blood, and well 25
Bound up, in a fair letter, too. Would I
Had her with all the errata!
    *Pla.*              She has not
An honourable fame.
    *Sec.*          Her fame! that 's nothing;
A little stain; her wealth will fetch again
The colour, and bring honour into her cheeks 30
As fresh; —
If she were mine, and I had her exchequer,
I know the way to make her honest;
Honest to th' touch, the test, and the last
        trial.
    *Pla.*  How, prithee?                35
    *Sec.*  Why,
First I would marry her, that 's a verb material;
Then I would print her with an *index
Expurgatorius*, a table drawn
Of her court heresies; and when she 's read, 40
*Cum privilegio*, who dares call her whore?
    *Pla.*  I 'll leave you, if you talk thus.
    *Sec.*              I ha' done;
Placentia, thou may'st be better company
After another progress; and now tell me,
Didst ever hear of such a patient madness 45
As my lady is possess'd with? She has rav'd
But twice: — an she would fright the Cardinal,
Or at a supper if she did but poison him,
It were a frenzy I could bear withal.
She calls him her dear governor. —

    *Enter Hernando disguised, having a letter*

    *Pla.*              Who is this?  50
    *Her.*  Her secretary! — Sir,
Here is a letter, if it may have so
Much happiness to kiss her grace's hand.
    *Sec.*                From whom?
    *Her.*  That 's not in your commission, sir,
To ask, or mine to satisfy; she will want 55
No understanding when she reads.

71 **libel:** make scurrilous comments     2 **all:** (not in Q)     26 **letter:** style of type

*Sec.*                                   Alas!
Under your favour, sir, you are mistaken;
Her grace did never more want understanding.
*Her.*   How?
*Sec.*   Have you not heard?   Her skull is
  broken, sir,                                    60
And many pieces taken out; she 's mad.
*Her.*   The sad fame of her distraction
Has too much truth, it seems.
*Pla.*                   If please you, sir,
To expect awhile, I will present the letter.
*Her.*   Pray do. —         *Exit Placentia.*  65
How long has she been thus distemper'd, sir?
*Sec.*   Before the Cardinal came to govern
  here,
Who, for that reason, by the king was made
Her guardian.   We are now at his devotion.
*Her.*   A lamb given up to a tiger!   May dis-
  eases                                           70
Soon eat him through his heart!
*Sec.*                   Your pardon, sir.
I love that voice; I know it, too, a little.
Are not you — ?   Be not angry, noble sir,
I can with ease be ignorant again,
And think you are another man; but if      75
You be that valiant gentleman they call ⌐
*Her.*   Whom? what?
*Sec.*   That kill'd — I would not name him,
  if I thought
You were not pleas'd to be that very gentleman.
*Her.*   Am I betray'd?
*Sec.*                   The devil sha' not  80
Betray you here: kill me, and I will take
My death you are the noble colonel.
We are all bound to you for the general's death,
Valiant Hernando!   When my lady knows
You are here, I hope 't will fetch her wits
  again.                                          85
But do not talk too loud; we are not all
Honest i' th' house; some are the Cardinal's
  creatures.
*Her.*   Thou wert faithful to thy lady.   I am
  glad
'T is night.   But tell me how the churchman
  uses
The duchess.                                      90

#### Enter Antonelli

*Sec.*   He carries angels in his tongue and face,
  but I
Suspect his heart: this is one of his spawns. —
Signor Antonelli.
*Anton.*   Honest Antonio!
*Sec.*   And how, and how — a friend of mine
  — where is                                      95
The Cardinal's grace?

*Her.* [*Aside.*]   That will be never answer'd.
*Anton.*   He means to sup here with the
  duchess.
*Sec.*   Will he?
*Anton.*   We 'll have the charming bottles at
  my chamber.                                     100
Bring that gentleman; we 'll be mighty merry.
*Her.* [*Aside.*]   I may disturb your jollity.
*Anton.*   Farewell, sweet —         [*Exit.*]
*Sec.*   Dear Antonelli! — A round pox con-
  found you!
This is court rhetoric at the back-stairs.       105

#### Enter Placentia

*Pla.*   Do you know this gentleman?
*Sec.*   Not I.
*Pla.*   My lady presently dismiss'd Valeria,
And bade me bring him to her bed-chamber.
*Sec.*   The gentleman has an honest face.
*Pla.*                   Her words  110
Fell from her with some evenness and joy. —
Her grace desires your presence.
*Her.*                   I 'll attend her.
                     *Exit* [*with Placentia*].
*Sec.*   I would this soldier had the Cardinal
Upon a promontory.   With what a spring
The churchman would leap down!   It were a
  spectacle                                       115
Most rare, to see him topple from the preci-
  pice,
And souse in the salt water with a noise
To stun the fishes; and if he fell into
A net, what wonder would the simple sea-gulls
Have, to draw up the o'ergrown lobster,   120
So ready boil'd!   He shall have my good wishes.
This colonel's coming may be lucky;   I
Will be sure none shall interrupt 'em.

#### Enter Celinda

*Cel.*                                   Is
Her grace at opportunity?
*Sec.*                   No, sweet madam;
She is asleep, her gentlewoman says.         125
*Cel.*   My business is but visit.   I 'll expect.
*Sec.*   That must not be, although I like your
  company.
*Cel.*   You are grown rich, Master Secretary.
*Sec.*   I, madam?   Alas!
*Cel.*   I hear you are upon another purchase.
*Sec.*   I upon a purchase!                       131
*Cel.*   If you want any sum —
*Sec.*   If I could purchase your sweet favour,
  madam.
*Cel.*   You shall command me, and my for-
  tune, sir.
*Sec.* [*Aside.*]   How 's this?                  135

---

⁶⁹ **at his devotion:** subject to him   ⁸⁷ **Honest:** loyal   ¹¹⁹ **sea-gulls:** foolish fishermen   ¹²⁰⁻¹²¹ **lob-ster . . . boil'd:** (alluding to the Cardinal's red robe)   ¹²⁴ **at opportunity:** willing to receive visi-tors

*Cel.* I have observ'd you, sir, a staid
And prudent gentleman — and I shall want —
*Sec.* Not me?
*Cel.* A father for some infant. He has credit
I' th' world. I am not the first cast lady    140
Has married a secretary. [*Aside.*]
*Sec.* Shall I wait upon you?
*Cel.* Whither?
*Sec.* Any whither.
*Cel.* I may chance lead you then —    145
*Sec.* I shall be honour'd to obey. My blood
Is up, and in this humour I 'm for anything.
*Cel.* Well, sir, I 'll try your manhood.
*Sec.*                    'T is my happiness;
You cannot please me better.
*Cel.* [*Aside.*]              This was struck
I' th' opportunity.
*Sec.*              I am made ιⱳr ever.    150
                    [*Exit, following her.*]


[SCENE III.  *Another Room*]

*Enter Hernando and Duchess*

*Her.* Dear madam, do not weep.
*Duch.* Y' are very welcome;
I ha' done; I wo' not shed a tear more
Till I meet Alvarez; then I 'll weep for joy.
He was a fine young gentleman, and sung
    sweetly;                              5
An you had heard him but the night before
We were married, you would ha' sworn he had
    been
A swan, and sung his own sad epitaph.
But we 'll talk o' the Cardinal.
*Her.*                    Would his death
Might ransom your fair sense! he should not
    live                                10
To triumph in the loss. Beshrew my manhood,
But I begin to melt.
*Duch.*              I pray, sir, tell me, —
For I can understand, although they say
I have lost my wits; but they are safe enough,
And I shall have 'em when the Cardinal dies; —
Who had a letter from his nephew, too,    16
Since he was slain?
*Her.*              From whence?
*Duch.* I know not where he is. But in some
    bower
Within a garden he is making chaplets,
And means to send me one; but I 'll not take it;
I have flowers enough, I thank him, while I live.
*Her.* But do you love your governor?    22
*Duch.* Yes, but I 'll never marry him; I am
    promis'd
Already.
*Her.* To whom, madam?
*Duch.*              Do not you

Blush when you ask me that? Must not you
    be                                  25
My husband? I know why, but that 's a secret.
Indeed, if you believe me, I do love
No man alive so well as you. The Cardinal
Shall never know 't; he 'll kill us both; and yet
He says he loves me dearly, and has promis'd 30
To make me well again; but I 'm afraid,
One time or other, he will give me poison.
*Her.* Prevent him, madam, and take noth-
    ing from him.
*Duch.* Why, do you think 't will hurt me?
*Her.*                    It will kill you.
*Duch.* I shall but die, and meet my dear-
    lov'd lord,                          35
Whom when I have kiss'd, I 'll come again and
    work
A bracelet of my hair for you to carry him,
When you are going to heaven; the posy shall
Be my own name, in little tears, that I
Will weep next winter, which congeal'd i' th'
    frost,                              40
Will show like seed-pearl. You 'll deliver it?
I know he 'll love, and wear it for my sake.
*Her.* She is quite lost.
*Duch.*              I pray, give me, sir, your pardon:
I know I talk not wisely; but if you had
The burthen of my sorrow, you would miss 45
Sometimes your better reason. Now I 'm well.
What will you do when the Cardinal comes?
He must not see you for the world.
*Her.*                    He sha' not;
I 'll take my leave before he come.
*Duch.*                    Nay, stay;
I shall have no friend left me when you go. 50
He will but sup; he sha' not stay to lie wi' me.
I have the picture of my lord abed;
Three are too much this weather.

*Enter Placentia*

*Pla.*                    Madam, the Cardinal.
*Her.* He shall sup with the devil.
*Duch.*                    I dare not stay;
The red cock will be angry. I 'll come again. 55
                    *Exeunt* [*Duchess and Placentia*].
*Her.* This sorrow is no fable. Now I find
My curiosity is sadly satisfied. —
Ha! if the duchess in her straggled wits
Let fall words to betray me to the Cardinal,
The panther will not leap more fierce to meet 60
His prey, when a long want of food hath parch'd
His starved maw, than he to print his rage,
And tear my heart-strings. Everything is fatal;
And yet she talk'd sometimes with chain of
    sense,
And said she lov'd me. Ha! they come not yet.
I have a sword about me, and I left    66
My own security to visit death.

⁵⁵ **red cock:** the Cardinal

Yet I may pause a little, and consider
Which way does lead me to 't most honourably.
Does not the chamber that I walk in tremble?
What will become of her, and me, and all 71
The world in one small hour?  I do not think
Ever to see the day again; the wings
Of night spread o'er me like a sable hearse-cloth;
The stars are all close mourners, too; but I 75
Must not alone to the cold, silent grave.
I must not. — If thou canst, Alvarez, open
That ebon curtain, and behold the man,
When the world's justice fails, shall right thy
    ashes,
And feed their thirst with blood!  Thy duchess
    is 80
Almost a ghost already, and doth wear
Her body like a useless upper garment,
The trim and fashion of it lost. — Ha!

*Enter Placentia*

*Pla.*  You need not doubt me, sir. — My
    lady prays
You would not think it long; she in my ear 85
Commanded me to tell you that when last
She drank, she had happy wishes to your health.
*Her.*  And did the Cardinal pledge it?
*Pla.*                          He was not
Invited to 't, nor must he know you are here.
*Her.*  What do they talk of, prithee?    90
*Pla.*  His grace is very pleasant
                    *A lute is heard.*
And kind to her; but her returns are after
The sad condition of her sense, sometimes
Unjointed.
*Her.*      They have music.
*Pla.*                  A lute only,  94
His grace prepar'd; they say, the best of Italy,
That waits upon my lord.
*Her.*              He thinks the duchess
Is stung with a tarantula.
*Pla.*              Your pardon;
My duty is expected.                *Exit.*
*Her.*          Gentle lady! —
A voice, too!

        SONG *within*

*Strep.*  *Come, my Daphne, come away,*  100
        *We do waste the crystal day;*
        *'T is Strephon calls.* Dap. *What*
            *says my love?*
*Strep.*  *Come, follow to the myrtle grove,*
        *Where Venus shall prepare*
        *New chaplets for thy hair.*  105
*Dap.*  *Were I shut up within a tree,*
        *I'd rend my bark to follow thee.*
*Strep.*  *My shepherdess, make haste.*
        *The minutes slide too fast.*
*Dap.*  *In those cooler shades will I,*  110
        *Blind as Cupid, kiss thine eye.*

*Strep.*  *In thy bosom then I'll stay;*
        *In such warm snow who would not*
            *lose his way?*
*Chor.*  *We'll laugh, and leave the world be-*
            *hind,*
        *And gods themselves that see,*  115
        *Shall envy thee and me,*
                *But never find*
        *Such joys, when they embrace a deity.*

[*Her.*]  If at this distance I distinguish, 't
    is not
Church music; and the air 's wanton, and no
    anthem  120
Sung to 't, but some strange ode of love and
    kisses.
What should this mean? — Ha! he is coming
    hither.            [*Draws his sword.*]
I am betray'd; he marches in her hand.
I'll trust a little more; mute as the arras,
My sword and I here.  125
        *He* [*conceals himself behind the arras,*
            *and*] *observes.*

*Enter Cardinal, Duchess, Antonelli, and*
        *Attendants*

*Car.*  Wait you in the first chamber, and let
    none
Presume to interrupt us. —
            *Exeunt* [*Antonelli and*] *servants.*
                She is pleasant;
Now for some art to poison all her inno-
    cence.
*Duch.* [*Aside.*]  I do not like the Cardinal's
    humour; he
Little suspects what guest is in my chamber. 130
*Car.*  Now, madam, you are safe.
                [*Embraces her.*]
*Duch.*              How means your lordship?
*Car.*  Safe in my arms, sweet duchess.
*Duch.*              Do not hurt me.
*Car.*  Not for the treasures of the world! You
    are
My pretty charge.  Had I as many lives
As I have careful thoughts to do you service, 135
I should think all a happy forfeit, to
Delight your grace one minute; 't is a heaven
To see you smile.
*Duch.*          What kindness call you this?
*Car.*  It cannot want a name while you pre-
    serve
So plentiful a sweetness; it is love.  140
*Duch.*  Of me?  How shall I know 't, my
    lord?
*Car.*  By this, and this, swift messengers to
    whisper
Our hearts to one another.        *Kisses* [*her*].
*Duch.*  Pray, do you come a-wooing?

---

⁹² returns: replies  ⁹⁷ tarantula: (the bite of which was supposed to produce a hysterical malady)

*Car.*                          Yes, sweet madam;
You cannot be so cruel to deny me.                    145
*Duch.*  What, my lord?
*Car.*                          Another kiss.
*Duch.*                          Can you
Dispense with this, my lord? — (*Aside.*) Alas;
    I fear
Hernando is asleep, or vanish'd from me.
    *Car.* [*Aside.*]  I have mock'd my blood into
        a flame; and what
My angry soul had form'd for my revenge, 150
Is now the object of my amorous sense.
I have took a strong enchantment from her
    lips,
And fear I shall forgive Columbo's death,
If she consent to my embrace. — Come, madam.
    *Duch.*  Whither, my lord?
    *Car.*              But to your bed or couch, 155
Where, if you will be kind, and but allow
Yourself a knowledge, love, whose shape and
    raptures
Wise poets have but glorified in dreams,
Shall make your chamber his eternal palace;
And with such active and essential streams 160
Of new delights glide o'er your bosom, you
Shall wonder to what unknown world you are
By some blest change translated.  Why d' ye
    pause,
And look so wild?  Will you deny your gov-
    ernor?
    *Duch.*  How came you by that cloven foot?
    *Car.*              Your fancy
Would turn a traitor to your happiness.    166
I am your friend; you must be kind.
    *Duch.*                          Unhand me,
Or I 'll cry out a rape.
    *Car.*              You wo' not, sure?
    *Duch.*  I have been cozen'd with Hernando's
        shadow;
Here 's none but heaven to hear me. — Help! a
    rape!                                    170
    *Car.*  Are you so good at understanding,
        then?
I must use other argument.
        *He forces her.* [*Hernando rushes from
            the arras.*]
    *Her.*  Go to, Cardinal.
                    *Strikes him.  Exit Duchess.*
    *Car.*  Hernando?  Murder! treason! help!
    *Her.*  An army sha' not rescue thee.  Your
        blood                                175
Is much inflam'd; I have brought a lancet wi'
    me
Shall open your hot veins, and cool your
    fever. —
To vex thy parting soul, it was the same
Engine that pierc'd Columbo's heart.
    *Car.*              Help! murder!  [*Stabs him.*]

179 **pierc'd:**  ('pinc'd' Q)

*Enter Antonelli and Servants*

    *Anton.*  Some ring the bell, 't will raise the
        court;                                180
My lord is murder'd!  'T is Hernando.
                    *The bell rings.*
    *Her.*  I 'll make you all some sport. — [*Stabs
        himself.*] — So; now we are even.
Where is the duchess?  I would take my leave
Of her, and then bequeath my curse among you.
                    *Hernando falls.*

*Enter King, Duchess, Valeria, Lords, Guard*

    *King.*  How come these bloody objects? 185
    *Her.*  With a trick my sword found out.  I
        hope he 's paid.
    1 *Lord.* [*Aside.*]  I hope so, too. — A surgeon
For my Lord Cardinal!
    *King.*  Hernando?
    *Duch.*  Justice! oh, justice, sir, against a rav-
        isher!                                190
    *Her.*  Sir, I ha' done you service.
    *King.*                          A bloody service.
    *Her.*  'T is pure scarlet.

*Enter Surgeon*

    *Car.* [*Aside.*]  After such care to perfect my
        revenge,
Thus bandied out o' th' world by a woman's
    plot!
    *Her.*  I have preserv'd the duchess from a
        rape.                                195
Good night to me and all the world for ever.
                    *Dies.*
    *King.*  So impious!
    *Duch.*  'T is most true; Alvarez' blood
Is now reveng'd; I find my brain return,
And every straggling sense repairing home. 200
    *Car.*  I have deserv'd you should turn from
        me, sir,
My life hath been prodigiously wicked;
My blood is now the kingdom's balm.  Oh, sir,
I have abus'd your ear, your trust, your people,
And my own sacred office; my conscience  205
Feels now the sting.  Oh, show your charity,
And with your pardon, like a cool soft gale,
Fan my poor sweating soul, that wanders
    through
Unhabitable climes and parched deserts.
But I am lost, if the great world forgive me, 210
Unless I find your mercy for a crime
You know not, madam, yet, against your life.
I must confess more than my black intents
Upon your honour: y' are already poison'd.
    *King.*  By whom?                        215
    *Car.*  By me,
In the revenge I ow'd Columbo's loss;
With your last meat was mix'd a poison that

By subtle and by sure degrees must let
In death.
*King.* Look to the duchess, our physicians!
*Car.* Stay;       221
I will deserve her mercy, though I cannot
Call back the deed. In proof of my repentance,
If the last breath of a now dying man
May gain your charity and belief, receive  225
This ivory box; in it an antidote
'Bove that they boast the great magistral med-
    icine:
That powder, mix'd with wine, by a most rare
And quick access to the heart, will fortify it
Against the rage of the most nimble poison.  230
I am not worthy to present her with it.
Oh, take it, and preserve her innocent life.
  *1 Lord.* Strange, he should have a good
    thing in such readiness.
  *Car.* 'T is that, which in my jealousy and
    state,
Trusting to false predictions of my birth,  235
That I should die by poison, I preserv'd
For my own safety. Wonder not, I made
That my companion was to be my refuge.

*Enter Servant with a bowl of wine*

  *1 Lord.* Here 's some touch of grace.
  *Car.* In greater proof of my pure thoughts,
    I take       240
This first, and with my dying breath confirm
My penitence; it may benefit her life,
But not my wounds. [*He drinks.*] Oh, hasten
    to preserve her;
And though I merit not her pardon, let not
Her fair soul be divorc'd.      245
    [*The Duchess takes the bowl and drinks.*]
  *King.* This is some charity; may it prosper,
    madam!
  *Val.* How does your grace?
  *Duch.* And must I owe my life to him,
    whose death
Was my ambition? Take this free acknowl-
    edgment;
I had intent, this night, with my own hand  250
To be Alvarez' justicer.
  *King.*      You were mad,
And thought past apprehension of revenge.
  *Duch.* That shape I did usurp, great sir, to
    give
My art more freedom and defence; but when
Hernando came to visit me, I thought  255
I might defer my execution;
Which his own rage suppli'd without my guilt,
And when his lust grew high, met with his
    blood.
  *1 Lord.* The Cardinal smiles.
  *Car.*      Now my revenge has met

With you, my nimble duchess! I have took  260
A shape to give my act more freedom, too,
And now I am sure she 's poison'd with that
    dose
I gave her last.
  *King.*      Th' art not so horrid?
  *Duch.* Ha! some cordial.
  *Car.*      Alas, no preservative
Hath wings to overtake it; were her heart  265
Lock'd in a quarry, it would search and kill
Before the aids can reach it. I am sure
You sha' not now laugh at me.
  *King.* How came you by that poison?
  *Car.*      I prepar'd it,
Resolving, when I had enjoy'd her, which  270
The colonel prevented, by some art
To make her take it, and by death conclude
My last revenge. You have the fatal story.
  *King.* This is so great a wickedness, it will
Exceed belief.
  *Car.*      I knew I could not live.  275
  *Surg.* Your wounds, sir, were not desperate.
  *Car.* Not mortal? Ha! were they not mor-
    tal?
  *Surg.* If I have skill in surgery.
  *Car.* Then I have caught myself in my own
    engine.
  *2 Lord.* It was your fate, you said, to die by
    poison.      280
  *Car.* That was my own prediction, to abuse
Your faith; no human art can now resist it:
I feel it knocking at the seat of life;
It must come in; I have wrack'd all my
    own
To try your charities: now it would be rare,  285
If you but waft me with a little prayer;
My wings that flag may catch the wind; but
    't is
In vain, the mist is risen, and there 's none
To steer my wand'ring bark.    *Dies.*
  *1 Lord.*      He 's dead.
  *King.*      With him
Die all deceived trust.
  *2 Lord.*      This was a strange  290
Impiety.
  *King.* When men
Of gifts and sacred function once decline
From virtue, their ill deeds transcend exam-
    ple.
  *Duch.* The minute 's come that I must take
    my leave, too.
Your hand, great sir; and though you be a
    king,      295
We may exchange forgiveness. Heaven for-
    give,
And all the world! I come, I come, Alvarez.
        *Dies.*

*King.* Dispose their bodies for becoming funeral.
How much are kings abus'd by those they take
To royal grace, whom, when they cherish most
By nice indulgence, they do often arm          301
Against themselves! from whence this maxim
  springs:
None have more need of perspectives than
  kings.                                    *Exeunt.*

## Epilogue

*Within.* Master Pollard! Where 's Master
  Pollard, for the epilogue?
        *He is thrust upon the stage, and falls.*
Epi. [Rising.] *I am coming to you, gentle-*
  *men. The poet*
*Has help'd me thus far on my way, but I 'll*
*Be even with him: the play is a tragedy,*
*The first that ever he compos'd for us,*          5
*Wherein he thinks he has done prettily,*

### Enter Servant

*And I am sensible. — I prithee, look,*
*Is nothing out of joint? Has he broke nothing?*

Serv. *No, sir, I hope.*
Epi. *Yes, he has broke his epilogue all to*
  *pieces.*                                        10
*Canst thou put it together again?*
Serv. *Not I, sir.*
Epi. *Nor I; prithee be gone.*   [Exit Serv.]
      *— Hum! — Master Poet,*
*I have a teeming mind to be reveng'd. —*
*You may assist, and not be seen in 't now,*       15
*If you please, gentlemen, for I do know*
*He listens to the issue of his cause;*
*But blister not your hands in his applause;*
*Your private smile, your nod, or hum! to tell*
*My fellows that you like the business well;*      20
*And when, without a clap, you go away,*
*I 'll drink a small-beer health to his second*
  *day;*
*And break his heart, or make him swear and*
  *rage*
*He 'll write no more for the unhappy stage.*
*But that 's too much; so we should lose. 'Faith,*
  *shew it,*                                       25
*And if you like his play, 't 's as well he knew*
  *it.*

---

²⁹⁸ **becoming:** suitable     Epilogue ¹ **Pollard:** Thomas Pollard of the King's Men, speaker of the epilogue.  (See list of Principal Actors on page 799.)

3  4  5  6  7  8  9